Contemporary Authors

Contemporary Authors

A BIO-BIBLIOGRAPHICAL GUIDE TO CURRENT AUTHORS AND THEIR WORKS

ANN EVORY

Editor

volumes **29-32**

first revision

GALE RESEARCH COMPANY • BOOK TOWER • DETROIT, MICHIGAN 48226

CONTEMPORARY AUTHORS

Published by
Gale Research Company, Book Tower, Detroit, Michigan 48226
Each Year's Volumes Are Revised About Five Years Later

Frederick G. Ruffner, *Publisher*   James M. Ethridge, *Editorial Director*

Christine Nasso, *General Editor, Contemporary Authors*

Ann Evory, *Editor*
Michael L. Auty, Robin Farbman, Peter M. Gareffa,
Victoria France Hutchinson, Margaret Mazurkiewicz, Linda Metzger,
Nancy M. Rusin, and Catherine Stadelman, *Assistant Editors*
Ellen Koral, *Editorial Assistant*
Michaeline Nowinski, *Production Manager*

Copyright © 1972, 1978 by
GALE RESEARCH COMPANY

Library of Congress Catalog Card Number 62-52046
ISBN 0-8103-0035-4

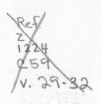

Preface

This volume represents a complete revision of bio-bibliographical material which originally appeared in *Contemporary Authors,* Volumes 29-32, published in 1972. The material is up-to-date, in most cases, through late 1977.

Questions and Answers About Revised Volumes
of
Contemporary Authors

How much change is undertaken when past volumes of *Contemporary Authors* are revised? Every part of every sketch is changed, if necessary. Present production techniques provide for fast, economical typesetting of all material used in revised volumes, and no attempt is made to minimize changes.

About 80-85% of all sketches in revised volumes have one or more changes from the original volume. The nature and extent of the revisions can be seen by comparing the original listings for Adolfo Bioy-Casares, Toni Morrison, and Thomas Tryon with the revised sketches in this volume.

How are revised volumes prepared? Clippings of previously published sketches are sent to authors at their last-known addresses. Authors mark material to be deleted or changed, and insert any new personal data, new affiliations, new books, new work in progress, new sidelights, and new biographical/critical sources. Gale makes great efforts to encourage responses from all authors, and has a toll-free telephone number so authors can conveniently reply by phone without personal expense.

How do you revise previously published sketches if the authors do not return marked clippings? First, every attempt is made to reach authors through previous home addresses, business affiliations, publishers, organizations, or other practicable means either by mail or telephone. When necessary, searches are made to determine whether the authors have died. A number of sources are checked for obituaries, including newspaper and magazine indexes.

If living authors fail to reply, or if authors are now deceased, work proceeds on verifying and updating the previously published information. Biographical dictionaries are checked (a task made easier through the use of Gale's *Biographical Dictionaries Master Index* and new *Author Biographies Master Index*), as are bibliographical sources, such as *Cumulative Book Index, The National Union Catalog,* etc. In other words, all steps are taken which can reasonably be expected to confirm or invalidate previous information, or to provide additional information. Sketches not personally verified by the authors are marked as follows:

> † Research has yielded new information which has been added to the sketch
> † † Research has yielded no new information

Do all sketches in a revised volume undergo some change? No, they do not. In a sense, however, *all* sketches in a revised volume are "revised" sketches, in that the authors have examined them and indicated that the information they furnished for the previous edition is currently correct, or a revision editor has checked as many facts as possible and made the same determination. Obviously, previously published information which is verified as still accurate is just as helpful to the reference user as information newly added.

How much revision takes place in an average volume? It is difficult to measure. Revised Volumes 1-4, for example, showed a net increase of about 70 pages, and Revised Volumes 5-8 an increase of 200 pages. These increases represented only the *net* change in the number of pages, however; they did not measure the total amount of change, since things like new addresses do not affect sketch length, and deletions of memberships or transfers of items from "Work in Progress" to the bibliography of published works usually result in decreases in space used.

Sketches of deceased and inactive authors have been removed from recent revision volumes and listed separately in the two volumes of *Contemporary Authors—Permanent Series*. Even with the substantial number of sketches which were transferred, however, recent revision volumes have been larger than the corresponding original volumes.

What is the rationale behind the *Permanent Series*? The purpose of the *Permanent Series* was to remove from the revision cycle entries for deceased authors and authors past normal retirement age who were presumed to be no longer actively writing. Since revised volumes of *Contemporary Authors* were consistently larger than original volumes, and since Gale knew that future revised volumes would continue to grow, it seemed reasonable to list separately in the *Permanent Series* those entries which would not require future revision. This procedure was both logical in itself and comparable to the practices of other biographical reference-book publishers. For example, sketches removed from *Who's Who in America* are published periodically in *Who Was Who in America*.

Will the *Permanent Series* be continued? No. Experience has proved that a cumulative series devoted entirely to authors cannot effectively be treated in the same way as a repetitive series devoted to noteworthy persons in general. The *Permanent Series* has, therefore, been discontinued with the publication of Volume 2. The two *Permanent Series* volumes are an integral part of the entire *Contemporary Authors* series and will be kept in print along with all other volumes in the series because they contain sketches of deceased and inactive authors drawn from volumes 9-36. In the future, all entries appearing in a given volume of *Contemporary Authors* will be retained in that volume when it is revised, whether the subjects of the sketches are active or inactive, living or dead.

Can any volumes of *Contemporary Authors* safely be discarded because they are obsolete? Following the publication of Revised Volumes 33-36 (scheduled for late 1978), users who have all the revised volumes published to that time *and* the two *Permanent Series* volumes will be able to discard the superseded volumes. Thereafter, an unrevised volume may be discarded each time a corresponding revised volume is published.

An unusual number of biographical publications have been appearing recently, and the question is now often asked whether a charge is made for listings in such publications. Do authors listed in *Contemporary Authors* make any payment or incur any other obligation for their listings? Some publishers charge for listings or require purchase of a book by biographees. There is, however, absolutely no charge or obligation of any kind attached to being included in *CA*. Copies of the volumes in which their sketches appear are offered at courtesy discounts to persons listed, but less than five percent of the biographees purchase copies.

Cumulative Index Should Always Be Consulted

Since *CA* is a multi-volume series, the cumulative index published in alternate new volumes of *CA* will continue to be the user's guide to the location of an individual author's listing. Authors not included in this revision will be indicated in the cumulative index as having appeared in specific original volumes of *CA* (for the benefit of those who do not hold *Permanent Series* volumes), *and* as having their finally revised sketches listed in a specific *Permanent Series* volume.

As always, suggestions from users concerning revision or any other aspect of *CA* will be welcomed.

CONTEMPORARY AUTHORS

† Research has yielded new information which has been added to the sketch, but the author has not personally verified the entry in this edition.

† † Research has yielded no new information, but the author has not personally verified the entry in this edition.

AARONSON, Bernard S(eymour) 1924-

PERSONAL: Born May 8, 1924, in Bronx, N.Y.; son of Zachary and Nettie (Brodsky) Aaronson; married Patricia Anderson, December 29, 1954. *Education:* Attended Brooklyn College (now Brooklyn College of the City University of New York), 1941-42, and Niagara University, 1943-44; University of Illinois, B.A., 1947; University of Minnesota, Ph.D., 1955. *Home:* 56 Merritt Dr., Trenton, N.J. 08638. *Office address:* New Jersey Bureau of Research in Neurology and Psychiatry, Box 1000, Princeton, N.J. 08540.

CAREER: U.S. Veterans Administration Regional Office, St. Paul, Minn., clinical psychologist, 1949-52; New Castle State Hospital, New Castle, Ind., chief psychologist, 1955-57; Trenton State Hospital, Trenton, N.J., director of psychology department, 1957-60; New Jersey Bureau of Research in Neurology and Psychiatry, Princeton, chief of section of clinical behavior science, 1960-63, chief of section of experimental psychology, 1963—. Certified psychologist in Minnesota, 1952, and New Jersey, 1959; private practice as psychologist in New Castle, 1955-57, and Princteon, 1957—. Lecturer at Rider College, 1959-65, and at Graduate School of Education, Rutgers University, 1964. *Military service:* U.S. Army, 1943-46.

MEMBER: American Association for the Advancement of Science (fellow), American Psychological Association, American Association for Humanistic Psychology, American Society of Clinical Hypnosis (fellow; chairman of liaison committee, 1967-70), Society for Clinical and Experimental Hypnosis, International Society for Clinical and Experimental Hypnosis, Inter-American Union of Scientific Psychology, International Society for the Study of Time, International Platform Association, Eastern Psychological Association, New York Academy of Sciences, New Jersey Academy of Sciences, New Jersey Psychological Association, Mercer County Psychological Association (president, 1960-61), Sigma Xi.

WRITINGS: (Contributor) Charles T. Tart, editor, *Altered States of Consciousness,* Wiley, 1969; (editor with Humphrey Osmund, and contributor) *Psychedelics: The Uses and Implications of Hallucinogenic Drugs,* Doubleday-Anchor, 1970. Also contributor to *Man's Place in Time,* edited by Henri Yaker, Frances E. Cheek, and Osmund, Doubleday. Has made two recordings produced by Big Sur Recordings, "Hypnosis, Perception and Altered States of Consciousness," 1967, and "Tantric Chant, Poetry and Hypnosis," 1969. Contributor of more than sixty articles to scientific journals. Consulting editor, *American Journal of Clinical Hypnosis.*

AVOCATIONAL INTERESTS: Meditation, mysticism, tantric yoga, and Zen Buddhism.

* * *

ABBOUSHI, W(asif) F(ahmi) 1931-

PERSONAL: Born July 26, 1931, in Nazareth, Palestine; naturalized American citizen; son of Fahmi Sherif and Nazlah Abboushi; married Leah Marie Russell (a librarian), September 9, 1960; children: Mark Sherif, Jenine Alice. *Education:* Great Lakes College, B.A., 1956; University of Detroit, M.A., 1957; University of Cincinnati, Ph.D., 1959. *Home:* 202 Greendale Ave., Cincinnati, Ohio 45220. *Office:* Department of Political Science, University of Cincinnati, Cincinnati, Ohio 45221.

CAREER: St. Francis College, Loretto, Pa., assistant professor of comparative government, 1960-61; Highland Park Community College, Highland Park, Mich., lecturer in social science, 1961-62; Wayne State University, Detroit, Mich., assistant professor of political science, 1962-65; University of Cincinnati, Cincinnati, Ohio, 1965—, began as assistant professor, now professor of political science. Consultant to Peace Corps. *Member:* American Society of International Law, International Studies Association, Arab-American Association (member of board, 1969), Omicron Delta Kappa.

WRITINGS: Political Systems of the Middle East in the Twentieth Century, Dodd, 1970; *The Angry Arabs,* Westminster Press, 1974. Contributor of articles in Arabic and English to journals.

WORK IN PROGRESS: The Legacy of Palestine.

* * *

ABDEL-MALEK, Anouar 1924-

PERSONAL: Born October 23, 1924, in Cairo, Egypt; son of Iskandar (a lawyer and diplomat) and Alice (Zaki Ibrahim) Abdel-Malek; children: Nadia-Alice. *Education:* Attended British Institute, Cairo, 1944; Ain-Shams University, B.A. (with honors), 1954; University of Paris, Sorbonne, Doctorat de sociologie, 1964, Doctorat es lettres (1st class honors), 1969. *Politics:* National Progressive. *Religion:* Christian (Copt). *Home:* Avenue d'Italie, N. 17, Paris, France. *Office:* Centre National de la Recherche Scientifique, 54 Boulevard Raspail, 75006 Paris, France.

CAREER: Worked in accounts department of National Bank of Egypt, 1940-42, legal department of Credit Foncier Egyptien, 1942-46, Cairo, Egypt; journalist, *Le Journal d'-Egypte,* 1950-52, *Rose el-Youssef,* 1956-57, and *Al-Massa,* 1957-59, acting editor, *Actualite,* 1952-54, Cairo; Lycee Francais, Cairo, professor of philosophy, 1956-57; Centre National de la Recherche Scientifique (C.N.R.S.; division of sociology-demography), Paris, France, attache, 1960-64, charge, 1964-70, research professor, 1971—. Writer, 1944—; lecturer at l'Ecole Pratique des Hautes Etudes, Sorbonne, Paris, 1966—; visiting professor, Ain Shams University, Cairo; lecturer at major universities in Europe, Africa, and Latin America.

MEMBER: International Sociological Association (vice-president), Association Internationale des Sociologues de Langue Francaise, Association Internationale de Science Politique, Institut des Civilisations Differentes, Societe Francaise de Philosophie, Societe Francaise de Sociologie (member of bureau), Association Francaise de Science Politique, Egyptian Historical Association, Egyptian Philosophical Association.

WRITINGS: (Translator to the Arabic) John Lewis, *Madkhal ila'l-falsafah* (title means "Introduction to Philosophy"), Al-Dar al-Micriyyah li'l-Koutoub (Cairo), 1957; *Maktabat al-afkar* (introduction to 1st volume of "Bibliotheque des Idees" collection), Al-Dar al-Micriyyah li'l-Koutoub, 1959; *Peuples d'Afrique,* Editions du Seuil (Paris), 1962, translation by Charles Lam Markmann published as *Egypt, Military Society: The Army Regime, the Left, and Social Change Under Nasser,* Random House, 1968; (compiler, translator, and editor) *Anthologie de la literature arabe contemporaineii: Les Essais,* Editions du Seuil, 1964; *Dirasat fi al-thaqafah al-wataniyah* (title means "Studies on National Culture"), Dar al-Tali'ah (Beirut), 1967; *Ideologie et renaissance national: L'Egypte moderne,* Editions Anthropos (Paris), 1969, also issued in Paris as doctoral thesis under title *La Formation de l'ideologie dans la renaissance nationale de l'Egypte,* 1969; *La Pensee politique arab contemporaine,* Le Seuil, 1970; (editor with A. A. Belal and H. Hanafi) *La Renaissance du monde arabe,* Duculo (Brussels), 1971; (editor) *Sociologie de l'imperialisme,* Anthropos, 1971; (editor) *L'Armee et nation dans les trois continents,* S.N.E.D. (Algiers), 1975; *La Dialectique sociale,* Le Seuil, 1972; *Specifite et theorie sociale,* Anthropos, 1976.

Contributor: *Kueltuer emperyalizmi,* Atac Kitabevi (Istanbul), 1967; *Actes du Colloque Robespierre,* Societe des Etudes Robespierristes (Paris), 1967. Also author of *Al-Fikr al-Arabi Li marakat al-Nahdah,* 1974, and of several radio scripts for programs on Balzac, Lorca, Moliere's "Don Juan," Jules Verne, contemporary Japanese tales, Chekov, Brecht, and others. Contributor of articles and essays to *Tiers Monde, Diogene, La Quinzaine litteraire, Cahiers Internationaux de Sociologie, Le Monde, Quaderni Critica Marxists, Nuovi Argomenti, New Left Review* (London), *Koelner Zeitschrift fuer Soziologie und Sozialpsychologie, Civilisations* (Brussels), *Combate* (Costa Rica), *Al-Hadaf, Dirassat Arabiyyah,* and numerous other periodicals in Paris, Rome, London, and Cairo. Film critic for *Al-Izaa,* 1958-59; Egyptian correspondent for *Horizons* Magazine.

WORK IN PROGRESS: Editing a series of volumes which

present the collective research activities of his scientific divisions; *L'Avenir de l'Egypte; Al-Scrabyiyah al-Hadariyah; The New World Order.*

SIDELIGHTS: Anouar Abdel-Malek told *CA* he was "born and educated in an old-established Cairo family of intellectuals, senior public servants and businessmen. Father took a leading part in the Egyptian Revolution of 1919-23, in the militant activist organization of the Wafd party, and in the trade-union movement." Abdel-Malek himself "took a central part in the formation and orientation of the Marxist movement in Egypt (1940-59), mainly in framing the 'national Marxist' school of thought and action which distinguishes the Egyptian Left ... today." Since he left Cairo in 1959 "because of the continued repression," he has been involved with "analysis of Egypt's national renaissance in the 19th century, and under Nasserism, and the prospects of evolution of society and ideology through a national and social revolution towards a genuine renaissance ... [and with] the criticism and re-structuration of the conceptual framework of Western-centered sociology, as from the dialectics of civilizations." This last activity he calls "the very center of my life-work, when life-experience and social philosophy unite."

BIOGRAPHICAL/CRITICAL SOURCES: Les Temps modernes (Paris), April, 1963; *Times Literary Supplement,* July 31, 1969; *Le Pensee,* autumn, 1971; *Revolution Africaine,* August, 1973.

* * *

ABDUL, Raoul 1929-

PERSONAL: Born November 7, 1929, in Cleveland, Ohio; son of Hamid and Beatrice (Shreve) Abdul. *Education:* Vienna Academy of Music, Diploma, 1962; additional study at Harvard University, summer, 1966, New School for Social Research, and at music schools, including Cleveland Institute of Music, New York College of Music, and Mannes College of Music; vocal training with Alexander Kipnis, Lola Hayes, Yves Tinayre, Adolf Vogel, and others. *Home and office:* 360 West 22nd St., New York, N.Y. 10011.

CAREER: Concert and opera singer; organizer of Coffee Concerts, Harlem's first subscription series of chamber music concerts, 1958-59, and director, 1958-63; sang abroad in Marlboro Music Festival, 1956, and Vienna Music Festival, 1962; made his New York debut with John Wustman in a recital of German lieder at Carnegie Hall, 1967; has appeared in other concerts on tours in United States, Canada, Austria, Netherlands, Hungary, and Germany; currently music critic, *New York Amsterdam News.* Had operatic roles in first American stage productions of Karl Orff's "Die Kluge" and Darius Milhaud's "Les Malheures d'Orphee" (title role); also appeared in seventeen performances of "Cosi fan Tutte" and twelve performances of "Amahl and the Night Visitors" at Cleveland's Karamu Theatre. At one time was editorial assistant to Langston Hughes. Member of various committees, Friends of Symphony of the New World.

WRITINGS—All published by Dodd: (Editor with Alan Lomax) *3000 Years of Black Poetry,* 1970; (editor) *The Magic of Black Poetry,* 1972; *Famous Black Entertainers of Today,* 1974; *Blacks in Classical Music,* 1977. Articles included in *Anthology of the American Negro in the Theatre* and *The Negro in Music and Art.* Writer of column, "The Cultural Scene," for Associated Negro Press. Cultural editor, *New York Age.*

WORK IN PROGRESS: Writing a book about great Black

performers in the theatre; researching a biography of Langston Hughes.

BIOGRAPHICAL/CRITICAL SOURCES: New York Times, September 27, 1970; *Publishers Weekly,* October 2, 1972; *Boston Globe,* October 22, 1972; *Examiner,* November 5, 1972; *Christian Science Monitor,* November 8, 1972; *Record,* June 6, 1974.†

* * *

ABRAM, H(arry) S(hore)   1931-1977

PERSONAL: Born March 25, 1931, in Roanoke, Va.; married Mary Combs (a medical doctor). *Education:* Northwestern University, B.S., 1952; University of Virginia, M.D., 1956; Washington Psychoanalytic Institute, Washington, D.C., additional study, 1961-68. *Home:* 2516 Fairfax Ave., Nashville, Tenn. 37212. *Office:* School of Medicine, Vanderbilt University, Nashville, Tenn. 37232.

CAREER: University of Virginia Hospital, Charlottesville, intern, 1956-57, assistant resident, 1957-58, chief resident in psychiatry, 1958-59; Harvard Medical School and Massachusetts General Hospital, Boston, clinical and research fellow in psychiatry, 1959-61; University of Virginia, School of Medicine, Charlottesville, instructor, 1961-64, assistant professor, 1964-67, associate professor of psychiatry, 1967-70; Vanderbilt University, School of Medicine, Nashville, Tenn., professor of psychiatry, 1970-77. *Member:* American Medical Association, American Psychiatric Association (fellow), American Psychosomatic Society, American Psychoanalytic Association, American Association for the Advancement of Science, Tennessee Medical Association, Washington Psychoanalytic Society, Nashville Academy of Medicine.

WRITINGS: (Editor) *Psychological Aspects of Surgery,* Little, Brown, 1967; (editor) *Psychological Aspects of Stress,* C. C Thomas, 1970; (contributor) C. A. Frazier, editor, *Should Doctors Play God,* Broadman, 1971; *Basic Psychiatry for the Primary Care Physician,* Little, Brown, 1976. Contributor of more than thirty articles and twenty reviews to medical journals. Abstracts editor, *Psychosomatic Medicine,* beginning 1969.†

(Died September 3, 1977)

* * *

ACCOLA, Louis W(ayne)   1937-

PERSONAL: Born September 16, 1937; married Kathleen Mae McMullen, July 3, 1976; children: (previous marriage) Terence Steven, Hans Louis. *Education:* Luther College, Decorah, Iowa, B.A., 1959; Luther Theological Seminary, St. Paul, B.D. (with highest honors), 1964; Princeton Theological Seminary, Th.M. (with honors), 1965. *Home:* 8100 32nd Ave. N., Minneapolis, Minn. 55427. *Office:* Parish Development, American Lutheran Church, 422 South Fifth St., Minneapolis, Minn. 55415.

CAREER: Ordained a Lutheran minister, 1965; Our Savior's Lutheran Church, Milwaukee, Wis., associate pastor, 1965-66, pastor, 1966-73; American Lutheran Church, Minneapolis, Minn., director of Parish Development, 1973—. Instructor for two years in Rhodesia; frequent lecturer on comparative religions, contemporary theology, and church renewal movement; guest lecturer, Alverno College, Marquette University. Board member of Milwaukee Conference Council; adult education chairman, Metropolitan Lutheran Council. *Member:* Common Cause, Center for the Study of Democratic Institutions.

WRITINGS: Personal Faith for Human Crises, Augsburg, 1970; *Life in Mission,* Augsburg, 1977.

Also writer of three adult education courses: "Prayer in the Life of Modern Man," "Living in the Spirit," and "What Mean These Words." Contributor to *Lutheran Standard, Event,* and *Mission '78 Youth Resource Manual.*

WORK IN PROGRESS: Research on the impact of science and technology upon faith-life, the concept of self, meaning of life and death, and the impact of science and technology on family-life; *A Global-Meal for a Global Family,* reflections on the Lord's Supper as a celebration of peace and oneness, from an ecumenical perspective.

* * *

ACKERMAN, Carl W.   1890-1970

January 16, 1890—October 9, 1970; American journalist, educator, and defender of freedom of the press. Obituaries: *New York Times,* October 10, 1970; *Washington Post,* October 10, 1970; *Newsweek,* October 19, 1970; *Time,* October 19, 1970; *Current Biography,* 1970.

* * *

ADAMS, Richard N(ewbold)   1924-
(Stokes Newbold)

PERSONAL: Born August 4, 1924, in Ann Arbor, Mich.; son of Randolph Greenfield (a historian) and Helen Constance (Spiller) Adams; married Betty Virginia Hannstein (a teacher and writer), November 4, 1951; children: Walter Randolph, Tani Marilena, Gina Constance. *Education:* University of Michigan, A.B., 1947; Yale University, M.A., 1949, Ph.D., 1951. *Home:* 1506 Westlake Dr., Austin, Tex. 78746. *Office:* Department of Anthropology, University of Texas, Austin, Tex. 78712.

CAREER: Ethnological research and consultation in Guatemala and other Central American countries for Institute of Social Anthropology, Smithsonian Institution, U.S. Department of State, World Health Organization, and U.S. Operations Mission Educational Program; Michigan State University, East Lansing, professor of sociology and anthropology, 1956-62, researcher for Institute of Overseas Research in Peru, Bolivia, and Chile, 1958; University of California, Berkeley, visiting professor of anthropology, 1960-61; University of Texas at Austin, assistant director of Institute of Latin American Studies, 1962-67, professor of anthropology and chairman of department, 1962—. Consultant, Institute of Nutrition of Central America and Panama, Peace Corps, Ford Foundation, Agency for International Development. Board member and president of Texas Ballet Concerto, Inc., 1966-67; volunteer fireman, Westlake Hills, Tex. *Military service:* U.S. Naval Reserve, 1943-46; became lieutenant.

MEMBER: American Anthropological Association (fellow; member of executive board, 1970-72; president, 1976-77), American Association for the Advancement of Science (fellow; vice-president and chairman of Section "H," 1972 and 1973), American Sociological Society, American Ethnological Society, Society for Applied Anthropology (regional vice-president, 1958; executive committee member, 1959-61; vice-president, 1961-62; president, 1962-63), Latin American Studies Association (vice-president, 1967; president, 1968), Sigma Xi (fellow).

WRITINGS: The Home Made Poems, [London], 1934; *Un Analisis de las enfermedades y sus curaciones en una poblacion indigena de Guatemala* (written but not published in

English), translation by Amalia G. de Ramirez, Instituto de Nutricion de Centro America y Panama, 1951, published as *Un Analisis de las creencias y practicas medicas en un pueblo indigena de Guatemala,* Ministerio de Educacion Publica (Guatemala), 1952; *Encuesta sobre la cultura de los ladinos en Guatemala,* translation by Joaquin Noval, Ministerio de Educacion Publica, 1956, 2nd edition, 1964; *Cultural Surveys of Panama-Nicaragua-Guatemala-El Salvador-Honduras,* Pan American Sanitary Bureau, 1957; *A Community in the Andes: Problems and Progress in Muquiyauyo,* University of Washington Press for American Ethnological Society, 1959.

(With Charles C. Cumberland) *United States University Cooperation in Latin America: A Study Based on Selected Programs in Bolivia, Chile, Peru, and Mexico,* Institute of Research on Overseas Programs, Michigan State University, 1960; (with others) *Social Change in Latin America Today: Its Implications for United States Policy,* introduction by Lyman Bryson, Harper for Council on Foreign Relations, 1960, published as *Social Change in Latin America Today,* Vintage Books, 1960; *Introduccion a la antropologia aplicada* (written but not published in English), translation and prologue by Jorge Skinner Klee, Ministerio de Educacion Publica, 1964; *Migraciones internas en Guatemala: Expansion agraria de los indigenas kekchies hacia El Peten* (written but not published in English), translation by Julio Vielman, Ministerio de Educacion Publica, 1965; *The Second Sowing: Power and Secondary Development in Latin America,* Chandler Publishing, 1967.

Crucifixion by Power: Essays on Guatemalan National Social Structure, 1944-1966, University of Texas Press, 1970; *Energy and Structure,* University of Texas Press, 1975; *Poder y control: la red de la expansion humana,* Mexico-CIS-INAN, 1977.

University of Texas Offprint series, published by the Institute of Latin American Studies: *The Community in Latin America: A Changing Myth* (originally published in *Centennial Review,* summer, 1962), 1963; *Rural Labor in Latin America* (originally published in *Continuity and Change in Latin America,* edited by John J. Johnson, Stanford University Press, 1964), 1964; *Politics and Social Anthropology in Spanish America* (originally published in *Human Organization,* spring, 1964), 1964; *The Pattern of Development in Latin America* [and] *Desarrollo acelerado* (the former originally published in *Annals* of the American Academy of Political and Social Science, July, 1965; the latter originally published as "Sudden Development: Growth Patterns in Latin America" in *Americas,* August, 1965), 1965; *Ethics and the Social Anthropologist in Latin America* (originally published in *American Behavioral Scientist,* June, 1967), 1967; *Nationalization* (originally published in *Handbook of Middle American Indians,* Volume VI, edited by Robert Wauchope, University of Texas Press, 1967), 1967; *Power and Power Domains* (originally published in *America Latina,* April-June, 1966), 1967; *Political Power and Social Structures* (originally published in *The Politics of Conformity in Latin America,* edited by Claudio Veliz, Oxford University Press, 1967), 1968.

Editor or compiler: *Political Changes in Guatemalan Indian Communities: A Symposium,* edited by Margaret W. Harrison and Robert Wauchope, Middle American Research Institute, Tulane University, 1957; (with Jack J. Preiss) *Human Organization Research: Field Relations and Techniques,* Dorsey for the Society for Applied Anthropology, 1960; (and author of introduction) *Responsibilities of the Foreign Scholar to the Local Scholarly Community,* Council

on Educational Cooperation with Latin American Education and World Affairs, and Latin American Studies Association, 1961; (and author of introduction and notes, with Dwight B. Heath) *Contemporary Cultures and Societies of Latin America: A Reader in the Social Anthropology of Middle and South America and the Caribbean,* Random House, 1965; (with Raymond Fogelson and contributor) *The Anthropology of Power,* Academic Press, 1977.

Contributor: Benjamin D. Paul and W. B. Miller, editors, *Health, Culture and Community,* Russell Sage, 1955; Jorge Luis Arriola, editor, *Cultura indigena de Guatemala: Ensayos de antropologia social,* Ministerio de Educacion Publica, 1956; (and author of introduction) *Integracion social en Guatemala,* Seminario de Integracion Social Guatemalteca, Publicacion 3, [Guatemala], 1956; Frederick B. Pike, editor, *Freedom and Reform in Latin America,* University of Notre Dame Press, 1959.

Gertrude E. Dole and Robert L. Carneiro, editors, *Essays in the Science of Culture in Honor of Leslie A. White,* Crowell, 1960; *Social Change in Latin America Today,* Harper for Council on Foreign Relations, 1960; Lago Gladston, editor, *Human Nutrition, Historic and Scientific,* Institute of Social and Historical Medicine, 1960; David G. Mandelbaum, Gabriel W. Lasker, and Ethel Albert, editors, *The Teaching of Anthropology,* American Anthropological Association, 1963; Donald M. Valdes and Dwight G. Dean, editors, *Sociology in Use,* Macmillan, 1965; Wauchope, editor, *Handbook of Middle American Indians,* Volume VI, University of Texas Press, 1967; Claudio Veliz, editor, *Latin America and the Caribbean: A Handbook,* Anthony Blond, 1968; David L. Sills, editor, *International Encyclopedia of the Social Sciences,* Macmillan, 1968; *Survey of the Alliance for Progress* (hearings before Subcommittee on American Republics Affairs of the Committee on Foreign Relations), U.S. Senate, Ninetieth Congress, Second Session, 1969.

Social Anthropology of Latin America: Essays in Honor of Ralph Leon Beals, Latin American Studies Center, University of California, Los Angeles, 1970; Stanley Ross, editor, *Latin America in Transition: Problems in Training and Research,* State University of New York Press, 1970; *Contemporary Cultures and Societies of Latin America,* Random House, 1970; B. M. DuToit and Helen I. Safa, editors, *Migration and Urbanization: Models and Adaptive Strategies,* Mouton & Co., 1975; Joseph Spielberg and Scott Whiteford, editors, *Forging Nations,* Michigan State University Press, 1976.

Contributor under pseudonym, Stokes Newbold, of an article to *Economic Development and Cultural Change.* Contributor of articles to numerous anthropology and sociology journals, including *American Anthropologist, Social Forces, Antropologia e Historia de Guatemala, Boletin de la Oficina Sanitaria Panamericana, Nutrition Reviews, Politica, Ethnohistory, Current Anthropology, Revista de Indias, Foro Internacional, Reviews in Anthropology,* and *Southwestern Journal of Anthropology.*

* * *

ADSHEAD, Gladys L(ucy) 1896-

PERSONAL: Born April 25, 1896, in Manchester, England; daughter of James Frederick and Bertha Wilson (Groome) Adshead. *Education:* Froebel Educational Institute, London.

CAREER: Teacher and headmistress in various private schools in England, and in Maryland, Massachusetts, and

Illinois, 1916-59; storyteller in libraries and for independent associations, 1921-27; trainer of apprentice teachers, 1927-59. Chairman, Advisory Board Finance, Mason, N.H., for five years. *Member:* Royal Society of Teachers (charter member), Historical Society (Hancock, N.H.).

WRITINGS—All juveniles; all published by Oxford University Press, except as indicated: *Brownies—Hush!,* 1938, reprinted, Walck, 1966; *Something Surprising,* 1939; *Casco, the Little Seal,* 1943; *What Miranda Knew,* 1944; (with George H. Shapiro) *Seventeen to Sing* (children's songs; music by Shapiro, lyrics by Adshead), 1946; (compiler with Annis Duff) *An Inheritance of Poetry,* Houghton, 1948; *Brownies—It's Christmas!,* 1955.

All published by Walck: *Brownies—Hurry!,* 1959; *Smallest Brownie's Fearful Adventure,* 1961; *Brownies, They're Moving,* 1970; *Where Is Smallest Brownie?,* 1971; *Smallest Brownie and the Flying Squirrel,* 1972.

WORK IN PROGRESS: Retelling of tales from Don Quixote.

SIDELIGHTS: Gladys Adshead told *CA:* "My English father read to me as a child and hoped I would be an author of books for children. . . . In my books, especially the Brownie books, I am inside a small child's skin and identify the characters with children I have known, who in turn identify with these little folk, their adventures, interest in one another and their cooperation when one of them is in trouble. My honors have been the recognition by retirement citations for my work in the field of education and as a writer for children, and a poem to me written by three 9-year-olds, which is the nicest tribute of all."

AVOCATIONAL INTERESTS: Natural science, photography, travel, classical music, theatre, symphonic concerts, walking, snow-shoeing, gardening.†

* * *

AEBY, Jacquelyn
(Jocelyn Carew, Vanessa Gray)

PERSONAL: Born in South Bend, Ind.; daughter of Ross (an educator) and Gladys (Kline) Aeby. *Education:* University of Chicago, B.A. *Religion:* Presbyterian. *Residence:* Howe, Ind.

CAREER: Has held secretarial positions in investment banking and real estate management. *Member:* Authors Guild, P.E.O. Sisterhood.

WRITINGS—All published by Dell, except as indicated: *Romance of the Turquoise Cat,* Avalon, 1969; *Wait for the Dawn,* Avalon, 1970; *Laurie's Legacy,* Avalon, 1971; *No Gentle Love,* Avalon, 1972; *The Trillium Cup,* Avalon, 1972; *Linnet's Folly,* 1973; *The Elusive Clue,* 1974; *Flight of Fancy,* Avalon, 1975; *Serena,* 1975; *Counterfeit Love,* 1975; *Diary of Danger,* 1975; *Companion to Danger,* Dell, 1975; *Sign of the Blue Dragon,* 1976; *Never Look Back,* 1976; *Falconer's Hall,* 1976; *Cottage on Catherina Cay,* 1976; (under pseudonym Jocelyn Carew) *The Golden Sovereigns,* Avon, 1976; (under pseudonym Vanessa Gray) *The Masked Heiress,* New American Library, 1977; *The Storm,* in press.

* * *

AGETON, Arthur Ainsley 1900-1971

October 25, 1900—April 23, 1971; American admiral, diplomat, and author. Obituaries: *New York Times,* April 30, 1971. (See index for *CA* sketch)

AGNIEL, Lucien D. 1919-

PERSONAL: Surname is pronounced An-*yell;* born April 23, 1919; son of Lucien A. (a salesman) and Marie (Duhring) Agniel; married Elizabeth Harms (an interior decorator), November 21, 1942 (died, 1973); married Madelyn Penn; children: (first marriage) Mrs. Laurent Sauerwein, Lucien D., Jr., Elizabeth W., Stephanie T. *Education:* Student at Missouri Valley College, 1935-36, and Central Missouri State College (now Central Missouri State University), 1937-38. *Politics:* Democrat. *Religion:* Presbyterian. *Home:* 112 Riverview Dr., Elkins, W.Va. 26241.

CAREER: Chattanooga Evening Times, Chattanooga, Tenn., tellegraph editor, 1940-41; U.S. Government, information officer for agencies in Berlin, Frankfurt, Paris, and Munich, 1946-53; *Charlotte News,* Charlotte, N.C., city editor, 1953-54; information officer, U.S. Information Agency, 1954-60; program manager, Radio Free Europe, 1961-64; *U.S. News & World Report,* Washington, D.C., associate editor, 1964-72; Rundfunk Im Amerikanischen Sektor Berlins (Radio in American Sector; RIAS), West Berlin, Germany, deputy director, 1973-77. *Military service:* U.S. Army, 1942-45; became first lieutenant; received Bronze Star, Purple Heart with oak-leaf cluster, and Croix de Guerre. *Member:* Washington Athletic Club.

WRITINGS: Code Name: Icy, Paperback Library, 1970; *Pressure Point,* Paperback Library, 1970; (with others) *Zeppelin* (novelization of Warner Brothers film of the same name), Paperback Library, 1971; *The Late Affair Has Almost Broke My Heart,* Chatham Press, 1972; *Rebels Victorious,* Mockingbird Books, 1975; "Father Ruffian" (three-act play), produced in Berlin, 1976. Writer of documentary films, "Men and Boats" and "Save Our Children," both 1958.

WORK IN PROGRESS: A novel for Viking based on "Father Ruffian."

* * *

AINSWORTH, Katherine 1908-

PERSONAL: Born November 15, 1908, in Los Angeles, Calif.; daughter of William Alson (inspector for a telephone company) and Alice (O'Neill) Lake; married Edward Maddin Ainsworth, June, 1931 (died June 15, 1968); children: Sheila Beth (Mrs. Robert S. Herron), Cynthia Kate (Mrs. Jerome Lengvel). *Education:* University of California, Los Angeles, B.A., 1930; University of Southern California, Library Certificate, 1932, State Teaching Credential, 1946. *Politics:* Republican. *Religion:* Protestant.

CAREER: Los Angeles (Calif.) Public Library, branch children's librarian, 1928-35; Los Angeles (Calif.) public schools, librarian, 1949-51; Monrovia (Calif.) Public Library, head librarian, 1953-67. Co-owner and developer, Palm Island Estates, Mecca, Calif. Founder and director, Monrovia Art Festival Association. *Member:* Quota Club, Delta Kappa Gamma (honorary member), North Shore Yacht Club.

WRITINGS: (With husband, Edward M. Ainsworth) *In the Shade of the Juniper Tree: A Life of Fray Junipero Serra,* Doubleday, 1970; *The McCallum Saga: The Story of the Founding of Palm Springs,* Palm Springs Desert Museum, 1973. Regular reviewer for *Los Angeles Times* and *Monrovia News Post.*

WORK IN PROGRESS: An adventure novel with Mexican setting; research for a novel on the period of the U.S.-Mexican War.

AVOCATIONAL INTERESTS: Western American art and American Indians.†

* * *

ALBERT, Harold A.

PERSONAL: Born in London, England. *Education:* Privately educated. *Home:* Milland, Liphook, Hants, England.

CAREER: Biographer, historian, and free-lance writer; with Ministry of Information, 1940-45; managing director, Harold Albert Ltd.

WRITINGS: The Queen and the Arts, W. H. Allen, 1963; *Queen Victoria's Sister: The Life and Letters of Princess Feodora,* R. Hale, 1967.

WORK IN PROGRESS: Further writing on British royal historical topics.

BIOGRAPHICAL/CRITICAL SOURCES: Times Literary Supplement, March 9, 1967.

* * *

ALBERTS, David Stephen 1942-

PERSONAL: Born December 4, 1942, in New York, N.Y.; son of Jack J. (an accountant) and Mirian (Pillisdorf) Alberts; married Mimi Ginsberg (a novelist and college instructor), January 29, 1965. *Education:* City College (now City College of the City University of New York), New York, N.Y., B.B.A., 1964; University of Pennsylvania, M.S., 1968, Ph.D., 1969. *Residence:* New York, N.Y.

CAREER: University of Pennsylvania, Philadelphia, management research analyst, 1965-67; New York University, New York City, assistant professor of operations research and director of computer science program, School of Commerce, 1968-71; special assistant to commander, New York Police Department, New York City, 1971—. *Member:* Institute of Management Sciences, American Institute of Planners, American Institute of Decision Sciences.

WRITINGS: A Plan for Measuring the Performance of Social Programs, Praeger, 1970; *Pantomime: Elements and Exercises,* Regents Publishing, 1971. Contributor to *Journal of Environmental Systems* and other journals.

WORK IN PROGRESS: Sun, Life, Environment; research into evaluation of social action, welfare, education, prisons, and urban planning.

AVOCATIONAL INTERESTS: Architecture, planning.†

* * *

ALEXANDER, Edwin P. 1905-

PERSONAL: Born August 14, 1905, in Belleville, N.J.; son of Alexander S. (an artist and designer) and Zenida (Jansen) Alexander; married Margaret Ploof, 1964. *Education:* Attended Columbia University, three years. *Home:* Upper Darby Rd., Box 333, Yardley, Pa. 19067.

CAREER: Propietor of his own business, 1930—, building scale models of original railroads for museums, except for a period during World War II when he was with the engineering department of the Pennsylvania Railroad. Seven museums including the Smithsonian Institution have his models on display, and motion picture producers, publishers, and museums use data and pictures from his extensive railroad research collection. *Member:* Philadelphia Art Alliance.

WRITINGS: Model Railroads, Norton, 1939; *Iron Horses,* Norton, 1942; *Pictorial History of the Pennsylvania Rail-*

road, Norton, 1947; *American Locomotives,* Norton, 1950; *Collector's Book of the Locomotive,* C. N. Potter, 1969; *Down at the Depot: American Railroad Stations from 1831 to 1920,* C. N. Potter, 1970; *On the Main Line: Pennsylvania Railroad in the Nineteenth Century,* C. N. Potter, 1971; *Civil War Railroads and Models,* C. N. Potter, 1977. Contributor to magazines.

WORK IN PROGRESS: Three books, *Pennsylvania (R.R.) Philadelphia, The General* (about a famous Civil War engine) for Bramhall House, and *United Railroads of New Jersey.*

SIDELIGHTS: C.B.B. Penrose of the *Pennsylvania Magazine of History and Biography* says of *On the Main Line: The Pennsylvania Railroad in the Nineteenth Century:* "For both the historian and the railroad enthusiast this is a first-rate book. For the Pennsylvania Railroad fan, it is a necessity." Another reviewer, Edison H. Thomas, comments, "This volume, tagged 'another one for Maggie,' takes you along the main line of the Pennsylvania Railroad, division by division, on one of the best trips to yesterday that we have ever enjoyed."

BIOGRAPHICAL/CRITICAL SOURCES: News (Wilmington, Del.), August 9, 1971; *L & N Magazine,* December, 1971; *Pennsylvania Magazine of History and Biography,* January, 1972; *Locomotive Engineer,* April 9, 1972.

* * *

ALFVEN, Hannes O(lof) G(oesta) 1908-
(Olof Johannesson)

PERSONAL: Surname is pronounced Al-vein; born May 30, 1908, in Norrkoeping, Sweden; son of Johannes (a physician) and Anna-Clara (a physician; maiden name, Romanus) Alfven; married Kerstin Erikson (a teacher of social science), June 18, 1935; children: Cecilia, Inger, Goesta, Reidun, Berenike. *Education:* University of Uppsala, Ph.D., 1934. *Home:* Lillaengsvaegen 3 183 64, Viggbyholm Taeby, Sweden; and 8110 El Paseo Grande, Apt. 403, La Jolla, Calif. 92037. *Office:* Department of Physics, University of California, San Diego, La Jolla, Calif. 92037.

CAREER: Royal Institute of Technology, Stockholm, Sweden, professor of physics, 1940-73; University of California, San Diego, La Jolla, professor of physics, 1967—. Member of Swedish Atomic Energy Commission, board of directors of Atomic Energy Company, and Natural Science Research Council, 1946-67. *Member:* Swedish Royal Academy of Sciences, Akademia Nauk (Moscow), U.S. National Academy of Sciences, and ten other academies. *Awards, honors:* Nobel Prize in Physics, 1970; Franklin Medal and Lomonosov Medal, both 1971.

WRITINGS: (With others) *Theory and Applications of Trochotrons,* Elanders, 1948; *Atomer och maenniskor* (addresses, essays, and lectures on science), Kooperativa Foerbundets Bokfoerlag, 1950, 2nd edition published as *Atomen maenniskan universum,* Aldus/Bonniers, 1964; *Cosmical Electrodynamics,* Clarendon Press, 1950, 2nd edition (with Carl-Gunne Faelthammar), 1963; *On the Origin of the Solar System,* Clarendon Press, 1954; *Magnetic Storms and Aurorae* (lecture), Institute for Fluid Dynamics and Applied Mathematics, University of Maryland, 1954; *Lectures on Magnetohydrodynamics and Cosmic Rays,* Tata Institute of Fundamental Research (Bombay), 1958; (with others) *Max-Planck Festschrift,* Deutscher Verlag der Wissenschaften, 1959; *Fisica del plasma: Esperimenti e tecniche* (report on course Alfven directed at Enrico Fermi Centre for Nuclear Studies), Zanichelli, 1960; (with others) *On the Oscillation of Electrons in Hyperbolic Magnetic Fields and Its Application to Microwave Generation,* Elanders, 1960; (with others) Ernst Aake Brunberg, editor, *Rymdforskning* (addresses, essays, and lectures on astronautics), Natur & Kultur, 1963; *Worlds-Antiworlds: Antimatter in Cosmology,* W. H. Freeman, 1966; (under pseudonym Olof Johannesson) *Sagan om den stora datamaskinen* (novel), Bonnier, 1966, translation by Naomi Wallford published as *The Tale of the Big Computer,* Coward, 1968 (translation published in England as *The Great Computer: A Vision,* Gollancz, 1968); *Atom, Man and the Universe,* W. H. Freeman, 1966; (with husband, Kerstin Alfven) *Living on the Third Planet,* W. H. Freeman, 1972; (with G. Arrhenius) *Structure and Evolutionary History of the Solar System,* D. Reidel, 1975. Also author with Arrhenius of *Origin of the Solar System,* 1976.

WORK IN PROGRESS: An essay on the sociological impact of science and technology.

BIOGRAPHICAL/CRITICAL SOURCES: New York Times Book Review, March 3, 1968; *Young Readers' Review,* April, 1968.

* * *

ALHAIQUE, Claudio 1913-

PERSONAL: Born August 23, 1913, in Naples, Italy; son of Aldo and Stefania (Luzzatto) Alhaique; married Maria Piovani (an art bibliographer), July 5, 1941; children: Franco. *Education:* University of Naples. *Religion:* Roman Catholic. *Home:* T. Taramelli 14, Rome, Italy. *Office:* Via Collina 27, Rome, Italy.

CAREER: National Productivity Council, Rome, Italy, manager, 1955-60; United Nations, Organization for Economic Co-operation and Development (OECD), expert in industrial development in Somalia, Brazil, Argentina, Ecuador, Costa Rica, and Portugal, 1960, 1961, 1964, 1965, 1967, 1970; Institute for Assistance to the Development of Southern Italy, Rome, manager, 1962-77; journalist. Adviser and consultant in the fields of handicraft development, industrial areas, productivity problems, and improvement of public administration services in depressed areas.

WRITINGS: Relazione sull'attivita della Compagnia nazionale arti giana nel 1950, [Rome], 1950; *L'Assistenza integrata strumento di sviluppo dell'artigianato,* E.N.A.P.I., 1963; *Italian Industry and International Technical Cooperation,* Bestetti, 1964, W. S. Heinman, 1965; *I Problemi dell'qssetto territoriale in Italia,* [Rome], 1967; *Italian Builders,* Bestetti, 1971; *Creation of an Industrial Promotion Service,* Organization for Economic Co-operation and Development, 1973.

* * *

ALLDRIDGE, James Charles 1910-

PERSONAL: Born October 16, 1910, in Calcutta, India; son of James Henry and Edith Mary (Baker) Alldridge. *Education:* St. Catherine's College, Oxford, M.A., 1937. *Home:* 2 Elmhurst, Harrowby Dr., Newcastle-under-Lyme, Staffordshire ST5 3JS, England. *Office:* Department of German, University of Keele, Keele, Staffordshire ST5 5BG, England.

CAREER: British Embassy, Office of the Cultural Attache, Bonn, Germany, universities officer and first secretary, 1952-57; The Grammar School, Long Eaton, Nottingham, England, head of German department, 1958-67; currently lecturer in German, University of Keele, Keele, Staffordshire, England. *Military service:* British Army, Royal Artillery, 1940-46; became major.

WRITINGS: (Editor and adaptor) Leo Wispler, *Wir sind durch Deutschland gefahren,* Oxford University Press, 1963; (editor and adaptor) Heinrich Rumpff, *Kommissar Hansen oeffnet sein Geheimarchiv,* Oxford University Press, 1963; (editor) Heinrich Boell, *Das Brot der fruehen Jahre,* Heinemann, 1965; (editor) Ilse Aichinger, *Selected Short Stories and Dialogue,* Pergamon, 1966; (translator and editor with Werner Rehfeld) *German Narrative Prose,* Volume III, Dufour, 1968; *Ilse Aichinger,* Dufour, 1969; (editor) Heinrich Boell, *Im Tal der donnernden Hufe,* Heinemann, 1970; (contributor) *Essays in Memory of Oswald Wolff,* O. Wolff, 1971. Also author of script "Modern German Poetry," for British Broadcasting Corp. schools broadcast, 1972. Contributor to *Mundus Artium.*

BIOGRAPHICAL/CRITICAL SOURCES: Books Abroad, winter, 1971.

* * *

ALLEN, Chris 1929-

PERSONAL: Born July 28, 1929, in Hyannis, Mass.; married Paul M. Allen (a professor of education at University of Arizona); children: Pamela, Gary. *Education:* Muskingum College, B.A., 1951; University of Arizona, M.Ed., 1958. *Home:* 529 South Downing Lane, Tucson, Ariz. 85711.

CAREER: Tucson (Ariz.) public schools, elementary teacher, 1957—.

WRITINGS: (With Edwin B. Kurtz, Jr.) *Adventures in Living Plants,* University of Arizona Press, 1965.

* * *

ALLEN, H(elena) G(ronlund)
(H. Fredericka Allen)

PERSONAL: Born in Prescott, Ariz.; daughter of Frederick J. (a mining engineer) and Helma (Larson) Gronlund; married Paul Franklin Allen (a college professor of history), February 23, 1946; children: Randall Lawrence. *Education:* University of California, Berkeley, B.A., 1942, graduate study, 1947. *Politics:* Republican. *Religion:* Christian Science. *Home:* 705 West Highland Ave., Redlands, Calif. 92373.

CAREER: U.S. Army, service club director, 1944; University of California, Berkeley, instructor in English, 1945-50; University of Redlands, Redlands, Calif., assistant professor of English, 1950-57; San Bernardino Valley College, San Bernardino, Calif., lecturer in English, 1958-66; California Baptist College, Riverside, associate professor of English, 1963-71. Young adult director, Young Women's Christian Association, San Bernardino, 1951-52. *Member:* International Platform Association.

WRITINGS: Grammar and Writing (college text), Kendall Hunt, 1962, revised as semi-programmed text, Parts I-II, W. C. Brown, 1965; *Writing Better* (college text), Kendall Hunt, 1963; *Fundamentals of English: Reading, Writing, and Grammar,* W. C. Brown, 1970. Also author of *San Bernardino County Museum,* commemorative edition, 1976. Editor, *Agreement: An Attitude of Prayer* by Virginia Stephenson, 1977. Author of radio scripts for "Woman's Forum." Contributor of more than five hundred articles, personal essays, short stories, and other items, including some under pseudonym, H. Fredericka Allen, to magazines and newspapers, including *Coronet, National Cats,* and religious and educational periodicals. West coast editor, *International House Quarterly.*

WORK IN PROGRESS: A biography of Lilioukalani,

queen of the Hawaiian islands; a nonfiction book on teaching; *College Handbook* (English).

* * *

ALLEN, Johannes 1916-

PERSONAL: Born May 16, 1916, in Copenhagen, Denmark; son of Poul and Karen (Schleisner) Allen; married Lise Luetzen, December 12, 1941. *Education:* Oestersoegades Gymnasium, graduate, 1935. *Home:* C.V.E. Knuthsvej 34, Hellerup DK-2900, Denmark. *Agent:* Kurt Michaels, Charlottenlund DK-2920, Denmark.

CAREER: Lived and studied in Paris, France, 1936-37; journalist with *Berlingske Tidende,* Copenhagen, Denmark, 1937-45, and *Politiken,* Copenhagen, 1945-49; novelist and playwright. Consultant to Danish television, 1965—. *Member:* Danish Journalists' Union, Danish Writers' Association (member of board, 1966-70), Danish Playwrights' Society, P.E.N. *Awards, honors:* Antonius Prize, Danish Society for Mental Hygiene, 1951, for the film, "Cafe Paradize."

WRITINGS—Novels, except as noted: *Det bor i os alle,* Schoenbergske, 1941; *Hinsides alle Droemme,* Schoenbergske, 1942; *Frihed, Lighed og—Louise,* Schoenbergske, 1943; *Mennesker ved en Graense* (play; first produced, 1953), Branner & Korch, 1953; *Ung Leg,* Branner & Korch, 1956, translation by Naomi Walford published as *Young Love,* Hogarth, 1958, Knopf, 1959; *I disse skoenne Tider,* Branner & Korch, 1961, translation by Keith Bradfield published as *It's a Swinging Life,* Hogarth, 1966; *Det aerede Medlem,* Branner & Korch, 1963; *Operation Charlie* (play; first produced, 1965), Arena, 1965; *Nu,* Branner & Korch, 1967, translation by Fred Marker published as *Tumult,* Hogarth, 1969, same translation published as *Relations,* World Publishing, 1970; *Data for din Doed,* Banner & Korch, 1970, translation by Marianne Rogers published as *Data for Death,* Hogarth, 1971; *TV-Kuppet,* Winther, 1971; *Manden med Krykkerne,* Banner & Korch, 1973.

Unpublished stage plays: "Vorherres Moerkekammer," first produced, 1947; "Harlekins Tryllestav," first produced, 1951.

Film plays: "My Name Is Petersen," 1946; "Passenger from London," 1948; "Naalen," 1950; "Cafe Paradize," 1950; (adapter) "Det sande ansigt," 1951; "Vejrhanen," 1952; "Farlig Ungdom," 1953; "Taxa K 1640 efterlyses," 1955; "Ung Leg," 1956; "Natlogi betalt," 1957; "Guld og groenne skove," 1958; "Pigen i Soegelyset," 1959; "Gymnasiepigen," 1960.

Radio plays: "Alt for Marie," 1943; "Hr. Adam smiler," 1953; "Pas paa Bruden," 1954; "For egen Domstol," 1964; "En venlig Hilsen til Gudrun," 1965.

SIDELIGHTS: Johannes Allen traveled in the United States in 1939, 1947, and 1961. *Avocational interests:* Playing chess and tennis.

BIOGRAPHICAL/CRITICAL SOURCES: Spectator, July 19, 1969.

* * *

ALLEN, Sydney (Earl), Jr. 1929-
(David Currie)

PERSONAL: Born August 17, 1929, in Fallon, Nev.; son of Sydney Earl (a farmer) and Irma Belle (Cushman) Allen; married Donna Lee (a teacher), June 25, 1950 (divorced); married Jean Neufeld, December 7, 1975; children: (first marriage) Earl, Eddy, Eric, Esther, Evan. *Education:* Loma Linda University, B.A., 1950; Andrews University, M.A., 1958; University of Nebraska, Ph.D., 1964. *Politics:* "Independent." *Home:* 627 Monterey, Redlands, Calif. 92373. *Office:* San Bernardino Valley College, San Bernardino, Calif.

CAREER: Pastor of various Seventh-day Adventist churches in Utah, California, and Nevada, 1950-57; Union College, Lincoln, Neb., 1957-64, began as instructor, became associate professor of religion; Philippine Union College, Manila, Philippines, director of graduate program in history and philosophy, 1964-70; University of California, Los Angeles, visiting scholar, 1969-70; Andrews University, Berrien Springs, Mich., General Conference of Seventh-day Adventists, department of education, textbook writer, 1970-71; Loma Linda Academy, Loma Linda, Calif., curriculum specialist, 1971-75; San Bernardino Valley College, San Bernardino, Calif., instructor, 1975—. *Member:* American Academy of Religion.

WRITINGS: Directional Signals, Southern Publishing, 1970; *One Week with a Modern Missionary,* Review & Herald, 1970; *Electric Grass Company,* Southern Publishing, 1974. Contributor of articles, poetry, and photographs to numerous periodicals, some under pseudonym, David Currie.

WORK IN PROGRESS: Classroom scripts in religion and history.

SIDELIGHTS: Sydney Allen told *CA* that he is "very much interested in a radical investigation of repressive church governments." *Avocational interests:* Fishing, photography.

* * *

ALLEN, Vernon L(esley) 1933-

PERSONAL: Born June 6, 1933, in Lineville, Ala.; son of Harvey N. (a businessman) and Hassie (Sims) Allen; married Patricia Shumake (a research associate), December 31, 1956; children: Derek R., Craig R. *Education:* University of Alabama, A.B., 1955; Tufts University, M.S., 1958; University of California, Berkeley, Ph.D., 1962. *Religion:* None. *Home:* 1106 Edgehill Dr., Madison, Wis. 53705. *Office:* Department of Psychology, University of Wisconsin, Madison, Wis. 53706.

CAREER: Stanford University, Stanford, Calif., National Institute of Mental Health research fellow, 1962-63; University of Wisconsin—Madison, assistant professor, 1963-66, associate professor, 1966-69, professor of psychology, 1969—. *Military service:* U.S. Army, 1956-58; became first lieutenant. *Member:* American Psychological Association, American Sociological Association, Society for the Psychological Study of Social Issues, Society for Experimental Social Psychology, American Association for the Advancement of Science. *Awards, honors:* Fulbright fellowship in England, 1969-70.

WRITINGS: (Editor) *Psychological Factors in Poverty,* Markham, 1970; (editor) *Children as Teachers: Theory and Research on Tutoring,* Academic Press, 1976; (editor with B. Levin) *Cognitive Learning in Children: Theories and Strategies,* Academic Press, 1976.

Contributor: Leonard Berkowitz, editor, *Advances in Experimental Social Psychology,* Volume II, Academic Press, 1965; Gardner Lindzey and Elliot Aronson, editors, *The Handbook of Social Psychology,* Volume II, Addison-Wesley, 1968. Contributor to psychology and sociology journals.

WORK IN PROGRESS: Two books; research on role theory and applied social psychology.

* * *

ALLISON, Anthony C. 1928-

PERSONAL: Born August 21, 1928, in East London, South Africa; married Helen Green (an administrator), August 11, 1952; children: Miles Clifford, Joseph Mark Clifford. *Education:* University of the Witwatersrand, B.Sc., 1947; M.Sc., 1960; Oxford University, D.Phil., 1950, B.M., B.Ch., and M.A., 1952. *Politics:* Socialist. *Religion:* Church of England. *Home:* 100 Wise Lane, London N.W.7, England.

CAREER: Oxford University, Christ Church, Oxford, England, medical tutor, 1955-57; National Institute for Medical Research, London, England, research scientist, 1957-67; Clinical Research Centre, Harrow, England, division head, 1967—. Member of Oxford University expedition to Mount Kenya, 1949, and expedition to Lapland, 1950; has done field work in anthropology in Africa, Alaska, the Near East, and the Basque country. *Member:* Royal College of Pathologists (fellow), Society for Experimental Biology, Experimental Pathology Club, and other scientific societies.

WRITINGS: (Editor) *Penguin Science Survey 1965,* two volumes, Penguin, 1966, and similarly titled volumes, 1966-69; (editor) *Population Growth,* Penguin, 1970.

WORK IN PROGRESS: Research in pathology and in methods of scientific discovery.

* * *

ALMQUIST, L. Arden 1921-

PERSONAL: Born September 4, 1921, in Nome, Alaska; son of missionary parents, Lars August (a clergyman) and Edith D. (Hall) Almquist; married Jo Ann EuVay Adell (a missionary), June 17, 1947; children: Leland Alden, Rebecca Jo Ann, Katherine Marie. *Education:* Clark University, B.A., 1944; Andover Newton Theological Seminary, B.D. (cum laude), 1945; University of Kansas, M.D., 1950.

CAREER: Clergyman of Evangelical Covenant Church of America; pastor of Congregational Church in Holden, Mass., 1942-45, and Methodist Church in Kansas City, Mo., 1948-50; Mission Evangelique de l'Ubangi, Wasolo, Congo, medical missionary, 1951-62 (also territorial health officer, Congo Republic, 1960-61); Evangelical Covenant Church of America, Chicago, Ill., executive secretary, department of world mission, 1963-70; Paul Carlson Foundation, Chicago, medical director, beginning 1970, and medical director of Medical Center, Loko, Congo, beginning 1970. *Member:* International College of Physicians, American Medical Association, Christian Medical Society, Illinois Medical Society, Kansas Medical Society, Chicago Medical Society, Royal Society of Tropical Medicine. *Awards, honors:* Distinguished Alumnus Award, University of Kansas, School of Medicine, 1963; Alumni Achievement Award, Midland Lutheran College, Fremont, Neb., 1971.

WRITINGS: Covenant Missions in Congo, Covenant Press, 1957; *Covenant Missions in Alaska,* Covenant Press, 1961; (contributor) C. P. Anderson, compiler, *There Was a Man, His Name: Paul Carlson,* Revell, 1965; *Missionary, Come Back!,* World Publishing, 1970. Contributor to religious journals and to *Journal of Practical Anthropology.*

WORK IN PROGRESS: Remembering the Forgotten Corner, for Covenant Press.

SIDELIGHTS: Paul Carlson, martyred in the Congo Rebellion, was L. Arden Almquist's successor at the Wasolo hospital; Almquist returned to the Congo to develop a hospital which bears Carlson's name.††

* * *

ALTMAN, Robert A. 1943-

PERSONAL: Born March 30, 1943, in Petersburg, Va.; son of Julian A. and Katherine (Goldschmidt) Altman; married Jane Rotman, June 13, 1965; children: Jennifer Anne, John Scott. *Education:* Harvard University, A.B., 1964; Columbia University, M.A., 1965, Ph.D., 1969. *Home:* 28 Merion Pl., Lawrenceville, N.J. 08648. *Office:* Educational Testing Service, Princeton, N.J. 08540.

CAREER: City University of New York, New York, N.Y., various administrative posts, including assistant to dean of Academic Development, 1966-70; Western Interstate Commission for Higher Education (WICHE), Boulder, Colo., director, special higher education programs, 1970-72; Educational Testing Service, Princeton, N.J., director of Graduate Record Examination Program, 1972-76, director of college and university programs, 1976—. Lecturer in higher education, Teachers College, Columbia University, 1969-70. *Member:* American Association for Higher Education, American Association for the Advancement of Science, Phi Delta Kappa. *Awards, honors:* U.S. Office of Education grant, 1968-69.

WRITINGS: The Upper Division College, Jossey-Bass, 1970; (editor with Patricia Snyder) *The Minority Student on the Campus,* Western Interstate Commission for Higher Education, 1971. Editor with Carolyn Byerly of *The Public Challenge and the Campus Response,* Western Interstate Commission for Higher Education; also editor with Quentin Jones of *Credit by Examination,* Western Commission for Higher Education. Also author of studies and research papers on education. Contributor of many articles to education journals.

* * *

ALYESHMERNI, Mansoor 1943-

PERSONAL: Surname is pronounced Al-yesh-mer-ni; born June 20, 1943, in Shiraz, Iran; son of Bashi (an exporter) and Mouness (Navie) Alyeshmerni; married Mahryam Daniels (a teacher of Spanish and Portuguese), March 6, 1971. *Education:* University of Minnesota, B.A., 1965, M.A., 1970. Summer study at University of Michigan, 1965, and University of California, Los Angeles, 1966. *Religion:* Jewish.

CAREER: University of Minnesota, Minneapolis, teaching associate in communication program, beginning 1968. *Member:* Linguistic Society of America, International Linguistic Association, American Council on the Teaching of Foreign Languages, Ivriyah Society.

WRITINGS: (With Paul Taubr) *Working with Aspects of Language,* Harcourt, 1970, 2nd edition, 1975. Editor, *B'yad Halashon Newsletter.*

WORK IN PROGRESS: Developing materials for the teaching of Hebrew.

* * *

AMADI, Elechi (Emmanuel) 1934-

PERSONAL: Born May 12, 1934, in Aluu, Nigeria; son of Daniel Wonuchuku and Enwere (Weke) Amadi; married Dorah Nwonne Ohale, December, 1957; children: Eberechi,

Chinyere, Ejimole, Nyege, Okachi, Aleru (all daughters). *Education:* University College of Ibadan (now University of Ibadan), B.Sc., 1959. *Politics:* Independent. *Religion:* Protestant. *Home:* Mbodo, Aluu c/o Isoba P.A., Port Harcourt, Nigeria. *Office address:* 7 Akomas St., Box 331, Port Harcourt, Nigeria.

CAREER: Surveyor in Enugu, Nigeria, 1959-60; science teacher in Nigerian schools, 1960-63, and headmaster, 1966-67; Government of the Rivers State of Nigeria, Ahoada and Port Harcourt, 1968—, government divisional officer and senior assistant secretary, currently an administrative officer (permanent secretary). *Military service:* Nigerian Army, 1963-66; became captain; rejoined in 1968 and served with Marine Commandos during the civil war.

WRITINGS: *The Concubine* (novel), Humanities, 1966; *The Great Ponds* (novel), Humanities, 1969; (with Obiajunwo Wali and Greensille Enyinda) *Okwukwo Eri* (hymnbook in Ikwerre), C.S.S. Printers (Port Harcourt), 1969; *Okpukpe* (prayerbook in Ikwerre), C.S.S. Printers, 1969; *Isiburu* (play; performed in Ibadan, Port Harcourt, and Aiyetoro), Heinemann, 1973; *Sunset in Biafra* (Civil War diary), Humanities, 1973; *Peppersoup* [and] *Ibadan* (plays), Onibonoje, 1977. Also author of twenty-two poems.

WORK IN PROGRESS: *Son of the Crab,* a novel; translating the entire Protestant prayerbook into Ikwerre; an expanded edition of the hymnal, *Okwukwo Eri.*

SIDELIGHTS: Amadi is "preoccupied with gods, matter, gravity, space, life's purpose (if any), and man." His novels, plays, and poems are set in his own country. He has traveled to Britain, Western Germany, and the United States. *Avocational interests:* Music, lawn tennis, table tennis, hockey.

BIOGRAPHICAL/CRITICAL SOURCES: *Spectator,* September 20, 1969; *West Africa,* March 14, 1970.

*   *   *

AMES, Norma 1920-

PERSONAL: Born August 17, 1920; daughter of Robert M. (a mail carrier) and Flora (Wiener) Knipple; married July 8, 1944 (divorced); children: Karyn. *Education:* Smith College, A.B. (magna cum laude), 1942; graduate study at Wellesley College, 1942, and at Institute of Arctic and Alpine Research, University of Colorado, 1964. *Home address:* P.O. Box 4233, Santa Fe, N.M. 87502. *Office:* New Mexico Department of Game and Fish, State Capitol, Santa Fe, N.M. 87503.

CAREER: Curtiss-Wright Aircraft, Buffalo, N.Y., time study engineer, 1942-44; free-lance advertising copywriter and artist in Buffalo, 1944, and Santa Fe, N.M., 1944-46; worked as bookkeeper, chicken farmer, and at other jobs in Santa Fe, 1946-54; New Mexico Taxpayers Association, Santa Fe, research assistant, 1954-56; New Mexico Department of Game and Fish, Santa Fe, wildlife management officer, 1956-74, assistant chief of game management and supervisor of endangered species program, 1974-76, publications director, 1976—. Member, New Mexico Environmental Education Committee; New Mexico representative to Western Regional Environmental Education Council, 1971-74; researcher and breeder of Mexican wolves, 1971—.

MEMBER: Wildlife Society (chairman of conservation education committee, Mexico-Arizona section, 1969-72), National Audubon Society, American Association for the Advancement of Science, National Wildlife Federation, American Society of Mammalogists, North American Wolf Society, Wild Canid Survival and Research Center, North American Wildlife Park Foundation, Phi Beta Kappa, Sigma Xi. *Awards, honors:* Conservation Education Award of the Wildlife Society for *New Mexico Wildlife Management.*

WRITINGS: (Editor, contributor, and illustrator) *New Mexico Wildlife Management,* New Mexico Department of Game and Fish, 1967; *My Path Belated* (novel), Avon, 1970; *Whisper in the Forest* (novel), Avon, 1971. Author of booklet series on mammals, birds, and fish, published by New Mexico Department of Game and Fish, 1960-64, and other department materials. Illustrator of *Woody Plants of New Mexico,* 1971, and *Woody Plants of the Southwest,* 1975. Contributor of articles to *New Mexico Wildlife, National Wildlife, Journal of North American Wolf Society,* and quarterly journal of American Association for the Advancement of Science; contributor of reviews to *Science Books.*

WORK IN PROGRESS: Books and articles (technical and popular) on wolves.

SIDELIGHTS: Norma Ames writes *CA:* "My acquisition of Mexican wolves in 1971 affected my whole life, including my literary output. Now, my work 'in progress' is, naturally, about wolves, but I lack time for speedy completion of such work. This, because I have added behavioral research and canid custodial chores to my continuing responsibilities....

"There is great need today for far more people to understand and cherish the natural world as it really is. The majority—who decide fates—still see the natural world as something expendable or exploitable or improvable or easily recreated by man. Direct exposure to nature is the best route to understanding and love, but most of urban America today can be exposed only through word and picture. Conveying understanding and love of nature will be a concern of my writing, whether nonfiction or fiction."

*   *   *

AMES, Ruth M(argaret) 1918-

PERSONAL: Born December 8, 1918, in New York, N.Y.; daughter of Jack and Julia (Fuerst) Ames; married Anthony Gelber (a delivery supervisor), April 8, 1938; children: Anthony, James, Mary, Catherine, Peter. *Education:* Hunter College (now Hunter College of the City University of New York), B.A., 1940; Columbia University, M.A., 1942, Ph.D., 1950. *Politics:* Independent. *Religion:* Roman Catholic. *Home:* 4440 De Reimer Ave., Bronx, N.Y. 10466. *Office:* Department of English, Queensborough Community College, Queens, N.Y.

CAREER: Taught at Hunter College (now Hunter College of the City University of New York), New York, N.Y., 1940-52; Queensborough Community College, Queens, N.Y., professor of English, 1968—. *Member:* Phi Beta Kappa.

WRITINGS: *The Fulfillment of the Scriptures: Abraham, Moses, and Piers,* Northwestern University Press, 1970; (contributor) Szarmach, editor, *The Alliterative Revival of the Fourteenth Century,* Franklin, 1977. Also contributor to a book on medieval studies.

WORK IN PROGRESS: *The Religious Spirit of Geoffrey Chaucer: An Interpretation.*

*   *   *

AMRAM, David (Werner III) 1930-

PERSONAL: Born November 17, 1930, in Philadelphia, Pa.; son of Philip Werner (a lawyer and writer) and Emilie

(Weyl) Amram. *Education:* Attended Oberlin Conservatory of Music, 1948-49; George Washington University, B.A., 1952; Manhattan School of Music, graduate study, 1955-56; studied composition with Vittorio Giannini, and French horn with Gunther Schuller. *Home:* 461 Sixth Ave., New York, N.Y. 10011. *Office:* c/o Barna Ostertag, 501 Fifth Ave., Room 1410, New York, N.Y. 10017.

CAREER: Composer, conductor, musician; worked at various odd jobs prior to stage assignments, including truck driver, gym teacher, and short order cook; played with various jazz groups, including those of Charlie Mingus, Sonny Rollins, and Oscar Pettiford, and his own group, Amram-Barrow Jazz Quartet, 1955; New York Shakespeare Festival, New York, N.Y., musical director, 1956-68. Guest conductor, Marlboro Music Festival, 1961; first composer-in-residence, New York Philharmonic Orchestra, 1966-67; performer at various benefit concerts. *Military service:* U.S. Army, 1952-54. *Member:* American Federation of Musicians. *Awards, honors:* Obie Award, *Village Voice,* 1959, for compositions for Phoenix Theatre and New York Shakespeare Festival.

WRITINGS: Vibrations: The Adventures and Musical Times of David Amram (autobiography), Macmillan, 1968.

Orchestral works: *Autobiography for Strings: String Orchestra* (first performed in New York by Washington Square Chamber Orchestra, June, 1959), C. F. Peters, 1964; *Shakespearean Concerto for Oboe, Two Horns, and Strings* (first performed in New York at Town Hall by Washington Square Chamber Orchestra, May 8, 1960), C. F. Peters, 1964; "Three Songs for America," first performed on National Educational Television, April 27, 1969. Also composer of "The American Bell" and "Three Dances for Oboe and Strings."

Wind symphonies: *King Lear Variations for Wind Symphony and Percussion* (first performed in New York by New York Philharmonic, March 23, 1967), C. F. Peters, 1967. Also composer of "Horn Concerto."

Chamber music; all published by C. F. Peters: *Overture and Allegro: Flute Solo* (first performed in New York at Carnegie Hall by Washington Square Chamber Orchestra, January 5, 1960), 1964; *The Wind and the Rain: Viola, Pianoforte* (based on the second movement of the *Shakespearean Concerto for Small Orchestra*), 1964; *Three Songs for Marlboro, Horn and Violincello,* 1964; *Dirge and Variations for Violin, Violincello and Pianoforte,* 1965; *Discussion for Flute, Cello, Piano and Percussion,* 1965; *Sonata for Violin and Piano,* 1965; *Trio for Tenor Saxophone, Horn and Bassoon,* 1965; *Fanfare and Processional for Brass Quintet,* 1968; *String Quartet* (first performed in New York at Town Hall by Beaux Arts Quartet, February 20, 1962), 1968.

Choral music: *Two Anthems for Mixed Voices A Cappella,* C. F. Peters, 1964; *Shir L'Erev Shabat: Friday Evening Service for Tenor Solo, SATB, and Organ* (first performed in New York at Town Hall by Beaux Arts Quartet with George Shirley, February 20, 1962), C. F. Peters, 1965; "A Year in Our Land," first performed in New York at Town Hall by Interracial Chorus and Orchestra, May 13, 1965. Also composer of "By the Rivers of Babylon," "Let Us Remember," "May the Words of the Lord," "Songs from Shakespeare," and "Thou Shalt Love the Lord, Thy God."

Keyboard music: *Sonata for Piano,* C. P. Peters, 1965.

Operas: (With Arnold Weinstein) "The Final Ingredient," first networked by ABC for "Directions '65," April 11, 1965, and performed yearly thereafter; "Twelfth Night,"

first produced in Lake George, N.Y., at Lake George Opera Festival, August 1, 1968.

Incidental music: "Titus Andronicus," first produced in New York at Emanuel Presbyterian Church, November, 1956; "Romeo and Juliet," first produced at Belvedere Lake Theatre, June, 1957; "Two Gentlemen of Verona," first produced in Belvedere Lake Theatre, July, 1957; "Richard III," first produced at Heckscher Theater, November 25, 1957; "As You Like It," first produced at Heckscher Theater, January 20, 1958; "The Sign of Winter," first produced Off-Broadway at Theater 74, May 7, 1958; "Othello," first produced at Belvedere Lake Theatre, July, 1958; "Twelfth Night," first produced at Belvedere Lake Theatre, August, 1958; "Death Watch," first produced Off-Broadway at Theatre East, October 9, 1958; "The Family Reunion," first produced Off-Broadway at Phoenix Theatre, October 20, 1958; "Comes a Day," first produced on Broadway at Ambassador Theatre, November 6, 1958; "The Power and the Glory," first produced Off-Broadway at Phoenix Theatre, December 10, 1958; "J.B.," first produced on Broadway at ANTA Theatre, December 11, 1958; "Antony and Cleopatra," first produced at Heckscher Theatre, January 13, 1959; "The Rivalry," first produced on Broadway at Bijou Theatre, February 7, 1959; "The Beaux Strategem," first produced Off-Broadway at Phoenix Theatre, February 24, 1959; "Kataki," first produced on Broadway at Ambassador Theatre, April 9, 1959; "Julius Caesar," first produced at Belvedere Lake Theatre, August 3, 1959; "Great God Brown," first produced on Broadway at Coronet Theatre, October 6, 1959; "Lysistrata," first produced Off-Broadway at Phoenix Theatre, November 24, 1959.

"Peer Gynt," first produced Off-Broadway at Phoenix Theatre, January 12, 1960; "Caligula," first produced on Broadway at 54th Street Theatre, February 16, 1960; "Henry IV, Part I," first produced Off-Broadway at Phoenix Theatre, April 18, 1960; "Henry V," first produced at Belvedere Lake Theatre, June 29, 1960; "Measure for Measure," first produced at Belvedere Lake Theatre, July 25, 1960; "Taming of the Shrew," first produced at Belvedere Lake Theatre, July 25, 1960; "Hamlet," first produced Off-Broadway at Phoenix Theatre, March 16, 1961; "Macbeth," first produced in Stratford, Conn., at American Shakespeare Festival, June 28, 1961; "Much Ado About Nothing," first produced in New York at Wollman Skating Rink, July 31, 1961; "A Midsummer Night's Dream," first produced in New York at Wollman Skating Rink, July 31, 1961; "Richard II," first produced in New York at Wollman Skating Rink, August 28, 1961; "The Merchant of Venice," first produced in New York at Delacorte Theatre, June 14, 1962; "The Tempest," first produced in New York at Delacorte Theatre, July 16, 1962; "King Lear," first produced in New York at Delacorte Theatre, August 13, 1962; "The Winter's Tale," first produced in New York at Delacorte Theatre, July 19, 1963; "After the Fall," first produced in New York at Delacorte Theatre, July 19, 1964; "The Passion of Joseph D.," first produced on Broadway at Ethel Barrymore Theatre, February 11, 1964; "Henry IV, Part II," first produced Off-Broadway at Phoenix Theatre. Also composed music for "All's Well That Ends Well," "Coriolanus," and "Troilus and Cressida."

Film scores: "Echo of an Era," 1957; "Pull My Daisy," G-String Productions, 1958; "The Young Savages," United Artists, 1959; "The Harmful Effects of Tobacco," 1959; "Splendor in the Grass," Warner Brothers, 1961; *The Manchurian Candidate* (United Artists, 1962), Sergeant Music Co., 1962; *We Are Young,* Edward B. Marks Music Corp.,

1967; "US," 1968; "The Arrangement," Warner-Seven Arts, 1969.

Television scores: "Turn of the Screw," networked by NBC for Ford Startime, October 20, 1959; "Something Special," networked by NBC, 1959; "The American," networked by NBC for Purex Special, 1960; "The Fifth Column," networked by CBS, 1960.

SIDELIGHTS: "I learn about music by walking through the woods watching the birds fly, the rhythm of the wind on the grass, the texture of the grass . . .," Amram once told an interviewer. "The body is the vessel of the soul. It has a certain rhythm. If it's in shape it tunes your mind." Praised by musical critics and musicians of various genres, Amram has been called by Victor Chaplin "a composer who may yet write the great American opera and has already created some of the best incidental theatre music of our time. . . ." In 1960, William Flanagan described Amram's works as "in a generally contemporary idiom untouched by the dictates of stylish fashion or, on the other hand, the opportunism that so often plagues the work of composers associated with the commercial theatre and cinema," adding that it was "everywhere musical, dedicated, and . . . passionately honest."

Amram's autobiography, *Vibrations,* has likewise received critical praise. Thomas Lask believes that "the great quality of his book is zest. He relishes everything. He is always moving forward to meet life. He is the least introspective of men; he never apologies for his existence; he never tries to explain it away; he enjoys it. His responses are infectious."

Amram does not share the distaste for popular music that marks many of his contemporaries. "Kids are always challenges," Amram has said. "They are real people, not yet brainwashed. They don't have to read or be told about something to know if they are moved or not." He adds: "Young people who avidly listen to rock 'n' roll will save American music. This is the first time a generation of children is tuned into sound produced by contemporaries, heroes and spokesmen—not something imposed on them by adults. They can listen and say, 'Yeah. That's mine.'"

AVOCATIONAL INTERESTS: Kayaking, sailing, skiing, running track, playing jazz, learning languages.

BIOGRAPHICAL/CRITICAL SOURCES: Life, August 11, 1967; David Amram, *Vibrations: The Adventures and Musical Times of David Amram,* Macmillan, 1968; *New York Times,* October 15, 1968, February 20, 1969; *Washington Post,* October 18, 1968, November 2, 1968; *Saturday Review,* November 16, 1968; *Nation,* December 9, 1968.†

* * *

ANDERS, Evelyn 1916-

PERSONAL: Born February 28, 1916, in Newark, New Jersey; daughter of Emil and Marie (Kalberer) Anders. *Education:* Rutgers University, B.A. *Religion:* Protestant. *Home:* 101 Stuyvesant Ave., Newark, N.J. 07106.

CAREER: H. C. Brill Co., Newark, N.J., secretary, 1935-40; War Manpower Commission, Training-Within-Industry Division, Newark, secretary, 1940-45; M & M Ltd., Newark, head of stenographic department, 1945-49; Colgate-Palmolive Co., New York, N.Y., secretary to vice-president and general counsel, 1949-74.

WRITINGS: (With Esther Becker) *The Successful Secretary's Handbook,* Harper, 1971.

AVOCATIONAL INTERESTS: Golf, playing the organ, painting.

ANDERSEN, Marion Lineaweaver 1912(?)-1971

1912(?)—May 24, 1971; American author and poet. Obituaries: *New York Times,* May 26, 1971; *Antiquarian Bookman,* June 7-14, 1971.

* * *

ANDERSEN, Wilhelm 1911-

PERSONAL: Born February 5, 1911, near Fleensburg, Germany; son of Johannes (a post office clerk) and Anna (Mathiesen) Andersen; married Ilse Langlo, August 14, 1936; children: Anke (Mrs. Norbert Klein), Hanfried, Wolfgang, Martje, Sigrid, Marlene, Heinke, Ute, Baerbel. *Education:* Studied theology at Universities of Rostock, Goettingen, Tuebingen, Bonn, and Kiel; Dr.Theol., 1939. *Home:* Neuwiesenstrasse 10, 8806 Neuendettelsau, Germany. *Office:* Augustana-Hochschule, Neuendettelsau, Germany.

CAREER: Clergyman of Evangelical Lutheran Church; pastor in Tetenbuell, Germany, 1936-46; lecturer at training college for missionaries and Kirchlichen Dienst, Breklum, Germany, 1946-55; director of preacher training, Preetz, Germany, 1955-56; Augustana-Hochschule, Neuendettelsau, Germany, professor of systematic theology, 1956—, headmaster, 1957-71. Vereinigten Evangelische Lutheische Kirche Deutschlands (VELK), member of ecumenical council, member of general synod.

WRITINGS: Der Existenzbegriff und das existenzielle Denken in der neueren Philosophie und Theologie, Bertelsman, 1940; *Moeglichkeiten und Grenzen einer Abendmahlsgemeinschaft heute,* C. Kaiser, 1947; *Vom Lob der Taufe,* Pressverband (Munich), 1950; *Das Wirkende Wort,* Pressverband, 1953; *Towards a Theology of Mission: A Study of the Encounter between the Missionary Enterprise and the Church and Its Theology,* S.C.M. Press, 1956; (editor) *Das Wort Gottes in Geschichte und Gegenwart,* C. Kaiser, 1957; (with F. W. Kantzenbach and G. F. Vicedom) *Lutherische Stimmen zur Frage der Atom-waffen* (booklet), C. Kaiser, 1958; *Law and Gospel: A Study in Biblical Theology,* Association Press, 1961; *Der Gesetzesbegriff in der gegenwaertigen theologischen Diskussion: Ueberlegungen zu G. Ebeling,* C. Kaiser, 1963; (contributor) *Jesus Christus und der Kosmos,* M.B.K. Verlag, 1963; (contributor) Helmut Lamparter, editor, *Das Wahrzeichen des Christenglaubens,* Aussaat Verlag, 1965; (compiler) *Vom Dienst der Theologie an Amt und Gemeinde* (collection of Lutheran writings), Claudius Verlag, 1965; *Die biblische Auferstehungsbotschaft als Frage an unseren Gottesglauben* (booklet), Calwer, 1967; *Der herausgeforderte Glaube,* Christian Jensen Verlag, 1972. Contributor to journals.

* * *

ANDERSEN, Yvonne 1932-

PERSONAL: Born September 7, 1932, in Long Beach, Calif.; daughter of Edward Owen (a dentist) and Josephine (Mengel) Andersen; married Dominic Falcone (a film distributor), September 7, 1954; children: Paul, Jean. *Education:* Louisiana State University, B.A., 1954.

CAREER: Yellow Ball Workshop (film animation classes and production of animated films), Lexington, Mass., director, beginning 1963. Film animation instructor in public schools of Newton, Mass. Film and educational consultant to Center for Understanding Media, New York, N.Y., and other educational groups. *Member:* American Federation of Film Societies, American Film Institute. *Awards, honors:* Animated films made by her students have won about thirty awards at International film festivals.

WRITINGS: Make Your Own Animated Movies, Little, Brown, 1970; *Teaching Film Animation to Children,* Van Nostrand, 1970.††

* * *

ANDERSON, Charles C. 1931-

PERSONAL: Born January 2, 1931, in Minneapolis, Minn.; son of George O. and Myrtle (Johnson) Anderson; married Dorothy Hanson, December 27, 1958; children: Curtis, Jeremy. *Education:* Bethel College and Seminary, St. Paul, Minn., B.A., 1954, B.D., 1957; University of Chicago, Ph.D., 1963. *Home:* 424 South Hickory, Ottawa, Kan. 66067. *Office:* Department of Religion, Ottawa University, Ottawa, Kan. 66067.

CAREER: Clergyman of American Baptist Churches; Ottawa University, Ottawa, Kan., assistant professor, 1961-66, associate professor, 1967-73, professor of religion, 1974—, chairman of department, 1967—.

WRITINGS: Critical Quests of Jesus, Eerdmans, 1969; *The Historical Jesus: A Continuing Quest,* Eerdmans, 1972.

WORK IN PROGRESS: Life after Death in Judaism and Christianity.

* * *

ANDERSON, Clarence William 1891-1971

April 12, 1891—March 26, 1971; American artist and author of horse stories. Obituaries: *Publishers' Weekly,* April 26, 1971; *Antiquarian Bookman,* May 17, 1971.

* * *

ANDERSON, Eugene N(ewton) 1900-

PERSONAL: Born July 24, 1900, in Tehuacana, Tex.; son of Jesse (a professor) and Luda Lee (Newton) Anderson; married Pauline Safford Relyea, June 25, 1932; children: Eugene Newton, Jr. *Education:* Trinity University, Waxahachie, Tex., student, 1918-19; University of Colorado, A.B., 1921; University of Berlin, graduate study, 1924-25; University of Chicago, Ph.D., 1928. *Politics:* Liberal. *Religion:* Protestant. *Home:* 552 Pintura Dr., Santa Barbara, Calif. 93111.

CAREER: University of Chicago, Chicago, Ill., instructor, 1925-32, assistant professor of European history, 1932-36; American University, Washington, D.C., professor of European history, 1936-41; U.S. Government, Washington, D.C., with Office of Strategic Services, 1942-45, assistant chief, Division of Cultural Cooperation, Department of State, 1945, associate chief, German-Austrian Activities, Division of Occupied Areas, Department of State, 1946-47; University of Nebraska, Lincoln, professor of European history, 1947-55; University of California, Los Angeles, professor of European history, 1955-68, professor emeritus, 1968—. Visiting professor, University of Peshawar, West Pakistan, summer, 1961; visiting professor of history, University of California, Santa Barbara, 1968-70. *Member:* American Historical Association, Phi Beta Kappa, Phi Delta Theta. *Awards, honors:* Social Science Research Council fellow in Germany, 1930-31.

WRITINGS: The First Moroccan Crisis, 1904-1906, University of Chicago Press, 1930, reprinted, Archon, 1966; (editor with James Lea Cate) *Medieval and Historiographical Essays in Honor of James Westfall Thompson,* University of Chicago Press, 1938, reprinted, Kennikat, 1966; *Nationalism and the Cultural Crisis in Prussia, 1806-1815,* Farrar &

Rinehart, 1939, reprinted, Octagon, 1967; (with others) *The Struggle for Democracy in Germany,* edited by Gabriel A. Almond, University of North Carolina Press, 1949; *The Humanities in the German and Austrian Universities* (report on survey he made for American Council of Learned Societies and the U.S. Army, 1949), American Council of Learned Societies, 1950; *Process Versus Power: Studies in Modern Culture,* University of Nebraska, 1952; (editor) *The Prussian Election Statistics, 1862 and 1863,* University of Nebraska, 1954; *The Social and Political Conflict in Prussia, 1858-1864,* University of Nebraska, 1954; *European Issues in the Twentieth Century,* Rinehart, 1958; *Modern Europe in World Perspective: 1914 to the Present,* Rinehart, 1958; *Nineteenth Century Europe, Crisis and Contribution* (booklet), Service Center for Teachers of History, 1959, 2nd edition, 1964; (editor with Stanley J. Pincetl, Jr. and Donald J. Ziegler) *Europe in the Nineteenth Century: A Documentary Analysis of Changes and Conflict,* Bobbs-Merrill, Volume I: *1815-1870,* Volume II: *1870-1914,* both 1961; (with wife, Pauline R. Anderson) *Political Institutions and Social Change in Continental Europe in the Nineteenth Century,* University of California Press, 1967; (editor and translator with P. R. Anderson) Eckart Kehr, *Battle Fleet Building and Party Politics in Germany 1894-1901: A Cross Section of the Political, Social, and Ideological Preconditions of German Imperialism,* University of Chicago Press, 1975. Contributor of articles and essays to journals. Member of board of editors, *Journal of Modern History,* 1952-55.

* * *

ANDREE, Robert G(erald) 1912-

PERSONAL: Born May 30, 1912, in Grand Rapids, Mich.; son of Gerrit N. and Wilhelmina (Rose) Andree; married Vaneta Grace Stoppels, August 25, 1937; children: Ross C. *Education:* Calvin College, B.A., 1933; University of Michigan, M.A., 1937; Harvard University, Ed.D., 1942. *Home:* 534 Oak Hill Dr., Edwardsville, Ill. *Office:* General Office Building, Southern Illinois University, Edwardsville, Ill. 62025.

CAREER: Teaching principal at high schools in New Holland, S.D., 1933-34, and Allendale, Mich., 1934-36; junior high school principal in Romulus, Mich., 1936-37; dean of boys at senior high school in Muskegon, Mich., 1937-41; director of guidance at high school in Schenectady, N.Y., 1942-44; senior high school principal in Oneonta, N.Y., 1944-46; Brookline High School, Brookline, Mass., headmaster, 1946-56; Rich Township High School District, Park Forest, Ill., superintendent, 1956-65; Southern Illinois University at Edwardsville, professor of educational administration and curriculum, 1965—. Summer professor at University of Rochester and University of Maine. *Member:* National Society for the Study of Education, Academy of Political Science, National Organization on Legal Problems of Education, Phi Delta Kappa, Kappa Delta Pi, Rotary. *Awards, honors:* Fulbright scholar in Rotterdam, 1954-55.

WRITINGS: (With John Ligtenberg) *Collective Bargaining in the Public Schools,* American Federation of Teachers, 1967; (editor with Harry H. Smith) *Collective Negotiation: A Symposium* (twelve lectures), Education Division, Southern Illnois University, 1967; (with George T. Wilkins) *School Construction,* Stipes, 1968; *Collective Negotiations: A Guide to School Board-Teacher Relations,* Heath, 1970; *The Art of Negotiation: Rules, Games, Logic,* Heath, 1971; *America's Secondary Schools: To Tell It Like It Is,* American Education Council, 1974; *America's Elementary Schools: To Tell It Like It is,* American Education Council,

1975; *P/R in Public Schools,* American Education Council, 1976. Author of monographs and articles on phases of educational administrative and collective bargaining. Member of editorial board, *Clearing House.*

WORK IN PROGRESS: Politics, Propaganda and Power Conflict Management.

* * *

ANDRES, Stefan 1906-1970

June 26, 1906—June 29, 1970; German novelist and poet. Obituaries: *New York Times,* July 31, 1970; *Books Abroad,* spring, 1971.

* * *

ANDREWS, J(ames) S(ydney) 1934-

PERSONAL: Born December 14, 1934, in Belfast, Northern Ireland; son of David (a company director) and Helene L. (Baud) Andrews; married Judith Ann McCartan, June 1, 1962; children: Rona Mary, Susan Helene, Eileen Pamela. *Education:* Attended Rossall School, Fleetwood, Lancashire, England. *Home:* Dunyvaig, Tarbert, Argyll, Scotland.

CAREER: Isaac Andrews & Sons Ltd. (millers) and associated companies, Belfast, Northern Ireland, director. *Member:* Society of Authors, Ulster Archaeological Society, Society of Antiquaries of Scotland (fellow), Amateur Yacht Research Society, Clyde Cruising Club.

WRITINGS: The Bell of Nendrum, Bodley Head, 1969, published as *The Green Hill of Nendrum,* Hawthorn, 1970; *The Man from the Sea,* Bodley Head, 1970, Dutton, 1971; *Catamarans for Cruising,* Hollis & Carter, 1974; *Simple Sailing,* World's Work, 1975. Contributor to yachting journals.

WORK IN PROGRESS: Two novels, one about the early Bronze Age in Ireland, and one about the Irish Sea in the thirteenth century.

AVOCATIONAL INTERESTS: Photography, archaeology, sailing.

BIOGRAPHICAL/CRITICAL SOURCES: Times Literary Supplement, June 26, 1969.

* * *

ANGEL, Marie 1923-

PERSONAL: Born March 15, 1923, in London, England; daughter of Cyril George (a stockbroker) and Mary (Potter) Angel. *Education:* Studied art at Croyden School of Art and Crafts, 1940-45; Royal College of Art, A.R.C.A., 1948. *Home:* Silver Ley, Oakley Rd., Warlingham, Surrey CR3 9BE, England.

CAREER: Calligraphist and illustrator. Exhibitions at Royal Academy, Crafts Center of Great Britain, Society of Scribes and Illuminators, and Arts and Crafts Exhibition. *Member:* Society of Designer Craftsmen (fellow), Society of Scribes and Illuminators.

WRITINGS—All self-illustrated: *A Bestiary,* Harvard University Library, 1960; *A New Bestiary,* Harvard University Library, 1963; *The Ark,* Harper, 1973; *Beasts in Heraldry,* Stephen Greene Press, 1974.

Illustrator: Aileen Fisher, *We Went Looking,* Crowell, 1968; Emily Dickinson, *Two Poems,* Walker & Co., 1968; Beatrix Potter, *The Tale of the Faithful Dove,* Warne, 1970; *The Twenty-third Psalm,* Crowell, 1970; Toby Talbot, *Two by Two,* Follett, 1974.

WORK IN PROGRESS: Calligraphy, to be published by Scribner's.

AVOCATIONAL INTERESTS: Small animals (particularly cats), birds, conservation, gardening (growing plants specially needed for her botanical drawings).

* * *

ANNETT, John 1930-

PERSONAL: Born July 11, 1930, in Kent, England; married, 1955; wife's name, Marian E. (a research psychologist); children: one son, one daughter. *Education:* Oxford University, B.A., 1953, M.A., 1957, Ph.D., 1959. *Office:* Department of Psychology, University of Warwick, Coventry CV4 7AL, England.

CAREER: University of Sheffield, Sheffield, England, senior research worker, 1960-63; University of Aberdeen, Aberdeen, Scotland, lecturer, 1963-65; University of Hull, Hull, Yorkshire, England, senior lecturer, 1965-68, reader in psychology, 1968-72; professor of psychology, Open University, 1972-74; University of Warwick, Coventry, England, professor of psychology, 1974—. Visiting scientist, U.S. Naval Training Devices Center, 1960. Member of education research board, Social Science Research Council, 1970-74; member of research committee, Central Training Council, 1968—, and Chemical Industry Training Board, 1970—. *Member:* British Psychological Society (council member, 1969-72), Experimental Psychology Society, Orgonomics Research Society, Ergonomics Research Society (chairman of training section, 1968-72), Association for Programmed Learning and Educational Technology. *Awards, honors:* G. H. Miles Prize for industrial training, National Institute for Industrial Psychology, 1968.

WRITINGS: Feedback and Human Behaviour, Penguin, 1969. Contributor to professional journals. Editor, *Programmed Learning and Educational Technology,* 1965-69; co-editor, *British Journal of Psychology,* 1970-73.

WORK IN PROGRESS: Research in acquisition of skill and industrial training.

* * *

ANTICO, John 1924-

PERSONAL: Born March 31, 1924, in Glassport, Pa.; son of John (a factory worker) and Frances (Marabito) Antico; married Alma Gasperson, August, 1945; married second wife, Jean Frances Peters (a stenographer), February, 1954; children: (second marriage) Carla Marie, Mary Frances. *Education:* Wayne State University, B.A., 1950, M.A., 1956; Michigan State University, additional study, 1958-59. *Home:* 1518 Loraine, Lansing, Mich. 48910. *Office:* Department of English, Lansing Community College, 419 North Capitol Ave., Lansing, Mich. 48914.

CAREER: Bigelow-Liptak Corp., Detroit, Mich., draftsman, 1953-55; General Motors Institute, Flint, Mich., instructor in English, 1955-58; Lansing Community College, Lansing, Mich., instructor in English, 1960—. *Member:* American Association of University Professors (president of Lansing chapter, 1965), Michigan College English Association.

WRITINGS: (With Meredith Hazelrigg) *Insight through Fiction: Dealing Effectively with the Short Story,* Cummings, 1970. Contributor to *Modern Fiction Studies.*

WORK IN PROGRESS: A book on J. D. Salinger; a poetry text; and a novel on World War II.†

ANTONOVSKY, Aaron 1923-

PERSONAL: Born December 19, 1923, in Brooklyn, N.Y.; son of Isaac (a laundryman) and Esther (Halperin) Antonovsky; married Helen Faigin (a psychologist), November 27, 1958; children: Avishai. *Education:* Brooklyn College (now Brooklyn College of the City University of New York), B.A., 1945; Yale University, M.A., 1952, Ph.D., 1955. *Politics:* Socialist. *Religion:* Jewish. *Home:* 10A Brosh St., Omer, Israel. *Office:* Israel Institute of Applied Social Research, P.O. Box 7150, Jerusalem, Israel; and Department of Health Sciences, Ben Gurion University of the Negev, Beersheva, Israel.

CAREER: Research associate, Yiddish Science Institute for Jewish Research, 1953-56; Brooklyn College (now Brooklyn College of the City University of New York), Brooklyn, N.Y., lecturer in sociology, 1955-59; research director of race relations, New York State Committee Against Discrimination, 1956-59; Israel Institute of Applied Social Research, Jerusalem, Israel, senior research associate, 1960—; Hebrew University of Jerusalem, Hadassah Medical School, Jerusalem, instructor in social medicine, 1962-73; Ben Gurion University of the Negev, Beersheva, Israel, Kunin-Lunenfeld Professor of Medical Sociology, 1973—. *Military service:* U.S. Army, 1943-45. *Member:* American Sociological Association, Israeli Sociological Association (national secretary, 1972-73). *Awards, honors:* Fulbright fellow, University of Tehran, 1959-60; U.S. Public Health Service fellow, Harvard University, 1965-66.

WRITINGS: (Editor with L. Lorwin) *Discrimination and Low Incomes,* New York State Committee Against Discrimination, 1960; (translator and reviser from original Yiddish edition) Elias Tcherikower, *The Early Jewish Labor Movement in the United States,* Yivo Institute for Jewish Research, 1961; (editor with John Kosa and I. K. Zola) *Poverty and Health: A Sociological Analysis,* Harvard University Press, 1969; (with A. M. Davies and Judith T. Shuval) *Social Functions of Medical Practice: A Study of Doctor-Patient Relationships in Israel,* Jossey-Bass, 1970; (with Alan Arian) *Hopes and Fears of Israelis,* Jerusalem Academic Press, 1971. Contributor of articles to *Journal of Chronic Diseases, Social Science and Medicine,* and other periodicals.

WORK IN PROGRESS: Extensive research in medical sociology; a book on ethnic factors in adjustment to menopause.

* * *

APPLEMAN, Mark J(erome) 1917-
(Mark Jerome)

PERSONAL: Born May 4, 1917, in Columbus, Ohio; son of Philip and Rose (Singer) Appleman; married Marguerite Reinhold (an artists' representative), December 13, 1958. *Education:* Attended City College (now City College of the City University of New York), 1934-36, and New York University, 1936-37. *Agent:* Phyllis Jackson, International Creative Management, 40 West 57th St., New York, N.Y. 10019.

CAREER: Writer in New York City, and Hollywood, Calif., 1938-41, 1945-46; J. Walter Thompson Co., New York City, group head, 1956-61; F. I. duPont, Glore, Forgan & Co. (investment brokers and bankers), New York City, general partner, 1961-71; DuPont, Glore, Forgan, New York City, vice-president, 1971—. Member of marketing advisory committee and public relations advisory committee, New York Stock Exchange; owner, Mark J. Appleman Co.; president, Corporate Shareholders, Inc., 1973—. *Military service:* U.S. Army, 1941-46; became captain. *Member:* Authors League, International Arts, Overseas Press Club.

WRITINGS: (With Edmond Demaitre) *The Liberation of Manhattan,* Doubleday, 1949; *The Winning Habit,* McCall Publishing, 1971; *Understanding Your Customer: Psychological Aspects of Investing,* New York Institute of Finance, 1973; (compiler) *Organizing and Managing the Marketing Function,* New York Institute of Finance, 1973; (editor) *Challenge 1977: Marketing for the Future,* New York Institute of Finance, 1973. Author, under pseudonym Mark Jerome, of a motion picture script, "Invitation to Happiness," 1939; also author of two plays, "Stockade," 1954, and "On Trial," 1976. Contributor to *Look, Intellectual Digest, Finance, Financial Analysts Journal,* and other periodicals. Editor, *Corporate Shareholder.*

BIOGRAPHICAL/CRITICAL SOURCES: Forbes, October 15, 1970.

* * *

APTER, Michael J(ohn) 1939-

PERSONAL: Original name, Michael Smith; name legally changed, 1964; born June 17, 1939, in Stockton-on-Tees, England; son of Kenneth Carl Pfeiffer (a psychiatrist) and Vera Blanche (Apter) Smith; married Claude Annik Raymonde Deburaux (a schoolteacher), June 29, 1964 (divorced, 1977); children: Carolyn Sophie. *Education:* University of Bristol, B.Sc. (honors), 1960, Ph.D., 1964; Princeton University, graduate study, 1960-61. *Home:* 6 St. Nicholas House, Seaview Court, Bradford Pl., Penarth, South Glamorgan, Wales. *Office:* Department of Psychology, University College, University of Wales, Cardiff, Wales.

CAREER: Teaching Programmes Ltd., Bristol, England, head of department of research and validation, 1964-67; University of Wales, University College, Cardiff, lecturer, 1967-73, senior lecturer in psychology, 1973—. Visiting professor, University of British Columbia, summers, 1974, 1975. *Member:* British Psychological Society, Association for Programmed Learning and Educational Technology.

WRITINGS: Cybernetics and Development, Pergamon, 1966; *An Introduction to Psychology,* Teaching Programmes (Bristol), 1967; *The New Technology of Education,* Macmillan (London), 1968; *The Computer Simulation of Behaviour,* Hutchinson, 1970, Harper, 1971; (editor with G. Westby) *The Computer in Psychology,* Wiley, 1973. Contributor to academic journals.

WORK IN PROGRESS: Research into cybernetics, structuralism, phenomenological psychology, "Reversal Theory."

SIDELIGHTS: Michael Apter wrote *CA:* "One of the central questions which generates much of my work is the question of how far one can take the mechanistic hypothesis in biology and psychology. I have approached this question by looking in particular at phenomena which appear difficult to explain in mechanistic terms e.g. phenomena related to biological development, to emotional and irrational behaviour (especially that related to humour, to religion, and to crime), and to consciousness. I have then attempted to interpret or model such phenomena mechanistically, especially using cybernetic principles. This has led me recently to develop (with Dr. K.C.P. Smith) a new general psychological theory which we call 'Reversal Theory'."

AVOCATIONAL INTERESTS: Writing poetry and novels (so far unpublished), music, collecting antiques (especially watercolors), golf, and tennis.

* * *

APTHEKER, Bettina 1944-

PERSONAL: Surname is pronounced *ap*-tek-er; born September 2, 1944, in Fort Bragg, N.C.; daughter of Herbert (a writer) and Fay (Aptheker) Aptheker; married Jack Kurzweil (a college professor), August 29, 1965; children: Joshua Mark, Jennifer Gloria Lucy. *Education:* University of California, Berkeley, A.B., 1967; San Jose State University, M.A., 1976. *Politics:* Communist. *Residence:* San Jose, Calif. 95112. *Office:* Women's Studies Program, San Jose State University, San Jose, Calif.

CAREER: Free-lance writer and lecturer, 1968—; *People's World,* San Francisco, Calif., editor and writer, 1969—; San Jose State University, San Jose, Calif., assistant instructor in speech, 1974-75, lecturer in Women's Studies Program, 1976—; San Jose City College, San Jose, instructor in speech, 1976—. Member of steering committee, Free Speech Movement, Berkeley, 1964-65; member of national administration committee, Mobilization Committee to End the War in Vietnam, San Francisco and Washington, D.C., 1966-68. Member of board of directors, Pacific Publishing Foundation, Inc. Member of Communist Party National Committee, 1966—; member of Angela Davis Defense Committee.

WRITINGS: (With Robert Kaufman and Michael Folsom) *F.S.M.: The Free Speech Movement at Berkeley,* W.E.B. DuBois Clubs of America, 1965; *Big Business and the American University* (pamphlet), New Outlook Publishers, 1966; *Columbia University, Inc.* (pamphlet), W.E.B. DuBois Clubs of America, 1968; *Higher Education and the Student Rebellion in the United States, 1966-69: A Bibliography,* American Institute for Marxist Studies, 1969, revised edition, 1970; (with Angela Davis) *If They Come in the Morning, Voices of Resistance,* New American Library, 1971; *The Academic Rebellion in the United States: A Marxist Appraisal,* Citadel, 1972; *The Morning Breaks: The Trial of Angela Davis,* International Publishers, 1975. Contributor of articles and book reviews to *California Law Review, Nation, Guardian, Political Affairs,* and other periodicals.

WORK IN PROGRESS: Research on the history of Afro-American Women in the United States; theoretical work in Marxism and feminism.

SIDELIGHTS: One of the leaders of the Free Speech movement at the University of California, Bettina Aptheker is also the daughter of Herbert Aptheker, who was described by *Time* as "the American Communist Party's leading theoretician." She has since endeavored to extend her work to various other causes, including the anti-war movement, asserting that "Communists are quite relevant to the peace movement, and play a modest role in it."

She still continues to research and write on the issue of student power in the university. In an article in *Nation* she states: "Many of the worst crises and confrontations on the University of California Campuses have been either provoked by the regents or aggravated by a punitive disciplinary policy. More important, very large numbers of students have been driven into a frustrated fury by the unresponsiveness of the regents, and of higher authorities in general, to their demands, concerns and aspirations." Bettina Aptheker told *CA* that, as a result of the personal impact of the Angela

Davis case, she "switched [her] emphasis from student movement to Afro-American and Woman's history." Her thesis ("Mary Church Terrell & Ida B. Wells: A Comparative Rhetorical/Historical Analysis") on the lives of two outstanding black women who lived and worked at the turn of the century led her to explore the lives of other black women. She has delivered several papers on the subject at scholarly conferences, and intends to further explore the contributions black women have made to the struggle of women's rights in the United States.

She has traveled to England, Hungary, Czechoslovakia, U.S.S.R., German Democratic Republic, Finland, West Germany, Denmark, and France.

AVOCATIONAL INTERESTS: Playing and watching sports, especially baseball and basketball, driving on trips through the U.S., and concerts.

BIOGRAPHICAL/CRITICAL SOURCES: New York Times, November 21, 1965; *Time,* December 3, 1965; *New Republic,* April 29, 1967, June 10, 1967; *Nation,* September 7, 1970; *Guardian,* November 7, 1970.

* * *

ARAPOFF, Nancy 1930-

PERSONAL: Born May 15, 1930, in Chicago, Ill.; divorced; children: Christopher, Andreya. *Education:* Santa Barbara College (now University of California, Santa Barbara), B.A., 1952; University of Hawaii, M.A., 1963. *Politics:* Liberal. *Home:* 1230 Aalapapa Dr., Kailua, Hawaii 96734. *Office:* University of Hawaii, Honolulu, Hawaii 96822.

CAREER: University of Hawaii, Honolulu, instructor, 1963-69, assistant professor of English as a second language, 1969—. *Member:* Modern Language Association of America, National Council of Teachers of English, Linguistic Society of America, Teachers of English to Speakers of Other Languages.

WRITINGS: Writing through Understanding, Holt, 1970.

WORK IN PROGRESS: A textbook on composition entitled, *Writing through Problem Solving.*

* * *

ARCHIBALD, William 1924-1970

March 7, 1924—December 27, 1970; Trinidad-born American playwright, actor, and choreographer. Obituaries: *New York Times,* December 29, 1970; *Washington Post,* December 30, 1970; *Variety,* December 30, 1970; *Antiquarian Bookman,* January 18, 1971; *Books Abroad,* spring, 1971.

* * *

ARESKOUG, Kaj 1933-

PERSONAL: Name is pronounced Kai *Ah*-re-skoog; born November 27, 1933, in Sweden; became U.S. citizen; son of Gustaf and Britta (Soederberg) Areskoug. *Education:* University of Lund, LL.M., 1957; University of Virginia, M.A., 1958; Columbia University, Ph.D., 1968. *Home:* 68 Bank St., New York, N.Y. 10014.

CAREER: Stockholms Enskilda Bank, Stockholm, Sweden, analyst in economic research department, 1958-59; Bank of America, San Francisco, Calif., research economist in international section of economic research department, 1961-64; Standard Oil Co., New York City, senior economic analyst in planning coordination department, 1967-69; New York University, School of Business, New York City, assistant professor, 1969-73, associate professor of banking, 1973-76.

Military service: Swedish Navy, midshipman, 1952-53. *Member:* American Economic Association. *Awards, honors:* Grant from Government of Sweden to do research at National University of Mexico, 1960.

WRITINGS: Economic Integration in Latin America (booklet), Bank of America, 1963; *External Public Borrowing: Its Role in Economic Development,* Praeger, 1969; *The Liberalization of U.S. Capital Outflows* (monographs), New York University, 1976. Contributor to economic journals.

WORK IN PROGRESS: Research on international capital markets; textbook on the financing of economic development.

SIDELIGHTS: Kaj Areskoug speaks Spanish, German, and French.

* * *

ARKHURST, Frederick S(iegfried) 1920-

PERSONAL: Born October 13, 1920, in Sekondi, Ghana; son of Frederick and Hagar (Crankson) Arkhurst; married Joyce Eileen Cooper (an author of children's books), November 4, 1959; children: Reginald, Cecile Nanaba. *Education:* University of Aberdeen, M.A., (first class honors), 1952. *Home:* 2500 Johnson Ave., Riverdale, N.Y. 10463.

CAREER: British Embassy, Rome, Italy, attache, 1955-56; Gold Coast Office, London, England, public relations officer, 1956-57; Ghana High Commission, London, second secretary, 1957; Permanent Mission of Ghana to United Nations, New York City, first secretary, 1957-59, counsellor, 1959-60; Ministry of Foreign Affairs, Accra, Ghana, principal secretary, 1962-65, permanent representative to United Nations, 1965-68; Adlai Stevenson Institute of International Affairs, Chicago, Ill., director of African programs, 1967-70; Phelps-Stokes Fund, New York City, vice-president, beginning 1970; currently affiliated with a United Nations agency in Africa. Associate, Royal Institute of International Affairs, London, 1950—. *Awards, honors:* Faculty fellow, Center for International Affairs, Harvard University, 1962-63; Eisenhower exchange fellow, 1964-65.

WRITINGS: (Editor) *Africa in the Seventies and Eighties: Issues in Development,* Praeger, 1970.

WORK IN PROGRESS: Research on the effect of military expenditures on economic development in developing countries, probably leading to a book.

AVOCATIONAL INTERESTS: Reading, tennis.

BIOGRAPHICAL/CRITICAL SOURCES: W. Scott Thompson, *Ghana's Foreign Policy,* Princeton University Press, 1969; *Africa Today,* May-June, 1969.†

* * *

ARLANDSON, Leone 1917-
(Lee Ryland)

PERSONAL: Surname is pronounced *Ar*-landson; born October 30, 1917, in Baker, Ore.; daughter of Frank and Ella (Wilbourn) Ryland; married second husband, Robert Andrew Arlandson (with Pacific Motor Trucking), December 25, 1953; children: (first marriage) Carolyn Cook, David Cook; (second marriage) John, James and Janis (twins). *Education:* Attended Lake Merritt Business College, 1939. *Politics:* Republican. *Religion:* Protestant. *Home:* 2170 Milford Dr., Medford, Ore. 97501.

CAREER: State of Oregon, Welfare Division, Portland, clerk, 1937-40; Pictsweet (food company), Albany, Ore., timekeeper, 1950-53. *Member:* Western Writers of America.

WRITINGS—Juvenile: *Mr. Puffer-Bill,* Golden Press, 1965; (under name Lee Ryland) *Gordon and the Glockenspiel,* Whitman Publishing, 1966; (under name Lee Ryland) *Whistle-Bell Train,* Whitman Publishing, 1967. Contributor to Harper's *SCOPE,* 1969, and to other anthologies. Contributor of more than fifty juvenile stories and adult articles to *Sunday Oregonian, Jack and Jill, Golden Magazine,* and to western journals including *Horseman, Western Life, True West,* and *Western Roundup.*

WORK IN PROGRESS: Four books, *Trail of the Spotted Horse, Cha-oo, the Magnificent,* boyhood of Chief Joseph, and an anthology about early western individuals and horses.

SIDELIGHTS: Leone Arlandson prefers to write non-fiction, and does fiction only for young people, from pre-school to teens. Her teen-aged daughter, Janis, has done all the map work and drawings for her mother's articles on Indian horse painting.

* * *

ARLEO, Joseph 1933-

PERSONAL: Born January 2, 1933, in Brooklyn, N.Y.; son of Dominick and Giovanna (Puca) Arleo; married Starr Taber, February 18, 1956; children: Michael, Adrian, Joseph, Jr. *Education:* Columbia University, B.A., 1954, M.A. 1956. *Agent:* Curtis Brown Ltd., 575 Madison Ave., New York, N.Y. 10022.

CAREER: Advertising copywriter in New York City, for J. Walter Thompson and then for Grey Advertising, 1956-60; Benton & Bowles (advertising agency), New York City, vice-president and associate creative director, 1960-69; Wm. Esty Co. (advertising agency), New York City, senior vice-president and creative director, 1969; full-time author, 1969—. *Member:* Authors Guild.

WRITINGS: The Grand Street Collector (novel), Walker & Co., 1970.

WORK IN PROGRESS: Two novels, *Home Late,* and *Errata.*

SIDELIGHTS: The Grand Street Collector was based on the 1943 assassination of Carlo Tresco, the editor of an Italian-language labor newspaper. This book was Joseph Arleo's third novel and the first to be published.

BIOGRAPHICAL/CRITICAL SOURCES: Book World, December 6, 1970.††

* * *

ARMBRUSTER, Francis E(dward) 1923-
(Frank Armbruster)

PERSONAL: Born April 9, 1923, in Wilkes-Barre, Pa.; son of Anthony (a telephone lineman) and Anna (Keller) Armbruster; married Irene Wojick, December 30, 1952; children: Francis (Frank), Jr., Ellen Anne, Janet. *Education:* George Washington University, B.A., 1948, graduate study, 1949-50; American University, graduate study, 1951. *Politics:* Democrat. *Religion:* Roman Catholic. *Home:* Lexow Ave., Upper Nyack, N.Y. 10960. *Office:* Hudson Institute, Quaker Ridge Rd., Croton-on-Hudson, N.Y. 10520.

CAREER: U.S. Air Force, Washington, D.C., analyst, 1950-57, unit chief, 1957-58; Boeing Aircraft Co., Seattle, Wash., research specialist, 1958-59; International Electric Corp., Paramus, N.J., chief of operations analysis, 1959-60; International Telephone & Telegraph Co., Nutley, N.J., manager of operations analysis in Advanced Systems Center, 1960-62; Hudson Institute, Croton-on-Hudson, N.Y., member of professional staff, 1962—, member of Research Management Council, 1964—, and lecturer. Also lecturer under auspices of other organizations. Member of Council on Foreign Relations study groups and of University of Chicago Academy for Policy Study Conference on China, the United States, and Asia. *Military service:* U.S. Army, Tenth Armored Division, 1943-46; served in Europe. *Member:* Operations Research Society of America, U.S. Naval Institute, Pi Gamma Mu, Delta Phi Epsilon.

WRITINGS: A Military and Police Security Program for South Vietnam, Hudson Institute, 1967; (contributor) Herman Kahn and Anthony Wiener, editors, *The Year 2000,* Macmillan, 1967; (with others) *China Briefing,* Center for Policy Study, University of Chicago, 1968; (contributor) Ping-ti Ho and Tang Tsou, editors, *China in Crisis,* University of Chicago Press, 1968; (with Raymond D. Gastil, Herman Kahn, William Pfaff, and Edmund Stillman) *Can We Win in Vietnam?,* Praeger, 1968; (contributor) Johan J. Holst and William Schneider, Jr., editors, *Why ABM? Policy Issues in the Missile Defense Controversy,* Pergamon, 1969; *The Forgotten Americans: The Values, Beliefs and Concerns of the Majority,* Arlington House, 1972; *Our Children's Crippled Future: How American Education Has Failed,* Quadrangle, 1977. Author of political-military area studies on Europe, Southeast Asia, and China, and of studies on Soviet-American trade, education and the work force in the United States, and present and future energy and transportation policies, all for Hudson Institute.

BIOGRAPHICAL/CRITICAL SOURCES: Listener, July 25, 1968.

*   *   *

ARMOUR, Lloyd R. 1922-

PERSONAL: Born May 17, 1922; son of William V. and Oma Belle (Rowland) Armour; married Joan Link, October 9, 1954; children: Christopher Link, Mark Richard. *Education:* Lambuth College, A.B., 1948; Vanderbilt University, graduate study, 1950. *Politics:* Democrat. *Religion:* Presbyterian. *Home:* 1105 Stonewall Dr., Nashville, Tenn. 37220. *Office:* 1100 Broad St., Nashville, Tenn. 37201.

CAREER: Commercial Appeal, Memphis, Tenn., bureau chief, 1947-48; *Nashville Tennessean,* Nashville, 1948—, vice-president, 1970—, executive editor, 1973—. *Military service:* U.S. Marine Corps, 1941-45; served in Pacific theater. *Member:* National Conference of Editorial Writers (president, 1973).

WRITINGS: . . . For All the Crying Children, Broadman, 1970.

*   *   *

ARMSTRONG, (A.) James 1924-

PERSONAL: Born September 17, 1924, in Marion, Ind.; son of Arthur J. and Frances (Green) Armstrong; married Phyllis Jeanne Schaeffer, February 26, 1942; children: James, Teresa Armstrong Etchison, John, Rebecca Armstrong Putens, Leslye. *Education:* Florida Southern College, A.B., 1948; Candler School of Theology, B.D., 1952; additional study at University of Chicago and Boston University. *Politics:* Democrat. *Home:* 1419 North Main, Aberdeen, S.D. 57401. *Office:* United Methodist Area Office, 405 Northwest 8th Ave., Aberdeen, S.D. 57401.

CAREER: Clergyman of United Methodist Church; currently bishop, United Methodist Church, Area Office, Ab-

erdeen, S.D. *Military service:* U.S. Navy, 1942. *Member:* Theta Phi. *Awards, honors:* Distinguished Service Award, Indianapolis Junior Chamber of Commerce, 1959; D.D. from Florida Southern College, 1960, DePauw University, 1964, and Westmar College, 1971; L.H.D. from Illinois Wesleyan University, 1970, and Dakota Wesleyan University, 1970.

WRITINGS: (Contributor) A. T. Davies, editor, *The Pulpit Speaks on Race,* Abingdon, 1966; *The Journey That Men Make,* Abingdon, 1969; (contributor) Judy McFadden, editor, *War Crimes and the American Conscience,* Holt, 1970; *The Urgent Now,* Abingdon, 1970; *Mission: Middle America,* Abingdon, 1971; *United Methodist Primer,* Tidings, 1973, revised edition, 1977; *Wilderness Voices,* Abingdon, 1974; *The Nation Yet to Be,* Friendship, 1975; *Telling Truth: The Foolishness of Preaching in a Real Word,* Word, Inc., 1977.

*   *   *

ARMSTRONG, Keith F(rancis) W(hitfield) 1950- (Carm Mac, Keith X)

PERSONAL: Born July 4, 1950, in Capetown, South Africa; son of John and Nina Armstrong. *Education:* Attended boarding school near Reading, England, 1959-66. *Religion:* None. *Address:* c/o The London Poetry Secretariat, 25/31 Tavistock Pl., London W.C.1, England.

CAREER: OXFAM, Oxford, England, member of education department, 1966; Circle Books, Oxford, publisher and editor, 1966—; free-lance disc jockey in Cheltenham, England, 1968-69, and part-time social worker in Oxford, 1969—. Director, The Trip Company of Great Britain Unlimited, Oxford and London, England, 1969-70; chairman and founder, Oxford Community Workshop, 1969. Former judge of poetry and short story competitions; organizer of free concerts, street theatre, poetry readings, benefits, happenings, and art and "concrete/poetry" exhibitions. Represented at exhibitions at Stroud College of Art, Arnolfini Gallery (Bristol), All Saints College (London), Rotunda Gallery (Cheltenham), Birmingham Arts Lab, Drury Lane Arts Lab, and Trinity College; one-man show at Midland Region Arts Council New Activities Festival. *Member:* Poets Conference, Poetry Society of Cheltenham. *Awards, honors:* Third prize, Manifold Fire Competition, for "Fire."

WRITINGS—All poetry; published by Circle Books, except as noted: *Dreams,* 1968; *Miniposterpoem,* 1969; (editor) J. Van Luik, *Jacob's Ladder to the Moon,* 1969; *Freepoemfolder,* 1970; *Image 41,* 1971; *Womb Wow,* Axis, 1971. Anthologized in *It's the World that Makes the Love Go Around,* Ken Geering, editor, Corgi Books, 1968, and *St. Ives Festival Books,* Niki Testor, editor, New Activities, 1970. Contributor of poetry and articles to *Breakthru, Expression One, The Journal, Riding West, Informer, Flame, Firebird, Oxford Mail, Second Aeon, Respronaut,* and many other periodicals and little magazines. Editor, *Informer,* 1966-72.

WORK IN PROGRESS: A book of poems.

SIDELIGHTS: Keith Armstrong told *CA:* "I work with words, part words, sounds, space, matter, machines, love, liberation, songs, and action. I like to use as few words as possible when I write. . . . I write for life and not for death. I write to help us breathe in a world where people die because of property. If people could not make a profit out of war there would be no war . . . and that is why I write . . . to help stop war."

Armstrong lists influences of his work as "D.S.H., William Burroughs, Karl Liebknecht, Reich, and Ravel." His main interests in relation to his work are the arts, "physic rock music/poetry," concrete and kinetic poetry.

BIOGRAPHICAL/CRITICAL SOURCES: Reading Mercury, July 15, 1967; *Tamarisk,* summer, 1968; *Oxford Mail,* July 10, 1969, August 6, 1969, February 17, 1971, May 6, 1971.

* * *

ARMSTRONG, (Daniel) Louis 1900-1971

July 4, 1900—July 6, 1971; American trumpeter, singer, and jazz bandleader. Obituaries: *New York Times,* July 7, 1971; *Washington Post,* July 7, 1971; *Time,* July 19, 1971.

* * *

ARMSTRONG, Robert L(aurence) 1926-

PERSONAL: Born April 6, 1926, in Bayonne, N.J.; son of Robert L. and Mary (Klein) Armstrong; married Diane Wales, September 8, 1951; married second wife, Betty Burnett, September 14, 1960; children: (second marriage) Benjamin Joseph, Marianne. *Education:* Antioch College, A.B., 1951; Roosevelt University, M.A., 1954; University of California, Berkeley, Ph.D., 1962. *Politics:* Independent. *Religion:* None. *Home:* 6118 Bougainvilla Cir., Pensacola, Fla. 32504. *Office:* Faculty of Philosophy, University of West Florida, Pensacola, Fla. 32504.

CAREER: University of Nevada, Reno, instructor, 1962-64, assistant professor of philosophy, 1964-67; University of West Florida, Pensacola, associate professor, 1967-69, professor of philosophy, 1969—, chairman of Faculty of Philosophy and Religion, 1967—. *Military service:* U.S. Navy, 1944-46. *Member:* American Philosophical Association, American Association of University Professors, Southern Society for Philosophy and Psychology, Florida Philosophical Association, Phi Kappa Phi.

WRITINGS: Metaphysics and British Empiricism, University of Nebraska Press, 1970. Contributor to philosophy journals.

WORK IN PROGRESS: Research in social philosophy and in the philosophy of science.

* * *

ARMSTRONG, Terence Ian Fytton 1912-1970
(John Gawsworth)

June 29, 1912—September 23, 1970; British itinerant poet, editor, and bibliographer. Obituaries: *New York Times,* September 27, 1970; *L'Express,* October 5-11, 1970. (See index for *CA* sketch)

* * *

ARNEZ, Nancy Levi 1928-

PERSONAL: Born July 6, 1928, in Baltimore, Md.; daughter of Milton Emerson and Ida (Rusk) Levi; married Juan Jose Arnez (divorced). *Education:* Morgan State College, A.B., 1949; Columbia University, M.A., 1954, Ed.D., 1958; additional study at Johns Hopkins University, Harvard University, and Loyola College, Baltimore, Md. *Office:* School of Education, Howard University, 2400 Sixth St. N.W., Washington, D.C. 20001.

CAREER: Baltimore (Md.) public schools, junior high teacher, 1949-62; Morgan State College, Baltimore, Md., associate professor of education, 1962-66; Northeastern Illinois State College (now Northeastern Illinois University), Chicago, professor of education, 1966-74, director of Center for Inner City Studies, 1969-74; Howard University, Washington, D.C., professor of educational administration and associate dean of School of Education, 1974—. *Member:* Association for Higher Education, National Education Association, National Council of Teachers of English, Association for Supervision and Curriculum Development, American Educational Research Association, National Council of Women in Educational Administration, American Association for Colleges of Teacher Education, American Association of University Professors, African Heritage Studies Association, Wisconsin Poetry Foundation, Kappa Delta Pi, Pi Lambda Theta.

WRITINGS: Operation Headstart: Projects and Projections, Cook County Office of Economic Opportunity, 1967; *The Rocks Cry Out* (poems), Broadside Press, 1969; (contributor) James A. Banks and William W. Joyce, editors, *Teaching Language Arts to Culturally Different Children,* Addison-Wesley, 1970; (contributor) Stanley Lehrer, editor, *The Desperate Dilemma of the Disadvantaged: Imperatives for Education,* School & Society Books, 1971; *Equality of Educational Opportuntiy,* National Urban League, 1975. Also author of *Partners in Urban Education: Teaching the Inner City Child,* 1973. Writer of study notes for *Moll Flanders,* Barnes & Noble, 1969. Poems included in *America Sings: Anthology of College Poetry, National Poetry Anthology,* and to periodicals including *Negro History Bulletin;* contributor of articles to education journals.

* * *

ARNOLD, William Robert 1933-

PERSONAL: Born May 4, 1933, in Salina, Kan.; son of Henry Clay (a farmer and custodian) and Ruby Belle (Hagler) Arnold; married Margaret Jean Smith (a college teacher of English), January 30, 1955; children: Janice, Bruce, Mark. *Education:* University of Kansas, A.B., 1955; University of Illinois, M.A., 1956; University of Chicago, Ph.D., 1963. *Politics:* Liberal Democrat. *Religion:* Baptist. *Home:* 2631 Missouri, Lawrence, Kan. 66044. *Office:* Department of Sociology, University of Kansas, Lawrence, Kan. 66044.

CAREER: Hanover College, Hanover, Ind., 1960-63, began as instructor, became assistant professor of sociology; University of Texas at Austin, assistant professor of sociology, 1963-68; University of Kansas, Lawrence, associate professor of sociology, 1968—. Director of research on self-reported delinquency in six cities, 1964—. *Military service:* U.S. Army Reserve, 1955-65, active duty, 1956; became captain. *Member:* American Sociological Association (fellow), Society for the Study of Social Problems, Society for Religion in Higher Education, National Council on Crime and Delinquency, Midwestern Sociological Association, Southwestern Sociological Association, Southwestern Social Science Association.

WRITINGS: (Contributor) Jay Hall and Martha Williams, editors, *Readings in Correctional Change,* Hogg Foundation for Mental Health, University of Texas, 1967; *Juveniles on Parole: A Sociological Perspective,* Random House, 1970. Contributor to *Journal of Thought, International Journal of Group Psychotherapy,* and to sociology journals.

WORK IN PROGRESS: Continuing work on self-reported juvenile delinquency.

ARONSON, James 1915-

PERSONAL: Born March 26, 1915, in Boston, Mass.; son of Victor and Mary Lilliam (Alpert) Aronson; married third wife, Grambs Miller (an illustrator), September 22, 1952; children: (previous marriages) Mary (Mrs. Graydon McCormick), Maggi. *Education:* Harvard University, A.B., 1936; Columbia University, M.S., 1937. *Politics:* Independent radical. *Religion:* None. *Home:* 244 East Fifth St., New York, N.Y. 10003. *Office:* Department of Communications, Hunter College of the City University of New York, 695 Park Ave., New York, N.Y. 10021.

CAREER: Member of editorial staff of Boston *Evening Transcript,* 1937-38, *New York Herald Tribune,* 1939-40, *New York Post,* 1940-46, and *New York Times,* 1946-48; founder of *National Guardian* (news weekly), 1948, editor, 1955-67; contributing editor, *Antioch Review,* 1969-73; National Emergency Civil Liberties Committee, New York City, editor of publications, 1970-75; Hunter College of the City University of New York, New York City, professor of communications, 1974—; contributing editor, *In These Times,* 1976—. Instructor in journalism at New York University and New School for Social Research, 1970-74. *Military service:* U.S. Army, 1945-46; chief of press, Western Military District, Germany, Information Control Division. *Member:* American Authors Guild, P.E.N., Society of Professional Journalists, Sigma Tau Alpha, American Center. *Awards, honors:* Alumni award, Columbia University Graduate School of Journalism, 1975.

WRITINGS: The Press and the Cold War, Bobbs-Merrill, 1970; *Packaging the News: A Critical Survey of Press, Radio and Television,* International Publishers, 1971; (contributor) *The Pentagon Papers,* Beacon Press, 1973; *Deadline for the Media,* Bobbs-Merrill, 1973.

WORK IN PROGRESS: With Cedric Belfrage, a history of the *National Guardian,* 1948-1967, entitled *An American Dissent.*

BIOGRAPHICAL/CRITICAL SOURCES: Best Sellers, January 15, 1971; *Nation,* January 25, 1971; *New Leader,* June 28, 1971; *Nieman Reports* (Harvard University), spring, 1975, summer, 1975.

*   *   *

ARTHUR, Don(ald) R(amsay) 1917-

PERSONAL: Born May 1, 1917, in Ammanford, Wales; son of Henry and Rachel (Davies) Arthur; married Doreen Gingell, March 3, 1945; children: Janet Elizabeth. *Education:* University of Wales, B.Sc., 1938, M.Sc., 1941; University of London, Ph.D., 1952, D.Sc., 1962. *Home:* 57 Rushgrove Ave., London N.W.9, England. *Office:* Department of Zoology, King's College, University of London, Strand, London W.C.1, England.

CAREER: Schoolmaster in London, England, 1938-39; scientist, Royal Ordnance Factory, 1939-42; University of Wales, College of South Wales and Monmouthshire, Cardiff, senior entomologist, 1943-47; senior biology master at high school in Cardiff, Wales, 1947-48; University of London, King's College, London, lecturer, 1948-59, reader, 1959-63, professor of zoology and head of department, 1963—, dean of Faculty of Science, 1968-70, fellow of King's College, 1972—, director of studies of School of Human Environmental Studies, 1974—. Visiting professor, University of Rhodesia, 1962; research professor, Rhodes University, 1972. Consultant to U.S. Naval Medical Research Unit, Cairo, Egypt, 1955-62.

MEMBER: Institute of Biology (fellow), Institution of Environmental Sciences (council member), British Society of Parasitology (council member, 1962-64), London Old Aberystwythians Society (president, 1966), London Carmarthenshire Society (president). *Awards, honors:* Leverhulme research award.

WRITINGS: (With Colin Burrow) *The Ixodes Rasus Group of African Ticks,* Museum of Comparative Zoology, Harvard University, 1957; *Ticks,* Part 5: *On the Genera Dermacentor, Anocentor, Cosmiomma Boophilus and Margaropus,* Cambridge University Press, 1960; (editor) *Aspects of Disease Transmission by Ticks,* Zoological Society (London), 1962; *Ticks and Disease,* Harper, 1962; *British Ticks,* Butterworth, 1963; *Ticks of the Genus Ixodes in Africa,* Athlone Press, 1965; (editor) *Looking at Animals Again,* W. H. Freeman, 1966; (editor with others) *The Biological Effects of Oil Pollution on Littoral Communities,* Field Studies Council, 1968; *Man and His Environment,* American Elsevier, 1969 (published in England as *Survival: Man and His Environment,* English Universities Press, 1969); (contributor) *Population and Polution,* Academic Press, 1972; (contributor) B. E. Dawson, editor, *Pollution in Nuffield Programme of Physical Science for A-level Students,* Penguin, 1974; (contributor) *Aquatic Biology,* Basil Blackwell, 1975; (contributor) C. R. Kennedy, editor, *Ecological Parasitology,* Elsevier, 1976. Editor, "Biological Science Texts," 1966—. Member of editorial board, *Parasitology,* 1964—, and *International Journal of Environment Studies.*

WORK IN PROGRESS: Research on environmental matters and on pollution of estuarine shores.

AVOCATIONAL INTERESTS: Don R. Arthur says he has a "fanatical interest" in Rugby football and a "deep hate" for gardening.

*   *   *

ARTOM, Guido 1906-

PERSONAL: Born June 15, 1906, in Turin, Italy; son of Alessandro (a physicist) and Elvira (Fubini) Artom; married Cristina Forges Davanzati (a translator), July 10, 1933; children: Elena (Mrs. Francesco Vicario), Sandra (Mrs. Giorgio Vigano), Alessandro. *Education:* University of Rome, Doctor in Law, 1930. *Religion:* Roman Catholic. *Home:* 37 Via Manin, Milan 20121, Italy. *Office:* Selezione dal *Reader's Digest,* 10 Via Alserio, Milan, Italy.

CAREER: Selezione dal *Reader's Digest,* Milan, Italy, books editor, 1948-71, general editorial consultant, 1971—. Delegate of Italian publishers to European Common Market. *Military service:* Italian Army, Reserve officer. *Member:* Italian Publishers Association (member of board), Italian Professional Journalists Association. *Awards, honors:* Knight Commander of the Order of the Italian Republic.

WRITINGS: (Editor) Henri Amedee Le Lorgne, Comte d'Ideville, *Il re, Il Conte e la Rosina,* Longanesi, 1959; *Napoleone e morto in Russia,* translation by Muriel Grindrod published as *Napoleon Is Dead in Russia,* Atheneum, 1970; *I Piemmtesi a Roma,* Longanesi, 1974; *Cinque bombe per l'Imperatore,* Mondadori, 1974; *I Giudici scomparsi,* Mondadori, 1977. Regular contributor to *Storia Illustrata* (a monthly), and *Tuttolibri* (a weekly).

SIDELIGHTS: Guido Artom travels frequently throughout Europe and in the United States. He speaks English, French, Spanish, and German.

BIOGRAPHICAL/CRITICAL SOURCES: Books, April, 1970; *New York Times Book Review,* April 19, 1970; *New Yorker,* May 23, 1970; *Best Sellers,* June 1, 1970.

* * *

ASHBROOK, William (Sinclair) 1922-

PERSONAL: Born January 28, 1922, in Philadelphia, Pa.; son of William Sinclair and Mildred (Janney) Ashbrook; married Florence Russell di Zerega, June 13, 1942; children: Lucy Janney (Mrs. Wayne W. Wenzel), William Sinclair III. *Education:* University of Pennsylvania, A.B., 1946; Harvard University, M.A., 1947. *Politics:* Independent. *Religion:* Episcopalian. *Home:* 310 Barberry Lane, Wayne, Pa. 19087. *Agent:* London Authors Representation Ltd., 235/241 Regent St., London W1A 2JT, England. *Office:* Department of Opera, Philadelphia College of the Performing Arts, 250 South Broad St., Philadelphia, Pa. 19102.

CAREER: Harvard University, Cambridge, Mass., teaching fellow in English, 1947-49; Stephens College, Columbia, Mo., assistant professor of humanities, 1949-55; Indiana State University, Terre Haute, assistant professor, 1955-59, associate professor, 1959-63, professor of humanities, 1963-73; Philadelphia College of the Performing Arts, Philadelphia, Pa., professor of opera, 1973—. *Military service:* U.S. Army, Mountain Infantry, 1942-45; became sergeant. *Member:* Modern Language Association of America. *Awards, honors:* Summer study grant from Italian Government, 1962; Indiana Authors' Day Award, 1966, for *Donizetti.*

WRITINGS: Donizetti, Cassell, 1965; *The Operas of Puccini,* Oxford University Press, 1968. Contributor to *Encyclopedia Americana* and to *Opera, Opera News,* and other publications.

WORK IN PROGRESS: Donizetti and His Operas; a critical biography of Arrigo Boito.

SIDELIGHTS: William Ashbrook writes: "I spend as much time as possible in Italy, particularly Bergamo, which serves as my headquarters for research on Italian operatic composers. Besides Italian, this work involves me in the French, German, and Spanish languages. My chief interest is to examine and present the field of opera in its cultural context *as it was,* rather than criticizing it for not being something else."

BIOGRAPHICAL/CRITICAL SOURCES: Spectator, May 9, 1969; *Virginia Quarterly Review,* summer, 1969.

* * *

ASHLOCK, Robert B. 1930-

PERSONAL: Born September 17, 1930, in Indianapolis, Ind.; son of Hobert Dean (an engineer) and Juanita (Kinzer) Ashlock; married Julia Ann Bronnenberg, December 23, 1951; children: Joli Ann, Alan Dean. *Education:* Attended Ball State University, 1948-51, and Wheaton College, Wheaton, Ill., 1955; Butler University, B.S., 1957, M.S., 1959; Indiana University, Ed.D., 1965. *Religion:* Presbyterian. *Home:* 1005 Roswell Dr., Silver Spring, Md. 20901. *Office:* College of Education, University of Maryland, College Park, Md. 20740.

CAREER: Elementary teacher and principal in Noblesville, Ind., 1957-64; University of Maryland, College Park, assistant professor, 1965-68, associate professor, 1968-73, professor of education, 1973—, director of Arithmetic Center, 1972—. *Member:* National Education Association (life member), National Council of Teachers of Mathematics, Central Association of Science and Mathematics Teachers, Phi Delta Kappa.

WRITINGS: (Editor with Wayne Herman) *Current Research in Elementary School Mathematics,* Macmillan, 1970; *Error Patterns in Computation,* Bobbs-Merrill, 1972, 2nd edition, 1976; (with James Humphrey) *Teaching Elementary School Mathematics through Motor Learning,* C. C Thomas, 1976. Contributor of about twenty-five articles and reviews to education journals.

SIDELIGHTS: Robert Ashlock told *CA:* "Most of my writings are concerned with helping children understand and enjoy success in arithmetic. I want them to perceive computation as a written record of observations in physical reality, something that makes sense. I also want the operations of arithmetic to make sense to children so they will know how to use them solving problems."

* * *

ASTIN, Helen S(tavridou) 1932-

PERSONAL: Born February 6, 1932, in Serras, Greece; naturalized U.S. citizen; daughter of Pericles and Soteria (Boukouvala) Stavrides; married Alexander W. Astin, 1956; children: John A., Paul A. *Education:* Adelphi University, B.A., 1953; Ohio University, M.S., 1954; University of Maryland, Ph.D., 1957. *Home:* 2681 Cordelia Rd., Los Angeles, Calif. 90049. *Office:* University of California, Los Angeles, Calif. 90024.

CAREER: U.S. Public Health Service Hospital, Lexington, Ky., clinical psychologist, 1957-59; University of Maryland Medical School, College Park, instructor in pediatrics, 1960; National College of Education, Evanston, Ill., instructor in psychology, 1961-65; Gallaudet College, Washington, D.C., associate professor of psychology, 1965; National Academy of Sciences, Washington, D.C., research associate, Commission on Human Resources and Advanced Education, 1965-67; Stanford University, Stanford, Calif., research associate and lecturer, Institute for the Study of Human Problems, 1967-68; Bureau of Social Science Research, Washington, D.C., research associate, 1968-70; University Research Corp., Washington, D.C., director of research, 1970-73; University of California, Los Angeles, professor of higher education, 1973—. Trustee of Hampshire College. *Member:* American Psychological Association, American Educational Resource Association, American Association for Higher Education.

WRITINGS: The Woman Doctorate in America: Origins, Career, and Family, Russell Sage, 1969; (with J. K. Folger and A. E. Bayer) *Human Resources and Higher Education,* Russell Sage, 1969; (with others) *Higher Education and the Disadvantaged Student,* Behavioral Publications, 1972; (with Nancy Suniewick and Susan Dweck) *Women: A Bibliography on Their Education and Careers,* Behavioral Publications, 1974; (editor) Allison Parelman and Anne Fisher, *Sex Roles: A Research Bibliography,* National Institute of Mental Health, 1975; *Some Action of Her Own,* Lexington Books, 1976. Also author with others of *The Power of Protest,* for Jossey-Bass, *Open Admissions at City University of New York,* for Prentice-Hall, and *Sex Discrimination in Career Guidance and Education,* for Praeger. Author of several studies, reports, and booklets on educational and women's problems. Contributor to psychology and education journals. Member of editorial board, *Journal of Vocational Behavior, Journal of Counseling Psychology, Signs, Psychology of Women Quarterly.*

ASTRO, Richard 1941-

PERSONAL: Born February 11, 1941, in New York, N.Y.; son of Ralph (a social worker) and Sylvia (Bach) Astro; married Betty Ann Lubinski (an administrative assistant), June 6, 1964. *Education:* Oregon State University, B.A., 1964; University of Colorado, M.A., 1965; University of Washington, Seattle, Ph.D., 1969. *Politics:* Independent. *Home:* 3360 Northwest Crest Dr., Corvallis, Ore. 97330. *Office:* Department of English, Oregon State University, Corvallis, Ore. 97331.

CAREER: Oregon State University, Corvallis, instructor, 1966-68, assistant professor, 1968-71, associate professor, 1971-77, professor of English, 1977—, chairman of department, 1975—, director of humanities development, 1976—. *Member:* Modern Language Association of America, John Steinbeck Society of America, Rocky Mountain Modern Language Association.

WRITINGS: (Editor with Tetsumaro Hayashi) *Steinbeck: The Man and His Work,* Oregon State University Press, 1971; *John Steinbeck and Edward F. Ricketts,* University of Minnesota Press, 1973; (editor with Jackson Benson) *Hemingway in Our Time,* Oregon State University Press, 1974; (editor with Benson) *The Fiction of Bernard Malamud,* Oregon State University Press, 1977. Contributor to literature journals. Associate editor, *Steinbeck Quarterly.*

WORK IN PROGRESS: Directing a major curriculum development program supported by the National Endowment for the Humanities and National Oceanic and Atmospheric Administration.

*   *   *

ATCHESON, Richard 1934-
(Charles Tressilian)

PERSONAL: Born August 10, 1934, in Houston, Tex.; son of William H. (in publishing business) and Dorothy (Williams) Atcheson; married Jean C. Nicholas (an editor), November 25, 1961; children: Dorothy, Katharine, Nicholas. *Education:* Princeton University, A.B., 1956. *Agent:* Don Gold, William Morris Agency, 1350 Avenue of the Americas, New York, N.Y. 10019.

CAREER: Time, Inc., New York City, executive trainee, 1956-57; *Chicago Daily News,* Chicago, Ill., general assignment reporter, 1959-61; *Show Business Illustrated* (magazine), Chicago, theater editor, 1961-62; *Show* (magazine), New York City, contributing editor, 1962-64; *Holiday* (magazine), New York City, senior staff editor, 1965-70. Movie critic, *Playboy* (magazine), 1966-68. *Military service:* U.S. Army, 1957-59. *Member:* Society of Magazine Writers, Society of American Travel Writers.

WRITINGS: What the Hell Are They Trying to Prove, Martha?: A Wary Convert's Report on the New Self-Expression in America Today, John Day, 1970; *The Bearded Lady: Going on the Commune Trip and Beyond,* John Day, 1971. Contributor to *Saturday Review, Cosmopolitan, Vista USA, Travel & Leisure,* and other magazines, occasionally under the pseudonym Charles Tressilian.

WORK IN PROGRESS: Research for a book on death and dying, "the last taboo subject in our society"; compiling materials on American attitudes toward nakedness (a continuing project).

SIDELIGHTS: Richard Atcheson has an enduring interest in human behavior, "particularly through the focus of the 'human potential movement.'" He adds: "The beauty of my profession, for me, is that it permits me to remain a gener-

alist without owing any apologies. This is, perhaps, why I have worked so long in travel. I remain eager to be in places where I am not, and to see what I have not seen, and do what I have not done, and no other field offers so open an invitation to new experience. I am drawn to the human potentials movement, to the radical life experiments of my time, because the adventurous spirit there never fails to jar my assumptions. . . ."††

*   *   *

AUMONT, Jean-Pierre 1913-

PERSONAL: Born January 5, 1913, in Paris, France; married Maria Montez (an actress), July 13, 1943 (died September 7, 1951); married Marisa Pavan (an actress), March 27, 1956; children: (first marriage) Maria-Christina; (second marriage) Jean-Claude, Patrick. *Agent:* International Famous Artists, 1301 Avenue of the Americas, New York, N.Y. 10019.

CAREER: Stage and screen actor and playwright. Made his stage debut in Paris in Jean Cocteau's "La Machine infernale," 1934; played in three other Paris productions before coming to America in a tour of "Rose Burke," 1942; had the role of Pierre Renault in his own play, "L'Empereur de Chine," in Paris, 1948, and the same part in the Broadway adaptation of the play, "My Name is Aquilon," 1949; from 1953 on, he more or less divided his time between the French and American stage, appearing in New York in "The Heavenly Twins," 1955, "Second String," 1960, "Tovarich," 1963, "Incident at Vichy," 1965, "The Tempest," 1966, "Camino Real," 1970, "Murderous Angels," 1971, and "Jacques Brel Is Alive and Well and Living in Paris," 1972. Had film roles in "Lac aux dames," 1936, "L'Equipage," 1936, "Hotel du Nord," 1938, "Le Deserteur," 1939, and a number of other films produced in France, Italy, and Argentina, 1936-60; his first Hollywood role was in Metro-Goldwyn-Mayer's "Assignment in Britanny," 1943, followed by "The Cross of Lorraine," 1943, "Scheherazade," 1945, "Atlantis," 1945, "Heartbeat," 1946, "Lili," 1953, "Charge of the Lancers," 1954, "Hilda Crane" 1956, "The Seventh Sin," 1957, "Royal Affairs in Versailles," 1957, "John Paul Jones," 1959, "The Devil at 4 O'Clock," 1961, "7 Capital Sins," 1962, "Castle Keep," 1969, "The Happy Hooker," 1975, and "Mahogany," 1975. He has also acted in television plays, including "No Time for Comedy," 1951, "Arms and the Man," 1952, "Crime and Punishment," 1953, and has been a guest on the Perry Como, Nanette Fabray, Sid Caesar, and other shows. He also appeared in a supper club act with his wife, Marisa Pavan, 1965-67. *Military service:* Free French Forces, World War II; received Legion of Honor and Croix de Guerre. *Member:* Screen Actors Guild, Artists Equity Association, American Federation of Television and Radio Artists. *Awards, honors:* Nominated by *Variety* New York Critics Poll for his 1963 performance as Mikail in "Tovarich."

WRITINGS: Souvenirs provisoires (reminiscences), Julliard, 1957; *La Pomme de son oeil* (short stories), Julliard, 1969.

Plays: *L'Empereur de Chine* (first produced in Paris at Theatre des Mathurins, January, 1948, adaptation by Philip Barry produced on Broadway at Lyceum Theatre as "My Name Is Aquilon" [titled "Figure of a Girl" in pre-Broadway tryouts]; published with a preface by Jean Cocteau), Nagel, 1948; "L'Ile heureuse," first produced in Paris at Theatre Edouard VII, January 23, 1951; "Un beau dimanche" (based on Pierre Corthomas' novel, *Recontre),* first produced at Theatre de la Michodiere, June 25, 1952, published in supplement to *France Illustration,* Number 119, 1952; "Ange le bienheureux," first produced in Nice at Theatre Municipal, December 21, 1956; "Farfada," first produced in Paris at Comedie Wagram, November 12, 1957; *Lucy Crown* (adapted from Irwin Shaw's novel of the same name; first produced in Paris at Theatre de Paris, September 22, 1958), published, 1958.

WORK IN PROGRESS: A novel.

BIOGRAPHICAL/CRITICAL SOURCES: L'Express (Paris), November 3-9, 1969.

* * *

AUSTIN, David E(dwards)   1926-

PERSONAL: Born March 20, 1926, in Bloomington, Ind.; son of Harmon O. and Bertha (Edwards) Austin; married Dorothy Lea Dodd (a teacher), September 3, 1949; children: Janet Louise, Paula Jean, Lois Eileen, Carol Elizabeth. *Education:* Lingnam University, Canton, China, student, 1948-49; Eastern Washington State College, A.B. (political science; with honors) and A.B. (education), 1949, M.A., 1951; Colorado State College (now University of Northern Colorado), Ed.D., 1955; University of California, Berkeley, additional study, 1955. *Home:* 2034 Alan Lane, Merced, Calif. 95340. *Office:* Merced County Department of Education, 632 West 13th St., Merced, Calif. 95340.

CAREER: Lingnam University, Canton, China, instructor in English department, 1948-49; primary teacher in Spokane, Wash., 1949-50, 1951-53; San Leandro (Calif.) public schools, teacher, 1954-55, vice-principal, 1955-56, general supervisor (elementary), 1956-61; Ministry of Education, Sudan, educational adviser, 1961-63; Merced County Department of Education, Merced, Calif., general consultant, 1963—. Visiting or part-time instructor at California State Colleges, 1959, 1964-66, University of California, Berkeley, 1964, Chapman College, 1966-69, and University of California, Davis, 1970-71; visiting summer professor at State University of New York at Cortland, California State University, Fresno, University of Nebraska, and Colorado State University. Member of firm, Technical Writers. *Military service:* U.S. Navy, Submarine Service, 1943-46.

MEMBER: National Education Association, Association for Supervision and Curriculum Development, American Academy of Political and Social Science, American Political Science Association, American Association of University Professors, National Council of Mathematics Teachers, California Teachers Association, California Association of Secondary School Administrators, Phi Delta Kappa, Kappa Delta Pi. *Awards, honors:* Exchange student scholarship in China, 1948-49.

WRITINGS: (With Velma Clark and Gladys Fitchett) *Reading Rights for Boys: Sex Role and Language Experience,* Appleton, 1970. Contributor to "Our Working World" series, Science Research Associates, 1967. Editorial consultant, "Supplemental Mathematics Program," Franklin Press.

* * *

AVERILL, Esther   1902-

PERSONAL: Born July 24, 1902, in Bridgeport, Conn.; daughter of Charles Ketchum (a civil engineer) and Helen (Holden) Averill. *Education:* Graduate of Vassar College, 1923; attended Brooklyn Museum Art School. *Religion:* Episcopalian. *Home:* 30 Joralemon St., Brooklyn, N.Y. 11201.

CAREER: Editor for *Women's Wear Daily,* New York City, beginning 1923; lived in Paris, France, 1925-35, working as free-lance journalist/photographer in field of fashion and decorative arts, later establishing The Domino Press and publishing books for children; returned to New York, working in children's section of New York Public Library, and studying painting; full-time free-lance writer and illustrator.

WRITINGS: (With Lila Stanley) *Powder: The Story of a Colt, a Duchess, and the Circus,* H. Smith, 1933; *Flash: The Story of a Horse, a Coach-Dog and the Gypsies,* Faber, 1934; *Political Propaganda in Children's Books of the French Revolution,* Hawthorn, 1935; *The Voyages of Jacques Cartier* (illustrated by Feodor Rojankovsky), Domino Press, 1937, revised edition published as *Cartier Sails the St. Lawrence,* Harper, 1956; *Daniel Boone* (illustrated by Rojankovsky), Harper, 1946; *King Philip: The Indian Chief* (illustrated by Vera Belsky), Harper, 1950; *Eyes on the World,* Funk, 1969.

Self-illustrated juveniles; all published by Harper: *The Cat Club,* 1944; *The Adventures of Jack Ninepins,* 1944; *The School for Cats,* 1947; *Jenny's First Party,* 1948; *Jenny's Moonlight Adventure,* 1949; *When Jenny Lost Her Scarf,* 1951; *Jenny's Adopted Brothers,* 1952; *How the Brothers Joined the Cat Club,* 1953; *Jenny's Birthday Book,* 1954; *Jenny Goes to Sea,* 1957; *Jenny's Bedside Book,* 1959; *The Fire Cat,* 1960; *The Hotel Cat,* 1969; *Captains of the City Streets,* 1972; *Jenny and the Cat Club,* 1973. Contributor of articles to *Colophon* and *Horn Book.*

SIDELIGHTS: The Cat Club, which introduced Jenny Linsky, the shy little black cat with the bright red scarf, "launched me on my cat career," wrote Esther Averill, "for these little books of mine, as they appeared over the years, have brought me in touch with that wonderful world of true cat lovers. I mean the people who not only care for their own pets, but also devote much time and effort to the humanitarian work of alleviating the suffering of the stray, abandoned cats of their communities. I wish that I might participate in such work more fully than I am able. It is sometimes heartbreaking work, and in no sense a 'hobby.'

"Jenny in real life was as shy as I have portrayed her. The number of books surprises me, for Jenny, when she was tiny, was so shy and plain that I felt that of all the cats I had had—many of them truly glamorous—she was the only one who would never have a 'story.' I did not suspect that Jenny's special brand of courage would carry her into so many adventures. The Cat Club, too, has expanded since she joined it in her first story—then there were only 12 members. Sometimes I feel that fate has made me a kind of Balzac of the Cat Club."

Esther Averill's Cat Club books have been published in German, Swedish, Danish, Afrikaans, and Japanese.

* * *

AVISON, N(eville) Howard   1934-

PERSONAL: Born Janaury 8, 1934; son of Ernest and Betty (Green-Simpson) Avison; married Margaret Mary F. Coonagh, April 29, 1959 (divorced, 1974); children: Katherine, Isobel, John. *Education:* Attended Trinity College, Dublin, B.A., 1960, M.A., 1963. *Home and office:* 612-257 Lisgar, Ottawa, Ontario, Canada K2P 0C7.

CAREER: Cambridge University, Cambridge, England, senior research officer, Institute of Criminology, 1960-66; University of Edinburgh, Edinburgh, Scotland, lecturer,

1966-70, senior lecturer in criminal law and criminology, 1970-74; research director, British Columbia Police Commission, 1974-76; Federal Department of Justice, Ottawa, Ontario, consultant, 1976—.

WRITINGS: (With F. H. McClintock) *Crime in England and Wales,* Heinemann, 1968, Humanities, 1969. Contributor to *Juridical Review.*

BIOGRAPHICAL/CRITICAL SOURCES: New Statesman, February 14, 1969.

* * *

AVRIL, Pierre 1930-

PERSONAL: Born November 18, 1930, in Pau, Basses-Pyrenees, France; son of Stanislas and Genevieve (Camion) Avril; married Malou Hillion, July 11, 1959; children: Pierre-Olivier. *Education:* University of Paris, Docteur en droit, 1962. *Home:* 48 rue Gay-Lussac, Paris 5, France. *Office:* University of Poitiers, Poitiers Cedex, France 86034.

CAREER: Cahiers de la Republique (monthly), Paris, France, editor-in-chief, 1957-62; Societe Generale de Presse, Paris, member of board of editors, 1962-68; University of Poitiers, Poitiers, France, assistant professor, 1970-75, professor of public law, 1975—. Assistant professor of political science, University of Paris, 1971—.

WRITINGS: La Regime politique de la Ve Republique, Librairie Generale de Droit et de Jurisprudence, 1964, 3rd edition, 1975; *Un President pour quoi faire?,* Editions du Seuil, 1965; *Le Gouvernement de la France,* Editions Universitaires, 1969, translation by John Ross published as *Politics in France,* Penguin, 1970; *L'Arrondissement devant la reforme administrative,* Berger-Levrault, 1970; *UDR et gaullistes,* Presses Universitaires de France, 1971; *Les francais et leur Parlement,* Casterman, 1972. Contributor to literary and legal journals.

* * *

AWOONOR, Kofi 1935-

PERSONAL: Born March 13, 1935, in Wheta, Ghana; son of Atsu E. and Kosiwo (Nyidevu) Awoonor; children: Sika, Dunyo, Kalepe. *Education:* University College of Ghana, B.A., 1960; University College, London, M.A., 1970; State University of New York at Stony Brook, Ph.D., 1972. *Religion:* Ancestralist. *Home address:* P.O. Box K.346, Accra, Ghana. *Agent:* Harold Ober Associates, Inc., 40 East 49th St., New York, N.Y. 10017. *Office:* Department of English, University of Cape Coast, Cape Coast, Ghana.

CAREER: University of Ghana, Accra, lecturer and research fellow, 1960-64; Ghana Ministry of Information, Accra, director of films, 1964-67; State University of New York at Stony Brook, assistant professor of English, 1968-75; arrested for suspected subversion, charged with harboring a subversionist, served one year in prison in Ghana, 1975-76; University of Cape Coast, Cape Coast, Ghana, assistant professor of English, 1976—. *Member:* African Studies Association of America. *Awards, honors:* Longmans fellow at University of London, 1967-68.

WRITINGS: Rediscovery, Northwestern University Press, 1964; (editor with G. Adoli-Mortty) *Messages: Poems from Ghana,* Heinemann, 1970, Humanities, 1971; *Ancestral Power and Lament,* Heinemann, 1970; *This Earth, My Brother,* Doubleday, 1971; *Night of My Blood,* Doubleday, 1971; *Ride Me Memory,* Greenfield Review Press, 1973; *Guardians of the Sacred Wand,* NOK, 1974; *The Breast of the Earth,* Doubleday, 1975. Contributor to *Africa Report* and *Books Abroad.* Associate editor, *Transition.*

WORK IN PROGRESS: A House by the Sea, poems; *Notes from Prison,* a personal account; *Alien Corn,* a novel; "The Lambezi Flows Here," a screenplay.

SIDELIGHTS: Kofi Awoonor wrote *CA:* "The written word came almost as if it had no forebears. So my poetry assays to restate the oral beginnings, to articulate the mysterious relation between the WORD and the magical dimensions of our cognitive world. I work with forces that are beyond me, ancestral and ritualized entities who dictate and determine all my literary endeavours. Simply put, my work takes off from the world of all our aboriginal instincts. It is for this reason that I have translated poetry from my own society, the Ewes, and sat at the feet of ancient poets whose medium is the voice and whose forum is the village square and the market place."

AVOCATIONAL INTERESTS: Politics, jazz, tennis, and herbal medicine (African).

BIOGRAPHICAL/CRITICAL SOURCES: Ariel, Volume VI, number 1, January, 1975.

* * *

AYARS, Albert L(ee) 1917-

PERSONAL: Surname rhymes with "cares"; born September 17, 1917, in Kettle Falls, Wash.; son of Glen Garrison (in motel management) and Ama Belle (Jennings) Ayars; married Frances Louise Schaaf, June 21, 1941; children: Cheron Marie (Mrs. Howard H. Holman), Judith Louise, Albert Lee, Jr., Danielle Jo (Mrs. Richard Alexander), Garrison Hubert, Theodore Ama, Virginia Darlene. *Education:* Washington State University, B.A., 1939, B.Ed., 1940, M.A.Ed., 1942, D.Ed., 1956. *Religion:* American Baptist. *Home:* 512 Mowbray Arch, Norfolk, Va. 23507. *Office:* Norfolk City Schools, 800 East City Hall Ave., Norfolk, Va. 23510.

CAREER: Teacher of English in Davenport, Wash., 1940-42; high school principal in Colville, Wash., 1942-45; superintendent of schools in Omak, Wash., 1945-49, and Sunnyside, Wash., 1949-52; Joint Council on Economic Education, New York City, associate director, 1952-53; Hill & Knowlton, Inc. (public relations counselors), New York City, director of education department, 1953-65; Spokane (Wash.) public schools, superintendent, 1965-72; Norfolk (Va.) public schools, superintendent, 1972—. Visiting professor at Washington State University, 1950-52, Michigan State University, 1958, University of Delaware, 1959, and at other universities. Member of board of directors of Northwest Regional Education Laboratory, 1968-72, and Joint Council on Economic Education, 1970—; member of advisory bodies to U.S. Office of Education, Association Internationale des Etudiants en Sciences Economiques et Commerciales, W. E. Upjohn Institute for Employment Research, National Training Laboratories, and other organizations.

MEMBER: Council of National Organizations for Adult Education (past president), National Association for Industry-Education Cooperation (past president; honorary life member), American Association of School Administrators (member of executive committee, 1970; vice-president, 1973-74), American Economic Association, American Association for the Advancement of Science, Washington State University Alumni Association (past national president), Inland Empire Education Association (president, 1968-69), Eastern Washington Historical Society (member of board of directors, 1968).

WRITINGS: How to Plan Your Community Resources

Workshop, Teachers Publishing Corp., 1954; *Administering the People's Schools,* McGraw, 1957; (with Gail G. Milgram) *The Teenager and Alcohol,* Richards Rosen, 1970; (with Corlan Bovee) *How to Plan a Community Resources Workshop,* National Association for Industry-Education Cooperation, 1975.

Contributor to *Handbook of Adult Education in the United States, Handbook of Public Relations,* and *Planning for Excellence in High School Science.* Member of editorial advisory board, *Public Relations News,* 1962-65.

* * *

AZUMI, Koya 1930-

PERSONAL: Born November 23, 1930, in Tokyo, Japan; became U.S. citizen; son of Tokuya and Masako (Kurata) Azumi; married Jann A. Eckert, November 26, 1960; children: Eric, Elise. *Education:* Haverford College, B.A., 1955; Columbia University, Ph.D., 1966. *Office:* Department of Sociology, Rutgers University, Newark, N.J. 07102.

CAREER: Rutgers University, New Brunswick, N.J., instructor in sociology, 1963-65; New York University, New York City, assistant professor of sociology, 1965-67; University of Wisconsin—Madison, assistant professor of sociology, 1967-70; Columbia University, New York City, visiting assistant professor of sociology and research associate, 1970-72; Rutgers University, Newark, N.J., associate professor, 1972-77, professor of sociology, 1977—. *Member:* American Sociological Association, Association for Asian Studies. *Awards, honors:* Fulbright grant for research in Japan, 1969-70.

WRITINGS: Higher Education and Business Recruitment in Japan, Teachers College Press, 1969; (with Jerald Hage) *Organizational Systems,* Heath, 1972; (contributor) Arthur E. Tiedemann, editor, *An Introduction to Japanese Civilization,* Columbia University Press, 1974; (with Charles McMillan) *Japan: The Paradox of Progress,* Yale University Press, 1976. Contributor of articles to journals in his field.

WORK IN PROGRESS: Organizations and Cultures, with Charles McMillan, David Hickson, and Dezso Horvath.

* * *

BACCHELLI, Riccardo 1891-

PERSONAL: Born April 19, 1891, in Bologna, Italy; son of Giuseppe (a lawyer) and Anna (Bumiller) Bacchelli; married Ada Fochesfati, 1966. *Home:* Borgonuovo 20, 20121 Milan, Italy.

CAREER: Writer since his early twenties. *Member:* Accademia Nazionale dei Lincei, Accademia della Crusca, Accademia delle Scienze (Bologna), Accademia delle Scienze (Ferrara), Instituto Lombardo di Scienze e Lettere. *Awards, honors:* Doctor honoris causa from University of Bologna and University of Milan; Grand Officer of Italian Republic, 1953.

WRITINGS: Poemi lirici, [Italy], 1914; *Lo sa il tonno: Ossia, Gli esemplari marini, favola mondana e filosofica,* Bottega di Poesia, 1923, subsequent editions to 1953 published with varying subtitles; *Il diavolo al Pontelungo* (historical novel), [Italy], 1927, translation by Orlo Williams published with an introduction by translator as *The Devil at the Long Bridge,* Longmans, Green, 1929; *Bella Italia* (stories), Ceschina, 1928; *La citta degli amanti* (novel), Ceschina, 1929, reprinted, Mondadori, 1966, translation by Williams published as *Love Town,* Duckworth, 1930.

Amore di poesia (includes *Poemi lirici* and other poems), Preda, 1930, reprinted, Mondadori, 1967; *Una passione coniugale* (novel), Ceschina, 1930; *Oggi, domani e mai* (novel), Treves-Treccani-Tumminelli, 1932; *Mal d'Africa* (historical novel), Fratelli Treves, 1934; *Il rabdomante* (novel), Fratelli Treves, 1936; *Iride* (novel), Fratelli Treves, 1937; (collaborator) Adriano Lualdi, *Der Hummer* (one-act opera), Ricordi (Milan and New York), 1937; *Il Mulino del Po* (trilogy; includes *Dio ti salvi, La miseria viene in barca,* and *Mondo vecchio, sempre nuovo*), Fratelli Treves, 1938-40, translation by Frances Frenaye of *Dio ti salvi* and *La miseria viene in barca* published as *The Mill on the Po,* Pantheon, 1950, reprinted, Greenwood Press, 1975, translation by Stuart Hood of *Mondo vecchio, sempre nuovo* published as *Nothing New under the Sun,* Pantheon, 1955.

Gioacchino Rossini, Unione Tipografico-Editrice Torinese, 1941, latest edition published as *Rossini e Esperienze rossiniane,* Mondadori, 1959; *La fine d'Atlantide* (stories), Garzanti, 1942; *Il fiore della Mirabilis* (novel), Garzanti, 1942; *La notte dell'8 settembre 1943* (World War II poetry), Garzanti, 1943; *Il pianto del figlio de Lais* (historical novel), Garzanti, 1945; *La politica di un impolitico, 1914-1945: Dieci anni di ansie* (on Italian politics and government), Garzanti, 1948; *L'alba dell'ultima sera* (tragedy in three acts), Garzanti, 1949.

La Cometa (novel), Rizzoli, 1951; *Italia per terra e per mare* (travel), Rizzoli, 1952; *L'incendio di Milano* (novel), Rizzoli, 1952, translation by Kathleen Nott published as *The Fire of Milan,* Secker & Warburg, 1958; (with Roberto Longhi) *Teatro e immagini del Settecento italiano* (on the Italian theater and art), Edizioni Radio Italiana, 1953; *Memorie del tempo presente* (includes *Poemi lirici* and later volumes of poems), Rizzoli, 1953; *Il figlio di Stalin* (novel), Mondadori, 1953, translation by Nott published as *Son of Stalin,* Secker & Warburg, 1956, same translation published as *Seed of Steel,* Walker & Co., 1963; (with Orio Vergani) *Bagutta: 122 tavole di Mario Vellani Marchi,* edited by Marino Parenti, Casini, 1955; *Tre giorni di passione* (novel), Rizzoli, 1955; (with others) *La Civilta veneziana del secolo di Marco Polo,* Sansoni, 1955; *Nel fiume della storia* (addresses, essays, and lectures), Mondadori, 1957; *Il tre schiavi di Giulio Cesare* (historical novel), Mondadori, 1957; *Viaggio in Greece* (travel), Ricciardi, 1959; *Ritorno sotto i portici* (guide to Bologna), Nuova Abes Editrice, 1959; *Non ti chiamero piu padre* (historical novel), Mondadori, 1959, 2nd edition, 1962.

(Author of essay on Machiavelli) Niccolo Machiavelli, *La Mandragola,* Tallone, 1960; *Garibaldi e i Mille,* Cordani, 1960; (author of libretto) *La notte di un nevrastenico* (one-act musical comedy; music by Nino Rota), Ricordi, 1960; *Leopardo: Commenti letterari,* Mondadori, 1962; *Teatro di Pietro Metastasio,* Edizioni RAI, 1962; *Secondo viaggio in Grecia* (travel), Ricciardi, 1963; *Le Bolognesi,* photographs by Antonio Masotti, Nuova Abes Editrice, 1964; *Manzoni: Commenti letterari,* Mondadori, 1964; *Teatro,* two volumes, Mondadori, 1965; (author of preface) *Riva di Po* (travel), photographs by Harold Null, Edizioni Valdonega, 1965; (with others) *Drammaturgia nuova: Raccolta di drammi e commedie scritte per la televisione,* edited by Sergio Pugliese, ERI (Torino), 1965; (with others) *Carducci et Croce,* edited by Giovanni Spadolini, Carlino, 1966; *Il coccio de terracotta,* Mondadori, 1966; *Giorno per giorno dal 1912 al 1922: Entusiasmi e passioni letterarie,* Mondadori, 1966; *America in confidenza* (travel), Ricciardi, 1966; *Rapporto segreto dall'inglese di mille parole* (novel), Mondadori, 1967; *Pagine bolognesi,* Almanacco Torriani, 1967; (author of introduction) Lodovico Ariosto, *Orlando furioso,* Electa, 1967; *L'Afrodite* (novel), Mondadori, 1969.

Africa tra storia e fantasia, Ricciardi, 1970; *Versi e rime,* Mondadori, Volume I: *La stella del mattino,* 1971, Volume II: *Bellezza e umanita,* 1972, Volume III: *Giorni da vita e tempo di poesia,* 1973; (with others) *Le Madri,* Bramante, 1972; *In Arqua Petrarco nel sesto centenario della morte del poeta,* Antenore, 1974; *Il progresso e un razzo: Un romanzo matto,* Mondadori, 1975; (with others) *Per l'Ariosto,* Marzorati, 1976.

Editor: *Le Piu belle pagine di Ippolito Nievo,* [Milan], 1929; Luca della Robbia, *La Morte di Pietro Paolo Boscoli,* [Florence], 1943; Allesandro Manzoni, *Opere,* Ricciardi, 1953, excerpts published as *Adelchi,* G. Einaudi, 1976, other excerpts published as *Poesi,* G. Einaudi, 1976; *Cantoni* (selected short stories and a novel by Alberto Cantoni), [Milan], 1953; (with others) *Emilia Romagna,* Electa, c.1975, translation by Rudolf Carpanini and Margaret Meringer published under same title, Electa, 1975.

Books and pamphlets: *Nel centenario di Giacomi Leopardi* (lectures by Bacchelli and Carl Vossler), [Padua], 1937; *Antonio Fogazzaro* (centenary tribute), [Rome], 1942; *Sull'amore delle arti e delle scienze, oggi e sempre,* [Rome], 1947; *Il fregio e la stele di Francesco Barbieri nel salone della Banco commerciale Italiana in Bari,* Tipografic Gregoriana, 1951; *Passeggiate orobiche,* Societa Anonima Orobia, 1956.

Collected works: *Tutte le novelle, 1911-1951,* two volumes, Rizzoli, 1952-53; *Tutte le opere,* Mondadori, twenty-eight volumes, 1958-74, Volume I: *Memorie del tempo presente,* Volume II: *Versi e rime,* Volume III: *Il diavola al Pontelungo,* Volume IV: *La citta degli amanti* [and] *Una Passione coniugale,* Volume V: *Oggi domani e mai,* Volume VI: *Mal d'Africa* [and] *Il rabdomante,* Volume VII: *Iride* [and] *Il fiore della Mirabilis,* Volume VIII: *Il mulino del Po,* Volume IX: *Il pianto del figlio di Lais* [and] *Lo sguardo di Gesu,* Volume X: *La Cometa* [and] *L'incendio di Milano,* Volume XI: *Il figlio di Stalin* [and] *Tre giorni di passione,* Volumes XII-XIII: *Tutte le novelle, 1911-1951,* Volume XIV: *Teatro,* Volume XV: *La congiura di Don Giulio d'Este, e altri scritti ariosteschi,* Volume XVI: *Rossini e altri scritti musicali,* Volume XVII: *Nel fiume della storia,* Volume XVIII: *Confessioni letterari,* Volume XIX: *Saggi critici,* Volume XX: *Italia per terra e per mare,* Volume XXI: *Viaggi all'estero e Vagabondaggi di fantasia,* Volume XXII: *Giorno per giorno dal 1912 al 1922: Entusiasm e passioni letterari,* Volume XXIII: *Giorno per giorno dal 1922 al 1966: Cronaca e storia estri, ricordi e riflessioni,* Volume XXVI: *I tre schiavi di Giulo Cesare,* Volume XXVIII: *L'Afrodite.*

Also author of *Amleto 1918* (Hamlet adaptations and parodies), 1923, reprinted by Mondadori, 1957; *La Congiura di Don Giulo d'Este,* 1931, *Il Brigante di tocca del lupo,* edited by Francesco Grisi, 1942, *L'Elmo di Tancredi,* 1942, *Le Bellissima fiaba di Rosa dei Venti,* 1948, *Lo Sguardo di Gesu,* 1948, and *Viaggi all'estero e vaga bondaggi di fantasia,* 1966.

SIDELIGHTS: Riccardo Bacchelli's fame probably rests most solidly on his historical novels, the first one published more than forty years ago. At the age of seventy-six, he attacked a theme that the *Times Literary Supplement* says borders on science fiction in *Rapporto segreto dall'inglese di mille parole,* a novel about space flight. The *Times* reviewer quotes Bacchelli on the genesis of *Rapporto segreto,* published so far only in Italian, but set in an unnamed country which is clearly America: "The novel began to take shape in me around an agonizing question: has the astronaut the right to cut short his agony, to kill himself, when he becomes aware, way out in space, that the instruments are no longer functioning, that the undertaking is a failure and the space-craft in which he is imprisoned continues on its crazy way, and there is no hope, perhaps for days and days."

Bacchelli has not been widely translated, but in Italy even his early poetry has endured, and the novels have been frequently reissued. In recent years Mondadori has brought most of the major works back into print separately in addition to publishing the twenty-eight volume *Tutte le opere.*

BIOGRAPHICAL/CRITICAL SOURCES: Dial, May, 1928; *Nuova Antologia,* September 1, 1936; *Mercure de France,* May 1, 1937; Aldo Andreoli and others, *Discorrendo di Riccardo Bachelli,* Ricciardi, 1966; *Times Literary Supplement,* January 18, 1968, July 18, 1968; Claudio Casoli, *Bacchelli, Betocchi, Cassola, Luzi, Quasimodo: Silone interpretano la societa in cui viviamo,* Citta nuova, 1969; *Books Abroad,* winter, 1970.†

*   *   *

BACON, Edward 1906-
(Francis Boon)

PERSONAL: Born July 6, 1906, in Normanby, England; son of Richard William (a schoolmaster) and Edith (Blewitt) Bacon; married Mary Patricia Jacques, February 17, 1941; married second wife, Doris Kate Wiseman, May 17, 1967; children: Jacqueline Mary (Mrs. Peter Hammond), Victoria Catherine Amanda. *Education:* Keble College, Oxford, B.A. (honors), 1929. *Religion:* Church of England. *Home:* Swift's Garden, Chelsworth, Ipswich, Suffolk, England. *Agent:* Maurice Michael, Chucks Cottage, Littleworth, Partridge Green, Sussex RH13 8EJ, England. *Office:* Illustrated London News, Elm House, Elm St., London W.C.1, England.

CAREER: Illustrated London News, London, England, archaeological editor, 1945-68, archaeological contributor, 1968—.

WRITINGS: Digging for History, A. & C. Black, 1960, John Day, 1961; (editor) *Vanished Civilizations of the Ancient World,* McGraw, 1963 (published in England as *Vanished Civilisations: Forgotten Peoples of the Ancient World,* Thames & Hudson, 1963); (with A. G. Galanopoulos) *Atlantis: The Truth Behind the Legend,* Bobbs-Merrill, 1969; *Archaeology: Discoveries in the 1960's,* Praeger, 1971; *Archaeology: A Survey,* Cassell, 1971; *The Great Archaeologists,* Bobbs-Merrill, 1976.

Novels under pseudonym Francis Boon: *Lord, What Fools,* John Long, 1936; *Ancient and Fishlike,* John Long, 1937; *A Cat Among the Rabbits,* John Long, 1940.

WORK IN PROGRESS: A book about Victorian Cyprus; a personal book about gardens.

SIDELIGHTS: Edward Bacon has traveled throughout Europe and the Middle East, and in India, Kashmir, Nepal, Ceylon, Thailand, and Cambodia.

BIOGRAPHICAL/CRITICAL SOURCES: Spectator, September 20, 1969; *Books,* October, 1969; *New York Review of Books,* December 4, 1969.

*   *   *

BACON, Elizabeth 1914-
(Betty Morrow)

PERSONAL: Born September 15, 1914, in Los Angeles,

Calif.; daughter of James Edwin (a teacher) and Elizabeth (Hodenpyl) Morrow; married George Richards Bacon (a printing estimator), September 8, 1939 (divorced, 1962); children: David Nathaniel, Daniel Carl. *Education:* Bryn Mawr College, A.B., 1935; University of California, Berkeley, M.L.S., 1958. *Home:* 1631 Channing Way, Berkeley, Calif. 94703.

CAREER: Did editorial work for publishing firms in New York, N.Y., 1935-53; Contra Costa County (Calif.) Library, children's librarian, 1958-70; Vallejo Public Library, Vallejo, Calif., supervisor of children's services, 1970—. Extension instructor in children's literature at Sonoma State College (now California State College, Sonoma) and at University of California, Berkeley. *Member:* Association of Children's Librarians of Northern California, Social Responsibilities Round Table.

WRITINGS—Under name Betty Morrow; juvenile books: (With Millicent E. Selsam) *See Through the Sea,* Harper, 1955; *See Up the Mountain,* Harper, 1958; (with Louis Hartman) *Jewish Holidays,* Garrard, 1967; *A Great Miracle: The Story of Hanukkah,* Harvey House, 1968. Contributor of poetry to *New Yorker* in the 1930's, reviews to *New York Times Book Review* in the 1940's, and more recently, articles to library journals.

WORK IN PROGRESS: "Four juvenile books on a variety of subjects. I am working especially hard on a book on a neglected subject—the extraordinary lifestyle and history of the Native Americans of the San Francisco Bay area."

SIDELIGHTS: Elizabeth Bacon told *CA:* "My deepest concerns are an end to war and to racism. I wrote about the Jewish holidays because they are very meaningful to me personally, both in their view of life and in their quality of celebration. I write about nature because I am constantly amazed and delighted by the beauty and variety of the natural world. As an armchair anthropologist, I am fascinated by the amazing adaptability of human beings."

* * *

BAER, John 1886-1970

March 29, 1886—February 18, 1970; American cartoonist, congressman, and journalist. Obituaries: *Washington Post,* February 23, 1970.

* * *

BAETZHOLD, Howard G(eorge) 1923-

PERSONAL: Surname is pronounced *Bates*-hold; born January 1, 1923, in Buffalo, N.Y.; son of Howard K. and Harriet (Hofheins) Baetzhold; married Nancy Cheesman, August 5, 1950; children: Howard King, Barbara Millard. *Education:* Brown University, A.B. (magna cum laude), 1944, A.M., 1948; University of Wisconsin, Ph.D., 1953. *Politics:* Independent. *Home:* 6723 Riverview Dr., Indianapolis, Ind. 46220. *Office:* Department of English, Butler University, Indianapolis, Ind. 46208.

CAREER: Brown University, Providence, R.I., assistant director, then director of Veterans College, 1947-48, admissions officer, 1948-50; University of Wisconsin—Madison, assistant to the associate dean, College of Letters and Science, 1951-53; Butler University, Indianapolis, Ind., assistant professor, 1953-57, associate professor, 1957-67, professor of English, 1967—. Visiting professor, University of Delaware, summer, 1963. *Military service:* U.S. Army Air Forces, Air Transport Command, 1943-46; served in India and China; became first lieutenant.

MEMBER: American Association of University Professors (vice-president, Indiana Conference, 1955), Modern Language Association of America, American Studies Association (national council member, 1973-76), Midwest Modern Language Association, Ohio-Indiana American Studies Association (vice-president, 1965-66; president, 1967-68), Indianapolis Urban League, Art Association of Indianapolis, Phi Kappa Phi, British Sub-Aqua Club. *Awards, honors:* American Philosophical Society grant, 1958; American Council of Learned Societies grant, 1967; *Mark Twain and John Bull: The British Connection* chosen for Scholar's Library List of Modern Language Association of America, 1970.

WRITINGS: Mark Twain and John Bull: The British Connection, Indiana University Press, 1970; (contributor) Robert Falk, editor, *Literature and Ideas in America: Essays in Memory of Harry Hayden Clark,* Ohio University Press, 1975. Contributor to professional journals.

WORK IN PROGRESS: Editing two volumes of short fiction and miscellaneous essays for the twenty-four volume Iowa-California edition of the works of Mark Twain.

BIOGRAPHICAL/CRITICAL SOURCES: American Literary Scholarship, 1970, 1972; *Nineteenth-Century Fiction,* June, 1971; *Modern Fiction Studies,* summer, 1971.

* * *

BAHLKE, George W(ilbon) 1934-

PERSONAL: Born June 20, 1934, in Chicago, Ill.; son of William Herbert (a chemical engineer) and Agnes (Wilbon) Bahlke; married Valerie Worth (a writer), December 28, 1955; children: Conrad George, Catherine Worth, Margaret Grey. *Education:* University of Chicago, B.A., 1953, M.A., 1956; Swarthmore College, B.A., 1955; Yale University, Ph.D., 1960. *Politics:* Democrat. *Home:* 19 Canterbury Dr., Clinton, N.Y. 13323. *Office:* Division of Humanities, Kirkland College, Clinton, N.Y. 13323.

CAREER: University of Virginia, Mary Washington College, Fredericksburg, instructor in English, 1957-60; Rutgers University, New Brunswick, N.J., instructor in English, 1960-61; Middlebury College, Middlebury, Vt., assistant professor of English, 1961-69; Kirkland College, Clinton, N.Y., associate professor of literature, 1969—. *Member:* Modern Language Association of America, English Institute.

WRITINGS: The Later Auden: From "New Year Letter" to "About the House," Rutgers University Press, 1970.

WORK IN PROGRESS: Studies on imagery in Virginia Woolf's novels and on the fiction of E. M. Forster and D. H. Lawrence.

AVOCATIONAL INTERESTS: Gardening, painting, playing the piano, reading.

BIOGRAPHICAL/CRITICAL SOURCES: Books Abroad, spring, 1971.

* * *

BAHR, Howard M. 1938-

PERSONAL: Born February 21, 1938, in Provo, Utah; son of Albert Frances (a soil scientist with U.S. Department of Agriculture) and Louie Jean (Miner) Bahr; married Rosemary Frances Smith, August 28, 1961; children: Bonnie Louise, Howard McKay, Rowena Ruth, Tanya Lavonne, Christopher Joseph, Laura Lee, Stephen Smith, Rachel Marie. *Education:* Brigham Young University, B.A. (with honors), 1962; University of Texas, M.A., 1964, Ph.D., 1965. *Religion:* Church of Jesus Christ of Latter-day Saints (Mormon). *Home:* 180 East 4320 N., Provo, Utah 84601. *Office:* Department of Sociology, Brigham Young University, Provo, Utah 84602.

CAREER: Columbia University, Bureau of Applied Social Research, New York, N.Y., project director of study on homelessness, 1965-68, research associate, 1966-67; Washington State University, Pullman, associate professor and associate rural sociologist, 1968-72, professor of sociology and rural sociologist, 1972-73, chairman of department, 1971-73; Brigham Young University, Provo, Utah, professor of sociology, 1973—, director of Family Research Institute, 1977—. Lecturer in sociology, New York University, 1966-68, Brooklyn College of the City University of New York, 1967; visiting lecturer, Columbia University, summer, 1968; visiting professor, University of Virginia, 1976-77. *Member:* American Sociological Association, National Council on Family Relations, Society for the Study of Social Problems, Rural Sociological Society, Pacific Sociological Association.

WRITINGS: (Editor and contributor) *Disaffiliated Man: Essays and Bibliography on Skid Row, Vagrancy, and Outsiders,* University of Toronto Press, 1970; (editor with Bruce A. Chadwick and Robert C. Day, and contributor) *Native Americans Today: Sociological Perspectives,* Harper, 1971; (editor with Chadwick and Darwin L. Thomas) *Population, Resources, and the Future: Non-Malthusian Perspectives,* Brigham Young University Press, 1972; (with Theodore Caplow) *Old Men Drunk and Sober,* New York University Press, 1973; *Skid Row: An Introduction to Disaffiliation,* Oxford University Press, 1973; (with Gerald R. Garrett) *Women Alone: The Disaffiliation of Urban Females,* Lexington Books, 1976. Contributor to *International Encyclopedia of the Social Sciences,* 1968, and to social science journals.

WORK IN PROGRESS: Monographs on widowhood, family role behavior, and divorce; a text on ethnic relations in America; co-investigator on four-year study of Middletown, 1976-80.

*   *   *

BAILY, Samuel L(ongstreth)   1936-

PERSONAL: Born May 9, 1936, in Philadelphia, Pa.; son of Nicholas Newlin (a railroad executive) and Arlene (Mack) Baily; married Joan Gaskill, September 3, 1960; children: Jennifer, Sarah, Benjamin. *Education:* Harvard University, A.B., 1958; Columbia University, M.A., 1963; University of Pennsylvania, Ph.D., 1964. *Home:* 58 Lake Side Dr. S., Piscataway, N.J. 08854. *Office:* Department of History, Rutgers University, New Brunswick, N.J. 08903.

CAREER: Served in Mexico with American Friends Service Committee, 1958-59; Cambridge Neighborhood House, Cambridge, Mass., program director, 1959-60; Rutgers University, New Brunswick, N.J., assistant professor, 1964-68, associate professor, 1968-77, professor of history, 1977—, associate director of Latin American Institute, 1967-70. Director, National Defense Education Act Summer Institute of Latin American History, 1967. *Member:* American Historical Association, Latin American Studies Association, Immigration History Group. *Awards, honors:* Rockefeller Foundation fellow, University of Pennsylvania, 1961-64; Social Science Research Council fellowship, 1968.

WRITINGS: Labor, Politics, and Nationalism in Argentina, Rutgers University Press, 1967; (editor) *Nationalism in Latin America,* Knopf, 1971; (editor with Ronald T. Hyman) *Perspectives on Latin America,* Macmillan, 1974; *The United States and the Development of South America,* F. Watts, 1976. Contributor to *International Migration Review, Journal of Social History,* and to other historical journals.

WORK IN PROGRESS: A study of Italian immigrants in Buenos Aires, Sao Paulo, and New York City.

*   *   *

BAIN, Chester A(rthur)   1912-

PERSONAL: Born November 21, 1912, in Lincoln, Neb.; son of Frederick A. and Naomi (Johnson) Bain; married June Wilson, 1942; children: Chester Arthur, Jr., James Robert, Lani. *Education:* Columbia University, A.B., 1946, M.A., 1948; American University, Ph.D., 1956.

CAREER: U.S. Navy, 1930-35, 1941-45, left service as chief photographer's mate; Idaho State College (now University), Pocatello, instructor in history, 1947-49; University of Bridgeport, Bridgeport, Conn., instructor in history 1949-51; Mutual Security Agency, Washington, D.C., consultant to work-study program, 1951-52; U.S. Department of Defense, Office of Naval Intelligence, Washington, D.C., analyst on Southeast Asia, 1952-53; Florida State University, Tallahassee, assistant professor of Far East history, 1953-55; American University, Washington, D.C., research associate, Human Relations Area Files, and assistant professor, 1955-56; Illinois State Normal University (now Illinois State University), Normal, associate professor of Far East history, 1956-59; U.S. Information Agency, assistant cultural affairs officer in Tehran, Iran, 1959-61, cultural affairs officer and cultural attaché in Seoul, Korea, 1962-64, program planning officer of joint U.S. Public Affairs Office, Saigon, Vietnam, 1964-65, research analyst with Vietnam unit, Washington, D.C., 1965-67; U.S. Department of State, Foreign Service Institute, Washington, D.C., chairman of operations support branch, Vietnam Training Center, 1967-69; American Cultural Center, Saigon, director, 1969-70; Whittier College, Whittier, Calif., professor of history, beginning 1970. Consultant to Center for Research in Social Systems, American University, 1967-68. *Member:* Association for Asian Studies, American Historical Association, Alpha Chi Rho.

WRITINGS: The Far East: An Outline History, Littlefield, 1952, 5th edition, 1972; (co-author) *Viet-Nam: Both Sides of the 17th Parallel,* Human Relations Area File Press, 1956; (co-author) *North Borneo, Brunei, Sarawak,* Human Relations Area File Press, 1956; (co-author) *Cambodia: Its People, Its Society, Its Culture,* Human Relations Area File Press, 1959; (co-author) *Laos: Its People, Its Society, Its Culture,* Human Relations Area File Press, 1960; *Vietnam: Roots of Conflict,* Prentice-Hall, 1967. Contributor to *Encyclopedia Americana, New Wonder World Encyclopedia,* and to journals, including *Transition, Texas Quarterly, South Atlantic Quarterly,* and *Virginia Quarterly Review.*

WORK IN PROGRESS: A book, *Ho Chi Minh and His Party: The Development of Communism in Vietnam;* also articles on Vietnamese culture.

AVOCATIONAL INTERESTS: Photography, hiking, swimming.

BIOGRAPHICAL/CRITICAL SOURCES: Times Literary Supplement, December 14, 1967.†

*   *   *

BAITY, Elizabeth Chesley   1907-

PERSONAL: Born March 5, 1907, in Hamilton, Tex.;

daughter of Hervey Edgar and Helen (Roddy) Chesley; married Herman Glenn Baity (an international sanitation engineer), March 16, 1930 (died, 1973); children: William Anthony, Philip Chesley. *Education:* College of Industrial Arts (now Texas Women's University), B.A. and B.S., 1928; University of North Carolina, M.A. (English) 1930, M.A. (educational psychology), 1945, M.A. (anthropology), 1962, Ph.D., 1968; also attended University of Geneva, 1963, University of Tehran, 1964, and University of London, 1965. *Politics:* Democrat. *Religion:* Presbyterian. *Home:* 1503 Mason Farm Rd., Chapel Hill, N.C. 27514; also maintains a summer residence in Mourex-par-Divonne, Ain, France.

CAREER: Independent researcher and writer. *Member:* American Anthropological Association (fellow). *Awards, honors: New York Herald Tribune* award for "best juvenile book of the year" and University of North Carolina Woman's Award for "best North Carolina book for young people," 1951, both for *Americans before Columbus.*

WRITINGS: The Modern Woman, University of North Carolina Press, 1937; *Man Is a Weaver* (Junior Literary Guild selection), Viking, 1942; *Americans before Columbus* (Junior Literary Guild selection), Viking, 1951, revised edition, 1961; *America before Man,* Viking, 1953, revised edition, 1964; (contributor) Anthony F. Aveni, editor, *Archeoastronomy in Pre-Columbian America,* University of Texas Press, 1975.

Editor of "Tanganyika Reading" series, which includes selections from *Village Improvement and Women's Reader,* and the full text of *Song of Rejoicing,* published by the Committee on World Literacy and Christian Literature, 1958. Contributor of poetry and articles to numerous magazines, including *Atlantic Monthly, American Scholar, Chatelaine, Ladies' Home Journal, Harper's, Saturday Review,* and *Current Anthropology.*

WORK IN PROGRESS: A protohistory of the Pontic Steppes, dealing largely with the life and arts of the Scythians and other nomadic horsemen, tentatively entitled *The Forgotten World of the Steppes;* a seminar for African Studies, with the title *Tanzania: Old Ways and New Voices;* a general reader's book on archaeoastronomy and ethnoastronomy.

SIDELIGHTS: Elizabeth Chesley Baity writes: "I also plan to revise my dissertation on the fire, bull, and solstice rituals of certain protohistoric societies of Asia, Africa, and Spain into a book for general readers. On a recent trip through Oceania and Asia I did research on the low-literacy productions dealing with family planning and family life, on a grant from a population study agency. This research covered family planning agencies in Fiji, New Zealand, New Guinea, Taiwan, Nepal, and India.

"The most fascinating employment I have had was as the director of literacy workshops served by the World Team of the Committee for Christian Literacy and Literature." These workshops produced readers for Pakistan (1953), the South Sudan (1953), and Tanganyika (1954).

"My most interesting anthropological research has been on ancient astronomy as revealed by megalithic and other structures built by prehistoric and prohistoric societies. Present research deals with alternative explanations for the Bronze Age site destructions and cultural discontinuities."

*   *   *

BAKER, James R(upert) 1925-

PERSONAL: Born May 18, 1925, in Freeport, Ill.; son of

Von C. and Ruth (Rupert) Baker; married Francoise Demerson, November 7, 1953; children: Christopher Demerson. *Education:* University of Denver, B.A., 1947, M.A., 1949, Ph.D., 1954. *Office:* Department of English, San Diego State University, San Diego, Calif. 92115.

CAREER: Colorado State University, Fort Collins, instructor in English, 1951; University of Idaho, Moscow, assistant professor of literature, 1954-56; San Diego State University, San Diego, Calif., assistant professor, 1956-61, associate professor, 1961-67, professor of literature, 1967—. Visiting professor, University of Missouri, 1967-68. *Military service:* U.S. Marine Corps Reserve, 1943. *Member:* Modern Language Association of America.

WRITINGS: (Contributor) William E. Morris and Clifford A. Nault, Jr., editors, *Portraits of an Artist,* Odyssey, 1962; (contributor) Marvin Magalaner, editor, *A James Joyce Miscellany: Third Series,* Southern Illinois University Press, 1962; (editor with Arthur P. Ziegler, Jr., of casebook edition) William Golding, *Lord of the Flies,* Putnam, 1964; *William Golding: A Critical Study,* St. Martin's, 1965. Contributor of articles to *Western Humanities Review* and other periodicals. Member of editorial board, *Twentieth Century Literature,* 1955—; advisory editor, *James Joyce Quarterly,* 1967—.

WORK IN PROGRESS: Research on contemporary literature, especially British.

*   *   *

BAKER, Liva 1930-

PERSONAL: Born June 25, 1930, in Plymouth, Pa.; daughter of Burton A. (a physician) and Dorothy (Fidell) Weil; married Leonard Baker (a writer), August 1, 1958; children: David Weil, Sara Dorothy. *Education:* Smith College, B.A., 1952; Columbia University, M.S.J., 1955. *Politics:* Independent. *Religion:* Episcopalian. *Residence:* Washington, D.C.

CAREER: Lamson's Department Store, Toledo, Ohio, advertising copywriter, 1953-54; *Newsday,* Garden City, N.Y., reporter, 1955-58; National Geographic Society, Washington, D.C., writer, 1959-63. *Member:* Smith College Club of Washington, National Cathedral Choral Society.

WRITINGS: World Faiths (young adult book), Abelard, 1967; *Felix Frankfurter* (juvenile), Coward, 1969; *I'm Radcliff! Fly Me!* (juvenile), Macmillan, 1976.

BIOGRAPHICAL/CRITICAL SOURCES: New York Times, October 17, 1976.

*   *   *

BAKER, Ross K(enneth) 1938-

PERSONAL: Born June 26, 1938, in Philadelphia, Pa.; son of Maurice and Augusta (Lieberman) Baker; married Carole C. Walker, September 3, 1966; children: Susannah, Sarah. *Education:* University of Pennsylvania, A.B. (cum laude), 1960, M.A., 1962, Ph.D., 1966; University of California, Berkeley, graduate student, 1962-63. *Home:* 119 Hill St., Highland Park, N.J. 08904. *Office:* Department of Political Science, Rutgers University, New Brunswick, N.J. 08903.

CAREER: American University, Washington, D.C., research scientist, Center for Research in Social Systems, 1965-66; Brookings Institution, Washington, D.C., research associate, 1966-68; Rutgers University, New Brunswick, N.J., assistant professor, 1968-70, associate professor, 1970-74, professor of political science, 1974—, chairman and graduate director of department of political science, 1971-74. Professorial lecturer, Catholic University of America, 1967-68; regular lecturer in course on the New Left, U.S. Department of State, Foreign Service Institute. Special assistant to Senator Walter Mondale, 1975, to Senator Birch Bayh, 1975-76; issues adviser to Senator Frank Church, 1976. Member of board, Eagleton Institute of Politics, 1971. *Member:* American Political Science Association, African Studies Association (fellow), Association of Social and Behavioral Scientists, Phi Beta Kappa.

WRITINGS: (Editor) *The Afro American: Readings,* Van Nostrand, 1970. Contributor to *Nation, Society, Middle Eastern Studies, Washington Post,* and other newspapers and journals.

*   *   *

BALCHIN, Nigel Marlin 1908-1970

December 3, 1908—May 17, 1970; British brigadier general and novelist. Obituaries: *New York Times,* May 18, 1970; *Antiquarian Bookman,* June 1, 1970; *Books Abroad,* spring, 1971.

*   *   *

BALDINGER, Stanley 1932-

PERSONAL: Born January 11, 1932, in St. Paul, Minn.; son of Samuel Charles (owner of a bakery) and Ethel S. (Yaffey) Baldinger; married Judith G. Altman (a teacher), December 20, 1970. *Education:* University of Minnesota, B.A., 1953, M.A., 1956; Columbia University, M.S.U.P., 1969. *Office:* D.C. Government Office of Housing Programs, Washington, D.C.

CAREER: U.S. Foreign Service, foreign service officer in Washington, D.C., and Rome, 1957-64; U.S. Social Security Administration, Washington, D.C., administrative assistant to chief of international training, 1964-66; National Capital Planning Commission, Washington, D.C., administrative assistant to director of current plans and programs, 1966-67; D.C. Government Office of Housing Programs, Washington, D.C., urban planner and chief of overall program design, 1970—. *Member:* American Institute of Planners (associate member). *Awards, honors:* Hawkins Award, 1969.

WRITINGS: Planning and Governing the Metropolis: The Twin Cities Experience, Praeger, 1971. Contributor to *American County.*

WORK IN PROGRESS: A revision of *Planning and Governing the Metropolis.*††

*   *   *

BALDUCCI, Ernesto 1922-

PERSONAL: Born August 6, 1922, in St. Fiora, Grosseto, Italy. *Education:* Attended University of Florence. *Home:* Baolia Fiesolsua, Santo Domenico di Fiesole, Florence, Italy.

CAREER: Roman Catholic priest.

WRITINGS: Antonio Fogazzaro, Morcelliana, 1952; *Concordanze spirituali,* Edizioni della Rai Radiotelevisione Italiana, 1959; *La verita e le occasioni,* Paoline, 1960; *Le stagioni di Dio,* Edizioni La Scoula, 1961; *Il seme e la pazienza,* Edizioni Esperienze, 1961; *L'esperienza religiosa,* Borla, 1962; *Perche i preti non si sposano?,* Nuova Accademia, 1963; *Cristianesimo e cristianita,* Morcelliana, 1963; *Papa Giovanni,* Vallecchi, 1964, translation by Dorothy White

published as *John, "The Transitional Pope,"* McGraw, 1965; *Per una nuova cristianita,* Ave, 1964; *Tempo e liturgia: Meditazioni evangeliche,* Morcelliana, 1965; *Il Vangelo secondo Giovanni,* Testimonianze, 1965; *La pietra in cammino,* Morcelliana, 1967; *Sono morte le missioni?* (booklet), Edizioni di Vicenza, 1968; *L'esistenza cristiana: Meditazione sulle virtu teologali,* Testimonianze, 1968; *La Chiesa come Eucaristia,* Queriniana, 1970; *I servi inutili,* Cittadella, 1970; *Dario dell'Esodo 1960/1970,* Vallecchi, 1971; *Vietnam, collera di Dio,* Piero Gribaudi, 1973; *La politica della fede,* Guaraldi, 1976. Also author of *La fede dalla fede,* Cittadella. Also author of *Mistero di Dio e mistero dell'uomo* (televised conversation), L'Arco, 1965.

*   *   *

BALDWIN, Anne Norris 1938-

PERSONAL: Born March 25, 1938, in Philadelphia, Pa.; daughter of Robert Fogg (a physician) and Mary (Scattergood) Norris; married Robert Lesh Baldwin (a professor of biochemistry), August 28, 1965; children: David Norris, Eric Lawrence. *Education:* Smith College, B.A. (summa cum laude), 1959; Harvard University, Ph.D., 1963; Stanford University, National Institute of Health postdoctoral fellow, 1963-65. *Home:* 1243 Los Trancos Rd., Portola Valley, Calif. 94025. *Agent:* William Reiss, 12 East 41st St., New York, N.Y. 10017.

CAREER: Stanford University, Stanford, Calif., National Science Foundation independent researcher in biochemistry, 1965-66. Author of books for children.

WRITINGS—For children: *The Sometimes Island,* Norton, 1969; *Sunflowers for Tina,* Four Winds, 1970; *Sunlight Valley,* Four Winds, 1971; *A Friend in the Park,* Four Winds, 1973; *Jenny's Revenge,* Four Winds, 1974. Contributor of scientific papers to *Proceedings of the National Academy of Science,* and to *Journal of Biological Chemistry.*

WORK IN PROGRESS: A book for older children.

*   *   *

BALIKCI, Asen 1929-

PERSONAL: Born December 30, 1929, in Istanbul, Turkey; son of Cosma and Nidela Balikci; married Verena Ossent (an editor), 1956; children: Nicolas, Anna. *Education:* University of Geneva, M.A., 1952; Columbia University, Ph.D., 1962. *Office:* Department of Anthropology, University of Montreal, P.O. Box 6128, Montreal, Quebec, Canada.

CAREER: National Museum of Canada, Ottawa, Ontario, anthropologist, 1954-61; University of Montreal, Montreal, Quebec, 1961—, began as assistant professor, professor of anthropology, 1969—. Research fellow at Peabody Museum, Harvard University, 1969; lecturer, Massachusetts Institute of Technology, 1971. Consultant, Education Development Center, Cambridge, Mass. Has done field work on expeditions in the Canadian Arctic, Senegal, and Ethiopia. *Member:* American Anthropological Association, Societe des Americanistes (Paris), Comite International du Film Ethnographique (Paris). *Awards, honors:* Christopher Award, 1970; Canadian Film Association Prize for 1970.

WRITINGS: Suicidal Behavior Among the Netsilik Eskimos (booklet), Department of Northern Affairs and National Resources (Ottawa), 1960; *Vunta Kutchin Social Change: A Study of the People of Old Crow, Yukon Territory,* Department of Northern Affairs and National Resources, 1963; *Development of Basic Socio-Economic Units in Two Eskimo Communities,* National Museum of Canada, 1964; *The Netsilik Eskimo,* Doubleday, 1970. Writer and producer of "Netsilik Eskimo" film series for National Film Board of Canada, and "Eskimos: Fight for Life," a Columbia Broadcasting System special.

WORK IN PROGRESS: Anthropological research on pastoral nomadism in Ethiopia and Afghanistan.

*   *   *

BALLOWE, James 1933-

PERSONAL: Surname is pronounced Ba-*loo;* born November 28, 1933, in Carbondale, Ill.; son of Frank Charles (a wholesaler) and Ruth (Maynard) Ballowe; married Jeanne Frances Sparks (a teacher), December 27, 1953; children: Jeffrey Craig, Mary Elizabeth. *Education:* Millikin University, A.B., 1954; University of Illinois, M.A., 1956, Ph.D., 1963. *Home:* 217 West Crestwood Dr., Peoria, Ill. 61614. *Office:* Graduate School, Bradley University, Peoria, Ill. 61615.

CAREER: Decatur (Ill.) public schools, teacher of English and history, 1954-55; Millikin University, Decatur, Ill., assistant professor of English, 1961-63; Bradley University, Peoria, Ill., assistant professor, 1963-67, associate professor, 1967-71, professor of English, 1971—, chairman of department, 1971-74, interim associate dean of college of liberal arts and sciences, 1971, dean of Graduate School, 1974—. *Military service:* National Guard, 1954-63; became sergeant. *Member:* Modern Language Association of America, American Studies Association, American Association of University Professors, Midwestern Association of Graduate Schools (member of executive committee), American Civil Liberties Union.

WRITINGS: (Editor) *George Santayana's America: Essays on Literature and Culture,* University of Illinois Press, 1967, revised edition, 1970; (with others) *A Sampler: New Poems and Some Poetry Talk,* Dunes House, 1976. Contributor of poetry to *Southern Review* and *Encounter;* contributor of articles to *American Quarterly, American Literature,* and other journals.

WORK IN PROGRESS: Writing essays on literature and graduate studies; working on poetry manuscript, *The Coal Miners.*

SIDELIGHTS: James Ballowe told *CA:* "I do not find that poetry conflicts with research or administration. It is a way of keeping aware of myself and surroundings while engaged in more technical and mechanical activities. Reading and writing poetry improve everything else I do."

BIOGRAPHICAL/CRITICAL SOURCES: Kenyon Review, Volume XXX, number 4, 1968.

*   *   *

BALTZ, Howard B(url) 1930-

PERSONAL: Born July 27, 1930, in St. Louis, Mo.; son of Arthur William (a banker) and Ollie (Batdorf) Baltz; married Sylvia Clayton (an assistant professor), June 23, 1968; children: Debra Lynn, Geoffrey Burl, Jami Elizabeth. *Education:* Baylor University, B.B.A., 1956, M.S., 1958; Oklahoma State University, Ph.D., 1964. *Home:* 718 Country Manor, Creve Coeur, Mo. 63141. *Office:* School of Business Administration, University of Missouri, St. Louis, Mo. 63121.

CAREER: Baylor University, Waco, Tex., instructor in sta-

tistics, 1957-59, assistant director of bureau of business and economic research, 1958-59; Oklahoma State University of Agricultural and Applied Sciences, Stillwater, teaching assistant, 1959-62; Midwestern University, Wichita Falls, Tex., assistant professor of statistics and director of Computer Center, 1962-64; University of Texas at Austin, assistant professor of statistics, 1964-68; University of Missouri—St. Louis, associate professor of statistics and quantitative management science, 1968—. Consultant, Texas Concrete Masonry Association, 1966-67. *Military service:* U.S. Air Force Reserve, management analysis officer and statistician, 1951—; current rank, lieutenant colonel. *Member:* American Statistical Association, Institute of Management Sciences, American Institute for Decision Sciences, Alpha Pi Omega, Delta Sigma Pi, Omicron Delta Epsilon. *Awards, honors:* Foundation for Economic Education fellow, 1970.

WRITINGS: (With Richard B. Baltz) *Fundamentals of Business Analysis,* and *Study Guide,* Prentice-Hall, 1970; *Statistics: A Study of Variation,* Edwards Brothers, 1976. Contributor to economic and business publications.

*   *   *

BAMBARA, Toni Cade
(Toni Cade)

PERSONAL: Born in New York, N.Y. *Education:* Queens College (now Queens College of the City University of New York), B.A., 1959; University of Florence, studied Commedia dell'Arte, 1961; student at Ecole de Mime Etienne Decroux in Paris, 1961, New York, 1963; City College of the City University of New York, M.A., 1964; attended post-degree courses in linguistics at New York University and New School for Social Research. Also attended Katherine Dunham Dance Studio, Syvilla Fort School of Dance, and Clark Center of Performing Arts, 1958-69, Studio Museum of Harlem Film Institute, 1970. *Office:* Spelman College, Atlanta, Ga. 30314.

CAREER: Social investigator, New York State Department of Welfare, 1959-61; Venice Ministry of Museums, Venice, Italy, free-lance writer, 1961-62; Metropolitan Hospital, New York City, director of recreation in psychiatry department, 1962-64; Colony House Community Center, New York City, program director, 1964-65; English instructor in SEEK Program, City College of the City University of New York, New York City, 1965-69, and in New Careers Program of Newark, N.J., 1969; Rutgers University, Livingston College, New Brunswick, N.J., director of pre-school summer program, 1969, assistant professor, 1969-71, associate professor of English, 1971-74; Duke University, Durham, N.C., visiting professor of African American studies, 1974; Stephens College, Columbia, Mo., visiting professor, 1975; consultant on Women's Studies, Emory University and Atlanta University, both Atlanta, Ga., 1976; Atlanta Public Schools, Atlanta, project coordinator for Arts-in-the-Schools Project, 1976; Spelman College, Atlanta, writer-in-residence, 1977—.

AWARDS, HONORS: Peter Pauper Press Award, 1958; John Golden Award for Fiction, Queens College (now Queens College of the City University of New York), 1959; Theatre of Black Experience award, 1969; Rutgers University research fellowship, 1972; Black Child Development Institute service award, 1973; Black Rose Award, *Encore* (magazine), 1973; Black Community Award, Livingston College, Rutgers University, 1974.

WRITINGS—Editor: (And contributor, under name Toni

Cade) *The Black Woman,* New American Library, 1970; (and contributor) *Tales and Stories for Black Folks,* Doubleday, 1971; *Gorilla, My Love* (short stories), Random House, 1972; *The Sea Birds Are Still Alive: Collected Stories,* Random House, 1977.

Contributor: A. Gayle, Jr., editor, *Black Expression: Essays by and about Black Americans in the Creative Arts,* Weybright, 1969; Jules Chametsky, editor, *Black and White in American Culture,* University of Massachusetts Press, 1970; Ruth Miller, *Backgrounds to Blackamerican Literature,* Chandler Publishing, 1971. Contributor to *What's Happnin, Somethin Else,* and *Another Eye,* readers, Scott, Foresman, 1969-70. Contributor of articles and book and film reviews to *Massachusetts Review, Negro Digest, Liberator, Prairie Schooner, Redbook, Audience, Black Works, Umbra, Onyx,* and other periodicals. Guest editor of special issue of *Southern Exposure,* summer, 1976, devoted to new southern black writers and visual artists.

WORK IN PROGRESS: A novel, for Random House, completion expected in 1978; a filmscript.

SIDELIGHTS: Toni Cade Bambara writes of "black women at the edge of a new awareness . . . who create their own choices about the kinds of women they will be," notes Mary Helen Washington in her review of *The Sea Birds Are Still Alive.* "The strongest features of this collection are the contemporaneity of these stories, their variety, and their daring to examine previously unexplored aspects of black women's lives." But, the reviewer continues, "the trouble with deliberately creating models is that they slip all too easily out of character . . . into being mouthpieces for the writer's ideology."

Other reviewers have also seen that the stories, though flawed, are fine. Of Bambara's characters, a *Newsweek* critic writes, "as drawn with spirit and subtlety, they are—even in their defeats—a pleasure to watch." Robie Macauley says: "Some of the stories fail because there is too much verbal energy, too much restless pursuit of random anecdote. But the fine title story ["The Sea Birds Are Still Alive"] . . . makes its meaning felt just by the diversity of sights and sounds and inferred lives."

BIOGRAPHICAL/CRITICAL SOURCES: New York Times, October 11, 1972; *New York Times Book Review,* October 15, 1972, December 3, 1972, March 27, 1977; *Sewanee Review,* November 18, 1972, December 2, 1972; *Village Voice,* April 12, 1973; *Black World,* July, 1973; *Newsweek,* May 2, 1977; *Ms.,* July, 1977.

* * *

BANCROFT, Griffing 1907-

PERSONAL: Born February 18, 1907, in San Diego, Calif.; son of Griffing (a scientist) and Ethel (Works) Bancroft; married Mary Jackson, 1936; married second wife, Jane Eads (a writer and artist), August 22, 1949. *Education:* University of Chicago, Ph.B., 1930. *Politics:* Democrat. *Religion:* None. *Address:* P.O. Box 93, Captiva, Fla. 33924. *Agent:* Julian Bach, Jr., 3 East 48th St., New York, N.Y. 10017.

CAREER: International News Service, reporter in California and in Washington, D.C., 1933-41; *Chicago Sun,* Chicago, Ill., Washington correspondent, 1941-48; Columbia Broadcasting System, Washington, D.C., commentator, 1948-58. *Wartime service:* Civilian in Psychological Warfare Service, World War II; received Medal of Freedom. *Member:* American Ornithologists' Union,

Wilson Ornithological Society, Sanibel-Captiva Conservation Foundation (vice-chairman), Sanibel-Captiva Audubon Society (vice-president). *Awards, honors:* Christopher Award, 1972, for *Vanishing Wings.*

WRITINGS: (Reviser) William J. Miller, *The Meaning of Communism,* Silver Burdett, 1968; *Snowy: The Story of an Egret* (juvenile), McCall Publishing, 1970; *Vanishing Wings: A Tale of Three Birds of Prey* (juvenile; Junior Literary Guild selection), F. Watts, 1972; *The White Cardinal,* Coward, 1973.

WORK IN PROGRESS: Writing on the early days of ornithology.

* * *

BANERJI, Ranan B(ihari) 1928-

PERSONAL: Surname is pronounced *Banner*-gee; born May 5, 1928, in Calcutta, India; came to United States in 1961, naturalized in 1969; son of Bijan Bihari (a professor) and Setabja (Chatterji) Banerji; married Purnima Purkayastha (a teacher), July 8, 1954; children: Anindita, Sunandita (daughters). *Education:* Patna University, B.Sc., 1947; University of Calcutta, M.S., 1949, D.Phil., 1956. *Politics:* Liberal. *Religion:* Quaker. *Home:* 7612 Woodlawn Ave., Melrose Park, Pa. *Office:* Department of Computer Science, Temple University, Philadelphia, Pa. 19122.

CAREER: Pennsylvania State University, University Park, visiting assistant professor of engineering research, 1953-56; Indian Statistical Institute, Calcutta, senior maintenance engineer, computer section, 1956-58; Case Institute of Technology (now Case Western Reserve University), Cleveland, Ohio, research associate, 1958-59; University of New Brunswick, Fredericton, assistant professor of engineering, 1959-61; Case Western Reserve University, assistant professor, 1961-62, associate professor, 1963-67, professor of engineering, 1968-73; Temple University, Philadelphia, Pa., professor of computer science, 1973—. *Member:* Institute of Electrical and Electronics Engineers, Association for Computing Machinery, Pattern Recognition Society, Common Cause, American Civil Liberties Union.

WRITINGS: Theory of Problem Solving: An Approach to Artificial Intelligence, American Elsevier, 1969; (editor with M. D. Mesarovic) *Theoretical Approaches to Non-Numerical Problem Solving* (proceedings of systems symposium), Springer-Verlag, 1970. Contributor to scientific journals. Editor, *Newsletter* of Association for Computing Machinery.

WORK IN PROGRESS: Research on complex information processing in computers.

* * *

BANHAM, (Peter) Reyner 1922-

PERSONAL: Born March 2, 1922, in Norwich, England; son of Percy (a gas engineer) and Violet (Reyner) Banham; married Mary Mullett, August 25, 1946; children: Deborah Ann, Benjamin John. *Education:* Courtald Institute of Art, University of London, B.A., 1952, Ph.D., 1958. *Politics:* "Non-organized left." *Religion:* "Undefined." *Home:* 274 Summer St., Buffalo, N.Y. 14222. *Office:* School of Architecture and Environmental Design, State University of New York, 2917 Main St., Buffalo, N.Y. 14214.

CAREER: Architectural Review, London, England, member of editorial staff, 1952-64, rising to assistant executive editor; University of London, University College, London, part-time lecturer at School of Architecture, 1960-64, lecturer, 1964-69, professor of history of architecture, 1969-76; State University of New York at Buffalo, professor and chairman of department of design studies, 1976—. Visiting or occasional lecturer at universities in England, United States, Argentina, France, Germany, Italy, and Norway; research fellow, Graham Foundation, Chicago, Ill., 1964-66. Chairman of Commission on Doctrine and Definition, International Council of Societies for Industrial Design, 1962-67; program chairman, International Design Conference, Aspen, Colo., 1968. Trustee, Institute for Research in Art and Technology, London. *Awards, honors:* Prix Jean Tschumi, International Union of Architects, 1975; International Award, American Society of Interior Designers, 1975.

WRITINGS: Theory and Design in the First Machine Age, Praeger, 1960, 2nd edition, 1970; *Guide to Modern Architecture,* Van Nostrand, 1962, revised edition published as *The Age of the Masters,* 1975; *The New Brutalism: Ethic or Aesthetic?,* Reinhold, 1966; *The Architecture of the Well-Tempered Environment,* University of Chicago Press, 1969; *Los Angeles* (architectural study), Penguin, 1970; *Megastructure,* Harper, 1977. Contributor of articles on architecture and design to *New Society* (London); contributor to architecture journals.

WORK IN PROGRESS: On-site investigations of U.S. industrial and handicraft architecture, 1900-1915.

SIDELIGHTS: Reyner Banham, the subject of an article titled "Profession: Enfant Terrible" in the *Guardian,* says that his interests lie wherever art and technology meet (he originally trained as a mechanical engineer). "Hence," he continues, "a range of professional interests running from industrial design through architecture to city planning—but hence, also, non-professional interests (at a consumer level) in automobile racing and pop-music. As a result of the latter I have a second 'reputation' as an authority on pop culture (and Los Angeles), and am regarded as a sort of background influence on British pop painting and sculpture."

BIOGRAPHICAL/CRITICAL SOURCES: New Statesman, March 10, 1967, April 9, 1971; *London Magazine,* April, 1967; *Times Literary Supplement,* April 27, 1967; *Nation,* May 15, 1967; *New York Times Book Review,* September 10, 1967; *Guardian,* October 26, 1968; *National Review,* August 12, 1969; *New York Times,* July 10, 1971; *Time,* August 9, 1971.

* * *

BANKS, Ronald F(illmore) 1934-

PERSONAL: Born January 24, 1934, in Bangor, Me.; son of Leon (a shoe-worker) and Nellie (Leadbetter) Banks; married Helena Thelma Poland, August 28, 1955; children: Philip, Katherine, Amy, Nancy. *Education:* Gorham State College (now University of Maine at Portland-Gorham), B.S., 1956; University of Maine, M.A., 1958, Ph.D., 1966. *Politics:* Democrat. *Home:* 156 Washington St., Brewer, Me. 04412. *Office:* 102 East Annex, University of Maine, Orono, Me. 04473.

CAREER: Aroostook State Teachers College (now University of Maine at Presque Isle), instructor in history, 1958-59; Farmington State College (now University of Maine at Farmington), instructor in history, 1959-60; high school teacher in Rockland, Me., 1960-61; University of Maine at Orono, assistant professor, 1963-67, associate professor of history, 1970—, assistant dean of College of Arts and Sciences, 1967-68, assistant to the president, 1968-73. Visiting professor of history, American College of Switzerland, 1971-72; historical consultant to Maine attorney-general on Indian

land claim cases, 1976—. Chairman, Maine State American Revolution Bicentennial Commission, 1972-77; member, Maine State Historic Preservation Commission, 1977—. *Member:* Maine Historical Society (member of governing board, 1965-67), Phi Kappa Phi.

WRITINGS: (Editor) *A History of Maine, 1600-1970,* Kendall-Hunt, 1969, 3rd revised edition, 1976; *Maine Becomes a State: The Movement to Separate Maine from Massachusetts, 1785-1820,* Wesleyan University Press, 1970.

WORK IN PROGRESS: New England and the War of 1812.

* * *

BANZ, George 1928-

PERSONAL: Born December 21, 1928, in Lucerne, Switzerland; son of Robert (a businessman) and Josephine (Simeon) Banz; married Josette Charmillot, September 3, 1958; children: Eric, Caroline. *Education:* Swiss Federal Institute of Technology, Dipl.Arch., 1951; Oklahoma State University, M.S., 1952. *Home:* 498 St. Clair Ave. E., Toronto, Ontario, Canada.

CAREER: Architect and planning consultant in Toronto, Ontario, 1957—. Part-time member of architecture faculty, University of Toronto, 1971-75. *Member:* Royal Architectural Institute of Canada, Royal Canadian Academy of Arts.

WRITINGS: Elements of Urban Form, McGraw, 1970.

WORK IN PROGRESS: A book on the potential of alternative settlement patterns; research into use of computers in urban planning and design.

* * *

BARBER, Benjamin R. 1939-

PERSONAL: Born August 2, 1939, in New York, N.Y.; married Naomi Weiss, 1962; children: Jeremy, Rebecca. *Education:* Albert Schweitzer College, Churwalder, Switzerland, Certificate, 1956; Grinnell College, B.A. (with honors), 1960; London School of Economics and Political Science, Certificate, 1959; Harvard University, A.M., 1963, Ph.D., 1966. *Office:* Department of Political Science, Rutgers University, New Brunswick, N.J. 08903.

CAREER: Albert Schweitzer College, Churwalder, Switzerland, lecturer in politics and ethics, 1963-65; University of Pennsylvania, Philadelphia, assistant professor of political science, 1966-69; Rutgers University, New Brunswick, N.J., assistant professor, 1969-70, associate professor, 1971-75, professor of political science, 1975—. Visiting assistant professor, Haverford College, 1968; visiting associate professor, Hunter College of the City University of New York, 1970; senior Fulbright-Hayes Research Scholar, Essex University, 1976-77. *Member:* American Political Science Association (co-chairperson of program committee, 1975-76), Conference for the Study of Political Thought, American Society for Political and Legal Philosophy, Academy of Political Science, International Political Science Association, Caucus for a New Political Science, Dramatists Guild.

WRITINGS: (With C. J. Friedrich and M. Curtis) *Totalitarianism in Perspective: Three Views,* Praeger, 1969; *Superman and Common Men: Freedom, Anarchy and the Revolution,* Praeger, 1971; *The Death of Communal Liberty: A History of Freedom in a Swiss Mountain Canton,* Princeton University Press, 1974; *Liberating Feminism,* Continuum Books, 1975. Also author of monograph, "Political Participation," for Poynter Foundation.

Contributor: I. Wallerstein and P. Starr, editors, *The University Crisis Reader*, Volume II, Random House, 1971; F. Fleron and E. Hoffman, editors, *The Conduct of Soviet Foreign Policy*, Aldine-Atherton, 1971; J. A. Ogilvy, editor, *Self and World: Readings in Philosophy*, Harcourt, 1973; R. Edwards, editor, *Relevant Methods in Comparative Education*, UNESCO, 1973; J. B. Williamson, editor, *Social Problems: The Contemporary Debate*, Little, Brown, 1974; C. Bennett, editor, *Comparative Studies in Education: An Anthology*, Publications in Continuing Education, Syracuse University, 1975; Norman Daniels, editor, *Reading Rawls*, Basic Books, 1975; R. Perruci, editor, *Introductory Sociology*, W. C. Brown, 1977; George Roberts, editor, *Bertrand Russell: The Memorial Volumes*, Allen & Unwin, in press; John Perry and Erna Perry, editors, *The Social Web*, 2nd edition, Canfield Press, in press; R. Horowitz, editor, *Collected Essays*, University Press of Virginia, in press.

Plays: "The People's Heart," first produced Off-Off Broadway at Theatre 3, November, 1969; "Delly's Oracle," first produced at Berkshire Theatre Festival, October, 1970; "Fightsong" (musical), produced in New York at Gene Frankel Theatre, 1975; "Journeys" (musical), produced in Hanover, N.H. at Hopkins Center, 1975. Also author of play, "The Bust."

Contributor of articles to *Journal of Politics, Government and Opposition, American Political Science Review, Political Studies, Comparative Education Review, Trans-Action, Politics and Society, Harper's, Worldview, Modern Occasions, Dissent, Progressive*, and other periodicals; contributor of book reviews to scholarly journals. Editor, *Political Theory: An International Journal of Political Philosophy*, 1974—.

BIOGRAPHICAL/CRITICAL SOURCES: U.S. News and World Report, February 9, 1975, July 7, 1975.

* * *

BARBER, Richard J. 1932-

PERSONAL: Born May 15, 1932, in Detroit, Mich.; son of Raymond L. and Elizabeth (McCann) Barber; married Elizabeth Schomer, August 19, 1967. *Education:* Wayne University (now Wayne State University), A.B. (with honors), 1953, J.D., 1955; University of Michigan, M.A., 1958; Yale University, LL.M., 1959. *Home:* 5511 Pollard Rd., Washington, D.C. 20016. *Agent:* Robert Lescher, 155 East 71st St., New York, N.Y. 10021.

CAREER: Admitted to Michigan Bar, 1956; Rutgers University, New Brunswick, N.J., professor of law, 1959-61; Southern Methodist Universtiy, Dallas, Tex., professor of law, 1962-64; Yale University, New Haven, Conn., professor of law, 1964-65; U.S. Senate, Washington, D.C. special counsel to Antitrust Subcommittee, 1965-67; U.S. Department of Transportaion, Washington, D.C., deputy assistant secretary for policy, and internal affairs, 1967-70; Richard J. Barber Associates, Inc., Washington, D.C., president, 1970—. *Military service:* U.S. Army, 1955-57. *Member:* American Economic Association.

WRITINGS: The Politics of Research, Public Affairs Press, 1966; *The American Corporation: Its Power, Its Money, Its Politics*, Dutton, 1970. Contributor to *New Republic, Nation, Challenge*, and to law journals. Editor, *Journal of Air Law and Commerce.*

WORK IN PROGRESS: Writing on government and business, on the challenges to democratic government presented by modern global business and technology, and on transportation and urban society.

BIOGRAPHICAL/CRITICAL SOURCES: Washington Post, February 13, 1970; *New York Times Book Review*, March 8, 1970; *Nation*, May 4, 1970; *New Republic*, May 9, 1970; *New Yorker*, June 27, 1970.

* * *

BARCLAY, Barbara 1938-

PERSONAL: Born April 1, 1938, in Pasadena, Calif.; daughter of William and LaVerne (Scott) Barclay. *Education:* University of California, Los Angeles, A.B. (cum laude), 1958, teaching credentials, 1960, M.Ed., 1974; San Fernando State College (now California State University, Northridge), graduate study, 1967-68. *Home:* 17337 Tramonto Dr., Pacific Palisades, Calif. 90272.

CAREER: Los Angeles Unified School District, Los Angeles, Calif., elementary school teacher, 1960—. Instructor in music and fine arts, Pepperdine University. *Member:* National Education Association, California Teachers Association, United Teachers of Los Angeles, Phi Delta Kappa, Phi Lambda Theta.

WRITINGS: Lamps to Light the Way, Bowmar, 1971; *Our Presidents*, Ottenheimer, 1976; (senior consulting editor) *Our Nation's Heritage*, Bowmar, 1976.

WORK IN PROGRESS: Researching a book on in-depth personality and character study of great names in American history.

SIDELIGHTS: Barbara Barclay told *CA*, "In my writings I am interested in getting the human touch, warmth, and sense of humor of my subject across to my readers." She has traveled extensively in Europe, the Middle East, and Africa.

* * *

BARKINS, Evelyn (Warner) 1919-

PERSONAL: Born April 28, 1919, in New York, N.Y.; daughter of Bennett and Anne (Kay) Warner; married M. John Barkins, May 19, 1939; children: Elizabeth, Martha, George, Bradley, Laura. *Education:* St. Lawrence University, B.A., LL.B.; Brooklyn Law School, J.D.

CAREER: Admitted to Bar of New York State. *Member:* Authors League of America.

WRITINGS: The Magic Pod, and Other Poems, Island Workshop Press, 1945; *The Doctor Has a Baby*, Creative Age Press, 1947; *I Love My Doctor*, Crowell, 1948; *The Doctor Has a Family*, Pelleorini & Cudahy, 1950; *Are These Our Doctors?* Fell, 1952; *Four Children for the Doctor*, Fell, 1955; *Hospital Happy* (poems), Fell, 1959; *Love Poems of a Marriage*, Fell, 1970; *A Grandparent's Garden of Verses*, Fell, 1973; *From an Understanding Heart*, Fell, 1977.†

* * *

BARNETT, George L(eonard) 1915-

PERSONAL: Born January 18, 1915, in Caldwell, N.J.; son of D'Arcy C. (a school superintendent) and Adelle (Leonard) Barnett; married Johanetta Louise Usinger, June 15, 1940; children: George Leonard, Jr., Mary. *Education:* Randolph-Macon College, A.B., 1936; Princeton University, A.M., 1939, Ph.D., 1942. *Religion:* Protestant. *Home:* 1615 East University St., Bloomington, Ind. 47401. *Office:* Department of English, Indiana University, Bloomington, Ind. 47401.

CAREER: Randolph-Macon College, Ashland, Va., instructor in English, French, and Latin, 1939-41; Indiana

University, Bloomington, instructor in English and naval correspondence, U.S. Naval Training School, 1942-43, supervisor, U.S. Naval Training School, 1943-44, instructor in English in the university, 1944-46, assistant professor, 1946-56, associate professor, 1956-63, professor of English, 1963—. *Member:* Modern Language Association of America, Charles Lamb Society (vice-president), Phi Beta Kappa.

WRITINGS: (With others) *The English Romantic Poets and Essayists: A Review of Research and Criticism,* Modern Language Association of America, 1957, revised edition, New York University Press, 1966; *Charles Lamb: The Evolution of Elia,* Indiana University Press, 1964; (editor) *Eighteenth-Century British Novelists on the Novel,* Appleton, 1968; (editor) *Nineteenth-Century British Novelists on the Novel,* Appleton, 1971; *Charles Lamb,* Twayne, 1976. Contributor to professional journals.

* * *

BARNETT, Leo 1925-

PERSONAL: Born January 3, 1925, in New York, N.Y.; son of Max (a grocer) and Fanny (Fagin) Barnett; married Betty Rudoy (an executive secretary), January 29, 1950; children: Neil, David, Matthew, Richard. *Education:* New York University, B.A., 1950, graduate study, 1967—. *Home:* 1364 Pennington Rd., Teaneck, N.J. 07666. *Office:* Information Processing Center, 31-10 Thompson Ave., Long Island, N.Y. 11101.

CAREER: New School for Social Research, New York, N.Y., director of information processing center, beginning 1967; currently affiliated with Information Processing Center, Long Island, N.Y. Registrar, City University of New York, 1970. Computer consultant, Metropolitan Applied Research Council. *Military service:* U.S. Army Air Forces, 1943-46; became staff sergeant. *Member:* Association for Computing Machinery.

WRITINGS: (With Lou Ellen Davis) *Careers in Computer Programming,* Walck, 1967.

BIOGRAPHICAL/CRITICAL SOURCES: Best Sellers, February 1, 1968.†

* * *

BARNUM, W(illiam) Paul 1933-
(Jon O'Brynt, Eric O'Neil)

PERSONAL: Born January 14, 1933, in Placerville, Calif.; son of Harry David and Blodwyn (Ellis) Barnum; married Doris Tompkins, May 10, 1951; married second wife, Peggie Gilbert, March 9, 1956; children: Terry, Jennifer, Bridgette, William, Michael. *Residence:* Tucson, Ariz.

CAREER: Spent much of his childhood in Alaska; began radio work as a disc jockey in 1952, and subsequently was a newsman, copy writer, and program director for radio stations; went to Alaska on a news assignment following the 1964 earthquake, entered the night club business in Alaska and remained there for some time. *Military service:* U.S. Army, Paratroops, 1949-52; became sergeant.

WRITINGS: Black Is the Sun (collection of free verse), Branden Press, 1969. Author of regular column, ''Profiles of Loneliness,'' in *Bachelor* (magazine); contributor of articles and poetry to newspapers.

WORK IN PROGRESS: Yesterday Follows Tomorrow, a volume of free verse.

AVOCATIONAL INTERESTS: Tennis, golf, hunting, continental cookery.††

BARRANGER, M(illy) S(later) 1937-

PERSONAL: Born February 12, 1937, in Birmingham, Ala.; daughter of C. C. (an engineer) and Mildred (Hilliard) Slater; married Garic Kenneth Barranger (an attorney), August 26, 1961; children: Heather D. *Education:* Alabama College (now University of Montevallo), B.A., 1958; Tulane University, M.A., 1959, Ph.D., 1964. *Home:* 1414 Jahncke Ave., P.O. Box 1268, Covington, La. 70433. *Office:* Department of Theatre and Speech, Tulane University, New Orleans, La. 70118.

CAREER: Louisiana State University in New Orleans, special lecturer in English, 1964-69; Tulane University, New Orleans, La., assistant professor, 1969-73, associate professor of theatre and speech, 1973—, chairman of department, 1971—. Executive director of Tulane Center Stage, 1973—. *Member:* American Theatre Association (vice-president of administration, 1975-77), Speech Communication Association, Southwest Theatre Conference.

WRITINGS: Barron's Simplified Approach to Ibsen, Barron's, Volume I: *Peer Gynt, A Doll's House, An Enemy of the People,* 1969, Volume II: *Ghosts, The Wild Duck, Hedda Gabler,* 1969; (editor with Daniel Dodson) *Generations: A Thematic Introduction to Drama,* Harcourt, 1971. Contributor to *Dictionary of Church History,* Westminster Press, 1971. Contributor of articles to *College Language Association Journal, Modern Drama,* and other journals.

WORK IN PROGRESS: Studies in Henrik Ibsen's late plays.

AVOCATIONAL INTERESTS: Music, films, travel.

* * *

BARRETT, Ward J. 1927-

PERSONAL: Born August 11, 1927, in Jersey City, N.J.; son of Carroll Lewis and Madeline (Rehorn) Barrett; married Carol Gibbs (a professor of geography), December 20, 1966. *Education:* Columbia University, B.A., 1948, M.A., 1949; University of California, Berkeley, Ph.D., 1959. *Home:* 651 Fairmount Ave., St. Paul, Minn. 55105. *Office:* Department of Geography, 414 Social Sciences, University of Minnesota, Minneapolis, Minn. 55455.

CAREER: Auckland University College, Auckland, New Zealand, visiting lecturer in geography, 1955; Samoa College, Apia, Western Samoa, teacher of social studies, 1956-58; University of Minnesota, Minneapolis, 1959—, began as assistant professor, professor of geography, 1969—. *Military service:* U.S. Navy, 1945-46. *Member:* Association of American Geographers, American Association for the Advancement of Science. *Awards, honors:* McKnight Award, 1970, for *The Sugar Hacienda of the Marqueses del Valle.*

WRITINGS: The Sugar Hacienda of the Marqueses del Valle, University of Minnesota Press, 1970; *Mission in the Marianas: An Account of Father Diego Luis de Sanvitores and His Companions, 1669-1670,* University of Minnesota Press, 1975.

WORK IN PROGRESS: Writing on various aspects of the historical geography of Morelos, Mexico, including the colonial sugar industry.

* * *

BARRY, Jackson G(ranville) 1926-

PERSONAL: Born November 4, 1926, in Boston, Mass.; son of John Francis (a stockbroker) and Edith Jenny (Grush) Barry; married Prudence Julia Broadley, November 16,

1956; children: Leigh John. *Education:* Yale University, B.A., 1950; Columbia University, M.A., 1951; Western Reserve University (now Case Western Reserve University), M.F.A., 1962, Ph.D., 1963. *Religion:* Episcopalian. *Home:* 5042 Eliot's Oak Rd., Columbia, Md. 21044. *Office:* Department of English, University of Maryland, College Park, Md. 20742.

CAREER: De Cordova Museum, Lincoln, Mass., director of adult drama program, 1953-56; Smith College, Northampton, Mass., instructor in drama, 1958-61; University of Miami, Coral Gables, Fla., assistant professor of humanities, 1963-64; Villanova University, Villanova, Pa., assistant professor of drama, 1964-67; State University of New York at Stony Brook, associate professor of drama, 1967-70; University of Maryland, College Park, associate professor of English, 1970—. *Military service:* U.S. Navy, 1945-46. *Member:* Modern Language Association of America, American Society for Aesthetics, Shakespeare Association of America.

WRITINGS: Dramatic Structure: The Shaping of Experience, University of California Press, 1970. Contributor of reviews and articles on art, film, poetry, and drama to academic journals; art critic, *Pictures on Exhibit,* 1957-58.

WORK IN PROGRESS: Research on the structure of language in its relation to the nature of the poem.

*   *   *

BARTH, Christoph F. 1917-

PERSONAL: Born September 29, 1917; son of Karl Barth (a professor); married Marie-Claire Frommel, December 24, 1957. *Education:* Educated at primary and secondary schools in Germany and Switzerland, 1924-36; University of Basel, Dr. theol., 1947. *Home:* Auf der Steig 4, D-65 Mainz, West Germany. *Office:* Faculty of Evangelical Theology, University of Mainz, 6500 Mainz, West Germany.

CAREER: Missionary of Reformed Church in Indonesia, 1947-65; University of Mainz, Faculty of Evangelical Theology, Mainz, West Germany, professor of Old Testament exegesis and theology, 1967—. Staff member of translation department, Indonesian Bible Society, 1954-63.

WRITINGS: Die Errettung vom Tode in den individuellen Klage-und Dankliedern des Alten Testamentes, Evangelischer Verlag, 1947; (translator into Indonesian) *Kitab mazmur* (Old Testament psalms), Badan Penerbit Kristen, 1960; *Einfuehrung in die Psalmen,* Neukirchener Verlag, 1961, translation by R. A. Wilson published as *Introduction to the Psalms,* Scribner, 1966; *Old Testament Theology* (in Indonesian), Part I, Jakarta, 1969; *Diesseits und Jenseits,* [Stuttgart], 1974.

WORK IN PROGRESS: Part II of *Old Testament Theology.*

SIDELIGHTS: Christoph Barth speaks five languages: English, Dutch, and French in addition to German and Indonesian.

*   *   *

BARTH, J(ohn) Robert 1931-

PERSONAL: Born February 23, 1931, in Buffalo, N.Y.; son of Philip C. (an attorney) and Mary K. (Eustace) Barth. *Education:* Fordham University, A.B., 1954, M.A., 1956; Bellarmine College, Ph.L., 1956; Woodstock College, S.T.L., 1962; Harvard University, Ph.D., 1967. *Home:* Newman Center, 701 Maryland Ave., Columbia, Mo.

65201. *Office:* Department of English, 231 Arts and Science, University of Missouri, Columbia, Mo. 65201.

CAREER: Entered the Society of Jesus (S.J.) in 1948, ordained Roman Catholic priest, 1961; Canisius High School, Buffalo, N.Y., teacher of English, Latin, and French, 1955-58; Canisius College, Buffalo, assistant professor of English, 1967-70; Harvard University, Cambridge, Mass., assistant professor of English, 1970-74; University of Missouri—Columbia, associate professor, 1974-77, professor of English, 1977—. *Member:* Modern Language Association of America, American Association of University Professors, Modern Humanities Research Association, English Institute, Conference on Christianity and Literature. *Awards, honors:* Howard Mumford Jones Prize, 1967; Dexter traveling fellowship from Harvard University, summer, 1967; National Endowment for the Humanities summer grant, 1969; American Council of Learned Societies grant, 1970; Harvard University faculty research grant, 1973-74.

WRITINGS: Coleridge and Christian Doctrine, Harvard University Press, 1969; *Religious Perspectives in Faulkner's Fiction: Yoknapatawpha and Beyond,* University of Notre Dame Press, 1972; *The Symbolic Imagination: Coleridge and the Romantic Tradition,* Princeton University Press, 1976. Contributor of articles to *America, Renascence, Thought, Studies in Romanticism,* and other journals.

WORK IN PROGRESS: A work tentatively entitled, *Varieties of Romantic Religion.*

*   *   *

BARTLETT, Charles (Leffingwell) 1921-

PERSONAL: Born August 14, 1921, in Chicago, Ill.; son of Valentine C. (a stockbroker) and Marie (Frost) Bartlett; married Martha Buck, December 12, 1950; children: Peter Buck, Michael Valentine, Robert Shubael, Helen Buck. *Education:* Yale University, B.A., 1942. *Politics:* Independent. *Religion:* Roman Catholic. *Home:* 4615 W St. N.W., Washington, D.C. 20007. *Office:* Suite 300, 1901 Pennsylvania Ave. N.W., Washington, D.C. 20006.

CAREER: Chattanooga Times, Chattanooga, Tenn., reporter, 1946-48, Washington correspondent, 1948-62; *Chicago Daily News* and Field Newspaper Syndicate, both Chicago, Ill., columnist, 1962—, with column, "News Focus," appearing in metropolitan dailies across the country. *Military service:* U.S. Navy, 1942-46; became lieutenant senior grade. *Member:* Gridiron Club, Federal City Club. *Awards, honors:* Pulitzer Prize for national reporting, 1956.

WRITINGS: (With Edward Weintal) *Facing the Brink: An Intimate Study of Crisis Diplomacy,* Scribner, 1967.

BIOGRAPHICAL/CRITICAL SOURCES: New York Times Book Review, March 12, 1967; *Book Week,* April 16, 1967; *Spectator,* September 8, 1967.

*   *   *

BARUCH, Ruth-Marion 1922-

PERSONAL: Born June 15, 1922, in Berlin, Germany; daughter of Max and Bertha (Zweigenhaft) Baruch; married Pirkle Jones (a photographer), January 15, 1949. *Education:* University of Missouri, B.A. and B.J., 1944; Ohio University, M.F.A., 1946; California School of Fine Arts, San Francisco, further study in photography, 1946-48. *Politics:* "Registered Peace and Freedom Party." *Religion:* Jewish. *Home:* 663 Lovell Ave., Mill Valley, Calif. 94941. *Agent:* William Webb, Route 1, Box 167, Carmel, Calif. 93921.

CAREER: Work as a photographer has been exhibited in numerous museums, including San Francisco Museum of Art, San Francisco, Calif., Amon Carter Museum of Western Art, Fort Worth, Tex., Museum of Modern Art, New York, N.Y., George Eastman House, Rochester, N.Y., M. H. de Young Museum of Art, San Francisco, and at Dartmouth College, University of California, Santa Cruz, and Indiana University.

WRITINGS: (Author of preface; photographer with husband, Pirkle Jones) *The Vanguard: A Photographic Essay on the Black Panthers,* Beacon Press, 1970; (photographer) *Language Lives,* McDougal, Littel, 1975. Photographs have been published in books and periodicals.

SIDELIGHTS: Alfred Frankenstein, reviewing Ruth-Marion Baruch's solo exhibition, "Haight-Ashbury, 1967," at the M. H. de Young Museum of Art, calls her "a photographer who has documented the pathos, comedy, wistfulness, and deep tragedy of the Haight-Ashbury district with superlative insight and magnificent camera-craft. This display is a highly significant contribution to our history and to the sociology of San Francisco and the 20th century, as well as a contribution of the highest importance to the record of the fine art of photography in this part of the world." In a review of another Baruch show, "A Retrospective," which highlights the photographs of her twenty year career, Joan Murray writes: "She says what *she* believes in her photographs, especially in the series on the Black Panthers. Photographically, the images are fine studies of selected persons within these various minority cultures. She has a knack for capturing the open, unguarded, totally human moment that binds all humans one to another."

Ruth-Marion Baruch told *CA:* "The urge to communicate; a compelling need to express either internal or external conditions, circumstances, relationships, states of being, in other words, the human condition, motivates me in photography. I feel that the craft, or technique as it is referred to, in photography is a necessary and beautiful means toward the perfection of expression, as it is in writing or any of the arts, but never an end in itself. Without it, the photograph is limited; but I feel that technique is still secondary. If the viewer becomes conscious of it first, long before absorbing the feelings and content, the photograph has failed. This applies to composition as well. 'Art,' as Edward Weston once said, 'is just the strongest way of seeing.' "

In 1976 Arthur Ollman and Rosana Felsenfeld made a ninety-minute film on the lives and work of Ruth-Marion Baruch and her husband, photographer Pirkle Jones, which will be available to museums, galleries, and educational institutions.

AVOCATIONAL INTERESTS: Writing poetry (she has given readings of her poems under the auspices of the Poetry Center of San Francisco State College but has not attempted to have any published).

BIOGRAPHICAL/CRITICAL SOURCES: Art Forum, May, 1964; *San Francisco Chronicle,* November 6, 1968; *New York Times,* December 16, 1968; *Artweek,* June 3, 1972.

*   *   *

BASCHE, James 1926-

PERSONAL: Born May 22, 1926, in Green Bay, Wis.; son of James Roland and Lena (Hannon) Basche. *Education:* Northwestern University, B.S., 1950; Columbia University, M.A., 1952, graduate study, 1957-58, 1962-63; attended University of Wisconsin, 1952-53, and University of Chicago, 1953-54. *Home:* 440 East 79th St., New York, N.Y. 10021. *Office:* The Conference Board, 845 Third Ave., New York, N.Y. 10022.

CAREER: University of Denver, Social Science Foundation, Denver, Colo., instructor in international relations, 1954-57; Foreign Policy Association, Inc., New York City, community consultant, 1958-59; Asia Foundation, San Francisco, Calif., staff member, 1959-65; Greater New York Council for Foreign Students, Inc., New York City, executive director, 1965-66; Nelson Associates, Inc., New York City, management consultant, 1966-69; The Conference Board, New York City, senior research associate in international affairs, 1970—. Part-time instructor at University of Wisconsin, 1952-53, School of General Studies, Hunter College (now Hunter College of the City University of New York), 1957-58, and at Thammasat University, Bangkok, Thailand, 1961-62. Member of final selection committee for Thai grantees, U.S. Educational Foundation (Fulbright) in Thailand, 1961; member-at-large of U.S. General Committee, World University Service, 1963-68. Trustee, United Board for Christian Higher Education in Asia, 1973-76. *Military service:* U.S. Army, 1944-46; became staff sergeant; received battle star for service in Asiatic-Pacific theater. *Member:* Asia Society (chairman of Thailand Council, 1971-75), Siam Society (Bangkok), Phi Beta Kappa, Phi Eta Sigma.

WRITINGS: (Author of introduction; photographs by Hubert Sieben) *Thailand: Land of Color,* Taplinger, 1969; *Thailand: Land of the Free,* Taplinger, 1971. Also author of fifteen reports on international business problems and activities for The Conference Board. Author of four television scripts for public affairs series, "Focus," on KLZ-TV, Denver, 1955-56. Contributor to education and other journals.

WORK IN PROGRESS: A novel set in contemporary Southeast Asia; research on the history of Manila.

*   *   *

BASS, Jack 1934-

PERSONAL: Born June 24, 1934, in Columbia, S.C.; son of Nathan (a merchant) and Esther (Cohen) Bass; married Carolyn McClung, March 3, 1957; children: Kenneth, David, Elizabeth. *Education:* University of South Carolina, A.B., 1956, M.A., 1976; Harvard University, further study, 1965-66. *Home:* 3508 Fox Hall Rd., Columbia, S.C. 29204. *Agent:* Liz Darhansoff, 52 East 91st St., New York, N.Y. 10028. *Office:* South Carolina State College, Orangeburg, S.C. 29115.

CAREER: State (newspaper), Columbia, S.C., governmental affairs editor, 1963-66; *Charlotte Observer,* Charlotte, N.C., bureau chief, Columbia, S.C., 1966-73; Duke University, Durham, N.C., research scholar, 1973-75; South Carolina State College, Orangeburg, S.C., writer-in-residence, 1975—. Part-time lecturer in journalism, University of South Carolina, 1967-71. *Military service:* U.S. Naval Reserve; became commander. *Member:* Sigma Delta Chi. *Awards, honors:* Nieman fellowship, Harvard University, 1965-66; named South Carolina newspaperman of the year, 1968 and 1972; Notable Books for Adults List, American Library Association, 1976, for *The Transformation of Southern Politics.*

WRITINGS: (With Jack Nelson) *The Orangeburg Massacre,* World Publishing, 1970; (contributor) *You Can't Eat Magnolias,* McGraw, 1972; *Porgy Comes Home: South*

Carolina after 300 Years, R. L. Bryan, 1972; (with Walter De Vries) *The Transformation of Southern Politics*, Basic Books, 1976. Contributor to *New York Times, Washington Post, Los Angeles Times,* and *New Republic.*

SIDELIGHTS: In a review of *The Orangeburg Massacre,* Jonathan Yardley exclaimed: ". . . Thank the Lord for Jack Nelson and Jack Bass. A passionate belief in the truth, their book demonstrates, is essential if one wishes to find out what happened at Orangeburg, for the smokescreen of official lies and evasions put up to hide it is nearly impenetrable. . . . Perhaps the publication of *The Orangeburg Massacre* will finally make their version more durable than the official version. It ought to. Their book is angry, honest, perceptive and profoundly disturbing; it stands out in the flood of civil rights books not merely because of its good reportage, but because it is a devastating case history of the misuse of law-enforcement authority and the perversion of justice."

Jack Bass wrote *CA:* "For more than a decade, I had thought and occasionally talked about the idea of updating V. O. Key's classic book, *Southern Politics in State and Nation.* As a southern-based journalist who covered politics and witnessed dramatic changes as they occurred, it seemed to me that a book that was both readable and academically sound could be produced by a political reporter teaming up with a political scientist. Others agreed. In the spring of 1973, a chance meeting with a visitor from the Ford Foundation to Columbia, S.C. got me moving. What evolved was a two-year project, funded by grants from the Ford and Rockefeller Foundations, in which Walter De Vries and I operated from a base at Duke University, traveled more than 40,000 miles in the 11 states of the old Confederacy, and conducted more than 360 interviews with elected officials, journalists, academic analysts, party officials, and others.

"Although our publisher managed to get the first books off the press the week after 5,000 delegates and alternates gathered in New York to nominate Jimmy Carter, our luck couldn't have been better in coming out the year that the South produced a president.

"It is not the kind of book that makes one wealthy, but there is a genuine payoff that can't be measured financially when a reviewer for *New Republic* writes: 'Were V. O. Key alive, I have no doubt that he would gladly endorse *Transformation* as a sequel to his own work.'"

BIOGRAPHICAL/CRITICAL SOURCES: Nation, September 28, 1970; *Time,* October 26, 1970; *Best Sellers,* November 15, 1970; *Washington Post,* November 30, 1970, August 22, 1976; *Commonweal,* December 25, 1970; *New York Times Book Review,* August 15, 1976; *New Republic,* September 11, 1976; *St. Louis Post-Dispatch,* October 19, 1976.

*　　　*　　　*

BASSIOUNI, M. Cherif 1937-

PERSONAL: Born in 1937, in Cairo, Egypt; became U.S. citizen; married Rosanna Cesari, 1962. *Education:* College of the Holy Family (Cairo, Egypt), A.A.B., 1955; University of Dijon, law student, 1955-57; University of Geneva, law student, 1957; University of Cairo, LL.B., 1961; Indiana University, J.D., 1964; John Marshall Lawyer's Institute, LL.M., 1966; George Washington University, S.J.D., 1973. *Home:* 1130 North Lake Shore Dr., Chicago, Ill. 60611. *Office:* College of Law, DePaul University, 25 East Jackson Blvd., Chicago, Ill. 60604.

CAREER: Member of Illinois and District of Columbia Bars; DePaul University, Chicago, Ill., assistant professor, 1964-67, associate professor, 1967-70, professor of law, 1970—. Fulbright visiting professor, University of Freiburg, summer, 1970; visiting professor of law, New York University School of Law, 1971; guest scholar, Woodrow Wilson International Center for Scholars, 1972; lecturer at other universities, including University of Michigan, Stanford University, University of Wisconsin, University of Denver, University of Colorado, University of Kansas, University of Illinois, University of Paris, University of Naples. *Member:* American Society of International Law, Association Internationale de Droit Penal (secretary-general), World Peace Through Law Center, American Bar Association, Illinois State Bar Association, Chicago Bar Association.

WRITINGS: Criminal Law and Its Processes: The Law of Public Order (textbook), C. C Thomas, 1969; *Crimes and Justice,* Law in American Society Foundation, 1969; *Juvenile Delinquency,* Law in American Society Foundation, 1969; *Crimes and Justice in Urban America,* Houghton, 1970; *Juvenile Delinquency in Urban America,* Houghton, 1970; (editor) *The Law of Dissent and Riots,* C. C Thomas, 1971; *Crimes and Criminal Justice,* University of Chicago, 1971; (with E. M. Fischer) *Storm Over the Arab World: A People in Revolution,* foreword by Arnold Toynbee, Follett, 1972; (with V. P. Vanda) *A Treatise on International Criminal Law,* two volumes, C. C Thomas, 1973; (with Thecia Sheil) *Youth and the Law,* Houghton, 1973; *International Extradition and World Public Order,* Sijthoff, 1974; *International Terrorism and Political Crimes,* C. C Thomas, 1975; (editor) *Issues in the Mediterranean,* Chicago Council on Foreign Relations, 1976; *The Law of Citizens Arrest,* C. C Thomas, 1977; *Substantive Criminal Law,* C. C Thomas, 1977. Also author of *Cases and Materials on Criminal Law.* Contributor of forty-five articles to scholarly, legal, and professional journals.

*　　　*　　　*

BATEMAN, Walter L(ewis) 1916-

PERSONAL: Born January 5, 1916, in Duluth, Minn.; son of Lewis William and Nancy (Lee) Bateman; married Sue Sturm (executive director of Y.W.C.A.), October 8, 1943; children: William Frederick, Neale Edward, Nancy Sue. *Education:* University of Chicago, B.A., 1937; University of Minnesota, M.A., 1942; additional study at University of Mexico, University of Oregon, University of Denver, University of Minnesota, University of Wisconsin, and Hamline University. *Politics:* Independent. *Religion:* Unitarian Universalist. *Home:* 615 Third St. S.W., Rochester, Minn. 55901. *Office:* Rochester State Community College, Rochester, Minn. 55901.

CAREER: High school teacher of history, English, and Spanish in Faribault, Minn., 1937-39, and Duluth, Minn., 1939-40; Rochester State Community College, Rochester, Minn., instructor in history, anthropology, and sociology, 1947—. Member, Planning and Zoning Commission of Rochester, 1963-69. *Military service:* U.S. Army, Infantry, 1942-46; served in Europe; became first lieutenant. *Member:* American Anthropological Association, Midwest Sociological Society, Central States Anthropological Society, Minnesota Junior College Faculty Association.

WRITINGS: (With Fred King) *How Our Government Began,* Benefic, 1965; *How Man Began,* Benefic, 1966; *The Navajo of the Painted Desert,* Beacon Press, 1970; *The Kung of the Kalahari,* Beacon Press, 1970; *Man the Culture*

Builder, Parts I-II, Beacon Press, 1970; (contributor) T. C. Aylesworth, editor, *Mysteries from the Past,* Natural History Press, 1971. Contributor to newspapers and magazines.

AVOCATIONAL INTERESTS: Photography, chess, wine making.

* * *

BAUER, Fred 1934-

PERSONAL: Born March 30, 1934, in Montpelier, Ohio; married Shirley L. Snyder, August 23, 1953; children: Laraine, Stephen, Christopher, Daniel. *Education:* Bowling Green State University, B.S., 1957. *Home:* 6 Littlebrook Rd., Princeton, N.J.

CAREER: Former newspaperman, working successively as sports editor in Montpelier, Ohio, editor in Bryan, Ohio, and copy editor in Fort Wayne, Ind.; Radio Station WONW, Defiance, Ohio, sports director; *Guideposts* (magazine), New York, N.Y., 1962—, executive editor and assistant director. *Military service:* U.S. Army, 1954-56.

WRITINGS: (With G. S. Shea) *Then Sings My Soul,* Revell, 1968; *How Many Hills to Hillsboro?,* Hewitt House, 1969; (editor) *Ev: The Man and His Words,* Hewitt House, 1969; (with Brooks Robinson) *Putting It All Together,* Hawthorn, 1971; *I Don't Live There Anymore,* Impact Books, 1973; *For Rainy Mondays and Other Dry Spells,* Prometheus Press, 1974; *Daily Guideposts,* Guideposts Books, 1977.

AVOCATIONAL INTERESTS: Politics, poetry, nature, bicycling, camping, hiking.

* * *

BAUER, George Howard 1933-

PERSONAL: Born December 31, 1933, in Cortez, Colo.; son of John Henry (a businessman) and Geraldene (Howard) Bauer; married Ellen Wood (a college teacher), October 26, 1962; children: Ellen Robinson, George Howard, Jr. *Education:* University of Colorado, A.B., 1955; University of Grenoble, graduate study, 1955-56; Indiana University, M.A., 1960, Ph.D., 1967. *Office:* Department of French and Italian, University of Minnesota, Minneapolis, Minn. 55455.

CAREER: Dartmouth College, Hanover, N.H., instructor in French, 1961-63; Northwestern University, Evanston, Ill., lecturer, 1963-64, instructor, 1964-67, assistant professor of French, 1967-70; University of Minnesota, Minneapolis, assistant professor of French, 1970-73, associate professor of French, humanities, and comparative literature, 1973—. Distinguished visiting professor of humanities, University of Wyoming, 1976-77. *Military service:* U.S. Army, Military Intelligence, 1956-58; became lieutenant colonel. *Member:* Modern Language Association of America, American Association of Teachers of French, College Art Association, American Association of University Professors, Phi Beta Kappa. *Awards, honors:* Fulbright scholar in France, 1955-56; American Council of Learned Societies study fellowship, 1968-69.

WRITINGS: Sartre and the Artist, University of Chicago Press, 1969.

WORK IN PROGRESS: A study of art and the artist in the contemporary French novel; with Michel Rybalka and Michel Contat, preparing the Pleiade edition of the novels of Jean-Paul Sartre.

BAUER, Yehuda 1926-

PERSONAL: Born April 6, 1926, in Prague, Czechoslovakia; son of Viktor (an engineer) and Uly (Fried) Bauer; married Shula White (a children's dress designer), December 20, 1955; children: Danit, Anat. *Education:* Hebrew University, student, 1945-46, Ph.D., 1960; University of Wales, B.A., 1948, M.A., 1950. *Home:* Kibbutz Shoval, Negev, Israel. *Office:* Institute of Contemporary Jewry, Hebrew University, Jerusalem, Israel.

CAREER: Lecturer at kibbutz seminars at Oranim and Giv'ath Haviva, Israel, 1954-61; Hebrew University, Jerusalem, Israel, professor, head of department of Holocaust Studies, and head of Institute of Contemporary Jewry, 1961—. Member, scientific advisory committee, Yad Vashem, Jerusalem. *Military service:* Palmach (Jewish underground force), 1945-46; Israeli Army, 1948-49.

WRITINGS: Diplomatyah u-mahteret, [Merhavya], 1963, translation by Alton Winters published as *From Diplomacy to Resistance: A History of Jewish Palestine, 1939-1945,* Jewish Publication Society, 1970; (compiler) *ha-Tenu'ah ha-tsiyonit,* Institute of Contemporary Jewry, Hebrew University, 1963; *Flight and Rescue,* Random House, 1970; *They Chose Life: Jewish Resistance in the Holocaust,* American-Jewish Committee, 1973; *My Brother's Keeper,* Jewish Publication Society, 1974. Contributor to *Midstream, Jewish Heritage, Middle East Journal, Yad Vashem Studies, Zion, Yalkut Moreshet,* and other publications. Editor of historical section, *Hebrew Encyclopedia of Social Sciences,* 1965-71; member of editorial board, *Yalkut Moreshet* and *Yad Voshem Studies.*

WORK IN PROGRESS: A book on rescue attempts during World War II by the American Jewish Joint Distribution Committee, tentatively entitled *A Friend in Need.*

* * *

BAUM, Willi 1931-

PERSONAL: Born March 10, 1931, in Biel, Bern, Switzerland; son of August and Johanna (Jseli) Baum. *Education:* Educated in Dresden, Germany. *Home:* 550 Marin Ave., Mill Valley, Calif. 94941. *Office:* Pier 39, San Francisco, Calif. 94133.

CAREER: Served apprenticeship as a designer in Bern, Switzerland, 1947-52; designer with South African advertising firm in Capetown, 1952-54; art director of Lintas, Hamburg, Germany, and London, England, 1956-58; freelance designer and illustrator in the United States, principally in San Francisco, Calif., 1959—. *Awards, honors:* Awards from Art Directors Club of New York and Art Directors Club of Los Angeles; award from Society of Illustrators, 1970.

WRITINGS—Self-illustrated: Birds of a Feather (juvenile), Addison-Wesley, 1969; *The Expedition* (juvenile), Emme Edizioni, 1975; *Kiboko* (juvenile), Abelard-Schuman, 1976; *Fred and Tom and the Golden Mountain* (juvenile), Otto Maier Verlag, 1976.

Illustrator: Rudyard Kipling, *The Miracle of the Mountain,* adapted by Caroline Beecher Leach, Addison-Wesley, 1969; R. E. Raspe, *Baron Munchausen (Fifteen Truly Tall Tales),* retold by Doris Orgel, Addison-Wesley, 1970.

WORK IN PROGRESS: A picture book of the East Asian epic "Ramayana" as told and performed in Bali.

SIDELIGHTS: Willi Baum has lived and traveled in Africa, Europe, and Asia.

BAUMANN, Walter 1935-

PERSONAL: Born November 10, 1935, in Winterthur, Switzerland; son of Max (a plumber) and Rosa (Geiger) Baumann; married Margaret E. Adam (a language teacher), August 7, 1961; children: Martin. *Education:* Kantonales Oberseminar, Zurich, Primary School Teacher's Diploma, 1957; attended University of Zurich, 1957-59, and University of Aberdeen, 1959-61; University of Zurich, Dr.Phil., 1964; also received Swiss Grammar School Teacher's Diploma, 1964. *Home:* 42 Northland Rd., Londonderry, Northern Ireland. *Office:* New University of Ulster, Coleraine, Northern Ireland.

CAREER: University of Toronto, Toronto, Ontario, lecturer in German, 1964-66; New University of Ulster, Coleraine, Northern Ireland, lecturer, 1966-73, senior lecturer in German, 1973—. *Member:* Conference of University Teachers of German of Great Britain and Ireland, International Association for Germanic Studies.

WRITINGS: (Contributor) Eva Hesse, editor, *New Approaches to Ezra Pound,* University of California Press, 1969; *The Rose in the Steel Dust: An Examination of the Cantos of Ezra Pound,* Francke (Berne), 1967, University of Miami Press, 1970; (contributor) Marie Henault and Charles E. Merrill, editors, *Studies in the Cantos,* [Columbus, Ohio], 1971. Contributor to language journals.

WORK IN PROGRESS: A study dealing with Pound, nature, Goethe; investigations of twentieth-century authors.

BIOGRAPHICAL/CRITICAL SOURCES: Journal of Modern Literature, Supplement, 1971; *Erasmus,* March 10, 1972; *American Literature,* June, 1972.

* * *

BAUSCH, William J. 1929-

PERSONAL: Born March 3, 1929, in Jamesburg, N.J.; son of Charles J. (a baker) and Colette (Perdoni) Bausch. *Education:* St. Mary's College of Maryland, A.B., 1951; St. Mary's Seminary and University, Baltimore, S.T.B., 1955. *Address:* Hwy. 34, Colts Neck, N.J. 07722.

CAREER: Roman Catholic priest. Parish priest and teacher in New Monmouth, Keyport, and Maple Shade, N.J., 1955-69; parish priest at St. Benedict's Church, Hazlet, N.J., 1969-73, and St. Mary's Church, Colts Neck, N.J., 1973—.

WRITINGS—All published by Fides: *A Boy's Sex Life* (juvenile), 1969; *It Is the Lord!: Sin and Confession Revisited,* 1970; *Renewal and the Middle Catholic,* 1971; *Pilgrim Church,* 1973; *Positioning: Belief in the Mid Seventies,* 1975; *The Sacraments: Of the People, by the People, for the People,* 1976. Contributor to Catholic journals.

* * *

BAXTER, John 1939-
(Martin Loran, a joint pseudonym)

PERSONAL: Born December 14, 1939, in Sydney, Australia; son of John Archibald William (a chef) and Cathleen (Konrad) Baxter; married Merie Elizabeth Brooker, September 1, 1962 (divorced, 1967). *Education:* Attended Waverly College, Sydney, Australia, 1944-54. *Politics:* None. *Religion:* None. *Agent:* E. J. Carnell, 17 Burwash Rd., London SE18 72Y, England.

CAREER: New South Wales State Government, Sydney, Australia, staff controller, 1957-67; Australian Commonwealth Film Unit, Sydney, director of publicity, 1967-70; spent 1970 visiting European film festivals and archives,

studying facilities for film research; writer. Member of board, Sydney Film Festival, 1968-69. *Member:* Royal Commonwealth Society (London), British Film Institute, Sydney Film Study Group (president, 1967-68). *Awards, honors:* Bronze Medal in Australian Film Awards, 1969, for script, "After Proust"; Silver Medal, Kranj Film Festival (Yugoslavia), 1970, for script, "Golf in Australia"; first prize, Benson and Hedges Australian Film Competition, 1970, for television documentary, "No Roses for Michael."

WRITINGS: The Off-Worlders, Ace Books, 1966; *The God Killers,* Ace Books, 1966; (compiler) *The Pacific Book of Australian Science Fiction,* Angus & Robertson, 1968, published as *The Pacific Book of Science Fiction,* 1969; *Hollywood in the Thirties,* A. S. Barnes, 1968.

Science Fiction in the Cinema, A. S. Barnes, 1970; (compiler) *The Second Pacific Book of Science Fiction,* Angus & Robertson, 1970; *The Australian Cinema,* Angus & Robertson, 1970; *The Gangster Film,* A. S. Barnes, 1970; *Adam's Woman* (novel; adaptation of screenplay), Horwitz, 1970; *The Cinema of Josef von Sternberg,* Zwemmer, 1970, A. S. Barnes, 1971; *The Cinema of John Ford,* Zwemmer, 1970, A. S. Barnes, 1971; *Hollywood in the Sixties,* A. S. Barnes, 1972; *Sixty Years of Hollywood,* A. S. Barnes, 1973; *An Appalling Talent: Ken Russell,* M. Joseph, 1973; *Stunt: The Story of the Great Movie Stunt Men,* Macdonald & Co., 1973, Doubleday, 1974; *King Vidor,* Monarch, 1975; *The Hollywood Exiles,* Taplinger, 1976; (with Thomas Atkins) *The Fire Came By: The Riddle of the Great Siberian Explosion,* introduction by Isaac Asimov, Doubleday, 1976.

Films: Scripts for documentary films for Australian Commonwealth Film Unit include "Beyond the Pack Ice," 1968, "Golf in Australia," 1969, "Top End," 1970, and a number of films in "Australian Diary" series; wrote script and co-produced "After Proust," 1969, and script of "No Roses for Michael," a documentary presented on Australian and British television networks, 1970. Also wrote scripts for and presented "Understanding Film," a series of thirteen half-hour television programs, 1969.

Author with Ron Smith, under joint pseudonym Martin Loran, of novelettes and short stories. Stories included in *New Writings in Science Fiction* and in *New Australian Writing,* Penguin, 1968. Regular contributor to most Australian magazines, including *Bulletin* (national weekly), *Nation, Masque,* and *Hemisphere.*

WORK IN PROGRESS: Two science fiction novels, *The Meadows of Capricorn* and *Tense* (working title); *The Tiger's Tail,* for MacDonald.

SIDELIGHTS: John Baxter was "drawn by an early fascination into science fiction and the cinema, fields which demand as the price of participation a heavy investment in the social life that surrounds them. I have little time for anything outside. I've hoped in my film books and scripts to show my devotion to the 'professional' cinema rather than to what passes for experiment these days, and to relate cinema to the other arts by taking subjects from literature, or in my books to adopt some of the terminology of art criticism." He is interested in avant garde music and "in the avant garde of other generations," including Proust and Cocteau.†

* * *

BAYNHAM, Henry (W. F.) 1933-

PERSONAL: Born July 21, 1933, in Wrexham, Wales; son of William Lewis (an army major) and Mignon (Forster) Baynham. *Education:* Peterhouse, Cambridge, B.A., 1957,

M.A., 1960. *Religion:* Church of England. *Home:* New Rusko, Gatehouse-of-Fleet, Kirkcudbrightshire, Scotland. *Agent:* Julian Bach, Jr., 3 East 48th St., New York, N.Y. 10017; and Anthony Sheil Associates Ltd., 52 Floral St., Covent Garden, London WC2E 9DA, England.

CAREER: Canford School, Wimborne, Dorsetshire, England, assistant master of Beaufort House, 1958-65, housemaster of Beaufort House, beginning, 1966. Fellow, Balliol College, Oxford University, 1965. *Military service:* Royal Navy, Submarine Service, 1952-54. Royal Naval Reserve, 1954—; current rank, lieutenant commander. *Member:* Historical Association, Past and Present Society, Society for Nautical Research, Naval Records Society, Wimborne Round Table. *Awards, honors:* Travel scholarship to Italy, summer, 1957, spent with British Council and at University of Florence; Goldsmith travelling fellow, 1971.

WRITINGS: From the Lower Deck: The Old Navy, 1780-1840, Hutchinson, 1969, published as *From the Lower Deck: The Royal Navy,* Barre, 1970; *Before the Mast,* Hutchinson, 1971; *Men from the Dreadnoughts,* Hutchinson, 1976. Contributor to *Mariner's Mirror* and *Naval Review.*

WORK IN PROGRESS: Anglo-American Naval Relations in the Nineteenth Century; writing on other aspects of nineteenth-century naval history.

AVOCATIONAL INTERESTS: Playing violin, singing, mountaineering in the Pyrenees and Lapland, rock climbing in England and Scotland.

BIOGRAPHICAL/CRITICAL SOURCES: Books and Bookmen, June, 1969; *Virginia Quarterly Review,* autumn, 1970.

* * *

BEAMAN, Joyce Proctor 1931-

PERSONAL: Born April 27, 1931, in Wilson, N.C.; daughter of Jesse David (a farmer) and Pauline (maiden name, Owens; a teacher) Proctor; married Robert Hines Beaman (a farmer), August 17, 1952; children: Robert David. *Education:* East Carolina University, B.S., 1951, M.A., 1952, B.S. in L.S., Masters in Supervision, 1970, Principal's Certificate, 1977. *Politics:* Democrat. *Religion:* Baptist. *Home address:* Route 2, Walstonburg, N.C. 27888.

CAREER: Snow Hill High School, Snow Hill, N.C., English and French teacher, 1953-59; Saratoga Central High School, Saratoga, N.C., English and French teacher and librarian, 1959-71, full-time librarian, 1971-77. Creative writing teacher, Wilson Technical Institute, Wilson, N.C., 1971. *Member:* National Education Association (life member), North Carolina Association of Educators, North Carolina English Teachers' Association, Delta Kappa Gamma, Kappa Delta Pi. *Awards, honors:* Terry Sanford Award, 1977, for creativity and innovation in teaching.

WRITINGS: Broken Acres, Blair, 1971; *All for the Love of Cassie* (novel), Moore Publishing, 1973; *Bloom Where You Are Planted* (nonfiction), Moore Publishing, 1975. Contributor of articles and essays to *North Carolina Education, Progressive Farmer,* and *Farm Journal.*

WORK IN PROGRESS: A "Victorian" novel, *To Love and Have Not,* for which the words and music to a theme song have been written.

* * *

BEARDSLEY, Elizabeth Lane

PERSONAL: Born in Ann Arbor, Mich.; daughter of Robert Porter (in social work) and Bess B. (Edwards) Lane; married Monroe Curtis Beardsley (a college professor), June 29, 1940; children: Philip Lane, Mark Monroe. *Education:* Swarthmore College, A.B., 1935; Columbia University, M.A., 1937; Yale University, Ph.D., 1940. *Politics:* Democrat. *Religion:* Unitarian Universalist. *Home:* 1916 Delancey Pl., Philadelphia, Pa. 19103. *Office:* Department of Philosophy, Temple University, Philadelphia, Pa. 19122.

CAREER: University of Delaware, Newark, lecturer in philosophy, 1949-52; Lincoln University, Lincoln University, Pa., professor of philosophy, 1953-60; Temple University, Philadelphia, Pa., associate professor, 1962-64, 1965-73, professor of philosophy, 1973—. Member of board of directors, Fair Housing Council of Delaware Valley, 1962—. *Member:* American Philosophical Association, American Society for Political and Legal Philosophy, American Association of University Professors, National Association for the Advancement of Colored People, American Civil Liberties Union.

WRITINGS: (With husband, Monroe Curtis Beardsley) *Philosophical Thinking: An Introduction,* Harcourt, 1965, abridged edition published as *Invitation to Philosophical Thinking,* 1972. Editor with M. C. Beardsley of Prentice-Hall's "Foundations of Philosophy" series, 1963—.

WORK IN PROGRESS: Research in ethical theory and philosophy of religion.†

* * *

BEATON, (Donald) Leonard 1929-1971

June 20, 1929—June 9, 1971; Canadian-born British journalist and defense authority. Obituaries: *New York Times,* June 16, 1971. (See index for *CA* sketch)

* * *

BEATTIE, Carol 1918-

PERSONAL: Born January 21, 1918; married Robert F. Beattie (a clergyman), March 25, 1940 (died April 10, 1976); children: Robert C., Brian C. *Education:* Wellesley College, B.A. (with honors), 1939. *Politics:* Conservative. *Religion:* Episcopalian. *Home:* 278 2H Crosse Dr., "Clearbrook," Cranbury, N.J. 07060.

CAREER: New York Times, New York, N.Y., employed in School Service Division, 1939-40; Holy Cross School, North Plainfield, N.J., directress, 1956-69. Teacher of adult education oil painting, Middlesex College and Monroe Township High School. Exhibited her paintings in three solo shows, 1975-76.

WRITINGS: For Goodness Sake, Prentice-Hall, 1954; *The Brier Affair,* Hewitt House, 1969. Contributor of articles and poetry to magazines.

WORK IN PROGRESS: Avanti or Europe with Josie, a travel book.

SIDELIGHTS: Carol Beattie has traveled in forty-five countries. Her first book was translated into Finnish and her second into Dutch.

* * *

BEAUCHAMP, Kenneth L(loyd) 1939-

PERSONAL: Born April 15, 1939, in Madera, Calif.; son of Harold R. (a truck driver) and Evelyn (Weld) Beauchamp; married Judy Reynolds, April 1, 1961; children: Karen Elaine, Geoffrey Alan. *Education:* Whitman College, A.B., 1962; Claremont University Center (now Claremont Graduate School), M.A., 1965, Ph.D., 1968. *Politics:* Liberal. *Home:* 1561 Stanton Way, Stockton, Calif. 95207. *Office:* Department of Psychology, University of the Pacific, Stockton, Calif. 95211.

CAREER: California State Polytechnic College, Pomona (now California State Polytechnic University, Pomona), instructor, 1965-67, assistant professor of psychology, 1967-69; University of the Pacific, Stockton, Calif., associate professor of psychology, 1969—, acting dean, 1974-76, associate dean, 1974-77. Staff experimental psychologist, Stockton State Hospital, 1969-73. *Member:* American Association for the Advancement of Science, American Association of University Professors, Western Psychological Association, New York Academy of Science.

WRITINGS: (Editor with J. L. Philbrick) *Readings in Contemporary Scientific Psychology,* Selected Academic Readings, 1966, 2nd edition, 1967; (editor with R. L. Bruce and D. W. Matheson) *Current Topics in Experimental Psychology,* Holt, 1970; (with Bruce and Matheson) *Introduction to Experimental Psychology,* Holt, 1970, 2nd edition, 1974. Contributor to psychology journals.

WORK IN PROGRESS: Research on the effect that amount of handling has on curiosity and emotional behavior in rats; research on cooperative/competitive behavior of children; third edition of *Introduction to Experimental Psychology.*

AVOCATIONAL INTERESTS: Gardening, bridge, athletics, teaching "Positive Parenting" classes at Y.M.C.A.

* * *

BEAUDOIN, Kenneth Lawrence   1913-
(Victor de Chatellerault, James de Todany)

PERSONAL: Surname is pronounced Bow-*dwan;* born December 12, 1913, in Elmira, Mich.; son of Arthur Joseph (a plant executive; one of the designers of the first Dodge car) and Ruth Helen Marie (Derrer) Beaudoin. *Education:* Memphis State University, B.S., 1935; further study at Louisiana State University, 1936, Loyola University, New Orleans, 1939, and New School for Social Research, 1942. *Politics:* Democrat. *Religion:* Roman Catholic. *Home:* 1298 Jefferson Ave., Memphis, Tenn. 38104. *Office:* 247 Washington Ave., Third Floor, Memphis, Tenn. 38104.

CAREER: Editor and publisher, *Iconograph* (quarterly), 1940-47; editor, Archangel Press, 1947-48; Memphis Police Department, Memphis, Tenn., chief clerk in criminal intelligence department, 1956-74. Director, Gallerie Neuf, New York, N.Y., 1944-47. President, Nodena Foundation, Wilson, Ark., 1953—. Vice-president, South & West, Fort Smith, Ark., 1967—. Secretary, Shelby County Historical Commission, Memphis, 1965—, Memphis Citizens-Police Community Relations Committee, 1969—. Member of liberal arts panel and literary advisory panel, Tennessee Arts Commission. *Member:* National Federation of State Poetry Societies (vice-chancellor, 1967-68), Smithsonian Associates, Societe Genealogique Francaise-Canadienne, Poetry Society of Tennessee (workshop director, 1953—). *Awards, honors: South & West* Award for major contribution to American poetry, 1967; Ruth Forbes Sherry Award, 1967; Olivant Press Award for Poetry, 1970, for *Selected Eye Poems, 1940-1970;* citation from World Poetry Society, 1971.

WRITINGS: Boll Weevils and Butterflies, privately printed, 1936; *City Suite,* Press of James A. Decker, 1940; *Incunabula,* Iconograph Press, 1943; *Six Eye Poems,* Ar-

changel Press, 1948; *Two Suites for Manhattan,* Attaturk, 1949; *Strange April,* Attaturk, 1950; *Hot Springs Holiday,* Salter House, 1950; *On Hot Summer Afternoons and Other Poems,* Bern Porter, 1956; *Sixteen Eye Poems,* Folio, 1963; (editor and author of foreword) *Memphis Tennessee Anthology,* Olivant, 1968; *Selected Poems and Eye Poems, 1940-1970,* Olivant, 1970; (with Lura Nowotny and Sue Abbott Boyd) *The New Look Trio: Eye Poems by Kenneth L. Beaudoin, Poems by Lura Nowotny, and Essays by Sue Abbott Boyd,* South & West, 1970. Also author of plays, "Richelieu" and "Lucia d'Alba," both 1939.

Also author, except as indicated, of numerous other books, including: *The Family of Napoleon Beaudoin,* 1949; (translator) *Four Sioux Myths,* 1950; (translator) *The Papago Genesis,* 1950; (translator) *The Wuwuchim,* 1950; (with Lawrence Lipton and James Boyer May) *Three American Poets,* 1954; *Bayou Gayoso,* 1954, Japanese translation by Beaudoin, 1958; *Cahokia Poems,* 1958; *Mississippi River Suite,* 1964; *A Book of the Hours* (holograph), 1965. Editor of southeast U.S. section of anthology, *American Poets,* World Poetry Society (Madras, India). Regular reviewer for *South & West* and *Human Voice Quarterly.*

WORK IN PROGRESS: Codex MM, a group of poems ("which may engage me the rest of my life"); *Babel,* poems; *Selected Prose, 1940-1975; Gems Ransom: An Anthology of Gem Award Winners, 1955-1975;* a group of love poems.

SIDELIGHTS: Kenneth Lawrence Beaudoin told *CA:* "I write because I like to believe I have something to say that is important to be said in my time. I write as tightly as I can for this is the way I have learned to write. I write as directly and honestly as I can for this is what I expect of writers I read, and I would offer nothing less than this in return." He has done translations from French, Spanish, German, Greek, Italian, and Japanese.

AVOCATIONAL INTERESTS: Archaeology, anthropology, collecting gem stones.

* * *

BECHT, J. Edwin   1918-

PERSONAL: Born July 20, 1918, in Oak Park, Ill.; son of John J. (a salesman) and Lois May (Cole) Becht; married Dorene L. Tams (a fabric saleswoman), July 12, 1942; children: Forrest L., Darrell A., Kimberley L., Bette L. *Education:* Southern Illinois University, B.S., 1947; University of Illinois, M.S., 1948, Ph.D., 1951. *Home:* 25 Royal Place Cir., Odessa, Tex. 79762. *Office:* Office of Academic Affairs, University of Texas of the Permian Basin, Odessa, Tex. 79762.

CAREER: Indiana University, Bloomington, assistant professor of geography, assistant to dean of College of Arts and Sciences, and student advisor for two years; University of Houston, Houston, Tex., associate professor, 1955-57, professor of transportation and resources, 1958-67, chairman of department of transportation, foreign trade and resources, 1958-61, and of department of transportation and international business, 1959-61, director of Center for Research in Business and Economics, College of Business Administration, 1961-67; Western Illinois University, Macomb, professor of marketing and international business, and chairman of business administration department, 1967-69, acting academic dean and provost, and acting president, 1969; University of Oklahoma, Norman, professor of geography and senior research associate of Bureau of Business and Economic Research, 1969-71; University of Arkansas, Fayetteville, Oren Harris Professor of Transportation, 1971-72;

University of Texas of the Permian Basin, Odessa, Tex., dean of College of Management, 1972-75, vice-president for academic affairs, 1975—. Licensed commercial pilot, 1945—; airway weather reader for U.S. Department of Commerce, 1946; licensed surveyor, State of Illinois, 1948; certified member of American Society for Traffic and Transportation, 1962. Consultant on transportation, development, and business administration for various government agencies and private firms. *Military service:* U.S. Army Air Forces, served as Artillery Pilot during World War II; served in Military Intelligence, became colonel; received eleven awards, including Air Medal.

MEMBER: American Geographical Society, American Marketing Association, Association of American Geographers, National Council for Geographic Education, National Council of University Research Administrators, Associated University Bureaus of Business and Economic Research, Regional Science Association, Delta Nu Alpha, Sigma Xi, Phi Kappa Phi.

WRITINGS: Commodity Origins, Traffic, and Markets Accessible to Chicago via the Illinois Waterway, Illinois River Carriers' Association, 1952; (with John N. Fry) *Ada Warehouse Site and Distribution Study,* Bureau of Business and Economic Research, University of Houston, 1960; (with Joel W. Sailors) *Growth of Houston and Investment Real Estate,* Gulf Coast Consultant, 1960; (with others) *Mantrap: Management Training Program,* Center for Research in Business and Economics, University of Houston, 1963; *The Noble Line* (monograph), Bureau of Business and Economic Research, University of Oklahoma, 1970; *A Geography of Transportation and Business Logistics,* edited by Robert Fuson, W. C. Brown, 1970. Also author, with Alan D. Carey and John P. Owen, of a special study, *Market and Industrial Location Analysis: North Central Houston,* published by Bureau of Business and Economic Research, University of Houston.

Contributor to numerous journals, including *Journal of Geography, Waterway Journal, Indiana Social Science Quarterly, Houston Business Review,* and *Journal of Soil and Water Conservation.*

WORK IN PROGRESS: A book, *Resource Dynamics/ Problems of Resource Mobilization.*

* * *

BECK, Hubert (F.) 1931-

PERSONAL: Born July 21, 1931, in Du Quoin, Ill.; son of Louis Carl (owner of a chicken hatchery) and Martina (Dierks) Beck; married Betty Lee Beaver, October 6, 1956; children: Kathleen Ann, Cynthia Sue, Mary Lee, John Mark. *Education:* Concordia Seminary, St. Louis, Mo., B.A., 1953, M.Div., 1961; additional study at Concordia Seminary, St. Louis, and Lutheran School of Theology, Chicago, Ill. *Home:* 1405 Francis, College Station, Tex. 77840. *Office:* University Lutheran Chapel, Texas A&M University, College Station, Tex. 77843.

CAREER: Minister of Lutheran Church; pastor of churches in Topeka, Charleston, and Des Plaines, Ill., 1956-67; Texas A&M University, College Station, pastor of University Lutheran Chapel, 1968—. *Member:* Lutheran Campus Ministers' Association, Kiwanis.

WRITINGS: The Christian Encounters the Age of Technology, Concordia, 1970; *The Way of God and the Ways of Men,* C.S.S. Publishing, 1972; *Thoughts for Today,* C.S.S. Publishing, 1972; *Why Can't the Church Be Like This?,*

Concordia, 1973; (with Robert Otterstad) *Into the Wilderness,* Fortress, 1975; *Fantasies for Fantastic Christians,* Concordia, 1977. Author of tracts, magazine articles, and theological papers.

WORK IN PROGRESS: Analyses of contemporary religious phenomena.

* * *

BECK, Robert H(olmes) 1918-

PERSONAL: Born November 25, 1918; son of Carl (a physician) and Pauline (Altman) Beck; married Maeve Butler (a teacher), 1943; children: Roger, Peggy, Carl. *Education:* Harvard University, A.B., 1939; Yale University, Ph.D., 1942. *Politics:* Democrat. *Religion:* None. *Home:* 1610 East River Ter., Minneapolis, Minn. 55414. *Office:* Department of Foundations of Education, University of Minnesota, 203-A Burton Hall, Minneapolis, Minn. 55455.

CAREER: University of Rochester, Rochester, N.Y., instructor in history and philosophy of education, 1942-43; University of Kansas City (now University of Missouri at Kansas City), assistant professor of history and philosophy of education, 1946-47; University of Minnesota, Minneapolis, associate professor, 1947-50, professor of history and philosophy of education, 1950—. Summer professor at University of Texas, University of Southern California, and University of Colorado. *Military service:* U.S. Army, 1942-46; became master sergeant.

MEMBER: Philosophy of Education Society (president, 1961), Society of Professors of Education (president, 1970-71), History of Education Society, Comparative and International Education Society, International Studies Association. *Awards, honors:* Fulbright research grant for the Netherlands, 1955-56; Hebrew University of Jerusalem fellowship, summer, 1960; Hill Family Foundation research grant for Europe, 1966-67.

WRITINGS: (With Walter Cook and Nolan C. Kearney) *Curriculum in the Modern Elementary School,* Prentice-Hall, 1953, second edition, 1960; (editor) *The Three R's Plus,* University of Minnesota Press, 1956; *A Social History of Education,* Prentice-Hall, 1965; (with John Turnbull, Harold Deutsch, Arnold Rose, and Philip Raup) *The Changing Structure of Europe: Economic, Social and Political Trends,* University of Minnesota Press, 1970; *Change and Harmonization in European Education,* University of Minnesota Press, 1971; *Aeschylus: Playwright, Educator,* Nijhoff, 1975. Contributor to professional journals.†

* * *

BECKER, Arthur P(eter) 1918-

PERSONAL: Born April 28, 1918, in Milwaukee, Wis.; son of Peter Joseph and Theresa (Hanacek) Becker; married Bernita M. Thompson, November 21, 1941; children: Bonita, Jan Peter, Lee Arthur, Nancy, Arthur Ernest, Karen. *Education:* University of Wisconsin, B.A., 1939, M.A., 1940, Ph.D., 1943. *Religion:* Christian. *Office:* Department of Economics, University of Wisconsin, Milwaukee, Wis. 53201.

CAREER: University of Connecticut, Storrs, instructor in economics, 1942-44; Eastern New Mexico University, Portales, assistant professor of economics and chairman of School of Business and Economics, 1944-45; Morningside College, Sioux City, Iowa, professor of economics and chairman of department, 1945-46; Ohio State University, Columbus, assistant professor of economics, 1946-48; University of Wisconsin—Milwaukee, associate professor in Extension Division, 1948-56, associate professor at university, 1956-57, professor of economics, 1957—, chairman of department, 1956-63. Founder and chairman, Economic Policy Association of Milwaukee, 1954-66; co-founder and chairman, Committee on Taxation, Resources, and Economic Development, 1962—. Member of board of directors, Robert Shalkenbach Foundation, 1962—, and Wisconsin Council on Economic Education, 1963-65. Commissioner, Redevelopment Authority of City of Milwaukee, 1963—; member of citizens advisory council, Milwaukee Common Council Committee on Development, 1965-70. University of Wisconsin—Milwaukee Credit Union, member of board of directors, 1965—, president, 1966—.

MEMBER: American Economic Association, National Tax Association-Tax Institute of America (counselor and advisor, 1972-76; member of board of directors, 1973-75; formerly Tax Institute of America [member of advisory council, 1968-71; member of board of directors, 1969-72] and National Tax Association), National Association of Housing and Redevelopment Officials, Municipal Finance Officers Association, International Association of Assessing Officers, American Association of University Professors, Midwest Economic Association, Southwestern Social Science Association, Alpha Kappa Psi. *Awards, honors:* Fulbright faculty research scholar in Mexico City, 1968.

WRITINGS: (With Elgie C. Marks) *Library Resources for Economics,* University of Wisconsin—Milwaukee, 1962; (contributor) *State and Local Problems,* University of Tennessee Press, 1969; (editor and contributor) *Land and Building Taxes: Their Effect on Economic Development,* University of Wisconsin Press, 1969; (editor and contributor) *The Erosion of the Ad Valorem Real Estate Tax Base,* National Tax Association-Tax Institute of America, 1973; (contributor) *Government Spending and Land Values,* University of Wisconsin Press, 1973. Also contributor to *Proceedings of the Annual Conference,* National Tax Association-Tax Institute of America, 1974. Author or co-author of a number of bulletins and technical reports for Management Research International, Robert Schalkenbach Foundation, and the cities of Dayton and Milwaukee. Contributor to *Collier's Encyclopedia* and to journals.

WORK IN PROGRESS: Research on property taxation, on methods of property tax research, and on land value taxation.

SIDELIGHTS: Arthur P. Becker told *CA:* "It is the responsibility of an active and effective scholar to write and convey his research and views to other scholars. I have tried to carry out this responsibility by writing on those subjects which I deem to be socially important rather than popular. To me, personal integrity is of greater value than the opportunity of greater financial gain."

*   *   *

BECKER, Harold K(auffman)   1933-

PERSONAL: Born September 16, 1933, in Los Angeles, Calif.; son of Harold K. and Hazel (Jumper) Becker; married; children: three. *Education:* Los Angeles City College, A.A., 1957; University of Southern California, B.A., 1959, M.S., 1963; University of California, Berkeley, Doctor of Criminology, 1971. *Home:* 9421 Tiki Circle, Huntington Beach, Calif. 92646. *Office:* Center for Criminal Justice, California State University, Long Beach, Calif. 90804.

CAREER: Los Angeles (Calif.) Police Department, police officer, 1959-63, administrative research officer, 1961-63;

California State University, Long Beach, assistant professor, 1963-66, associate professor of criminology, 1963—, director of Center for Criminal Justice, 1971—. Part-time instructor, Long Beach City College, 1964; visiting professor at University of Birmingham and at Bramshill Police College, England, 1970. Consultant to public, university, and industrial police programs. *Military service:* U.S. Coast Guard, 1953-55; became petty officer second class.

WRITINGS: (With G. T. Felkenes and P. M. Whisenand) *New Dimensions in Criminal Justice,* Scarecrow, 1968; (with Felkenes) *Law Enforcement: A Selected Bibliography,* Scarecrow, 1968, revised edition, 1976; *Issues in Police Administration,* Scarecrow, 1970; *Police Systems of Europe,* C. C Thomas, 1973; *Justice in Modern Sweden,* C. C Thomas, 1976. Contributor to police science and human relations journals.

WORK IN PROGRESS: Various texts and articles dealing with international criminal justice organizations.

*   *   *

BECKER, Lucille F(rackman)   1929-

PERSONAL: Born February 4, 1929; daughter of Mark (a lawyer) and Sylvia (Schwartz) Frackman; married Robert F. Becker (a pension consultant), February 27, 1954; children: David, Daniel, Michael, Andrew. *Education:* Barnard College, B.A. (magna cum laude), 1949; University of Aix-Marseilles, France, Fulbright scholar, 1949-50, diplome d'etudes francaises, 1950; Columbia University, M.A., 1954, Ph.D., 1958. *Office:* Department of French, Drew University, Madison, N.J. 07940.

CAREER: Columbia University, New York, N.Y., French instructor, 1954-58; Rutgers University, New Brunswick, N.J., French instructor, 1959-69; Drew University, Madison, N.J., associate professor of French, 1969—. *Member:* Modern Language Association, American Association of Teachers of French, American Association of University Professors, Phi Beta Kappa.

WRITINGS: (Contributor) *Montherlant vu par des jeunes,* La Table Ronde (Paris), 1959; (editor and author of introduction and notes with Alba della Fazia) Henry de Montherlant, *Le Maitre de Santiago,* Heath, 1965; *Henry de Montherlant: A Critical Biography,* Southern Illinois University Press, 1970; *Louis Aragon,* Twayne, 1971. Contributor of articles to *Books Abroad, Yale French Studies, Romance Notes, French Review, Romanic Review, Nation,* and reference books.

*   *   *

BECKHAM, Barry   1944-

PERSONAL: Born March 19, 1944, in Philadelphia, Pa.; son of Clarence and Mildred (Williams) Beckham; married Betty L. Hope, February 19, 1966; children: Brian Elliott, Bonnie Lorine. *Education:* Brown University, A.B., 1966. *Religion:* Episcopalian. *Home:* 236 Camp St., Providence, R.I. 02906. *Agent:* Mel Berger, William Morris Agency, 1350 Ave. of the Americas, New York, N.Y. 10019. *Office:* Department of English, Brown University, Providence, R.I.

CAREER: Employed in public relations by Chase Manhattan Bank, New York City, 1966-67, National Council of Young Men's Christian Associations, New York City, 1967-68, and Western Electric Co., New York City, 1968-69; Chase Manhattan Bank, urban affairs work, 1969-70; Brown University, Providence, R.I., visiting lecturer, 1970-72, assistant professor of English, 1972—. Visiting professor,

University of Wyoming, 1972. *Member:* Authors Guild, P.E.N. (member of executive board of American Center, 1970-71).

WRITINGS: My Main Mother (novel), Walker & Co., 1969; *Runner Mack* (novel), Morrow, 1972. Contributor to *Esquire, New York Times, New York Magazine, Black Review, Intellectual Digest,* and *Novel.*

WORK IN PROGRESS: I Am the God, a biography to be published by Quadrangle; a portrait of Chase Manhattan Bank to be published by Morrow.

SIDELIGHTS: Barry Beckham told *CA,* "I want to grow as Miles Davis and Stevie Wonder have, and to make the reader feel he has never read anything like 'that' before." *Avocational interests:* Photography, chess, film production.

BIOGRAPHICAL/CRITICAL SOURCES: New York Times, November 30, 1969; *Variety,* January 14, 1970.

* * *

BEEBE, H. Keith 1921-

PERSONAL: Born March 16, 1921, in Anaheim, Calif.; son of Marshall Earl (a businessman and insurance agent) and Anna (Ullrich) Beebe; married Wilma Kerr (an executive secretary), January 31, 1943; children: Sara, Lawrence. *Education:* Occidental College, B.A., 1943; Princeton Theological Seminary, B.D., 1945; Columbia University, E.D., 1951. *Politics:* Democrat. *Religion:* Christian. *Office:* Department of Religious Studies, Occidental College, Los Angeles, Calif. 90041.

CAREER: New York Giants (football team), New York, N.Y., fullback, 1943; ordained to the ministry of Presbyterian Church, 1946; Pasadena Presbyterian Church, Pasadena, Calif., minister to youth, 1946-48; Princeton University, Princeton, N.J., assistant dean of University Chapel, 1949-54; Occidental College, Los Angeles, Calif., assistant professor, 1954-57, associate professor, 1957-67, David B. and Mary H. Gamble Professor of Religion, 1967—. Visiting professor of religion, Beirut College for Women, Beruit, Lebanon, 1963-64. Part-time assistant football coach at Columbia University, 1948-49, and Princeton University, 1949-54. Chairman of committee on candidates for the ministry, Presbytery of San Gabriel, 1967-70.

MEMBER: Society of Biblical Literature, American Academy of Religion (secretary of Pacific Coast section, 1956-60; president of Pacific Coast section, 1960-61), Society for the Scientific Study of Religion. *Awards, honors:* American School of Oriental Research, Jerusalem, visiting scholar, 1965; Ford Foundation grant for research on archaeological book, 1969; annual professor, Albright Institute, for archaeological research in Jerusalem, 1970-71.

WRITINGS: The Old Testament: An Introduction to Its Literary, Historical, and Religious Traditions, Dickenson, 1970. Contributor to religious and archaeology journals.

WORK IN PROGRESS: Journal article on domestic architecture in Palestine from 550 B.C. to 325 A.D.; a monograph on the cities of ancient Palestine; *Archaeology and Biblical Interpretation,* for Dickenson; with Milo C. Connic, *Introduction to Biblical Literature,* also for Dickenson.

SIDELIGHTS: H. Keith Beebe lived in Lebanon for two years, Jordan for a year, and Israel for a year. He was a field supervisor for the joint American School of Oriental Research-Concordia Seminary excavations at Taanach the summers of 1963 and 1968, served in a similar position with the British School of Archaeology in Jerusalem, 1965, was

supervisor of a field in the joint Caesarea Expedition of the Albright Institute, 1971 and 1972, and was administrative director of this expedition in 1973 and 1974.†

* * *

BEHRMAN, Jack N(ewton) 1922-

PERSONAL: Born March 5, 1922, in Waco, Tex.; son of Mayes and Marguerite (Newton) Behrman; married Louise Sims, September 6, 1945; children: Douglas, Gayle, Andrea. *Education:* Davidson College, B.S., 1943; University of North Carolina, M.A., 1945; Princeton University, M.A., 1950, Ph.D., 1952. *Politics:* Democratic. *Religion:* Presbyterian. *Home:* 1702 Audubon Rd., Chapel Hill, N.C. 27514. *Office:* Graduate School of Business Administration, Carroll Hall, University of North Carolina, Chapel Hill, N.C. 27514.

CAREER: International Labor Office, Montreal, Quebec, research assistant, 1945; Davidson College, Davidson, N.C., assistant professor of economics, 1946-48; Princeton University, Princeton, N.J., instructor, 1949-50; Washington and Lee University, Lexington, Va., associate professor of economics and political science, 1952-57; University of Delaware, Newark, professor of economics and business administration, 1957-61; U.S. Department of Commerce, Washington, D.C., deputy assistant secretary for international affairs, 1961, assistant secretary for international affairs, 1961-62, assistant secretary for domestic and international business, 1962-64; University of North Carolina at Chapel Hill, professor of international business, 1964—. Visiting professor, Harvard Business School, 1967; lecturer on international investment and foreign licensing for American Management Association and at Salzburg Seminar in American studies. Consultant to Committee for Economic Development, National Planning Association, Pan American Union, United Nations, and U.S. Department of State. *Member:* Association for Education in International Business (secretary, 1959-60; president, 1966-68), Council on Foreign Relations, Beta Gamma Sigma.

WRITINGS: (With Gardner Patterson) *Survey of United States International Finance,* Princeton University Press, 1951, revised edition, 1952, second revised edition (also with John M. Gunn, and others), 1953; (with Wilson E. Schmidt) *International Economics,* Rinehart, 1957; (with Raymond F. Mikesell) *Financing of Free-World Trade with the Sino-Soviet Bloc,* Princeton Studies in International Finance, 1958.

(Contributor) Mikesell, editor, *U.S. Private and Government Investment Abroad,* University of Oregon Press, 1962; (with Roy Blough) *Regional Integration and the Trade of Latin America,* Committee for Economic Development, 1968; (contributor) Walter Krause and F. J. Mathis, editors, *International Economics and Business: Selected Readings,* Houghton, 1968; *Some Patterns in the Rise of the Multinational Enterprise* (monograph), Graduate School of Business Administration, University of North Carolina, 1969.

National Interests and the Multinational Enterprise, Prentice-Hall, 1970; *U.S. International Business and Governments,* McGraw, 1971; (with J. J. Boddewyn and A. Kapoor) *International Business-Government Communications,* Lexington Books, 1975; (with H. Wallender) *Transfers of Manufacturing Technology within Multinational Enterprises,* Ballinger, 1976. Writer of monographs for National Foreign Trade Council and Committee for Economic Development, and research studies for Pan American Union and Economic Council of Canada. Contributor to *American*

People's Encyclopedia and to professional journals and business magazines.

WORK IN PROGRESS: Research technology transfers and international research and development activities, on international industrial integration, and on foreign investment problems.

SIDELIGHTS: Jack Behrman has traveled widely in Latin America, Canada, Europe, and the Far East as a government delegate, consultant, and researcher. In 1970 he spent six months in Europe doing research for the Department of State.

* * *

BEILENSON, Laurence W. 1899-

PERSONAL: Surname is pronounced Beel-en-son; born May 31, 1899, in Helena, Ark.; son of Jacob and Julia (Meyer) Beilenson; married June 9, 1923; wife's name, Gerda M. (a lyricist). *Education:* Harvard University, A.B., 1920, LL.B., 1922. *Home:* 1946 North Gramercy Pl., Los Angeles, Calif. 90068.

CAREER: Private practice of law in San Francisco, Calif., Chicago, Ill., and Los Angeles, Calif., 1922-65. Organizing counsel for Screen Actors Guild, Screen Writers Guild, Screen Directors Guild, and one of organizing counsel of American Federation of Radio Artists; general counsel and negotiator for Screen Actors Guild, 1933-49. *Military service:* U.S. Army, 1918; became sergeant. U.S. Army, Infantry, World War II; served in China and Burma; became lieutenant colonel; received Silver Star, Bronze Star with oakleaf cluster, combat infantry badge, and Chinese medals. *Member:* Screen Actors Guild (honorary life member).

WRITINGS: The Treaty Trap, Public Affairs Press, 1969; *Power Through Subversion,* Public Affairs Press, 1972.

WORK IN PROGRESS: The Treaty Trap and *Power Through Subversion* are the first two books of a trilogy on the tools of statecraft; the third book is in preparation.

* * *

BEJA, Morris 1935-

PERSONAL: Surname is pronounced *Bay*-ja; born July 18, 1935, in New York, N.Y.; son of Joseph (a manufacturer) and Eleanor (Cohen) Beja; married Nancy Friedman, November 27, 1957; children: Andrew, Eleni. *Education:* City College (now City College of the City University of New York), B.A., 1957; Columbia University, M.A., 1958; Cornell University, Ph.D., 1963. *Home:* 79 Richards Rd., Columbus, Ohio 43214. *Office:* Department of English, Ohio State University, 164 West 17th Ave., Columbus, Ohio 43210.

CAREER: Ohio State University, Columbus, instructor, 1961-63, assistant professor, 1963-68, associate professor, 1968-71, professor of English, 1971—. Fulbright lecturer in American literature, University of Thessaloniki, 1965-66; Fulbright lecturer, University College, 1972-73. Member of board of editors, Ohio State University Press. *Military service:* U.S. Army, 1958. *Member:* Modern Language Association of America, James Joyce Foundation (member of board of trustees), Virginia Woolf Society (founder), American Committee for Irish Studies, Midwest Modern Language Association (chairman of modern literature section, 1971). *Awards, honors:* Guggenheim fellowship, 1972-73.

WRITINGS: (Editor) Virginia Woolf, *To the Lighthouse: A Casebook,* Macmillan, 1970; *Epiphany in the Modern*

Novel, University of Washington Press, 1971; (editor) *Psychological Fiction,* Scott, Foresman, 1971; (editor) *James Joyce's Dubliners and A Portrait of the Artist as a Young Man: A Selection of Critical Essays,* Macmillan, 1973. Contributor of articles on modern literature, short stories, and reviews to journals.

WORK IN PROGRESS: A study of dissociation in modern literature.

AVOCATIONAL INTERESTS: Photography and sketching.

* * *

BEJEROT, Nils 1921-

PERSONAL: Surname is pronounced Bay-yer-root; born September 21, 1921, in Stockholm, Sweden; son of Hugo Johanson (a bank clerk) and Linnea (Karlsson) Bejerot; married Carol Maurice; children: Eva, Lena, Susanne, Peter (deceased). *Education:* Karolinska Institute, Qualified Physician, 1957; London School of Hygiene and Tropical Medicine, specialized study in epidemiology and medical statistics, 1963. *Home:* Sunnerdahlsvaegen 13, 161 38 Bromma, Sweden. *Office:* Department of Social Medicine, Karolinska Institute, Stockholm 60, Sweden.

CAREER: Junior physician in practice of general psychiatry, Stockholm, Sweden, 1957-61; senior physician in practice of social psychiatry, Stockholm, 1962-66; Karolinska Institute, Stockholm, research fellow in drug dependence, 1966—. Psychiatric consultant to Stockholm Police Department, 1958—. *Member:* Swedish Medical Society, International Institute of Addictions, Swedish Union of Authors. *Awards, honors:* World Health Organization fellowship in London, 1963; Gold Medal of Mental Health Foundation, 1970.

WRITINGS: (With Ragnar Berfenstam) *Doedsolycksfallen i Sverige* (title means "Fatal Accidents in Sweden"), S.M.T., 1954; *Barn, Serier, Samhaelle* (title means "Children, Comics and Society"), Folket i Bild, 1954; *Narkotikafraagan och Samhaellet* (title means "The Drug Question and Society"), Aldus/Bonniers, 1968; *Narkotika och Narkomani,* Aldus/Bonniers, 1969, translation published as *Addiction and Society,* C. C Thomas, 1970; *Inlaegg i Narkotikadebatten* (title means "Contribution to the Addiction Debate"), [Sweden], 1970; *Addiction: An Artificially Induced Drive,* C. C Thomas, 1972; *Drug Abuse and Drug Policy,* Munksgaard, 1975.

WORK IN PROGRESS: A study on mortality and cause of death in addiction.

SIDELIGHTS: Nils Bejerot has made study trips to the United States, Mexico, England, Soviet Union, Israel, Iran, India, Thailand, Hong Kong, Japan, and the Philippines.

* * *

BELINKOV, Arkady Viktorovich 1922(?)-1970

1922(?)—May 14, 1970; Soviet writer and critic. Obituaries: *New York Times,* May 16, 1970; *Antiquarian Bookman,* June 1-8, 1970; *Books Abroad,* spring, 1971.

* * *

BELKIND, Allen 1927-

PERSONAL: Born March 27, 1927, in Milwaukee, Wis.; son of Norman and Betty (Jenkins) Belkind; married Francine Fishel (a teacher of English), September 6, 1959; children: Laraa. *Education:* University of California, Los Angeles, B.A., 1956, M.A., 1961; University of Southern California, Ph.D., 1966.

CAREER: Teacher in secondary schools and junior colleges in Los Angeles, 1959-61; University of Southern California, Los Angeles, lecturer, 1961-64; University of Nevada, Reno, assistant professor of English, 1964-71; California State College, Bakersfield, associate professor of American and modern literature, beginning 1971. Fulbright lecturer, Helsinki School of Economics, 1969-70, University of Haiti, 1974-75. *Military service:* U.S. Navy, 1944-46. *Member:* Modern Language Association of America, American Association of University Professors, Philological Association of the Pacific Coast. *Awards, honors:* Desert Research Institute Humanities grants, University of Nevada, 1965, 1967, 1968, 1970.

WRITINGS: (Compiler) *Jean-Paul Sartre: Sartre and Existentialism in English* (bibliography), Kent State University Press, 1970; (compiler and author of introduction and annotations) *John Dos Passos, the Critics, and the Writer's Intention,* Southern Illinois University Press, 1971. Contributor to *Journal of Modern Literature* and *Helsingin Sanomat.* Staff reviewer, *Books Abroad.*

WORK IN PROGRESS: John Dos Passos: Satirist and Seeker, and *John Dos Passos: A Checklist,* for Kent State University Press.

SIDELIGHTS: Allen Belkind has been a professional singer and musician. He enjoys the study of interdisciplinary subjects concerning interrelationships among the arts and other humanities. His vocational interests are American and modern world literature, comparative literature, Black studies, and literature and psychology.

AVOCATIONAL INTERESTS: Music, tennis, skiing.†

*   *   *

BELL, Carolyn Shaw   1920-

PERSONAL: Born June 21, 1920, in Framingham, Mass.; daughter of Clarence Edward (a business executive) and Grace (Wellington) Shaw; married Robert A. Solo, November 3, 1942; married second husband, Nelson Sibley Bell (a merchant), July 26, 1953; children: (first marriage) Tova Marie. *Education:* Mount Holyoke College, B.A. (magna cum laude), 1941; London School of Economics and Political Science, Ph.D., 1949. *Politics:* Independent. *Religion:* Unitarian Universalist. *Home:* 167 Clay Brook Rd., Dover, Mass. 02030. *Office:* Department of Economics, Wellesley College, Wellesley, Mass. 02181.

CAREER: U.S. Office of Price Administration, economist in Washington, D.C., 1941-42, and San Francisco, Calif., 1943-45; Harvard University, Cambridge, Mass., research economist, 1950-53; Wellesley College, Wellesley, Mass., 1951—, began as instructor, professor of economics, 1962—, Katharine Coman Professor, 1970. Member of board of advisors, Public Interest Economics; member of board of governors, Amos Tuck Graduate School of Business, Dartmouth College. Chairwoman, Federal Advisory Council on Unemployment Insurance. Commentator on radio and television. *Member:* American Economic Association, Association for Evolutionary Economics, American Association of University Professors, United Nations Association of the U.S.A. (member of economic policy council), Joint Council on Economic Education (trustee), Phi Beta Kappa. *Awards, honors:* Lucy Farr fellowship of American Association of University Women, 1961-62.

WRITINGS: (Contributor) Lucile Tomlinson, editor,

Those Having Torches, Department of Economics and Sociology, Mount Holyoke College, 1954; (with John Kenneth Galbraith, Richard Hoiton, and others) *Marketing in Puerto Rico,* Harvard University Press, 1955; (with Willard Cochrane) *The Economics of Consumption,* McGraw, 1960; *Consumer Choice in the American Economy,* Random House, 1967; *The Economics of the Ghetto,* Pegasus, 1970; (with Marion Just and others) *Coping in a Troubled Society,* Lexington Books, 1975. Contributor to professional economics journals, newspapers, and other periodicals. Member of board of editors, *Challenge* (magazine), *Journal of Economic Issues.*

WORK IN PROGRESS: Research on the appropriate micro-economic unit of analysis: family vs. individual.

*   *   *

BELL, Colin (John)   1938-

PERSONAL: Born April 1, 1938, in London, England; son of Alexander John (an antique dealer) and Regina (Knott) Bell; married Rose Thomson (an archaeologist), July 22, 1961; children: Rachel, Catherine, Alexander, Georgina. *Education:* King's College, Cambridge, B.A., 1959. *Religion:* Church of Scotland. *Home:* 7 Water St., Chesterton, Cambridge, England. *Agent:* Deborah Rogers Ltd., 29 Goodge St., London W1P 1FD, England.

CAREER: The Scotsman, Edinburgh, Scotland, reporter, 1960-61; *Scene,* London, England, managing editor, 1963; *London Life,* London, assistant editor, 1965-66; writer. Visiting lecturer, Morley College, London, 1965-67, and King's College, Cambridge, 1968-71. *Member:* National Union of Journalists.

WRITINGS: (Editor) *Boswell's Johnson,* Albany Books, 1969; (with wife, Rose Bell) *City Fathers: History of Town Planning in Britain,* Barrie & Rockliffe, 1969, published as *City Fathers: Town Planning in Britain from Roman Times to 1900,* Praeger, 1970; *Middle Class Families: Social and Geographical Mobility,* Humanities, 1969; *Making a Start in Life,* Heron Books, 1970; (with Howard Newby) *Community Studies: An Introduction to the Sociology of the Local Community,* Allen & Unwin, 1971, Praeger, 1972; (editor with Newby) *The Sociology of Community: A Selection of Readings,* Frank Cass & Co., 1974; (editor and author of introduction) *"The Times" Reports National Government, 1931: Extracts from "The Times",* Times Books, 1975; (editor with Newby) *Doing Sociological Research,* Free Press, 1977. Frequent contributor to *Sunday Times, Daily Telegraph, Guardian, Daily Mirror, Reader's Digest, Radio Times, New Statesman,* and other publications.

WORK IN PROGRESS: A biography of King William IV of England; a study of industrialization of the United Kingdom and Europe.†

*   *   *

BELL, Philip W(ilkes)   1924-

PERSONAL: Born October 24, 1924, in New York, N.Y.; son of Samuel Dennis (a physician) and Miriam (Wilkes) Bell; married Katharine Elizabeth Hubbard, June 16, 1945; children: Susan, Geoffrey, Mary Ellen, James. *Education:* Princeton University, A.B., 1947, Ph.D., 1954; University of California, Berkeley, M.A., 1949. *Home:* 6617 Bonny Doon Rd., Santa Cruz, Calif. 95060. *Office:* Merrill College, University of California, Santa Cruz, Calif. 95060.

CAREER: Council on Foreign Relations, New York, N.Y., research assistant to European aid study group directed by

Dwight D. Eisenhower, 1949-50; Princeton University, Princeton, N.J., instructor in economics, 1950-51; Institute for Advanced Study, Princeton, assistant, Institute of International Relations, 1951-52; Haverford College, Haverford, Pa., assistant professor of economics, 1952-56; University of California, Berkeley, associate professor of economics, 1957-60; Haverford College, associate professor, 1960-62, professor of economics, 1962-64; University of East Africa, Makerere University College, Kampala, Uganda, professor of economics, head of department, and dean of Social Science faculty, 1963-65; Fisk University, Nashville, Tenn., professor of economics and head of department, 1965-66; Lincoln University, Lincoln University, Pa., professor of economics and head of department, 1966-68; University of California, Santa Cruz, professor of economics, 1968—, provost of Merrill College, 1968-72. Visiting professor of economics, University of Nairobi, 1972-74. Lecturer, Salzburg Seminar in American Studies, 1955. Consultant to U.S. Treasury Department, 1961-63, Agency for International Development and Rockefeller Foundation, 1962-63, and U.S. Department of State, 1966-67. *Military service:* U.S. Army Air Forces, 1943-45; became second lieutenant. *Member:* American Economic Association, Royal Economic Society.

WRITINGS: The Sterling Area in the Postwar World, Clarendon Press, 1956; (with Edgar O. Edwards) *The Theory and Measurement of Business Income,* University of California Press, 1961; (with Michael P. Todaro) *Economic Theory,* Oxford University Press (Nairobi), 1969.

*   *   *

BELL, Raymond Martin 1907-

PERSONAL: Born March 21, 1907, in Weatherly, Pa.; son of Frank Thompson (a minister) and Marion E. (Seibert) Bell; married Lillian Kelly, March 28, 1942; children: Carol Ann (Mrs. Thomas Dennis Sullivan), Martha Jean (Mrs. George William Butler), Edward Frank. *Education:* Dickinson College, A.B., 1928; Syracuse University, A.M., 1930; Pennsylvania State University, Ph.D., 1937. *Politics:* Republican. *Religion:* United Methodist. *Home:* 413 Burton Ave., Washington, Pa. 15301. *Office:* Department of Physics, Washington and Jefferson College, Washington, Pa. 15301.

CAREER: Washington and Jefferson College, Washington, Pa., instructor, 1937-39, assistant professor, 1939-45, associate professor, 1945-46, professor of physics and astronomy and chairman of department, 1946-75, professor emeritus, 1975—. *Member:* American Physical Society, American Association of University Professors, American Association of Physics Teachers, American Society of Genealogists, Phi Beta Kappa, Sigma Xi. *Awards, honors:* Sc.D., Washington and Jefferson College, 1976.

WRITINGS: (With Oswald H. Blackwood and William C. Kelly) *General Physics,* 3rd edition (Bell was not associated with earlier editions), Wiley, 1963, 4th edition, 1973; *Your Future in Physics* (youth book), Richards Rosen, 1967; *Your Future in Astronomy* (youth book), Richards Rosen, 1970; *The Ancestry of Richard Milhous Nixon,* privately printed, 1970; *Television in the Thirties,* Xerox College Publishing, 1974. Editor of *New Century Book of Facts,* 1951-62. Also author with J. Martin Stroup of *The Genesis of Mifflin County, Pennsylvania,* and of *The People of Mifflin County, Pennsylvania,* both 1973. Contributor of articles to periodicals in United States, Great Britain, Germany, and New Zealand.

WORK IN PROGRESS: The Black Man in Early Southwestern Pennsylvania; Early Methodist Circuits on the Upper Ohio; Seventy Years on the Planet Earth; also writing on Pennsylvania families.

SIDELIGHTS: Raymond Martin Bell told *CA:* "I have always been interested in writing, as was my father before me. When I was nine, I started to publish a little neighborhood newspaper on my father's hand press. Much of my writing after age twenty-one was for newspapers and magazines. Later I got interested in college textbooks.

"As a teacher, I spent many hours with young people. A question often asked was: What shall I do when I finish school? As a result, two career books, *Your Future in Physics* and *Your Future in Astronomy,* were written telling something of the nature of the field and suggesting how to get into the field."

Bell continues: "My field of study has been physics and astronomy, but my hobby has always been history: local, church, and family." He explains that his family histories are intended "to show young people the story of their heritage. A need in teaching history today is to tie together local and national history, so that the student will feel that history is not remote."

*   *   *

BELL, (Caroline) Rose (Buchanan) 1939-

PERSONAL: Born April 6, 1939, in London, England; daughter of Sir George Paget (a physicist) and Kathleen Adam (Smith) Thomson; married Colin John Bell (a writer), July 22, 1961; children: Rachel, Catherine, Alexander, Georgina. *Education:* Attended Newnham College, Cambridge, 1957-60. *Home:* 7 Water St., Chesterton, Cambridge, England. *Agent:* Deborah Rogers Ltd., 29 Goodge St., London, W1P 1FD, England.

CAREER: Thames & Hudson Ltd. (publishers), London, England, editor, 1960-62. *Member:* Institute of Archaeology (London).

WRITINGS: (With husband, Colin Bell) *City Fathers: The Early History of Town Planning in Britain,* Barrie & Rockliff, 1969, published as *City Fathers: Town Planning in Britain from Roman Times to 1900,* Praeger, 1970.

WORK IN PROGRESS: Research and writing on industrial archaeology.

BIOGRAPHICAL/CRITICAL SOURCES: Spectator, April 18, 1970.††

*   *   *

BELMONT, Georges 1909-

PERSONAL: Born July 19, 1909, in Belley, France; son of Jean (an inspector of schools) and Marguerite (Monnet) Pelorson; married Eileen Graham, September, 1931 (divorced); married Josephine Caliot, June, 1954 (divorced); children: (first marriage) Sophie (Mrs. Guy Genovesi). *Education:* Attended Ecole Normale Superieure, Paris. *Politics:* "Never belonged to any party." *Religion:* Pantheism. *Home:* 20 Quai de la Megisserie, Paris 1, France. *Agent:* Boris Hoffmann and Georges Hoffmann, 77 Boulevard Saint-Michel, Paris 6, France. *Office:* Editions Robert Laffont, 6 Place Saint-Sulpice, Paris 6, France.

CAREER: Journalist, writing on foreign affairs for *Paris-Midi* and *Paris-Soir,* Paris, France, 1931-40; director of bilingual school, Paris, 1936-40; editor-in-chief of the Paris magazines, *Paris-Match,* 1953-54, *Jours de France,* 1954-56, and *Marie-Claire,* 1957-60; *Arts* (magazine), Paris, director, 1965-67; Editions Robert Laffont, Paris, editor and director of two foreign fiction series, 1967—. *Military service:* French Army, Infantry, 1939-40; taken prisoner by the Germans, 1940.

WRITINGS: Connaissance (poem), Fustier, 1937; *Jules Cesar* (tragedy in verse), Editions du Chene, 1939; *Le Grand pressoir* (novel), Laffont, 1957; *Chris* (novel), Rene Julliard, 1965; *Un Homme au crepuscule* (novel), Rene Julliard, 1966; *Ex* (novel), Denoel, 1969; *L'Honneur de vivre* (poems), Editions Poesie I, 1970; (with Celeste Albaret) *Monsieur Proust,* Laffont, 1973, McGraw, 1976. Also author of an essay, *De l'Enfant a la nation.* Translator of almost seventy books from English into French, including the works of Henry James, Henry Miller, Evelyn Waugh, Graham Greene, Nehru, and Gandhi.

WORK IN PROGRESS: Two novels, *Hicks* and *Les Eaux froides;* poems; research on Henry Miller and Samuel Beckett; accumulating material for memoirs.

SIDELIGHTS: Georges Belmont was influenced in his choice of vocation by a father who wrote poetry and urged his son to read such poets as Tasso and Goethe when the boy was eight, and by an uncle who spent all of his life in England. Other major influences: "Meeting J. Joyce in 1930 and becoming a friend of his; a valid friendship with Samuel Beckett dating back to 1928; meeting Henry Miller in 1937 and being his friend since then."

Regarding other writers and their work, Georges Belmont told *CA:* "I follow Joyce's advice to me. One day when we were walking along the Seine he said 'I don't read my contemporaries.'" He offers the following advice to aspiring writers: "Be merciless with yourself. Never write for money or in the hope of making money."

* * *

BELSLEY, David A(lan) 1939-

PERSONAL: Born May 24, 1939, in Chicago, Ill.; son of Gilbert Lyle (a political scientist) and Dorothy (Fricke) Belsley; married Judith Ann Walton, July 3, 1961; children: Karen Lise, Eric David. *Education:* Haverford College, B.A., 1961; Massachusetts Institute of Technology, Ph.D., 1965. *Office:* Department of Economics, Boston College, Chestnut Hill, Mass. 02167; and Computer Research Center, National Bureau of Economic Research, 575 Technology Sq., Cambridge, Mass. 02139.

CAREER: Dartmouth College, Hanover, N.H., assistant professor of economics, 1965-66; Boston College, Chestnut Hill, Mass., assistant professor, 1966-69, associate professor, 1969-74, professor of economics, 1974—. Senior research associate, Center for Economics and Management Services, National Bureau of Economic Research, 1972—. Fellow, Center for Advanced Study in the Behavioral Sciences, Stanford, Calif., 1971-72. Former mathematician, U.S. Patent Office. *Member:* Econometric Society, American Economic Association, Phi Beta Kappa.

WRITINGS: Industry Production Behavior: The Order-Stock Distinction, North-Holland Publishing, 1969; (editor with E. J. Kane, P. A. Samuelson, and R. M. Solow and contributor) *Inflation, Trade, and Taxes,* Ohio State University Press, 1976.

* * *

BELZ, Carl 1937-

PERSONAL: Born September 13, 1937, in Camden, N.J.;

son of Irvin Carl (in sales) and Ella (Engler) Belz; married Joan Kear, November 26, 1959; married second wife, Barbara Vetter, June 17, 1968; children: (first marriage) Melissa, Gretchen. *Education:* Princeton University, B.A., 1959, M.F.A., 1962, Ph.D., 1963. *Home:* 85 Ridge Rd., Waban, Mass. 02168. *Agent:* Julian Bach, Jr., 3 East 48th St., New York, N.Y. 10017. *Office:* Rose Art Museum, Brandeis University, Waltham, Mass. 02154.

CAREER: University of Massachusetts, Amherst, teacher of art history, 1963-65; Mills College, Oakland, Calif., teacher of art history, 1965-68; Brandeis University, Waltham, Mass., teacher of art history, 1968-74, director of Rose Art Museum, 1974—.

WRITINGS: The Story of Rock (on folk art), Oxford University Press, 1969, 2nd edition, 1972; *Cezanne,* McGraw, 1974. Regular contributor to *Artforum;* also contributor to other art journals.

WORK IN PROGRESS: A humanist history of contemporary art from 1945 to the present.

AVOCATIONAL INTERESTS: Tennis.

BIOGRAPHICAL/CRITICAL SOURCES: New York Times Book Review, November 9, 1969.

* * *

BENEDETTI, Robert L(awrence) 1939-

PERSONAL: Born February 27, 1939, in Chicago, Ill.; son of Dino R. and Lola (Chiostri) Benedetti; married Joan M. Howe, June 5, 1966; children: Benjamin Guiseppe, Nina Francesca; stepchildren: Kirsten L. Hermann. *Education:* Northwestern University, B.S., 1960, M.A., 1962, Ph.D., 1971; Indiana University, graduate study, 1965-66. *Office:* School of Theatre, California Institute of the Arts, Valencia, Calif. 91355.

CAREER: University of Chicago, Chicago, Ill., director of theatre, 1962-64; Second City Theatre, Chicago, actor, 1964-65; University of Wisconsin—Milwaukee, assistant professor of drama, 1966-68; Carnegie-Mellon University, Pittsburgh, Pa., assistant professor of drama, 1968-70; Yale University, School of Drama, New Haven, Conn., chairman of acting department, 1970-71; York University, Toronto, Ontario, associate professor and chairman of theatre department, 1971-73; University of California, Riverside, associate professor, 1973-74; California Institute of the Arts, Valencia, dean of School of Theatre, 1974—. Company director, Milwaukee Repertory Theatre, 1966-68; guest director at Colorado, Great Lakes and Oregon Shakespeare Festivals, Tyrone Guthrie Theatre, and Pacific Conservatory of the Performing Arts; director, "NET Playhouse." *Member:* American Theatre Association, National Theatre Conference.

WRITINGS: The Actor at Work: An Introduction to the Skills of Acting, Prentice-Hall, 1970, revised and enlarged edition, 1975; *Seeing, Being and Becoming: Acting in Our Century,* Drama Book Specialists, 1976.

WORK IN PROGRESS: Becoming: A Human Development Handbook.

SIDELIGHTS: Robert L. Benedetti wrote *CA:* "I started writing to make money. Now I am writing to work things out to objectify my own sense of growth, and to try to make my skills as a teacher of acting available to others in the broader context of personal change and development."

AVOCATIONAL INTERESTS: Food, wine, camping, psychotherapy.

BENES, Jan 1936-
(Milan Stepka)

PERSONAL: Born March 26, 1936, in Prague, Czechoslovakia; son of Bohumil (an officer) and Bohumila (Draska) Benes; married Savalieva Salchera Eristavi (a painter), August 4, 1966; children: Jan, Alice. *Education:* Umelecko prumyslova skola, student, 1950-55; Akademie Muzickych Umeni, student, 1956. *Religion:* Catholic.

CAREER: Writer; employed as development manager in a toy factory, 1955-56, 1958, miner, 1958-60, scenery technician in a theatre, 1960-62, and taxi driver, 1963. *Military service:* Czechoslovakian Army, Paratroops, 1956-58, 1961. *Member:* Union of Czechoslovak Writers. *Awards, honors:* Gold medal for sculpture, Brussels World Fair, 1958; Czechoslovak Literary Prize, 1963; Czechoslovak Short Story Prize, 1964; British Broadcasting Corp. Literary Prize, 1966.

WRITINGS: Drobna domovni udrzba, Statni nakl. technicke literatury (Prague), 1958; *Do Vrabcu jako kdyz streli* (short stories), Nase Vojsko (Prague), 1963; *Disproporce* (title means "Disproportions"), [Prague], 1964; *Situace* (short stories; title means "Situations"), Ceskoslovenky Spisovatel (Prague), 1969; *Trojuhelnik s madonou* (title means "Triangle with Madonna"), 1970; *The Blind Mirror* (short stories; originally written in Czech but published in English), translation by Jan Herzfeld, Orion Press, 1971; *Na miste: Zaznamy o principu skutecna,* [Toronto], 1972; *Az Se se mnou vyspis . . . budes plakat,* [Cologne], 1973; *Stavba garaze,* Prace (Prague), 1974; *Druhy dech* (novel), Konfrontation Verlag (Zurich), 1974, translation of original Czechoslovakian by Michael Montgomery published as *Second Breath,* Orion Press, 1969; *Tajemstvi pana Dawsona,* Blok (Brno), 1975.

Teleplays: "Cas Plyne i v nedeli" (title means "Time Also Passes on Sunday"), 1964; "Problem" (title means "Troubles"), 1968; "Tridni Nepritel" (title means "The Enemy of the Working Class"), 1969.

SIDELIGHTS: John Hughes sees Jan Benes' first novel, *Second Breath,* as an allegory about the pressing problems facing contemporary civilization. "That modern life is a tightrope-walk over the twin abyss of fanaticism and dogmatism; that the attempt to overthrow political repression should not result in the destruction of the age-old ordering devices established to control the animal in man; and that emotional freedom and emotional maturity are identical—these are the ideas informing Jan Benes' novel. Only a handful of modern thinkers and artists are as aware as Benes seems to be of the inescapable choice forcing itself into the consciousness of mankind."

In a review for the *New York Times,* John Leonard writes that Benes "appears to have begun *Second Breath* in 1963. In 1966, after collecting over 300 signatures from fellow writers on a petition protesting the Soviet imprisonment of Sinyavsky and Daniel, Mr. Benes was himself arrested and sentenced to five years in a camp. He was pardoned in 1968. I suspect, from the grittiness of details and the powerful evocation of place, that the novel might have been revised after his own inadvertent experience." Leonard also said that Benes had returned to Czechoslovakia after a visit to the U.S., "and intends to remain there." Benes and his wife spent only six weeks in their native country before they learned that the border was to be closed. They managed to obtain passports and left the country 58 minutes before the closing of the border, which had not been reopened since. Their two children, whom they were forced to leave behind, are living with grandparents in Prague.

BIOGRAPHICAL/CRITICAL SOURCES: New York Times, July 4, 1967, July 16, 1967, November 12, 1969; *Le Monde,* July 5, 1967, July 12, 1967, July 18, 1967; *London Times,* July 10, 1967, July 11, 1967, July 12, 1967; *New York Times Book Review,* November 16, 1969; *Publishers' Weekly,* November 24, 1969; *Atlantic Review,* December, 1969; *Best Sellers,* December 15, 1969; *Saturday Review,* January 3, 1970; *New Leader,* January 5, 1970.†

*   *   *

BEN-HORIN, Meir 1918-

PERSONAL: Born December 31, 1918, in Koenigsberg, East Prussia (now Kaliningrad, U.S.S.R.); came to United States in 1939, naturalized in 1943; son of Joseph and Dwoira (Polishuk) Schiffmann; married Alice Neugebauer, September 15, 1946; children: Judith, David, Gideon. *Education:* Hebrew University, student, 1937-39; Jewish Theological Seminary of America, B.J.P., 1941; Columbia University, M.A., 1948, Ph.D., 1952. *Home:* 634 West Upsal St., Philadelphia, Pa. 19119. *Office:* Horace M. Kallen Center for Jewish Studies, 69 Bank St., New York, N.Y. 10014.

CAREER: U.S. Department of the Army, Washington, D.C., investigator, 1946-48; Jewish Cultural Reconstruction, Inc., New York City, field director for western Europe, 1949-50; Hebrew Teachers College, Brookline, Mass., member of faculty and acting registrar, 1951-57; Dropsie University, Philadelphia, Pa., professor of education, 1957-75; Jewish Teachers Seminary, Horace M. Kallen Center for Jewish Studies, New York City, professor of modern Jewish thought and education and vice-president for academic affairs, 1976—. *Military service:* U.S. Army, 1943-46. U.S. Army Reserve, 1948-74; now colonel (retired).

MEMBER: American Association of University Professors, National Council for Jewish Education (former vice-president), Civil Affairs Association, Conference on Jewish Social Studies, Conference on Jewish Philosophy (founder), Reserve Officers Association of the United States, Religious Education Association of the United States, Zionist Organization of America, Kappa Delta Pi, Phi Delta Kappa.

WRITINGS: Max Nordau: Philosopher of Human Solidarity, Conference on Jewish Social Studies, 1956; (editor with Bernard Weinryb and Solomon Zeitlin) *Studies and Essays in Honor of Abraham A. Neuman,* Dropsie College Press, 1962; (editor with Judah Pilch) *Judaism and the Jewish School,* Bloch Publishing, 1966; *Common Faith—Emancipation and Counter-Emancipation,* Ktav, 1974. Contributor to scholarly and literary journals. Member of editorial boards, *Reconstructionist, Judaism, Jewish Education.* Managing editor, *Jewish Social Studies,* 1957-69.

WORK IN PROGRESS: Education as Religion; essays in modern Jewish theology; a critique of neo-mysticism; an intellectual biography of Mordecai M. Kaplan, founder of Jewish reconstructionism.

SIDELIGHTS: Meir Ben-Horin lists his professional interests as philosophies of education, modern theology, Zionism and Zionist history, nineteenth- and twentieth-century history, history of education, and modern Hebrew literature. He told *CA* that his work "seeks to develop the implications of Jewish religious naturalism which regards Judaism as the Jewish people's evolving civilization of 'the religious.'" He speaks German, Hebrew, Yiddish, in addition to English, and reads French, Italian, Latin, and Greek.

BENNETT, Gordon A(nderson) 1940-

PERSONAL: Born April 1, 1940, in Baltimore, Md.; son of James Lippincott (an aeronautical engineer) and Grace (Anderson) Bennett. *Education:* Pennsylvania State University, B.A., 1962; University of Wisconsin, M.S., 1964, Ph.D., 1973. *Home:* 3000 LaFayette, Austin, Tex. 78722. *Office:* Department of Government, University of Texas, Austin, Tex. 78712.

CAREER: University of California, Berkeley, visiting research political scientist at Center for Chinese Studies, 1969-70; University of Texas at Austin, assistant professor, 1971-75, associate professor of government, 1976—.

WRITINGS: (With Ronald N. Montaperto) *Red Guard: The Political Biography of Dai Siao-Ai,* Doubleday, 1971; *Yundong: Mass Campaigns in Chinese Communist Leadership,* University of California Center for Chinese Studies, 1976; (contributor) Sidney Greenblatt, Richard Wilson, and Amy Wilson, editors, *Social Control and Deviance in the People's Republic of China,* Praeger, 1977. Contributor to journals of Asian studies.

WORK IN PROGRESS: A book on financial and commercial issues in Chinese politics, completion expected in 1978.

SIDELIGHTS: Gordon Bennett lived in Taiwan, 1965-66, and in Hong Kong, 1967-69; he has traveled in Japan, South Vietnam, Thailand, India, and People's Republic of China.

*　　*　　*

BENNETT, John (Frederic) 1920-

PERSONAL: Born March 12, 1920, in Pittsfield, Mass.; son of John Frederic (a linesman) and Loretta (Simpson) Garrigan; name legally changed in 1929, after adoption by Gerald and Annie Bennett; married Elizabeth Mary Jones, August 20, 1960; children: Catherine, Jennifer. *Education:* Oberlin College, A.B., 1947; University of Wisconsin, M.A., 1950, Ph.D., 1956. *Politics:* Democrat. *Religion:* Episcopalian. *Home:* 526 Karen Lane, Green Bay, Wis. 54301. *Office:* Department of English, St. Norbert College, West DePere, Wis. 54178.

CAREER: Indiana University, Jeffersonville, instructor in English, 1953-58; Beloit College, Beloit, Wis., assistant professor of English, 1958-59; Rockford College, Rockford, Ill., associate professor, 1959-62, professor of English, 1962-68, chairman of department, 1960-68; St. Norbert College, West DePere, Wis., professor, 1968-70, Bernard H. Pennings Distinguished Professor of English, 1970—. Consultant in communications, Air War College, Maxwell Air Force Base, Ala., 1951; member of faculty advisory committee, Illinois Board of Higher Education, 1962-68. *Military service:* U.S. Army, 1942-46; served in Office of Strategic Services as liaison officer, Forces Francaises de l'Interieur; served in Field Artillery; became first lieutenant. *Member:* Melville Society, National Society of Literature and Arts, Amnesty International.

AWARDS, HONORS: Poetry prizes, Oberlin College, 1947 and 1948; Borestone Mountain Poetry awards, 1950 and 1967; Devins Memorial Award, Chicago Book Clinic Award, Printing Industries of America Award, Midwestern Book of the Year Award, American Association of University Presses Book Competition Award, all 1970, for *The Struck Leviathan;* Midland Poetry Award, 1971, for *Griefs and Exultations.*

*WRITINGS—*Poetry: (Editor) *Once We Thought: An Anthology of Oberlin Verse,* privately printed, 1941; *The Zoo Manuscript,* Sydon Press, 1968; *The Struck Leviathan:*

Poems on Moby Dick, University of Missouri Press, 1970; *Griefs and Exultations,* St. Norbert College Press, 1970; *Knights and Squires: More Poems on Moby Dick,* St. Norbert College Press, 1972; *Solstice Poems,* St. Norbert College Press, 1972; *A Quartet for the Seasons,* privately printed, 1974.

Poems anthologized in several collections, including: *Doors into Poetry,* edited by Chad Walsh, Prentice-Hall, 1962, 2nd edition, 1970; *Today's Poets: British and American Poetry since the 1930's,* edited by Walsh, Scribner, 1964, revised edition, 1972; *The New York Times Book of Verse,* edited by Thomas Lask, Macmillan, 1970; *Invitation to Poetry,* edited by Janet M. Cotter, Winthrop, 1971. Recorded reading of own poetry, *The Struck Leviathan: Poems on Moby Dick,* University of Missouri Press, 1976. Contributor of critical articles and poetry to professional journals. Co-editor, *Beloit Poetry Journal,* 1958-72.

*WORK IN PROGRESS—*Poetry: *Dinner in the Union Lunch; Quatrains from the Nixon Rubaiyats; Pequod Down: Last Poems on Moby Dick,* completion expected in 1978; *Old Shotgun's Book of Practical Dirties,* completion expected in 1978; *Candles and Cobwebs: A Vari-Gaited Congeries of 500 Aphorisms.*

SIDELIGHTS: John Bennett told *CA:* "I wrote *The Zoo Manuscript* partly because I am a frustrated zoologist. My other books I have written because I am (impossible description!) a Christian-Platonist-Existentialist-Humanist. . . . I try for the classical virtues of clarity and simplicity—in the best sense of the latter term. Images/metaphors should be accurate—and as evocative and startling as possible without disturbing the tenor of the poem. . . . I write blank verse, free verse, metric/rhymed/stanzaic verse—whatever suits the need of the poem as it forces its discovery on the page. But I insist on discipline, control, order, intelligence: I deeply loath the mass of so-called poetry which is really chopped-up prose (bad prose!) arrogantly hiding its inadequacies of thought, language, image and feeling under the barbaric yell 'It's my thing!' Hogwash and worse. And finally, I think that it is impossible to write well without being aware of one's predecessors, without holding for them variously a feeling of critical love and respect and honor.''

AVOCATIONAL INTERESTS: Rifle markmanship, amateur gunsmithing, fishing for muskellunge in western Wisconsin, visiting zoos with his wife and children.

*　　*　　*

BENSON, C. Randolph 1923-

PERSONAL: Born June 8, 1923, in Staunton, Va.; son of Charles R. and Nora (Branch) Benson. *Education:* University of Virginia, B.A. and M.A.; Louisiana State University, Ph.D. *Address:* P.O. Box 4103, Roanoke, Va. 24015. *Office:* Department of Sociology, Roanoke College, Salem, Va. 24153.

CAREER: Assistant professor of sociology at Arlington State College (now University of Texas at Arlington), Arlington, Tex., 1962-63, and Northwestern State College of Louisiana (now Northwestern State University of Louisiana), Natchitoches, 1963-64; Louisiana State University, Baton Rouge, special lecturer in sociology, 1964-65; New Mexico State University, University Park, assistant professor of sociology, 1965-66; Trinity University, San Antonio, Tex., assistant professor of sociology, 1966-68; Roanoke College, Salem, Va., associate professor, 1968-69, professor of sociology and chairman of department, 1969—. *Member:* American Anthropological Association, American

Sociological Association, Southern Sociological Association, Eastern Sociological Association, Phi Beta Kappa.

WRITINGS: Thomas Jefferson as Social Scientist, Fairleigh Dickinson University Press, 1971. Contributor to professional journals.

WORK IN PROGRESS: A text in sociological theory; research in deviant behavior and sociology of law.

* * *

BENSON, Robert G(reen) 1930-

PERSONAL: Born in 1930, in Nashville, Tenn.; son of John T., and Jimmy Lou (Root) Benson; married Peggy Siler (an interior decorator); children: Bob, Jr., Mike, Leigh, Tom, Patrick. *Education:* Trevecca Nazarene College, A.B., 1951; Nazarene Theological Seminary, B.D., 1955. *Home address:* Route 2, Bayshore Dr., Hendersonville, Tenn. 37075. *Office:* Benson Company, 365 Great Circle Rd., Nashville, Tenn. 37228.

CAREER: Benson Company, Nashville, Tenn., executive vice-presient, 1960—. Speaker at conferences, retreats, and colleges. Member of board of directors, Songtime, Inc. *Member:* National Academy of Recording Arts and Sciences, Church Music Publishers Association (former president), Gospel Music Association (member of board of directors).

WRITINGS: Laughter in the Walls, Impact Books, 1969; *Come Share the Being,* Impact Books, 1974; *Something's Going On Here,* Impact Books, 1977.

* * *

BENSON, Thomas W(alter) 1937-

PERSONAL: Born January 25, 1937, in Abington, Pa.; son of Walter A. (a civil servant) and Beatrice (Newton) Benson; married Margaret Sandelin (a nursery school teacher), September 3, 1960; children: Margaret, Sarah. *Education:* Hamilton College, A.B., 1958; Cornell University, M.A., 1961, Ph.D., 1966. *Home:* 327 McBath St., State College, Pa. 16801. *Office:* Department of Speech Communication, Pennsylvania State University, 227 Sparks Bldg., University Park, Pa. 16802.

CAREER: Cornell University, Ithaca, N.Y., assistant director of debate, 1962-63; State University of New York at Buffalo, instructor, 1963-66, assistant professor of speech, 1966-69, member of graduate faculty, 1968-71, associate professor of photographic studies, 1970-71; Pennsylvania State University, University Park, associate professor, 1971-75, professor of speech, 1975—. Instructor, Cornell University, summers, 1962, 1965; fellow of Cassirer College, State University of New York at Buffalo, 1968-71; visiting assistant professor of rhetoric, University of California at Berkeley, 1969-70; visiting associate professor of speech, Pennsylvania State University, 1971. Producer and director of films, "We Wish to Thank," 1971, and "Couples," 1975. Participant, Spring Arts Festival, 1966; production consultant and additional photography, "Have You Ever Considered Archaeology?" (film); participant in production of several single-concept films for teaching aids for courses in film history and theory; participant in television and experimental video-tape shows. Film critic, WBFO-FM, 1966-68; has given numerous lectures, participated on panels and juries, and acted as reviewer for television, movie theatres, schools, and colleges in the Buffalo, New York area. *Member:* International Communication Association, Speech Communication Association, Society for Cinema Studies, University Film Asso-

ciation, Society for the Anthropology of Visual Culture, Eastern Communication Association. *Awards, honors:* State University of New York at Buffalo Graduate School grant, 1968; summer fellowship, State University of New York, 1968.

WRITINGS: (Editor with Michael H. Prosser) *Readings in Classical Rhetoric,* Allyn & Bacon, 1969; *Medieval Rhethoric,* Indiana University Press, 1973. Author with K. Frandsen, *An Orientation to Nonverbal Communication,* 1976. Also author of film slide presentation, "Visual Literacy," 1971. Contributor of articles, reviews, and interviews to *Southern Speech Journal, Today's Speech, Colleague, Speech Monographs, Quarterly Journal of Speech, Theatre Design and Technology, Speech Teacher, Philosophy and Rhetoric,* and *Film Society Review.* Editor of column, "Cinema" for *Reports* of the New York State Speech Association, 1965-69. Editor, *Communication Quarterly,* 1976—. Associate editor, *Quarterly Journal of Speech,* 1971-74, and *Today's Speech,* 1972-75.

WORK IN PROGRESS: Work in film, rhetoric, and criticism.

* * *

BENTLEY, Sarah 1946-
(Sarah Bentley Doely)

PERSONAL: Born April 27, 1946, in Syracuse, N.Y.; daughter of Warren Robertson (a banker) and Dorothy (deNoyelles) Bentley; married David Owen Doely, June 21, 1969 (divorced). *Education:* Smith College, B.A. (magna cum laude), 1968; Columbia University, M.A., 1970; Union Theological Seminary, New York, N.Y., M.Div., 1975, Ph.D. candidate, 1975—. *Home:* 527 Riverside Dr., New York, N.Y. 10027. *Office:* National Council of Churches, 475 Riverside Dr., New York, N.Y. 10027.

CAREER: Church Women United, New York City, program assistant, 1970-71; IDOC-North America, Inc., New York City, managing editor of *International Documentation on the Contemporary Church,* 1971-72; National Council of Churches, New York City, staff member in news and information services, 1975-77, and office of general secretary, 1977—.

WRITINGS: (Editor under name Sarah Bentley Doely) *Women's Liberation and the Church,* Association Press, 1970.

WORK IN PROGRESS: Research on the role of pre-conscious perception in ethical judgment, the mind-body relationship in historical and contemporary Christian thought, and the use of movement and dance in theological education and worship.

* * *

BENTON, John W. 1933-

PERSONAL: Born August 29, 1933, in Seattle, Wash.; son of Eric (a minister) and Virginia (Trowbridge) Benton; married Margaret Whaley (an administrative assistant), December 19, 1952; children: Marji Eileen, Connie Jean, Jim Edwin. *Education:* Studied at Bethel Temple Bible School, Seattle, Wash., 1952-54. *Home and office address:* Walter Hoving Home, Box 194, Garrison, N.Y. 10524.

CAREER: Pastor of Assembly of God Church, 1958-63; Spokane Youth for Christ, Spokane, Wash., executive director, 1964; Teen Challenge, Inc., Brooklyn, N.Y., associate director, 1965—; Walter Hoving Home (rehabilitation home for girls), Garrison, N.Y., director, 1965—.

WRITINGS: Debs, Dolls and Dope, Revell, 1968; *Carmen,* Revell, 1970; *Teenage Runaway,* Revell, 1976; *Crazy Mary,* Revell, 1977.

WORK IN PROGRESS: Cindy.

* * *

BERBRICH, Joan D. 1925-

PERSONAL: Born May 12, 1925, in Richmond Hill, N.Y.; daughter of John Adam and Dorothy (Scharen) Berbrich. *Education:* New York College for Teachers (now State University of New York at Albany), B.A., 1946; Columbia University, M.A., 1949; New York University, Ph.D., 1964. *Politics:* Independent. *Religion:* Roman Catholic. *Home:* 5 Owen Ave., Glens Falls, N.Y. 12801.

CAREER: Mineola High School, Mineola, N.Y., English teacher, 1949-59, chairman of English department, 1959-75. Teacher of English, University of Connecticut, Storrs, summer, 1966; extension teacher of English, Nassau Community College, Garden City, N.Y., 1969-70.

WRITINGS: Three Voices from Paumanok: The Influence of Long Island on Cooper, Bryant, and Whitman, Friedman, 1969; (editor) *Sounds and Sweet Airs: The Poetry of Long Island,* Friedman, 1970; (editor) W. Oakley Cagney, *The Heritage of Long Island,* Friedman, 1970; *101 Ways to Learn Vocabulary,* Amsco School Publications, 1971; (with M. Hecht and C. Cooper) *The Women, Yes,* Holt, 1973; (editor) *Stories of Crime and Detection,* McGraw, 1974; (editor) *Heaven and Hell,* McGraw, 1975; *Wide World of Words,* Amsco School Publications, 1975; *Writing Practically,* Amsco School Publications, 1976; *Writing Creatively,* Amsco School Publications, 1977. Contributor to literary and popular journals.

WORK IN PROGRESS: Writing Logically, to be published by Amsco School Publications.

SIDELIGHTS: Joan Berbrich told *CA:* "Since I believe that writing is an art, not a happening, I have spent the last few years trying to understand and explain the 'how-to's' of writing. This seems important to me since good writing depends on clear thinking—and our contemporary world certainly needs *that.*"

* * *

BERDES, George R. 1931-

PERSONAL: Born February 12, 1931, in Milwaukee, Wis.; son of Frank R. and Johanna (Galubinski) Berdes; married Jane Baldauf (a free-lance writer), June 27, 1953; children: Celia, Beth, John, Madelyn. *Education:* Marquette University, B.A., 1953, M.A., 1962. *Politics:* Democrat. *Religion:* Roman Catholic. *Home:* 6025 Berkshire Dr., Bethesda, Md. 20014. *Office:* 2170 Rayburn House Office Building, Washington, D.C. 20515.

CAREER: Appleton Post-Crescent, Appleton, Wis., news reporter, 1955-57; WISN-TV, Milwaukee, Wis., radio and television news writer, 1957-58; Marquette University, Milwaukee, editorial director of University Press, 1959-62, assistant professor of journalism, 1960-65; administrative assistant to Congressman Clement J. Zablocki, U.S. House of Representatives, Washington, D.C., 1965-71; staff consultant, House International Relations Committee, 1971—. *Military service:* U.S. Army, 1953-55. *Member:* American Association of University Professors, Milwaukee Press Club. *Awards, honors:* Study and travel grants from Federal Republic of Germany, 1963, 1967; Gridiron Award of Milwaukee Press Club, 1964, for best story improving relations between the United States and foreign nations.

WRITINGS: Up from Ashes: An American Journalist Reports from Germany, Institute of German Affairs, Marquette University, 1964; *Friendly Adversaries: The Press and Government* (includes interviews with thirteen Washington newspapermen), Center for the Study of the American Press, Marquette University, 1969. Contributor to magazines.

* * *

BERGSTROM, Louise 1914-

PERSONAL: Born October 29, 1914, in Leavenworth, Wash.; daughter of William Basil (a merchant) and Mary (Lewis) Simpson; married Oscar F. Bergstrom, May 21, 1938; children: Loa Marta (Mrs. Quang Nguyen), Kristine Bergstrom Choate. *Education:* Attended Indiana State Teachers College (now Indiana University of Pennsylvania), one year, and a business college, two years. *Politics:* Nonpartisan. *Religion:* Agnostic. *Home:* 3308 Sunny Harbor Dr., Punta Gorda, Fla. 33950.

WRITINGS—Youth novels; all published by Bouregy, except as indicated: *Strange Legacy,* 1968; *The Pink Camellia,* 1968; *Claudia's Secret,* 1969; *Midsummer Eve,* 1970; *The Mockingbird Tree,* 1971; *The House of the Golden Dogs,* 1971; *The House of the Sphinx,* 1972; *The Mysterious Grotto,* 1973; *Night of the Fires,* 1973; *Giants in the Wings,* 1974; *Dangerous Paradise,* 1975; *The House of the Evening Star,* 1976; *My Heart Has Its Love,* 1977; *The Dragon's Pearls,* Dell, 1977. Contributor of short stories to *Co-Ed,* and articles to *Mobile Living.*

SIDELIGHTS: Louise Bergstrom spent a year in Sweden and has toured in Europe and America by camper. "I had no 'motivation' to be a writer," she says, "I just was one—whether anyone wanted to buy what I wrote or not. I am very glad, however, that I finally started to sell . . . I am fascinated by the workings of the Universe, and [am] an interested observer of life on our own little planet. I would like to be a profound writer—but I am afraid my talent only runs to entertaining my readers."

* * *

BERKOWITZ, Marvin 1938-

PERSONAL: Born October 8, 1938; children: four. *Education:* Rutgers University, B.S., B.A., 1961; University of East Africa, diploma in education, 1962; Columbia University, M.S., 1966, Ph.D., 1973. *Home:* 780 West End Ave., New York, N.Y. 10025.

CAREER: New York City Planning Commission, New York City, senior quantitative analyst, 1968-71; Hofstra University, Hempstead, N.Y., assistant professor of business statistics, 1968-71; New York University, New York City, professor in Graduate School of Public Administration, 1970-72; affiliated with New York City Police, 1971-74; American Foundation for the Blind, New York City, director of research and technological development, 1975—.

WRITINGS: The Conversion of Military-Oriented Research and Development to Civilian Uses, Praeger, 1970; *Social Costs of Human Undevelopment,* Praeger, 1974. Contributor of articles to various journals.

WORK IN PROGRESS: Empirical studies on public administration, social indicators, and use of public services.

* * *

BERLE, Adolf A(ugustus), Jr. 1895-1971

January 29, 1895—February 17, 1971; American lawyer,

economist, and diplomat. Obituaries: *Washington Post,* February 19, 1971; *Time,* March 1, 1971. (See index for *CA* sketch)

* * *

BERLEANT, Arnold 1932-

PERSONAL: Surname is pronounced *Ber*-le-ant; born March 4, 1932, in Buffalo, N.Y.; son of Bernard and Elizabeth (Barkun) Berleant; married Riva Schiller (an anthropologist), August 2, 1958; children: Jared, Andrea, Anne Nicole. *Education:* Attended New York State Teachers College, Fredonia (now State University of New York College at Fredonia), 1949-51; University of Rochester, B.M., 1953, M.A., 1955; State University of New York at Buffalo, Ph.D., 1962. *Home:* 25 Highfield Rd., Glen Cove, N.Y. 11542. *Office:* C. W. Post Center, Long Island University, P.O. Greenvale, N.Y. 11548.

CAREER: State University of New York at Buffalo, instructor, 1960-61, lecturer in philosophy, 1961-62; Long Island University, C. W. Post Center, Brookville, N.Y., assistant professor, 1962-65, associate professor, 1965-70, professor of philosophy, 1970—. Member of social science faculty, Sarah Lawrence College, 1966-68; visiting associate professor, San Diego State College (now University), summer, 1966. *Military service:* U.S. Army, 1954-56. *Member:* American Society for Aesthetics, American Society for Value Inquiry (member of executive committee, 1970-72), American Association of University Professors, Long Island Philosophical Society.

WRITINGS: (Contributor) R. S. Guttchen and Bertram Bandman, editors, *Philosophical Essays on Curriculum,* Lippincott, 1969; *The Aesthetic Field: A Phenomenology of Aesthetic Experience,* C. C Thomas, 1970; (contributor) D. Kiepe, editor, *Phenomenology and Natural Existence,* State University of New York Press, 1973. Contributor of more than sixty articles and reviews to philosophy and related journals.

WORK IN PROGRESS: Research on environmental aesthetics.

SIDELIGHTS: Arnold Berleant told *CA:* "Writing for me is an exploration into the experiences of living, both as felt and as understood. It is an effort to evoke and articulate problems and conditions that have not been deciphered to my satisfaction. Thus writing is a means of creative discovery that has led me from trying to find some order in the conditions of our encounter with art to puzzling more recently over the aesthetic dimensions of environmental experience."

* * *

BERLINER, Franz 1930-

PERSONAL: Born August 10, 1930, in Denmark; married Bibi Noergaard, 1952; children: Franz, Peter, Bolette. *Politics:* "As a human being, capable of thinking, I'm a pacifist." *Home:* Hoejland, Vrold, 8660 Skanderborg, Denmark.

CAREER: Author and journalist. Weekly columnist, writing about children and their parents, in *Soendags-BT,* Copenhagen, Denmark, 1965-71; television critic (on children's programs), writing daily in *Politiken,* Copenhagen, Denmark, 1968-71.

WRITINGS: Evelyn (short stories), Gyldendal, 1954; *Tingelingelater,* Nyt Nordisk, 1956; *Hundene,* Gyldendal, 1957; *Godnat Skipper* (juvenile), Borgen, 1962; *Maane over*

fjeldet (on Greenland), Borgen, 1964; *Stederne,* Borgen, 1966; *Boernene og vi* (child study), Berlingske, 1967; *Menneskenes Land* (juvenile), Bonniers, 1967, translation by Louise Orr published as *Summertime,* Collins, 1969; (with wife, Bibi Berliner) *Derude bag havet* (juvenile), Munksgaard, 1968; *Groenland,* Carit Andersen, 1968; *Vestgroenland,* Carit Andersen, 1970; *Soefolket* (juvenile), Gyldendal, 1970, translation by Lone Thygesen-Blecher published as *The Lake People,* Putnam, 1973; *En anden bog om Soefolket,* Gyldendal, 1972; *Alene hjemme,* Gyldendal, 1972; *Kaninoeen,* Gyldendal, 1973. Contributor to *Boerne- og ungdomsboeger* (a study of children's literature), Gyldendal, 1969. Writer of television adaptation of *Menneskenes Land* for Danmarks Radio, 1969; also has written for Greenland and Danish radio. Contributor of articles to magazines and newspapers, and book reviews to *Politiken.* Editor, *Refleks,* 1973—.

SIDELIGHTS: Franz Berliner spent five years in Greenland and has visited there three times since. He wrote the text of *Summertime* around drawings of Eskimo children done by Ingrid Vang Nyman, who was Danish but who did most of her work in Sweden. When she died in 1959 her son took her unpublished drawings to Berliner.

BIOGRAPHICAL/CRITICAL SOURCES: Times Literary Supplement, October 16, 1969; *Books,* October, 1969.

* * *

BERMAN, Marshall 1940-

PERSONAL: Born November 24, 1940, in New York, N.Y.; son of Murray (a journalist) and Betty (Shur) Berman; married Carole Greenman, May 18, 1969; children: Mare. *Education:* Columbia University, A.B. (summa cum laude), 1961; Oxford University, B.Litt., 1963; Harvard University, Ph.D., 1967. *Politics:* Radical. *Religion:* Jewish. *Home:* 838 West End Ave., New York, N.Y. 10025. *Office:* Department of Political Science, City College of the City University of New York, New York, N.Y. 10031.

CAREER: City College of the City University of New York, New York, N.Y., assistant professor, 1967-71, associate professor of political science, 1972—. *Awards, honors:* National Endowment for the Humanities senior fellowship, 1974. *Member:* Phi Beta Kappa.

WRITINGS: The Politics of Authenticity: Radical Individualism and the Emergence of Modern Society, Atheneum, 1970. Contributor of numerous articles to journals and magazines.

WORK IN PROGRESS: All That Is Solid Melts into Air, a study of relations between modernism in culture and modernization in economic and social life.

* * *

BERNARD, Kenneth A(nderson) 1906-

PERSONAL: Born February 1, 1906, in Everett, Mass.; son of Alexander A. (a builder) and Ida C. (Bemis) Bernard; married Dorothy F. Graham (a soprano soloist), September 4, 1927; children: Sylvia (Mrs. Robert N. Larson). *Education:* Boston University, S.B., 1927; Harvard University, A.M., 1935. *Religion:* Congregationalist. *Residence:* South Eaton, Mass. *Office:* Department of History, Boston University, 725 Commonwealth Ave., Boston, Mass. 02215.

CAREER: Teacher of history in Tilton, N.H., 1927-35, and Newtonville, Mass., 1935-37; Boston University, Boston, Mass., instructor, 1937-41, assistant professor, 1941-48, associate professor, 1948-53, professor of history, 1953-72, professor emeritus, 1972—, registrar of College of Liberal Arts, 1937-47. Visiting professor at Washington State University, 1953, 1957, 1961, and University of Idaho, 1959, 1968. Honorary member, U.S. Lincoln Sesquicentennial Commission, 1959-60. Trustee, Jackson Homestead, Newtonville, 1960-69. *Member:* Lincoln Group of Boston (president, 1960-69), Lincoln Group of District of Columbia, Phi Beta Kappa. *Awards, honors:* Benjamin Barondess Award of New York Civil War Round Table, 1967, for *Lincoln and the Music of the Civil War.*

WRITINGS: (Contributor) H. B. Kranz, editor, *Abraham Lincoln: A New Portrait,* Putnam, 1959; (contributor) R. G. Newman, editor, *Lincoln for the Ages,* Scribner, 1962; *Lincoln and the Music of the Civil War,* Caxton, 1966; *Abraham Lincoln: The Song in His Heart,* Achille J. St. Onge, 1970. Contributor to history journals.

WORK IN PROGRESS: History of the Lincoln Group of Boston.

*   *   *

BERNARD, Sidney 1918-

PERSONAL: Born February 4, 1918, in New York, N.Y. *Education:* Columbia University, student, 1946-47. *Politics:* "Activist and hopeful." *Home:* 319 West 75th St., New York, N.Y. 10023. *Agent:* Mary Yost Associates, 141 East 55th St., New York, N.Y. 10022. *Office:* The Smith, 5 Beekman St., New York, N.Y. 10038.

CAREER: Standard News Association, New York City, reporter and rewriter, 1947-53; Fenster Associates, New York City, public relations writer, 1959-61; *Literary Times,* Chicago, Ill., New York editor, 1963-67; *Smith* and *Newsletter,* New York City, roving editor, 1967—. *Member:* P.E.N. *Military service:* U.S. Army, 1942-45; served in Normandy invasion and Mediterranean campaigns; became technical sergeant.

WRITINGS: (Contributor) W. Lowenfels and N. Braymer, editors, *Where Is Vietnam?,* Doubleday, 1968; *This Way to the Apocalypse: The 1960's* (collection of articles and essays), Horizon Press, 1969. Also author of a poem reprinted in three anthologies. Contributor of more than five hundred articles, essays, and other pieces to *Nation, Commonweal, Ramparts, Evergreen Review, National Observer, New York Herald Tribune, Defiance, Realist, Smith, Rogue,* and other magazines, newspapers, and periodicals.

WORK IN PROGRESS: A collection of poems, *City Edition;* a second collection of essays.

SIDELIGHTS: In the foreword to *This Way to the Apocalypse* Sidney Bernard wrote: "As to one small note of self-assessment, I would say there's always a hole in my work, where my best should be. And I try to narrow that hole. Fitfully, nervously, rarely easily, and almost every day." To *CA,* he added: "Have an abiding interest in music (more Bach than rock); downtown and West Fifty-seventh Street galleries; film and theater (all off-Broadway, haven't tripped on-Broadway in years). Interest in sports—tennis (doubles easier than singles), fishing . . . billiards."

BIOGRAPHICAL/CRITICAL SOURCES: Village Voice, April 23, 1970.

*   *   *

BERNAUER, George F. 1941-

PERSONAL: Born August 5, 1941, in Madison, Wis.; son of George F. and Helen A. (Larscheid) Bernauer. *Educa-*

tion: Student at Georgetown University, 1959-60, and University of Lille, Lille, France, 1960-61; University of Wisconsin, B.A., 1964, M.A., 1965; Yale University, Ph.D. candidate. *Home:* 14 Green Mountain Pl., Middlebury, Vt. 05753. *Office:* Department of French, Middlebury College, Middlebury, Vt. 05753.

CAREER: Middlebury College, Middlebury, Vt., instructor in French, 1969—. *Member:* Modern Language Association of America, American Association of University Professors.

WRITINGS: (Editor with Germaine Bree) *Defeat and Beyond: An Anthology of French Wartime Writing, 1940-1945,* Pantheon, 1970.††

*   *   *

BERNHARDSEN, (Einar) Christian (Rosenvinge) 1923-
(Bris Bernhardsen)

PERSONAL: Born February 11, 1923, in Bergen, Norway; son of Einar (a clerk) and Ragna (Thomassen) Bernhardsen; married Helene Grieg Shetelig, June 24, 1949; children: Mette (daughter). *Education:* Left high school at seventeen to serve with partisans. *Politics:* Anarchist. *Religion:* None. *Home:* Soevej 18, Birkeroed, Denmark. *Agent:* A. Leonhardt, Loevstraede 8, Copenhagen, Denmark.

CAREER: Left Bergen after the liberation of Norway in 1945 and went to Denmark where he worked as culture reporter for *Information* (Danish underground newspaper that became a daily following the war); literary editor of *B.T.* (daily newspaper), Copenhagen, Denmark. *Wartime service:* Member of Norwegian partisan forces ("decorations: 23 scars"). *Member:* Norwegian Press Association, Danish Press Association, Danish Author's Society. *Awards, honors:* Danish Art Foundation Award for *Kampen paa fjeldet;* and "several general/uninteresting press prizes."

WRITINGS: Henrik og den doede mand, Vinten, 1967; *Henrik og doeden i sneen,* Vintin, 1967; *Henrik og doeden paa stranden,* Vinten, 1967; *Kampen paa fjeldet* (youth book), translation by Franey Sinding published as *Fight in the Mountains,* Harcourt, 1968; *Den store gade: Eventyret om P.V. Glob,* Vinten, 1970.

Under name Bris Bernhardsen: *Portraet af en oe* (travel), Vinten, 1966; *Lykkens hjul: En Mosaik,* Vinten, 1966; *Graenseland* (travel), Vinten, 1966.

Author of science fiction and other short stories; contributor of more than one thousand articles about literature and film to magazines and newspapers.

WORK IN PROGRESS: A book about Norway; a biography of Thor Heyerdahl.

SIDELIGHTS: Christian Bernhardsen says that if any book is ever written about him he will do the writing and the book "will not be nice." He thinks *Fight in the Mountains* probably is his best children's book, but the American edition depressed him, presumably because of its (nearly) happy ending. As a journalist Bernhardsen has traveled more than he cares to contemplate, visiting for varying periods in every country of Europe. He is fluent in the three Scandinavian languages ("and they are very different"), and speaks German, French, Spanish, Italian, Russian, and English. He is fond of French wines, orchids and Francois Villon.†

*   *   *

BERNSTEIN, Arnold 1920-

PERSONAL: Born December 19, 1920, in New York,

N.Y.; son of Max (a musician) and Mamie (Dembinsky) Bernstein; married Joan Hamilton. *Education:* City College (now City College of the City University of New York), B.S., 1942; Columbia University, A.M., 1946, Ph.D., 1952. *Home:* 26 West Ninth St., New York, N.Y. 10011. *Office:* Department of Psychology, Queens College of the City University of New York, Flushing, N.Y. 11367.

CAREER: City College (now City College of the City University of New York), New York City, lecturer in psychology, 1947-52; Queens College of the City University of New York, Flushing, N.Y., 1953—, began as instructor, professor of psychology, 1971—. Psychoanalyst in private practice, New York City, 1950—; chief of Psychological Clinic, Stuyvesant Polyclinic Hospital, New York City, 1958-65. *Military service:* U.S. Army, 1942-45. *Member:* American Psychological Association, American Association for the Advancement of Science, National Psychological Association for Psychoanalysis, Eastern Psychological Association.

WRITINGS: (With H. L. Lennard) *Anatomy of Psychotherapy,* Columbia University Press, 1960; *Patterns in Human Interaction,* Jossey-Bass, 1969; *Mystification and Drug Misuse,* Jossey-Bass, 1971.

*   *   *

BERNZWEIG, Eli P. 1927-

PERSONAL: Born November 17, 1927. *Education:* Rutgers University, B.S., 1950, J.D., 1953. *Home:* 9107 Shad Lane, Potomac, Md. 20854.

CAREER: Admitted to Bar of New York State and of U.S. Supreme Court; practicing attorney in Ellenville, N.Y., 1953-57; U.S. Department of Labor, Washington, D.C., staff attorney, 1957-62; U.S. Department of Health, Education, and Welfare, Washington, D.C., chief of health services branch, Office of the General Counsel, 1962-67, legislative planning officer, Bureau of Health Services, 1967-68, legislative attorney, Health Services and Mental Health Administration, 1968-69, special assistant for malpractice research and prevention, Community Health Service, beginning 1969. Lecturer on medico-legal subjects.

WRITINGS: Nurse's Liability for Malpractice: A Programmed Course, McGraw, 1969, 2nd edition, 1975. Author of monographs and manuals for U.S. Public Health Service. Contributor to law and medical journals.†

*   *   *

BERRIDGE, P(ercy) S(tuart) A(ttwood) 1901-

PERSONAL: Born June 10, 1901, in South Croydon, Surrey, England; son of Percy Herbert (a stockbroker) and Minnie (Stuart) Berridge; married Olga Fenin, August 14, 1939; children: Pamela Ann, Jennifer Valerie, Rosemary Patricia. *Education:* Royal Technical College, Glasgow, Diploma in Civil Engineering, 1923. *Politics:* Conservative. *Religion:* Church of England. *Home and office:* 26 Higher Holcombe Rd., Teignmouth, Devonshire TQ14 8RJ, England.

CAREER: Apprentice and draughtsman at Sir William Arrol & Co. Ltd., and Dalmarnock Iron Works, Glasgow, Scotland, 1919-24; Coode, Fitzmaurice, Wilson & Mitchell, Westminster, England, assistant engineer, 1924-26; bridge engineer, North Western Railway, India, 1926-46, and Great Western Railway and Western Region of British Railways, 1946-63; consulting engineer, 1964-68. *Member:* Institution of Civil Engineers (fellow), Institute of Welding (fellow). *Awards, honors:* Gold medal of Punjab Engineering Con-

gress, 1935; member of Order of the British Empire, 1945; Webb Prize, 1953, and Telford Premium, 1954, both from Institution of Civil Engineers.

WRITINGS: The Girder Bridge, after Brunel and Others, Maxwell & Co., 1969; *Couplings to the Khyber: The Story of the Northwestern Railway,* David & Charles, 1969; (contributor) *A History of Technology: The Twentieth Century,* Oxford University Press, 1976. Contributor to *Hamlyn Illustrated Modern Encyclopaedia,* 1970.

*   *   *

BERRIEN, F. Kenneth 1909-1971

December 22, 1909—February 9, 1971; American psychologist and author. Obituaries: *New York Times,* February 10, 1971. (See index for *CA* sketch)

*   *   *

BERRY, David (Ronald) 1942-

PERSONAL: Born April 12, 1942, in Bury St. Edmunds, England; son of Ronald and Olive (Baxter) Berry. *Education:* University of Liverpool, B.A., 1964, M.A., 1967. *Politics:* Labour. *Religion:* None. *Home:* 35 Llantarnam Rd., Cardiff CF4 3EF, Wales. *Office:* Department of Sociology, University College, University of Wales, Cardiff, Wales.

CAREER: University of Strathclyde, Glasgow, Scotland, lecturer in sociology, 1966-69; University of Wales, University College, Cardiff, lecturer, 1969-75, senior lecturer in sociology, 1975—. *Member:* British Sociological Association.

WRITINGS: The Sociology of Grass Roots Politics, St. Martin's, 1970; *Central Ideas in Sociology,* F. E. Peacock, 1975.

WORK IN PROGRESS: The Construction of the Social World: A Theoretical Introduction to Sociology.

*   *   *

BEST, Thomas W(aring) 1939-

PERSONAL: Born March 10, 1939, in Charlotte, N.C.; son of Emory (a businessman) and Elizabeth (Hardeman) Best; married Susan Burt, January 29, 1971. *Education:* Duke University, B.A., 1961; Indiana University, M.A., 1963, Ph.D., 1965. *Office:* Department of German, University of Virginia, Charlottesville, Va. 22903.

CAREER: University of Hamburg, Hamburg, Germany, lecturer, 1965-66; Duke University, Durham, N.C., assistant professor of German literature, 1966-67; University of Virginia, Charlottesville, associate professor of German, 1967—, chairman of department, 1972—. *Member:* Modern Language Association of America, American Renaissance Society, American Association of Teachers of German.

WRITINGS: The Humanist Ulrich von Hutten, University of North Carolina Press, 1969; *Eccius Dedolatus: A Reformation Satire,* University Press of Kentucky, 1971; *Macropedius,* Twayne, 1972; *Jacob Bidermann,* Twayne, 1975.†

*   *   *

BETHEL, Dell 1929-

PERSONAL: Born November 22, 1929, in Chicago, Ill.; son of Earl Francis (a sports artist) and Dolly (Bethel) Cowgill; married Pauline Dorothy Halter (a college receptionist), August 30, 1953; children: William Dell. *Education:* University of Minnesota, A.A., 1949; St. Cloud State College, B.S., 1955; Central Washington State College, M.Ed.,

1964, and additional graduate study. *Politics:* Democrat. *Religion:* Lutheran.

CAREER: Professional baseball player with New York Giants, 1949-53; coach and teacher in Pine City, Minn., Sunnyside, Wash., and Banning, Calif., 1953-66; Olivet College, Olivet, Mich., associate professor of physical education, head of department, and head baseball coach, 1966-71; City College of the City University of New York, New York, N.Y., assistant professor of physical education and head baseball coach, beginning 1971. Has taught baseball and English in Japanese schools. *Military service:* U.S. Army, Infantry, 1951-53; served in Korea; became sergeant; received Bronze Star and Purple Heart. *Member:* American Association of College Baseball Coaches (member of international committee), Lions Club, Knife and Fork Club.

WRITINGS: (Contributor) Stephen Jones and Marion Murphy, *Geography and World Affairs,* 2nd edition, Rand McNally, 1962; *Inside Baseball: Tips and Techniques for Coaches and Players,* Reilly & Lee, 1969; (contributor) *The Best in Baseball,* Scholastic Athletic Services, 1970. Contributor to coaching periodicals.

WORK IN PROGRESS: Baseball with the Pro's; and *Adventure in Living,* a novel.

AVOCATIONAL INTERESTS: Oil painting, chess, fishing, study of great people.

BIOGRAPHICAL/CRITICAL SOURCES: Strength and Health, April, 1962; *Saturday Review,* June 28, 1969.††

* * *

BEVILACQUA, Alberto 1934-

PERSONAL: Born June 27, 1934, in Parma, Italy; son of Mario and Giuseppina (Cantadori) Bevilacqua; married Marianna Bucchich (a poet), June 12, 1961. *Education:* University of Parma, law degree, 1956. *Religion:* Catholic. *Home:* Via Napoleone Colajanni 4, Rome, Italy.

CAREER: Author and journalist. *Member:* Sindacato Nazionale Scrittori, Comunita Europea Scrittori (both Rome). *Awards, honors:* Premio Campiello, 1966; Premio Strega, 1968, for *L'occhio del gatto;* Premio Banca Rella, 1972, for *Il viaggio misterioso.*

WRITINGS: La polvere sull'erba (nonfiction), Sciascia, 1955; *L'amicizia perduta* (poetry), Sciascia, 1961; *Una citta in amore* (novel), Sugar, 1962; *La Califfa* (novel), Rizzoli, 1964, translation by Harvey Fergusson II published as *The Califfa,* Atheneum, 1969; *Questa specie d'amore* (novel), Rizzoli, 1966; *L'occhio del gatto* (novel; title means "Eye of the Cat"), Rizzoli, 1968; *Il viaggio misterioso* (novel), Rizzoli, 1972; *L'indignazione* (poetry), Rizzoli, 1973; *Umana avventura* (novel), Garzanti, 1974; *La crudelta* (poetry), Garzanti, 1975. Also author of *Attenti al buffone,* 1975. Writer of film and television scripts. Literary correspondent for *Corriere della sera.*

WORK IN PROGRESS: A novel.

SIDELIGHTS: Alberto Bevilacqua adapted for the screen and directed *La Califfa,* 1970, *Questa specie d'amore,* 1971, and *Attenti al buffone,* 1975.

BIOGRAPHICAL/CRITICAL SOURCES: Saturday Review, September 20, 1969; *Book World,* July 27, 1969; *Spectator,* November 22, 1969.

* * *

BHAGAT, G(oberdhan) 1928-

PERSONAL: Born December 20, 1928, in Bhagalpur,

India; son of Raghunath and Rameshwari Bhagat; married Sheela Agarwal, June 24, 1961; children: Rekha. *Education:* Tej Narain Jubilee College, B.A., 1948; Patna University, M.A., 1950; University of Minnesota, M.A., 1955; Yale University, M.A., 1960, Ph.D., 1963. *Politics:* None. *Religion:* "Born Hindu." *Address:* P.O. Box 538, University, Miss. 38677. *Office:* Department of Political Science, University of Mississippi, University, Miss. 38677.

CAREER: Permanent Mission of India to the United Nations, New York, N.Y., adviser on economics and politics, 1956-63; University of Mississippi, University, assistant professor, 1964-66, associate professor, 1966-68, professor of international relations and Asian studies, 1969—. *Member:* American Political Science Association, Conference on British Studies.

WRITINGS: Americans in India, 1784-1860, New York University Press, 1970.

WORK IN PROGRESS: Two books, *John Foster Dulles and India,* and *Prime Minister Nehru and the American Press.*

* * *

BHAGAVATULA, Murty S. 1921-

PERSONAL: Born September 1, 1921, in Guntur, Andhra Pradesh, India; son of Sarma S. (a lawyer) and Nagabhushnamma Bhagavatula; married wife, Sundaramma, July 1, 1943; children: Mallikharjuna Sarma (son), Prabha (daughter), Ramakrishna (son), Somayaji Sarma (son). *Education:* Andhra University, B.A., 1940; Madras University, B.L., 1942, M.L., 1952; Yale University, LL.M., J.S.D., 1957. *Religion:* Hinduism. *Home:* 39 Siripuram, Vizagapatam 3, Andhra Pradesh, India. *Office:* University College of Law, Andhra University, Vizagapatam 3, Andhra Pradesh, India.

CAREER: Andhra University, Vizagapatam, India, professor of law. *Member:* American Society of International Law, Indian Society of International Law, Indian Institute of Public Administration. *Awards, honors:* Fulbright and Smith-Mundt grants, 1954.

WRITINGS: Propaganda and World Public Order, Yale University Press, 1968; (contributor) Max Soerenson, editor, *Manual of Public International Law,* St. Martin's, 1968.

WORK IN PROGRESS: International Diplomacy and World Public Order.

SIDELIGHTS: Murty S. Bhagavatula wrote *CA,* "I consider that legal inquiries which do not focus on values appropriate to upholding human dignity are useless."

* * *

BIELENBERG, Christabel 1909-

PERSONAL: Born June 18, 1909, in Totteridge, Hertfordshire, England; daughter of Percy Collingwood (an advertising director) and Christabel (Harmsworth) Burton; married Peter Bielenberg (formerly a lawyer in Germany; currently farms in Ireland), September 29, 1934; children: Nicholas Paul, John Peter, Christopher Albrecht. *Education:* Educated in Bushey, England. *Home:* Munny House, Tullow, County Carlow, Ireland.

AWARDS, HONORS: Richard Hillary Memorial Prize, 1968, for *The Past Is Myself.*

WRITINGS: The Past Is Myself (autobiographical), Chatto & Windus, 1968, published as *Ride Out the Dark* (Book-of-the-Month Club selection), Norton, 1971. Also author of *Guided Tour of Dublin,* Mercier Press.

SIDELIGHTS: From a comfortable British childhood and finishing school, Christabel Bielenberg went to Germany to live from 1934 to 1946 as the wife of a German lawyer. *Ride Out the Dark* is a series of sketches about life under the Nazis—gay incidents, according to Robert Birley, "like the marvelous party in 1940 in their house in Berlin, when all the guests were in the resistance and one of them . . . was persuaded to give his famous version of Goebbels' broadcast to the nation after the *Endsieg*—the final victory," and other, quite terrifying incidents, "like the account of the interrogation of the author by *Kriminalrat* Lange, after her husband had been arrested." Margot Lester writes, "The most extraordinary part of Mrs. Bielenberg's personal story is her brilliantly conceived and extremely dangerous plan to get her husband released from Ravensbruck; he had been imprisoned after the July plot on Hitler's life." Christabel Bielenberg told *CA* that she wrote the book because she felt that her experiences as an Englishwoman married to a German "might constitute a missing link in the mass of books, historical and otherwise, which have been written about that time."

BIOGRAPHICAL/CRITICAL SOURCES: New Statesman, November 29, 1968; *Spectator,* December 13, 1968; *Jewish Quarterly,* spring, 1969; *Variety,* January 28, 1970; *Newsday,* March 6, 1971.†

* * *

BIGIARETTI, Libero 1906-

PERSONAL: Born May 16, 1906, in Matelica, Italy; son of Lucano Bigiaretti; married Matilde Crespi (a journalist). *Education:* Attended Liceo Artistico, Rome. *Home:* Via Denza 66, Rome, Italy.

CAREER: Journalist and author, with principal vocational interest in contemporary arts. *Member:* Sindacato Nazionale Scrittori (Rome), Comunita Europea Scrittori, Societe Europeenne de Culture, P.E.N., Societa Italiana degli Autori ed Editori (councillor). *Awards, honors:* Viareggio Award, 1968, for *La Controfigura.*

WRITINGS: Una Amicizia difficile (novel), de Luigi, 1945, published as *Esterina: Un' Amicizia difficile,* Bompiani, 1962; *Incendi a Paleo,* Editrice Cultura Moderna, 1945; *Roma borghese,* Organizzazione Editoriale Tipografica, 1945; *Il villino* (novel), Garzanti, 1946, reprinted, Bompiani, 1974; *La Scuola dei ladri* (three short novels), Garzanti, 1952; *I Figli,* Vallecchi, 1955, reprinted, Bompiani, 1974; *Disamore* (novel), Nistri-Lischi, 1956; *Carlone: Vita di un italiano,* Avanti, 1956; *Etruskische Wandmalerei,* W. Klein, 1956; *Schedario,* All'Insegna del Pesce d'Oro, 1956; *Disegni e dipinti di Bruno Caruso, 1952-1955* (text in Italian, English, and French), Priulla, 1957; *Carte romane,* Societa Editrice Internazionale, 1957; *Leopolda,* Sodalizio del Libro, 1957; *Uccidi o muori,* Vallecchi, 1958; *I Racconti* (short stories; contains "Segreto di famiglia," "Lacrime e bugie," "Le Statue," "L'Oscuramento," "Un Altro destino") Vallecchi, 1961; *Il Congresso* (novel), Bompiani, 1963, translation by Joseph Green published as *A Business Convention,* Knopf, 1965 (translation published in England as *The Convention,* Macmillan, 1965); *Cattiva memoria,* Nuova Accademia, 1965; *Le Indulgenze* (novel), Bompiani, 1963; *Il Dito puntato: Lettera all'editore con una riposta del medesimo* (correspondence with Valentino Bompiani), Bompiani, 1967; (with others) *Giovanni Pintori* (text in Italian and English), Bassoli, 1967; *La Controfigura* (novel), Bompiani, 1968; *Il Dissenso,* Bompiani, 1969; *Dalla donna alla luna* (novel), Bompiani, 1972; *L'Uomo che mangia il leone* (short stories), Bompiani, 1974; *Le Stanze* (novel), Bompiani, 1976.

WORK IN PROGRESS: A novel, untitled.

SIDELIGHTS: Libero Bigiaretti told *CA* that, as a youth, he aspired to painting. Books, however, occupied much of his time and led him eventually from reading to writing. He found writing easy and developed no particular writing habits, composing as he went and where he could. As a reason for writing he says, "I wanted to write to learn and to elevate myself socially."

Senor Bigiaretti believes that modern literature has "overrated the contributions of psychoanalysis and sociology. Flaubert and Dostoevski did not study sociology. Dante, Kafka, Melville did not know of psychoanalysis. Zola, Verga, Dickens did not study sociology."

His books are widely read and have been translated into all the major languages. A filmscript based on his prize-winning novel, *La Controfigura,* has been written and produced.

* * *

BILKEY, Warren J(oseph) 1920-

PERSONAL: Born February 2, 1920, in Poynette, Wis.; son of Joseph W. (a farmer) and Lena (Truttschel) Bilkey; married F. Angelica Romero-Beltre (a statistician), September 10, 1949; children: Warren Joseph, Jr., Christopher, Peter, Martin, Maria. *Education:* University of Wisconsin, B.S., 1941; Harvard University, A.M., 1948, Ph.D., 1950. *Politics:* Democrat. *Religion:* Roman Catholic. *Home:* 6310 Woodington Way, Madison, Wis. 53711. *Office:* School of Business, University of Wisconsin, Madison, Wis. 53706.

CAREER: University of Connecticut, Storrs, 1949-58, began as instructor, became assistant professor of economics; University of Notre Dame, Notre Dame, Ind., associate professor of economics, 1958-63; University of Wisconsin—Madison, School of Business, associate professor, 1966-69, professor of business, 1969—. Economic adviser to President of Dominican Republic, 1963; economist, Central Bank of the Dominican Republic, 1963-65. *Military service:* U.S. Army, 1941-46; became captain. *Member:* American Economic Association, Society for International Development, Association for Social Economics.

WRITINGS: Industrial Stimulation, Heath, 1970.

WORK IN PROGRESS: Transportation in Costa Rica: A Multidisciplinary Analysis; and *Consumer Activity Analysis and New Product Development.*

* * *

BILLY, Andre 1882-1971

December 13, 1882—April 10, 1971; French journalist and author. Obituaries: *New York Times,* April 12, 1971; *L'Express,* April 19-25, 1971.

* * *

BINDER, Frederick M(elvin) 1931-

PERSONAL: Born June 19, 1931, in Chelsea, Mass.; son of Harry (a printer) and Beatrice (Seltzer) Binder; married Teris Weinberger, June 21, 1964; children: Abby Beth. *Education:* Boston University, B.S., 1953; Columbia University, M.A., 1954, Ed.D., 1962. *Home:* 880 Eastlawn Dr., Teaneck, N.J. 07666. *Office:* Department of Social and Psychological Foundations, City College of the City University of New York, New York, N.Y.

CAREER: Fairlawn High School, Fairlawn, N.J., social studies teacher, 1956-62; Ball State University, Muncie, Ind., assistant professor of U.S. history, 1962-65; City College of the City University of New York, New York, N.Y., assistant professor, 1965-68, associate professor, 1968-70, professor of history of education, 1970—, chairman, Department of Social and Psychological Foundations, 1968—. *Military service:* U.S. Army, 1954-56; became first lieutenant. *Member:* American Historical Association, Organization of American Historians, History of Education Society, American Studies Association (president, metropolitan New York chapter, 1970-71), American Educational Research Association, Phi Delta Kappa.

WRITINGS: The Color Problem in Early National America as Viewed by John Adams, Jefferson and Jackson, Mouton & Co. (The Hague), 1968, Humanities, 1969; (compiler) *Education in the History of Western Civilization: Selected Readings,* Macmillan, 1970; *The Age of the Common School, 1830-1865,* Wiley, 1974; (contributor) F. Cordasco and W. Brickman, editors, *A Bibliography of American Educational History,* AMS Press, 1975.

WORK IN PROGRESS: Research in the educational history of black people under slavery.

* * *

BINGHAM, Robert E. 1925-

PERSONAL: Born August 10, 1925, in Kansas City, Mo.; son of Carl E. (in transportation) and Bertha (Potter) Bingham; married Opha Mae Stump, April 3, 1947; children: Linda K., Nancy A. *Education:* Attended Columbia University and Union Theological Seminary, New York, N.Y., 1944, 1951; University of Kansas, B.S. in B.A., 1946; Furman University, additional study, 1953-55. *Religion:* Baptist. *Home and office:* 4017 Arden Way N.E., Atlanta, Ga. 30342.

CAREER: Black, Sivalls & Bryson (steel fabrication), Kansas City, Mo., market analyst, 1947-48; minister of education at Baptist churches in St. Joseph, Mo., 1948-52, Greenville, S.C., 1952-60, and Atlanta, Ga., 1960-71. Taught in Japan, 1966. Baptist Home Mission Board, member of board of directors, 1967—, second vice-president, 1971—, director of Services section and executive assistant, 1972—. *Military service:* U.S. Navy, 1944-46; became lieutenant junior grade. *Member:* Southwestern Religious Education Association (president, 1960), Georgia Religious Education Association (president, 1961).

WRITINGS: (Contributor) John Sisemore, editor, *Vital Principles in Religious Education,* Broadman, 1966; *New Ways of Teaching the Old Story,* Broadman, 1970; (with Ernest J. Loessner) *Serving with the Saints,* Broadman, 1970; *A Cup of Cold Water,* Convention Press, 1971; *Flight 1994,* HMB Press, 1975. Contributor of more than one hundred articles to religious journals.

WORK IN PROGRESS: Booby Trap, for Broadman.

* * *

BIOY-CASARES, Adolfo 1914-
(Martin Sacastru, Javier Miranda; joint pseudonyms: H[onorio] Bustos Domecq, B. Suarez Lynch)

PERSONAL: Born September 15, 1914, in Buenos Aires, Argentina; son of Adolfo and Marta (Casares) Bioy; married Silvina Ocampo (a writer); children: Marta. *Home:* Posadas 1650, Buenos Aires, Argentina.

CAREER: Writer since his late teens. *Awards, honors:* Premio Municipal de la Ciudad de Buenos Aires, 1940, for

La Invencion de Morel; 2nd Premio Nacional de Literatura, 1963, for *El Lado de la sombra;* 1st Premio Nacional de Literatura, 1969, for *El Gran serafin.*

WRITINGS: Prologo (miscellany), Editorial Biblos (Buenos Aires), 1929; (under pseudonym Martin Sacastru) *17 disparos contra lo porvenir* (short stories), Editorial Tor (Buenos Aires), 1933; *Caos* (short stories; includes "Claridad y sombra," "Caos," "Un Muchacho fuerte," "Un Punal en el sueno," "Un Dia extrano," "La Duda en el espacio," "Historia del hombre que se asoma a la nada," "El Prisionero y su fuga," "La Nueva Minerva," "Camino inutil," "La Sonrisa indecisa," and "Esto es un monstruo senores: Yo"), Viau & Zona (Buenos Aires), 1934; *La Nueva tormenta; o, La Vida multiple de Juan Ruteno* (novel), [Buenos Aires], 1935; *La Estatua casera* (miscellany), Ediciones del Jacaranda (Buenos Aires), 1936; *Luis Greve, muerto* (short stories), Editorial Destiempo (Buenos Aires), 1937.

La Invencion de Morel (novel), prologue by Jorge Luis Borges, Losada (Buenos Aires), 1940, 10th edition, Emece (Buenos Aires), 1975, translation by Ruth L. C. Simms published with stories from *La Trama celeste,* as *The Invention of Morel, and Other Stories from "La Trama celeste"* (also see below) University of Texas Press, 1964; *Plan de evasion* (novel), Emece, 1945, new edition, Galerna (Buenos Aires), 1969, translation by Suzanne J. Levine published as *A Plan for Escape,* Dutton, 1976; *La Trama celeste* (short stories; includes "En memoria de Paulina," "De los reyes futuros," "El Idolo," "La Trama celeste," "El Otro laberinto," and "El Perjurio de la nieve"), Sur (Buenos Aires), 1948, 3rd edition, 1969, translation by Simms published as *The Invention of Morel, and Other Stories from "La Trama Celeste"* (includes "The Invention of Morel," "In Memory of Pauline," "The Future Kings," "The Idol," "The Celestial Plot," "The Other Labyrinth," and "The Perjury of Snow"), University of Texas Press, 1964; *Las Visperas de Fausto* (short stories; includes "Las Visperas de Fausto," "En la torre," and "Orfeo"), illustrations by Hector Basaldua, La Perdiz (Buenos Aires), 1949; *El Sueno de los heroes* (novel), Losada, 1954, 4th edition, Emece, 1975; *Historia prodigiosa* (short stories; includes "Historia prodigiosa," "Clave para un amor," "Homenaje a Francisco Almeyra," "La Sierva ajena," and "Las Visperas de Fausto"), Obregon (Mexico), 1956, new edition with an additional story, "De los dos lados," Emece, 1961; *Guirnalda con amores* (miscellany about love; includes the short stories "Encrucijada," "Una Aventura," "Todos los hombres son iguales," "Todas las mujeres son iguales," "Triste historia del verdulero Delgado," "Un Sueno," "Los Regresos," "Reverdecer," "Mito de Orfeo y Euridice," "Casanova secreto," "Moscas y aranas," "Historia romana," and "Recuerdo de las sierras"), Emece, 1959.

El Lado de la sombra (short stories; includes "El Lado de la sombra," "La Obra," "Carta sobre Emilia," "El Calamar opta por su tinta," "Un Viaje, o, El Mago inmortal," "Un Leon en el bosque de Palermo," "Cavar un foso," "Paradigma," "Cuervo y paloma del doctor Sebastian Darres," and "Los Afanes"), Emece, 1962; *El Gran serafin* (short stories; includes "El Gran serafin," "Confidencias de un lobo," "Ad porcos," "El Don supremo," "La Tarde de un fauno," "Los Milagros no se recuperan," "El Solar," "Las Caras de la verdad," "El Atajo," and "Un Perro que se llamaba Dos"), Emece, 1967; *La Otra aventura* (critical essays), Galerna, 1968; *Diario de la guerra del cerdo* (novel), Emece, 1969, translation by Gregory Woodruff and Donald A. Yates published as *Diary of the War of the Pig,*

McGraw, 1972, 15th edition, 1976; *Memoria sobre la pampa y los gauchos* (essay), Sur, 1970; *Dormir al sol* (novel), Emece, 1973, 3rd edition, 1974.

Anthologies: *Adolfo Bioy Casares,* includes monograph on Bioy-Casares and his works by Ofelia Kovacci, Ministerio de Educacion y Justicia, Direccion General de Cultura (Buenos Aires), 1963; *Adversos milagros,* prologue by Enrique Pezzoni, Monte Avila (Caracas), 1969.

With Jorge Luis Borges: (Under joint pseudonym H. Bustos Domecq) *Seis problemas para don Isidro Parodi* (essay-parodies), Sur, 1942; (under joint pseudonym B. Suarez Lynch) *Un Modelo para la muerte* (novel), Oportet & Haereses (Buenos Aires), 1946; (under joint pseudonym H. Bustos Domecq) *Dos fantasias memorables* (short stories), Oportet & Haereses, 1946; *Los Orilleros* (film scripts; includes "Los Orilleros" and "El Paraiso de los ceyentes"), Losada, 1955; *Cronicas de Bustos Domecq* (short stories in form of "a discussion on writers, sculptors, architects, cooks and painters, who still don't exist, but who are dangerously possible"), Losada, 1967.

With S. Ocampo: *Los que aman, odian* (detective novel), Emece, 1946.

Editor with wife, Silvina Ocampo, and Borges: *Antologia de la literatura fantastica,* prologue by Bioy-Casares, Sudamericana (Buenos Aires), 1940, reprinted, 1971; *Antologia poetica argentina,* Sudamericana, 1941.

Editor or compiler with Borges: (And translator with Borges) *Los Mejores cuentos policiales* (detective and mystery stories, primarily English and American), Emece, 1943, 5th edition, 1965; *Poesia gauchesca,* two volumes, Fondo de Cultura Economica (Mexico), 1955; (and translator with Borges) *Cuentos breves y extraordinarios,* Raigal (Buenos Aires), 1955, new edition, Rueda (Buenos Aires), 1968, translation by Anthony Kerrigan published as *Extraordinary Tales,* Herder, 1971; *Libro del cjelo y del infierno,* Sur, 1960, new edition, 1970.

SIDELIGHTS: Adolfo Bioy-Casares' friend and co-author, Jorge Luis Borges, writes: "We hear sad murmurs that our century lacks the ability to devise interesting plots. But no one attempts to prove that if this century has any ascendancy over the preceding ones it lies in the quality of its plots.... I believe I am free from every superstition of modernity, of any illusion that yesterday differs intimately from today or will differ from tomorrow; but I maintain that during no other era have there been novels with such admirable plots as *The Turn of the Screw, Der Prozess, Le Voyageur sur la terre,* and [*The Invention of Morel*], which was written in Buenos Aires by Adolfo Bioy-Casares.... In Spanish, works of reasoned imagination are infrequent and even very rare.... *The Invention of Morel* (the title alludes filially to another island inventor, Moreau) brings a new genre to our land and our language. I have discussed with the author the details of his plot. I have reread it. To classify it as perfect is neither an imprecision nor a hyperbole."

In a *Books Abroad* review of *Cronicas de Bustos Domecq,* which was "a continuous best seller," H. Ernest Lewald cites Bioy-Casares' affiliation with the Argentine River Plate literary community, "a cultural island, equally far removed from the nerve centers of the United States and Western Europe, but at the same time completing a vital triangle." Lewald is especially appreciative of the cosmopolitan, highly literate background of the River Plate group, "all of which contributes greatly to a high level of sophistication and a search for universality in sharp contrast to the regionalism that dominated Latin American fiction earlier in the century."

David William Foster writes that Bioy-Casares "continues to fulfill ... the definition given him by one critic: a psychiatrist of the human experience.... [He] has long been a leading representative in Argentina of the 'metaphysical narrative' which probes aspects of the human experience by way of highly intellectualized plots and character delineation.... Bioy's intent is obvious: to deftly turn observable reality inside out, revealing within a context of humdrum daily circumstance the turbulent and desperate chaos of man's soul."

In a review of *Diary of the War of the Pig,* Michael Wood writes: "Bioy Casares is a close friend and collaborator of Borges, and Borges's influence is very clear in his work.... He is in one sense more inventive than Borges, better able to create a plot and sustain a narrative. But he appears to lack Borges's eeriest and most important gift: the ability to suggest the uncanny lurking in the quietest, most unlikely corner of a house or phrase." Martin Levin believes that "this hypnotic novel conjures up a Kafka-like nightmare each reader may interpret as he likes: an affirmation of life, of bestiality, or of love. It's all there, bubbling in rich profusion."

BIOGRAPHICAL/CRITICAL SOURCES: Ofelia Kovacci, monograph on Bioy-Casares accompanying anthology, *Adolfo Bioy Casares,* Ministerio de Educacion y Justicia, Direccion General de Cultura (Buenos Aires), 1963; Jorge Luis Borges, author of prologue, Adolfo Bioy-Casares, *The Invention of Morel and Other Stories, from "La Trama Celeste,"* University of Texas Press, 1964; *Books Abroad,* autumn, 1968, spring, 1969; *New York Times Book Review,* January 28, 1973; *Best Sellers,* February 1, 1973; *New York Review of Books,* April 19, 1973; *Contemporary Literary Criticism,* Volume IV, Gale, 1975.

* * *

BIRENBAUM, William M. 1923-

PERSONAL: Born July 18, 1923, in Macomb, Ill.; son of Joseph and Rose (Whiteman) Birenbaum; married Helen Bloch (an assistant professor at New York Community College), March 8, 1951; children: Susan, Lauren Amy, Charles. *Education:* Iowa State Teachers College (now University of North Iowa, Cedar Falls), 1941-43, 1945-46; University of Chicago, J.D., 1949. *Home:* 108 Willow St., Brooklyn, N.Y. 11201. *Agent:* Curtis Brown Ltd., 575 Madison Ave., New York, N.Y. 10022. *Office:* Office of the President, Antioch College, Yellow Springs, Ohio 45387.

CAREER: University of Chicago, Chicago, Ill., assistant dean of students, 1949-50, director of student affairs, 1950-55, dean of students at University College, 1955-57; Wayne State University, Detroit, Mich., assistant vice-president, 1957-61, assistant to president, 1959-61; New School for Social Research, New York, N.Y., dean, 1961-64; Long Island University Center, Brooklyn, N.Y., vice-president and provost, 1964-67; The Education Affiliate of the Bedford Stuyvesant Restoration and D. & S. Corporations, president, 1967-68; Staten Island Community College of the City University of New York, Staten Island, N.Y., president, 1968-76; Antioch College, Yellow Springs, Ohio, president, 1976—. Director, Detroit Adventure, 1958-61; chairman, Michigan Cultural Commission, 1960-61; member, New York City Board of Education, Districts 21-22, 1962-65. Member of board of advisers, Brooklyn Academy of Music, 1965—; trustee of Brooklyn Institute of Arts and Sciences, 1969—, and Friends World College, 1970-74. *Military service:* U.S. Army Air Forces, 1942-45. *Member:* American

Civil Liberties Union. *Awards, honors:* D.H.L., Columbia College, Chicago, 1970.

WRITINGS: Overlive: Power, Poverty, and the University, Delacorte, 1969; *Something for Everybody Is Not Enough,* Random House, 1972; (contributor) *New Directions for Community Colleges,* Jossey-Bass, 1974; (contributor) Thomas Harrington, editor, *Student Personnel Work in Urban College,* Intext Education, 1975.

BIOGRAPHICAL/CRITICAL SOURCES: New York Review, April 24, 1969; *Saturday Review,* May 17, 1969.

* * *

BJORNSTAD, James 1940-

PERSONAL: Surname is pronounced Be-yawn-stad; born December 23, 1940, in Brooklyn, N.Y.; son of Thomas (an engineer) and Gerda (Andersen) Bjornstad; married Rebecca Ann Leonard (a teacher), July 23, 1966. *Education:* Northeastern Bible Institute, B.R.E. and Th.B., 1967; New York Theological Seminary, M.R.E., 1969; New York University, Ph.D. candidate, 1969—. *Religion:* Conservative Baptist. *Residence:* North Haledon, N.J. *Office:* Institute of Contemporary Christianity, 410 Ramapo Valley Rd., Oakland, N.J. 07436.

CAREER: Ordained American Baptist minister, 1971; Van Riper-Ellis Memorial Church, Fair Lawn, N.J., minister of youth, 1966-70; Christian Research Institute, Wayne, N.J., assistant director, 1966-71; Institute of Contemporary Christianity, Oakland, N.J., executive director, 1971—. Assistant professor of philosophy and theology, Northeastern Bible College, 1972—. *Member:* Evangelical Theological Society, Society of Biblical Literature, American Teilhard de Chardin Association, Delta Epsilon Chi.

WRITINGS—All published by Bethany Fellowship: *Twentieth Century Prophecy,* 1969; *Stars, Signs and Salvation in the Age of Aquarius,* 1971; *The Transcendental Mirage,* 1975; *The Moon Is Not the Son,* 1975. Contributor to *Christianity Today* and other religious journals. Editor, *Religious Book Reviews;* book review editor, *On-Line.*

WORK IN PROGRESS: Two books, *The Theology of Teilhard de Chardin,* and *Reincarnation: The Gospel of Many Chances.*

* * *

BLACK, Angus 1943-

PERSONAL: Angus Black is a pseudonym; born May 1, 1943. *Education:* University of California, Berkeley, A.B. (summa cum laude), 1965. *Politics:* "Anarchal radical libertarian capitalist." *Religion:* "Zero." *Office:* c/o Holt, Rinehart and Winston, 383 Madison Ave., New York, N.Y. 10017.

CAREER: "Student of the world." *Member:* Phi Beta Kappa.

WRITINGS: A Radical's Guide to Economic Reality, Holt, 1970, new edition published as *A New Radical's Guide to Economic Reality,* 1971; *A Radical's Guide to Self-Destruction,* Holt, 1971.

WORK IN PROGRESS: How to Lose Money.

SIDELIGHTS: Angus Black described himself for *CA* as a "draft dodger" and "freak" who rides a bike to work and is "rich now, very poor before," and that his education includes a Ph.D. degree from the "School of Hard Knox." *Avocational interests:* Weightlifting, scuba diving, skiing, photography.†

BLACK, Margaret K(atherine) 1921-
(M. K. Howorth)

PERSONAL: Born September 22, 1921, in London, England; daughter of Humphrey Noel (a civil servant) and Gladys (Lewis) Howorth; married Robert Alastair Lucien Black (a professor), May 15, 1943 (deceased); children: Andrew Ian, Christopher James Robert. *Education:* Attended University of Witwatersrand and Sorbonne, University of Paris. *Religion:* Agnostic. *Home:* Flat 2, 34 Shepherds Hill, London, England. *Agent:* Laurence Pollinger Ltd., 18 Maddox St., London W1R 0EU, England.

MEMBER: Royal Institute of International Affairs, Society of Authors, National Union of Journalists, Wine and Food Society.

WRITINGS: Three Brothers: Two Young Explorers, Acorn Press, 1945; *Three Brothers and a Lady,* Acorn Press, 1947; *The Magic Way Readers,* three books, A.P.B. Bookstore (Johannesburg), 1950; *The Mabunga Family,* Institute of Race Relations, 1954; *The City Built on Gold,* Longmans, Green, 1957; (with others) *Happy Trek Readers,* five books, Longmans, Green, 1957; *A South African Holiday,* Longmans, Green, 1958; (editor with Lionel T. Bennett) *The Golden Journey: Anthologies of English Poetry for High Schools,* three books, A.P.B. Bookstore, 1959; *Johannesburg,* Longmans, Green, 1961; (with Molly Brearley) *Honey Family,* three books, Educational Supply Association (London), 1961; *No Room for Tourists* (on South Africa race question), preface by Angus Wilson, Secker & Warburg, 1965. Also author of *The Bennet Readers,* three books, *Giving Parties,* and a play, "The Kindly Islands." Author of radio plays for children, and articles and book reviews for South African and British newspapers.

WORK IN PROGRESS: A novel set in South Africa.

AVOCATIONAL INTERESTS: Cooking, economics, politics.†

* * *

BLAIR, Leon Borden 1917-

PERSONAL: Born October 26, 1917, in Dexter, Tex.; son of George Washington and Mattie (Wheeler) Blair; married Edith Witek; children: Christopher David, Peter Leon, David Irvin, Barbara Susan (Mrs. Raymond Stoudt), Michelle Edith (Mrs. David E. Jones), Matthew Curtis. *Education:* Texas Technological College (now Texas Tech University), B.A., 1940; Rice University, M.A., 1949; Texas Christian University, Ph.D., 1968. *Religion:* Christian Church (Disciples of Christ). *Home:* 3604 Kimberly Lane, Fort Worth, Tex. 76133. *Office:* Suite 1139, 611 Ryan Plaza Dr., Arlington, Tex. 76011.

CAREER: U.S. Navy, aviator, 1941-62, retiring as lieutenant commander; University of Texas at Arlington, instructor, 1967-68, assistant professor, 1968-71, associate professor of history, 1971-74; University of Plano, Plano, Tex., professor of history and dean of graduate studies, 1974-75. Vice-president and executive director, Texas Bureau for Economic Understanding, 1970—; executive director, Gifted Students Institute for Research and Development, 1974—. *Member:* American Historical Association, Middle East Studies Association. *Awards, honors*—Military: Legion of Merit, Air Medal (three times), Medaille Aeronovale (France). Civilian: George Washington Honor Medal, Freedoms Foundation of Valley Forge, 1963; Silver Medal, Arts-Sciences-Lettres (France), 1971, for *Western Window in the Arab World.*

WRITINGS: People to People Report, Iframar (Rabat), 1959, also published in English-Arabic edition, U.S. Information Service (Beirut), 1960; *Western Window in the Arab World,* University of Texas Press, 1970; (editor) *Essays on Russian Intellectual History,* University of Texas Press, 1971; (editor) *Essays on Radicalism in Contemporary America,* University of Texas Press, 1972. Editor of seventeen Navy technical reports, 1950-51, and of Walter Prescott Webb Memorial Lectures, 1970-72. Contributor to *U.S. Naval Institute Proceedings, Mid-East, This Week, Chasse et Chiens,* and historical journals.

WORK IN PROGRESS: La Presence americain au Maroc depuis 1942; The Diary of Rene Malevergne.

SIDELIGHTS: Leon Borden Blair has lived in France, Germany, and North Africa, and has traveled extensively throughout the Middle East. He believes "that our American society is in danger of losing its perspective, allowing itself to be overwhelmed with its problems, little realizing that this society has far more that is good than bad." He was technical adviser for the motion picture, "The Sixth Fleet," and aviation technical adviser for the television series, "Victory at Sea," 1952-53.

BIOGRAPHICAL/CRITICAL SOURCES: Christian Science Monitor, July 6, 1959; *New York Times,* May 23, 1960; *Time,* June 6, 1960.

* * *

BLANZACO, Andre C. 1934-

PERSONAL: Surname is pronounced Blan-*zack*-o; born July 28, 1934, in Philadelphia, Pa.; son of Laurent (a hairdresser) and Simone (Vurpillot) Blanzaco; married Jean Elizabeth Sturrock, June 23, 1956; married second wife, Geraldine Jablonski (a registered nurse), October 13, 1962; married third wife, Janet Ruth Keller (a registered nurse), June 7, 1974; children: (first marriage) David Paul, Suzanne Louise; (third marriage) Stephen Mark. *Education:* Ursinus College, B.S., 1955; University of Pennsylvania, M.D., 1959. *Politics:* Republican. *Religion:* Episcopalian. *Home:* 409 Washington Lane, Fort Washington, Pa. 19034. *Office:* 717 Bethlehem Pike, Philadelphia, Pa. 19118.

CAREER: Chestnut Hill Hospital, Philadelphia, Pa., intern, 1959-60, staff physician, 1965—, director of department of obstetrics and gynecology, 1975—; Germantown Dispensary and Hospital, Philadelphia, Pa., resident in obstetrics and gynecology, 1960-63, chief resident, 1962-63, staff physician, 1965—; Roxborough Memorial Hospital, Philadelphia, Pa., staff physician, 1965—. Clinical instructor in obstetrics and gynecology, Temple University School of Medicine, 1968-74. Director, Greater Philadelphia Alliance for the Eradication of Venereal Disease, 1969—. Diplomat of the American Board of Obstetrics and Gynecology. *Military service:* U.S. Army, Medical Corps, 1963-65; received Army Commendation Medal.

MEMBER: American College of Obstetricians and Gynecologists (fellow), American Medical Association, American Association of Gynecological Laparoscopists, American Fertility Society, Pennsylvania Medical Society, Philadelphia County Medical Society, Philadelphia Obstetrical Society.

WRITINGS: (With William F. Schwartz and Julius B. Richmond) *VD: Facts You Should Know* (juvenile), Scott, Foresman, 1970.

AVOCATIONAL INTERESTS: Photography, ice hockey, travel.

BLASS, Birgit A(nnelise) 1940-

PERSONAL: Born May 18, 1940, in Copenhagen, Denmark; came to U.S. in 1961; daughter of Arne and Elly (Pedersen) Knudsen; married John P. Blass (a doctor), December 20, 1960; children: Charles A., Louise C. *Education:* Columbia University, M.A., 1965. *Home:* 478 25th St., Santa Monica, Calif. 90402.

CAREER: Center for Applied Linguistics, Washington, D.C., research assistant, 1967-70. *Member:* Linguistic Society of America.

WRITINGS: (With Dora E. Johnson and William W. Gage) *A Provisional Survey of Materials for the Study of Neglected Languages,* Center for Applied Linguistics, 1970, new edition published as *Survey of Materials for the Study of the Neglected Languages,* 1976.

* * *

BLAUSHILD, Babette 1927-

PERSONAL: Born November 14, 1927, in Cleveland, Ohio; daughter of Louis and Florence (Smith) Rosen; married David Blaushild, December 25, 1946 (divorced); children: Eric, Steven, Lisa. *Education:* Western Reserve University (now Case Western Reserve University), student, 1961-62.

CAREER: Cleveland Press, Cleveland, Ohio, columnist, writing "Around the Town," 1969-72. National director of woman's political action in presidential campaign of Hubert H. Humphrey, 1972.

WRITINGS: (With Robert Pitcher) *Why College Students Fail,* Funk, 1970. Contributor to *Saturday Review.*†

* * *

BLOCH, Ernst 1885-1977

PERSONAL: Born July 8, 1885, in Ludwigshafen am Rhein, Germany; son of Max and Berta (Feitel) Bloch; married Elsa von Stritzky, June 17, 1913 (died, 1921); married Karola Piotrkowska, November 12, 1934; children: (second marriage) Jan Robert. *Education:* Attended University of Munich; University of Wuerzburg, Ph.D., 1908. *Home:* Im Schwanzer 35, Tuebingen, West Germany. *Office:* Department of Philosophy, University of Tuebingen, Tuebingen, West Germany.

CAREER: Free-lance writer, working primarily on *Das Prinzip Hoffnung* in New York, N.Y., and Cambridge, Mass., 1937-47; University of Leipzig, Leipzig, East Germany, professor of philosophy, 1949-61, director of Institute of Philosophy, 1949-56; University of Tuebingen, Tuebingen, West Germany, guest professor of philosophy, 1961-77. *Member:* Hegel-Gesellschaft (Heidelberg), P.E.N. *Awards, honors:* Kulturpreis des Deutschen Gewerkschaftsbundes, 1963, for *Literarische Aufsaetze;* Friedenspreistrager des Deutschen Buchhandels, 1967; Dr. honoris causa, University of Zagreb, 1969; Sigmund Freud Prize, Akademie fuer Sprache und Dichtung, 1975.

WRITINGS: Geist der Utopie (addresses, essays, and lectures on esthetics), Duncker & Humblot, 1918, translation published as *Spirit of Utopia,* Herder & Herder, 1970; *Thomas Muenzer als Theologe der Revolution,* Kurt Wolff, 1921, reprinted, Suhrkamp, 1960; *Durch die Wueste,* Paul Cassirer, 1923; *Spuren,* Paul Cassirer, 1930, reprinted, Suhrkamp, 1967; *Erbschaft dieser Ziet,* Oprecht & Hilbling, 1935.

Freiheit und Ordnung: Abriss der Sozial-Utopien, Aurora Verlag (New York), 1946; *Il Pensamiento de Hegel,*

[Mexico City], 1949; *Christian Thomasius: Ein deutscher Gelehrter ohne misere*, Aufbau-Verlag, 1953; *Das Prinzip Hoffnung*, Aufbau-Verlag, Volume I, 1954, Volume II, 1955, Volume III, 1959, Volume II published as *Das antizipierende Bewusstsein*, Suhrkamp, 1972; *Ernst Bloch: Wissen und Hoffen* (extracts from his works, 1918-1955, published for his seventieth birthday), Aufbau-Verlag, 1955; *Avicenna und die aristotelische Linke*, J. Fladung, 1958.

Zur Ontologie des Noch-Nicht Seins: Ein Vortrag und Zwei Abhandlungen, Suhrkamp, c. 1961; *Naturrecht und menschliche Wuerde* (also see below), Suhrkamp, 1961; *Philosophische Grundfragen*, Suhrkamp, 1961; *Verfremdunge*, Suhrkamp, Volume I, 1962, Volume II, 1964; *Tuebinger Einleitung in die Philosophie* (also see below), Suhrkamp, Volume I, 1963, Volume II, 1964, translation of Volume I by John Cumming published as *A Philosophy of the Future*, Herder & Herder, 1970; (compiler) Johann Peter Hebel, *Kalendergeschichten* (selections from *Schatzkaestlein des rheinischen Hausfreundes)*, Insel Verlag, 1965; *Literarische Aufsaetz*, Suhrkamp, 1965; *Religion im Erbe: Eine Auswahl aus seinen religions-philosophischen Schriften*, Siebenstern-Taschenbuch-Verlag, 1967; *Ernst Bloch: Vier Ansprachen anlaesslich der Verleihung des Friedenspreises des Deutschen Buchhandels*, Voersenverein des Deutschen Buchhandels, 1967; (with others) *Bildung und Konfessionalitaet*, Diesterweg, 1967; *Eine Auswahl aus seinen Schriften*, edited by Hans Heinz Holz, Fisher Buecherei, 1967; *Frieden im Nahen Osten: Zum arabisch-israelischen Konflikt* (booklet), Europaeische Verlagsanstalt, 1967; *Widerstand und Friede: Aufsaetze zur Politik*, Suhrkamp, 1968; *Atheismus im Christentum: Zur Religion des Exodus und des Reichs*, Suhrkamp, 1968, translation by J. T. Swann published as *Atheism in Christianity: The Religion of the Exodus and the Kingdom*, Herder & Herder, 1972; *Ueber Karl Marx* (excerpts from Bloch's previously published works), Suhrkamp, 1968, translation by John Maxwell published as *On Karl Marx*, Herder & Herder, 1971; *Karl Marx und die Menschlichkeit*, Rowohlt, 1969.

Marx und die Revolution (lectures), Suhrkamp, 1970; *Philosophische Aufsaetze zur objectiven Phantasia* (also see below), Suhrkamp, 1970; *Politische Aufsaetze*, Suhrkamp, 1970; *Ueber Methode und System bei Hegel*, Suhrkamp, 1970; *Man on His Own: Essays in the Philosophy of Religion*, translation by E. B. Ashton, Herder & Herder, 1970; *Paedagogica* (selections from *Philosophische Aufsaetze zur Objectiven Phantasie)*, Suhrkamp, 1971; *Recht, Moral, Staat* (selections from *Naturrecht und menschliche Wuerde)*, Neske, 1971; *Subjekt-Objekt*, Suhrkamp, 1971; *Differenzierungen im Begriff Fortschritt* (selections from *Tuebinger Einleitung in die Philosophie)*, Verlag der Arche, 1971; *Im Christentum steckt die Revolte*, Verlag die Arche, 1971; (contributor) Dietrich Mack, editor, *Ausgewaehlte Schriften: Richard Wagner*, Suhrkamp, 1971; *Vom Hasard zur Katastrophe: Politische Aufsaetze, 1934-1939* (lectures), Suhrkamp, 1972; *Vorlesungen zur Philosophie der Renaissance*, Suhrkamp, 1972; *Zur Philosophie der Musik*, Suhrkamp, 1974; *Aesthetik des Vor-Scheins*, Suhrkamp, 1974; *Ernst Blochs Wirkung: Ein Arbeitsbuch zum 90 Geburtstag*, Suhrkamp, 1975.

Gesamtausgabe (collected works), Suhrkamp, Volume I: *Spuren*, 1958, 5th edition, 1967, Volume II: *Thomas Muenzer als Theologe der Revolution*, 1958, Volume III: *Geist der Utopie*, 1958, Volume IV: *Erbschaft dieser Zeit*, 1958, enlarged edition, 1962, Volume V: *Das Prinzip Hoffnung*, 1958, Volume VI: *Naturrecht und menschliche Wuerde*, 1958, Volume VII: *Das Materialismusproblem*,

seine Geschichte und Substanz, 1958, Volume VIII: *Subjekt-Objekt, Erlaenterungen zu Hegel*, 1962, Volume IX: *Literarische Aufsaetze*, 1965, Volume X: *Philosophische Aufsaetze*, 1969, Volume XI: *Politische Messungen, Pestzeit, Vormaerz*, 1970, Volume XIII: *Tuebinger Einleitung in die Philosophie*, 1970, Volume XIV: *Atheismus in Christentum*, 1968, Volume XV: *Experimentum Mundi*, 1973, Volume XVI: *Geist der Utopie* (facsimile of 1918 edition), 1971.

Also author of *Gespraeche mit Ernst Bloch*, 1975. Contributor to journals.

WORK IN PROGRESS: Gesamtausgabe, for Suhrkamp, Volume XII: *Leipziger Vorlesungen zur Philosophie*.

BIOGRAPHICAL/CRITICAL SOURCES: Sinn und Form (Potsdam), July, 1955; Juergen Ruehle, *Literatur und Revolution: Die Schriftseller und der Kommunismus*, Kiepenheur & Witsch, 1960; Hellmuth G. Buetow, *Philosophie und Gesellschaft im Denken Ernst Bloch*, Osteuropa-Institut, 1963; Wolf Dieter Marsch, *Hoffnung worauf? Auseinandersetzung mit Ernst Bloch*, Furche-Verlag, 1963; Juergen Haberman, *Theorie und Praxis: Sozialphilosophische Studien*, Luchterhand, 1963; Siegfried Unseld, editor, *Ernst Bloch zu ehren: Beitraege zu seinem Werk*, Suhrkamp, 1965; Heinz Kimmerle, *Die Zunkunftsbedeutung der Hoffnung: Auseinandersetzung mit Ernst Blochs "Prinzip Hoffnung" aus Philosophischer und Theologischer sicht*, Bouvier, 1966; *Ueber Ernst Bloch*, Suhrkamp, 1968; *Times Literary Supplement*, December 11, 1969; Detlef Horster and others, editors, *Ernst Bloch zum 90 Geburstag: Es muss nicht immer Marmor sein*, Verlag Klaus Wagenbach, 1975; *Time*, August 15, 1977.†

(Died August, 1977)

* * *

BLOCH, Herman D(avid) 1914-

PERSONAL: Born May 8, 1914, in Brooklyn, N.Y.; son of Jack L. (a businessman) and Sadie (Manowitz) Bloch; married Joyce Cohn (a speech therapist), January 19, 1947; children: Leslie, Kate. *Education:* Brooklyn College (now Brooklyn College of the City University of New York), evening student, 1932-38, B.A., 1938; University of Chicago, graduate study, 1938-40, 1942-43; New School for Social Research, graduate study at evening school, 1941-45, Ph.D., 1950. *Politics:* Independent. *Home:* 16 Sachem St., East Rockaway, N.Y. 11518. *Office:* Department of Economics, St. John's University, Jamaica, N.Y. 11432.

CAREER: Economist with U.S. Bureau of Labor Statistics, 1943-44, and National War Labor Board, 1944-45; University of Toledo, Toledo, Ohio, assistant professor of economics, 1946-49; University of Bridgeport, Bridgeport, Conn., assistant professor, 1950-51, associate professor, 1951-55, professor of industrial relations and chairman of department, 1955-57; Howard University, Washington, D.C., Philip Murray Professor of Industrial Relations, 1957-60; State University of New York School of Industrial and Labor Relations at Cornell University, assistant director of New York City office, 1960-65; St. John's University, Jamaica, N.Y., professor of economics, 1965—. Consultant to New York Catholic Interracial Council, National Afro-American Committee, and other groups. *Member:* American Economic Association, American Sociological Association, Phi Gamma Mu.

WRITINGS: The Circle of Discrimination: An Economic and Social Study of the Black Man in New York, New York

University Press, 1969. Contributor to *The Encyclopedia of Black America*, McGraw, 1972; contributor to *Phylon, Journal of Social Psychology, Journal of Negro History, International Review of Social History,* and other professional journals.

WORK IN PROGRESS: The Locus of Discrimination in Local Craft Unions, 1833-1924; and *Colonialism and Discrimination in New York, 1625-1660.*†

* * *

BLOOMQUIST, Edward R. 1924-

PERSONAL: Born March 12, 1924, in Iowa City, Iowa; son of Edward William (a businessman) and Alice Katherine (Neal) Bloomquist; married Lila Mae Skadsheim (a registered nurse), December 29, 1949; children: Carol Diane, Roger Edward, Donald Edward. *Education:* Andrews University, B.S., 1948; Loma Linda University, M.D., 1949. *Address:* P.O. Box 22222, Los Angeles, Calif. 90022.

CAREER: Private practice of anesthesiology, Los Angeles, Calif.; University of Southern California, School of Medicine, Los Angeles, associate clinical professor of anesthesiology. Former director, County of Los Angeles, Drug Detoxification and Identification Center. Former chairman, California State Interagency Council on Drug Abuse and Los Angeles Mayors Committee on Drug Abuse. Member of advisory committee, Federal Bureau of Narcotics. Visiting professor and lecturer to numerous colleges. *Military service:* U.S. Air Force, Medical Corps, 1951-53; became captain.

MEMBER: American Medical Association, American Society of Anesthesiologists, American College of Anesthesiologists, American Medical Writers Association (fellow), International College of Surgeons, National Association of Science Writers, National Platform Association, Royal Society of Health (fellow), California Medical Association (vice-chairman of committee on dangerous drugs), California Society of Anesthesiologists, New York Academy of Sciences, Los Angeles County Medical Association (past chairman, committee on dangerous drugs).

WRITINGS—All published by Glencoe Press: *Marijuana,* 1968; (with John B. Williams) *Vice and Its Control,* 1970; *Marijuana: A Second Trip,* 1971. Contributor of chapters to books including: *The Marijuana World in a Perceptual Approach to College English,* Glencoe Press; *Amphetamines in Principals of Psychopharmacology,* Academy Press; *Cannabis in Drugs For and Against,* Hart; *Marijuana in Drug Awareness,* Avon. Also contributor of over fifty articles to journals and other periodicals. Former editor, *Illustrated Medical Lectures;* former contributing editor, *New Physician.* Former medical review columnist, *Medical Arts and Sciences.*

WORK IN PROGRESS: An Adult Understanding of Drug Abuse.

SIDELIGHTS: Edward Bloomquist told *CA:* "I began writing as a child, mainly because I like to express thoughts and work with words. I was active editorially and as a writer in both high school and college. I started writing 'professionally' while I was in the United States Air Force, mainly as a hobby and partly to see if I could really meet competition in the writing field. . . . The work I have done in drugs has been primarily to educate and, hopefully, to dissuade people from abusing drugs. I find, however, that most people prefer to have their opinions reenforced rather than their thoughts stimulated to new ideas. . . . I think books are improving,

that readership is growing, that people are growing tired of the pap of TV and returning once again to the fun of reading when, where and what they choose. And I think there is a good market for talented authors in all fields."

* * *

BLUME, Judy (Sussman) Kitchens 1938-

PERSONAL: Born February 12, 1938, in Elizabeth, N.J.; daughter of Rudolph (a dentist) and Esther (Rosenfeld) Sussman; married John M. Blume (an attorney), August 15, 1959 (divorced, 1975); married Thomas A. Kitchens (a physicist), May 8, 1976; children (first marriage): Randy Lee (daughter), Lawrence Andrew. *Education:* New York University, B.A., 1960. *Religion:* Jewish. *Residence:* Northern New Mexico. *Agent:* Harold Ober Associates, Inc., 40 East 49th St., New York, N.Y. 10017.

CAREER: Writer of juvenile and adult fiction. Former chairman, Greater Westfield (N.J.) Committee for UNICEF, 1960-71. *Member:* Society of Children's Book Writers, Women's National Book Association, Authors Guild. *Awards, honors:* Golden Archer Award, 1974; Nene Award, 1975, for *Are You There God?: It's Me, Margaret;* Pacific Northwest Young Readers Choice Award, 1975, for *Tales of a Fourth Grade Nothing;* Sequoyah Children's Book Award, 1975; Arizona Young Readers Book Award, 1977; Georgia Children's Book Award, 1977; South Carolina Children's Book Award, 1977; Massachusetts Children's Book Award, 1977.

WRITINGS—All juvenile, except as indicated: *The One in the Middle Is the Green Kangaroo,* Reilly & Lee, 1969; *Iggie's House,* Bradbury, 1970; *Are You There God?: It's Me, Margaret,* Bradbury, 1970; *Then Again, Maybe I Won't,* Bradbury, 1971; *Freckle Juice,* Four Winds, 1971; *Tales of a Fourth Grade Nothing,* Dutton, 1972; *Otherwise Known as Sheila the Great,* Dutton, 1972; *It's Not the End of the World,* Bradbury, 1972; *Deenie,* Bradbury, 1973; *Blubber,* Bradbury, 1974; *Forever* (young adult), Bradbury, 1975; *Starring Sally J. Freedman, As Herself,* Bradbury, 1977. Contributor to *Free to Be . . . You and Me,* for the *Ms* Foundation, 1974.

WORK IN PROGRESS: An adult novel and several book ideas for young readers.

SIDELIGHTS: Judy Blume told *CA:* "Writing is always exciting, especially once the torture of the first draft is over. It's the rewriting that I like best. I work on each book five or six times before publication. I like to watch it grow—I like to get to know my characters well. When a book is finished I feel sad. It's like saying goodbye to an old friend. But writing can be tough, lonely, frustrating work. Sometimes the efforts of a whole day wind up in the trash can. And the isolation of writing is difficult because I like to be with people. Every day I remind myself that I'm really not alone, that I share my books with my readers. And remembering that makes me smile." Blume goes on to say: "Writing about young people comes naturally to me because I am blessed with almost total recall. Often, young people will ask me how I know all their secrets. It's because I remember just about everything from third grade on, and many things that happened before that. I can tell you exactly what I was wearing on the spring day that one of my kindergarten classmates stepped on my little finger while I was sketching on the floor."

BIOGRAPHICAL/CRITICAL SOURCES: New York Times Book Review, May 24, 1970, December 9, 1970; *Publishers' Weekly,* January 11, 1971; *Boston Globe,* January 30, 1971; *Children's Literature Review,* Volume II, Gale, 1976.

BLUMENTHAL, Arthur L. 1936-

PERSONAL: Born December 4, 1936, in Cheyenne, Wyo.; son of Arthur F. (a businessman) and Mildred (Bollock) Blumenthal. *Education:* University of Redlands, B.A., 1959; University of Washington, Ph.D., 1964; attended Harvard University, 1964-67. *Home:* 48 Kirkland St., Cambridge, Mass. 02138. *Office:* Graduate School of Education, Harvard University, Cambridge, Mass. 02138.

CAREER: Harvard University, Cambridge, Mass., assistant professor in Graduate School of Education, 1968-73, lecturer in psychology department, 1973—. *Member:* American Association of University Professors, American Association for the Advancement of Science, Psychonomic Society.

WRITINGS: Language and Psychology: Historical Aspects of Psycholinguistics, Wiley, 1970; *The Process of Cognition,* Prentice-Hall, 1977.

WORK IN PROGRESS: A history of psychology.

* * *

BLUMENTHAL, Henry 1911-

PERSONAL: Born October 21, 1911, in Graudenz, Germany; son of Edwin and Regina (Cronheim) Blumenthal. *Education:* University of Berlin, A.B., 1933; University of California, Berkeley, M.A., 1943, Ph.D., 1949. *Home:* 171 Vose Ave., South Orange, N.J. 07079.

CAREER: Rutgers University, Newark, N.J., instructor, 1949-52, assistant professor, 1953-59, associate professor, 1959-63, professor of history, 1963-71, professor emeritus, 1971—, academic dean, 1969-71. *Military service:* U.S. Army, 1943-46; became sergeant. *Member:* American Historical Association, Organization of American Historians, Phi Beta Kappa. *Awards, honors:* Selman A. Waksman fellow in France, 1954-55; Rutgers University, alumni Outstanding Teacher award, 1960, faculty fellow, 1967-68.

WRITINGS: A Reappraisal of Franco-American Relations, 1830-1871, University of North Carolina Press, 1959; *France and the United States: Their Diplomatic Relations, 1789-1914,* University of North Carolina Press, 1970; *American and French Culture, 1800-1900: Interchanges in Art, Science, Literature, and Society,* Louisiana State University Press, 1975. Contributor of articles to *Pacific Historical Review, Journal of Negro History, Revue Politique et Parlementaire* (Paris), *Mississippi Valley Historical Review, Southern History, New England Quarterly, Southeastern Science Quarterly,* and *Annals* of American Academy of Political and Social Sciences.

AVOCATIONAL INTERESTS: Music.

* * *

BOARD, Joseph B(reckinridge), Jr. 1931-

PERSONAL: Born March 5, 1931, in Princeton, Ind.; son of Joseph Breckinridge (a miner) and Rachel (Unthank) Board; married Kjersti Danielson, December 31, 1955; children: Ian, Annika. *Education:* Indiana University, A.B. (with highest honors), 1953, J.D., 1958, Ph.D., 1962; Oxford University, B.A., 1955, M.A., 1961. *Politics:* Democrat. *Religion:* Episcopalian. *Home:* 15 Sunnyside Rd., Scotia, N.Y. 12302. *Office:* Department of Political Science, Union College, Schenectady, N.Y. 12308.

CAREER: Indiana University, Bloomington, lecturer in political science, 1958-59; Elmira College, Elmira, N.Y., assistant professor of political science, 1959-61; Cornell College,

Mount Vernon, Iowa, associate professor, 1961-64, professor of political science, 1964-65, chairman of department, 1961-65; Union College, Schenectady, N.Y., professor of political science and chairman of department, 1965—, Robert Porter Patterson Professor of Government, 1973—. Co-host, National Public Radio broadcast of Nobel prize ceremonies in Stockholm, Sweden, 1976. Member of Indiana Bar. Member of political science advisory committee, Fulbright-Hays Program; member of Woodrow Wilson Fellowship Regional (New York and Ontario) Selection Committee.

MEMBER: American Political Science Association, American Association of University Professors, American-Scandinavian Foundation, Schenectady County Historical Society (trustee), Schenectady Freedom Forum (member of board of directors), Phi Beta Kappa. *Awards, honors:* Rhodes scholar; Fulbright fellowship to Sweden; American Philosophical Society research grant, 1966-67.

WRITINGS: The Government and Politics of Sweden, Houghton, 1970. Contributor of articles and reviews to professional journals. Guest editor, *Scandinavian Review,* special issue on environmental protection in Scandinavia, 1976.

WORK IN PROGRESS: Research on systemic change in Swedish politics, on Swedish foreign policy, and on center parties.

SIDELIGHTS: Joseph B. Board, Jr. is competent in Swedish, German, French, Spanish, Portuguese, and Russian.

* * *

BOARDMAN, Charles C. 1932-

PERSONAL: Born October 18, 1932, in Duluth, Minn.; son of Howard Coit and Margaret (Tolen) Boardman; married Virginia Jones, April 3, 1953; married second wife, Erika Geberl (a college teacher), January 26, 1967; children: James C., C. Alan. *Education:* Virginia Commonwealth University, B.S., 1958; Rutgers University, M.Ed., 1964; University of Arkansas, Ed.D., 1969. *Politics:* Democrat. *Religion:* Unitarian Universalist. *Home:* 356 Shelton Woods Ct., Stone Mountain, Ga. 30088. *Office:* Department of Vocational Education, Georgia State University, 33 Gilmer St. S.E., Atlanta, Ga. 30303.

CAREER: Rider College, Trenton, N.J., instructor, 1961-65; Georgia Southwestern College, Americus, assistant professor of education, 1968-72; Georgia State University, Atlanta, associate professor of vocational and career development, 1972—. Interim director, Georgia Council on Economic Education, 1976-77. *Military service:* U.S. Navy, 1950-53. *Member:* American Council on Consumer Interests, National Association of Affiliated Economic Education Directors, National Business Education Association, Society of Consumer Affairs Professionals, Georgia Business Education Association, Georgia Council on the Social Studies, Phi Delta Kappa, Kappa Delta Pi, Delta Pi Epsilon.

WRITINGS: (With Rudyard K. Bent and H. H. Kronenberg) *Principles of Secondary Education,* 6th edition (Boardman was not associated with earlier editions), McGraw, 1970; (with Wilmer Maedke, Ross Lowe, and Charles Malouf) *Consumer Education,* Benziger, 1977. Contributor to education journals.

* * *

BOBINSKI, George S(ylvan) 1929-

PERSONAL: Born October 24, 1929, in Cleveland, Ohio;

son of Sylwian and Eugenia (Sarbiewski) Bobinski; married Mary Lillian Form (a librarian), February 20, 1953; children: George, Jr., Mary Anne. *Education:* Western Reserve University (now Case Western Reserve University), B.A., 1951, M.S.L.S., 1952; University of Michigan, M.A., 1960, Ph.D., 1966. *Home:* 40 Hamlin Sq., Williamsville, N.Y. 14221. *Office:* School of Information and Library Studies, State University of New York, Buffalo, N.Y. 14260.

CAREER: Cleveland Public Library, Cleveland, Ohio, reference assistant in Business Information Bureau, 1954-55; Royal Oak Public Library, Royal Oak, Mich., assistant director, 1955-59; State University of New York College at Cortland, director of libraries, 1960-67; University of Kentucky, School of Library Science, Lexington, professor and assistant dean, 1967-70; State University of New York at Buffalo, School of Information and Library Studies, Buffalo, professor and dean, 1970—. *Military service:* U.S. Army, 1952-54. *Member:* American Library Association (chairman, publishing committee), Association of American Library Schools, American Civil Liberties Union, New York Library Association, Beta Phi Mu. *Awards, honors:* Fulbright scholar in Poland, 1977.

WRITINGS: A Brief History of the Libraries of Western Reserve University, 1826-1952, University of Rochester Press, for Association of College and Reference Libraries, 1955; *Carnegie Libraries: Their History and Impact on American Public Library Development,* American Library Association, 1969; (contributor) Michael Harris, editor, *Reader in American Library History,* IHS-Microcard, 1971; (contributor) Mary B. Cassata and Herman L. Totten, *Administrative Aspects of Education for Librarianship,* Scarecrow, 1975; (executive editor) *Dictionary of American Library Biography,* Libraries Unlimited, 1977. Contributor to library journals.

AVOCATIONAL INTERESTS: Philately, hiking, travel.

*   *   *

BOCK, Harold I. 1939-
(Hal Bock)

PERSONAL: Born May 11, 1939, in New York, N.Y.; son of Milton and Sarah (Nieman) Bock; married Frances Elkin (a college instructor), November 4, 1961; children: Richard Allan. *Education:* New York University, B.S., 1961. *Home:* 396 Jackson Ave., Mineola, N.Y. 11501.

CAREER: New York Rangers Hockey Club, New York City, publicity writer, 1961-63; Associated Press, New York City, sports writer specializing in baseball, football, and hockey, 1963—. *Military service:* U.S. Army Reserve, 1961-67. *Member:* Professional Hockey Writers Association, Baseball Writers Association of America, Professional Football Writers Association of America, New York Hockey Writers Association (former president).

WRITINGS—Under name Hal Bock: (With Rod Gilbert and Stan Fischler) *Goal: My Life on Ice* (youth book), Hawthorn, 1968; (editor with Zander Hollander) *The Complete Encyclopedia of Ice Hockey,* Prentice-Hall, 1970; *Dynamite on Ice: The Bobby Orr Story,* Scholastic Book Services, 1972; *Save!: Hockey's Brave Goalies,* Avon, 1974; (with Bill Chadwick) *The Big Whistle,* Hawthorn, 1974. Contributor to *Encyclopedia Americana* and to sports magazines.

BIOGRAPHICAL/CRITICAL SOURCES: Saturday Review, April 19, 1969.

BOEGNER, Marc 1881-1970

February 21, 1881—December 20, 1970; French Protestant minister and author. Obituaries: *Christian Century,* January 6, 1971.

*   *   *

BOICE, James Montgomery 1938-

PERSONAL: Born July 7, 1938, in Pittsburgh, Pa.; son of G. Newton (an orthopedic surgeon) and Jean (Shick) Boice; married Linda Ann McNamara, June 9, 1962; children: Elizabeth Anne, Heather Louise, Jennifer Sue. *Education:* Harvard University, AB. (with high honors), 1960; Princeton Theological Seminary, B.D., 1963; University of Basel, D.Theol. (insigni cum laude), 1966. *Home:* 1827 Delancey Pl., Philadelphia, Pa. 19103. *Office:* Tenth Presbyterian Church, 1700 Spruce St., Philadelphia, Pa. 19103.

CAREER: Licensed in the Presbytery of Pittsburgh, Pa., 1963; *Christianity Today,* Washington, D.C., member of editorial staff, summers, 1962, 1963, assistant editor, 1966-68; Tenth Presbyterian Church, Philadelphia, Pa., pastor, 1968—. Speaker on "The Bible Study Hour" radio program originating in Philadelphia, 1969—.

WRITINGS—All published by Zondervan, except as indicated: *Witness and Revelation in the Gospel of John,* 1970; *Philippians: An Expositional Commentary,* 1971; *The Sermon on the Mount,* 1972; *How to Really Live It Up,* 1973; *How God Can Use Nobodies,* Victor, 1974; *The Last and Future World,* 1974; *The Gospel of John,* Volume I, 1975, Volume II, 1976, Volume III, 1977; (contributor) Frank E. Gaebelin, editor, *Expositor's Bible Commentary,* 1976; (editor) *Our Sovereign God,* Baker, 1977; *Jonah: The Prophet Who Ran Away,* Victor, 1977; *God the Creator,* Intervarsity Press, 1977. Contributor to religious periodicals.

WORK IN PROGRESS: Two additional volumes of *The Gospel of John.*

BIOGRAPHICAL/CRITICAL SOURCES: Time, December 26, 1969.

*   *   *

BOK, Cary W(illiam) 1905-1970

January 25, 1905—December 29, 1970; American publisher. Obituaries: *New York Times,* December 30, 1970.

*   *   *

BOLAND, Lillian C(anon) 1919-

PERSONAL: Born December 19, 1919, in Hinton, Okla.; daughter of Charles G. (a realtor) and Ruth (Lowry) Canon; married John L. Boland, Jr. (director of Oklahoma Psychological and Educational Center); children: Ann C., Michael C. *Education:* Oklahoma College for Women (now Oklahoma College of Liberal Arts), B.A., 1940; University of Michigan, M.A., 1949; further courses at Greeley College of Education, Rhode Island College, Oklahoma City University, and Central State University. *Politics:* Democrat. *Religion:* Unitarian. *Home:* 6703 Avondale, Oklahoma City, Okla. 73116. *Office:* Department of Speech, Central State University, Edmond, Okla. 73034.

CAREER: Dock Street Theatre, Charleston, S.C., acting apprentice, 1941-42; Martin Hall Institute for Voice Disorders, Bristol, R.I., intern, 1944-46; University of Michigan, Ann Arbor, assistant director of dysphasia division of speech clinic, 1947-49; Oklahoma City (Okla.) public schools, teacher of special class, 1949-51; Central State University, Edmond, Okla., lecturer in speech, 1958—. Commercial announcer, television station WKY, Edmond, 1969-70. *Member:* Oklahoma Education Association, Oklahoma Speech and Hearing Association, Zeta Phi Eta, Mummers.

WRITINGS: A Guide to Speech Improvement with the Mike and Cindy Stories (with pupil's workbook and set of sound cards), Steck, 1969; (editor with Joyce Turley) *The Zeta Phi Eta "As You Like It Cookbook,"* Oklahoma University Press, 1973.

SIDELIGHTS: Lillian C. Boland told *CA:* "Our books were developed from a classroom project in a speech methods and materials class at Central State University.... I am most interested in motivating teachers to try 'speech improvement' time. Would like to organize a workshop in this area...."

* * *

BOND, Geoffrey 1924-

PERSONAL: Born May 8, 1924, in Norfolk, England; son of Bertie Henry and Eunice May (Linton) Bond; married Joan Allen, August 20, 1949; children: Hilary Jane, Elizabeth, Richard Alan. *Education:* Attended King's College, London, 1941-42; Redland College, Bristol, Teacher's Certificate, 1950; Leicester School of Education, Diploma in the Sociology and Psychology of Education, 1969. *Home:* 16 College Close, Coltishall, Norfolk, England.

CAREER: Framingham Earl Secondary School, Norwich, Norfolk, England, headmaster, 1959-74.

WRITINGS—Books for young people, except as noted: *Echoes from Blakeney,* Glaven Press, 1949; *Portrait of Cromer,* Glaven Press, 1949; (editor) *One World,* University of London Press, Volume I: *People and Animals: An Anthology of Travel Writing,* 1968, Volume II: *The Face of the World: An Anthology of Travel Writing,* 1968. Contributor to *Times Educational Supplement.* Editor of "Life and Adventure" series, six books, Blackie & Son, 1948, and "The Wayfarer" series, five books, with L. F. W. White, Blackie & Son, 1957-63.

AVOCATIONAL INTERESTS: Photography, collecting watercolor drawings and contemporary oil paintings.

* * *

BOND, Ruskin 1934-

PERSONAL: Born May 19, 1934, in Kasauli, India; son of Aubrey Alexander (in Royal Air Force) and Edith (Clerke) Bond. *Education:* Attended Bishop Cotton School, Simla, India, 1943-50. *Home:* Maplewood Lodge, Bala Hissar, Mussoorie, Uttar Pradesh, India.

CAREER: Worked at one period for Cooperative for American Relief Everywhere (CARE), but has been a full-time writer since the age of twenty-two. *Awards, honors:* John Llewellyn Rhys Memorial Prize for the most memorable work of 1957 by a writer under thirty, for *The Room on the Roof.*

WRITINGS: The Room on the Roof (novel), Deutsch, 1956, Coward, 1957; *The Neighbour's Wife and Other Stories,* Higginbotham (Madras), 1967; *Grandfather's Private Zoo,* India Book House, 1967; *Panther's Moon,* Random House, 1969; *The Last Tiger,* Publications Division (New Delhi), 1970; *Angry River,* Hamish Hamilton, 1972; *The Blue Umbrella,* Hamish Hamilton, 1974. Stories included in *World's Best Contemporary Stories,* Ace Books, and *Young Winter's Tales 1970,* Macmillan. Contributor of short stories and articles to *Reader's Digest, Christian Science Monitor, Lady, Cricket, Short Story International, New Renaissance, Blackwood's, Statesman,* and other publications.

WORK IN PROGRESS: A novel; a children's book.

SIDELIGHTS: All of Ruskin Bond's books, to date, have dealt with life in India—*The Room on the Roof,* about growing up in a changing India, *The Last Tiger,* about the disappearance of wild life in India, and *Panther's Moon,* about a remote Himalayan village. "My interests (children, mountains, birds, trees, wild flowers) are embodied in these and other writings.... Once you have lived with the mountains, you belong to them, and must come back again and again. There is no escape," Bond says. He is an Indian national.

* * *

BONDI, Joseph C. 1936-

PERSONAL: Born August 15, 1936, in Tampa, Fla.; son of Joseph C. (a teacher) and Virginia (Colie) Bondi; married Patsy Hammer (a teacher), August 6, 1960; children: Pamela Jo, Beth Jana, Bradley Joseph. *Education:* University of Florida, B.S., 1958, M.Ed., 1964, Ed.D., 1968. *Politics:* Democrat. *Religion:* Presbyterian. *Home:* 207 Bannockburn, Temple Terrace, Fla. 33617. *Office:* Department of Education, University of South Florida, Tampa, Fla. 33620.

CAREER: University of South Florida, Tampa, assistant professor of education, 1965—. Elected mayor of Temple Terrace, Fla., 1974, re-elected, 1976. Member, Temple Terrace City Council. *Military service:* U.S. Naval Reserve, 1955-63. *Member:* Association for Supervision and Curriculum Development, American Educational Research Association, National Education Association, John Dewey Society, Florida Educational Research Association, Florida Association for Supervision and Curriculum Development (member of board of directors; vice-president; president), Phi Delta Kappa, Kappa Delta Pi.

WRITINGS: (Editor with Glen Hass and Kim Wiles) *Readings in Curriculum,* Allyn & Bacon, 1970; *Developing Middle Schools: A Guidebook,* MSS Information, 1972. Also author, with Glen Hass and Jon Wiles, of *Curriculum Planning,* and, with Wiles, of *Curriculum Development: A Guide to Practice.* Contributor to education journals.

* * *

BOORMAN, Scott A(rcher) 1949-

PERSONAL: Born February 1, 1949, in Peking, China; son of Howard Lyon (a professor) and Margaret (Echlin) Boorman. *Education:* Harvard University, B.A., 1970. *Office:* Department of Government, University of Pennsylvania, Philadelphia, Pa. 19104.

CAREER: Harvard University, Cambridge, Mass., junior fellow, Society of Fellows, beginning 1970; currently affiliated with department of government, University of Pennsylvania, Philadelphia. *Member:* American Mathematical Society, Association for Symbolic Logic, Institute for Strategic Studies (London).

WRITINGS: The Protracted Game: A Wei-ch'i Interpretation of Maoist Revolutionary Strategy, Oxford University Press, 1969.

WORK IN PROGRESS: Mathematical models in social and behavioral science; comparative strategic studies; Chinese strategy.

BIOGRAPHICAL/CRITICAL SOURCES: National Review, February 10, 1970.†

* * *

BOREA, Phyllis Gilbert 1924-

PERSONAL: Born October 12, 1924; daughter of Clinton W. (a newspaperman) and Pauline (a U.S. Government executive; maiden name, Clarke) Gilbert; married Raimondo Borea (a photographer), 1951; children: Roberto, Carla. *Education:* Attended Bryn Mawr College, 1942-44, Barnard College, 1944-45, New School for Social Research, 1962-66, and School of Visual Arts, 1966-68. *Home and office:* 245 West 104th St., New York, N.Y. 10025. *Agent:* John Meyer, 141 East 55th St., New York, N.Y. 10022.

CAREER: Editorial assistant, Dell Publishing Co., New York City, during the 1940's; Raimondo Borea Photography, New York City, associate, 1955—. *Member:* American Society of Picture Professionals.

WRITINGS: (With husband, Raimondo Borea) *First Thing in the Morning* (based on children's television photo story originally shown on NBC's "Today Show"), Cowles, 1970; (illustrator with R. Borea) Catherine Stern and Margaret B. Stern, *Children Discover Arithmetic,* revised edition (the Boreas were not associated with earlier editions), Harper, 1971; (with R. Borea) *Tino and Jamie,* Macmillan, 1972; (contributor with R. Borea) Margaret McElderry, *Seymour: A Gibbon,* Atheneum, 1973. Contributor to *Graphics Today, Popular Photography, Monday Morning,* and *Lady's Circle.* Editor, *American Society of Picture Professionals Newsletter,* 1971—.

SIDELIGHTS: Phyllis Borea lived and worked in Italy for three years.

* * *

BORNSTEIN, George (Jay) 1941-

PERSONAL: Born August 25, 1941, in St. Louis, Mo.; son of Harry and Celia (Price) Bornstein; married Christine Verzar (an art historian), December 21, 1967; children: Benjamin Jay. *Education:* Harvard University, B.A., 1963; Princeton University, Ph.D., 1966. *Office:* Department of English, University of Michigan, Ann Arbor, Mich. 48104.

CAREER: Massachusetts Institute of Technology, Cambridge, assistant professor of English, 1966-69; Rutgers University, New Brunswick, N.J., assistant professor of English, 1969-70; University of Michigan, Ann Arbor, associate professor, 1970-75, professor of English, 1975—. *Member:* Modern Language Association of America, American Association of University Professors, Phi Beta Kappa. *Awards, honors:* Woodrow Wilson fellowship, 1963; American Council of Learned Societies fellowship, 1972-73; Rackham fellowship, 1974.

WRITINGS: Yeats and Shelley, University of Chicago Press, 1970; (co-author) *British Periodicals of the 18th and 19th Centuries,* University Microfilm, 1972; (co-author) *Two Centuries of British Periodicals,* University Microfilm, 1974; *Transformation of Romanticism in Yeats, Eliot, and Stevens,* University of Chicago Press, 1976; (editor) *Romantic and Modern: Revaluations of Literary Tradition,* University of Pittsburgh Press, 1977. Contributor to literature journals.

WORK IN PROGRESS: The Postromantic Conciousness of Ezra Pound.

AVOCATIONAL INTERESTS: Travel, tennis.

BOROFF, David 1917-1965

March 28, 1917—May 16, 1965; American educator and critic. Obituaries: *New York Times,* May 16, 1965; *Publishers' Weekly,* May 31, 1965. (See index for *CA* sketch)

* * *

BORRELLO, Alfred 1931-

PERSONAL: Born January 17, 1931, in Brooklyn, N.Y.; son of Philip (a tailor) and Mary (Briglio) Borrello. *Education:* St. John's University, Jamaica, N.Y., B.A., 1952, Ph.D., 1965; New York University, M.A., 1956. *Home:* 280 Humboldt St., Brooklyn, N.Y. 11206. *Office:* Department of English, Kingsborough Community College of the City University of New York, Sheepshead Bay, Brooklyn, N.Y. 11235.

CAREER: Mercer County Community College, Trenton, N.J., chairman of English department and chairman of Division of Liberal Arts, 1967-69; Kingsborough Community College of the City University of New York, Brooklyn, 1969—, began as associate professor, currently professor of English. *Military service:* U.S. Army, 1953-55.

WRITINGS: (Editor) *A Concordance of the Poetry in English of Gerard Manley Hopkins,* Scarecrow, 1969; (compiler) *An E. M. Forster Dictionary,* Scarecrow, 1971; *An E. M. Forster Glossary,* Scarecrow, 1972; *H. G. Wells: Author in Agony,* University of Southern Illinois Press, 1972; *E. M. Forster: An Annotated Bibliography of Secondary Materials,* Scarecrow, 1973; *Gabriel Fielding,* Twayne, 1974. His annotated bibliography of H. G. Wells appeared in three parts in *English Literature in Transition,* 1968-70. Associate editor of *Evelyn Waugh Newsletter* and *School Press Review;* research consultant, *English Literature in Transition.*

WORK IN PROGRESS: Graham Greene: An Annotated Bibliography of Secondary Materials.

SIDELIGHTS: While Alfred Borrello has published only in the field of English literature, he would like to write mystery novels ("the two I have begun have never gone beyond the third chapter," he admits). *Avocational interests:* Painting (house and Sunday variety), music (especially opera), collecting antiques and paintings on a modest scale.

* * *

BORTON, John C., Jr. 1938-
(Terry Borton)

PERSONAL: Born August 25, 1938, in Washington, D.C.; married, June 18, 1960; wife's name, Deborah H.; children: Lynn, Mark. *Education:* Amherst College, B.A. (cum laude), 1960; University of California, Berkeley, M.A., 1962, General Teaching Certificate, 1964; Temple University, graduate study, 1964; Harvard University, Ed.D., 1970. *Home:* 59 Westview St., Philadelphia, Pa. *Office:* Time for Learning Project, Board of Education, Philadelphia, Pa.

CAREER: Berkeley (Calif.) Unified School District, assistant director of school resource volunteers, 1962-63; high school teacher of English in Richmond, Calif., 1963-66; Board of Education, Philadelphia, Pa., consultant to Curriculum Office, 1966-67, acting director of Affective Education Project, 1970-71, director of special projects, 1971—. Consultant to U.S. Office of Education and to Ford, Carnegie, and other foundations. *Member:* Phi Delta Kappa.

WRITINGS—Under name Terry Borton: *Herman Melville: The Philosophical Implications of Literary Techniques* in *"Moby Dick"* (booklet), Amherst College Press, 1960; (with Norman Newberg) *Education for Students Concerns* (curriculum guide), Philadelphia Public Schools, 1969; *Reach, Touch and Teach: Student Concerns and Process Education,* McGraw, 1970; (contributor) Mario Fantini and Gerald Weinstein, editors, *Toward Humanistic Education: A Curriculum of Affect,* Praeger, 1970. Contributor to *Harvard Educational Review, Saturday Review, Learning,* and other periodicals.

Educational films: (With James Morrow and Oliver Nuse) "Prelude," 1966; (with Morrow) "A Lot of Undoing to Do," 1967; (with Morrow) "Hard to Hang On To," 1968. Also has done tapes and two recordings, "Poetry, Like It or Not," and (with Norman Newberg and Joan Newberg) "All's Fair in Love and War," both issued by Educational Activities, Inc.

WORK IN PROGRESS: Development of theory and practice of "concomitant instruction," designed for out-of-classroom use.

AVOCATIONAL INTERESTS: Camping, skiing, travel, sculpture, poetry, carpentry.

* * *

BOSCH, William Joseph 1928-

PERSONAL: Born September 28, 1928, in Milwaukee, Wis.; son of Aloysius William (a maltster) and Anne (Gerstner) Bosch. *Education:* Loyola University, Chicago, Ill., A.B., 1952, Ph.L., 1954, A.M., 1956; Woodstock College, Th.L., 1961; University of North Carolina, Ph.D., 1966. *Home:* 317 Springfield Rd., Syracuse, N.Y. 13214. *Office:* Department of History, LeMoyne College, Syracuse, N.Y. 13214.

CAREER: Ordained priest; member of the Society of Jesus (Jesuits). University of North Carolina, Chapel Hill, instructor in modern civilization, 1964-66; LeMoyne College, Syracuse, N.Y., instructor, 1966-67, assistant professor, 1967-70, associate professor of history, 1971—. *Member:* American Historical Association, American Studies Association, Southern Historical Association, Jesuit Historical Association.

WRITINGS: Judgment on Nuremberg: American Attitudes toward the Major German War-Crime Trials, University of North Carolina Press, 1970.

WORK IN PROGRESS: Research on changing American attitudes toward science and technology.

* * *

BOULTON, James T(hompson) 1924-

PERSONAL: Born February 17, 1924, in Pickering, Yorkshire, England; son of Harry (a builder) and Annie M. P. (Thompson) Boulton; married Margaret H. Leary, August 6, 1948; children: Andrew J. M., Helen E. *Education:* University of Durham, B.A. (first class honors), 1948, Diploma in Education, 1949; Lincoln College, Oxford, B.Litt., 1952; University of Nottingham, Ph.D., 1960. *Office:* University of Birmingham, P.O. Box 363, Birmingham B15 2TT, England.

CAREER: University of Nottingham, Nottingham, England, assistant lecturer, 1951-53, lecturer, 1953-62, senior lecturer, 1962-63, reader in English, 1963-64, professor of English literature, 1964-75; University of Birmingham, Birmingham, England, professor of English studies and head of department, 1975—. John Cranford Adams Professor of

English, Hofstra University, Hempstead, N.Y., 1967. Member of executive committee, Anglo-American Associates, New York, 1968-75. *Military service:* Royal Air Force, pilot, 1943-46. *Member:* Royal Society of Literature (fellow), Royal Historical Society (fellow).

WRITINGS: (Editor) Edmund Burke, *Philosophical Enquiry into the ... Sublime and Beautiful,* Routledge & Kegan Paul, 1958, 2nd edition, 1968, University of Notre Dame Press, 1968; (editor) C. F. G. Masterman, *The Condition of England,* Methuen, 1960; *The Language of Politics in the Age of Wilkes and Burke,* Routledge & Kegan Paul, 1963, Greenwood Press, 1975; (editor) John Dryden, *Of Dramatick Poesie,* Oxford University Press, 1964; *Daniel Defoe,* Batsford, 1965; (editor with James Kinsley) *English Satiric Poetry: Dryden to Byron,* E. J. Arnold, 1966; (editor and author of introduction and notes) *Lawrence in Love: Letters to Louie Burrows,* University of Nottingham Press, 1968, 2nd edition, 1969, Southern Illinois University Press, 1969; (author of introduction) Daniel Defoe, *Memoirs of an English Officer,* Gollancz, 1970; *Samuel Johnson,* Routledge & Kegan Paul, 1971; (author of introduction) D. H. Lawrence, *Movements in European History,* Oxford University Press, 1971.

Contributor: *The Familiar Letter in the Eighteenth Century,* University of Kansas Press, 1966; *Renaissance and Modern Essays,* Routledge & Kegan Paul, 1966; *Essays on Rhetorical Criticism,* Random House, 1968. Contributor of articles and reviews to *Modern Drama, Essays in Criticism,* and other journals. Editor, *Renaissance and Modern Studies* (University of Nottingham), 1969-75; associate editor, *Studies in Burke and His Time* (Texas Tech University).

WORK IN PROGRESS: Editing *The Letters of D. H. Lawrence* and *The Works of D. H. Lawrence,* for Cambridge University Press.

BIOGRAPHICAL/CRITICAL SOURCES: New Statesman, January 24, 1969; *New York Times Book Review,* March 9, 1969; *New Yorker,* May 10, 1969; *London Magazine,* June, 1969; *Kenyon Review,* Volume XXXI, number 3, 1969.

* * *

BOUMAN, Pieter M(arinus) 1938-

PERSONAL: Born July 9, 1938, in Gent, Belgium; son of Jan-Arie (a bookkeeper) and Maria-Jozina (Moens) Bouman; married Jannetje Meijers (a secretary), October 26, 1961 (separated); children: Anne-Marie, Irene, Peter. *Education:* Protestant Theological Faculty, Brussels, Licencie in Protestant Theology, 1961; Protestant Theological Faculty, Paris, and University of Paris, Sorbonne, Institut des Hautes Etudes Religieuses, student, 1961-62. *Politics:* Socialist-Marxist. *Religion:* Reformed. *Office:* Ecumenical Centre, World Council of Churches, 150 Route de Ferney, CH-1211, Geneva, Switzerland.

CAREER: Ecumenical youth secretary for Belgium, Federation des Eglises Protestantes de Belgique, 1962-65; World Council of Churches, Geneva, Switzerland, and United Nations Food and Agriculture Organization, Rome, Italy, member of staff of Freedom from Hunger Campaign and Young World Program, 1965-68; general secretary, Ecumenical Youth Council for Europe, 1968-73; World Council of Churches, Geneva, Europe secretary, Programme Unit on Justice and Service, 1973—. Staff officer for adult education, Stichting Lodewyk de Raet. *Member:* Sjaloom-Group (founding member).

WRITINGS: Can the World Share the Wealth?, Friendship, 1969; Die Satten und die Habenichtse, Burckhardthaus (West Germany), 1970. Contributor to Diepgang, Dux, Op Vrije Voeten, Risk, and other ecumenical reviews.

WORK IN PROGRESS: Researching questions on church and society, development of education, and east-west problems.

SIDELIGHTS: Pieter M. Bouman has traveled in the Middle East, Africa, eastern and western Europe, United States, Canada, and Latin America.

* * *

BOUMAN, Walter Richard 1929-

PERSONAL: Born July 9, 1929, in Springfield, Minn.; son of Walter Herman (a clergyman) and Cordelia (Haar) Bouman; married Janet Ann Gundermann, August 17, 1957; children: Andrew, Lukas, Gregory. Education: Concordia Junior College, Fort Wayne, Diploma (cum laude), 1948; Union Theological Seminary, New York, further study, 1952-53; Concordia Seminary, St. Louis, B.D., 1954; University of Heidelberg, Dr.theol., 1963. Home: 1360 Millerdale Rd., Columbus, Ohio 43209. Office: Department of Theology, Lutheran Theological Seminary, Columbus, Ohio 43209.

CAREER: Pastor of Lutheran churches in Chatfield, Minn., 1956-60, and in Albany, N.Y., 1960-63; Concordia Teachers College, River Forest, Ill., assistant professor, 1963-67, associate professor of theology, 1967-71; Lutheran Theological Seminary, Columbus, Ohio, professor of systematic theology, 1971—. Visiting summer professor, Concordia Seminary, St. Louis, 1964, 1965; lecturer, Rosary College, River Forest, 1967-70; part-time instructor, Loyola University, Chicago, 1971. Member: American Society for Reformation Research, American Theological Society, American Society of Church History, American Academy of Religion, Lutheran Education Association, Lutheran Academy for Scholarship. Awards, honors: Fulbright scholar at University of Heidelberg, 1954-56.

WRITINGS: (Translator) Max Lackmann, The Augsburg Confession and Catholic Unity, Herder & Herder, 1963; Christianity American Style, Pflaum, 1970. Contributor to Lutheran Education Yearbook and Encyclopedia of the Lutheran Church, both 1965; contributor of articles and reviews to religious journals. Contributing editor, Lutheran Forum; member of editorial council, Dialog.

* * *

BOURKE-WHITE, Margaret 1904-1971

June 14, 1904—August 27, 1971; American photographer, journalist, and author of travel books. Obituaries: New York Times, August 28, 1971; Washington Post, August 28, 1971; Time, September 6, 1971; Saturday Review, September 11, 1971. (See index for CA sketch)

* * *

BOURRICAUD, Francois 1922-

PERSONAL: Born January 28, 1922, in St. Martin du Bois, France; son of Andre R. and Simone (Parraud) Bourricaud. Home: 41 Rue des Martyrs, Paris 9, France. Agent: Agence Pierre Quet, 20 Rue de la Michodiere, Paris 9, France. Office: Department of Sociology, University of Paris, Paris 5, France.

CAREER: Has taught at universities in Paris, Bordeaux,

Nanterre, and elsewhere in France; University of Paris, Paris, France, professor of sociology, 1968—.

WRITINGS: (Editor) Elements pour une sociologie de Cachon, Plon, 1955; Esquisse d'une theorie de l'autorite, Plon, 1961, 2nd edition, 1970; Changements a Puno: Etude de sociologie andine, Institut des Hautes Etudes de l'-Amerique Latine, University of Paris, 1962; Pouvoir et societe dans le Perou contemporain, A. Colin, 1967, translation by Paul Stevenson published as Power and Society in Contemporary Peru, Praeger, 1970; Universites a la derive, Stock, 1971; (with others) Intellectuals and Change, American Academy of Arts and Sciences, 1972.†

* * *

BOUSSARD, Jacques Marie 1910-

PERSONAL: Born April 24, 1910, in Paris, France; son of Leon and Germaine (Le Gambier) Boussard; married Renee Morette, 1936; children: Jean-Marc, Jean-Luc, Christine (Mrs. Christian Rey), Jean-Mathieu. Education: Studied at Facultes Catholiques d'Angers, 1927-28, Ecole Nationale des Chartes and Ecole Pratique des Hautes Etudes, 1928-32, King's College, London, 1933-34, and University of Paris, 1934-35; qualified as archiviste-paleographe, 1932; Ecole Pratique des Hautes Etudes, Eleve diplome, 1938. Home: 7 boulevard Saint-Germain, Paris 5, France.

CAREER: Librarian of the city of Orleans, France, 1935-43; National Library, Paris, France, librarian, 1943-50, curator, Library of the Arsenal (library specializing in literature and the theater), 1950-59, curator in charge, Library of the Arsenal, 1959-60; University of Poitiers, Faculty of Letters and Human Sciences, Poitiers, France, lecturer, 1960-63, professor of auxiliary sciences of medieval history, 1963-69; Ecole Pratique des Hautes Etudes, Paris, faculty member of historical and philological sciences division, 1965—. Member, Comite des Travaux historiques et scientifiques, and Commission internationale de Diplomatique. Military service: French Army, World War II; received Croix de guerre. Member: Societe des Antiquaires de France (president, 1970). Awards, honors: Laureate of the Institute of France (second place, Prix Gobert of the Academie des Inscriptions et Belles-Lettres, 1939, and first place, Prix Gobert, 1957; the prize is given for historical works).

WRITINGS: Le Comte d'Anjou sous Henri Plantegenet et ses fils (1151-1204), H. Champion, 1938; (contributor) Melanges Felix Grat, [Paris], 1946; Les Mercenaires au XIIe siecle (booklet), [Paris], 1947; (contributor) Melanges Louis Halphen, Presses Universitaires de France, 1951; (editor and annotator with Fernand Aubert and Henri Meylan) Un Premier recueil de poesies latines de Theodore de Beze, Droz (Geneva), 1954; (contributor) Histoire de France, Larousse, 1954; (contributor) Recueil de travaux offert a M. Clovis Brunel, Societe de l'Ecole des Chartes, 1955; Le gouvernement d'Henri II Plantegenet, Librairie d'Argences, 1956; (editor and annotator) Historia pontificum et comitum Engolismensium, Librairie d'Argences, 1957; Atlas historique et culturel de la France, Elsevier, 1957; (contributor) Histoire des institutions francaises au moyen age, Presses Universitaires de France, 1957.

Carte archeologique de la Gaule romaine, Presses Universitaires de France, 1960; (contributor) Melanges Frantz Calot, Librairie d'Argences, 1960; La France historique et culturelle, Meddens, 1965; (with J. Monicat) Recueil des actes de Philippe Auguste, roi de France, Volume III, Academie des Inscriptions et Belles-Lettres, 1966; (contributor) Melanges Rene Crozet, Societe d'Etudes Medievales

(Poitiers), 1966; *Charlemagne et son temps,* Hachette, 1968, translation by Frances Partridge published as *The Civilization of Charlemagne,* McGraw, 1968; (editor) *Ferdinand Lot, Naissance de la France,* Fayard, 1970; (contributor) *Melanges E.-R. Labande,* C.E.S.C.M. (Poitiers), 1974; (contributor) *Droit prive et institutions regionales: Etudes historiques offertes a Jean Yver,* Presses Universitaires de France, 1976; *Paris, de la fin du siege de 885-886 a la mort de Philippe Auguste,* Hachette, 1976. Contributor to *Encyclopedie de la Pleiade, Encyclopaedia Universalis,* and to library annals and historical journals.

WORK IN PROGRESS: Further research in the history of the late Middle Ages (ninth-to-eleventh centuries) in France and England.

* * *

BOVIS, H(enry) Eugene 1928-

PERSONAL: Born March 31, 1928, in Kenansville, Fla.; son of Henry P. and Vassie (Wright) Bovis; married Beatrice Wilfong, June 24, 1958; children: Henry E., Jr. *Education:* University of Florida, B.A. (cum laude), 1948, M.A., 1950; University of Grenoble, Certificats d'etudes francaises, 1951; American University, Ph.D., 1968. *Home:* 621 Avocado St., St. Cloud, Fla. 32769. *Office:* c/o American Embassy, Jidda, Department of State, Washington, D.C. 20521.

CAREER: U.S. Department of State, Foreign Service officer, 1956—, with assignments in Beirut, Tel Aviv, Haifa, and then Cairo, 1956-71, coordinator of political studies, Foreign Service Institute, 1973-77, counselor for political affairs, American Embassy, Jidda, 1977—. Visiting lecturer, U.S. Air Force Academy, Colorado Springs, Colo., 1971-73. *Member:* Middle East Institute, Middle East Studies Association, Phi Beta Kappa.

WRITINGS: The Jerusalem Question 1917-1968, Stanford University Press, 1971.

* * *

BOWDEN, J(ocelyn) J(ean) 1927-

PERSONAL: Born June 20, 1927, in El Paso, Tex.; son of Jocelyn Kennedy and Ruth (Holmes) Bowden; married Celia Zant; children: Rebecca, Jay, Janet, LaDonna, Scott, Cynthia, Van, Kent. *Education:* College of Mines and Metallurgy (now University of Texas at El Paso), B.A., 1948; University of Texas, LL.B., 1951; Texas Western University, M.A., 1952; Southern Methodist University, LL.M., 1969.

CAREER: Continental Oil Co., Houston, Tex., counsel, 1960—. Vice-President, Conoco Houston Federal Credit Union. *Military service:* U.S. Naval Reserve, 1945-46. *Member:* Phi Alpha Delta, Phi Alpha Theta.

WRITINGS: Private Land Claims in the Southwest, privately printed, 1969; *The Ponce de Leon Land Grant,* Texas Western Press, 1969; *Spanish and Mexican Land Grants in the Chihuahuan Acquisition,* Texas Western Press, 1971; *The Ascarate Grant,* Garland Publishing, 1974; *Surveying the Texas and Pacific Land Grant West of the Pecos River,* Texas Western Press, 1975.†

* * *

BOWEN, Zack (Rhollie) 1934-

PERSONAL: Born August 10, 1934, in Philadelphia, Pa.; son of Zack R. (an automobile dealer) and Mary (a singer;

maiden name, Upton) Bowen; married Patricia Lingsch (a teacher), June 23, 1957; children: Zack, Daniel, Patricia. *Education:* University of Pennsylvania, B.A., 1956; Temple University, M.A., 1960; State University of New York at Buffalo, Ph.D., 1964. *Home address:* Box 178, Buttonwood Rd., Landenburg, Pa. 19350. *Office:* Department of English, University of Delaware, Newark, Del. 19711.

CAREER: Temple University, Philadelphia, Pa., instructor, 1958-60; State University of New York College at Fredonia, assistant professor of English, 1960-64; State University of New York at Binghamton, 1964-76, began as assistant professor, became Distinguished Teaching Professor and chairman of English department; University of Delaware, Newark, professor of English and chairman of department, 1976—. Lecturer in poetry, drama, and English research, Philadelphia Museum College of Art, 1960; producer-director of works by James Joyce for Folkway Records, *Lestrygonians,* 1961, *Calypso,* 1963, *Lotus Eaters,* 1963, *Hades,* 1964, and *Sirens,* 1965. *Member:* Modern Language Association, James Joyce Society.

WRITINGS: Padraic Colum: A Biographical-Critical Introduction, preface by Harry T. Moore, Southern Illinois University Press, 1970; *Mary Lavin,* Bucknell University Press, 1975; *Musical Allusions in the Woods of James Joyce: Early Poetry through "Ulysses,"* State University of New York Press, 1975. Contributor of articles and essays to *Literary Monographs, Literature and Psychology, James Joyce Quarterly,* and *Eire-Ireland.*

WORK IN PROGRESS: A full-length study of the works of John Barth; a study of the music in Huxley's *Point Counter Point.*

* * *

BOWERS, C. A. 1935-

PERSONAL: Born June 4, 1935, in Portland, Ore.; married; wife's name, Mary Katharine; children: Elizabeth Adelle, Ann Elise. *Education:* Portland State College (now University), B.S., 1958; University of California, Ph.D., 1962. *Politics:* Democrat. *Home:* 250 East 37th, Eugene, Ore. *Office:* Department of Educational Foundations, University of Oregon, Eugene, Ore. 97403.

CAREER: University of Saskatchewan, Saskatoon, Saskatchewan, 1962-67, began as assistant professor, became associate professor; University of Oregon, Eugene, associate professor and chairman of department of educational foundations, 1967—.

WRITINGS: The Progressive Educator and the Depression: The Radical Years, Random House, 1969; (editor with Ian Housego and Doris Dyke) *Education and Social Policy: Local Control of Education,* Random House, 1970; *Cultural Literacy for Freedom,* Elan, 1974.

AVOCATIONAL INTERESTS: Competitive sailboat racing, 5-0-5 class.

BIOGRAPHICAL/CRITICAL SOURCES: Saturday Review, June 21, 1969.

* * *

BOWRA, (Cecil) Maurice 1898-1971

April 8, 1898—July 4, 1971; Chinese-born English authority on classical Greek literature. Obituaries: *New York Times,* July 5, 1971; *Washington Post,* July 5, 1971; *Publishers' Weekly,* August 2, 1971; *Antiquarian Bookman,* August 2-9, 1971. (See index for *CA* sketch)

BOYD, Waldo T. 1918-
(Ted Andersen, Robert Parker)

PERSONAL: Born February 4, 1918, in Wiergor Township, Wis.; son of Walter S. (a farmer) and Mary S. (Reid) Boyd; married Anna B. Anker (an accountant and bookkeeper), July 19, 1941; children: Tahirih Ann (Mrs. Lowell Bell), Anna Ruhiyyih (Mrs. John Vasquez). *Education:* Attended high school in West Des Moines, Iowa. *Politics:* None. *Religion:* Baha'i. *Address:* P.O. Box 86, Geyserville, Calif. 95441. *Agent:* Larry Sternig Literary Agency, 742 Robertson St., Milwaukee, Wis. 53213.

CAREER: U.S. Navy, 1936-40, 1941-45, served as warrant radio electrician (radar) in South Pacific during World War II; teacher of electronics at technical high school in Des Moines, Iowa, 1945-47; Philco Corp., field electronics engineer in Germany, 1948-50; Dianetic Foundation, Wichita, Kan., director of public relations and publications, 1950-53; Aerojet-General Corp., Sacramento, Calif., manager of publications department, 1956-65; Baha'i School, Geyserville, Calif., manager, 1967-71. Holds Federal Communications Commission radiotelephone operator's license, first class, and is a licensed radio amateur, advanced class. *Member:* Authors League of America, Science Fiction Writers of America, California Writer's Club (president, 1966).

WRITINGS: Your Career in the Aerospace Industry (Junior Literary Guild selection), Messner, 1966; *Your Career in Oceanology,* Messner, 1968; *The World of Cryogenics,* Putnam, 1968; *The World of Energy Storage,* Putnam, 1977; *Let's Look Into Geology,* Naturegraph, in press. Contributor to *Popular Electronics, Popular Science, IF Science Fiction,* and other publications, some articles under pseudonyms.

WORK IN PROGRESS: Baha'i: The Kingdom at Last, and *You Too Can Be Wealthy.*

SIDELIGHTS: Waldo Boyd says that he "has resigned from the race for riches" and is "now rich in interests and friendships and expanding horizons of understanding." As an avocation he is building an electric automobile and an external-combustion powered automobile, experimenting with electrical effects on plant growth, and conducting research into psi-functions of human beings, especially clairvoyance. He is currently founding an international association of DSK (Dvorak Simplified Keyboard) typists.

*   *   *

BOYDSTON, Jo Ann 1924-

PERSONAL: Born July 2, 1924, in Hugo, Okla.; married Donald N. Boydston (chairman of health education department at Southern Illinois University), May 8, 1943. *Education:* Oklahoma State University, B.A. (with high distinction), 1944, M.A., 1947; Columbia University, Ph.D., 1950. *Home:* 1200 West Sycamore, Carbondale, Ill. *Office:* Center for Dewey Studies, Southern Illinois University, Carbondale, Ill. 62901.

CAREER: High school and junior college teacher in Poteau, Okla., 1944-45; Columbia University, New York, N.Y., lecturer in Spanish, 1947-49; University of Mississippi, University, assistant professor of Spanish, 1950-51, School of Education, associate professor and supervisor of student teachers, 1952-55; Southern Illinois University, Carbondale, assistant director of teacher training, 1955-61, associate director, 1961-66, director, 1966—, Center for Dewey Studies, professor of library affairs, 1973—.

MEMBER: John Dewey Society (secretary-treasurer, 1962-70; president-elect, 1970), Modern Language Association of America, Bibliographical Society of America, Manuscript Society of America, American Association of University Professors, Bibliographical Society of the University of Virginia, Philosophy of Education Society, Midwest Modern Language Association, Midwest Philosophy of Education Society, Phi Kappa Phi, Mortar Board.

WRITINGS—All published by Southern Illinois University Press: (Editor) *The Early Works of John Dewey, 1882-1898,* Volume I: *Early Essays and Leibniz's New Essays Concerning the Human Understanding,* 1969, Volume II: *Psychology,* 1967, Volume III: *Early Essays and Outlines of a Critical Theory of Ethics,* 1970, Volume IV: *Early Essays and the Study of Ethics: A Syllabus,* 1971, Volume V: *Early Essays,* 1972; (with Robert E. Andresen) *John Dewey: A Checklist of Translations, 1900-1967,* 1969; (editor) *Guide to the Works of John Dewey,* 1970; (editor) George Dykhuizen, *The Life and Mind of John Dewey,* 1973; (with Kathleen Poulous) *Checklist of Writings about John Dewey, 1882-1973,* 1974; (editor) *The Middle Works of John Dewey,* four volumes, 1976-77; (editor and author of introduction) *The Poems of John Dewey,* 1977. Contributor to education and bibliography journals. General editor, "The Collected Works of John Dewey"; editor, *Dewey Newsletter,* 1967—.

WORK IN PROGRESS: Writing second edition of *Checklist of Writings about John Dewey, 1882-1976;* editing Volumes V-VIII of *Middle Works of John Dewey.*

*   *   *

BOYLE, Ann (Peters) 1916-

PERSONAL: Born January 21, 1916, in Independence, Mo.; daughter of Robert Mize (a pharmacist) and Lucy (Conway) Peters; married James Hancock Boyle (a lawyer), December 26, 1938; children: Eleanor Ann (Mrs. Richard Riley), Lucy Charlotte (Mrs. Robert E. Buschmann), Jean Boyle Dannenberg. *Education:* Chevy Chase Junior College, graduate, 1936; University of Kansas City (now University of Missouri—Kansas City), B.A., 1938. *Religion:* Protestant. *Home:* 15991 Bliss Lane, Apt. A, Tustin, Calif. 92680.

CAREER: Model for various women's clothing shops, Kansas City, Mo., 1936-38; Barstow School, Kansas City, teacher in primary grades, 1938-39. *Member:* P.E.N. (membership vice-president, 1977-78), Association of Junior Leagues of America, California Writers Guild, Long Beach Writers Workshop, Quill Pen (vice-president, 1971; president, 1972), Lambda Beta Writers Workshop. *Awards, honors:* Prize in *Writer's Digest* Short Short Story Contest, 1962, for "The Christmas Eve Surprise"; first and second prizes for short stories in Long Beach Writers Club annual contests.

WRITINGS: Stormy Slopes (young adult novel), Bouregy, 1971; *Sundown Girl,* Bouregy, 1971; *The Well of Three Echoes,* Avalon Books, 1972; *Rim of Forever,* Avalon Books, 1973; *One Golden Earring,* Avalon Books, 1974; *Dark Mountain,* Avalon Books, 1975; *Beyond the Wall,* Avalon Books, 1976; *The Snowy Hills of Innocence,* Avalon Books, 1977. Contributor of short stories and serials to *Jack and Jill, Wee Wisdom, Children's Activities, Highlights for Children,* and other juvenile magazines.

WORK IN PROGRESS: Viel of Sand (young adult adventure-romance); untitled teenage book; untitled adult Gothic.

SIDELIGHTS: Ann Boyle wrote *CA:* "For all its hard work and frequent frustrations, writing gives me great pleasure and is important to my personal life. Since I believe that the background or setting must be an integral, working part of a story, like another character, I fictionalize and use experiences from our own recreational activities as backgrounds for my novels and short stories. My husband and I spend much of our free time hiking, backpacking, and cross-country skiing in the mountains and deserts of the west, and these activities and settings play an important role in most of my fiction. My husband is patient when I stop on the trail to jot down an idea in my miniature notebook, but when I delay us too long, he sometimes says, 'If you stop to write the whole book, we'll never make it to the mountain's summit.'

"But there is also research, not only to check the accuracy and feasibility of the situations I create, but also the fields that are new to me. One of the reasons I like to write is that there are so many things I would like to do if I had time. By researching subjects that interest me and weaving them into the background of the story, I feel almost as if I had actually designed and cast jewelry by the lost wax method, as a character in *Beyond the Wall* did, or had actually spent a summer as a lookout with Charlie in *Sundown Girl,* in one of the fire towers we have visited in the wilderness. So, writing has given me a second, if vicarious, life and enabled me to enjoy twice as many experiences as could be packed into one lifetime."

AVOCATIONAL INTERESTS: Skiing, hiking, swimming, travel, sewing, music, art, collecting antiques.

* * *

BRACEY, John H(enry, Jr.) 1941-

PERSONAL: Born July 17, 1941, in Chicago, Ill.; son of John Henry, Sr. and Helen (Harris) Bracey; married Ingrid Babb; children: Kali Nneka (daughter). *Education:* Attended Howard University, 1959-60; Roosevelt University, B.A., 1964, graduate study, 1964-66; attended Chicago Teachers College (now Chicago State University), 1965; Northwestern University, N.D.E.A. fellow, 1966-69. *Home:* 7 Eaton Ct., Echo Hill, Amherst, Mass. 01002. *Office:* W. E. B. DuBois Department of Afro-American Studies, University of Massachusetts, Amherst, Mass. 01003.

CAREER: U.S.A. Signal Engineering Agency, Washington, D.C., mail clerk, 1960-61; University of Michigan Institute for Social Research, Ann Arbor, interviewer and consultant, 1965; Chicago Urban League, Chicago, Ill., research assistant, 1967-68; Northwestern University, Evanston, Ill., research assistant at Center for Urban Affairs, 1968-69; Northeastern Illinois State College (now Northeastern Illinois University), Chicago, lecturer in history, 1969; Northern Illinois University, DeKalb, lecturer, 1969-70, assistant professor of Afro-American history, 1970-71; University of Rochester, Rochester, N.Y., assistant professor of history, 1971-72; University of Massachusetts—Amherst, associate professor of Afro-American studies, 1972—, chairman of department, 1974—. Member of selection committee, William Starobin Memorial fellowship, 1971—. Consultant to several publishers on Afro-American history and culture. *Member:* American Historical Association, Association for the Study of Negro Life and History, Organization of American Historians (life member), Southern Historical Association, Phi Alpha Theta.

WRITINGS: (Author of foreword) T. Thomas Fortune, *Black and White: Land, Labor and Politics in the South,* Johnson Publishing Co. (Chicago, Ill.), 1970; (with August Meier and Elliott Rudwick) *Black Nationalism in America,* Bobbs-Merrill, 1970; (with Meier and Rudwick) *The Afro-Americans: Selected Documents,* Allyn & Bacon, 1971.

Contributor: N. Huggins, M. Kilson, and D. Fox, editors, *Key Issues in the Afro-American Experience,* Harcourt, 1971; Edward T. James, editor, *Notable American Women, 1607-1950: A Biographical Dictionary,* Volume III, Radcliffe College, 1972; J. T. Chase, editor, *The Study of American History,* Dushkin, 1974. General editor with Meier and Rudwick, "Explorations in the Black Experience" series, eight volumes, Wadsworth, 1971. Contributor to *Encyclopedia of World Biography,* McGraw, 1973, 1974, and *Dictionary of American History,* Scribner, 1976. Contributor of articles and reviews to *Graduate Journal, Midcontinent American Studies Journal, Nummo News,* and *Washington Star.* Contributing editor, *Journal of Ethnic Studies,* 1973—.

WORK IN PROGRESS: Toward a Black Sociology: A History and Critique; several book reviews and articles.

SIDELIGHTS: John Bracey, Jr. told *CA:* "I consider myself more a teacher and a student of the human experience (with a heavy emphasis on the Afro-American variant thereof) than a writer. I write articles, reviews, essays as part of an effort to clarify ideas and events for my students as well as myself. The books I have produced so far have presented examples of important historical documents and research in a form both interesting and accessible to students. Quite frankly I prefer reading and research to writing, and teaching is my first love."

* * *

BRADFIELD, Nancy 1913-

PERSONAL: Born November 4, 1913, in Hampstead, London, England; daughter of Archibald Thomas (a businessman) and Elsie May (a portrait painter; maiden name, Eves) Bradfield; married Harold Wilfred Sayer (a principal lecturer, painter, and etcher), October 29, 1938; children: Hazel Jean (deceased), Wendy Lynn. *Education:* Attended Willesden College of Art, London, 1930-33; Royal College of Art, London, A.R.C.A., 1936. *Politics:* Conservative. *Religion:* Church of England. *Home:* Elm Cottage, Far End, Sheepscombe, Stroud, Gloucestershire, England. *Office:* Gloucestershire College of Art, Cheltenham, England.

CAREER: East Barnet Grammar School, East Barnet, Hertfordshire, England, teacher of art, 1941-45; Gloucestershire College of Art, Cheltenham, England, lecturer on history of costume, 1965—. Adviser to National Trust on Charles Wade Collection of Costume. Lecturer at colleges and to study groups and women's clubs. *Member:* Costume Society.

WRITINGS—Self-illustrated: *Historical Costumes of England, 1066-1936,* Harrap, 1938, revised edition, 1958, Barnes & Noble, 1959, 3rd edition, revised and enlarged, published as *Historical Costumes of England from the Eleventh to the Twentieth Century, 1066-1968,* Harrap, 1970, Barnes & Noble, 1971; *Costume in Detail: Women's Dress, 1730-1930,* Plays, 1968. Contributor of articles to *Costume Society Journal* (London).

SIDELIGHTS: As an art student Nancy Bradfield gathered together about five hundred of her drawings of period dress (for men and women) and bound them for her own reference. This personal study evolved into her first book. In 1953 she started redrawing the illustrations for a second edition of *Historical Costumes,* which ran into five reprintings. All of the drawings for *Costume in Detail,* which took eight years to complete, were originally done for her own pleasure; they have been reproduced directly from her sketch books.

AVOCATIONAL INTERESTS: Collecting period books and dresses.

BIOGRAPHICAL/CRITICAL SOURCES: Drama, winter, 1968.

* * *

BRADLEY, John Lewis 1917-

PERSONAL: Born August 5, 1917, in London, England; son of Oscar and Jessie (Lewis) Bradley; married Elizabeth Pettingell, November 4, 1943; children: Robin Newell (daughter). *Education:* Yale University, B.A., 1940, Ph.D., 1950; Harvard University, M.A., 1946. *Home:* 7 The Manor Close, Shincliffe, Durham DH1 2NS, England. *Office:* Department of English, University of Durham, Durham, England.

CAREER: Instructor in English at Wellesley College, Wellesley, Mass., 1948-51, and University of Maryland, College Park, 1952-53; Clark University, Worcester, Mass., assistant professor of English, 1953-55; Mount Holyoke College, South Hadley, Mass., assistant professor, 1955-58, associate professor of English, 1958-64; Ohio State University, Columbus, visiting associate professor, 1963-64, professor of English, 1964-65; University of South Carolina, Columbia, professor of English, 1965-69; currently professor of English, University of Durham, Durham, England. Visiting lecturer, Smith College, 1962-63; visiting professor, Harvard University, summer, 1975, University of Maryland, second term, 1976-77. *Military service:* Royal Canadian Air Force, flying officer, 1943-46. *Member:* Association of University Teachers. *Awards, honors:* American Philosophical Society grants, 1957, 1959, 1964; Guggenheim fellow, 1961-62.

WRITINGS: An Introduction to Ruskin, Houghton, 1970.

Editor: *Ruskin's Letters from Venice, 1851-1852,* Yale University Press, 1955; *Letters of John Ruskin to Lord and Lady Mount-Temple,* Ohio State University Press, 1964; *Selections from Mayhew's London Labour and the London Poor,* Oxford University, 1965; *Rogue's Progress: An Autobiography of "Lord Chief Baron" Nicholson,* Houghton, 1965; John Ruskin, *Unto This Last* [and] *Traffic,* Appleton, 1967; (with Martin Stevens) *Masterworks of English Prose,* Holt, 1968. Contributor of articles and reviews to academic journals.

WORK IN PROGRESS: An edition of *Far from the Madding Crowd.*

AVOCATIONAL INTERESTS: Travel (especially in Italy), music.

* * *

BRANDENBERG, Franz 1932-

PERSONAL: Born February 10, 1932, in Zug, Switzerland; son of Franz and Marie (Sigrist) Brandenberg; married Aliki Liacouras (an author and illustrator under name Aliki), March 15, 1957; children: Jason, Alexa Demetria. *Education:* Attended school in Einsiedeln, Switzerland. *Home:* 473 West End Ave., New York, N.Y. 10024.

CAREER: Began apprenticeship with publisher and bookseller in Lucerne, Switzerland, 1949; continued in book trade, 1952-60, working in bookshops or publishing houses in London, Paris, and Florence; literary agent in New York, N.Y., 1960-72; writer for children, 1970—.

WRITINGS—All illustrated by wife, Aliki: *I Once Knew a Man,* Macmillan, 1970; *Fresh Cider and Pie,* Macmillan, 1973; *No School Today!,* Macmillan, 1975; *A Secret for Grandmother's Birthday,* Greenwillow Books, 1975; *A Robber! A Robber!,* Greenwillow Books, 1976; *I Wish I Was Sick, Too!,* Greenwillow Books, 1976; *What Can You Make of It?,* Greenwillow Books, 1977; *Nice New Neighbors,* Greenwillow Books, 1977.

WORK IN PROGRESS: Several children's books.

SIDELIGHTS: Several of Franz Brandenberg's books have been published in Japanese, Hebrew, French, German, Danish, and Swedish.

BIOGRAPHICAL/CRITICAL SOURCES: New York, December 17, 1973.

* * *

BRECKENRIDGE, Adam Carlyle 1916-

PERSONAL: Born July 10, 1916, in Turney, Mo.; son of Adam Carlisle and Mabel Ruth (Sheldon) Breckenridge; married Marion Marie Stenten Nickerson, April 13, 1963; children: (stepson) Thomas S. Nickerson. *Education:* Northwest Missouri State College (now University), A.B., 1936; University of Missouri, M.A., 1938; Princeton University, Ph.D., 1942. *Politics:* Independent. *Religion:* None. *Home:* 1545 East Manor Dr., Lincoln, Neb. 68506. *Office:* Department of Political Science, University of Nebraska, Lincoln, Neb. 68508.

CAREER: Christian College, Columbia, Mo., instructor, 1940; University of Nebraska at Lincoln, instructor, 1946-48, assistant professor, 1948-50, associate professor, 1950-55, professor of political science, 1955—, chairman of department, 1953-55, chancellor's assistant for academic affairs, 1955, dean of faculties, 1955-66, vice-chancellor, 1962-68, acting director of libraries, 1973-74, acting vice-chancellor for academic affairs, 1974-75, interim chancellor, 1975-76, vice-chancellor for academic affairs, 1975-77. Visiting professor at Pennsylvania State University, University Park, Pa., summers, 1948-49. Member of Lincoln City-Lancaster County Planning Commission, 1965-71. *Military service:* U.S. Naval Reserve, 1942—; became captain. *Member:* American Political Science Association, American Society for Public Administration, National Municipal League, American Association of University Professors, Nebraska Historical Society, Pi Sigma Alpha (member of national executive council, 1960-64).

WRITINGS: (With John Gilbert Heinberg) *Law Enforcement in Missouri,* University of Missouri Press, 1942; (editor with Lane W. Lancaster) *Readings in American State Government,* Rinehart, 1950; *One House for Two: The Nebraska Unicameral Legislature,* Public Affairs Press, 1957; *The Right to Privacy,* University of Nebraska Press, 1970; *Congress against the Court,* University of Nebraska Press, 1970; *The Executive Privilege,* University of Nebraska Press, 1974.

WORK IN PROGRESS: The Impact of Congressional Committees on the Executive Branch.

* * *

BREFFORT, Alexandre 1901-1971

November 22, 1901—February 23, 1971; French author and playwright. Obituaries: *New York Times,* February 24, 1971; *L'Express,* March 1-7, 1971; *Variety,* March 3, 1971; *Antiquarian Bookman,* May 17, 1971.

BRENDTRO, Larry K. 1940-

PERSONAL: Born July 26, 1940, in Sioux Falls, S.D.; son of A. Kenneth (a manager) and Bernice (Matz) Brendtro; married Janna Agena, July 14, 1973; children: Daniel Kenneth, Steven Lincoln. *Education:* Augustana College, Sioux Falls, B.A., 1961; South Dakota State University, M.S., 1962; University of Michigan, Ph.D., 1965. *Politics:* Independent. *Religion:* Lutheran. *Home and office:* Starr Commonwealth, Albion, Mich. 49224.

CAREER: University of Illinois, Urbana, assistant professor of special education, 1966-67; Starr Commonwealth for Boys, Albion, Mich., and Van Wert, Ohio, president, 1967—. Certified consulting psychologist. *Member:* National Association of Homes for Children (vice-president), Council for Exceptional Children, Council for Children with Behavioral Disorders.

WRITINGS: The Other 23 Hours, Aldine, 1969; (with Harry H. Vorroth) *Positive Peer Culture,* Aldine, 1974. Editor, *Residential Group Care.*

* * *

BRENER, Milton E. 1930-

PERSONAL: Born January 11, 1930, in New Orleans, La.; son of Rose (Feldman) Brener; married Isabel Feldstein, November 16, 1952; children: Lisa, Ann, Neil Sol, Matthew Joseph. *Education:* Tulane University, LL.B., 1952. *Religion:* Jewish. *Home:* 6038 St. Charles Ave., New Orleans, La. 70118.

CAREER: Garon, Brener, McNeely & Hart (law firm), New Orleans, La., partner, 1958—. *Military service:* U.S. Army, 1952-56; became first lieutenant. *Member:* Louisiana State Bar Association.

WRITINGS: The Garrison Case: A Study in the Abuse of Power, C. N. Potter, 1969.

BIOGRAPHICAL/CRITICAL SOURCES: New York Times Book Review, November 30, 1969.

* * *

BRESLAUER, George W. 1946-

PERSONAL: Born March 4, 1946, in New York, N.Y.; son of Henry Edward and Marianne (Schaeffer) Breslauer; married Yvette Assia, August 8, 1976. *Education:* University of Michigan, A.B., 1966, A.M. and Certificate in Russian Studies, 1968, Ph.D., 1973. *Office:* Department of Political Science, University of California, Berkeley, Calif. 94720.

CAREER: University of California, Berkeley, acting assistant professor, 1971-73, assistant professor of political science, 1973—. *Member:* American Political Science Association, American Association for the Advancement of Slavic Studies, Phi Kappa Phi, Pi Sigma Alpha.

WRITINGS: (With Alexander Dallin) *Political Terror in Communist Systems,* Stanford University Press, 1970; (with Stanley Rothman) *Soviet Politics and Society,* West Publishing, 1977; (contributor) Alexander Dallin, editor, *The Twenty-Fifth Congress of the CPSU,* Hoover Institution, 1977. Contributor to *Problems of Communism.*

WORK IN PROGRESS: Research on post-Stalin change in Soviet Russia.

* * *

BREWER, Margaret L. 1929-

PERSONAL: Born October 6, 1929, in Winthrop, Ark.; daughter of Manuel Labron (a carpenter) and Nora (McClain) Dossett; married Durward Brewer (a professor), 1948 (deceased). *Education:* Southern State College, Magnolia, Ark., student, 1946-48; Oklahoma State University, B.A., 1953; University of Missouri, M.Ed., 1956. *Address:* Box 231, Wickes, Ark. 71973. *Office:* Van-Cove High School, Cove, Ark. 71937.

CAREER: Elementary teacher in Arkinda, Ark., 1947-49; high school teacher and supervisor of school library, Gillham, Ark., 1949-51; Oklahoma State University, Stillwater, purchasing assistant, 1952-55; University of Missouri Library, Columbia, assistant librarian (for education and psychology), 1956-73; Columbia (Mo.) public schools, media coordinator, 1973-74; Van-Cove (Ark.) public schools, librarian, 1975—. *Member:* North Central Association of Colleges and Secondary Schools, Missouri State Historical Society, Missouri Library Association (secretary, 1970-71), American Association of University Women (president of Columbia, Mo. branch, 1965-67), Missouri Association of School Librarians (vice-president, 1970-71), Missouri State Teachers Association, University Community Teachers Association (president, 1960), Arkansas Education Association, Pi Gamma Mu, Delta Kappa Gamma, Order of the Eastern Star.

WRITINGS: (With Sharon O. Willis) *The Elementary School Library,* Shoe String, 1970; (collaborator) *School Media Standards,* Missouri Department of Education, 1970. Contributor to library and education journals. Editor, *Newsletter* of Missouri Association of School Librarians, 1968-70.

AVOCATIONAL INTERESTS: Philately, rock collecting, lapidary, playing the five-string banjo, fishing, boating, bowling, writing short stories for children.

* * *

BREZA, Tadeusz 1905(?)-1970

1905(?)—May 19, 1970; Polish author. Obituaries: *Washington Post,* May 22, 1970; *Books Abroad,* spring, 1971.

* * *

BRIAND, Rena 1935-

PERSONAL: Born November 12, 1935, near French-German border; now a Canadian citizen living in Australia; divorced; adopted a half-Vietnamese girl, Tuyen Bettina. *Education:* Attended primary and secondary schools in Europe; took English history and literature courses at McGill University. *Address:* Apollo Bay, Victoria, Australia.

CAREER: Researcher-writer for Canadian Broadcasting Corporation educational programs, 1959-61; went to Vietnam in 1965, worked as broadcaster for U.S. Armed Forces Radio Service, and as free-lance photographer and stringer for Associated Press in Vietnam, 1965-67; became feature writer for Southdown Press, Melbourne, Australia, 1968-69; free-lance journalist and author, 1969—.

WRITINGS: No Tears to Flow: Woman at War (a documentary on Vietnam), photographs by author, Heinemann, 1969, International Publications, 1970; *White Man in a Hole* (documentary on Coober Pedy, an opal mining town in the Australian desert), Phuong-Hoang Press, 1971; *The Waifs,* [Melbourne], 1973. Contributor of several free-lance feature articles to Australian magazines.

WORK IN PROGRESS: A novel; compiling material on Australian desert regions, including photographs.

SIDELIGHTS: According to an article in the Melbourne *Walkabout,* Rena Briand is a "Frenchwoman who went to Canada and married Jean, a rather shady adventurer, who dealt in information and who was eventually sent by the C.I.A. to a job in Viet Nam where he deserted Rena, left her penniless, and ordered her out of the country. She was so angry that she turned the official tables on him, and he had to get out instead." In order to avoid the soup lines in Saigon, Miss Briand became a photo-journalist for Associated Press, documenting the war and often becoming personally involved. *No Tears to Flow* is an autobiographical chronicle of her three years in Vietnam. "Briand's account," writes Michael Shmith of the *Melbourne Herald,* "is vastly different to other feminine accounts, Mary McCarthy, Susan Sontag and so on." A reviewer for the *Sydney Sun* notes that "as she wrote it in what is virtually a foreign language without any formal journalistic training, it is quite an achievement. Some of her anecdotes give a better picture of aspects of the war than anything else I've read." Briand's job often took her into dangerous situations; the Cairns *Post* reviewer mentions that "in one case a patrol she was with was ambushed by the Viet Cong and in another she acted as an emergency second gunner on an American helicopter.... Her keen observations and vivid characterisations serve to put the book in a class of its own dealing with an aspect of war so frequently forgotten in a narration of victories and reverses."

Rena Briand told *CA* of her experiences: "[I] always live among locals, board or stay in cheap hotels. Take odd jobs ... from dishwasher to opal miner. Affinity with so-called primitive peoples (Montagnards of Vietnam, aboriginals, etc.), I love to learn about different cultures firsthand. My books are for a general market, are without political or sociological overtones, and aimed towards international understanding." She also told *CA* that she is "interested in politics, but not committed," and that she "occasionally attends [religious] services of various denominations." The *Sun* writer calls her "an unusual woman," who has "lived with Montagnard tribesmen and shared their meals of dog and monkey and bullock blood ... [she went] to live in a dug-out at Coober Pedy and write a book about the opal-diggers," and who adopted an abandoned Vietnamese baby "'to put some meaning in my life.'"

BIOGRAPHICAL/CRITICAL SOURCES: Macleans (Toronto), April, 1967; *Melbourne Herald,* July 10, 1969; *Sun* (Sydney), October 4, 1969; *Post* (Cairns), October 30, 1969; *Age* (Melbourne), January 31, 1970; *Walkabout* (Melbourne), February, 1970; *People* (Sydney), February 25, 1970.†

* * *

BRIGGS, Austin (Eugene), Jr. 1931-

PERSONAL: Born May 4, 1931, in Highland Park, Mich.; son of Austin Eugene (an illustrator) and Ellen (Weber) Briggs; married Margaret Pearce, February 4, 1956; children: Christopher Austin. *Education:* Harvard University, B.A. (magna cum laude), 1954; Columbia University, M.A. (with high honors), 1955, Ph.D., 1963. *Home:* 302 College Hill Rd., Clinton, N.Y. 13323. *Office:* Department of English, Hamilton College, Clinton, N.Y. 13323.

CAREER: Hamilton College, Clinton, N.Y., instructor, 1957-64, assistant professor, 1964-68, associate professor of English, 1968—. *Member:* Modern Language Association of America, American Association of University Professors.

WRITINGS: The Novels of Harold Frederic, Cornell University Press, 1969.

WORK IN PROGRESS: A study of the Gothic novel.

BIOGRAPHICAL/CRITICAL SOURCES: American Literary Realism, spring, 1970; *American Literature,* May, 1970; *New Yorker,* June 6, 1970; *Nineteenth-Century Fiction,* September, 1970; *Modern Fiction Studies,* winter, 1970-71.

* * *

BRIGGS, Dorothy Corkille 1924-

PERSONAL: Born February 23, 1924; daughter of John D. and Helen (Young) Corkille; married James W. Briggs (an attorney), June 13, 1952; children: Laurie, Kerrie. *Education:* Whitman College, A.B., 1946; Washington State University, M.S., B.Ed., 1949; also attended Loyola University, Los Angeles, University of California, Los Angeles, University of Washington, Seattle, Claremont Graduate School, Western Behavior Sciences Institute, La Jolla, and Esalen Institute. *Politics:* Republican. *Religion:* Methodist. *Home and office:* 31213 Ganado Dr., Palos Verdes Peninsula, Calif. 90274.

CAREER: Teacher and girls dean in Port Townsend, Wash., 1946-47; part-time counselor in Pullman, Wash., 1947-49; school psychologist in Seattle, Wash. public schools, 1949-51; teacher in Hermosa Beach, Calif. schools, 1952-53; teacher, counselor, and school psychometrist in Santa Monica, Calif. schools, 1953-55; author, parent education teacher, lecturer, and marriage and child counselor in Whittier and Palos Verdes Peninsula, Calif., 1958—. Therapist for small children, Broadbent Psychiatric Clinic, Long Beach, Calif., 1968-70. Consultant for Dimension Films film project, "Feelings." *Member:* California State Marriage Counseling Association, Phi Beta Kappa, Pi Lambda Theta, Psi Chi.

WRITINGS: Your Child's Self-Esteem: The Key to His Life, Doubleday, 1970; *Celebrate Your Self,* Doubleday, 1977. Contributor of articles to *Woman's Day, California State Marriage Counseling Quarterly,* and *Parent Cooperative Preschools International Journal.*

SIDELIGHTS: Dorothy Corkille Briggs told *CA:* "I had taught parent education classes for ten years before my book was published *(Your Child's Self-Esteem)....* Over the years I saw and heard the same questions, concerns, worries if not at times agonies in the hearts of adults who were trying their best to nurture. Often these adults were struggling to break free of the negative aspects of the modeling provided by their own upbringing. Always there was the search for guidelines on how to do not just an adequate job but a truly fine one. The need seemed so great, the parents and teachers so sincere and the questions so pervasive.

"Although there were hundreds of child rearing books on the market, it was apparent to me that there wasn't one that gave parents and teachers my particular focal point—that is of how to build self-esteem in children. Since the literature was rife with data indicating that the high self-esteemer was not the problem child and since in my private practice as a family counselor I saw the pain caused by low self-esteem, it seemed imperative to me that what was and is known to clinicians needed to be spelled out to parents and teachers in lay terms....

"Since my primary mode of communicating was via the spoken word, my earliest struggle was teaching myself the skills of writing for the lay public. All those long hours of work were worth it when I consider that via the written word I have been able to reach far more people than I ever could have in the classroom. The need to reach a larger audience was the particular motivating point that sustained me during the long process. . . .

"Since self-esteem is contagious and affects how each of us connects with others—it is the most important characteristic about each human being, slating him or her for winning or losing in life—it has been important to me to reach out to others with whatever knowledge my present 30 years in the field of psychology and education has provided to share it with them. It has felt like my mission in life to share what I know that others might find help and ease from inner distress. My biggest hope is that in this way we can alleviate some of the apathy and distress so rampant in so many people today. . . ."

AVOCATIONAL INTERESTS: Painting, riding, swimming, art, theatre, dancing, hiking.

* * *

BRIGHAM, Besmilr 1923-

PERSONAL: Given name is pronounced Bess-miller; born September 28, 1923, in Pace, Mississippi; daughter of Monroe and Bessye (Emmons) Moore; married Roy C. Brigham; children: Heloise (Mrs. Keith Wilson). *Education:* Mary Hardin-Baylor College, Belton, Tex., degree in journalism; New School for Social Research, graduate study. *Politics:* "No commitment." *Religion:* "No formal affiliation." *Home:* Route 1, Horatio, Ark. 71842.

CAREER: Free-lance author and poet. Poet-resident, Bryan Public Schools, Bryan, Tex., 1974. *Awards, honors:* National Endowment for the Arts fellowship grant for continuance of her work in poetry.

WRITINGS: Agony Dance: Death of the Dancing Dolls, Winepress Publishing, 1969; *Heaved from the Earth,* Knopf, 1971. Also author of "The Thirteenth Mask: Games for an Easter Child" (script for dance/lyric drama), produced at Mythic Theatre, Phoenix, Ariz.

Contributor to anthologies: *31 New American Poets,* edited by Ron Schreiber, Hill & Wang, 1969; *New Directions #21,* New Directions, 1969; *New Directions #23,* New Directions, 1971; *Their Place in the Heat: Contemporary Poetry Statements,* Road Runner Press, 1971; *New Generation: Poetry,* edited by Fred Wolven, Ann Arbor Review Books, 1971; *I Love You All Day: It Is That Simple,* Abbey Press, 1971; *The Best American Short Stories of 1972,* edited by Martha Foley, Houghton, 1972; *The Best American Short Stories of 1973,* edited by Martha Foley, Houghton, 1973; *From the Belly of the Shark,* edited by Walter Lowenfels, Random House, 1973; *Rising Tides: Twentieth Century American Women Poets,* edited by Laura Chester and Sharon Barbra, Simon & Schuster, 1973; *Psyche: An Anthology of Modern American Women Poets,* edited by Barbara Segnitz and Carol Rainey, Dial Press, 1973; *I Hear My Sisters Saying,* edited by Dorothy Walters and Carol Konek, Crowell, 1976; *Arkansas Voices,* edited by Sarah M. Fountain, Rose Press, 1976.

Contributor of short stories to *Southern Review, Confrontation, Southwest Review, North American Review;* contributor of poetry to numerous journals and periodicals, including *Texas Quarterly, Atlantic, Harper's Bazaar, Confrontation, Prairie Schooner, Southwest Review, North American Review, New York Times, West Coast Review, Wisconsin Review, Beloit Poetry Journal, Granite, Minnesota Review.*

WORK IN PROGRESS: "I am now working on new poems, solidifying collections (poems) and compiling studies in fiction, in particular *Rainbow House* (fictions of Mexico). And, along with *Death of the Wild . . .,* another body of poems is taking shape as *The Firebird Heart.* The animal life, bird life, human life (present and past), surviving on toil, gallantry, courage . . . a kind of phosphorous that gives off and that we keep as memory. Magnified from another by our own experience."

SIDELIGHTS: Besmilr Brigham, who reports that a great grandfather on her mother's side was a Choctaw Indian and that there is also Choctaw blood in her father's family, writes in *Their Place in the Heat:* "We are all in some concept heaved from the earth or tied down to it, or come from it, or go to it (unless we are either burned or cut up in little chunks for the animals and birds like the people of Tibet do) and ad infinitum are the legends that grow from that connection. . . ."

Reviewers of *Heaved from the Earth* remark on Brigham's special feeling for the natural world and her ability to write of it. Halvard Johnson calls her poems "dense and powerful notations of a physical world, its human and animal life, its geography, its climate and natural processes." The Poetry Society of America *Bulletin* reviewer finds the book ". . . a sheer work of art with the color of earth and sky stained in it, and haunted with the pathos and joy of life." Phil Dacey writes that "what emerges strongly . . . is the sense that the observer who speaks these poems possesses maturity of the kind that comes from the wedding of an informed sensibility to natural events and essences."

Sandra Hutchins echoes and expands the thoughts and conclusions of other reviewers. She writes: "Besmilr sees the natural world for itself, with a kind of primitive innocence . . . the inner life is revealed through the tone of her poems, that of wonder, unflinching openness, and complete absorption in her central purpose, to describe what she senses outside herself. . . . Women's lives have not often been such that they could open themselves up to wilderness nature so completely, that they could experience the elemental world in its raw, fierce extremes with a clear sense of belonging in the environment. . . . Perhaps her Choctaw ancestry has provided her with a special sensibility."

BIOGRAPHICAL/CRITICAL SOURCES: Their Place in the Heat: Contemporary Poetry Statements, Road Runner Press, 1971; *Crazy Horse,* Number 7, June, 1971; *Wisconsin Review,* summer, 1971; *Minnesota Review,* fall, 1971; Poetry Society of America *Bulletin,* February, 1972; *Texas Woman,* April-May, 1974.

* * *

BRINKS, Herbert J(ohn) 1935-

PERSONAL: Born May 25, 1935, in South Holland, Ill.; married Ruth Kortenhoven, 1957; children: Timothy, Steven, Marie, John. *Education:* Calvin College, A.B., 1957; University of Michigan, M.A., 1961, Ph.D., 1965. *Office:* Department of History, Calvin College, Grand Rapids, Mich. 49506.

CAREER: Junior high school teacher in Allendale, Mich., 1957-60; University of Michigan, Michigan Historical Collection, Ann Arbor, research assistant, 1961-62; Calvin College, Grand Rapids, Mich., 1962—, began as instructor, professor of history, 1971—, curator of Colonial Origins Collection, 1962—. University of Michigan, teacher of extension courses in history at Grand Rapids, 1967, 1968, Flint and Detroit, 1970, and Dearborn Campus, 1971. *Member:* American Historical Association, Organization of American

Historians, Historical Society of Michigan (director, 1969—), Michigan Archival Association. *Awards, honors:* Earhart Foundation fellowship, 1965.

WRITINGS: (Editor) *Guide to the Dutch-American Historical Collections of Western Michigan,* Dutch American Historical Commission, 1967; *Peter White,* Eerdmans, 1970; (editor with George S. May) *A Michigan Reader: 11,000 B.C. to A.D. 1865,* Eerdmans, 1974. Contributor to history journals.†

* * *

BRINLEY, Bertrand R(ussell) 1917-

PERSONAL: Born June 19, 1917, in Hudson, N.Y.; son of Clarence Coapes and Susan (Finley) Brinley; married Euphemia Brown, December 24, 1938; children: Kendall Jayne (Mrs. Robert T. Boschert), Richard Sheridan. *Education:* Stanford University, student, 1935-37. *Politics:* "Generally a Democrat." *Religion:* None. *Home:* Boxwood Place, 120 High St., Luray, Va. 22835.

CAREER: Palo Alto Community Playhouse, Palo Alto, Calif., assistant director and publicity manager, 1937-39; Lockheed Aircraft Corp., Burbank, Calif., writer and procedures analyst, 1940-44; U.S. Army, troop officer in Special Services and aide de camp, 1944-48; Salvation Army, New England Region, fund raising and public relations, 1949-50; U.S. Army, public information officer, troop officer, and aide de camp, 1950-59, retiring as major; Martin Marietta Corp. (aerospace firm), Orlando, Fla., public relations representative, 1961-69; Bell Telephone Laboratories, Murray Hill, N.J., editor in public relations department, 1970-71. *Awards, honors*—Military: Bronze Star Medal.

WRITINGS: Rocket Manual for Amateurs, Ballantine, 1960; *The Mad Scientists' Club* (juvenile), Macrae, 1964; *The New Adventures of the Mad Scientists' Club* (juvenile), Macrae, 1968; *The Big Kerplop* (juvenile), Macrae, 1974. Also author of *The Big Chunk of Ice.*

WORK IN PROGRESS: Goodbye, Melissa, a novelette about a touring U.S.O. troupe in postwar Europe; *You Can't Get There from Here,* a study of the deterioration of public transportation facilities and the mail service in the United States.

SIDELIGHTS: Bertrand R. Brinley writes: "If I ever get down to serious writing, it will probably be largely concerned with the increasing inability of man—as his society becomes more sophisticated—to understand any of the lessons of the past and apply them to the present, or even to understand what occurs in his own lifetime, because of his susceptibility to propaganda, mass phobia, and the confusing effects of mass communication." He intends to write comedy scripts for television and wants eventually to write for the legitimate theater.

* * *

BRISKIN, Jacqueline 1927-

PERSONAL: Born December 18, 1927, in London, England; daughter of Spencer and Marjorie (Mendelsohn) Orgell; married Bert Briskin (an oil executive), May 9, 1948; children: Ralph Louis, Elizabeth Ann, Richard Paul. *Education:* Attended University of California, Los Angeles, 1946-47. *Residence:* Los Angeles, Calif.

MEMBER: P.E.N. (board member of Los Angeles center).

WRITINGS: California Generation (novel), Lippincott, 1970; *Afterlove* (novel), Bantam, 1973; *Rich Friends* (novel), Delacorte, 1976. Author of television scripts for "Insight." Contributor of short stories to *Seventeen, Southwest Review,* and other periodicals.

WORK IN PROGRESS: A novel, *The Founders.*

SIDELIGHTS: Columbia Pictures has bought the film rights to *California Generation.* The television rights to *Rich Friends,* originally titled "The Years Between," have been purchased by Lorimar for a series to be shown by Columbia Broadcasting System, Inc. *Avocational interests:* Travel, opera, golf, gourmet cooking, film-making.

BIOGRAPHICAL/CRITICAL SOURCES: San Francisco Examiner, June 1, 1970; *Best Sellers,* July 1, 1970; *New York Post,* July 9, 1970; *Boston Herald Traveler,* July 22, 1970; *San Francisco Chronicle,* August 2, 1970; *Evening Standard* (London), September 16, 1970; *Books,* November, 1970.

* * *

BRITTAN, Samuel 1933-

PERSONAL: Born December 29, 1933, in London, England; son of Joseph (a doctor) and Riva (Lipetz) Brittan. *Education:* Jesus College, Cambridge, M.A. (first class honors in economics), 1955. *Politics:* Liberal ("in old-fashioned English sense"). *Home:* Flat 10, Kensington Park Gardens, London W11 JHA, England. *Agent:* Andrew Best, Curtis Brown Ltd., 1 Craven Hill, Lancaster Gate, London W2 3EW, England. *Office: Financial Times,* 10 Cannon St., London E.C.4, England.

CAREER: Financial Times, London, England, member of editorial staff, 1955-61; *Observer,* London, economics editor, 1961-64; British Department of Economic Affairs, London, economic adviser, 1965; *Financial Times,* economics editor, 1966—, principal economic commentator, 1970. Member of executive committee, Political and Economic Planning, 1969-75; governor and member of executive committee, National Institute of Economic Affairs, 1970-74; visiting fellow, Nuffield College (Oxford), 1974—. *Member:* Royal Economic Society, Royal Institute of International Affairs. *Awards, honors:* Wincott Senior Award for Financial Journalists, 1971; Nuffield College Journalist Research fellowship, 1973-74.

WRITINGS: The Treasury under the Tories, Penguin, 1964, revised and enlarged edition published as *Steering the Economy: The Role of the Treasury,* Secker & Warburg, 1969, 3rd edition published as *Steering an Economy: The British Experiment,* Library Press, 1971; *Left or Right: The Bogus Dilemma,* Secker & Warburg, 1968; *The Price of Economic Freedom: A Guide to Flexible Rates,* Macmillan, 1970, St. Martin's, 1971; *Government and the Market Economy,* Institute of Economic Affairs, 1971; *Capitalism and the Permissive Society,* Macmillan, 1973; *Is There an Economic Concensus?: An Attitude Survey,* Macmillan, 1973; *Second Thoughts on Full Employment Policy,* Barry Rose, 1975; *Participation without Politics: Analysis of Nature and Role of Markets,* Institute of Economic Affairs, 1975; (with Peter Lilley) *The Delusion of Incomes Policy,* Temple Smith, 1977; *The Economic Consequences of Democracy,* Temple Smith, 1977.

Contributor: D. C. Watt, editor, *Survey of International Affairs,* Royal Institute of International Affairs and Oxford University Press, 1964; Richard Rose, *Policy-Making in Britain: The Reader in Government,* Free Press, 1969; M. Dogan and Rose, editors, *European Politics,* Little, Brown, 1970; *Symposium on Monopoly Policy,* H.M.S.O.,

1970; W. A. Robson, editor, *Taxation Policy,* Penguin, 1973. Contributor to economics journals.

BIOGRAPHICAL/CRITICAL SOURCES: Spectator, August 23, 1969.

* * *

BRITTON, Karl (William) 1909-

PERSONAL: Born October 12, 1909, in Scarborough, Yorkshire, England; son of James Nimmo (a minister) and Elsie Clare (Slater) Britton; married Sheila Margaret Christie, September 25, 1936; children: Margaret Clare, Andrew, Kate. *Education:* Clare College, Cambridge, M.A. (first class honors), 1932; Harvard University, A.M., 1934. *Religion:* Church of England.

CAREER: University College of Wales, Aberystwyth, lecturer in philosophy, 1934-37; University College of Swansea, Swansea, Wales, lecturer in philosophy, 1937-51; University of Newcastle upon Tyne, Newcastle upon Tyne, England, professor of philosophy, 1951-75. University of Durham, public orator, 1960-62, dean of Faculty of Arts, 1961-63, 1966-69. Served in Regional Commissioner's Office, Reading, 1941-45. *Member:* Mind Association (secretary, 1948-60; president, 1963), Cambridge Union Society (president, 1931). *Awards, honors:* Choate fellowship at Harvard University, 1932-34; D.Litt., University of Durham, 1976.

WRITINGS: Communication: A Philosophical Study of Language, Routledge & Kegan Paul, 1939, McGrath, 1970; *John Stuart Mill: An Introduction to the Life and Teaching of a Great Pioneer of Modern Social Philosophy and Logic,* Penguin, 1953, Dover, 1969; *The Paragon of Knowledge* (pamphlet; inaugural lecture), University of Durham, 1954; *Philosophy and the Meaning of Life,* Cambridge University Press, 1969. Contributor to collected papers on J. S. Mill, David Hume, and on communication.

WORK IN PROGRESS: Continuing studies on the life and philosophy of John Stuart Mill and on the philosophy of symbols in religion and poetry.

BIOGRAPHICAL/CRITICAL SOURCES: Times Literary Supplement, September 18, 1970.

* * *

BROCK, Betty 1923-

PERSONAL: Born August 31, 1923, in Biltmore, N.C.; daughter of Aleck R. and Kathleen (Lipe) Carter; married Clarence C. Brock (a captain in the U.S. Navy), June 9, 1943; children: Leslie Elizabeth, Alison Carter. *Education:* Attended University of North Carolina at Greensboro, 1941-42; George Washington University, Junior College Diploma, 1943. *Religion:* Episcopalian. *Home:* 5 Potomac Ct., Alexandria, Va. 22314.

MEMBER: Children's Book Guild of Washington, D.C., Pi Beta Phi.

WRITINGS: No Flying in the House (juvenile), Harper, 1970; *The Shades* (juvenile), Harper, 1971.

AVOCATIONAL INTERESTS: Art, antiques, gardens, travel.

BIOGRAPHICAL/CRITICAL SOURCES: New York Times Book Review, August 16, 1970, November 7, 1971.

* * *

BRODSKY, Stanley L. 1939-

PERSONAL: Born July 22, 1939, in Boston, Mass.; son of Harry and Selma (Cohen) Brodsky; married Annette Ratner (a psychologist), February 6, 1962; children: Michael, Rachel. *Education:* University of New Hampshire, B.A., 1960; University of Florida, M.A., 1962, Ph.D., 1964. *Politics:* Democrat. *Home:* 2726 33rd Ave. E., Tuscaloosa, Ala. 35401. *Office address:* Department of Psychology, P.O. Box 2968, University of Alabama, University, Ala. 35486.

CAREER: U.S. Army, 1963-67, serving as chief of Psychology Division, U.S. Disciplinary Barracks, Fort Leavenworth, Kan., 1964-67, left service as captain; Southern Illinois University, Center for the Study of Crime, Delinquency and Corrections, Carbondale, assistant professor, 1967-70, associate professor of psychology, 1971-72; University of Alabama, University, 1972—, began as associate professor, currently professor of psychology. *Member:* American Association of Correctional Psychologists (president, 1969-71), American Psychology-Law Society (member of board of directors), American Psychological Association (secretary-treasurer, Division of Psychologists in Public Service, 1975-78).

WRITINGS: (Editor with Norman Eggleston) *The Military Prison: Theory, Research and Practice,* Southern Illinois University Press, 1970; *Psychologists in the Criminal Justice System,* University of Illinois Press, 1973; *Families and Friends of Men in Prison,* Lexington Books, 1975; (editor with Marcia Walker) *Sexual Assault: The Victim and Rapist,* Lexington Books, 1976; (editor with Kenneth B. Melvin and Raymond D. Fowler) *Psy-Fi One,* Random House, 1977.

* * *

BROGAN, Gerald E(dward) 1924-

PERSONAL: Born August 15, 1924, in Bentonville, Ark.; son of Albert C. (a painter) and Emma Lee (Story) Brogan; married Coweta Maye Adkins, August 30, 1961. *Education:* Colorado State College (now University of Northern Colorado), A.B., 1950; University of Denver, M.A., 1951. *Home:* 1633 Russ St., Eureka, Calif. 95501. *Office:* Office of Head Librarian, College of the Redwoods, Eureka, Calif. 95501.

CAREER: Denver Public Library, Denver, Colo., reference librarian, 1951-54; Long Beach City College, Long Beach, Calif., assistant librarian, 1954-59, head librarian, Business and Technical Division, 1959-66; Community Colleges of Hawaii, Honolulu, library coordinator, 1966-67; Chico State College (now California State University, Chico), Chico, Calif., social science librarian, 1967-68; College of the Redwoods, Eureka, Calif., head librarian, 1968—. *Military service:* U.S. Army Air Forces, 1943-46; became master sergeant. *Member:* California Library Association, California Teachers Association, Audio Visual Education Association of California, Western Education Society for Telecommunications, Phi Delta Kappa.

WRITINGS: (With Jeanne Buck) *Using Libraries Effectively,* Dickenson, 1968.

WORK IN PROGRESS: Peter Wimsey and Philo Vance.

* * *

BROMBERGER, Serge Paul 1912-

PERSONAL: Born August 29, 1912, in Chatillon, France; son of Andre (a journalist) and Lucie (Mertz) Bromberger; married Noelle Gerber, June 8, 1950; married second wife, Marie Elbe (a writer), April 6, 1968; children: (first marriage) Sabine. *Education:* Educated in Aix-en-Provence, France.

Religion: Catholic. *Home:* 219 avenue du Versailles, Paris, France. *Office: Figaro,* Champs Elysees, Paris, France.

CAREER: Journalist, writing for *Matin* and *Intransigeant,* 1934, and *Journal,* 1935-39; *Figaro,* Paris, France, journalist, 1945—, chief deputy of reportage, 1965—. Served as war correspondent in Korean War, Suez operation, Indo Chinese War, Algerian War. *Military service:* French First Army, volunteer, 1939-45. *Member:* Association des Grands Reporters Francais. *Awards, honors:* Prix Albert Londres, 1948, for reportage; Officier de la Legion d'Honneur.

WRITINGS: Les Marquisards, Marguerat (Geneva), 1944; (with others) *Retour de Coree,* Julliard, 1951; (with brother, Merry Bromberger) *Les Secrets de l'expedition d'Egypte,* Editions des 4 Fils Aymon, 1957, translation by James Cameron with revision by the authors published as *Secrets of Suez,* Pan Books, 1957; *Les Rebelles algeriens,* Plon, 1958; *Les 13 Complots du 13 mai,* Fayard, 1959; *Barricades et Colonels,* Fayard, 1961; *En 1990,* Fayard, 1964; (with M. Bromberger) *Les Coulisses de l'Europe,* Presses de la Cite, 1968, translation by Elaine P. Halperin published as *Jean Monnet and the United States of Europe,* Coward, 1969.

* * *

BROOKHOUSE, (John) Christopher 1938-

PERSONAL: Born January 6, 1938, in Cincinnati, Ohio; married Diane Banks, June 14, 1959 (divorced, October, 1972); married Anne Ponder, March 3, 1973; children: (first marriage) Stephen, Nathaniel. *Education:* Stanford University, A.B., 1959; Harvard University, M.A., 1960, Ph.D., 1964. *Politics:* Independent. *Home:* Sunbear Woods, Pittsboro, N.C. *Agent:* John Hawkins, Paul R. Reynolds, Inc., 12 East 41st St., New York, N.Y. 10017. *Office:* Department of English, University of North Carolina, Chapel Hill, N.C. 27515.

CAREER: Harvard University, Cambridge, Mass., instructor in English, 1964-66; University of North Carolina at Chapel Hill, 1966—, began as assistant professor, currently associate professor of English. *Member:* Authors League of America, Phi Beta Kappa.

WRITINGS: (Editor) *Sir Amadace and the Avowing of Arthur,* Rosenkilde & Bagger, 1968; *Scattered Light* (poems), University of North Carolina Press, 1969; *Running Out,* Little, Brown, 1970; *Genesis House,* Loom Press, 1974; *If Lost, Return,* Loom Press, 1974.

WORK IN PROGRESS: A novel, *Down the Paths of Wintermute,* for Dutton.

BIOGRAPHICAL/CRITICAL SOURCES: New York Times Book Review, May 3, 1970.

* * *

BROOKS, Hugh C. 1922-

PERSONAL: Born June 19, 1922, in Seattle, Wash.; son of David Franklin and Emily (Campbell) Brooks; married Savina Vicini, June 16, 1950; children: Robert, Alison. *Education:* University of Washington, Seattle, B.A., 1947; Columbia University, M.A., 1952, Ed.D., 1954; also attended University of Geneva, 1948, and University of the Witwatersrand, 1953. *Home:* 513 Grove St., Upper Montclair, N.J. 07043. *Office:* Center for African Studies, St. John's University, Jamaica, N.Y. 11432.

CAREER: Instructor in geography at Oregon State University, Corvallis, 1950-51, and at Teachers College, Columbia University, New York City, 1952-54; University of the Witwatersrand, Johannesburg, South Africa, Fulbright lecturer in geography, 1955-58; Newark State College, Union, N.J., associate professor of geography, 1957-61; St. John's University, Jamaica, N.Y., associate professor of geography and director of African Institute, 1961—. Lecturer at Hunter College (now Hunter College of the City University of New York), 1952-54. Consulting editor, McGraw Hill Publishing Co., 1967-70, Nystrom Map Co., 1967-73, Grolier Publishing Co., 1967—, Sadlier Publishing Co., 1968—, Negro Universities Press, 1970-73, Hunter Development Co., 1971-73. *Military service:* U.S. Army, 1941-46; received Bronze Star, Purple Heart, and Silver Star. *Member:* American Geographic Association, Association of American Geographers, Royal Geographic Society, African Studies Association, African Academy of Arts and Research, American Association for the Advancement of Science. *Awards, honors:* New York State scholar incentive awards, Columbia University, 1965, and Syracuse University, 1968.

WRITINGS: College Geography, Appleton, 1957; *Africa Today,* Sadlier, 1968; *New Africa,* Sadlier, 1969; (editor with Yassin El-Ayouty) *Refugees South of the Sahara: An African Dilemma,* Negro Universities Press, 1970; (with El-Ayouty) *Africa & International Organization,* Nijhoff, 1973; (with Francis Lees) *Economic & Political Development of the Sudan,* Macmillan, 1976.

WORK IN PROGRESS: Geography of Africa.

* * *

BROWN, David S(pringer) 1915-

PERSONAL: Born December 27, 1915, in Bangor, Me.; son of Lyle Lincoln (a postal clerk) and Myra Jane (Springer) Brown; married Evelyn Lovett, May 1, 1943 (died May 22, 1967); married Anne Elizon, June 29, 1968; children: (first marriage) David Springer, Jr., Christopher L., Robert L., Adele Q. *Education:* University of Maine, A.B., 1936; Syracuse University, Ph.D., 1955. *Religion:* Protestant. *Home:* 5248 Macomb St. N.W., Washington, D.C. 20016. *Office:* George Washington University, Washington, D.C. 20006.

CAREER: Bangor Daily News, Bangor, Me., reporter, 1931-36; U.S. Department of Agriculture, Washington, D.C., member of staff of Office of Budget and Finance, 1940-42; Civil Aeronautics Administration, Placement Division, Washington, D.C., assistant chief, 1946-48; Air Coordinating Committee, Washington, D.C., member of staff, 1948-50; Economic Cooperation Administration, Washington, D.C., deputy director of executive secretariat, 1950-52; Mutual Security Agency, Washington, D.C., secretary of Public Advisory Board, 1950-53; Committee for a National Trade Policy, Washington, D.C., assistant director, 1953-54; George Washington University, Washington, D.C., associate professor of public administration, 1954-57, professor of public administration, 1957-69, professor of management, 1969—, chairman of department, 1971-75. President, Leadership Resources, Inc., Washington, D.C., 1969-74. Instructor, U.S. Department of Agriculture Graduate School, 1946-54; visiting professor, Royal College of Science and Technology, Glasgow, Scotland, 1958. Secretary, U.S. delegation to International Civil Aviation Organization, 1950; coordinator, U.S. Air Force Advanced Management Program, 1954-61; member, U.S. delegation to International Institute of Administrative Sciences, 1958; member of advisory committee, Internal Revenue Service,

1959-60; deputy chief, University of Southern California Party in Public Administration, Lahore, Pakistan, 1961-62. *Military service:* U.S. Navy, 1942-45; became lieutenant, naval aviator.

MEMBER: International Personnel Management Association, American Political Science Association, American Society for Public Administration, Academy of Management, American Association of University Professors. *Awards, honors:* Citation, Society for the Advancement of Management, 1967, for contributions to management theory.

WRITINGS: The Public Advisory Board and the Tariff Study, University of Alabama Press, 1956; *A Guide to the Use of Advisory Committees,* U.S. Department of Health, Education, and Welfare, 1959; *The Leader Looks at Authority and Hierarchy* (monograph), Leadership Resources, Inc., 1961; *The Leader Looks at Decision-Making* (monograph), Leadership Resources, Inc., 1961; (with A. M. Woodruff) *The Federal Government and the Cities,* George Washington University, 1963; *Delegating and Sharing Work,* Leadership Resources, Inc., 1966; *The Organization and Use of the Community Shelter Planning Council and Technical Advisory Committee,* Government Printing Office, 1966; *Understanding the Management Function,* Leadership Resources, Inc., 1966; (editor) *Federal Contributions to Management: Effects on the Public and Private Sectors,* Praeger, 1971. Contributor of articles to professional journals.

SIDELIGHTS: David S. Brown told *CA:* "The written word is still the most economical as well as the most long-lasting method of communicating with others. If we thought more often of *writing* in these dimensions, we would probably give more care to it. It has another virtue also: it encourages us to organize our thoughts, to develop them logically, to say what we want to say. Those who write badly often do so because their thinking is jumbled. Getting our thoughts down on paper forces us to think more clearly. If we would hope to have influence with others, we must give attention to the written word."

*   *   *

BROWN, Eleanor Frances 1908-

PERSONAL: Born May 28, 1908, in Spokane, Wash.; daughter of John Francis and Lucretia (Mack) Brown. *Education:* Washington State College (now University), B.A.Ed., 1931; Syracuse University, M.A.Ed., 1935; University of Texas, graduate study, 1938-39; University of Washington, Seattle, B.A., in L.S., 1941; further summer study at Washington State College and University of Idaho. *Politics:* Republican. *Religion:* Protestant. *Home:* 2092-D Ronda Granada, Laguna Hills, Calif. 92653.

CAREER: High school teacher of English and other subjects in Washington, Oregon, and New York, at intervals, 1931-40; Clackamas County Library, Oregon City, Ore., assistant county librarian, 1941-42; Deschutes County Library, Bend, Ore., head librarian, 1942-59, director of Central Oregon Regional Library, based in Bend, 1957-59; Montana State University (now University of Montana), Missoula, assistant professor of library science, 1959-60; Camas Public Library, Camas, Wash., head librarian, 1960-62; Santa Ana Public Library, Santa Ana, Calif., head of extension services and publicity, 1963-69; free-lance public library consultant and workshop director, 1969—. Teacher of summer courses in library science at University of Denver, 1956, Western Michigan University, 1970, and Southern Oregon College, 1971. *Member:* American Library Association, American Association of University Professors, American Association for Retired Persons (president of Springfield, Ore. chapter, 1971-72), Oregon Library Association (president, 1944-45), Phi Beta Kappa, Phi Kappa Phi, Theta Sigma Phi, Pi Lambda Theta.

WRITINGS—Juvenile books: *Golden Lady: The Story of an American Show Horse,* Lothrop, 1946; *A Horse for Peter,* Messner, 1950; *Wendy Wanted a Pony,* Messner, 1951; *The Colt from Horse Heaven Hills,* Messner, 1956; *Mountain Palomino,* Lothrop, 1956.

Nonfiction: *Bookmobiles and Bookmobile Service,* Scarecrow, 1967; *Modern Branch Libraries and Libraries in Systems,* Scarecrow, 1970; *Library Service to the Disadvantaged,* Scarecrow, 1971; *Bibliotherapy and Its Widening Applications,* Scarecrow, 1975. Contributor to *Author and Journalist, Wilson Library Bulletin, Science & Mechanics, Horse Lover,* and other journals; has also written more than one hundred feature stories for newspapers.

WORK IN PROGRESS: A book on cutting library costs, for Scarecrow; a story, for children, of a boy and dog.

AVOCATIONAL INTERESTS: Gardening, fishing, photography, woodworking, boating, buying and selling real estate, and oil painting.

*   *   *

BROWN, Frederick G(ramm) 1932-

PERSONAL: Born April 6, 1932, in Madison, Wis.; son of Fred E. (an accountant) and Meda (Gramm) Brown; married Barbara Ann Thaller (an art teacher), June 23, 1956; children: Jeffrey, Kirk, Daniel. *Education:* University of Wisconsin, B.A., 1954, M.A., 1955; University of Minnesota, Ph.D., 1958. *Religion:* Lutheran. *Home:* 2616 Kellogg, Ames, Iowa 50010. *Office:* Department of Psychology, Iowa State University, Ames, Iowa 50011.

CAREER: University of Missouri, Columbia, assistant professor of psychology and assistant director of testing and counseling, 1958-61; Iowa State University, Ames, assistant professor, 1961-64, associate professor, 1964-68, professor of psychology and education, 1968—. *Member:* American Psychological Association (fellow), American Educational Research Association, National Council on Measurement in Education, American Association for the Advancement of Science, Phi Beta Kappa. *Awards, honors:* National postdoctoral fellow, U.S. Office of Education, 1967-68; fellow, Center for Advanced Study in the Behavioral Sciences, 1967-68.

WRITINGS: Principles of Educational and Psychological Testing, Dryden Press, 1970, 2nd edition, Holt, 1976; *Measurement and Evaluation,* F. E. Peacock, 1971. Contributor to education and psychology journals.

*   *   *

BROWN, Irene Bennett 1932-

PERSONAL: Born January 31, 1932, in Topeka, Kan.; daughter of Paul Howard and Vesta (Helberg) Bennett; married Robert Ray Brown (a research chemist), November 2, 1951; children: Rourke Alan, Corey Wayne, Melia Elaine, Shana Leigh. *Education:* Attended high schools in Oregon. *Address:* Box 75, 149 West Union, Jefferson, Ore. 97352.

CAREER: Worked in Salem, Ore., as waitress, 1951, retail clerk, 1951-52, and long distance telephone operator, 1952-53; writer for children. *Member:* Society of Children's Book Writers (member of board of advisors), Western Writers of

America, Pacific Northwest Writers Conference, Kansas State Historical Society. *Awards, honors:* Pacific Northwest Writers Conference, editors award for juvenile stories, 1967, 1969, and for best children's book, 1975.

WRITINGS: To Rainbow Valley (juvenile), McKay, 1969; *Run from a Scarecrow* (juvenile), Concordia, 1978. Author of weekly column on children's activities for three Oregon newspapers. Contributor of adult articles to *Westways, Northwest Living, Portland Oregonian, Oregon Journal,* and other publications; contributor of children's short stories and serials to *Five/Six, Friends, Fun for Middlers, Children's Friend,* and other magazines. Woman's editor, *Capitol Press* (Oregon farm weekly).

WORK IN PROGRESS: Larnie, an adventure novel for girls set in the old West; other juvenile novels; Americana.

SIDELIGHTS: Irene Bennett Brown told *CA:* "When writing a book, I always pick a subject I care very much about, then read everything I can find about that subject. From this research a story line, or plot, will begin to build in my imagination, along with characters to people the plot. I then make a brief outline of the story, being sure I know how I want the story to end. I write each book manuscript through, from start to finish, three or more times. The manuscript I offer to a publisher is always the very best I can do.

"Why do I write? Because it is almost as necessary to me as breathing. Reading a good book, and I read constantly, always makes me want to *write* a good book.

"Those who like to read books hold a golden key—to knowledge, far journeys, adventure, and good friends. It is the same with writers of books—in our imagination we can go anywhere we like, be anyone we want to be, in any time or place we choose. There is no better life!"

* * *

BROWN, James Cooke 1921-

PERSONAL: Born July 21, 1921, in Tagbillarin, Bohol, Philippines; son of Bryan Burtis (a teacher) and Violet (Cooke) Brown; married Lujoye Fuller (a medical research technician), August, 1959; children: Jefferson, Jill, Jennifer. *Education:* University of Minnesota, B.A. (cum laude), 1946, Ph.D., 1952. *Politics:* Socialist. *Religion:* None. *Office:* Office of the Director, Loglan Institute, Gainesville, Fla.

CAREER: Wayne University (now Wayne State University), Detroit, Mich., instructor in sociology, 1949-50; Indiana University, Bloomington, instructor in sociology, 1950-52; Institute of Motivation Research, Croton, N.Y., director of statistical controls, 1954-55; University of Florda, Gainesville, assistant professor of humanities and sociology, 1955-62; Loglan Institute, Gainesville, Fla., director, 1962—. Visiting professor of philosophy, University of Florida, 1970-71. *Military service:* U.S. Army Air Forces, 1941-45; became first lieutenant; received Distinguished Flying Cross, Purple Heart, Air Medal with three oak-leaf clusters. *Member:* American Association for the Advancement of Science.

WRITINGS—All published by Loglan Institute, except as indicated: (With wife, Lujoye Fuller Brown) *Loglan 4: A Loglan-English Dictionary,* 1963; (with L. F. Brown) *Loglan 5: An English-Loglan Dictionary,* 1963; (with L. F. Brown) *Loglan 3: Speaking Loglan,* 1965; *Loglan 1: A Logical Language,* 1966, 3rd edition, 1975; *Loglan 2: Methods of Construction,* 1970; *The Troika Incident: A Tetralogue in Two Parts,* Doubleday, 1970; *Loglan 4 and 5: A Loglan-*

English/English-Loglan Dictionary (sole compiler; revised edition of *Loglan 4: A Loglan-English Dictionary* and *Loglan 5: An English-Loglan Dictionary),* 1975.

WORK IN PROGRESS: Books on interpersonal perception, on science and human ethics, and on the nature of man, the good, and the possible.

SIDELIGHTS: James Cooke Brown invented the Parker Brothers game, "Careers." He has lived in Mexico, France, Spain, England, Greece, and the Philippines.†

* * *

BROWN, James Patrick 1948-

PERSONAL: Born June 28, 1948, in St. Louis, Mo.; son of Robert L. and Anne C. (Donnelly) Brown. *Education:* Attended St. Louis University, 1967-70. *Politics:* Democrat. *Religion:* Roman Catholic. *Home:* 4537 Ravensworth, Annandale, Va. 22003. *Office:* United States Department of Transportation, Washington, D.C. 20590.

CAREER: Office of the Second Congressional District, St. Louis, Mo., administrative assistant to Representative James W. Symington, 1970-77; U.S. Department of Transportation, Washington, D.C., administrative assistant in Office of the Assistant Secretary, 1977—. *Military service:* National Guard, 1969-76. *Member:* University City Library Association.

WRITINGS: (With James A. Kearns III) *Era of Challenge,* edited by Herald M. Doxsee, B. Herder, 1970.

* * *

BROWN, Lee Dolph 1890-1971

July 25, 1890—March 20, 1971; American publisher, author, and editor. Obituaries: *Washington Post,* March 24, 1971; *Publishers' Weekly,* April 12, 1971.

* * *

BROWN, Michael John 1932-

PERSONAL: Born January 7, 1932, in Wallasey, England; became naturalized United States citizen, 1966; son of William H. (an office manager) and Nora (Sprigings) Brown; married Lee Hale (a teacher), December 17, 1955; children: Julie, Colin, Mary Kathryn. *Education:* La Grange College, B.A., 1956; Emory University, M.A., 1958, Ph.D., 1964. *Religion:* Methodist. *Home:* 333 South Candler St., Decatur, Ga. 30030. *Office:* Department of History, Agnes Scott College, Decatur, Ga. 30030.

CAREER: Agnes Scott College, Decatur, Ga., instructor in history, 1960-62; La Grange College, La Grange, Ga., assistant professor, 1962-65; Agnes Scott College, associate professor, 1965-71, professor and chairman of department of history and political science, 1971—, Charles A. Dana Professor of History, 1976—. *Military service:* British Army, Royal Artillery, 1950-52. *Member:* American Historical Association, Royal Historical Society (fellow), Southern Historical Association, Conference on British Studies. *Awards, honors:* Danforth fellow, 1956-64.

WRITINGS: Itinerant Ambassador: The Life and Career of Sir Thomas Roe, University Press of Kentucky, 1970.

WORK IN PROGRESS: Six short articles for inclusion in *Biographical Dictionary of British Radicals in the Seventeenth Century.*

* * *

BROWN, R(onald) G(ordon) S(clater) 1929-

PERSONAL: Born May 21, 1929, in Edinburgh, Scotland;

son of Gordon (a civil servant) and Tomima (Slater) Brown; married Jean Isobel Peebles (a teacher), August 2, 1952; children: Gordon David Alexander, Stuart Chester. *Education:* University of St. Andrews, M.A., 1951; University of Hull, Ph.D., 1972. *Home:* 16 Tranby Lane, Anlaby, Humberside, England. *Office:* Institute for Health Studies, University of Hull, Hull, Humberside, England.

CAREER: Ministry of Health and Local Government, Belfast, Northern Ireland, administrator, 1953-58; University of Manchester, Manchester, England, lecturer in social administration, 1958-62; Scottish Home and Health Department, Edinburgh, Scotland, administrator, 1962-65; University of Hull, Hull, Humberside, England, senior lecturer in social administration, 1965-74, director of Institute for Health Studies, 1974—. *Military service:* Royal Air Force, 1951-53; became flying officer. *Member:* Royal Institute of Public Administration. *Awards, honors:* Haldane Essay Prize of Royal Institute of Public Administration, 1964.

WRITINGS: The Administrative Process in Britain, Barnes & Noble, 1970; (contributor) K. Jones, editor, *The Yearbook of Social Policy in Britain, 1971,* Routledge & Kegan Paul, 1972; *The Changing National Health Service,* Routledge & Kegan Paul, 1973; (with R.W.H. Stones) *The Male Nurse,* G. Bell & Sons, 1973; *The Administrative Process as Incrementalism,* Open University Press, 1974; (contributor) W. D. Reekie and N. C. Hunt, editors, *Management in the Social and Safety Services,* Barnes & Noble, 1974; *The Management of Welfare,* Martin Robertson, 1975; (contributor) K. Jones, editor, *Yearbook of Social Policy in Britain, 1975,* Routledge & Kegan Paul, 1976. Contributor to public administration, hospital, and nursing journals.

WORK IN PROGRESS: Research on health care organization and administrative systems in the National Health Service.

* * *

BROWN, Stuart C. 1938-

PERSONAL: Born August 16, 1938, in Edinburgh, Scotland; son of John Duncan (a chartered accountant) and Violet (Creed) Brown; married Mavis Brownlee (a play-group supervisor), March 29, 1966; children: Frances, Jonathan. *Education:* University of St. Andrews, M.A., 1960; University of London, Ph.D., 1963. *Home:* 42 Park Rd., New Barnet, Hertfordshire, England. *Office:* Faculty of Arts, Walton Hall, Open University, Milton Keynes, Buckinghamshire MK7 6AA, England.

CAREER: University of London, Birkbeck College, London, England, lecturer in philosophy, 1965-72; Open University, Milton Keynes, Buckinghamshire, England, senior lecturer in philosophy, 1972—. Assistant director, Royal Institute of Philosophy.

WRITINGS: Do Religious Claims Make Sense?, Macmillan (New York), 1969.

* * *

BROWNE, Michael Dennis 1940-

PERSONAL: Born May 28, 1940, in Walton, England; son of Edgar Dennis and Winifred Browne. *Education:* University of Hull, B.A., 1962; University of Iowa, M.A., 1967. *Home:* 1525 Talmage Ave., S.E., Minneapolis, Minn. 55414. *Office:* Department of English, University of Minnesota, Minneapolis, Minn. 55455.

CAREER: Columbia University, School of the Arts, New York, N.Y., adjunct assistant professor, 1968; Bennington College, Bennington, Vt., member of English department, 1969-71; University of Minnesota, Minneapolis, visiting assistant professor, 1971-72, assistant professor, 1972-75, associate professor of English, 1975—. Visiting lecturer in creative writing at University of Iowa, 1967-68. *Awards, honors:* Borestone Mountain Poetry Award, 1974.

WRITINGS—Poems: *The Wife of Winter,* Scribner, 1970; *Sun Exercises,* Red Studio, 1976. Poetry included in several anthologies. Contributor of poetry to periodicals.

WORK IN PROGRESS: A song cycle for tenor and piano, an Easter cantata, a large choral work entitled "North Shore," and other songs and carols, all with Stephen Paulus.

SIDELIGHTS: Michael Dennis Browne told *CA:* "I especially enjoy writing for music, and years ago wrote four texts for the young English composer David Lord, three of them works for children, one a song cycle for Janet Baker. Now I have begun a collaboration with a young Minnesota composer, Stephen Paulus, and our first work was a group of children's songs.... It's challenging to write for music, and wonderfully exciting when the music is good and gives your words many more dimensions and implications."

* * *

BRUCE, Violet R(ose)

PERSONAL: Born in London, England; daughter of John and Emma (Rogers) Bruce. *Education:* Bergnan Osterberg College of Physical Education, Diploma; University of Leicester, Dip.Ed., M.Ed., and Ph.D. *Home:* Corner Cottage, Skeffington, Leicester, England.

CAREER: Teacher, physiotherapist, and adviser in education; City of Leicester College of Education, Leicester, England, principal lecturer and head of dance department.

WRITINGS: Dance and Dance Drama in Education, Pergamon, 1965; (with Joan D. Tooke) *Lord of the Dance: An Approach to Religious Education,* Pergamon, 1966; *Awakening the Slower Mind,* Pergamon, 1969; *Movement in Silence and Sound,* G. Bell, 1970.

WORK IN PROGRESS: With Joan D. Tooke, *Words into Dance;* research into expressive needs of handicapped children.††

* * *

BRUMM, Ursula 1919-

PERSONAL: Born October 24, 1919, in Berlin, Germany; daughter of Willi and Claere (Dillenseger) Brumm. *Education:* University of Berlin, Ph.D., 1943; Harvard University, postdoctoral study, 1953-55; Free University of Berlin, Habilitation, 1961. *Home:* Bismarckstrasse 1, 1000 Berlin 37, Germany. *Office:* John F. Kennedy Institute for North American Studies, Lansstrasse 7-9, 1000 Berlin 33, Germany.

CAREER: Monumenta Germaniae Historica, Berlin, Germany, research assistant, 1943-45; Free University of Berlin, Berlin, instructor in American literature, 1956-63, associate professor, 1963-66, professor of American civilization, 1966—. *Member:* German Association of American Studies (member of executive committee, 1965-72), European Association of American Studies (member of executive committee, 1966-71), Modern Language Association of America (member of Section I executive committee, 1972-74). *Awards, honors:* Commonwealth Fund fellowship at Harvard University, 1953-55.

WRITINGS: Die religioese Typologie im amerikanischen

Denken, E. J. Brill, 1963, translation by John Hoaglund published as *Religious Typology in American Thought,* Rutgers University Press, 1970; *Literatur des Puritanismus,* Wissenschaftliche Buchgesellschaft Darmstadt, 1973. Member of editorial board, *Jahrbuch fuer Amerikastudien,* 1966-75; European editor, *Early American Literature,* 1975—.

WORK IN PROGRESS: The American Writer and History.

*   *   *

BUCCO, Martin 1929-

PERSONAL: Born December 3, 1929, in Newark, N.J.; son of Mario and Ann (De Salvo) Bucco; married Edith Erickson, 1956; children: Tamara Lisa. *Education:* Rutgers University, student, 1948-49; Highlands University, B.A., 1952; Columbia University, M.A., 1957; University of California, Berkeley, further graduate study, 1957-58; University of Missouri, Ph.D., 1963. *Politics:* Independent. *Home:* Horsetooth Heights, Fort Collins, Colo. 80521. *Office:* Department of English, Colorado State University, Fort Collins, Colo. 80523.

CAREER: Junior high school English teacher in Las Vegas, N.M., 1954-55; high school English teacher in Raton, N.M., 1955-56; North Dakota State Teachers College, Valley City, instructor in English, 1958-59; University of Missouri, Columbia, instructor in English, 1959-63; Colorado State University, Fort Collins, assistant professor, 1963-67, associate professor, 1967-71, professor of English, 1971—, honors professor, 1975. *Military service:* U.S. Naval Reserve, 1947-49, U.S. Army, 1952-53. *Member:* Western Literature Association. *Awards, honors:* National Humanities Foundation summer grant, 1968. Recipient of numerous faculty research grants.

WRITINGS: The Voluntary Tongue (poems), Wurlitzer Foundation, 1957; (author of introduction) Thomas Bulfinch, *The Age of Fable,* Harper, 1966; *Frank Waters,* Steck, 1969; *Wilbur Daniel Steele,* Twayne, 1972; *An American Tragedy* (study guide), Cliff's Notes, 1974; *E. W. Howe,* Boise State College, in press. Contributor of poems, short stories, and criticism to numerous periodicals, including *Southwest Literature, Colorado State Review, Missouri Historical Review, Occident, Studies in the Novel, New Generation, Four Quarters, Denver Post,* and *Rocky Mountain News.* Assistant editor, *Ceramic Age,* 1953-54. *Western American Literature,* assistant editor, 1966-74, member of editorial advisory board, 1974—, member of executive council, 1976—.

WORK IN PROGRESS: Rene Wellek, for Twayne.

SIDELIGHTS: Martin Bucco told *CA* that he "began writing at age sixteen—journalism in high school, poetry and stories in college, and criticism in graduate school.... My teaching and my writing, my work and my play, form a whole, an outgrowth of my passion for literature and for literary studies."

*   *   *

BUCKINGHAM, James (William) 1932-
(Jamie Buckingham)

PERSONAL: Born March 28, 1932, in Vero Beach, Fla.; son of Walter S. (a businessman) and Elvira (Thompson) Buckingham; married Jacqueline Law, June 4, 1954; children: Bruce, Robin, Bonnie, Timothy, Sandy. *Education:* Mercer University, A.B., 1954; Southwestern Baptist Theological Seminary, B.D., 1957, postgraduate student, 1958.

Home: 1149 Sparkman, Melbourne, Fla. 32935. *Agent:* Evelyn Singer Agency, Inc., Box 163, Briarcliff Manor, N.Y. 10510. *Office:* Logos International, 201 Church St., Plainfield, N.J. 07061.

CAREER: Pastor of South Main Street Baptist Church, Greenwood, S.C., 1957-65, Harbor City Baptist Church, Eau Gallie, Fla., 1965-66, and Tabernacle Church, Melbourne, Fla., 1967—. Member of publisher's board, *Logos International.* Member of board of board of directors, Logos Fellowship, 1971—. *Military service:* U.S. Army Reserve, chaplain, 1954-58; became captain. *Member:* Exchange Club, Civil Air Patrol, Lions Club. *Awards, honors:* Named best columnist by Florida Press Association, 1974, and Evangelical Press Association, 1975.

WRITINGS—All published by Logos International, except as indicated: (With Nicky Cruz) *Run Baby Run,* 1968; (with Arthur Katz) *Ben Israel,* 1969; *Some Gall and Other Reflections on Life,* Word, Inc., 1969; *Your New Look,* 1970; *Coming Alive,* 1970; (with Cruz) *The Lonely Now,* 1971; (with Pat Robertson) *Shout It from the Housetops,* 1971; *O Happy Day,* Word, Inc., 1971; (contributor) Ben Johnson, editor, *Rebels in the Church,* Word, Inc., 1971; (with Aaron Johnson) *The End of Youngblood Johnson,* Chosen Books, 1972; *Into the Glory,* 1974; (with Corrie ten Boom) *Tramp for the Lord,* Revell, 1974; (with Juan Carlos Ortiz) *Call to Discipleship,* 1975; (with Father Sherwood) *Let's Begin Again,* 1975; *Risky Living,* 1976; *Daughter of Destiny,* 1976; (with ten Boom) *Don't Wrestle, Just Nestle,* Revell, 1976.

With Kathryn Kuhlman; all published by Bethany Fellowship, except as indicated: *God Can Do It Again,* Prentice-Hall, 1969; *Nothing Is Impossible,* Prentice-Hall, 1973; *Captain LeVrier Believes in Miracles,* 1973; *Ten Thousand Miles for a Miracle,* 1974; *How Big Is God?,* 1974; *Standing Tall,* 1975; *Never Too Late,* 1975; *Twilight to Dawn,* 1976; *Medicine to Miracles,* 1976.

Author of regular column, "The Last Word," *Logos Journal,* 1972—; editorial columnist, *Vera Beach Journal* and *National Courier.* Contributor of over 100 articles to national periodicals. Roving editor, *Guideposts,* 1972-74; executive editor, *Logos Journal,* 1975—.

SIDELIGHTS: James Buckingham told *CA* that he "has spent time in the Amazon jungles, behind the Iron Curtain, the islands of the South Pacific, the Orient, and into the Himalayas—collecting research for books and carrying the good news of the move of God as well."

*   *   *

BUCKINGHAM, Willis J(ohn) 1938-

PERSONAL: Born July 14, 1938, in Bismarck, N.D.; son of Tracy Willis (a physician) and Lorraine (Bohlig) Buckingham. *Education:* Harvard University, A.B., 1960; Union Theological Seminary, New York, graduate study, 1960-61, 1962-63; University of Wisconsin, M.S., 1962; Indiana University, Ph.D., 1971. *Home:* 7732 East Northland Dr., Scottsdale, Ariz. 85251. *Office:* Department of English, Arizona State University, Tempe, Ariz. 85281.

CAREER: Western Michigan University, Kalamazoo, instructor in English, 1963-65; Indiana University, Bloomington, teaching associate in English, 1965-68; Arizona State University, Tempe, assistant professor of English, 1969—. *Member:* Modern Language Association of America.

WRITINGS: (Editor) *Emily Dickinson, an Annotated Bibliography: Writings, Scholarship, Criticism and Ana, 1850-1968,* Indiana University Press, 1970; (contributor) James

Woodress, editor, *American Literary Scholarship: An Annual–1975,* Duke University Press, 1977.

WORK IN PROGRESS: A volume surveying Emily Dickinson's critical reception in the 1890's.

* * *

BUCKLEY, Thomas H(ugh) 1932-

PERSONAL: Born September 11, 1932, in Elkhart, Ind.; son of Bernard L. (a county office holder) and Martha B. (Swoveland) Buckley; married first wife, 1954; married second wife, Patricia, 1968; children: Christopher, Kathryn, Elizabeth, Thomas J., Barbara. *Education:* Northwestern University, student, 1950-53; Indiana University, A.B., 1955, M.A., 1956, Ph.D., 1961. *Politics:* Republican. *Religion:* Methodist. *Office:* Department of History, University of Tulsa, Tulsa, Okla. 74104.

CAREER: University of South Dakota, Vermillion, instructor, 1960-61, assistant professor, 1961-64, associate professor, 1964-68, professor of history, 1968-69; Indiana University, Bloomington, visiting professor of history, 1969-71; University of Tulsa, Tulsa, Okla., professor of history and chairman of department, 1971—, chairman of division of humanistic studies, 1974—. *Member:* American Historical Association, Society for Historians of American Foreign Relations, Organization of American Historians, Phi Alpha Theta, Lambda Chi Alpha. *Awards, honors:* Fulbright summer fellow in Taiwan, 1963; research fellow at Denver School of International Relations, 1964-65; postdoctoral fellow in Japanese language and history at Stanford University, 1968; Phi Alpha Theta national award for best first book by a historian, 1971, for *The United States and the Washington Conference, 1921-1922.*

WRITINGS: The United States and the Washington Conference, 1921-1922, University of Tennessee Press, 1970; (research associate) Thomas D. Clark, *Indiana University,* Indiana University Press, Volume I, 1970, Volume II, 1975; (contributor) Edward Bennett and Richard Burns, editors, *Diplomats in Crisis,* American Bibliographic Center-Clio Press, 1975. Contributor of reviews to historical journals.

WORK IN PROGRESS: Thomas F. Millard: American Journalist in Shanghai, 1913-1941; and *American Foreign Relations, 1913-1945.*

* * *

BUDGE, Ian 1936-

PERSONAL: Born October 21, 1936, in Leeds, Yorkshire, England; son of John Elder (a pharmacist) and Elizabeth (Barnet) Budge; married Judith Beatrice Ruth Harrison (a teacher), July 17, 1964; children: Gavin Elder, Eileen Elizabeth. *Education:* University of Edinburgh, M.A. (first class honors in history), 1959; Yale University, A.M. (with distinction), 1961, Ph.D., 1966. *Politics:* Scottish nationalist. *Religion:* Church of Scotland. *Home:* 4 Oxford Rd., Colchester, England. *Office:* Department of Government, University of Essex, Colchester, Essex, England.

CAREER: University of Edinburgh, Edinburgh, Scotland, assistant lecturer, 1962-64; University of Strathclyde, Glasgow, Scotland, assistant lecturer, 1963-64, lecturer, 1964-66; University of Essex, Colchester, England, lecturer, 1966-68, senior lecturer, 1968-71, reader, 1971-75, professor of government, 1975—, chairman of department, 1974-77. Co-director, Social Science Research Council project for a computer survey analysis package for social scientists, 1969-71; director, summer school of European Consortium for Political Research, 1971, 1972, 1973.

WRITINGS: (With D. W. Urwin) *Scottish Political Behaviour: A Case Study in British Homogeneity,* Longmans, Green, 1966; *Agreement and the Stability of Democracy,* Markham, 1970; (with M. Margolis, J. S. Brand, and A. L. M. Smith) *Political Stratification and Democracy,* Macmillan, 1972; (with C. O'Leary) *Belfast: Approach to Crisis,* Macmillan, 1973; (editor with I. Crewe and D. J. Farlie) *Party Identification and Beyond,* Wiley, 1976; (with Farlie) *Voting and Party Competition,* Wiley, 1977. Contributor to political science journals.

AVOCATIONAL INTERESTS: Opera, military architecture.

* * *

BUDGEN, Frank Spencer Curtis 1882-1971

1882—April 26, 1971; British author and associate of James Joyce. Obituaries: *New York Times,* April 29, 1971; *Antiquarian Bookman,* May 17, 1971.

* * *

BUFORD, Thomas O(liver) 1932-

PERSONAL: Born November 18, 1932, in Overton, Tex.; son of Oliver P. (a businessman) and Annie Doris (Smith) Buford; married Delores Jean Phife, December 27, 1954; children: Russell Warren, Robert Carl, Anna Louise. *Education:* North Texas State University, B.A., 1955; Southwestern Baptist Theological Seminary, B.D., 1958; Boston University, Ph.D., 1963. *Home:* 104 Abingdon Way, Greenville, S.C. 29607. *Office:* Department of Philosophy, Furman University, Greenville, S.C. 29613.

CAREER: Kentucky Southern College (now University of Louisville), Louisville, assistant professor of philosophy, 1962-68; North Texas State University, Denton, assistant professor of philosophy, 1968-69; Furman University, Greenville, S.C., 1969—, began as associate professor, now professor of philosophy. *Member:* American Philosophical Association, Philosophy of Education Society, South Atlantic Philosophy of Education Society, Southern Society for Philosophy and Psychology, South Carolina Society for Philosophy and Psychology.

WRITINGS: (Editor) *We Pass This Way But Once,* Southern Press, 1962; *Toward a Philosophy of Education,* Holt, 1969; *Essays on Other Minds,* University of Illinois Press, 1970; (with John Howie) *Contemporary Studies in Philosophical Idealism,* Claude Stark, 1976. Contributor to professional journals.

WORK IN PROGRESS: Research in philosophy of learning, the other minds problem, and methodology in Plato's later dialogues.

AVOCATIONAL INTERESTS: Playing trombone in local community orchestras, backpacking into wilderness areas.

* * *

BULLOCK, Paul 1924-

PERSONAL: Born November 6, 1924, in Pasadena, Calif.; son of Paul (a bookkeeper) and Eleanor (Galloway) Bullock; married Constance Strickland (a librarian), June, 1962. *Education:* Occidental College, B.A., 1948, M.A., 1949; University of California, Los Angeles, graduate study, 1948-50. *Politics:* Democrat. *Religion:* None. *Home:* 640 The Village, #117, Redondo Beach, Calif. 90277. *Office:* Institute of Industrial Relations, University of California, Los Angeles, Calif. 90024.

CAREER: El Camino College, Los Angeles, Calif., instructor in economics, 1949-50; Occidental College, Los Angeles, instructor in economics, 1950-51; Wage Stabilization Board, Los Angeles Region, Los Angeles, wage analyst, 1951-53; University of California, Los Angeles, research economist, Institute of Industrial Relations, 1953—. Consultant to McCone Commission, 1965, and Kerner Commission, 1967. Chairman of New Careers Task Force, Los Angeles County Commission on Delinquency and Crime, 1968-70. Member of board of directors, Central City Community Mental Health Center, Jazz Heritage Foundation, Transportation Opportunity Program, and other community organizations. *Military service:* U.S. Army, 1943-46. *Member:* Industrial Relations Research Association, Association for Evolutionary Economics, National Committee for Full Employment, Phi Beta Kappa, Pi Gamma Mu.

WRITINGS: Standards of Wage Determination, Institute of Industrial Relations, University of California, 1960; *Merit Employment,* Institute of Industrial Relations, University of California, 1960; *Equal Opportunity in Employment,* Institute of Industrial Relations, University of California, 1965; (with Fred H. Schmidt and Robert Singleton) *Hard-Core Unemployment and Poverty in Los Angeles,* U.S. Government Printing Office, 1965; (contributor) Irving Howe and Jeremy Larner, editors, *Poverty: Views from the Left,* Morrow, 1968; (editor and contributor) *Watts: The Aftermath, by the People of Watts,* Grove, 1969.

(Contributor) John H. Burma, editor, *Mexican-American Problems in the United States: A Reader,* Harper, 1970; *Aspiration vs. Opportunity: "Careers" in the Inner City,* University of Michigan Press, 1973; (editor and contributor) *A Full Employment Policy for America,* Institute of Industrial Relations, University of California, 1974; (editor and contributor) *Goals for Full Employment,* Institute of Industrial Relations, University of California, 1976; (editor) *Directory of Organizations in Greater Los Angeles,* Institute of Industrial Relations, University of California, 1976. Contributor of articles to *New Republic, Progressive, Journal of Negro Education,* and other journals.

WORK IN PROGRESS: Jerry Voorhis: The Idealist as Politician, a political biography; *Creative Careers: Minorities in the Arts;* a study of CETA programs in Orange County; policy studies in youth employment and training.

AVOCATIONAL INTERESTS: Jazz, sports, tennis.

*   *   *

BUNCH, David R.
(Darryl R. Groupe)

PERSONAL: Born in Lowry City, Mo.; son of David Henry and Bessie Edna (Barker) Bunch; children: Phyllis Elaine, Velma Lorraine. *Education:* Central Missouri State College (now University), B.S.; Washington University, St. Louis, Mo., M.A., further graduate study; also studied at Writer's Workshop, University of Iowa. *Home address:* P.O. Box 12233, Soulard Station, St. Louis, Mo. 63157. *Agent:* Virginia Kidd, P.O. Box 278, Milford, Pa. 18337. *Office:* Rusco Apartments, 2021 South Compton, St. Louis, Mo. 63104.

CAREER: U.S. Air Force Aeronautical Chart and Information Center, St. Louis, Mo., cartographer (civilian), beginning 1954. Judge for *Scimitar and Song*'s best poems of the year contest, 1970. *Military service:* U.S. Army Air Forces. *Member:* Science Fiction Writers of America, Alpha Phi Sigma. *Awards, honors:* Fourth place in *Promethean Lamp*

poetry contest, 1966; first prize in long poem category in *Scimitar and Song* awards for best poems of the year, 1969.

WRITINGS: Jones Very, A Child of God (critical study), Washington Universities Studies, 1950; *Moderan* (science fiction novel), Avon, 1971. Stories represented in numerous anthologies, including: *Annual of the Year's Best S-F,* Simon & Schuster, 1962, Dial Press, 1965, 1966; *Dangerous Visions,* edited by Harlan Ellison, Doubleday, 1967; *Protostars,* edited by David Gerrold, Ballentine, 1971; *Generation,* edited by Gerrold, Dell, Volume I, 1972, Volume II, 1974; *The Smith Fiction,* edited by Harry Smith, Horizon Press, 1972; *New Dimensions IV,* edited by Robert Silverberg, New American Library, 1974; *Future Pastimes,* edited by Scott Edelstein, Aurora, 1977. Contributor of more than 120 stories to *Southwest Review, New Mexico Quarterly, Smith, Fantastic Stories, Genesis West, San Francisco Review, Amazing Stories,* and other periodicals; contributor of more than fifty poems to newspapers and magazines, including *Fiddlehead, Flame, Poetry Digest, Epos, Washington Evening Star,* and *Aspects.*

WORK IN PROGRESS: Good Luck, Good Hanging and Good Kicking, an anthology of short stories; *Little Brother, Little Sister,* a novel; a collection of science fiction short stories; a book-length collection of poems.

SIDELIGHTS: David Bunch told *CA:* "I'm not in this business of writing primarily to describe or explain or entertain, you know. I'm here with the satirical comment, and the social statement and the grim assessment to make the reader think; I'm here to tear the utter shell off Sham and dynamite the facade from the lying face of Pretense. I'm here to solve and resolve the world. Even if I have to grab the reader up (with words, of course) and swing him through the air like a bat (baseball, that is), I WILL startle him (I hope) to awareness and pound his utter face (thinking) into the utter lampposts of all his flawed villages and towns. I hate almost everything now, I fear almost everything now, I mistrust almost everything now, I KNOW almost everything now is meaningless and drear. . . .''

Moderan has been accepted for publication in Argentina, France, Germany, and Italy.

AVOCATIONAL INTERESTS: The reading and study of the philosophical history of man, and the study and appreciation of the arts other than writing, especially painting and music.

BIOGRAPHICAL/CRITICAL SOURCES: Magazine of Fantasy and Science Fiction, December, 1972; *Amazing Stories,* January, 1973; *Son of WSFA Journal,* November, 1973.

*   *   *

BURCH, Francis F(loyd) 1932-

PERSONAL: Born May 15, 1932, in Baltimore, Md.; son of Thaddeus Joseph and Frances (Greenwell) Burch. *Education:* Attended Maryland Institute; Fordham University, A.B., 1956, M.A., 1958; Woodstock College, Ph.L., 1957, S.T.L., 1964; Sorbonne, University of Paris, Ph.D., 1967. *Home:* 54th and City Line Ave., Philadelphia, Pa. 19131. *Office:* Department of English, St. Joseph's College, Philadelphia, Pa. 19131.

CAREER: Entered Society of Jesus (Jesuits), 1950, ordained a priest, 1963; Gonzaga High School, Washington, D.C., English and French teacher, 1957-60; St. Joseph's College, Philadelphia, Pa., professor of English, 1967—, assistant dean, 1972-74. Trustee, St. Joseph's College, 1971-76.

WRITINGS: Tristan Corbiere: L'Originalite des "Amours jaunes" et leur influence sur T. S. Eliot, Nizet (Paris), 1970; (co-editor) *Charles Cros et Tristan Corbiere: Oeuvres completes,* Gallimard, 1970; *Sur Tristan Corbiere: Lettres inedites addressees au poete et premieres critiques le concernant,* Nizet (Paris), 1975. Contributor of articles to *American Literature, Downside Review, Modern Language Notes, Modern Language Review, Romance Notes,* and other periodicals.

BIOGRAPHICAL/CRITICAL SOURCES: Times Literary Supplement, September 18, 1970, September 10, 1976.

* * *

BURDETT, Winston 1913-

PERSONAL: Born December 12, 1913, in Buffalo, N.Y.; son of Owen and Elizabeth (White) Burdett; married Lea Schiavi, July 28, 1940 (died, 1942); married Giorgina Nathan, July 1, 1945; children: (second marriage) Cristina Sandra, Richard Michael. *Education:* Harvard University, B.A. (magna cum laude), 1933; Columbia University, graduate study, 1933-34. *Home:* Via Cassia Vecchia 15, Rome 00191, Italy. *Office:* CBS News, Via Condotti 61/A, Rome 00191, Italy.

CAREER: Prior to 1940 was reporter for *Brooklyn Eagle,* author of the column, "Sound Track," and associate editor of Sunday supplement, *Trend;* free-lance correspondent in Europe and Middle East, 1940-42; Columbia Broadcasting System News, New York City, staff correspondent, 1943—, reporting and broadcasting from New York City, Washington, D.C., and foreign capitols, presently as chief of Rome Bureau. Has covered assignments throughout western Europe, the Mediterranean, Africa, Middle East, India, and the Orient. *Member:* Association of Radio News Analysts (New York), Overseas Press Club (New York), Associazione Stampa Estera (Rome). *Awards, honors:* Headliner's Club award, 1948, for radio coverage of Bilbo hearings in Mississippi; Overseas Press Club award, 1958, for best television-radio reporting from abroad; Sigma Delta Chi award, 1966, for distinguished service in journalism.

WRITINGS: Encounter with the Middle East: An Intimate Report on What Lies behind the Arab-Israeli Conflict, Atheneum, 1969.

AVOCATIONAL INTERESTS: The theater, music.

* * *

BURDICK, Eric 1934-

PERSONAL: Born August 14, 1934, in Vancouver, British Columbia, Canada; son of Reginald Charleton (a businessman) and Lenore (Heinman) Burdick; married Angela Piercy (an artist), May 15, 1961; children: Dominic, Gray, Linus, Lucy, Ashling, Erica. *Education:* Attended high school in West Vancouver. *Residence:* London, England.

CAREER: The Ould Cod, Dublin, Ireland, owner, 1965-72; diplomatic speechwriter in London, England, 1973-75.

WRITINGS: I'm Coming Virginia (novel), Longmans, Green, 1962; *Old Rag Bone* (novel), Hutchinson, 1969; *How to Become a Complete Alcoholic: A Satire,* New English Library, 1974. Contributor of short stories to European publications.

WORK IN PROGRESS: A novel; a film; ghostwriting.

BIOGRAPHICAL/CRITICAL SOURCES: Times Literary Supplement, June 12, 1969; *Punch,* September 10, 1969.

BURGER, Robert S. 1913-

PERSONAL: Born November 13, 1913, in New York, N.Y.; son of Bernard (a merchant) and Pauline (Klein) Burger; married Ruth Kaplan, May 13, 1939 (died, 1943); married Elisabeth Gordon, August 12, 1946; children: (second marriage) Robert S., Jr., Grant Gordon, William Penn, James Oliver. *Education:* City College (now City College of the City University of New York), B.A., 1939; University of Minnesota, M.A., 1954. *Politics:* Democrat. *Religion:* Quaker. *Residence:* Glen Mills, Pa. 19342. *Office:* R. S. Burger & Associates, Inc., Glen Mills, Pa. 19432.

CAREER: Southern Illinois University, Carbondale, lecturer in journalism, 1954-55; *Louisville Courier-Journal,* Louisville, Ky., copy editor, 1955-56; Dartmouth College, Hanover, N.H., assistant professor, 1956-60; self-employed consultant on informative writing, Glen Mills, Pa., 1958-64, as president of R. S. Burger & Associates, 1964—.

WRITINGS: How to Write So People Can Understand You, Management Development Institute, 1969. Contributor to periodicals.

* * *

BURGESS, Robert L. 1938-

PERSONAL: Born June 24, 1938, in Long Beach, Calif.; son of Harry T. (a painter) and May (Armstrong) Burgess; married Judy Myers (a teacher), January 31, 1959; children: Lori L., Lynda L. *Education:* California State College at Long Beach (now California State University, Long Beach), B.A., 1962; Washington University, St. Louis, Mo., M.A., 1964, Ph.D., 1969. *Home:* 209 Elm St., Lemont, Pa. 16851. *Office:* College of Human Development, Pennsylvania State University, University Park, Pa. 16802.

CAREER: University of Washington, Seattle, acting assistant professor, 1965-68, assistant professor, 1968-69, associate professor of sociology, 1969-75; Pennsylvania State University, University Park, professor of human development, 1975—. *Military service:* U.S. Navy, 1956-58. *Member:* American Sociological Association, American Psychological Association, Association for the Advancement of Behavior Therapy, Society for Research in Child Development.

WRITINGS: (Compiler with D. G. Bushell) *Behavioral Sociology: The Experimental Analysis of Social Process,* Columbia University Press, 1969. Contributor of articles on drug use, criminal behavior, communication networks, social exchange, child abuse, and other topics to journals.

WORK IN PROGRESS: A book on exchange in developing relationships; research in observational and experimental analyses of child abuse and neglect and in the development of behavioral deterioration among the aged.

* * *

BURICH, Nancy J(ane) 1943-

PERSONAL: Born August 12, 1943, in Orange County, Calif.; daughter of William L. (a professor emeritus of ancient history at Kent State University) and Gladys (Meussner) Wannemacher; married Raymond L. Burich (a fellow in physiology at Cornell Medical Center), June 19, 1965. *Education:* Kent State University, B.A., 1965, M.L.S., 1968. *Home:* 10247 Hauser St., Lenexa, Kan. 66215. *Office:* Regent's Center, University of Kansas, Lawrence, Kan. 66044.

CAREER: Kent State University Library, Kent, Ohio, divisional assistant in the social sciences, 1965-67; Michigan State University, East Lansing, reference librarian, 1967-69, head of Business Library, 1969-70; Columbia University, Medical Library, New York, N.Y., reference librarian, 1970-71; University of Kansas, Regent's Center, Lawrence, librarian, 1976—. *Member:* American Library Association, Phi Alpha Theta, Alpha Gamma Delta.

WRITINGS: (Compiler) *Alexander the Great: A Bibliography,* Kent State University Press, 1970.

* * *

BURKHART, Robert E(dward) 1937-

PERSONAL: Born January 11, 1937, in Pittsburgh, Pa.; son of Edward Wendelin (a clerk) and Violet (Reichel) Burkhart; married Sylvia Davis (an associate professor of German), June 11, 1966; children: Heather Ellen. *Education:* University of Pittsburgh, B.B.A., 1958, M.A., 1963; University of Cincinnati, Ph.D., 1967. *Office:* Department of English, Eastern Kentucky University, Richmond, Ky. 40475.

CAREER: Bell Telephone Co., Richmond, Va., member of marketing staff, 1961-62; University of Kentucky, Lexington, instructor in English, 1965-67; Eastern Kentucky University, Richmond, assistant professor, 1967-69, associate professor, 1969-71, professor of English, 1971—. *Military service:* U.S. Army, 1959-61; became first lieutenant. U.S. Army Reserve, 1961-67; became captain. *Member:* International Shakespeare Association, Modern Language Association of America, Shakespeare Association of America, American Association of University Professors.

WRITINGS: (Editor with Francis X. Davy) *Perspectives on Our Time,* Houghton, 1970; *Shakespeare's Bad Quartos,* Mouton (The Hague), 1975. Contributor to literary publications.

WORK IN PROGRESS: A novel with a contemporary European setting; several short stories and suspense novels "in various stages of completion. Usually working on something Shakespearean as well."

AVOCATIONAL INTERESTS: Coin collecting.

* * *

BURKMAN, Katherine H. 1934-

PERSONAL: Born June 13, 1934, in Chicago, Ill.; daughter of Emil (an insurance salesman) and Beatrice (Reissman) Horween; married Allan M. Burkman (a professor of pharmacology), August 8, 1965; children: David Eric, Deborah Rae. *Education:* Radcliffe College, B.A., 1955; University of Chicago, M.A. and certificate of education, 1956; Ohio State University, Ph.D., 1968. *Religion:* Jewish. *Residence:* Columbus, Ohio. *Office:* Division of Comparative Literature, Ohio State University, 230 West 17th Ave., Columbus, Ohio 43210.

CAREER: Began as a high school teacher of English in Riverdale, N.Y., 1957-63; Harcourt, Brace, & World, Inc. (publisher), New York, N.Y., promotion writer, 1963-64; University of Iowa, Iowa City, teaching assistant, 1964-65; Butler University, Indianapolis, Ind., instructor in English, 1965-66; Ohio State University, Columbus, assistant professor of comparative literature, 1968—. *Member:* American Educational Theater Association, American Association of University Professors, Modern Language Association of America. *Awards, honors:* National Endowment for the Humanities grants, 1969-70, 1971-72.

WRITINGS: The Dramatic World of Harold Pinter: Its

Basis in Ritual, Ohio State University Press, 1971; (with Mark Auburn) *Drama Through Performance* (textbook), Houghton, 1977; *Literature Through Performance: "Shakespeare's Mirror" and "A Canterbury Caper,"* Ohio University Press, 1977. Contributor to *Modern Drama* and *New Directions in Teaching.*

SIDELIGHTS: Although Katherine Burkman teaches comparative literature, she received her doctorate in theater, and has done considerable work in directing. She received two grants from National Endowment for the Humanities, one to tour the program "Shakespeare's Mirror," which she wrote for a touring group of teacher-actors called The Collection, and another for a workshop to share The Collection's teaching approach with other teachers. She told *CA* that "[her] recent writing has centered around various uses of performance in teaching literature and the development of teaching scripts. [She is] presently involved in research for a book which approaches several Absurdist playwrights in terms of ritual and mythic structures."

* * *

BURKOWSKY, Mitchell R(oy) 1931-

PERSONAL: Born August 11, 1931, in Cooperstown, N.Y.; son of Edward and Fannie (Gertz) Burkowsky; married Diane Benowitz, June 24, 1956; children: Ruth, Joel, Rena. *Education:* New York State College for Teachers (now State University of New York at Albany), A.B., 1952; University of Paris, three certificates, 1954; Wayne State University, Ph.D., 1960. *Home:* 164 Temple St., Fredonia, N.Y. 14063. *Office:* State University of New York, Fredonia, N.Y. 14063.

CAREER: Speech correctionist in elementary schools, Washington, D.C., 1956-57; Detroit Institute of Technology, Detroit, Mich., assistant professor of speech and modern languages, 1959-61; University of North Dakota, Grand Forks, assistant professor of audiology and speech pathology, 1961-65; University of Florida, Gainesville, postdoctoral resident in communicative disorders, 1965-66; Syracuse University, Syracuse, N.Y., member of department of speech pathology, 1966-72; State University of New York College at Fredonia, professor of speech pathology and audiology and chairman of department, 1972—. *Military service:* U.S. Army, 1952-54; served in Europe. *Member:* American Speech and Hearing Association, American Cleft Palate Association, National Society for Autistic Children, New York State Speech and Hearing Association, New York State Society for Autistic Children.

WRITINGS: Teaching American Pronunciation to Foreign Students, Warren Green, 1969; (editor) *Parents' and Teachers' Guide to the Care of Autistic Children,* Systems Educators, 1970; *Orientation to Language and Learning Disorders,* Warren Green, 1973. Contributor to professional journals.

SIDELIGHTS: Mitchell Burkowsky told *CA:* "In high school I had a vague desire to enter the field of journalism. At age ten a poem I doodled in class was published in a county newspaper. At age sixteen I was honored by having a short poem printed in a national anthology of high school poets. So, working on the high school and college class newspapers seemed naturally progressive steps toward a journalistic goal. But, through a complicated chain of events, I became immersed in teacher education, which required 'scholarly' (and to me 'sterile') writing.

"'Publish or Perish' being the name of the game, I did just enough scholarly writing not to perish and aimed as much writing as possible to a less academic population, while still teaching concepts and procedures in a relatively simple fashion. Eventually I hope to write children's books for adults and children alike, which will take much trial and error. I believe that this is the most difficult form of writing because it necessitates highly delicate balancing of subject matter, word choice, action and examples to hit a wide population range without insulting anyone's intelligence.''

* * *

BURLEIGH, Anne Husted 1941-

PERSONAL: Born September 12, 1941, in Indianapolis, Ind.; daughter of Ralph W. (a lawyer) and Margaret (Walden) Husted; married William Robert Burleigh (a newspaper editor), November 28, 1964; children: David William, Catherine Anne, Margaret Walden. *Education:* DePauw University, B.A. (with honors), 1963; Indiana University, graduate study, 1963-64. *Religion:* Roman Catholic. *Home:* 405 Darby Dr., Newburgh, Ind. 47630.

CAREER: Writer. *Indianapolis Star,* Indianapolis, Ind., writer, summers, 1960-63. Member of parish school board, St. John's Church, Newburgh, Indiana. *Member:* Newburgh Women's Club (vice-president, 1968-70), Evansville Performing Arts Series of Musicians' Club (member of board of directors, 1970—), Delta Gamma. *Awards, honors:* Creative Writing Award, Indiana Federation of Women's Clubs, 1969-70.

WRITINGS: John Adams, Arlington House, 1969; (editor) *Education in a Free Society,* Liberty Fund, 1973. Contributor to *Analysis, Academic Reviewer, Intercollegiate Review, Evansville Press, Indianapolis Star.*

WORK IN PROGRESS: Book reviews; research on Edith Hamilton.

BIOGRAPHICAL/CRITICAL SOURCES: National Review, January 27, 1970.

* * *

BURMEISTER, Edwin 1939-

PERSONAL: Born November 30, 1939, in Chicago, Ill. *Education:* Cornell University, B.A., 1961, M.A., 1962; Massachusetts Institute of Technology, Ph.D., 1965. *Home address:* P.O. Box 149, Ivy, Va. 22945. *Office:* Department of Economics, 114 Rouss Hall, University of Virginia, Charlottesville, Va. 22901.

CAREER: University of Pennsylvania, Philadelphia, assistant professor, 1965-68, associate professor, 1968-71, professor of economics, 1972-76; University of Virginia, Charlottesville, professor of economics and member of Center for Advanced Studies, 1976—. Visiting professor, Duke University, Durham, N.C., 1971-72; visiting research professor, Australian National University, Canberra, Australia, 1974-75. *Member:* American Association of University Professors, American Economics Association, American Finance Association, Royal Economic Society, American Statistical Association, Econometric Society, Western Economic Association, Southern Economic Association, Canadian Economic Society. *Awards, honors:* Woodrow Wilson fellowship, 1961-62; National Science Foundation research grants, 1967-68, 1968-70, 1970-72, 1972-75, 1976-78; John Simon Guggenheim Memorial fellowship, 1974-75.

WRITINGS: (Contributor) Peter Newman, editor, *Readings in Mathematical Economics,* Volume I, Johns Hopkins Press, 1968; (with A. Rodney Dobell) *Mathematical Theories of Economic Growth,* Macmillan, 1970; (contributor)

Paul Kay, editor, *Explorations in Mathematical Anthropology,* M.I.T. Press, 1971; (editor with Lawrence R. Klein) *Econometric Model Performance: Comparative Simulation Studies of the U.S. Economy,* University of Pennsylvania Press, 1976. Contributor to economics journals. *International Economic Review,* acting editor, 1970-71, editor, 1971-76, associate editor, 1976—.

* * *

BURMEISTER, Jon 1933-

PERSONAL: Surname is pronounced Burr-mister; born May 25, 1933, in Stutterheim, South Africa; son of Paul Julius (an attorney) and Marjorie (Campbell) Burmeister; married Audrey James, February 13, 1957; children: Richard Paul, Penelope Ann. *Education:* St. Andrews College, Grahamstown, South Africa, matriculation and attorney's admission, 1950. *Religion:* Anglican. *Home:* 29 Vincent Gardens, East London, Cape Province, Republic of South Africa. *Agent:* Innes Rose, John Farquharson Ltd., 15 Red Lion Sq., London WC1R 4QW, England.

CAREER: Partner in law and notary public firm in East London, Republic of South Africa, 1960-70; full-time writer, 1970—.

WRITINGS—Novels: *The Edge of the Coast,* M. Joseph, 1968; *A Hot and Copper Sky,* M. Joseph, 1969; *The Darkling Plain,* M. Joseph, 1970; *Running Scared,* M. Joseph, 1972, St. Martin's, 1973; *The Unloved Ones,* M. Joseph, 1972; *Someone Else's War,* M. Joseph, 1973, St. Martin's, 1974; *The Weatherman Guy,* St. Martin's, 1975; *The Protector Conclusion,* St. Martin's, 1977.

SIDELIGHTS: Jon Burmeister writes that he dislikes ''bored people, people who waste words, and having to work on a day when I know the surf is running.'' *Avocational interests:* The sea, body-surfing, fishing, lobster thermidor, scotch whiskey, and good legs.

BIOGRAPHICAL/CRITICAL SOURCES: Times Literary Supplement, October 16, 1969.†

* * *

BURN, Doris 1923-

PERSONAL: Born April 24, 1923, in Portland, Ore.; daughter of Lage and Adele (Wilcox) Wernstedt; married South Burn (a builder), May 20, 1946 (divorced); children: Robin, Mark, Cameron, Lisa. *Education:* Attended Oregon State University and University of Hawaii; University of Washington, B.A. *Politics:* Independent. *Agent:* Dorothy Markinko, McIntosh & Otis, Inc., 475 Fifth Ave., New York, N.Y. 10017.

CAREER: Author and illustrator. *Awards, honors:* Pacific Northwest Bookseller's Award, 1965, for *Andrew Henry's Meadow;* Governor's Award, 1969, for *The Summer Folk.*

WRITINGS—Self-illustrated: *Andrew Henry's Meadow,* Coward, 1965; *The Summer Folk,* Coward, 1968; *The Tale of Lazy Lizard Canyon,* Putnam, 1977.

Illustrator: Joseph Jacobs, *Hudden and Dudden and Donald O'Neary,* Coward, 1968; Robert Nathan, *Tappy,* Knopf, 1968; Leisel Moak Skorpen, *We Were Tired of Living in a House,* Coward, 1969; Patricia Gauch, *My Old Tree,* Coward, 1970; Gauch, *Christina Katerina and the Box,* Coward, 1971; Skorpen, *Phipps,* Coward, 1972; Oscar Brand, *When I First Came to the Land,* Putnam, 1974.

SIDELIGHTS: ''The core of my life,'' Doris Burn says, ''has probably been the island where I have spent so many years. I have traveled little, because everytime responsibilities free me, I fly to my island like a homing pigeon. I can't resist it. But I have always loved to read, dream, draw, ski, boat, garden and visit for hours with close friends."†

* * *

BURNEY, Eugenia 1913-

PERSONAL: Born July 4, 1913, in Orangeburg, S.C.; daughter of John Henry and Eugene (Griner) Burney; married Gardell Dano Christensen (an author and artist), June 3, 1953; children: Barbara (Mrs. Glenn Collins), Gardell Dano, Jr., Peter Burch, Yahna (Mrs. Kimberly Ripley). *Education:* Attended University of South Carolina. *Address:* P.O. Box 577, Dubois, Wyo. 82513.

CAREER: G. P. Putnam's Sons, New York, N.Y., assistant editor, 1953-55; administrative assistant, Rajo Publications, 1968-70; writer.

*WRITINGS—*All published by Thomas Nelson: *Colonial South Carolina,* 1970; (with Clifford Capps) *Colonial Georgia,* 1972; (with husband, Gardell Dano Christensen) *Colonial Delaware,* 1974; *Colonial North Carolina,* 1975.

WORK IN PROGRESS: Biographies of John Colter and Nathaniel Wyeth, for children.

SIDELIGHTS: Eugenia Burney and her husband, Gardell Dano Christensen, present exhibits and programs at elementary schools, illustrating how books are made. Miss Burney plays the autoharp and sings children's folk songs, and her husband draws pictures to show how illustrations for children's books are designed and executed.

She told *CA:* "To me, writing for children is much more exciting than writing for adults. In the series of Colonial Histories we have written what we call 'Anecdotal Histories' of the colonies in which we have tried to tell what the people thought, what they did and why they did it. Because I hated history as a child, I have done my best to make history live through incidents and anecdotes so that the children who read my books can identify themselves with an historical experience. Having recently moved to Dubois, Wyoming, I am now looking for personalities and events that shaped the history of the west. I plan to continue writing in the children's field while at the same time I expand my own knowledge of our western heritage."

* * *

BURNS, Carol 1934-

PERSONAL: Born October 27, 1934, in London, England; daughter of Mordicai (a company director) and Julie (Shavick) Lynn (the surname originally was Zichlynsky); married Alan Burns (an author), January 5, 1954; children: Daniel, Alshamsha (both adopted). *Education:* Studied at Courtauld Institute, London, 1953-54, and Slade School of Art, 1955-59. *Politics:* Socialist. *Religion:* Jewish/Agnostic. *Home:* 26a Ladbroke Gardens, London W.11, England. *Agent:* Deborah Rogers Ltd., 29 Goodge St., London W1P 1FD, England.

CAREER: Painter in London, England, 1953-62, exhibiting at a one-woman show at New Art Centre, 1961, and at several galleries; teacher of art and English in London and Dorset, England, 1960-66; lecturer in creative writing, City Literary Institute, London, 1972-76. Graphics designer for *Resurgence, Limestone,* and *Christian Action. Awards, honors:* Arts Council grant, 1975.

WRITINGS: The Narcissist (novel), Calder & Boyars,

1967; (contributor) *New Writers,* Volume VI, Calder & Boyars, 1967, Transatlantic, 1968. Contributor of book reviews to *Tribune* and *Books and Bookmen.* Editor, *Matrix* and *More.*

WORK IN PROGRESS: Three novels, *Ha-Ha Happiness, Sfumato,* and *So Possessed.*

AVOCATIONAL INTERESTS: Art history, psychology, films, theater, music, politics.

BIOGRAPHICAL/CRITICAL SOURCES: Guardian, September 1, 1967; *Times Literary Supplement,* December 21, 1967.

* * *

BUROW, Daniel R(obert) 1931-

PERSONAL: Born April 26, 1931, in Kodai Kanal, India; son of Ralph Julius (a minister) and N. Ruth (Everett) Burow; married Marcia Caverly, May 26, 1958; children: Mark, Paul, Elizabeth. *Education:* Concordia Collegiate Institute, Bronxville, N.Y., A.A., 1951; Concordia Theological Seminary, St. Louis, Mo., B.A., 1953, B.D., 1969; St. Louis University, graduate study, 1971. *Home:* 3123 East 51st St., Minneapolis, Minn. 55417. *Office:* Augsburg Publishing House, 426 South Fifth St., Minneapolis, Minn. 55415.

CAREER: Minister of Lutheran Church; pastor of churches in Orlando, Fla., 1957-64, and Augusta, Ga., 1964-67; Lutheran Church, Missouri Synod, Board of Parish Education, St. Louis, Mo., editor, 1967-75; American Lutheran Church, Division for Life and Mission in the Congregation, Minneapolis, Minn., director for children's ministries, 1975-77; Augsburg Publishing House, Minneapolis, editor of curricular materials, 1977—. *Member:* National Association for the Education of Young Children, Lutheran Education Association.

*WRITINGS—*All published by Concordia: *I Meet God through the Strangest People,* 1970; (with Estelle Griffen) *Joyfully Alive,* 1971; (with Dorothy Hoyer) *Alive Together,* 1971; (with Marian Baden) *Always Alive,* 1972; *Sound of the Bugle* (novel), 1973; *A Peek at the Promise,* 1975; *Hail to Our Promised King,* 1975; *A Peek Inside God's Heart,* 1976; *The Spirit Moves,* 1976. Author of religious education filmstrips and kindergarten story books. Contributor to magazines. Editor, *My Devotions,* 1967-69; assistant editor, *His People,* 1967-69.

SIDELIGHTS: I Meet God through the Strangest People has been translated into German and published in Germany.

* * *

BURROWS, James C. 1944-

PERSONAL: Born February 3, 1944, in Buenos Aires, Argentina; son of Charles Robert (a diplomat) and Lucy (Mullin) Burrows; married Deann Beach (a rehabilitation counselor), July 5, 1966. *Education:* Harvard University, A.B. (magna cum laude), 1965; Massachusetts Institute of Technology, Ph.D., 1970. *Office:* Charles River Associates, 1050 Massachusetts Ave., Cambridge, Mass. 02138.

CAREER: Massachusetts Institute of Technology, Cambridge, Mass., instructor in economics, 1967-68; Charles River Associates, Cambridge, senior research associate, 1968—. *Member:* American Economic Association, Phi Beta Kappa. *Awards, honors:* National Science Foundation fellowship; Woodrow Wilson fellowship.

WRITINGS: (With Thomas A. Domencich) *An Analysis of*

the United States Oil Import Quota, Heath, 1970; (with Charles E. Metcalf and John B. Kaler) *Industrial Location in the United States: An Economic Analysis,* Heath, 1971; *Tungsten: An Industry Analysis,* Heath, 1971; *Cobalt: An Industry Analysis,* Heath, 1971.

WORK IN PROGRESS: Studies in environmental economics, fuel and power, natural resources, and the aluminum market; a manuscript, "Policy Implications of Producer Country Supply Disruptions."

* * *

BURT, John J. 1934-

PERSONAL: Born September 3, 1934, in Enfield, N.C.; son of Johnny Joseph (a farmer) and Pearl (Nevellie) Burt; married Ann Gillett (a teacher), December 28, 1956; children: Emelia, Keith, Joe. *Education:* Duke University, A.B., 1956; University of North Carolina, M.Ed., 1957; University of Oregon, M.S., 1960, Ed.D., 1962. *Office:* Department of Health Education, University of Maryland, East Education Annex, 117 Lehigh Rd., College Park, Md. 20742.

CAREER: Temple University, Philadelphia, Pa., member of teaching faculty; University of Toledo, Toledo, Ohio, professor; University of Maryland, College Park, professor of health education and chairman of department. *Member:* Association for the Advancement of Health Education (president).

WRITINGS: (With Benjamin Miller) *Good Health,* Saunders, 1966; (with Linda A. Brower) *Education for Sexuality: Concepts and Programs for Teaching,* Saunders, 1970.

* * *

BUSH, Martin H(arry) 1930-

PERSONAL: Born January 24, 1930, in Amsterdam, N.Y.; son of Martin J. and Louise (Surento) Bush; married Elinor Seward, August 6, 1955 (divorced, December 23, 1969); children: Lisa Vail, Jennifer Seward, Pamela Lynn. *Education:* New York College for Teachers (now State University of New York at Albany), B.A., 1958, M.A., 1959; Syracuse University, Ph.D., 1966. *Home:* 202 North Rock Rd., Apt. 109, Wichita, Kan. 67206. *Office:* Office of the Vice-President, Wichita State University, Wichita, Kan. 67208.

CAREER: New York State Department of Education, Albany, N.Y., acting senior historian, 1961-62, historical consultant, 1962-63; Syracuse University, Syracuse, N.Y., instructor in history, 1963-65, assistant dean, 1966-70; Wichita State University, Wichita, Kan., assistant vice-president, 1970-74, vice-president, 1974—, director of Edwin A. Ulrich Museum of Art, 1975—. *Military service:* U.S. Army, Intelligence, 1953-54.

WRITINGS: Francis Scott Key: Our National Anthem (brochure), New York State Education Department, 1964; (editor with H. L. Applegate and O. T. Barck) *Moses Dewitt Burnet, A Tour to the South: Travel Diary, 1815-1816,* Syracuse University, 1965; *American Political Cartoons: 1865-1965* (catalog), Syracuse University Library, 1966; *Boris Lovet-Lorski: The Language of Time* (catalog), introduction by Salvatore Quasimodo, Syracuse University Press, 1967; (author of introduction) *James Earle Fraser: American Sculptor* (catalog), Kennedy Galleries, 1969; *Ben Shahn: The Passion of Sacco and Vanzetti,* with an essay by Ben Shahn, Syracuse University Press, 1969; *Revolutionary Enigma: A Re-appraisal of General Philip Schuyler of New York,* Friedman, 1969; *Doris Caesar,* introduction by Marya

Zaturenska, preface by D. B. Wyndham Lewis, Syracuse University Press, 1970; *Goodnough,* commentary by Kenworth Moffett, Wichita State University, 1973; *Hanson,* Wichita State University, 1976. Contributor to *Notable American Women, School Letter, National Sculpture Review, Art News,* and *Art International.*

* * *

BUSHMILLER, Ernest Paul 1905-
(Ernie Bushmiller)

PERSONAL: Born August 23, 1905, in New York, N.Y.; son of Ernest George (an insurance man) and Elizabeth (Hall) Bushmiller; married Abby Bohnet, July 9, 1930. *Education:* Studied at National Academy of Design. *Religion:* Episcopalian. *Home:* 552 Haviland Rd., Stamford, Conn. *Office:* United Features Syndicate, 220 East 42nd St., New York, N.Y.

CAREER: Prior to 1931 was cartoonist on *New York World* and *New York Graphic,* New York City, and comedy writer for Harold Lioyd in Hollywood, Calif.; cartoonist with United Features Syndicate, New York City, 1931—, creating both the "Fritzi Ritz" and "Nancy" comic strips. "Nancy" presently appears in more than seven hundred newspapers in the United States and in over one hundred overseas newspapers including newspapers in Australia, Japan, Mexico, and Peru. Member of advisory board, Salvation Army. *Member:* National Cartoonists Society, Society of Illustrators, Artist and Writers Association, Dutch Treat Club, Banshees. *Awards, honors:* Voted best humor strip cartoonist by National Cartoonists Society, 1961.

WRITINGS: Nancy (cartoon anthology), Pocket Books, 1961. Also author and illustrator of monthly *Fritzi Ritz* and *Nancy* comic books.

SIDELIGHTS: Ernie Bushmiller remarked: "I'm always intrigued by the huge appeal of 'Nancy.' I guess there are kids all over the world and my gags being mostly visual there's no problem in understanding them." An illustration which shows the popularity and acceptance of "Nancy" is the use of a tiny inch-high sized "Nancy" by the *American Heritage Dictionary of the English Language* to accompany and illustrate its definition of the word comics. As an avid and long time lover of word games and crossword puzzles this delighted Bushmiller.

Bill Crouch, Jr. writes of Bushmiller: "Unlike many cartoonists, Bushmiller draws his strip backward. He starts with the last frame that contains the gag or punch line and then fills in what comes before." "I'm a very slow worker and a slow thinker," says Bushmiller, "and always late for my deadlines with the syndicate. When I draw, my lines don't have great flamboyance. 'Nancy' is the Lawrence Welk of the comic strip world." Bushmiller goes on to say, "I get up at the crack of noon and do most of my work at night. It takes the newspapers and about forty cups of coffee to get me started. But often I work until two in the morning."

When asked what advice he would give to aspiring cartoonists, Bushmiller suggests: "There's only one way to learn cartooning. It's like you can't go to school to learn to write a song. You just do it. I read humor strips when I was a kid and traced and swiped and developed my art work. The gag of course comes first and is more difficult than the drawing part of cartooning."

BIOGRAPHICAL/CRITICAL SOURCES: Pittsburgh Press, June 23, 1974.†

BUTTERWORTH, F(rank) Edward (Jr.)   1917-

PERSONAL: Born August 28, 1917; son of Frank Edward (a mechanic) and Ada (Reynolds) Butterworth; married Lilly Raye Howard, April 12, 1944; children: Gary, Cheryl, Janis. *Education:* Attended Oklahoma City University and Kansas City University. *Politics:* Independent. *Religion:* Reorganized Church of Jesus Christ of Latter-day Saints. *Home:* 1159 Lawton Dr., Chico, Calif. 95926. *Office:* The Auditorium, Independence, Mo. 64051.

CAREER: Montgomery Ward & Co., Kansas City, Mo., adjuster, 1939-40; appointed missionary, 1940—; currently president of Shasta-Sierra District.

WRITINGS: Adventures of a South Sea Missionary (autobiography), Herald House, 1961; *The Adventures of John Hawkins, Restoration Pioneer,* Herald House, 1963; *The Sword of Laban,* four volumes, Herald House, 1969-71; *Irby,* Herald House, 1976; *White Shadows among the Mighty Sioux,* Herald House, 1977. Translator of several books and periodicals into Polynesian.

WORK IN PROGRESS: Sons of the Sea; Sons of Destiny.

*   *   *

BYRD, Martha   1930-
(Martha Byrd Hoyle)

PERSONAL: Born September 25, 1930, in Morganton, N.C.; daughter of Samuel Jefferson (a postal employee) and Mattye (Harbison) Byrd; married Vinton Asbury Hoyle (a chemist), June 14, 1952 (divorced July 31, 1972); married Jerry Allan Roberts (a mathematics professor), June 19, 1976; children: (first marriage) Kenneth S., Katherine Susan. *Education:* University of North Carolina, B.S. (with honors), 1952; University of Tennessee at Knoxville, M.S., 1976. *Home address:* Box 2377, Davidson, N.C. 28036. *Office:* Davidson College, Davidson, N.C. 28036.

CAREER: Writer. Director of Communications, Davidson College, Davidson, N.C., 1974—. *Member:* Women in Communications, Council for the Advancement and Support of Education, American Committee on the History of the Second World War, Phi Beta Kappa, Phi Kappa Phi.

WRITINGS: A World in Flames: A History of World War II, Atheneum, 1970; *Saratoga: The Turning Point in the American Revolution,* Auerbach, 1973. Contributor to *Simon and Schuster Encyclopedia of World War II,* 1978; also contributor to *American History Illustrated.*

WORK IN PROGRESS: Researching U.S. prisoner of war policy and administration.

BIOGRAPHICAL/CRITICAL SOURCES: New York Times, June 23, 1970.

*   *   *

BYRNE, Edmund F(rancis)   1933-

PERSONAL: Born May 30, 1933, in Kansas City, Mo.; son of Edmund J. and Cecilia (Heili) Byrne; married Margaret Karen (a social worker), December 16, 1967; children: Coco Jeannine, Carl Robert. *Education:* Saint Joseph's College, Collegeville, Ind., B.A., 1955; Loyola University, M.A., 1956; Universite Catholique de Louvain, Louvain, Belgium, L.Phil., 1965, Ph.D., 1966; Indiana University, J.D., 1978. *Home:* 6451 Sunset Lane, Indianapolis, Ind. 46260. *Office:* Department of Philosophy, Indiana University—Purdue University at Indianapolis, Indianapolis, Ind. 46202.

CAREER: Michigan State University, East Lansing, Mich., assistant professor of philosophy, 1966-69; Indiana University—Purdue University at Indianapolis, assistant professor, 1969-71, associate professor, 1971-76, professor of philosophy, 1976—. *Member:* American Philosophical Association, American Association for the Advancement of Science, Society for the Study of Philosophy and Technology. *Awards, honors:* Fulbright-Hays grant, 1963-65.

WRITINGS: Probability and Opinion: A Study of the Medieval Presuppositions of Post-Medieval Theories of Probability, Nijhoff, 1968; (with Edward A. Maziarz) *Human Being and Being Human: Man's Philosophies of Man,* Appleton, 1969; (contributor) Rubin Gotesky and Ervin Laszlo, editors, *Evolution—Revolution,* Gordon & Breach, 1971; (contributor) Paul T. Durbin, editor, *Philosophy and Technology: An Annual Compilation of Research,* Jai Press, Volume I, 1977, Volume II, 1978. Contributor to various periodicals.

WORK IN PROGRESS: Publications dealing with mental illness and communications satellites; research on "the impact of science and technology on public policy, e.g., in the areas of aging, environment, and labor relations."

SIDELIGHTS: Edmund F. Byrne told *CA:* "My recent writings might be called philosophy of technology, but they have been heavily influenced by my ongoing study of law. No overarching synthesis has appeared on the horizon, but there are countless examples of how philosophical analysis can complement legal problem-solving, and vice versa. It is these examples that I have been exploring in my later work."

*   *   *

BYRNE, Edward M.   1935-

PERSONAL: Born September 10, 1935, in Watertown, Wis.; son of Edward Joseph (a publisher) and Rosalie A. (Bell) Byrne; married Dorothy Jane Schopp (an editor), September 19, 1958; children: Kathryn Ann, Edward Mark, Jr. *Education:* College of Wooster, student, 1953-55; Syracuse University, J.D., 1959; George Washington University, L.L.M. (highest honors), 1971. *Home:* 425 West Main St., Waterloo, N.Y. 13165.

CAREER: Gowanda News and Observer, Gowanda, N.Y., publisher, 1959-60; U.S. Navy, 1961—, attorney, with current rank of commander. *Member:* American Bar Association, New York State Bar Association.

WRITINGS: Military Law: A Handbook for the Navy and Marine Corps, edited by Louise Gerretson, U.S. Naval Institute, 1970, 2nd edition published as *Military Law,* edited by Veronica Amoss, Naval Institute Press, 1976. Contributor to journals and books concerning military matters.

SIDELIGHTS: Edward Byrne told *CA:* "One of the widespread false impressions of military justice is that an accused would be better off in the civilian criminal justice system. The truth is that military justice provides more practical rights to a military accused than would be available in state or federal criminal trials. Neither the military or civilian criminal justice systems adequately serve the needs of the society in which they are expected to function. Both systems reflect an unwarranted overconcern for the accused as against the interests of victims and potential victims. As a result, neither system sufficiently strengthens the goals, aspirations, morals and ethical values our country requires for its long-term survival. Both military and civilian criminal justice must provide foundations for a resurgence of concepts like community, fellowship, inner reliance, and fair dealing based upon good faith. A nation whose citizens lack morality and spiritual faith can never have a just legal system—no matter how many legal rights are accorded an accused."

*   *   *

CABOT, Robert (Moors) 1924-

PERSONAL: Born February 1, 1924, in Boston, Mass.; son of Thomas Dudley (a manufacturer) and Virginia (Wellington) Cabot; married Charlotte Fitzpatrick, December 17, 1949; married second wife, Maria Anagnostopulu, June 15, 1968; children: (first marriage) Kathleen Lawton, Sara. *Education:* Harvard University, A.B., 1945; Yale University, LL.B., 1950. *Politics:* "Anti." *Religion:* Greek Orthodox. *Home:* Via del Tempio 4, Rome, Italy.

CAREER: Began what he describes as "several careers in many parts of the world" as a lawyer, economist, and government official in Washington, D.C., 1951; worked in U.S. aid programs in Italy, Thailand, Ceylon, and Washington, D.C. Wrote his first novel while living in a trailer in California; now makes his home in Rome and aboard a small sailboat plying Greek waters. *Military service:* U.S. Army, 1942-45; served in North Africa and Europe; became sergeant.

WRITINGS: The Joshua Tree (novel), Atheneum, 1970. Contributor of "criticism and comment" to journals in United States and Italy.

WORK IN PROGRESS: Two novels, *The Cell* and *Nima.*

BIOGRAPHICAL/CRITICAL SOURCES: Harper's, September, 1970.††

*   *   *

CAHN, Edgar S. 1935-

PERSONAL: Born March 23, 1935, in New York, N.Y.; married Jean Camper, 1957; children: Jonathan Daniel, Reuben Camper. *Education:* Swarthmore College, B.A. (magna cum laude), 1956; Yale University, M.A., 1957, Ph.D., 1960, LL.B. (cum laude), 1963; Pembroke College, Cambridge, graduate study, 1958-59. *Home:* 5500 39th St. N.W., Washington, D.C. 20015.

CAREER: U.S. Department of Justice, Washington, D.C., special attorney in Office of Legal Counsel, 1963-64; U.S. Office of Economic Opportunity, Washington, D.C., special assistant to director, 1964-66; Field Foundation, New York, N.Y., associate research director, 1966-67; Planning Committee for a National Complaint Center, Washington, D.C., staff director, 1967; Citizens Advocate Center, Washington, D.C., executive director, 1967-71; Antioch School of Law, Washington, D.C., co-dean, 1971—. Consultant to Agency for International Development on manpower programs and community organization in Venezuela, 1966, and to President's Committee on Juvenile Delinquency. *Member:* Phi Beta Kappa, Order of the Coif. *Awards, honors:* Fulbright scholar in England, 1958-59; citation from the City Council of the District of Columbia.

WRITINGS: (Editor) *Hunger USA: A Report by the Citizens' Board of Inquiry into Hunger and Malnutrition in the United States,* New Community Press (Washington, D.C.), 1968; (editor and author of introduction) *Our Brother's Keeeper: The Indian in White America,* World Publishing, 1969; (with Tim Eichenberg and Roberta V. Rohrberg) *The Legal Lawbreakers: A Study of the Nonadministration of Federal Relocation Requirements,* Citizens Advocate Center, 1970; (editor and contributor) *Legal Services: Where Next? A Discussion of Legislative Alternatives,* Citizens Advocate Center, 1970; (editor with B. A. Passett, and con-

tributor) *Citizen Participation: Effective Community Change,* Praeger, 1971. Contributor to law journals. Former articles editor, *Yale Law Journal.*

BIOGRAPHICAL/CRITICAL SOURCES: Christian Science Monitor, December 18, 1969.

*   *   *

CAIDEN, Gerald E(lliot) 1936-

PERSONAL: Born June 2, 1936, in London, England; son of Morris and Rosa (Silverman) Caiden; married Naomi Joy Solomons (a university researcher); children: Miriam Hannah, Rachel Debra. *Education:* London School of Economics and Political Science, B.Sc., 1957, Ph.D., 1959. *Office:* Department of Political Science, Haifa University, Haifa 31999, Israel.

CAREER: West London College of Commerce, London, England, lecturer, 1957-58; University of London, London School of Economics and Political Science, London, tutor, 1958-59; Carleton University, Ottawa, Ontario, Canada Council fellow, 1959-60; Australian National University, Canberra, research fellow, 1961-66; Hebrew University of Jerusalem, Jerusalem, Israel, professor of political science, 1966-68; University of California, Berkeley, visiting professor of political science, beginning 1966; currently affiliated with department of political science, Haifa University, Haifa, Israel. Guest lecturer at Indian Institute of Public Administration, Delhi, and Hebrew University of Jerusalem, 1964, and at other universities and institutes in Canada, England, Israel, and United States. Has done field work in comparative public administration in the Philippines, Hong Kong, India, Israel, Greece, Italy, and France.

MEMBER: Royal Institute of Public Administration, American Society for Public Administration, Australian Political Science Association. *Awards, honors:* Canada Council fellowship, 1959-60; research grant from Institute of Personnel Administration, Melbourne, Australia, 1963; Storey Memorial Award of Australian Institute of Management, 1964.

WRITINGS: The Federal Civil Service of Canada [London], 1960; *Career Service: An Introduction to the History of Personnel Administration in the Commonwealth Public Service of Australia, 1901-1961,* Melbourne University Press, 1965; *The A.C.P.T.A.: A Study of White Collar Public Service Unionism in the Commonwealth of Australia 1885-1922,* Department of Political Science, Australian National University, 1966; *The Superannuation Act, 1922-1965,* A.C.O.A. (Sydney), 1966; *The Commonwealth Bureaucracy,* Melbourne University Press, 1967; *Assessing Administrative Performance: A Case Study of Israel's Administrative Culture,* Department of Political Science, University of California, Berkeley, 1968; *Administrative Reform,* Aldine, 1969; *Industrial Relations in the Australian Public Sector,* Institute of Industrial Labor Relations, University of Michigan Press, 1971; *Israel's Administrative Culture,* Institute of Governmental Studies, University of California, 1970; *The Dynamics of Public Administration,* Holt, 1971; *Public Employment Compulsory Arbitration in Australia,* Institute of Labor and Industrial Relations, University of Michigan-Wayne State University, 1971. Also author of several monographs on public institutions of Israel and Australia. Editorial consultant, *Public Personal Review,* 1964—; member of editorial board, *Public Administration in Israel and Abroad,* 1966-68.

WORK IN PROGRESS: Further studies in administrative reform, and depth research into Israeli political and administrative problems.†

CALDER, Angus 1942-

PERSONAL: Born February 5, 1942, in Sutton, Surrey, England; son of Ritchie (a writer) and Mabel (McKail) Calder; married Jenni Daiches (a writer), October 1, 1963; children: Rachel Elizabeth, Gowan Lindsay, Gideon James. *Education:* King's College, Cambridge, M.A., 1963; University of Sussex, D.Phil., 1968. *Politics:* "International Revolutionary Socialist." *Religion:* None. *Home:* 6 Buckingham Ter., Edinburgh, Scotland. *Agent:* A. D. Peters & Co., Ltd., 10 Buckingham St., London WC2N 6BV, England.

CAREER: University of East Africa, University College, Nairobi, Kenya, lecturer in literature, 1968-71; part-time tutor and counsellor, Open University, 1972—. Free-lance author. *Awards, honors:* Gregory Award, 1967, for an unpublished collection of poems; John Llewellyn Rhys Memorial Prize, 1970, for *The People's War: Britain, 1939-1945.*

WRITINGS: (Editor) Charles Dickens, *Great Expectations,* Penguin, 1965; (with wife, Jenni Calder) *Scott,* Evans Brothers, 1969; *The People's War: Britain, 1939-1945,* Pantheon, 1969; (co-editor) *Writers in East Africa,* East African Literature Bureau, 1974; (editor) Walter Scott, *Old Mortality,* Penguin, 1974; *Russia Discovered: Nineteenth Century Fiction from Pushkin to Chekhov,* Heinemann, 1976; (contributor) *Literature and Western Civilisation,* Volume VI, Aldus Books, 1976. Also author of television script, "Home Fires," for "World at War" series, 1973. Contributor of reviews to *New Statesman* and other publications, and of poems to journals.

WORK IN PROGRESS: A history of the British Empire, for Doubleday and Jonathan Cape.

SIDELIGHTS: American critics were almost unanimous in viewing *The People's War* as a marvelously comprehensive record of Britain's home front in World War II. Almost as unanimously, though, they implied that the book punctured the traditional picture—"the image," as Thomas Lask comments in the *New York Times,* "of a tight little island, without division or complaint, silently united under Churchill, stoic under the bombing, patient with shortages, girded only for war.... If this book has a thesis, it is that the average Briton's desire for change (a muted revolutionary impulse) was thwarted during the war."

Some explanation of that thesis may be found in what Angus Calder told *CA,* although he was not referring to *The People's War* but to all of his writing: "I try to express, as well as I can, my humanist values, which commit me to international, libertarian, revolutionary socialism. This is not narrowly 'political,' and I doubt if writers should get mixed up in political parties. My humanism involves every aspect of life which prose and poetry can cover. Ideology is, precisely, the writer's medium and his business. Writing is a form of action designed to affect the way people think. But it is also a form of exploration and research, and I think the acceptance as binding of any received set of ideas (Methodism, say, or a party political programme) is bound to hamper exploration and research...."

Eric Forbes-Boyd in the *Christian Science Monitor* mentions that at times in his "gripping narrative" of Britons under siege, Calder looks "back from the viewpoint of his own postwar, disillusioned generation" and "observes with a too sardonic eye that quite fails to perceive what is there." Forbes-Boyd also notes that *The People's War* was drawn and sifted from official documents, Mass Observation Reports, diaries, memoirs, newspapers, and anything that offered an authentic piece of evidence. But Calder regards

himself as a writer (from a family of writers), "not as a 'critic' or 'historian' or 'scholar' or any kind of specialist."

Calder's focus has changed somewhat since writing *The People's War.* He recently told *CA:* "I grow more and more interested in myth, its relationship to history and to human action in the present. My wife has recently published books on the American West and on Heroes in general, and her preoccupations greatly influence mine. Why do people create their heroes—Jefferson, Burns, Churchill, Lenin—and how do these creations affect the historical process? Like my wife, I value the art of story-telling which many scholars—though few ordinary people—seem to think old-fashioned and embarrassing. I am doing my best to practise it in my book in progress on the British Empire. It will seem pretentious to say that Scott and Tolstoy have latterly been the chief influences on my technique of which I am conscious, but I will be content if I can produce a large volume, like one of theirs, which people will read through, in sequence, from cover to cover. Narrative isn't in conflict with 'analysis'; for a historian, I think, it should be the means by which insight is conveyed."

AVOCATIONAL INTERESTS: Cookery, cricket, music of all kinds, cinema-going, and looking at paintings.

BIOGRAPHICAL/CRITICAL SOURCES: Observer Review, September 7, 1969; *Books,* November, 1969; *Christian Science Monitor,* November 1, 1969; *Nation,* November 24, 1969; *New York Times,* December 20, 1969; *New York Times Book Review,* December 21, 1969; *New Yorker,* January 17, 1970; *National Observer,* January 26, 1970; *New Leader,* February 2, 1970; *Time,* February 2, 1970; *Esquire,* April, 1970.

*   *   *

CALDWELL, Lynton (Keith) 1913-

PERSONAL: Born November 21, 1913, in Montezuma, Iowa; married Helen Walcher, 1940; children: Edwin Lee, Elaine Lynnette. *Education:* University of Chicago, Ph.B. (with honors), 1935, Ph.D., 1943; Harvard University, M.A., 1938. *Home address:* Cedar Crest, Box 197, R.R. 12, Heritage Woods Rd., Bloomington, Ind. 47401. *Office:* Department of Political Science, 213 Woodburn Hall, Indiana University, Bloomington, Ind. 47401.

CAREER: Indiana University, Bloomington, assistant professor of government and director of South Bend Center, 1938-44; Council of State Governments, Lexington, Ky., director of research and publications, 1944-47; Syracuse University, Maxwell Graduate School of Citizenship and Public Affairs, Syracuse, N.Y., professor of political science, 1947-55; University of California, Berkeley, visiting professor of political science, 1955-56; Indiana University, professor of political science, 1956—, Arthur E. Bentley Professor of Political Science, 1971—. Visiting member of faculty, University of Chicago, 1944-47. Co-director of Public Administration Institute in Turkey and the Middle East, United Nations, 1954-55; involved in other special assignments and technical assistance in Colombia, Pakistan, India, the Philippines, Thailand, Indonesia, and with Central Treaty Organization. Member of environmental advisory board, U.S. Army Corps of Engineers; member of environmental science review committee, National Institutes of Health, 1966-67; member of environmental studies board, National Research Council, 1973-76; consultant to National Aeronautics and Space Administration, Argonne National Laboratory, Oak Ridge National Laboratory, Office of Technology Assessment, and other government departments and agencies; served on National Commission on Materials Policy, 1971-73.

MEMBER: American Association for the Advancement of Science (fellow), American Society for Public Administration (member of council), Ecological Society of America, International Union for the Conservation of Nature and Natural Resources (life member), Society for General Systems Research, Society for International Development, International Council on Environmental Law, Indiana Academy of Sciences. *Awards, honors:* William E. Mosher Award of American Society for Public Administration, 1964, for article, "Environment: A New Focus for Public Policy"; National Science Foundation grants, 1965-76; guest scholar at Woodrow Wilson International Center for Scholars, Smithsonian Institution, 1970; Laverne Burchfield Award of the American Society for Public Administration, 1972, for book review essay "Environment: A Short Course in Semantics"; L.L.D., Western Michigan University, 1977.

WRITINGS: The Administrative Theories of Hamilton and Jefferson, University of Chicago Press, 1944, reprinted, Russell & Russell, 1964; *The Government and Administration of New York,* Crowell, 1954; *Government in Action: A Course of Training for Civic Leaders—Handbook for Universities* (booklet), American Foundation for Continuing Education, 1961; *Improving the Public Service through Training,* Agency for International Development, 1962; *Science, Technology, and Public Policy: A Syllabus for Advanced Study,* two volumes, Department of Government, Indiana University, 1968; *Science, Technology, and Public Policy: A Selective and Annotated Bibliography, 1945-1967,* two volumes, Department of Government, Indiana University, for National Science Foundation, 1968; *Environment: A Challenge to Modern Society* (selected as one of outstanding books of 1970, Indiana Writers Conference), Natural History Press, 1970; *In Defense of Earth: International Protection of the Biosphere,* Indiana University Press, 1972; *Man and His Environment: Policy and Administration,* Harper, 1975; (with Lynton R. Hayes and Isabel M. MacWhirter) *Citizens and the Environment: Case Studies in Popular Action,* Indiana University Press, 1976.

Contributor: *Toward the Comparative Study of Administration,* Department of Government, Indiana University, 1957; *University Education and Public Service,* International Association of Universities, 1959; *Politics and Public Affairs,* Institute of Training for Public Service, Indiana University, 1962; *Symposium on Management Training in Public Administrations,* Central Treaty Organization (Ankara, Turkey), 1964; Roscoe C. Martin, editor, *Public Administration and Democracy: Essays in Honor of Paul H. Appleby,* Syracuse University Press, 1965; Claude E. Hawley and Ruth G. Weintraub, editors, *Administrative Questions and Political Answers,* Van Nostrand, 1966; F. Fraser Darling and John P. Milton, editors, *Future Environments of North America,* Natural History Press, 1966; Bertram M. Gross, editor, *Action Under Planning: The Guidance of Economic Development,* McGraw, 1967; Richard A. Humphrey, editor, *Universities and Development Assistance Abroad,* American Council on Education, 1967; Jerry R. Hopper and Richard I. Levin, editors, *Turkish Administrator: A Cultural Survey,* U.S. Agency for International Development, 1967; James C. Charlesworth, editor, *Theory and Practice of Public Administration: Scope, Objectives, and Methods,* American Academy of Political and Social Science, 1968; *Social Sciences and Environment,* University of Colorado Press, 1968; William R. Nelson, editor, *The*

Politics of Science, Oxford University Press, 1968; George W. Rogers, editor, *Change in Alaska: People, Petroleum, and Politics,* University of Alaska Press and University of Washington Press, 1970; Lorne H. Russurm and Edward Sommerville, editors, *Readings on Man's Natural Environment: A Systems Approach,* Wadsworth, 1970; Phillip O. Foss, editor, *Public Land Policy,* Associated University Press, 1970; Richard A. Cooley and Geoffrey Wandesforde-Smith, editors, *Congress and the Environment,* University of Washington Press, 1970; William W. Murdoch, editor, *Man and Environment,* Sinauer Associates, 1971; *A Time to Hear and to Answer,* University of Alabama Press, 1977.

Editor: A. C. Conk and N. K. Savun, *Turkish Public Administration: A Report on the Rationalization of the State Organization,* Institute of Training for Public Service, Indiana University, 1961; *Environmental Studies: Papers on the Politics and Public Administration of Man-Environment Relationship,* Numbers I-IV, Institute of Public Administration, Indiana University, 1967; *Science and Public Policy in the American University,* Department of Government, Indiana University, 1969; (with Toufig A. Siddigi) *Environmental Policy, Law, and Administration: A Guide to Advanced Study,* with supplementary bibliographies and author index, School of Public and Environmental Affairs, Indiana University, 1976.

Contributor to *American Behavioral Scientist, Human Ecology, Yale Review, BioScience, Religious Humanism, Technology and Culture,* and a number of public administration, law, public personnel, history, and political science journals. Member of editorial board, *Public Administration Review,* 1948-51.

WORK IN PROGRESS: Research on international aspects of environmental policy, priority conflicts over energy, the economy and environment, and the management of "growth."

*   *   *

CALLCOTT, George H(ardy)   1929-

PERSONAL: Born March 6, 1929, in Columbia, S.C.; son of Wilfrid Hardy (a college professor) and Grace (Otter) Callcott; married Margaret Law (a writer), August 18, 1959; children: Wilfrid Hardy, Stephen Law. *Education:* University of South Carolina, A.B., 1950; Columbia University, M.A., 1951; University of North Carolina, Ph.D., 1956. *Home:* 4311 Clagett Rd., University Park, Md. *Office:* Department of History, University of Maryland, College Park, Md. 20742.

CAREER: Longwood College, Farmville, Va., instructor in history, 1954-55; University of Maryland, College Park, instructor, 1956-59, assistant professor, 1959-65, associate professor, 1965-69, professor of history, 1969—, vice-chancellor for academic affairs, 1970-76. Visiting professor, University of Virginia, 1968-69. *Member:* American Historical Association, Organization of American Historians, American Association of University Professors (president of Maryland branch, 1966-67), Southern Historical Association, Maryland Historical Association, Delta Delta Kappa, Pi Gamma Mu, Phi Alpha Theta. *Awards, honors:* Named outstanding faculty member at University of Maryland, 1966.

WRITINGS: A History of the University of Maryland, Maryland Historical Society, 1966; *History in the United States, 1800-1860: Its Practice and Purpose,* Johns Hopkins Press, 1970; *The Maryland Education Commissions,* State of Maryland, 1974. Contributor to history journals.

CALLISON, Brian 1934-

PERSONAL: Born July 13, 1934, in Manchester, England; son of Thomas T. and Kathleen Alice (Pounder) Callison; married Phyllis Joyce Jobson, May 12, 1958; children: Richard, Mark. *Education:* Attended Dundee College of Art, 1954-56. *Home:* 1 Margaret Crescent, West Ferry, Dundee, Scotland.

CAREER: British Merchant Navy, deck officer, 1951-54; managing director of a construction company, 1956-63; general manager of an entertainment center, 1963-67; full-time writer, 1967—. *Military service:* Royal Naval Auxiliary Service, 1965—; section officer and commander of Dundee Unit. *Member:* Society of Authors.

WRITINGS: A Flock of Ships, Putnam, 1970; *A Plague of Sailors,* Putnam, 1971; *The Dawn Attack,* Putnam, 1972; *A Web of Salvage,* Putnam, 1973; *Trapp's War,* Dutton, 1974; *A Ship Is Dying,* Dutton, 1975; *A Frenzy of Merchantmen,* Dutton, in press.

SIDELIGHTS: Brian Callison's work has been published in England, Germany, Iceland, Japan, Finland, and seven other countries of Europe.

BIOGRAPHICAL/CRITICAL SOURCES: Best Sellers, June 1, 1970; *New York Times Book Review,* June 14, 1970.

* * *

CALNAN, T(homas) D(aniel) 1915-

PERSONAL: Born December 16, 1915, in Malta; son of Arthur Daniel (a civil servant) and Teresa (Rowley) Calnan; married Timea Zoltan, June 1, 1940; married second wife, Rosella Vitolo, September 1, 1965; children: (second marriage) Martin Rowley. *Education:* Attended Wimbledon College, Wimbledon, England, 1930-33, and Royal Air Force College, Cranwell, England, 1934-36. *Politics:* Conservative. *Religion:* Roman Catholic. *Home:* 52040 Montanare di Cortona, Arezzo, Italy. *Agent:* Curtis Brown Ltd., 60 East 56th St., New York, N.Y. 10022.

CAREER: Royal Air Force, 1936-58, retiring as wing commander; *Aeroplane* (magazine), London, England, correspondent in Rome, Italy, 1958-69; resident representative in Italy of various aerospace manufacturers, 1959-64; *ABC Airways* (magazine), London, correspondent in Rome, 1969—. Former managing director, Paneuram Trade Establishment (exporters to the Middle East). *Member:* Royal Air Force Club, Royal Air Force Sailing Club, Ski Club of Great Britain.

WRITINGS: Free as a Running Fox, Dial, 1970; *The Reluctant Spy,* Curtis Books, 1973. Contributor to aviation journals and of articles on gastronomy to popular periodicals.

WORK IN PROGRESS: One autobiographical book tentatively entitled, *Letters to My Son.*

AVOCATIONAL INTERESTS: Skiing, sailing, farming (experimenting with production of grapes for wine with modern methods), preservation of wildlife in Italy.

BIOGRAPHICAL/CRITICAL SOURCES: Best Sellers, November 15, 1970.

* * *

CAMERON, John 1914-

PERSONAL: Born July 16, 1914, in Edinburgh, Scotland; son of Peter Sinclair (a police inspector) and Alexandrina (Robertson) Cameron; married Joyce Dearlove, July 13, 1940; children: Anne Elizabeth (Mrs. John Hemingway), Jane Marjorie (Mrs. Alexander Martin), Peter Sinclair. *Education:* Studied at University of Edinburgh; University of Leeds, B.A. (honors), 1939; University of London, Dip.Ed., 1947. *Religion:* Presbyterian. *Home:* Heron Rise, Lower Farm Rd., Effingham, Surrey, England. *Office:* Institute of Education, University of London, Bedford Way, London WC1H 0AL, England.

CAREER: Specialist in educational planning in Uganda and Tanzania, East Africa, 1957-64, with last post as assistant chief education officer for Tanzania; University of London, Institute of Education, London, England, senior lecturer on education in tropical areas, 1964—, currently on leave at Kenyatta University College. UNESCO specialist in educational planning, on special assignment in Malta, 1968-69. Consultant in Ethiopia, 1973, India, 1974, and Swaziland, 1975. *Military service:* British Army, Artillery, 1939-46; became captain. *Member:* African Studies Association (member of executive committee), Association of University Teachers, British Educational Administration Society, Royal High School Club, Malta Union Club.

WRITINGS: (With W. A. Dodd) *Tanzania: Society, Schools, and Progress,* Pergamon, 1970; *The Development of Education in East Africa,* Teachers College Press, 1970; (with J. Carver and M. Wallace) *English Learner's Dictionary,* Collins, 1971. Contributor of articles and reviews to education journals.

WORK IN PROGRESS: English as a Second Language; African Languages in Education.

* * *

CAMPBELL, John Lorne 1906-
(Fear Chanaidh)

PERSONAL: Born October 1, 1906, in Edinburgh, Scotland; son of Duncan and Ethel H. (Waterbury) Campbell; married Margaret Fay Shaw (an American-born folklorist), 1935. *Education:* St. John's College, Oxford, B.A., 1929, M.A., 1933. *Politics:* "Liberal Scottish Home-Ruler." *Religion:* Roman Catholic. *Home:* Isle of Canna, Scotland.

CAREER: Has owned and farmed the Isle of Canna in the Outer Hebrides, 1938—; folklorist. Secretary of Hebridean Sea League, 1933-38; president of Folklore Institute of Scotland, 1947-51; chief of Gaelic Society of Inverness, 1965. *Member:* National Farmers' Union, Society of Authors, Oxford Union. *Awards, honors:* Leverhulme research grant, 1949-51; LL.D., St. Francis Xavier University, 1953; D.Litt., University of Glasgow and Oxford University, both 1965.

WRITINGS: (Editor and translator) *Duain Ghaidhealach mu Bhliadhna Thearlaich: Highland Songs of the Forty-Five* (in Gaelic and English), John Grant, 1933; (editor) *The Book of Barra: Being Accounts of the Island of Barra in the Outer Hebrides* (written by various authors at various times, with chapters by Compton Mackenzie and Carl H. Borgstroem), G. Routledge & Sons, 1936; *Orain Ghaidhlig le Seonaidh Caimbeul,* privately printed, 1936; (editor and author of introduction) *Sia Sgialachdan* (six Gaelic stories), privately printed by T. & A. Constable, 1938; (with Alexander MacEwen) *Act Now for the Highlands and Islands,* Saltire Society, 1939; *Gaelic in Scottish Education and Life,* Saltire Society, 1945; (recorder; editor and translator with Annie Johnston and John MacLean) *Gaelic Folksongs from the Isle of Barra,* Folklore Institute of Scotland, 1950; *Fr. Allan McDonald of Eriskay, 1895-1905: Priest, Poet, and Folklorist* (booklet), Oliver & Boyd, 1954; (editor) *Gaelic*

Words from South Uist: Collected by Fr. Allan McDonald, Dublin Institute for Advanced Studies, 1958.

(Editor) *Tales from Barra: Told by the Coddy,* privately printed, 1960; (recorder and translator) *Stories from South Uist,* Routledge & Kegan Paul, 1961; (translator from tape recordings) *The Furrow Behind Me: The Autobiography of a Hebridean Crofter,* Routledge & Kegan Paul, 1962; (with Derick Thomson) *Edward Lhuyd in the Scottish Highlands,* Clarendon Press, 1963; (editor) *A School in South Uist: Memoirs of Frederick Rea,* Routledge & Kegan Paul, 1964; *Bardachd Mhgr Ailein: The Gaelic Poems of Fr. Allan McDonald,* privately printed, 1965; (with Trevor H. Hall) *Strange Things,* Routledge & Kegan Paul, 1968; (editor with Francis Collinson) Donald MacCormick, *Hebridean Folksongs,* Oxford University Press, Volume I, 1969, Volume II, 1977. Contributor of articles on Gaelic folklore and Hebridean entomology to journals.

WORK IN PROGRESS: Editing with Francis Collinson, Volume III of *Hebridean Folksongs.*

SIDELIGHTS: John Campbell has tape-recorded traditional Gaelic songs, legends, and stories in the Hebrides and on Cape Breton Island, Nova Scotia, where he collected with his wife in 1937. Their recordings were transcribed by Seamus Ennis for a manuscript in possession of the Irish Folklore Commission, Dublin. Campbell says that he is interested generally "in vindicating Scottish Gaeldom, particularly the Western Islands, economically, politically, historically, against the prejudices and misunderstandings of various politicians, bureaucrats and writers."

BIOGRAPHICAL/CRITICAL SOURCES: Books and Bookmen, January, 1969.

* * *

CAMPBELL, John W(ood) 1910-1971
(Arthur McCann, Don A. Stuart, Karl Van Campen)

June 8, 1910—July 11, 1971; American editor and science fiction writer. Obituaries: *New York Times,* July 13, 1971; *Antiquarian Bookman,* August 2-9, 1971. (See index for *CA* sketch)

* * *

CAMPBELL, Oscar James, Jr. 1879-1970

August 16, 1879—June 2, 1970; American Shakespearean scholar, author, and editor. Obituaries: *New York Times,* June 2, 1970; *Books Abroad,* spring, 1971.

* * *

CANARY, Robert H(ughes) 1939-

PERSONAL: Born February 1, 1939, in Providence, R.I.; son of Richard Lee (a teacher) and Margaret (Hughes) Canary; married Margaret Anne Cook (a teacher), June 12, 1961; children: Richard Douglas, Linda Anne. *Education:* Denison University, B.A., 1960; University of Chicago, M.A., 1962, Ph.D., 1963. *Politics:* Democrat. *Religion:* Protestant. *Home:* 420 Carlton Dr., Racine, Wis. 53402. *Office:* Department of English, University of Wisconsin—Parkside, Kenosha, Wis. 53140.

CAREER: San Diego State College (now University), San Diego, Calif., assistant professor of English, 1963-66; Grinnell College, Grinnell, Iowa, assistant professor of English, 1966-68; University of Hawaii, Honolulu, associate professor of English, 1968-70; University of Wisconsin—Parkside, Kenosha, associate professor, 1970-74, professor of English, 1974—, chairman of Humanities Division, 1976—. Visiting summer professor at University of Michigan, 1967, and Hofstra University, 1968. Songwriter; compositions include "To Catch the Blues," 1967, and "To Anthony Hecht," 1968. *Member:* Modern Language Association of America, American Historical Association, Organization of American Historians, American Association of University Professors, Catch Society of America (member of executive board, 1969—), Cabell Society, Society for the Study of Southern Literature.

WRITINGS: William Dunlap, Twayne, 1970; *George Bancroft,* Twayne, 1974. Contributor to literature journals. Coeditor, *Clio.*

WORK IN PROGRESS: Robert Graves; Footnotes to History: Civil War Diaries; The Cabillian Scene; T. S. Eliot; Notes toward a Poetics of History; co-editing *Structure of Historical Writing.*

SIDELIGHTS: Robert Canary told *CA:* "Like other scholarly authors, I find that my books, once accepted, move only slowly toward publication. The sales figures suggest that my publishers' delay is created by a reasonable instinct for self-preservation on their part."

* * *

CANNON, Lou(is S.) 1933-

PERSONAL: Born June 3, 1933, in New York, N.Y.; son of Jack and Irene (Kohn) Cannon; married Virginia Oprian, February 2, 1953; children: Carl, David, Judith, Jack. *Education:* Attended University of Nevada, 1950-52, and San Francisco State College (now University), 1952. *Religion:* Congregationalist. *Home:* 1934 Hull Rd., Vienna, Va. 22180. *Office:* Ridder Publications, 1325 E St. N.W., Washington, D.C.

CAREER: Worked as a truck driver, 1954-56, and as a reporter for various newspapers, 1956-59; *Contra Costa Times,* Walnut Creek, Calif., managing editor, 1959-65; *San Jose Mercury-News,* San Jose, Calif., copy editor, 1961-65, State Capitol bureau chief, 1965-69; Ridder Publications, Washington, D.C., correspondent, 1969—. *Military service:* U.S. Army, 1953-54. *Member:* National Press Club, American Political Science Association, Sacramento Press Club, Sigma Delta Chi. *Awards, honors:* American Political Science Association Award, 1968, for distinguished reporting of public affairs; California Taxpayers Award, 1969, for editorial writing.

WRITINGS: Ronnie and Jesse: A Political Odyssey, Doubleday, 1969; *The McCloskey Challenge,* Dutton, 1972; *Reporting An Inside View,* California Journal Press, 1977. Contributor to *Cry California* and other publications. Also author of monthly column, "Letter from Washington," for *California Journal* (Sacramento).

SIDELIGHTS: Louis Cannon mentions that "an exceptionally generous reviewer of *Ronnie and Jesse* [Ronald Reagan and Jessie Unruh] refers to the 'deeper contest' that underlies all political competition." "It is to this contest," Cannon writes, "that my interest is addressed. I care a good deal, or think I do, about our political system and my intention is to write books that contribute to the understanding of that system and those who inhabit it."

BIOGRAPHICAL/CRITICAL SOURCES: New York Times, November 11, 1969; *Los Angeles Times,* November 28, 1969; *National Review,* February 10, 1970.

CANNON, William (S). 1918-
(Bill Cannon)

PERSONAL: Born December 16, 1918, in Meridian, Miss.; son of Willis Street (an auto mechanic) and Angela (Schlevoight) Cannon; married Nelwyn Nesmith (a secretary), November 10, 1943; children: Pamela (Mrs. John Michael Willenbring), William N., Claire (Mrs. Dawon Parker). *Education:* University of Alabama, B.A., 1942; Southwestern Baptist Theological Seminary, Fort Worth, B.D., 1956. *Politics:* Independent. *Home:* 332 River St., Hartsville, Tenn. 37074.

CAREER: Meridian Star, Meridian, Miss., reporter, 1936-38; Sears, Roebuck & Co., advertising manager in Mississippi and North Carolina, 1946-53; pastor of Southern Baptist churches in North Carolina and Texas, 1954-65; Broadman Press, Nashville, Tenn., editor of inspirational books, beginning 1965. *Military service:* U.S. Navy, 1942-46.

WRITINGS—All published by Broadman: (Under name Bill Cannon) *One Last Christmas* (fiction), 1966; (editor) *Everyday, Five Minutes with God,* 1969; *How High Are the Stars!: Can a Man Live a Year of His Life Entirely Within the Will of God?* (fiction), 1970; *The Jesus Revolution: New Inspiration for Evangelists,* 1971.

WORK IN PROGRESS: A novel set in Tennessee of the 1890's, dealing with the effect of violence on the character of a young Army veteran.†

*   *   *

CANTINAT, Jean 1902-

PERSONAL: Born April 7, 1902, in Brest, Finistere, France. *Education:* Studied at University of Strasbourg, University of Lille, and Catholic Institute of Paris. *Home:* 95 rue de Sevres, Paris 6, France.

CAREER: Roman Catholic priest; teacher and writer.

WRITINGS: Au coeur de notre redemption, Tequi, 1953; (contributor) *The Introduction to the Bible,* Desclee-Cie, 1959, new edition, 1976-77; *La Pedagogie de Dieu dans la Bible,* Editions Ouvrieres, 1960; *Les Epitres de Saint Paul expliquees,* Gabalda, 1960, translation published as *The Epistles of St. Paul Explained,* Alba, 1967; *La Pedagogie du Christ,* Editions Ouvrieres, 1961; *Marie dans la Bible,* Mappus, 1963, translation by Paul Barrett published as *Mary in the Bible,* Newman, 1965; *Vie de Saint Paul apotre,* Apostolat des Editions, 1964; (translator and author of commentary) *Les Actes des apotres,* Mame, 1966; *Saint Paul et l'Eglise,* Mame, 1968; *L'Eglise de la Pentecote,* Mame, 1969; *Les Epitres de Saint Jacques et de Saint Jude,* Gabalda, 1973. Contributor to French reviews.

*   *   *

CANTOR, Arthur 1920-

PERSONAL: Born March 12, 1920, in Boston, Mass.; son of Samuel S. (a salesman) and Lillian (Landsman) Cantor; married Deborah Rosmarin, November 18, 1951 (deceased); children: David Jonathan, Jacqueline Hope, Michael Stephen. *Education:* Harvard University, A.B., 1940. *Religion:* Jewish. *Home:* 1 West 72nd St., New York, N.Y. 10023. *Office:* Arthur Cantor, Inc., 234 West 44th St., New York, N.Y. 10036.

CAREER: Publicist for Playwright's Company, New York City, 1947-51; president of Advance Public Relations, New York City, 1953—, and press representative for "Inherit the Wind," 1955, "The Most Happy Fellow," "Auntie Mame," and "Long Day's Journey into Night," 1956, "Two for the Seesaw," 1958, and "The Miracle Worker," 1959; president of Arthur Cantor, Inc., New York City, 1953—, producing about twenty plays in Manhattan. Productions include: "The Tenth Man" (co-producer, Saint Subber), 1959; "All the Way Home" (co-producer, Fred Coe), 1960; "Gideon," 1961; "A Thousand Clowns," 1962; "The Passion of Josef D.," 1964; "The World of Gunter Grass," 1966; "The Concept," 1968; "The Golden Bat," 1970; also co-producer of six plays in London, among them "Vivat! Vivat Regina!," "The Winslow Boy," and "Captain Brassbound's Conversion," starring Ingrid Bergman. *Military service:* U.S. Army Air Forces, 1942-46; became first lieutenant. *Member:* League of New York Theatres, Harvard Club of New York, Coffee House Club. *Awards, honors:* "All the Way Home," written by Tad Mosel, won the Pulitzer Prize in drama, 1961; American Jewish Congress Award, 1969.

WRITINGS: (With Stuart W. Little) *The Playmakers,* Norton, 1970.

BIOGRAPHICAL/CRITICAL SOURCES: Cue, March 7, 1970; *New York Times,* April 5, 1970; *Christian Science Monitor,* April 28, 1970; *Variety,* June 10, 1970.

*   *   *

CANTOR, Louis 1934-

PERSONAL: Born September 21, 1934, in Memphis, Tenn.; son of Paul and Libby (Mendelsohn) Cantor; married Alice C. Beck, September 19, 1960 (divorced). *Education:* Memphis State University, B.S., 1957; Duke University, M.A., 1961, Ph.D., 1963. *Politics:* Democrat. *Home:* 915 West Wayne St., Apt. 5, Fort Wayne, Ind. 46804. *Office:* Department of History, Indiana University at Fort Wayne, Fort Wayne, Ind. 46805.

CAREER: Southeast Missouri State College (now University), Cape Girardeau, assistant professor of history, 1963-68; Indiana University at Fort Wayne, associate professor of history, 1968—. *Military service:* National Guard and U.S. Army Reserve, 1953-61; became first lieutenant. *Member:* American Historical Association, Organization of American Historians, American Association of University Professors.

WRITINGS: A Prologue to the Protest Movement, Duke University Press, 1969. Contributor to historical journals.

WORK IN PROGRESS: Bob Dylan and the Protest Movement of the 1960's.

*   *   *

CANTORI, Louis J. 1934-

PERSONAL: Born June 29, 1934, in Haverhill, Mass.; son of Louis J. and Catherine Cantori; married Barbara-Joan Nye, December 19, 1953; children: Gregory, Eric, Nadia. *Education:* University of Massachusetts, B.A., 1959; University of Chicago, M.A., 1962, Ph.D., 1966. *Home:* 716 Dryden Dr., Baltimore, Md. 21229. *Office:* Department of Political Science, University of Maryland, Baltimore, Md. 21228.

CAREER: University of California, Los Angeles, assistant professor of political science, 1966-72; University of Maryland, Baltimore, associate professor of political science, 1972—. Adjunct associate professor, University of Pennsylvania, 1973—; visiting associate professor, American University in Cairo, 1974-76. Consultant, Office of Education, U.S. Department of Health, Education and Welfare, 1968-

72. *Military service:* U.S. Marine Corps, 1953-55; became sergeant. *Member:* International Studies Association, American Political Science Association, African Studies Association (fellow), Middle East Studies Association (fellow). *Awards, honors:* Fulbright fellowship for United Arab Republic, 1963-65; Ford Foundation grant for international studies in France and Morocco, 1967, 1968-69; Social Science Research Council grant for Morocco, 1968-69; Fulbright-Hays faculty research grant for Morocco, 1970; U.S. Office of Education International Studies grant, 1973-75.

WRITINGS: (With Steven L. Spiegel) *The International Politics of Regions: A Comparative Approach,* Prentice-Hall, 1970; (editor) *Comparative Political Systems,* Holbrook, 1974. Contributor to political science journals.

WORK IN PROGRESS: Political Mobilization in Pre-Revolutionary Egypt: The Wafd Party 1918-1924; with Peter Benedict, *Leadership and Local Development.*

*   *   *

CAPITAN, William H(arry)   1933-

PERSONAL: Born February 7, 1933, in Owosso, Mich.; son of Harry and Anthe (Sarris) Capitan; married Dolores Marie Randolph, September 19, 1959; children: Rita Anne, Edwin Andrew. *Education:* University of Michigan, B.A., 1954; Queen's University, Belfast, graduate study, 1954-55; University of Minnesota, M.A., 1958, Ph.D., 1960. *Religion:* Protestant/Episcopal. *Home:* 2 Lincoln Way, Buckhannon, W.Va. 26201. *Agent:* Educational Resources Corp., 128 East 74th St., New York, N.Y. 10021. *Office:* Office of Academic Affairs, West Virginia Wesleyan College, Buckhannon, W.Va. 26201.

CAREER: University of Minnesota, Minneapolis, instructor in philosophy, 1959-60; University of Maryland, College Park, instructor in philosophy, 1960-62; Oberlin College, Oberlin, Ohio, assistant professor, 1962-65, associate professor of philosophy, 1965-70, chairman of department of philosophy, 1968-70; Saginaw Valley College, University Center, Mich., director of fine arts, 1970-72, vice-president of academic affairs, 1972-74, acting president, 1974; West Virginia Wesleyan College, Buckhannon, vice-president for academic affairs and dean, 1974—. Visiting professor, State University of New York at Buffalo, 1967. Board member, Saginaw Symphony Orchestra, 1970—. Editorial consultant, World Publishing Co. *Member:* American Philosophical Association, American Society for Aesthetics, Academy of Academic Personnel Administrators (secretary-treasurer, 1973). *Awards, honors:* American Council of Learned Societies research fellowship, 1967-68.

WRITINGS: (Editor with D. D. Merrill) *Metaphysics and Explanation,* University of Pittsburgh Press, 1966; (editor with Merrill) *Art, Mind, and Religion,* University of Pittsburgh Press, 1967; *The Philosophy of Religion: An Introduction,* Pegasus, 1971. Anthologized in *Hume: A Collection of Critical Essays,* edited by Vere Claiborne Chappell, Doubleday, 1966. Contributor to *American Philosophical Quarterly, Monist, La Revue Internationale de Philosophie, Revista de Occidente, Social Studies, Activist,* and *Art Quarterly.*

WORK IN PROGRESS: The Concept of Art, a book-length work on the rise of impressionism as a case history for the study of aesthetic change.

SIDELIGHTS: William Capitan lists his major vocational interests as "the promotion of the arts, understand[ing] of the arts, [and] the arts as integral parts of the quality of American life." He told *CA:* "At present I am concerned to make available instruction in the arts to areas where this is not readily available. The arts must no longer be looked upon as frills for the rich, but as important ways for all people to gain self understanding."

*   *   *

CAPPS, Donald E(ric)   1939-

PERSONAL: Born January 30, 1939, in Omaha, Neb.; son of Holden F. (an accountant) and Mildred (Bildt) Capps; married Karen Docken, August 22, 1964; children: John Michael. *Education:* Lewis and Clark College, B.A., 1960; Yale University, Divinity School, B.D., 1963, S.T.M., 1965; University of Chicago, Divinity School, M.A., 1957, Ph.D., 1970. *Home:* 1901 Pawhuska Dr., Enid, Okla. 73701. *Office:* Graduate Seminary, Phillips University, Enid, Okla. 73701.

CAREER: University of Chicago, Divinity School, Chicago, Ill., assistant professor, 1969-74; University of North Carolina at Charlotte, associate professor of religious studies, 1974-76; Phillips University, Graduate Seminary, Enid, Okla., associate professor, 1976—.

WRITINGS: (Editor with brother, Walter H. Capps) *Religious Personality,* Wadsworth, 1970; (editor with Frank E. Reynolds) *The Biographical Process,* Mouton & Co., 1976; (editor with Lewis Rambo and Paul Ransohoff) *Psychology of Religion: A Guide to Information Sources,* Gale, 1976; (editor with W. H. Capps and Gerald Bradford) *Encounter with Erikson,* Scholars Press (Missoula, Mont.), 1976. Contributor of articles to *Journal for the Scientific Study of Religion, Journal for the History of Behavioral Sciences, Journal of Religion,* and *Social Research.*

*   *   *

CAPPS, Walter Holden   1934-

PERSONAL: Born May 5, 1934; son of Holden F. (an accountant) and Mildred Linnea Theresa (Bildt) Capps; married Lois Ragnhild Grimsrud, August 22, 1960; children: Lisa Margarit, Todd Holden. *Education:* Portland University, B.S., 1958; Augustana Theological Seminary, B.D. (summa cum laude), 1960; Yale University, S.T.M., 1961, M.A., 1963, Ph.D., 1965. *Home:* 531 Sussex Ct., Goleta, Calif. 93017. *Office:* Institute of Religious Studies, University of California, Santa Barbara, Calif. 93106.

CAREER: University of California, Santa Barbara, assistant professor, 1964-69, associate professor, 1969-73, professor of religious studies, 1973—, director of Institute of Religious Studies, 1970—. Visiting scholar, Warburg Institute, London, 1968-69. Member of senior common room, Mansfield College, Oxford University, 1971. Member of board of theological education, Lutheran Church in America; member of board of directors, Pacific Lutheran Theological Seminary; member of Collegium, Pacific Lutheran University; president, Council on the Study of Religion; member of advisory council, La Casa de Maria (Immaculate Heart College). *Member:* Society for Religion in Higher Education, American Academy of Religion, Society for the Scientific Study of Religion, American Association of University Professors. *Awards, honors:* Society for Religion in Higher Education fellow, 1968-69; University of California Humanities Institute fellow, 1971-72.

WRITINGS: (Editor and contributor) *The Future of Hope,* Fortress, 1970; (editor with brother, Donald E. Capps, and contributor) *The Religious Personality*, Wadsworth, 1970; (editor and contributor) *Ways of Understanding Religion*, Macmillan, 1972; *Time Invades the Cathedral*, Fortress, 1972; *Hope against Hope*, Fortress, 1976; (editor) *Seeing with a Native Eye*, Harper, 1976; (editor with D. E. Capps and Gerald Bradford) *Encounter with Erikson*, Scholars Press, 1976. Contributor to *Revue Philosophique de Louvain, Heythrop Journal, Humanitas*, and other journals.

WORK IN PROGRESS: The Horizon of Religion, analyses of approaches to religion.

*   *   *

CAPRON, William M(osher)   1920-

PERSONAL: Surname is pronounced *Kay*-pron; born July 30, 1920, in New York, N.Y.; son of Charles Alexander and Margaret Eleanor (Mosher) Capron; married Margaret Morgan, June 13, 1942; children: Alexander Mosher, Margaret Wells, Barry Lincoln, Seth Thompson. *Education:* Swarthmore College, A.B., 1942; attended Syracuse University, 1942; Harvard University, M.P.A., 1947, M.A., 1948. *Religion:* Unitarian. *Home:* 248 Gray St., Arlington, Mass. 02174. *Office:* John F. Kennedy School of Government, Harvard University, Littauer Center 110, Cambridge, Mass. 02138.

CAREER: U.S. Bureau of the Budget, Washington, D.C., fiscal analyst, 1945-46, assistant director, 1964-65; Harvard University, Cambridge, Mass., Economic Research Project, research associate, 1948-49; University of Illinois at Urbana-Champaign, Urbana, assistant professor of economics, 1949-51; RAND Corporation, Santa Monica, Calif., economist, 1951-56, consultant, 1956-62, 1966—; Stanford University, Stanford, Calif., assistant professor of economics, 1956-62; Council of Economic Advisors, Washington, D.C., senior staff member, 1962-64; Brookings Institution, Washington, D.C., senior fellow, 1965-69, co-director of Studies in Regulation of Economic Activity, 1967-69; Harvard University, Cambridge, Mass., John F. Kennedy School of Government, lecturer in politics and economics and associate dean, 1969—. Member of Commerce Technical Advisory Board, U.S. Department of Commerce, 1966-70, Social Science Advisory Board, Arms Control and Disarmament Agency, 1966—, and Research Advisory Committee, Economic Development Administration, 1967-69, all in Washington, D.C. *Military service:* U.S. Army, Infantry, 1942-45; became first lieutenant; awarded Purple Heart, Distinguished Service Cross.

MEMBER: American Association for the Advancement of Science, American Political Science Association, Federation of American Scientists, American Economic Association, Econometric Society, American Society for Public Administration, American Academy of Arts and Sciences, National Association of Student Personnel Administrators.

WRITINGS: (Editor) *Technological Change in the Regulated Industries*, Brookings Institution, 1971.††

*   *   *

CARBERY, Thomas F.   1925-

PERSONAL: Born January 18, 1925, in Glasgow, Scotland; son of Thomas Albert (a local government official) and Jean (Morrison) Carbery; married Ellen Donnelly (a teacher), August, 1954; children: Anne, Moira Jane, Thomas Anthony. *Education:* University of Glasgow, part-time student, 1949-52, Diploma in Public Administration, 1952; Scottish College of Commerce, part-time student, 1952-56;

University of London, B.Sc. (with honors; economics), 1956, M.Sc. (economics), 1962, Ph.D., 1966. *Politics:* Labour Party. *Religion:* Roman Catholic. *Home:* 32 Crompton Ave., Glasgow S.4, Scotland. *Office:* University of Strathclyde, Glasgow, Scotland.

CAREER: Executive in British civil service, 1947-61; Scottish College of Commerce, lecturer, 1961-63, senior lecturer in government and economics, 1963-64; University of Strathclyde, Glasgow, Scotland, senior lecturer in government and business relations, 1964-75, head of department of office organization, 1975—. Member of Independent Broadcasting Authority (formerly Independent Television Authority), 1970—, Royal Commission on Gambling, 1976—, Central Transport Users Consultation Committee, 1976—; chairman of Scottish Transport Users Consultation Committee, 1976—. *Military service:* Royal Air Force, 1943-47. *Member:* Public and Cooperative Enterprise (chairman of Scottish branch), Society for Cooperative Studies (past president).

WRITINGS: (Contributor) *Progress to Prosperity*, Scottish Council of Fabians, 1968; *Consumers in Politics*, Augustus M. Kelly, 1969; (contributor) Arend Lijphart, editor, *Politics in Europe: Comparisons and Interpretations*, Prentice-Hall, 1969.

WORK IN PROGRESS: Research on member participation in cooperative societies.

BIOGRAPHICAL/CRITICAL SOURCES: Times Literary Supplement, August 29, 1969.

*   *   *

CARIN, Arthur A.   1928-

PERSONAL: Born November 27, 1928, in Brooklyn, N.Y.; son of Samuel and Etta (Gaa) Carin; married Doris Terry Orkand (a teacher), December 23, 1951; children: Jill, Amy, Jon. *Education:* Oswego State Teachers College (now State University of New York at Oswego), B.S., 1951; Queens College of the City of New York (now Queens College of the City University of New York), M.A., 1954; University of Utah, Ed.D., 1958. *Home:* 12 Richmond Ave., Jericho, N.Y. 11753. *Office:* Queens College of the City University of New York, Kissena Blvd., Flushing, N.Y. 11367.

CAREER: Teacher in public schools in Great Neck, N.Y., 1951-55; University of Utah, Salt Lake City, instructor in elementary education, 1955-58; Queens College of the City University of New York, Flushing, N.Y., assistant professor, 1958-62, chairman of early childhood and elementary education department, 1962-66, associate professor and assistant dean, 1966-69, professor of teacher education and associate dean, 1969—. Visiting professor, State University of New York at New Paltz, summer, 1960, Adelphi University and Hofstra University, summer, 1961, Long Island University, 1966-69, University of Utah, summers, 1967, 1970. Guest lecturer and consultant, Council for Elementary Science International, Association for Supervision and Curriculum Development, National Science Teachers Association, 1955—. Director of In-Service Workshops, Portchester Public Schools, 1958-61; director of Science In-Service Workshops, public schools in New Hyde Park, N.Y., 1961-62, East Williston, N.Y., 1962-63, Floral Park, N.Y., 1964-65, North Merrick, N.Y., 1966-67, North Shore, N.Y. and Glen Cove, N.Y., 1967-71. Member of board of education, Jericho, N.Y., 1961-63, president of board of education, 1963-67; member of executive committee of Metropolitan New York Teacher Education and Professional Standards Committee, 1966-67; participant, Implementation Program of the Science Curriculum Improvement Study of University of California at Berkeley, 1968, and Implementation Program of Outdoor Biology Instructional Strategies of University of California at Berkeley, 1975. President and co-director of Kenwal Country Day School, Melville, N.Y., 1972-74. Consultant and reviewer of educational films, Texture Films, 1974—. *Military service:* U.S. Army, Medical Corps, 1946-48; became sergeant.

MEMBER: Association for Childhood Education International, Council for Elementary Science International, International Oceanographic Foundation, American Association for the Advancement of Science, American Association of University Professors, National Association for College Teachers of Education, National Education Association of University Professors, National Association for Teaching, National Oceanographic Data Center, National Science Teachers Association, Association for Student Teaching, Association for Supervision and Curriculum Development, New York State School Boards Association, New York State Teachers Association, Phi Delta Kappa, Kappa Delta Pi. *Awards, honors:* Grade Teacher's Education Book-of-the-Month award, 1971.

WRITINGS: (With Robert B. Sund) *Teaching Science through Discovery* (Educator's Book-of-the-Month Club selection), C. E. Merrill, 1964, 3rd revised edition, 1975, abridged edition published as *Discovery Teaching in Science,* C. E. Merrill, 1966, revised edition, 1975; *Teaching Science through Discovery Teacher's Guide,* C. E. Merrill, 1964, 3rd revised edition, 1975; (contributor) *Dimension 99* (Educator's Book-of-the-Month Club selection), New Dimensions in Education, 1968; (contributor) *Professional Teacher's Manual for Project Alpha,* New Dimensions in Education, Inc., 1969; *Teaching Modern Science,* C. E. Merrill, 1971; *Developing Questioning Techniques: A Self-Concept Approach,* C. E. Merrill, 1971, revised edition, 1977. Contributor to *Science and Children, Trends in Teaching.*

* * *

CARLISLE, Carol Jones 1919-

PERSONAL: Born May 11, 1919, in Tuscaloosa, Ala.; daughter of Richard Palmer (a business executive) and Pauline Vaughan (Overbey) Jones; married Douglas Hilton Carlisle (a professor of political science), August 20, 1942; children: Carol Diane (Mrs. John Russell Lindsey), Douglas Hilton, Jr. *Education:* Wesleyan College, Macon, Ga., B.A. (summa cum laude), 1940; University of North Carolina, M.A., 1941, Ph.D. 1951. *Politics:* Democrat. *Religion:* Protestant. *Home:* 1100 Gregg St., Columbia, S.C. 29201. *Office:* Department of English, University of South Carolina, Columbia, S.C. 29208.

CAREER: Pearl River Junior College, Poplarville, Miss., instructor in English, 1942-43; Wesleyan College, Macon, Ga., instructor in English, 1944; University of South Carolina, Columbia, instructor, 1946-50, assistant professor, 1950-58, associate professor, 1958-69, professor of English, 1969—. *Member:* Shakespeare Association of America, International Shakespeare Association, Modern Language Association of America, American Society for Theatre Research, International Theatre Federation, Society for Theatre Research (London), Renaissance Society of America, South Atlantic Modern Language Association, Southeastern Renaissance Conference, Mortarboard.

WRITINGS: Shakespeare from the Greenroom: Actors' Criticisms of Four Great Tragedies, University of North Carolina Press, 1969. Contributor to *Shakespeare Quarterly, Theatre Survey, Theatre Notebook,* and other journals. An editor, *Explicator,* 1954-66, 1977—.

WORK IN PROGRESS: Research for a biography of Helen Faucit, nineteenth-century English actress.

* * *

CARLSON, Andrew R(aymond) 1934-

PERSONAL: Born August 19, 1934, in Ludington, Mich.; son of Louis P. and Mabel (Genter) Carlson; married Linda Volfarts, September 5, 1959; children: Sharon Lee, Andrew Arthur. *Education:* Western Michigan University, B.A., 1960, M.A., 1961; Michigan State University, Ph.D., 1970. *Politics:* Independent. *Religion:* Protestant. *Home:* 924 124th Ave., Shelbyville, Mich. 49344. *Office:* Probate Court, Kalamazoo County Building, Kalamazoo, Mich. 49008.

CAREER: Teacher of modern languages in public schools of Galesburg, Mich., 1960-61; Michigan State University, East Lansing, teaching assistant in history, 1964-65; Kalamazoo Public Schools, Kalamazoo, Mich., substitute teacher, 1965-67; Eastern Kentucky University, Richmond, assistant professor of history, 1967-70; Ferris State College, Big Rapids, Mich., assistant professor of social sciences, 1970-73; Western Michigan University, Kalamazoo, member of social science faculty, 1973-75; employee of Probate Court in Kalamazoo County, 1976—. *Military service:* U.S. Army, 1954-57. *Member:* American Historical Association, American Library Association, Historische Commission zu Berlin, Institute of Contemporary History (London), Pi Gamma Mu, Phi Alpha Theta.

WRITINGS: German Foreign Policy 1890-1914, and Colonial Policy to 1914: A Handbook and Annotated Bibliography, Scarecrow, 1970; *Anarchism in Germany: The Early Years,* Scarecrow, 1971; *Wilhelm II and the Daily Telegraph Affair: A Study of the Disfunctionalism of Politics and Society in Wilhelminian Germany,* Scarecrow, 1977. Contributor to academic journals and popular magazines.

WORK IN PROGRESS: Anarchism in Germany: The Later Years; Hitler-Mussolini: Letters and Conversations; Working-Class Women in Imperial Germany; August Reinsdorf and the Niederwald Dynamite Plot: A Study of Justice in Imperial Germany; Bibliography of Writing on Working-Class Women in Imperial Germany; A Biographical Who Was Who in Imperial Germany, a biographical approach to history; *Gustav Landauer: A Bio-Bibliography;* and *Sergeant York Doughboy Hero.*

SIDELIGHTS: Andrew Carlson wrote to *CA:* "I started to write because I felt that I had something to say and wanted to address myself to a larger audience than a classroom holds. It is my firm belief that all aspiring authors should have something to say if they plan to write, if not, they should hang up their typewriter. If you plan to write with the idea that you will make a lot of money, forget it. I have published a number of books and articles and figure that the money I have made from my writing amounts to only a few cents an hour when you consider the enormous amount of work that goes into the creative process. If you need additional money, forget about writing, get a part-time job, you will be ahead in the long run."

AVOCATIONAL INTERESTS: Victorian objects and homes, collecting books.

CARLSON, John A(llyn) 1933-

PERSONAL: Born July 4, 1933, in Boston, Mass.; son of Valdemar E. (a professor) and Lilian (Deans) Carlson; married Jean Brown, June 22, 1957; children: Robin, Marjorie. *Education:* Denison University, B.S., 1955; Johns Hopkins University, Ph.D., 1961. *Religion:* Unitarian Universalist. *Home:* 132 Pawnee Dr., West Lafayette, Ind. 47906. *Office:* Department of Economics, Purdue University, Lafayette, Ind. 47907.

CAREER: Mutual of New York Insurance Co. (MONY), New York, N.Y., actuarial trainee, 1955-57; Princeton University, Princeton, N.J., research aide, 1960-61; Cornell University, Ithaca, N.Y., visiting assistant professor of economics, 1961-62; Purdue University, Lafayette, Ind., assistant professor, 1962-66, associate professor, 1966-69, professor of economics, 1969—. Guest scholar, Brookings Institution, 1967-68; research fellow, University of Manchester, Manchester, England, 1971-72. *Member:* American Economic Association, Econometric Society, Phi Beta Kappa.

WRITINGS: Macroeconomic Adjustments, Holt, 1970. Contributor to economic journals.

*   *   *

CARLSON, Ruth (Elizabeth) Kearney 1911-
(Ruth Elizabeth Kearney)

PERSONAL: Born June 2, 1911, in Ramona, Calif.; daughter of Mark C. and Jessie (Martin) Kearney; married Oscar Edward Carlson (a building contractor), July 20, 1945. *Education:* University of California, Berkeley, A.B., 1932, M.A., 1944, Ed.D., 1959. *Politics:* Republican. *Religion:* Lutheran. *Home:* 1718 Le Roy Ave., Berkeley, Calif. 94709. *Office:* California State University, Hayward, 25800 Hillary St., Hayward, Calif. 94542.

CAREER: Elementary school teacher, Ramona, Calif., 1933-37; high school teacher of English and history in California, Valencia, 1937-40, Fullerton, 1940-41, Nevada City, 1941-42, and San Diego, 1942-45; Pearl Harbor Naval Shipyard, Pearl Harbor, Oahu, Hawaii, civilian personnel assistant, 1945-48; teacher in Richmond, Calif., 1949-54; Contra Costa County, Calif., curriculum consultant, 1954-59; high school teacher in Orinda, Calif., 1959-60; California State University, Hayward, part-time teacher, 1959-60, assistant professor, 1960-61, associate professor, 1961-65, professor, 1965—. Teacher of creative writing at Nova Scotia Summer School, Halifax, for fourteen summers, and at University of Nevada workshop, 1970-74.

MEMBER: National Council of Teachers of English (member of board of directors, 1963-66; chairman of creativity and childrens writing, 1965-68; member of committee on composition in the elementary schools, 1976—), International Reading Association (chairman of library and literature committee, 1968—; member of library resources and reading committee, 1976-77), National Society for the Study of Education, Women's National Book Association (San Francisco chapter), International Folklore Society, American Folklore Society, Pi Lambda Theta, California Association of Teachers of English, California Writers Club, Central California Council of Teachers of English, University of California Education Alumni Society (president, 1969), Alpha Delta Kappa. *Awards, honors:* Certificate of Merit, Central California Council of Teachers of English, 1970.

WRITINGS: Sparkling Words: Two Hundred Practical and Creative Writing Ideas, privately printed, 1965, revised edition published as *Sparkling Words: Two Hundred Twenty Five Practical and Creative Writing Ideas,* Paladin, 1973; *Language Sparklers Through the Intermediate Grades,* privately printed, 1968; *Poetry for Today's Child,* Instructor Publications (Dansville, N.Y.), 1968; (contributor) Helen Huus, editor, *Evaluating Books for Children and Young People,* International Reading Association, 1968; *Literature for Children: Enrichment Ideas,* W. C. Brown, 1970, revised edition, 1976; *Writing Aids Through the Grades: One Hundred Eighty-Six Developmental Writing Activities,* Teachers College Press, 1970; (contributor) Jane Catterson, editor, *Children and Literature,* International Reading Association, 1970; *Emerging Humanity: Multiethnic Literature for Children and Adolescents,* W. C. Brown, 1972; (editor and contributor) *Folklore and Folktales Around the World,* International Reading Association, 1972; *Speaking Aids Through the Grades,* Teachers College Press, 1975. An address entitled "Literature for Personal Development" was published in the proceedings of the Fifth World Congress on Reading. Collaborator on instructional films and filmstrips produced by Coronet Films, including "Making Word Pictures" and "Haiku: An Introduction to Poetry." Contributor of more than sixty-five articles to professional journals, with those prior to 1945 published under name Ruth Elizabeth Kearney.

WORK IN PROGRESS: Literature sections for an English textbook series, for Harcourt.

SIDELIGHTS: Ruth Carlson was speaker at the Fifth World Congress on Reading sponsored by the International Reading Association in Vienna, Austria, August 12, 1974.

*   *   *

CARNAP, Rudolf P. 1891-1970

May 18, 1891—September 14, 1970; German-born American philosopher and founder of logical positivism. Obituaries: *New York Times,* September 15, 1970; *Washington Post,* September 16, 1970; *Time,* September 28, 1970. (See index for *CA* sketch)

*   *   *

CARPENTER, Patricia (Healy Evans) 1920-
(Patricia Healy Evans)

PERSONAL: Born May 22, 1920, in Milwaukee, Wis.; daughter of Harry Thomas and Ann (Barney) Healy; married Kenneth J. Carpenter (special collections director, University of Nevada Library); children: Judith Sherry (Mrs. Gershon Legman). *Education:* Attended San Francisco State College (now University), University of Arizona, and University of Nevada. *Home:* 1454 Exeter Way, Reno, Nev. 89503.

CAREER: Writer and illustrator of children's books. *Member:* California Folklore Society (former regional vice-president).

WRITINGS—Under name Patricia Healy Evans; self-illustrated, except as indicated: *The Mycophagists' Book* (adult), Peregrine Press (San Francisco), 1951; *An Alphabet Book,* Peregrine Press, 1953; (compiler) *Jump Rope Rhymes,* Porpoise Bookshop (San Francisco), 1954; *Hopscotch,* Porpoise Bookshop, 1955; *Who's It?,* Porpoise Bookshop, 1956; *Jacks,* Porpoise Bookshop, 1956; (compiler) *Sticks and Stones,* Porpoise Bookshop, 1960; (compiler) *Rimbles* (collection of children's games, rhymes, songs, and sayings), illustrated by Gioia Fiammenghi, Doubleday, 1961; *A Modern Herbal* (adult), illustrated by Rick Barton, Porpoise Bookshop, 1961.

Illustrator: Henry H. Evans, *First Duet,* Peregrine Press, 1956; Evans, *Small New Poems,* Porpoise Bookshop, 1957; Ernest Peninou and Sydney Greenleaf, *Winemaking in California,* two volumes, Peregrine Press, 1964.

* * *

CARR, Jess(e Crowe, Jr.) 1930-

PERSONAL: Born July 27, 1930, Bland County, Va.; son of Jesse Crowe and Flossie (Mitchell) Carr; married Lois Domazet (a choir director), June 17, 1955; children: Marsha Ainslie, Susan Kay, Catherine Rae. *Education:* Coyne Technical School, Chicago, Ill., graduate. *Politics:* Independent. *Religion:* Baptist. *Home:* 1401 Madison St., Radford, Va. 24141.

CAREER: Self-employed businessman in southwestern Virginia, 1949-51, 1953-56; Commonwealth Press, Inc., Radford, Va., sales manager, 1956-62, vice-president and general manager, 1962-67; Professional Printing Services Corp., Radford, division president, 1967-71; full-time writer, 1971—. Owner, Woodland Heights Sub-Division Co.; builder of homes and commercial buildings. *Military service:* U.S. Marine Corps, 1951-52. *Member:* Printing Industries of the Virginias (vice-president, 1967).

WRITINGS: A Creature Was Stirring and Other Stories, Commonwealth Press, 1970; *The Second Oldest Profession: An Informal History of Moonshining in America,* Prentice-Hall, 1972; *The Falls of Rabbor,* Moore Publishing, 1973; *The Saint of the Wilderness,* Commonwealth Press, 1974; *Birth of a Book,* Commonwealth Press, 1974; *The Frost of Summer,* Moore Publishing, 1975; *A Cabal of Knaves,* Aurora, 1977.

WORK IN PROGRESS: Shipride Down the Spring Branch and Other Stories; How a Book Is Written, Published, Printed, and Distributed; A Star Rising, an historical novel set in first century Asia Minor; *The Gift Horse and Other Stories; Encounter at Ararat.*

AVOCATIONAL INTERESTS: Fishing, water skiing, boating, photography, playing folk guitar, collecting books.

* * *

CARRINGTON, Paul D(eWitt) 1931-

PERSONAL: Born June 12, 1931, in Dallas, Tex.; son of Paul Carrington; married Bessie Meek, August 2, 1952; children: Clark, Mary, Will, Emily. *Education:* University of Texas, B.A., 1952; Harvard University, LL.B. (cum laude), 1955. *Home:* 3098 Newcastle Rd., Ann Arbor, Mich. 48104. *Office:* Law School, University of Michigan, Ann Arbor, Mich.

CAREER: Carrington, Johnson & Stephens, Dallas, Tex., attorney, 1955; Harvard University, Law School, Cambridge, Mass., teaching fellow, 1957-58; assistant professor at University of Wyoming, Laramie, 1958-60, and Indiana University, Bloomington, 1960-62; Ohio State University, Columbus, associate professor, 1962-64, professor, 1964-65; University of Michigan, Ann Arbor, professor of law, 1965—. Visiting professor at Columbia University, 1972-73, and University of California, Los Angeles, 1975. Director of American Bar Foundation Study of United States Court of Appeals, 1966-68. Trustee, Ann Arbor Board of Education, 1970-73. *Military service:* U.S. Army, active duty, 1955-57; U.S. Army Reserve, 1957-58.

MEMBER: American Bar Association, American Judicature Society, American Law Institute, Association of American Law Schools (director of curriculum committee, 1968-71), American Association of University Professors, American Civil Liberties Union, Texas Bar Association, Michigan Bar Association.

WRITINGS: Civil Procedure: Cases and Comments on the Process of Adjudication, Little, Brown, 1969, 2nd edition, with Barbara Babcock, 1977; (with others) *Justice on Appeal,* West Publishing, 1976. Contributor of many articles to law journals.

* * *

CARROLL, C(armal) Edward 1923-

PERSONAL: Born October 8, 1923, in Grahn, Ky.; son of Noah W. (a carpenter) and Jessie (Scott) Carroll; married Greta Seastrom, June 11, 1960. *Education:* University of Toledo, Ph.B., 1947, M.A., 1950, B.Ed., 1951; University of California, Los Angeles, M.L.S., 1961; University of California, Berkeley, Ph.D., 1969. *Politics:* Democrat. *Religion:* Episcopalian. *Home:* 2001 Country Club Dr., Columbia, Mo. 65201. *Office:* Department of Library Science, University of Missouri, Columbia, Mo.

CAREER: Public school teacher in Ohio and Illinois, 1947-56; University of California, Los Angeles, director of curriculum laboratory, 1956-60; University of Southern California, Los Angeles, reference librarian, 1961-62; University of California, Berkeley, reference librarian, 1962-65; Southern Oregon College, Ashland, head librarian, 1965-67; Wichita State University, Wichita, Kan., director of libraries, 1967-70; University of Missouri—Columbia, director of libraries and professor of library science, 1970—. *Member:* American Library Association, American Association of University Professors, International Platform Association, LARC Association, Phi Delta Kappa, Beta Phi Mu.

WRITINGS: The Professionalization of Education for Librarianship: With Special Reference to the Years 1940-1960, Scarecrow, 1970; (contributor) *Administrative Aspects of Education for Librarianship,* Scarecrow, 1975; *Microforms in Libraries,* Microform Review, 1976. Also contributor to *Encyclopedia of Library and Information Science,* 1976.

WORK IN PROGRESS: A book of readings on library education; research into the emergence of academic librarians as faculty members at large universities.

AVOCATIONAL INTERESTS: Reading, camping, gardening.

* * *

CARSBERG, Bryan Victor 1939-

PERSONAL: Born January 3, 1939, in London, England; son of Alfred Victor (a chartered secretary) and Maryllia (Collins) Carsberg; married Margaret Graham, December 10, 1960; children: Debbie Anne, Sarah Jane. *Education:* London School of Economics and Political Science, M.Sc., 1967. *Religion:* None. *Home:* 9 Cherington Close, Handforth, Cheshire, England. *Office:* University of Manchester, Manchester, England.

CAREER: Bryan Carsberg & Co. (public accounting firm), Amersham, England, public accountant, 1962-64; University of London, London School of Economics and Political Science, London, England, lecturer in accounting, 1964-69; University of Manchester, Manchester, England, professor of accounting, 1969—. Visiting professor of business administration, University of California, Berkeley, 1974. Visiting lecturer in accounting, University of Chicago, Graduate School of Business, 1968-69. *Member:* Royal Institution of Great Britain, Institute of Chartered Accountants in England and Wales. *Awards, honors:* W. B. Peat Medal and Prize, Institute of Chartered Accountants, 1960.

WRITINGS: An Introduction to Mathematical Programming for Accountants, Augustus M. Kelley, 1969; (editor with H. C. Edey) *Modern Financial Management,* Penguin, 1969; *Analysis for Investment Decisions,* Haymarket, 1974; (with E. V. Morgan and M. Parkin) *Indexation and Inflation,* Financial Times, 1975; *Economics of Business Decisions,* Penguin, 1975; (with A. Hope) *Investment Decisions under Inflation,* Institute of Chartered Accountants in England and Wales, 1976. Contributor to accounting and finance journals.

WORK IN PROGRESS: A book on comparative international accounting; research on the predictive value in financial accounting.

* * *

CARSE, Robert 1902-1971

July 9, 1902—January 14, 1971; American merchant mariner and author. Obituaries: *Publishers' Weekly,* February 8, 1971. (See index for *CA* sketch)

* * *

CARSON, Herbert L(ee) 1929-

PERSONAL: Born October 3, 1929, in Philadelphia, Pa.; son of Saul (a journalist) and Bertha (Shapiro) Carson; married Ada Lou Siegel (a college professor), May 31, 1953; children: William, Rosalyn, Bryan. *Education:* University of Pittsburgh, B.A., 1953; Columbia University, M.A., 1955; University of Minnesota, Ph.D., 1959. *Politics:* "Independent—Liberal." *Religion:* Jewish. *Residence:* Big Rapids, Mich. *Office:* Department of Humanities, Ferris State College, Big Rapids, Mich. 49307.

CAREER: Worked in Philadelphia, Pa., as a newspaper copy boy, and as an assistant theater manager, and in New York City for an advertising firm, 1944-50; high school teacher of English in Orange, N.J., 1953-55; University of Minnesota, Minneapolis, instructor in English, 1956-59, instructor in creative writing in Independent Study Department, 1957-59; University of Nebraska, Lincoln, instructor in speech and drama, 1959-60; Ferris State College, Big Rapids, Mich., assistant professor, 1960-64, associate professor, 1964-68, professor of humanities and literature, 1968—. Visiting professor, Youngstown University, 1966. Director, Institute on Blacks in Movies, National Endowment for Humanities, and Ford Foundation, 1969. Actor, designer, and director in about seventy-five stage productions; also gives poetry recitals, and lectures. *Military service:* U.S. Army, Infantry, 1946-48. *Member:* Poetry Society of America, Michigan Academy of Science, Arts and Letters, Kappa Phi Kappa.

WRITINGS: Steps in Successful Speaking, Van Nostrand, 1967; (contributor) John Graham, editor, *Great American Speeches,* Appleton, 1970; (editor with wife, Ada Lou Carson) *The Impact of Fiction,* Cummings, 1970; (with Ada Lou Carson) *Royall Tyler: A Critical Biography,* Twayne, 1978. Also author of *The Harrowing of Thebes* and *Greek Vases.* Contributor of over two hundred articles and reviews, about fifteen short stories and plays, and about ninety poems to literary and academic journals.

WORK IN PROGRESS: George Lillo; Greek Statuary; meditative poetry.

CARSON, Robert C(harles) 1930-

PERSONAL: Born January 6, 1930, in Providence, R.I.; son of Robert Earl and May (Oborne) Carson; married Mary Mako, June 25, 1955; children: David Allen, Carolyn Marie. *Education:* Brown University, B.A., 1953; Northwestern University, M.A., 1955, Ph.D., 1957. *Home:* 1315 Morreene Rd., Durham, N.C. 27705. *Office:* Department of Psychology, Duke University, Durham, N.C. 27706.

CAREER: U.S. Veterans Administration, Chicago, Ill., trainee in clinical psychology, 1954-57; Northwestern University, Evanston, Ill., lecturer, 1956-57; University of Chicago, Chicago, instructor, 1957-59, assistant professor of psychology, 1959-60; Duke University, Durham, N.C., assistant professor, 1960-64, associate professor, 1964-68, professor of psychology and medical psychology, 1968—, director of internship training in clinical psychology, University Medical Center, 1961-63, head of Division of Medical Psychology, University Medical Center, 1963-70. Diplomate in clinical psychology, American Board of Examiners in Professional Psychology, 1963; licensed psychologist, State of North Carolina, 1968. Consultant to Veterans Administration Hospital, Durham, 1961—, and to Durham County Health Center, 1968—. *Military service:* U.S. Navy, 1948-49.

MEMBER: American Psychological Association (chairman of membership committee, Division of Clinical Psychology, 1966-67), American Association for the Advancement of Science, Southeastern Psychological Association, North Carolina Psychological Association (president, 1967-68), Phi Beta Kappa, Sigma Xi. *Awards, honors:* U.S. Public Health Service fellowship, 1967-68.

WRITINGS: (Contributor) J. Eels, editor, *Jobs in Psychology,* Science Research Associates, 1962; (contributor) J. R. Newbrough, editor, *Training in Clinical Psychology,* Division of Clinical Psychology, American Psychological Association, 1964; (contributor) J. N. Butcher, editor, *MMPI: Research Developments and Clinical Applications,* McGraw, 1969; *Interaction Concepts of Personality,* Aldine, 1969; (contributor) T. Huston and R. Burgess, editors, *Social Exchange in Developing Relationships,* Academic Press, in press. Contributor of articles and reviews to professional journals.

WORK IN PROGRESS: With J. N. Butcher, *Contemporary Behavior Disorder,* for Scott, Foresman.

* * *

CARUTH, Donald L(ewis) 1935-

PERSONAL: Born September 22, 1935, in Dallas, Tex.; son of Ralph Waldo and Marguerite (Young) Caruth; married Sarah Beth Buck, April 3, 1959; children: Jennifer Anne, Trevor Lane. *Education:* Southern Methodist University, B.B.A., 1958; North Texas State University, Ph.D., 1970. *Politics:* No party preference. *Religion:* "Unity." *Home:* 2715 Peach Tree Dr., Carrollton, Tex. 75006. *Office:* Caruth Management Consultants, Inc., 11500 North Stemmons, Suite 105, Dallas, Tex. 75229.

CAREER: Republic National Bank, Dallas, Tex., cost accountant, 1959-61; U.S. Air Force, Dallas, management engineer (civilian), 1961-63; First National Bank, Dallas, work measurement analyst, 1963-65; Texas Instruments, Inc., Dallas, cost engineer, 1965-66; North Texas State University, Denton, instructor in management, 1966-69; University of Dallas, Braniff Graduate School of Management, Irving, Tex., assistant professor of management,

1969-75; Caruth & Rachel & Associates, Dallas, managing partner, 1975-76; Caruth Management Consultants, Inc., Dallas, president, 1976—. *Member:* American Management Association, American Society for Personnel Administration, American Society for Training and Development, American Society of Business and Management Consultants, Association for Systems Management (president, Dallas chapter, 1970-71), Dallas Sales and Marketing Executives, Industrial Relations Research Association (president, North Texas chapter, 1974), Beta Gamma Sigma, Sigma Iota Epsilon. *Awards, honors:* Association for Systems Management achievement award and merit award for service to the profession.

WRITINGS: (With Cleatice L. Littlefield and Frank M. Rachel) *Office and Administrative Management,* 3rd edition (Caruth was not associated with earlier editions), Prentice-Hall, 1970, 4th edition, 1978; *Planning for Clerical Work Measurement,* American Management Association, 1970; *Guidelines for Organizing a Work Measurement Program* (monograph), Association for Systems Management, 1971; *Work Measurement for Commercial Banks,* Bankers Publishing, 1971; (with Rachel) *Business Systems: Articles, Analyses, and Cases,* Canfield Press, 1972; (with James H. Filkins) *A Lexicon of American Business Terms,* Simon & Schuster, 1973; (with Rachel) *Study Guide to Accompany Business Systems,* Canfield Press, 1975; (with Rachel and Victor J. Rizzo) *Basic Supervision: A Work Book for First-Line Managers,* CMC Publications, 1977; (with Rachel Dunn and J. D. Dunn) *Wage and Salary Administration: Total Compensation Systems,* 2nd edition (Caruth was not associated with first edition), McGraw, in press. Contributor to business journals.

AVOCATIONAL INTERESTS: Sailing, bicycling, reading.

* * *

CARVELL, Fred J(ohn) 1934-

PERSONAL: Born June 22, 1934, in Brooklyn, N.Y.; son of Douglas and Ada (Cook) Carvell; married Joan Barnes (an urban planner), July 3, 1954; children: Lyndell, John. *Education:* Monterey Peninsula College, A.A., 1960; Fresno State College (now California State University, Fresno), B.A., M.A., 1963; Stanford University, additional study. *Home:* 577 Van Buren St., Los Altos, Calif. 94022.

CAREER: Fresno City College, Fresno, Calif., instructor, 1962-66; URS Research Co., Palo Alto, Calif., consultant in manpower and education, 1966-69; Tadlock Associates, Inc., Los Altos, Calif., vice-president, 1969-75; Carvell Educational Management Planning, Los Altos, independent educational consultant, 1975—. Consultant to various colleges and state departments of education, private industrial firms, and public agencies at the local and federal level. Project manager for various studies in occupational training. *Military service:* U.S. Naval Reserve, 1952-60. *Member:* National Academy of Management, California Association of Distributive Education, California Business Educators Association.

WRITINGS: Human Relations in Business: Social and Organizational Factors of Supervision, Macmillan, 1970, 2nd edition, 1975; (editor with Max Tadlock) *It's Not Too Late,* Glencoe Press, 1971; (contributor) *Maternity Nursing Today,* 2nd edition, McGraw, 1976.

WORK IN PROGRESS: Researching a book on parental and community attitudes toward public schools at the presecondary level.

AVOCATIONAL INTERESTS: Painting and sailing.

* * *

CARVER, Fred D(onald) 1936-

PERSONAL: Born September 10, 1936, in Suwannee County, Fla.; son of Fred B. (a farmer) and Lessie (Burney) Carver; married Helen Schofield (a teacher), June 23, 1957; children: Sheryl Lynn, Eric Fred. *Education:* Aurora College, B.A., 1957; University of Wisconsin, M.S., 1963, Ph.D., 1967. *Politics:* Democrat. *Religion:* United Methodist. *Home:* 1913 Vassar Dr., Edwardsville, Ill. 62025. *Office:* School of Education, Southern Illinois University at Edwardsville, Edwardsville, Ill. 62026.

CAREER: Teacher in public schools in St. Petersburg, Fla., 1957-62; Markesan Public Schools, Markesan, Wis., high school principal, 1963-64; University of Wisconsin—Madison, research assistant to dean of School of Education, 1964-66; University of Illinois, Urbana, assistant professor, 1966-70, associate professor, 1970-74, professor of educational administration, 1974-76; Southern Illinois University at Edwardsville, professor of educational administration and dean of School of Education, 1976—. *Member:* American Educational Research Association, American Association of University Professors, Phi Delta Kappa.

WRITINGS: (Editor with Thomas J. Sergiovanni) *Organizations and Human Behavior: Focus on Schools,* McGraw, 1969; (with Sergiovanni) *The New School Executive,* Dodd, 1972. Contributor to educational journals. *Educational Administration Quarterly,* associate editor, 1970-72, editor, 1973-76.

* * *

CARY, Lee J(ames) 1925-

PERSONAL: Born December 13, 1925, in Binghamton, N.Y.; son of John L. (a toolmaker) and Louise (Scheider) Cary; married Norma Trask (a special reading teacher), June 11, 1949; children: Paul, Keith, Mark. *Education:* College of the Holy Cross, B.S., 1948; University of Buffalo, M.S.S., 1949; Syracuse University, Ph.D., 1962. *Politics:* Democrat. *Religion:* Presbyterian. *Home:* 300 Mumford Dr., Columbia, Mo. 65201. *Office:* University Center for Aging Studies, University of Missouri, Columbia, Mo. 65201.

CAREER: Syracuse University, Syracuse, N.Y., associate director of Youth Development Center, associate professor of social work, 1959-66; University of Missouri—Columbia, professor and chairman of Department of Regional and Community Affairs, 1966-73, director of School of Social Work, 1973-75, director of University Center for Aging Studies, 1975—. Researcher in Central and East Africa for U.S. State Department, 1965. *Military service:* U.S. Marine Corps, 1946-47; became first lieutenant. Recalled to active duty, 1950-52; served in Korean War. *Member:* American Association of University Professors, American Association of Social Workers, Council on Social Work Education, Community Development Society (founder and first president).

WRITINGS: (Editor) *Community Development as a Process,* University of Missouri Press, 1970.

WORK IN PROGRESS: A book, *An Introduction to Community Development.*

* * *

CASTAGNOLA, Lawrence A. 1933-

PERSONAL: Surname is pronounced Cas-ta-*no*-la; born

June 3, 1933, in Sacramento, Calif.; son of Ferdinand (a certified public accountant) and Louise Castagnola. *Education:* Attended University of Santa Clara, 1951-54; Gonzaga University, B.A., M.A., 1957; Alma College, M.A., 1964. *Home:* 1345 Stewart Rd., Sacramento, Calif. 95825.

CAREER: Entered Society of Jesus (Jesuits) in 1951; ordained a priest in 1964. High school teacher in San Francisco, Calif., 1957-60; chaplain at Fort Worden Treatment Center for Juveniles, Port Townsend, Wash., 1965; teacher at Jesuit High School, Sacramento, Calif., 1965-71; founder and director of a home for emotionally disturbed boys, Sacramento, 1970—.

WRITINGS: Let Your Lamps Be Burning, St. Paul Publications, 1966; *Pastoral Reflections,* St. Paul Publications, 1967; *I Love Youth: It's Teenagers I Hate,* B. Herder, 1970; *Confessions of a Catechist,* Alba, 1970.

*   *   *

CASTILLO, Edmund L.   1924-

PERSONAL: Surname pronounced Cas-*ti*-yo; born November 13, 1924, in Toledo, Ohio; son of Carlos (a professor of Spanish literature) and Marian (Griffith) Castillo; married Jane Taylor, November 22, 1947; children: Edmund Christopher, James Carlos, Margaret Ann. *Education:* Northwestern University, B.S., 1945; Boston University, M.S., 1954; George Washington University, D.P.A., 1977. *Religion:* Catholic. *Home:* 204 East St. N.E., Washington, D.C. 20002. *Office:* Fairfax County Government, 4100 Chain Bridge Rd., Fairfax, Va. 22030.

CAREER: Commissioned in Naval Reserve, February, 1945; served in Pacific Fleet and transferred to regular Navy as public affairs specialist after World War II, various assignments including public affairs officer for U.S. Seventh Fleet, 1955, and U.S. Sixth Fleet, 1963-65; press officer for Department of Navy, 1959-62, and Department of Defense, 1967-68; retired in the grade of captain, U.S. Navy, 1968. Director of public affairs, County of Fairfax, Va., 1968—. Associate professorial lecturer in public administration, George Washington University, 1977—. *Member:* American Society for Public Administration, Public Relations Society of America, National Press Club, U.S. Naval Institute. *Awards, honors:* Legion of Merit for service in Office of Secretary of Defense, 1968.

WRITINGS—All published by Random House, except as indicated: *All about the United States Navy,* 1961; *The Seabees of World War II,* 1963; *Midway—Battle for the Pacific,* 1968; *Flat-Tops—The Story of Aircraft Carriers,* 1969; (contributor) Howard Stephenson, editor, *Handbook of Public Relations,* 2nd edition, McGraw-Hill, 1971. Author of various articles in U.S. Naval Institute *Proceedings,* 1959-63.

*   *   *

CATANESE, Anthony James (Jr.)   1942-

PERSONAL: Born October 18, 1942, in New Brunswick, N.J.; son of Anthony James, Sr. (an engineer) and Josephine (Barone) Catanese; married Sara Phillips, October 23, 1968; children: Mark Anthony, Mark Alexander, Michael Scott. *Education:* Rutgers University, B.A., 1963; Rider College, certificate in real estate, 1963; University of Washington, certificate in Computer Applications to Urban Analysis, 1964; New York University, M.U.P. (with honors), 1965; University of Wisconsin, Ph.D., 1968; also attended LaSalle Law School. *Politics:* Democrat. *Religion:* Methodist. *Office:* School of Architecture and Urban Planning, University of Wisconsin, Milwaukee, Wis. 53201.

CAREER: Rutgers University, New Brunswick, N.J., assistant to director, Rutgers Planning Service and Campus Planning Office, 1961-62; Middlesex County Planning Board, New Brunswick, planning assistant, 1962-63; senior planner, 1964-66; New Jersey Department of Conservation and Economic Development, Division of State and Regional Planning, Trenton, N.J., senior planner, 1963-64; Georgia Institute of Technology, School of Architecture, Atlanta, Ga., assistant professor, 1967-68, associate professor of city planning, director of Urban Systems Simulation Laboratory, 1968-73; University of Miami, Coral Gables, Fla., James A. Ryder Professor, 1973-77; University of Wisconsin—Milwaukee, dean of School of Architecture and Urban Planning, 1975—. State planning consultant, Wisconsin Department of Resource Development, Madison, Wis., 1966-67; president, A. J. Catanese & Associates, Atlanta, 1967—; vice-president for management, MRC Realty Joint Venture, 1968—; executive vice-president, PP&C Properties, 1970—. Lecturer on state planning at New York University, New York, N.Y., 1964; visiting lecturer at Clark College, Atlanta, 1968; visiting professor of urban and regional studies, Virginia Polytechnic Institute, Blacksburg, Va., 1969. Democratic Party, member of U.S. 4th Congressional District Caucus, 1970—, chairman of state 77th House District (member, DeKalb County Executive Committee), 1971—.

MEMBER: International Platform Association, American Academy of Political and Social Sciences, American Association of University Professors, American Institute of Planners (executive vice president of Georgia chapter, 1970-71), American Institute of Urban and Regional Affairs, American Society of Planning Officials, Association for Computing Machinery, Association of Collegiate Schools of Planning (secretary of executive board, 1970-71), National Association of Housing and Redevelopment Officials, National Urban Coalition, Urban America, Inc., Urban and Regional Information Systems Association (Southeast section, member of board of governors, 1970-71, president, 1971-72), Regional Science Association, National Geographic Society, Association of Wisconsin Planners, Georgia Planning Association, Regional Plan Association (New York-New Jersey-Connecticut region; group chairman, 1963), City Planners Section, Georgia Municipal Association, Wisconsin Alumni Union (Georgia chapter; member of board of governors, 1968-70), New York University Planners Organization (chairman, 1965), Organization of Rutgers Planning (president, 1962), University of Wisconsin Planning Club, Korean Karate Association (Purple Belt).

AWARDS, HONORS: National Defense Education Act research travel grant, 1967; Ford Foundation summer research grant, 1967; Automotive Safety Foundation research grant, 1967-68; Urban Mass Transportation Administration, U.S. Department of Transportation, research award, 1969-70; Georgia Tech Foundation, Inc., faculty European travel and research award, 1969; Fulbright-Hays Senior Lecturer at Universidad Nacional de Colombia, Bogota, Colombia, 1970.

WRITINGS: The Alternatives of the Horizon Planning Concept, New Jersey Division of State and Regional Planning, 1964; *A Statewide Planning Analysis of Utility Services in New Jersey,* New Jersey Division of State and Regional Planning, 1964; *The Residential Development of New Jersey: A Regional Approach,* New Jersey Division of State and Regional Planning, 1964; (editor) *The Myths and Realities of the Image of Greenwich Village: A Workshop Model of a Planning Process,* Graduate School of Public Administration, New York University, 1966; *Data Processing for*

State Planning, Wisconsin Department of Resource Development, 1967; *The Economy of Northwestern Wisconsin,* Wisconsin Department of Resource Development, 1967; *Comprehensive Plan for Cordele, Georgia,* Keck & Wood, 1969; *Alpharetta Plans for the Future,* Keck & Wood, 1969; *Systemic Planning: An Annotated Bibliography and Literature Guide,* Council of Planning Librarians (Monticello), 1969; *Scientific Methods of Urban Analysis,* University of Illinois Press, 1970; *Structural and Socioeconomic Factors of Commuting,* Clearinghouse for Federal Scientific and Technical Reports, 1971; *Planners and Local Politics: Impossible Dreams,* Sage Publications, 1973; *New Perspectives in Urban Transportation,* Heath, 1973; *Urban Transportation in South Florida,* University of Miami, 1974.

With others: *A Plan for Manasquan,* Rutgers University, 1963; (with Alan Walter Steiss) *Commercial Land Use in New Jersey,* New Jersey Division of State and Regional Planning, 1964; *The Stottsburg Plan: A Model of Growth and Factors Affecting Development,* Graduate School of Public Administration, New York University, 1965; *Wisconsin Development Plan,* Wisconsin Department of Resource Development, 1967; (editor with John L. Gann and Leo Jakobson) *Explorations into Urban Functions, Spatial Organization, and Environmental Form,* University of Wisconsin Board of Regents, 1967; (with Richard G. Poirier) *Planning for Recreation: A Methodology for Functional Planning,* Department of Planning and Economic Development (Honolulu), 1968; *A Survey of Student Planning Organizations,* American Institute of Planners, 1968; (with Roger J. Budke) *Urban Transportation: Problems and Potentials,* Atlanta Chamber of Commerce, Leadership Development Foundation, 1969; *An Information System for Fulton County, Georgia,* Fulton County Manager's Office, 1969; (with James B. Grant and Edward N. Kashuba) *Application of Computer Graphics to Urban and Regional Planning,* School of Architecture, Georgia Institute of Technology, 1969; (with Steiss) *Systemic Planning: Essays on Theory and Application,* Heath, 1970.

Contributor: Michael Sumichrast, editor, *What's Ahead in 1966?,* National Association of Homebuilders, 1965; *Proceedings of Midwest Seminar on Urban and Regional Research,* University of Wisconsin Board of Regents, 1967; *The Recreation Element of the General Plan Revision Program: State of Hawaii,* Donald Wolbrink & Assoc. (Honolulu), 1967; *Handerworterbuch der Raumforshung and Raumordnung,* Verlag, 1970. Also author of *Managing Hawaii's Coast,* 1976. Contributor of articles to *Jersey Plans, New Jersey Economic Review, Journal of Housing, Les Annales de l'economie collective, Annalen der Geminwirtschaft, Annals of Public and Co-operative Economy, Journal of the Town Planning Institute* (Great Britain), *Rotor & Wing: Magazine of Professional Helicopter Operations, Plan: Journal of the Town Planning Institute of Canada, Public Administration Review, Architectural Forum, Ekistics* (Greece), *Planning Outlook* (England), *Urban Georgia, Municipal South, Traffic Quarterly, Bulletin of the Association of Collegiate Schools of Planning,* and other periodicals and planning journals. Contributor to "New Ideas on Rapid Transit in Atlanta," a television series broadcast by WSB-TV in June, 1969. Editor for Southeast Chapter of American Institute of Planners, 1967—.

WORK IN PROGRESS: Editing book, *Comparative Urban Planning.*

SIDELIGHTS: Anthony Catanese told *CA:* "For too long we have been writing about cities and planning in only technical terms or in supercillious popular treatments. I intend to direct my writing on cities towards the intelligent citizen by combining technical matters with straightforward analysis in order to plan for solving problems." Catanese was an active adviser to President Jimmy Carter during his campaign.

AVOCATIONAL INTERESTS: Painting in oils and acrylics, karate.

* * *

CATES, Ray A., Jr. 1940-

PERSONAL: Born November 20, 1940, in Greeneville, Tenn.; son of Ray A. (a store owner) and Ellen (Earthman) Cates; married Barbara Fore (a legal secretary), June 10, 1961; children: Ray A. III. *Education:* Central Florida Junior College, A.A., 1961; University of Florida, B.A., 1964, M.A., 1977; Blackstone School of Law, LL.B., 1965; Stetson University, graduate study, 1965-69. *Politics:* Democrat. *Religion:* Baptist. *Home:* 723 Southeast 11th St., Ocala, Fla. 32670.

CAREER: High school teacher in Ocala, Fla., 1964-71; president, Cates Enterprises, Inc., 1971—. Counselor for delinquent teenagers, summer, 1969; bookstore owner, 1974—; financial counselor, 1975—; vice-president, Jury of the People. Inc., 1976—. *Military service:* U.S. Naval Reserve, 1959-64. *Member:* National Education Association, International Platform Association, American Civil Liberties Union, Florida Education Association (delegate, 1965-70), Central Florida Federation of Teachers (president, 1970-71), Marion County Education Association, Marion County Social Studies Council (president, 1966-68).

WRITINGS: Pure American Corn Humor, Adams Press, 1970; *The Confessions of a Real Estate Scavenger,* Adams Press, 1977. Contributor to *All Time Favorite Poetry,* Mark Press, to *Quote Magazine,* and to school journals.

WORK IN PROGRESS: Faulkner's Fictional Children; A Practical Guide to Florida's Flea Markets; a novel, *Sahara;* a book of children's poems.

* * *

CATTAN, Henry 1906-

PERSONAL: Born February 26, 1906, in Jerusalem, Palestine (now Israel); son of Michael and Hellen (Sayegh) Cattan; married Eva Guillemet. *Education:* University of London, diploma in journalism, 1929, M.L., 1932; University of Paris, Licence en Droit, 1929, Barrister-at-law. *Address:* P.O. Box 5150, Beirut, Lebanon.

CAREER: Lawyer, 1932—; member of Palestine and Syrian Bars.

WRITINGS: Law of Oil Concessions in the Middle East and North Africa, Oceana, for Parker School of Foreign and Comparative Law, 1967; *The Evolution of Oil Concessions in the Middle East and North Africa,* Oceana, for Parker School of Foreign and Comparative Law, 1967; (with Edward Selim Atiyah) *Palestine, terre de promesse et de sang,* Editions Cujas, c. 1968; *Palestine, the Arabs and Israel: The Search for Justice,* Longmans, Green, 1969, second edition, International Publications Service, 1970; *Palestine: The Road to Peace,* International Publications Service, 1971; *La Partage de la Palestine du point de vue jurudique,* Groupe d'Etude sur le Moyen-Orient (Geneva), 1971; *Palestine and International Law: The Legal Aspects of the Arab-Israeli Conflict,* Longman, 1973, 2nd edition, 1976. Pamphlets include *Plunder in the Holy Land,* Greek Convent Press, 1952, *The Dimensions of the Palestine Problem,* Institute for Palestine Studies, 1967, and *To Whom Does Palestine Belong?,* Institute for Palestine Studies, 1967.†

CAVITCH, David 1933-

PERSONAL: Born June 13, 1933, in Traverse City, Mich.; son of Sol and Bessie (Rabinovitch) Cavitch; married Joan Byrne, September 14, 1960; children: Max, Elizabeth. *Education:* University of Michigan, A.B., 1955; University of New Mexico, M.A., 1960; University of California, Berkeley, Ph.D., 1966. *Home:* 47 Yale St., Winchester, Mass. 01890. *Office:* Department of English, Tufts University, Medford, Mass. 02155.

CAREER: Idaho State College (now University), Pocatello, instructor in English, 1959-60; Smith College, Northampton, Mass., instructor, 1964-66, assistant professor, 1966-70, associate professor of English, 1970-72; Tufts University, Medford, Mass., associate professor of English, 1972-76, chairman of English department, 1976—. Visiting professor, University of California, Riverside, 1966-67. Researcher at Hampstead Clinic, London, England, on the application of psychoanalysis to literary criticism, 1970. *Military service:* U.S. Army, 1955-57. *Member:* Modern Language Association of America, Group for Applied Psychoanalysis. *Awards, honors:* American Philosophical Society summer grant, 1967, research grant, 1970.

WRITINGS: D. H. Lawrence and the New World, Oxford University Press, 1969. Contributor to literature journals.

WORK IN PROGRESS: A critical study of the work of Walt Whitman.

* * *

CAYTON, Horace R(oscoe) 1903-1970

April 12, 1903—January 22, 1970; American sociologist and author. Obituaries: *New York Times,* January 25, 1970; *Current Biography,* 1970. (See index for *CA* sketch)

* * *

CEBULASH, Mel 1937-
(Ben Farrell, Glen Harlan, Jared Jansen)

PERSONAL: Surname is pronounced *Seb*-yu-lash; born August 24, 1937, in Jersey City, N.J.; son of Jack (a mailman) and Jeanette (Duthie) Cebulash; married Deanna Penn, August 19, 1962 (divorced); children: Glen, Benjamin, Jeanette. *Education:* Jersey City State College, B.A., 1962, M.A., 1964; University of South Carolina, graduate study, 1964-65. *Religion:* Jewish. *Address:* c/o Bowmar Publishing Co., 4563 Colorado Blvd., Los Angeles, Calif. 90039.

CAREER: Junior high school teacher of reading in Teaneck, N.J., 1962-64; Fairleigh Dickinson University, Rutherford, N.J., instructor in reading clinic, 1965-67; Scholastic Magazines, Inc., New York, N.Y., editor for language arts, beginning 1966; currently affiliated with Bowmar Publishing Co., Los Angeles, Calif. *Military service:* U.S. Army, 1955-58. U.S. Army Reserve, 1958-61. *Member:* International Reading Association. *Awards, honors:* Author Award of New Jersey Association of Teachers of English, 1969, for *Through Basic Training with Walter Young.*

WRITINGS—All published by Scholastic Book Services, unless otherwise indicated: *Monkeys, Go Home* (adaptation of Walt Disney film script), 1967; *Through Basic Training with Walter Young,* 1968; *The Love Bug* (adaptation of Walt Disney film script), 1969; *Man in a Green Beret and Other Medal of Honor Winners,* 1969; *The Boatniks* (adaptation of Walt Disney film script), 1970; *The Ball That Wouldn't Bounce,* 1972; *Benny's Nose,* 1972; *The See-Saw,* 1972; *Willie's Pet,* 1972; (under pseudonym Glen Harlan) *Petey the Pup,* 1972; (under pseudonym Ben Farrell) *Nancy and Jeff,* 1972; (under pseudonym Jared Jansen) *Penny the Poodle,* 1972; *Baseball Players Do Amazing Things,* Random House, 1973; *Dic-tion-ar-y Skilz,* 1974; *Herby Rides Again* (adaptation of Walt Disney film script), 1974; *The Strongest Man in the World* (adaptation of Walt Disney film script), 1975; *Football Players Do Amazing Things,* Random House, 1975; *Basketball Players Do Amazing Things,* Random House, in press. Editor and author of much of the material in Scholastic Book Services "ACTION Reading Kit," 1970. Contributor of short stories to university literary journals. Contributing editor, *Scholastic Scope* (magazine).

WORK IN PROGRESS: Coming Close, a novel.

AVOCATIONAL INTERESTS: The literature and popular music of the 1930's, the works of James T. Farrell ("a friend and inspiration").

* * *

CERF, Bennett (Alfred) 1898-1971

May 25, 1898—August 27, 1971; American publisher, editor, and television personality. Obituaries: *New York Times,* August 29, 1971; *Time,* September 6, 1971; *Publishers' Weekly,* September 6, 1971; *Saturday Review,* September 11, 1971. (See index for *CA* sketch)

* * *

CHAFE, Wallace L. 1927-

PERSONAL: Surname rhymes with "wafe"; born September 3, 1927, in Cambridge, Mass.; son of Albert J. (a minister) and Nathalie (Amback) Chafe; married Mary Elizabeth Butterworth (a teacher), June 23, 1951; children: Christopher, Douglas, Stephen. *Education:* Yale University, B.A., 1950, M.A., 1956, Ph.D., 1958. *Home:* 636 Beloit Ave., Kensington, Calif. 94708. *Office:* Department of Linguistics, University of California, Berkeley, Calif. 94720.

CAREER: University of Buffalo (now State University of New York at Buffalo), Buffalo, N.Y., assistant professor of modern languages, 1958-59; Smithsonian Institution, Bureau of American Ethnology, Washington, D.C., linguist, 1959-62; University of California, Berkeley, professor of linguistics, 1962—. *Military service:* U.S. Navy, 1945-46. *Member:* Linguistic Society of America, American Anthropological Association, American Psychological Association. *Awards, honors:* National Science Foundation grant for Caddo language project, 1961-62, 1964-65; National Institute of Mental Health grant, 1975-77, for project on language and experience.

WRITINGS: Seneca Thanksgiving Rituals, Smithsonian Institution, 1961; *Handbook of the Seneca Language,* New York State Museum and Science Service, 1963; *Seneca Morphology and Dictionary,* Smithsonian Institution Press, 1967; *Meaning and the Structure of Language,* University of Chicago Press, 1970.

WORK IN PROGRESS: Research on semantic structure, with special reference to the semantics of discourse, and its relation to cognitive processes.

* * *

CHAMBERS, Dewey W. 1929-

PERSONAL: Born March 23, 1929, in King City, Calif.; son of Ned and Mabel (Woods) Chambers; married Judith A. McMillin (vice-president of student life, University of the Pacific), June 12, 1970. *Education:* San Jose State College (now University), A.B., 1952, M.A., 1960; Wayne State

University, Ed.D., 1965. *Religion:* Christian. *Home:* 3636 Merrimac Circle N., Stockton, Calif. 95207. *Office:* University of the Pacific, Stockton, Calif. 95204.

CAREER: San Francisco State College (now University), San Francisco, Calif., demonstration-laboratory teacher, 1959-62; Wayne State University, Detroit, Mich., instructor in education, 1962-65; University of the Pacific, Stockton, Calif., assistant professor, 1965-68, associate professor of education, 1968—. Professor of education, University of California, Davis, Extension, 1966-67, 1971-72. Visiting professor at Wisconsin State University—Platteville, 1966, and State University of New York College at Fredonia, 1970; guest professor, State University of Wisconsin, 1966. Producer, "The Frederick Burk Story" (television special) for KGO-TV, 1963. Lecturer, "University Classroom on the Air," for K.U.O.P. Radio, 1968-69. Member of board of trustees, Pacific Collegiate School, 1974-75. Consultant to television series, "The Wonderful World of Children's Literature," ABC-TV, 1967. Consultant to Xerox Microreading Libraries of Xerox Corp., 1971, Far West Regional Laboratory of Education Research, 1974, and Coronet Film Corp., 1974-75, 1976-77.

WRITINGS: Literature for Children: Storytelling and Creative Drama, W. C. Brown, 1970; *Children's Literature in the Curriculum,* Rand McNally, 1971; (contributor) *Elementary School Language Arts: Selected Readings,* edited by Paul C. Burns and Leo Schell, Rand McNally, 1969; (editor) *Adventuring with Books,* Citation Press, 1973; (editor) *Folk and Other Tales from the Mother Lode,* University of the Pacific Press, 1974; (with Heath Lowry) *The Language Arts: A Pragmatic Approach,* W. C. Brown, 1975; *The Oral Tradition: Storytelling and Creative Drama,* W. C. Brown, 1977. Also author with S. Jennings of monograph, *The Achievement Patterns of Eight Linguistic Sets of Children in a Pluralistic Community,* 1975. Contributor of many articles to education journals. Former book reviewer for *Elementary English,* 1964-65, and *Pacific Historian,* 1966.

* * *

CHAMBERS, W(illiam) Walker 1913-

PERSONAL: Born December 7, 1913, in Wishaw, Scotland; son of William (a merchant) and Agnes (Wilson) Chambers; married Mary Margaret Best, July 16, 1947; children: James Andrew, Janet Elizabeth. *Education:* University of Glasgow, M.A. (first class honors), 1937; University of Munich, Ph.D., 1939; University of Paris, L.esL., 1940. *Home:* 45 Newlands Rd., Glasgow S.3, Scotland. *Office:* University of Glasgow, Glasgow W.2, Scotland.

CAREER: University of Leeds, Leeds, England, assistant lecturer, 1946-47, lecturer in German, 1947-50; University College of North Staffordshire (now University of Keele), Keele, England, professor of modern languages, 1950-54; University of Glasgow, Glasgow, Scotland, William Jacks Professor of German, 1954—, dean of Faculty of Arts, 1960-64, vice-principal, 1972-76. Member of Commonwealth Scholarship Commission in Britian, 1962-66; vice-chairman of board of governors, Jordanhill College of Education, 1962-67. *Military service:* British Army, 1939-45; served on Intelligence Staff, Headquarters, 8th Army, in North Africa, Sicily, Italy, and Austria; became major; was mentioned in dispatches. *Member:* Association of University Teachers (president, 1962-63). *Awards, honors:* Membership of Order of the British Empire; Educational Institute of Scotland fellow, 1964; Bundes Verienstkreuz Erster Klasse (Germany), 1967; Ehrensenator of University of Freiburg, 1976.

WRITINGS: (Editor) *Paul Ernst: Selected Short Stories,* Basil Blackwell, 1953; (editor) Friedrich de la Motte Fouque, *Undine,* Thomas Nelson, 1956, Holt, 1959; (editor) Paul Ernst, *Erdachte Gesprache,* Thomas Nelson, 1958; (with John R. Wilkie) *A Short History of the German Language,* Methuen, 1970. General editor, Thomas Nelson's German texts.

WORK IN PROGRESS: Study of Lessing's dramas.

* * *

CHAMPION, R(ichard) A(nnells) 1925-

PERSONAL: Born January 6, 1925, in Largs Bay, South Australia; son of George Arthur (a bank manager) and Ethel (Annells) Champion; married Margaret Sturt, May 20, 1950; children: Rebecca, Stephen, Katherine, Sarah. *Education:* University of Sydney, B.A., 1947; University of Iowa, M.A., 1954. *Home:* 14 Waterview St., Mona Vale, New South Wales, Australia. *Office:* Department of Psychology, University of Sydney, Sydney, New South Wales, Australia.

CAREER: University of Sydney, Sydney, New South Wales, Australia, senior lecturer, 1955-63, associate professor, 1963-65, McCaughey Professor of Psychology, 1965—. *Member:* Australian Psychological Society (fellow), American Psychological Association (foreign affiliate), Academy of the Social Sciences in Australia (fellow).

WRITINGS: Learning and Activation, Wiley (Australia), 1969. Series editor, "Basic Topics in Psychology," Wiley (Australia). Contributor to psychology journals in Australia and United States. Member of editorial board, *Physiology and Behavior* (periodical), published by Pergamon.

WORK IN PROGRESS: Research in learning and motivation.

* * *

CHANDOR, (Peter John) Anthony 1932-

PERSONAL: Born November 9, 1932, in Moshi, Tanzania (then Tanganyika); son of Peter France (an author) and Eileen (Hives) Chandor; married Maryanne Bankes (an editor), September 6, 1958; children: Sarah Jane Murray, Nicholas Anthony Bankes. *Education:* Attended Epsom College, Surrey, England, 1946-51; New College, Oxford, B.A. (honors), 1956, M.A., 1967. *Politics:* Conservative. *Religion:* Church of England. *Home:* Blackdown Border, Haslemere, Surrey, England.

CAREER: Benn Brothers Ltd. (publishers), London, England, editor, 1956-58; International Computers Ltd., London, executive, 1958-75; National Computing Centre, London, director, 1975—. United Nations specialist in electronic data processing in Czechoslovakia, 1969-71, and in Malaysia, 1972. *Military service:* British Army, Royal Artillery, 1951-53; became lieutenant. *Member:* British Computer Society (member of council; fellow), English-Speaking Union.

WRITINGS: A Short Introduction to Computers, Arthur Barker, 1968; (editor) *A Dictionary of Computers,* Penguin, 1970, revised edition, 1977; (with John Graham and Robin Williamson) *Practical Systems Analysis,* Hart-Davis, 1970, Putnam, 1971; *Computers as a Career,* Hart-Davis, 1970; *Choosing and Keeping Computer Staff,* Allen & Unwin, 1976.

WORK IN PROGRESS: Data Processing.

SIDELIGHTS: "I believe that, as well as being a good deal

easier to manufacture, people are a great deal more important than computers," Anthony Chandor writes. "This is not always recognized in the computer field, especially by computers, and my books attempt to emphasize it. The only computer to have read a book by me, however, seemed to remain unmoved." Chandor goes on to write: "It is also true that while my books have been translated into Japanese, Italian, Hungarian, Slovak, Swedish, Spanish, and Portuguese, none has yet appeared in COBOL, FORTRAN, or any other computer language."

*   *   *

CHANOVER, E(dmond) Pierre   1932-

PERSONAL: Born December 10, 1932, in Paris, France; came to United States in 1950, naturalized in 1953; son of Jacques and Helene Chanover; married Susan Ansara (a college professor); children: Nancy Janet, Michael Jacques. *Education:* Brooklyn College (now Brooklyn College of the City University of New York), B.A., 1957; University of Kansas, M.A., 1959; New York University, Ph.D., 1974. *Home:* 6 Seton St., Huntington Station, N.Y. 11746.

CAREER: University of Kansas, Lawrence, instructor in French, 1957-59; Garden City High School, Garden City, Long Island, N.Y., teacher of French, 1959—. Professor of French, Institut Francais, evenings, 1960-63; professor of civilization, N.D.E.A. French Institute, summer, 1961, professor of composition and lecturer, summer, 1963; demonstration teacher, Regents Educational Television Project, WPIX, May, 1962; reader of French, Educational Testing Service, 1962-64; director of intermediate level and instructor of French, Peace Corps Training Program, Princeton University, summers, 1964, 1966; visiting instructor, Hofstra University, 1965, 1967, 1968; Dijon University, France, dean of students, 1970-71; guest speaker at professional conferences. *Military service:* U.S. Army, 1953-55.

MEMBER: American Academy of Poets, Modern Language Association of America, American Association of Teachers of French (president of Long Island chapter, 1964-67), Association Folklorique et Culturelle des Antilles Francaises, Association des Professeurs Francais en Amerique (member of executive council, 1964-67), New York State Federation of Foreign Language Teachers (associate director), New York State Teachers Association, Association of Foreign Language Chairmen and Supervisors of Long Island, Garden City Teachers Association, Pi Delta Phi. *Awards, honors:* First Prize, Walt Whitman Poetry Contest, 1970, for "An Offering"; Chevalier de L'ordre Des Palmes Academiques.

WRITINGS: (Contributor) *Chez les Francais,* Holt, 1969; (contributor) *Ce monde des Francais,* Holt, 1970; (contributor) *The World of Verse,* Regency Press, 1971; *Clapotis d'outre-mer* (poems), Editions de la Grisiere (Paris), 1971. Poems have been represented in many anthologies including *Anthologie de Poetes et Prosateurs Francophones de l'-Amerique Septentrional,* 1970, *The World of Verse,* 1971, *Poetes Face a la Vie Anthologie,* 1976, and others. Contributor to *Amenophis, Sequence, Perimetre, Poetry Venture, Psychoanalytic Review, Shantih, Voices International, New York Public Library Bulletin, American Imago, Baby John, Verticales 12, Cahiers de Poetisme,* and in numerous other journals, magazines, and periodicals. Editor and publisher, *Poesie-U.S.A.*

WORK IN PROGRESS: Georges Simenon: An International Bibliography; another volume of poetry.

CHAPMAN, Colin   1937-

PERSONAL: Born March 17, 1937, in Croydon, England; son of Norman Charles and Marjorie (Wakefield) Chapman. *Education:* Attended school in London, England, 1946-53. *Politics:* Unattached. *Religion:* None. *Agent:* John Farquharson Ltd., 15 Red Lion Sq., London WC1R 4QW, England. *Office:* British Broadcasting Corp., Bush House, Strand, London WC2, England.

CAREER: Times, London, England, staff writer, 1962-65; *Sunday Times,* London, England, education correspondent, 1965-67, foreign news editor, 1967-69; *Times,* Australian financial correspondent, 1969—; British Broadcasting Corp., Australia correspondent, 1969—; *Bulletin* (national news magazine), Sydney, Australia, assistant editor, 1969—. Frequent broadcaster for Australian Broadcasting Commission and British Broadcasting Corp. *Member:* Royal Institute of International Affairs. *Awards, honors:* Young British Journalist Award from National Council for Training of Journalists, 1963; Winston Churchill fellow, 1966.

WRITINGS: August 21: The Rape of Czechoslovakia, Lippincott, 1968.

SIDELIGHTS: Colin Chapman has traveled in the United States, Middle East, West Africa, India, and Southeast Asia.†

*   *   *

CHAPMAN, G(eorge) W(arren) Vernon   1925-
(Vernon Warren)

PERSONAL: Born June 30, 1925, in London, England; married, 1953; wife's name, Margaret; children: Carol, Robert. *Education:* Educated in London, England. *Residence:* Edmonton, Alberta, Canada.

CAREER: Osler, Hammond & Nanton Insurance Ltd., Edmonton, Alberta, assistant manager, beginning 1959. *Military service:* Royal Air Force Volunteer Reserve. *Member:* Rotary Club of West Edmonton (secretary).

WRITINGS—Under pseudonym Vernon Warren; all published by Gifford: *Brandon Takes Over,* 1953; *The Blue Mauritius,* 1954; *Brandon Returns,* 1954; *Bullets for Brandon,* 1955; *No Bouquets for Brandon,* 1955; *Appointment in Hell,* 1956; *By Fair Means or Foul,* 1956; *Stop-Over Danger,* 1959; *Back-Lash,* 1960; *Farewell by Death,* 1961; *Invitation to Kill,* 1963; *Mister Violence,* 1964.

WORK IN PROGRESS: Another thriller; a long-term work on the Spanish invasion of Peru.

AVOCATIONAL INTERESTS: World War I aviation and vintage aircraft.††

*   *   *

CHARMATZ, Bill   1925-

PERSONAL: Surname is pronounced Charm-ats; born November 15, 1925, in New York, N.Y.; son of Morris and Beckie Charmatz; married November 14, 1959; wife's name, Marianne; children: Katrina. *Education:* Attended Ecole des Beaux Arts, Fontainbleau, France, and Ecole de la Grande Chaumiere, Paris, France. *Home:* 25 West 68th St., New York, N.Y. 10023.

MILITARY SERVICE: U.S. Navy, 1944-46. *Member:* American Institute of Graphic Arts, Society of Illustrators, Graphic Arts Guild (member of board of directors; vice-president), Illustrators Guild (founding member).

WRITINGS—Self-illustrated: *The Little Duster* (juvenile),

Macmillan, 1967; *The Cat's Whiskers* (juvenile), Macmillan, 1969; *Endeerments*, Ballantine, 1971; *Troy St. Bus*, Macmillan, 1977.

SIDELIGHTS: Bill Charmatz told *CA:* "I regard myself as an image maker using words and pictures to convey my feelings and meanings. My ideal is for these words and pictures to move as one, and walk and talk to my reader, creating its own reality. Towards that end I'll try forever."

* * *

CHAROSH, Mannis 1906-

PERSONAL: Surname rhymes with "parish"; born November 9, 1906, in Brooklyn, N.Y.; son of Israel and Celia (Charmoy) Charosh; married Beatrice Meyers, August 30, 1930; children: Paul. *Education:* City College (now City College of the City University of New York), New York, N.Y., B.S., 1928; New York University, M.Sc., 1934. *Home:* 5207 20th Ave., Brooklyn, N.Y. 11204.

CAREER: New York (N.Y.) schools, teacher of mathematics, 1928-68, also coordinator of guidance, 1959-68. *Member:* Mathematical Association of America, National Council of Teachers of Mathematics, Association of Teachers of Mathematics of New York State, Association of Teachers of Mathematics of New York City. *Awards, honors: Number Games for One or Two* cited as "Outstanding Science Trade Book for Children," National Science Teacher's Association—Children's Book Council, 1972.

WRITINGS: (With others) *Selected Topics in Higher Mathematics for Teachers,* Association of Teachers of Mathematics of New York City, 1942; (editor and annotator) *Mathematical Challenges,* National Council of Teachers of Mathematics, 1965; *Straight Lines, Parallel Lines, Perpendicular Lines* (juvenile), Crowell, 1970; *The Ellipse,* Crowell, 1971; *Number Games for One or Two* (juvenile), Crowell, 1972; *Number Ideas through Pictures* (juvenile), Crowell, 1974. Associate editor, *A.T.M.* (publication of Association of Teachers of Mathematics of New York City), 1945-52, and *Mathematics Student Journal* (publication of National Council of Teachers of Mathematics), 1960-66.

WORK IN PROGRESS: Activity cards based on juvenile mathematic books.

AVOCATIONAL INTERESTS: Mathematical recreations, chess, checkers, music, philately.

* * *

CHASAN, Daniel Jack 1943-

PERSONAL: Born August 28, 1943, in New York, N.Y. *Education:* Harvard University, B.A., 1965. *Office: New Yorker,* 25 West 43rd St., New York, N.Y. 10036.

CAREER: New Yorker, New York, N.Y., writer, 1967—.

WRITINGS: Klondike '70: The Alaskan Oil Boom, Praeger, 1971; *A Primer of Dominion,* Madrona, 1977. Contributor to *Audubon, Pacific Search,* and *Smithsonian.*

BIOGRAPHICAL/CRITICAL SOURCES: Newsweek, January 18, 1971; *Christian Science Monitor,* March 13, 1971; *New York Times Book Review,* March 14, 1971.

* * *

CHAVCHAVADZE, Paul 1899-1971

June 27, 1899—July 9, 1971; Russian-born American author and translator. Obituaries: *New York Times,* July 10, 1971. (See index for *CA* sketch)

CHENEY, Lois A. 1931-

PERSONAL: Born May 2, 1931, in Cleveland, Ohio; daughter of Clark Wallace and Lillian (Burton) Cheney. *Education:* Muskingum College, B.A., 1954; Kent State University, M.A., 1957; Michigan State University, Ph.D., 1961. *Politics:* Republican. *Religion:* Presbyterian. *Home:* 602 Haskins Rd., Bowling Green, Ohio 43402. *Office:* Department of Speech, Bowling Green State University, Bowling Green, Ohio 43402.

CAREER: High school teacher of English and speech, Kent, Ohio, 1954-56; Tarkio College, Tarkio, Mo., professor of speech and drama and chairman of department of speech, 1956-64; Bowling Green State University, Bowling Green, Ohio, professor of speech, 1964—. *Member:* Speech Association of America, Central States Speech Association, Ohio Speech Association, Pi Kappa Delta.

WRITINGS: (Contributor) Otto Bauer, editor, *Introduction to Speech Communication,* W. C. Brown, 1968; *God Is No Fool,* Abingdon, 1969.

WORK IN PROGRESS: An oral interpretation textbook for Scott, Foresman.

* * *

CHESHAM, Sallie

PERSONAL: Born in Detroit, Mich.; daughter of Robert Henry and Margaret (Ebsary) Keeler; married Howard Chesham (director of Eastern Territory finance department and national treasurer of the Salvation Army); children: David Howard, Julie Margaret (Mrs. Alan Kennedy). *Education:* Studied journalism at Northwestern University. *Home:* 145 Claremont Ave., Mount Vernon, N.Y. 10550.

CAREER: Ordained minister of the Salvation Army (third generation Salvationist), with current rank of colonel; certified social worker; Salvation Army, Central Territory Headquarters, Chicago, Ill., former member of editorial department, head of historical research section, and director of "Old Hat" Inner City coffee house program, Eastern Territory Headquarters, New York, N.Y., head of special services section (creative writing and public speaking), 1971—. *Member:* Society of Midland Authors, Women's Press Club (London, England; honorary member). *Awards, honors:* Chicago Poetry Award, 1970, for *Walking with the Wind;* Chicago Publishers Award, 1973, for *Trouble Doesn't Happen Next Tuesday.*

WRITINGS: Born to Battle, Rand McNally, 1965; *Walking with the Wind,* Word Books, 1969; (editor) *Today Is Yours,* Word Books, 1972; *Trouble Doesn't Happen Next Tuesday,* Word Books, 1972. Salvation Army booklets and published reports include *The Contender,* 1958, *It Isn't So,* 1960, *Creators All,* 1960, *Plus and Minus,* 1963, *Combat Songs,* 1965, and *One Hand Upon Another,* 1976. Writer and producer of "Marching On," the Salvation Army 75th anniversary pageant, and the centennial pageant; also writer of more than 400 feature stories, short stories, serials, and poems.

WORK IN PROGRESS: A play, "Evangeline"; two musicals, "Jehovah," and "Combat," the story of the first five years of struggle by the Salvation Army.

* * *

CHESNEY, Kellow (Robert) 1914-

PERSONAL: Born March 3, 1914, in Whimple, Devonshire, England; son of Kellow (a soldier) and Vera (Moule) Chesney; married Anne M. H. Thackeray (a social worker),

March 19, 1951; children: Charlotte. *Education:* Attended Haileybury College and Wadham College, Oxford, 1928-33. *Home:* 10C Acol Rd., West Hampstead, London N.W.6, England.

CAREER: Journalist, publisher's reader, and editor; currently full-time writer. *Military service:* British Army, 1940-46; became lieutenant.

WRITINGS: (Translator) Jacques Decrest, *Body on the Bench,* Hammond, 1953; (editor and translator) Rene Roussin, *Royal Menus,* Hammond, 1960; *Crimean War Reader,* Muller, 1960; *The Anti-Society: An Account of the Victorian Underworld,* Gambit, 1970 (published in England as *The Victorian Underworld,* M. T. Smith, 1970). Contributor to *Observer* and other publications.

BIOGRAPHICAL/CRITICAL SOURCES: Punch, June 17, 1970; *Observer Review,* June 21, 1970; *Books and Bookmen,* August, 1970; *Best Sellers,* October 15, 1970.

*   *   *

CHETIN, Helen 1922-

PERSONAL: Born July 6, 1922; daughter of Guy Edward (a physician) and Helen (Collins) Campbell; married Adnan Chetin (a geologist); children: Timur, Sara. *Education:* Attended University of Texas, 1943-45. *Home:* 761 Oregon Ave., Palo Alto, Calif. 94303.

CAREER: Stanford University, Institute for Mathematical Studies in the Social Sciences, Stanford, Calif., writer, 1966-71; editor, New Seed Press (publisher of children's books), 1973—.

WRITINGS: Tales from an African Drum, Harcourt, 1971; *Perihan's Promise, Turkish Relatives and the Dirty Old Iman,* Houghton, 1973; *How Far Is Berkeley?,* Houghton, 1976. Editor, *The Wild Iris,* 1973—.

WORK IN PROGRESS: Stories, articles, and collective writings in both juvenile and adult areas; a three-part novel of 1930-50.

*   *   *

CHIBNALL, Marjorie (McCallum) 1915-
(Marjorie Morgan)

PERSONAL: Born September 27, 1915, in Shrewsbury, England; daughter of John Christopher (a farmer) and Maggie Morgan; married A. C. Chibnall (a former professor of biochemistry), June 4, 1947; children: Joan, Cicely, Mary, John. *Education:* Lady Margaret Hall, Oxford, B.Litt., 1937, M.A. and D.Phil., 1942; Sorbonne, University of Paris, graduate study, 1937-38. *Home:* 6 Millington Rd., Cambridge CB3 9HP, England. *Office:* Clare Hall, Cambridge University, Cambridge, England.

CAREER: University of Aberdeen, Aberdeen, Scotland, lecturer in history, 1943-47; Cambridge University, Cambridge, England, lecturer in history and fellow of Girton College, 1947-65, research fellow of Clare Hall, 1969-75, official fellow of Clare Hall, 1975—. *Member:* Royal Historical Society (fellow).

WRITINGS: (Under name Marjorie Morgan) *The English Lands of the Abbey of Bec,* Oxford University Press, 1946; (translator) John of Salisbury, *Historia Pontificalis,* Thomas Nelson, 1955; (translator) *The Ecclesiastical History of Orderic Vitalis,* Clarendon Press, Volume II, 1969, Volume III, 1972, Volume IV, 1973, Volume V, 1975. Contributor to *Encyclopaedia Britannica, New Catholic Encyclopedia,* and historical journals.

WORK IN PROGRESS: Translating Volumes I and VI of *The Ecclesiastical History of Orderic Vitalis;* editing estate surveys of Holy Trinity Abbey, Caen, for the British Academy; research in medieval historiography, ecclesiastical history of the Normans, and medieval economic history.

BIOGRAPHICAL/CRITICAL SOURCES: Virginia Quarterly Review, summer, 1969.

*   *   *

CHICKERING, Arthur W. 1927-

PERSONAL: Born April 27, 1927, in Framingham, Mass.; son of Rowell O. and Thelma (Wright) Chickering; married Joanne Nelson, November 22, 1951; children: Alan, Susan, Peri, Nancy. *Education:* Wesleyan University, Middletown, Conn., B.A., 1950; Harvard University, A.M.T., 1951; Columbia University, Ph.D., 1958. *Home:* 301 Deloach St., Memphis, Tenn. 38111. *Office:* Memphis State University, 202 Education Bldg., Memphis, Tenn. 38152.

CAREER: Junior high school teacher in Linden, N.J., 1952-53; school psychologist, Woodmore Hewlett (N.J.) public schools, 1955-58; Monmouth College, Long Branch, N.J., director of teacher education, 1958-59; Goddard College, Plainfield, Vt., professor of psychology and coordinator of evaluation, 1959-65; Project on Student Development, Plainfield, Vt., program director, 1965-70; American Council on Education, Office of Research, Washington, D.C., visiting scholar, 1970-71; State University of New York, Empire State College, Saratoga Springs, N.Y., professor of psychology and higher evaluation, vice-president for academic affairs, and director of strategies for change and knowledge utilization, 1971-77; Memphis State University, Memphis, Tenn., distinguished professor of higher education and director of Center for Higher Education, 1977—. *Military service:* U.S. Army, 1944-46. *Member:* American Educational Research Association, American Association for the Advancement of Science, American Psychological Association, Association for Institutional Research, Society for the Scientific Study of Religion, Vermont Psychological Association, Professional Ski Instructors of America. *Awards, honors:* Book Award of American Council on Education for *Education and Identity,* 1969.

*WRITINGS—*All published Jossey-Bass: *Education and Identity,* 1969; *Commuting Versus Resident Students: Overcoming the Educational Inequities of Living Off Campus,* 1974; *Experiential Learning–Rationale, Characteristics, Assessment,* 1976; *Individuality in Learning,* 1976.

WORK IN PROGRESS: Studies on student development in college and improvement of higher education.

*   *   *

CHIPMAN, Donald E(ugene) 1928-

PERSONAL: Born November 19, 1928, in Hill City, Kan.; son of Albert Cyril (a farmer) and Olive (Hemmy) Chipman; married Doris Thompson, December 27, 1955; children: Zachary Andrew, Jason Alaric. *Education:* Attended University of Kansas, 1948-51; Fort Hays Kansas State College, A.B., 1955, M.S., 1958; University of New Mexico, Ph.D., 1962. *Home:* 1120 Imperial Dr., Denton, Tex. 76201. *Office:* Department of History, North Texas State University, Denton, Tex. 76203.

CAREER: Secondary school teacher in Kansas, 1955-57; Fort Hays Kansas State College, Hays, Kan., assistant professor of history, 1962-64; North Texas State University,

Denton, Tex., associate professor, 1964-67, professor of history, 1967—. Visiting professor of history at University of Washington, Seattle, 1962, and University of San Francisco, San Francisco, Calif., 1970. Ranger naturalist for five summers in Yellowstone and Grand Canyon National Parks. *Military service:* U.S. Army, 1946-47. *Member:* Western History Association, Conference on Latin American History, Latin American Studies Association. *Awards, honors:* American Council of Learned Societies grant-in-aid, 1963; American Philosophical Society grant-in-aid, 1976. Contributor to *Handbook of Latin American Studies,* 1974, and 1976.

WRITINGS: Nuno de Guzman and the Province of Panuco in New Spain, 1518-1533, Arthur Clark, 1967; (with Randolph Campbell and Robert Calvert) *The Dallas Cowboys and the NFL,* University of Oklahoma Press, 1970.

Contributor: *Homenaje a Don Jose Maria de la Pena y Camara,* Ediciones Jose Porrua Turanzas, 1969; *Reflections of Western Historians* (Conference on the History of Western America), University of Arizona Press, 1969. Contributor of articles and reviews to *Americas, Hispanic American Historical Review, Journal of Southern History, New Mexico Historical Review,* and other periodicals.

WORK IN PROGRESS: The Descendants of the Aztec Emperor Moctezuma II.

* * *

CHISHOLM, Shirley (Anita St. Hill) 1924-

PERSONAL: Born November 30, 1924, in Brooklyn, N.Y.; daughter of Charles Christopher and Ruby (Seale) St. Hill; married Conrad Q. Chisholm (a social service investigator), October 8, 1949 (divorced February, 1977); married Arthur Hardwick (a businessman), November 26, 1977. *Education:* Brooklyn College (now Brooklyn College of the City University of New York), B.A. (cum laude), 1946; Columbia University, M.A., 1952. *Politics:* Democrat. *Religion:* Methodist. *Home:* 1355 President St., Brooklyn, N.Y. 11213. *Office:* U.S. House of Representatives, Washington, D.C. 20515.

CAREER: Nursery school teacher in metropolitan New York City area, 1946; Friends Day Nursery, Brownsville, N.Y., director, 1953-59; Bureau of Child Welfare, Division of Day Care, New York City, educational consultant, 1959-64; New York State Assembly, Albany, member, 1964-68; U.S. Congress, representative from 12th District, New York City, 1968—. Unsuccessful Democratic presidential primary candidate, 1972. Founding member, National Women's Political Caucus. Former member of board of directors, Brooklyn Home for Aged. *Member:* National Association of College Women, League of Women Voters, National Association for the Advancement of Colored People, Bedford-Stuyvesant Political League, Brooklyn College Alumnae, Delta Sigma Theta. *Awards, honors:* Award for Outstanding Work in Field of Child Welfare, from Women's Council of Brooklyn, 1957; Key Women of the Year Award, 1963; Women of Achievement Award, from Key Women, Inc., 1965; Youth in Action Humanitarian Award of family counselling, 1969; Albert Einstein College of Medicine achievement award, 1969; Deborah Gannett Award, from National Media Women, 1969. LL.D., from Talladega College, 1969, Wilmington College, 1970, LaSalle College, William Patterson College of New Jersey, University of Maine, and Capitol University, all 1971; L.H.D., North Carolina Central University, 1969, and Hampton Institute, 1970.

WRITINGS: Unbought and Unbossed, Houghton, 1970;

The Good Fight, Harper, 1973. Contributor of articles to newspapers and periodicals.

SIDELIGHTS: "Shirley Chisholm is true grit," Susan Brownmiller writes. "Her cometlike rise from clubhouse worker to Representative in the United States Congress was no accident of the political heavens. It was accomplished by the wiles of a steely politician with a belief in her own abilities which at times approaches an almost Messianic fervor." The title of her first book, *Unbought and Unbossed,* exemplifies the intense individualism of Shirley Chisholm's political life. Ignoring the political machines of her home district and the traditions of the U.S. Congress, she has constantly asserted her independence. Assemblyman Albert H. Blumenthal characterizes her as "a very tough lady, likeable but a loner. . . . She knew what she wanted to say and she said it well. She wasn't quick to make up her mind, but when she did, you couldn't blast her out of it. Enemies like Shirley, nobody needs in politics."

Among Shirley Chisholm's causes are better educational opportunities for minority groups, programs for the poor and disadvantaged, and a constant push for equality for ethnic minorities and for women. During her years in Congress, she has introduced, co-sponsored, and ardently supported and backed many Congressional measures including proposals to create a study commission on Afro-American history and culture, to enlarge the powers of the Department of Housing and Urban Development, to establish a Department of Consumer Affairs at a full Cabinet level, and several anti-poverty and welfare programs.

Chisholm has said that as "the first Black woman elected to Congress," she found that "being Black is much less of a drawback than being female in politics." In a speech in support of the Women's Rights Amendment to the Constitution, she said: "Prejudice against Blacks is becoming unacceptable although it will take years to eliminate it. But it is doomed because, slowly, white America is beginning to admit that it exists. Prejudice against women is still acceptable. There is very little understanding yet of the immorality involved in double pay scales and the classification of most of the better jobs as 'for men only.'" She adds: "That one sex needs protection more than the other is a male supremacist myth as ridiculous and unworthy of respect as the white supremacist myths that society is trying to cure itself of at this time."

In her second book, *The Good Fight,* Chisholm details her campaign for the Democratic presidential nomination in 1972. A reviewer for the *New York Times Book Review* reports that *The Good Fight* is "written in a hardnosed, straightforward style that suitably reflects the author's image as a politician. Wisely, Mrs. Chisholm focuses on the practical aspects of coalition politics as they relate to women and other minority groups; she deals realistically with over-optimistic political theories and avoids self-serving rhetoric."

In her typically direct manner, Chisholm has said: "I'd like them to say that Shirley Chisholm had *guts.* That's how I'd like to be remembered."

BIOGRAPHICAL/CRITICAL SOURCES: Ebony, February, 1969; *New York Times Magazine,* April 13, 1969; *Nation,* January 26, 1970; *McCall's,* August, 1970; *Washington Post,* October 10, 1970; *Atlantic,* November, 1970; Susan Brownmiller, *Shirley Chisholm,* Doubleday, 1970; *Congressional Digest,* January, 1971; *New York Times Book Review,* October 21, 1973.

CHRISTY, Joseph M. 1919-
(Joe Christy)

PERSONAL: Born July 17, 1919, in Lawton, Okla.; son of Joseph B. and Bess (Prickett) Christy; married Rene Van Cleave. *Education:* Attended University of Kansas. *Politics:* "Goldwater Republican." *Home:* 1705 Northwest 44th St., Lawton, Okla. 73501.

CAREER: Oklahoma Air Associates, Tillman County Oklahoma Airport, Okla., president, 1961-63; Sports Car Press, Ltd., East Norwalk, Conn., editor of aviation division, 1962—; Conde Nast Publications, New York, N.Y., contributing editor, *Air Progress* magazine, 1965-68, *Air Trails* magazine, 1970—. *Member:* American Aviation Historical Society, Air Force Association, Aviation/Space Writers Association, OX-5 Club of America. *Awards, honors:* Aviation/Space Writers Association award for best non-fiction aviation book of 1970, *Summon the Stars.*

WRITINGS: (With Clay Johnson) *Your Pilot's License,* Crown, 1960, revised edition, Sports Car Press, 1965; *Beechcraft Guide: Bonanza, Debonair, Musketeer,* Crown, 1962, reissued as *Single-Engine Beechcrafts,* Sports Car Press, 1970; *Racing Planes Guide,* Sports Car Press, 1963; (with Roy Wieden) *Lightplane Engine Guide,* Sports Car Press, 1963; (with Page Shamburger) *Aces and Planes of World War I,* Sports Car Press, 1968; (with Shamburger) *Command the Horizon: A Pictorial History of Aviation,* A. S. Barnes, 1968; (with Shamburger) *Summon the Stars,* A. S. Barnes, 1970; *Curtiss P-Thirty Six to P-Forty,* Sports Car Press, 1970; *The Single-Engine Cessnas,* Sports Car Press, 1971; (with Shamburger) *The Hawks,* Wolverine Publications, 1971; *Used Plane Buying Guide,* Sports Car Press, 1975; *Engines for Home-Built Aircraft,* Sports Car Press, 1976; *The P-Thirty Eight Lightning at War,* Ian Allen, 1977. Contributor of articles and stories to several periodicals, including *Argosy, Adventure, Flying,* and *Air Facts.*

WORK IN PROGRESS: A history of U.S. military aviation, 1907-1970, *Trail of Thunder.*

* * *

CHURCHILL, Guy E. 1926-

PERSONAL: Born April 8, 1926, in London, England; son of Frank (an engineer) and Grace (Dickens) Churchill; married Maria Magdalena Wieck (an insurance agent); children: Michael, Victor, Nicolette. *Education:* University of London, B.Sc., 1952. *Home:* 28 Cuikenburn, Penicuik, Midlothian, Scotland. *Office:* Napier College, Sighthill Court, Edinburgh EH11 4BN, Scotland.

CAREER: Manager of Lloyd's Agency in Sumatra, Indonesia, and head of insurance department, Harrisons & Crosfield Ltd., Belawan and Medan, Indonesia, 1959-60; Croydon Technical College, Croydon, England, lecturer in life assurance, 1960-66; Holborn College of Law, London, England, senior lecturer in insurance, 1966-70; The Polytechnic of Central London, London, senior lecturer in business studies, 1970-72; Ngee Ann Technical College, Singapore, visiting professor of business studies, 1972-75; Napier College, Edinburgh, Scotland, senior lecturer in banking and insurance, 1975—. Proprietor, Churchill & Co. (insurance brokers), West Croydon, England, 1963-66. *Member:* Chartered Insurance Institute (fellow), Institute of Arbitrators (fellow), British Institute of Management, Institute of Marketing, Royal Statistical Society (fellow), British Insurance Law Association. *Awards, honors:* Morgan Owen Gold Medallist, 1971; Ellis Carson Award, 1972, for "making a

significant contribution to forward thinking in the insurance industry."

WRITINGS: Compound Interest Simplified, Pergamon, 1969. Contributor of many articles on insurance and the insurance industry to British insurance journals.

WORK IN PROGRESS: Life Assurance Mathematics, publication expected in 1979; risk management consultancy assignments and seminars in Singapore and England.

BIOGRAPHICAL/CRITICAL SOURCES: Accountancy, October, 1969.

* * *

CLAGUE, Ewan 1896-

PERSONAL: Given name is pronounced Yuan; born December 27, 1896, in Prescott, Wash.; son of John (a farmer) and Eleanor (Cooper) Clague; married Dorothy Vermilya Whipple (a physician), May 29, 1923; children: Ewan (deceased), Anne Vermilya (Mrs. Leslie Farber), Llewellyn Whipple, Christopher Karran. *Education:* University of Washington, Seattle, A.B., 1917, M.A., 1921; University of Wisconsin, Ph.D., 1929. *Home:* 3821 Woodley Rd. N.W., Washington, D.C. 20016. *Office:* Leo Kramer, Inc., 1835 K St. N.W., Washington, D.C. 20006.

CAREER: U.S. Bureau of Labor Statistics, Washington, D.C., statistician, 1926-28; Metropolitan Life Insurance Co., New York, N.Y., research assistant in Business Research Bureau, 1928-29; University of Pennsylvania, School of Social Work, Philadelphia, professor of social research, 1931-35; U.S. Social Security Board, Washington, D.C., director of Bureau of Research and Statistics, 1936-40, director of Bureau of Employment Security, 1940-46; U.S. Department of Labor, Washington, D.C., commissioner of labor statistics, 1946-54, 1955-65, consultant, 1966—; Leo Kramer, Inc., Washington, D.C., senior associate, 1969—. Visiting professor at University of California, Los Angeles, Michigan State University, Columbia University, and other universities. Former consultant abroad for Ford Foundation and Agency for International Development. Member of U.S. National Commission on UNESCO, 1966-71; chairman of United Nations Expert Committee on Post Adjustments, 1959-70. *Military service:* U.S. Army, Ambulance Service, 1917-19.

MEMBER: American Economic Association, American Statistical Association, Society for Advancement of Management, Gerontological Society, National Association of Social Workers, National Conference of Social Welfare, Cosmos Club, International Club. *Awards, honors:* National Civil Service League Award as one of ten top men in U.S. Government service, 1958.

WRITINGS: (With Webster Powell) *Ten Thousand Out of Work,* University of Pennsylvania Press, 1933; (with Walter Couper and E. Wight Bakke) *After the Shutdown,* Institute of Human Relations, Yale University, 1934; *Seventeenth Century Poor Relief in the Twentieth Century,* Commonwealth of Pennsylvania, 1935; *Charitable Trusts,* University of Pennsylvania Press, 1935; *Statistics and Economic Policy* (booklet of lectures), Institute of Industrial Relations, University of California, Los Angeles, 1966; *The Bureau of Labor Statistics,* Praeger, 1968; *Unemployment: Past, Present, and Future,* American Enterprise Institute, 1969; (with Kim and Farrell) *The All-Volunteer Army,* Praeger, 1970; (with Palli and Kramer) *The Aging Worker and the Union,* Praeger, 1971; (with Kramer) *The Health Impaired Miner under the Black Lung Legislation,* Praeger, 1973. Also author with Kramer of *U.S. Manpower Policies, 1935-75,* Upjohn. Publications include various Department of Labor reports and a number of his speeches. Contributor to magazines.

* * *

CLAIBORNE, Robert (Watson, Jr.) 1919-

PERSONAL: Born May 15, 1919, in High Wycombe, Buckinghamshire, England; son of Robert W. (an attorney) and Virginia (McKenney) Claiborne; married Adrienne Aaron, August 26, 1945 (divorced, 1965); married Sybil Resnik (a writer), April 24, 1965; children: (first marriage) Amanda Susan, Samuel McKenney; (second marriage) Jan Stacy (stepson). *Education:* Attended Massachusetts Institute of Technology, 1936-37, Antioch College, 1937-39; New York University, A.B. (magna cum laude), 1942. *Agent:* Julian Bach Literary Agency, Inc., 3 East 48th St., New York, N.Y. 10017.

CAREER: Lathe operator, factory worker, and union official in New Jersey and New York, 1942-46; folksinger and music teacher in New York City, 1946-57; *Scientific American,* New York City, associate editor, 1957-60; *Medical World News,* New York City, associate, news, and managing editor, 1960-64; *Life Science Library,* New York City, editor, 1964-65. Lecturer on ecology for New School for Social Research, 1971-72. *Member:* Authors Guild, Greenwich Village Peace Center, National Association of Science Writers.

WRITINGS: (With Samuel Goudsmit) *Time,* Time, Inc., 1966; (with Walter Modell and Al Lansing) *Drugs,* Time, Inc., 1968; *Climate, Man and History,* Norton, 1970; *On Every Side the Sea,* American Heritage Press, 1971; *The First Americans,* Time-Life, 1973; (editor with Victor McKusick) *Medical Genetics,* HP Publishing, 1973; *God or Beast: Evolution and Human Nature,* Norton, 1974; *The Birth of Writing,* Time-Life, 1974; *The Summer Stargazer: Astronomy for Absolute Beginners,* Coward, 1975; (editor with Gerald Weissman) *Cell Membranes: Biochemistry, Cell Biology & Pathology,* HP Publishing, 1975.

Contributor of articles and reviews to *Harper's, Nation, New York Times, Book World, Village Voice,* and other periodicals. Part-time senior editor for *Hospital Practice,* 1966—.

WORK IN PROGRESS: With Lionel Casson and Bryan M. Fagan, *Mysteries of the Past,* for American Heritage Press; with Rainer Erhart, *Physical Geography: An Introduction,* for McGraw-Hill; and *Doctors, Drugs and Dollars: The High Cost of Medical Care.*

SIDELIGHTS: Robert Claiborne lists his major vocational interests as "ecology, interaction of science and society, human prehistory and archeology, and linguistics." Of his writings, he told *CA:* "Basically, I tend to think of myself as a teacher whose medium happens to be print rather than the classroom—and who (unlike most teachers) doesn't have a captive audience. For this reason, and because I believe in playing fair with the reader, I try (space permitting) to present not just conclusions but the facts and reasoning which produced the conclusions—and if the facts are inconclusive, to say so. I have an abiding hatred of writers who publish nonsense on serious subjects (names on request) and try to show them up when I get the chance."

AVOCATIONAL INTERESTS: Aikido, body-surfing, bird-watching, gardening, astronomy, travel, and writing letters to the editor.

BIOGRAPHICAL/CRITICAL SOURCES: Best Sellers, June 1, 1970; *Washington Post,* December 3, 1974.

* * *

CLAIR, Andree

EDUCATION: University of Paris, License-es-lettres, 1948; Education Nationale, Paris, certificat d'aptitude pedagogique and certificat d'aptitude a l'enseignement des enfants arrieres (C.A.E.A.). *Residence:* Paris, France.

CAREER: School teacher and professor in Paris, France; professor in Chad; Institut d'Etudes Centrafricaine de Brazzaville, Republic of the Congo, staff ethnologist, 1945-46; cultural counsellor, Presidency, Republic of Niger, 1961—.

*WRITINGS—*Juveniles; all published by La Farandole, except as indicated: *Moudaina; ou Deux enfants au coeur de l'Afrique* (novel), Bourrelier, 1952, translation by James Cleugh published as *Moudaina,* Muller, 1957; *Le Mur gris de toutes les couleurs* (novel), Bourrelier, 1955; (self-illustrated) *Bemba* (novel), 1957, translation by Marie Ponsot published as *Bemba: An African Adventure,* Harcourt, 1962; *Eau ficelee et ficelle de fumee* (picture book), 1957; *Aminatou* (picture book), 1959; *Tchinda, la petite soeur de Moudaina* (novel), Bourrelier, 1959; *Le Fabuleux Empire du Mali* (history of Mali, 10th through 17th centuries), Presence Africaine, 1959.

Bakari, enfant du Mali, Presence Africaine, 1960; *Rejoignons Moudaina!* (novel), Bourrelier, 1961; *Dije* (picture book), 1961; *Le Voyage d'Oumarou* (elementary school textbook), illustrations, photos, and letters by Clair, Bourrelier, 1963; *Les Decouvertes d'Alkassoum* (picture book), 1964; *Un, deux, trois* (picture book), 1966; *Le Babiroussa . . . et les autres* (poems), Istra, 1966; *Nicole au quinzieme etage* (picture book; chosen best children's book, 1969), 1968.

Nicole et l'ascenseur, 1971; (with Boubou Hama) *Le Baobab merveilleux* (picture book), 1971; (with Hama) *La Savane enchantee: Contes d'Afrique,* 1972, translation by Olive Jones published as *The Enchanted Savannah: Tales from West Africa,* Methuen, 1974; *Issilim,* 1972, revised edition, 1976; (with Hama) *L'aventure d'Albarka,* Julliard, 1972; (with Hama) *Kangue Ize,* 1974; (with Francoise Estachy) *Les duex etoiles,* Seneve, 1975; (with Beatrice Tanaka) *Escargotiques,* Ecole Loisirs, 1976. Also author of *Founya le vaurien, Nicole dans le grand pre,* and *Nicole ne voit pas rien;* author, with Tanaka, of *Farfelettis* and *Kangourourimes.*

Adult books: *Le Niger, pays a decouvrir,* Hachette, 1965; *Le Niger independent,* Istra, 1966.

Contributor of articles, stories, and poems to adult and children's journals and periodicals; children's book critic and reader of manuscripts on Africa for publishers. Stories, extracts from books, and poems anthologized in several collections, including *Et l'on raconte encore . . .,* edited by Mathilde Leriche, Bourrelier, 1969.

WORK IN PROGRESS: Several books on Africa for both children and adults.

SIDELIGHTS: Andree Clair calls herself an "Africaniste ou antiraciste." She has traveled throughout Europe and in ten African nations, and believes it is necessary to become acquainted with other peoples and life-styles in order to combat prejudice and racism.

BIOGRAPHICAL/CRITICAL SOURCES: Marc Soriano, editor, *Guide de la litterature enfantine,* Flammarion, 1959;

Natha Caputo, editor, *De quatre a quinze ans: Guide de lecture,* l'Ecole et la Nation, 1968; *Dictionnaire des Ecrivains pour la jeunesse, ausers de langue Francaise,* Seghers.†

*   *   *

CLARK, Anne 1909-

PERSONAL: Born May 19, 1909, in Metcalfe, Miss.; daughter of Clive (a cotton planter) and Anne (Poindexter) Metcalfe; married Edward Clark (a lawyer, banker, and former U.S. Ambassador to Australia), December 28, 1927; children: Leila Downs (Mrs. Douglas C. Wynn). *Education:* Attended Newcomb College, 1925-27; University of Texas, B.A., 1937. *Politics:* Democrat. *Religion:* Episcopalian.

WRITINGS: Australian Adventure: Letters from an Ambassador's Wife, University of Texas Press, 1969; (compiler and editor) *Historic Homes of San Augustine,* photographs by Jim Alvis, San Augustine Historical Society, 1972.†

*   *   *

CLARK, Charles E(dwin) 1929-

PERSONAL: Born April 28, 1929, in Brunswick, Me.; son of Clarence Hobart (a clergyman) and Beatrice (Wright) Clark; married Margery Anne Schumacher, June 28, 1952; children: Marilyn Anne, Douglas Edwin, Jonathan Charles, David Richard. *Education:* Bates College, A.B., 1951; Columbia University School of Journalism, M.S., 1952; Brown University, Ph.D., 1966. *Politics:* Independent. *Religion:* United Church of Christ. *Home:* 2 Thompson Lane, Durham, N.H. 03824. *Office:* Department of History, University of New Hampshire, Durham, N.H. 03824.

CAREER: Valley News, West Lebanon, N.H., reporter, 1952; *Providence Journal and Evening Bulletin,* Providence, R.I., reporter, 1956-61; Southeastern Massachusetts Technological Institute (now Southeastern Massachusetts University), North Dartmouth, assistant professor of history, 1965-67; University of New Hampshire, Durham, assistant professor, 1967-70, associate professor, 1970-75, professor of history, 1975—, chairman of department of history, 1977—. Researcher, Program for Loyalist Studies and Publications, 1970—. *Military service:* U.S. Navy, 1953-56; became lieutenant junior grade. U.S. Naval Reserve, 1956—; current rank, commander. *Member:* American Historical Association, American Studies Association, Organization of American Historians, Maine Historical Society, New Hampshire Historical Society (trustee, 1971—). *Awards, honors:* National Endowment for the Humanities fellow, 1968.

WRITINGS: The Eastern Frontier: The Settlement of Northern New England, 1610-1763, Knopf, 1970; *Maine During the Colonial Period: A Bibliographical Guide,* Maine Historical Society, 1974; (with C. W. Eastman, Jr.) *The Portsmouth Project: An Exercise in Inductive Historical Scholarship,* New Hampshire Publishing, 1974; (author of forward) John P. Adams, *Drowned Valley,* University Press of New England, 1976; *Maine: A Bicentennial History,* Norton, 1977. Contributor to *William & Mary Quarterly, New England Quarterly, Historical New Hampshire,* and other journals.

WORK IN PROGRESS: Research for a comparative study of English and American journalism in the eighteenth century, and for a social and cultural history of northern New England from 1760 to about 1830.

SIDELIGHTS: As a reporter who turned to history, Charles Clark has "tried to refine my craft rather than abandon it." "As a humanist," he says, "I am struggling dimly in my writing and teaching toward a cultural synthesis of life in early America without resort to cold scientism. I have few hobbies except my family and, when time affords, looking at the sky."

*   *   *

CLARK, Dennis E. 1916-

PERSONAL: Born October 24, 1916, in Bristol, England; son of Harold R. and Lorna (Rose) Clark; married Gladys M. Wright, October 11, 1941; children: Judith M. (Mrs. Arthur Loveless), Paul G., Martyn J., R. Michael. *Education:* Attended Bristol Grammar School; studied in Switzerland, India, and West Pakistan. *Religion:* Christian. *Home:* 410 Cedar Hill Rd., Victoria, British Columbia, Canada.

CAREER: Founded two publishing houses, MIK, Lahore, West Pakistan, for books on Urdu literature, and MSS, Delhi, India, for books on Hindi literature; traveller, evangelist, and bible teacher throughout Asia, 1940-66. Consultant in communications media to David C. Cook Foundation.

WRITINGS: Missions in the Seventies, Scripture Union, 1970, published as *Third World and Mission,* Word Books, 1971. Also author of *The Life and Teaching of Jesus the Messiah,* and *Jesus Christ: His Life and Teaching,* both published by Dove Bible Publications.

*   *   *

CLARK, Don(ald Henry) 1930-

PERSONAL: Born July 10, 1930, in Spring Lake, N.J.; son of Samuel Harrison and Hazel (Arlington) Clark; married Barbara Brown, January 24, 1958; children: Vicki, Andy. *Education:* Antioch College, B.A., 1953; Adelphi University, Ph.D., 1959. *Agent:* Mary Yost Associates, 141 East 55th St., New York, N.Y. 10022. *Office:* 1240 University Dr., Menlo Park, Calif. 94025.

CAREER: Licensed psychologist in California and certified psychologist in New York; served internship at Veterans' Administration Hospital, Palo Alto, Calif., 1958-59; post-doctoral fellow at Veterans' Administration Mental Hygiene Clinic, San Francisco, Calif., 1959; Philadelphia State Hospital, Philadelphia, Pa., coordinator of male rehabilitation, 1959-61; City University of New York, New York, N.Y., staff psychologist, Educational Clinic of Hunter College, 1961-64, assistant professor of education, 1965-67, director of Educational Clinic and associate professor of education, Herbert H. Lehman College, 1965-71; psychologist in private practice, Menlo Park, Calif., 1971—. Member of first governing board of Humanistic Psychology Institute. *Member:* American Psychological Association, Association of Gay Psychologists.

WRITINGS: (With Gerald S. Lesser and Gordon Fifer) *Mental Abilities of Children from Different Social-Class and Cultural Groups,* University of Chicago Press, for Society for Research in Child Development, 1965; (editor with Lesser) *Emotional Disturbance and School Learning,* Science Research Associates, 1965; (compiler) *The Psychology of Education,* Free Press, 1967; (with Arlene Goldsmith and Clementine Pugh) *Those Children: Case Studies from the Inner-City School,* Wadsworth, 1970; (with Asya L. Kadis) *Humanistic Teaching,* C. E. Merrill, 1971; *Loving Someone Gay,* Celestial Arts Press (Millbrae, Calif.), 1977.

Contributor: *Imperatives for Change,* New York State Education Department, 1968; Gerald Egan, editor, *Read-*

ings in Encounter, Brooks-Cole, 1971; L. Blank, G. Gottsegen, and M. Gottsegen, editors, *Confrontation,* Macmillan, 1971; L. Solomon and B. Berzon, editors, *New Perspectives on Encounter Groups,* Jossey-Bass, 1972. Contributor of articles to *Campus School Exchange, Young Children, Psychology in the Schools, British Journal of Social Psychiatry, Gay, Humanist,* and other periodicals.

* * *

CLARK, Joseph James   1893-1971

November 12, 1893—July(?), 1971; American retired admiral and pioneer in naval aviation. Obituaries: *Detroit News,* July 14, 1971; *New York Times,* July 14, 1971; *Washington Post,* July 14, 1971. (See index for *CA* sketch)

* * *

CLARK, (William) Ramsey   1927-

PERSONAL: Born December 18, 1927, in Dallas, Tex.; son of Tom C. (a former U.S. Supreme Court Justice) and Mary (Ramsey) Clark; married Georgia Welch, April 16, 1949; children: Ronda Kathleen, Tom C. *Education:* University of Texas, B.A., 1949; University of Chicago, M.A. and J.D., 1950. *Home:* 37 West 12th St., New York, N.Y. 10011.

CAREER: Admitted to the Bars of the State of Texas, 1951, U.S. Supreme Court, 1956, District of Columbia, 1969, and State of New York, 1970; Clark, Reed & Clark (law firm), Dallas, Tex., member of firm, 1951-61; U.S. Government, Department of Justice, Washington, D.C., assistant attorney general, 1961-65, deputy attorney general, 1966-67, attorney general, 1967-69; Paul, Weiss, Rifkind, Wharton & Garrison (law firm), New York, N.Y., and Washington, D.C., partner, 1969—. Adjunct professor, Howard University, 1969-72, Brooklyn Law School, 1973—. *Military service:* U.S. Marine Corps, 1945-46. *Member:* Federal Bar Association (president, 1964-65), American Bar Association, American Judicative Society (director, 1963), Southwest Legal Foundation. *Awards, honors:* LL.D., Loyola University, 1967.

WRITINGS: Crime in America: Observations on Its Nature, Causes, Prevention and Control, introduction by Tom Wicker, Simon & Schuster, 1970.

SIDELIGHTS: James Q. Wilson presents a typical description of Ramsey Clark when he describes the former attorney general as ''a soft-spoken Texan, thoughtful and liberal . . . [who] managed on many occasions to reveal a capacity for fairness combined with determination that was reassuring to those confused or angered by the excessively ideological nature of the public clamor about crime.''

Critical reaction to Clark's first book was, predictably, favorable in the liberal press, disparaging in the more conservative media. Ernest Van Den Haag of *National Review,* stated: ''If an ambitious politician has to write a campaign book, and is possessed of Clark's shortcomings, he might do better to hire a ghostwriter. To do so would disclose humility (all too well earned here) and an awareness of inadequacy—the beginning of wisdom. The ghostwriter might decently veil the politician's actual mind, a service to him, and even more to the reader.''

Herbert Packer, writing in *New Republic,* exemplifies the generally enthusiastic attitude, with some reservation, that the liberal establishment evinces toward Clark. ''[He] has written a modest and sensitive book about our current problems that deserves the widest readership. He scrupulously eschews the personal. . . . Mr. Clark shows a great deal of

insight into our crime problem and is obviously familiar with its most important facets, like the impotence of our correctional system and the anger that separates the police from their adversaries. Still, he resorts to most of the tired liberal cliches about crime that don't tell us anything. . . . Nonetheless, [his] book provides an excellent introduction from a 'liberal' standpoint to the problems that face law enforcement.''

Edward Bennett Williams writes that Clark ''combines toughness and idealism, pragmatism and optimism. Anyone who thinks being tough on crime and being compassionately concerned with civil liberties are mutually exclusive should hasten to his corner bookstore and get this able, literate, thoughtful and reasoned discussion of the problems of crime in America. . . . Ramsey Clark is one of the few visionary voices we have in a field desperately in need of vision, one of the rare men in law enforcement capable both of empathy toward the police, and recognition of the dehumanizing impact of slum life.''

BIOGRAPHICAL/CRITICAL SOURCES: Washington Post, June 3, 1970; *New York Times,* July 8, 1970, November 12, 1970; *Newsweek,* August 17, 1970, August 31, 1970, March 22, 1971; *New Republic,* November 7, 1970; *Life,* November 13, 1970; *Book World,* November 15, 1970; *Saturday Review,* November 28, 1970; *New York Times Book Review,* November 29, 1970; *Time,* November 30, 1970; *New Leader,* December 14, 1970; *Best Sellers,* January 1, 1971; *National Review,* January 12, 1971, March 9, 1971, March 23, 1971; *Commentary,* March, 1971; *Commonweal,* March 19, 1971.

* * *

CLARK, William (Donaldson)   1916-

PERSONAL: Born July 28, 1916, in Haltwhistle, England; son of John McClure and Marion (Jackson) Clark. *Education:* Oriel College, Oxford, M.A. (first class honors), 1938. *Home:* 3407 Rodman St. N.W., Washington, D.C. 20008. *Office:* World Bank, 1818 H St., Washington, D.C. 20433.

CAREER: University of Chicago, Chicago, Ill., lecturer in humanities, 1938-40; British Information Services, Chicago, staff member, 1942-44; British Embassy, Washington, D.C., press attaché, 1945-46; *Encyclopaedia Britannica,* London, England, London editor, 1946-49; *Observer,* London, diplomatic correspondent, 1950-55; public relations adviser to Prime Minister Anthony Eden, 1955-56; toured Africa and Asia for British Broadcasting Corp. and *Observer,* 1957; *Observer,* editor of ''The Week,'' 1958-60; Overseas Development Institute, London, director, 1960-68; World Bank, Washington, D.C., vice-president of external relations, 1968—. *Member:* Athenaeum Club and Savile Club (both London), Tavern Club (Chicago).

WRITINGS: Less than Kin: A Study of Anglo-American Relations, Houghton, 1957; *What Is the Commonwealth?,* Newman Neame, 1958; *After Independence in East Africa* (pamphlet), Overseas Development Institute (London), 1962; *Number 10* (novel), Heinemann, 1966, Houghton, 1967; *Special Relationship* (novel), Heinemann, 1968, Houghton, 1969.

SIDELIGHTS: Ronald Millar's dramatization of *Number 10* was produced, under the original title, on the West End at Strand Theatre, 1967.

BIOGRAPHICAL/CRITICAL SOURCES: Christian Science Monitor, March 23, 1967; *Punch,* November 22, 1967, November 6, 1968; *Drama,* spring, 1968.

CLARKE, Jack Alden 1924-

PERSONAL: Born February 20, 1924, in Bay City, Mich.; son of Harry and Olivia (Bence) Clarke; married Anna Holler, February 1, 1951; children: David, Cynthia. *Education:* Michigan State University, B.A., 1949; University of Wisconsin, M.A., 1950, M.A.L.S., 1952, Ph.D., 1954; also attended Universite de Poitiers, Poitiers, France, 1949. *Home:* 4326 Herrick La., Madison, Wis. 53711. *Office:* Graduate School of Library Science, University of Wisconsin, 425 Henry Mall, Madison, Wis. 53706.

CAREER: Library of Congress, Washington, D.C., intern, 1952-53; director of Washington Cathedral Library, Washington, D.C., 1953-55, and Doane College Library, Crete, Neb., 1955-56; University of Wisconsin—Madison, assistant librarian, 1956-62; Wisconsin State University (now University of Wisconsin—Eau Claire), Eau Claire, director of libraries and professor of library science, 1962-65; University of Wisconsin—Madison, Graduate School of Library Science, professor, 1965—, assistant director, 1965-68, acting director, 1968-69, 1970-71. *Military service:* U.S. Army, 1943-45; became sergeant. *Member:* American Library Association, American Association of University Professors, Wisconsin Library Association (chairman, College and University Libraries Section, 1963-64), Association of Wisconsin State College Faculties (chairman, Library Section, 1964-65), Wisconsin Academy of Sciences, Arts and Letters (librarian, 1964—).

WRITINGS: (Compiler) *Research Materials in the Social Sciences,* University of Wisconsin Press, 1959, 2nd edition, 1967; *Huguenot Warrior: The Life and Times of Henri de Rohan, 1579-1638,* Nijhoff Press (The Hague), 1967; *Gabriel Naude, 1600-1653,* Archon, 1970; (co-compiler) *Modern French Literature and Language: A Bibliography of Homage Studies,* University of Wisconsin Press, 1976.

WORK IN PROGRESS: A History of European Librarianship: 1500-1800; a biography of Jean Paul Bignon.

AVOCATIONAL INTERESTS: Conservation education, camping in northern Canada.

* * *

CLARKSON, Paul S(tephen) 1905-

PERSONAL: Born October 2, 1905, in Worcester, Mass.; son of Henry (an envelope manufacturer) and Carrie (Pendell) Clarkson; married Wilma West, November 30, 1930; children: Richard West (deceased), Paul Stephen, Jr. *Education:* Clark University, A.B. (with honors), 1925; Harvard University, J.D., 1928. *Home:* 3 Lowell Ave., Holden, Mass. 01520. *Office:* Robert H. Goddard Library, Clark University, Worcester, Mass. 01610.

CAREER: Admitted to Maryland bar, 1929; Baltimore Gas & Electric Co., Baltimore, Md., research attorney, 1929-69; Clark University, Worcester, Mass., curator of special collections and rare books, 1969—. Lecturer on literary and historical themes. *Military service:* U.S. Naval Reserve, 1943-46; became lieutenant. *Member:* Maryland Historical Society, Phi Beta Kappa, Baltimore Bibliophiles, Trial Table Law Club (Baltimore), Tudor and Stuart Club (Baltimore), Baker Street Irregulars (New York), Six Napoleons of Baltimore. *Awards, honors:* Andrew White Medal, Loyola College (Baltimore), 1969; Double Shilling award, Baker Street Irregulars, 1975.

WRITINGS: A Bibliography of William Sydney Porter (O. Henry), Caxton, 1938; (with Clyde T. Warren) *The Law of Property in Shakespeare and the Elizabethan Drama,* Johns Hopkins Press, 1942, 2nd edition, Gordian, 1968; *The Liberal Arts and the Future* (address given at Clark University, April 5, 1943), Clark University Library, 1943; (with R. Samuel Jett) *Luther Martin of Maryland,* Johns Hopkins Press, 1970. Author with Joseph H. Purdy of a play, "Tom Jones: A Romantic Comedy," after the work by Fielding, first produced at Tryout Theater, Seattle, Wash., August, 1949. Also editor and author of *The Goddard Bibliolog,* 1971—.

* * *

CLAUDE, Richard (P.) 1934-

PERSONAL: Born May 20, 1934, in St. Paul, Minn.; son of Charles J. and Rose Elizabeth Claude; married Colette Anne Germann (a French and remedial reading teacher), June 15, 1963; children: Eric Jean-Baptiste, Christine Rose, Gregor Pierre. *Education:* College of St. Thomas, St. Paul, Minn., B.A., 1956; Florida State University, M.S., 1960; Harvard University, special research, 1961; University of Virginia, Ph.D., 1964. *Home:* 5107 Moorland Lane, Bethesda, Md. 20014. *Office:* Department of Government and Politics, University of Maryland, College Park, Md. 20742.

CAREER: Vassar College, Poughkeepsie, N.Y., instructor in political science, 1962-64; College of William & Mary, Williamsburg, Va., visiting assistant professor of government, 1964-65; University of Maryland, College Park, assistant professor, 1965-69, associate professor of government and politics, 1969—. Consultant to American Public Health Association, *Congressional Quarterly,* Maryland Human Relations Center, and other public and private organizations. *Military service:* U.S. Air Force Reserve, 1956-59; became captain.

MEMBER: American Political Science Association, National Municipal League, Society for Study of Negro History, American Association of University Professors, American Civil Liberties Union (member of board of governors of Maryland branch), Southern Political Science Association, Washington Urban League, District of Columbia Political Science Association (member of executive council, 1967-68). *Awards, honors:* Ford Foundation grant, 1963; National Science Foundation grant, 1969, 1971; *The Supreme Court and the Electoral Process* was nominated for a Pulitzer Prize in 1970.

WRITINGS: The Supreme Court and the Electoral Process, Johns Hopkins Press, 1970; *The University of Maryland Guide to Political Science Research,* 3rd revised edition (Claude was not associated with earlier editions), Department of Government and Politics, University of Maryland, 1970; (editor) *Comparative Human Rights,* Johns Hopkins Press, 1976. Contributor of articles and reviews to political science and law journals.

WORK IN PROGRESS: Research in comparative human rights.

AVOCATIONAL INTERESTS: Oil painting, travel.

* * *

CLAYES, Stanley A(rnold) 1922-

PERSONAL: Born July 4, 1922, in Brookline, Mass.; son of Stanley Arnold (a dentist) and Elizabeth (Slaymaker) Clayes. *Education:* Ursinus College, A.B., 1947; University of Pennsylvania, M.A., 1950, Ph.D., 1951. *Religion:* Episcopalian. *Residence:* Chicago, Ill. *Office:* Department of English, Loyola University, 820 North Michigan Ave., Chicago, Ill. 60611.

CAREER: Assistant professor of literature at Oregon State College (now University), Corvallis, 1951-60, and San Francisco State College (now University), San Francisco, Calif., 1960-62; Loyola University, Chicago, Ill., assistant professor, 1962-64, associate professor, 1964-70, professor of English literature, 1970—. *Military service:* U.S. Army, World War II; served in Germany. *Member:* Modern Language Association of America.

WRITINGS: (Editor with David G. Spencer) *Contemporary Drama: Thirteen Plays, American, English, and European,* Scribner, 1962, 2nd edition, 1970; (editor with Spencer) *Contexts for Composition,* Prentice-Hall, 1965, 4th edition, 1976; (editor) *Drama and Discussion,* Prentice-Hall, 1967; (editor with John Gerrietts) *Ways to Poetry,* Harcourt, 1975.

WORK IN PROGRESS: Revisions of earlier books.

AVOCATIONAL INTERESTS: Skiing (coached ski team at Oregon State College).

* * *

CLAYTON, (Francis) Howard 1918-

PERSONAL: Born May 20, 1918, in St. John's, Newfoundland; son of Arthur (an Anglican minister) and Ella (Warren) Clayton; married Helen Margaret Doig, July 29, 1942; children: Elizabeth, Margaret, John. *Education:* University of Birmingham, Birmingham, England, Bachelor of Commerce, 1949; University of London, teaching certificate, 1957. *Politics:* Conservative. *Religion:* Anglican. *Home:* 34 Wissage Rd., Lichfield, Staffordshire, England.

CAREER: Birmingham Regional Hospital Board, Birmingham, England, hospital administrator, 1949-56; lecturer at Wednesbury College of Commerce, 1957-63, and Tamworth College of Further Education, 1963-67, both Staffordshire, England; writer and free-lance lecturer, 1967—. Elected councillor on Lichfield District Council, 1976. *Military service:* British Army, 1939-45; served in Royal Artillery; became lieutenant; lost left leg in action during World War II. *Member:* Newcomen Society (London), Victorian Society (London).

WRITINGS: The Atmospheric Railways, privately printed, 1966; *The Duffield Bank and Eaton Railways,* Oakwood Press, 1968; *Atlantic Bridgehead: The Story of Transatlantic Communications,* Garnstone Press, 1968; (with M. Jacot and R. Buttrell) *Miniature Railways,* Volume I, Oakwood Press, 1971; *Coaching City: A Glimpse of Georgian Lichfield,* Dragon Press (Bala, Wales), 1971. Contributor to *Country Life* and *Railway Magazine.*

WORK IN PROGRESS: A book about Victorian Lichfield, 1837-1900; and a book about the Swinfen vs. Swinfen lawsuit of 1856.

SIDELIGHTS: Howard Clayton told *CA:* "I began by lecturing and giving talks on subjects which interested me—mainly local history, industrial history and railway history. This naturally involved a good deal of research. It seemed sensible to use this material for writing—first for magazine articles and then for books. I found I enjoyed writing and so I have continued."

* * *

CLAYTON, James L. 1931-

PERSONAL: Born July 28, 1931, in Salt Lake City, Utah; son of Ernest (an educator) and Olita (Melville) Clayton; married Geraldine Horsley, June 13, 1957; children: Creed,

Catherine, Andrea. *Education:* University of Utah, B.A., 1958; Cornell University, Ph.D., 1964. *Home:* 1445 Arlington Dr., Salt Lake City, Utah 84103. *Office:* University of Utah, Salt Lake City, Utah 84112.

CAREER: Hamilton College, Clinton, N.Y., instructor, 1962-63; University of Utah, Salt Lake City, instructor, 1963-64, assistant professor, 1964-66; associate professor, 1967-71, professor, 1971—, director of honors programs, 1967-70. Member of Utah State Medical Schools Admissions Board, 1968-69. Visiting professor, U.S. Air Force bases in Germany and Greece, 1975. *Military service:* U.S. Army, 1953-55. *Member:* Economic History Association, Organization of American Historians. *Awards, honors:* Voelker Foundation grant, New York University, 1960; Social Science Research Council travel grant, 1962; Distinguished Teaching Award, University of Utah, 1966; Solon J. Buck Prize, 1967, for best article published in *Minnesota History* in 1967; American Philosophical Society grant, 1970.

WRITINGS: (Editor with Alfred Cave) *American Civilization: A Documentary History,* W. C. Brown, 1966, revised edition, 1969; (editor) *The Economic Impact of the Cold War,* Harcourt, 1970.

Contributor: Davis Bobrow, editor, *Components of Defense Policy,* Rand McNally, 1965; David Ellis, editor, *The Frontier in American Development,* Cornell University Press, 1969; Seymour Melman, editor, *The War Economy,* St. Martin's, 1971. Contributor of articles to *Western Political Quarterly, Dialogue: A Journal of Mormon Thought, Minnesota History, Pacific Historical Review, Financial Post, Nation, Playboy,* and other periodicals.

WORK IN PROGRESS: A monograph, *The Economic Consequences of American Wars; The Limits of Greatness,* a monograph on the rise and limitations of the American welfare state.

SIDELIGHTS: James Clayton told *CA:* "My primary purpose in what I write is to alert Americans to the limitations of what government can accomplish, either in warfare or welfare, without diminishing the faith to try to improve the lot of the less fortunate. This purpose is rooted in the belief that America tends to follow England more than any other country and England's current problems may be ours before long."

AVOCATIONAL INTERESTS: Skiing.

* * *

CLEMENS, Diane S(haver) 1936-

PERSONAL: Born September 5, 1936, in Cincinnati, Ohio; daughter of Gilbert Jerome (a lawyer) and Elizabeth (Schwab) Shaver; married Walter Clark Clemens, Jr. (a professor of political science), 1960; children: Iolani. *Education:* University of Cincinnati, B.A., B.S. (summa cum laude), 1958, M.A., 1960; attended University of Frankfurt, 1959-60; University of California, Santa Barbara, Ph.D., 1966. *Office:* Department of History, University of California, Berkeley, Calif. 94720.

CAREER: University of Hawaii, Honolulu, lecturer, assistant to dean of East-West Center, 1960-61; Santa Barbara City College, Santa Barbara, Calif., lecturer, 1961-63; Boston University, Boston, Mass., lecturer in Russian history, 1964-66; Massachusetts Institute of Technology, Cambridge, Mass., assistant professor of history, 1966-72; University of California, Berkeley, associate professor of history, 1972—. Consultant, in Soviet affairs, Special Operations Research Office, American University, Washington, D.C., Pacific and Asian Affairs Council, Honolulu, Hawaii, 1960-61, EduTech, Inc., Washington, D.C., 1964.

MEMBER: International Platform Association, American Historical Association, Society for Historians of American Foreign Relations, Union of Concerned Scientists, American Association for the Advancement of Slavic Studies, American Political Science Association, Foreign Relations Study Group on Law and Politics (member of council), Strategy for Peace, Phi Beta Kappa, Pi Delta Epsilon, Pi Sigma Alpha, Kappa Delta Pi, Tau Kappa Alpha. *Awards, honors:* History fellow, Deutscher Akademische Austauschdieust, 1958-60; West German Government research grant, University of Frankfurt, 1959-60; travel grants to Moscow, 1967-68, and to Budapest, 1968.

WRITINGS: Yalta, Oxford University Press, 1970. Contributor of articles on methodological approach to wartime diplomacy to *Peace Research Society, Mezinarodni Vztahy,* and other periodicals. Author of numerous papers presented at seminars and conferences throughout the world.

WORK IN PROGRESS: A History of Soviet-American Diplomacy, for Oxford University Press; *Joseph Stalin: Profile of the Diplomat,* near completion, to be published either as a short monograph or two long articles.

BIOGRAPHICAL/CRITICAL SOURCES: Best Sellers, February 1, 1971.†

* * *

CLEMENT, George H. 1909-
(G. Henri)

PERSONAL: Surname is pronounced Cle-*ment;* born November 15, 1909, in Hamilton, Ontario, Canada; son of Herbert Benson (a merchant) and Alice (Blake) Clement; married Pearl Mildred Nuell (a piano teacher), August 27, 1937; children: Lawrence G., Carolyn P. (Mrs. Calvin Coolidge), Marlene M. (Mrs. John Waters). *Education:* Studied at Ontario Bible College for three years; Galilean Bible Seminary, B.A., 1949, B.Th., 1950. *Politics:* Progressive Conservative. *Home:* 4001 Steele Ave., Apt. 1107, Downsview, Ontario, Canada M3N 2T8.

CAREER: Baptist clergyman, 1936—; minister in Montreal, Quebec, and Hamilton, Ontario, before he gave up his church and salary to go to the Cumberland Mountain area of Virginia as a missionary, 1951-58; minister in Peterborough, Ontario, 1959-63; Arthur Fellowship Baptist Church, Arthur, Ontario, minister, 1963-74; Black Creek Pioneer Village, Downsview, Ontario, minister-in-residence, 1974—. When his funds ran thin, he also painted signs and houses, worked as a mail clerk, sharpened skates, and other jobs.

WRITINGS: Untangling the Line in Fishing for Souls, Union Gospel Press, 1947; *Versatile Object Lessons,* Zondervan, Book I, 1961, Book II, 1971; *The ABC's of the Prophetical Scriptures,* Broadman, 1970. Contributor of more than a thousand short stories to several dozen religious periodicals in the United States, occasionally using the pseudonym G. Henri.

WORK IN PROGRESS: Three books, *Cumberland Mountain Adventures, Sixty-Six Devotional Studies in Revelation,* and *The Concise Encyclopedia of the Prophetical Scriptures.*

SIDELIGHTS: In his early teens George H. Clement was Canadian champion in the 100-yard and 220-yard dashes; he skied until several years ago, and still skates regularly. *Avocational interests:* Oil painting, astronomy (he owns a 500x telescope), gardening, bird watching, jogging.

BIOGRAPHICAL/CRITICAL SOURCES: Kitchener Record, May 3, 1969; *Hamilton Spectator,* September 19, 1970.

* * *

CLEMENTS, A(rthur) L(eo) 1932-

PERSONAL: Born April 15, 1932, in Brooklyn, N.Y.; married Irma Kellner, November 19, 1955 (divorced, 1976); children: Margaret, Stephen, Michael, Thomas. *Education:* Princeton University, A.B. (cum laude), 1954; University of Connecticut, M.A., 1958; Syracuse University, Ph.D., 1964. *Home address:* Box 351, R.D. 2, Binghamton, N.Y. 13903. *Office:* Department of English, State University of New York, Binghamton, N.Y. 13901.

CAREER: Syracuse University, Syracuse, N.Y., lecturer in English, 1962-64; State University of New York at Binghamton, assistant professor, 1964-69, associate professor of English, 1969—. *Military service:* U.S. Army, 1954-56. *Member:* Modern Language Association of America, American Association of University Professors, Phi Kappa Phi. *Awards, honors:* National Endowment for the Humanities fellowship, 1967-68.

WRITINGS: John Donne's Poetry, Norton, 1966; *The Mystical Poetry of Thomas Traherne,* Harvard University Press, 1969. Contributor to *Thoth, Criticism,* and other journals.

WORK IN PROGRESS: A study of seventeenth-century poetry in relation to medieval contemplative tradition and a novel.

AVOCATIONAL INTERESTS: Gardening, cooking, yoga, walking in woods, and "unpremeditated meditations, trips of the imagination."

* * *

CLEVERDON, (Thomas) Douglas (James) 1903-

PERSONAL: Born January 17, 1903, in Bristol, England; son of Thomas Silcox and Louisa (James) Cleverdon; married Elinor Nest Lewis, June 7, 1944; children: Julia, Lewis, Francis. *Education:* Attended Jesus College, Oxford. *Home:* 27 Barnsbury Sq., London N.1, England. *Agent:* David Higham Associates Ltd., 5-8 Lower John St., London W1R 4HA, England.

CAREER: Proprietor of bookselling and publishing firm, Bristol, England, 1926-39; British Broadcasting Corp., London, England, free-lance actor and writer for West Region, 1935-39, features producer for West Region, 1939-43, features producer in London, 1943-68, mainly working on productions for Third Programme, correspondent in Burma, 1945; publisher, Clover Hill Editions (fine illustrated editions), 1964—; free-lance radio producer, 1968—. Co-director of stage productions of "Under Milk Wood" in Edinburgh and London, 1955, and on Broadway, 1957; compiler and director for numerous recitals of poetry and drama for Apollo Society, Stratford-on-Avon Festivals, Globe Theatre, Cheltenham Festival, and others, 1965—. *Member:* Savile Club, Double Crown Club. *Awards, honors:* Halea Prize for first radio productions of "Under Milk Wood" by Dylan Thomas and "The Face of Violence" by Jacob Bronowski.

WRITINGS: Engravings by Eric Gill, Douglas Cleverdon (the publishing firm), 1929; *The Growth of Milk Wood,* New Directions, 1969; (compiler with Nicolas Barker) *Stanley Morrison, 1889-1967,* Cowell, 1969; (author of introduction) Theocritus, *Six Idyllia,* Chilmark, 1971; (editor and author of introduction) Dylan Thomas, *Under Milk Wood: A Play for Voices,* Folio Society, 1972. Author of numerous radio scripts and play adaptations for British Broadcasting Corp., 1939-68.

WORK IN PROGRESS: His autobiography.

AVOCATIONAL INTERESTS: Book collecting.

BIOGRAPHICAL/CRITICAL SOURCES: Drama, fall, 1969.

* * *

CLEVIN, Joergen 1920-

PERSONAL: Surname is pronounced Cle-*vin;* born April 24, 1920 in Copenhagen, Denmark; son of Peter and Ellen (Larsen) Petersen; married Gudrun Bondgaard, June 27, 1945; children: Helle, Janne, Lotte (all daughters). *Education:* Training College for Teachers, Copenhagen, graduate, 1941. *Religion:* Protestant. *Home:* Marielystvej 14, Copenhagen, Denmark.

CAREER: Teacher at a municipal school in Frederiksberg, Denmark, 1943—, and at Training College for Teachers, Copenhagen, Denmark, 1947—. Producer of television programs for children, 1952—; conductor of his own weekly television program for children, 1967—. *Member:* Danish Authors' Association, Danish Council of Educational Toys.

WRITINGS—Self-illustrated books for children: *Rasmus,* Gyldendal, 1945; *Historien om Brille,* Gyldendal, 1946; *Rasmus faar Besoeg,* Gyldendal, 1948; *Mads og Mikkel,* Gyldendal, 1966; *Jakob og Joakim,* Gyldendal, 1966, translation by Elisabeth Boas published as *Jacob and Joachim,* Benn, 1969, same translation published as *Pete's First Day at School,* Random House, 1973; *Nicki,* Gyldendal, 1966; *Nikkolajsen,* Gyldendal, 1967; *Clevins legebog,* Samleren, 1968; *Kom og Se,* Gyldendal, 1969; *Kom og se Mere,* Gyldendal, 1970; *Jakob og Joakims redningskorps,* Gyldendal, 1971, translation published as *Pete and Johnny to the Rescue,* Random House, 1974. Author of *Kom og loer, Kom og loer mere, Kom og se hvorfan,* and *Kom og se hvordan,* all published by Gyldendal; also writer and illustrator of more than thirty other books for children, including six editions of playbooks, 1963-70, hobby books, school texts, and drawing books.

BIOGRAPHICAL/CRITICAL SOURCES: Times Literary Supplement, June 26, 1969; *Top of the News,* January, 1973.

* * *

CLOUSE, Robert Gordon 1931-

PERSONAL: Born August 26, 1931, in Mansfield, Ohio; son of Garry R. (a teacher) and Marian (Culp) Clouse; married Bonnidell A. Barrows (a professor of psychology), June 18, 1955; children: Gary R., Kenneth D. *Education:* William Jennings Bryan College, B.A., 1954; Grace Theological Seminary, B.D. and M.Div., 1957; University of Iowa, M.A., 1960, Ph.D., 1963. *Politics:* Republican. *Home:* 2122 South 21st St., Terre Haute, Ind. 47802. *Office:* Department of History, Indiana State University, Terre Haute, Ind. 47809.

CAREER: Minister of Church of the Brethren; pastor in Cedar Rapids, Iowa, 1957-60; Indiana State University, Terre Haute, associate professor, 1963-70, professor of history, 1970—. Visiting professor, Indiana University, 1964-65, 1968-69. *Member:* National Fellowship of Brethren Ministers, American Historical Association, American Society

of Church History, Society for Reformation Research, Central Renaissance Conference (president, 1968-69). *Awards, honors:* Grants from Folger Shakespeare Library, 1964, American Philosophical Society, 1968, Institute for Advanced Christian Studies, 1970, Newberry Library, 1972, Lilly Library, 1976.

WRITINGS: (With Robert D. Linder and Richard V. Pigrard) *Protest and Politics: Christianity and Contemporary Affairs,* Attic Press, 1968; (with Peter Toon) *Puritans, the Millennium, and the Future of Israel,* James Clarke, 1970; (with Linder and Pierard) *The Cross and the Flag,* Creation House, 1972; (editor) *The Meaning of the Millennium: Four Views,* Inter-Varsity Press, 1977. Contributor to theology journals.

WORK IN PROGRESS: History of Indiana State University, 1870-1970.

* * *

CLOW, Martha deMey 1932-

PERSONAL: Born November 16, 1932, in Columbus, Ohio; daughter of Charles Frederic (an engineer) and Amelia (Smith) deMey; married John Warner Clow (a certified public accountant), April 10, 1956; children: John Frederic deMey, Gregory Vincent, Amelia Bayley, Guy Rowan, Louise Crankshaw. *Education:* Smith College, B.A., 1954. *Politics:* Libertarian. *Religion:* Episcopalian. *Address:* P.O. Box 1448, Ross, Calif. 94957.

CAREER: Artist for department stores in California, including commercial art for Macy's, 1954-56, and layout work for Joseph Magnin, 1956-57; free-lance artist, 1957—. Designer of playgrounds for Ross (Calif.) School District.

WRITINGS: Starbreed (fiction), Ballantine, 1970.

WORK IN PROGRESS: Alien Earth, a science fiction book; *Neptune's Quest,* a children's play.

* * *

CLUNE, Francis Patrick 1893-1971
(Frank Clune)

November 27, 1893—March 11, 1971; Australian author. Obituaries: *Antiquarian Bookman,* May 17, 1971. (See index for *CA* sketch)

* * *

CLYTUS, John 1929-
(Monongo)

PERSONAL: Born July 18, 1929, in Temple, Okla.; son of Willis (a Baptist minister) and Ruth (Lewis) Clytus; married Gertrude Tucker (a secretary), September 19, 1968; children: Rashid, Radiclani. *Education:* Attended City College of San Francisco, 1952-54, Mexico City College, 1954-55.

MILITARY SERVICE: U.S. Air Force, 1947-51.

WRITINGS: (With Jane Reicker) *Black Man in Red Cuba,* University of Miami Press, 1970.

SIDELIGHTS: John Clytus has lived in Mexico City and Cuba and traveled to Haiti, Paris, and Rome. He told *CA:* "The racial conflict in the U.S. motivated me to write the book. Many Blacks were being misinformed about the racial harmony in communist Cuba; it is a racist country."

BIOGRAPHICAL/CRITICAL SOURCES: National Review, January 12, 1971.†

CNUDDE, Charles F. 1938-

PERSONAL: Born February 12, 1938, in Macomb County, Mich.; son of Francis Alva and Lucille (Neering) Cnudde; married Susan Beamer, June 10, 1961; children: Katherine, Emily. *Education:* University of Michigan, A.B., 1960; University of North Carolina, Ph.D., 1967. *Office:* Department of Political Science, Michigan State University, East Lansing, Mich. 48823.

CAREER: Wayne State University, Detroit, Mich., research associate, 1962-63; University of California, Irvine, assistant professor of political science, 1966-68; University of Wisconsin—Madison, visiting lecturer, 1967, assistant professor, 1968-70, associate professor of political science, 1970-73; Michigan State University, East Lansing, professor of political science and head of department, 1973—. California election analyst, Institute for Social Science Research, University of North Carolina, 1968; member of executive committee, Inter-University Consortium for Political Research, Ann Arbor, Mich., 1968-69. *Member:* American Political Science Association, American Association for Public Opinion Research.

WRITINGS: (Contributor) Robert E. Crew, Jr., editor, *State Politics: A Behavioral Reader,* Wadsworth, 1968; (editor with Deane E. Neubauer and contributor) *Empirical Democratic Theory,* Markham, 1969; *Democracy in the American South,* Markham, 1970. Articles written for *American Political Science Review* have been reprinted in four books; contributor of articles and reviews to other professional journals.

WORK IN PROGRESS: Research on theories and measures of power and influence and on application of econometric methods to political data; an analysis of presidential power and leadership.†

*   *   *

COCHRANE, James D(avid) 1938-

PERSONAL: Born September 4, 1938, in Cherokee, Iowa; son of George T. and Gertrude (Hallbauer) Cochrane. *Education:* Morningside College, B.A., 1960; University of Iowa, M.A., 1961, Ph.D., 1964. *Home:* 801 Henry Clay Ave., Apt. 215, New Orleans, La. 70118. *Office:* Department of Political Science, Tulane University, New Orleans, La. 70118.

CAREER: U.S. House of Representatives, legislative assistant, 1961-62; Brookings Institution, Washington, D.C., fellow, 1964-65; Western Michigan University, Kalamazoo, assistant professor of political science, 1965-66; Tulane University of Louisiana, New Orleans, assistant professor, 1966-68, associate professor, 1968-74, professor of political science, 1974—. *Member:* American Political Science Association.

WRITINGS: The Politics of Regional Integration: The Central American Case, Tulane Studies in Political Science, Tulane University, 1969. Contributor to professional journals.

*   *   *

CODY, John J. 1930-

PERSONAL: Born June 10, 1930, in La Crosse, Wis.; son of James D. (a factory worker) and Mary (Murphy) Cody; married Donna Morgan, August 20, 1956; children: Lisa Marie, Mary Patrice, Thomas John, Timothy James. *Education:* Wisconsin State College—La Crosse (now University of Wisconsin—La Crosse), B.S., 1956; University of Iowa,

M.A., 1959; University of Wisconsin, Ph.D., 1961. *Religion:* Roman Catholic. *Home:* 201 Rod Lane, Carbondale, Ill. 62901. *Office:* Guidance Department, Southern Illinois University, Carbondale, Ill. 62901.

CAREER: Indiana University, Bloomington, assistant professor of education, 1961-65; Southern Illinois University, Carbondale, professor of guidance and educational psychology, 1965—, chairman of department, 1971—.

WRITINGS: (With Frances Kelly) *Educational Psychology,* C. E. Merrill, 1969.

*   *   *

COFFIN, Arthur B. 1929-

PERSONAL: Born April 24, 1929, in Berlin, N.H.; son of Alfred Chandler and Dora (Bonneau) Coffin; married Gertrude Dupuis (a bank teller), January 10, 1956; children: Cathleen Ann. *Education:* University of New Hampshire, B.A., 1951; Boston College, M.A., 1958; University of Wisconsin, Ph.D., 1965. *Religion:* Roman Catholic. *Home:* 908 South Willson St., Bozeman, Mont. 59715. *Office:* Department of English, Montana State University, Bozeman, Mont. 59715.

CAREER: St. Vincent College, Latrobe, Pa., instructor in English, 1958-60; Washington State University, Pullman, assistant professor, 1965-71, associate professor of English, 1971-72; Montana State University, Bozeman, professor of English and department head, 1972—. *Military service:* U.S. Navy, 1951-56. U.S. Naval Reserve, 1956—; present rank, lieutenant commander. *Member:* Modern Language Association of America, Association of Departments of English, Rocky Mountain Modern Language Association.

WRITINGS: Robinson Jeffers: Poet of Inhumanism, University of Wisconsin Press, 1971. Contributor to *Encyclopedia of World Literature in the 20th Century,* Ungar, 1968.

WORK IN PROGRESS: Work in structuralist and phenomenological criticism with respect to poets such as Wallace Stevens, Robert Lowell, Theodore Roethke, Jeffers, and others.

*   *   *

COHEN, Bernard Lande 1902-

PERSONAL: Born June 6, 1902, in Montreal, Quebec, Canada; son of Judah Isaac and Rose (Lande) Cohen; married Alyce Shapiro, December, 1942; children: Richard, Susannah (Mrs. Charles Dalfen). *Education:* McGill University, degree in arts, 1924, and degree in law, 1927. *Home:* 5160 Macdonald Ave., Apt. 509, Montreal, Quebec, Canada.

CAREER: Insurance broker, author, and lawyer. Active since early youth in the Zionist organization of Canada. *Awards, honors:* First prize, Province of Quebec Literary Awards, 1954, for *The Case for Conservatism.*

WRITINGS: The Case for Conservatism, Exposition, 1952; *Introduction to the New Economics,* Philosophical Library, 1959; *Law Without Order: Capital Punishment and the Liberals,* Arlington House, 1970; *Jews among the Nations: A Political and Economic Survey,* Philosophical Library, 1977.

SIDELIGHTS: Bernard Lande Cohen began to write during the Hitler-Stalin era by contributing a number of articles to the *North American Review* on the international affairs of that time. He told *CA* that "the trend in all my writings, economic, political, and legal, has been in the direction of anti-radicalism. My first two books contain criticism of Marxist Socialism; but they deal more broadly with economics generally. As an economist I am to be associated with the rejection of professorial economics, non-Socialist as well as Socialist. In place of the traditional preoccupation with 'schools' and 'economic systems' I have attempted to explain the man-made world in terms of the 'cellular theory,' which has, for well over a century, been accepted as proven in the fields of botany and zoology. I have attempted to adapt this interpretation of the natural world to the artificial world of man's creation. The entire world-wide apparatus of production, transportation, marketing, and finance, despite variability as to time, place, and function, is conceived as being made up of a vast collectivity of 'cells,' all having a basic identity, and corresponding somewhat to the cells of plant and animal organisms.

"In *Law Without Order* I revert to my earlier training as a lawyer. It is an extensive defence of capital punishment, taking note of . . . objections to the practice. . . . The book goes on to criticize a number of features of criminal procedure currently accepted as sacrosanct, including the Fifth Amendment, trial by jury, and defence of insanity. The book ends with a proposal for curbing the propensity of the courts to overturn legislation."

*　　*　　*

COHEN, Edgar H. 1913-

PERSONAL: Born October 28, 1913, in Montreal, Quebec, Canada; son of Abraham Zebulon (a merchant and manufacturer) and Malca (Vineberg) Cohen; married Ruth Goldberg, April 3, 1949; children: Lenore, Judith, Andrew. *Education:* McGill University, B.A., 1934, graduate study, 1969-70. *Religion:* Jewish. *Home:* 4817 Cedar Crescent, Montreal, Quebec, Canada. *Agent:* A. Watkins, Inc., 77 Park Ave., New York, N.Y. 10016.

CAREER: L. Cohen & Son Ltd. (fuel firm), Montreal, Quebec, president, 1937-61; F. A. Price Coal & Oil Ltd., Montreal, secretary-treasurer, 1937—; Yarco Building Corp., Montreal, president, 1950—. Real estate consultant in Montreal, 1970—. Former national director of Oil Heat Institute of Canada; former chairman, Better Business Bureau, fuel division. *Member:* International P.E.N. (treasurer, Canadian chapter).

WRITINGS: Mademoiselle Libertine: A Portrait of Ninon de Lenclos, Houghton, 1970. Contributor to *Canadian Forum, Jewish Frontier,* and *Montreal Star.*

WORK IN PROGRESS: A novel, *Don't Marry Money But . . .*

SIDELIGHTS: Edgar Cohen has made sixteen trips to Europe. He cites his chief literary influences as the Bible, Shakespeare, Keats, G. B. Shaw, Thomas Mann, Saul Bellow and told *CA* that he "respect[s] Bertrand Russell, Albert Schweitzer, and Dr. Benjamin Spock." *Avocational interests:* Sailing, skiing, travel, Romanesque, Gothic and Renaissance churches, walled cities, history, civil rights, World Federalism, chamber music, and literature.

BIOGRAPHICAL/CRITICAL SOURCES: Best Sellers, November 15, 1970.

*　　*　　*

COHEN, Jozef 1921-

PERSONAL: Born July 21, 1921, in Brookline, Mass.; son of David (a grocer) and Dora (Levin) Cohen; married Huguette Schachnovitch, July 31, 1958. *Education:* University of Chicago, B.S., 1942; Cornell University, Ph.D., 1945. *Politics:* Democrat. *Religion:* Jewish. *Home:* 303 Burkwood Ct. W., Urbana, Ill. 61801. *Office:* 81 Psychology Building, University of Illinois at Urbana-Champaign, Urbana, Ill. 61820.

CAREER: University of Illinois at Urbana-Champaign, Urbana, assistant professor, 1947-51, currently professor of psychology. *Member:* American Psychological Association (fellow), American Association for the Advancement of Science (fellow), Psychonomic Society, Sigma Xi.

WRITINGS: "Eyewitness Series in Psychology," Rand McNally, 1969-71, volume titles include: *Complex Learning* (two books), 1969; *Operant Behavior and Operant Conditioning,* 1969; *Personality Assessment,* 1969; *Sensation and Perception,* 1969; *Secondary Motivation* (two books), 1970; *Thinking,* 1971. Contributor to *Encyclopaedia Britannica* and to journals.

*　　*　　*

COHEN, Robert 1938-

PERSONAL: Born July 14, 1938; son of Lester Ellis (an attorney) and Lydia (Goldblatt) Cohen; married Lorna Buck, November 13, 1972; children: (previous marriage) Michael Geoffrey. *Education:* University of California, Berkeley, B.A., 1961; Yale University, D.F.A., 1965. *Home:* 1360 Bluebird Canyon Dr., Laguna Beach, Calif. 92651. *Agent:* Robert Freedman, Harold Freedman Brandt & Brandt Dramatic Department, Inc., 101 Park Ave., New York, N.Y. 10017. *Office:* School of Fine Arts, University of California, Irvine, Calif. 92664.

CAREER: Connecticut College, New London, drama director, 1964-65; University of California, Irvine, 1965—, began as assistant professor, currently professor of drama and chairman of drama department. Actor and director.

WRITINGS: Giraudoux: Three Faces of Destiny, University of Chicago Press, 1969; *Acting Professionally,* Mayfield, 1972, 2nd edition, Barnes & Noble, 1976; (with John Harrop) *Creative Play Direction,* Prentice-Hall, 1974; *Acting Power,* Mayfield, 1977. Contributor to *Educational Theatre Journal, Drama Review,* and *Los Angeles Times.*

*　　*　　*

COHEN, S. Alan 1933-

PERSONAL: Born April 22, 1933, in Boston, Mass.; son of Samuel and Bessie Cohen; married Rita Palan, December 21, 1952; children: Shelley Ilene, Stuart Benjamin, Jerri. *Education:* Suffolk University, B.S., 1953; Harvard University, Ed.M., 1956; graduate study at New School for Social Research, 1956-58, and Rutgers University, 1958-61; Boston University, Ed.D., 1965. *Politics:* Democrat. *Religion:* Jewish. *Home:* 422 Main St., Fort Lee, N.J. *Office:* 201 East 50th St., New York, N.Y. 10002.

CAREER: Elementary teacher, 1956-61; Jersey City State College, Jersey City, N.J., assistant professor of education and director of reading laboratory, 1961-62; Mobilization for Youth, New York City, director of reading, 1963-65, director of materials development unit, 1964-65; Center for Urban Education, New York City, associate director of research project on development of disadvantaged preschoolers, 1966-67; Ferkauf Graduate School of Humanities and Social Sciences, New York City, associate professor in department of curriculum and instruction and director of Reading and Language Arts Center, 1965—. Consultant to public and private groups, 1962—, including U.S. Office of

Education, 1965-67, and Job Corps, 1965-66; consulting education editor, Random House. Vice-president of Urban Ed Inc. *Awards, honors:* U.S. Office of Education research grant, 1966-67.

WRITINGS: Teach Them All to Read: Theories, Methods, and Materials for Teaching the Disadvantaged, Random House, 1969. Writer of educational materials.

Contributor: M. Jerry Weiss, editor, *An English Teacher's Reader,* Odyssey, 1962; A. J. Reiss, editor, *Schools in a Changing Society,* Free Press, 1966; *Recreation and Socialization for the Brain Injured Child,* New Jersey Association for Brain Injured Children, 1966. Also contributor to *Reading in the Elementary School,* Odyssey, and *Teaching Reading to a Linguistically Different Child,* Harcourt. Contributor of articles to education journals.

*   *   *

COHEN, Stanley 1928-

PERSONAL: Born March 3, 1928, in Shelbyville, Tenn.; son of Jacob (a merchant) and Estelle (Elterman) Cohen; married Marilyn Goodman (a schoolteacher), June 18, 1950; children: Edward, Jodi, Stephen. *Education:* Vanderbilt University, B.E. (chemical engineering), 1948; M.S., 1950. *Religion:* Jewish. *Home:* 322 Pine Tree Dr., Orange, Conn. 06477. *Agent:* Whitehall, Hadlyme & Smith, 140 East 57th St., New York, N.Y. 10019.

CAREER: May Hosiery Mills, Nashville, Tenn., process development, 1950-52; Oak Ridge National Laboratory, Oak Ridge, Tenn., nuclear research engineer, 1952-57; Olin Corp., supervisor of product development in Packaging Division, New Haven, Conn., 1958-64, product manager, Plastics Division, Stamford, Conn., 1964—. *Member:* Society of Plastics Engineers, Scientific Research Society of America, Mystery Writers of America (member of board of directors, 1972-76), Writer's Guild of America, Authors Guild, Mensa. *Awards, honors:* Olin Research Award for patented plastics development, 1969.

WRITINGS: Taking Gary Feldman, Putnam, 1970 (published in England as *The Abduction,* Constable, 1971); *The Diane Game,* Stein & Day, 1973; *Tell Us, Jerry Silver,* Bobbs-Merrill, 1973.

Work represented in anthologies, including *Every Crime in the Book,* edited by R. L. Fish, Putnam, 1975, and *Best Detective Stories of the Year—1975,* edited by Allen Hubin, Dutton, 1975. Contributor of short stories to *Ellery Queen Mystery Magazine, Mystery Monthly, Alfred Hitchcock Mystery Magazine;* also contributor of articles to *Nuclear Science, Modern Packaging,* and other periodicals.

WORK IN PROGRESS: A work about police procedures dealing with a large caper in New York City, for Putnam.

SIDELIGHTS: Stanley Cohen, the holder of several patents in his career field, began writing as a hobby about ten years ago, joined a creative writing workshop, "wrote and sent out countless short stories, placed three of them." Since he sold his first novel, most of his writing time goes into novels. *Gary Feldman* is under option by an independent film producer.

*   *   *

COHN, Stanley H(arold) 1922-

PERSONAL: Born December 2, 1922, in Portland, Ore.; son of Edward E. (a salesman) and Ethel (Enkeles) Cohn. *Education:* Reed College, B.A., 1947; University of Chi-

cago, M.A., 1949, Ph.D., 1952. *Home:* 5 Riverside Dr., Apt. 307, Binghamton, N.Y. 13905. *Office:* Department of Economics, State University of New York at Binghamton, Binghamton, N.Y. 13901.

CAREER: International Monetary Fund, Washington, D.C., economist, 1950-51; U.S. Government, Washington, D.C., economist, 1951-63; Research Analysis Corp., McLean, Va., economist, 1963-66; State University of New York at Binghamton, professor of economics, 1966—. Lecturer, University of Maryland, 1964-66. Consultant, Research Analysis Corp., 1966, U.S. Bureau of Labor Statistics, 1972-73, Stanford Research Institute, 1973—. *Military service:* U.S. Army, 1943-46; became sergeant. *Member:* American Economic Association, Association for Comparative Economic Studies (member of executive committee, 1971—), Association for the Study of Soviet-Type Economics.

WRITINGS: The Gross National Product in the Soviet Union: Comparative Growth Rates, U.S. Government Printing Office, 1963; (contributor) Peter Gutmann, editor, *Economic Growth: An American Problem,* Prentice-Hall, 1964; *Derivation of 1959 Value-added Weights for Originating Sectors of Soviet Gross National Product,* Research Analysis Corp., 1966; (contributor) Vladimir Treml, editor, *The Development of the Soviet Economy: Plan and Performance,* Praeger, 1968.

(Contributor) *The Economic Burden of Soviet Defense Outlays,* U.S. Government Printing Office, 1970; (contributor) Morris Bornstein and Daniel R. Fusfeld, editors, *The Soviet Economy: A Book of Readings,* Irwin, 1970; *Economic Development in the Soviet Union,* Heath, 1970; (contributor) Vladimir Treml, editor, *Soviet Economic Statistics,* Duke University Press, 1972; (contributor) *Economic Burden of Soviet Defense Expenditures: An Econometric Analysis,* U.S. Government Printing Office, 1973; (contributor) Ellen Mickiewicz, editor, *Handbook of Soviet Social Science Data,* Free Press, 1973; (contributor) *Deficiencies in Soviet Investment Policies and the Technological Imperative,* U.S. Government Printing Office, 1976; (contributor) *Ukrainian Economic Growth in a National Perspective,* Praeger, 1977. Contributor to *Bulletin* of the Association for the Study of Soviet-Type Economics, *Michigan Business Review, Review of Income and Wealth,* and *Soviet Studies.*

WORK IN PROGRESS: Estimation of Military Durables Procurement from Machinery Production and Sales Data; Rationality of Soviet Investment Maintenance, Retirement, and Replacement Policies.

*   *   *

COHON, Baruch J(oseph) 1926-
(Barry Cohon)

PERSONAL: Born April 28, 1926, in Chicago, Ill.; son of Samuel S. (a rabbi and professor) and A. Irma (Reinhart) Cohon; married Claire Stollman (a teacher), August 27, 1950; children: Rachel, Deborah, Samuel, Jonathan. *Education:* Attended Cincinnati College of Music (now part of University of Cincinnati), 1943, 1946-47; University of California, Los Angeles, B.A., 1950; University of Judaism, graduate study, 1969-70. *Politics:* Independent. *Home:* 6500 Whitworth, Los Angeles, Calif. 90035.

CAREER: Rabbinical ordination, 1969; cantor in synagogues in Pasadena, Calif., Los Angeles, Calif., and Hollywood, Calif., 1947-62; free-lance writer, story editor, and production manager for various motion picture studios in Hollywood, 1953-62; State of California, Los Angeles, member of Department of Public Information, 1962-65; Valley Beth Israel, North Hollywood, Calif., cantor, 1962-73; Temple Emanuel, Beverly Hills, Calif., cantor, 1973—. Organizer and teacher of cantorial classes, Hebrew Union College-Jewish Institute of Religion, Los Angeles, 1953-54; instructor, Rhea Hirsch School of Education, 1969—; part-time faculty member, University of Judaism, 1960-70. Music coordinator, Jewish Centers Association of Los Angeles, 1968-70; founder and proprietor of Shalom Concert Bureau, Los Angeles. Free-lance concert and lecture appearances. *Military service:* U.S. Navy, 1943-46.

MEMBER: American Society of Composers, Authors and Publishers (A.S.C.A.P.), Writer's Guild of America (voluntary withdrawal), Cantor's Assembly. *Awards, honors:* Cantorial Certification from Hebrew Union College-Jewish Institute of Religion, 1963; Cantorial Commission from Cantor's Assembly, 1970.

WRITINGS—Books: (Musical editor) A. Z. Idelsohn, *The Jewish Song Book,* Publications for Judaism, 1951; (editor) *Jewish Existence in an Open Society,* two volumes, Ward Ritchie Press, 1970.

Musicals and television scripts: "Stars Over Shnipishok" (musical), first produced in Los Angeles at Jewish Center Association, 1960; "A Melody Reborn" (television script), for CBS "Lamp Unto My Feet" series, 1960; "Howdy, Miss Rosen" (musical), first produced in Los Angeles at Jewish Centers Association, 1961; "Bialik, Poet of the People" (television script), for CBS "Insight" series, 1962; "The Great Yarid" (musical), first produced in Los Angeles at Temple Isaiah, 1967; "Under the Canopy" (musical), first produced in Los Angeles at Westside Center Theatre, 1968; "Book of Life" (television script), for KNBC-TV, 1970.

Cantatas: *Let There Be Light* (first performed by Cincinnati Symphony Orchestra, 1954), Publications for Judaism, 1962; *I Never Set Foot on the Ladder,* V.B.I., 1965; *Beware the Avenger,* V.B.I., 1965; *Waiting for Moses,* Los Angeles Bureau of Jewish Education, 1966; *Not in Heaven,* Los Angeles Bureau of Jewish Education, 1967.

Synagogue music: *Avodas Simchoh* (title means "Service of Joy"), Publications for Judaism, 1960; *I Give This House,* V.B.I., 1964.

Recordings: "We Wish you Love," SCB Records, 1973; "The Seventh Day," Elektra, 1977. Also author of many segments of "Cisco Kid," "Sea Hunt," "Maverick," and other series under pseudonym Barry Cohon.

WORK IN PROGRESS: New songs and script for a live production for an upcoming tour.

SIDELIGHTS: Baruch J. Cohon told *CA:* "I have a life-long urge to reach people, hopefully to 'turn them on' to some of the great adventure of daily life. I find that kind of adventure in my Jewish heritage, and I know that others can find it in their own identity, once they've established it. I express my adventure—my climb up the mountain that has no top—in words and music."

* * *

COLE, Michelle 1940-

PERSONAL: Born August 21, 1940, in Los Angeles, Calif.; daughter of Henry and Joyce (Raskin) Goldman; married Laurence S. Cole (a writer and director of a youth organization), August 31, 1959. *Education:* Attended University of California, Santa Barbara, 1958, and University of California, Los Angeles, 1959.

CAREER: Playboy Magazine, New York City, assistant men's fashion director, 1962-67; Lower East Side Action Project (L.E.A.P.), New York City, co-director, beginning 1962, director of L.E.A.P. school, beginning 1968.

WRITINGS: (With Stuart Black) *Checking It Out: Some Lower East Side Kids Discover the Rest of America,* Dial, 1971; (contributor) *Educational Psychology,* CRM Books, 1971; (contributor) *HiSchool,* Simon & Schuster, 1971.

WORK IN PROGRESS: Researching alternative methods of education, documentation of an alternative high school, changing laws regarding children, designing children's environments.

AVOCATIONAL INTERESTS: Designing environmental furniture called "portadorms," to be marketed to large institutions.††

* * *

COLE, Stephen 1941-

PERSONAL: Born June 1, 1941, in New York, N.Y.; son of Richard (an actor) and Sylvia (Dym) Cole; married Ann H. Brawerman (a sociologist), June 4, 1969. *Education:* Columbia University, B.A. (magna cum laude), 1962, Ph.D., 1967. *Home:* 1 Evans Ct., Setauket, N.Y. 11733. *Office:* Department of Sociology, State University of New York, Stony Brook, N.Y. 11790.

CAREER: State University of New York at Stony Brook, assistant professor, 1968-70, associate professor, 1970-72, professor of sociology, 1972—. *Member:* American Sociological Association, American Association for the Advancement of Science, Eastern Sociological Society, Phi Beta Kappa. *Awards, honors:* Ford Foundation faculty research grant, 1971-72.

WRITINGS: The Unionization of Teachers: A Case Study of the U.F.T., Praeger, 1969; *Social Stratification in Science,* University of Chicago Press, 1973; *The Sociological Method,* Markham, 1972, 2nd edition, Rand McNally, 1976; *The Sociological Orientation,* Rand McNally, 1975.

* * *

COLEMAN, Clayton W(ebster) 1901-
(Webster Smith)

PERSONAL: Born November 26, 1901, in Baldwin, La.; son of Sidney Horace (a lumberman) and Sara Elizabeth (Petrie) Coleman; married Maurice Benton, June 24, 1937; children: Elizabeth Benton, Clayton W., Jr., *Politics:* Democrat. *Religion:* Episcopalian.

CAREER: Louisiana Public Service Commission, Baton Rouge, executive secretary, 1932-65; Louisiana State Science Foundation, Baton Rouge, director, 1965—. *Military service:* U.S. Army, World War I. *Member:* City Club of Baton Rouge.

WRITINGS: (Under pseudonym Webster Smith) *The Kingfish,* Putnam, 1932; *Timbalier,* Dell, 1969; (under pseudonym Webster Smith) *The Farnese Hours,* Braziller, 1976.

WORK IN PROGRESS: A novel.†

* * *

COLEMAN-NORTON, P(aul) R(obinson) 1898-1971

February 28, 1898—May 9, 1971; American classicist, linguist, and author of books on Roman law. Obituaries: *New York Times,* May 11, 1971.

COLES, John M(orton) 1930-

PERSONAL: Born March 25, 1930, in Woodstock, Ontario, Canada; son of John L. (an investment broker) and Alice (Brown) Coles; married Mona Shiach, December 20, 1958; children: Joanne, Steven, Alison, Ian. *Education:* University of Toronto, B.A., 1952; Cambridge University, diploma, 1957; University of Edinburgh, Ph.D., 1959. *Home:* 89 Long Rd., Cambridge, England. *Office:* Department of Archaeology, Cambridge University, Cambridge, England.

CAREER: Cambridge University, Cambridge, England, lecturer in archaeology and anthropology, 1960-75, reader in European prehistory, 1976—.

WRITINGS: (Editor with D. A. Simpson) *Studies in Ancient Europe: Essays Presented to Stuart Piggott,* Leicester University Press, 1968, Humanities, 1969; (with E. S. Higgs) *The Archaeology of Early Man,* Praeger, 1969; *Field Archaeology in Britain,* Methuen, 1972; *Archaeology by Experiment,* Scribner, 1973. Contributor to *Proceedings* of Prehistoric Society, *Proceedings* of Society of Antiquaries of Scotland, *Antiquity,* and other journals. Editor, *Proceedings* of the Prehistoric Society, and Somerset Levels *Papers.*

WORK IN PROGRESS: With A. F. Harding, *The Bronze Age in Europe,* for Methuen.

*   *   *

COLLINGWOOD, Charles (Cummings) 1917-

PERSONAL: Born June 4, 1917, in Three Rivers, Mich.; son of George Harris (a conservationist) and Jean (Cummings) Collingwood; married Louise Allbritton, May 13, 1946. *Education:* Deep Springs College, student, 1935-37; Cornell University, A.B., 1939; New College, Oxford, further study, 1939-40. *Agent:* International Famous Agency, Inc., 1301 Avenue of the Americas, New York, N.Y. 10019. *Office:* CBS News, 524 West 57th St., New York, N.Y. 10019.

CAREER: United Press, war correspondent in London, England, 1939-40; Columbia Broadcasting System News, war correspondent in Europe, 1941-46, United Nations correspondent, 1946-47, West Coast correspondent, 1947-49, White House correspondent, 1949-51, radio and television commentator, 1952—, chief of News Bureau, New York, N.Y., 1957-60, chief foreign correspondent, 1966—. Special assistant to director Averell Harriman, Mutual Security Agency, 1952.

MEMBER: Association of Radio News Analysts, Institute of World Affairs (member of board of directors), National Press Club (Washington, D.C.), Century Association (New York), Garrick Club and Savile Club (both London). *Awards, honors:* Headliners Award, 1942, 1948; George Foster Peabody Award for best foreign reporting, 1943, and for White House tour with Mrs. John Kennedy, 1963; Alexander Hadden Medal for promoting world understanding, 1954; English-Speaking Union Award for promoting better understanding, 1957; Chevalier, Legion of Honor (France); Commander, Order of the British Empire.

WRITINGS: The Defector (novel), Harper, 1970. Contributor to national magazines.

AVOCATIONAL INTERESTS: Archaeology, especially of pre-Columbian America, Southeast Asia, and the Middle East; collecting modern painting and sculpture.

BIOGRAPHICAL/CRITICAL SOURCES: Washington Post, February 7, 1970.

COLLINS, David 1940-

PERSONAL: Born February 29, 1940, in Marshalltown, Iowa; son of Raymond A. (an educator) and Mary Elizabeth (Brecht) Collins. *Education:* Western Illinois University, B.S., 1962, M.S., 1966. *Politics:* Democrat. *Religion:* Roman Catholic. *Home:* 3403 45th St., Moline, Ill. 61265. *Office:* Woodrow Wilson Junior High School, 1301 48th St., Moline, Ill. 61265.

CAREER: Woodrow Wilson Junior High School, Moline, Ill., teacher of English, 1962—. President, Friends of the Moline Public Library, 1965-67. *Member:* National Education Association (life member), Illinois Education Association, Illinois Congress of Parents and Teachers (life member), Illinois State Historical Society (life member), Children's Reading Roundtable, Society of Children's Book Writers, Author's Guild, Juvenile Forum (president, 1975—), Writers' Studio (president, 1968-72), Mississippi Valley Writers Conference (founder; director, 1974—), Blackhawk Division of Teachers of English (president, 1967-68), Quad City Writers Club, Quad City Arts Council, Phi Delta Kappa, Kappa Delta Pi, Delta Sigma Pi. *Awards, honors:* Outstanding Juvenile Writer Award, Indiana University, 1970; Judson College Writing Award, 1971; Writer of the Year Award, Writers' Studio, 1971; Writer of the Year Award, Quad City Writers Club, 1972; Western Illinois University Alumni Achievement Award, 1973.

WRITINGS—Juvenile: *Kim Soo and His Tortoise,* Lion Press, 1970; *Great American Nurses,* Messner, 1971; *Walt Disney's Surprise Christmas Present,* Broadman, 1971; *Linda Richards, America's First Trained Nurse,* Garrard, 1973; *Harry S. Truman, People's President,* Garrard, 1975; *Football Running Backs,* Garrard, 1976; *Abraham Lincoln,* Mott Media, 1976; *Illinois Women: Born to Serve,* DeSaulniers, 1976; *Joshua Poole Hated School,* Broadman, 1977; *Charles Lindbergh, Flying Ace,* Garrard, 1977; *George Washington Carver,* Mott Media, 1977; *The Spirit of Giving,* Mott Media, in press. Contributor to *Plays, Modern Woodman, Junior Discoveries, Catholic Boy, Catholic Miss, Vista,* and other periodicals.

WORK IN PROGRESS: Research on great American doctors, for a collective biography.

SIDELIGHTS: David Collins stated: "Children are curious, their minds open and flexible. A child is eager to enjoy new adventures. Anyone choosing to write for young readers faces an exciting challenge and a great responsibility. He must remember that his words and ideas may have a lasting effect on his reader's imagination, personality, even his entire character. Young readers deserve the best in reading. . . .

"Why did I decide to write for children? Probably because some of my best childhood adventures were discovered in books. . . . I owe a tremendous debt to the realm of children's literature. Perhaps if I can offer something worthwhile to young readers, part of that debt will be repaid."

*   *   *

COLSON, Howard P(aul) 1910-

PERSONAL: Born April 18, 1910, in Moline, Ill.; son of Philip E. (a postal clerk) and Minnie (Johnson) Colson; married Mary Wilder, August 16, 1934; children: Rosemary, Rachel (Mrs. Robert W. Gilmer, Jr.), William. *Education:* Augustana College, Rock Island, Ill., A.B., 1931; Southern Baptist Theological Seminary, Th.M., 1934, Ph.D., 1938. *Home:* 2919 Compton Rd., Nashville, Tenn. 37215. *Office:*

Department of Seminary Extension, Southern Baptist Convention, Nashville, Tenn.

CAREER: Baptist clergyman; pastor in Indiana, Tennessee, and Missouri, 1934-49; University of Missouri, Columbia, professor, holding Baptist Chair of Bible, 1948-49; Southern Baptist Convention, Nashville, Tenn., Sunday School Board, editor-in-chief of Sunday school lesson courses, 1952-64, director of editorial services, 1964-67, editorial services staff consultant, 1967-69, editorial secretary, 1969-75, Department of Seminary Extension, assistant to director, 1975—.

WRITINGS: Living in the Faith, Broadman, 1954; *Preparing to Teach the Bible,* Convention Press, 1959; *The Practical Message of James,* Broadman, 1969; (with Raymond M. Rigdon) *Understanding Your Church's Curriculum,* Broadman, 1969; (with Robert J. Dean) *The Letter to the Galatians: Freedom through Christ,* Convention Press, 1972; *I Recommend the Bible,* Convention Press, 1976. Writer of articles and curriculum units for Southern Baptist Sunday School Board.

*   *   *

COLWELL, Eileen (Hilda) 1904-

PERSONAL: Born June 16, 1904, in Robin Hoods Bay, Yorkshire, England; daughter of Richard Harold (a Methodist minister) and Gertrude (Mason) Colwell. *Education:* University College School of Librarianship, London, Diploma of Librarianship, 1924. *Religion:* Christian. *Home:* 60 Priory Rd., Loughborough, Leicester, England.

CAREER: Children's librarian in Bolton, Lancaster, England, 1924-26; Borough of Hendon, London, England, children's librarian, 1926-67; Loughborough School of Librarianship, Loughborough, Leicester, England, lecturer on children's literature, 1967-69. *Member:* Youth Libraries Group of Library Association (founding member; chairman at various times), International Federation of Library Associations. *Awards, honors:* Member, Order of British Empire, 1965, for service to children in libraries and in the book world; honorary Doctor of Literature, 1975.

WRITINGS: How I Became a Librarian, Nelson, 1956; *Eleanor Farjeon: A Monograph,* Bodley Head, 1961; (editor) *Tell Me a Story,* Penguin, 1962; (editor and contributor) *Storyteller's Choice,* Bodley Head, 1963; (editor and contributor) *Tell Me Another Story,* Penguin, 1964; (editor and contributor) *A Second Storyteller's Choice,* Bodley Head, 1965; (editor and contributor) *Hallowe'en Acorn,* Bodley Head, 1966; (editor and contributor) *Time for a Story,* Penguin, 1967; (editor and contributor) *Youngest Storybook,* Bodley Head, 1967; (editor) *The Princess Splendour,* Longmans, Green, 1969; (editor and contributor) *Bad Boys,* Penguin, 1972; *Roundabout and Long Ago,* Longman Young Books, 1972; *Tales from the Islands,* Kestrel Books, 1975; (editor and contributor) *The Magic Umbrella,* Bodley Head, 1976. Contributor to professional library and reviewing journals.

WORK IN PROGRESS: Another Puffin collection of stories; and a possible autobiography.

SIDELIGHTS: Eileen Colwell told *CA:* "My main interests throughout my life have been children and their natural complement, storytelling. I became a children's librarian at a time when children's libraries were rare in this country, with the resolve that as many children as possible should have an opportunity to know books, not just *any* books but the best I could find. . . . Nearly everything interesting in my life has been bound up with my chosen career. I read manuscripts for publishers, review books and travel about the country lecturing on children's literature and storytelling. These activities have taken me to most European countries and across the Atlantic and to Japan and, most important of all, brought me valued friendships with people of like interests.''

BIOGRAPHICAL/CRITICAL SOURCES: Nancy Larrick, *A Parent's Guide to Children's Reading,* 3rd edition, Doubleday, 1969.

*   *   *

COMPTON, James V(incent) 1928-

PERSONAL: Born July 5, 1928, in Perth Amboy, N.J.; son of Lewis (assistant Secretary of the Navy under Franklin D. Roosevelt) and Beatrice (Vincent) Compton. *Education:* Princeton University, B.A., 1950; University of Chicago, M.A., 1952; graduate study at Cornell University, 1952-53, University of Munich, 1954-55, and University of Heidelberg, 1955-56; University of London, Ph.D., 1964. *Politics:* Liberal Democrat. *Religion:* Roman Catholic. *Home:* 170 Diamond St., San Francisco, Calif. 94114. *Office:* History Department, San Francisco State University, 1600 Holloway Ave., San Francisco, Calif. 94132.

CAREER: University of Maryland, European Division, Germany, lecturer in history and government, 1955-61; University of London, London, England, lecturer in history and international relations in extramural department, 1961-63; University of Edinburgh, Edinburgh, Scotland, lecturer in American history and chairman of program in North American studies, 1964-68; Trinity College, Hartford, Conn., assistant professor of history, 1968-69; San Francisco State University, associate professor, 1969-72, professor of history, 1972—. Visiting professor, Doshisha University, Kyoto, Japan. Consultant, British Broadcasting Co., and Southwest German Radio. *Member:* British Association for American Studies, Organization of American Historians. *Awards, honors:* Konrad Adenauer fellowship in international affairs at University of Munich, 1954-55.

WRITINGS: The Swastika and the Eagle: Hitler, the United States, and the Origins of World War II, Houghton, 1967; (editor) *America and the Origins of the Cold War,* Houghton, 1971; (contributing editor with O. Bullitt) *For the President: Personal and Secret,* Houghton, 1972; *The New Deal,* Viking, 1972.

WORK IN PROGRESS: Contributing editor of *Ordeals of Loyalty and Betrayal: Hiss, Chambers, Nixon;* and *The Politics of Obsession: Anti-Communism, Civil Liberty and The Cold War in America, 1945-55.*

SIDELIGHTS: After fourteen years' residence abroad, James Compton has "rather a mid-Atlantic mentality." "Am fascinated," he writes, "with general problems of America in world perspective. . . . I do not subscribe to any scheme or philosophy of history and do not believe it [history] can repeat itself, though parallels are frequently useful." He has traveled extensively in Europe, Africa, the Middle and Far East. In addition to fluency in German, he has a fair knowledge of French and Spanish.

AVOCATIONAL INTERESTS: Music, folklore, linguistics, natural science, swimming, horseback riding, mountain climbing.

BIOGRAPHICAL/CRITICAL SOURCES: Book Week, July 2, 1967; *New York Times Book Review,* July 2, 1967; *Atlantic Monthly,* August, 1967; *New Yorker,* September 2, 1967; *New York Review,* February 15, 1968.

CONAN DOYLE, Adrian Malcolm 1910-1970

November 19, 1910—June 3, 1970; British travel writer and author of books on the works of his father (Sir Arthur Conan Doyle). Obituaries: *Variety,* June 10, 1970. (See index for *CA* sketch)

* * *

CONANT, Ralph W(endell) 1926-

PERSONAL: Born September 7, 1926, in Hope, Me.; son of Earle Raymond (a business executive) and Margaret (Long) Conant; married Audrey Karl (a teacher), August 27, 1950; children: Beverlie Elaine, Lisa Audrey, Jonathan Arnold. *Education:* University of Vermont, B.A., 1949; University of Chicago, M.A., 1954, Ph.D., 1959. *Politics:* Democrat. *Religion:* Unitarian. *Address:* Box 104, North Vassalboro, Me. 04962. *Office:* Office of the President, Shimer College, Mt. Carroll, Ill. 61053.

CAREER: Staff associate, National Municipal League, 1957-59; director, Citizens for Michigan, 1959-60; University of Denver, Denver, Colo., assistant professor, 1960-62; Joint Center for Urban Studies, Massachusetts Institute of Technology and Harvard University, Cambridge, Mass., assistant to director, 1962-66; Brandeis University, Lemberg Center for the Study of Violence, Waltham, Mass., associate director, 1967-69; University of Houston, Houston, Tex., professor of political science and director of Institute for Urban Studies, 1969-75; Rice University, Houston, professor of urban studies and president of Southwest Center for Urban Research, 1969-75; Shimer College, Mt. Carroll, Ill., president, 1975—. Member of Regional Health Advisory Committee, Department of Health, Education and Welfare. *Military service:* U.S. Army, 1943-45, 1951-53. U.S. Army Reserves, 1945-68; became major. *Member:* American Political Science Association, Community Welfare Planning Association (board member).

WRITINGS: (Editor) Milton Greenburg and Sherrill Cleland, *State Constitutional Revision in Michigan,* [Detroit], 1960; *Politics of Regional Planning in Greater Hartford,* Greater Hartford Chamber of Commerce, 1964; (editor) *The Public Library and the City,* M.I.T. Press, 1965; *The Politics of Community Health,* Public Affairs Press, 1968; *Civil Disobedience, Rioting and Insurrection,* Lincoln Filene Center for Citizenship and Public Affairs, 1968; (editor with Molly Apple Levin) *Problems in Research on Community Violence,* Praeger, 1969; *The Prospects for Revolution: A Study of Riots, Civil Disobedience and Insurrection in Contemporary America,* Harper's Magazine Press, 1971; *The Metropolitan Library,* M.I.T. Press, 1972; (with Alan Shank) *Urban Perspectives: Politics and Policies,* Holbrook, 1975. Contributor to *American Scholar, Urban Affairs Quarterly, Library Journal, Wilson Library Bulletin, A.L.A. Bulletin, International Journal of Health Education, American Behavioral Scientist,* and other journals.

WORK IN PROGRESS: The Education of Librarians, for American Library Association.

AVOCATIONAL INTERESTS: Mountain climbing, skiing, European travel.

BIOGRAPHICAL/CRITICAL SOURCES: Nation, June 14, 1971.

* * *

CONARROE, Joel (Osborne) 1934-

PERSONAL: Born October 23, 1934, in West Orange, N.J.; son of Elvin Hamm (a businessman) and Helen (Lofland) Conarroe. *Education:* Davidson College, A.B., 1956; Cornell University, M.A., 1957; New York University, Ph.D., 1966. *Home:* 203 St. Mark's Sq., Philadelphia, Pa. 19104. *Office:* Department of English, University of Pennsylvania, Philadelphia, Pa. 19104.

CAREER: Davidson College, Davidson, N.C., instructor in English, 1957-58; University of Pennsylvania, Philadelphia, instructor, 1963-66, assistant professor, 1966-71, associate professor, 1971-77, professor of English, 1977—, chairman of Department of English, 1973-77, university ombudsman, 1971—. Reader for Educational Testing Service, 1966—; interviewer; Danforth Foundation. *Military service:* U.S. Army, 1958-59. *Member:* Modern Language Association of America, American Association of University Professors, American Studies Association, Phi Beta Kappa. *Awards, honors:* Danforth fellowship, 1960-64; University of Pennsylvania research grant, 1966-67; Lindback Teaching Award, University of Pennsylvania, 1968; Yaddo fellowship, 1970-71.

WRITINGS: William Carlos Williams' Paterson: Language and Landscape, University of Pennsylvania Press, 1970; *John Berryman: An Introduction to the Poetry,* Columbia University Press, 1977. Contributor to literary journals.

WORK IN PROGRESS: A cultural and critical study of five modern American poets.

* * *

CONNERS, Kenneth Wray 1909-

PERSONAL: Born November 12, 1909, in Minotola, N.J.; son of William Henry (a school superintendent and real estate executive) and Evelyn (Brown) Conners; married Christine M. Rosenberger, August 10, 1940. *Education:* University of Pennsylvania, B.S., 1930, A.M., 1932, further study, 1941-42; also studied at Temple University, 1937-38, Mansfield College, Oxford, summer, 1966, and University of St. Andrews, summer, 1970. *Religion:* Methodist. *Home:* 1601 Meadowbrook Rd., Meadowbrook, Pa. 19046.

CAREER: Free-lance writer, 1932-34; Leeds & Northrup Co., North Wales, Pa., advertising copywriter, 1934-42, advertising supervisor, 1942-47, manager of advertising division, 1947-69, director of public relations, 1969-74. Special lecturer in department of journalism, University of Pennsylvania, 1954-60. Guest preacher (lay) and conductor of seminars and retreats in United States, Canada, and England; member of board, Wellsprings Ecumenical Center, 1965-71. Member of executive board, Junior Committee of Philadelphia Orchestra, 1946-50, 1958-63; vice-president, Philadelphia Science Council, 1960—; Covenant House, member of board, 1964, chairman of board, 1967-70, president, 1970—; member of board, Kirkridge Retreat/Study Center, 1974—, and Metropolitan Boys' Club of Philadelphia, 1976—. *Member:* English-Speaking Union, Philadelphia Art Alliance.

WRITINGS: Pro, Con and Coffee, Howell, Soskin, 1942; (contributor) *Church Creative,* Abingdon, 1967; *Stranger in the Pew,* Judson, 1970; *Who's In Charge Here?,* Judson, 1973. Contributor to *The Upper Room Disciplines 1975;* also contributor to *American Mercury, Christian Herald, London Studio, Author and Journalist, Church Management, Pulpit Digest,* and other periodicals.

WORK IN PROGRESS: Writing on the parish, theological attitudes versus cultural values, problems of ministers, and other topics.

CONQUEST, Edwin Parker, Jr. 1931-
(Ned Conquest)

PERSONAL: Born June 13, 1931, in Richmond, Va.; son of Edwin Parker (an engineer and building contractor) and Eugenia Tennant (Fairfax) Conquest. *Education:* Princeton University, B.A., 1953, Ph.D. 1967; New College, Oxford, B.A., 1955, M.A., 1959; Harvard University, LL.B., 1960. *Politics:* Independent. *Religion:* Episcopalian. *Home:* 1547 33rd St. N.W., Washington, D.C. 20007.

CAREER: Barter Theatre, Abingdon, Va., apprentice actor, summer, 1953; Hunton, Williams, Gay, Powell & Gibson (law firm), Richmond, Va., clerk, summer, 1959; Milbank, Tweed, Hadley & McCloy (law firm), New York, N.Y., associate, 1960-64; Georgetown University, Washington, D.C., assistant professor of English literature, 1967-73. *Military service:* U.S. Army, Artillery, 1955-57; served in Germany; became first lieutenant. U.S. Army Reserve, 1957-62. *Member:* Phi Beta Kappa, Harvard Club of New York, Country Club of Virginia, Metropolitan Club of Washington, D.C., Potomac Hunt (Maryland), Rappahannock Hunt (Virginia). *Awards, honors:* Rhodes scholar at Oxford University, 1953-55.

WRITINGS: (Under name Ned Conquest) *The Gun and Glory of Granite Hendley* (novel), Doubleday, 1969. Contributor to *Harvard Law School Bulletin*, and other periodicals.

WORK IN PROGRESS: Two novels, *A Woman, a Dog, and a Hanging Tree*, and *Without Assenting Gods; The Perfect Fool*, a collection of short stories; research for a critical work on Joseph Conrad.

*   *   *

CONRAD, Andree 1945-
(L. K. Conrad)

PERSONAL: Born March 18, 1945; daughter of Peter Paul and Blanche (Valois) Conrad. *Education:* Attended University of Colorado, 1962-63, and Trinity College, Hartford, Conn., 1964; Smith College, A.B., 1965. *Residence:* New York, N.Y.

CAREER: Doubleday & Co., Inc., New York, N.Y., editorial assistant, 1965-67; Farrar, Straus & Giroux, New York, N.Y., editorial assistant, beginning 1967.

WRITINGS—Translator under pseudonym L. K. Conrad: Gaia Servadio, *Melinda*, Farrar, Straus, 1968; Giovanni Guareschi, *Duncan and Clotilda*, Farrar, Straus, 1968; Gaia Servadio, *Salome and Don Giovanni: Notes for a New Novel and Notes for a Revised Opera*, Farrar, Straus, 1969; *The Murder of Allende: And the End of the Chilean Way to Socialism*, Harper, 1976. Also has done translations of nonfiction and fiction from the Spanish.

WORK IN PROGRESS: Novels, stories, and essays of her own.†

*   *   *

COOK, William J(esse), Jr. 1938-

PERSONAL: Born July 22, 1938, in Piedmont, Ala.; son of William J. and Genevieve (Putnam) Cook; married Judy M. Wallace, February 21, 1959; children: Vonda, Jennifer, Jill. *Education:* Jacksonville State University, A.B., 1960; Auburn University, M.A., 1965, Ph.D., 1968. *Politics:* Republican. *Religion:* Christian. *Address:* Box 385, Pike Rd., Ala. 36064. *Office:* Hudson-Thompson, Inc., Montgomery, Ala. 36105.

CAREER: Ordained minister of the Church of Christ, 1963; Auburn University, Auburn, Ala., instructor in English, 1967-68; Jacksonville State University, Jacksonville, Ala., associate professor of English, 1968-69; Auburn University, Montgomery, Ala., assistant professor, 1969-71, associate professor of English, 1971-75, coordinator of English program, 1969-71, assistant to Vice President, 1970-73, vice president for development, 1973-75; Hudson-Thompson, Inc., Montgomery, vice-president, 1975-77. Auburn University, Auburn, director of Christian Student Center and associate minister of Auburn Church of Christ, 1963-68, director of University Relations at Montgomery campus, 1970; director, School of Biblical Studies and Christian Student Center, Jacksonville State University, 1968-69; minister, Highland Church of Christ at Carriage Hills, Montgomery, 1969-76. Member of board of directors, Montgomery Rotary Club; frequent speaker at civic, youth, and professional programs. *Military service:* U.S. Army, 1960-63; became lieutenant. *Member:* International Platform Association, Modern Language Association, South Atlantic Modern Language Association, Sigma Tau Delta, Phi Kappa Phi, Kappa Phi Kappa.

WRITINGS: The Church and Her Responsibility to the Young (booklet), Christian Publishing Co., 1967; *The Bible Chair* [and] *The Great Commission* (booklet), Quality Printing Co., 1968; *Confidence in Fact*, Quality Printing Co., 1970; *Masks, Modes and Morals: The Art of Evelyn Waugh*, Fairleigh Dickenson University Press, 1971; *The British Short Story*, Twayne, 1978. Contributor to *Readers Encyclopedia of English Literature*. Also contributor to *Notre Dame English Journal, Mission, Conradiana, Gospel Advocate, Firm Foundation, Campus Journal, 20th Century Christian, Christian Chronicle*, and *Bible Chair Journal*. Chairman of editorial board, *Campus Journal*; contributing editor, *Christian Bible Teacher;* editor, *Modern Catholic Novelists, Thesis Bibliography Series*.

WORK IN PROGRESS: Two book-length religious studies and a novel of the urban south.

*   *   *

COOPER, C(hristopher) D(onald) H(untington) 1942-

PERSONAL: Born June 14, 1942, in Sydney, New South Wales, Australia; son of Ronald Walter (a sales and marketing executive) and Florrice (Brabin) Cooper; married Francisca Elisabeth Valkenburg (an obstetric sister), February 6, 1965; children: Christopher, Julian, Louise, Simone. *Education:* University of Sydney, B.Sc. (honors), M.Sc., 1965; University of London, Ph.D., 1968. *Religion:* Methodist. *Home:* 31 Epping Ave., Eastwood, New South Wales 2122, Australia. *Office:* School of Mathematics and Physics, Macquarie University, New South Wales 2113, Australia.

CAREER: Sir John Cass College, London, England, lecturer in mathematics, 1967-68; Macquarie University, New South Wales, Australia, lecturer, 1968-70, senior lecturer in mathematics, 1971—. Methodist Local Preacher. *Member:* American Mathematical Society, Mathematical Association of America, London Mathematical Society, Australian Mathematical Society.

WRITINGS—All published by J. Murray: *Computer Programming*, 1969; *Infinite Numbers*, 1975; *Numbers: Their Personalities and Properties*, 1975; *Permutations and Groups*, 1975. Contributor to *Mathematische Zeitschrift* and *Journal of the Australian Mathematical Society*.

WORK IN PROGRESS: Research papers on "verbally related groups."

SIDELIGHTS: Christopher Cooper's major areas of vocational interests are algebra ("particularly Group Theory") and set theory. *Avocational interests:* Managing singing career of mezzo-soprano Maria-Louise Valkenburg (sister-in-law); collecting old books.

* * *

COOPER, Chester L. 1917-

PERSONAL: Born January 13, 1917, in Boston, Mass.; son of Israel (a businessman) and Hannah (Levenson) Cooper; married Orah Pomerance (an economist), June 8, 1941; children: Joan Lawrence, Susan Louise. *Education:* Attended Massachusetts Institute of Technology, New York University, and Columbia University; American University, Ph.D. *Home:* 7514 Vale St., Chevy Chase, Md. 20015. *Office:* Institute for Energy Analysis, 11 Dupont Circle N.W., Washington, D.C. 20036.

CAREER: Central Intelligence Agency, Washington, D.C., member of staff, 1945-52; National Security Council, Washington, D.C., staff assistant, 1953-55; United States Embassy, London, England, liaison officer, 1955-58; Office of National Estimates, Washington, D.C., chief of estimates staff, 1958-63; U.S. Government, Washington, D.C., deputy director of intelligence, 1963-64, senior member of staff of McGeorge Bundy, 1964-66; Institute for Defense Analysis, Arlington, Va., director of International and Social Studies Division, beginning 1967; currently director of Washington office, Institute for Energy Analysis. Consultant to former Ambassador Averell Harriman on a negotiated settlement of the Vietnam War. Frequent lecturer, participant in panels and conferences on international affairs. *Military service:* U.S. Army, served in infantry, and intelligence.

MEMBER: Council on Foreign Relations, P.E.N., District of Columbia Tuberculosis Society (member of board of directors), Beacon Hill Mutual Fund (member of board of directors), Bath Club (London), Cosmos Club (Washington, D.C.). *Awards, honors:* Intelligence Medal, Central Intelligence Agency; Woodrow Wilson fellow.

WRITINGS: (Contributor) Richard M. Pfeffer, editor, *The War and the Future of American Foreign Policy,* Harper, 1968; (contributor) Keith C. Clark and Laurence J. Legere, editors, *The President and the Management of National Security,* Praeger, 1969; (contributor) A. D. Barnett and E. D. Reischauer, editors, *United States and China: The Next Decade,* Praeger, 1970; *The Lost Crusade: America in Vietnam* (Book-of-the-Month Club selection), Dodd, 1970; (editor) *Growth in America,* Greenwood Press, 1976; *Suez, 1956,* Putnam, in press. Contributor to *Foreign Affairs, Foreign Policy,* and *New Republic.*

SIDELIGHTS: Chester Cooper states: "During the course of my professional experience in foreign affairs I have had some rather unique experiences. I have attended, as an advisor to the head of the American delegation, virtually every major international conference dealing with Asian problems since the Far East Conference of 1954. I was closely involved in the Suez crisis of 1956 and during the height of the problems between the United States and the United Kingdom was designated as the sole American contact with the British Government.... During the Cuban missile crisis I was dispatched secretly to London to brief Prime Minister Macmillan and other members of the British Government on the situation in Cuba and on President Kennedy's inten-

tions.... In early 1963 I was sent on a special mission by the National Security Council to Vietnam for the purpose of assessing the advisability of continued American support to President Diem. In 1964 I was sent to London in advance of Prime Minister Wilson's trip to Washington to present President Johnson's views on the multilateral force—an issue which up to then had been sharply dividing the two Governments. During the period 1965 through 1967 I carried out a variety of high level and sensitive missions in pursuit of a negotiated settlement in Vietnam, the most dramatic of which was my mission to London in February of 1967 during Kosygin's visit."

AVOCATIONAL INTERESTS: Sailing, sculpting, music, gardening, and eighteenth-century American and English furniture and ceramics.

* * *

COOPER, Susan 1935-

PERSONAL: Born May 23, 1935, in Burnham, Buckinghamshire, England; came to United States in 1963; daughter of John Richard and Ethel May (Field) Cooper; married Nicholas J. Grant (a college professor), August 3, 1963; children: Jonathan, Katharine; stepchildren: Anne, Bill, Peter. *Education:* Somerville College, Oxford, M.A., 1956.

CAREER: Writer; *Sunday Times,* London, England, reporter and feature writer, 1956-63. *Member:* Society of Authors (United Kingdom), Author's Guild. *Awards, honors: Boston Globe, Horn Book* award, for *The Dark Is Rising;* Newberry Medal and Tirna Nog Award (Wales), for *The Grey King.*

WRITINGS: (Contributor) Michael Sissons and Philip French, editors, *The Age of Austerity: 1945-51,* Hodder & Stoughton, 1963, Penguin, 1965; *Mandrake* (novel), J. Cape, 1964, Penguin, 1966; *Behind the Golden Curtain: A View of the U.S.A.* (Book Society Alternative Choice), Hodder & Stoughton, 1965, Scribner, 1966; *Over Sea, under Stone* (*Horn Book* Honor List; first children's novel in five-part series, *The Dark Is Rising*), J. Cape, 1965, Harcourt, 1966; (editor and author of preface) J. B. Priestley, *Essays of Five Decades,* Little, Brown, 1968; *J. B. Priestley: Portrait of an Author,* Heinemann, 1970, Harper, 1971; *Dawn of Fear* (children's novel; *Horn Book* Honor List, ALA Notable Book), illustrations by Margery Gill, Harcourt, 1970; *The Dark Is Rising* (ALA Notable Book), Atheneum, 1973; *Greenwitch* (ALA Notable Book), Chatto & Windus, 1973, Atheneum, 1974; *The Grey King* (*Horn Book* Honor List, ALA Notable Book), Chatto & Windus, 1974, Atheneum, 1975; *Silver on the Tree,* Atheneum, 1977.

SIDELIGHTS: Susan Cooper lives in the United States, but visits Britain once a year and also travels to a remote island in the Caribbean where she and her husband maintain a small house. She told *CA,* "All my fiction tends toward fantasy and—so far—has its roots in my very English background and Anglo-Celtic racial mixture."

BIOGRAPHICAL/CRITICAL SOURCES: New York Times Book Review, October 27, 1968, November 8, 1970; *Times Literary Supplement,* September 18, 1970; *Bookseller,* September 19, 1970; *Books,* November, 1970; *Best Sellers,* June 15, 1971; *Children's Literature Review,* Volume III, Gale, 1977.

* * *

COOX, Alvin D(avid) 1924-

PERSONAL: Surname rhymes with "books"; born March

8, 1924, in Rochester, N.Y.; son of Irving (a portrait photographer) and Ruth (Werner) Coox; married Hisako Suzuki, April 4, 1954; children: Roy Alan. *Education:* New York University, B.A. (magna cum laude), 1945; Harvard University, M.A., 1946, Ph.D., 1951. *Politics:* Independent. *Religion:* "No preference." *Address:* P.O. Box 15544, San Diego, Calif. 92115. *Office:* Department of History, San Diego State University, San Diego, Calif. 92182.

CAREER: Johns Hopkins University, Operations Research Office, Washington, D.C., senior historian, 1949-54; U.S. Army, Japanese Research Division, Tokyo, Japan, historian, 1955-57; U.S. Air Force, Japan, analyst, 1957-63; University of Maryland, Far East Division, Tokyo and Misawa, Japan, lecturer in history, 1963-64; San Diego State University, San Diego, Calif., assistant professor, 1964-67, associate professor, 1967-69, professor of history, 1969—. Visiting professor of history at Shiga National University, Hikone, Japan, 1954-55; part-time lecturer in history at Far East Divisions of University of California and University of Maryland, 1954-63. *Member:* American Historical Association, Association for Asian Studies, American Military Institute, Perstare et Praestare (New York University), Phi Beta Kappa. *Awards, honors:* Postdoctoral grants, Rockefeller Foundation, 1961-64; faculty research grants, San Diego State University Foundation, 1965—.

WRITINGS: (Editor and translator) Saburo Hayashi, *Kogun: The Japanese Army in the Pacific War*, U.S. Marine Corps Association, 1959; *Year of the Tiger*, Orient/West Press, 1964; (editor with Maurice Schneps) *The Japanese Image*, two volumes, Orient/West Press, 1965-66; *Japan: The Final Agony*, Ballantine, 1970, hardcover edition, Macdonald & Co., 1971; *Tojo*, Ballantine, 1975; *The Anatomy of a Small War: The Soviet-Japanese Struggle for Changkufeng-Khasan, 1938*, Greenwood Press, 1977; (editor with H. Conroy) *China and Japan: Search for Balance Since World War I*, Clio Press, 1977.

Contributor: S. Chawla and others, editors, *Southeast Asia under the New Balance of Power*, Praeger, 1974; R. D. Burns and E. M. Bennett, editors, *Diplomats in Crisis: U.S.-Chinese-Japanese Relations, 1919-1941*, ABC-Clio Press, 1974; D. MacIsaac, editor, *The Military and Society*, U.S. Government Printing Office, 1975; R. F. Weigley, editor, *New Dimensions in Military History*, Presidio Press, 1975; N. Frankland and C. Dowling, editors, *Decisive Battles of the Twentieth Century: Land-Sea-Air*, Sidgwick & Jackson, 1976; J. W. Morley, editor, *Deterrent Diplomacy: Japan, Germany, and the U.S.S.R., 1935-1940*, Columbia University Press, 1976.

Contributor of many articles, book reviews, and monographs to professional journals. *Orient/West*, 1958-64, began as associate editor, became managing editor; member of editorial board, *Military Affairs*, 1970—.

WORK IN PROGRESS: Preparing books on the Japanese versus Soviet Russian power confrontation, 1931-45, with special reference to the activities of the Kwantung Army, and an evidence of antimilitarism in prewar and wartime Japan.

SIDELIGHTS: Alvin Coox told *CA:* "I studied, wrote, and taught in Japan for about 13 years after World War II. I developed a particular interest in oral history, and traveled very extensively in Japan and Korea, intensively interviewing knowledgeable officials, diplomats, and soldiers about prewar and wartime affairs in the Far East.... Since returning from Japan to San Diego in 1964, I have retained my professional and personal attachment to matters Japa-

nese, but am also very interested in military history and national security. At San Diego State University, for example, I have developed a two-semester upper division course for undergraduates and graduates on the subject of war and civilization. Though my main personal interest is in the twentieth century, I trace war back to the Assyrians and Babylonians. At present I am exercised by the growing alienation of the military from the society which it serves, and my attention has been increasingly focused upon solutions to the problem of the armed forces as [a] mirror of civilization."

*   *   *

COPELAND, Miles 1916-

PERSONAL: Born July 16, 1916, in Birmingham, Ala.; son of Miles Axe (a physician) and Leonore (Armstrong) Copeland; married Elizabeth Lorraine Adie (an archaeologist), September 25, 1942; children: Miles III, Lorraine Leonore, Ian Adie, Stewart Armstrong. *Politics:* Republican. *Religion:* Unitarian. *Home:* 21 Marlborough Pl., London N.W.8, England. *Agent:* Jonathan Clowes Ltd., 19 Jeffrey's Pl., London NW1 9PP, England.

CAREER: Jazz arranger for name bands during the thirties; U.S. Department of Defense, Washington, D.C., specialist on intelligence matters, 1945-47, 1950-53; U.S. Department of State, political attache in Damascus, Syria, 1947-50; Booz-Allen & Hamilton, management consultant to Egyptian Government, Cairo, 1953-55; U.S. Department of State, Washington, D.C., consultant, 1955-57; Kermit Roosevelt Associates, Inc. (government relations consultants specializing in the Middle East and Africa), Washington, D.C., senior partner, 1957—. Chairman of the board, Interser, Inc., New York; president, SCOPE Ltd., Geneva, Switzerland. *Military service:* U.S. Army, 1940-45; enlisted to play in Glenn Miller's orchestra and then was transferred to Office of Strategic Services; became major; received Legion of Merit, Croix de Guerre, and Presidential Citation.

WRITINGS: Staffs and Staff Work, U.S. Army, 1950; *The Game of Nations: The Amorality of Power Politics*, Weidenfeld & Nicolson, 1969, Simon & Schuster, 1970; *Without Cloak and Dagger*, Simon & Schuster, 1975; *The Real Spy World*, Weidenfeld & Nicolson, 1976; *Beyond Cloak and Dagger: Inside the CIA*, Pinnacle Books, 1976. Co-author of television film on the British spy, Kim Philby. Contributor to magazines, newspapers, and management journals.

WORK IN PROGRESS: Steve, Baby, Your Country Needs You, about an American "political action" operation in an Afro-Asian country; with Marcia McDonald, *The Feathermuckers*, for Harcourt.

SIDELIGHTS: During World War II Copeland was known to various intelligence services as Major Lincoln, an alias under which he negotiated with the German Army's Paris command on behalf of Allen Dulles. He has made a special study of the organization of intelligence and information systems, both of governments and of business organizations.

BIOGRAPHICAL/CRITICAL SOURCES: Spectator, August 30, 1969; *Christian Science Monitor*, September 3, 1969, July 2, 1970; *Economist*, September 6, 1969; *New Republic*, May 23, 1970; *Saturday Review*, May 23, 1970; *Washington Post*, May 28, 1970.

*   *   *

COPPARD, Audrey 1931-

PERSONAL: Born July 5, 1931; daughter of Alexander Sherwood and Doris (Beamont) Begbie; married Christopher Coppard (an editor); children: Harriet, Tim, Abbie. *Politics:* "Conservative revolutionary." *Agent:* Sheila Watson, 8 Storey's Gate, London S.W.1, England.

WRITINGS—All published by Heinemann, except as indicated: *Who Has Poisoned the Sea?* (science fiction for young people), S. G. Phillips, 1970; *This Could be the Start of Something,* 1970; *Sending Secrets,* 1972; *Nancy of Nottingham,* 1974; *Don't Panic,* 1975; *Get Well Soon,* 1978. Collaborated on recording of English folksongs produced by Folkways. Contributor of poems to periodicals.

*　　*　　*

CORBETT, J(ack) Elliott 1920-

PERSONAL: Born November 27, 1920, in Oak Park, Ill.; son of Elliott and Clara (Fraehlich) Corbett; married Sara Anne Rapp (a social worker); children: Kathleen, Marjorie, Stephen. *Education:* Temple University, B.A., 1950; Crozer Theological Seminary, B.D., 1950; American University, Ph.D., 1967. *Home:* 6006 Milo Dr., Bethesda, Md. 20016.

CAREER: Minister at Methodist churches in McHenry, Ill., 1950-58, and Oregon, Ill., 1958-61; Methodist Board of Christian Social Concerns, Washington, D.C., staff member of educational and legislative programs, 1961-68, director of church-government relations, 1968—. Secretary, National Council for a Responsible Firearms Policy, 1966—; cofounder and president, Pax World Foundation, 1971—; cofounder and vice-president, Pax World Fund, 1971—; administrator, Committee for Congressional Reform, 1973; chairman of Washington Interreligious Staff Council, 1975, and National Coalition to Ban Handguns, 1975-77; coordinator, Interfaith Coalition on Energy, 1977. *Member:* American Society of Christian Ethics, United Nations Association, Northern Illinois United Methodist Annual Conference.

WRITINGS: The Prophets on Main Street, John Knox, 1964; *Christians Awake,* Harper, 1970; *Turned On by God,* John Knox, 1971. Contributor to religious periodicals.

AVOCATIONAL INTERESTS: Tennis, swimming.

*　　*　　*

CORBETT, Ruth 1912-

PERSONAL: Born January 24, 1912, in Northville, Mich.; daughter of Howard James (a sheet metal patternmaker) and Rhoda (Fuller) Corbett; married Chester Janczarek, May 16, 1934; married second husband, Roy Brent (an actor), February 23, 1958; children: Jana Loi Janczarek Paton. *Education:* Studied at Cranbrook Academy of Art and Meinzinger Art School; private tutoring in art. *Politics:* Republican. *Religion:* Methodist-Episcopal. *Home:* 25681 Sun City Blvd., Sun City, Calif. 92381.

CAREER: Advertising illustrator in Detroit, Mich., 1934-56; Universal Pictures, Universal City, Calif., illustrator, 1956-74; currently free-lance writer. Art teacher and judge; has exhibited watercolors in group shows and had one-woman show in Montrose, Calif. *Awards, honors:* Commercial art awards, and awards from art clubs and exhibitions; award from National Writers Club, 1976.

WRITINGS: Daddy Danced the Charleston, A. S. Barnes, 1970. Contributor of articles and personality profiles to trade journals and nostalgia magazines.

WORK IN PROGRESS: Two books on World War II, *Johnny Went Marching Out,* and *Here Today, Gone to*

War; memoirs, *Gone Forever Again; Art as a Living; Fuss 'n Feathers,* observations of birds.

SIDELIGHTS: Ruth Corbett told *CA:* "When I went into writing after a long career as an advertising illustrator, the differences in these allied fields was soon apparent. An illustration is a one-dimensional story, a momentary action frozen on canvas or board, but it goes no farther than your imagination might carry it. Writing goes all around the subject in a completely dimensional way that's more satisfying to me. . . . It's challenging to try to launch a new career after retirement from another of longstanding."

BIOGRAPHICAL/CRITICAL SOURCES: Illustrator (now *Illustrator/Writer*), summer, 1958, fall, 1968.

*　　*　　*

CORBIN, Charles B. 1940-

PERSONAL: Born October 20, 1940, in Toledo, Ohio; son of Don E. (a school principal) and D'Esta June (Wolford) Corbin; married Mary Catherine Milligan, June 12, 1964; children: Charles, Jr., John David, William Robert. *Education:* University of New Mexico, B.S., 1960, Ph.D., 1965; University of Illinois, M.S., 1962. *Religion:* Protestant. *Home:* 770 Midland, Manhattan, Kan. 66502. *Office:* Department of Physical Education, Kansas State University, Manhattan, Kan. 66502.

CAREER: Albuquerque (N.M.) public schools, teacher, 1960-61; assistant professor of health and physical education at College of Santa Fe, Santa Fe, N.M., 1964-65, and University of Toledo, Toledo, Ohio, 1965-67; Texas A&M University, College Station, associate professor of health and physical education, 1967-71, and director of health and physical education research laboratory; Kansas State University, Manhattan, professor of physical education, 1971—, head of department, 1971-75, director of motor development research lab, 1975—. *Member:* American Alliance for Health, Physical Education and Recreation, American College of Sports Medicine, National College Physical Education Association, North American Society for Psychology of Sport and Physical Activity, Phi Epsilon Kappa, Phi Delta Kappa.

WRITINGS: (With Linus Dowell and Carl Landiss) *Concepts and Experiments in Physical Education,* Kendall Hunt, 1968; *Becoming Physically Educated in the Elementary School,* Lea & Febiger, 1969, 2nd edition, 1976; (with Dowell, Homer Tolson, and Ruth Lindsey) *Concepts of Physical Education,* W. C. Brown, 1970, 3rd edition, 1978; *Inexpensive Games Equipment,* W. C. Brown, 1973; *A Textbook of Motor Development,* W. C. Brown, 1974. Creator of record albums in physical education for Education Activities, Inc. Contributor to professional journals and magazines. Associate editor, *Physical Educator.*

WORK IN PROGRESS: Concepts in Physical Activity for High School Students, for Scott, Foresman; *Introduction to Physical Education,* for W. C. Brown.

*　　*　　*

CORCORAN, Gertrude B(eatty) 1922-

PERSONAL: Born September 19, 1922, in Torrington, Wyo.; daughter of Frank Stinson (a music teacher) and Jessie (Macdonald) Beatty; married James Tait Corcoran (an industrial engineer), July 1, 1952. *Education:* Colorado Women's College (now Temple Buell College), A.A., 1941; San Jose State College (now University), B.A., (magna cum laude), 1950, M.A., 1952; Stanford University, Ed.D., 1960. *Home:* 16025 Greenridge Ter., Los Gatos, Calif. 95030. *Of-*

fice: Department of English, San Jose State University, San Jose, Calif. 95114.

CAREER: Teacher in public schools in San Jose, Calif., 1950-55; San Jose State University, San Jose, assistant professor, 1955-60, associate professor, 1960-65, professor of English, 1965—. Instructor on television station, KNTV. Consultant to KTEH-TV, Campbell Union School District, California Department of Education, language arts and creative writing workshops, and various school districts in California. *Member:* National Council of Teachers of English, National Council for Social Studies, Association for Student Teaching, Association for State College Professors, American Association of University Professors, National Education Association, Association for Supervision and Curriculum Development, California Teachers Association, California State Employees Association, Kappa Delta Pi, Pi Lambda Theta. *Awards, honors:* Faculty Research Grant, San Jose State College, 1965-66.

WRITINGS: Language Arts in the Elementary School: A Modern Linguistic Approach, Ronald, 1970; *Language Experience for Nursery and Kindergarten Children,* F. E. Peacock, 1975.

WORK IN PROGRESS: With Betty Grand, *Reading Principles and Practices for Elementary School Teachers;* with Estrella Calimog, *Reading Handbook: Decoding for Teacher.*

* * *

CORKRAN, Herbert, Jr. 1924-

PERSONAL: Born January 16, 1924, in Baltimore, Md.; son of Herbert (a railroad accountant) and Florence (Sutherland) Corkran; married Shirley Stoddard, October 17, 1948; children: Louise Ann, Robert Edward. *Education:* Johns Hopkins University, B.A. (with honors), 1945, M.A., 1946; Indiana University, Ph.D., 1961. *Religion:* Baptist. *Home:* 3324 Milton Ave., Dallas, Tex. 75205. *Office:* Political Science Department, Southern Methodist University, Dallas, Tex. 75275.

CAREER: U.S. Department of State, Washington, D.C., foreign service officer, 1945-58, serving as foreign affairs analyst, 1945-50, vice-consul at American consulate in Le Havre, France, 1950-52, estates and notarials officer, 1952-56, and as visa officer at American consulate in Aruba, Netherlands Antilles, 1956-58; Southern Methodist University, Dallas, Tex., assistant professor, 1961-65, associate professor of political science, 1965—, acting chairman of department, 1967-68. *Member:* American Political Science Association, American Academy of Political and Social Science, Caribbean Studies Association, Southern Political Science Association, Western Association of Africanists, Phi Beta Kappa.

WRITINGS: From Formal to Informal Cooperation in the Caribbean (booklet), Arnold Foundation, Southern Methodist University, 1966; *Patterns of International Cooperation in the Caribbean, 1942-1969,* Southern Methodist University Press, 1970; *Mini-Nations and Macro-Cooperation: The Caribbean and the South Pacific,* North American International, 1977. Contributor to political science journals.

* * *

CORNISH, W(illiam) R(odolph) 1937-

PERSONAL: Born in 1937, in Adelaide, South Australia. *Education:* University of Adelaide, LL.B., 1960; Oxford University, B.C.L., 1962. *Office:* London School of Economics and Political Science, London W.C.2, England.

CAREER: University of London, London, England, lecturer in law at London School of Economics and Political Science, 1962-68, reader in law at Queen Mary College, 1969-70, professor of English law at London School of Economics and Political Science, 1970—.

WRITINGS: The Jury, Allen Lane, 1968, revised edition, Penguin, 1971; (editor with A. L. Diamond, A. S. Grabiner, and R. S. Nock) *Sutton and Shannon on Contracts,* 7th edition, Butterworth & Co., 1970.

WORK IN PROGRESS: English Law and Society, 1800-1945, completion expected in 1979; research in the field of patent, copyright, and trade mark law.

BIOGRAPHICAL/CRITICAL SOURCES: New Statesman, February 14, 1969.

* * *

COSGROVE, Carol Ann 1943-

PERSONAL: Born May 7, 1943, in Slough, Buckinghamshire, England; daughter of Thomas Jack (an engineer) and Gay (Killick) Cosgrove; married Kenneth Joseph Twitchett (a university lecturer), July 16, 1966; children: Robin, Andrew. *Education:* London School of Economics, B.Sc. (honors), 1965, M.Sc., 1966, Ph.D., 1976. *Politics:* "Vaguely liberal." *Religion:* Christian. *Home:* 154 Craven Rd., Newbury, Berkshire, England. *Office:* University of Surrey, Guildford, Surrey GU2 5XH, England.

CAREER: University of Reading, Berkshire, England, lecturer in politics, 1966-68; Aberdeen College of Education, Aberdeen, Scotland, lecturer in politics, 1968-72; University of Surrey, Guildford, Surrey, England, associate professor, 1976—. Lecturer for European Communities' Information Service.

WRITINGS: (Editor with husband, Kenneth J. Twitchett) *The New International Actors: The United Nations and the European Economic Community,* St. Martin's, 1970; *A Reader's Guide to Britain and the European Communities,* Chatham House, 1970. Contributor to *International Relations, World Today, Journal of Contemporary History, European Community, Europa-Archiv,* and other journals. Literary editor, *Journal of Common Market Studies.*

WORK IN PROGRESS: A research project, *The EEC and Developing Countries: The Lome Convention of 1975; British Police and the EEC.*

* * *

COUROUCLI, Jennifer 1922-

PERSONAL: Born August 22, 1922, in Watford, Hertfordshire, England; daughter of William James (a regular officer, British Army) and Molly (Fusedale) Clark; married Evangelos C. Couroucli (an importer), February 17, 1950; children: Katerina Teresa; stepchildren: Maria (Mrs. Kostas Mavromatis), Charlambos. *Education:* Attended Watford Girls' School, 1931-38. *Politics:* Liberal ("British variety"). *Religion:* Church of England. *Home:* 32 Anast Tsocha, Athens 601, Greece.

MILITARY SERVICE: British Army, Auxiliary Territorial Service, World War II.

WRITINGS: On This Athenian Hill (poems), Chatto & Windus, 1969.

SIDELIGHTS: Jennifer Couroucli writes poems about Greece from an Irish-English-Greek background; her father was Irish and she spent many holidays in Ulster. In writing poetry, she says, "one finds, apart from the technique, that only the most scrupulous honesty can achieve anything of value. One tries to penetrate to the bone and then beyond, where, perhaps, one may catch a glimpse of eternity. If this sounds pretentious it is also sincere. . . .''

BIOGRAPHICAL/CRITICAL SOURCES: Books and Bookmen, June, 1969; *Times Literary Supplement,* July 24, 1969.

* * *

COWAN, James C(ostello) 1927-

PERSONAL: Born September 16, 1927, in Albany, Ga.; son of James C. (a pecan farmer) and Elizabeth B. (Browne) Cowan; married Judith H. Ryder (a psychiatrist), January 29, 1960; children: Catherine Nancy, Cynthia Mary, Christina Judith, Michael James. *Education:* Mercer University, A.B., 1950; Oklahoma State University, M.A., 1956; University of Oklahoma, Ph.D., 1964. *Religion:* Episcopalian. *Home:* Route 1, Fayetteville, Ark. 72701. *Office:* Department of English, University of Arkansas, Fayetteville, Ark. 72701.

CAREER: Tulane University, New Orleans, La., instructor, 1963-64, assistant professor of English, 1964-66; University of Arkansas, Fayetteville, assistant professor, 1966-67, associate professor, 1967-72, professor of English, 1972—. *Military service:* U.S. Army, 1952-54. *Member:* Modern Language Association of America, South Central Modern Language Association (vice-president, 1976-77, president, 1977-78).

WRITINGS: D. H. Lawrence's American Journey: A Study in Literature and Myth, Press of Case Western Reserve University, 1970. Contributor of articles to literary journals. Founding editor, *D. H. Lawrence Review,* 1968—.

WORK IN PROGRESS: D. H. Lawrence: An Annotated Bibliography of Writings about Him, for Northern Illinois University Press; further research on Lawrence.

* * *

COX, Edward Finch 1946-

PERSONAL: Born October 2, 1946, in Southampton, N.Y.; son of Howard Ellis (a lawyer) and Anne (Finch) Cox; married Patricia Nixon (daughter of former President of U.S.), June, 1971. *Education:* Princeton University, B.A., 1968; Yale University, graduate student, 1968-69; Harvard University, J.D., 1972. *Home:* 351 East 84th St., New York, N.Y. 10028. *Office:* Crovath, Swain & Moore (law firm), New York, N.Y.

CAREER: Has traveled and worked in Europe and South America; currently associate lawyer with Crovath, Swain & Moore (law firm), New York, N.Y. *Military service:* U.S. Army Reserve; current rank, captain.

WRITINGS: (With John Schulz and Robert Fellmeth) *The Nader Report on the Federal Trade Commission,* preface by Ralph Nader, Baron, 1969. Contributor to *New Republic.*

BIOGRAPHICAL/CRITICAL SOURCES: New York Times Book Review, October 19, 1969; *Washington Post,* October 24, 1969; *Village Voice,* November 13, 1969.

* * *

COX, Frank D. 1933-

PERSONAL: Born February 16, 1933, in Los Angeles, Calif.; married Brigitte Klunker, December 22, 1957; married second wife Pamela Slagle, August, 1976; children:

(first marriage) Randall, Michelle. *Education:* Occidental College, B.A., 1954, M.A., 1958; University of California, Santa Barbara, Ph.D., 1971. *Office:* Santa Barbara City College, Santa Barbara, Calif. 93105.

CAREER: Glendale College, Glendale, Calif., instructor in psychology, 1957-62; Santa Barbara City College, Santa Barbara, Calif., professor of psychology, 1962—. Lecturer, University of California, Santa Barbara, 1962—. *Military service:* U.S. Army, 1954-56. *Member:* American Psychological Association, National Council on Family Relations, Psi Chi.

WRITINGS: Youth, Marriage, and Seductive Society, W. C. Brown, 1967, 2nd edition, 1974; *Psychology,* W. C. Brown, 1970, 2nd edition, 1973; *American Marriage: A Changing Scene?,* W. C. Brown, 1972, 2nd edition, 1976. Contributor to *Voices* and other journals.

WORK IN PROGRESS: Human Destiny and Its Meaning, for West Publishing.

* * *

COX, John Roberts 1915-
(Jack Cox; David Roberts, a pseudonym)

PERSONAL: Born January 15, 1915, in Worsley, Lancashire, England; son of Frank Clarkson (a local educational official) and Elizabeth (Roberts) Cox; married Kitty Margaret Forward, August 26, 1943; children: David John, Martin Andrew, Lindsay Robert. *Education:* University of Geneva, traveling scholar, 1936; Manchester University, B.A., 1941. *Religion:* Anglican/Methodist. *Home:* 43 Hill View Rd., Llandrhos via Llandudno, North Wales.

CAREER: Manchester Guardian, Manchester, England, news and feature reporter, 1937-40; Lutterworth Press, London, England, editor of *Boy's Own Paper,* 1946-67, managing editor, Lutterworth Periodicals, Ltd., 1953-63; Purnell Group/B.P.C., London, editor of *Family Pets,* 1964-67, general editor of book department, 1966-68, editor of *Boy's Own Annual,* 1959-76, currently *Boy's Own Anthology,* 1977—; International Publishing Corp., Hamlyn Group, London, managing editor of Practical Books Division, 1968-71; consultant editor and author, 1971—. Geographer. *Military service:* British Army, 1940-46, served in Royal Engineers; became captain. *Member:* National Union of Journalists, British Society of Authors, Association of Radio Writers, London Press Club, Guildsman (London), Sports Writers Club, Wasps Rugby Football Club (vice-president, 1951), Manchester University Convocation (treasurer, 1948-58; chairman, 1958-68; vice-president, 1969—), Surrey University Rugby Club (vice-president, 1966).

WRITINGS—Nonfiction: Camping for All, Ward Lock, 1951; *Ideas for Rover Scouts,* Jenkins, 1953, 5th edition, 1959; *Ideas for Scout Troops,* Jenkins, 1954, 8th edition, 1963; *The Outdoor Series,* Lutterworth, 1954, 7th edition, 1975; *Camp and Trek,* foreword by Lord Hunt, Lutterworth, 1956, 3rd new and revised edition, 1971; *Portrait of B-P.: The Life Story of Lord Baden-Powell,* Lutterworth, 1957; *The Hike Book,* Lutterworth, 1960, 3rd revised edition, 1968; *Don Davies: "An Old International"* (biography), Hutchinson, 1962; *Camping in Comfort,* Lutterworth, 1963; *The Rugby Union Football Book,* Purnell, *Volume 1,* 1968, *Volume 2,* 1970; *Modern Camping,* Hutchinson, 1968; *The World of Rugby,* two volumes, Purnell, 1970-72; *Lightweight Camping,* Lutterworth, 1971; *Fun and Games Outdoors,* Pan Books, 1971; *Fun and Games Indoors,* Pan Books, 1973; *The Outdoor Cookbook,* Lutterworth, 1976;

Camping Skills, Wolfe Publishing, 1977; *The Outdoor Handbook,* Hamlyn, 1977. Also author of *Richard Hakluyt* (Elizabethan play for schools), 1937; author of radio and television scripts, and documentaries for the BBC and I.T.A. programs, including two educational series in geography; author of a BBC documentary on Lord Baden-Powell for the 1957 Centenary of his birth.

Fiction for young people: *Dangerous Waters* (originally written and broadcast as a BBC radio serial), Lutterworth, 1955; *Calamity Camp,* Lutterworth, 1957; *Majorca Moon,* Lutterworth, 1960; (under pseudonym David Roberts) *The Mushroom God,* Parrish, 1961.

Editor: *World Rover Moot Handbook,* Munro Press, 1939; *The Boy's Book of Popular Hobbies,* Burke, 1954, revised edition, 1968; *The Boy's Own Book of Hobbies,* Lutterworth, 1957, revised edition published as *The Boy's Book of Hobbies,* 1966, 2nd revised edition, 1968; (and contributor) Frank Showell Styles, *Getting to Know Mountains,* George Newnes, 1958; *The Boy's Own Companion, Volumes 1-5,* Lutterworth, 1959-64; *Serve by Conserving: A Study of Conservation,* UNESCO [Paris], amended edition by Arco Publications, 1959; *The Boy's Own Book of Outdoor Hobbies,* Lutterworth, 1960, revised edition, 1968; *They Went to Bush: Forestry in Ghana,* MacGibbon & Kee, 1961; *Fred Buller's Book of Rigs and Tackles,* Purnell, 1967; (and reviser) Stuart Petre Brodie Mais, *An English Course for Everybody,* 5th edition, Frewin Publishers, 1969; *The Motorists Touring Maps & Gazetteer,* Hamlyn, 1970; Douglas Gohn, *Tropical Fish: Aquaria,* Hamlyn, 1970; *Quotations for Speakers & Writers,* Hamlyn, 1970; Gilbert Salteritwaite, *Encyclopedia of Astronomy,* Hamlyn, 1970. Editor, with Enid Blyton, of the "Children's Library of Knowledge" series, published by Odhams Books, 1957-62.

Editor of books by Gilbert Davey; all published by Kaye & Ward: *Fun with Radio,* 1957, *Fun with Short Wave Radio,* 1960, *Fun with Electronics,* 1962, *Fun with Transistors,* 1964, *Fun with Hi-Fi,* 1965; *Scout Camping,* Scout Association, 1973; revised editions of all titles, 1974-77.

Author of weekly columns for children in the *Daily Graphic* (Kemsley), 1946-59, *Sunday Graphic,* 1959-61, *Birmingham Weekly Post,* 1957-58, and *Manchester Evening News,* 1975—. Also author of column on adult leisure for *Manchester Evening News,* 1977—, and of monthly feature *Outdoors with Jack Cox* (official journal of the Scout Association), 1975—. Contributor of sport and recreation articles, book reviews, and interviews to the (London) *Sunday Times,* 1951-68, *Daily Telegraph,* 1956-72, *The Guardian,* 1960-72, *Smith's Trade News,* and various periodicals.

WORK IN PROGRESS: A detailed history of *Boy's Own Paper,* founded in 1879, with all original source material and illustrations for important authors 1879-1979; a series of practical books based on conservation in practice for youth groups of all kinds.

SIDELIGHTS: John Cox wrote to *CA:* "I hope to influence young people especially, to whose welfare and interests I have largely devoted my life, along the lines of worthwhile endeavour in outdoor leisure, recreation and achievement. I try always to encourage youngsters and get them to learn from their own mistakes and the mistakes of others, including myself. Conservation of natural resources is all-important today in all parts of the world and I do my utmost to get young people conservation-minded and really active. Enthusiasm then comes naturally. Achievement follows." To aspiring authors he gives this advice: "Young writers: do not be discouraged by rejects. Keep trying to find your niche; have confidence in your own thing once you have found what it is; build on that and you will impress others through your skill and enthusiasm. Never be afraid to ask for advice or to learn from others."

AVOCATIONAL INTERESTS: Music of all kinds; playing the piano; conservation, ornithology, gardening and outdoor interests.

* * *

COX, R(obert) David 1937-

PERSONAL: Born January 4, 1937, in Evansville, Ind.; son of Warren M. (a research chemist) and Ruby (Diehl) Cox; married Shirley Stephenson (an actress), September 9, 1958. *Education:* University of Colorado, B.A., 1958, M.A., 1960. *Home:* 22-10 Pond Way, Manorville, N.Y. 11949. *Office:* Suffolk County Community College, Eastern Campus, Riverhead, N.Y. 11901.

CAREER: McGraw-Hill Book Co., New York, N.Y., assistant director of advertising, 1960-61; Friends Academy, Locust Valley, N.Y., teacher of English, 1961-66; Rutgers University, Newark, N.J., lecturer in English, 1965-67; Suffolk County Community College, Selden, N.Y., chairman of department of English, 1967-73, executive assistant to the president, 1973-76, executive dean of Eastern Campus, Riverhead, N.Y., 1976—. President, David Prints, Inc. (greeting card firm), 1970—.

WRITINGS: Where Home Is (poetry), Keller-Crescent, 1966; *Composition: Getting the Job Done,* Holbrook, 1970; *Composition Calisthenics,* Holbrook, 1971; (with wife, Shirley Cox) *Themes in the One Act Play* (includes one-act play, "The Beer Can Tree," broadcast by CBS-TV, 1966), McGraw, 1971; (with Stephen Lewis) *The Student Critic,* Winthrop Publishing, 1974; *Build Yourself an A-Frame,* Reston, 1977.

Unpublished plays: "Charlie and Friday" (two one-act plays), first produced Off-Broadway at Players Theatre, 1965; "As the Lion Does" (three one-act plays), first produced in New York at Triangle Theatre, 1966; "Thanks Courteous Wall," produced in New York, 1973. Also author of film documentary, "Circus," broadcast by ABC-TV, 1966.

WORK IN PROGRESS: The Feeling of the Man, a series of thirty-six one-act plays, each dealing with one American president.

AVOCATIONAL INTERESTS: Building houses.

* * *

CRAMER, Harold 1927-

PERSONAL: Born June 16, 1927, in Philadelphia, Pa.; son of Aaron Harry and Blanche (Greenberg) Cramer; married Geraldine Hassuk, July 14, 1957; children: Patricia Gail. *Education:* Temple University, A.B., 1948; University of Pennsylvania, J.D. (cum laude), 1951. *Religion:* Jewish. *Home:* 1361 Wright Dr., Huntingdon Valley, Pa. 19006. *Office:* Mesirov, Gelman, Jaffe, Cramer & Jamieson, Fidelity Bldg., 123 South Broad St., Philadelphia, Pa. 19109.

CAREER: Law clerk in several private offices and to judge of Court of Common Pleas prior to 1954; University of Pennsylvania Law School, Philadelphia, associate director of Institute of Legal Research, 1954; Shapiro, Rosenfeld, Stalberg & Cook (now Shapiro, Stalberg, Cook, Murphy & Kalodner), Philadelphia, Pa., associate, 1955, partner, 1956-67; Mesirov, Gelman, Jaffe & Levin, Philadelphia, partner,

1967-74; Mesirov, Gelman, Jaffe, Cramer & Jamieson, Philadelphia, partner, 1974—. American Bar Foundation, trustee, 1970-72, fellow; president, Theodore F. Jenkins Memorial Law Library Co., 1974—; lecturer, Practicing Law Institute and National Institute for Trial Advocacy; chairman of board, Eastern Pennsylvania Psychiatric Institute, 1974—; trustee, Delaware Valley College of Science and Agriculture, 1974—; member of board, Federation of Jewish Agencies, 1974—; member of board, Citizens Crime Commission of Philadelphia, 1975—; trustee, Jewish Publication Society, 1976—. Board member of various community and religious organizations. *Military service:* U.S. Army, 1951-53; became first lieutenant; served in Korea; received Bronze Star Medal, three battle stars, and Presidential Unit Citation (twice).

MEMBER: American Bar Association, American Arbitration Association (member of national panel), American Law Institute, Pennsylvania Bar Association (member of house of delegates, 1966-75; member of board of governors, 1975—), Philadelphia Bar Association (member of committee of censors, 1964, chairman of committee, 1966; member of board of governors, 1966-69, chairman of board, 1969; vice-chancellor, 1970; chancellor, 1972), University of Pennsylvania Law Alumni Society (member of board of managers, 1959-64; president, 1968-70), Order of the Coif (member of national executive committee, 1974-76), Tau Epsilon Rho, Locust Club, Old York Road Ice Skating Club, Philmont Country Club, Midday Club.

WRITINGS: Trial Advocacy, Foundation Press, 1968. Editor, *University of Pennsylvania Law Review,* 1950-51; *Shingle* (journal of Philadelphia Bar Association), associate editor, 1961-69, editor, 1970.

* * *

CRAMER, J(an) S(olomon) 1928-

PERSONAL: Born April 26, 1928, in The Hague, Netherlands; son of P.J.S. (a botanist) and A. P. (van Deventer) Cramer; married M. J. van Gogh, October 24, 1953; children: four. *Education:* University of Amsterdam, B.A., 1950, M.A., 1953, Ph.D., 1961. *Home:* Oud Loosdrechtse Dijk 274A, Loosdrecht, Netherlands. *Office:* University of Amsterdam, Amsterdam, Netherlands.

CAREER: Worked for Centraal Plan Bureau, The Hague, Netherlands, 1953-56, Cambridge University, Cambridge, England, 1956-59, and Centre de Recherches et de Documentation sur la Consommation, Paris, France, 1959-62; University of Amsterdam, Amsterdam, Netherlands, professor of econometrics, 1962—. Member of Scientific Council for Government Policy, 1973—. *Member:* Royal Statistical Society, Econometric Society.

WRITINGS: The Ownership of Major Consumer Durables, Cambridge University Press, 1962; *Empirical Econometrics,* North-Holland Publishing, 1969.

* * *

CRAMER, Richard S(eldon) 1928-

PERSONAL: Born October 8, 1928, in Bandon, Ore.; son of John Francis (an educator) and Mabel (Oesterling) Cramer; married Beverly L. Grace, August 26, 1950; children: Cynthia Elizabeth, Cary Margaret, Richard Seldon II. *Education:* University of Oregon, B.S., 1950, M.S., 1952; attended George Washington University, 1953, San Francisco State College (now University), 1954, and San Jose State College (now University), 1955; Stanford University,

Ph.D., 1960. *Politics:* Democrat. *Home:* 755 De Soto Dr., Palo Alto, Calif. 94303. *Office:* Department of History, San Jose State University, San Jose, Calif. 95114.

CAREER: Teacher of history at high schools in Oswego, Ore., and Palo Alto, Calif., 1951-58; Stanford University, Stanford, Calif., instructor in history, 1960-61; San Jose State University, San Jose, Calif., assistant professor, 1961-65, associate professor, 1965-70, professor of history, 1970—. Instructor, Foothill College, 1964—. *Military service:* U.S. Air Force, 1952-54; became first lieutenant. *Member:* American Historical Association, Organization of American Historians, Southern Historical Association, Oregon Historical Society. *Awards, honors:* College Foundation research grant, 1962.

WRITINGS: (With John Wintterle) *Portraits of Nobel Laureates in Peace* (juvenile), Abelard, 1971. Also author with Wintterle and Billie B. Jensen of *American Humor and Humorists,* Volume I, 1970, Volume II, 1971. Contributor to academic journals.

WORK IN PROGRESS: A study of Civil War humor; a work on the Chief Justices of the United States.

AVOCATIONAL INTERESTS: Reading, philately.

* * *

CRAMER, Stanley H. 1933-

PERSONAL: Born October 1, 1933, in Brooklyn, N.Y.; son of Louis and Sophie (Zimmerman) Cramer; married Rosalind Faber (an acting teacher), November 26, 1959; children: Elizabeth, Lauren, Matthew. *Education:* University of Massachusetts, B.A., 1955; New York College for Teachers (now State University of New York at Albany), M.A., 1957; Columbia University, Ed.D., 1963. *Home:* 21 Foxboro Lane, East Amherst, N.Y. 14051. *Office:* Department of Education, State University of New York, Buffalo, N.Y. 14260.

CAREER: State University of New York at Buffalo, professor of education and associate provost, 1965—. *Member:* American Personnel and Guidance Association, American School Counselor Association, Association for Measurement and Evaluation in Guidance, Association for Counselor Education and Supervision, National Vocational Guidance Association.

WRITINGS: (With Edwin L. Herr) *Guidance of the College Bound: Problems, Practices, and Perspectives,* Appleton, 1968; (with Herr, C. N. Morris, and T. T. Frantz) *Research and the School Counselor,* Houghton, 1970; (with James C. Hansen) *Group Guidance and Counseling in the Schools: Selected Readings,* Appleton, 1971; (with Herr) *Career Development and Vocational Guidance in the Schools: Toward a Systems Approach,* Houghton, 1972.

SIDELIGHTS: Stanley Cramer told *CA* that he has a "general interest in vocational, educational, and personal-social guidance and counseling of youth."

* * *

CRAWFORD, T(erence Gordon) S(harman-) 1945-

PERSONAL: Born May 23, 1945, in Birmingham, England; son of Robert Hugh and Violet (Williams) Sharman-Crawford. *Education:* Attended Marlborough College, 1959-63. *Politics:* Right-wing. *Home:* 1 Mapledurham View, Reading, England. *Office:* Central Office of Information, Reading, England.

CAREER: Free-lance writer, 1963-70; British Civil Service

Commission, Basingstoke, Hampshire, England, editor, 1970-73; Central Office of Information, Reading, England, press officer, 1974—.

WRITINGS: A History of the Umbrella, Taplinger, 1970.

SIDELIGHTS: T. S. Crawford told *CA:* "My current job as press officer for the British Government measures to combat unemployment provides a good wage but does not fulfil any creative writing urge. I plan to resume freelance writing on general interest matters in my spare time."

* * *

CRECHALES, Anthony George 1926-
(Tony Crechales; pseudonyms: Tony Kent, Tony Trelos)

PERSONAL: Born May 27, 1926, in Hoboken, N.J.; son of George Anthony (a restaurateur and columnist for Greek newspapers) and Irene (Worth) Crechales. *Education:* Trained for stage at drama schools in New York and Hollywood. *Politics:* Democrat. *Religion:* "Greek Orthodox turned Roman Catholic turned Greek Orthodox." *Home:* 12031 Hoffman St., Studio City, Calif. 91604. *Agent:* William Morris Agency, 1350 Avenue of the Americas, New York, N.Y. 10019.

CAREER: Actor in films and on television under the professional name of Tony Kent between 1948-53; stage manager for National Road Co. tour of "The Teahouse of the August Moon," 1955-56; appeared in summer stock in a series of shows, 1956, 1957; partner in talent publicity agency, Crechales & Stemler, Hollywood, Calif., 1958-65; full-time writer, 1965—; currently affiliated with Dimension Pictures, Inc. as story reader and film consultant. Had film roles in "Just for You," a Paramount film starring Bing Crosby and Jane Wyman, and in "Fixed Bayonets," produced by Twentieth-Century Fox; also appeared in fifteen live television shows during his acting days and many commercials. *Military service:* U.S. Navy, 1944-46; served aboard a destroyer. *Member:* Screen Actors Guild, Writers Guild of America, West.

WRITINGS—Under pseudonym Tony Trelos; all published by Brandon House: *Cindy Baby,* 1965; *Reluctant Gay Girls,* 1965; *Sophisticated Sinner,* 1966; *The Lavendar Runway,* 1966; *The Stray Pussycat,* 1966; *A Lesbian Happening,* 1966; *Love Arena,* 1967; *Anytime for Love,* 1967; *Corruption of Linda,* 1968; *Hired Lover,* 1968; *Sex Happenings of Margo Turner,* 1968; *The Twisted Drives of Victoria McCall,* 1968; *Lisa's Sweet Body,* 1969; *King Sex for President,* 1969; *Four Wheeling Bastard,* 1969; *Blood Lust,* 1970.

Under name Tony Crechales; all screenplays: "Blood Mania," Crown International; "Point of Terror," Crown International; "Love Thy Murderer"; "Impulse"; "The Killing Kind."

WORK IN PROGRESS: Three screenplays, "Barracuda," "Bunky and Mae," and "The Widow."

* * *

CREEVEY, Lucy E. 1940-
(Lucy Creevey Behrman)

PERSONAL: Born July 2, 1940, in Cambridge, N.Y.; daughter of Kennedy (a physician) and Margaret (Brundage) Creevey. *Education:* Smith College, B.A., 1962; Boston University, M.A., 1963, Ph.D., 1967. *Home:* 4232 Regent, Philadelphia, Pa. 19104. *Office:* Urban Studies Program, 3400 Walnut St., University of Pennsylvania, Philadelphia, Pa. 19174.

CAREER: University of Pennsylvania, Philadelphia, 1967—, began as assistant professor of political science, currently associate professor of city planning and director of urban studies program. *Member:* American Political Science Association, African Studies Association, Phi Beta Kappa.

WRITINGS—Under name Lucy Creevey Behrman: *Muslim Brotherhoods and Politics in Senegal,* Harvard University Press, 1970.

Contributor: Jeffrey Butler and A. A. Castagno, editors, *Boston University Papers on Africa: Transition in African Politics,* Praeger, 1967; Butler, Daniel F. McCall, Norman R. Bennett, editors, *Western African History,* Praeger, 1969; D. E. Smith, editor, *Religion and Modernization,* Yale University Press, 1974. Also author of special report for the National Science Foundation, 1975. Also contributor of articles and reports to journals.

* * *

CRENA de IONGH, Daniel 1888-1970

April 21, 1888—November 26, 1970; Dutch bank executive and author. Obituaries: *New York Times,* November 28, 1970. (See index for *CA* sketch)

* * *

CRETAN, Gladys (Yessayan) 1921-

PERSONAL: Born November 11, 1921, in Reedley, Calif.; daughter of Vahan Hodge (a minister) and Annig (Keleshian) Yessayan; married Clarence A. Cretan (a school administrator), August 16, 1943; children: Clifford Vahan, Lawrence Diran. *Education:* Attended University of California, Berkeley, 1939-40, 1946-47. *Religion:* Protestant. *Home:* 717 Barneson Ave., San Mateo, Calif. 94402.

CAREER: Writer. Executive director, San Mateo Foundation, 1970-74; director of annual workshop for freelance writers, Canada College, Redwood City, Calif., 1975—.

WRITINGS: A Gift from the Bride, Atlantic-Little, Brown, 1964; *All Except Sammy* (Junior Literary Guild selection), Atlantic-Little, Brown, 1966; *Runaway Habeeb,* Abingdon, 1968; *Lobo,* Lothrop, 1969; *Me, Myself, & I,* Morrow, 1969; *Because I Promised,* Abingdon, 1970; *Lobo and Brewster,* Lothrop, 1971; *Messy Sally,* Lothrop, 1972; *A Hole, a Box and a Stick,* Lothrop, 1972; *Sunday For Sona,* Lothrop, 1973; *Ten Brothers with Camels,* Western Publishing, 1975.

SIDELIGHTS: Gladys Cretan told *CA:* "Two of my books (*Gift* and *Promised*) have Armenian backgrounds, which I am familiar with from my parents who came from Armenia when they were young. Our home was always an interesting conglomeration of people from the near-east, and of theologians of all sorts of backgrounds." Mrs. Cretan speaks the Armenian language, which has brought about interesting and unusual experiences in her travels.

* * *

CRIM, Keith R(enn) 1924-
(Casey Renn)

PERSONAL: Born September 30, 1924, in Winchester, Va.; son of Harry Marshall (a clergyman) and Grace (Renn) Crim; married Evelyn Ritchie (a teacher), August 26, 1947; children: Deborah, Gregory, Edward, Julia, Martin. *Education:* Bridgewater College, Bridgewater, Va., B.A., 1947; Union Theological Seminary, Richmond, Va., B.D., 1950, Th.M., 1951, Th.D., 1959; University of Basel, graduate study, 1951-52. *Politics:* Democrat. *Home:* 5000 East Seminary Ave., Richmond, Va. 23227. *Office:* Department of Philo-Religious Studies, Virginia Commonwealth University, 901 West Franklin St., Richmond, Va. 23220.

CAREER: Clergyman of Presbyterian Church; Taejon College, Taejon, Korea, assistant professor, 1956-59, associate professor, 1959-62, professor of English, 1962-65, acting president, 1958-59, 1964-65; John Knox Press, Richmond, Va., senior book editor, 1967-69; American Bible Society, New York, N.Y., Bible translator, beginning 1969; currently affiliated with department of philo-religious studies, Virginia Commonwealth University, Richmond, Va. Visiting professor of world religions, Austin Presbyterian Seminary, Austin, Tex., 1962-63. Teacher in seminars for translators in Asia, North America, and Europe; consultant on translation projects in Korea and Curacao, and in Amerindian languages. *Military service:* U.S. Army, Military Intelligence, 1943-46; served in Europe; became staff sergeant.

WRITINGS: The Royal Psalms, John Knox, 1962; (under pseudonym Casey Renn) *Limericks—Lay and Clerical,* John Knox, 1969; (with George A. Buttrick and others) *The Interpreter's Dictionary of the Bible,* Abingdon, 1976.

Translator from the German; all published by John Knox, except as indicated: *The Praise of God in the Psalms,* 1964; Dietrich Bonhoeffer, *I Loved This People,* 1965; Karl Barth, *Selected Prayers,* 1966; Barth, *Ad Limina Apostolorum,* 1968; Hans W. Wolff, *The Old Testament: A Guide to Its Writings,* Fortress, 1973. Contributor of news reports from Korea to *Christian Century,* 1959-62, 1964-66.

WORK IN PROGRESS: Translating, under auspices of the American Bible Society, the Old Testament in *Today's English Version,* including the Book of Job, which is to be published separately; a novel dealing with tensions between Americans and Koreans on an army base in South Korea.

SIDELIGHTS: In addition to fluency in German and Korean, Keith Crim reads French, and has some ability in Japanese, Dutch, Italian, and the classical European languages.†

* * *

CRINKLEY, Richmond 1940-

PERSONAL: Born January 20, 1940, in Richmond, Va.; son of James Epes (a commissioner of revenue) and Sarah (Beck) Crinkley. *Education:* University of Virginia, B.A. (with honors), 1961, M.A., 1962, Ph.D., 1966; Oxford University, graduate study, 1965-67. *Home:* 59 West 71st St., New York, N.Y. 10023. *Office:* American National Theatre, 245 West 52nd St., New York, N.Y. 10019.

CAREER: University of North Carolina, Chapel Hill, assistant professor of English, 1967-69; Folger Theatre Group, Washington, D.C., artistic director, 1969-73; Kennedy Center for the Performing Arts, New York City, theatre producer, 1973-76; American National Theatre, New York City, executive director, 1976—. Member of board of directors, WETA-TV, Washington, D.C. *Member:* Raven Society, Phi Beta Kappa, Pi Delta Epsilon.

WRITINGS: Walter Pater, Humanist, University Press of Kentucky, 1971. Drama critic, *National Review,* 1968—. Contributor of articles and reviews to periodicals.

* * *

CRITCHLEY, T(homas) A(lan) 1919-

PERSONAL: Born March 11, 1919, in London, England; son of Thomas (an analytical chemist) and Annie (Darvell) Critchley; married Margaret Robinson, July 25, 1942; chil-

dren: Carol Mary (Mrs. A. W. Mathieson), Barbara Jean (Mrs. D. G. Porteous-Butler), Alan James. *Education:* Educated in England. *Home:* 26 Temple Fortune Lane, London N.W.11, England.

CAREER: Commonwealth Prime Ministers' Conference, London, England, member of secretariat, 1956; Home Secretary, London, principal private secretary, 1957-60; Royal Commission on Police, London, secretary, 1960-62; Lord Denning's Enquiry into the Profumo Affair, secretary, 1963; Home Office, Police Department, London, senior civil servant, 1963-71; director of Uganda Resettlement Board, 1972-74. *Military service:* British Army, 1940-46; became lieutenant. *Member:* London Library, Reform Club.

WRITINGS: The Civil Service Today, Gollancz, 1951; *A History of Police in England and Wales 900-1966,* Constable, 1967; *The Conquest of Violence: Order and Liberty in Britain,* Schocken, 1970.

AVOCATIONAL INTERESTS: Mountain climbing, swimming, chess, tennis.

BIOGRAPHICAL/CRITICAL SOURCES: New Statesman, October 20, 1967; *Spectator,* March 7, 1970.

* * *

CROSBY, Alexander L. 1906-

PERSONAL: Born June 10, 1906, in Catonsville, Md.; son of Philip B. and Bessie (Clayton) Crosby; married Dorothy Christensen, June, 1930; married second wife, Lucretia Prentiss, December, 1951; married third wife, Nancy Larrick (a writer), February 15, 1958; children: (first marriage) Alexander C., Philip B. *Education:* Attended San Diego State University; University of California, Berkeley, B.A., 1928. *Politics:* Independent radical. *Home:* Route 4, Quakertown, Pa. 18951. *Agent:* Joan Daves, 515 Madison Ave., New York, N.Y. 10022.

CAREER: Newspaperman in New York, N.Y., and Paterson, N.J., 1929-42; editor of *New Jersey Guide* in American Guide Series, 1936-38; executive director of National Housing Conference, 1942-44; free-lance writer of pamphlets and children's books, 1944—. *Awards, honors: The Rio Grande* and *Steamboat Up the Colorado* were included in *Scientific American*'s list of best children's books of the year.

WRITINGS: (With wife, Nancy Larrick) *Rockets into Space,* Random House, 1959; *The Junior Science Book of Beavers,* Garrard, 1960; *The Colorado, Mover of Mountains,* Garrard, 1961; *The Junior Science Book of Pond Life,* Garrard, 1964; *Steamboat Up the Colorado,* Little, Brown, 1965; *The World of Rockets,* Random House, 1965; *The Junior Science Book of Canada Geese,* Garrard, 1966; *The Rimac, River of Peru,* Garrard, 1966; *The Rio Grande, Life for the Desert,* Garrard, 1966; *Old Greenwood,* Talisman, 1967; *Go Find Hanka!,* Golden Gate, 1970; *One Day for Peace,* Little, Brown, 1971.

WORK IN PROGRESS: A fantasy in which animals conspire to block construction of an interstate highway through a wildlife sanctuary.

BIOGRAPHICAL/CRITICAL SOURCES: The Children's Bookshelf, Bantam, 1965; Nancy Larrick, *A Teacher's Guide to Children's Books,* Merrill, 1966; *Books for Children, 1960-1965,* American Library Association, 1966; Nancy Larrick, *A Parent's Guide to Children's Reading,* 3rd edition, Doubleday, 1969.

CROSS, Aleene Ann 1922-

PERSONAL: Born January 19, 1922, in Ocilla, Ga.; daughter of John Gordon and Mae (Baker) Cross. *Education:* Georgia State College for Women (now Georgia College), B.S.H.E., 1943; University of Georgia, M.Ed., 1952; Columbia University, Ed.D., 1959. *Politics:* Democratic. *Religion:* Methodist. *Home:* 320 South Pope, Athens, Ga. 30605. *Office:* University of Georgia, Aderhold Hall, Athens, Ga. 30602.

CAREER: Teacher of home economics at high schools in Nashville, Ga., Fitzgerald, Ga., and College Park, Ga., 1943-54; University of Georgia, Athens, instructor in home economics, 1954-57, professor of home economics education and head of department, 1959—. Visiting instructor, Columbia University, 1958. *Member:* American Vocational Association (president of home economics division, 1972-73), Phi Delta Kappa, Kappa Delta Pi, Omicron Nu, Pi Lambda Theta, Phi Upsilon Omicron.

WRITINGS: Suggestions for Teaching Foods and Nutrition, Department of Homemaking Education, University of Georgia, 1958, revised edition, 1965; (project director) *A Post-High School Program in Child Care Services and Food Services,* Department of Home Economics Education, University of Georgia, 1966; *Enjoying Family Living,* Lippincott, 1967; *Introduction to Homemaking,* Lippincott, 1970; *Home Economics Evaluation,* C. E. Merrill, 1973.

*   *   *

CROSS, Jennifer 1932-

PERSONAL: Born May 10, 1932, in London, England; daughter of Thomas Reginald and Ruth (Neil) Cross; married Ellis Myron Gans (a house-mender), July 10, 1965; children: Jason David Mycroft. *Education:* King's College, London, B.A. (honors), 1953. *Politics:* Left of center. *Religion:* "Nominally, Church of England." *Home:* 301 Surrey St., San Francisco, Calif. 94131.

CAREER: Tatler, London, England, sub-editor, 1953-54; Hamish Hamilton Ltd. (publishers), London, secretary, 1954-55; William Collins Sons & Co. Ltd. (publishers), London, secretary, 1955-56; *British Medical Journal,* London, staff member, 1956-57; Napper, Stinton, Woolley (advertising agency), London, public relations executive, 1958-63; free-lance journalist, writer, and teacher of consumer economics. Consultant to Consumer Action, San Francisco, Calif., 1975—; public member, State Board of Dental Examiners, 1976—.

WRITINGS: (Contributor) Carey McWilliams, *The California Revolution,* Grossman, 1968; *The Supermarket Trap: The Consumer and the Food Industry,* Indiana University Press, 1970, revised edition, 1976; *Justice Denied: A History of the Japanese in America* (juvenile), Scholastic Book Services, 1973; (with Eli Djeddah) *Now that I Know Which Side Is Up,* Ten Speed Press, 1976. Regular contributor to *Nation* and *San Francisco Bay Guardian;* contributor to *Times* (London), *Sunday Times* (London), *New Statesman, Punch,* and trade journals. Editor, *California Consumer.*

AVOCATIONAL INTERESTS: Jewelry making.

BIOGRAPHICAL/CRITICAL SOURCES: Harper's, October, 1970; *Nation,* December 28, 1970.

*   *   *

CROUDACE, Glynn 1917-
(Peter Monnow)

PERSONAL: Surname is pronounced *Crowd*-us; born April 22, 1917, in Monmouth, England; son of Harry and Gertrude (Athow) Croudace; married Lynette Jooste, 1948; children: Jeremy, David, Clare. *Education:* Attended schools in Monmouth, England. *Politics:* Progressive. *Religion:* Anglican. *Home:* Westwinds, Rowan Ave., Kenilworth, Cape Town, South Africa. *Agent:* J. F. Gibson's Literary Agency, 4-5 Vernon House, Sicilian Ave., London WC1 2QH, England.

CAREER: Began as furnishing trade apprentice, Hereford, England; worked as free-lance journalist; joined *Cape Times,* Cape Town, South Africa, 1947; has worked for *Cape Argus* and *Sunday Tribune,* both Cape Town. *Military service:* Indian Army, 1939-46; served in India, Burma, and Malaya; became major. *Member:* Crime Writers' Association (London), P.E.N. (South Africa).

WRITINGS—Fiction: *The Dark Tide,* R. Hale, 1967; *The Silver Grass,* R. Hale, 1968; *The Black Rose,* R. Hale, 1968; (under pseudonym Peter Monnow) *Fire Opal,* Jenkins, 1968; (under pseudonym Peter Monnow) *The Killing of Alquin Judd,* Jenkins, 1968; *Blackadder,* Macmillan, 1969; *The Scarlet Bikini,* Macmillan, 1970; *The Hooded Skull,* R. Hale, 1971. Writer of about one-hundred broadcasted radio plays, 1974-76.

*   *   *

CROUT, George C(lement) 1917-

PERSONAL: Born February 10, 1917, in Middletown, Ohio; son of Ebert (a policeman) and Myrtle M. (a teacher; maiden name, Williamson) Crout. *Education:* Miami University, Oxford, Ohio, B.S., 1938, M.A., 1941, M.E., 1948, Specialist in Ed., 1955; further graduate study at Bowling Green University, 1962, Appalachian State University, 1963, University of Michigan, 1964, and George Peabody College for Teachers, 1965. *Politics:* Independent. *Religion:* Methodist. *Home:* 48-A Miami Dr., Monroe, Ohio 45050.

CAREER: Middletown (Ohio) public schools, teacher, 1938-42, 1946-48, principal of elementary schools, 1948-75; free-lance writer, 1975—. Instructor in Evening College, Miami University, Oxford, Ohio, 1946-47. *Military service:* U.S. Army Air Forces, 1942-45; served in Pacific theater; became staff sergeant; received six battle stars. *Member:* National Education Association, National Association of Elementary School Principals, Ohio Education Association, Ohio Department of Elementary School Principals, Ohio Historical Society, Canal Society of Ohio, Butler County Historical Society, Middletown Historical Society (curator), Phi Beta Kappa, American Legion. *Awards, honors:* American Educators Medal of Freedoms Foundation.

WRITINGS—Children's books, except as noted: (With illustrator Herbert W. Fall) *Stories of Our School Community,* Perry Printing Co., 1960, 5th edition, 1977; Wilfred D. Vorhis, editor, *Middletown U.S.A.: All American City* (adult), Perry Printing Co., 1960; (with Edith McCall) *Where the Ohio Flows,* Benefic, 1960; *Ohio Caravan* (poems), Perry Printing Co., 1961; *Seven Lives of Johnny B. Free,* Denison, 1961; *Middletown Diary* (adult), privately printed, 1965; *Lincoln's Littlest Soldier,* Denison, 1969; *Lucky Cloverleaf of the 4-H,* Denison, 1971; (with McCall) *You and Ohio,* Benefic, 1971; *Middletown Landmarks* (adult), Perry Printing Co., 1974; *You and Dayton,* News Publishing Co., 1976; *Old Middletown* (adult), KGI Printing Co., 1976; *Ohio: Its People and Culture,* Denison, 1977.

Plays for children: *Do It Yourself Christmas Plays,* Eldridge Publishing Co., 1960; *Little Star Lost,* Eldridge Publishing Co., 1960; *The Tinsel Fairy,* Eldridge Publishing Co., 1964;

Santa's Christmas Satellite, Eldridge Publishing Co., 1970. Contributor to journals and newspapers.

WORK IN PROGRESS: Jungle Air Force, a story of World War II; *Valley Vignettes.*

SIDELIGHTS: George C. Crout wrote *CA:* "Each book represents basic historical research utilizing previously unpublished manuscript material, presented simply for the young reader. An underlying theme is explored that may provide a young person with background in solving a problem he may face. *The Seven Lives of Johnny B. Free* shows how life has changed for youth searching for economic independence, while *Ohio: Its People and Culture* explores planning a career today in a state with a diverse culture, made up of many ethnic groups. Local and regional history is presented against a backdrop of national events, for American culture is a composite of its many localities."

* * *

CROVITZ, Herbert F(loyd)   1932-

PERSONAL: Born May 21, 1932; in Providence, R.I.; son of Jack (a salesman) and Natalie (Turick) Crovitz; married Esther Handelman, June, 1954 (annulled); married Elaine Kobrin (a clinical psychologist), December 19, 1957 (divorced August, 1973); children: (second marriage) Gordon, Deborah, Sara Pi. *Education:* Clark University, Worcester, Mass., A.B., 1953, M.A., 1954; Duke University, Ph.D., 1960. *Home:* 3600 Tremont Dr., Durham, N.C. 27705. *Office:* Veterans Administration Hospital, Durham, N.C. 27705.

CAREER: Veteran's Administration Hospital, Durham, N.C., research psychologist, 1961—. Duke University, Durham, N.C., lecturer in psychology, 1961—, Medical Center, associate professor, 1961-73, professor of psychology, 1973—. *Member:* American Psychological Association, Psychonomic Society, Optical Society of America, American Association for the Advancement of Science.

WRITINGS: Galton's Walk: Methods for the Analysis of Thinking, Intelligence, and Creativity, Harper, 1970. Contributor to *Journal of Experimental Psychology, American Journal of Psychology, Science, Vision Research,* and other professional journals.

WORK IN PROGRESS: Research in human binocular vision, analogies between sensation and cognition, heuristics, memory.

SIDELIGHTS: Herbert F. Crovitz told *CA* that one of his major areas of vocational interest is "trying to understand the disorders of memory."

* * *

CROWELL, Pers   1910-

PERSONAL: Surname is pronounced with long "o"; born March 28, 1910, in Pasco, Wash.; son of Willis Watson (a farmer) and Carrie May (Smith) Crowell; married Donna Stamper Osborne, July 15, 1952; children: Donna (Mrs. Donald Lynch). *Education:* Attended Phoenix Art Institute, 1931-32, Chouinard's School of Art, 1933-34, University of Oregon, 1940-41. *Politics:* Independent. *Home and office:* 1845 Southwest 170th Ave., Beaverton, Ore. 97005.

CAREER: Began career as free-lance advertising artist in Portland, Ore., in 1937; later served as art director for various advertising agencies in Portland, as account executive for Carvel, Nelson & Powell Advertising Agency, Portland; GAF Corp. (formerly Sawyer's, Inc.), Portland, former

creative director, and consulting art director; free-lance illustrator and writer.

WRITINGS: Beau Dare: American Saddle Colt, McGraw, 1946; *Six Good Friends,* McGraw, 1947; (self-illustrated) *The First Horseman,* McGraw, 1948; (self-illustrated) *Cavalcade of American Horses,* McGraw, 1951; *What Can a Horse Do That You Can't Do?,* McGraw, 1954; (self-illustrated) *The Thought Book,* Coward, 1959; (self-illustrated) *King Moo, the Wordmaker,* Caxton, 1976. Contributor of articles to *American Shetland Pony Journal, Western Horseman, Portland Oregonian,* and *Oregon Journal.*

Illustrator: Isabel M. McMeekin, *First Book of Horses,* F. Watts, 1949; Leland Silliman, *Golden Cloud: Palomino of Sunset Hill,* Winston, 1950; Joan Beckman, *Skylark Farm,* McGraw, 1950; Eleanor Frances Brown, *Horse for Peter,* Messner, 1950; Brown, *Wendy Wanted a Pony,* Messner, 1951; George Sullivan, *Pass to Win,* Garrard, 1968; Charles P. Graves, *William Tecumseh Sherman,* Garrard, 1968; Alice Thorne, *Anna Sewell's Black Beauty,* World Distributors, 1969; Wyatt Blassingame, *William F. Halsey,* Garrard, 1970; Rutherford Montgomery, *Big Red, a Wild Stallion,* Caxton, 1970; William E. Sanderson, *Nez Perce Buffalo Horse,* Caxton, 1971; John W. Ball, *Casting and Fishing the Artificial Fly,* Caxton, 1971; Dorothy Grunbock Johnston, *Pounding Hooves,* David C. Cook, 1976.

WORK IN PROGRESS: Horse stories for young people; paintings with Western Americana themes.

SIDELIGHTS: Pers Crowell told *CA:* "The themes which I am most interested in presenting to young people are ones which point out man's basic accomplishments. Anthropology and early man's ability to innovate and creatively cope with his environment interest me. Also the belief that the true spark of creativity is largely an individual process is touched on in *The Thought Book.* While I respect tradition and recognize its importance to human development, I deplore political and economic trends which stifle individual freedom and potentiality of thought.

AVOCATIONAL INTERESTS: Horses. ("My wife and I raise American Shetland ponies and my relaxation and diversion lies in training and showing ponies.")

BIOGRAPHICAL/CRITICAL SOURCES: Illustrators of Children's Books: 1946-1956, Horn Book, 1958.

* * *

CRUMBLEY, D. Larry   1941-

PERSONAL: Born January 18, 1941, in Kannapolis, N.C.; son of Carl Donald and Velvia Crumbley; married Donna D. Loflin; children: Stacey, Dana, Heather. *Education:* Pfeiffer College, B.S. (cum laude), 1963; Louisiana State University, Baton Rouge, M.S., 1965, Ph.D., 1967. *Home address:* P.O. Box 9027, College Station, Tex. 77840. *Office:* Department of Accounting, School of Business, Texas A & M University, College Station, Tex. 77843.

CAREER: Seidman & Seidman, Baton Rouge, La., staff accountant, 1967; Pennsylvania State University, University Park, assistant professor of accounting, 1967-69; Arthur Andersen & Co., New York, N.Y., faculty resident, 1969-70; certified public accountant in the state of North Carolina, 1970; University of Florida, Gainesville, associate professor of accounting, 1970-75; Texas A & M University, School of Business, College Station, faculty member in department of accounting, 1975—. Adjunct assistant professor, Graduate School of Buisness, New York University, 1970. *Member:* American Institute of Certified Public Accountants, National Tax Association, American Taxation Association (former president), American Accounting Association, Texas Society of Certified Public Accountants, Phi Kappa Phi, Beta Gamma Sigma, Beta Alpha Psi. *Awards, honors:* Ford Foundation grant, 1966-67; Humble Oil Company fellowship, 1966-67.

WRITINGS: (With Michael Davis) *Organizing, Operating and Terminating Subchapter S Corporations,* Estate Tax Publishing Co. (Aberdeen), 1970, revised edition, Lawyers & Judges Publishing, 1975; (with Ronald Copeland and Joseph Wojdak) *Advanced Accounting,* Holt, 1971; *A Practical Guide to the Preparation of Gift Tax Returns,* Estate Tax Publishing Co., 1971, revised edition, Lawyers & Judges Publishing, 1977; *A Practical Guide to Preparing an Estate Tax Return,* Lawyers & Judges Publishing, 1977. Coauthor of a column, "Tax Notes for the Young Practitioner," in *Taxation for Accountants.* Contributor of about eighty-five articles on accounting and taxation to professional journals. Editor of *Oil and Gas Tax Quarterly;* also editor of various hobby-related columns for *Coin World, Philatelic Reporter and Digest,* and *Linn's World Stamp Almanac.*

* * *

CRUNDEN, Robert M. 1940-

PERSONAL: Born December 23, 1940, in Jersey City, N.J.; son of Allan B., Jr. (an obstetrician and gynecologist) and Marjorie (Morse) Crunden; children: Wendy. *Education:* Yale University, B.A., 1962; Harvard University, Ph.D., 1967. *Politics:* Independent. *Religion:* None. *Home:* 117 Laurel Lane, Austin, Tex. 78705. *Office:* Department of American Civilization, Garrison Hall 303-A, University of Texas, Austin, Tex. 78712.

CAREER: University of Texas at Austin, assistant professor, 1967-70, associate professor of history and American studies, 1970—. Bicentennial Professor of American Studies, University of Helsinki, Finland, 1975-76. *Member:* American Historical Association, American Studies Association, Organization of American Historians.

WRITINGS: The Mind and Art of Albert Jay Nock, Regnery, 1964; *A Hero in Spite of Himself: Brand Whitlock in Art, Politics, and War,* Knopf, 1969; *From Self to Society: Transition in American Thought,* Prentice-Hall, 1972; (editor with F. Freidel and N. Pollack) *Builders of American Institutions,* Rand McNally, 1972; *The Superfluous Men: Conservative Critics of American Culture,* University of Texas Press, 1977; *Progressivism,* Schenkman, 1977.

WORK IN PROGRESS: "*The Progressive Experience in American Culture, 1889-1919,* an interdisciplinary work that will expand conventional definitions of the term 'progressivism.'"

* * *

CUBAN, Larry 1934-

PERSONAL: Born October 31, 1934, in Passaic, N.J.; son of Morris (a jobber) and Fanny (Janoff) Cuban; married Barbara Joan Smith (a secretary), June 15, 1958; children: Sondra, Janice. *Education:* University of Pittsburgh, B.A., 1955; Western Reserve University (now Case Western Reserve University), M.A., 1958; Yale, graduate student, 1958-63; Stanford University, Ph.D., 1974. *Religion:* Jewish. *Home:* 1436 Holly St. N.W., Washington, D.C. 20012.

CAREER: Teacher in public schools in Pennsylvania and

Ohio, 1955-63; Cardozo Project in Urban Teaching, Washington, D.C., master teacher of history, 1963-65, director, 1965-67; Roosevelt High School, Washington, D.C., teacher of history, 1967-68; District of Columbia Public Schools, Washington, D.C., director of staff development, 1969-70; Roosevelt High School, teacher of history, 1970-71; Virginia Public Schools, Arlington, superintendent, 1974—. Member, President's Advisory Committee for Teacher Corps, 1967-69; director, U.S. Commission on Civil Rights, 1968. Consultant to National Institute for Education, National Teacher Corps, and various public school systems, colleges, and universities, 1964—.

WRITINGS: The Negro in America, Scott, Foresman, 1964, revised edition published as *The Black Man in America,* 1971; *To Make a Difference: Teaching in the Inner City,* Free Press, 1970; (contributor) V. Haubrich, editor, *Freedom, Bureaucracy and the Schools,* National Education Association, 1971; (with Philip Roden) *The Promise of America,* Scott, Foresman, 1971; (editor) *Youth as a Minority,* National Council for the Social Studies, 1972; *Urban School Chiefs under Fire,* University of Chicago Press, 1976.

Editor of "Contemporary Civilization" series; all published by Scott, Foresman: *Japan,* 1970; *India,* 1971; *Russia,* 1972; *Kenya,* 1972; *Mexico,* 1972. Contributor to *D.C. Gazette, Social Education, Harvard Educational Review, Education Project Review, Saturday Review, Educational Leadership, Journal of Negro Education, Phylon, Washington Post, Social Studies,* and *Negro History Bulletin.*

* * *

CULLEN, Patrick (Colborn) 1940-

PERSONAL: Born October 7, 1940, in Crisfield, Md.; son of Reginald (a farmer) and Hope (Colborn) Cullen. *Education:* Washington College, Chestertown, Md., B.A., 1962; Brown University, M.A., 1964, Ph.D., 1967. *Home:* 300 West 108th St., New York, N.Y. 10025. *Office:* Department of Humanities, College of Staten Island of the City University of New York, 130 Stuyvesant Pl., Staten Island, N.Y. 10301.

CAREER: College of Staten Island of the City University of New York, Staten Island, N.Y., assistant professor, 1967-71, associate professor of English, 1971—, faculty member of Graduate Center, 1971—. *Member:* Modern Language Association of America, Renaissance Society of America, Milton Society, Spenser Society, Modern Humanities Research Association, Medieval Academy of America, North Eastern Modern Language Association.

WRITINGS: Spenser, Milton, and Renaissance Pastoral, Harvard University Press, 1970; *Infernal Triad: The Flesh, the World, and the Devil in Spenser and Milton,* Princeton University Press, 1974.

WORK IN PROGRESS: The Pastoral Mode and Renaissance Epic; co-editing *Spenser Studies* for University of Pittsburgh Press.

* * *

CULP, John H(ewett, Jr.) 1907-

PERSONAL: Born August 31, 1907, in Meridian, Miss.; son of John Hewett and Nelle (Hoyle) Culp; married Elizabeth Price, June 25, 1934 (deceased). *Education:* University of Oklahoma, A.B., 1934. *Home and office:* 1805 North Louisa, Shawnee, Okla. 74801.

CAREER: Teacher in public schools of Norman, Okla.,

1934-41; owner of music store in Ardmore, Okla., 1941-42, and Shawnee, Okla., 1946-68; full-time writer, 1968—. *Military service:* U.S. Army Air Forces, 1943-45; became sergeant. *Member:* Phi Beta Kappa.

WRITINGS: Born of the Sun, Sloane, 1959; *The Men of Gonzales,* Sloane, 1960; *The Restless Land,* Sloane, 1962; *The Bright Feathers,* Holt, 1965; *A Whistle in the Wind,* Holt, 1968; *Timothy Baines,* Holt, 1969; *The Treasure of the Chisos,* Holt, 1972; *Oh, Valley Green!,* Holt, 1972.

BIOGRAPHICAL/CRITICAL SOURCES: New York Times Book Review, June 28, 1968; *Best Sellers,* August 15, 1968.

*   *   *

CURRAN, Stuart (Alan) 1940-

PERSONAL: Born August 3, 1940, in Highland Park, Mich.; son of Lawrence Charles (an engineer) and Margaret (a social worker; maiden surname Dalton) Curran. *Education:* University of Michigan, B.A., 1962, M.A., 1963; attended Cornell University, 1963-64; Harvard University, Ph.D., 1967. *Home:* 320 South 16th St., Philadelphia, Pa. 19102. *Office:* Department of English, University of Pennsylvania, Philadelphia, Pa. 19104.

CAREER: University of Wisconsin—Madison, associate professor of English, 1967-74; University of Pennsylvania, Philadelphia, professor of English, 1974—, chairman of English department, 1977-80. *Member:* Modern Language Association of America, Keats-Shelley Association, Byron Society, American Blake Foundation (member of board of directors). *Awards, honors:* American Philosophical Society research grant, 1968; National Endowment for the Humanities junior fellowship, 1970-71; Huntington Library fellowships, 1970, 1972; John Simon Guggenheim Foundation grant, 1973-74.

WRITINGS: Shelley's "Cenci": Scorpions Ringed with Fire, Princeton University Press, 1970; (editor and author of introduction) *Le Bossu and Voltaire on the Epic,* Scholars Facsimiles & Reprints, 1970; (editor with Joseph Anthony Wittreich, Jr.) *Blake's Sublime Allegory: Essays on "The Four Zoas," "Milton," and "Jerusalem,"* University of Wisconsin Press, 1973; *Shelley's "Annus Mirabilis": The Maturing of an Epic Vision,* Huntington Library Press, 1975.

Author of annual bibliography for Shelley and Keats, "Bibliography of Romanticism" for *English Language Notes;* contributor of articles to *Keats-Shelley Journal, Keats-Shelley Memorial Bulletin, Blake Studies,* and *Nineteenth-Century Fiction.*

WORK IN PROGRESS: Poetic Genres and English Romanticism.

*   *   *

CURRY, Leonard Preston 1929-

PERSONAL: Born March 23, 1929, in Cave City, Ky.; son of Daniel Preston (a professor) and Ruby (Downey) Curry; married Mary Prichard, June 25, 1959; children: Fletcher, Justin. *Education:* Western Kentucky State College (now Western Kentucky University), A.B., 1951; University of Kentucky, M.A., 1956, Ph.D., 1961. *Politics:* Democrat. *Religion:* Presbyterian. *Home:* 1801 Spring Dr., Louisville, Ky. 40205. *Office:* Department of History, University of Louisville, Louisville, Ky. 40208.

CAREER: Memphis State University, Memphis, Tenn.,

instructor, 1958-60, assistant professor of history, 1960-62; University of Louisville, Louisville, Ky., assistant professor, 1962-66, associate professor, 1966-69, professor of history, 1969—. Visiting professor at University of Maine, 1964-65, and University of Maryland, 1968-69; visiting postdoctoral research associate, Smithsonian Institution, 1970-71. *Military service:* U.S. Air Force, 1951-53. U.S. Air Force Reserve, 1953; current rank, captain. *Member:* American Historical Association, Organization of American Historians, Southern Historical Association, Phi Alpha Theta. *Awards, honors:* Research grants from American Philosophical Society, 1962, 1972, 1976, and American Council of Learned Societies, 1976.

WRITINGS: Blueprint for Modern America: Nonmilitary Legislation of the First Civil War Congress, Vanderbilt University Press, 1968; *Rail Routes South: Louisville's Fight for Southern Commerce, 1865-1872,* University of Kentucky Press, 1969; (contributor) J. Winston Coleman, editor, *The Pictorial History of Kentucky,* University Press of Kentucky, 1971; *Urban Life in the Old South* (essay), Forum Press, 1976. Contributor to historical journals.

WORK IN PROGRESS: A book-length study of U.S. urban development, 1800-1850; a book-length study of urban blacks in the United States, 1800-1850.

*   *   *

CURTIS, (Hubert) Arnold 1917-

PERSONAL: Born May 20, 1917, in London, England; son of Frank Hubert and Elizabeth Ethel (Ward) Curtis; married Almaria Daphne Wingfield Digby, March 9, 1948; children: Stephanie, Jill. *Education:* New College, Oxford, B.A., 1939, M.A., 1959. *Address:* P.O. Box 10, Limuru, Kenya.

CAREER: International Refugee Organization, chief of East Africa Mission, 1947-50; British Council for Aid to Refugees, staff member, 1951; Keyna Ministry of Education, Nairobi, 1952-74, secretary, Institute of Education, 1964-66, inspector of teacher education, 1966—. *Wartime service:* Friends Ambulance Unit, 1940-44; UNRAA, Middle East and Greece, 1944-47.

WRITINGS: Africa (youth book), Oxford University Press, 1969; *Conversation Practice,* East Africa Publishing House, 1970; *Write Well* (junior composition textbook), Oxford University Press, 1975. Co-author of "New Peak" juvenile series, Oxford University Press, 1962-65, and "Pivot English Course," Longmans (Kenya), 1965-69; also editor of two East African series of civics and English readers.

BIOGRAPHICAL/CRITICAL SOURCES: Times Literary Supplement, June 26, 1969.

*   *   *

CUSHING, Jane 1922-

PERSONAL: Born June 7, 1922, in Chicago, Ill.; daughter of John Leo (an auditor) and Adelaide (McPartlin) Cushing. *Education:* Saint Xavier College, Chicago, Ill., B.S., 1955; University of Notre Dame, M.A., 1965; Northern Arizona University, M.A., 1977. *Home:* 1713 North 42nd St., Phoenix, Ariz. 85008.

CAREER: Roman Catholic religious in order of Institute of Blessed Virgin Mary (I.B.V.M.); elementary teacher in Chicago, Ill., 1943-50, and in Phoenix, Ariz., 1950-54; Loretto High School and Loretto Academy, Chicago, Ill., librarian and teacher of English and communication arts, 1954-64; Loretto Adult Education Center, Chicago, Ill., director of young adult program, 1964-66; Loretto Extension Service, Chicago, Ill., director, 1966—. Teacher of communication arts, College of DuPage, 1967-76, Northern Arizona University, 1976-77, and Scottsdale Community College, 1977. *Member:* Screen Education Society (speaker's bureau).

WRITINGS: 101 Films for Character Growth, Fides, 1969.

WORK IN PROGRESS: A revised edition of *101 Films for Character Growth.*

* * *

CUTTLER, Charles D(avid) 1913-

PERSONAL: Born April 8, 1913, in Cleveland, Ohio; son of Morris Joseph and Nettie (Wolff) Cuttler; married Mary Cecilia Fuller, December 17, 1941 (divorced); children: Judith Ann. *Education:* Ohio State University, B.F.A., 1935, M.A., 1937; New York University, Ph.D., 1952. *Politics:* Independent. *Religion:* Unitarian Universalist. *Home:* 1691 Ridge Rd., Iowa City, Iowa 52240. *Office:* School of Art and Art History, University of Iowa, Iowa City, Iowa 52242.

CAREER: University of Colorado, Boulder, instructor in art history, 1938; engineering designer for several firms in Detroit, Mich., 1940-47; Michigan State University, East Lansing, assistant professor of art history, 1947-57; University of Iowa, Iowa City, associate professor, 1957-65, professor of art history, 1965—, research professor, 1965-66. Assistant professor, Indiana University, summers, 1952, 1953. *Member:* College Art Association of America, Renaissance Society of America, Mediaeval Academy of America, International Center for Medieval Art, American Association of University Professors, Midwest Art History Society (president, 1973-77). *Awards, honors:* Carnegie fellow at University of Paris, 1937; fellow at University of Brussels, 1939; Committee for Relief in Belgium senior fellow in Brussels, 1953-54; senior Fulbright fellow in Brussels, 1965-66.

WRITINGS: (With others) *An Introduction to Literature and the Fine Arts,* Michigan State College Press, 1950; *Northern Painting from Pucelle to Bruegel,* Holt, 1968. Also compiler of a catalogue of Flemish and German primitives for Detroit Institute of Arts. Contributor to art journals.

WORK IN PROGRESS: Repertoire de la peinture flamande du quinzieme et seizieme siecles: Midwest Collections; a monograph, *The Paintings and Drawings of Hieronymus Bosch.*

* * *

D'ALFONSO, John 1918-

PERSONAL: Born February 20, 1918, in Rochester, N.Y.; son of Angelo (a physician) and Djalma (Vurinoff) D'Alfonso; married Ruth Walker, July 7, 1943; married second wife, Mabel Ellen Baity, January 13, 1951; children: (second marriage) Bartley, Drake; stepchildren: Craig Stewart. *Education:* Attended Aquinas Institute, Rochester, 1932-36. *Home:* 4332 Randolph Ter., San Diego, Calif. 92103. *Office:* John D'Alfonso & Associates, 4033 El Cajon Blvd., San Diego, Calif. 92105.

CAREER: Convair Aircraft Corp., San Diego, Calif., member of planning staff, 1940-45; commentator on radio station KSDJ, San Diego, and reporter and columnist for *San Diego Daily Journal,* 1945-49; California-Western States Life (insurance company), San Diego, assistant manager, 1949-55; John D'Alfonso & Associates, San Diego, owner, 1955—; American Family Life Assurance Co., San Diego, state manager, 1970-75; Alert Enterprises, Inc., San Diego, president, 1974—. President of San Diego Salvation Army Citadel Board, 1956, and San Diego Stamp Out Crime Crusade, 1969-70; executive director, Leaf Foundation, 1976—. *Military service:* U.S. Navy, 1936-40; became petty officer. *Member:* National Association of Securities Dealers, Independent Insurance Agents Association, National Exchange Club (California state president, 1968-69). *Awards, honors:* San Diego Newspaper Guild award, 1947, for exposure of conditions leading to construction of a new facility for juveniles.

WRITINGS: The Crime Game, Viewpoint Books, 1969.

SIDELIGHTS: D'Alfonso was featured in the world press in 1948, when he tested Marine Corps security during maneuvers at Camp Pendelton while disguised as a Russian colonel. *The Crime Game* resulted from what he terms his outrage at the "molleycoddling of chronic vicious repeat criminals by the Warren Supreme Court, which in its zeal to protect the right of the accused, trampled on the rights of the law-abiding."

* * *

D'AMATO, Anthony A. 1937-

PERSONAL: Born January 10, 1937, in New York, N.Y.; son of Anthony A. (a teacher) and Mary (DiNicholas) D'Amato; married Barbara Steketee (a writer), September 4, 1958; children: Brian, Paul. *Education:* Cornell University, A.B. (with distinction and high honors), 1958; Harvard University, J.D. (magna cum laude), 1961; Columbia University, Ph.D., 1968. *Home:* 5807 Lake Shore Ave., Holland, Mich. 49423. *Office:* School of Law, Northwestern University, Chicago, Ill. 60611.

CAREER: Wellesley College, Wellesley, Mass., instructor in political science, 1964-67; Misco Management Co., Ann Arbor, Mich., Social Science Research Council fellow in statistics, 1967-68; Northwestern University, Evanston, Ill., assistant professor, 1968-70, associate professor, 1970-73, professor of law, 1973—. Visiting professor of law, Oregon Law School, 1973-74. Consultant to Hudson Institute, 1962-63, and to International League for the Rights of Man. Assistant counsel to Ethiopia and Liberia in "The South West Africa Cases," International Court of Justice, 1965-66. Trustee Museum of the Media, New York, N.Y. *Member:* American Society of International Law, American Political Science Association, International Studies Association, American Bar Association, New York Bar Association, Phi Beta Kappa. *Awards, honors:* National Endowment for the Humanities fellow, 1973.

WRITINGS: Law of the Use of Force Short of War, Hudson Institute, 1963; (editor with Christopher W. Beal) *The Realities of Vietnam,* Public Affairs Press, 1968; *The Concept of Custom in International Law,* Cornell University Press, 1971; (editor with Robert M. O'Neil) *The Judiciary and Vietnam,* St. Martin's, 1972; (with Hargrove) *Environment and the Law of the Sea,* West Publishing, 1975; *Desegregation from Brown to Alexander: An Exploration of Supreme Court Strategies,* Southern Illinois University Press, 1977. Also author of lyrics and music for a musical comedy based on *The Magic Man,* a book by his wife Barbara D'Amato. Contributor of more than forty articles to scholarly journals.

WORK IN PROGRESS: Studies of jurisprudence, ethics, and constitutional and international law, aiming toward book-length explorations of the philosophy and ethics of law.

SIDELIGHTS: Anthony D'Amato wrote to *CA:* "Why write about such a mundane subject as law? If one agrees with the prevailing legal philosophy (positivism), writing about law is just serving to make more efficient the power wishes of the central government—even if the government is democratic. Since I believe in the primacy of human liberty against any government, what I hope to accomplish in my research and writing is further understanding of the notion of a government limited by law. Legal limitations on government can make human liberty possible. Even if everyone else in society wants to deprive you of your natural rights and freedoms, you should be able to resist by invoking legal limitations that the others have previously consented to follow. Your natural rights and freedoms existed long before there were gangs or governments. You do not owe these freedoms to the government—even to a totally democratic government—and the government should not ever be acknowledged to have the right to take them away from you."

BIOGRAPHICAL/CRITICAL SOURCES: Christian Science Monitor, June 27, 1968.

*   *   *

DANIELL, Jere Rogers 1932-

PERSONAL: Born November 28, 1932, in Millinocket, Me.; son of Warren F. (an engineer) and Mary (Holway) Daniell; married Sally Wellborn, December 17, 1955; married second wife, Elena Lillie (a leather worker), July 17, 1969; children: (first marriage) Douglas, Alexander, Matthew; stepchildren: Breena, Clifford. *Education:* Dartmouth College, A.B., 1955; Harvard University, M.A., 1961, Ph.D., 1964. *Home:* 11 Barrymore Rd., Hanover, N.H. 03755. *Office:* Reed Hall, Dartmouth College, Hanover, N.H. 03755.

CAREER: Dartmouth College, Hanover, N.H., assistant professor, 1964-69, associate professor, 1969-74, professor of history, 1974—. Chairman, Dartmouth Committee on Equal Opportunity. *Military service:* U.S. Navy, 1955-58; became lieutenant junior grade. *Member:* National Humanities Faculty, Colonial Society of Massachusetts, New Hampshire Historical Society, New Hampshire Council of Humanities. *Awards, honors:* American Association of State and Local History research grant, 1968.

WRITINGS: Experiment in Republicanism: New Hampshire Politics and the American Revolution, 1741-1794, Harvard University Press, 1970.

WORK IN PROGRESS: History of Colonial New Hampshire; Small Town England.

*   *   *

DANIELS, Anna Kleegman 1893-1970

June 10, 1893—March 22, 1970; Ukrainian-born American gynecologist, obstetrician, and author. Obituaries: *New York Times,* March 23, 1970.

*   *   *

DANIELS, Arlene Kaplan 1930-

PERSONAL: Born December 10, 1930, in New York, N.Y.; daughter of Jacob (a store-keeper) and Elizabeth (Rathstone) Kaplan; married Richard Rene Daniels (a hospital administrator), June 9, 1956. *Education:* University of California, Berkeley, B.A. (with honors), 1952, M.A., 1954, Ph.D., 1960. *Politics:* Democrat. *Religion:* Agnostic. *Home:* 3404 Lodge Dr., Belmont, Calif. 94002. *Office:* Department of Sociology, Northwestern University, Evanston, Ill. 60201.

CAREER: University of California, Berkeley, private investigator for School of Public Health, 1957-58, instructor in speech, 1959-61; Mental Research Institute, Palo Alto, Calif., research associate, 1961-66; San Francisco State College (now University), San Francisco, Calif., associate professor of sociology, 1966-69; Scientific Analysis Corp., San Francisco, research associate, 1968—; Northwestern University, Evanston, Ill., professor of sociology and director of program on women, 1974—. *Member:* American Sociological Association, Society for the Study of Social Problems. *Awards, honors:* U.S. Army Research and Development Command grant, 1963-66; National Institute of Mental Health fellowship in law and psychiatry at School of Criminology, University of California, Berkeley, 1965-66, child health and human development grant, 1967-70; Social Science Research Council, faculty research award, 1970-71; Ford Foundation fellowship, 1975-76.

WRITINGS: (Contributor) Gideon Sjoberg, editor, *Politics, Ethics and Social Research,* Schenkman, 1967; (editor with Rachel Kahn-Hut) *Academics on the Line,* Jossey-Bass, 1970; (contributor) Tamotsu Shibutani, editor, *Human Nature and Collective Behavior,* Prentice-Hall, 1970; (contributor) Hans P. Dreitzle, editor, *Recent Trends in Sociology,* Macmillan, 1970; (contributor) Eliot Freidson and Judith Lorber, editors, *Medical Men and Their Work,* Atherton, 1971; *A Survey of Research Concerns on Women's Issues,* Association of American Colleges, 1975; (contributor) Marcia Millman and Rosabeth Kanter, editors, *Another Voice,* Doubleday, 1975. Contributor to psychiatry and sociology journals.

WORK IN PROGRESS: The Development of a Female Power Elite, completion expected in 1978.

*   *   *

DANIELS, George M(orris) 1927-

PERSONAL: Born July 9, 1927, in St. Louis, Mo.; son of Stafford Cecil and Hattie (Nichols) Daniels; married Cecille Adams (a teacher), 1960; married second wife, June Smith (a teacher), July 5, 1961; children: (first marriage) Margaret Ann; (second marriage) Lisa. *Education:* Drake University, B.A., 1951; Columbia University, M.A., 1970. *Politics:* Independent Liberal Republican. *Religion:* Methodist. *Home:* 392 Central Park W., New York, N.Y. 10025.

CAREER: Associated Negro Press, Chicago, Ill., rewrite man, 1951; *Chicago Daily Defender,* Chicago, reporter, 1951-57; *Together Magazine,* Chicago, news and feature writer, 1957-61; United Methodist Board of Missions, New York, N.Y., director of interpretive service, 1961—. Publications consultant; consultant-writer, Agency for International Development, U.S. State Department, 1976; freelance writer on African affairs; lecturer on the Black press in America and ghetto communications. *Military service:* U.S. Army Air Forces, 1945-47. *Member:* American Committee on Africa (member of board of directors), American Association for the United Nations, American Academy of Political and Social Science, Sigma Delta Chi, Alpha Phi Alpha. *Awards, honors: Vision Magazine* Award, Columbia University, 1970; Sigma Delta Chi Front Page Award for Reporting.

WRITINGS: This Is the Church in the New Nations, Friendship, 1964; (editor) *Southern Africa: A Time for Change,* Friendship, 1969; (editor) *Drums of War: The Continuing Crisis in Rhodesia,* Third Press, 1974. Contributor to *Black World, Black Enterprise, New World, Outlook, Together,* and *Tuesday.* Editor, *Sphinx.*

WORK IN PROGRESS: Researching book on the Black press in America; researching Black power in the Caribbean; editing, *Comprehensive Guide to Black Colleges.*

* * *

DANNER, Margaret (Essie) 1915-

PERSONAL: Born January 12, 1915, in Chicago, Ill.; daughter of Caleb and Nomi Danner; married Cordell Strickland; married second husband, Otto Cunningham; children: Naomi (Mrs. Sterling Montrose Washington). *Education:* Attended YMCA College and Roosevelt University; also studied under Karl Shapiro and Paul Engle. *Religion:* Baha'i. *Home:* 626 East 102nd Pl., Chicago, Ill. 60628.

CAREER: Poet. *Poetry* magazine, Chicago, Ill., editorial assistant, 1951-55, assistant editor, 1956-57; Wayne State University, Detroit, Mich., poet-in-residence, 1961-62; touring poet, Baha'i Teaching Committee, 1964-66; Whitney fellow in Senegal, Africa and Paris, France, 1966; Virginia Union University, Richmond, poet-in-residence, 1968-69.

MEMBER: Writers, Inc. (president), Nologonya African Cultural Organization. *Awards, honors:* Poetry Workshop Award, Midwestern Writers Conference, 1945; Women's Auxiliary of Afro-American Interests grant, 1950; African Studies Association grant, 1950; Harriet Tubman Award, 1956; John Hay Whitney Foundation award, 1959; American Society of African Culture grant, 1960; awards from African Studies Association, 1961, and Poets in Concert, 1968.

WRITINGS—All poetry: *Impressions of African Art Forms in the Poetry of Margaret Danner,* Broadside Press, 1960; *To Flower: Poems,* Counterpoise Series, 1963; (with Dudley Randall) *Poem Counterpoem,* Broadside Press, 1966, revised edition, 1969; *Iron Lace,* Poets Press, 1968; (editor) *Brass Horses* (anthology), Virginia Union University, 1968; (editor) *Regroup* (anthology), Virginia Union University, 1969; *The Down of a Thistle: Selected Poems, Prose Poems, and Songs,* Country Beautiful, 1976. Work represented in *La Poesie Negro-Americaine,* edited by Langston Hughes, Editions Seghers, 1966, and *Kaleidoscope,* edited by Robert Hayden, Harcourt, 1967. Contributor to *Negro Digest, Baha'i World Order, Poetry, Accent,* and *Chicago Review.*

SIDELIGHTS: Margaret Danner writes: "I have for many years been involved in the study of Africana, especially African Art, because I feel that man reveals a sensitivity through his creative work that is a clue to his present day reactions to problems and pleasures. . . ."

In response to the question of Black writers directing their output toward Black audiences, Danner said: "A writer should write what he feels, and yet I believe that we should help each other. If our talent is writing, we can help in this way—by deliberately directing some of our work toward black audiences. Because of the predicament that the black man is in, and faces, those of us who are black should unite to extricate ourselves and each other."

BIOGRAPHICAL/CRITICAL SOURCES: Negro Digest, January, 1968.†

* * *

DANSKA, Herbert 1928-

PERSONAL: Born October 16, 1928; son of Lazar and Ruth (Hakas) Danska; married Lorraine Triquere; married second wife, Dolores Elizabeth Ondra Friedman (a television associate producer), July, 1967; children: (first marriage) Jeffrey, Jane. *Education:* Art Students League, student, 1944-45; Pratt Institute, student, 1949-51. *Home:* 240 West 98th St., New York, N.Y. 10025. *Agent:* (Literary) McIntosh & Otis, 475 Fifth Ave., New York, N.Y. 10017; (art) Helen Wohlberg Inc., 331 East 50th St., New York, N.Y. 10025.

CAREER: Graphic artist, painter, and illustrator, 1952—; motion picture director and writer, 1962—, has directed "The Gift," 1962, "Sweet Love, Bitter," 1966, "Right On!," 1971. Consultant, Lincoln Hospital and Yeshiva University community psychiatry program, 1965-67, Bloomingdale Neighborhood Program, 1966, Weston Woods Cinemobile Tour, 1966, Urban Coalition, 1967, and Mobilization for Youth arts program, 1968-69. Guest lecturer, Cooper Union, Pratt Institute, School of Visual Arts, Boston University, City College of the City University of New York, Millenium Film Workshop, Urban Coalition, New York School of Social Work, Einstein College, Rockefeller Foundation, and others. *Military service:* U.S. Air Force, 1945-47.

MEMBER: Director's Guild of America, Film-Makers Cooperative. *Awards, honors:* Thirty-one citations from American Institute of Graphic Art, Society of Illustrators, and Art Directors Club; eight film awards from Vancouver, Edinburgh, Venice, and American film festivals; two Cine Golden Eagles; International Critics Prize and Interfilm Prize, Mannheim Festival; Artist's Equity Medal; two awards from American Society of Watercolors; Herald Tribune Medal, 1954, for best book illustration for *Story of People.*

WRITINGS: (Self-illustrated) *The Street Kids,* Knopf, 1971.

Illustrator: M. M. Edel, *Story of People,* Little, Brown, 1954; Virginia Haviland, *Favorite Fairy Tales Told in Russia: Retold from Russian Storytellers,* Little, Brown, 1961; Oscar Wilde, *The Selfish Giant,* Quist, 1967; Evelyn M. Begley, *Rory, the Red,* Van Nostrand, 1968; Ethel S. Sandowsky, *Francois and the Langouste,* Little, Brown, 1969; Midge Turk, *Gordon Parks,* Crowell, 1971; Franklyn Mansfield Branley, *Pieces of Another World: The Story of Moon Rocks,* Crowell, 1972; *The Other Side of Tomorrow,* Random House, 1973.

Screenplays: "The Gift" (featurette), Joseph Burstyn release, 1962; "It Won't Rub Off, Baby" (feature-length; originally titled "Sweet Love, Bitter"), U.M.C., 1969; "The Nest," Nexus Films, Inc., 1969; "The Minimaid and the Demigod," Danska Films, 1970. Also writer of a screenplay based on his own novel, *The Street Kids.*

Plays: (With Robert Somerfeld) "Funnin," 1969, produced Off-Off-Broadway at Fortune Theatre Workshop, 1970.

WORK IN PROGRESS: A children's book, *Yours Truly, Hieronymus;* a novel, *Last Daughter, First Son;* and "Motherblammer—A Chronicle," an account of the making of feature film "Right On!"

SIDELIGHTS: Herbert Danska has traveled extensively in Europe and Mexico. He told *CA,* "Both my children were born in autos (Chevy and Ford, in that order)."

BIOGRAPHICAL/CRITICAL SOURCES: Best Sellers, December 1, 1970.†

* * *

DARY, David A. 1934-

PERSONAL: Born August 21, 1934, in Manhattan, Kan.;

son of Milton Russell and Ruth (Long) Dary; married Carolyn Sue Russum, June 2, 1956; children: Cathy, Carol, Cindy, Cris. *Education:* Kansas State University, B.S., 1956; University of Kansas, M.S., 1970. *Religion:* Episcopalian. *Home:* 1101 West 27th St., Lawrence, Kan. 66044. *Agent:* Lurton Blassingame, 60 East 42nd St., New York, N.Y. 10017. *Office:* William Allen White School of Journalism, University of Kansas, Lawrence, Kan. 66044.

CAREER: Columbia Broadcasting System, Washington, D.C., reporter and editor, 1960-63; National Broadcasting Corp., Washington, D.C., manager of local news, 1963-67; free-lance writer, Topeka, Kan., 1967-69; University of Kansas, Lawrence, assistant professor, 1969-75, associate professor of journalism, 1975—. *Member:* Radio and Television News Directors Association, Association for Education in Journalism, Western History Association, Kansas State Historical Society (member of board of directors, 1972—), Kansas Corral of the Westerners, Sigma Delta Chi, Kappa Tau Alpha, Mason.

WRITINGS: Radio News Handbook, TAB Books, 1967, 2nd edition, 1970; *Television News Handbook,* TAB Books, 1971; *How to Write News for Print and Broadcast,* TAB Books, 1973; *The Buffalo Book,* Swallow Press, 1974; *Comanche,* University of Kansas, Museum of Natural History, 1976. Contributor of newspaper and magazine articles dealing with the Old West and articles and book reviews related to broadcast journalism to various publications.

*   *   *

DAVID, Anne 1924-

PERSONAL: Born July 4, 1924, in New York, N.Y.; daughter of William (a printer) and Florence (Korn) Rauchman; married Harold (Hal) David (a songwriter and lyricist), December 24, 1946; children: James Andrew, Craig Warren. *Education:* New York University, B.E., 1945. *Home:* Elm Dr., East Hills, Long Island, N.Y. 11576.

CAREER: Elementary teacher in public schools in Baldwin, N.Y., 1945-48, and Valley Stream, N.Y., 1949; Roslyn Public Schools, Roslyn, N.Y., volunteer worker as chairman of various parent groups, teacher, tutor of disadvantaged children, 1956—; chairman of legislation for Coordinated Council, 1970-71. Member of board of directors, League of Women Voters, Roslyn, 1961-69; Commissioner to Commemorate U.N. Day, Roslyn Village Government, 1968-70. Organizer of community service programs for high school seniors, Roslyn.

WRITINGS: A Guide to Volunteer Services: Help Yourself by Helping Others, Cornerstone Library, 1970. Editor of local news column for Roslyn Public Schools Coordinated Council, 1965-69.

SIDELIGHTS: Anne David told *CA:* "In 1971, based on research done for *A Guide to Volunteer Services,* I opened a clearinghouse for volunteers and agencies utilizing the services of volunteers. We operated this successful community service (never a fee) as volunteers, by volunteers, for volunteers until 1976 having placed more than 1,500 people in more than 300 agencies throughout Nassau County, N.Y."

*   *   *

DAVIDSON, Alastair 1939-

PERSONAL: Born November 2, 1939, in Nausori, Fiji Islands; son of William Lambert (a barrister) and Celeste (Walker) Davidson; first wife, Joan Helen Morgan; second wife, Maryellen Galbally; children: (first marriage) Rachel,

Nicola; (second marriage) Francesca. *Education:* Australian National University, B.A., 1962, Ph.D., 1965; University of Rome, Certificate of Historical Studies, 1963. *Politics:* Revolutionary socialist. *Office:* Department of Political Science, Monash University, Melbourne, Victoria, Australia.

CAREER: Office of the Prime Minister, Canberra, Australia, clerk, 1958-60; Australian National University, Canberra, tutor, 1965; Monash University, Melbourne, Australia, lecturer in politics, 1965—. Visiting professor, University of Turin, 1970. *Member:* Dante Alighieri Society (executive member).

WRITINGS: Antonio Gramsci: The Man, His Ideas (first published as series in *Australian Left Review,* 1967-68, under title "Gramsci's Marxism"), Left Review Publications, 1968; *The Communist Party of Australia: A Short History,* Hoover Institution, 1969; *Antonio Gramsci: Towards an Intellectual Bibliography,* Humanities, 1977. Editor, *Australian Left Review.*

WORK IN PROGRESS: A book on the Mafia as a form of social culture.†

*   *   *

DAVIDSON, Chalmers Gaston 1907-

PERSONAL: Born June 6, 1907, in Chester, S.C.; son of Zeb Vance (a mayor and probate judge) and Kate (Gaston) Davidson; married Alice Graham Gage, March 20, 1937; children: Robert Gage, Alice Graham (Mrs. William H. Sims III), Mary Gage. *Education:* Davidson College, B.A., 1928; Harvard University, M.A., 1930, Ph.D., 1942; University of Chicago, M.A., 1936.

CAREER: Instructor in history at Chamberlain Hunt Military Academy, Port Gibson, Miss., 1928-29, Blue Ridge School for Boys, Hendersonville, N.C., 1933-34, and The Citadel, Charleston, S.C., 1934-35; Davidson College, Davidson, N.C., professor of history and director of library, 1936-76. Lecturer, Piedmont University Center, 1967-68. Member, North Carolina Governor's Carolina Tercentenary Commission, beginning 1963. *Military service:* U.S. Naval Reserve, 1944-46; served in Pacific; became lieutenant junior grade.

MEMBER: North Carolina Literary and Historical Association (president, 1961-62), Historical Society of North Carolina (president, 1966-67), Mecklenburg County Historical Association (president, 1956-57), Phi Beta Kappa, Omicron Delta Kappa, Beta Theta Pi, Society of the Cincinnati. *Awards, honors:* Charles A. Cannon Award, 1951, for contribution to North Carolina history.

WRITINGS: Major John Davidson of "Rural Hill," Lassiter Press, 1943; (with William P. Cumming) *Davidson College Library Handbook,* Davidson College, 1948; *Cloud over Catawba,* Mecklenburg Historical Society, 1949; *Friend of the People* (biography of Peter Fayssoux), Medical Association of South Carolina, 1950; *Piedmont Partisan* (biography of William Lee Davidson), Davidson College, 1951; *Mid-Point for '28* (class history), Davidson College, 1953; *Gaston of Chester,* privately printed, 1956; *The Plantation World Around Davidson,* Mecklenburg Historical Association, 1969; *The Last Foray: The South Carolina Planters of 1860,* University of South Carolina Press, 1971. Contributor to *Dictionary of American Biography* and to scholarly and popular periodicals.

SIDELIGHTS: The campus of Davidson College originally was part of the plantation owned by Davidson's great-great uncle. About once every ten years Davidson gets out a booklet, *The Generations of Davidson College,* which lists those families represented in the student body for three or more generations.

BIOGRAPHICAL/CRITICAL SOURCES: Raleigh News and Observer, December 14, 1952.

* * *

DAVIDSON, Diane 1924-

PERSONAL: Born March 6, 1924, in Los Angeles, Calif.; daughter of Charles C. (a lieutenant colonel, U.S. Cavalry) and Stella (a journalist; maiden name, Bateman) Winnia; married February 1, 1948 (divorced); children: William E. Davidson, Ronald M. Davidson. *Education:* University of California, Berkeley, A.B., 1943, general secondary teaching credential, 1944; Sacramento State College (now California State University, Sacramento), M.A., 1959. *Politics:* Democrat. *Religion:* Episcopalian. *Home:* 8146 Toyon Ave., Fair Oaks, Calif. 95628. *Agent:* Ruth Cantor, 156 Fifth Ave., New York, N.Y. 10010; (motion pictures) Kevin Casselman, Kurt Frings Agency, 9025 Wilshire Blvd., Beverly Hills, Calif. 90211. *Office:* El Camino High School, 4300 El Camino Ave., Sacramento, Calif. 95821.

CAREER: Teacher in California schools, 1944-45; Pasadena Playhouse, Pasadena, Calif., student-actor, 1945-46; United Service Organizations (USO) Camp Shows, New York, N.Y., ingénue and character actress, 1946-47; Nara Dependent School, Kurokamiyama, Nara, Japan, acting principal, 1947-48; teacher in California schools, 1951—, teaching English and film at El Camino High School, Sacramento, 1954—. Actress, appearing in "Blithe Spirit," 1968; writer-producer of a satiric film, "3.1416." *Member:* National Education Association, Authors Guild, California Teachers Association, Phi Beta Kappa, Pi Lambda Theta, California Writers Club.

WRITINGS: Feversham (novel), Crown, 1969.

WORK IN PROGRESS: The Comedy of Earth, fiction based on Dante's *Divine Comedy;* a transcription of the medieval *Wardmote Book of Feversham, 1540-1556;* a screenplay of *Feversham;* other fiction and also poetry.

AVOCATIONAL INTERESTS: Camping, gardening, skiing.†

* * *

DAVIDSON, F(rank) G(eoffrey) 1920-

PERSONAL: Born April 9, 1920, in Manchester, England; son of William Joseph (a commercial traveler) and Ethel (Wardle) Davidson; married Margaret May Godward, April 3, 1951; children: Julia, Christopher, Elizabeth. *Education:* King's College, Cambridge, M.A., 1949. *Politics:* Leftish. *Religion:* Atheist. *Home:* 150 Marshall St., Ivanhoe, Victoria 3079, Australia. *Office:* Department of Economics, La Trobe University, Bundoora, Victoria 3083, Australia.

CAREER: Political and Economic Planning, London, England, research assistant, 1946-49; Ministry of Town and Country Planning, London, research officer, 1949-51; National Institute of Economic and Social Research, London, research associate, 1951-54; University of Melbourne, Melbourne, Victoria, Australia, lecturer, 1954-57, senior lecturer in economics, 1957-60; Commonwealth Department of Labour and National Service, Melbourne, assistant secretary, 1960-62, first assistant secretary, 1962-66; La Trobe University, Bundoora, Victoria, professor of economics, 1966—, dean of social sciences, 1970-71, dean of economics 1977-78. Visiting professor of economics, Universite de

Saint-Etienne, France, 1973. *Military service:* British Army, 1940-45; became sergeant. *Member:* Economic Society of Australia and New Zealand.

WRITINGS: The Industrialization of Australia, Melbourne University Press, 1957, 4th edition, 1969; *Economics and Economic Policy* (inaugural lecture at La Trobe University), F. W. Cheshire, for La Trobe University, 1967; (with B. R. Stewardson) *Economics and Australian Industry,* Longman, 1974. Contributor to economic journals.

AVOCATIONAL INTERESTS: French language and literature, and to some extent the German.

* * *

DAVIDSON, Gustav 1895-1971

December 25, 1895—February 7, 1971; Polish-born American editor, music and book critic, and author. Obituaries: *New York Times,* February 10, 1971; *Publishers' Weekly,* March 1, 1971.

* * *

DAVIDSON, Michael Childers 1897-

PERSONAL: Born February 24, 1897, in London, England. *Education:* Attended Cambridge University, 1914. *Agent:* Anthony Sheil Associates Ltd., 52 Floral St., Covent Garden, London WC2E 9DA, England.

CAREER: Has traveled most of the time since 1919, more often abroad than in England; war correspondent for newspapers during eight wars "of varying size, including the Korean"; foreign correspondent for *Observer* and *News Chronicle,* London, England, and for *New York Times* and *Christian Science Monitor,* 1947-58. *Military service:* British Army, 1914-19.

WRITINGS: The World, the Flesh, and Myself (correspondence and reminiscences), Guild Press (Washington, D.C.), 1962; *Some Boys,* David Bruce & Watson, 1970; (with David M. Rorvick) *Sex Surrogates,* Geis, 1972; *Two Views of Pears,* Sand Dollar Press, 1973; *The Karma Machine,* Popular Library, 1975.

Translator from the German: Klaus Mehnert, *Youth in Soviet Russia,* Harcourt, 1933; Ernst Henri, *Hitler over Europe?,* Simon & Schuster, 1934; Anna Seghers (pseudonym of Netty Radvanyi), *Ernst Thaelmann,* Workers' Bookshop (London), 1934; Walter Schoenstedt, *Shot Whilst Escaping,* Wishart Books, 1935; Egon E. Kosch, *Secret China,* John Lane, 1935; R. Braun, *Communist: Fascism, Make or Break?,* International Publishers, 1935; (with Dona Torr) Georgi Dimitrov, *Letters from Prison,* International Publishers, 1935; Ernst Henri, *Hitler over Russia?,* Simon & Schuster, 1936.

WORK IN PROGRESS: A book on Sicily, commissioned by Arthur Barker.†

* * *

DAVIES, J. Clarence III 1937-

PERSONAL: Born November 16, 1937, in New York, N.Y.; son of J. Clarence, Jr. (a real estate consultant) and Helen (Wolfe) Davies; married Barbara Schonfeld, December 20, 1959; children: Elizabeth, Eric. *Education:* Dartmouth College, B.A., 1959; Columbia University, Ph.D., 1965. *Home:* 10307 Dickens Ave., Bethesda, Md. 20014. *Office:* The Conservation Foundation, 1717 Massachusetts Ave. N.W., Washington, D.C. 20036.

CAREER: Bowdoin College, Brunswick, Me., instructor in

government, director, Bureau of Municipal Government, 1963-65; Executive Office of the President, Bureau of the Budget, Washington, D.C., examiner, 1965-67; Princeton University, Princeton, N.J., assistant professor of politics and public affairs, 1967-70; Executive Office of the President, Council on Environmental Quality, Washington, D.C., senior staff member, 1970-73; Resources for the Future, Inc., Washington, D.C., assistant director of Institutions and Public Decisions Divisions, 1973-76; The Conservation Foundation, Washington, D.C., executive vice-president, 1976—.

WRITINGS: Neighborhood Groups and Urban Renewal, Columbia University Press, 1966; *The Politics of Pollution,* Bobbs-Merrill, 1970, 2nd edition, 1975.

BIOGRAPHICAL/CRITICAL SOURCES: Best Sellers, July 15, 1970.

* * *

DAVIES, Ruth A(nn) 1915-

PERSONAL: Born June 28, 1915, in Pittsburgh, Pa.; daughter of William Tarleton (a locomotive engineer) and Ruth Ann (Crawford) Davies. *Education:* Pennsylvania College for Women, B.A., 1939; University of Pittsburgh, M.Litt., 1940; Carnegie Institute of Technology, B.S.L.S., 1941. *Home:* 156 McIntyre Rd., Pittsburgh, Pa. 15237. *Office:* Graduate School of Library Science, University of Pittsburgh, Pittsburgh, Pa. 15213.

CAREER: Carnegie Institute of Technology (now Carnegie-Mellon University), Pittsburgh, Pa., instructor in library science, 1947-62; University of Pittsburgh, Pittsburgh, department of education, member of research staff, 1956-58, Graduate School of Library Science, instructor, 1963—. North Hills School District, Pittsburgh, coordinator of library services, beginning 1950. Chairman of advisory committee, Pennsylvania Department of Public Instruction. *Member:* American Library Association (chairman of standards implementation program for Pennsylvania), National Education Association, Association for Supervision and Curriculum Development, Pennsylvania Library Association, Pennsylvania School Library Association, Pennsylvania State Education Association. *Awards, honors:* Received citation from Pennsylvania Department of Public Instruction, 1964; Distinguished Service Award, Pennsylvania Library Association, 1968; Outstanding Alumnus Award, University of Pittsburgh School of Library Science, 1969; Citation of Merit, Pennsylvania School Library Association, 1970.

WRITINGS: Bibliography: Revitalizing American History through Primary Sources, Pennsylvania Department of Public Instruction, 1968; *The School Library: A Force for Educational Excellence,* Bowker, 1969, 2nd edition published as *The School Library Media Center: A Force for Educational Excellence,* 1973. Contributor to *World Book Encyclopedia, Encyclopedia of Library and Information Science,* and library journals. Member of editorial staff, *School Instructional Materials Center,* Pennsylvania Department of Public Instruction, 1963.

WORK IN PROGRESS: Programmed Learning Guides: Social Studies.†

* * *

DAVIS, Grant Miller 1937-

PERSONAL: Born May 26, 1937, in Tuscaloosa, Ala.; son of Theoren Wilburn (a bus driver) and Mary (Craton) Davis;

married Susan Bridgens Riden, February 17, 1966; children: Susan Louise, Grant II. *Education:* Georgia State College (now University), B.B.A., 1963; University of Alabama, M.A., 1966, Ph.D., 1968. *Religion:* Episcopal. *Home:* 2217 Juneway Ter., Fayetteville, Ark. 72701. *Office:* Center for Transportation Research, University of Arkansas, Fayetteville, Ark. 72701.

CAREER: Manager of traffic, Mason & Dixon Line, Inc., 1958-60; Ford Motor Co., Atlanta, Ga., manager of inbound freight distribution, 1961-65; University of Alabama, University, research associate in economics, 1965-66, instructor in finance, 1966-68; Arizona State University, Tempe, assistant dean, 1968-70; Auburn University, Auburn, Ala., associate professor, 1970-72; University of Arkansas, Fayetteville, Oren Harris Professor of Transportation and director of Center for Transportation Research, 1972—. Consultant, Vertico Manufacturing Co., Inc., 1968-71, Sperry-Rand Corp., 1968—, Arrow Trucking Co., Inc., 1970—. *Military service:* U.S. Army, 1955-58. *Member:* Association of Interstate Commerce Commission Practitioners, American Society of Traffic and Transportation, Society of Logistics Engineers, American Economic Association, American Marketing Association, Beta Gamma Sigma.

WRITINGS: The Department of Transportation, Heath, 1970; (with Stephen W. Brown) *Logistics Management,* Lexington Books, 1974; (with Charles S. Sherwood) *Rate Bureaus and Antitrust Conflicts in Transportation: Public Policy Issues,* Praeger, 1975; (with Martin T. Farris, and Jack J. Holder, Jr.) *Management of Transportation Carriers,* Praeger, 1975; (editor) *Transportation Regulation: A Pragmatic Assessment,* Interstate, 1976; (with John E. Dillard, Jr.) *Increasing Motor Carrier Productivity: An Empirical Analysis,* Praeger, 1977. Contributor to *Alabama Business, Transportation Journal, Quarterly Review of Economics and Business, Journal of Purchasing, Arizona Business Bulletin, Public Utility Forthnightly, Logistics Review, Alphian, Journal of Economic Issues, ICC Practitioners' Journal,* and other professional journals and newspapers.

* * *

DAVIS, James W(arren, Jr.) 1935-

PERSONAL: Born September 14, 1935, in Chillicothe, Mo.; son of James Warren (a lawyer) and Jennie (Cox) Davis; married Jean Ludwig, June 29, 1963; children: Warren, Clare. *Education:* Harvard University, A.B. (cum laude), 1957; University of Michigan, M.P.A., 1962, Ph.D., 1964. *Home:* 600 West Polo, St. Louis, Mo. 63105. *Office:* Department of Political Science, Washington University, St. Louis, Mo. 63130.

CAREER: Worked in Washington, D.C., with Washington Metropolitan Regional Conference, summer, 1961, and U.S. Bureau of the Budget, summer, 1962; University of Wisconsin—Madison, assistant professor of political science, 1964-68; Washington University, St. Louis, Mo., associate professor, 1968-74, professor of political science, 1974—. Consultant, National Advisory Commission on Selective Service, 1966; adviser in School of Public Administration, National Institute of Development Administration, Bangkok, Thailand, 1968-69. Visiting lecturer, University of Wisconsin, 1970. *Military service:* U.S. Army, Security Agency, 1957-60. *Member:* American Political Science Association, American Association for the Advancement of Science, American Society for Public Administration, Midwest Political Science Association, Phi Kappa Phi, Pi Sigma Alpha.

WRITINGS: (Contributor) Austin Ranney, editor, *Political Science and Public Policy,* Markham, 1968; (with Kenneth Dolbeare) *Little Groups of Neighbors: The Selective Service System,* Markham, 1968; (editor) *Politics, Programs, and Budgets: A Reader in Government Budgeting,* Prentice-Hall, 1969; (contributor) Roger W. Little, editor, *Selective Service and American Society,* Russell Sage, 1969; *The National Executive Branch: An Introduction,* Free Press, 1970; *An Introduction to Public Administration,* Free Press, 1974. Contributor to political science and public administration journals.

WORK IN PROGRESS: A book on the analysis and evaluation of public policy.

* * *

DAVIS, John D(avid) 1937-

PERSONAL: Born March 31, 1937, in London, England; son of Louis (a tambour beader) and Lily (Koch) Davis; married Marcia Lee Dackman (a clinical psychologist), August 18, 1963; children: Jonathan Wystan, Meredith Tristan. *Education:* New College, Oxford, B.A. (honors in mathematics), 1960, B.A. (honors in philosophy and psychology), 1962; Indiana University, Ph.D., 1968. *Home:* 36 Sterndale Rd., Sheffield S7 2LD, England. *Office:* Department of Psychology, University of Sheffield, Sheffield S10 2TN, England.

CAREER: University of California Medical School, Langley Porter Neuropsychiatric Institute, San Francisco, Calif., fellow in medical psychology, 1966-67, research psychologist, 1967-68; Oxford Polytechnic, Oxford, England, senior lecturer in psychology, 1968-69; University of Sheffield, Sheffield, England, lecturer in psychology, 1969—. Honorary clinical psychologist, United Sheffield Hospitals. *Military service:* Royal Air Force, 1955-57. *Member:* British Psychological Society (associate member), American Psychological Association (foreign affiliate), Sigma Xi. *Awards, honors:* New College, Oxford, Open Scholarship and State Scholarship, 1957-62; Fulbright travel award, 1962-68; honorable mention, Creative Talent Awards Program, American Institutes for Research, 1970.

WRITINGS: (Translator) G. Y. Shilov, *Mathematical Analysis: A Special Course,* Pergamon, 1965; (contributor) Lawrence Litwack, Russell Getson, and Glenn Saltzman, editors, *Research in Counseling,* F. E. Peacock, 1968; *The Interview as Arena: Strategies in Standardized Interviews and Psychotherapy,* Stanford University Press, 1971; (contributor) Teodor Shanin, editor, *The Rules of the Game: Crossdisciplinary Essays on Models in Scholarly Thought,* Tavistock Publications, 1972; *Experimental Studies of Interview Behaviour and Therapeutic Behaviour Modification,* National Lending Library (Wetherby, England), 1974; (contributor) G. R. Patterson, I. M. Marks, J. D. Matarazzo, R. A. Myers, G. E. Schwartz, and H. H. Strupp, editors, *Behavior Change 1974: An Aldine Annual on Psychotherapy, Counseling, and Behavior Modification,* Aldine, 1975; (contributor) C. D. Spielberger and I. G. Sarason, editors, *Stress and Anxiety,* Volume V, Wiley, in press. Contributor to *Journal of Consulting Psychology, Journal of Consulting and Clinical Psychology, Journal of Personality and Social Psychology,* and *British Journal of Social and Clinical Psychology.*

WORK IN PROGRESS: Research in self-disclosure, social construction processes, learned helplessness, and marital interaction.

SIDELIGHTS: John Davis told *CA:* "Like the novelist and the historian, I am endlessly fascinated by human behavior. Only my approach to unraveling its mysteries is different. I write for the most skeptical of audiences, one that abjures rhetoric, so I must arrange for my observations to speak for themselves. My writing allows me to pursue the studies that allow me to write."

AVOCATIONAL INTERESTS: Music, theatre, cinema, food, and wine.

* * *

DAVIS, John H(erbert) 1904-

PERSONAL: Born October 9, 1904, in Wellsville, Mo.; son of Ollie W. (a farmer) and Mabel (Buchanan) Davis; married Edna Frazier, December 25, 1928; children: James F., H. Lowell. *Education:* Iowa State University of Science and Technology, B.S., 1928; University of Minnesota, M.A., 1935, Ph.D., 1940. *Politics:* Republican. *Religion:* Protestant. *Home:* 2500 Massachusetts Ave. N.W., Washington, D.C. 20008. *Office:* American Near East Refugee Aid, Inc., 733 15th St. N.W., Washington, D.C. 20005.

CAREER: Teacher of agriculture, principal, and then superintendent of schools in Iowa, 1928-35; U.S. Department of Agriculture, Washington, D.C., economist, 1936-38; Story City (Iowa) public schools, superintendent, 1938-40; Farm Credit Administration, Washington, D.C., economist, 1941-42; Commodity Credit Corp., Washington, D.C., chief of wheat section, 1942-44; National Council of Farmer Cooperatives, Washington, D.C., executive vice-president, 1944-52; U.S. Department of Agriculture, assistant secretary of Agriculture, 1953-54; Harvard University, Graduate School of Business Administration, Boston, Mass., director of program in agribusiness, 1954-59; United Nations Relief and Works Agency for Palestine Refugees, commissioner-general, 1959-64; American University of Beirut, vice-chairman of board of trustees and director of U.S. office, New York, N.Y., 1965-67; American Near East Refugee Aid, Inc., Washington, D.C., president, 1968—. Member of Food and Nutrition Board, National Research Council, 1956-59; consultant to United Nations Food and Agriculture Organization, U.S. Secretary of State, and other government offices.

AWARDS, HONORS: Knight, Order of St. John of Jerusalem (England); First Officer, Order of Merit (Syria); Grand Officer, Order of Cedar (Lebanon); Grand Officer, Order of the Star (Jordan); and other foreign and U.S. Government awards.

WRITINGS: An Economic Analysis of the Tax Status of Farmer Cooperatives, American Institute of Cooperation, 1950; (with Ray A. Goldbert) *A Concept of Agribusiness,* Graduate School of Business Administration, Harvard University, 1957; (with Kenneth Hinshaw) *Farmer in a Business Suit,* Simon & Schuster, 1957; *The Evasive Peace: A Study of the Zionist-Arab Problem,* J. Murray, 1968, New World Press, 1971, revised edition, Dillon-Liederbach, 1976. Also compiler of *Selected Bibliography: Burma and Adjacent Regions, Agriculture,* 1961.

WORK IN PROGRESS: Research on the essentials for economic development in the Middle East.

SIDELIGHTS: The Evasive Peace has been translated and published in German, Finish, Polish, Arabic, and Japanese.

* * *

DAVIS, Marc 1934-

PERSONAL: Born November 12, 1934, in Chicago, Ill.; son of Sol A. (a newspaper photographer) and Rose

(Schwartz) Davis; married Judy Axelrod, March 15, 1961; children: Kevin, Laura. *Education:* Studied at University of Illinois, 1952, Roosevelt University, 1952-54, and New York University, 1957-58. *Residence:* Highwood, Ill. *Agent:* Max Gartenberg, 331 Madison Ave., New York, N.Y. 10017.

CAREER: Chicago Tribune, Chicago, Ill., employed in sports department, 1952-55; City News Bureau, Chicago, reporter, 1957; *World News of the Week,* Chicago, writer/editor, 1958-59; *El Paso Herald-Post,* El Paso, Tex., general assignment reporter, 1959-60; *Physician's Management,* Evanston, Ill., editor, 1960-63; free-lance advertising and publicity writer; book reviewer for *Chicago Sun-Times* and *Chicago Tribune.* Painter and former teacher of art; work has been exhibited in Chicago and the Southwest. *Military service:* U.S. Army, 1955-57. *Member:* Authors Guild.

WRITINGS: Spector (novel), Scribner, 1970; *Man's History of Law,* Legal Heritage Society, 1973. Also author of *Strokes* (novel), 1976. Contributor to *Compton's Yearbook.*

WORK IN PROGRESS: A long novel with a Chicago setting.

SIDELIGHTS: Marc Davis wrote *CA:* "My writing has been influenced by everything: movies, comic strips; the entire history of art and music—modern, ancient, primitive; great spontaneous talkers and storytellers; fabulous characters both real and fictional; graffiti; fragments of conversation overheard on subway, in saloons, in banks and brokerage houses, at rock concerts, at the crap table, in unemployment lines; etc.; and of course, other writers. Advice to young writers: Stay healthy. Develop innovative methods of earning money with minimal effort and maximum return. Use everything useable. Don't marry or live with the wrong person. Don't be afraid to start all over when necessary. Discount 90% of all praise and criticism. Don't con yourself. Be a gambler. Don't get talked out of or into anything. Learn all survival tactics. Get a good agent. Nothing's too tough if you've got the drive."

BIOGRAPHICAL/CRITICAL SOURCES: New Yorker, July 4, 1970.

*   *   *

DAVIS, Nuel Pharr   1915-

PERSONAL: Born October 21, 1915, in Fort Worth, Tex.; son of John Owen and Pearl (Pharr) Davis. *Education:* University of Texas, M.A., 1940; University of Illinois, Ph.D., 1955; also studied at Texas Christian University. *Home:* 805 South Walnut St., Urbana, Ill. 61801. *Agent:* Sterling Lord Agency, 660 Madison Ave., New York, N.Y. 10021. *Office:* Department of English, 306 E.B., University of Illinois, Urbana, Ill. 61801.

CAREER: University of Illinois, Urbana, assistant professor of English, 1957—, associate professor of narrative writing, 1960—. *Member:* Authors Guild. *Awards, honors:* Texas Writers' Award, 1969.

WRITINGS: The Life of Wilkie Collins, University of Illinois Press, 1956; *Lawrence and Oppenheimer,* Simon & Schuster, 1968.

SIDELIGHTS: "Nuel Pharr Davis . . . has stepped boldly into the world of physics and produced a book of broader scope than the title indicates," Lauri Fermi, widow of the physicist Enrico Fermi told *Life* Magazine. She mentions that Davis interviewed 100 of the protagonists' associates before writing *Lawrence and Oppenheimer,* but "over-edited his notes, occasionally distorting the information." She

comments, "Davis has brilliantly and plausibly caught for the lay public the excitement and *feeling* of dedicated scientists at work under the tremendous moral and political burden of responsibilities they did not seek and bore as well as they could."

Alexander Zucker, himself a nuclear physicist, notes that *"Lawrence and Oppenheimer* reads like a novel . . . not biography, not history, but more of a journalistic account of two famous scientists." He finds the book "generally accurate; and in view of the large amount of technical material Davis presents, this can only be the result of long and effective research." Zucker does take issue with the characterizations of Lawrence and some of the other scientists, Fermi, Alvarez, Teller, and Groves: "Davis sees Lawrence as a slow-witted driver of men. . . . On the other hand, Davis' Oppenheimer is a brooding saint, a man of unquestionable brilliance, the foremost American theoretical physicist of his time who is also a devoted student of the Indian holy books."

John Leonard, while predicting that *Lawrence and Oppenheimer* would enrage many of the people who appear in its pages, takes a different view of the characterizations, calling the book "a triumph on at least four counts: as a character study of scientists in action; as the story of the creation of the atom bomb; as a reminder of a nation's disgrace; and as a trenchant analysis of the growth of 'big science,' its Byzantine relationship with government and policies arising from that relationship."

BIOGRAPHICAL/CRITICAL SOURCES: New York Times, September 20, 1968; *Newsweek,* September 23, 1968; *Book World,* September 29, 1968; *Best Sellers,* October 1, 1968; *Washington Post,* October 3, 1968; *New York Times Book Review,* October 6, 1968; *Life,* October 18, 1968; *New Republic,* November 16, 1968; *Nation,* December 9, 1968; *Punch,* July 2, 1969; *Spectator,* August 2, 1969; *Virginia Quarterly Review,* winter, 1969; *Times Literary Supplement,* December 18, 1969.

*   *   *

DAVIS, Samuel   1930-

PERSONAL: Born September 2, 1930, in Cleveland, Ohio; son of David J. and Sara (Kolinsky) Davis; married Marlene Moot, September 11, 1954; children: Teri Ann, Jeffrey Alan, Dana Joy. *Education:* Ohio State University, student, 1952-53; Case Western Reserve University, B.S.E.E., 1956. *Politics:* Independent. *Religion:* Hebrew. *Home:* 23616 Mariano St., Woodland Hills, Calif. 91364. *Office:* c/o Cahners Publishing Co., 89 Franklin St., Boston, Mass. 02110.

CAREER: Engineer, Rocketdyne Division, North American Aviation, 1956-57; engineer, Clevite Corp., 1957-61; Aerospace Corp., El Segundo, Calif., member of technical staff, 1961; Litton Industries, Data Systems division, Van Nuys, Calif., senior engineering specialist, 1961-68; Bunker Ramo Corp., Westlake Village, Calif., member of technical staff, 1968; Hughes Aircraft Co., Culver City, Calif., senior project engineer, 1968-70; Litton Industries, Data Systems Div., Van Nuys, program manager, 1970-74; CMP Publications, Great Neck, N.Y., Western editor, based in California, 1974-77; Cahners Publishing Co., Boston, Mass., manager of Western editorial office based in California, 1977—. *Military service:* U.S. Army, Signal Corps, 1948-52. *Member:* Society for Information Display (secretary-treasurer of Los Angeles chapter, 1959). *Awards, honors:* Institute of Radio Engineers Prize Papers Contest, second prize, 1955, first prize, 1956.

WRITINGS: Computer Data Displays, Prentice-Hall, 1969. Contributor to *Computer Design, Proceedings* of the Society for *Information Design, Information Display, Datamation, Electronic Engineering Times, Electronic Buyers News, EDN Magazine,* and *Electronic Business.* Editor, *Proceedings* of the Society for Information Display, 1974—.

*   *   *

DAVISON, Edward   1898-1970

July 28, 1898—February 8, 1970; Scottish-born American poet and educator. Obituaries: *New York Times,* February 9, 1970; *Books Abroad,* spring, 1971.

*   *   *

DAVY, Francis X(avier)   1916-

PERSONAL: Born January 24, 1916, in Los Angeles, Calif.; son of Francis X. and Ivy Ann (Edwards) Davy; married Betty Louise Chene, November 22, 1947; children: Dianne, Paul, Mark, Christine, Peter. *Education:* St. Mary's College of California, A.B., 1941; University of California, Berkeley, M.A., 1944; Johns Hopkins University, graduate study, 1946; Columbia University, Ph.D., 1958. *Home:* Lancaster Woods, Richmond, Ky. 40475. *Office:* 213 Wallace Bldg., Eastern Kentucky University, Richmond, Ky. 40476.

CAREER: St. Mary's College of California, Moraga, instructor in Latin, 1942-46; Manhattan College, New York, N.Y., instructor, 1946-51, assistant professor, 1951-59, associate professor of English, 1959-63; C. W. Post College, Brookville, N.Y., adjunct associate professor of English, 1959-66; Nassau Community College, Garden City, N.Y., associate professor of English, 1963-66; Sullivan County Community College, South Fallsburg, N.Y., professor of English and chairman of department of humanities, 1966-67; Eastern Kentucky University, Richmond, professor of English, 1967—, chairman of department of humanities, 1967-68. *Member:* International Benjamin Franklin Society, Modern Language Association of America, National Council of Teachers of English, American Association of University Professors, International Association of Torch Clubs, College Council on English in the Central Atlantic States, South Atlantic Modern Language Association, Phi Kappa Phi.

WRITINGS: (With Paul Cortissoz) *Perspectives for College,* W. C. Brown, 1963; *Swift's Gulliver's Travels,* Barrister Books, 1966; (with Robert Burkhart) *Perspectives on Our Times,* Houghton, 1970.

WORK IN PROGRESS: Two books, *No Uncertain Sound: The Environmental Crisis* and *Gulliver's Travels: Swift's Ideal for Man;* studies on Dryden's religious poetry, Franklin's satire and understanding of rhetoric, and on structure and style in *Billy Budd.*

*   *   *

DAWSON, Christopher (Henry)   1889-1970

October 12, 1889—May 25, 1970; British Catholic theologian and historian. Obituaries: *Christian Century,* June 10, 1970. (See index for *CA* sketch)

*   *   *

DAY, R(oss) H(enry)   1927-

PERSONAL: Born March 20, 1927, in Albany, Western Australia; son of Harold Lindsay and Dorothy (Currer)

Day; married Grecian T. Snooke (a schoolteacher), July 3, 1951; children: Christine Grecian, Helen Louise, Philip Harold. *Education:* University of Western Australia, B.Sc., 1950; University of Bristol, Ph.D., 1954. *Politics:* None. *Religion:* None. *Home:* 6 Quinton Ct., Melbourne, Victoria 3149, Australia. *Office:* Psychology Department, Monash University, Melbourne, Victoria 3168, Australia.

CAREER: University of Bristol, Bristol, England, lecturer in psychology, 1951-54; University of Sydney, Sydney, New South Wales, Australia, lecturer, 1955-58, senior lecturer, 1959-62, reader in psychology, 1962-64; Monash University, Melbourne, Victoria, Australia, professor of psychology, 1965—. *Member:* Australian Psychological Society (fellow; president, 1966-67), British Psychological Society (fellow).

WRITINGS: Perception, W. C. Brown, 1966; *Human Perception,* Wiley, 1969. Contributor of about seventy-five technical and scholarly papers to journals. Associate editor, *Australian Journal of Psychology;* consulting editor, *Perceptual and Motor Skills.*

WORK IN PROGRESS: The Nature of Human Perception.

*   *   *

DEAN, Warren   1932-

PERSONAL: Born October 17, 1932, in Passaic, N.J.; son of Warren Kempton (a salesman) and Gabrielle (Roykovich) Dean; married Judith Thomas, January 26, 1960; children: Thomas, Julia. *Education:* University of Miami, B.A., 1953; University of Florida, M.A., 1961, Ph.D., 1964. *Office:* Department of History, New York University, New York, N.Y. 10003.

CAREER: University of Texas at Austin, assistant professor of history, 1965-70; New York University, New York, N.Y., associate professor of history, 1970—. *Member:* American Historical Association, Latin American Studies Association.

WRITINGS: Industrialization of Sao Paulo, 1880-1945, University of Texas Press, 1969; *Rio Claro: A Brazilian Plantation System,* Stanford University Press, 1976. Co-author of film script, "Pancho Villa." Contributor to *Nation* and other publications.

WORK IN PROGRESS: A study of the histories of multinational corporations.

*   *   *

DEANE, Nancy H(ilts)   1939-

PERSONAL: Born December 27, 1939, in Detroit, Mich.; daughter of Roy Ellis (a factory worker) and Helen (Ludwig) Hilts; married Robert H. Deane (a college teacher), August 1, 1964. *Education:* Albion College, B.A., 1962; University of Wisconsin—Madison, M.A., 1964.

CAREER: Portage Senior High School, Portage, Wis., senior English teacher, 1964-66; University of New Hampshire, Durham, instructor, 1966-69, director of freshman English, 1969-71, assistant professor of English, beginning 1970, chairman of faculty caucus and member of senate executive council, 1971-72. Reviewer of new manuscripts for three publishers. *Member:* American Association of University Professors, National Council of Teachers of English, College Composition and Communication, Phi Beta Kappa.

WRITINGS: (Editor and author of analytical instructor's manual) *Voices of Revelation* (collection of contemporary essays), text edition, Little, Brown, 1970; (author of creative teaching manual) James McCrimmon, *Writing with a Purpose* (textbook), 5th edition (Deane was not associated with earlier editions), Houghton, 1971; *In the Mind of the Writer*, Canfield Press, 1973.

WORK IN PROGRESS: Editing an anthology of short stories and a book on composition.†

* * *

DeBOER, John C(harles) 1923-

PERSONAL: Born May 23, 1923, in Kodaikanal, India; son of John (a clergyman, educator, and missionary) and Erma E. (Eardley) DeBoer; married Clara L. Merritt (a professor of history), April 29, 1944; children: John L., Katharine L., David C. *Education:* University of Michigan, B.S., 1944; New Brunswick Theological Seminary, B.D., 1950; Drew University, S.T.M., 1954. *Office:* United Church, 287 Park Ave. S., New York, N.Y. 10010.

CAREER: Clergyman of United Church of Christ; Grumman Aircraft Co., Bethpage, N.Y., flight test engineer, 1944-47; minister of Congregational churches in Union, N.J., 1949-53, and Maple Shade, N.J., 1953-59; Vermont Congregational Conference, Burlington, associate minister, 1959-65; United Church of Christ Board for Homeland Ministries, New York, N.Y., chairman of department of church development, 1965—. Chairman of Church Development Task Force, Joint Strategy Action Committee (twelve Protestant denominations). Vice-president, Boston Seamen's Friend Society, 1963-65. *Member:* Sigma Xi, Tau Beta Pi.

WRITINGS: Discovering Our Mission, United Church Board for Homeland Ministries, 1966, revised edition, 1969; *Let's Plan: A Guide to the Planning Process for Voluntary Organizations*, Pilgrim Press, 1970; *How to Succeed in the Organization Jungle without Losing Your Religion*, Pilgrim Press, 1972; (co-editor with Alexander Greendale) *Are New Towns for Lower Income Americans, Too?*, Praeger, 1974. Contributor to church periodicals.

* * *

DE CAUX, Leonard Howard 1899-
(Len De Caux)

PERSONAL: Born October 14, 1899, in Westport, New Zealand; came to United States in 1921; naturalized in 1928; son of Howard Percival (a clergyman) and Helen (Branfill) De Caux; married Caroline Abrams, July 14, 1928 (deceased); children: Shirley Marie (Mrs. F. Gordon Turner). *Education:* Attended Oxford University, 1919-21, and Brookwood Labor College, 1922-24. *Home:* 800-B East Windsor Rd., Glendale, Calif. 91205. *Agent:* Barthold Fles, 507 Fifth Ave., New York, N.Y. 10017.

CAREER: Illinois Miner, Springfield, Ill., assistant editor, 1925; *Locomotive Engineers Journal*, Cleveland, Ohio, assistant editor, 1926-34; Federated Press, Washington, D.C., bureau chief, 1934-35; Congress of Industrial Organizations, Washington, D.C., national publicity director and editor of *C.I.O. News*, 1935-47.

WRITINGS—Under name Len De Caux: *Labor Radical: From the Wobblies to C.I.O.—a Personal History*, Beacon Press, 1970; *The Living Spirit of the Wobblies*, International Publishers, 1977.

WORK IN PROGRESS: All My Kids—Old Man Among the Little People.

DE GREGORI, Thomas R(oger) 1935-

PERSONAL: Born May 5, 1935, in Cleveland, Ohio; son of James V. (an engineer) and Mary Anne (Tambascio) De Gregori; married Gayle Sutherland, October 22, 1960; children: Alice, James, Roger. *Education:* University of New Mexico, B.A., 1959, M.A., 1960; University of Texas, Ph.D., 1965. *Politics:* Democrat. *Religion:* None. *Home:* 2327 Goldsmith, Houston, Tex. 77030. *Office:* Department of Economics, University of Houston, Houston, Tex. 77004.

CAREER: University of Khartoum, Khartoum, Sudan, visiting lecturer, 1962-63; Case Institute of Technology (now Case Western Reserve University), Cleveland, Ohio, assistant professor of economics, 1963-67; University of Houston, Houston, Tex., associate professor, 1967-75, professor of economics, 1975—, chairman of department, 1969-71. *Military service:* U.S. Marine Corps Reserve. *Member:* American Economic Association, Society for the History of Technology, African Studies Association, Economic History Association.

WRITINGS: (With Oriol Pi-Sunyer) *Economic Development: The Cultural Context*, Wiley, 1969; *Technology and the Economic Development of the Tropical African Frontier*, Press of Case Western Reserve University, 1970; *Technology and Economic Change: Essays and Inquiries*, McLouglin Associates, 1977; (contributor) Z. A. Konczacki and J. M. Konczacki, editors, *The Economic History of Tropical Africa*, Frank Cass & Co., in press. Also author, with June Hendricks, of a four-act play, "Only Connect."

Contributor of articles and book reviews to *Journal of Economic Issues, Technology and Culture, Journal of Developing Areas, Administration and Society, Topic: A Journal of the Liberal Arts, American Journal of Economics and Sociology, Forum, Journal of Economic History, Growth and Change: A Journal of Regional Development*, and other journals. Member of editorial board, *Journal of the American Studies Association of Texas*, 1975-76, *Journal of Economic Issues*, 1976.

WORK IN PROGRESS: Two books, *The African Slave Trade to the Gulf Coast* and *Limits of Economic Growth: A Challenge to Orthodoxy*.

SIDELIGHTS: Technology and the Economic Development of the Tropical African Frontier has been widely and favorably reviewed in scholarly journals. Ian Parker calls the book "a powerful work of synthesis, which integrates a vast amount of primary and secondary source material and brings it imaginatively to bear on some of the more challenging problems of African economic development. The wide-ranging bibliography in De Gregori's study is 87 pages in length, and the text itself displays in abundance the rare and valuable scholarly gift of a disciplined eclecticism."

Michael T. Pledge finds the book "an important addition to the growing literature on Africa and on economic development. It is important for economic development, not because of its departure from traditional analysis, but because of its scholarly investigation of African development and its insights into the process of development in general. Its value is enhanced by its interdisciplinary presentation of the topic and can be profitably read by individuals in many different disciplines."

BIOGRAPHICAL/CRITICAL SOURCES: Journal of Developing Areas, Volume V, number 2, January, 1971; *World Affairs Bulletin*, Volume V, number 6, March, 1971; *Professional Geographer*, Volume XXIII, number 2, April,

1971; *Technology and Culture,* Volume XII, number 2, April, 1971; *American Anthropologists,* Volume LXXIII, number 4, August, 1971; *Journal of Modern African Studies,* Volume IX, number 3, October, 1971; *Political Science Quarterly,* Volume LXXXVII, number 1, March, 1972; *American Political Science Review,* Volume LXVI, number 2, June, 1972; *Agricultural History,* Volume XLVI, number 4, October, 1972; *Economic Development and Cultural Change,* Volume XXI, number 2, January, 1973; *Africa Today,* Volume XX, number 4, fall, 1973.

* * *

DEHR, Dorothy 1915-

PERSONAL: Surname is pronounced "dare"; born June 23, 1915, in San Francisco, Calif.; daughter of William Leonard and Lillian (Baker) Carr; married Albert Dehr (an engineer), July 26, 1942; children: Albert William, David Dawson (died September 16, 1975), Daniel Timothy. *Education:* San Francisco State College (now University), A.B. and M.A., 1952; graduate study at University of California, Berkeley, University of San Francisco, University of California, Sacramento, and University of the Pacific. *Politics:* Republican. *Religion:* Protestant. *Home:* 6313 Parkview Way, Citrus Heights, Calif. 95610.

CAREER: American River College, Sacramento, Calif., instructor in management communications and business machines, 1963-76, professor emeritus, 1976—. Visiting lecturer, Kapiolani Community College, Honolulu, Hawaii, 1971. Member, State Advisory Committee on Program and Cost Effectiveness, 1970. *Member:* Women Flyers of America (national president), International Society for Business Education (secretary, U.S. chapter), American Association of University Women (Lodi, Calif. branch president), National Business Education Association, Western Business Education Association, California Business Education Association (northern section secretary), American Arbitration Association (member of Panel of Arbiters, commercial area), Delta Pi Epsilon.

WRITINGS: (With Flora Locke) *Office Calculating and Adding Machines,* Wiley, 1964, 3rd edition, 1969; (with Locke) *Machine Accounting,* Locke Publications, 1964, 3rd edition, 1969.

SIDELIGHTS: Mrs. Dehr has traveled throughout Canada and in Mexico, and since June, 1970, has visited West Germany, Austria, Hungary, Yugoslavia, Italy, Switzerland, Norway, Sweden, Denmark, Finland, England, Scotland, Ireland, Wales, France, Greece, Turkey, Egypt, Israel, Ethiopia, Uganda, Kenya, South Africa, Australia, New Zealand, Fiji, Japan, Formosa, Philippines, Hong Kong, and South Korea.

* * *

deKRUIF, Paul (Henry) 1890-1971

March 2, 1890—February 28, 1971; American microbiologist, writer, and popularizer of medical science. Obituaries: *Detroit Free Press,* March 2, 1971; *New York Times,* March 2, 1971; *Washington Post,* March 3, 1971; *Variety,* March 10, 1971; *Newsweek,* March 15, 1971; *Time,* March 15, 1971; *Antiquarian Bookman,* March 17, 1971. (See index for *CA* sketch)

* * *

De La IGLESIA, Maria Elena 1936-

PERSONAL: Born July 9, 1936, in Madrid, Spain; daughter of Federico (a teacher) and Laura (Keller) De La Iglesia; married Andre Schiffrin (managing director of Pantheon Books), June 14, 1961; children: Anya, Natalia. *Education:* Newnham College, Cambridge, B.A., 1959, M.A., 1968. *Home:* 250 West 94th St., New York, N.Y. 10025.

CAREER: Penguin Books, London, England, reviews editor, 1960.

WRITINGS: (Translator and adapter) *The Cat and the Mouse and Other Spanish Tales* (juvenile), Pantheon, 1966; (translator and adapter) *The Oak That Would Not Pay* (juvenile), Pantheon, 1968; *The Catalogue of Catalogues,* Random House, 1972; *The Catalogue of American Catalogues,* Random House, 1973; *The New Catalogue of Catalogues,* Random House, 1975.

* * *

DELANY, Paul 1937-

PERSONAL: Born July 18, 1937, in London, England; son of George F. and Claire (Parfait) Delany; children: Nicholas, Lev. *Education:* McGill University, B.Comm., 1957; Stanford University, A.M., 1958; University of California, Berkeley, M.A., 1961, Ph.D., 1965. *Politics:* New Democratic Party (Canada). *Home:* 1962 East Sixth Ave., Vancouver, British Columbia, Canada. *Office:* English Department, Simon Fraser University, Burnaby, British Columbia, Canada V5A 1S6.

CAREER: Columbia University, New York, N.Y., assistant professor of English, 1964-70; Simon Fraser University, Burnaby, British Columbia, associate professor, 1970-76, professor of English, 1977—. Guggenheim fellow, 1975-76. *Member:* Modern Language Association.

WRITINGS: British Autobiography in the Seventeenth Century, Columbia University Press, 1969; (editor with R. W. Hanning and J. Ford) *Sixteenth Century English Literature: A Selective Anthology,* Holt, 1976. Contributor of articles to *Philological Quarterly, Chaucer Review, Modern Language Quarterly, Massachusetts Review, New York Times Book Review, AMLA,* and other periodicals.

WORK IN PROGRESS: The Nightmare: D. H. Lawrence and His Circle in the Years of the Great War, for Basic Books; a study of John Berger.

* * *

DELGADO, Jose Manuel R(odriguez) 1915-

PERSONAL: Born August 8, 1915, in Ronda, Spain; son of Rafael Amerigo (a physician) and Amada (Delgado) Rodriguez; married Caroline Stoddard (an associate in psychiatric research), June 26, 1956; children: Jose Carlos, Linda Amada. *Education:* University of Madrid, M.D., 1940, D.Sc., 1942. *Office:* Department of Physiological Sciences, School of Medicine, Autonomous University of Madrid, Arzobispo Morcillo 1, Madrid 34, Spain.

CAREER: University of Madrid, School of Medicine, Madrid, Spain, instructor, 1940-42, associate professor of physiology, 1942-46; Yale University, School of Medicine, New Haven, Conn., senior fellow, 1946-47, Brown fellow, 1950-52, instructor, 1952-53, assistant professor, 1953-55, associate professor, 1955-60, professor of physiology in department of psychiatry, 1966-73; Autonomous University of Madrid, School of Medicine, Madrid, professor and chairman of department of physiological sciences, 1973—; Patronato Santiago Ramon y Cajal (research institute in the biological and medical sciences), Madrid, director of research, 1973—. Clinical and research fellow, Massachusetts

General Hospital, Boston, 1951-52; researcher, Rockland State Hospital, Orangeburg, N.Y., 1973—. *Member:* American College of Neuropsychopharmacology (charter fellow), New York Academy of Sciences (fellow). *Awards, honors:* Spanish National Research Council senior fellow, 1943-45; Countess of Maudes Prize, 1944, and Roel Prize, 1945, both for outstanding scientific research; Ramon y Cajal Prize of Spanish Government, 1952, for scientific research; Guggenheim fellow, 1963.

WRITINGS: Physical Control of the Mind: Toward a Psychocivilized Society, edited by Ruth N. Anshen, Harper, 1969; *Planificacion cerebral del hombre futuro,* Publicaciones de la Fundacion Juan March, 1973; (editor with F. V. DeFeudis) *Behavioral Neurochemistry,* Halsted Press, 1977. Contributor of more than two hundred scientific papers to journals. Member of editorial board, *International Review of Neurobiology, Psychosomatic Medicine,* and *Journal of Nervous and Mental Diseases.*†

* * *

DEMSKE, James Michael 1922-

PERSONAL: Born April 10, 1922, in Buffalo, N.Y.; son of Albert J. (a musician) and Augusta (Nagel) Demske. *Education:* Canisius College, A.B. (summa cum laude), 1947; Woodstock College, Ph.L., 1951, University of Innsbruck, S.T.L., 1958; University of Freiburg, Ph.D., 1962. *Home and office:* Office of the President, Canisius College, 2001 Main St., Buffalo, N.Y. 14208.

CAREER: Entered Society of Jesus (Jesuits), 1947, ordained Roman Catholic priest, 1957; Federal Bureau of Investigation, Washington, D.C., technician, 1942-43; St. Peter's College, Jersey City, N.J., instructor in philosophy, 1951-54; Bellarmine College, Plattsburgh, N.Y., director of seminarians, 1963-66; Canisius College, Buffalo, N.Y., president, 1966—. Member of board of directors, Buffalo Chamber of Commerce. Trustee, Buffalo United Fund, Buffalo Philharmonic, Studio Arena Theater, WNED-TV. *Military service:* U.S. Army, 1943-46; became captain. *Member:* National Conference of Christians and Jews (former board member), Association of Colleges and Universities of the State of New York, University Club, Buffalo Club. *Awards, honors:* Educator of the Year, University Club of Buffalo, 1970; Centennial Regents Award, Canisius College, 1970; University Award, State University of New York at Buffalo, 1971; Urban Center Distinguished Educators Award, 1971; *Courier Express* Goodfellow of the Year, 1971; *Buffalo Evening News* Outstanding Citizen of the Year, 1971; Law Day Award, American Bar Association, 1973; Brothers of Mercy Award, 1976.

WRITINGS: (With Avery Dulles and Robert O'Connell) *Introductory Metaphysics: A Course Combining Matter Treated in Ontology, Cosmology, and Natural Theology,* Sheed, 1955; (translator) Karl Rahner, *Encounters with Silence,* Newman, 1960; *Sein, Mensch und Tod: Das Todesproblem bei Martin Heidegger,* K. Alber (Freiburg), 1963, translation by the author published as *Being, Man and Death: A Key to Heidegger,* University Press of Kentucky, 1970; *A Promise of Quality: The First One Hundred Years of Canisius College* (originally an address), Princeton University Press, 1970. Also author of series, "Irish and I," Buffalo *Courier Express,* 1976.

* * *

DENNY, Ludwell 1894-1970

November 18, 1894—October 12, 1970; American journalist

and editor. Obituaries: *New York Times,* October 13, 1970; *Washington Post,* October 14, 1970; *Newsday,* October 17, 1970.

* * *

DENZIN, Norman K(ent) 1941-

PERSONAL: Born March 24, 1941, in Iowa City, Iowa; son of Kenneth F. (a foreman) and Betty (Townsley) Denzin; married Evelyn K. Hurlbut, February 1, 1963; children: Johanna, Rachel. *Education:* University of Iowa, A.B., 1963, Ph.D., 1966. *Home:* 803 West Indiana, Urbana, Ill. 61801. *Office:* Department of Sociology, University of Illinois, Urbana, Ill. 61801.

CAREER: University of Illinois, Urbana, assistant professor of sociology, 1966-69; University of California, Berkeley, assistant professor of sociology, 1969-71; University of Illinois, associate professor, 1971-73, professor of sociology, 1973—. Consulting sociologist, Federal Offenders Rehabilitation Project, Seattle, Wash., 1967-68. Referee on grant applications, National Foundation on the Arts and Humanities, 1970. *Member:* American Sociological Association, American Anthropological Association, American Psychological Association, American Association for Public Opinion Research, Society for the Sociological Study of Social Problems, Society for the Psychological Study of Social Issues, Society for the Study of Applied Anthropology, Pacific Sociological Society, Midwest Sociological Society.

WRITINGS: (Editor and contributor with Stephen P. Spitzer) *The Mental Patient: Studies in the Sociology of Deviance,* McGraw, 1968; *The Research Act: A Theoretical Introduction to Sociological Methods,* Aldine, 1970, 2nd edition, McGraw, 1977; (contributor) Eliot Freidson and Janet Lobeser, editors, *Medical Men and Their Work,* Atherton, 1970; (contributor) Anthony L. Guenther, editor, *Criminal Behavior and Social Systems: Contributions of American Society,* Rand McNally, 1970; (editor and contributor) *Sociological Methods: A Sourcebook,* Aldine, 1970, 2nd edition, McGraw, 1977; (editor and contributor) *The Values of Social Science,* Aldine, 1970; (with others) *Social Relationships,* Aldine, 1970; (contributor) Gregory P. Stone and Harvey A. Farberman, editors, *Social Psychology through Symbolic Interaction,* Ginn-Blaisdell, 1970; (contributor) Jack D. Douglas, editor, *Understanding Everyday Life,* Aldine, 1970; (contributor) Douglas, editor, *Deviance and Respectability: The Social Construction of Moral Meanings,* Basic Books, 1970; (contributor) Douglas, editor, *Situations and Structures: Introduction to Sociology,* Free Press, 1970; (with Alfred R. Lindesmith and A. R. Strauss) *Social Psychology,* 4th edition, Dryden, 1975; (with Lindesmith and Strauss) *Readings in Social Psychology,* 2nd edition, Dryden, 1975; *Childhood Socialization,* Jossey-Bass, 1977.

Contributor to *Social Forces, Journal of Health and Social Behavior, Mental Hygiene, Sociological Quarterly, Social Problems, American Sociological Review, American Sociologist, American Journal of Sociology, Newsociety, Pacific Sociological Review, Word, Quest,* and *Slavic Review.* Special issue editor, *Trans-action,* June-July, 1971; associate editor, *Sociological Quarterly, Contemporary Sociology;* editorial referee, *American Journal of Sociology.*

WORK IN PROGRESS: Long term analysis of symbolic interactionism as a distinct theoretical orientation in sociology, for Aldine.

SIDELIGHTS: Norman K. Denzin told *CA:* "[My] basic

position is that human conduct can only be understood by grasping the perspectives, languages and points of view of those the sociologist wishes to understand. Instrumental works have been by G. H. Mead, C. H. Cooley, H. Blumer and Manford Kuhn. [The] basic question guiding my work is 'How is society possible and how does the self develop out of the interaction process?' I am attempting to spell out the theoretical and methodological implications of pragmatism, symbolic interactionism and naturalism.''

* * *

DERLETH, August (William) 1909-1971
(Stephen Grendon, Tally Mason)

February 24, 1909—July 4, 1971; American novelist, poet, mystery writer, and author of books on Wisconsin. Obituaries: *New York Times,* July 6, 1971; *Washington Post,* July 8, 1971; *Antiquarian Bookman,* July 19-26, 1971; *Publishers' Weekly,* August 2, 1971. (See index for *CA* sketch)

* * *

DeROSIER, Arthur H(enry), Jr. 1931-

PERSONAL: Born February 18, 1931, in Norwich, Conn.; son of Arthur Henry and Rose Rita (Raymond) DeRosier; married Dora Delores Jordan (a nurse), February 23, 1952; children: Deborah Ann, Marsha Carol, Charles Arthur, Melissa Estelle. *Education:* University of Southern Mississippi, B.S., 1954; University of South Carolina, M.A., 1955, Ph.D., 1959. *Politics:* Democrat. *Religion:* Presbyterian. *Home:* Shelbridge, Johnson City, Tenn. 37601. *Office:* President's Office, East Tennessee State University, Johnson City, Tenn. 37601.

CAREER: The Citadel, Charleston, S.C., assistant professor of history, 1956-57; Converse College, Spartanburg, S.C., assistant professor of history, 1957-59; University of Southern Mississippi, Hattiesburg, assistant professor, 1959-60, associate professor, 1960-64, professor of history, 1964-65; University of Oklahoma, Norman, associate professor of history, 1965-67, assistant dean of graduate school, 1966-67; East Tennessee State University, Johnson City, professor of history and dean of School of Graduate Studies, 1967-72, director of Research Advisory Council, 1968-74, vice-president for administration, 1972-74; University of Mississippi, Oxford, vice chancellor for academic affairs, 1974-76, vice chancellor, 1976-77; East Tennessee State University, president, 1977—. Director, Title XI Institute on Economic History, summer, 1966; director, Title XI Institute for Teachers of Indian Children, summer, 1967; co-executive director, Appalachian Consortium, Inc., 1971. *Military service:* U.S. Air Force, 1948-52; became sergeant.

MEMBER: American Historical Association, Organization of American Historians, American Association of State Colleges and Universities, Southern Historical Association, Western History Association, Mississippi Historical Society, Phi Beta Kappa, Pi Gamma Mu, Phi Alpha Theta, Kappa Sigma. *Awards, honors:* American Philosophical Society grant, 1964; Award of Merit, American Association for State and Local History, 1971, for *The Removal of the Choctaw Indians;* Eagle Feather award, *American Indian Review,* 1971, for *The Removal of the Choctaw Indians;* Freedom Foundation of Valley Forge award, 1973, for educational radio series, ''An Analysis of the Constitution of the United States''; George Washington Medallion.

WRITINGS: Through the South with a Union Soldier, Research Advisory Council, East Tennessee State University, 1969; *The Removal of the Choctaw Indians,* University of Tennessee Press, 1970; *Four Centuries of Southern Indians,* University of Georgia Press, 1975; *Appalachia: Family Traditions in Transition,* Research Advisory Council, East Tennessee State University, 1975; *Forked Tongues and Broken Treaties,* Caxton, 1975. Contributor to many journals, including *Journal of Mississippi History, Historian, Chronicles of Oklahoma, Southern Quarterly, Publications of the South Carolina Historical Association, Journal of the West, Cherokee One Feather, Choctaw Times, Proceedings of the Oklahoma Academy of Science.* Editor, *Southern Quarterly,* 1962-65; assistant editor, *Journal of Mississippi History,* 1962-63.

SIDELIGHTS: Arthur H. DeRosier told *CA:* ''I am an American Indian historian who spends most of his time working on and with the Indian problem in America. I would like to write a multi-volume work on the removal of all American Indian tribes from the time Spaniards first set foot on American soil. I have started this task by my Choctaw removal book.... My main interest is in the removal of the Indian: Why we did it; how we did it; what the results have been.''

AVOCATIONAL INTERESTS: Travel (''especially to different Indian reservations and areas of the country''), sports, and people.

* * *

DERVIN, Brenda 1938-

PERSONAL: Born November 20, 1938, in Beverly, Mass.; daughter of John J. (a salesman) and Marjorie (Sullivan) Dervin. *Education:* Cornell University, B.S., 1960; Michigan State University, M.A., 1968, Ph.D., 1971. *Home:* 9126 First Ave. N.E., Seattle, Wash. 98115. *Office:* School of Communications, DS-40, University of Washington, Seattle, Wash. 98195.

CAREER: American Home Economics Association, Washington, D.C., public relations assistant, 1962-64; University of Wisconsin—Milwaukee, communications specialist, 1964-66; Michigan State University, East Lansing, instructor, 1966-68, senior research assistant, 1968-70, resident lecturer in communication, 1970; Syracuse University, Syracuse, N.Y., assistant professor of library science, 1971-73; University of Washington, Seattle, assistant professor of communications, 1973—. *Member:* International Communications Association, Association for Education in Journalism.

WRITINGS: (Editor) *The Spender Syndrome,* University of Wisconsin Extension Service, 1965; (with Bradley S. Greenberg) *The Use of the Mass Media by the Urban Poor,* Praeger, 1970. Contributor to communications journals.

WORK IN PROGRESS: Research on the development of communication-based systems for information and human service delivery.

* * *

DESAI, P(rasannavadan) B(hagwanji) 1924-

PERSONAL: Born October 2, 1924, in Surat, Gujarat, India; son of B. K. and R. B. Desai; married, February 16, 1951; wife's name, Lina; children: Neelam, Daksha, Asha, Himanshu. *Education:* University of Bombay, B.Com., M.A. *Religion:* Hindu. *Home:* Staff Quarters, Institute of Economic Growth, Delhi 7, India. *Office:* Institute of Economic Growth, University Campus, Delhi 7, India.

CAREER: Institute of Economic Growth, Delhi, India, senior fellow and chief of Demographic Research Centre,

1961—. *Member:* Population Council of India (founder member), Population Council (New York; fellow), Indian Association for the Study of Population (founder member), Institute for Economic Growth Society (secretary).

WRITINGS: (With Vljayendra K.R.V. Rao) *Greater Delhi: A Study in Urbanisation,* Asia Publishing House, 1966; *Size and Sex Composition of Population in India, 1901-1961,* Asia Publishing House, 1969; (editor-in-chief) *Regional Perspective of Urban and Industrial Growth,* Macmillan, 1969; (compiler) *Studies in Demography,* University of North Carolina Press, 1970; *A Survey of Research in Demography,* InterCulture Associates, 1976.

WORK IN PROGRESS: Evolution of Population Policy in India; a fertility survey of the Delhi metropolitan population.†

*   *   *

de SAINT PHALLE, Therese   1930-

PERSONAL: Born March 7, 1930, in New York, N.Y.; daughter of Alexandre and Helen Georgia (Harper) de Saint Phalle; married Jehan de Drouas (a bank manager), December 30, 1950; children: Henri. *Education:* Attended the Sorbonne, University of Paris. *Politics:* Liberal ("for peace"). *Religion:* Roman Catholic. *Home:* 46 Blvd. Emile Augier, Paris 16, France. *Agent:* Mrs. Bradley, 18 quai de Bethune, Paris 4, France. *Office:* Flammarion, 26 rue Racine, Paris 6e, France.

CAREER: Fayard (publishers), Paris, France, member of editorial staff, 1948-63; Presses de la Cite (publishers), Paris, editor, 1963-70; Flammarion (publishers), Paris, editor, 1971—. Novelist. *Awards, honors:* Prix le Bec et la Plume for *La Mendigote.*

WRITINGS: La Mendigote, Gallimard, 1966; *La Chandelle,* Gallimard, 1967, translation by Antonia White published as *The Candle,* Harrap, 1968; *Le Tournesol,* Gallimard, 1968, translation published as *The Sunflower,* Harrap, 1970; *Le Souverain,* Gallimard, 1970; *La Clairiere,* Gallimard, 1974. Author of television play, "A Trois Temps," produced in 1971. Contributor to *Le Monde, Le Figaro, Revue de Paris, Publishers' Weekly, Spectacle du Monde,* and other periodicals.

WORK IN PROGRESS: Le Jardin des grands Augustins, a novel; a film script.

SIDELIGHTS: "My American blood is very important to me," Therese de Saint Phalle writes, mentioning a grandfather, Donald A. Harper, who practiced before the U.S. Supreme Court and two American cousins, Willie Morris, former editor-in-chief of *Harper's,* and author William Styron. And American background seeps into her novels—the central figure in *The Candle* is the managing editor of a fictional New York newspaper.

She also told *CA:* "I am working as editor full time, taking care about other people's writings. For a woman, to work means communicating with others. My own novelist work takes place from 5 a.m. to 8 a.m. Then I go down into myself, like a coal worker, to pick up word after word in the coal mine of my mind."

Therese de Saint Phalle's novels have been published in ten countries. *La Chandelle, Le Mendigote,* and *Le Tournesol* were adapted for television films in France.

BIOGRAPHICAL/CRITICAL SOURCES: Books and Bookmen, November, 1968.

DEUTSCHKRON, Inge   1922-

PERSONAL: Born August 23, 1922, in Finsterwalde, Germany; daughter of Martin (a teacher) and Ella (Mannhalt) Deutschkron. *Education:* "Due to persecution as a Jewess hardly any education. Just few years at school." *Home:* Raw Ashi St. 6, Ramat Aviv, Israel.

CAREER: Journalist, 1955—; correspondent of Israeli newspaper, *Maariv,* in Bonn, Germany, 1958-72; staff-writer, Tel-Aviv newspaper, 1972—. *Member:* Deutscher Journalistenverband, Verein der Auslands-presse (Bonn), Israeli Journalist Association.

WRITINGS: (With Fritz Heine) *Die Internationale,* J.H.W. Dietz, 1965; *. . . denn ihrer war die Hoelle* (title means ". . . For Theirs Was the Hell"), Verlag Wissenschaft & Politik, 1965; *Israel und die Deutschen,* Verlag Wissenschaft & Politik, 1970, translation published as *Bonn and Jerusalem: The Strange Coalition,* Chilton, 1970.

WORK IN PROGRESS: Memoirs of her experiences living underground in Berlin during World War II.

SIDELIGHTS: Inge Deutschkron writes in both English and German, speaks French, and has a working knowledge of Spanish and Italian. She has traveled extensively in Southeast Asia.

*   *   *

DEVER, Joseph   1919-1970

September 1, 1919—December 13, 1970; American author and biographer. Obituaries: *Books Abroad,* spring, 1971. (See index for *CA* sketch)

*   *   *

de VOSJOLI, Philippe L. Thyraud   1920-

PERSONAL: Surname is pronounced Vos-jo-*lee;* born November 30, 1920, in Chalon-sur-Saone, Saone-et-Loire, France; son of Lucien Thyraud (an attorney) and Louise (Montaigut) de Vosjoli; married Monique Morgan, 1968; children: Philippe L., Jr., Patrick. *Education:* College de Pont-Levoy, B.A., 1939; Ecole des Sciences Politiques, Diploma.

CAREER: French Military Mission in China, Chungking, inspector, 1944-45; Presidence du Conseil, Paris, France, attache, 1945-47; Prime Minister's Office, Paris, chef de cabinet, 1947-50; French Embassy, Washington, D.C., attache, 1951-63; consultant to *Life* Magazine, 1968-70. *Military service:* Free French Forces, Cavalry, World War II; became captain. *Member:* Jockey Club, Ocean Reef Club (both Miami).

WRITINGS: Lamia, Little, Brown, 1970. Contributor to *Life, Reader's Digest, Sunday Times* (London), and other publications.

WORK IN PROGRESS: The Huguenots, a novel based on the settlement of Florida by French Huguenots; *Subversion,* a book on the underground movements in the world.

BIOGRAPHICAL/CRITICAL SOURCES: Look, May 14, 1968; P. de Villemarest, *L'Espionnage sovietique en France, 1944-1969,* Nouvelles Editions Latines, 1969; *Best Sellers,* November 15, 1970; Leroy Finville, *Heurs et Malheurs d'un agent secret,* Plon, 1970.††

*   *   *

de WAAL, Victor (Alexander)   1929-

PERSONAL: Born February 2, 1929, in Amsterdam, Netherlands; son of Hendrik and Elizabeth (Ephrussi) de Waal; married Esther Moir (a lecturer in history and author), September 3, 1960; children: John, Alexander, Edmund, Thomas. *Education:* Cambridge University, B.A., 1949, M.A., 1954; Ely Theological College, further study, 1950-52. *Residence:* Canterbury, England.

CAREER: Clergyman of Church of England; Ely Theological College, Ely, England, lecturer in theology, 1956-59; Cambridge University, King's College, Cambridge, England, succentor, 1959-63; University of Nottingham, Nottingham, England, Anglican chaplain, 1963-69; Lincoln Cathedral and Theological College, Lincoln, England, chancellor, 1969-76; Canterbury Cathedral, Canterbury, England, dean, 1976—.

WRITINGS: What Is the Church?, S.C.M. Press, 1969, Judson, 1970.

Contributor: John Coulson, editor, *Theology and the University,* Helicon, 1964; *Stages of Experience: The Year in the Church,* Helicon, 1965; Laurence Bright, editor, *The Committed Church,* Darton, Longman & Todd, 1966; G. R. Dunstan, editor, *The Sacred Ministry,* S.P.C.K., 1970. Contributor to theology journals.

*　　*　　*

DEWEY, Bradley R. 1934-

PERSONAL: Born October 25, 1934, in Detroit, Mich.; son of Richard S. and Viola K. Dewey; married Marcia Althaus; children: Anne D., Jane R. *Education:* University of Michigan, B.S., 1957; Yale University, B.D., 1960, M.A., 1961, Ph.D., 1964. *Office:* Department of Religion, Franklin and Marshall College, Lancaster, Pa. 17603.

CAREER: Methodist clergyman. Franklin and Marshall College, Lancaster, Pa., assistant professor, 1964-68, associate professor in department of religious studies, 1968—. Has conducted study series on theological trends for church groups. *Member:* American Academy of Religion, American-Scandinavian Foundation, American Association of University Professors, Soeren Kierkegaard Selskab. *Awards, honors:* Fulbright research fellow in Denmark, 1962-63; F. and M. Lindback Award for Distinguished Teaching, 1966; National Endowment for the Humanities research fellow in Denmark, 1969-70.

WRITINGS: The New Obedience: Kierkegaard on Imitating Christ, World Publishing, 1968. Contributor to theological journals.

*　　*　　*

DEWOLF, Rose (Doris) 1934-

PERSONAL: Born July 18, 1934, in Reading, Pa.; daughter of Lewis Marcus (a merchant) and Pauline (Hirshout) DeWolf; married Bernard Ingster (a management consultant), September 30, 1967; children: Carole. *Education:* Temple University, B.S., 1956. *Home:* 2226 Lombard St., Philadelphia, Pa. 19146. *Office: Philadelphia Evening and Sunday Bulletin,* 30th and Market Sts., Philadelphia, Pa. 19101.

CAREER: Daily Intelligencer, Doylestown, Pa., writer, 1956-60; *Camden Courier-Post,* Camden, N.J., writer, 1960-61; *Philadelphia Inquirer,* Philadelphia, Pa., columnist, 1961-68; *Philadelphia Evening and Sunday Bulletin,* Philadelphia, columnist, 1969—; free-lance magazine writer. Television interviewer, WFIL-TV, Philadelphia, 1968-69, and WCAU-TV, Philadelphia, 1976—; commentator, KYW-TV, Philadelphia, 1971; lecturer.

WRITINGS: The Bonds of Acrimony, Lippincott, 1970; (with Joel Moldorsky) *The Best Defense,* Macmillan, 1975. Contributor to periodicals.

*　　*　　*

DHRYMES, Phoebus J(ames) 1932-

PERSONAL: Born October 1, 1932, in Cyprus; came to United States in 1951, naturalized in 1954; son of Demetrios and Kyriaki (Neophytou) Dhrymes; married Beatrice Bell Fitch, 1972; children: Phoebus, Jr. *Education:* University of Texas, B.A., 1957; Massachusetts Institute of Technology, Ph.D., 1961. *Religion:* Greek Orthodox. *Home:* 445 Riverside Dr., New York, N.Y. 10027. *Office:* Department of Economics, Columbia University, New York, N.Y. 10027.

CAREER: Harvard University, Cambridge, Mass., assistant professor of economics, 1962-64; University of Pennsylvania, Philadelphia, associate professor, 1964-67, professor of economics, 1967-73; Columbia University, New York, N.Y., professor of economics, 1973—, Wesley Clair Mitchell Research Professor, 1977. *Military service:* U.S. Army, 1952-54. *Member:* American Economic Association, American Statistical Association (fellow), Economic Studies Society, Econometric Society (fellow). *Awards, honors:* Natural Science Foundation fellowship, 1961-62; Guggenheim fellowship, 1965-66; Ford Foundation faculty research fellowship, 1968-69.

WRITINGS: Distributed Lags: Problems of Formulation and Estimation, Holden-Day, 1970; *Econometrics: Statistical Foundations and Applications,* Harper, 1970, new edition, Springer-Verlag, 1974. Editor, *International Economic Review,* 1964-71; co-editor, *Journal of Econometrics,* 1972—.

*　　*　　*

DICKEY, R(obert) P(reston) 1936-

PERSONAL: Born September 24, 1936; son of Delno Miren (a lead miner) and Naomi (Jackson) Dickey; married Victoria McCabe (a college instructor), February 1, 1969 (divorced May 18, 1976); children: Shannon Ezra. *Education:* University of Missouri, B.A., 1968, M.A., 1969; Walden University, Ph.D., 1975. *Agent:* Charles R. Byrne, 1133 Avenue of the Americas, New York, N.Y. 10036. *Office:* Pima College, West Campus, Tucson, Ariz. 85709.

CAREER: University of Missouri, Columbia, instructor in creative writing, 1967-69; Southern Colorado State College, Pueblo, assistant professor of creative writing, 1969-73; Pima College, Tucson, Ariz., assistant professor of creative writing, 1975—. Has given more than 500 readings of his poems at colleges and high schools across the country; operates his own press, Poetry Bag Press. *Military service:* U.S. Air Force, 1954-56. *Awards, honors:* Two prizes in Kansas City Poetry Contests, 1966.

WRITINGS—Poems: (With Donald Justice, Donald Drummond, and Thomas McAfee) *Four Poets,* CUI Press (Pella, Iowa), 1967; *Running Lucky,* Swallow Press, 1969; *Acting Immortal,* University of Missouri Press, 1970; *Concise Dictionary of Lead River, Mo.,* Black Bear Press, 1972; *McCabe Wants Chimes,* Silver Mountain Press, 1973; *Life-Cycle of Seven Songs,* Silver Mountain Press, 1974; "Minnequa" (opera libretto), first produced January, 1976. Contributor to *Sewanee Review.* Founder and editor, *Poetry Bag* (magazine).

WORK IN PROGRESS: Two novels; a biography of publisher Alan Swallow; two opera libretti; a book of children's poems.

SIDELIGHTS: R. P. Dickey lists his chief literary influences as "Yeats, Pound, and now Lawrence, although I'm not at all certain that would be very apparent to a casual reader of my work—maybe not even a close reader! Schools and trends are mostly very dull. I love to read and try to write all kinds of poetry—indirect, direct, objective, subjective, all kinds of lines and structures, and all kinds of combinations. Either Lawrence's *Fantasia of the Unconscious* or Pound's *Cantos* is the greatest book of the twentieth century."

Dickey adds that "the books I write help keep me in touch with reality and help keep me sane. When on any book manuscript I work from 5 am until about 10:30 or so for five or six days a week."

BIOGRAPHICAL/CRITICAL SOURCES: Poetry, July, 1971.

* * *

DIERKS, Jack Cameron 1930-

PERSONAL: Born June 1, 1930, in Evanston, Ill.; son of Wilford Rudolph (a banker) and Margaret (MacLaren) Dierks. *Education:* Beloit College, A.B., 1951; Northwestern University, M.S.J., 1957. *Religion:* Presbyterian. *Home:* 1360 North Lake Shore Dr., Chicago, Ill. 60610. *Office:* Porter, Gould & Dierks, 215 West Ohio St., Chicago, Ill. 60610.

CAREER: Public relations and advertising executive with Prudential Insurance Co., Chicago, Ill., 1957-59, Allstate Insurance Co., Skokie, Ill., 1959-61, and TransUnion Corp., Chicago, 1961-63; *Food Business,* Chicago, editor, 1963-64; Sweetwood Corp., Houston, Tex., advertising consultant, 1964; free-lance writer, 1965—; Porter, Gould & Dierks (authors' agents), Chicago, partner, 1972—. *Military service:* U.S. Navy, 1951-55. *Member:* Sigma Delta Chi, Chicago Headline Club.

WRITINGS: A Leap to Arms: The Cuban Campaign of 1898, Lippincott, 1970; (contributor) *The Writer's Manual,* ETC Publications, 1977. Contributor of feature material to newspapers and of articles to trade magazines.

WORK IN PROGRESS: A book on the Hague peace conferences of 1899 and 1907.

SIDELIGHTS: "In a visual age," Dierks writes, "I still maintain a tenacious interest in the printed word, and in the continuing value of history in its traditional role of lesson-teacher. The claim that life changes too quickly today for the past to be of value is a popular and youthful view, but not my own. If things are changing faster, we must learn faster."

* * *

DIETZ, Elisabeth H. 1908-
(Betty Warner Dietz)

PERSONAL: Born May 12, 1908, in Chicago, Ill.; daughter of Bernhard Theodore (an ophthalmologist) and Auguste (Erasmi) Hoffman; married Ernest W. Warner, December 18, 1926 (deceased); married Thomas S. Dietz, December 24, 1953 (divorced); children: (first marriage) Nadine (Mrs. John Rea, Jr.), Theodore B. *Education:* Northwestern University, B.S., 1940, M.A., 1942; New York University, Ed.D., 1955; Columbia University, additional study, 1965-66. *Home:* 9939 Pleasant Valley Rd., Sun City, Ariz. 85351. *Office:* School of Education, Brooklyn College of the City University of New York, Brooklyn, N.Y. 11210.

CAREER: Teacher in Deerfield, Ill., 1940-42, in New Orleans, La., 1942-44, and in Scarsdale, N.Y., 1944-50; Brooklyn College (now Brooklyn College of the City University of New York), Brooklyn, N.Y., assistant professor of education, 1950-52; American Education Mission to Korea, professor, 1952-53; Brooklyn College of the City University of New York, assistant professor, 1954-64, associate professor, 1964-70, professor of education, 1971-73, professor emeritus, 1973—. Trustee and member of board of directors, Fellowship Day Care Center, Inc., Garden City, N.Y. Consultant, American-Korean Foundation, 1954.

MEMBER: Association for Supervision and Curriculum Development, Association for Childhood Education International, Society for Ethnomusicology, National Society for the Study of Education, International Reading Association, National Council of Teachers of English, International Folk Music Council, Music Educators National Conference, Asia Society, Society for the Preservation of Samaritan Culture (member of board of directors), Society for Asian Music, Tagore Society. *Awards, honors:* Scroll of appreciation from Republic of Korea, 1953.

WRITINGS—Under name Betty Warner Dietz: (With Thomas Choonbai Park) *Folk Songs of China, Japan, Korea,* John Day, 1964; (with Michael Babatunde Olatunji) *Musical Instruments of Africa: Their Nature, Use, and Place in the Life of a Deeply Musical People,* and phonodisc recorded by Colin M. Turnbull, John Day, 1965; *You Can Work in the Health Services,* John Day, 1968; *You Can Work in the Education Services,* John Day, 1968; *You Can Work in the Transportation Industry,* John Day, 1969; *You Can Work in the Communications Industry,* John Day, 1970; (editor) *Folk Melodies of the Orient for Soprano and Alto Recorders and Percussion,* Consort Music, 1972. Contributor to music and education journals.

Editor: Betty Atwell Wright, "Urban Education Studies," eight albums of photographs with teachers guides, John Day, 1965-66, and a sub-series, "Big City," nine books with teachers guide, 1965-71; Nancy Schueler and Mark Feldstein, "The City Is My Home" series, four books with teachers guide, John Day, 1966-68; Wright, "Rural Education Studies," eight books with teachers guide, John Day, 1967; Charles Hofmann, *American Indians Sing,* John Day, 1967.

WORK IN PROGRESS: You Can Work in the Utilities Services and *You Can Work in the Protective Services,* both for John Day; further research on musical instruments and folk music of non-western cultures.†

* * *

DIMICK, Kenneth M. 1937-

PERSONAL: Born June 27, 1937, in Corvallis, Ore.; son of Roland E. (a college professor) and Mary Dimick; married Janice M. Wirth, August 15, 1959; children: Julia E., Jeffrey M. *Education:* Oregon State University, B.S., 1960, M.Ed., 1962; University of Arizona, Ed.D., 1966. *Home:* 2107 Lincolnshire Dr., Muncie, Ind. 47904. *Office:* Department of Psychology, Ball State University, Muncie, Ind. 47906.

CAREER: Teacher and counselor in public schools in Troutdale, Ore., and Albany, Ore., 1960-64; University of Arizona, Tucson, assistant professor of counseling, 1966-67; Ball State University, Muncie, Ind., counseling psychologist, 1967—. *Member:* American Personnel and Guidance Association, Sigma Delta Chi, Kappa Delta Pi, Phi Delta Kappa.

WRITINGS: (With Vaughn E. Huff) *Child Counseling,*

W. C. Brown, 1970; (with Frank H. Krause) *Practicum Manual for Counseling and Psychotherapy*, 3rd edition (Dimick was not associated with earlier editions), Accelerated Development, 1975.†

* * *

DIONISOPOULOS, P(anagiotes) Allan 1921-

PERSONAL: Born May 9, 1921, in St. Paul, Minn.; son of George Peter (a janitor) and Katherine (Allan) Dionisopoulos; married Christine Nasios, September 15, 1946; children: Regina, James, George, Michael, Catherine. *Education:* University of Minnesota, B.A., 1948, B.S. and M.A., 1950; University of California, Los Angeles, Ph.D., 1960. *Politics:* Democrat. *Religion:* Greek Orthodox. *Home:* 124 Manor Dr., DeKalb, Ill. 60115. *Office:* Department of Political Science, Northern Illinois University, DeKalb, Ill. 60115.

CAREER: Indiana University, Bloomington, lecturer in political science, 1955-60, director of Institute of Training for Public Service, 1957-60; University of Arizona, Tucson, assistant professor of political science, 1960-61; University of Wisconsin—Milwaukee, assistant professor of political science and coordinator of extension courses in Letters and Science, 1961-62; Northern Illinois University, DeKalb, associate professor, 1962-66, acting head of department of political science, 1963-64, professor of political science, 1966—. Director, Peace Corps, Northern Illinois University, 1964-65. Served on various committees including Indiana University Governor's Conference for Legislators, 1957, 1959, Governor's Conference on Urban Problems, 1959. Consultant to Indiana Municipal League, 1959, League of Women Voters, and organized labor education programs in Indiana, Wisconsin, and Illinois. Appeared on educational television at Indiana University, 1956-60, University of Arizona, 1960, and University of Wisconsin, 1962. *Military service:* U.S. Navy, 1941-45, 1950-52. *Member:* American Political Science Association.

WRITINGS: (Contributor) Kazuo Ichien, *Fundamental Problems of the Japanese Constitution*, [Japan], 1959; (editor) *Challenge to State Righters*, University of Wisconsin, 1962; *The Government of the United States*, Scribner, 1970; *Rebellion, Racism, and Representation: The Adam Clayton Powell Case and Its Antecedents*, Northern Illinois University Press, 1970; (with Dan Wit) *Our American Government and Political System*, Laidlaw Brothers, 1972; (editor) *Racism in America*, Northern Illinois University Press, 1972; (with Craig Ducat) *The Right of Privacy*, West Publishing, 1976. Contributor to *Collier's Encyclopedia*, *Indiana Law Journal*, *Journal of Law and Politics* (Japan), *Midwest Journal of Political Science*, *Western Political Quarterly*, *Insight and Outlook*, *Chicago-Kent Law Review*, *Journal of Public Law*, *Minnesota Law Review*, *Buffalo Law Review*, *Akron Law Review*. Editor, *Grassroots* and *DEA News*.

* * *

DI PALMA, Ray(mond) 1943-

PERSONAL: Born September 27, 1943, in New Kensington, Pa. *Education:* Duquesne University, B.A., 1966; University of Iowa, M.F.A., 1968. *Home:* 226 West 21st St., Apt. 4-R, New York, N.Y. 10011.

CAREER: Bowling Green University, Bowling Green, Ohio, instructor in English and creative writing, 1968-75; adjunct professor, Union Graduate School, 1976-77. Founder, Doones Press and *Doones Magazine*, 1969.

WRITINGS: Max, Body Press, 1969; (with Stephen Shrader) *Macaroons*, Doones Press, 1969; *Between the Shapes*, Zeitgeist, 1970; *Clinches*, Abraxas Press, 1970; *The Gallery Goers*, Ithaca House, 1971; *All Bowed Down*, Burning Deck Press, 1972; *Works in a Drawer*, Blue Chair Press, 1972; *Borgia Circles*, Sand Project Press, 1972; (with Asa Benveniste and Tom Raworth) *Time Being*, Trigram Press, 1972; *Five Surfaces*, Tottel's no. 12, 1974; *The Sargasso Transcries*, 'X' Editions, 1974; *Max, a Sequel*, Burning Deck Press, 1974; *Soli*, Ithaca House, 1974; *Accidental Interludes*, Turkey Press, 1975; *Marquee*, 'X' Editions, 1976. Editor, Doones Press and *Doones Magazine*, 1969—.

* * *

DOBNER, Maeva Park 1918-
(Maeva Park)

PERSONAL: Born February 17, 1918, in Elmira, N.Y.; daughter of Walter William (a newspaperman and insurance broker) and Olive (Brown) Park; married Charles Adam Dobner (publisher of a shopping news), April 21, 1951; children: Christopher Adam; stepchildren: Victor Charles. *Education:* Attended schools in Elmira, N.Y. *Politics:* "Lean toward Republicans." *Religion:* Protestant. *Home:* 146 Averill Ave., Rochester, N.Y. 14620. *Agent:* Curtis Brown Ltd., 575 Madison Ave., New York, N.Y. 10022.

CAREER: Democrat & Chronicle, Rochester, N.Y., classified advertising desk, 1942-44; L. M. Berry (advertising firm), Rochester, trademark manager, 1947-50; Redpath Lecture Agency, Rochester, secretary, 1953-58. Instructor, Brighton Writers' Workshop. *Military service:* Women's Army Corps (WAC), assigned to Army Air Forces, 1944-46. *Awards, honors:* Awards in *Writer's Digest* short story contest and in *Author and Journalist* fiction contest.

WRITINGS—Novels; all published by Dell: *The Woman in the Maze*, 1970; *Heather*, 1970; *The Gingerbread House*, 1974; *Sea Wind*, 1976. Also author of *Call to a Stranger*, a suspense novella. Contributor of short stories to *Ingenue*, *Co-Ed*, *Redbook*, *Chatelaine*, *Good Housekeeping*, *Dude*, and other magazines.

WORK IN PROGRESS: A novel, *The Singles Company*.

SIDELIGHTS: Maeva Dobner wrote to *CA:* "Although I had always 'written', I had written without direction, until that old cliche, a broken ankle, happened to me. Then I began to write in earnest. An intensive YWCA writers' workshop, conducted by Leonard Snyder of New York City, helped immeasurably. I began to sell short stories, then novels. (A TV show featuring James Michener spurred me on. He said that anyone who hadn't sold a book by the time he/she was 40, undoubtedly never would sell one. I had reached that age, and was determined to prove him wrong. I did.)

"When Sidney Beckerman took an option on 'Call to a Stranger', my suspense novella published in *Redbook*, it made up for many rejections. The film wasn't made, but the thrill remains.

"My stories and books have been translated into German, Italian, Spanish, Norwegian, Swedish, and Danish, and have been anglicized for England, Scotland, and Australia."

* * *

DOBSON, James (Clayton, Jr.) 1936-

PERSONAL: Born April 21, 1936, in Shreveport, La.; son of James C. and Myrtle (G.) Dobson; married Shirley

Deere, August 27, 1960; children: Danae, Ryan. *Education:* Pasadena College, B.A., 1958; University of Southern California, M.S., 1962, Ph.D., 1967; graduate study, University of California, Berkeley, 1963, University of California, Los Angeles, 1964. *Home:* 348 Harvard Dr., Arcadia, Calif. 91006. *Office:* Children's Hospital of Los Angeles, Los Angeles, Calif. 90027.

CAREER: Teacher and counselor in public schools in Hacienda, Calif. and Covina, Calif., 1960-64; Charter Oak Unified School District, Covina, Calif., psychologist and coordinator of Pupil Personnel Services, 1964-66; University of Southern California, School of Medicine, Los Angeles, 1966—, began as assistant professor, currently associate clinical professor of pediatrics. Co-director of Research, Division of Medical Genetics, Children's Hospital of Los Angeles. *Member:* American Psychological Association, American Association on Mental Deficiency, National Council for Measurement in Education, California Association of Guidance and Counseling, California Educational Research and Guidance Association, California Teachers Association, Sigma Phi Mu.

WRITINGS: Dare to Discipline, Tyndale, 1970; (editor and contributor with Richard Koch) *The Mentally Retarded Child and His Family: A Multidisciplinary Handbook,* Brunner, 1971; *Symposium on Phenylketonuria: Present Status and Future Developments,* Verlag Thieme Publications (Heidelberg), 1971; *Hide or Seek,* Revell, 1974; *What Wives Wish Their Husbands Knew About Women,* Tyndale, 1975. Contributor to *Educational and Psychological Measurement, Journal of Developmental Reading, New England Journal of Medicine, Hospital Topics, Lancet,* and *Journal of Pediatrics.* Consulting editor, *Journal of International Neurosciences Abstracts.*

SIDELIGHTS: James Dobson told *CA:* "My mission in writing is to help preserve the health and vitality of the American family, which is undergoing a serious threat to its survival. It is my view that our society can be no more stable than the foundation of individual family units upon which it rests. Our government, our institutions, our schools . . . indeed, our way of life are dependent on healthy marriages and loyalty to the vulnerable little children around our feet. Thus, my professional life is devoted to the integrity of the family and the God who designed it."

*   *   *

DODD, Thomas J. 1907-1971

May 15, 1907—May 24, 1971; U.S. Senator from Connecticut. Obituaries: *New York Times,* May 25, 1971; *Time,* June 7, 1971.

*   *   *

DODGE, H(arry) Robert 1929-

PERSONAL: Born September 17, 1929, in St. Louis, Mo.; son of Harry Varnum (a sales manager) and Jeanne (Groeinger) Dodge; married Donna Broughman, August 6, 1960; children: Melody Jean, Kevin Robert. *Education:* Ohio State University, B.Sc., 1951, M.B.A., 1954, Ph.D., 1962. *Politics:* Republican. *Religion:* Presbyterian. *Home:* 17 Golfview Pl., De Kalb, Ill. 60115. *Office:* Department of Marketing, Northern Illinois University, De Kalb, Ill. 60115.

CAREER: University of Nebraska, Lincoln, instructor in business organization, 1954-55; Ohio State University, Columbus, instructor in business organization, 1955-57; Florida State University, Tallahassee, assistant professor of marketing, 1957-58; Knox Associates, Inc. (consultants), Toledo, Ohio, research associate, 1958-59; California State College, Los Angeles (now California State University, Los Angeles), assistant professor of marketing, 1959-64; Arlington State College (now University of Texas at Arlington), associate professor of marketing, 1964-65; Memphis State University, Memphis, Tenn., professor of marketing, 1965-76; Northern Illinois University, De Kalb, professor of marketing and chairman of department, 1976—. Officer and managing director, Market Consultants, Inc., 1967-69; vice-president, Curriculum Aids, 1975-76. Consultant to various businesses, banks and civic organizations. *Military service:* U.S. Army, 1951-53. U.S. Army Reserve, 1953-59; became captain. *Member:* American Marketing Association (vice-president of industrial marketing, 1974-75), American Institute of Decision Sciences, Southern Marketing Association, Phi Kappa Tau, Beta Gamma Sigma.

WRITINGS: Industrial Marketing, McGraw, 1970; *Field Sales Management,* Business Publications, 1973; (co-author) *Professional Selling,* Business Publications, 1976. Contributor to *Journal of Retailing, A.I.D.S. Journal, Journal* of Bank Public Relations and Marketing Association.

WORK IN PROGRESS: New Production Management, for Grid Publishing; *Positioning Selling Strategies to the Product-Life Cycle; The Corporate Life Cycle and Attendant Management Decisions; Faculty Ratings of Marketing and Management Publications.*

SIDELIGHTS: H. Robert Dodge told *CA:* "Books are an expression of self and the ultimate in professionalism. Authors are those who are better disciplined, not necessarily more intelligent."

*   *   *

DODSON, Fitzhugh (James) 1923-

PERSONAL: Born October 28, 1923, in Baltimore, Md.; son of Fitzhugh J. (a stockbroker) and Lillian (Northam) Dodson; married Grace Goheen (a preschool director), August 1, 1958; children: Robin Ellyn, Randall James, Rustin Fitzhugh. *Education:* Johns Hopkins University, A.B. (cum laude), 1944; Yale University, B.D. (magna cum laude), 1948; University of Southern California, Ph.D., 1957. *Agent:* Sterling Lord, 660 Madison Ave., New York, N.Y. 10021. *Office:* 1801 South Catalina, Redondo Beach, Calif. 90277.

CAREER: Lewis and Clark College, Portland, Ore., lecturer, 1949-52; director of counseling centers in Los Angeles, Calif., and Portland, Ore., 1957-58; private practice in clinical psychology, Redondo Beach, Calif., 1959—; La Primera Schools, Torrance, Calif., owner and administrator, 1963-70. Lecturer, Claremont College, 1959; instructor, El Camino College, 1959-60; assistant professor, Long Beach State College, 1962-63; lecturer, Chadwick School, 1964-1970. Consultant, Project Head Start, Long Beach, Calif., 1966-67.

MEMBER: American Psychological Association, American Group Therapy Association, American Anthropological Association, American Sociological Association, American Association for the Advancement of Science, Academy of Religion and Mental Health, Society for the Study of Religion, Western Psychological Association, California Psychological Association, Los Angeles Psychological Association, Los Angeles Society of Clinical Psychologists, Phi Beta Kappa.

WRITINGS: How to Parent, Nash Publishing, 1970; *Dr. Dodson's Whiz-Bang, Super-Economy Parent's Survival Kit*, New American Library, 1971; *How to Father*, Nash Publishing, 1974; *The You That Could Be*, Follett, 1976.

WORK IN PROGRESS: Sex Education for Parents and *How to Cope with Your Teen-ager.*

AVOCATIONAL INTERESTS: Camping, backpacking, painting, papier-mache, sculpture, and travel.

* * *

DODSON, Tom 1914-

PERSONAL: Born October 27, 1914, in Little Rock, Ark.; married Ruth Elizabeth Pera, May 17, 1948; children: Thomas Pera, Timothy Daniel. *Education:* Attended public schools in Little Rock, Ark. *Politics:* "Ultra conservative." *Religion:* "Protestant Fundamental." *Home:* 9812 Barlow Rd., Fairfax, Va. 22030.

CAREER: United States Navy, radio operator, 1932-40; Federal Communications Commission, worked in radio intelligence, 1940-42; Federal Aviation Agency, Washington, D.C., program control division chief for air traffic control automation, 1942-70.

WRITINGS: Pilots Radio Handbook, U.S. Government Printing Office, 1953; *Working in a Washington Wonderland*, Adams Press, 1969. Contributor to *Aviation Encyclopedia* and to *Horizons.*

* * *

DODWELL, Peter C(arpenter) 1930-

PERSONAL: Born March 13, 1930, in Ootacamund, India; son of David William (an Indian civil servant) and Marcia (Bradley) Dodwell; married Hanna Junge, 1953 (divorced, 1972); married Sharon M. Williams, 1974; children: (first marriage) Nicholas, Karen, Tobias; (second marriage) Andrea Helen. *Education:* Balliol College, Oxford, B.A. (honors), 1953; Oxford University, D.Phil., 1958. *Home:* 20 Hatter St., Kingston, Ontario, Canada. *Office:* Department of Psychology, Queen's University, Kingston, Ontario, Canada.

CAREER: Queen's University, Kingston, Ontario, assistant professor, 1958-63, associate professor, 1963-65, professor of psychology, 1965—. Visiting professor, Harvard University, 1970; visiting fellow, Wolfson College, Oxford, 1975. *Military service:* British Army, Royal Electrical and Mechanical Engineers, 1949-50; became lieutenant. *Member:* Canadian Psychological Association (director, 1972-77), Psychonomic Society, British Experimental Psychology Society. *Awards, honors:* C. D. Howe Fellowship, 1966-67; Guggenheim Fellowship, 1967-68; fellowship, Center for Advanced Study of Behavioral Science, 1968-69; Canada Council Fellowship, 1975-76.

WRITINGS: Visual Pattern Recognition, Holt, 1970; (editor) *Perceptual Learning and Adaptation*, Penguin, 1970; *Perceptive Processing*, Appleton, 1972; (editor) *New Horizons in Psychology, No. 2*, Penguin, 1973; (contributor) Carterette and Friedman, editors, *Handbook of Perception*, Vol. V, Academic Press, 1975; *Introduction to Statistics and Experimental Design*, Holt, in press; (contributor) R. Held, H. Leibowitz, and H. Teuber, editors, *Handbook of Sensory Physiology*, Vol. VIII, Springer-Verlag, in press. Contributor to many journals, including *Science, Nature, Canadian Journal of Psychology, British Journal of Psychology*, and *Psychological Review.* Assistant editor, *Canadian Journal of Psychology*, 1960-64; assistant editor,

Canadian Journal of Behavioral Science, 1970-74; editor, *Canadian Journal of Psychology.*

WORK IN PROGRESS: Research on visual perception, discrimination learning, and perceptual theory.

SIDELIGHTS: Peter C. Dodwell told *CA:* "[I am] interested in cognitive psychology generally, also epistemology and the philosophy of science. [I] started as a mathematician, moved to logic, philosophy and then psychology as [my] field of main research." *New Horizons in Psychology, No. 2* has been translated into Italian and Portuguese.

AVOCATIONAL INTERESTS: Music, literature, travel.

* * *

DOEHRING, Donald G(ene) 1927-

PERSONAL: Surname rhymes with "scoring"; born April 7, 1927, in Pittsburgh, Pa.; son of Walter A. and Francis (Mehnert) Doehring; married Jean M. Kick (a teacher), August 5, 1950; children: Nancy, Carrie, Carl, Laura, Peter. *Education:* University of Buffalo (now State University of New York at Buffalo), B.A., 1949; University of New Mexico, M.A., 1951; Indiana University, Ph.D., 1954. *Home:* 300 Somervale Gardens, Apt. 9, Pointe Claire, Quebec, Canada. *Office:* Department of Human Communications Disorders, McGill University, Beatty Hall, Montreal, Quebec, Canada.

CAREER: Central Institute for the Deaf, St. Louis, Mo., research associate, 1954-59; Indiana University Medical Center, Indianapolis, 1959-63, began as assistant professor, became associate professor of neurology and research associate; McGill University, Montreal, Quebec, 1963—, began as associate professor, currently professor of psychology and human communication disorders, director of School of Human Communication Disorders, 1963-68. *Military service:* U.S. Army, 1944-47. *Member:* American Psychological Association, Canadian Psychological Association, Psychonomic Society, International Reading Association. *Awards, honors:* Paper on automated method of dental instruction by Doehring and P. E. Starkey received $300 prize from *Journal of Dental Education*, 1963; Medical Research Council Visiting Scientist Award, 1971-72, to Cambridge University.

WRITINGS: Patterns of Impairment in Specific Reading Disability: A Neuropsychological Investigation, Indiana University Press, 1968; (contributor) S. E. Gerber, editor, *Introductory Hearing Science*, Saunders, 1974; (contributor) R. M. Knights and D. J. Bakker, editors, *The Neuropsychology of Learning Disorders*, University Park Press, 1976. Also author of research reports published by Central Institute for the Deaf and Naval School of Aviation Medicine. (Contributor) *Monograph of the Society for Research in Child Development*, 1976. Contributor of more than fifty articles to psychology and medical journals.

WORK IN PROGRESS: Research on sub-types of reading disability.

AVOCATIONAL INTERESTS: Music, reading, camping.

* * *

DOLPHIN, Robert, Jr. 1935-

PERSONAL: Born June 7, 1935, in Richmond, Va.; son of Robert Dolphin; married Nancy Wentworth, 1962; children: William Robert, Christina Ann. *Education:* Indiana University, B.S., 1960, M.B.A., 1961; Michigan State University, D.B.A., 1964; Harvard Business School, graduate study,

1965. *Home:* 4125 Breckenridge Rd., Kettering, Ohio 45429. *Office:* School of Graduate Studies, Wright State University, Colonel Glenn Hwy., Dayton, Ohio 45431.

CAREER: Florida State University, Tallahassee, assistant professor of finance, 1964-67; Wright State University, Dayton, Ohio, professor of finance, 1967—, dean of school of graduate studies, 1969-71. *Member:* American Finance Association, Financial Management Association, Academy of Management, Midwest Finance Association. *Awards, honors:* Ford Foundation research grant, 1965.

WRITINGS: An Analysis of Economic and Personal Factors Leading to Consumer Bankruptcy, Graduate School of Business Administration, Michigan State University, 1965; *Self-Correcting Problems in Personal Finance,* Allyn & Bacon, 1970. Contributor to *Business, Banking, Personal Finance Law Quarterly Report, Report Accounting Review, Consumer Finance News.*

WORK IN PROGRESS: Evaluation of professional development of financial executives.

*   *   *

DOMENCICH, Thomas A.

OFFICE ADDRESS: RFD 3, Montpelier, Vt. 05602.

CAREER: Charles River Associates (economic research), Cambridge, Mass., vice-president, 1965-73; currently freelance consultant.

WRITINGS: (With J. C. Burrows) *An Analysis of United States Oil Import Quota,* Heath, 1970; (with Gerald Kraft) *Free Transit,* Heath, 1970; (with Daniel McFadden) *Urban Travel Demand: A Behavioral Analysis,* North-Holland Publishing, 1975.

WORK IN PROGRESS: The Economics of the Panama Canal, for American Enterprise Institute for Public Policy Research.

*   *   *

DONIS, Miles   1937-

PERSONAL: Born December 6, 1937, in Scranton, Pa. *Education:* Dartmouth College, B.A., 1958; Columbia University, M.F.A., 1975. *Home:* 2135 North Ivar Ave., Hollywood, Calif. 90068. *Agent:* Mary Yost Associates, 141 East 55th St., New York, N.Y. 10022; Stuart Miller, 8693 Wilshire Blvd., Beverly Hills, Calif. 90211.

CAREER: Columbia Pictures, New York, N.Y., free-lance writer, 1969—. *Military service:* U.S. Army. *Member:* Authors Guild.

WRITINGS: Falling Up, McKay, 1970; *The Fall of New York,* McKay, 1971; *Cloud Eight,* Warner Paperback, 1975. Also author of screen adaptation of *Falling Up.*

WORK IN PROGRESS: A new novel; a screenplay.

SIDELIGHTS: Miles Donis told *CA:* "Writing fiction is a difficult, frustrating, business, and usually underpaid as well. I'm grateful for the small victories, the occasional satisfactions of style or craft. If there is a goal in mind, it is simply to write my own life, to work through my own experience, and hope it has enough relevance and insight to touch someone who reads it."

A *New York Times* critic says that in *Falling Up* Donis "reveals noticeable talents. He has a nice feeling for the absurd and the outrageous and a good ear for current argot, especially for those conditioned responses that pass for speech. The incidents are funny, the details exaggerated, but the purpose is serious."

BIOGRAPHICAL/CRITICAL SOURCES: New York Times Book Review, August 16, 1970; *New York Times,* August 29, 1970.

*   *   *

DONNELLY, James H(oward), Jr.   1941-

PERSONAL: Born December 24, 1941, in Brooklyn, N.Y.; son of James H. (a policeman) and Helene (Servais) Donnelly. *Education:* Pace College, B.B.A., 1963; Long Island University, M.B.A., 1964; University of Maryland, D.B.A., 1968. *Office:* Department of Business Administration, University of Kentucky, Lexington, Ky. 40506.

CAREER: University of Kentucky, Lexington, 1968—, began as associate professor, currently professor of business administration. *Member:* American Marketing Association. *Awards, honors:* American Marketing Association award, 1963; Association for Education in International Business Doctoral Dissertation Competition, third place, 1968; University of Kentucky Alumni Association Great Teachers Award, 1971.

WRITINGS: Analysis for Marketing Decisions, Irwin, 1970; *New Dimensions in Retailing,* Wadsworth, 1970; *Fundamentals of Management: Functions, Behavior, Models,* Business Publications, 1971, revised edition, 1975; (editor) *Fundamentals of Management: Selected Readings,* Business Publications, 1971, revised edition, 1975; *Workbook for Elements of Business Enterprise,* 3rd edition, Ronald, 1971. Also author of *Organizations: Behavior, Structure, Processes,* 1973, revised edition, 1976, and of *Readings in Organizations: Behavior, Structure, Processes,* 1973, revised edition, 1976.

*   *   *

DORE, Anita Wilkes   1914-

PERSONAL: Surname rhymes with "more"; born December 16, 1914, in New York, N.Y.; daughter of Abraham P. (a lawyer) and Rose (Hirsch) Wilkes; married Robert M. Dore (an advertising executive), June 26, 1938; children: Marjorie Dore Allen, Elizabeth. *Education:* Vassar College, B.A., 1935; Columbia University, M.A., 1937. *Politics:* Independent. *Home:* 36 East 36th St., New York, N.Y. 10016.

CAREER: Teacher of English at various high schools prior to 1965; New York (N.Y.) Board of Education, head of English department at a high school, 1965-68, Bureau of English, assistant director, 1968-72, director, 1972—. Producer and consultant for Educational Television programs. *Member:* National Council of Teachers of English, New York State English Council (vice-president), New York City Teachers of English (member of executive board), National Organization for Women.

WRITINGS: (Editor) *Premier Book of Major Poets,* Fawcett, 1970; *The Emerging Woman,* Globe, 1975. Contributor to test books for "Adventures for Readers" series, Harcourt, 1963, and to education journals.

WORK IN PROGRESS: A textbook, *The Distrust of Authority and the Cannonization of the Rebel in America,* for Hayden.

AVOCATIONAL INTERESTS: Peace, women's rights.

*   *   *

DORFMAN, Eugene   1917-

PERSONAL: Born April 27, 1917, in Newark, N.J.; son of

Joseph and Fannie (Grubman) Dorfman; married Sylvia Farber, July 30, 1939; children: David Lawrence, Joseph Richard, Michael Victor. *Education:* New Jersey College of Jewish Studies, student, 1933-34; Montclair State College, B.A., 1938; Columbia University, M.A., 1947, Ph.D., 1950. *Religion:* Jewish. *Home:* 13907 109th Ave., Edmonton, Alberta, Canada. *Office:* Department of Romance Languages, University of Alberta, Edmonton, Alberta, Canada T6G 2E6.

CAREER: Columbia University, New York, N.Y., lecturer in French, 1947-51, lecturer in linguistics, 1950-55; University of Washington, Seattle, assistant professor of Romance linguistics, 1955-64; University of Iowa, Iowa City, associate professor of Romance languages, 1964-65; University of Alberta, Edmonton, associate professor, 1965-68, professor of Romance linguistics, 1968—. Fulbright lecturer, University of Montpellier, 1960-61; Fulbright lecturer at Central University of Ecuador and coordinator of English program for Ecuador, 1963-64; Fulbright professor, University of Tel Aviv, 1966-67; visiting professor, Hebrew University of Jerusalem, 1971-72. Delegate, National Conference of Applied Linguistics, Pennsylvania State University, 1959; specialist, National Defense Education Act Summer Language Institute, 1959-60; director of first Linguistic Institute, Ecuador, summer, 1963, and second Linguistic Institute, winter, 1964; language consultant on English curriculum in secondary schools, Department of Integral Educational Planning, Ministry of Public Education, Ecuador, 1963-64; consultant, Canada Council, 1969—. Member of executive board, Edmonton Association for Retarded Children, 1970-71.

MEMBER: International Linguistic Association (treasurer, 1951-56; second vice-president, 1973—), Linguistic Society of America, Modern Language Association of America, Canadian Linguistic Association, Canadian Association of Applied Linguistics, Latin American Association of Linguistics and Philology, Canadian Association of University Teachers, Pacific Northwest Conference of Foreign Language Teachers, Linguistic Society of Paris, Alberta Linguistic Association (president, 1970-71), Linguistic Circle of Columbia (president, 1947-51), Phi Sigma Iota. *Awards, honors:* University of Washington graduate research grant, 1957; Fulbright grants to Chile, Uruguay, 1964; Canada Council and Humanities Research Council publication grant, 1969, for *The Narreme in the Medieval Romance Epic.*

WRITINGS: The Narreme in the Medieval Romance Epic: An Introduction to Narrative Structures, University of Toronto Press, 1969. Contributor to journals. Member of editorial board, *Word,* 1950-55.

WORK IN PROGRESS: A Narremic Guide for the Perplexed: Parody and Parable in Aucassin et Nicolette; research on diachronic phonology, comparative Romance linguistics, and on the relation between linguistics and literature.

* * *

DORLIAE, Peter Gondro 1935-
(Saint Dorliae)

PERSONAL: Born February 22, 1935, in Mehnla, Nimba County, Liberia; son of Weh (a paramount chief) and Lerkolie (Boanyen) Dorliae; married Kou Sitan Hawa in a native ceremony, 1958; children: three sons, one daughter. *Education:* Schooling began at the age of ten at the only school in a district of five large chiefdoms; later went to

Catholic schools in Kakata and Monrovia but was forced to drop out of high school for two years by illness (much later diagnosed as malaria); after finishing high school in 1958, attended University of Liberia, 1959-60, before illness again disrupted his studies. *Religion:* Catholic. *Home:* Mehnla, Nimba County, Liberia. *Office:* Mehnla Headquarters, Yarwin-Mehnsonoh Chiefdom, Nimba County, Liberia.

CAREER: Worked for the Government of Liberia as a typist for the administrative assistant to the President at the Executive Mansion in Monrovia, 1961-65, and as a news reporter at the Department of Information, 1965-66; on the death of his father he became acting paramount chief of the Yarwin-Mehnsonoh Chiefdom, 1966-68; paramount chief of the Yarwin-Mehnsonoh Chiefdom (elected under the provisions of the Constitution of Liberia), 1968—. Former president of United Geh-Mah Association (inter-tribal organization). *Military service:* Captain in Armed Forces of Liberia.

WRITINGS: Folk Tales and Proverbs, Carlton Press, 1965; *Animals Mourn For Da Leopard and Other West African Tales,* Bobbs-Merrill, 1970.

WORK IN PROGRESS: Inside Geh-Mah, a history of the Gio and Mano tribes; *Mr. Paramount Chief,* an autobiographical book; *Witchcraft and Superstition,* a book on superstitious practices in his land.

SIDELIGHTS: "One's birthplace," Peter Dorliae believes, "is [more] superb to him than the moon trip to the astronauts." As a chief he wants his people to have better school facilities and roads (lack of both used to worry his father). "In all writings," he continues, "I prefer fictions, because fiction which is a brother of lie is also a grandparent to science, scientific thinkings. I like this also because I am a born artist who had no privilege to practice same." His hobby is carpentry.

BIOGRAPHICAL/CRITICAL SOURCES: New York Times Book Review, June 14, 1970.††

* * *

DORN, Frank 1901-

PERSONAL: Born June 25, 1901, in San Francisco, Calif.; son of Walter E. (a lawyer) and Ellen J. (O'Reilly) Dorn; married Phyllis Moore Gallagher, February 24, 1964. *Education:* San Francisco Institute of Art, student, 1915-18; U.S. Military Academy at West Point, B.S., 1923; College of Chinese Studies, Peking, further study, 1934-35. *Religion:* Roman Catholic. *Residence:* Washington, D.C.

CAREER: U.S. Army, cadet, 1919-23, commissioned officer, 1923-53, retiring as brigadier general, 1953; General Logging Co., Santa Rosa, Calif., president, 1954-57. Painter, with one-man shows in Paris, Madrid, Majorca, Mexico City, Washington, D.C., and five shows in California. *Member:* Various officers associations and clubs; Georgetown Club (Washington, D.C.), Old Capital Club (Monterey, Calif.). *Awards, honors*—Military: Distinguished Service Medal, Silver Star, Bronze Star, Legion of Merit, two decorations from China, and eight other awards and campaign ribbons.

WRITINGS: Forest Twilight (novel of the Philippines), Harrap, 1935; (self-illustrated) *The Dorn Cookbook: A Treasury of Fine Recipes from All Around the World,* Regnery, 1953; *Good Cooking with Herbs and Spices,* Harvey House, 1958; *The Forbidden City: The Biography of a Palace,* Scribner, 1970; *Walkout,* Crowell, 1971; *The Sino-Japanese War, 1937-41,* Macmillan, 1974. Contributor to magazines and military publications.

WORK IN PROGRESS: A book tentatively entitled *People and Places.*

SIDELIGHTS: Frank Dorn spent more than seven years in China, and has traveled throughout the Far East, western Europe, and in Mexico. He has been consultant and assistant to the director of three motion pictures.

*   *   *

DORRIS, R(obert) T.   1913-

PERSONAL: Born June 26, 1913, in Vinson, Okla.; son of Clio C. (a merchant) and Addie (Thompson) Dorris; married Helen Mayo, August 1, 1937; divorced second wife; married Helen Harlin (a counselor); children: (first marriage) Gail (Mrs. James Shoop), Robert T., Jr. *Education:* Yale University Summer School of Alcohol Studies, Certificate, 1948; additional study at University of Utah and University of California, Los Angeles. *Home and office:* 29500 Heathercliff Rd. No. 224, Malibu, Calif. 90265.

CAREER: Minneapolis-Moline Power Implement Co., Hopkins, Minn., zone manager, 1937-42; U.S. Civil Service, administrative assistant to post engineer at U.S. Army Air Forces Base, Clovis, N.M., 1942-45; Dorris Distributing Co. (farm machinery), Clovis, vice-president and general manager, 1945-54; Orendorff Manufacturing Co. (farm supplies), Los Angeles, Calif., sales manager, 1954-64; North American Rockwell, Power Systems Division, Canoga Park, Calif., employee counselor, 1964-70; member of staff, McDonnell-Douglas Corp., Long Beach, Calif., 1970-74; Robert T. Dorris & Associates (consultants), founder and president, 1974—. Arrested his own case of alcoholism in 1945 and has done volunteer and professional work since that time on the problem of alcoholism; former member, New Mexico Commission on Alcoholism; staff member, Alcoholism Foundation of Alberta, 1959-60; founder and first president, Counselors on Alcoholism and Related Disorders, 1967—. *Military service:* U.S. Army, 1932-33.

WRITINGS: (With D. F. Lindley) *Counseling in Alcoholism and Related Disorders,* Glencoe Press, 1968; *Am I Drinking too Much?,* World Publishing, 1969.

*   *   *

DOS PASSOS, John (Roderigo)   1896-1970

January 14, 1896—September 28, 1970; American novelist and social critic. Obituaries: *New York Times,* September 29, 1970; *Washington Post,* September 29, 1970; *L'Express,* October 5-11, 1970; *Variety,* October 7, 1970; *Time,* October 12, 1970; *Current Biography,* 1970; *Books Abroad,* spring, 1971. (See index for *CA* sketch)

*   *   *

DOSS, Margot Patterson

PERSONAL: Born in St. Paul, Minn.; daughter of Eugene Northrop (a certified public accountant) and Irene (Watson) Patterson; married John Whinham Doss (a pediatrician), June 7, 1947; children: Richard, Alexander, Jock, Gordon. *Education:* Illinois Wesleyan University, B.A.; graduate study at New School for Social Research and University of Chicago. *Politics:* Democrat. *Religion:* Episcopalian. *Home:* 1331 Greenwich St., San Francisco, Calif. 94109; and Box 447, Bolinas, Calif. 94924. *Office: San Francisco Chronicle,* San Francisco, Calif. 94119.

CAREER: Feature writer for *Baltimore Sun, Milwaukee Sentinel, Peoria Journal Transcript,* and *Bloomington* (Ill.) *Pantagraph,* 1943-60; *San Francisco Chronicle,* San Fran-

cisco, Calif., weekly columnist, 1960—. Instructor in nature, University of California Outdoor Environmental classes, 1969—, and Pacific Heights Community College, 1972—. Hostess of weekly television show on KDIX-TV, "Friday Evening Show." *Member:* San Francisco Press Club, Sierra Club (life member).

WRITINGS: San Francisco at Your Feet, Grove, 1962, revised edition, 1974; *Bay Area at Your Feet,* Chronicle Publishing, 1970; *Golden Gate Park at Your Feet,* Chronicle Publishing, 1970; *Walks for Children in San Francisco* (juvenile), Grove, 1970; *Paths of Gold,* Chronicle Books, 1974; (contributor) *Richtig Reisen,* Dumont, 1976. Contributor to magazines.

AVOCATIONAL INTERESTS: Conservation and ecology, history of California, letterpress printing, wild herbs and gardening, trail finding and trail building.

*   *   *

DOW, J(ose) Kamal   1936-

PERSONAL: Born September 3, 1936, in Ibague, Colombia; came to United States in 1964, naturalized in 1970; son of Fuad (a businessman) and Renee (Mawad) Dow; married Teresa Salazar, December 9, 1962; children: Fuad, Renee. *Education:* University of Illinois, B.S., 1961; University of Missouri, M.S., 1965, Ph.D., 1967. *Politics:* Democrat. *Religion:* None. *Home address:* P.O. Box 12742, Gainesville, Fla. 32601. *Office:* Department of Food and Resource Economics, University of Florida, Gainesville, Fla. 32601.

CAREER: Colombian Agriculture Research Institute, Monteria, administrator, 1961-62; Colombian Planning Department, Bogota, engineer in charge of agricultural projects, 1962-64; John Deere & Co., Moline, Ill., market economist, 1967-68; University of Florida, Gainesville, assistant professor of agricultural economics, 1968—; chief of party economics, Ecuador, 1971—. Consultant to Weilz-Hettelsaller Engineers, 1965, and Ford Foundation, 1966. *Member:* American Economic Association, American Agricultural Economics Association, Ecuadorian Agricultural Economic Association.

WRITINGS: The Impact of Mechanical Harvesting on the Demand for Labor in the Florida Citrus Industry, Department of Economics, University of Florida, 1970; *Colombia's Foreign Trade and Economic Integration in Latin America,* University of Florida Press, 1971.†

*   *   *

DOWLER, James R(oss)   1925-

PERSONAL: Born April 19, 1925, in Royal, Ill.; son of Emery Ross (a teacher) and Ethel (Burroughs) Dowler; married Helen Jean Ernst, February 19, 1950; children: Ross Matthew. *Education:* University of Illinois, B.S., 1949, M.S., 1950. *Religion:* Protestant. *Home:* 3303 Riverlawn Dr., Kingwood, Tex. 77339. *Agent:* August Lenniger Literary Agency, 437 Fifth Ave., New York, N.Y. 10016. *Office:* Shell Chemical Co., One Shell Place, Houston, Tex. 77001.

CAREER: Champaign News-Gazette, Champaign, Ill., reporter, 1949-50; *Adams County Republican,* Brighton, Colo., publisher, 1950-51; Shell Chemical Co., New York, N.Y., advertising manager, 1954-70, Atlanta, Ga., advertising manager, 1970-75, San Ramon, Calif., advertising and promotion manager, 1975-77, Houston, Tex., advertising and promotion manager, 1977—. *Military service:* U.S. Army Air Forces, pilot, 1943-45; became second lieutenant;

U.S. Air Force, 1951-53; became first lieutenant. U.S. Air Force Reserves, 1953-68; became major (retired).

WRITINGS: Partner's Choice, Arcadia House, 1958; *Fiddle Foot Fugitive,* Crown, 1970; *Laredo Lawman,* Crown, 1970; *Copperhead Colonel,* Crown, 1972.

WORK IN PROGRESS: An international mystery, intrigue novel.

AVOCATIONAL INTERESTS: Inventing games; created two for Parker Brothers, "Dai Jobi" and "Moon Tag."

* * *

DOWLING, Allen 1900-
(Jack King)

PERSONAL: Born December 17, 1900, in New Orleans, La.; son of John Mark and Louise (Phelan) Dowling; married Nellie Ann Shaw, March 31, 1934; children: Kathleen Elizabeth (Mrs. John W. Hite, Jr.). *Education:* Attended public schools in New Orleans. *Residence:* New Orleans, La.

CAREER: Housing Authority of New Orleans, La., public relations consultant, 1938—. *Member:* National Association of Housing and Redevelopment Officials, Press Club of New Orleans.

WRITINGS: (Under pseudonym Jack King) *Confessions of a Poker Player,* Washburn, 1940; (under pseudonym Jack King) *Play Winning Poker,* privately printed, 1955; (under pseudonym Jack King) *Under the Round Table,* Dorrance, 1961; *The Great American Pastime: Notes on Poker, the Game and the Players,* A. S. Barnes, 1970; *Confessions of a Winning Poker Player,* Gamblers, 1970; *Concrete Walkways Project,* Audel, 1974; *Play Winning Poker,* Gamblers, 1974. Editor, *Choctaw Democrat* (weekly political newspaper), New Orleans, 1933.

WORK IN PROGRESS: A revision of *Under the Round Table.*†

* * *

DOWNING, A(rthur) B(enjamin) 1915-

PERSONAL: Born December 1, 1915, in Sheffield, England; son of Arthur (an engineer) and Gertrude (Stephenson) Downing; married Ruth Holt (an orthoptist), November 27, 1954; children: Naomi, Adam. *Education:* Studied at University of Manchester and Unitarian College, Manchester; received B.A., 1940, M.A., 1947, B.D. (London), 1957. *Home:* 10 Southway, Guiseley, West Yorkshire LS20 8HX, England.

CAREER: Unitarian minister, 1953-62; *Inquirer* (religious weekly), London, England, editor, 1962-67; Educational Interchange Council, London, staff member, 1968-69; National Adult School Union, London, tutor and organizer, 1969-72; Bradford Unitarian Church, West Yorkshire, England, minister, 1973—. Chairman of international and general purposes committee, General Assembly of Unitarian and Free Christian Churches, 1965-67, 1976—. Member of court, City University, London, 1966—; Unitarian College, Manchester, honorary secretary, 1955-65, college visitor, 1976-77; trustee, Dr. Williams's Library and Charity, 1965-73; member of council, Manchester College, Oxford University, 1973—. Participant in university, public, and television debates on voluntary euthanasia. *Military service:* British Army, Intelligence Corps, 1941-45. Royal Air Force, Education Branch, 1949-53; became flight lieutenant; mentioned in dispatches, Malaya, 1951. *Member:* International Asso-

ciation for Religious Freedom (chairman, European Free Religious Commission, Frankfurt, Germany, 1973—), Voluntary Euthanasia Society (chairman, 1965-75; vice-president, 1976—), British Society of Recorder Players, Bradford Library and Literary Society (committee member, 1974—), Bradford Civic Society (committee member, 1976—).

WRITINGS: Unitarianism: Some Questions Answered, Lindsey Press, 1962; (editor and contributor) *Euthanasia and the Right to Death,* P. Owen, 1969, Humanities, 1970; *From Max Mueller to Karl Marx: A Study of E. M. Geldart, 1844-1885, Scholar of Balliol College, Oxford,* English Unitarian Historical Society, 1970; *A Death of One's Own* (study handbook), National Adult School Union, 1972; *Beyond the Horizon: Dissent, Independence and the Future of the Free Religious Tradition,* Lindsey Press, 1976. Contributor to *Faith and Freedom,* National Adult School Union study handbooks, *Hibbert Journal,* and other publications. English correspondent, *Protestant de Geneve,* 1955-60. Assistant editor, *Faith and Freedom* (Manchester College quarterly), 1972—.

BIOGRAPHICAL/CRITICAL SOURCES: Punch, July 2, 1969; *Guardian,* June 4, 1969; *British Medical Journal,* August 30, 1969.

* * *

DOZIER, Edward P. 1916-1971

April 23, 1916—May 2, 1971; American Indian anthropologist and linguistics authority. Obituaries: *Antiquarian Bookman,* May 17, 1971.

* * *

DRACHMAN, Edward Ralph 1940-

PERSONAL: Born October 25, 1940, in New York, N.Y.; son of Norman and Marion Drachman; married Linda Sargon; children: Joy. *Education:* Harvard University, B.A., 1961, M.A.T., 1963; University of Pennsylvania, M.A., 1962, Ph.D., 1968. *Office:* Department of Social Studies, Ipswich High School, 130 High St., Ipswich, Mass. 01938.

CAREER: Boston University, Boston, Mass., instructor, 1966-68, assistant professor of political science, 1968-72; Ipswich High School, Ipswich, Mass., chairman of department of social studies, 1972—.

WRITINGS: United States Policy toward Vietnam, 1940-1945, Fairleigh Dickinson University Press, 1970; (contributor) A. Gyorgy and H. Gibbs, editors, *Problems in International Relations,* Prentice-Hall, 1970.†

* * *

DRIVER, C(harles) J(onathan) 1939-

PERSONAL: Born August 19, 1939, in Cape Town, South Africa; son of Kingsley Ernest (an Anglican priest) and Phyllis (Gould) Driver; married Ann Elizabeth Hoogewerf, June 8, 1967; children: Dominic, Thackwray, Tamlyn. *Education:* University of Cape Town, B.A. (honors) and B.Ed., 1962; Trinity College, Oxford, B.Phil., 1967. *Politics:* Member of Labour Party. *Home and office:* 11 Rowston St., Cleethorpes, South Humberside, England. *Agent:* John Johnson, 12-13 Henrietta St., London WC2E 8LF, England.

CAREER: National Union of South African Students, president, 1963-64; left South Africa in 1964 after being detained in solitary confinement under the 90 Day Detention Law, and was deprived of his South African passport in 1966;

Sevenoaks School, Sevenoaks, Kent, England, teacher of English, 1964-73, housemaster of International Sixth Form Centre, 1968-73; director of sixth form studies, Matthew Humberstone Comprehensive School, 1973—. Research fellow, University of York, 1976. Member of literature panel, Arts Council of Great Britain, 1975—.

WRITINGS—All published by Faber, except as indicated: *Elegy for a Revolutionary* (novel), 1969, Morrow, 1970; *Send War in Our Time, O Lord* (novel), 1970; *Death of Fathers* (novel), 1972; *A Messiah of the Last Days* (novel), 1974. Verse has been included in a number of anthologies, including *London Magazine Poems, 1961-1966,* Alan Ross, 1966, *Seven South African Poets,* Heinemann, 1969, and *Penguin Book of South African Verse,* Penguin, 1969; a short story was included in *Penguin Modern Stories,* Number 8, Penguin, 1971. Also author of monthly review of new fiction for *Guardian.* Contributor to *Contrast, New Review,* and other periodicals.

WORK IN PROGRESS: A novel, *In a Green Tree;* a biography, *Patrick Duncan, 1918-1967;* a collection of poems, *Some Light.*

SIDELIGHTS: A reviewer for the *Times Literary Supplement* calls *Elegy for a Revolutionary* "a first novel of remarkable power and promise: an understated yet immensely telling study of political activists restricted by their own conflicts." In another review of the book, Oscar A. Bouise says: "The subject matter of this novel is timely. It presents in detail the formation, activities, and final apprehension of a group of young men who organize to sabotage with explosives the 'racist system' of South Africa. Each of the young saboteurs is studied microscopically; his home background, his parents, his associates, his girl friends, his habits—all are examined carefully by the narrator in an attempt to explain why such a group is formed and what kind of men undertake such a 'societal role.'"

Of *Send War in Our Time, O Lord,* Vernon Scannell writes: "The novel is well organised, very exciting, and running through it is a sense of justice and charity, a stern honesty that I find moving." A *Times Literary Supplement* reviewer feels that "where Mr. Driver's first novel was concerned with the weakness of avowed liberals, this one is more widely—and subtly—occupied with the problem of the survival of ordinary humanity itself in a brutalized society. The message is not hopeful."

AVOCATIONAL INTERESTS: Playing cricket and rugby football, holidays in France, and carpentry.

BIOGRAPHICAL/CRITICAL SOURCES: Best Sellers, March 15, 1970; *Times Literary Supplement,* September 2, 1970; *New Statesman,* September 18, 1970.

*   *   *

DUCKAT, Walter Benjamin 1911-

PERSONAL: Born July 22, 1911, in Philadelphia, Pa.; son of Max (a merchant) and Mollie (Tiskowitz) Duckat; married Esther Lubliner (a high school teacher), July 3, 1938; children: Gila Lipton, Hillel. *Education:* Brooklyn College (now Brooklyn College of the City University of New York), B.A., 1935; Columbia University, M.A., 1943. *Politics:* Independent. *Religion:* Jewish. *Home:* 1091 East 19th St., Brooklyn, N.Y. 12230.

CAREER: Certified psychologist, State of New York; Federation Employment and Guidance Service, New York City, director of Guidance Division, 1943-76. Vocational consultant, New York City Board of Education; consultant

to Stern College, Yeshiva University, 1960-70. Jewish Guild for the Blind, chaplain, 1931-76, chaplain emeritus, 1976—. *Member:* American Psychological Association, American Personnel and Guidance Association. *Awards, honors:* Israel Cummings Award, 1972, for distinguished contributions to social service.

WRITINGS: Opportunities in Jewish Religious Vocations, Vocational Guidance Manuals, 1952; *Jewish Contributions to the American Economy,* Jewish Occupational Council, 1954; *Beggar to King: All the Occupations of Biblical Times,* Doubleday, 1968; *A Guide to Professional Careers,* Messner, 1970. Contributor of more than 150 articles to national publications in the United States and abroad. Contributing editor, *Universal Jewish Encyclopedia, Inc.,* New York City, 1939-43.

WORK IN PROGRESS: Writing on vocational and personal adjustment, mental health and religion.

SIDELIGHTS: Walter B. Duckat writes *CA:* "Having advised over 15,000 persons in their personal and vocational problems I've been profoundly impressed with the far reaching impact of vocational satisfaction on our mental health and total functioning. I plan to devote more of my writing to this theme as well as the relationship of mental health to religion."

BIOGRAPHICAL/CRITICAL SOURCES: New York Times Book Review, June 28, 1968; *New York Times,* September 6, 1968; *Saturday Review,* April 19, 1969.

*   *   *

DUGGAN, Joseph J(ohn) 1938-

PERSONAL: Born September 8, 1938, in Philadelphia, Pa.; son of Bart J. (a mechanic) and Mary (Boyce) Duggan; married Mary Kay Conyers (a musicologist), March 3, 1962; children: Marie Christine, Kathleen. *Education:* University of Paris, Sorbonne, student, 1958-59; Fordham University, B.A., 1960; Ohio State University, Ph.D., 1964. *Home:* 2229 Marin Ave., Berkeley, Calif. 94707. *Office:* Department of Comparative Literature, University of California, Berkeley, Calif. 94720.

CAREER: University of California, Berkeley, instructor in French, 1964-65, assistant professor, 1965-71, associate professor of French and comparative literature, 1971—. *Member:* Modern Language Association of America, Mediaeval Academy of America. *Awards, honors:* National Humanities Foundation fellowship, 1968-69.

WRITINGS: (Editor) *A Concordance of the "Chanson de Roland,"* Ohio State University Press, 1970; *"The Song of Roland": Formulaic Style and Poetic Craft,* University of California Press, 1973; *Oral Literature: Seven Essays,* Barnes & Noble, 1975. Contributor to *Romania, Orbis Litterarum, University of Southern California Studies in Comparative Literature, Revue,* and *Romance Philology.* Member of editorial board, *Forum for Modern Language Studies.*

SIDELIGHTS: Joseph Duggan has lived in Paris and Madrid.†

*   *   *

DULLES, Foster Rhea 1900-1970

January 24, 1900—September 11, 1970; American educator, historian, and scholar of U.S.-Asian foreign relations. Obituaries: *New York Times,* September 12, 1970; *Washington Post,* September 14, 1970. (See index for *CA* sketch)

DUMARCHAIS, Pierre 1882-1970
(Pierre MacOrlan)

February 26, 1882—June 27, 1970; French poet and novelist. Obituaries: *New York Times,* June 29, 1970; *Washington Post,* June 30, 1970; *Antiquarian Bookman,* September 7-14, 1970; *Books Abroad,* spring, 1971.

* * *

DUNCOMBE, David C(ameron) 1928-

PERSONAL: Born July 14, 1928, in New York, N.Y.; son of Herbert Sydney, Jr. (a colonel, U.S. Army) and Frances (writer of children's books; maiden name, Riker) Duncombe; married Sarah Stevens Morton, June 21, 1958; children: Elizabeth Anne, Jane Alexandra, Stephen Ross. *Education:* Dartmouth College, B.A., 1953; Union Theological Seminary and Columbia University, M.A., 1955; Yale University, B.D., 1962, S.T.M., 1963, M.A., 1965, Ph.D., 1966. *Politics:* Democrat. *Home:* 270 Sam Hill Rd., Guilford, Conn. 06437. *Office:* School of Medicine, Yale University, 333 Cedar St., New Haven, Conn. 06510.

CAREER: Taft School, Watertown, Conn., chaplain and instructor in religion, 1955-60; ordained minister in United Church of Christ (Congregational), 1958; Yale University, Divinity School, New Haven, Conn., acting lecturer in psychology of religion, 1965; Norwich State Hospital, Norwich, Conn., clinical training intern in chaplaincy department, 1966-67; Yale University, lecturer in psychology of religion at Divinity School, 1968-70, chaplain to School of Medicine, 1970—. *Military service:* U.S. Army, 1946-48, 1950-52; served in Germany; became sergeant. *Member:* Society for the Scientific Study of Religion, Society for Health and Human Values.

WRITINGS: (Contributor) Kenneth W. Underwood, editor, *The Church, the University, and Social Policy,* Wesleyan University Press, 1969; *The Shape of the Christian Life,* Abingdon, 1969.

WORK IN PROGRESS: Research in theology and personality testing and in the theological dimensions of health.

AVOCATIONAL INTERESTS: Skiing, bicycling, folk music, stone wall-building.

* * *

DUNHAM, John L. 1939-

PERSONAL: Born March 4, 1939, in Charleston, W.Va.; son of George and Mary (Summers) Dunham; married Margaret J. Mobley, October 1, 1960 (divorced). *Education:* Studied at Wilson Branch of Chicago City Junior College, Roosevelt University, I.B.M. (International Business Machines) schools, and at American Savings and Loan Institute. *Home:* 8747 South Cornell Ave., Chicago, Ill. 60617. *Office:* U.S. League, 111 East Wacker Dr., Chicago, Ill. 60601.

CAREER: Has worked in both data processing and savings and loan fields; associated with U.S. League, Chicago, Ill., 1964—. *Member:* Systems/Programmers' Society (Chicago; board chairman).

WRITINGS: (With Gene Klinger) *Someday I'm Going to Be Somebody* (juvenile), Childrens Press, 1970.

AVOCATIONAL INTERESTS: Working with Boy Scouts, skiing, boating, table tennis.

* * *

DUNN, Marion Herndon 1920-

PERSONAL: Born October 24, 1920, in Nashville, Tenn.; married E. L. Dunn (a contractor), April 12, 1968. *Education:* Attended high school in Nashville and studied creative writing privately. *Home:* Waldron Dr., La Vergne, Tenn. 37086.

CAREER: Clements Paper Co., Nashville, Tenn., cost analyst, 1951. *Member:* Press and Author's Club (Nashville; secretary).

WRITINGS: Tenase Brave (juvenile), Aurora Publishing, 1971. Contributor to local newspapers and periodicals.

WORK IN PROGRESS: A juvenile book, tentatively entitled *Brother Stevie,* dealing with the problems and attitudes of a white brother and sister and an eleven-year-old Negro slave boy during the battle of Nashville; research into the founding of Nashville.††

* * *

DURFEE, David A(rthur) 1929-

PERSONAL: Born January 31, 1929, in Glenside, Pa.; son of Elbert Foster and Ethel (Howell) Durfee; married Gertrude Jameson, June 21, 1952; children: Suzanne Robertson, Edmund Howell, Kenneth Jameson, Rachel Elaine. *Education:* Harvard University, A.B., 1951, M.A.T., 1955; further courses at New School for Social Research, 1956-63, and Fordham University, 1969-71. *Home:* 43 Wilton Rd., Pleasantville, N.Y. 10570.

CAREER: Teacher of social studies in public schools in Great Neck, N.Y., 1955-63; social studies coordinator in public schools in North Tarrytown, N.Y., 1963—. *Military service:* U.S. Navy, 1951-54; became lieutenant. *Member:* National Council for the Social Studies, National Education Association, Association for Supervision and Curriculum Development, New York State Teachers Association, New York State Council for the Social Studies, Westchester Council for the Social Studies, Phi Beta Kappa. *Awards, honors:* John Hay fellowship in the humanities, 1965.

WRITINGS: Poverty in an Affluent Society, Prentice-Hall, 1970; (editor) *William Henry Harrison, 1773-1841, and John Tyler, 1790-1862,* Oceana, 1970; *Power in American Society,* Allyn & Bacon, 1976.

WORK IN PROGRESS: Research in strategies to promote inductive learning and materials to contribute to such strategies.

* * *

DURHAM, John I 1933-

PERSONAL: Born May 29, 1933, in Bucyrus, Ohio; son of John Isaac (a businessman) and Frances (Jackson) Durham; married Judith Allen Harvell, June 16, 1957; children: Gwynne Jocelyn, John Jeremy. *Education:* Wake Forest College, B.A., 1955; Southeastern Baptist Theological Seminary, B.D., 1959, Th.M., 1961; Oxford University, D.Phil., 1963. *Home:* 321 West Juniper Ave., Wake Forest, N.C. 27587. *Office:* Southeastern Baptist Theological Seminary, Wake Forest, N.C. 27587.

CAREER: Ordained Baptist minister, 1955; Sharon Baptist Church, Chinquapin, N.C., pastor, 1955-61; Meredith College, Raleigh, N.C., instructor in ancient languages, 1956-57; Southeastern Baptist Theological Seminary, Wake Forest, N.C., instructor, 1959-60, visiting professor, 1963-64, assistant professor, 1964-65, associate professor, 1965-70, professor of Old Testament interpretation, 1970-76, professor of Hebrew and Old Testament, 1976—, acting academic dean, 1963-66, administrative associate to president of seminary, 1966-69, director of summer school at Oxford, 1975. *Member:* Society for Old Testament Study, Society of Biblical Literature, Phi Beta Kappa. *Awards, honors:* American Association of Theological Studies faculty fellowship, 1969-70; Baptist Theological Seminary scholar in Switzerland, 1976-77.

WRITINGS: (Editor, contributor, and translator with J. Roy Porter) *Proclamation and Presence: Old Testament Essays in Honour of Gwynne Henton Davies,* John Knox, 1970; (contributor) Robert B. Laurin, editor, *Contemporary Old Testament Theologians,* Judson, 1970; (editor, contributor, and translator with Porter) *Psalms Commentary, Broadman Bible Commentary IV,* Broadman, 1971; (contributor) William Pinson, Jr. and Clyde E. Fant, Jr., editors, *Contemporary Christian Trends: Perspectives on the Present,* Word Books, 1972; (contributor) *Interpreter's Dictionary of the Bible,* Volume V, Abingdon, 1976; (contributor) Brooks, editor, *Adult Bible Study: The Living God and His People,* Baptist Southeastern Seminary Board, 1976; (contributor) Brooks, editor, *Advanced Bible Study: The Ten Commandments,* Baptist Southeastern Seminary Board, 1977; (editor and contributor) *Towards the Year 2000: Emerging Directions in Christian Ministry,* Edwards & Broughton, 1977. Consulting editor and contributor, *Broadman Bible Commentary,* twelve volumes, 1967-74.

WORK IN PROGRESS: Theological Rhetoric and the Credos of the Old Testament.

SIDELIGHTS: John Durham indicated that his major areas of vocational interest are biblical studies, Old Testament literature and theology, the Pentateuch, and the Psalms. He has traveled to the United Kingdom and Europe, lived in England for three years, in Switzerland for one year, and in Germany for six months. He has competence in biblical Hebrew, Greek, classical and ecclesiastical Latin, German, and French.

AVOCATIONAL INTERESTS: Classical music, gardening, art.

* * *

DUSHNITZKY-SHNER, Sara 1913-
(Sara Neshamith)

PERSONAL: Born March 12, 1913, in Seiny, Poland; daughter of Moshe-Shlomo (an engineer and surveyor) and Lisa (Fink) Dushnitzky; married Zvi Shner, December, 1946; children: Avner, Giora, Moshe. *Education:* Lithuanian National University, student, 1931-33; University of Vilno, M.A., 1940. *Politics:* Labour Party. *Home and office:* Kibbutz Lohame-Hagetaot, Israel.

CAREER: Teacher in school for oligophrenic children in Lithuania, 1938-39; Hebrew Pedagogical Institute, Vilno, Lithuania, head of school, 1939-40; cared for Jewish war orphans in Lodz, Poland, 1945-47; Ghetto Fighters Kibbutz, Western Galilee, Israel, researcher, 1948—. *Member:* Archivistice Society, Society of Museum Workers.

*WRITINGS—*All published under name, Sara Neshamith: *Ha-Yeladim me-rehov Mapu* (title means "The Children of Mapu Street"), Kibbutz Meuchad, 1958; *L'Toldot hashoa V-hamered* (title means "On Behalf of the History of the Holocaust and Resistance"), Kibbutz Meuchad, 1961; *Maavako shel hagetto* (title means "The Struggle of the Ghetto"), Ministry of Education and Culture, 1968. Contributor to periodicals.

WORK IN PROGRESS: Working on the subject of the ideological roots of Nazism; a book for children; *The Hechalutz, 1929-1940,* movement in Lithuania.

SIDELIGHTS: With the Nazi invasion of Lithuania in 1941, Sara Neshamith attempted to reach safety in the U.S.S.R. Failing to cross the fighting lines, she stayed in a ghetto in White Russia for several months, and was caught and sent to a concentration camp. After a year she escaped and joined a partisan unit.

Her writings concentrate mainly on various problems of World War II and, to some extent, reflect her own wartime experiences.

* * *

DUSTER, Troy 1936-

PERSONAL: Born July 11, 1936, in Chicago, Ill.; son of Benjamin Cecil and Alfreda (Barnett) Duster; married Ellen Marie Johansson (a ceramicist), May 16, 1964. *Education:* Northwestern University, B.S., 1957, Ph.D., 1962; University of California, Los Angeles, M.A., 1959; University of Uppsala, postdoctoral study, 1962-63. *Home:* 3031 Benvenue Ave., Berkeley, Calif. 94705. *Office:* Institute for the Study of Social Change, University of California, Berkeley, Calif. 94720.

CAREER: National Academy of Sciences, Washington, D.C., research associate, 1961; Northwestern University, Evanston, Ill., lecturer, 1962; University of California, Riverside, assistant professor of sociology, 1963-66; University of Stockholm, Stockholm, Sweden, visiting lecturer, 1966-67; University of California, Berkeley, lecturer, 1967-69, associate professor of sociology, 1969—, director of the Institute for the Study of Social Change, 1976—. Visiting associate professor, University of British Columbia, summer, 1969. Consultant to Pacific State Hospital, Pomona, Calif., and California Rehabilitation Center, Corona, 1964-66. *Member:* American Sociological Association, National Academy of Sciences (member of Assembly of Behavioral and Social Sciences, 1973—). *Awards, honors:* Postdoctoral research grant from Swedish government, 1962-63; Guggenheim fellow, London School of Economics, 1971-72.

WRITINGS: (Contributor) Raymond W. Mack, editor, *Our Children's Burden,* Random House, 1968; (contributor) R. B. Edgerton and S. C. Plog, editors, *Changing Perspectives in Mental Illness,* Holt, 1969; *The Legislation of Morality: Law, Drugs, and Moral Judgment,* Free Press, 1970; (contributor) J. D. Douglas, editor, *Crime and Justice in American Society,* Bobbs-Merrill, 1970; (contributor) Kenneth Blum, Sanford Feinglass, and Arthur Briggs, editors, *Social Meaning of Drugs: Principles of Social Pharmacology,* Basic Books, 1977. Contributor to *Encyclopedia of Education, American Sociologist,* and to professional journals.

* * *

DYE, Harold E(ldon) 1907-

PERSONAL: Born April 5, 1907, in Tulsa, Okla.; son of Harvey Smith and Pearl Belle (Upton) Dye; married Ina Pearl Hollaway, December 21, 1927; children: Lila Belle (Mrs. Richard Hopkins), Joyce (Mrs. Robert Lowry), Jeanne (Mrs. Charles Hightower), Leland Eldon. *Education:* Attended Montezuma Baptist College, 1925-27. *Politics:* Democrat. *Home:* 1193 East Fewtrell Dr., Campbell, Calif.

CAREER: Pastor of Baptist churches in Las Cruces, N.M., 1934-44, Clovis, N.M., 1946-49, and Bakersfield, Calif., 1949-52; Baptist Temple, San Jose, Calif., pastor, 1952—. Trustee of Golden Gate Baptist Theological Seminary, 1950—, and California Southern Baptist Board of Christian

Higher Education, 1959—. *Member:* California Writers Club.

WRITINGS: Robes of Splendor, Broadman, 1944; *Shining Like the Stars,* Baptist Home Mission Board, 1947; *Through God's Eyes,* Broadman, 1947; *The Prophet of Little Cane Creek,* Baptist Home Mission Board, 1949; *The Weaver,* Broadman, 1952; *Under the North Star,* Baptist Home Mission Board, 1954; *This Gold Is Mine,* Broadman, 1958; *His to Command,* Baptist Home Mission Board, 1960; *Stories to Remember,* Broadman, 1962; *Pablo and the Magi,* Broadman, 1967; *The Weaver,* Broadman, 1974; *No Rocking Chair for Mel,* Broadman, 1976. Also author of *The World in Her Hands.* Contributor to Southern Baptist Sunday School Board publications for more than twenty-five years and to other Baptist publications. Editor, *Baptist New Mexican,* 1944-46.†

*   *   *

DZIEWANOWSKI, M(arian) Kamil 1913-

PERSONAL: Born June 27, 1913, in Zhitomir, Ukraine, Russia; came to United States in 1947; naturalized in 1953; son of Kamil A. (a landowner) and Sophie (Kamienska) Dziewanowski; married Ada Karczewska (a dance teacher), October 4, 1946; children: Barbara, John. *Education:* University of Warsaw, LL.M., 1937; French Institute of Warsaw, Licencie en Droit, 1937; Harvard University, M.A., 1948, Ph.D., 1951. *Home:* 41 Katherine Rd., Watertown, Mass. 02172. *Office:* Department of History, Boston University, 226 Bay St. R.R., Boston, Mass. 02215.

CAREER: British Broadcasting Corp., London, England, news commentator, 1942-44; Harvard University, Russian Research Center, Cambridge, Mass., research fellow, 1949-52; Massachusetts Institute of Technology, Center of International Studies, Cambridge, research fellow, 1952-53; Boston College, Boston, Mass., assistant professor, 1954-56, associate professor, 1956-62, professor of history, 1962-65; Harvard University, Russian Research Center, Cambridge, associate, 1960—; Boston University, Boston, professor of history, 1965—. Ford Exchange Professor, Poland, 1958; visiting professor, Brown University, 1961-62; lecturer at various American and European universities, including Oxford University, Cambridge University, University of Heidelberg, and London School of Economics; lecturer, Peace Corps. *Military service:* Polish Army, 1940-45; became second lieutenant; received two Crosses of Valor. *Member:* American Historical Association, American Association for the Advancement of Slavic Studies, Polish Institute of Arts and Sciences in America. *Awards, honors:* American Philosophical Society research fellowships, 1959-60; Inter-University Committee for Travel Grants research fellowship, 1960; Hoover Institution research fellowships, 1961-62, 1967.

WRITINGS: Vienna Appeasement, Library of Fighting Poland, 1945; (editor) *Poland To-day as Seen by Foreign Observers,* Polish Freedom Movement, 1946; (with others) *Cohesive Forces and Tensions in the European Satellites,* Center for International Studies, Massachusetts Institute of Technology, 1952; (contributor) A. Ulam, editor, *The Communist Take-Over in Eastern Europe,* Center for International Studies, Massachusetts Institute of Technology, 1954; (with A. Gyory and P. Zinner) *East Central Europe Under Communism,* Praeger, 1957; (with others) *Russian Thought and Politics,* Harvard University Press, 1957; *The Communist Party of Poland: An Outline of History,* Harvard University Press, 1959, revised edition, 1976; (contrib-

utor) Adam Bromke, editor, *The Communist States at the Crossroads,* Praeger, 1964; (with others) *Bibliography of Soviet Foreign Relations,* Princeton University Press, 1965; (with others) *Eastern Europe: Czechoslovakia, Hungary, Poland,* Life World Series, 1965; *A European Federalist: Joseph Pilsudski and Eastern Europe, 1918-1922,* Stanford University Press, 1969; (with others) *Bibliography of East Central Europe,* Chicago University Press, 1969; (contributor) P. Horecky, editor, *Studies for a New Eastern Europe,* Queens College (New York), 1970; (editor) *The Russian Revolution: An Anthology,* Crowell, 1970; *Poland in the Twentieth Century,* Columbia University Press, 1977.

Contributor to *Journal of Central European Affairs, Current History, American Slavonic Review, Problems of Communism, Soviet Survey, Forum, Mankind, American Historical Review, East European Quarterly, Erasmus,* and other scholarly journals.

WORK IN PROGRESS: A History of Soviet Russia; and *Snobless Oblige! Limericks for a Sophisticated Set in Five Languages.*

*   *   *

EBEJER, Francis 1925-

PERSONAL: Surname is pronounced Eb-*ey*-er; born August 28, 1925, in Malta; son of Joseph (a head teacher) and Josephine (Cutajar) Ebejer; married Jane Cauchi-Gera, September 5, 1948 (divorced); children: Francis Joseph (deceased), Mary Jane. *Education:* Studied at Royal University of Malta, 1942-43, St. Mary's College, Twickenham, England, 1948-50, and University of Utah, 1961. *Religion:* Roman Catholic. *Home:* 140 Upper rue d'Argens, Msida, Malta. *Agent:* A. M. Heath & Co., 40-42 William IV St., London WC2N 4DD, England.

CAREER: British Military Administration, Tripoli, Libia, English-Italian interpreter, 1943-44; principal and educationist in drama and creative writing in Malta; novelist, playwright, and poet. Producer of amateur and professional theatre in Malta; member of drama group, Manoel Theatre (national theater of Malta); drama adviser, Malta Television and Broadcasting. Honorary president, Movement for the Promotion of Literature in Malta. *Member:* International P.E.N., Malta Academy of Letters. *Awards, honors:* Fulbright travel grant in United States, 1961-62; Manoel Awards and Cheyney Award for Plays; other first prizes for stage and radio plays; television script, "An Eye to Reckon With," received special mention for third place, at Golden Harp Award International Festival in Dublin, Ireland, 1969; Malta's Best Publication of the Year award, 1971.

WRITINGS—Novels: A Wreath for the Innocents, MacGibbon & Kee, 1958; *Evil of the King Cockroach,* MacGibbon & Kee, 1960 (published in Malta as *Wild Spell of Summer,* 1968); *In the Eye of the Sun,* Macdonald & Co., 1969; *Come Again in Spring,* Union Press, 1973.

Produced plays: "Menz" produced in Tokyo, Japan, 1971; "Hefen Plus Zero," produced on Third Programme of Spain's National Radio, 1974.

Other plays: "Bwani"; "Iz-Zjara"; "Tx-Xorti ta'Mamzell"; "Is-Sejha ta' Sarid"; "Vagazi tas- Sajf"; "Boulevard"; "Il-Hadd Fuq Il-Bejt"; "L-Omnarja Zmien it-Qtil"; "L-imwarrbin"; "Hitan"; "Meta Morna tal-Mellieha"; "Vum-Barala-Zun gare"; "Karnival"; "The Cliffhangers"; "Saluting Battery"; "BB or Bloody in Bolivia"; "Cleopatra Slept (Badly) Here." Also author of *Requiem for a Malta Blackshirt,* and *Leap of Dolphins.* Author of poem in English recited to music at Expo '70 in Osaka, Japan.

WORK IN PROGRESS: The Inverts.

SIDELIGHTS: Francis Ebejer told *CA:* "I write or I'll burst with indignation, frustration and downright rudeness. And anyone of my own fellow creatures on this sorry planet doesn't deserve such treatment. All my anger distils itself through the typewriter keys into a properly modulated and subtlized comment with people still recognizable as people largely unscathed by the hot wind of my wrath."

BIOGRAPHICAL/CRITICAL SOURCES: Times Literary Supplement (London), October 16, 1969; *Nagens Nyheter,* January 14, 1974; *Canadian Theatre Review,* summer, 1975.

* * *

EDEL, Matthew (David) 1941-

PERSONAL: Born October 5, 1941, in New York, N.Y.; son of Abraham (a philosopher) and May (an anthropologist; maiden name, Mandelbaum) Edel; married Candace Kim Dye, 1972; children: Nathan Keir. *Education:* Harvard University, B.A., 1962; Columbia University, M.A., 1965; Yale University, Ph.D., 1968. *Office:* Department of Urban Studies, Queens College of the City University of New York, Flushing, N.Y. 11367.

CAREER: Massachusetts Institute of Technology, Cambridge, assistant professor of economics, 1967-72; Queens College of the City University of New York, Flushing, N.Y., associate professor of urban studies, 1972—. *Member:* Union of Radical Political Economists, American Economic Association, Latin American Studies Association. *Awards, honors:* Foreign Area fellowship, 1966; National Science Foundation research grant, 1972—.

WRITINGS: Food Supply and Inflation in Latin America, Praeger, 1969; (editor with Jerome Rothenberg) *Readings in Urban Economics,* Macmillan, 1972; *Economies and the Environment,* Prentice-Hall, 1973; (contributor) Roger Alcaly and David Mermelstein, editors, *The Fiscal Crisis of American Cities,* Vintage Books, 1977. Contributor to economic and Latin American studies journals. Editor, *Review of Radical Political Economics.*

WORK IN PROGRESS: With Elliott Sclar and Daniel Luria, a study of the suburbanization of Boston; research on economic aspects of urban growth and problems in the United States and Latin America.

SIDELIGHTS: Matthew Edel has done research in Colombia, Cuba, Mexico, and other Latin American countries.

* * *

EDGERTON, William B(enbow) 1914-

PERSONAL: Born March 11, 1914, in Winston-Salem, N.C.; son of Paul Clifton (a real estate broker) and Annie Maud (Benbow) Edgerton; married Jewell Mock Conrad, June 6, 1935; children: Susan Edgerton Bradshaw, David. *Education:* Guilford College, B.A., (with high honors), 1934; Haverford College, M.A., 1935; Columbia University, Ph.D., 1954. *Politics:* Democrat. *Religion:* Quaker. *Home:* 1801 East Maxwell Lane, Bloomington, Ind. 47401. *Office:* Ballantine 502, Indiana University, Bloomington, Ind. 47401.

CAREER: Language teacher in preparatory schools in Pennsylvania, 1935-37, 1938-39; assistant in English at a secondary school in France, 1937-38; Guilford College, Greensboro, N.C., 1939-47, began as assistant professor, became associate professor of French and Spanish; Quaker

relief worker in Egypt and Europe, 1944-46; Pennsylvania State University, University Park, assistant professor of Russian, 1950-56; Columbia University, New York, N.Y., assistant professor, 1956-57, associate professor of Slavic languages, 1957-58; Indiana University, Bloomington, professor of Slavic languages and literatures, 1958—, chairman of department, 1958-65, 1969-73. Visiting professor, University of Michigan, 1954-55; exchange research scholar in Moscow and Leningrad, 1963-64. Ford Foundation consultant, 1953-57, 1958-61; American Council of Learned Societies-Social Science Research Council joint committee on Slavic studies, member, 1951-62, chairman, 1957-60. Member of board of directors, American Friends Service Committee, 1956-59; member of board of trustees, Guilford College, 1970—.

MEMBER: Modern Language Association of America (member of executive council, 1963-65), American Committee of Slavists (chairman, 1958—), International Committee of Slavists (American representative, 1958—), American Association for the Advancement of Slavic Studies (president, 1961), American Comparative Literature Association, American Association of Teachers of Slavic and East European Languages. *Awards, honors:* American Council of Learned Societies fellow, 1948-50; Guggenheim fellow, 1963-64; Josef Dobrovsky Silver Medal, Czechoslovak Academy of Sciences, 1968, for "merit in encouraging scholarship in the humanities."

WRITINGS: (With others) *The United States and the Soviet Union: Some Quaker Proposals for Peace* (booklet), Yale University Press, 1950; (translator) *A Soviet History of Philosophy,* Public Affairs Press, 1950; (with others) *Steps to Peace: A Quaker View of American Foreign Policy,* American Friends Service Committee, 1951; (with others) *Speak Truth to Power: A Quaker Search for an Alternative to Violence,* American Friends Service Committee, 1955; (editor and contributor) *Meeting the Russians: American Quakers Visit the Soviet Union,* American Friends Service Committee, 1956; (editor and contributor) *American Contributions to the Fifth International Congress of Slavists, Sofia, September, 1963,* Mouton & Co., 1963; (contributor) *Orbis Scriptus: Dmitrij Tschizewskij zum 70 Geburtstag,* Wilhelm Fink Verlag, 1966; (contributor) *To Honor Roman Jakobson: Essays on the Occasion of His Seventieth Birthday,* Mouton & Co., 1967; (translator) *Satirical Stories of Nikolai Leskov,* Pegasus, 1969. Co-editor, *Indiana Slavic Studies,* Volume III, 1963; editor and contributor, *Indiana Slavic Studies,* Volume IV, 1967. Contributor to other symposia, to *Collier's Encyclopedia, Encyclopedia Judaica,* and about thirty articles to scholarly publications in the United States and Europe. Member of editorial committee of *Slavic and East European Journal* and *Yearbook of Comparative and General Literature;* associate editor, *Columbia Dictionary of Modern European Literature.*

WORK IN PROGRESS: A critical biography of Nikolai Leskov; a study of Leo Tolstoy in European and American literature; editing unpublished Gorky documents.

SIDELIGHTS: William Edgerton has made eighteen visits to the Slavic countries of eastern Europe, eleven of them to the Soviet Union. Three of his trips to the Soviet Union were made as a representative of the Inter-University Committee on Travel Grants, which he helped found. He speaks Russian, French, German, Polish, Serbo-Croatian, Spanish, and Italian.

BIOGRAPHICAL/CRITICAL SOURCES: New Republic, March 1, 1969; *Saturday Review,* March 8, 1969.

EDGLEY, Roy 1925-

PERSONAL: Born June 19, 1925, in Northampton, England; son of Edwin (a shoemaker) and Annie (Coles) Edgley; married Elizabeth Boxer (an actress), August 20, 1960; children: Alison, Katherine. *Education:* University of Manchester, B.A. (honors in philosophy), 1952; Oxford University, B.Phil., 1954. *Politics:* Socialist. *Religion:* None. *Home:* 18 Montpelier Villas, Brighton BN1 3DG, England. *Office:* Arts Building, University of Sussex, Falmer, Brighton, England.

CAREER: University of Bristol, Bristol, England, assistant lecturer, 1954-57, senior lecturer, 1964-70; University of Sussex, Brighton, England, professor of philosophy, 1970—. Visiting lecturer, University of Ghana, 1960; Ellis Visiting Professor of Philosophy, Reed College, 1969. *Military service:* Royal Air Force, 1944-48. *Member:* Aristotelian Society, Mind Association.

WRITINGS: Reason in Theory and Practice, Hutchinson, 1969. Contributor to *Mind, Proceedings* of the Aristotelian Society, *Philosophy, Essays in Criticism, Radical Philosophy,* and other professional journals. Editor, *Philosophy Now* (Sussex University Press).

WORK IN PROGRESS: The concept of reason, rationality and science, especially social science, Marxism, and dialectic.

* * *

EDSON, J(ohn) T(homas) 1928-
(Rod Denver, Chuck Nolan)

PERSONAL: Born February 17, 1928, in Worksop, Nottinghamshire, England; son of Thomas John (a coal miner) and Eliza Charlotte (Gill) Edson; married Dorothy Mary Thompson, December 14, 1957 (divorced, 1974); children: Leslie Brian, Raymond, Steven, Peter John, Samantha Diane, Mark William James. *Education:* Attended schools in Nottinghamshire. *Politics:* None ("against all organised political groups"). *Religion:* Church of England ("nominally"). *Home:* 1 Cottesmore Ave., Melton Mowbray, Leicestershire LE13 0HY, England. *Agent:* Rosica Colin, 4 Hereford Sq., London SW7 4TU, England.

CAREER: Haulage hand at a stone quarry in Steetley, England, 1943-46; British Army, Royal Army Veterinary Corps, dog trainer, 1946-58, serving as sergeant in Germany, Malaya, Hong Kong, North Africa, Kenya, and Cyprus (combat duty in Kenya and Cyprus); owner of a fish and chip shop in Melton Mowbray, England, 1958-62; also worked in Mowbray, as a production hand in Petfoods Industries, 1962-65, and as a postman, 1965-68; writer of western novels. *Member:* Western Writers of America, Royal Army Veterinary Corps Old Comrades Association, Northampton Lower Forty Club (honorary member). *Awards, honors:* Second prize in western section of Brown, Watson's Literary Contest, for *Trail Boss.*

WRITINGS—All published by Brown, Watson, except as indicated: *Trail Boss,* 1961; *The Hard Riders,* 1962; *The Texan,* 1962; *Rio Guns,* 1962; *The Ysabel Kid,* 1962; *Sagebrush Sleuth,* 1962; (under pseudonym Rod Denver) *Arizona Ranger,* 1962, later reprinted under his own name; (under pseudonym Chuck Nolan) *Quiet Town,* 1962, later reprinted under his own name; *Waco's Debt,* 1962; *The Rio Hondo Kid,* 1963; *Apache Rampage,* 1963; *The Fastest Gun in Texas,* 1963; *The Drifter,* 1963; *The Half Breed,* 1963; *Gun Wizard,* 1963; *Gunsmoke Thunder,* 1963; *Wagons to Backsight,* 1964; *Waco Rides In,* 1964; *The Rushers,* 1964; *The*

Rio Hondo War, 1964; *Trigger Fast,* 1964; *The Wildcats,* 1965; *The Peacemakers,* 1965; *Troubled Range,* 1965; *The Fortune Hunters,* 1965; *Slaughter's Way,* 1965, Bantam, 1969; *The Man from Texas,* 1965; *The Trouble Busters,* 1965; *Trouble Trail,* 1965; *The Cowthieves,* 1965; *The Bull Whip Breed,* 1965, Bantam, 1969; *Guns in the Night,* 1966; *A Town Called Yellowdog,* 1966; *The Devil Gun,* 1966, Bantam, 1969; *The Colt and the Sabre,* 1966; *The Law of the Gun,* 1966; *Return to Backsight,* 1966; *The Fast Gun,* 1967; *The Big Hunt,* 1967; *Terror Valley,* 1967; *Comanche,* 1967; *Hound Dog Man,* 1967; *Sidewinder,* 1967.

All published by Corgi Books, except as indicated: *The Floating Outfit,* 1967; *The Rebel Spy,* 1968; *The Bad Bunch,* 1968; *The Hooded Riders,* 1968; *Calamity Spells Trouble,* 1968; *Rangeland Hercules,* 1968; *McGraw's Inheritance,* 1968; *The Making of a Lawman,* 1968, Bantam, 1971; *The Professional Killers,* 1968; *The Town Tamers,* 1969, Bantam, 1973; *Cold Deck, Hot Lead,* 1969; *The Bloody Border,* 1969; *The Small Texan,* 1969; *The ¼ Second Draw,* 1969; *Cuchilo,* 1969; *The Deputies,* 1969; *Goodnight's Dream,* 1969; *From Hide and Horn,* 1969, Bantam, 1974; *Under the Stars and Bars,* 1970; *Kill Dusty Fog,* 1970; *Back to the Bloody Border,* 1970; *White Stallion: Red Mare,* 1970; *Point of Contact,* 1970; *The Owlhoot,* 1970; *A Horse Called Mogallon,* 1971; *Hell in the Palo Duro,* 1971; *Slip Gun,* 1971; *Run for the Border,* 1971; *Bad Hombre,* 1971; *Go Back to Hell,* 1972; *The South Will Rise Again,* 1972; *Two Miles to the Border,* 1972; *You're in Command Now Mr. Fog,* 1973; *The Big Gun,* 1973; *Set Texas Back on Her Feet,* 1973; *.44 Calibre Man,* 1973; *Blonde Genius,* 1973; *The Hide and Tallow Men,* 1974; *The Quest for Bowie's Blade,* 1974; *Sixteen Dollar Shooter,* 1974; *Young Ole Devil,* 1975; *Bunduki and Dawn,* 1975; *Sacrifice for the Quagga God,* 1975; *Get Urrea,* 1975; *Ole Devil and the Caplocks,* 1976; *Ole Devil and the Mule Train,* 1976; *Doc Leroy, M.D.,* 1977; *Ole Devil at San Jacinto,* 1977; *Mr. J. G. Reeder, Meet Cap. Fog!,* 1977; *Texas Ranger,* 1977; *Set A-Foot,* 1977; *Beguinage,* 1978; *Fearless Master of the Jungle,* 1978; *Beguinage Is Dead,* 1978.

Writer of serials, series, short stories, and nonfiction for *Rover, Hotspur,* and *Victor.*

WORK IN PROGRESS: The Whip and the War Lance; The Amazons of Zillikian; J. T.'s Hundredth, an anthology of Edson's main protagonists.

SIDELIGHTS: A wire service photograph of J. T. Edson brandishing two plastic guns appeared in American newspapers in the spring of 1970 under the caption "Paper Cowboy," with the explanation that "England's answer to Zane Grey" was forced to work out action scenes for his books with fake revolvers because British police claim he doesn't need real ones. Edson says that his writing "is of action, adventure, escapist variety, written purely for the enjoyment of people who like that kind of a story . . . while also earning a comfortable living for myself . . . I have become hooked on the fictionist genealogy style of writing perfected by Philip Jose Farmer. This allows me to tie in various of my Western characters with the protagonists of the "Bunduki" series of books . . . All my work is action-escapism-adventure motivated and I try to steer clear of the 'message' style of writing." Edson goes on to say: "I refuse to accept the frequently made statement that the traditional type of Western novel is not wanted by the reading public and my sales figures seem to prove me correct. One thing I will not do is produce books featuring the 'liberal' anti-hero. My pet hate is journalists who label me a 'postman-turned-author,' or pretend to think I need to dress in 'cowboy' clothes to write.

To me, this is merely an extension of their middle class 'liberal' snobbery. I was a moderately, if not financially successful writer before I became a postman. If they have to use a label, I would prefer to be called any ex-regular soldier turned author which is correct.''

J. T. Edson was made a honorary admiral in the Texas Navy, and honorary deputy sheriff of Travis County, Texas, and of Thurston County, Washington. Edson's books have been translated into Danish, Dutch, Swedish, Norwegian, German, Afrikaans, and Serbo-Croation.

AVOCATIONAL INTERESTS: Fishing, clay pigeon shooting, collecting police concealment holsters, ''adding to my collection of Japanese replica-nonfiring firearms,'' and building up his reference library.

BIOGRAPHICAL/CRITICAL SOURCES: Times, February 24, 1968; *Sunday Mirror,* April 28, 1968.

* * *

EDWARDS, Charlotte

PERSONAL: Born in Erie, Pa.; daughter of Edward Judson (a plant manager) and Florence (Vail) Walrath; married Donald Thomas Edwards (a photographer), December 15, 1934; children: Thomas Edward Edwards. *Education:* Lake Erie College, B.M., 1931. *Politics:* Republican. *Religion:* Episcopalian. *Home:* 636 West Seventh St., Erie, Pa. 16502. *Agent:* James Brown Associates, Inc., 22 East 60th St., New York, N.Y. 10022.

CAREER: Rochester Journal, Rochester, N.Y., woman's editor, 1934-35; WHEC, Rochester, continuity director, 1935-41; *Dayton Daily News,* Dayton, Ohio, reporter and feature writer, 1943-45; presented solo programs of dramatic readings while living in Pomona, Calif., 1957-62; teacher of music at a country school near Easton, Md., and teacher of creative writing at Chesapeake College, Wye Mills, Md., 1969; adult and college-level teacher at Gannon College, Erie, Pa.

WRITINGS: The Right Place for Love, McGraw, 1953; *Heaven on the Doorstep,* Hawthorn, 1958; *Heaven in the Home,* Hawthorn, 1959; *Let Yourself Go: Try Creative Sunday School,* Morehouse, 1969; *View through the Window,* Hawthorn, 1975. Contributor of more than 150 short stories and novelettes to popular magazines. Contributing editor, *Erie Today.*

WORK IN PROGRESS: A novel, *Pity the Strong; Learning to Write from the Inside Out;* a travel book.

SIDELIGHTS: Charlotte Edwards told *CA:* ''As I grow older . . . not only do I realize that all living is grist for a writer's mill, all observation of life and people, all empathy—but no words are ever lost, no matter what the field. Newspaper for conciseness, radio for dialogue, teaching for understanding—they all interweave to make a professional whole. And it has become my firm belief that practically anyone can write, given a sincere idea and firm discipline.''

AVOCATIONAL INTERESTS: Knitting, needlepoint, reading, cooking.

* * *

EGAN, Ferol   1923-

PERSONAL: Born July 25, 1923, in Sonora, Calif.; son of Ferol Ruoff and Verna (Maddox) Egan; married Martha Toki Oshima (a research assistant), March 6, 1965. *Education:* College of the Pacific (now University of the Pacific), A.B., 1946, M.A., 1950; University of California, Berkeley,

additional study, 1947-48, 1958-59. *Residence:* Berkeley, Calif.

CAREER: Teacher of English at high school in Arcata, Calif., 1948-49; Yuba College, Marysville, Calif., instructor in English, 1950-51; Matson Navigation Co., San Francisco, Calif., cargo checker and timekeeper, 1951-52; teacher of English at high school in Reno, Nev., 1952-53; slot machine keyman at Harold's Club, Reno, 1953; Stockton College, Stockton, Calif., instructor in English and history, 1953-55; California College of Arts and Crafts, Oakland, associate professor of humanities, 1956-61; University of California, Berkeley, science writer (biology), 1961-65; presently freelance writer in Berkeley, Calif. Consultant, designer, and writer for California Indian Exhibit, Oakland Museum, 1969. *Member:* Western History Association, California Historical Society, Friends of Bancroft Library. *Awards, honors:* Commonwealth Club of California, Californiana Silver Medal, Medal for General Nonfiction, 1971, for *The El Dorado Trail,* 1973, for *Sand in a Whirlwind.*

WRITINGS: The El Dorado Trail: The Story of the Gold Rush Routes across Mexico, McGraw, 1970; *Sand in a Whirlwind: The Paiute Indian War of 1860,* Doubleday, 1972; *Fremont: Explorer for a Restless Nation,* Doubleday, 1977; *The Taste of Time,* McGraw, 1977.

Editor and author of introduction and notes: *Incidents of Travel in New Mexico,* Lewis Osborne, 1969; *A Sailor's Sketch of the Sacramento Valley in 1842,* Friends of Bancroft Library, 1971; *California, Land of Gold, or Stay at Home and Work Hard,* Book Club of California, 1971; *A Dangerous Journey,* Lewis Osborne, 1972; *Overland Journey to Carson Valley and California,* Book Club of California, 1973; *With Fremont to California and the Southwest,* Lewis Osborne, 1975. Contributor of articles and reviews to *The American West, California Historical Society Quarterly, California Monthly, Nevada Historical Society Quarterly, San Francisco Magazine, Sierra Club Bulletin, Westways,* and to various newspapers. Film critic, *Imagery: American Journal of Cinematic Art,* 1961-63. *The American West,* associate editor, 1970-72, contributing editor, 1972—.

WORK IN PROGRESS: Goodby God, a novel.

SIDELIGHTS: His youth in a wide-open California mining town and on his father's cattle ranch inspired Ferol Egan with a love for the American West and a desire to record it in history and fiction. For all his books, he has made extensive field trips to capture the look of the land in all seasons.

BIOGRAPHICAL/CRITICAL SOURCES: New York Times, February 12, 1977.

* * *

EGAN, Gerard   1930-

PERSONAL: Born June 17, 1930, in Chicago, Ill. *Education:* Loyola University, Chicago, A.B., 1953; M.A. (philosophy), 1959, M.A. (clinical psychology), 1963, Ph.D., 1969. *Office:* Department of Psychology, Loyola University, Chicago, Ill. 60626.

CAREER: Loyola University, Chicago, Ill., assistant professor of psychology, 1969—. *Member:* American Psychological Association, American Association for Humanistic Psychology, American Personnel and Guidance Association.

WRITINGS—All published by Brooks/Cole: *Encounter: Group Processes for Interpersonal Growth,* 1970; (editor) *Encounter Groups: Basic Readings,* 1971; *Face to Face: The Small-Group Experience and Interpersonal Growth,*

1973; *The Skilled Helper: A Model for Helping and Human Relations Training*, 1975; *Exercises in Helping Skills*, 1975; *Interpersonal Living: A Skills/Contract Approach to Human Relations Training in Groups*, 1976; *You and Me: The Skills of Human Communication in Everyday Life*, 1977.

* * *

EGG, Maria 1910-
(Maria Egg-Benes)

PERSONAL: Born February 21, 1910, in Budapest, Hungary; became a Swiss citizen in 1937; daughter of Imre (a proprietor of hotels and lodgings) and Fanny Benes; married Gotthard Egg (an engineer), March 25, 1937; children: Reinhard, Barbara (Mrs. Alexander Jaecklin). *Education:* Maria Theresia Gymnasium, Budapest, B.A., 1927; Kindergarten-Teachers' College, Berlin, Diploma, 1931; University of Berlin, Ph.D., 1932. *Religion:* Roman Catholic. *Home:* Voltastrasse 64, Zurich, Switzerland 8044.

CAREER: Director of city schools for the retarded, Zurich, Switzerland, 1937-75, of vocational training workshops for the retarded, 1953—, and of sheltered workshops for retarded adults, 1959—. Lecturer on education of the retarded at the school for parents, Zurich, 1954—, and at Training College for Special Education, Zurich, 1956-75; also has given about forty lectures annually since 1945 at the invitation of governments, universities, and associations throughout Europe and the United States. Former consultant to World Health Organization; consultant on special education to government agencies in Europe, Middle East, India, and Africa. Member of board of directors of several residential homes for the retarded in Switzerland. Member of State Parliament, 1971—.

MEMBER: Swiss Association for the Welfare of Retarded (member of executive committee), Swiss Federation of Parents of Retarded (member of executive committee), Swiss Teachers' Association, Swiss Association of University Women, American Association on Mental Deficiency (honorary member), Zurich Association of Parents of Retarded (honorary member).

AWARDS, HONORS: International Award, Joseph P. Kennedy Foundation (Washington, D.C.), for outstanding service to the retarded; International Prize, FONEME Foundation (Milan, Italy), for pioneer research in the psychology of retarded adolescents; award from the Government of Zurich for contribution to the cultural life of the community; Doctor honoris causa, University of Zurich.

WRITINGS: Die Heilpaedagogische Hilfsschule der Stadt-Zurich: Ihre Wege und Ziele, Verlag der Schul- und Bueromaterialverwaltung der Stadt Zurich, 1952; *Das geistesschwache Kind daheim und in der Schule*, Schulamt der Stadt Zurich, 1956; *Ein Kind ist anders: Ein Wegweiser fuer Eltern, Betreuer und Freunde geistig gebrechlicher Kinder*, Schweizer Spiegel, 1959, translation published as *When a Child Is Different: A Basic Guide for Parents and Friends of Mentally Retarded Children*, introduction by Eunice Kennedy Shriver, John Day, 1964; *Andere Kinder, andere Erziehung*, Schweizer Spiegel, 1965, translation by Shelton B. Hicock published as *Educating the Child Who Is Different*, introduction by Shriver, John Day, 1968; *Andere Menschen, anderer Lebensweg*, Schweizer Spiegel, 1966, translation by Marietta Moskin published as *The Different Child Grows Up*, John Day, 1969; *Diesen gehoert mein Herz* (autobiography), Schweizer Spiegel, 1970; *Behinderte Kindererziehen*, Walter Verlag, 1975; *Lebensweg der Behinderten*, Walter Verlag, 1976.

SIDELIGHTS: Dr. Egg has given her life "to forward a way of life in human dignity for the retarded." Some decades ago this meant pioneering, but now, as she points out, "these aims are more and more acknowledged all over the world." *When a Child Is Different* has been published in nine languages, *Educating the Child Who Is Different*, in four, and *The Different Child Grows Up*, in three.

* * *

EGGERS, William T. 1912-

PERSONAL: Born April 27, 1912, in Tacoma, Wash.; son of William A. and Rosette (Pritzlaff) Eggers; married Marcella Nohos, 1938; children: William C., Mary Ann (Mrs. James Wiertzema), Joan (Mrs. Donald C. Wendelburg). *Education:* Attended Concordia College, Milwaukee, Wis., 1925-31; Concordia Seminary, St. Louis, Mo., graduate, 1935; Marquette University, further study, 1935-36. *Home:* 2510 North Swan Blvd., Wauwatosa, Wis. 53226. *Office:* Home for Aged Lutherans, 7500 West North Ave., Wauwatosa, Wis. 53213.

CAREER: Lutheran clergyman of the Missouri Synod; held pastorates in Illinois and Wisconsin, 1937-53; Home for Aged Lutherans, Wauwatosa, Wis., administrator, 1954—. Pulpit assistant, Oklahoma Avenue Lutheran Church, Milwaukee, 1956-62. Chairman of board, Oconomowoc Memorial Hospital, 1951-55; former member of board of directors, Milwaukee Council on Aging; member, Wisconsin State Council on Aging; member of long-term care council, Joint Commission on Accreditation of Hospitals. *Member:* American Association of Homes for the Aging (president, 1968), American Hospital Association (member of board of approval), Wisconsin Association of Homes for the Aging (member of executive committee), Employers Association of Milwaukee (member of board). *Awards. honors:* Award of Merit, Wisconsin Council of Homes for the Aging, 1968; Award of Honor, American Association of Homes for the Aging, 1968; Dr.D., Concordia Seminary, 1977.

WRITINGS: Space of Joy, Concordia, 1968. Writer of monthly article, "Accents in Aging," for *Professional Nursing Home* (magazine), and columnist in *Badger Lutheran*. Contributor to other denominational periodicals. Former contributing editor, *Lutheran Witness;* editor of *Affirm*, 1971—, and *Concern*, 1974-77.

* * *

EGLER, Frank E(dwin) 1911-

PERSONAL: Born April 26, 1911, in New York, N.Y.; son of Charles John and Florence Edna (Wilshusen) Egler; married Happy Kitchel Hamilton, June 6, 1968. *Education:* Attended State College of Forestry at Syracuse University (now State University of New York College of Environmental Science and Forestry), 1929-31, University of Michigan Biological Station, 1931, and Columbia University, 1932; University of Chicago, B.S., 1932; University of Minnesota, M.S., 1934; Yale University, Ph.D., 1936; Sorbonne, University of Paris, certificate in French, 1936; also attended University of Hawaii, 1937. *Address:* Aton Forest, Norfolk, Conn. 06058.

CAREER: Research fellow at Yale University, New Haven, Conn., and Bishop Museum, Honolulu, Hawaii, 1936-37; State College of Forestry at Syracuse University (now State University of New York College of Environmental Science and Forestry), Syracuse, N.Y., assistant professor of forest botany, 1937-44; Chicle Development Co., director of experiment station in British Honduras, 1941-44; Aton

Forest, Norfolk, Conn., director and president, 1943—. Associate professor of botany, University of Connecticut, Waterbury, 1947-48; consulting vegetationist, 1949—; research associate, Department of Conservation, American Museum of Natural History, 1951-55; guest lecturer and visiting professor at various institutes and universities, 1959—. Technical advisor, R/W Maintenance Corp., 1949-54. *Wartime service*—As civilian: U.S. Army Air Forces, 1943-44; U.S. Navy, 1944-45; U.S. Army, 1945.

MEMBER: American Association for the Advancement of Science (fellow), American Geographical Society (fellow), Ecological Society of America, National Audubon Society, Nature Conservancy, Wilderness Society, American Association of University Professors, Connecticut Botanical Society. *Awards, honors:* Eaton Scholar, Yale University, 1935; Guggenheim fellowship, 1956-58.

WRITINGS: The Way of Science: A Philosophy of Ecology for the Layman, Hafner, 1971; *The Plight of the Right-of-way Domain: Victim of Vandelism,* Futura Media Services, 1975; *The Nature of Vegetation, Its Management and Mismanagement: An Introduction to Vegetation Science,* Connecticut Conservation Association, 1977.

*　　*　　*

EHRHARDT, Reinhold 1900-

PERSONAL: Born July 28, 1900, in Potsdam, Germany; married Christa Gildemeister, June 18, 1930; children: Hans-Alfred, Christiane Ehrhardt von Bonin. *Religion:* Evangelical. *Home:* Hans Thomastrasse 50, Bremen, West Germany.

WRITINGS—Juvenile: *Kikeri,* Nord-Sued Verlag, 1970, translation published as *Kikeri; or, The Proud Red Rooster,* World Publishing, 1970; *Die Turmuhr* (title means "The Tower Clock"), Nord-Sued Verlag, 1971.

WORK IN PROGRESS: Two books, one title means "Postman Hinnerk," and the other title means "Our Little Town," both for Nord-Sued Verlag.†

*　　*　　*

EICHHORN, Werner 1899-

PERSONAL: Born July 1, 1899, in Theuern, Germany; son of Richard (a forestry commissioner) and Elsbeth (Sachtleben) Eichhorn. *Education:* Studied at Universities of Heidelberg, Berlin, Goettingen, Leipzig, Paris, Peking, and Bonn; University of Goettingen, Dr.Phil., 1926; University of Bonn, Dr.Phil.Habil., 1937. *Religion:* "Would be inclined to become a Quaker." *Home:* 7406 Moessingen, Karl-Jaggy-Str. 19, Germany.

CAREER: Tsing-hua University, Peking, China, lecturer, 1933-34; docent in Germany at Universities of Bonn, Goettingen, Frankfurt, and in Austria at University of Vienna, 1937-49; Oxford University, Bodleian Library, Oxford, England, assistant librarian, 1949-61; University of Tuebingen, Tuebingen, Germany, professor of Sinology and director of Seminar for East Asian Philology, 1960-70.

WRITINGS: T'ung-su des Ceu-tsi, China-Bibliothek, Bd. 3, 1932; *Chou Tun-1: Ein chinesisches Gelehrtenleben aus dem 11 Johrhundert,* Abhandluengen der Deutschen Morgenlaendischen Gesellschaft, 1936; *Die Westinschrift des Chang Tsai: Ein Beitrag zur geistesgeschichte der noerdlichen Sung* (text in Chinese, with Manchu and German translation), Abhandluengen der Deutschen Morgenlaendischen Gesellschaft, No. 71, Kommissionsverlag F. A. Brockhaus, 1937; (translator) Hsiung Fo-hsi, *Chinesisches*

Bauernleben, Kommissionsverlag O. Harrassowitz, 1938; *Unter Blueten eine Weile* (short stories), E. Roeth, 1958; *Kulturgeschichte Chinas,* Kohlhammer Verlag, 1964, translation by Janet Seligman published as *Chinese Civilization: An Introduction,* Praeger, 1969; *Beitrag zur rechtlichen Stellung des Buddhismus und Taoismus im Sung-Staat,* E. J. Brill, 1968; *Heldensagen aus dem unteren Yantse-Tal,* Deutsche Morgenlaendische Gesellschaft, 1969; *Die Religionen Chinas,* Verlag Kohlhammer, 1973; *Die alte chinesische Religion und das Staatskultwesen,* E. J. Brill, 1976. Contributor to journals.

WORK IN PROGRESS: Further research in Chinese religion and history.

SIDELIGHTS: Werner Eichhorn, a modest scholar, supplied the briefest of information to *CA,* listing six book titles and no other publications, explaining that it "would be too long a list . . . and some are no good." He said too: "I think I am able to speak English fairly fluently. Being a stammerer I hate languages. Sometimes I like travelling, if I am able to overcome my inborn immovableness and sense for economy. I do not like to be shown up in public." Eichhorn also wrote *CA* that his career covered such varied occupations as bank clerk, cemetery gardener, and farmhand, "in between."

*　　*　　*

EIDELBERG, Ludwig 1898-1970

December 27, 1898—November 13, 1970; Austrian-born psychoanalyst and author. Obituaries: *New York Times,* November 14, 1970. (See index for *CA* sketch)

*　　*　　*

EINSEL, Mary E. 1929-

PERSONAL: Born April 18, 1929, in Coldwater, Kan.; daughter of Wilford and Lucille (Jackson) Betzer; married Ralph D. Einsel, January 14, 1947; children: Christine (Mrs. Eric Sprado II), Karen. *Education:* Attended public schools in Coldwater, Kan. *Residence:* Coldwater, Kan.

WRITINGS: Stagecoach West to Kansas: True Stories of the Kansas Plains, Pruett, 1970, revised edition published as *Kansas, the Priceless Prairie,* 1976.

*　　*　　*

EISNER, Betty Grover 1915-
(Rev. B.)

PERSONAL: Born September 29, 1915, in Kansas City, Mo.; daughter of John Carpenter (an attorney) and Helen (Weber) Grover; married Willard David Eisner, 1937 (died, 1965); married William R. Micks (a teacher and engineer), 1965; children: (first marriage) Maleah, David Barth. *Education:* Stanford University, B.A., 1937; University of California, Los Angeles, M.A., 1955, Ph.D., 1956. *Residence:* Santa Monica, Calif. *Office:* 1237 Seventh St., No. 111, Santa Monica, Calif. 90401.

CAREER: Private practice in psychotherapy, 1955—. *Member:* American Psychological Association, Western Psychological Association, California State Psychological Association, Los Angeles Society of Clinical Psychologists, Phi Beta Kappa.

WRITINGS: (Contributor) Harold Abramson, editor, *The Use of LSD in Psychotherapy and Alcoholism,* Bobbs-Merrill, 1969; *The Unused Potential of Marriage and Sex,* Little, Brown, 1970. Contributor to medical journals in England

and the United States. Writer of song lyrics under pseudonym, Rev. B.

WORK IN PROGRESS: I Can't, You Can't, But We Can!; song albums.

SIDELIGHTS: Mrs. Micks (Dr. Eisner professionally) has travelled extensively in Europe, Asia, Mexico, and the South Pacific. For the last six years, she has managed a summer school in Mexico which teaches English, art, and sports. Mrs. Micks and her husband maintain a business in Puerto Vallarta and employ students from the school. She told *CA* that she "writes of these experiences [in Mexico] and of deep insights from her psychotherapy practice."

* * *

EKWALL, Eldon E(dward) 1933-

PERSONAL: Born August 28, 1933, in Geneva, Neb.; son of Arthur Clarance (a farmer) and Bessie G. (Ingels) Ekwall; married Maxine Rains, January 26, 1956 (divorced, 1974); children: Dwight, Cindy. *Education:* University of Nebraska, B.Sc., 1959, Ed.M., 1961; University of Arizona, Ed.D., 1966. *Religion:* Methodist. *Home:* 299 Kings Point, #25, El Paso, Tex. 79912. *Office:* Department of Curriculum and Instruction, University of Texas, El Paso, Tex. 79968.

CAREER: Public school teacher and administrator in Benedict, Neb. and San Manuel, Ariz., 1959-67; New Mexico Highlands University, Las Vegas, assistant professor of education, 1967-68; University of Kansas, Lawrence, assistant professor of education, 1968-69; University of Texas at El Paso, 1969—, began as associate professor, currently professor of education. Reading and language arts consultant to many school districts in Midwest, South, and southwestern United States. *Military service:* U.S. Army, 1953-55. *Member:* International Reading Association (former president and former member of board of directors of Arizona State chapter), National Education Association (life member), Texas Education Association, Arizona Reading Association (member of board of directors, 1965-67), Trans Pecos Education Association, Phi Delta Kappa.

WRITINGS: Locating and Correcting Reading Difficulties, C. E. Merrill, 1970, 2nd edition, 1977; *Psychological Factors in the Teaching of Reading,* C. E. Merrill, 1973; *Diagnosis and Remediation of the Disabled Reader,* Allyn & Bacon, 1976; *Teachers Handbook on Diagnosis and Remediation in Reading,* Allyn & Bacon, 1977. Senior author and co-inventor of *Rx Reading Program;* also author of *Corrective Reading System,* Psychotechnics, Inc., 1976. Author of several monographs on effective reading skills. Contributor of articles to *Arizona Teacher, Science Teacher, Reading Teacher, Reading Quarterly, Phi-Delta Kappan,* and others.

WORK IN PROGRESS: Conducting research study entitled "The Use of the Polygraph to Determine Students' Frustration Reading Level."

SIDELIGHTS: Eldon Ekwall told *CA* that he is interested "especially in the use of audio-visual materials and techniques in teaching . . . and in the validity of group vs. individual testing techniques in reading."

* * *

EKWENSI, Cyprian (Odiatu Duaka) 1921-
(C.O.D. Ekwensi)

PERSONAL: Born September 26, 1921, in Minna, Nigeria; married Eunice Anyiwo; children: five. *Education:* Attended Achimota College, Ghana, and Ibadan University; received B.A.; further study at Chelsea School of Pharmacy, London. *Home:* Nkwelle, near Onitsha, Eastern Nigeria. *Mailing address:* P.O. Box 317, Enugu, Nigeria.

CAREER: Novelist, writer of short stories, and stories for children. Lecturer in biology, chemistry, and English, Igbodi College, Lagos, Nigeria, 1947-49; lecturer in pharmacognosy and pharmaceutics, School of Pharmacy, Lagos, 1949-56; pharmacist for Nigerian Medical Service and head of features, Nigerian Broadcasting Corp., 1956-61; director of information, Federal Ministry of Information, Lagos, 1961-66; chairman of Bureau for External Publicity during Biafran secession, 1967-69, and director of an independent Biafran radio station; chemist for a plastics firm in Enugu, Nigeria; currently managing director of Star Printing & Publishing Co. (publishers of *Daily Star*). Chairman of East Central State Library Board, 1972-75. *Member:* Society of Nigerian Authors, P.E.N. (London), Pharmaceutical Society of Great Britain, Institute of Public Relations (London), Institute of Public Relations (Nigeria; fellow). *Awards, honors:* Dag Hammarskjold International Award, 1968.

WRITINGS: People of the City, Andrew Dakers, 1954, Northwestern University Press, 1967, revised edition, Fawcett, 1969; *Jagua Nana,* Hutchinson, 1961, Fawcett, 1969; *Burning Grass,* Heinemann, 1962; *Beautiful Feathers,* Hutchinson, 1963; *Lokotown and Other Stories,* Heinemann, 1966; *Iska,* Hutchinson, 1966; *Coal Camp Boy,* Longman, 1971; *Samankwe in the Strange Forest,* Longman, 1973; *The Restless City; and Christmas Gold,* Heinemann, 1975; *Samankwe and the Highway Robbers,* Evans Africa Library, 1975; *Rainbow-Tinted Scarf,* Evans Africa Library, 1975; *Survive the Peace,* Heinemann, 1976.

Children's books: *The Drummer Boy,* Cambridge University Press, 1960; *The Passport of Mallam Ilia,* Cambridge University Press, 1960; *An African Night's Entertainment* (folklore), African Universities Press, 1962; *Yaba Roundabout Murder* (short novel), Tortoise Series Books (Lagos, Nigeria), 1962; *The Great Elephant-Bird,* Thomas Nelson, 1965; *The Rainmaker and Other Stories,* African Universities Press, 1965; *Juju Rock,* African Universities Press, 1966; *The Boa Suitor,* Thomas Nelson, 1966; *Trouble in Form Six,* Cambridge University Press, 1966.

Under name C.O.D. Ekwensi: *When Love Whispers* (short novel), Tabansi Bookshop (Onitsha, Nigeria), 1947; *Ikolo the Wrestler and Other Ibo Tales,* Thomas Nelson, 1947; *The Leopard's Claw,* Thomas Nelson, 1950.

Writer of plays and scripts for B.B.C. radio and television, Radio Nigeria, and other communication outlets. Contributor of stories, articles, and reviews to magazines and newspapers in Nigeria and England, including *West African Review, Times* (London), *Black Orpheus, Flamingo,* and *Sunday Post.*

SIDELIGHTS: Reviewing *Beautiful Feathers* John F. Povey writes: "The very practice of writing, the developing professionalism of his work, makes us find in Ekwensi a new and perhaps important phenomenon in African writing. By constant productivity, his style is becoming purged of its derivative excess and his plots begin to take on a less picaresque structure. Ekwensi is interesting because he is concerned with the present, with the violence of the new Lagos slums, the dishonesty of the new native politicians. Other Nigerian novelists have sought their material from the past, the history of missionaries and British administration as in Chinua Achebe's books, the schoolboy memoirs of Onuora

Nzekwu. Ekwensi faces the difficult task of catching the present tone of Africa, changing at a speed that frighteningly destroys the old certainties. In describing this world, Ekwensi has gradually become a significant writer.''

Cyprian Ekwensi states that his life in government and quasi-government organizations like the Nigerian Broadcasting Corp. has prevented him from expressing any strong political opinions, but adds, ''I am as much a nationalist as the heckler standing on the soap-box, with the added advantage of objectivity. . . .'' During the Biafran war. Ekwensi visited the United States more than once to help raise money for Biafra and to purchase radio equipment for the independent Biafran radio station of which he was director. He has also traveled in western Europe.

His novel, *Jagua Nana,* has been translated into Italian, German, Serbo-Croatian, and Portuguese, while *Burning Grass* has been translated into Russian. One of his short novels, *The Passport of Mallam Ilia,* has been published in Dutch. The short novels have been used primarily in schools as supplementary readers.

AVOCATIONAL INTERESTS: Hunting game, swimming, photography, motoring, and weight-lifting.

BIOGRAPHICAL/CRITICAL SOURCES: Critique, October, 1965; *Books Abroad,* autumn, 1967; *Contemporary Literary Criticism,* Volume IV, Gale, 1975.

* * *

EL-AYOUTY, Yassin 1928-

PERSONAL: Born April 14, 1928, in Kanayat, Sharkia, Egypt; son of Shaikh El-Sayed Mohammad (a teacher and farmer) and Aziza El-Sayed Ahmad (El-Shareef) El-Ayouty; married Grace A. Lasser (a teacher), June 17, 1970. *Education:* Teachers Institute, Zeitoun, Cairo, Egypt, Diploma, 1948; Trenton State College, B.S., 1953; Rutgers University, M.A., 1954; New York University, Ph.D., 1966. *Religion:* Muslim. *Home:* 2 Peter Cooper Rd., New York, N.Y. 10010. *Office:* Secretariat, United Nations, New York, N.Y. 10017.

CAREER: Teacher of social studies in Cairo, Egypt, 1948-52; United Nations Secretariat, New York, N.Y., staff member, 1958—, presently senior political officer. St. John's University, Jamaica, N.Y., adjunct associate professor, 1966-72, adjunct professor of African and Middle Eastern studies, 1972-73; State University of New York at Stony Brook, professor of political science, 1972—. Consultant to several colleges and universities, and to International Peace Academy Committee (IPAC). *Member:* American Political Science Association, African Studies Association (fellow), Middle East Studies Association (fellow of North American branch), American Society of International Law, Egyptian Society of Political Science. *Awards, honors:* Fulbright fellow, 1952-53; Founders Day Award, New York University, 1966.

WRITINGS: Dajjal fi Karia (novel), [Cairo], 1948; (editor with Hugh Brooks) *Refugees South of the Sahara: An African Dilemma,* Negro Universities Press, 1970; (contributor) *Report from Vienna: An Appraisal of the International Peace Academy 1970 Pilot Projects,* IPAC (New York), 1970; *The United Nations and Decolonization: The Role of Afro-Asia,* Nijhoff, 1971; (editor with Hugh Brooks) *Africa and International Organization,* Nijhoff, 1974; *The Organization of African Unity after Ten Years: Comparative Perspectives,* Praeger, 1975. Contributor to *Grolier's Encyclopedia* and to Middle Eastern and African journals published in Egypt, France, Netherlands, Switzerland, United Kingdom, and the United States.

* * *

ELCOCK, Howard J(ames) 1942-

PERSONAL: Born June 6, 1942, in Shrewsbury, England; son of George (a coal merchant) and Marion S. (Edge) Elcock. *Education:* Queen's College, Oxford, B.A., 1964, B.Phil., 1966, M.A., 1968. *Politics:* Labour Party. *Religion:* Anglican. *Home:* 30 Mizzer Rd., Hull, Humberside, England. *Agent:* M. Sissons, A. D. Peters & Co., 10 Buckingham St., London WC2N 6BU, England. *Office:* Department of Political Studies, University of Hull, Hull, Yorkshire, England.

CAREER: University of Hull, Hull, Yorkshire, England, lecturer, 1966-77, senior lecturer in political studies, 1977—. *Member:* Political Studies Association, Royal Institute of Public Administration, Fabian Society, Royal Yachting Association, Elgar Society, Yorkshire Ouse Sailing Club, Colemere Sailing Club.

WRITINGS: Administrative Justice, Longmans, Green, 1969; *Portrait of a Decision: The Council of Four and the Treaty of Versailles,* Methuen, 1972; *Political Behavior,* Methuen, 1976. Contributor to *Historical Journal, Public Administration, Public Administration Bulletin,* and *Political Studies.*

WORK IN PROGRESS: A book on local governments in England and a study of members of regional health authorities.

AVOCATIONAL INTERESTS: Dingy sailing, music.

* * *

ELIOT, George Fielding 1894-1971

June 22, 1894—April 21, 1971; American military correspondent and analyst. Obituaries: *New York Times,* April 22, 1971; *Washington Post,* April 22, 1971; *Variety,* April 28, 1971; *Antiquarian Bookman,* May 17, 1971.

* * *

ELKINS, Dov Peretz 1937-

PERSONAL: Born December 7, 1937, in Philadelphia, Pa.; married Elaine Rash, June 12, 1960; children: Hillel Michael, Jonathan Saul. *Education:* Gratz College, Teacher's Diploma, 1958; Temple University, B.A., 1959; Jewish Theological Seminary of America, M.H.L., 1962, Rabbi, 1964; Hebrew University of Jerusalem, additional study, 1962-63; Colgate Rochester Divinity School, D.Min., 1976. *Office address:* Growth Associates, Box 8429, Rochester, N.Y. 14618.

CAREER: Rabbi at Har Zion Temple, Philadelphia and Radnor, Pa., 1966-70, at Jacksonville Jewish Center, Jacksonville, Fla., 1970-72, and at Temple Beth El, Rochester, N.Y., 1972-76; Growth Associates (human relations consulting firm), Rochester, president, 1976—. Jewish chaplain, Haverford State Hospital, 1967-70; faculty member of department of theology, Villanova University, 1969-70. Consultant in couple and family therapy, individual and group counseling, and consulting for educational and industrial organizations. Member of commission of Jewish chaplaincy, National Jewish Welfare Board, 1967-70; member of board, Philadelphia Zionist Organization, 1968—. *Military service:* U.S. Army, chaplain, 1964-66. *Awards, honors:* Siegel Prize of Jewish Book Council of America for best juvenile work of

1964, for *Worlds Lost and Found: Discoveries in Biblical Archaeology;* honorary doctorate, from Colgate Rochester Divinity School, 1976.

WRITINGS: (With Azriel Eisenberg) *Worlds Lost and Found: Discoveries in Biblical Archaeology* (juvenile), Abelard, 1964; *So Young to Be a Rabbi* (essay collection), Yoseloff, 1969; (with Eisenberg) *Treasures from the Dust,* Abelard, 1972; *Rejoice with Jerusalem,* Media Judaica, 1972; *A Tradition Reborn: Sermons and Essays on Liberal Judaism,* A. S. Barnes, 1973; *God's Warriors: Heroic Stories of Jewish Military Chaplains,* Jonathan David, 1974; *Proud to Be Me: Raising Self-Esteem in Individuals, Families, Schools and Minority Groups,* Growth Associates, 1975, revised edition published as *Glad to Be Me: Raising Self-Esteem in Yourself and Others,* Prentice-Hall, 1976; *Shepherd of Jerusalem: A Biography of Chief Rabbi Abraham Isaac Kook,* Shengold, 1976; *Humanizing Jewish Life: Judaism and the Human Potential Movement,* A. S. Barnes, 1976; *Teaching People to Love Themselves: A Leader's Handbook of Theory and Technique for Self-Esteem and Affirmation Training,* Growth Associates, 1977; *Clarifying Jewish Values,* Growth Associates, 1977; *Jewish Conciousness Raising,* Growth Associates, 1977.

Sermons included in *Best Jewish Sermons,* Jonathan David, 1966 and 1968, in *Sermons on Jewish Holidays and Festivals,* National Jewish Welfare Board, 1966, and in *Sermons for Special Occasions,* Jonathan David, 1967. Columnist for Seven Arts Feature Syndicate. Contributor of articles to numerous periodicals. Editor, *Benineinu;* contributing editor, *Judaica Book Guide.* Book review editor, *Torch;* regular reviewer, *The Jewish Exponent* and *The Jewish Advocate.*

WORK IN PROGRESS: Meeting Your Jewish Self: Personal Growth for Jews; Self Concept Sourcebook, for Prentice-Hall.

SIDELIGHTS: Dov Peretz Elkins is a certified instructor for Parent Effectiveness Training (P.E.T.) and Teacher Effectiveness Training (T.E.T.).

*   *   *

ELLIOTT, E(scalus) E(mmert) III 1945-
(Chip Elliott)

PERSONAL: Born June 21, 1945, in Columbus, Ohio; son of Escalus Emmert, Jr. (an engineer) and Janet Patricia (a television director; maiden name, Berry) Elliott. *Education:* Ohio State University, B.A., 1968; Stanford University, graduate study, 1968-69. *Politics:* "R. D. Laing/Norman O. Brown/Democratic." *Religion:* "Combination Episcopal/Judaic-Unitarian/McLuhan Tim Leary and Wm. Buckley."

CAREER: Columbus Dispatch, Columbus, Ohio, reporter and assistant to city editor, 1966-68; Ohio State University, lecturer in humanities and fiction theory, 1969-70; *San Francisco Chronicle,* San Francisco, Calif., reporter, beginning 1971. *Member:* Authors Guild, Authors League of America, Sigma Delta Chi, Sigma Chi. *Awards, honors:* First place, Book-of-the-Month Club/National English Association Creative Writing Fellowship, for *Tomorrow Come Sunrise,* 1969.

WRITINGS: Tomorrow Come Sunrise, Harper, 1970. Also author of "Retrograde," an unpublished novel.

WORK IN PROGRESS: "A huge novel about the midwest—an American Comedy," titled *Scioto County.*

SIDELIGHTS: E. E. Elliott told *CA:* "I became a writer—or began writing novels—because there simply was no

other choice; it is as though I was always to do this, and I guess I knew it (I did know it) when I was about fifteen years old—which may be the Abraham Maslow self-fulfilling prophecy thing, but somewhere down in it all I have a strong belief, irrational, absurd . . . but still there, that I'm here for a purpose, and it seems as though every few months I'm struck by that belief again just to make sure I don't forget it. . . . I feel as though I haven't really started yet, that the books so far have merely been to learn how. . . . I have a stubborn but multifaceted mind—interested in literally everything—have trouble staying interested in one thing except when I ground my intelligence in a work of fiction or journalism. I tend to think in huge panoramic simultaneously occurring bits [and] fragments of experience/events that have continuity, and I write it all down."

He adds: "I love it all—I feel like I'm in an enormous hurry. But not as much of a hurry as a couple of years ago. . . . I've led a complex and wild life. . . . I harbor wonderful escapist fantasies that I know will never come true. . . . (i.e. 'disappearing' into Wyoming or the Everglades.) I'm very much against the drug/youth subculture, which I think is absurd and elitist—but I'm not necessarily against drugs. . . . I think the midwestern growing-up experience, which I lived idyllically, has contributed to what I'm about more than anything else—though that idea may be a short-lived one for me. That is, growing up 'out there' you are . . . imbued with a sense of timelessness, and the insignificance of man. A building there falls into disuse, and no one tears it down to make room for something else—time, wind, and weather change it . . . but it is still there—and you watch that effect in many ways, see it happen all around you for years. Because of that, I think, I want to write novels."

AVOCATIONAL INTERESTS: American and Russian literature, photography, film, theatre, acting, oceanography, wilderness, painting, "used to be in a folk-rock group—have pounds of poetry and half-finished songs."††

*   *   *

ELLIOTT, Kit 1936-

PERSONAL: Born October 27, 1936; son of Robert Arthur (a civil engineer) and Sybil (Scott) Elliott; married Constance Webb (a teacher), June 18, 1960; children: Nicholas, Elizabeth, Sarah, Catherine. *Education:* Attended St. John's College, Cambridge, 1955-58. *Politics:* Socialist. *Religion:* Roman Catholic. *Agent:* Curtis Brown Ltd., 1 Craven Hill, London W2 3EW, England. *Office:* Department of History, Kingswood School, Tower Hill Rd., Corby, Northampshire, England.

CAREER: Kingswood School, Corby, England, head of history department, 1967—.

WRITINGS: An African School: A Record of Experience, Cambridge University Press, 1970; *Benin,* Cambridge University Press, 1973. Also author of television and radio scripts.

WORK IN PROGRESS: Textbooks for African history; a study of Roman Catholic education in the United Kingdom.†

*   *   *

ELLISON, Jerome 1907-
(N. Emorey)

PERSONAL: Born October 29, 1907, in Maywood, Ill.; son of Earl J. (a heating and ventilation engineer) and Vera D. (Engmark) Ellison; married, 1934 (divorced, 1949); married

Miriam Train Neftel, 1950 (divorced, 1970); children: (first marriage) Jerome III (deceased), Judith; (second marriage) Julie. *Education:* Attended University of Wisconsin, 1925-26; University of Michigan B.A., 1930; Southern Connecticut State College, M.S., 1966. *Politics:* Democrat. *Religion:* Episcopalian. *Home:* 43 Wallingford Rd., Cheshire, Conn., 06410.

CAREER: Life, New York City, assistant editor and columnist, 1932-34; *Reader's Digest,* Pleasantville, N.Y, associate editor, 1935-42; *Liberty,* New York City, editor-in-chief, 1942-43; *Collier's,* New York City, managing editor, 1943-44; U.S. Office of War Information, Bureau of Overseas Publications, editorial director in New York, Washington, and London, 1944-45; New York University, New York City, lecturer at Washington Square Writer's Center, 1946; editor, *Magazine of the Year,* 1946-47; *Saturday Evening Post,* Philadelphia, Pa., article writer, 1948-62; Indiana University, Bloomington, associate professor of journalism, 1955-60; *Best Articles & Stories,* Bloomington, editor, 1957-61; University of Connecticut, Storrs, lecturer in continuing education, 1963-64; University of New Haven, West Haven, associate professor, 1964-70, professor of English and humanities, 1970-74. *Member:* Phoenix Society (president, 1973—).

WRITINGS: The Run for Your Money, Dodge Publishing, 1935; *The Prisoner Ate a Hearty Breakfast* (novel), Random House, 1939; *The Dam* (novel), Random House, 1941; *John Brown's Soul* (novel), Duell, Sloan & Pearce, 1952; *Report to the Creator* (autobiography), Harper, 1955; *Twelve,* Older Member Press, 1964; (under pseudonym N. Emorey) *A Serious Call to an American (R)Evolution,* Bulldog Books, 1967, published under own name, Berkley, 1971; *God on Broadway,* John Knox, 1971; (with Arthur Ford) *The Life Beyond Death,* Putnam, 1971; *The Last Third of Life Club,* Pilgram Publications, 1973. Contributor of short stories and articles to *McCall's, Nation, New Republic, Southwest Review, University Review,* and other periodicals; his articles have been reprinted in more than twenty anthologies.

WORK IN PROGRESS: A novel; a new book on creative aging.

SIDELIGHTS: Jerome Ellison told *CA:* "Those who labor in any form of literary creativity, and do so in good conscience and with unswerving purpose to understand and communicate the truth, are engaged in enterprise that is more than local, more than national, more than global. It is cosmic. The great labor of the cosmos is the evolution of human consciousness, and literature is the prime carrier of that upward thrust."

*   *   *

ELLWOOD, Gracia-Fay 1938-

PERSONAL: Born July 17, 1938, in Lynden, Wash.; daughter of George Lambert and Alice M. (Kok) Bouwman; married Robert Ellwood, Jr. (a professor of religion), August 28, 1965; children: Richard Scott Lancelot. *Education:* Attended Western Washington State College (now Western Washington University), 1956-57; Calvin College, B.A., 1961; University of Chicago, M.A., 1964. *Politics:* Democrat. *Religion:* Christian. *Residence:* Los Angeles, Calif.

CAREER: University of Evansville, Evansville, Ind., instructor in English; now full-time writer. *Member:* American Society for Psychical Research, Parapsychological Association, Mythopoeic Society (member of board, 1971-72; member of board of advisors, 1973—); Southern California Society for Psychical Research (board member, 1971-73).

WRITINGS: Good News from Tolkien's Middle Earth, Eerdmans, 1970; *Psychic Visits to the Past,* New American Library, 1971; *Seek a Spired Castle,* Pegana Press, 1977. Contributor to *Journal of the American Society for Psychical Research, International Journal of Parapsychology, Reformed Journal,* and *Queen of All Hearts.*

WORK IN PROGRESS: A screenplay, "Blind Journey."

SIDELIGHTS: Gracia-Fay Ellwood told *CA* that her "chief interests are psychical research, theology, and fantasy. All these are involved in my novel, *Seek a Spired Castle,* which presents the central religious symbol of rebirth, the hero-adventure, in a context of psychic events. I consider myself a generalist, a synthesizer ... the chief influence on my thought has been the writings of the English poet and novelist, Charles Williams, whose central concerns have been the place of the romantic love experience and of supernormal events in the great unity of beings."

*   *   *

ELWARD, James (Joseph) 1928-
(R. James)

PERSONAL: Surname is pronounced *el*-word; born November 22, 1928, in Chicago, Ill.; son of Joseph F. and Dasianne (Lenert) Elward. *Education:* Attended Loyola University, 1946-48; Catholic University, A.B., 1950. *Politics:* Democrat. *Religion:* Roman Catholic. *Home:* 14 Bank St., New York, N.Y. 10014. *Agent:* Joan Stewart, William Morris Agency, 1350 Avenue of the Americas, N.Y. 10019.

CAREER: Head writer and assistant writer for various television programs on all three major networks, 1956—; actor and director at various summer stock theatres, 1955-70. *Military service:* U.S. Army, 1950-52. *Member:* Actor's Equity, Players Club. *Awards, honors:* Award from Writers' Guild, 1956, for best comedy script of the year.

WRITINGS—Plays: (Contributor) *Writers Guild Anthology of Prize Television Plays* (contains television script, *Paper Foxhole*), Random House, 1956; *Upbeat* (three-act), Dramatic Publishing Co., 1960; (author of libretto) *The Man on the Bearskin Rug* (one-act opera), Boosey & Hawkes, 1963; *Friday Night* (contains three one-acts, "The River," "Passport," and "Mary Agnes Is 35," first produced Off-Broadway at Pocket Theatre, February, 1965), Dramatists Play Service, 1970; *Best of Friends* (three-act; first produced in London at Strand Theatre, February, 1970), Dramatists Play Service, 1970. Also author of two-act play, *Hallelujah!* first produced in New York at Lambs Club.

Unproduced film scripts: "Grand Alliance," "Before I Wake," and "The Long Night."

Television scripts: "The Remittance Man," produced on "Matinee Theatre," 1956; "Upbeat," produced on "U.S. Steel Hour," 1957; "Victim," produced on "U.S. Steel Hour," 1957; "Hide Me in the Mountains," networked by CBC (Canada), 1960; "Music Power," networked by ABC, September, 1968.

Television serial scripts: "Look Up and Live," and "Lamp Unto My Feet," networked by CBS, 1961-63; "The Secret Storm," networked by CBS, 1963-67; "The Young Marrieds," networked by ABC, 1964; "Love Is a Many Splendored Thing," networked by CBS, 1968; "The Guiding Light," networked by CBS, 1969; "The Doctors," networked by NBC, 1970; "Where the Heart Is," networked by CBS, 1970.

Novels; under pseudonym, R. James: *Storms End,* Doubleday, 1975; *The House Is Dark,* Doubleday, 1976.

WORK IN PROGRESS: A third novel.

*   *   *

ELY, Donald P(aul)   1930-

PERSONAL: Born September 3, 1930, in Buffalo, N.Y.; son of Paul B. and Florence (Fuller) Ely; married Martha L. Spencer (a religious educator), September 6, 1952; children: Mark, Scott, Christopher. *Education:* New York College for Teachers (now State University of New York at Albany), B.A., 1951; Syracuse University, M.A., 1953, Ph.D., 1961. *Religion:* Presbyterian. *Home:* 704 Hamilton Pkwy., Dewitt, N.Y. 13214. *Office:* School of Education, Syracuse University, Syracuse, N.Y. 13210.

CAREER: State Teachers College (now State University of New York College at New Paltz), New Paltz, N.Y., assistant professor of education, 1952-55; Hicksville Public Schools, Hicksville, N.Y., director of audiovisual education, 1955-56; Syracuse University, Syracuse, N.Y., instructor, 1956-61, assistant professor, 1961-64, associate professor, 1964-70, professor of education, 1970—, director of Center for Study Information and Education, 1972—, associate director of Audio-Visual Center, 1956-59, director, 1959-62, director of Center for Instructional Communication, 1962-71. Senior Fulbright professor, University of Chile, 1963, Consejo Nacional de la Universidad Peruana, 1976; visiting professor of education, University of Colorado, summer, 1962, Arizona State University, 1968. Member of board of trustees, Dewitt Community Library Association, 1971—. *Military service:* U.S. Army Reserve, 1951-54. *Member:* Association for Educational Communications and Technology (president, 1964-65), American Library Association, American Society for Information Science, New York State Educational Communications Association (president, 1955-56).

WRITINGS: (Editor) *The Changing Role of the Audiovisual Process in Education: A Definition and a Glossary of Related Terms,* National Education Association, 1963; (editor) *Technology-Education,* Syracuse University Press, 1967; (with James E. Alexander and Edward A. George) *Audiovisual Equipment and Facilities for Churchmen,* edited by B. F. Jackson, Volume III, Abingdon, 1970; (with Vernon S. Gerlach) *Teaching and Media: A Systematic Approach,* Prentice-Hall, 1971; (with Margaret E. Chisholm) *Media Personnel in Education: A Competency Approach,* Prentice-Hall, 1976. Contributor to *Encyclopedia of Education.* Also contributor to *Education Researcher, Audiovisual Instruction,* and other periodicals.

SIDELIGHTS: Donald Ely told *CA* that he is "active in communicating religious concepts through contemporary media." He has traveled in Europe, Latin America, and the Philippines.

*   *   *

EMANUEL, James A.   1921-

PERSONAL: Born June 14, 1921, in Alliance, Neb.; son of Alfred A. (a farmer and railroad worker) and Cora Ann (Mance) Emanuel; married Mattie Etha Johnson, 1950 (divorced, 1974); children: James A., Jr. *Education:* Howard University, A.B. (summa cum laude), 1950; Northwestern University, M.A., 1953; Columbia University, Ph.D., 1962. *Politics:* Democrat. *Office:* Department of English, City College of the City University of New York, Convent Ave. at 138th St., New York, N.Y. 10031.

CAREER: Canteen steward in Civilian Conservation Corps, Wellington, Kan., 1939-40; weighmaster with an iron company, Rock Island, Ill., 1941-42; U.S. War Department, Office of the Inspector General, Washington, D.C., confidential secretary to assistant inspector general of the Army, 1942-44; Army and Air Force Induction Station, Chicago, Ill., chief of pre-induction section (as civilian), 1950-53; YWCA Business and Secretarial School, New York City, teacher of English and commercial subjects, 1954-56; City College of the City University of New York, New York City, instructor, 1957-62, assistant professor, 1962-70, associate professor, 1970-73, professor of English, 1973—. Fulbright professor, University of Grenoble, France, 1968-69, and University of Warsaw, Poland, 1975-76. Visiting professor, University of Toulouse, France, 1971-73. Has given readings of his poetry in universities, schools, and before civic groups in America and Europe. Consultant on Black literature with New York State Education Department and boards of education, 1970. *Military service:* U.S. Army, Infantry, 1944-46; served in Netherlands, East Indies, and the Philippines; became staff sergeant; received Army Commendation Ribbon.

MEMBER: American Association of University Professors, National Association for the Advancement of Colored People. *Awards, honors:* John Hay Whitney Foundation Opportunity fellowship, 1952-54; Eugene F. Saxton Memorial Trust fellowship, 1964-65.

WRITINGS: Langston Hughes, Twayne, 1967; *The Treehouse and Other Poems,* Broadside Press, 1968; (editor with Theodore Gross) *Dark Symphony: Negro Literature in America,* Free Press, 1968; *At Bay,* Broadside Press, 1968; *Panther Man,* Broadside Press, 1970; (with McKinley Kantor and Lawrence Osgood) *How I Write/2,* Harcourt, 1972, new edition, 1975.

Poems anthologized in *Sixes and Sevens* (London), 1962, *American Negro Poetry,* 1963, *New Negro Poets: U.S.A.,* 1964, *Anthologie de la Poesie Negro-Americaine: 1770-1965* (Paris), 1966, *Kaleidoscope: Poems by American Negro Poets,* 1967, and about seventy-five other volumes. General editor, "Broadside Critics" series on Black poetry. About ninety poems have been published in periodicals, including *Phylon, Negro Digest, Renaissance,* and *Imprints Quarterly;* also contributor of book reviews to *Books Abroad* and *New York Times Book Review,* and of articles to scholarly journals.

WORK IN PROGRESS: A book on selected Black poets, developing from the course in Negro poetry he introduced at City College of the City University of New York; a third volume of poems, tentatively entitled *Black Tender.*

SIDELIGHTS: James Emanuel told a *Black World* writer: "A writer's best art will always be a rendering of his most profound experience. For a Black writer who is honest, that experience is essentially molded by his race at the most crucial point of his life. 'Black experience' is the most 'American' experience that a Black writer can have. The moral meaning of the America of the future will reveal itself first to Black writers in the act of facing themselves." Emanuel's poems have been read on a British Broadcasting Corp. program in England, on the Voice of America program, "The Whole World Is Listening," used in the Broadway show, "A Hand Is on the Gate," and included in dramatic presentations on the college circuit. His greatest satisfaction, though, came from writing *Langston Hughes,* "a book evolving from my racial pride."

Emanuel's own readings have taken him to Africa, England, France, Austria, Poland, Hungary, Romania, and elsewhere in Europe, where much of his poetry and prose since 1970 has been written. "My European experiences," he now says, "have confirmed my faith in literary art and in Blackness as one of its deepest sources."

BIOGRAPHICAL/CRITICAL SOURCES: Negro Digest, April, 1965, June, 1966, January, 1968, January, 1969; *Times Literary Supplement,* July 8, 1965; *Negro American Literature Forum,* Volume I, number 1, fall, 1967; *Nation,* December 4, 1967; *New York Times Book Review,* November 26, 1968; *Ramparts,* October, 1969; *Road Apple Review,* winter, 1971-72; *The Paperback,* University of Warsaw, June, 1976.

*   *   *

EMERY, David A(mos)   1920-

PERSONAL: Born August 4, 1920, in Des Moines, Iowa; son of Amos Barton (an architect) and Alice (Cusson) Emery; married Gertrude Courant, May 5, 1944; married second wife, Beatrice Landshoff, March 11, 1950; children: Richard, Joan, Susan, Christopher, Laurie. *Education:* Haverford College, B.S., 1942; Swarthmore College, M.A., 1945; Massachusetts Institute of Technology, Ph.D., 1948.

CAREER: New School for Social Research, New York City, associate professor of psychology, 1947-51; Research Institute of America, New York City, editor and psychologist, 1951-54; conference director, American Management Association, 1954-55; General Electric Co., Ossining, N.Y., consultant, 1955-61; Kepner-Tregoe Associates, Princeton, N.J., associate, 1961-65; International Business Machines Corp., Sands Point, N.Y., program director, 1966-75; director, National Development Corp., Tanzania, beginning 1975. Professor of industrial psychology, Long Island University, 1969-70; professor of management communications, Fairfield University, 1970. *Military service:* American Field Service, warrant officer, 1942-43. *Member:* American Psychological Association, New York State Psychological Association, New York Academy of Science, Sigma Xi.

WRITINGS: The Complete Manager: Combining the Humanistic and Scientific Approaches to the Management Job, McGraw, 1970. Also author of *Executive Communication Dynamics,* 1972. Contributor of numerous publications in scientific and business journals.

WORK IN PROGRESS: The Mature Executive, for McGraw.

SIDELIGHTS: David A. Emery told *CA* that his primary work objective is to improve man's work environment to increase productivity *and* intrinsic value of [the] task for the individual. *Avocational interests:* Surfing, skiing, flying.†

*   *   *

EMMITT, Robert (P.)   1925-

PERSONAL: Born February 8, 1925, in Akron, Ohio; son of Stanley William (a civil engineer) and Helen (Parker) Emmitt; married Ann Roy, December 8, 1946; married second wife, Jean Heith, August 26, 1955; children: Marta Ellen, David Heith, Andrew Gordon Treat, Susannah Ruth. *Education:* Attended University of Colorado, 1941-45. *Politics:* Independent. *Religion:* Episcopalian. *Home:* 1544 Lee Hill Rd., Boulder, Colo. 80302.

CAREER: New York Herald Tribune, New York, N.Y., copy editor, 1954-58; *Toronto Telegram,* Toronto, Ontario, copy editor, 1958-60; *Tucson Citizen,* Tucson, Ariz., copy editor, 1961-65; Vanderbilt University Press, Nashville, Tenn., managing editor, beginning 1965.

WRITINGS: The Last War Trail: The Utes and the Settlement of Colorado, University of Oklahoma Press, 1954; *The Legend of Ogden Jenks,* McNally & Loftin, 1970.

WORK IN PROGRESS: Actaeon Homeward (working title), a novel.

SIDELIGHTS: "I consider myself a follower of Unamuno, Berdyaev, and Tillich," Robert Emmitt writes, "although I like to think that I am not a slavish follower of anybody.... As a 'Christian existentialist' (a term I reject on the face of it but use for succinct communication here), I am concerned with the total condition of estrangement and, as an American historian, with the problem of man's estrangement from his natural environment as the tragedy re-enacted in the 300 years of American history."

AVOCATIONAL INTERESTS: Hunting, fishing, archery, horsemanship, camping, and other outdoor pursuits.†

*   *   *

EMPEY, LaMar T.   1923-

PERSONAL: Born April 9, 1923, in Price, Utah; son of Claudius M. (a banker) and Mabel (Taylor) Empey; married Betty Mitchell, August 25, 1949; children: John, Kathleen, Martha, James. *Education:* Brigham Young University, B.A., 1950, M.A., 1951; Washington State University, Ph.D., 1955. *Politics:* Democrat. *Religion:* None. *Home:* 5170 Veronica, Los Angeles, Calif. 90008. *Office:* Department of Sociology, University of Southern California, Los Angeles, Calif. 90007.

CAREER: Brigham Young University, Provo, Utah, assistant professor, 1955-57, associate professor of sociology, 1958-62; University of Southern California, Los Angeles, associate professor, 1962-67, professor of sociology, 1967—, chairman of department of sociology, 1967-71, research director of Gerontology Center, 1971-74. Senior research associate, Youth Studies Center, 1963-64, director, 1964-67. Consultant, President's Committee on Juvenile Delinquency and Youth Crime, 1961-64, President's Commission on Law Enforcement and Administration of Justice, 1966-67; also consultant to various state and federal government departments and commissions. Member, research advisory committee, California Department of Mental Hygiene. *Military service:* U.S. Army, infantry, 1943-46; became first lieutenant. U.S. Army Reserves, 1946-52; became captain.

MEMBER: American Sociological Association, American Society of Criminology, Society for the Study of Social Problems, Pacific Sociological Association (vice-president, 1967-68, 1970-71), Phi Beta Kappa, Phi Kappa Phi. *Awards, honors:* Research grants, Ford Foundation, Rosenberg Foundation, Office of Juvenile Delinquency, National Science Foundation, and National Institute of Mental Health, 1959-77.

WRITINGS: Alternatives to Incarceration, U.S. Government Printing Office, 1967; (with Anthony J. Manocchio and Jimmy Dunn) *The Time Game: Two Views of a Prison,* Sage Publications, 1970; (with Steven G. Lubeck) *The Silverlake Experiment: Testing Delinquency Theory and Community Intervention,* Aldine, 1971; (with Lubeck) *Explaining Delinquency,* Heath, 1971; (with Maynard L. Erickson) *The Provo Experiment: Impact and Death of an Innovation,* Lexington Books, 1972. Contributor to *American Sociological Review, Sociological Problems, Journal of Research in Crime and Delinquency.* Associate editor, *American Sociological Review, Sociology and Social Research.*

WORK IN PROGRESS: American Delinquency: Its Meaning and Construction; editing *Juvenile Justice: The Progressive Legacy and Current Reforms.*

SIDELIGHTS: LaMar T. Empey told *CA:* "[I] have been interested primarily in youth and their problems. Like many of my contemporaries, I have concentrated on the scientific study of delinquency and juvenile justice. My recent work, however, convinces me that we have often been off target because of our failure to grasp the significance of broad historical and cultural changes. Our current preoccupation with childhood in Western Civilization is a product of the last two or three centuries. Furthermore, that preoccupation is now undergoing radical change. As a result, the status of youth will be altered and, with it, will come sharp changes in our perceptions of, and reactions to, them."

* * *

ENDO, Shusaku 1923-

PERSONAL: Born March 27, 1923, in Tokyo, Japan; son of Tsunehisa and Iku (Takei) Endo; married Junko Okada, September 3, 1955; children: Ryunosuke (son). *Education:* Keio University, Tokyo, B.A., 1949; Lyon University, Lyon, France, student in French literature, 1950-53. *Religion:* Roman Catholic. *Home:* 2-3-35 Tamagawa-gakuen, Machidashi, Tokyo, Japan 194.

MEMBER: International P.E.N. (member of executive committee of Japanese centre, 1969), Association of Japanese Writers (member of executive committee, 1966). *Awards, honors:* Akutagawa prize (Japan), 1955, for *Shiroihito;* Tanizaki prize (Japan), 1967, and Gru de Oficial da Ordem do Infante dom Henrique (Portugal), 1968, both for *Chinmoku;* Sancti Silvestri, awarded by Pope Paul VI, 1970.

WRITINGS: Shiroihito (novel), Kodansha (Tokyo), 1955; *Umi to Dokuyaku* (novel), Bungeishunju, 1958, translation by M. Gallagher published as *The Sea and Poison,* P. Owen, 1971; *Chinmoku* (novel), Shinkosha (Tokyo), 1966, translation by William Johnston published as *Silence,* P. Owen, 1969; *Seisho no Naka no Joseitachi* (essay; title means "Women in the Bible"), Shinkosha, 1968; *Ougon no Kuni* (play), Shinkosha, 1969, translation by Francis Mathy published as *The Golden Country,* Tuttle (Tokyo), 1970; *Bara no Yakata* (play), Shinkosha, 1969.

WORK IN PROGRESS: A novel, *Shikai no Hotori* (title means "By the Dead Sea").

SIDELIGHTS: Shusaku Endo told *CA* he is interested in the "confrontation and harmony of the oriental 'climat' and Christianity, [and the] difference in conception between the Orient and the Occident."

BIOGRAPHICAL/CRITICAL SOURCES: Tomoju Takeda, *Endo Shusaku no Sekai,* Chuo Suppansha (Tokyo), 1969; *Contemporary Literary Criticism,* Volume VII, Gale, 1977.

* * *

ENGDAHL, Sylvia Louise 1933-

PERSONAL: Born November 24, 1933, in Los Angeles, Calif.; daughter of Amandus J. and Mildred Allen (a writer under her maiden name of Butler) Engdahl. *Education:* Attended Pomona College, 1950, Reed College, 1951, and University of Oregon, 1951-52; University of California, Santa Barbara, A.B., 1955; University of Oregon Extension, additional study, 1956-57. *Religion:* Episcopalian. *Address:* Box 153, Garden Home P.O., Portland, Ore. 97223.

CAREER: Elementary teacher in Portland, Ore., 1955-56; System Development Corp. (computer programming for SAGE Air Defense System), 1957-67, began as programmer, became computer systems specialist, working in Lexington, Mass., Madison, Wis., Tacoma, Wash., and Santa Monica, Calif.; full-time writer, 1967—. *Awards, honors: Enchantress from the Stars* was a 1971 Newbery honor book.

WRITINGS—Novels for young people, except as indicated; all published by Atheneum: *Enchantress from the Stars* (Junior Literary Guild selection), 1970; *Journey between Worlds,* 1970; *The Far Side of Evil,* 1971; *This Star Shall Abide,* 1972; *Beyond the Tomorrow Mountains,* 1973; *The Planet-Girded Suns: Man's View of Other Solar Systems* (nonfiction), 1974; (co-editor) *Universe Ahead: Stories of the Future* (anthology), 1975; (editor) *Anywhere, Anywhen: Stories of Tomorrow* (anthology), 1976; (co-author) *The Subnuclear Zoo: New Discoveries in High Energy Physics* (nonfiction), 1977.

WORK IN PROGRESS: A novel for young people; a more scholarly presentation of the historical research material summarized in *The Planet-Girded Sun,* for possible university press publication.

SIDELIGHTS: As a writer, Sylvia Engdahl aims to "bring present-day issues into perspective through speculation about the future as related to the past, with particular emphasis on space exploration, which I believe to be the most significant challenge facing the human race and the only long-range goal that will unite mankind in peace.... It is also my belief that today's tendency to equate realism with pessimism is invalid. My science fiction is not intended for fans of that genre; rather, it is directed primarily to young people, who are less interested in the typical space adventure than in the problems that might confront individuals of hypothetical worlds, and deals not so much with technological progress as with the human values I consider important."

BIOGRAPHICAL/CRITICAL SOURCES: Children's Literature Review, Volume II, Gale, 1976.

* * *

ENGLISH, (Emma) Jean M(artin) 1937-

PERSONAL: Born July 5, 1937, in Young Harris, Ga.; daughter of Sim Hoover (a minister) and Ruby (Welch) Martin; married John Clifford English (a businessman), June 20, 1959 (divorced, 1974). *Education:* Attended Truett-McConnell Junior College, 1955-56; Tift College, B.A., 1959; University of Georgia, M.F.A., 1965; Florida State University, Ph.D., 1969. *Home:* 1212 Francisco Dr., Tallahassee, Fla. 32304. *Office:* Department of Fine Arts, Tallahasse Community College, 444 Appleyard Dr., Tallahassee, Fla. 32304.

CAREER: Greenville County Schools, Greenville, S.C., teacher of English, 1959-62; Young Harris College, Young Harris, Ga., director of theater and instructor in speech and English, 1962-66; Western Carolina University, Cullowhee, instructor in English, speech, and journalism, 1966-67; Florida State University School, Tallahassee, director of theater and instructor in English, 1967-68; Tallahassee Community College, Tallahassee, Fla., director of drama and theater and instructor in English, 1968—. Member, State of Florida Art Educational Television Committee, 1968—. *Member:* American Educational Theatre Association, Southern Speech Association, Southeastern Theatre Conference, Florida Film Study Conference, Tallahassee Little

Theatre (member of board of directors), Delta Kappa Gamma. *Awards, honors:* First place award, Georgia Fine Arts Festival, 1965.

WRITINGS: Handbook for Readers and Writers, C. E. Merrill, 1968; *From Thesis to Theme,* Scott, Foresman, 1970. Also author of *Strindberg's Women,* 1965, and *Edward Albee: Theory Theme, and Technique,* 1969.

WORK IN PROGRESS: How to Write and Sell Textbooks; Blue Prints for Writing.

*   *   *

ENGQUIST, Richard 1933-

PERSONAL: Born April 26, 1933, in Scandia, Minn.; son of Albert Rodney and Anna (Monson) Engquist; married Jane E. Brody (a medical writer), October 2, 1966; children: Lee Erik and Lorin Michael (twins). *Education:* Hamline University, B.A. (magna cum laude), 1954. *Politics:* Independent. *Religion:* Christian. *Home:* 536 Third St., Brooklyn, N.Y. 11215.

CAREER: Gustavus Adolphus Lutheran Church, New York City, parish secretary, 1956-58; Faith at Work, Inc. (inter-church agency), New York City, associate editor, 1958-63, 1966-71. *Member:* American Guild of Authors and Composers, Dramatists Guild, Broadcast Music Incorporated.

WRITINGS: (Editor) *Living the Great Adventure,* Word, Inc., 1967; (editor) *The Emerging Church,* Word, Inc., 1970; (with Jane E. Brody) *Secrets of Good Health,* Popular Library, 1970; (editor) *Is Anyone for Real?,* Word, Inc., 1971; (editor) *Today Is All You Have,* Zondervan, 1971; (co-author) *The Miracle Goes On,* Zondervan, 1976.

*   *   *

ENTWISTLE, Harold 1923-

PERSONAL: Born December 24, 1923, in Manchester, England; married Winifred Hartley (a teacher), July 23, 1955; children: David Giles. *Education:* Institute of Education, University of Sheffield, Certificate in Education, 1949; University of London, B.Sc., 1953, Academic Diploma in Education (distinction), 1955, Ph.D., 1956; University of Manchester, M.Ed., 1958. *Home:* 149 Westminster Ave., Montreal West, Quebec, Canada H4X 123. *Office:* Sir George Williams University, Montreal 107, Quebec, Canada.

CAREER: Teacher in primary and secondary schools in Manchester, England, 1949-58; City of Leeds Training College, Leeds, England, lecturer in education, 1958-60; James Graham College of Education, Leeds, England, senior lecturer in education and head of department, 1960-62; University of Manchester, Manchester, England, lecturer in education, 1962-69; Sir George Williams University, Montreal, Quebec, associate professor, 1969-73, professor of education, 1973—. Visiting professor, University of Bristol, 1975-76. *Military service:* British Army, Royal Tank Regiment, 1942-47; served in Italy and northwestern Europe. *Member:* Philosophy of Education Society (Great Britain; founding member), Philosophy of Education Society (United States; fellow), Canadian Association of Professors in Education, American Education Association, Comparative Education Society (Canada), Comparative Education Society (United States), Comparative Education Society of Europe.

WRITINGS: Education, Work and Leisure, Humanities, 1970; *Child-Centered Education,* Barnes & Noble, 1970; *Political Education in a Democracy,* Routledge & Kegan Paul, 1971; *Class, Culture and Education,* Methuen, 1977.

Contributor: *Teaching Economics,* Economics Association (London), 1967; D. B. Heater, editor, *The Teaching of Politics,* Methuen, 1969; J. W. Tibble, editor, *Education: An Outline for the Intending Student,* Routledge & Kegan Paul, 1971; Hartnett and Naish, editors, *The Theory and Practice in Education,* Heinemann, 1976. Contributor to *Times Educational Supplement* and education journals. Member of editorial board, *Research in Education* (University of Manchester).

SIDELIGHTS: Harold Entwistle has generally been on the progressive and liberal wing of religious, political, social and cultural issues, but now is "convinced of value of traditional culture as basis of education, but equally convinced that this ought not to be the esoteric possession of an elite. . . ."

*   *   *

EPP, Frank H(enry) 1929-

PERSONAL: Born May 26, 1929, in Lena, Manitoba, Canada; son of Henry M. (a minister) and Anna (Enns) Epp; married Helen L. Dick (a secretary), June 27, 1953; children: Marianne, Esther, Marlene. *Education:* Attended Vancouver Teachers College, 1948-49; Canadian Mennonite Bible College, B.Th., 1953; Bethel College, North Newton, Kan., B.A., 1956; University of Minnesota, M.A., 1960, Ph.D., 1965, LL.D., 1975. *Office:* Conrad Grebel College, University of Waterloo, Waterloo, Ontario, Canada.

CAREER: Elementary school teacher in British Columbia, 1949-50; *Canadian Mennonite,* Winnipeg, Manitoba, editor and general manager, 1953-67; free-lance writer and lecturer, Ottawa, Ontario, 1967-71; University of Waterloo, Conrad Grebel College, Waterloo, Ontario, associate professor of history and communications, 1971—, president of college, 1973—. Member of advisory board for the Adjustment of Immigrants of the Minister for Manpower and Immigration. Has lectured throughout Canada, and in United States and eight foreign countries at colleges, and for civic and religious organizations. *Member:* World Federalists of Canada, Mennonite Central Committee, Mennonite World Conference Praesidium.

WRITINGS: Mennonite Exodus: The Rescue and Resettlement of the Russian Mennonites since the Communist Revolution, D. W. Frieson, 1962; *Your Neighbour as Yourself: A Study on Responsibility in Immigration,* Mennonite Central Committee, 1968; *The Glory and the Shame: Editorials on the Past, Present, and Future of the Mennonite Church,* Canadian Mennonite Publishing Co., 1968; *I Would Like to Dodge the Draft-Dodgers, But . . .,* [Winnipeg], 1970; *Whose Land Is Palestine?: The Middle East Problem in Historical Perspective,* Eerdmans, 1970; *Strategy for Peace,* Eerdmans, 1970; *Mennonites in Canada: The History of a Separate People,* Macmillan, 1974; *Education with a Plus,* Conrad Press, 1975; *The Palestinians: Portrait of a People in Conflict,* McClelland & Stewart, 1976; *Mennonite Peoplehood: A Plea for New Initiatives,* Conrad Press, 1977.

Contributor: Cornelius J. Dyck, editor, *An Introduction to Mennonite History: A Popular History of the Anabaptists and the Mennonites,* Herald Press, 1967; John A. Lapp, editor, *Peacemakers in a Broken World,* Herald Press, 1969; Richard Marshall, editor, *Aspects of Religion in the Soviet Union,* University of Chicago Press, 1970; John H. Redekop, editor, *Canada and the U.S.,* Peter Martin, 1971.

Contributor to *Canadian Mennonite, Mennonite Quarterly Review, Mennonite Life, World Federalist, Winnipeg Free Press, Ottawa Citizen,* and other publications.

WORK IN PROGRESS: Mennonites in Canada, 1921-50; The Israelis: Portrait of a People in Conflict.

SIDELIGHTS: Frank Epp's interests lie with twentieth-century issues, including Canadian immigration minorities, the U.S.S.R., the Middle East, and the mass media. He has traveled abroad annually since 1966, visiting various countries in Asia, Europe, the Middle East, Latin America, and the Far East.

* * *

EPSTEIN, Cynthia Fuchs 1933-

PERSONAL: Born November 9, 1933, in New York, N.Y.; daughter of Jesse I. and Birdie (Seider) Fuchs; married Howard Epstein (an editor), July 3, 1954; children: Alexander Maxim. Education: Antioch College, B.A., 1955; University of Chicago, law student, 1955-56; New School for Social Research, M.A., 1960; Columbia University, Ph.D., 1968. Home: 425 Riverside Dr., New York, N.Y. 10025. Office: Department of Sociology, Queens College of the City University of New York, Flushing, N.Y. 11367.

CAREER: Researcher for Science Research Associates, New York City, 1956-57, and Save the Children Federation, New York City, 1957; Hadassah, the Women's Zionist Organization of America, New York City, program writer, 1957-60; instructor in sociology at Finch College, New York City, 1961-62, and Barnard College, New York City, 1965; Queens College of the City University of New York, Flushing, N.Y., instructor, 1966-67, became assistant professor, 1968, now professor of sociology. Senior research associate, Columbia University, Bureau of Applied Social Research; research associate, Center for Policy Research, New York. Member: American Sociological Association, American Association for the Advancement of Science, Eastern Sociological Society.

WRITINGS: Woman's Place: Options and Limits of Professional Careers, University of California Press, 1970; (editor with William J. Goode) The Other Half: Roads to Women's Equality, Prentice-Hall, 1971. Contributor to Dissent and Social Policy and to sociology journals.

* * *

EPSTEIN, Erwin H(oward) 1939-

PERSONAL: Born January 2, 1939, in Chicago, Ill.; son of Louis Nathan (an attorney) and Charlotte (Kozin) Epstein; married Barbara Robbin (a teacher), September 3, 1961; children: Jack, Eric, Maury. Education: University of Illinois, B.A. (with honors), 1960; University of Chicago, M.A.T., 1962, Ph.D., 1966. Religion: Jewish. Residence: Rolla, Mo. Office: Department of Social Sciences, University of Missouri, Rolla, Mo. 65401.

CAREER: Public school teacher in Skokie, Ill., 1961-62; University of Wisconsin—Madison, assistant professor of education, 1965-71; Kearney State College, Kearney, Neb., associate professor and head of sociology department, 1971-73; University of Missouri—Rolla, professor of sociology and chairman of department of social sciences, 1973—. Director, Workshop on Educational Problems of Minority Children, University of Wisconsin Extension Program, 1970. Participant in seminars and commissions on education. Lecturer to professional, student, and civic groups. Member: American Sociological Association, Comparative and International Education Society, American Educational Studies Association, Council on Anthropology and Education, Rural Sociological Society, Latin American Studies Association. Awards, honors: Research grant, University of Wisconsin Graduate School and Ibero-American Studies Program, 1966-67; Rockefeller Foundation grant, 1967-69; University of Wisconsin Graduate School grant, 1969-70; National Research Council grant, 1971-73.

WRITINGS: Value Orientation and the English Language in Puerto Rico: Attitudes toward Second Language Learning among Ninth-Grade Pupils and Their Parents, Cooperative Research Branch, U.S. Office of Education, 1966; (editor with Andreas Michael Kazamias) Schools in Transition: Essays in Comparative Education, Allyn & Bacon, 1968; (editor) Politics and Education in Puerto Rico: A Documentary Survey of the Language Issue, Scarecrow, 1970; Extra-Societal Effects on Academic Performance, UNESCO Institute for Education (Hamburg), 1970; (contributor) Ayers Bagley, editor, Making Teacher Education More Relevant, Society of Professors of Education, 1970; (with Burton A. Weisbrod and others) Disease and Economic Development, University of Wisconsin Press, 1973. Anthologized in Education in Latin America and the Caribbean, edited by Thomas J. LaBelle, Latin American Center, University of California, 1971. Contributor to Comparative Education Review, International Journal of Comparative Sociology, Educational Forum, Educational Studies, Cuadernas Vieus, Interamericana Review, Education and Urban Society, Theory and Society, Social and Economic Studies, and International Review of Social Economics.

WORK IN PROGRESS: Parasitic Disease and Academic Performance of School Children; American Educational Colonialism in Cuba; and The Nation Indivisible: Public Education and the Decline of Pluralism.

SIDELIGHTS: Erwin Epstein lists his academic interests as comparative education and sociology, colonialism, human ecology, nationalism, and ethnic minorities. He has traveled to Puerto Rico to "study sense of nationality among school children, Peru and Bolivia to study acculturation among Indian school children, [and] West Indies to study effects of disease on academic performance." He is also the author of the "filter-effect" theory in education, a hypothesis "which postulates that schools at the periphery of national culture are likely to be relatively effective in screening out unfavorable images of the national society."

* * *

ERDMAN, Nikolai R. 1902(?)-1970

1902(?)—August 10, 1970; Soviet playwright and author of film scripts. Obituaries: New York Times, August 12, 1970; Variety, August 19, 1970.

* * *

ERDOS, Paul L(ouis) 1914-

PERSONAL: Born April 11, 1914, in Budapest, Hungary; son of Armand (a publisher) and Aranka (Hartmann) Erdos; married Helen Weiss (a designer), April 22, 1950. Education: Attended University of Heidelberg, University of Zurich, Sorbonne, University of Paris, and University of Exeter, 1932-35; University of Pecs, Ph.D., 1937. Home: 3 Sheridan Sq., New York, N.Y. 10014. Office: Erdos & Morgan, Inc., 114 Fifth Ave., New York, N.Y. 10011.

CAREER: Held various positions as literary agent and in market research, data processing, and publishing, 1939-42; Fact Finders, Inc. (market research firm), New York City, office manager, 1942-47; Erdos & Morgan, Inc. (market research firm), New York City, president and partner, 1947—.

Part-time lecturer, Graduate School of Business Administration, University of Michigan. *Member:* World Association for Public Opinion Research, Sociedad Mexicana de Antropologia (Mexico), American Marketing Association, American Association for Public Opinion Research, Advertising Research Foundation, Archaeological Institute of America.

WRITINGS: (Contributor) Parker M. Holmes, *Marketing Research Principles and Readings,* South-Western, 1960; (with A. J. Morgan) *Professional Mail Surveys,* McGraw, 1970; (contributor) Robert Ferber, editor, *Handbook of Marketing Research,* McGraw, 1974. Contributor to trade publications in U.S. and Mexico.

AVOCATIONAL INTERESTS: Pre-Columbian archaeology, collector of Pre-Columbian, Greek, and Etruscan pottery.

*   *   *

ERICKSEN, Gerald L(awrence) 1931-

PERSONAL: Born October 13, 1931, in Chicago, Ill.; son of Edwin L. and Edith D. (Tyrrell) Ericksen; married Claire Grady, July 11, 1953; children: Joan Nancy, Karl Frederick. *Education:* Macalester College, student, 1949-51; University of North Dakota, Ph.B., 1951; University of Minnesota, M.A., 1953, Ph.D., 1962. *Residence:* Northfield, Minn. *Office:* Department of Psychology, St. Olaf College, Northfield, Minn. 55057.

CAREER: Sperry Rand Corp., St. Paul, Minn., mathematician, 1953-62; University of Nebraska, Omaha, assistant professor of psychology, 1962-63; St. Olaf College, Northfield, Minn., assistant professor, 1963-67, associate professor, 1967-71, professor of psychology, 1971—, chairman of department of psychology, 1967—. Consulting statistician, Minnesota State Department of Education. *Member:* American Psychological Association, American Association of University Professors, American Educational Research Association, National Council of Measurement in Education.

WRITINGS: Scientific Inquiry in the Behavioral Sciences: An Introduction to Statistics, Scott, Foresman, 1970. Contributor to sixth and seventh editions, *Mental Measurements Yearbook.*

WORK IN PROGRESS: Curriculum development centering on experimental designs for undergraduates.

SIDELIGHTS: Gerald L. Ericksen lists his major vocational interests as statistics, research design, and introductory psychology. He has traveled in South America, Europe, and the Canary Islands. *Avocational interests:* Sailing, golf, hiking.

*   *   *

ERICKSON, Donald A(rthur) 1925-

PERSONAL: Born June 27, 1925, in Saskatoon, Saskatchewan, Canada; son of Joseph A. and Pearl (Stephenson) Erickson; married Phyllis Mundt, November 29, 1949; children: Roddy Wayne. *Education:* Bob Jones University, B.A., 1954; University of Chicago, M.A., 1960, Ph.D., 1962. *Office:* Faculty of Education, Simon Fraser University, Burnaby, British Columbia, Canada V5A 156.

CAREER: Florida State University, Tallahassee, assistant professor of education, 1962-63; University of Chicago, Chicago, Ill., assistant professor, 1963-67, associate professor, 1967-73, professor of education, beginning 1973; cur-

rently member of faculty of education, Simon Fraser University, Burnaby, British Columbia, Canada. Consultant to U.S. Office of Economic Opportunity, beginning 1966, to Educational Testing Service, 1969, and to Bureau of Indian Affairs and public school systems. *Member:* American Educational Research Association, American Association of School Administrators, National Conference of Professors of Educational Administration, National Organization on Legal Problems in Education, National Committee for Amish Religious Freedom, Phi Delta Kappa. *Awards, honors:* Danforth Foundation grants, 1966, 1967; U.S. Office of Economic Opportunity grant to study Rough Rock Demonstration School on a Navaho Reservation, 1968; State of Illinois grant to study nonpublic schools in the state, 1970; U.S. Office of Education grant for national study of nonpublic schools for President's Commission on School Finance, 1971.

WRITINGS: (Editor) *Public Controls for Nonpublic Schools,* University of Chicago Press, 1969; (editor and contributor) *Crisis in Illinois Nonpublic Schools,* [Springfield], 1970; (with John D. Donovan) *The Three R's of Nonpublic Education in Louisiana: Race, Religion, and Region,* Office of Education, U.S. Department of Health, Education, and Welfare, 1972. Also author of numerous reports on education to various federal, state, and local government agencies.

Contributor: Erwin Miklos, editor, *Program and Personnel: The Lecture Series of the 1965 Leadership Course for School Principals,* University of Alberta Press, 1965; Richard I. Miller, *The Nongraded School: Analysis and Study,* Harper, 1967; Robert J. Havighurst, editor, *Metropolitanism: Its Challenge to Education,* National Society for the Study of Education, 1968; Richard W. Saxe, editor, *Perspectives on the Changing Role of the Principal,* C. C Thomas, 1968; J. Alan Thomas, *School Finance and Educational Opportunity in Michigan,* Michigan Department of Education, 1968; Henry M. Brickell, *Nonpublic Education in Rhode Island: Alternatives for the Future,* Rhode Island Special Commission to Study the Entire Field of Education, 1969; John D. Donovan, editor, *The Social and Religious Sources of the Crisis in Catholic Schools,* Center for Field Research and School Services, Boston College, 1971. Contributor of about forty articles to magazines and professional journals. Editor, *1965 Program Abstracts,* American Educational Research Association; has done editorial work on other education journals.

WORK IN PROGRESS: Editing a volume of research readings on educational organization and administration, for Wiley; editing and writing a section for *Major Studies of Nonpublic Education;* a book on the issue of aid to nonpublic schools; case studies of conflicts between the Amish and educational authorities.

BIOGRAPHICAL/CRITICAL SOURCES: Saturday Review, June 21, 1969.†

*   *   *

ERICKSON, Keith V. 1943-

PERSONAL: Born June 30, 1943, in Vancouver, Wash.; son of Keith M. and Rosamond E. Erickson; married Susan E. Berkowitz (a teacher), September 27, 1967. *Education:* Washington State University, B.A., 1965; Pennsylvania State University, M.A., 1967; University of Michigan, Ed.D., 1972. *Office:* Department of Speech, Texas Tech University, Lubbock, Tex. 79409.

CAREER: University of Houston, Houston, Tex., instructor in speech, 1969-70; University of Michigan, Ann

Arbor, instructor in speech, 1970-73; Texas Tech University, Lubbock, associate professor of speech, 1973—. *Member:* Speech Communication Association, American Forensics Association, Central States Speech Association, Delta Sigma Rho, Pi Kappa Alpha, Pi Kappa Phi.

WRITINGS: Communicative Rhetoric, McCutcheon, 1968; *Dimensions of Oral Communication Instruction: Readings in Speech Education,* W. C. Brown, 1970; *Aristotle: The Classical Heritage of Rhetoric,* Scarecrow, 1974; *Aristotle's Rhetoric: Five Centuries of Philological Research,* Scarecrow, 1975; *Plato: True and Sophistic Rhetoric,* Editions Rodopi (Netherlands), in press.

* * *

ERVIN, Janet Halliday 1923-

PERSONAL: Born May 29, 1923, in Muncie, Ind.; daughter of Everett Clayton and Lois (Kidnocker) Halliday; married Howard G. Ervin (a sales manager), July 3, 1946; children: Howard III, Dennis, David. *Education:* University of Chicago, Ph.B., 1946. *Religion:* Presbyterian. *Home:* 2450 North 97th St., Wauwatosa, Wis. 53226. *Agent:* Scott Meredith Literary Agency, Inc., 845 Third Ave., New York, N.Y. 10022.

CAREER: Muncie Evening Press, Muncie, Ind., reporter, 1941-44; free-lance writer. *Member:* Mensa, Council for Wisconsin Writers, Women in Communications, University of Chicago Alumni, Milwaukee Fictioneers. *Awards, honors: Vogue* Prix de Paris, 1946; Friends of American Writers juvenile book award, 1972.

WRITINGS: The White House Cook Book, Follett, 1964; *The Last Trip of the Juno* (juvenile), Follett, 1970; *More than Half Way There* (juvenile), Follett, 1970. Author of column, "Keeping Up with Janet," for the *Toledo Blade;* guest editor-in-chief, *Mademoiselle,* 1945; contributor of teen-age fiction and articles to women's magazines.

AVOCATIONAL INTERESTS: Art, antiques, American history, conservation, the Head Start program.

* * *

ERVINE, St. John Greer 1883-1971

December 28, 1883—January 24, 1971; Irish playwright, novelist, biographer, and critic. Obituaries: *New York Times,* January 25, 1971; *Variety,* January 27, 1971; *Publishers' Weekly,* February 8, 1971.

* * *

ERWIN, Edward (James) 1937-

PERSONAL: Born December 4, 1937, in Brooklyn, N.Y.; son of Joseph W. and Ruth (McGee) Erwin; married Patricia Summers, December 31, 1969. *Education:* City College of the City University of New York, B.B.A., 1960, M.A., 1966; Johns Hopkins University, Ph.D., 1969. *Home:* 9143 Southwest 77th Ave., Miami, Fla. 33156. *Office:* Department of Philosophy, University of Miami, Coral Gables, Fla. 33124.

CAREER: State University of New York at Stony Brook, assistant professor of philosophy, 1968-73; University of Miami, Coral Gables, Fla., professor of philosophy, 1973—. *Member:* American Philosophical Association.

WRITINGS: The Concept of Meaninglessness, Johns Hopkins Press, 1970. Contributor to *Philosophical Studies, Canadian Journal of Philosophy, Boston Studies in the Philosophy of Science,* and *Australian Journal of Philosophy.*

WORK IN PROGRESS: Behavior Therapy: Philosophical and Empirical Foundations.

* * *

ESSER, Robin 1933-

PERSONAL: Born May 6, 1933, in Harrow, England; son of Charles and Winifred (Grantham) Esser; married Shirley Irene Clough; married second wife, Lyn Lee-Hargreaves; children: (first marriage) Sarah-Jane, Daniel, Tobias, Rebecca. *Education:* Wadham College, Oxford, B.A. (honors), 1955, M.A., 1957. *Home:* 39 Moore Park Rd., London S.W.6, England. *Agent:* Curtis Brown Ltd., 1 Craven Hill, London W2 3EW, England. *Office: Daily Express,* London, England.

CAREER: Daily Express, London, England, assistant editor, 1960—. *Military service:* British Army, 1953-55; became captain.

WRITINGS: The Hot Potato (espionage novel), M. Joseph, 1969; *The Paper Chase* (spy novel), M. Joseph, 1971. Contributor to periodicals.

WORK IN PROGRESS: A novel about American people.

BIOGRAPHICAL/CRITICAL SOURCES: Punch, September 3, 1969.

* * *

ESTES, Winston M. 1917-

PERSONAL: Born October 31, 1917, in Quanah, Tex.; son of Thomas Marvin (a railroad employee) and Grace (Newsom) Estes; married Sarah Hamlin Spears, February 23, 1946; children: Richard Hawley, Elizabeth Meade. *Education:* Attended Texas Technological College (now Texas Tech University). *Religion:* Episcopalian. *Home:* 5302 Ravensworth Rd., Springfield, Va. 22151.

CAREER: U.S. Air Force, career officer, 1941-69, retiring as lieutenant colonel; served two years in the Pacific during World War II, and in Germany, 1955-58. *Member:* Authors Guild, Retired Officers Association.

WRITINGS—Novels; all published by Lippincott, except as indicated: *Winston in Wonderland,* Eagle Press, 1956; *Another Part of the House,* 1970; *A Streetful of People,* 1972; *A Simple Act of Kindness,* 1973; *Andy Jessup,* 1975; *Homefront,* 1976. Author of military manuals, handbooks, and textbooks.

WORK IN PROGRESS: A novel, as yet untitled.

SIDELIGHTS: After seven unsuccessful book manuscripts and more than one hundred short pieces Winston Estes came to the conclusion that he is a story-teller, that "a story will tell itself if allowed to unfold on its own terms." He adds: "Looking back, I can see that my unsuccessful stories were those I wrote as I *wanted* them to be or thought they *should* be, rather than as they actually are. A story has its own life, its own integrity, its own reason for being. . . ."

BIOGRAPHICAL/CRITICAL SOURCES: New York Times Book Review, July 26, 1970.

* * *

ESTRADA, Jacquelyn (Ann) 1946-

PERSONAL: Born September 10, 1946, in Bainbridge, Md.; daughter of John Walter (a businessman) and Ruth E. (Coleman) Harper; married Dave Estrada, August 17, 1968. *Education:* San Diego State College (now University), B.A., 1968. *Politics:* "Libertarian (laissez-faire capitalist)."

Religion: None. *Home:* 3528 Luna Ave., San Diego, Calif. 92117.

CAREER: CRM Books, Del Mar, Calif., editor, 1969-75; free-lance editor and writer, 1975—.

WRITINGS: (Editor and contributor) *The University under Siege,* Nash Publishing, 1971; (contributor) *Go to Health,* Dell, 1973; (co-author) *Instructor's Manual for Life and Health,* 2nd edition (Estrada was not associated with earlier edition), 1976; (co-editor) *The Future of Being Human,* Canfield Press, 1977; (co-author) *Psychology Today and Tomorrow,* Canfield Press, 1977.

WORK IN PROGRESS: Researching the cinema in the 1930's and 1940's; co-authoring a college textbook for Canfield Press; compiling science fiction anthologies as texts for social science courses.

SIDELIGHTS: Jacquelyn Estrada told *CA:* "At the moment I am moving in two totally different directions. First, I am firmly entrenched as a writer/editor for college texts, especially in psychology. This field can be very rewarding. . . . Second, I am doing magazine pieces on the popular arts, a particular interest of mine."

* * *

ETTINGER, Elzbieta 1925-

PERSONAL: Born September 19, 1925, in Poland. *Education:* University of Warsaw, M.A., Ph.D.; Academy of Political Science, Warsaw, additional study. *Home:* 83 Brattle St., Cambridge, Mass. 02138. *Agent:* Mary Yost Associates, 141 East 55th St., New York, N.Y. 10022. *Office:* Massachusetts Institute of Technology, 14N-328, Cambridge, Mass. 02139.

CAREER: Affiliated with Radcliffe Seminars, Harvard Extension, beginning 1970, senior fellow at Radcliffe Institute, 1972-74; Massachusetts Institute of Technology, Cambridge, Mass., assistant professor, 1973—.

WRITINGS: Kindergarten (novel), Houghton, 1970. Also author of critical articles and essays published in Polish. Translator of numerous works from the English and German into Polish.

WORK IN PROGRESS: A sequel to *Kindergarten.*

BIOGRAPHICAL/CRITICAL SOURCES: New York Times Book Review, February 8, 1970.†

* * *

ETTINGER, Richard Prentice 1893-1971

September 26, 1893—February 24, 1971; American publisher and business writer. Obituaries: *New York Times,* February 25, 1971; *Publishers' Weekly,* March 8, 1971.

* * *

EVANS, Humphrey (Marshall, Jr.) 1914-

PERSONAL: Born December 27, 1914, in Los Angeles, Calif.; son of Humphrey Marshall and Winifred (Craig) Evans; married Doris Portwood (a researcher), June 7, 1941; married second wife, Mechtild Countess von Podewils, April 18, 1967; children: (first marriage) Humphrey Marshall III.

CAREER: McGraw-Hill Book Co., New York, N.Y., an editor, 1950-53; professional writer.

WRITINGS: (With wife, Doris Evans) *Seven Pillars of Foolishness,* Educational Publishing, c. 1960; *Thimayya of India: A Soldier's Life,* Harcourt, 1960; (by Robert Loh as

told to Humphrey Evans) *Escape from Red China,* Coward, 1962; (with Tung Chi Ping) *The Thought Revolution,* Coward, 1966; *The Adventures of Li Chi: A Modern Chinese Legend,* Dutton, 1967. Also author of fifteen other books, some written for the government and some published under various undisclosed pseudonyms. Contributor of articles and short stories to periodicals.††

* * *

EVANS, Idella M(arie Crowe) 1924-

PERSONAL: Born March 15, 1924, in Leavenworth, Wash.; daughter of Joe and Madeline (Van de Grift) Crowe; married James Hudson Evans, November 23, 1945 (divorced). *Education:* Everett Junior College, A.A., 1947; University of Washington, B.S., 1949; University of Oregon, M.S., 1952, Ph.D., 1955. *Home address:* Box 1619, Los Gatos, Calif. 95030.

CAREER: Northwest Psychological Services, Portland, Ore., founder and clinical psychologist, 1955-62; Santa Clara County Mental Health Center, San Jose, Calif., clinical psychologist, 1962-65; San Jose State College (now University), San Jose, assistant professor of psychology, 1965-68; Saratoga County Mental Health Clinic, Saratoga Springs, N.Y., supervising clinical psychologist, 1968-70. Consultant, Santa Clara Valley Medical Center, 1962—. Member of board of directors, Foundation to Aid Mentally Ill Children. *Military service:* U.S. Marine Corps, Women's Reserve, 1944-45. *Member:* International Council for Exceptional Children, American Psychological Association, National Rehabilitation Association, National Academy for Religion and Mental Health, American Association of University Women, California Psychological Association, Bay Area Society of Clinical Psychologists, Sigma Xi, Psi Chi, Zonta.

WRITINGS: (With Patricia A. Smith) *Psychology for a Changing World,* Wiley, 1970.†

* * *

EVEREST, Allan S(eymour) 1913-

PERSONAL: Born October 9, 1913, in South Shaftsbury, Vt.; son of Charles Seymour (a merchant) and Clara (Hawkins) Everest; married Elsie Hathaway Lewis, October 10, 1942; children: Martha Everest Lockwood. *Education:* University of Vermont, Ph.D., 1936; Columbia University, M.A., 1937, Ph.D., 1948. *Home:* 26 South Catherine St., Plattsburgh, N.Y. 12901. *Office:* Department of History, State University of New York College, Plattsburgh, N.Y. 12901.

CAREER: Green Mountain Junior College, Poultney, Vt., instructor in social science, 1938-41; State University of New York College at Plattsburgh, professor of American history, 1947—. *Military service:* U.S. Army Air Forces, 1941-46; became captain. *Member:* New York State Historical Association, Vermont Historical Society, Clinton County Historical Association (former president), Phi Beta Kappa, Pi Gamma Mu.

WRITINGS: Morgenthau, the New Deal and Silver: A Story of Pressure Politics, King's Crown Press, 1950; *British Objectives at the Battle of Plattsburgh,* Moorsfield Press, 1960; (editor) David Sherwood Kellogg, *Recollections of Clinton County and the Battle of Plattsburgh, 1800-1840,* Clinton County Historical Association, 1964; *Pioneer Homes of Clinton County, 1790-1820,* Clinton County Historical Association, 1966; (editor) Kellogg, *A Doctor at All*

Hours: A Private Journal of a Small-Town Doctor's Varied Life, 1886-1909, Greene, 1970; *Our North Country Heritage: Architecture Worth Saving in Clinton and Essex Counties,* Tundra Books, 1972; (editor) Charles Carroll, *The Journal of Charles Carroll of Carrollton,* Champlain-Upper Hudson Bicentennial Committee, 1976; *Moses Hazen and the Canadian Refugees in the American Revolution,* Syracuse University Press, 1976. Editor, *North County Notes.*

WORK IN PROGRESS: Rum Along the Border.

SIDELIGHTS: Allan Everest has traveled extensively in the British Isles, Western Europe, and Canada.

* * *

EYSTER, C(harles) William 1917-

PERSONAL: Born June 14, 1917, in Hanover, Pa.; son of Charles Hoke and Clara (Wright) Eyster; married Beverly Vollmer (a college professor), August, 1949; children: Charles V. *Education:* Shippensburg State College, B.S.Ed., 1939. *Address:* Box 1149, Litchfield Park, Ariz. 85340.

CAREER: Professional airline pilot, 1940-46; business pilot, 1946-69. Spends summers flying tanker aircraft in forest fire control work; has U.S. Forestry Service "initial attack" rating and has logged 186 jumps; spent summer of 1971 working with Apache Indians on their reservation in Whiteriver, Ariz.

WRITINGS: Thataway: The Story of the Magnetic Compass, A. S. Barnes, 1970. Contributor to aviation magazines.

WORK IN PROGRESS: Writing and illustrating a manual for aerial applicators and agricultural students.††

* * *

FAAS, Larry A(ndrew) 1936-

PERSONAL: Born September 25, 1936, in Iowa City, Iowa; son of Merlin Andrew (a farmer) and Lavone (Cheney) Faas; married Patricia Middleton, December 18, 1962; children: Anna Rachel, Eric Andrew. *Education:* Iowa State University, B.A., 1959; Colorado State College (now University), M.A., 1961; Brigham Young University, graduate study, 1962; Utah State University, Ed.D., 1967. *Religion:* Church of Jesus Christ of Latter-day Saints. *Home:* 519 East Del Rio Dr., Temple, Ariz. 85281. *Office:* Department of Education, Arizona State University, Tempe, Ariz. 85281.

CAREER: Teacher and psychologist in public schools in North English, Iowa and Decorah, Iowa, 1959-65; University of Nevada, Reno, director of special education and assistant professor of education, 1966-67; Arizona State University, Tempe, assistant professor, 1967-70, associate professor of education, 1970—. *Member:* Council for Exceptional Children, Phi Delta Kappa.

WRITINGS: (Editor) *Children and Youth with Special Learning and Behavior Problems,* University of Nevada, 1967; (contributor) *Work Experience Programs,* Department of Public Instruction, Division of Special Education, Arizona State University, 1968; (editor) *The Emotionally Disturbed Child: A Book of Readings,* C. C Thomas, 1970; (editor) *Learning Disabilities: A Book of Readings,* C. C Thomas, 1972; *Learning Disabilities: A Competency Based Approach,* Houghton, 1976.

* * *

FABER, Charles F(ranklin) 1926-

PERSONAL: Born December 6, 1926, in Monroe County, Iowa; son of Richard A. (a farmer) and Inez (McAlister) Faber; married Patricia Jane Utt, June 8, 1947; children: Deborah, Daniel, Melinda. *Education:* Coe College, B.A., 1948; Columbia University, M.A., 1952; Northern Illinois University, graduate study, 1957-58; University of Chicago, Ph.D., 1961. *Home:* 3569 Cornwall Dr., Lexington, Ky. *Office:* Department of Administration and Supervision, University of Kentucky, Lexington, Ky. 40506.

CAREER: Principal and teacher in public schools in Bethany, Ill. and Geneva, Ill., 1949-59; University of Chicago, Chicago, Ill., instructor in education, 1959-61; Iowa State University, Ames, assistant professor of education, 1961-64; George Peabody College for Teachers, Nashville, Tenn., professor of education and chairman of department of educational administration, 1964-71; University of Kentucky, Lexington, professor of education and chairman of department of educational administration and supervision, 1971—. Member of various school survey teams from University of Chicago, Iowa State University, and George Peabody College for Teachers; member of various committees on educational improvement and finance; coordinator, Study of Administrative Organization, Chattanooga Public Schools, 1969. Lecturer to and participant in panel discussions for educational and civic organizations. *Member:* National Association of Elementary School Principals, Phi Delta Kappa.

WRITINGS: (With Walter Hartrick) *School Program Characteristics Opinionnaire,* Midwest Administration Center, University of Chicago, 1960; (editor) *Tenth Annual Report of the Midwest Administration Center,* Midwest Administration Center, University of Chicago, 1961; *Toward Improved School Administration,* W. K. Kellogg Foundation, 1962; (with Virgil S. Lagomarcina and Glenn E. Holmes) *A Proposed Plan for School District Reorganization in Poweshiek, Iowa, Mahaska, Keokuk, Washington, and Jefferson Counties,* privately printed, 1962; (with Holmes and Daryl Hobbs) *An Analysis of Factors Related to School District Quality in TENCO,* Iowa State University Extension Service, 1962; (with Hobbs and Holmes) *Comparison of Measures of School District Quality in TENCO—1961-62 and 1962-63,* Iowa State University Extension Service, 1963; *Education Holds Our Future,* State of Iowa, Department of Public Instruction, 1964; *Project MID-TENN,* Metropolitan Nashville-Davidson County School System, 1966; (with James C. LaPlant and Robert A. Pittillo, Jr.) *School Organization in Chattanooga, Tennessee,* privately printed, 1969; (with Gilbert Shearron) *Elementary School Administration: Theory and Practice,* Holt, 1970; (with Shearron) *Administracion Escolar: Teoria y Practica,* Paraninfo (Madrid), 1974; *A Manual for School Board Members,* Center for Professional Development, University of Kentucky, 1976.

Contributor: *School District Organization in St. Louis County, Missouri,* Department of Education, University of Chicago, 1960; *An Educational Survey of the Palos Community Consolidated School District #118,* Department of Education, University of Chicago, 1961; *Organization of School Systems in Georgia,* Division of Surveys and Field Services, George Peabody College for Teachers, 1965; David B. Guralnik and Richard H. Hinze, editors, *Webster's New World Dictionary and Student Handbook,* elementary edition, Southwestern Co., 1966; Ernest Q. Campbell, editor, *Problems in Urban Educational Planning,* Central Midwestern Regional Educational Laboratory, 1967; *Vermilion Parish Public Schools,* Division of Surveys and Field Services, George Peabody College for Teachers, 1969; *Stanly County Public Schools,* Division of Surveys and Field Services, George Peabody College for Teachers, 1971; *Monroe Public Schools,* Division of Surveys and Field Services, George Peabody College for Teachers, 1971; *Charlottesville Pattern for School Improvement,* Division of Surveys and Field Services, George Peabody College for Teachers, 1973; *Alleghany County Public Schools,* Division of Surveys and Field Services, George Peabody College for Teachers, 1973; *Little Rock Public Schools,* Division of Surveys and Field Services, George Peabody College for Teachers, 1974; *Fort Wayne Public Schools,* Division of Surveys and Field Services, George Peabody College for Teachers, 1975.

Contributor to *Peabody Journal of Education, Phi Delta Kappan, Journal of Teacher Education, Journal of Educational Research, American School Board Journal, Educational Forum, Journal of Collective Negotiations, Clearing House,* and *Review of Educational Research.*

*   *   *

FADIMAN, Edwin, Jr. 1925-
(Edwina Mark)

PERSONAL: Born November 3, 1925; son of Edwin Miles (an entrepreneur) and Celeste (Frankel) Fadiman; married Susan Thorne (a psychological consultant), May 14, 1949; children: Mar, Kenneth. *Education:* Attended Columbia University and Middlebury College. *Politics:* None. *Religion:* None. *Home and office:* 141 Woodbine Rd., Stamford, Conn. 06903. *Agent:* John Starr, 232 West End Ave., New York, N.Y.

CAREER: Novelist. *Military service:* U.S. Army, World War II. *Member:* Authors Guild, Authors League of America.

*WRITINGS—*Novels, except as noted: *The Voice and the Light,* Crown, 1949; (under pseudonym Edwina Mark) *My Sister, My Beloved,* Citadel, 1955; *The Glass Playpen: The Story of a New York Call Girl,* New American Library, 1956; (author of introduction) Marcelle Maurette, *Anastasia* (play), New American Library, 1956; *An Act of Violence,* New American Library, 1957; *The 21″ Screen,* Doubleday, 1958; (under pseudonym Edwina Mark) *The Sinful One,* Hillman Books, 1959; *The One-Eyed King,* Geis, 1971; *Who Will Watch the Watchers?,* Pyramid Publications, 1971; *The Feast Day,* illustrations by Charles Mikolaycak, Little, Brown, 1973; *The Professional,* Fawcett, 1975. Free-lance reviewer, *Saturday Review.*

WORK IN PROGRESS: The Voice and the Light (juvenile), for Little, Brown; *The Children's Crusade,* for Dodd.

SIDELIGHTS: Edwin Fadiman told *CA,* "If at all possible, [I] advise *not* ever becoming a free-lance novelist, as a method of making a full-time living."†

*   *   *

FAIR, James R(utherford), Jr. 1920-

PERSONAL: Born October 14, 1920, in Charleston, Mo.; son of James Rutherford and Georgia (Case) Fair; married Merle Innis, January 14, 1950; children: James Rutherford III, Elizabeth, Richard I. *Education:* Citadel, student, 1938-40; Georgia Institute of Technology, B.S. in Ch.E., 1942; University of Michigan, M.S. in Ch.E., 1949; University of Texas, Ph.D., 1954. *Politics:* Republican. *Religion:* Presbyterian. *Home:* 661 West Polo Dr., Clayton, Mo. 63105.

CAREER: Monsanto Co., Marshall, Tex., chemist and research engineer, 1942-43, research and design engineer, 1943-45, development associate, 1945-47, project leader and

engineer in Texas City, 1947-52; Shell Development Corp. of Calif., process design engineer, 1954-56; Monsanto Co., St. Louis, Mo., research group leader and section leader, 1956-61, engineering manager, 1961-69, director of engineering, 1969—; Washington University, St. Louis, affiliate professor of engineering, 1964—. *Member:* American Chemical Society, American Institute of Chemical Engineers, National Society of Professional Engineers, American Society for Engineering Education, Faculty Club of Washington University. *Awards, honors:* McGraw-Hill Professional Achievement Award, 1968; D.Sc., Washington University, 1977; Walker Award and Founders Award from American Institute of Chemical Engineers.

WRITINGS: The North Arkansas Line, Howell-North Books, 1969; *Distillation,* International Textbook Co., 1971. Contributor of about fifty articles and chapters to journals and books in the field of chemical engineering.

WORK IN PROGRESS: A history of the Kansas City Southern-Louisiana & Arkansas railway system.

AVOCATIONAL INTERESTS: Travel, collecting books.

*   *   *

FAIR, Ray C(larence) 1942-

PERSONAL: Born October 4, 1942, in Fresno, Calif.; son of Clarence and Goldie (Smith) Fair. *Education:* Fresno State College (now California State University, Fresno), B.A., 1964; Massachusetts Institute of Technology, Ph.D., 1968. *Home:* 20 East Stanworth Dr., Princeton, N.J. 08540. *Office:* Department of Economics, Yale University, New Haven, Conn. 06520.

CAREER: Princeton University, Princeton, N.J., assistant professor of economics, 1968-74; Yale University, New Haven, Conn., associate professor of economics, 1974—. *Member:* American Economic Association, American Statistical Association, Econometric Society.

WRITINGS: The Short-run Demand for Workers and Hours, North-Holland Publishing, 1969; *A Short-run Forecasting Model of the United States Economy,* Heath, 1971; *A Model of Macroeconomic Activity,* Balinger, Volume I: *The Theoretical Model,* 1974, Volume II: *The Empirical Model,* 1976. Contributor to *Econometrica, Quarterly Journal of Economics, Review of Economics and Statistics, Journal of Money, Credit and Banking,* and *Federal Reserve Bank of St. Louis Review.*

WORK IN PROGRESS: Work in econometrics and macroeconomics.

*   *   *

FAIRLEY, Peter 1930-

PERSONAL: Born November 2, 1930, in Kuala Lumpur, Malaya; son of Frank and Ethel (Griggs) Fairley; married Vivienne Richards, June 4, 1954; children: Josephine, Alastair, Duncan, Simon. *Education:* Sidney Sussex College, Cambridge, B.A. (honors), 1953. *Politics:* None. *Religion:* Church of England. *Home:* Pacific, 149 Hayes Lane, Bromley, Kent, England. *Office:* Independent Television Network, ITN House, 48 Wells St., London W.1, England.

CAREER: Science editor, *Evening Standard,* London, England, Independent Television Network News, London, and *TV Times.* Appears regularly on several television programs and produces the British Broadcasting Corp. science program, "Tomorrow's World." *Military service:* British Army, 1949-51; became captain. *Member:* Association of

British Science Writers, Medical Journalists Association, Sportsman Club (London). *Awards, honors:* Glaxo traveling fellowship, 1967, for best science writing of the year.

WRITINGS: This Is Cambridge, Metcalfe, 1953; *Man on the Moon,* Arthur Barker, 1969; *The ABC of Space,* Independent TV Books, 1969; *Project X: The Exciting Story of British Invention,* Mayflower Books, 1970, revised edition published as *British Inventions of the 20th Century,* Hart-Davis, 1972; *Peter Fairley's Space Annual,* Independent TV Books, 1970; *Peter Fairley's World of Wonders Annual,* Independent TV Books, 1970; *Is There Life in Outer Space?,* Independent TV Books, 1975; *TV—Behind the Screen,* Independent TV Books, 1976; *North Sea Bonanza,* Hart-Davis, 1977; *The A-Z of Space,* Hart-Davis, 1977. Author of television scripts. Contributor to magazines.

WORK IN PROGRESS: Two books, *Behind the Ballyhoo* and *The Name on the Bullett.*

AVOCATIONAL INTERESTS: Swimming, tennis, cricket, woodworking.

BIOGRAPHICAL/CRITICAL SOURCES: Times Literary Supplement, October 16, 1969.

*   *   *

FAIRWEATHER, Virginia 1922-

PERSONAL: Born January 25, 1922, in London, England; daughter of Cyril Charles and Jessie Amelia (Thorpe) Winter; married Leslie Julian-Jones (a television director and composer), July 8, 1939; married second husband, David Fairweather (a theater publicist), July 24, 1963. *Education:* Attended a private school in St. John's Wood, London, England, for seven years, and studied in France for one year. *Politics:* Conservative. *Religion:* Agnostic. *Home:* Flat 7, 98 Marylebone High St., London W.1, England; and 8 Russell St., Chichester, Sussex, England.

CAREER: Former actress; left the stage to be press agent for Sir Laurence Olivier and the National Theatre of Great Britain. First appeared as a child actress at the Old Vic Theatre in London, later played throughout England with repertory companies; returned to London in a revue, "Come Out of Your Shell," at the Criterion Theatre; subsequently had roles in "Rise above It" (revue) at the Comedy Theatre, "My Sister Eileen" at the Savoy Theatre, and in "Brighton Rock," and then played opposite Beatrice Lillie in "Better Late" at the Garrick Theatre; also has appeared on radio and television programs and in the film version of "Brighton Rock."

WRITINGS: Sir Laurence Olivier: An Informal Portrait, Coward, 1969 (published in England as *Cry God for Larry,* Calder & Boyars, 1969); *Some Do It Every Night* (professional autobiography), J. Calder, 1977. Author of several scripts performed by British Broadcasting Corp.

WORK IN PROGRESS: "What's the Matter with Daddy, Mummy?", a controversial play for BBC-TV.

SIDELIGHTS: Virginia Fairweather's "intimate memoir" of Sir Laurence Olivier was published in a two-part serialization in London's *Sunday Times.* According to *Variety,* Sir Laurence was "not happy" about the chatty book, which "shows an obvious admiration and affection for Olivier" although the author was fired from her publicity post with the National Theatre prior to starting the memoir.

She recently told *CA:* "Approaching the exciting emergent chrysalis age of fifty-five—according to the gospel of the everlastingly optimistic late Sophie Tucker—I've been pre- vailed upon to record (thank heavens blest with a memory tabulated 'total recall') my close associations with many of the great personalities of this post-war century on both sides of the Atlantic. Since I am a-racial, a-political, at least militantly, agnostic, except in total inherent belief, and a-moral in bed, which should be my own affair, I nevertheless have future plans to follow up my professional with my personal autobiography. Who needs a head-shrinker if you're happy on your own couch? No, that won't be the title."

BIOGRAPHICAL/CRITICAL SOURCES: Variety, June 11, 1969; *Show,* February, 1970.

*   *   *

FAKHRY, Majid 1923-

PERSONAL: Born January 6, 1923, in Zerarieh, Lebanon; son of Fakhreddine (a landowner) and Khashia (Yahia) Fakhry; married Alice Shiber, June 25, 1955; children: Samir, Bassen, Rima. *Education:* Attended Gerard Institute, 1934-36, American University of Beirut, 1939-47, and University of Edinburgh, 1947-49. *Office:* Department of Philosophy, American University of Beirut, Beirut, Lebanon.

CAREER: University of London, London, England, lecturer in Arabic philosophy, 1949-54; American University of Beirut, Beirut, Lebanon, assistant professor, 1954-65, associate professor, 1966-68, professor of philosophy, 1968—. Visiting associate professor, Georgetown University, 1965-67. *Member:* Societe International pour l'Etude de la Philosophie Medievale, Institut International de Philosophie, American Association of University Professors, P.E.N. (Lebanon).

WRITINGS: Islamic Occasionalism and Its Critique by Averroes and Aquinas, Allen & Unwin, 1958; (translator into Arabic) John Locke, *Two Treatises on Civil Government,* UNESCO Commission for the Translation of World Classics, 1959; *Ibn Rushd,* Catholic Press (Beirut), 1960; (translator into Arabic) Arthur O. Lovejoy, *The Great Chain of Being,* Franklin Publications (Beirut), 1964; *Aristotle,* Catholic Press, 1968; *Ibn Bajjah, Opera Metaphysica,* Dar an-Nahar, Beirut, 1968; *Studies in Arabic Thought,* Dar an-Nahar, Beirut, 1970; *A History of Islamic Philosophy,* Columbia University Press, 1970; (editor) Ibn Bajjah, *Paraphrase of Aristotle's Physics,* Dar an-Nahar, Beirut, 1973. Contributor to *Muslim World, Journal of International Affairs, Journal of History of Ideas, Journal of History of Philosophy, Mediaeval Studies, Al-Mashriq, Al-Abhath, Hiwar, Le Museon,* and *Studia Islamica.* Member of advisory board, *Al-Abhath;* member of international advisory board, *International Journal for Philosophy of Religion.*

WORK IN PROGRESS: Trends in Contemporary Arabic Thought; an Arabic translation of John Locke's *An Essay Concerning the Human Understanding;* and *Ethical Theories in Islam.*

*   *   *

FARBER, Donald C.

PERSONAL: Born in Columbus, Neb.; son of Charles and Sarah (Epstein) Farber; married Ann Eis (a mathematics professor), December 28, 1947; children: Seth, Patricia. *Education:* University of Nebraska, B.S., 1948, J.D., 1950. *Politics:* Independent. *Religion:* Jewish. *Home:* 14 East 75th St., New York, N.Y. 10021.

CAREER: Theatrical attorney in private practice, 1950—, currently affiliated with firm of Kuh, Shapiro, Goldman, Cooperman & Levitt; professor of law at Hofstra University, Hempstead, N.Y., 1974-75; presently teaching courses in theatre law at New School for Social Research, New York, N.Y. Visiting professor York University, Toronto, Ontario, 1970-73; chairman of Practicing Law Institute seminar in theatre law, 1972. Guest lecturer or speaker at Brooklyn College of the City University of New York, New York University, Iowa Arts Council Seminar, Hofstra Institute for the Arts and National Theatre Conference. *Military service:* U.S. Army, Infantry, World War II; became sergeant. *Member:* Order of the Coif.

WRITINGS: From Option to Opening, DBS Publications, 1968, 3rd edition, 1976; *Producing on Broadway: A Comprehensive Guide,* DBS Publications, 1969; *Actor's Guide: What You Should Know About the Contracts You Sign,* DBS Publications, 1971; (with Paul Baumgarten) *Producing, Financing and Distributing Film,* DBS Publications, 1973.

SIDELIGHTS: Reviewing *Producing on Broadway,* a *Variety* critic writes: "Farber has not only done his homework brilliantly, but he has also delivered a highly readable, sometimes wryly amusing work that is simultaneously a handbook and an encyclopedia. . . . Farber and his publisher are to be commended on providing profession and reading public with a book that likely will remain for some time to come the authoritative reference in its field."

BIOGRAPHICAL/CRITICAL SOURCES: Variety, April 26, 1968, September 3, 1969; *After Dark,* August, 1968; *New York Law Journal,* November 1, 1968.

*   *   *

FARIDI, Shah Nasiruddin Mohammad 1929-
(S. N. Faridi; Jareed, a pseudonym)

PERSONAL: Born April 23, 1929, in Nooruddinpura, Ghazipur, Uttar Pradesh, India; son of S. M. Hosain (a teacher) and Majidun (Nisa) Faridi; married Salma Ansari, October 24, 1964; children: Shah Najam Iqbal (son), Tabassum (daughter), Shah Meraj (son). *Education:* Attended Ewing Christian College, Allahabad; Aligarh Muslim University, B.A., 1947, M.A. (economics), 1949, M.A. (English), 1957, M.A. (sociology), 1973. *Religion:* Islam. *Home:* Astana Hazrat Asi, Nooruddinpura, Ghazipur, Uttar Pradesh, India. *Office:* Department of Economics, Shuaib Mohammadia College, Agra, Uttar Pradesh, India.

CAREER: Shuaib Mohammadia College, Agra, Uttar Pradesh, India, lecturer in economics, 1950—. Writer and translator. Broadcaster on All-India Radio from Delhi and Lucknow stations.

WRITINGS: Tanveer (novel), Agra Akhbar Press, 1952; *Unchi Nichi Lehrain* (short stories), Ram Prasad, 1954; (editor) *Watan ke Geet* (collection of patriotic Urdu poems), Vinod Pustak Mandir, 1956; *Haan Haan Teri Dunia Main* (novel; title means "Yes, in Thy World"), Jan Pirya Prakashan, 1960; (editor) *Urdu ki Prasidh Hindu Kavitrianian* (title means "The Hindu Poetesses of Urdu"), Ram Prasad, 1961; (editor) *Guldadastai Shairi* (poems by Urdu poets), Modern Book Depot (Agra), 1962; *Jiwan Jhanki* (short stories), Nav Jyoti Prakashan, 1962; *Economic Welfare of Indian Moslems,* Ram Prasad, 1965; *Hindu History of Urdu Literature,* Ram Prasad, 1966; *Tarziati Khaakey* (imaginary interviews with Urdu poets; in Urdu), Agra Akhbar Press, 1969; *Girti Shabnam Khilte Phool* (short stories), Mahesh Book Depot, 1970; *Islam and Non-Moslem Intellectuals,* Grimf & Co., 1973.

Textbooks: *Popular Set of General English,* three parts, Sharma Book Depot, 1953; *Arth Shastra ka Navin Perder-*

shan (economics), Hansraj Sharma, 1956; *Spotlight* (English prose), Pustak Bhawan, 1956; *Navin Bhugol Darshan* (geography), four parts, Hari Book Depot, 1958; *Bharat ka Arthik Bhugol* (economic geography), Hasraj Sharma, 1971. Also author of *Gayan Vigayan Arthshastra Ka* (economics text).

Translator of political literature of All India Swantantra Party from English into Urdu. Contributor of articles in Hindi, Urdu, and English to periodicals, including a series of fourteen critical and satirical articles in *Fankaar* (Bombay weekly), 1958-59; he has used pseudonym Jareed for some articles. Former sub-editor, *Citizen* (English-language weekly published in Agra).

WORK IN PROGRESS: Reworking his doctoral thesis for resubmission to Agra University.

SIDELIGHTS: Shah Nasiruddin Mohammad Faridi told *CA:* "Personally I feel that a book not only serves as a weapon of self-defence but is also an instrument of unlocking the gates and doors. The sufferings of the Indian Moslems pained me, and I could have the privilege of writing the *first* book on the subject of Indian Moslems, i.e. *Economic Welfare of Indian Moslems.* The Moslems of India received this book as a gospel of their welfare. Likewise it has shown the path of progress to the other minorities of the world. . . ." Faridi goes on to mention that there exists a "lot of misunderstanding about Urdu language in India." He continues: "Only to remove the misunderstanding and to show the real picture of Urdu I have written the book *Hindu History of Urdu Literature.* And indeed this was also the *first* book on the subject in its own way."

Commenting on the motivating factors and circumstances important to his career, Faridi writes: "This is an irony with me in life that I have never found clear position of choice. Only the circumstances have guided me to this way and that way. But a craze for learning and reading and a temptation to find a place among the . . . intellectuals of the world enabled me to labour hard, to think correctly and to rise upward. Now, in many parts of the world and in many advanced countries my books are read with interest."

Faridi's first short story in English, "Was She a Flower?," appeared in a college magazine; his first short story in Hindi was published in the monthly *Samaj* in Delhi. He wrote his first novel, *Tanveer,* in seventeen days, at times identifying himself so much with the sentiments of the book that he found "tears in my own eyes." Among the influences he mentions are the short stories of Tagore and the poems of Iqbal. Many of his books were originally written in Hindi; some have been reissued in Urdu.

*   *   *

FARR, Judith 1937-

PERSONAL: Born March 13, 1937, in New York, N.Y.; daughter of Russell John (a musician) and Frances (Wissell) Banzer; married George F. Farr, Jr. (a college professor), June 30, 1962; children: Alec Winfield. *Education:* Marymount Manhattan College, B.A., 1957; Yale University, M.A., 1959, Ph.D., 1965. *Politics:* Democrat. *Religion:* Episcopalian. *Home address:* Moores Mills, R.D. 1, Pleasant Valley, N.Y. 12569. *Office:* Department of English, State University of New York, New Paltz, N.Y. 12561.

CAREER: Vassar College, Poughkeepsie, N.Y., instructor in English, 1961-63; St. Mary's College, St. Mary's, Calif., assistant professor of English, 1964-68; State University of New York College at New Paltz, assistant professor, 1968-71, associate professor of English, 1971—.

WRITINGS: (Editor) *Twentieth Century Interpretations of "Sons and Lovers,"* Prentice-Hall, 1970. Work represented in anthologies, *Riverside Poetry Three: An Anthology of Student Poetry,* edited by Marianne Moore and others, Twayne, 1958, and *New Campus Writing #4,* edited by Nolan Miller and Judson Jerome, Grove, 1963. Contributor to *American Literature* and *Minnesota Review.*

WORK IN PROGRESS: 'Language from Spirit': The Art of Elinor Wylie.

SIDELIGHTS: Judith Farr told *CA:* "There is little to say about my writing except that, apart from my husband and child, it absorbs me most." *Avocational interests:* Eighteenth-century French art, history, and decoration, French literature, collecting eighteenth-century English china and furniture.

* * *

FARR, Michael 1924-

PERSONAL: Born October 24, 1924, in Bristol, England; son of William Bryant and Helena Farr; married Daphne Mary Johnson, May 10, 1952; children: Christopher, Simon, Briony, Guy. *Education:* Cambridge University, B.A. (honors), 1949.

CAREER: Design (magazine), London, England, editor, 1952-59; Council of Industrial Design, London, chief information officer, 1959-61; design management consultant in London, 1962—; director of Michael Farr (Design Integration) Ltd., 1962—, and director of Farr Ergonomics Ltd., 1968—. *Military service:* Royal Air Force, 1943-47. *Member:* Design and Industries Association (general secretary, 1962-66), Ergonomics Research Society. *Awards, honors:* Design Centre awards.

WRITINGS: Design in British Industry: A Mid-Century Survey, Cambridge University Press, 1955; *Design Management,* Hodder & Stoughton, 1966; *Control Systems for Industrial Design,* Cahners, 1973; *Security for Computer Systems,* National Computing Centre, 1973.†

* * *

FARRAR, Larston Dawn 1915-1970

February 25, 1915—September 21, 1970; American freelance writer and publisher. Obituaries: *Washington Post,* September 26, 1970. (See index for *CA* sketch)

* * *

FARRISON, William Edward 1902-

PERSONAL: Born August 19, 1902, in Orangeburg County, S.C.; son of Jacob Fletcher (a farmer) and Eliza (Goldson) Farrison; married Alice Marie Norris (a college teacher of English), August 4, 1932. *Education:* Lincoln University, Lincoln University, Pa., B.A., 1926; University of Pennsylvania, M.A., 1928; Ohio State University, Ph.D., 1936. *Religion:* African Methodist Episcopal Church. *Home:* 905 Dupree St., Durham, N.C. 27701.

CAREER: Lincoln University, Lincoln University, Pa., instructor in English, 1926-28; West Virginia State College, Institute, instructor in English, 1928-31; Bennett College, Greensboro, N.C., professor of English, 1932-39; North Carolina Central University, Durham, professor of English, 1939-70. *Member:* College Language Association (president, 1938-39), Modern Language Association of America, National Council of Teachers of English, Association for the Study of Negro Life and History, National Association for the Advancement of Colored People.

WRITINGS: (Editor with H. M. Gloster and N. P. Tillman) *My Life, My Country, My World,* Prentice-Hall, 1952; *William Wells Brown, Author and Reformer,* University of Chicago Press, 1969; (editor) William Wells Brown, *Clotel: Or, The President's Daughter,* Citadel, 1969; (editor) Brown, *The Negro in the American Rebellion,* Citadel, 1971. Contributor of about seventy articles and reviews to *Phylon, South Atlantic Quarterly, Journal of Negro History,* and other educational and historical journals.

* * *

FASOLD, Ralph W(illiam August) 1940-

PERSONAL: Surname is pronounced *Fah*-sold; born April 8, 1940, in Passaic, N.J.; son of Ewald Conrad Dietrich (a controller for Sears, Roebuck & Co.) and Ruth (Morgan) Fasold; married Gae Garman, August 22, 1964; children: Judd G. A., Ward B. R. *Education:* Wheaton College, Wheaton, Ill., A.B., 1962; University of Chicago, M.A., 1965, Ph.D., 1968. *Residence:* Alexandria, Va. *Office:* School of Languages and Linguistics, Georgetown University, Washington, D.C. 20007.

CAREER: Center for Applied Linguistics, Washington, D.C., research associate, 1967-70; Trinity College, Washington, D.C., lecturer on urban dialectology, 1968-69; Georgetown University, Washington, D.C., lecturer, 1968-70; assistant professor of linguistics, 1970—. Instructor in linguistics at missionary training programs. *Member:* Linguistic Society of America, National Council of Teachers of English.

WRITINGS: (Contributor) Joan C. Baratz and Roger W. Shuy, editors, *Teaching Black Children to Read,* Center for Applied Linguistics, 1969; (editor with Shuy and contributor) *Teaching Standard English in the Inner City,* Center for Applied Linguistics, 1970; *Tense Marking in Black English,* Center for Applied Linguistics, 1972; (with Walt Wolfram) *The Study of Social Dialects in American English,* Prentice-Hall, 1974. Contributor to *Language* and other journals.

WORK IN PROGRESS: An introductory textbook on sociolinguistics.

* * *

FAUROT, Jean H(iatt) 1911-

PERSONAL: Born October 11, 1911, in Missouri; son of Ira N. (a clergyman) and Grace (Hiatt) Faurot; married Louise Johnson, March 3, 1941; children: Anne (Mrs. Carl Edwards), Jeannette Louise, Mary Ruth. *Education:* Park College, A.B., 1933; Westminster Theological Seminary, Philadelphia, Th.B., 1936, Th.M., 1937; McGill University, M.A. and B.D., 1940; University of Toronto, Ph.D., 1946. *Office:* California State University, Sacramento, Calif. 95819.

CAREER: Clergyman; minister with Presbyterian Church in Canada, 1937-45, and with Presbyterian Church in United States, 1945—; Missouri Valley College, Marshall, professor of philosophy, 1947-54; California State University, Sacramento, professor of philosophy, 1954-75, professor emeritus, 1975—.

WRITINGS: Problems of Political Philosophy, Chandler Publishing, 1970; *The Philosopher and the State: An Introduction to Modern Philosophy,* Chandler Publishing, 1971.

* * *

FAZAL, M(uhammad) A(bul) 1939-

PERSONAL: Born January 1, 1939, in Pakistan; son of

Munshi Golam Rahman and Khairunnesa Bibi (Mollah) Fazal. *Education:* University of Dacca, B.A. (honors), 1959, M.A., 1960, LL.B., 1963; Oxford University, D.Phil., 1967. *Religion:* Islam. *Home:* Majhpara, P.O. Sengram, District Kushtia, Bangladesh (permanent). *Office:* Trent Polytechnic, Burton St., Nottingham NH1 4BU, England.

CAREER: Barrister-at-law of Inner Temple, 1970; Nottingham College of Technology, Nottingham, England, lecturer, 1967-68, senior lecturer in law, 1968-75; Trent Polytechnic, Nottingham, principal lecturer in law, 1975—. *Member:* Royal Institute of International Affairs, British Institute of International and Comparative Law, Association of Law Teachers in United Kingdom, Oxford Society, Balliol Society.

WRITINGS: Judicial Control of Administrative Action in India and Pakistan: A Comparative Study of Principles and Remedies, Oxford University Press, 1969.

WORK IN PROGRESS: The United Kingdom Federal Constitution and a Bill of Rights.

SIDELIGHTS: M. A. Fazal told *CA:* "Pursuit of knowledge for its own sake is a pleasure that I could not seek in this life. I was born and brought up in circumstances in which one has to address oneself to the basic needs and problems of life. Consequently my writings are problems oriented. Motivating factor in my case is the response from me towards the challenge of human problems and issues. The writings may have the effect of advancing my career but ultimately my aim is to contribute to human efforts in dealing with problems and thereby enrich the cultural heritage of the mankind. My writings have so far been in an objective field (public law) but in my experience the process of finding a solution to problems (in the intellectual sense) is analogous to that of a poet, a philosopher or a spiritual meditator. A searcher of a solution is surrounded by facts which he uses as his tools but his own ideas are the result of an inspiration that comes to him from a source beyond the material world. In my field I have found the works of other writers useful. Much of it is factual and a few original. My opinion of the contemporary literary scene (using the expressions in a broad sense so as to include academic works in humanities) is that massive amount of facts and data, valuable though they are in themselves, are multiplying quantity at the cost of quality."

*   *   *

FEAGUE, Mildred H.   1915-

PERSONAL: Surname is pronounced Fayg; born May 30, 1915, in Sharon, Pa.; daughter of Carl Isaac (a patternmaker) and Mildred (Jones) Hickox; married Robert Feague, July 11, 1941 (deceased); children: Robert Carl. *Education:* Hiram College, A.B., 1937; Westminster College, New Wilmington, Pa., M.S.Ed., 1947. *Residence:* Prescott, Ariz.

CAREER: Elementary teacher in Prescott, Ariz., 1952-55; U.S. Bureau of Indian Affairs, Gallup, N.M., counselor, 1955-57; teacher of English, French, and Latin at Orme School, Mayer, Ariz., 1957-58, at Leelanau School, Glen Arbor, Mich., 1958-60, in Traverse City, Mich., 1960-67; Arizona State University, Tempe, administrator, 1967-68. *Member:* American Association of University Women.

WRITINGS—Juvenile; all published by Childrens Press: *Little Indian and the Angel,* illustrations by Ted DeGrazia, 1970; *Little Sky Eagle and the Pumpkin Drum,* illustrations by DeGrazia, 1971; *True Book of Rodeos,* 1972.

WORK IN PROGRESS: Other juvenile fiction and nonfiction books based on authentic Indian history and lore.†

*   *   *

FEARON, Peter (Shaun)   1942-

PERSONAL: Born March 20, 1942, in Liverpool, England; son of Thomas and Isabelita (Domenech) Fearon; married Patricia Mullen (a librarian), July, 1966. *Education:* University of Liverpool, B.A., 1964. *Office:* Department of Economic History, University of Leicester, Leicester, England.

CAREER: University of Leicester, Leicester, England, lecturer in economic history, 1966—. Visiting associate professor of history, University of Kansas, 1977-78. *Member:* Economic History Society.

WRITINGS: (Editor with Derek H. Aldcroft) *Economic Growth in Twentieth Century Britain,* Macmillan, 1969, Humanities, 1970; (editor with Aldcroft) *Growth and Fluctuations in the British Economy, 1790-1939,* Macmillan, 1971. Contributor to *Business History Review, Economic History Review,* and *Journal of Transport History.*

WORK IN PROGRESS: Research on the British aircraft industry before 1939, on western Europe's economy, 1919-39, on the economic history of the United States in the twentieth century, and on other aspects of business history.

*   *   *

FEAVER, George (Arthur)   1937-

PERSONAL: Born May 12, 1937, in Hamilton, Ontario, Canada; son of Harold (a trucker) and Doris (Senior) Feaver; married Nancy Alice Poynter Stephenson, June 12, 1963; children: Catherine Fergusson. *Education:* University of British Columbia, B.A. (honors), 1959; London School of Economics and Political Science, Ph.D., 1962. *Home:* 5775 Toronto Rd., Apt. 807, Vancouver, British Columbia, Canada V6T 1X4. *Office:* Department of Political Science, University of British Columbia, Vancouver, British Columbia, Canada V6T 1W5.

CAREER: Mount Holyoke College, South Hadley, Mass., assistant professor of political science, 1962-65; University of London, London, England, visiting lecturer at London School of Economics and Political Science, 1965-66, research associate of University College, 1966-67; Georgetown University, Washington, D.C., visiting associate professor, 1967-68; Emory University, Atlanta, Ga., associate professor of political science, 1968-71; University of British Columbia, Vancouver, associate professor, 1971-74, professor of political science, 1974—. *Member:* International Political Science Association, American Political Science Association, American Association of University Professors, Canadian Political Science Association, Society of Authors. *Awards, honors:* Canada Council Leave fellowship in humanities and the social sciences, 1970-71, 1974-75; American Council of Learned Societies fellow, 1974-75.

WRITINGS: From Status to Contract: A Biography of Sir Henry Maine, 1822-1888, Longmans, Green, 1969, Humanities, 1970; (contributor) Maurice Cranston, editor, *The New Left,* Bodley Head, 1970, Library Press (New York), 1971; (author of introduction) Beatrice Webb, *Our Partnership,* edited by Barbara Drake and Margaret I. Cole, Cambridge University Press, 1975. Contributor to political science journals.

WORK IN PROGRESS: Sir James Fitzjames Stephen: A Biography; The Political Thought of Sidney Webb.

BIOGRAPHICAL/CRITICAL SOURCES: Times Literary Supplement, June 12, 1969.

* * *

FEINBERG, Barry (Vincent) 1938-

PERSONAL: Born December 26, 1938, in South Africa; married; children: three sons. Education: Johannesburg School of Art, Fine Art Diploma, 1959, National Art Teacher's Certificate, 1960; Slade School of Fine Art, London, Fine Art Diploma, 1965. Politics: African National Congress of South Africa. Religion: None. Home: 36 Clifton Gardens, London N.W.11, England.

CAREER: Teacher and artist in South Africa, 1959-60; teacher, artist, and writer in London, England, 1961-66; Bertrand Russell Archives, London, editor, 1966-74; International Defence and Aid Fund for Southern Africa, London, designer, 1975—. Has had exhibitions of his paintings and graphic work at Lidchi Gallery, Johannesburg, 1960, New End Gallery, London, 1966, Rotunda Gallery, London, 1970, and Erica Bourne Gallery, London, 1973; work has also been included in many group exhibitions.

WRITINGS: (Editor) The Archives of Bertrand Russell, Continuum, 1967; (editor with Ronald Kasrils) Dear Bertrand Russell: A Selection of His Correspondence with the General Public, 1950-1968, Houghton, 1969; (editor) The Collected Stories of Bertrand Russell, Simon & Schuster, 1972; (with Kasrils) Bertrand Russell's America, Volume I: 1896-1944, Viking, 1974; (editor) Poets to the People: South African Freedom Poems, Allen & Unwin, 1974. Contributor of poetry, articles, and reviews to South African and international journals; some of his poems have been included in anthologies.

WORK IN PROGRESS: Bertrand Russell's America, Volume II: 1944-1970.

SIDELIGHTS: Barry Feinberg has traveled extensively in Africa, America, Asia, and Europe.

BIOGRAPHICAL/CRITICAL SOURCES: Publishers' Weekly, June 30, 1969; Los Angeles Times, September 17, 1969; Washington Star, September 26, 1969; New Yorker, November 1, 1969; Nation, November 10, 1969; Progressive, December, 1969; Book World, December 7, 1969.

* * *

FEINGOLD, Henry L(eo) 1931-

PERSONAL: Born February 6, 1931, in Ludwigshaven, Germany; son of Marcus M. (a merchant) and Frieda (Singer) Feingold; married Vera Schiff (an artist), February 7, 1954; children: Margo R., Judith E. Education: Brooklyn College (now Brooklyn College of the City University of New York), B.A., 1953, M.A., 1954; New York University, Ph.D., 1966. Religion: Jewish. Home: 280 Ninth Ave., New York, N.Y. 10001. Office: Department of History, Bernard M. Baruch College of the City University of New York, New York, N.Y. 10010.

CAREER: Bernard M. Baruch College of the City University of New York, New York, N.Y., 1968—, began as assistant professor, professor of history, 1976—. Military service: U.S. Army, Intelligence, 1954-57.

WRITINGS: The Politics of Rescue: The Roosevelt Administration and the Holocaust, 1938-44 (Commentary Book Club selection), Rutgers University Press, 1970; Zion in America: The Jewish Experience from Colonial Times to the Present (Commentary Book Club selection), Twayne, 1975. Contributor to periodicals.

WORK IN PROGRESS: The Limits of Ethnic Power: Jews and the Jewish Question in American Foreign Relations.

BIOGRAPHICAL/CRITICAL SOURCES: National Review, December 15, 1970.

* * *

FEINSILVER, Lillian Mermin 1917-

PERSONAL: Born October 15, 1917, in New Haven, Conn.; daughter of Charles (a merchant) and Nechame (Rosen) Mermin; married Alexander Feinsilver (a rabbi and marriage counselor), September 23, 1946; children: David, Ruth. Education: University of Chicago, student, 1941, 1942; New School for Social Research, student, 1945. Religion: Jewish. Home: 510 McCartney, Easton, Pa. 18042.

CAREER: Yale University, New Haven, Conn., assistant in university secretary's office, 1937-39; Yale University, School of Medicine, assistant secretary for the Committee on the Hygiene of Housing of the American Public Health Association, 1939-44; John Wiley & Sons, New York, N.Y., research assistant, 1944-46; free-lance writer and editor, 1943—. Board member of Mansfield Co-op, 1948-49, Easton Planned Parenthood Center, 1957-58, and Penn-Jersey Co-op, 1959-62. Program chairman of B'nai B'rith Women, Lafayette (Ind.) chapter, 1954-55. Member: Deborah, Hadassah, Sisterhood, Temple Covenant of Peace (publicity chairman, 1956-73). Awards, honors: Prize in story-ending contest, Ellery Queen Mystery Magazine, 1947.

WRITINGS: The Taste of Yiddish, A. S. Barnes, 1971. Contributor of articles, features, book reviews, and verse to American Mercury, American Speech, Chicago Jewish Forum, Commentary, Hadassah Magazine, Hebrew Union College Monthly, Humanist, Internal Affairs, Jewish Digest, Jewish Heritage, Jewish Post and Opinion, National Jewish Monthly, New Republic, Philadelphia Bulletin Sunday Magazine, and Present Tense.

WORK IN PROGRESS: Miscellaneous material in the fields of language, sociology, public health, and consumer problems.

* * *

FEJTO, Francois (Philippe) 1909-

PERSONAL: Born August 31, 1909, in Nagykanizsa, Hungary; son of Louis (a bookseller) and Ida (Bonyhadi) Fischel; married Rose Hilmayer, December 3, 1933; children: Charles. Education: Studied at University of Pecs, 1927-29, and University of Budapest, 1929-32. Home: 49 Blvd. Victor-Hugo, Neuilly-sur-Seine, France. Office: Il Gioruale, 29 rue Tronchet, Paris 8e, France.

CAREER: Professor of German language and literature in Hungary, 1930-32; co-editor of Szep Szo (literary review), Budapest, Hungary, 1935-38; active in the Socialist movement in Hungary before taking up residence in France, 1938; correspondent in France for the Hungarian journal, Nepszava, 1938-39; commentator on European and Communist affairs for Agence France-Press, Paris, 1944-74. Military service: French Army, volunteer, 1939-40. Member: Association Francaise de Politique Etrangere, P.E.N.

WRITINGS: Henri Heine, Marechal, 1946, translation by Mervyn Savill published as Heine: A Biography, Wingate, 1946; (editor) Le Printempts des peuples: 1848 dans le monde, two volumes, Editions de Minuit, 1948, translation by Hugh Shelley and others published in one volume as The Opening of an Era, 1848: An Historical Symposium, Wingate, 1948, published with introduction by A.J.P. Taylor,

Fertig, 1966; *Un Habsbourg revolutionnaire: Joseph II*, Plon, 1953; *La Tragedie hongroise*, preface by Jean Paul Sartre, P. Horay, 1956, translation by Norbert Guterman published as *Behind the Rape of Hungary*, McKay, 1957; (author of introductory sketch on Nagy) Imre Nagy, *Un Communisme n'oublie pas l'homme*, Plon, 1957; (author of preface) *La Revolte de la Hongrie d'apres les emissions de radios hongroises, Octobre-Novembre 1956*, P. Horay, 1957.

Dieu et son Juif, Grasset, 1960; *Les Juifs et l'antisemitisme dans les pays communistes, entre l'integration et la secession*, Plon, 1960; *Chine—USSR: La Fin d'une hegemonie*, Plon, 1964; *Budapest 1956*, Julliard, 1966; *Le Conflit: Le Developpement du grand schisme communiste, 1956-66*, Plon, 1966; *The French Communist Party and the Crisis of International Communism*, M.I.T. Press, 1967; *Histoire des democraties populaires apres Staline*, Editions du Seuil, revised edition, two volumes, 1969, translation by Daniel Weissbort published as *A History of the People's Democracies: Eastern Europe since Stalin*, Penguin, 1974; *Dictionnaire des partis communistes et mouvements revolutionnaires*, Casterman, 1971; *L' heritage de Lenine*, Casterman, 1973; *Le Coup de Prague de 1948*, Editions du Seuil, 1976.

SIDELIGHTS: Francois Fejto is "what better-known writers merely purport to be: a connoisseur of the world of Communism," George Lichtheim wrote in the *New York Review of Books*. Fejto speaks English but usually writes in French. His study on the French Communist Party was edited by William E. Griffith for the "Studies in International Communism" series of the Center for International Studies at Massachusetts Institute of Technology. There have been several German and Italian translations of his books.

BIOGRAPHICAL/CRITICAL SOURCES: Francois Fejto, *La Tragedie hongroise*, preface by Jean Paul Sartre, P. Horay, 1956; *New York Review of Books*, June 1, 1967, July 13, 1967.

* * *

FELDMAN, Herbert (H. S.) 1910-
(Ross McLeod)

PERSONAL: Born November 5, 1910, in London, England; son of Harry (a manufacturer) and Mary (Goddard) Feldman; married Nishat Hyat; children: Guy. *Education:* Attended Gray's Inn, London. *Politics:* Independent. *Religion:* "Non-institutional." *Home:* 14 Kutchery Rd., Karachi 4, Pakistan. *Agent:* Anthony Sheil Associates Ltd., 52 Floral St., Covent Garden, London WC2E 9DA, England.

CAREER: Called to the Bar; before World War II was employed in the legal department of an oil company; after the war was a temporary civil servant in the pre-partition government of India, and went to Pakistan in the same capacity in 1947; later entered business, mostly contracting; still active in business but is devoting increasing time to writing. *Military service:* British Army, Royal Artillery, 1940-46; became major.

WRITINGS: A Constitution for Pakistan, Oxford University Press, 1955; *Clubs Are Trumps*, W. J. Jeffrey, 1956; *Karachi through a Hundred Years: The Centenary History of the Karachi Chamber of Commerce and Industry, 1860-1960*, Oxford University Press, 1960, 2nd edition, 1970; *Pakistan: An Introduction*, Oxford University Press, 1961, 2nd edition, 1968; *The Land and People of Pakistan*, Macmillan, 1965; *Revolution in Pakistan: A Study of the Martial Law Administration*, Oxford University Press, 1967; *From Crisis to Crisis: Pakistan, 1962-69*, Oxford University Press, 1972;

The End and the Beginning, Oxford University Press, 1976. Contributor to *International Affairs* (London). Has written a few short stories published under the pseudonym Ross McLeod.

WORK IN PROGRESS: A novel set in pre-partition India; gathering material for a political study of General Yahya Khan's administration.

SIDELIGHTS: Herbert Feldman went to the Indo-Pakistan area as a soldier in 1941 and has remained there since "except for such breaks at home as are usual." He says that he resisted the impulse to write for many years, but eventually succumbed, adding that he has not been successful with fiction but would like to be. He speaks the Urdu language "fairly well."

BIOGRAPHICAL/CRITICAL SOURCES: Times Literary Supplement, April 6, 1967; *Virginia Quarterly Review*, autumn, 1967.†

* * *

FELDMAN, Kenneth A. 1937-

PERSONAL: Born October 6, 1937, in Saginaw, Mich.; son of Evener and Sarah (Caplan) Feldman; married June F. Tiefenbrun (a social worker), June 14, 1964; children: Elena Kay, Daniel Jason. *Education:* Bay City Junior College, A.A., 1957; University of Michigan, B.A., 1959, M.A., 1961, Ph.D., 1965. *Politics:* Democrat. *Religion:* Jewish. *Home:* 4 Robert Townsend Dr., Setauket, N.Y. 11733. *Office:* Department of Sociology, State University of New York, Stony Brook, N.Y. 11794.

CAREER: University of Michigan, Ann Arbor, study director at Institute for Social Research, 1965-68, assistant professor of sociology, 1966-68; State University of New York at Stony Brook, assistant professor, 1968-69, associate professor of sociology, 1969—. *Member:* American Sociological Association, American Psychological Association, American Educational Research Association, Sigma Xi, Phi Theta Kappa, Phi Kappa Phi.

WRITINGS: (With Theodore M. Newcomb) *The Impact of College on Students*, two volumes, Jossey-Bass, 1969; (editor) *College and Student: Selected Readings in the Social Psychology of Higher Education*, Pergamon, 1972. Also coauthor with John O'Connor of study guide for *Social Psychology*, Holt, 1965.

* * *

FENSTERMAKER, J(oseph) Van 1933-

PERSONAL: Born July 4, 1933, in Columbus, Ga.; son of Fred C. and Inez (Smith) Fenstermaker; married Joan Mach Griffin, September 15, 1955; children: Joseph Van, Jr., Jo Ann. *Education:* Kent State University, B.S., 1958, M.A., 1959; University of Illinois, Ph.D., 1963. *Home:* 238 St. Andrews Cir., Oxford, Miss. 38655. *Office:* Department of Economics, University of Mississippi, 208 Conner Hall, University, Miss. 38677.

CAREER: Federal Reserve Bank of New York, New York, N.Y., research economist, 1962-64; Kent State University, Kent, Ohio, assistant professor of economics, 1964-66; Southern Illinois University, Carbondale, associate professor of finance and chairman of department of finance, 1966-69; University of Mississippi, University, professor of economics and holder of the Chair of Banking, 1969—. Part-time assistant professor of economics at Hunter College of the City University of New York and City College of the City University of New York, 1963. Vice-president, Van

Stone Associates. Director, Mississippi School of Banking; case coordinator, Banking School of the South.

MEMBER: American Economic Association, American Finance Association, Economic History Association, Business History Conference, Midwest Finance Association (secretary-treasurer, 1968-69), Appalachian Finance Association (vice-president, 1968-69), Phi Kappa Phi, Pi Gamma Mu, Phi Alpha Theta, Kappa Delta Pi, Omicron Delta Epsilon, Alpha Kappa Psi.

WRITINGS: A Century of Service: History of the Trevett-Mattis Banking Company, [Champaign], 1965; (editor) *Papers Presented at the Annual Business History Conference, February 26-27, 1965,* Bureau of Economic and Business Research, Kent State University, 1965; *A Statistical Summary of the Commercial Banks Incorporated in the United States Prior to 1819,* Bureau of Economic and Business Research, Kent State University, 1965; *The Development of American Commercial Banking: 1782-1837* (monograph), Bureau of Economic and Business Research, Kent State University, 1965; *Cash Management: Managing the Cash Flows, Bank Balances, and Short-Term Investments of Non-Profit Institutions,* Kent State University Press, 1967; *A Technique of Determining a Firm's Minimum Bank Balances,* Bureau of Business Research, Southern Illinois University, 1967; *Readings in Financial Markets and Institutions,* Appleton, 1969. Contributor to *Appalachian Financial Review, Business and Government Review, Southern Journal of Business, Business History Review, Educational Record, Journal of Economic History,* and other professional journals. Editor of *Appalachian Financial Review,* 1968-69, and *Business Perspectives.*

WORK IN PROGRESS: Research project, "A Growth Model of the Life Insurance Industry"; *What Prerequisites Best Prepare a College Student for the Basic Course in Business Finance?;* "The Extension of Bank Charge Card Programs to Small Cities through Correspondent Relationships," article submitted for publication; *Financial Markets and Institutions,* a textbook; and "Flows of Funds through the Life Insurance Industry," article submitted for publication.†

*   *   *

FENTON, Carroll Lane 1900-1969

February 12, 1900—November 16, 1969; American naturalist, editor, and educator. Obituaries: *New York Times,* November 17, 1969; *Antiquarian Bookman,* December 1, 1969; *Publishers' Weekly,* January 5, 1970. (See index for *CA* sketch)

*   *   *

FERLITA, Ernest (Charles) 1927-

PERSONAL: Born December 1, 1927, in Tampa, Fla.; son of Giuseppe R. (a macaroni manufacturer) and Vicenta (Ficarrotta) Ferlita. *Education:* Spring Hill College, B.S., 1950; St. Louis University, M.A., 1964; Yale University, D.F.A., 1969. *Home and office:* Department of Drama and Speech, Loyola University, New Orleans, La. 70118.

CAREER: Entered Order of Society of Jesus (Jesuits), 1950, ordained Roman Catholic priest, June 13, 1962; high school teacher in New Orleans, La., 1956-59; Spring Hill College, Mobile, Ala., instructor in English and speech, 1964-65; Loyola University, New Orleans, La., assistant professor of drama and chairman of department of drama and speech, 1969—. Member of board of directors, Loyola University,

1970—. *Military service:* U.S. Army, Medical Corps, 1946-47; became sergeant.

WRITINGS: The Hills Send Off Echoes (one-act play), Baker's Plays, 1962; "The Ballad of John Ogilvie" (three-act play), first produced Off-Broadway at Blackfriars' Theatre, October 9, 1968; *The Theatre of Pilgrimage,* Sheed, 1971; (with John R. May) *Film Odyssey,* Paulist/Newman, 1976; (with May) *Man in Disorder: The Parables of Lina Wertmueller,* Paulist/Newman, 1977; *The Way of the River: A Book of Scriptural Meditations,* Paulist/Newman, 1977. Contributor to *Drama Critique* and *New Orleans Review.*

SIDELIGHTS: Father Ferlita told *CA,* "Both as teacher and writer, I am very interested in the dialectic between religion and drama."

*   *   *

FERRISS, Abbott Lamoyne 1915-

PERSONAL: Born January 31, 1915, in Jonestown, Miss.; son of Alfred William O. and Grace Childs (Mitchell) Ferriss; married Ruth Elizabeth Sparks, December 21, 1940; children: John Abbott, William Thomas. *Education:* Attended University of Mississippi, 1933-35; University of Missouri, B.J., 1937; University of North Carolina, M.A., 1943, Ph.D., 1950; also attended Furman University, George Washington University, and U.S. Department of Agriculture Graduate School. *Politics:* Democrat. *Religion:* Episcopalian. *Home:* 1273 Oxford Rd. N.E., Atlanta, Ga. 30306. *Office:* Department of Sociology and Anthropology, Emory University, Atlanta, Ga. 30322.

CAREER: University of North Carolina at Chapel Hill, junior research assistant at Institute for Research in Social Science, 1942, research assistant, 1942-43, instructor in sociology, 1946-48; Berea College, Berea, Ky., instructor in sociology, 1946; Vanderbilt University, Nashville, Tenn., assistant professor of sociology, 1949-51; Human Resources Research Institute, Maxwell Air Force Base, Montgomery, Ala., social scientist and chief of various divisions, 1951-54; Air Force Personnel and Training Research Center, Lackland Air Force Base, San Antonio and Randolph Air Force Base, Universal City, both in Texas, chief of various branches, 1954-57; U.S. Census Bureau, Washington, D.C., chief of Health Statistics Branch, 1957-59; Outdoor Recreation Resources Review Commission, Washington, D.C., supervisory survey statistician, 1959-62; National Science Foundation, Office of Economic and Manpower Studies, Washington, D.C., associate study director of Science Education Studies Group, 1962-67; Russell Sage Foundation, New York, N.Y., research sociologist in Washington, D.C., 1967-70; Emory University, Atlanta, Ga., professor of sociology and chairman of department of sociology and anthropology, 1970—. Lecturer at George Washington University, Washington, D.C., 1958, University of Maryland, 1958-59, and Northern Virginia Center, University of Virginia, Charlottesville, 1959-70. Consultant to directorate of life sciences, U.S. Air Force Office of Scientific Research, Washington, D.C., 1959-60. Member of social science committees and advisory boards of various universities and institutions. *Military service:* U.S. Army Air Corps, 1943-46.

MEMBER: American Sociological Association, American Association for the Advancement of Science, American Statistical Association, Population Association of America, Sociological Research Association, Southern Sociological Society (second vice president, 1966-67), District of Columbia Sociological Society (secretary-treasurer, 1965-68; president, 1969-70), Sigma Alpha Epsilon, Phi Eta Sigma, Algonquin Wildlands League, Cosmos Club.

WRITINGS: Indicators of Trends in American Education, Russell Sage, 1969; *Indicators of Change in the American Family,* Russell Sage, 1970; *Indicators of Trends in the Status of American Women,* Russell Sage, 1971.

Government reports and technical memoranda: (Contributor) *Symposium on Electronics Maintenance PPT 202/4,* Office of the Assistant Secretary of Defense, Research and Development, 1955; *The Allocation of Material Control Functions in Six Armament-Electronics Maintenance Squadrons, SAC,* Air Force Personnel and Training Research Center, Randolph Air Force Base, 1956; (with Charles Proctor and others) *National Recreation Survey* (ORRRC Study Report 19), U.S. Government Printing Office, 1962; (contributor) *Recreation Research* (collected papers from the National Conference on Recreation Research, November 7-10, 1965), American Association for Health, Physical Education and Recreation, 1966; (editor) *Research and the 1970 Census,* Southern Regional Demographic Group, Oak Ridge Associated Universities (Oak Ridge, Tenn.), 1971. Member of abstract staff of *Sociological Abstracts,* 1958-61. Contributor of articles, book reviews, and abstracts to numerous sociological journals, including *American Sociologist, Social Forces, Science, Rural Sociology, Public Opinion Quarterly, College and University, Social Indicators Research,* and *Annals.*

*   *   *

FERRO, Robert Michael 1941-

PERSONAL: Born October 21, 1941, in Cranford, N.J.; son of Michael Jerome (a corporation president) and Gaetana (Panzera) Ferro. *Education:* Rutgers University, B.A., 1963; University of Iowa, M.F.A. and M.A., 1967. *Residence:* New York, N.Y. *Agent:* John Cushman Associates, Inc., 25 West 43rd St., New York, N.Y. 10036.

CAREER: Full-time writer.

WRITINGS: (With Michael Grumley) *Atlantis: The Autobiography of a Search,* Doubleday, 1970; *The Others,* Scribner, 1977.

BIOGRAPHICAL/CRITICAL SOURCES: New York Times, January 23, 1969, January 25, 1970; *Best Sellers,* November 1, 1970; *Chicago Tribune Sunday Magazine,* February 14, 1971.

*   *   *

FIEDLER, Jean(nette Feldman)

PERSONAL: Born in Pittsburgh, Pa.; daughter of Harry (a businessman) and Dina (Diness) Feldman; married Harold Fiedler (a painter), July 5, 1949; children: Judith, Joan. *Education:* University of Pittsburgh, B.A., 1945; graduate study at New York University, 1955-57, and New School for Social Research, 1960-61. *Politics:* Democrat. *Home:* 69-23 Bell Blvd., Bayside, N.Y. 11364.

CAREER: Children's Aid Society, Pittsburgh, Pa., social worker, 1945; high school teacher of English in Pittsburgh, 1946-48; Gimbel's Department Store, Pittsburgh, copywriter, 1948; Brooklyn Public Library, Brooklyn, N.Y., librarian, 1949-50; free-lance writer and editor in New York City, 1950—; substitute teacher in New York City high schools, 1961—; librarian in private high school in Queens, N.Y., 1967—. City University of New York, teacher of juvenile writing at Queens College, 1964, teacher of creative

writing at Queensborough Community College, 1975—; teacher of creative writing in Bayside, N.Y., 1964-67. *Member:* Authors League of America, Women's National Book Association.

WRITINGS—Children's and young adult books, except as noted: *The Green Thumb Story,* Holiday House, 1952; *Big Brother Danny,* Holiday House, 1953; *Teddy and the Ice Cream Man,* Abelard, 1957; (with Carol Reuter) *The Last Year,* McKay, 1962; *A Yardstick for Jessica,* McKay, 1964; *Jill's Story,* McKay, 1965; *Lassie, Sand Bar Rescue,* Whitman Publishing, 1965; *New Brother, New Sister,* Golden Press, 1966; *Great American Heroes,* Hart Publishing, 1966; *Lassie and the Deer Mystery,* Whitman Publishing, 1967; *My Special House,* Whitman Publishing, 1967; *My Special Day,* Whitman Publishing, 1967; *Call Me Juanita,* McKay, 1968; *In Any Spring,* McKay, 1969; *I Know What a Farm Is,* Whitman, 1970; *A Break in the Circle,* McKay, 1971; *Atone with Evil* (gothic novel), Bantam, 1976. Writer of two filmstrips, "Reading," 1974, and "And Then What Happened," 1975. Contributor of stories and articles to magazines.

SIDELIGHTS: Jean Fiedler has been writing since childhood, and first published at the age of eleven. *Avocational interests:* Music, travel, transcendental meditation.

BIOGRAPHICAL/CRITICAL SOURCES: Best Sellers, April 1, 1969; *Commonweal,* May 23, 1969.

*   *   *

FIELD, Joyce W(olf) 1932-

PERSONAL: Born October 1, 1932, in Bronx, N.Y.; daughter of Abraham and Bella (Kestenbaum) Wolf; married Leslie A. Field (a college professor), January 25, 1953; children: Jeffrey H., Linda K. *Education:* Wayne University (now Wayne State University), B.A., 1955; Indiana University, student, 1955-56, 1959; Purdue University, M.A., 1959. *Home:* 625 Avondale Dr., West Lafayette, Ind. 47906.

CAREER: Purdue University, Lafayette, Ind., instructor in industrial management, 1964-75; Tippecanoe County Manpower Department, Lafayette, administrative assistant, 1975—. Founder, Purdue Women's Caucus. *Member:* Women's Equity Action League, Phi Beta Kappa.

WRITINGS: (Editor with husband, Leslie A. Field) *Bernard Malamud and the Critics,* New York University Press, 1970; (with L. A. Field) *Bernard Malamud: A Collection of Critical Essays,* Prentice-Hall, 1975. Contributor to *Journal of Popular Culture* and *Modern Fiction Studies.* Assistant editor, *Journal of Reading,* 1964-67.

*   *   *

FIELD, Leslie A. 1926-

PERSONAL: Surname originally Sheinfeld; born September 19, 1926, in Montreal, Quebec, Canada; son of Harry (a grocer) and Rose (Youlis) Sheinfeld; married Joyce Wolf (a county administrator), January 25, 1953; children: Jeffrey H., Linda K. *Education:* Attended Asumption College, Windsor, Ontario, University of Detroit, and University of California, Los Angeles; Wayne University (now Wayne State University), B.A., 1953, M.A., 1955; Indiana University, further graduate courses, 1955-63. *Home:* 625 Avondale Dr., West Lafayette, Ind. 47906. *Office:* Department of English, Purdue University, West Lafayette, Ind. 47907.

CAREER: Purdue University, West Lafayette, Ind., instructor in English and American literature, 1956-57, research editor at Agriculture Experiment Station, 1957-58, instructor, 1958-65, assistant professor, 1965-72, associate professor of English and American literature, 1972—. Senior fellow and lecturer, Bar-Ilan University, Ramat-Gan, Israel, 1969-70. *Military service:* Royal Canadian Navy, 1944-45. *Member:* Modern Language Association of America, American Professors for Peace in the Middle East (national vice-president; Purdue chapter president), Academic Committee on Soviet Jewry. *Awards, honors:* Purdue Research Foundation travel grant to France, 1961.

WRITINGS: (Editor with William Braswell) *Thomas Wolfe's Purdue Speech: Writing and Living,* Purdue University Studies, 1964; (editor with Maurice Beebe) *Robert Penn Warren, All the King's Men: A Critical Handbook,* Wadsworth, 1966; (editor) *Thomas Wolfe: Three Decades of Criticism,* New York University Press, 1968; (editor with wife, Joyce W. Field) *Bernard Malamud and the Critics,* New York University Press, 1970; (with J. W. Field) *Bernard Malamud: A Collection of Critical Essays,* Prentice-Hall, 1975. Contributor of articles and reviews to literary journals. Advisory editor, *Modern Fiction Studies, Journal of Popular Culture,* and *Thomas Wolfe Newsletter.*

WORK IN PROGRESS: Further research and writing on Thomas Wolfe and Bernard Malamud; ethnic studies in literature.

* * *

FIELD, Michael 1915-1971

February 21, 1915—March 22, 1971; American author and editor of cookbooks. *Obituaries: New York Times,* March 24, 1971; *Variety,* March 31, 1971; *Newsweek,* April 5, 1971; *Publishers' Weekly,* April 19, 1971.

* * *

FIGURITO, Joseph 1922-

PERSONAL: Born November 24, 1922, in Gaeta, Italy; son of Salvatore L. (in produce business) and Maria L. (Romano) Figurito; married Mary T. Calarese, June 17, 1956. *Education:* Boston College, A.B., 1947; Middlebury College, A.M., 1949, D.M.L., 1953. *Religion:* Roman Catholic. *Home:* 110 Sycamore St., Roslindale, Mass. 02131. *Office:* Department of Romance Languages, Boston College, Chestnut Hill, Mass. 02167.

CAREER: Boston College, Chestnut Hill, Mass., instructor in French and Italian, 1947-54, assistant professor, 1954-67, associate professor of Romance languages, 1968—. Harvard University Extension, assistant professor, 1957-68, associate professor of Spanish, 1968—. *Military service:* U.S. Army, Military Intelligence, 1943-46. *Member:* Modern Language Association of America, American Association of Teachers of Italian (president of New England chapter, 1964-66), Dante Society of America (member of council, 1964-67), Mediaeval Academy of America, American Association of University Professors. *Awards, honors:* Silver Medal of Culture, 1962, and Cross of Knight of Order of Merit, 1968, both from Republic of Italy.

WRITINGS: (Compiler and editor) *A Student's Guide to Dante's "Divina Commedia,"* Eaton Press, 1959; (contributor) E. H. Wilkins and others, editors, *A Concordance to the "Divine Comedy" of Dante Alighieri,* Harvard University Press, 1965; Dante, *Divine Comedy* (book notes), Barnes & Noble, 1968.

Plays: "Lo Sposalizio," 1950; "La Congiura delle Fidanzate," 1954; "Possiamo Essere Immortali," 1955. Contributor to *Italica.*

WORK IN PROGRESS: Translation of a critical edition of Giacomo Leopardi's *Lo Zibaldone;* research on Italian-American contributions to the United States.

AVOCATIONAL INTERESTS: Music, spotter at football games.

* * *

FINDLEY, Paul 1921-

PERSONAL: Born June 23, 1921, in Jacksonville, Ill.; son of Joseph S. and Florence Mary (Nichols) Findley; married Lucille Gemme, January 8, 1946; children: Craig Jon, Diane Lillian. *Education:* Illinois College, Jacksonville, B.A., 1943, LL.D., 1973. *Politics:* Republican. *Religion:* Congregational. *Home:* 7207 Normandy Lane, Falls Church, Va. 22042. *Office:* 2442 Rayburn House Office Building, Washington, D.C. 20515.

CAREER: Pike Press, Inc., Pittsfield, Ill., president and publisher, 1947—; member of 87th-94th U.S. Congress representing 20th Illinois District, Washington, D.C., 1962—, presently serving as member of House subcommittees on Europe, international organizations, and national security. Secretary, International Movement for Atlantic Union; member of board of directors, Federal Union, Inc. Trustee, Illinois College. *Military service:* U.S. Naval Reserve, active duty; served in South Pacific; became lieutenant junior grade. *Member:* American Academy of Political and Social Science, American Legion, Veterans of Foreign Wars, Lincoln Group of the District of Columbia (board of directors), Phi Beta Kappa, Lions Club. *Awards, honors:* D.H.L. from Lindenwood College.

WRITINGS: The Federal Farm Fable, Arlington House, 1968. Contributor to *Reader's Digest.*†

* * *

FINE, Ralph Adam 1941-

PERSONAL: Born February 14, 1941, in New York, N.Y.; son of Sidney (a New York Supreme Court justice) and Libby (Poresky) Fine; married Kay Prange (a teacher), July, 1971. *Education:* Tufts University, A.B., 1962; Columbia University, LL.B., 1965. *Religion:* Jewish. *Office:* 111 East Wisconsin Ave., Milwaukee, Wis. 53202.

CAREER: Admitted to the State Bar of New York, 1965; law clerk for U.S. district court judge, Brooklyn, N.Y., 1965-67; joined U.S. Department of Justice, Washington, D.C., prepared briefs for U.S. Supreme Court cases, practiced before various U.S. Courts of Appeals, 1967-70; full-time professional writer, 1970-74; admitted to the State Bar of Wisconsin, 1973; involved with television news programs, 1974-75; host of television talk show, Milwaukee, Wis., 1975-77; attorney in private practice, Milwaukee, 1976—.

WRITINGS: Mary Jane versus Pennsylvania, McCall Publishing, 1970; *The Great Drug Deception,* Stein & Day, 1972.

WORK IN PROGRESS: General fiction.

BIOGRAPHICAL/CRITICAL SOURCES: Milwaukee Journal, November 8, 1970; *Milwaukee Sentinel,* March 11, 1971; American Bar Association *Journal,* December, 1973.

* * *

FINLAYSON, Ann 1925-

PERSONAL: Born March 25, 1925, in New York, N.Y.; daughter of Frank Lathrop and Anna (Neacy) Finlayson. *Education:* Northwestern University, B.S.J., 1945. *Politics:*

Usually Democratic. *Religion:* Roman Catholic. *Home and office:* 33 North Western Hwy., Blauvelt, N.Y. 10913.

CAREER: Popular Publications, New York City, editor, 1950-51, editor and staff writer for *True Story,* 1951-60; freelance writer, mostly for confession magazines, 1960-63; Rutledge Books, Inc., New York City, editor, 1963-64; free-lance copy editor and proofreader for book publishers, and free-lance writer, mostly for young people, 1965—.

WRITINGS: Runaway Teen, Doubleday, 1963; *A Summer to Remember,* Doubleday, 1964; *Animal Habits,* Golden Press, 1965; *Decathlon Men,* Garrard, 1966; *Stars of the Modern Olympics,* Garrard, 1967; *Champions at Bat: Three Power Hitters,* Garrard, 1970; *Redcoat in Boston,* Warne, 1971; *Rebecca's War,* Warne, 1972; (with Harold B. Gill, Jr.) *Colonial Virginia,* Thomas Nelson, 1973; *House Cat,* Warne, 1974; *Greenhorn on the Frontier,* Warne, 1974; *Colonial Maryland,* Thomas Nelson, 1974.

WORK IN PROGRESS: More Olympic Stars, for Garrard.

AVOCATIONAL INTERESTS: Walking, reading, watching television, knitting, talking, browsing in hardware and stationery stores.

* * *

FINN, Jonathan   1884(?)-1971

1884(?)—June 4, 1971; American novelist, playwright, and screenwriter. Obituaries: *New York Times,* June 5, 1971; *Antiquarian Bookman,* July 19-26, 1971.

* * *

FINNERAN, Richard J(ohn)   1943-

PERSONAL: Born December 19, 1943, in New York, N.Y.; son of Edward G. and Maude Florence (Rudden) Finneran; married Mary M. Fitzgerald, 1976. *Education:* New York University, B.A., 1964; University of North Carolina, Ph.D., 1968. *Home:* 1024 Lowerline St., New Orleans, La. 70118. *Office:* Department of English, Newcomb College, Tulane University, New Orleans, La. 70118.

CAREER: University of Florida, Gainesville, instructor in English, 1967-68; New York University, New York, N.Y., instructor in English, 1968-70; Tulane University, Newcomb College, New Orleans, La., assistant professor, 1970-74, associate professor of English, 1974—. *Member:* International Association for the Study of Anglo-Irish Literature (member of executive committee, 1973—), American Association of University Professors, Modern Language Association of America (chairman of Celtic group, 1972, and Anglo-Irish Group, 1979), South Atlantic Modern Language Association, (chairman of Irish studies section, 1977), South Central Modern Language Association (chairman of Anglo-Irish group, 1972). *Awards, honors:* Centenary fellowship to Yeats International Summer School at Sligo, Ireland, 1965; National Endowment for the Humanities summer stipend, 1975.

WRITINGS: (Editor) William Butler Yeats, *John Sherman and Dhoya,* Wayne State University Press, 1969; *William Butler Yeats: The Byzantium Poems,* C. E. Merrill, 1970; *The Prose Fiction of W. B. Yeats,* Dolmen Press, 1973; (editor) *Letters of James Stephens,* Macmillan, 1974; (editor and contributor) *Anglo-Irish Literature: A Review of Research,* Modern Language Association of America, 1976; (co-editor) *Letters to W. B. Yeats,* Macmillan, 1977; (editor) *The Correspondence of Robert Bridges and W. B. Yeats,* Macmillan, 1977; *The Olympian and the Leprachaun: W. B. Yeats and James Stephens,* Dolmen Press, in press. Contributor to language journals.

WORK IN PROGRESS: Editing a new and comprehensive edition of *The Complete Poems of W. B. Yeats,* for Macmillan.

AVOCATIONAL INTERESTS: Tennis, basketball, football, music.

* * *

FINOCCHIARO, Mary (Bonomo)   1913-

PERSONAL: Born April 21, 1913, in New York, N.Y.; daughter of Anthony and Josephine (Billone) Bonomo; married Santo Finocchiaro (a surgeon), September 21, 1940; children: Salvatore, Rosemary (Mrs. Andreas Bartsch). *Education:* Hunter College (now Hunter College of the City University of New York), B.A., 1932, M.A., 1934; additional study at Sorbonne, University of Paris, 1934; Columbia University, Ph.D., 1948. *Office:* Department of Education, Hunter College of the City University of New York, 695 Park Ave., New York, N.Y. 10021.

CAREER: New York (N.Y.) public schools, began as elementary and secondary teacher, and was subsequently supervisor of instruction for non-English speaking pupils, and curriculum assistant, Division of Curriculum Research; Hunter College of the City College of New York, New York, N.Y., currently professor of education. Fulbright professor in Italy and Spain; director, associate director, or speaker at language-teaching seminars in Morocco, Turkey, Poland, Spain, and Germany. Co-director, U.S. Government's Bilingual Readiness Project, educational consultant to Migration Division, Commonwealth of Puerto Rico. *Member:* American Association of University Professors, New York State Association for Curriculum Development, State Federation of Foreign Language Teachers (member of board), Administrative Women in Education (vice-president), Foreign Language Chairman's Association, Experimental Society (New York).

WRITINGS: (With Theodore Huebener) *English for Spanish Americans,* Henry Holt, 1950; *Teaching English as a Second Language in Elementary and Secondary Schools,* Harper, 1958, revised edition, 1974; *Children's Living Spanish Illustrated Lesson Book,* Crown, 1960; *Children's Living Spanish Picture Dictionary,* Crown, 1960; *Teaching Children Foreign Languages,* McGraw, 1964; *English as a Second Language: From Theory to Practice* (synthesis of her lectures and demonstrations for U.S. Department of State, 1960-64), Regents Publishing, 1964; (with Harold J. McNally) *Educator's Vocabulary Handbook for Administrators, Supervisors, Teachers, Students, and Others, Learning and Using English as a Foreign Language,* American Book Co., 1965; *Teachers Manual for Learning to Use English,* two books, Regents Publishing, 1966; *Learning to Use English,* two books, Regents Publishing, 1967; *Let's Talk,* Regents Publishing, 1968; *Aablemos,* Regents Publishing, 1976. Contributor to education journals.

WORK IN PROGRESS: College Subjects Self-Taught; and *Tales from Everywhere.*†

* * *

FIORINO, A(ngelo) John   1926-

PERSONAL: Born September 9, 1926, in Cleveland, Ohio; son of John and Mary (DiCarlo) Fiorino; married Mary Vallese, April 15, 1950; children: Michael, Mary Ann. *Education:* State Teachers College at Brockport (now State University of New York College at Brockport), B.S., 1953; Rutgers University, Ed.M., 1956; University of Buffalo (now State University of New York at Buffalo), Ed.D., 1961. *Home:* 2705 Salem Ct., Cinnaminson, N.J. 08077. *Office:* Division of Curriculum and Instruction, Temple University, Philadelphia, Pa. 19122.

CAREER: University of Detroit, Detroit, Mich., assistant professor of supervision and curriculum, 1961-64; University of Massachusetts, Amherst, assistant professor of elementary curricula, 1964-67; Eastern Kentucky University, Richmond, coordinator of Appalachia Teacher Education Project, 1967-68; Temple University, Philadelphia, Pa., 1968—, began as associate professor, currently professor of curriculum and instruction. *Military service:* U.S. Army, 1944-46. *Member:* American Association of University Professors, Society for General Systems Research, Association for Supervision and Curriculum Development, Phi Delta Kappa, Kappa Delta Pi.

WRITINGS: (With Kathryn Feyereisen and Arlene Nowak) *Supervision and Curriculum Renewal: A Systems Approach,* Appleton, 1970; *Differentiated Staffing: A Flexible Instructional Organization,* Harper, 1972. Also author of a monograph, *Differentiated Staffing.*

WORK IN PROGRESS: Work on systems planning.

* * *

FIRESIDE, Harvey 1929-

PERSONAL: Born December 28, 1929, in Vienna, Austria; son of Norbert (a photographer) and Sidy (Nagel) Fireside; married Bryna Joan Levenberg (a free-lance writer), December 12, 1959; children: Leela Ruth, Douglas Leonard, Daniel Ephraim. *Education:* Harvard University, B.A., 1952, A.M., 1955; Free University of Berlin, exchange fellow, 1953; New School for Social Research, Ph.D., 1968. *Politics:* Democrat. *Religion:* Jewish. *Home:* 105 Valentine Pl., Ithaca, N.Y. 14850. *Office:* Department of Political Science, Ithaca College, Ithaca, N.Y. 14850.

CAREER: Palmerton Publishing Corp., New York City, editor, 1959-60; American Cyanamid Co., New York City, editor, 1960-61; Foreign Policy Association, Inc., New York City, writer and editor, 1961-62; free-lance editor, New York City, 1962-64; New York Institute of Technology, New York City, instructor in social science, 1964-68; Ithaca College, Ithaca, N.Y., Charles A. Dana Professor of Politics, 1968—. *Military service:* U.S. Army, 1955-57. *Member:* American Political Science Association, International Political Science Association, American Association for the Advancement of Slavic Studies, American Association of University Professors (Ithaca College vice-president, 1968-70), American Civil Liberties Union (board member of Tompkins County chapter, 1970—), Amnesty International (founder of Ithaca branch, 1974).

WRITINGS: Icon and Swastika: The Russian Orthodox Church under Nazi and Soviet Control, Harvard University Press, 1971. Contributor to *Review of Politics, Russian Review, Journal of Modern History, Annals* of American Academy of Political and Social Science, *Epoch, Nation, New Republic, Commonweal, New Leader,* and *Problems of Communism.*

WORK IN PROGRESS: Researching political themes of current Soviet literature.

SIDELIGHTS: Harvey Fireside told *CA* that he has an "ongoing interest in cultural facets of [the] Soviet political system.... A tour of the USSR in 1974 made me face the bureaucratic callousness of a system that throttles free expression. Since then, writing about dissidents who value

their individualism above survival has been a labor of love as well as duty I urge other Western writers to share." He has also traveled in England, France, Germany, Switzerland, and Italy.

AVOCATIONAL INTERESTS: Writing poetry.

* * *

FISH, Kenneth L(loyd) 1926-

PERSONAL: Born August 25, 1926, in Woodsville, N.H.; son of Lloyd Samson (a railroad telegrapher) and Beulah (Green) Fish; married Joyce Marshall (a teacher), June 26, 1951; children: David, Cheryl, Brenda. *Education:* University of New Hampshire, B.A., 1950, Ed.M., 1951; Harvard University, Ed.D., 1959. *Politics:* Democrat. *Religion:* Protestant. *Office:* Northwestern Community High School, Carpenter Rd., Flint, Mich. 48505.

CAREER: Began as high school teacher in Highland Falls, N.Y., later was teacher-principal in Ashland, Me.; high school principal in Madrid, Spain (Air Force dependents' school), 1955-58, in Millville, N.J., 1958-60, in Haddonfield, N.J., 1960-64, and in Montclair, N.J., 1964-69; Northwestern Community High School, Flint, Mich., principal, 1969—. Member of board of advisers, American Institute for Foreign Study. *Military service:* U.S. Army, 1944-46; became sergeant. *Member:* National Education Association, National Association of Secondary School Principals, Michigan Association of Secondary School Principals. *Awards, honors:* Ford Foundation grant for study of student unrest in high schools, 1969.

WRITINGS: Conflict and Dissent in the High School, Bruce Publishing, 1970. Contributor to education journals.

WORK IN PROGRESS: Research on methods of training educators to adapt their behavior to racially integrated schools.††

* * *

FISZEL, Henryk 1910-

PERSONAL: Surname is pronounced Fish-el; born February 15, 1910, in Bendzin, Poland; son of Salomon (a clerk) and Rozalia (Donski) Fiszel; married Irene Kon (a writer), July 27, 1949. *Education:* Institute of Social Sciences, Warsaw, Poland, Ph.D., 1954. *Home:* Wilcza 13, Warsaw, Poland. *Office:* Faculty of Political Economy, University of Warsaw, Krakowski Przedmiescie, Warsaw, Poland.

CAREER: Polish Commission of Planning, Warsaw, Poland, vice-director, 1954-58; University of Warsaw, Faculty of Political Economy, Warsaw, professor of economics, 1954—. Lecturer at universities abroad. *Member:* Polish Economic Association. *Awards, honors:* Ford Foundation fellowship in Germany, Switzerland, Netherlands, and England, 1960; fellowship of French Government for work in Paris, 1961; Polish Economic Association Prize, 1964, for *Efektywnosc inwestycji i optimum produkcji w gospodarce socjalistycznej;* Oskar Lange Award, 1967, for *Szkice z teorii gospodarowania.*

WRITINGS: Czynniki i rezerwy przyspieszenia krazenia srodkow obrotowych w gospodarce Polski Ludowej (title means "Factors and Reserves of Turnover Acceleration in the Economy of Polish People's Republic"), Ksiazka i Wiedza, 1954; *Koszty wlasne i ceny produkcji przemyslowej* (booklet; title means "Costs and Prices of Industrial Production"), Ksiazka i Wiedza, 1955; *Prawo wartosci a problematyka cen w przemysle socjalistycznym* (title means "The Law of Value and Problems of Prices in the Socialist Industry''), Panstwowe Wydawnictwo Naukowe, 1956; *Zagadnienie cen i rachunku ekonomicznego w gospodarce socjalistycznej* (title means ''Problems of Prices and Economic Evaluation in a Socialist Economy''), Panstwowe Wydawnictwo Naukowe, 1958; *Efektywnose inwestycji i optimum produkcji w gospodarce socjalistycznej,* Ksiazka i Wiedza, 1960, 2nd edition with summaries in Russian, English, and German, 1963, translation by Olgierd Wojtasiewicz published as *Investment Efficiency in a Socialist Economy,* Pergamon, 1966; *Szkice z teorii gospodarowania* (title means ''Essays on the Theory of Economics''; summaries in Russian and English included), Panstwowe Wydawnictwo Ekonomiczne, 1965; *Teoria efektywnosci inwestycji i jej zastosowania* (title means ''Theory of Investment Efficiency and its Applications''), Panstwowe Wydawnictwo Naukowe, 1969; *Wstep do teorii gospodarowania* (title means ''Introduction to Theory of Economics''), Panstwowe Wydawnictwo Ekonomiczne, 1970; *Teoria gospodarowania* (title means ''The Theory of Management''), Panstwowe Wydawnictwo Naukowe, 1973. Contributor of more than sixty articles to journals in Poland and abroad.

WORK IN PROGRESS: Further work on the economic problems in a socialist economy.

SIDELIGHTS: Henryk Fiszel told *CA:* ''[From] my youth I have had an interest in the questions of economics and mathematics. I was always keen on being engaged in scientific research in one of these fields. The war, the military service and the difficulties after war caused a delay in accomplishment of my plans. Early in [the] fifties I took my doctor's degree and started to work in the University of Warsaw. I have devoted mostly to research the questions of the planning in socialist economy . . . in my works—in accordance with the second direction of my interests—I employed the mathematical methods.''

* * *

FITCH, Stanley K. 1920-

PERSONAL: Born November 4, 1920, in Canada; son of Mary Fitch; married Tess Ladonna; children: Bill, Debbie, Brian, Gina. *Education:* University of Manitoba, B.A., B.Ed., M.Ed., 1954; University of Southern California, Ed.D., 1962. *Home:* 15643 South Aravaca Dr., Paramount, Calif. 90723. *Office:* Department of Behavioral Sciences, El Camino College, Torrance, Calif. 91306.

CAREER: El Camino College, Torrance, Calif., professor of psychology, 1965—. *Military service:* Canadian Army.

WRITINGS: *Insights into Human Behavior,* Holbrook, 1970, 2nd edition, 1974.

* * *

FITTING, Melvin (Chris) 1942-

PERSONAL: Born January 24, 1942, in Troy, N.Y.; son of Chris and Helen (Van Denburg) Fitting; married Greer Russell, January 17, 1971. *Education:* Rensselaer Polytechnic Institute, B.S., 1963; Yeshiva University, M.A. and Ph.D., 1968. *Home:* Star Route, Stephentown Center, N.Y. 12169. *Office:* Herbert H. Lehman College of the City University of New York, Bronx, N.Y. 10468.

CAREER: Herbert H. Lehman College of the City University of New York, Bronx, N.Y., 1968—, began as assistant professor, currently associate professor of mathematics. *Member:* American Mathematical Society, Association for Symbolic Logic. *Awards, honors:* Research Foundation of City University of New York grants, 1970, 1971.

WRITINGS: *Intuitionistic Logic Model Theory and Forcing,* North Holland Publishing, 1969; (with wife, Greer Fitting) *In Praise of Simple Things,* McKay, 1975. Contributor to *Journal of Symbolic Logic, Notre Dame Journal of Formal Logic, Theoria,* and *West Coast Review.*

WORK IN PROGRESS: Researching modal logic, and recursion theory.

AVOCATIONAL INTERESTS: Writing poetry, photography, and homesteading.

* * *

FITZ, Jean DeWitt 1912-

PERSONAL: Born February 12, 1912, in Oak Park, Ill.; daughter of Charles Irwin (a Western Electric Corporation executive) and Gladys (Bowen) DeWitt; married Morgan Hiller Fitz (a photographer), October 17, 1941. *Education:* Skidmore College, A.B., 1933. *Politics:* Democratic. *Religion:* Unitarian Universalist. *Residence:* Augusta, Ga.

CAREER: Skidmore College, Saratoga Springs, N.Y., instructor in English and director of college bookstore, 1935-38; *Department Store Buyer* (magazine), New York, N.Y., assistant editor, 1939-40; *R.N.* (nursing journal), Rutherford, N.J., associate editor, 1940-43; free-lance writer, 1943—. *Member:* Dixie Council of Authors and Journalists, Georgia Writers Association.

WRITINGS: *The Viper's Bite,* Geron-X, 1969; *The Devon Maze,* Geron-X, 1969; *Graven Image,* Pyramid Communications, 1975. Contributor of articles to professional journals and short stories to U.S. and Canadian magazines, including *American, Mademoiselle, Charm.*

* * *

FITZGERALD, Ernest A. 1925-

PERSONAL: Born July 24, 1925, in Crouse, N.C.; son of James Boyd (a minister) and Hattie (Chaffin) Fitzgerald; married Frances Perry, August 25, 1945; children: James Boyd, Patricia Anne. *Education:* Western Carolina College (now University), A.B. (cum laude), 1947; Duke University, B.D., 1951. *Home:* 1921 Virginia Rd., Winston-Salem, N.C. 27104. *Office address:* Centenary United Methodist Church, Box 608, Winston-Salem, N.C. 27102.

CAREER: Has served pastorates in Methodist churches in Sylva, Liberty, Asheboro, Asheville, Charlotte, and Greensboro, North Carolina; currently senior minister of Centenary United Methodist Church, Winston-Salem, N.C. Joined Western North Carolina Conference in 1946, served as chairman of Television, Radio and Film Commission for four years, member of Commission on Christian Social Concerns and Board of Pensions. Official visitor to World Methodist Conference in London, England, 1966. Member of board of trustees of Pfeiffer College, Misenheimer, N.C., and board of visitors, Duke University Divinity School, Durham, N.C. *Member:* Masons, Rotary Club (Winston-Salem), Torch Club (secretary). *Awards, honors:* Distinguished Alumni Award from Pfeiffer College, 1965, and Duke University, 1973; D.D., High Point College, 1968.

WRITINGS: *There's No Other Way,* Abingdon, 1970; *The Structures of Inner Peace,* Fisher-Harrison Corp., 1973; *Living under Pressure,* Fisher-Harrison Corp., 1975; *You Can Believe!,* Abingdon, 1975.

AVOCATIONAL INTERESTS: Flying, woodworking, reading, boating, operating ham radio, water skiing, amateur mechanics, playing guitar, collecting epitaphs.

FLAKE, Chad J(ohn) 1929-

PERSONAL: Born December 28, 1929, in Snowflake, Ariz.; son of John Taylor (a rancher) and Carrie (Lindsay) Flake. Education: Northern Arizona University, student, 1947-49; Brigham Young University, B.A., 1953; University of Denver, M.A., 1955. Religion: Church of Jesus Christ of Latter-day Saints (Mormon). Home: 261 South Third St. E., Provo, Utah 84601. Office: Brigham Young University Library, Provo, Utah 84601.

CAREER: Brigham Young University Library, Provo, Utah, assistant reference librarian, 1953-54, documents librarian, 1955-57, special collections librarian, 1957-68, curator of special collections, 1959—, university instructor in library science, 1957—. Member: American Library Association, Western Historical Society, Utah Library Association (president, 1964), Utah Historical Society, Utah Valley Historical Society (past president), Utah Westerners.

WRITINGS: (Editor) Mormon Bibliography, 1830-1930, University of Utah Press, 1971. Co-author of The Brescia Danti. Contributor to professional journals. Editor, Mormon Americana, 1960—.

WORK IN PROGRESS: Periodical articles on Mormonism, 1830-1930, pre-Utah Mormon printing, 1830-1846, and on Mormonism and the National Reform Association; the journal of Lucy Hannah White Flake.

*   *   *

FLEISCHER, Manfred P(aul) 1928-

PERSONAL: Born June 26, 1928, in Peilau, Silesia, Germany; naturalized U.S. citizen; son of Alfred Hermann (a farmer) and Hilda (Herzog) Fleischer; married Margarete Breuninger (a professor of German literature), December 27, 1962; children: Maria, Monica, Martina. Education: Wagner College, B.A., 1955; Lutheran Theological Seminary, Philadelphia, B.D., 1959; University of Pennsylvania, M.A., 1961; University of Erlangen, Ph.D., 1965. Office: Department of History, University of California, Davis, Calif. 95616.

CAREER: Wagner College, Staten Island, N.Y., lecturer in philosophy, 1955-56; pastor of Lutheran church in Lyons, N.Y., 1959-61; Wagner College, lecturer in philosophy and religion, 1961; University of California, Riverside, associate, 1963-64, acting instructor in history, 1964-65; University of California, Davis, assistant professor, 1965-71, associate professor of history, 1971—. Member: American Historical Association, American Society of Church History, Gesellschaft fuer Geistesgeschichte. Awards, honors: Fulbright research scholar at University of Strasbourg, 1967-68.

WRITINGS: Katholische und lutherische Ireniker: Unter besonderer Beruecksichtigung des 19. Jahrhunderts, Musterschmidt-Verlag, 1968; (editor) The Decline of the West, Holt, 1970; (contributor) Lewis W. Spitz, editor, Discord, Dialog and Politics, Fortress, 1977. Contributor to Archive for Reformation History, Church History, Historische Zeitschrift, Jahrbuch fuer Schlesische Kirchengeschichte, Zeitschrift fuer Religions und Geistesgeschichte.

WORK IN PROGRESS: Research on the interrelationship of Humanism, Reformation, and Counter-Reformation in Silesia.

*   *   *

FLEMING, Miles 1919-

PERSONAL: Born August 14, 1919, in Northern Ireland.

Education: Queen's University of Belfast, B.Com.Sc., 1940. Home: 15 Southover Close, Bristol BS9 3NG, England. Office: Department of Economics, University of Bristol, Bristol, England.

CAREER: University of Manchester, Manchester, England, Drummond-Fraser research fellow, 1945-46; University of Bristol, Bristol, England, lecturer in economics, 1946-69, professor of economics, 1969—. Economic adviser to H. M. Treasury, 1952-54. Visiting lecturer, University of Pennsylvania, 1962-63, summer, 1967.

WRITINGS: Introduction to Economic Analysis, Allen & Unwin, 1969, Schocken, 1970; Monetary Theory, Macmillan, 1972.

*   *   *

FLORY, Julia McCune 1882-1971

February 2, 1882—April 23, 1971; American illustrator, author, and co-founder of Cleveland Playhouse. Obituaries: New York Times, April 26, 1971; Variety, May 5, 1971. (See index for CA sketch)

*   *   *

FLOWERS, Charles 1942-

PERSONAL: Born November 12, 1942, in Knoxville, Tenn.; son of Howard Fischer (an electrician) and Rose (Sullins) Flowers. Education: Harvard University, A.B. (magna cum laude), 1964; University of California, Los Angeles, graduate study, 1966. Politics: Democrat. Home: 13 Buckingham St., Rochester, N.Y. 14607. Agent: Jill Dargeon Agency, 160 East 48th St., New York, N.Y. 10016. Office: Department of English, University of Rochester, Rochester, N.Y. 14627.

CAREER: Chattanooga Times, Chattanooga, Tenn., reporter, 1960-64; head of English department at high school in Avalon, Calif., 1965-67; drama coach at school in Palmdale, Calif., 1967-68; audiovisual coordinator at school in Los Angeles, Calif., 1968-69; full-time writer, 1969-71; Television Information Office, New York, N.Y., associate editor, 1971-73; University of Rochester, Rochester, N.Y., assistant professor in English department, 1974—. Drama reviewer for WXXI-TV, Rochester. Member: Authors Guild. Awards, honors: Fellowship to Bread Loaf Writers' Conference; Thomas R. Coward Memorial Award in Fiction, Coward-McCann, Inc., 1970, for It Never Rains in Los Angeles; fellowship to MacDowell Colony; outstanding English Teacher in New York State, 1975.

WRITINGS: It Never Rains in Los Angeles, Coward, 1970. Also author of Laguna, Coward, and "Watson," a two-act play. Writer of television scripts for Appalachian Educational Laboratory, and radio scripts for C. P. MacGregor Productions.

WORK IN PROGRESS: A three-act play on Akhenaton.

BIOGRAPHICAL/CRITICAL SOURCES: Saturday Review, December 26, 1970; New York Times, December 28, 1970; Best Sellers, January 15, 1971; New York Times Book Review, January 17, 1971.

*   *   *

FLOYD, William Anderson 1928-

PERSONAL: Born December 5, 1928, in Akron, Ohio; son of Elmer Anderson (a rubber worker) and Mary (Surber) Floyd; married Sally Souther (a university professor), September 4, 1948; married second wife, Deloris Butler (a staff psychologist), December 21, 1973; children: Sally Ann, William A., Jr., Regina, Remona, Scott Anderson. *Education:* Eastern Kentucky University, A.B., 1949; University of Akron, M.A., 1953; Southern Methodist University, B.D., 1956; North Texas State University, Ed.D., 1962. *Home:* 320 Windsor Cir., Bowling Green, Ky. 42101. *Office:* Western Kentucky University, Bowling Green, Ky. 42101.

CAREER: Licensed psychologist in Kentucky and South Carolina; Western Kentucky University, Bowling Green, professor of psychology and child development and family living, and head of department, 1968—. *Member:* American Psychological Association, American Personnel and Guidance Association, National Vocational Guidance Association, American Association of Marriage Counselors, Southeastern Psychological Association, Southeastern Council on Family Relations, Kentucky Psychological Association, South Carolina Psychological Association. *Awards, honors:* National Institute of Mental Health fellow, 1967-68.

WRITINGS: A Definitive Study of Your Future as a Minister, Rosen Press, 1969. Contributor of articles to vocational guidance, counseling, marriage, and family journals.

WORK IN PROGRESS: Research on the screening and selection of police officers.

* * *

FLYNN, Donald R(obert) 1928-

PERSONAL: Born November 18, 1928, in St. Louis, Mo.; son of George Joseph and Mary (Foley) Flynn; married Charlotte J. Bayton, October 26, 1957; children: Kevin, Christopher, Colin. *Education:* University of Missouri, B.A., 1952. *Home:* 303 Lantana Ave., Englewood, N.J. 07631. *Agent:* Francie Hidden, 229 West 42nd St., New York, N.Y. 10021. *Office: New York Daily News,* 220 East 42nd St., New York, N.Y. 10017.

CAREER: Newspaper reporter, *St. Joseph Gazette,* St. Joseph, Mo., 1953-54, *Topeka State-Journal,* Topeka, Kan., 1955-56, *Kansas City Star,* Kansas City, Mo., 1956, *Chicago Daily News,* Chicago, Ill., 1957-58, and *New York Journal-American,* 1959-65, and *New York Herald Tribune,* 1966, both New York City; *New York Daily News,* New York City, reporter and writer, 1967—. *Member:* Authors League of America, Dramatists Guild. *Awards, honors:* First prize in spot news, Uniformed Firemen's Association Award, 1963.

WRITINGS—All plays: "Now It Makes Sense" (three-act comedy), first produced in Bellport, L.I., at Gateway Playhouse, August 26, 1969; "Pull the Covers Over My Head" (three-act drama), first produced in New York at Actor's Place, fall, 1969; "A Money-Back Guarantee" (one-act comedy), first produced in New York at American Theatre, fall, 1969; "The Petition" (one-act comedy), first produced in Waterford, Conn., at Eugene O'Neill Memorial Theatre Center, summer, 1970; "The Man Who Raped Kansas" (two-act comedy), first produced at Gilford Playhouse, August 3, 1970 (rewritten version, "Up the Creek," first produced in Corning, N.Y., at Corning Summer Theatre, August 17, 1971).

WORK IN PROGRESS: A two-act comedy; a two-act drama.††

* * *

FLYNN, Robert (Lopez) 1932-

PERSONAL: Born April 12, 1932, in Chillicothe, Tex.; son of James Emmett (a farmer) and Gladys (Wilkinson) Flynn;

married Jean Sorrels (a teacher), June 1, 1953; children: Deirdre Siobhan, Brigid Erin. *Religion:* Baptist. *Residence:* San Antonio, Tex. *Agent:* Robert Lescher, 155 East 71st St., New York, N.Y. 10021. *Office:* Department of Drama, Trinity University, San Antonio, Tex. 78212.

CAREER: Trinity University, San Antonio, Tex., assistant professor of drama, 1963—. *Military service:* U.S. Marine Corps, 1950-52. *Member:* Writers Guild of America, Authors Guild, Authors League of America, Texas Institute of Letters. *Awards, honors:* Special Jury Award, Theater of Nations, 1964, for "Journey to Jefferson"; Texas Institute of Letters Award, and Western Heritage Award, both 1968, for *North to Yesterday.*

WRITINGS—Novels: *North to Yesterday,* Knopf, 1967; *In the House of the Lord,* Knopf, 1969; *The Sounds of Rescue, The Signs of Hope,* Knopf, 1970. Author of play, "Journey to Jefferson," produced by Dallas Theater Center, 1964, and of television script, "Cowboy Legacy," for American Broadcasting Company.

SIDELIGHTS: Brian Garfield called *North to Yesterday* "a powerful first novel . . . a thoughtful, tragicomic parable of all America . . . and ungentle satire on the foolishness of those who live in the past, as well as the blindness of those who turn their backs on it."

A *Best Sellers* critic, reviewing *The Sounds of Rescue, The Signs of Hope,* writes: "Despite the fact that my natural reading interests would strongly deter me from reading this or any other 'war' novel, I was hooked on the first paragraph of this book and read it through in an almost uninterrupted single sitting. I read totally immersed, with pity, horror, pain, compassion, disbelief, . . . wishing I had never started, unable to stop. This is a moving and, I suspect, unforgettable story of a man revealed to his very marrow, to the deepest center of his *self,* an average young man, no hero, no superman."

BIOGRAPHICAL/CRITICAL SOURCES: Best Sellers, June 15, 1967, October 1, 1970; *New York Times Book Review,* June 25, 1967, March 30, 1969; *Saturday Review,* July 22, 1967; *Time,* October 5, 1970.

* * *

FOLEY, (Anna) Bernice Williams 1902-

PERSONAL: Born November 20, 1902, in Wigginsville, Ohio; daughter of Karl Howland (president of a wholesale grocers' concern) and Bertye (a poet; maiden name Young) Williams; married Warren Massey Foley (deceased); children: Williams Massey, Karlanne (Mrs. William Scully Hauer). *Education:* Attended University of Cincinnati, 1920-24, Nanking Language College, Nanking, China, 1925-26, and Columbia University, 1931; Jesus College, Oxford, graduate school certificate, 1969. *Politics:* Conservative. *Religion:* Christian Fundamentalist. *Home:* 3440 Olentangy River Rd., Columbus, Ohio 43202. *Office:* 1105 Ohio Departments Bldg., Columbus, Ohio 43215.

CAREER: Fashion commentator for WKRC, 1934, WSAI, 1938, and WCPO-TV, 1947-50, all in Cincinnati, Ohio; Mabley & Carew Department Store, Cincinnati, special events coordinator, 1951-66; Martha Kinney Cooper Ohioana Library, Columbus, Ohio, director, 1966—. Lecturer at Evening College, University of Cincinnati, 1948-49; lecturer on creative writing for American Association of University Women and other groups; member of board of directors of Ohio Poetry Day, 1968—.

MEMBER: American Women in Radio and Television (Educational Foundation Hi-O chapter chairman, 1970), English Speaking Union (Columbus branch president, 1966-69), National League of American Pen Women, Overseas Press Club, Freedoms Foundation of Valley Forge, Women in Communications, Society of Ohio Archivists, Ohio Historical Society, Ohio Academy of History, Ohio Arts Council (member of literary advisory panel, 1966-70), Ohio Press Women, Ohio Press Club, Faculty Club of Ohio State University, Theta Sigma Phi, Kappa Kappa Gamma, Sigma Delta Chi. *Awards, honors:* First Award, Ohio Press Women, 1975, for *Ohioana Quarterly;* Freedoms Foundation of Valley Forge award and First Award, Ohio Press Women, both 1976, for *Ohioana Year Book.*

WRITINGS: Star Stories (juvenile), McCall Publishing, 1970.

Columnist for *Forest Hills Journal* and *Community Journal,* 1970—. Editor of *Ohioana Quarterly,* 1966—, and *Ohioana Year Book,* 1966—; book reviewer for Sunday edition of *Columbus Dispatch.*

WORK IN PROGRESS: Another juvenile book, *Sky Stories.*

AVOCATIONAL INTERESTS: Swimming, hiking, travel in Europe.

*   *   *

FONER, Eric 1943-

PERSONAL: Born February 7, 1943, in New York, N.Y.; son of Jack Donald (a professor) and Liza (Kraitz) Foner; married Naomi Achs (an associate producer of a children's television workshop), June 20, 1965 (divorced, 1977). *Education:* Columbia University, B.A., 1963, Ph.D., 1969; Oxford University, B.A., 1965. *Home:* 606 West 116th St., New York, N.Y. 10027. *Office:* Department of History, City College of the City University of New York, New York, N.Y. 10031.

CAREER: Columbia University, New York City, assistant professor of history, 1969-73; City College of the City University of New York, New York City, associate professor of history, 1973—. *Member:* American Historical Association, Southern History Association, Phi Beta Kappa. *Awards, honors:* American Council of Learned Societies fellowship, 1972-73; Guggenheim fellowship, 1975-76.

WRITINGS: Free Soil, Free Labor, Free Men: The Ideology of the Republican Party before the Civil War, Oxford University Press, 1970; (editor) *America's Black Past: A Reader in Afro-American History,* Harper, 1971; *Nat Turner,* Prentice-Hall, 1971; *Tom Paine and the American Revolution,* Oxford University Press, 1976. Contributor of reviews to *New York Times* and *New York Review of Books;* contributor of articles to *Journal of American History, Journal of Negro History,* and *New York History.*

WORK IN PROGRESS: A volume on Reconstruction for "New American Nation" series; a book on nineteenth-century American radicalism.

*   *   *

FORD, Edsel 1928-1970

December 30, 1928—February 19, 1970; American poet and lecturer. Obituaries: *New York Times,* February 21, 1970; *Antiquarian Bookman,* March 16, 1970; *Publishers' Weekly,* March 16, 1970; *Books Abroad,* spring, 1971. (See index for *CA* sketch)

FORD, James L(awrence) C(ollier) 1907-
(Collier Ford)

PERSONAL: Born April 7, 1907, in Foochow, China; son of American citizens, Eddy L. (a clergyman and educator) and Effie (Collier) Ford; married Elsa E. Grimmer (a university mathematics instructor), December 23, 1929; children: James L. C. III, Frederick Eddy. *Education:* Lawrence College (now University), B.A., 1928; University of Wisconsin, M.A., 1939; University of Minnesota, Ph.D., 1948. *Home:* 807 Skyline Dr., Carbondale, Ill. 62901. *Office:* Department of Journalism, Southern Illinois University, Carbondale, Ill. 62903.

CAREER: Chicago Tribune, Chicago, Ill., cable editor in New York bureau, 1928-30; Fairchild Publications, New York City, writer, 1930; United Press, New York City, wire editor and cable editor, 1931-37; University of Oregon, Eugene, assistant professor of journalism, 1939-40; University of California, Berkeley, assistant professor of journalism, 1940-42; Associated Press, San Francisco, Calif., news analyst, 1941-42; University of Montana, Missoula, professor and dean of School of Journalism, 1942-55; Southern Illinois University, School of Communications, Carbondale, professor of journalism, 1955-73, professor emeritus, 1973—. Visiting professor of journalism, University of Montana, 1976. *Member:* American Association of University Professors, Phi Beta Kappa, Sigma Delta Chi, Phi Delta Kappa, Pi Delta Epsilon, Sigma Phi Epsilon, Kappa Tau Alpha. *Awards, honors:* Coffman Memorial fellowship, University of Minnesota, 1945.

WRITINGS: (With others) G. F. Mott, editor, *Survey of Journalism,* Barnes & Noble, 1937, also published as *Outline Survey of Journalism,* 1937, enlarged and revised edition published as *New Survey of Journalism,* 1950, 7th edition, Harper, 1976; (with others) *Careers for Journalism,* 3rd revised edition (not associated with earlier editions), Quill and Scroll Society, 1956; *Magazines for Millions: The Story of Specialized Publications,* Southern Illinois University Press, 1969. Contributor of articles to periodicals. Consulting editor, *Focus/Midwest.*

SIDELIGHTS: James Ford writes *CA:* "To me, writing is a lifelong profession—and one occupies himself at different times with articles, stories, poems, books depending on material, markets, personal desire."

AVOCATIONAL INTERESTS: Travel, conservation.

*   *   *

FORER, Lois G(oldstein) 1914-

PERSONAL: Born March 22, 1914, in Chicago, Ill.; daughter of Harry and Lorraine (Beilman) Goldstein; married Morris Leon Forer (an attorney), June 30, 1940; children: Stuart, John, Hope Abigail. *Education:* Northwestern University, A.B. (with honors), 1935, J.D., 1938. *Politics:* Democrat. *Religion:* Jewish. *Home:* 622 West Hortter St., Philadelphia, Pa. 19119. *Agent:* Curtis Brown Ltd., 575 Madison Ave., New York, N.Y. 10022.

CAREER: Admitted to Illinois Bar, 1938, to Bar of U.S. Supreme Court, 1942, to Pennsylvania Bar, 1943; attorney for U.S. Senate Committee on Education and Labor, 1938-39, and for Rural Electrification Administration, 1940-41; U.S. Court of Appeals Third Circuit, Philadelphia, Pa., law clerk, 1942-46; private practice as an attorney, Philadelphia, 1943—. Lecturer, University of Pennsylvania Law School, 1950-55; deputy attorney general, Commonwealth of Pennsylvania, 1955-63; attorney in charge of office for juveniles,

Community Legal Services, 1966-68; judge, Court of Common Pleas, Philadelphia. Member of board of directors, Philadelphia City Policy Committee, Philadelphia Anti-Defamation League, Philadelphia Planned Parenthood, Camp William Penn, and Pennsylvania Liberties Union.

MEMBER: American Bar Association, National Association of Women Lawyers, International Federation of Women Lawyers, American Civil Liberties Union (member of national board), Pennsylvania Bar Association, Philadelphia Bar Association, Philadelphia Conference of Jewish Women's Organizations (president, 1966-67). *Awards, honors:* Ross Essay Prize of American Bar Association, 1953.

WRITINGS: No One Will Listen: How Our Legal System Brutalizes the Youthful Poor, John Day, 1970; *The Death of the Law,* Mckay, 1975. Contributor to legal journals and to *Horizon, Philadelphia Bulletin, Philadelphia Magazine,* and other publications.

BIOGRAPHICAL/CRITICAL SOURCES: Atlantic, December, 1970; *Best Sellers,* February 1, 1971.

* * *

FORNARI, Franco 1921-

PERSONAL: Born April 18, 1921, in Piacenza, Italy; son of Attilio and Maria (Vermi) Fornari; married Bianca Bertonazzi (a teacher), December 27, 1947; children: Gigliola, Maurizio, Silvia, Massimo, Ilaria. *Education:* University of Milan, graduate in medicine and surgery, libero Docente of psychology. *Home and office:* Via Plinio 63, Milano, Italy 21029.

CAREER: University of Milan, Milan, Italy, resident professor, School of Psychology, 1961—, founder of l'Instituto di Polemologia. *Member:* Societa Psicanalitica Italiana, Societa Italiana de Psicologia, Societa Italiana di Psichiatria, International Psychoanalytical Society. *Awards, honors:* Premio Letterairo S. Dona di Piave, 1969, for *Angelo a capofitto.*

WRITINGS: La Vita affettiva originaria del bambino, Feltrinelli (Milan), 1963; *Psicanalisi della guerra atomica,* Comunita (Milan), 1964; *Nuovi orientamenti della psicanalisi,* Feltrinelli, 1966, revised edition, 1970; *Psicanalisi della guerra,* Feltrinelli, 1966, translation by Alenka Pfeifer published as *The Psychoanalysis of War,* Anchor Press, 1974; (compiler) *Dissacrazione della guerra,* Feltrinelli, 1969; *Angelo a capofitto,* Rizzoli, 1969; *Mussolini's Gadfly,* Vanderbilt University Press, 1971; *Genialita e cultura,* Feltrinelli, 1975. Author of numerous scientific papers on psychoanalysis and related subjects.†

* * *

FORSYTH (OUTRAM), Anne 1933-

PERSONAL: Born March 17, 1933, in Dunfermline, Scotland; daughter of James Whyte and Catherine (Marshall) Forsyth; married D. H. Outram. *Education:* University of St. Andrews, M.A., 1953. *Home:* 4 East Ridgeway, Cuffley, Hertsfordshire, England. *Office:* Evans Brothers Ltd., Montagu House, Russell Sq., London WC1B 5BX, England.

CAREER: Fife Herald, Cupar, Fife, Scotland, reporter, 1953-55; *Manchester Evening News,* Manchester, England, reporter, 1955-57; Halle Concerts Society, Manchester, secretary to Sir John Barbirolli, 1957-59; *Woman's Own,* London, England, sub-editor, then assistant home editor, 1959-64; Macmillan & Co., London, editor in overseas depart-

ment, 1964-69; Routledge & Kegal Paul Ltd., London, editorial manager, 1969-70; Evans Brothers Ltd., London, managing editor of Overseas and English Language Teaching Books, 1970—.

WRITINGS: English for Everyone, Macmillan, 1969; *Cheap and Cheerful, Homemaking on a Budget,* Mills & Boon, 1973; *Table Settings for All Occasions,* Mills & Boon, 1975. Has done adaptations for Macmillan's "Favourite Tales for Children" series, 1969-70, and of Sherlock Holmes stories for Macmillan's "Stories to Remember" series, 1971.

BIOGRAPHICAL/CRITICAL SOURCES: Books and Bookmen, September, 1969.

* * *

FOSTER, Jack Donald 1930-

PERSONAL: Born September 21, 1930, in Dixon, Ill.; son of William H. and Alma (Frye) Foster; married second wife, Peggy Skrtic, November 26, 1975; children: (first marriage) Steven Kent, Karyl Ann. *Education:* Kent State University, B.A., 1953, M.A., 1959; Oberlin Graduate School of Theology, graduate study, 1954-55; Ohio State University, Ph.D., 1971. *Office:* Council of State Governments, Iron Works Pike, Lexington, Ky. 40511.

CAREER: Ordained Congregational minister, 1952; Congregational minister in Akron, Ohio, 1950-56, and Youngstown, Ohio, 1956-60; Youngstown State University, Youngstown, instructor, 1957-65, assistant professor of sociology, 1965-71, associate professor of criminal justice, 1971-74, chairman of department of criminal justice, 1969; Council of State Governments, Lexington, Ky., project director, 1974—. Lecturer, Kent State University, 1961, University of Pennsylvania, 1968, Toledo University, 1968-69, Bowling Green State University, 1969. Director, Police Juvenile Training Institute, 1961-62; consultant, Mahoning County Juvenile Court, 1962-68; assistant director and lecturer, Inner-City Education Workshop, School of Education, Youngstown State University, 1968-69. Manuscript reviewer and editorial consultant, John Wiley & Sons, Random House, Canfield Press, Anderson Publishing Co., Charles Merrill Publishing Co., 1969-74. Member, Ohio Criminal Justice Supervisory Commission, 1971-75. *Member:* Academy for Criminal Justice Sciences, Alpha Kappa Delta. *Awards, honors:* Distinguished Professor Award, Youngstown State University, 1967.

WRITINGS: (Editor) *Readings in Criminal Justice,* McCutchan, 1969; (contributor with G. Roy Sumpter) *Introduction to the Administration of Justice,* Wiley, 1974; (with Sumpter) *Adolescent Lawbreaking: Delinquency in Social and Legal Context,* Canfield Press, 1977. Also author of research reports.

* * *

FOSTER, Julian F(rancis) S(herwood) 1926-

PERSONAL: Born July 27, 1926, in London, England; son of George Sherwood (an artist) and Norah (Langford) Foster; married Beatrice Joerer-Lindner, February 22, 1957; children: Hugh Christopher Sherwood, Fiona Eileen, Jennifer Anne. *Education:* New College, Oxford, B.A., 1951, M.A., 1955; University of California, Los Angeles, Ph.D., 1963. *Office:* Political Science Department, California State University, Fullerton, Calif. 92634.

CAREER: University of Santa Clara, Santa Clara, Calif., assistant professor of political science, 1957-61; California

State University, Fullerton, assistant professor, 1963-64, associate professor, 1964-70, professor of political science, 1970—. *Military service:* Royal Navy, 1945-47. *Member:* American Political Science Association, Western Political Science Association, Sierra Club, Friends of the Earth. *Awards, honors:* Fulbright scholarship, 1953-54; American Council on Education fellow in academic administration at Princeton University, 1967-68.

WRITINGS: The Impact of a Value-Oriented University on Student Attitudes and Thinking, U.S. Office of Education, 1961; (contributor) Robert Hassenger, editor, *The Shape of Catholic Higher Education,* University of Chicago Press, 1967; (editor with Durward Long) *Protest! Student Activism in America,* Morrow, 1970. Contributor to political science journals. Founder and editor, *Reason: A Review of Politics,* 1965-66.

WORK IN PROGRESS: Research in contemporary political philosophy.

* * *

FOSTER, Virginia Ramos

PERSONAL: Born in St. Louis, Mo.; daughter of Raoul Leon (a physician) and Virginia (Maynard) Ramos; married David W. Foster (a professor of Spanish), May 31, 1966. *Education:* University of Missouri, B.A., 1958, M.A., 1964, Ph.D., 1966. *Religion:* Catholic. *Home:* 928 West Palm Lane, Phoenix, Ariz. 85007. *Office:* Phoenix College, 1202 West Thomas Rd., Phoenix, Ariz. 85013.

CAREER: University of Missouri, Kansas City, Spanish instructor for Peace Corps, 1964; Phoenix College, Phoenix, Ariz., professor of Spanish, 1968—. *Member:* Modern Language Association of America, American Association of Teachers of Spanish and Portuguese, Hispanic Institute of the United States, Dante Society of America, Rocky Mountain Council on Latin American Studies, Arizona Cello Society. *Awards, honors:* Organization of American States research grant to Argentina, 1970.

WRITINGS: (Compiler with husband, David W. Foster) *Manual of Hispanic Bibliography: An Annotated Handbook of Basic Sources,* University of Washington Press, 1970; (with D. W. Foster) *Research Guide to Argentine Literature,* Scarecrow, 1970; (with D. W. Foster) *Luis de Gongora,* Twayne, 1973; (editor with D. W. Foster) *Modern Latin American Literature,* two volumes, Ungar, 1975; *Baltasar Gracian,* Twayne, 1975.

* * *

FOX, Mary Virginia 1919-

PERSONAL: Born November 17, 1919, in Richmond, Va.; daughter of George Henry (a realtor) and Leila Virginia (Merrell) Foster; married Richard Earl Fox (a manufacturer); children: Phillip Richard, Thomas George, William Earl. *Education:* Northwestern University, B.S. (honors), 1940. *Politics:* "Very flexible." *Religion:* United Church of Christ.

CAREER: Writer. *Member:* National League of American Pen Women, Wisconsin Writers, Suburban Writers, Children's Reading Round Table of Chicago, Alpha Phi.

WRITINGS—All juveniles: *Apprentice to Liberty,* Abingdon, 1960; *Treasure of the Revolution,* Abingdon, 1961; *Ambush at Fort Dearborn,* St. Martin's, 1962; *Ethel Barrymore: A Portrait,* Reilly & Lee, 1970; *Pacifists: Adventures in Courage,* Reilly & Lee, 1971; *Lady for the Defense: A Biography of Belva Lockwood,* Harcourt, 1975. Writer of

material for other publishers, including Harper, Science Research Associates, Lyons & Carnahan, and David Cook. Contributor to *Encyclopaedia Britannica;* author of radio scripts and travel articles.

SIDELIGHTS: Mary Virginia Fox traveled with her husband, Richard Earl Fox, who was advising industry in undeveloped countries, 1966-69, living in the Philippines, Iran, Colombia, and Tunisia.†

* * *

FOX, Stephen R. 1945-

PERSONAL: Born February 28, 1945, in Boston, Mass.; son of Kenneth R. (a textile engineer) and Eleanor (a librarian; maiden name, Pihl) Fox. *Education:* Williams College, A.B., 1966; Brown University, Ph.D., 1971. *Politics:* Democratic socialist. *Religion:* None.

MEMBER: American Historical Association, Organization of American Historians.

WRITINGS: The Guardian of Boston, William Monroe Trotter, Atheneum, 1970.††

* * *

FRAENKEL, Jack R(unnels) 1932-

PERSONAL: Born April 4, 1932, in Chicago, Ill.; son of Herbert Charles and Bessie (Ratcliffe) Fraenkel; married Marjorie Jean Hansen, December 1, 1961. *Education:* University of Nebraska, B.A., 1953; San Francisco State College (now University), M.A., 1965; Stanford University, Ph.D., 1966. *Home:* 201 Edgehill Way, San Francisco, Calif. 94127. *Office:* Ised School of Education, San Francisco State University, San Francisco, Calif. 94132.

CAREER: Teacher in public schools in San Francisco, Calif. and Pacifica, Calif., 1959-64; San Francisco State University, San Francisco, Calif., associate professor, 1966-71, professor of interdisciplinary studies in education, 1971—. Associate director, Teachers Corps, Taba Curriculum Development Project in Social Studies, 1966-69; coordinator, National Defense Education Act Institute on Teaching Disadvantaged Children, 1968; associate director, National Competency-Based Educational Research and Development Project, 1970-71. Consultant to National Science Foundation, 1966-67, World Law Fund, 1968-71, American Institutes for Research, 1969, University of California Medical Center, 1969-70, Children's Book Council, 1973—, and other educational organizations and programs; consulting editor, Wadsworth Publishing Co., 1973-76. Participant, Seminar on World Order, World Law Fund, 1968, and Working Conference on World Affairs, Foreign Policy Association, 1968. Member, Program Committee, American Council on Educational Simulation and Games, 1970. *Military service:* United State Air Force, 1953-55; became captain.

MEMBER: American Association of College and University Professors, National Council for the Social Studies, American Educational Research Association, Association for Supervision and Curriculum Development, California Teachers Association, California Council for the Social Studies (chairman of research committee, 1966-68), San Francisco Council for the Social Studies, Phi Delta Kappa, Pi Gamma Mu, Alpha Kappa Delta.

WRITINGS: (Contributor) *Professional Growth for Teachers,* Croft Educational Publications, 1964; (author of teaching guide with Malcolm Mitchell) *Charles Rhind Joy, Emerging Africa: An Introduction to the History, Geogra-*

phy, Peoples, and Current Problems of the Multi-National African Continent on Its Way from Colonialism to Independence, revised edition (Fraenkel was not associated with previous edition), Scholastic Book Services, 1965; (author of teaching guide with Mitchell) Human Kublin, *The Rim of Asia—Japan and Southeast Asia: An Introduction to the Geography, Peoples, History, Cultures and Problems of the Mainland and Island Countries of East Asia,* revised edition (Fraenkel was not associated with previous edition), Scholastic Book Services, 1965; (contributor) Mary C. Durkin and Patricia Hardy, editors, *Teaching Strategies for Developing Children's Thinking,* Addison-Wesley, 1968; *The U.S. War with Spain, 1898: Was Expansion Justified?,* Scholastic Book Services, 1969; (editor with Richard Gross and Walter McPhie) *Teaching the Social Studies: What, Why, and How,* Crowell, 1969.

Crime and Criminals: What Can We Do about Them?, Prentice-Hall, 1970, second edition, 1976; (with Margaret Carter and Betty Reardon) *Peacekeeping: Problems and Possibilities,* World Law Fund, 1970; (editor) *Inquiry into Crucial American Problems,* sixteen volumes, Prentice-Hall, 1970-73, 2nd edition, eighteen volumes, 1976; (with Hilda Taba, Mary C. Durkin, and Anthony H. McNaughton) *A Teacher's Handbook to Elementary Social Studies,* revised edition (Fraenkel was not associated with previous edition), Addison-Wesley, 1971; *Helping Students Think and Value: Strategies for Teaching the Social Studies,* Prentice-Hall, 1973; (with Carter and Reardon) *The Struggle for Human Rights: A Question of Values,* Random House, 1974; (editor) *Inquiry into World Cultures,* six volumes, Prentice-Hall, 1974-76; (editor) *Crucial Issues in American Government,* fifteen volumes, Allyn & Bacon, 1975-77; (editor with Carl Ubbelohde and contributor) *Values of the American Heritage: Challenges, Case Studies, and Teaching Strategies,* National Council for the Social Studies, 1976; (contributor) *Values Concepts and Techniques,* National Education Association, 1976; *Decision-Making in American Government,* Allyn & Bacon, 1977; *How to Teach about Values: An Analytic Approach,* Prentice-Hall, 1977; (contributor) M. Eugene Gilliam, editor, *Sourcebook for the Social Studies Teacher,* Wadsworth, 1977.

Contributor to *California Social Science Review, Clearing House, Social Education, NEA Journal, Journal of Educational Research, Elementary School Journal, Phi Delta Kappan, High School Journal, Intercom, Professional Growth for Teachers, Social Science Record, Social Studies Journal,* and *Today's Education.* Member of editorial board, *Theory and Research in Social Education,* 1973—.

SIDELIGHTS: Jack R. Fraenkel told *CA:* "The purpose underlying everything I write is to make people think. If my books and articles do even a bit of that, they will have served their purpose, and I shall be pleased."

*   *   *

FRAKES, George Edward 1932-

PERSONAL: Born May 12, 1932, in Los Angeles, Calif.; son of Samuel Franklin (a petroleum engineer) and Frances (Fountaine) Frakes; married Catherine Davis (a home and hospital teacher), August 7, 1954; children: James B., Laura L., Robert M. *Education:* Stanford University, B.A., 1954, M.A., 1958; University of California, Santa Barbara, Ph.D., 1966. *Religion:* Episcopalian. *Home:* 735 Willow Glen Rd., Santa Barbara, Calif. 93105. *Office:* Department of History, Santa Barbara City College, 721 Cliff Dr., Santa Barbara, Calif. 93105.

CAREER: Teacher of social studies in public schools in Santa Barbara, Calif., 1958-62; Santa Barbara City College, Santa Barbara, Calif., instructor, 1962-65, assistant professor, 1966-69, associate professor of history, 1969—, chairman of department. Supervisor of student teachers, University of California, Santa Barbara, 1965-66. Member, Citizens Planning Association of Santa Barbara. *Military service:* U.S. Air Force, 1954-57; became first lieutenant. *Member:* American Historical Association, Organization of American Historians, American Studies Association, Sierra Club, South Carolina Historical Society, Santa Barbara Scholarship Foundation, Channel City Club.

WRITINGS: Laboratory for Liberty: The South Carolina Legislative Committee System, 1719-1776, University Press of Kentucky, 1970; (editor with Curtis B. Solberg) *Pollution Papers,* Appleton, 1971; (editor with Solberg) *Minorities in California History,* Random House, 1971; (with W. Royce Adams) *Columbus to Aquarius: An Interpretive History,* two volumes, Dryden, 1976.

WORK IN PROGRESS: Biographical research concerning Peter Timothy, South Carolina publisher during the colonial and revolutionary period.

SIDELIGHTS: George Edward Frakes told *CA,* "I am particularly interested in colonial history, the history of the American West, and the importance of the geographic environment in history." *Avocational interests:* Reading, tennis, volleyball, camping, and gardening.

*   *   *

FRANCIS, Pamela (Mary) 1926-

PERSONAL: Born September 4, 1926, in Ipswich, England; daughter of Jack Lincoln (a metallurgist) and Anna May (Hughes) Francis. *Education:* King's College, London, B.A. (honors), 1947. *Home:* 29 Turnberry Way, Crofton Place, Orpington, Kent, England. *Office:* Imperial Chemical Industries Ltd., Millbank, London S.W.1, England.

CAREER: Imperial Chemical Industries Ltd., London, England, employed in secretarial position, 1948-55, 1971-74, editor of house magazine, 1969-71, officer of Americas zone, international coordination, 1975—. Lived in Argentina, 1955, Peru, 1955-57, and 1959-69, and was Lima correspondent for *Times* (London), 1959-69, and for *Statist,* 1965-67. *Awards, honors:* Prize awarded by Editorial Doncel (Madrid), 1964, for folktale in Spanish; Award of Merit from CRAV (Chile) in contest sponsored by UNESCO, 1968, also for folktale in Spanish.

WRITINGS—All for young people: *Spanish Conquest in America,* Wheaton & Co., 1964; *Life in Ancient Peru,* Wheaton & Co., 1965; (contributor) *Cuentos peruanos,* Editorial Doncel, 1965; *What Became of the Mayas?,* Wheaton & Co., 1969; *Ricardo Palma: Tradiciones peruanas* (text), Pergamon, 1969.

BIOGRAPHICAL/CRITICAL SOURCES: Times Literary Supplement, October 16, 1969.

*   *   *

FRANKFORT, Ellen 1936-

PERSONAL: Born October 6, 1936, in New York, N.Y.; daughter of Jack and Sylvia (Slote) Frankfort; divorced. *Education:* Barnard College, B.A., 1958; attended Yeshiva University, 1965, Brandeis University, 1968-69. *Politics:* "Towards a radical center." *Religion:* Jewish. *Home:* 175 West 12th St., New York, N.Y. 10011.

CAREER: English teacher in New York schools, 1958-64; Yeshiva University, Albert Einstein College of Medicine, New York City, researcher in psychiatry department, 1964-65; Harvard University, Medical School, Cambridge, Mass., researcher in psychiatry department, 1967-69; Medical Committee for Human Rights, New York City, city coordinator, 1970; Bantam Lecture Bureau, New York City, lecturer, 1972-76; Brooklyn College of the City University of New York, New York City, professor of journalism, 1975-76. *Member:* Women's Health Collective, Chelsea Village Health Council.

WRITINGS: The Classrooms of Miss Ellen Frankfort: Confessions of a Private School Teacher, Prentice-Hall, 1970; *Vaginal Politics,* Quadrangle, 1972; *The Voice: Life at "The Village Voice",* Morrow, 1976. Columnist for *Village Voice,* 1970-71. Contributor of articles to *Barnard Alumnae Magazine, Urban Underground, American Journal of Orthopsychiatry, New York Times, Washington Post,* women's magazines, and other periodicals.

WORK IN PROGRESS: A book about women and success.

AVOCATIONAL INTERESTS: Piano, dogs; travel in Europe, Caribbean, Haiti, and Puerto Rico.

* * *

FRANKLIN, Harold   1926-

PERSONAL: Surname originally Feigenbaum; born August 4, 1926, in Detroit, Mich.; son of Isidore (a barber) and Bessie (Hutman) Feigenbaum; married Frances Bogner; children: Beth Ann, Laura Susan. *Education:* Attended New York University, 1946-48, New School for Social Research, 1949-52, and Workshop School of Art, 1953-55. *Religion:* Jewish. *Home:* 1323 East 55th St., Brooklyn, N.Y. 11234. *Agent:* Henry Morrison, Inc., 58 West 10th St., New York, N.Y. 10011.

CAREER: Graystone Press, Inc., New York, N.Y., project director, 1959-64; free-lance book designer, 1964—. *Military service:* U.S. Army Air Forces, served during World War II.

WRITINGS: Run a Twisted Street (juvenile), Lippincott, 1970. Also author of an adult novel, *One-at-a-Time.* Writer of plays for young people, including *Black Explorer, General Moses* and *First to Die,* published by Youth Discovers, 1971.

WORK IN PROGRESS: Meeting the Enemy, a novel; "The Holdout," a play; researching and writing a series of plays for young people, featuring black Americans, American Indians, Mexican-Americans, and Puerto Ricans.

* * *

FRANKLIN, Marc A.   1932-

PERSONAL: Born March 9, 1932, in Brooklyn, N.Y.; married Ruth E. Korzenik, June 29, 1958; children: Jonathan, Alison. *Education:* Cornell University, A.B., 1953, LL.B., 1956. *Home:* 2870 Pacific Ave., San Francisco, Calif. 94115. *Office:* School of Law, Stanford University, Stanford, Calif. 94305.

CAREER: Columbia University, School of Law, New York, N.Y., assistant professor, 1959-61, associate professor of law, 1961-62; Stanford University, School of Law, Stanford, Calif., associate professor, 1962-64, professor of law, 1964-76, Frederick I. Richman Professor, 1976—. Fellow, Center for Advanced Study in the Behavioral Sciences,

1968-69; Fulbright research scholar, Victoria University, Wellington, 1973.

WRITINGS—All published by Foundation Press: *Dynamics of American Law: Courts, Legal Process, and Freedom of Expression,* 1968; *Biography of a Legal Dispute,* 1968; *Injuries and Remedies: Cases and Materials on Tort Law and Alternatives,* 1971, supplement, 1976; *Mass Media Law,* 1977; *The First Amendment and the Fourth Estate,* 1977. Contributor to law reviews.

* * *

FRANZBLAU, Abraham N(orman)   1901-

PERSONAL: Born July 1, 1901, in New York, N.Y.; son of Manes (a merchant) and Esther Eva (Blau) Franzblau; married Rose Nadler (a psychologist and columnist), December 21, 1923; children: Michael, Jane (Mrs. Richard A. Isay). *Education:* Jewish Theological Seminary, Hebrew Teaching License, 1919; City College (now City College of the City University of New York), B.S., 1921; Columbia University, Ph.D., 1934; University of Cincinnati, M.D. and M.B., 1937. *Politics:* Democrat. *Religion:* Jewish (Reform). *Home and office:* 1 Gracie Ter., New York, N.Y. 10028.

CAREER: Teacher and principal in Jewish religious schools, 1917-19; City College (now City College of the City University of New York), New York City, psychologist in Educational Clinic, 1920-23; Hebrew Union College School for Teachers, New York City, founder, 1923, principal, 1923-31; Hebrew Union College-Jewish Institute of Religion, Cincinnati, Ohio, dean of summer session, 1925-35, professor of psychology and religious education, 1931-37, professor of pastoral psychiatry, 1937-46; Hebrew Union College-Jewish Institute of Religion, New York City, professor of pastoral psychiatry, 1946-58, and dean and founder of Schools of Education and Sacred Music, dean emeritus, 1958—; Mount Sinai Hospital, New York City, member of staff, 1949—, associate attending psychiatrist, 1958-62, preceptor in psychiatry, 1962—. Private practice in psychoanalytically oriented psychotherapy, New York City, 1946—. Director of Commission on Research, Union of American Hebrew Congregations, 1928-30; professor of pastoral psychiatry, Graduate School of Applied Religion (Episcopalian), Cincinnati, 1935-43; member of board of visitors, New York State Rehabilitation Hospital, 1962—. Vice-chairman and member of board, Arts of the Theatre Foundation; member of Commission on Jewish Education, National Council for Jewish Education, and National Conference of Jewish Communal Service. Established Department of Pastoral Psychiatry at Hebrew Union College, Cincinnati, 1937, School of Education, 1946, and School of Sacred Music, 1948, at Hebrew Union College—Institute of Religion, New York City, and American Conference of Cantors, 1951; founder of Sacred Music Press, 1953, and with Lou Lister, New Methods 'Publishing Co., 1954. *Military service:* U.S. Public Health Service, psychiatric consultant to Surgeon-General on civilian affairs, 1943-46; became surgeon (major).

MEMBER: American Psychiatric Association (fellow; delegate to national assembly; chairman, Task Force on Religion and Psychiatry), American Psychosomatic Society, American Geriatrics Society, American Medical Association, Israel Medical Society, Society for the Scientific Study of Religion, New York Academy of Medicine, New York Society for Clinical Psychiatry (president, 1970-72), New York State Medical Society, Central Conference of American Rabbis, New York Association of Reform Rabbis, Alpha

Omega Alpha, Kappa Delta Pi. *Awards, honors:* L.H.D. from Hebrew Union College-Jewish Institute of Religion, 1958; Maimonides Award, Wisconsin Mount Sinai Medical Center, 1973.

WRITINGS: Reform Judaism in the Large Cities, Union of American Hebrew Congregations, 1930; *The Teaching of Jewish History,* Hebrew Union College (Cincinnati), 1931; *Organization, Supervision and Administration of the Jewish Religious School,* Hebrew Union College, 1932; *The Curriculum of the Jewish Religious School,* Hebrew Union College, 1932; *An Introduction to Jewish Education,* Hebrew Union College, 1932; *A Quarter Century of Training Rabbis,* Hebrew Union College Press, 1933; (editor) *Stories from Hebrew and Yiddish Sources,* two volumes, Hebrew Union College Press, 1934; *Religious Belief and Character,* Columbia University Press, 1935; *Jews in the World Today,* Hebrew Union College Press, 1935; *The Road to Sexual Maturity,* Simon & Schuster, 1954; *A Primer of Statistics for Non-Statisticians,* Harcourt, 1958, revised edition, Wiley, 1977; (with wife, Rose N. Franzblau) *A Sane and Happy Life: A Family Guide,* Harcourt, 1963; (editor) *Psychiatrists' Viewpoints on Religion,* American Psychiatric Association, 1975.

Contributor: *Why You Do What You Do,* Random House, 1956; Simon Noveck, editor, *Judaism and Psychiatry,* Basic Books, 1956; David Max Eichhorn, editor, *Conversion to Judaism: A History and Analysis,* Ktav, 1965; (author of foreword) Jack S. Spiro, *A Time to Mourn,* Block Publishing, 1967; Norman Kiell, editor, *The Psycho-Dynamics of American Jewish Life,* Twayne, 1967; Carl F. Hereford, *Basic Descriptive Statistics and Psychological Measurement for Teachers,* W. C. Brown, 1970; Alfred M. Freedman and Harold I. Kaplan, editors, *Comprehensive Textbook of Psychiatry,* 2nd edition, Williams & Wilkins, 1975; Freedman, Kaplan, and Sadock, editors, *The Sexual Experience,* Williams & Wilkins, 1976; (author of introduction) *Erotic Art of China,* Crown, 1977. Contributor of more than fifty articles and papers to medical, educational, and other periodicals, including *Saturday Review* and *This Week.*

WORK IN PROGRESS: "Psychiatry and Religion," a historical review for *New York State Medical Journal;* writing the introduction for *Erotic Art of Japan,* for Abrams.

* * *

FRANZBLAU, Rose N(adler) 1905-

PERSONAL: Born January 1, 1905, in Vienna, Austria; brought to United States the year of her birth; daughter of Meyer (a manufacturer) and Rachael (Breitfeld) Nadler; married Abraham Norman Franzblau (a psychiatrist), December 21, 1923; children: Michael, Jane (Mrs. Richard A. Isay). *Education:* Hunter College (now Hunter College of the City University of New York), B.A., 1926; Columbia University, M.A., 1931, Ph.D., 1935; additional study at University of Heidelberg, summer, 1924, and Sorbonne, University of Paris, summers, 1926-28. *Politics:* Democrat. *Religion:* Jewish (Reform). *Home:* 1 Gracie Ter., New York, N.Y. 10028.

CAREER: Teacher and principal in religious high schools, New York City, 1917-35; National Youth Administration, personnel worker in Cincinnati, Ohio, 1935-40, director of personnel in Cincinnati and Columbus, Ohio, 1940-43, national director of training of girls in Washington, D.C., 1943-44; United Nations Relief and Rehabilitation Administration (UNRRA), Washington, D.C., director of placement and training of overseas personnel, 1944-46; U.S. Office of Price Administration, New York City, regional training officer, 1946-47; United Nations Educational, Scientific and Cultural Organization (UNESCO), associate director of International Tensions Research Project, 1947-51; newspaper columnist, 1948—, conductor of daily column, "Human Relations," in *New York Post,* New York City, 1951—; radio commentator, presenting a daily program, "The World of Children," on WCBS, New York City, 1965-70. Licensed psychologist; lecturer and consultant on human relations problems. American chairman, Girls Town of Italy, 1960—; member of advisory board to psychology department, University of Jerusalem, 1967—. Member of board of directors, Lorge School; chairman and member of advisory council, Home Term Courts of New York, 1957—.

MEMBER: Hadassah (honorary life member), National Association for the Advancement of Colored People (honorary life member), Sigma Xi. *Awards, honors:* Awards from Albert Einstein College of Medicine, Asthma Research Institute, Child Guidance League, and Bar Ilan University (Israel).

WRITINGS: Race Differences in Mental and Physical Traits, Studied in Different Environments, Columbia University Press, 1935; (with Marie Lane) *National Youth Administration: Final Report,* War Manpower Commission, Federal Security Agency, 1944; (with Otto Klineberg) *Tensions Affecting International Understanding,* Social Science Research Council, 1950; (with husband, Abraham N. Franzblau) *A Sane and Happy Life: A Family Guide,* Harcourt, 1963; *The Way It Is Under Twenty,* Avon, 1964; (contributor) Seymour M. Farber and Roger H. L. Wilson, editors, *Sex and the Mass Media,* Diablo, 1967; *Your Budding Adolescent* (monograph), Station WCBS, 1967; *The Middle Generation,* Holt, 1971; (author of foreword) Sheldon H. Cherry, *The Menopause Myth,* Ballentine, 1976.

Writer of series, "Searchlight on Delinquency," in *New York Post Magazine,* 1954-55, and monthly feature, "Your Family and You," in *Family Circle,* 1967-69; also wrote a series, "How to Avoid the Tyranny of Executive Tensions," in *Sales Management,* 1967-68. Contributor of a monthly feature to *Pageant,* 1971—; contributor to *Cosmopolitan, Seventeen,* and other popular magazines and professional journals.

WORK IN PROGRESS: An autobiography, *A View from the Rosy Side.*

SIDELIGHTS: Dr. Franzblau made a survey of guidance techniques for youth in France, Denmark, Sweden, and England, 1958, and a study of court procedures in handling juvenile delinquents in London, Paris, Rome, and Tel Aviv, 1960. She has been a guest on a number of network television programs, among them "Contact," "Girl Talk," "Noonday Live," and the Johnny Carson, Mike Douglas, and Merv Griffin shows.

* * *

FRANZEN, Nils-Olof 1916-

PERSONAL: Born August 23, 1916, in Oxeloesund, Sweden; son of Frans Waldemar (an organizing secretary) and Elma (Loefstedt) Franzen; married Birgit Levihn (a civil servant), August 31, 1940; children: Berit (Mrs. Kjell Engdahl), Bo (son), Gerd (daughter). *Education:* University of Stockholm, B.A., 1942, M.A., 1960. *Home:* Luetzengatan 4, 115 23 Stockholm, Sweden.

CAREER: Sveriges Radio (Swedish Broadcasting Corp.),

Stockholm, 1940-73, began as announcer, staff of magazine, 1941-43, producer in talks department, 1943-49, head of talks department, 1950-55, director of radio, 1956-73.

WRITINGS: Se, daa kom daer en kvinna (historical novel about Don Juan), Ljus Foerlag, 1944; *Den aattonde doedssynden* (novel), Ljus Foerlag, 1945; *Hur stora foerfattare arbeta* (essays on authorship), Natur & Kultur, 1947; *Den groena manteln* (historical novel), Ljus Foerlag, 1948; *Rossini*, Bonnier, 1951; *Emile Zola*, Natur & Kultur, 1958; *Zola et la joie de vivre* (thesis; published in French), Almqvist & Wiksell, 1958; *Moliere*, Natur & Kultur, 1960; *Brunkebergsmorden* (crime novel), Bonnier, 1971; *Doedens aengel* (crime novel), Bonnier, 1972; *Svea Soeder* (crime novel), Bonnier, 1973; *Stina* (novel), Bonnier, 1974; *Christina Nilssonen svensk saga* (biography), Bonnier, 1976.

Children's books; "Agaton Sax" series; all Deutsch translations by author and Pamela Royds: *Agaton Sax klipper till*, Bonnier, 1955; *Agaton Sax och den ljudloesa spraengaemnesligan*, Bonnier, 1956, published as *Agaton Sax and the League of Silent Exploders*, Deutsch, 1974; *Agaton Sax och vita moess-mysteriet*, Bonnier, 1957, published as *Agaton Sax and the Haunted House*, Deutsch, 1975; *Agaton Sax och de slipade diamanttjuvarna*, Bonnier, 1959, translation by Evelyn Ramsden published as *Agaton Sax and the Diamond Thieves*, Deutsch, 1965, Delacorte, 1967; *Agaton Sax och det gamla pipskaegget*, Bonnier, 1961, his own translation published as *Agaton Sax and the Scotland Yard Mystery*, Dell, 1969; *Agaton Sax och Bykoepings gaestabud*, Bonnier, 1963, published as *Agaton Sax and the Criminal Doubles*, Deutsch, 1971; *Agaton Sax och Broederna Max*, his own translation published as *Agaton Sax and the Incredible Max Brothers*, Dell, 1970; *Agaton Sax och den bortkomne Mr. Lispington*, Bonnier, 1966, published as *Agaton Sax and the Colossus of Rhodes*, Deutsch, 1972; *Agaton Sax och de okontanta miljardaererna*, Bonnier, 1967, published as *Agaton Sax and the Big Rig*, Deutsch, 1976; *Agaton Sax och den svaellande rotmos-affaren*, Bonnier, 1970, published as *Agaton Sax and the London Computer Plot*, Deutsch, 1973.

Other children's books: *Sammansvaerjningen* (historical adventure), Raben & Sjoegren, 1955; *Den hemlighetsfulle ryttaren* (historical adventure), Raben & Sjoegren, 1956; *Goeran Ulv* (historical adventure), Bonnier, 1960; *Goeran Ulv och faangarna i Bastiljen* (historical adventure), Bonnier, 1962; *Herr Zippo och den tjuvaktiga skatan*, Bonnier, 1968; *Fred Y. och den farlige Dr. Snook*, Bonnier, 1968; *Herr Zippo och barnen i byn*, Bonnier, 1969.

Translator into Swedish: Grimmelshausen, *Der abentheurelich Simplicissimus*, Ljus Foerlag, 1944; *La Sage: Gil Blas*, Ljus Foerlag, 1945; (translation and abridgement with wife, Birgit Franzen) Edward Gibbon, *Decline and Fall of the Roman Empire*, three volumes, Ljus Foerlag, 1946-50.

WORK IN PROGRESS: Another story in "Agaton Sax" series; a biography of Mozart.

SIDELIGHTS: Some of the Agaton Sax adventures also have been published in Germany, Austria, Netherlands, Denmark, Finland, Norway, Poland, and Czechoslovakia. *Avocational interests:* Listening to Mozart's music and reading books about the composer, whom he considers "mankind's greatest genius."

* * *

FRASER, John 1931-

PERSONAL: Born March 18, 1931; son of John Alexander (an engineer) and Christina (McDonald) Fraser. *Education:* Attended secondary school in Glasgow, Scotland. *Politics:* Socialist. *Religion:* Agnostic. *Home:* 87 Blenheim Crescent, London W.11, England. *Agent:* Peter Schlesinger, Hart-Davis Macgibbon Ltd., 3 Upper James St., Golden Square, London W1R 48P, England.

CAREER: Actor for twenty years, appearing at Old Vic, on television, and in twenty films; the films include "Trials of Oscar Wilde," "Waltz of the Toreadors," "Tunes of Glory," "El Cid," "Repulsion," and "Isadora." Organiser of London Shakespeare Group (theatrical company) for the British Council. *Military service:* British Army, Royal Signals, 1949-51; became second lieutenant.

WRITINGS: The Babysitter, Putnam, 1969 (published in England as *Clap Hands If You Believe in Fairies,* Collins, 1969). Author of play, "Cannibal Crackers," performed at Hampstead Theatre, London, 1969. Also author of *Palimpset,* a novel, *Jungle Greenroom,* a travel book, and "Pure Filth," a play.

WORK IN PROGRESS: Collecting material for a second travel book.

SIDELIGHTS: John Fraser told *CA,* "Want to direct a movie and write a best seller, but suffer from inertia and fits of pessimism." He likes to travel in the more exotic and distant countries.

* * *

FRAZIER, Claude A(lbee) 1920-

PERSONAL: Born April 15, 1920, in Knoxville, Tenn.; son of Claude (a physician) and Nina (Toney) Frazier; married Karen Bryson, August 31, 1957. *Education:* West Virginia Institute of Technology, B.S. (cum laude); Medical College of Virginia, M.D. *Religion:* Baptist. *Home:* 347 Vanderbilt Rd., Asheville, N.C. 28801. *Office:* 4C Doctors Park, Asheville, N.C. 28801.

CAREER: Licensed to practice medicine in North Carolina; internship at Medical College of Virginia, Richmond; residency at Johns Hopkins University, Baltimore, Md; residency in pediatrics at Children's Hospital, Washington, D.C.; now in private practice in Asheville, N.C.; St. Joseph's Memorial Hospital, Asheville, N.C., staff member; Memorial Mission Hospital, Asheville, N.C., staff member, 1971—. Regional consultant, Children's Asthma Hospital and Research Institute. Diplomate, American Board of Allergy and Immunology. Host of weekly television Sunday school program on WSPA-TV, Spartanburg, S.C., and of weekly radio program, "Teachers' Tips" on WMIT and WFGW radio, Black Mountain, N.C. *Member:* International Association of Allergology (fellow), American College of Allergists (fellow), American Academy of Allergy (fellow), American College of Chest Physicians, American Academy of Pediatrics (fellow), American Medical Writers Association. *Awards, honors:* Hal M. Davison Memorial Award, Southeastern Allergy Association, 1964; West Virginia Institute of Technology alumnus of the year award, 1970; American Medical Association award for continuing studies to physicians, 1970; numerous awards for scientific exhibits.

WRITINGS: Insect Allergy: Allergic and Toxic Reactions to Insects and Other Arthropods, Warren H. Green, 1969; *Devotionals by a Physician,* C. C Thomas, 1970; *Surgery and the Allergic Patient,* C. C Thomas, 1971; *Through the Bible with a Physician,* C. C Thomas, 1971; *Parents' Guide to Allergy in Children,* Doubleday, 1973; *Coping with Food*

Allergy, Quadrangle, 1974; *Psychosomatic Aspects of Allergy*, Van Nostrand, 1977.

Editor: *Should Doctors Play God?*, Broadman, 1971; *What Did the Bible Mean?*, Broadman, 1971; *Notable Personalities and Their Faith*, Independence Press, 1972; *Should Preachers Play God?*, Independence Press, 1973; *Games Doctors Play*, C. C Thomas, 1973; *Dentistry and the Allergic Patient*, C. C Thomas, 1973; *Is It Moral to Modify Man?*, C. C Thomas, 1973; *Faith Healing: Finger of God? or, Scientific Curiosity?*, Thomas Nelson, 1973; *Doctor's Guide to Better Tennis and Health*, Crowell, 1974; *Current Therapy of Allergy*, Medical Examination Publishing, 1974; *Mastering the Art of Winning Tennis*, Pagurian Press, 1974; *Politics and Religion Can Mix!*, Broadman, 1974; *Healing and Religious Faith*, United Church Press, 1974; *What Faith Has Meant to Me*, Westminster Press, 1975; *Self Assessment of Current Knowledge in Allergy*, Medical Examination Publishing, 1976.

Contributor to *Current Therapy*, edited by Howard F. Conn, published by Saunders, *Allergy and Immunology, Current Diagnosis*, edited by Howard F. Conn and Rex B. Conn, Jr., published by Saunders, and *Current Pediatric Therapy*, edited by Sydney S. Gellis and B. M. Kagan, also published by Saunders, and many others.

Writer of weekly Sunday school lessons for *Asheville Citizen and Times, Ironton Tribune*, and *Biblical Recorder*. Contributor to religious and medical publications. Former editor of allergy section, *Southern Medical Journal*; editor, *Annual Review of Allergy*; religious books editor, *Asheville Citizen and Times*; guest editor, *CUTIS*, July, 1968, and *Clinical Symposia*, July-September, 1968; member of editorial board, *Clinical Toxology*.

WORK IN PROGRESS: Sniff, Sniff, Al-er-gee; Progress, Polution, and Personality; and editing several books.

* * *

FREDMAN, Henry John 1927-
(John Fredman)

PERSONAL: Born January 22, 1927, in Plymouth, England; son of David (a company director) and Lily Fredman; married Susan Dering, April 4, 1967; children: Jenny. *Education:* Trinity College, Cambridge, M.A., 1944, LL.B., 1945. *Politics:* Conservative. *Religion:* Jewish. *Home:* White House, Waytown, North Bridport, Dorsetshire, England. *Agent:* A. D. Peters & Co., 10 Buckingham St., Strand, London WC2N 6BU, England.

CAREER: Formerly a solicitor; now active in property investment.

WRITINGS—Fiction: The Fourth Agency, Hutchinson, 1969, Bobbs-Merrill, 1970; *The False Joanna*, Hutchinson, 1970, Bobbs-Merrill, 1971; *Epitaph to a Bad Cop*, R. Hale, 1973.

WORK IN PROGRESS: Two Roman historical novels set in the times of the first and second Jewish revolt.

* * *

FREEDMAN, Mervin B. 1920-

PERSONAL: Born March 6, 1920, in Brooklyn, N.Y.; son of Eli and Rose (Weithorn) Freedman; married Marjorie Ellingson, February 16, 1952; children: Eric Ellingson, Kristin Charlotte, Rolf Edward Harold, Anne Marie. *Education:* City College (now City College of the City University of New York), B.S., 1940; University of California, Berkeley,

Ph.D., 1950. *Home:* 866 Spruce St., Berkeley, Calif. 94707. *Office:* Department of Psychology, San Francisco State University, San Francisco, Calif. 94132; and Graduate Division, Wright Institute, 2728 Durant Ave., Berkeley, Calif. 94704.

CAREER: University of California, Berkeley, lecturer in department of psychology, 1950-53; Vassar College, Poughkeepsie, N.Y., research associate, 1953-58, director of Mary Conover Mellon Foundation for the Advancement of Education, 1958-60; Stanford University, Stanford, Calif., assistant dean of undergraduate education, 1962-65; San Francisco State University, San Francisco, Calif., professor of psychology and chairman of department, 1965—; Wright Institute, Berkeley, Calif., dean of Graduate Division, 1969—. *Military service:* U.S. Army, 1941-45; became second lieutenant; served in North Africa, Italy, and Austria; awarded battlefield commission; received Bronze Star.

MEMBER: American Psychological Association (fellow), American Association for Higher Education, American College Personnel and Guidance Association, Western Psychological Association, California State Psychological Association. *Awards, honors:* Co-recipient of annual research award of American Personnel and Guidance Association, 1956; fellow of Center for Advanced Study in the Behavioral Sciences, 1960-61; Fulbright research scholar at University of Oslo, 1961-62.

WRITINGS: The College Experience, Jossey-Bass, 1967; (editor with G. K. Smith) *Stress and Campus Response*, Jossey-Bass, 1968; (editor with Smith) *Agony and Promise*, Jossey-Bass, 1969; (with Joseph Axelrod and others) *Search for Relevance: The Campus in Crisis*, Jossey-Bass, 1969; (with others) *Academic Culture and Faculty Development*, Montaigne Press (Berkeley, Calif.), in press. Writer of monographs, and contributor of sixty articles to *Nation* and other periodicals.

WORK IN PROGRESS: A book on personality development in adult women; a book on innovation in higher education.

SIDELIGHTS: Mervin B. Freedman speaks Spanish, French, German, Swedish, and Norwegian, "none fluently." *Avocational interests:* Tennis, squash racquets, badminton.

* * *

FREEMAN, Darlene 1934-

PERSONAL: Born March 25, 1934, in Turlock, Calif.; daughter of Ernest I. (a farmer) and Effie (Smith) Freeman. *Education:* Sacramento State College (now California State University, Sacramento), A.B., 1955; University of California, Los Angeles, M.A., 1959. *Politics:* Republican. *Religion:* Methodist. *Home:* 620 Palacia Ct., Turlock, Calif. 95380. *Office:* Modesto Junior College, Modesto, Calif. 95350.

CAREER: Business instructor, Castro Valley High School, Castro Valley, Calif., 1956-58, Cabrillo College, Aptos, Calif., 1959-65, and Modesto Junior College, Modesto, Calif., 1965—. *Member:* California Business Education Association, California Teachers Association.

WRITINGS: (With Toma K. Tyler) *Business Education Teaching Tricks*, second edition (Freeman not associated with previous edition), Interstate, 1969. Contributor of articles to *Business Education World* and other periodicals.††

FREIRE-MAIA, Newton 1918-

PERSONAL: Born June 29, 1918, in Boa Esperanca, Brazil; son of Belini Augusto and Maria Castorina (Freire) Maia; married Flavia Leite Naves, September 27, 1948 (died, 1972); married Eleidi A. Choutard, 1974; children: (first marriage) Regina, Fatima, Newton, Marco Domiciano. *Education:* Federal University of Rio de Janeiro, Ph.D., 1960. *Home:* Praca Rui Barbosa, 795, Apt. 33, Curitiba, Parana, Brazil. *Office:* Human Genetics Lab, Federal University of Parana, Curitiba, Parana, Brazil.

CAREER: University of Sao Paulo, assistant researcher, 1946-47, teacher and researcher, 1948-50; Federal University of Parana, Human Genetics Lab, Curitiba, Parana, Brazil, 1951—, began as instructor, now professor of human genetics and chief of the department. Honorary researcher-lecturer for Brazilian National Research Council in various locations, 1954—. Member of study group on effect of radiation on human genetics, World Health Organization, Copenhagen, Denmark, 1956; participant in Cold Spring Harbor Symposium, N.Y., 1964. *Member:* Brazilian Society of Genetics (former vice-president; president, 1961-62; president of executive council), Brazilian Society for the Advancement of Science (member of executive council). *Awards, honors:* Rockefeller Foundation fellow, University of Michigan, 1956-57; National Prize for Genetics (Brazil), 1968.

WRITINGS: Genetica Medica, University of Sao Paulo Press, Volume I: (with brother, Ademar Freire-Maia) *Teoria do aconselhamento,* 1966, Volume II: *Pratica de aconselhamento,* 1966; (with Francisco Mauro Salzano) *Populacoes brasileiras: Aspectos demograficos, geneticos e antropologicos,* Editora Nacional and University of Sao Paulo Press, 1967, translation published as *Problems of Human Biology: A Study of Brazilian Populations,* text edition, Wayne State University Press, 1970; *Radiogenetica humana,* Editora Edgard Bluecher and University of Sao Paulo Press, 1972; *Brazil-Laboratorio Racial,* Editora Vozes, 1973, 3rd edition, 1976; *Genetica de Populacoes Humanas,* Editora HUCITEC and University of Sao Paulo Press, 1974; *Topicos de Genetica Humana,* Editora HUCITEC and University of Sao Paulo Press, 1976. Also author of 250 scientific papers on animal and human genetics; contributor of chapters to scientific books.

SIDELIGHTS: Newton Freire-Maia, who has visited about twenty-five countries in the Americas, Europe, and Asia, told *CA* he "favors ecumenic activities, pacific solution of international problems and absolute right to self-determination of nations." *Avocational interests:* Classical music, jazz, plastic arts.

* * *

FREIXEDO, Salvador 1923-

PERSONAL: Born April 23, 1923, in Orense, Spain; son of Salvador and Maria (Tabares) Freixedo. *Education:* Attended Colegio Mayor St. Estanislao, Salamanca, for three years as Bachelor in classical studies; Pontifical University of Comillas, Santander, Bachelor of Philosophy and Theology; also studied psychology at Loyola University, Los Angeles, for one year, and Fordham University for three years.

CAREER: Catholic priest, member of Society of Jesus (Jesuits) for thirty years; founder and counselor of Young Christian Workers (labor-oriented action group) in Puerto Rico, 1958-69, vice-national chaplain of Young Christian Workers in Cuba for two years.

WRITINGS: Cuarenta casos de injusticia social: Examen de conciencia para cristianos distraidos, Centro de Informacion y Accion Social (Havana), 1958; *Mi iglesia duerme,* privately printed in Mexico, 1969, translation by Thomas Dorney published as *My Church Is Sleeping,* Baron, 1970; *When UFO's Land Dogmas Fly,* Baron, 1971.

WORK IN PROGRESS: Two books, *The Logical Violence,* and *The Rotten Authority.*

SIDELIGHTS: Salvador Freixedo told *CA* that he is interested in "the social instability going on all over the world. Also I have travelled the world over to study the UFO phenomenon and to establish its significance in relation with human values and culture. After the publication of my second book I've been suspended from the ministry by the four Bishops of Puerto Rico and I had to leave the Society of Jesus under a friendly agreement. Also I have been in jail and then chased out by the Authorities of Venezuela and the Dominican Republic. Reason given by Government, influenced by Catholic Bishops: 'Too controversial,' 'dangerous.'"

My Church Is Sleeping, first printed in Mexico without the church imprimatur as *Mi iglesia duerme,* has stirred bitter controversy between liberals and authorities of the Catholic Church in Puerto Rico. The book was also banned in Spain. According to a 1969 *New York Times* article on Freixedo, the book, "subtitled 'Not Apt for Satisfied Christians'—strongly criticizes the church hierarchy, clergy and doctrine. In describing the church's 'monetary concern,' he calls bingo 'the new apostolate.' 'Christ,' he says, 'could not be a Christian if he came down to earth right now'.... A spokesman for Bishop Aponte [Archbishop of San Juan] said, 'Father Freixedo was not banned because of his book. He was banned for some of the things he has said on radio, television and to the newspapers. The bishop himself says that many of the things in the book are worthwhile. But Father Freixedo has publicly made some statements which contradict basic church doctrine." These issues involve the credibility of the gospel, the infallibility of the Pope, the Holy Trinity, and divorce and remarriage.

Freixedo says that he speaks "Galician (my native tongue), Spanish (in which I write my books), French, Portuguese, Italian and Un-Shakespearean English."

BIOGRAPHICAL/CRITICAL SOURCES: El Mundo (San Juan), August 2, 5, 6, and 9, 1969, September 10, 1969; *New York Times,* August 17, 1969.††

* * *

FRENCH, Fiona 1944-

PERSONAL: Born June 27, 1944, in Bath, England; daughter of Robert Douglas (an engineer) and Mary G. (Black) French. *Education:* Croyden College of Art, N.D.D., 1966. *Residence:* London, England.

CAREER: Psychiatric Hospital, Epsom, Surrey, England, teacher of art therapy, 1967-69; free-lance illustrator, London, England, 1967—. Teacher of design at Wimbledon School of Art, 1970-71, and at Leicester and Brighton Polytechnics, 1973-74. *Awards, honors:* Children's Book Showcase award, 1973, for *The Blue Bird.*

WRITINGS—Self-illustrated juveniles; published by Oxford University Press, except as indicated: *Jack of Hearts,* Harcourt, 1970; *Huni,* 1971; *The Blue Bird,* 1972; *King Tree,* 1973; *City of Gold,* 1974; *Aio the Rainmaker,* 1975; *Matteo,* 1976; *Hunt the Thimble,* 1977.

AVOCATIONAL INTERESTS: Collecting "blue and white" china and old editions of children's books.

BIOGRAPHICAL/CRITICAL SOURCES: New York
Times Book Review, November 8, 1970.

*   *   *

FRENZ, Horst 1912-

PERSONAL: Born June 29, 1912, in Oberlauringen, Germany; came to United States in 1937, naturalized in 1948; son of Paul and Betty (Oestreicher) Frenz; married Evelyn Anna Haerting, December 23, 1939; children: Paul Dieter, Sigred Frenz Insull. *Education:* Studied at University of Breslau, 1930-31, University of Heidelberg, 1931-32, University of Goettingen, 1932-33, 1934-36, and University of London, 1933-34; University of Goettingen, Ph.D., 1936; Allegheny College, fellow, 1937-38; University of Illinois, M.A., 1939. *Home:* 421 Blue Ridge Dr., Bloomington, Ind. 47401. *Office:* 402 Ballantine Hall, Indiana University, Bloomington, Ind. 47401.

CAREER: University of Illinois, Urbana, teaching and research assistant, 1938-40; Indiana University, Bloomington, instructor, 1940-45, assistant professor, 1945-49, associate professor, 1949-54, professor of English and comparative literature, 1954—, distinguished professor, 1969—, chairman of comparative literature program, 1949—, associate director of School of Letters, 1964-72. Fulbright professor at University of Hamburg, 1954-55, at Universities of Hamburg and Goettingen, 1962-63, and at University of Erlangen, summer, 1969; visiting lecturer at University of Wisconsin, spring, 1948; visiting professor at New York University, summers, 1950, 1960; holder of Mary Moody Northern Chair in the Humanities, Virginia Military Institute, fall, 1974. Consultant, National Endowment for the Humanities, 1973—; delegate, American Council of Learned Societies, 1974—; examiner-consultant, North Central Association of Colleges and Universities.

MEMBER: International Comparative Literature Association (vice-president, 1961-64; president, 1973-76), American Comparative Literature Association (vice-president, 1968-71; president, 1971-73), Modern Language Association of America, National Council of Teachers of English, American Society for Theatre Research. *Awards, honors:* Ford Foundation fellow, 1952-53; Guggenheim Foundation fellow, 1968-69; grants from American Council of Learned Societies, American Philosophical Society, Japan Foundation, and German Academic Exchange Service.

WRITINGS: Die Entwicklung des Sozialen Dramas in England vor Galsworthy, Carl Nieft, 1938; (translator, and author of introduction and notes) Gerhart Hauptmann, *The Weavers, Hannele,* [and] *The Beaver Coat,* Rinehart, 1951, new edition, Unger, 1977; (editor) *Whitman and Rolleston: A Correspondence,* Indiana University, 1951, special trade edition with foreword by Roger McHugh, Browne & Nolan, 1952; (editor) Clarence Addison Hibbard, *Writers of the Western World,* 2nd edition (Frenz was not associated with 1st edition), Houghton, 1954, revised edition, 1967; (editor with G. L. Anderson) *Indiana University Conference on Oriental-Western Literary Relations,* University of North Carolina Press, 1955; (editor) *Asia and the Humanities* (proceedings of Second Indiana University Conference on Oriental-Western Literary Relations), Indiana University, 1959; (editor with Newton P. Stallknecht, and contributor) *Comparative Literature: Method and Perspective,* Southern Illinois University Press, 1961, revised edition, 1971; (editor, and author of notes and introduction) *Amerikanische Dramaturgie,* Rowohlt, 1962; *Eugene O'Neill,* Colloquium Verlag, 1965, revised edition, Ungar, 1971; (editor and au-

thor of introduction) *American Playwrights on Drama,* Hill & Wang, 1965; (editor and author of introduction) *Nobel Lectures: Literature, 1901-1967,* Elsevier, 1969; (editor with H. J. Lang, and contributor) *Nordamerikanische Literatur im deutschen Sprachraum seit 1945,* Winkler, 1973.

Contributor: *Good Reading: A Guide to the World's Best Books,* New American Library, 1954; Gay Wilson Allen, editor, *Walt Whitman Abroad,* Syracuse University Press, 1955; *A Reader's Companion to World Literature,* Dryden, 1956.

With Joseph Mileck did a revised translation of Hermann Hesse's *Steppenwolf,* Rinehart, 1963. His translations of Gerhart Hauptmann's plays have been included in *Makers of the Modern Theater,* edited by B. Ulanov, McGraw, 1961, *Modern Drama,* Random House, 1961, and *Seeds of Modern Drama,* Dell, 1963. Contributor of over fifty articles to *Theatre Annual, Die Neuren Sprachen, Theatre Arts, Helikon* (Budapest), *Queen's Quarterly, Rising Generation* (Tokyo), and other literature journals in America and abroad.

Yearbook of Comparative and General Literature, associate editor, 1952-60, editor, 1961—; member of advisory board, *Papers on Language and Literature,* 1965—, and *Comparative Drama,* 1967—; member of editorial board, *Modern International Drama,* 1967—.

WORK IN PROGRESS: Eugene O'Neill and Europe, American Literature in Post-War Germany, and *The Nobel Prize in Literature.*

*   *   *

FREY, Leonard H(amilton) 1927-

PERSONAL: Born February 27, 1927, in Philadelphia, Pa.; son of George L. (an insurance underwriter) and Mary (Haines) Frey; married Kathryn Thurston, May 30, 1959; children: Ruth, Margaret, Judith. *Education:* Dartmouth College, A.S., 1949; University of Oregon, M.A., 1953, Ph.D., 1959. *Politics:* Independent. *Office:* San Diego State University, 5420 College Ave., San Diego, Calif. 92115.

CAREER: San Diego State University, San Diego, Calif., instructor, 1956-58, assistant professor, 1958-62, associate professor, 1962-66, professor of English, 1966-73, professor of linguistics, 1973—, chairman of department of English, 1968-70. Visiting professor at Universites d'Aix Marseille and Rouen, 1971-72; visiting professor at Universite Clermont-Ferrand, 1976-77. Lecturer in Yugoslavia, 1977. *Member:* Phi Beta Kappa. *Awards, honors:* Edwin Perkins Prize for Literature, 1949.

WRITINGS: (Editor) *Readings in Early English Language History,* Odyssey, 1966; *An Introduction to Early English Grammar,* Odyssey, 1970. Contributor to journals and newspapers.

WORK IN PROGRESS: Research in the relationship of epic poetry and myth.

SIDELIGHTS: Leonard Frey has traveled to the Far East in connection with teaching assignments for the U.S. Navy.

*   *   *

FRIED, Charles 1935-

PERSONAL: Born April 15, 1935, in Prague, Czechoslovakia; brought to United States in 1941, naturalized in 1948; son of Anthony (an executive) and Marta (Winterstein) Fried; married Anne Summerscale (a high school teacher), June 13, 1959; children: Charles Gregory, Antonia Catherine. *Education:* Princeton University, A.B., 1956; Oxford University, B.A. Juris, 1958, M.A., 1961; Columbia University, LL.B., 1960. *Office:* Law School, Harvard University, Cambridge, Mass. 02138.

CAREER: Admitted to District of Columbia and Massachusetts Bars; U.S. Supreme Court, Washington, D.C., law clerk to Associate Justice John M. Harlan, 1960-61; Harvard University, Law School, Cambridge, Mass., assistant professor, 1961-65, professor of law, 1965—. Visiting professor at University of California, Berkeley, summer, 1968, and Massachusetts Institute of Technology, 1968-69. Associate reporter, model code pre-arraignment procedure, American Law Institute, 1964. Special consultant to U.S. Treasury Department, 1961-62; consultant and member of steering committee, School of Public Health, Harvard University, 1972—. *Member:* American Society for Political and Legal Philosophy (vice-president), Phi Beta Kappa. *Awards, honors:* Guggenheim fellow, 1971-72.

WRITINGS: An Anatomy of Values: Problems of Personal and Social Choice, Harvard University Press, 1970; *Medical Experimentation: Personal Integrity and Social Policy,* American Elsevier, 1974. Contributor to law journals.

WORK IN PROGRESS: Right and Wrong.

*   *   *

FRIED, Eleanor L. 1913-

PERSONAL: Born February 20, 1913, in New York, N.Y.; married second husband, Sylvan S. Furman (assistant commissioner of New York State Department of Mental Hygiene), 1961; children: (first marriage) Ellen J. Sklar; stepchildren: Emily, Laura, Hester. *Education:* Barnard College, B.A., 1933. *Home:* 680 West End Ave., New York, N.Y. 10025.

CAREER: State University of New York, Fashion Institute of Technology, New York, director of placement, 1947-73, professor emeritus, 1973—. Secretary-treasurer and member of board, Bill of Rights Foundation. *Member:* National Vocational Guidance Association, American College Personnel Association, Personnel Association of New York.

WRITINGS: Is the Fashion Business Your Business?, Fairchild, 1958, 3rd edition, 1970; (with Catherine Avent) *Starting Work,* Parrish, 1965.

*   *   *

FRIEDRICH, Paul 1927-

PERSONAL: Born October 22, 1927, in Cambridge, Mass.; son of Carl Joachim and Lenore (Pelham) Friedrich; married Lore Enig, January 9, 1950; married second wife, Margaret Hardin (a college professor), February 26, 1966; married third wife, Deborah Gordon (doctoral candidate, Scandinavian languages); children: (first marriage) Maria Elizabeth, Susan Guadalupe, Peter Roland. *Education:* Harvard University, B.A., 1950, M.A., 1951; Yale University, Ph.D., 1957. *Home:* 5550 South Dorchester, Chicago, Ill. 60637. *Office:* Department of Anthropology, University of Chicago, 1126 East 59th, Chicago, Ill. 60637.

CAREER: University of Connecticut, Storrs, instructor in anthropology and sociology, 1956-57; Harvard University, Cambridge, Mass., instructor in anthropology, 1957-58; Deccan College, Poona, India, junior linguistic scholar, 1958-59; University of Pennsylvania, Philadelphia, assistant professor of anthropology and linguistics, 1959-62; University of Chicago, Chicago, Ill., associate professor, 1962-67, professor of anthropology and linguistics, 1967—. Associate

professor of linguistics, University of Michigan, summers, 1960, 1961, and University of Indiana, summer, 1964. *Military service:* U.S. Army, 1946-47. *Member:* Linguistic Society of America, American Anthropological Association. *Awards, honors:* Social Science Research Council fellow in Mexico, 1966-67.

WRITINGS: Agrarian Revolt in a Mexican Village, Prentice-Hall, 1970; *Proto-Indo-European Trees,* University of Chicago Press, 1970; *The Tarascan Suffixes of Locative Space: Meaning and Morphotactics,* University of Indiana Press, 1971; *A Phonology of Tarascan,* University of Chicago Press, 1975. Also author of *Neighboring Leaves Ride This Wind* (poems), 1976, and *The Meaning of Aphrodite,* in press.

WORK IN PROGRESS: Researching general mythology, Ancient Greek, and various aspects of linguistics; work on a second volume of poetry.

SIDELIGHTS: Paul Friedrich has competence in Spanish, Greek, German, Russian Tarascan, and reads French and several other languages.

*   *   *

FUCHS, Erich 1916-

PERSONAL: Born March 16, 1916, in Stuttgart, Germany; son of Friedrich Wilhelm and Maria (Faul) Fuchs; married Hilde Hermann (a master hand weaver), August 30, 1952; children: Andrea, Olaf. *Education:* Attended Kunstgewerbeschule (School of Applied Arts), 1935-37; Staatliche Akademie der Bildende Kuenste (State Academy of Fine Arts), Stuttgart, qualified architect, 1948. *Home:* Gruenewaldstrasse 45, Stuttgart, West Germany.

CAREER: State Academy of Fine Arts, Stuttgart, Germany, instructor in weaving, material design, and tapestry weaving, 1949-58; free-lance artist and author, 1958—. *Military service:* German Army, 1939-45. *Awards, honors:* Fourth prize in modern art competition at Darmstadt, Germany; Primero Graphico die Fiera, Bologna, 1970, for *Moonwalk.*

WRITINGS—Self-illustrated: *Nawai,* Ellermann, 1965; *Hier Apollo II,* Ellermann, 1969, translation published as *Moonwalk: The Story of Apollo II,* Abelard, 1969; *Journey to the Moon* (Horn Book honor list; American Library Association Notable Book), Seymour Lawrence-Delacorte, 1970; *Wie Arbeitet ein Kernkraftwerk,* Ellermann, 1971, translation published as *What Makes a Nuclear Power Plant Work,* Seymour Lawrence-Delacorte, 1971; *Hier Studio 7,* Ellermann, 1972; *Looking for Maps,* Abelard, 1976.

Illustrator: Brothers Grimm, *Vom Fischer und seriner Frau,* Ellermann, 1971; *Niki wohortin Ubikum,* Ellermann, 1976.

WORK IN PROGRESS: Illustrating *Was Papa werden wollte als Papa Klein war,* by Alexander Borisowitsch Raskin.

SIDELIGHTS: Erich Fuchs wrote *CA:* "My fantasies get into motion and one idea follows another. The beginning of a book is a small, still not ripened idea, which in the cadence of work, develops. Discoveries and surprises generate the fun which for me is very important.

"The present scene is distinguished by uncertainty. Uncertainty of people and uncertainty of artists. We must free ourselves from so much nonsense and form ourselves significantly."

Erich Fuchs' children's books have been published in Germany, United States, Great Britain, Japan, South Africa, Holland, and Denmark.

BIOGRAPHICAL/CRITICAL SOURCES: New York Times Book Review, April 5, 1970.

* * *

FUKUI, Haruhiro 1935-

PERSONAL: Born February 19, 1935, in Tokyo, Japan; son of Kunihiro (a teacher) and Hisako (Umezu) Fukui; married Junri Ohshima, November 9, 1958; children: Toshiya, Hisaya. *Education:* Tokyo University of Foreign Studies, B.A., 1957; Tokyo University, M.A., 1961; Australian National University, Ph.D., 1968. *Home:* 371 Lexington Ave., Goleta, Calif. 93017. *Office:* Department of Political Science, University of California, Santa Barbara, Calif. 93106.

CAREER: University of Michigan, Center for Japanese Studies, Ann Arbor, research assistant, 1961-64; University of California, Santa Barbara, assistant professor, 1968-72, associate professor of political science, 1972—. Visiting lecturer, University of Adelaide, 1967; visiting professor, University of Sydney, 1977. *Member:* Association for Asian Studies, American Political Science Association. *Awards, honors:* Fulbright exchange scholar, University of Michigan, 1962-63; visiting fellow, Australian National University, 1976.

WRITINGS: (Contributor) Dan F. Henderson, editor, *The Constitution of Japan: Its First Twenty Years, 1947-67,* University of Washington Press, 1968; *Jiyuminshuto to Seisakukettei,* Fukumura Shuppan (Tokyo), 1969; *Party in Power: The Japanese Liberal-Democrats and Policy Making,* University of California Press, 1970; (co-author) *Managing an Alliance: The Politics of U.S.-Japanese Relations,* Brookings Institution, 1976; (contributor) Robert A. Scalapino, editor, *The Foreign Policy of Modern Japan,* University of California Press, 1977; (contributor) Frank P. Belloni and Dennis C. Beller, editors, *Faction Politics,* ABC-Clio Press, 1977; (contributor) T. J. Pempel, editor, *Policy-making in Contemporary Japan,* Cornell University Press, 1977; (co-author) *The Textile Wrangle: Conflict in Japanese-American Relations, 1969-1971,* Cornell University Press, in press.

Contributor to *Papers on Modern Japan, 1965,* and *Papers on Modern Japan, 1968,* edited by David Carlisle Stanley Sissons, both published by the Australian National University, Department of International Relations.

WORK IN PROGRESS: Decision-Making in Negotiations for Basic Treaty between Australia and Japan; editing *Encyclopedia of Political Parties of Asia,* for Greenwood Press; also writing two articles, "Foreign Policy Planning in Japan," and "The Japanese Communist Party."

* * *

FULLER, Catherine Leuthold 1916-

PERSONAL: Born December 31, 1916, in Bucyrus, Ohio; daughter of Godfrey (a lawyer) and Mila (Bomgardner) Leuthold; married Leonard F. Fuller, Jr. (an engineer), November 24, 1952. *Education:* Mount Holyoke College, B.A., 1938; Oberlin College, M.A., 1945. *Politics:* Independent. *Religion:* Christian. *Home:* 1135 Hillcrest Blvd., Millbrae, Calif. 94030.

CAREER: Worked as an art historian at Dudley Peter Allen Memorial Art Museum of Oberlin College, Oberlin, Ohio, and at National Gallery of Art, Washington, D.C.; employed in the fields of economics and history with several organizations and projects including Republic Steel Corp., Cleveland Council on World Affairs, and Stanford Study of

Undergraduate Education. *Member:* The Print Club of Cleveland, Phi Beta Kappa.

WRITINGS: Beasts: An Alphabet of Fine Prints (introduction to fine prints for young people), Little, Brown, 1968.

BIOGRAPHICAL/CRITICAL SOURCES: New York Times Book Review, November 3, 1968; *Chicago Tribune Children's Book World,* November 3, 1968.

* * *

GABRIELSON, James (Brashear) 1917-

PERSONAL: Born May 2, 1917, in Santa Monica, Calif.; son of John (a minister) and Pearl (Stephens) Gabrielson; married Gena C. Sampson (a teacher), July 1, 1939; children: Kristin C. (Mrs. John Webster), Jan C. *Education:* Attended Santa Monica City College, 1935-37; University of Southern California, B.A., 1950, M.S., 1961. *Politics:* Democrat. *Religion:* Methodist. *Home:* 1124 Walnut Grove, Rosemead, Calif. 91770. *Office:* Montebello Unified School District, 123 South Montebello Blvd., Montebello, Calif. 90640.

CAREER: Worked as teller, flight radio officer, and carpenter in Santa Monica, and San Francisco, Calif., 1937-50; Montebello Unified School District, Montebello, Calif., child welfare worker, 1950-64, Neighborhood Youth Corps coordinator, 1964-65, public relations officer, 1965-69, administrative assistant for special services, 1969—. *Military service:* U.S. Navy, inactive duty, 1943-45. *Member:* National Education Association, National School Public Relations Association (president of southern California chapter, 1969-70), Family Service Association (chairman), California Teachers Association, Montebello Teachers Association.

WRITINGS: The Small Activity Group Project (booklet), Montebello Unified School District, 1961; *The Hooky Cop,* Hewitt House, 1970. Contributor of articles and stories to education periodicals.

WORK IN PROGRESS: A novel, tentatively entitled *Eleven Days of Panic.*

SIDELIGHTS: James Gabrielson lists his literary influences as Carson McCullers and D. H. Lawrence.†

* * *

GADDIS, Thomas E(ugene) 1908-

PERSONAL: Born September 14, 1908, in Denver, Colo.; son of T. E. and Alice Catherine Gaddis. *Education:* University of Minnesota, B.A., 1932; University of Oregon, M.A., 1959, Ed.D., 1962. *Home:* 4730 Southwest Taylor's Ferry Rd., Portland, Ore. 97219. *Agent:* Bertha Klausner, 71 Park Ave., New York, N.Y. 10022.

CAREER: Author; educator in field of correction. Reed College, Portland, Ore., co-director of department of education, 1962-64; assistant professor in Oregon State System of Higher Education, 1964-67; University of Portland, Portland, associate professor, 1967-69. Founding director, National Newgate Prison Projects. Member of national advisory committee, Upward Bound, Office of Education, Washington, D.C.; member of board, Halfway House, Seattle, Wash.; advisor, Citizen's Inquiry Parole, New York, N.Y.

WRITINGS: Birdman of Alcatraz: The Story of Robert Stroud, Random House, 1955; (with James O. Long) *Killer: A Journal of Murder* (originally titled *Panzram the Obsessed*), Macmillan, 1970; (author of introduction) *In Prison: Writings and Poems about the Prison Experience* (anthology), edited by James E. Trupin, Fawcett, 1975; (author of introduction) *Prison Experience: An Anthology,* Delacorte, 1976. Contributor to *True, Writer's Digest, Coronet, Pageant, Oregonian, Scientific American, Northwest Magazine, California Probation Journal, Nation,* and *New York Times.*

WORK IN PROGRESS: Editing the manuscripts of Robert F. Stroud; corrections research; and a book, *Alcatraz.*

SIDELIGHTS: Thomas E. Gaddis was technical director for the United Artists film production of *Birdman of Alcatraz* in 1962.

BIOGRAPHICAL/CRITICAL SOURCES: Washington Post, December 22, 1971.

*   *   *

GAITSKELL, Charles D(udley) 1908-

PERSONAL: Born May 28, 1908, in Herne Bay, Kent, England; son of Gregory Herbert and Iris (Newman) Gaitskell; married Kathleen Harte, March 16, 1933 (died, 1949); married Margaret R. McCormack, November 3, 1951; children: Adrienne (Mrs. Al. Edward), Susan, Victoria. *Education:* University of British Columbia, B.A., 1938, M.A., 1939; University of Toronto, D.Paed., 1948; also attended Otis Art Institute, Los Angeles, Calif., and Victoria Normal School, British Columbia, Canada. *Religion:* Anglican. *Home:* 349 Blythwood Rd., Toronto, Ontario, Canada M4N 1A7.

CAREER: British Columbia Department of Education, teacher in one-room rural school, 1933, principal of junior-senior school, Dawson Creek, 1934-37, supervisor of art, Peace River Educational Area, 1938, supervisor of art, Powell River Educational Area, 1939-44, art instructor of Teachers-in-Service, Department of Education summer school, 1940-42; Ontario Department of Education, principal of Summer Courses in Art, 1944-73, director of art, 1945-65, advisor to winter courses in art, 1964-73, assistant superintendent of curriculum, 1965-73. Director of UNESCO seminar on education, Bristol, England, 1951; member of Committee on Art Education Council, Museum of Modern Art, New York, N.Y., 1952-55; educational consultant to "Creative Hands" film series, Crawley Films Ltd., 1955-56; appointed to council of Ontario College of Art, 1956-71; consultant to the art department of Metropolitan Separate School Board, Toronto, Ontario, 1975—. Visiting lecturer at art associations, universities, and teacher-training institutions in Canada, Netherlands, England, Japan, Philippines, France, and the United States.

MEMBER: International Society for Education Through Art (first vice-president, 1955-61; president, 1961-63; member of council, 1964-70), National Art Education Association, Canadian Education Association (chairman, Art Education Group, 1952), Canadian Society for Education Through Art (founding president, 1955-56; honorary president, 1957-73), National Junior Red Cross (member of advisory committee, 1966-70). *Awards, honors:* Stone Award, Vancouver Gallery, 1944, for painting; Centennial Medal (Canada), 1967.

WRITINGS: Art Education in the Province of Ontario, Ryerson, 1948; *Art and Crafts in the Schools of Ontario,* Ryerson, 1949, 12th edition, 1966; *Art and Crafts in Our Schools,* Charles A. Bennett, 1949, 11th edition, 1961; *Children and Their Pictures,* International Film Bureau (Chicago), 1951, 9th edition, Ryerson, 1965; *The Visual Arts in General Education* (seminar report), UNESCO, 1952; *Children and Their Art: Methods for the Elementary School,* Harcourt, 1958, 2nd edition, with Al Herwitz, 1970, 3rd edition, 1970.

With wife, Margaret R. Gaitskell: *Art Education in the Kindergarten,* Charles A. Bennett, 1952, 6th edition, 1958; *Art Education for Slow Learners,* Charles A. Bennett, 1953, 8th edition, Ryerson, 1964; *Art Education During Adolescence,* Harcourt, 1954, 3rd edition, Ryerson, 1964.

Contributor of articles on art and art education to *Canadian Art, School Arts, Instructor, Biiku Bunka* (Japan), and other periodicals. Associate editor, *School Arts,* 1950-60; advisory editor, *Discovering Art* (London), 1964-70; art consultant, *Book of Knowledge,* 1966-70; editor, *Curriculum Bulletin* (Ontario Board of Education), 1967-73.

WORK IN PROGRESS: Art Education in Catholic Elementary Schools.

SIDELIGHTS: Charles D. Gaitskell told *CA:* "After retirement from government jobs, I found it necessary to continue working. Retirement is not a time for idleness and waste of whatever knowledge one has gained over the years. My job and my writing (and my family) still challenge me as an elderly person should be challenged."

*   *   *

GALEANO, Eduardo H(ughes) 1940-

PERSONAL: Born September 3, 1940, in Montevideo, Uruguay; son of Eduardo Hughes and Ester (Galeano Munoz) Roosen; married Silvia Brando, 1959; married second wife, Graciela Berro (a lawyer), 1962; married third wife, Helena Villagra, 1976; children: (first marriage) Veronica; (second marriage) Florencia, Claudio. *Education:* Attended high school in Uruguay. *Politics:* Socialist, Marxist. *Religion:* None. *Address:* Apartado postal 2446, Barcelona, Spain.

CAREER: Marcha (weekly), Montevideo, Uruguay, editor-in-chief, 1961-64; *Epoca* (daily), Montevideo, director, 1964-66; University Press, Montevideo, editor-in-chief, beginning 1965; *Crisis* (magazine), Buenos Aires, Argentina, founder, 1973, director, 1973-76. *Awards, honors:* Premio Casa de las Americas, 1975, for *La cancion de hosotros.*

WRITINGS: China 1964: Cronica de un desafio, Jorge Alvarez, 1961; *Los Dias siguientes,* Alfa, 1967; *Los Fantasmas del dia del leon,* Arca, 1967; *Guatemala: Clave de Latinoamerica,* [Uruguay], 1967, translation by Cedric Belfrage published as *Guatemala: Occupied Country,* Monthly Review Press, 1969; *Reportajes,* Tauro, 1968; *Las Venas Abiertas de America Latina* (title means "Open Veins of Latin America"), Monthly Review Press, 1971. Also author of *Vagamundo* (short stories), 1973, and *La cancion de nosotros* (novel), 1975.

WORK IN PROGRESS: Days and Nights of Love and War, a testimonial work.

SIDELIGHTS: Eduardo H. Galeano wrote *CA:* "Perhaps I write because I see that I will die and I want to preserve myself. And I know that the people and the things I care about are going to die and I would like the permanence of everything. Perhaps I write because I don't believe the human condition is a sewer and there is courage and happiness that is worth the pain. Perhaps I write because I feel that my private memory is in a certain way the memory of a generation; and because this is my way of fighting against the machine that picks at human flesh and because I'm sure that there are things stronger than whatever unhappiness or dictatorship exists."

Las Venas Abiertas de America Latina has been translated into eleven languages. Galeano has traveled in western Europe, in Russia, China, Cuba, and Mexico.

BIOGRAPHICAL/CRITICAL SOURCES: Nation, June 30, 1969.

*   *   *

GAMST, Frederick C(harles) 1936-

PERSONAL: Born May 24, 1936, in New York, N.Y.; son of Rangvald Julius and Aida (Durante) Gamst; married Marilou Swanson, January 28, 1961; children: Nicole Christina. *Education:* Pasadena City College, A.A., 1959; University of California, Los Angeles, A.B. (with highest honors), 1961; University of California, Berkeley, Ph.D., 1967. *Politics:* Democrat. *Religion:* None. *Home:* 73 Forest Ave., Cohasset, Mass. 02025. *Office:* Department of Anthropology, University of Massachusetts, Boston, Mass. 02125.

CAREER: Railroad engineman, operating in California, Nevada, and Utah, 1955-61; Rice University, Houston, Tex., instructor, 1966-67, assistant professor, 1967-71, associate professor of anthropology, 1971-75, associate of Lovett College, 1967-75; University of Massachusetts, Boston, professor of anthropology, 1975—, chairman of department, 1976—. *Military service:* U.S. Army Reserve, 1955-63; became sergeant. *Member:* American Anthropological Association (fellow), Royal Anthropological Institute (fellow), Society for Applied Anthropology (fellow), International African Institute, American Association for the Advancement of Science (fellow), British Institute of History and Archaeology in East Africa, American Association of University Professors (Rice University chapter; secretary-treasurer, 1968-69; president, 1973-74), Sigma Xi, Pi Gamma Mu. *Awards, honors:* Woodrow Wilson National fellowship, 1961-62; Ford Foundation foreign area fellowship, 1962-63; Social Science Research Council and American Council of Learned Societies fellowships for field research in Ethiopia, 1963-64, 1964-65, 1966; Rice University grant-in-aid for research in Ethiopia, summer, 1967; Center for Research in Social Change and Economic Development grants-in-aid for research in Ethiopia, Rice University, summers, 1968 and 1969; National Science Foundation grant for research on railroad enginemen, 1970-71; National Institute of Mental Health grant for research on railroads, 1972-74.

WRITINGS: The Qemant: A Pagan-Hebraic Peasantry of Ethiopia, Holt, 1969; *Peasants in Complex Society,* Holt, 1974; (editor) *Studies in Cultural Anthropology,* Rice University Studies, 1975; (editor with Edward Norbeck) *Ideas of Culture: Sources and Uses,* Holt, 1976. Contributor to professional journals in America and Ethiopia and to *Trains* and *Railroad* (magazines).

WORK IN PROGRESS: Articles and a book based on research on social consequences of marked technological change upon railroad enginemen.

*   *   *

GANGEMI, Kenneth 1937-

PERSONAL: Surname is pronounced Gan-jemmy; born November 23, 1937, in Bronxville, N.Y.; son of Frank and Marjorie (Wesstrom) Gangemi; married Jana Fisher (an artist), March, 1961. *Education:* Rensselaer Polytechnic Institute, B.Mgt.E., 1959; further study at San Francisco State College (now San Francisco State University). *Home:* 211 East 5th St., New York, N.Y. 10003. *Agent:* Betty Anne Clarke, International Creative Management, 40 West 57th St., New York, N.Y. 10019.

CAREER: Writer. *Military service:* U.S. Navy, 1960-61. *Awards, honors:* Stegner fellowship in creative writing, Stanford University, 1968-69; P.E.N. grant, 1975; Creative Artists Public Service fellowship, 1976.

WRITINGS: Olt (novel), Grossman/Viking, 1969; *Lydia* (poems), Black Sparrow Press, 1970; *Pilote de chasse* (novel), Flammarion (Paris), 1975; *Corroboree* (novel), Assembling Press, 1977. Contributor of poetry and fiction to literary magazines.

WORK IN PROGRESS: A novel.

SIDELIGHTS: Kenneth Gangemi has had the audacity to write a fifty-five-page novel, and one reviewer guesses that *Olt* may be "a finger exercise for the long novel [he] is writing." Reviewed in the *Times Literary Supplement, Olt* is there described as "[lacking] the cohesion and formal tightness which make brevity a virtue. It reads, in fact, like a fragment . . . [however] it can at least be said that *Olt* is more interesting, as a failure, than the qualified successes to which we have become accustomed."

BIOGRAPHICAL/CRITICAL SOURCES: Times Literary Supplement, December 11, 1969; *Life,* December 12, 1969; *New York Times,* December 16, 1969; *Esquire,* December, 1970.

*   *   *

GARDNER, Joseph L. 1933-

PERSONAL: Born January 26, 1933, in Willmar, Minn.; son of Elmer Joseph (a railroad executive) and Margaret Eleanor (Archer) Gardner; married Sadako Miyasaka, February 25, 1967; children: Miya Elise, Justin Lawrence. *Education:* University of Oregon, B.A. (with honors), 1955; University of Wisconsin, M.A., 1956. *Home:* 17 Cohawney Rd., Scarsdale, N.Y. 10583. *Agent:* William Reiss, Paul R. Reynolds, Inc., 12 East 41st St., New York, N.Y. 10017. *Office:* General Books, *Reader's Digest,* 750 Third Ave., New York, N.Y. 10017.

CAREER: American Heritage Publishing Co., Inc., New York City, editor, Book Division, 1959-65, editor of juvenile books, 1965-68; Newsweek, Inc., New York City, editor, Book Division, 1968-76; *Reader's Digest,* New York City, senior staff editor of General Books, 1977—. *Military service:* U.S. Army, 1956-58. *Member:* P.E.N., Phi Beta Kappa.

WRITINGS: (Managing editor) *American Heritage History of World War I,* American Heritage Press, 1964; (editor) S. L. A. Marshall, *Swift Sword,* American Heritage Press, 1967; *Labor on the March,* American Heritage Press, 1969; *Departing Glory: Theodore Roosevelt as Ex-President,* Scribner, 1973. Editor of "American Heritage Junior Library" and "Horizon Caravel Books," 1965-68; editor of Newsweek's "Wonders of Man" series, "Founding Fathers" series, and "World of Culture" series, 1971-76.

WORK IN PROGRESS: A biography of Gilbert Stuart.

*   *   *

GARFIELD, Sol L(ouis) 1918-

PERSONAL: Born January 8, 1918, in Chicago, Ill.; son of Julius (a grocer) and Rebecca (Friedman) Garfield; married Amy L. Nusbaum, December 25, 1945; children: Ann, Joan, Stanley, David. *Education:* Northwestern University, B.S., 1938, M.A., 1939, Ph.D., 1942. *Home:* 419 Polo Dr., Clayton, Mo. 63105. *Office:* Department of Psychology, Washington University, St. Louis, Mo. 63130.

CAREER: Veterans Administration, Mendota, Wis., chief psychologist, 1946-47, Mental Hygiene Clinic, Milwaukee, Wis., chief psychologist, 1949-51, Downey, Ill., chief of psychology service, 1951-57; University of Connecticut, Storrs, associate professor of psychology, 1947-49; University of Nebraska College of Medicine, Omaha, associate professor, 1957-59, professor of medical psychology, 1959-63; Missouri Institute of Psychiatry, St. Louis, principal research scientist, 1963-64; Columbia University, Teachers College, New York, N.Y., professor of psychology, 1964-70; Washington University, St. Louis, Mo., professor of psychology, 1970—. Lecturer, Northwestern University, 1952-57. Consultant, Veterans Administration, 1958—, National Institute of Mental Health, 1961-64, Peace Corps, 1964-70. *Military service:* U.S. Army, 1942-46; became second lieutenant. *Member:* American Association for the Advancement of Science (fellow), American Psychological Association (fellow; president of Division of Clinical Psychology, 1965-66).

WRITINGS: Introductory Clinical Psychology: An Overview of the Functions, Methods and Problems of Contemporary Clinical Psychology, Macmillan, 1957; (editor with A. E. Bergin) *Handbook of Psychotherapy and Behavior Change: An Empirical Analysis,* Wiley, 1971; *Clinical Psychology: The Study of Personality and Behavior,* Aldine, 1974.

Contributor: A. Burton and R. E. Harris, editors, *Clinical Studies of Personality,* Harper, 1955; J. M. Wepman and R. W. Heine, editors, *Concepts of Personality,* Aldine, 1963; N. Ellis, editor, *Theory and Research in Mental Deficiency,* McGraw, 1963; B. B. Wolman, editor, *Handbook of Clinical Psychology,* McGraw, 1965; E. F. Hammer, editor, *Use of Interpretation in Treatment,* Grune, 1968; *Psychology of the Educational Process,* McGraw, 1970.

Consulting editor, *Journal of Abnormal Psychology,* 1964-70, and *Journal of Consulting and Clinical Psychology,* 1964—.

WORK IN PROGRESS: Revising *Handbook of Psychotherapy and Behavior Change,* for Wiley.

*   *   *

GARNER, William   1920-

PERSONAL: Born in 1920, in Grimsby, Lincolnshire, England; married Gwen Owen, 1944. *Education:* University of Birmingham, B.Sc. (honors), 1941. *Agent:* Jonathan Clowes Ltd., 19 Jeffrey's Pl., London NW1 9PP, England.

CAREER: Free-lance writer, London, England, 1947-49; public relations director, Monsanto Co., London, 1949-64, and Massey-Ferguson Ltd., Toronto, Ontario (corporate staff based in London), 1964-66; full-time novelist, 1967—. *Military service:* Royal Air Force, 1941-46; became flight lieutenant. *Member:* Writer's Guild of Great Britain.

WRITINGS: Overkill, New American Library, 1966; *The Deep, Deep Freeze,* Putnam, 1968; *The Us or Them War,* Putnam, 1969; *The Manipulators,* Bobbs-Merrill, 1970 (published in England as *The Puppet-Masters,* Collins, 1970); *Strip Jack Naked,* Bobbs-Merrill, 1971 (published in England as *The Andra Fiasco,* Collins, 1971); *Ditto, Brother Rat,* Collins, 1973; *A Big Enough Wreath,* Putnam, 1975.

WORK IN PROGRESS: A novel.

SIDELIGHTS: Anthony Horner writes: "In [two of Garner's] previous novels, *Overkill* and *The Deep, Deep Freeze,* William Garner showed himself more than adept at creating characters that live and breathe . . ., and [*The Us or Them War*] is a worthy successor. . . . This is not only a competent but a highly intelligent novel."

Of one of Garner's recent works, a *New York Times Book Review* critic states: "Once one recovers from the shock of reading an espionage novel that has poetry quotations, that uses Latin and is familiar with the 'Urn Burial' one can settle back and have a very good time with William Garner [who] handles everything with the finesse of Anatoly Karpov in a convulsive Sicilian Defense. *A Big Enough Wreath* is one of the best of the year."

Garner's novels also have been published in hardback, paperback, and book club editions in England and continental Europe. He writes: "Strongly motivated. Views on almost everything that matters. Views on what matters might differ from those of many."

Film options have been sold on five out of seven books.

BIOGRAPHICAL/CRITICAL SOURCES: New York Times Book Review, June 9, 1968, January 18, 1976.

*   *   *

GARRETT, Lillian

PERSONAL: Born in Beatrice, Neb.; daughter of Harry Mead and Ethel (Johnson) Garrett; married Samuel K. Workman (a professor of English), March 12, 1953. *Education:* University of Nebraska, B.S., 1937; Illinois Institute of Technology, M.S., 1955; also studied with Archipenko, Moholy-Nagy, and Gyorgy Kepes. *Home address:* RD 1, Box 195, Riegelsville, Pa. 18077.

CAREER: New Trier High School, Winnetka, Ill., teacher of art, 1942-43; University of Wisconsin—Madison, instructor in related arts, 1944-46; Layton School of Art, Milwaukee, Wis., teacher of basic design, 1947-49; Walker Art Center, Minneapolis, Minn., acting curator of Everday Art Gallery, 1949-50; Minneapolis School of Art, Minneapolis, chairman of interior design, 1950-52; Layton School of Art, teacher of basic Design, 1954-59; Parsons School of Design, New York, N.Y., teacher of basic design, 1965-73. Chief designer, Louisville Textiles, Inc., 1946-51. Has had one-woman shows of her paintings at Milwaukee Art Institute, 1944, University of Wisconsin, 1945, of her weaving at University of Nebraska, 1952, and of her "light" constructions at Fairweather-Hardin Gallery, Chicago, 1962, Architectural League, New York, 1963, and West Broadway Gallery, New York, 1973; her painting and weaving have also been exhibited in group shows at Museum of Modern Art, Cranbrook Academy of Art, Museum of Contemporary Crafts, Institute of Design, Chicago, Alumi Exhibition, and elsewhere. Lecturer on design and juror of design exhibitions. *Awards, honors:* Louis W. and Maude Hill Foundation grant for research in visual fundamentals, 1952-53; honorable mention for power-loomed fabrics she designed in two annual American Institute of Decorators competitions; Department of Housing and Urban Development National Community Art Competition bronze fountain-sculptor winner, 1974.

WRITINGS: (Self-illustrated) *Visual Design: A Problem-Solving Approach,* Reinhold, 1966. Acting editor, *Everyday Art Quarterly,* Walker Art Center, 1949-50.

SIDELIGHTS: Lillian Garrett makes use of contemporary materials and methods in her work, doing "light" painting-construction with acrylics, synthetic polymers, metal, and wood. Her private commissions for industrial buildings include a mural in plexiglass, a polished brass and polymer sculpture, a bronze sculpture-fountain, and models of an aluminum screen and of a plexiglass and walnut screen.

GARSON, Noel George 1931-

PERSONAL: Born December 3, 1931, in Johannesburg, South Africa; son of George (a journalist) and Winifred (Turner) Garson; married Yvonne Kamp, February 2, 1957; children: Lisa, Catherine Mary, Fiona, Philippa. Education: University of the Witwatersrand, B.A. (honors), 1952, M.A., 1955; Cambridge University, B.A., 1956, M.A., 1963. Home: 135 Dundalk Ave., Greenside East, Johannesburg, South Africa. Office: Department of History, University of the Witwatersrand, Jan Smuts Ave., Johannesburg, South Africa.

CAREER: University of the Witwatersrand, Johannesburg, South Africa, temporary lecturer in history and economic history, 1957-59, lecturer in history, 1960-64, senior lecturer, 1964-66, professor of history and head of department, 1967—. Member: South African Historical Society (chairman, 1971-73), South African Institute of Race Relations.

WRITINGS: What Is History For? (inaugural lecture; pamphlet), Witwatersrand University Press, 1968; Louis Botha or John X. Merriman: The Choice of South Africa's First Prime Minister, Athlone Press, for Institute of Commonwealth Studies, University of London, 1969. Contributor to Archives Year Book of South African History, Part II, 1957, and of articles in the field of modern South African history to journals.

WORK IN PROGRESS: A historical study of party politics in South Africa, 1910-1924.

*   *   *

GARVEY, Mona 1934-

PERSONAL: Born November 1, 1934, in Omaha, Neb.; daughter of William John (a railroad agent) and Clara (a teacher; maiden name, Spain) Garvey. Education: University of Iowa, B.A., 1956; Atlanta University, M.S. in L.S., 1967.

CAREER: Palmer House Art Gallery, Chicago, Ill., assistant director, 1956-57; American Airlines, Chicago, reservations agent, 1957-61; Arts and Crafts Shop, La Rochelle and Fontainebleau, France, director, 1961-66; Brooklyn Public Library, Brooklyn, N.Y., librarian, 1967-68; Hebrew Academy of Atlanta, Atlanta, Ga., librarian, 1969-70; freelance artist, writer, and lecturer on library and educational displays, 1970—. Member: American Library Association, Georgia Library Association, Beta Phi Mu.

WRITINGS: Library Displays: Their Purpose, Construction, and Use, H. W. Wilson, 1969; Teaching Displays: Their Purpose, Construction, and Use, Shoe String, 1972. Contributor to library and education journals.†

*   *   *

GARWOOD, Darrell (Nelson) 1909-

PERSONAL: Born October 8, 1909, in Fort Wayne, Ind.; son of Levi Nelson (a businessman) and Dora Pearl (Roberts) Garwood; married Helen Parizek, June 9, 1934 (deceased); married Martha Butler, July 22, 1974. Education: University of Iowa, B.A., 1933. Home: 131 West Park Lane, Cocoa Beach, Fla. 32931. Agent: A. L. Fierst, 630 Ninth Ave., New York, N.Y. 10036.

CAREER: United Press International, Washington, D.C., reporter, 1948-71. Member: Sigma Delta Chi, Delta Upsilon. Awards, honors: Iowa Library Association Award for "outstanding contribution to literature by an Iowa author in 1945-46," for Artist in Iowa: A Life of Grant Wood.

WRITINGS: Artist in Iowa: A Life of Grant Wood, Norton, 1945, reprinted, Greenwood Press, 1971; Crossroads of America: The Story of Kansas City, Norton, 1948; The Arbaugh Affair, Macrae, 1970.

WORK IN PROGRESS: The Case against the CIA.

*   *   *

GASTIL, Raymond D(uncan) 1931-

PERSONAL: Born April 13, 1931, in San Diego, Calif.; son of Russell Chester and Frances (Duncan) Gastil; married Jeannette Carr, 1955; children: Leila, Raymond. Education: Harvard University, A.B., 1953, A.M., 1956, Ph.D., 1958. Home: 425 Pelham Manor Rd., Pelham, N.Y. 10803. Office: Freedom House, 20 West 40th St., New York, N.Y. 10018.

CAREER: Harvard University, Cambridge, Mass., research associate, Center for International Affairs, 1958-59; University of Oregon, Eugene, assistant professor of anthropology, 1959-62; Hudson Institute, Croton, N.Y., research analyst, 1962-69; Battelle Seattle Research Center, Seattle, Wash., fellow, 1969-76; Freedom House, New York, N.Y., director of Comparitive Survey of Freedom, 1977—. Member: American Anthropological Association, Royal Central Asian Society, International Institute for Strategic Studies, Middle East Institute. Awards, honors: Fulbright grant for work in Pakistan, 1953-54; Ford Foundation grant for work in Iran, 1957-58.

WRITINGS: (With Frank E. Ambruster and others) Can We Win in Vietnam?, Praeger, 1968; (contributor) Johan J. Holst and William Schneider, Jr., editors, Why ABM?, Pergamon, 1969; Cultural Regions of the United States, University of Washington Press, 1975; Social Humanities, Jossey-Bass, 1977. Contributor to American Anthropologist, American Sociological Review, Policy Sciences, Ethics, and other journals.

WORK IN PROGRESS: Continuing production of the comparitive survey of Freedom House published annually in Freedom at Issue; a volume on America's international responsibilities.

*   *   *

GAT, Dimitri V(sevolod) 1936-

PERSONAL: Born October 5, 1936, in Pittsburgh, Pa.; son of John Dimitri and Anne (a librarian; maiden name, Prunte) Gat; married Margaret Moses, June 24, 1967; children: Christine, Alexandra. Education: Carnegie Institute of Technology (now Carnegie-Mellon University), student, 1954-57; University of Pittsburgh, B.A., 1960, M.A. in L.S., 1963. Politics: "Indifferent." Religion: None. Agent: Curtis Brown, Ltd., 575 Madison Ave., New York, N.Y. 10022. Office: Institute for Governmental Services, Middlesex House, University of Massachusetts, Amherst, Mass. 01002.

CAREER: Hagan Chemicals and Controls, Pittsburgh, Pa., advertising assistant, 1960-62; Harvard University, Cambridge, Mass., cataloger and administrator in Harvard Library, 1963-66, assistant librarian in Graduate School of Education Library, 1967-69; Mount Holyoke College, South Hadley, Mass., assistant librarian, 1969-71; University of Massachusetts, Amherst, assistant professor of English and technical communication, 1971-76, editorial associate, Institute for Governmental Services, 1976—. Member: Science Fiction Writers of America. Awards, honors: Honorable mention, Atlantic short story contest for college students,

1959, for "Queen's Gambit Declined"; fourth prize, *Atlantic* short story contest for college students, 1960, for "Nancynancynancynancy."

WRITINGS: *The Shepherd Is My Lord,* Doubleday, 1971; (with Bill Heward) *Some Are Called Clowns: A Season with the Last of the Great Barnstorming Baseball Teams,* Crowell, 1974; (with Arthur Eve) *Municipal Grants: How to Get and Administer Them,* Institute for Governmental Services, University of Massachusetts, 1977. Editor, *Harvard Librarian,* 1966-67.

WORK IN PROGRESS: A science fiction novel and a novel with contemporary setting.

SIDELIGHTS: Dimitri V. Gat wrote *CA:* "I've discovered years of writing fiction with little success is good training for non-fiction. Now I do both—and well, too.... George Plimpton said about *Some Are Called Clowns*—'one of the best sports books in the last ten years....'" *Avocational interests:* Music, golf, squash racquets, gardening, film, poker.

*   *   *

GATCH, Milton McC(ormick, Jr.) 1932-

PERSONAL: Born November 22, 1932, in Cincinnati, Ohio; son of Milton M. (a banker) and Mary (Curry) Gatch; married Ione G. White (a religious councillor), August 25, 1956; children: Ione W., Lucinda McC., George C. W. *Education:* Haverford College, A.B., 1953; University of Cincinnati, law student, 1953-55; Episcopal Theological School, B.D., 1960; Yale University, M.A., 1961, Ph.D., 1963. *Politics:* Democrat. *Home:* 206 East Ridgeley Rd., Columbia, Mo. 65201. *Office:* Department of English, University of Missouri, Columbia, Mo. 65201.

CAREER: Episcopal clergyman; Wooster School, Danbury, Conn., master in Latin and acting chaplain, 1963-64; Shimer College, Mount Carroll, Ill., member of humanities faculty and chaplain, 1964-66, chairman of humanities faculty, 1966-67; Northern Illinois University, DeKalb, associate professor of English, 1967-68; University of Missouri, Columbia, associate professor, 1968-72, professor of English, 1972—, chairman of department, 1971-74. Senior fellow, National Endowment for the Humanities and associate, Clare Hall, Cambridge University, 1974-75. *Military service:* U.S. Army, 1965-67. *Member:* Modern Language Association of America (member of executive committee for Old English, 1975—; chairman, 1977), Mediaeval Academy of America, Early English Text Society, American Society of Church History, American Association of University Professors, Midwest Modern Language Association (president, 1974).

WRITINGS: *Death: Meaning and Mortality in Christian Thought and Contemporary Culture,* Seabury, 1969; (contributor) Liston O. Mills, editor, *Perspectives on Death,* Abingdon, 1969; *Loyalties and Traditions: Man and His World in Old English Literature,* Pegasus, 1971; *Preaching and Theology in Anglo-Saxon England: Aelfric and Wulfstan,* University of Toronto Press, 1977. Contributor to literary and religious journals.

WORK IN PROGRESS: Studies of the relationship of literature to the liturgy in the Anglo-Saxon period.

*   *   *

GAVRON, Daniel 1935-

PERSONAL: Born December 7, 1935, in London, England; son of Nathan (a patent attorney) and Lily (Ettman) Gavron; married Angela Jacobs (a teacher of blind children), September 20, 1957; children: Etan, Ilana, Assaf. *Education:* Attended School of Oriental and African Studies, London, 1955-59. *Politics:* Social Democrat. *Religion:* "Jewish-Agnostic." *Home:* Motza Elite, Jerusalem, Israel.

CAREER: Regional Tourist Office, Arad, Israel, tourist officer, 1961-63; Kaiser Engineers, Sdom, Israel, secretary, 1963-67; University of the Negev, Beersheba, Israel, public relations officer, 1967-71; Israel National Radio, Jerusalem, news editor and senior reporter, 1971—. Founder-settler of Arad, new town in the Negev, chairman of Arad Settlers Committee, 1963; former leader in Habonim youth movement and former kibbutz member. *Military service:* Israel Defense Forces (Reserves), 1961—.

WRITINGS: *The End of Days* (historical novel), Jewish Publication Society (Philadelphia), 1970. Contributor to a number of journals, including *Commentary.* Former staff member, *Jerusalem Post.*

WORK IN PROGRESS: A historical novel, *Jonathan;* and a series novel of modern Israel, *Towers in the Desert.*

SIDELIGHTS: Daniel Gavron wrote *CA:* "My present project, *Towers in the Desert,* is seen as a series of at least six novels, presenting a fictional panorama of modern Israel. My object is to bring to life real Israelis, the good and the bad and to tell the epic story of the creation of a new country, not as propaganda, but as a human story, 'warts and all.' The first novel deals with a new town in the Negev desert. Subsequent volumes will deal with the army, politics, and so on. The project will take at least a decade to complete."

*   *   *

GEACH, Patricia Sullivan 1916-

PERSONAL: Born April 26, 1916, in Bon Aqua, Tenn.; daughter of Joseph Z. (a farmer) and Lona (Davidson) Sullivan; married Robert W. Geach (a teacher), February 25, 1945; children: Robert W., Jr., Cheryl Ann (Mrs. Gary L. Long), Daniel Ray, Roger Wayne. *Education:* Southern Missionary College, summer student, 1939, 1940; University of Toledo, B.A., 1967. *Religion:* Seventh-day Adventist. *Home:* Route 1, Lancaster, Tenn. 38569.

CAREER: Seventh-day Adventist teacher in Miami, Fla., 1940-46, in Toledo, Ohio, 1957-67, in Nashville, Tenn., 1967-71. Former critic teacher at Southern Adventist College and Madison College.

WRITINGS: *Joe's Palomino Pal* (juvenile), Southern Publishing, 1970. Contributor of articles and poems to *Review and Herald.*

WORK IN PROGRESS: Children's books; research on the boyhood of William Miller.

*   *   *

GEARING, Fred(erick) O(smond) 1922-

PERSONAL: Born October 17, 1922, in Morgantown, W. Va.; son of Raymond Dewey (a minister) and Winifred (Osmond) Gearing; married Marjorie Dodd (a teacher), December 28, 1951; children: David, Lisa, Adam. *Education:* University of Chicago, A.B., 1951, M.A., 1953, Ph.D., 1956. *Office:* Department of Anthropology, State University of New York, Buffalo, N.Y. 14226.

CAREER: University of Chicago, Chicago, Ill., assistant director of Tama Indian program, 1954-56, instructor in anthropology, 1956-57; University of Washington, Seattle, assistant professor of anthropology, 1957-61; University of

Chicago, research associate in anthropology, 1961-62; University of California, Riverside, assistant professor, 1962-64, associate professor of anthropology, 1964-70; State University of New York at Buffalo, professor of anthropology, 1970—, chairman of department, 1975—. *Military service:* U.S. Army Air Forces, 1942-45; became technical sergeant. *Member:* American Anthropological Association (fellow), Council on Anthropology and Education, Current Anthropology.

WRITINGS: Priests and Warriors: Social Structures for Cherokee Politics in the Eighteenth Century, American Anthropological Association, 1962; *The Face of the Fox,* Aldine, 1970; *A Cultural Theory of Education and Schooling* (with commentaries), Mouton, 1977. Contributor to anthropology journals.

WORK IN PROGRESS: Social structural analysis of a rural Greek village; development of public schools curricula with cross-cultural emphasis; anthropological research in U.S. schools.

*   *   *

GEIWITZ, P(eter) James 1938-

PERSONAL: Surname is pronounced *Guy*-wits; born June 9, 1938, in Minneota, Minn.; son of Peter H. (a hardware dealer) and Hansina (a teacher; maiden name, Johanssen) Geiwitz; married Judith Haefele, 1963 (divorced); married Roberta Klatzky, 1972; children: (first marriage) Charles Paul. *Education:* St. Olaf College, B.A., 1960; University of Michigan, Ph.D., 1964. *Home and office:* 1122 Olive St., Santa Barbara, Calif. 93101.

CAREER: Had his own business, the Gopher Stamp Co., at age fourteen, worked as a garage mechanic and on a road crew to pay for his education, and wrote sports and political columns for a local newspaper; University of Michigan, Ann Arbor, instructor in psychology, 1964; Stanford University, Stanford, Calif., assistant professor of psychology, 1965-69; free-lance writer, 1969—; University of California, Santa Barbara, lecturer in psychology, 1971-72. *Member:* Gerontological Society, Society for the Psychological Study of Social Issues, Phi Beta Kappa.

WRITINGS: Non-Freudian Personality Theories, Brooks/Cole, 1969; (with P. Mussen, M. Rosenzweig, and others) *Psychology: An Introduction,* Heath, 1973, 2nd edition, 1977; *Looking at Ourselves,* Little, Brown, 1976. Contributor to professional journals.

WORK IN PROGRESS: A textbook on psychological development through the life-span.

SIDELIGHTS: P. James Geiwitz is one-eighth Sioux. He mentions a baseball record, of sorts, he set in high school when he was charged with six errors on one play.

*   *   *

GELLNER, John 1907-

PERSONAL: Born May 18, 1907, in Trieste, Austria-Hungary (now Italy); son of Gustav (a physician) and Maria (Tomassi) Gellner; married Herta Michel, June 26, 1937. *Education:* Attended the classical high school in Olomouc, Czechoslovakia; Masaryk University, D.iur., 1930. *Politics:* "Small 'l' liberal without party association." *Religion:* Roman Catholic. *Home:* R.R.#3, Caledon E., Ontario, Canada. *Office:* Baxter Publishing Co., Suite 401, 150 King St. W., Toronto, Ontario, Canada.

CAREER: Junior partner in a law firm in Brno, Czechoslo-

vakia, 1932-39; Royal Canadian Air Force, pilot, 1940-58, leaving service with rank of wing commander; writer and lecturer, 1958—; Baxter Publishing Co., Toronto, Ontario, editor of *Commentator* (monthly magazine of opinion), 1964-69, editor of *Canadian Defense Quarterly,* 1970—. Visiting professor of political science, York University, Toronto, 1972—. Chairman of Toronto branch, Canadian Institute of International Affairs, 1967-69. *Member:* Royal Canadian Military Institute. *Awards, honors*—Military: Distinguished Flying Cross, Czechoslovak Military Cross, and other medals.

WRITINGS: (With Frantisek Kroutil) *Vysoke Tatry, Horolezecky Pruvodce* (title means "Climber's Guide through the High Tatra Mountains"), four volumes, Orbis, (Prague), 1936-38; (with John Smerek) *The Czechs and Slovaks in Canada,* University of Toronto Press, 1968; *Canada in NATO,* Ryerson, 1970; *Bayonets in the Streets,* Collier-Macmillan, 1974.

Editor; books in "Canadian Heritage" series, Baxter Publishing: Volume I: *Sketch of His Majesty's Province of Upper Canada,* 1961; Volume II: *Simcoe's Military Journal,* 1962; Volume III: *Travels of Thomas Simpson,* 1963; Volume IV: *Recollections of the War of 1812,* 1964; Volume V: *Cheadle's Journal,* 1965. Regular contributor to *Toronto Globe and Mail;* contributor of articles, including travel features to *Saturday Night, Passport, Canadian Aviation,* and other magazines.

SIDELIGHTS: John Gellner speaks French, Italian, and German in addition to Czech. *Avocational interests:* Mountain climbing (has climbed in the Alps, Pyrenees, Carpathians, Rocky Mountains, and in Mexico, and still is active as a climber).

*   *   *

GELVEN, (Charles) Michael 1937-

PERSONAL: Born June 22, 1937, in Rolla, Mo.; son of Charles E. (a florist) and Katherine (Parker) Gelven. *Education:* Quincy College, B.A., 1960; Washington University, Ph.D., 1966. *Home:* 523 Fisk Ave., DeKalb, Ill. 60115. *Agent:* Charles Sherover, Educational Resources Corp., 128 East 74th St., New York, N.Y. 10021. *Office:* Department of Philosophy, Northern Illinois University, DeKalb, Ill. 60115.

CAREER: Northern Illinois University, DeKalb, associate professor of philosophy, 1965—. *Member:* American Association of University Professors, American Philosophical Association, Heidegger Circle. *Awards, honors:* Fulbright fellow at Albert-Ludwigs University at Freiburg, 1963-65.

WRITINGS: A Commentary on Heidegger's "Being and Time," Harper, 1970; *Winter, Friendship and Guilt: The Sources of Self-Inquiry,* Harper, 1972. Contributor to *Intercollegiate Review, Humanitas, Southwestern Journal of Philosophy, Man and World,* and *Journal of Existential Psychiatry.*

WORK IN PROGRESS: Eros and Tragedy; A Commentary on the Later Heidegger.

SIDELIGHTS: Michael Gelven told *CA* that he has been "profoundly influenced by Plato, especially in theories of education." *Avocational interests:* Classical music, theatre, and opera.

*   *   *

GENTHE, Charles V(incent) 1937-

PERSONAL: Born May 23, 1937, in Detroit, Mich.; son of

Earl Robert (a business executive) and Helen (Vairo) Genthe; married Anna Carlile, August 15, 1963; children: Julia, Jean. *Education:* Rutgers University, A.B., 1959; University of Wyoming, M.A., 1960; Washington State University, Ph.D., 1965. *Home:* 629 Poplar St., Chico, Calif. 95926. *Office:* Department of English, California State University, Chico, Calif. 95926.

CAREER: Instructor in English at Miami-Dade Junior College, Miami, Fla., 1961-63, and Long Beach State College (now California State University, Long Beach), 1965-66; California State University, Chico, assistant professor, 1966-73, associate professor, 1973, professor of English, 1973—. *Military service:* U.S. Army Reserve, 1960—; now major. *Member:* Modern Language Association of America, American Studies Association, Philological Association of Central California (secretary, 1969—). *Awards, honors:* W. R. Coe fellowship in American studies.

WRITINGS: American War Narratives, 1917-1918, David Lewis, 1969; *Reflection/Perception* (college text), Blaisdell, 1971; *Themes in American Literature,* Heath, 1973. Contributor to literary journals.

* * *

GENTLES, Frederick (Ray) 1912-

PERSONAL: Born November 12, 1912, in Winnipeg, Manitoba, Canada; son of Robert Frederick (a realtor) and Florence (Truthwaite) Gentles; married Marian Louise Bubb, October 9, 1941; children: Michael E., Anne Louise (Mrs. Glenn Gray Pillubury), Karen R., Robert F., Mary C. (Mrs. Joel J. Garcia). *Education:* Long Beach Junior College, student, 1932-33; San Diego State College (now University), A.B., 1937; University of California, Berkeley, M.A., 1938; Columbia University, graduate study, 1952-53. *Politics:* Democrat. *Religion:* "Formerly Episcopalian." *Home:* 1079 Le Roy St., San Diego, Calif. 92106. *Office:* Department of History, San Diego Mesa College, 7250 Artillery Dr., San Diego, Calif. 92111.

CAREER: High school teacher of science, mathematics, and history in San Diego, Calif., 1938-56; San Diego City College, San Diego, instructor in history and geography, 1956-59, 1960-63; High Pavement Grammar School, Nottingham, England, Fulbright exchange teacher, 1959-60; San Diego Mesa College, San Diego, instructor in geography and history, 1963-67, instructor in history, 1968—. *Military service:* U.S. Army, 1943-45. *Member:* American Federation of Teachers.

WRITINGS: (With Melvin Steinfield) *Hangups from Way Back: Historical Myths and Canons,* two volumes, Canfield Press, 1970, 2nd edition, 1974; (with Steinfield) *Dream On, America,* two volumes, Canfield Press, 1971.

AVOCATIONAL INTERESTS: Chinese history and culture, rock collecting.

* * *

GEORGE, Mary Yanaga 1940-

PERSONAL: Born August 15, 1940, in Berkeley, Calif.; daughter of Chitoshi (a professor and writer) and Clara (Sato) Yanaga; married Lawrence C. George (a law professor), June 9, 1962; children: Laura Keiko, Matthew Bruce. *Education:* Smith College, A.B. (cum laude), 1962; attended University of Munich, 1960-61; Claremont Graduate School, M.A. in Ed., 1968. *Home:* 418 North Ride, Tallahassee, Fla. 32303.

CAREER: Claremont Unified School District, Claremont,

Calif., teacher, 1964-67; Claremont Graduate School, Claremont, instructor in education, 1969-70; Florida State University, Tallahassee, instructor in department of education, 1971-74; Asolo Touring Theater, Sarasota, Fla., theatre pedagogue, 1976—. *Member:* Pi Lambda Theta.

WRITINGS: Language Art: An Ideabook, Chandler Publishing, 1970.

WORK IN PROGRESS: A teleplay adaptation of Machado De Assis' *Epitaph of a Small Winner;* a play, *Re-rise.*

AVOCATIONAL INTERESTS: Crafts, travel.

* * *

GERARD, Albert S(tanislas) 1920-

PERSONAL: Born July 12, 1920, in Namur, Belgium; son of Arthur (a teacher) and Gabrielle (Dupon) Gerard; married Madeleine Bultot (a teacher), November 19, 1942; children: Michele, Christiane. *Education:* University of Liege, Licence en philosophie et lettres (great distinction), 1941, Ph.D. (great distinction), 1942, Agregation de l'enseignement superieur, 1956. *Home:* 51/23 rue Louvrex, Liege, Belgium. *Office:* Faculty of Philosophy and Letters, University of Liege, Place DU 20-AOUT 7, Liege, Belgium.

CAREER: Teacher of Germanic languages in secondary schools of Jodoigne, Rochefort, and Seraing, Belgium, 1941-56; University of Elisabethville, Elisabethville, Democratic Republic of Congo (now Republic of Zaire), professor of English and comparative literature, 1956-63, dean of Faculty of Philosophy and Letters, 1961-63; National Foundation for Scientific Research, Brussels, Belgium, research associate, 1963-67; University of Liege, Liege, Belgium, assistant professor, 1966-67, ordinary professor of modern and comparative literature, 1968—. Research scholar, University of Manchester, 1948-49; visiting professor, University of Minnesota, 1958, University of Wisconsin, 1963-64, and Harvard University, 1966-67; research fellow of Institute for the Arts and Humanistic Studies, Pennsylvania State University, 1968.

MEMBER: Modern Language Association of America (co-head of African literature section of bibliography committee), International Association of University Professors of English, International Association of University Professors and Lecturers, Association Internationale de Litterature Comparee, African Studies Association (United States; associate member), Academie Royale des Sciences d' Outremer (associate member), Congres des Africanistes (Belgian representative on permanent council). *Awards, honors:* British Council scholarship for research at University of Manchester, 1948-49.

WRITINGS: Aldous Huxley, Editions la Sixaine, 1947; *John Steinbeck,* Editions la Sixaine, 1947; *L'enigme poetique,* Office de Publicite (Brussels), 1947; *Education et democratie,* Editions Amis de l'Ecole Publique (Seraing), 1948; *L'Idee romantique de la Poesie en Angleterre,* Les Belles Lettres (Paris), 1955.

(Contributor) R. F. Sleckner and G. E. Glencoe, editors, *Romanticism: Points of View,* Prentice-Hall, 1962; (contributor) G. Willan and V. B. Reed, editors, *A Casebook on Shakespeare's Sonnets,* Crowell, 1964; (contributor) D. N. Baker and G. W. Fasel, editors, *Landmarks in Western Culture,* Prentice-Hall, 1968; *English Romantic Poetry: Ethos, Structure and Symbol in Coleridge, Wordsworth, Shelley, and Keats,* University of California Press, 1968; *Les Tambours du neant: Essai sur le probleme existentiel dans le roman americain,* Renaissance du Livre, 1969.

(Contributor) B. Weber, editor, *Sense and Sensibility in Twentieth-Century Writing,* Southern Illinois University Press, 1970; *Four African Literatures: Xhosa, Sotho, Zulu, Amharic,* University of California Press, 1971; (contributor) A. R. Jones and W. Tydeman, editors, *Wordsworth: Lyrical Ballads,* Macmillan, 1972; (contributor) Raymond Cowell, editor, *Critics on Wordsworth,* Allen & Unwin, 1973; (contributor) H. Maes-Jelinek, editor, *Commonwealth Literature and the Modern World,* Didier, 1975. Also author of *Charles Morgan,* Editions Langues Vivante, and translator with M. Gerard-Bultot of an edition of *Macbeth* published in Brussels.

Contributor to *New International Yearbook;* contributor of more than one hundred articles to *Faulkner Studies, English Studies, Africa Report, New York Times Book Review, Diogenes, Research in African Literatures, Review of National Literatures,* and to other professional journals in Belgium, Germany, Netherlands, France, Great Britain, Canada, Congo, South Africa, and Australia.

WORK IN PROGRESS: Research on creative writing in black Africa and on seventeenth-century tragedy in Europe.

*   *   *

GERARD, Charles (Franklin)   1914-

PERSONAL: Born December 17, 1914, in Lincoln, Ill.; son of Cloyd Francis (a postal clerk) and Ethel (Crull) Gerard; married Janis Ernst, May 23, 1959; children: Craig. *Education:* Lincoln Junior College, Lincoln, Ill., A.S., 1935; Bradley University, B.S.M.E., 1949. *Home:* Cree 5, 2011 Aztec Dr., North Little Rock, Ark. 72116.

CAREER: Letter carrier in Lincoln, Ill., 1941-42; Caterpillar Tractor Co., Peoria, Ill., inspector, 1946; Hart-Carter Co. (grain moving), Peoria, machinist, 1947; U.S. Geological Survey, hydraulic engineer in Illinois, 1949-51; U.S. Government, quality assurance inspector in Chicago, Ill., 1951-76. *Military service:* U.S. Army Air Forces, 1943-46. *Member:* Society of Midland Authors, Sons and Daughters of Pioneer Rivermen, Counter Intelligence Corps Association, Arkansas Authors, Composers, and Artists Society, Cross and Cockade Society (society of World War I Aero International Historians).

WRITINGS: Illinois River Hokey Pokey (novel), Doubleday, 1969. Contributor of short stories to *Minnesota Review, Forum, Husk, New Mexico Quarterly, Mississippi Review, Coe Review,* and other journals.

WORK IN PROGRESS: Writing more stories about the Illinois River.

SIDELIGHTS: Charles Gerard has traveled along the Illinois, Mississippi, and Ohio Rivers looking for paddlewheel boats and old hotels. *Avocational interests:* Tennis.

*   *   *

GERBER, Douglas E(arl)   1933-

PERSONAL: Born September 14, 1933, in North Bay, Ontario, Canada; son of Earl Jacob (a postmaster) and Bertha (Cox) Gerber; married Shirley Baker, August 31, 1957; children: Allison. *Education:* University of Western Ontario, B.A., 1955, M.A., 1956; University of Toronto, Ph.D., 1959. *Politics:* Liberal. *Religion:* Anglican. *Home:* 1521 Richmond St., London, Ontario, Canada. *Office:* Department of Classics, University of Western Ontario, London, Ontario, Canada.

CAREER: University of Toronto, University College, To-ronto, Ontario, lecturer in Greek, 1958-59; University of Western Ontario, London, lecturer, 1959-60, assistant professor, 1960-64, associate professor, 1964-69, professor of classics, 1969—. *Military service:* Royal Canadian Naval Reserve, 1952-66; became lieutenant. *Member:* Classical Association of Canada (treasurer, 1960-62), American Philological Association, Classical Association (Great Britain), Classical Association of the Middle West and South, Ontario Classical Association (president, 1968-70).

WRITINGS: A Bibliography of Pindar, 1513-1966, American Philological Association, 1969; (editor, and author of introduction and commentary) *Euterpe: An Anthology of Early Greek Lyric, Elegiac, and Iambic Poetry,* A. M. Hakkert, 1970; *Emendations in Pindar, 1513-1972,* A. M. Hakkert, 1976. Contributor to classical journals. Editor, *Transactions* (annual publication of American Philological Association), 1974.

WORK IN PROGRESS: Studies in Greek Lyric Poetry.

*   *   *

GEROULD, Daniel C.   1928-

PERSONAL: Surname is pronounced *Ger*-ald; born March 28, 1928, in Cambridge, Mass.; son of Russell (a newspaper editor) and Virginia (Vaughan) Gerould; married Eleanor A. Southwick (a teacher of music and collaborator with her husband on some translations), August 16, 1955; children: Alexander L. *Education:* University of Chicago, A.B., 1946, M.A., 1949, Ph.D., 1959; Harvard University, graduate study, 1953; University of Paris, Diplome, 1955. *Politics:* None. *Religion:* None. *Address:* c/o Mrs. Virginia Gerould, 2240 Green St., San Francisco, Calif. 94123. *Agent:* (Plays) Toby Cole, 234 West 44th St., New York, N.Y. 10036.

CAREER: University of Arkansas, Fayetteville, instructor in English and humanities, 1949-51; University of Chicago, Chicago, Ill., instructor in humanities, 1955-59; San Francisco State College (now University), San Francisco, Calif., assistant professor, 1959-61, associate professor, 1963-67, professor of English and world literature, 1967-71, chairman of department of world literature, 1961-71. Fulbright lecturer in American literature, University of Warsaw, 1968-70; has also taught at City University of New York, Graduate Center, and lectured at Moscow State University, 1967, Charles University, Prague, 1969, and Poznan University, Poland, 1970. *Military service:* U.S. Army, 1951-53; instructor in English language and American literature on Okinawa, 1951-52.

MEMBER: Phi Beta Kappa. *Awards, honors:* French Government scholarship at University of Paris, 1953-54; first prize in San Francisco Poetry Center national poetic drama competition, 1963, for "The Games of Narcissus"; Marian Kister Memorial Award of Roy Publishers, for best Polish-into-English translation, 1969, for *The Madman and the Nun and Other Plays.*

WRITINGS: (Editor and translator with C. S. Durer) *The Madman and the Nun and Other Plays by Stanislaw Ignacy Witkiewicz,* University of Washington Press, 1968; (editor and author of introduction with Bernard F. Dukore) *Avant-Garde Drama between World Wars* (includes two plays and four essays translated by Gerould and others), Bantam, 1969; (with Dukore) *Avant-Garde Drama: A Casebook,* Crowell, 1976.

Plays: "The Games of Narcissus" (verse), 1963; "Candaules, Commissioner" (published in *First Stage,* fall, 1965;

first performed on radio by Actors Workshop of San Francisco, 1966; produced Off-Broadway at Mercer-Hansberry Theatre, May, 1970 [closed after five performances]), published in *Drama and Revolution*, Holt, 1970; "Explosion," 1969, published in *BREAKOUT! In Search of New Theatrical Environments*, Swallow Press, 1971; "Tripstych," 1970, published in *Drama and Theatre;* "The Travels of Perseus," 1970.

Translator with wife, Eleanor S. Gerould, of Witkiewicz play, "The Cuttlefish," in *Treasury of the Theatre*, edited by John Gassner, 4th edition, Holt, 1970, and of Konstanty Ildefons Galczynski's "Twenty Short Plays from The Little Theatre of the Green Goose" published in special English-language edition of *Dialog*, 1971. Has done other translations and articles for theater journals.

WORK IN PROGRESS: A critical study on Stanislaw Ignacy Witkiewicz, for Twayne; *The Metaphysics of a Two-Headed Calf: Five Plays by Witkiewitz;* an original play, *Eva von Buttlar.*

BIOGRAPHICAL/CRITICAL SOURCES: Drama, fall, 1969; *Village Voice*, February 12, 1970, June 4, 1970; *Show Business*, February 21, 1970, June 13, 1970; *New York Times*, April 29, 1970; *Cue*, June 6, 1970; *Variety*, June 10, 1970.†

* * *

GERT, Bernard 1934-

PERSONAL: Born October 16, 1934, in Cincinnati, Ohio; son of Max and Celia (Yarnovsky) Gert; married Esther Libbye Rosenstein, August 3, 1958; children: Heather Joy, Joshua Noah. *Education:* University of Cincinnati, B.A., 1956; Cornell University, Ph.D., 1962. *Religion:* Jewish. *Office:* Department of Philosophy, Dartmouth College, Hanover, N.H. 03755.

CAREER: Dartmouth College, Hanover, N.H., instructor, 1959-62, assistant professor, 1962-66, associate professor, 1966-70, professor of philosophy, 1970—. Visiting associate professor, Johns Hopkins University, 1967-68. *Member:* American Philosophical Association, American Society for Political and Legal Philosophy. *Awards, honors:* National Endowment for the Humanities fellowship, 1969-70.

WRITINGS: The Moral Rules: A New Rational Foundation for Morality, Harper, 1970, 2nd edition, 1975; (translator with T. S. K. Scott-Craig and Charles Wood, and author of introduction) Thomas Hobbes, *Man and Citizen*, Doubleday, 1972. Contributor to philosophy journals.

* * *

GERTZOG, Irwin N(orman) 1933-

PERSONAL: Born May 18, 1933, in Brooklyn, N.Y.; son of Ben (a grocer) and Sonia (Posnack) Gertzog; married Alice Solomon (a librarian), November 22, 1956; children: Joshua B., Rachel L. *Education:* Union College, Schenectady, N.Y., B.A., 1954; Georgetown University, graduate study, 1958-61; University of North Carolina, Ph.D., 1965. *Politics:* Democrat. *Religion:* Jewish. *Home:* 468 Gilmore St., Meadville, Pa. 16335. *Office:* Department of Political Science, Allegheny College, Meadville, Pa. 16335.

CAREER: Union Star, Schenectady, N.Y., sports reporter, 1953-54; J. Walter Thompson Co., New York, N.Y., copy writer, 1954-55; U.S. Department of the Navy, Bureau of Supplies and Accounts, Washington, D.C., editor and writer in department of technical information, 1959-61; Yale University, New Haven, Conn., instructor, 1964-65, assistant professor of political science, 1965-71; Allegheny College, Meadville, Pa., Arthur E. Braun Professor of Political Science, 1971—. *Military service:* U.S. Army, 1956-58. *Member:* American Political Science Association, American Civil Liberties Union. *Awards, honors:* American Political Science Association congressional fellow, 1963-64; Social Science Research Council grant, 1969-70.

WRITINGS: (Contributor) *The City in American History*, Yale University, 1967; (editor) *Readings on State and Local Government*, Prentice-Hall, 1970. Contributor to political science journals.

WORK IN PROGRESS: The President at Midterm: The Nature and Impact of Presidential Activity in Midterm Congressional Elections; The Freshman Experience: The Adjustment of First Term House Members to Congressional Life; research on women in the U.S. House of Representatives.

AVOCATIONAL INTERESTS: Tennis, philately, hiking, reading fiction.

BIOGRAPHICAL/CRITICAL SOURCES: New York Times, February 12, 1970.

* * *

GESCH, Dorothy K(atherine) 1923-

PERSONAL: Born June 20, 1923, in Alton, Ill.; daughter of William C. (a clergyman) and Katherine (Laux) Gesch; married Roy G. Gesch (a clergyman), April 8, 1945; children: Gary Richard. *Education:* Santa Ana College, student, 1941-42. *Politics:* "Depends on candidate." *Religion:* Lutheran. *Home:* 1572 Skyline Dr., Laguna Beach, Calif. 92651.

CAREER: Has traveled extensively with her husband in Europe, Asia, and North America; travel agent with travel firm, 1973—. Regular church organist for fifteen years; has done choral work with choirs and small choral groups.

WRITINGS: Make Me Aware, Lord, Augsburg, 1971; (with husband, Roy G. Gesch) *Lord of the Young Crowd*, Concordia, 1971; *Discover Europe*, Concordia, 1973. Wrote background teaching material booklets on world areas for International Express Travel School. Contributor to travel and religious journals.

WORK IN PROGRESS: Europe for the First-Timer; a series of books on individual countries of the world.

AVOCATIONAL INTERESTS: Oil painting, particularly landscape and seascape.

* * *

GESNER, Carol 1922-

PERSONAL: Born July 7, 1922, in Colon, Panama; U.S. citizen; daughter of Ralph Lawrence (a businessman) and Elsie (White) Gesner. *Education:* New Jersey State College, B.S., 1944; University of New Hampshire, M.A., 1949; Louisiana State University, Ph.D., 1956. *Politics:* "Ordinary AMERICAN." *Religion:* Episcopalian. *Office:* 863 Berea College, Berea, Ky. 40403.

CAREER: Berea College, Berea, Ky., instructor, 1954-56, assistant professor, 1956-61, associate professor, 1961-67, professor of English, 1967—. *Member:* Modern Language Association of America, American Association of University Professors.

WRITINGS: Shakespeare and the Greek Romance: A Study of Origins, University Press of Kentucky, 1970; *Plymouth Exploration* (long narrative poem), Modern Language

Association of America, 1976. Contributor of articles to *Modern Language Notes, Shakespeare Quarterly, Louisiana State University Studies in English Renaissance Literature,* and of poems to *Quartet, Pulpit, Coracle, Approaches, Twigs,* and *Wind.*

* * *

GETZ, Gene A(rnold) 1932-

PERSONAL: Born March 15, 1932, in Francisville, Ind.; son of John A. (a farmer) and Matilda (Honegger) Getz; married Elaine Holmquist, June 11, 1956; children: Renee Elaine, Robyn Lynn, Kenton Gene. *Education:* Moody Bible Institute, Diploma, 1952; Eastern Montana College of Education (now Eastern Montana College), student, 1952-53; Rocky Mountain College, B.A., 1954; Wheaton College, Wheaton, Ill., M.A., 1958; New York University, Ph.D., 1969. *Home:* 10929 Fernald, Dallas, Tex. 75218. *Office:* Dallas Theological Seminary, 3909 Swiss, Dallas, Tex. 75204.

CAREER: Engaged in radio ministry with Montana Gospel Crusade and youth director of Church of the Air, Billings, Mont., 1952-54; assistant pastor of community church, Hinsdale, Ill., 1954; director of Christian education at Bible church, Lisle, Ill., 1956-58; Moody Bible Institute, Chicago, Ill., instructor in Christian education, 1956-68, director of Evening School, 1963-68; Dallas Theological Seminary, Dallas, Tex., associate professor of Christian education, 1968—. Pastor, Fellowship Bible Church, Dallas, 1972—. Visiting professor, Word of Life Summer Institute of Camping, Schroon Lake, N.Y., 1964-68. President, Space Age Communications, Dallas. *Member:* National Association of Professors of Christian Education, National Sunday School Association (past president of Research Commission).

WRITINGS: Audio-Visuals in the Church, Moody, 1959, revised edition published as *Audiovisual Media in Christian Education,* 1972; *The Vacation Bible School in the Local Church,* Moody, 1962; *The Christian Home,* Moody, 1967; (with Roy B. Zuck) *Christian Youth: An In-Depth Study,* Moody, 1968; *The History of the Moody Bible Institute,* Moody, 1969; *The Story of the Moody Bible Institute,* Moody, 1969; (editor with Zuck) *Adult Education in the Church,* Moody, 1970; (with Zuck) *Ventures in Family Living,* Moody, 1971; *Sharpening the Focus of the Church,* Moody, 1974; *The Measure of a Man,* Regal Books (Glendale), 1974; *The Measure of a Church,* Regal Books, 1975; *Philippeans: A Profile of Christian Maturity,* Zondervan, 1976; *Abraham: Trials and Triumphs,* Regal Books, 1976; *Moses: Moments of Glory, Feet of Clay,* Regal Books, 1976; *The Measure of a Family,* Regal Books, 1976; *Building Up One Another,* Victor, 1976. Contributor to religious journals.

WORK IN PROGRESS: The Measure of a Woman, for Regal Books.

* * *

GEYER, Georgie Anne 1935-

PERSONAL: Born April 2, 1935, in Chicago, Ill.; daughter of Robert George (a dairy owner) and Georgie Hazel (Gervens) Geyer. *Education:* Northwestern University, B.S., 1956. *Home and office:* 800 25th St. N.W., Washington, D.C. 20037.

CAREER: Chicago Daily News, Chicago, Ill., foreign correspondent, 1964-75; syndicated columnist, Los Angeles Times Syndicate, 1975—. Member of board, Chicago Council on Foreign Relations. *Member:* Overseas Writers, Overseas Press Club, Women in Communications, Sigma Delta Chi. *Awards, honors:* Fulbright scholarship, University of Vienna, 1956-57; American Newspaper Guild, human interest award, Chicago, 1st place, 1962; Seymour Berkson Foreign Assignment grant, 1964; Overseas Press Club award for Latin American reporting, 1966; alumnae merit award, Northwestern University, 1966; national merit award, Theta Sigma Phi, 1967; Maria Moors Cabot award, Columbia University, 1971; National Council of Jewish Women award, 1971.

WRITINGS: The New Latins: Fateful Change in South and Central America, Doubleday, 1970; *The New 100 Years War,* Doubleday, 1972; *The Young Russians,* ETC Publications, 1975. Contributor of articles to *Saturday Review, Atlantic, New Republic, Progressive, Nation, Wildlife, Kiwanis Magazine, True,* and other periodicals.

SIDELIGHTS: Georgie Anne Geyer, who speaks German, Spanish, Portuguese, and Russian, told *CA* that she has a "deep motivation in wanting to illuminate other parts of the world—and the rationales for living there—for American readership. My writing I see as a combination of straight journalism, personal journalism and sociological insight. I attempt to bring to life . . . other countries . . . and peoples, but in particular the trends of attitudes and ideas in these countries. . . . My entire writing career has been dedicated to the idea of explaining one cultural group in the world to another."

Seldon Rodman called *The New Latins* "affirmative, optimistic, compassionate and truth-seeking. . . . Miss Geyer is most trenchant when discussing the absolutism of the student-intellectuals, and that sick love-hate relationship with the United States which makes self-criticism and the practical solution of problems so difficult. 'The lower classes,' Miss Geyer adds cogently, 'can absorb anti-Americanism, as in Cuba, but they have to be taught it.' It is from these 'marginal' people, their pragmatic 'Nasserite' leaders, and such radical but non-Marxist priests as Vekemans, that Georgie Anne Geyer sees a new Latin America emerging."

AVOCATIONAL INTERESTS: Archeology, swimming, water skiing.

BIOGRAPHICAL/CRITICAL SOURCES: National Review, October 6, 1970.

* * *

GIBSON, E(rnest) Dana 1906-

PERSONAL: Born April 5, 1906, in Worthington, Minn.; son of James and Genevieve (Robinson) Gibson; married Rosemary Pierce, June 16, 1956. *Education:* University of Minnesota, B.S., 1936; Colorado State College (now University), Greeley, M.A., 1939; New York University, Ed.D., 1944. *Religion:* Presbyterian. *Address:* Box 411, Anza, Calif. 92306.

CAREER: New Mexico Highlands University, Las Vegas, 1939-42, 1944-47, began as associate professor, professor, 1947, chairman of department of business administration, 1939-47; City College (now City College of the City University of New York), New York, N.Y., part-time instructor, 1942-44; San Diego State University, San Diego, Calif., associate professor, 1947-52, professor of information systems management, 1953-71. Consultant, American Telephone & Telegraph Co., 1964-65. Member, Southern Presbyterian Board, Los Angeles. *Member:* Society for Automation in Business Education (co-founder; president,

1960-68; executive director, 1968-69), Data Processing Management Association (member of board), National Business Education Association, Association of California State College Professors, California State Employees Association, California Business Education Association (president, 1954-55), Delta Pi Epsilon, Pi Omega Pi, Phi Delta Kappa.

WRITINGS: One-Minute Gregg Shorthand Tests, Gregg, 1944; *Integrated and Electronic Data Processing in Relation to Schools of Business Administration* (monograph), South-Western, 1957; (with Esta Stuart) *Typing Employment Tests,* Prentice-Hall, 1958; (with Leroy Pemberton) *Progressive Advanced Typing Tests,* W. C. Brown, 1959; (with Lura Lynn Straub) *Liquid Duplicating Systems: A Manual of Operations,* W. C. Brown, 1960, 2nd edition, 1974; (with Straub) *Stencil Duplicating Systems: A Manual of Operations,* W. C. Brown, 1960, 2nd edition, 1974; *Adding Machine Systems: Manual,* W. C. Brown, 1960; *Trends in the Educational Use of Computers in Schools of Business* (monograph), Bureau of Business and Economic Research, San Diego State College, 1960; (with Ruth I. Anderson) *The Prentice-Hall Word Finder,* Prentice-Hall, 1960, 3rd edition, 1969; *Calculating Machine Systems Manual,* W. C. Brown, 1961; *International Data Processing,* Business Press (Elmhurst, Ill.), 1965; *Audio-Visual Aids for Automation* (monograph), Bureau of Business and Economic Research, San Diego State College, 1965, revised edition, SDE (Society of Data Educators) Press, 1967; *An Introduction to Automated Data Processing,* Business Press, 1966; (with Pemberton) *Administrative Systems Management,* Wadsworth, 1968; *Educational Data Processing* (monograph), SDE Press, 1969; *Latin American Data Processing,* Bureau of Business and Economic Research, San Diego State University, 1971; *World Information Systems,* Xerox College Publishing, 1976.

Co-author of film scripts for ''Mimeographing Techniques,'' Bailey Films, 1958, and ''Duplicating by the Spirit Method,'' Bailey Films, 1960. Writer of filmstrips on business subjects, test manuals, and papers on data processing. Contributor of more than seventy articles to professional publications.

WORK IN PROGRESS: Latin American Data Processing.

SIDELIGHTS: Some of E. Dana Gibson's management books have been published in Spanish and Japanese.

* * *

GIEGLING, John A(llan) 1935-

PERSONAL: Surname is pronounced Guy-gling: born January 23, 1935, in Sioux Falls, S.D.; son of Ernest Henry and Helen (Freese) Giegling. *Education:* Augustana College, Sioux Falls, student, 1953-55; South Dakota State University, B.S., 1960. *Home:* 600 South Kiwanis Ave., Apt. 119, Sioux Falls, S.D. 57104. *Agent:* Jane Jordan Browne, Multimedia Product Development, Inc., 170 South Beverly Dr., Suite 314, Beverly Hills, Calif. 90212.

CAREER: During his college years worked summers for South Dakota Department of Game, Fish and Parks; National Audubon Society, teacher at camp for adults in Greenwich, Conn., and librarian at national headquarters, New York, N.Y., 1961-65; *Purple Martin News,* Griggsville, Ill., associate editor, 1970-72; Public Library, Sioux Falls, S.D., assistant librarian, 1973-76; Pettigrew Museum, Sioux Falls, natural science curator, 1976-77. *Military service:* National Guard, 1955-57. *Member:* Authors Guild, National Writers Club, Society for the Preservation of Birds of Prey (field director and biologist), Saskatchewan Natural

History Society, Los Angeles Audubon Society, Sioux Falls Audubon Society (president), Griggville Wild Bird Society.

WRITINGS: Warrior of the Skies (nature novel), Doubleday, 1970; *Black Lightning* (nature novel), Coward, 1975. Monthly columnist on wildlife for *Purple Martin News.* Contributor to *National Wildlife, California Condor, Twelve/Fifteen, Colorado Outdoors, Golden Magazine, Dakota Farmer, Canadian Audubon, Pennsylvania Game News, Sierra Club Bulletin,* and other magazines.

WORK IN PROGRESS: A nature novel about a wolf, a prairie falcon, and a purple martin.

AVOCATIONAL INTERESTS: Hiking, bird trips, canoeing, reading, and travel.

* * *

GIL, David G(eorg) 1924-

PERSONAL: Surname legally changed, 1952; born March 16, 1924 in Vienna, Austria; came to United States in 1957, naturalized in 1963; son of Oskar and Helene (Weisz) Engel; married Eva A. Bresslauer, August 2, 1947; children: Daniel, Gideon. *Education:* Hebrew University, Jerusalem, Israel, B.A., 1957; University of Pennsylvania, M.S.W., 1958; D.S.W., 1963. *Politics:* Socialist. *Home:* 29 Blossomcrest Rd., Lexington, Mass. 02173. *Office:* Florence Heller Graduate School, Brandeis University, Waltham, Mass. 02154.

CAREER: Teacher at Village for Dependent, Neglected, and Delinquent Boys, Department of Social Welfare, Jewish Community Council for Palestine, 1943-45; probation officer, Department of Social Welfare, Government of Palestine, 1945-48; Ministry of Social Welfare, Tel Aviv, Israel, senior probation officer, 1950-51, assistant director, 1951-53, chief supervisor, 1955-57; Jewish Family Service, Philadelphia, Pa., family counselor, 1957-59; Association for Jewish Children, Philadelphia, supervisor, 1959-63; Massachusetts Society for the Prevention of Cruelty to Children, Boston, director of research, 1963-64; Brandeis University, Waltham, Mass., assistant professor, 1964-66, associate professor, 1966-69, professor of social policy, 1969—. Part-time lecturer, Hebrew University, 1955-57; member of professional advisory committee, Martha Eliot Center, 1967-68; member of steering committee, Program for Advanced Social Work Training in Teaching and Consultation in Child Treatment, Judge Baker Guidance Center, 1967-71; cochairman of Committee to Develop an Adequate Standard of Living for Massachusetts, 1971; Boston University School of Social Work, member of faculty, Division of Continuing Education, 1972, member of research curriculum review committee, 1972; member of faculty, Commission on Extension Courses, Harvard University, 1973—; member of national advisory board, National Committee to Abolish Corporal Punishment in Schools, 1973; member of Massachusetts Committee for National Health Insurance, 1973—; member of advisory committee on child abuse legislation, American Bar Association, 1974-75; member of panel on Vietnam, Laos, and Cambodia, Asia Society, 1974—; member of board of directors, American Parents Committee, 1974—; member of professional advisory board, National Committee for Prevention of Child Abuse, 1974—; member of external review committee, University of Minnesota School of Social Development, 1975; member of program committee, Consortium on Peace Research, Education, and Development, 1975-76; member of Langdon Associates, 1975—. Consultant to National Commission on the Causes and Prevention of Violence, 1968, National Science Foundation, 1973-74, Minnesota Systems Research,

Inc., 1974-75, National Incidence of Child Abuse Study, 1975, Metropolitan College, Boston University, 1975, and to Westat, Inc., 1976. *Military service:* Israeli Army, 1948-49; conscientious objector, served as welfare officer.

MEMBER: National Association of Social Workers, Academy of Certified Social Workers, American Sociological Association, American Ortho-Psychiatric Association, National Conference on Social Welfare, American Association of University Professors (member of executive committee, Brandeis University chapter, 1968), American Association for the Advancement of Science, American Civil Liberties Union, Union of Radical Political Economists, Association for Humanist Sociology, Radical Alliance of Social Service Workers, New American Movement, American Humanist Association, War Resisters League, Child Welfare League of America (member of publications advisory committee, 1964-71; member of research committee, 1968-71).

WRITINGS: Implications for Doctoral Education in Social Welfare of an Examination of the Concept of Motivation, Brandeis University, Papers in Social Welfare, 1965; (contributor) H. Aptekar, editor, *Social Work Practice, 1966,* National Conference on Social Welfare, Columbia University Press, 1966; *Doctoral Dissertations in Social Work Related to the Field of Child Welfare,* U.S. Department of Health, Education, and Welfare, Children's Bureau, 1966; (with John H. Noble) *Public Knowledge, Attitudes and Opinions about Physical Child Abuse in the United States,* Brandeis University, Papers in Social Welfare, 1967; (contributor) Ray E. Helfer and C. H. Kempe, editors, *The Battered Child,* University of Chicago Press, 1968; *Nationwide Survey of Legally Reported Physical Abuse of Children,* Brandeis University, Papers in Social Welfare, 1968; *Physical Abuse of Children: One Manifestation of Violence in American Society,* National Commission on the Causes and Prevention of Violence, 1968.

Abusing Parents: Cultural and Class Factors, Virginia Commonwealth University, 1970; *Violence Against Children: Physical Child Abuse in the United States,* Harvard University Press, 1970; (contributor) *Social Security: The First 35 Years,* University of Michigan Press, 1972; (contributor with Victor DeFrancis) Mason P. Thomas, Jr., editor, *Proceedings of the Second Governor's Conference on Child Abuse and Neglect,* University of North Carolina, Institute of Government, 1972; (contributor) *Hearings before the Subcommittee on Children and Youth of the Committee on Labor and Public Welfare,* U.S. Government Printing Office, 1973; *Unravelling Social Policy: Theory, Analysis, and Political Action towards Social Equality,* Schenkman, 1973, revised and enlarged edition, 1976; (contributor) Alvin L. Schorr, editor, *Children and Decent People,* Basic Books, 1974; *The Challenge of Social Equality: Essays on Policy, Social Development, and Political Practice,* Schenkman, 1976. Also editor of *Child Abuse and Violence,* American Orthopsychiatric Association.

Contributor to professional journals, including *Journal of Health and Social Behavior, Social Service Review, American Education, Journal of Marriage and the Family, Journal of Education for Social Work, Social Service Outlook, Social Work Practice,* and *Social Work.* Member of editorial board, *American Journal of Ortho-psychiatry,* 1973-77; consulting reader, *American Sociological Review,* 1973—; associate editor, *Journal of Sociology and Social Welfare,* 1974—.

GILBERT, Herman Cromwell 1923-

PERSONAL: Born February 23, 1923, in Mariana, Ark.; son of Van Luther (a minister) and Cora (Allen) Gilbert; married Ivy McAlpine, July 19, 1949; children: Dorthea, Vincent Newton. *Education:* Completed two years of a three-year correspondence course in law, LaSalle Extension University, 1941; IBM Educational Center, student in computer technology. *Politics:* Independent Democrat. *Religion:* Protestant. *Home:* 11539 South Justice St., Chicago, Ill. 60643. *Office:* Illinois Department of Labor, 165 North Canal, Chicago, Ill. 60606.

CAREER: AFL-CIO, United Packinghouse Workers of America, Chicago, Ill., program coordinator, 1955-57; Illinois Department of Labor, Bureau of Employment Security, Chicago, manager of automated systems section, 1957-70, assistant administrator, 1970—. Executive vice-president, Path Press, Chicago, 1968—. Member of joint Federal-State Committee on Automated Systems, Interstate Conference of Employment Security Agencies. Publicity director for Chicago League of Negro Voters, and Protest at the Polls. *Military service:* U.S. Army Air Forces, 1943-46; attended Armed Forces Institute, 1944-45; became staff sergeant.

WRITINGS: The Uncertain Sound (novel), Path Press, 1969. Author of column, "This Needs Saying," in Chicago's *Westside Booster,* 1959-60. Managing editor of Citizen Newspapers, 1965-67.

WORK IN PROGRESS: Two novels, *The Campaign,* which deals with attempts of black independent politicians to gain political power in Chicago, and *The Negotiations,* concerning efforts of blacks to negotiate a separate state in the late 1980's.

*   *   *

GILBERT, James 1935-

PERSONAL: Born April 28, 1935, in Croydon, England; son of Alan and Mary Margaret Elisabeth (Campion) Gilbert; married Lucretia Simonds, 1964 (annulled); married Elizabeth Richmond, 1972. *Education:* Attended Radley College, 1948-53. *Politics:* "Don't care for them." *Religion:* None. *Home:* 1 Grafton Sq., London SW4 0DE, England. *Office: Pilot,* The White House, Church Rd., Claygate, England.

CAREER: Flying (magazine), New York, N.Y., 1964-70, began as associate editor, became senior editor; *Pilot* (magazine), Claygate, England, editor, 1970—. *Military service:* Royal Air Force, controller, 1953-55. *Member:* Aviation and Space Writers Association. *Awards, honors:* Award of Merit, New York Society of Publication Designers, 1967, for best use of photography; United Press International newspapers monthly contest award, 1973; Aviation and Space Writers Association photojournalism award, 1974.

WRITINGS: The Great Planes, Grosset, 1970; *The World's Worst Aircraft,* St. Martin's, 1974; *The Flier's World,* Random House, 1976; *Skywriting: An Aviation Anthology,* St. Martin's, 1977. General editor, "Literature and History of Aviation" series, thirty-six volumes, Arno, 1971. Contributor to *Flying, Air Progress, Business and Commercial Aviation,* and other publications.

WORK IN PROGRESS: Make Angels, a novel set in 1940 during the Battle of Britain.

SIDELIGHTS: Gilbert is a specialist in film flying; he was a pilot for the movies "The Red Baron," "The Little Prince," "Aces High," and "Wings." He told *CA* that he also specializes in "aviation history, general aviation, sport flying and aerobatics, and aviation photography."

GILBERTS, Helen 1909-

PERSONAL: Born March 14, 1909, in South Boardman, Mich.; daughter of George W. (a businessman) and Etta (Hanson) Stover; married Elliott W. Gilberts (a millwright), June 18, 1932; children: John H., Richard A. *Education:* Graceland College, A.A., 1930; also attended Everett Community College and University of Washington. *Home:* 307 Pecks Dr., Everett, Wash. 98203.

CAREER: Writer.

WRITINGS: Sariah, Herald House, 1970. Contributor of articles to magazines.

WORK IN PROGRESS: A second book.

SIDELIGHTS: Helen Gilberts told *CA:* "I am an idealist and believe that in the future my voice will be heard. I feel that I have a contribution to make to my community and the best way is to write that which is real to me and which will be of value to others."

* * *

GILBOA, Yehoshua A. 1918-

PERSONAL: Surname originally Globerman; born May 13, 1918, in Pinsk, Poland (Pinsk now is in Soviet territory); son of Isaac and Rachel (Futerman) Globerman; married Dina Firstenberg (a teacher), December, 1948; children: Shuvit (daughter), Avishai (son). *Education:* Boston University, M.A., 1967; Tel-Aviv University, Ph.D., 1975. *Religion:* Jewish. *Residence:* Tel-Aviv, Israel. *Office: Maariv,* Karli-bach, Tel-Aviv, Israel; and Diaspora Research Institute, Tel-Aviv University, Ramat-Aviv, Tel-Aviv, Israel.

CAREER: Davar (daily newspaper), Tel-Aviv, Israel, member of editorial board, 1950-53; *Zmanim* (daily newspaper), Tel-Aviv, assistant editor and then editor-in-chief, 1953-55; *Maariv* (daily newspaper), Tel-Aviv, member of editorial board, 1955—. Brandeis University, Waltham, Mass., senior research associate at Institute of East European Studies, 1965-67; Tel-Aviv University, Tel-Aviv, research associate at Diaspora Research Institute, 1969—, and editor of *Shvut* (scholarly journal).

WRITINGS—Originally published in Hebrew, except as noted: (Editor and author of introduction) *Gehalim Lo-hashot* (title means "Glowing Embers"; anthology of Hebrew and Yiddish literature in the Soviet Union), Newman (Tel-Aviv), 1954; *Al Horvot ha-Tarbut* (on the ruins of Jewish culture in the Soviet Union), Peretz, 1959; *Li-Shemor la-Netsah* (title means "Hold Forever"), Massadah, 1963, translation by Dov Ben Aba published as *Confess! Confess! Eight Years in Soviet Prisons,* Little, Brown, 1968; *Uhuru: Days and Nights in Africa* (travel in Africa), Massadah, 1965; *Hebreisher Bikher-Shank* (title means "A Hebrew Bookshelf"; essays on twenty-eight Hebrew writers; in Yiddish), Hamenora, 1966; *The Black Years of Soviet Jewry, 1939-1953,* Little, Brown, 1971; *The Kibbutz Sitting Pretty,* Sifriat Poalim, 1973; *Hebrew Octobrists: History of an Illusion,* Tel-Aviv University Press, 1974; *Fight for Survival: Hebrew Culture in the Soviet Union,* Sifriat Poalim, 1977. Also editor with Y. Barzilay and M. Gefen of a book of short stories in Hebrew (title means "Contemporary Soviet Stories") published by Am Hasefer, 1962.

SIDELIGHTS: Yehoshua A. Gilboa is competent in Polish, Russian, and German in addition to Hebrew, Yiddish, and English.

GILCHER, Edwin L. 1909-

PERSONAL: Born August 9, 1909, in Republic, Ohio; son of Frederick C. (a physician) and Nellie (Horton) Gilcher; married Elizabeth M. Cipperly (a school secretary; maiden name, Carr), June 21, 1957; stepchildren: Mrs. Ellen Neaton, Stephen L. Cipperly. *Education:* American Academy of Dramatic Arts, student, 1927-29; took further courses at City College (now City College of the City University of New York), New York University, New School for Social Research, Albany Law School, and St. Lawrence University. *Politics:* Independent Republican. *Religion:* Episcopalian ("nominally"). *Home:* Folly Farm, Cherry Plain, N.Y. 12040. *Office address: Hemmings Motor News,* Box 380, Bennington, Vt. 05201.

CAREER: Formerly an actor on stage and in radio, and a puppeteer. Between theatrical engagements worked as a tester in a glue factory, production manager in a costume jewelry shop, an assistant steward in a New York City hotel, a farmer, a teacher in a one-room schoolhouse, and a proofreader; justice of the town of Berlin, N.Y., 1952-76; *Bennington Banner* (daily newspaper), Bennington, Vt., wire editor, 1965-74; *Hemmings Motor News,* Bennington, proofreading coordinator, 1974—. *Member:* Bibliographical Society of America, Society of Bibliophiles (treasurer, 1975—), New York Magistrates Association, Rensselaer County Magistrates Association (past secretary; president).

WRITINGS: A Bibliography of George Moore, Northern Illinois University Press, 1970. Contributor of articles and reviews to *Antiquarian Bookman, Modern Language Quarterly, English Literature in Transition, Serif,* and other journals and newspapers.

WORK IN PROGRESS: A revised and enlarged edition of *A Bibliography of George Moore.*

SIDELIGHTS: Compiling a George Moore bibliography has been Edwin L. Gilcher's avocation for more than thirty years. The project began as notes of textual differences in various editions and finally grew into a full-scale study, based to a large extent on Gilcher's personal collection but checked against copies in other libraries here and abroad (the latter with the help of cooperative correspondents). Since publication of the bibliography, he has continued correspondence with librarians, scholars, and collectors in the United States and abroad in an effort to assemble information to correct and enlarge the Moore bibliography in a future edition. He recently "visited England and Ireland to see as many sites as possible connected with George Moore, including several places he lived, his birthplace at Moore Hall and where his ashes are buried on Castle Island in Lough Carra, near Moore Hall."

* * *

GILDEN, Bert 1915(?)-1971
(K. B. Gilden, a joint pseudonym)

1915(?)—April 4, 1971; American novelist and writer of television scripts, short stories, and screenplays. Obituaries: *Publishers' Weekly,* May 3, 1971; *Antiquarian Bookman,* May 17, 1971. (See index for *CA* sketch)

* * *

GILDERSLEEVE, Thomas R(obert) 1927-

PERSONAL: Born October 27, 1927, in Middletown, N.Y.; son of Robert Wallace (a banker) and Marguerite (Bradley) Gildersleeve; married Beverly Kenworthy, July 5, 1952; children: Mark David, Robert James. *Education:* Brown

University, A.B., 1952; Columbia University, graduate study, 1954-55. *Politics:* Republican. *Religion:* None. *Home:* 56 Witch Lane, Rowayton, Conn. 06853. *Office:* Equitable Life Assurance, 1285 Avenue of the Americas, New York, N.Y. 10019.

CAREER: Equitable Life Assurance, New York, N.Y., manager of Fiscal Analysis and Control and Corporate Computer Services. *Military service:* U.S. Navy, 1945-47.

WRITINGS: (With Hyman N. Laden) *System Design for Computer Applications,* Wiley, 1963; *Computer Data Processing and Programming,* Prentice-Hall, 1970; *Decision Tables and Their Practical Application in Data Processing,* Prentice-Hall, 1970; *Design of Sequential File Systems,* Wiley, 1971; *Basic Computer Concepts,* N.G.P. Associates, 1971; *Data Processing Project Management,* Van Nostrand, 1974.

WORK IN PROGRESS: Organizing and Documenting Data Processing Information, for Hayden; *How to Succeed in the Data Processing System Analyst's World,* for Prentice-Hall.

SIDELIGHTS: Thomas R. Gildersleeve told *CA:* "I don't feel I have sufficient mastery of a subject unless I can express myself on it in the written word. I also believe that books are a more potent educational tool than is generally conceded, and I enjoy trying to format information so it can be most readily communicated."

* * *

GILES, Carl H(oward) 1935-
(William C. Gale)

PERSONAL: Born March 13, 1935, in Big Stone Gap, Va.; son of William Carl (an advertising employee) and Thelma (a bookkeeper; maiden name, Fields) Giles; married Shelby Jean Ball, November 24, 1956 (divorced, 1974); married Barbara Ann Williams (a writer), March 18, 1975; children: (first marriage) Sheldon Carl. *Education:* Florida Southern College, B.S.J., 1962; attended University of Georgia, 1963; West Virginia University, M.S.J., 1965. *Politics:* Republican. *Religion:* Protestant. *Home:* 564 East Main St., Jackson, Tenn. 38301. *Office:* Department of Journalism, University of Tennessee, Martin, Tenn. 38237.

CAREER: Employed as factory worker in Ohio and Florida, construction worker in Virginia, milk company employee, store clerk, and book peddler, 1956-61; Terry Parker High School, Jacksonville, Fla., journalism teacher, school newspaper adviser, 1962-64; West Virginia University, Morgantown, instructor in journalism, 1964-65; University of Tennessee at Martin, assistant professor of journalism, 1965—. *Member:* Association for Education in Journalism, National Council of College Publications Advisers, Kappa Tau Alpha, Sigma Delta Chi. *Awards, honors:* Writers Digest contest awards, 1966, 1969, and 1970.

WRITINGS: Seduction on Location, Novel Books, 1964; *All about Booze* (documentary on whiskey), United Graphics Inc., 1966; (under pseudonym, William C. Gale) *The Fight to Legalize Narcotics,* Publishers Export Co., 1967; *1927: A Picture Story of a Wonderful Year* (Nostalgia Book Club selection), Arlington House, 1971; *Underground Movie Revue,* Stearn Publishing, 1972; *Bewitching Jewelry,* A. S. Barnes, 1976.

Journalism textbooks: *The Student Journalist and Feature Writing* (grade 7 and up), Rosen Press, 1969; *Writing Right: To Sell,* A. S. Barnes, 1970; *Feature Writing,* University of Tennessee, 1970; *Advising Advisors,* UT Correspondence

Press, 1972; *Journalism: Dateline, The World,* Rosen Press, 1973.

Contributor of over 500 articles and short stories to men's magazines, general editorial and specialty magazines, and religious journals, including *National Enquirer, National Tattler, True, Coronet, Ace, Bachelor, Cavalcade, Consumer Confidential, Dude, Rampage, Holiday, Adult Bible Study, Auto-Driver, Progressive Farmer,* and *Success.* Contributor of feature articles to King Features Syndicate.

WORK IN PROGRESS: John Wayne Lacy Story.

BIOGRAPHICAL/CRITICAL SOURCES: Muscle Training Illustrated, January, 1967.

* * *

GILL, David (Lawrence William) 1934-

PERSONAL: Born July 3, 1934, in Chislehurst, Kent, England; son of Donald James Walton and Marjorie Maud (Paramor) Gill; married Irene Zuntz (a lecturer), July 5, 1958; children: Thomas, Nicholas, Jaquetta. *Education:* University College, London, B.A. (honors in German), 1955; University of Birmingham, Certificate in Education, 1960; University of London (external), B.A. (honors in English), 1970. *Home:* 25 Redriff Close, Maidenhead, Berkshire, England. *Office:* Newland Park College of Education, Chalfont St., Giles, Buckinghamshire, England.

CAREER: Bedales School, Hampshire, England, teacher of German and English, 1960-62; Nyakasura School, Fort Portal, Uganda, teacher of English, 1962-64; Magdalen College School, Oxford, England, teacher of German and English, 1965-71; Newland Park College of Education, Buckinghamshire, England, lecturer, 1971—. Vice-chairman for Oxford area, Campaign for Nuclear Disarmament. *Military service:* British Army, Royal Signals, 1955-57. *Awards, honors:* Birmingham Post poetry prize, 1960.

WRITINGS: Men without Evenings (poems), Chatto & Windus, 1966, Wesleyan University Press, 1967; *The Pagoda and Other Poems,* Chatto & Windus, 1969, Wesleyan University Press, 1970; *Peaches and Apercus,* Poet & Peasant Books, 1974; *In the Eye of the Storm: Fifty Years of Ondva Iysohorsky,* Hub Publications, 1976. Poems have appeared in *Listener, Observer, Critical Quarterly, Country Life,* and other periodicals.

WORK IN PROGRESS: A fourth collection of his poems; *We Are Utopia,* an opera based on the Digger leader, Gerrard Winstanley.

SIDELIGHTS: David Gill wrote *CA:* "We had the booming sixties in Britain and poetry was all right. Now the pound is sliding down somebody else's greasy pole, the publishers are telling us to be quiet—the people don't need poetry any more. They still need everything else, but not poetry. Poetry's froth. So we must become self-reliant, become our own publishers, our own performers. A good many poets have seen this already; mine's a delayed reaction, typically. I say to younger poets: you are the D.I.Y. [do-it-yourself] generation. Do you mind if I join you?"

* * *

GILLQUIST, Peter E. 1938-

PERSONAL: Born July 13, 1938, in Minneapolis, Minn.; son of William Parker Gillquist (with Minnesota State Highway Department); married Marilyn Grinder, May 14, 1960; children: Wendy Jo, Gregory Ray, Ginger Ann, Terri Beth, Heidi Lou, Peter Jon. *Education:* University of Minnesota, B.A., 1960; further study at Dallas Theological Seminary, 1960-61, and Wheaton College, Wheaton, Ill., 1961-62. *Politics:* "A-political!" *Religion:* Christian. *Home:* Paupers Alley, Grand Junction, Tenn. 38039. *Office:* Thomas Nelson, Inc., 407 Seventh Ave. S., Nashville, Tenn. 37203.

CAREER: Campus Crusade for Christ, district director, later regional director in Illinois, 1960-68; Memphis State University, Memphis, Tenn., director of development, 1969-72; Thomas Nelson, Inc. (publishers), Nashville, Tenn., editor, 1976—. *Member:* Alpha Delta Sigma, Sigma Alpha Epsilon.

WRITINGS: Love Is Now (study manual), Zondervan, 1970; *Farewell to the Fake I.D.,* Zondervan, 1972; *Let's Quit Fighting about the Holy Spirit,* Zondervan, 1975. Managing editor, *Collegiate Challenge,* 1962-68.

WORK IN PROGRESS: I'm Glad I'm Turning 40; A Popular Theology on the Holy Spirit.

*   *   *

GILMORE, Don 1930-
(Gil Davis)

PERSONAL: Born December 9, 1930; son of Donald Henry and Ladymay (Adams) Gilmore; married Betty Jo Bullard (a researcher), February 2, 1957; children: Maria Consuelo, Jesus Guadalupe (both adopted). *Education:* Ohio Christian College, Ph.D. *Home:* 3808 Douglas, Suite 3, Des Moines, Iowa 50310. *Agent:* Warren Bayless, W B Agency, Inc., 156 East 52nd St., New York, N.Y. 10022.

CAREER: Writer. *Member:* Instituto Cultural Mexicano Norte Americano (member of board of directors of Guadalajara chapter), Salvation Army (member of men's advisory board), Concert Guild, American Society of Jalisco (president of Guadalajara chapter, 1970-71).

WRITINGS: Adam Clayton Powell, P.E.C., 1966; *Was Oswald Alone?,* P.E.C., 1967; *A Guide to Living in Mexico,* Putnam, 1971.

WORK IN PROGRESS: Several historical works.

*   *   *

GIONO, Jean 1895-1970

March 30, 1895—October 8 (or 9), 1970; French poet, novelist, and playwright. Obituaries: *New York Times,* October 10, 1970; *Washington Post,* October 10, 1970; *L'Express,* October 12-18, 1970; *Books Abroad,* spring, 1971. (See index for *CA* sketch)

*   *   *

GIOVANNI, Nikki 1943-

PERSONAL: Given name, Yolande Cornelia, Jr.; born June 7, 1943, in Knoxville, Tenn.; daughter of Jones (a probation officer) and Yolande Cornelia (a social worker; maiden name, Watson) Giovanni; children: Thomas Watson. *Education:* Fisk University, B.A. (honors), 1967; also attended University of Pennsylvania, Social Work School, and Columbia University, School of the Arts. *Residence:* Cincinnati, Ohio.

CAREER: Poet, writer, lecturer; Queens College of the City University of New York, Flushing, N.Y., assistant professor of Black studies, 1968; Rutgers University, Livingston College, New Brunswick, N.J., associate professor of English, 1968-72; founder of publishing firm, Niktom Ltd., 1970. Has made television appearances on "Soul!," produced on National Educational Television, and on nu-

merous talk shows; participated in "Soul at the Center," Lincoln Center for the Performing Arts, 1972.

MEMBER: National Council of Negro Women, Society of Magazine Writers. *Awards, honors:* Grants from Ford Foundation, 1967, National Endowment for the Arts, 1968, and Harlem Cultural Council, 1969; named one of ten most admired Black women, *Amsterdam News,* 1969; *Mademoiselle* award for outstanding achievement, 1971; Omega Psi Phi Fraternity award for outstanding contribution to arts and letters, 1971; Meritorious Plaque for Service, Cook County Jail, 1971; Life membership and scroll, National Council of Negro Women, 1972; keys to the cities of Lincoln Heights, Ohio, Dallas, Tex., and Gary, Ind., all 1972; National Association of Radio and Television Announcers award for best spoken word album, 1972, for "Truth Is on Its Way"; Woman of the Year—Youth Leadership Award, *Ladies Home Journal,* 1972; Doctorate of Humanities, Wilberforce University, 1972; National Book Award nomination, 1973, for *Gemini;* American Library Association commendation for one of the best books for young adults, 1973, for *My House;* Doctorate of Literature, University of Maryland, Princess Anne Campus, 1974, Ripon University, 1974, Smith College, 1975.

WRITINGS: Black Feeling, Black Talk (poems; also see below), Broadside Press, 1968, 3rd edition, 1970; *Black Judgement* (poems; also see below), Broadside Press, 1968; *Black Feeling, Black Talk, Black Judgement* (contains *Black Feeling, Black Talk* and *Black Judgement*), Morrow, 1970; *Re: Creation,* Broadside Press, 1970; (editor) *Night Comes Softly: Anthology of Black Female Voices,* Niktom, 1970; *Poem of Angela Yvonne Davis,* Niktom, 1970; *Spin a Soft Black Song: Poems for Children,* Hill & Wang, 1971; *Gemini: An Extended Autobiographical Statement on My First Twenty-Five Years of Being a Black Poet,* Bobbs-Merrill, 1971; *My House* (poems), Morrow, 1972; (with James Baldwin) *A Dialogue: James Baldwin and Nikki Giovanni,* Lippincott, 1972; *Ego Tripping and Other Poems for Young Readers,* Lawrence Hill, 1973; (with Margaret Walker) *A Poetic Equation: Conversations between Nikki Giovanni and Margaret Walker,* Howard University Press, 1974; *The Women and the Men* (poems), Morrow, 1975.

Recordings of her poetry include: "Truth Is on Its Way," Right On Records, 1971; "Like a Ripple on a Pond," Atlantic Records, 1973; "The Way I Feel," Atlantic Records, 1974; "Legacies," Folkways Records, 1975; "The Reason I Like Chocolate," Folkways Records. Work has been represented in numerous anthologies. Author of columns, "One Woman's Voice," for Anderson-Moberg Syndicate of the *New York Times,* and "The Root of the Matter," in *Encore American and Worldwide News.* Contributor to *Black Creation, Black World, Ebony, Essence, Freedom Ways, Journal of Black Poetry, Negro Digest,* and *Umbra.* Editorial consultant, *Encore American and Worldwide News.*

WORK IN PROGRESS: Cotton Candy on a Rainy Day, a book of poems; *So the Little Old Lady Can Get Home Tonight,* an extended essay on America during the Bicentennial; *Snowflakes and Daffodils,* a book of poems for children.

SIDELIGHTS: From a childhood which she has said was happy, Nikki Giovanni went to Fisk University where she fought to restore the campus chapter of the Student Nonviolent Coordinating Committee. After Giovanni led a group of two hundred students in a demonstration for the political organization's right to exist on campus, the chapter was reinstated in 1964. But Giovanni noticeably changed her outlook, and ten years after the campus event Paula Brookmire writes of a poetry reading in Milwaukee: "It was not the student activist here that night. It was Nikki Giovanni the mother, the lover, the woman. The only remembrance of her days at Nashville's Fisk University during the '60's was a poem about a black revolutionary she fell in love with. . . ."

Giovanni herself said that night: "I am an individualist. And groups are formed and function because of the individual needs. A lot of the needs in the black community at this point are really very personal needs and are not going to be satisfied by group involvement." Peter Bailey further explains her individualistic outlook: "Nikki's attitude on many issues is better understood when one realizes that one of the people whose philosophy she admires most is Ayn Rand whose concept of rational self-interest and extreme individualism is so way-out that even arch-conservatives of the William Buckley ilk reject its implications."

This outlook has led to Giovanni standing apart from the mainstream of Black poetry in the 1960's and early 1970's. Although some of her poetry includes militant Black revolutionary sentiment, she more often writes of love and life and the individual's fight for survival. As John W. Conner notes: "The poet Nikki Giovanni looks upon her world with a wide open penetrating gaze. She sees her world as an extension of herself, she sees problems in the world as an extension of her problems, she sees herself existing amidst tension, heartache, and marvelous expressions of love. But the tension, heartaches, and expressions of love do not overwhelm the poet. She controls her environment—sometimes with her mind, often with her heart."

Bailey comments: "Nikki's poetry is about what she sees, what she feels and experiences [and she often deals in her poems with her own happy childhood and with her family]. . . . Besides dealing with her childhood, Nikki's poetry and essays deal also with, among other things, the black liberation movement, revolution, love among all black people and between individual black man and black woman, Angela Davis . . . , and rhythm and blues music and its interpreters. . . . Nikki's language ranges from angry to bitter to sensuous to melancholy to joyful. . . ."

Nikki Giovanni has added to her diverse following through lecturing on college campuses, reading her poetry on television, and recording her poetry on five albums which have been popular with all age groups. "Truth Is on Its Way," her first record album, has gospel music as accompaniment to her poetry partly because, as Giovanni has explained, she wanted the record to appeal to her grandmother as well as her contemporaries. She has become a major figure in the Black oral poetry movement. Thomas Lask, reviewing her appearance at Lincoln Center, reports that she "controlled the reading with her presence and her reading gave the evening its character of informality and joyousness." Don L. Lee comments: "Nikki is at her best in the short, personal poem. She is definitely growing as a poet. Her effectiveness is in the area of the 'fast rap.' She says the right things at the right time. Orally this is cool, but it doesn't come across as printed poetry."

Whatever the medium, Nikki Giovanni remains a strong voice in contemporary poetry. Reviewing *My House,* John W. Conner comments that the book "is the poetic expression of a vibrant black woman with a special way of looking at things. A strong narrative line runs through many of the poems: a familiar scene is presented, and the poet comments upon the people or the events. The poems are short, the language is simple; each poem contains a single

poignant image. . . . When a reader enters *My House,* he is invited to savor the poet's ideas about a meaningful existence in today's world."

A reviewer for *Choice* comments on her latest book, *The Women and the Men:* "Giovanni has mellowed, at least poetically. She has dropped her honky-hating attacks which marred some of her past work and has become more optimistic, loving, gentle, concerned. She still can turn out an arresting thought."

In a review of *Gemini,* Martha Duffy writes that Giovanni "is one of the most talented and promising black poets. She is also one of the most visible, not only because she is beautiful but because she is a shrewd and energetic propagandist. . . . Hers is a committed social rage. She is capable of scalding rhetoric, but the artist in her keeps interrupting. . . . She keeps sending out bulletins—in poetry, prose, children's books—whether they are neat or messy, rash or reasoned. But one senses a dynamic intelligence behind the shrillest page of *Gemini.* It is a report about a life in progress that demands to be seen."

AVOCATIONAL INTERESTS: Travel, music, painting.

BIOGRAPHICAL/CRITICAL SOURCES: New York Times, April 25, 1969, July 26, 1972; *Time,* April 6, 1970, January 17, 1972; *Christian Science Monitor,* June 4, 1970, June 19, 1974; *Black World,* December, 1970, January, 1971, February, 1971, April, 1971, August, 1971, August, 1972, July, 1974; Don L. Lee, *Dynamite Voices I: Black Poets of the 1960's,* Broadside Press, 1971; Nikki Giovanni, *Gemini: An Extended Autobiographical Statement on My First Twenty-Five Years of Being a Black Poet,* Bobbs-Merrill, 1971; *CLA Journal,* September, 1971; *Publishers' Weekly,* October 18, 1971, September 11, 1972, November 18, 1972, December 31, 1973, April 1, 1974, September 15, 1975; *New York Times Book Review,* November 7, 1971, November 28, 1971, February 13, 1972, June 4, 1972, December 3, 1972, May 5, 1974; *Ebony,* February, 1972, August, 1972; *Encore,* spring, 1972; *Choice,* May, 1972, March, 1973, September, 1974, January, 1976; *Harper's Bazaar,* July, 1972; *Ingenue,* February, 1973; *English Journal,* April, 1973, January, 1974; *Mademoiselle,* May, 1973, December, 1973, September, 1975; *Best Sellers,* September 1, 1973, January, 1976; *Contemporary Literary Criticism,* Gale, Volume II, 1974, Volume IV, 1975; *Milwaukee Journal,* November 20, 1974.

*   *   *

GISH, Arthur G.   1939-

PERSONAL: Born August 15, 1939; son of Paul A. (a school custodian) and Ruth (Greiner) Gish; married Peggy Faw, June 2, 1962; children: Dale Martin, Daniel Paul. *Education:* Manchester College, B.A. (magna cum laude), 1964; Bethany Theological Seminary, M.Div. (cum laude), 1968. *Religion:* Church of the Brethren. *Home address:* New Covenant Fellowship, Route 3, Box 213A, Athens, Ohio 45701.

CAREER: Free-lance writer and lecturer; Akron Church of the Brethren, Akron, Ind., pastor, 1963-65. Founder, Brethren Action Movement; member of New Covenant Fellowhip, an intentional community related to the Church of the Bretheran..

WRITINGS: The New Left and Christian Radicalism, Eerdmans, 1970; *Beyond the Rat Race,* Herald Press, 1973.

WORK IN PROGRESS: A book on Christian community.

SIDELIGHTS: Arthur Gish told *CA:* "[I] come from an

Anabaptist background [and am] interested in radical Christianity and the relation of religion to social issues. [I] do a lot of street preaching, spend much of my time traveling and speaking to churches and colleges. [I] have been active in the peace and civil rights movements.''

* * *

GITLIN, Todd 1943-

PERSONAL: Born January 6, 1943, in New York, N.Y.; son of Max (a teacher) and Dorothy (Siegel) Gitlin. *Education:* Harvard University, B.A., 1963; University of Michigan, M.A., 1966. *Home:* 4348 26th St., San Francisco, Calif. 94131.

CAREER: San Francisco Express Times, San Francisco, Calif., writer, 1968-69; San Jose State College (now University), San Jose, Calif., instructor in politics and poetry, 1970-71.

WRITINGS: (Contributor) Andrew Kopkind, editor, *Thoughts of the Young Radicals,* New Republic, 1966; (contributor) David Horowitz, editor, *Containment and Revolution,* Beacon Press, 1967; (contributor) Hans Dreitzel, editor, *Recent Sociology,* Macmillan, 1969; (with Nanci Hollander) *Uptown: Poor Whites in Chicago,* Harper, 1970; (editor) *Campfires of the Resistance: Poetry from the Movement,* Bobbs-Merrill, 1971; (with Robert Paul Wolff) *1984 Revisited: Prospects for American Politics,* University of Massachusetts Press, 1973; *Busy Being Born* (poems), Straight Arrow Books, 1974. Contributor to *Nation, Liberation, Christian Century, Commonweal, New Republic, Progressive, Hard Times, Nickel Review,* and other publications.

WORK IN PROGRESS: History of the New Left; utopian possibilities of liberation; a play; a book of poetry.

BIOGRAPHICAL/CRITICAL SOURCES: Nation, September 28, 1970; *Best Sellers,* December 1, 1970.

* * *

GIUTTARI, Theodore Richard 1931-

PERSONAL: Born February 4, 1931, in Jersey City, N.J.; son of Anthony and Giovanna (Santamaria) Giuttari. *Education:* Fordham University, B.A., 1952, LL.B., 1958; Columbia University, M.I.A., 1954, M.A., 1958, Ph.D., 1969. *Religion:* Roman Catholic. *Home:* 2111 Third Ave., Spring Lake, N.J. *Office:* American Home Products Corp., 685 Third Ave., New York, N.Y. 10017.

CAREER: Norwich Pharmacal Co., New York City, counsel with International Division, 1969-73; American Home Products Corp., New York City, international attorney, 1973—. *Member:* International Law Association (member of executive committee of American branch).

WRITINGS: The American Law of Sovereign Immunity: An Analysis of Legal Interpretation, Praeger, 1970.

* * *

GLADSTONE, Gary 1935-

PERSONAL: Born July 8, 1935, in Philadelphia, Pa.; son of Milton Stanley (an advertising man) and Bernice (Bayuk) Gladstone; married Meredith Townsend (a fashion designer), July 7, 1967; children: Gregory Townsend. *Education:* Attended Art Students' League of New York, 1952-54. *Agent:* McIntosh & Otis, 475 Fifth Ave., New York, N.Y. 10017. *Office:* Gladstone Studio Ltd., 237 East 20th St., New York, N.Y. 10003.

CAREER: Westchester News, White Plains, N.Y., photographer and columnist, 1955-56; *New York Daily News,* New York City, photographer, 1957-58; Norton O'Neil Co., Inc. (industrial theater), New York City, producer, 1962-68. *Member:* American Society of Magazine Photographers. *Awards, honors: New York Daily News* annual free-lance award, 1956; *Popular Photography* yearbook design and photography award, 1960, 1961; Printing Industries of America yearbook design and photography award, 1964, 1965, 1966; Art Directors Club of New York Merit Award, 1975; Certificate of Merit, *Art Direction Magazine,* 1976.

WRITINGS: Hey, Hey, Can't Catch Me, Van Nostrand, 1970; *Dune-Buggies,* photographs by author, Lippincott, 1972; (with wife, Meredith Gladstone) *The Needlepoint Alphabet Book,* Morrow, 1973; (with M. Gladstone) *Kids' Clothes by Meredith Gladstone: A Sewing Book,* Morrow, 1976. Member of editorial board, *Infinity* (American Society of Magazine Photographers publication), 1961-62.

* * *

GLASGOW, Gordon H(enry) H(arper) 1926-

PERSONAL: Born October 8, 1926, in Leeds, England; son of William Ewart (a civil servant) and Sybil Maud Thompson (Harper) Glasgow. *Education:* Emmanuel College, Cambridge, M.A., 1951, LL.M., 1962. *Home:* 152 Lord St., Birkdale, Southport, Merseyside, England.

CAREER: Solicitor in private practice, 1953—. Visiting lecturer in law at City of Liverpool College of Commerce, 1962-67. *Member:* Law Society.

WRITINGS: A Modern View of Conveyancing, Pergamon, 1969. Contributor to *Law Times* and other law journals.

WORK IN PROGRESS: Guide to Mental Health Acts.

* * *

GLASSE, Robert Marshall 1929-

PERSONAL: Born April 3, 1929, in New York, N.Y.; married Bernadette Bucher, 1966. *Education:* City College (now City College of the City University of New York), B.S.S. (with honors), 1951; Australian National University, Ph.D., 1962. *Office:* Department of Anthropology, Queens College of the City University of New York, Flushing, N.Y. 11367.

CAREER: Australian School of Pacific Administration, Sydney, lecturer in anthropology, and Adelaide University, department of genetics, research fellow, 1961; Territory of New Guinea, visiting specialist in anthropology, 1962-63; Pakistan-Southeast Asia Treaty Organization, Dacca, East Pakistan, anthropologist, 1963-64; Queens College of the City University of New York, Flushing, N.Y., assistant professor, 1965-66, associate professor, 1967-71, professor of anthropology, 1971—. Did field work in Papua, New Guinea, 1955-56, 1959-60, 1961-63, 1969, in New Ireland, 1956, in Bangladesh, 1963-64, and in East Bengal, 1963-64. *Military service:* U.S. Army, 1951-53. *Member:* American Anthropological Association (fellow), American Ethnological Society, Royal Anthropological Institute (fellow).

WRITINGS: (Contributor) Peter Lawrence and M. J. Meggitt, editors, *Gods, Ghosts, and Men in Melanesia,* Oxford University Press (Melbourne), 1965; *Huli of Papua,* Mouton & Co. (The Hague), 1968; (editor with Meggitt) *Pigs, Pearlshells, and Women: Marriage Arrangements in the New Guinea Highlands,* Prentice-Hall, 1969. Contributor to *Encyclopedia of Papua and New Guinea;* contributor of about twenty-five articles and reviews to *Australian Outlook, Lancet, Oceania, L'Homme,* and other anthropology and medical journals.

WORK IN PROGRESS: Volcanoes and Virtue: The Social and Cultural Consequences of Ash Falls in the Southern Highlands of Papua New Guinea.

* * *

GLASSER, Paul H(arold) 1929-

PERSONAL: Born August 21, 1929; son of David (a businessman) and Rae (Startz) Glasser; married Lois Naefach (a lecturer), November 25, 1954; children: Heather Denise, Frederick Naefach. *Education:* City College (now City College of the City University of New York), B.A., 1949; Columbia University, M.S., 1951; University of North Carolina, Ph.D., 1961. *Religion:* Jewish. *Home:* 4141 Woodland Dr., Ann Arbor, Mich. 48103. *Office:* School of Social Work, University of Michigan, Ann Arbor, Mich. 48109.

CAREER: University of Cincinnati, Medical School, Cincinnati, Ohio, instructor in psychiatric group work, 1953-55; North Carolina Memorial Hospital, Chapel Hill, psychiatric social worker, 1956; University of Michigan, Ann Arbor, 1958—, began as assistant professor, currently professor of social work. Assistant director of residence, Child Guidance Home, Cincinnati, 1953-55; part-time psychiatric social worker, Alcoholism Clinic, City of Cincinnati, 1954-55. Fulbright-Hays lecturer in sociology at University of the Philippines, 1966-67, in social work in Italy, 1971, and at University of New South Wales, Sydney, Australia, 1973-74. Member of board of directors, Family and Children's Service of Washtenaw County, 1964-66, 1968-72; member of divisional board for Social Science and Education, Graduate School of University of Michigan; member of advisory board, University of Michigan Fresh Air Camp and University of Michigan Institute for Mental Retardation, 1969-72. Consultant to Office of Economic Opportunity, Children's Bureau, Michigan Department of Mental Health, Michigan Department of Social Services, Ohio Youth Commission, Grand Rapids Veterans Administration Hospital, Ann Arbor Veterans Administration Hospital, Lapeer State Home and Training School, Australian Department of Social Services. Has lectured to American Psychiatric Association, National Conference on Social Welfare, and other professional organizations. *Military service:* U.S. Army, Medical Corps, 1952-53; became first lieutenant.

MEMBER: International Conference on Social Welfare, National Conference on Social Welfare, American Sociological Society, National Council on Family Relations, Council on Social Work Education, American Orthopsychiatric Association, National Association of Social Workers, Academy of Certified Social Workers, American Public Welfare Association, Groves Conference on Marriage and the Family, Ohio Valley Sociological Society, Michigan Sociological Society. *Awards, honors:* Research grant, Children's Bureau, U.S. Department of Health, Education, and Welfare, 1962-66.

WRITINGS: (With Sallie R. Churchill) *Small Groups in the Hospital Community* (monograph), Department of Mental Health, State of Michigan, 1967; *New Careers in Community Service,* University of Michigan, Center for Continuing Education for Women, 1968; (editor with wife, Lois N. Glasser, and contributor) *Families in Crisis,* Harper, 1970; (editor and contributor) *1971 Encyclopedia of Social Work,* National Association of Social Work, 1971; *La Ricerca Valutative* (title means "Evaluative Research"), Emanuela Zancon Foundation (Italy), 1972; (with Helen Hunter and Henry Meyer) *Social Work Education for Family and Population Planning: Topical Outlines and Annotated Refer-

ences,* Social Work Education and Population Planning Project, University of Michigan, 1973; (editor and contributor with Rosemary Sarri and Robert D. Vinter) *Individual Change through Small Groups,* Free Press, 1974; *Social Work Roles and Functions in Family and Population Planning: Some Implications for Social Work Education,* Social Work Education and Population Planning Project, University of Michigan, 1974.

Contributor: Vinter, editor, *Readings in Group Work Practice,* Campus Publishers, 1967; Edwin Thomas, editor, *Behavioral Science for Social Workers,* Free Press, 1967; J. Ross Eshelman, editor, *Perspectives in Marriage and the Family: Text and Readings,* Allyn & Bacon, 1969; Ruth S. Cavan, editor, *Marriage and Family in the Modern World: A Book of Readings,* 3rd edition (Glasser was not associated with earlier editions), Crowell, 1969; *Social Work Practice, 1970,* Columbia University Press, 1970; Robert W. Roberts and Helen Northen, editors, *Theories of Social Work with Groups,* Columbia University Press, 1976.

Contributor to professional journals, including *Journal of Marriage and the Family, Social Work, General Education Journal* (Philippines), *Exchange, Journal of Social Issues, International Social Work,* and *Social Forces.* Member of editorial committee, *Journal of Social Work,* 1965-69, *Journal of Health and Social Behavior,* 1970-73, *Journal of Marriage and Family Counseling,* 1974—.

Anthologized in *Group Method and Services in Child Welfare,* Child Welfare League of America, 1963, and *Poverty: A Psychological Analysis,* edited by Lawrence E. Sneelen II, McCutchan, 1970.

WORK IN PROGRESS: With Lois Glasser and Catherine Chilman, *Family Policy;* with Charles Garvin, *Family Community Intervention: Abuse and Neglect.*

SIDELIGHTS: Paul H. Glasser told *CA:* "My career in writing and teaching has emphasized the utility of the social and behavioral sciences for human betterment. Emphasis has been on means to strengthen family life and eliminate or reduce poverty and the problems associated with this social problem throughout the world by applying the latest available knowledge from the social and behavioral sciences, and doing studies which will increase the fund of knowledge in this endeavor."

* * *

GLAUBER, Uta (Heil) 1936-

PERSONAL: Born June 8, 1936, in Pirmasens, Germany; daughter of Paul (a purchasing agent) and Gudula (Schmoll) Heil; married Heinrich Glauber (an electronics engineer), October 6, 1957; children: Vanna, Lucca, Mattia. *Education:* Attended Academy of Fine Arts, Berlin, 1950-54. *Politics:* None. *Religion:* Protestant. *Home:* Via Belvedere, Lipomo, Como, Italy.

CAREER: Free-lance illustrator and graphic artist.

WRITINGS: (Illustrator) Gertrud von Walther, *Heile, heile Segen* (children's picture book), Herder, 1967; (illustrator) von Walther, *The Four Seasons* (originally written but never published in German), translated by Patricia Crampton, Abelard, 1968; (and illustrator) *How the Willow Wren Became King: Story and Pictures* (juvenile, based on a story by the brothers Grimm), Abelard, 1970; *Petruska,* Emme, 1971. Also author of *Il Lungo viaggio dell'acqua,* for Monadori, and *Abends wenn ich schlafen geh,* for Herder.

WORK IN PROGRESS: Text and illustrations for two children's books.

AVOCATIONAL INTERESTS: Child psychotherapy in an institution for orphans.†

* * *

GLAZEBROOK, Philip 1937-

PERSONAL: Born April 3, 1937, in London, England; son of Kirkland (a judge) and Winifred (Davison) Glazebrook; married Clare Gemmell, October 5, 1968. *Education:* Trinity College, Cambridge, B.A., (honors), 1959. *Home:* Strode Manor, Bridport, Dorsetshire, England. *Agent:* Richard Scott Simon, 32 College Cross, London N.I., England.

CAREER: British Embassy, Rome, Italy, honorary attache, 1959-61; advertising copywriter, 1963-64, and film scriptwriter, 1965.

WRITINGS: Try Pleasure (novel), Longmans, Green, 1969; (contributor) *Winters' Tales,* Macmillan, 1975; *The Eye of the Beholder* (novel), Gollancz, 1975, Atheneum, 1976; *The Burr Wood* (novel), Gollancz, 1977. Contributor of short stories and articles to *London Daily Telegraph Magazine* and *Cornhill Magazine.*

WORK IN PROGRESS: A novel.

SIDELIGHTS: Philip Glazebrook wrote *CA:* "My intention in writing is to investigate the lies people tell each other, and themselves, in their attempt to create a reality they can tolerate."

Glazebrook traveled in Mexico and Central America in 1969, gathering background material for his writing, and in East Africa, the Seychelles, and India in 1970.

AVOCATIONAL INTERESTS: Fishing, gardening, and travel.

* * *

GLEN, Robert S. 1925-

PERSONAL: Born June 23, 1925, in Edinburgh, Scotland; son of Douglas James (a doctor) and Doris (Sawers) Glen. *Education:* Cambridge University, M.A. and Diploma in Classical Archaeology, 1954; National School of Opera, production course, 1959. *Religion:* Church of England. *Home:* Devan Haye, North Rd., Sherborne, Dorsetshire, England. *Office:* Sherborne School, Sherborne, Dorsetshire, England.

CAREER: Cranleigh School, Surrey, England, assistant master, 1951-58; Shrewsbury School, Shrewsbury, Shropshire, England, assistant master, 1960; Sherborne School, Sherborne, Dorsetshire, England, head of classics, 1960—, housemaster, 1973—. *Military service:* British Army, Royal Indian Artillery, 1943-47; became captain. *Member:* Classical Association.

WRITINGS: The Two Muses: An Introduction to Fifth-Century Athens by Way of the Drama, Macmillan, 1968.

WORK IN PROGRESS: Writing on Euripides.

SIDELIGHTS: Robert S. Glen produces three or four operas and plays a year with amateur groups, and is active in a project for a Shakespearean Globe Theatre in Sherborne.

* * *

GLESSING, Robert J(ohn) 1930-

PERSONAL: Born December 14, 1930; son of Leo Herman (a printer) and Rose (Richardell) Glessing; married Martha Meinert (a journalist); children: Erica Marie, Gerard Robert. *Education:* Marquette University, B.A., 1961; University of California, Berkeley, M.A., 1968. *Politics:* Independent. *Home:* 430 Addison St., Palo Alto, Calif. 94301. *Office:* Department of Journalism, Canada College, Redwood City, Calif. 94601.

CAREER: Ross Valley Times (newspaper), San Anselmo, Calif., editor, 1962-63; *Reveille* (newspaper), Seneca Falls, N.Y., editor-publisher, 1963-67; Canada College, Redwood City, Calif., instructor in journalism, 1968—. *Military service:* U.S. Air Force Reserve, 1950-56. *Member:* Sigma Delta Chi. *Awards, honors:* Two New York Press Association awards, 1966.

WRITINGS: The Underground Press in America, Indiana University Press, 1970; (with William P. White) *Mass Media: The Invisible Environment Revisited,* Science Research Associates, 1973, revised edition, 1976.

WORK IN PROGRESS: The future of media.

BIOGRAPHICAL/CRITICAL SOURCES: Nation, October 26, 1970†

* * *

GLICK, Thomas F(rederick) 1939-

PERSONAL: Born January 28, 1939, in Cleveland, Ohio; son of Lester G. and Ruth (Rothstein) Glick; married Elizabeth Ladd (a potter), November 10, 1963; children: Rachel, Amos. *Education:* Harvard University, B.A., 1960, Ph.D., 1968; University of Barcelona, graduate study, 1960-61; Columbia University, M.A., 1963. *Home:* 3 Hill St., Medway, Mass. 02053. *Office:* Department of History, Boston University, Boston, Mass. 02215.

CAREER: University of Texas at Austin, assistant professor, 1968-71, associate professor of history, 1971-72; Boston University, Boston, Mass., associate professor of history and geography, 1972—. *Member:* American Historical Association, Mediaeval Academy of America, Society for the History of Technology, History of Science Society, Association of American Geographers, Gerontological Society (member of history and archives committee). *Awards, honors:* Social Science Research Council fellowship, 1970-71; American Council of Learned Societies fellowship, 1974-75.

WRITINGS: Irrigation and Society in Medieval Valencia, Harvard University Press, 1970; *The Old World Background of the Irrigation System of San Antonio, Texas,* Texas Western Press, 1972; *Darwinism in Texas,* University of Texas Humanities Research Center, 1972; *The Comparitive Reception of Darwinism,* University of Texas Press, 1974.

WORK IN PROGRESS: Comparative History of Islamic and Christian Spain, to be published by Ediciones Grijalbo (Barcelona); co-editing *Historical Dictionary of Modern Science in Spain.*

SIDELIGHTS: Thomas F. Glick told *CA:* "My interest in Spanish culture continues in two areas: intercultural and ethnic relations in medieval and early modern times, and the reception of modern scientific ideas. In the latter area, I have organized a group of American scholars interested in Spanish science which is working in tandem with a group at the University of Valencia medical school. Science has been a touchstone of ideological division in Spain for the past 200 years (with progressives identifying strongly with modern scientific ideas, like Copernican astronomy and Darwinian evolution, and conservatives opposing them). As such, science seems to afford a particularly insightful observation post for evaluating the impact of modernity upon Spanish society and culture."

BIOGRAPHICAL/CRITICAL SOURCES: Times Literary Supplement, October 20, 1970; *Virginia Quarterly Review,* winter, 1971.

*   *   *

GLIEWE, Unada (Grace)   1927-
(Unada)

PERSONAL: Given name is pronounced You-*nay*-dah; born July 10, 1927, in Rochester, N.Y.; daughter of Edwin Herman (a carpenter) and Unada (Hinckley) Gliewe. *Education:* Syracuse University, B.F.A. (magna cum laude), 1949. *Politics:* Democrat (usually). *Religion:* Lutheran. *Residence:* Philadelphia, Pa.

CAREER: O'Brien Advertising Agency, Rochester, N.Y., staff artist, 1950-54; Lutheran Board of Parish Education, Philadelphia, Pa., staff artist, 1954-67; free-lance illustrator and writer. *Member:* Philadelphia Art Alliance, Plays and Players (associate arts member).

WRITINGS—Self-illustrated children's books: *Ricky's Boots,* Putnam, 1970; *Andrew and the Boxes,* Putnam, 1971; *Andrew's Amazing Boxes,* Putnam, 1971.

Illustrator under name Unada: Patricia Miles Martin, *Dolley Madison,* Putnam, 1967; Ruby L. Radford, *Sequoya,* Putnam, 1967; Martha M. Welch, *Saucy,* Coward, 1968; Bayard Dominick, *Joe, a Porpoise,* Astor-Honor, 1968; Ned Hoopes, *Ali Baba and the Forty Thieves,* Dell, 1968; Lynn Gessner, *Trading Post Girl,* Fell, 1968; Oren Arnold, *The Great Sleepy Gun Animal Hunt,* Fell, 1968; Gertrude Weaver, *The Emperor's Gift,* Thomas Nelson, 1969; Patricia M. Martin, *That Cat: One, Two, Three,* Putnam, 1969; Anne Malcolmson, *Captain Ichabod Paddock: Whaler of Nantucket,* Walker & Co., 1970; Peggy Mann, *Twenty-Five Cent Friend,* Coward, 1970; Marion E. Gridley, *Pontiac,* Putnam, 1970; *Our Gifts* (children's prayers), C. R. Gibson, 1971; N.J.W. Sellers, *Charley's Clan,* Albert Whitman, 1973; Jo Anne Wold, *Well, Why Didn't You Say So?,* Albert Whitman, 1975; Dorothy Hamilton, *Rosalie,* Herald Press, 1977; Jo Anne S. Hoffman, *Martin's Invisible Invention,* Judson, 1977. Illustrator of textbooks and readers for Lippincott, Fortress, Judson, and Westminster.

*   *   *

GLYNN, Jeanne Davis   1932-

PERSONAL: Born April 13, 1932, in Oak Park, Ill.; daughter of William Charles (an electrical engineer) and Harriet (Barber) Davis; married Malachy McMahon Glynn (a fund-raiser), June 25, 1960; children: John, Liam. *Education:* Catholic University of America, B.A., 1954. *Religion:* Roman Catholic. *Home:* 70 Park Ter. W., New York, N.Y. 10034. *Agent:* Ann Elmo Agency, Inc., 52 Vanderbilt Ave., New York, N.Y. 10017. *Office:* The Christophers, 12 East 48th St., New York, N.Y. 10017.

CAREER: The Christophers, New York, N.Y., executive producer and host of "Christopher Closeup," syndicated public service television and radio series.

WRITINGS: My Name Is Mary, Guild Press, 1966; *If I Were an Angel,* Guild Press, 1967; *Diary of a New Mother,* Abbey, 1968; *Answer Me, Answer Me!,* Bruce, 1970.

Plays: *Santa's Spectacles,* Baker's Plays; *Sunshine for the Queen,* Baker's Plays.

WORK IN PROGRESS: Women Who Make a Difference, for Harper.

GOBLE, (Lloyd) Neil   1933-

PERSONAL: Born August 21, 1933, in Oklahoma City, Okla.; son of Lloyd Earl (a businessman) and Thena (Felts) Goble; married Ann Broadhurst (a teacher), November 22, 1954; children: Thena, Tana, Sara. *Education:* Oklahoma State University, B.S., 1955; University of Oklahoma, special writing courses, 1965, 1967. *Agent:* Nicholas Literary Agency, 161 Madison Ave., New York, N.Y. 10016. *Office:* Detachment 550, AFROTC, Rensselaer Polytechnic Institute, Troy, N.Y. 12181.

CAREER: Newspaper reporter in Oklahoma City, Okla., 1955-56; U.S. Air Force, regular officer, 1956—, currently with rank of major. Stationed in Tokyo, Japan, as electronic warfare officer, 1958-61, and as developmental engineer and electronics test officer, 1963-67; assistant professor of aerospace studies, Air Force Reserve Officers Training Corps at Rensselaer Polytechnic Institute, Troy, N.Y., 1967—. *Member:* Armed Forces Writers League (president of Tokyo branch, 1959-60; Far East regional director, 1960-61), Sigma Delta Chi, Kappa Sigma. *Awards, honors*—Military: Air Force Commendation Medal (twice). Literary: All-Pacific winner in U.S. Air Force Short Story Contest, 1958, and three-time winner of first prize in the annual contest at Air Force bases.

WRITINGS: Condition Green: Tokyo, Tuttle, 1967; *Asimov Analyzed,* Mirage Press, 1972. Contributor to *ANALOG Science Fact and Fiction, Highway,* and *Armed Forces Writer.* Editor, *Daily O'Collegian,* Oklahoma State University, 1954-55.

WORK IN PROGRESS: A collection of science fiction stories, *The Cloud-Shaped Mushroom;* a short novel, *Preposterous Adventure,* a science fiction spoof in an adult Tom Swift style.

AVOCATIONAL INTERESTS: String music (had own band in high school, played guitar and ukulele with college bands during student days, and guitar and banjo with a trio at various military clubs).†

*   *   *

GODDARD, J(ack) R.   1930-

PERSONAL: Born February 14, 1930, in Fresno, Calif.; son of Jack R. (an editor) and Doris (Hutchison) Goddard. *Education:* University of California, Berkeley, B.A., 1952. *Politics:* Democrat ("usually"). *Residence:* San Patricio, N.M.

CAREER: Lived in Paris, France, 1952-53; worked with family race horses in San Francisco Bay area of California, 1953-54; advertising writer in New York City, 1955-59; reporter for *Village Voice* and free-lance writer for magazines, New York City, 1959-66; writer of fiction, 1967—, currently in San Patricio, N.M.; Partington Ridge Road and Water Co-operative, Big Sur, Calif., manager, 1967-70. *Member:* Authors Guild, Sierra Club, American Civil Liberties Union. *Awards, honors:* National Editorial Association Award for news feature in *Village Voice,* 1961.

WRITINGS: The Night Crew (novel), Little, Brown, 1970. Contributor to men's magazines, U.S. Information Agency publications, and other magazines.

WORK IN PROGRESS: Vados, an episodic novel, for Little, Brown.

AVOCATIONAL INTERESTS: Conservation, hiking, history.†

GODWIN, Gail 1937-

PERSONAL: Born June 18, 1937, in Birmingham, Ala.; daughter of Mose Winston and Kathleen (Krahenbuhl) Godwin. *Education:* Attended Peace Junior College, 1955-57; University of North Carolina, B.A., 1959; University of Iowa, M.A., 1968, Ph.D., 1971. *Residence:* Woodstock, N.Y. *Agent:* John Hawkins, Paul R. Reynolds, Inc., 12 East 41st St., New York, N.Y. 10017.

CAREER: Miami *Herald,* Miami, Fla., reporter, 1959-60; U.S. Embassy, London, England, with U.S. Travel Service, 1962-65; University of Iowa, Iowa City, instructor in English literature, 1967-71; University of Illinois, Center for Advanced Studies, Champaign-Urbana, fellow, 1971-72. *Member:* Modern Language Association of America, National Book Critics Circle, P.E.N., Authors Guild. *Awards, honors:* National Endowment for the Arts grant, 1974-75; Guggenheim fellowship, 1975-76.

WRITINGS: The Perfectionists (novel), Harper, 1970; *Glass People* (novel), Knopf, 1972; *The Odd Woman* (novel), Knopf, 1974; *Dream Children* (short stories), Knopf, 1976. Contributor of essays and short stories to *Antaeus, Ms., Harper's, Writer, McCalls, Cosmopolitan, North American Review, Paris Review,* and *Esquire.* Reviewer for *North American Review, New York Times Book Review,* and *Chicago Tribune Book World.*

WORK IN PROGRESS: A novel entitled *Violet Clay.*

SIDELIGHTS: Anatole Broyard of the *New York Times* says of *Glass People:* "I have been crying out, in this column, for contemporary woman's 'new consciousness' to express or define itself in a good novel. O.K., here it is: 'Glass People' by Gail Godwin." Jonathan Yardley makes this comment about *Dream Children,* "*Dream Children* is the work of a writer who, though still young and still testing the range of her powers, is moving confidently to the forefront of contemporary American fiction." Reviewer Lore Dickstein says, "Her new book 'The Odd Woman,' could be compared, in sensitivity and brilliance, to the best of Doris Lessing and Margaret Drabble." Joyce Carol Oates finds *The Perfectionists* "an engrossing and mysterious first novel, . . . a perfectly structured story. . . . It is a most intelligent and engrossing novel and introduces a young writer of exciting talent." Gail Godwin has lived in Spain and Denmark as well as in England.

BIOGRAPHICAL/CRITICAL SOURCES: New York Times Book Review, June 7, 1970; *New York Times,* September 21, 1972; Miami *Herald,* February 29, 1976; *Contemporary Literary Criticism,* Volume V, Gale, 1976.

* * *

GOEDECKE, W(alter) Robert 1928-

PERSONAL: Born March 14, 1928, in Gary, Ind.; son of Walter Scott (a certified public accountant) and Mary M. (Kinnard) Goedecke; married Virginia Stoddard Hornor, September 19, 1950; married second wife, Gloria Lorrayne Ziatz, June 12, 1965; children: (first marriage) Richard Scott, Anne Parker, Martha Nancy; (second marriage) Tracy, Stephanie, Mary, Robert, Ellen. *Education:* University of Chicago, B.A., 1946, Ph.D., 1958; Harvard University, M.A., 1954. *Politics:* Republican. *Religion:* Methodist. *Home:* 1106 A St., Ellensburg, Wash. 98926. *Office:* Department of Philosophy, Central Washington State College, Ellensburg, Wash. 98926.

CAREER: Washington University, St. Louis, Mo., part-time instructor, 1950-51; University of Chicago, University College, Chicago, Ill., lecturer in humanities, 1954-58; Central College (now Central University of Iowa), Pella, Iowa, instructor, 1958-59, assistant professor of philosophy, 1959-60; Southern Methodist University, Dallas, Tex., assistant professor of philosophy, 1960-62; Kansas State University, Manhattan, assistant professor of philosophy, 1962-65; Southern Illinois University, Carbondale, associate professor of humanities, 1965-67; Florida State University, Tallahassee, associate professor of philosophy, 1967-70; Central Washington State College, Ellensburg, professor of philosophy, 1970—. *Member:* American Philosophical Association, Metaphysical Society of America.

WRITINGS: Change and the Law, Florida State University Press, 1969. Contributor of essays and reviews to learned journals.

WORK IN PROGRESS: A second book on the law; a general book on humanities; a book on structuralism focusing on the ideas of Emile Durkheim and Claude Levi-Strauss.

AVOCATIONAL INTERESTS: Hiking, mountain climbing, reading novels, travel.

* * *

GOETTEL, Elinor 1930-

PERSONAL: Surname is pronounced Go-*tell;* born August 14, 1930, in Bangkok, Siam (now Thailand); daughter of Otto (assistant postmaster general under President Woodrow Wilson and known as the "father of airmail") and Carrie Will (Coffman) Praeger; married Gerard Goettel (a U.S. district judge), June 4, 1951; children: Sheryl, Glenn, James. *Education:* Duke University, A.B., 1951. *Home:* 6 Chamberlain St., Rye, N.Y. 10580.

MEMBER: Phi Beta Kappa.

WRITINGS: Eagle of the Philippines: President Manuel Quezon (juvenile), Messner, 1970; *America's Wars—Why?* (juvenile text), Messner, 1972. Also author of an eleven-part film strip, "The United States as World Leader," 1968, and of a four-part film strip, "The Civil War: Two Views," 1976, both for Educational Audio-Visual Co. Contributor to *Columbia Encyclopedia, Merit Student Encyclopedia, Columbia Viking Desk Encyclopedia,* and *Reader's Digest Almanac.*

SIDELIGHTS: Elinor Goettel told *CA:* "I love to work with primary sources and visit historical places. The Civil War and World War II are my primary areas of interest. Have toured and re-toured most of the Civil War Battlefields."

* * *

GOLD, Martin 1931-

PERSONAL: Born February 28, 1931, in Bronx, N.Y.; son of David M. (an advertising executive) and Sadie (Ratner) Gold. *Education:* Dartmouth College, A.B., 1953; University of Michigan, A.M., 1955, Ph.D., 1962. *Office:* Research Center for Group Dynamics, Institute of Social Research, University of Michigan, Box 1248, Ann Arbor, Mich. 48106.

CAREER: University of Michigan, Ann Arbor, instructor, 1957-62, assistant professor, 1962-68, associate professor of psychology, 1968—, assistant program director at Research Center for Group Dynamics, Institute of Social Research, 1962-65, program director, 1965—. Before and while attending college he worked summers as stock clerk, machine operator, counterboy, camp director, and on a newspaper. Consultant, Washtenaw County (Mich.) Office of Economic

Opportunity, 1965-68. Member of Advisory Committee on Youth Services, Michigan Department of Social Service, 1967-70. *Member:* American Psychological Association (fellow), American Sociological Association (fellow), Society for the Psychological Study of Social Issues (program chairman, 1964), American Association of University Professors, American Civil Liberties Union (member of National Planning Committee, 1967—).

WRITINGS: Status Forces in Delinquent Boys, University of Michigan, Institute for Social Research, 1963; (contributor) M. L. Hoffman and L. W. Hoffman, editors, *Review of Research in Child Development,* Volume II, Russell Sage, 1966; (editor with E. M. Douvan) *Adolescent Development: Readings in Theory and Research,* Allyn & Bacon, 1967; *Delinquent Behavior in an American City,* Brooks/Cole, 1969; (with Hans W. Mattick) *Experiment in the Streets,* University of Michigan, Institute for Social Research, 1974; (with Robert J. Berger and others) *Experiment in a Juvenile Court,* University of Michigan, Institute for Social Research, 1975. Contributor to *Encyclopaedia Britannica* and *Encyclopedia of Social Work;* also contributor of articles and reviews to professional journals and camping publications.

* * *

GOLDENSON, Robert M(yar) 1908-

PERSONAL: Born February 2, 1908, in Albany, N.Y.; son of Samuel H. (a rabbi) and Claudia (Myar) Goldenson; married Irene Herz, June 25, 1940; children: Ronald, Daniel. *Education:* Princeton University, B.A. (magna cum laude), 1930; University of Pittsburgh, M.A., 1932; Harvard University, Ph.D., 1940. *Home and office:* 50 Dearborn Ave., Rye, N.Y. 10580.

CAREER: Black Mountain College, Black Mountain, N.C., instructor in philosophy, 1934-37; Hunter College (now Hunter College of the City University of New York), New York City, assistant professor of psychology, 1939-59; Book-of-the-Month Club, New York City, educational director, 1960-68; psychotherapist in Harrison, N.Y., 1960—. Psychologist, United Cerebral Palsy Association of Westchester County, N.Y., 1969—. Educational director, Resource Publications, Princeton, N.J., 1965—. Consultant to National Broadcasting Co., 1951-55, and Institute for Child Mental Health, New York, 1965—. Conductor and writer of veterans readjustment series, "When He Comes Home," WMCA and Armed Forces Network, 1945-46; panel member of television program, "It's a Problem," NBC, 1951-52; conductor of NBC, ABC television series, "Keep Up to Date," 1953-54. Member of mental health education committee, International Mental Health Congress, 1951. *Member:* American Psychological Association, New York State Psychological Association, Tri-State Council on Family Relations (president, 1953), Phi Beta Kappa. *Awards, honors:* Award from National Institute for Education by Radio and Television for "When He Comes Home."

WRITINGS: (With Ruth Edith Hartley and L. K. Frank) *Understanding Children's Play,* Columbia University Press, 1952; *Helping Your Child to Read Better,* Crowell, 1957; (with Hartley) *The Complete Book of Children's Play,* Crowell, 1957, 3rd edition, 1970; *All About the Human Mind,* Random House, 1963; *Encyclopedia of Human Behavior: Psychology, Psychiatry, and Mental Health,* two volumes, Doubleday, 1970; *Mysteries of the Mind,* Doubleday, 1973; *The Disability Handbook,* McGraw, 1977. Also

author with Luther Woodward of radio series, "Inquiring Parent," 1946-50. Contributor to education and psychology journals and to popular magazines, including *Look, Good Housekeeping,* and *Parents' Magazine.*

AVOCATIONAL INTERESTS: Tennis and do-it-yourself projects.

* * *

GOLDFADER, Edward H. 1930-

PERSONAL: Born June 30, 1930, in Worcester, Mass.; son of Emanuel and Marion (Cohen) Goldfader; married Paula Eisenberg, June 20, 1954; children: Laura, David, Ellen. *Education:* Brandeis University, B.A., 1954; New York University, graduate study, 1956-57. *Home:* 14 Cord Pl., East Norwich, N.Y. 11732. *Office:* Tracers Company of America, Inc., 509 Madison Ave., New York, N.Y. 10022.

CAREER: Tracers Company of America, Inc. (private investigators), New York, N.Y., executive vice-president, 1952—. *Military service:* U.S. Army, 1955-56.

WRITINGS: Tracer! The Search for Missing Persons, Nash Publishing, 1970.

* * *

GOLDMAN, Irving 1911-

PERSONAL: Born September 2, 1911, in New York, N.Y.; son of Louis and Golda (Levine) Goldman; married Hannah Stern (a professor of literature). *Education:* Brooklyn College (now Brooklyn College of the City University of New York), B.S., 1933; Columbia University, Ph.D., 1941. *Politics:* Independent. *Religion:* Jewish. *Residence:* New York, N.Y. *Office:* Department of Anthropology, Sarah Lawrence College, Bronxville, N.Y. 10708.

CAREER: Brooklyn College (now Brooklyn College of the City University of New York), Brooklyn, N.Y., tutor, 1940-42; U.S. Department of State, Washington, D.C., Office of Coordinator of Inter-American Affairs, research analyst, 1944-45, Office of Research and Analysis, chief of Latin America Branch, 1945-47; Sarah Lawrence College, Bronxville, N.Y., professor of anthropology, 1947—. Has done field work in the South American tropical forest, the Andes, Mexican highlands, and among the Indians of British Columbia and Oregon. Trustee, Sarah Lawrence College. *Military service:* U.S. Army, 1942-45; served with Office of Strategic Services, 1944-45; became second lieutenant.

MEMBER: American Anthropological Association (fellow), American Ethnological Society, American Association for the Advancement of Science, Polynesian Society (fellow). *Awards, honors:* Bollingen Foundation fellowship, 1960-62; American Philosophical Society research grant, 1968; Social Science Research Council fellowship, 1969-70.

WRITINGS: (With wife, Hannah Goldman) *First Men,* Collier Books, 1962; *The Cubeo: Indians of the Northwest Amazon,* University of Illinois Press, 1963; *Ancient Polynesian Society,* University of Chicago Press, 1970; *The Mouth of Heaven: An Introduction to Kwakiutl Religious Thought,* Wiley, 1975. Contributor to *Collier's Encyclopedia* and to anthropology journals.

WORK IN PROGRESS: A book based on field studies of Indians of the Vaupes in Columbia, completion expected in 1978.

* * *

GOLDMAN, Phyllis W. 1927-

PERSONAL: Born April 15, 1927, in New York, N.Y.;

daughter of Henry (a physician) and Rae (Tuchman) Wolin; married Robert P. Goldman (a film producer), August 16, 1951; children: Joshua, Matthew. *Education:* Eastern Michigan University, B.S., 1948; New York University, graduate study, 1965-66. *Home and office:* 60 East 96th St., New York, N.Y. 10028.

CAREER: Junior high school teacher of health education and modern dance in public schools of New York City, 1949-56; designer of felt toys and president of a toy manufacturing firm, New York City, 1962-64; television researcher, New York City, 1966—. Secretary-treasurer, R. G. Production Co. (television and educational films).

WRITINGS: (With husband, Robert P. Goldman, and Mary Calderone) *Release from Sexual Tensions,* Random House, 1960; (with Grace Jaffe) *Whatever Happened to Yes?,* Walker & Co., 1971; *Make It from Felt,* Crowell, 1971; *Decorate with Felt,* Crowell, 1973. Contributor to *Look, Better Homes and Gardens, Pageant, Glamour,* and *New York Times.*

WORK IN PROGRESS: Three children's books, a storybook, a cookbook, and a teen-age novel; a television musical.†

* * *

GOLDRING, Patrick (Thomas Zachary) 1921-

PERSONAL: Born February 21, 1921, in Dublin, Ireland; son of Douglas (a writer) and Beatrix (Duncan) Goldring; married Joan Goldsmith (a short story writer), August 31, 1946; children: Polly, Hugh, Zachary, Sarah. *Education:* Attended secondary school in London, England. *Politics:* Socialist. *Home:* Ship Cottage, Riverside, Reedham, Norfolk, England. *Agent:* Rupert Crew Ltd., King's Mews, London WC1N 2JA, England.

CAREER: Journalist in England, 1938—. *Military service:* British Army, 1941-46; served in Middle East; became sergeant. *Member:* National Union of Journalists (chairman of London free-lance branch, 1965-67).

WRITINGS: Yugoslavia (holiday guide), Rand McNally, 1967, 4th revised edition, 1974; *The Broilerhouse Society,* Weybright, 1969; *Friend of the Family,* Barnes & Noble, 1973; *Multipurpose Man,* Taplinger, 1974. Contributor to magazines and newspapers.

WORK IN PROGRESS: A Lovely Place to Live.

AVOCATIONAL INTERESTS: Exploring towns, looking at buildings, arguing over drinks, railways, boats.

BIOGRAPHICAL/CRITICAL SOURCES: Saturday Review, December 27, 1969; *Chicago Tribune,* January 26, 1970.

* * *

GOLDSCHMIDT, Yaaqov 1927-

PERSONAL: Born October 15, 1927, in Germany; son of Martin J. and Gertrude (Kochman) Goldschmidt; married Rachel Yasemska, July 15, 1965; children: Asaf-Moshe, Nitzan, Nadav. *Education:* Attended Hebrew University of Jerusalem, 1953-56; University of Arizona, B.A., 1959, M.S., 1959; Cornell University, Ph.D., 1968. *Home:* 6 Rambam, Ramat Hasharon, Israel. *Office address:* Heshev, P.O.B. 40021, Tel Aviv, Israel.

CAREER: Heshev, Inter-Kibbutz Economic Advisory Unit, Tel Aviv, Israel, general director, 1960—; Tel Aviv University, Tel Aviv, assistant professor of business administration, 1968—; Hebrew University, Rehovot, Israel, assistant professor of business administration, 1970—.

WRITINGS: Introduction to Production Economics on the Farm (written in Hebrew), Hakibbutz-Hameuchad, 1963; *Information for Management Decisions: A System for Economic Analysis and Accounting Procedures,* Cornell University Press, 1970; *Costing and Budgeting Theory—Accounting, Economic and Behavioral Aspects* (written in Hebrew), Heshev, 1974; (with K. Admon) *Profit Measurement During Inflation—Accounting, Economic and Financial Aspects,* Wiley, 1977.

* * *

GOLDSMITH, Carol Evan 1930-
(Carol Evan)

PERSONAL: Born April 29, 1930, in New York, N.Y.; daughter of Harold Francis (an engineer) and Rose Hannah (Shapera) Goldsmith; married Nigel McKeand, February 20, 1971. *Education:* Attended Queens College (now Queens College of the City University of New York), Flushing, N.Y. *Politics:* "Not conservative." *Religion:* Jewish.

CAREER: Began work in television with Sid Caesar Production Co., New York City, 1954-60; television producer with Virginia Graham Show, New York City, 1962-64, Les Crane Production Co., New York City and Los Angeles, Calif., 1964-68, and Erwin Wasey Advertising, Los Angeles, 1968-69; also has worked on other television programs in various production capacities.

WRITINGS: (Under name Carol Evan) *Glad and Sorry Seasons* (novel), Harper, 1970; *Compost: A Cosmic View with Practical Suggestions,* Harper, 1973.

WORK IN PROGRESS: A novel, a motion picture script.

SIDELIGHTS: Carol Evan Goldsmith began to write because "a friend shamed me into activity while I was unemployed. . . . The novel interests me most," she says, "and, as it has been with most other things, I chose to become interested in it just as it chose to go out of style."†

* * *

GONZALEZ, Justo L(uis) 1937-

PERSONAL: Born August 9, 1937, in Havana, Cuba; son of Justo Bernardino (a professor, minister, and author) and Luisa (a teacher and author; maiden name Garcia) Gonzalez; married second wife, Catherine Gunsalvs (a theologian), December 18, 1973; children: (first marriage) Juana Luisa. *Education:* University of Havana, student, 1954-57; Union Theological Seminary, Matanzas, Cuba, S.T.B., 1957; Yale University, S.T.M., 1958, M.A., 1960, Ph.D., 1961; University of Strasbourg, graduate study, 1958-59. *Religion:* Methodist. *Home and office:* 511 South Columbia Dr., Decatur, Ga. 30021.

CAREER: Evangelical Seminary of Puerto Rico, professor of historical theology, 1961-69; Emory University, Candler School of Theology, Atlanta, Ga., associate professor of world Christianity, 1969-77; full-time writer.

WRITINGS: Revolucion y encarnacion, La Reforma, 1965; *Historia del pensamiento cristiano,* Methopress, Volume I, 1965, Volume II, 1972; (editor) *Por la renovacion del entendimiento,* La Reforma, 1965; *The Development of Christianity in the Latin Caribbean,* Eerdmans, 1969; *A History of Christian Thought,* Abingdon, Volume I: *From the Beginnings to the Council of Chalcedon,* 1970, Volume II: *From Augustine to the Eve of the Reformation,* 1971, Volume III: *From the Protestant Reformation to the Present,* 1975; *Historia de las Misiones,* Methopress, 1970; *Ambrosio de*

Milan, Centro de Publicaciones Cristianas, 1970; *Jesucristo es el Senor*, Caribe, 1971; *Itinerario de la teologia cristiana*, Caribe, 1974; *Luces bajo el almud*, Caribe, 1977; (with wife, Catherine G. Gonzalez) *Their Souls Did Magnify the Lord*, Knox, 1977; *Sus Almas Engrandecieron el Senor*, Caribe, 1977.

Translator into Spanish: H. R. Macintosh, *Types of Modern Theology*, Methopress, 1964; Bernard Ramn, *Special Revelation and the Word of God*, Methopress, 1968; Seward Hiltner, *Pastoral Counselling*, Methopress, 1971.

WORK IN PROGRESS: Three Types of Early Christian Theology.

SIDELIGHTS: Besides Spanish and English, Justo Gonzalez is competent in French, Danish, German, Portuguese, Italian, Greek, Hebrew, and Latin.

*   *   *

GOODMAN, David S. 1917-

PERSONAL: Born February 28, 1917, in Racine, Wis.; son of Julius (a property manager) and Esther (Sanderson) Goodman; married Phyllis Steinberg (assistant to dean of School of Education, University of Wisconsin—Milwaukee), April 6, 1941; children: Jeffrey, Kathy (Mrs. Charles Aller), Laurie (Mrs. Steven Horowitz), Theodore. *Education:* Attended University of Wisconsin, 1933-36, and Northwestern University, 1936-37. *Home:* 8915 North Bayside Dr., Milwaukee, Wis. 53217. *Office:* Barkin, Herman, Solochek & Paulsen, Inc., 777 East Wisconsin Ave., Milwaukee, Wis. 53202.

CAREER: Waukegan Post, Waukegan, Ill., reporter and real estate editor, 1939-41; *Wall Street Journal*, reporter in Chicago, Ill., 1941-43; Ziff-Davis Publishing Co., Chicago, associate editor, 1943-45; General Electric Co., Milwaukee, Wis., public relations director of medical systems department, 1945-58; Barkin, Herman, Solochek & Paulsen, Inc. (public relations counsel), Milwaukee, account executive, 1958—. Vice-president, Darrs Realty Co., Milwaukee. *Member:* Public Relations Society of America, National Association of Science Writers.

WRITINGS: The President's Letterbook, Prentice-Hall, 1970; (with M. C. Maultsby) *Emotional Well-Being through Rational Behavior Training*, C. C Thomas, 1975.

BIOGRAPHICAL/CRITICAL SOURCES: Milwaukee Journal, July 5, 1970.

*   *   *

GOODWIN, R(ichard) M(urphey) 1913-

PERSONAL: Born February 24, 1913, in New Castle, Ind.; son of William Murphey (a farmer) and Mary (Florea) Goodwin; married Jacqueline Wynmalen, June 24, 1937. *Education:* Harvard University, B.A. (summa cum laude), 1934, Ph.D., 1941; Oxford University, B.A., 1936, B.Litt., 1937. *Politics:* "Formerly Communist, now Socialist (member British Labour Party)." *Religion:* None. *Home:* 1 Belvoir Ter., Cambridge, England. *Office:* Peterhouse, Cambridge University, Cambridge, England.

CAREER: Harvard University, Cambridge, Mass., instructor, 1942-45, assistant professor of economics, 1945-50; Cambridge University, Cambridge, England, lecturer and fellow, 1952-67, reader in economics, 1967—. Painter. *Member:* Econometric Society (fellow), Royal Economic Society. *Awards, honors:* Rhodes scholar.

WRITINGS: Elementary Economics from the Higher Standpoint, Cambridge University Press, 1970.

SIDELIGHTS: R. M. Goodwin spends approximately half his time painting, pointing out that "this is not an avocation but of equal importance in my life to the writing and teaching of economics."

*   *   *

GOONERATNE, (Malini) Yasmine 1935-

PERSONAL: Born December 22, 1935, in Colombo, Ceylon; daughter of Samuel James Felix (an estate owner and proprietor) and Esther Mary (Ramkeesoon) Dias Bandaranaike; married Brendon W. M. Gooneratne (a doctor, medical researcher, and university lecturer), December 31, 1962; children: Channa Brendon Randhiren (son), Esther Malathi Devika. *Education:* University of Ceylon, B.A. (honors), 1958; Cambridge University, Ph.D., 1962. *Office:* Department of English, University of Ceylon, Peradeniya, Ceylon.

CAREER: University of Ceylon, Peradeniya, assistant lecturer, 1962-65, lecturer, 1966-67, senior lecturer in English, 1968—, acting head of department of English, 1970—. Member, University Arts Council, 1970—. *Member:* Association for the Study of Commonwealth Literature and Language. *Awards, honors:* Senkadalaga Memorial Prize for Poetry, 1954; Pettah Library Prize for English, 1955; Leigh Smith Prize for English Literature, 1958; Mary E. Woolley Research fellowship, Education Foundation of American Association of University Women, 1968-69; Leon Bequest Award, University of London, 1968-69.

WRITINGS: (Contributor) Alan Lindsey McLeod, editor, *The Commonwealth Pen: An Introduction to the Literature of the British Commonwealth*, Cornell University Press, 1961; *English Literature in Ceylon 1815-1878*, Tisara Press, 1968; (author of introduction) John Davy, *An Account of the Interior of Ceylon and of Its Inhabitants*, edited by S. Saparamady, Ceylon Historical Journal, 1969; (contributor) Rosalie Murphy, editor, *Contemporary Poets of the English Language*, St. James Press, 1970; *Jane Austen*, Cambridge University Press, 1970; (editor and contributor) *New Ceylon Writing*, [Kandy], 1970; *Word, Bird, Motif* (poetry), [Kandy], 1971; *The Lizard's Cry* (poems), [Kandy], 1972; *Alexander Pope*, Cambridge University Press, 1976. Also contributor to *Encyclopedia of World Literature*, Cassell. Contributor to *English, Hemisphere, Community, NESC, Ceylon Journal of Historical and Social Studies, Historical Journal* (formerly *Cambridge Historical Journal*), *University of Ceylon Review, Journal of Commonwealth Literature*, and other literary and historical journals. Member of editorial board, *Ceylon Journal of Humanities*, 1970—.

WORK IN PROGRESS: The Lovely Land, an anthology of Ceylon verse, 1744-1972.

SIDELIGHTS: Yasmine Gooneratne lists her major vocational interests as "the imaginative literature of Ceylon, and of nineteenth-century Britain, American and Australian literature, especially poetry." She stopped writing verse in 1963 to pursue research interests in nineteenth-century literature. She returned to writing poetry in 1970.†

*   *   *

GORDON, Bernard Ludwig 1931-

PERSONAL: Born November 6, 1931, in Westerly, R.I.; son of Julius and Mollie (Meltzer) Gordon; married Esther Saranga (a teacher), July 19, 1959; children: Jocelyn Fay, Zimra Joy. *Education:* University of Rhode Island, B.Sc., 1955, M.S., 1958; also attended graduate programs at University of Massachusetts, Brown University, and Boston University. *Home:* 29 Old Colony Rd., Newton, Mass. *Agent:* Toni Strassman, 130 East 18th St., 7-D, New York, N.Y. 10003. *Office:* Department of Earth Sciences, Northeastern University, 360 Huntington Ave., Boston, Mass. 02115.

CAREER: Teacher in public school in Ware, Mass., 1955-56; Rhode Island College, Providence, instructor in biology, 1956-60; Northeastern University, Boston, Mass., instructor, 1961-65, became assistant professor, 1965, currently associate professor of biology. Lecturer at Graduate School, University of Connecticut and at Boston University. Member of Education and Research Committee, Governor's Conference on Oceanography, 1968; member of advisory committee, oceanography program, St. George's School, Newport, R.I. Participant in numerous international scientific congresses, 1968-72. Consultant, Massachusetts Department of Education, 1963—, Wally Sea Products, 1967—, and Marine Careers Conference at Boston University.

MEMBER: International Oceanographic Foundation, International Society of Limnologists, American Society of Limnology and Oceanography, Marine Technology Association (chairman of New England section, 1971—), Junior American Littoral Society (national director, 1962—), American Institute of Biological Sciences, American Society of Icthyologists and Herpetologists, American Association for the Advancement of Science, Marine Historical Association, National Association of Biology Teachers, American Society for Oceanography, National Oceanography Association, New England Biology Association, Southern New England Marine Sciences Association (director, 1967-71, chairman, 1971—), New England Biology Association, Rhode Island Wildlife Federation (director, 1959-62), Sigma Xi, Phi Sigma, Phi Delta Kappa.

WRITINGS: Guide Book to the Marine Fishes of Rhode Island, Book & Tackle Shop, 1960; *Handbook for Advisors of American Littoral Society,* American Littoral Society, 1964; *Guide to Historical Southern New England,* Book & Tackle Shop, 1967; *Marine Careers,* Northeastern University, 1970; (editor) *Man and the Sea: Classic Accounts of Marine Explorations,* Doubleday, 1970; *Marine Resource ... Perspectives,* Book & Tackle Shop, 1974; (with wife, Esther Gordon) *There Really Was a Dodo,* Walck, 1974; *Hurricane in Southern New England: An Analysis of the Great Storm of 1938,* Book & Tackle Shop, 1976; *Once There Was a Passenger Pigeon,* Walck, 1976; *If an Auk Could Talk,* McKay, 1977; *Secret Lives of Fishes,* Grosset, 1977.

Contributor to many journals and periodicals, including *Sea Frontiers, Natural History, Nature, Biologist, Fisherman, Frontiers, Outdoor Life,* and *Underwater Naturalist.* Correspondent, *Salt Water Sportsman, Southern Fisherman,* and *National Fisherman.*

WORK IN PROGRESS: A glossary; and children's books.

*   *   *

GORDON, Leonard H(erman) D(avid)   1928-

PERSONAL: Born August 8, 1928, in New York, N.Y.; son of Herman (a businessman) and Ray (Keidan) Gordon; married Marjorie J. Hunt, June 11, 1951; children: Herman J., David B. *Education:* Indiana University, B.A., 1950, M.A., 1953; further study at U.S. Army Language School, 1954-55, Taiwan Normal University, 1958-59, and at Tokyo University, 1959-60; University of Michigan, Ph.D., 1961.

Office: Department of History, Purdue University, West Lafayette, Ind. 47907.

CAREER: U.S. Department of State, Washington, D.C., diplomatic historian, 1961-63; University of Wisconsin—Madison, assistant professor of Chinese history, 1963-67; Purdue University, West Lafayette, Ind., associate professor of Chinese history, 1967—. *Military service:* U.S. Army, 1953-56. *Member:* Association for Asian Studies, Society for Historians of American Foreign Relations. *Awards, honors:* Inter-University fellowship, Taiwan, 1958-59, for field training in Chinese; Fulbright research fellowship in Japan, 1959-60; American Philosophical Society grants, 1963, 1967.

WRITINGS: (Editor) *Taiwan: Studies in Chinese Local History,* Columbia University Press, 1970; (editor and compiler with Frank J. Shulman) *Doctoral Dissertations on China: A Bibliography of Studies in Western Languages, 1945-1970,* University of Washington Press, 1972. Contributor to *Historian, Journal of Modern History, Journal of Asian Studies, Smithsonian Journal of History,* and *Pacific Historical Review.* Editor, *Newsletter* of the Association for Asian Studies, 1968-71.

WORK IN PROGRESS: The Asian Heritage; Confrontation Over Taiwan: Nineteenth-Century China and the Powers.

SIDELIGHTS: Gordon has traveled to Japan and Taiwan (Formosa) in researching his books.

*   *   *

GORDON, Lillian L.   1925-1977

PERSONAL: Born September 12, 1925, in Baltimore, Md.; daughter of Charles J. and Pauline (Powell) Hardesty; married Melvin G. Gordon (an engineer), February 16, 1946; children: Gay V. (Mrs. John Shaw), Gloria D. (Mrs. Val Huber), Dorothy Lynn, Charles H. *Education:* El Camino College, A.A., 1955; California State University, B.S., 1957; graduate study at University of California, Los Angeles and Loyola University at Baltimore. *Politics:* Democrat. *Religion:* Methodist. *Office:* Catonsville Community College, Catonsville, Md. 21228.

CAREER: Catonsville Community College, Catonsville, Md., beginning 1964, began as lecturer, became assistant professor of reading. *Member:* International Reading Association, National Reading Association, College Reading Association, American Association of University Professors, North East Reading Association (former area director), Maryland Corrective Reading Association.

WRITINGS—With Patricia S. Buck: *Communication Skills: A Laboratory Manual,* Little, Brown, 1970; *Instructor's Guide to Communication Skills,* Little, Brown, 1970. Contributor to *Journal of the Reading Specialist.*

WORK IN PROGRESS: A revision of *Communication Skills: A Laboratory Manual.*†

(Died August 1, 1977)

*   *   *

GORDON, Richard L(ewis)   1934-

PERSONAL: Born June 19, 1934, in Portland, Me.; son of Benjamin M. and Sara (Israelson) Gordon; married Nancy Ellen Helfand, June 8, 1958; children: David, Benjamin. *Education:* Dartmouth College, A.B. (magna cum laude), 1956; Massachusetts Institute of Technology, Ph.D., 1960. *Religion:* Jewish. *Home:* 429 Kemmerer Rd., State College,

Pa. 16801. *Office:* 219 Envir, Pennsylvania State University, University Park, Pa. 16802.

CAREER: Massachusetts Institute of Technology, Cambridge, instructor in economics, 1959-60; Pennsylvania State University, University Park, assistant professor, 1962-66, associate professor, 1966-70, professor of mineral economics, 1970—. Economic analyst for New England Mutual Life Insurance Co., 1957-58, Union Carbide Corp., 1959-64, and First National City Bank of New York, 1964. Consultant, Public Land Law Review Commission, 1967-69, U.S. Department of Interior, 1971, and U.S. Department of State, 1971—. *Member:* American Economic Association, Royal Economic Society, Econometric Society, American Institute of Mining, Metallurgical and Petroleum Engineers (chairman of council on economy, 1973), Phi Beta Kappa.

WRITINGS: The Evolution of Energy Policy in Western Europe: The Reluctant Retreat from Coal, Praeger, 1970; *U.S. Coal and the Electric Power Industry,* Johns Hopkins Press, 1975; *Economic Analysis of Coal Supply: An Assessment of Existing Studies,* Electric Power Research Institute, Volume I, 1975, Volume II, 1976; (contributor) W. A. Vogely, editor, *Economics of the Mineral Industries,* 3rd edition, American Institute of Mining, Metallurgical and Petroleum Engineers, 1976. Contributor to technical journals.

WORK IN PROGRESS: Continued research on coal economics.

*   *   *

GORDON, Sydney 1914-

PERSONAL: Born July 9, 1914, in Liverpool, England; married Pearl Newman (died June 5, 1974); children: Geoffrey Spencer. *Education:* Teachers' Training College, Liverpool, Teacher's Certificate, 1948. *Home:* 5 St. Mary's Garden, Worsbrough Village, near Barnsley, England.

CAREER: Began as primary teacher, became deputy headmaster, at schools in Lancashire, England, 1949-67; adviser in primary mathematics and science to schools in Barnsley, England, 1967—. Member of lecture team conducting primary science course for teachers in Nigeria, 1965. Justice of the peace, 1958—. *Military service:* British Army, Royal Artillery and Army Educational Corps, 1941-46; became sergeant. *Awards, honors:* Officer of Order of the British Empire, 1968, for services to local government.

WRITINGS: "Pageant of Scientists" series, published by Basil Blackwell: *Leonardo da Vinci,* 1966; *Thomas Alva Edison,* 1966; *Galileo Galilei; 1564-1642: His Life, Work, and Experiments,* 1968; *Isaac Newton, 1642-1727,* 1968; *Michael Faraday, 1791-1867: His Life, Work, and Experiments,* 1969; *Wilbur Wright, 1867-1912, Orville Wright, 1871-1948: Their Life, Work, and Experiments,* 1969; *Archimedes,* 1971; *Jean Henri Fabre,* 1971.

New Pence for Young Children, Galt, 1971; *Decimal Money,* Philip & Tacey, 1971.

BIOGRAPHICAL/CRITICAL SOURCES: Times Literary Supplement, June 26, 1969.

*   *   *

GORDON, Thomas 1918-

PERSONAL: Born March 11, 1918, in Paris, Ill.; son of Allan T. and Florence (Masteller) Gordon; married, wife's name Linda; children: Judith, Michele. *Education:* DePauw University, A.B., 1939; Ohio State University, M.A., 1941;

University of Chicago, Ph.D., 1949. *Office:* 531 Stevens Ave., Solana Beach, Calif. 92075.

CAREER: American Institutes for Research, Pittsburgh, Pa., director of aviation research, 1947-49; University of Chicago, Chicago, Ill., assistant professor, 1949-54, associate professor, 1954; Edward Glaser & Associates, Pasadena, Calif., consultant, 1954-58; private practice as psychological consultant, 1958-64; Effectiveness Training, Inc., Solana Beach, Calif., president, 1968—. Member, board of overseers, California School of Professional Psychology. *Military service:* U.S. Army Air Forces, 1942-46; became captain. *Member:* American Psychological Association, California State Psychological Association (former president). *Awards, honors:* Outstanding Research Award, American Personnel and Guidance Association, 1955.

WRITINGS: (With Dugald Sinclair Arbuckle) *Industrial Counseling,* Bellman Publishing, 1949; *Group-Centered Leadership: A Way of Releasing the Creative Power of Groups,* Houghton, 1955; *Parent Effectiveness Training: The No-Lose Way to Raise Responsible Children,* Peter H. Wyden, 1970; *T.E.T.: Teacher Effectiveness Training,* Peter H. Wyden, 1974; *P.E.T. in Action,* Wyden Books, 1976.

WORK IN PROGRESS: Effective Leadership.

*   *   *

GORDON WALKER, Patrick (Chrestien) 1907-

PERSONAL: Born April 7, 1907, in Worthing, Sussex, England; son of Alan Lachlan (a High Court judge) and Dora (Chrestien) Gordon Walker; married Audrey Rudolf, December 21, 1934; children: Judith, Caroline, Ann, Alan and Robin (twins). *Education:* Christ Church, Oxford, M.A., 1929, B.Litt., 1930. *Politics:* Labour. *Office:* House of Commons, London S.W.1, England.

CAREER: Oxford University, Christ Church College, Oxford, England, student and tutor, 1931-40; British Broadcasting Corp., London, England, staff of European Service, 1940-44; chief editor, Radio Luxemburg, 1944; British Broadcasting Corp., assistant director of German Service, 1945; House of Commons, London, member of Parliament for Smethwick, 1945-64, and for Leyton, 1966-74, with posts as Parliamentary Under-Secretary of State, Commonwealth Relations Office, 1947-50, Secretary of State for Commonwealth Relations, 1950-51, Secretary of State for Foreign Affairs, 1964-65, Minister without Portfolio, 1967, and Secretary of State for Education, 1967-68; member, European Parliament, 1975—. Privy counsellor, 1950—. Leader of United Kingdom delegation to Council of Europe, 1966. Chairman, British Film Institute, 1946; vice-chairman, British Council, 1947; chairman, Book Development Council, 1965-67; adviser, Initial Teaching Alphabet Foundation, 1965-67. *Awards, honors:* Companion of Honour, 1968; created a Baron (Life Peer) of Leyton, 1974.

WRITINGS: The Sixteenth and Seventeenth Centuries: The Rise of the Nations, Gollancz, 1935; *An Outline of Man's History,* N.C.L.C. Publishing Society, 1939; *The Lid Lifts,* Gollancz, 1945; *Restatement of Liberty,* Hutchinson, 1951; *The Commonwealth,* Secker & Warburg, 1962, Fernhill, 1965; *The Cabinet: Political Authority in Britain,* Basic Books, 1970 (published in England as *The Cabinet,* J. Cape, 1970, revised edition, 1972); (with Max Beloff) *Change and Decay* (phonotape), Holt Information Systems, 1972.

WORK IN PROGRESS: A life of Sir Robert Peel.

SIDELIGHTS: According to a reviewer for the *Times Lit-*

erary Supplement, certain information contained in *The Cabinet* caused a minor political scandal when published in the *Daily Mail* in 1970. "The truth is," the reviewer writes, "that Mr. Gordon Walker's study must be reckoned easily the most revealing of recent books about British politics simply because he illustrates his constitutional argument with a wealth of modern instances. Even before he brings his key to the principal characters into the light of day he uses a narrative method that is as gossipy as Creevey. He is not merely the insider confirming much that outsiders have guessed about some of the important decisions of the Wilson Cabinet and the sharp conflicts that preceded the decisions; he also lets slip a surprising amount of information that is quite new."

AVOCATIONAL INTERESTS: Reading.

BIOGRAPHICAL/CRITICAL SOURCES: Times Literary Supplement, April 23, 1970.†

* * *

GORMAN, Burton W(illiam) 1907-

PERSONAL: Born March 29, 1907, in Mitchell, Ind.; son of William James and Minnie Rose (Burton) Gorman; married Rebecca Evelyn Tolle, December 29, 1931; children: Benjamin Lee, Joseph Tolle, John Burton. *Education:* Indiana University, A.B., 1930, 1936; Purdue University and University of Chicago, graduate study, 1942-46; George Peabody College for Teachers, Ph.D., 1953. *Home:* R.R.2, DeLand, Fla. 32720. *Office:* Department of Education, Stetson University, DeLand, Fla. 32720.

CAREER: Teacher and principal in public schools in Bardstown, Ky., Rising Sun, Ind., Lawrenceburg, Ind., Connersville, Ind., and Indianapolis, Ind., 1930-51; DePauw University, Greencastle, Ind., professor of education and chairman of department of education, 1953-54; Kent State University, Kent, Ohio, professor of education and chairman of department of secondary education, 1954-69, professor of school administration and supervision, 1969-72; George Peabody College for Teachers, Nashville, Tenn., professor of education, 1972-74; Stetson University, DeLand, Fla., professor of education, 1975—. Visiting professor at Butler University, summer, 1946, George Peabody College for Teachers, summers, 1948-53, 1961, Indiana University, summer, 1954, University of North Carolina, 1966-67, University of Vermont, summer, 1968. Participant in projects on school studies under auspices of Indiana University, George Peabody College for Teachers, and Kent State University. Consultant to state and local governments. Participant in foreign field seminars.

MEMBER: National Education Association, American Association of University Professors, National Association of Secondary School Principals, Ohio Education Association, Ohio Association of Secondary School Principals, Indiana Schoolmen's Club (president, 1948), Phi Delta Kappa, Kappa Delta Pi, Acacia, Kiwanis International (president of Connersville, Ind. chapter, 1946; lieutenant governor of ninth district Indiana chapter, 1947). *Awards, honors:* Distinguished Alumnus award, George Peabody College for Teachers, 1972.

WRITINGS: The Wit and Wisdom of A. C. Burton, privately printed, 1934; *Education for Learning to Live Together,* Kendall/Hunt, 1971; *Secondary Education: The High School America Needs,* Random House, 1971. Contributor to *American School Board Journal, Nation's Schools, Phi Delta Kappan, Clearing House, School Review, Indiana Teacher, Ohio Schools, Educational Forum,*

National Association of Secondary School Principals Bulletin, School Progress, and *Educational Leadership.*

WORK IN PROGRESS: A book on teaching and learning, completion expected in 1978.

SIDELIGHTS: Burton Gorman told *CA:* "The greatest need of education today is that it become much more personal and personalized. Every youth is entitled to a teacher who believes in his possibilities and who will work to get him to believe in his possibilities."

* * *

GOSNELL, Elizabeth Duke Tucker 1921-
(Betty Gosnell)

PERSONAL: Born April 21, 1921, in Little Rock, Ark.; daughter of Henry Hennegin (a president of a hardware company) and Katherine (Duke) Tucker; married William Burton Gosnell (an insurance agency owner), September 24, 1943; children: Katharine Amanda. *Education:* Duke University, B.A., 1942. *Politics:* Independent. *Religion:* Reformed Presbyterian. *Residence:* Monticello, Ark.

CAREER: Writer. Founder, Holiday School, Drew, Ark., 1964. Chairman, South and West Poetry Workshop, 1969—; instructor, Creative Writing Camp, Southeast Arkansas Arts and Science Center, 1970. Broadcaster of radio program, "Afterglow: The World of Poetry," over station KHBM, 1971—. Teacher of creative writing, Monticello High School, 1975. *Member:* World Poetry Society Intercontinental (director, 1969—), International Biographical Association, International Poetry Society (founding fellow), United Poets Laureate International, League of American Pen Women, Poetry Society of America, National Federation of State Poetry Societies, Authors, Artists, and Composers Society, South and West, Inc. (secretary, 1967—), Kentucky State Poetry Society, Arkansas Historical Society, Poet's Roundtable of Arkansas, Illinois Poetry Society, Drew County Historical Association (member of board of directors), Delta Delta Delta. *Awards, honors:* South and West Festival, award for winning quatrain, 1966, Certificate of Merit, 1968; Select Poem Cum Laude, 1970, Pancontinentla Premier Poets; International Woman of the Year, with laureate honors, 1975, from United Poets Laureate International.

WRITINGS: The Poet Who Was a Painter of Souls: Poems, edited by Sue A. Boyd, South & West, 1969. Also author of *Silk and Silence* (poems), 1971. Represented in several anthologies, including *Poems of Patriotism and Peace,* edited by Geneva Booher, Rubert Publications, 1966, *Contemporary Poets of Arkansas,* edited by Sue A. Boyd, South & West, 1969, *Pancontinental Premier Poets, 1969-70,* edited by Orville Crowder Miller, World Poetry Society, Intercontinental, 1970. Editor of "Muse," poetry column in *Advance Monticellonian* and *McGehee Times,* 1966-74.

SIDELIGHTS: Elizabeth Gosnell told *CA:* "When you are a housewife everything fits into your vocation—plants, people, politics, cooking, religion, community service education. It's a Renaissance occupation. As the kids apparently were driven to pot by the modern world, I was driven to poetry." *Avocational interests:* Outdoors, conservation.

* * *

GRABILL, Joseph L. 1931-

PERSONAL: Born July 21, 1931, in Bluffton, Ohio; married Doris Evelyn Davis, 1957 (divorced, 1976); children: three.

Education: Fort Wayne Bible College, B.A., 1954; Taylor University, B.A., 1956; Indiana University, M.A., 1959, Ph.D., 1964. *Office:* Department of History, Illinois State University, Normal, Ill. 61761.

CAREER: Malone College, Canton, Ohio, assistant professor, 1960-65, associate professor of history, 1965-68; Illinois State University, Normal, associate professor, 1968-72, professor of history, 1972—. *Awards, honors:* McKnight Foundation Award, 1972, for *Protestant Diplomacy and the Near East.*

WRITINGS: Protestant Diplomacy and the Near East: Missionary Influence on American Policy, 1810-1927, University of Minnesota Press, 1971. Contributor to religious and historical journals.

*   *   *

GRADE, Arnold (Edward) 1928-

PERSONAL: Born December 12, 1928, in Newton, Mass.; son of Arnold Eugene (a retail executive) and Katharine (Pendergast) Grade; married Mary Anne Menard, June 13, 1959; children: Christopher, Anne Marie, Andrew, Jeremy. *Education:* Rutgers University, student,1947-49; University of Massachusetts, Amherst, B.A., 1955; Andover Newton Theological School, student, 1955-56; Bread Loaf School of English, M.A., 1960; University of Iowa, Ph.D., 1967. *Home:* 189 Hollybrook Rd., Brockport, N.Y. 14420. *Office:* Department of English, State University of New York College at Brockport, Brockport, N.Y. 14420.

CAREER: Teacher of English in private schools in Canaan, N.H. and New Hampton, N.H., 1955-58; College of St. Thomas, St. Paul, Minn., instructor, 1958-61, assistant professor of English, 1962-65; Bentley College, Boston, Mass., associate professor of English, 1961-62; State University of New York College at Brockport, assistant professor, 1967-70, associate professor, 1970-73, professor of English, 1973—. *Military service:* U.S. Air Force, 1950-51. *Member:* New York State English Council. *Awards, honors:* State University of New York faculty fellowship, 1970, 1971.

WRITINGS: The Outset and Other Poems, St. Thomas Press, 1959; *A Robert Frost Folio,* privately printed, 1960; (editor with Lawrance Thompson) *New Hampshire's Child: The Derry Journals of Lesley Frost,* State University of New York Press, 1969; *Guide to Early Juvenile Literature,* C. E. Merrill, 1970; (editor) *Family Letters of Robert and Elinor Frost,* State University of New York Press, 1972. Contributor of reviews, articles, and poetry to *Choice, Ann Arbor Review, Liberal Education, Yankee, Country Journal, Americana, Bulletin of the New York Public Library,* and other periodicals and journals.

WORK IN PROGRESS: A Guide to Paper Americana; a children's book.

SIDELIGHTS: Arnold Grade told *CA:* "I write irregularly but intensely—eight or ten hours at a clip when I am motivated. The typewriter is my notebook. Maddeningly, my 'final, final draft' turns out to be simply another in a series. I am very seldom really pleased with my writing; it finally gets sent-off out of a perverse need to be free of it. Then it becomes someone else's burden, at least for a few weeks. I labor in the midst of disorder, invariably. It may be that the crisp blankness of paper challenges me, finally, to some semblance of order and good sense."

AVOCATIONAL INTERESTS: "Things-old," New England, hand carpentry, photography, and excursions to old bookshops.

GRAFF, Gerald (Edward) 1937-

PERSONAL: Born June 28, 1937, in Chicago, Ill.; son of David R. and Mollie (Newman) Graff. *Education:* University of Chicago, A.B., 1959; Stanford University, Ph.D., 1963. *Politics:* Left-radical. *Religion:* Jewish. *Home:* 932 Judson Ave., Evanston, Ill. 60202. *Office:* English Department, Northwestern University, Evanston, Ill. 60201.

CAREER: University of New Mexico, Albuquerque, assistant professor of English, 1963-66; Northwestern University, Evanston, Ill., assistant professor, 1966-70, associate professor of English, 1970—.

WRITINGS: Poetic Statement and Critical Dogma, Northwestern University Press, 1970. Contributor to literary journals.

*   *   *

GRAHAM, Ada 1931-

PERSONAL: Born August 22, 1931, in Dayton, Ohio; daughter of James D. and Jeannette (Steller) Cogan; married Frank Graham, Jr. (a writer), October 31, 1953. *Education:* Bowling Green State University, student, 1949-52; Hunter College (now Hunter College of the City University of New York), A.B., 1957. *Residence:* Milbridge, Me. 04658. *Agent:* Jane Wilson, John Cushman Associates, 25 West 43rd St., New York, N.Y. 10036.

CAREER: Teacher in public schools of New York, N.Y., 1957-58, 1964-65, at Baldwin School, New York, 1958-59, and in Sullivan, Me., 1965-67; Summer Head Start Program, Washington County, Me., teacher, 1967-70; researcher; free-lance writer of juvenile books, 1968—. Organizer and supervisor of summer nature program in Milbridge, Me., 1967-70; member of Maine State Commission on the Arts and Humanities, 1976—. *Awards, honors:* Outstanding Science Books for Children citation, Children's Book Council and National Association of Science Teachers, 1972, for *The Mystery of the Everglades,* 1974, for *Dooryard Garden,* 1975, for *The Careless Animal,* 1976, for *The Milkweed and Its World of Animals;* honorable mention, New York Academy of Science's Annual Children's Science Book award, 1977, for *The Milkweed and Its World of Animals.*

WRITINGS—All juveniles: *Foxtails, Ferns and Fish Scales,* Four Winds Press, 1976.

With husband, Frank Graham, Jr.: *The Great American Shopping Cart,* Simon & Schuster, 1969; *Wildlife Rescue,* Cowles, 1970; *Puffin Island* (juvenile), Cowles, 1971; *The Mystery of the Everglades,* Random House, 1972; *Dooryard Garden,* Four Winds Press, 1974; *The Careless Animal,* Doubleday, 1975; *The Milkweed and It's World of Animals,* Doubleday, 1976.

"The Audubon Primers" series; with F. Graham, Jr.; all published by Golden Press: *Let's Discover: The Floor of the Forest,* 1974; . . .: *Birds in Our World,* 1974; . . .: *The Winter Woods,* 1974; . . .: *Changes Everywhere,* 1974.

WORK IN PROGRESS: Two juveniles for Four Winds Press, *Six Little Chickadees: The Field Studies of a Naturalist* and *Clown: How to Be One;* juveniles with Frank Graham, Jr. for "The Audubon Readers" series, for Dell, *The Clever Coyote, Whale Watch, Learning to Be Wild,* and *The Wily Wasps;* another juvenile with F. Graham, Jr. for Doubleday, *Seabirds.*

*   *   *

GRAHAM, Harry Edward 1940-

PERSONAL: Born September 20, 1940; son of Samuel (a

teacher) and Lilian (Pokras) Graham; married Joyce Noth-mann, August 15, 1965; children: Aaron, Liliann. *Education:* Hunter College of the City University of New York, B.A., 1962, M.A., 1964; University of Wisconsin, Ph.D., 1967. *Office:* Department of Education, Elizabethtown College, Elizabethtown, Pa. 17022.

CAREER: University of Iowa, Iowa City, affiliated with Center for Labor and Management, 1967-70; Northern Illinois University, DeKalb, member of faculty, beginning 1970; currently associate professor of education and coordinator of secondary education, Elizabethtown College, Elizabethtown, Pa. *Member:* Industrial Relations Research Association, Association for Evolutionary Economics.

WRITINGS: The Paper Rebellion: Development and Upheaval in Pulp and Paper Industry Unionism, University of Iowa Press, 1970. Contributor to labor, industrial relations, and business journals.

WORK IN PROGRESS: Research on unionism in proprietary health care facilities and on unionism in higher education.†

* * *

GRAHAM, Jory 1925-

PERSONAL: Born February 7, 1925, in Chicago, Ill.; daughter of Ralph A. (a physician) and Rose-Frances (Kramer) Reis; married former husband, Stephen Geoffrey Graham. *Education:* Attended University of Chicago, 1940-43; Northwestern University, graduate courses in journalism. *Politics:* Independent. *Religion:* Episcopalian. *Home and office:* 1560 North Sandburg Terrace, Chicago, Ill. 60610. *Agent:* Dominick Abel Literary Services, 498 West End Ave., New York, N.Y. 10024.

CAREER: Needham, Louis & Brorby, Inc., Chicago, Ill., copywriter, 1952-55; John W. Shaw, Chicago, senior copywriter, 1955-58; Cunningham & Walsh, Chicago, senior copywriter, 1959; free-lance writer and editor, 1959—. Stringer for *Time* and other magazines published by Time, Inc., 1959-62, and for *World Wide Medical News,* 1961-62; Chicago area feature writer for *America Illustrated* (published by U.S. Information Agency), and assignment writer for Press & Publications Service, 1961-65; editor of *Movie Guide,* 1964; project director, Curriculum Resources, Inc., and editorial consultant to Urban Child Center, University of Chicago, 1965-66; columnist for *Chicago Sun-Times,* writing "Jory Graham's City," 1969—; columnist for *Chicago Daily News,* writing "A Time to Live," 1975—. Author, 1956—; lecturer, 1969—; public relations counsel, Field Museum of Natural History, 1975—. *Member:* American Society of Journalists and Authors, Society of Midland Authors, Sigma Delta Chi, Arts Club of Chicago. *Awards, honors:* Designated Chicago Ambassador, 1974, by Mayor Richard J. Daley; received first annual Jory Graham Award for most creative programs for city parks, from the Chicago Friends of the Parks.

WRITINGS: (Ghost-writer for William Menninger) *Growing Up Emotionally,* Science Research Associates, 1956; *I'm Driving My Analyst Crazy,* Citadel, 1959 (published in England as *I'm Driving My Psycho-Analyst Crazy,* Hammond & Hammond, 1960); *Children on a Farm* (juvenile), Encyclopaedia Britannica, 1962; *Katie's Zoo* (juvenile), Encyclopaedia Britannica, 1964; *Chicago: An Extraordinary Guide,* Rand McNally, 1968; *Instant Chicago: How to Cope,* Rand McNally, 1973. Editor of *The Wagon and the Star: A Study of American Community Initiative,* 1966.

Contributor to "Basic Reader Series," Level H, Science Research Associates. Writer of *New Twentieth Century Citizens* for U.S. Information Agency, 1964, and other monographs, booklets, and brochures for Science Research Associates, National Safety Council, Urban Child Center of University of Chicago, and for corporations. Also has written radio scripts and ghost-written speeches.

Contributor of articles to *America Illustrated, Saturday Evening Post, Venture, Pageant, Chicago Scene, Ladies' Home Journal, Argosy,* and other magazines. Associate editor, *Smart Motoring,* 1961-62; contributing editor, *Dental Progress,* 1960-61, *Chicago Scene,* 1961-63, and *Physician's Management, Pediatrics Management,* and *OB-Gyne Management,* 1963-66.

BIOGRAPHICAL/CRITICAL SOURCES: New York Times, December 18, 1968; *Book World,* December 20, 1968.

* * *

GRAHAM, Richard 1934-

PERSONAL: Born November 1, 1934, in Anapolis, Brazil; U.S. citizen; son of F. F. and Jean (Porter) Graham; married Ann Hartness (a librarian), September 2, 1956; children: Jonathan, Stephen, Andrew. *Education:* College of Wooster, B.A., 1956; University of Texas, M.A., 1957, Ph.D., 1961. *Home:* 8712 Tallwood Dr., Austin, Texas. 78759. *Office:* Department of History, University of Texas, Austin, Tex. 78712.

CAREER: Cornell University, Ithaca, N.Y., assistant professor of history, 1961-68; University of Utah, Salt Lake City, associate professor of history, 1968-70; University of Texas at Austin, associate professor, 1970-73, professor of history, 1973—. *Member:* American Historical Association, Conference on Latin American History, Latin American Studies Association. *Awards, honors:* American Philosophical Society grant, 1962, 1971; Rockefeller Foundation international relations fellowship, 1964-65; Social Science Research Council faculty grant, 1964-65, 1966, Bolton prize, 1969; Guggenheim fellowship, 1972-73; Fulbright-Hays senior scholar, 1974.

WRITINGS: Britain and the Onset of Modernization in Brazil, 1850-1914, Cambridge University Press, 1968; (editor) *A Century of Brazilian History since 1865: Issues and Problems,* Knopf, 1969; (with William Rogers) *Cornell-Brazil Project: An Experiment in Learning,* Centro Intercultural de Documentacion, 1969; (with Virginia Valiela) *Brazil in the London "Times," 1850-1905: A Guide,* Latin American Institute, Southern Illinois University, 1969; *Independence in Latin America: A Comparative Approach,* Knopf, 1972; (editor with Peter H. Smith) *New Approaches to Latin American History,* University of Texas Press, 1974. Contributor to *Handbook of Latin American Studies;* contributor of articles and reviews to journals.

WORK IN PROGRESS: Nineteenth- and twentieth-century Brazilian history; slavery in the Americas; interest-group politics in Brazil.

SIDELIGHTS: Britain and the Onset of Modernization in Brazil has been translated into Portuguese.

* * *

GRAVES, Leon B(erneil) 1946-

PERSONAL: Born November 29, 1946, in Beaver, Okla.; son of George Kester (a farmer and industrial worker) and Vera (Ozenberger) Graves. *Education:* University of Kansas, B.A., 1968, M.P.A., 1972, J.D., 1975; Texas A&M University, graduate study, 1969-70. *Politics:* Republican. *Religion:* Baptist. *Home:* 635 Harrison, Topeka, Kan. 66603. *Office:* Colmery, McLure, Funk, Letourneau & Wilkinson, Attorneys-at-Law, 1000 First National Bank Bldg., Topeka, Kan. 66603.

CAREER: Admitted to Bar and to U.S. District Court, State of Kansas, 1975; Colmery, McLure, Funk, Letourneau & Wilkinson, Attorneys-at-Law, Topeka, Kan., associate, 1976—. Budget analyst, State of Kansas Budget Division, 1971-72. Legislative counsel and research assistant to League of Kansas Municipalities, Kansas State Legislature, 1976; assistant city attorney, Topeka, 1976—. *Military service:* U.S. Army, Intelligence Command, 1968-71, special agent, 1969-71. *Member:* American Bar Association, Kansas Bar Association, Phi Beta Kappa, Phi Delta Phi, Pi Sigma Alpha.

WRITINGS: (With William H. Cape and Burton M. Michaels) *Government by Special Districts,* Governmental Research Center, University of Kansas, 1969. Contributor to *Search* and *Southwesterner.*

WORK IN PROGRESS: An article, with Mike Meacham, on esthetic factors in land-use controls for the *Bar Journal.*

SIDELIGHTS: Leon B. Graves told *CA:* "My relatives on both sides were always involved in local government in some minor way: Two great-grandfathers were toilers in the Republican vineyards, a grandfather who has been on the cemetary district board since 1939, an uncle who ran for county sheriff. I think this heritage had a lot to do with my gravitating, first to the academic study of political science and public administration and the practice of law, with emphasis on municipal and constitutional law themes."

*　　*　　*

GRAY, John Milner   1889-1970

July 7, 1889—January 8, 1970; British pioneer East African historian and writer. Obituaries: *Antiquarian Bookman,* March 2, 1970.

*　　*　　*

GRAY, Oscar S(halom)   1926-

PERSONAL: Born October 18, 1926, in New York, N.Y.; son of Samuel Z. and Esther M. (Grynberg) Gray; married Sara Sheila Hafter (a physician), April 8, 1967. *Education:* Yale University, B.A., 1948, J.D., 1951. *Residence:* Washington, D.C. *Office:* 1225 19th St. N.W., Washington, D.C. 20007; and 500 West Baltimore St., Baltimore, Md. 21201.

CAREER: Admitted to Maryland Bar, 1951, and to District of Columbia Bar, 1952; U.S. Department of State, Washington, D.C., attorney-adviser in Legal Adviser's Office, 1951-57; Nuclear Materials and Equipment Corp., Apollo, Pa., secretary, 1957-64, treasurer, 1957-67, vice-president, 1964-71; U.S. Department of Transportation, Washington, D.C., acting director of Office of Environmental Impact, 1968-70; attorney in private practice, Washington, D.C., 1970—, and Baltimore, Md., 1971—; University of Maryland, School of Law, Baltimore, associate professor, 1971-74, professor of law, 1974—. Secretary-treasurer and director, Nuclear Decontamination Corp., 1962-71; secretary-treasurer, Isotopes and Radiation Enterprises Ltd., Israel, 1964-70. Special council, President's Task Force on Communications Policy, 1967-68. Adjunct professor of law, Georgetown University Law Center, Washington, 1970-71; lecturer, School of Law, Catholic University of America, Washington, D.C., 1970;

visiting professor of law, College of Law, University of Tennessee, Knoxville, 1977. Consultant on telecommunications to office of Secretary of Transportation, 1967-68, and to Environmental Protection Agency, 1971. *Military service:* U.S. Naval Reserves, 1945-46. *Member:* American Trial Lawyers Association (faculty member), Maryland Bar Association, Phi Beta Kappa.

WRITINGS: Cases and Materials on Environmental Law, Bureau of National Affairs, 1970, 2nd edition, 1973; (with H. Shulman and F. James, Jr.) *Cases and Materials on the Law of Torts,* 3rd edition (Gray was not associated with earlier editions), Foundation Press, 1976. Contributor to law reviews.

WORK IN PROGRESS: A revision, with others, of Harper and James, *The Law of Torts,* for Little, Brown.

*　　*　　*

GRAY, Patricia (Clark)
(Patsey Gray, Virginia Clark)

PERSONAL: Born in San Mateo, Calif.; daughter of Charles (a copper mine owner and operator) and Celia (Tobin) Clark; married Gerald Gray (a surgeon), February 17, 1934; children: Gerald Clark, Celia (Mrs. Jon Cummings), Alice (Mrs. Louis Coelho), Tim. *Home:* Ten Acre Ranch, Walnut Creek, Calif. 94595. *Agent:* Curtis Brown, Ltd., 575 Madison Ave., New York, N.Y. 10022.

CAREER: Breeds and shows horses. Author.

*WRITINGS—*Juveniles, except as indicated; published by Coward, except as noted: *The Doggone Roan,* 1957; *4-H Filly,* 1958; *Galloping Gold,* 1958; *Challenger,* 1959; (under pseudonym Virginia Clark) *The Mysterious Buckskin,* Macmillan, 1960; *Diving Horse,* 1960; *Horse in Her Heart,* 1960; *Loco, the Bronc,* 1961; *The Horse Trap,* 1962; *Show Ring Rogue,* 1963; *Show and Tell* (adult), A. S. Barnes, 1976.

Under name Patsey Gray; published by Norton, except as indicated: *Heads Up,* Coward, 1956; *Star Bright,* 1964; *Star Lost,* 1965; *Jumping Jack,* 1965; *Horsepower,* 1966; *Norah's Ark,* 1966; *Lucky Star,* 1967; *Blue Ribbon Summer,* 1968; *Star, the Sea Horse,* 1968; *The Flag Is Up,* Nelson, 1970.

Contributor of more than thirty-five short stories to various magazines.

WORK IN PROGRESS: A book of fiction, for young adults, on Apaches, with an Indian boy as protagonist; an adult suspense novel; two articles on horses.

*　　*　　*

GREAN, Stanley   1920

PERSONAL: Surname is pronounced *Gree*-on; born April 3, 1920, in New York; son of Alexander Michael (a designer and manufacturer) and Anna (Kurtz) Grean; married Patricia Anthony, July 25, 1944; children: Nicholas (deceased). *Education:* Columbia University, B.A. (with honors), 1941, Ph.D., 1961; Union Theological Seminary, New York, N.Y., B.D., 1944. *Politics:* Democrat. *Religion:* Episcopalian. *Home:* 163 B, Pine Grove Hts., Athens, Ohio 45701. *Office:* Department of Philosophy, Ohio University, Athens, Ohio 45701.

CAREER: Unitarian Universalist minister in Mount Vernon, N.Y., 1945-46; University of Connecticut, New London Campus, instructor in philosophy, 1947-49, Storrs Campus, instructor in philosophy, 1949-53; Howard University, Washington, D.C., visiting lecturer in humanities,

1954; Ohio University, Athens, assistant professor, 1955-65, associate professor, 1965-69, professor of philosophy, 1969—, chairman of department, 1971-76, member of board of editors, Ohio University Press, 1965—. *Member:* American Philosophical Association, American Academy of Religion, Ohio Philosophical Association (secretary-treasurer, 1965-69), Phi Beta Kappa. *Awards, honors:* Baker Fund research grant, 1964.

WRITINGS: (Author of introduction) Earl of Shaftesbury, *Characteristics of Men, Manners,* edited by J. M. Robertson, Bobbs-Merrill, 1964; *Shaftesbury's Philosophy of Religion and Ethics: A Study in Enthusiasm,* Ohio University Press, 1967. Contributor to religion and philosophy journals. *Ohio University Review,* member of board of editors, 1958-71, chief editor, 1965-70.

WORK IN PROGRESS: The Philosophy of Love.

BIOGRAPHICAL/CRITICAL SOURCES: Times Literary Supplement, February 1, 1968; *Journal of the History of Philosophy,* January, 1969; *Studia Leibnitiania,* October, 1969.

* * *

GREBSTEIN, Lawrence C(harles) 1937-

PERSONAL: Born February 17, 1937, in Providence, R.I.; son of Sigmund (a house painter) and Sylvia (Scotkin) Grebstein; married Ellen Jean Levitt, June 5, 1966; children: Laurie Beth, Ari Nathan. *Education:* Brown University, A.B., 1958; University of Kentucky, M.A., 1961, Ph.D., 1964. *Religion:* Jewish. *Home:* 66 Spring Dale Dr., Kingston, R.I. 02881. *Office:* Department of Psychology, University of Rhode Island, Kingston, R.I. 02881.

CAREER: University of Rhode Island, Kingston, 1964—, began as associate professor, became professor of psychology and director of Psychological Consultation Center, director of clinical training, 1964—, assistant dean of College of Arts and Sciences, 1969-70. Visiting professor, University of Bergen, Bergen, Norway, 1970-71. *Member:* American Psychological Association, Eastern Psychological Association, New England Psychological Association, Rhode Island Psychological Association.

WRITINGS: Toward Self-Understanding: Studies in Personality and Adjustment, Scott, Foresman, 1969. Contributor to psychology journals.

* * *

GREEN, Joseph 1931-

PERSONAL: Born January 14, 1931, in Compass Lake, Fla.; son of Francis Marion and Mattie (Carlisle) Green; married Juanita Henderson (a secretary), March 3, 1951 (divorced December 16, 1975); married Patrice Milton, December 24, 1975; children (first marriage): William Merritt, Rose-Marie. *Politics:* Democrat. *Religion:* None. *Home:* 1390 Holly Ave., Merritt Island, Fla. 32952. *Agent:* Lurton Blassingame, 60 East 42nd St., New York, N.Y. 10017. *Office:* John F. Kennedy Space Center, Merritt Island, Fla.

CAREER: International Paper Co., Panama City, Fla., laboratory technician, 1949-51; Civil Service shop worker and welder in Panama City, 1952-54; construction millwright in Florida, Texas, and Alabama, 1955-58; Boeing Co., Seattle, Wash., senior supervisor, 1959-63; John F. Kennedy Space Center, Merritt Island, Fla., engineering writer, 1965—. *Member:* American Association for the Advancement of Science, Science Fiction Writers of America, American Civil Liberties Union, Authors Guild.

WRITINGS: The Loafers of Refuge, Ballantine, 1965; *An Affair with Genius* (short story collection), Gollancz, 1969; *Gold the Man,* Gollancz, 1971; *Concience Interplanetary,* Doubleday, 1973; *Star Probe,* Millington, 1975; *The Horde,* Laser, 1975. Contributor of short stories to science fiction magazines.

WORK IN PROGRESS: A second science fiction novel on the conscience of mankind in the future world; several short stories and novelettes.

SIDELIGHTS: Joseph Green told *CA:* "I note with pleasure that my chosen field, science-fiction, looms ever larger on the modern scene. Today major novelists sometimes reside for a time in our little ghetto, or use science-fiction concepts in their contemporary works. The average science-fiction novel now outsells the average mainstream novel (though only a few s-f novels become best-sellers). Futurology is now a struggling young science, born of our fiction. We live in a science-fiction world. Welcome aboard."

* * *

GREEN, Maury 1916-

PERSONAL: Born May 10, 1916, in Raleigh, N.C.; son of Henry Lee (a salesman) and Ethel (Emmerson) Green; married Evelyn Taggart, August 11, 1940; children: Barbara (Mrs. John Hager), Lee (son). *Education:* University of Illinois, B.A. (summa cum laude), 1937.

CAREER: Chicago Herald-Examiner, Chicago, Ill., reporter and editor, 1937-39; *Chicago Tribune,* Chicago, reporter and editor, 1939-56; *Los Angeles Times,* Los Angeles, Calif., reporter, 1957; KNXT News (television), Los Angeles, reporter and producer, 1959-69; KNBC (television), Los Angeles, host of "Inquiry," and producer of documentaries, beginning 1970; Maury Green Enterprises, Inc. (film and television production and consultation), Encino, Calif., president, beginning 1970. Lecturer in department of journalism, University of California, Los Angeles, beginning 1968. *Military service:* U.S. Naval Reserve, 1943-46; became lieutenant.

MEMBER: National Academy of Television Arts and Sciences, Screen Actors Guild, American Federation of Television and Radio Artists, Radio and Television News Association of Southern California, Greater Los Angeles Press Club (member of board of directors, 1968-71; president, 1970-71), Sigma Delta Chi. *Awards, honors:* "Golden Mikes" award from Radio and Television News Association of Southern California for best spot news story for television, 1962-63, and for best television news writing, 1965; "Emmy" from Hollywood chapter of National Academy of Television Arts and Sciences, 1964, for documentary drama, "Tell Me Not in Mournful Numbers," broadcast by KNXT, 1963; Broadcast Preceptor Award at Annual Broadcast Industry Conference at San Francisco State College (now University), 1970, for *Television News: Anatomy and Process.*

WRITINGS: Television News: Anatomy and Process, Wadsworth, 1969; (with Lyn Franklin) *Sawed-off Justice,* Putnam, 1976. Author of screenplay, "This Rebel Breed," released by Warner Brothers, 1958, and of television documentaries for KNTX, 1959-69, and KNBC, 1970. Writer with William Walker of radio plays for Columbia Broadcasting System "Suspense" series; also has done episodes for "Zane Grey Theater" and "Bonanza."

WORK IN PROGRESS: The Intimate Eye (tentative title),

a book on television communication; *Black and Blue,* a book of humor on the experiences of a black policeman; *Tangents,* a novel; and a stage play.†

*   *   *

GREENBERG, Daniel S. 1931-

PERSONAL: Born May 5, 1931, in New York, N.Y.; son of Max and Bertha (Rosenberg) Greenberg; divorced; children: Julie, Margaret, Cathryn, Ellen. *Education:* Columbia University, A.B., 1953. *Home:* 3736 Kanawha St., N.W., Washington, D.C. 20015. *Agent:* John Schaffner, 425 East 51st St., New York, N.Y. 10022. *Office address: Science and Government Report,* P.O. Box 21123, Washington, D.C. 20005.

CAREER: Wilmington Journal-Every Evening, Wilmington, Del., general assignment reporter, 1955-57; *Washington Post,* Washington, D.C., general assignment reporter, 1957-60; American Association for the Advancement of Science, Washington, D.C., news editor of *Science* (weekly), 1961-70; publisher of *Science and Government Report,* a newsletter, 1969—; Washington correspondent for *New Scientist,* a British periodical. Research fellow, Department of History of Science, Johns Hopkins University, 1965-67. *Military service:* U.S. Naval Reserve, active duty, 1953-55; became lieutenant. *Awards, honors:* Medal of Excellence, Columbia University, 1970.

WRITINGS: The Politics of Pure Science, New American Library, 1967 (published in England as *The Politics of American Science,* Pelican, 1969). Contributor to *Harper's, New York Times, Reader's Digest, Saturday Evening Post, Public Interest,* and other publications.

BIOGRAPHICAL/CRITICAL SOURCES: New York Times Book Review, October 6, 1968.

*   *   *

GREENBERG, Selma 1930-

PERSONAL: Born September 11, 1930, in Brooklyn, N.Y.; daughter of Benjamin (a businessman) and Anna (Amarant) Weintraub; married William Greenberg (a certified public accountant), June 22, 1952; children: Lisa, Andrew, Ellen. *Education:* State University of New York College at Oswego, B.S., 1951; Queens College of the City University of New York, M.A., 1958; Columbia University, Ed.D., 1966. *Home:* 93 Myrtle Dr., Great Neck, N.Y. 10021. *Office:* Department of Education, Hofstra University, Hempstead Turnpike, Hempstead, N.Y. 11550.

CAREER: Hofstra University, Hempstead, N.Y., 1966—, began as associate professor, currently professor of education, affirmative action officer, 1977. Director, Classroom Materials Co. *Member:* American Educational Research Association.

WRITINGS: Selected Studies of Classroom Behavior: A Comparative Analysis, International Textbook Co., 1970; (with Greta Morine and Robert Spaulding) *New Directions in the Teaching Process,* International Textbook Co., 1971; *Right from the Start,* Houghton, 1978. Author of educational material for films, recordings, and visual aids.

WORK IN PROGRESS: A book on the teaching of logic to young children; a study in spontaneous verbal interaction; research in mother-infant initial interaction.

*   *   *

GREENLEAF, Barbara Kaye 1942-

PERSONAL: Born July 1, 1942, in New York, N.Y.; daughter of Louis C. (a builder) and Alice (Ginsburg) Kaye; married Jonathan W. Greenleaf (an advertising executive), July 29, 1965; children: Caroline Kaye, Catherine Kaye. *Education:* Vassar College, B.A., 1963. *Home:* 5 Birch Grove Dr., Armonk, N.Y. 10504.

CAREER: Grolier, Inc., New York City, assistant editor of *New Book of Knowledge,* 1963-64; *New York Times,* New York City, writer, 1964-66. Technical writer and editorial consultant, Rockland Psychiatric Research Institute, 1974-76.

WRITINGS: America Fever: The Story of American Immigration, Four Winds, 1970; *Forward March to Freedom: The Story of A. Philip Randolph* (juvenile), Grosset, 1971; *Children of All Ages: A History of Childhood,* McGraw, 1978; *Help!,* Crowell, 1978. Contributor to *Newsday, Bride and Home, Westchester, Vassar Quarterly, Bride's Magazine,* and other publications.

SIDELIGHTS: Barbara Kaye Greenleaf told *CA:* "For people aspiring to write nonfiction, I advise against rushing ahead with any project. Let it sit on your back burner for at least several months. If, after that time the topic is still simmering, then you know it's for you. If it isn't, you've saved yourself a lot of wasted motion, because the topic obviously was not vital enough to sustain your interest through to completion. Don't feel you have to earn money from your work. Never give up. Work as hard as you think you are capable of working and then work some more. No results without hard work. Be clear, clearer, clearest. Learn grammatical English. Speak it, write it."

*   *   *

GREENWOOD, Edward Alister 1930-
(Ted Greenwood)

PERSONAL: Born December 4, 1930, in Melbourne, Victoria, Australia; son of George Frederick (an architect) and Ilma (McDonald) Greenwood; married Florence Lorraine Peart (a kindergarten director), January 15, 1954; children: Catherine, Meredith, Alister, Emma. *Education:* Melbourne Teachers' College, Primary Teaching Qualification, 1949; Royal Melbourne Institute of Technology, Diploma of Art, 1959. *Politics:* Uncommitted. *Religion:* "Personal." *Home and office:* Hilton Rd., Ferny Creek, Victoria 3786, Australia.

CAREER: Education Department of Victoria, Melbourne, Australia, primary teacher, 1948-56; lecturer in art education at Melbourne Teachers' College, Melbourne, 1956-60; and at Toorak Teachers' College, Toorak, Melbourne, 1961-68; writer, illustrator, and painter, also working in a plant nursery to help support the other three endeavors. *Awards, honors:* Picture Book of the Year Award of Children's Book Council of Australia, 1968, for illustrations in *Sly Old Wardrobe;* Book Council commendation, 1969, for *Obstreperous;* high commendation from Children's Book Council, and Hans Christian Anderson Honours List, 1974, both awards for *Joseph and Lulu and the Prindiville House Pigeons;* Visual Arts award for illustration from Australian Council for the Arts, and Children's Book Council of Australia commendation, 1976, both for *Teddy's Brrrmmm GT.*

WRITINGS—Self-illustrated children's books under name Ted Greenwood; all published by Angus & Robertson, except as indicated: *Obstreperous,* 1969, Atheneum, 1970; *Aelfred,* 1970; *V.I.P.,* 1971; *Joseph and Lulu and the Prindiville House Pigeons,* 1972; *Terry's Brrrmmm GT,* 1975; *Curious Eddie,* 1977.

Illustrator; under name Ted Greenwood: Ivan Southall, *Sly Old Wardrobe,* F. W. Cheshire, 1968, St. Martin's, 1970; *Children Everywhere* (Australian section; text by Southall), Field Enterprises Education Corp., 1970. Craft reviewer, *Age.*

WORK IN PROGRESS: A short novel, *The Pochetta Coat;* a set of four short stories about a small girl, *Ginnie;* an adult film script.

SIDELIGHTS: Edward Alister Greenwood is particularly interested in cultivating the senses of children "in an age where so many experiences come to them in a vicarious form." "Although the illustrated book is such a form," he says, "I hope my books will act as catalysts for activity by those who read and look at them."

* * *

GREENWOOD, Theresa 1936-

PERSONAL: Born December 28, 1936, in Cairo, Ill.; daughter of Hubert Augustus (a postal employee) and Lillian (Williams) Winfrey; married Charles Huddie Greenwood (a college professor), June, 1960; children: Lisa Renee, Marc Charles. *Education:* Millikin University, B.Mus.Ed., 1959; Ball State University, M.A.Ed., 1963, Ed.D., 1976. *Religion:* Methodist. *Residence:* Muncie, Ind.

CAREER: Teacher of music in public schools of East Chicago, Ind., 1959-61; elementary teacher in Muncie, Ind., 1962-67; Ball State University, Muncie, academic counselor, 1971. Member of board of directors, EIC-TV (Muncie public broadcasting station); member of board, Huffer Children's Center. *Member:* National League of American Pen Women, Kappa Delta Pi, Pi Lambda Theta, Sigma Alpha Iota.

WRITINGS: Psalms of a Black Mother, Warner Press, 1970. Contributor of short stories and poetry to *Saturday Evening Post, English Journal,* and to religious publications; author of weekly newspaper column, "The Magic of Learnin!" Co-editor, *Human Rights Yearbook,* 1971.

WORK IN PROGRESS: A collection of poems.

BIOGRAPHICAL/CRITICAL SOURCES: Muncie Evening Press, August 26, 1970.

* * *

GREGG, Andrew K. 1929-
(Sneed Hearn, Tom Vinegar)

PERSONAL: Born October 12, 1929, in Chippewa Falls, Wis.; son of Burt A. and Freda (Beaudette) Gregg; married Fay Alice Sherwood (a teacher), January 30, 1955; children: Andrew K., Jr., Tanley Alison. *Education:* Attended Eau Claire State Teachers College (now University of Wisconsin—Eau Claire), 1948-49, and University of Wisconsin, 1953-55. *Politics:* None. *Reliigion:* None. *Home:* 2119 Gardenia S.W., Albuquerque, N.M. 87105. *Office address:* Vinegar Tom Press, P.O. Box 12142, Albuquerque, N.M. 87105.

CAREER: Eau Claire State Tribune, Eau Claire, Wis., photographer, 1952; *Albuquerque Tribune,* Albuquerque, N.M., photographer, 1956-65; Vinegar Tom Press (handprinted books), Albuquerque, owner. *Military service:* U.S. Army, 1949-52.

WRITINGS: New Mexico in the Nineteenth Century: A Pictorial History, University of New Mexico Press, 1968; *Drums of Yesterday: The Forts of New Mexico,* Press of the Territorian, 1969; (under pseudonym Tom Vinegar) *A New*

Mexico Christmas, Vinegar Tom Press, 1969; (under pseudonym Tom Vinegar) *A Walk Around Old Town, Albuquerque,* Vinegar Tom Press, 1970.

Contributor of fiction, articles, and photographs to *Newsweek, Writer's Digest, Mankind,* and other magazines.

WORK IN PROGRESS: Fiction, nonfiction, humor, and plays.

* * *

GREGORIAN, Vartan 1935-
(V. Herian)

PERSONAL: Born April 7, 1935, in Tabriz, Iran; son of Samuel B. (a government employee) and Shushan (Mirzaian) Gregorian; married Clare Russell, March 25, 1960; children: Vahe, Raffi, Dareh (all sons). *Education:* College Armenien, Beirut, Lebanon, Diploma in Armenian Studies, 1956; Stanford University, B.A., 1958, Ph.D., 1964. *Home:* 408 Drew Ave., Swarthmore, Pa. 19081. *Office:* Office of the Dean, Faculty of Arts and Sciences, University of Pennsylvania, Philadelphia, Pa. 19104.

CAREER: Stanford University, Stanford, Calif., assistant foreign student adviser, 1959-60; University of California, Berkeley, instructor in Armenian history and culture, 1960; San Francisco State College (now University), San Francisco, Calif., instructor, 1962-64, assistant professor, 1964-66, associate professor of history, 1966-68; University of California, Los Angeles, visiting associate professor of history, 1968; University of Texas at Austin, associate professor, 1968-70, professor of history, 1970-72; University of Pennsylvania, Philadelphia, professor of history and Tarzian Professor of Armenian and Caucasian History, 1972—, faculty assistant to president and provost, 1973-74, dean of Faculty of Arts and Sciences, 1974—.

MEMBER: American Historical Association (program chairman, 1971), American Association for the Advancement of Slavic Studies, American Civil Liberties Union, Middle East Studies Association, Academy of Political Science, Far Western Slavic Conference (program chairman, 1968), World Affairs Council of Philadelphia, Fellowship Commission of Pennsylvania, Sierra Club. *Awards, honors:* Ford Foundation foreign area fellowship, 1960-62; American Council of Learned Societies-Social Science Research Council fellow, 1965-66, 1971-72; Danforth Foundation Award for outstanding teaching, 1969; John Simon Guggenheim fellowship, 1972-72; American Council of Education fellow, 1972-73; Golden Medal of Honor, City and Province of Vienna, Austria, 1976.

WRITINGS: (Editor) Simon Vratzian, *Hin Tghter Nor Patmutian Hamar* (in Armenian; title means "Old Papers for the New History"), [Beirut], 1962; (editor) Vratzian, *Kianki Oughinerov* (in Armenian; memoirs), Volume V, [Beirut], 1966; *The Emergence of Modern Afghanistan: Politics of Reform and Modernization, 1880-1946,* Stanford University Press, 1969. Contributor, sometimes under pseudonym V. Herian, to encyclopedias and to journals in United States, Iran, and Lebanon.

WORK IN PROGRESS: Three books, *Defense of Baku: 1918, National Culture in Soviet Armenia (1928-1970),* and *Social Darwinism in France,* listed in order of expected completion.

SIDELIGHTS: Vartan Gregorian is competent in Turkish, Arabic, and French, in addition to his native Persian, English, and Armenian.

GREGORY, Robert Lloyd 1892-

PERSONAL: Born July 23, 1892, in Harlan, Ky.; son of Walter Zink (a businessman) and Rella (Turner) Gregory; married Mina Clare Williams, October 22, 1922 (died, 1959); children: Robert Granville, Walter Eugene, George G. *Education:* University of Kentucky, B.C.E., 1914, M.C.E., 1933. *Home:* 9945 Beverly Grove Dr., Beverly Hills, Calif. 90210.

CAREER: Interstate Commerce Commission, junior engineer, 1914-18; J. G. White Engineering Corp., New York, N.Y., assistant engineer on government projects in Virginia and Alabama, 1918-19; State Highway Department of Colorado, 1919-22, began as assistant field engineer, became resident engineer; County of Los Angeles, Calif., 1925-55, began as chief of survey party for the County Surveyor's Office, became chief deputy, Department of County Engineers. *Military service:* U.S. Army, 1917; became second lieutenant. *Member:* American Society of Civil Engineers (fellow), International Platform Association, Tau Beta Pi.

WRITINGS: Rays of Hope: The Universe-Life-Man, Philosophical Library, 1969. Contributor to *Transactions* of American Society of Civil Engineers.

WORK IN PROGRESS: A biographical novel concerning the lives of four men, including himself, who were born and reared in the mountains of eastern Kentucky; *The Third Choice.*

SIDELIGHTS: Robert L. Gregory told *CA:* "It seems that I have always possessed a natural bent toward philosophical thinking, but finding it necessary to earn my own living ('from scratch'), I needed to equip myself for immediate employment ... I have no regrets for having spent 41 years as an engineer—they were fruitful, and besides they prepared me well for the work of future years. . . . Upon retiring from the active practice of engineering at the age sixty-three, realizing the need for broadening my horizon, I embarked upon a self-charted, intensive study of the leading sciences, the philosophies and the humanities."

*   *   *

GREGORY, Ross 1933-

PERSONAL: Born February 11, 1933, in Washington, Ind.; son of Norrell (a writer) and Bertha B. (Jones) Gregory; married Shirley Ann Heines, December 15, 1961; children: Theresa M., Graham T., Darren M. *Education:* Indiana University, A.B., 1959, M.A., 1961, Ph.D., 1964. *Politics:* Democrat. *Religion:* Protestant. *Home:* 2812 Romence Rd., Kalamazoo, Mich. 49002. *Office:* History Department, Western Michigan University, Kalamazoo, Mich. 49001.

CAREER: West Virginia Institute of Technology, Montgomery, assistant professor of history, 1963-66; Western Michigan University, Kalamazoo, assistant professor, 1966-69, associate professor, 1969-73, professor of history, 1973—. *Military service:* U.S. Army, 1954-56. *Member:* American Historical Association, Organization of American Historians. *Awards, honors:* Summer research grant from American Philosophical Society for work in London, England, 1967; Frederick Jackson Turner Prize of Organization of American Historians, 1969, for *Walter Hines Page: Ambassador to the Court of St. James.*

WRITINGS: Walter Hines Page: Ambassador to the Court of St. James, University Press of Kentucky, 1970; *Origins of American Intervention in the First World War*, Norton, 1971; (contributor) Frank J. Merli and Theodore A. Wilson, editors, *Makers of American Diplomacy*, Scribner, 1974. Contributor to history journals.

WORK IN PROGRESS: A social history of the United States during World War II.

*   *   *

GREGORY, William King 1876-1970

May 19, 1876—December 29, 1970; American anthropologist, ichthyologist, and author. Obituaries: *New York Times*, December 30, 1970; *Washington Post*, December 31, 1970; *Antiquarian Bookman*, January 18, 1971.

*   *   *

GRENDAHL, J(ay) Spencer 1943-

PERSONAL: Born October 7, 1943, in Lewiston, Idaho; son of Jay H. and Mildred (Spencer) Grendahl. *Education:* Whitworth College, B.A. (cum laude), 1965; Brown University, A.M., 1967; Harvard University, Ed.M., 1969. *Politics:* Independent. *Religion:* Independent. *Home:* 2408 North Benchwood Dr., Hollywood, Calif. 90068.

CAREER: Teacher in government high school, Peace Corps, Yola, Nigeria, 1967-68; teacher of English, Bellevue High School, Seattle, Wash., 1969-72; free-lance writer and educational consultant, 1972—; staff writer for *Viva* (magazine), 1977—. *Member:* Writers Guild. *Awards, honors:* Woodrow Wilson fellow, 1965; named Literary Find of the Year, G. P. Putnam's Sons, 1970.

WRITINGS: The Mad Dog Press Archives, Putnam, 1970.

WORK IN PROGRESS: Two books, *God Is a Funky Piano Player*, and *Push the Button When I Die.*

SIDELIGHTS: J. Spencer Grendahl told *CA:* "I have traveled in Europe and Africa. In Africa I discovered the novel wasn't dead—I met it in Morocco ... NEWSFLASH—A couple of my friends and I are getting it together. We're going to pull off a literary scene called The Seventies."

*   *   *

GRENIER, Mildred 1917-

PERSONAL: Born February 1, 1917, in Maysville, Mo.; daughter of Clarence W. (a farmer) and Mary Ann (Bottorff) Bromley; married Joseph G. Grenier (a public school teacher), December 24, 1942; children: Joseph Kent (killed in Vietnam), Candace Jeanette. *Education:* Attended Maryville State Teachers College and Furman University. *Politics:* Republican. *Religion:* Methodist.

CAREER: Public school teacher in Fairport, Mo., 1936-39, and in Osborn, Mo., 1939-43; nursery school teacher in Columbia, S.C., 1944-46. *Member:* National League of American Pen Women (president, 1960-62; Missouri state president, 1962-64; historian, 1964-66; treasurer, 1966-68; secretary, 1970-72), Missouri Writers Guild. *Awards, honors:* First prize in International Instructor Stories for Children Awards, 1965; has won four awards in *Writer's Digest* contests, two from Freedoms Foundation, and local, state, regional, and national awards from National League of American Pen Women.

WRITINGS: Christmas Every Day, A. D. Freese, 1961; *How High Is the Sky?* (juvenile), Herald House, 1968; *How Kids Can Earn Cash*, Fell, 1970; *The Wagon and the Star*, Standard Publishing, 1971; *God Made Our World*, C. R. Gibson, 1972; *The Quick and Easy Guide to Making Money at Home*, Fell, 1974. Has sold more than two thousand items to more than one hundred publications, including *Ladies' Home Journal, Saturday Evening Post, Wee Wisdom, Jack and Jill, Writer, Together, Coronet, New York Herald Trib-*

une, Denver Post, Kansas City Star and Times, Chicago Tribune, and *Christian Herald.*†

* * *

GRESSER, Seymour 1926-
(Sy Gresser)

PERSONAL: Born May 9, 1926, in Baltimore, Md.; son of Simon Solomon and Sara (Williams) Gresser; married Evangeline Wilson (an art teacher), July 4, 1950 (divorced); children: Jeffrey, Terence, Rachel, Daniel. *Education:* Institute of Contemporary Arts, Washington, D.C., student, 1949-50; George Washington University, student, 1950-53; University of Maryland, B.S., 1949, M.A., 1972. *Politics:* "Apolitical, except in my art." *Religion:* "In my art." *Home and office:* 1015 Ruatan St., Silver Spring, Md. 20903.

CAREER: Sculptor and writer; employed in various positions, including doing research on American Indians, technical writing and editing, and teaching art. Instructor in sculpture, Sculptor's Studio, evenings, 1958-63, and Paint Branch Unitarian Church; sculptor-in-residence, Yale University, 1969. Works exhibited in one-man shows and group exhibitions in U.S., Europe, and Mexico since 1951, including Smithsonian Exhibition, 1952. Washington Irving Gallery, New York, N.Y., 1956, San Angel Exhibition, Mexico, 1960, Capricorn Gallery, New York, N.Y., 1967, Harvard University, 1971, Fordham University, Berkeley Center at Yale University, and Athena Gallery, New Haven, Conn. *Military service:* U.S. Merchant Marine, radio operator, 1944-46. *Awards, honors:* Organization of American States fellowship, 1960-61.

WRITINGS—All poetry: *Stone Elegies,* H. H. Walters, 1955; *Coming of the Atom,* Hennypenny Press, 1957; *Letters from Mexico,* Goosetree Press, 1964; *Voyages,* Quixote Press, 1969; *A Garland for Stephen,* Olivant House, 1970; *A Departure for Sons,* Daedal Press, 1973. Contributor of over two hundred poems, short stories, reviews, and essays to *Hopkins Review, Trace, Antioch Review,* and other quarterlies and little magazines.

WORK IN PROGRESS: A novel, *These Last Men;* a new volume of poems.

SIDELIGHTS: Seymour Gresser told *CA:* "I have been a sculptor in stone and wood, as well as a poet and prose writer, for over twenty years. [I] am very hostile to [the] anti-art movement [and] consider myself old hat in writing and sculpture—namely, the stellar importance of content over any other consideration. [I] consider spirituality—the way people love or hate one another—to be seminal in all my work. I also believe poetry and sculpture are very similar in the manner in which they are derived from human experience."

* * *

GRETZ, Susanna 1937-

PERSONAL: Born September 27, 1937, in New York, N.Y.; daughter of George G. (a lawyer) and Helen (White) Tennant; married Guenter Gretz (an industrial designer), 1966. *Education:* Smith College, B.A., 1959. *Home:* 6 Frankfurt 90, Damaschke-Anger 51, West Germany.

CAREER: Writer and illustrator.

WRITINGS—All self-illustrated: *Teddy Bears 1 to 10,* Follett, 1969; *The Bears Who Stayed Indoors,* Follett, 1970; *The Bears Who Went to the Seaside,* Benn, 1972; *Teddy Bears ABC,* Follett, 1975; *Ten Green Bottles,* Penguin, 1976.

Illustrator: Helen Cresswell, *Rug Is a Bear,* Benn, 1968; Cresswell, *Rug Plays Tricks,* Benn, 1968; *Rug Plays Ball,* Benn, 1968; *Rug and a Picnic,* Benn, 1968; *Rillsby-Rill,* O'Hara, 1972; *The Book of Kalila and Dimna,* Societe Nationale des Editions (Algeria), 1973.

WORK IN PROGRESS: Teddy Bears' Cookbook, for Benn.

* * *

GREY, Anthony 1938-

PERSONAL: Born July 5, 1938, in Norwich, England; son of Alfred (a tradesman) and Agnes (Bullent) Grey; married Shirley McGuinn (a college lecturer), April 4, 1970. *Education:* Attended secondary school in England. *Home:* Marylebone, London, N.W.1, England. *Agent:* A. D. Peters, 10 Buckingham St., London WC2N 6BU, England; and Peter Matson, Harold Matson Co., Inc., 22 East 40th St., New York, N.Y. 10016.

CAREER: Reporter for *Eastern Daily Press,* England, 1960-64; correspondent for Reuters News Agency in East Berlin, 1965-67, and in Peking, China, 1967-69, where he was interned by the Chinese; writer; currently host of daily international current affairs program, "Twenty-Four Hours," for British Broadcasting Corp. world service. Also host of such television documentaries as "The Lure of the Dolphins," broadcast in Britain and United States, 1976. *Awards, honors:* Member, Order of the British Empire, 1969; International Publishing Corporation Journalist of the Year Award, 1970.

WRITINGS: Hostage in Peking, M. Joseph, 1970, Doubleday, 1971; *A Man Alone* (short stories), M. Joseph, 1971; *Crosswords from Peking,* Penguin, 1971; *Some Put Their Trust in Chariots,* M. Joseph, 1973; *The Bulgarian Exclusive,* M. Joseph, 1976, Dial Press, 1977. Writer of radio play, "Himself," broadcast in Britain, Australia, New Zealand, and Switzerland.

WORK IN PROGRESS: A history of Canada's biggest coal company, tentatively entitled *The Luscar Story.*

SIDELIGHTS: Anthony Grey's internment in Peking consisted of 806 days as a solitary prisoner, locked in a small room of his home. Accused of no crime, he was held while Britain was pressured for the release of thirteen Chinese journalists jailed in Hong Kong. *Hostage in Peking* is based on the diary which Grey kept secret from his captors. Al Phillips writes, "Having been caught in the middle of an international dispute between Britain and Red China, correspondent Anthony Grey tells a poignant story as he tries 'to set out the historical, political and emotional background to the long, isolated imprisonment . . . and the vindictive and intentionally humiliating treatment meted out to me.' He vividly depicts humility and human suffering and it is almost unbelievable that anyone should be subjected to such treatment." Harry Schwarz states that "there is probably no more bizarre chapter in the history of modern journalism than Anthony Grey's ordeal. . . . His absorbing book describes how he survived the nightmare . . . [and] is devoted to the inspiring account of how Grey overcame the terrors that invaded his mind and being."

Reviewing "The Lure of the Dolphins," Shaun Usher of the *Daily Mail* highlights Grey's abilities in television. He writes: "I hope that Grey makes more programmes, for his wide ranging approach is more common in books than on television. He has respect for facts but also finds room for humane matters."

BIOGRAPHICAL/CRITICAL SOURCES: Times Literary Supplement, September 11, 1970; Newsday, March 6, 1971; Time, March 29, 1971; Best Sellers, April 15, 1971; Saturday Review, June 26, 1971; Daily Mail (London), June 1, 1976.

* * *

GRIBBLE, James 1938-

PERSONAL: Born September 5, 1938, in Melbourne, Victoria, Australia; son of Charles Harry (an inspector) and Florence (Gannon) Gribble; married Jennifer Maud Dallimore (a university lecturer), January 9, 1961; children: Daniel Walter. Education: University of Melbourne, B.A., 1960, Ph.D., 1976; University of London, Ph.M., 1965. Religion: None. Home: 4 Kiora Ave., Mosman, Sydney, New South Wales, 2088, Australia. Office address: University of New South Wales, P.O. Box 1, Kensington, New South Wales, Australia.

CAREER: Lecturer at University of Leicester, Leicester, England; University of Melbourne, Melbourne, Victoria, Australia, lecturer in philosophy of education, 1967-74; University of New South Wales, Kensington, New South Wales, Australia, senior lecturer in philosophy of education, 1975—. Member: Philosophy of Education Society of Great Britain, Philosophy of Education Society of Australia.

WRITINGS: (Editor and author of introduction) D. H. Lawrence, Kangaroo, Heinemann, 1963; (editor and author of introduction) Matthew Arnold, Collier-Macmillan, 1967; Introduction to Philosophy of Education, Allyn & Bacon, 1969. Contributor to Melbourne Critical Review, British Journal of Aesthetics, and education journals.

WORK IN PROGRESS: A book on the philosophy of library criticism and education.

AVOCATIONAL INTERESTS: Reading novels and poetry; classical music, surfing.

* * *

GRIBBONS, Warren D(avid) 1921-

PERSONAL: Born June 23, 1921, in Worcester, Mass.; son of John B. and Mary E. (Leary) Gribbons; married Jean P. Cote, August 30, 1947. Education: Boston University, A.B., 1955; Harvard University, Ed.D., 1959. Residence: Weston, Mass. Office: Department of Psychology, Regis College, Weston, Mass. 02193.

CAREER: Regis College, Weston, Mass., instructor in psychology, 1957-59; Clark University, Worcester, Mass., assistant professor of education and guidance, 1959-62; Regis College, associate professor, 1962-66, professor of psychology, 1966—. Consultant, Educational Testing Service, 1958-59. Military service: U.S. Army Air Forces, 1942-45; became sergeant. Member: American Psychological Association, American Personnel and Guidance Association, Psi Chi, Phi Delta Kappa. Awards, honors: U.S. Office of Education research grants, 1961-72.

WRITINGS—With Paul R. Lohnes: Career Development, U.S. Office of Education, 1966; Emerging Careers, Teachers College, Columbia University, 1968; Career Development from Age 13 to Age 25, U.S. Office of Education, 1969. Contributor to professional journals.

* * *

GRIEB, Kenneth J. 1939-

PERSONAL: Born April 3, 1939, in Buffalo, N.Y.; son of Joseph J. and Ida Grieb. Education: University of Buffalo, B.A., 1960, M.A., 1962; Indiana University, Ph.D., 1966. Home: 312 A Rosalia St., Oshkosh, Wis. 54901. Office: Department of History, University of Wisconsin, Oshkosh, Wis. 54901.

CAREER: Indiana University, South Bend Campus, resident lecturer in history, 1965-66; University of Wisconsin—Oshkosh, assistant professor, 1966-70, associate professor, 1970-74, professor of history, 1974—, coordinator of Latin American studies, 1968—. Member: American Historical Association, Organization of American Historians, Latin American Studies Association, Conference on Latin American History, Society for Historians of American Foreign Relations, Midwest Association for Latin American Studies (president, 1972-73), Wisconsin Council of Latin Americanists (president, 1970-71), Phi Alpha Theta. Awards, honors: Doherty Foundation fellow in Mexico, 1964-65.

WRITINGS: The United States and Huerta, University of Nebraska Press, 1969; (co-editor) Latin American Government Leaders, Arizona State University Press, 1970, 2nd edition, 1975; (co-author) Essays on Miguel Angel Asturias, Latin American Center, University of Wisconsin—Milwaukee, 1973; (contributor) Richard E. Greenleaf and Michael C. Meyer, editors, Research in Mexican History: Topics, Methodology, Sources, and a Practical Guide to Field Research, University of Nebraska Press, 1973; The Latin American Policy of Warren G. Harding (monograph), Texas Christian University Press, 1976; (contributor) Jules David, editor, Perspectives in American Diplomacy, Arno Press, 1976. Contributor of articles and reviews to historical journals.

WORK IN PROGRESS: The Regime of General Jorge Ubico (Guatemala, 1931-1944); United States Relations with Central America, 1930-1945.

* * *

GRIFFIN, Glen C. 1934-

PERSONAL: Born August 2, 1934, in Asnieres, France; U.S. citizen; son of Smith Ben and Marion (Hussey) Griffin; married Mary Ella Page, December 23, 1957; children: Janelle, Joan, Mark, Gary, Jill, Greg. Education: Texas Western College, B.A., 1954; University of Texas, M.D., 1958. Politics: Republican. Religion: Church of Jesus Christ of Latter-day Saints (Mormon). Home: 421 Indian Springs Rd., Bountiful, Utah 84010. Office: College of Medicine, University of Utah, Salt Lake City, Utah 84112.

CAREER: Former positions include: pediatrician at South Davis Medical Center, Bountiful, Utah; president of Medical Practice Systems, Inc., Bountiful; and vice-president of Child Health Centers of America, Jackson, Tenn.; currently pediatrician in private practice. University of Utah, College of Medicine, Salt Lake City, clinical instructor in pediatric department, 1970—. Diplomate of American Board of Pediatrics. National adviser, American Association of Medical Assistants. Military service: U.S. Army, 1961-63; became captain. Member: American Academy of Pediatrics (fellow), American Medical Association, American Thoracic Society, American College of Allergists (associate fellow), Utah State Medical Association, Davis County Medical Association.

WRITINGS: About Life and Love, Deseret, 1968; (with W. Dean Belnap) About Marriage and More, Deseret, 1968; (with Lynn Eric Johnson) What's Up?, Deseret, 1970; You Were Smaller than a Dot, Better Books, 1972. Writer of patient education filmstrips and other educational materials.

WORK IN PROGRESS: A new book for teenagers.

SIDELIGHTS: Dr. Griffin told *CA* that he "has developed numerous efficiency systems for the improvement of health care delivery, including his unique medical office for the care of children and teens. In this office there is no waiting room. Patients drive into a covered parking place and enter their own examining or surgery room. Closed circuit televisions and electric eye beams and thirteen tape recording units welcome patients, and instruct them in interesting ways, many automatically. Even the examining rooms are unconventional—designed like mini-living rooms to avoid a 'sterile doctor's office appearance and setting.'"

* * *

GRIFFIN, James A. 1934-

PERSONAL: Born June 13, 1934, in Cleveland, Ohio; son of Thomas A. and Margaret M. (Hanousek) Griffin. *Education:* Borromeo Seminary, B.A., 1956; St. Mary Seminary, Cleveland, Ohio, graduate study, 1956-60; Pontifical Lateran University, Rome, Italy, J.C.L., 1963; Cleveland State University, J.D. (summa cum laude), 1972. *Home and office:* 1007 Superior Ave., Cleveland, Ohio 44114.

CAREER: Roman Catholic priest, ordained in 1960; Roman Catholic Diocese of Cleveland, Cleveland, Ohio, associate pastor of St. Jerome Church, 1960-61, secretary-notary of Diocesan Tribunal, 1963-65, assistant diocesan chancellor, 1965-68, vice-chancellor, 1968-73, chancellor, 1973—, promoter of justice, Diocesan Tribunal, 1969—. Member of advisory board, Diocesan Family Life Bureau; member of Diocesan Clergy Relations Board. *Member:* Canon Law Society of America.

WRITINGS—All published by Alba: (With A. James Quinn) *Thoughts for Our Time,* 1969; (with Quinn) *Thoughts for Sowing: Reflections on the Liturgical Readings for Sundays and Holydays,* 1970; *Ashes from the Cathedral,* 1973; *Sackcloth and Ashes,* 1976. Contributor to newspapers and religious journals.

* * *

GRIPARI, Pierre 1925-

PERSONAL: Born January 7, 1925, in Paris, France. *Politics:* Neo-facist. *Religion:* Epicurism. *Home:* 13 Boulevard de Port Royal, 75013 Paris, France.

CAREER: Writer. Has worked as a farm hand, dance hall pianist, and at clerical jobs.

WRITINGS: Lieutenant Tenant (three-act comedy; based on Youri Tynianov's short story, "Sous Lieutenant Kije"), [Paris], 1962; *Pierrot la lune,* La Table Ronde, 1963; *L'-Incroyable equipee de Phosphore Noloc et de ses compagnons* (novel), La Table Ronde, 1964; *Diable, Dieu et autres contes de menterie,* La Table Ronde, 1965; *Contes de la rue Broca* (juvenile), La Table Ronde, 1967, translation in part by Doriane Grutman published as *Tales of the Rue Broca,* Bobbs-Merrill, 1969; *La Vie, la mort et la resurrection de Socrate-Marie Gripotard* (novel), La Table Ronde, 1968; *L'arriere monde* (short stories), Editions Robert Morel, 1972; *Gueule d'Aminche,* Editions Robert Morel, 1973; *Le Solilesse* (poems), L'Age d'homme, 1975; *Frere Gaucher ou le voyage en Chine* (novel), L'Age d'homme, 1975; *Reveries d'un Martien en exil* (short stories), L'Age d'homme, 1976.

* * *

GRIPE, Maria (Kristina) 1923-

PERSONAL: Surname is pronounced *Gree*-per; born July 25, 1923, in Vaxholm, Sweden; married Harald Gripe (an artist), 1946; children: Camilla. *Education:* Stockholm University, student; received General Certificate of Education. *Home:* Fruaengsgatan 37, 611 00 Nykoeping, Sweden.

CAREER: Free-lance writer. *Awards, honors:* Association of Swedish Libraries' Nils Holgersson Plaque for the best children's book of the year for *Hugo och Josefin;* Lewis Carrol Shelf Award, Wisconsin Book Conference, for *Pappa Pellerin's Daughter;* honor book, *New York Herald Tribune's* Children's Spring Book Festival, for *Pappa Pellerin's Daughter; Expressen* (Swedish evening newspaper) "Heffaklumpen" Award, 1966, for *Hugo;* Litteraturfraamjandets stipendium, 1968, for *Nattpappan;* Sveriges foerfattarfonds konstnaars stipendium, 1970-71; Astrid Lindgren-priset, 1972; Hans Christian Andersen Medal, 1974; Sveriges foerfattarfonds premium foer litteraar foertjaanst, 1974.

WRITINGS—All published by Bonniers, except as noted: *I vaar lilla stad,* 1954; *Kung Laban Kommer,* 1956; *Kvarteret Labyrinten,* 1956; *Sebastian och Skuggan,* 1957; *Stackars Lilla Q,* 1957; *Tappa inte Masken,* 1959; *Glastunneln,* 1969; *Tanten* (based on radio play "The Aunt"; also see below), 1970; *. . . ellen dellen . . .,* 1974.

With illustrations by husband, Harald Gripe: *Naar det snoeade,* 1955; *De smaa roeda,* 1960; *Josefin,* 1961, translation by Paul Britten Austin published as *Josephine,* Delacorte, 1970; *Hugo och Josefin,* 1962, translation by Austin published as *Hugo and Josephine,* Delacorte, 1969; *Pappa Pellerins dotter,* 1963, translation by Kersti French published as *Pappa Pellerin's Daughter,* John Day, 1966; *Glasblaasarns Barn,* 1964, translation by Sheila La Farge published as *The Glassblower's Children,* Delacorte, 1974; *I Klockornas Tid,* 1965, translation by La Farge published as *In the Time of the Bells,* Delacorte, 1976; *Hugo,* 1966, translation by Austin published under same title, Delacorte, 1970; *Landet utanfoer,* 1967, translation by La Farge published as *The Land Beyond,* Delacorte, 1974; *Nattpappan,* 1968, translation by Gerry Bothmer published as *The Night Daddy,* Delacorte, 1971.

Julias hus och Nattpappan, 1971, translation by Bothmer published as *Julia's House,* Delacorte, 1975; *Elvis Karlsson,* 1972, translation by La Farge published as *Elvis and His Secret,* Delacorte, 1976; *Elvis!, Elvis!,* 1973, translation published as *Elvis and His Friends,* Delacorte, 1976; *Den riktige Elvis,* 1976.

Author of screenplays for a movie version of *Hugo and Josephine,* 1968, and for a film based on the Elvis Karlsson books, 1976; also author of radio plays, "The Night Daddy," "Elvis Karlsson," 1973, "Elvis! Elvis!," 1974, and a television play based on *The Night Daddy,* 1971.

SIDELIGHTS: Maria Gripe told *CA* that she had been warned by her father that there was but one person worthy to be called an *author:* Hans Christian Andersen, that "light years behind him come all the poor wretches who were just 'writers'." Her father, she said, told her one day, "In order to write you need (a) to have something to write about, and (b) to know how to write. While waiting for (a) learn (b)." Such was his judgment. "And so I began to wait . . . and wait. Till I had my little daughter. Then there was no getting away from it—I had something to write about—and somebody to write *for*."

BIOGRAPHICAL/CRITICAL SOURCES: Christian Science Monitor, November 6, 1969; *New Statesman,* June 4, 1971.

GROLLMES, Eugene E. 1931-

PERSONAL: Surname is pronounced *Gro*-mes; born November 9, 1931, in Seneca, Kan.; son of Edward Anthony (a businessman) and Josephine (Roeder) Grollmes. *Education:* St. Louis University, A.B., 1957, M.A., 1961; Boston College, Ph.D., 1969; Harvard University, postdoctoral study, 1969. *Office:* St. Louis University, 221 North Grand Blvd., St. Louis, Mo. 63103.

CAREER: Roman Catholic priest of Jesuit order (S.J.); Regis College, Denver, Colo., academic dean, 1970-73; St. Louis University, St. Louis, Mo., associate professor of education and assistant dean of College of Arts and Sciences, 1974—. *Member:* American Association for the Advancement of Science, National Catholic Education Association (member of executive committee), American Association for Higher Education, American Conference of Academic Deans, American Educational Studies Association.

WRITINGS—Editor: *Vows But No Walls,* B. Herder, 1967; *Catholic Colleges in the Secular Mystique,* B. Herder, 1970. Also editor of *Human Dignity and American Democracy,* 1976. Contributor to *Jesuit Educational Quarterly.*

* * *

GROSS, Beverly 1938-

PERSONAL: Born May 5, 1938, in New York, N.Y.; daughter of Alex and Justine (Klein) Gross. *Education:* University of Michigan, B.A., 1959; University of Chicago, M.A., 1960, Ph.D., 1966. *Home:* 10 Downing St., New York, N.Y. 10014. *Office:* Department of English, Queens College of the City University of New York, Flushing, N.Y. 11367.

CAREER: Northwestern University, Evanston, Ill., instructor in English, 1963-66; Vassar College, Poughkeepsie, N.Y., assistant professor of English, 1966-67; Queens College of the City University of New York, Flushing, N.Y., assistant professor, 1967-70, associate professor of English, 1970—, director of Special Studies and Honors, 1972-76. *Member:* Modern Language Association of America.

WRITINGS: (Editor with Richard Giannone) *The Shapes of Fiction: Open and Closed,* Holt, 1970. Also fiction editor of *A Shout in the Street,* 1976. Contributor to *Antioch Review, South Atlantic Quarterly,* and other journals. Fiction editor, *Chicago Review,* 1962-64; literary editor, *Nation,* 1969-70.

BIOGRAPHICAL/CRITICAL SOURCES: Nation, July 7, 1969.

* * *

GROSS, Feliks 1906-

PERSONAL: Born June 17, 1906, in Cracow, Poland; son of Adolf (a lawyer) and Augusta (Alexander) Gross; married Priva Baidaff (a professor of art history), 1937; children: Eva Helena Gross Friedman. *Education:* University of Cracow, Magister Juris, 1929, Dr.Juris, 1930; University of Paris, further study, 1931. *Home:* 310 West 85th St., New York, N.Y. 10024. *Office:* Graduate Center, City University of New York, 33 West 42nd St., New York, N.Y. 10036.

CAREER: Active in Workers University Association (adult education movement in Poland), 1925-39, and director of its Labor Social Science School, Cracow, 1934-38; University of London, London School of Economics and Political Science, London, England, appointed occasional lecturer in social anthropology, 1939-40; *New Europe and World Reconstruction* (monthly journal), New York City, editor, 1942-45; City University of New York, Brooklyn College, Brooklyn, N.Y., and Graduate Center, New York City, professor of sociology and anthropology, 1946—. Secretary-general, Central-East European Planning Board (Czechoslovakia, Greece, Yugoslavia, and Poland), 1942-45. Visiting professor, New York University, 1945-68; University of Wyoming, visiting professor and director of Institute of International Affairs, summers, 1945-52; also visiting professor at Woodrow Wilson School of Foreign Affairs, University of Virginia, 1951, 1954-56, University of Vermont, 1957, and at Columbia University, 1973; senior Fulbright lecturer at University of Rome, 1957-58, 1964-65, 1974, and lecturer at other European and American universities. Member of research council, Foreign Policy Research Institute, Philadelphia, Pa., 1966—. President, Taraknath Das Foundation; member of board of directors, International League of Human Rights. Consultant, National Committee for Prevention and Causes of Violence, 1969.

MEMBER: International Academy of Political Science, American Sociological Association, American Association for the Advancement of Slavic Studies, Academy of Political Science, Polish Institute of Arts and Sciences in America, New York Academy of Sciences, Authors League of America, Sigma Xi. *Awards, honors:* Carnegie scholar in Paris, 1931; Order of Phoenix (Greece) for scholarly work, 1963; grants from Public Affairs Foundation, New York University, 1962-63, Sloane Foundation, 1963, Research Foundation of the City University of New York, 1966-67, 1971, 1974, American Council of Learned Societies, 1969, National Science Foundation, 1972, Rockefeller Foundation, 1974, Italian National Research Council, 1974, and Brooklyn College Foundation, 1975.

WRITINGS: (With Zygmunt Gross) *Sojologia Partii Politycznej* (title means "Sociology of Political Parties"), [Cracow], 1928, 2nd edition, Czytelnik, 1946; *Koczownictwo: Studja nad Nomadyznem i nad Wyply wem Tegoz na spoleczenstwo* (title means "Nomadism: Studies on Nomadism and Its Influence on Society"; summaries in English included), Instytyt Popierania Nauki, 1936; (editor with Zygmunt Myslakowski) *Robotnicy Pisza,* (title means "Biographies of Workers"), Ksiegarnia Powszechna, 1937; *Proletariat i Kultura* (title means "Proletariat and Culture"), Proletariatum Ksiegarnia Powszechna, 1938.

Cross Roads of Two Continents: A Democratic Federation of East-Central Europe, Columbia University Press, 1945; *The Polish Worker: A Study of a Social Stratum* (large part written in Polish), translation by Norbert Guterman, Roy, 1945; *Socjalism Humanistyczny* (title means ((Humanistic Socialism")), Polish Socialist Alliance (New York), 1946; (editor) *European Ideologies: A Survey of 20th Century Political Ideas,* introduction by Robert M. MacIver, Philosophical Library, 1948; (editor with Rex Hopper and Samuel Koenig) *Sociology* (readings), Prentice-Hall, 1954; (editor with Basil J. Vlavianos) *The Struggle for Tomorrow: Modern Political Ideologies of the Jewish People,* Arts (New York), 1954; *Foreign Policy Analysis,* preface by Adolf A. Berle, Jr., Philosophical Library, 1954; *The Seizure of Political Power in a Century of Revolutions,* Philosophical Library, 1958, portions of this book with added chapters by Rex D. Hopper published in Spanish as *Un Siglo de Revolucion,* National Autonomous University of Mexico, 1959; *Druga Rewolucja Przemyslowa* (title means "Second Industrial Revolution"), Swiatlo (Paris), 1958.

O Wartosciach Spolecznych (title means "On Social Values''), Polish Institute of Arts and Sciences in America, 1961; *Uwagi o Zmianie Spolecznej,* introduction by Norman Thomas, Democratic Press and Liberty Publications (London), 1964; *World Politics and Tension Areas,* New York University Press, 1966; *Valori Sociale e Struttura* (title means "Social Values and Structure"), Institute of Empirical Research, University of Rome, 1967; *Violence in Politics,* Mouton, 1973; *Il Paese: Values and Social Change in an Italian Village,* New York University Press, 1974; *Contadini, Rocche, Contrade,* University of Rome, 1974; *The Revolutionary Party: Essays in the Sociology of Politics,* Greenwood Press, 1974.

Contributor: Joseph E. Roucek, editor, *Central-Eastern Europe,* Prentice-Hall, 1946; Roucek, *Contemporary Sociology,* Philosophical Library, 1958; *La Fonction publique internationale et l'action internationale d'assistance technique,* [Paris], 1958; Kirkham, Levy, and Croty, editors, *Assassination and Political Violence,* U.S. Government Printing Office, 1970; *Boundaries and Regions,* Lint, 1973; Sidney Hook and others, editors, *The Philosophy of the Curriculum,* Prometheus Press, 1975; L. Pellicani, editor, *Sociologia dei mutamenti rivoluzionari,* Vallecchi, 1976. Associate editor and contributor, *Slavonic Encyclopedia,* Philosophical Library, 1949. Syndicated columnist for Asian and Latin American newspapers, Foreign News Service, 1962-63. Contributor to journals in United States, Belgium, Sweden, India, Mexico, Germany, Poland, Costa Rica, Italy, and France.

WORK IN PROGRESS: Ethics in the Borderland: Slavs and Latins in a Border Region, a study of the causes of peace based on fieldwork on the Italian-Yugoslav border in 1974; *Values and Social Change,* completion expected in 1978.

SIDELIGHTS: Many of Feliks Gross's books have been published in Italian, Japanese, Polish, Spanish, and Chinese.

*   *   *

GROSS, Franz B(runo) 1919-

PERSONAL: Born July 29, 1919, in Vienna, Austria; naturalized American citizen; son of Max and Alice (Koref) Gross; married Margaret Chappell, December 7, 1952; children: Christopher John. *Education:* Undergraduate study in Vienna and Rome; Harvard University, M.A., 1943, Ph.D., 1952; also studied at Graduate Institute of International Relations, Geneva, 1947-50, and University of Heidelberg, summer, 1948; Academy of International Law, Diploma, 1958. *Home:* 5404 Plainfield St., Pittsburgh, Pa. 15217. *Office:* Graduate School of Arts and Sciences, Dequesne University, Pittsburgh, Pa. 15219.

CAREER: Grinnell College, Grinnell, Iowa, lecturer, 1943-44; *Des Moines Register and Tribune,* Des Moines, Iowa, member of editorial staff, 1944; U.S. Military Government, Stuttgart, Germany, press officer, 1946-47; *Look,* correspondent at United Nations Headquarters, Geneva, Switzerland, 1947-50; *United Nations Bulletin,* New York City, editor-writer, 1950-51; visiting professor at Babson Institute of Business Administration, Babson Park, Mass., 1951-52, and Queens College (now Queens College of the City University of New York), Flushing, N.Y., 1953; City College (now City College of the City University of New York), New York City, assistant professor of government, 1953-54; Bradford College, Bradford, Mass., professor of political science and acting chairman of department of social science, 1954-59; Widener College, Chester, Pa., professor of polit-

ical science, 1959-71, distinguished professor, 1967-71, chairman of Liberal Arts Division, 1962-67, chairman of department of political science, 1967-71; Duquesne University, Pittsburgh, Pa., professor of international affairs and African studies, 1971—, dean of Graduate School of Arts and Sciences, 1971-76. Member of faculty, Cambridge Center for Adult Education, Cambridge, Mass., 1951-54; staff writer, *New York Times,* summer, 1960; visiting professor at University of Pennsylvania, 1961-63, Institute on Indian Civilization, Mysore, 1965, University of Dakar, 1966-67, Center for Arms Control and International Security Studies, University of Pittsburgh, 1976-77, and at John F. Kennedy Institute for North American Studies, Free University of Berlin, summer, 1977; visiting lecturer at University of Oslo, University of Louvian, University of Bujumbura, Burundi, and Academy of International Law and Relations, Bucharest, Romania. Consultant on United Nations, Foreign Policy Research Institute, University of Pennsylvania, 1962-67. Member of board, Delaware County Research Council. *Military service:* U.S. Army, Intelligence, 1944-46.

MEMBER: International Society for Educational, Cultural, and Scientific Exchange (executive secretary), Middle Atlantic International Studies Association (member of executive committee), American Political Science Association, American Society of International Law, American Association of University Professors, American Professors for Peace in the Middle East (vice-chairman), International Studies Association (president, Philadelphia area), Northeastern Political Science Association (vice-president), Pennsylvania Political Science Association (member of executive committee; vice-president, 1974-76; president, 1976-78), African Studies Association (fellow). *Awards, honors:* Research fellow at Academy of International Law, 1958; Fulbright fellow in India, 1965; Outstanding Teaching award, Widener College, 1966; Social Science Research Council grant, 1974-75; Fulbright grant, 1975.

WRITINGS: (Editor) Waldo Chamberlin and others, *The United States and the United Nations,* University of Oklahoma Press, 1964; (contributing editor) Joseph Dunner, editor, *Dictionary of Political Science,* Philosophical Library, 1964; (contributor) R. J. Tresolini and R. T. Frost, editors, *Cases in American National Government and Politics,* Prentice-Hall, 1966; (contributor) Dunner, editor, *Handbook of World History,* Philosophical Library, 1967; *Relations between National and City Government and Administration in Francophone West Africa,* Institute of African Government, Lincoln University (Pa.), 1968. Contributor to professional journals, including *Middle East Review, Journal of American Professors for Peace in the Middle East, African Report,* and *Orbis.* Also contributor of reviews to periodicals, including *Perspectives, World Affairs, Pittsburgh Sunday Press,* and *Duquesne Law Review.*

WORK IN PROGRESS: A research project, "Egypt and Arms Control."

SIDELIGHTS: Franz B. Gross regularly visits western Europe. He has travelled to all of the countries in eastern Europe, western Europe, and the Mediterranean area (except Albania and Libya), most countries of Africa and the Caribbean, as well as the Far East and South America. He has appeared on television and radio as an expert on international affairs, and is a frequent member of panels devoted to this subject.

The United States and the United Nations has been translated into Portugese.

GROSS, Joel 1949-

PERSONAL: Born March 22, 1949, in New York, N.Y.; son of David Charles (an editor) and Esther (Pearl) Gross; married Linda Sanders, May, 1973. *Education:* Queens College of the City University of New York, B.A. (with high honors in English), 1971; Columbia University, M.A. (with high honors), 1972. *Politics:* Liberal Democrat. *Religion:* Jewish. *Home:* 245 East 63rd St., New York, N.Y. 10021.

CAREER: Writer. *Awards, honors:* John Golden Annual Award, Queens College of the City University of New York, 1970, for *Bubble's Shadow.*

WRITINGS: *Bubble's Shadow,* Crown, 1970; *The Young Man Who Wrote Soap Operas,* Scribner, 1975. Contributor of stories to *Seventeen* and *New Yorker.* Fiction editor, *Whereas.*

* * *

GROSS, Johannes Heinrich 1916-

PERSONAL: Born September 13, 1916, in Bonn, Germany; son of Michael (a farmer) and Anna Maria (Pung) Gross. *Education:* Theological Faculty of Trier, student, 1937-39, 1945-48, Habilitation in Old Testament, 1955; University of Bonn, Dr.Theol., 1951; Biblical Institute, Rome, Italy, Lic.Bibl., 1953. *Home:* Agnesstrasse 13, 84 Regensburg, Germany. *Office:* University of Regensburg, 84 Regensburg, Germany.

CAREER: Secular priest; Theological Faculty of Trier, Trier, Germany, assistant professor, 1953-57, ordinary professor of theology, 1957-68; University of Saarbruecken, Saarbruecken, Germany, assistant professor of theology, 1957-68; University of Regensburg, Regensburg, Germany, ordinary professor, 1968—, dean of Theological Faculty, 1968-69. *Military service:* German Army, 1939-45. *Member:* Society of Biblical Literature, Organisation Beirat der Goerresgesellschaft.

WRITINGS: *Weltherrschaft als religioese Idee,* Hanstein, 1953; *Weltfrieden im Alten Testament und Alten Orient,* Paulinus-Verlag, 1956, 2nd edition, 1967; *Kleine Bibelkunde zum Alten Testament,* Koesel, 1967, translation published as *Biblical Introduction to the Old Testament,* University of Notre Dame Press, 1968.

WORK IN PROGRESS: Commentary on the Psalms.

* * *

GROSS, John 1935-

PERSONAL: Born March 12, 1935, in London, England; son of Abraham (a physician) and Muriel Gross; married Miriam May (a journalist), 1965; children: Thomas, Susanna. *Education:* Wadham College, Oxford, M.A., 1955; Princeton University, graduate study, 1958-59. *Home:* 25 Platts Lane, London N.W.3, England. *Agent:* A. D. Peters Ltd., 10 Buckingham St., London WC2N 6BU, England.

CAREER: Victor Gollancz Ltd. (publishers), London, England, editor-in-chief, 1956-58; University of London, Queen Mary College, London, England, lecturer in English, 1959-62; Cambridge University, King's College, Cambridge, England, fellow, 1962-65; *Encounter,* London, England, assistant editor, 1963-65; editorial consultant, *Observer,* 1965—. Rutgers University, visiting professor, 1969. Member of committee, London Library. *Awards, honors:* Harkness fellow at Princeton University, 1958-59; Duff Cooper Memorial Prize, 1969, for *The Rise and Fall of the Man of Letters.*

WRITINGS: (Editor with Gabriel Pearson, and contributor) *Dickens and the Twentieth Century,* Routledge & Kegan Paul, 1962; *The Rise and Fall of the Man of Letters: A Study of the Idiosyncratic and the Humane in Modern Literature,* Macmillan, 1969; *James Joyce,* Viking, 1970; (editor) *The Age of Kipling,* Simon & Schuster, 1971 (published in England as *Rudyard Kipling: The Man, His Work, and His World,* Wiedenfeld & Nicholson, 1972). Contributor to *Commentary, New York Review of Books, New Statesman, Observer, Listener, Times Literary Supplement,* and other publications.

WORK IN PROGRESS: A study of the literature and culture of imperialism.

BIOGRAPHICAL/CRITICAL SOURCES: *Punch,* June 11, 1969; *London Magazine,* June, 1969; *Book World,* July 20, 1969; *New Leader,* September 29, 1969; *New York Times Book Review,* October 5, 1969; *Esquire,* November, 1969; *Commentary,* February, 1970; *Harper's,* March, 1971.†

* * *

GROSSHANS, Henry 1921-

PERSONAL: Born March 19, 1921, in Cheyenne, Wyo.; married Donna Adams, January 21, 1945; children: Geoffrey, Katherine. *Education:* Doane College, A.B., 1943; University of Iowa, A.M., 1947; Oxford University, B.Litt., 1950. *Home:* 830 Southeast Pullman, Wash. 99163. *Office:* Department of History, Washington State University, Pullman, Wash. 99163.

CAREER: Bowling Green University, Bowling Green, Ohio, instructor in history, 1951-52; Washington State University, Pullman, university editor and lecturer in history, 1952—. *Military service:* U.S. Navy, 1943-46; commissioned officer. *Awards, honors:* Rhodes scholar at Oxford University, 1948-50.

WRITINGS: (Editor) *To Find Something New,* Washington State University Press, 1969; *The Search for Modern Europe,* Houghton, 1970. Contributor to historical and other journals. Editor, *Research Studies.*

WORK IN PROGRESS: *The American Intellectual Impulse* (tentative title); "Adolf Hitler: The Artist in Politics," a monograph.

* * *

GROVER, Linda 1934-

PERSONAL: Born January 28, 1934, in Nashua, N.H.; daughter of Fred W. (an inventor) and Mildred (Clarke) Rauskolb; married Stanley Grover (a singer and actor), April 7, 1956 (divorced); children: Cynthia, Steven, Jamie. *Education:* High school graduate in Las Vegas, Nev., 1950. *Politics:* Independent liberal Democrat. *Religion:* Unitarian. *Home:* 325 Central Park W., New York, N.Y. 10025. *Agent:* Owen Laster, William Morris Agency, 1350 Avenue of the Americas, New York, N.Y. 10019.

CAREER: U.S. House of Representatives, Washington, D.C., clerk of Indian Affairs Subcommittee, 1954-56; occasionally acts in television. Staff member of National Committee for an Effective Congress, 1956, and International Rescue Committee, 1956-58. *Member:* Authors Guild, Screen Actors Guild.

WRITINGS: *The House Keepers,* Harper, 1970. Contributor of material to CBS-TV; also contributor to *McCall's, New York Times, New York Post,* and *Cue.*

WORK IN PROGRESS: A book on cooking without waste; television scripts.

AVOCATIONAL INTERESTS: Water skiing, cooking.

* * *

GRUBBS, Frank Leslie, Jr. 1931-

PERSONAL: Born June 21, 1931, in Lynchburg, Va.; son of Frank Leslie and Grace Louise (Smith) Grubbs; married Carolyn Barrington (a college instructor), July 31, 1965; children: Thomas Ashby, Robert Barrington. *Education:* Lynchburg College, B.A. (cum laude), 1959; University of Virginia, M.A., 1960, Ph.D., 1963. *Religion:* Episcopalian. *Home:* 1706 Baker Rd., Raleigh, N.C. *Office:* Department of History, Meredith College, Raleigh, N.C. 27602.

CAREER: Meade Corp., Lynchburg, Va., laboratory assistant, 1949-52, 1954-59; Meredith College, Raleigh, N.C., assistant professor, 1963-68, associate professor, 1968-73, professor of American history, 1973—, director of American Civilization Program, 1971—. Lecturer for In-School Television, University of North Carolina, 1964-68; lecturer, St. Michael's Church. *Military service:* U.S. Army, 1952-54; served in Korea; became sergeant; received Meritorious Unit Citation. *Member:* American Historical Association, Organization of American Historians, American Association of University Professors, Southern Historical Association, Torch International. *Awards, honors:* Meredith College, named by students as most popular professor, 1964, 1969, trustee's Outstanding Professor Award, 1974; selected one of the Outstanding Young Men of America by U.S. Junior Chamber of Commerce, 1968; National Humanities grant, 1970.

WRITINGS: The Struggle for Labor Loyalty: Gompers, the A.F. of L. and the Pacifists, 1917-1920, Duke University Press, 1968. Contributor to *Labor History, Science and Society, Torch Magazine;* contributor of editorials to Raleigh *News & Observer;* contributor of reviews to *Virginia Quarterly Review, North Carolina Historical Review, American Quarterly, Journal of Southern History,* and *Richmond Newsleader.*

WORK IN PROGRESS: Protecting Labor's Standards: Organized Labor and World War One, for Duke University Press; studies on labor history, socialist history, pacificism, and radical-minority problems.

* * *

GRUENHAGEN, Robert W. 1932-

PERSONAL: Born January 20, 1932, in Great Falls, Mont.; son of William Henry (a machinist) and Helen (Jaraczeski) Gruenhagen; married Jean Shirley Law, July 4, 1952; children: Susan, Stephanie. *Education:* Attended public schools in Great Falls, Mont. *Home:* 707 Red Oak Lane, Arlington, Tex. 76012. *Agent:* Evelyn Oppenheimer, 4505 Fairway Ave., Dallas, Tex. 75219.

CAREER: Montana Air National Guard, Great Falls, aircraft maintenance technician, 1950-51, jet engine maintenance supervisor, 1954-60, aircraft maintenance officer, 1960-66; Texas Air National Guard, Dallas, aircraft maintenance officer, 1966—. *Military service:* U.S. Air Force, 1951-54; became captain. *Member:* Air Force Association, Confederate Air Force.

WRITINGS: Mustang: The Story of the P-51 Fighter, Arco, 1970.

WORK IN PROGRESS: Research on development of the jet engine and development of the Messerschmitt Me-262 fighter.

* * *

GRUMLEY, Michael 1941-

PERSONAL: Born July 6, 1941, in Bettendorf, Iowa; son of Charles Francis (vice-president, J. I. Case) and Elizabeth Mary (Nowak) Grumley. *Education:* Attended University of Denver, Mexico City College, University of Wisconsin—Milwaukee, and School of Visual Arts, New York, N.Y.; graduate study at City College of the City University of New York and University of Iowa. *Residence:* New York, N.Y. and Wisconsin. *Agent:* Candida Donadio & Associates, Inc., 111 West 57th St., New York, N.Y. 10019.

CAREER: Principally occupied in writing and drawing.

WRITINGS: (With Robert Ferro) *Atlantis: The Autobiography of a Search,* Doubleday, 1970; *There Are Giants in the Earth,* Doubleday, 1974; *Hard Corps,* Dutton, 1977; *Night People,* Scribner, 1978.

WORK IN PROGRESS: A novel, *A World of Men.*

BIOGRAPHICAL/CRITICAL SOURCES: Il Messaggero, September 26, 1968; *New York Times,* January 23, 1969, January 25, 1970; *Chicago Tribune Magazine,* February 14, 1971; *Milwaukee Sentinel,* February 19, 1975; *London Evening News,* May 21, 1975; *London Daily Mirror,* May 26, 1975; *Chicago Sun-Times,* January 2, 1976; *Village Voice,* March 14, 1977.

* * *

GRUNWALD, Stefan 1933-
(Eric Ludwig, Frederic Ludwig)

PERSONAL: Born November 28, 1933, in Berlin, Germany; son of Michael (a psychiatrist) and Rut (Lowe) Grunwald; married Harriet Zwerdling, June 16, 1957; children: Eric Michael David, Susan-Joy. *Education:* Hunter College (now Hunter College of the City University of New York), B.A., 1961; University of Colorado, M.A., 1962, Ph.D., 1965. *Home:* 7332 Elvin Ct., Norfolk, Va. 23505. *Office:* Department of Foreign Languages, Old Dominion University, Norfolk, Va. 23508.

CAREER: Old Dominion University, Norfolk, Va., 1968—, began as associate professor, currently professor of comparative literature. *Scope* (magazine), Norfolk, Va., managing editor, 1970—. *Military service:* U.S. Army, 1954-56. *Member:* Modern Language Association of America.

WRITINGS: A Biography of Johann Michael Moscherosch, 1601-1669, Lange (Berne), 1969; (editor) *Osten und Westen,* Harcourt, 1970; (editor with Bruce A. Beattie, and contributor) *Theorie und Kritik: Zur vergleichenden und neueren deutschen Literatur,* Francke (Munich), 1974. Regular contributor to *Virginian Pilot;* contributor to *Washington Post, Manhattan East,* and to scholarly journals.

WORK IN PROGRESS: Two novels, *By Trial and Error* and *No Time for Answers;* a third book, *Bertold Brecht in Hollywood;* a translation of a seventeenth-century novel by J. H. Moscherosch, for Ungar.

SIDELIGHTS: "My true vocational interest is in writing prose," Stefan Grunwald told *CA,* "an area in which I have had the least success up to now. But everything I do revolves about the question of social problems affecting me and others...."

GRUSKIN, Alan D(aniel)   1904-1970

December 28, 1904—October 7, 1970; American art dealer and author. Obituaries: *New York Times,* October 8, 1970. (See index for *CA* sketch)

*   *   *

GRUTZMACHER, Harold M(artin), Jr.   1930-

PERSONAL: Born November 17, 1930, in Chicago, Ill.; son of Harold Martin and Irene (Kowalski) Grutzmacher; married Marjorie Sharlene Andersen, 1955; children: Stephen Robert, Sharon Lynn. *Education:* Beloit College, B.A., 1952; Northwestern University, M.A., 1953, Ph.D., 1962. *Address:* Box 153, Ephraim, Wis. 54211.

CAREER: Carthage College, Carthage, Ill., assistant professor of English, 1958-60; Knox College, Galesburg, Ill., 1960-65, began as instructor, became assistant professor of English; Parsons College, Fairfield, Iowa, chairman of department of rhetoric, 1965-67; University of Tampa, Tampa, Fla., vice-president of academic affairs, 1967-70; Beloit College, Beloit, Wis., dean of students, beginning 1970. Has given poetry readings and served as judge in poetry competitions. *Military service:* U.S. Army, 1956-68. *Member:* American Association of University Professors, Modern Language Association of America, Tau Kappa Epsilon.

WRITINGS: A Giant of My World, Golden Quill, 1960. Poems have been published in *Cornucopia, American Weave, Approach, Epos, Wormwood Review, Northwestern Tri-Quarterly,* and a number of other literary periodicals. Book reviewer, *Chicago Tribune,* 1961-65.†

*   *   *

GRYNBERG, Henryk   1936-

PERSONAL: Born July 4, 1936, in Warsaw, Poland; son of Abraham (a dairy merchant) and Sofia (Stolik) Grynberg; married Ruth Maria Meyers, January 24, 1964 (divorced, 1966); married Krystyna Walczak (an actress), July 30, 1967; children: (second marriage) Deborah Maria. *Education:* University of Warsaw, Master in Journalism, 1959; University of California, Los Angeles, M.A., 1971. *Politics:* None.

CAREER: Jewish State Theatre, Warsaw, Poland, actor and translator, 1959-67, secretary, Union of Workers of Culture and Art, 1966-67; University of California, Los Angeles, teaching assistant in Russian language and literature, beginning 1971. *Member:* Union of Polish Writers (Warsaw, 1965-69), Union of Polish Writers Abroad. *Awards, honors:* Annual literary prize of Koscielski Foundation (Switzerland), 1966, for *Zydowska wojna;* Tadeusz Borowski fellowship (Poland), 1966.

WRITINGS: Ekipa "Antygona" (short stories), Panstwowy Instytut Wydawniczy (Warsaw), 1963; *Swieto kamieni* (poems), Instytut Wydawniczy "Pax" (Warsaw), 1964; *Zydowska wojna* (novella), Czytelnik (Warsaw), 1965, translation by C. Wieniewska published in England as *Child of the Shadows,* Vallentine, Mitchell, 1969; *Zwyciestow,* Institut Litteraire (Paris), 1969; *Antynostalgia* (poems), Oficyna Poetow i Malarzy (London), 1971.

Contributor and translator from English to the Polish for *Kultura* (Paris), *Wiadomosci* (London), and *America Illustrated.*

SIDELIGHTS: Henryk Grynberg told *CA:* "My original writing is inspired by my being one of the very few child-survivors of the Jewish holocaust in Eastern Europe and recently by the revival of Jewish persecution in my homeland which forced me to self-exile. My writing is concerned with ethics, including its religious and ideological aspects, problems of identity. My stories are realistic and so are my poems."

BIOGRAPHICAL/CRITICAL SOURCES: C. Wieniewska, editor, *Polish Writing Today,* Penguin (London), 1967; *Yiddisher Kemfer,* December 15, 1967; *New York Times,* December 31, 1967; *Los Angeles Times,* December 31, 1967; *Forward,* January 8, 1968; *Hadassah,* March, 1968; *Volksbote* (Munich), May 17, 1969; *L'Arche* (Paris), June/July, 1970.†

*   *   *

GUENTHER, Charles (John)   1920-

PERSONAL: Born April 29, 1920, in St. Louis, Mo.; son of Charles R. and Hulda C. (Schuessler) Guenther; married Esther Klund, April 11, 1942; children: Charles John, Jr., Cecile and Christine (twins). *Education:* Jefferson College, St. Louis, Mo., student, 1937-38; Harris Teachers College, A.A., 1940; Webster College, B.A., 1973, M.A., 1974. *Home:* 2935 Russell Blvd., St. Louis, Mo. 63104.

CAREER: Clerk, U.S. Employment Service, St. Louis, Mo., 1941-42, U.S. Corps of Engineers, St. Louis, 1942-43; U.S. Air Force Aeronautical Chart and Information Center, St. Louis, 1943-75, began as clerk, 1943, assistant chief librarian with dual assignments as historian, translator, and geographer, 1948-59, supervisory librarian and chief of Technical Library, 1959-75. Poet and translator of poetry mainly from the Italian, French, and Spanish, with his work appearing in more than two hundred American and foreign periodicals. Has given readings of his own and translated poetry at colleges in the Middle West and West. Instructor in creative writing at People's Art Center, St. Louis, 1953-56; poetry workshop leader at McKendree Writer's Conference, Lebanon, Ill., Green Lake Writers' Conference, Green Lake, Wis., Upper Peninsula Creative Writers' Conference, Marquette, Mich., and in St. Davids, Penn., Cape Cod, Hyannis, Mass., and conferences elsewhere, 1955—; McKendree Writer's Conference, assistant director, 1966, director, 1969-73; instructor, McKendree College, 1976. St. Louis Poetry Center, chairman of board of chancellors, 1969-72, president, 1974-76.

MEMBER: Poetry Society of America, Missouri Writers' Guild (president, 1973-74), Special Libraries Association (president of Greater St. Louis chapter, 1969-70), St. Louis Writers' Guild (president, 1959, 1976), Rose Society of Greater St. Louis. *Awards, honors:* Commander, Order of Merit of the Italian Republic, 1973; James Joyce Award, Poetry Society of America, 1974, for poem "Missouri Woods"; Missouri Library Association Literary Award, 1974; American Bicentennial Medal, French government, 1976.

WRITINGS: (Translator) *Modern Italian Poets,* Inferno Press, 1961; (translator with Samuel Beckett, Edouard Roditi, and Ruth Whitman) *Selected Poems of Alain Bosquet,* New Directions, 1963; (translator) *Paul Valery in English,* Olivant, 1970; *Phrase/Paraphrase* (original poems and translations), Prairie Press, 1970; (translator) Juan Ramon Jimenez, *High Sundowns: Twelve Poems of Death and Resurrection,* St. Louis University, 1974; *Voices in the Dark,* The Printery, 1974.

Contributor: Angel Flores, editor, *An Anthology of Spanish Poetry,* Doubleday, 1961; *The French in the Mississippi Valley,* University of Illinois Press, 1965; David Ray, editor, *From the Hungarian Revolution,* Cornell University

Press, 1966; Willis Barnstone, editor, *Modern European Poetry*, Bantam, 1966; Robert Bly, editor, *The Sea and the Honeycomb*, Sixties Press, 1966; Donald Junkins, editor, *Contemporary World Poets*, Harcourt, 1976; Hardie St. Martin, editor, *Roots and Wings*, Harper, 1976. His own poems have appeared in *New Directions, Literary Review, Nation, Poetry*, and other periodicals in America; translations of his poetry also have been published in Greece, Italy, Japan, and other countries abroad. Reviewer of poetry and criticism for *St. Louis Post-Dispatch*, 1953—, and *St. Louis Globe-Democrat*, 1972—. Poetry editor, *Weid: The Sensibility Revue*, 1972-78; contributing editor, *Webster Review*, 1976—; consulting editor, *Poet Lore*.

WORK IN PROGRESS: "Although I plan to write and publish more of my own poetry than translations . . . I'll continue to work on the major (and even neglected) foreign poets: Rene Char, Alain Bosquet, Pierre Emmanuel, L. S. Senghor, V. Aleixandre, Franco Fortini, Ugo Fasolo, Nelo Risi—the list is endless."

SIDELIGHTS: Charles Guenther writes that he "began writing and translating poetry at the age of 17, and vowed I'd stop translating at 25—but never did stop. The challenge of poetry in other languages than English is so persistent that any poet who knows other languages ought to work in them to improve his own poetry. Although editing has occupied much of my time (until 1978), I plan to devote more time to writing after that time."

Guenther received the Order of Merit of the Italian Republic for his work in translating Italian poets into English. James Boyer writes of the translations of eleven poets included in the volume *Modern Italian Poets:* "Without benefit . . . of the originals these (in English) are undeniably beautiful; Guenther, to be sure *is* a poet, and makes poetry . . . a statement which (in the light of an admitted prejudice against translations generally) is intended as a commendation. The credit due Guenther, *as poet,* is verified by the fact that there is much less variety in manners than should be anticipated from many different individuals with the widely-varied backgrounds Guenther outlines."

The original poetry of Charles Guenther has appeared in many magazines, but it wasn't until the publication of *Phrase/Paraphrase* that they were published in book form. In reviewing this volume, Peter L. Simpson writes: "His vast range of interests testifies to the random, occasional nature of contemporary experience. The feelings are like phrases, fragmentary, suggestive of any number of possible relations. The burden of his art is to produce a syntax that can articulate essences. He reflects one of the great concerns of all modern art (the list of allusions shows how many great names he is at home with): the process by which suggestion moves to affirmation. . . . It is clear that his deepest ecstacy has always been in the act of poetry itself. That is where he has found and given his richest fulfillment."

In his acceptance of the Order of Merit of the Italian Republic, Charles Guenther remarked: ". . . Even in a world which tends to be imitative, regimented and standardized, each poet is his own definition of poet, his own conscience, his own value, held in abeyance perhaps for a more solicitous appraisal by a generation later than his own. And strangely in this world even the universal poet or artist . . . often goes long unacknowledge by a society which judges part of his work for the whole, or rashly condemns him for a few mistakes or failures and ignores some overwhelming weight of the success of his genius."

BIOGRAPHICAL/CRITICAL SOURCES: St. Louis Post-Dispatch, June 30, 1957, April 28, 1961, January 24, 1971; *Trace*, April-June, 1961; *Focus/Midwest*, September, 1962; *Bulletin of the New York Public Library*, October, 1968; *St. Louis Globe-Democrat*, April 25-26, 1970, January 9-10, 1971, March 31-April 1, 1973, January 22, 1974, September 28-29, 1974; *Special Libraries*, May-June, 1971; *Show-Me Libraries*, Volume XXIV, number 1, October, 1973, Volume XXV, number 10, July, 1974; *American Libraries*, March, 1974.

*   *   *

GUERRIER, Dennis 1923-

PERSONAL: Surname rhymes with "terrier"; born December 19, 1923, in London, England; son of Henry Benjamin and Dorothy (Carter) Guerrier; married Betty Ruth Bell, June 3, 1950; children: Yvonne Ruth, John Dennis. *Education:* Attended schools in England until fourteen and then continuation classes. *Home:* 505 Willoughby House, Barbican, London EC2, England. *Agent:* Curtis Brown Ltd., 1 Craven Hill, London W2 3EW, England. *Office:* Department of Health and Social Security, State House, High Holborn, London W.C.1, England.

CAREER: British Civil Service, London, England, 1942—, staff training officer, 1964-70, senior executive officer in Department of Health and Social Security, 1970—. *Military service:* British Army, Royal Artillery, 1943-48, served in Italy and Africa.

WRITINGS: (With Joan Richards) *State of Emergency: A Novel of Alternatives*, Heinemann, 1969, Houghton, 1970; (with John Garforth) *Sleep, and the City Trembles*, Panther Books, 1970; *Solo Noughts and Crosses*, Panther Books, 1970; *Solo Boxes*, Panther Books, 1970. Writer of four books on basic physics published by Blond Educational, 1970.

WORK IN PROGRESS: A novel, *Shadows and the Substance;* television plays for BBC-TV.

BIOGRAPHICAL/CRITICAL SOURCES: Books and Bookmen, June, 1969, July, 1969; *New York Times*, July 20, 1970.

*   *   *

GUILFORD, Joan S. 1928-

PERSONAL: Born September 28, 1928, in Lincoln, Neb.; daughter of J. Paul (a psychologist) and Ruth (Burke) Guilford; married Franklin B. McClung, September 1, 1951 (divorced); married Frederick L. McGuire, November 16, 1972; children: Jacqueline M., Scott S., Michael P. *Education:* University of Nebraska, B.A., 1949; University of Southern California, M.A., 1951, Ph.D., 1963. *Politics:* Democrat. *Religion:* Episcopalian. *Home:* 220 City Blvd. W., Apt. 112, Orange, Calif. 92668.

CAREER: Sheridan Supply Co., Beverly Hills, Calif., psychologist, 1951-62; American Institutes for Research, Pittsburgh, Pa., research scientist in Los Angeles (Calif.) office, 1962-64, director of Los Angeles office, 1964-66; McDonnell-Douglas Corp., Douglas Aircraft Division, Long Beach, Calif., director of industrial research, 1966-67; Holy Cross Hospital, Mission Hills, Calif., director of hospital operations and training research project, 1967-69; General Behavioral Systems, Inc., Torrance, Calif., senior behavioral scientist, 1969-72; Sheridan Psychological Services, Inc., Orange, Calif., executive director, 1972—.

MEMBER: American Psychological Association, Human Factors Society, Western Psychological Association, Psi

Chi, Sigma Xi, Phi Kappa Phi. *Awards, honors:* U.S. Public Health Service research grants, 1963-67; Metropolitan Life-National Safety Council Award of Merit for research in accident prevention, 1966; U.S. Office of Education contracts, 1970-72.

WRITINGS: (Contributor) S. V. Zagona, editor, *Studies and Issues in Smoking Behavior,* University of Arizona Press, 1967; (contributor) E. F. Borgatta and R. R. Evans, editors, *Smoking, Health, and Behavior,* Aldine, 1969; (with D. E. Gray) *Motivation and Modern Management,* Addison-Wesley, 1970; (with J. P. Guilford and W. S. Zimmerman) *The Guilford-Zimmerman Temperament Survey Handbook,* Robert R. Knapp, 1976. Author of research reports, a number of them for Douglas Aircraft; contributor of about twenty articles to psychological journals.

AVOCATIONAL INTERESTS: Reading, theater, gourmet cooking.

* * *

GUITHER, Harold D. 1927-

PERSONAL: Surname is pronounced *Guy*-ther; born June 16, 1927, in Walnut, Ill.; son of Benjamin E. and Alma (Attig) Guither; married Jo Marie Jackson, November 1, 1953 (died May 17, 1973); married Lois Downey, August 16, 1975; children: (first marriage) Bruce, Victoria, Glenn. *Education:* University of Illinois, B.S., 1949, M.S., 1950, Ph.D., 1962; Washington University, St. Louis, Mo., graduate study, 1951. *Politics:* Independent. *Religion:* Presbyterian. *Home:* 613 Harding Dr., Urbana, Ill. 61801. *Office:* Department of Agricultural Economics, University of Illinois, Urbana, Ill. 61801.

CAREER: Doane Agricultural Service, Inc. (agricultural publications and research), St. Louis, Mo., agricultural economist and editor, 1950-56; University of Illinois, Urbana, assistant professor, Agricultural Extension, 1956-63, chief of party, University of Illinois-U.S. Agency for International Development contract in Jordan, 1964-66, associate professor, 1966-74, professor of agricultural economics, 1974—. *Military service:* U.S. Naval Reserve, 1945-46. *Member:* American Agricultural Economics Association, Agricultural History Society, Gamma Sigma Delta, Exchange Club of Urbana. *Awards, honors:* Agricultural communications award, American Association of Agricultural College Editors, 1961; American Agricultural Economics Association, Distinguished Extension Publication Award, 1973, Distinguished Extension Program Award, 1976.

WRITINGS: (With W. N. Thompson) *Mission Overseas: A Handbook for U.S. Families in Developing Countries,* University of Illinois Press, 1969; *Heritage of Plenty: A Guide to the Economic Development of U.S. Agriculture,* Interstate, 1972. Contributor to agricultural journals.

AVOCATIONAL INTERESTS: Photography, Middle East affairs.

* * *

GUNDERS, Henry 1924-

PERSONAL: Born June 30, 1924, in Munich, Germany; son of Paul L. (an accountant) and Rose (Cheikowsky) Gunders; married Elaine L. Schantz; children: Susan R., David A., Joan M. *Education:* Boston University, B.S. in B.A. (cum laude), 1950; New York University, M.B.A., 1953. *Home:* Mead's Point, Greenwich, Conn. 06830. *Office:* Price Waterhouse & Co., 60 Broad St., New York, N.Y.

CAREER: S. D. Leidesdorf & Co. (certified public accoun-

tants), New York City, staff accountant, 1950-51; Price Waterhouse & Co. (certified public accountants), New York City, accountant, 1951-60, partner, 1960—. *Military service:* U.S. Army; became sergeant. *Member:* American Institute of Certified Public Accountants, National Association of Accountants, American Management Association. *Awards, honors:* Lybrand Gold Medal of National Association of Accountants, 1965, for outstanding article of the year.

WRITINGS: Financial Planning and Control in the Meat Packing Industry, American Meat Institute, 1965; (with Raymond A. Hoffman) *Inventories: A Guide to Their Control, Costing and Effect upon Income and Taxes,* 2nd edition, Ronald, 1970.

* * *

GUNDERSON, Doris V.

PERSONAL: Born in Glyndon, Minn.; daughter of B. J. and Rena (Jerpseth) Gunderson; married Carlton M. Singleton (an educator), October 2, 1963. *Education:* University of Minnesota, Ph.D., 1960. *Religion:* Lutheran. *Home:* 2111 Jefferson Davis Hwy., Arlington, Va. 22202. *Office:* U.S. Office of Education, Washington, D.C. 20202.

CAREER: U.S. Office of Education, Washington, D.C., chief of reading section, 1966-68; Center for Applied Linguistics, Washington, D.C., executive director of interdisciplinary committee on reading problems, 1968-69; U.S. Office of Education, education specialist, 1970—. *Member:* International Reading Association (member of commission on quality teacher education), National Council of Teachers of English (associate chairman of committee on research), American Educational Research Association, National Association for Bilingual Education, Teachers of English to Speakers of Other Languages.

WRITINGS: Language and Reading: An Interdisciplinary Approach, Center for Applied Linguistics, 1970.

* * *

GUNDRY, Robert H(orton) 1932-

PERSONAL: Born October 15, 1932, in Los Angeles, Calif.; son of Norman Clifton (a minister) and Lolita (Hinshaw) Gundry; married Lois Obenchain, July 1, 1954; children: Judith, Connie, Mark. *Education:* Los Angeles Baptist College and Seminary, B.A., 1954, B.D., 1957; University of Basel, graduate study, 1960; University of Manchester, Ph.D., 1961. *Home:* 611 Cowles Rd., Santa Barbara, Calif. 93103. *Office:* Westmont College, 955 La Paz, Santa Barbara, Calif. 93103.

CAREER: Westmont College, Santa Barbara, Calif., assistant professor, 1962-66, associate professor of biblical studies, 1966-70, professor of New Testament and Greek, 1970—, chairman of department of religious studies and philosophy, 1966—. *Member:* Studiorum Novi Testamenti Societas, Society of Biblical Literature, American Academy of Religion, Evangelical Theological Society.

WRITINGS: The Use of the Old Testament in St. Matthew's Gospel, E. J. Brill, 1967; *A Survey of the New Testament,* Zondervan, 1970; *The Church and the Tribulation,* Zondervan, 1973; *Soma in Biblical Theology,* Cambridge University Press, 1976. Contributor to *Pictorial Bible Encyclopedia,* Zondervan, and to professional journals in the United States and Europe.

WORK IN PROGRESS: A commentary on the Gospel of Matthew; contributions for *New International Standard Bible Encyclopedia.*

SIDELIGHTS: Robert H. Gundry has reading and research competence in German, French, Greek, Hebrew, and Aramaic, and some ability in Latin and Syriac.

* * *

GUNJI, Masakatsu 1913-

PERSONAL: Born July 7, 1913, in Sapporo, Japan; son of Ichisaburo (a businessman) and Ai (Shioya) Gunji; married Tetsuko Nomoto, March 4, 1949 (died, 1963); married Chiyoe Matsumoto (a professor), April 4, 1970; children: (first marriage) Keiko (Mrs. Mamoru Miyasaka), Yoshiko. *Education:* Waseda University, graduate. *Home:* 2-48-2 Otsuka, Bunkyo-ku, Tokyo, Japan. *Office:* Department of Literature, Waseda University, Totsukacho, Shinjuku-ku, Tokyo, Japan.

CAREER: Waseda University, Tokyo, Japan, staff of Tsubouchi Memorial Theatre Museum, 1939-49, lecturer, 1949-55, assistant professor, 1955-60, professor of literature, 1960—, councilor of Tsubouchi Memorial Theatre Museum, 1965—. Member of experts committee, National Theatre of Japan, 1966—, and National Commission for Protection of Cultural Property, Board of Culture of Japanese Ministry of Education, 1967—. *Member:* Japanese Society for Theatre Research, (officer, 1963—), Society of History of Folk Customs of Japan (councilor and officer, 1967—). *Awards, honors:* Award of Art in the Kabuki, 1954, and Art Festival Encouragement Prize for recording, "Nihonbuyo Taikei," both from Minister of Education.

WRITINGS: Kabuki, translation by John Bester, Kodansha Publishers, 1969; *Buyo: The Classical Dance,* translation by Don Kenny, Weatherhill, 1970. Author of fifteen books on Kabuki published in Japanese.

WORK IN PROGRESS: History of Kabuki; Dictionary of Japanese Dance.

AVOCATIONAL INTERESTS: Painting, travel.

* * *

GUNTER, (J.) Bradley (Hunt) 1940-

PERSONAL: Born December 8, 1940, in Norfolk, Va.; son of J. A. and Mary Virginia (Whalen) Gunter; married Susan Hart, December 27, 1962 (divorced); married Elizabeth Beale, July 16, 1977; children: (first marriage) Bradley Hunt, Valerie Mason. *Education:* University of Richmond, A.B. (with honors), 1962; University of Virginia, M.A., 1963, Ph.D., 1969. *Politics:* Democrat. *Religion:* Episcopalian. *Home:* 4800 Charmian Rd., Richmond, Va. 23226. *Office:* Federal Reserve Bank of Richmond, 9th and Franklin, Richmond, Va. 23219.

CAREER: University of Virginia, Charlottesville, instructor and junior instructor in English, 1964-67; Washington and Lee University, Lexington, Va., instructor in English, 1967-69; Boston College, Chestnut Hill, Mass., assistant professor of modern literature, 1969-71; Federal Reserve Bank of Richmond, Richmond, Va., editor of special publications, 1971-76, assistant cashier and secretary, 1973-74, assistant vice-president and secretary, 1975—. First vice-president, Federated Arts Council of Richmond; member of board, Memorial Guidance Clinic; secretary, member of executive committee, and trustee, St. Paul Endowment Fund, Inc.; judge, William Faulkner Foundation First Novel Award, 1967-69. Consultant, National Endowment for the Humanities, 1973-77. *Member:* Modern Language Association of America, American Association of University Professors, English Institute, Society of American Archivists, Biblio-

graphical Society of University of Virginia, Virginia Society of Mayflower Descendants (librarian and member of board), Phi Beta Kappa, Omicron Delta Kappa. *Awards, honors:* Faculty research grant, Washington and Lee University, 1968.

WRITINGS: Checklist of T. S. Eliot, C. E. Merrill, 1969; *Guide to T. S. Eliot,* C. E. Merrill, 1970; (editor) *Studies in "The Waste Land,"* C. E. Merrill, 1971. Contributor to *Queen's Quarterly* and other journals; contributor of reviews to numerous periodicals, including *Virginia Quarterly Review.* Editorial adviser to *Rapier: A Magazine of Satire and Broad Discussion,* 1966-67; editorial consultant to *American Quarterly,* 1970; editor, *Economic Review,* 1971-75.

WORK IN PROGRESS: T. S. Eliot and Anglicanism; Handbook to T. S. Eliot; a textual edition of Hemingway's *Green Hills of Africa;* a critical book on the American personal narrative.

AVOCATIONAL INTERESTS: Travel, hiking, squash, tennis, handball, book-collecting.

* * *

GUNTHER, A(lbert) E(verard) 1903-

PERSONAL: Born November 27, 1903, in Heacham, Norfolk, England; son of Robert Theodore (a writer on the history of science) and Amy (Neville-Rolfe) Gunther. *Education:* Magdalen College, Oxford, B.A., 1925. *Home:* 35 Rudall Crescent, Hampstead, London N.W.3, England.

CAREER: Shell International Petroleum Co., employed as geologist, petroleum engineer, and in various administrative positions in United States, West Indies, Venezuela, Netherlands, Rumania, Germany, and England, 1925-61; full-time writer, 1961—. *Military service:* British Army, 1945-47; became major, General List. *Member:* Geological Society and Royal Geographical Society (both London).

WRITINGS: The German War for Crude Oil in Europe, Petroleum Times (London), 1948; *Rolfe Family Records,* Volumes I-III, privately printed, 1962; *Early Science in Oxford,* Volume XV: *Robert T. Gunther* (biography of his father), Oxford University Press, 1967; *A Century of Zoology of the British Museum, 1815-1914,* Dawson & Sons, 1975; *The Life of William C. M'Intosh, Marine Zoologist of St. Andrews, Scotland,* St. Andrews University Press, 1977. Contributor to *Alpine Journal.*

AVOCATIONAL INTERESTS: History of art; mountaineering, with expeditions in the Sierra Nevada, Venezuelan Andes, Alps, Carpathians, and the Himalaya area of Punjab; gardening, bricklaying; upkeep of century-old property at Heacham in Norfolk.

BIOGRAPHICAL/CRITICAL SOURCES: Times Literary Supplement, October 19, 1967.

* * *

GUSSOW, Joan Dye 1928-

PERSONAL: Born October 4, 1928, in Alhambra, Calif.; daughter of Chester H. (a civil engineer) and M. Joyce (Fisher) Dye; married Alan M. Gussow (an artist and conservationist), October 21, 1956; children: Adam Stefan, Seth James. *Education:* Pomona College, B.A., 1950; Yeshiva University, graduate study, 1965-67; Columbia University, M.Ed., 1974, Ed.D., 1975. *Politics:* "Democrat-liberal." *Home:* 121 New York Ave., Congers, N.Y . 10920. *Office:* Teachers College, Columbia University, New York, N.Y. 10027.

CAREER: Time, Inc., New York City, researcher, 1950-56; Street & Smith Publications, New York City, free-lance writer, 1956-58; Yeshiva University, New York City, editorial and research assistant, 1964-66, editorial and research assistant at Albert Einstein College of Medicine, Bronx, N.Y., 1966-69; Columbia University, Teachers College, New York City, instructor in nutrition, 1970-75, assistant professor of nutrition and education and chairperson of nutrition program, 1975—. *Member:* American Association for the Advancement of Science, American Dietetic Association (member of board of directors), Community Nutrition Institute (vice-president and member of board of directors), Society for Nutrition Education, Consumer Action Now.

WRITINGS: (With Herbert G. Birch) *Disadvantaged Children: Health, Nutrition and School Failure,* Grune, 1970. Contributor of articles to professional journals.

WORK IN PROGRESS: Nutritional Ecology: A Book of Readings; various projects related to nutrition miseducation in America.

SIDELIGHTS: Joan Dye Gussow told *CA:* "My principal area of specialization so far as subject matter is concerned is nutrition; however, my overall focus of interest is in bringing about social and economic change before it is too late. I question the value of writing 'just another book' in pursuing this end—but have concluded that books influence opinion leaders and opinion leaders *may* influence the course of events. I continue to be interested in the 'massest' of the mass media—television."

* * *

GUTERMAN, Stanley S(anford) 1934-

PERSONAL: Born February 19, 1934, in Texarkana, Ark.; son of Joseph and Mary (Pinsker) Guterman; married Marilyn Lefkowitz, June 30, 1960; children: Adam J., Damon G. *Education:* University of Chicago, A.B. (with honors), 1956; Columbia University, Ph.D., 1967. *Home:* 24151 Ridgedale, Oak Park, Mich. 48237. *Office:* Department of Sociology, Wayne State University, Detroit, Mich. 48202.

CAREER: Carleton University, Ottawa, Ontario, assistant professor of sociology, 1965-69; Rutgers University, New Brunswick, N.J., assistant professor of sociology, 1969-72; Long Island University, Southampton, N.Y., associate professor of sociology, 1972-73; Wayne State University, Detroit, Mich., associate professor of sociology, 1973—. *Member:* American Sociological Association, American Association of University Professors.

WRITINGS: The Machiavellians: A Social Psychological Study of Moral Character and Organizational Milieu, University of Nebraska Press, 1970; (contributor) Donald G. McTavish and Herman Loether, editors, *Statistical Analysis: A Laboratory Manual for Sociologists,* Allyn & Bacon, 1970; (contributor) J. John Palen, editor, *Urban America: Conflict and Change,* Holt, 1971; (editor) *Black Psyche: The Modal Personality Patterns of Black Americans,* Glendessary, 1972. Contributor to sociology journals.

SIDELIGHTS: Stanley Guterman told *CA:* "My major interest as a social scientist is in the influences that social structure and personality have on each other. This topic, I believe, holds the key to understanding what changes are needed in order to evolve a society that fosters the psychological well-being of its members."

* * *

GUTHRIE, (William) Tyrone 1900-1971

July 2, 1900—May 15, 1971; Irish actor, director, and au-

thor. Obituaries: *New York Times,* May 16, 1971; *Time,* May 24, 1971; *L'Express,* May 24-30, 1971.

* * *

GUTTMANN, Alexander

PERSONAL: Born in Budapest, Hungary; came to United States in 1940; son of Michael (president of Budapest and Breslau Jewish Theological Seminaries) and Camilla (Schnuerer) Guttmann; married Manya Kampf; children: Ariel, Naomi, Esther Whitman, Judy. *Education:* University of Breslau, Ph.D., 1924; Jewish Theological Seminary, Breslau, Rabbi, 1927; University of Berlin, post-graduate student, 1927-28. *Home:* 960 Lenox Pl., Cincinnati, Ohio 45229. *Office:* Hebrew Union College—Jewish Institute of Religion, Clifton Ave., Cincinnati, Ohio 45220.

CAREER: Jewish Home for the Blind, Berlin, Germany, director, 1927; lecturer on Talmud and history at Juedisches Lehrhaus, Rambam Lehrhaus, and Talmud schools of higher learning, Berlin, 1927-32; professor at Berlin Jewish Teachers' College, Berlin, 1932-35, Lehranstalt fuer de Wissenschaft des Judentums, Berlin, 1935-40, and Hebrew Union College—Jewish Institute of Religion, Cincinnati, Ohio, 1940—. *Member:* World Union of Jewish Studies (Jerusalem), Central Conference of American Rabbis, Society of Jewish Bibliophiles (Cincinnati), Academic Committee for the Hebrew University (New York). *Awards, honors:* Israel Lewy Prize, Jewish Theological Seminary (Breslau), 1928, for *Das redaktionelle und sachliche Verhaeltnis zwischen Mischna und Tosephta;* Guggenheim fellowship, 1969.

WRITINGS: Das redaktionelle und sachliche Verhaeltnis zwischen Mischna und Tosephta, M. & H. Marcus (Breslau), 1928; *Enthuellte Talmudzitate,* Philo Verlag Press (Berlin), 1930; *Rabbinic Judaism in the Making: A Chapter in the History of the Halakhah from Ezra to Judah I,* Wayne State University Press, 1970; *Studies in Rabbinic Judaism,* Ktav, 1976; *The Struggle over Reform in Rabbinic Literature of the Last Century and a Half,* World Union for Progressive Judaism, 1977.

Contributor: *Festschrift zum 75 Jaehrigen Bestehen des Juedisch-Theologischen Seminars,* II, [Breslau], 1929; *Juedische Gestalten und ihre Zeit,* [Berlin], 1936; *Festschrift fuer Leo Baeck,* [Berlin], 1938; *Jewish Studies in Memory of Michael Guttmann,* [Budapest], 1946; *Essays in Honor of Solomon B. Freehof,* [Pittsburgh], 1964; Moses Mielziner, *Introduction to the Talmud,* 4th edition, Bloch Publishing, 1968. Contributor of articles and essays to various yearbooks, Jewish memorial volumes, and periodicals, including *Bericht* der Lehranstalt fuer die Wissenschaft des Judentums, *Hebrew Union College Annual, Bitzaron, Jewish Quarterly Review, Tradition udn Erneuerung* (St. Gallen), and *Jewish Chronicle* (London). Member of editorial board, *Hebrew Union College Annual.*

* * *

GWIRTZMAN, Milton S. 1933-

PERSONAL: Born March 17, 1933, in Rochester, N.Y.; son of Louis George (an optician) and Stella (Silverstein) Gwirtzman; married Elisabeth Ten Eyck Lansing, May 19, 1968; children: Matthew Michael, Daniel Gordon. *Education:* Harvard University, A.B. (summa cum laude), 1954; Yale University, LL.B., 1958. *Home:* 33 Oxford St., Chevy Chase, Md. *Office:* 1150 17th St. N.W., Washington, D.C.

CAREER: Member of the Bar of District of Columbia; U.S.

Senate, Washington, D.C., legislative assistant, 1959-63; Dutton, Gwirtzman, Zumas & Wise (attorneys), Washington, D.C., partner, 1964-73. Chairman of the board, Overseas Information Systems (publications), Paris, France, 1970-73. Assistant director of research for John F. Kennedy's presidential campaign, 1960; political consultant to Senator Robert Kennedy, 1964-68, and Governor Jimmy Carter, 1976. *Member:* Federal City Club.

WRITINGS: (With William van den Heuvel) *On His Own: Robert F. Kennedy, 1964-1968,* Doubleday, 1970; *The Bloated Branch,* New York Times, 1974; *Is Bribery Defensible?,* New York Times, 1975.

WORK IN PROGRESS: The relationship of politicians, the press, and the public on the major national issues over the past twenty years; changing relationships between government and business.

BIOGRAPHICAL/CRITICAL SOURCES: National Observer, March 16, 1970; *Washington Post,* April 15, 1970.

*　　　*　　　*

HAAS, Harold I(rwin) 1925-

PERSONAL: Born September 26, 1925, in Buffalo, N.Y.; son of Elmer J. and Gladys (Ford) Haas; married Ruth Miller, September 6, 1952; children: Rachel, Peter, Sara, Elizabeth, Lois. *Education:* Concordia Seminary, St. Louis, Mo., B.A., 1946, M.Div., 1949; Washington University, St. Louis, Mo., M.A., 1949; University of Buffalo (now State University of New York at Buffalo), Ph.D., 1956. *Home:* 1914 Wendmere Lane, Fort Wayne, Ind. 46825. *Office:* Department of Psychology, Concordia Senior College, Fort Wayne, Ind. 46825.

CAREER: Lutheran clergyman, 1949—; pastor in Rochester, N.Y., 1956-57; Concordia Senior College, Fort Wayne, Ind., assistant professor, 1957-59, associate professor, 1959-66, professor of psychology, 1967—, dean of students, 1960-62. Private practice as clinical psychologist. Diplomate of American Board of Professional Psychology. *Member:* American Psychological Association, American Group Psychotherapy Association, Indiana Psychological Association. *Awards, honors:* U.S. Public Health Service postdoctoral fellowship to University of Colorado Medical Center, 1963-64; Lutheran World Federation stipend, West Germany, 1969.

WRITINGS: Mental Illness, Concordia, 1966; *Pastoral Counseling with People in Distress,* Concordia, 1970.

WORK IN PROGRESS: Mental Health: A Christian View.

*　　　*　　　*

HABENSTREIT, Barbara 1937-

PERSONAL: Born February 17, 1937, in New York, N.Y.; daughter of Irving (a shopkeeper) and Beatrice (Millman) Ziegler; married Abraham I. Habenstreit (director of remedial programs, College of Staten Island of the City University of New York), August 24, 1958; children: David, Shelly. *Education:* City College (now City College of the City University of New York), B.A., 1958; Long Island University, M.A., 1966. *Politics:* Independent. *Religion:* Jewish. *Home:* 101 Clark St., Brooklyn, N.Y. 11201. *Office:* Hopkinson & Blake Publishers, 329 Fifth Ave., New York, N.Y. 10016.

CAREER: Riverdale Press (newspaper), Bronx, N.Y., reporter and editor, 1956-58; *Food Topics Magazine,* New York City, writer and editor, 1958-61; Long Island University, Brooklyn, N.Y., instructor in government, 1966; Hopkinson & Blake (publishers), New York City, editorial director, 1974—.

WRITINGS: Changing America and the Supreme Court (juvenile), Messner, 1970, revised edition, 1975; *The Making of Urban America* (juvenile), Messner, 1970; *Eternal Vigilance: The American Civil Liberties Union in Action* (juvenile), Messner, 1971; *Men Against War* (juvenile), Doubleday, 1972; *To My Brother Who Did a Crime: Former Prisoners Tell Their Stories in Their Own Words,* Doubleday, 1973; *Cities in the March of Civilization,* F. Watts, 1974; *Fort Greene, U.S.A.,* Bobbs-Merrill, 1975. Contributor to *Common Cents.*

*　　　*　　　*

HABER, Louis 1910-

PERSONAL: Born January 12, 1910, in New York, N.Y.; son of Jacob (in real estate) and Lena (Turim) Haber; married Blanche Steinberg, December 27, 1937; children: Richard Jay. *Education:* City College (now City College of the City University of New York), B.S., 1932, M.S., 1939; New York University, Ed.D., 1960. *Home:* 3000 Bronx Park E., New York, N.Y. 10467.

CAREER: Woodlands High School, Hartsdale, N.Y., chairman of science department, 1960-73; Pace College Westchester (now Pace University Westchester Campus), Pleasantville, N.Y., adjunct professor of sciences, 1965-74; College of White Plains (now College of White Plains of Pace University), White Plains, N.Y., director of teacher education, 1973-75. *Military service:* U.S. Army, 1943-46; became captain. *Member:* National Science Teachers Association, National Education Association, New York State Sciences Supervisors Association. *Awards, honors:* U.S. Office of Education research grant, 1966.

WRITINGS: (Editor) *Discovery Problems in Biology,* College Entrance Publications, 1958; (with Lawrence Samuels) *How to Study Science,* College Entrance Publications, 1959; *Black Pioneers of Science and Invention* (juvenile), Harcourt, 1970. Contributor to science education journals.

WORK IN PROGRESS: Collaborating on a textbook in general chemistry; research and writing in the history of science.

*　　　*　　　*

HACK, Walter G. 1925-

PERSONAL: Born May 29, 1925, in Jefferson, Wis.; son of George Fredrick (a minister) and Melvina (Frey) Hack; married Barbara Gast (a teacher), June 18, 1950; children: Susan Barbara, Diane Marie. *Education:* North Central College, B.A., 1947; Northwestern University, M.A., 1952; Northern Illinois University, M.S., 1955; Ohio State University, Ph.D., 1959. *Home:* 2620 York Rd., Columbus, Ohio 43221. *Office:* Center for Educational Administration, Ohio State University, 29 West Woodruff, Columbus, Ohio 43210.

CAREER: High school teacher, Alexis, Ill., 1947-48; elementary school principal, Glen Ellyn, Ill., 1949-50; school district superintendent, Hillside, Ill., 1950-57; Miami University, Oxford, Ohio, assistant professor of educational administration, 1959; Ohio State University, Columbus, assistant professor, 1959-62, associate professor, 1962-65, professor of educational administration, 1966—. *Member:* National Conference of Professors of Educational Administration, American Association of School Administrators, American Education Finance Association, Phi Delta Kappa.

WRITINGS: (Editor) *Educational Administration: Selected Readings,* Allyn & Bacon, 1965, 2nd edition, 1971; (with Francis O. Woodard) *Economic Dimensions of Public School Finance: Concepts and Cases,* McGraw, 1971; (editor) *Educational Futurism: 1985,* McCutchan, 1971; (with Carl Candoli, John Ray, and Dewey Stollar) *School Business Administration: A Planning Approach,* Allyn & Bacon, 1973; (editor) *Educational Administration: The Developing Decades,* McCutchan, 1977. Contributor to education journals.

*   *   *

HACKETT, Donald F. 1918-

PERSONAL: Born November 8, 1918, in Wakefield, Mich.; son of Fred H. (a teacher) and Cunnie (Kraft) Hackett; married Mary Ann Hynes, June 6, 1942; children: Ann, Michael, Mary, David. *Education:* University of Illinois, B.S., 1940; University of Missouri, M.Ed., 1947, Ed.D., 1953. *Home:* 405 Donehoo St., Statesboro, Ga. 30458. *Office:* Industrial Technology Division, Georgia Southern College, Statesboro, Ga. 30458.

CAREER: Teacher in public schools in Missouri and Illinois, 1940-41, and in California, 1946; Murray State College (now University), Murray, Ky., teacher of metals and drafting, 1947-48; Georgia Southern College, Statesboro, 1948—, began as associate professor, professor of industrial technology, 1954—, chairman of division, 1948—. Visiting professor, State University of New York College at Oswego, summer, 1965; wood technology consultant, *Industrial Arts and Vocational Magazine,* 1970—. *Military service:* U.S. Naval Reserve, active duty, 1942-46; became lieutenant. *Member:* American Industrial Arts Association (chairman of public and professional relations committee, 1962-65; chairman of publications committee, 1971-73; president, 1973-74), American Council of Industrial Arts Teacher Education, National Education Association, Society for the History of Technology, American Society for Engineering Education, Society of Manufacturing Engineers, Southeastern Industrial Arts Conference (chairman, 1962-63; historian, 1967-76), Georgia Industrial Arts Association, Georgia Education Association, Epsilon Pi Tau (laureate member).

WRITINGS: (With Patrick E. Spielman) *Modern Wood Technology,* Bruce, 1968; (contributor) *Industrial Arts in Senior High School* McKnight, 1973. Author of courses of study for Georgia State Department of Education; editor of *Industrial Arts for Georgia Schools,* 1958, and *Industrial Arts for the Middle Grades,* 1960, revised edition, 1967. Contributor to education journals.

AVOCATIONAL INTERESTS: Golf, bridge, and chess.

*   *   *

HACKETT, Paul 1920-

PERSONAL: Born July 19, 1920, in Boston, Mass.; son of William Francis (an engineer) and Margaret (Dorsey) Hackett; married Marie Gannon (a learning psychologist), September 27, 1944; children: Christine Marie, Regina (Mrs. Paul O'Neil), John, Paula. *Education:* Boston College, B.A., 1941; Boston University, law student, 1941; Fordham University, further study, 1945. *Politics:* Radical Democrat. *Religion:* Roman Catholic. *Agent:* McIntosh & Otis, Inc., 475 Fifth Ave., New York, N.Y. 10017.

CAREER: Commercial pilot, New York, N.Y., 1946-48;

writer in New York, California, and then Florida, 1950—. *Military service:* U.S. Army Air Corps Reserve, 1937-41. U.S. Army Air Forces, pilot, 1941-46.

WRITINGS: The Cardboard Giants, Putnam, 1952; *Children of the Stone Lions,* Putnam, 1955; *Palmetto Springs,* New American Library, 1962; *Obscenity Trial,* New American Library, 1964; *The Faded Elegance,* Bobbs-Merrill, 1970. Writer of television scripts; contributor to newspapers.

WORK IN PROGRESS: A novel, *View from the Mountain;* research in the areas of theology, law, sociology, and psychology.

SIDELIGHTS: Paul Hackett is a compulsive writer who is most interested "in survival of man." His first book, *The Cardboard Giants,* was published in England and the Netherlands, produced as a film by Paramount Pictures, and condensed in several magazines. *Avocational interests:* History, politics, dogs.††

*   *   *

HACKMAN, Martha L. 1912-

PERSONAL: Born August 10, 1912, in Lincoln, Neb.; daughter of Henry F. and Lillian (Cooper) Hackman. *Education:* University of Nebraska, B.S., 1932, M.A., 1935; University of Denver, B.S. in L.S., 1940. *Home:* 1207 South Los Robles, Pasadena, Calif. 91106.

CAREER: High school English and Latin teacher in Roca, Neb., 1932-33; junior high school English teacher in Central City, Neb., 1935-39; Des Moines Public Library, Des Moines, Iowa, reference assistant, 1940-42; New York Public Library, New York, N.Y., reference assistant in Economics Division, 1942-45; University of Illinois Library, Urbana, assistant reference librarian, 1946-51; Occidental College Library, Los Angeles, Calif., reference librarian, 1952-60; California State University at Los Angeles Library, reference librarian, 1960-67, 1969-77. *Member:* American Library Association, California Library Association, Phi Beta Kappa.

WRITINGS: The Practical Bibliographer, Prentice-Hall, 1970.

*   *   *

HADLEY, Eleanor M(artha) 1916-

PERSONAL: Born July 17, 1916, in Seattle, Wash.; daughter of Homer More (a civil engineer) and Margaret (Floyd) Hadley. *Education:* Mills College, Oakland, Calif., B.A., 1938; Radcliffe College, M.A., 1943, Ph.D., 1949. *Home:* 5040 Klingle St. N.W., Washington, D.C. 20016. *Office:* U.S. General Accounting Office, 441 G St. N.W., Washington, D.C. 20548.

CAREER: U.S. Office of Strategic Services, Washington, D.C., intelligence analyst, 1943-44; economist with U.S. Department of State, Washington, D.C., 1944-46, General MacArthur's Headquarters, Tokyo, Japan, 1946-47, President Truman's Commission on Migratory Labor, Washington, D.C., 1950-51, and Subcommittee on Migratory Labor, U.S. Senate Committee on Labor and Public Welfare, Washington, D.C., 1951-52; National Association of Social Workers, Washington, D.C., Washington representative, 1953-56; Smith College, Northampton, Mass., 1956-65, began as visiting lecturer, became associate professor of economics, dean, class of 1962; U.S. Tariff Commission, Washington, D.C., economist, 1967-74; U.S. General Accounting Office, International Division, Washington, D.C., assistant director, 1974—. Professorial lecturer in economics, George Washington University, 1972—.

MEMBER: American Economic Association, Association for Asian Studies, National Consumers League, American Association of University Women, Phi Beta Kappa. *Awards, honors:* Fulbright research scholar in Japan, 1962-63; Asia Foundation grant, 1964.

WRITINGS: Antitrust in Japan, Princeton University Press, 1970. Contributor to economics journals and to journals of Asian studies.

SIDELIGHTS: Antitrust in Japan has been translated into Japanese.

* * *

HAEBERLE, Erwin J(akob) 1936-

PERSONAL: Born March 30, 1936, in Dortmund, Germany; son of Erwin Clemens (a salesman) and Hedwig (Hertling) Haeberle. *Education:* Attended University of Cologne, 1956-57, University of Freiburg, 1957-60, and University of Glasgow, 1960-61; Cornell University, M.A., 1964; University of Heidelberg, Ph.D. (magna cum laude), 1966; Institute for Advanced Study of Human Sexuality, San Francisco, Calif., D.A., 1976. *Office:* Institute for Advanced Study of Human Sexuality, 1523 Franklin St., San Francisco, Calif. 94109.

CAREER: Private tutor for the family of the late Prince of Hohenzollern, 1961-62; University of Heidelberg, Heidelberg, Germany, lecturer in English, 1964-66; Yale University, New Haven, Conn., research fellow in American studies, 1966-68, 1970-71; University of California, Berkeley, Center for Japanese and Korean Studies, research fellow, 1968-69, 1971-72; Herder & Herder, New York, N.Y., editor, 1969-70; Institute for Advanced Study of Human Sexuality, San Francisco, Calif., faculty member, 1976—.

WRITINGS: Das szenische Werk Thornton Wilders, Carl Winter Universitaetsverlag (Heidelberg), 1967; (with Martin Goldstein and Will McBride) *The Sex Book,* Herder & Herder, 1971; (contributor) H.-J. Lang, editor, *Der Amerikanische Roman* [Duesseldorf, Germany], 1972; (contributor) K. Schubert and U. Mueller-Richter, editors, *Geschichte und Gesellschaft in der Amerikanischen Literatur,* Quelle & Meyer, 1975; (contributor) H. Gochros and J. Gochros, editors, *The Sexually Oppressed,* Association Press, 1977; *The Sex Atlas,* Seabury, 1977. Editor of English language edition, *The Collected Works of Karl May,* Seabury, 1977—. Contributor to *Jahrbuch fuer Amerikastudien* und *Neue Rundschau.*

* * *

HAGEN, Clifford (Warren, Jr.) 1943-

PERSONAL: Born February 22, 1943, in Bradenton, Fla.; son of Clifford Warren and Frankie Elizabeth (Richards) Hagen; married Cynthia Kay Watson (an interior decorator), December 28, 1963 (divorced); children: Clifford Warren III. *Education:* Attended Manatee Junior College, summer, 1962, and University of Florida, 1961-63; Troy State University, B.S., 1966; Florida State University, graduate study. *Politics:* None. *Religion:* None.

CAREER: High school teacher in Tampa, Fla., 1967-68; Montgomery Ward & Co., Tampa, personnel manager, 1968—.

WRITINGS: Sunshine (novel), Harper, 1971.

WORK IN PROGRESS: Two books, *Orange Blossom Special* and *The Silver Cup Awards;* short stories and a short novel.††

HAIGHT, John McVickar, Jr. 1917-

PERSONAL: Born May 31, 1917, in Highland Falls, N.Y.; son of John McVickar (an Episcopalian priest) and Elsie (Stanton) Haight; married Edith Farwell; married second wife, Deborah Dunlap Smith, June 12, 1948; children: (first marriage) John McVickar III; (second marriage) Virginia T. (Mrs. Richard Stevenson), Catherine H. (Mrs. Stephen Petty), Elizabeth S. *Education:* Princeton University, A.B., 1940; Yale University, M.A., 1947; Northwestern University, Ph.D., 1953. *Home:* 55 East Church St., Bethlehem, Pa. 18018. *Office:* Department of History, Lehigh University, Bethlehem, Pa. 18015.

CAREER: Lehigh University, Bethlehem, Pa., instructor, 1949-54, assistant professor, 1954-65, associate professor, 1965-67, professor of European history, 1967—. *Military service:* U.S. Army, 1942-46. *Member:* American Historical Association, Society for French Historical Studies, Society for Historians of American Foreign Relations. *Awards, honors:* American Philosophical Society grants, 1961, 1966, 1971; Social Science Research Council grant, 1963-64; North Atlantic Treaty Organization (NATO) fellowship, 1971.

WRITINGS: American Aid to France, 1938-1940, Atheneum, 1970. Contributor to political science and history journals.

WORK IN PROGRESS: American Aid to Britain: From Dunkirk to Pearl Harbor, researched at Public Record Office, London, 1971-72.

* * *

HAIR, William Ivy 1930-

PERSONAL: Born November 19, 1930, in Monroe, La.; son of Walter Ivy (a merchant) and Annabell (James) Hair; married Emily Karolyn Stevens, December 27, 1957; children: Steven, Walter. *Education:* Louisiana State University, B.A., 1952, M.A., 1953, Ph.D., 1962. *Politics:* Independent. *Religion:* Presbyterian. *Home:* 500 North Tattnall St., Milledgeville, Ga. 31061. *Office:* Department of History, Box 686, Georgia College, Milledgeville, Ga. 31061.

CAREER: Florida State University, Tallahassee, instructor, 1957-63, assistant professor, 1963-69, associate professor of history, 1969-73; Georgia College at Milledgeville, Callaway Professor of Southern History, 1973—. Visiting assistant professor, Louisiana State University, 1962. *Military service:* U.S. Army, 1954-56; became sergeant. *Member:* Organization of American Historians, Southern Historical Association, Louisiana Historical Association, Georgia Association of Historians.

WRITINGS: Bourbonism and Agrarian Protest: Louisiana Politics, 1877-1900, Louisiana State University Press, 1969; *Carnival of Fury: Robert Charles and the New Orleans Race Riot of 1900,* Louisiana State University Press, 1976.

WORK IN PROGRESS: Research for a book, *Louisiana Politics and Society, 1900-1928.*

* * *

HAITHCOX, John Patrick 1933-

PERSONAL: Born February 6, 1933, in Gaffney, S.C.; son of James Franklin and Margaret Angelle (Lowe) Haithcox; married Marilyn Mattina, 1957; children: Kevin, Steffan, Kiran. *Education:* Oberlin College, B.A., 1955; University of California, Berkeley, M.A., 1959, Ph.D., 1965. *Home:* 2410 Thayer St., Evanston, Ill. 60201. *Office:* Office of the

Vice-President, Associated Colleges of the Midwest, 60 West Walton St., Chicago, Ill. 60610.

CAREER: University of Chicago, Chicago, Ill., Carnegie Teaching Fellow in Indian Civilization, 1963-64; University of Michigan—Dearborn, assistant professor of political science, 1964-67; Carleton College, Northfield, Minn., 1967-72, began as assistant professor, became associate professor of government and international relations; Associated Colleges of the Midwest, Chicago, vice-president, 1972—. *Military service:* U.S. Army, 1955-57. *Member:* American Institute of Indian Studies (trustee, 1969-71), American Political Science Association, Association for Asian Studies, International Studies Association, American Association of University Professors, Midwest Political Science Association, Minnesota Political Science Association. *Awards, honors:* Ford Foundation fellow in India, 1961-63; Research Institute on Communist Affairs senior fellow, 1967; honorable mention, Watumull Foundation Biennial Book Prize, American Historical Association, 1972, for *Communism and Nationalism in India: M. N. Roy and Comintern Policy, 1920-1939.*

WRITINGS: Communism and Nationalism in India: M. N. Roy and Comintern Policy, 1920-1939, Princeton University Press, 1971. Contributor to *Journal of Asian Studies* (Calcutta) and other journals of Asian studies.

WORK IN PROGRESS: Studies on Congress Party politics and non-Brahmin movement in Maharashtra, on India Hindu-Muslim relations and British colonial policy in India, and on the Indian nationalist movement and World War II.

* * *

HAJ, Fareed 1935-

PERSONAL: Born November 14, 1935, in Haifa, Palestine (now Israel); son of Eid and Rawand (Marcus) El-Haj; married Nadia Karam, July 2, 1961; children: George, Joseph, James. *Education:* University of London, B.A. (external), 1956; Hebrew University of Jerusalem, B.A., 1957; Hunter College (now Hunter College of the City University of New York), M.S., 1959; New York University, Ph.D., 1968; also studied at Columbia University, 1965-69, and took summer courses at Fordham University, 1963, Florida State University, 1967, and Harvard University, 1970. *Religion:* Catholic. *Home:* 12333 Southwest 32nd Ter., Miami, Fla.

CAREER: Itinerant teacher of the blind in Israel under direction of Ministry of Education of Israel and Hebrew University of Jerusalem, 1957-58; high school teacher of English in Galilee, Israel, 1960-61; St. Joseph School for the Blind, Jersey City, N.J., teacher, 1963-67, director of prevocational rehabilitation program, 1964-67; Dade Board of Public Instruction, Miami, Fla., special education teacher, 1967—.

WRITINGS: Disability in Antiquity, Philosophical Library, 1970. Contributor to journals on the blind.

WORK IN PROGRESS: Life of a Man (tentative title), an autobiography.

SIDELIGHTS: Fareed Haj told *CA,* "Although I have been blind since childhood, I have found that the typewriter, Braille system, and good memory enable me to work effectively both as a teacher and counselor."

* * *

HALL, Gimone 1940-

PERSONAL: Given name is pronounced Ja-*mone;* born April 30, 1940, in Highland Park, Ill.; daughter of Timothy L. and Gladys (Gimon) McNamara; married Lawrence C. Hall (a ghost writer), July 13, 1963; children: Shannon Michelle. *Education:* University of Texas, B.A., 1962. *Home:* 110 North Clinton St., Doylestown, Pa. 18901. *Agent:* Donald MacCampbell, Inc., 12 East 41st St., New York, N.Y. 10017.

CAREER: Corpus Christi Caller-Times, Corpus Christi, Tex., news reporter, 1962.

WRITINGS—Novels: *The Blue Taper,* Macfadden, 1970; *Witch's Suckling,* Macfadden, 1970; *The Silver Strand,* Dell, 1974; *The Juliet Room,* Manor, 1974; *Hide My Savage Heart,* Pyramid Publications, 1977. Also author of *Devil's Walk.* Contributor of short stories to magazines.

WORK IN PROGRESS: An historical romance, tentatively entitled *Rapture's Mistress,* for New American Library.

SIDELIGHTS: Gimone Hall told *CA:* "What I enjoy most about writing is the adventure and friendship I experience from good characters. Like real people, good characters reveal themselves more and more the longer the writer lives with them. Capable of tumbling plots, they are also the ones to come to a writer's aid in time of trouble. The best solution to a problem in a book is usually provided by a good character."

* * *

HALL, Mary Anne 1934-

PERSONAL: Born September 17, 1934, in Kimberly, W.Va.; daughter of Edward J. (a teacher) and Frances (Stahl) Hall. *Education:* Marshall University, B.A. (cum laude), 1955; University of Maryland, M.Ed., 1959, Ed.D., 1965. *Religion:* Presbyterian. *Office:* Department of Curriculum and Instruction, Georgia State University, 33 Gilmer St., Atlanta, Ga. 30303.

CAREER: Elementary teacher in Prince Georges County, Md., 1955-58; State University of New York College at New Paltz, assistant professor of education and supervising teacher, 1958-62; University of Maryland, College Park, instructor, 1962-65, assistant professor, 1965-68, associate professor of education, 1968-73; Georgia State University, Atlanta, professor of reading, 1973—. Lecturer, Graduate School of Education, University of Pennsylvania, summer, 1968. *Member:* International Reading Association, College Reading Association, National Reading Conference, National Council of Teachers of English.

WRITINGS: (With Robert M. Wilson) *Programmed Word Attack for Teachers,* C. E. Merrill, 1968; *Teaching Reading as a Language Experience,* C. E. Merrill, 1970, 2nd edition, 1976; (with Wilson) *Reading and the Elementary School Child,* Van Nostrand, 1971; *The Language Experience Approach for the Culturally Disabled,* International Reading Association, 1972. Contributor to education journals.†

* * *

HALL, Roger (Wolcott) 1919-

PERSONAL: Born May 20, 1919, in Baltimore, Md.; son of Wolcott Ellsworth (a U.S. Navy captain) and Kathryn (Rogers) Hall; married Linda Texter (a poet). *Education:* University of Virginia, B.A., 1941. *Religion:* Episcopalian. *Home:* 49 West 53rd St., New York, N.Y. 10019.

CAREER: Sports announcer for radio, Baltimore, Md., 1946-50; free-lance journalist, New York, N.Y., 1950-56;

writer and journalist, 1957—. *Military service:* U.S. Army, Parachute Infantry, 1942-46; became captain; on duty with Office of Strategic Services, 1943-46. *Awards, honors:* Fletcher Pratt Fellowship in Prose, Bread Loaf Writers' Conference Endowment Fund, 1968.

WRITINGS: You're Stepping on My Cloak and Dagger, Norton, 1957; *All My Pretty Ones,* Norton, 1959; *19,* Norton, 1970.

*   *   *

HALL, Tord (Erik Martin) 1910-

PERSONAL: Born January 7, 1910, in Joenkoeping, Sweden; son of Frithiof (a lecturer) and Anna (Larsson) Hall; married Britt Torell, June 28, 1949; children: Torun, Martin. *Education:* University of Uppsala, Fil.kand, 1931, Fil.mag., 1933, Fil.lic., 1937, Fil.dr., 1950. *Home:* Fyrisgatan 14, Uppsala 75222, Sweden.

CAREER: Teacher and lecturer at several secondary schools and colleges in Sweden, 1933-59; University of Uppsala, Uppsala, Sweden, lecturer in mathematics, 1959-75, docent, 1971. Scientific writer, *Svenska Dagbladet* (newspaper), 1950—.

WRITINGS: Atomer och stjaernor, Norstedt, 1956; *Vaar tids stjaernsaang,* Bonnier, 1958, 2nd edition, 1961; *Satelliter och rymdfaerder,* Bonnier, 1958, 2nd edition, 1960; *Analys I-II,* Biblioteksforlaget, 1961; *Gauss: Matematikernas konung,* Bokforlaget Prisma, 1965, translation by Albert Froderberg published as *Carl Friedrich Gauss,* M.I.T. Press, 1970; *Entropi* (poems), Wahlstroem & Widstrand, 1966; *Maenniskan infoer Kosmos,* Wahlstroem & Widstrand, 1966; *Fraan Ginnungagap till saapbubbla,* Laeromedelsfoerlagen, 1970; *Matematikens utveckling,* Gleerup, 1970; *En matematisk tragedi,* Scientia Bromberg, 1977.

Co-author with, Bo Pederby and Bo Elmgren of about twenty physics textbooks for elementary schools, 1966—. Author of scientific papers and of more than one thousand articles on science, art, and poetry, 1950—, the majority published in *Svenska Dagbladet.*

*   *   *

HALL, Trevor H(enry) 1910-

PERSONAL: Born May 28, 1910, in Wakefield, Yorkshire, England; son of Harold Roxby and Maude (Boardman) Hall; married Dorothy Keningley, June 10, 1937; children: Kathryn Elizabeth (Mrs. C.S.G. Liversedge), Richard Roxby. *Education:* Attended Trinity College, Cambridge, 1954-56; University of Leeds, M.A., Ph.D. *Politics:* Conservative. *Religion:* Church of England. *Home:* Carr Meadow, Thorner, near Leeds, Yorkshire, England. *Office:* V. Stanley Walker & Son, Albion Pl., Leeds, Yorkshire, England.

CAREER: V. Stanley Walker & Son (chartered surveyors), Leeds, England, partner, 1945—; Huddersfield Building Society, Huddersfield, England, director, 1958—, vice-president, 1967-71, president, 1972—; Legal & General Assurance Society, London, England, director, 1962—, deputy chairman, 1974—. Justice of the peace, Leeds, 1959—. University of Leeds, member of Brotherton Committee, 1967—, Cecil Oldman Memorial Lecturer in bibliography and textual criticism, 1972-73; Leeds Library, president and trustee, 1969—. *Military service:* British Army, 1939-45; became major. *Member:* Royal Institution of Chartered Surveyors (fellow), Cambridge Society (appointed Founder Life Member), Magic Circle of London (honorary vice-president).

WRITINGS: The Testament of Ralph H. Hull, Academy of Recorded Crafts, Arts, and Sciences (London), 1945; *Nothing Is Impossible* (book of card tricks), Academy of Recorded Crafts, Arts, and Sciences, 1946; *Reading Is Believing,* Goodliffe, 1947; (with Eric J. Dingwall and K. M. Goldney) *The Haunting of Borley Rectory,* Duckworth, 1956; *A Bibliography of Books on Conjuring in English from 1580 to 1850,* C. W. Jones (Minneapolis), 1957; (with Dingwall) *Four Modern Ghosts,* Duckworth, 1958; *The Spiritualists: The Story of Florence Cook and William Crookes,* Duckworth, 1962, Helix Press, 1963; *The Strange Case of Edmund Gurney,* Duckworth, 1964; *The Mystery of the Leeds Library* (booklet), [Leeds], 1965; *New Light on Old Ghosts,* Duckworth, 1965; (with John Lorne Campbell) *Strange Things: The Story of Fr. Allan McDonald and Ada Goodrich Freer,* Routledge & Kegan Paul, 1968; *Mathematical Recreations, 1633: A Study in Seventeenth Century Bibliography,* Leeds University Press, 1969; *Sherlock Holmes: Ten Literary Studies,* Duckworth, 1969, St. Martin's, 1970; *The Late Mr. Sherlock Holmes,* St. Martin's, 1971; *Old Conjuring Books: A Bibliographical and Historical Study,* Duckworth, 1972, St. Martin's, 1973; *The Early Years of the Huddersfield Building Society,* W. S. Maney, 1974; *The Winder Sale of Old Conjuring Books,* W. S. Maney, 1975; (with Percy H. Muir) *Some Printers and Publishers of Conjuring Books and Other Ephemera, 1800-1850,* W. S. Maney, 1976; *Search for Harry Price,* Duckworth, 1977; *Sherlock Holmes and His Creator,* Duckworth, 1977.

SIDELIGHTS: Trevor Hall told *CA:* "Writing (on which I am not financially dependent) like book-collecting, has always been a relief from business activity and professional practice. Now, as retirement gradually approaches, it is a great delight to know that I can always be happily occupied as an established author and devote as much time to it as I wish. I shall never write a best-seller, for fiction is not my field, but my books have a steady, modest sale in Britain and America, exemplified by my first *Sherlock Holmes....* It has not made my fortune, but it did cause my publisher to make the journey from London to the wilds of Yorkshire to persuade me to write Sherlock Holmes III, ... *Sherlock Holmes and His Creator.*"

Trevor Hall, besides his interest in bibliography, has made a lifelong study of odd happenings, seeking to find an explanation for them. *The Strange Case of Edmund Gurney* was presented on British Broadcasting Corp. television in October, 1967.

BIOGRAPHICAL/CRITICAL SOURCES: Books and Bookmen, January, 1969; *Times Literary Supplement,* May 7, 1971; *New Statesman,* May 21, 1971.

*   *   *

HALLORAN, Richard (Colby) 1930-

PERSONAL: Born March 2, 1930, in Washington, D.C.; son of Paul James (an engineer) and Catherine (Lenihan) Halloran; married Carol Prins (a teacher), June 21, 1958 (divorced); children: Christopher, Laura, Catherine. *Education:* Dartmouth College, A.B. (with distinction), 1951; University of Michigan, M.A., 1957; Columbia University, graduate study, 1965. *Politics:* "Wildly independent." *Religion:* Roman Catholic. *Home:* 4740 Connecticut Ave. N.W., Washington, D.C. 20008. *Office: New York Times,* 1920 L St. N.W., Washington, D.C. 20036.

CAREER: Business Week, New York City, staff writer with Philadelphia Bureau, 1957-59, assistant foreign editor, 1959-61, Far East Bureau chief, Tokyo, Japan, 1962-64;

Washington Post, Washington, D.C., specialist on Asian affairs, 1965-66, Northeast Asia correspondent, based in Tokyo, 1966-68, economic correspondent, 1968-69; *New York Times,* New York City, diplomatic correspondent, Washington Bureau, Washington, D.C., 1969-70, general assignment correspondent, Washington Bureau, 1970-72, Tokyo Bureau chief, Tokyo, 1972-76, special projects correspondent, Washington Bureau, 1976—. *Military service:* U.S. Army, paratrooper, 1952-55; served in Korea, Japan, Okinawa, Taiwan, and Vietnam; became first lieutenant. *Member:* Foreign Correspondents Club of Japan. *Awards, honors:* Ford Foundation fellowship to East Asia Institute, Columbia University, 1965; Overseas Press Club citation for coverage of the Pueblo crisis in Korea, 1968.

WRITINGS: Japan: Images and Realities, Knopf, 1969; *Conflict and Compromise: The Dynamics of American Foreign Policy,* Quadrangle, 1973. Contributor to *Saturday Review, Commonweal,* and to Japanese and Korean publications.

BIOGRAPHICAL/CRITICAL SOURCES: Saturday Review, November 15, 1969; *Los Angeles Times,* November 16, 1969; *Book World,* November 30, 1969; *Washington Post,* December 18, 1969; *New York Times Book Review,* March 1, 1970.

* * *

HALPERIN, Irving. 1922-

PERSONAL: Born January 17, 1922, in New York, N.Y.; son of Herman and Bertha (Kleban) Halperin; married Tam Greene (a social worker), February, 1956; children: Daniel, Dina, Jon. *Education:* Roosevelt University, B.A., 1948; University of Iowa, M.A., 1950; Washington University, St. Louis, Mo., Ph.D., 1957. *Religion:* Jewish. *Home:* 17 Marcela Ave., San Francisco, Calif. 94116. *Agent:* Julian Bach, Jr., 249 East 48th St., New York, N.Y., 10017. *Office:* Department of English, San Francisco State University, San Francisco, Calif. 94132.

CAREER: University of Illinois, Chicago, instructor in English, 1955-56; Northwestern University, Evanston, Ill., instructor in English, 1956-57; San Francisco State University, San Francisco, Calif., assistant professor, 1957-65, professor of English, 1965—. Fulbright teacher in India, 1953-54; Fulbright lecturer, University of Erlangen, 1963-64; visiting professor, Hebrew University, 1964-65, and Sir George Williams University, 1975. *Military service:* U.S. Army Air Forces, 1943-45. *Member:* Modern Language Association of America, American Jewish Congress. *Awards, honors:* National Curriculum Research Institute grant, 1965-66; National Foundation for Jewish Culture research grant, 1966-67.

WRITINGS: Messengers from the Dead: Literature from the Holocaust, Westminster, 1970; *Here I Am: A Jew in Today's Germany,* Westminster, 1971. Contributor of articles, literary critiques, and short stories to numerous periodicals, including *Christian Century, Commonweal, Judaism, Reconstructionist, Conservative Judaism, English Journal, Kansas Quarterly, South Dakota Review, Saturday Review, Nation, Chronicle of Higher Education,* and *Phi Delta Kappan.*

WORK IN PROGRESS: A book on the teaching of literature in the post-Auschwitz age.

* * *

HALTRECHT, Montague 1932-

PERSONAL: Born February 27, 1932, in London, England; son of Philip (a businessman) and Deborah Kate (Oslof) Haltrecht. *Education:* Wadham College, Oxford, M.A., 1954. *Religion:* Jewish. *Agent:* Deborah Rogers Ltd., 29 Goodge St., London W1P 1FD, England.

CAREER: Novelist. *Awards, honors:* Henfield Foundation Award, 1967.

WRITINGS—Novels, except as noted: *Jonah and His Mother,* Deutsch, 1964; *A Secondary Character,* Deutsch, 1965; *The Devil Is a Single Man,* Collins, 1969; *The Edgware Road,* Collins, 1970; *The Quiet Showman: The Story of Sir David Webster and the Royal Opera House* (biography), Collins, 1975. Theater and book reviewer for *Sunday Times, Scotsman, Queen,* and other publications.

BIOGRAPHICAL/CRITICAL SOURCES: Books and Bookmen, September, 1965, July, 1969, September, 1969; *Spectator,* July 7, 1969; *Guardian,* July 21, 1970; *Observer Review,* June 21, 1971.

* * *

HAMBURGER, Kaete 1896-

PERSONAL: Born September 21, 1896, in Hamburg, Germany; daughter of John (a banker) and Hertha Hamburger. *Education:* Studied philosophy and literature at University of Berlin and University of Munich, 1917-22, received Dr.phil., 1922. *Home:* Hegelstrasse 51, Stuttgart, Germany.

CAREER: University of Stuttgart, Stuttgart, Germany, professor of literature, beginning 1957. *Member:* Goethe-Gesellschaft, Deutsche Schiller-Gesellschaft, Thomas Mann-Gesellschaft, International Federation of University Women, International P.E.N., Verdienstkrewz der Bundesrepublik Deutschland.

WRITINGS: (Editor) Betty Heimann, *System und Methode in Hegel's Philosophie,* [Leipzig], 1927; *Thomas Mann und die Romantik,* Junker & Duennhaupt, 1932; *Thomas Mann's Roman "Joseph und seine Brueder,"* Bermann-Fischer, 1945, 2nd edition published as *Der Humor bei Thomas Mann,* Nymphenburger Verlagshandlung, 1965; *Schiller: Problemen i hans verk* (in Swedish), Natur & Kultur, 1947; *Leo Tolstoi: Gestalt und Problem,* L. Lehnen, 1950, 2nd edition, Vandenhoeck & Ruprecht, 1963; *Die Logik der Dichtung,* Ernst Klett, 1957, 2nd edition, 1968, translation by Marilynn Rose published as *The Logic of Literature,* Indiana University Press, 1973; *Von Sophokles zu Sartre: Griechische Dramenfiguren antik und modern,* Kohlhammer, 1962, translation by Helen Sebba published as *From Sophocles to Sartre: Figures from Greek Tragedy, Classical and Modern,* Ungar, 1969; (editor) Thomas Mann, *Das Gesetz,* Ullstein, 1964; *Philosophie der Dichter: Novalis, Schiller, Rilke,* Kohlhammer, 1966; (editor and contributor) *Rilke in neuer Sicht,* Kohlhammer, 1971; *Rilke: Eine Einfuehrung,* Ernst Klett, 1976.

Contributor: H. W. Seiffert and B. Zeller, editors, *Festgabe fuer Eduard Berend,* Hermann Boehlaus Nachfolger, 1959; H. Holtzhauer and Zeller, editors, *Studien zur Goethezeit: Festschrift fuer Lieselotte Blumenthal,* Hermann Boehlaus Nachfolger, 1968; H. Kreuzer, editor, *Gestaltungsgeschichte und Gesell schaftsgeschichte,* J. B. Metzlersche Verlagsbuchhandlung, 1969; B. Hueppauf and D. Sternberger, editors, *Ueber Literatur und Geschichte: Festschrift fuer Gerhard Storz,* Athenaeum, 1973; V. J. Guenther and H. Koopmann, editors, *Untersuchungen zur Literatur als Geschichte: Festschrift fuer Benno V. Wiese,* Erich Schmidt, 1973; H. Ruediger, editor, *Literatur und Dichtung,* Kohlhammer, 1973; U. Schweikert, editor, *Jean Paul,* Wissenschaftliche Buchgesellschaft, 1974; Koopmann, editor, *Thomas Mann,* Wissenschaftliche Buchgesellschaft, 1975; H. J. Schrimpf, editor, *Gerhart Hauptmann,* Wissenschaftliche Buchgesellschaft, 1976; W. Keller, editor, *Beitraege zur Poetik des Dramas,* Wissenschaftliche Buchgesellschaft, 1976; G. Gillespie and E. Lohner, editors, *Herkommen und Erneuerung: Festschrift fuer Oskar Seidlin,* Max Niemeyer, 1976.

Contributor to *Jahrbuch der deutschen Schillergesellschaft, Handbuch der deutschen Gegenwartsliteratur,* and of more than ninety papers and articles to professional journals, magazines, and newspapers in Germany, England, Sweden, Netherlands, and United States.

* * *

HAMES, (Alice) Inez 1892-

PERSONAL: Born January 8, 1892, in Paparoa, New Zealand; daughter of Rowland (a farmer) and Clara (Hutchinson) Hames. *Education:* Auckland Teachers College, Teachers' Certificate, 1912. *Politics:* Left. *Religion:* Methodist. *Home address:* King's Rd., Suva, Fiji; and Box 40, Nausori, Fiji.

CAREER: Teacher in New Zealand schools, 1914-19, and in Methodist Church schools, 1920-64; Nausori Tutorial College, Nausori, Fiji, teacher of history, English, and literature, 1965-69. *Member:* Pan-Pacific and South-East Asia Women's Association, Fiji Society. *Awards, honors:* Certificate of Honour from Queen Elizabeth II for long and faithful service to the community.

WRITINGS: Legends of Fiji and Rotuma, privately printed, 1960; (with Alexander Wyclif Reed) *Myths and Legends of Fiji and Rotuma,* A. H. & A. W. Reed, 1967; *Folk Tales of the South Pacific,* University of London Press, 1969; *I Remember . . . Personal Memories of a New Zealand Missionary in Fiji,* privately printed, 1972. Occasional contributor to *New Zealand Observer, Australasian Missionary Review,* and other periodicals.

BIOGRAPHICAL/CRITICAL SOURCES: Times Literary Supplement, October 16, 1969.†

* * *

HAMILTON, David (Boyce, Jr.) 1918-

PERSONAL: Born August 31, 1918, in Pittsburgh, Pa.; son of David Boyce (a lawyer) and Nell (Blackburn) Hamilton; married Elizabeth Teal, December 21, 1946; children: Elizabeth Nell (Mrs. Tod Delaney), David Teal. *Education:* University of Pittsburgh, A.B., 1940, M.A., 1941; University of Texas, Ph.D., 1951. *Politics:* Democrat. *Home:* 4844 Southern Ave. S.E., Albuquerque, N.M. 87108. *Office:* Department of Economics, University of New Mexico, Albuquerque, N.M. 87106.

CAREER: University of Pittsburgh, Pittsburgh, Pa., instructor in economics, 1946-47; University of Texas, Main University (now University of Texas at Austin), instructor in economics, 1947-49; University of New Mexico, Albuquerque, assistant professor, 1949-56, associate professor, 1956-62, professor of economics, 1962—. Carnegie intern and visiting professor, Columbia University, 1956-57. *Military service:* U.S. Army Air Forces, 1941-45, U.S. Air Force, 1951-52; became major. *Member:* Association for Evolutionary Economics, American Economic Association, Southwestern Social Science Association.

WRITINGS: Newtonian Classicism and Darwinian Institutionalism: A Study of Change in Economic Theory, Univer-

sity of New Mexico Press, 1953, revised edition published as *Evolutionary Economics: A Study of Change in Economic Thought,* 1970; *Consumer Cooperation in New Mexico,* University of New Mexico Press, 1955; *The Consumer in Our Economy,* Houghton, 1962; *A Primer on the Economics of Poverty,* Random House, 1968. Contributor to *Nation, Frontier, New Mexico Independent, Colorado Quarterly,* and to economics journals.

WORK IN PROGRESS: The Rise of the Industrial Economy.

* * *

HAMILTON, Michael (Pollock) 1927-

PERSONAL: Born January 28, 1927, in Belfast, Northern Ireland; son of Hugh Pollock and Blanche (Webb) Hamilton; married Sarah Clippinger, November 23, 1956; children: Patrick, Katrina. *Education:* University of Toronto, B.A., 1951; Protestant Episcopal Theological Seminary in Virginia, B.D., 1955. *Home:* 3509 Woodley Rd. N.W., Washington, D.C. 20016. *Office:* Washington Cathedral, Mount St. Alban, Washington, D.C. 20016.

CAREER: Episcopal priest; University of Southern California, Los Angeles, chaplain, 1958-64; Washington Cathedral, Washington, D.C., canon, 1964—. Chairman, Washington Coalition for Clean Air, 1973-75. Consultant, National Institute of Health Volunteer Research Committee, 1974-76. *Military service:* British Army, Airborne, 1945-48; became lieutenant. *Member:* Church Society for College Work.

WRITINGS: (Editor) *The Vietnam War: Christian Perspectives,* Eerdmans, 1967; (editor) *This Little Planet,* introduction by Edmund Muskie, Scribner, 1970; (editor) *The New Genetics and the Future of Man,* Eerdmans, 1972; (editor) *The Charismatic Movement,* Eerdmans, 1974; (editor with Nancy S. Montgomery) *The Ordination of Women: Pro and Con,* Morehouse, 1975.

WORK IN PROGRESS: Editing *To Avoid Catastrophe,* a study of future nuclear arms policy, for Eerdmans.

AVOCATIONAL INTERESTS: Sailing, hiking.

* * *

HAMMER, Emanuel F(rederick) 1926-

PERSONAL: Born August 15, 1926, in New York, N.Y.; son of Isadore (a dress designer) and Bella (Scherer) Hammer; married Lila King (a psychoanalyst), June 4, 1950; children: Diane Robin, Cary Mark. *Education:* Attended Brooklyn College (now Brooklyn College of the City University of New York), 1944-45, 1946-47; Syracuse University, B.A. (magna cum laude), 1948; New York University, Ph.D., 1951. *Religion:* Hebrew. *Home:* 381 West End Ave., New York, N.Y. 10024.

CAREER: Lynchburg State Colony, Lynchburg, Va., director of intern training, 1951-52; private practice as psychologist, New York City, 1952—; New York State Psychiatric Institute, New York City, senior research scientist, 1952-55; New York City Criminal Courts, Psychiatric Clinic, New York City, director of psychology department, 1955-72. Diplomate in clinical psychology, American Board of Examiners in Professional Psychology, 1962. Psychologist, Child Guidance League, 1952-62; faculty member, National Psychological Association for Psychoanalysis, 1962—; director of training, Metropolitan Academy of Psychoanalytic Training, 1966-75; adjunct associate professor of psychology, New York University, Graduate School of Arts and Science, 1968—. *Military service:* U.S. Army Air Forces, 1945-46.

MEMBER: Society for Projective Techniques and Personality Assessment (secretary, 1963-64), American Psychological Association (fellow), American Anthropological Association (liaison fellow, 1954-58), New York Society of Clinical Psychologists (president, 1964-65), New York State Psychological Association (member of executive committee of clinical division, 1967-70).

WRITINGS: The H-T-P Clinical Research Manual, Western Psychological Services, 1954; *The Clinical Application of Projective Drawings,* C. C Thomas, 1958; *Creativity,* Random House, 1960; *The Use of Interpretation in Treatment,* Grune, 1968; (with John N. Buck) *Advances in the House-Tree-Person Technique,* Western Psychological Services, 1970; *Antiachievement: Perspectives on School Dropouts,* Western Psychological Services, 1971. Contributor to psychological and psychiatric journals.

WORK IN PROGRESS: Research and writing on psychoanalytic techniques and on the creative process.

SIDELIGHTS: Emanuel Hammer told *CA:* "With the requirements of a full time psychotherapy private practice, supplemented by part-time teaching, I have either to write in the crumbs of time around my other work or not write at all. I carry index cards with me, and once I get into a book I'm writing, the writing spills over into the time on the subway to the university where I teach, as long as I can get a seat, . . . into the gifts of time provided by a patient being late for his appointment, into the waiting time I previously used to spend on one foot while my wife finished dressing before we went out, into the spaces of boredom between the more vital parts of professional meetings and conventions, and even at times while waiting for an elevator or a waiter. The trick, I guess, is not waiting, as is often said, until I have the time to write."

*   *   *

HANEY, John B.   1931-

PERSONAL: Born May 2, 1931, in Milwaukee, Wis.; son of Earl McKinley (a teacher) and Edith (Heizer) Haney; married Diane Dutton (a teacher), July 18, 1959; children: Steven Arthur, John Frederic. *Education:* Miami University, Oxford, Ohio, B.S., 1952; University of Michigan, M.A., 1954, Ph.D., 1960. *Home:* 39 Hawthorne Pl., Manhassett, N.Y. 11030. *Office:* Department of Communication Arts and Sciences, Queens College of the City University of New York, Flushing, N.Y. 11367.

CAREER: U.S. Air Force, 1954-64, leaving service as captain; Air Force assignments were in teaching, as instructor in communication technology at Air University, Maxwell Air Force Base, Montgomery, Ala., 1954-57, instructor at U.S. Air Force Academy, Colorado Springs, Col., 1959-61, assistant professor, 1961-64, associate professor of English, 1964; University of Illinois at Chicago Circle, associate professor, 1964-68; professor of speech, 1968-71, director of Office of Instructional Resources, 1964-71; Queens College of the City University of New York, Flushing, N.Y., director of instructional development and professor of communication arts and sciences, 1971—. Consultant to Michigan State University, 1965-67, Ford Foundation Educational Facilities Laboratory and U.S. Office of Education, 1968—, National Fire Prevention and Control Administration, 1975—, and to Middle States Association Higher Education Accreditation panel, 1976—. *Member:* International Communications Association (president, 1962), National Society for the Study of Communication, Speech Association of America, Speech Communication Association, So-

ciety for Programmed and Automated Learning (president, 1967-68).

WRITINGS: (With Charles J. McIntyre) *Planning for Instructional Resources,* University of Illinois, 1967; (with Eldon J. Ullmer) *Educational Media and the Teacher,* W. C. Brown, 1970, second edition published as *Educational Communications and Technology,* 1975. Contributor to communications and education journals.

WORK IN PROGRESS: Video Project.

*   *   *

HANNIBAL, Edward   1936-

PERSONAL: Born August 24, 1936, in Manchester, Mass.; son of Joseph Leary (a ship's mechanic) and Loretta (McCarthy) Hannibal; married Margaret Twomey, June 14, 1958; children: Mary Ellen, Edward J., Eleanor, John, Julia. *Education:* Boston College, B.A., 1958. *Religion:* "Roman Catholic, but . . ." *Home:* 118 Pantigo Rd., East Hampton, N.Y. 11937. *Agent:* Helen Brann Agency, 14 Sutton Pl. S., New York, N.Y. 10022. *Office:* Grey Advertising, Inc., 777 Third Ave., New York, N.Y. 10017.

CAREER: Kenyon & Eckhardt (advertising agency), New York City, copywriter, 1962-64; Norman, Craig & Kummel (advertising agency), New York City, copywriter, 1964-65; Benton & Bowles (advertising agency), New York City, associate creative director, 1965-68; Wayne Jervis & Associates (advertising agency), New York City, creative director, 1968-69; Grey Advertising, Inc., New York City, copywriter, 1975—. *Military service:* U.S. Army, Intelligence Corps, 1958-62; became first lieutenant. *Awards, honors:* Houghton Mifflin Literary fellowship, 1970, for manuscript of *Chocolate Days, Popsicle Weeks;* Bread Loaf Writers' Conference fellowship, 1971.

WRITINGS: Chocolate Days, Popsicle Weeks (novel), Houghton, 1970; *Dancing Man* (novel), Simon & Schuster, 1973. Contributor to *Writer.*

WORK IN PROGRESS: A novel set in the peacetime army.

SIDELIGHTS: Edward Hannibal told *CA:* "Just as there's no longer any such thing as a 'B' movie, you can't just write 'a novel' any more. If it isn't a blockbuster, forget it. But, as serious fiction shrinks steadily toward 'endangered species' status, the committed novelist does not despair. He begins to feel—Underground. It's a good place from which to write. Also, Underground has a way of turning Exotic, then, gradually, vaguely, Forbidden. Which is when it becomes Attractive again, and the cycle begins anew, freshened by the process. So, to save literature in our time, stop reading the hard stuff now."

*   *   *

HANSEN, Chadwick (Clarke)   1926-

PERSONAL: Born February 15, 1926, in Benton Harbor, Mich.; son of Herbert Winston (a clergyman) and Louise (Clarke) Hansen; married Betty Jane Richards, June 21, 1947; children: Cynthia Jane, Judith Walker, Kirsten Shaw, Katherine Clarke. *Education:* Yale University, B.A., 1948; University of Minnesota, M.A., 1951, Ph.D., 1956. *Agent:* Henriette Neatrour, Curtis Brown Ltd., 575 Madison Ave., New York, N.Y. 10022; and A. P. Watt & Son, 26/28 Bedford Row, London WC1R 4HL, England. *Office:* Department of English, University of Illinois at Chicago Circle, Box 4348, Chicago, Ill. 60680.

CAREER: Pennsylvania State University, University Park, instructor, 1955-60, assistant professor, 1960-65, associate professor of English, 1965-70, professor of English and American studies, 1970-71; University of Minnesota, Minneapolis, professor of English and American studies, 1971-74; University of Illinois at Chicago Circle, Chicago, professor of English, 1974-75; University of Iowa, Iowa City, professor of English and American civilization and director of American Civilization Program, 1975-76; University of Illinois at Chicago Circle, professor of English, 1976—. *Military service:* U.S. Naval Reserve, 1943-46. *Member:* Modern Language Association of America, American Studies Association, American Historical Association.

WRITINGS: (With D. S. Austin and R. W. Condee) *Modern Fiction: Form and Idea in the Contemporary Novel and Short Story,* Pennsylvania State University Center for Continuing Liberal Education, 1959; (with Martin Abbott and others) *The American Renaissance: The History and Literature of an Era,* Verlag Moritz Diesterweg, 1961; *Witchcraft at Salem,* Braziller, 1969; (editor with Art Hodes) *Selections from the Gutter: Portraits from the Jazz Record,* University of California Press, 1977. Contributor to *American Quarterly, Massachusetts Review, New England Quarterly,* and other journals.

WORK IN PROGRESS: A Documentary History of Negro Music; and *The 54th Massachusetts Volunteer Infantry.*

SIDELIGHTS: Reviewing *Witchcraft at Salem,* a *Time* critic wrote: "Hansen has done two things admirably well: he has suggested how nearly impossible it is to see another era clearly through the accretion of prejudice and the changes of time. And he has demonstrated that in the Salem witch hunt, as in many others since, it was really the people who led the leaders." *Avocational interests:* Music and photography.

BIOGRAPHICAL/CRITICAL SOURCES: Christian Century, April 30, 1969; *Atlantic,* May, 1969; *Time,* May 2, 1969; *New York Times Book Review,* July 6, 1969; *Saturday Review,* September 27, 1969; *New England Quarterly,* December, 1969; *New York Review of Books,* December 2, 1971; *Journal of American Studies,* Volume VI, number 3, 1972.

*   *   *

HANSEN, Joseph 1923-
(Rose Brock, James Colton, James Coulton)

PERSONAL: Born July 19, 1923, in Aberdeen, S.D.; son of Henry Harold (operator of a retail business) and Alma (Rosebrock) Hansen; married Jane Bancroft (a teacher and translator), August 4, 1943; children: Barbara Bancroft. *Education:* Attended public schools in Aberdeen, S.D., Minneapolis, Minn., and Pasadena, Calif., 1929-42. *Residence:* Los Angeles, Calif. *Mailing address:* c/o Harper & Row Publishers, Inc., 10 East 53rd St., New York, N.Y. 10022.

CAREER: Author and lecturer. Teacher of fiction writing at Beyond Baroque Foundation, Venice, Calif. *Member:* Mystery Writers of America. *Awards, honors:* National Endowment for the Arts grant, 1974; British Arts Council grant for lecture tour of Northumberland, 1975.

WRITINGS—All books are fiction: *Fadeout,* Harper, 1970; *Death Claims,* Harper, 1973; *Troublemaker,* Harper, 1975.

Under pseudonym Rose Brock: *Tarn House,* Avon, 1971; *Longleaf,* Harper, 1974.

Under pseudonym James Colton: *Lost on Twilight Road,* National Library, 1964; *Strange Marriage,* Argyle Books, 1965; *The Corruptor,* Greenleaf Classics, 1968; *Known Homosexual,* Brandon House, 1968; *Cocksure,* Greenleaf Classics, 1969; *Hang-Up,* Brandon House, 1969; *The Outward Side,* Olympia, 1971; *Todd,* Olympia, 1971.

Under pseudonym James Coulton: *Gard,* Award Books, 1969.

Stories have been anthologized in *Killers of the Mind,* Random House, 1974, *Different,* Bantam, 1974, and *Literature of South Dakota,* University of South Dakota Press, 1976. A number of poems have been published under his own name since the 1950's, appearing in *Harper's, Atlantic, Saturday Review, New Yorker,* and other magazines. Contributor of fiction to *South Dakota Review, Tangents, Bachy, Transatlantic Review,* and other literary reviews and articles to *Writer.*

SIDELIGHTS: Joseph Hansen told *CA:* "In most of my novels and short stories my intent has been to deal as honestly as I know how with homosexuals and homosexuality as an integral part of the fabric of contemporary life, rather than something bizarre and alien. I chose the mystery novel form as a way to keep readers turning pages while I gave as faithful a picture as I could of a side of life I believe I understand and that needs no apology. Brainy people read mysteries and by and large reviewers seem to think I've presented a touchy subject in a straightforward way yet without special pleading. *Fadeout, Death Claims,* and *Troublemaker* have been published not only in the U.S. but in England, France, Holland and Japan as well. I believe in the mystery form as a viable one whose potential for dealing with real and deep and moving human problems has only begun to be tapped by a few writers. I hope mightily for its future."

BIOGRAPHICAL/CRITICAL SOURCES: Mystery and Detection Annual, 1977.

*   *   *

HANSEN, Norman J. 1918-

PERSONAL: Born June 22, 1918, in Omaha, Neb.; son of Peder (a grocer) and Barbara (Cutler) Hansen; married Mary E. Johnson, September, 1955; married second wife, Mary G. Wagner (a legal secretary), December, 1969; children: James T., Jan Elaine, Mark C., John N., Paul C. *Education:* University of Nebraska, B.S., 1943, M.A., 1949; graduate study at University of Chicago, 1950, University of Colorado, 1952-55; Central Lutheran Theological Seminary, B.Th., 1959; University of Missouri, further study, 1962-63. *Politics:* Republican.

CAREER: Clergyman of Lutheran Church; high school teacher in Holdrege, Neb., 1943-44, in Kearney, Neb., 1944-45; superintendent of schools, Ericson, Neb., 1945-47; Doane College, Crete, Neb., assistant professor of speech, 1947-52; University of Colorado, Boulder, instructor in speech and English, 1952-55; Lutheran pastor in Hot Springs, Ark., New Carlisle and Brandt, Ohio, Corydon, Ind., and Kansas City, Mo., 1959-64; high school teacher of social studies, Kansas City, 1964-65; Kansas Wesleyan University, Salinas, chairman of speech department, 1965-68; Hiram Scott College, Scottsbluff, Neb., chairman of speech department, beginning 1968. *Member:* Speech Communication Association of America, Nebraska Educational Association of Speech Teachers (past president), Elks, Delta Sigma Rho.

WRITINGS: The Discussion Approach to Speech, Mc-Cutchan, 1969.

WORK IN PROGRESS: Prose and poetry.

AVOCATIONAL INTERESTS: Hunting, fishing, hiking, camping.††

* * *

HANSEN, W(illiam) Lee   1928-

PERSONAL: Born November 8, 1928, in Racine, Wis.; son of William R. and Gertrude (Spillum) Hansen; married Sally Porch (a college teacher), December 26, 1955; children: Ellen, Martha. *Education:* University of Wisconsin, B.A., 1950, M.A., 1955; Johns Hopkins University, Ph.D., 1958. *Religion:* Unitarian Universalist. *Office:* Department of Economics, University of Wisconsin, Madison, Wis. 53706.

CAREER: Johns Hopkins University, Baltimore, Md., instructor in economics, 1955-56; Brookings Institution, Washington, D.C., fellow, 1957-58; University of California, Los Angeles, assistant professor, 1958-63, associate professor of economics, 1963-65; University of Wisconsin—Madison, professor of economics, 1965—. Postdoctoral fellow, University of Chicago, 1961-62; senior staff economist, President's Council of Economic Advisers, 1964-65; Hill Family Foundation Visiting Professor of Economics and Education, University of Minnesota, 1975. *Military service:* U.S. Army, 1951-53; became sergeant. *Member:* International Union for the Scientific Study of Population, Population Association of America, American Economic Association, Industrial Relations Research Association, Conference on Research in Income and Wealth (member of executive committee, 1968-71). *Awards, honors:* Guggenheim fellowship, 1969-70.

WRITINGS: (With Charles Tiebout and R. Thayne Robson) *Markets for California Products,* State of California, 1961; (with Burton A. Weisbrod) *Benefits, Costs, and Finance of Public Higher Education,* Markham, 1969; (editor) *Education, Income and Human Capital,* National Bureau of Economic Research, 1970; (with Glen G. Cain and Richard B. Freeman) *The Labor Market for Scientists and Engineers,* Johns Hopkins University Press, 1973; (editor with Donald Wentworth and Sharryl Hawke) *Perspectives on Economic Education,* Joint Council on Economic Education, 1977. Contributor to economics, labor, and other journals. Member of editorial board, *Journal of Human Resources;* associate editor, *Comparative Education Review.*

WORK IN PROGRESS: Research on schooling and earnings, on supply and demand in the professions, and on social and economic determinants of demand for education.

* * *

HANSON, Peggy   1934-

PERSONAL: Born December 3, 1934, in Shreveport, La.; daughter of Paul David and Edna (Alexander) Pugh; married H. P. Hanson, August 15, 1955; married second husband, Nicolas P. Stein (a major, U.S. Army Aviation), June 17, 1970; children: (first marriage) Michael Lee, Patricia Suzanne. *Education:* Attended Trinity University, San Antonio, one year. *Religion:* Protestant. *Home:* 4826 West 16th St., Lubbock, Tex. 79416.

CAREER: Spent fifteen years in data processing as operator, supervisor, and teacher; lived two years in Saigon, Vietnam as a civilian technical representative for U.S. Army, and three years in Germany; University of Texas Medical Branch at Galveston, assistant to director of Data Processing Center, 1973-76.

WRITINGS: Keypunching, Prentice-Hall, 1966, third edition, 1977; *Operating Data Entry Systems,* Prentice-Hall, 1977.

WORK IN PROGRESS: A journal-diary of her two years in Vietnam; nonfiction of a nontechnical nature.

SIDELIGHTS: Peggy Hanson has retired to Houston, Texas where she owns a design studio creating custom designs for needlepoint canvases.

* * *

HARBOTTLE, Michael (Neale)   1917-

PERSONAL: Born February 7, 1917, in Littlehampton, England; son of Thomas Cecil Benfield (a naval officer) and Kathleen (Kent) Harbottle; children: Simon Neale, Carolyn Daphne. *Education:* Attended Marlborough College, 1931-35, and Royal Military College, Sandhurst, 1936-37. *Religion:* Church of England. *Home:* 860 Hamilton Ter., London NW8 QUL, England. *Agent:* Campbell Thompson & McLaughlin Ltd., 31 Newington Green, London N16 9PU, England.

CAREER: British Army, career officer, 1937-68, retiring as a brigadier general from last assignment as chief of staff, United Nations Force in Cyprus; Sierra Leone Selection Trust Ltd. (British-owned diamond mining company), London, England, and Yengema, Sierra Leone, chief security officer, 1969-70. Consultant and director of studies, International Peace Academy. Visiting senior lecturer, School of Peace Studies, University of Bradford. Sponsor, British-Kurdish Friendship Society. Churchwarden, St. Marks, Hamilton Terrace, London. *Member:* Royal Institute of International Affairs. *Awards, honors:* Order of the British Empire.

WRITINGS: The Impartial Soldier, Oxford University Press, 1970; *The Blue Berets,* Leo Cooper, 1972, revised edition, 1975; (with Rikhye and Eage) *The Thin Blue Line: International Peacekeeping and Its Future,* Yale University Press, 1974; *The Knaves of Diamonds,* Leo Cooper, 1976. Contributor to military journals in Canada and United States.

WORK IN PROGRESS: Miranda, a children's book about a kitten; *A Peacekeeper's Handbook,* a work "on behalf of the International Peace Academy, to assist in the preparation of soldiers of all countries for U.N. third party peacekeeping roles."

SIDELIGHTS: Michael Harbottle writes: "My experience in Cyprus showed me the potential value of peaceful third party intervention, hence my concentration on this subject in my writings. Now retired, my interest is in furthering the teaching of techniques which will improve the international peacekeeping machinery."

AVOCATIONAL INTERESTS: Travel, people, sport.

* * *

HARDING, Jack   1914-

PERSONAL: Born February 7, 1914, in La Porte, Ind.; son of John Egbert and Sadie Jo (Rogers) Harding; married Lela Loudder, December 27, 1946; children: Jacqueline (Mrs. David T. Blake), Jill (Mrs. William N. McDonald III), Benjamin Rogers, Jane (Mrs. R. T. Strader), John Philip. *Education:* Agricultural and Mechanical College of Texas (now Texas A&M University), B.S. in E.E., 1934. *Politics:* Republican. *Religion:* Christian. *Home:* 6401 North Sterling, Oklahoma City, Okla. 73132. *Office:* Big "D" Chemical Co., 1708 West Main St., Oklahoma City, Okla. 73106.

CAREER: Kelvinator Corp., Detroit, Mich., designer, 1934-37; Canada Dry Ginger Ale, Dallas, Tex., division sales manager, 1937-40; Skillern Drug Stores, Dallas, general manager, 1946-50; Southland Corp., Dallas, vice-president, 1950-56; Tracy-Locke Advertising Agency, Dallas, account executive, 1956-58; self-employed lecturer and consultant, Dallas, 1958-67; Big "D" Chemical Co., Oklahoma City, Okla., chief executive, 1967—. Licensed minister in Christian Church. *Military service:* U.S. Army, 1940-46; became major.

WRITINGS: Retail Selling Is Fun!, Interstate, 1970; *Professional Selling,* McNair-Dorland, 1976.

WORK IN PROGRESS: Thus Saith the Lord, a book of sermons; *The Fall of a Great Nation,* a book on democracy.

* * *

HARDY, Leroy C(lyde) 1927-

PERSONAL: Born March 29, 1927, in Welch, Okla.; son of Howard L. (a foundry worker) and Pearl (Headley) Hardy. *Education:* University of California, Santa Barbara, A.B., 1949; University of California, Los Angeles, Ph.D., 1955. *Politics:* Independent. *Religion:* Methodist. *Home:* 15182 Jackson St., Midway City, Calif. 92655. *Office:* Department of Political Science, California State University, 1250 Bellflower Blvd., Long Beach, Calif. 90840.

CAREER: California State University, Long Beach, instructor, 1953-55, assistant professor, 1955-59, associate professor, 1959-63, professor of political science, 1963—, head of department, 1956. Consultant to California Assembly, 1960-61, mayor of Los Angeles, 1962, governor of California, 1964-65, California congressional delegations, 1965, 1967, 1971, 1973. *Military service:* U.S. Navy, 1945-46. *Member:* American Political Science Association, British Political Science Association, Southern Political Science Association, Western Political Science Association, Midwestern Political Science Association, Northeastern Political Science Association, Pi Sigma Alpha, Pi Gamma Mu, Pi Alpha Theta.

WRITINGS: California Government, Harper, 1964, 4th edition, Canfield Press, 1973; (with Robert L. Morlan) *Politics in California,* Dickenson, 1968. Contributor of articles and book reviews to *Western Political Science Quarterly, San Diego Law Review,* and *Pepperdine Law Review.* Member of board of editors, Western Political Science Association, 1962-64.

WORK IN PROGRESS: California Voting Behavior; Introduction to Political Science; California Reapportionment; and *Districting as a Political Process.*

* * *

HARDYCK, Curtis D(ale) 1929-

PERSONAL: Born July 5, 1929, in Mitchell, S.D.; son of Henry B. (a cabinetmaker) and Helen (Ensminger) Hardyck; married Jane Allyn (divorced); children: Allyn. *Education:* Phoenix College, B.A., 1950; University of California, Berkeley, A.B., 1952, Ph.D., 1960. *Office:* School of Education, University of California, Berkeley, Calif. 94720.

CAREER: University of California Medical Center, San Francisco, assistant professor of psychology, 1960-67; University of California, Berkeley, research associate, Institute of Human Learning, 1967, professor of educational psychology, 1968—. *Member:* American Psychological Association, American Association for the Advancement of Science, Society for Psychophysiological Research, Society for Re-

search in Child Development. *Awards, honors:* National Institute of Health Career Development Award, University of California, Berkeley, 1968-72.

WRITINGS: (With L. F. Petrinovich) Introduction to *Statistics for the Behavioral Sciences,* Saunders, 1969, 2nd edition, 1976, with student's workbook, 1969, 2nd edition, 1976; *Understanding Research in the Social Sciences,* Saunders, 1975.

* * *

HARKINS, Philip 1912-
(John Blaine, a joint pseudonym)

PERSONAL: Born September 29, 1912, in Boston, Mass.; son of E. F. Harkins; married Anita Nash, 1953; children: Joan, Arthur Dodge. *Education:* Attended University of Grenoble, 1931-32, and School of Political Science, Paris, 1932-33. *Home:* 2628 Hidden Valley Rd., La Jolla, Calif.

CAREER: Traveled on his own in North Africa and Europe after finishing high school; reporter, and semi-pro hockey player; free-lance writer.

WRITINGS—Mainly junior books: *Coast Guard, Ahoy!,* Harcourt, 1943; *Bomber Pilot,* Harcourt, 1944; *Lightning on Ice,* Morrow, 1946; *Touchdown Twins,* Morrow, 1947; *The Big Silver Bowl,* Morrow, 1947; *Southpaw from San Francisco,* Morrow, 1948; *Punt Formation,* Morrow, 1949; *Son of the Coach,* Holiday House, 1950; *Knockout,* Holiday House, 1950; *Double Play,* Holiday House, 1951; (with Paul Donal Harkins) *The Army Officers Guide,* McGraw, 1951; *Center Ice,* Holiday House, 1952; *Road Race,* Crowell, 1953; *Blackburn's Headhunters,* Norton, 1955; *Young Skin Diver,* Morrow, 1956; *Game, Carol Canning!,* Morrow, 1953; *Breakaway Back,* Morrow, 1959; *The Day of the Drag Race,* Morrow, 1960; *Fight Like a Falcon,* Morrow, 1961; *Argentine Road Race,* Morrow, 1962; *Where the Shark Waits,* Morrow, 1963; *No Head for Soccer,* Morrow, 1964; (with Harold Leland, under joint pseudonym John Blaine), *Danger Below,* Grosset, 1968.

SIDELIGHTS: Blackburn's Headhunters was filmed as "Surrender—Hell," in 1958.†

* * *

HARKNESS, D(avid) W(illiam) 1937-

PERSONAL: Born October 30, 1937, in Dublin, Ireland; son of William Frederick Samuel (a bank official) and Rita Alice (Barrett) Harkness; married Hilary Katherine Margaret Land, August 29, 1964; children: Emma Katherine, Lucy Roisin, Patrick John William. *Education:* Attended Campbell College, Belfast, 1951-56; Corpus Christi College, Cambridge, B.A., 1961; University of Dublin, Ph.D., 1967. *Home:* 84 Marleborough Pk. N., Belfast, Northern Ireland. *Agent:* A. D. Peters & Co., 10 Buckingham St., London WC2N 6BU, England. *Office:* Department of Modern History, Queen's University, Belfast, Northern Ireland.

CAREER: University of Kent at Canterbury, Canterbury, Kent, England, lecturer in history, 1965-75; Queen's University, Belfast, Northern Ireland, professor of Irish history, 1975—. Visiting professor, University of Ibadan, Ibadan, Nigeria, 1971-72. *Military service:* British Army, Royal Engineers, 1956-58; became lieutenant. *Member:* Historical Association, Royal Historical Society (fellow), Royal Commonwealth Society.

WRITINGS: The Restless Dominion: The Irish Free State and the British Commonwealth of Nations, 1923-31, Macmillan, 1969, New York University Press, 1970; *The Post-*

War World, Macmillan, 1974; (contributor) G. Peele and C. Cook, editors, *The Politics of Reappraisal 1918-39,* Macmillan, 1975. Also author of *History and the Irish,* 1976. Contributor to *Journal of Commonwealth Political Studies, Irish Times, History, Historical Journal, Historical Times.*

WORK IN PROGRESS: A biographical study of Patrick MacGilligan.

SIDELIGHTS: D. W. Harkness told *CA:* "We Irish need to view our history with compassion and without anachronism so that it may serve as a medium of understanding, not as an excuse for bitterness. It is my hope to teach and write in this spirit."

*   *   *

HARRELL, Allen W(aylan) 1922-

PERSONAL: Surname rhymes with "barrel"; born December 24, 1922, in Bertie County, N.C.; son of Britton (a farmer) and Bessie (Owens) Harrell; married Irene Burk (a writer and editor), June 22, 1952; children: Thomas, Alice, James, Susan, Marguerite, Maria. *Education:* University of North Carolina, B.S., 1950, J.D., 1953. *Politics:* Democrat. *Religion:* Christian Church (Disciples of Christ). *Home:* 408 Pearson St., Wilson, N.C. 27893.

CAREER: Allsbrook & Benton, Attorneys, Roanoke Rapids, N.C., attorney, 1953-55; private practice of law, Wilson, N.C., 1955-68; City of Wilson, N.C., solicitor, 1957-61; judge of Recorders Court, 1961-68; State of North Carolina (7th Judicial District), Wilson, district judge, 1968—. *Military service:* U.S. Army, Infantry, 1944-46; became staff sergeant; received Purple Heart. *Member:* North Carolina State, district, and county bar associations.

WRITINGS: Splinters from My Gavel: Confessions of a Judge, Zondervan, 1970; (with wife, Irene B. Harrell) *The Opposite Sex,* Word, Inc., 1972; (contributor) Irene B. Harrell, *Security Blankets Family Size,* Word, Inc., 1973. Contributor to *Home Life, Sunday Digest,* and other journals.

AVOCATIONAL INTERESTS: Sunday School teaching, organic gardening.

*   *   *

HARRIS, Bertha 1937-

PERSONAL: Born December 17, 1937, in Fayetteville, N.C.; daughter of John Holmes (a salesman) and Mary (Jones) Harris; divorced; children: Jennifer Harris Wyland. *Education:* University of North Carolina at Greensboro, A.B., 1959, M.F.A., 1969. *Home:* 54 Seventh Ave. S., New York, N.Y. 10014. *Agent:* Elizabeth McKee, Harold Matson Co., Inc., 22 East 40th St., New York, N.Y. 10016. *Office:* Department of Social Science, College of Staten Island of the City University of New York, Staten Island, N.Y. 10301.

CAREER: Formerly taught literature at Eastern Carolina University, Greenville, N.C.; University of North Carolina at Charlotte, instructor in English, 1969-73; College of Staten Island of the City University of New York, Staten Island, N.Y., assistant professor of performing and creative arts, and director of women's studies, 1973—. *Member:* American Association of University Professors.

WRITINGS: Catching Saradove (novel), Harcourt, 1969; *Confession of Cherubino,* Harcourt, 1972; *Traveller in Eternity,* Regency Press, 1975; *Lover,* Daughters, Inc., 1976; (with Emily L. Sisley) *The Joy of Lesbian Sex,* Crown, 1977. Contributor to *Red Clay Reader* and *Greensboro Reader.*

WORK IN PROGRESS: Two novels, one "based very loosely on the central theme of Euripides' *The Bacchae.*"

BIOGRAPHICAL/CRITICAL SOURCES: New York Times Book Review, March 9, 1969; *Nation,* May 19, 1969; Maurice Leonard, *Battling Bertha: A Biography of Bertha Harris,* Regency Press, 1975.

*   *   *

HARRIS, Chauncy D(ennison) 1914-

PERSONAL: Born January 31, 1914, in Logan, Utah; son of Franklin Stewart (a university president) and Estella (Spilsbury) Harris; married Edith Young, September 5, 1940; children: Margaret. *Education:* Brigham Young University, A.B., 1933; Oxford University, B.A., 1936, M.A., 1943; London School of Economics and Political Science, graduate study, 1936-37; University of Chicago, Ph.D., 1940. *Home:* 5649 Blackstone Ave., Chicago, Ill. 60637. *Office:* Center for International Studies, University of Chicago, 5828 University Ave., Chicago, Ill. 60637.

CAREER: Indiana University, Bloomington, instructor in geography, 1939-41; University of Nebraska, Lincoln, assistant professor of geography, 1941-43; University of Chicago, Chicago, Ill., assistant professor, 1943-46, associate professor, 1946-47, professor, 1947-69, Samuel N. Harper Distinguished Service Professor of Geography, 1969—, chairman of department, 1967-69, dean of Graduate Division of Social Sciences, 1954-60, director of Center for International Studies, 1966—, assistant to the President, 1973-75, vice-president for academic resources, 1975—. Visiting professor at University of Frankfurt, 1950-51, and Columbia University, 1954. Served in Office of Geographer, U.S. Department of State, 1943-44, and as chief of urban studies section, Far East Division, U.S. Office of Strategic Services, 1944-45. Member of board of directors, Social Science Research Council, 1959-70; member of executive board, Division of Behavioral Sciences of National Research Council, 1967-70, and of International Council of Scientific Unions, 1969-72. Member of Joint Committee on Slavic Studies, 1954-65, Inter-University Committee on Travel Grants, 1956-65, Joint Committee on the Foreign Area Fellowship Program, 1962-70, and International Research and Exchanges Board, 1968-71.

MEMBER: Association of American Geographers (president, 1957-58), American Association for the Advancement of Slavic Studies (president, 1962), American Geographical Society (vice-president, 1969-74), International Geographical Union (vice-president, 1956-64; secretary-general, 1968-76). *Awards, honors:* Honorary member of geographical societies in London, Paris, Berlin, Frankfort, Rome, Florence, and Warsaw; Rhodes scholar at Oxford University and University of London, 1934-37; D.Econ. (h.c.), Catholic University of Santiago, Chile, 1956; Distinguished Service Award of Geographic Society of Chicago, 1965; Alexander Csoma de Korosi Memorial Medal of Hungarian Geographical Society, 1971; D.Litt., Oxford University, 1973; Honors Award, Association of American Geographers, 1976; Laureat d'Honneur, International Geographical Union, 1976.

WRITINGS: Salt Lake City, a Regional Capital, private edition distributed by University of Chicago Libraries, 1940; (compiler with Jerome D. Fellmann) *A Comprehensive Checklist of Serials of Geographic Value,* Part I, Department of Geography, University of Chicago, 1949, revised and expanded edition published as *A Union List of Geographical Serials,* 1950, further revised edition published as

International List of Geographical Serials, 1960, 2nd edition, 1971; (editor of American edition) S. S. Bal'zak and others, editors of original Russian edition, *Economic Geography of the U.S.S.R.,* translation by Robert M. Hankin and Olga Adler Titelbaum, Macmillan, 1949; (editor with Max Horkheimer) *Universitaet und moderne Gesellschaft: Referate und Diskussionsbeitraege zum dem im Sommer 1957 vom Chicago-Ausschuss der Johann Wolfgang Goethe-Universitaet in Frankfurt am Main veranstalteten Seminar* [Frankfurt am Main], 1959.

An Annotated World List of Selected Current Geographical Serials in English, Department of Geography, University of Chicago, 1960, third edition, expanded and revised, published as *Annotated World List of Selected Current Geographical Serials in English, French and German,* 1971; (editor of American edition) *Soviet Geography: Accomplishments and Tasks* (symposium of fifty chapters), translation by Lawrence Ecker, American Geographical Society, 1962; *Cities of the Soviet Union: Studies in Their Functions, Size, Density and Growth,* Association of American Geographers, 1970; *Guide to Geographical Bibliographies and Reference Works in Russian or on the Soviet Union,* Department of Geography, University of Chicago, 1975; *Bibliography of Geography,* Volume I: *Introduction to General Aids,* Department of Geography, University of Chicago, 1976. Contributing editor, *Geographical Review,* 1960-72; editor, *IGU Bulletin,* 1969-76.

* * *

HARRIS, John S(harp) 1917-

PERSONAL: Born August 5, 1917, in Richmond, Va.; son of James Davis (an elementary school principal and superintendent of schools) and Janet (Sharp) Harris; married Lois Staffelbach (a university instructor), September 4, 1948; children: James Thomas, Steven John. *Education:* University of Richmond, B.S. in B.A., 1939; College of William and Mary, M.A., 1941; Syracuse University, M.S., 1942; University of Chicago, Ph.D., 1951. *Religion:* Methodist. *Home:* R.R. 2, Marshall, Ill. 62441.

CAREER: State of Virginia, Division of the Budget, Richmond, research assistant, 1939-41; Reynolds Metals Co., Richmond, Va., advertising assistant, 1941-42; University of Cincinnati, Cincinnati, Ohio, instructor in political science, 1946-47; University of Chicago, Chicago, Ill., instructor in political science, 1947; University of Southern California, Los Angeles, assistant professor of public administration, 1949-51; University of Tennessee, Knoxville, associate professor of political science, 1951-52; Wayne State University, Detroit, Mich., assistant professor of political science, 1952-56; University of Massachusetts, Amherst, professor of government and head of department, 1956-63, Commonwealth Professor of Government, 1960-70; University of Wisconsin—Parkside, Kenosha, vice-chancellor for academic affairs, 1970-71; University of Wisconsin—Madison, professor of arts administration and public management, 1971-72; Indiana State University, Terre Haute, dean of College of Arts and Sciences, 1972-73, university professor, 1973-75; president, Distributors Terminal Corp., 1975—. *Military service:* U.S. Naval Reserve, 1942-46; became lieutenant senior grade. *Member:* American Political Science Association, American Society for Public Administration, Appalachian Mountain Club, Wilderness Society, Sierra Club, Phi Beta Kappa, Phi Kappa Phi, Omicron Delta Kappa, Pi Sigma Alpha, Pi Delta Epsilon. *Awards, honors:* Rockefeller Foundation research grants, 1964-65, 1967.

WRITINGS: British Government Inspection as a Dynamic Process: The Local Services and the Central Departments, Praeger, 1955; (contributor) J. D. Montgomery and A. O. Hirschman, editors, *Public Policy,* Harvard University Press, 1967; *Government Patronage of the Arts in Great Britain,* University of Chicago Press, 1970. Contributor of about twenty articles to professional journals.

WORK IN PROGRESS: Articles on public administration, British government and politics, and Canadian government and politics.

AVOCATIONAL INTERESTS: Conservation of natural resources, mountain climbing, amateur ornithology, and travel.

* * *

HARRIS, Michael R(ichard) 1936-

PERSONAL: Born August 23, 1936, in Boise, Idaho; son of Sydney and Merle (Meadows) Harris. *Education:* Stanford University, B.A., 1958, M.A., 1962, Ph.D., 1966. *Home:* 2155 Outpost Dr., Los Angeles, Calif. 90068. *Office:* 250 South Rossmore St., Los Angeles, Calif. 90004.

CAREER: Pomona College, Claremont, Calif., administrator and instructor, 1964-68, assistant professor of history, 1968-69; Claremont Graduate School, Claremont, director of Institute for Study of Change in the Four-Year College, 1969-70, assistant dean and assistant professor of history and education, 1970-72; Marlborough School, Los Angeles, Calif., instructor in history, 1972-77. Member of advisory board, Los Angeles Clearing House for Minority Students, 1966-68. *Member:* American Historical Association, American Association for Higher Education, Organization of American Historians, Mormon History Association (member of board of directors), Town Hall of California.

WRITINGS: Five Counterrevolutionists in Higher Education, Oregon State University Press, 1970. Member of national editorial board, *Dialogue,* 1966-76.

WORK IN PROGRESS: Historical screenplays.

* * *

HARRIS, Stephen L(eRoy) 1937-

PERSONAL: Born February 5, 1937, in Aberdeen, Wash.; son of Glenn Edwin and Ruby O. (Bell) Harris; married Marjorie B. Miller (a college instructor), September 4, 1965; children: Geoffrey Edwin, Jason Mark. *Education:* University of Puget Sound, B.A. (with honors), 1959; Cornell University, M.A., 1961, Ph.D., 1964. *Politics:* Liberal Democrat. *Home:* 3630 Maplewood Lane, Sacramento, Calif. 95825. *Office:* Department of Humanities, California State University, 6000 J St., Sacramento, Calif. 95819.

CAREER: Acting librarian, Washington State Historical Society, 1963; Washington State University, Pullman, assistant professor of English, 1964-65; California State University, Sacramento, assistant professor, 1965-69, associate professor of English, 1969-72, director of interdepartmental humanities program, 1970—, chairman of department of humanities, 1972-76, professor of humanities, 1974—. *Member:* California Classics Association, California Humanities Association, Philological Association of Central California (president), Mu Sigma Delta. *Awards, honors:* Woodrow Wilson fellow, 1960-61.

WRITINGS: (Editor and author of critical essays) *The Humanist Tradition in World Literature: An Anthology of Masterpieces from Gilgamesh to "The Divine Comedy,"*

C. E. Merrill, 1970; *Fire and Ice: The Cascade Volcanoes,* Mountaineers, 1976, revised edition, 1977. Drama, movie, and music critic, *Sacramento Union,* 1968-75.

WORK IN PROGRESS: Island Summer, Island Death, a mystery novel.

AVOCATIONAL INTERESTS: The ancient Near East, archaeology, religion, mountain climbing, reading English mystery novels.

*   *   *

HARRIS, Walter A. 1929-

PERSONAL: Born September 28, 1929, in New York, N.Y.; son of Harold I. and Jean (Jacobs) Harris; married June 19, 1955; wife's name, Barbara. *Education:* City College (now City College of the City University of New York), New York, N.Y., B.S.S., 1950; New School for Social Research, M.A., 1952. *Politics:* Democrat. *Religion:* Jewish. *Home:* 86-11 151st Ave., Howard Beach, N.Y. 11414.

CAREER: Port Richmond High School, Staten Island, N.Y., chairman of social studies department, 1965-74; Sheephead Bay High School, Brooklyn, N.Y., principal, 1974—. *Military service:* U.S. Army, Infantry, 1950-54; served in Korea. *Member:* New York City Council on Economic Education (member of board of directors), Phi Beta Kappa.

WRITINGS: (Author of workbook) Albert Alexander and others, *Modern Economy in Action,* Pitman, 1968; *Introductory Economics: Analysis and Practice,* Burgess, 1970; (co-author) *Economics for Everybody,* AMSCO School Publications, 1973; *Current Issues in American Democracy,* AMSCO School Publications, 1975.

WORK IN PROGRESS: Collaborating on a textbook on Western civilization, completion expected in 1978.

AVOCATIONAL INTERESTS: Travel.

*   *   *

HARRISON, Barbara 1941-

PERSONAL: Born January 22, 1941, in New York, N.Y.; daughter of Alexander (in hotel management) and Ann (Sukulak) Harrison. *Education:* Attended schools in New York and Vermont, receiving a B.A. degree. *Politics:* Liberal Democrat. *Religion:* Roman Catholic. *Home and office:* 400 East 57th St., New York, N.Y. 10022.

CAREER: Playboy Organization, New York, N.Y., publicity director, 1963-68; former public relation consultant for a film production firm, Cinegraphique, and volunteer worker in political campaigns.

WRITINGS—Novels; all published by Avon: *The Pagans,* 1970; *City Hospital,* 1975; *The Gorlin Clinic,* 1975.

WORK IN PROGRESS: Researching for a sports novel.†

*   *   *

HARRISON, Chip 1952-

PERSONAL: Born September 12, 1952, in Chicago, Ill.; son of John Wesley (a criminal) and Dorothy (Leigh) Harrison. *Education:* Attended Upper Valley Preparatory Academy, 1968. *Religion:* Pantheist. *Home:* "No fixed address." *Agent:* Henry Morrison, Inc., 58 West Tenth St., New York, N.Y. 10011.

CAREER: Held odd jobs as assistant pavement photographer, salesman for a termite exterminating company, fruit picker, busboy, handyman, and deputy sheriff in a South Carolina house of prostitution; currently employed as assistant to private detective Leo Haig.

WRITINGS: No Score (originally entitled *Lecher in the Rye*), Fawcett, 1970; *Chip Harrison Scores Again,* Fawcett, 1971; *Make Out with Murder,* Fawcett, 1973; *The Topless Tulip Caper,* Fawcett, 1974.

SIDELIGHTS: Chip Harrison told *CA:* "I suppose I'll be writing another book but what it's about will depend on what happens in the next year." When asked for comments on his work, he said, "I don't really want to go into all this now because actually this is the sort of thing I put in the books, except for changing the names which you have to do for legal reasons."

*   *   *

HARRISON, Fred 1917-

PERSONAL: Born April 30, 1917, in Syracuse, Kan.; son of Charles F. (a physician) and Bessie (Manker) Harrison; married Berniece Robb, November, 1952. *Education:* Attended New Mexico Military Institute, 1935-37.

CAREER: U.S. Weather Bureau, weather observer in Washington, D.C., and then in Amarillo, Tex., 1957-61; *Amarillo Citizen,* Amarillo, reporter and editor, 1962-64; owner of farming interests in Kansas and free-lance writer in Amarillo, 1964—. *Military service:* U.S. Army Air Forces, 1942-46; became sergeant; received Asiatic-Pacific Theater Medal with two Bronze Stars and Air Medal.

WRITINGS: Hell Holes and Hangings, Clarendon Press, 1968. Contributor of about seventy-five short stories to western magazines.

WORK IN PROGRESS: Army-Indian Battles of the West.††

*   *   *

HARSH, Wayne C. 1924-

PERSONAL: Born November 13, 1924, in WaKeeney, Kan.; son of Douglas David (a plasterer) and Ocia (Yarborough) Harsh; married Diane Regez (divorced). *Education:* Colorado State College (now University), B.A., 1950; University of Denver, M.A., 1953; University of Groningen, additional study, 1959-60; University of California, Berkeley, Ph.D., 1963. *Home:* Rd. 97, Russell Blvd., Davis, Calif. 95616. *Office:* Department of English, University of California, Davis, Calif. 95616.

CAREER: High school teacher in California, 1953-57; Ohio University, Athens, assistant professor of English, 1962-64; University of California, Davis, assistant professor, 1964-66, associate professor, 1967-73, professor of English and linguistics, 1973—. Visiting summer professor at University of Southern California, 1964, and University of California, Berkeley, 1967; Fulbright professor, University of Athens, 1968-69. Guest lecturer at University of Poznan, University of Hull, University of York, University of Mainz, Aristotelian University, and for U.S. Information Service in Berlin and Greece. Consultant-reader for publishers, including Doubleday, Heath, and Scott, Foresman. *Military service:* U.S. Army, 1943-46; became sergeant.

MEMBER: Modern Language Association of America, National Council of Teachers of English, Philological Association of the Pacific Coast, California Association of Teachers of English. *Awards, honors:* Fulbright scholar at University of Groningen, 1959-60.

WRITINGS: (Contributor) Samuel Everett and Christian

O. Arndt, editors, *Teaching World Affairs in American Schools: A Case Book,* Harper, 1956; (author of introduction to teacher's edition) Anne Kirby, *Elementary School English,* Addison-Wesley, 1967; *The Subjunctive in English,* University of Alabama Press, 1968; *Introduction to Linguistics: A Guidebook for Teachers,* McCutchan, 1968; (with C. H. Marrah, R. V. Marsh, and H. G. Shane) *New Approaches to Language and Composition,* Laidlaw Brothers, Book 7, 1969, Book 8 (with T. H. Wetmore as additional author), 1969; "Laidlaw Linguistic" series, Grades 3-6, 9-10, Laidlaw Brothers, 1972; (contributor) Porter G. Perrin and Wilma R. Ebbit, *Writer's Guide and Index to English,* revised edition (Harsh was not associated with earlier edition), Scott, Foresman, 1972; (editor with Helen Mills) *Commanding Sentences,* Scott, Foresman, 1974. Author of monographs on the teaching of English and grammar; contributor to education journals.

WORK IN PROGRESS: Meaning and Convention in Punctuation and Printing: A Linguistic Analysis; error analysis in English by Greek speakers.

* * *

HART, Ray L(ee) 1929-

PERSONAL: Born March 22, 1929, in Hereford, Tex.; son of Albert Mann and Ruby Douglas (Bracken) Hart; married Juanita Fern Morgan, 1951; children: Douglas Morgan, Stuart Bracken. *Education:* University of Texas, B.A., 1949; Southern Methodist University, B.D., 1953; Yale University, Ph.D., 1959. *Home:* 16 Carriage Way, Missoula, Mont. 59801. *Office:* Department of Religious Studies, University of Montana, Missoula, Mont. 59801.

CAREER: Drew University, Theological School, Madison, N.J., instructor, 1956-59, assistant professor of philosophy and theology, 1959-63; Vanderbilt University, Divinity School, Nashville, Tenn., associate professor of theology, 1963-69; University of Montana, Missoula, professor of religious studies and chairman of department, 1969—. *Member:* American Academy of Religion, Society for the Scientific Study of Religion, Society for Religion in Higher Education, Metaphysical Society of America, Foundation for the Arts, Religion and Culture, American Association of University Professors, New Haven Theological Society. *Awards, honors:* American Association of Theological Schools faculty research fellow at American Academy in Rome, 1962-63; Society for Religion in Higher Education grant, 1967-68.

WRITINGS: (Editor; translation into Chinese by N. Z. Zia) *Sheng to mo ti shen hsueh* (title means "Selections from Thomas Aquinas"), Foundation for Theological Education in Southeast Asia, 1966; *Unfinished Man and the Imagination: Toward an Ontology and a Rhetoric of Revelation,* Herder & Herder, 1968. Contributor to *Britannica Junior Encyclopaedia;* contributor of about fifteen articles and reviews to theology and humanities journals. Editor, *Journal of American Academy of Religion,* 1969—.

BIOGRAPHICAL/CRITICAL SOURCES: Christian Century, September 3, 1969.

* * *

HARTCUP, Guy 1919-

PERSONAL: Born May 30, 1919, in Reading, England; son of Montagu (a mining engineer) and Winifred Hartcup; married Henrietta Greaves, May 30, 1953; children: two stepsons. *Education:* St. Catharine's College, Cambridge, B.A. (honors), 1947. *Religion:* Church of England. *Home:* 3 Chestnut Ave., East Sheen, London S.W. 14, England.

CAREER: British Air Ministry, Air Historical Branch, London, England, historian, 1948-59; International Atomic Energy Agency, Vienna, Austria, English editor, 1960-62; British Cabinet Office, Historical Section, London, assistant historian, 1962-64; H. M. Treasury, Historical Section, London, historian, 1964-76; general editor, Royal Commission on Civil Liability and Compensation, 1976—. *Military service:* British and Indian Armies, 1939-46; became lieutenant. *Member:* International Institute for Strategic Studies, Council of the Airship Association (vice-chairman).

WRITINGS: Origins and Development of Operational Research in the Royal Air Force, H.M.S.O., 1963; *The Challenge of War: Britain's Scientific and Engineering Contributions to World War Two,* Taplinger, 1970; *The Achievement of the Airship,* David & Charles, 1975; *Mulberries: The Planning, Construction, and Operation of the Normandy Harbours,* David & Charles, 1977. Contributor to Purnell's *History of the Second World War.*

AVOCATIONAL INTERESTS: Painting in watercolor and gouache (work has been exhibited at Royal Academy and other London galleries).

* * *

HART-DAVIS, Duff 1936-

PERSONAL: Born June 3, 1936, in London, England; son of Rupert (a publisher and author) and Comfort (Turner) Hart-Davis; married Phyllida Barstow, April 22, 1961; children: Alice, Guy. *Education:* Attended Eton College, 1949-54; Oxford University, B.A. (second class honors), 1960. *Home:* Bromsden Farm, Henley-on-Thames, England. *Agent:* Curtis Brown Ltd., 575 Madison Ave., New York, N.Y. 10022. *Office: Daily Telegraph,* Fleet St., London E.C.4, England.

CAREER: Worked as a deckhand on a cargo boat on the West African coast and pioneered a motor route to Moscow and Crimea, 1957; *Sunday Telegraph,* London, England, feature writer, 1969-75, literary editor, 1975-76, assistant editor, 1977—. *Military service:* British Army, 1955-57; became second lieutenant.

WRITINGS: Behind the Scenes on a Newspaper, Dent, 1964; *The Megacull,* Constable, 1968; *The Gold Trackers,* Doubleday, 1970 (published in England as *The Gold of St. Matthew,* Constable, 1970); *Spider in the Morning,* Doubleday, 1972; *Ascension: The Story of a South Atlantic Island,* Doubleday, 1973; *Peter Fleming* (biography), J. Cape, 1974.

WORK IN PROGRESS: Monarchs of the Glen: A History of Deerstalking in the Scottish Highlands, for J. Cape.

SIDELIGHTS: Duff Hart-Davis spent eighteen months in Germany, 1955-56, visited Ascension Island, 1966 and 1969, and on assignment for the *Sunday Telegraph* has reported from many parts of the world, including Nepal, India, Afghanistan, Iran, the Persian Gulf, Turkey, Europe, and the Caribbean. *Avocational interests:* Deer (study, conservation, and hunting).

* * *

HARTFORD, Claire 1913-

PERSONAL: Born November 28, 1913, in Brooklyn, N.Y.; daughter of Bernard B. (a manufacturer) and Rose (Mutterperl) Brown; married Ben Iceland, June 8, 1935; married second husband, Ken H. Hartford (a business manager), April 11, 1943 (died November 16, 1973); married Aaron Hornstein (a dentist), May 2, 1976; children: (second marriage) Bruce A., Daniel C. *Education:* Attended City College (now City College of the City University of New York), two years, Los Angeles City College, one year, and Southern Connecticut State College, one year. *Politics:* Democrat. *Religion:* Jewish. *Home:* 1170 Whitney Ave., Hamden, Conn. 06517. *Agent:* Barthold Fles Literary Agency, 507 Fifth Ave., New York, N.Y. 10017.

CAREER: Employed in medical public relations, Los Angeles, Calif., 1947-53, in union public relations, Los Angeles, 1953-60, in public service broadcasting, Los Angeles, 1960-63, in academic public relations, Hamden, Conn., 1963-64, and in academic research, New Haven, Conn., 1964-68; Miller & Fink Publications, Greenwich, Conn., staff writer, 1969-71; Quinnipiac College, Hamden, director of public relations, 1971-76. Professional actress, appearing in stage plays and television programs, including ''Divorce Court'' and ''Youth Court.'' Executive secretary, California Broadcasters Association, 1962-63. *Member:* American Federation of Radio and Television Artists.

WRITINGS: (With Milton J. E. Senn) *The First Born: Experiences of Eight American Families,* Harvard University Press, 1968. Contributor of about twenty articles and short stories to *Coronet, Health, Patient Care,* and other magazines.

WORK IN PROGRESS: A novel, *The Pitied One;* short stories; research for a possible novel about the labor movement in the thirties and forties.

* * *

HARTMAN, Olov 1906-

PERSONAL: Born May 7, 1906, in Stockholm, Sweden; son of Carl August (a Salvation Army officer) and Anna (Karlsson) Hartman; married Ingrid Ohlsson, July 14, 1929; children: Lars, Anna-Britta (Mrs. Sten-Bertil Risberg), Per, Ingrid (Mrs. Per Soederberg), Hans, Sven, Karin. *Education:* University of Uppsala, teol.cand., 1932. *Home:* Kaerrvaegen 19, Sigtuna, Sweden.

CAREER: Church of Sweden, clergyman assigned to pastoral work in different dioceses and parishes, 1932-38; perpetual curate in Naessjoe, Sweden, 1938-48; Sigtuna Foundation, Sigtuna, Sweden, director, doing pastoral counseling and leading conferences, 1948-70; associate court chaplain, Sweden, 1965—. *Member:* Sveriges Foerfattarefoerening, Sveriges Dramatikerfoerbund. *Awards, honors:* Gustaf VI Adolf's Minnesmedalj; Nordstjerneorden; D.D. from University of Lund; Wallin Prize, 1972; Prize of the Nine, 1976.

WRITINGS: Opium foer folket, Sveriges kristliga Studentroerelses Bokfoerlag, 1935; *Dopets gaava foerpliktar,* Svenska kyrkans Diakonistyrelses Bokfoerlag, 1939.

Ett heligt arv, Svenska kyrkans Diakonistyrelses Bokfoerlag, 1940; *I tid och otid,* Svenska kyrkans Diakonistyrelses Bokfoerlag, 1941; *Att bedja Guds ord,* C.W.K. Gleerup Bokfoerlag, 1943; *I noed och lust,* Svenska kyrkans Diakonistyrelses Bokfoerlag, 1943; *Att foelja en stjaerna,* Svenska kyrkans Diakonistyrelses Bokfoerlag, 1945; *Stormvarning,* Svenska kyrkans Diakonistyrelses Bokfoerlag, 1948; *Doed med foerhinder* (novel), Norlin, 1948; *Helig maskerad* (novel), Norlin, 1949, translation by Karl A. Olsson published as *Holy Masquerade,* Eerdmans, 1963.

Maenniskor i roett (novel), Norlin, 1950, translation by Eric J. Sharpe published as *Marching Orders,* Eerdmans, 1970; *Natten skulle lysa saasom dagen* (sermons), Svenska kyrkans Diakonistyrelses Bokfoerlag, 1951; *Aer Gud moralisk?* (booklet of radio sermons), Radiotjaenst, 1951; *Medmaenskligt* (essays), Raben & Sjoegren, 1952; *Den heliga staden* (drama), Raben & Sjoegren, 1953; *Saasom i en spegel* (sermons), Svenska kyrkans Diakonistyrelses Bokfoerlag, 1953; *Kunst und Christentum* (booklet of essays), [Hamburg], 1953; *Profet och timmerman* (church drama) Raben & Sjoegren, 1954; *Stenfisken* (short stories), Raben & Sjoegren, 1954; *Borg och bro: En bok om Sigtunastiftelsen,* Svenska kyrkans Diakonistyrelses Bokfoerlag, 1955, translation by Margareta Angstroem published as *The Sigtuna Foundation,* S.C.M. Press, 1955; *Oxens tecken* (sermons), Svenska kyrkans Diakonistyrelses Bokfoerlag, 1955; *Jordiska ting* (essays), Raben & Sjoegren, 1956, translation and introduction by Eric J. Sharpe published as *Earthly Things,* Eerdmans, 1968; *Livets krona* (church drama), Raben & Sjoegren, 1956; *Adam och Eva: En Studie i biblisk aektenskapssyn,* Svenska kyrkans Diakonistyrelses Bokfoerlag, 1957; *Den brinnande ugnen* (church drama), Raben & Sjoegren, 1958; *Innanfoer* (novel), Raben & Sjoegren, 1958, translation by Elsa Kruuse published as *The Sudden Sun,* Fortress, 1964; *Oeppna kyrkan* (essays), Svenska kyrkans Diakonistyrelses Bokfoerlag, 1958; *Brusande Vaag* (autobiographical novel; also see below), Raben & Sjoegren, 1959; *Tre kyrkospel,* Raben & Sjoegren, 1959, translation by Brita Stendahl published as *Three Church Dramas,* Fortress, 1966.

Gud i nattens timmar (sermons), Svenska kyrkans Diakonistyrelsens Bokfoerlag, 1960; *Staellet om toernbusken* (essays on Christianity and theology), Raben & Sjoegren, 1961; *Korsfararen* (three-act miracle play), Raben & Sjoegren, 1962; *Marias oro* (church drama), Raben & Sjoegren, 1961, translation by Sharpe published as *Mary's Quest,* Faith Press, 1963; *Ett fritt evangelium* (essays), Svenska kyrkans Diakonistyrelsens Bokfoerlag, 1963; *Vad aer det: En katekes i ord och bild,* Raben & Sjoegren, 1965; *Medan synagogfoerestaandaren vaentar* (sermons), Svenska kyrkans Diakonistyrelsens Bokfoerlag, 1966; *Eld och Kontrapunkt* (two plays), Raben & Sjoegren, 1967; *Den borttraengda himlen* (sermons, 1951-67), Svenska kyrkans Diakonistyrelsens Bokfoerlag, 1967; (compiler) *Bibeln laest i dag* (essays), Raben & Sjoegren, 1967; (compiler) *Att bli gammal* (lectures), Verbum, 1967; *Baeraren* (drama), Raben & Sjoegren, 1968, translation by Brita Stendahl published as *On That Day,* Fortress, 1968; *Jordbaevningen i Lissabon,* Raben & Sjoegren, 1968.

Efter oss (drama), Raben & Sjoegren, 1970; *Miljoevesper Maessa och Meditation* (two liturgies), Verbum, 1971; *Vad aer da en maenniska* (sermons), Verbum, 1972; *Tva spel* (two plays), Verbum, 1972; *Trefaldighetsmaessa* (liturgy), Hakan Ohlssons, 1973; *Massa for rattvisan* (liturgy), Hakan Ohlssons, 1973; *En ay Manniskosonens dagar* (meditations), Verbum, 1973; *Den korsfasta skapelsen* (meditations), Verbum, 1973; *Profeten Jesus och hans vaenner* (essays), Verbum, 1975; *Med Gud och hans vaenskap* (liturgy), Nordiska Musikfoerlaget, 1976; *Brusande vag* (first part of memoirs; adaptation of autobiographical novel of same title), Raven & Sjoegren, 1977; *Livstecken* (second part of memoirs), Raben & Sjoegren, 1977.

Omnibus volumes: *The Crucified Answer: The Fortress Press Book for Lent and Easter,* translation by Gene L. Lund, Fortress, 1967; *The Birth of God: Readings for Advent, Christmas, and Epiphany,* translation by Lund, Fortress, 1969.

AVOCATIONAL INTERESTS: Fishing (''although today I have not time for that''), ornithology (''which I can cultivate in a couple of hours now and then''), music (''with an accent on baroque'').

BIOGRAPHICAL/CRITICAL SOURCES: Kai Henmark, *Orden foervandlas till haender Om Olov Hartman som pros-aberaettre, in En fagel av eld,* Raben & Sjoegren, 1962; *Vaar Loesen,* Number 5-6, 1966 (issue honoring Hartman on his sixtieth birthday); *Earthly Things,* introduction by Eric J. Sharpe, Eerdmans, 1968; *Kirkens Verden,* August, 1971; George Robert Jacks, ''Five Dramas of the Swedish Church-Drama Movement Discussed with Reference to Hartman's Theology and Symbolism'' (doctoral dissertation), Columbia University, 1972; *Svenska Dagbladet,* December 5, 1972.

* * *

HARWOOD, Edwin 1939-

PERSONAL: Born January 4, 1939, in Pasadena, Calif.; son of Edwin T. (a businessman) and Marie (Evans) Harwood; married Susan Rosenthal, June 10, 1965; children: Brina Jennifer, Alexander Edwin. *Education:* Stanford University, B.A., 1962; University of Chicago, M.A., 1963, Ph.D., 1966. *Politics:* Republican. *Home:* 2512 Alameda Ave., Sarasota, Fla. 33580. *Office:* New College, University of South Florida, Sarasota, Fla. 33580.

CAREER: Rice University, Houston, Tex., instructor in sociology, 1966-71; Harvard University, Cambridge, Mass., visiting lecturer, 1971-72; Kenyon College, Gambler, Ohio, associate professor, 1972-73; University of Texas, Odessa, professor, 1973-75; University of South Florida, Sarasota, associate professor at New College, 1975—. *Military service:* U.S. Army, 1957-60. *Member:* American Sociological Association, Phi Beta Kappa.

WRITINGS: (With W. C. McCord and John Howard) *Life Styles in the Black Ghetto,* Norton, 1969. Contributor to *Contemporary Social Problems,* Harcourt, 1976; also contributor to *The Public Interest* and *Wall Street Journal.*

* * *

HASLAM, Gerald W. 1937-

PERSONAL: Born March 18, 1937, in Bakersfield, Calif.; son of Fred M. (an oil worker) and Lorraine (Johnson) Haslam; married Janice E. Pettichord, July 1, 1961; children: Frederick, Alexandra, Garth, Simone, Carlos. *Education:* San Francisco State College (now University), A.B., 1963, M.A., 1965; Washington State University, additional study, 1965-66. *Home:* 1100 G St., Petaluma, Calif. 94952. *Office:* California State College, Sonoma, 1801 East Cotati Ave., Rohnert Park, Calif. 94928.

CAREER: Before and during his college years, Haslam worked as a roustabout in oilfields, picked, plowed, irrigated, and packed crops in the San Joaquin Valley, and was employed in stores, banks, and shops; San Francisco State College (now University), San Francisco, Calif., instructor in English, 1966-67; California State College, Sonoma, Rohnert Park, professor of English, 1967—. *Military service:* U.S. Army, 1958-60. *Member:* College Language Association, National Council of Teachers of English, Western Literature Association, California Teachers Association, California Association of Teachers of English, Sierra Club, Trout Unlimited, Valley of the Moon Track Club, Napa Valley Runners' Club, Little Hills Striders. *Awards, honors:* *Arizona Quarterly* nonfiction award, 1969, for ''The Subtle Thread''; General Semantics Foundation grant; Joseph Henry Jackson Award, 1970, for *Okies.*

WRITINGS: (Editor) *Forgotten Pages of American Literature,* Houghton, 1970; *William Eastlake,* Steck, 1970; (trans-

lator) Alexander Ecker, *The Anatomy of the Frog,* Lubrecht & Cramer, 1971; *The Language of the Oilfields,* Old Adobe Press, 1972; *Okies: Selected Stories,* New West Publications, 1973, revised and enlarged edition, Peregrine Smith, 1975; (editor) *Western Writings,* University of New Mexico Press, 1974; *Jack Schaefer,* Boise State College Western Writers, 1976; *Masks: A Novel,* Old Adobe Press, 1976; (editor with John S. Bullen) *Critics West,* Everett/Edwards, 1978; (editor with James D. Houston) *California Heartland,* Capra, 1978. Short stories included in anthologies, including *The Far Side of the Storm,* edited by Gary Elder, Holmgangers, 1975, *Father Me Home Wind,* and *American Ethnic Stories.* General editor, ''Western American Writers'' series, Everett/Edwards. Contributor to *Arizona Quarterly, College English, Western American Literature, Negro American Literature Forum, The Nation, American History Illustrated, New Society, Southwest Review, Mother Jones,* and other journals; has had many short stories and poems published. Former production editor, *ETC: A Review of General Semantics.* Editor, *Ecolit.*

WORK IN PROGRESS: Hawk Flights: Stories from the West; Big Hunk, a novel; continued forays into interpretative journalism.

AVOCATIONAL INTERESTS: Backpacking, flyfishing, competitive running.

* * *

HASLER, Joan 1931-

PERSONAL: Born June 11, 1931, in Hutton, Essex, England; daughter of William George (a company director) and Elsie (Wentworth) Hasler. *Education:* Lady Margaret Hall, Oxford, B.A. (honors in modern history), 1952; Institute of Education, London, Postgraduate Certificate in Education, 1953. *Religion:* Christian. *Home:* 17 Albany Gardens West, Clacton on Sea, Essex, England.

CAREER: Bedford High School, Bedford, England, head of history department, 1959-66; Colchester County High School, Colchester, England, headmistress, 1967-76.

WRITINGS: The Making of Russia (juvenile), Longmans, Green, 1969, Delacorte, 1970. Contributor to *History of Parliament Trust* and *Victoria County History of Essex.*

* * *

HAUSSIG, Hans Wilhelm 1916-

PERSONAL: Born October 3, 1916, in Berlin, Germany; son of Hans (an architect) and Elisabeth (Boderke) Haussig; married Margarete Nicksch, 1957; children: Hans Michael. *Education:* Friedrich-Wilhelm-University, Berlin, Ph.D., 1939. *Home:* 1 Berlin 33, Meisenstrasse 14, West Berlin, Germany. *Office:* Leiter der Abteilung fuer Byzantinische Geschichte, Geschicte Vorder-und Mittelasiens, Ruhr-Universitaet Bochum, 463 Bochum, Germany.

CAREER: Freie Universitaet Berlin, West Berlin, Germany, docent, 1956—, professor of Byzantine history, 1968—; Ruhr-Universitaet Bochum, Bochum, Germany, professor and head of department of Byzantine history and history of Western and Central Asia, 1969—. *Member:* Deutsche Morgenlaendische Gesellschaft, Societe Asiatique (Paris).

WRITINGS: (Editor and author of commentary) *Herodot, Historien,* Kroener Verlag (Stuttgart), 1955; (with Franz Altheim) *Die Hunnen in Osteuropa,* Verlag fuer Kunst und Wissenschaft B. Grimm (Baden-Baden), 1958; *Kulturgeschichte von Byzanz,* Kroener Verlag, 1959, 2nd edition,

1966, translation by Joan Hussey published as *History of Byzantine Civilization*, Praeger, 1971; *Byzantinische Geschichte*, Kohlhammer Verlag, 1970.

Editor of "Mythologisches Woerterbuch der alten Kulturvoelker," published by Ernst Klett Verlag (Stuttgart), 1958—.

SIDELIGHTS: Kulturgeschichte von Byzanz has also been translated into Italian and Polish.

*   *   *

HAVLICE, Patricia Pate   1943-

PERSONAL: Born February 2, 1943, in Cleveland, Ohio; daughter of Edward A. (a machinist) and Theresa (Makuc) Pate; married Richard F. Havlice (a chemical engineer), September 9, 1967. *Education:* Ursuline College for Women, B.A., 1965; University of Michigan, M.A.L.S., 1966. *Home:* 333 Ellen Lane, Batavia, Ill. 60510.

CAREER: Cuyahoga County Public Library, Cleveland, Ohio, adult services librarian, 1966-67; Ohio State University Library, Columbus, junior reference librarian, 1967-68; Indiana University, Northwest Regional Campus Library, Gary, senior reference librarian, 1969-70.

WRITINGS—All published by Scarecrow: *Art in Time* (index to all the pictures in the art section of *Time* magazine), 1970; *Index to American Author Bibliographies*, 1971; *Index to Artistic Biography*, 1973; *Index to Literary Biography*, 1975; *World Painting Index*, 1977.

WORK IN PROGRESS: First supplement of *Popular Song Index*.

AVOCATIONAL INTERESTS: Needlework of all kinds.

*   *   *

HAWKESWORTH, Eric   1921-
(The Great Comte)

PERSONAL: Born May 22, 1921, in Heanor, Derbyshire, England; son of William (a builder) and Lucy (Hill) Hawkesworth; married Margaret Flook, February 15, 1958; children: Helen, Hazel. *Education:* Attended secondary school in Derbyshire, England. *Religion:* Church of England. *Home:* 31 St. John's Priory, Lechlade, Glos GL7 3EZ, England.

CAREER: Conjurer since his school days; during World War II service performed (in addition to his regular duties) for troops in many parts of the world; professional entertainer, 1946—, presenting music hall illusion shows as The Great Comte: began to write magazine articles in 1950, later expanding the writing to give him more time at home with less disruption of family life. Inventor of more than two hundred illusions. *Military service:* Royal Air Force, aero engineer, 1941-46. *Member:* Belongs to a number of British and international magician's societies and was founder member of several.

WRITINGS—All published by Faber, except as noted: (With Norman Hunter) *Successful Conjuring,* 2nd edition (Hawkesworth had no connection with the 1st edition), C. Arthur Pearson, 1963; *Practical Lessons in Magic,* 1967, Meredith, 1968; (self-illustrated) *Making a Shadowgraph Show* (juvenile), 1969; *The Art of Paper Tearing* (juvenile), 1970; *Conjuring,* 1971; *Puppet Shows to Make,* 1972; *A Magic Variety Show,* 1973; *Rag Picture Shows,* 1974; *Pleated Paper Folding,* 1975; *Paper Cutting,* 1976, S. G. Phillips, 1977. Contributor to magazines of do-it-yourself articles on model steam locomotives, vintage cars, caravan-

ning, and conjuring; contributor of action stories for children to *Tarzan Adventures*.

SIDELIGHTS: Eric Hawkesworth told *CA:* "I first became interested in magic while still in junior grade at school and used to present backyard theatre with a stage built from old boxes and a pair of Mum's old curtains for the front tabs. All the kids of the neighbourhood used to come and watch the show. . . . All my tricks and illusions were home-built from material culled out of books on loan from our town's lending library. I well remember the thrill of finding a whole shelf full of books on conjuring and magic . . . works by Houdini, Maskelyne and Devant and Will Blythe . . . all great artists of the past . . . and their writings and guidance encouraged this young magician into a lifetime of pleasureable entertainment. I have always carried a picture of keen, young beginners finding [my] books on the shelves of their libraries and being entranced with the work in the same way I was."

AVOCATIONAL INTERESTS: Building live steam locomotives (1½-inch scale) big enough to haul passengers; also maintains a 1929 Rolls-Royce Phantom II, which is used daily for family transport.

BIOGRAPHICAL/CRITICAL SOURCES: Times Literary Supplement, October 16, 1969.

*   *   *

HAYES, E(ugene) Nelson   1920-

PERSONAL: Born October 19, 1920, in Salem, Mass.; son of Eugene (a clerk) and Helen Fuller (Sargent) Hayes; married Nena Polulech (a teacher), June 18, 1946; married second wife, Alexia K. Selig (an architectural secretary), May 14, 1960; children (first marriage): Tanya, Arthur, Deirdre; stepchildren: Carla Herwitz, Alexander Herwitz. *Education:* Cornell University, A.B., 1942, graduate study, 1942-45. *Home:* 34 Hume Ave., Medford, Mass. 02155.

CAREER: Instructor in English at Cornell University, Ithaca, N.Y., 1942-45, and Union College, Schenectady, N.Y., 1945-58; Skidmore College, Saratoga Springs, N.Y., assistant professor of English, 1948-50; Sylvania, Salem, Mass., technical writer for applications laboratory, 1950-51; Porter Sargent, Inc. (publishers), writer, editor, and education consultant, 1951-58; Smithsonian Astrophysical Observatory, Cambridge, Mass., senior editor, 1959-73; currently freelance writer, editor and book reviewer. Member of faculty at Tufts University. *Member:* American Academy of Political and Social Science.

WRITINGS: (Editor) *The Directory for Exceptional Children,* Sargent, 1953, 5th edition, 1965; *Trackers of the Skies,* Smithsonian Institution, 1967; (editor with William Kvaraceus) *If Your Child Is Handicapped,* Sargent, 1969; (editor with daughter, Tanya Hayes) *Claude Levi-Strauss: The Anthropologist as Hero,* M.I.T. Press, 1970; (editor with James C. Cornell) *Man and Cosmos,* Norton, 1975. Columnist for Citizen Group Publications. Contributor of articles and reviews to *Nineteenth Century Fiction, Progressive, New Leader, Philosophical Review, Washington Post, New York Review,* and other journals and newspapers. Associate book editor, *Quincy Patriot Ledger.*

WORK IN PROGRESS: Revised edition of *If Your Child Is Handicapped;* research for an extensive study of alcoholism and twentieth-century American writers.

*   *   *

HAYES, Edward L(ee)   1931-

PERSONAL: Born September 26, 1931, in Modesto, Calif.;

son of G. Lester (a farmer) and Sylvia (Utzinger) Hayes; married Marilyn Elizabeth Bjorklund, July 31, 1954; children: Carla, Darryl, Bryan. *Education:* Westmont College, B.A., 1953; Dallas Theological Seminary, Th.M., 1957; University of Denver, Ph.D., 1966; Stanford University, additional study, 1969. *Politics:* Republican. *Home:* 4701 East Fremont Pl., Littleton, Colo. 80120. *Office:* Conservative Baptist Theological Seminary, P.O. Box 10,000, University Park Station, Denver, Colo. 80210.

CAREER: Baptist clergyman; Biola College, La Mirada, Calif., assistant professor of Christian education, 1957-60; Conservative Baptist Theological Seminary, Denver, Colo., professor of Christian education, 1961—, assistant dean, 1970-72, academic dean, 1972—. Member of board of directors, Evangelical Teacher Training Association and Westmont College. *Member:* Evangelical Theological Society, American Association for Higher Education, Association of Professors of Christian Education. *Awards, honors:* Association of Theological Schools and Lilly Foundation faculty fellowship, 1969, and administrative development grant, 1976.

WRITINGS: Words to Live By, Moody, 1968.

Contributor: Paul Loth, editor, *The Church's Educational Ministry,* Evangelical Teacher Training Association, 1967; Roy G. Irving and Roy B. Zuck, editors, *Youth and the Church,* Moody, 1968, revised edition, 1976; Zuck and Gene A. Getz, editors, *Adult Education in the Church,* Moody, 1970; Bruce Shelley, editor, *A Call to Christian Character,* Zondervan, 1970; Marvin Taylor, editor, *Foundations for Christian Education in an Era of Change,* Abingdon, 1976. Contributor to religious journals.

*   *   *

HAYES, James T(homas) 1923-

PERSONAL: Born December 3, 1923, in Franklin, Ky.; son of Vaude O'Neal and Lola (Barrett) Hayes; married Jessica Shanklin, May 17, 1947 (divorced, 1972); children: Marcus, Marcia. *Education:* Austin Peay State University, B.S., 1950; Western Kentucky University, M.A., 1953; Michigan State University, additional graduate study, 1960-61. *Politics:* Republican. *Religion:* Congregational. *Home:* 1605 Belmonte Dr., Murray, Ky. 42071. *Office:* English Department, Murray State University, Murray, Ky. 42071.

CAREER: High school teacher in Kentucky, 1946-53, in Michigan, 1953-62; Central Michigan University, Mount Pleasant, lecturer, 1961-62; Murray State University, Murray, Ky., assistant professor, 1962-65, associate professor of English, 1965—. *Military service:* U.S. Army, 1943-46, 1950-51; became technical sergeant. *Member:* National Council of Teachers of English, American Association of University Professors, Conference on College Composition and Communication, Council for Basic Education, American Federation of Astrologers, International Society for Astrological Research. *Awards, honors:* L.H.D., Geneva College, 1967.

WRITINGS: Rhetoric: Then and Now, Holbrook, 1970; *Introduction to Natal Astrology,* University Books, 1974. Columnist for National Features Syndicate, 1973-76. Contributor to education journals, and about one hundred articles annually on astrology and parapsychology to other publications. Contributing editor, *Future Star Horoscope,* 1976—.

WORK IN PROGRESS: Textbook in intermediate and advanced classical astrology.

SIDELIGHTS: James T. Hayes wrote to *CA:* "My motivation to write is to share with others that which I have discovered through study and research. Actually, my purpose is always to inform or to teach; and I realize the greatest of satisfaction from a letter or a telephone call from someone who tells me that he has indeed found the process of learning to be easy and pleasurable through the study of that which I have written."

*   *   *

HAYES, Louis D. 1940-

PERSONAL: Born December 12, 1940, in Durango, Colo.; son of Clarence O. and Martha (Metzgar) Hayes; married Carol Samsel, August 21, 1962; children: Douglas, Kristin. *Education:* University of Colorado, B.A., 1962; University of Arizona, M.A., 1964, Ph.D., 1966. *Home:* 615 Evans, Missoula, Mont. 59801. *Office:* Department of Political Science, University of Montana, Missoula, Mont. 59801.

CAREER: University of Wisconsin—Milwaukee, assistant professor of political science, 1968; University of Montana, Missoula, assistant professor, 1968-71, associate professor, 1971-75, professor of political science, 1975—, chairman of department, 1972-77, director of Bureau of Government Research. *Awards, honors:* Fulbright lecturer in Nepal, 1970-71, and in Afghanistan, 1977.

WRITINGS: (Editor with Ronald D. Hedlund) *The Conduct of Political Inquiry: Behavioral Political Analysis,* Prentice-Hall, 1970; *American Foreign Policy and the Kashmir Crisis,* University of Arizona Press, 1970; *Federalism: One American Experience,* Bureau of Government Research, University of Montana, 1976.

WORK IN PROGRESS: Coal Development in Montana: Politics and Public Policy.

*   *   *

HAYTER, Alethea 1911-

PERSONAL: Born November 7, 1911, in Cairo, Egypt; daughter of Sir William and Alethea (Slessor) Hayter. *Education:* Lady Margaret Hall, Oxford, B.A., 1932. *Religion:* Church of England. *Home:* 1 Montagu Sq., London W1H 1RA, England.

CAREER: Country Life, London, England, member of editorial staff, 1934-38; held wartime positions in Gibraltar, Bermuda, Trinidad, and London, 1939-45; British Council, London, assignments in London, Athens, and Paris, 1945-67, representative and cultural attache with British Embassy for Belgium and Luxembourg, 1967-71. Governor, Old Vic Theatre. *Member:* Society of Authors (member of committee of management), Royal Society of Literature (fellow). *Awards, honors:* W. H. Heinemann Award, Royal Society of Literature, 1962, for *Mrs. Browning: A Poet's Work and Its Setting;* Rose Mary Crawshay Prize, British Academy, 1969, for *Opium and the Romantic Imagination;* Officer of Order of the British Empire, 1970.

WRITINGS: Mrs. Browning: A Poet's Work and Its Setting, Barnes & Noble, 1962; *A Sultry Month: Scenes of London Literary Life in 1846,* Faber, 1965; *Elizabeth Barrett Browning,* Longmans, Green, 1965; *Opium and the Romantic Imagination,* University of California Press, 1968; *Horatio's Version,* Faber, 1972; *A Voyage in Vain: Coleridge's Journey to Malta in 1804,* Faber, 1973. Also author of introduction and notes for *Confessions of an English Opium Eater,* by Thomas De Quincey, and *Melmath the Wanderer,* by C. R. Maturin, both for Penguin. Contributor of articles and reviews to *Times, Country Life, Ariel, History Today, Times Literary Supplement,* and *New Statesman.*

WORK IN PROGRESS: Selected Letters of Edward Fitzgerald.

SIDELIGHTS: "So many acid-heads and speed-freaks have come lurching through Huxley's Doors of Perception in search of poetic inspiration," a *New Republic* critic writes, "that it is good to have a book that unsensationally traces the effects of opium—the daddy of all 'consciousness-expanders'—on a previous generation of romantics. With the exception of that shaky pillar of rectitude, Wordsworth, every major and most minor English romantic writers at least dabbled with opium, Miss Hayter maintains, and two of them—Coleridge and De Quincey—wrote eloquently about their addictions." Her major theme in *Opium and the Romantic Imagination,* according to the *New Republic,* is that "opium will not of itself supply the imagination with anything that was not already dormant there. At best the poet may *think* it has done so. . . ."

But Geoffrey Grigson in the *Listener* mentions another of Alethea Hayter's conclusions: that "opium might—to begin with—prolong sensations normally evanescent. Coleridge's laudanum above the Dead Sea of the Bristol Channel and Colbone's inky ravine perhaps helped him, says Miss Hayter, to prolong his reverie, his sleep, at any rate of the external senses, into the writing down of 'Kubla Khan.'" *Opium and the Romantic Imagination* makes clear, as a *Time* reviewer explains, that "for most of the 19th century's mind blowers, opium meant laudanum, an alcoholic solution of the drug used as a common painkiller. Laudanum was cheaper than beer and regarded as scarcely more harmful. . . . Under such names as 'Mother Bailey's Quieting Syrup' and 'Venice Treacle,' it was prescribed for children more or less as aspirin is today. . . . In the end, Alethea Hayter makes obvious, all writers have to face the banal truth that confronts everyone: in art, as in life, there are few long-term shortcuts."

BIOGRAPHICAL/CRITICAL SOURCES: Punch, December 4, 1968; *Listener,* December 12, 1968; *New Republic,* February 15, 1969; *Book World,* March 2, 1969; *Time,* May 30, 1969; *Virginia Quarterly Review,* summer, 1969.

*   *   *

HEAD, Bessie 1937-

PERSONAL: Born July 6, 1937, in South Africa; married Harold Head (separated); children: Howard. *Education:* Educated in South Africa as a primary teacher. *Politics:* None ("dislike politics"). *Religion:* None ("dislike formal religion"). *Address:* P.O. Box 15, Serowe, Botswana, Africa.

CAREER: Taught small children in South Africa for about six years.

WRITINGS—All novels: *When Rain Clouds Gather,* Simon & Schuster, 1969; *Maru,* McCall, 1971; *A Question of Power,* Pantheon, 1973. Contributor to *New African, Transition,* and other periodicals.

WORK IN PROGRESS: A collection of short stories; book about Botswana Village life; historical novel on the founding of the old British Bechuanaland Protectorate.

SIDELIGHTS: Fittingly enough, Bessie Head set her first novel in a Botswana village named Golema Mmidi, which means "to grow crops." Fittingly, because much of her daily activity is absorbed by the care of a seedling nursery in her yard, geared mainly toward vegetable production. "My life has been very haphazard," she writes. "I've done many things [primary teaching was her only professional post], and . . . I find eventually that work with crops/plant life interests me deeply. Perhaps I like food so much because I've been poor. . . . But there are deeper causes for human suffering and starvation—perhaps found in the realm of the spirit and I'd record these causes in books. I am generally interested in all people. And in a new age, of peace and happiness." She added that she had filled out the *CA* form "because I am usually terrorized by various authorities into accounting for my existence; and filling in forms, under such circumstances, acquires a fascination all its own."

BIOGRAPHICAL/CRITICAL SOURCES: Best Sellers, March 15, 1969.

*   *   *

HEARD, (Henry Fitz) Gerald 1889-1971 (H. F. Heard)

October 6, 1889—August 14, 1971; English-born philosopher, educator, and author of books on religion and man. Obituaries: *New York Times,* August 19, 1971; *Washington Post,* August 20, 1971; *Time,* August 30, 1971; *Publishers' Weekly,* September 6, 1971. (See index for *CA* sketch)

*   *   *

HEATH, Jim F(rank) 1931-

PERSONAL: Born April 9, 1931, in Clarendon, Tex.; son of James Frank (a furniture salesman) and Texie (Hukel) Heath; married Carole Wilson (a high school teacher), January 25, 1951 (divorced, 1973); married Judith A. Letcher, January 11, 1975; children: Nancy B., Ann F. *Education:* Attended Amarillo Junior College, 1949-51; University of New Mexico, B.B.A., 1953, M.A., 1955; Stanford University, Ph.D., 1967. *Politics:* Independent. *Home:* 4400 Southwest Dickinson, Portland, Ore. 97219. *Office:* Department of History, Portland State University, Portland, Ore. 97207.

CAREER: Portland State University, Portland, Ore., assistant professor, 1967-70, associate professor, 1970-74, professor of history, 1974—. Teaching associate, Danforth Foundation, 1970-72. *Military service:* U.S. Air Force, 1955-57; became captain. *Member:* American Historical Association, Organization of American Historians, American Association of University Professors. *Awards, honors:* American Council of Learned Societies grant, 1973-74; Outstanding Educators of America award, 1974-75.

WRITINGS: John F. Kennedy and the Business Community, University of Chicago Press, 1969; *Decade of Disillusionment: The Kennedy-Johnson Years,* Indiana University Press, 1975.

WORK IN PROGRESS: Business-government relationships during World War II.

*   *   *

HECHT, Henri Joseph 1922- (Henri Maik)

PERSONAL: Born March 27, 1922, in Paris, France; son of Joseph (a painter and engraver) and Ingrid (Morssing) Hecht; married Irma Chevalier (director of a school), January 22, 1946; children: Sylvain, Frederic, Ingrid. *Education:* Attended primary and secondary schools in France. *Home:* 25 rue lu Moulin, La Vierge, Paris 14, France.

CAREER: Painter with his own studio in Paris, France, 1956—.

WRITINGS—Self-illustrated children's books under pseudonym Henri Maik: *L'Oiseau charmant,* Desclee de Brouwer, 1966, translation published in America as *The Foolish Bird,* Luce, 1968; *Flegmatique le Lion,* Desclee de Brouwer, 1967, translation published in England as *Livingstone the Lion,* Evans Brothers, 1969, and in America as *The Flying Lion,* Putnam, 1970; *Hermes le Crocodile bleu,* Desclee de Brouwer, 1968; *Bismuth le Tigre,* Desclee de Brouwer, 1972.

SIDELIGHTS: Henri Hecht traveled in the United States and Mexico, 1967.

BIOGRAPHICAL/CRITICAL SOURCES: Times Literary Supplement, October 16, 1969.

* * *

HECHT, Joseph C. 1924-

PERSONAL: Born August 26, 1924, in Brooklyn, N.Y.; son of Abraham (a businessman) and Tillie (Druckman) Hecht; married Phyllis Miller, December 25, 1950; children: Idette Cary, Devorah Leslie, Bennett Lowell. *Education:* Long Island University, B.S., 1948; New York University, M.A., 1950, Ed.D., 1964. *Religion:* Hebrew. *Home:* 145 Linden Ave., Verona, N.J. 07044. *Office:* Montclair State College, Upper Montclair, N.J. 07043.

CAREER: Department store salesman in New York, N.Y., 1945-47, in Brooklyn, N.Y., 1947-48, in Poughkeepsie, N.Y., 1952-60; high school coordinator of distributive education, Millville, N.J., 1948-50, Poughkeepsie, N.Y., 1950-59; Dutchess Community College, Poughkeepsie, chairman of retail business management program, 1959-64; Montclair State College, Upper Montclair, N.J., professor of distributive education, 1964—. *Military service:* U.S. Army, Airborne, 1943-45; served in European theatre of operations and France. *Member:* American Vocational Association, National Association of Distributive Education Teachers, Association of Two Year Colleges Marketing and Retailing Educators (president, 1959), Delta Pi Epsilon, Epsilon Delta Epsilon.

WRITINGS: (With Karen R. Gillespie) *Retail Business Management,* McGraw, 1970, revised edition published as *Retail Business Management: Two,* 1977. Contributor to marketing and educational journals.

* * *

HECHTLINGER, Adelaide 1914-

PERSONAL: Born October 23, 1914, in New York, N.Y.; daughter of Philip and Jennie Pruss; married Irving Hechtlinger (in manufacturing), 1948; children: Phyllis. *Education:* New York University, B.Sc., 1934; Adelphi University, graduate study, 1960-63. *Religion:* Jewish. *Home:* 149 Island Parkway N., Island Park, N.Y. 11558.

CAREER: New York (N.Y.) Board of Education, teacher, 1957—; Far Rockaway High School, Queens, N.Y., member of science staff, 1960—.

WRITINGS: Modern Science Dictionary, Franklin Publishing Co. (Palisade, N.J.), 1959; (with Harold Visner) *Simple Science Experiments for the Elementary Grades,* Franklin Publishing Co., 1960; *Q + A Biology,* Arco, 1962; *A Simple Soupbook,* Branden Press, 1969; *Cooking with Bread,* Greene, 1970; (editor) *The Great Patent Medicine Era; or, Without Benefit of Doctor,* Grosset, 1970; (with Wilbur Cross) *The Complete Book of Paper Antiques,* Coward, 1973; *American Quilts, Quilting, and Patchwork,* Stackpole, 1975; *Historic Homes and Sights of Revolutionary*

America, Volume I, Pelican, 1976; *The Seasonal Hearth: The Woman at Home in Early America,* Overlook Press, 1977. Domestic science editor, *Early American Life.*

SIDELIGHTS: All trips Adelaide Hechtlinger makes are geared to her interest in early American history and life. She has an extensive collection of all sorts of materials relating to this interest.

* * *

HEDGES, Ursula M. 1940-

PERSONAL: Born January 9, 1940, in Lucknow, Uttar Pradesh, India; daughter of Vere (a clergyman) and Gwen (Carrau) Wood-Stotesbury; married Allan George Hedges (a teacher), January 12, 1961; children: Kenneth Allan, Dwane Robert, Linelle Ursula. *Education:* Longburn College, New Zealand, diploma for secretarial course, diploma in Bible instructor's course, and certificate of theological normal training, 1958. *Religion:* Seventh-day Adventist. *Address:* c/o Seventh-day Adventist Conference of Northern New Zealand, 591 Dominion Rd., Balmoral, Auckland, New Zealand.

CAREER: Seventh-day Adventist Conference of Northern New Zealand, Auckland, secretarial work and Bible instructor, 1959-60; Price Waterhouse & Co., Auckland, secretary-receptionist, 1960; leader and teacher of youth groups in Australia, New Zealand, and New Guinea; free-lance interior decorator; teacher of creative art in adult education programs, 1971—.

WRITINGS: Sasa Rore: Little Warrior (juvenile), Review & Herald, 1966; *Carol and Johnny Go to New Guinea* (juvenile), Review & Herald, 1967; *Down Under with Carol and Johnny* (juvenile), Review & Herald, 1973. Editor of monthly, "Adventist School Journal," printed in Warburton, Australia. Author of plays for young people, and stories and poems for religious periodicals.

WORK IN PROGRESS: Birth of a School, a book about her experiences in helping start a boarding school in the New Guinea jungles; a juvenile, *Australian Days, Panim Appointment,* and *Something Out of Nothing,* for Review & Herald.

* * *

HEERWAGEN, Paul K. 1895-

PERSONAL: Born November 29, 1895, in Little Rock, Ark.; married Adele Ramsey (a bridge teacher), June 11, 1918; children: Paul K., Jr., William Ramsey. *Education:* University of Arkansas, B.S.A., 1918. *Politics:* Democrat. *Religion:* Presbyterian. *Home and office:* 338 Washington Ave., Fayetteville, Ark. 72701.

CAREER: War Production Board, Fort Smith, Ark., manager, 1943-44; Heerwagen Acoustic Co., Fayetteville, Ark., owner and manager, 1946-59. *Member:* Westerners (Chicago Corral).

WRITINGS: Snowball (juvenile), Pioneer Press (Little Rock, Ark.), 1957; *Indian Scout, Western Painter: Captain Charles L. von Berg,* Pioneer Press, 1969. Contributor of feature stories to magazines and newspapers.

WORK IN PROGRESS: The Grace of the Dunes.

* * *

HEILNER, Van Campen 1899-1970

July 1, 1899—July 12, 1970; American editor, author, and explorer. Obituaries: *New York Times,* July 13, 1970; *Washington Post,* July 14, 1970.

HEIMBECK, Raeburne S(eeley) 1930-

PERSONAL: Born September 25, 1930, in Rock Island, Ill.; son of Harold Holmyard (an architect) and Dulce (Seeley) Heimbeck; married Joye Marcoe, August 30, 1953 (divorced 1972); children: Bryn Evan, Reid Deverin. *Education:* Stanford University, B.A., 1952, Ph.D., 1963; Fuller Theological Seminary, B.D., 1955; additional study at Victoria University of Wellington, 1958-59, and University of Zurich, 1964-65. *Home:* 910 East 9th Ave., Apt. 1, Ellensburg, Wash. 98926. *Office:* Central Washington State College, Ellensburg, Wash. 98926.

CAREER: Stanford University, Stanford, Calif., instructor, 1959-61, acting assistant professor of speech and drama, 1961-64; Episcopal Theological Seminary of the Southwest, Austin, Tex., associate professor of theology, 1965-67; Central Washington State College, Ellensburg, associate professor, 1967-69, professor of humanities, 1969-74, professor of religious studies, 1974—. William H. Bonsall Visiting Professor of Humanities, Stanford University, 1976. *Awards, honors:* Fulbright fellow in New Zealand, 1958-59; Church Society for College Work faculty fellow in Switzerland, 1964-65.

WRITINGS: Theology and Meaning: A Critique of Metatheological Scepticism, Stanford University Press, 1969. Contributor to theology journals.

WORK IN PROGRESS: Enigmatic Man: Meditations on Human Self-understanding.

AVOCATIONAL INTERESTS: Participant sports.

* * *

HEIMER, Melvin Lytton 1915-1971

July 5, 1915—February 8, 1971; American columnist and writer of short stories and novels. Obituaries: *New York Times,* February 9, 1971; *Variety,* February 10, 1971. (See index for *CA* sketch)

* * *

HEIRICH, Max 1931-

PERSONAL: Surname is pronounced Hy-rick; born May 13, 1931, in Aurora, Ill.; son of Charles A. (a contractor) and Virginia (Lea) Heirich; married Jane Ruby (a musician), June 12, 1956; children: Douglas, Alan, Julia, Deborah. *Education:* Attended College of Emporia, 1949-50; Earlham College, B.A., 1953; University of California, Berkeley, M.A., 1963, Ph.D., 1967. *Religion:* Society of Friends. *Home:* 2229 Hilldale, Ann Arbor, Mich. 48105. *Office:* Department of Sociology, University of Michigan, Ann Arbor, Mich. 48105.

CAREER: Warren Wilson College, Swannanoa, N.C., instructor in sociology, 1953-54; American Friends Service Committee, projects director in Richmond, Ind., 1954-57, college secretary for seven southeastern states with headquarters in High Point, N.C., 1957-60; University of California, Berkeley, acting instructor in sociology, 1965-66; University of Michigan, Ann Arbor, assistant professor, 1967-70, associate professor in department of sociology and in Residential College, 1970—, associate director of Residential College, 1972—. Consultant, President's Advisory Commission on the Causes and Prevention of Violence, 1968-70. *Member:* American Sociological Association, Society for the Study of Religion in Higher Education. *Awards, honors:* Woodrow Wilson fellow, 1960-61; Rackham research fellow, summer, 1969.

WRITINGS: (Contributor) S. M. Lipset and S. S. Wolin, editors, *The Berkeley Student Revolt,* Doubleday, 1966; *The Beginning: Berkeley, 1964-1965,* Columbia University Press, 1970; *The Spiral of Conflict: Berkeley, 1964-1965,* Columbia University Press, 1971. Contributor to sociology journals.

WORK IN PROGRESS: Asking Sociological Questions, a textbook, for Prentice-Hall; research on religious conversion and commitment.

AVOCATIONAL INTERESTS: Music—performing and occasional composing; camping.

BIOGRAPHICAL/CRITICAL SOURCES: Nation, May 10, 1971.†

* * *

HELMERICKS, Harmon R. 1917-
(Bud Helmericks)

PERSONAL: Born January 18, 1917, in Gibson, Ill.; son of Clarence James (owner of a store) and Abbie (Cornelius) Helmericks; married Constance Chittenden, April 27, 1941 (divorced); married Martha M. Morlang, February 22, 1953; children: (first marriage) Constance Jean, Carol Ann; (second marriage) Mark H., Jeffrey T., James W. *Education:* University of Arizona, M.E. *Politics:* Republican. *Religion:* Presbyterian. *Residence:* Colville River Delta via Barrow, Alaska 99723.

CAREER: Writer about Alaska, 1947—; founder and owner of Arctic Tern Fish Co., Barrow, Alaska, 1952-65; Arctic research director for Eastman Kodak Co., 1962-65; director of western Arctic operation for Northern Transportation Co.; pilot. Arctic consultant to Gulf Oil Co. and Union Oil Co. Master guide licensed by Alaska Game Commission. *Military service:* U.S. Army, Corps of Engineers. *Member:* Explorers Club, Circumnavigators Club, Airplane Owners and Pilots Association.

WRITINGS—With former wife, Constance Helmericks; all published by Little, Brown, except as indicated: *We Live in the Arctic,* 1947; *Our Summer with the Eskimos,* 1948; *Our Alaska Winter,* 1949; *The Flight of the Arctic Tern,* 1952.

Sole author under name Bud Helmericks: *Arctic Hunter,* 1955; (self-illustrated with photographs) *Arctic Bush Pilot,* 1956; *Oolak's Brother,* 1963; *The Last of the Bush Pilots,* Knopf, 1969. Contributor to *Life, Reader's Digest, Sports Afield,* and other magazines.

WORK IN PROGRESS: Research in Arctic flying history and Arctic fish resources; a study of the polar bear; a book on arctic oil and conservation.

SIDELIGHTS: Harmon Helmericks was the originator of the arctic ice island method of drilling for oil in the Arctic ocean and considered a leading authority on arctic ice and arctic conservation and resources. He has made two trips around the world to study conservation practices, concentrating mainly on Africa, India, and Europe.

* * *

HELMORE, G(eoffrey) A(nthony) 1922-

PERSONAL: Born December 26, 1922, in Herne Bay, Kent, England; son of Leonard (a printer) and Alice (Gush) Helmore; married Joan Parker (a newspaper proofreader), May 4, 1943; married second wife, Jean Martin (a teacher), January 20, 1963 (died April, 1975); married Jean Evelyn Dawes (a teacher), May 1, 1975; children: (first marriage) John Christopher, Jennifer Mary; (second marriage) Damelza Jane, Piran Mark. *Education:* St. Luke's College, Exeter, teacher's certificate, 1942; University of Leeds, Advanced Diploma in Primary Education, 1961. *Religion:* Church of England. *Home:* Nampara, Lowertown, Helston, Cornwall, England.

CAREER: Assistant teacher at schools in Romford, Essex, England, 1946-49, and Rainham, Essex, England, 1949-53; head teacher at St. Buryan, Penzance, Cornwall, England, 1953-60, and Portscatho, Truro, Cornwall, England, 1962-65; head teacher at Parc Eglos County Primary School, Helston, Cornwall, England, 1965—. *Military service:* Royal Navy, 1942-46; became lieutenant.

WRITINGS: Piaget–a Practical Consideration of the General Theories and Work of Jean Piaget, with an Account of a Short Follow Up Study of His Work on the Development of the Concept of Geometry, Pergamon, 1969.

WORK IN PROGRESS: A professional biography, illustrating what educational change has meant in the day-to-day life of the teacher in England; a four year plan of religious services for school children aged seven to eleven years based upon the pattern of school year.

* * *

HELPS, Racey 1913-1971

February 2, 1913—January 25, 1971; British antiquarian bookseller and children's author and illustrator. Obituaries: *Publishers' Weekly,* March 29, 1971. (See index for *CA* sketch)

* * *

HEMMING, John (Henry) 1935-

PERSONAL: Born January 5, 1935, in Vancouver, British Columbia, Canada; son of Henry Harold and Alice (Weaver) Hemming. *Education:* Attended Eton College, Windsor, England, 1948-53, and McGill University, 1953-54; Oxford University, B.A., 1957, M.A., 1960. *Politics:* None. *Religion:* None. *Office:* Municipal Journal Ltd., 178-202 Great Portland St., London W.1, England; and Royal Geographical Society, 1 Kensington Gore, London SW7, England.

CAREER: Maclean-Hunter Publishing Co., Toronto, Ontario, assistant editor, 1957-59; deputy leader in Brazil, Iriri River Exploration Party, 1961; Brintex Exhibitions Ltd., London, England, managing director, 1963-70; Municipal Journal Ltd., London, deputy chairman, 1965-76, chairman, 1976—. Trustee of *Geographical Magazine* and *Survival International,* both London. *Military service:* Canadian Army, Militia Artillery, 1958-59; became first lieutenant. *Member:* Royal Geographical Society (director and chairman, 1976—), Anglo-Brazilian Society (council member), Travellers Club, Beefsteak Club. *Awards, honors:* Robert Pitman Literary Prize, 1970, and Christopher Award, 1971, both for *The Conquest of the Incas.*

WRITINGS: The Conquest of the Incas, Harcourt, 1970; (co-author) *Tribes of the Amazon Basin in Bazil,* Charles Knight, 1973; *Red Gold: The Conquest of the Brazilian Indians,* Macmillan, 1977. Contributor to *Sunday Times, Observer, Sunday Telegraph,* and other publications in England. *Assistant editor,* Civic Administration (*Toronto*).

SIDELIGHTS: "The great merit of John Hemming's fascinating book," according to J. H. Plumb in *Book World,* "is that he keeps all the complex issues to the fore.... Hemming sacrifices the full dramatic intensity of this story [of Pizarro, the Spanish conqueror of Peru] in order to explore the world of the Incas and the tangled issues which its capture brought to trouble the conscience of the Spanish court.... To say that it replaces the *Conquest of Peru* would be absurd, but it is worthy to stand by the side of Prescott's masterpiece." An *Economist* critic also made a Hemming-Prescott comparison: "Anyone who rides into Prescott country today has to decide whether he is going to tread in the same tracks or turn a scholarly gaze in the directions that Prescott overlooked. Mr. Hemming has managed to do something of both.... Eminently readable, Mr. Hemming's book is most valuable because it brings the multi-faceted collision between two civilisations into the clearest light of common day."

Hemming told *CA* that he has "a deep concern with the fate of original or primitive tribes clashing with modern society. The Spanish conquest of Inca Peru was one of the first colonial invasions of the Americas; but lesser invasions are still taking place, as native peoples find their homelands occupied in the name of progress."

He has traveled quite widely in all continents, including a crossing of an unusual part of the Sahara and of the Syrian desert, a major exploration of an unknown part of Brazil, and visits to remote tribes in Brazil, Peru, and central Africa.

BIOGRAPHICAL/CRITICAL SOURCES: New Statesman, July 10, 1970; *Economist,* July 11, 1970; *Observer Review,* August 9, 1970; *Book World,* October 11, 1970.

* * *

HENDERSON, G(eorge) P(atrick) 1915-

PERSONAL: Born April 22, 1915, in Alves, Moray, Scotland; son of George Aitchison (a clergyman) and Violet (Mackenzie) Henderson; married Hester Lowry Douglas McWilliam (a driving instructor), August 9, 1939. *Education:* University of St. Andrews, M.A. (first class honors in philosophy), 1936; Oxford University, B.A., 1938, M.A., 1943. *Politics:* Liberal. *Religion:* Protestant. *Home:* "The Pendicle," Invergowrie, by Dundee DD2 5DQ, Scotland. *Office:* Department of Philosophy, University of Dundee, Dundee DD1 4HN, Scotland.

CAREER: University of St. Andrews, St. Andrews, Scotland, assistant lecturer in logic and metaphysics, 1938-40; University of Edinburgh, Edinburgh, Scotland, Shaw fellow in mental philosophy, 1939-41; University of St. Andrews, lecturer, 1946-53, senior lecturer in logic and metaphysics, 1953-59; University of Dundee, Dundee, Scotland, professor of philosophy, 1959—, dean of the faculty of arts and social sciences, 1973-76. Corresponding member, Academy of Athens, 1972. *Military service:* British Army, Royal Artillery, 1940-46; became captain. *Member:* Mind Association, Aristotelian Society, British Society of Aesthetics, Scots Philosophical Club, Scottish-Hellenic Society, National Trust for Scotland.

WRITINGS: The Revival of Greek Thought, 1620-1830, State University of New York Press, 1970. Contributor to philosophical journals. Editor, *Philosophical Quarterly,* 1962-72.

WORK IN PROGRESS: The Ionian Academy, 1824-64.

* * *

HENDERSON, Stephen E. 1925-

PERSONAL: Born October 13, 1925, in Key West, Fla.; son of James and Lenora (Sands) Henderson; married Jeanne Holman, June 14, 1958; children: Stephen E., Jr.,

Timothy A., Philip L., Alvin Malcolm. *Education:* More-house College, A.B., 1949; University of Wisconsin, M.A., 1950, Ph.D., 1959. *Home:* 1703 Lebanon St., Langley Park, Md. 20783. *Office:* Institute for the Arts and the Humanities, P.O. Box 723, Howard University, Washington, D.C. 20059.

CAREER: Taught at Virginia Union University, Richmond, 1950-62; Morehouse College, Atlanta, Ga., professor of English and chairman of department, 1962-71; Howard University, Washington, D.C., professor of Afro-American studies, 1971—, director of Institute for the Arts and the Humanities, 1973—. *Military service:* U.S. Army, 1944-45. *Member:* National Council of Teachers of English, American Association of University Professors, College Language Association, South Atlantic Modern Language Association, Phi Beta Kappa. *Awards, honors:* Danforth research grant; Southern Fellowships Fund grant; American Council of Learned Societies, General Education Board, grant.

WRITINGS: (With M. Cook) *The Militant Black Writer in Africa and the United States,* University of Wisconsin Press, 1969; *Understanding the New Black Poetry,* Morrow, 1973. Contributor of articles to *Ebony, Black World, New Directions.*

WORK IN PROGRESS: Long essay on contemporary black poetry; critical anthology of blues poetry.

AVOCATIONAL INTERESTS: Art (paints in water colors), folk and classical music, following current scientific developments.

*   *   *

HENDRICKSON, Robert A(ugustus) 1923-

PERSONAL: Born August 9, 1923, in Indianapolis, Ind.; son of Robert A. (a lawyer) and Eleanor Riggs (Atherton) Hendrickson; married Virginia Reiland Cobb (an actress), February 3, 1951; children: Alexandra Kirk, Robert Augustus III. *Education:* Attended Yale University, 1941-43, and University of Bescancon, 1945; Sorbonne, University of Paris, Certificat, 1946; Harvard University, LL.B., 1948. *Office:* Lovejoy, Wasson, Lundgren & Ashton, 250 Park Ave., New York, N.Y. 10017.

CAREER: Admitted to Indiana Bar, 1948, and New York Bar, 1949; Lord, Day & Lord (law firm), New York City, attorney, 1948-52; Surrogates of New York County, New York City, law assistant, 1952-54; Breed, Abbott, Morgan (law firm), New York City, attorney, 1954-67; Lovejoy, Wasson, Lundgren & Ashton (law firm), New York City, partner, 1967—. Visiting professor of law, University of Miami, 1976. Lecturer on estate planning and other subjects at law institutes in a number of states. Member of board of directors, St. Martin's Press, Inc., and Mason/Charter Publishers, Inc.; trustee of Institute for the Crippled and Disabled, and St. Hilda's and St. Hugh's School. President, The Church Club of New York, Inc., 1976—. Chairman of board of governors, New York Young Republican Club, 1954. *Military service:* U.S. Army, 1943-46; became first lieutenant; received Bronze Star, Purple Heart with oak-leaf cluster, Presidential Unit Citation, and battle stars for the Ardennes, Rhineland, and Central Europe campaigns. *Member:* American Bar Association, Maritime Law Association, American Foreign Law Association, Consular Law Society, New York State Bar Association, Indiana Bar Association, Bar Association of the City of New York.

WRITINGS: Interstate and International Estate Planning,

Practising Law Institute, 1968; (contributor) *Successful Estate Planning Ideas and Methods,* Prentice-Hall, 1968; *The Future of Money,* Prentice-Hall, 1970; (contributor) Jacob K. Lasser, *J. K. Lasser's Estate Tax Techniques,* [New York], 1970; *Estate Planning for the Migrant Executive,* Practising Law Institute, 1971; *The Cashless Society,* Dodd, 1972; *Hamilton,* Mason/Charter, Volume I: *1757-1789,* Volume II: *1789-1804,* 1976. Contributor to law journals.

SIDELIGHTS: The Future of Money has been published in British, German, and Japanese editions.

*   *   *

HENDRY, J(ames) F(indlay) 1912-

PERSONAL: Born September 12, 1912, in Glasgow, Scotland; son of John McEwan and Christina (Findlay) Hendry; married Theodora Ussai, May 1, 1935 (deceased); married Dorothy Stainton, July 3, 1944; children: (first marriage) David; (second marriage) Darya (Mrs. Lawrence Robert Cooper), Dorian. *Education:* Attended University of Paris, 1934-35; University of Glasgow, M.A. (honors), 1952; University of London, Certificate of Proficiency in German, 1953. *Politics:* Nonparty. *Religion:* Nondenominational. *Home:* 79 Sheldrake Blvd., Toronto, Ontario, Canada. *Agent:* E. P. S. Lewin & Partners, 7 Chelsea Embankment, London S.W.3, England. *Office:* School of Translators and Interpreters, Laurentian University of Sudbury, Sudbury, Ontario, Canada.

CAREER: British Intelligence Corps, service in Yugoslavia, 1939-40; Allied Commission for Austria, Vienna, translator and interpreter, 1945-50; affiliated with British Embassy, Vienna, 1950-52; free-lance translator and author, 1952-54; language teacher and university lecturer, Education Authority of Glasgow and University of Glasgow, Glasgow, Scotland, 1954-60; translator for International Atomic Energy Agency, Vienna, 1960-63, International Labour Office, Geneva, Switzerland, 1963-64, International Telecommunication Union, Geneva, 1964-66, and various other European agencies; Laurentian University of Sudbury, Sudbury, Ontario, professor of modern languages, 1965, head of department, 1965, director of School of Translators and Interpreters, 1967—. *Military service:* British Army, 1940-45; became major. *Member:* Association of International Conference Translators, Canadian Association of Slavists, Canadian Linguists Association. *Awards, honors:* Atlantic Award for Literature, 1950.

WRITINGS: (Editor with Henry Treece, and contributor) *The New Apocalypse* (anthology of criticism, poems, and stories), Routledge, 1939; (editor with Treece) *The White Horseman* (poems and prose by Dylan Thomas, Norman McCaig, and others), Routledge, 1941; *Bombed Happiness* (poems), Routledge, 1942; *The Orchestral Mountain* (poems), Routledge, 1943; (editor with wife, Theodora Hendry) *Scottish Short Stories,* Penguin, 1943, 2nd edition (with Hendry as editor and contributor), 1969; (editor with Treece) *The Crown and the Sickle* (anthology), P. S. King & Staples, 1944; *The Blackbird of Ospo; Stories of Jugoslavia,* W. Maclellan, 1945; *Fernie Brae* (novel), W. Maclellan, 1947; *Your Future in Translating and Interpreting,* Rosen Press, 1969; (translator) Y. Gentilhomme, *Russian for Scientists,* Dunod, 1969; (translator) Robert Haardt, *Gnosis,* E. J. Brill, 1971.

Poems represented in many anthologies including, *Little Reviews Anthology,* Allen & Unwin, 1943, *Poems of Today: Fourth Series,* Macmillan, 1951, *The Guinness Book of Po-*

etry, Putnam, 1958, *The Oxford Book of Scottish Verse*, Clarendon Press, 1966, *I Burn for England*, Frewin, 1966, and *Scottish Love Poems: A Personal Anthology*, Canongate Publishing, 1975. Short stories represented in *A Map of Hearts*, Lindsay Drummond, 1944, *English Story: First Series*, Collins, 1944, and *Scottish Stories*, Faber, 1947. Critical essays represented in *Herbert Read: A Symposium*, Faber, 1943, *Robert Burns*, W. Maclellan, 1947, and *James Joyce: Two Decades of Criticism*, Vanguard, 1948. Also author of several other long poems not yet published. Contributor to *New Statesman*, *Nation* (London), *New Yorker*, *Poetry* (Chicago), *Prism International*, *Imago* (Paris), *Saturday Night*, *Canadian Forum*, and other periodicals.

WORK IN PROGRESS: A volume of short stories; *Keeper of the Light*, a long poem; research work on scientific terminology; novels.

SIDELIGHTS: J. F. Hendry told *CA* that his "view of the current scene in art and literature is generally that it is formless, incompetent and organically decadent. As Yeats put it 'the worst is preferred'. All the 'pushers' are pushing 'drugs'." He added that he "dislikes 'I' poetry, prose poetry, 'descriptive' poetry and all poetry that does not create a world of its own." Hendry himself has written "mostly poetry, but long poems, which are not wanted by publishers."

Hendry is especially interested in semiology and its relation to the arts, especially painting, and in the development of a poetic technique akin to music; his future aims include furthering of world consciousness instead of national. Major vocational interest for Hendry is in syntax and semantics of scientific terminology and its storage, and in the establishment of an international bureau of terminology. He is proficient in French, German, Italian, Spanish, Russian, Slovene, Persian, and other languages.

BIOGRAPHICAL/CRITICAL SOURCES: Francis Scarfe, *Auden and After*, Routledge, 1942; Jack Lindsay, *Perspective for Poetry*, Fore, 1944; Stephen Spender, *Poetry since 1939*, Longmans, Green, 1946; Henry Treece, *How I See Apocalypse*, Drummond, 1946; William York Tindall, *Forces in Modern British Literature*, Knopf, 1947; Babette Deutsch, *Poetry in Our Time*, Holt, 1952; Duncan Glen, *Hugh MacDiarmid and the Scottish Renaissance*, Chambers, 1964.

* * *

HENISSART, Paul 1923-

PERSONAL: Born August 23, 1923, in New York, N.Y.; son of Albert and Eva (Grinoch) Henissart; married Sylvie Maugras (a department store executive), August 24, 1953. *Education:* Kenyon College, B.A., 1947; Sorbonne, University of Paris, additional study, 1947-48. *Residence:* Ibiza, Spain. *Agent:* Marcia Higgins, William Morris Agency, 1350 Avenue of the Americas, New York, N.Y. 10019.

CAREER: National Broadcasting Co., New York City, writer, 1959-60; Radio Free Europe, New York City, bureau chief, 1960-63; American Broadcasting Co., New York City, writer, 1964-65; Mutual Broadcasting System, New York City, correspondent, 1966—. *Military service:* U.S. Army, 1943-46. *Member:* Phi Beta Kappa.

WRITINGS: Wolves in the City: The Death of French Algeria, Simon & Schuster, 1970; *Narrow Exit*, Simon & Schuster, 1973; *The Winter Spy*, Simon & Schuster, 1977. Contributor to *Saturday Evening Post*, *Reader's Digest*, *New York Times*, *International Herald Tribune*, and *Travel & Camera*.

WORK IN PROGRESS: Two novels.

SIDELIGHTS: Paul Henissart has been traveling for twenty-five years, "with varying degrees of comfort and sometimes total lack thereof, in Europe, the Middle East, North and Black Africa and Central America, by jet, Trans-Europe Express, passenger liners, cargos, military truck, helicopter, Volkswagen, Mercedes-Benz, C-47 Transport, jeep and caique."

BIOGRAPHICAL/CRITICAL SOURCES: Newsweek, September 14, 1970; *Publishers Weekly*, November 1, 1976.

* * *

HENNESSEY, R(oger) A(nthony) S(ean) 1937-

PERSONAL: Born November 22, 1937, in Fulham, London, England; son of S. J. (a captain in the Royal Navy) and W. I. Hennessey; married Penelope A. Coningham; children: one daughter, two sons. *Education:* Attended Epsom College, 1951-56, and Downing College, Cambridge, 1958-61. *Home:* 40 Linden Rd., Gosforth, Newcastle upon Tyne 3, England.

CAREER: Royal Grammar School, Newcastle upon Tyne, England, assistant master and head of economics department, 1962-73; Her Majesty's Inspector of Schools, England, 1973—. *Military service:* National Service, 1956-58; later commissioned captain in Territorial Army.

WRITINGS: Transport, Batsford, 1966, 2nd edition, 1969; *Factories*, Batsford, 1969; *The Electric Railway That Never Was: York-Newcastle, 1919*, Oriel Press, 1970; *Power*, Batsford, 1971; *The Electric Revolution*, Oriel Press, 1972; *Railways*, Batsford, 1973; *Dragon and the Rising Sun, the Sino-Japanese War 1894-1895*, in press.

BIOGRAPHICAL/CRITICAL SOURCES: Times Literary Supplement, February 2, 1967, October 16, 1969; *Times Educational Supplement*, March 10, 1967, January 2, 1970.

* * *

HENWOOD, James N. J. 1932-

PERSONAL: Born April 17, 1932, in Upper Darby, Pa.; son of Harry Francis and Esther (Peterson) Henwood. *Education:* West Chester State College, B.S. in Ed., 1954; University of Pennsylvania, A.M., 1958, Ph.D., 1975. *Home:* 7 Media Ave., Havertown, Pa. 19083. *Office:* Department of History, East Stroudsburg State College, East Stroudsburg, Pa. 18301.

CAREER: Marple-Newtown School District, Newtown Square, Pa., high school teacher, 1958-66; East Stroudsburg State College, East Stroudsburg, Pa., professor of history, 1966—. *Military service:* U.S. Army, radio operator, 1955-56. *Member:* American Historical Association, Organization of American Historians, National Railway Historical, Railway and Locomotive Historical Society, U.S. Naval Institute, Historical Society of Pennsylvania, Phi Alpha Theta.

WRITINGS: A Short Haul to the Bay, Greene, 1969.

WORK IN PROGRESS: History of Delaware Valley Railroad; History of Pennsylvania Redding Seashore Lines.

* * *

HEPNER, Harry W(alker) 1893-

PERSONAL: Born February 1, 1893, in Freeburg, Pa.; son of William A. (a teacher and farmer) and Katherine (Schnee) Hepner; married Edna Carnahan, November 23, 1920; married second wife, Hazel Virginia Miller (an administrator for American Association of Retired Persons and National Retired Teachers Association), April 4, 1970; children: (first marriage) F. Alyse (Mrs. Walter F. Arnold). *Education:* Muhlenberg College, A.B., 1916; graduate study at Cornell University, 1916, and Carnegie Institute of Technology (now Carnegie-Mellon University), 1918-19; Syracuse University, M.A., 1924; Harvard University, graduate study, 1931. *Politics:* Republican. *Religion:* Protestant. *Home and office:* 194 26th Ave. N., St. Petersburg, Fla. 33704.

CAREER: Personnel research with Kaufmann's Department Store, Pittsburgh, Pa., 1918-19, Philadelphia Co. and affiliated corporations, Philadelphia, Pa., 1919-20, and Goodyear Tire & Rubber Co., Akron, Ohio, 1920-21; Syracuse University, Syracuse, N.Y., instructor, 1921-24, assistant professor, later associate professor, 1924-35, professor of psychology, 1941-59, professor emeritus, 1959—. Director of consumer research panels, Batten, Barton, Durstine & Osborn, New York, N.Y., 1942-61; consultant to other corporations, such as Carborundum Co., Crosley Corp., and Air Preheater Corp. *Military service:* U.S. Army, 1917-18; became second lieutenant. *Member:* American Psychological Association (fellow), American Marketing Association, Phi Beta Kappa, Sigma Xi. *Awards, honors:* First prize in B. C. Forbes book contest, 1953, for *The Best Things in Life.*

WRITINGS: Psychology in Modern Business, Prentice-Hall, 1930; *Human Relations in Changing Industry,* Prentice-Hall, 1934; *Finding Yourself in Your Work: A Guide for Career and Personality,* Appleton, 1937; *It's Nice to Know People Like You,* Appleton, 1939; *Effective Advertising,* McGraw, 1941, 3rd edition published as *Modern Advertising: Practices and Principles,* 1956, 4th edition published as *Advertising: Creative Communication with Consumers,* 1964 (all editions have *Student Workbook* and *Teacher's Manual*); *Psychology Applied to Life and Work,* Prentice-Hall, 1941, 5th edition, 1973, also adapted by the editorial staff of U.S. Armed Forces Institute for two-volume edition, 1944; *How to Live and Work Successfully with People in Business,* Prentice-Hall, 1952; *The Best Things in Life,* B. C. Forbes, 1953; *Modern Marketing: Dynamics and Management,* McGraw, 1955; *Perceptive Management and Supervision: Social Responsibilities and Challenges,* Prentice-Hall, 1961, 2nd edition, 1971; *Psychology in Marketing,* International Correspondence Schools, 1966; *Retirement—A Time to Live Anew,* McGraw, 1969.

Author of manuals for private industry, including the booklets, *How to Learn Quickly,* American Business Builders, 1924, and *Your Career as an Appliance Salesman,* General Electric Co., 1945. Occasional contributor to magazines and journals.

WORK IN PROGRESS: Revising his textbooks "to show that college students who wish to make constructive contributions to our changing social order can do so in business as well as in certain other fields that are usually chosen . . . to 'improve the world.'"

SIDELIGHTS: Harry Hepner still is functioning "in terms of a Messiah complex, developed in childhood and accentuated in my college years, the so-called 'crusading tendency of youth.'"

* * *

HEPPLE, Bob (Alexander) 1934-

PERSONAL: Born August 11, 1934, in South Africa; son of Alexander (a journalist) and Josephine (Zwarenstein) Hepple; married Shirley Goldsmith (a secretary), July 7, 1960; children: Brenda, Paul Alexander. *Education:* University of the Witwatersrand, B.A., 1954, LL.B., 1957; Cambridge University, LL.B., 1966. *Religion:* None. *Office:* Regional Office of the Industrial Tribunals, Tufton House, Tufton St., Ashford, Kent, England.

CAREER: University of the Witwatersrand, Johannesburg, South Africa, lecturer in law, 1959-62; attorney in private practice and advocate of Supreme Court of South Africa, 1958-63; detained and imprisoned for ninety days without trial in 1963 on grounds of political activities against apartheid policies of the South African Government; upon his release he took refuge in England; Gray's Inn, London, England, barrister-at-law, 1966—; University of Nottingham, Nottingham, England, lecturer in law, 1966-68; Cambridge University, Cambridge, England, lecturer in law and fellow of Clare College, 1968-76; chairman of Industrial Tribunals, England and Wales, 1975—. Honorary professor of comparative social and labour law, University of Kent at Canterbury, 1976—.

WRITINGS: Race, Jobs, and the Law in Britain, Allen Lane, 1968, 2nd edition, Penguin, 1970; (with Paul O'Higgins) *Public Employee Unionism in the United Kingdom: The Legal Framework,* Institute of Labor and Industrial Relations, University of Michigan and Wayne State University, 1971; (with M. H. Matthews) *Tort: Cases and Materials,* Butterworth & Co., 1974; (with Glanville Williams) *Foundations of the Law of Tort,* Butterworth & Co., 1976; (with O'Higgins) *Employment Law,* second edition, Sweet & Maxwell, 1976; (with J. Loewenberg and others) *Compulsory Arbitration,* Lexington Books, 1976. Contributor to *International Encyclopedia of Labor Law and Industrial Relations;* contributor to *Race* and to legal journals. Founding editor, *Industrial Law Journal,* 1972-77.

WORK IN PROGRESS: Books on labor relations law.

BIOGRAPHICAL/CRITICAL SOURCES: Statesman, June 21, 1968; *Listener,* July 18, 1968; *Cambridge Law Journal,* November, 1970; *British Journal of Industrial Relations,* March, 1971.

* * *

HERAVI, Mehdi 1940-

PERSONAL: Born September 10, 1940, in Tehran, Iran. *Education:* Utah State University, B.S., 1963, M.A., 1964; American University, School of International Service, Ph.D., 1967.

CAREER: Utah State University, Logan, teaching assistant in American National Government, 1964-65; Tennessee Technological University, Cookeville, assistant professor, 1967, associate of graduate faculty, 1968-69, member of graduate faculty, 1969, associate professor of political science, beginning 1970. *Member:* International Political Science Association, Middle East Institute, Middle East Studies Association of North America, American Political Science Association, American Academy of Political and Social Sciences, American Society for Public Administration, American Association of University Professors.

WRITINGS: Iranian-American Diplomacy, Gaus, 1969; (compiler and editor) *Concise Encyclopedia of the Middle East,* Public Affairs Press, 1973. Contributor of articles to *Muslim World* and other periodicals.

WORK IN PROGRESS: An article, "An American Campaign: 1970."†

HERBERT, Don 1917-
(Mr. Wizard)

PERSONAL: Born July 10, 1917, in Waconia, Minn.; son of Herbert Geoffrey and Lydia (Peopple) Kemske; married Maraleita Dutton, October 12, 1939 (divorced, 1972); married Norma Nix Kasell, 1972; children: Jeffrey, Jay, Jill. *Education:* Wisconsin State University (now University of Wisconsin—LaCrosse), LaCrosse, B.S., 1940. *Address:* P.O. Box 83, Canoga Park, Calif. 91305.

CAREER: Prism Productions, Inc., Canoga Park, Calif., television and film producer, president, 1951—. Writer-performer. Performed title role on television show, "Mr. Wizard," N.B.C., 1951-65, 1971—. *Military service:* U.S. Air Force, became captain; awarded D.F.C. Air Medal. *Awards, honors:* George Foster Peabody Award, Ohio State Institute, and Thomas Alva Edison Award for "Mr. Wizard."

WRITINGS: Mr. Wizard's Science Secrets, Hawthorne, 1952, first revised edition, E. M. Hale, 1968; *Mr. Wizard's Experiments for Young Scientists,* Doubleday, 1959; (with Hy Ruchlis) *Mr. Wizard's 400 Experiments in Science,* Book-Lab, 1968; (with Fulvio Bardossi) *Kilauea, Case History of a Volcano,* Harper, 1968; (with Bardossi) *Secret in the White Cell: Case History of a Biological Search,* Harper, 1969; *Mr. Wizard's Science Activities,* Book-Lab, 1973.

BIOGRAPHICAL/CRITICAL SOURCES: Charlotte S. Huck and D. A. Young, *Children's Literature in the Elementary School,* Holt, 1961; *The Children's Bookshelf,* Child Study Association of America, Bantam, 1965.

* * *

HERINGTON, C. J(ohn) 1924-

PERSONAL: Born November 23, 1924, in Isleworth, England; son of C. E. E. (a physician) and Celia M. (Hewes) Herington; married Helen J. Rose, April 9, 1949; married second wife, Nancy L. Hamilton, June 12, 1969; children: (first marriage) David John, Christina Mary, Elizabeth Clare. *Education:* Exeter College, Oxford, B.A. and Diploma in Classical Archaeology, 1949, M.A., 1960. *Religion:* Anglican. *Home:* 463 Whitney, Apt. 1, New Haven, Conn. 06511. *Office:* Department of Classics, Yale University, New Haven, Conn. 06510.

CAREER: University of Manchester, Manchester, England, assistant lecturer, 1949-52, lecturer in classics, 1952-55; University of Toronto, Toronto, Ontario, associate professor of classics, 1962-65; University of Texas at Austin, professor of classics and chairman of department of classics, 1965-70; Stanford University, Stanford, Calif., professor of classics, 1970-72; Yale University, New Haven, Conn., professor of classics and Talcott Professor of Greek, 1972—. Visiting lecturer, Smith College, 1960-62. Member, University of Manchester Archaeological Expedition to Cyrene, 1955. Associate director, National Humanities Institute, Yale University, 1976. *Military service:* Royal Air Force, 1943-46. *Member:* Society for the Promotion of Hellenic Studies (member of council, 1957-60), Classical Association of Canada, American Philological Association. *Awards, honors:* Cromer Prize for Greek, British Academy, 1958; American Council of Learned Societies grant, 1967; Guggenheim fellowship, 1968-69.

WRITINGS: Athena Parthenos and Athena Polias: A Study in the Religion of Periclean Athens, Manchester University Press, 1955, Barnes & Noble, 1956; *The Author of Prometheus Bound,* University of Texas Press, 1970; *The Older Scholia on the "Prometheus Bound",* Brill, 1972; (translator with James Scully) *Prometheus Bound,* Oxford University Press, 1975. Contributor to *Journal of Hellenic Studies, Arion, Rheinisches Museum,* and other learned journals. Editor, *Arion.*

WORK IN PROGRESS: A new edition of *Prometheus Bound; Poetry into Tragedy: Aeschylus and the Greek Poetic Tradition;* studies in the tragedies and prose works of Seneca.

SIDELIGHTS: C. J. Herington lists his chief motivation as the "belief that the Greek and Roman civilizations have something to say that does not date." *Avocational interests:* Canoeing, sailing, poetry, biography, archaeology.

* * *

HERMAN, Simon N(athan) 1912-

PERSONAL: Born April 9, 1912, in Port Elizabeth, South Africa; son of Abraham (a merchant) and Anne (Benn) Herman; married Segula Benyosef (a teacher), June 24, 1951; children: Ephraim, Benzion, Avital. *Education:* University of Capetown, B.A., 1932, LL.B., 1934; University of the Witwatersrand, M.A., 1943, Ph.D., 1949; graduate study at Columbia University, 1944-45, and at Harvard University and Research Center for Group Dynamics (then located at Massachusetts Institute of Technology), 1945-47. *Religion:* Jewish. *Home:* 62 Nayot, Jerusalem, Israel. *Office:* Department of Psychology, Hebrew University, Jerusalem, Israel.

CAREER: South African Zionist Federation, South Africa, director of information and organization department, 1936-42; Jewish Agency, New York, N.Y., assistant to the director, 1947-48; Jewish Agency, Jerusalem, Israel, director of summer and winter institutes, 1949-54; Hebrew University of Jerusalem, Jerusalem, Israel, began as lecturer, currently associate professor of psychology. *Member:* Israel Psychological Association.

WRITINGS: The Reaction of Jews to Anti-Semitism, Witwatersrand University Press, 1945; *American Students in Israel,* Cornell University Press, 1970; *Israelis and Jews: The Continuity of an Identity,* Random House, 1971; *The Social Psychology of Jewish Identity,* Sage Publications, 1977. Contributor to social science journals in Great Britain, Israel, and the United States.

WORK IN PROGRESS: Research on the social psychological determinants of the Israel/Diaspora relationship, and on the impact of the memory of the "holocaust" (the destruction of European Jewry by the Nazis) on contemporary Jewish life.

* * *

HERNER, Charles H. 1930-

PERSONAL: Born November 6, 1930, in Clarkdale, Ariz.; son of Harlan R. (a metallurgist) and Thelma (Jenkins) Herner; married Beryl S. Srigley, June 24, 1956; children: Harlan Louis, Katherine Louise. *Education:* University of Arizona, B.A. and M.A., 1965. *Home:* 1065 West Oleta Dr., Tucson, Ariz. 85704.

CAREER: Canyon Del Oro High School, Tucson, Ariz., teacher of American history, 1963—. *Military service:* U.S. Army, 1953-55; served in Korea. U.S. Army Reserve, 1953—; present rank, lieutenant colonel.

WRITINGS: The Arizona Rough Riders, University of Arizona Press, 1970.

WORK IN PROGRESS: Research on American mining activities in Northern Sonora in the nineteenth century.

SIDELIGHTS: Charles Herner lived in Nacozari, Sonora, Mexico, where his father was superintendent of a copper reduction plant, 1941-44.

* * *

HERRIOT, Peter 1939-

PERSONAL: Born February 24, 1939, in Woodford, Essex, England; son of Frank Henry (an accountant) and Ada (Wagland) Herriot; married Barbara Lane, August 29, 1965; children: Russell, Martin, Alison. *Education:* Oxford University, B.A., 1964; Queens University of Belfast, M.Ed., 1966; University of Manchester, Ph.D., 1969. *Office:* Hester Adrian Research Centre for the Study of Learning Processes in the Mentally Handicapped, Victoria University of Manchester, Manchester M13 9PL, England.

CAREER: Queens University of Belfast, Belfast, Northern Ireland, assistant lecturer in psychology, 1966-67; Victoria University of Manchester, Manchester, England, lecturer in psychology, 1967-69, research lecturer in subnormality, 1969—. *Member:* British Psychological Society (associate member).

WRITINGS: An Introduction to the Psychology of Language, Methuen, 1970; *Language and Teaching: A Psychological Approach,* Barnes & Noble, 1971 (published in England as *Language and Teaching: A Psychological View,* Methuen, 1971); (with Josephine M. Green and Roy McConkey) *Organisation and Memory: A Review and a Project in Subnormality,* Methuen, 1973; *Attributes of Memory,* Methuen, 1974. General editor, "Essential Psychology" series, Methuen, 1976. Contributor to *American Journal on Mental Deficiency* and to psychology and child development journals.†

* * *

HERRON, Shaun 1912-

PERSONAL: Born November 23, 1912, in Carrickfergus, County Antrim, Northern Ireland; son of Thomas and Maire (Johnstone) Herron; married Marghanita Duncan; children: Niall, Virginia, Shaun, Siobhan. *Education:* Educated at Queen's University of Belfast, University of Edinburgh, and Princeton University, B.A., B.D., M.A. *Agent:* Curtis Brown Ltd., 575 Madison Ave., New York, N.Y. 10022.

CAREER: Ordained minister of Scottish Congregational Churches, 1940; *British Weekly,* Edinburgh, Scotland, editor, 1949-58; United Church of Canada, minister, 1958—; F. P. Publications (Canadian newspaper chain), Winnipeg, Manitoba, U.S. correspondent, 1962-65, editorial writer, beginning 1965. Smith Lecturer at Union College, University of British Columbia, 1952; Cole Lecturer at Vanderbilt University, 1956; Wilson Lecturer at Oklahoma City University, 1957; Chancellor's Lecturer at Queen's University at Kingston, 1959. *Military service:* British Army, 1940-45.

WRITINGS—Novels: *Miro,* Random House, 1969; *The Hound and the Fox and the Harper,* Random House, 1970; *Through the Dark and Hairy Wood,* Random House, 1972; *The Whore-Mother,* M. Evans, 1973; *The Bird in Last Year's Nest,* M. Evans, 1974. Writer of radio and television scripts for British Broadcasting Corp., and Canadian Broadcasting Commission. Contributor of articles and essays to periodicals and newspapers.

WORK IN PROGRESS: Two novels, *The Mac Donnell* and *The Clearance.*

SIDELIGHTS: Shaun Herron told *CA:* "Why do I write? Probably most writers of fiction are neurotic and need to complete themselves by creating people and the events and relationships that make them real. . . . Perhaps that's why I wrote *The Whore-Mother* which isn't a dirty book—as many people suppose—but a novel about a young Catholic who got himself involved with the Provisional IRA before he understood what sort of people they are. But I had another reason which applies also to *The Bird in Last Year's Nest:* In both cases they were written for my son to read so that, if he heeded them, he would not in his youth be the sort of fool his father was when he was young. One is set in my native Ireland, the other in Spain and is about the tragedy of a family that was involved in the Civil War. Both books are about the sort of naive idiot my son's father was when he was young."

Herron also wrote that what he hopes to achieve through his novels is the "life I live now: relaxed, leisured, peaceful, quiet, self-determined and very very comfortable. And of course, as Richard Condon says of himself: 'I am an entertainer, a story-teller' and I hope I write well, tell good stories well, do in fact what every good novelist ought to do, and be adequately rewarded for doing it. What else is there? I do not write to change people or societies, I write, I suppose, because I want it to be seen that I can do well what I have chosen to do—write—and if that contradicts what I said about novelists being neurotics, so be it. If one were consistent one couldn't write good novels, for consistency in a writer of fiction is the mark of death."

There have been German, Italian, Swedish, Dutch, Finnish, and Turkish editions of Shaun Herron's books.

* * *

HERZOG, John P(hillip) 1931-

PERSONAL: Born August 28, 1931, in Canton, Ohio; son of Phil Charles and Frances Lillian (Norris) Herzog; married Eleanor Lee Winters, December 22, 1956; married second wife, Sharon Lee Prosser, June 27, 1969; children: (first marriage) Jan Alan, Julie Ann, Brian Scott, Gregory Stephen; stepchildren: Lisa Michelle. *Education:* University of California, Berkeley, B.S. (honors), 1958, Ph.D., 1962. *Home:* 219 Harvard Dr., Port Moody, British Columbia, Canada. *Office:* Department of Economics and Commerce, Simon Fraser University, Burnaby, British Columbia, Canada V5A 156.

CAREER: University of California Extension, Berkeley, instructor in economics, 1960-61; University of Wisconsin—Madison, assistant professor of commerce, 1961-65; Claremont Graduate School, Claremont, Calif., associate professor of business economics, 1965-69, chairman of department of business economics, 1967-68; Simon Fraser University, Burnaby, British Columbia, professor of economics and commerce, 1969—, and acting chairman of department of economics and commerce, 1970-71. Visiting associate professor, University of California, Los Angeles, summer, 1968, and University of California, Riverside, winter, 1968. Lecturer in commerce extension and management institute programs and to business, professional, and alumni organizations. Member of research staff, National Bureau of Economic Research, 1963-70. Consultant to businesses and charitable organizations. Incorporator and board member, C.I.R.A.D., 1968-69. Participant in workshops, seminars, and professional commissions. *Military service:* U.S. Air Force, Intelligence, 1950-54.

MEMBER: American Economic Association, American

Finance Association, American Real Estate and Urban Economics Association, Financial Management Association, Western Economics Association, Western Finance Association (president, 1975-76), Phi Beta Kappa, Beta Gamma Sigma (president, University of California, Berkeley chapter, 1958-59).

WRITINGS: Trends and Factors Influencing Real Estate, University of California, 1958; *The Dynamics of Large-Scale Housebuilding,* Institute of Business and Economic Research, University of California, 1963; (contributor) William L. C. Wheaton and others, editors, *Urban Housing,* Free Press, 1966; (with James S. Earley) *Home Mortgage Delinquency and Foreclosure,* Columbia University Press, 1970; (contributor) *Recent Perspectives in Urban Land Economics,* Urban Land Economics Divison, University of British Columbia, 1976. Contributor to *Western City, Journal of Economic Abstracts, Journal of Finance, Land Economics, Journal of Financial and Quantitative Analysis,* and *California Builder.*

WORK IN PROGRESS: The Management of Corporate Financial Resources, for Wadsworth; *The Performance of Individual Investment Fund Managers.*

*   *   *

HESS, Robert L. 1932-

PERSONAL: Born December 18, 1932, in Asbury Park, N.J.; son of Henry and Ada (Davis) Hess; married Frances Aaron, April 9, 1960; children: Carl, Laura, Jonathan, Roger. *Education:* Yale University, B.A. (magna cum laude), 1954, M.A., 1955, Ph.D., 1960; University of Rome, additional study, 1956-58. *Home:* 648 Country Lane, Glencoe, Ill. 60022. *Office:* Office of Vice-Chancellor for Academic Affairs, University of Illinois at Chicago Circle, Chicago, Ill. 60680.

CAREER: Carnegie Institute of Technology (now Carnegie-Mellon University), Pittsburgh, Pa., instructor, 1958-60, assistant professor of history, 1960-61; Mount Holyoke College, South Hadley, Mass., assistant professor of history, 1961-64; Northwestern University, Evanston, Ill., assistant professor of history, 1964-65; University of Illinois at Chicago Circle, associate professor, 1966-71, professor of history, 1971—, associate dean, 1970-72, associate vice-chancellor for academic affairs, 1970—. Visiting assistant professor in African studies program, Boston University, 1962-63. Consultant to University of Chicago Press, Northwestern University Press, Cornell University Press, *Encyclopaedia Britannica,* and *Encyclopedia Americana.* President, Center for Study of Democratic Institutions, 1966-68.

MEMBER: African Studies Association (fellow), Middle East Studies Association of North America (fellow), American Historical Association, Society for Italian Historical Studies. *Awards, honors:* Fulbright fellow at University of Rome, 1956-58; Guggenheim fellow in Italy, 1968-69.

WRITINGS: Italian Colonialism in Somalia, University of Chicago Press, 1966; *Ethiopia: The Modernization of Autocracy,* Cornell University Press, 1970; (with D. M. Coger) *Semper ex Africa: Bibliography of Primary Sources for Nineteenth-Century Africa,* Hoover Institution, 1972. Contributor to history and political science journals. Editor, *Dictionary of Ethiopian Biography,* Volume I, 1977.

WORK IN PROGRESS: A book on the origins of Italian colonialism in Ethiopia, 1870-1890; research for a book on Falasha ("Black Jews") in Ethiopian history; and editing memoirs of Giacomo Naretti in Ethiopia, 1871-1886.

SIDELIGHTS: Robert Hess is fluent in Italian, proficient in French, Spanish, German, and Hebrew, and reads Portuguese, Latin, and some Amharic.

*   *   *

HESS, William N. 1925-

PERSONAL: Born September 1, 1925, in Shreveport, La.; son of C. G. and Bessie (Boylston) Hess; married Antoinette Fontana, April 2, 1955; stepchildren: Linda B. (Mrs. Charles Lundgren), Edward Biggs. *Education:* Louisiana Polytechnic Institute, B.S., 1953. *Religion:* Episcopalian. *Home address:* P.O. Box 61268, Houston, Tex. 77208. *Agent:* Stanley W. Ulanoff, 17 The Serpentine, Roslyn, Long Island, N.Y. *Office:* United Gas Pipe Line Co., Houston, Tex. 77001.

CAREER: U.S. Air Force, 1943-45, 1946-49, 1951-52; served in Italy, became staff sergeant, spent seven months as German prisoner of war, received Air Medal and Purple Heart; United Gas Pipe Line Co., Shreveport, La., employed in natural gas proration, most recently in Texas, 1954—. *Member:* American Fighter Aces Association (recording secretary and assistant historian), American Aviation Historical Society, Society of World War I Aero Historians (also known as Cross and Cockade), Air Force Historical Foundation, Veterans of Foreign Wars, Air Force Association.

WRITINGS: Allied Aces of World War II, Arco, 1966; *American Aces of World War II and Korea,* Arco, 1968; (with Kenn C. Rust) *Slybird,* Aero, 1968; (with E. R. McDowell) *Checkertail Clan,* Aero, 1969; *Fighting Mustang: The Chronicle of the P-51,* Doubleday, 1970; *Escort Fighter: P-51 Mustang,* Ballantine, 1971; *B-17: Flying Fortress,* Ballantine, 1974; *Pacific Sweep: The 5th and 13th Fighter Commands in World War II,* Doubleday, 1974; (with Christopher Shores and Hans Ring) *Fighters over Tunisia,* Neville Spearman, 1975; *P-47: Thunderbolt at War,* Ian Allan, 1976. Contributor to *Journal of the AAHS* (American Aviation Historical Society).

WORK IN PROGRESS: History of 8th Fighter Command; Aces's Album.

*   *   *

HEWITSON, John Nelson 1917-

PERSONAL: Born October 6, 1917, in Aspatria, Cumberland, England; son of Joseph Barnes (a miner) and Mary Hannah (Nelson) Hewitson; married Jean Mary Laydon, November 30, 1943; children: Elizabeth Mary. *Education:* Christ's College, Cambridge, B.A., M.A. *Religion:* Church of England. *Home:* 450 Unthank Rd., Norwich, England. *Office:* City of Norwich School, Eaton Rd., Norwich, England.

CAREER: City of Coventry Training College for Teachers, Coventry, England, lecturer in English, 1946-48; Manchester Grammar School, Manchester, England, assistant master, 1948-54; Ilkeston Grammar School, Ilkeston, England, headmaster, 1956-61; City of Norwich School, Norwich, England, headmaster, 1961—. Justice of the peace. *Military service:* British Army, Intelligence Corps and Royal Army Education Corps, 1960-66; became major. *Member:* Headmasters' Association. *Awards, honors:* Schoolmaster fellow commoner at Downing College, Cambridge University, 1967.

WRITINGS: The Grammar School Tradition in a Comprehensive World, Routledge & Kegan Paul, 1969, Humanities,

1970. Free-lance script writer and broadcaster for British Broadcasting Corp.

WORK IN PROGRESS: Research on general educational topics.

* * *

HICKS, Wilson 1897-1970

January 7, 1897—July 5, 1970; American editor and photo-journalist. Obituaries: *New York Times,* July 7, 1970; *Antiquarian Bookman,* July 20-27, 1970.

* * *

HIGGINBOTHAM, John E. 1933-

PERSONAL: Born February 28, 1933, in Bradford, Yorkshire, England; son of Alick (a company director) and Winifred Mavis (Eagle) Higginbotham; married Clarissa Elizabeth Beloe, July 29, 1963; children: Lydia Clare, Robert Charles Trant. *Education:* Trinity Hall, Cambridge, B.A. (first class honors), 1957, M.A., 1961. *Politics:* "Radical Conservative." *Religion:* Church of England. *Home:* Teme House, Lancing College, Sussex, England.

CAREER: Lancing College, Sussex, England, assistant master, 1957—, head of department of classics, 1963—, housemaster of Teme House, 1970—. School master-fellow, Selwyn College, Cambridge, 1969. Qualified Russian interpreter. *Military service:* Royal Air Force, Intelligence Branch, 1952-54. *Member:* Sussex Association of Classical Teachers (president, 1967-71; chairman, 1971—).

WRITINGS: (Translator, and author of introduction and commentary) *Cicero on Moral Obligation: A New Translation of Cicero's "De Officiis,"* University of California Press, 1967; (editor and contributor) *Greek and Latin Literature: A Comparative Study,* Methuen, 1969, Barnes & Noble, 1973; (contributor) *A Dictionary of Mnemenics',* Methuen, 1972. Contributor to classical journals.

WORK IN PROGRESS: An edition of the works of the second-century satirist, Lucian; a television play.

BIOGRAPHICAL/CRITICAL SOURCES: Times Literary Supplement, November 23, 1967, July 31, 1969; *New York Times Book Review,* October 12, 1969.

* * *

HIGGINS, Jean C. 1932-

PERSONAL: Born January 27, 1932, in Camden, S.C.; daughter of Joseph Loran (president of Duralith Corp.) and Josephine (Weixeldorfer) Carley; married Willard Lester Higgins, Jr. (a salesman), May 6, 1950 (deceased); children: Linda Sue, Willard Lester III. *Education:* Attended Presbyterian Hospital School of Nursing, Philadelphia, one year; currently attending Charles Morris Price School of Advertising and Journalism, Philadelphia. *Politics:* Independent. *Home:* 267 Washington Ave., Phoenixville, Pa. 19460.

MEMBER: National Federation of State Poetry Societies, Mensa, Pennsylvania Poetry Society.

WRITINGS: Lindy (verse with prose inserts), Judson, 1970. Work represented in anthologies, including *Clover Collection of Verse,* 1969, 1970, *Spring Anthology 1970, Mitre Press* (London), and other collections. Her poems have been published in *Accent on Living, Haiku Highlights, Adventure Time, American Bard,* and similar periodicals.

WORK IN PROGRESS: A novel, *Under the Influence.*

SIDELIGHTS: Jean Higgins wrote to *CA* that she began writing "to cope with traumatic happenings (2 handicapped children) and my bad background." She states that she writes "purely by inspiration—the words flow when *they* will," and her advice to aspiring writers is "whenever an inspiration moves you, write *then.*"

AVOCATIONAL INTERESTS: Acting and directing in amateur theatricals, giving poetry readings, helping the retarded to help themselves.

* * *

HILL, John P(aul) 1936-

PERSONAL: Born July 20, 1936, in Michigamme, Mich.; son of William A. and Vieno (Kulju) Hill. *Education:* Stanford University, A.B. (with great distinction), 1958; Harvard University, Ph.D., 1964. *Home:* 1 William Way, Newfield, N.Y. 14867. *Office:* NG-14 VanRensselaer Hall, Cornell University, Ithaca, N.Y. 14853.

CAREER: Massachusetts General Hospital, Department of Psychiatry, Boston, Mass., and Wellesley Human Relations Service, Wellesley, Mass., psychologist, 1962-63; University of Minnesota, Institute of Child Development, Minneapolis, assistant professor, 1963-67, associate professor of child psychology and of psychology, 1967-70; Cornell University, New York State College of Human Ecology, Ithaca, associate dean for research and graduate education, professor of human development and family studies, and assistant director, experiment station, 1971—, chairman of department of human development and family studies, 1973—. Minneapolis Institute of Arts, member of advisory committee for Children's Theatre Company, 1964-70, chairman, 1966-69. Consultant, Lincoln Center for the Performing Arts, 1971—, Ford Foundation, 1975—. *Member:* American Psychological Association (fellow), Society for Research in Child Development, American Association of University Professors, American Association for the Advancement of Science, Phi Beta Kappa, Psi Chi, Delta Sigma Rho. *Awards, honors:* Woodrow Wilson fellow, 1958-59; U.S. Public Health Service research grant, 1966-70.

WRITINGS: (Editor) *Minnesota Symposia on Child Psychology,* University of Minnesota Press, Volume I, 1967, Volumes II-III, 1969, Volume IV, 1970, Volume V, 1971; (with Jev Shelton) *Readings in Adolescent Development and Behavior,* Prentice-Hall, 1971; (contributor) D. W. Allen and E. Seifman, editors, *Teacher's Handbook,* Scott, Foresman, 1971; (with Franz Moenks) *Adolescence and Youth in Prospect,* IPC Science and Technology Press, 1977. Contributor of about fifteen articles to psychology journals. Associate editor, *Developmental Psychology,* 1970-75.

WORK IN PROGRESS: With Clara Mayo, *Screening Children: The Practice, Design and Evaluation of Programs for the Early Identification of Children with Problems; Adolescence.*

* * *

HILL, Winfred F(arrington) 1929-

PERSONAL: Born May 23, 1929, in Chelsea, Mass.; son of Roy Wesley (a school administrator) and Lura (Cole) Hill; married Libby M. Kaplan (a school librarian), June 14, 1957; children: Alison, Linda. *Education:* Yale University, A.B., 1950; Northwestern University, M.A., 1951; Stanford University, Ph.D., 1954. *Home:* 2715 Woodland Rd., Evanston, Ill. 60201. *Office:* Psychology Department, Northwestern University, Evanston, Ill. 60201.

CAREER: Harvard University, Cambridge, Mass., instructor in psychology, 1956-57; Northwestern University, Evanston, Ill., assistant professor, 1957-62, associate professor, 1962-68, professor of psychology, 1968—. Fellow, Center for Advanced Study in the Behavioral Sciences, Stanford, Calif., 1966-67. Research consultant, Veterans Administration Hospital, Downey, Ill., 1963—. *Military service:* U.S. Army, 1954-56. *Member:* American Psychological Association, Psychonomic Society, American Association for the Advancement of Science (council member, 1970-72), American Association of the University Professors, Midwestern Psychological Association (secretary-treasurer, 1970-73; president, 1974-75), Phi Beta Kappa, Sigma Xi.

WRITINGS: Learning: A Survey of Psychological Interpretations, Chandler Publishing, 1953, 3rd edition, Crowell, 1977; *Psychology: Principles and Problems,* Lippincott, 1970. Contributor to psychology journals.

WORK IN PROGRESS: Research on animal learning and motivation.

* * *

HILLERMAN, Tony 1925-

PERSONAL: Born May 27, 1925; son of August Alfred (a farmer) and Lucy (Grove) Hillerman; married Marie Unzner, August 16, 1948; children: Anne, Janet, Anthony, Monica, Stephen, Daniel. *Education:* Oklahoma State University, student, 1943; University of Oklahoma, B.A., 1946; University of New Mexico, M.A., 1966. *Politics:* Democrat. *Religion:* Roman Catholic. *Home:* 2729 Texas N.E., Albuquerque, N.M. 87110. *Office:* Department of Journalism, University of New Mexico, Albuquerque, N.M. 87106.

CAREER: Borger News Herald, Borger, Tex., reporter, 1948; *Morning Press-Constitution,* Lawton, Okla., city editor, 1948-50; United Press International, political reporter in Oklahoma City, Okla., 1950-52, bureau manager in Santa Fe, N.M., 1952-54; *New Mexican,* Santa Fe, political reporter, later editor, 1954-63; University of New Mexico, Albuquerque, assistant to the president, 1963-66, chairman of department of journalism, 1966—. *Military service:* U.S. Army, 1943-45; received Silver Star, Bronze Star, and Purple Heart. *Member:* Sigma Delta Chi, Phi Kappa Phi, Albuquerque Press Club. *Awards, honors:* Edgar Allen Poe Award, Mystery Writers of America, 1974, for *Dance Hall of the Dead.*

WRITINGS: The Blessing Way, Harper, 1970; *The Fly on the Wall,* Harper, 1971; *The Boy Who Made Dragonfly,* Harper, 1972; *Dance Hall of the Dead,* Harper, 1973; *The Great Taos Bank Robbery,* University of New Mexico Press, 1973; *New Mexico,* Portland Graphic Arts Center, 1975; *Rio Grande,* Portland Graphic Arts Center, 1975; (editor) *The Spell of New Mexico,* University of New Mexico Press, 1976; *Listening Woman,* Harper, 1977. Contributor to *True, New Mexico Quarterly,* and other periodicals.

SIDELIGHTS: Tony Hillerman, who had Indians as playmates and friends, says that he is interested in what can be done, in the literary sense, with the contrast of cultures. His mystery novels are concerned with the culture and values of contemporary Navajo and Pueblo Indians.

BIOGRAPHICAL/CRITICAL SOURCES: New Yorker, May 23, 1970; *Variety,* August 19, 1970.

* * *

HILLIER, Bevis 1940-

PERSONAL: Born March 28, 1940, in Redhill, Surrey, England; son of Jack Ronald (an author) and Mary (an author; maiden name, Palmer) Hillier. *Education:* Attended Magdalen College, Oxford, 1959-62. *Home:* Goldbeaters House, Manette St., London W.1, England. *Agent:* A. D. Peters, 10 Buckingham St., London WC2N 6BU, England.

CAREER: Times, London, England, home news reporter, 1963-65, sale room correspondent, 1965-69, antiques correspondent, 1970—; British Museum, London, public relations officer, 1969-70; full-time writer, 1970-73; *Connoisseur,* London, editor, 1973—. Guest curator and organizer of Art Deco exhibition for Minneapolis Institute of Arts, 1971. *Member:* Society of Authors, Royal Society of Arts (fellow), English Ceramic Circle, Beefsteak Club and Garrick Club (both London). *Awards, honors:* Gladstone Memorial prize, 1961.

WRITINGS: Master Potters of the Industrial Revolution, Cory, Adams & Mackay, 1965; *Pottery and Porcelain, 1700-1914,* Meredith Corp., 1968; *Art Deco of the Twenties and Thirties,* Dutton, 1968; *Posters,* Stein & Day, 1969; *Cartoons and Caricatures,* Dutton, 1970; *The World of Art Deco,* Dutton, 1971; (compiler) *100 Years of Posters,* Harper, 1972; *The Decorative Arts of the Forties and Fifties: Austerity Binge,* C. N. Potter, 1975 (published in England as *Austerity Binge: The Decorative Arts of the Forties and Fifties,* Studio Vista, 1975); *Travel Posters,* Dutton, 1976; *Victorian Studio Photographs,* David R. Godine, 1976; (editor) *Dead Funny,* Ash & Grant, 1976; *Punorama, or the Best of the Worst Victorian Puns,* Whittington Press, 1976. Regular reviewer for *Sunday Times;* contributor to *Connoisseur, Apollo, Cornhill, Daily Telegraph,* and *Guardian.* Editor, *British Museum Society Bulletin,* 1968-70.

WORK IN PROGRESS: A biography of Gerard Manley Hopkins, for J. Murray.

SIDELIGHTS: Bevis Hillier's ultimate ambition "is to be a great—not just a competent or even popular—novelist." He adds, "This may sound arrogant, and may indeed be delusory; but it is what I feel. . . ."

Posters has been published in a French translation.

AVOCATIONAL INTERESTS: Piano, collecting antiques.†

* * *

HILLING, David 1935-

PERSONAL: Born February 21, 1935, in Eastbourne, Sussex, England; son of William Roderick (a travel agent) and Jessie (Hobbs) Hilling; married Wendy Elizabeth Hubbard, September 8, 1962; children: Hugh Richard, Christopher James. *Education:* University College of Wales, Aberystwyth, B.Sc. (upper second class honors), 1957; University of London, Postgraduate Certificate in Education, 1958, Ph.D., 1974; University of Wales, M.Sc., 1961. *Home:* Torrington Rd., Berkhamsted, Hertfordshire, England. *Office:* Bedford College, University of London, Regent's Park, London NW1 4NS, England.

CAREER: University of Ghana, Legon, lecturer in geography, 1961-66; University of London, Bedford College, London, England, lecturer in geography, 1966—. Transport consultant for United Nations Economic Commission for Africa and for shipping lines. *Member:* Royal Geographical Society (fellow), Geographical Association, Institute of British Geographers, Maritime Economists Group, Chartered Institute of Transport, Royal Society of Arts.

WRITINGS: (Contributor) C. A. Fisher, editor, *Essays in Political Geography,* Methuen, 1968; (editor with Brian

Stewart Hoyle, and contributor) *Seaports and Development in Tropical Africa,* Macmillan, 1970; (contributor) J. I. Clarke, editor, *An Advanced Geography of Africa,* Hulton Educational Publications, 1975. Contributor to encyclopedias and directories; contributor of about twenty articles to geography journals.

WORK IN PROGRESS: Report on barge-carrying systems in maritime transport, for Inland Waterways Association.

* * *

HILTON, Alice Mary 1924-

PERSONAL: Born June 18, 1924, in New York, N.Y.; daughter of Frederick O. (an architect) and Thea (Weber) Hilton; married Herbert Layton Hayward (an orthodontist and biologist), September, 1958; children: Barbara-Mary Hilton Hayward, Kathryn-Anne Hilton Hayward. *Education:* St. Hugh's College, Oxford, B.A. (honors); graduate study at Sorbonne, University of Paris, University of Heidelberg, and at Claremont Graduate School; University of California, Los Angeles, Ph.D. *Politics:* "Independent leaning towards Democrat." *Religion:* Episcopalian. *Residence:* New York, N.Y.

CAREER: ElectroData Corp., Pasadena, Calif., director of publications, 1952-56; Underwood Corp., New York City, director of publications, 1956-58, consulting editor, 1958—; Conover-Mast Publications, New York City, associate editor, 1959-61; A. M. Hilton & Associates (consultants on cybernetics and automation), New York City, president, beginning 1958; Institute for Cybercultural Research, New York City, founder, president, and chairman of board of directors, beginning 1964. Organizer of First Conference on the Cybercultural Revolution, New York, 1964. Lecturer on the impact of science and technology.

MEMBER: American Association for the Advancement of Science, Federation of American Scientists, American Academy of Political and Social Science, Mind Association, Society for General Systems Research, Institute of Electrical and Electronics Engineers, American Mathematical Society, Association for Computing Machinery, Society for Social Responsibility in Science, International Federation of Information Processing Societies, American Federation of Information Processing Societies, Institute of Management Sciences, Simulations Councils, Operations Research Society of America, British Association for the Advancement of Science, American Society for Cybernetics (charter member), Authors League of America, Fellowship of Reconciliation, Emergency Civil Liberties Committee.

WRITINGS: Computing Machines in Control Systems, Conover-Mast Publications, 1961; *Logika i tsepi perekliucheniia* (on symbolic and mathematical logic), [Moscow], 1962; *Logic, Computing Machines, and Automation,* Spartan, 1963; (editor) *The Evolving Society,* Institute for Cybercultural Research, 1966; (editor) *Against Pollution and Hunger,* Wiley, 1974. Also author of *The Available Commitment.*

Writer of television documentaries and scripts for "You Are There," "Twentieth Century," and other programs. Contributor of scientific papers to professional journals, and articles to *New York Times Magazine, Cooperative Forum, Liberation,* and other journals. Editor, "Age of Cyberculture" series, World Publishing, 1962—; consulting editor, Spartan Books and *Data Processing* (magazine).†

HILTON, Ralph 1907-

PERSONAL: Born September 10, 1907, in Mendenhall, Miss.; son of R. T. (an attorney) and Myrtis (Cruise) Hilton; married Mary Jane Kendall, February 20, 1935 (deceased); married Dorothy M. Asnip, April 27, 1972; children: (first marriage) Mary Jane (Mrs. John F. Field). *Education:* George Washington University, B.A., 1929. *Home:* 167 North Sea Pines Dr., Hilton Head Island, S.C. 29928. *Agent:* A. Watkins, Inc., 77 Park Ave., New York, N.Y. 10016.

CAREER: Newspaper correspondent in Mexico City, Mexico, 1931-32; Associated Press, staff writer and editor in New Orleans, New York, Dallas, Richmond, and Washington, D.C., 1933-43; U.S. Department of State, Foreign Service officer, 1943-64, with posts in Lima, Peru, 1943-45, San Jose, Costa Rica, 1946, Buenos Aires, Argentina, 1947-49, and as public affairs adviser, assistant Secretary of State for Inter-American Affairs, 1955-57, American Embassy, Asuncion, Paraguay, counselor, 1957-58, director of UNESCO relations staff, 1959, special assistant to administrator, Bureau of Security and Consular Affairs, 1960, executive secretary, Joint Board of Examiners, U.S. Information Agency, 1962-64, Consul-General, 1964. *Member:* Foreign Service Association, National Press Club (Washington, D.C.), Overseas Press Club of America (New York).

WRITINGS: Worldwide Mission: The Story of the United States Foreign Service, World Publishing, 1970; (editor) *The Gentlemanly Serpent,* University of South Carolina Press, 1974; (editor) *Tales of the Foreign Service,* University of South Carolina Press, 1977. Co-founder and editor, "The Island Packet," 1970—.

* * *

HILTON, Ronald 1911-

PERSONAL: Born July 31, 1911, in Torquay, England; naturalized U.S. citizen in 1946; son of Robert and Elizabeth Alice (Taylor) Hilton; married Mary Bowie, May 1, 1939; children: Mary Alice Hilton Huyck. *Education:* Oxford University, B.A., 1933, M.A., 1936; studied at Sorbonne, University of Paris, 1933-34, University of Madrid, 1934-35, University of Perugia, 1935-36, and University of California, 1937-39. *Politics:* "Mugwump." *Home:* 766 Santa Ynez, Stanford, Calif. 94305.

CAREER: Comite Hispano Ingles Library, Madrid, Spain, director, 1936; University of British Columbia, Vancouver, assistant professor of modern languages, 1939-41; Stanford University, Stanford, Calif., associate professor, 1942-49, professor of Romantic languages, 1949-76, professor emeritus, 1976—. Director of Hispanic-American and Luso-Brazilian studies, 1944-64, executive director of California Institute of International Studies, 1965—. Honorary professor at University of San Marcos and visiting professor at University of Brazil, 1949; cultural director, University of the Air, KGEI, San Francisco, 1953-56; honorary professor, Foundation University of America, Bogota, 1957; visiting professor at Universities in France, 1970, 1976-77.

MEMBER: Hispanic Society of America, American Association of Teachers of Spanish and Portuguese. *Awards, honors:* Zaharoff traveling fellow, 1933-34; Howard traveling fellow, 1934-35; Commonwealth Fund fellow and honorary research fellow at University of California, 1937-39; Cruzeiro do Sul (Brazil), 1948.

WRITINGS: Campoamor, Spain, and the World, University of Toronto Press, 1940; (editor) *Handbook of Hispanic*

Source Materials and Research Organizations in the United States, University of Toronto Press, 1942, 2nd edition, Stanford University Press, 1956; *Four Studies in Franco-Spanish Relations,* University of Toronto Press, 1943; (editor) *Who's Who in Latin America,* seven parts, Stanford University Press and Marquis, 1946-51; *Joaquim Nabuco e a civilizacao anglo-americana* (booklet), Instituto Brasil-Estados Unidos, 1949; (translator and editor) *The Life of Joaquim Nabuco,* Stanford University Press, 1950, reprinted, Greenwood Press, 1968; (editor) *Jose Vasconcelos, Ulises Criollo,* Heath, 1960; (editor) *The Movement Toward Latin American Unity,* Praeger, 1969; *La America Latina de ayer y de hoy,* Holt, 1970; *The Scientific Institutions of Latin America,* California Institute of International Studies, 1970; *The Latin Americans: Their Heritage and Their Destiny,* Lippincott, 1973.

Associate editor for southern republics, *Who's Who in America,* 1943—. Contributor to *Columbia University Forum Anthology.* Editor and contributor on Soviet affairs, *World Affairs Report* (quarterly), and contributor to other periodicals. Editor, *Hispanic American Report,* 1948-64.

WORK IN PROGRESS: A book tentatively entitled *Let Us Now Damn Famous Men,* an account of the author's experiences in Spain from the last days of the monarchy (1931) to the first days of the Civil War (1936).

SIDELIGHTS: Ronald Hilton wrote *CA:* "A scholarship took me to Spain in early 1931, and I spent most of the period 1931 to 1936 there. I was evacuated during the early days of the Civil War, in which some of my best friends were killed on the right or on the left. I am one of the very few people who lived through the whole Republican period and who knew most of the leading intellectuals. Garcia Lorca lived in the same building with me, and I developed a scorn for him as an individual and as a writer. Most literary reputations are the results of political circumstances, and they should not be regarded as reflecting inherent values. The Civil War made a deep impression on me. While I admired men like Madariaga and Ortega y Gasset, most of the famous Spanish writers of the period impressed me as being a crowd of irresponsible weirdos . . . I had earlier reached the conclusion that the established literary forms (Poetry, Drama, Novel) are anachronisms."

*   *   *

HILTON, Suzanne 1922-

PERSONAL: Born September 3, 1922, in Pittsburgh, Pa.; daughter of Edwin P. (an insurance broker) and Helen (McFeely) McLean; married Warren Mitchell Hilton (an insurance engineeer), June 15, 1946; children: Edwin Bruce, Diana Lester. *Education:* Attended Pennsylvania College for Women (now Chatham College), 1940-43; Beaver College, B.A., 1945. *Religion:* Methodist. *Home:* 301 Runnymede Ave., Jenkintown, Pa. 19046.

CAREER: Former researcher and copywriter for advertising department of Westminster Press, Philadelphia, Pa.; currently working as public relations director for Jenkintown School District, Jenkintown, Pa. Researcher and writer of local history. *Member:* Philadelphia Children's Reading Round Table. *Awards, honors: How Do They Get Rid of It?* and *How Do They Cope with It?* were selected books of the year by Child Study Association; *The Way It Was—1876* was selected as one of the best books of the year, 1975, by *New York Times.*

WRITINGS—Young adult books; all published by Westminster: *How Do They Get Rid of It?* (Junior Literary Guild selection), 1970; *How Do They Cope with It?,* 1970; *It's Smart to Use a Dummy* (Junior Literary Guild selection), 1971; *It's a Model World* (Junior Literary Guild selection), 1972; *Beat It, Burn It, and Drown It,* 1974; *The Way It Was—1876,* 1975; *Who Do You Think You Are?: Digging for Your Family Roots,* 1976. Contributor of short stories and articles to periodicals. Editor, Old York Road Historical Society *Bulletin.*

WORK IN PROGRESS: A book on history using resources rarely read before.

SIDELIGHTS: Suzanne Hilton told *CA:* "Writing for young people is exciting—but some of my most fulfilling days happen in dusty libraries or from a search through the musty boxes stashed away in a historical society. Some days the research is just pure struggle, with a dutiful recording of facts on note cards. Then there are the days when a faded diary page can open a whole new view on those old facts and dates. Luckily, I live near Philadelphia—a city of libraries. There are special collections like those in the medical or historical or philosophical libraries. A college library usually stores the most recent books on a subject while a high school library will have already pre-selected the information of interest to the age group I write for. Although a large library contributes much in variety, sometimes the small local library makes up for its small number of volumes by allowing the author to roam through the stacks. Since I enjoy writing history for young people, these dusty shelves are my hunting grounds and the librarians who maintain them are my best helpers."

AVOCATIONAL INTERESTS: "Sailing around Chesapeake Bay and traveling anywhere. Also genealogy—since my latest book sparked the interest."

*   *   *

HINES, Paul (David) 1934-

PERSONAL: Born March 5, 1934, in Kansas City, Mo.; son of Jesse Paul (an auto worker) and Coramae (Patterson) Hines; married Pauline Laflen, May 14, 1954; children: Scot, Bruce, Mary, Susan, Kathleen (deceased). *Education:* Central Missouri State College (now University), B.S., 1959; Missouri University, M.A., 1962; Ball State University, Ed.D., 1964. *Politics:* Republican. *Religion:* United Methodist. *Residence:* Huntington, W.Va. *Office:* Office of the Vice-President, Marshall University, Huntington, W.Va. 25701.

CAREER: Hillsdale College, Hillsdale, Mich., assistant professor of education, 1964-65; Indiana University, Bloomington, assistant professor of education, 1965-68; School of the Ozarks, Point Lookout, Mo., vice-president for academic affairs, 1968-69; Marshall University, Huntington, W.Va., director of special programs, 1969-71; Barton County Community College, Great Bend, Kan., dean, 1971-75; Marshall University, Huntington, W.Va., vice-president, 1976—. Consultant to various counties in West Virginia and to National Advisory Council for the Education of Disadvantaged Children, 1968. *Military service:* U.S. Army, 1953-56. *Member:* National Council for the Social Studies, Phi Delta Kappa. *Awards, honors:* Outstanding Education Book of 1968-69, Pi Lambda Theta, 1969, for *A Guide to Human Rights Education.*

WRITINGS: (With Felix Snider) *Workbook in Missouri History,* Ramfre Press, 1962; (contributor) C. Benjamin Cox and Bryon Massialas, editors, *Social Studies in the United States: A Critical Appraisal,* Harcourt, 1967; (with Leslie Wood) *A Guide to Human Rights Education,* National

Council for the Social Studies, 1969. Contributor to *Indiana Elementary Principals Bulletin.*

WORK IN PROGRESS: Inquiry Units in Elementary Social Studies.

AVOCATIONAL INTERESTS: History, sports, and current affairs.

* * *

HINGORANI, R(up) C. 1925-

PERSONAL: Born September 10, 1925; son of Chandumal Nanikram (an advocate) and Savitri Hingorani; married wife, Kamla, December, 1959; children: Mohan (son), Chitra (daughter). *Education:* Bombay University, LL.B., 1945; Delhi University, LL.M., 1949; Yale University, J.S.D., 1955. *Home:* Rani Ghat, Patna-6, India. *Office:* Law Department, Patna University, Patna-6, India.

CAREER: Instructor of law in Universities of Agra, Lucknow, and Gorakhpur, India, 1951-63; Delhi University, Delhi, India, reader, 1963-64; Patna University, Patna, India, professor of international law and head of law department, 1964—, dean of faculty of law. *Member:* International Law Association, World Association of Law Professors (member of executive committee), International Institute of Human Rights, International Institute of Humanitarian Law (member of scientific committee), World Peace Through Law Center, Indian Law Institute, Association of Law Teachers and Schools in Southeast Asia.

WRITINGS: Prisoners of War, N. M. Tripathi (Bombay), 1963; *Indian Extradition Law,* Asia Publishing House (Bombay), 1969; (editor) *International Law through United Nations,* N. M. Tripathi, 1972. Editor-in-chief of *Journal* of All India Law Teachers Association, 1969-70.

WORK IN PROGRESS: International Law of the Developing States.

* * *

HIRAOKA, Kimitake 1925-1970
(Yukio Mishima)

January 14, 1925—November 25, 1970; Japanese novelist, playwright, and short story writer. Obituaries: *New York Times,* November 25, 1970; *Books Abroad,* spring, 1971.

* * *

HIRSHFIELD, Daniel S. 1942-

PERSONAL: Born February 11, 1942, in New York, N.Y.; son of Victor (an attorney) and Esther (Bender) Hirshfield; married Susan Hertz, June 17, 1963; children: Miriam, Rebecca. *Education:* Brandeis University, A.B., 1962; Harvard University, M.A., 1963, Ph.D., 1967.

CAREER: Worked in Washington, D.C., as writer and staff assistant for the President and the Department of Health, Education, and Welfare, 1969-70; Brandeis University, Waltham, Mass., assistant professor of history, 1970-71; Radio Corporation of America (RCA), New York, N.Y., director of creative services, beginning 1971. *Member:* American Historical Association, Ripon Society, Phi Beta Kappa. *Awards, honors:* Woodrow Wilson fellow, 1962, 1967.

WRITINGS: The Lost Reform: The Campaign for Compulsory Health Insurance in the United States from 1932 to 1943, Harvard University Press, 1970.††

HJELTE, George 1893-

PERSONAL: Surname is pronounced Jelt-*ay;* born July 4, 1893, in San Francisco, Calif.; son of Anton and Augusta (Pihlgren) Hjelte; married Frances Smith, June 12, 1920; children: George S., Helen Anne (Mrs. Woody Grey), Dorothy Virginia (Mrs. Harvey John Meyer). *Education:* University of California, Berkeley, B.S., 1917; Cambridge University, graduate study, 1917. *Politics:* Republican. *Religion:* Protestant. *Home:* 4468 Dundee Dr., Los Angeles, Calif. 90027.

CAREER: State of California, assistant supervisor of physical education, 1919-21; City of Berkeley, Calif., superintendent of recreation, 1921-26; City of Los Angeles, Calif., general manager, department of playgrounds and recreation, 1926-30; County of Westchester, N.Y., superintendent of recreation, 1930-33; City of Los Angeles, general manager, department of recreation and parks, 1933-62. Consultant on parks and recreation, 1962—, including consultant to National Recreation and Park Association on master study for New York City, 1965-66, and special consultant to Recreation and Youth Services Council of Los Angeles, 1966-67. Director of Civil Defense, Los Angeles, 1941-45. *Military service:* U.S. Army, Infantry, 1917-18; served in France; became captain; received Belgian Croix de Guerre. U.S. Navy, Special Services, 1937-41; became lieutenant commander.

MEMBER: American Recreation Society (fellow; president, 1937-41), National Recreation and Park Association (fellow), American Academy of Physical Education, California Recreation and Park Association, Phi Delta Kappa, Lambda Alpha, Pi Sigma Epsilon.

WRITINGS: Administration of Public Recreation, Macmillan, 1942; (contributor) *Sports and Recreation Facilities for School and Community,* Prentice-Hall, 1958; (with Jay S. Shivers) *Public Administration of Park and Recreational Services,* Macmillan, 1963; (with Shivers) *Planning Recreational Places,* Fairleigh Dickinson University Press, 1971; (with Shivers) *Administration of Park and Recreational Services,* Lea & Febiger, 1972. Contributor to *Yearbook* of American Association for Health, Physical Education and Recreation, 1951.

* * *

HOADLEY, Irene Braden 1938-
(Irene A. Braden)

PERSONAL: Born September 26, 1938, in Hondo, Tex.; daughter of Andrew H. (a farmer) and Theresa (Lebold) Braden; married Edward E. Hoadley (a realtor), February 21, 1970. *Education:* University of Texas, B.A., 1960; University of Michigan, A.M.L.S., 1961, Ph.D., 1967; Kansas State University, M.A., 1965. *Politics:* Republican. *Religion:* Roman Catholic. *Home:* 1031 Rose Circle, College Station, Tex. 77840. *Office:* Texas A & M University Library, College Station, Tex. 77843.

CAREER: Sam Houston State Teachers College Library (now Sam Houston State University Library), Huntsville, Tex., cataloger, 1961-62; Kansas State University Library, Manhattan, head of circulation department, 1962-64; Ohio State University Libraries, Columbus, librarian for general administration and research, 1966-73, assistant director of libraries for administrative services, 1973-74; Texas A & M University Library, College Station, director of libraries, 1974—. *Member:* American Library Association, Ohio Library Association (secretary, 1970-71), Phi Kappa Phi, Phi

Alpha Theta, Pi Lambda Theta. *Awards, honors:* Scarecrow Press Award, American Library Association, 1971; Distinguished Alumnus Award, School of Library Science, University of Michigan, 1976.

WRITINGS: (Under name Irene A. Braden, with Yvonne Wulff, F. H. Shillito, and J. F. Tomashefski) *Physiological Factors Relating to Terrestrial Altitudes: A Bibliography,* Ohio State University Libraries, 1968; (under name Irene A. Braden) *The Undergraduate Library,* American Library Association, 1970; (editor) *Natural Resources Bibliography,* Ohio State University Libraries, 1970; (editor with Alice S. Clark) *Quantitative Methods in Librarianship: Standards, Research, Management,* Greenwood Press, 1970; (with A. Robert Thorson) *An Automated On-Line Circulation System: Evaluation, Development, Use,* Ohio State University Libraries, 1973. Contributor to library journals.

* * *

HOCH, Edward D. 1930-
(Irwin Booth, Stephen Dentinger, Pat McMahon, Mister X, R. L. Stevens)

PERSONAL: Surname rhymes with "coke"; born February 22, 1930, in Rochester, N.Y.; son of Earl G. (a banker) and Alice (Dentinger) Hoch; married Patricia McMahon, June 5, 1957. *Education:* University of Rochester, student, 1947-49. *Politics:* Liberal Republican. *Religion:* Roman Catholic. *Home:* 2941 Lake Ave., Rochester, N.Y. 14612.

CAREER: Rochester Public Library, Rochester, N.Y., researcher, 1949-50; Pocket Books, Inc., New York, N.Y., staff member in adjustments department, 1952-54; Hutchins Advertising Co., Rochester, copy writer, 1954-68; full-time author, 1968—. *Military service:* U.S. Army, Military Police, 1950-52. *Member:* Mystery Writers of America. *Awards, honors:* Edgar Allan Poe ("Edgar") Award of Mystery Writers of America for best mystery short story of 1967, for "The Oblong Room."

WRITINGS: The Shattered Raven, Lancer, 1969; *The Transvection Machine,* Walker & Co., 1971; *The Judges of Hades,* Leisure Books, 1971; *The Spy and the Thief,* Davis Publications, 1971; *City of Brass,* Leisure Books, 1971; (editor) *Dear Dead Days,* Walker & Co., 1973; *The Fellowship of the Hand,* Walker & Co., 1973; *The Frankenstein Factory,* Warner Books, 1975; (editor) *Best Detective Stories of the Year—1976,* Dutton, 1976; (editor) *Best Detective Stories of the Year—1977,* Dutton, 1977. Contributor of more than four hundred short stories to *Antaeus, Argosy, Ellery Queen's Mystery Magazine, Alfred Hitchcock's Mystery Magazine,* and other periodicals; some of the stories have appeared under one of five pseudonyms.

SIDELIGHTS: Six of Edward Hoch's stories have been adapted for television, including three for the NBC-TV series "MacMillan and Wife." *Avocational interests:* The contemporary motion picture as an art form.

BIOGRAPHICAL/CRITICAL SOURCES: New York Times Book Review, June 29, 1968; *Rochester Democrat & Chronicle,* September 7, 1969; *Writer,* April, 1974; *Ellery Queen's Mystery Magazine,* August, 1976.

* * *

HOCHWAELDER, Fritz 1911-

PERSONAL: Born May 28, 1911, in Vienna, Austria; son of Leonhard (an upholsterer) and Therese (Koenig) Hochwaelder; married Ursula Buchi, July 26, 1951; married second wife, Susan Schreiner, July 20, 1960; children: (second marriage) Monique. *Education:* Attended elementary school in Vienna, Austria, and later studied in evening classes. *Home:* Am Oeschbrig 27, 8053 Zurich, Switzerland.

CAREER: Playwright. Served apprenticeship as an upholsterer in Vienna, Austria, where his first plays were performed in small theaters, 1932, 1936; emigrated to Switzerland in 1938; writer in Zurich, Switzerland, 1945—. *Member:* P.E.N. (Austrian center), Societe des Auteurs (Paris), Schweizer Schriftsteller-Verein, Vereinigung oesterreichischer Dramatiker. *Awards, honors:* Literary Prize of City of Vienna, 1955; Grillparzer Prize of Austrian Academy of Sciences, 1956; Anton Wildgans Prize of Austrian Industry, 1963; Austrian State Prize for Literature, 1966; Oesterreichisches Ehrenkreuz fuer Kunst und Wissenschaft 1971; Ehrenring der Stadt Wien, 1972.

WRITINGS—Plays: Das heilige Experiment (five-act; first produced, 1943, subsequently presented in Paris in two acts as "Sur la Terre comme au Ciel," and then in London and New York as "The Strong Are Lonely"), Volksverlag Elgg (Zurich), 1947, translation of the French play by Eva le Gallienne published as *The Strong Are Lonely,* Samuel French, 1954, German version published in *Oesterreichisches Theater,* Buechergilde Gutenberg, 1964; *Der Unschuldige* (title means "The Innocent"; three-act comedy; first produced, 1958), privately printed in Zurich, 1949, Volksverlag Elgg, 1958.

Donadieu (three-act; first produced, 1953), Paul Zsolnay (Hamburg), 1953, edition in German with introduction by Richard Thieberger published in England by Harrap, 1967; *Der oeffentliche Anklaeger* (three-act; first produced, 1948), Paul Zsolnay, 1954, acting edition with translation by Kitty Black published as *The Public Prosecutor,* Samuel French, 1958, television adaptation by Theodore Apstein, produced on "U.S. Steel Hour," 1958, edition in German with introduction and notes by J. R. Foster in English published under original title, Methuen, 1962; *Hotel du commerce* (comedy; first produced, 1944), Volksverlag Elgg, 1954; *Der Fluechtling* (title means "The Fugitive"; taken from a scenario by George Kaiser; first produced, 1945), Volksverlag Elgg, 1955; *Die Herberge* (title means "The Shelter"; three-act; first produced, 1956), Volksverlag Elgg, 1956; *Meier Helmbrecht* (first produced, 1946), Volksverlag Elgg, 1956; *Dramen I* (includes "Das heilige Experiment," "Die Herberge," and "Donnerstag" [a modern miracle play]; "Donnerstag" produced at Salzburg Festival, 1959), Albert Langen/Georg Mueller (Munich and Vienna), 1959.

Esther (an old tale dramatized; first produced, 1940), Volksverlag Elgg, 1960; *Dramen II* (includes "Der oeffentliche Anklaeger," "Der Unschuldige," and "1003" [three-act]; "1003" produced, 1963), Albert Langen/Georg Mueller, 1964; *Der Himbeerpfluecker* (three-act comedy; first produced, 1964; translation by Michael Bullock produced in London as "The Raspberry Picker," June, 1967; a translation published in Martin Esslin, *The New Theatre of Europe,* ["Das heilige Experiment," "Der oeffentliche Anklaeger," "Donadieus" "Die Herberge," and "Der Himbeerpfluecker"], Delta, 1970), Albert Langen/Georg Mueller, 1965; *Der Befehl* (title means "The Command"; commissioned for television by Eurovisions-Zentrale; book contains notes by the author and by Franz Theodor Csokor and Theodor W. Adorno; translation by Robin Hirsch published in *Modern International Drama,* Volume III, number 2, Pennsylvania State University Press, 1970), Stiasny (Graz), 1967.

Dramen, Albert Langen/Georg Mueller, 1958; *Dramen* (contains "Esther," "Das heilige Experiment," "Hotel du commerce," "Meier Helmbrecht," "Der oeffentliche Anklaeger," "Donadieu," "Die Herberge," "Der Unschuldige," "Der Himbeerpfluecker," and "Der Befehl"), two volumes, Verlag Styria (Graz), 1975; *Lazaretti: oder, Der Sae beltiger* (three-act; produced at Salzburg Festival, 1975), Verlag Styria, 1975.

SIDELIGHTS: Fritz Hochwaelder presents unusual twists of religious and moral themes in "Das heilige Experiment" and most of his later plays. According to Frederick Lumley, the Viennese-born playwright first attracted attention in 1952 when "Das heilige Experiment" was presented in Paris, where it "caused an immediate stir through the relationship of its theme with that of the worker-priest controversy then topical." Lumley mentions Hochwaelder's constant experiment both in ideas and form; the play "1003," for instance, has only two characters—the author and his imagination, with the author in the process of losing his creation, who seems more alive than himself. The development of Hochwaelder, Lumley says, "makes him not only an important dramatist for the German-speaking theatre, but together with Duerrenmatt and Frisch, also living in Switzerland, and Peter Weiss, another 'exile' living in Sweden, it may be said that the most interesting living dramatists anywhere to-day are to be found in these [four] representatives of the German language." Three of Hochwaelder's plays have been published in Buenos Aires, and several in Paris.

BIOGRAPHICAL/CRITICAL SOURCES: H. M. Feret, *"Sur la terre comme au ciel," le vrai drame de Hochwaelder,* Edition du Cerf, 1953; *Litteratur du xxe siecle,* Volume IV, Casterman, 1960; George Wellwarth, *The Theater of Protest and Paradox,* New York University Press, 1964; Frederick Lumley, *New Trends in 20th Century Drama,* Oxford University Press, 1967; Peter Demetz, *Post-War German Literature,* Western Publishing, 1970.

*   *   *

HOCKLEY, G(raham) C(harles) 1931-

PERSONAL: Born October 21, 1931, in England; son of Charles Alfred and Phyllis (Spinks) Hockley; married Irene Florence Holland, 1964; children: Andrew Charles, Corinne Jean. *Education:* University of Nottingham, B.A., 1959; Cambridge University, M.A., 1962. *Religion:* "Humanist." *Home:* 43 Woodvale Ave., Cyncoed, Cardiff CF2 6RE, Wales. *Office:* Department of Economics, University of Wales, Cardiff CF1 1XL, Wales.

CAREER: Cambridge University, Cambridge, England, junior research officer, 1959-62; University of Nottingham, Nottingham, England, lecturer in economics, 1962-64; University of Wales, Cardiff, lecturer, 1964-72, senior lecturer in economics, 1972—.

WRITINGS: (With Jack Revell and John Moyle) *The Wealth of the Nation: The National Balance Sheet of the United Kingdom, 1957-61,* Cambridge University Press, 1967; *Monetary Policy and Public Finance,* Routledge & Kegan Paul, 1970. Contributor to *British Tax Review, Times* (London), *Local Government Finance, Banker, Local Finance, Building Societies Gazette, Britannica Year Book.*

WORK IN PROGRESS: A revision of *Monetary Policy and Public Finance.*

*   *   *

HODGINS, Eric 1899-1971

March 2, 1899—January 7, 1971; American editor and author. Obituaries: *New York Times,* January 8, 1971; *Washington Post,* January 9, 1971; *Newsweek,* January 18, 1971; *Publishers' Weekly,* January 18, 1971.

*   *   *

HODGSON, Peter Crafts 1934-

PERSONAL: Born February 26, 1934, in Oak Park, Ill.; son of Jack E. and May (Crafts) Hodgson; married Eva Fornady, June 18, 1960; children: David, Jennifer. *Education:* Princeton University, A.B. (summa cum laude), 1956; Yale University, B.D. (cum laude), 1959, M.A., 1960, Ph.D., 1963; University of Tuebingen, postdoctoral research, summer, 1963. *Politics:* Democrat. *Home:* 71 Brookwood Ter., Nashville, Tenn. 37205. *Office:* Divinity School, Vanderbilt University, Nashville, Tenn. 37240.

CAREER: Ordained clergyman of the United Presbyterian Church in the U.S.A.; Trinity University, San Antonio, Tex., assistant professor of religion, 1963-65; Vanderbilt University, Divinity School, Nashville, Tenn., assistant professor, 1965-68, associate professor, 1969-73, professor of theology, 1973—, chairman of graduate department of religion, 1975—. On academic leave for research at University of Tuebingen, 1968-69. *Member:* Society for Religion in Higher Education (fellow), American Academy of Religion, Phi Beta Kappa. *Awards, honors:* Woodrow Wilson fellow, 1956-57; American Association of Theological Schools faculty fellow at University of Tuebingen, 1968-69; Guggenheim fellow, 1974-75.

WRITINGS: The Formation of Historical Theology: A Study of Ferdinand Christian Baur, Harper, 1966; (editor and translator) *Ferdinand Christian Baur on the Writing of Church History,* Oxford University Press, 1968; *Jesus—Word and Presence,* Fortress, 1971; (editor) David Friedrich Strauss, *The Life of Jesus Critically Examined,* Fortress, 1972; *Children of Freedom: Black Liberation in Christian Perspective,* Fortress, 1974; *New Birth of Freedom: A Theology of Bondage and Liberation,* Fortress, 1976. Contributor to religious and historical journals.

WORK IN PROGRESS: Translating G. W. F. Hegel's *Philosophy of Religion.*

BIOGRAPHICAL/CRITICAL SOURCES: Spectator, May 9, 1969.

*   *   *

HOENIG, J(ulius) 1916-

PERSONAL: Born April 11, 1916, in Prague, Czechoslovakia; married Inge Greve (a painter), 1942; children: Elisabeth (Mrs. Ray Rogers), Peter. *Education:* Charles University, M.D., 1943; Maudsley Hospital and National Hospital for Nervous Disorders, London, England, further study, 1947-53, D.P.M., 1951. *Politics:* None. *Religion:* None. *Residence:* St. John's, Newfoundland, Canada. *Office:* Department of Psychiatry, Memorial University of Newfoundland, St. John's, Newfoundland, Canada.

CAREER: World Health Organization, Bangalore, India, consultant, 1955-56; Manchester University, Manchester, England, reader in psychiatry, 1957-68; Memorial University of Newfoundland, St. John's, professor of psychiatry and chairman of department, 1969—. Visiting professor, All India Institute of Mental Health, Bangalore, 1955-56; honorary consultant, Royal Infirmary, Manchester, 1957-68. *Military service:* Royal Army Medical Corps, 1944-47. *Member:* Royal College of Physicians.

WRITINGS: (Contributor) Hugh Freeman and James

Farndale, editors, *New Aspects of the Mental Health Service,* Pergamon, 1967; (with Marian W. Hamilton) *The Desegregation of the Mentally Ill,* Routledge & Kegan Paul, 1969.

Translator with Hamilton: Karl Jaspers, *General Psychology,* Manchester University Press, 1962, University of Chicago Press, 1963; Jaspers, *The Nature of Psychotherapy,* Manchester University Press, 1964. Contributor of more than forty articles to medical journals.

* * *

HOFFELD, Donald R(aymond) 1933-

PERSONAL: Born September 12, 1933, in Baltimore, Md.; son of Jacob and Edna (Smith) Hoffeld; married Sharon Lytle, May 21, 1965; children: Rachel Elizabeth, Scott Lytle. *Education:* George Washington University, A.B. (cum laude), 1955; University of Wisconsin, M.S., 1956, Ph.D., 1958. *Politics:* Independent. *Home:* 2245 Glendale Ave., Baton Rouge, La. 70808. *Office:* Department of Psychology, Louisiana State University, Baton Rouge, La. 70803.

CAREER: Research scientist, Psychological Research Associates, 1958; Louisiana State University, Baton Rouge, assistant professor, 1960-63, associate professor, 1963-73, professor of psychology, 1973—. Member of Control of Forces Conference, National Research Council, 1959. *Military service:* U.S. Air Force, 1958-60; became first lieutenant. U.S. Air Force Reserve, 1960-68; became captain. *Member:* American Association for the Advancement of Science, Midwestern Psychological Association, Phi Beta Kappa, Sigma Xi.

WRITINGS: A Student Guide to Introductory Psychology, McCutchan, 1969; *Introductory Psychology,* McCutchan, 1972. Contributor to *Nature* and psychology journals.

WORK IN PROGRESS: A book on the history of psychology, completion expected in 1979; research on stimulus variables in perception of illusions.

* * *

HOFFERBERT, Richard I(ra) 1937-

PERSONAL: Born April 2, 1937, in Grant County, Ind.; son of Ernest A. (a sales manager) and Margaret (Stover) Hofferbert; married Rosemarie Besemer, September 7, 1957; children: Mark Richard, Samuel Carter. *Education:* Indiana University, A.B., 1959, Ph.D., 1962. *Politics:* Republican. *Religion:* Atheist. *Office:* Center for Social Analysis, State University of New York, Binghamton, N.Y. 13901.

CAREER: Williams College, Williamstown, Mass., instructor, 1962-64, assistant professor of political science, 1964-67; Cornell University, Ithaca, N.Y., assistant professor, 1962-68, associate professor of political science, 1968-70; University of Michigan, Ann Arbor, associate professor of political science, 1970-75; State University of New York at Binghamton, professor of political science, 1975—. Executive director, Inter-University Consortium for Political Research, 1970-75. *Member:* American Political Science Association, International Studies Association, Midwest Political Science Association. *Awards, honors:* National Center for Education in Politics fellow, 1965-66; Social Science Research Council fellow, 1967-69.

WRITINGS: (Editor with Ira Sharkansky) *State and Urban Politics: Readings in Public Policy,* Little, Brown, 1970; *The Study of Public Policy,* Bobbs-Merrill, 1974. Contributor to social science journals.

HOFFMAN, Adeline M(ildred) 1908-

PERSONAL: Born May 13, 1908, in Richmond Hill, N.Y.; daughter of Francis (a building specialties dealer) and Helena (Schimmer) Hoffman. *Education:* Trenton State College, Diploma, 1928; University of Missouri, B.S., 1930; Columbia University, M.A., 1935; Pennsylvania State University, Ph.D., 1956. *Politics:* Republican. *Religion:* Presbyterian. *Home:* 7 Gilmore Ct., Iowa City, Iowa 52240.

CAREER: High school teacher of home economics in Bel Air, Md., 1930-35, and Freehold, N.J., 1935-36; county home demonstration agent in Maryland, 1936-43; senior nutritionist, New York State Emergency Food Commission, 1943-45; University of Delaware Cooperative Extension Service, Newark, specialist in clothing, textiles, and home furnishings, 1945-49; University of Connecticut, Storrs, assistant professor of textiles and clothing, 1949-53; U.S. Department of Health, Education, and Welfare, Washington, D.C., clothing specialist with Defense Welfare Services, 1956-57; Southern Illinois University, Carbondale, professor of textiles and clothing and chairman of department, 1957-61; University of Iowa, Iowa City, professor in charge of teaching and research in textiles and clothing, department of home economics, 1962-76, professor emeritus, 1976—. Member of board of directors, Christian Retirement Services, Inc., Iowa City; member of women's committee, Japan International Christian University.

MEMBER: American Gerontological Society, American Home Economists Association (life member), International Graphoanalysis Society (life member), International Home Economics Federation, American Association of University Professors, American Association of University Women, Fashion Group, Inc., National League of American Pen Women (national fourth vice-president), Phi Upsilon Omicron, Omicron Nu, Phi Kappa Phi, Pi Lambda Theta, Delta Kappa Gamma, Soroptimist International. *Awards, honors:* University of Missouri, Women's Centennial Award, 1967, citation of merit, and Gold Medal Award, both 1970.

WRITINGS: (With Iva M. Balder) *Social Science Aspects of Clothing for Older Women: An Annotated Bibliography,* Department of Home Economics and Institute of Gerontology, University of Iowa, 1964; (contributor) W. W. Morris and H. Lee Jacobs, editors, *Nursing and Retirement Home Administration,* Iowa State University Press, 1966; (editor) *The Daily Needs and Interests of Older People,* C. C Thomas, 1970. Contributor to professional journals.

WORK IN PROGRESS: Clothing for the Physically Handicapped and the Aged; The Role of the Federal Government in the Textile and Apparel Industries; and a second edition of *The Daily Needs and Interests of Older People.*

SIDELIGHTS: Adeline Hoffman wrote to *CA:* "It was my doctoral dissertation that phased in my serious professional writing, but lesser writing started with my high school paper, quarterly and yearbook. At the time, I couldn't afford to subscribe to the high school publications and the pressure of 'school spirit' dictated that I do something to express my school spirit. So, I went out and got ads for the school paper, and as a reward for having brought in the most ad money, I was given a place on the editorial staff. From then on, I have never stopped writing." Believing in the importance of good writing, she comments, "I have concentrated on establishing writing awards to help focus attention on excellence in writing among university students."

HOFFMAN, Lisa 1919-
(Candida)

PERSONAL: Born May 19, 1919, in Essen, Germany; daughter of Otto (a businessman) and Elsa (Weis) Hoffman. *Education:* Attended secondary school in Frankfurt, Germany. *Politics:* Democrat. *Religion:* Jewish. *Home:* 445 West 23rd St., New York, N.Y. 10011. *Agent:* Max Gartenberg, 331 Madison Ave., New York, N.Y. 10017.

CAREER: Free-lance journalist and photographer. Correspondent for *Schweizer Illustrierte,* Zurich, Switzerland, and *Jasmin,* Germany; publicist for Prentice-Hall and translator of subtitles for film companies, chiefly Metro-Goldwyn-Mayer. *Member:* Overseas Press Club, Foreign Press Association.

WRITINGS: (With Denison Hatch and Mary Eleanor Browning) *Reigning Cats and Dogs,* Prentice-Hall, 1964; (with Lucy Freeman) *The Ordeal of Stephen Dennison,* Prentice-Hall, 1970. Contributor to *National Observer, Chicago Tribune Syndicate, Playbill, Elle, Harvest Years,* and other publications here and abroad.

WORK IN PROGRESS: A cookbook.††

*   *   *

HOFFMAN, Michael J(erome) 1939-

PERSONAL: Born March 31, 1939, in Philadelphia, Pa.; son of Nathan P. (a consolidator) and Sara (Perlman) Hoffman; married Dianna Bukey, June 12, 1960 (divorced February 8, 1972); married Diane Turner, February 18, 1972; children: (first marriage) Cynthia Joy, Matthew Stephen; (second marriage) Kimberly, Correy. *Education:* University of Pennsylvania, A.B. (cum laude), 1959, A.M., 1960, Ph.D., 1963. *Agent:* Joan Daves, 515 Madison Ave., New York, N.Y. 10022. *Office:* Department of English, University of California, Davis, Calif. 95616.

CAREER: Washington College, Chestertown, Md., instructor in English, 1962-64; University of Pennsylvania, Philadelphia, instructor, 1964-66, assistant professor of English, 1966-67; University of California, Davis, assistant professor, 1967-71, associate professor, 1971-75, professor of English, 1975—, assistant vice chancellor of academic affairs, 1976—. *Military service:* U.S. Army Reserve, 1957-61. *Member:* Modern Language Association of America, American Studies Association. *Awards, honors:* Summer faculty fellowships, University of Pennsylvania, 1967, and University of California, Davis, 1969, 1970, 1972, 1973.

WRITINGS: The Development of Abstraction in the Writings of Gertrude Stein, University of Pennsylvania Press, 1965; *The Buddy System* (novel), Holt, 1971; *The Subversive Vision: American Romanticism in Literature,* Kennikat, 1973; *Gertrude Stein,* Twayne, 1976. Contributor of articles, fiction, and reviews to *Era, Yale Review, Georgia Review, American Literature.*

WORK IN PROGRESS: A book on "modernism"; a chapter, "Themes, Topics, Criticism," for *American Literary Scholarship.*

*   *   *

HOFFMAN, Phyllis M(iriam) 1944-

PERSONAL: Born September 7, 1944, in Brooklyn, N.Y.; daughter of Morris and Bertha (Levine) Hoffman. *Education:* State University of New York at Binghamton, B.A. (magna cum laude), 1965; Bank Street College of Education, M.A., 1974. *Home:* 49 Eighth Ave., New York, N.Y. 10014.

CAREER: Harper & Row Publishers, Inc., New York City, children's book editor, 1966-70; Abelard-Schuman Ltd., New York City, children's book editor, 1970-72; Little Star of Broome Day Care Center, New York City, group teacher, 1975-77.

WRITINGS: Steffie and Me (juvenile), Harper, 1970.

WORK IN PROGRESS: Several children's books.

AVOCATIONAL INTERESTS: Dance, music, cooking, photography, anthropology, psychology.

*   *   *

HOFFMAN, Richard L(ester) 1937-

PERSONAL: Born February 28, 1937, in Philadelphia, Pa.; son of Lester Samuel (a machinist) and Helena (Forrest) Hoffman; married Marie Aileen Regina Golden, July 5, 1968. *Education:* University of Pennsylvania, A.B., 1959; Princeton University, A.M., 1961, Ph.D., 1964. *Office:* Department of English, Virginia Polytechnic Institute and State University, Blacksburg, Va. 24061.

CAREER: University of Pennsylvania, Philadelphia, instructor, 1963-65, assistant professor of English, 1965-68; Queens College of the City University of New York, Flushing, N.Y., associate professor of English, 1968-71; Virginia Polytechnic Institute and State University, Blacksburg, Va., professor of English, 1971—. *Member:* Modern Language Association of America, Modern Humanities Research Association, Mediaeval Academy of America, Early English Text Society, Phi Beta Kappa, Eta Sigma Phi. *Awards, honors:* Woodrow Wilson fellow, 1959-60; Danforth fellow, 1959-63; Scribner fellow at Princeton University.

WRITINGS: Ovid and the Canterbury Tales, University of Pennsylvania Press, 1967; (editor) *History of the English Language: Selected Texts and Exercises,* Little, Brown, 1968, 2nd edition (with L. M. Myers), published as *The Roots of Modern English: Selected Texts and Exercises,* 1971; (editor with Paul Elledge), *Romantic and Victorian: Studies in Memory of William H. Marshall,* Fairleigh Dickinson University Press, 1971; (editor with Maxwell Luria) *Middle English Lyrics,* Norton, 1975.

Contributor: Shirley E. Marshall, editor, *A Young American's Treasury of English Poetry,* Washington Square, 1967; Beryl Rowland, editor, *A Companion to Chaucer Studies,* Oxford University Press, 1968; R. M. Lumiansky and Herschel Baker, editors, *Critical Approaches to Six Major English Works,* University of Pennsylvania Press, 1968. Contributor of more than twenty articles to language journals.

WORK IN PROGRESS: A new edition of *The Tale of Beryn,* for Early English Text Society (Oxford); editing with Maxwell Luria, two "Norton Critical Editions" of Middle English poetry (romances, drama), for Norton; *The Tale of Melibee* for the University of Oklahoma Press; *The Variorum Chaucer.*

*   *   *

HOFSTADTER, Richard 1916-1970

August 6, 1916—October 24, 1970; American political historian. Obituaries: *New York Times,* October 25, 1970; *Newsday,* October 26, 1970; *Washington Post,* October 26, 1970; *Newsweek,* November 2, 1970; *Current Biography,* 1970. (See index for *CA* sketch)

HOGE, Phyllis 1926-
(Phyllis Rose, Phyllis Hoge Thompson)

PERSONAL: Born November 15, 1926, in Elizabeth, N.J.; daughter of Philip Barlow (an engineer) and Dorothy (Anderson) Hoge; married John Creighton Rose (a geophysicist), October 6, 1951; married second husband, Noel James Thompson (an electrical engineer), June 4, 1964 (divorced); children: (first marriage) Mead Anderson, William Scoffield, John C., Jr., Katherine Blair. *Education:* Connecticut College, B.A., 1948; Duke University, M.A., 1949; University of Wisconsin, Ph.D., 1957. *Religion:* Quaker. *Home:* 2520 Rainbow Dr., Honolulu, Hawaii 96822. *Office:* Department of English, University of Hawaii, Honolulu, Hawaii 96822.

CAREER: University of Wisconsin Extension—Madison, special instructor, 1957-62; Milton College, Milton, Wis., professor of English, 1962-64; University of Hawaii, Honolulu, assistant professor, 1964-69, associate professor, 1969-73, professor of English, 1973—. Member of board, Hawaii Literary Arts Council, and Hawaii Council for Culture and the Arts. *Member:* National Council of Teachers of English, Modern Language Association, Historic Hawaii Foundation, Phi Beta Kappa. *Awards, honors:* National Endowment for the Humanities grant to conduct poetry workshops in schools in Hawaii, 1968-69.

WRITINGS: Artichoke, and Other Poems, University of Hawaii Press, 1969; (under name Phyllis Hoge Thompson) *The Creation Frame,* University of Illinois Press, 1973; (under name Phyllis Hoge Thompson) *The Serpent of the White Rose,* Petronium, 1975. Contributor to literary journals, poetry magazines, and teaching periodicals. Editor, *Festival,* 1966, and *Any Direction.* Phyllis Hoge used the name Phyllis Rose for poetry and prose until 1968; and now uses it on song lyrics only.

WORK IN PROGRESS: The Truth, a book of poems; *The Song that Belongs to the Land,* based on Hawaiian myth and religion chants.

SIDELIGHTS: Phyllis Hoge told *CA:* "I am fragmented among teaching, mothering, writing. I love all of these. Poetry is central, and is closely bound to the place where I am. I have a strong sense of place and of how human emotions are evoked from natural surroundings. I love travel, but have rarely been able to go far and long because of four young children.... Yeats was crucial to me and Rilke is, and most recently, James Wright. I think long practice in traditional meters yields a flexible, ready music to poetry—even when the form becomes free. My work is devoted now almost entirely to Hawaiian themes, centered in aloha aina, love of the land, and draws as deeply as possible upon the mona, the sacred power, gathered in the islands."

* * *

HOGG, Ian V(ernon) 1926-

PERSONAL: Born October 29, 1926, in Durham, England; son of William Vernon (an attorney) and Mary Eleanor (Whalley) Hogg; married Anna Teresa Trebinska, March 10, 1962; children: George, Leslie, Alexandra. *Education:* Attended schools in Durham and St. Albans, Hertfordshire, England, 1932-40. *Politics:* Conservative. *Religion:* Protestant. *Home and office:* 15 Packers Hill, Upton-upon-Severn, Worchestershire, England. *Agent:* Bolt & Watson, 8 Storey's Gate, London S.W.1, England.

CAREER: British Army, 1945-72; served in Europe, Hong Kong, and in the Korean War, 1950-52; Royal Military College of Science, Shrivenham, Swindon, Wiltshire, England,

member of instructional staff of Royal Artillery, 1953-72, retired as master gunner. *Member:* Royal Artillery Historical Society.

WRITINGS: Military Pistols and Revolvers: The Handguns of the Two World Wars, Arco, 1970; *The Guns, 1939-1945,* Ballantine, 1970; *German Secret Weapons of World War II,* Arms & Armour Press, 1970; *Barrage: The Guns in Action,* Ballantine, 1971; *The Guns, 1914-1918,* Ballantine, 1971; *German Pistols and Revolvers,* Arms & Armour Press, 1971; (with J. S. Weeks) *Military Small Arms of the Twentieth Century,* Arms & Armour Press, 1973; (with L. F. Thurston) *British Artillery of the First World War,* Ian Allen, 1973; *Artillery,* MacDonald & Janes, 1973; *Rail Gun,* John Batchelor, 1973; *Weapons of the Arab-Israeli War,* Phoebus Publishing, 1973; *Coast Defences of England and Wales,* David & Charles, 1974; *Grenades and Mortars,* Ballantine, 1974; *A History of Artillery,* Hamlyn, 1974; *Infantry Weapons,* Phoebus Publishing, 1974; *German Secret Weapons,* Phoebus Publishing, 1974.

German Artillery of World War Two, Arms & Armour Press, 1975; *Gas: The Story of Chemical Warfare,* Ballantine, 1975; *Fortress: The History of Military Defence,* MacDonald, 1975; (with J. H. Batchelor) *Armies of the American Revolution,* Leo Cooper, 1975; *Allied Secret Weapons,* Phoebus Publishing, 1975; *Modern Soviet Weapons,* Phoebus Publishing, 1975; *The Machine Gun,* Phoebus Publishing, 1975; *The Guns of World War Two,* MacDonald, 1976; *Encyclopedia of Infantry Weapons,* Bison Books, 1977; *World Pistols,* Arms & Armour Press, 1977; *British and American Artillery of World War Two,* Arms & Armour Press, in press.

Contributor to *The Japanese War Machine,* Bison Books, 1977, *The Russian War Machine,* Bison Books, 1977, and *Hitler's Decisive Battles,* Quarto Publications, 1977; also contributor to *War Monthly, Weapons & Warfare,* and *Guns Review.*

WORK IN PROGRESS: The Steel Umbrella, a survey of air defense from Napoleon's time to the present day, for MacDonald & Janes.

SIDELIGHTS: Ian Hogg told *CA:* "After retiring from the Army in 1972 I went, as I intended, to live in Portugal, but for a number of reasons I found it necessary to return to England in 1975. If nothing else, it makes life easier because of the more ready access to libraries, museums and military acquaintances. Although my work has so far been principally about military hardware I hope to broaden the field somewhat, as I have tried to do in writing about fortification and tactical problems. But as long as the demand continues to be there, I shall continue to respond, leaving my other ideas in pickle until I can find time to work on them."

* * *

HOLLAND, Alma Boice

PERSONAL: Born in Parkersburg, W.Va.; daughter of Charles E. and Lyda (Showalter) Boice; married Thurl O. Holland (vice-president of O. Ames Co.; now retired); children: Robert, Donald, John, Alma, Jr. *Education:* After graduation from Parkersburg High School attended a southern finishing school for one year. *Politics:* Republican. *Religion:* Baptist. *Home:* 5523 Second Ave., Island Lane, Vienna, W.Va. 26101.

CAREER: Free-lance writer. Editorial associate, *Writer's Digest,* and writer of "Second Thoughts" column, 1962—. Member of advisory board for creative writing course, La Salle Extension University.

WRITINGS: Second Thoughts, Writer's Digest, 1969. Work included in collection, *The Articulate Woman,* Droke, 1968, and in college texts published by Science Research Associates and Heath; plays originally published in *Players* have been included in a text published by Row, Peterson & Co. Contributor to national magazines ranging from *Saturday Evening Post* to *Woman's Day;* columnist for eight years in *Woman's World.*

WORK IN PROGRESS: Magazine articles.

SIDELIGHTS: Alma Holland told *CA* that through her work she has found "two types of writers—those who *want* to write and those who *have* to write. Most of the former are influenced by the idea of author-prestige and the possibility of financial gain. The latter *must* write down the things in their minds regardless of whether publication is achieved or there are monetary rewards. Those are the real writers who invariably attain ultimate success in the profession. A compulsion accompanies in-born talent which won't be denied."

*   *   *

HOLLINGSWORTH, Paul M. 1932-

PERSONAL: Born February 29, 1932, in Preston, Idaho; son of Austin Earl (a car dealer, service station owner, and farmer) and Blanche (Merrill) Hollingsworth; married Colleen Black, April 26, 1955; children: Debra, Kendal, Janae. *Education:* Brigham Young University, B.S., 1951; Arizona State University, M.A., 1961, Ed.D., 1963. *Politics:* Conservative. *Religion:* Church of Jesus Christ of Latter-day Saints. *Home:* 1606 Byrd Dr., Sparks, Nev. 89431. *Office:* Department of Education, University of Nevada, Reno, Nev. 89507.

CAREER: Elementary and junior high teacher in Arizona public schools, 1956-61; Arizona State University, Tempe, instructor, 1962-65, assistant professor of education, 1965-66; University of Nevada, Reno, associate professor, 1966-70, professor of education and director of Reading Study Center, 1970—. Educational consultant for twelve California and Nevada county school districts. *Military service:* U.S. Navy, 1953-55. *Member:* International Reading Association, National Council of Teachers of English, Sierra Reading Council (president, 1969-70), Western College Reading Association (president, 1971-72; director, 1973—), Phi Delta Kappa, Alpha Phi Omega.

WRITINGS: (With G. M. Chronister) *A Longitudinal View of Development,* Arizona State University College of Education, 1965; (with others) *Reading Programs and Practices in Elementary and Secondary Schools in Arizona* (bulletin), Arizona State University College of Education, 1965; (with J. Patrick Kelly) *Basic Reading Instruction,* MSS Educational Publishing Co., 1969; (with Kenneth H. Hoover) *Learning and Teaching in the Elementary School,* Allyn & Bacon, 1970, 2nd edition, 1975; (with Hoover) *A Handbook for Elementary School Teachers,* Allyn & Bacon, 1973. Contributor of articles on reading to *Reading Teacher, Education, Instructor, Journal of Communication, Elementary English,* and other educational journals.

*   *   *

HOLMES, Charles M(ason) 1923-

PERSONAL: Born August 25, 1923, in North Dartmouth, Mass.; son of Harold Denison (a cotton goods salesman) and Margaret (Macfarlane) Holmes; married Carolyn Lyons, June 25, 1960; children: Anne, Elizabeth, John. *Education:* Cornell University, B.S. in Chem.E., 1944,

A.B., 1947, Columbia University, M.A., 1950, Ph.D., 1959. *Residence:* Lexington, Ky. *Office:* Department of English, Transylvania University, Lexington, Ky. 40508.

CAREER: Merck & Co., Inc., Rahway, N.J., technical assistant in chemical purchasing, 1947-49; Tufts College, Medford, Mass., instructor in English, 1950-52; Duke University, Durham, N.C., instructor in English, 1953-55; Washington University, St. Louis, Mo., instructor, 1956-59, assistant professor of English, 1959-60; Transylvania University, Lexington, Ky., associate professor, 1960-65, professor of English, 1965—, chairman of department, 1971-75, 1976—, acting director of humanities, 1976—, acting vice-president and dean of College, 1975-76. Consultant, Danforth Foundation, 1966-67. *Military service:* U.S. Navy, 1944-45. *Member:* American Civil Liberties Union, Phi Beta Kappa. *Awards, honors:* Andrew Mellon postdoctoral fellow at University of Pittsburgh, 1967-68.

WRITINGS: Aldous Huxley and the Way to Reality, Indiana University Press, 1970. Contributor of articles and reviews to *Western Humanities Review, Modern Fiction Studies,* and other journals.

BIOGRAPHICAL/CRITICAL SOURCES: Nation, November 30, 1970; *Times Literary Supplement,* April 19, 1971; *Modern Fiction Studies,* XVII, no. 2, 1971, XVIII, no. 2, 1972.

*   *   *

HOLMES, W(ilfred) J(ay) 1900-
(Alec Hudson)

PERSONAL: Born April 4, 1900, in Stockport, N.Y.; son of John Eric and Esther (Moett) Holmes; married Isabelle West, June 17, 1922 (died March 25, 1972); married Elizabeth B. Carr, January 2, 1976; children: (first marriage) John Eric. *Education:* U.S. Naval Academy, B.S., 1922; Columbia University, M.S., 1929. *Home:* 1434 Punahou St., Apt. 1133, Honolulu, Hawaii 96822. *Agent:* Paul R. Reynolds, Inc., 12 East 41st St., New York, N.Y. 10017.

CAREER: U.S. Navy, midshipman, 1918-22, regular officer, 1922-36, 1941-46, retired with rank of captain; University of Hawaii, Honolulu, assistant professor of engineering and mathematics, 1936-41, professor of engineering, 1946-66, dean of College of Applied Science, 1951-54, vice-president, 1954-59, dean of College of Engineering, 1959-66, dean emeritus of College of Engineering, 1966—. *Member:* American Society for Engineering Education, Phi Kappa Phi, Epsilon Chi. *Awards, honors—*Military: Distinguished Service Medal, Legion of Merit, and Navy Unit Citation.

WRITINGS: (Under pseudonym Alec Hudson) *Battle Stations,* Macmillan, 1940; (under pseudonym Alec Hudson) *Enemy Sighted,* Macmillan, 1941; (under pseudonym Alec Hudson) *Rendezvous,* Macmillan, 1942; *Undersea Victory,* Doubleday, 1966. Contributor to *U.S. Naval Institute Proceedings;* and contributor of a number of short stories on undersea warfare, under pseudonym Alec Hudson, to *Saturday Evening Post.*

WORK IN PROGRESS: An account of Intelligence activity in the Central Pacific during World War II, completed and under review for clearance by the Navy Department.

*   *   *

HOLMQUIST, Anders 1933-
(Ostrowsky)

PERSONAL: Born March 30, 1933, in Stockholm, Sweden; son of Goeran Fredrik and Ulla (Brambeck) Holmquist;

children: Eva E., Tristan. *Education:* Kunsthandwerk-school Saarbrucken, Diploma in Photography, 1958.

CAREER: Free-lance photographer, doing creative photography and films.

WRITINGS: (Photographs by Holmquist; text by Peter Marin) *The Free People,* Outerbridge & Dienstfrey, 1969. Contributor to magazines in Europe under pseudonym Ostrowsky.

WORK IN PROGRESS: A book about the discovery of several unknown Maya temples in Mexico.††

* * *

HOLT, Thelma Jewett 1913-

PERSONAL: Born August 17, 1913; daughter of Harry Francis (an insurance broker) and Isabelle (Turner) Jewett; married Frederick Burton Holt (a pharmacist), June 27, 1936; children: David Jewett, Gary Kendrick, Jonathan Turner. *Education:* New Haven Normal School (now Southern Connecticut State College), Certificate. *Politics:* Republican. *Religion:* Episcopalian. *Home:* 131 Elmwood Dr., Cheshire, Conn. 06140.

CAREER: Cheshire (Conn.) public schools, elementary teacher, 1934-65, teacher-tutor of disadvantaged children, 1965-78. *Member:* National Education Association, Connecticut Education Association.

WRITINGS—Juvenile: *Mr. Tic,* John Day, 1970.

* * *

HOLTZ, Avraham 1934-

PERSONAL: Born May 26, 1934, in New York, N.Y.; son of Leon and Pauline (Nadel) Holtz; married Toby Esther Berger; children: Shalom Eliezel. *Education:* Herzliah Hebrew Teacher Institute, Teachers Diploma, 1952; Brooklyn College (now Brooklyn College of the City University of New York), B.A., 1955; Jewish Theological Seminary of America, M.H.L., 1959, D.H.L., 1962. *Residence:* New York, N.Y. *Office:* Department of Hebrew Literature, Jewish Theological Seminary of America, 3080 Broadway, New York, N.Y. 10027.

CAREER: Rabbi; Jewish Theological Seminary of America, New York, N.Y., associate professor, 1968-73, professor of Hebrew literature, 1973—. *Member:* Rabbinical Assembly, Modern Language Association of America, American Association of University Professors. *Awards, honors:* Advanced studies fellowship at Hebrew University of Jerusalem, 1969; Jewish Cultural Foundation award, 1974-75.

WRITINGS: (Editor) *The Holy City: Jews on Jerusalem,* Norton, 1971; *Isaac Dov Berkowitz: Voice of the Uprooted,* Cornell University Press, 1973. Contributor to religious and literary journals in United States and Israel.

WORK IN PROGRESS: Writing on Agnon and on Hillel Zeitlin.

* * *

HOLYER, Erna Maria 1925-
(Ernie Holyer)

PERSONAL: Born March 15, 1925, in Weilheim, Germany; came to United States in 1956, naturalized citizen; daughter of Mathias (a hotel, theater, and farm owner) and Anna (Goldhofer) Schretter; married Friedrich Rupp, May 27, 1943; married second husband, Gene Wallace Holyer (president, Holyer Construction Co.), August 24, 1957. *Educa-*

tion: San Jose Junior College, A.A., 1964; attended San Mateo College, San Jose State University, and University of Santa Cruz, 1965-74. *Home:* 1314 Rimrock Dr., San Jose, Calif. 95120.

CAREER: Free-lance writer, mainly for children; painter, with several one-woman shows. Teacher of creative writing in San Jose adult education program. *Member:* California Writers Club.

WRITINGS—Juveniles under pseudonym Ernie Holyer: *Rescue at Sunrise, and Other Stories,* Review & Herald, 1965; *Steve's Night of Silence, and Other Stories,* Review & Herald, 1966; *A Cow for Hansel,* Review & Herald, 1967; *At the Forest's Edge,* Southern Publishing, 1969; *Song of Courage,* Southern Publishing, 1970; *Lone Brown Gull, and Other Stories,* Review & Herald, 1971; *Shoes for Daniel,* Southern Publishing, 1974; *Sigi's Fire Helmet,* Pacific Press Publishing Association, 1974; *The Southern Sea Otter,* Steck, 1975. Also contributor to *Und Wieder Scheint de Sonne* (three volume anthology), edited by G. Tobler, Advent Verlag (Zurich). Contributor of several book-length serials and 200 short stories and articles to magazines.

WORK IN PROGRESS: Reservoir Road, a junior novel about Mexican-American migrants; *Elisha Brooks,* a biography of a backwoods boy who became a leading educator; and *North American Mammals.*

SIDELIGHTS: Fifteen of Erna Holyer's children's stories have been translated into German for publication in Switzerland, a quirk of success, since she worked so hard to learn to write in English. She had nine years of schooling in Germany, entered a public high school in California as a regular student when she was over thirty, spent three more years attending high school evening classes to earn her diploma, and another three in classes at San Jose Evening Junior College for an Associate in Arts degree. She has sold paintings as well as stories, despite a rare condition that necessitated open heart surgery for the second time in 1969 to remove calcium deposits around her heart.

Erna Holyer told *CA:* "Following my 1969 open-heart surgery, I wrote *Sigi's Fire Helmet* entirely in bed. At predawn, my husband rigged up the typewriter on a special table across my lap and I worked propped up on pillows. Recuperating, I drafted *Shoes for Daniel* during the doctor-prescribed walks and worked out details during necessary stays in bed. It was a good way to write. *Reservoir Road,* my most recent project, first took shape on notebooks during daily heart-strengthening hikes in the Pacific Coast Range. *Reservoir Road* aims to show the trauma, challenge, and necessity of change. I try to make human problems and possible solutions understandable to youngsters in hopes of giving them inspiration and guidance on their journey into adulthood. After much inner and outer conflict Daniel, the migrant boy, reflects, 'The road, is it not like life itself? Sometimes beautiful, sometimes ugly? One needs courage to travel such a road, but in the end it is worth it.'"

BIOGRAPHICAL/CRITICAL SOURCES: Valley Journal, May 29, 1974; *PHP,* May, 1975.

* * *

HOMZE, Alma C. 1932-

PERSONAL: Surname is pronounced Home-ze; born October 28, 1932; daughter of J. Glenn and Edith (Carland) Cross; married Edward L. Homze (a professor of history at University of Nebraska), March 21, 1959; children: Eric, Heidi. *Education:* Wilson Teachers College (now District of

Columbia Teachers College), Washington, D.C., B.S., 1954; Pennsylvania State University, M.Ed., 1957, D.Ed., 1963. *Home:* 3450 Woodshire Pkwy., Lincoln, Neb. 68502. *Office:* Teachers College, University of Nebraska, Lincoln, Neb. 68508.

CAREER: Elementary teacher in Washington, D.C., Richmond, Va., Emporia, Kan., and Schweinfurt, Germany; Kansas State Teachers College, Emporia, lecturer in education, 1961-65; University of Nebraska, Lincoln, assistant professor of education, 1965—. Visiting reading consultant, Curriculum Research and Development Center, University of Rhode Island, 1975-77. *Member:* International Reading Association, National Council of Teachers of English, Childhood Education International.

WRITINGS: (With husband, Edward L. Homze) *Germany: The Divided Nation* (juvenile), Thomas Nelson, 1970; *Willy Brandt* (juvenile), Thomas Nelson, 1975. Contributor to education journals.

WORK IN PROGRESS: A young people's book of German legends.

* * *

HOOPER, John W(illiam) 1926-

PERSONAL: Born November 6, 1926, in Laona, Wis.; son of Frank Arnold (a lawyer) and Myldred (Barlement) Hooper; married Eva Salmang, August 14, 1959; children: Ellen, Carol, Joan. *Education:* Stanford University, A.B., 1950, Ph.D., 1956; University of Washington, Seattle, graduate study, 1951-52. *Home:* 5878 Soledad Rd., La Jolla, Calif. 92037. *Office:* Department of Economics, University of California at San Diego, La Jolla, Calif. 92038.

CAREER: Stanford University, Stanford, Calif., instructor in economics, 1955-56; Fulbright scholar and fellow at Netherlands School of Economics, Rotterdam, 1957-58; Rand Corp., Santa Monica, Calif., economist, 1958-59; Yale University, New Haven, Conn., instructor, 1959-60, assistant professor, 1960-62, associate professor of economics, 1962-66, assistant director of Cowles Foundation, 1961-66; University of California at San Diego, La Jolla, professor of economics, 1966—, chairman of department, 1967—. *Military service:* U.S. Navy, 1944-46. *Member:* American Economic Association, Royal Economic Society, Econometric Society. *Awards, honors:* Social Science Research Council senior fellow, 1964-65.

WRITINGS: (Editor with Marc Nerlove) *Selected Readings in Econometrics from Econometrica,* M.I.T. Press, 1970. Contributor to economics journals.

* * *

HOOVER, Hardy 1902-

PERSONAL: Born January 28, 1902, in Port Huron, Mich.; son of Roy E. (a businessman) and Sylvia (Smith) Hardy; married Ruth Van Court, September 1, 1956; children: (former marriage) Nancy (Mrs. William Dufresne), Charlotte (Mrs. Earl Anders), Tom Hardy; stepchildren: Nancy (Mrs. Cliff Harwood). *Education:* Attended University of Michigan, 1919-22; Harvard University, B.A. (magna cum laude), 1926, M.A., Ph.D., 1929. *Politics:* "General Democrat." *Religion:* "Protestant-agnostic." *Home:* 20421 Lorne St., Canoga Park, Calif. 91306.

CAREER: Lockheed Aircraft Corp., Burbank, Calif., production control dispatcher, 1943-44; Bendix Aviation Corp., North Hollywood, Calif., report writer, 1944-45; Fernando Valley Insulation Co., North Hollywood, Calif., sales man-

ager, 1945-50; Los Angeles City School System, Los Angeles, Calif., teacher of evening courses for adults, 1950-63; Los Angeles Pierce College, Woodland Hills, Calif., teacher of philosophy and psychology, 1952-58; Autotechnics, Downey, Calif., service analyst, 1956-58; Atomics International, Canoga Park, Calif., service analyst and associate publications analyst, 1958-67; Hydraulic Research and Manufacturing Co., Valencia, Calif., publications supervisor, 1968-71. Teacher of extension and correspondence courses for University of California, Berkeley, and University of California, Los Angeles. *Member:* Society of Technical Writers and Publishers (senior member), Sigma Delta Chi, Delta Chi.

WRITINGS: (Editor) *Electronic Circuit Analysis,* McGraw, 1960; *Essentials for the Technical Writer,* Wiley, 1970.

WORK IN PROGRESS: Plays; writing on the philosophy of history.

* * *

HOPE, Marjorie (Cecelia) 1923-

PERSONAL: Born January 15, 1923, in Lakewood, Ohio; daughter of Carl Augustus (a lawyer) and Ethel (Jones) Hope; married Yuksel Turkmen, 1958 (divorced); married James Young (a professor), August 7, 1971. *Education:* Sarah Lawrence College, B.A., 1944; Columbia University, M.A., 1954; New York University, M.S.W., 1959. *Politics:* Radical pacifist. *Religion:* "Quaker-oriented Pan-theist." *Home:* 1129 Hoskins Rd., Wilmington, Ohio 45177. *Office:* Wilmington College, Wilmington, Ohio 45177.

CAREER: Former grade and high school teacher in France and the United States; did library work, 1951-53; taught sociology and social work at East Stroudsburg State College; did social work in New York, N.Y.; currently instructor at Wilmington College, Wilmington, Ohio. *Member:* Society of Magazine Writers, American Sociological Association, Association for Humanistic Sociology.

WRITINGS: Youth Against the World, Little, Brown, 1970, paperback edition published as *The New Revolutionaries,* 1971; (with James Young) *The Struggle for Humanity: Agents of Nonviolent Change in a Violent World,* Orbis, 1977. Contributor of articles on social revolution, youth revolt, and other topics to *Commonweal, Village Voice, Antioch Review, Redbook, Courier,* and other periodicals.

SIDELIGHTS: Marjorie Hope wrote *CA:* "I have traveled in sixty-five countries. Speak French, German, Italian, Spanish, and a 'smidgin' of Russian. Always travel on a shoestring, staying in third-class hotels, hostels, schools, or homes—trying to know the people and to see the world as *they* see it. Am a strong advocate of a nonviolent radical restructuring of our society."

BIOGRAPHICAL/CRITICAL SOURCES: Yale Review, autumn, 1970.

* * *

HOPE, Welborn 1903-

PERSONAL: Born July 8, 1903, in Ada, Okla.; son of Tom (a banker) and Minnie (Welborn) Hope. *Education:* East Central State College, student, 1916-21.

CAREER: "Tramp poet since 1940." *Awards, honors:* Pegasus Award of Oklahoma Writers Foundation for the year's best book of poetry, 1970.

WRITINGS: The Great River and Small, and Other

Poems, Oklahoma University Press, 1970; *Four Men Hanging: The End of the Old West,* Century Press, 1974.

WORK IN PROGRESS: An autobiography.

BIOGRAPHICAL/CRITICAL SOURCES: Daily Oklahoman, January 3, 1971.†

* * *

HOPKINS, Harry 1913-

PERSONAL: Born March 26, 1913, in Preston, Lancashire, England; son of Thomas and Mary (Bilsborough) Hopkins; married Endla Kustlov, 1948. *Education:* Merton College, Oxford, B.A., 1935. *Home and office:* 61 Clifton Hill, St. John's Wood, London NW8 OJN, England. *Agent:* Julian Bach Literary Agency, Inc., 3 East 48th St., New York, N.Y. 10017.

CAREER: Birmingham Gazette, Birmingham, England, assistant editor, 1936-38; toured United States writing features, 1938-39; *Manchester Evening News,* Manchester, England, diplomatic correspondent in London office, 1946-47; *John Bull* (magazine), London, England, feature writer, 1947-60; free-lance journalist and author, London, 1961—. *Military service:* British Army, Royal Army Ordnance Corps, 1940-42, Indian Army, 1942-45; *Contact* (British troop newspaper, Indian Command), editor and war reporter in Burma Campaign; became captain. *Member:* National Union of Journalists.

WRITINGS: New World Arising: A Journey of Discovery through the New Nations of South East Asia, Hamish Hamilton, 1952; *England Is Rich,* Harrap, 1957; *The New Look: A Social History of the Forties and Fifties in Britain,* Secker & Warburg, 1963, Houghton, 1964; *Egypt, the Crucible: The Unfinished Revolution in the Arab World,* Houghton, 1969; *The Numbers Game: The Bland Totalitarianism,* Little, Brown, 1973; *The Strange Death of Private White,* Weidenfeld & Nicolson, 1977.

WORK IN PROGRESS: A reconstruction of a minor *cause celebre* arising out of that curious feudal survival, the English "Game Laws" of the nineteenth century.

SIDELIGHTS: "As a British private soldier at the fall of Singapore in 1942, I watched the curtain coming down on the British Empire," Harry Hopkins writes. "Later, in India, I saw it rising, decisively at last, on the revolution of Asia. In my first book, based on a return to South East Asia, and in my book on the New Egypt, I tried to dispel a little of the blank indifference with which the affluent West regards the great mass of mankind."

* * *

HOPKINS, Mark W(yatt) 1931-

PERSONAL: Born June 29, 1931, in Peoria, Ill.; son of Walter Harvey (in advertising) and Mary (Vaughn) Hopkins; married Mary Jean Doherty, August 27, 1955; children: Jon, Elizabeth, Paul, Amy. *Education:* Middlebury College, B.A., 1956; University of Wisconsin, M.A., 1958, Certificate in Russian Studies, 1963; University of Leningrad, Certificate in Journalism, 1964. *Office:* East European Bureau, Voice of America, Ludwigstrasse 2, 8000 Munich 22, West Germany.

CAREER: Milwaukee Journal, Milwaukee, Wis., journalist, 1960-62, Soviet and East European affairs specialist, 1964-69, staff member, beginning 1970; Soviet and East European correspondent, Voice of America, 1971—. *Military service:* U.S. Air Force, 1951-55. *Member:* American Asso-

ciation for the Advancement of Slavic Studies. *Awards, honors:* Ford Foundation fellow at University of Leningrad, 1963-64; Overseas Press Club citation for interpretative reporting, 1968; Alicia Patterson Fund fellowship for study and travel in eastern Europe, 1969-70.

WRITINGS: Mass Media in the Soviet Union, Pegasus, 1970; (contributor) *International Communication,* Hastings House, 1970. Editor and translator, *The Soviet Press in Translation,* University of Wisconsin, 1965-69. Contributor to *New Leader* and other periodicals.

WORK IN PROGRESS: Research on Yugoslav mass communications.

SIDELIGHTS: On reporting trips to the Soviet Union, Mark Hopkins traveled through the Ukraine and central and northern Russia, 1965 and 1967, and through Siberia by train in 1967. Yugoslavia was his base in 1969-70, with travel to Poland and Czechoslovakia.

BIOGRAPHICAL/CRITICAL SOURCES: New Republic, November 15, 1969; *Columbia Journalism Review,* Spring, 1970; *Journalism Quarterly,* Summer, 1970.

* * *

HOPKINSON, Diana 1912-

PERSONAL: Born November 26, 1912, in London, England; daughter of Francis William and Eva Marian (Spielman) Hubback; married David Martin Hopkinson (a civil servant), May 2, 1939; children: Thomas, Andrea, Nicholas. *Education:* Attended Lady Margaret Hall, Oxford, 1931. *Address:* c/o Routledge & Kegan Paul Ltd., 39 Store St., London WC1E 7DD, England.

WRITINGS: Family Inheritance: A Life of Eva Hubback, Staples, 1954; *The Incense Tree* (autobiography), Routledge & Kegan Paul, 1968. Contributor of articles to newspapers and magazines.

WORK IN PROGRESS: Lives of Jane Austen's family members, concentrating on her niece, Catharine Hubback, a nineteenth-century novelist and Mrs. Hopkinson's great-grandmother.

BIOGRAPHICAL/CRITICAL SOURCES: New Statesman, November 29, 1968.

* * *

HORBACH, Michael 1924-

PERSONAL: Born January 13, 1924, in Aachen, Germany; son of Jean and Else (Porschen) Horbach; married Ursula Schaake (a novelist writing under the name Ursula Horbach-Schaake), June 13, 1958. *Education:* Attended Kaiser Karl Gymnasium in Aachen until he was called up for military duty at eighteen. *Religion:* Roman Catholic.

CAREER: DENA (news agency), reporter in Bad Nauheim, Germany, 1946-50; Associated Press, political and military correspondent in Bonn, Germany, 1951-57; *Der Stern* (newspaper), Hamburg, Germany, assistant chief editor, 1957-59; free-lance writer, 1959—. *Military service:* German Army, officer, 1942-45; served on Russian front.

WRITINGS: Die verratenen Soehne (novel), Rowohlt, 1957, translation by Robert Kee published as *The Great Betrayal,* Bodley Head, 1958, same translation published as *The Betrayed,* Coward, 1959; *Gestern war der Juengste Tag* (novel), Desch, 1960, translation by Norman Denny published as *Yesterday Was Doomsday,* Random House, 1961 (translation published in England as *The Reckoning,* Bodley Head, 1961); *Bevor die Nacht begann* (novel), Desch, 1960;

Liebe in Babylon (novel), Desch, 1961; *Wenige: Zeugnisse der Menschlichkeit, 1933-1945* (fictionized reportage), Kindler, 1964, translation by Nina Watkins published as *Out of the Night,* Vallentine, Mitchell, 1967, Fell, 1970; *Gespraech mit dem Moerder: Zwoelf Interviews mit Lebenslaenglichen* (reportage), Hestia, 1965; *Die Titanen* (novel), Axel Juncker-Verlag (Munich), 1970; *Der Kampf um die ietzten Tier-Paradiese in Afrika,* Desch, 1972; *Die Kanzlerreise,* Scherz, 1974. Contributor to *Bunte Illustrierte, Stern, Neue Illustrierte,* and other publications in Germany.

SIDELIGHTS: Michael Horbach considers *The Betrayed,* a war novel, and *Out of the Night* ("against violence and persecution during the Nazi regime, 1933-45") his most important books. He and his wife have traveled extensively through Europe, Asia, and Africa, and have visited South America. *Avocational interests:* Collecting African art, hiking in the forests near his home, rifle-shooting.

BIOGRAPHICAL/CRITICAL SOURCES: Jewish Quarterly, autumn, 1968.†

*   *   *

HORKA-FOLLICK, Lorayne Ann 1940-

PERSONAL: Born February 20, 1940, in Hackensack, N.J.; daughter of Lawrence (in traffic and transportation) and Hazel (DuHaime) Horka. *Education:* Whittier College, B.A. (history), 1961; California State College at Los Angeles (now California State University, Los Angeles), M.A., 1964; Free International Protestant-Episcopal University, London, England, Ph.D., 1968; Blackstone School of Law, LL.B., 1969, J.D., 1971; Los Angeles College of Chiropractic, B.A. (biology), 1971, candidate for D.C.; additional study at University of Copenhagen, 1960-61, McGill University, 1965, and University of Southern California, 1966-69. *Address:* c/o Westernlore Press, 5117 Eagle Rock Blvd., Los Angeles, Calif. 90041.

CAREER: El Rancho Unified School District, Pico Rivera, Calif., history teacher, 1961-67; California State College at Los Angeles (now California State University, Los Angeles), instructor in history, 1967; Pepperdine University, Los Angeles, instructor in history, 1969; Los Angeles (Calif.) City School District, staff member of examination and selection department, 1969. *Member:* Phi Delta Gamma, Phi Alpha Theta, Pi Lambda Theta, Governor Pio Pico Mansion Society.

WRITINGS: Los Hermanos Penitentes, Westernlore, 1969.

WORK IN PROGRESS: Chiropractic and the California Law from Its Inception to the Present; Governor Pio Pico's Littlest Rancho: Paso de Bartolo; also writing on the Philippine Independent Church.†

*   *   *

HORMAN, Richard E. 1945-

PERSONAL: Born October 25, 1945, in Philadelphia, Pa.; son of Max B. (a salesman) and Cecile (Erlichman) Horman; married Cathy Friedman (a teacher), June 30, 1969. *Education:* Temple University, A.B., 1967, Ed.M., 1969; Illinois Institute of Technology, Ph.D., 1971.

CAREER: Temple University, Philadelphia, Pa., director of drug education program, 1967-69; Cook County School of Nursing, Chicago, Ill., psychologist, 1969-71; Northeastern Illinois University, Chicago, instructor in psychology, beginning 1971; University of Chicago, Chicago, coordinator of drug abuse training, beginning 1971.

WRITINGS: (Editor with Alan M. Fox) *Drug Awareness: A Collection of Literature,* Volume I, Temple University, 1969, revised and expanded edition, Avon, 1970. Contributor of articles on drug use and drug education to journals.

WORK IN PROGRESS: Drug Awareness, Volume II, concerning stimulants and depressants and the drug culture.†

*   *   *

HORN, Robert M. 1933-

PERSONAL: Born September 7, 1933, in Addis Ababa, Ethiopia; son of Eric Stringer (a missionary) and Syvilla E. (Ferron) Horn; married Joyce Madeleine Wilkinson (a research assistant at Institute of Historical Research, University of London), May 21, 1960; children: Timothy Robert, Catherine Ruth, Alistair Martin. *Education:* Downing College, Cambridge, M.A. (with honors), 1956; Lincoln College and Regent's Park College, Oxford, B.A. (with honors), 1959. *Home:* 54 Russell Hill, Purley, Surrey, England.

CAREER: Baptist clergyman; Inter-Varsity Fellowship, London, England, universities' secretary, 1959-62, theological secretary, 1962-66; Horley Baptist Church, Horley, Surrey, England, minister, 1966-72; editor, *Evangelical Times,* 1973—. *Military service:* British Army, Royal Artillery, 1951-53.

WRITINGS—All published by Inter-Varsity Press: *The Book that Speaks for Itself,* 1969; *Student Witness and Christian Truth,* 1971; *Go Free,* 1976.

AVOCATIONAL INTERESTS: Climbing and hill-walking, cricket, photography, bird-watching.

*   *   *

HORNBACK, Bert G(erald) 1935-
(Gerald Frascatoro, Norman D. Plumm)

PERSONAL: Born December 22, 1935, in Bowling Green, Ky.; son of Vernon Theodore (an athletic director) and Elizabeth (Borrone) Hornback. *Education:* University of Notre Dame, A.B., 1957, A.M., 1961, Ph.D., 1964; Trinity College, Dublin, graduate study, 1961-62. *Politics:* Liberal. *Home:* 1717 South University, Ann Arbor, Mich. 48104. *Office:* Department of English, University of Michigan, Ann Arbor, Mich. 48104.

CAREER: University of Notre Dame, Notre Dame, Ind., instructor in English, 1963-64; University of Michigan, Ann Arbor, instructor, 1964-65, assistant professor, 1965-70, associate professor, 1970-75, professor of English, 1975—. Founder, Lord Chamberlain's Players, Ann Arbor. Member of board of directors, Poetry Ann Arbor, 1969-74; member, Foster Parents Plan. *Military service:* U.S. Marine Corps, 1957-60. U.S. Marine Corps Reserve, 1961-66; became captain (resigned in protest against the Indochina War). *Member:* Modern Language Association of America, Dickens Society, Interfaith Council for Peace. *Awards, honors:* Rotary Foundation fellowship, 1961-62; Horace H. Rackham fellowship, 1965, 1971-72; Distinguished Faculty Achievement Award, University of Michigan, 1970.

WRITINGS: (Editor) Thomas Hardy, *Scenes from "The Dynasts,"* University of Michigan, 1968; "A Game of Chess" (one-act play), first produced in Ann Arbor by Lord Chamberlain's Players, December, 1970; "A Dickens Christmas," first produced on WUOM Radio, December 24, 1970.

The Metaphor of Chance: Vision and Technique in the

Works of Thomas Hardy, Ohio University Press, 1971; "Tom and Mary Courting" (one-act play), first produced in Ann Arbor by Lord Chamberlain's players, February 20, 1971; *King Richard the Catsup,* Porridge Press, 1972; *Noah's Architecture: A Study of Dickens's Mythology,* Ohio University Press, 1972; *A Critical Edition of Middlemarch,* Norton, 1977; "Yes to the Universe" (one-act play), first produced in Ann Arbor by Lord Chamberlain's Players, April 5, 1977. Also author of "The Dickens World," ten half-hour television programs, produced by University of Michigan Television Center, 1974. Contributor to *Studies in English Literature, Papers on Language and Literature, Criticism, Journal of English and Germanic Philology, Victorian Poetry, Michigan Quarterly Review, Victorian Newsletter,* and as Gerald Frascatoro to *Malahat Review.*

WORK IN PROGRESS: The Hero of My Life: Essays on "David Copperfield," completion expected by 1979; four essays on James Joyce and Albert Einstein, completion expected by 1979.

SIDELIGHTS: Bert G. Hornback participates in amateur theatricals, and has produced, directed, or played in several plays, including *MacBird, A Game of Chess, The Drunkard, Ubu Cocu, The Rising of the Moon, Don Giovanni,* and *The Three Penny Opera.*

*   *   *

HORTON, Frank E. 1939-

PERSONAL: Born August 19, 1939, in Chicago, Ill.; son of Elba E. and Mae (Prahaska) Horton; married Nancy Yocum, August 26, 1961; children: Kimberley, Pamela, Amy, Kelly. *Education:* Western Illinois University, B.S., 1963; Northwestern University, M.S., 1964, Ph.D., 1966. *Home address:* Route 3, Box 42C, Carbondale, Ill. 62901. *Office:* Vice–President for Academic Affairs and Research, Southern Illinois University at Carbondale, Carbondale, Ill. 62901.

CAREER: Lake Forest College, Lake Forest, Ill., instructor in geography, 1964-65; University of Iowa, Iowa City, assistant professor, 1966-68, associate professor, 1968-70, professor of geography, 1970-75, director of Institute of Urban and Regional Research, 1968-72; dean for advanced studies, 1972-75; Southern Illinois University at Carbondale, professor of geography and vice-president for academic affairs and research, 1975—. Lecturer in urban transportation program, Carnegie-Mellon University, 1970—. *Member:* American Association for the Advancement of Science (member of national council), Association of American Geographers, Urban and Regional Information Systems Association, Regional Science Association, Sigma Xi.

WRITINGS: (With Brian Joe Lobley Berry and others) *Geographic Perspectives on Urban Systems: With Integrated Readings,* Prentice-Hall, 1970; (editor) *Geographical Perspectives and Urban Problems,* National Academy of Sciences, 1973; (editor and contributor with Berry) *Urban Environmental Management: Planning for Pollution Control,* Prentice-Hall, 1974. Also author of monographs and course manuals. Contributor of about sixty articles to geography journals in the United States and Europe. Associate editor, *Regional Science Perspectives,* 1970—; member of editorial advisory board, *Transportation.*

*   *   *

HORVATH, Violet M. 1924-

PERSONAL: Born July 5, 1924, in New York, N.Y.; daughter of George and Anna (Hubert) Horvath. *Education:* Stanford University, B.A. (with great distinction), 1953; University of Rome, graduate study, 1953-55; University of Paris, degre superieur, 1954; Radcliffe College, M.A., 1957; summer study at Middlebury College, 1959, and University of Mexico, 1960; Columbia University, Ph.D., 1967. *Religion:* Roman Catholic. *Home:* 79 West 12th St., New York, N.Y. 10011. *Office:* Department of French, Spanish, and Italian, Bernard M. Baruch College of the City University of New York, New York, N.Y.

CAREER: Harvard University, Cambridge, Mass., teaching fellow in French, 1955-56; Texas Technological College (now Texas Tech University), Lubbock, instructor in French, 1956-59; Bronx Community College (now Bronx Community College of the City University of New York), Bronx, N.Y., lecturer in French and Spanish, 1959-60; Bernard M. Baruch College of the City University of New York, New York, N.Y., lecturer, 1960-67, instructor, 1967-68, assistant professor, 1968-69, associate professor, 1970-76, professor of French, Spanish, and Italian, 1976—, chairperson of French, Spanish, and Italian, 1969-75. *Member:* Modern Language Association of America, American Association of Teachers of French, American Translators Association, Malraux Society, French Institute, Societe des Professeurs Francais en Amerique, Phi Beta Kappa, Pi Delta Phi.

WRITINGS: Andre Malraux: The Human Adventure, New York University Press, 1969; (translator) Edmund J. Cantilli and John Guernelli, editors, Furioso, *There Is No Death That Is Not Ennobled by So Great a Cause: Anecdotes of the American Patriots,* Obranoel Press, 1976. Contributor to *Malraux Miscellany* and literature journals.

WORK IN PROGRESS: The Antimemoires of Andre Malraux: Interviews with the Author, 1970-1976.

AVOCATIONAL INTERESTS: Music (operatic), dancing, art, theater, hiking.

BIOGRAPHICAL/CRITICAL SOURCES: Books Abroad, Volume I, winter, 1971.

*   *   *

HOSKINS, Robert 1933-
(Grace Corren, Susan Jennifer, Jennifer Redfield)

PERSONAL: Born May 26, 1933; son of Frederic M. (a builder) and Irene (Clune) Hoskins. *Education:* Albany State College for Teachers, student, 1951-52. *Residence:* Canoga Park, Calif. *Agent:* Richard Curtis, 156 East 52nd St., New York, N.Y. 10022.

CAREER: Employed in family business, 1952-64; child care worker, New York State Department of Mental Hygiene, 1964-66; Brooklyn Home for Children, New York City, child care worker, 1966-68; Scott Meredith Literary Agency, Inc., New York City, sub-agent, 1967-68; Lancer Books, Inc., New York City, senior editor, 1969-72; free-lance writer, 1972—. *Member:* Science Fiction Writers of America, American Numismatic Society, American Numismatic Association, Canadian Numismatic Association.

WRITINGS—Science fiction: The Shattered People, Doubleday, 1975; *Master of the Stars,* Laser Books, 1976; *To Control the Stars,* Ballantine, 1977; *Tomorrow's Son,* Doubleday, 1977; *Jack-in-the-Box Planet* (young adult), Westminster Press, in press; *To Escape the Stars,* Ballantine, in press.

Editor of science fiction anthologies: *First Step Outward,* Dell, 1969; *The Stars around Us,* New American Library,

1970; *Swords against Tomorrow,* New American Library, 1970; *Infinity One,* Lancer Books, 1970; *Infinity Two,* Lancer Books, 1971; *Tomorrow: One,* New American Library, 1971; *The Far Out People,* New American Library, 1971; *Infinity Three,* Lancer Books, 1972; *Wondermakers,* Fawcett, 1972; *Strange Tomorrows,* Lancer Books, 1972; *Infinity Four,* Lancer Books, 1972; *Infinity Five,* Lancer Books, 1973; *The Edge of Never,* Fawcett, 1973; *Wondermakers Two,* Fawcett, 1974; *The Liberated Future,* Fawcett, 1974; *The Future Now,* Fawcett, 1977; *Wondermakers Three,* Fawcett, in press; *Gamma,* Popular Library, in press.

Gothic novels; under pseudonym Grace Corren: *The Darkest Room,* Lancer Books, 1969; *A Place on Dark Island,* Lancer Books, 1971; *Evil in the Family,* Lancer Books, 1972; *Mansion of Deadly Dreams,* Popular Library, 1973; *Dark Threshold,* Popular Library, 1977.

Under pseudonym Susan Jennifer: *The House of Counted Hatreds,* Avon, 1973; *Country of the Kind,* Avon, 1975.

Contributor of eight short stories to Globe Books' textbook series, "Living Cities," 1970. Short stories have been published in *Ellery Queen's Mystery Magazine, Alfred Hitchcock's Mystery Magazine, Mike Shayne's Mystery Magazine, Mystery Monthly, Magazine of Fantasy and Science Fiction, Galaxy Science Fiction,* and others. Writer of "Birthday Party" episode for the television series, "Kojak."

WORK IN PROGRESS: Numerous novels in several areas, including gothic, suspense, and science fiction.

*　　　*　　　*

HOSKYNS-ABRAHALL, Clare (Constance Drury) (Clare Hoskyns Abrahall, Clare Marie Drury)

PERSONAL: Born in London, England; daughter of Richard Fredrick (a lieutenant colonel in British Army) and Gertrude (Holt) Drury; married Sir Chandos Hoskyns-Abrahall (divorced); children: Priscila Le Bas, Robin, Follett. *Education:* Attended Royal College of Music, London, for two years. *Politics:* Conservative. *Religion:* Church of England. *Home:* 67 Lancaster Rd., St. Albans, Hertfordshire, England. *Agent:* Hope Leresche & Steele, 11 Jubilee Pl., Chelsea, London S.W.3, England.

CAREER: Writer. Once traveled around the world on concert tours with Eileen Joyce; former producer of amateur dramatics in London and an exhibiting painter in oils. Driver in Parachute Section of Women's Royal Air Force during World War I; commandant in British Red Cross during World War II. *Member:* Arts Theatre Club (London), Hovenden Theatre Club (London; director).

WRITINGS—Under name Clare Hoskyns Abrahall, except as noted; juvenile books: (Under name Clare Marie Drury) *Kit Norris: Schoolgirl Pilot,* Juvenile Productions, 1937; *From Serf to Page,* Harrap, 1939; *Priscilla's Caravan,* Epworth, 1939; *Prelude: The Early Life of Eileen Joyce,* Oxford University Press, 1947, 2nd edition, 1950; *Boadicea: Queen of the Iceni,* Harrap, 1949; *The Young Marie Curie,* Roy, 1961; *The Young Elizabeth Barrett,* Roy, 1963; *The Young Louis Braille,* Parris, 1964, Roy, 1965; *The Young John Bunyan,* Roy, 1968; *Looking after Wild Birds,* Corgi Books, 1971. Also author of *Kate Fox and the Princesses.*

Adult books: (With Adeline De Lara) *Finale,* Burke Publishing, 1955; *Amateur Dramatics,* Collins, 1963. Plays produced: "The Light Within"; "Pitchblend"; "Butler in a Box"; "Florence Nightingale"; "Palissy the Potter." Con-

tributor of articles and short stories to magazines. Former editor, *Road* and *Guide.*

WORK IN PROGRESS: Work on her memoirs.

*　　　*　　　*

HOSOKAWA, William K. 1915- (Bill Hosokawa)

PERSONAL: Born January 30, 1915, in Seattle, Wash.; son of Setsugo and Kimiyo (Omura) Hosokawa; married Alice Tokuko Miyake, August 28, 1938; children: Michael C., Susan (Mrs. Warren Boatright), Peter E., Christie (Mrs. Lloyd C. Harveson). *Education:* University of Washington, Seattle, B.A., 1937. *Politics:* Independent. *Religion:* Protestant preference. *Home:* 140 South Upham Ct., Denver, Colo. 80226. *Agent:* Paul R. Reynolds, Inc., 12 East 41st St., New York, N.Y. 10017. *Office: Denver Post,* Denver, Colo. 80201.

CAREER: Writer for *Singapore Herald,* Singapore, 1938-40, and *Shanghai Times and Far Eastern Review,* Shanghai, China, 1940-41; *Des Moines Register,* Des Moines, Iowa, an editor, 1943-46; *Denver Post,* Denver, Colo., associate editor, 1946—. *Member:* American Association of Sunday and Feature Editors (president, 1956), Denver Press Club, Rotary. *Awards, honors:* Western Heritage Award from Cowboy Hall of Fame, 1966; named Outstanding Colorado Journalist by University of Colorado School of Journalism, 1967; named Outstanding Journalist by the Colorado chapter of Sigma Delta Chi, 1976.

WRITINGS—Under name Bill Hosokawa; all published by Morrow: *Nisei: The Quiet Americans,* 1969; *The Two Worlds of Jim Yoshida,* 1972; *Thunder in the Rockies* (a history), 1976.

SIDELIGHTS: In *The Quiet Americans,* Hosokawa has reconstructed the story of the Nisei, their history in America and their forcible removal to "relocation centers" during the days following Pearl Harbor. Gladwin Hill calls the book, "[a] searching and dramatic inquiry into the genesis of the evacuation program." He states that, "Hosokawa . . . in stark dispassionate reporting limns a classic laboratory case of government and human fallibilities suddenly converging in monstrous injustice . . . an absorbing chronicle of this important slice of history."

William Hosokawa describes *Thunder in the Rockies* as "the no-holds-barred story of the *Denver Post,* a colorful, controversial, newspaper." Marshall Sprague writes, "Hosokawa knows and tells far more than he ought to."

The Two Worlds of Jim Yoshida is the story of an American drafted by the Japanese to fight against his own country. Born of Japanese-American parents Yoshida grew up in Seattle, Washington. While abroad war with the United States broke out and Jim was conscripted to fight against the country of his birth. The work has been adapted into a movie script and a producer is being sought.

BIOGRAPHICAL/CRITICAL SOURCES: Saturday Review, November 15, 1969; *New York Times Book Review,* December 21, 1969; *New Yorker,* January 2, 1970; *America,* March 14, 1970; *Detroit News,* August 27, 1972.

*　　　*　　　*

HOSS, Marvin Allen 1929-

PERSONAL: Born February 1, 1929, in Philadelphia, Pa.; son of Jack R. and Esther (Goldberg) Hoss; married Ilene Scheaffer, September 17, 1950; children: Leonard, Susan.

Education: University of Florida, A.A., 1950; University of Miami, Coral Gables, A.B., 1953, J.D., 1957, M.Ed., 1964, Ed.D., 1976; further study at Michigan State University, 1967-68, and Florida State University. *Home:* 242 Gralan Road, Catonsville, Md. 21228. *Office:* Office of Director of Student Development, Catonsville Community College, Catonsville, Md.

CAREER: Florida Industrial Commission, supervisor of special services, 1954-62; instructor and group counseling leader in Florida at North Miami Adult Center and Miami Jackson Adult Center, 1958-62; Miami-Dade Junior College-North, Miami, Fla., counselor, 1962-64, associate professor of counseling services, beginning 1964, chairman and coordinator of counseling services, 1968-70; Catonsville Community College, Catonsville, Md., 1970—, began as associate professor and director of counseling and advisement, currently professor and director of student development. Lecturer at Morgan State University, Antioch College, and Johns Hopkins University. *Member:* American Personnel and Guidance Association, National Vocational Guidance Association, American College Personnel Association, Royal Society of Health (fellow), Maryland Personnel and Guidance Association, Maryland Vocational Guidance Association (past president), Maryland Academy of Science, Phi Delta Kappa.

WRITINGS: (With Joseph B. Cook and Robert Vargas) *The Search for Independence ... An Orientation for the Junior College Student,* Brooks/Cole, 1968.

* * *

HOUCK, John W(illiam) 1931-

PERSONAL: Born April 16, 1931, in Beloit, Wis.; son of Walter and Gertrude (Coakley) Houck; married Mary Dooley, December 27, 1955; children: Christopher, Monica, Gregory. *Education:* University of Notre Dame, A.B., J.D.; University of North Carolina, M.B.A.; Harvard University, LL.M. *Office:* College of Business Administration, University of Notre Dame, Notre Dame, Ind. 46556.

CAREER: University of Notre Dame, College of Business Administration, Notre Dame, Ind., began as instructor, currently professor of management. President, St. Joseph County Mental Health Association; member of board of directors, South Bend Urban League, 1960-62; president, Catholic Interracial Council, 1962. *Member:* American Association of University Professors (member of panel of consultants, 1967—). *Awards, honors:* Ford Foundation summer fellowship, 1961; Danforth teacher's fellowship, 1962-63.

WRITINGS: (Editor with Edward Manier) *Academic Freedom and the Catholic University,* Fides, 1967; (editor) *Outdoor Advertising: History and Regulation,* University of Notre Dame Press, 1969; (editor with William Heisler) *A Matter of Dignity: Inquiries into the Humanization of Work,* University of Notre Dame Press, 1977. Contributor to *St. Louis Times-Democrat, Review of Politics, Notre Dame Magazine, Sign,* and other publications.

* * *

HOWARD, C(hester) Jeriel 1939-

PERSONAL: Born March 14, 1939, in Wharton, Tex.; son of Chester (a service manager for B. F. Goodrich) and Alma Howard. *Education:* Union College, Lincoln, Neb., B.A., 1961; Texas Christian University, M.A., 1962, Ph.D., 1967. *Home:* 7047 Freemont St., Dallas, Tex. 75231. *Office:* Department of English, Bishop College, 3837 Simpson-Stuart Rd., Dallas, Tex. 75241.

CAREER: Southwestern Union College, Keene, Tex., instructor in English, 1962-64; Union College, Lincoln, Neb., assistant professor of English, 1964-66; Texas Christian University, Fort Worth, instructor in English, 1966-67; Tarrant County Junior College, Fort Worth, Tex., chairman of English department, 1967-69; Bishop College, Dallas, Tex., associate professor of English, 1970—. Guest instructor, Texas Wesleyan College, 1967; guest professor, East Texas State University, summer, 1968. *Member:* Modern Language Association of America, National Council of Teachers of English, Conference on College Composition and Communication, College English Association, Texas College English Association.

WRITINGS: (With Coramae Thomas) *Contact: A Textbook in Applied Communications,* Prentice-Hall, 1970, 2nd edition, 1974; (compiler with Richard F. Tracz) *The Responsible Man: Essays, Short Stories, Poems,* Canfield Press, 1970, 2nd edition published as *The Responsible Person,* 1975; (with Tracz) *Tempo: A Thematic Approach to Sentence-Paragraph Writing,* Canfield Press, 1971; (with Donald Gill) *Desk Copy: Modern Business Communications,* Canfield Press, 1971; *The Age of Anxiety,* Allyn & Bacon, 1972; *Technique,* Canfield Press, 1972, 2nd edition, 1977; *—30—A Journalistic Approach to Freshman Composition,* Goodyear Publishing, 1973; *Reprise: A Review of the Basics in Grammar and Composition,* Goodyear Publishing, 1975; *Writing Effective Paragraphs,* Winthrop Publishers, 1976; *Writing for a Reason,* Wiley, in press.

WORK IN PROGRESS: Revised edition of *Reprise: A Review of the Basics in Grammar and Composition;* third edition of *Contact.*

* * *

HOWARD, Jane Temple 1935-

PERSONAL: Born May 4, 1935, in Springfield, Ill.; daughter of Robert Pickrell (a newspaper reporter) and Eleanor (Nee) Howard. *Education:* University of Michigan, B.A., 1956. *Residence:* New York, N.Y. *Office:* c/o Sterling Lord Agency, 660 Madison Ave., New York, N.Y. 10021.

CAREER: Life, New York, N.Y., reporter, 1958-63, assistant editor, 1963-65, associate editor, 1965-67, staff writer, 1967—. Visiting lecturer, University of Iowa Writer's Workshop, 1974-75, University of Georgia, 1975, Yale University, 1976.

WRITINGS: Please Touch: A Guided Tour of the Human Potential Movement, McGraw, 1970; *A Different Woman,* Dutton, 1973.

SIDELIGHTS: "As a guided tour of the human potential movement, *Please Touch* seems flawless," according to Webster Schott, who continues, "Jane Howard tells you where the action is, how it happens, what it feels like and what it costs (about $150 a weekend). . . . She writes beautifully. She has the gift of language and the intelligence to crown it. . . . [The book] shows how thousands of Americans are trying to break their cycles of emotional crisis, kick the past and escape from cold isolation. It also shows why the human potential movement may reach millions of persons before this century is over." And in his review Richard Schickel says: "At the simplest level, it tells the common reader all and exactly what he needs to know about it and does so with perceptiveness, wit, sympathy, and understanding that are hard come by anywhere and are near miraculous to discover in a book about a subject as amorphous, elusive, and controversial as this one." Agreeing is Robert Kirsch, who reports, "There is good hard information here as well as an evocation of experience that may come close to the best reporting Miss Howard has ever done."

BIOGRAPHICAL/CRITICAL SOURCES: New York Times, June 1, 1970; *Washington Post,* June 24, 1970; *New York Times Book Review,* June 28, 1970; *Show,* July 23, 1970; *Saturday Review,* July 25, 1970; *Time,* July 27, 1970; *Harper's,* August, 1970; *Book World,* August 2, 1970; *Nation,* October 19, 1970.

*   *   *

HOWE, Daniel Walker 1937-

PERSONAL: Born January 10, 1937, in Ogden, Utah; son of Maurice (a newspaperman) and Lucie (Walker) Howe; married Sandra Shumway, September 3, 1961; children: Rebecca, Christopher, Stephen. *Education:* Harvard University, A.B. (magna cum laude), 1959; Oxford University, M.A., 1962; University of California, Berkeley, Ph.D., 1966. *Home:* 3814 Cody Rd., Sherman Oaks, Calif. 91403. *Office:* Department of History, University of California, Los Angeles, Calif. 90024.

CAREER: Yale University, New Haven, Conn., instructor, 1966-68, assistant professor, 1968-72, associate professor of history, 1972-73; University of California, Los Angeles, associate professor of history, 1973—. Fellow of Charles Warren Center for Studies in American History, Harvard University, 1970-71. *Military service:* U.S. Army, 1959-60. *Member:* American Historical Association, American Studies Association, Society for Religion in Higher Education, Phi Beta Kappa. *Awards, honors:* Frank S. and Elizabeth D. Brewer Prize of American Society of Church History, 1970, for *The Unitarian Conscience;* National Endowment for the Humanities fellow, 1975-76.

WRITINGS: The Unitarian Conscience: Harvard Moral Philosophy, 1805-1861, Harvard University Press, 1970; (editor) *The American Whigs: An Anthology,* Wiley, 1973; (contributor) Conrad Wright, editor, *A Stream of Light: A Sesquicentennial History of American Unitarianism,* Unitarian Universalist Association, 1975; (editor) *Victorian America,* University of Pennsylvania Press, 1976. Contributor to *New England Quarterly,* and *Comparative Studies in Society and History.*

*   *   *

HOWE, Jonathan Trumbull 1935-

PERSONAL: Born August 24, 1935, in San Diego, Calif.; son of Hamilton Wilcox (a retired rear admiral in U.S. Navy) and Margaret (Backus) Howe; married Harriet Mangrum, June 21, 1957; children: Richard, Jonathan, David, Katharine, Paul, Margaret. *Education:* U.S. Naval Academy, B.S., 1957; Tufts University, Fletcher School of Law and Diplomacy, M.A., 1968, M.A.L.D. and Ph.D., 1969. *Home:* 5443 31st St. N.W., Washington, D.C. 20015.

CAREER: U.S. Navy, officer, beginning 1957; served on a cruiser, a diesel submarine and the Polaris submarine "George Washington," and was training officer of Naval Nuclear Power Training Unit, West Milton, N.Y.; "U.S.S. Patrick Henry" (nuclear-powered Polaris submarine), engineer officer, 1963-67; military assistant to the assistant to the President of the United States for national security affairs, beginning 1969, with current rank of commander.

WRITINGS: Multicrises: Seapower and World Politics in the Missile Age, M.I.T. Press, 1971. Frequent contributor to naval and military journals.††

*   *   *

HOWE, W(arren) Asquith 1910-

PERSONAL: Born June 16, 1910, in Custar, Ohio; son of David Newton (a professor and minister) and Clara (Werking) Howe; married Edith Lucille Miller (a real estate developer), February 2, 1936. *Education:* Bowling Green State University, B.S., 1943; University of Toledo, M.B.A, 1946; Ohio State University, Ph.D., 1954. *Religion:* Protestant. *Home:* 218 Crews Ct., Port Charlotte, Fla. 33952.

CAREER: National Supply Co., Toledo, Ohio, procurement officer, 1943-46; assistant professor of accounting at University of Toledo, Toledo, 1946-54, and Bowling Green State University, Bowling Green, Ohio, 1954-55; Temple University, Philadelphia, Pa., 1955-77, began as associate professor of accounting and department chairman, professor of accounting, 1958-77. *Member:* American Accounting Association, National Accounting Association, Institute of Internal Auditors, Financial Executives Institute, American Association of University Professors, Beta Alpha Psi, Beta Gamma Sigma.

WRITINGS: (With Carlson) *Workbook of Study Guides,* South-Western Publishing, c. 1955, 5th edition, 1977; *Cost Accounting,* International Textbook, 1969; *Intermediate Accounting,* Barnes & Noble, 1974. Contributor of articles to *Encyclopedia Americana* and other publications.

*   *   *

HOWELL, Clinton T. 1913-

PERSONAL: Born July 28, 1913, in Skinnerton, Ala.; son of William Horace (a farmer) and Narcissa (Brooks) Howell; married Peggy Lou Huffman (a legal secretary), September 17, 1964; children: (prior marriage) William B., Gloria; (present marriage) Brooke, Clinton T., Jr.; (stepchildren) Greg, Clyde, Delilah, Joey. *Education:* University of Alabama, A.B., 1935; further study in law. *Religion:* Methodist. *Home:* 6645 Cabot Dr., Nashville, Tenn. 37209.

CAREER: Editor of weekly magazines and newspapers in the South most of his adult life; United Methodist Church, General Board of Publication, Nashville, Tenn., member, 1948-60; Howell Publications, Nashville, founder, beginning 1967. Delegate to Ecumenical Conference at Oxford University, 1951.

WRITINGS: (Compiler) *Lines to Live By,* Grosset, 1968; *Design for Living,* Grosset, 1970; (editor) *Better than Gold,* Thomas Nelson, 1970; *A Garden of Jewels,* Fudge Book Co. (Athens, Ala.), 1970; (compiler and editor) *Nelson's Patriotic Scrapbook,* Thomas Nelson, 1974; (compiler) *Seasons of Inspiration,* Thomas Nelson, 1974. Editor of *Prominent Personalities in American Methodism,* 1945, and author of *You Can Go to College,* 1950, *Don't Quit,* 1978, and *Joyous Journey.*

*   *   *

HOWES, Paul Griswold 1892-

PERSONAL: Born September 30, 1892, in Stamford, Conn.; son of L. Townsend and Annie (Landon) Howes; married Lucy Churchill. *Education:* Studied at King School, Stamford, Conn., and with private tutors from Harvard and Heidelberg Universities. *Home:* West View Lane, South Norwalk, Conn. 06854.

CAREER: Member of American Museum of Natural History's Colombian Andean Expedition, 1913; New York Zoological Society, New York, N.Y., research assistant in tropical research department, 1916, 1922; Bruce Museum, Greenwich, Conn., assistant curator, 1919-38, curator-director, 1938-66, curator emeritus, 1968—. *Military service:* U.S. Naval Reserve Force, Senior Medical Department laboratory, 1918. *Member:* American Museum of Natural History (fellow), Explorers Club (emeritus member).

WRITINGS—All but first book illustrated with drawings, photographs, or sketches by the author: (With William Beebe and G. Inness Hartley) *Tropical Wild Life in British Guiana,* Volume I, New York Zoological Society, 1917; *Insect Behavior,* R. G. Badger, 1920; *Backyard Explorations,* Doubleday, 1927; *Hand Book for the Curious,* Putnam, 1936; *The Giant Cactus Forest and Its World: A Brief Biology of the Giant Cactus Forest of Our American Southwest,* Duell, Sloan & Pearce, 1954; *The Cactus World,* Doubleday, 1958; *This World of Living Things,* Duell, Sloan & Pearce, 1959; *Photographer in the Rain-Forests,* Sylvanus Books, 1970; *Mini-Wood Community,* Sylvanus Books, 1975.

WORK IN PROGRESS: An ecological succession study of New England area returning to woodland.

SIDELIGHTS: Paul Howes wrote *CA:* "Motivating factors in my career have been association in the field with American Museum men, including Dr. Frank M. Chapman, Louis Agassiz Fuertes, George K. Cherrie; at the British Guiana jungle research station of New York Zoological Society with William Beebe, G. Inness Hartely, and Theodore Roosevelt. Began writing (magazine articles) on natural history 1907. Through my books, lucidly written and lavishly illustrated, I hope to help others working in similar lines. Working habits in laboratory; writing, research, illustrating, photography and motion picture work 7 hours a day, beginning at 9 a.m. Advice to aspiring writers: Keep at it, pay no attention to rejects except to rewrite, send material out again. Favorite museum work: collecting materials for, construction and painting backgrounds in fifty dioramas at the Bruce Museum, Greenwich, Connecticut."

* * *

HOWTON, F(rank) William 1925-

PERSONAL: Born April 1, 1925, in Portland, Ore.; son of Frank Lawson and Geraldine (Hill) Howton; married Louise Gottesman (a college teacher), December 2, 1954; children: Erica Isabel, Joseph Conrad. *Education:* Attended University of Arizona, 1946-48; University of California, Berkeley, B.A., 1949, M.A., 1952, Ph.D., 1959. *Home:* 255 Nassau St., Princeton, N.J. 08540. *Office:* Department of Sociology, City College of the City University of New York, Convent at 139th St., New York, N.Y. 10031.

CAREER: Contra Costa County, Martinez, Calif., probation officer, 1954-55; College of Idaho, Caldwell, assistant professor of sociology, 1955-57; System Development Corp., Santa Monica, Calif., human factors scientist, 1957-60; Los Angeles State College (now California State University, Los Angeles), Los Angeles, Calif., assistant professor of sociology, 1960-61; City College of the City University of New York, New York, N.Y., assistant professor, 1961-67, associate professor, 1967—, chairman of department of sociology, 1967-70. *Military service:* U.S. Army, 1943-46. *Member:* American Sociological Association, Society for the Study of Social Problems, Eastern Sociological Society.

WRITINGS: (Editor with Bernard Rosenberg and Israel Gerver) *Mass Society in Crisis,* Macmillan, 1964; *Functionaries,* Quadrangle, 1969. Contributor to sociology journals. Former associate editor, *Berkeley Journal of Sociology.*

WORK IN PROGRESS: Continuing studies focused on future studies and science fiction in their bearing on sociological doctrine.

* * *

HOYT, Herman A(rthur) 1909-

PERSONAL: Born March 12, 1909, in Greenfield, Iowa; son of Clarence Lymann (a sheetmetal worker) and Anna Leola (Dorsey) Hoyt; married Harriet Lucille Fitz, August 30, 1930; children: Joseph Paul, Edwin Max. *Education:* Ashland College, A.B., 1932, B.Th. (summa cum laude), 1935; University of Michigan, summer graduate study, 1935; Grace Theological Seminary, B.D., 1938, M.Th., 1939, D.Th., 1946. *Politics:* Republican. *Home address:* Box 785, Winona Lake, Ind. 46590. *Office:* Grace Theological Seminary and Grace College, Winona Lake, Ind. 46590.

CAREER: Clergyman of the Brethren Church; Ashland College, Theological Seminary, Ashland, Ohio, professor of New Testament and Greek, 1935-37; Grace Theological Seminary and Grace College, Winona Lake, Ind., professor of New Testament and Greek, 1937-62, dean, 1948-62, president and professor of Christian theology, 1962-76, chancellor, 1976—. Member of Town Board of Winona Lake, 1945-51. Trustee of Bryan College, American Association for Jewish Evangelism, and Christian League for the Handicapped. *Member:* American Association for Higher Education, Evangelical Theological Society, Indiana Conference of Higher Education, Kiwanis Club. *Awards, honors:* LL.D., Bryan College, 1963.

WRITINGS—All published by Brethren Missionary Herald, except as indicated: *This Do in Remembrance of Me,* 1946; *All Things Whatsoever I Have Commanded,* 1950; *Exposition of Romans,* 1950; *Exposition of Hebrews,* 1951; *Exposition of Revelation,* 1953; *Then Would My Servants Fight,* 1956; *The New Birth,* Dunham Publishing Co., 1961; *The End Times,* Moody, 1969; *Expository Messages on the New Birth,* Baker Book, 1971; *The First Christian Theology: Studies in Romans,* Baker Book, 1977. Also author of *The Attributes of God,* 1978. Contributor to *Wycliffe Bible Encyclopedia.*

WORK IN PROGRESS: Editing a book on *The Epistle to the Romans; Redeemed in the Eternal State;* a volume on *Revelation,* completion expected in 1978.

AVOCATIONAL INTERESTS: Photography.

* * *

HUBBELL, Harry M. 1881-1971

August 30, 1881—February 24, 1971; American classicist and educator. Obituaries: *New York Times,* February 26, 1971.

* * *

HUBER, Thomas 1937-

PERSONAL: Born March 23, 1937, in Berlin, Germany; son of Eugen and Cecilie (Grundmann) Huber; married Ulla-Maija Halonen (a teacher), August 4, 1962; children: Peter Thomas, Michael. *Education:* Studied at University of Tuebingen, University of Vienna, and University of Berlin, 1956-60, and passed first State Boards Examination; University of Vermont, M.A., 1962; Princeton University, M.A.,

1964, Ph.D., 1965. *Residence:* Middlebury, Vt. *Office:* Middlebury College, Middlebury, Vt. 05753.

CAREER: Instructor in German at University of Vermont, Burlington, 1961-62, and Princeton University, Princeton, N.J., 1964-65; University of Bergen, Bergen, Norway, lecturer in German, 1965-66; Middlebury College, Middlebury, Vt., associate professor of German, 1966—, director of Graduate School of German in Germany, 1965-66, 1969-70, 1972-73. Consultant, Institute of International Education. *Member:* Modern Language Association of America, Deutsche Schiller-Gesellschaft, Freies deutsches Hochstift, Goethe-Gesellschaft.

WRITINGS: Studien zur Theorie des Uebersetzens, Hain, 1967; *U.S. Programs in Germany: Problems and Perspectives,* Institute of International Education, 1968; (with Kimberly Sparks and Van Horn Vail) *Modern German,* Harcourt, 1971; (with Sparks and Vail) *Thomas Mann's "Tonio Kroger,"* Harcourt, 1974.

WORK IN PROGRESS: A critical profile of F. Nicolai's work.

SIDELIGHTS: Thomas Huber speaks French, Norwegian, and some Finnish in addition to being bilingual in German and English. *Avocational interests:* Railroading (model and prototype).

* * *

HUDSON, Liam 1933-

PERSONAL: Given name is pronounced *Lee*-um; born July 20, 1933, in London, England; son of Cyril and Kathleen Hudson; married Elizabeth Ward, 1955; married second wife, Bernadine Jacot de Boinod, 1965; children: three sons, one daughter. *Education:* Attended Exeter College, Oxford, 1954-57. *Home:* 30 Dick Pl., Edinburgh 9, Scotland. *Office:* Research Unit on Intellectual Development, University of Edinburgh, Edinburgh, Scotland.

CAREER: Cambridge University, Cambridge, England, researcher at Psychological Laboratory, 1957-65, fellow of King's College, 1966-68; University of Edinburgh, Edinburgh, Scotland, professor of educational sciences and director of Research Unit on Intellectual Development, 1968—. Member, Institute for Advanced Study, Princeton, N.J., 1974-75.

WRITINGS: Contrary Imaginations, Methuen, 1966, Penguin, 1968; *Frames of Mind: Ability, Perception and Self-Perception in the Arts and Sciences,* Methuen, 1968, Norton, 1970; (editor) *The Ecology of Human Intelligence,* Penguin, 1970; *The Cult of the Fact,* J. Cape, 1972, published as *The Cult of the Fact: A Psychologists Autobiographical Critique of His Discipline,* Doubleday, 1973; *Human Beings: The Psychology of Human Experience,* Doubleday, 1975.

AVOCATIONAL INTERESTS: Painting.

BIOGRAPHICAL/CRITICAL SOURCES: New Statesman, January 17, 1969.

* * *

HUFF, Vaughn E(dward) 1935-

PERSONAL: Born November 7, 1935, in Chatham, Ontario, Canada; naturalized U.S. citizen; son of Lewis E. (a builder) and Alice (McLarty) Huff; married Gretchen Fuller, August 23, 1964; children: Christopher, Jennifer. *Education:* University of Arizona, B.A., 1958, M.Ed., 1963, Ph.D., 1966. *Home:* 4340 North Camino Vinorama, Tuc-

son, Ariz. 85718. *Office:* Student Counseling Service, University of Arizona, Tucson, Ariz. 85721.

CAREER: High school teacher in Arizona, 1961-63; Ball State University, Muncie, Ind., assistant professor, 1966-70, associate professor of psychology, 1970-72; University of Arizona, Tucson, counseling psychologist and director of honors program, 1972—. Counseling psychologist in Tucson, 1965, and in Muncie, 1966-72. *Military service:* U.S. Army, Dental Corps, 1958-60. *Member:* International Association for Transactional Analysis, American Personnel and Guidance Association, American Psychological Association, Association for Humanistic Psychology, Academy of Parapsychology and Medicine, Association for Research and Enlightenment, Southern Arizona Psychological Association. *Awards, honors:* U.S. Office of Education grant, 1968-70; National Institute of Mental Health grant, 1972—.

WRITINGS: (With K. M. Dimick) *Child Counseling,* W. C. Brown, 1970. Contributor to psychology journals.

* * *

HUFFMAN, Franklin E(ugene) 1934-

PERSONAL: Born January 28, 1934, in Harrisonburg, Va.; son of Rudolph Bernard and Stella (Zigler) Huffman; married Marcia Russell, June 9, 1962 (divorced); married Sandra Isliescu, January 14, 1974; children: (first marriage) Russell Franklin, David Kenneth; (second marriage) Christopher Gregory. *Education:* Bridgewater College, B.A., 1955; American University, summer graduate study, 1960; Cornell University, graduate study, 1960-64; School of Oriental and African Studies, London, graduate study, 1964-65; Cornell University, Ph.D., 1967. *Home:* 520 Chestnut St., Ithaca, N.Y. 14850. *Office:* Department of Modern Languages and Linguistics, 414 Morrill Hall, Cornell University, Ithaca, N.Y. 14853.

CAREER: High school teacher of French, history, and geography in Weyers Cave, Va., 1958-60; Yale University, New Haven, Conn., assistant professor of Southeast Asian languages, 1967-1972; Cornell University, Ithaca, N.Y., associate professor of Southeast Asian Linguistics, 1972—. *Military service:* Conscientious objector; served as French interpreter with International Voluntary services in Laos, Indochina, 1956-58.

MEMBER: Linguistic Society of America, Association for Asian Studies, Siam Society, American Oriental Society. *Awards, honors:* London-Cornell Project fellow at University of London, 1964-65; Fulbright research fellow in Thailand and Cambodia, 1964-66; Guggenheim fellowship for research in Southeast Asia, 1970-71.

WRITINGS: Cambodian System of Writing and Beginning Reader with Drills and Glossary, Yale University Press, 1970; *Modern Spoken Cambodian,* Yale University Press, 1970; *Intermediate Cambodian Reader,* Yale University Press, 1972; *Cambodian Literary Reader and Glossary,* Yale University Press, 1977.

WORK IN PROGRESS: English-Cambodian Dictionary; Bibliography of Mainland Southeast Asian Linguistics; Intermediate Spoken Vietnamese.

SIDELIGHTS: In addition to his fluency in Thai, Cambodian, and French, Franklin Huffman speaks some German, Spanish, Burmese, and Lao.

* * *

HUGGINS, Nathan Irvin 1927-

PERSONAL: Born January 14, 1927, in Chicago, Ill.; son of

Winston John and Marie (Warsaw) Huggins; married Brenda Carlita Smith, July 18, 1971. *Education:* University of California, Berkeley, A.B., 1954, M.A., 1955; Harvard University, A.M., 1959, Ph.D., 1962. *Home:* 410 Riverside Dr., Apt. 122, New York, N.Y. 10025. *Office:* History Department, Columbia University, New York, N.Y. 10027.

CAREER: Long Beach State College (now California State University), Long Beach, Calif., assistant professor of history, 1962-64; Lake Forest College, Lake Forest, Ill., assistant professor of history, 1964-66; University of Massachusetts, Boston Campus, assistant professor, 1966-69, associate professor of history, 1969-70; Columbia University, New York, N.Y., professor of history, 1970—. Visiting associate professor, University of California, Berkeley, 1969-70; Fulbright senior lecturer in Grenoble, France, 1974-75. President, American Museum of Negro History, Boston, 1966-69; member, Council of the Smithsonian Institution, 1973—; vice-president, Howard Thurman Educational Trust. Adviser to Danforth Foundation on black studies fellowships and to Educational Testing Service. *Military service:* U.S. Army, 1945-46. *Member:* American Historical Association, Organization of American Historians, Society for the Study of Negro Life and History. *Awards, honors:* Guggenheim fellow, 1971-72.

WRITINGS: Protestants against Poverty: Boston's Charities, Greenwood Press, 1971; (editor with Martin Kilson and Daniel Fox) *Key Issues in the Afro-American Experience,* two volumes, Harcourt, 1971; *Harlem Renaissance,* Oxford University Press, 1971; (contributor) Daniel Aaron and others, editors, *American Issues Forum,* Volume I, Publishers, Inc., 1975; (editor) *Voices from the Harlem Renaissance,* Oxford University Press, 1976.

WORK IN PROGRESS: A social history of slavery in the United States.

*   *   *

HUGHES, Douglas A(llan) 1938-

PERSONAL: Born February 15, 1938, in Chicago, Ill.; son of Howell Thomas and Gweneith (Davies) Hughes; married Carole Hurley, June 25, 1963; children: Lisa Ann, Douglas Allan, Jr. *Education:* University of Idaho, B.A., 1961, M.A., 1965; University of Colorado, Ph.D., 1971. *Politics:* Democrat. *Religion:* None. *Home:* 861 North Lincoln, Moscow, Idaho 83843. *Office:* Department of English, Washington State University, Pullman, Wash. 99163.

CAREER: Washington State University, Pullman, assistant professor of English, 1969—. *Military service:* U.S. Army, 1961-62. *Member:* Modern Language Association of America.

WRITINGS—Editor: The Way It Is: Readings in Contemporary American Prose, Holt, 1970; (and author of introduction) *Perspectives on Pornography,* St. Martin's, 1970; *From a Black Perspective: Contemporary Black Essays,* Holt, 1970; *Studies in Short Fiction,* Holt, 1971, 2nd edition, 1975; *The Man of Wax: Critical Essays on George Moore,* New York University Press, 1971; *George Moore's Art of Fiction,* University of Colorado Press, 1971.

WORK IN PROGRESS: A critical study of George Moore; an edition of George Moore's three-volume autobiography, *Hail and Farewell.*

BIOGRAPHICAL/CRITICAL SOURCES: New Statesman, September 25, 1970.†

HUGHES, Mary Louise 1910-

PERSONAL: Born May 3, 1910; daughter of George Laurence (a locomotive engineer) and Mary Elizabeth (Sullivan) Hughes. *Education:* Teachers College, Cincinnati, Ohio, B.Sc. in Ed., 1941; St. Louis University, M.A., 1965. *Home and office:* 701 East Columbia Ave., Cincinnati, Ohio 45215.

CAREER: Teacher in elementary schools, 1930-57; high school teacher of speech and theater, 1957-62; private teacher in own studio, Cincinnati, Ohio, 1965-77. Part-time curator in museum in Cincinnati area. Program director in the arts and home visiting for senior citizens and shut-ins. *Member:* International Graphoanalysis, International Mission Radio Association, Queen City Writers.

WRITINGS: Teenager: Speechmaking and Debating, Richards Rosen, 1969. Also author of *The Joy of Speaking* and *Let Me See.* Scripts include "The Good News Train" for television. Contributor to education and religious journals.

WORK IN PROGRESS: Two scripts, "The Joy of Learning" and "The Joy of Moving"; a book on puppetry for children.

SIDELIGHTS: Mary Louise Hughes told *CA:* "I have added the study of graphoanalysis to my heretofore accomplishments because of my involvement in a questioned will. I have used this latest scientific knowledge of handwriting to assist teachers with students having problems; also, to help people to know their potential better." She went on to say "I am now working with older people developing skills of painting, writing, needlework and forming friendships ... I was also involved in setting up a museum showing various phases of development in equipment in teaching and students' work from the period of 1840-1975. I show visitors through at times."

AVOCATIONAL INTERESTS: Amateur radio (holds Federal Communications Commission license), photography, painting, and handwriting analysis (certified graphoanalyst).

*   *   *

HUGHES, (James) Quentin 1920-

PERSONAL: Born February 28, 1920, in Liverpool, England; son of James Stanley (an estate agent) and Marjory (Edwards) Hughes; married Margaret Olwen Evans, April 27, 1947; children: Ceridwen, Deborah Sian. *Education:* Attended Rydal School, Cowyn Bay, Wales, 1933-37; University of Liverpool, B.Arch. (honors), 1946; University of Leeds, Ph.D., 1952. *Home:* Loma Linda, Cricieth, Caernarvonshire, North Wales; and 10a Fulwood Park, Liverpool, 17 England. *Office:* University of Liverpool, Liverpool, England.

CAREER: Leeds School of Architecture, Leeds, England, lecturer, 1947-55; University of Liverpool, School of Architecture, Liverpool, England, senior lecturer, 1955-67, reader in architecture, 1967-68; Royal University of Malta, Msida, dean of faculty and professor in department of architecture, beginning 1968; currently member of faculty at University of Liverpool. Architect and planning consultant in Liverpool and Chester, England. Chairman, Chester Civic Trust, 1963-66. *Military service:* British Army, 2nd Special Air Service, 1940-45; became captain; received Military Cross and bar. *Member:* Royal Institute of British Architects (fellow), Victorian Society (Liverpool; chairman, 1966-68), Athenaeum Club (Liverpool), Union Club (Malta), Special Forces Club (London). *Awards, honors:* Civic Trust commendation, 1969.

WRITINGS: The Building of Malta, Tiranti, 1956; (with Norbert Lynton) *History of Architectural Development,* Volume IV: *Renaissance Architecture,* McKay, 1962; *Seaport,* Lund Humphries, 1964; *Liverpool,* Studio Vista, 1968; *Fortress: Architecture and Military History in Malta,* Lund Humphries, 1969; *Malta,* Prestel-Verlag, 1972; *Military Architecture,* St. Martin's, 1974. Contributor to *Times* and to architectural journals.

WORK IN PROGRESS: British Defense of the Mediterranean; The Age of Gunpowder.

BIOGRAPHICAL/CRITICAL SOURCES: Times Literary Supplement, July 24, 1969.

* * *

HUGHES, Thomas Parke   1923-

PERSONAL: Born September 13, 1923, in Richmond, Va.; son of Hunter R. (a lumber merchant) and Mary (Quisenberry) Hughes; married Agatha Chipley, August 7, 1948; children: Thomas (deceased), Agatha, Lucian. *Education:* University of Virginia, B.M.E., 1947, M.A., 1950, Ph.D., 1953. *Home:* 8330 Millman St., Philadelphia, Pa. 19118. *Office:* Department of History and Sociology of Science, University of Pennsylvania, Philadelphia, Pa. 19174.

CAREER: University of Virginia, Charlottesville, instructor in engineering, 1952-54; Sweet Briar College, Sweet Briar, Va., assistant professor of modern European history, 1954-56; Washington and Lee University, Lexington, Va., assistant professor, 1956-59, associate professor of history, 1959-63; Massachusetts Institute of Technology, Cambridge, associate professor of history, 1963-66; Johns Hopkins University, Baltimore, Md., visiting associate professor of history, 1966-69; Southern Methodist University, Institute of Technology, Dallas, Tex., professor of history of technology, 1969-73; University of Pennsylvania, Department of History and Sociology of Science, Philadelphia, professor, 1973—. Visiting professor, University of Wisconsin, 1963; visiting scholar, University Center of Virginia, 1966; fellow of Center for Recent American History, Johns Hopkins University, 1966-69; research associate, Smithsonian Institution, 1968-69. *Military service:* U.S. Navy, 1943-46; became lieutenant junior grade. U.S. Naval Reserves; became lieutenant commander.

MEMBER: Society for the History of Technology (vice-president, 1977-79), American Historical Association, History of Science Society (member of council). *Awards, honors:* Fulbright research fellow in Germany, 1958-59; American Council of Learned Societies fellowship, 1968-69; Social Science Research Council grant, 1971; Rockefeller Humanities Grant, 1976.

WRITINGS: Medicine in Virginia, 1607-1699, Virginia 350th Anniversary Celebration Corp., 1957; (editor) *Development of Western Technology since 1500,* Macmillan, 1964; (editor and author of introduction) *Lives of Engineers: Selections from Samuel Smiles,* M.I.T. Press, 1966; *Elmer Sperry: Inventor and Engineer,* Johns Hopkins Press, 1971; *Edison: Professional Inventor,* Science Museum (London, England), 1976. Contributor to *Dictionary of American Biography, Dictionary of Scientific Biography,* and to history, business, and technology journals.

WORK IN PROGRESS: A history of electric light and power systems in Germany, Britain, and the United States.

* * *

HULL, Helen (Rose)   1888(?)-1971

1888(?)—July 15, 1971; American author and educator. Obit-

uaries: *New York Times,* July 17, 1971; *Variety,* July 21, 1971; *Antiquarian Bookman,* August 2-9, 1971. (See index for *CA* sketch)

* * *

HULL, Katharine   1921-

PERSONAL: Born July 18, 1921; daughter of Hubert Hull; married Paul Buxton (a British diplomat). *Education:* Educated at St. Mary's Convent, Ascot, England, and Lady Margaret Hall, Oxford University, England. *Address:* c/o Sir Hubert Hull, 59 Campden Hill Rd., London W.8, England; and c/o British Embassy, 3100 Massachusetts Ave. N.W., Washington, D.C. 20008.

MILITARY SERVICE: Served in the Royal Air Force during World War II; became captain.

WRITINGS—With Pamela Whitlock: *The Far-Distant Oxus* (juvenile), illustrations by Whitlock, J. Cape, 1937, Macmillan, 1938, reprinted with afterword by Arthur Ransome, 1969; *Escape to Persia,* illustrations by Whitlock, J. Cape, 1938, Macmillan, 1939; *Oxus in Summer,* illustrations by Whitlock, J. Cape, 1939, published with illustrations by Charles E. Pont, Macmillan, 1940; *Crowns,* illustrations by Whitlock, J. Cape, 1947.†

* * *

HULSE, (Herman) LaWayne   1922-

PERSONAL: Born June 12, 1922, in Wanette, Okla.; son of James Anderson and Mabel Mildred (Klinglesmith) Hulse; married Vanita Holland, April 10, 1946; children: LaRonna Joyce, James David, Kris Philip, Karen Denise. *Education:* Southern Methodist University, B.S., 1949; Southwestern Baptist Theological Seminary, graduate student, 1959; Texas Christian University, M.A., 1967; Texas A&M University, Ph.D. candidate. *Home:* 2131 Hermanson Dr., Waco, Tex. 76710. *Office:* Texas State Technical Institute, Building 34-3, Waco, Tex. 76705.

CAREER: Snyder Daily News, Snyder, Tex., 1949-55, began as reporter, became assistant editor; *San Angelo Standard-Times,* San Angelo, Tex., reporter and photographer, 1956-57; affiliated with Southern Baptist organizations in Mason and Fort Worth, Tex., 1957-64; Baptist Standard Publishing Co., Dallas, Tex., assistant editor, 1964-68; Texas State Technical Institute, Waco, professor of technical writing, 1968—. Marriage counselor in Dallas, Tex., 1964-68. *Military service:* U.S. Army Air Forces, 1942-45; served in South Pacific theater; received Presidential Unit Citation and battle star. *Member:* American Technical Education Association, American Association of University Professors, Texas Technical Society.

WRITINGS: Meditation Programs, Zondervan, 1969.

WORK IN PROGRESS: Communications in Technology; A Dozen Roads, religious devotionals; *Background for Psychology; The Miry Clay,* a novel.

AVOCATIONAL INTERESTS: Study of geography and tribes of New Guinea, mechanics and aviation, antique automobiles.

* * *

HUME, Robert D.   1944-

PERSONAL: Born July 25, 1944, in Oak Ridge, Tenn.; son of David Newton (a college professor) and Aloyse (Bottenwiser) Hume; married Kathryn Irvine (a college teacher), June 18, 1966. *Education:* Haverford College, B.A. (with honors), 1966; University of Pennsylvania, Ph.D., 1969. *Politics:* Independent. *Religion:* None. *Office:* Department of English, Cornell University, Ithaca, N.Y. 14853.

CAREER: Cornell University, Ithaca, N.Y., assistant professor, 1969-74, associate professor of English, 1974—. *Member:* Modern Language Association of America, American Society for Eighteenth-Century Studies, Society for Theatre Research, Phi Beta Kappa. *Awards, honors:* Woodrow Wilson fellow, 1966.

WRITINGS: Dryden's Criticism, Cornell University Press, 1970; *The Development of English Drama in the Late Seventeenth Century,* Clarendon Press, 1976; (co-editor) *"The Country Gentleman": A "Lost" Play and Its Background,* University of Pennsylvania Press, 1976; (co-editor) Elizabeth Polwhele, *The Frolicks; or, the Lawyer Cheated,* Cornell University Press, 1977. Editor for English and American literature annual eighteenth-century bibliography in *Philological Quarterly,* 1971-74.

WORK IN PROGRESS: Revision of Parts I and II of *The London Stage, 1660-1800;* an Oxford English text, *Buckingham;* an edition of Vice Chamberlain Coke's *Theatrical Papers.*

*   *   *

HUMPHREY, Michael (Edward) 1926-

PERSONAL: Born May 6, 1926, in London, England; son of Edward and Doris (Carter) Humphrey; married Heather Ferris (a secretary), October 6, 1956; children: Elaine Fiona, Russell Edward Mark. *Education:* Attended Balliol College, Oxford, 1947-51. *Home:* The Ruffetts, Outwood Lane, Chipstead, Surrey, England. *Office:* St. George's Hospital Medical School, University of London, Blackshaw Rd., Tooting, London S.W.17, England.

CAREER: Clinical psychologist in National Health Service, 1951-64, became principal psychologist at Warneford & Park Hospitals, Oxford, England; University of Essex, Essex, England, research fellow in department of sociology, 1964-66; University of Bristol, Bristol, England, lecturer in department of mental health, 1967-69; University of London, St. George's Hospital Medical School, London, England, senior lecturer in psychology, 1969—. *Member:* British Psychological Society (fellow).

WRITINGS: The Hostage Seekers: A Study of Childless and Adopting Couples, Humanities, 1969. Contributor to medical and psychology journals.

WORK IN PROGRESS: The effects of head injury in young adults with special reference to the family.

SIDELIGHTS: Michael Humphrey's main vocational interest is "the new look in medical education." *Avocational interests:* Music and drama.

*   *   *

HUMPHREYS, (Robert Allan) Laud 1930-

PERSONAL: Born October 16, 1930, in Chickasha, Okla.; son of Ira Denver (an Oklahoma state legislator) and Stella Bernice (Smith) Humphreys; married Nancy Margaret Wallace, October 1, 1960; children: Clair Elizabeth, David Wallace. *Education:* Attended University of Virginia, 1948-49; Colorado College, B.A., 1952; Seabury-Western Theological Seminary, B.D., 1955; Washington University, St. Louis, Mo., M.A., 1967, Ph.D., 1968. *Politics:* Democrat. *Religion:* Episcopalian. *Office:* Department of Sociology, Pitzer College, Claremont, Calif. 91711.

CAREER: Colorado Springs Free Press, Colorado Springs, Colo., reporter, 1950-52; ordained Episcopal priest, 1955, and served as parish priest in Guymon, Okla., 1955-56, Cripple Creek, Colo., 1956-59, Bartlesville, Okla., 1959-61, Guthrie, Okla., 1961-63, and Wichita, Kan., 1963-65; became "one of the activist clergy drop-outs," 1965; Washington University, St. Louis, Mo., instructor in sociology, 1967-68; Southern Illinois University, Edwardsville Campus, assistant professor of sociology, 1968-70; State University of New York at Albany, School of Criminal Justice, associate professor, 1970-72; Pitzer College, Claremont, Calif., professor of sociology, 1972—. Board member, National Committee for Sexual Liberties, 1970—. Consultant, Harvard-M.I.T. Joint Center for Urban Studies.

MEMBER: American Sociological Association, Society for the Study of Social Problems, American Society of Criminology, International Academy of Sex Research, Pacific Sociological Association. *Awards, honors:* C. Wright Mills Award of Society for the Study of Social Problems, 1969, for *Tearoom Trade: Impersonal Sex in Public Places,* as "outstanding book in the area of social problems."

WRITINGS: Tearoom Trade: Impersonal Sex in Public Places, Aldine, 1969, revised edition, 1975; *Out of the Closets: Homosexual Liberation,* Prentice-Hall, 1972. Contributor to *Encyclopedia Americana;* contributor of articles and reviews to sociology journals. Member of editorial board, *Archives of Sexual Behavior,* and *Journal of Homosexuality.*

WORK IN PROGRESS: The ecology of sexual deviance in a sample of American cities; study of murder and sexual orientation.

BIOGRAPHICAL/CRITICAL SOURCES: Trans-Action, May, 1970; *Washington Post,* July 30, 1970.

*   *   *

HUNNEX, Milton D(eVerne) 1917-

PERSONAL: Born October 16, 1917, in Walla Walla, Wash.; son of Charles E. and Annabel (Lee) Hunnex; married Jeanne Ilabelle Chapman, October 12, 1940 (divorced, 1971); married Minnie Flora Neuharth, March 17, 1973; children: (first marriage) Diane Lee (Mrs. Anthony Dorsch), James Edward, Richard Milton. *Education:* University of Redlands, A.B., 1952, M.A., 1954; Claremont Graduate School, Ph.D., 1957. *Religion:* Baptist. *Office:* Department of Philosophy, Willamette University, Salem, Ore. 97301.

CAREER: San Bernardino Valley College, San Bernardino, Calif., instructor in philosophy, 1946-58; Willamette University, Salem, Ore., professor of philosophy and head of department, 1958—. Visiting professor, summers, at Idaho State University, 1962, Pacific Philosophy Institute, 1964, and Oregon State University, 1968. *Member:* American Philosophical Association, National Education Association, Mind Association, Oregon Education Association.

WRITINGS: Philosophies and Philosophers, Chandler Publishing, 1961, revised edition, 1971; *Existentialism and Christian Belief,* Moody, 1969. Contributor of articles and reviews to *Philosophy Forum, Philosophy East and West, Christianity Today,* and to other philosophy and religious journals.

*   *   *

HUNT, Gladys M. 1926-

PERSONAL: Born October 23, 1926, in Michigan; daughter of Wilbur J. and Clara (DeWeerd) Schriemer; married

Keith L. Hunt (national director of Inter-Varsity Christian Fellowship); children: Mark Earl. *Education:* Michigan State University, B.A., 1948. *Religion:* Protestant. *Residence:* Ann Arbor, Mich.

CAREER: Involved in working with university students as a counselor-friend for twenty-five years; lecturer; writer. *Member:* American Association of University Women, League of Women Voters.

WRITINGS: Does Anyone Here Know God, Zondervan, 1966; *Honey for a Child's Heart,* Zondervan, 1969; *Listen to Me!,* Inter-Varsity Press, 1969; *Focus on Family Life,* Baker Book, 1970; *The Christian Way of Death,* Zondervan, 1971; *Eyewitness: John's View of Jesus,* H. Shaw, 1971; *It's Alive,* H. Shaw, 1971; *The God Who Understands Me,* H. Shaw, 1971; *The Lamb Who Is the Lion,* H. Shaw, 1972; *Ms Means Myself,* Zondervan, 1972. Contributor to magazines.

WORK IN PROGRESS: A book on the Christian view of sex; another book on relationships, with husband Keith L. Hunt.

SIDELIGHTS: Gladys Hunt writes: "I find writing a hard discipline. I don't wait for inspiration. I find it comes best when I sit down with pad and pen and simply begin. The first paragraph is terribly important to me; it develops the rhythm and flow which are so important in the making of good sentences and the communication of ideas."

*   *   *

HUNTER, Norman Charles   1908-1971

September 18, 1908—April 19, 1971; British playwright and novelist. Obituaries: *Variety,* April 28, 1971; *Antiquarian Bookman,* May 17, 1971.

*   *   *

HUNTER BLAIR, Pauline (Clarke)   1921-
(Pauline Clarke; Helen Clare, a pseudonym)

PERSONAL: Born May 19, 1921, in Kirkby-in-Ashfield, England; daughter of Charles Leopold (a minister of religion) and Dorothy Kathleen (Milum) Clarke; married Peter Hunter Blair (a university instructor), February, 1969. *Education:* Somerville College, Oxford, B.A. (with honors), 1943. *Home:* 62 Highsett, Hills Rd., Cambridge, England. *Agent:* Curtis Brown Ltd., 1 Craven Hill, London W2 3EP, England; and John Cushman Associates, Inc., 24 East 38th St., New York, N.Y. 10016.

CAREER: Free-lance writer, 1948—. Lecturer; adaptor of own stories and writer of educational material for the British Broadcasting Corporation in England. *Member:* British Society of Authors, National Book League (England). *Awards, honors:* Library Association Carnegie Medal (England), 1962, Lewis Carroll Shelf Award (United States), and Deutsche Jugend Buchpreis (Germany), 1968, all for *The Twelve and the Genii.*

WRITINGS—All juveniles; under name Pauline Clarke: *Pekinese Princess,* J. Cape, 1948; *Great Can,* Faber, 1952; *The White Elephant,* Faber, 1952, Abelard, 1957; *Smith's Hoard,* Faber, 1955, published as *The Golden Collar,* 1967; *Sandy, the Sailor,* Hamish Hamilton, 1956; *The Boy with the Erpingham Hood,* Faber, 1956; *Hidden Gold,* Abelard, 1957; *James, the Policeman,* Hamish Hamilton, 1957; *James and the Robbers,* Hamish Hamilton, 1959; *Torolv the Fatherless,* Faber, 1959; *The Lord of the Castle,* Hamish Hamilton, 1960; *The Robin Hooders,* Faber, 1960; *James and the Smugglers,* Hamish Hamilton, 1961; *Keep the Pot*

Boiling, Faber, 1961; *Silver Bells and Cockle Shells* (verse), Abelard, 1962; *The Twelve and the Genii,* Faber, 1962, published as *The Return of the Twelves,* Coward, 1963; *James and the Black Van,* Hamish Hamilton, 1963; *Crowds of Creatures,* Faber, 1964; *The Bonfire Party,* Hamish Hamilton, 1966; *The Two Faces of Silenus,* Coward, 1972.

Under pseudonym Helen Clare: *Five Dolls in a House,* Bodley Head, 1953, Prentice-Hall, 1965; *Merlin's Magic,* Bodley Head, 1953; *Bel, the Giant, and Other Stories,* Bodley Head, 1956; *Five Dolls and the Monkey,* Bodley Head, 1956, Prentice-Hall, 1967; *Five Dolls in the Snow,* Bodley Head, 1957, Prentice-Hall, 1967; *Five Dolls and Their Friends,* Bodley Head, 1959, Prentice-Hall, 1968; *Seven White Pebbles,* Bodley Head, 1960; *Five Dolls and the Duke,* Bodley Head, 1963, Prentice-Hall, 1968; *The Cat and the Fiddle, and Other Stories From Bel, the Giant,* Prentice-Hall, 1968.

Omnibus volumes, under pseudonym Helen Clare: *Five Dolls and Their Friends, and Other Stories* (includes *Five Dolls in the Snow, Five Dolls and Their Friends,* and *Five Dolls and the Duke*), Bodley Head, 1967; *Five Dolls in a House, and Other Stories* (includes *Five Dolls in a House* and *Five Dolls and the Monkey*), Bodley Head, 1967.

Also author of short stories and several plays for adults. Book reviewer for *Times Literary Supplement.* Contributor to *My England,* Heinemann, 1973; also contributor to *Eastern Daily Press.*

AVOCATIONAL INTERESTS: Music, theatre, films, history, archaeology, gardening, walking, travel.

*   *   *

HUNTLEY, James Robert   1923-

PERSONAL: Born July 27, 1923, in Tacoma, Wash.; son of Wells James (a business executive) and Laura (Berquist) Huntley; married Colleen Grounds, May 27, 1967; children: Mark Edward, David Farrington, Virginia Christine, Jean Elizabeth. *Education:* University of Washington, Seattle, B.A. (magma cum laude), 1948, graduate student, 1951; Harvard University, M.A., 1956. *Home:* Treetops West, 8748 Sand Point Way N.E., Seattle, Wash. 98115.

CAREER: Variously employed as community recreation director, YMCA secretary, and technician for Pan American World Airways, Seattle, Wash., 1942-49; consultant, State of Washington Parks and Recreation Commission, 1949-52; U.S. Foreign Service, exchange-of-persons officer in Frankfurt and Nuremburg, Germany, 1952-54, director of U.S. Information Agency information center, Hof/Saale, Germany, 1954-55, assistant to U.S. President's Coordinator for Hungarian Relief, 1956, European regional affairs officer for U.S. Information Agency, Washington, D.C., 1956-58, and deputy public affairs officer for U.S. Mission to the European Communities, Brussels, Belgium, 1958-60; Atlantic Institute, Paris, France, founder and executive secretary, 1960-63, director of North American office, Washington, D.C., 1963-65; Ford Foundation, New York, N.Y., program associate in International Affairs Division, 1965-67; Council of the Atlantic Colleges, London, England, secretary general, 1967-68; free-lance writer and consultant on international affairs, 1968-74; Battelle Memorial Institute, Seattle, Wash., fellow and head of research in advanced international systems, 1974—. Consultant to Atlantic Council of the United States, IBM, Regional Council for International Education, Iliffe Publications, and other organizations. *Military service:* U.S. Navy, 1943-46. *Member:* English-Speaking Union, American Friends of Wilton Park, Phi Beta Kappa, DACOR Club (Washington, D.C.).

WRITINGS: (Co-editor) *The Atlantic Community: A Force for Peace,* National Association of Secondary School Principals, 1963; *The NATO Story,* Manhattan Publishing, 1965, 2nd edition, 1969; (with W. R. Burgess) *Europe and America: The Next Ten Years,* Walker & Co., 1970. Contributor to *Orbis, Futures, European Community, Atlantic Community Quarterly, Dialogue,* and other journals.

WORK IN PROGRESS: Research on the relationships between the developed democracies of North America, Europe, Japan, and Australia.

*   *   *

HUPPERT, George   1934-

PERSONAL: Born February 2, 1934, in Tesin, Czechoslovakia; naturalized U.S. citizen; son of Edmund Huppert (a chemist); married Loretta Louise Porter, June 22, 1956; children: Aimee, Joshua, Joseph, Anne Marie, Jacob. *Education:* University of California, Berkeley, B.A., 1958, Ph.D., 1962; University of Wisconsin, M.A., 1959. *Home:* 943 Oak, Winnekta, Ill. *Office:* Department of History, University of Illinois at Chicago Circle, Chicago, Ill. 60680.

CAREER: Alameda State College (now California State University, Hayward), Hayward, Calif., assistant professor of history, 1962-65; University of Illinois at Chicago Circle, Chicago, assistant professor, 1965-70, associate professor, beginning 1970, currently professor of history. *Military service:* U.S. Army, 1953-55. *Member:* American Historical Association, Society for French Historical Studies, Renaissance Society of America. *Awards, honors:* Woodrow Wilson fellow, 1958-59; American Council of Learned Societies fellow, 1965-66; Social Science Research Council faculty grant, 1970; Guggenheim fellow, 1972-73.

WRITINGS: The Idea of Perfect History: Historical Erudition and Historical Philosophy in Renaissance France, University of Illinois Press, 1970; *Les Bourgeois Gentilshommes: An Essay on the Definition of Elites in Renaissance France,* University of Chicago Press, 1977. Contributor to historical journals in the United States and Europe.

WORK IN PROGRESS: A study of public secondary schools in Renaissance France.

BIOGRAPHICAL/CRITICAL SOURCES: University of Illinois Press Catalogue, spring, 1970; *New York Review of Books,* October 22, 1970; *Virginia Quarterly Review,* winter, 1971.

*   *   *

HURD, Clement   1908-

PERSONAL: Born January 12, 1908, in New York, N.Y.; son of Richard M. (a mortgage banker) and Lucy (Gazzam) Hurd; married Edith Thacher (an author), June 24, 1939; children: John Thacher Hurd. *Education:* Yale University, Ph.B., 1930; studied painting in Paris with Fernand Leger, 1931-33. *Home:* 80 Mountain Lane, Mill Valley, Calif. 94941. *Agent:* Curtis Brown Ltd., 575 Madison Ave., New York, N.Y. 10022.

CAREER: Illustrator and writer. *Military service:* U.S. Army, 1942-46.

WRITINGS: Town, W. R. Scott, 1939; *Country,* W. R. Scott, 1939; *The Race,* Random House, 1940, published as *The Race between the Monkey and the Duck,* Wonder Books, 1946; *The Merry Chase,* Random House, 1941; *Run, Run, Run,* Harper, 1951.

Illustrator: Margaret Wise Brown, *Bumble Bugs and Ele-*

phants, W. R. Scott, 1938, revised edition, 1941; Gertrude Stein, *The World Is Round,* limited autographed edition, W. R. Scott, 1939; Edith Thacher Hurd, *Engine, Engine, No. 9,* Lothrop, 1940; E. T. Hurd, *Sky High,* Lothrop, 1941; E. T. Hurd, *The Annie Moran,* Lothrop, 1942; E. T. Hurd, *Speedy, the Hook and Ladder Truck,* Lothrop, 1942; Brown, *Runaway Bunny,* Harper, 1942; Brown, *Goodnight Moon,* Harper, 1947; Brown, *The Bad Little Duckhunter,* W. R. Scott, 1947; E. T. Hurd, *Benny the Bulldozer,* Lothrop, 1947; Morrell Gipson, *Hello Peter,* Doubleday, 1948; E. T. Hurd, *Toughy and His Trailer Truck,* Lothrop, 1948; E. T. Hurd, *Willy's Farm,* Lothrop, 1949; Brown, *My World,* Harper, 1949.

E. T. Hurd, *Caboose,* Lothrop, 1950; Brown, *The Peppermint Family,* Harper, 1950; E. T. Hurd, *Old Silversides,* Lothrop, 1951; E. T. Hurd, *St. George's Day in Williamsburg, Va.,* Colonial Williamsburg, 1952; Jane Siepmann, *Lion on Scott Street,* Oxford University Press, 1952; E. T. Hurd, *Somebody's House,* Lothrop, 1953; E. T. Hurd, *Nino and His Fish,* Lothrop, 1954; E. T. Hurd, *The Devil's Tail: Adventures of a Printer's Apprentice in Early Williamsburg,* Doubleday, 1954; E. T. Hurd, *The Cat from Telegraph Hill,* Lothrop, 1955; Brown, *Little Brass Band,* Harper, 1955; E. T. Hurd, *Mr. Charlie's Chicken House,* Lippincott, 1955; E. T. Hurd, *Mr. Charlie's Gas Station,* Lippincott, 1956; E. T. Hurd, *Windy and the Willow Whistle,* Sterling, 1956; E. T. Hurd, *Mary's Scary House,* Sterling, 1956; E. T. Hurd, *It's Snowing,* Sterling, 1957; E. T. Hurd, *Mr. Charlie's Camping Trip,* Lippincott, 1957; E. T. Hurd, *Johnny Littlejohn,* Lothrop, 1957; E. T. Hurd, *Fox in a Box,* Doubleday, 1957; E. T. Hurd, *Mr. Charlie, the Fireman's Friend,* Lippincott, 1958; E. T. Hurd, *The Faraway Christmas: A Story of the Farallon Islands,* Lothrop, 1958; E. T. Hurd, *Mr. Charlie's Pet Shop,* Lippincott, 1959; E. T. Hurd, *Last One Home Is a Green Pig,* Harper, 1959.

E. T. Hurd, *Mr. Charlie's Farm,* Lippincott, 1960; E. T. Hurd, *Hurry, Hurry,* Harper, 1960; Brown, *Diggers,* Harper, 1960; E. T. Hurd, *Stop, Stop,* Harper, 1961; E. T. Hurd, *Come and Have Fun,* Harper, 1962; E. T. Hurd, *Christmas Eve,* Harper, 1962; E. T. Hurd, *No Funny Business,* Harper, 1962; E. T. Hurd, *Follow Tomas,* Dial, 1963; E. T. Hurd, *The Day the Sun Danced,* Harper, 1965; E. T. Hurd, *Johnny Lion's Book,* Harper, 1965; May Garelick, *Winter's Birds,* W. R. Scott, 1965; E. T. Hurd, *The So-So Cat,* Harper, 1965; E. T. Hurd, *What Whale? Where?,* Harper, 1966; E. T. Hurd, *Little Dog Dreaming,* Harper, 1967; E. T. Hurd, *The Blue Heron Tree,* Viking, 1968; Edna Mitchell Preston, *Monkey in the Jungle,* Viking, 1968; E. T. Hurd, *Rain and the Valley,* Coward, 1968; E. T. Hurd, *This Is the Forest,* Coward, 1969.

E. T. Hurd, *Johnny Lion's Bad Day,* Harper, 1970; E. T. Hurd, *Catfish,* Viking, 1970; E. T. Hurd, *The Mother Beaver,* Little, Brown, 1971; E. T. Hurd, *Wilson's World,* Harper, 1971; E. T. Hurd, *The Mother Deer,* Little, Brown, 1972; E. T. Hurd, *The Mother Whale,* Little, Brown, 1973; E. T. Hurd, *The Mother Owl,* Little, Brown, 1974; E. T. Hurd, *Catfish and the Kidnapped Cat,* Harper, 1974; Ginny Cowles, *Nicholas,* Seabury, 1975; E. T. Hurd, *The Mother Kangaroo,* Little, Brown, 1976; E. T. Hurd, *The Mother Chimpanzee,* Little, Brown, 1977; E. T. Hurd, *Look for a Bird,* Harper, 1977.

BIOGRAPHICAL/CRITICAL SOURCES: Charlotte S. Huck and D. A. Young, *Children's Literature in the Elementary School,* Holt, 1961; *The Children's Bookshelf,* Child Study Association of America, Bantam, 1965.

HURLEY, Neil 1925-

PERSONAL: Born August 3, 1925, in New York, N.Y. *Education:* Fordham University, B.S., 1945, M.A., 1946, Ph.D., 1956; Bellarmine College, Plattsburgh, N.Y., Ph.L., 1954; University of Innsbruck, additional study, 1956-60. *Office:* Casilla 10445, Santiago, Chile.

CAREER: Roman Catholic priest; Instituto de Comunicaciones Sociales, Santiago, Chile, founder and director, 1965; Universidad Catolica de Santiago, Santiago, lecturer and communications consultant, 1971—. *Member:* World Academy of Arts and Sciences.

WRITINGS: Theology through Film, Harper, 1970, published as *Toward a Film Humanism,* Dell, 1975. Also author of *Sacred Communications in a Secular Society.* Contributor to *America, Commonweal, Land Economics,* and other journals.

WORK IN PROGRESS: Film Parables; a book on film as a means of religious insight.

SIDELIGHTS: Neil Hurley speaks Spanish, German, and French; he reads Italian, Portuguese, Latin, and biblical Greek.†

* * *

HURST, James M(arshall) 1924-

PERSONAL: Born September 2, 1924, in Salina, Kan.; son of Carl L. and Neva G. (Beltz) Hurst; married Patricia D. Selnic, April 22, 1966. *Education:* Studied at Kansas State College (now University), Manhattan, 1942-43, 1946, Brown University, 1943-44, Washington University, St. Louis, 1952, and University of California, Los Angeles, 1957. *Home:* 645 Shelter Creek Lane, Apt. 137, San Bruno, Calif. 94066. *Office address:* P.O. Box 1202, Los Gatos, Calif. 95030.

CAREER: Radar technician with U.S. War Department, Kansas City, Kan., 1946-47; electronics technician with U.S. Department of Commerce, 1947-48; McDonnell Aircraft, St. Louis, Mo., electronics research engineer, 1948-49; Salina TV & Radio, Salina, Kan., owner, 1949-54; Douglas Aircraft Co., Culver City, Calif., branch chief, 1954-68; Investment Facilities, Playa Del Rey, Calif., owner, 1968-69; Decision Models, Inc., Tiburon, Calif., president, 1969-74. *Military service:* U.S. Army Air Forces, 1943-46.

WRITINGS: The Profit Magic of Stock Transaction Timing, Prentice-Hall, 1971; *Understanding Marketing Cycles,* Decision Models, Inc., 1974. Writer of more than 150 technical reports (titles classified).

WORK IN PROGRESS: Research in the mechanism of human irrational decision processes.

AVOCATIONAL INTERESTS: Sailing, skiing, camping.

* * *

HURWITZ, Abraham B. 1905-

PERSONAL: Born July 22, 1905, in Lithuania; came to United States, 1914; son of Benjamin and Sarah Hurwitz; married Ann L. Ritz, June 21, 1930; children: Shari Lewis Hurwitz Tarcher (a puppeteer under name Shari Lewis), Barbara Ruth Hurwitz Okun. *Education:* City College (now City College of the City University of New York), B.S., 1927; Columbia University, M.A., 1928; New York University, Ph.D., 1933. *Religion:* Jewish. *Home:* 3800 South Ocean Dr., Hollywood, Fla. 33019. *Agent:* Jeremy Tarcher, 603 Alta Dr., Beverly Hills, Calif. 90210. *Office:* Yeshiva University, New York, N.Y. 10033.

CAREER: Yeshiva University, New York City, instructor, 1927-35, assistant professor, 1935-45, associate professor, 1945-53, professor of creative recreations, 1953—, director of health education. Director of creative education, Division of Recreation, New York City Park Department, 1930-49. Camp director in New York area camps, 1927-60. Hurwitz describes himself as one of the "most knowledgable magicians in the world," and as the developer of hundreds of talented performers. *Member:* International Guild of Prestidigitators (president), Knights of Magic (president), International Brotherhood of Magicians, Society of American Magicians, Future American Magical Entertainers, Dolphins Magic Club. *Awards, honors:* Supreme Knight Medal and fourteen plaques from Knights of Magic, for developing talented entertainers.

WRITINGS: (Contributor) *Ed McMahon's Barside Companion,* World Publishing, 1969; (with Arthur Goddard) *Games to Improve Your Child's English,* Simon & Shuster, 1969; *Number Games to Improve Your Child's Arithmetic,* Funk, 1975; *Number Games For Children,* Hodder & Stoughton, 1975; (with daughter, Shari Lewis) *Magic for Non-Magicians,* J. P. Tarcher, 1975; *More Number Games: Mathematics Made Easy Through Play,* Funk, 1976; (contributor) Harry Blackstone, Jr., *There's One Born Every Minute,* J. P. Tarcher, 1976. Also author of *Puzzle Fun for Everyone,* and of *Elastrix and Other Novel Tease.* Author of more than seventy pamphlets on methods in Jewish education. Contributor to *Sphinx, Huggards Annual, Seventeen, Magic Around the World, Linking Ring, Recreation Magazine,* and other magazines and newspapers.

WORK IN PROGRESS: Games to improve a child's mathematics and games to develop a child's creativity, memory, and judgment; books on recreation and creative education.

* * *

HUSON, Paul (Anthony) 1942-

PERSONAL: Surname is pronounced Hew-sun; born September 19, 1942, in London, England; son of Edward Richard (an author) and Olga (a motion picture art director; maiden name, Lehmann) Huson. *Education:* University College, London, Slade Diploma of Fine Art, 1964, graduate study in cinema arts, 1964-65. *Residence:* Los Angeles, Calif. *Agent:* William Morris Agency, 1350 Avenue of the Americas, New York, N.Y. 10019.

CAREER: Toured United States and opened an exhibition of his paintings in Houston, Tex., 1965; assistant designer for a London play and a Vienna State Opera production, 1965-66; designer with British Broadcasting Corp. Television, London, England, 1966-67; assistant art director for Columbia Pictures-BCC Films Ltd. production of "Otley," and visual coordinator of Columbia Pictures "The Virgin Soldiers," London, England, 1967-68; emigrated to United States to live, 1968. Played the part of Edward V in the film version of Shakespeare's "Richard III" starring Laurence Olivier, 1956. *Member:* Writers Guild of America West, Academy of Television Arts and Sciences, American Society for Psychical Research, Association of Cinematograph, Television and Allied Technicians (London).

WRITINGS—Self-illustrated: Mastering Witchcraft: A Practical Guide for Witches, Warlocks and Covens, Putnam, 1970; *The Devil's Picturebook: The Complete Guide to Tarot Cards, Their Origins and Their Usage,* Putnam, 1971; *The Coffee Table Book of Witchcraft and Demonology,* Putnam, 1973; *Mastering Herbalism: A Practical Guide,* Stein & Day, 1974; *How to Test and Develop Your*

ESP, Stein & Day, 1975. Also author of two teleplays, "The Bermuda Triangle," Playboy Productions, and "Ghost Riders," Talent Associates. Contributor to *Witches Almanac*, 1974, 1976, 1977.

SIDELIGHTS: Paul Huson told *CA:* "I didn't begin writing professionally until I emigrated to the United States in 1968. Having difficulty finding work in the area of film art direction here was a marvellous excuse to try my hand at writing. I suppose writing and illustrating my own books has given me the greatest creative satisfaction I have known. I haven't as yet cracked the field of fiction, but I fully intend to. The goal, literary that is, in all my writing so far is enchantment—I attempt to evoke in my readers my own sense of wonder and involvement in the occult or paranormal, to guide them into those mysterious realms." He has this advice for aspiring writers: "Write about your obsessions and try and share them with your reader. Write clearly and unpretentiously." Many of Paul Huson's books have been translated into French, Italian, Danish, and Spanish.

BIOGRAPHICAL/CRITICAL SOURCES: Modern Screen, August, 1970; *True,* October, 1970; *Boston Morning Globe,* July 16, 1974; *Journal of Parapsychology,* Volume XXXIX, number 4, December, 1975.

*　　*　　*

HUTCHINSON, Arthur Stuart Menteth 1879-1971

June 2, 1879—March 14, 1971; British novelist. Obituaries: *New York Times,* March 15, 1971; *Bookseller,* March 20, 1971; *Antiquarian Bookman,* May 17, 1971.

*　　*　　*

HUTCHINSON, C(ecil) Alan 1914-

PERSONAL: Born March 13, 1914, in Lowestoft, England; naturalized U.S. citizen; son of Ernest Boyd (a businessman) and Elizabeth (Tennant) Hutchinson; married Margaret Funk, June 24, 1951; children: Jean, Robert, Mary. *Education:* Dartmouth College, student, 1932-34; Cambridge University, B.A., 1937, M.A., 1941; University of Texas, Ph.D., 1948. *Home:* 216 High View Lane, Charlottesville, Va. 22901. *Office:* Department of History, University of Virginia, Charlottesville, Va. 22901.

CAREER: Ferguson Brothers Ltd., Carlisle, England, executive trainee, 1937-38; Dartmouth College, Hanover, N.H., instructor in Romance languages, 1938-40; University of Virginia, Charlottesville, assistant professor, 1948-56, associate professor, 1956-70, professor of history, 1970—. *Member:* American Historical Association, Western History Association, Conference on Latin American History.

WRITINGS: (With C. D. Eaves) *Post City, Texas,* Texas State Historical Association, 1952; *Frontier Settlement in Mexican California: The Hijar-Padres Colony and Its Origins,* Yale University Press, 1969. Also translator and author of introduction and explanatory notes, Jose Figueroa, *Manifesto to the Mexican Republic,* University of California Press. Contributor to historical journals.

WORK IN PROGRESS: A biography of Valentin Gomez Farias; further research in Mexican history of the first half of the nineteenth century and in Spanish borderlands history.

*　　*　　*

ILARDI, Vincent 1925-

PERSONAL: Born May 15, 1925, in Newark, N.J.; son of Vincenzo and Filippa (Giannazzo) Ilardi; married Antoinette Ficarra (a psychologist), 1952; children: Vincent Michael. *Education:* Rutgers University, A.B., 1952; Harvard University, A.M., 1953, Ph.D., 1958. *Home:* North Main St., Sunderland, Mass. 01375. *Office:* Department of History, University of Massachusetts, Amherst, Mass. 01002.

CAREER: Carnegie Institute of Technology (now Carnegie-Mellon University), Pittsburgh, Pa., instructor in history, 1956-57; University of Massachusetts, Amherst, instructor, 1957-59, assistant professor, 1960-61, associate professor, 1961-69, professor of history, 1969—. Chairman, Fulbright National Screening Committee for Greece and Italy, 1963-64. *Wartime service:* U.S. Military Sea Transportation Service, 1943-45. *Member:* American Historical Association, Renaissance Society of America, American Society for Reformation Research, Society for Italian Historical Studies. *Awards, honors:* Fulbright research scholar in Italy, 1959-60; American Philosophical Society research grant, 1960-63; Rockefeller Foundation research grants, 1961-63, 1963-64; Guggenheim Foundation research grant, 1970-71; National Endowment for the Humanities research grant, 1976-78.

WRITINGS: (Editor with Paul M. Kendall) *Dispatches with Related Documents of Milanese Ambassadors in France and Burgundy, 1450-1483,* Ohio University Press, Volume I, 1970, Volume II, 1971; (contributor) L. Martines, editor, *Violence and Civil Disorder in Italian Cities, 1200-1500,* University of California Press, 1972; (contributor) D. H. Thomas and L. M. Case, editors, *The New Guide to the Diplomatic Archives of Western Europe,* University of Pennsylvania Press, 1975. Contributor to academic journals.

WORK IN PROGRESS: Co-editing *Dispatches of Milanese Ambassadors in France and Burgundy,* Volume III: *1466,* for Northern Illinois University Press.

SIDELIGHTS: Vincent Ilardi is competent in Latin, Italian, French, Spanish, and German.

*　　*　　*

ILLWITZER, Elinor G. 1934-

PERSONAL: Born September 23, 1934, in Summit, N.J.; daughter of John (a lawyer) and Maud (Gilbert) Howard; children: Robert (deceased), Carl, Eric. *Education:* Cornell University, B.A., 1955; Middlebury College, student at Russian Summer School, 1955, 1957; Georgetown University, M.S., 1958. *Religion:* Roman Catholic. *Office:* Scott, Foresman & Co., Glenview, Ill.

CAREER: U.S. Government, Washington, D.C., cryptanalyst, 1955-57; Georgetown University, Washington, D.C., instructor in Russian, 1957-58; volunteer tutor and religious teacher in Washington, D.C., and vicinity, 1960-68; Scott, Foresman & Co., Glenview, Ill., editor, 1968—.

WRITINGS: (With Virginia B. Wilson) *For You and Me* (kindergarten religion program), Sadlier, 1968. Author with V. B. Wilson of *Home Notebook I,* a workbook to accompany *Our Life with God,* Grade 1, Sadlier, 1968. Contributor of articles on religious education to *Living Light* and *Marriage.*

WORK IN PROGRESS: With Virginia B. Wilson, an innovative program of religious preparation for three- and four-year-olds, also religious education materials to accompany Sadlier programs.

BIOGRAPHICAL/CRITICAL SOURCES: National Catholic Reporter, January 12, 1966.

INCH, Morris Alton 1925-

PERSONAL: Born October 21, 1925, in Wytopitlock, Me.; son of Clarence S. and Blanche (Mix) Inch; married Joan Parker (a secretary), December 16, 1950; children: Deborah, Lois, Thomas, Joel, Mark. *Education:* Houghton College, A.B., 1949; Gordon Divinity School, M.Div., 1951; Boston University, Ph.D., 1955. *Home:* 201 West Lincoln, Wheaton, Ill. 60187. *Office:* Department of Biblical, Religious, and Archeological Studies, Wheaton College, Wheaton, Ill. 60187.

CAREER: Pastor of Baptist churches in Massachusetts, 1951-60; Gordon College, Wenham, Mass., member of faculty, 1955-62; Wheaton College, Wheaton, Ill., administrator, 1960-62; Wheaton College, Wheaton, Ill., professor of theology, 1962—, chairman of department of biblical, religious, and archeological studies, 1964-65, 1969—. *Member:* Evangelical Theological Society, American Academy of Religion.

WRITINGS: (Contributor) *Introduction to Evangelical Christian Education,* Moody, 1964; (contributor) *Church Educational Agencies,* Evangelical Teacher Training Association, 1968; *Psychology in the Psalms,* Word Books, 1969; (contributor) *Adult Education in the Church,* Moody, 1970; *Christianity without Walls,* Creation House, 1972; *Paced by God,* Word Books, 1973; *Celebrating Jesus as Lord,* Moody, 1974; (co-editor with Schutte) *Interpreting the Word of God,* Moody, 1976. Contributor to religion and education journals.

SIDELIGHTS: Morris Alton Inch wrote to *CA:* "My purpose in writing has generally been to address some issue being faced by my students. It likewise rises out of a Christian perspective on life and tends to have both confessional and apologetic implications."

* * *

INGLE, Clifford 1915-

PERSONAL: Born January 12, 1915, in Howard, Kan.; son of Jesse Newton (a carpenter) and Martha (Gadberry) Ingle; married Theda Smith (a teacher), June 17, 1941; children: John Barry, Thomas Lynn. *Education:* Southwest Baptist College, A.A., 1936; William Jewell College, B.A., 1938; Southwestern Baptist Theological Seminary, B.D., 1947, M.R.E., 1948, D.R.E., 1952, D.E., 1973; also studied at Divinity School, University of Chicago and Lutheran Theological Seminary of Chicago, 1967-68. *Politics:* Independent. *Home:* 4916 Chouteau Dr., Kansas City, Mo. 64119. *Office:* Department of Religious Education & Church Administration, Midwestern Baptist Theological Seminary, 5001 North Oak, Kansas City, Mo. 64118.

CAREER: Baptist minister. Held student pastorates, 1934-41; U.S. Army chaplain, Pacific and European Theatres, 1942-46; Walnut Creek Baptist Church, Fort Worth, Tex., pastor, 1949-51; Southwest Missouri State College, Springfield, Mo., teacher and director of Baptist Student Center, 1951-59, professor of philosophy and ethics, 1957-59; Midwestern Baptist Theological Seminary, Kansas City, Mo., professor of religious education and church administration, 1959—. *Military service:* U.S. Army Reserves, chaplain, 1942-60; became major; awarded Purple Heart and Regimental Commendation. *Member:* American Academy of Religion, Southwestern Baptist Religious Education, National Religious Education Association, Association of Seminary Professors in the Practical Fields.

WRITINGS: The Military Chaplain as a Counselor, Central Seminary Press, 1953; *A New Commitment,* Broadman,

1965, revised edition, 1970; (editor) *Children and Conversion,* Broadman, 1970. Also author of *Organizing for Ministry,* and *Basic Principals of Church Administration,* both 1972. Contributor of numerous articles to Southern Baptist periodicals.

WORK IN PROGRESS: Editing a book (ecumenical in approach) for seminary students on, *An Introduction to Creative Church Administration.*

SIDELIGHTS: Clifford Ingle told *CA* that he edited *Children and Conversion,* "because of pressure put upon our younger son by his S.S. teacher to become a Christian; (2) lowering age of conversion and church membership in Southern Baptist churches; (3) confusion as to religious status of children."

With regard to his present work in progress he wrote: "Since leading a Doctoral level seminar on the Ministry of Administration, I have become convinced of the need for a book on Church Administration written for graduate level students. Such [a] book should be ecumenical in approach, edited and care given to securing the best authorities possible for each chapter."

* * *

INMAN, Billie (Jo) Andrew 1929-

PERSONAL: Born May 16, 1929, in Thurber, Tex.; daughter of Robert A. (an oilfield worker) and Gussie (Oyler) Andrew; married George D. Inman (an elementary school principal), May 23, 1950; children: Paul David, Laura Lou. *Education:* Midwestern University, B.A., 1950; Tulane University, M.A., 1951; Texas Technological College (now Texas Tech University), graduate study, summer 1954; University of Texas, Austin, Ph.D., 1961. *Religion:* Unitarian-Universalist. *Home:* 5531 East North Wilshire Dr., Tucson, Ariz. 85711. *Office:* Department of English, University of Arizona, Tucson, Ariz. 85721.

CAREER: Teacher of English in public schools in Lubbock, Tex. and Borger, Tex., 1951-54; West Texas State College (now University), Canyon, instructor in English, 1955-57; University of Texas, Austin, special instructor, 1961-62; University of Arizona, Tucson, instructor, 1962-63, assistant professor, 1963-68, associate professor, 1968-72, professor of English, 1972—, director of graduate studies, 1973—, director of freshman English, 1967-71. Director of National Defense Education Act Institute in English, University of Arizona, 1965. *Member:* Modern Language Association of America.

WRITINGS: (With Ruth Gardner) *Aspects of Composition,* Harcourt, 1970. Contributor to *Philological Quarterly, Texas Studies in Literature and Language, 19th Century Fiction, Victorian Newsletter,* and *Papers on Language and Literature.*

WORK IN PROGRESS: A monograph on Walter Pater's reading, based on his borrowings from libraries in Oxford; a revision of *Aspects of Composition.*

SIDELIGHTS: Billie Inman's major area of vocational interest is the study of Victorian literature.

* * *

IRVINE, Keith 1924-

PERSONAL: Surname is pronounced *Ir*-vin; born August 7, 1924, in Ipswich, England; son of Frederick Robert (a botanist) and Dorothy Stuart (Gilchrist) Irvine; married Marie Aline Hekimian, April 9, 1949; children: Mary Lilian,

Marie Dominique, Madeline Maya, John David. *Education:* Studied at Achimota College, Accra, Gold Coast, at intervals prior to 1935, Friends' School, Saffron Walden, England, 1935-41, University of Manchester, 1941-42, Birkbeck College, London, 1942, University of Edinburgh, 1946-47, and Sorbonne, University of Paris, 1947-48. *Religion:* Quaker. *Home:* 218 St. Clair River Dr., Algonac, Mich. 48001. *Agent:* Gunther Stuhlmann, Becket, Mass. 01223.

CAREER: Edinburgh Evening News, Edinburgh, Scotland, sub-editor, 1947; *East Anglican Daily Times* Group (weeklies), Suffolk, England, assistant editor, 1948-52; *Africa Today,* New York City, editor, 1954-56; American Foundation for Political Education, New York City, assistant executive director, 1956-58; *Africa Weekly,* New York City, editor and publisher, 1957-61; Permanent Mission of Ghana to United Nations, New York City, attache, 1958-69; *Encyclopaedia Britannica,* Chicago, Ill., principal editor (geography), 1969-73; Scholarly Press, Saint Clair Shores, Mich., general editor for encyclopaedias, 1973-75; president, Reference Publications Inc., 1975—. *Military service:* Royal Navy (British), 1943-46.

WRITINGS: The Rise of the Colored Races, Norton, 1970; (editor) *Encyclopaedia of Indians of the Americas,* Scholarly Press, 1974; (editor) *World Encyclopedia of Black Peoples,* Scholarly Press, 1975; (general editor) *Encyclopaedia Africana "Dictionary of African Biography,"* Volume I, Reference Publications, 1977.

SIDELIGHTS: Keith Irvine told *CA:* "If I do not do some writing every day, I feel not so much unfulfilled as out of order, like a machine that has not been properly oiled, and that therefore does not run well. The early morning is the best time. I do not find Anthony Trollope, the novelist, and especially extraordinary writer, but find his routine of rising early to write before breakfast is the discipline that brings the most productive results.

"At first I wanted to be another Conrad—that is to say I wanted both to follow the sea and to write books at the same time. But my family believed that a nomadic seafaring life would spoil any chance of a stable married life, and at an early age I was shipped out to West Africa for a time instead. This made a lasting impression on me, and much of my writing has been an attempt to communicate, in one form or another, an intimation that there is a spirit, or essence, of things African whose existence still remains largely unsuspected on our side of the Atlantic. When the existence of this spirit, so different from those of popular myth, is realized, I think that the world will be a better place. This is a blind article of faith with me, much as Livingstone believed that the troubles of the world would be on the way to a cure if only the source of the Nile could be discovered. This is, no doubt, not an entirely rational belief, but then few beliefs are, and in any case some element of blind faith is necessary to achieve works. If one tries too hard to understand and explain everything to oneself, nothing worthwhile gets done. On another plane I also believe that it is important to make as much information as possible generally available in the form of reference books. Being a Scot, I share the traditional national belief in the virtue of both democracy and education, and the production of reference books seems to me to forward both causes at once by making knowledge accessible to all."

* * *

IRWIN, Ruth Beckey 1906-

PERSONAL: Born January 8, 1906, in Linwood, Kan.; daughter of Earl Durwood and Ann Girton (Springer) Beckey; married Harry Power Irwin (a doctor of osteopathy), August 12, 1940. *Education:* Emporia State Teachers College (now College of Emporia), B.S., 1929; State University of Iowa, M.A., 1936; University of Southern California, Ph.D., 1940. *Religion:* Congregationalist. *Home:* 2685 Henthorne Rd., Columbus, Ohio 43221. *Office:* Speech and Hearing Science Section, Department of Communication, Ohio State University, 154 North Oval Mall, Columbus, Ohio 43210.

CAREER: Teacher in public schools in Kansas, and colleges in Washington and Tennessee, 1924-36; William Penn College, Oskaloosa, Iowa, head of speech department, 1936-37; Nebraska State Teachers College (now Kearney State College), Kearney, instructor in speech, 1937-38; Ohio University, Athens, instructor and director of speech clinic, 1940-42; private practice, 1942-45; State Department of Education, Columbus, Ohio, supervisor of speech and hearing therapy, 1945-49; Ohio State University, Columbus, assistant professor, 1949-54, associate professor, 1954-63, professor, 1963-76, professor emeritus, 1976—, head of Speech and Hearing Science Section, 1973-76. Instructor in speech, Washington State University, summer, 1939. Consultant, Shaw University. *Member:* American Speech and Hearing Association (fellow), American Psychological Association (fellow), International Council for Exceptional Children (president of Ohio chapter, 1955-56), Society for Research in Child Development, Ohio Speech and Hearing Association (president, 1951-52), Delta Kappa Gamma.

WRITINGS: Special Education of Children with Speech and Hearing Disorders (pamphlet), Division of Special Education, Ohio Department of Education, 1948; *Make Your Career Speech and Hearing Therapy* (pamphlet), Division of Special Education, Ohio Society for Crippled Children, 1949, revised edition, 1958; *Speech and Hearing Therapy in the Public Schools of Ohio* (pamphlet), Division of Special Education, Ohio Department of Health, 1951; *Speech and Hearing Therapy,* Prentice-Hall, 1953; (contributor) Merle E. Frampton and Elena D. Gall, editors, *Special Education for the Exceptional,* Sargent, 1955; (contributor) N. M. Levin, editor, *Voice and Speech Disorders: Medical Aspects,* C. C Thomas, 1962; *A Speech Pathologist Talks to Parents and Teachers,* Stanwix, 1962; *Speech and Hearing Therapy: Clinical and Educational Principles and Practices,* Stanwix, 1969; (with J. W. Black) *Voice and Diction: Applied Phonation and Phonology,* C. E. Merrill, 1969. Contributor to over twenty scholarly journals and periodicals. Associate editor, *Exceptional Children;* editor, *Bulletin* of Delta Kappa Gamma, 1953-70.

WORK IN PROGRESS: Books on *Clinical Speech Pathology,* and *Toward Effective Supervision in Speech Pathology: Theory, Research, and Application;* research in microsupervision and microtherapy in speech pathology.

* * *

ISAIS, Juan M. 1926-

PERSONAL: Surname rhymes with "ice"; born March 8, 1926, in Zacatecas, Mexico; married Elisabeth Fletcher, January 21, 1955; children: Raquel, Cynthia, Sally, Juan, David. *Education:* Central American Bible Institute, Guatemala, Diploma, 1951; further study at Northeastern Collegiate Bible Institute, 1956-57, Wheaton College, Wheaton, Ill., 1963-64, and University of the Americas, 1966-67. *Home:* Priv. de Agustin Gutierrez 67, Mexico 13, D.F., Mexico. *Office:* Latin America Mission, Inc., Bogota, N.J. 07603.

CAREER: Latin America Mission, Inc., Bogota, N.J., missionary in various parts of Latin America, 1952—.

WRITINGS: El Otro lado de la Moneda, Christian Service Fellowship, 1966, translation by wife, Elisabeth Isais, published as *The Other Side of the Coin,* Eerdmans, 1966; *Manual practico de evangelismo a fondo,* Latin America Mission, 1969; *Como tener exito en evangelismo a fondo,* Latin America Mission, 1970; (compiler) *The Other Revolution,* Word Books, 1971; *Invierno y ostros poemas,* Editorial CLIE, 1976. Director, *Prisma* (Spanish magazine). Composer of hymns in Spanish.

* * *

ISRAEL, Jerry (Michael) 1941-

PERSONAL: Born September 20, 1941, in New York, N.Y.; son of Arthur Joseph and Sylvia (Herzberg) Israel; married Carol S. Schiller, August 16, 1968; children: Deborah Ann, Jeffrey Bruce, Mark Aaron. *Education:* New York University, B.A. (magna cum laude), 1962; University of Michigan, M.A., 1963; Rutgers University, Ph.D., 1967. *Office:* Department of History, Illinois Wesleyan University, Bloomington, Ill. 61701.

CAREER: University of Pittsburgh, Pittsburgh, Pa., assistant professor of history, 1967-68; University of Texas at El Paso, assistant professor of history, 1968-70; Northern Illinois University, De Kalb, associate professor of history, 1970-74; Illinois Wesleyan University, Bloomington, chairman of history department and director of social science programs, 1974—.

WRITINGS: Progressivism and the Open Door: America and China, 1905-1921, University of Pittsburgh Press, 1971; (editor) *Building the Organizational Society,* Free Press, 1972. Contributor to historical journals.

WORK IN PROGRESS: Open Door to Cold War: American Images and Interests in China in the Twentieth Century.

* * *

IVANCEVICH, John M. 1939-

PERSONAL: Born August 16, 1939, in Chicago, Ill.; married Margaret Karsner; children: Daniel, Jill, Dana. *Education:* Purdue University, B.S., 1961; University of Maryland, M.B.A., 1965, D.B.A., 1968. *Religion:* Eastern Orthodox. *Home:* 17011 Hillview Lane, Spring, Tex. 77379. *Office:* College of Business Administration, University of Houston, Houston, Tex. 77004.

CAREER: Republic Steel, Chicago, Ill., industrial engineer, 1960-61; University of Maryland, College Park, instructor in management, 1964-68; University of Kentucky, Lexington, assistant professor, 1968-70, associate professor of management, 1970-74; University of Houston, Houston, Tex., professor and associate dean for research, 1974—. Consultant to hospitals, banks, and industrial firms. *Military service:* U.S. Army, 1961-63; became first lieutenant. *Member:* Academy of Management, American Psychological Association, American Institute of Decision Sciences, Beta Gamma Sigma.

WRITINGS: (Author of workbook) D. L. Gentry and C. A. Taff, *Elements of Business Enterprise,* 2nd edition, Ronald, 1966; (editor, with J. K. Ryans, Jr. and Donnelly) *New Dimensions in Retailing,* Wadsworth, 1970; (with Donnelly) *Analyses for Marketing Decisions,* Irwin, 1970; (editor, with Donnelly and Gibson) *Fundamentals of Management: Selected Readings,* Business Publications, 1971;

(with Donnelly and Gibson) *Fundamentals of Management: Functions, Behavior, Models,* Business Publications, 1971; *Organizations,* Business Publications, 1973; *Management Science in Organizations,* Goodyear Publishing, 1976; *Organizational Behavior and Performance,* Goodyear Publishing, 1977. Also author of over seventy professional papers.

* * *

IZARD, Barbara 1926-

PERSONAL: Born May 8, 1926, in Gulfport, Miss.; daughter of Fred H. and Camille (West) Sinquefield; married Carroll E. Izard (a professor of psychology at Vanderbilt University); children: Carroll E., Jr., Camille Sinquefield, Ellen Ashley. *Education:* Yale University, B.M., 1948; Syracuse University, M.Mus., 1950; additional study at Cleveland Playhouse, 1954-55, Vanderbilt University, 1958-60, and Centre Universitaire International, University of Paris, 1966-67. *Home:* 1701 Graybar Lane, Nashville, Tenn. 37215. *Office:* Aquinas Junior College, Nashville, Tenn. 37205.

CAREER: Belmont College, Nashville, Tenn., instructor in drama, 1960-62; Vanderbilt University, Nashville, director of summer theater, 1965; St. Cecilia Academy, Nashville, drama director, 1969—; Aquinas Junior College, Nashville, instructor in speech and drama, 1970—. Member of board of directors, Circle Theatre, Nashville. *Member:* Daughters of the American Revolution, Colonial Dames of America.

WRITINGS: (Co-author with Clara Hieronymus) *Requiem for a Nun: On Stage and Off,* Aurora, 1970.

WORK IN PROGRESS: "Ten Minutes with a Four-Year-Old," a song cycle for children.††

* * *

JACKMAN, Leslie (Arthur James) 1919-

PERSONAL: Born December 23, 1919, in London, England; son of Arthur James and Lilian (Abrey) Jackman; married Cynthia Rudge, July, 1942; children: Diane, Paul, Rodger, Lynne. *Education:* Attended Weymouth Training College, 1946-47. *Home:* 44 Old Torquay Rd., Paignton, Devonshire, England.

CAREER: Schoolmaster in Torquay, Devonshire, England, 1947-63; Devonshire County Council, Devonshire, England, schools museum officer, 1963—. Maker of natural history films for British Broadcasting Corp. "Look" series, and producer of other educational television films for BBC-TV. *Military service:* British Army, 1939-46. *Member:* Zoological Society (London; fellow), Marine Biological Association.

WRITINGS: Marine Aquaria, Cassell, 1957, Transatlantic, 1969; (editor) *Hobbies for Boys,* Evans Brothers, 1968; *Exploring a Woodland,* Evans Brothers, 1970; *Exploring the Park,* Evans Brothers, 1970; *Exploring the Hedgerow,* Evans Brothers, 1970; *Exploring the Seashore,* Evans Brothers, 1970; *The Field,* Evans Brothers, 1972; *The Beach,* photographs by author, Evans Brothers, 1974. Also author of *Exploring a Pond* and *Exploring a Garden.*

WORK IN PROGRESS: Larus; The Herring Gull; Exploring a Canal; Exploring the Town.

BIOGRAPHICAL/CRITICAL SOURCES: Books and Bookmen, November, 1968.

* * *

JACKSON, Gabriele Bernhard 1934-

PERSONAL: Born November 17, 1934, in Berlin, Germany; naturalized U.S. citizen; daughter of Ernest George (a businessman) and Ruth (Friedlander) Bernhard; married Thomas H. Jackson (a college teacher), December 16, 1961; children: Olivia, Emily. *Education:* Hunter College (now Hunter College of the City University of New York), student, 1951-52; Bard College, B.A., 1955; Lady Margaret Hall, Oxford, further study, 1955-56; Yale University, M.A., 1958, Ph.D., 1961. *Residence:* Philadelphia, Pa. *Office:* Department of English, Temple University, Philadelphia, Pa. 19122.

CAREER: Yale University, New Haven, Conn., instructor in English, 1960-63; Wellesley College, Wellesley, Mass., assistant professor of English, 1963-68; Temple University, Philadelphia, Pa., associate professor, 1968-70, professor of English, 1970—. Visiting associate professor, University of Pennsylvania, 1968, 1970. *Awards, honors:* Fulbright fellow at Oxford University, 1955-56; junior leave grant from Wellesley College, 1966-67, to complete work on Ben Jonson's *Every Man in His Humor;* American Council of Learned Societies fellowship, 1971-72.

WRITINGS: Vision and Judgment in Ben Jonson's Drama, Yale University Press, 1968; (editor) Ben Jonson, *Every Man in His Humor,* Yale University Press, 1970; (contributor) Alvin Kernan, editor, *Jonson and Marlowe,* Johns Hopkins Press, 1977.

WORK IN PROGRESS: Byron and the Problem of Romantic Formal Structure.

SIDELIGHTS: In addition to German, Gabriele Jackson is competent in Spanish, French, and Latin, and knows some Italian. *Avocational interests:* Dressmaking, gourmet cooking.

*   *   *

JACKSON, Joy J(uanita)   1928-

PERSONAL: Born October 8, 1928, in New Orleans, La; daughter of Oliver Daniel (a Mississippi River pilot) and Oneida (Drouant) Jackson. *Education:* Tulane University of Louisiana, B.A., 1951, M.A., 1958, Ph.D., 1961. *Politics:* Democrat. *Religion:* Lutheran. *Home:* 1411 University Dr., Hammond, La. 70401. *Office:* Box 761, College Station, Southeastern Louisiana University, Hammond, La. 70401.

CAREER: New Orleans Times-Picayune, New Orleans, La., feature writer, 1951-56; Nicholls State College (now University), Thibodaux, La., instructor, 1961-62, assistant professor of history, 1962-66; Southeastern Louisiana University, Hammond, associate professor, 1966-73, professor of history, 1973—. *Member:* Organization of American Historians, Southern Historical Association, Louisiana Historical Association (member of board of directors, 1966-69; vice-president, 1976), Southeast Louisiana Historical Association (vice-president).

WRITINGS: New Orleans in the Gilded Age: Politics and Urban Progress, 1880-1896, Louisiana State University Press, 1969. Contributor to regional history journals.

WORK IN PROGRESS: Research on James Bryce and his interpretation of American democracy and on New Orleans in the Progressive Era.

*   *   *

JACKSON, Robert S(umner)   1926-

PERSONAL: Born January 25, 1926, in New York, N.Y.; son of Sumner Allen and Jean (Roy) Jackson; married Jacqueline Dougan (a college professor and writer), June 17,

1950 (divorced, 1973); children: Damaris, Megan, Gillian, Elspeth. *Education:* Beloit College, B.A., 1949; Oxford University, graduate study, 1953-54; Harvard University, S.T.B., 1956; University of Michigan, Ph.D., 1959. *Politics:* Democrat. *Religion:* Christian. *Home:* 1914 Orrington Ave., Evanston, Ill. 60201. *Office:* 845 Chicago Ave., Evanston, Ill. 60202.

CAREER: Ordained priest of Episcopal Church, 1960. Yale University, New Haven, Conn., instructor in religion, 1957-58, instructor in English, 1958-61; Kent State University, Kent, Ohio, assistant professor of English, 1961-68; Rockford College, Rockford, Ill., associate professor of English and philosophy, 1968-70; Sangamon State University, Springfield, Ill., professor of humanities, 1970-74; Robert Jackson & Associates (career development agency), Evanston, Ill., founder and director, 1974—. Chicago area coordinator, Campus Free College, 1975—. *Military service:* U.S. Naval Reserve, 1944-46; became petty officer first class. *Member:* Modern Language Association of America, American Academy of Religion, American Association of University Professors, American Association of Higher Education, Association for Humanistic Psychology, National Organization for Self-Supporting Ministry, Professional and Organizational Development Network in Higher Education, Analytic Psychology Club of Chicago.

WRITINGS: John Donne's Christian Vocation, Northwestern University Press, 1970. Contributor to literary and religious journals.

WORK IN PROGRESS: University and Human Life; Career-Sighting Keys; Clear-Fork Meditations.

SIDELIGHTS: Robert Jackson told *CA:* "The late 60's at Kent State University was the setting for writing *John Donne's Christian Vocation.* I was well aware of the widening gap between the faculty's ideal of high intellectualism and the ordinary human concerns of the students. Meditation, depth psychology and support groups strengthened me to walk in one piece between these two camps. The insights gained in the process helped me link up the vocational and psychic struggle of the 17th-century man of letters who said 'no man is an island entire unto himself.' Lately, vocation matters more to me than academics. I have founded an agency for personal and professional growth, especially career development, in which academics participate but don't dominate. Hence, my recent writing includes a theoretical statement of professional development in universities and coauthoring a 'how to' book on career-shifting."

*   *   *

JACOB, Nancy L(ouise)   1943-

PERSONAL: Born January 15, 1943, in Berkeley, Calif.; daughter of Irvin Carl and Ruby (Roberts) Feustel. *Education:* University of Washington, B.A., 1966; University of California, Irvine, Ph.D., 1970. *Home:* 2515 East Roanoke, Seattle, Wash. 98112. *Office:* Department of Finance, Business Economics, and Quantitative Methods, University of Washington, Seattle, Wash. 98105.

CAREER: Center for Naval Analyses, Arlington, Va., researcher, 1969; University of Washington, Seattle, professor of finance, 1970—. *Member:* American Economic Association, American Finance Association.

WRITINGS: (With William Forsyth Sharpe) *BASIC: An Introduction to Computer Programming Using the Basic Language,* revised edition, Free Press, 1970.

WORK IN PROGRESS: Studies on portfolio theory and

security markets; an investments textbook, completion expected in 1979.

* * *

JACOBS, Glenn 1940-

PERSONAL: Born October 14, 1940, in Brooklyn, N.Y.; son of Morris (a retailer) and Jean (Hoffman) Jacobs; married Ada Janow (an elementary teacher), May 1, 1966; children: Brian Lee. *Education:* Brooklyn College of the City University of New York, B.A., 1963, M.A., 1966; New School for Social Research, further study. *Politics:* "Existential Humanist."

CAREER: New York City Department of Welfare, Brooklyn, N.Y., caseworker, 1965-66; University of Wisconsin, instructor in sociology and anthropology at Wausau Campus, 1966-69, and at Janesville Campus, 1969-71. *Member:* American Sociological Association, Sigma Xi.

WRITINGS: (Contributor) Thomas E. Lasswell, John H. Burma, and Sidney H. Aronson, editors, *Readings in Sociology: Life in Society,* Scott, Foresman, 1965; (editor and contributor) *The Participant Observer,* Braziller, 1970; (editor with Joel Emery Gerstl) *Professions for the People: The Politics of Skill,* Halsted Press, 1976. Contributor of articles and reviews to sociology journals. Abstractor, *Sociological Abstracts,* 1964-65.

WORK IN PROGRESS: Research on sociology and mysticism, on introspection in sociological fieldwork, on participant observation as an educational technique in non-sociological contexts, on relation between sociology and the arts, and on photography as a sensory expander.†

* * *

JACOBS, Harvey 1930-

PERSONAL: Born January 7, 1930, in New York, N.Y.; son of Louis (a dentist) and Laura Jacobs; married Estelle Rose (an artist), October 18, 1956; children: Adam. *Education:* Syracuse University, B.A., 1950; Columbia University, graduate study, 1950-51. *Residence:* New York, N.Y.

CAREER: Weizman Institute of Science, New York City, public relations, 1954-55; *Village Voice* (newspaper), New York City, staff member, 1955-56; *East* (newspaper), New York City, publisher, 1956-57; American Broadcasting Co., New York City, director of industry affairs, 1958-73. Instructor in writer's workshop, Syracuse University, 1958-59. *Member:* Writers Guild of America, P.E.N., Dramatists Guild. *Awards, honors: Playboy* Fiction Award for story, "The Lion's Share"; Earplay Award for Drama from Writers Guild of America.

WRITINGS: The Egg of the Glak (short stories), Harper, 1969; *Summer on a Mountain of Spices* (novel), Harper, 1976. Also author of scripts of specials for ABC-TV, NBC-TV, and Children's Television Workshop. Contributor of short stories to *Transatlantic Review, Esquire, Playboy, Mademoiselle, Cosmopolitan, New Worlds, Realist, Midstream, Paris Review,* and other periodicals.

WORK IN PROGRESS: A novel, *Comet News.*

SIDELIGHTS: Syracuse University Library has a collection of Harvey Jacobs's manuscripts.

* * *

JACOBS, Jerry 1932-

PERSONAL: Born July 5, 1932, in New York, N.Y.; son of Alex and Sarah (Rosen) Jacobs. *Education:* University of

California, Los Angeles, B.A., 1959, Ph.D., 1967. *Residence:* Syracuse, N.Y. *Office:* Department of Sociology, Syracuse University, Syracuse, N.Y. 13210.

CAREER: University of Southern California, School of Medicine, Los Angeles, research associate, 1964-67; University of California, San Francisco Medical Center, San Francisco, assistant professor of medical sociology, 1967-69; University of California, Riverside, assistant professor of sociology, 1969-72; Syracuse University, Syracuse, N.Y., associate professor of sociology, 1972—. *Member:* American Sociological Association, Society for the Study of Social Problems, Alpha Kappa Delta.

WRITINGS: The Search for Help: A Study of the Retarded Child in the Community, Brunner, 1969; (contributor) Simon Dinitz and others, editors, *Deviance: Studies in the Process of Stigmatization and Societal Reaction,* Oxford University Press, 1969; (contributor) Jack Douglas, editor, *Deviance and Respectability: The Social Construction of Moral Meanings,* Basic Books, 1970; *Adolescent Suicide,* Wiley, 1971; (editor) *Getting By: Studies in Marginal Living,* Little, Brown, 1972; (contributor) Douglas, editor, *Introduction to Sociology: Situations and Structures,* Free Press, 1973; (editor) *Deviance: Field Studies and Self Disclosures,* Mayfield, 1974; *Fun City: An Ethnographic Study of a Retirement Community,* Holt, 1974; *Case Studies in Social Gerontology,* C. C Thomas, 1975; (contributor) Roy Bryce-LaPorte, editor, *Alienation and Contemporary Society,* Praeger, 1976; (contributor) Cary S. Kart and Barbara Manard, editors, *Aging in America,* Alfred Publishing, 1976; (with Howard Schwartz) *Qualitative Sociology,* Free Press, in press; (contributor) Douglas, editor, *Deviance in American Society,* Basic Books, in press. Contributor to sociology and psychiatry journals.

* * *

JACOBS, Linda C. 1943-
(Tom Austin, Claire Blackburn)

PERSONAL: Born January 22, 1943, in Winston-Salem, N.C.; daughter of Lloyd Daniel and Elizabeth (Parker) Blackburn; married Thomas D. Austin (a psychiatric technician), September 16, 1965 (divorced, 1970); married Joseph D. Jacobs (a former social worker), October 9, 1972; children: (first marriage) Brian Vincent. *Education:* Attended high school in San Bernardino, Calif. *Agent:* Jane Jordon Browne, 170 South Beverly Dr., Suite 314, Beverly Hills, Calif. 90212.

WRITINGS—Young adults; all published by EMC Corp.; "Women Who Win" series (biography): *Janet Lynn: Sunshine on Ice,* 1974; *Olga Korbut: Tears and Triumph,* 1974; *Shane Gould: Olympic Swimmer,* 1974; *Chris Evert: Tennis Pro,* 1974; *Laura Baugh: Golf's Golden Girl,* 1975; *Wilma Rudolph: Run for Glory,* 1975; *Evonne Goolagong: Smiles and Smashes,* 1975; *Cathy Rigby: On the Beam,* 1975; *Mary Decker: Speed Records and Spaghetti,* 1975; *Joan Moore Rice: The Olympic Dream,* 1975; *Annemarie Proell: Queen of the Mountain,* 1975; *Rosemary Casals: The Rebel Rosebud,* 1975; *Cindy Nelson: North Country Skier,* 1976; *Robyn Smith: In Silks,* 1976; *Martina Navratilova: Tennis Fury,* 1976; *Robin Campbell: Joy in the Morning,* 1976.

"Winners All" series (fiction): *Ellen the Expert; In Tennis, Love Means Nothing; For One—Or For All, Go for Six;* all published 1974.

"Really Me" series (fiction): *A Candle, a Feather, a Wooden Spoon; Will the Real Jeannie Murphy Please Stand*

Up; Everyone's Watching Tammy; Checkmate; Julie; all published 1974.

"Women behind the Bright Lights" series (biography): *Olivia Newton-John: Sunshine Supergirl; Valerie Harper: The Unforgettable Snowflake; Roberta Flack: Sound of Velvet Melting; Cher: Simply Cher;* all published 1975.

"Men behind the Bright Lights" series (biography): *Stevie Wonder: Sunshine in the Shadow; John Denver: A Natural High; Elton John: Reginald Dwight and Company; Jim Croce: The Feeling Lives On;* all published 1975.

"Black American Athletes" series (biography): *Madeline Manning Jackson: Running on Faith; Julius Erving: Dr. J. and Julius W.; Lee Elder: The Daring Dream; Arthur Ashe: Alone in the Crowd;* all published 1976.

Under pseudonym Claire Blackburn; all published by Bouregy: *Return Engagement,* 1970; *A Teacher for My Heart,* 1972; *Rainbow for Clari,* 1973; *Heart on Ice,* 1976. Contributor of articles to magazines under pseudonyms, Tom Austin and Claire Blackburn.

SIDELIGHTS: Linda Jacobs told *CA:* "I believe that balance is important to me as a writer and as a human being. When I first started writing, I simply wanted to make a decent living doing what I like most. Now I find my goals are expanding and the projects buzzing in my head are increasingly aimed at exploring and sharing my own 'interior landscape.' Because this exploration requires both intuitive insight and intellectual acuity, I find my activities are changing. I'm going back to school, taking courses in religion, philosophy and literature. I'm an avid student of Tai Chi Chuan, the Chinese 'moving meditation.' I'm also learning to take great enjoyment in things I formerly considered trivial. I do my own housework, groom my three Lhasa apsos instead of sending them to a professional—the little things count."

* * *

JAEN, Didier Tisdel 1933-

PERSONAL: Surname is pronounced High-in; born May 12, 1933, in Santiago, Panama; son of Rodolfo (a businessman) and Jacinta (Gonzalez) Jaen-Luna. *Education:* University of Texas, Main University (now University of Texas at Austin), B.A., 1956, M.A., 1959, Ph.D., 1965. *Home address:* P.O. Box 603, Davis, Calif. 95616. *Office:* Department of Spanish, University of California, Davis, Calif. 95616.

CAREER: Texas Southern University, Houston, assistant professor of Spanish literature, 1965; University of California, Davis, 1965—, began as assistant professor, currently associate professor of Spanish literature. *Member:* International Institute of Ibero American Literature, American Association of Teachers of Spanish and Portuguese, Modern Language Association of America, American Association of University Professors.

WRITINGS: (Translator and annotator) *Homage to Walt Whitman: A Collection of Poems from the Spanish,* foreward by Jorge Luis Borges, University of Alabama Press, 1969. Contributor to language journals.

WORK IN PROGRESS: Translating and editing *King John II of Castile and Don Alvaro de Luna.*†

* * *

JAFFE, Harold 1938-

PERSONAL: Born July 8, 1938, in New York, N.Y.; son of Lester and Blanche (Weber) Jaffe. *Education:* Grinnell College, B.A., 1960; New York University, Ph.D. (with honors), 1967. *Politics:* "Humane." *Office:* Department of English, Long Island University, Brooklyn Center, Brooklyn, N.Y. 11201.

CAREER: Long Island University, Brooklyn Center, Brooklyn, N.Y., assistant professor, 1965-71, associate professor of English, 1971—. Fulbright professor, University of Kerala, Kerala, India, 1971-72; guest lecturer, New School for Social Research, 1972-73. *Military service:* U.S. Army Reserve, 1961-62. *Member:* Modern Language Association of America, American Civil Liberties Union. *Awards, honors:* Founder's Day Award, New York University, 1968.

WRITINGS: (Editor with John Tytell and contributor) *The American Experience: A Radical Reader,* Harper, 1970; (editor with Tytell) *Affinities: A Short Story Anthology,* Crowell, 1970; (editor) Richard Maurice Burke, *Walt Whitman,* Johnson Reprint, 1971. Author of one-act play, *Assassination,* included in *The American Experience.* Contributor to literary journals.

WORK IN PROGRESS: A book on his experience in India; a collection of poems.

AVOCATIONAL INTERESTS: Skydiving, shark fishing, auto racing.†

* * *

JAIN, Ravindra Kumar 1937-

PERSONAL: Born January 31, 1937, in Delhi, India; son of Lakshmi Chandra (an author and editor) and Kuntha Jain; married Shobhita Dharmishtha Sharma (a researcher), January 1, 1961; children: Kajri (daughter), Shirish (son). *Education:* University of Lucknow, B.A., 1956, M.A., 1958; Australian National University, Ph.D., 1965. *Religion:* Jainism. *Home:* 105 New Campus, Jawaharlal Nehru University, New Delhi, India. *Office:* School of Social Sciences, Jawaharlal Nehru University, New Delhi, India.

CAREER: University of Lucknow, Lucknow, India, assistant professor of anthropology, 1958-61; Australian National University, Canberra, research scholar, 1961-65; University of New England, Armidale, Australia, lecturer in sociology, 1965-66; Oxford University, Oxford, England, lecturer in Indian sociology, 1966-74, official fellow of Wolfson College, 1970-74; Jawaharlal Nehru University, New Delhi, India, professor of social anthropology, 1975—. Fellow, Indian Institute of Advanced Study, Simla, 1968-70. Official representative of Oxford University, Eighth International Congress of the Anthropological and Ethnological Sciences, Tokyo and Kyoto, Japan, 1968. *Member:* Royal Anthropological Institute of Great Britain and Ireland (fellow), Malaysian Sociological Research Institute (honorary life fellow). *Awards, honors:* M.A., Oxford University, 1967.

WRITINGS: South Indians on the Plantation Frontier in Malaya, Yale University Press, 1970.

WORK IN PROGRESS: Status and Power in the Bundelkhand Region of Central India, with special reference to economic networks and social change, completion expected in 1978.

* * *

JAMES, Cary A(mory) 1935-

PERSONAL: Born December 17, 1935, in Richmond, Va.; son of Alvin Orlando (a dentist) and Frances (Laughlin)

James; married Elaine Martin, June 4, 1960; children: Maya, Susanna. *Education:* College of William and Mary, A.B., 1956; University of California, Berkeley, B.Arch., 1960. *Home:* 342 Tamalpais Ave., Mill Valley, Calif. 94941.

CAREER: Cary James, Architect, Mill Valley, Calif., owner, 1968—. *Military service:* U.S. Army Reserve, 1960-66. *Member:* American Institute of Architects.

WRITINGS: (Self-illustrated with photographs) *The Imperial Hotel: Frank Lloyd Wright and the Architecture of Unity,* Tuttle, 1968.

WORK IN PROGRESS: A novel, tentatively entitled *The Lightning Flash.*

BIOGRAPHICAL/CRITICAL SOURCES: Book World, December 29, 1968.

*   *   *

JAMES, Charles L(yman) 1934-

PERSONAL: Born April 12, 1934, in Poughkeepsie, N.Y.; son of Stanley and E. Romaine (Cooley) James; married R. Jane Fisher (assistant to Equal Opportunity Office at Swarthmore College), August 6, 1960; children: Sheila Ellen, Terri Lynn. *Education:* State University of New York College at New Paltz, B.S., 1961; State University of New York at Albany, M.S., 1969; Yale University, further study, 1971. *Home:* 402 Laurel Lane, Wallingford, Pa. 19086. *Office:* Department of English Literature, Swarthmore College, Swarthmore, Pa. 19081.

CAREER: Spackenkill School District, Poughkeepsie, N.Y., elementary teacher, 1961-65, high school teacher of English, 1965-67; Dutchess Community College, Poughkeepsie, instructor in English, 1967-69; State University of New York College at Oneonta, assistant professor, 1969-72, associate professor of English, 1972-73, acting chairman of Black-Hispanic studies program, 1969-73; Swarthmore College, Swarthmore, Pa., associate professor of English, 1973—. Neighborhood Service Organization, Poughkeepsie, director of summer program, 1964-65, secretary of board, 1968-69. *Military service:* U.S. Army, Special Services, 1955-57; became sergeant. *Member:* American Association of University Professors, African Studies Association, Modern Language Association of America, Conference of African and African-American Studies.

WRITINGS: (Editor) *From the Roots: Short Stories by Black Americans,* Dodd, 1970; (contributor) *Contemporary Poets of the English Language,* St. James Press, 1976. Also contributor to *Pennsylvania Ethnic Heritage Studies Dissemination Project,* 1977.

WORK IN PROGRESS: Revision of *From the Roots: Short Stories by Black Americans,* for Harper.

*   *   *

JAMES, D(orris) Clayton 1931-

PERSONAL: Born February 13, 1931, in Winchester, Ky.; son of Dorris Clayton and Opal (Shetter) James; married Erlene Downs, June 2, 1953; children: Dorris Sherrod, Newell Edmund, Judith Erlene, Allie Brady. *Education:* Southwestern at Memphis, B.A., 1953; Louisville Presbyterian Theological Seminary, B.D., 1956; University of Cincinnati, graduate study, 1956-57; University of Texas, M.A., 1959, Ph.D., 1964. *Home:* 1702 Linden Dr., Starkville, Miss. 39759. *Office:* Department of History, Mississippi State University, Starkville, Miss. 39762.

CAREER: Presbyterian minister in Union, Ky., 1954-56,

and in Cameron, Tex., 1957-59; Louisiana State University, Alexandria, instructor in history, 1960-64; Mankato State College, Mankato, Minn., assistant professor of history, 1964-65; Mississippi State University, Starkville, assistant professor, 1965-68, associate professor, 1968-71, professor of history, 1971—. Chief technical advisor on motion picture, "MacArthur," for Universal Studios, 1976-77. *Military service:* U.S. Naval Reserve, 1956-62; became lieutenant. *Member:* American Historical Association, American Military Institute, U.S. Naval Institute, Organization of American Historians, Southern Historical Association, Omicron Delta Kappa, Alpha Tau Omega. *Awards, honors:* National Endowment for the Humanities research grant, 1968.

WRITINGS: Antebellum Natchez, Louisiana State University Press, 1968; *The Years of MacArthur,* Houghton, Volume I: *1880-1941,* 1970, Volume II: *1941-45,* 1975; (editor) *South to Bataan, North to Mukden: The Prison Diary of Brigadier General W. E. Brougher,* University of Georgia Press, 1971. Contributor to historical journals.

WORK IN PROGRESS: The Years of MacArthur, Volume III: *1945-64.*

BIOGRAPHICAL/CRITICAL SOURCES: New York Times, September 25, 1970.

*   *   *

JAMES, Denise

PERSONAL: Born in New York, N.Y.; daughter of William M. (a clerical worker) and Katherine (Hurley) Petty; married Stephen D. James (founder of Citizen Exchange Corps), July 2, 1955; children: Timothy, Megan, Caitlin. *Education:* Hunter College (now Hunter College of the City University of New York), B.A.; took creative writing courses a total of four years at Columbia University and Stanford University. *Politics:* Registered Democrat. *Home:* 9 Wilson Dr., Rye, N.Y. 10580.

CAREER: Doherty, Clifford, Steers & Shenfeld and its successor firm, Needhem, Harper & Steers, New York, N.Y., advertising copywriter, 1959-64. *Awards, honors:* Creative writing fellowship at Stanford University; story, "Subway," included on honor roll of *Best American Short Stories.*

WRITINGS: Henry James: "The American," Barnes & Noble, 1968; *Henry James: "The Portrait of a Lady,"* Barnes & Noble, 1969. Contributor of articles to *Good Housekeeping, Esquire,* and *Pageant;* has also ghostwritten articles.

WORK IN PROGRESS: A novel.†

*   *   *

JAMES, Norah C(ordner)

PERSONAL: Born in London, England; daughter of John H. Cordner-James (a consulting mining engineer). *Education:* Attended Francis Holland School for Girls, London, and Slade School of Art. *Politics:* Labour. *Religion:* Church of England. *Agent:* Curtis Brown Ltd., 1 Craven Hill, London W2 3EW, England.

CAREER: Former designer of book jackets, organizing secretary for the Civil Service Clerical Association in England, and advertising and publicity manager for Jonathan Cape Ltd. (publishers), London, England; novelist, 1929—. Borough councillor for Finsbury, 1945-46. *Military service:* Auxiliary Territorial Service, World War II. *Member:* National Book League.

WRITINGS: *Sleeveless Errand,* Scholartis Press, 1929; *Hail! All Hail!,* Scholartis Press, 1929.

Shatter the Dream, Constable, 1930, Morrow, 1931; *To the Valiant,* Morrow, 1930; *The Wanton Way,* Morrow, 1931 (published in England as *Wanton Ways,* Duckworth, 1931); *Hospital,* Duckworth, 1932; *Tinkle the Cat: An Animal Story,* Dent, 1932; *Jake the Dog: An Animal Story,* Dent, 1933; *Nurse Adriane,* Covici, Friede, 1933; *Jealousy,* Covici, Friede, 1933; *Sacrifice,* Covici, Friede, 1934 (published in England as *Strap-Hangers,* Duckworth, 1934); *Mrs. Piffy,* Dent, 1934; *Cottage Angles* (nonfiction), Dent, 1935; *The Return,* Duckworth, 1935; *The Lion Beat the Unicorn,* Duckworth, 1935; *By a Side Wind,* Jarrolds, 1936; *Two Divided by One,* Macaulay, 1936; *Sea View,* Jarrolds, 1936; *The Stars Are Fire,* Cassell, 1937; *Women Are Born to Listen,* Macaulay, 1937; *As High as the Sky,* Macaulay, 1938; *The House by the Tree,* Cassell, 1938; *I Live in a Democracy* (autobiography), Longmans, Green, 1939; *Mighty City,* Cassell, 1939.

The Gentlewoman, Cassell, 1940; *The Hunted Heart,* Cassell, 1941; *The Long Journey,* Cassell, 1941; *Two Selfish People,* Cassell, 1942; *Enduring Adventure,* Cassell, 1944; *One Bright Day,* Cassell, 1945, modernized edition, Hurst & Blackett, 1964; *The Father,* Cassell, 1946; *There Is Always To-morrow,* Macdonald & Co., 1946; *Penny Trumpet,* Macdonald & Co., 1947; *Brittle Glory,* Macdonald & Co., 1948; *Swift to Sever,* Macdonald & Co., 1949; (with Barbara Beauchamp) *Greenfingers and the Gourmet* (cookbook), Nicholson & Watson, 1949.

Pay the Piper, Macdonald & Co., 1950; *Pedigree of Honey,* Macdonald & Co., 1951; *So Runs the River,* Macdonald & Co., 1952; *Cooking in Cider* (cookbook), World's Work, 1952; *A Summer Storm,* Macdonald & Co., 1953; *Silent Corridors,* Hutchinson, 1953, McGraw, 1955; *Over the Windmill,* Hutchinson, 1954; *Wed to Earth,* Hutchinson, 1955; *Mercy in Your Hands,* Hutchinson, 1956; *The Flower and the Fruit,* Hutchinson, 1957; *The True and the Tender,* Hutchinson, 1958; *Portrait of a Patient,* Hutchinson, 1959.

The Uneasy Summer, Hutchinson, 1960; *The Wind of Change,* Hurst & Blackett, 1961; *A Sense of Loss,* Hutchinson, 1962; *The Green Vista,* Hurst & Blackett, 1963; *Sister Veronica Greene,* Hurst & Blackett, 1963; *Small Hotel,* Hurst & Blackett, 1965; *Hospital Angels,* Hurst & Blackett, 1966; *Double Take,* Hurst & Blackett, 1967; *Point of Return,* Hurst & Blackett, 1968.

There Is No Why, Hurst & Blackett, 1970; *Ward of Darkness,* Hurst & Blackett, 1971; *The Doctor's Marriage,* Hurst & Blackett, 1972; *If Only,* Hurst & Blackett, 1972; *The Bewildered,* Hurst & Blackett, 1973; *Love,* Hurst & Blackett, 1975.

Short stories have been published in *Woman's Realm, Woman's Own, Sunday Mirror,* and other magazines and newspapers in England.

SIDELIGHTS: Norah James's novels have been translated into French, German, Dutch, Swedish, and Spanish.

* * *

JAMISON, Andrew 1948-

PERSONAL: Born August 22, 1948, in Santa Monica, Calif.; son of Saunders Eliot (a chemist) and Barbara (Berch) Jamison. *Education:* Harvard University, B.A. (magna cum laude), 1970; University of Lund, graduate study, 1970—. *Home:* Framnas Gard, S230, 47 Akarp, Sweden. *Office:* Research Policy Program, Solvegatan 8A, Lund, Sweden.

CAREER: Free-lance journalist; university teacher.

WRITINGS: *The Steam-Powered Automobile: An Answer to Air Pollution,* Indiana University Press, 1970. Also contributor, Daniel S. Greenberg, editor, *Science and Government Report International Almanac, 1977,* 1977. Contributor to *Science, New Scientist,* and *Technology Review.*

WORK IN PROGRESS: Research and magazine writing on science policy in Scandinavia, resulting in a book.

SIDELIGHTS: Andrew Jamison told *CA:* "[I] am interested in science and technology and the interactions with people and with societies in general; I am interested in finding out about and describing alternatives, either real or theorized, to the current societal ways of dealing with and using science and technology."

* * *

JANGER, Allen R(obert) 1932-

PERSONAL: Born September 5, 1932, in Chicago, Ill.; son of Max and Myrtle (Levy) Janger; married Inez Kurn, September 11, 1960; children: Edward, Matthew, Michael. *Education:* Attended University of Chicago, 1949-55, and London School of Economics and Political Science, 1955-56. *Office:* The Conference Board, 845 Third Ave., New York, N.Y. 10022.

CAREER: The Conference Board (formerly National Industrial Conference Board), New York, N.Y., senior specialist in organization and developmental research, 1960—. *Military service:* U.S. Army, 1957-59.

WRITINGS: (With Harold Steiglitz) *Top Management Organization in Divisionalized Companies,* National Industrial Conference Board, 1965; *Personnel Administration: Changing Scope and Organization,* National Industrial Conference Board, 1966; *Managing Programs to Employ the Disadvantaged,* National Industrial Conference Board, 1970; (with Ruth G. Shaeffer) *Employing the Disadvantaged: A Management Perspective,* The Conference Board, 1972; *Corporate Organization Structures,* The Conference Board, Volume I: *Manufacturing,* 1973, Volume II: *Financial Enterprises,* 1974; *The Personnel Function: Changing Objectives and Organization,* The Conference Board, 1977.

* * *

JASEN, David A(lan) 1937-

PERSONAL: Born December 16, 1937, in New York, N.Y.; son of Barnet (a dentist) and Gertrude (Cohen) Jasen; married Susan Pomerantz (a registered nurse), December 30, 1963; children: Raymond Douglas. *Education:* American University, B.A., 1959; Long Island University, M.S., 1972. *Home:* 225 East Penn St., Long Beach, N.Y. 11561. *Office:* C. W. Post Center, Long Island University, Brookville, N.Y.

CAREER: Columbia Broadcasting System, New York City, supervisor of news videotape, 1959-66; American Educational Theatre Association, Washington, D.C., administrative assistant, 1967; Florists' Transworld Delivery Association, Detroit, Mich., field service representative, 1968-69; Reading Development Center, Inc., New York City, assistant to president, 1969-70; Long Island University, C. W. Post Center, Brookville, N.Y., assistant professor, 1971-77, associate professor in School of Art, 1977—, director of communication arts, 1975—. Ragtime pianist; record producer; public speaker. *Member:* American Library Association, Ragtime Society, Maple Leaf Club, Pi Delta Epsilon, Alpha Psi Omega.

WRITINGS: *Bibliography and Reader's Guide to the First*

Editions of P. G. Wodehouse, Archon, 1970; *Recorded Ragtime, 1897-1958,* Archon, 1973; *P. G. Wodehouse: A Portrait of a Master,* Mason & Lipscomb, 1974; (editor) *The Uncollected Wodehouse,* Seabury, 1976; *Ragtime: An Original American Music,* Seabury, 1978. Contributor of articles to *Ragtimer.*

SIDELIGHTS: David Jasen is a composer and ragtime historian. He writes *CA:* "I am particularly fond of the Classic Period (1750-1830) in orchestral music, collecting first editions (Wodehouse, Arnold Bennett, W. W. Jacobs), mystery stories, Wedgwood, records and sheet music." Jasen is featured on a Euphonic Sound album (1206), "Creative Ragtime," and on "Fingerbusting Ragtime" and "Rompin', Stompin' Ragtime," for Blue Goose Records.   •

*   *   *

JEEVES, Malcolm A(lexander) 1926-

PERSONAL: Born November 16, 1926, in Stamford, England; son of Alexander F. T. and Helena M. (Hammond) Jeeves; married Ruth E. Hartridge, April 7, 1955; children: Sarah M. E., Joanna M. H. *Education:* St. John's College, Cambridge, B.A. (honors), 1951, M.A., 1954, Ph.D., 1956; Harvard University, additional study, 1953-54. *Religion:* Protestant. *Home:* 7 Hepburn Gardens, St. Andrews, Scotland. *Office:* Department of Psychology, University of St. Andrews, St. Andrews, Scotland.

CAREER: University of Leeds, Leeds, Yorkshire, England, lecturer in psychology, 1956-59; University of Adelaide, Adelaide, Australia, professor of psychology and head of department, 1959-69, dean of Faculty of Arts, 1963-64; University of St. Andrews, St. Andrews, Scotland, professor of psychology and head of department, 1969—. Inter-Varsity Fellowship, president of Australia branch, 1969, president of Great Britain branch, 1974. *Military service:* British Army of the Rhine, 1945-48; became lieutenant. *Member:* Experimental Psychology Society, British Psychological Society (fellow), Australian Psychological Society (fellow). *Awards, honors:* Rotary Foundation fellow at Harvard University, 1953-54.

WRITINGS: (Co-author) *Where Science and Faith Meet,* Inter-Varsity, 1952; *Contemporary Psychology and Christian Belief and Experience* (pamphlet), Tyndale Press, 1960; (with Zoltan Paul Dienes) *Thinking in Structures,* Hutchinson, 1965; *Scientific Psychology and Christian Belief,* Inter-Varsity, 1966; (editor) *The Scientific Enterprise and Christian Faith,* Tyndale Press, 1969; (with Dienes) *The Effects of Structural Relations upon Transfer,* Hutchinson, 1970; *Experimental Psychology: An Introduction for Biologists,* Arnold, 1974; *Psychology and Christianity: The View Both Ways,* Inter-Varsity, 1976. Contributor to scientific journals.

WORK IN PROGRESS: The Analysis of Structural Thinking, for Academic Press; neuropsychological studies of interhemispheric relations.

AVOCATIONAL INTERESTS: Music, hockey, tennis, squash,

*   *   *

JENNER, W(illiam) J(ohn) F(rancis) 1940-

PERSONAL: Born October 5, 1940, in Birmingham, England; first wife, Delia Davin; second wife, Eileen Candler (a teacher); children: (first marriage) Lucy; (second marriage) Rachel, Matthew. *Education:* Oxford University, B.A., 1962, D.Phil., 1976. *Home:* 2 Balbec Ave., Leeds LS6

2BB, England. *Office:* Department of Chinese Studies, University of Leeds, Leeds LS2 9JT, England.

CAREER: Foreign Languages Press, Peking, China, translator, 1963-65; University of Leeds, Leeds, England, lecturer in Chinese studies, 1965—.

WRITINGS: (Translator) Aisin Gioro Pu Yi, *From Emperor to Citizen* (autobiography of last emperor of China), Foreign Languages Press (Peking), Volume I, 1964, Volume II, 1965; (editor and translator, with additional translations by Gladys Yang) *Modern Chinese Stories,* Oxford University Press, 1970; (contributor) *Movements populares et societes secretes en Chine aux xue et xxe siecles,* Maspero, 1970. Contributor of reviews and articles on China to periodicals.

WORK IN PROGRESS: Memories of Loyang, a study of early Chinese medieval history, to be published by Oxford University Press; translating the Chinese classic novel, *Journey to the West;* long-term research on Chinese history and literature.

*   *   *

JENNINGS, Edward M(orton III) 1936-

PERSONAL: Born April 4, 1936, in Boston, Mass.; son of E. Morton, Jr. and Mary (Sabine) Jennings; married Sally Swayne, August 31, 1957; children: Anne G., Katherine D., Eleanor S. *Education:* Dartmouth College, A.B., 1957; University of Wisconsin, Ph.D., 1965. *Office:* Department of English, State University of New York, Albany, N.Y. 12222.

CAREER: Duke University, Durham, N.C., assistant professor of English, 1965-68; State University of New York at Albany, assistant professor of English, 1968—, assistant to president, 1972-75. *Military service:* U.S. Navy, 1957-60; became lieutenant junior grade. *Member:* Modern Language Association of America, National Council of Teachers of English, American Society for Eighteenth-Century Studies, American Association of University Professors.

WRITINGS: (Editor) *Science and Literature: New Lenses for Criticism,* Doubleday-Anchor, 1970. Contributor to literary journals.

WORK IN PROGRESS: Writing on the changing temporal paradigms of seventeenth- and eighteenth-century Europe.

*   *   *

JENSEN, Mary Ten Eyck Bard 1904-1970

November 21, 1904—November 29, 1970; American author. Obituaries: *New York Times,* December 4, 1970; *Newsday,* December 5, 1970; *Books Abroad,* spring, 1971. (See index for *CA* sketch)

*   *   *

JEZARD, Alison 1919-

PERSONAL: Born September 7, 1919, in Mayfield, Sussex, England; daughter of Stormont (an army colonel) and Alice (Angel) Bisset; divorced; children: Vanessa, Hilary, Gillian. *Education:* Educated in Edinburgh, Scotland. *Politics:* Conservative. *Religion:* Atheist. *Home and office:* Garden Flat, 57 Earl's Ave., Folkestone, England.

CAREER: Teacher in private schools in Folkestone, England, seventeen years; now part-time teacher at School of English Studies (for foreign students), and author of children's books.

WRITINGS: Stories of Willy Mouse, British Broadcasting Corp. Publications, 1969.

"Albert" juvenile series; published by Gollancz: *Albert*, 1968; *... in Scotland*, 1969; *... and Henry*, 1970; *Albert's Christmas*, 1970; *... up the River*, 1971; *... and Digger*, 1972; *... and Tum Tum*, 1973; *... Goes to Sea*, 1974; *... Police Bear*, 1975; *... Goes Trekking*, 1976, *Albert's Circus*, 1977.

Contributor of humorous articles to magazines.

WORK IN PROGRESS: Albert's Antiques; research for a science fiction work.

SIDELIGHTS: Alison Jezard told *CA:* "My writing career came about by sheer chance when I discovered the ability to write about the funny side of life. My stories are based on reality, laced with a little fantasy, as with talking animals and teddy bears. I am very strongly influenced by A. A. Milne and have deliberately tried to create a Pooh who lives in today's world—a teddy bear children can identify with. I try hard to amuse at the same time as stimulating interest and I research very carefully.

"Albert is a cheerful, friendly bear, who plods along while exciting things happen around him. His cousin Angus, from Scotland, Digger a Koala, and Tum Tum a panda, are all friends of Albert's. Each one has a different personality.

"My greatest pleasure has been meeting children who had a block against reading until they met Albert. My greatest disappointment has been the lack of interest in America."

AVOCATIONAL INTERESTS: Embroidery, carving alabaster, travel.

BIOGRAPHICAL/CRITICAL SOURCES: Listener, November 14, 1968; *Times Literary Supplement*, October 16, 1969; *Books and Bookmen*, December, 1969.

* * *

JIDEJIAN, Nina 1921-

PERSONAL: Born December 14, 1921, in Boston, Mass.; daughter of Mihran Nicholas (a businessman) and Eugenie (Coumarian) Nazaretian; married Yervant Jidejian (a clinical professor of surgery at American University of Beirut), June 10, 1948; children: Denise. *Education:* American University of Beirut, B.A., 1963, M.A., 1965. *Religion:* Armenian Gregorian. *Address:* c/o American University of Beirut, Beirut, Lebanon.

CAREER: Researcher and writer on ancient Phoenicia. Founding member and member of executive committee, Baalbeck-International Festival, Beirut; member of Beirut advisory committee, Jinishian Foundation, New York; president, Friends of Needy Children Society, Beirut; founding member and president, Anjar Festival Association, 1974—. *Awards, honors:* Said Akl Prize (first prize at Arab Book Exposition, Beirut), 1968, for *Byblos Through the Ages;* Chevalier, Ordre du Cedre, 1974, for publications on Lebanon's archeological sites.

WRITINGS: Byblos Through the Ages, Dar El-Mashreq, 1968, New York Graphic Society, 1969, 2nd edition, Dar El-Mashreq, 1971, International Publications Service, 1973; *Tyre Through the Ages*, Dar El-Mashreq, 1969; *Sidon Through the Ages*, Dar El-Mashreq, 1971; *Beirut Through the Ages*, Dar El-Mashreq, 1973; *Baalbek-Heliopolis* (title means "City of the Sun"), Dar El-Mashreq, 1975; *Tripoli Through the Ages*, Dar El-Mashreq, in press.

SIDELIGHTS: George M. A. Hanfmann, professor of fine arts at Harvard University, says of Nina Jidejian's book *Byblos Through the Ages:* "Lebanon is a very small and beautiful country, rich in archeological sites. On its coast are the remains of five Phoenician cities known to us from biblical and ancient sources: Byblos, Tyre, Sidon, Beirut and Tripolis. A motivating aim was to make known the history of the Phoenicians, seafarers of antiquity, to a wider public. At the same time ample bibliographical references were intended to guide the student and the reader to the original sources on which these books are based. Mrs. Jidejian has written a book which meets the highest standards of up-to-date scholarship while yet presenting an admirably lucid account of the millenial life of this remarkable city (Byblos)."

Nina Jidejian is fluent in French, speaks Arabic and Armenian, and knows some classical Greek.

* * *

JOELSON, Annette 1903-1971

February 16, 1903—May 14, 1971; South African radio commentator, biographer, and novelist. Obituaries: *New York Times*, May 21, 1971; *Antiquarian Bookman*, July 19-26, 1971.

* * *

JOHANNSEN, Hano D. 1933-

PERSONAL: Born December 26, 1933, in Hamburg, Germany; son of Ernst (an author and playwright) and Roselolte (Blank) Johannsen; married Grace Blaker, December, 1958; children: Helen, Paul, Ruth, Naomi. *Education:* Attended Polytechnic Management School, London, 1954-57. *Home:* 43 Brodrick Rd., London SW17 70X, England.

CAREER: British Institute of Management, London, England, research officer, 1961-64, head of information department, 1964-68, manager of surveys and publications, 1968—. *Member:* Organisation and Methods Society, Institute of Linguists.

WRITINGS: (Compiler with A. B. Robertson) *Management Glossary*, Longmans, Green, 1968, American Elsevier, 1969; *Inside Information on Careers in Management*, Dickens Press, 1964; *Company Organization Structure*, British Institute of Management, 1970; (with Stephanie Birch) *Achieving Computer Profitability*, British Institute of Management, 1971; (with G. Terry Page) *The International Dictionary of Management*, Houghton, 1975. Editor, *Management Abstracts.*

AVOCATIONAL INTERESTS: Gardening, mountains.

* * *

JOHN, Robert

PERSONAL: Born in Nice, France; son of Andrias McNab (a merchant) and Victoria (Stephen) John; children: Dane, Haig. *Education:* Attended King's College, London. *Politics:* "Social Darwinian." *Religion:* Protestant. *Home:* 1080 Park Ave., New York, N.Y. 10028.

CAREER: International Council for Rhodesia, New York, N.Y., president, 1966-70, advisor to the council on American affairs, 1975—. *Member:* American Political Science Association, New York Academy of Sciences, Honourable Society of the Middle Temple (London).

WRITINGS: (With Sami Hadawi) *The Palestine Dairy*, New World Press, 1970, Volume I: *Britain's Involvement, 1914-1945*, Volume II: *United Nations Intervention, 1945-1948.* Contributor of several articles to *Middle East International.*

WORK IN PROGRESS: Rediscovering the American traditon in foreign policy; research on pre-revolutionary Russian science, on racial differences, and on eugenics.

* * *

JOHNSON, Alvin 1874-1971

December 18, 1874—June 7, 1971; American educator and humanist. Obituaries: *New York Times*, June 9, 1971; *Antiquarian Bookman*, July 19-26, 1971.

* * *

JOHNSON, Clive (White, Jr.) 1930-

PERSONAL: Born November 12, 1930, in Los Angeles, Calif.; son of Clive White (an attorney) and Gwendolyn (Peifer) Johnson. *Education:* University of California, Los Angeles, A.B., 1953; University of Missouri, M.A., 1959; Oxford University, special studies, 1964. *Religion:* Hindu. *Home:* 10866 Fruitland D.C., Studio City, Calif. 91604.

CAREER: United Press International, San Francisco, Calif., reporter, 1959-60; Pasadena Chamber of Commerce, Pasadena, Calif., publicity manager, 1960-61; *La Habra Star,* La Habra, Calif., reporter, 1961-63; teacher in public school in Ventura, Calif., 1963-64; University of California, Santa Barbara, instructor in English, 1964-65; monastic member of Vedanta Society of Southern California, Trabuco Canyon, 1965-75. *Military service:* U.S. Navy, 1953-56; became lieutenant junior grade.

WRITINGS: (Editor with Swami Prabhavananda) *Prayers and Meditations from the Scriptures of India,* Vedanta Press, 1967; (editor) *Vedanta: An Anthology of Hindu Scripture, Commentary and Poetry,* Harper, 1971. Also author of *The Way of Vedanta.* Contributor to *Ayran Path, Main Currents,* and *Prabuddha Bharata.* Former assistant editor, *Vedanta and the West.* Contributing editor, *Science of Mind Magazine,* 1976—.

SIDELIGHTS: Clive Johnson told *CA:* "If one can call one's 'career' God-realization, then indeed I have one. I lived for ten years at the Ramakrishna Monastery with this end uppermost in my mind; essentially, then, writing has been an avocation for me. I have hoped that through it I can perhaps transmit a few of the basic religious and philosophical concepts that have not only influenced my own life but are, I feel, rapidly gaining prominence in the lives of others. My attempt has always been, wherever possible, to present the practical in preference to the vaguely philosophical; the concrete in place of the abstract. The primary features of Vedanta are practical and concrete, I believe, and I have attempted to adhere to this in my writing and thinking.... At the present time I am hoping to combine my secular pursuits and strong spiritual interests into a viable and meaningful way of life."

* * *

JOHNSON, E(dward) W(arren) 1941-

PERSONAL: Born April 8, 1941, in Jamestown, N.Y.; son of Edward and Dorothy (Rowe) Johnson; married Leigh Koffman (divorced); children: Shane, Stacy. *Education:* Florida State University, B.S.; University of Iowa, M.F.A. *Home:* 204 Beltrees St., Dunedin, Fla.

CAREER: Western Illinois University, Macomb, instructor, 1965-69; free-lance writer, 1969—.

WRITINGS: Sinclair, Division of Public Services, Western Illinois University, 1967; (editor) *Contemporary American Thought: Readings for Composition,* Free Press, 1968;

(compiler) *Short Stories International,* Houghton, 1969; *Geoffrey: Power and the Image,* Division of Public Services, Western Illinois University, 1969; *The Winner,* Carthage Press, 1971; (with Tom Wolfe) *The New Journalism,* Harper, 1973.

WORK IN PROGRESS: A Rhetoric Book, to be published by Harper; *A Sliver of Glass,* a novel.

* * *

JOHNSON, H(arold) B(enjamin), Jr. 1931-

PERSONAL: Born March 17, 1931, in Hastings, Neb.; son of Harold Benjamin and Patricia (Armstrong) Johnson. *Education:* Cambridge University, B.A., 1953, M.A., 1960; University of Chicago, Ph.D., 1963. *Politics:* Republican. *Religion:* Presbyterian. *Office:* Department of History, University of Virginia, Charlottesville, Va. 22903.

CAREER: Yale University, New Haven, Conn., lecturer in history, 1965-68; University of Virginia, Charlottesville, assistant professor of colonial Latin American history, 1969-72, associate professor of Iberian history, 1972—, director of Center for Latin American Studies, 1970—. *Military service:* U.S. Army, 1953-55. *Member:* American Historical Association, Mediaeval Academy of America, Conference on Latin American History, American Association of University Professors, Phi Beta Kappa. *Awards, honors:* Social Science Research Council fellowships, 1964, 1970; Ford Foundation fellowship, 1965-66; Foreign Area Training fellowship, 1966; Fulbright-Hays fellowship, 1968.

WRITINGS: (Editor) *From Reconquest to Empire: The Iberian Background to Latin American History,* Knopf, 1970; *Rio de Janeiro: A Preliminary Inquiry into Money, Prices, and Wages, 1763-1823,* [Berkeley], 1973. Contributor of articles and reviews to *Annales, E.S.C., Hispanic American Historical Review, Americas,* and *American Historical Review.*

WORK IN PROGRESS: A study of social structure and change in Portuguese Estremadura from 1309-1369; research in European demography, 1600-1800.

SIDELIGHTS: H. B. Johnson spends his summers either in Rio de Janeiro, Brazil or Lisbon, Portugal. He told *CA* that he is a "strong supporter of Zero Population Growth (important movement)." *Avocational interests:* Sailing, swimming, fishing.†

* * *

JOHNSON, Harry L. 1929-

PERSONAL: Born April 18, 1929, in Saltville, Va.; son of Jerry Donald (a farmer) and Zella (Henderson) Johnson; married Carolyn F. Batson, March 17, 1973. *Education:* Emory and Henry College, B.A., 1952; University of Virginia, M.A., 1957, Ph.D., 1959. *Religion:* Methodist. *Home:* 4301 Franklin Rd., Nashville, Tenn. 37204. *Office:* Department of Finance, University of Tennessee, Knoxville, Tenn. 37916.

CAREER: Louisiana Polytechnic Institute, Ruston, associate professor of economics, 1959-60; University of Alabama, University, associate professor, 1960-61, professor of finance, 1961-64; University of Texas at Austin, associate professor of finance, 1964-66; University of Tennessee, Knoxville, professor of finance and head of department, 1966—. *Military service:* U.S. Army, 1950-54. *Member:* American Economic Association, Royal Economic Society, American Finance Association, Southern Finance Association, Southern Economic Association. *Awards, honors:* Ayres fellow at Stonier Graduate School of Banking, 1968.

WRITINGS: (With David G. Edens and Lorin A. Thompson) *The Labor Force in Virginia,* Bureau of Population and Economic Research, University of Virginia, 1959; (editor with Ernest W. Walker) *Monetary Issues of the 1960's,* Bureau of Business Research, University of Texas, 1968; (editor) *State and Local Tax Problems,* University of Tennessee Press, 1969. Contributor to economic, banking and tax journals.

WORK IN PROGRESS: A textbook, *Money and Banking.*

*   *   *

JOHNSON, Herbert J.   1933-

PERSONAL: Born March 25, 1933; son of Bernard F. and Grace A. (Roben) Johnson; married Carla V. Bruch, August 29, 1960; children: Sheridan Michelle, Michael Douglas. *Education:* University of Houston, B.B.A., 1956, M.B.A., 1958; Ohio State University, Ph.D., 1965. *Politics:* Independent. *Religion:* Roman Catholic.

CAREER: Certified public accountant in Texas, 1956-71; University of Texas at Arlington, chairman of department of business administration, beginning 1970. *Member:* Academy of Management.

WRITINGS: (With Billy J. Hodge) *Management and Organizational Behavior: A Multidimensional Approach,* Wiley, 1970.

WORK IN PROGRESS: With Hodge, *Management and Organization Behavior: Cases and Incidents.*††

*   *   *

JOHNSON, Keith B(arnard)   1933-

PERSONAL: Born January 5, 1933, in California, Pa.; son of Everett (a carpenter) and Fannie June (Barnard) Johnson; married Marietta Welch, August 24, 1962; children: Seth Yen, Bradley Keith. *Education:* State University of New York College of Environmental Science Forestry at Syracuse University, B.S., 1955; Washington University, St. Louis, Mo., M.B.A., 1959, D.B.A., 1963. *Politics:* Independent. *Home:* Mulberry Rd., Mansfield Center, Conn. 06250. *Office:* School of Business Administration, University of Connecticut, Storrs, Conn. 06268.

CAREER: University of Connecticut, School of Business Administration, Storrs, assistant professor, 1963-67, associate professor, 1967-74, professor of finance, 1974—, acting head of finance department, 1967-69. Staff economist and assistant director, Institute Investor Study, U.S. Securities and Exchange Commission, 1969-70. *Military service:* U.S. Army, 1955-57. U.S. Army Reserve, 1957-59; became sergeant. *Member:* American Finance Association, Financial Management Association (vice-president, 1976), Hartford Society of Financial Analysts, Eastern Finance Association (president, 1975-76). *Awards, honors:* Ford Foundation summer research fellow at Harvard University, 1964, 1967.

WRITINGS: (Editor with Donald E. Fischer) *Readings in Contemporary Financial Management,* Scott, Foresman, 1969. Also author of *A Profile of Real Estate Financing by Large Commercial Banks in Connecticut;* author of study report for the U.S. Government Securities and Exchange Commission, 1971. Consulting editor, *Treasurer's Handbook,* Dow Jones-Irwin, 1976.

WORK IN PROGRESS: A research project on financing real estate; textbook on corporate finance and financial institutions.

JOHNSON, Nicholas 1934-

PERSONAL: Born September 23, 1934, in Iowa City, Iowa; son of Wendell A. L. (a professor of speech at University of Iowa) and Edna (Bockwoldt) Johnson; married Karen Mary Chapman, 1952; children: Julie, Sherman, Gregory. *Education:* University of Texas, B.A., 1956, LL.B. (with honors), 1958. *Politics:* Democrat. *Religion:* Unitarian Universalist. *Office:* National Citizens Committee for Broadcasting, 1346 Connecticut Ave. N.W., Washington, D.C. 20036.

CAREER: Admitted to Texas Bar, 1958, and to District of Columbia Bar and Bar of U.S. Supreme Court, both 1963; law clerk for Circuit Judge John R. Brown of U.S. Court of Appeals, 1958-59, and for U.S. Supreme Court Justice Hugo L. Black, 1959-60; University of California, Berkeley, acting associate professor of law, 1960-63; Covington & Burling (law firm), Washington, D.C., associate, 1963-64; U.S. Department of Commerce, Maritime Administration, Washington, D.C., administrator appointed by President Lyndon B. Johnson, 1964-66; Federal Communications Commission, Washington, D.C., commissioner, also appointed by President Johnson, 1966-73; National Citizens Committee for Broadcasting, Washington, D.C., chairperson and director, 1974—, director of Communications Lobby, 1975—. Adjunct professor of law, Georgetown University, 1971-73.

MEMBER: International Society for General Semantics (member of board of directors), Texas Bar Association, Phi Beta Kappa, Order of the Coif, Phi Delta Phi. *Awards, honors:* Named one of the ten outstanding young men of 1967 by U.S. Junior Chamber of Commerce; *New Republic* Public Defender Award, 1970.

WRITINGS: How to Talk Back to Your Television Set, Little, Brown, 1970; *Life before Death in the Corporate State,* University of California, Berkeley, 1970; *Test Pattern for Living,* Bantam, 1972. Also author of *Broadcasting in America,* 1973. Editor, *Texas Law Review,* 1957-58; member of board of editors, International Society for General Semantics.

SIDELIGHTS: "Nicholas Johnson doesn't affect all broadcasters the same way," Lawrence Laurent writes in the *Washington Post.* "At the mention of his name, some turn purple with rage, others lapse into eloquent profanity; some shout in outrage.... In private Nicholas Johnson is a most pleasant man. He has a wry, intelligent sense of humor, a courteous manner, and a respect for the opinions of others."

John Leonard of the *New York Times* comments on *How to Talk Back to Your Television Set:* "What this book makes clear is that Mr. Johnson is committed to the idea of broadcast licenses as a public trust; and to a role as regulatory commissioner or 'public defender' instead of industry apologist.... He is, in a sense, the last of the New Frontiersmen, young, bright, brash, apparently convinced that all our problems are simply social dysfunctions, susceptible to systems analysis and conventional democratic redress of grievances."

BIOGRAPHICAL/CRITICAL SOURCES: Newsweek, April 10, 1967; *New York Times,* March 5, 1970, June 12, 1971; *Washington Post,* March 9, 1970; *New Republic,* March 14, 1970; *Best Sellers,* March 15, 1970; *National Observer,* March 30, 1970; *Commentary,* June, 1970; *New York Times Book Review,* June 21, 1970; *Christian Science Monitor,* July 8, 1970.†

*   *   *

JOHNSON, Oliver A(dolph)   1923-

PERSONAL: Born February 16, 1923, in Everett, Wash.;

son of Gustaf A. and Olga (Toll) Johnson; married Carol Jeanne Pence, March 21, 1946; children: Julie Mae, Stuart Earle, Elizabeth Ann, Melinda Jean. *Education:* Linfield College, B.A., 1944; Yale University, M.A., 1950; Ph.D., 1951; Oxford University, graduate study, 1950-51. *Home:* 4381 Picacho Dr., Riverside, Calif. 92507. *Office:* Department of Philosophy, University of California, Riverside, Calif. 92502.

CAREER: Yale University, New Haven, Conn., instructor in philosophy, 1951-52; Institute for Philosophical Research, San Francisco, Calif., fellow, 1952-53; University of California, Riverside, assistant professor, 1953-59, associate professor, 1959-65, professor of philosophy, 1965—, chairman of department, 1963-71. *Military service:* U.S. Naval Reserve, active duty, 1943-46; became lieutenant junior grade. *Member:* American Philosophical Association (secretary-treasurer, Pacific division), Royal Institute of Philosophy.

WRITINGS: Ethics: A Source Book, Holt, 1958, published as *Ethics: Selections from Classical and Contemporary Writers,* 1965, 3rd edition, 1974; (editor with John Louis Beatty) *Heritage of Western Civilization,* Prentice-Hall, 1958, 3rd edition, 1971; *Rightness and Goodness,* Nijhoff, 1959; (editor) *Man and His World,* McKay, 1964; *Moral Knowledge,* Nijhoff, 1966; *The Moral Life,* Allen & Unwin, 1969, Humanities, 1970; *The Problem of Knowledge,* Nijhoff, 1974.

WORK IN PROGRESS: Scepticism and Cognitivism.

*   *   *

JOHNSON, R(obbin) S(inclair)   1946-

PERSONAL: Born September 13, 1946, in Minneapolis, Minn.; son of Melvin Leonard and Evelyn (Osterberg) Johnson; married Maren Swanson, June 27, 1970. *Education:* Yale University, B.A., 1968, graduate study in law; Oxford University, graduate study, 1968-70. *Religion:* Protestant. *Home:* 310 Wayside Rd., Hopkins, Minn. 55343.

AWARDS, HONORS: Rhodes scholar at Oxford University, 1968-70.

WRITINGS: More's "Utopia": Ideal and Illusion, Yale University Press, 1969; *Foreign Theses in British Libraries,* Standing Conference of National and University Libraries (Cardiff, Wales), 1971.

WORK IN PROGRESS: A thesis in political philosophy for Oxford University on concepts of authority, obligation, and rights; an article concerning the forms of argument and their correspondence to philosophies of action in Thomas More's *Utopia,* for publication in *Moreana,* a journal.†

*   *   *

JOHNSON, S(amuel) Lawrence   1909-

PERSONAL: Born August 16, 1909, in Tyne Dock, England; brought to United States in 1910, naturalized in 1930; son of Samuel and Florence (Woody) Johnson; married Alice Duncan, November 9, 1935; children: S. Thomas, Mrs. Robert Foulks, Lawrice Kay. *Education:* Carleton College, B.A., 1930; Andover Newton Theological School, M.Div., 1933; attended New England Conservatory of Music, Harvard University, and Hebrew University, Jerusalem. *Home:* 1430 John Wesley Cir., Birmingham, Ala. 35210.

CAREER: Ordained minister of Congregational Church, 1933; Pilgrim Congregational Church, Birmingham, Ala., pastor, beginning 1961, currently pastor emeritus. *Member:*

Philosophical Society of England (fellow), Society of Biblical Literature, National Association of Professors of Hebrew, Southern Association of Marriage Counselors, Masons, Rotary, Hi 12. *Awards, honors:* D.D., Piedmont College, 1954.

WRITINGS: "Come Unto Me," Said the Master, Department of the Ministry of Congregational Churches, 1949; *The Pig's Brother, and Other Children's Sermons,* Abingdon, 1970; *The Squirrel's Bank Account,* Abingdon, 1972; *Cats and Dogs Together,* Abingdon, 1975; *Captain Ducky,* Abingdon, 1976. Contributor of articles to *Christian Sun, Upper Room Disciplines,* and other periodicals.

WORK IN PROGRESS: Children's sermons.

*   *   *

JOHNSTON, A(aron) Montgomery   1915-

PERSONAL: Born December 26, 1915, in Harrisonburg, Va.; son of James Chapman (a professor and author) and Althea (a professor; maiden name, Loose) Johnston; married Pauline Brown (a teacher), November 20, 1941; children: James, John, Jane, Joseph. *Education:* Columbia University, B.S., M.A., 1939; University of Exeter, graduate study, 1936-37; University of Chicago, Ph.D., 1948. *Politics:* Democrat. *Religion:* Episcopalian. *Home:* 118 Herron Dr., Knoxville, Tenn. 37919. *Office:* Department of Education, University of Tennessee, Knoxville, Tenn. 37916.

CAREER: University of Tennessee, Knoxville, assistant professor, 1948-51, associate professor, 1951-56, professor of education, 1956—. Visiting professor at Pennsylvania State University, University of Maine, and San Jose State College (now University). Spent three months observing open curriculum schools in Britain, 1973. *Military service:* U.S. Army, 1942-46; became captain; received Bronze Star. *Member:* National Council for the Social Studies, National Education Association, National Society for the Study of Education, American Association of University Professors, Tennessee Education Association, Common Cause.

WRITINGS: The Relationship of Various Factors to Democratic and Autocratic Classroom Practices, University of Chicago Press, 1948; *Arithmetic in Tennessee: A Study of Teaching Practices Grades 1-8,* University of Tennessee, 1960; (editor with John U. Michaelis) *The Social Sciences: Foundations of the Social Studies,* Allyn & Bacon, 1965; (editor) *Priorities for Schools in Tennessee,* University of Tennessee Press, 1965; (with Paul C. Burns) *Research in Elementary School Curriculum,* Allyn & Bacon, 1970. Contributor to education journals.

WORK IN PROGRESS: Nation-wide survey and research on "teaching practices related to holidays and special events grades K-6"; research in procedures for humanizing education.

SIDELIGHTS: A. Montgomery Johnston told *CA:* "Strong emotions stemming from both real and vicarious experiences with children, teachers, and learning situations impel my writing in order to probe, clarify, and organize my thoughts and share them with others. Others of my writings start with university students' questions which I feel deserve careful and detailed answers. These answers expand into 'handouts', are hammered on the anvil of student discussions, and emerge as articles for publication.

"Too, I guess I gain understanding better through reading than through listening to talk, so I assume there are others, like me, who need to read and re-read a sentence and spin out its implications, and who are stimulated to activity through the printed word. Speech seems to be drowned out by trivia of radio, television, and conversation, while the written word remains to be re-read and shared with others. I lecture, make speeches, but I feel I reach so many more, and more effectively through my written words."

AVOCATIONAL INTERESTS: Tennis, stamps, coins, travel, music, crafts, politics.

* * *

JONAS, George 1935-

PERSONAL: Born June 15, 1935, in Budapest, Hungary; emigrated to Canada, 1956; son of George Maurice (a lawyer and composer) and Magda (Klug) Hubsch; married Sylvia Nemes (an assistant industrial psychologist), September, 1960 (divorced, 1974); married Barbara Amiel (a journalist); children: (first marriage) Alexander. *Education:* Attended Lutheran Gymnasium, Budapest, Hungary, eight years, and Institute of Art and Folklore, Budapest, two years. *Agent:* Katharine Brown, International Creative Management, 40 West 57th St., New York, N.Y. 10019. *Office:* c/o Canadian Broadcasting Corp., Box 500, Terminal A, Toronto, Ontario, Canada.

CAREER: Radio Budapest, Budapest, Hungary, editor, 1955-56; Canadian Broadcasting Corp., Toronto, Ontario, producer, 1962—, currently producer of television specials. *Member:* League of Canadian Poets (treasurer, 1969-70), Composers, Authors and Publishers Association of Canada, Poets and Writers, New York State Council on the Arts. *Awards, honors:* Canada Council short term grant, 1968, 1971, and 1974.

WRITINGS—Poems; all published by House of Anansi: *The Absolute Smile,* 1967; *The Happy Hungry Man,* 1970; *Cities,* 1973.

Plays: (Adaptor) "Of Mice and Men" (radio; adaptation of John Steinbeck's novel), produced on "CBC Stage," 1963; "To Cross a Bridge" (original radio script), produced on "CBC Matinee Theatre," 1964; "The Major" (television; based on story by Milovan Djilas), produced on "CBC Shoestring Theatre," 1964; "The European Lover" (libretto for comic opera), produced by Jason Ensemble for tour in Canada, 1966; "The Redl Affair" (original radio script), produced on "CBC Summer Stage," 1966; "The Agent Provocateur" (original radio script), produced by "CBC Summer Stage," 1966; "Fasting Friar" (radio; based on a novel by Edward McCourt), produced on "CBC Summer Stage," 1967; "Master and Man" (radio; based on a story by Tolstoy), produced on "CBC-FM Theatre," 1967; (adaptor) "Mr. Pym Passes By" (radio; from the play by A. A. Milne), produced on "CBC Summer Stage," 1967; "First and Vital Candle" (radio; based on a novel by Rudy Wiebe), produced on "CBC Stage," 1967; "Catullus" (original radio script), produced by CBC, 1967; "Tell His Majesty . . ." (original radio script), produced on "CBC Summer Stage," 1968; (translator and adaptor) "Ave Luna, Morituri Te Salutant" (from a poem by George Faludy), produced on "CBC Anthology," 1970; "The Glove" (libretto), first produced by The Canadian Opera Company, 1975, produced by CBC, 1975.

Contributor of poems, articles, and reviews to *Saturday Review, Prism International, Saturday Night, Tamarack Review, Canadian Forum, Exchange, Kayak, Quarry, Toronto Star, Maclean's, Books In Canada,* and other periodicals.

WORK IN PROGRESS: Peaceville North, a novel; *Push-*

kin, a stage play; *By Persons Unknown,* a documentary novel to be published by Macmillan; a fourth collection of poems, *New and Selected Poems.*

SIDELIGHTS: George Jonas told *CA:* "Politically, I've always felt that most of our problems in the West are nothing that a month in the Gulag wouldn't cure. The trick is not to conclude from this that we need the Gulag, but that we can only avoid it by seeing our problems in perspective."

Writing about George Jonas and three other Canadians in *Poetry* magazine, Margaret Atwood points out their differing techniques but unmistakable Canadian imprint, "something to do with space, sensed as vast, open, unconfining, and oppressive." About the *Absolute Smile,* she notes: "The spaces are between people. George Jonas's usual subject is himself, but he moves from an individual self with private histories to the self as representative urbanite . . . to the self as the very society under attack."

In Canada, Jonas has been the subject of two educational television films, "Robert Fulford in Conversation with George Jonas," 1968, and "Dennis Lee in Conversation with George Jonas," 1970, and a Canadian Broadcasting Corp. film, "Adrianne Clarkson Talks with George Jonas," 1970.

BIOGRAPHICAL/CRITICAL SOURCES: University of Toronto Quarterly, January, 1968; *Poetry,* June, 1969; *Canadian Literature,* summer, 1969.

* * *

JONES, Carolyn (Sue) 1932-

PERSONAL: Born April 28, 1932, in Amarillo, Tex.; daughter of John Joseph and Jeanette (Southern) Jones; married Aaron Spelling, April 2, 1953 (divorced, August 8, 1964); married Herbert Greene, December 19, 1968. *Education:* Studied at Pasadena Playhouse, three years. *Religion:* Jewish. *Residence:* Beverly Hills, Calif. *Agent:* Paul Gitlan, New York, N.Y.

CAREER: Actress on television, radio, stage, and in films. Has had major roles in "The Bachelor Party," "Marjorie Morningstar," "Man in the Net," "Last Train from Gun Hill," "A Hole in the Head," "Career," "Ice Palace," "How the West Was Won," "Heaven with a Gun," and other films; played Morticia for two seasons in the television series "The Addams Family," and has appeared in guest roles in other drama series; played Elvira in the musical "High Spirits," and toured for almost a year in the national company of Pinter's "The Homecoming." *Awards, honors:* Nominated for Academy Award (Academy of Motion Picture Arts and Sciences), 1957-58, for the role in "The Bachelor Party."

WRITINGS: Twice Upon a Time (novel), Trident, 1971; *Diary of a Food Addict* (novel), Grosset, 1974.

WORK IN PROGRESS: Collaborating with her husband, Herbert Greene, on a screenplay.

* * *

JONES, D(ouglas) G(ordon) 1929-

PERSONAL: Born January 1, 1929, in Bancroft, Ontario, Canada; son of Gordon W. and Arlene (Ford) Jones; married Betty Jane Kimbark; married second wife, Sheila Fischman (a translator), June 11, 1969; married third wife, Monique Baiel-Grandmangin; children: (first marriage) Stephen, Skyler, Tory, North. *Education:* McGill University, B.A., 1952; Queen's University at Kingston, M.A., 1954.

Religion: Anglican ("lapsed"). *Home address:* Box 356, Houghton St., North Hatley, Quebec, Canada. *Office:* Department of English, Faculty of Arts, University of Sherbrooke, Sherbrooke, Quebec, Canada.

CAREER: Royal Military College of Canada, Kingston, Ontario, lecturer in English, 1954-55; Ontario Agricultural College, Guelph, assistant professor of English, 1955-61; Bishop's University, Lennoxville, Quebec, assistant professor of English, 1961-63; University of Sherbrooke, Sherbrooke, Quebec, associate professor of English, 1963—.

WRITINGS: Frost on the Sun (poems), Contact Press, 1957; *The Sun Is Axeman* (poems), University of Toronto Press, 1960; *Phrases from Orpheus* (poems), Oxford University Press, 1967; *Butterfly on Rock: A Study of Themes and Images in Canadian Literature,* University of Toronto Press, 1970; *Synapses and Synaptosomes: Morphological Aspects,* Halsted, 1975. Also author of *Ellipse #13,* 1973.

*   *   *

JONES, F(rank) Lancaster   1937-

PERSONAL: Born January 12, 1937; son of Edgar Frederick and Olga (Jackson) Jones; married Rosemary Beadle, March 7, 1959; children: Bronwyn Ruth, Philip Lancaster, Penelope Anne. *Education:* University of Sydney, B.A. (honors), 1958; Australian National University, Ph.D., 1962. *Office:* Australian National University, P.O. Box 4, Canberra, Australian Capital Territory 2600, Australia.

CAREER: Australian Institute of Aboriginal Studies, Canberra, research officer in demography, 1962; Australian National University, Research School of Social Sciences, Canberra, 1963—, began as research fellow, currently professor, head of department of sociology, 1970-72. *Member:* International Sociological Association, American Sociological Association, Academy of Social Sciences in Australia. *Awards, honors:* Cavaliere dell-ordine al Merito della Repubblica Italiana.

WRITINGS: (Contributor) C. A. Price, editor, *The Study of Immigrants in Australia,* Australian National University Press, 1960; *A Demographic Survey of the Aboriginal Population of the Northern Territory, with Sepcial Reference to Bathurst Island Mission,* Australian Institute of Aboriginal Studies, 1963; *Dimensions of Urban Social Structure: The Social Areas of Melbourne,* University of Toronto Press, 1969; *The Structure and Growth of Australia's Aboriginal Population* (booklet), Australian National University Press, 1970; (with L. Broom) *A Blanket a Year,* Australian National University Press, 1973; (with Brown) *Opportunity and Attainment in Australia,* Stanford University Press, 1976. Contributor of more than twenty articles to Australian, American, and British sociology journals. Editor, *Australian and New Zealand Journal of Sociology;* member of editorial board, *International Journal of Comparative Sociology.*

WORK IN PROGRESS: A book on social mobility in Australia, based on large national survey.

*   *   *

JONES, Pirkle   1914-

PERSONAL: Born January 2, 1914, in Shreveport, La.; son of Alfred C. Jones (a fine cabinet maker); married Ruth-Marion Baruch (a photographer and writer), January 15, 1949. *Education:* San Francisco Art Institute (formerly California School of Fine Arts), photography major for three years, received certificate. *Politics:* Peace and Freedom Party. *Religion:* "None at this time." *Home and office:* 663 Lovell Ave., Mill Valley, Calif. 94941.

CAREER: Professional photographer; photography instructor, 1953-58; conducted and participated in many photographic workshops at University of California, Santa Cruz and Ansel Adams workshops in Yosemite, Calif.; represented in several major art museums, including Metropolitan Museum of Art and Museum of Modern Art, New York, N.Y., Amon Carter Museum of Western Art, Tex., Chicago Art Institute, and San Francisco Museum of Art. Member of Mill Valley Architectural Advisory Committee, 1963-67. *Military service:* U.S. Army, 1941-46; served as a warrant officer.

WRITINGS: (With wife, Ruth-Marion Baruch) *The Vanguard: A Photographic Essay on the Black Panthers,* Beacon Press, 1970. Also co-author with Dorothea Lange of photographic essay *Death of a Valley,* published as special issue of *Aperture* (magazine), August 3, 1960.

Producer of two portfolios of photography in limited editions, the first in commemoration of the tenth anniversary of the signing of the United Nations Charter, San Francisco, Calif., June 20, 1955, and the second with a foreword by Ansel Adams, Mill Valley, Calif., 1968.

WORK IN PROGRESS: A photographic study in depth on a counter culture community known as Gate Five in Sausalito, Calif., containing literary work by several people and over 150 photographs.

BIOGRAPHICAL/CRITICAL SOURCES: U.S. Camera Magazine, October, 1952; *Aperture,* Number 2, 1956; *Image,* March, 1957.

*   *   *

JONES, Robert O(wen)   1928-

PERSONAL: Born October 5, 1928; son of Morris Owen (in insurance) and Lillian (Strickland) Jones; married Norah Larsen, June 15, 1953; children: Mark, Donna, Nancy, Barbara, Robert. *Education:* Northwestern University, B.S., 1949, M.D., 1953. *Religion:* Episcopalian. *Address:* P.O. Box 1059, Georgetown, S.C. 29440. *Office:* Georgetown County Memorial Hospital, Georgetown, S.C.

CAREER: Georgetown County Memorial Hospital, Georgetown, S.C., radiologist, 1959—. *Military service:* U.S. Naval Reserve, 1955-57; became lieutenant. *Member:* Radiological Society of North America.

WRITINGS: A Theory of Thought Processes, Philosophical Library, 1959.

WORK IN PROGRESS: A Theory of Social Processes.

*   *   *

JONES, Scott N.   1929-

PERSONAL: Born June 23, 1929, in Salina, Kan.; son of Nathan Edward and Blanche Mary Jones; married Martha Craven (a painter), June 14, 1957; children: Scott Craven, Douglas Edward. *Education:* Ripon College, B.A., 1951; Virginia Theological Seminary, M.Div., 1954; Divinity School, University of Chicago, graduate study, 1954-55; St. Augustine's College, Canterbury, England, diploma (with honors), 1964. *Home:* 709 Foster, Evanston, Ill. 60201. *Office:* Episcopal Church, Northwestern University, 2010 Orrington, Evanston, Ill. 60201.

CAREER: Episcopal chaplain and lecturer at Northwestern University, Evanston, Ill., 1956—. *Member:* Academy of Religion and Mental Health, American Association for Higher Education, Episcopal Society for Ministry in Higher Education. *Awards, honors:* Danforth Foundation fellowship, 1963.

WRITINGS: Sex and the Now Generation, John Knox, 1969.

WORK IN PROGRESS: The Significant Sinner (a Christian apologetic for modern man).

SIDELIGHTS: Scott Jones has led several student study tours to Europe. He told *CA* that he is "motivated to communicate with the young and to unclutter Christianity from the countless wrong impressions concerning it. I take a moderate to liberal position on most things." *Avocational interests:* Politics.††

* * *

JONES, Thomas M(artin) 1916-

PERSONAL: Born November 18, 1916, in Yonkers, N.Y.; son of C. Hubert (a teacher) and Marian (Turnure) Jones; married Dorothy Simons (a secretary), February 1, 1941; children: Susan H., Martin C. *Education:* Earlham College, A.B., 1938; Haverford College, M.A., 1939; University of Pennsylvania, Ph.D., 1952. *Politics:* Democrat. *Religion:* Society of Friends. *Address:* Box 109, Lincoln University, Pa. 19352. *Office:* Department of History, Lincoln University, Lincoln University, Pa. 19352.

CAREER: Pacific College, Fresno, Calif., instructor in history, 1941-42; Reed College, Portland, Ore., instructor in history, 1942-43; Lincoln University, Lincoln University, Pa., 1946—, began as assistant professor, professor of history, 1959—, director of curriculum development, 1966—. *Member:* American Historical Association, Mediaeval Academy of America, American Association of University Professors. *Awards, honors:* Linbach Award for outstanding teaching, 1962; research travel grants, 1966, 1970.

WRITINGS: (Editor) *The Becket Controversy,* Wiley, 1970.

WORK IN PROGRESS: The Revolt of 1173-1174, a study of the revolt against Henry II led by his sons.

* * *

JORDAN, Robert Paul 1921-

PERSONAL: Born July 6, 1921, in Omaha, Neb.; son of Paul Hyde (a lawyer and newspaperman) and Lillian (Walters) Jordan; married Jane Carol Taylor, September 8, 1956; children: Robert, Jr., Meredith, Julia. *Education:* Attended Marquette University, 1940-42; George Washington University, B.A., 1947; American University, additional study, 1953-54. *Politics:* Independent. *Religion:* Presbyterian. *Home:* 9717 Brimfield Ct., Potomac, Md. 20854. *Office:* National Geographic Society, 17th and M Sts. N.W., Washington, D.C. 20036.

CAREER: Washington Post, Washington, D.C., 1947-61, began as copy boy, successively reporter, desk man, and assistant Sunday editor; *National Geographic,* Washington, D.C., assistant editor, 1962—. *Military service:* U.S. Army, Signal Corps, 1942-45. U.S. Air Force, 1951-53, became first lieutenant. *Member:* White House Correspondents Association, Sigma Delta Chi, Overseas Writers, Washington Press Club.

WRITINGS: (Contributor) Paul M. Angle, compiler and editor, *Prairie State,* University of Chicago Press, 1968; *The Civil War,* National Geographic Society, 1969. Contributor to magazines.

* * *

JORDAN, Stello 1914-

PERSONAL: Born December 17, 1914, in New York, N.Y.; son of Michael (a manufacturer) and Ida (Schmid) Jordan; married Matilda Campagna (a legal secretary), August 17, 1941. *Education:* Attended City College (now City College of the City University of New York), 1931-33; Roosevelt Aviation School, diplomas in aircraft design and mechanics, 1940; attended Columbia University, New York University, and Queens College of the City University of New York. *Politics:* Independent. *Religion:* Roman Catholic (far east rite). *Home:* 87-15 204th St., Hollis, N.Y. 11423.

CAREER: American Export Airlines, La Guardia Field, N.Y., airline inspector, 1943-44; Sperry Rand Corp., Great Neck, N.Y., department head of reports and parts documentation, 1944-67; Data Communication, Inc., New York, N.Y., head of management services, 1967-70; housing manager for large residential developments, 1974—. Real estate trustee, 1954—. Human communications specialist, teacher and lecturer on technical publications, and symposium director for various national trade associations. Major awards judge for science fairs, 1958—. *Member:* Society of Technical Writers and Publishers (former president, 1964-65), Society of Logistics Engineers (charter member), Society for Technical Communication (associate fellow).

WRITINGS: (Editor with others) *Handbook of Technical Writing Practices,* two volumes, Wiley, 1970. Contributor to journals. Member of editorial board, *Journal of Technical Writing and Communication.*

AVOCATIONAL INTERESTS: Investments.

* * *

JORSTAD, Erling (Theodore) 1930-

PERSONAL: Born October 13, 1930, in Kenyon, Minn.; son of Oscar Edwin and Laura (Voxland) Jorstad; married Helen Haban (a college teacher), August 25, 1956; children: Eric, Laura. *Education:* St. Olaf College, B.A., 1952; Harvard University, M.A., 1953; University of Wisconsin, Ph.D., 1957. *Religion:* Lutheran. *Home:* 1300 Washington, Northfield, Minn. 55057. *Office:* Department of History, St. Olaf College, Northfield, Minn. 55057.

CAREER: St. Olaf College, Northfield, Minn., instructor, 1956-58, assistant professor, 1958-61, associate professor, 1961-69, professor of history, 1969—. *Military service:* Minnesota National Guard, 1955-57; became second lieutenant. *Member:* American Historical Association, Organization of American Historians, American Association of University Professors, American Society of Church History, Society for Religion in Higher Education, Upper Midwest Historical Society (secretary, 1958-60), Phi Beta Kappa. *Awards, honors:* Minnesota Historical Society research fellowship, 1959; American Association of State and Local History grant-in-aid, 1960; Danforth Foundation research fellowship, 1963-64; American Philosophical Society research grant, 1970-71.

WRITINGS: The Politics of Doomsday: The Fundamentalists of the Far Right, Abingdon, 1970; *The Instant Giant: American Radicalism in the 1960's,* College Notes, 1970; *Love It Or Leave It?: A Dialog on Loyalty,* Augsburg, 1972; *That New-Time Religion: The Jesus Revival in America,* Augsburg, 1973; *The Holy Spirit in Today's Church,* Abingdon, 1973; *Bold in the Spirit: Lutheran Charismatic Renewal in America,* Augsburg, 1974. Contributor to *Dialog, Christian Scholar, Lutheran Quarterly, Reason, Concern, Event, Catholic World,* and *Minnesota History;* also contributor of reviews to *Journal of Presbyterian History, Lutheran Quarterly, Christianity Today,* and *Fides et Historia.*

WORK IN PROGRESS: The Frontier within Me: Christian Resources for Pilgrimhood.

SIDELIGHTS: Erling Jorstad's teaching fields are American intellectual history and American Christianity. *Avocational interests:* Classical music, aquatic sports, and chess.

* * *

JOSE, James R(obert) 1939-

PERSONAL: Surname rhymes with "those"; born January 7, 1939, in Pittsburgh, Pa.; son of J. Fred (a physician) and Helen (Hunter) Jose; married Joyce Ann Mosser, June 10, 1961; children: Anna Mansfield, Andrew Douglass. *Education:* Mount Union College, B.A., 1960; American University, M.A., 1962, Ph.D., 1968. *Home:* 1508 Elmira St., Williamsport, Pa. 17701. *Office:* Lycoming College, Williamsport, Pa. 17701.

CAREER: Mount Union College, Alliance, Ohio, instructor in political science, registrar, and administrative assistant to academic dean, 1963-65; American University, School of International Service, Washington, D.C., assistant professor of international relations and assistant dean, 1965-70; Lycoming College, Williamsport, Pa., dean of the college, 1970—. Part-time faculty member, University of Maryland, 1968-69; lecturer at U.S. Military Academy and U.S. Foreign Service Institute. *Military service:* U.S. Army Reserve, 1962-68. *Member:* American Political Science Association, Phi Kappa Phi, Pi Gamma Mu, Pi Sigma Alpha, Delta Phi Epsilon. *Awards, honors:* Named one of Outstanding Young Men in America by U.S. Junior Chamber of Commerce, 1967.

WRITINGS: An Inter-American Peace Force Within the Framework of the Organization of American States: Advantages, Impediments, and Implications, Scarecrow, 1970; (contributor) A. A. Said, editor, *America's World Role in the 70's,* Prentice-Hall, 1970. Contributor, *Liberal Education,* 1974.

WORK IN PROGRESS: The Political Dynamics of International Organization, a textbook.

* * *

JOSEY, E(lonnie) J(unius) 1924-

PERSONAL: Born January 20, 1924, in Norfolk, Va.; son of Willie J. and Frances (Bailey) Josey; married Dorothy Johnson, September 11, 1954 (divorced); children: Elaine Jacqueline. *Education:* Howard University, A.B., 1949; Columbia University, M.A., 1950; State University of New York at Albany, M.S.L.S., 1953. *Politics:* Democrat. *Religion:* Protestant. *Home:* 12C Old Hickory Dr., Albany, N.Y. 12204. *Office:* Bureau of Specialist Library Services, Division of Library Development, New York State Education Department, Albany, N.Y. 12230.

CAREER: Columbia University Libraries, New York City, desk assistant, 1950-52; New York Public Library, New York City, technical assistant, 1952; Free Library of Philadelphia, Philadelphia, Pa., librarian, 1953-54; Savannah State College, Savannah, Ga., instructor in social science, 1954-55; Delaware State College, Dover, librarian and assistant professor of library science, 1955-59; Savannah State College, librarian and associate professor of library science, 1959-66; New York State Education Department, Division of Library Development, Albany, associate in academic and research libraries, 1966-68, chief of Bureau of Academic and Research Libraries, 1968-76, chief of Bureau of Specialist Library Services, 1976—. Member of board of managers,

Savannah Public Library, 1962-66. *Military service:* U.S. Army, 1943-46.

MEMBER: American Library Association (member of council, 1970-74; chairman of black caucus, 1970-71), Association of College and Research Libraries (chairman of committee on community use of academic libraries, 1965-69), Association for the Study of Afro-American Life and History, American Academy of Political and Social Science, National Association for the Advancement of Colored People (Georgia State youth adviser, 1960-66), New York Library Association, Kappa Phi Kappa, Alpha Phi Omega. *Awards, honors:* Award from national office of National Association for the Advancement of Colored People, 1965, and from Georgia Conference, 1966, for service to youth; Savannah State College Award, 1967, for distinguished service to librarianship; award from *Journal of Library History,* 1970, for best piece of historical research to appear in the *Journal* in 1969; L.H.D., Shaw University, 1973.

WRITINGS: The Black Librarian in America, Scarecrow, 1970; (contributor) Charles Trinker, editor, *Teaching for Better Use of Libraries,* Shoe String, 1970; *What Black Librarians Are Saying,* Scarecrow, 1972; *New Dimensions for Academic Library Service,* Scarecrow, 1975; (co-editor) *A Century of Service: Librarianship in the United States and Canada,* American Library Association, 1976. Publications include library directories and surveys. Contributor of about 125 articles and reviews to *Savannah Tribune, Savannah Herald,* and to library, history, and education journals.

WORK IN PROGRESS: Black Librarians and Libraries: A Source Book, for Books Unlimited.

* * *

JOSHUA, Wynfred 1930-

PERSONAL: Born December 23, 1930, in Djakarta, Indonesia; daughter of David (a businessman) and Mathilde (de Vries) Joshua. *Education:* University of Amsterdam, B.A., 1953; Western Reserve University (now Case Western Reserve University), M.A., 1956; University of Pittsburgh, Ph.D., 1964. *Religion:* Roman Catholic. *Home:* 4000 Cathedral Ave. N.W., Apt. 731B, Washington, D.C., 20016. *Office:* Stanford Research Institute, 1611 North Kent St., Arlington, Va. 22209.

CAREER: Brookings Institution, Washington, D.C., research associate, 1964-66; Georgetown Research Project, Washington, D.C., senior research analyst, 1966-68; Stanford Research Institute, Arlington, Va., senior political scientist, 1968—. *Member:* American Political Science Association, U.S. Naval Institute.

WRITINGS: (With Stephen P. Gibert) *Arms for the Third World: Soviet Military Aid Diplomacy,* Johns Hopkins Press, 1969; *Soviet Military Aid Diplomacy,* Johns Hopkins Press, 1969; *Soviet Penetration into the Middle East,* National Strategy Information Center, 1970, revised edition, 1971; (with Gibert) *Guns and Rubles,* American-Asian Educational Exchange, 1970; (with Walter F. Hahn) *Nuclear Politics: America, France, and Britain,* Sage Publications, 1973; *Nuclear Weapons and the Atlantic Alliance,* National Strategy Information Center, 1973. Contributor of articles to professional journals.†

* * *

JOYCE, Mary Rosera 1930-

PERSONAL: Born June 20, 1930, in Coleman, Wis.; daughter of Paul E. (a farmer) and Saba (Ausloos) Rosera;

married Robert E. Joyce (a professor of philosophy), August 12, 1961. *Education:* Mount Mary College, Milwaukee, part-time student, 1948-54; Saint Xavier College, Chicago, B.A., 1957; Loyola University, Chicago, M.A., 1959; St. Louis University, additional study, 1959-61. *Religion:* Roman Catholic. *Home:* 1248 13th Ave. N., St. Cloud, Minn. 56301.

CAREER: College of St. Benedict, St. Joseph, Minn., instructor in philosophy, 1963-65; St. Cloud School of Nursing, St. Cloud, Minn., instructor in psychology and sociology, 1965-67. Minnesota Citizens Concerned for Life, member of board of directors, 1968—, coordinator for central Minnesota region, 1970-73.

WRITINGS: (With husband, Robert E. Joyce) *New Dynamics in Sexual Love: A Revolutionary Approach to Marriage and Celibacy,* St. Johns University Press, 1970; *The Meaning of Contraception,* Alba, 1970; (with R. Joyce) *Let Us Be Born: The Inhumanity of Abortion,* Franciscan Herald, 1970; *Love Responds to Life: The Challenge of Humanae Vitae,* Prow Books, 1971. Contributor to *America, Marriage,* and other periodicals.

WORK IN PROGRESS: The Friendship of Man and Woman.

AVOCATIONAL INTERESTS: Art, music, poetry.

* * *

JOYCE, Robert E(dward) 1934-

PERSONAL: Born May 13, 1934, in Chicago, Ill.; son of Peter J. (an electrician) and Mildred (Wurtz) Joyce; married Mary Rosera (a writer), August 12, 1961. *Education:* St. Mary of the Lake Seminary, Mundelein, Ill., B.A., 1957; University of Notre Dame, additional study, 1959-61; DePaul University, M.A., 1960. *Religion:* Roman Catholic. *Home:* 1248 13th Ave. N., St. Cloud, Minn. 56301. *Office:* Department of Philosophy, St. John's University, Collegeville, Minn. 56321.

CAREER: University of Notre Dame, Notre Dame, Ind., instructor in philosophy, 1961-62; St. John's University, Collegeville, Minn., assistant professor, 1962-70, associate professor of philosophy, 1970—, chairman of joint department of philosophy, St. John's University/College of St. Benedict, 1971-74. *Member:* Metaphysical Society of America, American Catholic Philosophical Association, Minnesota Philosophical Society (president, 1966-67).

WRITINGS: (With wife, Mary Joyce) *New Dynamics in Sexual Love: A Revolutionary Approach to Marriage and Celibacy,* St. John's University Press, 1970; (with M. Joyce) *Let Us Be Born: The Inhumanity of Abortion,* Franciscan Herald, 1970. Contributor to education and religious journals.

WORK IN PROGRESS: Metaphysics for Christian Renewal; also a study of the ethical in human life issues: origin, termination, organ transplantation, and others; development of the philosophy of natural family planning.

* * *

JUCKER, Sita 1921-

PERSONAL: Born April 21, 1921, in Switzerland; daughter of Hans (manager of a factory) and Delly (Kaehr) Bruder; married Werner Jucker (an architect), October 11, 1947; children: Andreas, Thomas. *Education:* Studied at Ecole des Beaux Arts, Geneva, Ecole Paul Colin, Paris, and Kunstgewerbeschule, Basel. *Home:* Greifenseestrasse 56, Schwerzenbach, Switzerland.

CAREER: Artist and illustrator; does book illustrating and bookcovers. *Member:* Gesellschaft Schweizerischer Malerinnen, Verband Schweizerischer Grafiker.

WRITINGS: Squaps, der Mondling (picture book with text by Ursina Ziegler), Artemis-Verlag, 1969, translation by Barbara Kowal Gallob published as *Squaps, the Moonling,* Atheneum, 1969; (with Ziegler) *Peppino,* Artemis-Verlag, 1971, translation published by Atheneum, 1971; *Omepul* (picture book with text by H. C. Artmann), Artemis Verlag, 1973, translation published as *Angus,* Methuen, 1973; *Hen Laugfuss* (picture book with text by Regine Schindler), Artemis Verlag, 1975, published as *Mr. Longfoot,* Methuen, 1975.

Illustrator: Dino Larese, *Regula,* Verlag Sauerlaender; Margrit Studer, *Mein Buch,* Flamberg Verlag; Hans Schranz, *Was kuemmert mich Maeni,* Flamberg Verlag; Annemarie Meyer-Dalbert, *Hexlein hilftsuchen,* Rascher-Verlag; Alois Dickerhoff, *Wendelau und Gueldenhaar,* Fussli-Verlag; Ursula Geiger, *Komm bald Christine,* Blaukreuz-Verlag; Colette Buechergilde Gutenberg, *Die Fessel;* Gobi Walter, *D'Wiehnachtsgschicht,* Zwingli-Verlag; Gunvor Fossum, *In Kukeberg geschieht etwas,* Verlag H. R. Sauerlaender & Co.; Roman Brodmann, *Tagebuch mit Aphrodite,* Turicum-Verlag; Johanna Stratenwerth, *Arma und der Reiter,* Verlag Ernst Kaufman; Olga Meyer, *Tapfer und treu,* Verlag Sauerlaender; Heinrich Ryssel, *Sterne und Sternchen,* Werner Classen-Verlag; Regine Schindler, *Auf der Shassenach Weihnachteh,* Kaufmann Verlag. Also illustrator of seven books by Jenifer Wayne for Albert Mueller-Verlag, and Heinemann; illustrator of elementary texts and other books.

* * *

JUDD, Gerrit P(armele) 1915-1971

May 15, 1915—April 16, 1971; American historian and author of books on Hawaii. Obituaries: *Washington Post,* April 17, 1971; *New York Times,* April 17, 1971. (See index for *CA* sketch)

* * *

JUKES, (James Thomas) Geoffrey 1928-

PERSONAL: Born August 28, 1928, in Accrington, England; son of Walter James (a mechanic) and Margaret (Herbert) Jukes; married Eunice M. Young, January 9, 1954; children: Michael, David, Anthony. *Education:* Wadham College, Oxford, M.A., 1953. *Politics:* "Noisy Centre." *Home:* 24 Hawker St., Torrens, Australian Capital Territory 2607, Australia. *Office:* Australian National University, Canberra, Australian Capital Territory 2601, Australia.

CAREER: Was in public service in England, working in Ministry of Defense and Foreign Office, until 1967; senior fellow in international relations at Institute of Advanced Studies, Australian National University, Canberra, 1967—. Vice-president, Australian Commission for Military History. *Military service:* British Army, Royal Electrical and Mechanical Engineers, 1947-49. *Member:* International Institute for Strategic Studies, Australian Political Science Association, Australian Society of Authors.

WRITINGS: The Strategic Situation in the 1980's, Australian National University Press, 1968; *Stalingrad: The Turning Point,* Ballantine, 1968; *Kursk: The Clash of Armor,* Ballantine, 1969; *The Defense of Moscow,* Ballantine, 1970; *Carpathian Disaster,* Ballantine, 1971; *The Development of Soviet Strategic Thinking since 1945,* Australian

National University, 1972; *The Soviet Union in Asia,* University of California Press, 1973. Contributor to Purnell's *History of the First World War* and *History of the Second World War;* contributor of articles and reviews to *Canberra Times, Australian, Australian Outlook, World Review,* and other journals.

WORK IN PROGRESS: Research on arms control and the strategic balance, and Soviet foreign policy.

SIDELIGHTS: Geoffrey Jukes told *CA* he is "interested in the prevention of war." He speaks six languages—Russian, German, French, Italian, modern Greek, and Japanese— and can read Bulgarian, Serbo-Croat, Polish, Latin, as well as ancient, New Testament, and medieval Greek. Jukes' books have been published in French, Dutch, Italian, Swedish, Portuguese, Spanish, and Japanese. He has been a successful rowing coach in both England and Australia.

*   *   *

KADLER, Eric H(enry) 1922-

PERSONAL: Born May 17, 1922, in Pilsen, Czechoslovakia; naturalized U.S. citizen in 1956; son of Thomas (an engineer) and Mary (Marik) Kadler; married Christine Ross (a professor), October 18, 1952; children: Karen, Marcia. *Education:* University of Prague, M.S., 1948; University of London, graduate study, 1949-52; University of Michigan, M.A., 1957, Ph.D., 1959. *Religion:* Episcopal. *Home:* 895 Hiawatha Dr., Mt. Pleasant, Mich. 48858. *Office:* Department of Foreign Languages, Central Michigan University, Mt. Pleasant, Mich. 48858.

CAREER: St. Christopher's, Hove, Sussex, England, French teacher, 1949-51; J. L. Hudson Co., Detroit, Mich., assistant buyer, 1952-54; Ohio University, Athens, Ohio, assistant professor of French and Spanish, 1959-60; Lycoming College, Williamsport, Pa., professor of linguistics, Russian, and French, 1960-70; Central Michigan University, Mt. Pleasant, professor of French and linguistics and chairman of department of foreign languages, 1970—. *Member:* American Association of Teachers of French (secretary-treasurer, 1964-65, president, 1966-68), American Council on Teaching Foreign Languages, Modern Language Association of America, American Association of University Professors, Rotary Club (Williamsport). *Awards, honors:* Fulbright fellowship, 1964.

WRITINGS: Literary Figures in French Drama (1784-1834), Nijhoff, 1969; *Linguistics and the Teaching of Foreign Languages,* Van Nostrand, 1970. Contributor to *French Review, Romance Notes, Lock Haven Bulletin, Modern Language Journal,* and *Etudes de linguistique appliquee.*

WORK IN PROGRESS: Studies in contrastive grammar and applied linguistics.

*   *   *

KAHLER, Erich Gabriel 1885-1970

October 14, 1885—June 28, 1970; Czech-born cultural historian and educator. Obituaries: *New York Times,* June 30, 1970; *Antiquarian Bookman,* July 20-27, 1970; *Books Abroad,* spring, 1971. (See index for *CA* sketch)

*   *   *

KAHNWEILER, Daniel-Henry 1884-
(Daniel Henry)

PERSONAL: Born June 25, 1884, in Mannheim, Germany;

became a French citizen in 1937 but was deprived of his citizenship during the Petain regime; son of Julius (a stockbroker) and Betty (Neumann) Kahnweiler; married Lucie Godon, November 4, 1904 (deceased). *Education:* Attended schools in Stuttgart, Germany, where his family moved in 1889. *Home:* 53 bis quai des Grands-Augustins, Paris 6, France. *Office:* Galerie Louise Leiris, 47 rue de Monceau, Paris 8, France.

CAREER: Art dealer, 1907—, and art historian. Kahnweiler started collecting the prints of Manet, Lautrec, Cezanne, and other painters while employed as a stockbroker's clerk in Paris, 1902-05; lived in London, 1905-07, working for an uncle who had mining interests in South Africa; refusing to go to South Africa on business, he returned to Paris in 1907 to open his first gallery on rue Vignon, where he came to know Derain, Picasso, Braque, Gris, Leger, and the sculptor Manolo; war broke out while Kahnweiler was traveling in Italy in 1914, and he and his wife spent the next six years in Switzerland; back in Paris he opened a gallery with Andre Simon and Louise Godon Leiris, his sister-in-law, which operated under Simon's name, 1920-41; the Kahnweilers left Paris once again during the German Occupation and Vichy regime, this time living more or less secretly in the south of France from 1940 until 1944 when they returned to Paris; Galerie Simon closed in 1941, but Louise Leiris subsequently reopened it under her own name with Kahnweiler as director, 1944-57, and co-director with Maurice Jardot, 1957—.

AWARDS, HONORS: An exhibition of Jaun Gris' works was organized in London by Marlborough Fine Art Ltd. in 1958 in recognition of Kahnweiler's fifty years in the art world; Prix Broquette-Gonin of the French Academy, 1964; received the title of professor from the Government of Baden-Wuertemberg, Germany, 1964; an exhibition, "Hommage a D.-H. Kahnweiler," was held in Mannheim, 1970; Dr. H. C., University of Kaiserslautern, 1974.

WRITINGS: (Under name Daniel Henry) *Der Weg zum Kubismus,* Delphin Verlag, 1920, enlarged edition (under name Daniel-Henry Kahnweiler) with a new preface by the author and an added chapter on Juan Gris, Verlag Niggli and Verlag Hatje, 1958; (under name Daniel Henry) *Maurice de Vlaminck,* Klinkhardt & Biermann, 1920; (under name Daniel Henry) *Juan Gris,* Klinkhardt & Biermann, 1929; *Juan Gris: Sa vie, son oeuvre, ses ecrits,* Gallimard, 1946, revised edition, 1968, translation by Douglas Cooper published as *Juan Gris: His Life and Work,* Curt Valentin (New York), 1947, revised edition, Abrams, 1969; (contributor) Maurice Jardot and Curt Martin, *Die Meister Franzoesischer Malerei der Gegenwart,* Woldemar Klein, 1947; *The Rise of Cubism* (booklet; translation by Henry Aronson of Kahnweiler's writings), Wittenborn, 1949; *Les Sculptures de Picasso,* Editions du Chene, 1949, translation by A.D.H. Sylvester published as *The Sculptures of Picasso,* Rodney Phillips (London), 1949.

Paul Klee, 1879-1940 (text in French, English, and German), Braun, 1950; *Les Annees heroiques du cubisme* (text in French, English, and German), Braun, 1950; (compiler and editor) *Letters of Juan Gris: 1913-1927,* translation by Douglas Cooper, limited edition privately printed in London, 1955; *Picasso: Keramik, Ceramic* (text in German, English, and French), Fackeltraeger-Verlag, 1957; (with others) *Picasso at Vallauris* (translation by Serge Huges of special edition of *Verve,* "Picasso a Vallauris"), Raynal, 1959; *Mes Galeries et mes Peintres: Entretiens avec Francis Cremieux* (autobiographical), Gallimard, 1961, translation by Helen Weaver published as *My Galleries and Painters,* introduction by John Russell, Viking, 1971; *Confessions esthetiques* (collection of published and unpublished writings), Gallimard, 1963; (contributor) Mario de Micheli, *Scritti di Picasso,* Feltrinelli, 1964; (contributor) Hannes Reinhardt, *Das Selbstportrait,* Christian Wegner, 1967; *Aesthetische Betrachtungen* (includes many of the selections in *Confessions esthetiques* and others), Dumont Schauberg, 1968; *Der Gegenstand der Aesthetik,* introduction by Wilhelm Weber, Heinz Moos Verlag (Munich), 1971.

Author of preface or postface: Gertrude Stein, *Painted Lace and Other Pieces,* Yale University Press, 1955; Gertrude Stein, *Autobiographie d'Alice Toklas,* Lucien Mazenod, 1965; Kay Helen, *Picasso's World of Children,* Doubleday, 1965; Werner Hoffmann, *Henri Laurens: Sculptures* (text in German, French, and English), Hatje (Stuttgart), 1971.

Work represented in many anthologies, including *From Baudelaire to Surrealism,* Wittenborn, 1950, and *Pablo Picasso: Wort und Bekenntis,* Verlag der Arche, 1954. Author of preface, notes, or essays for many exhibition catalogues, including many in recent years for Picasso shows; the catalogues cover exhibitions at his and other galleries in France, at New York galleries and San Francisco Museum, and shows in most major European cities, Jerusalem, Japan, Australia, and New Zealand.

Contributor to *Dictionnaire Benezit, Art News Annual* (New York), *Jahrbuch der Jungen Kunst,* and other yearbooks. Articles include interviews with Picasso published in *Observer,* and contributions to the major French art and architecture journals and to other periodicals in United States, England, Germany, Switzerland, Sweden, and Spain.

SIDELIGHTS: Daniel-Henry Kahnweiler's parents had intended him for banking, but he was so immersed in the art world by the age of twenty-three that his biographical notes for that period make mention of each artist he met and sometimes even the circumstances of the meeting. In 1907, for instance, he bought the works of Derain, Vlaminck, Van Dongen, and Braque, and made the acquaintance of Picasso, which led to Kahnweiler becoming his dealer in Paris. In 1908, in connection with his exhibition of Braque's pictures (rejected by the Salon d'Automne), the word "cubes" was used for the first time. The following year he published Guillaume Apollinaire's *L'Enchanteur pourrisant,* with illustrations by Derain, the first of almost forty titles issued under the names of galleries he has directed. The bibliography of his own writings extends to more than 160 items, excluding the multiple translations and reprints of many.

BIOGRAPHICAL/CRITICAL SOURCES: Werner Spies, editor, *Pour Daniel-Henry Kahnweiler,* Wittenborn, 1965; Hannes Reinhardt, *Das Selbstportrait,* Christian Wegner, 1967; *New York Times,* July 9, 1971.

*　　*　　*

KAIN, John F(orrest) 1935-

PERSONAL: Born November 9, 1935, in Fort Wayne, Ind.; son of Forrest Morgan and Bessie (Wilder) Kain; married Mary Fan Kiracofe, August 17, 1957; children: Mary Jo, Joanna. *Education:* Bowling Green State University, A.B. (with honors in economics and political science), 1957; University of California, Berkeley, M.A. and Ph.D., 1961. *Home:* 66 Watson Rd., Belmont, Mass. 02178. *Office:* Department of Economics, 235 Littauer Center, Harvard University, Cambridge, Mass. 02138.

CAREER: University of California, Berkeley, Extension

Division, lecturer in business administration and economics, 1959-61; RAND Corp., Santa Monica, Calif., research economist, 1961-62; U.S. Air Force Academy, Colorado Springs, Colo., associate professor of economics with rank of first lieutenant, 1962-65; Harvard University, Cambridge, Mass., assistant professor, 1966-67, associate professor, 1968-69, professor of economics, 1969—. Senior staff member, National Bureau of Economic Research, 1967—; consultant to Department of Housing and Urban Development, 1966-68, and to Department of Health, Education, and Welfare and U.S. Commission on Civil Rights, 1968. *Member:* American Economic Association, American Statistical Association, Econometric Society, Regional Science Association.

WRITINGS: (With John R. Meyer and Martin Wohl) *The Urban Transportation Problem,* Harvard University Press, 1965; (editor) *Race and Poverty: The Economics of Discrimination,* Prentice-Hall, 1969; (editor with Meyer) *Essays in Regional Economics,* Harvard University Press, 1971; (with Gregory K. Ingram and Royce Ginn) *The Detroit Prototype of the NBER Urban Simulation Model,* National Bureau of Economic Research, 1972; (with John M. Quigley) *Housing Markets and Racial Discrimination: A Micro-Economic Analysis,* National Bureau of Economic Research, 1975; *Essays on Urban Spatial Structure,* Ballinger, 1975.

Contributor: *Transportation Economics,* Columbia University Press, 1965; Thomas A. Goldman, editor, *Cost-Effectiveness Analysis: New Approaches in Decision Making,* Praeger, 1967; Leo F. Schnore and Henry Fagin, editors, *Urban Research and Policy Planning,* Sage Publications, 1967; James Q. Wilson, editor, *The Metropolitan Enigma: Inquiries into the Nature and Dimensions of America's Urban Crisis,* Harvard University Press, 1968; *Rural Poverty in the United States,* U.S. Government Printing Office, 1968; Daniel P. Moynihan, editor, *Toward a National Urban Policy,* Basic Books, 1970; D. P. Moynihan and Frederick Mosteller, editors, *On Equality of Educational Opportunity,* Random House, 1970.

Author or co-author of urban transportation reports for U.S. Government, RAND Corp., and Commonwealth Bureau of Roads, Melbourne, Australia. Contributor to economic, statistical, and planning journals.

*　　*　　*

KAITZ, Edward M. 1928-

PERSONAL: Born January 3, 1928, in Winthrop, Mass.; son of Aaron M. and Rose (Biller) Kaitz; married Lorrie Kopelman, May 3, 1953; children: James A., D. Jane. *Education:* United States Military Academy, graduated, 1950; Boston College, M.B.A., 1963; Harvard University, Ph.D., 1967. *Home:* 5706 Mohican Rd., Washington, D.C. 20016. *Office:* Laidlaw-Coggeshall, Inc., 1775 K St. N.W., Washington, D.C. 20006.

CAREER: Northeastern University, Boston, Mass., lecturer in finance, 1965-66; Brandeis University, Waltham, Mass., assistant professor, 1966-67; Arthur D. Little, Inc., Boston, senior staff associate, 1967-69; Boston College, Chestnut Hill, Mass., associate professor; Georgetown University, Washington, D.C., dean of school of business, 1970-76; currently member of staff, Laidlaw-Coggeshall, Inc., Washington, D.C. Special consultant, Health Care Planning, Boston, 1964-67; consultant, Rhode Island State Department of Education, 1965-68, Model City Planning, City of New York, 1967. *Military service:* U.S. Army, Counter Intelligence, 1946-53. *Member:* American Association of University Professors, American Economic Association, American Finance Association, American Academy of Political and Social Science, Regional Planning Association, Financial Management Association.

WRITINGS: Pricing Policy and Cost Behavior in the Hospital Industry, Praeger, 1968; (with Herbert H. Hyman) *Urban Planning for Social Welfare: A Model Cities Approach,* Praeger, 1970.

*   *   *

KALOW, Gert 1921-

PERSONAL: Born August 20, 1921, in Cottbus, Germany; son of Johannes and Maria K. (Heyde) Kalow. *Education:* Studied at University of Jena, University of Hamburg, and University of Heidelberg; Goethe University, Ph.D. *Home:* Im alten Brueckentor, Heidelberg, Germany.

CAREER: Hochschule fuer Gestaltung, Ulm, Germany, lecturer, 1957-63, provost, 1961-62; Hessischer Rundfunk (broadcasting), Frankfurt, Germany, head of department, 1963—. *Member:* P.E.N. (vice-president, 1976). *Awards, honors:* Rockefeller Foundation fellowship, 1962-63.

WRITINGS: Zwischen Christentum und Ideologie, W. Rothe, 1956; (editor) *Sind wir noch das Volk der Dichter und Denker?,* Rowohlt, 1964; *Hitler, das gesamtdeutsche Trauma,* Piper, 1967, revised edition, 1975, translation by Betty Ross published as *The Shadow of Hitler: A Critique of Political Consciousness,* Rapp & Whiting, 1968, Quadrangle, 1970; *Erdgaleere* (poem), Piper, 1969; *Poesie ist Nachricht,* Piper, 1975. Essays have appeared in English, French, Italian, and Japanese publications.

BIOGRAPHICAL/CRITICAL SOURCES: Books and Bookmen, December, 1968.

*   *   *

KALUGER, George 1921-

PERSONAL: Born September 20, 1921, in Tataria, Rumania; son of Niculae (an employee of U.S. Steel) and Valeria (Sutue) Kaluger; married O. Meriem Fair (a psychological consultant), June 11, 1947. *Education:* Slippery Rock State College, B.S., 1946; University of Pittsburgh, M.Ed., 1948, Ph.D., 1950; postdoctoral study at Pennsylvania State University, 1951, 1952, 1964, and University of Denver, 1960. *Home:* 625 Brenton Rd., Shippensburg, Pa. 17257. *Office:* Department of Psychology, Shippensburg State College, Shippensburg, Pa. 17257.

CAREER: Butler (Pa.) public schools, teacher, 1946-48, counselor, 1948-53; Shippensburg State College, Shippensburg, Pa., professor of psychology, 1953—, chairman of department, 1972-75. Private practice in clinical psychology and learning disabilities. *Military service:* U.S. Army Air Forces, 8th Air Force, 1942-45; became captain; received Purple Heart, Air Medal with four oak-leaf clusters, European Theater Ribbon with four battle stars, and Presidential Citation.

MEMBER: American Psychological Association, American Educational Research Association, Council for Exceptional Children, International Reading Association, Association for Children with Learning Disabilities, National Rehabilitation Association, National Education Association, Eastern Psychological Association, Pennsylvania State Education Association, Pennsylvania Psychological Association (secretary-treasurer, Academic Division), Shippensburg Historical Society (president, 1964-66), Rotary International (president, 1963-64), Phi Delta Kappa, Alpha Phi

Omega. *Awards, honors:* Humanitarian Citation from United Cerebral Palsy Association of Pennsylvania; Distinguished Teacher Award from Pennsylvania State University and *Butler Eagle;* Outstanding Educator Award, 1971, 1973, 1975.

WRITINGS: (With C. J. Kolson) *Clinical Aspects of Remedial Reading,* C. C Thomas, 1963; (with William H. Burkhart and Samuel L. Daihl) *Shippensburg in the Civil War,* Shippensburg Historical Society, 1965; (with C. M. Unkovic) *Psychology and Sociology: Integrated Approach to Understanding Human Behavior,* Mosby, 1969; (with Kolson) *Reading and Learning Disabilities,* C. E. Merrill, 1969; (with wife, Meriem F. Kaluger) *Human Development: The Span of Life,* Mosby, 1974; (with M. F. Kaluger) *Profiles in Human Development,* Mosby, 1976. Contributor of more than twenty articles to professional journals.

WORK IN PROGRESS: Human Behaviour: A Psychological Study, for Mosby; revision of *Reading and Learning Disabilities; Teaching Learning Disabled Children;* research in cross-cultural patterns of behavior and development; research in perceptual-motor development through body symmetry, posture and weight-shift.

AVOCATIONAL INTERESTS: Nature study, research on the nature of humor, reading, and worldwide travel.

*   *   *

KAMMEYER, Kenneth C(arl) W(illiam) 1931-

PERSONAL: Born October 26, 1931, in Clarksville, Iowa; son of Emil Henry (a farmer) and Lucinda (Ellerman) Kammeyer; married Alyce M. Kimberley, June 5, 1953 (divorced); children: Leslie Anne, Robert Craig. *Education:* University of Northern Iowa, B.A., 1953; University of Iowa, M.A., 1958, Ph.D., 1960. *Office:* Department of Sociology, University of Maryland, College Park, Md. 20740.

CAREER: University of California, Davis, instructor, 1960-61, assistant professor of sociology, 1961-68; University of Kansas, Lawrence, associate professor, 1968-70, professor of sociology, 1970-74; University of Maryland, College Park, professor of sociology and chairman of department, 1974—. *Military service:* U.S. Navy, 1953-56. U.S. Naval Reserve, 1956-66; became lieutenant junior grade. *Member:* American Sociological Association, Population Association of America, National Council on Family Relations. *Awards, honors:* National Institute of Mental Health grant, 1966; National Institute of Child Health and Human Development research grant, 1971, 1973.

WRITINGS: (With Charles D. Bolton) *The University Student: A Study of Behavior and Values,* College & University Press, 1967; (contributor) Terry N. Clark, editor, *Community Power and Decision Making: Comparative Analyses,* Chandler Publishing, 1967; *Population Studies: Selected Essays and Research,* Rand McNally, 1969, 2nd edition, 1975; *An Introduction to Population* (textbook), Chandler Publishing, 1971; *Confronting the Issues: Sex Roles, Marriage and the Family,* Allyn & Bacon, 1975. Contributor of about fifteen articles and reviews to sociology journals.

*   *   *

KANE, H. Victor 1906-

PERSONAL: Born June 10, 1906, in Derryneil, Ireland; son of Hugh and Jeanie (Burrows) Kane; married Maryn Elaine Bennington, July 29, 1926; married second wife, Marjorie Louise Abendschein, June 4, 1955; children: (first marriage) H. Victor, Jr., Nancy Marilyn (Mrs. Warren Hoffman).

Education: Northern Baptist Theological Seminary, Th.B., 1932; Syracuse University, B.A., 1940. *Politics:* Democrat. *Home:* 5 Watson Ave., Binghamton, N.Y. 13901.

CAREER: Clergyman of American Baptist Convention, 1927—; New York State Baptist Convention, Syracuse, N.Y., executive secretary, 1957-62; American Baptist Convention, Valley Forge, Pa., associate director of Ministers and Missionaries Benefit Board, 1962-66; First Baptist Church, Binghamton, N.Y., pastor, 1966-71; currently doing interim pastoral work and serving as church and public relations representative for Upstate Home for Children, Oneonta, N.Y. President of board of directors, ABC Housing Development Fund Co., Inc. *Member:* Rotary Club. *Awards, honors:* D.D., Keuka College, 1957.

WRITINGS: Devotions for Dieters, Judson, 1967; *Tell It to the Children,* Judson, 1970; *Horse Sense and Horsepower,* Judson, 1975. Contributor of poems and articles to magazines and religious journals. Editor, *New York State Baptist,* 1957-61.

AVOCATIONAL INTERESTS: Gardening, fishing.

* * *

KANOF, Abram 1903-

PERSONAL: Born December 25, 1903, in Russia; came to United States in 1908, naturalized in 1925; son of Philip and Miriam (Weil) Kanof; married Frances Pascher (a physician), June 28, 1931; children: Elizabeth (Mrs. Ronald Levine), Margaret (Mrs. Carl Norden). *Education:* Columbia University, student, 1921-24; Long Island College Hospital, M.D., 1928. *Religion:* Jewish. *Office:* Department of Pediatrics, College of Medicine, State University of New York Downstate Medical Center, Brooklyn, N.Y. 11226.

CAREER: Licensed to practice medicine in New York; certified by American Board of Pediatrics, 1937; Long Island College Hospital, Brooklyn, N.Y., intern, 1928-29; Jewish Hospital of Brooklyn, Brooklyn, resident, 1929-31; Mount Sinai Hospital, New York City, resident, 1931; private practice in pediatrics, New York City, 1931-65; Jewish Chronic Disease Hospital, New York City, director of pediatrics, 1951-61; State University of New York Downstate Medical Center, Brooklyn, clinical instructor, 1946-55, clinical assistant professor, 1955-57, clinical associate professor, 1957-63, clinical professor, 1963-66, professor of pediatrics, 1966-73, professor emeritus, 1973—. Attending pediatrician, Jewish Hospital of Brooklyn. Former member, Pediatric Advisory Board, Department of Health, New York City. Former chairman, Brooklyn Physicians Drive, United Jewish Appeal, and Bonds for Israel. Member of board of overseers, Jewish Theological Seminary of America; chairman, Jewish Museum of New York. *Military service:* U.S. Navy, Medical Corps, 1942-46; became commander. Served in U.S. Naval Reserve.

MEMBER: American Medical Association, National Tay-Sachs Association, National Committee on Mentally and Physically Handicapped Children, American Academy of Pediatricians, American Academy for Cerebral Palsy, American Board of Pediatricians, American Jewish Historical Society, New York Academy of Medicine, Kings County Medical Society, Long Island Historical Society, Brooklyn Academy of Pediatricians. *Awards, honors:* Louis Marshall Award, Jewish Theological Seminary of America.

WRITINGS: (With A. J. Weil) *Immunology of Infections,* Year Book Medical Publishers, 1946; (with B. Kramer) *Vitamin D Group,* Academic Press, 1954; (with others) *Vi-*

tamin and Avitaminoses, Saunders, 1959; (with others) *Principles and Practices on a Ward for Children with Tay-Sachs Disease,* Academic Press, 1962; *American Jewish History in Literature* (originally published in *Chicago Jewish Forum,* volume 20, number 4), American Jewish Historical Society, 1963; *Jewish Ceremonial Art and Religious Observances,* Abrams, 1970; (author of introduction and catalogue notes) *Ceremonial Art in the Judaic Tradition: An Exhibition Organized by the North Carolina Museum of Art, Raleigh, April 27 through June 15, 1975,* North Carolina Museum of Art, 1975. Contributor to *Journal of Pediatrics, Journal of Laboratory and Clinical Medicine, Journal of Disturbed Children, Journal of the American Medical Association, Pediatrics, Quarterly Review of Pediatrics, American Journal of Medicine,* and other professional journals.

WORK IN PROGRESS: A chapter on Jewish art for an anthology.†

* * *

KAPLAN, Irma 1900-

PERSONAL: Born June 17, 1900, in Gothenburg, Sweden; daughter of Mathias (managing director of a textile factory) and Selma (Friedland) Kaplan. *Education:* Etisk-Pedegogiska Institutet, Uppsala, student, 1922-23; studied at University of Hamburg, and University of London, 1924, 1925. *Home:* Jakobsdalsgatan 3, Gothenburg 412 68, Sweden.

CAREER: On her return from studying languages abroad in 1925, she began entertaining children from neighboring villas with story evenings, and arranged a children's theater; after the death of her father in 1927, was employed as a governess for a number of years; teacher of English and German at a girls' boarding school in Sweden, 1942-44; teacher of Swedish, English, and German at another private school in Sweden, 1944-47; teacher of Swedish history and English at Nya Elementarskolan (first grade through examinations to a university), Stockholm, Sweden, 1948-69.

WRITINGS: (Adapted from a collection of folk tales originally compiled by Gunnar O. Hylten-Cavallius and George Stephens) *Swedish Fairy Tales,* Muller, 1953, published as *Fairy Tales from Sweden,* Follett, 1967; (compiler, translator, and adaptor) *Old European Fairy Tales,* Muller, 1969; (translator) Zacharias Topelius, *Fairy Tales from Finland,* Muller, 1973; *Heroes from Kalevala* (adapted selections from the folk epic "Kalevala"), Muller, 1973.

Also author of two children's plays in Swedish, *Paask Haxorna* (title means "The Easter Witches"; first produced at Barnteatern, 1941) and *Kvaellen foere Julafton* (title means "The Night Before Christmas"; first produced at Barnteatern, 1943), both published by Barnbiblioteket Saga.

WORK IN PROGRESS: Stories from East and West; Legends from Three Epochs.

* * *

KARL, Jean E(dna) 1927-

PERSONAL: Born July 29, 1927, in Chicago, Ill.; daughter of William (a salesman) and Ruth (Anderson) Karl. *Education:* Mount Union College, B.A., 1949. *Home:* 300 East 33rd St., New York, N.Y. 10016.

CAREER: Scott, Foresman and Co., Chicago, Ill., junior editorial assistant and assistant editor, 1949-56; Abingdon Press, New York City, children's book editor, 1956-61; Atheneum Publishers, New York City, director of children's book department, 1961—, vice-president, 1964—. Chairman, American Library Association/Children's Book

Council joint committee, 1963-65; president, Children's Book Council, 1965; co-director of seminar on children's publications, School of Library Science, Case Western Reserve University, 1969; trustee, Mount Union College, 1974—. *Member:* American Association of Publishers (member of Freedom to Read Committee, 1974—; member of executive board, General Trade Division, 1975-77). *Awards, honors:* D.Litt., Mount Union College, 1969.

WRITINGS: From Childhood to Childhood: Children's Books and Their Creators, John Day, 1970; *The Turning Place: Stories of a Future Past,* Dutton, 1976. Contributor of articles to *Publishers' Weekly, Wilson Library Bulletin, Writer,* and other professional and educational periodicals.

*   *   *

KASPERSON, Roger E. 1938-

PERSONAL: Born March 29, 1938, in Worcester, Mass.; son of Carl G. and Ethel (Anderson) Kasperson; married Jeanne Xanthakos, 1959; children: Demetri A., Kyra E. *Education:* Clark University, A.B., 1959; University of Chicago, M.A., 1962, Ph.D., 1966. *Home:* R.R. 1, 168AA Joy Rd., Woodstock, Conn. *Office:* Department of Government, Clark University, Worcester, Mass. 01610.

CAREER: Instructor at Massachusetts State College at Bridgewater (now Bridgewater State College), 1962-63, and University of Connecticut, Storrs, 1964-66; Michigan State University, East Lansing, assistant professor of geography, 1966-68; Clark University, Worcester, Mass., associate professor, 1968-76, professor of government and geography, 1976—. Consultant to Center for Educational Research, University of Puerto Rico, 1968-70. *Member:* Association of American Geographers, American Political Science Association, Association for the Advancement of American Sciences.

WRITINGS: The Dodecanese: Diversity and Unity in Island Politics, Department of Geography, University of Chicago, 1966; (editor with Julian V. Minghi) *The Structure of Political Geography,* Aldine, 1969; *Geography in an Urban Age: Political Geography,* Macmillan, 1970. Also co-author with Myrna Breitbart of *Participation, Decentralization and Advocacy Planning,* 1975, and co-editor with wife, Jeanne X. Kasperson, of *Water Re-use and the Cities,* University Press of New England.

WORK IN PROGRESS: Research on risk assessment, public response to nuclear energy, and societal management of technological hazards.

*   *   *

KASRILS, Ronald 1938-

PERSONAL: Born November 15, 1938; son of Issy (a salesman) and Rene (Cohen) Kasrils; married Eleanor Logan, December 12, 1964; children: Andrew, Christopher. *Education:* Studied at London School of Economics and Political Science, 1966-70. *Politics:* Marxist. *Religion:* Atheist. *Home:* 81A Golders Green Rd., London N.W.11, England.

WRITINGS: (Editor with Barry Feinberg) *Dear Bertrand Russell: A Selection of His Correspondence with the General Public 1950-1968,* Houghton, 1969; (with Feinberg) *Bertrand Russell's America: His Transatlantic Travels and Writings; A Documented Account,* Volume I: *1896-1945,* Allen & Unwin, 1973, Viking, 1974.

BIOGRAPHICAL/CRITICAL SOURCES: Nation, November 10, 1969; *Books,* November, 1969.†

KASS, Norman 1934-

PERSONAL: Born July 26, 1934, in Cleveland, Ohio; son of Albert and Gertrude (Bernstein) Kass; married Linda Thornquest, May 30, 1969. *Education:* Western Reserve University (now Case Western Reserve University), B.A., 1956, M.A., 1957, Ph.D., 1960. *Home:* 4523 West Point Loma Blvd., San Diego, Calif. 92107. *Office:* Department of Psychology, San Diego State University, San Diego, Calif. 92115.

CAREER: Western Reserve University (now Case Western Reserve University), Cleveland, Ohio, instructor in child psychology, 1957, therapist in remedial reading center, 1957-59; University of Minnesota, Minneapolis, instructor in child development, 1960-61; San Diego State University, San Diego, Calif., assistant professor, 1961-66, associate professor, 1966-70, professor of psychology, 1970—. *Member:* American Psychological Association, Society for Research in Child Development. *Awards, honors:* National Institute of Mental Health fellow, 1960-61.

WRITINGS: (Editor with Thomas D. Spencer) *Perspectives in Child Psychology: Research and Review,* McGraw, 1970.†

*   *   *

KATCHADOURIAN, Vahe 1928-
(Vahe Katcha)

PERSONAL: Born April 1, 1928; son of Karnik and Louise Katchadourian. *Education:* Studied drama in Paris. *Religion:* Christian. *Agent:* Bernheim, 16 ave. Hoche, Paris, France.

CAREER: Critic, journalist, scenarist, and novelist. *Awards, honors:* Prix Rivarol (now called Prix de l'Universalite de la Langue Francaise), Librairie Bonaparte, 1957, for *Oeil pour oeil.*

WRITINGS—All under pseudonym Vahe Katcha: Les Megots de dimanche (novel), Gallimard, 1953; *Oeil pour oeil* (novel), Plon, 1955, translation published with translation of *L'Hamecon* as *The Hook* [and] *An Eye for an Eye,* Hart-Davis, 1961; *L'Hamecon* (novel), Plon, 1957, translation by Alexander Torok published as *The Hook,* Simon & Schuster, 1958; *Ne te retourne pas, Kipian* (novel), Plon, 1958, translation by David Hughes published as *Don't Look Down,* Hart-Davis, 1962; *Les Poings fermes* (novel), Plon, 1959; *Le Huitieme jour du monsieur* [suivi de] *Le Repas des fauves* (two novelettes), Plon, 1960; *L'Homme qui troubla la fete* (novel), Plon, 1962; *La Canne* (novel), Julliard (Paris), 1963; *Se reveiller demon* (novel), Plon, 1964; *Un Bateau de singes,* Presses de la Cite (Paris), 1966; *A coeur joie,* R. Solar (Paris), 1967; *Galia* (Novel of the Month selection), E. Nalis (Paris), 1967, reprinted as *Quitte ou double, Galia,* 1968; *Dix filles qui se levent a midi,* E. Nalis, 1968; *La Mort d'un juif,* Julliard, 1968; *Un Negre sur le statue de Lincoln,* Julliard, 1970; *Un homme est tombe dans la rue,* Fayard, 1975.

Screenplays: "Death of a Jew" (based on Katchadourian's novel of same title), Israfilm Production Services, 1969; "The Burglars" (based on novel by David Goodis), Columbia, 1972.

WORK IN PROGRESS: A novel about Americans in Paris, tentatively entitled *Super Relation.*

SIDELIGHTS: Vahe Katchadourian told *CA* he has had fifteen novels published in France, which have been translated into English, Dutch, Portuguese, Swedish, Italian, Russian, and German.

KATZ, Elias 1912-

PERSONAL: Born September 22, 1912, in New York, N.Y.; son of Samuel and Fannie (Huss) Katz; married Florence Ludins (an artist), December 7, 1937; children: Jonathan George. *Education:* City College (now City College of the City University of New York), B.A., 1932, M.S., 1933; Columbia University, Ph.D., 1942. *Home:* 3 Los Altos Dr., San Rafael, Calif. 94901. *Office:* Center for Training in Community Psychiatry and Mental Health Administration, 2045 Dwight Way, Berkeley, Calif. 94704.

CAREER: U.S. Veterans Administration, Regional Office, New York City, clinical psychologist with Mental Hygiene Service, 1946-48; U.S. Naval Disciplinary Barracks, San Pedro, Calif., chief clinical psychologist, 1948-50; Sonoma State Hospital, Eldridge, Calif., chief psychologist, 1951-53; University of California Medical Center, San Francisco, psychologist, 1953-70; Center for Training in Community Psychiatry and Mental Health Administration, Berkeley, Calif., assistant director, 1968—. San Francisco Aid to Retarded Children, director of Work-Training Center, 1957-61, director of Independent Living Rehabilitation Program, 1961-66, consultant, 1966-67. Instructor, City College (now City College of the City University of New York), New York City, 1947-48; lecturer at University of California, Berkeley, 1949-65, San Francisco State College (now University), 1951-52, 1955, 1957, 1967, and at College of Marin, 1952-58; lecturer for Extension Division of University of California, Berkeley, 1959-70; professor at Sonoma State College (now California State College, Sonoma), summer, 1967. Chairman of vocational rehabilitation committee, California Council for Retarded Children, 1957-66; founder and officer, San Francisco Coordinating Council on Mental Retardation, 1961-66; founder and president, California Association of Rehabilitation Workshops, 1963-65; consultant on mental retardation facilities, 1965-69. *Military service:* U.S. Army, 1943-46; became second lieutenant.

MEMBER: American Psychological Association (fellow), American Association on Mental Deficiency (fellow), Society for Child Development, Council for Exceptional Children.

WRITINGS: Children's Preferences for Traditional and Modern Paintings, Teachers College Press, 1944; *The Retarded Adult in the Community,* C. C Thomas, 1968; *The Retarded Adult at Home: A Guide for Parents,* Special Child, 1970; *Mental Health Services for the Mentally Retarded,* C. C Thomas, 1972. Contributor to psychology journals.

WORK IN PROGRESS: With wife, Florence Ludins-Katz, "The Wonder Box" series.†

* * *

KATZ, Ellis 1938-

PERSONAL: Born November 1, 1938, in Camden, N.J.; son of Charles (a businessman) and Frances (Gelb) Katz; married Barbara Ann Usatch (a speech therapist), June 11, 1961; children: Cindy Arla, Eric David. *Education:* Rutgers University, B.A. (honors), 1960; Columbia University, M.A., 1962, Ph.D., 1966. *Politics:* Radical. *Religion:* None. *Home:* 1084 Sherman Ave., Huntingdon Valley, Pa. 19006. *Office:* Department of Political Science, Temple University, Broad and Montgomery Ave., Philadelphia, Pa. 19122.

CAREER: Temple University, Philadelphia, Pa., instructor, 1962-66, assistant professor, 1966-71, associate professor of political science and foundations of education,

1971—, director, General Education Program for Teachers, 1970—. *Member:* American Political Science Association, Law and Society Association, Center for the Study of Federalism.

WRITINGS: (Editor with Harry A. Bailey, Jr.) *Ethnic Group Politics,* C. E. Merrill, 1969. Contributor to scholarly journals.††

* * *

KA-TZETNIK 135633

PERSONAL: Ka-Tzetnik 135633, a pseudonym, is the author's concentration camp number; born in Poland. *Residence:* Israel. *Agent:* Curtis Brown Ltd., 575 Madison Ave., New York, N.Y. 10022.

CAREER: Writer; was imprisoned in concentration camp by Nazis during World War II.

WRITINGS—All novels; all published under pseudonym Ka-Tzetnik 135633: *Salamandra,* Dvir Publishing, 1946, reprinted, 1973; *Bet ha-bubot,* Dvir Publishing, 1953, translation published as *House of Dolls,* Simon & Schuster, 1955; *Kohav haefer,* Bialak Institute, 1960, translation published as *Star of Ashes,* Gershon Kispel Lithographs (Tel Aviv), 1967, published as *Star Eternal,* Arbor House, 1971; *Kar'u lo Pipl,* Am Ha'Sefer (Tel Aviv), 1961, translation published as *They Called Him Piepel,* Anthony Blond, 1961, published as *Atrocity,* edited by Lyle Stuart, Lyle Stuart, 1963; *Kehol Me-efer,* Am Oved, 1966, translation published as *Phoenix over the Galilee,* Harper, 1969.

SIDELIGHTS: Eisig Silberschlag, reviewing *Phoenix over the Galilee,* writes: "The simple, conservative, realistic art of Ka-Tzetnik revives a desperate hope: inhumanity of man to man may change to empathy and sympathy. Love, not weaponry, is the key to humane metamorphosis."

A *Nation* reviewer said of *House of Dolls:* "Here is prose at once memorable and merciless, controlled and explosive. This novel, in a fine translation from the Hebrew . . . , records a degeneration of humanity the world has too soon forgotten."

A. H. Friedlander writes of Ka-Tzetnik, "A man who has obliterated his past identity under a name that means 'concentration camp inmate,' is a person with only one aim in life. He wants to be a witness, a remembrancer of the Holocaust. . . . Basically [*Star Eternal*] records no incidents that other accounts of the death camps have not supplied. Yet there are times when the concentrated horror of this work forges a language for itself that brings the utmost limits of the human agony into focus. We see the victims in the transports; we see them standing in the selection line, and we witness their death. . . . Ka-Tzetnik survives."

The House of Dolls has been published in over eleven languages.

BIOGRAPHICAL/CRITICAL SOURCES: Nation, August 6, 1955; *Books Abroad,* autumn, 1970; *Saturday Review,* March 13, 1971.†

* * *

KATZMAN, Allen 1937-

PERSONAL: Born April 27, 1937, in Brooklyn, N.Y.; son of Benjamin and Ruth (Greenhouse) Katzman. *Education:* City College (now City College of the City University of New York), B.A., 1958. *Home:* Westbeth, 463 West St., Apt. D603, New York, N.Y. 10014.

CAREER: Poet, teacher, journalist, producer, and publisher for the American underground; founded *The East Village Other,* New York City, in 1965, publisher, 1965—; founded Underground Press Syndicate, a fraternal organization of over 200 underground newspapers, in 1966; innovator in publishing of underground cartoons and cartoonists, first in *EVO* and later in *Zodiac Mind Warp* (now defunct) and *Gothic Blimp Works;* producer for Swift Comics, published by Bantam, 1970—; first syndicated columnist writing on the counter culture, Bell-McClure Syndicate, North American Newspaper Alliance, Inc., 1971—. Minister of Information for the Yippie Party and key witness in Chicago Conspiracy Trial, 1969-70. Instructor in underground journalism at Columbia University, Graduate School of Journalism, and New School for Social Research, both in New York City; producer of video tapes alone and with Jackie Cassen and Global Village, 1969—; created the first closed circuit community television station, Westbeth TV, 1971; lecturer on U.S. college campuses about the alternate media and culture and the crime of America. *Military service:* U.S. Army, 1958-60; became sergeant. *Awards, honors:* New York State Council on the Arts grant for poetry, 1971.

WRITINGS—All poetry: *Poems from Oklahoma, and Other Poems,* Hesperidian Press, 1962; *The Bloodletting,* Renegade Press, 1964; *The Comanche Cantos,* Sign of the Gun Press, 1966; *The Immaculate: Poems,* Doubleday, 1970.

Editor: Jerry Rubin, *We Are Everywhere,* Harper, 1971; *Our Time: An Anthology of Interviews from "The East Village Other",* Dial, 1972.

Poems represented in several anthologies, including *Notes from the New Underground,* edited by Jesse Kornbluth, Viking, 1968, *The Hippie Papers,* edited by Jerry Hopkins, New American Library, 1968, and *The Open Conspiracy: What America's Angry Generation is Saying,* edited by Ethel G. Romm, Giniger, 1970. Contributor of poetry, essays, and articles to numerous Underground publications, including *Los Angeles Free Press.*

WORK IN PROGRESS: Editing an anthology of prose and poetry from *The East Village Other;* and a collection of journalism, *Poor Paranoid's Almanac.*

SIDELIGHTS: As a pioneer publisher of the New Comic Art, Allen Katzman has presented the work of Kim Deitch, Artie Spiegelman, Trina Robbins, and Allan Shenker in Swift Comics. In 1966 he produced the first *Electric Newspaper,* now a collector's item, for ESP Records. A recognized authority on underground journalism, Katzman has said that his paper, *The East Village Other,* "has been an active force in the creation of alternate solutions to the military/industrial complex of American 'hypocracy.'"

BIOGRAPHICAL/CRITICAL SOURCES: Washington Post, April 5, 1972.

*　　*　　*

KAUFMAN, Donald D(avid)   1933-

PERSONAL: Born January 10, 1933, in Marion, S.D.; son of David Daniel and Hulda (Graber) Kaufman; married Eleanor Wismer, August 30, 1958; children: Kendra Janean, Galen David, Nathan Dean. *Education:* Freeman Junior College, A.A., 1953; Bethel College, North Newton, Kan., B.A., 1955; Mennonite Biblical Seminary, Chicago, Ill., B.D., 1958; Mennonite Biblical Seminary, Elkhart, Ind., M.Div., 1969. *Home:* 609 Central Ave., Newton, Kan. 67114.

CAREER: Clergyman of Mennonite Church; ministry to

agricultural migrants in Blue Earth, Minn., summer, 1951; Beacon Neighborhood House, Chicago, Ill., community service worker, summer, 1957; Prairie View Hospital, Newton, Kan., psychiatric aide, 1958-59; Mennonite Central Committee, Pati, Java, Indonesia, field director, 1959-67; Bethel Mennonite Church, Mountain Lake, Minn., associate pastor, 1968-71; Faith Mennonite Church, Minneapolis, Minn., pastor, 1971-74; General Conference of Mennonite Church, Commission on Home Ministries, Newton, personnel coordinator, 1974-77; currently home insulator with private company. President, Mennonite Intercollegiate Peace Fellowship, 1954-55; vice-president, Chicago Midwest Region Interseminary Movement, 1955-56; member, Retreat Committee of North District Conference, 1968-69; secretary, Peace and Social Concerns Committee, 1969-72; volunteer, Fish, 1971-74; member of Mutual Care Commission of Bethel College Mennonite Church and Mennonite Voluntary Service Reference Council. *Member:* Fellowship of Reconciliation, American Civil Liberties Union, Clergy and Laymen Concerned about Vietnam, War Tax Resistance, Minneapolis Ministerial Association.

WRITINGS: What Belongs to Caesar? A Discussion on the Christian's Response to Payment of War Taxes, Herald Press, 1969, reprinted with enlarged bibliography, 1973. Also author of two papers on the conflict between the Christian and payment of war taxes. Contributor to religious journals.

WORK IN PROGRESS: Nationalism, Patriotism, and "The Flag".

SIDELIGHTS: Donald Kaufman writes: "In order for my Christian faith to have integrity I found it necessary to seek a resolution to the war tax dilemma. In this quest it has been gratifying to find help through the experience of others and to discover that I was not alone in this struggle over the propriety of paying taxes that are used essentially for military purposes. The concern has mushroomed as new alternatives are developed."

AVOCATIONAL INTERESTS: Leathercraft, the outdoors.

*　　*　　*

KAUFMAN, Wolfe   1905(?)-1970

1905(?)—November 24, 1970; Polish-born critic, press agent, and theatre writer. Obituaries: *New York Times,* November 27, 1970; *Washington Post,* November 28, 1970; *Books Abroad,* spring, 1971.

*　　*　　*

KAVANAUGH, Robert E.   1926-

PERSONAL: Born August 5, 1926, in Kalamazoo, Mich.; son of Frank Paul (an insurance salesman) and Hazel (Wendell) Kavanaugh; married Patricia A. Griffin McWilliams (a rehabilitation nurse), October, 1969; step-children: Suzanne. *Education:* Sacred Heart Seminary, B.A., 1947; Catholic University of America, M.A., 1955; United States International University, San Diego, Ph.D., 1970. *Home:* 10985 Negley, San Diego, Calif. 92131. *Agent:* Foley Agency, 34 East 38th St., New York, N.Y. 10016. *Office:* University of California, San Diego, La Jolla, Calif. 92038.

CAREER: Ordained Catholic priest, 1951; St. Thomas Church, East Lansing, Mich., asst. pastor, 1951-57; Michigan State University, East Lansing, member of faculty, 1955-66, co-founder and director of St. John Student Parish, 1958-66; San Diego County, Calif., social worker in child welfare department, 1966-67; University of California, San Diego, La Jolla, counselling psychologist, 1967—. Vice-president, Kavanaugh Center (psychological service), Encinitas, Calif., 1972—. Consultant on death and dying to United States Navy, 1971-72.

WRITINGS: The Grim Generation, Trident, 1970.

WORK IN PROGRESS: A novel; research in thanatology for a University of California, San Diego extension course.

AVOCATIONAL INTERESTS: Gardening, cooking, golf.†

* * *

KEANE, John B. 1928-

PERSONAL: Born July 21, 1928, in Listowel, County Kerry, Ireland; son of William B. (a teacher) and Hannah (Purtill) Keane; married Mary O'Connor, January 1, 1955; children: William Joseph, Conor Anthony, John Mary, Joanna Mary Colette. *Education:* St. Michael's College, Listowel, Ireland, graduate, 1946. *Politics:* Fine Gael. *Religion:* Roman Catholic. *Home:* 37 William St., Listowel, County Kerry, Ireland. *Agent:* William Keane, 37 William St., Listowel, County Kerry, Ireland.

CAREER: Chemist's assistant in Ireland, 1946-51; emigrated to England and worked as a laborer, street-sweeper, and then as a furnace operator with British Timken; returned to Listowel, Ireland, where he bought and ran a public bar; free-lance journalist and playwright. *Awards, honors:* Honorary doctorate in literature, Trinity College, Dublin, 1977.

WRITINGS—Published by Mercier Press, except as noted: *The Street,* Progress House, 1960; *Self Portrait,* 1963; *Strong Tea,* 1964; (contributor) *Seven Irish Plays,* edited by Robert Hogan, University of Minnesota Press, 1967; *Letters of a Successful T.D.,* 1968; *Letters of an Irish Parish Priest,* 1972; *The Gentle Art of Matchmaking,* 1973; *Letters of an Irish Publican,* 1974; *Letters of a Love-Hungry Farmer,* 1974; *Letters of a Matchmaker,* 1975; *Letters of a Civic Guard,* 1976; *Is the Holy Ghost Really a Kerryman?,* 1976; *Letters of a Postman,* 1977.

Plays: *Sive,* Progress House, 1959; *Sharon's Grave,* Progress House, 1960; *The Highest House on the Mountain,* Progress House, 1961; *Many Young Men of Twenty,* Progress House, 1962; *The Man from Clare,* 1963; *The Year of the Hiker,* 1964; *The Field,* 1965; *The Rain at the End of the Summer,* Progress House, 1967; *Hut 42,* Proscenium Press, 1967; *Big Maggie,* 1969; *The Change in Mame Fadden,* 1972; *Moll,* 1973; *Values,* 1973; *The Crazy Wall,* 1974. Southern Theatre Group presented a season of Keane's plays in Killarney; plays also produced at Abbey Theatre in Dublin. Weekly columnist for *Dublin Herald* and *Limerick Leader.*

BIOGRAPHICAL/CRITICAL SOURCES: After the Irish Renaissance, University of Minnesota Press, 1967; *Seven Irish Plays,* edited by Robert Hogan, University of Minnesota Press, 1967; *Drama,* summer, 1968.

* * *

KEARNS, Francis E(dward) 1931-

PERSONAL: Born August 10, 1931, in Brooklyn, N.Y.; son of George A. (a prizefighter) and Gertrude F. (Pearsall) Kearns; married Ann Sherlock Polhemus, December 26, 1960; children: Ellen, Edward. *Education:* New York University, A.B., 1953; University of Chicago, A.M., 1954; University of North Carolina, Ph.D., 1961. *Office:* Depart-

ment of English, Herbert H. Lehman College of the City University of New York, Bedford Park Blvd. W., Bronx, N.Y. 10468.

CAREER: U.S. Central Intelligence Agency, Washington, D.C., case officer, 1955-56; University of North Carolina, Chapel Hill, instructor in English, 1956-60; Georgetown University, Washington, D.C., assistant professor of American literature, 1960-65; Herbert H. Lehman College of the City University of New York, Bronx, N.Y., associate professor of American literature, 1965—. Fulbright professor, University of Bergen, 1965-66; visiting professor, University of Nancy, 1969-70; U.S. Information Service lecturer in Zambia, Kenya, Somali, Ghana, Morocco, and at University of Heidelberg, University of Cologne, and University of Braunschweig, 1970. *Member:* Modern Language Association of America, Phi Beta Kappa. *Awards, honors:* American Philosophical Society summer research grant, 1962; Edward Douglas White Award for faculty excellence, Georgetown University, 1965; City University Research Foundation grants, 1968, 1971.

WRITINGS: (Contributor) Bradford Daniel, editor, *Black, White, and Gray: Twenty-One Points of View on the Race Question,* Sheed, 1964; (contributor) Daniel Callahan, editor, *The Generation of the Third Eye,* Sheed, 1965; (contributor) Robert Hassenger, editor, *The Shape of Catholic Higher Education,* University of Chicago Press, 1967; (editor) *The Black Experience: An Anthology of American Literature for the 70's,* Viking, 1970; (editor) *Black Identity,* Holt, 1970; (contributor) Alfred Weber, editor, *Geschichte und Fiktion: Amerikanische Prosa im 19 Jahrhundert,* Vandenhoeck & Ruprecht, 1972. Contributor to *Commonweal, Yale Review, Ramparts, America,* and other journals. Editor, *Chicago Review,* 1953-54.

WORK IN PROGRESS: A study of the literary relationship of Margaret Fuller and Ralph Waldo Emerson.

BIOGRAPHICAL/CRITICAL SOURCES: Daniel Callahan, editor, *The Generation of the Third Eye,* Sheed, 1965.

* * *

KEARNS, James A(loysius) III 1949-

PERSONAL: Born August 25, 1949, in St. Louis, Mo.; son of James Aloysius, Jr. (an investment broker) and Mary E. (Hoffmeister) Kearns. *Education:* University of Notre Dame, B.S.E.E. (summa cum laude), 1971, J.D. (cum laude), 1974. *Politics:* Independent. *Religion:* Roman Catholic. *Home:* 4300 Garrison St. N.W., Washington, D.C. 20016.

CAREER: Sverdrup & Parcel and Associates, Inc. (engineers-architects), St. Louis, Mo., draftsman, 1968-70; Missouri State Highway Department, Kirkwood, intermediate computer-draftsman, 1971; Smithsonian Astrophysical Observatory, Cambridge, Mass., research assistant, 1973; Cadwalader, Wickersham & Taft, Washington, D.C., attorney, 1974—. *Member:* American Bar Association, New York State Bar Association, District of Columbia Bar, Tau Beta Pi, Eta Kappa Nu.

WRITINGS: (With James Patrick Brown) *Era of Challenge,* B. Herder, 1970. Contributor to *Notre Dame Scholastic.*

WORK IN PROGRESS: A book concerning the rationale and implications of the Supreme Court's abortion decisions of 1973 and 1976.

KEARNY, Edward N. III 1936-

PERSONAL: First syllable of surname rhymes with "car"; born May 5, 1936, in New Orleans, La.; son of Edward N., Jr. (a businessman) and Cecil (Mooney) Kearny; married Mary Ann Warner (a university instructor), June 15, 1968; children: Lisa. *Education:* Southwestern at Memphis, B.A., 1958; Louisiana State University, M.A., 1962; American University, Ph.D., 1968. *Politics:* "Democratic party preference." *Religion:* Methodist. *Home:* 2007 Price St., Bowling Green, Ky. 42101. *Office:* Department of Government, Western Kentucky University, Bowling Green, Ky. 42101.

CAREER: Western Kentucky University, Bowling Green, assistant professor of government, 1968—. *Member:* American Political Science Association, American Studies Association, Southern Political Science Association.

WRITINGS: Thurman Arnold, Social Critic: The Satirical Challenge to Orthodoxy, University of New Mexico Press, 1970; *Mavericks in American Politics: Eight Men Who Forced the Issues of Their Day,* Mimir Publishers, 1976.

BIOGRAPHICAL/CRITICAL SOURCES: Louisville Courier Journal & Times, September 5, 1976; *Tennessean,* September 12, 1976.

* * *

KEATING, Leo Bernard 1915-
(Bern Keating)

PERSONAL: Born May 14, 1915, in Fassett, Quebec, Canada; son of John Julian (an engineer) and Laure (Lalonde) Keating; married Marian Frances West (a photographer), June 10, 1939; children: John Geoffrey, Kate Maulding (deceased). *Education:* Student at New York University; University of Arkansas, B.A. (summa cum laude), 1938. *Politics:* Democratic Party (liberal branch). *Religion:* None. *Home:* 141 Bayou Rd., Greenville, Miss. 38701.

CAREER: Full-time professional writer; has worked as reporter for a newspaper and a radio station. *Military service:* U.S. Naval Reserve, 1941-46; became lieutenant. *Member:* Society of Magazine Writers, Authors Guild, Society of American Travel Writers, Society of Journalists and Authors, Outdoor Writers of America, Overseas Press Club.

WRITINGS—Under name Bern Keating: *The Mosquito Fleet,* Putnam, 1963; *The Horse that Won the Civil War* (juvenile), Putnam, 1964; *Life and Death of the Aztec Nation* (juvenile), Putnam, 1964; *Zebulon Pike: Young America's Frontier Scout* (juvenile), Putnam, 1965; *The Invaders of Rome* (juvenile), Putnam, 1966; *Chaka, King of the Zulus* (juvenile), Putnam, 1968; *The Grand Banks,* photographs by Dan Guravich, Rand McNally, 1968; *Alaska,* National Geographic Society, 1969; *The Northwest Passage: From the Mathew to the Manhattan, 1497-1969,* Rand McNally, 1969.

The Mighty Mississippi, National Geographic Society, 1971; *Gulf of Mexico,* Viking, 1972; *Famous American Explorers* (juvenile), Rand McNally, 1972; *Florida,* Rand McNally, 1972; *Texas Rangers,* Rand McNally, 1975; *Inside Passage to Alaska,* Doubleday, 1976; *Chopper: The Illustrated Story of Helicopters in Action,* Rand McNally, 1976. Ghost writer of other books under various pseudonyms. Regular contributor to *National Geographic, Travel and Leisure, Smithsonian,* and other magazines.

WORK IN PROGRESS: Famous American Cowboys, for Rand McNally; a biography of Samuel Colt, for Doubleday;

a novel on the Mississippi slave revolt of 1835; continuing research on world population—food problems.

SIDELIGHTS: Leo Bernard Keating has traveled in more than ninety countries and circled the globe four times.

* * *

KEEBLE, John 1944-

PERSONAL: Born November 24, 1944, in Winnipeg, Manitoba, Canada; son of Raymond Charles William and Olivia (Wallace) Keeble; married Claire Sheldon (a violist), September 4, 1964; children: Jonathan Sheldon, Ezekiel Jerome, Carson R. C. *Education:* University of Redlands, B.A. (magna cum laude), 1966; University of Iowa, M.F.A., 1969. *Politics:* "No comment." *Religion:* "No comment." *Address:* P.O. Box 7, Four Lakes, Wash. 99014. *Agent:* John Sterling, c/o Paul R. Reynolds, Inc., 12 East 41st St., New York, N.Y. 10017.

CAREER: Grinnell College, Grinnell, Iowa, writer-in-residence, 1971-72; Eastern Washington State University, Cheney, Wash., assistant professor of English, 1973-77.

WRITINGS: Crab Canyon (novel), Grossman, 1971; (with Ransom Jeffery) *Mine* (novel), Grossman, 1974; (contributor) Theodore Solotaroff, editor, *American Review, No. 25,* Bantam, 1976.

WORK IN PROGRESS: A novel, *Yellow Fish,* for Bantam.

* * *

KEETON, Elizabeth B(aker) 1919-

PERSONAL: Born January 2, 1919, in Renville, Minn.; daughter of Harold (a judge) and Pearl (Morris) Baker; married Robert E. Keeton (a professor of law), May 28, 1941; children: Katherine (Mrs. Dale Carter), William R. *Education:* University of Texas, B.A., 1951; Boston University, M.Ed., 1958. *Home:* 25 Avon St., Cambridge, Mass. 02138.

CAREER: Teacher, mainly of remedial reading, in elementary schools of Acton, Mass., 1955-57, Lynnfield, Mass., 1959-61, and Boston, Mass., 1964-66.

WRITINGS: Esmeralda (juvenile), Little, Brown, 1970; *Friday Nights and Robert* (juvenile), Little, Brown, 1972.

* * *

KELLER, Allan 1904-

PERSONAL: Born August 3, 1904, in South Windham, Conn.; son of Harry Howard (an engineer) and Anna (Stedman) Keller; married Ima Elberfeld, May 10, 1926; children: Barbara (Mrs. Gerald Dolan), Katharine (Mrs. Roger A. Hood). *Education:* Columbia University, B.Litt., 1926; New York University, M.A., 1953. *Religion:* Congregationalist. *Home:* 27 Raymond St., Darien, Conn. 06820.

CAREER: New York World-Telegram, New York, N.Y., writer and columnist, 1933-67. Adjunct professor, Graduate School of Journalism, Columbia University, 1947-68. Director, James Gordon Bennett Foundation, 1966—. Editorial consultant, Sleepy Hollow Restorations, Inc. *Military service:* U.S. Navy, 1942-46; became commander. *Member:* Confrerie de la Chaine des Rotisseurs (member of board of directors), Civil War Round Table (Fairfield County; vice-president).

WRITINGS: (With Anne Putnam) *Madami,* Prentice-Hall, 1954; *Grandma's Cooking,* Prentice-Hall, 1955; *Thunder at Harper's Ferry,* Prentice-Hall, 1958; *Morgan's Raid,* Bobbs-Merrill, 1961; *The Spanish-American War: A Com-*

pact History, Hawthorn, 1969; *Colonial America*, Hawthorn, 1971; *Life along the Hudson*, Sleepy Hollow Restorations, 1976. Formerly author of weekly column, "The Roving Gourmet." Contributor to *Reader's Digest*, *Saturday Evening Post*, *Collier's*, *McCall's*, *Pageant*, *Argosy*, *Yankee*, and other periodicals.

WORK IN PROGRESS: A novel set in West Virginia.

AVOCATIONAL INTERESTS: Travel, gourmet food and wines.

* * *

KELLEY, Donald R(eed) 1931-

PERSONAL: Born February 17, 1931, in Elgin, Ill.; son of Walter Louis and Helen (Davis) Kelley; married Nancy Lief (a teacher), June 4, 1962; children: John Reed. *Education:* Harvard University, B.A., 1953; Columbia University, M.A., 1956, Ph.D., 1962; University of Paris, graduate study, 1958-59. *Home:* 132 Clintwood Ct., Rochester, N.Y. 14620. *Office:* Department of History, University of Rochester, Rochester, N.Y. 14627.

CAREER: Queens College of the City University of New York, Flushing, N.Y., lecturer in history, 1960-63; Southern Illinois University, Carbondale, assistant professor of history, 1963-65; State University of New York at Binghamton, assistant professor, 1965-68, associate professor, 1968-71, professor of modern European history, 1971-72; Harvard University, Cambridge, Mass., visiting professor, 1972-73; University of Rochester, Rochester, N.Y., professor of history, 1973—. *Military service:* U.S. Army, 1953-55. *Member:* American Historical Association, Renaissance Society of America, Mediaeval Academy of America. *Awards, honors:* Fulbright fellowship, 1958-59; American Philosophical Society grant, 1964, 1971; Newberry Library grant, 1965; American Council of Learned Societies fellowship, 1967-68; Institute for Advanced Study, fellow, 1969-70, 1977-78; Folger Shakespeare Library Grant, 1970; Guggenheim fellowship, 1974-75; National Endowment for the Humanities fellowship, 1977-78.

WRITINGS: Foundations of Modern Historical Scholarship, Columbia University Press, 1970; *Francois Hotman: A Revolutionary's Ordeal*, Princeton University Press, 1973. Contributor to a number of professional journals.

WORK IN PROGRESS: Views of History: Antiquity to the Enlightenment; a study of early modern propaganda; a book on law and the beginnings of modern social science.

SIDELIGHTS: Donald R. Kelley told *CA:* "I have made a hobby (though it is also the focus of my work) of trying to build intellectual bridges from my field, history, over to other disciplines, including philosophy, literature, religion, law, political science and sociology. Judging by the hospitality of various scholarly journals, the efforts seem to me to be successful for every case except the last, and even sociology I haven't yet given up on."

* * *

KELLNER, Bruce 1930-

PERSONAL: Born March 17, 1930, in Indianapolis, Ind.; son of Gordon (in insurance business) and Lillian (Zumbrunn) Kellner; married Margaret Wilcox, December 28, 1961; children: Hans Carl, Kate Hein. *Education:* Colorado College, B.A., 1955; University of Iowa, M.F.A., 1958. *Politics:* Democrat. *Religion:* None. *Home:* 514 North School Lane, Lancaster, Pa. 17603. *Agent:* Robert Lescher, 159 East 64th St., New York, N.Y. 10014. *Office:* Department of English, Millersville State College, Lancaster, Pa.

CAREER: Coe College, Cedar Rapids, Iowa, assistant professor of English, 1955-60; Hartwick College, Oneonta, N.Y., assistant professor of English and drama director, 1960-69; Millersville State College, Lancaster, Pa., associate professor of English, 1969—. *Military service:* U.S. Navy, 1951-54. *Member:* Modern Language Association of America, American Association of University Professors, Parent-Teacher Association (president of Lancaster area council), Alpha Psi Omega, Pi Delta Kappa, Kappa Sigma.

WRITINGS: Carl Van Vechten and the Irreverent Decades, University of Oklahoma Press, 1968.

WORK IN PROGRESS: An annotated bibliography of the published and unpublished work of Carl Van Vechten; an anthology of Carl Van Vechten's writings about the Negro, 1914-1964, *The Harlem Renaissance;* a textbook with scripts for reader's theater, *The Bookshelf Onstage.*

SIDELIGHTS: Discussing *Carl Van Vechten and the Irreverent Decades*, W. G. Rogers wrote: ". . . another valuable perspective, with Van Vechten as focal point, of the lush creative world that climaxed in the 1920's and still echoes excitingly today." *Variety's* critic reports that "[Kellner] has put his own vivid memories of a friendship with Van Vechten together with reflections of the thoughts and affections of others for his subject and has emerged with an important full-length portrait. As a social document indexing the mores of the more than half century Van Vechten flourished, this tome is also a valuable document. In all, a penetrating, rewarding effort; readable, handsomely produced, and indispensable as a reference source."

BIOGRAPHICAL/CRITICAL SOURCES: New York Times Book Review, February 16, 1969; *Variety*, March 26, 1969.

* * *

KELLY, Charles Patrick Bernard 1891(?)-1971

1891(?)—June 21, 1971; American lawyer and criminologist. Obituaries: *New York Times*, June 23, 1971.

* * *

KELLY, David M(ichael) 1938-

PERSONAL: Born June 23, 1938, in Grand Rapids, Mich.; son of Peter Earl (a laborer) and Margaret (Weisel) Kelly; married Sylvia Hayden Neahr (an English teacher), September 12, 1960; children: Jordu, Colette, Willow (all daughters). *Education:* Michigan State University, B.A. (journalism), 1961, M.A., 1962; University of Iowa, M.F.A., 1966. *Politics:* "Yes." *Religion:* "No." *Home address:* P.O. Box 53, Geneseo, N.Y. 14454. *Office:* Department of English, State University of New York College, Genesco, N.Y.

CAREER: State University of New York College at Geneseo, poet-in-residence and associate professor of English, 1967—. *Awards, honors:* State University of New York faculty fellowship in poetry, 1969; National Endowment for the Arts Discovery Grant, 1970, 1976; New York State Council on the Arts grant, 1975.

WRITINGS—All poetry: The Night of the Terrible Ladders, Hors Commerce Press (Torrance, Calif.), 1966; *All Here Together*, Lillabulero Press, 1969; *Summer Study*, Runcible Spoon Press, 1969; *Dear Nate*, Runcible Spoon Press, 1969; *Instruction for Viewing a Solar Eclipse*, Wesleyan University Press, 1972; *At a Time*, Basilisk, 1972; *Did You Hear They're Beheading Bill Johnson Today?*, The Stone Press, 1974; *The Flesh-Eating Horse*, Bartholomew's Cobble Press, 1976; *In These Rooms*, Red Hill Press, 1976.

Contributor of poetry to *Lillabulero, Nation, Meatball, Choice, Sumac, December, Poetry Review, Westigan Review, Kaleidoscope, Trace,* and other periodicals.

WORK IN PROGRESS: Several 50- and 60-poem "slim volumes"; a 200-page collected volume.

SIDELIGHTS: David Kelly told *CA:* "I am occasionally seized by the unhappy conviction that I belong to a species on the verge of its extinction and deserving of it. This of course colors my recent enjoyment of hobbies and pastimes including raising and running sled dogs, swimming, enjoying the sun, cooking and eating after somewhat of a gourmet fashion and faulty guitar playing. Important writers include, among many, Neruda, Lorca, Merwin, Chambers, Logan."

BIOGRAPHICAL/CRITICAL SOURCES: December, 1969; *Nickel Review* (Syracuse University), November 25, 1969; *Democrat and Chronicle* (Rochester), March 22, 1970; *Westigan Review* (Western Michigan University), Number 3, 1970 (special issue dedicated to Kelly's work).

*   *   *

KELLY, Gerald R(ay)   1930-

PERSONAL: Born January 18, 1930, in Milwaukee, Wis.; son of Walter W. and Grace M. (Gilbertson) Kelly. *Education:* Attended University of Wisconsin, 1954-56; Mexico City College, B.A., 1958. *Politics:* Independent. *Religion:* None. *Home address:* Box 57, West Tisbury, Mass. 02575.

CAREER: McCrindle Literary Agency, New York, N.Y., agent, 1961-63; *This Month,* Mexico City, Mexico, editor, 1963-65; Kelly, Bramhall & Ford Literary Agency, Boston, Mass., agent, 1965-68; Red Cat Books, West Tisbury, Mass., manager, 1968-69; free-lance editor and writer, 1969—. *Military service:* U.S. Navy, 1951-54; served as photographer's mate.

WRITINGS: (With William Spratling) *File on Spratling,* Little, Brown, 1967; (with Elizabeth Anderson) *Miss Elizabeth: A Memoir,* Little, Brown, 1969. Editor, *The Grapevine* (a weekly newspaper on Martha's Vineyard).

WORK IN PROGRESS: The Secession of Martha's Vineyard from the U.S. of A. Who We Don't Like No More, "a nonfiction book that turns into a novel when it has to."

SIDELIGHTS: Gerald Kelly collaborated in writing *Miss Elizabeth: A Memoir,* the autobiography of Elizabeth Anderson, Sherwood Anderson's third wife. A *New Yorker* reviewer of the book notes that "the writing is clearly that of Mr. Kelly, a professional journalist, but Mrs. Anderson's observations on her celebrated friends are just as clearly her own: 'Others might eat an apple; Sherwood *experienced* it'; 'Edna St. Vincent Millay . . . always had a coterie of followers but did not care about them one way or the other'; 'Bill Faulkner's studied courtesies and Southern mannerisms were a pose.'"

*   *   *

KELMAN, Steven   1948-

PERSONAL: Born May 1, 1948, in New York, N.Y.; son of Kurt (a patent agent) and Sylvia (an attorney; maiden name, Etman) Kelman. *Education:* Harvard University, B.A. (summa cum laude), 1970, Ph.D. candidate, 1972—. University of Stockholm, graduate study, 1970-71. *Politics:* "Democratic socialist." *Religion:* Jewish. *Home:* 21 Stoner Ave., Great Neck, N.Y. 11021.

MEMBER: Democratic Socialist Organizing Committee (member of national board), American Council on Germany (member of board of directors). *Awards, honors:* Fulbright scholar in Sweden, 1970-71.

WRITINGS: Push Comes to Shove: The Escalation of Student Protest, Houghton, 1970; *Behind the Berlin Wall,* Houghton, 1972. Contributor to *New Republic, Public Interest, New Yorker, Commentary, Harper's, New Leader,* and *Life.*

WORK IN PROGRESS: Research projects in health care and regulatory areas.

AVOCATIONAL INTERESTS: Learning of foreign languages (has mastered French, German, and Swedish).

BIOGRAPHICAL/CRITICAL SOURCES: Washington Post, May 27, 1970; *New Leader,* July 6, 1970; *New Republic,* September 26, 1970; *Commentary,* October, 1970.

*   *   *

KELTNER, John W(illiam)   1918-

PERSONAL: Born June 20, 1918, in Literberry, Ill.; son of Claude Eugene (a minister and salesman) and Geno Blanche (Lewis) Keltner; married Alberta I. Cochran (a teacher), January 1, 1941; children: Mary Jean (Mrs. Frank Rounds), Lewis Dean. *Education:* Illinois State Normal University (now Illinois State University), B.Ed., 1940; Northwestern University, M.A., 1943, Ph.D., 1947. *Politics:* Independent. *Home:* 2770 Southwest DeArmond Way, Corvallis, Ore. 97330. *Office:* Department of Speech Communication, Oregon State University, Corvallis, Ore. 97331.

CAREER: Junior high and high school teacher in Illinois, 1940-44; Northwestern University, Evanston, Ill., instructor in speech, 1944-46; Iowa State Teachers College (now University of Northern Iowa), Cedar Falls, assistant professor of speech, 1946-48; University of Oklahoma, Norman, assistant professor, 1948-51, associate professor of speech, 1951-54; Kansas State University of Agriculture and Applied Science (now Kansas State University), Manhattan, professor of speech and head of department, 1954-58; Federal Mediation and Conciliation Service, Washington, D.C., commissioner and training officer, 1958-63, consultant, 1963—; Oregon State University, Corvallis, professor of speech communication, 1963—, chairman of department, 1963-71. Principal, Consulting Associates, Corvallis, 1960—.

MEMBER: International Communication Association (member of board of directors, 1969—), American Arbitration Association (member of arbitration panel), Speech Communication Association of America (member of legislative assembly, 1956-59), National Society for the Study of Communication (second vice-president, 1954-56), National Council of Teachers of English, Adult Education Association of the U.S.A., American Association of University Professors, Central States Speech Association (president, 1951), Western States Communication Association (president, 1972), Oregon Education Association, Delta Sigma Rho, Pi Kappa Delta, Theta Alpha Phi.

WRITINGS: Group Discussion Processes, Longmans, Green, 1957; *Interpersonal Speech Communication,* Wadsworth, 1970; *Elements of Interpersonal Communication,* Wadsworth, 1973. Contributor to education, management, and speech journals. Associate editor, *Central States Speech Journal,* 1952-54, and *Journal of Communications,* 1953-55.

WORK IN PROGRESS: A study of self awareness and interpersonal communications; a revision of *Group Discussion Processes* for paperback publication; a basic reference book on dispute settlement through mediation; a study of the effect of organizational patterns of oral communication on task efficiency; a study of processes and techniques in resolving intergroup and interpersonal conflicts.

* * *

KENDALL, David Evan 1944-

PERSONAL: Born May 2, 1944, in Franklin, Ind.; son of Evan Perry (a commodities broker) and Eunice (Reagan) Kendall; married Anne N. Laybourne (a high school teacher), August 31, 1968. *Education:* Wabash College, B.A. (summa cum laude), 1966; Worcester College, Oxford, Rhodes scholar, B.A. and M.A., 1968; Yale University, LL.B., 1971. *Politics:* Registered Democrat. *Religion:* Quaker. *Home address:* 227 Lincoln Rd., Brooklyn, N.Y. 11225.

MEMBER: Phi Beta Kappa.

WRITINGS: (With Leonard Ross) *The Lottery and the Draft: Where Do I Stand?*, Harper, 1970. Contributor to *New Republic* and *Yale Law Journal.*††

* * *

KENEZ, Peter 1937-

PERSONAL: Born April 5, 1937, in Budapest, Hungary; son of Laszlo and Ilona (Harsanyi) Kenez; married Penelope Dalby, December 30, 1959. *Education:* Princeton University, B.A., 1960; Harvard University, M.A., 1962, Ph.D., 1967; St. Antony's College, Oxford, graduate study, 1963-64. *Home:* 810 Pine Tree Lane, Aptos, Calif. 95003. *Office:* Department of History, Stevenson College, University of California, Santa Cruz, Calif. 95064.

CAREER: University of California, Santa Cruz, assistant professor, 1966-71, associate professor, 1971-75, professor of history, 1975—. *Awards, honors:* Woodrow Wilson fellowship, 1960-61; International Research and Exchange Board study grant in U.S.S.R., 1969-70; Hoover Institute national fellow, 1973-74.

WRITINGS—All published by University of California Press: *Civil War in South Russia, 1918*, 1971; (contributor) *Revolution in Perspective*, 1972; *Civil War in South Russia, 1919-1920*, 1977. Contributor to *Slavonic Review, California Slavic Studies*, and other journals.

* * *

KENNEDY, David M. 1941-

PERSONAL: Born July 22, 1941, in Seattle, Wash.; son of Albert John and Millicent (Caufield) Kennedy; married Judith Osborne (a social worker), March 14, 1970; children: Ben Caufield, Elizabeth Margaret. *Education:* Stanford University, B.A. (with honors), 1963; Yale University, M.A., 1964, Ph.D., 1968. *Politics:* Registered Democrat. *Religion:* Roman Catholic. *Home:* 715 Salvatierra St., Stanford, Calif. 94305. *Office:* Department of History, Stanford University, Stanford, Calif. 94305.

CAREER: Stanford University, Stanford, Calif., assistant professor, 1967-72, associate professor of history, 1972—. Visiting professor, University of Florence, Italy, 1976-77. Member of National Planning Group, American Issues Forum, 1974; chief humanities consultant, "American Issues Radio Forum," National Public Radio, 1975-76. *Member:* American Historical Association, Organization of American Historians, American Studies Association. *Awards, honors:* John Gilmary Shea Prize of American Catholic Historical Association, 1970, and Bancroft Prize of

Columbia University, 1971, both for *Birth Control in America: The Career of Margaret Sanger;* American Council of Learned Societies fellow, and Hoover Institute of War, Revolution & Peace fellow, both 1971-72; John Simon Guggenheim fellow, 1975-76.

WRITINGS: Birth Control in America: The Career of Margaret Sanger, Yale University Press, 1970; (compiler with Paul A. Robinson) *Social Thought in America and Europe: Readings in Comparative Intellectual History*, Little, Brown, 1970; (editor) *Progressivism: The Critical Issues*, Little, Brown, 1971; (editor) *The American People in the Depression*, Pendulum Press, 1973; (editor) *The American People in the Age of Kennedy*, Pendulum Press, 1973.

WORK IN PROGRESS: World War I and American Society for Oxford University Press.

* * *

KENT, Rockwell 1882-1971
(Hogarth, Jr.)

June 21, 1882—March 13, 1971; American architect, carpenter, contractor, dairy farmer, artist, and writer. Obituaries: *Newsweek*, March 22, 1971; *Antiquarian Bookman*, May 17, 1971. (See index for *CA* sketch)

* * *

KENTON, Warren 1933-
(Z'ev ben Shimon Halevi)

PERSONAL: Born January 8, 1933; son of Simon and Esther (Barnet) Kenton. *Education:* Attended St. Martins School of Art, London, 1950-54, and Royal Academy Schools, London, 1956-58. *Home:* 44 Lansdowne Rd., London W.11, England.

CAREER: During his earlier career was a hospital worker, teacher, lecturer, and spent three years in a theater workshop; free-lance writer and graphic designer. Royal Academy of Dramatic Art, London, England, lecturer, 1963—; Architectural Association School of Architecture, London, tutor, 1966-71.

WRITINGS: Stage Properties and How to Make Them, Pitman, 1964; *As Above, So Below: A Study in Cosmic Progression*, Stuart & Watkins, 1969; *The Play Begins* (novel), Elek, 1971; *Astrology*, Thames & Hudson, 1974; *The Celestial Mirror*, Avon, 1974.

Under name Z'ev ben Shimon Halevi; all published by Rider & Co.: *Tree of Life: Introduction to the Kabbalah*, 1972; *Adam and Kabbalistic Tree*, 1974; *Way of Kabbalah*, 1976; *A Kabbalistic Universe*, 1977.

WORK IN PROGRESS: A novel, *The White Ship;* a play, "Don Immanuel"; for Rider & Co., *The Anatomy of Fate*, a philosophical study of the metaphysics of astrology.

SIDELIGHTS: Warren Kenton's books have been published in English, German, French, Dutch, Portuguese, Spanish, Japanese, and Hebrew.

BIOGRAPHICAL/CRITICAL SOURCES: Times Literary Supplement, June 26, 1969.

* * *

KERENSKY, Oleg 1930-

PERSONAL: Born January 9, 1930, in London, England; son of Oleg Alexander (a chartered civil engineer) and Nathalie (Bely) Kerensky. *Education:* Attended Westminster School, London, England, 1943-48; Christ Church, Oxford,

B.A. (honors), 1951, M.A., 1953. *Home:* 44 Pont St., London S.W.1, England. *Agent:* Curtis Brown Ltd., 575 Madison Ave., New York, N.Y. 10022.

CAREER: British Broadcasting Corp., London, England, sub-editor for BBC News, 1953-55, diplomatic correspondent, 1955-63, deputy editor of *Listener*, 1963-68; *Daily Mail*, London, ballet critic, 1957-71; *New Statesman*, London, ballet critic, 1968—; *International Herald Tribune*, Paris, France, London ballet critic, 1971—.

WRITINGS: World of Ballet, Coward, 1970 (published in England as *Ballet Scene*, Hamish Hamilton, 1970); *Anna Pavlova*, Dutton, 1973; *The New British Drama*, Hamish Hamilton, 1977. Contributor to *Times, Guardian, Dancing Times*, and other publications.

SIDELIGHTS: Oleg Kerensky, grandson of Alexander Fedorovitch Kerensky, who was prime minister of Russia in 1917, is "very interested in Soviet affairs and politics generally." His interests extend to all aspects of the theater, including opera.

BIOGRAPHICAL/CRITICAL SOURCES: New Statesman, September 18, 1970.

*   *   *

KERESZTY, Roch A(ndrew)   1933-

PERSONAL: Born February 6, 1933, in Budapest, Hungary; naturalized U.S. citizen; son of Odon (a career officer) and Margit (Csighy) Kereszty. *Education:* Eotvoes Lorant University, Budapest, M.A. in L.S., 1956; Sant'Anselmo University, Rome, Italy, S.T.L., 1960, S.T.D., 1963. *Home address:* Route 2, Box 1, Irving, Tex. 75062. *Office:* Department of Theology, University of Dallas, Irving, Tex. 75062.

CAREER: Roman Catholic priest of Cistercian Order (S.O.Cist.), ordained 1960; University of Dallas, Irving, Tex., chaplain and instructor, 1963-65, assistant professor, 1965-70, associate professor, 1970-76, adjunct professor of theology, 1976—. Teacher of theology, Cistercian Preparatory School, Irving, 1968—. *Member:* College Theology Society.

WRITINGS: God Seekers for a New Age: From Crisis Theology to Christian Atheism, Pflaum, 1970. Contributor to theology journals in the United States and Europe.

*   *   *

KERIGAN, Florence   1896-
(Frances Kerry)

PERSONAL: Born December 4, 1896, in Haverford, Pa.; daughter of John Joseph and Elizabeth (Harvey) Kerigan. *Education:* Educated in Lower Merion, Pa. *Politics:* Democrat ("usually voting independently"). *Religion:* Presbyterian. *Home and office:* 128 Arnold Rd., Ardmore, Pa. 19003.

CAREER: American Sunday School Union, Philadelphia, Pa., editorial work, 1924-45; David C. Cook Publishing Co., Elgin, Ill., editor of juvenile works, 1945-46; free-lance writer in Haverford, Pa., 1946-59; Family Service of Chester County, West Chester, Pa., secretary, 1959-66; secretary for a social service group, Philadelphia, 1966-67; free-lance writer, 1967—. *Member:* Professional Writers' Club of Philadelphia (current president), Penn Laurel Poets, Philadelphia Writers' Conference (founder and past president), Main Line Writers' Club (current vice-president).

WRITINGS: June's Quest (juvenile), Lothrop, 1931; *The Secret of the Maya Well* (teen book), Dodd, 1936; (under

pseudonym Frances Kerry) *Three on a Honeymoon*, Gramercy House, 1942; *Inspirational Talks for Women's Groups*, Standard Publishing, 1951; *Time and the Rivers*, Concordia, 1960; *Runaway from Romance*, Avalon Books, 1971; *Romance of the Moss Agate*, Avalon Books, 1972; *Passion Under the Flamboyante*, Avalon Books, 1974; *Hearts in Jeopardy*, Avalon Books, 1974. Contributor of poetry, plays, articles, fiction, and travel pieces (more than one thousand items in all) to magazines.

AVOCATIONAL INTERESTS: Music, travel, photography, gardening.

*   *   *

KETCHAM, Carl H(untington)   1923-

PERSONAL: Born October 3, 1923, in Ossining, N.Y.; son of Smith Carl (an engineer) and Eleanor (Huntington) Ketcham; married Edith Royal, June 10, 1950; children: William Christopher. *Education:* Williams College, B.A., 1944; Harvard University, M.A., 1947, Ph.D., 1951. *Politics:* Democrat. *Religion:* Episcopalian. *Home:* 7337 East Sabino Vista Dr., Tucson, Ariz. 85715. *Office:* Department of English, University of Arizona, Tucson, Ariz. 85721.

CAREER: Georgia Institute of Technology, Atlanta, instructor in English, 1945-46; New York University, New York, N.Y., instructor in English, 1948-50; University of Arizona, Tucson, instructor, 1950-55, assistant professor, 1955-61, associate professor, 1961-67, professor of English, 1967—, associate dean of Graduate College, 1970-74. *Member:* Modern Language Association of America, American Association of University Professors.

WRITINGS: (Editor) *The Letters of John Wordsworth*, Cornell University Press, 1969. Also author of articles and notes on nineteenth-century British literature.

WORK IN PROGRESS: The unpublished journals of Dorothy Wordsworth.

BIOGRAPHICAL/CRITICAL SOURCES: Georgia Review, Volume XXIII, number 3, fall, 1969.

*   *   *

KETCHAM, Charles B(rown)   1926-

PERSONAL: Born March 5, 1926, in Oberlin, Ohio; son of Charles Burgess (a college president) and Lucile (Brown) Ketcham; married Joyce A. Parker (a librarian), June 29, 1950; children: Merrick Scott. *Education:* Mount Union College, B.A. (magna cum laude), 1949; graduate study at University of Edinburgh, 1949-51, and University of Zurich, 1951; Drew Theological Seminary, B.D. (magna cum laude), 1953; University of St. Andrews, Ph.D., 1956. *Politics:* Independent. *Home:* 369 Henry St., Meadville, Pa. 16335. *Agent:* James Oliver Brown, James Brown Associates, Inc., 22 East 60th St., New York, N.Y. 10022. *Office:* Department of Philosophy and Religion, Allegheny College, Meadville, Pa. 16335.

CAREER: Minister of Methodist church in Rockaway Valley, N.J., 1956-57; Drew University, Madison, N.J., lecturer in philosophy, 1957; Allegheny College, Meadville, Pa., assistant professor, 1957-59, associate professor, 1960-64, James Mills Thoburn Professor of Religion and head of department of philosophy and religion, 1964—. *Military service:* U.S. Army, 10th Armored Division, 1944-46; served in Europe. *Member:* American Academy of Religion, American Association of University Professors. *Awards, honors:* Fulbright scholar at University of Edinburgh, 1949-50.

WRITINGS: The Search for Meaningful Existence, Weybright & Talley, 1968; (editor with James F. Day) *Faith and Freedom,* Weybright & Talley, 1969; *Federico Fellini,* Paulist/Newman, 1976. Also author of *The Theology of Encounter.*

WORK IN PROGRESS: Ingmar Bergman.

AVOCATIONAL INTERESTS: Hiking, photography.

* * *

KETTELKAMP, Larry 1933-

PERSONAL: Born April 25, 1933, in Harvey, Ill.; son of Gilbert Clarence (a teacher and administrator) and Ona (Webb) Kettelkamp; married Florence Goy, June 6, 1954; children: Lauren Lynn, Keith Allan, Karl William, Marianne. *Education:* University of Illinois, B.F.A. in painting, 1953; attended Pratt Institute, 1953-54. *Religion:* "Truth!" *Home:* 2 Wynnewood Dr., Cranbury, N.J. 08512.

CAREER: Spencer Press, Champaign, Ill., developed curriculum resource materials, 1956-58; Garrard Press, Champaign, Ill., art director, 1959-60; *Highlights for Children,* Honesdale, Penn., staff artist, 1962-67; Cranbury School, Cranbury, N.J., teacher, 1968—. Member of a baroque ensemble, The Cranbury Consort. *Military service:* Army Security Agency, 1954-56. *Member:* American Society for Psychic Research.

WRITINGS—All self-illustrated; all published by Morrow, except as noted: *Magic Made Easy,* 1954; *Spooky Magic,* 1955; *The Magic of Sound,* 1956; *Shadows,* 1957; *Singing Strings,* 1958; *Kites,* 1959; *Drums, Rattles and Bells,* 1960; *Gliders,* 1961; *Flutes, Whistles and Reeds,* 1962; *Puzzle Patterns,* 1963; *Spirals,* Prentice-Hall, 1964; *Horns,* 1964; *Spinning Tops,* 1966; *Song, Speech and Ventriloquism,* 1967; *Dreams,* 1968; *Haunted Houses,* 1969; *Sixth Sense,* 1970; *Investigating UFOs,* 1971; *Religions East and West,* 1972; *Astrology: Wisdom of the Stars,* 1973; *Tricks of Eye and Mind: The Story of Optical Illusion,* 1974; *Hypnosis: The Wakeful Sleep,* 1975; *A Partnership of Mind and Body: Biofeedback,* 1976; *Investigating Psychics: Five Life Histories,* 1977.

Illustrator: Herbert S. Zim, *The Sun,* Morrow, 1953, new edition with new illustrations, 1975; H. S. Zim, *Parrakeets,* Morrow, 1953; *Some Are Small,* Garrard, 1959; *When I Have a House,* Guideways, 1961; *Explorations in Chemistry,* Highlights for Children, 1967.

WORK IN PROGRESS: A guitar method book, *Folk-Classic Guitar.*

SIDELIGHTS: Larry Kettelkamp told *CA:* "Since I do a number of things—draw, write prose and poetry, compose and perform music—I am interested in the creative base for such activities. The key seems to be the understanding of consciousness itself. Recent research (as well as ancient traditions) suggests that consciousness has diverse levels of experience and expression, some quite divorced from the common physical world. Indeed consciousness seems quite free of the body at times and able to transcend the usual ideas of time and space. Consciousness itself is a creator of reality. This is the motivation behind the preparation of my books for young readers on such subjects as illusion, hypnosis, religion, biofeedback and extrasensory perception. The world is much more than it seems on the surface and a true and deep understanding is just beginning to unfold. I want to encourage young people to join in this unfolding, and they will have to reexamine everything in order to do this—history, science, and the materialistic view of personality. They will need all the help they can get. But such help is on hand if it can be made available to them in a form they can handle."

BIOGRAPHICAL/CRITICAL SOURCES: Charlotte S. Huck and D. A. Young, *Children's Literature in the Elementary School,* Holt, 1961; *The Children's Bookshelf,* Child Study Association of America, 1965; *Illustrators of Children's Books: 1957-1966,* Horn Book, 1968; *New York Times Book Review,* May 11, 1969, February 21, 1971.

* * *

KHRUSHCHEV, Nikita Sergeyevich 1884-1971

April 17, 1884—September 11, 1971; Russian leader; first secretary of Central Committee and chairman of Council of Ministers of U.S.S.R.; became premier. Obituaries: *New York Times,* September 12, 1971; *Detroit News,* September 12, 1971; *Washington Post,* September 13, 1971, September 14, 1971; *Time,* September 20, 1971.

* * *

KIANTO, Ilmari 1874-1970

1874—April 27, 1970; Finnish novelist, essayist, and poet. Obituaries: *New York Times,* April 29, 1970; *Antiquarian Bookman,* May 25, 1970; *Books Abroad,* spring, 1971.

* * *

KIBLER, Robert J(oseph) 1934-

PERSONAL: Born October 6, 1934, in Dayton, Ohio; son of Robert Joseph and Pauline (McFann) Kibler; married Sharon McCollum, June 27, 1954; children: Valerie Deanne, Vance Aric, Lora Megan. *Education:* Ohio State University, B.Sc., 1957, M.A., 1959, Ph.D., 1962. *Home:* 2936 Brandermere Dr., Tallahassee, Fla. 32303. *Office:* Department of Communication, Florida State University, Tallahassee, Fla. 32306.

CAREER: Southern Illinois University, Carbondale, assistant professor of communication, 1962-64, assistant professor of educational psychology, 1964-66, associate professor, 1966-67, director of Educational Research Bureau, 1964-67; Purdue University, Lafayette, Ind., associate professor of communication and associate director of Communication Research Center, 1967-69; Florida State University, Tallahassee, professor of communication, 1969—. Distinguished visiting professor, University of Montana, summer, 1969. Field reader, U.S. Office of Education, 1966-71. Consultant, Educational Testing Service; consulting editor for communication, Prentice-Hall, 1969—. *Military service:* U.S. Army, 1957-58; became first lieutenant.

MEMBER: Speech Communication Association of America (chairman of research board, 1969; member of finance board, legislative council, and administrative committee, 1970-73; member of administrative committee, 1976; member of educational policy board, 1976-79), International Communication Association (vice-president of Instructional Communication Division; member of board of directors, 1975-80; president, 1977-78), American Psychological Association, American Educational Research Association. *Awards, honors:* Outstanding Young Teacher Award from Central States Speech Association, 1964.

WRITINGS: (Contributor) Ronald Reid, editor, *An Introduction to the Field of Speech,* Scott, Foresman, 1965; (editor with Larry L. Barker) *Conceptual Frontiers in Speech Communication,* Speech Communication Association, 1969; (contributor) Philip Emmert and William Brooks, editors,

Methods of Research in Communication, Houghton, 1970; (with Barker and David T. Miles) *Behavioral Objectives and Instruction,* Allyn & Bacon, 1970; (with Barker) *Speech Communication Behavior,* Prentice-Hall, 1971; (with Donald J. Cegala, Barker, and Miles) *Objectives for Instruction and Evaluation,* Allyn & Bacon, 1974; (contributor) Leslie J. Briggs, editor, *Introduction to Instructional Design,* Educational Technology Publications, 1977. Contributor to communication, education, and psychology journals. Contributing editor, *Dramatics,* 1962-63; associate editor, *Southern Speech Journal,* 1969-71, 1975-77, *Human Communication Research,* 1974-77, *Contemporary Psychology,* 1975—.

WORK IN PROGRESS: With Barker, Cegala, and Kathy Wohlers, *Small Group Communication,* completion expected in 1978.

*   *   *

KIDD, Harry 1917-

PERSONAL: Born August 30, 1917, in Edinburgh, Scotland; son of Harry (a ship surveyor) and Annie (Fage) Kidd; married Marie Williams, August 5, 1944; children: Susan Penelope Rhys (Mrs. Ian James Parker), Victoria Mair Rhys. *Education:* Oxford University, M.A., 1945; Cambridge University, M.A., 1945. *Home:* 30 Staverton Rd., Oxford, England. *Office:* Office of the Bursar, St. John's College, Oxford University, Oxford OX1 2JD, England.

CAREER: Affiliated with British Ministry of Labour and National Service, London, England, 1940-45; Cambridge University, Cambridge, England, first assistant registrary, 1945-54; University of London, London School of Economics and Political Science, London, secretary, 1954-67; Oxford University, St. John's College, Oxford, England, bursar, 1967—.

WRITINGS: The Trouble at L.S.E., 1966-1967, Oxford University Press, 1969.

*   *   *

KIDDELL, John 1922-

PERSONAL: Surname is pronounced Kid-*dell;* born January 23, 1922, in Melbourne, Australia; son of John Herbert (a business executive) and Elizabeth A.G.M. (Farr) Kiddell; married Beb Thornton (a company director), January 8, 1949; children: Elizabeth Ann, David John. *Education:* Attended Wesley College, Melbourne, and Royal Melbourne Institute of Technology. *Address:* P.O. Box 71, Hunter's Hill, New South Wales 2110, Australia. *Agent:* Jo Stewart, 201 East 66th St., New York, N.Y. 10021.

CAREER: Worked in marketing and administration for several corporations prior to 1965; "vacated industry . . . most happily" to write; also managing director of Tarban Holdings Pty. Ltd. Life governor of Burwood Boys Home, Melbourne, 1959—. *Military service:* Australian Imperial Forces, 1st Australian Armoured Division, World War II. *Member:* Australian Society of Authors, Authors Guild, Authors League of America. *Awards, honors: Euloowirree Walkabout* was included on the *School Library Journal* (United States) list of the best books of 1968.

WRITINGS: Day of the Dingo, Thomas Nelson, 1955; *Giant of the Bush,* Bobbs-Merrill, 1962; *Euloowirree Walkabout* (teen book), Chilton, 1968; *Tod* (teen book), Chilton, 1968; *A Community of Men,* Chilton, 1969; *Choogoowarra: Australian Sheep Station,* Macmillan, 1972. Devised and wrote several early episodes for Australian television series,

"The Battlers," 1968, a television play "'D' Is for Destruction," produced, 1969, and a play produced twice by Australian Broadcasting Commission and British Broadcasting Commission on radio as "Totem Pole," 1969, and on television as "The Catalyst," 1970. Also author of screenplay, "Giant of the Bush," Samson Productions, 1977. Contributor of short stories and articles to Australian magazines, 1936-55.

WORK IN PROGRESS: An untitled novel.

BIOGRAPHICAL/CRITICAL SOURCES: Book World, May 5, 1968; *Best Sellers,* October 1, 1968; *Children's Book World,* November 3, 1968.

*   *   *

KIENIEWICZ, Stefan 1907-

PERSONAL: Born September 20, 1907, in Dereszewicze, Poland; son of Antoni (a government official) and Magdalena (Grabowska) Kieniewicz; married Zofia Sobanska, October 18, 1937; children: Jan, Andrzej, Teresa. *Education:* University of Poznan, M.A., 1930; University of Warsaw, Dr.Ph., 1934. *Religion:* Roman Catholic. *Home:* 83/87 Wiktorska Str., Warsaw 12, Poland. *Office:* Faculty of History, University of Warsaw, Warsaw, Poland.

CAREER: Financial Archive, Warsaw, Poland, archivist, 1937-44; University of Warsaw, Warsaw, professor of modern history, 1946—. *Member:* Polish Academy of Sciences, Polish Historical Association, Polish National Committee of Historical Sciences (president, 1969).

WRITINGS: Ignacy Dzialynski, 1754-1797, Kornickej, 1930; *Adam Sapieha,* Ossolinskich, 1939; *Oblicze ideowe wiosny ludow* (economic history, 1750-1918), Szkolnych, 1948; *Konspiracje galicyjskie, 1831-1845* (on Galicia), Ksiazka & Wiedza, 1950; *Rewolucja polska 1846 roku: Wybor zrodel* (on 1846 revolution), Ossolinskich, 1950; *Ruch chlopski w Galicji w 1846 roku* (title means "The Peasant Movement in Galicia in 1846"), Ossolinskich, 1951; *Sprawa wloscianska w powstaniu styczniowym* (title means "The Agrarian Problem in the January Insurrection"), Ossolinskich, 1953; *Warszawa w powstaniu styczniowym* (on Warsaw and the revolution, 1863-64), Wiedza Powszechna, 1954, 3rd edition, 1965; *Legion Mickiewicza, 1848-1849* (title means "The Legion of Mickiewicz, 1848-1849"), Panstwowe Wydawnictwo Naukowe, 1955; *Adam Mickiewicz jako polityk,* [Warsaw], 1955; (co-author and editor) *Historia Polski, 1795-1864,* Skolnych, 1956; *Samotnik brukselski: Opowiesc o Joachimie Lelewelu,* Wiedza Powszechna, 1960, 2nd edition, 1964; *Spoleczenstwo polskie w powstaniu poznanskim 1848 roku* (title means "The Polish Society in the Poznan Insurrection 1848"), Panstwowe Wydawnictwo Naukowe, 1960; (with Kalikst Morawski) *La Polonia e il Risorgimento Italiano* (booklet on Italian relations with Poland), Signorelli (Rome), 1961; *Miedzy ugoda a rewolucja* (title means "Between Compromise and Revolution"), Panstwowe Wydawnictwo Naukowe, 1962; *Dramat trzezwych entuziastow* (title means "The Drama of Sober Enthusiasts"), Wiedza Powszechna, 1964; *Wiek XIX* (collection of Kieniewicz's writings and lectures), edited by Barbara Grochulska, Boguslaw Lesnodorski, and Andrzej Zahorski, Panstwowe Wydawnictwo Naukowe, 1967; *Historia Polski 1795-1918,* Panstwowe Wydawnictwo Naukowe, 1968, 3rd edition, edited by Irena Tatarczuk, 1970, translation published as *A History of Poland 1795-1918,* Arthur Vanous, 1969; *The Emancipation of the Polish Peasantry,* University of Chicago Press, 1970; *Powstanie styczniowe* (title means "The January Insurrection of 1863"), Panstwowe Wydawnictwo Naukowe, 1972.

Editor: *Rok 1848 w Polsce,* Ossolinskich, 1948; *Przemiany spoleczne i gospodarcze w Krolestwie Polskin, 1815-1830,* Ksiazka & Wiedza, 1951; *Galicja w dobie autonomicznej, 1850-1914,* Ossolinskich, 1952; Z. Janczewski and others, *Zezania sledcze o powstaniu styczniowym,* Ossolinskich, 1956; (with Iza Biezunska-Malowiat and Antoni Maczak), *Z epoki Mickiewicza* (includes summaries in Russian and French), Ossolinskich, 1956; (with Tadeusz Mencel and Wyladyslaw Rostocki) *Wybor tekstow zrodlowych z historii Polski w latach 1795-1864,* Panstwowe Wydawnictwo Naukowe, 1956; *Chlopi i sprawa chlopska w powstaniu styczniowym* (contains documents in Polish and Russian), Ossolinskich, 1962; *Powstanie styczniowe 1863,* Polskie Towarzystwo Naukowe, 1963; *Ruch rewolucyjny 1861 roku w Krolestwie Polskim* (contains documents in Polish and Russian), Ossolinskich, 1963; *Korespondencja namiestnikow Krolestwa Polskiego z 1861 roku* (contains documents in Russian and French), Ossolinskich, 1964; *Zbior zeznan sledczych o przebiegu powstania styczniowego* (contains documents in Polish and Russian), Ossolinskich, 1965; (with I. S. Miller) *Prasa tajna z lat 1861-1864,* Ossolinskich, 1966; *Spiskowcy i partyzanci 1863 roku,* Panstwowe Wydawnictwo Naukowe, 1967; (with W. Koroluk) *Zabor pruski w powstaniu styczniowym* (text in German; preface also in Polish and Russian), Ossolinskich, 1968; (editor with I. Miller) *Dokumenty Wydzialu Wojny Rzadu Narodowego, 1863-1864,* Ossolinskich, 1973. Editor-in-chief, *Przeglad Historyczny* (historical review), Warsaw, 1952—.

WORK IN PROGRESS: A history of Warsaw in the nineteenth century.

SIDELIGHTS: Stefan Kieniewicz writes and reads English, French, German, and Russian.†

*   *   *

KIESLING, Christopher (Gerald) 1925-

PERSONAL: Surname is pronounced Keys-ling; born August 15, 1925, in Chicago, Ill.; son of Edward Joseph (in advertising) and Florence (Fiset) Kiesling. *Education:* Pontifical Philosophical Faculty of St. Thomas, River Forest, Ill., Ph.L., 1950; University of St. Thomas Aquinas, Rome, Italy, S.T.L., 1956; Pontifical Theological Faculty of Immaculate Conception, Washington, D.C., S.T.D., 1965. *Home and office:* Aquinas Institute of Theology, 2570 Asbury St., Dubuque, Iowa 52001.

CAREER: Entered Order of Preachers (Dominicans), 1947, ordained Roman Catholic priest, 1954; Aquinas Institute of Theology, Dubuque, Iowa, professor of theology, 1956—. Research fellow, Divinity School, Yale University, 1970-71. Director of formation, Province of St. Albert, 1975—. Lecturer and retreat master. *Member:* North American Academy of Liturgy, North American Academy of Ecumenists, Catholic Theological Society of America.

WRITINGS: (Contributor) Reginald Masterson, editor, *Seeking the Kingdom,* B. Herder, 1961; (contributor) Masterson, editor, *Theology in the Catholic College,* Priory Press, 1961; (contributor) T. A. O'Meara and C. D. Weisser, editors, *Paul Tillich in Catholic Thought,* Priory Press, 1964; *Before His Majesty,* Aquinas Library, 1965; *The Spirit and Practice of the Liturgy,* Priory Press, 1965; *The Future of the Christian Sunday,* Sheed, 1970; (contributor) James Michael Lee and Patrick C. Rooney, editors, *Toward a Future for Religious Education,* Pflaum Standard, 1970; *Any News of God?,* Pflaum Standard, 1971; *Confirmation and Full Life in the Spirit,* St. Anthony Messenger Press, 1973. Contributor to *McGraw's New Catholic Encyclopedia for Home and School;* contributor to *Worship, Review for Religious, Cross and Crown, Theological Studies, Living Light, Chicago Studies, Journal of Ecumenical Studies, Pastoral Life,* and other journals. Associate editor, *Cross and Crown.*

WORK IN PROGRESS: A book on celibacy, prayer, and friendship.

SIDELIGHTS: Father Kiesling told *CA:* "My writing satisfies my need to approach life creatively rather than passively. I prefer to write my thoughts than read others'—and certainly to write rather than watch TV. My writing is also a way for me to help others find their way through life."

*   *   *

KIM, K(wan) H(o) 1936-

PERSONAL: Born June 21, 1936, in Yosu, Korea; son of In Che and Soon-ye (Cho) Kim; married Kyung Ae Kim, August 27, 1966 (divorced); married Susan F. Farrell, September, 1972; children: Mimi. *Education:* Attended University of Pennsylvania and Stanford University. *Home:* 8315 North Brook Lane, Bethesda, Md. 20014. *Office:* Mathematica, Inc., 4630 Montgomery Ave., Bethesda, Md. 20014.

CAREER: Battelle Memorial Institute, Columbus, Ohio, senior economist, 1965-69, director of Washington, D.C. office, 1968-69; Leo Kramer, Inc., Washington, D.C., director of economics department, 1969-70; Jack Faucett Associates, Inc., Silver Spring, Md., director of research, 1970-71; TEMPO Center for Advanced Studies, Washington, D.C., full-time consultant, 1971-74; General Research Corp., McLean, Va., full-time consultant, 1975-76; Mathematica, Inc., Bethesda, Md., full-time consultant, 1976—. Consultant, U.S. Department of Defense, 1970—; advisor to Governor's Task Force on Employment Expansion, Columbus, Ohio, 1971-73. *Member:* Econometric Society, American Economic Association, American Statistical Association.

WRITINGS: (With Susan Farrell and Ewan Clague) *The All-Volunteer Army: An Analysis of Demand and Supply,* Praeger, 1971. Author of research papers on economics and defense planning.

*   *   *

KIM, Kyung-Won 1936-

PERSONAL: Born June 12, 1936, in Chinnampo, Korea; son of Soong-Key (a physicist) and Choon-Ran (Lee) Kim; married Akyong Park (a musician), 1960; children: Hunsoo, Eusoo (sons). *Education:* Williams College, B.A., 1959; Harvard University, Ph.D., 1963. *Home:* 36-8 Hongchi-dong, Seoul, Korea. *Office:* Ch'ong Wa Dae, Seoul, Korea.

CAREER: York University, Toronto, Ontario, assistant professor of political science, 1963-66; New York University, New York, N.Y., associate professor of political science, 1967-71; Korea University, Seoul, professor of political science, 1971-75; special assistant on international affairs to the president of the Republic of Korea, 1975—. *Member:* International Institute for Strategic Studies, Phi Beta Kappa. *Awards, honors:* Canada Council senior research fellow, 1966-67.

WRITINGS: Revolution and International System, New York University Press, 1970. Also author of articles and reports on U.S. foreign policy and Asian affairs.

*   *   *

KIM, Richard C(hong) C(hin) 1923-

PERSONAL: Born December 16, 1923, in Maui, Hawaii;

son of Young Cho and Pil Soo (Kim) Kim; married Frances M. Tokunaga, December, 1940; children: Toni (Mrs. Hollis Coleman), Melinda (Mrs. Dan Trammell), Jacque (Mrs. Nick de Vries). *Education:* Oklahoma Baptist University, B.A., 1956; University of Oklahoma, M.A., 1958, Ph.D., 1963. *Politics:* Liberal. *Home:* 3710 South St., Nacogdoches, Tex. 75961. *Office:* Department of Political Science, Stephen F. Austin State University, Nacogdoches, Tex. 75961.

CAREER: American Can Co., Kahului, Hawaii, clerk, 1945-50, supervisor of quality control, 1950-53; University of Oklahoma, Norman, instructor in political science, 1959-61; Hardin-Simmons University, Abilene, Tex., assistant professor, 1961-62, associate professor, 1962-64, professor of political science and chairman of Division of Social Science, 1964-67; Stephen F. Austin State University, Nacogdoches, Tex., associate professor of political science, 1967—. Fulbright lecturer in India, 1965-66; visiting professor, Inter-American University of Puerto Rico, 1967; consultant to junior colleges, National Defense Education Act, 1967; lecturer in Japan, University of Maryland Overseas, 1968. *Military service:* U.S. Army, 1942-45; served in Japan as interpreter for Army Intelligence. *Member:* American Political Science Association, American Association of University Professors, Southwestern Social Science Association, Rocky Mountain Social Science Association, Pi Sigma Alpha, Phi Alpha Theta.

WRITINGS: (Editor) *Politics and Polemics,* McCutchan, 1968; *Kimbrations,* R. F. Publishers, 1976. Contributor to social science and education journals.

WORK IN PROGRESS: Eastern Political Thought.

SIDELIGHTS: Richard Kim is fluent in Korean in addition to Japanese. *Avocational interests:* Art (mainly graphic), travel.

* * *

KIM, Seung Hee 1936-

PERSONAL: Born May 31, 1936, in Seoul, Korea; son of Dong Yun and Namsung (Hyun) Kim; married Kyung-sun Choi, 1966; children: Jason C., Lesley. *Education:* Juniata College, B.S., 1960; New York University, M.B.A., 1963, Ph.D., 1969. *Home:* 56 Berrywood Dr., St. Louis, Mo. 63122. *Office:* School of Commerce and Finance, St. Louis University, St. Louis, Mo. 63108.

CAREER: Manufacturers Hanover Trust, New York, N.Y., in international banking department, 1960-61; Canisius College, Buffalo, N.Y., instructor in finance and international economics, 1968-70; St. Louis University, St. Louis, Mo., 1970—, began as instructor, currently professor of finance and international finance. *Member:* American Economic Association, American Finance Association, Financial Management Association, American Institute of Decision Sciences.

WRITINGS: Foreign Capital for Economic Development: A Korean Case Study, Praeger, 1970. Contributor to economics and finance journals.

WORK IN PROGRESS: A book, *International Business Finance.*

* * *

KING, Coretta Scott 1927-

PERSONAL: Born April 27, 1927, in Marion, Ala.; daughter of Obie (a pulpwood dealer) and Bernice (Mc-Murry) Scott; married Martin Luther King, Jr. (civil rights leader and winner of Nobel Peace Prize, 1964), June 18, 1953 (assassinated April 4, 1968, in Memphis, Tenn.); children: Yolanda Denise, Martin Luther III, Dexter Scott, Bernice Albertine. *Education:* Antioch College, B.A.; New England Conservatory of Music, Mus.B. *Religion:* Baptist. *Home and office:* 234 Sunset Ave. N.W., Atlanta, Ga. 30314. *Agent:* Joan Daves, 515 Madison Ave., New York, N.Y. 10022.

CAREER: Voice instructor at Morris Brown College, Atlanta, Ga., 1962; sometimes substituted for her husband as a civil rights speaker during his lifetime, and also appeared as a concert artist and speaker in her own right; her particular contribution to the civil rights movement is the freedom concert, inaugurated at Town Hall in New York, November, 1964; since then has presented more than thirty freedom concerts in which she sings, recites poetry, and lectures, with benefits going to the Southern Christian Leadership Conference, its affiliates, and (more recently) the Martin Luther King, Jr. Memorial Center, Atlanta; narrator of Aaron Copland's "A Lincoln Portrait" at concerts performed by Washington National Symphony Orchestra in Washington, D.C., and New York, 1968, and by San Francisco Symphony, 1970; speaker in India on 1969 visit to accept the Nehru Award for International Understanding, presented posthumously to her husband; first woman to preach at a statutory service at St. Paul's Cathedral, London, 1969. President of Martin Luther King, Jr. Foundation and Martin Luther King, Jr. Memorial Center, Atlanta. Member of board of directors, Southern Christian Leadership Conference, and National Organization for Women. Co-chairman, Clergy and Laymen Concerned about Vietnam, and National Commission for Full Employment, 1974. Trustee, Robert F. Kennedy Memorial Foundation. Member of board of fellows, Boston University.

MEMBER: Women's International League for Peace and Freedom, National Council of Negro Women, Women Strike for Peace, Links, Inc., United Church Women, Alpha Kappa Alpha. *Awards, honors:* Annual Brotherhood Award, National Council of Negro Women, 1957; Distinguished Achievement Award, National Association of Colored Women's Clubs, 1968; Woman of the Year Award, National Association of Radio and Television Announcers, 1968; Wateler Peace Prize, 1968; selected in national college student poll as most admired woman, 1968, 1969; Pacem in Terris Award of International Overseas Service Foundation, 1969; Dag Hammarskjoeld Award and diploma as academicien, World Organization of the Diplomatic Press-Academie Diplomatique de la Paix, 1969. Honorary doctorates from Boston University, Marymount Manhattan College, and Brandeis University, 1969; University of Bridgeport, Wilberforce University, Bethune-Cookman College, Morgan State College, Morehouse College, Princeton University, and Keuka College, 1970; Northeastern University and Bates College, 1971.

WRITINGS: (Author of foreword) Martin Luther King, Jr., *Where Do We Go from Here: Chaos or Community?,* memorial edition, Bantam, 1968; (author of foreword) Martin Luther King, Jr., *Trumpet of Conscience,* Harper, 1968; *My Life with Martin Luther King, Jr.* (Book-of-the-Month Club selection), Holt, 1969. Contributor to a book about Robert Kennedy. Contributor to *Good Housekeeping, New Lady, McCall's, Theology Today,* and other periodicals.

SIDELIGHTS: Following her husband's assassination on April 4, 1968, Coretta King honored her husband's previously-made speaking commitments. It was during this period that Mrs. King's contributions to the civil rights cause as an effective and influential leader earned her the respect and admiration of people both involved with the movement and apart. Mrs. King's actions and speeches reflect her late husband's belief in nonviolent social change and a strong personal conviction to seeing this change take place.

Reviewers found *My Life with Martin Luther King, Jr.* flawed only by the portrayal of Dr. King as a man without human weaknesses. "Understandably enough," Patricia Canham writes in the *Christian Science Monitor,* "it is the public image, the 'noble servant of humanity' that Mrs. King wishes to perpetuate." A *Time* critic concurs: "Dispassionate reportage is not her real purpose. Rather, she has undertaken to bear witness to his life, and she has done so with great warmth and skill." The book, unlike many memorials, was not ghost-written. It was a best seller in America, led the British best seller list for some weeks, and sold well in Germany, Netherlands, Sweden, and Finland. It has been translated into a total of twelve languages, serialized in *Life* and metropolitan American newspapers, and included in *Reader's Digest Condensed Books,* fall, 1969.

BIOGRAPHICAL/CRITICAL SOURCES: Life, April 19, 1968, September 19, 1969; *Newsweek,* April 22, 1968, March 24, 1969, May 12, 1969; *Ladies' Home Journal,* June, 1968; *Ebony,* September, 1968; *Vogue,* May, 1969; *Christian Science Monitor,* September 25, 1969; *National Observer,* September 29, 1969; *Time,* October 3, 1969; *New Republic,* October 11, 1969; *Books,* March, 1970.

* * *

KING, Cynthia 1925-

PERSONAL: Born August 27, 1925, in New York, N.Y.; daughter of Adolph (a metallurgical engineer) and Elsie (a psychologist; maiden name, Oschrin) Bregman; married Jonathan King (an architect), July 26, 1944; children: Gordon, Austin, Nathaniel. *Education:* Attended Columbia University, Bryn Mawr College, 1943-44, University of Chicago, 1944-46; also attended writers' workshops at New York University, 1967-69, and University of Houston, 1974-76. *Home:* 2659 Englave Dr., Ann Arbor, Mich. 48103.

CAREER: Associate editor, Hillman Periodicals, New York City, 1946-51; managing editor, Fawcett Publications, New York City, 1951-56; former lecturer and speaker on writing and mythology in Houston (Tex.) public and private schools, libraries, and colleges; currently full-time writer. Coordinator of exhibition on children's book art, Contemporary Arts Museum, Houston, 1975; chairman, Houston Writers Workshop, 1975-76. *Member:* Associated Authors of Children's Literature, Society of Children's Book Writers, Teachers and Writers Collaborative, American-Scandinavian Foundation, Audubon Society, Sierra Club.

WRITINGS: In the Morning of Time: The Story of the Norse God Balder (juvenile), Four Winds, 1970; (contributor) James White and Walter McDonald, editors, *Texas Stories and Poems 1,* Texas Center for Writers Press, 1977; *The Year of Mr. Nobody* (juvenile), Harper, 1978. Contributor of book reviews to *New York Times Book Review, Houston Chronicle,* and *Opera Cues.*

WORK IN PROGRESS: Nonfiction juvenile books.

SIDELIGHTS: Cynthia King writes: "I have two memos posted over my desk. The first says, 'Writing is something you do, not just something you think about.' The other says (and I am not sure of the source) 'Why is a turnip like a free lance writer?' The first haunts me when I am doing all of those things that have to be done, and postponing the writing. The second reminds me that in everything I write the unanswered questions are as important as the answered ones. Writing is always, for me, like life—a treasure hunt. Or as the little boy in my recently completed juvenile says when he turns over a log, 'You never know what you'll find in the woods.'"

* * *

KING-HALL, Magdalen 1904-1971

July 22, 1904—March 1, 1971; British author and novelist. Obituaries: *Antiquarian Bookman,* June 24, 1971. (See index for *CA* sketch)

* * *

KING-HELE, Desmond (George) 1927-

PERSONAL: Surname is pronounced King-Heeley; born November 3, 1927, in Seaford, England; son of Sydney George (in government service) and Bessie (Sayer) King-Hele; married Marie Therese Newman, August 31, 1954; children: Carole, Sonia. *Education:* Trinity College, Cambridge, B.A. (first class honors), 1948, M.A., 1952. *Home:* 3 Tor Rd., Farnham, Surrey, England. *Office:* Royal Aircraft Establishment, Farnborough, Hampshire, England.

CAREER: Royal Aircraft Establishment, Farnborough, England, member of scientific research staff, 1948—, research concentrated on space, 1955—, deputy chief scientific officer, space department, 1968—. Bakerian lecturer, Royal Society, 1974; Halley Lecturer, Oxford University, 1974. *Member:* Royal Society (London; fellow), Royal Astronomical Society (fellow), Institute of Mathematics and Its Application (fellow), International Academy of Astronautics. *Awards, honors:* Eddington Gold Medal of Royal Astronomical Society, 1971; Charles Chree Medal and Prize of Institute of Physics, 1971.

WRITINGS: Shelley, the Man and the Poet, Yoseloff, 1960 (published in England as *Shelley, His Thought and Work,* Macmillan, 1960), 2nd edition, Barnes, 1971; *Satellites and Scientific Research,* Routledge & Kegan Paul, 1960, 2nd edition, revised, Dover, 1962; *Erasmus Darwin,* Macmillan, 1963, Scribner, 1964; *Theory of Satellite Orbits in an Atmosphere,* Butterworth & Co., 1964; (editor) *Space Research V,* North-Holland Publishing, 1965; *Observing Earth Satellites,* Macmillan, 1966; (editor, and author of linking commentary) *The Essential Writings of Erasmus Darwin,* MacGibbon & Kee, 1968, Hillary, 1969; *The End of the Twentieth Century?,* St. Martin's, 1970; *Poems and Trixies,* Mitre Press, 1972; *Doctor of Revolution,* Faber, 1977.

Published technical reports for Royal Aircraft Establishment include *Average Rotational Speed of the Upper Atmosphere from Changes in Satellite Orbits,* 1970, and *The Shape of the Earth,* 1970. Contributor to *Nature, Keats-Shelley Memorial Bulletin, Proceedings of Royal Society, Planetary and Space Science,* and other scientific journals.

AVOCATIONAL INTERESTS: Tennis, walking in the countryside, enjoying natural beauties.

* * *

KINGSBURY, Arthur 1939-

PERSONAL: Born August 20, 1939, in Joplin, Mo.; son of Charles H. and Beatrice (Rich) Kingsbury; married Mary Dell Harden (a teacher), July 3, 1963. *Education:* Daytona Beach Junior College, A.A., 1964; Florida State University,

B.S., 1966; Michigan State University, M.S., 1968; Wayne State University, Ph.D., 1976. *Office:* Macomb County Community College, Mount Clemens, Mich. 48043.

CAREER: U.S. Department of Treasury, Washington, D.C., agent in criminal investigation, 1966; Wisconsin State University, Platteville, (now University of Wisconsin—Platteville), assistant director of department of police science and administration, 1968-69; Macomb County Community College, Mt. Clemens, Mich., chairman of public services, 1969-75, associate dean of business and public service programs, 1975—. Vice-president of Security Management Services Ltd. *Military service:* U.S. Army, intelligence, 1964-66. U.S. Army Reserve, 1957-69. *Member:* American Society for Industrial Security.

WRITINGS: (With Richard Post) *Security Administration: An Introduction,* C. C Thomas, 1970, 3rd edition, 1977; *Law Enforcement Academic Guidelines,* Macomb County Community College, 1970; *Academic Security Guidelines for Community Colleges,* American Association of Junior Colleges, 1971. Contributor to *Industrial Security* and *Environmental Control and Safety Management.*

SIDELIGHTS: Arthur Kingsbury lived in Central America for several years. Lecture tours have afforded him the opportunity to reside in or visit over thirty-two nations.

* * *

KINTSCH, Walter 1932-

PERSONAL: Born May 30, 1932, in Temeschwar, Rumania; son of Christof (a teacher) and Irene (Hollerbach) Kintsch; married Eileen Hoover, June 26, 1959; children: Anja Sophia, Julia A. *Education:* University of Kansas, M.A., 1956, Ph.D., 1960; attended University of Vienna, 1957-58. *Office:* Department of Psychology, University of Colorado, Boulder, Colo. 80304.

CAREER: University of Indiana, Bloomington, U.S. Public Health Service research fellow, 1960-61; University of Missouri, Columbia, assistant professor of psychology, 1961-65; University of California, Riverside, associate professor of psychology, 1965-67; Stanford University, Stanford, Calif., visiting associate professor, 1967-68; University of Colorado, Boulder, professor of psychology, 1968—. Member of small grants study section, Institute of Mental Health, 1969-73. *Member:* American Psychological Association, Psychonomic Society. *Awards, honors:* Fulbright scholarship, 1955-56; National Institute of Mental Health fellowship, 1960-61.

WRITINGS: Learning, Memory, and Conceptual Processes, Wiley, 1970; (contributor) D. A. Norman, editor, *Models of Human Memory,* Academic Press, 1970; (contributor) Endel Tulning and Wayne Donaldson, editors, *Organization of Memory,* Academic Press, 1972; (with Edward Crothers and others) *The Representation of Meaning in Memory,* Erlbaum, 1974; *Memory and Cognition,* Wiley, 1977. Contributor to psychology journals. Editor, *Journal of Value Learning and Verbal Behavior,* 1972—.

* * *

KIPPLEY, John F(rancis) 1930-

PERSONAL: Born November 6, 1930, in Minneapolis, Minn.; son of Frank F. (in business management) and Hazel E. (Forth) Kippley; married Sheila K. Matgen, April 27, 1963; children: Jennifer, Mary, Margaret, Karen. *Education:* St. Paul Seminary, St. Paul, Minn., B.A., 1952; University of Minnesota, M.A. (industrial relations), 1956; University of San Francisco, M.A. (theology), 1967; Graduate Theological Union, Berkeley, Calif., M.A. (applied theology), 1970. *Politics:* Centrist. *Religion:* Roman Catholic. *Office address:* Couple to Couple League, P.O. Box 11084, Cincinnati, Ohio 45211.

CAREER: Sales representative for data processing systems in Omaha, Neb., and San Francisco, Calif., 1957-62; director-teacher of parish adult religious education programs in Santa Clara, Calif., and then in Regina, Saskatchewan, 1963-69; Marymount College, Salina, Kan., assistant professor of theology, 1969-71; Church of St. Odilia, St. Paul, Minn., professional coordinator, 1971-72; College of Mount St. Joseph, Cincinnati, Ohio, assistant professor of theology, 1972-74; Couple to Couple League, Cincinnati, executive director, 1974—.

WRITINGS: Covenant, Christ, and Contraception, Alba, 1970; (with wife, Sheila Kippley) *The Art of Natural Family Planning,* Couple to Couple, 1975; *Birth Control and the Marriage Covenant,* Liturgical Press, 1976. Contributor to *Ave Maria, America, Linacre Quarterly, St. Anthony Messenger,* and *Theological Studies.*

WORK IN PROGRESS: Research in the theology behind the sexual revolution for a book tentatively entitled *Two Packages of Sex;* continuing research about natural family planning.

SIDELIGHTS: John Kippley told *CA:* "I have been unable to remain indifferent to the overall decline of sexual morality that has accompanied the acceptance and practice of contraception; nor can I remain indifferent to past declines in sexual morality and overall declines in civilization, relationships that seem to be occurring once again. Therefore, in the wake of the well publicized rejection of *Humanae Vitae* by some, I wrote *Covenant, Christ and Contraception* which both analyzed (and found wanting) the reasons given for marital contraception and also provided a case for the traditional Christian teaching using a theology of personalism."

* * *

KIRCHNER, Glenn 1930-

PERSONAL: Born February 12, 1930; married October 28, 1972; wife's name, Diane Marie; children: (previous marriage) Grant, Mark, Brian, Paul. *Education:* University of British Columbia, B.P.E., 1954; University of Oregon, M.Sc., 1956, Ed.D., 1958. *Home:* 6083 Blink Bonnie, West Vancouver, British Columbia, Canada. *Office:* Department of Education, Simon Fraser University, Burnaby, British Columbia, Canada.

CAREER: Simon Fraser University, Burnaby, British Columbia, professor of education, 1965—. Member of first study mission to People's Republic of China, 1971. *Member:* American Association for Health, Physical Education and Recreation, Canadian Association for Health, Physical Education and Recreation.

WRITINGS: Physical Education for Elementary School Children: An Illustrated Program of Activities for Kindergarten to Grade Six, W. C. Brown, 1966, 4th edition published as *Physical Education for Elementary School Children: A Humanistic Approach,* 1978; (with Jean Cunningham and Eileen Warrell) *Introduction to Movement Education: An Individualized Approach to Teaching Physical Education,* W. C. Brown, 1970, 2nd edition, 1977. Author or co-author of twenty-seven educational films on movement education, physical education and related topics.

WORK IN PROGRESS: New book on physical education and continuation of educational film series.

* * *

KIRK, David 1935-

PERSONAL: Born March 12, 1935, in Kirkville, Miss.; son of Leo C. (a cotton grower) and Ruth (Clay) Kirk. *Education:* University of Alabama, B.S., 1957; Columbia University, M.A., 1961; Beda College, Rome, Italy, theological student, 1961-64; Union Theological Seminary, New York, further theological study. *Politics:* Socialist. *Home and office:* Emmaus House, 241 East 116th St., New York, N.Y. 10029.

CAREER: Became a Catholic convert (Melkite rite) while attending University of Alabama; teacher in Alabama public schools, 1957-59, and participant in the interracial movement in the South, taking part in the first sit-ins in Atlanta; taught school in New York while completing his work at Columbia University and also opened a hospitality house for overflow from the Catholic Worker Movement Center; entered Beda College to study for the priesthood under sponsorship of the Melkite Patriarch and was ordained in Basilica of St. Anne in Jerusalem in August, 1964; with a Beda College companion, Lyle Young, taught and counseled delinquents in East Harlem parishes while raising money to found Emmaus House, an interdenominational community in New York; director of Emmaus House and a leader in the movement variously called the New Church or the Underground Church, 1966—. Professor of theology or lecturer at St. John's University, Jamaica, College of New Rochelle, and other institutions. *Member:* Southern Christian Leadership Conference, National End of the War Committee, Farm Workers Committee, New York City Clergy Coalition.

WRITINGS: (Editor with Malcolm Boyd) *Underground Church,* Sheed, 1968; (editor) *Quotations from Chairman Jesus: The Good News of Revolution,* foreword by Daniel Berrigan, Templegate, 1969. Contributor to *Commonweal* and a number of other religious periodicals. Co-editor, *Bread Is Rising* (publication of and also the motto of Emmaus House), 1966-70.

WORK IN PROGRESS: Quotations from God's Revolutionaries; and *The Third Alternative to Western Christian Chaos: Eastern Christianity.*

AVOCATIONAL INTERESTS: Handicrafts, carpentry, bicycling, regular fasting (for health and spiritual good).

BIOGRAPHICAL/CRITICAL SOURCES: New Yorker, January 25, 1969; Francine D. Gray, *Divine Disobedience: Profiles in Catholic Radicalism,* Knopf, 1970.††

* * *

KIRSCHNER, Allen 1930-

PERSONAL: Born June 7, 1930, in Port Washington, N.Y.; son of Jack Louis and Frances (Gardner) Kirschner; married Linda Heinlein (a writer), December 20, 1968; children: Stephen, Michael, Scott, Kenneth, Edward. *Education:* University of Colorado, B.A., 1953; New York University, M.A., 1955; Columbia University, M.A., 1957. *Home:* 32 Randall Rd., Princeton, N.J. 08540.

CAREER: English teacher in public schools of Greenwich, Conn., 1954-62; Princeton (N.J.) Regional Schools, chairman of department of English, 1962-71; Hun School, Princeton, N.J., chairman of department of English, 1971—. Adjunct professor of English, Jersey City State College, 1965-68.

WRITINGS—Editor, except as noted: (With Mark Shorer, Arno Jewett, and Walter Havighurst) *American Literature,* Houghton, 1965; *Great Sports Reporting,* Dell, 1969; *Voices of Poetry,* Dell, 1970; (with Alfred Ferguson) Herman Melville, *Billy Budd and Other Stories,* Houghton, 1970; (with Philip McFarland, Morse Peckam, and Ferguson) *Themes in American Literature,* Houghton, 1971; (with wife, Linda Kirschner) *Film: Readings in the Mass Media,* Bobbs-Merrill, 1971; (with L. Kirschner) *Radio and Television: Readings in the Mass Media,* Bobbs-Merrill, 1971; (with L. Kirschner) *Journalism: Readings in the Mass Media,* Bobbs-Merrill, 1971; (with L. Kirschner) *Blessed Are the Peacemakers,* Popular Library, 1971; (with Peckham and McFarland) *Perceptions in Literature,* Houghton, 1971.

* * *

KISSIN, Eva H. 1923-

PERSONAL: Born February 12, 1923, in New York, N.Y.; daughter of Samuel A. (an architect) and Rose (Rubenstein) Hertz; married Benjamin Kissin (a medical doctor and professor), July 1, 1950; children: Ruth. *Education:* Syracuse University, B.A. (magna cum laude), 1943; New York University, M.A., 1949, M.A., 1970. *Home:* 25 Grace Ct., Brooklyn Heights, N.Y. 11201. *Agent:* Curtis Brown Ltd., 575 Madison Ave., New York, N.Y. 10022.

CAREER: Teacher in the public schools of New York City, 1946-52; English teacher at Ramaz School, New York City, beginning 1973. Brooklyn Museum, Brooklyn, N.Y., consultant on junior membership, 1961-69, vice-president of community committee. *Member:* Phi Beta Kappa.

WRITINGS: (Editor) *Stories in Black and White* (juvenile), Lippincott, 1970.

WORK IN PROGRESS: A second short story anthology.

* * *

KITANO, Harry H. L. 1926-

PERSONAL: Born February 14, 1926, in San Francisco, Calif.; married; wife's name, Y. Lillian; children: Keith, Kimberly, Kraig, Kerrily. *Education:* University of California, Berkeley, B.A., 1948, M.S.W., 1951, Ph.D., 1958. *Home:* 10500 Sandal Lane, Los Angeles, Calif. 90024. *Office:* Department of Sociology, University of California, Los Angeles, Calif. 90024.

CAREER: University of California, Los Angeles, 1958—, began as assistant professor, currently professor of social welfare and sociology, academic affirmative action officer, 1976—.

WRITINGS: The Child Care Center: Interaction among One Parent Family, Teachers and Children, University of California Press, 1962; *Japanese Americans: The Evolution of a Subculture,* Prentice-Hall, 1969, revised edition, 1976; (with Roger Daniels) *American Racism: Exploration of the Nature of Prejudice,* Prentice-Hall, 1970; *Race Relations,* Prentice-Hall, 1974. Also writer of filmstrip, "The Wartime Evacuation of the Japanese," for Social Studies School Service, 1970.

* * *

KLAAS, Joe 1920-

PERSONAL: Surname is pronounced klass; born March 24, 1920, in San Francisco, Calif.; son of Otto Henry (a transportation executive) and Isabel Emma (Schwesinger) Klaas;

married Betty Jane Stanley, June 8, 1947; children: Marc, Anthony, Marianna, Juliet, Jonathon, Hero. *Education:* University of Washington, B.A., 1946, M.A., 1952. *Politics:* Democrat. *Religion:* Protestant. *Office:* American Broadcasting Co., 277 Golden Gate Ave., San Francisco, Calif. 94102.

CAREER: Alaska Broadcasting System, Anchorage, news director, 1947-49; KUJ, Walla Walla, Wash., program director, 1949-50; Fisher Broadcasting Co., Seattle, Wash., account executive, 1954-56; KITO, San Bernardino, Calif., general manager, 1957-59; Crowell-Collier Broadcasting Co., Oakland, Calif., sales manager, 1959-61; Churchill Broadcasting Co., San Francisco, Calif., account executive, 1961-67; American Broadcasting Co., San Francisco, account executive, 1967—. Talent scout and screenwriter for Mardi Gras Productions, 1957-59. *Military service:* Royal Air Force, pilot, 1941-42; became sergeant; received Distinguished Service Medallion. U.S. Army Air Forces, 1942-45; became lieutenant colonel; received Air Medal with six oak leaf clusters, Purple Heart. U.S. Air Force Reserve, 1945-70. *Member:* International Platform Association, Authors Guild, Air Force Association, Sigma Delta Chi.

WRITINGS: Maybe I'm Dead, Macmillan, 1955; *Amelia Earhart Lives: A Trip Through Intrigue to Find America's First Lady of Mystery,* McGraw, 1970. Contributor to periodicals.

WORK IN PROGRESS: A novel, *Where in Hell Is Moses?,* completion expected in 1978.

SIDELIGHTS: Joe Klaas has traveled widely in England, France, Belgium, Germany, Czechoslovakia, Hungary, Austria, Switzerland, Italy, Spain, Tunisia, Algeria, Morocco, and islands in the South Pacific. He told *CA:* "[I] firmly believe that each of us can turn his will and his life over to the care of God and thereby achieve the freedom to do everything he wants to do. When you do what you want to do, you are a success. I believe everyone should do what he wants to do in total freedom. Any compromise of one's own wants is failure. Most people, starting with childhood, form a pattern of turning themselves down, which is a habit of failure. I do what I want to do and am free and successful. I fought for freedom, gave up to God, and won it."

AVOCATIONAL INTERESTS: Skin diving, riding horses.

*   *   *

KLAYMAN, Maxwell Irving 1917-

PERSONAL: Born April 30, 1917, in Boston, Mass.; son of Joseph (a businessman) and Lena (Seidenberg) Klayman; married Alice Budd (a computer scientist); children: Judith Ann, Daniel Budd, Naomi Jean. *Education:* University of Massachusetts, B.S. (cum laude), 1938; Iowa State University, M.S., 1941; Harvard University, M.A., 1951, Ph.D., 1968. *Politics:* Democrat. *Home:* 115 Melbourne Ave., Akron, Ohio 44313. *Office:* Department of Marketing, University of Akron, Akron, Ohio 44304.

CAREER: U.S. Department of Agriculture, Bureau of Agricultural Economics, Washington, D.C., economist in Division of Marketing and Transportation Research, 1939-41; U.S. Department of Labor, Bureau of Labor Statistics, Washington, D.C., economist, 1946-48; U.S. Department of Agriculture, Bureau of Agricultural Economics, sugar analyst, 1948-49; United Nations Food and Agriculture Organization, Rome, Italy, economist, 1951-68 (spent 1962-64 on special fund project in Cali, Colombia); State University of New York College at New Paltz, professor of economics,

1968-70; University of Akron, Akron, Ohio, professor of marketing and international business, 1970—. Faculty research associate, Graduate School of Public and International Affairs, University of Pittsburgh, 1965, 1966; visiting professor, University of Maryland, 1967-68; professor of business administration, Pahlavi University, Smiraz, Iran, 1974-77. Consultant, Inter-American Development Bank, 1967-69. *Military service:* U.S. Army, 1941-45.

MEMBER: Association for Education in International Business, American Marketing Association, American Economic Association, American Agricultural Economic Association, Society for International Development.

WRITINGS: The Moshav in Israel: A Case Study of Institution-Building for Agricultural Development, Praeger, 1969; *Data Needs for Agricultural Sector and Project Analyses,* Inter-American Development Bank, 1970. Contributor of articles and papers in English and Spanish to journals in the fields of economic development, international economics, agricultural development and policy, marketing, and statistics.

WORK IN PROGRESS: Continued research on the Moshav in Israel and the economy of Israel; research on international business in Canada, and on decision-making in domestic and international marketing.

*   *   *

KLEIN, Muriel Walzer 1920-

PERSONAL: Born September 15, 1920, in Hempstead, N.Y.; daughter of Isadore (a civil engineer) and Jennie (Flaxman) Walzer; married Leo Klein (a certified public accountant), April 24, 1955 (deceased); children: Gerald Alan, Jonathan David. *Education:* Attended Adelphi University, 1938-39; New York University, B.S., 1942; Columbia University, M.A., 1947. *Politics:* Independent. *Religion:* Jewish. *Home:* 14 Margaret Ct., Great Neck, N.Y. 11024.

CAREER: Elementary teacher in Roslyn, N.Y., 1942-48, in Manhasset, N.Y., 1948—; Long Island University, graduate Library School, Greenvale, N.Y., 1958—, began as adjunct assistant professor, currently adjunct associate professor. Summer instructor, State University of New York College at New Paltz, 1955, 1957, 1958; master teacher in summer program and instructor in children's literature, Adelphi University, summers, 1964-68. *Member:* National Council of Teachers of English, International Reading Association, New York State United Teachers, New York Library Association.

WRITINGS: (With Gerald G. Glass) *From Plays into Reading,* Allyn & Bacon, 1969. Her adaptation of "Ali Baba and the Forty Thieves" is included in *Entrances and Exits,* Dodd, 1960, and a shortened version in *Treasure Gold,* Heath, 1964.

WORK IN PROGRESS: A collection of plays adapted from the great stories of children's literature, for use in the middle school.

SIDELIGHTS: Muriel Klein writes: "I believe that the children's theatre children enjoy most are well-produced plays written for children to perform for other children. I have spent many years adapting great stories into plays that children could bring to life on stage. Even though most of the children in the audience will never read the classic the play was adapted from, at least they will have been exposed to great literature."

KLEINE-AHLBRANDT, W(illiam) Laird 1932-

PERSONAL: Born June 17, 1932, in Cincinnati, Ohio; son of Ernst Henry (a mechanical engineer) and Emma (a teacher; maiden name, Mithoefer) Kleine; married Cornelia K. Bodde (a professional counselor), April 20, 1963; children: Trevor, Stephanie, Courtenay. *Education:* University of Cincinnati, B.A., 1954, M.A., 1959; University of Geneva, Dr. es Sciences Politiques, 1962. *Home:* 140 Thornbush Dr., West Lafayette, Ind. 47906. *Office:* University Hall, Purdue University, West Lafayette, Ind. 47907.

CAREER: College of William and Mary, Richmond Professional Institute, Richmond, Va., instructor in history and political science, 1962-63; Purdue University, West Lafayette, Ind., assistant professor, 1963-69, associate professor of modern European history, 1969—. *Military service:* U.S. Air Force, 1954-57; became first lieutenant. *Member:* American Historical Association, Society for French Historical Studies, Phi Alpha Theta.

WRITINGS: The Policy of Simmering: A Study of British Policy during the Spanish Civil War (1936-1939), Nijhoff, 1963; (editor) *Appeasement of the Dictators: Crisis Diplomacy,* Holt, 1970; *Ploughshares into Swords,* Dryden, 1977. Contributor to *Opera News* and scholarly journals.

WORK IN PROGRESS: A history of Europe in the twentieth century.

AVOCATIONAL INTERESTS: Collecting old maps and modern paintings; "a fanatic about grand opera."

* * *

KLENK, Robert W(illiam) 1934-

PERSONAL: Born May 18, 1934, in Sandusky, Ohio; son of William and Louise (Wein) Klenk; married Eula Day, June 16, 1956; children: Cynthia Ann. *Education:* Ohio University, B.S. in Ed., 1956; Ohio State University, M.S.W., 1962; additional study at George Warren Brown School of Social Work, 1965-66, and University of Chicago Summer Institute, 1966. *Home address:* Route 2, Townline Rd., Norwalk, Ohio 44857. *Office address:* Huron County Mental Health and Mental Retardation Board, P.O. Box 531, Norwalk, Ohio 44857.

CAREER: Marion Correctional Institution, Marion, Ohio, social worker and acting supervisor of social services department, 1962-63; Veterans Administration Hospital, Chillicothe, Ohio, clinical social worker, 1963-65; Boys Town of Missouri, St. James, director of social services and field instructor, 1965-67; Region V Comprehensive Mental Health Retardation Center, Bowling Green, Ky., chief social worker, 1967-68; Western Kentucky University, Bowling Green, assistant professor of social work, 1967-70; Huron County Mental Health and Mental Retardation Board, Norwalk, Ohio, executive director, 1970—. Special instructor in sociology, Ashland College, 1971—. Consultant, Southern Kentucky Economic Opportunity Council and Purchase Area Economic Opportunity Council, 1967-68, Kentucky Institute for Community Development, 1968, Bowling Green Model City Demonstration Agency, 1968-69. *Military service:* U.S. Marine Corps, 1957-59; became sergeant. U.S. Army Reserve, Medical Service Corps, social work officer, 1964-66; became first lieutenant. *Member:* National Association of Social Workers, Academy of Certified Social Workers, Council on Social Work Education.

WRITINGS: (With Robert M. Ryan) *The Practice of Social Work,* Wadsworth, 1970, 2nd edition, 1974.†

KLEWIN, W(illiam) Thomas 1921-
(Tom Matthews)

PERSONAL: Born January 31, 1921, in Sheboygan, Wis.; son of Emil H. and Minnie (Gottowski) Klewin; married Jean S. McDaniel, February 8, 1947; children: Diana, Michael, Leslie Ellen, Matthew, Shelley. *Education:* Attended Concordia Junior College, Milwaukee, Wis., 1935-41; Concordia Seminary, St. Louis, Mo., A.B., 1943, B.D., 1945, S.T.M., 1971; Washington University, St. Louis, A.M., 1945; further graduate study at Drew University, 1948-50, Perkins Seminary, Dallas, Tex., 1958-59, and University of New Hampshire, 1967-68; Stockton State College, B.S. (anthropology), 1977. *Residence:* Crapaud, Prince Edward Island, Canada.

CAREER: Ordained a Lutheran minister, 1946; minister in Morristown, N.J., 1947-51; U.S. Air Force, chaplain, 1951-73, became lieutenant colonel; Southshore Health Plan, Atlantic City, N.Y., health educator, 1975-76. Instructor in history, Ricker College, Houlton, Me., 1964-65; instructor in European history with the overseas branch of University of Maryland, 1969.

WRITINGS: Love Thy Teenager, Ave Maria Press, 1970. Also author of booklets, *Coping with Stress,* 1974, and *Preparing for Retirement,* 1975, for National Research Bureau, and *Teens and Alcohol,* Liguorian Press, 1977. Contributor of more than five hundred articles to religious journals, occasionally under pseudonym Tom Matthews. Contributing editor, *Pastoral Life.*

WORK IN PROGRESS: Today's Children, Tomorrow's World; research on family and youth problems.

* * *

KLIEVER, Lonnie D(ean) 1931-

PERSONAL: Born November 18, 1931, in Corn, Okla.; son of David R. (a mechanic) and Amanda (Warkentine) Kliever; married Arthiss Laughman, August 14, 1964; children: Launa Deane, Marney Marie. *Education:* Hardin-Simmons University, B.A. (magna cum laude), 1955; Union Theological Seminary, New York, N.Y., B.D. (cum laude), 1959; Duke University, Ph.D., 1963. *Home:* 9549 Spring Branch, Dallas, Tex. 75238. *Office:* Department of Religion, Southern Methodist University, Dallas, Tex. 75275.

CAREER: University of Texas, El Paso Campus, assistant professor, 1962-63, associate professor of philosophy, 1963-65; Trinity University, San Antonio, Tex., associate professor of religion, 1965-69; University of Windsor, Windsor, Ontario, associate professor, 1969-71, professor of theology, 1971-75; Southern Methodist University, Dallas, Tex., professor of religion and chairman of department, 1975—. Member, Human Relations Council of El Paso, 1964-65. *Member:* American Academy of Religion, American Association of University Professors, Society for the Scientific Study of Religion, Canadian Society for the Study of Religion, Canadian Theological Society.

WRITINGS: (With John H. Hayes) *Radical Christianity: The New Theologies in Perspective,* Droke, 1968. Contributor to *Journal of Religion, Harvard Theological Review, Religion in Life,* and *Christian Century.*

WORK IN PROGRESS: Two books, *Religion as a Symbol System,* and *H. Richard Niebuhr.*

SIDELIGHTS: Lonnie D. Kliever has traveled in the Soviet Union as well as in western Europe and Mexico. *Avocational interests:* Politics, woodworking.

KLING, Robert E(dward), Jr. 1920-

PERSONAL: Born May 29, 1920, in York, Pa.; son of Robert Edward (a printer) and Gladys (Kinneman) Kling; married Doris M. Gilroy, June 11, 1943 (deceased); married Mary Apostolou (a personnel officer), May 29, 1969; children: (first marriage) Robert E. III, Stephen C.; (second marriage) Jonathon B., Susan M. *Education:* University of Maryland, student, 1937-38, 1952-54. *Home:* 701 Notley Rd., Silver Spring, Md. 20904.

CAREER: United States Government Printing Office, Washington, D.C., photoengraver, 1946-52, division superintendent, 1952-60, assistant to director of engineering, 1961-62, special assistant, 1962-70, superintendent of documents, 1970-73. Art and advertising consultant; commercial artist. President of city council, Hyattsville, Md., 1959-69. *Military service:* U.S. Army, Corps of Engineers, 1944-46, 1950-52; became lieutenant colonel.

WRITINGS: The Government Printing Office, Praeger, 1970.

WORK IN PROGRESS: A novel on German occupation.

* * *

KLUCKHOHN, Frank L. 1907-1970

November 24, 1907—October 2, 1970; American government advisor, newspaperman, and author. Obituaries: *New York Times,* October 4, 1970; *Washington Post,* October 5, 1970. (See index for *CA* sketch)

* * *

KLUGER, James R. 1939-

PERSONAL: Born November 11, 1939, in Davenport, Iowa; son of Frank F. (a truck driver) and Vera (Neyens) Kluger. *Education:* St. Ambrose College, B.A., 1961; University of Arizona, M.A., 1965, Ph.D., 1970. *Home:* 1700 East Lester St., Tucson, Ariz. 85719. *Office:* Pima College, Tucson, Ariz.

CAREER: Midwestern College, Denison, Iowa, instructor in humanities, 1965-67; University of Utah, Salt Lake City, assistant professor of history, 1970-71; Texas College, Tyler, associate professor of history, 1971-75; Pima College, Tucson, Ariz., instructor, 1975—. *Military service:* U.S. Army Reserve. *Member:* Organization of American Historians, Western History Association, Phi Alpha Theta, Delta Epsilon Sigma. *Awards, honors:* Outstanding Teacher Award, Midwestern College, 1966.

WRITINGS: (Assistant to editor John Alexander Carroll) *Reflections of Western Historians,* University of Arizona Press, 1969; *The Clifton-Morenci Strike: Labor Difficulty in Arizona, 1915-1916,* University of Arizona Press, 1970.

WORK IN PROGRESS: A biography of Elwood Mead.

* * *

KNAPPER, Christopher (Kay) 1940-

PERSONAL: "K" in surname is silent; born March 4, 1940, in Crewe, England; son of Harold Alfred Kay (a tool-fitter) and Hilda (Nevitt) Knapper; married Jean Mary Haywood, December 30, 1966 (divorced, 1976). *Education:* University of Sheffield, B.A. (honors), 1961; University of Saskatchewan, Ph.D., 1969. *Politics:* Socialist. *Religion:* Atheist. *Home:* 630 Rockway Dr., Kitchener, Ontario, Canada. *Office:* Department of Psychology, University of Waterloo, Waterloo, Ontario, Canada, N2L 3G1.

CAREER: Cutlery Research Council, Sheffield, England, editorial, information, and liaison officer, 1961-62; University of Sheffield, Sheffield, England, independent research worker in department of psychology, 1962-66; University of Regina, Regina, Saskatchewan, instructor and special lecturer, 1966-69, assistant professor, 1969-71, associate professor, 1971-76, professor of psychology, 1976, chairman of department, 1969-76; University of Waterloo, Waterloo, Ontario, professor of psychology and environmental studies, and teaching resource person, 1976—. University of Regina, co-chairman of M.A. program in communications, 1971-72, chairman of advisory committee to school of social work, 1971-73. External examiner, Ph.D. theses, York University, 1972. Canada Council, referee of research grant applications, 1972-75, member of doctoral fellowship selection committee, 1975, chairman of committee, 1976. Visiting scientist, University of Lethbridge, 1973. Research fellow, University of Waikato (New Zealand), 1974. Consultant for film series on post-secondary education, Association of Universities and Colleges of Canada, 1975—.

MEMBER: British Psychological Society (fellow), Canadian Psychological Association, Society for the Psychological Study of Social Issues, American Psychological Association (foreign affiliate), Canadian Association of University Teachers (chairman of professional orientation committee, 1971-73; member of curriculum, research, and education committee, 1971-73; treasurer and chairman of finance and management committee, 1972-73; member of executive committee, 1972-73; member of board, 1972-73, 1974—; member of teaching effectiveness subcommittee, 1973—; member of academic freedom and tenure committee, 1974—), Rocky Mountain Psychological Association, Midwestern Psychological Association, Saskatchewan Psychological Association, Psychological Society of Saskatchewan (secretary, 1967-69), Regina Campus Faculty Association (chairman, 1970-71), Regina Film Society (executive president, 1969-70). *Awards, honors:* Canada Council fellowship for work on psychology of clothes, 1968; Federal Department of Transportation grant, 1973, for investigation of psychological factors in automobile safety; Canada Council grant, 1973-74, to study teaching effectiveness and training strategies in Commonwealth universities.

WRITINGS: (Contributor) P. Heilmann, editor, *Materialen zur Einfuehrung in die Publizistik-Wissenschaft,* Volume I, Institute of Publicity, Free University of Berlin, 1966; (with Peter B. Warr) *Perception of People and Events,* Wiley, 1968; (with A. J. Cropley and R. J. Moore) *A Quasi-Clinical Strategy for Safety Research: A Case Study of Attitudes to Seat Belts,* Federal Department of Transportation (Ottawa), 1973; (contributor with Cropley) *Proceedings of the First International Conference on Driver Behaviour,* International Drivers' Behaviour Research Association (Paris), 1974; (with Cropley) *Property and Insurance: A Study of Public Opinion,* University of Regina, 1975; (editor) *Scaling the Ivory Tower: Appraising College and University Teaching,* Clarke, 1976; (contributor with Cropley) P. Stringer and H. Wenzel, editors, *Transportation and Urban Life,* Plenum, 1976; (editor) *If Teaching Is Important . . .,* Clarke, 1977. Contributor to professional journals and to newspapers. Editor, *Design in Sheffield,* 1964-66; referee, *Canadian Journal of Behavioural Science,* 1974, 1975; abstracter, *Psychological Abstracts.*

WORK IN PROGRESS: A book on personality and dress; an introductory text in psychology; work on training of university teachers for Canadian Association of University

Teachers; developing an innovative strategy for measuring public attitudes to important national issues.

SIDELIGHTS: Christopher Knapper feels that "in spite of the television age, it is important for academics to be able to communicate clearly in writing—both to their students and the public at large." He is competent in French and German.

*   *   *

KNOLL, Gerald M.   1942-

PERSONAL: Born October 7, 1942, in St. Louis, Mo.; son of Donald M. and Mary (Mattingly) Knoll; married Carol Davis, June 20, 1964; children: Kirsten, Sarah, Tobias. *Education:* St. Louis University, B.S., 1964; University of California, Santa Barbara, M.A., 1966. *Home address:* P.O. Box 392, Dale, Ind. 47523. *Office:* Abbey Press, St. Meinrad, Ind. 47577.

CAREER: Abbey Press, St. Meinrad, Ind., assistant director, product development, 1971-74, creative director, 1974—.

WRITINGS: (Editor with Philip Dacey) *I Love You All Day/It Is That Simple: Modern Poems of Love and Marriage,* Abbey Press, 1970; *The Living Book,* Abbey Press, 1975.

*   *   *

KNOP, Werner   1912(?)-1970

1912(?)—October 22, 1970; German-born economic writer and foreign correspondent. Obituaries: *New York Times,* October 23, 1970; *Washington Post,* October 23, 1970.

*   *   *

KNOWLES, Asa S(mallidge)   1909-

PERSONAL: Born January 15, 1909, in Northeast Harbor, Me.; son of Jerome Henry and Lilla Belle (Smallidge) Knowles; married Edna Irene Worsnop, March 24, 1930; children: Asa Worsnop, Margaret Anne Knowles Browning. *Education:* Bowdoin College, A.B., 1930; Harvard University, additional study, 1930-31; Boston University, A.M., 1935. *Politics:* Republican. *Religion:* Episcopalian. *Home:* 388 Beacon St., Boston, Mass. 02116. *Office:* Northeastern University, 360 Huntington Ave., Boston, Mass. 02115.

CAREER: Northeastern University, Boston, Mass., instructor, 1931-35, assistant professor and head of department of industrial engineering, 1936-39, professor of industrial engineering, dean of College of Business Administration, and director of Bureau of Business Research, 1939-42; University of Rhode Island, Kingston, professor of industrial administration and dean of School of Business Administration, 1942-46; Associated Colleges of Upper New York (Mohawk, Champlain, and Sampson Colleges), president, 1946-48; Cornell University, Ithaca, N.Y., vice-president for development, 1948-51; University of Toledo, Toledo, Ohio, president, 1951-58; Northeastern University, president, 1958-75, chancellor, 1975—. National Commission for Cooperative Education, vice-chairman, 1962-75, chairman, 1975—. Chairman, Massachusetts Commission on Postsecondary Education, 1975-76. Member of board of directors, Shawmut Association, Inc., National Shawmut Bank of Boston, Arkwright-Boston Insurance Co., and other government groups.

MEMBER: American Academy of Arts and Sciences (fellow), Association of American Colleges, American Council on Education, Association of Independent Colleges and Universities in Massachusetts (vice-chairman, 1973-74; chairman, 1974-75), New England Association of Colleges and Secondary Schools (president, 1971-72), Pershing Rifles, Tau Beta Pi, Chi Psi, Phi Kappa Phi, and a number of other honorary and social fraternities.

AWARDS, HONORS: LL.D. from Bowdoin College, 1951, Northeastern University, 1957, Emerson College and University of Toledo, 1960, and Brandeis University, 1968; Litt.D. from Western New England College, 1961; Sc.D. from New England College of Pharmacy, 1962, and Lowell Technological Institute, 1966; D.B.A. from University of Rhode Island, 1967, and Bryant College, 1967. Awards for distinguished service include Distinguished Service Medal and Citation, U.S. Army, 1966; Albert S. Bard Award of Chi Phi, 1964; Tiffany Glass Flame, American College Public Relations Association, 1974; Herman Schneider Award, 1977.

WRITINGS: Industrial Management: Principles and Problems, Macmillan, 1944; (with Robert D. Thomson) *Management of Manpower,* Macmillan, 1943; (with Thomson) *Production Control,* Macmillan, 1943; (with Thomson) *Industrial Management* (includes *Management of Manpower, Production Control,* and other material), Macmillan, 1944; *Handbook of College and University Administration,* two volumes, McGraw, 1970; (co-author and editor) *Handbook of Cooperative Education,* Jossey-Bass, 1971. Author or co-author of *Salary Evaluation, Merit Rating in Industry,* and other bulletins of Bureau of Business Research, Northeastern University, 1940-41. Contributor to educational journals. Editor, *International Encyclopedia of Higher Education,* 1977.

*   *   *

KNOWLES, Louis L(eonard)   1947-

PERSONAL: Born January 4, 1947, in Volga, S.D.; son of Louis Edward (a minister and teacher) and Velma (Fusby) Knowles; married Ruby Takanishi (a research assistant at Stanford University), August 23, 1969. *Education:* Stanford University, A.B., 1968; University of Chicago, M.Th., 1970; San Francisco Theological Seminary, M.Div., 1971, D.Min., 1973. *Residence:* Los Angeles, Calif. *Office:* Christian Church Regional Office, 3126 Los Feliz Blvd., Los Angeles, Calif. 90064.

CAREER: Presbyterian minister. Seminarians Organized for Racial Justice, Chicago, Ill., organizer, 1968-70; Mid-Peninsula Community House, East Palo Alto, Calif., acting director, 1970-71; consultant, Center of Metropolitan Mission In-service Training, 1973-75; coordinator of Christian Concerns for Christian Church (Disciples of Christ) in southern California, 1975—.

WRITINGS: (Editor with Kenneth Prewitt) *Institutional Racism in America,* Prentice-Hall, 1969. Columnist, *Stanford Daily,* 1967-68. Contributor to journals in his field.

BIOGRAPHICAL/CRITICAL SOURCES: Washington Post, February 24, 1970.

*   *   *

KNOX, Edmund George Valpy   1881-1971 (EVOE)

1881—January 2, 1971; British journalist and editor. Obituaries: *Antiquarian Bookman,* January 18, 1971.

KNOX-JOHNSTON, Robin 1939-

PERSONAL: Born William Robert Patrick Knox-Johnston, March 17, 1939, in Putney, England; son of David Robert (a company director) and Elizabeth Mary (Cree) Knox-Johnston; married, 1962 (divorced); children: Sara. *Education:* Attended Berkhamstead School, 1952-56. *Politics:* Conservative, and Unionist Party. *Religion:* Church of England. *Home:* Cherry Trees, School Lane, Hamble, Hampshire, England. *Agent:* John Farquharson Ltd., 15 Red Lion Sq., London WC1R 4QW, England.

CAREER: Lived in India, 1960-65; sailed from India in the thirty-two-foot ketch "Suhaili" to England via the Cape of Good Hope, 1965-67; made a 35,000-mile solo voyage around the world in "Suhaili," 1968-69, the first and only man to sail around the world non-stop single-handed; director of the British firms, Knoxmore, Ltd., D. R. Knox-Johnston & Sons Ltd., London, Knox-Johnston Marine Ltd., Port Hamble Ltd., Hoo Marina Ltd., Terminist Ltd., and Flagtime Ltd. Chairman, British Olympic Yachting Appeal. Freeman of Borough of Bromley. *Military service:* Royal Naval Reserve, 1961—; current rank, lieutenant commander.

MEMBER: Royal Yachting Association (member of Olympic committee), Ocean Cruising Club, Naval Club (London), Royal Irish Yacht Club, Royal Harwich Yacht Club, Benfleet Yacht Club, County Wicklow Yacht Club, Royal Naval Sailing Association, Little Ship Club, Royal Motor Yacht Club, Southampton Master Mariners Club, Cape Horners Club. *Awards, honors:* Commander, Order of the British Empire; *Sunday Times* Golden Trophy as yachtsman of the year, 1970; Sir Francis Chichester Award of Royal Yacht Squadron, 1970; Royal Cruising Club Seamanship Medal; Riposto Silver Galleon Award, 1969.

WRITINGS: A World of My Own: The Single-Handed Non-Stop Circumnavigation of the World in Suhaili (autobiographical), Cassell, 1969, Morrow, 1970; *Robin Round the World,* Cassell, 1970; *Sailing,* F. Watts, 1976. Contributor to *True, Rudder,* and other magazines.

SIDELIGHTS: A World of My Own is a detailed account of Robin Knox-Johnston's epic trip around the world and his reactions to the long months when he was out of radio contact, and navigating by the stars and the sea. He used a tape recorder to facilitate his daily diary of the voyage. Edward B. Garside writes: "This is a book that will go down in the literature of the sea." The autobiography has been translated into six languages.

BIOGRAPHICAL/CRITICAL SOURCES: Books and Bookmen, July, 1969; *New York Times Book Review,* July 12, 1970.

* * *

KNUDSEN, Hans August Heinrich 1886-1971

December 2, 1886—February 4, 1971; Polish-born German theatre historian. Obituaries: *Variety,* February 17, 1971.

* * *

KOCH, Richard 1921-

PERSONAL: Surname is pronounced coke; born November 24, 1921, in Dickinson, N.D.; son of Valentine and Barbara (Fisher) Koch; married Kathryn Jean Holt, October 2, 1943; children: Jill, Christine, Tom, Martin, Leslie. *Education:* Attended San Jose State College (now University), 1945-46; University of California, Berkeley, A.B., 1948; University of Rochester, M.D., 1951. *Home:* 2125 Ames

St., Los Angeles, Calif. 90027. *Office:* 4650 Sunset Blvd., Los Angeles, Calif. 90027.

CAREER: Licensed to practice medicine in California; Children's Hospital, Los Angeles, Calif., 1951—, head of division of child development, 1955-75, medical evaluator, 1976—. Professor of pediatrics, University of Southern California, 1955—. Member, Health Planning Council of California, 1969-71; deputy director, California Health Department, 1975-76. *Military service:* U.S. Army Air Forces, 1941-45; received Air Medal with oak-leaf cluster. *Member:* National Association for Retarded Children, American Association on Mental Deficiency, American Academy of Pediatrics.

WRITINGS: (Editor with James Dobson) *The Mentally Retarded Child and His Family: Handbook and Multidisciplinary Approach,* Brunner-Mazel, 1970, revised edition, 1976; (with wife, Kathryn Jean Koch) *Understanding the Mentally Retarded Child: A New Approach,* Random House, 1974. Contributor of more than one hundred articles to professional journals.

SIDELIGHTS: Richard Koch has participated in the production of five films on mental retardation.

* * *

KOENIG, Laird

PERSONAL: Born in Seattle, Wash.; son of Rowland Hill and Betty (Roeder) Koenig. *Education:* University of Washington, Seattle, B.A., 1950; additional study at University of California, Los Angeles, and New York University. *Politics:* "More or less liberal." *Religion:* None.

CAREER: Full-time writer. *Military service:* U.S. Army. *Member:* Writers Guild of America West, Authors Guild, Dramatists Guild, Beta Theta Pi.

WRITINGS: (With Peter L. Dixon) *The Children Are Watching* (novel), Ballantine, 1970; *The Little Girl Who Lives Down the Lane,* Coward, 1973. Writer of television plays and screenplays, including "The Cat" and "Red Sun."

Plays: "The Rubaiyat of Sophie Klein"; "The Dozens," produced on Broadway, 1968; "California Wine" (comedy), produced on Broadway at Booth Theater, 1969.

Screenplays: *The Little Girl Who Lives Down the Lane* (based on Koenig's novel of the same title), American International Pictures, 1977.

WORK IN PROGRESS: Stage and screen plays.

BIOGRAPHICAL/CRITICAL SOURCES: New Yorker, March 22, 1969.†

* * *

KOESIS, Robert 1935-

PERSONAL: Born September 1, 1935, in South Ozone Park, N.Y.; son of Frank J. and Mary (Ondyke) Koesis. *Education:* Hofstra College (now University), B.A. in drama, 1957. *Home:* 118 West 69th St., New York, N.Y. 10023. *Agent:* Ninon Tallon Karlweis, 250 East 65th St., New York, N.Y. 10021; and Judy Abbott, William Morris Agency, 1350 Avenue of the Americas, New York, N.Y. 10019.

MEMBER: Actors' Equity Association, Dramatists Guild.

WRITINGS—Unpublished plays: "A Dash of Spirits," first produced on West End at Wyndham's Theatre by Repertory Players, March 22, 1964; "Some Winter Games," first produced at Red Barn Theatre, August 17, 1965; "The Seven Deadly Arts," first produced in Westport, Conn., at County Playhouse, August 14, 1967; "The Wolves" (three-act), first produced in Washington, D.C., at the Washington Theatre Club, January 21, 1970; "A Place Without Mornings," first produced in Stratford, Conn., at American Shakespeare Festival, August 18, 1971.

WORK IN PROGRESS: Three plays, "Visit of Angels," "Circus of Dreams," and "Red, White and Very Blue."

SIDELIGHTS: "The Wolves" has also been produced in Hamburg, Germany, and Vienna, Austria.

BIOGRAPHICAL/CRITICAL SOURCES: Washington Post, January 23, 1970; *Variety,* February 18, 1970.††

* * *

KOESTENBAUM, Peter 1928-

PERSONAL: Born April 6, 1928, in Berlin, Germany; married Phyllis Orgel, 1952; children: Joshua, Wayne, Elissa, Ian. *Education:* Stanford University, B.A., 1949; Harvard University, M.A., 1950; Boston University, Ph.D., 1958. *Office:* Department of Philosophy, San Jose State University, San Jose, Calif. 95192.

CAREER: San Jose State University, San Jose, Calif., professor of philosophy, 1954—. *Awards, honors:* Trustees' Outstanding Professor Award, 1970, from California State Universities and Colleges.

WRITINGS: (Translator) Edmund Husserl, *The Paris Lectures,* Nijhoff, 1964; *Philosophy: A General Introduction,* Van Nostrand, 1968; *The Vitality of Death: Essays in Existential Psychology and Philosophy,* Greenwood, 1971; *Managing Anxiety: The Power of Knowing Who You Are,* Prentice-Hall, 1974; *Existential Sexuality: Choosing to Love,* Prentice-Hall, 1974; *Is There an Answer to Death?,* Prentice-Hall, 1976.

* * *

KOHLER, Foy D(avid) 1908-

PERSONAL: Born February 15, 1908, in Oakwood, Ohio; son of Leander David and Myrtle (McClure) Kohler; married Phyllis Penn, August 7, 1935. *Education:* University of Toledo, student, 1924-27; Ohio State University, B.S., 1931; graduate study at Cornell University and National War College, 1946. *Politics:* Independent. *Religion:* Protestant. *Home:* 215 Golf Club Cir., Tequesta, Fla. 33458. *Office address:* University of Miami, P.O. Box 8123, Coral Gables, Fla. 33124.

CAREER: Bank teller in Toledo, Ohio, 1924-27; U.S. Department of State, Foreign Service officer, 1931-67, serving as vice-consul in Windsor, Ontario, 1932-33, Bucharest, Rumania, 1933-35, and Belgrade, Yugoslavia, 1935, legation secretary and vice-consul in Bucharest, 1935-36, Athens, Greece, 1936-41, and Cairo, Egypt, 1941, serving in Washington, D.C. as country specialist, 1941-44, and as assistant chief of Division of Near Eastern Affairs, 1944-45, serving with U.S. Embassy, Moscow, Soviet Union, as first secretary and counselor, 1947-48, and minister plenipotentiary, 1948-49, director of "Voice of America" broadcasts, 1949-52, member of Department of State policy planning staff, 1952-53, counselor with U.S. Embassy in Ankara, Turkey, 1953-56, detailed to International Cooperation Administration, 1956-58, deputy assistant Secretary of State for European Affairs, 1958-59, assistant Secretary of State for European Affairs, 1959-62, U.S. Ambassador to Soviet Union, 1962-66, deputy Undersecretary of State for Political Af-

fairs, 1966-67, retiring with rank of career ambassador; University of Miami, Center for Advanced International Studies, Coral Gables, Fla., professor of international studies, 1968—. Consultant to Department of State, 1968—. Member, Board for International Broadcasting, 1974—; member of advisory council, National Convocation of the Challenge for Building Peace.

MEMBER: American Foreign Service Association, American Academy of Political and Social Science, Council on Foreign Relations, American Institute for Free Labor Development (member of board), Phi Beta Kappa, Delta Upsilon. *Awards, honors:* D.H.L., Ohio State University, 1962.

WRITINGS—All published by Center for Advanced International Studies, University of Miami, except as noted: *Understanding the Russians: A Citizen's Primer,* Harper, 1970; (author of foreword) *Science and Technology as an Instrument of Soviet Policy,* 1972; (co-author) *Soviet Strategy for the Seventies: From Cold War to Peaceful Coexistence,* 1973; (co-author) *Convergence of Communism and Capitalism: The Soviet View,* 1973; (co-author) *The Role of Nuclear Forces in Current Soviet Strategy,* 1974; (co-author) *The Soviet Union and the October 1973 Middle East War: Implications for Detente,* 1974; (author of foreword) *U.S.-Soviet Cooperation in Space,* 1974; (co-editor) *The Soviet Union: Yesterday, Today, Tomorrow; A Colloquy of American Long-Timers in Moscow,* 1975; (author of introduction) *Custine's Eternal Russia,* 1976; (author of foreword) *War Survival in Soviet Strategy: USSR Civil Defense,* 1976.

Contributor to *Orbis, Science, Interplay,* and other journals and newspapers. Co-editor, *Soviet World Outlook,* 1976.

WORK IN PROGRESS: Research on Soviet political, economic, social, scientific, military and foreign affairs.

BIOGRAPHICAL/CRITICAL SOURCES: Washington Post, July 22, 1970; *Best Sellers,* September 1, 1970; *Virginia Quarterly Review,* winter, 1971.

* * *

KOHN, Hans 1891-1971

September 15, 1891—March 16, 1971; Czech-born antinationalist, historian, and educator. Obituaries: *New York Times,* March 17, 1971; *Newsweek,* March 29, 1971.

* * *

KOLB, Harold H(utchinson), Jr. 1933-

PERSONAL: Born January 16, 1933, in Boston, Mass.; son of Harold Hutchinson (a commercial artist) and Ottille (Moss) Kolb; married Jean Burgin, March 9, 1957; children: Kathryn, Leigh. *Education:* Amherst College, B.A., 1955; University of Michigan, M.A., 1960; Indiana University, Ph.D., 1968. *Politics:* "Northern Democrat." *Religion:* "Eclectic Humanism." *Home:* Boaz Mountain, Covesville, Va. 22931. *Office:* Department of English, Wilson Hall, University of Virginia, Charlottesville, Va. 22901.

CAREER: Valparaiso University, Valparaiso, Ind., instructor in English, 1960-62; Indiana University, Bloomington, teaching associate, 1962-65, fellow, 1965-67; University of Virginia, Charlottesville, assistant professor, 1967-70, associate professor of English, 1970—. *Military service:* U.S. Navy, aviator, 1955-59, Naval Reserve, 1959-76; became commander. *Member:* Modern Language Association of America. *Awards, honors:* Armstrong Prize (Amherst); James A. Work Prize (Indiana); Guggenheim fellowship, 1970-71.

WRITINGS: The Illusion of Life: American Realism as a Literary Form, University Press of Virginia, 1969; *Field Guide to the Study of American Literature,* University Press of Virginia, 1976. Also author of various articles and reviews.

WORK IN PROGRESS: Mark Twain and the Pudd'n heads, and *American Literary Realism.*

* * *

KOLBREK, Loyal 1914-

PERSONAL: Born June 25, 1914, in Fairfax, S.D.; son of Louis (a farmer) and Emma (Anderson) Kolbrek; married Ida Mae Hansen, December 31, 1936; children: Dennis, Jan, Patricia (Mrs. Stanley Pickard), James. *Education:* Attended public schools and business college in South Dakota. *Politics:* Republican. *Religion:* Baptist. *Address:* R.R. 2, Box 112, Sioux Falls, S.D. 57101.

CAREER: John Morrell and Co., Sioux Falls, S.D., sheep buyer, 1948-65, cattle buyer, 1965-71. *Member:* Siouxland Writers Club (Sioux Falls, S.D.; president, 1967).

WRITINGS: (With Chris Larsen) *Samson's Secret,* Concordia, 1970; *The Man Who Changed His Name,* Concordia, 1972; *The Day God Made it Rain,* Concordia, 1977. Contributor of poetry to *Nuggets, Pasque Petals,* devotional magazines, and local newspapers.

SIDELIGHTS: Loyal Kolbrek told *CA:* "I enjoy writing poetry with a humorous twist but have submitted very little for publication. A recent trip to the southwest filled me with plans for a travel article—I have kept a diary for 24 years which I hope to use as a basis for family type articles. Have many ideas for cartoons but have no talent for drawing."

* * *

KONEFSKY, Samuel J. 1915-1970

January 15, 1915—July 18, 1970; Russian-born American political scientist and biographer of Supreme Court justices. Obituaries: *New York Times,* July 20, 1970.

* * *

KOPKIND, Andrew D(avid) 1935-

PERSONAL: Born August 24, 1935, in New Haven, Conn.; son of Bernard Philip (an attorney) and Esther (Aaronson) Kopkind. *Education:* Cornell University, A.B., 1957; London School of Economics and Political Science, M.Sc. (Econ.), 1961. *Agent:* Robert Lescher, 155 East 71st St., New York, N.Y. 10021.

CAREER: Washington Post, Washington, D.C., reporter, 1958-59; *Time,* New York, N.Y., correspondent, mainly on the Pacific coast, 1961-65; *New Republic,* Washington, D.C., associate editor, 1965-67; *New Statesman,* London, England, U.S. correspondent, 1965-69; *Hard Times,* Washington, D.C., founder, and editor, 1968-70; *Ramparts,* Berkeley, Calif., editor, beginning 1970.

WRITINGS: America: The Mixed Curse (collection of his magazine articles), Penguin, 1969; (editor with James Ridgeway) *Decade of Crisis: America In the Sixty's,* World Publications, 1972. Writer of film, "Head Start in Mississippi," for National Educational Television. Contributor of numerous articles to many magazines.

BIOGRAPHICAL/CRITICAL SOURCES: Times Literary Supplement, July 24, 1969.†

KOPP, Anatole 1915-

PERSONAL: Born November 1, 1915, in Saint Petersburg (now Leningrad), Russia; son of Alexandre and Helene (Margulis) Kopp; married Claudine Retail (a lawyer), June 24, 1953; children: Pierre. *Education:* Graduate of Ecole Speciale d'Architecture, Paris, 1936, and Ecole des Beaux Arts, Paris, 1939; Massachusetts Institute of Technology, M.Arch., 1943. *Politics:* "Extreme left." *Religion:* "Jewish origin; no religion." *Home:* 119 rue Notre Dame des Champs, Paris VI, France, *Office:* 16 rue de Chatillon, Paris XIV, France.

CAREER: Architect and planner, Paris, France, 1953—. B.E.R.U. (planning agency), Paris, associate member, 1960—; professor in department of planning, University of Paris VIII, Paris. *Military service:* French Army, 1939-45; became sergeant. *Member:* Cercle d'etudes d'Architecture.

WRITINGS: Ville et Revolution, Anthropos, 1967, translation by Thomas E. Burton published as *Town and Revolution: Soviet Architecture and City Planning, 1917-1935,* Braziller, 1970; *Changer la Vie—Changer la Ville,* Union Generale d'Editions (Paris), 1975. Director, *Espaces et Societes* (quarterly).

WORK IN PROGRESS: Monograph on Soviet architecture and planning; a work on the architecture of the Staline period.

AVOCATIONAL INTERESTS: Photography; Russian contemporary literature and life.

* * *

KOTLER, Milton 1935-

PERSONAL: Born March 15, 1935, in Chicago, Ill.; son of Maurice (a businessman) and Betty (Bubar) Kotler; married Janet Oldt, 1966; children: Anthony, Joshua. *Education:* University of Chicago, B.A., 1954, M.A., 1957, additional graduate study, 1957-61. *Politics:* "Ancient!" *Religion:* Jewish. *Home:* 3505 McKinley St. N.W., Washington, D.C.

CAREER: Institute for Policy Studies, Washington, D.C., resident fellow, 1963-74; Institute for Neighbor Studies, Washington, D.C., director, 1971—. Consultant and lecturer. *Military service:* Illinois Air National Guard. *Member:* American Political Science Association.

WRITINGS: Neighborhood Government: Local Foundations of Political Life, Bobbs-Merrill, 1969. Contributor to *Liberation, Ramparts, Boston Globe,* and other publications.

WORK IN PROGRESS: Three books, *Modern Political Rhetoric, The Rise and Fall of City Government,* and *The Gentlemen from Rochester,* the last a book of political epigrams.

AVOCATIONAL INTERESTS: "Summer in the garden in Vermont, with family, violin, and Latin."

BIOGRAPHICAL/CRITICAL SOURCES: Best Sellers, October 1, 1969; *Ramparts,* December, 1969.†

* * *

KOTZ, Nick 1932-

PERSONAL: Born September 16, 1932, in San Antonio, Tex.; son of Jacob (a physician) and Tybe (Kallison) Kotz; married Mary Lynn Booth (a free-lance writer), 1960; children: Jack Mitchell. *Education:* Dartmouth College, A.B., 1955; London School of Economics, 1956-57. *Residence:* Chevy Chase, Md. *Office: Washington Post,* 1500 L St. N.W., Washington, D.C.

CAREER: Des Moines Register, Des Moines, Iowa, reporter, 1958-64, Washington correspondent, 1964-70; *Washington Post,* Washington, D.C., reporter, 1970—. *Military service:* U.S. Marine Corps Reserve, 1956-58; became first lieutenant. *Member:* National Press Club, Sigma Delta Chi. *Awards, honors:* Raymond Clapper Awards, 1966, 1968; Pulitzer Prize for national reporting, 1968; the first Robert Kennedy Memorial Award in journalism, 1969.

WRITINGS: Let Them Eat Promises: The Politics of Hunger in America, introduction by George S. McGovern, Prentice-Hall, 1969; *The Unions,* Simon & Schuster, 1972; (with wife, Mary Lynn Katz) *A Passion for Eternity,* Norton, 1977. Contributor to *Look, Harper's, Nation, Progressive, Washington Monthly,* and other publications.

BIOGRAPHICAL/CRITICAL SOURCES: New York Times Book Review, January 15, 1970; *Atlantic,* February, 1970; *Nation,* May 25, 1970.

*   *   *

KOUTS, Anne 1945-

PERSONAL: Surname rhymes with *shouts;* born July 3, 1945, in Washington, D.C.; daughter of Herbert (a physicist) and Hertha (a writer; maiden name Pretorius) Kouts. *Education:* Antioch College, B.A., 1967. *Politics:* "Moderately left-wing." *Religion:* "None." *Home:* 152 West 20th St., New York, N.Y. 10011.

CAREER: Viking Press, Inc., New York City, began as secretary, became copy editor for Viking Junior Books, 1967-70; Harper & Row, Publishers, Inc., New York City, copy editor for Harper Junior Books, 1971-74; District 65, publishing division, New York City, organizer for trade union, 1974-75; currently attending law school. *Member:* SANE (National Committee for a Sane Nuclear Policy), American Museum of Natural History, Common Cause.

WRITINGS: Kenny's Rat (juvenile), Viking, 1970.

WORK IN PROGRESS: An article on developments in criminal law for *Rutger's Law Review.*

SIDELIGHTS: Anne Kouts told *CA* she has many avocational interests "but all I do these days is law." *Avocational interests:* Anthropology, sociology, psychology, child development, art, Far Eastern cultures, biology, typography, layout and design, wilderness, logic, humor, and plants.

*   *   *

KOVARSKY, Irving 1918-

PERSONAL: Born August 27, 1918, in Chicago, Ill.; son of Benjamin (a garment worker) and Sarah (Gedanowsky) Kovarsky; married Esther Rabinovitz, April 6, 1943; children: Joel, Dana. *Education:* Chicago-Kent College of Law (now Illinois Institute of Technology), LL.B., 1942; Loyola University, Chicago, M.A., 1953; University of Iowa, Ph.D., 1956; Yale University, LL.M., 1960. *Religion:* Jewish. *Home:* 1333 Bristol Dr., Iowa City, Iowa 52240. *Office:* College of Business Administration, University of Iowa, Iowa City, Iowa 52240.

CAREER: University of Oregon, Eugene, assistant professor of industrial relations and law, 1955-57; Southern Illinois University, Carbondale, associate professor, 1957-63, professor of business administration, 1963-64; University of Iowa, Iowa City, professor of business administration, 1964—. *Military service:* U.S. Army, 1942-45. *Member:* Academy of Management, American Arbitration Association, American Economic Association.

WRITINGS: (With William Albrecht) *Black Employment: The Impact of Religion, Economic Theory, Politics and Law,* Iowa State University Press, 1970; (with Vernon Hauck) *Epilepsy and Employment,* Center for Labor and Management, University of Iowa, 1975; *Discrimination in Employment,* Center for Labor and Management, University of Iowa, 1976.

Contributor: Baake, Kerr, and Anrod, editors, *Business Law,* 2nd edition (Kovarsky was not associated with earlier edition), Pitman, 1966; *Research in Apprentice Training,* University of Wisconsin, 1967; Edward B. Jakubauskas and C. P. Baumel, editors, *Human Resources Development,* Iowa State University Press, 1967. Also contributor to *Unions, Management and the Public.* Contributor of about fifty articles to law and management journals.

WORK IN PROGRESS: Research pertaining to the employment rights of cancer victims.

*   *   *

KOVEL, Joel S. 1936-

PERSONAL: Born August 27, 1936, in Brooklyn, N.Y.; son of Louis and Rose (Farber) Kovel; married Virginia Ryan, April 13, 1962; children: Jonathan, Erin. *Education:* Yale University, B.S. (summa cum laude), 1957; Columbia University, M.D., 1961. *Home:* 321 West 78th St., New York, N.Y. 10024. *Office:* Albert Einstein College of Medicine, Yeshiva University, New York, N.Y.

CAREER: Bronx Municipal Hospital Center, Bronx, N.Y., intern in medical service, 1961-62; assistant resident, later resident in psychiatry at Albert Einstein College of Medicine, Yeshiva University, New York, N.Y., and Bronx Municipal Hospital Center, 1962-64, chief resident in psychiatry at both institutions, 1964-65; Yeshiva University, Albert Einstein College of Medicine, instructor, 1967-69, assistant professor, 1969-74, associate professor of psychiatry, 1974—. *Member:* American Psychoanalytic Association.

WRITINGS: White Racism: A Psychohistory, Pantheon, 1970; (contributor) Jean Strouse, editor, *Women in Analysis: Dialogues on Psychoanalytic Views of Femininity,* Grossman, 1974; *A Complete Guide to Therapy,* Pantheon, 1976. Contributor of articles and reviews to *Telos, Social Research, Social Policy, New York Times Book Review,* and *Psychoanalytic Review.* Editorial associate, *Telos* (magazine).

WORK IN PROGRESS: The American Mental Health Industry, a critical history and survey of American Psychiatry; *Things and Hands,* a monograph on basic psychoanalytic theory; *Psychoanalysts and Socialism,* a book on the interrelations between the Freudian and the Marxist views of man and society; studies on the work of William Blake.

SIDELIGHTS: Joel Kovel wrote to *CA:* "My two intellectual heroes are Marx and Freud, and I am eternally fascinated by the paradoxes each sets for the other. My work is devoted to exploring these paradoxes. In the spirit of Marx and Freud, it is critical of the existing society, and aims toward a vision adequate for the society yet to be born."

*   *   *

KOVRIG, Bennett 1940-

PERSONAL: Born September 8, 1940, in Budapest, Hungary; married Marina Kuchar (a teacher), June 10, 1967. *Education:* University of Toronto, B.A., 1962, M.A., 1963;

University of London, Ph.D., 1967. *Home:* 48 Wilgar Rd., Toronto, Ontario, Canada. *Office:* Department of Political Science, University of Toronto, Toronto, Ontario, Canada.

CAREER: University of Toronto, Toronto, Ontario, assistant professor, 1968-70, associate professor, 1970-74, professor of political science, 1974—. *Member:* Canadian Institute of International Affairs.

WRITINGS: The Hungarian People's Republic, Johns Hopkins Press, 1970; (contributor) Peter A. Toma, editor, *The Changing Face of Communism in Eastern Europe,* University of Arizona Press, 1970; *The Myth of Liberation: East-Central Europe in U.S. Diplomacy and Politics Since 1941,* Johns Hopkins Press, 1973; (contributor) Charles Gati, editor, *The International Politics of Eastern Europe,* Praeger, 1976; (contributor) Richard F. Starr, editor, *Yearbook on International Communist Affairs, 1972-1976,* Hoover Institution, 1977.

WORK IN PROGRESS: A history of the Hungarian communist party for Hoover Institution.

* * *

KRAFT, Leonard E(dward) 1923-

PERSONAL: Born November 7, 1923, in Detroit, Mich.; son of William Joseph and Marie (Probst) Kraft; married Wilma Luckhard (a teacher); children: Wayne, Kurt. *Education:* Loughborough College, Loughborough, England, certificate, 1945; Eastern Michigan University, B.S., 1948; Purdue University, M.S., 1949; Michigan State University, Ed.D., 1962. *Home:* 69 Hamden Dr., Hudson, Ohio 44236. *Office:* Cuyahoga Community College—Eastern Campus, Warrensville Township, Ohio 44122.

CAREER: Elementary and high school teacher in Michigan public schools, 1949-54; Harper Woods Public Schools, Harper Woods, Mich., supervising elementary principal, 1954-59; Laingsburg Public Schools, Laingsburg, Mich., superintendent, 1960; Michigan State University, East Lansing, assistant instructor in educational administration, 1960-62; Southern Illinois University, Carbondale, assistant and associate professor, 1962-66, assistant director of student teaching, 1966-67; University of Georgia, Athens, associate professor, assistant chairman of graduate studies, College of Education, 1967-68, director of graduate studies, 1968-73; North Adams State College, North Adams, Mass., dean of graduate and continuing education, 1973-75; Cuyahoga Community College—Eastern Campus, Warrensville Township, Ohio, assistant to the president, 1975—. Illinois state delegate to National Conference on Education of the Disadvantaged, Washington, D.C., 1966; chairman of graduate section of Visitation Team for Georgia State Department of Education to Georgia Southern College, 1969; participant in National Foreign Policy Conference for Leaders in Teacher Education in Department of State, 1970; chairman, consultant, and member of various boards and committees on teacher education. *Member:* National Education Association, Michigan Education Association, Georgia Education Association, American Association of Higher Education, Kappa Delta Pi, Phi Delta Kappa.

WRITINGS: (Editor) *Compilation of Reactions to Proposed Revision of State Teacher Certification Code,* State of Michigan, 1961; (with John P. Casey) *Roles in Off-Campus Student Teaching,* Stipes, 1967; (contributor) *Readings in Student Teaching,* W. C. Brown, 1969; (with Luther Bradfield) *The Elementary School Principal in Action,* Intext Educational Publishers, 1970; *The Secondary School Principal in Action,* W. C. Brown, 1971. Also author,

with Thelbert L. Drake, of an unpublished work, "An Institute for Teachers of Disadvantaged Youth ... An In-Service Model." Contributor of book reviews to *Choice,* and of articles on teacher education to *NEA Journal, National Elementary Principal, National School Board Journal, Teachers College Journal, Peabody Journal, Journal of Negro Education,* and other journals. Editor of a quarterly newsletter, *Lamplighter,* published by the Southern Illinois University Phi Delta Kappa campus chapter, 1964-66.

* * *

KRAJENKE, Robert William 1939-

PERSONAL: Born May 7, 1939, in Detroit, Mich.; son of Clarence R. (an executive) and Wilma (Chase) Krajenke; children: Robert William, Jr. *Education:* University of Arizona, student, 1961-63; University of California, Berkeley, student, 1963. *Politics:* "Non-partisan." *Religion:* Quaker. *Home:* 305 East Farmington Rd., Virginia Beach, Va. 23454. *Office address:* P.O. Box 149, Virginia Beach, Va. 23458.

CAREER: Advertising executive; author; artist.

WRITINGS: The Call to Israel, A.R.E. Press, 1969; *Stand Like Stars,* A.R.E. Press, 1970; *Suddenly, We Were,* A.R.E. Press, 1970; *Footprints on the Water: Snapshots from the Journey of the Mental Traveler,* Create-A-Book Press, 1971; *A Million Years to the Promised Land: Edgar Cayce's Story of the Old Testament,* three volumes, Bantam, 1973; *The Psychic Side of the American Dream,* A.R.E. Press, 1976.

AVOCATIONAL INTERESTS: Meditation, diet, prayer, and spiritual healing.

* * *

KRASILOVSKY, Phyllis 1926-

PERSONAL: Born August 28, 1926, in Brooklyn, N.Y.; daughter of Richard and Florence Manning; married William Krasilovsky (an attorney and author), September 14, 1947; children: Alexis, Jessica, Margaret, Peter. *Education:* Attended Brooklyn College (now Brooklyn College of the City University of New York), 1944-47, and Cornell University, 1949-50. *Home:* 1177 Hardscrabble Rd., Chappaqua, N.Y. 10514. *Agent:* Marilyn Marlowe, Curtis Brown Ltd., 575 Madison Ave., New York, N.Y. 10022.

CAREER: Marymount College, Tarrytown, N.Y., teacher of children's literature, 1969-70; teacher of creative writing, Katonah Library, 1970-72.

WRITINGS—Juveniles; all published by Doubleday: *The Man Who Didn't Wash Dishes,* 1953; *The Very Little Girl,* 1955; *The Cow Who Fell in the Canal,* 1957; *The Very Little Boy,* 1964; *The Girl Who Was a Cowboy,* 1965; *The Very Tall Little Girl,* 1969.

Other juvenile books: *Scaredy Cat,* Macmillan, 1960; *Benny's Flag,* World Publishing, 1960; *Susan Sometimes,* Macmillan, 1962; *The Shy Little Girl,* Houghton, 1971; *Popular Girls Club,* Simon & Schuster, 1973; *L. C. Is the Greatest,* Thomas Nelson, 1975.

Contributor of travel articles to numerous periodicals including *Travel, Saturday Evening Post, Cosmopolitan, Washington Post, Boston Globe, San Diego Union, New York Times, American Home,* and various women's magazines. Travel editor, *Westchester* and *Long Island* (magazines), 1975—.

WORK IN PROGRESS: Several picture-books; an adult novel.

KRASLOW, David 1926-

PERSONAL: Born April 16, 1926, in New York, N.Y.; son of Frank and Goldie (Sirota) Kraslow; married Bernice Schonfeld, September 18, 1949; children: Ellen, Karen, Susan. *Education:* City College (now City College of the City University of New York), New York, N.Y., student, 1943-44; University of Miami, Coral Gables, Fla., A.B., 1948; graduate study at Harvard University, 1961-62, and at Columbia University. *Religion:* Hebrew. *Home:* 2316 North Gate Ter., Silver Spring, Md. 20906. *Office:* Cox Newspapers, 1901 Pennsylvania Ave. N.W., Washington, D.C. 20006.

CAREER: Miami Herald, Miami, Fla., reporter, 1948-56; Washington correspondent, Knight Newspapers, 1956-63; *Los Angeles Times,* Los Angeles, Calif., Washington Bureau reporter, news editor, bureau chief, 1963-72; *Washington Star,* Washington, D.C., assistant managing editor, 1972-74; Washington Bureau chief, Cox Newspapers, 1974—. *Military service:* U.S. Army Air Forces, 1944-46; became sergeant. *Member:* National Press Club, Authors League, Sigma Delta Chi, Gridiron Club, Federal City Club. *Awards, honors:* Nieman fellow at Harvard University, 1961-62; George Polk and Dumont awards for international reporting; Raymond Clapper Award for Washington correspondence.

WRITINGS: (With Robert S. Boyd) *A Certain Evil,* Little, Brown, 1965; (with Robert J. Donovan and others) *Six Days in June,* New American Library, 1967; (with Stuart H. Loory) *The Secret Search for Peace in Vietnam,* Random House, 1968.

BIOGRAPHICAL/CRITICAL SOURCES: New York Times Book Review, July 7, 1968; *New York Times,* August 5, 1968; *Time,* August 9, 1968; *New Yorker,* August 24, 1968.

*   *   *

KRESS, Paul F(rederick) 1935-

PERSONAL: Born September 10, 1935, in Stoughton, Wis.; son of Frederick Raymond and Mabelle (Paulson) Kress.; married Charlotte Belshe, August 17, 1959. *Education:* University of Wisconsin, B.S., 1956, M.S., 1958; University of California, Berkeley, Ph.D., 1964. *Home:* 904 Ridgecrest Dr., Chapel Hill, N.C. 27514. *Office:* Department of Political Science, University of North Carolina, Chapel Hill, N.C. 27514.

CAREER: Northwestern University, Evanston, Ill., assistant professor of political science, 1964-70; University of North Carolina, Chapel Hill, associate professor, 1970-75, professor of political science, 1975—. Visiting summer professor, University of Hawaii, 1967—.

WRITINGS: (Contributor) James Gould and Vincent Thursby, editors, *Contemporary Political Thought,* Holt, 1969; *Social Science and the Idea of Process: The Ambiguous Legacy of Arthur F. Bently,* University of Illinois Press, 1970; (contributor) Roderick Aya and Norman Miller, editors, *The New American Revolution,* Free Press, 1971; (contributor) Donald Freeman, editor, *Introduction to the Science of Politics,* Free Press, 1977. Contributor to social science and philosophy journals. Member of editorial board, *Journal of Politics,* 1971—.

WORK IN PROGRESS: Writing on contemporary political theory.

AVOCATIONAL INTERESTS: Chess, music.

KREUTER, Kent 1932-

PERSONAL: Born June 24, 1932, in Milwaukee, Wis.; son of Warner (an artist) and Ruth (Turner) Kreuter; married Gretchen von Loewe (an historian), December 1, 1958; children: David, Betsy. *Education:* University of Wisconsin, B.A., 1954, M.S., 1958, Ph.D., 1963. *Politics:* Democratic. *Religion:* None. *Home:* 2158 Commonwealth Ave., St. Paul, Minn. 55108. *Office:* Department of History, Hamline University, St. Paul, Minn. 55101.

CAREER: Colgate University, Hamilton, N.Y., instructor, 1961-63, assistant professor of history, 1963-66; Hamline University, St. Paul, Minn., associate professor, 1966-71, professor of history, 1971—. *Military service:* U.S. Army, 1955-57; became first lieutenant. U.S. Army Reserve, 1957—. *Member:* American Historical Association, Organization of American Historians. *Awards, honors:* Woodrow Wilson fellowship, 1960-61; grants from Littauer Foundation, 1963, and Hill Foundation, 1968-69; McKnight Foundation Prize in history and biography, 1967, for manuscript of *An American Dissenter: The Life of Algie Martin Simons, 1870-1950.*

WRITINGS: (With wife, Gretchen von Loewe Kreuter) *An American Dissenter: The Life of Algie Martin Simons, 1870-1950,* University of Kentucky Press, 1969. Contributor to *Saturday Review, Modern Fiction Studies,* and other journals.

WORK IN PROGRESS: A biography of Frank Billings Kellogg.††

*   *   *

KRIESBERG, Louis 1926-

PERSONAL: Born July 30, 1926, in Chicago, Ill.; son of Max (a furrier) and Bessie (Turner) Kriesberg; married Lois Ablin (an anthropologist), 1959; children: Daniel, Joseph. *Education:* University of Chicago, Ph.B. (with honors), 1947, M.A., 1950, Ph.D., 1953; attended summer sessions at Columbia University, 1946, University of California, Berkeley, 1947, Johns Hopkins University, School of Advanced International Studies, 1953. *Religion:* Jewish. *Home:* 247 Kensington Pl., Syracuse, N.Y. 13210. *Office:* Department of Sociology, Syracuse University, Syracuse, N.Y.

CAREER: Columbia University, New York, N.Y., instructor in sociology, 1953-56; University of Cologne, Cologne, Germany, Fulbright research scholar, 1956-57; University of Chicago, Chicago, Ill., senior fellow in law and behavioral sciences, 1957-58, research associate and senior study director of National Opinion Research Center, 1958-62; Syracuse University, Syracuse, N.Y., associate professor, 1962-66, professor of sociology, 1966—, chairman of department, 1974—, research associate at Youth Development Center, 1962-68. Research associate in International Relations Program, Northwestern University, 1968. *Member:* American Sociological Association (chairman, world conflicts section, 1976), Society for the Study of Social Problems (member, C. Wright Mills Award Committee, 1965-66; chairman, Committee on Standards and Freedom of Research Publication and Teaching, 1966-67; chairman, International Tensions Committee, 1969-71), American Association for Public Opinion Research, World Association for Public Opinion Research, American Association of University Professors, Eastern Sociological Society. *Awards, honors:* Marshall Field fellowship, 1950-51; Ford Research Training fellowship, 1952-53.

WRITINGS: (With Beatrice R. Treiman) *Public Attitudes*

Toward Prepaid Dental Care Plans, National Opinion Research Center (report Number 76), 1960; *Mental Health and Public Health Personnel and Programs: Their Relations in the Fifty States,* National Opinion Research Center (report Number 83), 1962; (with Seymour S. Bellin) *Fatherless Families and Housing: A Study in Dependency,* Syracuse University Youth Development Center, 1965; (editor and author of introduction) *Social Processes in International Relations: A Reader,* Wiley, 1968; *Mothers in Poverty: A Study of Fatherless Families,* Aldine, 1970; *Sociology of Social Conflicts,* Prentice-Hall, 1973.

Contributor: Hans L. Zetterberg, editor, *Sociology in the United States of America,* UNESCO, 1956; Richard L. and Ida Harper Simpson, editors, *Social Organization and Behavior: A Reader in General Sociology,* Wiley, 1964; Perry Bliss, editor, *Readings in Behavioral Sciences and Marketing,* 2nd edition, Allyn & Bacon, 1967; Howard S. Becker, David Riesman, Blanche Geer, and Robert Weiss, editors, *Institutions and the Person: Essays Presented to Everett C. Hughes,* Aldine, 1968; Kenneth E. Boulding, editor, *Peace and the War Industry,* Aldine, 1970; Charles V. Willie, editor, *The Negro Family,* C. E. Merrill, 1970; W. Heydebrand, editor, *Comparative Organizations,* Prentice-Hall, 1973; Michael Haas, editor, *Behavioral International Relations,* Chandler Publishing, 1974. Also contributor of articles to numerous periodicals, including *American Journal of Sociology, International Social Science Journal, Christian Century, Journal of the American Medical Association, Public Opinion Quarterly, Social Forces,* and *Journal of the American College of Dentists.* Book review editor, *American Journal of Sociology,* 1962; associate editor, *Social Problems,* 1967-69.

WORK IN PROGRESS: A study on the change and persistance of social inequalities, to be published by Prentice-Hall; editing a series, *Research in Social Movements, Conflicts, and Change.*

* * *

KRISTEIN, Marvin M(ichael) 1926-

PERSONAL: Born April 13, 1926, in New York, N.Y.; son of Aaron and Fannie (Rokeach) Kristein; married Barbara Frank, November 14, 1959 (died December 1, 1965); married Bernice Wolf Gordon, April 26, 1973. *Education:* City College (now City College of the City University of New York), New York, N.Y., B.S.S., 1947; Columbia University, M.A., 1949; New School for Social Research, Ph.D., 1955; Netherlands School of Economics, additional study, 1955-56. *Home:* 7 Tudor Dr., Stony Brook, N.Y. 11790. *Office:* Department of Economics, State University of New York, Stony Brook, N.Y. 11790.

CAREER: City College (now City College of the City University of New York), New York, N.Y., lecturer in economics, 1949-55; Harpur College, Binghamton, N.Y. (now State University of New York at Binghamton), assistant professor of economics, 1956-59; State University of New York at Stony Brook, associate professor of economics, 1959—, director of economic research bureau, 1970-76. Director, Anametrics, Inc. Consultant on investment management and security analysis, 1968-70; consulting health economist, 1974—. *Military service:* U.S. Army, 1944-46. *Member:* American Economic Association, American Statistical Association, Econometric Society, American Public Health Association, Phi Beta Kappa, Stony Brook Rotary Club. *Awards, honors:* Fulbright grant to study in the Netherlands, 1955-56.

WRITINGS: Corporation Finance, Barnes & Noble, 1969, 2nd edition, 1975. Contributor to professional journals in the United States and abroad.

WORK IN PROGRESS: Writing on health economics and hospital costs, financial markets, and on security analysis.

* * *

KRISTOF, Jane 1932-

PERSONAL: Born May 25, 1932, in Chicago, Ill.; daughter of Donald Saxon McWilliams (a lawyer) and Mary (Shakespeare) McWilliams; married Ladis K. D. Kristof (a professor of political science), December 29, 1956; children: Nicholas. *Education:* University of Chicago, B.A., 1950, M.A., 1956; University of Edinburgh, graduate study, 1951-52; Columbia University, Ph.D., 1972. *Politics:* "Ardent Democrat." *Religion:* Presbyterian. *Home address:* Route 2, Box 430, Gaston, Ore. 97119. *Office:* Department of Art and Architecture, Portland State University, Portland, Ore. 97207.

CAREER: Chicago City Junior College, Amundsen-Mayfair Branch, Chicago, Ill., lecturer in art history, 1957-59; University of Waterloo, Waterloo, Ontario, lecturer in art history, 1970-71; Mt. Hood Community College, Gresham, Ore., instructor, 1972-73; Portland State University, Portland, Ore., lecturer in art history, 1973—.

WRITINGS: Steal Away Home (juvenile), Bobbs-Merrill, 1969.

BIOGRAPHICAL/CRITICAL SOURCES: National Observer, November 3, 1969; *New York Times Book Review,* November 9, 1969.

* * *

KUBICEK, Robert V(incent) 1935-

PERSONAL: Born November 19, 1935, in Drumheller, Alberta, Canada; son of Frederick and Roxanna (MacKenzie) Kubicek; married, 1970, wife's name, Mila; children: Brett Booth. *Education:* University of Alberta, B.Ed., 1956, M.A., 1958; London School of Economics and Political Science, graduate study, 1958-59; Duke University, Ph.D., 1964. *Home:* 3755 West 13th, Vancouver, British Columbia, Canada V6R 257. *Office:* Department of History, University of British Columbia, Vancouver, British Columbia, Canada V6R 257.

CAREER: University of British Columbia, Vancouver, instructor, 1963-65, assistant professor, 1965-69, associate professor of history, 1969—. *Member:* Canadian Historical Association, Canadian Association of University Teachers, Canadian Association of African Studies. *Awards, honors:* Canadian Council summer research grants, 1966 and 1970, fellowships, 1968-69 and 1973-74.

WRITINGS: The Administration of Imperialism: Joseph Chamberlain at the Colonial Office, Duke University Press, 1969. Contributor to history journals.

WORK IN PROGRESS: Capitalization of the South African Goldmining Industry, 1886-1914; Technological Determinism and the New Imperialism.

* * *

KUGEL, James 1945-

PERSONAL: Born August 22, 1945, in New York, N.Y.; son of John Hans and Adelaide (Roth) Kugel; married Rachel B. Epstein, March 18, 1975; children: Jotham. *Education:* Yale University, B.A., 1968; Harvard University, graduate study, 1973-76; City University of New York, Ph.D., 1977. *Religion:* Jewish. *Home:* 110 West 96th St., New York, N.Y. 10025.

CAREER: U.S. Department of State, Washington, D.C., interpreter, 1969; Dispatch News Service, Washington, Boston correspondent, 1970-71; *Boston Phoenix,* Boston, Mass., editor, 1971-72; *Harper's,* New York, N.Y., poetry editor, 1973-75. *Member:* Phi Beta Kappa. *Awards, honors:* Woodrow Wilson, Danforth, and Fulbright fellowships.

WRITINGS: Issues of Educational Reform, privately printed, 1968; *Techniques of Strangeness in Symbolist Poetry,* Yale University Press, 1971. Contributor to *Poetry, Harper's, Rolling Stone, New York Quarterly, Antioch Review, Midstream,* and *Response.*

WORK IN PROGRESS: The Assemblyman, fiction.

* * *

KULKARNI, R(amchandra) G(anesh) 1931-

PERSONAL: Born February 4, 1931, in Poona, India; son of Ganesh S. (a government servant) and Saraswati (Beke) Kulkarni; married Nalini Joshi, June 24, 1955; children: Nitin, Sachin (both sons). *Education:* Sir Parashrambhau College, B.A. (honors), 1952; University of Poona, M.A., 1954, Ph.D., 1961. *Religion:* Hindu.

CAREER: R. A. Podar College of Commerce and Economics, Bombay, India, lecturer in economics, 1954-55; Government of Bombay, research assistant in Bureau of Economics and Statistics, 1955-56; Government College of Engineering, Poona, India, professor of economics, 1956-62; Arts and Commerce College, Wai, Satara, India, principal, 1962-64; M/S Kirloskav Oil Engines Ltd., Kirkee, Poona, purchase executive, beginning 1964. *Member:* National Association of Purchasing Executives (national vice-president).

WRITINGS: Deficit Financing and Economic Development, with Special Reference to Indian Economic Development, Asia Publishing House (Bombay), 1966. Contributor of articles on current economic problems to journals and newspapers. Former editor of engineering college magazine for four years.

WORK IN PROGRESS: A book on materials management in India; world economic developments.

AVOCATIONAL INTERESTS: Drama (has acted in and also directed more than twenty plays), and music (both Indian and western).†

* * *

KUPFERBERG, Herbert 1918-

PERSONAL: Born January 20, 1918, in New York, N.Y.; son of Moses (an importer) and Augusta (Lasserwitz) Kupferberg; married Barbara Gottesman (a teacher), January 24, 1954; children: Seth, Joel, Natalie. *Education:* Cornell University, A.B., 1939; Columbia University, M.A., 1940, M.S., 1941. *Religion:* Jewish. *Home:* 113-14 72nd Rd., Forest Hills, N.Y. 11375. *Agent:* Shirley Burke, 370 East 76th St., Suite B-704, New York, N.Y. 10021. *Office: Parade,* 733 Third Ave., New York, N.Y. 10017.

CAREER: New Bedford Standard Times, New Bedford, Mass., copy editor, 1941-42; *New York Herald Tribune,* New York City, copy editor, 1942-46, assistant to editor of European edition, 1946-47, reporter, 1948-50, editorial writer, 1950-62, record critic, 1952-66, lively arts editor, 1962-66; *Parade,* New York City, senior editor, 1967—. Instructor in journalism, Fordham University, 1960-68. Music

critic, *Atlantic,* 1958-68, *National Observer,* 1968—; advisory editor, *Dance News,* 1972—. *Member:* Overseas Press Club of America (chairman of music committee), Authors' League of America.

WRITINGS: These Fabulous Philadelphians: The Life and Times of a Great Orchestra, Scribner, 1969; *The Mendelssohns: Three Generations of Genius,* Scribner, 1972; *Felix Mendelssohn: His Life, His Family, His Music,* Scribner, 1973; *A Rainbow of Sound: The Instruments of the Orchestra and Their Music,* Scribner, 1974; *A History of Opera,* Newsweek, 1975; *Tanglewood,* McGraw, 1976. Contributor to *Harper's, Atlantic,* and other national magazines.

BIOGRAPHICAL/CRITICAL SOURCES: New York Times, October 18, 1969; *Book World,* November 2, 1969; *Times Literary Supplement,* July 16, 1970; *Detroit News,* February 20, 1972; *Washington Post,* March 18, 1972.

* * *

KURTZ, Katherine 1944-

PERSONAL: Born October 18, 1944, in Coral Gables, Fla.; daughter of Frederick Harry (in electronics) and Margaret Frances (Carter) Kurtz. *Education:* University of Miami, Coral Gables, B.S., 1966; University of California, Los Angeles, M.A., 1971. *Office:* Los Angeles Police Academy, 1880 North Academy Dr., Los Angeles, Calif. 90012.

CAREER: Los Angeles Police Department, Los Angeles, Calif., junior administrative assistant, 1969-71, training technician, 1971-74, senior training technician, 1974—. *Member:* Science Fiction Writers of America, Swordsmen & Sorcerors Guild of America, Society for Creative Anachronism, Phi Alpha Theta, Alpha Epsilon Delta, Mortar Board.

WRITINGS—All published by Ballantine: *Deryni Rising,* 1970; *Deryni Checkmate,* 1971; *High Deryni,* 1973; *Camber of Culdi,* 1976. Contributor to *Flashing Swords: Warriors and Wizards,* Number 4, Dell, 1977.

WORK IN PROGRESS: Saint Camber, for Ballantine.

AVOCATIONAL INTERESTS: Manuscript illumination, woodcarving, riding, hypnosis.

* * *

KURTZMAN, Joel 1947-

PERSONAL: Born June 25, 1947, in Los Angeles, Calif.; son of Samuel (a dentist) and Roselle (a sculptress; maiden name, Rosencranz) Kurtzman; married Susan Gross (a literary agent), December 28, 1969. *Education:* University of California, Berkeley, A.B., 1971. *Agent:* Harold Matson Co., Inc., 22 East 40th St., New York, N.Y. 10016.

MEMBER: Authors Guild, Writers Guild West. *Awards, honors:* Eisner Prize of Eisner Memorial Fund for creative achievement.

WRITINGS: Crown of Flowers (novel), Dutton, 1970; *Sweet Bobby* (novel), McGraw, 1974; (with Phillip Gordon and J. P. Tarcher) *No More Dying: The Conquest of Aging and the Extension of Human Life,* Hawthorne, 1976.

WORK IN PROGRESS: A new novel; a series of books on science.

SIDELIGHTS: A *Virginia Quarterly Review* book reviewer praised Joel Kurtzman's first novel for the methods by which the author "quite expertly evokes an atmosphere of dread, foreboding, and infinite sadness, revealing just enough to mystify and tantalize readers patient enough to comprehend his subtleties and appreciate his poetical though precious approach to simple tragedy."

Joel Kurtzman told *CA:* "I want to be involved with my subject, I want to know how my characters breathe and move, what it looks like to see through their eyes. While researching and writing *Sweet Bobby,* I worked in the violent wards of two mental hospitals. I needed to know my subjects firsthand." Kurtzman has recently begun writing non-fiction about science. He feels that "science is the true philosophy. The facts we know about the universe tell us both about where we live and about the human mind. Knowing about quarks and stars confirms Plato. The true dialectic is the equation between matter, energy, and mind. With non-fiction writing, I am interested in occupying the space between the actual and the possible. I want to observe things as they become. With fiction I want to straddle that point where the cosmos touches the heart."

BIOGRAPHICAL/CRITICAL SOURCES: Virginia Quarterly Review, summer, 1970.

*   *   *

KURZ, Mordecai 1934-

PERSONAL: Born November 29, 1934, in Nathanya, Israel; son of Moses and Sarah (Krauss) Kurz. *Education:* Hebrew University of Jerusalem, B.A., 1957; Yale University, M.A., 1958, Ph.D., 1961; Stanford University, M.S., 1960. *Home:* 931 Casanueva Pl., Stanford, Calif. 94305. *Office:* Department of Economics, Stanford University, Stanford, Calif. 94305.

CAREER: Stanford University, Stanford, Calif., research associate of Institute for Mathematical Studies in the Social Sciences, 1961-62, assistant professor of economics, 1962-63; Hebrew University of Jerusalem, Jerusalem, Israel, lecturer, 1963-64, senior lecturer in economics, 1964-65; Stanford University, visiting associate professor, 1966-67, associate professor, 1967-69, professor of economics, 1969—, economic consultant to Stanford Research Institute. Economic consultant to government of Canada. *Military service:* Israeli Armed Forces, 1952-54. *Member:* Econometric Society (fellow), American Economic Association.

WRITINGS: (Contributor) H. W. Kuhn and G. P. Szegoe, editors, *Mathematical Systems Theory and Economics,* Springer-Verlag, 1968; (with K. J. Arrow) *Public Investment, the Rate of Return, and Optimal Fiscal Policy,* Johns Hopkins Press, 1970. Contributor of about thirty articles to economics journals.

*   *   *

KURZ, Paul Konrad 1927-

PERSONAL: Born April 4, 1927, in Bad Schussenried, Germany; son of Paul and Paula (Hingele) Kurz. *Education:* Stanislaus College, Ireland, Lic.phil., 1953; Innsbruck University, Lic.theol., 1957; University of Munich, Dr.phil., 1964. *Religion:* Roman Catholic. *Home:* Josef-Gerstner-strasse 3, 8033 Planegg near Munich, West Germany.

CAREER: Roman Catholic priest, member of Society of Jesus (Jesuits), 1947-72; lecturer in modern German literature at University of Munich, Munich, Germany, 1964-72; free-lance writer in Munich, 1972—. *Member:* Verband deutscher Schriftsteller, International P.E.N. *Awards, honors:* Golden Quill Award, 1973, from International Conference of Weekly Newspaper Editors.

WRITINGS: Denn Er ist da: Verse zu Advent und Weihnacht (poems), Ehrenwirth, 1963; *Wer bist Du? Verse des Anfanga* (poems), Ehrenwirth, 1964; *Gegen die Mauer: Verse zu Passion und Ostern* (poems), Ehrenwirth, 1966;

Kuenstler, Tribun, Apostel: Heinrich Heines Auffassung vom Beruf des Dichters, W. Fink, 1967; *Ueber moderne Literatur,* Knecht, Volume I, 1967, Volume II, 1969, Volume III, 1971, Volume IV, 1973, translation by Sister Mary Frances McCarthy published as *On Modern German Literature,* University of Alabama Press, Volume I, 1970, Volume II, 1971, Volume III, 1973, Volume IV, 1976; (with others) *Moderne Literatur und christlicher Glaube,* Echter-Verlag, 1968; *Strukturen christlicher Existenz,* Echter-Verlag, 1968; (with others) *La Nueva novela europea,* Ediciones Guardarama, 1969; *Zwischen Entfremdung und Utopie,* Knect, 1975; *Wir wissen dass wir sterben muessen,* Gueterscloher Verlaghaus, 1975. Also author of *Nichts und doch alles haben,* Evangelischer Verlag, and of *Gott in der Literatur,* Oberoesterreischer Landesverlag.

WORK IN PROGRESS: Niemand knetet uns wieder: Lyrik und Psalm im 20 Jahrhundert for Krenz-Verlag and Koesel-Verlag.

SIDELIGHTS: Paul Kurz tries "to observe, interpret and diagnose contemporary German literature, with a special view on the antagonism of modern literature and Christianity."

*   *   *

KYTLE, Ray(mond) 1941-

PERSONAL: Born January 29, 1941, in Oklahoma City, Okla.; son of Raymond and Juanita (Smith) Kytle; married Annette Peterson (an instructor), July 14, 1969. *Education:* University of Oklahoma, B.A., 1962; Southern Illinois University, M.A., 1964. *Politics:* Independent. *Religion:* Atheist. *Home:* 112 Oak Ave., Roscommon, Mich. 48659. *Office:* Department of English, Central Michigan University, Mount Pleasant, Mich. 48858.

CAREER: Mankato State College, Mankato, Minn., instructor, 1966-68; Southern Illinois University, Carbondale, instructor, 1968-69; Central Michigan University, Mount Pleasant, 1969—, began as assistant professor, currently associate professor of English. *Member:* National Council of Teachers of English, Authors Guild.

WRITINGS: Clear Thinking for Composition, Random House, 1969; *Composition: Discovery and Communication,* Random House, 1970; (editor) *Confrontation: Issues of the '70s,* Random House, 1971; (with Juanita Lyons) *Reading and Writing about Literature,* Dickenson, 1972; *Prewriting: Strategies for Exploration and Discovery,* Random House, 1972; *The Comp Box,* Aspen, 1972; (with wife, Annette Kytle) *The Complex Vision,* Harcourt, 1972; *Concepts in Context: Aspects of the Writer's Craft,* Wiley, 1974; *Fire and Ice* (novel), McKay, 1975; *Meltdown* (novel), McKay, 1976.

WORK IN PROGRESS: Sea Stalk and *Duane and Cynthia,* novels; with Jack Stock, M.D., *The Doctor Will See You Now.*

SIDELIGHTS: Ray Kytle told *CA:* "I find great difficulty with highly restrictive, elitist and exclusive definitions of 'creative writing' (an invidiously judgmental label that could be profitably abandoned in favor of descriptive terminology). Integrity in writing is crucial. But that sense of integrity must both come from and be evaluated in terms of the author's own purpose and audience and attitude toward his craft—and special abilities. Ego is the only barrier between the writer and scribal impotence. For the writer, tragedy is not writing a book that gets bad reviews, it is not writing at all. I am highly judgmental in terms of craft, nonjudgmental in terms of 'literary merit' and 'ultimate significance.' What victory is there in labeling another as a hack, what justification in denigrating another's source of satisfaction and livelihood? It's so easy to sneer, and so suspect. The teacher of writing must facilitate writing, not inhibit it. He must praise the strengths, suggest the weaknesses and, above all, encourage the apprentice writer's commitment to his craft and his faith in his ability to master it. The role of the teacher of writing is that of 'feedback provider.' Informed feedback: craft-oriented, judgmentally neutral, ego-supportive.''

* * *

LABIN, Suzanne (Devoyon) 1913-

PERSONAL: Born May 6, 1913, in Paris, France; daughter of Louis Leon (a metal worker) and Marie-Eugenie (Leplatre) Devoyon; married Edouard Labin (an electronic engineer), April 4, 1935. *Education:* Ecole des hautes etudes internationales et de journalisme, Diplomee, 1935; Sorbonne, University of Paris, Licenciee es sciences, 1936. *Religion:* Roman Catholic. *Home and office:* 3 rue Thiers, Paris 16, France.

CAREER: Journalist, 1940—, author, and lecturer. Founder and president of International Conference on Political Warfare, with headquarters in Paris, 1960—; chairman of League of Freedoms; chairman of French chapter of the World Anti-Communist League; has launched campaigns in support of the Hungarian Revolution, in support of the Tibetan uprising against the Chinese invasion, in support of the South Vietnamese and their U.S. allies, and against the policy of the West in Katanga. Lecturer (in French, English, and Spanish) in most countries of Asia, Africa, Latin America, and North America; member of the Asian Speakers Bureau (United States) and of the Church League of America Speakers Bureau; producer of film, "Freedom Is at Stake in Berlin," for French television, 1962. *Member:* League of Freedom (president), Societe des gens de lettres, European Freedom Council (president of Committee for Information), Federacion Argentina Entidades Democraticas Anti-Communistas (honorary member), Association for the Study of the Problems of Public Opinion (honorary member of the board). *Awards, honors:* Freedom Prize for *Les Entretiens de Saint-Germain—Liberte aux Liberticides?;* Golden Cross of European merit; Golden Cross of cultural and philanthropic merit; Freedom Award of the Assembly of Captive Nations; Freedom Award of the Freedom Foundation of Valley Forge.

WRITINGS: Staline le terrible: Panorama de la Russie sovietique, Editions Self, 1948, translation by Edward Fitzgerald published as *Stalin's Russia,* Gollancz, 1950; *Le Drame de la democratie,* Horay, 1954, translation by Otto E. Albrecht published as *The Secret of Democracy,* Vanguard, 1955; *La Conspiration communiste, l'Hydre totalitaire: Comment la museler,* Spartacus, 1957; *Les Entretiens de Saint-Germain: Liberte aux liberticides?,* Spartacus, 1957; *La Condition humaine en Chine communiste,* La Table Ronde, 1959, translation by Edward Fitzgerald published as *The Anthill: The Human Condition in Communist China,* Stevens & Sons, 1960, Praeger, 1961; *The Technique of Soviet Propaganda* (pamphlet; originally written in French as a report for the tenth anniversary of the North Atlantic Treaty Organization), [London], 1959, expanded version prepared for U.S. Senate published as *The Techniques of Soviet Propaganda,* U.S. Government Printing Office, 1960, revised publication, 1965, also published as *The Unrelenting War: A Study of the Strategy and Tech-*

niques of Communist Propaganda and Infiltration, American-Asian Educational Exchange, 1960.

Il Est moins cinq: Propagande et infiltration sovietiques (further expansion of her report on Soviet propaganda), Berger-Levrault, 1960; (editor) *Vie ou mort de monde libre* (principal speeches at International Conference on Political Warfare, 1960), La Table Ronde, 1961; *Competition U.S.S.R.—U.S.A.: Economique, militaire, culturelle,* La Table Ronde, 1962; *Counter Attack: A Plan to Win the Political Warfare of the Soviets,* American-Asian Educational Exchange, 1963; *Reconnaissance Chine communiste, Ambassades pour subversions,* Editions de la Ligue de la Liberte, 1963, translation published, with an introduction by Senator Thomas J. Dodd as *Embassies of Subversion,* American Afro-Asian Education Exchange, 1965; *Le Tiers monde entre l'est et l'ouest: Vivre en dollars, voter en roubles,* La Table Ronde, 1964, translation published as *Red Foxes in the Chicken Coop,* Crestwood, 1966; *Vietnam: An Eye-Witness Account,* Crestwood, 1964, updated and enlarged edition published as *Sellout in Vietnam?,* Crestwood, 1966; (contributor) *Trouble Abroad,* Crestwood, 1965; *La Liberte se joue a Saigon,* Editions de la Ligue de la Liberte, 1965; *Les Colonialistes chinois en Afrique,* Editions de la Ligue de la Liberte, 1965; *DeGaulle ou la France enchainee,* Editions de la Ligue de la Liberte, 1965; *Menaces chinoises sur l'Asie,* La Table Ronde, 1966; *50 Annees de communisme,* Berger-Levrault, 1967, translation published as *Promise and Reality: 50 Years of Soviet "Achievements,"* John Graham, 1967; *Goliath and David: Justice pour la Chine libre,* Editions de la Ligue de la Liberte, 1967; *Le Petit livre rouge: Arme de guerre,* La Table Ronde, 1969.

Hippies, drogues et sexe, La Table Ronde, 1970, translation published as *Hippies, Drugs and Promiscuity,* Arlington House, 1970; *Le Monde des drogues,* France Empire, 1975; *Les Mille forces de la violence,* France Empire, 1977. Contributor of articles to magazines and newspapers in many countries.

SIDELIGHTS: Suzanne Labin's book on Stalin was translated into seven languages, and three later books—*La Condition humaine en Chine communiste, Il est moins cinq,* and *Competition U.S.S.R.—U.S.A.*—into eight languages. Her writings and anti-communist activities have made her the frequent target of diatribes in the press of the Soviet Union and its satellite countries.

AVOCATIONAL INTERESTS: Collecting unusual sculpture, riding horseback, swimming, skiing.

BIOGRAPHICAL/CRITICAL SOURCES: American Legion Magazine, December, 1962.

* * *

LACEY, Douglas R(aymond) 1913-

PERSONAL: Born April 29, 1913, in Easton, Pa.; son of Raymond H. (a professor) and Rosalind (Runyon) Lacey; married Mary Millington Moore (a teacher), January 3, 1946; children: Jack Cobb Moore, Mary C. Moore, Raymond, Pamela. *Education:* Illinois College, Jacksonville, A.B., 1935; Rutgers University, M.A., 1937; Columbia University, graduate study, 1937-41, Ph.D., 1959; University of London, graduate study, 1946-47. *Home:* 113 Wardour Dr., Annapolis, Md. 21401. *Office:* Department of History, U.S. Naval Academy, Annapolis, Md. 21402.

CAREER: Part-time instructor in history at Rutgers University, New Brunswick, N.J., 1937-38, City College (now City College of the City University of New York), New York,

N.Y., 1938-40, and Sarah Lawrence College, Bronxville, N.Y., 1939; U.S. Naval Academy, Annapolis, Md., instructor, 1941-42, associate professor, 1947-55, professor of history, 1955—, chairman of department, 1970—. Summer lecturer, University of Alberta, 1960; has also taught at University of Maryland and St. John's College, Annapolis. Member of board of directors of Anne Arundel County Citizens Committee, 1950-53, and Annapolis Citizens Committee, 1953-55. *Military service:* U.S. Navy, 1942-46; became lieutenant commander; received Presidential Unit Citation.

MEMBER: Conference on British Studies (chairman of development committee, 1965-68; chairman of nominating committee, 1968-70), International Commission for the History of Representative and Parliamentary Institutions, American Historical Association, American Association of University Professors, Southern Historical Association. *Awards, honors:* Rockefeller Foundation postwar fellowship in the humanities, 1946-47; Folger Library senior research fellowship, 1971-72.

WRITINGS: Dissent and Parliamentary Politics in England 1661-1689, Rutgers University Press, 1969.

WORK IN PROGRESS: An edition of the journal of Roger Morrice (1678-1691).

AVOCATIONAL INTERESTS: Playing the cello, fishing.

BIOGRAPHICAL/CRITICAL SOURCES: Washington Post, September 23, 1969.†

* * *

LA CHARITE, Virginia Anding 1937-

PERSONAL: Born January 18, 1937, in Philadelphia, Pa.; daughter of Claude Ellis, Jr. (an organic chemist) and Virginia (Nelson) Anding; married Raymond Camille La Charite (an associate professor of French), May 9, 1964; children: Claude Anding. *Education:* College of William and Mary, A.B., 1957, M.A., 1962; University of Besancon, graduate study, 1957-58; University of Pennsylvania, M.A., 1965, Ph.D., 1966. *Religion:* Episcopalian. *Home:* 1830 Cantrill Dr., Lexington, Ky. 40505. *Office:* Department of French, University of Kentucky, Lexington, Ky. 40506.

CAREER: College of William and Mary, Williamsburg, Va., instructor in French, 1959-62; University of North Carolina at Chapel Hill, lecturer in French, 1966-69; University of Kentucky, Lexington, associate professor, 1969-74, professor of French, 1974—, chairman of comparative literature curriculum, 1970—. *Member:* Modern Language Association of America, American Association of Teachers of French, South-Atlantic Modern Language Association, Midwest Modern Language Association, Phi Beta Kappa, Pi Delta Phi, Eta Sigma Pi, Kappa Delta Pi. *Awards, honors:* Fulbright fellowship, 1957-58; University of North Carolina research grant, 1968-69; Outstanding Faculty Woman, University of Kentucky, 1970-71; University of Kentucky research grant, 1970-72.

WRITINGS: The Poetics and the Poetry of Rene Char, University of North Carolina Press, 1968; (translator and editor with husband, Raymond C. La Charite), Bonaventure Des Periers, *Novel Pastimes and Merry Tales,* University Press of Kentucky, 1973; *Henri Michaux,* Twayne, 1977. Contributor to professional journals.†

* * *

LACKMANN, Ron(ald) 1934-

PERSONAL: Born May 8, 1934, in New York, N.Y.; son

of Frederick and Minerva (Morlock) Lackmann. *Education:* Hofstra College (now University), B.A., 1959, M.A., 1962; University of Hull, drama certificate, 1967-71.

CAREER: Central High School, Valley Stream, N.Y., speech and drama consultant, 1960—. Drama instructor in adult education program, Hofstra University, 1970-71. Host-moderator, "Education in Action," W.H.L.I. radio station, 1974-75; narrator, Pan Am's "Music in the Air." Actor on radio, television, and stage; playwright. *Military service:* U.S. Army, 1957-59; served as personnel and broadcast specialist. *Member:* Actors Equity Association, Screen Actors Guild.

WRITINGS: "Under the Angel's Wing" (play), first produced at Hofstra College, 1958; (with Barbara Gelman) *Bonnie and Clyde Scrapbook,* Personality Posters, 1968; *Remember Radio,* Putnam, 1970; "Hadrian's Wall" (a play about the Roman Empire), first produced at Showcase Theatre, May, 1970; *Remember Television,* Putnam, 1971; *TV Soap Opera Almanac,* Berkley Publishing, 1976. Author of several short stories and children's plays. Contributor of articles to magazines.

WORK IN PROGRESS: Two screenplays, "Back Off," which is about the Andy Warhol shooting, and a western, "Massacre at Lake Shetak"; a book, *Wild Women of the Wild West.*

BIOGRAPHICAL/CRITICAL SOURCES: Best Sellers, November 15, 1970, July 15, 1971.

* * *

LACKNER, Stephan 1910-

PERSONAL: Born April 21, 1910, in Paris, France; married Margaret Pernkopf, 1940; children: three. *Education:* University of Giessen, Ph.D. *Home:* 601 Bosque Rd., Santa Barbara, Calif. 93103.

CAREER: Journalist and author. *Military service:* U.S. Army, 1943-45. *Member:* P.E.N. (London).

WRITINGS: Die Weite Reise (poems), Oprecht (Zurich), 1937; *Der Mensch ist kein Haustier* (drama; lithographs by Max Beckmann), Editions Cosmopolites (Paris), 1938; *Jan Heimatlos* (novel), Verlag Die Liga (Zurich), 1939; *Das Lied des peckvogels* (novel), Suedverlag Konstanz, 1950; *Discover Your Self: A Practical Guide to Autoanalysis,* Merlin Press, 1956; *Max Beckmann, 1884-1950* (pamphlet), Safari-Verlag (Berlin), 1962; (editor) Max Beckmann, *Die neun Triptychen* (booklet), Safari-Verlag, 1965; *The Fables and Foibles of Professor Nimbus,* Noel Young, 1966; *Ich erinnere mich gut an Max Beckmann,* Kupferberg, 1967, translation published as *Max Beckmann: Memories of a Friendship,* University of Miami Press, 1969; *Max Beckmann,* Abrams, 1977. Contributor of short stories and articles in German and English to periodicals.

BIOGRAPHICAL/CRITICAL SOURCES: Henning Bock, *Max Beckmann: Germalde und Aquarelle der Sammlung Stephan Lackner, U.S.A.,* [Bremen], 1966.

* * *

LAIDLER, Harry W(ellington) 1884-1970

February 18, 1884—July 14, 1970; American author, economist, and socialist leader. Obituaries: *New York Times,* July 15, 1970; *Current Biography,* 1970. (See index for *CA* sketch)

LAKOFF, George 1941-

PERSONAL: Born May 24, 1941; son of Herman and Ida (Rosenfeld) Lakoff; married Robin Tolmach (a professor), June 9, 1963; children: Andrew. *Education:* Massachusetts Institute of Technology, B.S., 1962; Indiana University, Ph.D., 1966. *Politics:* "Yes." *Religion:* "No." *Office:* Department of Linguistics, University of California, Berkeley, Calif. 94720.

CAREER: Harvard University, Cambridge, Mass., research fellow and lecturer, 1965-69; University of Michigan, Ann Arbor, associate professor of linguistics, beginning 1969; currently faculty member in department of linguistics at University of California, Berkeley.

WRITINGS: Pronouns and Reference, Indiana University Linguistics Club, 1968; *Deep and Surface Grammar,* Indiana University Linguistics Club, 1968; *On Generative Semantics,* Indiana University Linguistics Club, 1969; *Irregularity in Syntax,* Holt, 1970; *Linguistik und natuerliche Logik,* translated from the original English by Udo Frie and Harald Mittermann, Athenaeum, 1971. Contributor to scholarly journals.†

* * *

LaMARSH, Julia Verlyn 1924-
(Judy LaMarsh)

PERSONAL: Born December 20, 1924, in Chatham, Ontario, Canada; daughter of Wilfred Clayton (an attorney) and Rhoda Elizabeth (Conibear) LaMarsh. *Education:* University of Toronto, B.A., 1947; Osgoode Hall Law School, LL.B., 1950. *Home:* 5992 Corwin Ave., Niagara Falls, Ontario, Canada.

CAREER: Called to Ontario Bar, 1950; practiced law in Niagara Falls, Ontario, 1950-63; member of Parliament representing Niagara Falls, 1960-68; appointed Queen's Counsel, 1963; minister of National Health and Welfare, 1963-65; Secretary of State, 1965-68; resigned from cabinet in April, 1968; host of radio program, "Person to Person," for station CJRN, and of television program, "LaMarsh Show," for CJOH-TV, both 1969; currently senior partner, specializing in litigation, of law firm, LaMarsh, MacBain, Slovak, Sinclair & Nicoletti, Niagara Falls and St. Catharines, Ontario. Budget chairman, Greater Niagara Community Chest, 1955-57; vice-president, Ontario Association of Rural-Urban Municipalities, 1957-59. Director of Scott-LaSalle Ltd.; former director of Greater Niagara General Hospital. *Military service:* Canadian Women's Army Corps, 1943-46; Japanese linguist in Pacific Military Intelligence Research section, 1945-46; became sergeant. *Member:* Canadian Bar Association, Council of Canada, Royal Canadian Legion, Planning Association of Canada. *Awards, honors:* LL.D., D'Youville College, 1967; named Canada's woman of the year and most newsworthy woman of the decade.

WRITINGS: (Under name Judy LaMarsh) *The Memoirs of a Bird in a Gilded Cage,* McClelland & Stewart, 1969. Contributor to magazines and the Canadian press.

SIDELIGHTS: "Controversy" was the word largely associated with Julia LaMarsh during her parliamentary career in Ottawa. A vocal Liberal from her university days on, she was the first woman in Canada to be a municipal corporation counsel and the only woman member of the official opposition in the House of Commons, 1960-63. Much of the controversy centered on her activity in behalf of pensions, medicare, and grants for the arts, and her support of broadcasting legislation, including the appointment of a Canadian Radio Television Commission to oversee broadcasting.

According to an official biography, LaMarsh has been living quietly in Niagara Falls. But not without some controversy. Ed Murphy, a former member of the Ottawa Press Gallery filed a libel suit against her, charging that his reputation was damaged by a statement in *Memoirs of a Bird in a Gilded Cage.* Testifying in Vancouver, where the case was tried in 1970, LaMarsh described her book as "honest impressions but not history." The book was a best seller in Canada.

BIOGRAPHICAL/CRITICAL SOURCES: Canadian Forum, March, 1969; *Variety,* February 4, 1970.†

* * *

LAMB, Robert (Boyden) 1941-

PERSONAL: Born June 19, 1941, in Washington, D.C.; son of Robert Keen (a professor) and Helen (Boyden) Lamb; married Rosemarie Wittman (a writer), July 11, 1965 (divorced); married Nancy Axelrod; children: Corinna Natasha Elizabeth Wittman, Robert Kenneth Wittman. *Education:* University of Chicago, B.A., 1963; London School of Economics and Political Science, Ph.D., 1970; Columbia University, M.B.A., 1976. *Politics:* Democrat. *Home:* 2210 Locust St., Philadelphia, Pa. 19103.

CAREER: Writer. Lecturer, London School of Economics and Political Science, University of London, 1967-71; assistant professor of political economy, Columbia University, 1971-75; visiting professor, Wharton School of Finance, University of Pennsylvania, 1976-77. Consultant in economics and business, 1971-76.

WRITINGS: The Plug at the Bottom of the Sea, Allen & Unwin, 1967, Bobbs-Merrill, 1968; *Fireblind,* Allen & Unwin, 1968; *The Rape,* Bantam, 1974; (with Robert Gilmour) *Political Alienation in Contemporary America,* Macmillan, 1976; (with Charles Frankel) *Equality,* Columbia University Press, 1977; *Market Man in the Market State,* Cambridge University Press, 1977.

Plays: (With Peter Brook and others) "U.S.," produced in London by Royal Shakespeare Co., 1967; "Reparation," produced on the West End at St. Martin's Lane, 1968; "Chain of Command," produced on the West End at St. Martin's Lane, 1969; "Raas," produced on the West End at St. Martin's Lane, 1972; "Fight Song," produced in New York at Gene Frankel Foundation Theater, 1975.

Television Plays: "Reparation," BBC-TV, 1970-72; "A Minor Operation," BBC-TV, 1971; "Raas," BBC-TV, 1973; "Feeling Good," NET-TV, 1975.

Contributor to *Atlantic Monthly, London Sunday Times, Current History, Oxford Economic Papers, Political Science Quarterly, Social Research, Political Science, Journal of the History of Ideas.* Associate editor, *Fortune.*

BIOGRAPHICAL/CRITICAL SOURCES: New Statesman, November 3, 1967; *Best Sellers,* March 1, 1968; *Young Readers' Review,* April, 1968.

* * *

LAMBO, Thomas Adeoye 1923-

PERSONAL: Born March 23, 1923, in Abeokuta, Nigeria; son of David Babatunde (a tribal chief) and Felicia B. (Akinlotan) Lambo; married Dinah Violet Adams (a teacher), February 10, 1945; children: David, Richard, Roger. *Education:* University of Birmingham, M.B. and Ch.B., 1948, M.D., 1953; University of London, D.P.M., 1953, F.R.C.P., 1963. *Religion:* Christian. *Home:* 27 Chemin des Chataigniers, 1292 Chambesy, Switzerland.

Office: World Health Organization, 1211 Geneva 27, Switzerland.

CAREER: House surgeon and house physician in Birmingham, England, 1949-50; medical officer in Lagos, Zaria, and Gusau, Nigeria, 1950-52; Western Region Ministry of Health, Nigeria, specialist, 1957-59, senior specialist at Neuro-Psychiatric Centre, 1960-63; University of Ibadan, Ibadan, Nigeria, professor of psychiatry and head of department of psychiatry and neurology, 1963-68, dean of medical faculty, 1966-68, vice-chancellor of university, 1968-71; World Health Organization, Geneva, Switzerland, assistant director-general, 1971-73, deputy director-general, 1973—. Chairman, International College of Tropical Medicine; member of advisory panel on mental health, World Health Organization, 1959-71.

MEMBER: International Hospital Federation (member of international advisory panel), International Epidemiological Association, World Federation for Mental Health (member of executive committee), World Future Studies Federation (member of scientific council), International Society for the Study of Human Development (co-chairman), World Association of Social Psychiatry (vice-president), International College of Psychosomatic Medicine (founding fellow), International Association for Child Psychiatry and Allied Professions (associate member), Centre for Advanced Study in the Development Sciences (member of advisory scientific panel), Ciba Foundation (member of advisory scientific panel), EARTHSCAN (member of advisory board), Association of Psychiatrists in Africa (vice-patron), Royal Medico-Psychological Association (corresponding member), Swiss Academy of Medical Sciences (honorary member), Mexican Institute of Culture (fellow, corresponding in Nigeria), Nigeria Medical Council.

AWARDS, HONORS: Officer, Order of the British Empire, 1962; D.Sc., Ahmadu Bello University, 1965, Long Island University; LL.D., Kent State University, 1969, Birmingham University, 1971; Haile Selassie African Research Award, 1970; D. honoris causa, University of Dahomey, 1973, University of Aix-Marseille, 1974, University of Louvan, 1976; first African appointed to Pontifical Academy of Sciences, 1974.

WRITINGS: (Editor) *Pan-African Psychiatric Conference Report,* [Ibadan], 1961; (with others) *Psychiatric Disorder among the Yorubas,* Cornell University Press, 1963; *Witch-doctoring,* Thomas Nelson, 1968. Contributor of more than one hundred monographs and articles to medical and other scientific journals.

BIOGRAPHICAL/CRITICAL SOURCES: Books and Bookmen, November, 1968.

*   *   *

LAMENSDORF, Leonard   1930-

PERSONAL: Born June 22, 1930; son of Maurice and Gertrude (Hellman) Lamensdorf; married Joyce Greenbaum, August 5, 1952 (divorced, October, 1974); married Barbara Witkowski, March 16, 1975; children: (first marriage) Lauren, Mark. *Education:* University of Chicago, B.A., 1948, J.D., 1952. *Home:* 3001 Long Valley Rd., Santa Ynez, Calif. 93460. *Agent:* Curtis Brown Ltd., 575 Madison Ave., New York, N.Y. 10022.

CAREER: Research associate on American Law Institute federal tax reform report, working at Harvard University, Cambridge, Mass., 1952-53; attorney and real estate developer, 1953—, building, owning, and managing stores, office

buildings, and regional shopping centers in various cities from coast to coast. Managing editor, *University of Chicago Law Review,* while attending law school at the university, Chicago, Ill.

WRITINGS: Kane's World (novel), Simon & Schuster, 1968; *In the Blood* (novel), Dell, 1974. Also author and executive producer of screenplay, "Cornbread, Earl and Me," filmed by American International Pictures, 1975.

WORK IN PROGRESS: Two novels and a screenplay.

*   *   *

LANDE, Henry F(rank)   1920-

PERSONAL: Born March 21, 1920, in Munich, Germany; married Marie-Luise Scheuer, March 31, 1951; children: Robert, Bettina, Diane. *Education:* Berlin Technical University, M.S., 1949; Western Reserve University (now Case Western Reserve University), M.B.A., 1956, Ph.D., 1965. *Home:* 35 Ave. Sainte Foy, Neuilly Sur Seine, France.

CAREER: Sealy Mattress Co., Cleveland, Ohio, various engineering and management positions in planning and control functions, 1951-56; International Business Machines Corp., Armonk, N.Y., 1956—, presently manager of planning systems for European division. Part-time lecturer at Graduate School of Business, New York University, 1967-68 and Pace University, 1970-75. *Member:* American Economic Association, National Planning Association, Verband Deutscher Wirtschaftsingenieure.

WRITINGS: How to Use the Computer in Business Planning, Prentice-Hall, 1969.

WORK IN PROGRESS: Research on how to structure systems for planning, measurement, and control.

*   *   *

LANDECKER, Manfred   1929-

PERSONAL: Born September 19, 1929, in Germany; son of Norbert (a physician) and Hildegard (Casper) Landecker; married Eva Landauer (a teacher), December 27, 1953; children: David, Lisa Jenny. *Education:* Syracuse University, B.A., 1952; Johns Hopkins University, School of Advanced International Studies, M.A., 1953, Ph.D., 1965. *Religion:* Jewish. *Home:* 903 South Taylor Dr., Carbondale, Ill., 62901. *Office:* Department of Political Science, Southern Illinois University, Carbondale, Ill. 62901.

CAREER: Johns Hopkins University, School of Advanced International Studies, Bologna (Italy) Center, research assistant, 1956-58; Southern Illinois University, Carbondale, 1959—, began as lecturer, associate professor of international affairs, 1969—. *Military service:* U.S. Army, 1953-55. *Member:* American Political Science Association, International Studies Association, American Association of University Professors. *Awards, honors:* Johns Hopkins University, School of Advanced International Studies fellowship, 1955; Alexander von Humboldt Foundation fellowship for research in Bonn, Germany, 1966-67.

WRITINGS: The President and Public Opinion: Leadership in Foreign Affairs, Public Affairs Press, 1968.

WORK IN PROGRESS: Research on German foreign policy.

*   *   *

LANDON, Michael de L(aval)   1935-

PERSONAL: Born October 8, 1935, in Saint John, New Brunswick, Canada; son of Arthur H. W. (a brigadier general in the Canadian Army) and Elizabeth (Fair) Landon; married Doris Lee Clay (an attorney), December 31, 1959; children: Clay de Laval, Letitia Elizabeth. *Education:* Worcester College, Oxford, B.A., 1958, M.A., 1961; University of Wisconsin—Madison, M.A., 1962, Ph.D., 1966. *Politics:* Republican. *Religion:* Episcopalian. *Home address:* P.O. Box 172, University, Miss. 38677. *Office:* Department of History, University of Mississippi, University, Miss. 38677.

CAREER: Manor House School, Horsham, Sussex, England, history teacher, 1957; Dalhousie Preparatory School, Ladybank, Fife, Scotland, history teacher, 1958; Lakefield College School, Lakefield, Ontario, English teacher, 1958-60; University of Mississippi, University, assistant professor, 1964-67, associate professor, 1967-72, professor of history, 1972—. Visiting associate professor, University of Wisconsin—Madison, 1971. *Member:* American Historical Association, American Association of University Professors, Royal Historical Society (London; fellow), Conference on British Studies, Eta Sigma Phi, Phi Alpha Theta. *Awards, honors:* American Philosophical Society research grant, 1966-67, 1973-74.

WRITINGS: The Triumph of the Lawyers, University of Alabama Press, 1970. Contributor to *Per Se, Enlightenment Essays, Proceedings* of the American Philosophical Society, and other journals.

WORK IN PROGRESS: The Mississippi State Bar Association, 1906-1976; The Political Career of Sir John Maynard, Serjeant-at-Law, 1604-1690.

SIDELIGHTS: Michael Landon writes: "I am competent in French and Spanish and am learning German. . . . I have been very frustrated by the fact that a history of Anglo-Irish relations from the earliest times to the present has been turned down by some twenty publishers who say it is interesting and well-written but that there is no market for such works."

AVOCATIONAL INTERESTS: Gardening, cooking.

* * *

LANDSHOFF, Ursula 1908-

PERSONAL: Born May 17, 1908, in Berlin, Germany; American citizen; daughter of Siegfried (a businessman) and Selma (Fernbach) Nothmann; married Herman Landshoff (a free-lance photographer), June 4, 1941. *Education:* Attended German lycee in Berlin, ten years, School of Applied Arts, Munich, three years, and one year at Academy in Berlin. *Home:* 227 East 57th St., New York, N.Y. 10022.

CAREER: Illustrator and writer.

WRITINGS—All juvenile: (Illustrator) Liesel Mark Skorpen, *If I Had a Lion,* Harper, 1967; (self-illustrated) *Daisy and Doodle,* Bradbury, 1969; (self-illustrated) *Daisy and the Stormy Night,* Bradbury, 1970; (illustrator) Claire Huchet Bishop, *Georgette,* Coward, 1974; (illustrator) Cynthia Jameson, *Mr. Wolf Gets Ready for Supper,* Coward, 1975.

WORK IN PROGRESS: Children's books.

* * *

LANE, Allen 1902-1970

September 21, 1902—July 7, 1970; British educator and founder of Penguin Books. Obituaries: *New York Times,* July 8, 1970; *Antiquarian Bookman,* July 20-27, 1970; *Current Biography,* 1970.

LANE, Carolyn 1926-

PERSONAL: Born June 4, 1926, in Providence, R.I.; daughter of Harry T. (president, Blocker Air Conditioning Corp.) and Margaret (Breitenfeld) Blocker; married M. Donald Lane, Jr. (an architect), April 28, 1951; children: Jay Donald. *Education:* Connecticut College, B.A., 1948. *Home:* Ward Rd., Salt Point, N.Y. 12578.

CAREER: Artist and writer. Has been a professional greeting card designer, paints, and does silk screen work; during the past ten years has designed and executed eight sets for local theatrical organizations, three of them for productions of her own plays. *Member:* Authors Guild. *Awards, honors:* Community Children's Theatre, Kansas City, Mo., 12th annual merit award, 1963, and Pioneer Drama Service award, 1967, both for play, *Turnabout Night at the Zoo;* Pioneer's Best Children's Play, 1969, for *The Wayward Clocks;* Theatre Guild of Webster Groves, Mo., one-act play contest, first prize, 1969, for *The Last Grad.*

WRITINGS—Juvenile books: Uncle Max and the Sea Lion, Bobbs-Merrill, 1970; *Turnabout Night at the Zoo* (based on play of same title; also see below), Abingdon, 1971; *The Voices of Greenwillow Pond,* Houghton, 1972; *The Winnemah Spirit,* Houghton, 1975.

Plays: *Turnabout Night at the Zoo* (juvenile), Pioneer Drama Service, 1967; *The Wayward Clocks* (juvenile), Pioneer Drama Service, 1969; *The Last Grad* (one-act adult drama), Baker's Plays, 1970; *Child of Air* (one-act adult drama), Pioneer Drama Service, 1972.

WORK IN PROGRESS: Several children's books, varied magazine pieces, and a book of Hudson Valley legends, for old and young readers alike.

SIDELIGHTS: Carolyn Lane told *CA:* "My writing career began when my husband and I were designing sets for a local children's play production. 'I could write a better play than that,' I kept sniffing haughtily at each rehearsal, and finally my husband surprised me by asking: 'Then why don't you?' So I did—and to my amazement it not only got published, but won two prizes, and later turned into a book as well! Not only had I shown my husband a thing or two, but I had learned for myself the inescapable truth that no one ever becomes a writer simply by talking about 'What I'm going to write some da.. ' 't r̄k-s hard work, discipline—and a whole lot of suffering. Somehow, though, the children make it all worthwhile. The joy of seeing a child laugh or cry over words I wrote is the great·st reward imaginable."

AVOCATIONAL INT 'K 'STS: Art, including serigraphs, painting, and set design.

* * *

LANE, David (Stuart) 1933-

PERSONAL: Born April 24, 1933, in Fleur-de-Lys, Monmouthshire, England; son of Reginald (a bench hand) and Mary (Maud) Lane; married Christel Noritzsch (a teacher), 1962; children: Christopher, Julie. *Education:* University of Birmingham, B.Soc.Sc., 1960; Nuffield College, Oxford, D.Phil., 1966. *Politics:* Labour Party. *Office:* Emmanuel College, Cambridge University, Cambridge, England.

CAREER: University of Essex, Colchester, England, lecturer and reader in sociology, 1967-73, chairman of department, 1973; Cambridge University, Cambridge, England, lecturer and fellow of Emmanuel College, 1974—, tutor, 1975—. *Military service:* Royal Air Force, 1951-53. *Member:* Association of University Teachers, British Sociological Association, American Sociological Association, British Political Studies Association.

WRITINGS: *Roots of Russian Communism: A Social and Historical Study of Russian Social-Democracy, 1898-1907,* Van Gorcum, 1969, Humanities, 1970; *Politics and Society in the U.S.S.R.,* Weidenfeld & Nicolson, 1970, Random House, 1971; *The End of Inequality?: Social Stratification under State Socialism,* Penguin, 1971; (with G. Kolankiewicz) *Social Groups in Polish Society,* Macmillan, 1973; *The Socialist Industrial State,* Allen & Unwin, 1976; (contributor) R. Scase, *Studies in Industrial Society,* Allen & Unwin, 1977. Contributor to sociology, political science, and Soviet studies journals.

WORK IN PROGRESS: With F. O'Dell, *Industrial Workers in the USSR: Education, Opportunity and Control,* for Martin Robertson.

AVOCATIONAL INTERESTS: Music, soccer, travel.

BIOGRAPHICAL/CRITICAL SOURCES: *Times Literary Supplement,* October 16, 1969.

*   *   *

LANE, William L.   1931-

PERSONAL: Born January 16, 1931, in New Britain, Conn.; son of William J. (a production supervisor) and Evelyn (Moore) Lane; married Lillian Christopherson, June 5, 1954 (divorced, 1974); married Brenda Whitaker, August 7, 1974; children: William John, Kristine Ruth, Mark Timothy, David Eric. *Education:* Wesleyan University, Middletown, Conn., B.A., 1952; Gordon Divinity School, B.D., 1955; Westminster Theological Seminary, Th.M., 1956; Harvard University, Th.D., 1962. *Politics:* Republican. *Religion:* American Baptist. *Home:* 1338 Park St., Bowling Green, Ky. 42101. *Office:* Department of Philosophy and Religion, Western Kentucky University, Bowling Green, Ky. 42101.

CAREER: Hebrew Union College-Jewish Institute of Religion, Cincinnati, Ohio, Christian research fellow, 1959-60; Gordon Divinity School (now Gordon-Conwell Theological Seminary), South Hamilton, Mass., assistant professor, 1960-63, associate professor, 1963-68, professor of New Testament and Judaic studies, 1968-73; Western Kentucky University, Bowling Green, Ky., professor of religious studies, 1974—. *Member:* Society of Biblical Literature, Evangelical Theological Society, Studiorum Novi Testamenti Societas, Near East Archeological Society, Phi Beta Kappa, Phi Alpha Chi.

WRITINGS: (With Glenn W. Barker and J. Ramsey Michaels) *The New Testament Speaks,* Harper, 1969; *Ephesians—2 Thessalonians* (Bible study book), Scripture Union (London), 1969; *Righteousness in Christ,* Scripture Union, 1973; *The New International Commentary on the Gospel of Mark,* Eerdmans, 1974; (contributor) R. N. Longenecker and M. C. Tenney, editors, *New Dimensions in New Testament Study,* Zondervan, 1974; (contributor) J. H. Skilton, editor, *The New Testament Student and Theology,* Presbyterian & Reformed, 1976. Bibliographical editor, *The Encyclopedia of Christianity,* Christian Educational Foundation, 1964; associate editor, *The Encyclopedia of Modern Christian Missions,* Thomas Nelson, 1967.

WORK IN PROGRESS: *Paul in the Perspective of His Mission,* completion expected in 1979.

SIDELIGHTS: William Lane told *CA:* "I have gradually come to understand that my primary task as a writer of technical biblical studies is to listen to the text, and to the discussion it has prompted over the course of the centuries, as a child who needs to be made wise. I view my writing as a response to the discipline of responsible listening." *Avoca-*

tional interests: Stamp collecting, with emphasis on Scandinavia.

*   *   *

LANGE, Suzanne   1945-

PERSONAL: "E" in surname is silent; born April 30, 1945, in Dallas, Tex.; daughter of Raymond Emil (with U.S. Navy) and Doris Faye (Ledbetter) Lange; married Kirt E. Duffy, December 8, 1972; children: Megen Corin. *Education:* University of Texas at Arlington, student, 1963-65; Southern Methodist University, B.A. (summa cum laude), 1970; Trinity University, M.A., 1971; Pittsburg State University, M.S., 1977. *Religion:* Existential humanism. *Home:* 1805 North Broadway, Pittsburg, Kan. *Office:* Pittsburg State University, Pittsburg, Kan. 66762.

CAREER: Southwest Production Co., Dallas, Tex., production accountant, 1968-69; Wenchel, Shulman & Manning, Washington, D.C., legal secretary, 1969; Children's Learning Center, San Antonio, Tex., teacher-therapist and assistant director, 1971; elementary school teacher in Parsons, Kan.; currently instructor at Pittsburg State University.

WRITINGS: *The Year,* S. G. Phillips, 1970.

WORK IN PROGRESS: *Alderian Psychology and Career Development,* an academic review.

*   *   *

LANGER, William L(eonard)   1896-

PERSONAL: Born March 16, 1896, in Boston, Mass.; son of Rudolph E. (a florist) and Johanna (Rockenbach) Langer; married Susanne Knauth (an art authority), September 3, 1921 (divorced August, 1942); married Rowena Allen Morse Nelson, April 9, 1943; children: (first marriage) Leonard Charles Rudolph, Bertrand Walter. *Education:* Harvard University, A.B., 1915, A.M., 1920, Ph.D., 1923; University of Vienna, graduate study, 1921-22. *Home:* 1 Berkeley St., Cambridge, Mass. 02138. *Office:* Department of History, Harvard University, Cambridge, Mass.

CAREER: Worcester Academy, Worcester, Mass., teacher of modern languages, 1915-17; Clark University, Worcester, assistant professor, 1923-25, associate professor of history, 1925-27; Harvard University, Cambridge, Mass., assistant professor, 1927-31, associate professor of history, 1931-36, Archibald Cary Coolidge Professor of History, 1936-64, professor emeritus, 1964—, director of Russian Research Center, 1954-59, and of Center for Middle East Studies, 1954-56. Visiting professor, Columbia University, 1931; Harvard lecturer, Yale University, 1933; professor, Fletcher School of Law and Diplomacy, 1933-34, 1936-41; fellow, Center for Advanced Study in the Behavioral Sciences, 1959-60. U.S. Government, Washington, D.C., member of board of analysts, Office of the Coordinator of Information, 1941-42, chief of research and analysis branch, Office of Strategic Services, 1942-45, director of Office of Intelligence Research, Department of State, 1945-46, special assistant to Secretary of State, 1946, assistant director for national estimates, Central Intelligence Agency, 1950-52, member of President's Foreign Intelligence Advisory Board, 1961-69. Editorial adviser to Houghton, Mifflin Co., Harper & Row Publishers, and American Heritage Press. *Military service:* U.S. Army, 1917-19; served in France; became master engineer junior grade.

MEMBER: American Historical Association (president, 1957), American Philosophical Society, American Academy of Arts and Sciences, Organization of American Historians, Council on Foreign Relations, Massachusetts Historical Society, Harvard Club (New York). *Awards, honors:* LL.D. from Harvard University, 1945, and Mills College, 1960; D.Phil. from University of Hamburg, 1955; L.H.D. from Yale University, 1956; Litt.D. from Alma College, 1961. Medal of Merit for wartime service with Office of Strategic Services, 1946; Bancroft Prize of Columbia University (shared with S. Everett Gleason), 1955, for *The Undeclared War, 1940-1941;* Golden Plate Award of American Academy of Achievement, 1966.

WRITINGS: With "E" of the First Gas, printed for members of his World War I unit, 1919, published as *Gas and Flame in World War I,* Knopf, 1965; *The Franco-Russian Alliance, 1890-1894,* Harvard University Press, 1929, reprinted, 1967; *European Alliances and Alignments, 1871-1890,* Knopf, 1931, 2nd edition with supplementary bibliographies, 1950; (editor with Hamilton Fish Armstrong) *Foreign Affairs Bibliography, 1919-1932,* Harper, 1933, reprinted, 1960; *The Diplomacy of Imperialism, 1890-1902,* Knopf, 1935, 2nd edition with supplementary bibliographies, 1951; (compiler and editor, with the assistance of others) *The Encyclopedia of World History: Ancient, Medieval and Modern* (revised and modernized version of Karl J. Ploetz's *Epitome of Ancient, Mediaeval and Modern History*), Houghton, 1940, 5th edition, revised and enlarged, 1972; *Our Vichy Gamble,* Knopf, 1947; (with S. Everett Gleason) *The Challenge to Isolation, 1937-1940,* Harper, for Council on Foreign Relations, 1952, reissued in two volumes, 1964; (with Gleason) *The Undeclared War, 1940-1941,* Harper, for Council on Foreign Relations, 1953; (contributor) Arthur P. Dudden, *Woodrow Wilson and the World of Today,* University of Pennsylvania Press, 1957; (contributor) *Goals for Americans,* Prentice-Hall, 1960; (contributor) Evelyn M. Acomb and Marvin L. Brown, editors, *French Society and Culture Since the Old Regime,* Holt, 1966; (editor) *Western Civilization,* Harper, Volume I: *Paleolithic Man to the Emergence of European Powers,* Volume II: *Struggle for Empire to Europe in the Modern World,* 1968; Carl E. Schorske and Elizabeth Schorske, editors, *Explorations in Crisis: Papers on International History,* Belknap Press, 1969; *Political and Social Upheaval, 1832-1852,* Harper, 1970, published as *Revolutions of 1848: Chapters from Political and Social Upheaval,* 1971; *Perspectives in Western Civilization,* two volumes, Harper, 1972; *The New Illustrated Encyclopedia of World History,* two volumes, Abrams, 1975.

Booklets (mainly separate reprints from journals): *A Critique of Imperialism,* 1935; *Die Innenseite der amerikanischen Aussenpolitik,* Steiner, 1956; *The Next Assignment,* 1958; *Farewell to Empire,* 1962; *Red Rag and Gallic Bull: The French Decision for War, 1870,* 1962; *Europe's Initial Population Explosion,* 1963.

General editor of Harper's twenty-volume series, "The Rise of Modern Europe," 1934—. Member of editorial board, *Journal of Modern History,* 1929-1933, *American Historical Review,* 1936-39, and *Foreign Affairs,* 1955—; member of editorial advisory board, *Historical Abstracts,* 1955—.

WORK IN PROGRESS: Studies of the European population in the time of Malthus.

SIDELIGHTS: Most of the books Langer has written and edited over half a century still are in print, due to reissues of the early works in the 1960's. William Langer has traveled and lectured extensively in Europe and the Near East, to a lesser degree in East Africa and Central America. Music is

his principal hobby (he plays viola in an amateur quartet and was president of the Harvard-Pierian Foundation, 1969-73), but he also is "devoted to golf and bowling."

BIOGRAPHICAL/CRITICAL SOURCES: Carl E. Schorske's introduction to *Explorations in Crisis,* Belknap Press, 1969.

* * *

LAQUIAN, Aprodicio A(rcilla)   1935-

PERSONAL: Born March 23, 1935, in Pampanga, Philippines; son of Narciso Cruz (a tailor) and Crisanta (Arcilla) Laquian; married Eleanor del Rio (a journalist), October 24, 1962; children: George Edwardo R., Agnes Helen R. *Education:* University of the Philippines, B.A. (cum laude), 1959; Massachusetts Institute of Technology, Ph.D., 1965. *Religion:* Roman Catholic. *Home:* 51 Bignay St., Project 2, Quezon City, Philippines. *Address:* c/o Regional Director, International Development Research Centre, P.O. Box 30677, Nairobi, Kenya.

CAREER: Associate professor of political science, University of the Philippines, Manila; University of Hawaii, East-West Center, Honolulu, senior specialist, 1968-69; International Association for Metropolitan Research and Development, Toronto, Ontario, director of research, 1969—. Lecturer, Faculty of Environmental Studies, York University, 1970—. Consultant, United Nations, 1970. *Member:* Society for Public Administration of the Philippines, American Association for the Advancement of Science, American Society for Public Administration, American Political Science Association, Canadian Association for Asian Studies, Canadian Association for African Studies, Asia Society, Phi Kappa Phi.

WRITINGS: The City in Nation-Building: Politics and Administration in Metropolitan Manila, School of Public Administration, University of the Philippines, 1966; *Slums Are for People: The Barrio Magsaysay Pilot Project in Urban Community Development,* College of Public Administration, University of the Philippines, 1968, 2nd edition, 1969, revised edition, East-West Center, 1971; (editor) *Rural-Urban Migrants and Metropolitan Development,* Intermet, 1971; *Administrative Aspects of Urbanization,* United Nations, 1971. Managing editor, *Philippine Journal of Public Administration,* 1962-64; editor-in-chief, *Local Government Bulletin,* 1965-68.

WORK IN PROGRESS: Town Drift: Policy Implications of Internal Migration in Developing Countries, tentative title, a comparative study of slums and squatters in Bandung, Caracas, Ibadan, Istanbul, Kuala Lumpur, Lima, Manila, and Seoul; *Housing Asia's Millions,* a comparative study of housing strategies in Hong Kong, Indonesia, Laos, Malaysia, Philippines, Singapore, Sri Lanka, and Thailand.

SIDELIGHTS: Aprodicio Laquian told *CA:* "My interest in slums and squatters in developing countries is rooted in the fact that until I was twenty-five years old, I lived in the slums of Manila. . . . To me, slums and squatter areas are necessary parts of urbanization—they make it possible for many migrants from the countryside to live in the city and find their place in society."

* * *

LARKIN, Oliver Waterman   1896-1970

August 17, 1896—December 18, 1970; American art historian. Obituaries: *New York Times,* December 19, 1970; *Books Abroad,* spring, 1971. (See index for *CA* sketch)

LARSEN, Peter 1933-

PERSONAL: Surname originally Lehrburger; born October 24, 1933, in England; son of Egon (an author; pen name, Egon Larsen) and Helen (Boetz) Lehrburger; married Lydia Guth (a teacher), January 25, 1956; married second wife, Elaine Lewis (a writer), June 25, 1965. *Education:* Attended secondary school in England; studied at Brodovitch Design Workshop, New York, N.Y., 1961, and at University of Missouri Photo-Journalism Workshop. *Politics:* None. *Address:* P.O. Box 7680, Jerusalem, Israel.

CAREER: Writer and photographer. Emigrated to Australia at age seventeen, and became interested in photography while working on a sheep station; after military service traveled to Africa and worked on *Drum Magazine;* in 1960, Larsen went to the United States and worked as an assistant to a photographer in public relations, industrial, and advertising photography, later becoming a free-lance photographer; with his wife, Larsen made a three-year world trip, 1966-69, traveling sixty thousand miles in two motor caravans, and visiting Europe, Asia, and the American continents from Canada to Argentina; during the journey, Larsen worked on photographic assignments for the United Nations, Red Cross, *World Book Encyclopedia, New York Times,* and other groups and publications. *Military service:* Royal Australian Air Force, 1952-58. *Member:* Royal Geographical Society (fellow), Royal Photographic Society (associate), National Union of Journalists.

WRITINGS: (With wife, Elaine Larsen) *Boy of Nepal,* Dodd, 1970; (with Elaine Larsen) *Boy of Dahomey,* Dodd, 1970; *United Nations: At Work around the World,* edited by father, Egon Larsen, Dent, 1970, Lathrop, 1971; (with Elaine Larsen) *Boy of Bolivia,* Dodd, 1971. Photographs included in *Young Africa,* edited by Egon Larsen, Phoenix House, 1964, and *Boy of the Masai.* Photo editor and chief photographer, *World Book Encyclopedia.*

WORK IN PROGRESS: Several books.

AVOCATIONAL INTERESTS: Dancing, water-skiing, travel.†

* * *

LARSON, Gustive O. 1897-

PERSONAL: Born August 18, 1897, in Salt Lake City, Utah; married Virginia Bean, February 12, 1926; children: G. Olof, Patricia Ann (Mrs. Elroy Nelson), Tanja Virginia (Mrs. George R. Cannon). *Education:* University of Utah, B.A., 1920, M.A., 1927; additional study at Columbia University, 1928, University of California, 1932, 1948. *Politics:* Democrat. *Religion:* Mormon. *Home:* 1234 Cherry Lane, Provo, Utah 84601. *Office:* Department of History, Brigham Young University, Provo, Utah 84601.

CAREER: Latter-day Saints Seminary, Cedar City, Utah, principal, 1924-36; president of Latter-day Saints Mission in Sweden, 1936-39; Latter-day Saints Institute of Religion, Cedar City, director, 1939-54; Brigham Young University, Provo, Utah, associate professor of religion, 1954-67, associate professor of history, 1954-72, associate professor emeritus, 1972—. Chairman of history committee, Utah Heritage Foundation, 1968-71. *Member:* American Historical Association, National Society of the Sons of Utah Pioneers (national historian, 1960-63), Western History Association, Utah State Historical Society (fellow; life member), Utah Academy of Sciences, Arts, and Letters (life member), Utah Westerners. *Awards, honors:* Brigham Young University grant for travel in Europe and research in National Archives

and Library of Congress, 1959-60, and summer research grants to National Archives, 1962, 1967, and to Huntington Library, 1964, 1974; Mormon History Association Book Award, 1971, for *The "Americanization" of Utah for Statehood;* American Association of University Professors faculty service award, 1972; D.Litt., Southern Utah State College, 1974; Merit Honor Award, University of Utah, 1975.

WRITINGS: Prelude to the Kingdom, Marshall Jones, 1947; *Outline History of Utah and the Mormons,* Deseret, 1958, 3rd edition, 1965; *The "Americanization" of Utah for Statehood,* Huntington Library, 1971. Contributor to *Mississippi Valley Historical Review, Utah Historical Quarterly, American West,* and other journals.

WORK IN PROGRESS: A book studying Mormon emigration activities.

AVOCATIONAL INTERESTS: Making river runs on the Colorado and its tributaries, tracing historic trails.

BIOGRAPHICAL/CRITICAL SOURCES: Provo Daily Herald, Provo, Utah, April 20, 1971; *Deseret News,* Salt Lake City, Utah, April 21, 1971.

* * *

La SALLE, Donald (Philip) 1933-

PERSONAL: Born March 14, 1933, in Corona, N.Y.; son of Rocco and Theresa (Chiliano) La Salle; married Nancy Haniewski, November 9, 1957; children: Christopher, Gregory, Donna Marie. *Education:* Central Connecticut State College, B.S., 1956; University of Virginia, additional study, 1960-61; University of Connecticut, M.A., 1964, doctoral candidate, 1969—; Columbia University, additional study, 1964. *Politics:* Democrat. *Religion:* Catholic. *Home and office:* 59 Beechwood Lane, Bristol, Conn. 06010. *Agent:* Mary Walsh, 257 Park Ave. South, New York, N.Y.

CAREER: Former high school science teacher and science coordinator in Avon, Conn.; Talcott Mountain Science Center for Student Involvement, Avon, director, 1966—. Member of staff at national workshops in science and nongraded schools at University of North Carolina, 1966, and University of Hartford, 1967. *Member:* National Science Teachers Association, Connecticut Association for the Gifted (president), Phi Delta Kappa.

WRITINGS: (With John McGavack) *Guppies, Bubbles and Vibrating Objects,* John Day, 1969; (with McGavack) *Crystals, Insects, and Unknown Objects,* John Day, 1971. Contributor to magazines and professional periodicals.

* * *

LASLETT, John H(enry) M(artin) 1933-

PERSONAL: Born May 7, 1933, in Watford, England; son of George H. R. (a minister) and Evelyn (Alden) Laslett; married Barbara R. Tauber (a sociologist), September 26, 1959; children: Michael, Sarah. *Education:* Oxford University, B.A., 1957, M.A., and D.Phil., 1962; Northwestern University, additional study, 1958-59. *Office:* Department of History, University of California, Los Angeles, Calif. 90024.

CAREER: University of Liverpool, Liverpool, England, assistant lecturer in political theory and institutions, 1961-62; University of Chicago, Chicago, Ill., assistant professor of social sciences, 1962-64, assistant professor of history, 1964-68; University of California, Los Angeles, associate professor, 1968-75, professor of history, 1975—. *Military service:* British Army, Intelligence, 1952-54. *Member:* American

Historical Association, Society for the Study of Labour History. *Awards, honors:* George W. Ochs-Oakes senior scholar in American history, Queen's College, Oxford, 1957-58; Willett Faculty Research Award from University of Chicago, 1964; Social Science Research Council fellow, 1970-71.

WRITINGS: The Workingman in American Life, Houghton, 1968; *Labor and the Left: A Study of Radical and Socialist Influences in the American Labor Movement, 1881-1924,* Basic Books, 1970; (with Seymour M. Lipset) *Failure of a Dream? Essays in the History of American Socialism,* Doubleday-Anchor, 1974. Contributor to historical journals.

WORK IN PROGRESS: A Short Comparative History of American Socialism, for Harper; research into comparative coal mining communities in Britain and America; research into U.S. working class history and culture.

*   *   *

LASSNER, Jacob 1935-

PERSONAL: Born March 15, 1935; son of Kalman (a furrier) and Ruth (Friedman) Lassner. *Education:* University of Michigan, A.B., 1955; Brandeis University, M.A., 1957; Yale University, Ph.D., 1963. *Office:* Department of Near Eastern Languages and Literatures, Wayne State University, Detroit, Mich. 48202.

CAREER: Wayne State University, Detroit, Mich., assistant professor, 1963-67, associate professor of Near Eastern languages and literatures, 1967—, chairman of department, 1967, 1969—. *Member:* American Oriental Society, Middle East Studies Association, American Historical Association. *Awards, honors:* Wayne State University faculty research fellowships, summer, 1964, 1967; archaeological fellow at Hebrew Union College—Jewish Institute of Religion, Biblical and Archaeological School, Jerusalem, 1968-69; Social Science Research Council grant, 1968-69.

WRITINGS: The Topography of Baghdad in the Early Ages: Text and Studies, Wayne State University Press, 1969; (contributor) A. H. Hourani and S. M. Stern, editors, *The Islamic City: A Colloquium,* University of Pennsylvania Press, 1970. Contributor to *Encyclopedia of Islam* and to journals in his field.

WORK IN PROGRESS: With M. Sharon, *Chrestomathia Historicorum Arabicorum; The Caliphate of Sammarra.*††

*   *   *

LASTER, Ann A(ppleton) 1936-

PERSONAL: Born August 10, 1936, in Water Valley, Miss.; daughter of Brinson DeWitt and Ludie (McGonagill) Appleton; married Bob Lee Laster (a superintendent for Allis Chalmers), June 11, 1961; children: Ann Lee. *Education:* Mississippi College, B.A., 1957; attended University of Mississippi, 1958-60, M.A., 1966. *Office address:* Box 424, Hinds Junior College, Raymond, Miss. 39154.

CAREER: Flora High School, Flora, Miss., English teacher and librarian, 1957-61; West Point High School, West Point, Miss., English and Latin teacher, 1961-62; Clarksdale-Coahoma High School, Clarksdale, Miss., English teacher, 1962-64; Hinds Junior College, Raymond, Miss., English teacher, 1964—. *Member:* National Council of Teachers of English, American Association of University Women (secretary, 1967-68), Southeast Regional English in Two-Year College (chairman, regional convention, 1974; chairman, regional executive committee, 1974-77), College Composition and Communication, Mississippi Education Associa-

tion (member of board of directors, 1973-75), Mississippi Association of English Teachers, Hinds Junior College Education Association (vice-president, 1966; president, 1967), Hinds County Association for Mental Health, Culture Club (vice-president, 1965; president, 1966; member of board of directors, 1967-69), Kappa Kappa Iota (state secretary, 1971; chairman, national convention, 1975; state president, 1975-77).

WRITINGS—All with Nell A. Pickett; published by Harper: *Writing and Reading in Technical English,* 1970; *The Student's Handbook for Writing,* Harper, 1971; *Writing for Occupational Education,* 1974; *Technical English,* 1975.

WORK IN PROGRESS: Refining English curriculum; revising *The Student's Handbook for Writing.*

*   *   *

LATIMER, H(enry) C. 1893-

PERSONAL: Born April 7, 1893; son of Thomas H. (an engineer) and Matilda (Speer) Latimer; married Stella Wilson, April 20, 1940; children: Susan W. *Education:* Attended Cornell University, one year. *Religion:* Presbyterian. *Home:* 44 Witch Lane, Rowayton, Conn. 06853. *Office address:* P.O. Box 68, Rowayton, Conn. 06853.

CAREER: Lithographers National Association, New York City, educational director, 1944-52; Metropolitan Lithographers Association, New York City, executive director, 1952-62. *Military service:* U.S. Army, World War I. *Member:* Cornell Club of New York.

WRITINGS: Survey of Lithography, Lithographic Technical Foundation, 1952; *Advertising Production Planning and Copy Preparation for Offset Printing,* Art Directions Book, 1969; *Advertising Graphics: A Guide to New Creative Preparation and Production Techniques,* McGraw, 1977. Also author of *Preparation of Art and Camera Copy for Printing,* McGraw. Offset editor, *Inland Printer.*

WORK IN PROGRESS: Another book.

*   *   *

LAUER, Evelyn G(erda) 1938-

PERSONAL: Born September 15, 1938, in Vienna, Austria; daughter of Erwin Peter (an optician) and Berta (Feyfarek) Lauer; married Richard E. Allen, June 9, 1962 (divorced). *Education:* University of Buffalo, B.A., 1960; Columbia University, M.S., 1961. *Politics:* "Usually Democratic but not registered member." *Religion:* Roman Catholic. *Office:* School of Library Service, Columbia University, New York, N.Y.

CAREER: Columbia University, New York, N.Y., librarian in reference department, 1961-68, librarian in School of Library Service, 1968—.

WRITINGS: (Compiler) *Index to Little Magazines 1964-65,* Swallow Press, 1966; (compiler) *Index to Little Magazines 1966-67,* Swallow Press, 1969. Contributor of reviews to *Slavic Review* and library journals.

SIDELIGHTS: Evelyn Lauer lived in Hungary for eighteen months. In addition to German and Hungarian, she is competent in French, Italian, and Russian.†

*   *   *

LAURENCE, Ester Hauser 1935-

PERSONAL: Born July 27, 1935, in Charleston, N.Y.; daughter of John and Edna (Stead) Hauser; married Joseph P. Laurence (a geophysicist), June 17, 1955; children: Daniel, William, John and Jeff (twins). *Education:* University of Wisconsin, B.S., 1957. *Politics:* Democrat. *Religion:* Unitarian Universalist. *Home:* 2858 Stevens St., Madison, Wis. 53705. *Agent:* Ruth Cantor, 156 Fifth Ave., New York, N.Y. 10010.

CAREER: Writer of fantasy books for children; teacher of writing at University of Wisconsin extension, 1972—. Cochairman, Madison Interracial Study Group, 1969. *Member:* Council for Wisconsin Writers, Madison Area Writers' Workshop. *Awards, honors:* Honorable mention for children's book, Council for Wisconsin Writers, 1970.

WRITINGS—Children's books: *We're Off to Catch a Dragon,* Abingdon, 1969; *B-9, the Hungry Metal Eater,* Rand McNally, 1972. Also author of *The Princess Book,* 1974.

WORK IN PROGRESS: The Bird-Berry Bread Boat, a novel for older children; *I.M.P.S.,* an adult fantasy novel; several picture books.

SIDELIGHTS: Ester Laurence has made up fantasy songs and stories as long as she can remember. She feels that it is significant that she was "a welfare kid and a foster child," mentioning this in the hope that it may encourage some other disadvantaged child to achieve his goal.†

* * *

LAYTON, Edwin T(homas), Jr. 1928-

PERSONAL: Born September 13, 1928, in Los Angeles, Calif.; son of Edwin Thomas and Virginia (Yarnell) Layton; married Barbara Wyman, May 2, 1952; children: George. *Education:* University of California, Los Angeles, B.A., 1950, M.A., 1953, Ph.D., 1956. *Home:* 3651 Latimore Rd., Shaker Heights, Ohio 44122. *Office:* Department of History of Science and Technology, Case Western Reserve University, Cleveland, Ohio 44106.

CAREER: University of Wisconsin—Madison, instructor in history, 1956-57; Ohio State University, Columbus, instructor in history, 1957-60; Purdue University, Lafayette, Ind., assistant professor of history, 1961-64; Case Western Reserve University, Cleveland, Ohio, associate professor of the history of science and technology, 1965—. *Member:* Society for Social Studies of Science, Society for the History of Technology, History of Science Society.

WRITINGS: The Revolt of the Engineers: Social Responsibility and the American Engineering Profession, Press of Case Western Reserve University, 1971; *A Regional Union Catalog of Manuscripts Relating to the History of Science and Technology,* [Cleveland], 1971; *Technology and Social Change in America,* Harper, 1973. Contributor to academic journals.

WORK IN PROGRESS: A monograph on the hydraulic turbine in America, part of a larger study of the interaction of science and technology.

* * *

LEAB, Daniel Josef 1936-

PERSONAL: Born August 29, 1936, in Berlin, Germany; son of Leo (a salesman) and Herta (Marcus) Leab; married Katharine Kyes (an editor), August 17, 1964; children: Abigail Elizabeth, Constance Martha. *Education:* Columbia University, B.A., 1957, M.A., 1961, Ph.D., 1969; Harvard University, additional study, 1957-58. *Religion:* Jewish. *Home address:* P.O. Box 216, Washington, Conn. 06793. *Agent:* Wallace, Aitken & Shiel, 118 East 61st St., New York, N.Y. 10021. *Office:* Department of History, Seton Hall University, South Orange, N.J. 07079; and 121 East 78th St., New York, N.Y. 10021.

CAREER: Columbia University, New York, N.Y., instructor, 1966-68, assistant professor of history, 1969-74, associate dean of Columbia College, 1969-71, assistant dean of faculties, 1971-73, special assistant to executive vice-president, 1973-74; Seton Hall University, South Orange, N.J., associate professor of history, 1974—, director of American studies, 1974—. Director, Bancroft Parkman Corp., 1973—. Lecturer, graduate seminar in American studies, Falkenstein, West Germany, 1970, 1972, 1975. *Member:* American Historical Association, Organization of American Historians, American Association of University Professors, Labor Historians, British Film Institute, Columbia Grolier Club. *Awards, honors:* Council for Research in Economic History grant, 1969; Lawrence Chamberlain fellowship, 1973; Fulbright-Hays fellowship, 1977.

WRITINGS: (Contributor) A.J.P. Taylor, editor, *History of the Twentieth Century,* Purnell & Sons, 1969; *A Union of Individuals: The Formation of the American Newspaper Guild, 1933-36,* Columbia University Press, 1970; (contributor) Richard B. Morris and Graham W. Irwin, editors, *Harper Encyclopedia of the Modern World: A Concise Reference History from 1760 to the Present,* Harper, 1970; *From Sambo to Superspade: The Black Motion Picture Experience,* Houghton, 1975. Contributor to *Monthly Labor Review, Gazette: International Journal for Mass Communications Studies, Labor History, Cultural Affairs, Midcontinent American Studies Journal, Journalism Quarterly, Columbia Journalism Review,* and *New England Quarterly.* Editor, *Labor History,* 1974—, and *American Book Prices Current,* 1974—. Editor, American history, *Columbia Encyclopedia,* 3rd edition, 1960-63; *Columbia Journalism Review,* assistant editor, 1963-66, research associate, 1967-69, contributing editor, 1971—; contributing editor, *Atlas World Press Review,* 1973—.

WORK IN PROGRESS: The American Film Industry, for Basic Books.

SIDELIGHTS: Daniel Leab told *CA:* "My interests professionally are based on my personal interests. These stem from work done as a graduate student, as a free-lance writer, and as a professional historian and teacher. My wife and I spend considerable time in Europe. . . . I have participated as a lecturer in American Studies programs for German graduate students and teachers at Falkenstein, West Germany, where each summer under U.S.I.S. auspices a two week seminar is held. I found that their problems are our problems, except that theirs have not yet reached crisis proportions. If anything underlies my writing, research, and other professional activities, it is that reasonable men can get together."

* * *

LEACH, Joseph (Lee) 1921-

PERSONAL: Born May 2, 1921, in Weatherford, Tex.; son of Austin Felix (a physician) and Eula Lee (Gose) Leach; married Dorothy Ann Stuart, June 5, 1958; children: Joseph Lee, Jr., Jonathan Stuart, Anne Stuart. *Education:* Southern Methodist University, B.A., 1942; Yale University, Ph.D., 1948. *Politics:* Republican. *Religion:* Episcopalian. *Home:* 735 De Leon St., El Paso, Tex. 79912. *Office:* Department of English, University of Texas, El Paso, Tex. 79968.

CAREER: University of Texas at El Paso, assistant professor, 1947-50, associate professor, 1950-55, professor of English, 1955—, head of department, 1960-66. President, Festival Theatre of El Paso, 1966. *Military service:* U.S. Army, 1946-47. *Member:* Modern Language Association of America, National Council of Teachers of English, Conference of College Teachers of English, American Folklore Society, Sierra Club (president of El Paso regional group, 1970—), Texas Institute of Letters, El Paso County Historical Society (president, 1961). *Awards, honors:* Honorable mention in Theatre Library Association annual award, 1970, for *Bright Particular Star.*

WRITINGS: The Typical Texan, Southern Methodist University Press, 1952; *Bright Particular Star: The Life and Times of Charlotte Cushman,* Yale University Press, 1970. Contributor of articles and stories to literary reviews; book reviewer for journals and newspapers.

AVOCATIONAL INTERESTS: Mountain climbing, conservation work, collecting Spanish colonial art.

* * *

LEACH, Robert J. 1916-

PERSONAL: Born February 4, 1916, in Reading, Mass.; son of A. Judson (a clergyman) and Mary (Kennedy) Leach; married Jean Francis (a secretary), March 28, 1953; children: David, Felicity. *Education:* Marietta College, A.B., 1938; Ohio State University, M.A., 1939; University of Geneva, graduate study, 1950-53. *Politics:* Liberal Democrat. *Religion:* Religious Society of Friends (Quakers). *Home:* 20 Arpillieres, Chene-Bougeries, Geneva, Switzerland 1224; and Chalet "Gigi," Morgins, Valais, Switzerland 1875. *Office:* Ecole Internationale, 62 Route de Chene, Geneva, Switzerland.

CAREER: Pendle Hill School, Wallingford, Pa., secretary of publications, 1939-42; Salem College, Winston-Salem, N.C., assistant professor of history, 1946-50; Ecole Internationale, Geneva, Switzerland, head of history department, 1950—. Consultant, International Schools Association, 1951-63. *Wartime service:* Civilian public service as conscientious objector. *Member:* Friends Historical Association, Dukes County Historical Association, Phi Beta Kappa, Phi Lambda Theta, Nantucket Historical Association.

WRITINGS: (With Arle Brooks) *Help Wanted! The Experiences of Some Quaker Conscientious Objectors,* American Friends Service Committee, 1940; *Yearly Meetings of Society of Friends,* Pendle Hill, 1942; (editor) Isaac Penington, *Inward Journey* (an abridgement of Penington's work), Pendle Hill, 1944; *International Schools and Their Role in the Field of International Education,* Pergamon, 1969. Contributor of about seventy-five articles to periodicals. Contributing editor, *Friends Journal,* 1955-1961; editor, International School Association *Bulletin,* 1961-64.

WORK IN PROGRESS: Nantucket Monthly Meeting, Volumes I and II, for Nantucket Historic Trust; Volume III in preparation; "Why Nantucket Quakers", cassette tapes.

* * *

LEAMER, Edward E(mery) 1944-

PERSONAL: Born May 24, 1944, in LaCrosse, Wis.; son of Laurence Eugene and Helen (Burkey) Leamer; married Cheryl Knowles, August 13, 1966 (divorced, 1974); children: Stephanie Joy, Abigail Marie. *Education:* Princeton University, A.B., 1966; University of Michigan, M.A., 1969, Ph.D., 1970. *Office:* Department of Economics, University of California, Los Angeles, Calif. 90024.

CAREER: Wayne State University, Detroit, Mich., assis-

tant professor of economics, 1970; Harvard University Cambridge, Mass., assistant professor of economics, 1970-73; University of California, Los Angeles, associate professor, 1973-75, professor of economics, 1975—. *Member:* American Economic Association, American Statistical Association.

WRITINGS: (With Robert M. Stern) *Quantitative International Economics,* Allyn & Bacon, 1970; *Specification Searches,* Wiley, 1976. Contributor to economics journals.

WORK IN PROGRESS: Bayesian Analysis of Nonexperimental Data.

* * *

LEAN, Garth Dickinson 1912-
(Tenax)

PERSONAL: Born December 26, 1912, in Cardiff, Wales; son of Frederick John and Myra (Dickinson) Lean; married Margaret Mary Appleyard, June 29, 1946; children: Geoffrey Kenneth, Jenifer Mary. *Education:* Worcester College, Oxford, B.A., 1934, M.A., 1950. *Religion:* Church of England. *Home:* 5 Marston Ferry Rd., Oxford OX2 7EF, England.

CAREER: Free-lance journalist and editor; writer of political column in *Time and Tide,* under pseudonym Tenax, 1965—. Member of council of management of Moral Rearmament, Britain. *Member:* Institute of Journalists.

WRITINGS—All published by Blanford, except as noted: *Brave Men Choose,* 1961; *John Wesley, Anglican,* 1964; (with Arnold Henry Moore Lunn) *The New Morality,* 1964, revised and enlarged edition, 1967; *The Cult of Softness,* 1965; (with Lunn) *Christian Counter-Attack,* Arlington House, 1969; (with Sydney Cook) *The Black and White Book: A Handbook of Revolution,* 1972; *Good God, It Works!: An Experiment in Faith,* 1974; *Rebirth of a Nation,* 1976. Editor of more than sixty books.

BIOGRAPHICAL/CRITICAL SOURCES: Anne Worige Gordon, *Peter Howard: Life and Letters,* Hodder & Stoughton, 1969.†

* * *

LEARY, Edward A(ndrew) 1913-

PERSONAL: Born May 3, 1913, in Bridgeport, Conn.; son of Edward J. (a printer) and Edna (Hill) Leary; married Rosemary Waters, July 4, 1942; married Linda Wohlfeld (an executive of Blue Cross/Blue Shield), March 9, 1961; children: Tim, Karen, Regina, Andrew. *Education:* "Left college the summer of enrollment with a touring stock company," 1943. *Politics:* Independent. *Religion:* "Nonsectarian." *Home:* 2625 North Meridian St., Indianapolis, Ind. 46208.

CAREER: Ed Leary & Associates (public relations counselors), Indianapolis, Ind., president, 1962-71. Creative director and account supervisor of major accounts for advertising agencies in New York, Cleveland, and Chicago. *Military service:* U.S. Army, 1942-45. *Member:* Indianapolis Press Club. *Awards, honors:* Indiana University award, 1967, for *The Nineteenth State, Indiana.*

WRITINGS: The Nineteenth State, Indiana, E. Leary, 1966, revised edition, 1977; *Indianapolis: The Story of a City,* Bobbs-Merrill, 1970; (editor) *Indiana Almanac and Fact Book,* E. Leary, 1977; *A Hoosier Scrapbook,* Sycamore Press, in press; *Pictorial History of Indianapolis,* Downing, in press. Columnist for *Indianapolis Sunday Star.*

Also author of motion picture documentaries, booklets, and public relations brochures.

AVOCATIONAL INTERESTS: Motion pictures, U.S. history (especially the Civil War, 1920's, and New Deal era), radio and TV, Lincoln, U.S. government, ecology, and the youth movement.

* * *

LEBESON, Anita Libman 1896-

PERSONAL: Born July 4, 1896, in Vilna, Lithuania; came to United States in 1907; daughter of Morris (a merchant) and Leah Elizabeth (Oleiski) Libman; married Hermon Lebeson (a chemist), August 7, 1921 (died, 1967); children: David R. (deceased), Mariamne (Mrs. David Goldstein). *Education:* University of Illinois, B.A., 1918; Northwestern University, M.A., 1935, Ph.D., 1969. *Religion:* Jewish. *Home:* 611 Wesley Ave., Evanston, Ill. 60202. *Agent:* Max Siegel & Associates, 154 East Erie St., Chicago, Ill. 60611.

CAREER: Illinois Historical Survey, custodian, 1918-19; high school teacher of American history, Chicago, Ill., 1921-23, 1926-29; College of Jewish Studies, Chicago, instructor in American Jewish history, 1951-52; lecturer in history, literature, and sociology, Adult Education Council, Chicago, 1950-62; lecturer for Jewish Theological Seminary "Living Books" series and for Jewish Center Lecture Bureau, 1954—. Chairman, Educational Fund for War Foster Children, 1945-52. Board member and officer, Chicago Travelers Aid Society, 1936-56.

MEMBER: American Jewish Historical Society (member of executive council, 1950—), Women's American ORT, Women's Trade Union League, Authors League, American Technion Society, Hadassah, Phi Beta Kappa, Kappa Delta Pi. *Awards, honors:* Chicago Foundation of Literature Award for outstanding nonfiction book, 1950, for *Pilgrim People;* College of Jewish Studies and Women's American ORT awards, 1955; American Jewish Congress award, 1958; D.Ph., Northwestern University, 1969.

WRITINGS: Jewish Pioneers in America, 1492-1848, Brentano, 1931; *Pilgrim People,* Harper, 1950; (contributor) Louis Finkelstein, editor, *The Jews,* Harper, 1950; (contributor) *Jewish People, Past and Present: History of the Jews in the United States,* Volume IV, Jewish Encyclopedia Handbooks, 1955; *Recall to Life: A Jewish Woman in America,* Barnes-Yoseloff, 1971. Also author of *A Live Flame,* 1977. Contributor to *Junior Jewish Encyclopedia,* 1957, and to *Historia Judaica, Congress Weekly,* and other periodicals. Co-editor, *Standard Jewish Encyclopedia,* 1959.

WORK IN PROGRESS: Updating *Pilgrim People* and *Jewish Pioneers in America.*

* * *

LEE, Edward N(icholls) 1935-

PERSONAL: Born April 1, 1935, in New York, N.Y.; son of Richard (a civil engineer) and Dorothy (Nicholls) Lee. *Education:* Cornell University, B.A., 1956; Princeton University, Ph.D., 1961. *Office:* Department of Philosophy, University of California, San Diego, La Jolla, Calif. 92093.

CAREER: Johns Hopkins University, Baltimore, Md., assistant professor of philosophy, 1961-67; University of Texas at Austin, associate professor of philosophy, 1968-70; University of California, San Diego, La Jolla, associate professor of philosophy, 1970—. *Military service:* U.S. Army, 1956-58; became first lieutenant.

WRITINGS: (Editor with Maurice Mandelbaum) *Phenomenology and Existentialism,* Johns Hopkins Press, 1967; (editor with R. Rorty and A. Mourelatos) *Exegesis and Argument,* Van Gorcum, 1973; (contributor) W. Werkmeister, editor, *Facets of Plato's Philosophy,* Van Gorcum, 1976. Contributor, *Essays in Greek Philosophy,* State University of New York Press, 1971. Contributor to philosophy journals.

WORK IN PROGRESS: Writing on Plato's metaphysics and political philosophy.

BIOGRAPHICAL/CRITICAL SOURCES: Encounter, summer, 1968.

* * *

LEE, Manfred B(ennington) 1905-1971
(Ellery Queen, Ellery Queen, Jr., and Barnaby Ross, all joint pseudonyms)

January 11, 1905—April 3, 1971; American mystery writer. Obituaries: *New York Times,* April 4, 1971; *Variety,* April 14, 1971; *Publishers' Weekly,* April 19, 1971; *Time,* April 19, 1971; *Antiquarian Bookman,* May 17, 1971. (See index for *CA* sketch)

* * *

LEE, Mary 1949-

PERSONAL: Born May 6, 1949, in Los Angeles, Calif.; married R. A. Rosenberg, January 18, 1975 (divorced, 1977). *Education:* Attended Santa Monica City College, 1968-69. *Office:* 609 Hightree Rd., Santa Monica, Calif.

CAREER: Formerly co-owner of small import business; currently director of a private beach club.

WRITINGS—Poetry: Tender Bough, photographs by Alice Gowland and Peter Gowland, Crown, 1969; (self-illustrated) *Hand in Hand,* Crown, 1971; *The Guest,* Hightree Books, 1973. Also author of screenplay, "The Actress."

WORK IN PROGRESS: Mama Told Me So, a book of interviews; *Mood Menus,* a cookbook; a poetry book with photographs by Alice Gowland and Peter Gowland.

SIDELIGHTS: Mary Lee told *CA:* "I study philosophy, astrology, and metaphysics. I love animals, especially cats, and the beach, and I am a student of Mandarin Chinese language."

* * *

LEE, Polly Jae 1929-

PERSONAL: Born November 26, 1929, in Toledo, Ohio; daughter of Jonathan Wheeler Stead (an electrical engineer) and Ona (a religious education director; maiden name, Grunder) Stead Gardiner; married Richard Lee (a clinical psychologist), April 7, 1945; children: Mary Kay, Karin, Ona Gwynne, Laurie Brett, Robin. *Education:* Attended University of Hawaii, 1944-46. *Politics:* Democrat. *Religion:* Society of Friends.

CAREER: Ohio State University, Columbus, counselor, 1958-59; Annie Whittemyer Home (orphanage), Davenport, Iowa, writer of technical manuals, 1960; Grand Rapids Public Library, Grand Rapids, Mich., technical processor, 1960-61; Waterford Library, Waterford, Mich., director, 1962-65; Pontiac Public Library, Pontiac, Mich., acquisition librarian, beginning 1965. Member of Michigan Area Committee of American Friends Service Committee, 1965-68. *Member:* Clergy and Laymen Concerned About Vietnam,

Another Mother for Peace, Michigan Library Association, Fellowship of Reconciliation, American Folklore Society, Friends of the Library (Pontiac; vice president, 1970-71).

WRITINGS: Giant: The Pictorial History of the Human Colossus, A. S. Barnes, 1970. Author of plays and pageants for local schools and churches, and short stories for children.

WORK IN PROGRESS: Saints: 20th Century Style; King Arthur of Cromwell: Reality vs. Legend.

AVOCATIONAL INTERESTS: Ecology, politics.†

* * *

LEE, Terence R(ichard) 1938-

PERSONAL: Born December 8, 1938, in Birmingham, England; son of Arthur Edward (an insurance agent) and Amy (Richards) Lee; married Francis Ray (an economist), September, 1970; children: Mary, Elizabeth. *Education:* London School of Economics and Political Science, B.Sc., 1961; University of Alberta, M.A., 1963; University of Toronto, Ph.D., 1967. *Religion:* None. *Home:* Luis Thayer Oseda 1071, Santiago, Chile. *Office:* Economic Commission for Latin America, Santiago, Chile.

CAREER: York University, Toronto, Ontario, lecturer in geography, 1966-67; Canada Department of Energy, Mines and Resources, Ottawa, Ontario, resources planning officer, 1967-70; Canada Centre for Inland Waters, Burlington, Ontario, head of Lakes Management Research Section, 1970-72; Economic Commission for Latin America, Santiago, Chile, adviser of water resources, 1972—. Training associate attached to Calcutta Metropolitan Planning Organization, Ford Foundation, 1964-66. *Member:* Canadian Association of Geographers, Association of American Geographers, American Water Resources Association.

WRITINGS: Residential Water Demand and Economic Development, University of Toronto Press, 1969. Writings include Canadian Government, World Health Organization, and United Nations reports.

WORK IN PROGRESS: Water management in Latin America; studies on the relationship between environmental quality and the process of social and economic development.

* * *

LEE, Yur Bok 1934-

PERSONAL: Born November 15, 1934, in Seoul, Korea; became U.S. citizen, 1966; son of Won Koo (a government official) and Ka-soon (Kim) Lee; married Ae-Hyung, June 15, 1966; children: Grace, Edward. *Education:* La Grange College, B.A., 1958; University of Georgia, M.A., 1960, Ph.D., 1965; Columbia University, additional study, 1966. *Religion:* Unitarian Universalist. *Office:* Department of History, North Dakota State University, Fargo, N.D. 58102.

CAREER: Virginia Polytechnic Institute, Blacksburg, visiting assistant professor of history, 1965-66; Little Rock University, Little Rock, Ark., assistant professor of history, 1966-67; North Dakota State University, Fargo, associate professor, 1967-73, professor of history, 1974—. *Member:* Association for Asian Studies, American Association for the Advancement of Slavic Studies, American Historical Association, Organization of American Historians, American Association of University Professors.

WRITINGS: Diplomatic Relations between the United States and Korea, 1866-1887, Humanities, 1970. Contributor of articles to journals in his field.

LEECH, Geoffrey N(eil) 1936-

PERSONAL: Born January 16, 1936, in Gloucester, England; son of Charles Richard (a bank employee) and Dorothy (Foster) Leech; married Frances Berman, July 29, 1961; children: Thomas, Camilla. *Education:* University College, London, B.A., 1959, M.A., 1962, Ph.D., 1969; Massachusetts Institute of Technology, additional study, 1964-65. *Religion:* Church of England. *Home:* 12 Clougha Ave., Lancaster, England. *Office:* Department of Linguistics and Modern English Languages, University of Lancaster, Bailrigg, Lancaster, England.

CAREER: Clarendon School, South Oxhey, Hertfordshire, England, assistant schoolmaster, 1960-61; University of London, University College, London, England, assistant lecturer, 1962-65, lecturer in English, 1965-69; University of Lancaster, Bailrigg, Lancaster, England, reader in English, 1969-74, professor of linguistics and modern English languages, 1974—. Assistant secretary, Communication Research Centre, 1962-69; director, Computer Archive of Modern English Texts, 1970—. *Military service:* Royal Air Force, 1954-56; became senior aircraftsman. *Member:* Philological Society, Linguistic Society of America, Linguistic Association of Great Britain. *Awards, honors:* Harkness fellow at Massachusetts Institute of Technology, 1964-65.

WRITINGS: English in Advertising: A Linguistic Study of Advertising in Great Britain, Longmans, Green, 1966; *A Linguistic Guide to English Poetry,* Humanities, 1969; *Towards a Semantic Description of English,* Longmans, Green, 1969, Indiana University Press, 1970; *Meaning and the English Verb,* Longman, 1971; (with Randolph Quirk, Sidney Greenbaum, and Jan Svartorik) *A Grammar of Contemporary English,* Longman, 1972; (with Jan Svantvik) *A Communicative Grammar of English,* Longman, 1975. Contributor of articles and essays to journals.

AVOCATIONAL INTERESTS: Music (playing piano and organ), conservation.

* * *

LEEDS, Barry H. 1940-

PERSONAL: Born December 6, 1940, in New York, N.Y.; son of Andrew (a teacher) and Paula (a teacher; maiden name, Stark) Leeds; married Robin Cornwell (a teacher), April 20, 1968; children: Brett Ashley (daughter). *Education:* Columbia University, B.A., 1962, M.A., 1963; Ohio University, Ph.D., 1967. *Home:* Jerome Ave., R.F.D. 3, Burlington, Conn. 06013. *Office:* Department of English, Central Connecticut State College, New Britain, Conn. 06050.

CAREER: Worked at manual jobs, 1957-62, mainly as ordinary seaman on U.S. Merchant Service freighters and tankers; *New York Times,* New York City, credit checker, 1963; City University of New York, New York City, lecturer in English, 1963-64; University of Texas at El Paso, instructor in English, 1964-65; Central Connecticut State College, New Britain, assistant professor, 1968-71, associate professor, 1971-76, professor of English, 1976—. *Member:* American Association of University Professors.

WRITINGS: The Structured Vision of Norman Mailer, New York University Press, 1969. Contributor of more than sixty reviews and articles to numerous magazines, journals, and other periodicals, including *Saturday Review, Modern Fiction Studies,* and *Journal of Modern Literature.*

WORK IN PROGRESS: A critical study of Ken Kesey, for Twayne.

SIDELIGHTS: Barry Leeds told *CA:* "In both my writing and my teaching, I am fascinated by the confluence of popular and high culture. I believe that everything in our culture is contingent on everything else, and that in the study of literature no digression is unproductive."

* * *

LEFFLAND, Ella 1931-

PERSONAL: Born November 25, 1931, in Martinez, Calif.; daughter of Sven William (an auto painter) and Emma (Jensen) Leffland. *Education:* San Jose State College (now University), B.A., 1953. *Residence:* San Francisco, Calif. *Agent:* Lois Wallace, 118 East 61st St., New York, N.Y. 10021.

CAREER: Writer and painter. Lived two years in Europe.

WRITINGS: Mrs. Munck, Houghton, 1970; *Love Out of Season,* Atheneum, 1974. Contributor to *Best Short Stories of 1970,* and *O. Henry Best Short Stories of 1976;* short stories have been published in *Harper's, New Yorker, Cosmopolitan, Epoch, Quarterly Review of Literature.*

SIDELIGHTS: Christopher Lehmann-Haupt praised Ella Leffland's novel, stating that "anyone with the smallest spark of indignation over the second-class status of women in modern society is going to read Leffland's novel with eyes blazing, adrenalin flowing and heart pounding."

Ella Leffland has described her intention in *Mrs. Munck* as wanting "to show . . . a woman—that is, specifically a female character—from the inside of her heart and mind. I wanted her to start off a free soul, an individual, unstamped by convention. . . . I wanted to give this girl a universality, and then show the difficulty she has in preserving it, in escaping from the roles thrust upon her. That's what I was *trying* to do, but I didn't succeed. I don't think Rose Munck makes it, but if not, she makes an attempt, and I'm not sorry to see her in print."

The film rights to *Mrs. Munck* have been sold to Cinema Center Films, and the rights to *Love Out of Season* have been sold to Metro-Goldwyn-Mayer.

BIOGRAPHICAL/CRITICAL SOURCES: New York Times, August 10, 1970; *Variety,* December 16, 1970.

* * *

LEFKOE, Morty R. 1937-

PERSONAL: Born May 17, 1937, in Miami Beach, Fla.; son of Herman (a financier) and Irene (Weiss) Lefkoe; married Virginia Vestoff (an actress), May 30, 1965. *Education:* University of Chicago, A.B., 1958, and additional graduate study. *Office:* Manning, Selvabe, & Lee, 660 Fifth Ave., New York, N.Y.

CAREER: Jesup & Lamont (member of New York Stock Exchange), New York City, security analyst, 1960-61; Trans-World Financial Co., Los Angeles, Calif., assistant vice-president, 1961-63; Lefkoe Consulting, Inc., New York City, president, 1964-72; Manning, Selvabe, & Lee (public relations firm), New York City, account executive, 1973—. Consultant on construction industry labor problems and on community and employee relations in various other industries. *Military service:* U.S. Army, 1954.

WRITINGS: The Crisis in Construction: There Is an Answer, Bureau of National Affairs, 1970. Contributor of more than one hundred articles to *Fortune, Pageant, Human Events,* and other magazines and financial publications. Former staff writer for *Wall Street Journal;* former col-

umnist for *Santa Monica Evening Outlook* and *Commercial and Financial Chronicle.*

SIDELIGHTS: Morty Lefkoe is in the process of producing a Broadway musical play. He says that "I expect to spend most of my time in the future producing and directing theater. If I do any writing, it probably will be either a play or nonfiction about some aspect of theater."†

* * *

LEFKOWITZ, Bernard 1937-

PERSONAL: Born August 24, 1937, in New York, N.Y.; son of Edward and Ann (Fishbein) Lefkowitz; married Abigail Johnston (an illustrator), June 16, 1963. *Education:* City College (now City College of the City University of New York), New York, N.Y., B.A., 1959. *Residence:* New York, N.Y. *Agent:* Monica McCall, International Creative Management, 40 West 57th St., New York, N.Y. 10019.

CAREER: New York Post, New York City, reporter, later assistant city editor, 1961-66; free-lance writer in New York City, 1966-67; Peace Corps, Washington, D.C., evaluation officer, with travel in Latin America, North Africa, the South Pacific, and Asia, 1968-69; free-lance writer in New York City, 1970—. Teacher at New School for Social Research, 1963-65, and City College of the City University of New York, 1970-71. Consultant to Ford Foundation, 1970-71. *Awards, honors:* Award of Silurian Society of New York for best feature article, 1965; Edgar Allan Poe Award of Mystery Writers of America for best nonfiction, 1970, for *The Victims.*

WRITINGS: (With Kenneth G. Gross) *The Victims: The Wylie-Hoffert Murder Case and Its Strange Aftermath,* Putnam, 1969 (published in England as *The Sting of Justice: The Wylie Hoffert Murder Case and Its Strange Aftermath,* W. H. Allen, 1971). Contributor of articles to *Look, Esquire, Nation, Village Voice,* and other publications.

WORK IN PROGRESS: A study of a professional revolutionary in the United States, for Putnam tentatively entitled *The Broken Connection;* a critical study of the international press.

BIOGRAPHICAL/CRITICAL SOURCES: Saturday Review, June 28, 1969.†

* * *

LEFLAR, Robert A(llen) 1901-

PERSONAL: Born March 22, 1901, in Siloam Springs, Ark.; son of Lewis D. (a drayman) and Viva (Pilkenton) Leflar; married Doris Drake, June 20, 1928; married second wife, Helen Finger, October 18, 1946; children: (first marriage) Helen Larcom (foster daughter); (second marriage) Robert B., Charles J. F. *Education:* University of Arkansas, B.A., 1922; Harvard University, LL.B. (cum laude), 1927, S.J.D., 1932. *Politics:* Democrat. *Religion:* Methodist. *Home:* 1717 West Center St., Fayetteville, Ark. 72701. *Office:* School of Law, University of Arkansas, Fayetteville, Ark. 72701.

CAREER: John E. Brown College (now John Brown University), Siloam Springs, Ark., professor of journalism, 1923-24; admitted to Arkansas Bar, 1928, and Bar of U.S. Supreme Court, 1943; University of Arkansas, School of Law, Fayetteville, 1927—, began as instructor, professor of law, 1933-54, distinguished professor, 1956—, dean of School of Law, 1943-54; New York University, School of Law, New York City, professor of law, 1954—, director of Seminar for Appellate Judges, Institute of Judicial Administration, 1956—. Consultant practice of law, 1928-42; visiting professor of law at University of Kansas, 1932-33, University of Colorado, 1952, University of Oklahoma, 1972, 1973-74, and Vanderbilt University, 1972-73; associate justice of Arkansas Supreme Court, 1949-51. U.S. War Relocation Authority, regional attorney, then head attorney and assistant solicitor, 1942-44; public member, Regional War Labor Board, 1944-45. Member, Arkansas Commissioner on Uniform State Laws, 1945—; president, Arkansan Constitutional Convention, 1969-70. President, Southwest Athletic Conference, 1948-49.

MEMBER: American Bar Association (member of judicial administration section), American Association of University Professors, American Association of Law Schools (executive committee member, 1951-52), American Judicature Society, Arkansas Bar Association, Phi Beta Kappa. *Awards, honors:* American Bar Foundation award for legal research, 1968; named Arkansas Man of Year, 1968; Scribes Best Legal Book of the Year Award, 1975.

WRITINGS: Arkansas Law of Conflict of Laws, privately printed, 1938; *The Law of Conflict of Laws,* Bobbs-Merrill, 1959, revised edition published as *American Conflicts Law,* Bobbs-Merrill, 1968, 2nd revised edition, 1977; *The First 100 Years* (centennial history of University of Arkansas), University of Arkansas Foundation, 1972; *Internal Operating Procedures of Appellate Courts,* American Bar Foundation, 1976. Also author of *Appellate Judicial Opinions,* 1974. Contributor to legal journals. First editor of *Arkansas Law Review,* 1947.

SIDELIGHTS: Robert A. Leflar told *CA:* "For more than fifty years I have been working with the law, especially in the fields of conflict of laws, torts, and jurisprudence. In the latter field my main interest has been the improvement of the judicial process in American appellate courts. Much of my writing and thinking has been directed to that end. Even my books on conflict of laws, though they deal with a specific area of the common law, are directed largely to the improvement of the law through the agency of appellate courts engaging wisely in their judicial function." Leflar went on to say, "Apart from my work with the law, I am a loyal alumnus of the University of Arkansas, and my centennial history of the University of Arkansas constituted a labor of love."

*   *   *

LEHMAN, Yvonne 1936-

PERSONAL: Born April 3, 1936, in Piedmont, S.C.; married Howard N. Lehman (retired employee of Federal Bureau of Prisons), September 28, 1958; children: Lori Susan, Lisa Kay, David Andrew, Cindy Carol. *Education:* Attended high school in Easley, S.C., and a business school; attended John A. Logan College as a part-time student. *Religion:* Southern Baptist. *Residence:* Black Mountain, N.C. 28711.

MEMBER: Western North Carolina Christian Writer's Conference (founder and director of Blue Ridge Assembly, 1976).

WRITINGS: Red Like Mine (novel), Zondervan, 1970; *Dead Men Don't Cry* (novel), Zondervan, 1973. Contributor of short stories to journals; weekly columnist, *Illinois Baptist,* 1970.

WORK IN PROGRESS: An occult novel, and a novel about slavery.

LEHN, Cornelia 1920-

PERSONAL: Born December 15, 1920, in Leonidavka, Russia; became a Canadian citizen; daughter of Gerhard G. (a farmer) and Sara (Ens) Lehn. *Education:* Bethel College, North Newton, Kan., B.A., 1957; Mennonite Biblical Seminary, student, 1958-59; University of Iowa, M.A., 1969. *Religion:* Mennonite. *Home:* 403 West 24th, North Newton, Kan. 67117. *Office:* Central Office, General Conference Mennonite Church, 722 Main, Newton, Kan. 67114.

CAREER: Did relief work under the Mennonite Central Committee for four years, working in Germany, 1950, 1951; General Conference Mennonite Church Central Office, Commission on Education, Newton, Kan., editor, 1959-70, director of children's work, 1970—.

WRITINGS: God Keeps His Promise: A Bible Story Book for Kindergarten Children, Herald Press, 1969. Editor of kindergarten curriculum materials published by Faith & Life and Herald Press. Editor, *Der Kinderbote* and *Junior Messenger,* published by Faith & Life. General editor, "Foundation" series, published by Evangel, Faith and Life, and Mennonite Brethren Publishing.

*   *   *

LEHRER, Adrienne (Joyce) 1937-

PERSONAL: Born January 16, 1937, in Minneapolis, Minn.; daughter of Julius and Evelyn (Hill) Kroman; married Keith Edward Lehrer (a professor of philosophy), 1957; children: Mark, David. *Education:* University of Minnesota, B.S. (with high distinction), 1957; Brown University, M.A., 1960; University of Edinburgh, graduate study, 1966-67; University of Rochester, Ph.D., 1968. *Office:* Department of Linguistics, University of Arizona, Tucson, Ariz. 85719.

CAREER: University of Rochester, Rochester, N.Y., instructor, 1967-68, assistant professor of linguistics, 1968-74; University of Arizona, Tucson, associate professor of linguistics, 1974—. *Member:* Linguistic Society of America, Phi Beta Kappa. *Awards, honors:* Fulbright fellow at University of Edinburgh, 1966-67; fellow at Center for Advanced Study in the Behavioral Sciences, Stanford, 1973-74.

WRITINGS: (Editor with husband, Keith Lehrer) *The Theory of Meaning,* Prentice-Hall, 1970; *Semantic Fields and Lexical Structure,* North-Holland, 1974. Contributor to academic journals.

*   *   *

LEISER, Burton M. 1930-

PERSONAL: Surname is pronounced *lee*-sur; born December 12, 1930, in Denver, Colo.; son of Nathan (in retail furniture business) and Eva Mae (Newman) Leiser; married Miriam Waid (a teacher), August 10, 1954 (divorced); married C. Barbara Hurowitz Tabor, June 9, 1967; children: Shoshana Yafah, Illana Devorah, Phillip B.; stepchildren: Ellen Beth Tabor, David Lawrence Tabor, Susan Ruth Tabor. *Education:* University of Chicago, B.A., 1951; University of Colorado, graduate study, 1951-52; Yeshiva University. M.Heb.Lit., 1956; New York University, graduate study, 1955-57; Brown University, Ph.D., 1968. *Politics:* Democrat. *Religion:* Jewish. *Home:* 900 45th St., West Des Moines, Iowa 50265. *Office:* 219 Medbury Hall, Drake University, Des Moines, Iowa 50311.

CAREER: Teacher and principal at Hebrew schools in Rhode Island and Massachusetts, 1957-64; University of Denver, Denver, Colo., instructor in philosophy, 1962-63;

Fort Lewis College, Durango, Colo., instructor in philosophy, 1963-65; State University of New York at Buffalo, assistant professor, 1965-68, associate professor of philosophy, 1968-70; Sir George Williams University, Montreal, Quebec, visiting associate professor, 1969-70, associate professor of Judaic studies, 1970-72; Drake University, Des Moines, Iowa, professor of philosophy and chairman of department of philosophy, 1972—.

MEMBER: International Society of Legal and Social Philosophy, American Philosophical Association, American Academy of Religion, Society for Political and Legal Philosophy, Society for Philosophy and Public Policy, University Centers for Rational Alternatives, American Association of University Professors, Authors Guild, American Professors for Peace in the Middle East. *Awards, honors:* Research grants from State University of New York Research Foundation and Memorial Foundation for Jewish Culture, 1966-68, 1970-71, and from Exyon Education Foundation, 1975-77.

WRITINGS: Custom, Law, and Morality: Conflict and Continuity in Social Behavior, Doubleday, 1969; *Liberty, Justice, and Morals: Contemporary Value Conflicts,* Macmillan, 1973; *Genocide,* Free Press, in press. Contributor to philosophy, religion, and law journals.

WORK IN PROGRESS: Fundamental Concepts of Judaism.

*   *   *

LEISER, Erwin   1923-

PERSONAL: Born May 16, 1923, in Berlin, Germany; son of Hermann (a lawyer) and Emmy (Abrahamsohn) Leiser; married Vera Wagner (a journalist), October 2, 1960; children: Marion, Sandra. *Education:* University of Lund, B.A., 1946. *Home:* 44 Zurichbergstrasse, CH 8028 Zurich, Switzerland.

CAREER: Left Germany to live in Sweden, 1939; journalist, author, and editor in Sweden, 1945-59; director and producer of documentary films in Sweden, 1959-62, and in Switzerland, 1962—. Films include "Mein Kampf," 1960, "Murder through Signature," 1961, "Choose Life," 1963, "Germany Awake," 1968, "NPD," 1969, "The World Is Not for Children," 1972, "From Bebel to Brandt," 1974, "Because They Are Women" and "Women of the Third World," both 1975. Also author of film portraits "Hans Richter," 1973, "Fernando Botero," 1976, and "Edward Kienholz," 1977. *Member:* Swedish P.E.N. *Awards, honors:* Awards at San Francisco, Berlin, Moscow, and Melbourne film festivals; Film Award of city of Zurich.

WRITINGS: (Contributor) *Bertolt Brecht,* Det Norske Studentersamfunds Kulturatvalg, 1958; *"Mein Kampf": Documenti su Hitler e il Terzio Reich* (book of the film), Feltrinelli, 1961, translation published as *A Pictorial History of Nazi Germany,* Penguin, 1962; (editor) *Flykt och foervandling* (Swedish translations of Nelly Sachs' poems with original German text of some of the poems), FIB:s lyrikklub, 1961; *Waehle das Leben* (book of the film, "Choose Life"), Hans Duetsch, 1963; *Om dokumentaerfilm,* Norstedt, 1967; *Deutschland Erwache! Propaganda im Film des Dritten Reiches,* Rowohlt, 1968, published as *Nazi Cinema,* Macmillan, 1975; *Samtal i Berlin,* Norstedt, 1969; *Gud har ingen vaxel,* Norstedt, 1977. Contributor to *Expressen* (Stockholm), *Weltwoche* (Zurich), and other Swedish and Swiss magazines and newspapers.

SIDELIGHTS: Erwin Leiser speaks English and French in addition to German and the Scandinavian languages.

BIOGRAPHICAL/CRITICAL SOURCES: Jay Leyda, *Films Beget Films,* Allen & Unwin, 1964; *Variety,* October 22, 1969.

*   *   *

LEMBO, John M(ario)   1937-

PERSONAL: Born May 24, 1937, in Vineland, N.J.; son of Joseph Anthony (a businessman) and Antoinette (Paolino) Lembo; married Judith J. Layton, June 27, 1964; children: Anthony, Daniel. *Education:* La Salle College, Philadelphia, Pa., B.A., 1961; Xavier University, Cincinnati, Ohio, M.Ed., 1964; Case Western Reserve University, Ed.D., 1966. *Office:* Department of Psychology, Millersville State College, Millersville, Pa. 17551.

CAREER: St. John College of Cleveland, Cleveland, Ohio, instructor in psychology, 1964-66; St. Bonaventure University, Olean, N.Y., assistant professor of psychology, 1966-67; St. John Fisher College, Rochester, N.Y., chairman of department of psychology, 1967-68; Millersville State College, Millersville, Pa., professor of psychology, 1968—, chairman of department, 1970.

WRITINGS: The Psychology of Effective Classroom Instruction, C. E. Merrill, 1969; (editor) *Purpose and Process in School Learning: Selected Academic Readings,* Simon & Schuster, 1970; *Why Teachers Fail,* C. E. Merrill, 1971; *Learning and Teaching in Today's Schools,* C. E. Merrill, 1972; *When Learning Happens,* Schocken, 1972; *Help Yourself,* Argus, 1974; *The Counseling Process: A Cognitive-Behavioral Approach,* Libra, 1976.

WORK IN PROGRESS: A book entitled, *You Can Cope! You Can Change!.*

SIDELIGHTS: John Lembo told *CA,* "I have found writing one of the most effective ways of evaluating ideas, refining them and bringing them into sharper focus in problem solving."

*   *   *

LEMME, Janet E(llen)   1941-

PERSONAL: Surname is pronounced Lem-may; born June 14, 1941; daughter of LeRoy B. (a businessman) and Virginia Fay (Morgan) Kemmis; married Busso Volker Lemme (a landscape architect), December 15, 1961; children: Christine Jeannette, Forrest B. N. *Education:* Attended University of Washington, Seattle. *Home:* 3046 Northeast 182nd St., Seattle, Wash. 98115.

CAREER: Evergreen Landscaping (husband's firm), Seattle, Wash., executive secretary, 1961—. *Member:* National League of American Pen Women, Shoreline Jaycee Wives (president, 1970).

WRITINGS: Conviction, Norton, 1970.

WORK IN PROGRESS: Investor Beware, a guide for the small investor; *Free to Choose,* collected biographies of Iron-Curtain escapees and their present life styles.

SIDELIGHTS: Janet Lemme has traveled extensively in Europe, the Near East, and North Africa and feels a strong bond to the peoples of these areas. "My earnest hope is that two events will develop in my lifetime," she writes, "the elimination of the Berlin Wall . . . and a longlasting settlement to the Arab-Israeli conflict."

*   *   *

LENNART, Isobel   1915-1971

May 18, 1915—January 24, 1971; American author and

screenwriter. Obituaries: *Newsday,* January 27, 1971; *Washington Post,* January 27, 1971.

* * *

LENT, John A(nthony) 1936-

PERSONAL: Born September 8, 1936, in East Millsboro, Pa.; son of John (a railroad worker) and Rose Marie (Marano) Lent; married Martha Meadows, June 17, 1961; children: Laura, Andrea, John Vincent, Lisa, Shahnon. *Education:* Sophia University, Tokyo, certificate, 1956; Ohio University, B.S.J. (with honors), 1958, M.S. (with highest honors), 1960; University of Guadalajara, student, summer, 1961; University of Oslo, certificate, 1962; Syracuse University, graduate study, 1962-64; University of Iowa, Ph.D. (with highest honors), 1972. *Home:* 669 Ferne Blvd., Drexel Hill, Pa. 19026. *Office:* Department of Communications, Temple University, Philadelphia, Pa. 19122.

CAREER: West Virginia Institute of Technology, Montgomery, instructor in English and journalism and director of public relations, 1960-62, 1965-66; Wisconsin State University, Eau Claire (now University of Wisconsin—Eau Claire), assistant professor of journalism, 1966-67; Marshall University, Huntington, W.Va., assistant professor of journalism, 1967-69; University of Iowa, Iowa City, teaching assistant and associate editor of *International Communications Bulletin,* 1970-72; Universiti Sains Malaysia, Penang, Malaysia, coordinator and lecturer in mass communications, 1972-74; Temple University, Philadelphia, Pa., associate professor, 1974-76, professor of communications, 1976—. Visiting lecturer, De La Salle College, Manila, Philippines, 1964-65; visiting associate professor, University of Wyoming, Laramie, 1969-70.

MEMBER: International Association of Mass Communication Research, Inter-American Press Association, World Association for Public Opinion Research, Association for Education in Journalism, Association for Asian Studies, Asia Mass Communication Research and Information Centre, Latin American Studies Association, Caribbean Studies Association, Malaysia/Singapore/Brunei Studies Group (founding chairman), Philippine Studies Group, Sigma Delta Chi, Sigma Tau Delta, Phi Alpha Theta, Kappa Tau Alpha. *Awards, honors:* Fulbright scholar to Philippines, 1964-65; Benedum Research Award; Vice-chancellor research awards, Universiti Sains Malaysia.

WRITINGS: Journalism Study of New York Colleges and High Schools, Newhouse Communications Research Center, Syracuse University, 1963; (editor) *Readings on the Foreign Press,* West Virginia Institute of Technology, 1965; *Philippine Mass Communications Bibliography: First Cumulation of Sources on Areas of Advertising, Journalism, Newspaper, Magazine, Public Relations, Radio, Television, Movies,* [Fort Worth], 1966; *Newhouse, Newspapers, Nuisances: Highlights in the Growth of a Communications Empire,* Exposition Press, 1966; *3 Research Studies,* West Virginia Institute of Technology, 1966.

(Editor) *The Asian Newspapers' Reluctant Revolution,* Iowa State University Press, 1971; *Before 1811, after 1966: Philippine Mass Communications,* Philippine Press Institute, 1971; (contributor) Alan Wells, *Mass Communications: A World View,* National Press, 1974; *Commonwealth Caribbean Mass Communications,* State University of New York Press, 1975; *Asian Mass Communications: A Comprehensive Bibliography,* Temple University Press, 1975; *Broadcasting in Asia and the Pacific,* Temple University Press, 1976; *Third World Mass Media and Their Search for*

Modernity: The Case of Commonwealth Caribbean, 1717-1976, Associated University Presses, 1977.

Contributor to *Journalism Quarterly, Television Quarterly, Quill, Gazette* (Amsterdam), *Asian Studies, Philippine Studies, European Broadcast Review, Silliman Journal* (Philippines), *Estudios Orientales* (Mexico), and other journals. Bibliographer for *Journalism Quarterly.* Founding editor, *Berita: Newsletter of Malaysia/Singapore/Brunei Studies Group,* and *Asian Studies at Temple Newsletter.* Associate editor, *International Communications Bulletin.* Director of United High School Press, 1967-69. Co-author of filmstrip, "Pied Type, A Load of Coal and the Laser"; compiler of slide presentations on Asia and Caribbean, Vis-Com, Inc., 1972, 1975.

WORK IN PROGRESS: Books on Asian films; *Asian Newspapers: Contemporary Trends and Problems;* updated version of Caribbean and Asian bibliographies on mass media; pop culture in Asia; *International Communications Textbook.*

SIDELIGHTS: John Lent has traveled in Europe, Asia, Latin America, and the Caribbean. He developed and taught the first international communications courses at Wisconsin State University—Eau Claire, Marshall University, University of Wyoming, and Universiti Sains Malaysia. He has also supervised archeological excavations in Canada, edited an underground newspaper, and helped organize FREE, a group for racial equality in West Virginia. Lent has chaired and organized panels, lectured, presented papers and spoken at national and international conferences and symposia in United States, England, Mexico, St. Lucia, Jamaica, Philippines, Malaysia, Laos, India, Thailand, Singapore, East Germany, Trinidad, Tobago, and Canada. He feels writing comes from rigid discipline; he writes at long stretches—usually going on an all-night schedule for months.

* * *

LEOPOLD, Nathan F. 1904-1971
(William F. Lanne, Richard A. Lawrence)

November 19, 1904—August 29, 1971; American ornithologist and medical researcher convicted of murder in the 1920's. Obituaries: *New York Times,* August 31, 1971; *Washington Post,* August 31, 1971. (See index for *CA* sketch)

* * *

LERNER, Warren 1929-

PERSONAL: Born July 16, 1929, in Boston, Mass.; son of Max and Rebecca (Rudnick) Lerner; married Francine Pickow (an editor), August 16, 1959; children: Suzanne Rachel, Amy Florence, Daniel Joseph. *Education:* Boston University, B.S., 1952; Columbia University, M.A. and Certificate of Russian Institute, 1954, Ph.D., 1961. *Politics:* Registered Democrat. *Religion:* Jewish. *Residence:* Durham, N.C. *Office:* Center for International Studies, Duke University, Durham, N.C. 27706.

CAREER: Roosevelt University, Chicago, Ill., assistant professor of history, 1959-61; Duke University, Durham, N.C., assistant professor, 1961-65, associate professor, 1965-72, professor of history, 1972—. Visiting research fellow, Hoover Institution, Stanford, Calif., 1968-69. *Military service:* U.S. Army, 1954-56. *Member:* Southern Conference on Slavic Studies. *Awards, honors:* Named outstanding professor by Associated Students of Duke University (student government association), 1968; American Philosophical

Society award, 1972; National Endowment for the Humanities senior fellow, 1974-75.

WRITINGS: (Contributor) *Essays in Russian and Soviet History,* Columbia University Press, 1963; (editor with Clifford M. Foust) *The Soviet Union in Flux,* Southern Regional Education Board, 1967; *Karl Radek: The Last Internationalist,* Stanford University Press, 1970; (editor) *Studies in the Development of Soviet Foreign Policy,* Duke University Press, 1973. Member of editorial board, *Studies in Comparative Communism,* 1973—.

WORK IN PROGRESS: A monograph, *The Marxist Revolutionary Left, 1905-1914.*

* * *

Le SHANA, David C(harles) 1932-

PERSONAL: Born November 15, 1932, in Lucknow, India; came to United States in 1949, naturalized in 1958; son of Newman John (a missionary) and Gwendolyn Beatrice (White) Le Shana; married Rebecca Ann Swander, June 8, 1951; children: Deborah Lynn, James David, Catherine Ann, Christine Joy. *Education:* Taylor University, A.B., 1953; Ball State University, A.M. in Ed., 1959; University of Southern California, Ph.D., 1967. *Home:* 410 North College St., Newberg, Ore. 97132. *Office:* George Fox College, Newberg, Ore. 97132.

CAREER: Society of Friends (Quakers), minister, 1953—; pastor in Ypsilanti, Mich., 1953-54; Taylor University, Upland, Ind., served in a number of capacities, including college chaplain, director of public relations, and assistant to the president, 1954-61; pastor in Long Beach, Calif., 1961-67; George Fox College, Newberg, Ore., vice-president and acting president, 1967-68, executive vice-president, 1968-69, president, 1969—. Member of board of advisors, Earlham School of Religion, Earlham College, 1967—; Council for Advancement of Small Colleges, member of board of directors, 1971—, vice-chairman, 1975—; chairman of commission on higher education, National Association of Evangelicals, 1973—. *Member:* Oregon Independent Colleges Association (secretary-treasurer, 1970; president, 1971), Newberg Rotary Club.

WRITINGS: Quakers in California, Barclay Press, 1969. Contributor to Quaker periodicals.†

* * *

LESLIE, Conrad 1923-

PERSONAL: Born September 3, 1923, in Springfield, Ohio; son of Royal C. and Emily (Messenger) Leslie; married Cynthia Adams; children: Bruce Alan, Lynda Ann, Elizabeth. *Education:* Miami University, Oxford, Ohio, B.S., 1947. *Religion:* Presbyterian. *Office:* Leslie Analytical Organization, 141 West Jackson Blvd., Chicago, Ill. 60604.

CAREER: Merrill Lynch, Pierce, Fenner & Smith, Inc., New York City, broker, 1949-54; F. I. du Pont & Co., New York City, broker, 1955-60; Bache & Co., New York City, broker, 1960-65; Lamson Bros. & Co., Chicago, Ill., general partner, 1965-69; Leslie Analytical Organization, Chicago, president, 1969—.

WRITINGS: Conrad Leslie's Guide for Successful Speculating, Dartnell, 1970.

SIDELIGHTS: Conrad Leslie told *CA* that his book is "one of the few books about the financial markets to receive public endorsement from presidents of three financial exchanges."

BIOGRAPHICAL/CRITICAL SOURCES: Chicago Tribune, April 19, 1970, October 13, 1976; *Journal of Commerce,* April 24, 1970; *New York Times,* September 24, 1976.

* * *

LETTERMANN, Edward John 1926-

PERSONAL: Born June 4, 1926, in Pittsburgh, Pa.; son of Henry Christof and Anna (Gerstacker) Lettermann; married Aldine Beatrice Ahrens (curator of Gibbs House), June 14, 1947; children: John Wallace. *Education:* Concordia Teachers College, River Forest, Ill., student, two years. *Politics:* Republican. *Religion:* Lutheran. *Home:* 2097 West Larpenteur, St. Paul, Minn. 55113. *Office:* Ramsey County Historical Society, 2097 West Larpenteur, St. Paul, Minn. 55113.

CAREER: E. Hoiby Body Co., Minneapolis, Minn., spray painter, 1955-65; Ramsey County Historical Society, St. Paul, Minn., curator of Gibbs Farm Museum, 1965—.

WRITINGS: Farming in Early Minnesota, Ramsey County Historical Society, 1966, revised edition, 1971; *From Whole Log to No Log: A History of the Indians Where the Mississippi and the Minnesota Rivers Meet,* Dillon, 1970.

WORK IN PROGRESS: A Pioneer Family: Gibbs of Rose Township, Ramsey County, Minnesota, for Ramsey County Historical Society.†

* * *

LEVENDOSKY, Charles (Leonard) 1936-

PERSONAL: Born July 4, 1936, in Bronx, N.Y.; son of Charles Leonard (an army officer) and Laura (Gregorio) Levendosky; married Charlotte Anne Jaeger (an elementary teacher), July 15, 1961; children: Alytia Akiko, Ixchel Nicole. *Education:* University of Oklahoma, B.S., 1958, B.A., 1960, graduate study, 1960-61; New York University, M.A. in Ed., 1963. *Address:* (Permanent) c/o Mrs. Charles Levendosky, 4841 Crisp Way, San Diego, Calif. 92117. *Office address:* Poetry Programs of Wyoming, P.O. Box 3033, Casper, Wyo. 82602.

CAREER: Full-time writer. High school teacher of mathematics and science in Christiansted, St. Croix, U.S. Virgin Islands, 1963-65, in New York City, 1966-68; New York University, New York City, part-time instructor for Project Apex, 1967-68, instructor, 1968-70, assistant professor of English, 1970-71; Georgia Southern College, poet-in-residence and associate director of Project Radius of Georgia Commission on the Arts, summers, 1971, 1972; Wyoming Council on the Arts, poet-in-residence and director of Poetry Programs of Wyoming, 1972-77. *Military service:* U.S. Army, 1961-62 ("given a discharge after proving my reluctance to be made into a killing machine"). *Member:* P.E.N., International Platform Association. *Awards, honors:* Teacher of the Year Award, 1965; National Education Association fellowship, 1974-75.

WRITINGS: perimeters (an extended poem), Wesleyan University Press, 1970; (contributor) R. Kostelanetz, editor, *Breakthrough Fictioneers* (anthology), Something Else Press, 1972; *small town america* (poem; engravings by Bernard Solomon), Boxwood Press, 1974; *words & fonts* (poster poems; graphics by Solomon), Council on the Arts, 1975; *The Breton Dream Letters,* Rocky Mountain Creative Arts Chapbooks, 1977. Also author of *aspects of the vertical* (poetry), and *of love and lust* (poetry); author of libretto entitled "From Hell to Breakfast." Contributor of poetry and reviews to *Parnassus, Poetry in Review, Paintbrush,* and other magazines. Member of advisory board, *New York Quarterly.*

WORK IN PROGRESS: The third volume of a projected quartet tentatively entitled *boomtown wyoming,* to be a continuation of *perimeters* and *aspects of the vertical.*

SIDELIGHTS: Charles Levendosky wrote to *CA:* "In the past ten years I have collaborated with film-makers, composers, graphic artists, choreographers, and musicians acting on my belief that the range and concept of poetry must be expanded. Each of these collaborations, conversely, has taught me something about the possibilities of poetry on the page. I have learned as much about 'language' from these experiments as I have writing poetry for fifteen years."

* * *

LEVENSON, Christopher 1934-

PERSONAL: First syllable of surname rhymes with "heaven"; born February 13, 1934; naturalized Canadian citizen in 1973; son of Maurice Rene (a teacher) and Ellen Ethel (Pinner) Levenson; married Ursula Frieda Lina Fischer, April 12, 1958 (divorced); children: Martin Roger, Michael Patrick, Sebastian Roderick, Sean Dominic. *Education:* Downing College, Cambridge, B.A. (honors), 1957; University of Iowa, M.A., 1970, Ph.D. candidate, 1970—. *Politics:* "Democratic socialist; in England would vote Labour." *Religion:* "Agnostic; brought up as Quaker." *Home:* 38 First Ave., Ottawa, Ontario, Canada K1S 2G2. *Agent:* A. D. Peters, 10 Buckingham St., London W.C.2, England. *Office:* Department of English, Carleton University, Ottawa, Ontario, Canada.

CAREER: As a conscientious objector worked in forestry, as a hospital orderly, and in Dutch flood relief with Friends Ambulance Unit International Service, in lieu of military service, 1952-54; International Quaker School, Eerde, Ommen, teacher, 1957-58; University of Muenster, Muenster, Germany, lecturer in English, 1958-61; Rodway Technical High School, Mangotsfield, Gloucestershire, England, teacher, 1962-64; Carleton University, Ottawa, Ontario, assistant professor of English, 1968—. *Member:* Modern Language Association of America, League of Canadian Poets. *Awards, honors:* Eric Gregory Trust Fund Award, 1961, for group of poems, "In Transit."

WRITINGS: (Editor) *Poetry from Cambridge,* Fortune Press, 1958; (contributor) Edwin Muir, editor, *New Poets, 1959: Iain Crichton Smith, Karen Gershon, Christopher Levenson* (includes Levenson's group, "In Transit"), Eyre & Spottiswoode, 1959; (translator) Peter Weiss, *The Leavetaking and Vanishing Point,* Calder & Boyars, 1966; (translator) Peter Weiss, *The Golden Casket,* Penguin, 1967; *Cairns* (poems), Chatto & Windus, 1969; *Stills* (poems), Chatto & Windus, 1972; *Into the Open* (poems), Golden Dog Press, 1977. Translator of stories and articles for *Delta* (Amsterdam).

WORK IN PROGRESS: Translations of seventeenth-century Dutch poetry, and of post-war German poets.

SIDELIGHTS: Christopher Levenson is concerned "with relativity and with the difficulty, often the impossibility, for many people to imagine a situation other than their own." "I want my poetry to *communicate* to a wide audience," he writes, "and to help, firstly myself then my potential reader, to realize what one really feels. . . . Any creative literature's main task today is to assert the value of the individual."

BIOGRAPHICAL/CRITICAL SOURCES: London Magazine, October, 1969.

LEVINE, Bernard 1934-

PERSONAL: Born July 15, 1934; son of Henry and Rose (Wernon) Levine; married Deborah Brown, August 31, 1963. *Education:* Harvard University, A.B., 1956; Brown University, Ph.D., 1963. *Home:* 2121 Highland, Ann Arbor, Mich. 48104. *Office:* Department of English, Wayne State University, Detroit, Mich. 48202.

CAREER: Wayne State University, Detroit, Mich., instructor, 1963-65, assistant professor, 1965-71, associate professor of English, 1971—. *Awards, honors:* ANTA Award, 1968, for "Death of Samson."

WRITINGS: The Dissolving Image: The Spiritual-Aesthetic Development of W. B. Yeats, Wayne State University Press, 1970. Also author of "Death of Samson," a three-act verse drama. Contributor to *James Joyce Quarterly, Bucknell Review,* and other literary periodicals.

* * *

LEVITIN, Sonia 1934-

PERSONAL: Born August 18, 1934, in Berlin, Germany; daughter of Max (a manufacturer) and Helene (Goldstein) Wolff; married Lloyd Levitin (a business executive), December 27, 1953; children: Daniel Joseph, Shari Diane. *Education:* University of California, Berkeley, student, 1952-54; University of Pennsylvania, B.S., 1956; San Francisco State College (now University), graduate study, 1957-60. *Residence:* Palos Verdes Estates, Calif. *Agent:* International Creative Management, 40 West 57th St., New York, N.Y. 10019.

CAREER: Elementary teacher in Mill Valley, Calif., 1956-57; adult education teacher in Daly City, Calif., 1962-64; Acalanes Adult Center, Lafayette, Calif., teacher, 1965-72; teacher of creative writing, Palos Verdes Peninsula, Calif., 1973-76. *Member:* P.E.N., Society of Children's Book Writers, California Writer's Guild, Moraga Historical Society (founder and past president). *Awards, honors:* Charles and Bertie G. Schwartz Award, Jewish Book Council of America, 1971, for *Journey to America.*

*WRITINGS—*Juveniles, except as indicated: *Journey to America,* Atheneum, 1970; *Rita the Weekend Rat,* Atheneum, 1971; *Who Owns the Moon,* Parnassus, 1973; *Roanoke: A Novel of the Lost Colony,* Atheneum, 1973; *Jason and the Money Tree,* Harcourt, 1974; *A Single Speckled Egg,* Parnassus, 1975; *The Mark of Conte,* Atheneum, 1976; *Beyond Another Door,* Atheneum, 1977; *The No-Return Trial,* Harcourt, 1978; *Reigning Cats and Dogs* (adult), Atheneum, 1978. Contributor to *Parents' Magazine, San Francisco Magazine,* and other magazines and newspapers.

SIDELIGHTS: Sonia Levitin has traveled in Europe, Hawaii, Indonesia, and Japan. *Avocational interests:* Travel, piano, painting.

* * *

LEWIS, George 1941-

PERSONAL: Born July 15, 1941, in Lubbock, Tex.; son of Willis Jack (a clergyman) and Mary (Mueller) Lewis; married Suzanne Sloan, August 26, 1964 (divorced, 1975); married Karla Ann Baker, 1976; children: Gabriel Sloan. *Education:* University of Texas, B.A., M.A.; attended Free University of Berlin, 1961-62, University of Vienna, 1962-63. *Address:* P.O. Box 77, Dunlap, Calif. 93621. *Agent:* Miss Elaine Markson, Knox Burger Associates, 39½ Washington Square S., New York, N.Y. 10012. *Office:* Department of English, California State University, Fresno, Calif. 93710.

CAREER: Randolph-Macon College, Ashland, Va., assistant professor of English, 1966-70; California State University, Fresno, associate professor of English and creative writing, 1970—.

WRITINGS: Luminous Night (novel), Dial, 1970.

WORK IN PROGRESS: A novel, *The Grayeye.*

BIOGRAPHICAL/CRITICAL SOURCES: New York Times Book Review, May 31, 1970; *Time,* June 29, 1970; *Nation,* October 12, 1970.

* * *

LEWIS, H. Warren 1924-

PERSONAL: Born February 11, 1924, in Detroit, Mich.; son of Alfred Harold (a machinist) and May (Haflett) Lewis; married Justine Patricia Sager, July 10, 1945; children: Gregory, Deanna (Mrs. Donald Allcorn). *Education:* Rensselaer Polytechnic Institute, B.S.M.E., 1949. *Home:* 2570 Nightingale Dr., San Jose, Calif. 95125.

CAREER: International Business Machines Corp., San Jose, Calif., staff engineer, 1949—. *Military service:* U.S. Army, 1943-46. *Member:* Sierra Club, California Writers' Club.

WRITINGS: You're Standing on My Fingers!, Howell-North Books, 1969.

* * *

LEWIS, James, Jr. 1930-

PERSONAL: Born March 7, 1930, in Newark, N.J.; son of James and Marie (Wilkerson) Lewis; married Valdmir M. Cummins, August 17, 1954; children: Michael, Patricia, Terence. *Education:* Hampton Institute, B.S., 1953; Columbia University, M.A., 1957; East Coast University, Ed.D., 1970; Harvard University, postdoctoral study, 1970-71; Antioch College, Ph.D., 1971. *Office:* Office of Superintendant, Central Berkshire Regional School District, Dalton, Mass. 01226.

CAREER: Industrial arts teacher in Jersey City, N.J., 1956-57; Wyandanch (N.Y.) public schools, special education teacher, 1957-59, director of special education, 1959-66, elementary principal, 1966-67, district principal, 1967-70; Harvard University, Graduate School of Education, Cambridge, Mass., Alfred North Whitehead fellow, 1970-71; Villanova University, Villanova, Pa., associate professor of education, 1972-73; Medgar Evers College of the City University of New York, Brooklyn, N.Y., professor of education, and chairman of division of technical education, 1973-74; Central Berkshire Regional School District, Dalton, Mass., superintendant of schools, 1974—. Consultant to National Center for Education Research and Development, New York State Department of Education, 1970-71. *Military service:* U.S. Army Reserve, 1955-57; became major. *Member:* American Association of School Administrators, National Education Association, Individualizing Teaching and Learning Worldwide Association (regional representative, 1968-69), New York State Council of School District Administrators, New York State Teachers Association.

WRITINGS: A Contemporary Approach to Nongraded Education, Parker Publishing, 1970; *The Tragedies in American Education,* Exposition, 1970; *Administering the Individualized Instruction Program,* Parker Publishing, 1971; (with Robert M. Bookbinder and Raymond R. Bauer) *Critical Issues in Education: A Problem-solving Guide for School Administrators,* Prentice-Hall, 1972; *Appraising*

Teacher Performance, Parker Publishing, 1973; *School Management by Objectives,* Parker Publishing, 1974; *Administrator's Complete Guide to Individualized Instruction: A Professional Handbook,* Prentice-Hall, 1977. Also author of *Differentiating the Teaching Staff,* for Parker Publishing.

BIOGRAPHICAL/CRITICAL SOURCES: School Management, March, 1969; *Think,* October, 1969.†

* * *

LEWIS, Michael Arthur 1890-1970

January 3, 1890—February 27, 1970; British naval historian and author. Obituaries: *Antiquarian Bookman,* March 16, 1970. (See index for *CA* sketch)

* * *

LEWIS, Oscar 1914-1970

December 25, 1914—December 16, 1970; American anthropologist and social critic. Obituaries: *New York Times,* December 18, 1970; *Washington Post,* December 18, 1970; *Newsweek,* December 28, 1970; *Publishers' Weekly,* December 28, 1970; *Books Abroad,* spring, 1971. (See index for *CA* sketch)

* * *

LEWIS, Ralph F(erguson) 1918-

PERSONAL: Born January 21, 1918, in Dayton, Ohio; son of Mark C. (a civil engineer) and Marguerite (Ferguson) Lewis; married Thelma Linke, October 27, 1941; children: John L., Barbara (Mrs. Frank Venutolo), Virginia. *Education:* Amherst College, A.B. (cum laude), 1939; Harvard University, M.B.A., 1941. *Home:* 1010 Memorial Dr., Cambridge, Mass. 02138; and Smith's Parish, Bermuda. *Office: Harvard Business Review,* Soldiers Field, Boston, Mass. 02163.

CAREER: Federal Bureau of Investigation, New York City, special agent, 1941-45; Time, Inc., New York City, assistant controller, 1945-51; *Fortune,* New York City, assistant managing editor, 1951-52; Booz, Allen & Hamilton (management consultants), New York City, management consultant, 1952-54; Arthur Young & Co. (certified public accountants), New York City, national director of management services, 1954-61, managing partner, New York office, 1962-69, senior partner, New York office, 1969-71; *Harvard Business Review,* Boston, Mass., editor and publisher, 1971—. Director, Houghton Mifflin Company, Paine, Webber, Jackson & Curtis, Inc., Twentieth Century-Fox Film Corp., and others. Treasurer, Berkshire Farm for Boys, 1965-71. Harvard Business School, member of executive council, 1961-69, and member of visiting committee. Member of Presidential Commission on Electronic Fund Transfers. Trustee, Babson College.

MEMBER: American Institute of Certified Public Accountants, New York State Society of Certified Public Accountants, Harvard Club of New York, Sky Club of New York, Metropolitan Club of the City of Washington, Sleepy Hollow Club, Mid-Ocean Club (Bermuda), Brae Burn Country Club (Boston). *Awards, honors:* Distinguished Service Award from Harvard Business School, 1970.

WRITINGS: Management Uses of Accounting, Harper, 1961, revised edition published as *Planning and Control for Profit,* 1970. Contributor to accounting and management journals.

LEWIS, Thomas P(arker) 1936-

PERSONAL: Born July 1, 1936, in Mt. Vernon, N.Y.; son of Thomas and Mary (Parker) Lewis; married Elizabeth Sloan, May 8, 1965; children: Abigail, Peter, Emily. *Education:* Attended Milton Academy, 1944-53, Princeton University, 1953-54, 1955-56; Columbia University, B.S., 1961. *Politics:* Democrat/Independent. *Home:* 63 Prospect St., White Plains, N.Y. 10606. *Office:* Harper & Row, Publishers, Inc., 10 East 53rd St., New York, N.Y. 10022.

CAREER: Harper & Row, Publishers, Inc., New York, N.Y., assistant manager of school and library promotion department, 1964—. *Military service:* U.S. Army, 82nd Airborne Division, 1956-59.

WRITINGS: Hill of Fire, Harper, 1971; *The Dragon Kite,* Holt, 1973.

WORK IN PROGRESS: Clipper Ship, to be published by Harper; adult fiction and philosophy; a music reference text entitled *Catalog of Music.*

* * *

LEWITON, Mina 1904-1970
(Mina Lewiton Simon)

March 22, 1904—February 11, 1970; American novelist and educator. Obituaries: *New York Times,* February 14, 1970; *Publishers' Weekly,* March 23, 1970.

* * *

LIDDELL, Brendan E(dwin) A(lexander) 1927-

PERSONAL: Surname pronounced Li-*dell;* born June 27, 1927, in Atlanta, Ga.; son of Edwin Carey and Rose (Bindewald) Liddell; married Elizabeth Holmgren, June, 1956; married second wife, Phyllis Fugle (a lawyer), June, 1959; children: (first marriage) Guy (deceased), Rose Ann, Eric; (second marriage) Bruce. *Education:* St. Vincent College, B.A., 1950; University of Michigan, M.A., 1957, Ph.D., 1961. *Politics:* Democrat. *Religion:* "Radical Christian." *Home:* 1113 North Elmwood, Peoria, Ill. 61606. *Office:* Department of Philosophy, Bradley University, Peoria, Ill. 61606.

CAREER: University of Michigan, Ann Arbor, instructor in philosophy, 1960-61; University of Oregon, Eugene, instructor in philosophy, 1961-64; Bradley University, Peoria, Ill., assistant professor, 1964-68, associate professor, 1968-73, professor of philosophy, 1973—. Member, Peoria Civil Defense Organization. *Military service:* U.S. Air Force, pilot, 1952-56; became major, U.S. Air Force Reserves, 1956—. *Member:* American Civil Liberties Union, National Cystic Fibrosis Research Foundation.

WRITINGS: Kant on the Foundation of Morality, Indiana University Press, 1970. Contributor to proceedings; contributor of articles to *Mind* and *Rendezvous.*

WORK IN PROGRESS: Research on the "new masculinity."

* * *

LIDZ, Theodore 1910-

PERSONAL: Born April 1, 1910, in New York, N.Y.; son of Israel (a merchant) and Esther (Shedlin) Lidz; married Ruth Wilmanns (a psychiatrist), November 23, 1939; children: Victor Meyer, Charles Wilmanns, Jerome Shedlin. *Education:* Attended University of Munich, 1929-30; Columbia University, A.B., 1931, M.D., 1936. *Politics:* Democrat. *Religion:* Jewish. *Home:* 60 Orchard Rd., Woodbridge, Conn. 06525. *Office:* School of Medicine, Yale University, 25 Park St., New Haven, Conn. 06519.

CAREER: New Haven Hospital, New Haven, Conn., intern, 1936-38; National Hospital, London, England, clinical clerk in neurology, 1938; Johns Hopkins Hospital, Baltimore, Md., resident in psychiatry at Phipps Clinic, 1938-41; Johns Hopkins University, Baltimore, instructor, 1940-46, assistant professor, 1946-47, associate professor of psychiatry and assistant professor of medicine, 1947-51, lecturer in preventive medicine, 1948-51; Yale University, School of Medicine, New Haven, professor of psychiatry, 1951—, head of department, 1967-69. Psychiatrist-in-chief, Grace-New Haven Hospital and Yale Psychiatric Institute, 1951-61. Consultant in psychiatry, Army Medical Center, 1946-51; consultant to the Office of the Surgeon General, 1958-72. Fellow, Center for Advanced Study in the Behavioral Sciences, 1965-66. Member of committee on psychiatry, National Research Council, 1948-54; National Institute of Mental Health, member of grants committees, 1952-56, 1959-63, career investigator, 1961—, member of mental health program-project committee, 1963-67; consultant, U.S. Army, 1966-74. Member of visiting committee to Center for Behavioral Sciences, Harvard University, 1966-74. Acting Master, Ezra Stiles College, 1976-77. Diplomate, American Board of Psychiatry and Neurology Examiner, 1946-51. *Military service:* U.S. Army, Medical Corps, 1942-46; became lieutenant colonel.

MEMBER: American Psychiatric Association (life-fellow; chairman of committee on medical education, 1949-55; chairman of Hofheimer Award Committee, 1956-57), American Psychosomatic Society (secretary-treasurer, 1952-56; president, 1957-58), American Psychoanalytic Association, American College of Psychiatrists (fellow), American College of Psychoanalysts (fellow), American Association of University Professors, Western New England Psychoanalytic Society, Sigma Xi (president of Yale chapter, 1964-65), Alpha Omega Alpha. *Awards, honors:* M.A. from Yale University, 1951; Frieda Fromm-Reichman Award, Academy of Psychoanalysis, 1961, for research in schizophrenia; Salmon Lecturer Medal, 1967, for outstanding lectures in psychiatry; William C. Menninger Award, American College of Physicians, 1972; Van Giesen Award, New York State Psychiatric Institute, 1973; Stanley R. Dean Award, American College of Psychiatrists, 1973; Association of Psychiatric Outpatient Centers of America annual award, 1975.

WRITINGS: The Family and Human Adaptation, International Universities Press, 1963; (with S. Fleck and A. Cornelison) *Schizophrenia and the Family,* International Universities Press, 1965; *The Person: His Development Throughout the Life Cycle,* Basic Books, 1968, revised edition, 1976; (editor with Marshall Edelson) *Training Tomorrow's Psychiatrists: The Crisis in Curriculum,* Yale University Press, 1970; *The Origin and Treatment of Schizophrenic Disorders,* Basic Books, 1973; *Hamlet's Enemy: Myth and Madness in Hamlet,* Basic Books, 1974. Contributor of more than 150 articles to medical journals. Member of editorial boards of *Family Process, Journal of Nervous and Mental Disease, Psychosomatic Medicine,* 1965-72, *Connecticut Medicine,* 1966-71, *Psychoanalysis and Contemporary Science,* and *Familiendynamik.*

BIOGRAPHICAL/CRITICAL SOURCES: Saturday Review, November 16, 1968

LIEBER, Joel   1937-1971

1937—May 3 (or 4), 1971; American author, critic, and screenwriter. Obituaries: *New York Times,* May 6, 1971; *Washington Post,* May 7, 1971; *Publishers' Weekly,* May 17, 1971; *Antiquarian Bookman,* June 24, 1971.

*   *   *

LIEBER, Robert J(ames)   1941-

PERSONAL: Born September 29, 1941, in Chicago, Ill.; son of Nathan R. and Beatrice (Bespalow) Lieber; married Nancy Lee Isaksen, June 20, 1964; children: Benjamin Yves, Keir Alexander. *Education:* University of Wisconsin, B.A. (with honors), 1963; University of Chicago, NDEA Title IV fellow in political science, 1963-64; Harvard University, Ph.D., 1968, Knox traveling fellow in London, 1966-67; St. Antony's College, Oxford, visiting fellow, 1969-70. *Office:* Department of Political Science, University of California, Davis, Calif. 95616.

CAREER: United Nations Student Intern, New York, N.Y., 1962; University of California, Davis, assistant professor, 1968-72, associate professor of political science, 1972—, chairman of Committee on International Relations, 1970, acting chairman of department of political science, 1975-76, vice chairman, 1976-77. Visiting scholar, Inter-University Consortium for Political Research, Ann Arbor, Mich., summer, 1968; research associate, Harvard University Center for International Affairs, 1974-75. *Member:* American Political Science Association, American Civil Liberties Union, International Studies Association, British Political Studies Association, Phi Beta Kappa. *Awards, honors:* Social Science Research Council postdoctoral Research Training fellowship, 1969-70; Council on Foreign Relations International Affairs fellowship, 1972; Guggenheim fellowship, 1973.

WRITINGS: British Politics and European Unity: Parties, Elites, and Pressure Groups, University of California Press, 1970; *Theory and World Politics,* Winthrop Publishing, 1972; (co-author) *Contemporary Politics: Europe,* Winthrop Publishing, 1976; *Oil and the Middle East War,* Harvard University Center for International Affairs, 1976.

Contributor of articles to *International Affairs* (London), *New Leader, American Political Science Review, Foreign Policy,* and other periodicals.

WORK IN PROGRESS: A research project to be titled *Contemporary European-American Relations.*

*   *   *

LIEBERMAN, Mark   1942-

PERSONAL: Born October 24, 1942, in Passaic, N.J.; son of Irving I. (a lawyer) and Patricia (Gropper) Lieberman; married Susan Jane Bornstein, March 17, 1968. *Education:* Southern Colorado State College, B.A., 1969. *Politics:* Independent. *Religion:* Jewish. *Home:* 26 Lockwood Dr., Clifton, N.J. 07013.

CAREER: Pueblo Chieftain, Pueblo, Colo., reporter, 1968-69; *Cambridge Phoenix* (literary magazine), Cambridge, Mass., senior editor, 1969. *Military service:* U.S. Army, 1966-68. *Member:* American GI Forum.

WRITINGS: Hidalgo: Mexican Revolutionary, Praeger, 1970; *The Dope Book,* Praeger, 1971; *Soldiers Without Guns: A History of Pacifism in America,* Praeger, 1972; *The Reporters* (novel), Playboy Press, 1976. Contributor to *Nation, Colorado Quarterly,* and *Motive.*

WORK IN PROGRESS: The Jewish-American Prince, nonfiction.

*   *   *

LIGGETT, Clayton E(ugene)   1930-

PERSONAL: Born February 23, 1930, in Aberdeen, S.D.; son of Joseph Roland and Irene G. (Brannon) Liggett; married Martha Ann Baldy (a registered nurse), December 28, 1952; children: Marcia Ann, Mark Edward. *Education:* Buena Vista College, B.A., 1952; graduate study at University of Iowa and San Diego State University. *Religion:* Methodist. *Home:* 1078 Evergreen Dr., Encinitas, Calif. 92024. *Office:* 800 Santa Fe Dr., Encinitas, Calif. 92024.

CAREER: Speech and English teacher in public schools of Montezuma, Iowa, 1952-56, and Spencer, Iowa, 1956-65; San Dieguito Union High School District, Cardiff, Calif., drama instructor at San Dieguito High School, Encinitas, 1965—, district chairman of department of fine arts, 1968-71, of department of speech and theatre, 1974—. Member of board of directors, Spencer Entertainment, Inc., 1963-65, San Dieguito Little Theatre Association, 1965-68. Has directed more than one hundred and fifty school and little theater plays. *Member:* International Thespian Society, American Theatre Association (member of board of secondary school association, 1961-64), Secondary School Theatre Association (national publicity chairman, 1964-66), National Education Association (life member), California Teachers Association, Pi Kappa Delta, Alpha Psi Omega, Sigma Tau Delta, Masons, Benevolent and Protective Order of Elks.

WRITINGS: The Theatre Student: Concert Theatre, Rosen Press, 1970.

WORK IN PROGRESS: Techniques of Rehearsal, completion expected in 1978; *Literature for the Concert Theatre,* completion expected in 1979.

*   *   *

LIGOMENIDES, Panos A.   1928-

PERSONAL: Born April 3, 1928, in Pireaus, Greece; naturalized U.S. citizen; son of Aristides P. and Sonia (Acritides) Ligomenides; married; wife's name, Danae; children: Katerina. *Education:* University of Athens, Diploma in Physics (highest honors), 1951, Graduate Special Degree in Radio Engineering, 1952; Stanford University, M.Sc.E.E., 1956, Ph.D., 1958. *Home:* 8537 Greenbelt Rd., T3, Greenbelt, Md. 20770; and 10 Nireos St., Palaion Faliron, Athens, Greece. *Office:* Electrical Engineering Department, University of Maryland, College Park, Md. 20742.

CAREER: Development engineer on radiotelephone communication for Greek Tel & Tel, 1954-55, directing installation of new Athens-USA radiotelephone circuit; International Business Machines Corp. (I.B.M.), researcher in Poughkeepsie, N.Y., and San Jose, Calif., 1958-64, consultant, 1964-69; University of California, Los Angeles, professor of electronics, 1964-69; Stanford University, Stanford, Calif., professor of electronics and computers, 1969-70; University of Maryland, College Park, professor of electrical and computer engineering, 1971—. Part-time professor at San Jose State College (now University), 1960-62, and University of Santa Clara, 1962-64; Fulbright professor at University of Athens, Greece, 1970-71, teaching in Greek universities and serving as consultant to Ministry of Education on establishment of educational television and computer education and training; Alumni Visiting Distinguished Professor in electrical engineering, University of Maryland,

1971-72. Technical director, STD International Corp., Pasadena, Calif. Consultant to industry and to government agencies in United States, Brazil, Gautemala, and Greece. *Military service:* Greek Royal Navy, 1952-54; became second lieutenant.

MEMBER: Institute of Electrical and Electronics Engineers (senior member), American Physical Society, Society for Social Responsibility in Science, Sigma Xi. *Awards, honors:* Greek Government scholarship for study in United States, 1955; Organization for Economic Cooperation and Development fellowship for research in Greece, 1965; Organization for Economic Co-operation and Development (O.E.C.D.) fellow, 1965, 1974; Ford Foundation fellowship for work in Brazil, 1966, 1968.

WRITINGS: Information Processing Machines, Holt, 1969; *Computer Structures and Assembly Programming,* Kendall/Hunt, 1977. Writer of tutorial programs for educational television in Greece. Contributor to electronics journals.

WORK IN PROGRESS: Intelligent Machines.

* * *

LILLY, Doris 1926-

PERSONAL: Born December 26, 1926, in South Pasadena, Calif.; daughter of Otto and Edith (Humphries) Lilly. *Education:* Attended public schools in Santa Monica, Calif. *Home:* 150 East 69th St., New York, N.Y. 10021.

CAREER: Film actress under contract to Cecil B. De Mille, later beauty editor of *Town and Country,* and then press agent; society columnist for *New York Post* for eight years, and columnist for *Daily Mirror.* Regular guest on "Merv Griffin Show"; panelist on other television programs; currently starring in her own nightly gossip show for WPIX-TV in New York.

WRITINGS: How to Marry a Millionaire, Putnam, 1951; *How to Make Love in Five Languages,* Bobbs-Merrill, 1965; *Those Fabulous Greeks: Onassis, Niarchos and Livanos,* Cowles, 1970. Author of film scripts for De Sica. Contributor to *McCall's, Ladies' Home Journal,* and *Cosmopolitan.* Gossip columnist for McNault Syndicate.

WORK IN PROGRESS: Love Life of a Glamour Girl, a novel in blank verse.

SIDELIGHTS: Doris Lilly lived in Europe for ten years and has traveled in the Far East, Asia, and Africa.

* * *

LINDEMANN, Herbert Fred 1909-

PERSONAL: Born April 17, 1909, in Brooklyn, N.Y.; son of Paul (a clergyman) and Dorette (Mattfeld) Lindemann; married Ruth Zelle (a study hall clerk), June 25, 1944; children: Stephanie (Mrs. John Mood), Elizabeth (Mrs. Frank Malone), Paul. *Education:* Attended Concordia College, 1924-28, Concordia Seminary, 1928-32; Evangelical Lutheran Theological Seminary, M.S.T., 1957. *Politics:* Democrat. *Home:* 302 Las Marias Dr., Rio Rancho, N.M. 87124.

CAREER: Ordained Lutheran minister, 1932. Pastor of Capitol Drive Lutheran Church, Milwaukee, Wis., 1932-33, of Redeemer Lutheran Church, St. Paul., Minn., 1933-51, and of Redeemer Lutheran Church, Ft. Wayne, Ind., 1951-74; Valparaiso University, Valparaiso, Ind., housemaster and visiting lecturer, 1974-76. *Member:* Inter-Lutheran Commission on Worship (chairman, 1966-68; member of

Liturgical Texts Committee); Societas Liturgica (charter member). *Awards, honors:* LL.D. from Concordia Teachers College.

WRITINGS: The Psalter (of the authorized version of the Scriptures), Augsburg, 1940; *Dead or Alive* (sermons), Concordia, 1955; *The Sunday Psalter,* edited and harmonized by Newman W. Powell, Concordia, 1961, psalm tone accompaniments also published separately under same title; (editor) *The Daily Office* (adapted from the breviary), Concordia, 1965; *A Sick World and the Healing Christ,* Concordia, 1970; *A New Mood in Lutheran Worship,* Augsburg, 1971; *The Cross in Agony and Ecstasy,* Concordia, 1973. Contributor to *Lutheran Forum, Lutheran Witness,* and *Concordia Theological Monthly.*

WORK IN PROGRESS: Liturgical Handbook to the Lutheran Book of Worship, for Augsburg.

AVOCATIONAL INTERESTS: Travel.

* * *

LINDSAY, James Martin 1924-

PERSONAL: Born February 5, 1924, in Aberdeen, Scotland; son of James Martin (a salesman) and Jessie (Milne) Lindsay; married Morfudd Lewis (a schoolmistress), December 22, 1947; children: Alexander David, Elizabeth Jane, Hugh Malcolm, Catherine Gwen. *Education:* Attended Robert Gordon's College, 1933-37, and Banff Academy, 1937-40; University of Aberdeen, M.A., 1944, Ph.D., 1950. *Politics:* "Well to the right but still democratic." *Religion:* Presbyterian. *Home:* 86 Watkins Rd., Dalkeith, Western Australia 6009, Australia. *Office:* University of Western Australia, Nedlands, Western Australia 6009, Australia.

CAREER: University of Aberdeen, Aberdeen, Scotland, assistant lecturer in German, 1950-52; University of St. Andrews, St. Andrews, Scotland, lecturer in German, 1952-69; University of Western Australia, Nedlands, professor of German, 1969—. *Military service:* British Army, 1944-47; became warrant officer. *Member:* Modern Humanities Research Association.

WRITINGS: Thomas Mann, Basil Blackwell, 1954; *Gottfried Keller: Life and Works,* Oswald Wolff, 1968, Dufour, 1969. Contributor to modern language journals.

WORK IN PROGRESS: Studies of seventeenth-century German history and literature.

* * *

LINDSAY, Zaidee 1923-

PERSONAL: Born August 18, 1923, in Reading, Berkshire, England; daughter of George Edward and Maud (Crosby) Lindsay. *Education:* Studied at Brighton Municipal Training College for Teachers, 1940-42; Brighton College of Art, Diploma (with distinction), 1943. *Home:* Dovercourt, 31 Northcourt Ave., Reading, Berkshire RG2 7HE, England.

CAREER: Reading Education Authority, Reading, England, specialist art teacher in primary, secondary, selective, and special schools, and in further education classes for adults, 1943—. Spastics Society Staff Training College, lecturer.

WRITINGS: Art for Spastics, Mills & Boon, 1966; *Art Is for All: Arts and Crafts for Less Able Children,* International Publications Service, 1967; *Learning about Shape: Creative Experience for Less Able Children,* Taplinger, 1969; *Art and the Handicapped Child,* Van Nostrand, 1972. Contributor to *Art & Craft in Education* (periodical).

WORK IN PROGRESS: Research and writing on art, directed toward a wider field of handicaps; study of the childhood art of other races (immigrant pupils of Asiatic and African origin), handicapped by change of cultures.

AVOCATIONAL INTERESTS: Designer and exhibitor of fabrics, pottery, and collage/embroidery pictures.†

* * *

LINEBACK, Richard H(arold) 1936-

PERSONAL: Born June 5, 1936, in Cincinnati, Ohio; son of Harold C. (a grocer) and Emma (Schoenberger) Lineback; married Carolyn M. Deckebach, August 24, 1957; children: Anne Marie, Lynn Renee. *Education:* University of Cincinnati, B.A., 1958; Indiana University, M.A., 1962, Ph.D., 1963. *Home:* 317 Knollwood Dr., Bowling Green, Ohio 43402. *Office:* Department of Philosophy, Bowling Green State University, Bowling Green, Ohio 43403.

CAREER: Wichita State University, Wichita, Kan., assistant professor of philosophy, 1963-65; Bowling Green State University, Bowling Green, Ohio, assistant professor, 1965-68, associate professor of philosophy and chairman of department, 1968—. *Member:* American Philosophical Association.

WRITINGS: (Editor with Ramona Cormier and Ewing Chinn) *Encounter: An Introduction to Philosophy,* Scott, Foresman, 1970. Editor, *Philosopher's Index.*

* * *

LINK, Ruth 1923-

PERSONAL: Born September 27, 1923, in Pittsburgh, Pa.; married Per Bergstroem (a medical journalist), October 31, 1951; children: Dennis, Peter, Henry. *Education:* Sociology student at Columbia University. *Home:* Ringparksvaegen 6, Saltsjoebaden, Sweden. *Office:* Sweden NOW, Box 5703, 11487 Stockholm, Sweden.

CAREER: Columnist for newspaper *Aftonbladet,* Stockholm, Sweden, 1953-63; free-lance writer, 1963-68; associate editor and feature writer for Sweden NOW, Stockholm, 1968—.

WRITINGS: Huset fullt med moess (juvenile), illustrated by Marianne Dombret, Svenska Laeraretidning (Stockholm), 1968, her own translation, published as *A House Full of Mice,* Atheneum, 1970; *Taking Part—the Power and the People in Sweden,* Engineer's Press, 1973. Writer of movies, booklets and articles on population in relation to environment for Swedish International Development Authority (SIDA).

* * *

LINNEMAN, Robert E. 1928-

PERSONAL: Born December 9, 1928, in Bloomington, Ill.; son of William L. (a farmer) and Bertha (Ummel) Linneman; married Annabelle Witt, February 29, 1952; children: Robert D., Kurt E. *Education:* Illinois Wesleyan University, Ph.B., 1950; University of Illinois, M.S., 1962, Ph.D., 1964. *Home:* Jug Hollow Rd., Phoenixsville, Pa. 19460. *Office:* Office of Undergraduate Affairs, School of Business Administration, Temple University, Philadelphia, Pa. 19122.

CAREER: Worked in industrial sales and farm management, Bloomington, Ill., 1955-60; Temple University, Philadelphia, Pa., associate professor of marketing, 1964—, associate dean, 1972—. Lecturer, American Management

Association, 1970—. *Military service:* U.S. Air Force, 1951-55; became first lieutenant. U.S. Air Force Reserve, 1955-57; became captain. *Member:* American Marketing Association (president of Philadelphia chapter, 1972-73, National Director, 1973-75).

WRITINGS: Turn Yourself On: Goal Planning for Success, Rosen Press, 1970. Contributor to professional journals.

* * *

LIPPITT, Gordon L(eslie) 1920-

PERSONAL: Born August 20, 1920, in Fergus Falls, Minn.; son of Walter Otis and Lois (Garvey) Lippitt; married Phyllis E. Parker, June 6, 1942; children: Anne (Mrs. Thomas Rarich), Mary (Mrs. Bruce Burner), Constance J. (Mrs. Robert Ridgway). *Education:* Springfield College, Springfield, Mass., B.S., 1942; Yale University, B.D., 1946; University of Nebraska, M.A., 1947; American University, Ph.D., 1959. *Politics:* Democrat. *Home:* 5605 Lamar Rd., Washington, D.C. 20016. *Office:* School of Government and Business Administration, George Washington University, Washington, D.C. 20006.

CAREER: Director, Industrial Recreation Federation, Young Men's Christian Associations, New Haven, Conn., 1942-45, executive secretary, University of Nebraska YMCA, 1945-49; Union College, Schenectady, N.Y., assistant professor of psychology, 1949-50; program director, White House Conference on Children and Youth, 1950; National Education Association, Washington, D.C., program director of National Training Laboratories and assistant director of Division of Adult Education Service, 1950-59; George Washington University, Washington, D.C., professor of behavioral science, 1959—, founder and director of Center for the Behavioral Sciences, 1960-65. Mutual Security Agency, Productivity Division, Paris, France, education and training specialist, 1952-53, chief of industrial training and education branch, 1953-54. Rufus Jones Lecturer, American Friends Service Committee, 1966; visiting scholar, University of California, Los Angeles, 1967. Leadership Resources, Inc., Washington, D.C., president, 1960-67, chairman of board, 1967-68; member of board of directors, Washington YMCA, 1965-73, Petroleum Exploration and Drilling Fund, Abilene, Tex., 1968-70, Data Financial Corp., Washington, D.C., 1969; chairman of the board, International Consultants Foundation, Washington, D.C., 1973—, Organization Renewal Inc., Washington, D.C., 1974—; president, Glenwood Manor Estates, Deland, Fla., 1968—, Franklin Parker Corp., 1970-73, Project Associates Inc., Washington, D.C., 1973—.

MEMBER: American Psychological Association, National Education Association (life member), Academy of Management, American Society for Public Administration, Society for the Psychological Study of Social Issues, American Management Association, American Society for Training and Development (president, 1969; member of board of directors, 1965-69), Society for Personnel Administration, American Association of University Professors, World Futurist Society. *Awards, honors:* National Award of Young Men's Christian Associations, 1942; Distinguished Civilian Service Award, U.S. Army, 1962; Dow Leadership Award, Hillsdale College, 1970; LL.D., Springfield College, 1971; Annual Authors Award, Training Officers Conference, 1974; Torch Award, American Society for Training and Development, 1975.

WRITINGS: (Editor) *Leadership in Action,* National Institute of Applied Behavioral Science, 1957; (with Edith W. Seashore) *The Leader and Group Effectiveness,* Association Press, 1962; *Quest for Dialogue,* Friends General Conference, 1966; *Organization Renewal,* Prentice-Hall, 1969; (with others) *Optimizing Human Resources: Reading in Individual and Organization Development,* Addison-Wesley, 1971; *Visualizing Chance,* University Associates, 1973; (with F. Taylor) *Management Development and Training Handbook,* McGraw, 1975. Also author of more than two hundred articles and pamphlets; guest columnist for *Nation's Cities,* 1967-68. Editor, *Journal of Social Issues,* 1960.

SIDELIGHTS: Gordon Lippitt wrote to *CA:* "In the early phases of my writing I seemed to feel a need to fulfill . . . ego, impress your colleagues, . . . leaving a memory for your grandchildren. It soon became evident, however, that the real criteria was whether one communicates in a manner that the reader can understand, use, and judge. This is a continuing challenge."

*   *   *

LIPSCOMB, F(rank) W(oodgate) 1903-
(Commander F. W. Lipscomb)

PERSONAL: Born August 27, 1903, in Monmouth, England; son of Frank and Annie (Oliver) Lipscomb; married Theodora Cary, December 11, 1934; children: Alan, Peter, Robert. *Education:* Studied at Royal Naval Colleges at Osborne and Dartmouth, 1917-21. *Religion:* Church of England. *Home:* Dolphins Overbrook, West Horsley, Surrey, England.

CAREER: Royal Navy, became commander; general secretary, Ex Services Mental Welfare Society (national charity operating throughout United Kingdom), 1949—. *Member:* Army and Navy Club (London), Old Student's Association (Faraday House; life member). *Awards, honors:* Order of the British Empire; Honorary Diploma of Faraday House, 1973, for *Wise Men of the Wires.*

WRITINGS—Under name Commander F. W. Lipscomb: *The British Submarine,* A. & C. Black, 1954, revised edition, Corway Maritime Press, 1975; (with John Davies) *"Up She Rises": The Story of Naval Salvage,* Hutchinson, 1966; *The D-Day Story,* Barrell, 1966; *Heritage of Sea Power: The Story of Portsmouth,* Hutchinson, 1967; *Historic Submarines,* Evelyn, 1970; *One Hundred Years of the America's Cup,* illustrations by John Gardner, Evelyn, 1971; *Wise Men of the Wires: The Story of Faraday House,* Hutchinson, 1973. Contributor of articles tc *Navy International* and other periodicals.

WORK IN PROGRESS: A book on a naval subject with full assistance from the British Board of Admiralty.

SIDELIGHTS: F. W. Lipscomb's *The British Submarine,* the *"only"* British standard work on the subject, maintains this status with a revised edition. The Board of Admiralty issued it to all major ships and select shore establishments. His book *Heritage of Sea Power: The Story of Portsmouth* has been accepted as the official history of the city of Portsmouth.

*   *   *

LIPTON, Dean 1919-

PERSONAL: Surname legally changed, 1943; born October 3, 1919, in Detroit, Mich.; son of Isadore and Dora Lipsitz; married Shirley Mills (a secretary), December 5, 1943 (divorced); children: Judy (Mrs. Bradley West), Linda (Mrs. Orville Perry). *Education:* San Francisco City College, stu-

dent, 1938-40; Woodbury College, B.A., 1948. *Politics:* Democratic. *Religion:* Jewish. *Home:* 737 Woolsey, San Francisco, Calif. 93134.

CAREER: Los Angeles Daily News, Los Angeles, Calif., reporter, 1946-68; *Truth* (newspaper), San Francisco, Calif., editor, 1948-50; *Jewish Record,* San Francisco, editor and publisher, 1953-56. Served as publicist for various political campaigns. Moderator, San Francisco Writer's Workshop, 1960-71. *Military service:* U.S. Army, historian, 1941-45. *Member:* San Francisco Press Club (1950-67, formerly historian and member of admissions committee).

WRITINGS: Faces of Crime and Genius: The Historical Impact of the Genius-Criminal, A. S. Barnes, 1970. Contributor to *National Review, General Politics, Editor & Publisher, Frontier, Industrial Marketing, Tomorrow, Science Digest, Freeman,* and other periodicals. Editor, *Engineer's Newsletter;* co-editor, *Machine Age.* Editorial writer and financial and economic correspondent for *Argonaut.* Book reviewer for *San Francisco Chronicle* and *Berkeley Daily Gazette.* Art critic for *Alameda Times-Star* and *San Francisco Progress.*

WORK IN PROGRESS: Malpractice, a personal account, and a novel titled *Land of the Canes;* also working on revision of three books, one about the Pueblo uprising in New Mexico, a satire on pacifism, and a publicist's guide.

SIDELIGHTS: Dean Lipton told *CA:* "It has been said that I am the only writer in the United States who has been both an art critic and a financial commentator. My published writings have ranged literally from A (art) to Z (zoology). This background made the writings of *Faces of Crime and Genius* possible. The book ranges from French poetic symbolism to Dampier's scientific discoveries. One of my main interests at the moment is an investigation into the possibility of silicon—instead of carbon—based life."

*   *   *

LITTLE, David 1933-

PERSONAL: Born November 21, 1933, in St. Louis, Mo.; son of Henry, Jr. (a minister) and Agathe (Daniel) Little; married Priscilla Cortelyou, August 18, 1956; children: Jonathan, Martha, Kathryn. *Education:* College of Wooster, B.A., 1955; Union Theological Seminary, New York, N.Y., B.D., 1958; Harvard University, Th.D., 1963. *Office:* Department of Religious Studies, University of Virginia, Charlottesville, Va. 22904.

CAREER: Harvard University, Divinity School, Cambridge, Mass., instructor, 1963; Yale University, Divinity School, New Haven, Conn., assistant professor, 1963-69, associate professor of Christian ethics, beginning 1969; currently member of department of religious studies, University of Virginia, Charlottesville. *Awards, honors:* Kennedy traveling fellowship of Harvard University, 1961-62; Morse fellowship of Yale University, 1968-69.

WRITINGS: American Foreign Policy and Moral Rhetoric: The Example of Vietnam, Council on Religion and International Affairs (New York), 1969; *Religion, Order and Law: A Study in Pre-Revolutionary England,* Harper, 1969; (with Summer B. Twiss, Jr.) *Comparative Religious Ethics,* Harper, 1976. Also author of *Tabernacle in the Wilderness,* for Loizeaux.†

*   *   *

LITTLE, Roger W(illiam) 1922-

PERSONAL: Born February 3, 1922, in Moose Lake,

Minn.; son of Emmet Joseph (a farmer) and Frances (Spencer) Little; married Irmgard Schmidtmann, September 11, 1948; children: Thomas, Anne, Mary Frances, Erika. *Education:* Harvard University, A.B. (cum laude), 1948; University of Chicago, M.A., 1949; Michigan State University, Ph.D., 1954. *Home:* 226 Tenth St., Wilmette, Ill. 60091. *Office:* Department of Sociology, University of Illinois at Chicago Circle, Chicago, Ill. 60680.

CAREER: U.S. Army, 1940-46, 1949-66, primarily research sociologist on various assignments, 1949-62, assistant director of military psychology and leadership at U.S. Military Academy, West Point, N.Y., 1963-66, retired as lieutenant colonel, 1966; University of Illinois at Chicago Circle, associate professor, 1966-67, professor of sociology, 1967—. While in the Army was lecturer in sociology at Catholic University of America, Washington, D.C., 1957, American University, Washington, D.C., 1956, and University of Maryland, European Division, 1958-61. *Member:* American Sociological Association. *Awards, honors—* Military: Bronze Star, Purple Heart, and Army Commendation Medal.

WRITINGS: (With Morris Janowitz) *Sociology and the Military Establishment,* Russell Sage, 1965; (editor and contributor) *Selective Service in American Society,* Russell Sage, 1969; *Handbook of Military Institutions,* Sage Publications, 1971.

Contributor: David Rioch, editor, *Symposium on Preventive and Social Psychiatry,* U.S. Government Printing Office, 1957; Morris Janowitz, editor, *The New Military,* Russell Sage, 1964; Donald Eberly, editor, *National Service,* Russell Sage, 1968; N. A. B. Wilson, editor, *Manpower Research: A NATO Symposium,* American Elsevier, 1968; Stanton Wheeler, editor, *On Record: Files and Dossiers in American Life,* Russell Sage, 1969; Robert Habenstein and Howard Becker, editors, *Pathways to Data,* Aldine, 1970. Contributor to social science and military journals.

BIOGRAPHICAL/CRITICAL SOURCES: Washington Post, July 26, 1969.

*   *   *

LITTLEWOOD, Thomas B.   1928-

PERSONAL: Born November 30, 1928, in Flint, Mich.; son of Thomas N. (a salesman) and Louise (Grebenkemper) Littlewood; married Barbara E. Badger, June 9, 1951; children: Linda S., Lisa L., Thomas S., Leah J. *Education:* Attended DePauw University, 1949-51; Northwestern University, B.S., 1952, M.S., 1953. *Home:* 7141 Rice St., Falls Church, Va. 22042. *Office:* 1901 Pennsylvania Ave. N.W., Washington, D.C.

CAREER: Chicago Sun-Times, Chicago, Ill., correspondent, 1953—, with Springfield (Ill.) bureau, 1955-64, and Washington bureau, 1965—. *Member:* National Press Club, Sigma Delta Chi. *Awards, honors:* American Political Science Association Award for distinguished reporting of state and local government, 1957.

WRITINGS: Horner of Illinois, Northwestern University Press, 1969; *The New Politics of Population,* University of Notre Dame Press, 1977.

*   *   *

LIU, Jung-Chao   1929-

PERSONAL: Born February 9, 1929, in China; son of Chuang-lai Liu; married; wife's name, Marlita; children: James, Jean, Mark. *Education:* Educated in Taiwan, received B.A., 1950; University of Washington, M.A., 1955; University of Michigan, Ph.D., 1960. *Office:* Department of Economics, State University of New York at Binghamton, Vestal Parkway East, Binghamton, N.Y. 13901.

CAREER: McGill University, Montreal, Quebec, associate professor of economics, 1966-71; State University of New York at Binghamton, associate professor of economics, 1971—. *Member:* American Economic Association, Econometric Society.

WRITINGS: China's Fertilizer Economy, Aldine, 1970.†

*   *   *

LIVESEY, Claire Warner   1927-

PERSONAL: Born April 7, 1927, in Los Angeles, Calif.; daughter of Roy Phillip (a real estate broker) and Meteah (Smartt) Warner; married Herbert Loyd Livesey, August 9, 1958 (died January, 1962). *Education:* Attended University of California, Los Angeles, 1945-46; Mills College, Oakland, Calif., B.A., 1949; University of California, Berkeley, B.L.S., 1953. *Politics:* Democrat. *Religion:* Protestant. *Home:* 21 South Calcite, Tucson, Ariz. 85705.

CAREER: Alameda Free Library, Alameda, Calif., children's librarian, 1954-66, head of children's services, 1967-71; currently full-time writer. *Member:* California Library Association, Association of Childrens' Librarians of Northern California, Sierra Club.

WRITINGS: At the Butt End of a Rainbow, and Other Irish Tales, Harvey House, 1970.

WORK IN PROGRESS: Working on several stories to be published as picture books; also, a "long fantasy" for older children.

SIDELIGHTS: Claire Livesey has traveled to Canada, England, France, Italy, Spain, Austria, and Ireland. She told *CA:* "My chief interest is in writing tellable short stories for boys and girls as well as longer stories—fantasies—that will in some way form a bridge between the inner and outer worlds of experience."

*   *   *

LLORET, Antoni   1935-

PERSONAL: Born May 13, 1935, in Barcelona, Spain; son of Nicholas (a physician) and Maria (Orriols) Lloret; married Maria Roja Flotats (employed in public relations), December 29, 1959; children: Eva. *Education:* University of Barcelona, Licence de Physique, 1958; University of Paris, Doctorat en sciences, 1969.

CAREER: National Center of Scientific Research, Paris, France, researcher, 1960-67; Junta Evegia Nuclea, Madrid, Spain, director of laboratory, 1967-70; National Center of Scientific Research, Strasbourg, France, chief of research, beginning 1970. *Military service:* Spanish Navy.

WRITINGS: (With Paul Musset) *Dictionnaire de l'atome,* Libraire Larousse, 1966, translation published as *Concise Encyclopedia of the Atom,* Follett, 1968.

WORK IN PROGRESS: Research in high elementary physics.††

*   *   *

LO, Samuel E.   1931-

PERSONAL: Born November 23, 1931, in Tainan, Taiwan, China; son of Shiong (a Presbyterian minister) and Khi (Kho) Lo; married Betty S. Chen (a public school music teacher), December 23, 1956; children: Calvin Eric, Erica Alexandria (deceased), Burton Judson. *Education:* Tainan College, Th.B. (cum laude), 1953; Pasadena College, A.B., 1956; Boston University, M.T.S., 1962; Harvard University, Certificate in Divinity, 1963; New York University, Ph.D., 1968. *Politics:* Independent. *Home:* 36 Glen Ave., Roseland, N.J. 07068. *Office:* Seton Hall University, South Orange, N.J. 07079.

CAREER: Clergyman of Presbyterian Church; minister in South Kortright, N.Y., 1960-62, Bethel, N.Y., 1962-69, and Andover, N.J., 1969-70; Seton Hall University, South Orange, N.J., assistant professor, 1968-71, research professor of Asian studies, 1971—. Director of East-West Counseling Center, Roseland, N.J., 1971—; president of East-West Who?, Inc. (publishers), Roseland, 1971—. Member of advisory board, American Security Council. *Member:* American Academy of Religion, American Philosophical Association, Religious Education Association, American Association of University Professors, Chinese Language Teachers Association. *Awards, honors:* Fellowship to Westminster College, Cambridge, England; American Historical Association grant.

WRITINGS: Tillichian Theology and Educational Philosophy, Philosophical Library, 1970; (compiler and editor) *Asian Who? in America,* Seton Hall University Press, 1971. Author of religious plays and contributor to religious journals.

WORK IN PROGRESS: Theistic Philosophy West to East; Who? in Asian Affairs in America; Who? from Abroad in U.S. Higher Education.

SIDELIGHTS: In addition to Chinese, Taiwanese, and English, Samuel Lo is competent in Japanese, Greek, and Hebrew; he also has some ability in German. *Avocational interests:* Singing, conducting, soccer, chess, tennis, judo, and karate.

* * *

Lo BELLO, Nino 1921-

PERSONAL: Born September 8, 1921, in Brooklyn, N.Y.; son of Joseph and Rosalie (Moscarelli) Lo Bello; married Irene Helen Rooney, February 22, 1948; children: Susan, Thomas. *Education:* Queens College (now Queens College of the City University of New York), B.A., 1947; New York University, M.A., 1948, graduate study, 1948-50. *Politics:* Liberal. *Home:* 24 Lenaugasse, 3400 Weidling bei Vienna, Austria. *Agent:* Paul Gitlin, 7 West 51st St., New York, N.Y. 10019.

CAREER: Newspaper reporter in Brooklyn, N.Y., 1946-50; instructor in sociology at University of Kansas, Lawrence, 1950-56; Rome correspondent for *Business Week* and McGraw-Hill's *World News,* 1957-62, and *New York Journal of Commerce,* 1962-64; *New York Herald Tribune,* New York, N.Y., economic correspondent in Vienna, Austria, 1964-66; free-lance writer. Visiting professor at Denison University, 1956, and University of Alaska, 1974. *Military service:* U.S. Army, 1942-46. *Member:* Overseas Press Club of America, American Society of Authors and Journalists, Foreign Press Club of Rome, Press Club of Vienna.

WRITINGS: The Vatican Empire, Trident, 1969; *Vatican, U.S.A.,* Simon & Schuster, 1972. Contributor of more than 1,000 articles to periodicals.

WORK IN PROGRESS: Two books.

SIDELIGHTS: "The extent of the Vatican's financial holdings is one of the big unwritten (and unwritable) stories of our day," Edward B. Fiske points out in his *New York Times* review of *The Vatican Empire.* Fiske says that Lo Bello has tracked down most of the obvious leads available on Vatican wealth (estimated at more than five billion in stocks alone). Robert Doty writes, "The author's basic thesis, interestingly presented and garnished with history and anecdotes, is the unassailable one that the Vatican rates among the top economic powers in Italy and, possibly, in the world." The *Saturday Review* describes *The Vatican Empire* as a work of popular journalism, but withal "the first approach to an extremely delicate field—one of absorbing interest."

AVOCATIONAL INTERESTS: Opera ("opera buff supreme").

BIOGRAPHICAL/CRITICAL SOURCES: New York Times, February 3, 1969; *Saturday Review,* February 8, 1969; *Commonweal,* February 28, 1969; *New York Times Book Review,* June 29, 1969; *Christian Science Monitor,* July 31, 1969.

* * *

LOBERG, Mary Alice 1943-

PERSONAL: Born August 26, 1943, in Amherst, Wis.; daughter of Chester Julian (a truck driver) and Alice (a librarian; maiden name, Smith) Loberg. *Education:* Wisconsin State College (now University of Wisconsin—Stevens Point), student for two years. *Home:* 9126 West 73rd, Shawnee Mission, Kan. 66204.

CAREER: Hallmark Cards, Inc., Kansas City, Mo., 1964—, began as writer and editor, currently writing manager.

WRITINGS—All published by Hallmark Editions: The World of Horses, 1967; *The Terrible Lizards,* 1967; *The Kingdom of the Sea,* 1967; *The Backyard Zoo,* 1967; *A Little Book of Cheer,* 1968; *I Wish You Bluebirds: Seasons of Friendship and Love,* 1970; *I Think of You So Much,* 1971; *The Beautiful Legends of Christmas,* 1971; *A Friend in Deed,* 1971; *Cats! Cats! Cats!,* 1973; *People at Work,* 1975.

* * *

LOBLEY, Robert (John) 1934-

PERSONAL: Born May 17, 1934, in London, England; son of Robert William (a surveyor) and Winifred (Duffy) Lobley; married Priscilla Elmore-Jones (a writer and designer), July 28, 1956; children: Benjamin. *Education:* St. Martin's College of Art, National Diploma in Design, 1954; University of London, Art Teacher's Certificate, 1955. *Religion:* None. *Home:* 33 Sunnyside Rd., Ealing, London W.5, England. *Office:* Chiswick School, Burlington Lane, Chiswick, London W.4, England.

CAREER: Hospital worker as "humanitarian objector" to military service, 1956-58; John Kelly Boys' School, London, England, head of art department, 1958-68; Chiswick School, London, head of art department, 1968—. Partner, Priscilla Lobley Flower Kits, 1968—. *Member:* National Union of Teachers.

WRITINGS—Self-illustrated children's books: Circus, privately printed, 1961; *Farm,* privately printed, 1961; *Toys,* privately printed, 1961; *Tom and Peter,* Faber, 1968; (with wife, Priscilla Lobley) *Your Book of Patchwork,* Faber, 1974. Designer of Christmas and birthday cards printed by Magpie Press, 1960-64. Contributor to *Visual Education* and to children's television.

WORK IN PROGRESS: A book on film-making for children; *The Grubblings,* a children's book.

AVOCATIONAL INTERESTS: English canals, mountain walking, industrial architecture.

BIOGRAPHICAL/CRITICAL SOURCES: Books and Bookmen, July, 1968.†

* * *

LOCHMAN, Jan Milic 1922-

PERSONAL: Born April 3, 1922, in Nove Mesto, Czechoslovakia; son of Josef and Marie (Jelinek) Lochman; married Eliska Jerabek, September 19, 1952; children: Vera, Tomas, Marek. *Education:* Studied at Hus Faculty of Theology, Prague, 1945-46, University of St. Andrews, 1946-47, and University of Basel, 1947-48; Hus Faculty of Theology, Th.D., 1948. *Home:* Largitzenstrasse 62, 4056, Basel, Switzerland. *Office:* University of Basel, Basel, Switzerland.

CAREER: Clergyman of Czech Brethren Church; Comenius Faculty of Theology, Prague, Czechoslovakia, professor of theology, 1950-68; Union Theological Seminary, New York, N.Y., professor of theology, 1968-69; University of Basel, Basel, Switzerland, professor of theology, 1969—. Noble lecturer, Harvard University, 1970-71; visiting lecturer at other universities in the United States and in many European countries. Member of central committee, World Council of Churches; chairman of theological department, World Alliance of Reformed Churches, 1970—. *Awards, honors:* D.D., University of Aberdeen, 1973.

WRITINGS: Nabozenske mysleni ceskeho obrozeni (title means "Religious Thought of the Czech Enlightenment"), Kalich, 1952; *Theologie und kalter Krieg* (booklet), Hefte aus Burgscheidungen, 1960; (with Gerhard Bassarak) *Gemeinde in der veraenderten Welt,* Evangelische Verlagsanstalt, 1963; *Die Bedeutung geschichtlicher Ereignisse fuer ethische Entscheidungen,* EVZ Verlag, 1963; *Die Not der Versoehnung,* Herbert Reich Evangelischer Verlag, 1963; *Duchovni odkaz obrozeni: Dobrovsky, Bolzano, Kollar, Palacky* (title means "Legacy of the Enlightenment"), Kalich, 1964; *Herrschaft Christi in der saekularisierten Welt* (booklet), EVZ Verlag, 1967; (with M. R. Shaull and Charles C. West) *Zur Theologie der Revolution,* Kaiser Verlag, 1967; *Church in a Marxist Society: A Czechoslovak Church,* Harper, 1970; *Perspektiven politischer Theologie,* TVZ Verlag, 1971; *Das radikale Erbe,* TVZ Verlag, 1972; *Christus oder Prometheus?,* Furche Verlag, 1972; (with Fritz Buri and Heinrich Ott) *Dogmatik im Dialog,* three volumes, Guetersloher Verlagshaus, 1973-76; *Traegt oder truegt die christliche Hoffnung?,* TVZ Verlag, 1974; *Marx begegnen,* Guetersloher Verlagshaus, 1975.

WORK IN PROGRESS: An English translation of *Marx begegnen,* for Fortress Press.

* * *

LOCKE, Hubert G. 1934-

PERSONAL: Born April 30, 1934, in Detroit, Mich.; son of Hubert H. and Willa (Hayes) Locke; married Antasha Linder, June 30, 1955; married second wife, Jane Ellen Greene (a teacher), December 29, 1962; children: (first marriage) Gayle. *Education:* Wayne University (now Wayne State University), B.A., 1955; attended University of Chicago and Chicago Theological Seminary; received B.D., 1959; University of Michigan, M.A., 1961. *Politics:* Democrat. *Office:* Office of the Provost, AH-20, University of Washington, Seattle, Wash. 98195.

CAREER: Clergyman of Church of Christ; Downtown Detroit Young Men's Christian Association, Detroit, Mich., associate youth work secretary, 1956-57; Wayne State University, Detroit, Mich., director of religious affairs, 1957-62, assistant professor of urban education, 1967-72, Leo M. Franklin Memorial Professor in Human Relations, 1969-70; University of Nebraska at Omaha, dean of College of Public Affairs, beginning 1972; currently vice-provost for academic affairs, University of Washington, Seattle. Member, board of directors, Police Foundation, Washington, D.C., 1968—. *Awards, honors:* D.D., Payne Theological Seminary of Wilberforce University, 1968; Liberty Bell Award of Michigan State Bar Association, 1966, for outstanding community service; L.H.D., University of Akron, 1971.

WRITINGS: The Detroit Riot of 1967, Wayne State University Press, 1969; (contributor) *The Urban Crisis,* Zondervan, 1969; *The Care and Feeding of White Liberals: The American Tragedy and the Liberal Dilemma,* Paulist/Newman, 1970; (contributor) *Students, Religion, and the University Community,* Eastern Michigan University Press, 1970; (with Franklin H. Littell) *The German Church Struggle and the Holocaust,* Wayne State University Press, 1974. Contributor to *Kerygma, Journal of Urban Law,* and other journals; former writer of weekly column, "As I See It," in *Michigan Chronicle.*

* * *

LOCKWOOD, W(illiam) B(urley) 1917-

PERSONAL: Born April 13, 1917, in South Bank, Yorkshire, England. *Office:* Faculty of Letters and Social Science, University of Reading, Whiteknights, Reading, RG6 2AA England.

CAREER: Humboldt University, Berlin, Germany, professor of Indo-European philology, 1961-65; University of Reading, Reading, England, professor of Indo-European philology, 1967—.

WRITINGS: Introduction to Modern Faroese, Munksgaard (Copenhagen), 1955; *The Faroese Bird Names,* Munksgaard, 1961; *An Informal History of the German Language,* Heffer, 1965, 2nd edition, Deutsch, 1976; *Historical German Syntax,* Clarendon Press, 1968; *Indo-European Philology, Historical and Comparative,* Hutchinson, 1969; *A Panorama of Indo-European Languages,* Hutchinson, 1972; *Languages of the British Isles Past and Present,* Deutsch, 1975. Contributor of articles on linguistic subjects to journals.

WORK IN PROGRESS: Linguistics and philology.

* * *

LOEB, Robert H., Jr. 1917-

PERSONAL: Born November 1, 1917, in New York, N.Y.; son of Robert H. (a stockbroker) and Irma (Fried) Loeb; first marriage, 1937, ended in divorce; married Bette Harmon, September 6, 1943 (deceased); married Jeanne Starr (a dance teacher), July 2, 1964; children: (second marriage) Karen, Robert H. III. *Education:* Attended schools in Switzerland for four years as a boy; student at Brown University for three and one-half years (quit in senior year); later took courses at Columbia University. *Politics:* "Christian-Marxist." *Religion:* Episcopalian. *Home address:* R.R. 2, Box 88, Pomfret Center, Conn. 06259. *Agent:* Raines & Raines, 475 Fifth Ave., New York, N.Y. 10017.

CAREER: Worked on Wall Street for several years; *Esquire,* Chicago, Ill., 1944-47, began as promotion man, became aviation, games, cook, and drink editor; Pegasus Books, Inc. (mail order publishing business), Chicago, president, 1947-50; Norman, Craig & Kummel Agency, New York City, copywriter, 1952-54; Ted Bates & Co., New York City, copywriter, 1954-66; full-time writer, 1966—. *Military service:* Royal Canadian Air Force and U.S. Army Air Forces during World War II (long since a pacificist). *Member:* Episcopal Peace fellowship.

WRITINGS: Wolf in Chef's Clothing: The Picture Cook and Drink Book for Men, Wilcox & Follett, 1950, published as *The New Wolf in Chef's Clothing,* Follett, 1958; *Date Bait: The Younger Set's Picture Cookbook,* Wilcox & Follett, 1952; *She Cooks to Conquer,* Funk, 1952; *He-Manners* (juvenile), Association Press, 1954, revised edition, 1970; *Nip Ahoy: The Picture Bar Guide,* Wilcox & Follett, 1954; *Mary Alden's Cook Book for Children,* Wonder Books, 1955; *She-Manners* (juvenile), Association Press, 1959, revised edition, 1970; *Manners for Minors,* Association Press, 1964; *How to Wine Friends and Affluent People,* Follett, 1965; *Manners at Work: How They Help You Toward Career Success,* Association Press, 1967; *The Sins of Bias* (juvenile), M. Evans, 1970; *His and Hers Dating Manners* (juvenile), Association Press, 1970; *Manners to Love by for Young Couples,* Association Press, 1971; *Your Legal Rights as a Minor,* F. Watts, 1974; *New England Village: Everyday Life in 1810,* Doubleday, 1976; *Your Guide to Voting,* F. Watts, 1977.

WORK IN PROGRESS: Ms. or His: Your Right to Be You, a book for young adults about the biological and social pressures which determine one's gender, for F. Watts; a satirical novel subsidized by a small grant from the Connecticut Commission on the Arts; an adult nonfiction work which describes the social conditions of mill workers in the Northeast in the early nineteenth century.

SIDELIGHTS: Robert Loeb wrote to *CA:* "The motivating purpose of the books I now write for young adults is to acquaint them with the realities of existence which schooling does not teach them; which most parents cannot teach them. In short, to try to awaken them from the coma which schooling, parental inertia, and the mass media (especially TV) have placed them in. This evaluation is based upon numerous and continuous in-depth interviews with junior and senior high school students. Such topics, for this market, do not even flirt with 'the best-seller' list. I have been greatly influenced in my approach by the late Professor Ernest Becker. I consider my nonfiction writing as ninety percent research and scholarship and ten percent writing craftsmanship. My creative outlet is fiction writing, none of which has ever been published. Why? I look at the current, popular fiction list and shudder. And still hope to find a sensative, literate editor who'll take a chance and possibly lose his job."

*   *   *

LOEPER, John J(oseph)   1929-
(Jay Lowe, Jr.)

PERSONAL: Born July 9, 1929, in Ashland, Pa.; son of Peter H. (a jeweler) and Mary (Monaghan) Loeper; married Jane B. Knawa, June 13, 1959. *Education:* Pennsylvania State University, A.B.S.; Trenton State College, B.S., M.A.; Protestant Episcopal University, London, Ph.D. *Religion:* Roman Catholic. *Residence:* New Hope, Pa.

CAREER: Teacher in Lambertville, N.J., 1952-56, and Princeton, N.J., 1956-59; Hatboro (Pa.) public schools, guidance counselor, 1959-61, administrator, 1961—. Guest lecturer, Bergische Universitat, 1975. President, New

Hope-Solebury Board of Education; member of board of directors, New Hope Public Library. *Member:* National Education Association, Pennsylvania State Education Association. *Awards, honors:* American Educators Medal, Freedoms Foundation, 1965.

WRITINGS: Men of Ideas (juvenile), Atheneum, 1970; *Understanding Your Child Through Astrology,* McKay, 1970; *Going to School in 1776,* Atheneum, 1975; *The Flying Machine,* Atheneum, 1976. Contributor of articles to education journals and to *Gourmet, Coronet,* and *Cats Magazine;* also contributor of drama reviews to newspapers.

WORK IN PROGRESS: The Shop on High Street, for Atheneum.

AVOCATIONAL INTERESTS: Paintings in oils and watercolors.

*   *   *

LOFTHOUSE, Jessica   1916-

PERSONAL: Born November 9, 1916, in Clitheroe, Lancashire, England; daughter of John (a shopkeeper) and Jemima (Read) Lofthouse. *Education:* Studied at Whitelands Teacher Training College two years; King's College, London, English Diploma; additional study at City School of Art, Liverpool. *Politics:* Conservative. *Religion:* Church of England. *Home:* Low Hollins, York Lane, Langho Blackburn, Lancashire BB6 8DW, England.

CAREER: Schoolmistress in Liverpool, Blackburn, and Clitheroe, England, 1937-59; free-lance journalist, 1937—; lecturer, 1940—, speaking on local history and topography in many cities and towns of England; also lecturer for Workers' Educational Association and University of Manchester extramural department. During World War II gave orientation talks to American troops station in England. Founder-president, Women's Institute, 1960—. *Member:* Society of Yorkshire Bookmen (vice-president, 1950—).

WRITINGS—Most books self-illustrated; all published by R. Hale, except as noted: *The Rediscovery of the North: Exploration on Foot and by Car,* Times Printing Service, 1939; *Three Rivers,* 1946; *Off to the Lakes: A Lakeland Walking Year,* 1949; *Off to the Dales: Walking by the Aire, Wharfe, Ure and Swale,* 1950; *Lancashire Landscape,* 1951; *Lancashire's Fair Face,* 1952; *Lancashire-Westmorland Highway,* 1953; *West Pennine Highway,* 1954; *The Curious Traveller through Lakeland,* 1954; *The Curious Traveller, Lancaster to Lakeland,* 1956; *Lancashire Countrygoer,* 1962; *Countrygoer in the Dales,* 1964; *Countrygoers' North,* 1965; *Portrait of Lancashire,* 1967; *North Wales for the Countrygoer,* 1970; *Lancashire's Old Families,* 1972; *Lancashire Villages,* 1973; *North Country Folklore,* 1976. Also author of a television series on the North West of England entitled "Look North", 1974-76, for British Broadcasting Corp.; author of travel brochure "Lancashire's Valley and Villages," 1975. Regular contributor to *Blackburn Times, Evening Telegraph,* and *Lancashire Life,* 1939—. Also contributor to "Liverpool Echo" series, 1975-77.

WORK IN PROGRESS: Tracing Scandinavian links in northern England and Celtic links in many parts of Great Britain.

SIDELIGHTS: Educating townsfolk to enjoy the countryside and its history and lore is Miss Lofthouse's consuming interest—she dwells on prehistory, landscape, legend, tradition, and Celtic, Anglo-Sacon, Danish, and Norwegian influences. Her landscape drawings and paintings are done mainly to illustrate her books. She wrote to *CA,* "B.B.C.

T.V. series have passed on my enthusiasms to many millions of viewers.''

BIOGRAPHICAL/CRITICAL SOURCES: Times Literary Supplement, October 19, 1967.

*   *   *

LOMAS, Derek   1933-

PERSONAL: Born August 25, 1933, in Manchester, England; married Pauline Charles, May 16, 1958. *Education:* Studied at Bretton Hall College of Education, 1953-55; University of London, B.Sc. *Office:* Department of English, Lakes County Secondary School, Dukinfield, Cheshire, England.

CAREER: Lakes County Secondary School, Dukinfield, Cheshire, England, teacher of English language and literature, drama, and head of English department, 1968—. Playwright; active in amateur theater movement, particularly children's theater.

WRITINGS: The Lord of the Amber Mountain (three-act play for children), Evans Brothers, 1967; *There's No Business* (one-act play), Evans Brothers, 1968; *Tom Sawyer,* Macmillan, 1976.

WORK IN PROGRESS: ''The Client,'' a contemporary one-act play; ''The Sorcerer and His Apprentice,'' a children's play.

BIOGRAPHICAL/CRITICAL SOURCES: Drama, winter, 1968.†

*   *   *

LONDON, Hannah R.   1894-

PERSONAL: Born January 2, 1894, in Boston, Mass.; daughter of Abraham (a traveling salesman) and Goldie (Freedman) London; married Benjamin M. Siegel (an attorney), June 14, 1923; children: Robert E. (killed in action in World War II). *Education:* Radcliffe College, B.A., 1916. *Home:* 97 Toxteth St., Brookline, Mass. 02146.

CAREER: After finishing college was assistant to Frank W. Bayley, antiquarian, at Copley Gallery, Boston, Mass.; supervisor of federal survey on silhouettes done by early American artists, 1938; lecturer on early American art. *Member:* American Jewish Historical Society, Society for the Preservation of New England Antiquities, China Students Club. *Awards, honors:* Recipient of $1,000 prize, given anonymously, 1927, for *Portraits of Jews by Gilbert Stuart and Other Early American Artists.*

WRITINGS: Portraits of Jews by Gilbert Stuart and Other Early American Artists, W. E. Rudge, 1927, reprinted, Tuttle, 1969; *Shades of My Forefathers,* Pond-Ekberg, 1941, reprinted with *Miniatures and Silhouettes of Early American Jews* under that title (see below); *Immortal Son* (one-act play; produced in Boston at Emerson College, 1958), privately printed, 1948; *Miniatures of Early American Jews,* Pond-Ekberg, 1953, reprinted with *Shades of My Forefathers* as *Miniatures and Silhouettes of Early American Jews,* Tuttle, 1969. Contributor to *Antiques* and other periodicals.

WORK IN PROGRESS: An autobiography entitled *A Girl from Boston.*

*   *   *

LONG, Priscilla   1943-

PERSONAL: Born March 17, 1943, in Quakertown, Pa.; daughter of Winslow N. (an accountant and farmer) and Barbara (a psychologist; maiden name, Henry) Long; married Peter H. Irons (a teacher), March 8, 1969. *Education:* Antioch College, B.A., 1966.

WRITINGS: (Editor) *The New Left: A Collection of Essays,* introduction by Staughton Lynd, Sargent, 1969.

WORK IN PROGRESS: A biography of labor organizer, ''Mother'' Mary Harris Jones.††

*   *   *

LONGACRE, William A(tlas) II   1937-

PERSONAL: Born December 16, 1937, in Hancock, Mich.; son of William A. (a professor) and Doris (Green) Longacre. *Education:* Attended Michigan College of Mining and Technology (now Michigan Technological University), 1955-56; University of Illinois, B.A., 1959; University of Chicago, M.A., 1962, Ph.D., 1963. *Home:* 2133 West Window Rock Dr., Tucson, Ariz. 85705. *Office:* Department of Anthropology, University of Arizona, Tucson, Ariz. 85721.

CAREER: Field Museum of Natural History, Chicago, Ill., field assistant in anthropology, 1959-61, research assistant, 1961-64; University of Illinois (now University of Illinois at Urbana-Champaign), Urbana, visiting assistant professor of anthropology, 1964, visiting lecturer at Chicago Undergraduate Division, summer, 1964; University of Arizona, Tucson, assistant professor, 1964-68, associate professor, 1968-72, professor of anthropology, 1973—, director of Archaeological Field School, 1966—. Visiting associate professor, Yale University, 1971-72; visiting professor, University of the Philippines, 1975-76. *Member:* American Anthropological Association (fellow), American Association for the Advancement of Science (fellow), Society for American Archaeology, Arizona Academy of Science, Sigma Xi. *Awards, honors:* Woodrow Wilson fellowships, 1959-60, 1960-61, 1963.

WRITINGS: (Contributor) Lewis R. and Sally R. Binford, editors, *New Perspectives in Archeology,* Aldine, 1968; (editor and contributor) *Reconstructing Prehistoric Pueblo Societies,* University of New Mexico Press, 1970. Contributor to *International Encyclopedia of the Social Sciences;* also contributor of about twenty-five articles to anthropology journals.

WORK IN PROGRESS: Multi-Disciplinary Research at Grasshopper Pueblo, Arizona, for University of Arizona Pres.

*   *   *

LOOKER, Antonina (Hansell)
(Antonina Hansell, Nina Hansell Macdonald; pseudonym: Orlando Jones)

PERSONAL: Given name is pronounced An-to-*nee*-na; born in Atlanta, Ga.; daughter of Andrew Jackson (a banker) and Annis Elise (Compton) Hansell; married John Elwood Macdonald, October 10, 1920; married second husband, (Reginald) Earle Looker (a free-lance writer), February 5, 1947 (died May 22, 1976); children: (first marriage) James Ross. *Education:* Attended Harvard University Summer School, 1918, Pennsylvania School of Social Work, 1929-31, Breadloaf School of English (writer's conference), 1933. *Home:* Hillhouse, Lakemont, Ga. 30552. *Agent:* Harold Ober Associates, Inc., 40 East 49th St., New York, N.Y. 10017; and Laurence Pollinger Ltd., 18 Maddox St., London W1R 0EU, England.

CAREER: Teacher of French in Atlanta, Ga., 1916-19; *Savannah Morning News,* Savannah, Ga., reviewer, 1926; St. Christopher's Hospital for Children, Philadelphia, Pa., medical and psychiatric social worker, 1929-31; employed as a medical and psychiatric aide for psychiatrist and pediatricians in Atlanta, 1932-34; Lenox Hill Hospital, New York City, director of psychiatric social service, 1934-35; psychiatric aide for various physicians in New York City, 1935-42; Duell, Sloan & Pearce (publishers), New York City, member of staff, 1942-43; American Red Cross, Pacific Ocean Area, AIEA Naval Hospital, Honolulu, Hawaii, medical and psychiatric social service, 1943-45. *Member:* Authors Guild, Georgia Writers Association.

WRITINGS: (With husband, Earle Looker) *Revolt* (novel), Hart-Davis, 1968. Poetry anthologized in *The Poetry Society of Georgia: Twenty-fifth Anniversary, 1923-48,* University of Georgia Press, 1949. Contributor of poetry to *New York Times, New York Sun, Scribner's.*

WORK IN PROGRESS: Three novels, *A Branch Cut Off,* co-authored with her late husband, Earle Looker, *The Seventh Vote,* and a novel tracing the fortunes of a Southern family from the end of the Civil War to the start of World War II; work on a synopsis and dramatisation outline of her late husband's first book, *The White House Gang,* for a film producer; poetry and short stories under the name Antonina Hansell.

SIDELIGHTS: Antonina Looker wrote to *CA:* "Since the death of my husband, Earle Looker, in May, 1976, I have become increasingly aware of the high privilege we enjoyed in our experience of harmonious collaboration. I was at first surprised that such a collaboration was possible, for creative writing had always seemed to me an essentially private matter. While this remains true, I now appreciate more fully the depth and height of that dimension which may be added by collaboration. It is a unique experience to see one's own idea so fully and immediately understood that another mind can at once augment and enrich the essential import. Between us this flow, this exchange, was mutual, perhaps because my husband's abilities lay in a different sphere from my own, so that in approach and development of a situation we complemented each other. He could take a scene I felt not quite conclusive and with one correlating emphasis give it power; I could sometimes bring a character who persisted in remaining at a distance into a closer, warmer focus. That we seldom disagreed was chiefly due, I believe, to the fact that neither had a personal, ego axe to grind, that each was intent only on the best development of the work at hand. I shall be forever grateful for what was 'a fearful joy'."

*   *   *

LOPEZ-REY (y Arrojo), Manuel 1902-

PERSONAL: Born September 30, 1902, in Spain; son of Leocadio (a doctor) and Filomena (Arrojo) Lopez-Rey; married, May, 1953; wife's name, Grace; children: (previous marriage) Diana. *Education:* University of Madrid, LL.D. (with highest honors), 1933; University of Munich, Criminology certificate (summa cum laude); attended postgraduate courses in criminology, criminal law, criminal sociology, and psychology at Universities of Berlin, Vienna, and Paris. *Politics:* "Left Republican Party in Spain." *Religion:* Roman Catholic. *Home and office address:* Greenhaven, Alston, Axminster, England.

CAREER: Criminal county judge and director general of prisons in Spain, 1928-39; professor of criminal law at University of Madrid, Madrid, Spain, University of Salamanca, Salamanca, Spain, 1931-35, and University of La Paz, La Paz, Bolivia, 1939-44; Minister Plenipotentiary of the Spanish Republic to Bucharest, Rumania, 1937-39; legal adviser in charge of drafting new penal and criminal procedures code for Bolivian Government, 1941-44; United Nations, New York, N.Y., director of and participant in various seminars in Europe and Latin America, 1946-65, chief of Research and Treaties Section, Narcotics Division, 1946-52, chief and principal adviser of Section of Social Defense and Prevention of Crime and Treatment of Offenders, Bureau of Social Affairs, 1952-65, senior adviser on Social Defense to Governments in the Middle and Far East, 1960-64; University of Puerto Rico, Rio Piedras, director of Criminological Research at Social Science Research Center. Visiting professor at Institute of Criminology, Cambridge, England, 1965—; also visiting professor and lecturer on criminal law and criminology at universities, bar associations, conferences, and research institutes, throughout the world. Member, International Advisory Committee for Comparative Criminal Law Project, University of New York. Delegate or adviser to several international law conferences, 1933-69.

MEMBER: International Society of Criminal Prophylaxy (president, 1967—), International Committee for the Study of Genocide (president, 1967—), American International Law Association, Institute for the Study of Crime and Delinquency, U.S.A. (member of advisory body), Bureau International pour l'Unification du Droit Penal (Geneva), L'Association Internationale du Droit Penal (Paris), Asociacion Francisco de Vitoria (Madrid), American Society of Criminology, Mexican Academy of Penal Sciences. "Honoris Causa" member of several Schools of Law.

WRITINGS—Books: (With others) *Elementos de derecho politico, administrativo y penal,* Editorial Reus (Madrid), 1933; *Derecho penal,* Editorial Reus, 1933; (with F. Alvarez Valdes) *El Nuevo codigo penal: Comentarios y jurisprudencia,* Revista de Derecho Privado (Madrid), 1933; (with others) *Actes de la cinquieme conference internationale pour l'unification de droit penal,* Pedone (Paris), 1934; (author of introduction and commentary) Antonio de la Pena, *Un Practico castellano del siglo XVI,* Tipografia de Archivos (Madrid), 1935; *Derecho penal: Parte especial,* Editorial Reus, 1936; *Proyecto oficial de codigo penal boliviano,* Bolivian Government, 1943; *Introduccion al estudio de la criminologia,* Editorial El Ateneo (Buenos Aires), 1945; *Proyecto oficial de codigo procesal penal para Bolivia* (mimeographed), Comision Codificadora Nacional de Bolivia (La Paz), 1946; *Que es el delito?,* Editorial Atlantida (Buenos Aires), 1947; (editor with Charles Germain, and contributor) *Studies in Penology,* Nijhoff, for International Penal and Penitentiary Foundation, 1964; *El Tratamiento de los reclusos y los derechos humanos* (title means "The Treatment of Prisoners and Human Rights"), Commission of Human Rights (Puerto Rico), 1970; *Crime: An Analytical Appraisal,* Praeger, 1970; *Criminology,* Aguilar, 1973.

Reports, articles, and pamphlets: *Justicia, poder civil,* Editorial Morata (Madrid), 1931; *Un Delito de asesinato,* E. F. Fe (Madrid), 1936; *Masas, literatura y politica,* Editorial Nascimento, 1940; *Endocrinologia y Criminalidad,* Editorial Nascimento (Santiago), 1941; *Consideraciones generales para la redaccion de bases de un anteproyecto de codigo penal* (mimeographed), Comision Codificadora Nacional de Bolivia, 1941; *Bases para la redaccion de un anteproyecto de codigo penal boliviano* (mimeographed), Comision Codificadora Nacional de Bolivia, 1941; *Programa de derecho penal,* Universidad de La Paz, 1942; *Programa de criminologia,* Universidad de La Paz, 1942; *La Criminologia,* Imprenta de la Universidad de Cordoba (Argentina), 1944; *El Dictamen criminologico,* Imprenta Universitaria (Cochabamba), 1945; *Proyecto oficial de codigo de menores delincuentes para Bolivia* (mimeographed), Comision Codificadora Nacional de Bolivia, 1946; (author of prologue) *Anales de criminologia y derecho penal,* Volume 1, School of Law, University of La Paz, 1946; *La Reforma procesal penal en Bolivia* (originally published in *Revista de Derecho Procesal, 11*), EDIAR (Buenos Aires), 1947; *Valor procesal penal de los "sueros de la verdad"* (originally published in *Revista de Derecho Procesal, VII*), EDIAR, 1949; *La Politica criminal de las Naciones Unidas,* Departamento de la Imprensa Nacional (Rio de Janeiro), 1953; *Concepto y limites de la readaptacion en penologia,* Departamento de la Imprensa Nacional, 1954; *Cuestiones penologicas,* Editorial Richardet (Tucuman), 1955; *Some Considerations on the Institutional Treatment of Juvenile Offenders,* United Nations Publication V. 58, 1955; *Guerra y criminalidad* (originally published in *Revista de Criminologia*), Direccion General de Institutos Penales (Montevideo), 1958; *Police and Juvenile Delinquency,* All India Crime Prevention Society (Lucknow), 1961; *The Functions of Social Workers in Penal Institutions,* Ram Prasad Gupta, for All India Crime Prevention Society, 1964; *La Reforma penal en Puerto Rico,* Centro de Investigaciones Sociales, Universidad de Puerto Rico, 1967; *La Prevencion del delito y la pena de muerte,* Universidade Coimbra, 1967; *Fundamento, consideraciones y sugestiones para un programa de investigacion criminologica,* Centro de Investigaciones Sociales, Universidad de Puerto Rico, 1968; *Estudio penal y criminologico del proyecto oficial de codigo penal de 1967 para Puerto Rico,* Comision de Derechos Civiles (San Juan), 1969; *The Different Kinds of Criminology and Their Respective Functions and Problems,* International Convention on Criminology (Mendoza), 1969.

Contributor: *La Vie Juridique des Peuples,* Delagrave (Paris), 1934; H. Manheim, editor, *Pioneers in Criminology,* Library of Criminology (London), 1960; G.O.W. Mueller, editor, *Essays in Criminal Science,* School of Law, New York University, 1960; *Encyclopaedia Britannica,* Book of the Year, 1968. Contributor to *The Planning of Social Defense* published by the United Nations, 1972. Also contributor of over 100 papers and articles to numerous university and government publications and criminology and sociology journals, including *Cuadernos Criminalia* (Mexico), *La Justicia Uruguaya* (Montevideo), *Revista Juridica* (Caracas), *Annals* of the American Academy of Political and Social Sciences, *Revue Penitentiaire* (Athens), *Siyasal Bilgiler Fakultesi Dergisi* (Ankara), *Revue Internationale de Criminologie et de Police Technique* (Geneva), *Journal of Correctional Work* (Lucknow), and *Kriminologischen Aktualitat* (Mainz).

WORK IN PROGRESS: A book on criminal justice; and another on the problems of crime.

SIDELIGHTS: Manuel Lopez-Rey told *CA:* "I am in favour of a radical change of contemporary sociopolitical and economic structures, including those of the socialist people's democracies and detest every ideology from right to left which tries to reduce human dignity and freedom. I am in favour of protest and disconformity but reject brutality and sheer violence. I left Spain after Franco's victory. . . . [I am] sceptical about scientism, technocracy and meritocracy. [I am] always in favour of Human Rights and against war."

AVOCATIONAL INTERESTS: Outdoor life, walking, swimming.

LOUIS, Debbie 1945-

PERSONAL: Born June 20, 1945, in New York, N.Y.; daughter of Melville (an artist) and Rebecca (Broadwell) Bernstein; married Joseph Louis, July 7, 1966; children: Simone Katiya. *Education:* University of Cincinnati, student, 1963-64; Columbia University, student, 1965. *Politics:* "Left." *Religion:* None. *Agent:* Mrs. Sylvia Miller, 433 North Palm Dr., Apt. 403, Beverly Hills, Calif. 90210.

CAREER: Free-lance writer. Congress of Racial Equality, assistant program director in New Orleans, La., 1965, director of southern resources in New York City, 1965; free-lance researcher for Urban Coalition, local unions, political candidates and organizations. *Member:* Council of Federated Organizations (state secretary, 1964), Assembly of Men and Women in the Arts Concerned with Vietnam (executive secretary, 1967-68).

WRITINGS: And We Are Not Saved: A History of the Movement as People, Doubleday, 1970.

WORK IN PROGRESS: A novel concerning "what drives young people to blow things up"; and a "comprehensive examination of American women [with] realistic social solutions."

SIDELIGHTS: Debbie Louis told *CA:* "As with any vocation, when skills are unpractised and tools unused, they deteriorate. Every hour spent typing or sewing for money is an hour not spent flexing and applying the mind, is an hour's-worth of reading, considering, keeping-up-with-the-world and progress in one's field, is an hour lost forever in the making of one's own contribution. As with the dancer or pianist or football player who must practice three hours to make up for one hour lost the day before, to reach the same point of proficiency and sharpness already acquired in order to reach a point beyond, the weeks and months I am forced to spend, of financial necessity, on unrelated tasks are that many weeks and months in which my skills are left unexercised, to die a little."††

*   *   *

LOVE, Glen A. 1932-

PERSONAL: Born July 4, 1932, in Seattle, Wash.; son of Ellsworth E. and Martha (Bartel) Love; married Rhoda Moore (a biology teacher), June 14, 1956; children: Stanley, Jennifer. *Education:* University of Washington, Seattle, B.A. (with honors), 1954, M.A., 1959, Ph.D., 1964. *Home:* 393 Ful Vue Dr., Eugene, Ore. 97405. *Office:* Department of English, University of Oregon, Eugene, Ore. 97403.

CAREER: Teacher in secondary schools of Seattle, Wash., 1955-59; University of Washington, Seattle, assistant dean of students, 1960-63; San Diego State College (now University), San Diego, Calif., assistant professor of English, 1963-65; University of Oregon, Eugene, assistant professor, 1965-68, associate professor, 1968-74, professor of English, 1974—, director of composition, 1965-70, 1973-74, associate dean of Graduate School, 1970-71, acting chairman of department of English, 1977-78. *Member:* National Council of Teachers of English, Conference on College Composition and Communication (member of executive committee, 1968-70), American Association of University Professors, Western Literature Association (member of governing council, 1975-77), Oregon Council of Teachers of English (president, 1969-70), Phi Beta Kappa.

WRITINGS: (Chief rhetoric author) *The Oregon Curriculum: Language/Rhetoric,* Volumes I-VI, with teachers' guides, Holt, 1968-70; (editor with Michael Payne) *Contem-*

porary Essays on Prose Style: Rhetoric, Linguistics, Criticism, Scott, Foresman, 1969; (editor with wife, Rhoda M. Love) *Ecological Crisis: Readings for Survival,* Harcourt, 1970. Writer of syllabi and instructor's manuals for University of Oregon Composition Program, 1965-70. Contributor to journals on composition and American literature.

WORK IN PROGRESS: "*New Americans,* a study of the hero in the post-industrial/post-frontier American novels, and focusing upon the works of Willa Cather, Hamlin Garland, Frank Norris, Sherwood Anderson, and Sinclair Lewis."

* * *

LOVE, Iris Cornelia 1933-

PERSONAL: Born August 1, 1933, in New York, N.Y.; daughter of Cornelius Ruxton, Jr. and Audrey Barbara Love. *Education:* Smith College, student, 1951-53, 1954-55, B.A., 1955; University of Florence, student, 1953-54; New York University, Ph.D. candidate. *Religion:* Episcopalian. *Home address:* R.F.D. 1, Box 301, Bristol, Vt. 05443. *Office:* C. W. Post College, Long Island University, Brookville, N.Y. 11548.

CAREER: Cooper Union, New York, N.Y., instructor in Greek and Roman art, 1963; Smith College, Northampton, Mass., instructor in Greek and Roman art and archaeology, 1964-65; Long Island University, C. W. Post College, Brookville, N.Y., assistant professor of art history and archaeology, 1966-67, research assistant professor, 1967—, director of archaeological expedition to Knidos, Turkey, 1967—. Instructor and coordinator of three lecture series, School of Continuing Studies, New York University, 1968-70; instructor in community education, Hofstra University, 1969; Distinguished Froman Professor, Russell Sage College, spring, 1972; Robert Sterling Clark Lecturer in Art History, Williams College, winters, 1973, 1974; John Hamilton Fulton Lecturer, Middlebury College, winter, 1974; research associate, Carnegie Museum of Natural History, 1976—. Staff member of archaeological expedition to Greek island of Samothrace, sponsored by Institute of Fine Arts, New York University, 1955-65; collaborator with British School in Rome on excavation of Quattro Fontanile, 1962. *Member:* Archaeological Institute of America, Society of Women Geographers, American Association of University Professors, American-Turkish Society. *Awards, honors:* D.Litt., Dowling College, 1971; recipient of citation from Republic of Turkey, 1973.

WRITINGS: (Contributor) *Samothrace,* Institute of Fine Arts, New York University, Part I: *Hall of Votive Gifts,* 1961, Part II: *The Altar Court,* 1965, Part III: *The Hieron,* 1969, Part IV: *The Temenos and the Central Terrace Precinct,* 1969; (author of text and captions) *Greece, Gods and Art,* photographs by Alexander Liberman, Viking, 1968. Contributor to archaeology journals. Member of editorial board, *Marsyas,* 1958-62.

WORK IN PROGRESS: Articles for archaeological journals on the excavations at Knidos.

SIDELIGHTS: Iris Cornelia Love is fluent in Italian, modern Greek, and French, and knows some German, Turkish, ancient Greek, and Latin. In addition to her work in the Near East, she has traveled extensively throughout Europe and South America. *Avocational interests:* Classical music (opera and concerts), ballet, gourmet cooking and wine tasting, photography, skiing, tennis, horseback riding, swimming, and Greek and Turkish folk dancing.

BIOGRAPHICAL/CRITICAL SOURCES: New York Times, December 31, 1968; *New Yorker,* January 4, 1969; *Harper's Bazaar,* August, 1969.

* * *

LOVE, Jean O. 1920-

PERSONAL: Born February 27, 1920, in York, S.C.; daughter of Walter Brown and Julia (Foster) Love. *Education:* Erskine College, B.A., 1941; Winthrop College, M.A., 1949; University of North Carolina, Ph.D., 1953; postdoctoral study at Oxford University and Clark University. *Politics:* Democrat. *Religion:* United Presbyterian. *Home:* 217 West Sheridan Ave., Annville, Pa. 17003. *Office:* Lebanon Valley College, Annville, Pa. 17003.

CAREER: Institute of Living, Hartford, Conn., vocational counselor, 1949-51, 1953-54; Lebanon Valley College, Annville, Pa., professor of psychology, 1954—. *Military service:* U.S. Naval Reserve, WAVES, 1943-46; became lieutenant. *Member:* American Psychological Association, American Association of University Professors, Eastern Psychological Association, Pennsylvania Psychological Association (secretary, 1965-66). *Awards, honors:* Penelope McDuffie fellowship of American Association of University Women, 1965-67; fellow of Heinz Werner Institute of Developmental Psychology, 1967.

WRITINGS: Worlds in Consciousness: Mythopoetic Thought in the Novels of Virginia Woolf, University of California Press, 1970; *Virginia Woolf: Sources of Madness and Art,* University of California Press, in press. Contributor to psychology journals.

WORK IN PROGRESS: A psychobiography of Virginia Woolf's adult years.

AVOCATIONAL INTERESTS: Art (has exhibited regionally and locally and won local awards).

* * *

LOVE, Joseph L. (Jr.) 1938-

PERSONAL: Born February 28, 1938, in Austin, Tex.; son of Joseph L. and Virginia (Ellis) Love; children: James Alexander, Stephen Nathaniel. *Education:* Harvard University, A.B., 1960; Stanford University, M.A., 1963; Columbia University, Ph.D., 1967. *Home:* 805 South Mattis, Champaign, Ill. 61820. *Office:* Department of History, University of Illinois at Urbana-Champaign, Urbana, Ill. 61801.

CAREER: University of Illinois at Urbana-Champaign, Urbana, instructor, 1966-67, assistant professor, 1967-69, associate professor of history, 1969—. *Member:* American Historical Association, Conference on Latin American History, Latin American Studies Association. *Awards, honors:* Social Science Research Council grant, 1968; Fulbright research grant, 1969.

WRITINGS: Rio Grande do Sul and Brazilian Regionalism, 1882-1930, Stanford University Press, 1971; (editor with Robert S. Byars) *Quantitative Social Science Research on Latin America,* University of Illinois Press, 1973. Contributor to journals on Latin American history.

WORK IN PROGRESS: Writing on regional bases of modern Brazilian politics, with special emphasis on Sao Paulo State, 1889-1937.

* * *

LOVELL, John P(hilip) 1932-

PERSONAL: Born August 12, 1932, in Racine, Wis.; son of

Frank H. (a newspaper editor) and Nyla (Metcalf) Lovell; married Joanne Creighton Granger, August 30, 1958; children: Sara Louise, David Frank. *Education:* U.S. Military Academy, B.S., 1955; University of Wisconsin, M.A., 1959, Ph.D., 1962. *Religion:* Protestant. *Home address:* R.R. 11, Box 129, Bloomington, Ind. 47401. *Office:* Department of Political Science, Indiana University, Bloomington, Ind. 47401.

CAREER: U.S. Army, cadet, 1951-55, artillery officer, 1955-58, served two years in Germany and left service as first lieutenant; Indiana University, Bloomington, instructor, 1962-64, assistant professor, 1964-67, associate professor, 1967-71, professor of political science, 1971—. Visiting professor at Vassar College, 1968-69, and U.S. Naval Academy, 1971-72. *Member:* International Studies Association (chairman of section on military studies, 1970-74; president of Midwest Region, 1974-76), American Political Science Association, American Civil Liberties Union, Inter-University Seminar on Armed Forces and Society.

WRITINGS: Foreign Policy in Perspective: Strategy, Adaptation, Decision Making, Holt, 1970; (editor and contributor) *The Military and Politics in Five Developing Nations,* Center for Research in Social Systems, 1970; (co-editor and contributor) *New Civil-Military Relations: The Agonies of Adjustment to Post-Vietnam Realities,* Transaction Books, 1974.

Contributor: Morris Janowitz, editor, *The New Military: Changing Patterns of Organization,* Russell Sage, 1964; Andrew C. Nahm, editor, *Studies in the Developmental Aspects of Korea,* School of Graduate Studies and Institute of International and Area Studies, Western Michigan University, 1969; Monte Palmer and Larry Stern, editors, *Political Development in Changing Societies,* Heath, 1971; Charles L. Cochran, editor, *Civil-Military Relations: Changing Concepts in the Seventies,* Free Press, 1974; Edward R. Wright, Jr., editor, *Korean Politics in Transition,* Royal Asiatic Society, 1975; Lawrence J. Korb, editor, *The System for Educating Military Officers in the U.S.,* International Studies Association, 1976; John Chay, editor, *The Problems and Prospects of American-East Asian Relations,* Westview Press, 1977; Franklin D. Margiotta, editor, *The Changing American Military Profession,* Westview Press, in press. Contributor of articles and reviews to political science journals.

WORK IN PROGRESS: Neither Athens Nor Sparta?: The American Service Academies in Transition.

AVOCATIONAL INTERESTS: Tennis, squash.

*   *   *

LOWBURY, Edward (Joseph Lister) 1913-

PERSONAL: Born December 6, 1913, in London, England; son of Benjamin William (a physician) and Alice (Halle) Lowbury; married Alison Young (a musician), June 12, 1954; children: Ruth, Pauline, Miriam. *Education:* University College, Oxford, B.A., 1936, B.M. and B.Ch., 1939; London Hospital Medical College, University of London, M.A., 1940, D.M., 1957. *Home:* 79 Vernon Rd., Birmingham 16, England.

CAREER: Member of scientific staff, Medical Research Council of Great Britain, 1947—; Birmingham Accident Hospital, Birmingham, England, bacteriologist in Burns Research Unit, 1949—. Honorary research fellow, University of Birmingham, 1950—; adviser in bacteriology, Birmingham Regional Hospital Board, 1960—; Hospital Infec-

tion Research Laboratory, Birmingham, honorary director, 1966—. Consultant to United States on hospital-acquired infection, World Health Organization, 1965. *Military service:* Royal Army Medical Corps, 1943-47; became major. *Member:* Royal College of Pathologists (fellow), Royal College of Physicians, Royal Society of Literature (fellow), Society for General Microbiology, Society for Applied Bacteriology, Pathological Society of Great Britain and Ireland, British Medical Association. *Awards, honors:* John Keats Memorial Lecturer award, 1973; Everett Evans Memorial Lecturer award, 1977.

WRITINGS—Poetry, except as noted: *Fire,* [Oxford], 1934; *Crossing the Line,* Hutchinson, 1947; *Metamorphoses,* Keepsake Press, 1958; (with Terence Heywood) *Facing North,* Mitre Press, 1960; *Time for Sale,* Chatto & Windus, 1961; *New Poems,* Keepsake Press, 1965; *Daylight Astronomy,* Wesleyan University Press, 1968; *Figures of Eight,* Keepsake Press, 1969; (with wife, Alison Young, and Timothy Salter) *Thomas Campion: Poet, Composer, Physician* (biography), Barnes & Noble, 1970; *Green Magic* (poems for young people), Chatto & Windus, 1972; *The Night Watchman,* Chatto & Windus, 1974; (with G. A. Ayliffe) *Drug Resistance in Antimicrobial Therapy* (technical), C. C Thomas, 1974; (editor with others) *Control of Hospital Infection: A Practical Handbook* (technical), Chapman & Hall, 1975; *Poetry and Paradox: Poems and an Essay,* Keepsake Press, 1976; (with others) *Troika: A Selection of Poems,* Daedalus Press, 1977; *Selected Poems,* Celtion Press, 1977.

Contributor of chapters and articles to numerous medical books, among them *Drug Resistance in Antimicrobial Therapy, The Scientific Basis of Medicine, Textbook of British Surgery, Recent Advances in Surgery, Recent Advances in Clinical Pathology,* and *Chamber's Encyclopedia.*

Poems included in Palgrave's *Golden Treasury,* Oxford University Press, 1964, *A Map of Modern Verse,* "The Poet Speaks" (recordings), and other collections. Contributor to *Encyclopedia of Poets.* Poems have been published in *Encounter, London Magazine, Times Literary Supplement, New York Times, Southern Review,* and elsewhere. Also contributor to medical and scientific journals. Editor, *Equator* (Nairobi), 1945-46.

SIDELIGHTS: The two sides of the double life Edward Lowbury leads as a medical man and as a poet are "excitingly contrasted," he notes, adding "I write at weekends and on holiday, but store up memories and experiences for use at these times. The collaborative study on Thomas Campion reflects an interest of many years in Elizabethan music and poetry, and incidentally gave me an insight into the divided life of a 17th century doctor-poet who was also a fine composer." While a student at Oxford Lowbury received the Newdigate Prize for English verse and the Matthew Arnold Memorial Prize for literary criticism.

BIOGRAPHICAL/CRITICAL SOURCES: Southern Review, Volume VI, 1970.

*   *   *

LOWE, C(arrington) Marshall 1930-

PERSONAL: Born October 22, 1930, in New York, N.Y.; son of James T. (an electrical engineer) and Constance (Marshall) Lowe; married Betty Meyers, August 28, 1960; children: David, Peter, Stephen. *Education:* Princeton University, A.B., 1952, Princeton Theological Seminary, B.D., 1955; Ohio State University, M.A., 1958, Ph.D., 1961. *Politics:* Independent Democrat. *Home and office:* Route 1, Chesterhill, Ohio 43728.

CAREER: Pastor of Presbyterian church in Newark, Ohio, 1955-58; Veterans Administration Hospital, Chillicothe, Ohio, trainee in psychology, 1958-60; Maryville College, Maryville, Tenn., assistant professor of psychology, 1960-61; Veterans Administration Hospital, Brecksville, Ohio, psychologist, 1961-66; University of California, Berkeley, School of Education, assistant professor of counseling psychology, 1966-73; partner, Joy Valley Farms, 1973—.

WRITINGS: (Contributor) E. C. Evans, editor, Children: Readings in Behavior and Development, Holt, 1968; Value-Orientations in Counseling and Psychotherapy, Intext, 1969, 2nd edition, Carroll Press, 1976. Contributor to professional journals.

* * *

LUBBOCK, (Mary Katherine) Adelaide 1906-

PERSONAL: Born May 30, 1906, in London, England; daughter of Lord Stanley of Alderley and Margaret Evans-Gordon Stanley; married Maurice Fox Pitt Lubbock, January 9, 1926 (died April 26, 1957); children: Olivia Lubbock Keighley, Eric (4th Lord Avebury, suceeded peerage 1971). Education: Privately educated. Politics: Liberal Party. Religion: Agnostic. Home: High Elms Clock House, Downe, Orpington, Kent, England. Agent: A. D. Peters, 10 Buckingham St., Adelphi, London WC2N 6BW, England.

CAREER: Trained in London, England, as a musician and opera singer; appeared in leading roles on West End stages in musicals, opera, and revues, 1935-39; served with Civil Defense in London, 1939-45, and as health and welfare officer with Allied Commission for Austria, 1945-47. President of Norwood Society for the Preservation, Protection, and Improvement of Physical and Cultural Amenities.

WRITINGS: Australian Roundabout, Heinemann, 1963; Owen Stanley RN: Captain of the Rattlesnake, Heinemann, 1968; Shall I Tell Them: Growing Up in Government House (autobiography), Thomas Nelson, Volume I: 1906-1920, 1977. Contributor of historical articles to periodicals.

WORK IN PROGRESS: Second volume of autobiography.

BIOGRAPHICAL/CRITICAL SOURCES: Spectator, June 7, 1969.

* * *

LUBECK, Steven G. 1944-

PERSONAL: Born May 23, 1944, in Salt Lake City, Utah; son of Glenn H. (a doctor) and Artha (Wood) Lubeck; married Diane Trimble, August 26, 1964. Education: Brigham Young University, B.S., 1964, M.S., 1965; University of Southern California, Los Angeles, Ph.D., 1969. Address: 4220 Newdale Dr., Los Angeles, Calif. 90027.

CAREER: University of Southern California, Law School, Los Angeles, research associate, 1965-71, instructor, 1971; California State College at Los Angeles (now California State University, Los Angeles), instructor in sociology, 1967; Washington State University, Pullman, assistant professor of sociology, beginning 1971. Consultant. Member: American Sociological Association, Society for the Study of Social Problems, Pacific Sociological Association, Alpha Kappa Delta.

WRITINGS—With LaMar T. Empey: Delinquency Prevention Strategies, Youth Development and Delinquency Prevention Administration, 1970; The Silverlake Experiment, Aldine-Atherton, 1971; Explaining Delinquency: Construction, Test, and Reformulation of a Sociological

Theory, Heath, 1971. Co-founder and associate editor, Et Al (sociology journal), 1966-70.

WORK IN PROGRESS: With Empey, Delinquency and Official Response; Dynamic Self Analysis; Theory Construction in Sociology.

AVOCATIONAL INTERESTS: Painting, photography, tennis, music, reading.†

* * *

LUBIS, Mochtar 1922-

PERSONAL: Born March 7, 1922, in Padang, Sumatra; son of Raja Pandapotan (a district commissioner) and Siti Madinah; married Siti Halimah, July 1, 1945; children: Indrawan, Arman, Yana Zamira. Education: Studied at School of Economics, Kayutanam, Indonesia. Religion: Islam. Home: 17 Jalan Bonang, Djakarta III/24, Indonesia. Office: Indoconsult Associates, 11 Medan Merdeka Timur, Djakarta, Indonesia.

CAREER: Indonesia Raya (daily), Djakarta, Indonesia, publisher and editor, 1950—; Indoconsult Associates, Djakarta, chairman, 1969—. Chairman, Indonesia Foundation, 1968—; president, Press Foundation of Asia. Member: International Press Insitute (director), International Association for Cultural Freedom (board member), Insitute for Science of Indonesia, Press Council of Indonesia, Djakarta Academy. Awards, honors: Indonesian National Award for the Novel, National Culture Council, 1954, for Djalan tak ada Udjung; co-winner of Ramon Magsaysay Foundation award for journalism and literature, the Philippines, August, 1958; Journalist's Prize Award, Indonesian Journalists Association; Golden Pen of Freedom, International Federation of Publishers, 1967; Best Novel Award, Indonesia Good Books Foundation, 1976.

WRITINGS: (Editor) Tehnik mengarang (addresses, essays, and lectures on journalism), Balai Pustaka, 1950; Pers dan Wartawan (about the press in Indonesia), Balai Pustaka, 1950, 3rd edition, 1963; Tidak ada esok (novel on the Indonesian revolution), Gapura, 1950; Indonesia dimata dunia: Dan goresan-goresan perdjalanan (on Indonesia politics and foreign relations and his travel in Europe), National Publishing House (Djakarta), c. 1950; Perkenalan di Asia Tenggara (on his travel in Asia), Gapura, 1951; Parlawatan ke Amerika Serikat (on his travels in America), Gapura, 1952; Perempuan (novel; title means "The Woman"), Timun Mas, 1956; Twilight in Djakarta, translated from the Indonesian by Clare Holt for initial publication in English, Hutchinson, 1963, Vanguard, 1964; Tanah gersang (novel; title means "The Burnt Earth"), Pembangunan, 1964; Djalan tak ada Udjung (novel on the Indonesian revolution), [Indonesia], 1964, translation by Anthony H. Johns published as A Road with No End, Hutchinson, 1968, Regnery, 1970. Also author of Tiga laporan perdjalan djurnalistik, with S. Tasuf and Roshan Anwar, 1953. A play, "Prince Wiraguna," has been published in Horison (magazine).

WORK IN PROGRESS: A new novel, Love and Death, on the Indonesian revolution for freedom; translating his prison diary into English.

SIDELIGHTS: Mochtar Lubis' prison diary dates from 1956 when he was arrested by Indonesian Military Police for editorials critical of the government and army and imprisoned without trial for several weeks. On his release he was placed under house arrest on undisclosed charges. Avocational interests: Growing orchids and roses, sailing, painting, sculpture, and ceramics.

BIOGRAPHICAL/CRITICAL SOURCES: Albert Roland, *Profiles from the New Aisa,* Macmillian, 1970.

* * *

LUCE, Don 1934-

PERSONAL: Born September 20, 1934, in East Calais, Vt.; son of Collins Andrew (a farmer) and Margaret (Sanders) Luce. *Education:* University of Vermont, B.S., 1957; Cornell University, M.S., 1958. *Religion:* Congregationalist. *Home:* East Calais, Vt. 05650.

CAREER: International Voluntary Services, director in Saigon, Vietnam, 1958-67; Cornell University, Ithaca, N.Y., research associate, 1968; World Council of Churches, Geneva, Switzerland, executive secretary, 1969; Clergy and Laity Concerned, Inc., New York, N.Y., director, 1974—.

WRITINGS: (With John Sommer) *Viet Nam: The Unheard Voices,* foreword by Edward M. Kennedy, Cornell University Press, 1969; (with Holmes Brown) *Hostages of War,* Clergy & Laity Concerned, Inc., 1973; (editor with Cora Weiss and author of afterword) Van Tien Dung, *Our Great Spring Victory,* Monthly Review Press, 1977; *Oh Freedom,* Clergy & Laity Concerned, Inc., 1977. Editor with Jacqui Chagnon, *Of Quiet Courage: Poems from the Viet War,* 1974.

BIOGRAPHICAL/CRITICAL SOURCES: Saturday Review, June 28, 1969; *New York Times Book Review,* July 20, 1969.

* * *

LUDER, William Fay 1910-

PERSONAL: Born October 19, 1910, in Caro, Mich.; son of Louis W. and Laura (Fisher) Luder; married Grace H. Farnsworth, June 14, 1937; children: Hope Elizabeth, Faith Cynthia. *Education:* Kalamazoo College, A.B., 1933; Brown University, Ph.D., 1937. *Politics:* "Jeffersonian liberal." *Religion:* Christian. *Office:* Department of Chemistry, Northeastern University, Boston, Mass. 02115.

CAREER: Northeastern University, Boston, Mass., instructor, 1937-40, assistant professor, 1940-44, associate professor, 1944-49, professor of chemistry, 1949—. Registered as pacifist conscientious objector in World War II. *Member:* Sigma Xi.

WRITINGS: (With Saverio Zuffanti) *The Electronic Theory of Acids and Bases,* Wiley, 1946, 2nd revised edition, Dover, 1961; (with Zuffanti and Arthur A. Vernon) *General Chemistry,* Saunders, 1951, 3rd edition (with Zuffanti, Vernon, and R. A. Shepard), 1965, laboratory manual (with Zuffanti and Vernon), 1965; *One Pearl of Great Price* (fiction), Farnsworth Books, 1958; *A New Approach to Sex,* Farnsworth Books, 1966; *A Different Approach to Thermodynamics,* Reinhold, 1967; *The Electron-Repulsion Theory of the Chemical Bond,* Reinhold, 1967. Author of more than sixty scientific papers; contributor to religious magazines.

WORK IN PROGRESS: Papers and an eventual book on his new theory of atomic structure; a travelog, *Adventures in Search of Roman Britain.*

SIDELIGHTS: William Luder and his wife have made trips to Rome and Israel and have visited Britain four times in researching *Adventures in Search of Roman Britain.* He writes: "My fundamental motivation is educating myself and others for everyday citizenship in the Kingdom of God here and now.... My non-chemistry articles and non-chemistry books are to that end."

AVOCATIONAL INTERESTS: Building waterfront cottages, his most recent one on St. Helena Island off South Carolina.

* * *

LUETHI, Max 1909-

PERSONAL: Born March 11, 1909, in Bern, Switzerland; son of Paul (a commercial traveler) and Marie (Ruegg) Luethi; married Toni Treppenhauer, March 27, 1937. *Education:* University of Bern, Dr.phil., 1943. *Religion:* Protestant. *Home:* Sonneggstrasse 60, Zurich, Switzerland. *Office:* University of Zurich, Zurich, Switzerland.

CAREER: Town of Zurich Toechterschule, Zurich, Switzerland, professor of German language and literature, 1936-68; University of Zurich, Zurich, professor of European folk-literature, 1968—. *Member:* International Society for Folk-Narrative Research, Internationale Vereinigung fuer Germanische Sprach-und Literaturwissenschaft.

WRITINGS: (With Hans von Greyerz, Max Moser, and Hans Sommer) *Deutschland und die Schweiz in ihren kulturellen und politischen Beziehungen waehrend der ersten Haelfte des 19. Jahrhunderts,* edited by Werner Naef, Herbert Lang & Cie, 1936; *Die Gabe im Maerchen und in der Sage: Ein Beitrag zur Wesenserfassung und Wesensscheidung der beiden Formen,* Francke, 1943; *Das europaeische Volksmaerchen: Form und Wesen,* Francke, 1947, 5th revised and enlarged edition, 1976; *Europaeische Volksmaerchen,* Manesse Verlag, 1951, 5th edition, 1976; *Shakespeares Dramen,* de Gruyter, 1957, 2nd edition, 1966; *Volksmaerchen und Volkssage,* Francke, 1961, 3rd edition, 1975; *Maerchen,* Metzler, 1962, 6th revised and enlarged edition, 1976; *Es war Einmal: Vom Wesen des Volksmaerchens,* Vandenhoeck & Ruprecht, 1962, 4th edition, 1973, translation by Lee Chadeayne and Paul Gottwald, with additions by the author and introduction and reference notes by Francis Lee Utley, published as *Once Upon a Time: On the Nature of Fairy Tales,* Ungar, 1970; *Shakespeare: Dichter des Wirklichen und des Nichtwirklichen,* Francke, 1964; (with Lutz Roehrich, George Fohrer, and Will Erich Peuckert) *Sagen und ihre Deutung,* Vandenhoeck & Ruprecht, 1965; *So leben sie noch heute: Betrachtungen zum Volksmaerchen,* Vandenhoeck & Ruprecht, 1969, 2nd edition, 1976; (with Wolfgang Clemen, Dieter Mehl, and Rudolf Stamm) *Shakespeare—Verstaendnis heute,* Vandenhoeck & Ruprecht, 1969; *Volksliteratur und Hochliteratur,* Francke, 1970; *Das Volksmaerchen als Dichtung: Aesthetik und Anthropologie,* Diederichs, 1975; (contributor) Dan Ben-Amos, editor, *Folklore Genres,* University of Texas Press, 1976; (contributor) *Folklore Today: A Festschrift for Richard M. Dorson,* Indiana University Press, 1976.

Monographs included in *Volksmaerchen und Volkssage* and *Volksliteratur und Hochliteratur* also have been published separately, and a section of the latter book was translated into English and published in *Journal of the Folklore Institute,* Indiana University, Volume IV, number 1. Other articles have been published in German journals, one in English translation in *Genre.*

WORK IN PROGRESS: Further research in the domain of folk literature; and contributions to the *Enzyklopaedie des Maerchens.*

SIDELIGHTS: Max Luethi wrote to *CA:* "Writing is a means not only to clarify observations and reflexions but to advance, to develop them, and at the same time to confront others with what we have seen, thought and felt and so to animate further investigations and reflexions, perhaps even to influence behaviour. One side of the anthropology present in Shakespeare's plays as well as in those of other Elizabethans and in folktales impressed me particularly: Man is permanently in danger of harming himself, of losing himself, of destroying himself. And: Everyone is in some way alone. But isolation is not a mere deficiency, it is, fairy tales tend to demonstrate this in their own peculiar way, also a chance. Man is free to communicate, to come in contact with all kinds of helpers, partners and antagonists, to accept their faith and to react upon their attacks. Isolation is a condition for communication. The portrait of a man contained in Shakespeare's works and in folktales may help us to find our own way."

* * *

LUGO, James O. 1928-

PERSONAL: Born June 5, 1928, in Santiago, Dominican Republic; son of Fred (a businessman) and Lillian (Perez) Lugo; married Maria Elisa Campillo, July 26, 1952; children: James, Anthony, John. *Education:* Attended City College (now City College of the City University of New York), 1947-50; University of California, Los Angeles, B.A., 1951, M.A., 1958; University of Southern California, Ph.D., 1970. *Religion:* Roman Catholic. *Home:* 1409 Kensington Dr., Fullerton, Calif. 92631. *Office:* Department of Psychology, Fullerton College, Fullerton, Calif. 92634.

CAREER: University of California, Los Angeles, Fernald School, reading instructor, 1953-58; Camarillo State Hospital, Camarillo, Calif., intern in psychology, 1956-57; director of reading at Taft High School and Taft College, Taft, Calif., 1958-61; Fullerton College, Fullerton, Calif., instructor in psychology, 1961—. Co-director, Educational and Psychological Associates (school consultants); research project director, Galton Institute. *Military service:* U.S. Army, 1951-53. *Member:* International Reading Association, American Psychological Association. *Awards, honors:* Grants from Rosenberg Foundation, through Galton Institute, for bilingual research.

WRITINGS: (With Frieda Libaw and William Kimbal) *The Lingua Plan* (monograph), Galton Institute, 1968; (editor with Gerald L. Hershey) *Problems of Teaching at the Two-Year College* (monograph), Macmillan, 1970; (with Hershey) *Living Psychology: An Experiential Approach to Behavior,* with teacher's manual and student workbook, Macmillan, 1970, 2nd edition published as *Living Psychology: Research in Action,* 1976; (with Hershey) *Human Development: A Multidisciplinary Approach to the Psychology of Individual Growth,* Macmillan, 1974.

* * *

LUKACS, Gyorgy 1885-1971

April 13, 1885—June 4, 1971; Hungarian philosopher, Marxist, and critic. Obituaries: *New York Times,* June 5, 1971; *Time,* June 14, 1971; *Antiquarian Bookman,* July 19-26, 1971.

* * *

LUMIAN, Norman C. 1928-

PERSONAL: Born January 5, 1928, in Boston, Mass.; son of Barrett (a dentist) and Florence (Luchnik) Lumian; married Geraldine Irene Richmond (a teacher), September 17, 1950; children: David, Jonathan. *Education:* University of New Hampshire, B.A., 1951; Harvard University, A.M.T., 1953. *Home:* 2016 Tustin Ave., Newport Beach, Calif.

92660. *Office:* Department of History, Orange Coast College, Costa Mesa, Calif. 92626.

CAREER: Orange Coast College, Costa Mesa, Calif., instructor, 1959-66, assistant professor, 1966-68, associate professor of history, 1970—. Fulbright consultant to Nigerian Ministry of Education, 1963-64. *Military service:* U.S. Marine Corps, 1946-47, 1951-52. *Member:* American Historical Association, California Teachers' Association.

WRITINGS—All published by Orange Coast College, except as indicated: *Living America,* with student's manual and instructor's manual, Van Nostrand, 1970; *The Louisiana Purchase,* 1970; *The Monroe Doctrine,* 1970; *Laying the Political Basis of the Nation,* 1970; *Essential Concepts in Political Science,* 1973.

WORK IN PROGRESS: Research on emigration from Europe to America.

AVOCATIONAL INTERESTS: Long distance running and gardening.

* * *

LUSSU, Joyce (Salvadori) 1912-
(Joyce Salvadori)

PERSONAL: Born May 8, 1912, in Florence, Italy; daughter of Guglielmo and Giacinta (Galletti) Salvadori; married Emilio Lussu (an Italian senator and writer), June 10, 1944; children: Giovanni. *Education:* University of Heidelberg, student, 1931-32; University of Lisboa, Diplome of Portuguese Literature, 1940; Sorbonne, University of Paris, Licence es Lettres, 1941. *Home:* San Tommaso, Fermo (Ascoli Piceno), Italy.

CAREER: Writer; translator of poetry. *Wartime service:* Captain in the Italian Liberation Corps, 1943-45, received Silver Medal. *Member:* Writers Trade Union.

WRITINGS: (Under name Joyce Salvadori) *Liriche,* Ricciardi, 1939; *Fronti e frontiere: Collana della liberazione,* Edizioni U, 1945, 2nd edition, Laterza, 1967, translation by William Clowes published as *Freedom Has No Frontier,* M. Joseph, 1969; (editor) *Donne come te: Inchieste di Luciano della mea,* Edizioni Avanti, 1957; *Poesie d'amore di Nazim Hikmet,* Mondadori, 1965; *Tradurre poesia* (includes poetry translated from various languages), Mondadori, 1967; *Le Inglesi in Italia,* Lerici, 1970; (with Gianfranco Azzurro and Giuseppe Colasanti) *Storia del Fermano,* Lerici, 1970; *Padre, Padrone, Padreterno,* Mazzotta, 1976. Has translated the work of poets from Portugal, Guinea, Angola, Mozambique, Turkey, Albania, and Vietnam.

SIDELIGHTS: Joyce Lussu has traveled in Africa, Turkey, and the Middle East, searching out poets not yet known. She is chairman of the associations for cultural exchanges and friendship with China and Albania.

BIOGRAPHICAL/CRITICAL SOURCES: Spectator, August 2, 1969.

* * *

LUTHANS, Fred 1939-

PERSONAL: Born June 28, 1939, in Clinton, Iowa; son of Carl H. and Leona (Stichter) Luthans; married Katharine Meldahl, June 9, 1963; children: Kristin, Brett, Kyle, Paige. *Education:* University of Iowa, B.A., 1961, M.B.A., 1962, Ph.D., 1965. *Home:* 501 Haverford Dr., Lincoln, Neb. 68510. *Office:* College of Business, University of Nebraska, Lincoln, Neb. 68588.

CAREER: University of Iowa, Iowa City, instructor in

management, 1963-65; University of Nebraska at Lincoln, College of Business, Regents Professor of Management and assistant dean, 1967—. Consultant on government, hospitals, and industry. *Military service:* U.S. Army, member of West Point faculty, 1965-67; became captain. *Member:* Academy of Management, Midwest Business Administration Association, Lincoln Personnel Association.

WRITINGS: The Faculty Promotion Process, Bureau of Business and Economic Research, University of Iowa, 1967; (editor with Max S. Wortman, Jr.) *Emerging Concepts in Management,* Macmillan, 1969; *Cases, Readings and Review Guide for Principles of Management,* Wiley, 1969; (with Richard Hodgetts) *Social Issues in Business,* Macmillan, 1972, 2nd edition, 1977; (editor) *Contemporary Readings in Organizational Behavior,* McGraw, 1972, 2nd edition, 1977; *Organizational Behavior Modification,* Scott, Foresman, 1975; *Introduction to Management,* McGraw, 1976. Contributor of more than forty articles to professional journals.

WORK IN PROGRESS: Research on behavioral science in management and the General Contingency Theory (GCT) of management.

*   *   *

LUZZATI, Emanuele 1921-

PERSONAL: Born June 6, 1921, in Genoa, Italy; son of Guido and Fernanda Vita (Finzi) Luzzati. *Education:* Ecole des Beaux Arts, Lausanne, Switzerland, Diploma. *Religion:* Jewish. *Home:* Via Caffaro 12A, Genoa, Italy.

CAREER: Stage desinger, designer of animated cartoons, and ceramic artist, 1945—. Has done more than 150 designs for theater sets, primarily for Italian theaters, including La Scala at Milan, but also for Chicago Lyric Opera, the Glyndebourne Festival Opera in London, the English Opera Group, and for productions in Paris, Munich, and Lisbon; director as well as designer of animated cartoons he has produced in Rome, Italy; his ceramics and decorations have been commissioned for the *Leonardo da Vinci* and other Italian luxury liners. *Member:* Academy of Motion Picture Arts and Sciences. *Awards, honors:* Academy Award nominations for animated cartoons, 1966, for "The Thieving Magpie," and 1973, for "Pulcinella"; also honored for his work at the Bratislava Illustration Biennial, 1967.

WRITINGS—Self illustrated: (Adaptor) Giovanni Boaccaccio, *Chichibio and the Crane,* Obolensky, 1961; *I Paladini di Francia: Ovvero il tradimento di Gano Dimaganza* (title means "The Paladius of France: Or the Betrayal of Gano Dimaganza"), Mursia, 1972; *La Gaza ladra* (title means "The Thieving Magpie"), Mursia, 1964, produced as an animated cartoon, 1966; (adaptor) *Ali Baba e i quaranta ladroni,* Emme Edizioni, 1968, translation by Robert Mann published as *Ali Baba and the Forty Thieves,* Pantheon, 1969; (adaptor from a medieval puppet show) *Ronald and the Wizard Calico,* Hutchinson, 1969; *Bimbo Recita,* Emme Edizioni, 1973; *C'Erano 3 Fratelli,* Emme Edizioni, 1977.

Illustrator: Gianni Rodari, *Castello di carte,* Mursia, 1963; William Ivan Martin, *When It Rains . . . It Rains,* Holt, 1970; Martin, *Whistle, Mary, Whistle,* Holt, 1970; *Pulcinella,* Emme Edizioni, 1971, translation published as *Punch and the Magic Fish,* Pantheon, 1972; *The Magic Flute,* Basil Blackwell, 1971; *Iviaggi of Marco Polo,* Emme Edizioni, 1972; *Luccellin bel Verde* (Italian tales), Edizioni Einaudi, 1972; *Bimbo Recita,* Emme Edizioni, 1973; *Il Principe granchio* (Italian tales), Edizioni Einaudi, 1974; *Italian Folk Tales,* Dent, 1975; *The Travels of Marco Polo,* Dent, 1975; *Gli Uomini del libro,* Adelphi, 1975.

BIOGRAPHICAL/CRITICAL SOURCES: Times Literary Supplement, October 16, 1969.

*   *   *

LYMAN, Stanford M(orris) 1933-

PERSONAL: Born June 10, 1933, in San Francisco, Calif.; son of Arthur H. (a grocer) and Gertrude (Kramer) Lyman. *Education:* University of California, Berkeley, A.B., 1955, M.A., 1957, Ph.D., 1961. *Politics:* Democrat. *Religion:* Jewish. *Home:* 60 East Eighth St., 29N, New York, N.Y. 10003. *Office:* Department of Sociology, New School for Social Research, 66 West 12th St., New York, N.Y. 10011.

CAREER: University of British Columbia, Vancouver, instructor, 1960-62, assistant professor of sociology, 1962-63; University of California Extension, Berkeley, associate professor and head of liberal arts department, 1963-64; Sonoma State College (now California State College, Sonoma), Rohnert Park, associate professor of sociology and chairman of department, 1964-68; University of Nevada at Reno, 1968-70, began as associate professor, became professor of sociology; University of California, San Diego, associate professor of sociology, 1970-72; New School for Social Research, New York, N.Y., professor of political and social science and chairman of department of sociology, 1972—. Lecturer in Southeast Asia for United States Information Service, 1975. Senior member, Linacre College, Oxford University, 1975. *Member:* American Sociological Association, Chinese American Historical Society, Center for Japanese American Studies, Society for the Study of Symbolic Interaction, Eastern Sociological Society, Phi Beta Kappa.

WRITINGS: (With Marvin B. Scott) *Sociology of the Absurd,* Appleton, 1970; (with Scott) *The Revolt of the Students,* C. E. Merrill, 1970; *The Asian in the West,* Desert Research Institute, University of Nevada, 1970; *The Black American in Sociological Thought: A Failure of Perspective,* edited by Herbert Hill, Putnam, 1972; *Chinese Americans,* Random House, 1974; (with Scott) *The Drama of Social Reality,* Oxford University Press, 1975; (editor with Richard Harvey Brown) *Structure, Consciousness and History,* Cambridge University Press, 1977. Advisory editor, *Pacific Sociological Review.*

WORK IN PROGRESS: With Marvin B. Scott, *The Seven Deadly Sins,* for St. Martin's; *The Asian in North America,* for American Bibliographic Center-Clio Press; editing *Asia in America: Stewart Culin's Essays.*

*   *   *

LYNCH, Lorenzo 1932-

PERSONAL: Born May 27, 1932, in Bessemer, Ala.; son of Ollie (a railroad worker) and Clara (Oliver) Lynch; married Catherine Lockett, November, 1956; children: Walter, Christopher, Andrew, Eyvette, Angela. *Education:* Took correspondence course from Art Instruction, Inc., Minneapolis, 1946-50; attended Art Students League, New York, 1950, and School of Visual Arts, New York, 1956-60. *Home and office:* 99 Powell St., Brooklyn, N.Y. 11212.

CAREER: Fisher Advertising, Brooklyn, N.Y., staff artist, 1961-65; Olivetti & Underwood, New York City, staff artist, 1966-67; Martins Department Store, Brooklyn, production manager, 1967-68; Annivette Studios (art and advertising), New York City, owner and artist, 1968-74. *Military service:* U.S. Army, 1953-55.

WRITINGS: (Self-illustrated) *The Hot Dog Man* (juvenile), Bobbs-Merrill, 1970.

Illustrator: James Holding, *A Bottle of Pop*, Putnam, 1972; C. E. Palmer, *Baba and Mr. Big*, Bobbs-Merrill, 1972; Phylis Green, *The Fastest Quitter in Town*, Addison-Wesley, 1972; Melba Miller, *The Black Is Beautiful Beauty Book*, Prentice-Hall, 1974; Arnold Adoff, *Big Sister Tells Me That I'm Black*, Holt, 1976.

WORK IN PROGRESS: A junior book, *The Coming Together.*

SIDELIGHTS: Lynch told *CA:* "I've always been interested in writing since reading Richard Wright's *Black Boy* when I was a child. I feel that writing, art and acting are very much in tune with each other. Also, the nourishment of a child's mind is the most important endeavor [in] which we can engage."

*   *   *

LYNCH, Owen M(artin) 1931-

PERSONAL: Born January 4, 1931, in New York, N.Y.; son of John Sylvester and Mary E. (O'Neill) Lynch. *Education:* Fordham University, A.B., 1956; Columbia University, Ph.D., 1966. *Politics:* None. *Religion:* None. *Office:* Department of Anthropology, New York University, New York, N.Y. 10003.

CAREER: State University of New York at Binghamton, 1966-71, began as assistant professor, became associate professor of anthropology; New York University, New York, N.Y., Charles F. Noyes Professor of Urban Anthropology, 1972—. *Member:* American Anthropological Association (fellow), American Ethnological Association, Royal Anthropological Institute of Great Britain and Ireland. *Awards, honors:* American Council of Learned Societies research grant, 1970; American Institute of Indian Studies grant, 1970.

WRITINGS: (Contributor) *India and Ceylon: Unity and Diversity*, Oxford University Press, 1967; *The Politics of Untouchability: Social Mobility and Social Change in a City of India*, Columbia University Press, 1969; (contributor) J. M. Mahar, editor, *The Untouchables in Contemporary India*, University of Arizona Press, 1972; (contributor) *Aspects of Political Mobilization in South Asia*, Syracuse University Press, 1976; (contributor) Kenneth David, editor, *The New Wind: Changing Identities in South Asia*, Aldine, 1977.

WORK IN PROGRESS: A study of a squatters' settlement in a city of India.

*   *   *

LYND, Robert S. 1892-1970

September 26, 1892—November 1, 1970; American sociologist and author. Obituaries: *New York Times*, November 3, 1970; *Washington Post*, November 3, 1970; *Time*, November 16, 1970.

*   *   *

LYONS, Arthur (Jr.) 1946-

PERSONAL: Born January 5, 1946, in Los Angeles, Calif.; son of Arthur and Shirley (Hamilton) Lyons. *Education:* University of California, Santa Barbara, B.A., 1967. *Residence:* Palm Springs, Calif.

CAREER: Proprietor of a restaurant and gift shop in Palm Springs, Calif., 1967—.

WRITINGS: The Second Coming: Satanism in America, Dodd, 1970; *The Dead Are Discreet*, Mason/Charter, 1974;

All God's Children, Mason/Charter, 1975; *The Killing Floor*, Mason/Charter, 1976.

WORK IN PROGRESS: You Kill the Body and the Head Dies, for Quadrangle.

*   *   *

LYONS, F(rancis) S(tewart) L(eland) 1923-

PERSONAL: Born November 11, 1923, in Londonderry, Northern Ireland; son of Stewart and May (Leland) Lyons; married Jennifer McAlister, April 2, 1954; children: John, Nicholas. *Education:* Trinity College, Dublin, B.A., 1945, Ph.D., 1947, M.A., 1951. *Religion:* Anglican (Church of Ireland). *Agent:* Michael Sissons, A. D. Peters & Co., 10 Buckingham St., London WC2N 6BU, England. *Office:* Provost's House, Trinity College, University of Dublin, Dublin, Ireland.

CAREER: University of Hull, Hull, England, lecturer in history, 1947-51; University of Dublin, Trinity College, Dublin, Ireland, fellow, 1951-64; University of Kent, Canterbury, England, professor of modern history, 1964-74, master of Eliot College, 1969-72; University of Dublin, Trinity College, provost, 1974—. *Member:* British Academy (fellow), Royal Irish Academy, Royal Historical Society (fellow). *Awards, honors:* Litt.D., Trinity College, University of Dublin, 1966; D.Litt., University of Pennsylvania, 1975.

WRITINGS: The Irish Parliamentary Party 1890-1910, Faber, 1951; *The Fall of Parnell, 1890-1891*, University of Toronto Press, 1960; *Internationalism in Europe, 1815-1914*, Humanities, 1963; *John Dillon: A Biography*, Routledge & Kegan Paul, 1968, University of Chicago Press, 1969; *Ireland since the Famine*, Scribner, 1971; *Charles Stewart Parnell*, Oxford University Press, 1977.

WORK IN PROGRESS: Ford lectures to be given at Oxford University, 1978; a book on the life of W. B. Yeats, for Oxford University Press.

BIOGRAPHICAL/CRITICAL SOURCES: New Statesman, November 22, 1968; *Spectator*, December 13, 1968; *Observer*, May 9, 1971.

*   *   *

LYONS, John T. 1926-

PERSONAL: Born January 13, 1926, in New York, N.Y.; son of John S. (a salesman) and Mary (Aylward) Lyons; married Margaret Hamilla, January 24, 1959; children: Nancy, John K. *Education:* St. Charles College (now St. Mary's Seminary and University), Catonsville, Md., student, 1943-45; St. Paul's College, Washington, D.C., A.B., M.A., 1951; St. John's University, Jamaica, N.Y., J.D., 1955. *Religion:* Roman Catholic.

CAREER: Employee of First National City Bank, New York City, and City Bank Farmers Trust Co., 1951-59; Schroder Trust Co., New York City, beginning 1959, began as trust officer, later vice-president.

WRITINGS: (Editor) *Personal Financial Planning for Executives*, American Management Association, 1969.††

*   *   *

LY-QUI, Chung 1940-

PERSONAL: Born September 1, 1940, in Mytho, Vietnam; son of Phat and Guong (Le Kiem) Ly-Qui; married Nguyen Thi Quynh Nga, April 4, 1962; children: Hung, Dung, Trung, Kim-Trinh, Chanh. *Education:* National Institute of

Administration, student, 1962. *Politics:* "Leader of 'People's Bloc' in Lower House." *Religion:* "Ancestors Culte." *Home and office:* 13 Place Lam-Son, Saigon, South Vietnam.

CAREER: National Constituent Assembly, Saigon, South Vietnam, deputy and leader of Restoration Bloc, 1967-68, deputy of Lower House, beginning 1968, leader of People's Bloc, 1968-69; *Voice of the People,* Saigon, editor and publisher, 1969-70; *Dien Tin Daily News,* Saigon, editor, beginning 1970. Adviser, Confederation of Labor. *Member:* Vietnam Council on Foreign Relations (founding member).

WRITINGS: (Editor) *Between Two Fires: The Unheard Voices of Vietnam,* introduction by Frances FitzGerald, Praeger, 1970. Contributor to *Voice of the People, Tin Sang Daily News.*

WORK IN PROGRESS: American Advisers at Vietnam.†

* * *

LYTTON-SELLS, Iris (Esther) 1903-

PERSONAL: Born October 29, 1903, in Adelaide, Australia; daughter of Frederick (a newspaper editor) and Clara (Jagoe) Robertson; married Arthur L. Lytton-Sells (a professor of Romance languages and author), September 2, 1929; children: Christopher Cedric. *Education:* University of Adelaide, M.A., 1925; Sorbonne, University of Paris, Diplome du Cours de Civilisation, 1926, Diplome l'Ecole de Preparation des professeurs de francais a l'etranger, 1927; Newnham College, Cambridge, philosophy course. *Politics:* Conservative. *Religion:* Church of England. *Home:* Dunster House, The Avenue, Durham, England.

CAREER: Training College, Darlington, England, lecturer in French, 1933-38; University of Durham, Durham, England, lecturer in French, 1940-44.

WRITINGS: (Editor) *Manual of French Translation and Composition for Advanced Students,* Oxford University Press, 1934, key to manual (with husband, Arthur Lytton-Sells), 1937; *Matthew Arnold and France: The Poet,* Macmillan, 1935, revised and enlarged edition, Octagon, 1970; (translator from the French) Emile Mireaux, *Daily Life in the Time of Homer,* Allen & Unwin, 1959; (with A. Lytton-Sells) *Oliver Goldsmith: His Life & Works,* Barnes & Noble, 1975. Also collaborator with husband on *Thomas Gray,* in press. Contributor to language journals.

WORK IN PROGRESS: A book on Matthew Arnold, as critic, and France.

AVOCATIONAL INTERESTS: Science (formerly specialist in crystallography), music, philosophy.

* * *

MAAS, Jeremy 1928-

PERSONAL: Born August 31, 1928, in Penang, Malaya; son of Henry Oscar (a businessman) and Marjorie (Pope) Maas; married Antonia Armstrong Willis, November 10, 1956; children: Athena, Rupert, Jonathan. *Education:* Pembroke College, Oxford, M.A. (honors), 1952. *Religion:* Church of England. *Home:* 10 Montpelier Row, Twickenham, Middlesex, England. *Office:* Maas Gallery, 15A Clifford St., London W.1, England.

CAREER: Advertising and printing executive in London, England, 1952-58; art auctioneer, London, 1958-60; Maas Gallery, London, owner, 1960—. *Military service:* British Army, national service; became second lieutenant. *Member:* Society of Authors, Society of London Art Dealers.

WRITINGS: Victorian Painters, Putnam, 1969; *Gambart: Prince of the Victorian Art World,* Barrie & Jenkins, 1976; *The Prince of Wales's Wedding,* Cameron & Taylem, 1977. Contributor to *Times Literary Supplement, Punch, Arts Review, Connoisseur, Queen,* and other publications.

WORK IN PROGRESS: Research on aspects of Victorian painting for several books.

BIOGRAPHICAL/CRITICAL SOURCES: Spectator, September 6, 1969; *Vogue,* March 1, 1970; *Harper's,* April, 1970.

* * *

MAAS, Willard 1911-1971

June 24, 1911—January 2, 1971; American poet and pioneer film maker. Obituaries: *New York Times,* January 13, 1971; *Variety,* January 20, 1971. (See index for *CA* sketch)

* * *

MABBETT, I(an) W(illiam) 1939-

PERSONAL: Born April 27, 1939, in London, England; son of F. W. (a Royal Air Force officer) and P. M. (Mack) Mabbett; married Jacqueline Towns, December 11, 1971. *Education:* Oxford University, B.A. (honors), 1960, D.Phil., 1963. *Politics:* Liberal. *Religion:* Church of England. *Home:* Serendipity, Tremont, Victoria 3785, Australia. *Office:* Department of History, Monash University, Clayton, Victoria 3168, Australia.

CAREER: Thanet Technical College, Ramsgate, Kent, England, assistant lecturer in English, 1963-64; Monash University, Clayton, Victoria, Australia, lecturer, 1965-71, senior lecturer in history, 1972—. *Member:* South Asian Studies Association, Australian Society of Authors.

WRITINGS: A Short History of India, Cassell, 1968, Praeger, 1969; (contributor) S. Ray, editor, *Gandhi, India and the World,* Temple University Press, 1970; *Truth, Myth, and Politics in Ancient India,* Thomson (Delhi), 1971. Contributor to journals of Asian studies.

WORK IN PROGRESS: Research on the history of Buddhism.

SIDELIGHTS: I. W. Mabbett completed his doctoral dissertation on Sanskrit. He has made extended visits to Southeast Asia, Hong Kong, and India. *Avocational interests:* Indian cookery.

* * *

MABLEY, Edward (Howe) 1906-
(John Ware)

PERSONAL: Born March 7, 1906, in Binghamton, N.Y.; son of Clarence Ware (a film technician) and Mabelle (a musician; maiden name Howe) Mabley. *Education:* Attended Wayne University (now Wayne State University), 1923. *Residence:* New York, N.Y. *Agent:* Robert Freedman, Brandt & Brandt Dramatic Dept., 101 Park Ave., New York, N.Y. 10017.

CAREER: Worked in various theatrical enterprises in Detroit, Mich., and Cleveland, Ohio, 1923-37; research writer for industrial designer Walter Dorwin Teague, New York City, 1937-42; U.S. Navy civilian employee, New York City, 1944-45; free-lance writer and director, New York City, 1945-52; instructor in playwriting under John Gassner at Dramatic Workshop, New School for Social Research, New York City, 1946-49; television director for Columbia Broadcasting System, Inc., 1952-69, and National Broadcasting Company, Inc., 1969; playwriting instructor at New School for Social Research, 1960—. Village of Pomona, N.Y., trustee and deputy mayor, 1967-71, mayor, 1971-73. *Military service:* U.S. Army, Signal Corps, 1942-43; became sergeant. *Member:* Dramatists Guild, American Society of Composers, Authors and Publishers, Writers Guild of America, Directors Guild of America. *Awards, honors:* Naval Ordnance Development Award for exceptional service, 1945; National Theatre Conference fellowships in playwriting, 1947 and 1948.

WRITINGS—Books: *The Motor Balloon "America"* (account of the first attempt, in 1910, to fly the Atlantic), Stephen Greene Press, 1969; *Dramatic Construction,* Chilton, 1972.

Plays: (With Leonard Mins) "Temper the Wind," first produced on Broadway at Playhouse Theatre, December 27, 1946; *Discrimination for Everybody* (adaptation for stage of his radio play, "Created Equal"), Samuel French, 1948; (under pseudonym John Ware, with Dorothy Evans) *June Dawn* (three-act comedy), Samuel French, 1949; (under pseudonym John Ware, with Graham) *Spring Journey,* Samuel French, 1950; *Glad Tidings* (originally entitled "All About Love"; first produced in Somerset, Mass., at Somerset Playhouse, June 3, 1951; produced on Broadway at Lyceum Theatre, October 11, 1951), Samuel French, 1952; (with Joanna Roos) "Red Sky at Morning," first produced in Olney, Md. at Olney Theatre, 1953.

Musical plays; text and lyrics: *The Mermaid in Lock No. 7* (jazz opera; first performed in Pittsburgh by American Wind Symphony, 1958), music by Elie Siegmeister, Henmar Press, 1958; "Dublin Song" (selections from "The Plough and the Stars"; also see below), first performed at Washington University, St. Louis, Mo., May 15, 1963; *Dick Whittington and His Cat* (symphonic story for narrator and orchestra; first performed in Philadelphia by Philadelphia Orchestra, 1967), MCA Music, 1968; *I Have a Dream* (cantata based on speech by Martin Luther King; first performed in United States, 1967), music by Siegmeister, MCA Music, 1968; "The Plough and the Stars"(grand opera based on Sean O'Casey's play of same title; originally written as musical drama), first performed in United States, 1969, music by Siegmeister; "Night of the Moonspell" (grand opera), first performed in Shreveport, La., November 14, 1976, music by Siegmeister; "Bon Voyage" (musical version of 1860 Labiche comedy, "Le Voyage de Monsieur Perrichon"), first performed in Woodstock, N.Y., August, 1977, music by Vera Brodsky.

Author of more than seventy-five produced plays for radio and television, including: "Created Equal" (radio play), broadcast by CBS, December 8, 1947; (adaptor) Sidney Howard's "The Silver Cord," broadcast by CBS-TV in 1949; (adaptor) J. B. Priestley's "Laburnum Grove," broadcast by CBS-TV in 1949; (with Joanna Roos) *Borderline of Fear* (teleplay broadcast by CBS-TV for "Danger," November 1, 1950; radio version beamed behind Iron Curtain by U.S. State Department over Station RIAS, Berlin. c. 1951), published in *The Best Television Plays, 1950-51,* edited by William Irving Kaufman, Merlin Press, 1952; (author of book) "The Box Supper" (original television musical), music by Otis Clements, broadcast by CBS-TV in 1950; (author of book) "Jasper" (original television musical), music by Clements, broadcast by NBC-TV in 1950; "The Woman at High Hollow," broadcast by NBC-TV in 1958. Author, with Ruth Friedlich, of "The O'Neill's," a family situation comedy on the Dumont Television Network, 1949-50. Also author of several industrial shows and motion picture

scripts, including "A Thousand Times Neigh" for Ford Motor Company's ballet at the New York World's Fair in 1940.

WORK IN PROGRESS: Two musical plays, *The Ascent of George W. Twitchell* and *Lysistrata.*

*   *   *

MACAROV, David 1918-

PERSONAL: Born November 20, 1918, in Savannah, Ga.; son of Isaac (a manufacturer) and Fannie (Schoenberg) Macarov; married Frieda Rabinowitz (a registered nurse), December 5, 1946; children: Varda, Frances, Raanan, Annette. *Education:* University of Pittsburgh, B.Sc., 1951; Western Reserve University (now Case Western Reserve University), M.Sc., 1954; Brandeis University, Ph.D., 1968. *Religion:* Jewish. *Home:* Nayot 8, Jerusalem, Israel. *Office:* School of Social Work, Hebrew University, Jerusalem, Israel.

CAREER: Hebrew University of Jerusalem, Paul Baerwald School of Social Work, Jerusalem, Israel, senior lecturer of social welfare and planning, 1959—, director, Joseph J. Schwartz Graduate Program for Training Directors and Senior Personnel for Community Centers, 1970-75. Visiting professor at Adelphi University, 1975-77, and University of Melbourne, 1977. *Military service:* U.S. Army Air Forces, 1942-45; served in China and Burma; received Distinguished Unit Citation and battle cluster. Israel Defence Forces, 1947-49; became squadron leader. *Member:* National Association of Social Workers, American Council on Social Work, National Conference of Jewish Communal Service, International Association of Social Workers, Council on Social Work Education, International Association for Social Economics (board member), Society for Human Development, Industrial Relations Research Association.

WRITINGS: Incentives to Work: The Effects of Unearned Income, Jossey-Bass, 1970; *The Short Course in Development Training,* Massadah, 1973; (contributor) D. Thursz and J. L. Vigilante, editors, *Meeting Human Needs: An Overview of Nine Countries,* Sage Publications, Volume I, 1975, Volume II, 1977; *Administration in the Social Work Curriculum,* Council on Social Work Education, 1976; *The Design of Social Welfare,* Praeger, in press.

*   *   *

MacCRACKEN, Henry Noble 1880-1970

November 19, 1880—May 7, 1970; American educator and historian. Obituaries: *New York Times,* May 8, 1970; *Washington Post,* May 9, 1970. (See index for *CA* sketch)

*   *   *

MACDONALD, Dwight 1906-

PERSONAL: Born March 24, 1906, in New York, N.Y.; son of Dwight (a lawyer) and Alice (Hedges) Macdonald; married Nancy Rodman, about 1935 (divorced); married Gloria Kaufman, about 1950; children: (first marriage) Michael Cary Dwight, Nicholas Gardner. *Education:* Yale University, B.A., 1928. *Politics:* "Conservative anarchist." *Religion:* None. *Home:* 56 East 87th St., New York, N.Y. 10028.

CAREER: Fortune Magazine, New York City, staff writer, 1929-36; *Partisan Review,* New York City, editor, 1938-43; *Politics,* New York City, editor and publisher, 1944-49; *New Yorker,* New York City, staff writer, 1951-66; *Esquire,* New York City, film critic, 1960-66, political columnist, 1966-68.

Visiting professor, University of Texas, 1966, University of California at Santa Cruz, 1969, University of Wisconsin—Milwaukee, 1970, University of Massachusetts, Amherst, 1971, State University of New York at Buffalo, 1973-74, and John Jay College of Criminal Justice of the City University of New York, 1974-76. Chairman, Spanish Refugee Aid, beginning 1968. *Member:* National Institute of Arts and Letters. *Awards, honors:* Guggenheim fellow, 1962; Litt.D., Wesleyan University, 1964.

WRITINGS: The Root Is Man: Two Essays in Politics, Cunningham Press, 1953; *Henry Wallace, the Man and the Myth,* Vanguard, 1948; *The Ford Foundation: The Men and the Millions,* Reynal, 1956; *Memoirs of a Revolutionist: Essays in Political Criticism,* Farrar, Straus, 1957; (editor) *Parodies: An Anthology from Chaucer to Beerbohm and After,* Random House, 1960; *Masscult and Midcult,* Partisan Review, 1961; *Our Invisible Poor* (originally published in *New Yorker*), Sidney Hillman Foundation, c. 1962; *Against the American Grain,* Random House, 1962; (compiler) *The Poems of Edgar Allan Poe,* Crowell, 1965; *Dwight Macdonald on Movies,* Prentice-Hall, 1969; *Politics Past,* Grossman, 1969; (editor) *My Past and Thoughts: The Memoirs of Alexander Herzen,* Knopf, 1973; *Discriminations,* Grossman, 1974. Also author of introduction, *The Tales of Hoffman,* edited by Mark L. Levine, George C. McNamee, and Daniel Greenberg. Contributor to many periodicals, including *Encounter, Symposium, Commentary, Partisan Review, Politics, Diogenes, New York Review of Books, Esquire, New Yorker, New International,* and *Nation.*

SIDELIGHTS: Respected as a critic both in the U.S. and abroad, Dwight Macdonald has undergone a variety of political stances since his journalistic career began in 1929. He once remarked, "The speed with which I evolved from a liberal into a radical and from a tepid Communist sympathizer into an ardent anti-Stalinist still amazes me." In 1944 he started his own political periodical, *Politics,* a publication in which he wished "to create a center of consciousness on the Left, welcoming all varieties of radical thought. . . ." Among the contributors were Albert Camus, Victor Serge, Simone Weil, Nicolo Tucci, C. Wright Mills, Bruno Bettelheim, Paul Goodman, James Agee, John Berryman, Meyer Schapiro, Mary McCarthy, and Daniel Bell. Hannah Arendt later said of *Politics,* "For if this was a one-man magazine, it was never the magazine of one man's opinion, not only because of the great generosity and hospitality which made it possible for many voices and viewpoints to have their say but, more importantly, because the editor himself never was a one-opinion man or, perhaps, had ceased to be opinionated when he felt the need to have a magazine of his own."

Most of Macdonald's fellow critics have found his work appealing both in content and style. A. C. Ames describes Macdonald's work as "both a treat and a treatment. He is so funny and so clever that he is a joy to read on any subject whatever. But he has found the incongruities on which his humor feeds in some of the most important political figures of our time." Others, like Benjamin DeMott, although they find weaknesses in his prose, appreciate Macdonald's skill in expressing his opinions. "As a commentator on masterpieces," DeMott says, "the author is brisk but crude. He speaks often of the critic's need for 'sensibility,' but he himself offers Midcult substitutes for the real thing. . . . [However], the issues Macdonald raises are not bogus issues. . . . Less than the sage that his current tone indicates he aspires to be, livelier than dozens of writers in the coherent English literary world that he extravagantly admires,

this critic stands forth at his best as a keen, effective witness against meretriciousness, and, as such, an invaluable literary man." Charles Rolo agrees, "While his reasoning strikes me as frequently fallacious, perverse, or merely a matter of hair splitting, his writing is an unfailing delight; he is quite possibly the wittiest and liveliest polemicist on the American scene."

AVOCATIONAL INTERESTS: Reading, talking, brooding.

BIOGRAPHICAL/CRITICAL SOURCES: New Yorker, February 21, 1948, May 20, 1956, September 28, 1957, September 16, 1961; *New York Times,* February 22, 1948, September 22, 1957, August 26, 1969, March 12, 1970; *New Republic,* March 1, 1948; *Nation,* March 6, 1948, April 29, 1961; *Saturday Review,* March 6, 1948, November 16, 1957, December 15, 1962; *New York Herald Tribune Book Review,* March 17, 1948; *Canadian Forum,* June, 1948; *Atlantic,* July, 1956, November, 1957, February, 1961; *Christian Science Monitor,* September 13, 1957; *Chicago Sunday Tribune,* September 15, 1957; *New York Times Book Review,* December 25, 1960, July 16, 1969, September 21, 1969; *Time,* January 13, 1961; *New York Herald Tribune Lively Arts,* February 5, 1961; *New Statesman,* November 24, 1961; *Times Literary Supplement,* November 24, 1961; *Spectator,* December 22, 1961; *Commonweal,* December 28, 1962, October 17, 1969; *Harper's,* January, 1963; *Yale Review,* March, 1963; *New York Review of Books,* August 1, 1968; *Esquire,* August, 1969; *Book World,* August 17, 1969; *Newsday,* September 13, 1969; *New Leader,* September 15, 1969; *Antioch Review,* spring, 1971.

*   *   *

MacDOUGALL, Mary Katherine

PERSONAL: Born in Mount Auburn, Ill.; daughter of F. D. (a newspaper editor and publisher) and Kitty May (Alexander) Slate; married Wayne Fox McMeans (deceased); married Harold Alexander MacDougall (deceased); children: (first marriage) David, Nancy MacDougall Richey; (second marriage) Alexander, Kent, Alan Ross. *Education:* Alma College, student, one year; University of Michigan, B.A. and graduate study; University of Texas, graduate study. *Home:* 2511 Hartford Rd., Austin, Tex. 78703.

CAREER: Former teacher in secondary schools and at University of Texas, editor of trade journal, and member of editorial staff of newspapers in Port Huron, Mich., Abilene, Tex., and Austin, Tex.; currently national lecturer.

WRITINGS: Black Jupiter, Broadman, 1960; *What Treasure Mapping Can Do for You,* Unity Books, 1968; *Prosperity Now,* Unity Books, 1969; *Healing Now,* Unity Books, 1970; *Making Love Happen,* Doubleday, 1970; *Happiness Now,* Unity Books, 1971. Contributor of short stories and several hundred articles to magazines.

WORK IN PROGRESS: Three books.

SIDELIGHTS: Mary Katherine MacDougall writes: "For as long as I have any memory, I have had the consistent desire: to be a channel of help to others, to learn more about God and me, and to write. . . . People are my vocation and avocation. They have seemed to be delayers but delays that come to us and that we do not instigate are always for good, for the better or for our protection in some way. . . . As teachers always learn more from teaching that the students, writers get more benefit from their writing than readers can. This is one reason why a writer should never write anything that is not helpful to his own growth and progress."

MacGREGOR, Alasdair Alpin (Douglas) 1899-1970
(Francis Featherstonehaugh)

March 20, 1899—April 15, 1970; Scottist journalist, poet, and world traveler. Obituaries: *Antiquarian Bookman*, June 1-8, 1970. (See index for *CA* sketch)

*   *   *

MACGREGOR-MORRIS, Pamela 1925-

PERSONAL: Born September 25, 1925, in London, England; daughter of William (a surgeon) and Maybelle Juliet (Mullen) Macgregor-Morris; married Rudolf Jurkschat (a stud owner and horse trainer), September 11, 1956; children: Gavin, Fiona, Angus. *Education:* Educated in Summit, N.J. *Politics:* Conservative. *Religion:* Church of England. *Home:* Stonelands, Bovey Tracey, Devonshire, England. *Agent:* Curtis Brown Ltd., 1 Craven Hill, London W2 3EW, England.

CAREER: Writer. *Times,* London, England, equestrian correspondent, 1954—.

WRITINGS: Topper, Carrington, 1947; *High Honours: The Story of an International Show-Jumper,* Witherby, 1948; *Lucky Purchase,* Gryphon Books, 1949; *Exmoor Ben,* Gryphon Books, 1950; *Blue Rosette,* Witherby, 1950; *Great Show Jumpers, Past, Present, and to Come,* Allen & Unwin, 1950; *Not Such a Bad Summer: A Story of Dartmoor,* Latimer House, 1950; *The Amateur Horse-Dealers,* Gryphon Books, 1951; *The World's Show Jumpers,* Hanover House, 1956, revised edition, Macdonald & Co., 1966, A. S. Barnes, 1967; *Chipperfields' Circus,* Faber, 1957; *Spinners of the Big Top,* Chatto & Windus, 1959; *Sawdust and Spotlight,* Witherby, 1960; *Show Jumping on Five Continents,* Heinemann, 1960; *Look at Ponies,* Hamish Hamilton, 1960; *Riding for Children,* Arthur Barker, 1961; (compiler) *Great Horse Stories,* Hill & Wang, 1961; *Clear Round,* Collins, 1962; *The Hunter,* Country Life, 1972. Co-editor of *Horse and Rider Yearbook,* 1973—.

*   *   *

MACHADO, Manuel Anthony, Jr. 1939-

PERSONAL: Born June 4, 1939, in Nogales, Ariz.; son of Manuel and Cruz (Martinez) Machado; married Marcia Elizabeth Morgan, December 28, 1959; children: Anna Maria, Paul Antonio, Travis Marcos, Alicia Catarina. *Education:* University of California, Santa Barbara, B.A., 1961, M.A., 1962, Ph.D., 1964. *Politics:* Republican. *Religion:* Episcopalian. *Home:* Star Route Potomac, Bonner, Mont. 59823. *Office:* Department of History, University of Montana, Missoula, Mont. 59801.

CAREER: State University of New York College at Plattsburgh, assistant professor of history, 1964-68; University of Dallas, Dallas, Tex., associate professor of history, 1968-69; University of Montana, Missoula, associate professor of history, 1969—. Consultant to Center for Advanced Studies in International Business, Pepperdine College. *Member:* American Historical Association, Agricultural History Society, Conference on Latin American History, Rocky Mountain Latin American Studies Association (member of executive council), International Arabian Horse Association, Montana Livestock Growers Association, Phi Alpha Theta, Sigma Delta Pi. *Awards, honors:* Organization of American States fellowship to Mexico, 1963; State University of New York grant-in-aid, 1965, and research fellowships, 1967, 1968; University of Montana research stipend, 1970; Social Science Research Council grant, for research in Mexico, 1971-72.

WRITINGS: An Industry in Crisis: Mexican-United States Cooperation in the Control of Foot-and-Mouth Disease, University of California Press, 1968; *AFTOSA: A Historical Survey of Foot-and-Mouth Disease and Inter-American Relations,* State University of New York Press, 1969; *A Personal History of the Mexican American,* Nelson-Hall, 1977. Contributor of articles and reviews to professional journals.

WORK IN PROGRESS: A book on United States-Mexican relations from 1919 to 1924; research in the Mexican cattle industry, especially after 1920.

SIDELIGHTS: Manuel Machado, Jr. writes: "For the historian, writing must remain the final expression of his thought and research. A historian who does not write may be an excellent classroom teacher, but he is incomplete as a practitioner of Clio's craft. An emphasis on good writing needs reintroduction in all college and university curricula. The field of history—be it penguins in Antarctica, the Civil War, French Revolution, or colonial Mexico—must reassert itself as the matrix discipline of both the humanities and the social sciences. It must abandon scientific sterilization and espouse instead the artful communication of a living past. History and historians lose ground because of their seeming irrelevance, a dreadful term when applied to the academic world. Yet, such a loss of territory could easily be avoided if the writers of history would make their material alive and vivid rather than reducing it to scientific equations and postulations."

*   *   *

MACHOTKA, Otakar (Richard) 1899-1970

October 29, 1899—July 29, 1970; Czech-born sociologist and government official of free Czechoslovakia. Obituaries: *New York Times,* July 30, 1970. (See index for *CA* sketch)

*   *   *

MacKAY, D(onald) I(ain) 1937-

PERSONAL: Born February 27, 1937, in Kobe, Japan; son of William and Rhona (Cooper) MacKay; married Deana Marjory Raffan, July 31, 1961; children: Deborah Jane, Paula Claire, Gregor Donald Raffan. *Education:* University of Aberdeen, M.A. (first class honors), 1959. *Home:* 14 Gamekeeper's Rd., Edinburgh, Scotland. *Office:* Department of Economics, Heriot-Watt University, Edinburgh, Scotland.

CAREER: Systems analyst for an electric company in England, 1959-62; University of Aberdeen, Aberdeen, Scotland, lecturer, 1962-66; University of Glasgow, Glasgow, Scotland, lecturer, 1966-68, senior lecturer in applied economics, 1968-71; University of Aberdeen, professor of political economy, 1971-76; Heriot-Watt University, Edinburgh, Scotland, professor of economics, 1976—.

WRITINGS: Geographical Mobility and the Brain Drain: A Case Study of Aberdeen University Graduates, G. Allen, 1969; (contributor) Derek Robinson, editor, *Local Labor Markets and Wage Structures,* Gower Press, 1970; *Labor Markets under Different Employment Conditions,* Allen & Unwin, 1971; *The Political Economy of North Sea Oil,* Martin Robertson, 1975.

AVOCATIONAL INTERESTS: Chess, bridge, all ball games, reading history and historical novels.

*   *   *

MacKAY, Donald M(acCrimmon) 1922-

PERSONAL: Born August 9, 1922, in Lybster, Scotland;

son of Henry and Janet (McHardy) MacKay; married Valerie Wood (a physicist), July 16, 1955; children: Robert, Eleanor, Janet, Margaret, David. *Education:* St. Andrew's University, B.Sc., 1943; King's College, London, Ph.D., 1951. *Religion:* Christian. *Home:* The Croft, Highway Lane, Keele, Staffordshire ST5 5AN, England. *Office:* Department of Communication, University of Keele, Keele, Staffordshire ST5 5BG, England.

CAREER: Radar researcher in the Admiralty, England, 1943-46; University of London, King's College, London, England, assistant lecturer, 1946-48, lecturer, 1948-59, reader in physics, 1959-60; University of Keele, Keele, England, Granada Research Professor of Communication, 1960—. Rockefeller fellow in United States, 1951; Eddington Lecturer, University of Cambridge, 1967; Herter Lecturer, Johns Hopkins University, 1971; Drummond Lecturer, University of Stirling, 1975; Fremantle Lecturer, Balliol College, Oxford University, 1975. *Member:* Institute of Physics, Physiological Society, Experimental Psychology Society, Electroencephalographic Society, Neurosciences Research Program.

WRITINGS: Science and Christian Faith Today, Falcon Press (London), 1960; (with Michael E. Fisher) *Analogue Computing at Ultra-High Speed: An Experimental and Theoretical Study,* Wiley, 1962; (editor) *Christianity in a Mechanistic Universe,* Inter-Varsity Fellowship (London), 1965; *Freedom of Action in a Mechanistic Universe* (Arthur Stanley Eddington Memorial Lecture 21), Cambridge University Press, 1967; *Information, Mechanism and Meaning,* Massachusetts Institute of Technology, 1969; *The Clockwork Image: A Christian Perspective on Science,* Inter-Varsity Press, 1974.

Contributor: W. Jackson, editor, *Communication Theory,* Academic Press, 1953; C. Cherry, editor, *Information Theory,* Butterworth, 1956; G. Wolstenholme, editor, *Man and His Future,* Little, Brown, 1963; J. E. Brierley, editor, *Science in its Context,* Humanities, 1964; R. W. Gerard and J. W. Duyff, editors, *Information Processing in the Nervous System,* Excerpta Medica Foundation, 1964; J. C. Eccles, editor, *Brain and Conscious Experience,* Springer-Verlag, 1966; C. Von Euler and others, editors, *Structure and Function of Inhibitory Neuronal Mechanisms,* Pergamon, 1968; F. O. Schmitt, editor, *The Neurosciences,* Rockefeller University Press, 1970; R. A. Hinde, editor, *Non-Verbal Communication,* Cambridge University Press, 1972; R. Jung, editor, *Handbook of Sensory Physiology,* Volumes VII/3A-VII/3B, Springer-Verlag, 1973.

Contributor to *Encyclopaedia Italiana;* contributor of numerous papers to scientific and philosophical journals and symposium volumes. Joint editor, *Experimental Brain Research;* member of editorial board, *Handbook of Sensory Physiology,* Springer-Verlag, 1971—.

WORK IN PROGRESS: Books on brain research and the mind-brain relationship.

SIDELIGHTS: Donald M. MacKay told *CA:* "Most of my writing is scientific and technical, but because brain research is so often misunderstood as some kind of threat to human dignity and moral and religious values, I have felt an obligation to write also on its philosophical implications (and nonimplications). I believe that the re-integration of science and Christian faith is not just possible but long over-due."

*   *   *

MACKELWORTH, R(onald) W(alter) 1930-

PERSONAL: Born April 7, 1930, in London, England; son

of William James (a company director) and Lillian (Andrews) Mackelworth; married Shiela Elizabeth Kilpatrick, June 1, 1957; children: David William, Siona Elizabeth, Mhairi Elizabeth. *Education:* Attended secondary school in England, 1940-48. *Politics:* Conservative ("with reservations"). *Religion:* Protestant. *Home:* 3, Glendale, Rowlands Castle, Hampshire, England. *Agent:* E. J. Carnell Agency, 17 Burwash Rd., London SE18 7QY, England. *Office:* Legal & General, Kings House, Kings Rd., Portsmouth, Hampshire, England.

CAREER: Employed by Thomas Cook (travel agency) in London, England, 1950; Legal & General (insurance establishment), employed as inspector in London, 1951-66, sales manager in Leeds, England, 1966-72, sales manager in Portsmouth, England, 1972—. *Military service:* British Army, Intelligence, 1948-50; became sergeant. Territorial Army, Intelligence, 1953-57. *Member:* Chartered Insurance Institute, Institute of Sales Management (fellow), Intelligence Corps Comrades Association, Spur Rugby Football Club.

WRITINGS: Firemantle (novel), R. Hale, 1968, published as *The Diabols,* Paperback Library, 1969; *Tiltangle* (novel), Ballantine, 1970; *Starflight 3000* (novel), Ballantine, 1972; *Year of the Painted World,* R. Hale, 1975. Contributor of about thirty short stories to periodicals, some of them anthologized; also contributor to business journals.

WORK IN PROGRESS: Shakehole-Revolution in '80, a political suspense novel; a science fiction novel about the distant future.

AVOCATIONAL INTERESTS: Painting, debate, rugby football coach and manager.

*   *   *

MacKENZIE, Louise (Wilks) 1920-

PERSONAL: Born February 8, 1920, in Cassville, Mo.; daughter of Beuford Dale (a merchant) and Gladys (Henry) Wilks; married Scott MacKenzie, Jr. (a professor of chemistry), June 14, 1947; children: Susan Wilks, Pamela Dee, Scott III. *Education:* University of Missouri, B.S., 1941; University of Minnesota, M.S., 1946; additional graduate study at Cornell University, University of Rhode Island, and University of Massachusetts, 1964-71. *Politics:* Republican. *Religion:* Protestant. *Home:* 35 Little Rest Rd., Kingston, R.I. 02881. *Office:* Department of Home Economics, University of Rhode Island, Kingston, R.I.

CAREER: High school home economics teacher in Carrollton, Mo., 1941-45; University of Minnesota, Minneapolis, instructor in home economics, 1946-49; Hunter College (now Hunter College of the City University of New York), New York, N.Y., instructor in home economics, 1950-52; University of Rhode Island, Kingston, assistant professor of home economics education, 1963—. *Member:* American Home Economics Association, American Vocational Association, Omicron Nu, Pi Lambda Theta, Alpha Pi.

WRITINGS: Evaluation in the Teaching of Home Economics, Interstate, 1970. Contributor to vocational education journals.

WORK IN PROGRESS: Home Economics in Grades One through Six.

*   *   *

MACLEAN, Fitzroy (Hew) 1911-

PERSONAL: Born March 11, 1911, in Cairo, Egypt; son of Charles Wilberforce (a British Army officer) and Gladys

(Royle) Maclean; married Veronica Fraser (daughter of 16th Baron of Lovat), January 12, 1946; children: Charles, James. *Education:* University of Cambridge, B.A., 1932, M.A. (first class honors). *Politics:* Conservative. *Religion:* Church of Scotland. *Home:* Strachur House, Strachur, Argyllshire, Scotland.

CAREER: Diplomatic Service, third secretary, 1933, transferred to Paris, 1934, transferred to Moscow, 1937, second secretary, 1938, transferred to Foreign Office, 1939; resigned from Diplomatic Service and enlisted as private in Cameron Highlanders, 1941, became second lieutenant, joined First Special Air Service Regiment and became captain, 1942, lieutenant-colonel and brigadier, 1943, commander of British Military Mission to Yugoslavia Partisans, 1943-45, head of Special Refugee Commission, Germany, Austria, and Italy, 1947; member of Parliament, Lancaster Division, 1941-59, Bute and North Ayrshire, 1959-74; War Office, parliamentary under-secretary of state and financial secretary, 1954-57. Lee Knowles Lecturer at University of Cambridge, 1953. Chairman of Great Britain-U.S.S.R. Association, 1959; chairman of military committee of NATO Parliamentarians.

MEMBER: Cable Television Association (president), Great Britain—U.S.S.R. Association (past president), British Yugoslav Society (president). *Awards, honors*—Military: Croix de Guerre (France), 1943; Commander, Order of the British Empire, 1944; Order of Kutusov (U.S.S.R.), 1944; Partisan Star 1st Class, 1945. Civilian: Created Baronet of Strachur and Glensmain, 1957; LL.D., Glasgow University, 1969; D.Litt., Acadia University, 1970; LL.D., Dalhousie University.

WRITINGS: Eastern Approaches (Book Society choice in England), J. Cape, 1949, published as *Escape to Adventure,* Little, Brown, 1950, special edition with new introduction by Charles W. Thayer, Time, 1964; *The Heretic: The Life and Times of Josip Broz-Tito,* Harper, 1957, published as *Tito, the Man Who Defied Hitler and Stalin,* Ballantine, 1957 (published in England as *Disputed Barricade: The Life and Times of Josip Broz-Tito, Marshal of Jugoslavia,* J. Cape, 1957); *A Person from England, and Other Travelers to Turkestan,* Harper, 1958; *Back to Bokhara,* Harper, 1959; (author of introduction) *Yugoslavia,* photographs by Toni Schneiders and others, Thames & Hudson, 1969; *A Concise History of Scotland,* Viking, 1970; *The Battle of the Neretva,* Panther Books, 1970; *To the Back of Beyond,* Little, Brown, 1975; *To Caucasus: The End of All the Earth,* Little, Brown, 1976.

WORK IN PROGRESS: Holy Russia; an anthology of spies, *Take Nine Spies;* and a life of Bonny Prince Charlie.

SIDELIGHTS: Fitzroy Maclean has traveled widely in the Balkans, the Caucasus, Near East, Middle East, Central Asia, Mongolia, and in European Russia.

BIOGRAPHICAL/CRITICAL SOURCES: New Yorker, May 30, 1970.

* * *

MacNEIL, Neil 1891-1969

February 6, 1891—December 30, 1969; American newspaper editor and author of books on journalism. Obituaries: *New York Times,* December 31, 1969; *Washington Post,* December 31, 1969; *Time,* April 27, 1970. (See index for *CA* sketch)

MACPHERSON, Kenneth 1903(?)-1971

1903(?)—June 14, 1971; Scottish novelist and editor. Obituaries: *New York Times,* June 18, 1971; *Washington Post,* June 19, 1971; *Publishers' Weekly,* June 28, 1971; *Antiquarian Bookman,* July 19-26, 1971.

* * *

MACRO, Eric 1920-

PERSONAL: Surname is pronounced *Mac*-ro; born March 5, 1920, in London, England; son of Harvey Lancelot (a pilot, Royal Air Force) and Margaret (Parkins) Macro; married Joan Bulmer, June 17, 1944; children: Howard, Jane. *Education:* Attended Cadet College, Cranwell, 1938-39, and Staff College, Bracknell, 1949. *Religion:* Church of England. *Home:* Boxford House, Eaton Park, Cobham, Surrey, England.

CAREER: Commissioned in Royal Air Force, 1939, and served continuously on active duty until 1969, when he resigned with rank of wing commander. *Member:* Royal Central Asian Society, British Institute of Management (associate). *Awards, honors*—Military: Order of the British Empire and various war campaign medals.

WRITINGS: Bibliography of the Arabian Peninsula, University of Miami Press, 1960; *Bibliography of Yemen and Notes on Mocha,* University of Miami Press, 1962; *Yemen and the Western World since 1571,* Praeger, 1968. Contributor of articles and reviews to *Middle East Journal* (Washington, D.C.), *Royal Central Asian Journal, Geographical Journal, New Middle East, Arab World, Port of Aden Annual,* and to government publications.

WORK IN PROGRESS: Research on the overland route to India and on the topography of Mocha.

AVOCATIONAL INTERESTS: Siena and Tuscany, Sienese painting and architecture, the Spanish Civil War, Yugoslavia, and his own specialized research library on Arabia and other subjects.†

* * *

MADGWICK, P(eter) J(ames) 1925-

PERSONAL: Born August 15, 1925, in London, England; son of Frederick Martin (manager of printing firm) and Ellen (Miller) Madgwick; married Olive Hoskins (a research assistant), August 16, 1947; children: Rupert, Julia, Clare. *Education:* Magdalen College, Oxford, B.A. and M.A., 1950, Diploma in Education, 1951. *Home:* 60 Danycoed, Aberystwyth, Wales. *Office:* University College of Wales, University of Wales, Aberystwyth, Wales.

CAREER: University of Nottingham, Nottingham, England, lecturer in political science, 1952-65; University of Wales, University College of Wales, Aberystwyth, senior lecturer, 1965-74, reader in political science, 1974—. *Military service:* Royal Air Force, 1944-47; became sergeant.

WRITINGS: (With Jonathan D. Chambers) *Conflict and Community: Europe since 1750,* George Philip & Son, 1968; *American City Politics,* Humanities, 1970; *Introduction to British Politics,* Hutchinson, 1970, 2nd revised edition, 1976; *The Politics of Rural Wales,* Hutchinson, 1973; (contributor) M. Beloff and V. Vale, editors, *American Political Institutions in the 1970's,* Macmillan, 1975.

WORK IN PROGRESS: Contributing to *European Integration and Welsh Devolution,* for Manchester University Press, *Linguistic Conflict as a Problem in Government,* for Routledge & Kegan Paul, and *Leadership in Local Govern-*

ment, for Charles Knight; research in linguistic conflict and electoral behavior in Wales.

*   *   *

MAITLAND, Derek   1943-

PERSONAL: Born April 17, 1943, in Chelmsford, Essex, England; son of James and Constance (Smallridge) Maitland. *Education:* Attended secondary schools in England and Australia. *Politics:* Liberal socialist. *Religion:* Christian. *Home:* 12 Judith St., Seven Hills, New South Wales, Australia.

CAREER: Script writer, reporter, and sub-editor for television stations in Sydney, Australia, prior to 1965; employed with Australian Broadcasting Commission, 1965; reporter for *South China Morning Post,* Hong Kong, newscaster for Rediffusion Television, Hong Kong, and feature editor for *Bangkok Post,* Bangkok, Thailand, 1965-68; Copley News Service, San Diego, Calif., staff correspondent in Saigon, 1968; British Broadcasting Corp., London, England, subeditor and script writer, 1970; free-lance correspondent in Beirut, Lebanon, for Copley News Service, *San Francisco Chronicle,* and *Toronto Daily Star,* 1971—.

WRITINGS: The Only War We've Got, Morrow, 1970; *T-Minus Tower,* MacGibbon & Kee, 1971; *The Alpha Experience,* W. H. Allen, 1974.

WORK IN PROGRESS: The Sheik, a novel based on the life of a Bedouin sheik in Jordan's Wadi Rum who is trying to protect his corrupted tribe from modern civilization.

SIDELIGHTS: Derek Maitland's interest in writing began in childhood. "Hemingway and Salinger provided the emotional element, and first expedition in 1965 to Southeast Asia . . . provided the material," he says. "Vietnam itself added fear, anger, new political awareness and motivation for *The Only War We've Got.* Since my twelve months there I have been fascinated, almost obsessed, by man's capacity for violence, his own obsession with war and the thin red line of mentality that separates warrior from peacenik. . . . During the three years I spent in London after Saigon, this old horror returned over a three-month period covering the Northern Ireland crisis for the BBC. In my third expedition, covering the Middle East from Beirut, the Arab-Israeli conflict has shown me the ridiculous lengths to which men will go to prove they are men."

BIOGRAPHICAL/CRITICAL SOURCES: Time, November 16, 1970.†

*   *   *

MAJONICA, Ernst   1920-

PERSONAL: Born October 29, 1920, in Soest, Germany; son of Ernst (a lumber merchant) and Josepha (Hagen) Majonica; married Ursula Dullin, January 6, 1961. *Education:* Studied at University of Freiburg and University of Muenster; assessorexamen in Duesseldorf, 1950; University of Munich, Ph.D., 1971. *Politics:* Christian Democratic Union. *Religion:* Catholic. *Home:* Im Buschacker 18, D-5300 Bonn-Bad Godesberg, Germany. *Office:* Bundeshaus, D-5300 Bonn, 12 Germany.

CAREER: Lawyer, 1950—. Member of German Federal Parliament, Bonn, 1950-72, chairman of foreign policy circle, 1959-69, German Council, Pan-European Movement, president, 1966-76, currently vice-president. Christian Democratic Union, national chairman of youth group, 1950-55, member of executive council, 1953-72. Lecturer in international relationships, University of Bonn, 1973-76. Advisor

on mineral oil trade, 1973—. *Military service:* Germany Army, 1942-46 (prisoner-of-war in latter part of service). *Awards, honors:* Awarded Grobes Bundesverdienstkreuz, 1969.

WRITINGS: Deutsche Aussenpolitik: Probleme und Entscheidungen, Kohlhammer, 1965, translation published as *East-West Relations: A German View,* Praeger, 1969; *Moeglichkeiten und Grenzen deutscher Aussenpolitik,* Kohlhammer, 1969; *Bonn-Peking: Die Beziehungen der Bundesrepublik Deutschland zur Volksrepublik China,* Kohlhammer, 1971. Contributor to periodical and newspapers.

SIDELIGHTS: Ernst Majonica has traveled in the United States, South America, the Far East, and in the Soviet Union. He speaks English and French. *Avocational interests:* Books, East-Asiatic art.

*   *   *

MAJOR, Reginald W.   1926-

PERSONAL: Born February 8, 1926, in New York, N.Y.; son of Wilford Reginald and Ethel (Allman) Major; married Helen Ruth Gabriel, August 3, 1949; children: David Robert, Deborah Ann. *Education:* Attended University of Chicago, 1946-50. *Politics:* "Black liberation." *Religion:* None. *Residence:* San Francisco, Calif. *Agent:* Robert P. Mills Ltd., 156 East 52nd St., New York, N.Y. 10022.

CAREER: State of California, Department of Motor Vehicles, Sacramento, driver improvement analyst, 1963-68; San Francisco State College (now University), San Francisco, Calif., director of educational opportunity program, 1968-70. *San Francisco Sun-Reporter,* part-time journalist, 1964—. Correspondent for Pacific News Service. *Member:* National Association for the Advancement of Colored People (education chairman of San Francisco chapter, 1963-65). *Military service:* U.S. Navy, 1943-46.

WRITINGS: A Panther Is a Black Cat, Morrow, 1971; *Justice in the Round: The Trial of Angela Davis,* Third Press, 1973.

*   *   *

MALAVIE, M. J.   1920-

PERSONAL: Born September 14, 1920, in Bethune, France; daughter of Rene (a jeweler) and Louise (Cornesse) Malavie; married Henry Duffus Hadden (a certified public accountant), September 15, 1960. *Education:* University of Clermont-Ferrand, License-es-lettres, 1943. *Religion:* Roman Catholic. *Home:* Chateau de Vodable, 63 Vodable, France.

CAREER: Former teacher of French in England, Scotland, Sweden, and France.

WRITINGS—For young people: L'Ile aux phoques, Presses de la Cite, 1964; *Le Secret du dragon,* Presses de la Cite, 1966, translation by Thelma Niklaus published as *The Canary Tree,* Bodley Head, 1969; *L'Artiste de Santiago,* Presses de la Cite, 1971; *Maria des Volcans,* Gautier-Languereau, 1972. Contributor of stories to French magazines for children.

BIOGRAPHICAL/CRITICAL SOURCES: Times Literary Supplement, June 26, 1969.

*   *   *

MALEFAKIS, Edward E(manuel)   1932-

PERSONAL: Born January 2, 1932, in Springfield, Mass.; son of Emanuel A. and Despina (Sophoulakis) Malefakis;

married Mary Anne Wilson, June 15, 1960 (divorced, 1975); children: Michael, Laura. *Education:* Bates College, A.B., 1953; Johns Hopkins School of Advanced International Studies, M.A., 1955; Columbia University, Ph.D., 1965. *Home:* 601 West 113th St., New York, N.Y. 10025. *Office:* Department of History, Columbia University, New York, N.Y. 10027.

CAREER: Northwestern University, Evanston, Ill., instructor in history, 1962-63; Wayne State University, Detroit, Mich., assistant professor of history, 1963-64; Columbia University, New York, N.Y., assistant professor of history, 1964-68; Northwestern University, associate professor of history, 1968-71; University of Michigan, Ann Arbor, professor of history, 1971-74; Columbia University, professor of history, 1974—. *Military service:* U.S. Army, 1955-57. *Member:* American Historical Association, Society for Spanish and Portuguese Historical Studies, Modern Greek Studies Association, Society for Italian Historical Studies. *Awards, honors:* Herbert Baxter Adams Prize, American Historical Association, 1971, for *Agrarian Reform and Peasant Revolution in Spain;* Faculty Teaching Award, Northwestern University, 1971; Guggenheim fellowship, 1974.

WRITINGS: Agrarian Reform and Peasant Revolution in Spain: Origins of the Civil War, Yale University Press, 1970; (contributor) Raymond Carr, editor, *The Republic and the Civil War in Spain,* Macmillan, 1971; (contributor) Robin Higham, editor, *Civil War in the Twentieth Century,* University Press of Kentucky, 1972; (contributor) Robert Bezucha, editor, *Modern European Social History,* Heath, 1972; (editor) *Indalecio Prieto: Discursos Fundamentales,* Turuer (Madrid), 1975.

WORK IN PROGRESS: A comparative history of Portugal, Spain, Italy, and Greece since 1800.

* * *

MALOF, Joseph F(etler) 1934-

PERSONAL: Surname is pronounced *mail*-off; born May 26, 1934, in Riga, Latvia; naturalized American citizen; married Delores Ann Kildare, 1957; children: Andrew, Jessica, Peter. *Education:* Kenyon College, B.A., 1956; University of California, Los Angeles, M.A., 1957, Ph.D., 1962. *Home address:* Box 8617, Austin, Tex. 78712. *Office:* Department of English, University of Texas, Austin, Tex. 78712.

CAREER: University of Texas at Austin, instructor, 1961-65, assistant professor, 1965-68, associate professor of English, 1968—. *Member:* Modern Language Association of America. *Awards, honors:* Woodrow Wilson fellow, 1956-57; Harbison Prize for Danforth Foundation for outstanding teaching, 1969.

WRITINGS: (Contributor) *Ezra Pound: Perspectives,* Regnery, 1965; *A Manual of English Meters,* Indiana University Press, 1970. Contributor to *Poetry Northwest, Modern Language Quarterly, Texas Studies,* and other journals.

WORK IN PROGRESS: Research and writing on prosody, modern poetry and literary structures.

* * *

MALONE, Michael P. 1940-

PERSONAL: Born April 18, 1940, in Pomeroy, Wash.; son of John A. (a merchant) and Doris (Cheyne) Malone; married Gail E. Wilcox, August 4, 1962; children: John Thomas, Molly Christine. *Education:* Gonzaga University, B.A., 1962; Washington State University, Ph.D., 1966. *Politics:* Democrat. *Religion:* Catholic. *Home:* 502 North 18th St., Bozeman, Mont. 59715. *Office:* Department of History, Montana State University, Bozeman, Mont. 59715.

CAREER: Texas A & M University, College Station, assistant professor of history, 1966-67; Montana State University, Bozeman, 1967—, began as assistant professor, professor of history, 1974—, head of department of history and science, 1976—. *Member:* Organization of American Historians, Pacific Northwestern History Association, Western History Association. *Awards, honors:* National Science Foundation summer grants, 1971, 1972.

WRITINGS: (Editor with Richard B. Roeder) *The Montana Past: An Anthology,* University of Montana Press, 1969, 2nd edition, 1973; *C. Ben Ross and the New Deal in Idaho,* University of Washington Press, 1970; (with Roeder) *Montana: A History of Two Centuries,* University of Washington Press, 1976. Contributor to *Pacific Historical Review, Idaho Yesterdays, Montana,* and *Pacific Northwest Quarterly.* Member of editorial board of *Pacific Historical Review* and *Pacific Northwest Quarterly;* member of editorial board and book review editor, *Montana: The Magazine of Western History.*

WORK IN PROGRESS: The Battle for Brute: Copper and Politics in America, 1869-1906.

* * *

MALTIN, Leonard 1950-

PERSONAL: Born December 18, 1950, in New York, N.Y.; son of Aaron I. and Jacqueline (Gould) Maltin; married Alice Tlusty, 1975. *Education:* New York University, student, 1968-72. *Religion:* Jewish. *Home:* 200 West 79th St., New York, N.Y. 10024. *Office:* New School for Social Research, 66 West 12th St., New York, N.Y. 10011.

CAREER: Film Fan Monthly (magazine), Teaneck, N.J., editor and publisher, 1966-75; general editor, Popular Library film series, 1973—; member of faculty, New School for Social Research, New York City, 1973—. Curator, American Academy of Humor, 1975-76; guest programmer, film department, Museum of Modern Art, New York City, 1976. Consultant and writer, showtime division of Viacom International, 1976—. *Member:* Society for Cinephiles, Sons of the Desert.

WRITINGS: TV Movies, New American Library, 1969, revised edition, 1974; *Movie Comedy Teams,* New American Library, 1970, revised edition, 1974; *Behind the Camera: The Cinematographer's Art,* New American Library, 1971; *The Great Movie Shorts,* Crown, 1972; *The Disney Films,* Crown, 1973; *Carole Lombard,* Pyramid Publications, 1976; (with Richard W. Bann) *Our Gang: The Life and Times of the Little Rascals,* Crown, 1977.

Editor: *The Real Stars,* Curtis Books, 1973; *The Laurel and Hardy Book,* Curtis Books, 1973; *The Real Stars #2,* Curtis Books, 1973; *Hollywood: The Movie Factory,* Popular Library, 1976; *Hollywood Kids,* Popular Library, 1977.

Contributor: *A Concise History of the Cinema,* A. S. Barnes, 1971; *The Compleat Guide to Film Study,* National Council of Teachers of English, 1972; *The American Film Heritage,* Acropolis Books, 1972; *Directors in Action,* Bobbs-Merrill, 1973; *The Movie Buff's Book,* Volume II, Pyramid Publications, 1977. Contributor to *Esquire, New York Times, Saturday Review, TV Guide, Film Comment, Variety, American Film, Millimeter, Print,* and other periodicals.

WORK IN PROGRESS: Pictorial History of Comedy, for Crown; *History of Animated Cartoons*, for New American Library; *The Real Stars #3*, for Popular Library.

SIDELIGHTS: Leonard Maltin, an ultra-dedicated film buff, started his own magazine at sixteen. He writes: "I am trying to shed light on various aspects of film history which have been neglected—the field of short subjects, for example. . . . I don't think one should discuss film as a cold, museum piece. Film is *alive.* . . ."

BIOGRAPHICAL/CRITICAL SOURCES: Saturday Review, September 17, 1967; *Variety*, October 29, 1969, April 5, 1972; *New York Daily News*, January 23, 1974, December 20, 1975; *New York Times*, May 6, 1976.

* * *

MANN, Kenneth Walker 1914-

PERSONAL: Born August 22, 1914, in Nyack, N.Y.; son of Arthur Hungerford (a mechanical engineer) and Ethel Livingston (Walker) Mann. *Education:* Princeton University, A.B., 1937; General Theological Seminary, S.T.B., 1942; University of Michigan, M.S., 1950, Ph.D., 1956. *Politics:* Republican. *Home:* 32 Tallman Ave., Nyack, N.Y. 10960.

CAREER: Ordained Episcopal priest, 1941; pastor of several churches in Episcopal Diocese of New York, New York City, 1941-45; Episcopal Diocese of Los Angeles, Calif., director of youth work and Christian education, 1945-47; All Saints' Church, Beverly Hills, Calif., curate, 1947-49; Cathedral of St. John the Divine, New York City, priest-therapist and concurrently chaplain and clinical psychologist at St. Luke's Hospital, 1952-55, 1956-58; Hospital of the Good Samaritan, Los Angeles, associate chaplain, 1958-65; Office of Pastoral Services of the Episcopal Church, New York City, national executive, 1965-70; Academy of Religion and Mental Health, New York City, program officer, 1970-72; senior advisor for professional affairs, Institutes of Religion and Health, 1972-74; Silver Hill Foundation, New Canaan, Conn., senior psychological staff member, 1974—. Licensed psychologist and marriage, family, and child counselor in California; licensed clinical psychologist in Connecticut. Consultant and member of professional advisory committee, Institutes of Religion and Health. Trustee, North Conway Institute.

MEMBER: American Psychological Association, Assembly of Episcopal Hospitals and Chaplains, American Protestant Hospital Association (member of College of Chaplains), American Association of Pastoral Counselors (diplomate), Association for Clinical Pastoral Education, National Council on Family Relations, American Association for the Advancement of Science (fellow), Western Psychological Association, California State Psychological Association, Los Angeles County Psychological Association.

WRITINGS: On Pills and Needles, Seabury, 1969; *Deadline for Survival: A Survey of Moral Issues in Science and Medicine*, Seabury, 1970. Contributor of articles to professional journals.

* * *

MANOS, Charley 1923-

PERSONAL: Name originally Alkiviadis Moustakas; born May 28, 1923, in Detroit, Mich.; son of Michael and Dinosia Moustakas; married Mara Panos; children: Mickey, John, Melinda, Melanie. *Education:* Attended Wayne State University. *Residence:* Grosse Pointe Farms, Mich. 48236. *Office: Detroit News*, Detroit, Mich. 48226.

CAREER: Days as a seaman ended when his ship was wrecked in a hurricane off Okinawa; police reporter and feature writer for *Detroit Free Press*, Detroit, Mich., 1951-57, and *Detroit Times*, Detroit, 1958-60; *Detroit News*, Detroit, member of editorial staff, 1968—, writer of daily column, "by Charley Manos," 1970—. Founder and director, Manos' Young Work in Press Corps, Detroit, 1974—. *Awards, honors:* National Broadcasting Co. Big Story Award, for story in *Detroit Free Press;* Associates Press and Detroit Newspaper Guild awards for feature writing.

WRITINGS: The Patch in Santa's Pants, Quill, 1966; *Sex and the Single Dog*, Quill, 1968; *Where's God, Daddy?*, Judson, 1969; "The Patch in Santa's Pants" (play adaptation from his own novel), first produced in Detroit, Mich., at Southland Shopping Center, November 14, 1976. Contributor, chiefly of humorous articles, to *Reader's Digest, This Week, McCall's, Saturday Review, Car Life*, and other magazines.

WORK IN PROGRESS: A collection of stories.

SIDELIGHTS: Charley Manos' experience as a Sunday school teacher in a suburban Episcopal church supplied the material for *Where's God, Daddy?*. Now he is thinking of doing a children's book based on his adventures with Rosey, the mongrel who accompanied her owner to the Rose Bowl in 1970, and the Kentucky Derby later that year. Manos' coverage of the two sports classics featured Rosey, who rode in the Rose Bowl Parade and turned up in the winner's circle at Churchill Downs.

Manos' Young Work in Press is a press conference for young journalists. Manos, to encourage these young writers, has arranged conferences and interviews with Henry "The Fonz" Winkler, Elton John, William G. Milliken, Mark "The Bird" Fidrych, and many others, so that high school students can get on-the-job-training press conferences for their high school newspapers.

Manos told *CA* that he prefers to look at the bright side of life. Through his humor in his writing, he achieves the feeling of accomplishment and hopes to provide enjoyment not only for himself but for others as well. His advice to aspiring writers is to "keep writing."

* * *

MANOSEVITZ, Martin 1938-

PERSONAL: Born June 22, 1938, in Minneapolis, Minn.; son of Julius (a pharmacist) and Ethel (Cohen) Manosevitz; married Carolyn H. Margulius, September 17, 1959; children: Bradley Sergei, Jason Uri. *Education:* University of Minnesota, B.A., 1960, Ph.D., 1964. *Home:* 3703 Kennelwood Rd., Austin, Tex. 78703. *Office:* Department of Psychology, University of Texas, Austin, Tex. 78712.

CAREER: Rutgers University, New Brunswick, N.J., assistant professor of psychology, 1964-67; University of Texas at Austin, assistant professor, 1967-69, associate professor, 1969-75, professor of psychology, 1975—, College of Arts and Sciences, assistant dean, 1971-72. *Member:* American Association for the Advancement of Science, American Psychological Association, Society for Research in Child Development.

WRITINGS: (Editor with Gardner Lindzey and Delbert D. Thiessen) *Behavioral Genetics: Method and Research*, Appleton, 1969; (editor with Lindzey and Calvin Hall) *Theories of Personality: Primary Sources and Research*, Wiley, 1973. Contributor to professional journals.

MANRY, Robert 1918-1971

June 2, 1918—February 21, 1971; Indian-born American adventurer and author. Obituaries: *New York Times*, February 22, 1971; *Washington Post*, February 23, 1971. (See index for *CA* sketch)

* * *

MANSFIELD, John M(aurice) 1936-

PERSONAL: Born December 5, 1936, in Swansea, Wales; son of John Lawford (a merchant) and Muriel (Liddle) Mansfield; married Fiona Boyd, June 20, 1968; children: Laura, Tessa. *Education:* Jesus College, Cambridge, M.A., 1959. *Home:* 135 Dalling Rd., London W.6, England. *Agent:* Jonathan Clowes Ltd., 19 Jeffrey's Place, London NW1 9PP, England. *Office:* BBC TV, Kensington House, Richmond Way, London W.14, England.

CAREER: British Broadcasting Corp., London, England, writer and producer of television documentaries, including the science program, "Tomorrow's World," 1960—. *Military service:* Royal Air Force, National Service; became pilot officer. *Awards, honors:* Prix Futura (Berlin), 1972, for film, "The Writing on the Wall."

WRITINGS: Man on the Moon, Stein & Day, 1969; *Self-scape*, Weidenfeld & Nicolson, 1975. Television films include "Out of This World," "A Case of Priority," "The Million Ton Ship," "Square Pegs," "The Secrets of Sleep," "The Other Way," "Lumbared," "Medicine 2000," "A Lesson for Teacher," and "The Writing on the Wall."

WORK IN PROGRESS: A film biography of Isaac Newton; a novel set in the world of television.

BIOGRAPHICAL/CRITICAL SOURCES: Times Literary Supplement, October 16, 1969.

* * *

MANSO, Peter 1940-

PERSONAL: Born December 22, 1940, in New York, N.Y.; son of Leo (a painter) and Blanche Manso; married Susan Beges (a professor and medievalist), September 8, 1962. *Education:* Antioch College, A.B., 1961; Johns Hopkins University, M.A., 1962; University of California, Berkeley, Ph.D., 1968. *Home:* 3 Sheridan Sq., New York, N.Y. 10014; and Treetops, Provincetown, Mass. 25609. *Agent:* Scott Meredith Literary Agency, Inc., 845 Third Ave., New York, N.Y. 10022.

CAREER: Has taught at University of California, Berkeley, and Rutgers University, New Brunswick, N.J.; free-lance writer. *Awards, honors:* Atlanta Film Festival Gold Prize, 1974, for "One by One."

WRITINGS: (Editor) *Running against the Machine: The Mailer-Breslin Campaign*, Doubleday, 1969; *Vroom!!: Conversations with the Grand Prix Champions*, Funk, 1969; (with Jackie Stewart) *Faster!*, Farrar, Straus, 1972. Also author of a documentary film, "One by One," 1974. Contributor to *Harper's, Playboy, Oui, Sports Illustrated, Sunday Times* (London), and other periodicals.

WORK IN PROGRESS: A critical biography of Norman Mailer, for Doubleday.

BIOGRAPHICAL/CRITICAL SOURCES: New York Times Book Review, November 9, 1969; *National Review*, January 13, 1970; *Carleton Miscellany*, spring, 1970; *San Francisco Examiner and Chronicle*, July 2, 1972; *National Observer*, August 19, 1972.

MANSON, Richard 1939-

PERSONAL: Born January 10, 1939, in New York, N.Y.; son of Aaron Lawrence and Aillene (Loeb) Manson; married Nancy Turel (a librarian), May 23, 1965. *Education:* University of Pittsburgh, B.A., 1960; New School for Social Research, graduate study, 1961-66; Columbia University, M.A., 1968. *Politics:* Liberal Democrat. *Religion:* Jewish. *Home:* 200 West 86th St., New York, N.Y. 10024. *Office:* American Language Program, Columbia University, New York, N.Y. 10027.

CAREER: Librarian, marketing research trainee, free-lance writer, and teacher of English in New York City, 1964-66; Pet Books, Inc., Maywood, N.J., staff writer, 1965; Columbia University, New York City, American Language Program, associate, 1966—.

WRITINGS: The Theory of Knowledge of Giambattista Vico, Archon Books, 1969. Also author of an unpublished novel, "Men Like Gods," 1961. Contributor to periodicals.

WORK IN PROGRESS: Two books, *A University in Exile: A History of the Graduate Faculty of Political and Social Science of the New School for Social Research, 1933-45;* and *Points of View*, a collection of short stories.

AVOCATIONAL INTERESTS: Creative writing, philosophy, political science, zoology, botany, gardening, carpentry, painting; travel to Scotland, England, Portugal, Bermuda, Mexico, Puerto Rico, Kentucky, and eastern United States.†

* * *

MANZALAOUI, Mahmoud (Ali) 1924-

PERSONAL: Surname is pronounced *Man-za-la-wee*; born May 13, 1924, in London, England; son of Hussein Sadek (a landowner) and Fatma (Deif) Manzalaoui; married M. H. Kirkley. *Education:* University of Cairo, B.A., 1944; Oxford University, B.Litt., M.A., D.Phil. *Home:* 4258 West 14th Ave., Vancouver, British Columbia, Canada. *Office:* Department of English, University of British Columbia, Vancouver, British Columbia, Canada V6T 1W5.

CAREER: University of Alexandria, Alexandria, Egypt, assistant lecturer, 1949-54, lecturer, 1954-61, associate professor, 1961-68, professor of English, 1968-69; University of British Columbia, Vancouver, professor of English, 1969—. Visiting fellow, Clare Hall, Cambridge University, 1968-69; visiting senior member, St. Anthony's College, Oxford University, 1974-75. Landowner with a small estate in the Egyptian delta. Member of Committee for Encouragement of Tourism, Alexandria, Egypt, 1966-67. *Member:* Amici Thomae Mori, Oxford and Cambridge Club (London).

WRITINGS: (Editor) *Arabic Writing Today: The Short Story*, American Research Center in Cairo, 1969, University of California Press, 1970; (contributor) D. Brewer, editor, *Writers and Their Background: Geoffrey Chaucer*, G. Bell, 1974, Ohio University Press, 1975. Contributor to *Times Educational Supplement, Etudes anglaises*, and other publications.

WORK IN PROGRESS: Arabic Writing Today: The Drama; "Secretum Secretorum": Nine English Versions and cognate articles.

* * *

MARCINIAK, Ed(ward) 1917-

PERSONAL: Born December 21, 1917, in Chicago, Ill.; son of Walter and Hattie (Kleszcz) Marciniak; married Virginia

Volini, April 25, 1953; children: Catherine Vianney, Christina Maria, Francesca Louise, Claudia Noel. *Education:* Loyola University, Chicago, Ill., A.B., 1939, Master of Social Administration, 1942. *Politics:* Democratic. *Religion:* Roman Catholic. *Home:* 1341 West Catalpa Ave., Chicago, Ill. 60640. *Office:* Institute of Urban Life, 14 East Chestnut St., Chicago, Ill. 60611.

CAREER: Loyola University, Chicago, Ill., instructor in sociology, 1939-49; Sheil School of Social Studies, Chicago, director of Labor Division, 1943-53; American Newspaper Guild, Chicago, international vice-president, 1955-60; Chicago Commission on Human Relations, Chicago, director, 1960-67; City of Chicago, deputy commissioner of department of development and planning, 1967-72; Institute of Urban Life, Chicago, president, 1973—. Instructor in Great Books Program, University of Chicago; lecturer in labor relations, Rosary College. Member of advisory board of school of education, Roosevelt University, 1973—. Founder, National Catholic Social Action Conference, 1953. *Member:* U.S. Catholic Conference (member of committee on social development, 1967-71). *Awards, honors:* Clarence Darrow Humanitarian Award; LL.D. from St. Joseph's College (Indiana).

WRITINGS: Tomorrow's Christian, Pflaum Standard, 1969; *Reviving an Inner City Community,* Loyola University Press, 1977. Contributor to *America, Commonweal, Crisis, New Republic,* and to religious and sociological journals. Editor, *Work* (Catholic Council on Working Life), 1943-60.

*   *   *

MARGOLIS, Richard J(ules) 1929-

PERSONAL: Born June 30, 1929, in St. Paul, Minn.; son of Harry Sterling (a rabbi) and Clara (Brunner) Margolis; married Diane Rothbard (a sociologist), April 3, 1954; children: Harry Sterling, Philip Eliot. *Education:* University of Minnesota, B.A., 1952, M.A., 1953. *Home and office address:* R.D. 1, Georgetown, Conn.

CAREER: Brooklyn Heights Press, Brooklyn, N.Y., editor and publisher, 1956-60; Lerner Newspapers, Chicago, Ill., editorial director, 1960-62; free-lance writer, 1962—. National chairman, Rural Housing Alliance; founding chairman, Rural America, Inc.; consultant at various times to Ford Foundation, Stern Fund, U.S. Civil Rights Commission, U.S. Office of Economic Opportunity, U.S. Bureau of Indian Affairs, and other government and private agencies. Member of library board, Wilton, Conn. *Awards, honors:* George Polk Memorial Award for achievement in journalism, 1959; National Editorial Association Award for editorial writing, 1962.

WRITINGS: Something to Build On (nonfiction), American Friends Service Committee, 1966; *Only the Moon and Me* (poetry for children), Lippincott, 1968; *Looking For a Place* (poetry for young people), Lippincott, 1969; *The Upside-Down King* (children's story), Windmill Books, 1971; *Wish Again, Big Bear* (children's story), Macmillan, 1971; *Homer the Hunter* (children's fable), Macmillan, 1972; *Big Bear to the Rescue* (children's story), Greenwillow Books, 1975. Contributor of articles and reviews to *Life, New Leader, Redbook, New York Times Magazine, Nation, Country Journal,* and many other periodicals.

WORK IN PROGRESS: A children's book on health, *Where Does It Hurt?,* for Holt.

MARIANI, Paul L(ouis) 1940-

PERSONAL: Born February 29, 1940, in New York, N.Y.; son of Paul Patrick (a day-camp foreman) and Harriet (Green) Mariani; married Eileen Spinosa (a grade school teacher), August 24, 1963; children: Paul, Mark, John. *Education:* Manhattan College, Bronx, N.Y., B.A., 1962; Colgate University, M.A., 1964; City University of New York, Ph.D., 1968. *Politics:* Democrat. *Religion:* Roman Catholic. *Office:* Department of English, Bartlett Hall, University of Massachusetts, Amherst, Mass. 01002.

CAREER: Colgate University, Hamilton, N.Y., instructor in English, 1963-64; John Jay College of Criminal Justice of the City University of New York, New York, N.Y., assistant professor of English, 1967-68; University of Massachusetts—Amherst, assistant professor, 1968-71, associate professor, 1971-75, professor of English, 1975—. *Member:* Modern Language Association of America, Hopkins Society. *Awards, honors:* National Endowment for the Humanities fellowship, 1973.

WRITINGS: A Commentary on the Complete Poems of Gerard Manley Hopkins, Cornell University Press, 1970; *William Carlos Williams: The Poet and His Critics,* American Library Association, 1975. Contributor to *Massachusetts Review, Month, Victorian Poetry, Paintbrush, Poetry Miscellany, Nation, Iowa Review, Parnassus, Twentieth Century Literature, Prairie Schooner,* and other journals. Associate editor, *William Carlos Williams Newsletter.*

WORK IN PROGRESS: A methodology for placing Hopkins in the Victorian milieu; a study of the long poem in English from the Romantics on; a critical study of *Paterson, Timing Devices,* and *Cliometrics* (poetry).

SIDELIGHTS: Paul Mariani told *CA:* "Nearly everything I write is an attempt, a failing attempt, to articulate in my own voice the public and private time and space which I find myself inhabiting. I have already spent half my life working out the ramifications of accepting, theologically, philosophically, aesthetically, the fact of incarnation."

*   *   *

MARIOTTI, (Raffaello) Marcello 1938-

PERSONAL: Born May 25, 1938, in Florence, Italy; son of Amedeo Siro (a city official) and Ada (Boschi) Mariotti. *Education:* Porta Romana Institute of Art, Florence, student, 1949-52. *Home:* Via Santo Spirito 29, Florence, Italy.

CAREER: Window decorator, 1953-55, and interior decorator, 1956-60, working throughout Italy; cartoonist for Rizzoli Publishing in Italy and for *Horizon* (magazine), in the United States, 1962-65; free-lance movie cartoonist and designer of graphics, fabric, fashions, and interiors in Italy and the United States, 1966-69; set designer for National Broadcasting Corp. in the United States and Radiotelevisione Italiana (RAI-TV) in Italy, 1969-71; held exhibitions of his Anti Designe wood carvings at Centro Domus, Milan, Italy, 1974, in Ulm, Germany, 1975, and at Artecronaca, Citta di Vinci, Italy, 1976; art director and designer for ceramics factory, Florence, Italy, 1976-77. *Military service:* Italian Army, Infantry, 1960-62.

WRITINGS: (Self-illustrated) *The Three Kings* (juvenile), Knopf, 1969; (self-illustrated) *Storielle a quadretti* (juvenile), six volumes, Vallecchi, 1972; (illustrator) *Verso il mondo,* three volumes, Edipem, 1973.

WORK IN PROGRESS: A self-illustrated educational children's book, *Contatutto,* for Einaudi; books for blind children made in carved wood.

MARKO, Katherine D(olores)

PERSONAL: Born in Allentown, Pa.; daughter of Charles A. and Nellie (Lafferty) McGlade; married Alex S. Marko (an employee of a teletype firm); children: Monica, John, Joel. *Residence:* Elgin, Ill.

CAREER: Free-lance writer.

WRITINGS: The Sod Turners (juvenile), Criterion, 1970. Contributor to *Encyclopaedia Britannica Junior.*

WORK IN PROGRESS: A children's book set in the era of the French and Indian War.

* * *

MARKS, Sema 1942-

PERSONAL: Born December 15, 1942, in Cleveland, Ohio; daughter of Morris and Rose (Kanarek) Fichtenbaum; married Peter Marks, December 31, 1965 (divorced). *Education:* Harvard University, M.A.T., 1965, Ed.D., 1970. *Religion:* Jewish. *Office:* Westinghouse Learning Corp., 100 Park Ave., New York, N.Y. 10017.

CAREER: Harvard University, Cambridge, Mass., research assistant in Program on Technology and Society, 1966-69; Westinghouse Learning Corp., New York, N.Y., project director, 1969—. Consultant to RAND Corp., to Bolt, Beranek & Newman, and to Creative Studies, Inc. *Member:* Association for Computing Machinery, American Association for the Advancement of Science, National Council of Teachers of Mathematics, Phi Beta Kappa, Kappa Delta Phi, Pi Lambda Theta.

WRITINGS: (With Anthony G. Oettinger) *Run, Computer, Run: The Mythology of Educational Innovation,* Harvard University Press, 1969.

WORK IN PROGRESS: A high school text on computer simulation.

BIOGRAPHICAL/CRITICAL SOURCES: Nation, September 1, 1969; *New York Times Book Review,* September 14, 1969.†

* * *

MARKS, Stan(ley) 1929-
(Martin King)

PERSONAL: Born April 25, 1929, in London, England; taken to Australia at the age of two; son of Sidney (in clothing business) and Sally (Bernstein) Marks; married Eve Mass (a designer of toys), July 15, 1951; children: Lee (daughter), Peter. *Education:* Attended University of Melbourne. *Home:* 348 Bambra Rd., Caulfield, Melbourne, Victoria, Australia 3162. *Office:* Australian Tourist Commission, St. Kilda Rd., Melbourne, Victoria, Australia 3004.

CAREER: Began working for an Australian country newspaper at the age of seventeen; later a reporter and theater critic for *Melbourne Herald,* Melbourne, Australia; reporter for newspapers in England, 1951, and in Montreal, Quebec, and Toronto, Ontario, 1952-53; correspondent for Australian newspapers in New York, N.Y., 1954-55; returned to Australia to become public relations officer of Trans Australia Airlines, 1965-67; Australian Broadcasting Commission, Melbourne, public relations supervisor, 1958-64; Australian Tourist Commission, Melbourne, public relations manager, 1968—. *Member:* Australian Journalists Association, Australian Society of Authors.

WRITINGS: God Gave You One Face (novel), R. Hale, 1964; *Graham Is an Aboriginal Boy,* photographs by Brian

McArdle, Methuen, 1968, Hastings House, 1969; *Fifty Years of Achievement,* Methuen, 1972; *Animal Olympics* (stories), Methuen, 1972-76; *Rarua Lives in Papua New Guinea,* Methuen, 1974; *Ketut Lives in Bali,* Methuen, 1976. Author of a play, "Everybody Out" and of a collection of scripts, "Is She Fair Dinkum?"; also author of stories for two records for children, "Animal Olympics" and "Montague the Mouse Who Sailed with Captain Cook." Work included in *Walkabout's Book of Best Australian Stories,* Lansdowne Press, 1968. Co-originator of a comic strip, "Ms.," for Australian newspapers including *Melbourne Herald, Auckland Star,* and *Christchurch Star,* 1975—. Contributor of feature stories and articles to Australian and overseas journals; some of the articles were published under the pseudonym Martin King.

WORK IN PROGRESS: A novel, *Who Speaks for Tommy?*

SIDELIGHTS: Stan Marks has a strong interest in arts and youth and promoting better understanding between nations. As early as 1951 he suggested that an All-British Commonwealth Arts Festival should be held regularly; later he began urging that a Youth Council be established at the United Nations to get the world's young closer to policy making. A Commonwealth Arts Festival eventually was held, and the Youth Council idea brought him an invitation to the 1960 White House Conference on Youth. He also has advocated an "Ideas Bank" for international peace, where people might send suggestions to be sifted for possible discussion ("just one good idea might save that button being pushed"). His books reflect those concerns and his interest in aborigines. While researching *Graham Is an Aboriginal Boy* he lived for ten days with the Arunta tribe near Alice Springs in the Northern Territory, learned to hunt with a boomerang and to enjoy a diet of bush bananas and figs. He has also lived in other villages while completing research for his books.

* * *

MARKSTEIN, David L. 1920-

PERSONAL: Born in 1920, in New Orleans, La.; son of Joseph Carl and Genevieve (Liberman) Markstein; married Elizabeth Gough, February 14, 1944; children: Donald, Genevieve, Anne, Robert. *Education:* Graduate of Louisiana State University, 1940. *Office:* 8208 East Vista Dr., Scottsdale, Ariz. 85253.

CAREER: Financial analyst. *Markstein Letter* (investment service), New Orleans, La., publisher, beginning 1966. Teacher of estate-planning course, Loyola University, New Orleans, 1958-68. *Member:* Financial Analysts of New Orleans (past president).

WRITINGS: How to Chart Your Way to Stock Market Profits, Parker Publishing, 1967; *How to Make Money with Mutual Funds,* McGraw, 1969; *Practical Ways to Build a Fortune in the Stock Market,* Cornerstone Library, 1969; *Six Steps to Successful Investing,* Cornerstone Library; *Nine Roads to Wealth,* McGraw, 1970; *How You Can Beat Inflation,* McGraw, 1970; *How to Make Your Money Do More,* Trident, 1971; *Investing in the 70's,* Crowell, 1972; *How to Invest and Retire Rich,* Arco, 1973; *Small Business,* Regnery, 1974; *Markstein's Guide to Much Bigger Investment Income,* Pay Day Press, 1976. Contributor of articles to professional journals.

MARLO, John A.   1934-

PERSONAL: Born May 9, 1934, in San Francisco, Calif.; son of John A. and Frances (Bouchine) Marlo; married Patricia A. Nock, August 26, 1956; children: Kimber, Kamala, Craig, John A. III. *Education:* San Jose State College (now University), B.A., 1956; University of Santa Clara, J.D., 1961. *Politics:* Republican. *Religion:* Roman Catholic. *Residence:* Aptos, Calif. *Office:* Municipal Court, 1430 Freedom Blvd., Watsonville, Calif.

CAREER: Police (patrolman), San Jose, Calif., 1955-61; attorney in general practice of law, Santa Cruz, Calif., 1961-73; city attorney, Capitola, Calif., beginning 1965; municipal court judge, County of Santa Cruz (Calif.), 1973—. Instructor in law enforcement, Cabrillo Community College, 1964. Chairman, Santa Cruz County Civil Service Commission. *Military service:* U.S. Army Reserve, 1956-61; became captain in Judge Advocate General's Corps. *Member:* American Bar Association, California Bar Association, California Association of Judges.

WRITINGS: (With Robert Gene Wright) *The Police Officer and Criminal Justice,* McGraw, 1970.

AVOCATIONAL INTERESTS: Deep sea fishing, skiing, big game hunting.

*   *   *

MARMOR, T(heodore) R(ichard)   1939-

PERSONAL: Born February 24, 1939, in New York, N.Y.; son of James and Mira (Karpf) Marmor; married Jan Schmidt, October 20, 1961; children: Laura Carleton, Sarah Rogers. *Education:* Harvard University, B.A., 1960, Ph.D., 1965; attended Wadham College, Oxford, 1961-62. *Politics:* Democrat. *Home:* 1345 East Madison Pk., Chicago, Ill. 60615. *Office:* Department of Political Science, University of Chicago, Chicago, Ill.

CAREER: Harvard University, Cambridge, Mass., instructor, 1965-66; research fellow at University of Essex, Colchester, England, and Nuffield College, Oxford University, Oxford, England, 1966-67; University of Wisconsin—Madison, 1967-69, began as assistant professor, became associate professor of political science; fellow at Adlai Stevenson Institute, Chicago, Ill., 1969, and John F. Kennedy Institute, Cambridge, 1970; University of Minnesota, Minneapolis, associate professor of political science, 1970-73; University of Chicago, Chicago, associate professor of political science, 1973—. Consultant to U.S. Department of Health, Education and Welfare, Senator Ribicoff (Conn.), and state of Illinois governor's office. *Member:* American Political Science Association.

WRITINGS: (With wife, Jan S. Marmor) *The Politics of Medicare,* Humanities, 1970; (editor and contributor) *Poverty Policy,* Aldine-Atherton, 1971. Contributor to *American Political Science Review* and other periodicals.

WORK IN PROGRESS: A book on the politics of national health insurance.

SIDELIGHTS: T. R. Marmor told *CA* he is interested in the "American version of the welfare state, which means learning about what non-America has done.... As a citizen, I am concerned about the state of urban living, the near impossibility of finding places where residing, walking, buying, meeting, eating, bussing, seeing commerce, etc. can take place in one environment.... Will try, ... to see if I can help re-create such a neighborhood in Minneapolis near Loring Park."

MAROKVIA, Mireille (Journet)   1918-

PERSONAL: Born December 7, 1918, in France; came to United States in 1950; naturalized U.S. citizen, 1955; daughter of Gabriel (a teacher) and Genevieve (Lafond) Journet; married Artur Marokvia (a painter and illustrator), May 23, 1939. *Education:* College Chartres, B.A.; Sorbonne, University of Paris, Certificat, 1938.

CAREER: Teacher in Paris, France, and then translator, 1946-49; dressmaker and designer in United States, 1954-56.

WRITINGS—Juvenile books; illustrations by husband, Artur Marokvia: *Jannot, A French Rabbit,* Lippincott, 1959; *Nanette, a French Goat,* Lippincott, 1960; *Grococo, a French Crow,* Lippincott, 1961; *Belle Arabelle,* Lippincott, 1962; *A French School for Paul,* Lippincott, 1963. Author of short stories, articles, and poetry for French periodicals prior to 1950; also did editing, and translating from the German, in France.

WORK IN PROGRESS: Two children's books with Mexican background; an autobiographical book about her years in Germany (1939-46); short stories.†

*   *   *

MARRISON, L(eslie) W(illiam)   1901-
(D. M. Dowley)

PERSONAL: Born December 11, 1901, in County Mayo, Ireland; son of William Dowley (a sailor) and A. E. (Carlisle) Marrison; married Edith M. Hallam, September 1, 1934. *Education:* University of London, B.Sc., 1923. *Home:* Claverham Way, Battle, Sussex, England.

CAREER: Research chemist in England and Burma, 1924-62.

WRITINGS: (Translator from the Italian) M. Sartori, *War Gases,* Churchill, 1939; *Wines and Spirits,* Penguin, 1957; *Crystals, Diamonds, and Transistors,* Penguin, 1966; *Wines for Everyone,* David & Charles, 1970, St. Martin's, 1971.

Novels; under pseudonym D. M. Dowley: *Charley,* P. Davies, 1950; *The Beach,* P. Davies, 1951; *Dr. Ischenasch,* P. Davies, 1952. Contributor to scientific journals.

WORK IN PROGRESS: A history of wine.

BIOGRAPHICAL/CRITICAL SOURCES: Books and Bookmen, January, 1969.

*   *   *

MARSHALL, Anthony D(ryden)   1924-

PERSONAL: Born May 30, 1924; son of John Dryden (an insurance broker) and Brooke (Russell) Kuser; married Elizabeth Cryan, June, 1947; married second wife, Thelma Hoegnell, December, 1962; children: (first marriage) Alexander Russell and Philip Cryan (twins). *Education:* Brown University, B.A., 1950. *Politics:* Republican. *Religion:* Episcopalian. *Home and office address:* American Embassy, P.O. Box 30137, Nairobi, Kenya.

CAREER: U.S. Government, Washington, D.C., employed in various assignments, 1950-59; president, African Research & Development Co., Inc., 1959-69; NIDOCO Ltd., Lagos, Nigeria, chairman of board, 1961-69; Tucker, Anthony, & R. L. Day (stockbrokers), New York, N.Y., limited partner, 1961—; U.S. Ambassador to Malagasy Republic, 1969-71, Trinidad and Tobago, 1972-74, and Kenya, 1974—, nonresident ambassador to Seychelles, 1976—. Trustee of New York Zoological Society, Vincent Astor Foundation, Seamans Church Institute, Astor Home for Children, and International Medical and Research Foundation. *Military service:* U.S. Marine Corps Reserve, 1942-56; active service, 1942-44; became captain; received Purple Heart.

WRITINGS: Africa's Living Arts (juvenile), F. Watts, 1969; *The Malagasy Republic: Madagascar,* F. Watts, 1972; *Trinidad and Tobago,* F. Watts, 1974. Contributor to *Explorers Club Journal* and *Focus* (journal of American Geographical Society).

SIDELIGHTS: Anthony Marshall is competent in French and has some ability in Spanish, Italian, Swahili, and Turkish. *Avocational interests:* Photography.

*   *   *

MARSHALL, Donald S(tanley) 1919-

PERSONAL: Born September 10, 1919, in Danvers, Mass.; son of Thomas Stanley and Mildred Eliza (Titus) Marshall; married Shirley Morrow, January 1, 1945; children: Mira Nan, Lance Martin, Shirley Moana, Anabel Jean. *Education:* Harvard University, A.B. (magna cum laude), 1950, A.M., 1951, Ph.D., 1956; advanced study at Auckland University College (now University of New Zealand), 1951-52, and Indiana University, 1953; also attended U.S. Army Command and General Staff College, 1957, Industrial College of the Armed Forces, 1961 (honor graduate), Army War College, 1962-63, and a number of other military schools. *Home:* Far Lands House, 3414 Halcyon Dr., Alexandria, Va. 22305.

CAREER: Began as salesman for firms in Malden, Mass., 1936-39, and operated a photography studio in Malden, 1938-42; Lafayette Camera Co., Boston, Mass., manager, 1939-42; Auckland University College (now University of New Zealand), Auckland, New Zealand, lecturer in anthropology, 1951-52; Peabody Museum of Salem, Salem, Mass., research anthropologist for Polynesia, 1953-58; Far Lands House, Alexandria, Va. (research and publishing firm), owner and general anthropologist, 1959—. U.S. Army, active duty, 1942-46, and periodically Reserve officer, 1946-63; continuous active duty, 1963-76, assigned to General Staff, Department of the Army, Washington, D.C., 1963-68, chief of Long Range Planning Task Group, Headquarters, Military Assistance Command, Vietnam, 1968-70, assistant for Vietnam, Office of the Assistant Secretary of Defense, International Security Affairs, 1970-71, military assistant to the assistant to the secretary and deputy secretary of defense, 1971-73, deputy director of SALT Task Force, 1973-74, special assistant for policy to the assistant to the secretary of defense, 1974-76; retired as colonel, 1976; currently consultant and advisor to Office of the Secretary of Defense. Public lecturer in anthropology, 1949—; professional lecturer at Department of State Foreign Service Institute, to government officials and service groups, and at universities in various parts of the world, 1951—. Make expeditions to Polynesia in 1951-53, 1954-55, 1957-58, 1959; did field work in Tahiti in 1960, 1961, 1963, 1967, 1973, 1976, and Southeast Asia, 1965-71.

MEMBER: American Anthropological Association (fellow), American Association for the Advancement of Science (fellow), Royal Anthropological Institute of Great Britain and Ireland (fellow), Society for Applied Anthropology (fellow), American Geographical Society (fellow), American Academy of Political and Social Science, American Association of Physical Anthropologists, American Ethnological Society, Linguistic Society of America, International Linguistic Association, Linguistic Society of New Zealand, Society for the Scientific Study of Religion, Polynesian Society (New Zealand; life member), Societe des Etudes Oceanienes (Tahiti), Societe des Oceanistes (Paris), Societe des Etudes Indo Chinoises (Saigon), Far Eastern Prehistory Association, Association for Social Anthropology in Eastern Polynesia, International Oceanographic Foundation, Institute for the Advancement of Sailing, Amateur Yacht Research Society (England), International Amateur Boat Building Society, Slocum Society, Association of the United States Army, Military Government Association, U.S. Naval Institute, United Nations Association of the U.S.A., American Judicature Society, National Rifle Association, British Museum Society, Hakluyt Society (England), Phi Beta Kappa.

AWARDS, HONORS—Scholarly: Fulbright award to New Zealand, 1951-52; McConnaughey fellowship for Polynesian research, 1952-57; National Research Council grant, 1957; Guggenheim fellowship, 1957-58; research fellowship in linguistics at Harvard University, 1960; Peabody Museum Polynesian fellowship, 1962; Kircher grant-in-aid, Peabody Museum of Salem, 1965-66. Military: Vietnam Service Medal with eleven campaign stars, 1965; Army Commendation Medal, 1968; Legion of Merit, 1969; Joint Service Commendation Medal, 1969, with added oak-leaf cluster and valor device, 1970; Bronze Star Medal, 1970; and decorations from the Republic of Vietnam, including Army Distinguished Service Medal (military), 1970 and Revolutionary Development Medal (civilian), 1970; Political Warfare Medal, Republic of China, 1976.

WRITINGS: (Editor and arranger) *Songs and Tales of the Sea Kings,* Peabody Museum of Salem, 1957; *Ra'ivavae: An Expedition to the Most Fascinating and Mysterious Island in Polynesia,* Doubleday, 1961 (published in England as *Island of Passion: Ra'ivavae,* Allen & Unwin, 1962); (with J. Frank Stimson) *A Dictionary of Some Tuamotuan Dialects of the Polynesian Language,* Peabody Museum of Salem, 1964; (editor with Robert C. Suggs) *Human Sexual Behavior: Variations across the Ethnographic Spectrum,* Basic Books, 1971.

Editor of and contributor to the following Department of the Army publications: *Program for the Pacification and Long Term Development of South Vietnam,* two volumes, 1966; *REPOST,* three volumes, 1967; *Comprehensive Army Study for Thailand,* three volumes, 1968; *MACV Objectives Plan,* three volumes, 1969; *JGS/MACV Combined Strategic Objectives Plan,* 1970; *Strategic Alternatives for Southeast Asia,* 1971. Also editor and contributor to several documents published by the Department of Defense, including *Net Assessment of East Asia,* 1973, and *U.S. Civil Defense Policy,* 1976.

Author of four manuals on Polynesia distributed by Department of Anthropology, Auckland University College, 1951, 1953, journals of eight Polynesian trips, and research papers. Contributor to *Encyclopaedia Britannica* and to *Scientific American, American Antiquity, Journal of Austronesian Studies,* and anthropology journals.

WORK IN PROGRESS: Editing and contributing sections to *Anthropology and Austronesia,* by the colleagues of E. S. Craighill Handy; *Parau Tahiti! Speak Tahitian!; The Face of His Desire: A Biography of Stimson of the South Seas; The Village of God: An Ethnography of Mangaia; High Island: An Ethnology of Ra'ivavae;* a dictionary of the Ra'ivavaean dialect of the Polynesian language and a dictionary and grammar of the Cook Island dialects of the Polynesian language; a comparison of the national strategies of six nuclear powers, and other works on national strategy.

SIDELIGHTS: Donald Marshall writes that he "is concerned with long-range strategic planning for national security, using an inter-disciplinary approach to such defense-related policy problems as 'Where is our nation to go? Where are we now? . . . What is the role of nuclear weapons?'" Marshall plans to make another voyage among the South Sea Islands in a "twin-hulled Polynesia ship of reformulated design and [my] own construction."

* * *

MARSHALL, Edison 1894-1967

August 29, 1894—October 2, 1967; American novelist, explorer, and short story writer. Obituaries: Washington Post, October 31, 1967. (See index for CA sketch)

* * *

MARSHALL, Mel(vin) 1911-
(Ray Cory)

PERSONAL: Born October 8, 1911, in San Antonio, Tex.; son of Carl S. and Della (Duncan) Marshall; married Aldine Thompson, May 22, 1937. Home: 330 First St., Phillips, Tex. 79071. Agent: August Lenninger, Lenninger Literary Agency, Inc., 437 Fifth Ave., New York, N.Y. 10016.

CAREER: Active in newspapers and broadcasting in South and Southwest, 1929-46; Pittsburg News (weekly), Pittsburg, Calif., owner and publisher, 1946-47; Pittsburg Broadcasting Co., Inc. (KECC), Pittsburg, secretary-treasurer and general manager, 1946-57; Pittsburg Daily News Publishing Co., Pittsburg, director and publisher, 1947-49; president and general manager of Humboldt Broadcasters, Inc., Arcata, Calif., 1957-64, and Del Norte Broadcasters, Inc., Crescent City, Calif., 1958-64; free-lance writer and photographer, 1965—. Consultant on news and editorial presentation for radio and television stations. Member: Western Writers of America (president, 1976-77).

WRITINGS—Western fiction, except as noted: Longhorn North, Ballantine, 1969; Buffalo!, Ballantine, 1969; McQuade, Ballantine, 1971; The Long Rider, Ballantine, 1971; Steelhead (nonfiction; Field & Stream Book Club selection), Winchester Press, 1971; Drift Fence, Ballantine, 1971; Two Funerals for Tombstone, Ballantine, 1973; Buffalo Hunt, Ballantine, 1975; The Care and Repair of Fishing Tackle (nonfiction), Winchester Press, 1976; How to Make Your Own Lures and Flies (nonfiction), Funk, 1976; Gato, Ballantine, in press; Forests to the Sea (California historical), Putnam, in press.

Cookbooks: The Delectable Egg, Simon & Schuster, 1968; Cooking over Coals, Winchester Press, 1971; Fish Cookery, Harper, 1971; The Family One-Pot Cookbook, Ace Books, 1973; The Family Poultry and Fowl Cookbook, Ace Books, 1973; The Family Cookout Cookbook, Ace Books, 1973; Real Living with Real Foods, Fawcett, 1974; The Perfect Host, Winchester Press, 1975.

Under pseudonym Ray Cory; all Western fiction: Valley of Death, Avalon, 1966; Trail of Venegeance, Avalon, 1966; Guns on the Pedernales, Avalon, 1967; Riders of Tierra Roja, Avalon, 1969; Hell Canyon, Award, 1973.

Contributor to Argosy, Gourmet, Outdoor Life, Sports Afield, Ladies' Home Journal, and to trade and regional periodicals.

WORK IN PROGRESS: How to Make All Kinds of Fishing Rods.

MARTIN, Charles-Noel 1923-

PERSONAL: Born December 25, 1923, in Paris, France; son of Charles Antoine (an engineer) and Jeanne Louise (Saupin) Martin; married Huguette Oddo, June 20, 1963. Education: Attended Lycee Carnot in Tunis for fourteen years and University of Algiers for three years; theorist of nuclear physics at Institut du Radium and Institut Henri Poincare, University of Paris, 1950-58; National Center of Scientific Research, Paris, Doctorat es Sciences. Office: 5 rue de la Baume, Paris 8, France.

CAREER: Le Figaro and Le Figaro Litteraire (newspapers), Paris, France, scientific editor and consultant, beginning 1961; Science et Vie (magazine), Paris, scientific editor and consultant, 1969—. Member: American Physical Society, American Institute of Physics, American Association for the Advancement of Science; and eleven other scientific societies in France, Great Britain, Japan, Italy, and Switzerland. Awards, honors: Nautilus Prize (France), 1959; Prize of French Academy, 1961, for La Recherche scientifique, 1968, for Feerie du monde invisible, and 1972, for Jules Verne, sa vie et son oeuvre.

WRITINGS: Numerical Tables of Nuclear Physics: Tables numeriques de physique nucleaire (text in English and French), Gauthier-Villars, 1954; L'Heure H a-t-elle sonne pour le monde?, preface by Albert Einstein, Grasset, 1955; L'Atome, maitre du monde, Centurion, 1956, augmented edition, Productions de Paris, c.1960; Les Satellites artificiels, Presses Universitaires de France, 1958, revised edition, 1964, translation by T. Schoeters published as Satellites Into Orbit, Harrap, 1967; Les Treize marches vers l'atome, Horizons de France, 1958, translation by B. B. Rafter published as The Thirteen Steps to the Atom: A Photographic Exploration, F. Watts, 1959; Les Vingt sens de l'homme devant l'inconnu (addresses, essays, and lectures on science and philosophy), Gallimard, 1958, translation by A. J. Pomerans published as The Role of Perception in Science, Hutchinson, 1963; La Recherche scientifique, Fayard, 1959.

Promesses et menaces de l'energie nucleaire, Presses Universitaires de France, 1960, translation by Schoeters published as The Atom: Friend or Foe?, F. Watts, 1962; L'Univers devoile, d'un infini a autre, Plon, 1961, translation by Schoeters published as The Universe of Science, Hill & Wang, 1963 (translation published in England as The Realm of Science, Harrap, 1963); L'Energie, moteur du monde, Presses Universitaires de France, 1962; Feerie du monde invisible, Hachette, 1967; Mille et une semaines de science, SODI, 1968; Le Cosmos et la vie, Livre de Poche, 1970; L'Annee scientifique, Hachette, 1971; Jules Verne, sa vie et son oeuvre, Editions Rencontre, 1971; L'annee scientific et medicale, Hachette, 1971; La Conquette spatiale, Bordas, 1972. Contributor to newspapers and television in France.

WORK IN PROGRESS: A bio-bibliography of Albert Einstein with his work explained for the layman.

SIDELIGHTS: Charles-Noel Martin is able to work in English, Russian, and Italian; he is less competent in reading German and Spanish. There have been more than fifty translations of his books in twelve languages.

* * *

MARTIN, Herbert 1913-

PERSONAL: Born February 5, 1913, in Felgentreu, Brandenburg, Germany; son of Ernst (a clergyman) and Margarete (Evenius) Martin; married Erika Hartwig, May 21,

1940; children: Ernst, Werner, Renate (Mrs. Wolfgang Wilhelm), Karl, Helmut, Hans. *Education:* Studied at University of Vienna, 1932, University of Heidelberg, 1933, University of Halle-Wittenberg, 1933-36, and at a seminary in Berlin, 1937. *Politics:* None. *Home:* Schuetzenhofstrasse 7, 62 Wiesbaden, Germany.

CAREER: Evangelical Lutheran clergyman; assistant at cathedral in Naumburg, Germany, 1940-41; imprisoned by the Gestapo in 1941, "later persecuted from Naumburg," and fined, 1944; parson in Genthin, Germany, 1941-55, and East Berlin, 1955-61; went into retirement for personal security, after three warnings from the Communist Party, 1961-66; with his family was taken safely into West Germany in 1966; prison priest in Wiesbaden, West Germany, 1966-68; parson in Wiesbaden, at Market Church, 1969—.

*WRITINGS—*All illustrated: *Offene Tueren,* Evangelisch Verlagsanstalt, 1958; *Leuchtende Kette,* Evangelisch Verlagsanstalt, 1960, translation by Inge Bash published as *Advent Chain of Stars: Devotions and Activities for the Family,* Augsburg, 1968; *Heilige Strasse* (title means "The Holy Street"; passion meditations for adults), Evangelisch Verlagsanstalt, 1963; *Vom Kind zum Koenig* (title means "From Child to King"; guide for parents), Evangelisch Verlagsanstalt, 1963. Illustrator of religious calendar for Verlag Kaufman Lahr.

WORK IN PROGRESS: Ein Passionsfenster entsteht: Wir sind dabei; an illustrated text on the Passion with map and a kit of materials for children to use.

SIDELIGHTS: Herbert Martin's plans to become a painter were hampered by poor vision, but in his work as a clergyman he became interested in visual representation of religious themes, resulting in his illustrated writings and other works.

* * *

MARTIN, Roderick 1940-

PERSONAL: Born October 18, 1940, in Lancaster, England; son of Reginald (a mechanic) and Edna (Josephson) Martin; married Jan Sergeant, August 17, 1963; children: Catherine Susannah, Sarah Frances, James Nicholas Alexander. *Education:* Balliol College, Oxford, B.A. (first class honors), 1961; University of Pennsylvania, graduate study, 1961-62; Nuffield College, Oxford, D.Phil., 1965. *Home:* 62 Lonsdale Rd., Oxford, England. *Office:* Trinity College, Oxford University, Oxford, England.

CAREER: University of York, Heslingdon, England, lecturer in modern history, 1964-66; Oxford University, Oxford, England, lecturer at Jesus College, 1966-69, university lecturer in politics and sociology, and fellow of Trinity College, 1969—. Visiting senior lecturer, Monash University, 1975. *Member:* British Sociological Association. *Awards, honors:* Arthur Andersen travelling fellow.

WRITINGS: Communism and the British Trade Unions 1924-1933: A Study of the National Minority Movement, Oxford University Press, 1969; (editor with D. E. H. Whiteley) *Sociology, Theology and Conflict,* Barnes & Noble, 1969; (with R. H. Fryer) *Redundancy and Paternalist Capitalism,* Allen & Unwin, 1973; *The Sociology of Power,* Routledge & Kegan Paul, 1977.

WORK IN PROGRESS: A research project on the introduction of new technology in the British national newspaper industry.

MARTINEAU, Gilbert 1918-

PERSONAL: Born July 26, 1918, in Rochefort, Charente-Maritime, France; son of Roger and Bertha (Bourlat) Martineau. *Education:* Lycee of Saint-Etienne, Loire, France, classical studies. *Religion:* Roman Catholic. *Address:* Consul of France, Island of St. Helena, South Atlantic Ocean; and 5 rue du Corneau, 17590 Ars-en-Re, France.

CAREER: French Navy, served with Fleet Air Arm squadron attached to U.S. Navy, 1944-45; French Diplomatic Service, 1956—, consul on the Island of St. Helena, 1957—. *Member:* Societe de Gens de Lettres (France), Society of Authors (England). *Awards, honors:* Knight, Legion of Honor; Order of Merit (France); Croix de Guerre; Member, Order of the British Empire.

WRITINGS: La vie quotidienne a Sainte-Helene au temps de Napoleon, Hachette, 1966, translation by Frances Partridge published as *Napoleon's St. Helena,* J. Murray, 1968, Rand McNally, 1969; (co-author) *Napoleon et l'empire,* Hachette, 1968; *Napoleon se rend aux Anglais,* Hachette, 1969, translation by Partridge published as *Napoleon Surrenders,* J. Murray, 1971; *Napoleon's Last Journey,* J. Murray, 1976; *Madame Mere, Napoleon's Mother,* J. Murray, 1977. Translator into French of Gore Vidal's *The City and the Pillar,* Deux Rives, 1948. Writer of scripts for French radio and British Broadcasting Corp. programs.

WORK IN PROGRESS: A history of Franco-British relations in the nineteenth century; a biography of Lord Byron; a book on the making of Europe; a history of the Entente Cordiale.

AVOCATIONAL INTERESTS: Film-making.

BIOGRAPHICAL/CRITICAL SOURCES: Le Figaro, May 31, 1967.

* * *

MARTON, George 1900-

PERSONAL: Born June 3, 1900, in Budapest, Hungary; son of Alexander and Albertine (Kovacs) Marton; married Rose Keledi, January 6, 1921; married second wife, Hilda Hess, September 1, 1949; children: (first marriage) Eva (Mrs. Jack Lafer), Marieclaire Marton Mulholland. *Education:* Sorbonne, University of Paris, Ph.D., 1924. *Politics:* Democrat. *Religion:* Jewish. *Home:* 15 Avenue Paul Doumer, Paris 16, France. *Agent:* Elizabeth Marton, 96 Fifth Ave., New York, N.Y. 10011.

CAREER: Literary agent in Vienna, Austria, 1925-37, and Paris, France, 1937-39; president of Playmarket Agency, Los Angeles, Calif., 1939-44; film producer under contract to Metro-Goldwyn-Mayer Studio, Culver City, Calif., 1944-45; producer of film, "The Fortress," in Canada for J. Arthur Rank, 1948; European story editor for Twentieth Century-Fox Film Co. in Paris, 1948-63. *Military service:* California National Guard, 1942-45; became lieutenant. *Member:* American Club of Paris. *Awards, honors:* Knight of French Legion of Honor.

WRITINGS: Schenk mir eine Insel, Kindler Verlag, 1964; (with Tibor Meray) *The Raven Never More,* Neville Spearman, 1965; (with Meray) *Catch Me a Spy,* Harper, 1969; "Mademoiselle Spaghetti" (play), adapted by Robert Thomas, produced in Paris at Theatre Capucinco, 1969; (with James McCargar) *Three Cornered Cover,* Holt, 1973; (with M. Burren) *The Obelisk Conspiracy,* Citadel, 1976; *Alarum,* W. H. Allen, in press. Also author, with Ladislas Fodor, of an unproduced play, "Bedside Manners," and a screenplay, "The Man from Medici," with Theodore J. Flicker.

WORK IN PROGRESS: A biography of Alexander Mackenzie; with Tibor Meray, *Monologue for Two,* a spy book.

SIDELIGHTS: Catch Me a Spy was made into a film with the same title, produced by Steve Pallos and Pierre Braunberger, and starred Kirk Douglas, 1971; an original story by Marton was adapted by Lotte Coline and Melvyn Bragg for the film, "Play Dirty," produced by Harry Saltzman. In addition to his native Hungarian and English, Goerge Marton is fluent in French, German, Italian, and Spanish.

BIOGRAPHICAL/CRITICAL SOURCES: New Yorker, September 13, 1969.

*   *   *

MARWICK, Arthur   1936-

PERSONAL: Born February 29, 1936, in Edinburgh, Scotland; son of William Hutton (a lecturer) and Maeve (Brereton) Marwick. *Education:* University of Edinburgh, M.A. (first class honors), 1957; Balliol College, Oxford, B.Litt., 1960. *Home:* 67 Fitzjohn's Ave., London N.W.3, England. *Office:* Department of History, Open University, Bletchley, Buckinghamshire, England.

CAREER: University of Aberdeen, Aberdeen, Scotland, assistant lecturer in history, 1959-60; University of Edinburgh, Edinburgh, Scotland, lecturer in history, 1960-69, director of studies, 1964-69; Open University, Bletchley, England, professor of history, 1969—. Visiting professor, State University of New York at Buffalo, 1966-67.

WRITINGS: The Explosion of British Society, 1914-1962, Pan Books, 1963; *Clifford Allen: The Open Conspirator,* Oliver & Boyd, 1964; *The Deluge: British Society and the First World War,* Bodley Head, 1965, Little, Brown, 1966; *Britain in the Century of Total War: War, Peace, and Social Change, 1900-1967,* Little, Brown, 1968; *The Nature of History,* Macmillan, 1970, Knopf, 1971; (contributor) Karl Miller, editor, *Memoirs of a Modern Scotland,* Faber, 1970; *War and Social Change in the Twentieth Century,* Macmillan, 1976; *The Home Front: The British and the Second World War,* Thames & Hudson, 1976; *Women at War 1916-1918,* Fontana, 1977. Contributor of articles and reviews to learned and popular journals.

WORK IN PROGRESS: Images of Class: Britain, France and the U.S. Since 1930; Dictionary of British History, for Thames & Hudson; *Penguin Social History of Britain, 1965 to the Present.*

BIOGRAPHICAL/CRITICAL SOURCES: New York Times, December 27, 1965; *Observer,* May 12, 1968; *Books and Bookmen,* July, 1968; *Christian Science Monitor,* October 22, 1968; *Book World,* October 27, 1968; *Punch,* March, 1969; *New York Review of Books,* December 16, 1969.

*   *   *

MARX, Anne

PERSONAL: Born in Bleicherode, Germany; came to United States in 1936, naturalized in 1938; daughter of Jakob (a physician) and Susanne (Weinberg) Loewenstein; married Frederick E. Marx (a real estate consultant), February 12, 1937; children: Thomas J., Stephen L. *Education:* Graduated from University of Heidelberg Medical School; University of Berlin Medical School, M.S., 1933; attended Orthopedic Clinic of University of Frankfurt/Main, 1934-35. *Home:* 315 The Colony, Tallwood Lane, Hartsdale, N.Y. 10530. *Office:* Frederick E. Marx Corp., Inc., 200 Park Ave., New York, N.Y. 10017.

CAREER: Vice-president of Frederick E. Marx Corp., New York City. Fairleigh Dickinson University, Madison, N.J., staff member of poetry workshop, 1962-64; Iona College, Writers' Conference, New Rochelle, N.Y., director of poetry workshop, 1964-70; Wagner College, New York City Writers' Conference, fellow, 1965; Arkansas Writers' Conference and South & West Conventions, principal speaker, 1966-71; Poetry Society of America Poetry Workshop, New York City, guest critic, 1970-71; Council for the Arts in Westchester, Inc., Westchester, N.Y., chairman of poetry division, 1970; New York Public Library, Donnell Library Center, New York City, director of poetry reading series, 1970-74; workshop leader at conventions, National League of American Pen Women, 1974, 1976, 1977.

MEMBER: Poetry Society of America (fellow, 1964; member of executive board, 1965-70; vice-president, 1970-72), Poetry Society of Great Britain, National League of American Pen Women (president of Westchester County branch, 1962-64; North Atlantic regional chairman, 1964-66), Academy of American Poets, National Federation of State Poetry Societies, Composers, Artists and Authors of America, Inc. (poetry editor, 1974—), Poetry Society of Pennsylvania, New York Poetry Forum. *Awards, honors:* National Sonnet prizes, 1959 and 1968; poetry awards from National Federation of Women's Clubs, 1957, 1958, 1959, and National Federation of State Poetry Societies, 1962, 1965, 1966; American Weave Chapbook award, 1960, for *Into the Wind of Waking;* annual Braithwaite Contest, 1960; Countess d'Esternaux gold medal, 1965; Greenwood prize (Great Britain), 1966; South & West Publications award, 1966, for *By Grace of Pain;* award, Ivan Franko Memorial Competition, 1966; Atlantic Award, 1967; Mason Sonnet Prizes, 1970, 1971, 1972, 1974, 1975; Cecil Hamely Memorial Prize, Poetry Society of America, 1974; numerous other awards in American and English poetry contests.

WRITINGS—Poetry: Ein Buechlein: German Lyrics, Kaufman Verlag, 1935; *Into the Wind of Waking,* foreword by John Holmes, American Weave Press, 1960; *The Second Voice,* Fine Editions Press, 1963; *By Grace of Pain,* South & West Publications, 1966; *By Way of People,* Golden Quill Press, 1970; *A Time to Mend: Selected Poems, 1960-1970,* Living Poets Library, 1973; *Hear of Israel and Other Poems,* Golden Quill Press, 1975. Also co-editor of an anthology, *Pegasus in the Seventies,* 1975.

Work represented in many anthologies, including: *The World's Love Poetry,* Bantam, 1960; *Discourses on Poetry,* South & West Publications, 1967; *The Illustrated Treasury of Poetry for Children,* edited by David Ross, Grosset, 1970; *Spring World, Awake,* edited by M. C. Luckhardt, Abingdon, 1970; *From Deborah and Sappho to the Present,* New Orlando Publications, 1976; *Americana Anthology,* Cross-Cultural Communications, 1976; *American Women Poets,* Olivant Press, 1976. Contributor of poetry to magazines, and to such journals as *Poet Lore, Midwest Review, Poet/India, Ukranian Review,* and *New York Quarterly.* Poetry editor, *Pen Woman,* 1974—.

WORK IN PROGRESS: A study of the angels in Klopstock's "Der Messias"; articles on contemporary poetry and poets; a collections of new poems, *Family Gatherings;* "A Practical Workshop for Impractical Poets."

SIDELIGHTS: Anne Marx told *CA:* "As a bi-lingual poet, I am especially intrigued with the mystery of language communicating in the unique way we call poetry. Born and educated in Germany, I always knew poetry to be a spontaneous natural activity for me. Being expelled from my homeland meant giving up not only a beloved language but also the writing of poetry, my most meaningful means of communication. It took twenty years until English became my most natural voice, the preferred tool for writing. The differences in my two languages, as well as in my two backgrounds, intrigue me now. Aided by a thorough early foundation in Latin, a fair command of French, and by my present extensive annual travel abroad, I am searching for new ways to overcome language barriers, especially in poetry. Translations are never enough.''

BIOGRAPHICAL/CRITICAL SOURCES: Beaux Arts, spring, 1957; *Poetry Society Bulletin,* October, 1959, October, 1963, November, 1964, November, 1966, November, 1968, November, 1970; *Villager,* October, 1960, February, 1971; *Il Giornale Dei Poetei,* April, 1961; *Essence,* winter, 1967-68; *Poet Lore,* spring, 1968, winter, 1971, summer, 1974; *Pen Woman,* May, 1969; *Book Exchange* (London), November, 1970; *Encore,* November, 1975, January, 1976.

* * *

MASLOW, Abraham H. 1908-1970

April 1, 1908—June 8, 1970; American psychologist. Obituaries: *New York Times,* June 10, 1970; *Time,* June 22, 1970. (See index for *CA* sketch)

* * *

MASON, George E(van) 1932-

PERSONAL: Born March 9, 1932, in Cortland, N.Y.; son of Evan E. and Norma (Barnes) Mason; married Gloria M. Gulino, July 3, 1953; children: Victoria, Joseph, Elizabeth, William, Christopher. *Education:* Cortland State Teachers College (now State University of New York College at Cortland), B.S., 1953; Syracuse University, M.S., 1958, Ph.D., 1963. *Politics:* Democrat. *Home:* 235 Pine Forest Dr., Athens, Ga. 30601. *Office:* College of Education, University of Georgia, Athens, Ga. 30601.

CAREER: Elementary teacher in North Syracuse, N.Y., 1955-57; Board of Cooperative Educational Services, Theresa, N.Y., reading specialist, 1957-60; Florida State University, Tallahassee, associate professor and head of department of elementary education, 1963-66; University of Georgia, Athens, associate professor, 1966-71, professor of reading, 1971—. *Military service:* U.S. Army, 1953-55. *Member:* National Society for the Study of Education, American Educational Research Association, International Reading Association, National Reading Conference, College Reading Association, Phi Delta Kappa.

WRITINGS: (With Edwin H. Smith) *Teaching Reading in Adult Basic Education,* Florida State Department of Education, 1965; (with William D. Sheldon) *Winner's Circle,* Allyn & Bacon, 1970; *On the Level,* Allyn & Bacon, 1975; *Full Count,* Allyn & Bacon, 1975.

WORK IN PROGRESS: Research on television and reading.

* * *

MASSA, Ann 1940-

PERSONAL: Born June 24, 1940, in Nottingham, England; daughter of Cyril Chapman (an accountant) and Phyllis (Ruff) Massa. *Education:* University of Edinburgh, M.A., 1962; Brown University, additional study, 1962-63; University of Manchester, Ph.D., 1965. *Politics:* ''Pragmatic.'' *Religion:* Roman Catholic. *Office:* School of English, University of Leeds, Leeds, Yorkshire, England.

CAREER: University of Nottingham, Nottingham, England, lecturer in American studies, 1965-67; University of Essex, Colchester, England, research fellow in American studies, 1967-70; University of Chicago, Chicago, Ill., American Council of Learned Societies fellow, 1970-71; University of Leeds, Leeds, Yorkshire, England, lecturer in American literature, 1971—. Visiting professor at College of William and Mary, 1976-77. *Member:* British Association of American Studies. *Awards, honors: Vachel Lindsay* was nominated for a National Book Award.

WRITINGS: Vachel Lindsay: Field Worker for the American Dream, Indiana University Press, 1970; *The American Novel since 1945,* National Book League, 1975.

WORK IN PROGRESS: A biography of Harriet Monroe; a study of the reciprocal relationship between women and Chicago in the nineteenth century.

* * *

MASSEY, James Earl 1930-

PERSONAL: Born January 4, 1930, in Ferndale, Mich.; son of George Wilson (a minister) and Elizabeth (Shelton) Massey; married Gwendolyn Inez Kilpatrick (a registered nurse), August 4, 1951. *Education:* Attended Detroit Conservatory of Music, 1946, University of Detroit, 1949-50, 1953-54, and Salzburg Mozarteum, Austria, 1952; Detroit Bible College, B.R.E., B.Th., 1961; Oberlin College, M.A., 1964; University of Michigan, graduate study, 1967-68. *Politics:* Democrat. *Home:* 700 Chestnut, Anderson, Ind. 46012. *Office:* Mass Communications Board of the Church of God, 1303 East Fifth St., Anderson, Ind. 46011.

CAREER: Ordained to the ministry of the Church of God, 1951; Church of God of Detroit, Detroit, Mich., associate pastor, 1953-54; Metropolitan Church of God, Detroit, founder and senior pastor, 1954-76, honorary pastor-at-large, 1976—; Jamaica School of Theology, Kingston, president, 1963-66; Anderson College and School of Theology, Anderson, Ind., professor of religion, campus pastor, 1969-77; Church of God, Mass Communications Board, Anderson, speaker, ''Christian Brotherhood Hour'' (international radio broadcast of the Church of God), 1977—. Member of board of directors, Detroit Council of Churches, 1967-69. Member of board of directors, Warner Press, Inc. *Military service:* U.S. Army, 1951-63.

MEMBER: National Association of the Church of God (historian, 1957—; chairman, commission on higher education, 1968—; vice-chairman, publication board, 1968—; chairman, committee on Christian unity, 1969—), National Negro Association of Evangelicals (member of board of directors, 1969—), Inter-Varsity Christian Fellowship (corporation member, 1970—), National Committee of Black Churchmen, National Association of College and University Chaplains. *Awards, honors:* D.D., Asbury Theological Seminary, 1972; Danforth Foundation Underwood fellow, 1972; Staley Distinguished Christian Scholar, 1977.

WRITINGS: The Growth of the Soul, privately printed, 1955; *An Introduction to the Negro Churches in the Church of God Reformation Movement,* Shining Light Survey Press, 1957; ''*When Thou Prayest*'': An Interpretation of Christian Prayer according to the Teachings of Jesus, Warner Press, 1960; *The Worshiping Church: A Guide to the Experience of Worship,* Warner Press, 1961; *Raymond S. Jackson: A Portrait,* Warner Press, 1967; *The Soul Under Siege (A Fresh Look at Christian Experience),* Warner Press, 1970; *The Hidden Disciplines,* Warner Press, 1972; *The Responsible Pulpit,* Warner Press, 1974; *The Sermon in Perspective,* Baker Book, 1976.

Contributor to periodicals and journals, including *Christianity Today, Methodist Herald, Christian Century, Pulpit,* and *Covenant Quarterly*. Member of editorial board, *Christian Scholar's Review;* contributing editor, *Vital Christianity.*

WORK IN PROGRESS: Howard Thurman: A Theological Biography; a revision of *An Introduction to the Negro Churches in the Church of God Reformation Movement,* with the new title *The Church of God and the Negro; Christian Theology and Social Experience.*

AVOCATIONAL INTERESTS: Beethoven's music, stamp collecting, oil painting, travel.

* * *

MASSEY, Joseph Earl 1897-

PERSONAL: Born October 22, 1897, in Reidsville, N.C.; son of William Graham (a farmer) and Nancy Ella (Pritchett) Massey; married Marguerite Youmans, July 15, 1929; children: Martha Anne (Mrs. Giles E. Walker), Kay Louise (Mrs. George C. Lyon, Jr.), Stephen Graham. *Education:* Elon College, A.B., 1918; Columbia University, B.Lit., 1922. *Politics:* Republican (independent). *Religion:* Protestant. *Home:* 165 Keating Dr. S.W., Largo, Fla. 33540.

CAREER: Newsman in New Haven, Conn., Utica, N.Y., and New York City, 1922-29; New York Telephone Co., New York City, copywriter and editor, 1929-62; East Hudson Parkway Authority, Pleasantville, N.Y., public relations director, 1963-69. *Member:* American Numismatic Society, American Numismatic Association, Sigma Delta Chi, Kiwanis Club, Deadline Club (New York). *Awards, honors:* Award of Merit of National Association of State and Local Historians, 1952, for *Historic Landmark Journeys in New York State.*

WRITINGS: Historic Landmark Journeys in New York State, New York Telephone Co., 1952; *America's Money: The Story of Our Coins and Currency,* Crowell, 1968; (contributor) *Studies on Money in Early America,* American Numismatic Society, 1976.

AVOCATIONAL INTERESTS: Amateur photography, coin collecting and numismatic study, fishing, and gardening.

* * *

MASSIS, Henri 1886-1970

March 21, 1886—April 17, 1970; French essayist and right-wing intellectual. Obituaries: *New York Times,* April 20, 1970; *Washington Post,* April 20, 1970; *Antiquarian Bookman,* May 4, 1970.

* * *

MATHISON, Stuart L. 1942-

PERSONAL: Born April 21, 1942, in Brooklyn, N.Y.; son of Ralph P. and Eleanor (Savage) Mathison; married June Goldstein (a teacher), September 14, 1968. *Education:* Cornell University, B.S., 1965; Massachusetts Institute of Technology, M.S., 1968. *Home:* 1976 Lancashire Dr., Potomac, Md. 20854. *Office:* Telenet Communications Corp., 1050 17th St. N.W., Washington, D.C. 20036.

CAREER: International Business Machines Corp., New York, N.Y., systems engineer, 1965-66; Arthur D. Little, Inc., Management Sciences Division, Cambridge, Mass., management consultant, 1968-73; Telenet Communications Corp., Washington, D.C., vice-president of corporate plan-

ning, 1973—. Part-time instructor in computer systems, Northeastern University, 1969-71. *Member:* Association for Computing Machinery, Institute of Electrical and Electronics Engineers (chairman of committee on computer communication).

WRITINGS: (With Philip M. Walker) *Computers and Telecommunications: Issues in Public Policy,* Prentice-Hall, 1970; (contributor) Norman Abramson and Franklin F. Kuo, editors, *Computer Communication Networks,* Prentice-Hall, 1970. Contributor of articles to technological periodicals.

WORK IN PROGRESS: Research in computer-communication networks, communication satellites, communication industry regulation, and global telecommunications.

* * *

MATSUNAGA, Alicia 1936-

PERSONAL: Surname is pronounced with even stress on each syllable; born May 25, 1936, in Livermore Valley, Calif.; daughter of Henry S. and Elvira (Holm) Orloff; married Daigan Lee Matsunaga (a college professor and Buddhist priest), April, 1964. *Education:* College of Agriculture (now University of California, Davis), A.B., 1958; University of Redlands, M.A., 1961; Otani University, graduate study, 1962-64; Claremont Graduate School, Ph.D., 1964. *Religion:* Buddhist. *Home:* 11761 Preston Trails Ave., Northridge, Calif. 91324.

CAREER: University of California, Los Angeles, assistant professor of Oriental languages, 1965-73. *Awards, honors:* Ford Foundation grant, 1968-69; Cultural Award of Japanese National Broadcasting Co., 1970, for *The Buddhist Philosophy of Assimilation.*

WRITINGS: The Buddhist Philosophy of Assimilation, Tuttle, 1969; (with husband, Daigan Matsunaga) *The Buddhist Concept of Hell,* Philosophical Library, 1971; (with Daigan Matsunaga) *Foundation of Japanese Buddhism,* Buddhist Books International, Volume I: *The Aristocratic Age,* 1974, Volume II: *The Mass Movement,* 1975.

* * *

MATTER, Joseph Allen 1901-

PERSONAL: Born March 13, 1901, in Watertown, S.D.; son of Arthur Guy (a lawyer) and Clyda (Allen) Matter; married May Finch, March 31, 1923; children: Allen P., Jean (Mrs. George Mandler). *Education:* Hastings College, B.A. (magna cum laude), 1921; University of Chicago, graduate study, 1921, 1927; Northwestern University, J.D., 1926. *Religion:* Protestant. *Address:* P.O. Box 889, Sedona, Ariz. 86336.

CAREER: High school teacher in Brady, Neb., 1922-24, and Glen Ellyn, Ill., 1924-25; admitted to Illinois Bar, 1926, and practiced law as associate and then as senior partner with firm of Chapman & Cutler, Chicago, 1926-66. Lecturer and writer on legal and financial subjects, 1935—. Union League Civic and Arts Foundation, Chicago, founder, 1952, president, 1954-55. *Member:* International Wine and Food Society, Western History Association, Westerners (Chicago Corral), Boswell Club of Chicago, Chicago Literary Club, Cliff Dwellers Club, Caxton Club (president, 1958-60), Union League Club (president, 1951-52), First Zen Institute (New York), Cultural Integration Fellowship (San Francisco), World Congress of Faiths (London).

WRITINGS: Henry Blake Fuller: A Biography, Chicago Literary Club, 1965; *My Lords and Lady of Essex: Their

State Trials, Regnery, 1969; *Love, Altruism and World Crisis: The Challenge of Pitirim Sorokin,* Nelson-Hall, 1974. Contributor to periodicals.

WORK IN PROGRESS: "At the suggestion of Harvard University, a book on my 40 years spent in the practice of municipal bond law"; research at Newberry Library in Chicago and in England for a book dealing with late Tudor history, biography, and state trials.

SIDELIGHTS: Joseph Matter told *CA:* "I have found my principal non-business satisfaction in reading and collecting books. I suppose my principal objective in writing my first book was to find out whether I could write anything that anyone would want to publish. However, I do enjoy the writing of books, although I am afraid I must admit that I enjoy the research involved more than the actual writing."

AVOCATIONAL INTERESTS: World travel (has visited about one hundred countries), wines, book collecting, Oriental art (and collecting Oriental antiques), philosophy of religions, music, western history.

* * *

MATTHEWS, Patricia (A.) 1927-
(Patty Brisco)

PERSONAL: Born July 1, 1927, in San Fernando, Calif.; daughter of Roy Oliver and Gladys (Gable) Ernst; married Marvin Owen Brisco, December 21, 1946 (divorced); married Clayton Matthews, November 3, 1971; children: (first marriage) Michael Arvie, David Roy. *Education:* Attended Pasadena Junior College and California State University, Los Angeles. *Home:* 3783 Latrobe St., Los Angeles, Calif. 90031. *Office:* California State University, Los Angeles, Calif. 90032.

CAREER: California State University, Los Angeles, secretary to general manager of Associated Students, 1959—. *Member:* Mystery Writers of America.

WRITINGS: (Under name Patty Brisco) *The Other People,* Powell Publications, 1970; (under name Patty Brisco) *The Carnival Mystery* (juvenile), Scholastic Book Services, 1974; (under name Patty Brisco) *The Campus Mystery* (juvenile), Scholastic Book Services, 1977; *Love's Avenging Heart,* Pinnacle Books, 1977; *Love's Wildest Promise,* Pinnacle Books, 1977; *Love Forever More,* Pinnacle Books, 1977.

With husband, Clayton Matthews; published under single name, Patty Brisco: *Merry's Treasure,* Avalon Books, 1970; *Horror at Gull House* (Gothic mystery), Belmont-Tower, 1973; *House of Candles* (Gothic mystery), Manor, 1973; *The Crystal Window* (Gothic mystery), Avon, 1973; *Mist of Evil* (Gothic mystery), Manor, 1976.

Short stories represented in *Action,* edited by Dolly Hasinbiller, Scholastic Book Services, 1977. Contributor of short stories to *Ladies' Home Journal, Escapade, Dude, Alfred Hitchcock's Mystery Magazine,* and *Mike Shayne's Mystery Magazine;* contributor of poetry to *American Bard, Oregonian,* and *Poetry.*

WORK IN PROGRESS: Love's Proud Captive, for Pinnacle Books.

SIDELIGHTS: Patricia Matthews told *CA:* "People ask us what it is like being married to another writer—and for us it has been great. We have not only worked together on several books, but we each are available for ideas, advice, editing, and other input for the books that we do separately. Talking over ideas with each other often engenders *new* ideas, and

triggers the creative process. We live a relatively quiet life with our large, spoiled Burmese cat, Pyewacket (who is also my familiar, as I am very interested in the occult). . . ."

* * *

MATTHEWS, William 1942-

PERSONAL: Born November 11, 1942, in Cincinnati, Ohio; son of William P., Jr. and Mary E. (Sather) Matthews; married Marie Harris (a teacher), May 4, 1963; children: William, Sebastian. *Education:* Yale University, B.A., 1965; University of North Carolina at Chapel Hill, M.A., 1966. *Home address:* Jamestown Star Route, Boulder, Colo. 80302. *Office:* Department of English, University of Colorado, Boulder, Colo. 80309.

CAREER: Wells College, Aurora, N.Y., instructor in English, 1968-69; Cornell University, Ithaca, N.Y., assistant professor of English, 1969-74; University of Colorado, Boulder, associate professor of English, 1974—. Visiting lecturer, University of Iowa, 1976-77. Co-director of Lillabulero Press and co-editor of *Lillabulero* (poetry journal), 1966-74; member of editorial board for poetry, Wesleyan University Press, 1969-74; advisory editor, L'Epervier Press, 1976—. Member of literature panel, National Endowment for the Arts, 1976—; member of board of directors, Associated Writing Programs, 1977—. *Awards, honors:* National Endowment for the Arts, 1974.

WRITINGS: Broken Syllables (poems), Lillabulero Press, 1969; *Ruining the New Road* (poems), Random House, 1970; *The Cloud,* Barn Dream Press, 1971; *Sleek for the Long Flight,* Random House, 1972; *An Oar in the Old Water* (pamphlet), Stone Press, 1974; *Sticks and Stones,* Pentagram Press, 1975; (with Mary Feeney, translator from the French) Jean Follain, *Removed from Time* (pamphlet), Tideline Press, 1977. Advisory editor, *Tennessee Poetry Journal,* 1970-72; poetry editor, *Iowa Review,* 1976-77; contributing editor, *Gumbo,* 1977—.

WORK IN PROGRESS: Rising and Falling, for Little, Brown; a book of Follain translations.

* * *

MAXWELL, Patricia 1942-
(Jennifer Blake, Elizabeth Treahearne)

PERSONAL: Born March 9, 1942, in Winn Parish, La.; daughter of John H. (an electrician) and Daisy (Durbin) Ponder; married J. R. Maxwell (a retail automobile dealer), August 1, 1957; children: Ronnie, Ricky, Delinda, Kathy. *Home address:* Rural Route 1, Box 203, Quitman, La. 71268.

CAREER: Writer. Member of board of directors, Deep South Writers and Artists Conference. *Member:* National League of American Pen Women, Les Beaux Arts Club.

WRITINGS: The Secret of Mirror House, Fawcett, 1970; *Stranger at Plantation Inn,* Fawcett, 1971; (under pseudonym Elizabeth Treahearne) *Storm at Midnight,* Ace Books, 1973; *Dark Masquerade,* Fawcett, 1974; *The Bewitching Grace,* Popular Library, 1974; *The Court of the Thorn Tree,* Popular Library, 1974; *Bride of a Stranger,* Fawcett, 1974; (under pseudonym Jennifer Blake) *Love's Wild Assault,* Popular Library, 1977; *The Notorious Angel,* Fawcett, 1977. Contributor of poetry, short stories, and articles to newspapers; contributor to *Vignettes of Louisiana History* and *Louisiana Leaders.*

MAY, Gita 1929-

PERSONAL: Born September 16, 1929, in Brussels, Belgium; came to United States, 1947, naturalized in 1950; daughter of Albert and Blima (Sieradska) Jochimek; married Irving May (an executive), December 21, 1947. Education: Hunter College (now Hunter College of the City University of New York), B.A. (magna cum laude), 1953; Columbia University, M.A., 1954, Ph.D., 1957. Home: 404 West 116th St., New York, N.Y. 10027. Office: 501 Philosophy Hall, Columbia University, New York, N.Y. 10027.

CAREER: Hunter College (now Hunter College of the City University of New York), New York City, lecturer in French, 1953-56; Columbia University, New York City, instructor, 1956-58, assistant professor, 1958-61, associate professor, 1961-68, professor of French, 1968—, departmental representative, 1968—. U.S. Education Commission lecturer in Great Britain, 1965. Member: Modern Language Association of America, American Society for Eighteenth-Century Studies, American Association of Teachers of French, Phi Beta Kappa. Awards, honors: Columbia University Council for Research in the Humanities grants, 1960, 1967, 1969; American Council of Learned Societies grant, 1961; Hunter College Outstanding Achievement Award, 1963; Fulbright and Guggenheim grants, 1964-65; decorated Chevalier dans l'Ordre des Palmes Academiques, 1968; National Endowment for the Humanities senior fellowship, 1971; Columbia University Van Amringe Distinguished Book Award, 1971, for Madame Roland and the Age of Revolution; Two Thousand Women of Achievement Distinguished Achievement Award, 1971.

WRITINGS: Diderot et Baudelaire: Critiques d'art, Droz, 1957, 3rd edition, 1973; (editor with Otis Fellows) Diderot Studies III, Droz, 1961; De Jean-Jacques Rousseau a Madame Roland: Essai sur la sensibilite preromantique et revolutionnaire, Droz, 1964, 2nd edition, 1974; Madame Roland and the Age of Revolution, Columbia University Press, 1970. Contributor to literary reviews and academic journals. Member of editorial board, French Review and Eighteenth-Century Studies.

WORK IN PROGRESS: Stendhal: A Critical Biography.

AVOCATIONAL INTERESTS: Painting, the history of art and art criticism, and travel.

BIOGRAPHICAL/CRITICAL SOURCES: Virginia Quarterly Review, autumn, 1970.

*   *   *

MAY, Robert Stephen 1929-
(Robin May)

PERSONAL: Born December 26, 1929, in Deal, Kent, England; son of Robert Cyril (a naval surgeon) and Mary (Robertson) May; married Dorothy Joan Clarke, June 7, 1958; children: Michael Robert, Elizabeth Magda, David Peter. Education: Attended Central School of Speech and Drama, 1950-53. Religion: Church of England. Home: 23 Malcolm Rd., Wimbledon, London S.W. 19, England. Agent: Rupert Crew Ltd., Kings Mews, London WC1N 2JA, England. Office: Look and Learn, I.P.C. Magazines Ltd., King's Reach Tower, Stamford St., London S.E.1, England.

CAREER: Actor, under name Robin May, in British Isles, 1953-63; commercial artists' agent in London, England, 1963-66; free-lance writer and journalist in London, 1966—; I.P.C. Magazines Ltd., London, feature writer and sub-editor of Look and Learn, 1970—. Military service: Royal Artillery, 1948-50; became second lieutenant. Member: National Union of Journalists, Society of Authors, English Westerners, Kansas Historical Society, Wyoming Historical Society, South Dakota Historical Society, Montana Historical Society.

WRITINGS—Under name Robin May: Operamania, Vernon & Yates, 1966; Theatremania, Vernon & Yates, 1967; (compiler) The Wit of the Theatre, Frewin, 1969; Who's Who in Shakespeare, Elm Tree, 1972; Companion to the Theatre, Lutterworth, 1973; Who Was Shakespeare?, David & Charles, 1974; Wolfe's Army, Osprey, 1974; The British Army in the American Revolution, Osprey, 1974; The Wild West, Look-In, 1975.

WORK IN PROGRESS: Books on opera and the western gold rushes.

SIDELIGHTS: Opera and America are May's most intense interests, along with the theatre.

BIOGRAPHICAL/CRITICAL SOURCES: Variety, December 10, 1969.

*   *   *

MAYBRAY-KING, Horace 1901-
(Horace Maybray King)

PERSONAL: Name legally changed to Horace Maybray-King, 1971; born May 25, 1901, in Grangetown, Yorkshire, England; son of John William and Margaret Ann King; married Victoria Florence Harris, 1924 (died, 1966); married Una Porter, 1967; children: (first marriage) one daughter. Education: King's College, London, B.A. (first class honors), 1922, Ph.D., 1940. Address: House of Lords, London S.W.1, England; and 37 Manor Farm Rd., Southampton SO9 3FQ, England.

CAREER: Taunton's School, Southampton, England, head of English department, 1930-47; Regent's Park Secondary School, London, England, headmaster, 1947-50; House of Commons, London, member of Parliament from Test Division of Southampton, 1950-55, from Itchen Division, 1955-70, chairman of Ways and Means and Deputy Speaker, 1964-65, Speaker, 1965-70; House of Lords, London, Deputy Speaker, 1971—. Privy councillor, 1965—. Member, BBC Complaints Committee, 1971-74; president, Spina Bifida Association, 1971—; honorary treasurer, Help the Aged, 1972—. Awards, honors: LL.D., University of Southampton, 1967, University of London, 1967, Bath University of Technology, 1969; D.C.L., University of Durham, 1968; D.Soc.Sc., University of Ottawa, 1969; D.Litt., Loughborough University of Technology, 1971; created a baron (life peer) of Southampton, 1971; fellow, King's College, University of London.

WRITINGS—Under name Horace Maybray King: (Editor and author of introduction and notes) Selections from Macaulay's Essays, Blackie & Son, 1930; (editor) Selections from Homer, Macmillan, 1935; (editor) Selections from Sherlock Holmes, J. Murray, 1950; Parliament and Freedom, J. Murray, 1953, revised edition, 1966; State Crimes, Dent, 1967; (compiler) Before Hansard, Dent, 1968, Barnes & Noble, 1969; (with others) To Church with Enthusiasm, Morgan & Scott, 1968; Songs in the Night: A Study of the Book of Job, illustrations by William Blake, Transatlantic, 1968; James Edward Oglethorpe's Parliamentary Career, Georgia College (Milledgeville), 1968. Also author of "Peter Wentworth" (radio play), 1968, and The Speaker and Parliament, 1973.†

MAYER, Ralph 1895-

PERSONAL: Born August 11, 1895, in New York, N.Y.; son of Moritz (a manufacturer) and Leonora (Toch) Mayer; married Bena Frank (an artist), July 25, 1927. Education: Attended Rensselaer Polytechnic Institute, 1913-16; studied painting at Art Students' League of New York, 1926-28. Home: 207 West 106th St., New York, N.Y. 10025.

CAREER: Chemist with industrial firms manufacturing paints, pigments, and varnishes, 1917-27; painter. Lecturer and teacher in art schools and colleges since 1932, conductor of courses in materials and techniques of creative painting at Columbia University, 1944-64, and at New School for Social Research, 1959-65. Director, Artists Technical Research Institute, 1958—. Military Service: U.S. Army, Chemical Warfare Service, 1917-18. Member: American Institute of Chemists (fellow), American Society of Contemporary Artists (member of board of directors), International Institute for Conservation (fellow), Artists Equity Association. Awards, honors: Guggenheim Fellowship, 1952; Painting fellowships from Yaddo, MacDowell Colony, and Huntington Hartford Foundation; Grumbacher Awards for paintings in 1966, 1974, and 1975 exhibitions of American Society of Contemporary Artists; Nassau Community College, retrospective exhibition, 1967; National Art Materials Trade Association award as man of the year in art, 1969.

WRITINGS: The Artists Handbook of Materials and Techniques, Viking, 1940, 3rd edition, 1970; The Painter's Craft, Van Nostrand, 1948, 3rd edition, 1975; A Dictionary of Art Terms and Techniques, Crowell, 1969. Contributor to art journals and other periodicals. Technical editor, Arts (formerly Art Digest), 1950-55, and American Artist, 1962—.

* * *

MAYS, Cedric Wesley 1907-
(Spike Mays)

PERSONAL: Born August 5, 1907, in Glemsford, Suffolk, England; son of John (a farm laborer) and Elizabeth Amy (Ford) Mays; married Vera Jones (a children's nurse), March 30, 1936; children: John Leslie, Glyn. Education: Boyhood schooling ended at fourteen, but resumed his education at Newbattle Abbey College, 1951-52, and University of Edinburgh, 1952-54 (graduate in social science). Politics: None. Religion: Church of England. Home: 39 Nield Rd., Hayes, Middlesex, England. Agent: Campbell Thomson & McLaughlin Ltd., 31 Newington Green, London N16 9PU, England.

CAREER: Worked as pantry boy at a manor house, Walton's Park, before leaving school; joined the British Army at sixteen, serving with the Royal Dragoons, 1924-32, Royal Signals, 1932-36, 1938-45, and rising to sergeant; later civil servant with General Post Office, British Ministry of Aviation, and finally with British Airports Authority as press and public relations officer at Heathrow Airport, London. Director, Current Affairs Productions Ltd. (producers of television documentaries on travel and on India). Awards, honors: Best First Work of 1969 award, Yorkshire Post, for Reuben's Corner.

WRITINGS—Under name Spike Mays: Reuben's Corner (autobiography), Eyre & Spottiswoode, 1969; Fall Out the Officers (autobiography), Eyre & Spottiswoode, 1969; No More Soldiering for Me (autobiography), Eyre & Spottiswoode, 1971; (with Christopher Ketteridge) Five Miles from Bunkum: A Village and its Crafts, Eyre Methuen, 1972; Last Post, Eyre Methuen, 1974; The Band Rats, P. Davies, 1975. Contributor to the British press.

SIDELIGHTS: In Reuben's Corner, Spike Mays tells of his childhood in a corner of East Anglia, an account described by a Spectator critic as "a clearly apprehended, unbitter record . . . that gives the true feel of the pre-1914 era in the arable eras of England" during one of the lowest dips in farming depression. Fall Out the Officers is the story of Mays' life in the Army.

BIOGRAPHICAL/CRITICAL SOURCES: Spectator, July 19, 1969; Observer Review, July 27, 1969; Books and Bookmen, March, 1970.†

* * *

MAYSLES, Albert 1926-

PERSONAL: Born November 26, 1926, in Boston, Mass.; son of Philip and Ethel (Epstein) Maysles. Education: Syracuse University, A.B., 1950; Boston University, M.A., 1952. Home: 1 West 72nd St., New York, N.Y. Office: Maysles Films, Inc., 1697 Broadway, New York, N.Y. 10019.

CAREER: Maysles Films, Inc. (makers of motion picture films), New York, N.Y., president, 1962—. Military service: U.S. Army, 1944-46.

WRITINGS: (With David Maysles) Salesman, New American Library, 1969.

* * *

McCABE, Victoria 1948-

PERSONAL: Born May 29, 1948, in Clare, Iowa; daughter of Raymond William (a farmer) and Ruby (Egli) McCabe; married Robert P. Dickey (an assistant professor of creative writing), December 22, 1968 (divorced May, 1976); children: Shannon Ezra. Education: University of Missouri, student, 1966-69; Southern Colorado State College, B.A., 1970; Western State College of Colorado, M.A., 1971; University of Denver, graduate study, 1976—. Religion: Roman Catholic. Home: 321 North El Paso, Colorado Springs, Colo. 80903.

CAREER: Western State College of Colorado, Gunnison, instructor in English, beginning 1970; currently teaching at University of Colorado. Awards, honors: Prizes in Stephens College Poetry Contest, 1969, for "Toward Kansas City," and Southern Colorado State College Contest, 1970, for "Cafeteria Scene Two"; Hallmark Honor Prize, 1970, for "Raymond's Letter."

WRITINGS: Victorian Poems, Poetry Bag Press (Pueblo, Colo.), 1970; John Keats Porridge: Favorite Recipes of Contemporary American Poets, University of Iowa Press, 1975. Poetry anthologized in The Missouri Poets, Out of This World, Poems One Line and Longer, The Basic Stuff of Poetry, and Full House of Poets. Poems have appeared in Folio, Latitudes, Oregonian, South Dakota Review, Hollins Critic, Kansas City Star, Poetry Now, Monument, and other literary magazines.

WORK IN PROGRESS: Two collections of poems, Divorce: A Handbook for Beginners and The Dirt Book.

SIDELIGHTS: Victoria McCabe writes poems "out of jolly desperation—some of life has got to be made permanent, holdable." She wrote CA that "the older I get the less jolliness there seems to be. . . . I live in a big old house with son Shannon Ezra ('Ez'), dog Molly Bloom, and cat Dante. These days I deal mostly in poems, food, and stubborn hope."

McCALL, Marsh H(oward), Jr. 1939-

PERSONAL: Born March 11, 1939, in New York, N.Y.; son of Marsh Howard (a cardiologist) and Josephine (Suddards) McCall; married Martha Terrell (a cellist), August 27, 1960; children: Marsh Terrell, Thomas Suddards, Ross William. *Education:* Harvard University, B.A., 1960, Ph.D., 1965. *Politics:* Democrat. *Religion:* Protestant. *Home:* 1017 Vernier Pl., Stanford, Calif. 94305. *Office:* Department of Classics, Stanford University, Stanford, Calif. 94305.

CAREER: Harvard University, Cambridge, Mass., instructor in classics, 1965-68; Center for Hellenic Studies, Washington, D.C., fellow, 1968-69; Johns Hopkins University, Baltimore, Md., assistant professor, 1969-70, associate professor of classics, 1970-75, chairman of department, 1971-73; Stanford University, Stanford, Calif., associate professor of classics, 1976—, chairman of department, 1977—. Visiting professor, University College, University of London, London, England, 1973-74; visiting associate professor of classics, University of California, Berkeley, 1975-76. *Member:* American Philological Association, Hellenic Society, American Association of University Professors, California Classical Association. *Awards, honors:* American Council of Learned Societies fellowship, 1973-74.

WRITINGS: Ancient Rhetorical Theories of Simile and Comparison, Harvard University Press, 1969; (editor and author of introduction) *Aeschylus: A Collection of Critical Essays,* Prentice-Hall, 1972. Also contributor to classical and philological journals in United States, England, and Germany. Associate editor and book review editor, *American Journal of Philology,* 1970-75.

WORK IN PROGRESS: The Manuscript and Scholia of Aeschylus' Supplices, for E. J. Brill; *Literary Criticism,* for E. J. Brill; *Literary Criticism,* for the "Aspects of Antiquity" series, for Hakkert.

AVOCATIONAL INTERESTS: Classical music, tennis.

*   *   *

McCARTHY, Clarence F. 1909-

PERSONAL: Born November 30, 1909, in Chicago, Ill.; son of James J. and Mary Agnes (McGann) McCarthy; married Lillian E. O'Brien, October 23, 1939; children: Maribeth (Mrs. Norman D. Schmidt), Neil R., Carol A., Gerald J. *Education:* De Paul University, LL.B., 1933, A.B., 1935; Northwestern University, graduate study, 1939-44. *Home:* 2728 Iroquois Rd., Wilmette, Ill. 60091.

CAREER: Admitted to the Bar of Illinois State, 1933; private law practice in Chicago, Ill., 1933-40; Arthur Andersen & Co. (accounting firm), Chicago, partner, 1941-72. Lecturer, Northwestern University, 1970—. *Member:* American Bar Association, American Institute of Certified Public Accountants (member and officer, Federal Tax Committee, 1958-65; member of board of examiners, 1966-70).

WRITINGS: (With others) *The Federal Income Tax: Its Sources and Applications,* Prentice-Hall, 1968, 3rd edition, 1974.

*   *   *

McCLELLAND, Ivy Lilian 1908-

PERSONAL: Born May 18, 1908, in Liverpool, England; daughter of William Henry and Selina (Foxall) McClelland. *Education:* University of Liverpool, B.A., 1930, M.A., 1932. *Office:* Department of Hispanic Studies, University of Glasgow, Glasgow G12 8QQ, Scotland.

CAREER: University of Glasgow, Glasgow, Scotland, 1930—, began as assistant, currently senior research fellow in Spanish.

WRITINGS: The Origins of the Romantic Movement in Spain, Liverpool University Press, 1937; *Tirso de Molina: Studies in Dramatic Realism,* Liverpool University Press, 1948; *Benito Jeronimo Feijoo,* Twayne, 1969; *Spanish Drama of Pathos, 1750-1808,* Liverpool University Press, Volume I: *High Tragedy,* 1970, Volume II: *Low Tragedy,* 1970; *Ignacio de Luzan,* Twayne, 1973; *Diego de Torres Villarroel,* Twayne, 1976. Contributor to *Encyclopaedia Britannica, Chambers's Encyclopaedia,* and to professional journals.

*   *   *

McCOMB, David G(lendinning) 1934-

PERSONAL: Born October 26, 1934, in Kokomo, Ind.; son of John F. (in civil service) and Jennie (Glendinning) McComb; married Mary Alice Collier, September 6, 1957; children: Katherine, Susan, Joe. *Education:* Southern Methodist University, B.A., 1956; Stanford University, M.B.A., 1958; Rice University, M.A., 1962; University of Texas, Ph.D., 1968. *Religion:* Unitarian Universalist. *Home:* 2024 Manchester Dr., Fort Collins, Colo. 80521. *Office:* Department of History, Colorado State University, Fort Collins, Colo. 80521.

CAREER: South Texas Junior College, Houston, instructor in history, 1962; San Antonio College, San Antonio, Tex., assistant professor of history, 1962-66; University of Houston, Houston, instructor in history, 1966-68; University of Texas at Austin, research associate in oral history, 1968-69; Colorado State University, Fort Collins, assistant professor, 1969-72, associate professor of history, 1972—. *Member:* American Association for State and Local History, Organization of American Historians, Oral History Association, State Historical Society of Colorado, Texas State Historical Association. *Awards, honors:* Tullis Prize of Texas State Historical Association, 1969, for *Houston: The Bayou City.*

WRITINGS: Houston: The Bayou City, University of Texas Press, 1969.

WORK IN PROGRESS: Research in the urban history of Texas; oral history in Colorado.

*   *   *

McCONKEY, Clarence 1925-

PERSONAL: Born July 17, 1925; son of Clarence Marion (a physician) and Ocie T. McConkey; married Joanne Myers, August 13, 1950; children: Celia, Joel, Amy, Anne. *Education:* McPherson College, B.A., 1949; Iliff School of Theology, Th.M., 1952. *Home:* 776 San Pablo, Balboa, Canal Zone. *Office:* Balboa Union Church, Balboa, Canal Zone.

CAREER: Clergyman of United Methodist Church, 1952—; pastor of Balboa Union Church, Balboa, Canal Zone. *Military service:* U.S. Marine Corps, 1943-46; received Presidential Unit Citation. *Member:* Society for Personnel Administration, National Conference of Christians and Jews, Masons.

WRITINGS: A Burden and an Ache, Abingdon, 1970; *When Cancer Comes.* Westminster, 1974.†

*   *   *

McCOY, Alfred W. 1945-

PERSONAL: Born June 8, 1945, in Concord, Mass.; son of

Alfred Mudge (a systems engineer) and Margarita (chairman of Urban Planning Department, California Polytechnic University; maiden name, Piel) McCoy; married Glenita M. Formoso. *Education:* Columbia University, B.A., 1968; University of California, Berkeley, M.A., 1969; Yale University, graduate student, 1969—. *Home:* 291-G Mansfield St., New Haven, Conn. 06511. *Agent:* David Obst, 3213 Macomb St., Washington, D.C. 20008.

MEMBER: Association of Asian Studies.

WRITINGS: (With Nina S. Adams) *Laos War and Revolution,* Harper, 1970; *The Politics of Heroin in Southeast Asia,* Harper, 1972; (contributor) Luis Simmons and Abdul Said, editors, *Drugs, Politics and Diplomacy: The International Connection,* Sage Publications, 1974. Contributor to journals.

WORK IN PROGRESS: A book on the role of urban growth and the development of sugar plantations in the history of the modern Philippines.

* * *

McCOY, Roy 1935-

PERSONAL: Born October 3, 1935, in Fort Worth, Tex.; son of Clint (a cook) and Mae (Birdwell) McCoy. *Education:* San Francisco State College (now University), writing and literature courses for four years. *Politics:* Independent. *Religion:* None. *Home:* 935 North Madison, Stockton, Calif. 95202.

CAREER: Served in the U.S. Navy, 1954-55, then hitchhiked around the United States, living briefly in Chicago, New Orleans, and New York, and working part-time in restaurants; shipped out twice with the Sailor's Union of the Pacific as a messman, traveling to Japan and the Persian Gulf; since 1968, when he was injured in an automobile accident, he has been reading and writing in California (with the exception of one short period of residence in San Juan, Puerto Rico).

WRITINGS: Entrapment, Argyle Books (Los Angeles), 1965; *Merchants of Venus,* Brandon House, 1967; *Caress Unseen,* Brandon House, 1967.

WORK IN PROGRESS: More fiction.†

* * *

McCRINDLE, Joseph F(eder) 1923-

PERSONAL: Born March 27, 1923, in New York, N.Y.; son of John Ronald (a lawyer) and Odette Fuller (Feder) McCrindle. *Education:* Harvard University, A.B., 1943; Yale University, LL.B., 1948. *Politics:* Democrat. *Religion:* Episcopalian. *Office: Transatlantic Review,* 33 Ennismore Gardens, London S.W.7, England.

CAREER: Editor with Eyre & Spottiswoode, Inc., London, England, Julian Messner, Inc., New York City, and William Morrow & Co., Inc., New York City; Henfield Foundation, New York City, president, 1958—; *Transatlantic Review,* New York City, publisher and editor, 1959—. Director, M. Evans & Co., Inc., New York City; governor of Brooklyn Museum, Brooklyn, N.Y.; trustee of Little Red Schoolhouse, New York City. *Military service:* U.S. Army, 1943-45; became first lieutenant. *Member:* P.E.N., Grolier Club, Yale Club (New York), University Club (Washington), Racquet & Tennis Club (New York), Boodle's (London), St. James' Club (London).

WRITINGS: (Translator from the French) Philip Reynolds, *When and If,* Eyre & Spottiswoode, 1951, Sloane, 1952; (editor) *Stories from the "Transatlantic Review,"* Holt, 1970; (editor) *Behind the Scenes: Theater and Film Interviews from the "Transatlantic Review,"* Holt, 1971.

WORK IN PROGRESS: With B. S. Johnson, editing a collection of poetry from the *Transatlantic Review.*†

* * *

McDONALD, Claude C(omstock), Jr. 1925-

PERSONAL: Born June 2, 1925, in St. Joseph, Mo.; son of Claude Comstock and Dorothy (Wing) McDonald; married Juanice Barnes (a secretary), August 12, 1951; children: Mike, Jeff. *Education:* St. Joseph Junior College, Certificate, 1946; University of Missouri, B.S., 1949; Phillips University, B.D., 1959.

CAREER: Teacher in on-the-farm training program in Albany and Stanberry, Mo., and manager of his own farm, 1949-56; ordained clergyman of Disciples of Christ; First Christian Church, Iowa Park, Tex., minister, 1959—. *Military service:* U.S. Army, 1943-45. *Awards, honors:* Disciples of Christ Town and Country Minister of the Year Award, 1965.

WRITINGS: There's Comfort in His Love, Revell, 1970.

WORK IN PROGRESS: Right On, a book about teen-age rebellion, rejection, and reconciliation; *For the Love of Mike,* a novel.†

* * *

McDONALD, Ian A(rchie) 1933-

PERSONAL: Born April 18, 1933, in Trinidad, West Indies; son of John Archie (a businessman) and Thelma (Seheult) McDonald; married Myrna Camille Foster, December 5, 1959 (divorced); children: Keith Ian. *Education:* Attended Queens Royal College, Trinidad, 1941-51; Cambridge University, B.A. (honors), 1955, M.A., 1959. *Home:* 16 Bel Air Gardens, East Coast, Demerara, Guyana, South America. *Office:* c/o Guyana Sugar Corp., 22 Church St., Georgetown, Guyana, South America.

CAREER: Bookers Group Committee, Georgetown, Guyana, secretary, 1955-59; Bookers Sugar Estates Ltd., Georgetown, Guyana, company secretary, 1959-64, administrative secretary, 1964-70; currently director, Guyana Sugar Corp., Georgetown. Director of Bookers Shipping (Demerara) Ltd., Port Mourant Ltd., West Bank Estates Ltd., Bookers Demerara Sugar Estates Ltd., and Demerara Foundry Ltd. Committee member, National Public Library Committee, Guyana. *Member:* Royal Society of Literature (London; fellow), Royal Agricultural and Commercial Society (Georgetown; director). *Awards, honors:* Winifred Holtby Memorial Prize of Royal Society of Literature, 1969, for best regional novel, *The Humming-Bird Tree.*

WRITINGS: The Humming-Bird Tree (novel), Heinemann, 1969. Contributor of short stories and poems to *Penthouse, Bim, Outposts, Chicago Tribune,* and other publications.

WORK IN PROGRESS: The Hook in the Flesh (tentative title), a novel; short stories and poems.

AVOCATIONAL INTERESTS: Tennis (captained the Cambridge University team and the West Indian Davis Cup team and has played at Wimbledon).

BIOGRAPHICAL/CRITICAL SOURCES: Books and Bookmen, June, 1969.

McDONALD, Julie 1929-
(Julie Jensen)

PERSONAL: Born June 22, 1929, in Audubon County, Iowa; daughter of Alfred J. (a farmer) and Myrtle (Faurschou) Jensen; married Elliott R. McDonald, Jr. (an attorney), May 6, 1952; children: Beth, Elliott R. III. *Education:* University of Iowa, B.A. and Certificate in Journalism, 1951. *Politics:* Republican (moderate). *Religion:* Presbyterian. *Home:* 2802 East Locust St., Davenport, Iowa 52803.

CAREER: Women's editor of newspaper in Rockford, Ill., 1951-52; *Davenport Times-Democrat,* Davenport, Iowa, feature writer and fine arts critic, 1962—. Black Hawk College, Moline, Ill., teacher of English, 1965; St. Ambrose College, Davenport, lecturer in journalism, 1974—. Clarinetist, formerly playing with Rockford Symphony Orchestra, currently with Bettendorf Community Band. Chairman and writer-in-the-schools, Iowa Arts Council, 1969-73. Liaison director, Scott County Association for Mental Health, 1956-58; secretary, Scott County Republican Central Committee, 1957-74. *Member:* National League of American Pen Women (Quad-Cities branch), Authors Guild, P.E.O. Sisterhood, Davenport Writers' Club, Questers Study Club, Phi Beta Kappa. *Awards, honors:* Honorary doctor of letters, St. Ambrose College, 1972.

WRITINGS: Baby Black, Angus Journal, 1960; *Amalie's Story,* Simon & Schuster, 1970. Author of a fifty part historical series, "Pathways to the Present," *Quad-City Times,* 1976. Author of two three-act plays for Davenport Junior Theatre and a three-act play, "High Rise," produced by Playcrafters, Moline; also author of a historical play, "Time and the River," produced by Quad-City Center for Performing Arts. Contributor of two short novels to *Redbook.* Uses maiden name, Julie Jensen, for newspaper articles.

WORK IN PROGRESS: A Mosaic Woman, non-fiction.

SIDELIGHTS: Julie McDonald wrote *CA:* "Though I have enjoyed fictional exploration of the 18th and 19th centuries, I always deny that I write historical novels, insisting that I'm interested in lives, not times. Even as I say this, I know that times do shape lives, and that I, myself, was turned to the past by the anomy of the 1960's. However, I am now ready to face the fictional present; even the future, perhaps. Thousands of authors have given me pleasure, and I'd like to pass it on. Actually, I have to write to feel at home in my own skin, and I'll do it until I die, with or without the readers I earnestly desire."

AVOCATIONAL INTERESTS: Paintings, drawings, and prints ("collect modestly"), Afghan hounds, cats.

* * *

McFARLAND, C(harles) K(eith) 1934-

PERSONAL: Born May 12, 1934, in Frostburg, Md.; son of Charles Marshall and Marie (Fike) McFarland; married second wife, Linda Miller, May 30, 1970. *Education:* Bridgewater College, Bridgewater, Va., B.A., 1960; University of Arizona, M.A., 1962, Ph.D., 1965. *Home:* 144 Maple St., Frostburg, Md. 21532. *Office:* Department of History, Arkansas State University, State University, Ark. 72467.

CAREER: University of Southwestern Louisiana, Lafayette, assistant professor of history, 1965-66; Texas Christian University, Fort Worth, assistant professor, became associate professor of history, 1966-71; Arkansas State University, State University, professor of history and chairman of department, 1971—. *Military service:* U.S. Navy, 1954-56.

Member: American Historical Association, Labor Historians, Organization of American Historians, Western Social Science Association, Southwestern Social Science Association, Arkansas Association of College History Teachers (president, 1976-78), Phi Alpha Theta.

WRITINGS: (Compiler) *Readings in Intellectual History: The American Tradition,* Holt, 1970; *Demand for Dignity: The Rise of Organized Labor,* edited by D. C. Worcester, Steck, 1970; *Roosevelt, Lewis, and the New Deal, 1933-1940* (monograph), Texas Christian University Press, 1970; *The Modern American Tradition: Readings in Intellectual History,* Holt, 1972. Contributor to history journals.

WORK IN PROGRESS: The Labor Press in the Age of Jackson, with Robert Thistlethwaite; contributing author to *United States History,* a textbook.

* * *

McGINNIS, Dorothy Jean 1920-

PERSONAL: Born May 28, 1920, in Dowagiac, Mich.; daughter of John C. (a manager for Western Union) and Wava (Vail) McGinnis. *Education:* Western Michigan University, B.S., 1943; Ohio State University, M.A., 1948; Michigan State University, Ph.D., 1963. *Religion:* Episcopalian. *Home:* 2238 Lorraine Ave., Kalamazoo, Mich. 49008. *Office:* Teacher Education Department, Western Michigan University, Kalamazoo, Mich. 49001.

CAREER: Western Michigan University, Kalamazoo, psychometrist in Psycho-Educational Clinic, 1942-44, instructor, 1944-48, assistant professor of psychology, 1948-64, associate professor of psychology and education, 1964-68, professor of education, 1968—, associate director of Psycho-Educational Clinic, 1948-64, director, 1964-75. *Member:* International Reading Association, American Psychological Association, Michigan Psychological Association, Michigan Reading Association, Michigan Academy of Science, Arts and Letters, Altrusa Club of Kalamazoo.

WRITINGS—All with Homer L. J. Carter: *Reading Manual and Work Book,* Prentice-Hall, 1949; *Learning to Read,* McGraw, 1953; *Effective Reading for College Students,* Dryden, 1957; *Teaching Individuals to Read,* Heath, 1962; *Building a Successful College Career,* W. C. Brown, 1965, 4th edition, 1971; *Reading: A Key to Academic Success,* W. C. Brown, 1976; *Diagnosis and Treatment of the Disabled Reader,* Macmillan, 1970. Contributor to professional journals.

* * *

McGRADY, Patrick M(ichael), Jr. 1932-

PERSONAL: Born July 17, 1932, in Shelton, Wash.; son of Patrick Michael (a journalist) and Grace Helen (Robinson) McGrady; married Elizabeth Rosenbaum, March 4, 1964; married second wife, Colleen Yvonne Bennett (a painter), January 7, 1967 (divorced, 1976); children: (first marriage) Ilya Andreas; (second marriage) Vanessa Veveya Totote, Ian Bennett Franklin. *Education:* Institut d'Etudes Politiques de Paris, Certificat d'etudes politiques, 1953; Yale University, B.A., 1954. *Home and office:* 221 West 82nd St., New York, N.Y. 10024. *Agent:* Julian Bach Literary Agency, 3 East 48th St., New York, N.Y. 10017.

CAREER: Associated Press, newsman in Minneapolis, Minn., 1954-55; United Press, newsman in Boston, Mass., 1954, and Albany, N.Y., 1954; *Chicago Sun-Times,* Chicago, Ill., newsman, 1955-56; news editor, Congress for Cultural Freedom, Paris, France, 1956-57; National Broadcasting Company, New York City, television editor, "Briefing Session," 1957-58; Fund for the Republic, New York City, consultant, 1958-59; Immedia, Inc. (broadcasting productions), New York City, president, 1959-62; *New Leader*, New York City, promotion manager, 1962; *Newsweek*, bureau chief in Moscow, Soviet Union, 1963; Young & Rubicam, New York City, consultant on international programming, 1965; free-lance writer and journalist, 1966—. Member of board of lay advisors, Whitestone Hospital, 1976—. Frequent guest on radio and television talk programs; lecturer and consultant. *Member:* American Society of Journalist and Authors (president, 1975-76), American Association for the Advancement of Science, Gerontological Society, American Aging Association (member of board of directors), American Geriatrics Society, National Association of Science Writers, Yale Club of New York. *Awards, honors: The Youth Doctors* was included on *Book World's* list of the one hundred best books of 1968.

WRITINGS: Television Critics in a Free Society, Fund for the Republic, 1960; *The Youth Doctors,* Coward, 1968; *The Love Doctors,* Macmillan, 1972; (editor) *Emily Wilkens' Secrets from the Super Spas,* Grosset, 1976. Contributor to *Esquire, Ladies' Home Journal, True, Vogue, Look, Holiday, Coronet, London Sun, Status, Book World, Woman's Day, Stern, Quick,* and other publications.

* * *

McGRATH, J. H. 1923-

PERSONAL: Born January 4, 1923, in Adams County, Iowa; son of James R. (a farmer) and Carolyn (Holbrook) McGrath; married Darlene Harlow, August 26, 1945; children: Michael Douglas, Stephanie Sue. *Education:* Buena Vista College, B.A., 1947; University of Iowa, M.A., 1956, Ph.D., 1962. *Residence:* Bloomington, Ill. *Office:* Illinois State University, Normal, Ill. 61761.

CAREER: Elementary and high school teacher, 1947-53; Manning General Hospital, Manning, Iowa, administrator, 1953-57; superintendent of public schools in Stanton, Iowa, 1957-59, and Henry County, Iowa, 1959-63; University of Utah, Salt Lake City, associate professor of school administration, 1963-68; Illinois State University, Normal, professor of school administration, 1968—. *Member:* American Association of School Administrators, National Society for the Study of Education, America Educational Research Association, World Future Society, Phi Delta Kappa.

WRITINGS: (contributor) E. T. De Mars, editor, *Utah School Organization and Administration,* University of Utah Press, 1964; (with Stephen P. Hencley and Lloyd McCleary) *Elementary School Principalship,* Dodd, 1970; (with D. Gene Watson) *Research Methods and Designs for Education,* International Textbook Co., 1970; *Planning Systems for School Executives: The Unity of Theory and Practice,* International Textbook Co., 1971; (contributor) Stephen P. Hencley and James R. Yates, editors, *Futurism in Education,* McCutchan, 1974.

WORK IN PROGRESS: Further writing in the fields of futurism, systems and long-range planning.

* * *

McGRATH, Lee Parr 1933-

PERSONAL: Born September 1, 1933, in Robstown, Tex.; daughter of James Carl (a farmer and cotton buyer) and Margaret (Russ) Parr; married Richard James McGrath, Jr. (employed in the shipping industry), November 5, 1955; children: John Parr, Margaret Lee, Maureen Alison. *Education:* Southern Methodist University, B.A., 1954. *Religion:* Roman Catholic. *Home:* 717 The Parkway, Mamaroneck, N.Y. 10543. *Agent:* John Cushman Associates, Inc., 25 West 43rd St., New York, N.Y. 10036. *Office:* McGrath/Power Associates, 489 Fifth Ave., New York, N.Y. 10017.

CAREER: Writer; McGrath/Power Associates (public relations firm), New York, N.Y., chairman of the board. *Member:* Public Relations Society of America, Fashion Group, Phi Beta Kappa.

WRITINGS—With Joan Scobey, except as noted: *Creative Careers for Women,* Essandess, 1968; (sole author) *Housekeeping with Antiques,* Dodd, 1971; *Do-It-All-Yourself Needlepoint,* Essandess, 1971; *Celebrity Needlepoint,* Dial, 1972.

With Scobey: "What Is a" series; published by Essandess: *What Is a Mother?,* 1968; *... Father?,* 1969; *... Brother?,* 1970; *... Sister?,* 1970; *... Grandmother?,* 1970; *... Grandfather?,* 1970; *... Friend?,* 1971; *... Pet?,* 1971.

SIDELIGHTS: Lee McGrath writes: "My approach to my work is a very contemporary one; I try to reach above all, today's woman; this woman is conscious of her commitments to family, career interests, her home and her social life. I try to write for the woman who wants to understand—in basic language—today's changing fashions and lifestyles. Additionally, if I can give her a good grip on her own creativity and talents, I feel I have really eased, to some extent, problems overwhelming women today: inflation, single and widow-hood, and simply put: an over-mechanized society. She perhaps can realize, through my books and articles, ways in which she can do and be her best, in modern terms."

* * *

McGRAW, Harold Whittlesey, Sr. 1890(?)-1970

1890(?)—July 3, 1970; American editor and publisher. Obituaries: *Antiquarian Bookman,* July 20-27, 1970; *Publishers' Weekly,* July 27, 1970.

* * *

McGRAW, William Corbin 1916-
(William Corbin)

PERSONAL: Born January 22, 1916, in Des Moines, Iowa; son of Frank Irving (an insurance executive) and Grace (Corbin) McGraw; married Eloise Jarvis (a fiction writer), January 31, 1940; children: Peter Anthony, Lauren Lynn (Mrs. J. Robert Wagner). *Education:* Attended Principia College, 1934-36, and University of Missouri, 1936-37; Drake University, A.B., 1938; Harvard University, graduate study, 1938-39. *Home and office:* 1970 Indian Trail, Lake Oswego, Ore. 97034. *Agent:* Curtis Brown Ltd., 575 Madison Ave., New York, N.Y. 10022.

CAREER: Athens Messenger, Athens, Ohio, reporter, 1939-40; *Cleveland Plain Dealer,* Cleveland, Ohio, copyreader, 1940-41; *Oklahoma City Times,* Oklahoma City, Okla., copyreader, 1942-45; *Union-Tribune,* San Diego, Calif., reporter, feature writer, and columnist, 1946-51; writer. Orchardist (grower of filberts) for twenty years. *Military service:* U.S. Navy, 1945-46. *Awards, honors:* Children's Book Award of Child Study Association of America and Junior Book Award of Boys' Clubs of America, 1955, for *High Road Home;* Young Reader's Choice Award of Pacific Northwest Library Association, 1958, for *Golden Mare,* and 1970, for *Smoke.*

WRITINGS—All juveniles; all under name William Corbin: *Deadline,* Coward, 1952; *High Road Home,* Coward, 1954; *Pony for Keeps,* Coward, 1955; *Golden Mare,* Coward, 1958; *Horse in the House,* Coward, 1963; *Smoke,* Coward, 1967; *The Everywhere Cat,* Coward, 1970; *The Day Willie Wasn't,* Coward, 1971; *The Prettiest Gargoyle,* Coward, 1971; *Pup with the Up-and-Down Tail,* Coward, 1972.

WORK IN PROGRESS: A book for younger readers, tentatively entitled, *Superchief, the Trufflepup.*

SIDELIGHTS: William Corbin McGraw writes: "In my view, story-telling is the most ancient and honorable of the arts, and I'm happy to have spent much of my life as a practitioner of it, on however modest a scale."

Smoke was made into a television movie for "World of Disney," on NBC-TV, 1970.

AVOCATIONAL INTERESTS: Listening to music, travel, reading.

*   *   *

McHARG, Ian L(ennox)   1920-

PERSONAL: Born November 20, 1920, in Clydebank, Scotland; came to United States in 1946, naturalized citizen in 1960; son of John Lennox and Harriet (Bain) McHarg; married Pauline Crena de Iongh, August 30, 1947; children: Alistair Craig, Malcolm Lennox. *Education:* Harvard University, B.L.A., 1949, M.L.A., 1950, M.C.P., 1951. *Politics:* Democrat. *Religion:* Presbyterian. *Home:* 725 Davidson Rd., Philadelphia, Pa. 19118. *Office:* Department of Landscape Architecture and Regional Planning, University of Pennsylvania, Philadelphia, Pa. 19104; and Wallace-McHarg, Roberts & Todd, 1737 Chestnut St., Philadelphia, Pa. 19103.

CAREER: Planner, Department of Health for Scotland, 1950-54; University of Pennsylvania, Philadelphia, 1954—, began as assistant professor, professor of landscape architecture, 1960—, chairman of department of landscape architecture and regional planning, 1957—; Wallace-McHarg, Roberts & Todd (architects, landscape architects, and planners), Philadelphia, partner, 1962—. Projects include Town Center Park, Washington, D.C., and Southwark Housing, Philadelphia; also has worked on a landscape plan for Washington, D.C., Inner Harbor plan, Baltimore, ecological study for Staten Island, Lower Manhattan plan, and other projects. Horace Albright Memorial Lecturer, University of California, Berkeley, 1969; member, White House Conference on Children and Youth, 1970; Danz Lecturer, University of Washington, Seattle, 1971; Brown and Haley Lecturer, University of Puget Sound, 1972. Trustee, National Parks Association; member of Art Commission, City of Philadelphia. *Military service:* British Army, Airborne Engineers, 1939-46; became major. *Member:* American Society of Landscape Architects (fellow), Institute of Landscape Architects, Town Planning Institute (England). *Awards, honors:* Bradford Williams Medal of American Society of Landscape Architects, 1968; L.H.D., Amhurst College, 1970; H.H.D., Lewis and Clark College, 1970; B. Y. Morrison Medal, North American Wildlife Management Association, 1971; Creative Arts award, Brandeis University, 1972; Allied Professions medal, American Institute of Architects, 1972.

WRITINGS: Design with Nature, Natural History Press, 1969; *Man: Planetary Disease,* U.S. Agricultural Research Service, 1971.

Contributor: Leonard Duhl, editor, *The Urban Condition,* Basic Books, 1963; F. Fraser Darling, editor, *The Future Environments of North America,* Natural History Press, 1966; *Challenge for Survival,* Columbia University Press, 1970. Contributor to *Annals* of the American Academy of Political and Social Science, to architecture journals, and to *Audubon Magazine.*

SIDELIGHTS: "Man is a blind, witless, low-brow, anthropocentric clod who inflicts lesions upon the earth," Ian McHarg told a reporter from *Life.* As an ecological planner, believed by many to be a successor to Rachel Carson, McHarg attempts to design with nature rather than against it; he has little patience with those who dare to upset its delicate balance. According to the reporter "a Philadelphia matron recently complained to [McHarg] about air pollution. 'Do you know the president of Pennsylvania Electric?' he asked her. 'Yes,' she replied. 'Well,' he said, 'the next time you see him don't shake hands. Leap upon him and bite his jugular vein!'" H. D. S. Greenway writes that McHarg "called the Pentagon a planetary disease become institutionalized, the merchant a man who would turn redwoods into tomato stakes, American cities the 'most inhumane and ugliest . . . ever made by man.'"

Former Secretary of the Interior, Stewart L. Udall says: "When I first met McHarg, he was sort of a voice in the wilderness. I think he's come out of the wilderness now." Udall feels that ecological planning "has really revolutionized landscape planning in this country and may soon begin to revolutionize land use. . . . [McHarg] has such verve and color, he's so bright, his mind moves so rapidly, that he has a way of overwhelming people. . . . He also has a kind of damn-the-torpedoes approach. But I admire this quality. I just wish we had had a whole bushel basket of McHargs fifteen years ago."

Greenway writes: "Now that McHarg has achieved prominence, one of his biggest problems is the flamboyant rhetoric that helped get him there. Carried over from the lecture podium to the planning process, it can alienate the very people whose cooperation is essential—state highway departments, for example. Moreover, some say that McHarg's plans suffer from too much rhetoric; they are all wrapped up in a kind of theological approach and lack down-to-earth directions for their implementation." David Wallace, one of McHarg's partners, concedes that there is some truth in this. However, he explains, "It is somewhat below Ian's level of attention to get down to detailed site planning." Greenway feels that, in contrast to his earlier style, McHarg is now "polemicizing much less and concentrating instead on refining his methodology, testing it against a diverse range of planning problems."

In an interview with an *Atlantic* reporter, McHarg says: "I regard myself as a teacher. It's absolutely the most important thing I do. . . . I'd like to see ecological planning become the only form of planning. But *human* ecological planning." According to Greenway, McHarg has said: "We have a great inheritance of enormous beauty, wealth, and variety. It is aching for glorious cities of civilized and urbane men. . . . We could build a thousand new cities in the most wonderful locations. . . . We can manage the land to ensure its health, productivity, and beauty. All of these things are within the capacity of this people now." The *Life* reporter writes that McHarg asks us to "abandon the self-mutilation which has been our way and give expression to the potential harmony of man-nature. The world is abundant, we require only a deference born of understanding to fulfill man's promise. Man is that uniquely conscious creature who can perceive and express. He must become the steward of the biosphere.''

BIOGRAPHICAL/CRITICAL SOURCES: Greater Philadelphia Magazine, October, 1965; Life, August 15, 1969; Time, October 10, 1969; Reader's Digest, August, 1970; Atlantic, January, 1974; Science, January 28, 1977.†

* * *

McILWRAITH, Maureen Mollie Hunter 1922-
(Mollie Hunter)

PERSONAL: Born June 30, 1922, in Longniddry, East Lothian, Scotland; daughter of William George and Helen Eliza Smeaton (Waitt) McVeigh; married Thomas ''Michael'' McIlwraith (a hospital catering manager), December 23, 1940; children: Quentin Wright, Brian George. Education: Educated in Scotland. Politcs: Scottish Nationalist. Religion: Episcopalian. Home: ''The Shieling,'' Milton, near Drumnadrochit, Inverness-shire, Scotland. Agent: A. M. Heath & Co., Ltd., 40-42 William IV St., London WC2N 4DD, England; and McIntosh & Otis, Inc., 475 Fifth Ave., New York, N.Y. 10017.

CAREER: Writer. Member: ''Congenital nonjoiner.'' Awards, honors: The Lothian Run was named an honor book, Book World Children's Spring Festival, 1970; Scottish Arts Council Literary Award, 1972, for The Haunted Mountain; Child Study Association of America Literary Award, 1972, for A Sound of Chariots; Carnegie Medal, 1975, for The Stronghold; May Hill Arbuthot lectureship, 1975.

WRITINGS—Under name Mollie Hunter; juveniles, except as noted: Patrick Kentigern Keenan, Blackie & Son, 1963, published as The Smartest Man in Ireland, Funk, 1965; The Kelpie's Pearls, Blackie & Son, 1964, Funk, 1966; Thomas and the Warlock, Funk, 1967; The Ferlie, Funk, 1968; The Bodach, Blackie & Son, 1970, published as The Walking Stones: A Story of Suspense, Harper, 1970; The Haunted Mountain, Harper, 1972; A Sound of Chariots, Harper, 1972; A Stranger Came Ashore, Harper, 1975; Talent Is Not Enough: Mollie Hunter on ''Writing for Children'' (nonfiction), Harper, 1976; The Wicked One, Harper, 1977.

Historical juveniles: Hi Johnny, Evans, 1963; The Spanish Letters, Evans, 1964, Funk, 1967; A Pistol in Greenyards, Evans, 1965, Funk, 1968; The Ghosts of Glencoe, Evans, 1966, Funk, 1969; The Lothian Run, Funk, 1970; The Thirteenth Member, Harper, 1971; The Stronghold, Harper, 1974.

Also author of two plays, ''A Love Song for My Lady,'' 1961, and ''Stay for an Answer,'' 1962. Contributor of articles to Scotsman and Glasgow Herald.

WORK IN PROGRESS: Research into Scottish history, folk-lore, and witchcraft as social phenomenon in the fifteenth and sixteenth centuries.

SIDELIGHTS: Maureen McIlwraith told CA, ''I write because I enjoy it and because my mind works that way.'' Avocational interests: Theatre, music. ''Like dogs (useful ones only) and places without people. Company preferred—children.''

* * *

McKAY, John P(atrick) 1938-

PERSONAL: Born August 27, 1938, in St. Louis, Mo.; son of John Price (a government official) and Eleanor (Jeffrey) McKay; married Jo Ann Ott (a church organist), April 21, 1961; children: Philip, Thomas. Education: Wesleyan University, Middletown, Conn., B.A., 1961; Fletcher School of Law and Diplomacy, M.A., 1962; University of California, Berkeley, Ph.D., 1968. Home: 915 West Charles St., Champaign, Ill. 61820. Agent: Gerard McCauley Agency, 551 Fifth Ave., New York, N.Y. 10017. Office: Department of History, University of Illinois at Urbana-Champaign, Urbana, Ill. 61801.

CAREER: University of Illinois at Urbana-Champaign, Urbana, assistant professor, 1966-70, associate professor of European economic history, 1970-76, professor of history, 1976—. Member: American Historical Association, Economic History Association, Economic History Society, American Association for the Advancement of Slavic Studies, American Association of University Professors. Awards, honors: Herbert Baxter Adams Award of American Historical Association, 1970, for Pioneers for Profit; Guggenheim fellowship, 1970; Fulbright-Hays senior research scholar to Soviet Union, 1974.

WRITINGS: Pioneers for Profit: Foreign Entrepreneurship and Russian Industrialization, 1885-1913, University of Chicago Press, 1970; (translator from the French and author of introduction) Jules Michelet, The People, University of Illinois Press, 1973; Tramways and Trolleys: The Rise of Urban Mass Transport in Europe, Princeton University Press, 1976. Contributor to history journals.

WORK IN PROGRESS: Research on the economic development of Europe from early times, Russian economic history, and European social history.

* * *

McKEMY, Kay 1924-

PERSONAL: Born November 24, 1924, in Trenton, Mo.; daughter of William Joseph and Ethel (Smith) McReynolds; married James Stanley McKemy (manager of banking for Texaco, Inc.), January 18, 1946; children: Kathryn Anne, Timothy James. Education: University of Missouri, A.B., 1946; Lamar State College of Technology (now Lamar University), graduate study, 1960-61; Columbia University, M.A., 1963. Politics: Conservative. Religion: Methodist. Home: 4 Megan Lane, Armonk, N.Y. 10504. Office: Department of English, Westchester Community College, Valhalla, N.Y. 10595.

CAREER: Hughen School, Port Arthur, Tex., director of public relations, 1953-59; Briarcliff College, Briarcliff Manor, N.Y., instructor in English, 1962-63; Westchester Community College, Valhalla, N.Y., 1963—, began as associate professor, currently professor of English. Member: Phi Beta Kappa.

WRITINGS: Samuel Pepys of the Navy (biographical novel for young adults), Warne, 1970. Poetry represented in anthologies, including The Owl Book, Warne, 1970, The Fox Book, Warne, 1971, and The Frog Book, Warne, 1972. Contributor of poetry to Ball State Forum and Hartford Courant; also contributor of articles to Dental Survey, Northeast Outdoors, Family Motor Coach Magazine, and other periodicals.

WORK IN PROGRESS: Articles on travel, theater, religion, and capital punishment; poetry.

AVOCATIONAL INTERESTS: Needlework, knitting, gardening, and motorhome travel.

McKENZIE, Leon R(oy) 1932-

PERSONAL: Born March 20, 1932, in Chicago, Ill.; son of Robert and Jeannette (Welch) McKenzie. *Education:* Glennon College, B.A., 1954; graduate study at Kenrick Seminary, 1954-58, Kansas State Teachers College, 1958, and Union Theological Seminary, New York, N.Y.; Fordham University, M.A., 1967; Indiana University, Ed.D., 1973. *Home:* 4277 Woodsage Trace, Indianapolis, Ind. 46227. *Office:* Department of Human Resource Development, Indiana University Hospitals, 384 Clinical Building, 1100 West Michigan St., Indianapolis, Ind. 46202.

CAREER: Roman Catholic priest; teacher at parochial high schools in Parsons, Kan., 1958-61, in Wichita, Kan., 1961-65, and at Sacred Heart College, Wichita, 1965; Carroll High School, Wichita, instructor in sociology, film arts, and psychology, 1967-70; Indiana University, Bloomington, assistant professor of adult education, 1973-75; Indiana University Hospitals, Indianapolis, coordinator of human resource development and associate professor of adult education, 1975—. Guest lecturer at Loyola University, Chicago, Ill., 1973, Indiana Professional Guidance Association, 1974, Southern Illinois University, 1974, and Vincennes University, 1974. Director of St. Jude Experimental School, Wichita, 1954-65, Young Adults Association, Wichita, 1961-63, Adult Study Program, Armonk, N.Y., 1966-67, and Title III funded project of Indiana Commission on Aging and the Aged, 1974-75. Associate superintendent of schools, Wichita Catholic Diocese, 1967-69. Consultant to universities and government agencies.

MEMBER: Adult Education Association of the U.S.A., American Academy of Religion, Commission of Professors of Adult Education, American Academy of Political and Social Science, American Hospital Association, American Society for Hospital Education and Training, Adult Education Association of Indiana (member of board of directors), Indiana Association of Public and Continuing Adult Education, Indiana Society for Hospital Education and Training. *Awards, honors:* Indiana University, Lilly fellow, 1971-72, Bergevin fellow, 1973.

WRITINGS: Minitations for Teens, Daughters of St. Paul, 1964; *Designs for Progress,* St. Paul Editions, 1967; *Process Catechetics: Basic Directions for Catechists,* Paulist/Newman, 1970; *Christian Education in the 70's,* Alba, 1971; (editor) *Community Teamwork,* Bureau of Studies in Adult Education, Indiana University, 1971; *Adult Religious Education,* [West Mystic, Conn.], 1975; *Adult Education and the Burden of the Future,* University Press of America, 1978. Also author of *Creative Learning for Adults,* 1977. Writer of over fifty articles, filmstrips, and audio tapes. Associate editor and columnist, *Pastroal Life;* guest editor with John McKinley of one issue of *Viewpoints.*

WORK IN PROGRESS: A New God for New Men; a chapter, "Teacher Decision Styles in Adult Education," in a book edited by Phillip J. Sleeman, for Baywood; research on adult religious education in its ecumenical aspects.

*   *   *

McLAREN, John (David) 1932-

PERSONAL: Born November 7, 1932, in Armidale, Victoria, Australia. *Education:* University of Melbourne, B.A., 1954. *Politics:* "Conservative Anarchist." *Religion:* "Christian Agnostic." *Residence:* North Carlton, Victoria, Australia. *Office:* Footscray Institute of Technology, Footscray, Victoria, Australia.

CAREER: High school teacher of English in Wodonga, Victoria, Australia, 1956-63; Secondary Teachers' College, Melbourne, Victoria, lecturer in English, 1966-70; full-time writer and lecturer, 1971; Darling Down Institute of Advanced Education, Towoomba, Queensland, Australia, head of department of humanities, 1972-76; Footscray Institute of Technology, Footscray, Victoria, head of department of humanities, 1976—. Chairman, Victorian Secondary English Syllabus Revision Committee. *Member:* Australian Society of Authors, Victorian Association for the Teaching of English.

WRITINGS: Our Troubled Schools, Verry, 1968; *Libraries for the Public,* Hill of Content, 1969; (editor) *Towards a New Australia,* Cheshire, 1972; *Dictionary of Australian Education,* Penguin, 1974; (with E. R. Treyvaud) *Equal but Cheaper,* Melbourne University Press, 1976. Associate editor, *Overland.*

WORK IN PROGRESS: A critical study of Patrick White and Australian realist fiction.

*   *   *

McLAREN, Robert Bruce 1923-

PERSONAL: Born July 13, 1923, in Springfield, Ill.; son of Homer D. (a lawyer) and Matilda (Rose) McLaren; married Althea Bernhard (a professor of art), August 6, 1951; children: Craig, Kirk, Christina. *Education:* Park College, A.B., 1945; McCormick Theological Seminary, B.D., 1948; University of Houston, M.A., 1951; University of Southern California, Ph.D., 1971. *Home:* 900 East Union, Fullerton, Calif. 92631. *Office:* California State University, Fullerton, Calif. 92631.

CAREER: University of Houston, Houston, Tex., instructor in philosophy, 1949-53; minister of Presbyterian churches in Houston, 1953-61, and Fullerton, Calif., 1961-66; Fullerton Junior College, Fullerton, instructor in philosophy, 1966-67; California State University, Fullerton, 1967—, began as assistant professor of philosophy of education, professor of human development, 1977—. Chaplain, Whittier College, 1967. Summer lecturer, University of Hawaii, 1969; lecturer in Germany, Holland, and Belgium, 1975-76. Speaker on tour in England at invitation of British Council of Churches, 1965. *Member:* American Philosophical Association, Philosophy of Education Society, American Association of University Professors, Far Western Philosophy of Education Society (president, 1976—), Fullerton Ministerial Association (president, 1963-65), Phi Theta Kappa, Phi Kappa Phi, Phi Delta Kappa.

WRITINGS: What's Special about Jesus?, Association Press, 1963; (with father, Homer D. McLaren) *All to the Good: A Guide to Christian Ethics,* World Publishing, 1969; *Science and Religion in 21st Century,* Paulist/Newman, 1973. Contributor to *American Educators Encyclopedia, World Topics Yearbook, Christian Century, Bulletin of the Atomic Scientists, Philosophy of Education, American Horseman,* and *International Gymnast.*

WORK IN PROGRESS: A textbook, *The World of Philosophy;* a novel, *Colony of Heaven.*

AVOCATIONAL INTERESTS: Fencing, hiking in mountains.

*   *   *

McLEISH, Kenneth 1940-

PERSONAL: Surname is pronounced McLeesh; born October 10, 1940, in Glasgow, Scotland; son of John (a professor at University of Victoria) and Stella (Tyrrell) Mc-Leish; married Valerie Heath, May 30, 1967; children: Simon, Andrew. *Education:* Worcester College, Oxford, B.A., 1963, B.Mus., 1965, M.A., 1971. *Residence:* Lincolnshire, England. *Agent:* Curtis Brown Ltd., 1 Craven Hill, London W2 3EP, England; and William Morris Agency, 1350 Avenue of the Americas, New York, N.Y. 10019.

CAREER: Watford Grammar School, Watford, Hertfordshire, England, teacher of classics, 1963-67; Leeds Grammar School, Leeds, Yorkshire, England, teacher of classics, 1967-68; Walsall Grammar School, Walsall, Staffordshire, England, teacher of classics, 1968-69; Bedales School, Petersfield, Hampshire, England, head of classics department, 1969-73; free-lance script writer for films and television, 1973—. Composer of musical works, some of them performed on radio.

WRITINGS—All published by Longmans, Green prior to 1971, Longman, 1971 and after, except as indicated: (Editor and translator) *Four Greek Plays: Sophocles, "Oedipus the King" and "Antigone," Aristophanes, "The Acharnians" and "Peace,"* 1964; (editor and translator) *"The Frogs" and Other Greek Plays,* 1970; *Greek Theatre,* 1970; *The Greeks and the Sea,* 1971; (with Roger Nichols) *Through Greek Eyes,* Cambridge University Press, 1975; (with Nichols) *Through Roman Eyes,* Cambridge University Press, 1976; *Roman Comedy,* Macmillan, 1976.

Juveniles: *The Story of Aeneas,* 1968; *Land of the Eagles,* 1969; *Chicken Licken,* 1973; *The Peace Players,* Heinemann, 1976; *Odysseus Returns,* 1976; *The Robe of Blood,* 1976.

Also author of film and television screenplays, including "Tony," and with Frederic Raphael, "The Oresteia" and "The Clouds." Has translated for radio the works of Plautus, Terence, Aristophanes, Ibsen, and Feydeau. Editor of series, *Aspects of Greek Life,* Longman, 1972—.

WORK IN PROGRESS: A series, *Composers and Their World,* for Heinemann, a series of classical translations for Cambridge University Press; a critical study, *The Theatre of Aristophanes.*

BIOGRAPHICAL/CRITICAL SOURCES: Times Literary Supplement, June 26, 1969; *Books and Bookmen,* September, 1969.

* * *

McMILLAN, Colin 1923-

PERSONAL: Born November 13, 1923, in Birmingham, England; son of Kenneth (a surgeon) and Elizabeth (Smythe) McMillan; married Pamela Hurndall (a laboratory technician), July 28, 1944; married second wife, Lavender Ashwell, July 27, 1957; children: (first marriage) Seamus, Iona, Sean; (second marriage) Sophie, Alexander, James. *Education:* Attended Downing College, Cambridge, 1947-48. *Religion:* Christian. *Home:* 12 Park Ave., London N.W. 11, England. *Office:* Muscovy Co., 12 Park Ave., London N.W.11, England.

CAREER: Royal Navy, 1940-55, with rank of lieutenant commander when he was invalided from active service in 1955 because of injury in Korea (mentioned in dispatches, 1953); Imperial Chemical Industries Ltd., production engineering and method study in Plastics Division, 1955-57, export executive, 1957-61; Management Selection Ltd., senior consultant, 1960-65, managing director of affiliate company, Export Services Ltd., 1966-68; Overseas Marketing Corp., director of East European department, 1968-69; Muscovy Co. (trade with Eastern Europe, principally Yugoslavia, on behalf of British and American companies), London, England, principal, 1969—. *Member:* Great Britain-USSR Association (member of executive committee, 1958—).

WRITINGS: (With Sydney Paulden) *Export Agents: A Complete Guide to Their Selection and Control,* Gower Press, 1968, second edition published as *Sales Manager's Guide to Selection and Control of Export Agents,* Cahners, 1969.

AVOCATIONAL INTERESTS: Landscape painting.

* * *

McMURRIN, Sterling M(oss) 1914-

PERSONAL: Born January 12, 1914, in Woods Cross, Utah; son of Joseph W., Jr. (a government employee) and Gertrude (Moss) McMurrin; married Natalie Barbara Cotterel, June 8, 1938; children: Gertrude Ann (Mrs. William Howard), Joseph Cotterel, Sterling James, Natalie Laurie, Melanie. *Education:* Attended University of California, Los Angeles, 1931-32; University of Utah, A.B., 1936, M.A., 1937; University of Southern California, Ph.D., 1946. *Home:* 2969 Devonshire Circle, Salt Lake City, Utah 84108. *Office:* Graduate School, University of Utah, Salt Lake City, Utah 84112.

CAREER: University of Southern California, Los Angeles, assistant professor of philosophy, 1945-48; University of Utah, Salt Lake City, professor of philosophy, 1948-64, E. E. Ericksen Distinguished Professor of Philosophy, 1964—, professor of history, 1970—, dean of College of Letters and Science, 1954-60, academic vice-president, 1960-61, provost, 1965-66, dean of Graduate School, 1966—. Chancellor and adviser, University of Tehran, 1958-59. U.S. Government, Washington, D.C., Commissioner of Education, 1961-62. Member of U.S. Commission for UNESCO and Board of Foreign Scholarships, 1961-62; vice-president, twenty-fifth annual International Conference on Education, Geneva, 1962; member of U.S. delegation, U.S.-Japan Conference on Education and Cultural Exchange, 1962. Visiting scholar, Columbia University and Union Theological Seminary. Trustee of Carnegie Foundation, 1963—; president of Park City Institute for the Arts and Sciences. Consultant to Committee for Economic Development, 1962—, to American Telephone and Telegraph Co., and to IBM Corp.

MEMBER: American Philosophical Association, Phi Beta Kappa, Phi Kappa Phi. *Awards, honors:* Ford Foundation fellowship, 1952-53; LL.D. from University of Utah, 1961, University of Southern California, 1962, Clark University, 1962, Delaware State College, 1962, and Pepperdine College, 1967; L.H.D., University of Puget Sound, 1963.

WRITINGS: (Editor with James Louis Jarrett) *Contemporary Philosophy: A Book of Readings,* Henry Holt, 1954; *The Patterns of Our Religious Faiths* (F. W. Reynolds lecture), Extension Division, University of Utah, 1954; (with Benjamin A. G. Fuller) *A History of Philosophy,* 3rd edition revised (McMurrin was not associated with earlier editions), Henry Holt, 1955; *The Philosophical Foundations of Mormon Theology* (address delivered at various universities), University of Utah Press, 1959.

Reason, Freedom, and the Individual (Riecker memorial lecture), University of Arizona Press, 1964; *The Theological Foundations of the Mormon Religion,* University of Utah Press, 1965; *Philosophy for the Study of Education,* Houghton, 1968; *The Schools and the Challenge of Innovation,* Committee for Economic Development, 1969.

(With others) *Conditions for Educational Equality,* Committee for Economic Development, 1971; (editor) *Functional Education for Disadvantaged Youth,* Committee for Economic Development, 1971; *Resources for Urban Schools: Better Use and Balance,* Committee for Economic Development, 1971; *On the Meaning of the University,* University of Utah Press, 1976. Contributor to *Saturday Evening Post, Saturday Review,* and a number of philosophy and education journals.

WORK IN PROGRESS: A book on the concept of the individual in oriental and occidental thought.†

* * *

McNALL, P(reston) E(ssex) 1888-

PERSONAL: Born February 1, 1888, in Gaylord, Kan.; son of Webb and Christina A. (Woodward) McNall; married first wife, Mabel Dunlap; married second wife, Eugenia Fairman, July 22, 1923; married third wife, Mary A. Davies, July 20, 1969; children: (first marriage) Preston Essex, Jr., John Fairman, James Arthur. *Education:* Kansas State Agricultural College (now Kansas State University), B.S. (electrical engineering), 1909, B.S. (agriculture) and M.S., 1915; Cornell University, graduate study, 1919-20; University of Wisconsin, Ph.D., 1927. *Politics:* Republican. *Religion:* Congregationalist. *Home:* 2423 Kimball Ave., Manhattan, Kan. 66502.

CAREER: Kansas State Agricultural College (now Kansas State University), Manhattan, assistant professor of agriculture economics, 1915-19; University of Wisconsin—Madison, professor of agriculture economics, 1920-56. *Member:* American Economic Association, American Farm Management Association.

WRITINGS: Agricultural Bookkeeping, Longmans, Green, 1937; *Our Natural Resources.* Interstate, 1954, 4th edition (with Harry B. Kircher), 1976. Contributor of section on dairy production to 1954 Agriculture Census report.

* * *

McNAUGHT, Kenneth (William Kirkpatrick) 1918-

PERSONAL: Born November 10, 1918, in Toronto, Ontario, Canada; son of Carlton (an advertising man) and Eleanor (Sanderson) McNaught; married Beverley Argue, June 13, 1942; children: Christopher, Allison, Andrew. *Education:* Upper Canada College, graduate, 1937; University of Toronto, B.A., 1941, M.A., 1946, Ph.D., 1950. *Politics:* New Democratic Party. *Religion:* Anglican. *Home:* 121 Crescent Rd., Toronto, Ontario, Canada. *Office:* Department of History, University of Toronto, Toronto, Ontario, Canada.

CAREER: United College, Winnipeg, Manitoba, assistant professor, 1947-54, associate professor, 1954-56, professor of history, 1956-59; University of Toronto, Toronto, Ontario, assistant professor, 1959-61, associate professor, 1961-64, professor of modern history, 1964—. Summer visiting professor at University of Manitoba, University of British Columbia, Queen's University at Kingston, and St. Francis Xavier University (Antigonish, Nova Scotia); lecturer at Oxford University, Macalester College, Duke University, Franklin and Marshall College, Michigan State University, and at London School of Economics and Political Science, University of London. Chairman of "Round Table," Canadian Broadcasting Corp.-TV, Winnipeg, 1954-58. Member of advisory panel, Canadian Studies Foundation, Toronto, 1970—. *Military service:* Canadian Army, 1942-45; became warrant officer second class.

MEMBER: Canadian Historical Association (member of council, 1955-58), Organization of American Historians, American Historical Association. *Awards, honors:* Canada Council senior research fellow, 1963-64, 1970-71.

WRITINGS: A Prophet in Politics: A Biography of J. S. Woodsworth, University of Toronto Press, 1959, 2nd edition, 1963; (with John H. S. Reid and Harry Crowe) *A Source-Book of Canadian History,* Longmans/Canada, 1959, 2nd edition, 1963; (with Ramsay Cook) *Canada and the United States,* Clarke, Irwin, 1963; *Manifest Destiny: A Short History of the United States,* Clarke, Irwin, 1965; *The History of Canada,* Heinemann, 1969, Praeger, 1970 (paperback edition published in England as *The Pelican History of Canada,* Pelican, 1969); *The Winnipeg Strike: 1919,* Longman, 1975.

Contributor: Michael K. Oliver, editor, *Social Purpose for Canada,* University of Toronto Press, 1961; Peter Russell, editor, *Nationalism in Canada,* McGraw (Toronto), 1966; *The Canadians,* Macmillan (Toronto), 1967; Stephen Clarkson, editor, *An Independent Foreign Policy for Canada?,* McClelland & Stewart, 1968; Alfred F. Young, editor, *Dissent: Explorations in the History of American Radicalism,* University of Illinois Press, 1968.

Editor, "Canadian Studies in History and Government" series, University of Toronto Press, 1959-66. Contributor of articles on current affairs, review articles, and book reviews to *Canadian Forum, Dalhousie Review, India Quarterly, Journal of American History* and other periodicals. Contributing editor, *Saturday Night,* 1959-60; member of editorial board of *Canadian Welfare* (Toronto), 1961-65, and *Christian Outlook* (Montreal), 1961-66.

WORK IN PROGRESS: A History of Collective Violence in Canada.

* * *

McNEILLY, Wilfred Glassford 1921-
(Wilfred Glassford; pseudonyms: William Howard Baker, W. A. Ballinger, Martin Gregg, Joe Hunter, Errol Lecale, Desmond Reid)

PERSONAL: Born March 8, 1921, in Renfrewshire, Scotland; son of William Henry and Christina Glassford (Aitkenhead) McNeilly; married Margaret Ferguson Macdonald Miller, March 7, 1946; children: Colin J.R.G., John H. R., Christopher A. P., Duncan F. S., Quentin K. C. *Education:* "Some." *Politics:* "Anarcho/Conservative/Liberal." *Religion:* "Presbyterian/Agnostic." *Home and office:* Glassford House, Ardglass, County Down, Northern Ireland. *Agent:* Albert Zuckerman, Writer's House, 132 West 31st St., New York, N.Y. 10001.

CAREER: Journalist for *Northern Whig,* Belfast, Northern Ireland, 1938-40; says he was a snake charmer with an Indian circus, 1946-47; journalist for *Belfast Newsletter,* Belfast, and part-time author, 1947-52; full-time author, occasional fisherman, and cameraman (film and still), for British Broadcasting Corp., 1952—. Founder and first honorary secretary, Ardglass Town Committee; member of East Down development and tourist committees. *Military service:* British Army, later Indian Army, and then Royal Indian Navy, 1940-46; became captain in Second Royal Lancers, Indian Army, and lieutenant commander in Royal Indian Navy. *Member:* P.E.N., Downe Society, Royal Naval Sailing Association, Irish Kennel Club, British Legion.

WRITINGS: The Case of the Stag at Bay, Mayflower

Books, 1965; *Death in the Top Twenty*, Mayflower Books, 1965; *The Case of the Muckrakers*, Mayflower Books, 1966; *No Way Out*, World Distributors, 1966; *Land of the Free*, Howard Baker, 1968; *The War Runners*, New English Library, 1970.

Under name Wilfred Glassford: *Alpha-Omega*, New English Library, 1977.

Under pseudonym William Howard Baker: *The Cellar Boys*, World Distributors, 1965; *Cry from the Dark*, World Distributors, 1965; *Departure Deferred*, World Distributors, 1965; *Destination Dieppe*, Mayflower Books, 1965; *The Fugitive* (originally entitled *Frightened Lady*), Mayflower Books, 1965; *Storm over Rockall*, World Distributors, 1965; *Take Death for a Lover*, World Distributors, 1965; *The Rape of Berlin*, World Publishers, 1965, published as *The Girl, the City, and the Soldier*, Howard Baker, 1969; *Blood Trail*, Mayflower Books, 1966; *The Dogs of War*, Mayflower Books, 1966; *Every Man an Enemy*, Mayflower Books, 1966, Macfadden, 1967; *Fire over India* (originally entitled *The Angry Night*), Mayflower Books, 1966; *The Inexpendable*, World Distributors, 1966; *The Dead and the Damned*, Mayflower Books, 1967; *The Girl in Asses' Milk*, Mayflower Books, 1967; *The Guardians*, Mayflower Books, 1967, published as *The Dirty Game*, Howard Baker, 1970; *Treason Remembered*, Mayflower Books, 1967; *Night of the Wolf*, Howard Baker, 1969; *Quintain Strikes Back*, Howard Baker, 1969; *Judas Diary*, Howard Baker, 1970; *The Treasure Hunters*, Mayflower Books, 1970; *The Charge Is Treason*, Howard Baker, 1973.

Under pseudonym W. A. Ballinger: *Unfriendly Persuasion*, World Distributors, 1964; *I, the Hangman*, Mayflower Books, 1965; *Call It Rhodesia*, Mayflower Books, 1966; *Drums of the Dark Gods*, Mayflower Books, 1966; *The Exterminator*, World Distributors, 1966; *Rebellion*, Mayflower Books, 1966; *A Starlet for a Penny*, Mayflower Books, 1966; *Women's Battalion*, Mayflower Books, 1967; *Down among the Ad Men*, Mayflower Books, 1968; *The Galaxy Lot*, Mayflower Books, 1968; *The Green Grassy Slopes*, Corgi Books, 1969; *Congo*, Mayflower Books, 1970; *The Shark Hunters*, Howard Baker, 1970; *Six-Day Loving*, Mayflower Books, 1970; *The Carrion Eaters*, M. Joseph, 1971; *The Waters of Madness*, New English Library, 1974; *The Voyageurs: A Novel*, New English Library, 1976.

Under pseudonym Martin Gregg: *Dark Amazon*, Macmillan, 1957.

Under pseudonym Joe Hunter; "Attack Force" series; all published by New English Library: *French Assignment*, 1976; *Mission to the Gods*, 1976; *Roman Holiday*, 1976; *Vampire Mission*, 1977.

Under pseudonym Errol Lecale; "Specialist" series; all published by New English Library: *The Tigerman of Terrahpur*, 1973; *Castledoom*, 1974; *The Death Box*, 1974; *The Severed Hand*, 1974; *Zombie*, 1975; *Blood of my Blood*, 1976.

Under pseudonym Desmond Reid: *The Babcock Boys*, Mayflower Books, 1966; *The Deadliest of the Species*, Mayflower Books, 1966; *Death Waits in Tucson*, Mayflower Books, 1966; *Frenzy in the Flesh*, Mayflower Books, 1966; *The Man from Pecos*, Mayflower Books, 1966; *The Snowman Cometh*, Mayflower Books, 1966; *Dead Respectable*, Mayflower Books, 1967; (editor) Peter Saxon, *The Slave Brain*, Mayflower Books, 1967; *The Abductors*, Mayflower Books, 1968; *The Case of the Renegade Agents*, Mayflower Books, 1968; *The Slaver*, Mayflower Books, 1969.

Work represented in many anthologies including: *Danger Man Omnibus*, Number 1, Howard Baker, 1965; and *Sexton Blake Omnibus*, Howard Baker, Number 2, 1968, Number 3, 1968, Number 5, 1969, Number 8, 1970, Number 9, 1972.

Writer of radio and television plays and verse.

WORK IN PROGRESS: "Too many books in progress to list."

SIDELIGHTS: "I don't have a vocation, I just write books," McNeilly insists, [and] I get better at it as I go along. Mostly I'm interested in sailing boats, archery, Irish wolfhounds, Siamese cats and sitting around boozers talking to people instead of working. I am motivated better by a pile of bills than anything else though occasionally I strike a vein of pure lyric genius that has to be carefully excised afterwards. The vital thing for a writer to do is to write. A paragraph on paper beats the hell out of a chapter in the mind."

BIOGRAPHICAL/CRITICAL SOURCES: New York Times Book Review, May 26, 1968; *Best Sellers*, May 1, 1969.

* * *

McNIVEN, Malcolm A(lbert) 1929-

PERSONAL: Born December 8, 1929, in Oceanside, N.Y.; son of William and Hazel (Summers) McNiven; married Elaine Vellacott, June 12, 1954; children: Geoffrey David, Susan Leslie, Jane Elizabeth. *Education:* Denison University, B.A., 1951; Ohio University, M.S., 1952; Pennsylvania State University, Ph.D., 1955. *Home:* 161 South Ferndale Rd., Wayzata, Minn. 55391. *Office:* Pillsbury Co., 608 Second Ave. S., Minneapolis, Minn. 55402.

CAREER: University of Maryland, College Park, assistant professor of psychology, 1955-56; Pennsylvania State University, University Park, supervisor of industrial testing, 1956-57; E. I. du Pont de Nemours, Wilmington, Del., research psychologist, 1957-59, manager of advertising research section, 1959-67; Coca-Cola Co., Atlanta, Ga., manager of marketing research department, 1967-68, Coca-Cola USA, Atlanta, vice-president and manager of marketing research department, 1968-71, vice-president of marketing services, 1971-72, vice-president and director of planning, 1972-74; Pillsbury Co., Minneapolis, Minn., vice-president of marketing services, 1975—. Visiting professor at University of Pennsylvania and Georgia Institute of Technology. Trustee, Denison University. *Member:* American Psychological Association (fellow), Audit Bureau of Circulations (director), National Industrial Conference Board (member of council on marketing research), Institute of Management Sciences, Lambda Chi Alpha.

WRITINGS: (Editor) *How Much to Spend for Advertising?: Methods for Determining Advertising Expenditure Levels*, Association of National Advertisers, 1969.

* * *

McPHERSON, Hugo (Archibald) 1921-

PERSONAL: Given name originally Hugh; born August 28, 1921, in Sioux Lookout, Ontario, Canada; son of Peter Gordon (a clergyman) and Nettie L. (Perrin) McPherson; married Louise Guertin (an assistant in an art gallery), June 12, 1951. *Education:* Provincial Normal School, Edmonton, Alberta, Diploma (first class honors), 1940; University of Manitoba, B.A. (honors in English and philosophy), 1949; University of Western Ontario, M.A. (first class honors), 1950; University of Toronto, Ph.D. (first class honors), 1956. *Home:* 4300 de Maisonneuve W., Apt. 1201, Montreal

215, Quebec, Canada. *Office:* Department of English, McGill University, P.O. Box 6070, Montreal, Quebec, Canada.

CAREER: Teacher at junior high school in Alberta, 1940-42; lecturer in English at McGill University, Montreal, Quebec, 1952-53, University of Manitoba, Winnipeg, 1953-55, and at University of British Columbia, Vancouver, 1955-56; University of Toronto, Toronto, Ontario, assistant professor, 1956-60, associate professor, 1960-65, professor of English, 1965-66; University of Western Ontario, London, professor of Canadian and American studies, 1966-70; McGill University, honorary lecturer, 1967-70, professor of Canadian and American literature, 1970—, Grierson Professor of Communications, 1976. Canadian Government film commissioner and chairman of the board of National Film Board of Canada, 1967-70; member of the board, National Arts Centre of Canada, Ottawa, 1967-70, and Canadian Film Development Corp., 1968-70; chairman of the board, Society for Art Publications, 1968-69, vice-chairman, 1969-70; member of administrative council, Fusion des Arts, Montreal, 1968-70; member of Governor General's Awards Committee for Literature, 1970—. Lecturer on literary subjects and on Canadian painting and sculpture; has given numerous talks for Canadian Broadcasting Corp. on subjects ranging from Whitman to recent Canadian novelists, and done reviewing in literature and art for Columbia Broadcasting System on "Critically Speaking" and other programs.

MEMBER: Association of Canadian University Teachers of English (secretary, 1957-58), Canadian Association of University Teachers, Canadian Association for American Studies, Humanities Association of Canada. *Awards, honors:* Humanities Research Council of Canada summer grants, 1953-57, for work at Harvard University; Canada Council postdoctoral fellowship, 1961-62, for work at British Museum; Commonwealth fellow at Yale University, 1966; Canadian Centennial Medal, 1967; LL.D. from University of Manitoba, 1970; Canada Council leave fellowship, 1976-77, for work on Joseph Conrad.

WRITINGS: Hawthorne as Myth-Maker: A Study in Imagination, University of Toronto Press, 1969.

Contributor: A.J.M. Smith, editor, *Masks of Fiction,* McClelland & Stewart, 1961; Abraham Rotstein, editor, *The Prospect of Change,* McGraw, 1965; C. F. Klinck, editor, *The Literary History of Canada,* University of Toronto Press, 1965; George Woodcock, editor, *A Choice of Critics,* Oxford University Press, 1966; J.M.S. Careless and R. Craig Brown, editors, *The Canadians: 1867-1967,* Macmillan (Canada), 1967; *Architecture and Sculpture in Canada,* Queen's Printer, for Expo '67, 1967.

Author of foreword: Gabrielle Roy, *The Tin Flute,* McClelland & Stewart, 1958; Hugh MacLennan, *Barometer Rising,* McClelland & Stewart, 1959; Morley Callaghan, *More Joy in Heaven,* McClelland & Stewart, 1960; Jeremy Adamson, editor, *Canadian Paintings in the Hart House Collection,* 2nd edition, University of Toronto Press, 1969.

General editor with Gary Geddes, "Studies in Canadian Literature," Copp Clark, 1969—, with nine books published and ten more titles planned. Contributor to *Ontario/67,* and of about thirty articles and twenty reviews to *Queen's Quarterly, Canadian Art, Tamarack Review,* and other journals. Member of editorial advisory board, *Canadian Art,* 1960-66.

WORK IN PROGRESS: A critical study of Joseph Conrad; directing an undergraduate program in communications at McGill University.

McPHERSON, Sandra 1943-

PERSONAL: Born August 2, 1943, in San Jose, Calif.; daughter of Walter James (a college physical education professor) and Frances (Gibson) McPherson; married Henry D. Carlile (a university English professor and poet), July 22, 1966; children: Phoebe. *Education:* Attended Westmont College, 1961-63; San Jose State College (now University), B.A., 1965; University of Washington, Seattle, graduate study, 1965-66. *Home:* 7349 Southeast 30th Ave., Portland, Ore. 97202.

CAREER: Honeywell, Inc., Seattle, Wash., technical writer, 1966; poet. Member, Forum on Individuality, White House Conference on Children, 1970; member of faculty, Writers Workshop, University of Iowa, 1974-76. Has given poetry readings at universities and schools around the United States. *Awards, honors:* Helen Bullis Prize of *Poetry Northwest,* 1968; Ingram Merrill Foundation grant, 1972; Bess Hokin prize for poetry, 1972; Emily Dickinson Prize from Poetry Society of America, 1973; National Endowment for the Arts grant, 1974-75; Blumenthal-Leviton-Blonder prize for poetry, 1975; Guggenheim Foundation fellowship, 1976-77; recipient of Northwest Booksellers Prize for *Radiation; Elegies for the Hot Season* was one of the first three books of verse chosen for National Council on the Arts program to aid university presses.

WRITINGS: Elegies for the Hot Season (poems), Indiana University Press, 1970; *Radiation* (poems), Ecco Press, 1973. Poetry represented in many anthologies, including *Best Poems of 1968,* The Borestone Mountain Poetry Awards, 1969, *American Literary Anthology III,* Viking, 1970, *Rising Tides: Twentieth Century American Women Poets,* Washington Square Press, 1973, *No More Masks! No More Mythologies!,* Doubleday, 1973, *Modern Poetry of Western America,* Brigham Young University Press, 1975, *The American Poetry Anthology: Poets Under Forty,* Avon, 1975. Contributor of poetry to various periodicals including *Nation, New Yorker, Poetry, New Republic, Field, Iowa Review, Harper's, Ironwood, Poetry Northwest,* and *Antaeus.*

WORK IN PROGRESS: A third collection of original poetry.

* * *

McPHIE, Walter E(van) 1926-

PERSONAL: Surname is pronounced McFee; born March 20, 1926, in Ogden, Utah; son of Walter Gordon and Heva (Galbraith) McPhie; married Marilyn Norma Jones, July 6, 1951; children: Susan, Mark, Brent, Jill. *Education:* Weber Junior College, Ogden, Utah, A.S., 1950; Utah State University, B.S., 1952; University of Utah, M.A., 1953; Stanford University, Ed.D., 1959. *Home:* 4996 Moor Mont Circle, Salt Lake City, Utah 84117. *Office:* MBH 142, University of Utah, Salt Lake City, Utah 84112.

CAREER: Teacher in Ogden, Utah, 1953-54, and Redwood, Calif., 1954-57; Brigham Young University, Provo, Utah, assistant professor of education, 1959-63; Haile Selassie I University, Addis Ababa, Ethiopia, associate professor of education and chairman of department of secondary education (representing University of Utah), 1963-65; University of Utah, Salt Lake City, associate professor, 1965-70, professor of education, 1970—, assistant chairman of department of secondary education, 1968-70, chairman of department, 1973—. Chief of University of Utah contract party to Ethiopia and associate dean of Faculty of Education, Haile Selassie I University, 1967-68. Seminar director, Robert A.

Taft Institute on Government, 1970. Member of contract team, American Association of Colleges for Teacher Education—United States Agency for International Development Materials Center Feasability Study, Lesotho, Africa, 1975. *Member:* National Education Association, Association for Higher Education, National Council for the Social Studies (chairman of research committee, 1966-67), Utah Council for the Social Studies (executive secretary), Phi Delta Kappa.

WRITINGS: (Editor with Richard E. Gross and Jack Fraenkel) *Teaching the Social Studies, What, Why, and How?,* International Textbook Co., 1969. Contributor of articles and reviews to education journals.

SIDELIGHTS: Walter E. McPhie has traveled in more than thirty countries of Africa, Europe, and Southeast Asia. *Avocational interests:* Sports, particularly hunting and fishing.

* * *

McREYNOLDS, David 1929-

PERSONAL: Born October 25, 1929; son of Charles F. and Elizabeth Grace (Tallon) McReynolds. *Education:* University of California, Los Angeles, B.A.S., 1953. *Politics:* "Socialist/Pacifist." *Religion:* "Bessie Smith." *Home:* 60 East Fourth St., New York, N.Y. 10012.

CAREER: Held odd jobs as typist, ditch digger, meter reader, shipping clerk, and hot dog stand server in New York, N.Y.; *Liberation,* New York, N.Y., editorial secretary; War Resisters League, New York, N.Y., co-secretary, 1961—. *Member:* War Resisters International, International Confederation for Disarmament and Peace, Fellowship of Reconciliation (member of national and executive committees), American Civil Liberties Union (member of free speech committee).

WRITINGS: We Have Been Invaded by the Twenty-first Century: A Radical View of the Sixties, Praeger, 1970. Contributor to *Village Voice, WIN,* and other publications.

* * *

McWHINNEY, Edward 1926-

PERSONAL: Born May 19, 1926, in Sydney, New South Wales, Australia; son of Matthew Andrew and Evelyn Annie (Watson) McWhinney; married Emily Ingalore (an economist and stockbroker), June 27, 1951. *Education:* University of Sydney, LL.B., 1949; Yale University, LL.M., 1951, Sc.Jur.D., 1953; Academy of International Law, The Hague, Diploma in International Law, 1951. *Home:* 1949 Beach Ave., Vancouver, British Columbia, Canada V6G IZ2. *Office:* Department of Politics, Simon Fraser University, Burnaby, Vancouver, British Columbia, Canada V5A 156.

CAREER: Yale University, New Haven, Conn., lecturer in law, 1951-53, assistant professor of political science and fellow of Silliman College, 1953-55; University of Toronto, Toronto, Ontario, professor of international and comparative law and member of Centre for Russian Studies, 1955-66; McGill University, Montreal, Quebec, professor of law and director of Institute of Air and Space Law, 1966-71; Indiana University, Bloomington, professor of law and director of international and comparative legal studies, 1971-74; Simon Fraser University, Vancouver, British Columbia, professor of international law and relations and chairman of department of politics, 1974—. Visiting professor at Ecole Libre des Hauts Etudes, 1952, New Luxembourg, 1959, 1960, University of Heidelberg and Max-Planck Institut, 1960-61,

National University of Mexico, 1965, University of Paris and University of Madrid, 1968, University d'Aix-Marseille, 1969, Institut Universitaire, Luxembourg, 1972, 1974, 1976, The Hague Academy of International Law, 1973, Aristotelian University of Thessalonik, 1975, and University of Nice, 1976-77. Queen's counsel, Canada, 1967—; royal commissioner, Quebec, 1968-72; royal commissioner, British Columbia, 1974-75. Legal consultant to United Nations, 1953-54, U.S. Naval War College, 1961-68, Government of Ontario, 1965-71, and Government of Quebec, 1969-70, 1974-75. *Military service:* Australian Air Force, 1943-45; became flying officer (first lieutenant).

MEMBER: American Society of International Law (member of executive council, 1965-68), Canadian Society of International Law (chairman of executive committee, 1972-75), Institut de Droit International (Paris; membre titulaire), American Foreign Law Association. *Awards, honors:* Rockefeller Foundation fellowship, 1960-61, 1966-68; Canada Council fellowship, 1960-61.

WRITINGS: Judicial Review in the English-Speaking World, University of Toronto Press, 1956, 4th edition, 1969; (editor and contributor) *Canadian Jurisprudence: The Civil Law and Common Law in Canada,* University of Toronto Press, 1958.

Foederalismus und Bundesverfassungsrecht, Quelle & Meyer, 1961; *Constitutionalism in Germany,* Sijthoff, 1962; *Comparative Federalism,* University of Toronto Press, 1962, 2nd edition, 1965; *Peaceful Coexistence and Soviet-Western International Law,* Sijthoff, 1964; (editor and contributor) *Law, Foreign Policy, and the East-West Detente,* University of Toronto Press, 1964; *Federal Constitution-Making for a Multi-National World,* Sijthoff, 1966; *International Law and World Revolution,* Sijthoff, 1967; (editor with Martin A. Bradley) *The Freedom of the Air,* Oceana, 1968; *Conflict ideologique et Ordre public mondial,* A. Pedone (Paris), 1969; (editor with Bradley) *New Frontiers in Space Law,* Oceana, 1969.

(Editor and contributor) *The International Law of Communications,* Oceana, 1971; (editor and contributor) *Aerial Piracy and International Law,* Oceana, 1971; (editor and contributor with P. Pescatore) *Federalism and Supreme Courts and the Integration of Legal Systems,* Editions UGA (Brussels), 1973; *The Illegal Diversion of Aircraft and International Law,* Sijthoff, 1975; (editor and contributor with Pescatore) *Parliament and Parliamentary Power Today,* Sijthoff, 1977; (editor and contributor with Pescatore) *The Executive and Executive Power Today,* Sijthoff, 1978.

Contributor to *International Encyclopaedia of the Social Sciences* and *Encyclopaedia Britannica;* contributor of articles and essays to *Harvard Law Review, Revue Generale de Droit, International Public,* and other journals in the United Kingdom, United States, France, Germany, Spain, and India.

WORK IN PROGRESS: Federalism and Nationalism; studies on relations between the West, the Communist countries, and the Third World; science and technology and international law; communications and broadcasting and international law.

SIDELIGHTS: Edward McWhinney is fluent in French and German and competent in Russian, Italian, and Spanish. *Avocational interests:* Golf, tennis, swimming, walking.

* * *

MEADOW, Charles T(roub) 1929-

PERSONAL: Born December 16, 1929, in Paterson, N.J.;

son of Abraham (a textile worker and union leader) and Florence (Troub) Meadow; married Harriet Riess, September 9, 1956 (divorced); married Mary Louise Shinskey, June 24, 1972; children: (first marriage) Debra Lynne, Sandra Lee; (second marriage) Alison Maria, Benjamin Niland. *Education:* University of Rochester, A.B., 1951; Rutgers University, M.S., 1954. *Home:* 214 West Mt. Airy Ave., Philadelphia, Pa. 19119. *Office:* Graduate School of Library Science, Drexel University, Philadelphia, Pa. 19104.

CAREER: U.S. Department of the Navy, Bureau of Ships, Washington, D.C., mathematician at David Taylor Model Basin, 1954-55; RAND Corp., Santa Monica, Calif., assistant mathematician in Systems Development Division, 1955-56; General Electric Co., Phoenix, Ariz., and Washington, D.C., unit manager, 1956-59, consulting analyst, 1959-60; International Business Machines Corp. (IBM), Federal Systems Division, Gaithersburg, Md., development mathematician, 1960-62, senior programmer, 1962-67, manager of information sciences, Center for Exploratory Studies, 1967-68; National Bureau of Standards, Center for Computer Sciences and Technology, Washington, D.C., chief of Systems Development Division, 1968-71; Atomic Energy Commission, Washington, D.C., assistant director of Division of Management Information and Telecommunications, 1971-74; Drexel University, Philadelphia, Pa., professor of information science, 1974—. Adjunct lecturer, University of Maryland, School of Library and Information Services, 1967-72. Executive secretary, Committee on Scientific and Technical Information, Federal Council for Science and Technology, 1970-71; member of advisory committee, Office of Library, Personnel Resources, American Library Association, 1970-77. *Military service:* U.S. Marine Corps, 1951-53; became first lieutenant. *Member:* Association for Computing Machinery, American Society for Information Science (vice-president, commission on long range planning, 1974-76). *Awards, honors:* Honorable mention, Children's Science Book Award, 1976, from New York Academy of Science for *Sounds and Signals: How We Communicate.*

WRITINGS: The Analysis of Information Systems, Wiley, 1967, 2nd edition, 1973; *The Story of Computers* (juvenile), Harvey House, 1970; *Man-Machine Communication,* Wiley, 1970; *Sounds and Signals: How We Communicate* (juvenile), Westminster, 1975; *Applied Data Management,* Wiley, 1976. Contributor to *Annual Review of Information Science and Technology,* Encyclopaedia Britannica, 1970, and to other publications.

AVOCATIONAL INTERESTS: Hiking, travel.

*   *   *

MEDLICOTT, Margaret P(aget)   1913-
(Margaret Paget)

PERSONAL: Born March 14, 1913, in Wallington, Surrey, England; daughter of William Norton (editor of a London newspaper) and Margaret (McMillan) Medlicott. *Education:* King's College, London, English Diploma, 1930; studied privately, 1930-31, and received the Royal Society of Arts Medal for English literature, 1931. *Religion:* Church of England. *Home:* 8 Hampstead Gardens, Golders Green, London N.W.11, England.

CAREER: Journalist and publicist in London, England, prior to 1952; EMI Film Productions Ltd., London, England, secretary to legal advisor, 1952—.

WRITINGS—All published by Hurst & Blackett, except as indicated: (Under name Margaret Paget) *Fortune Came Smiling* (novel), 1959; (under name Margaret Paget) *Stars*

Going Round (novel), 1960; (under name Margaret Paget) *Interval for Orchids* (novel), 1961; (editor) *No Hero, I Confess* (autobiography of Christopher Norton Wright), Pelham Books, 1969, Taplinger, 1970. Writer of "London Letter" for provincial newspapers, 1937-42.

WORK IN PROGRESS: A biography of her mother's eventful life, from her Victorian childhood to her career as a welfare worker in London factories after the death of her editor-husband.

SIDELIGHTS: In editing *No Hero, I Confess,* Margaret Medlicott fulfilled her great-grandfather's wish to have his life story published—a century after the nineteenth-century bookseller and publisher wrote it. In her own work she considers most vital "the portrayal of human beings as they really are, to prove that the virtues are as acceptable and normal as the vices and to provide humor (it is not only England which 'hath need of mirth' these days)."

AVOCATIONAL INTERESTS: Exploring her own country, studying its folklore and absorbing the atmosphere of ancient buildings and unspoiled places like the coast of Cornwall and the Scottish Highlands; reading, drawing and painting, gardening, playing the piano, and interior decorating.

BIOGRAPHICAL/CRITICAL SOURCES: New York Times, April 10, 1970.

*   *   *

MEEHAN, Thomas Edward   1932-

PERSONAL: Born August 14, 1932, in Ossining, N.Y.; son of Thomas Edward (a businessman) and Helen (O'Neill) Meehan; married Karen Termohlen (a writer and editor), June 22, 1963. *Education:* Hamilton College, B.A., 1951. *Home address:* R.D. 1, Sherman, Conn. 06784. *Agent:* Candida Donadio, 111 West 57th St., New York, N.Y. 10019. *Office: New Yorker,* 25 West 43rd St., New York, N.Y. 10036.

CAREER: New Yorker, New York, N.Y., staff writer for "Talk of the Town." Staff writer for television program, "That Was the Week That Was," 1964-65. *Military service:* U.S. Army, 1951-53; counterintelligence agent in Germany. *Awards, honors:* Tony Award, 1977, for "Annie."

WRITINGS: Yma, Ava; Yma, Abba; Yma, Oona; Yma, Ida; Yma, Aga . . . and Others, Simon & Schuster, 1967. Also author of book "Annie" the basis for the Broadway musical of the same title. Contributor of humor to *Esquire* and other magazines.

BIOGRAPHICAL/CRITICAL SOURCES: National Observer, December 4, 1967; *Christian Science Monitor,* December 7, 1967; *New Yorker,* December 9, 1967.

*   *   *

MEGSON, Barbara   1930-

PERSONAL: Born January 2, 1930; daughter of Norman Joseph Lane (a government scientist) and Gladys (a teacher; maiden name, Phillips) Megson. *Education:* Girton College, Cambridge, M.A. (2nd class honors), 1956. *Home:* 8 Stonebridge Way, Fauersham, Kent, England. *Office:* Department of Education and Science, London W.1, England.

CAREER: Professorial research assistant and library classifier, London, England, 1951-53; history teacher at Ladies' College, Cheltenham, England, 1953-62, Tornes High School, Tornes, England, 1962-64, and Devon Centre for Further Education, Dartington, England, 1965; Oakley Secondary Modern School, Cheltenham, England, governor, 1956-62; Riding Education Committee, Wakefield, England, administrative assistant, 1966-68; Department of Education and Science, Kent and London, England, Her Majesty's Inspector of schools, 1968—. Affiliated with catalogued archives, 1346-1840, of Uppark, Sussex, at intervals, 1949-62. *Member:* Historical Associations, British Federation of University Women, Commonwealth Society.

WRITINGS: A History of The Lady Eleanor Holles School, 1711-1945, privately printed, 1947; (with J. O. Lindsay) *Girton College, 1869-1959: An Informal History,* published for the Girton Historical and Political Society by Heffer, 1960; *English Homes and Housekeeping, 1700-1960,* Routledge & Kegan Paul, 1968; (with Alex Clegg) *Children in Distress,* Penguin, 1970.

WORK IN PROGRESS: Research into current educational practice and problems.†

* * *

MELBER, Jehuda 1916-

PERSONAL: Born May 3, 1916, in Berlin, Germany; came to United States in 1956; son of Samuel and Dina (Hirsch) Melber; married; wife's name, Mimi; children: Miriam Melber Perman, Samuel. *Education:* Yeshiva Chachmei, Lublin, Poland, Rabbi, 1934; Tufts University, M.A., 1960; Yeshiva University, Ph.D., 1965. *Home:* 83-40 Daniel St., Jamaica, N.Y. 11435. *Office:* Briarwood Jewish Center, 139-06 86th Ave., Jamaica, N.Y. 11435.

CAREER: Resident of Israel, 1948-54; chief rabbi of Jewish Community, Havana, Cuba, 1954-56; rabbi in Boston, Mass., 1956-57, and Brighton, Mass., 1957-60; Briarwood Jewish Center, Jamaica, N.Y., rabbi and principal of school, 1960—. Board member, Operation Yorkville (aimed to stem the amount of pornography and obscene literature available to youth). *Military service:* Israeli Defense Forces, chaplain, 1948-50; received Ben Gurion Award. *Member:* Religious Zionists of America (regional vice-president, 1956-58), Rabbinical Council of America, New York Board of Rabbis.

WRITINGS: The Universality of Maimonides, privately printed, 1960, Jonathan David, 1967; *Hermann Cohen's Philosophy of Judaism,* Jonathan David, 1968.

WORK IN PROGRESS: The Eternal Value of the Decalogue.

* * *

MELLON, Matthew T(aylor) 1897-

PERSONAL: Born July 6, 1897, in Pittsburgh, Pa.; son of William L. (a financier) and Mary (Taylor) Mellon; married Gertrud Altegoer, November 30, 1931; married second wife, Jane Kirkland, March 11, 1953; children: Karl N., James R. *Education:* Princeton University, A.B., 1922; Harvard University, A.M., 1928; University of Freiburg, Ph.D., 1934. *Politics:* Republican. *Home:* Snapper Creek Lakes, 10201 Southwest 55th Ave., Miami, Fla. 33156; (summers) Haus Mellon, Kitzbuehel, Tirol, Austria. *Office:* Mellon Bank Bldg., Mellon Sq., Pittsburgh, Pa. 15230.

CAREER: Manager of specialty department, Golf Oil Corp., 1922-26; University of Freiburg, Freiburg, Germany, lecturer in philosophy, 1929-38. Has made expeditions to Central America, the Bahamas, and East Africa for Carnegie Museum, Pittsburgh. Served for ten years on board of overseers for department of Germanic languages and literatures at Harvard College and for the Bush-Reisinger Museum. *Military service:* U.S. Naval Reserve, active duty,

1917-19; became ensign. *Member:* Phi Beta Kappa, New York Yacht Club, Rolling Rock Club, Pittsburgh Golf Club. *Awards, honors:* Litt.D., College of the Ozarks; Commander, German Order of Merit, 1950; D.Litt., New University of Ulster.

WRITINGS: Student Essays in Philosophy, privately printed, 1922; *How God Became Moral,* privately printed, 1922; *Early American Views on Negro Slavery: From the Letters and Papers of the Founders of the Republic,* Meador Publishing, 1934, 2nd edition, Bergman, 1969; (translator) Theodor Storm, *Immensee,* Random House, 1934; (editor) *Selections from "Thomas Mellon and His Times,"* Stanhope House (Belfast), 1970; (editor) *William Penn: His Life and Views,* privately printed, 1972; *The Grand Tour,* privately printed, 1972; *War Log 1917-18,* privately printed, 1975; *Essays in Philosophy,* privately printed, 1977. Also author of *Zwei Vortage Von Matthew Mellon,* 1972 and *The Watermellons,* 1974. Associate editor, *German-American Review.*

* * *

MENDELS, Joseph 1937-

PERSONAL: Born October 29, 1937, in Cape Town, South Africa; married Ora Kark (a writer), January 10, 1959; children: Gilla Avril, Charles Alan, David Ralph. *Education:* University of Cape Town, M.B. and Ch.B., 1960; University of the Witwatersrand, M.D., 1965. *Office:* U.S. Veterans Administration Hospital, University and Woodland Aves., Philadelphia, Pa. 19104.

CAREER: University of Pennsylvania, Philadelphia, assistant professor, 1967-70, associate professor, 1970-72, professor of psychiatry, 1973—; U.S. Veterans Administration Hospital, Philadelphia, director of Depression Research Unit operated jointly by the hospital and University of Pennsylvania. *Member:* American Psychopathological Association, American Psychiatric Association, Association for the Psychophysiological Study of Sleep, American Psychosomatic Society, American Association for the Advancement of Science, American College of Clinical Pharmacology (fellow), American College of Neuropharmacology, Congressium Internationale Neuropsychopharmacologia, International Society of Psychoneuroendocrinology, Psychiatric Research Society, Royal College of Psychiatry, Society of Biological Psychiatry, Philadelphia Psychiatric Society.

WRITINGS: Concepts of Depression, Wiley, 1970; (editor with Steven K. Secunda) *Lithium in Medicine,* Gordon & Breach, 1972; (editor) *Biological Psychiatry,* Wiley, 1973; (editor) *Psychobiology of Depression,* Spectrum, 1975; (editor with John Paul Brady, Martin Orne, and Wolfram Rieger) *Psychiatry: Areas of Promise and Advancement,* Spectrum, 1977. Contributor to scientific journals. Editor, *Comments on Contemporary Psychiatry.*

* * *

MENDELSOHN, Felix, Jr. 1906-
(Franklin Mayfair)

PERSONAL: Born August 20, 1906, in Chicago, Ill.; son of Felix (an expositions promoter) and Rose (Despres) Mendelsohn. *Education:* Attended University of Chicago, 1923-24. *Politics:* Socialist (registered Democrat). *Home:* 1815 Arizona Ave., Santa Monica, Calif. 90404.

CAREER: Meyer, Both Co., Chicago, Ill., advertising copywriter, 1927-32; free-lance writer, 1932-42; *Chicago Sun* (now *Sun-Times*), Chicago, rewrite man, 1945-46; Chi-

cago Journal of Commerce, Chicago, editorial writer and columnist, 1946-51; Illinois Bell Telephone Co., Chicago, member of public relations staff, 1951-52; Twentieth Century-Fox Film Corp., Los Angeles, Calif., publicist, 1952-53; free-lance publicist on public relations campaigns for Southern California Gas Co. and the film and entertainment business, 1953-58; RAND Corp., Santa Monica, Calif., editorial consultant, 1958-59; Bozell & Jacobs (advertising agency), Los Angeles, copywriter and publicist, 1960; free-lance writer, 1961-62; Ettinger-Mapes & Co., Los Angeles, publicist, 1963-65; free-lance writer and publicist, 1966—. *Military service:* U.S. Army, Signal Corps, cryptanalyst, 1942-45; served overseas in London and Paris.

WRITINGS: Max Henius: A Biography (published anonymously), Max Henius Memoir Committee, 1937; (under pseudonym Franklin Mayfair) *Over My Dead Body,* Book Co. of America, 1965; *Club Tycoon Sends Man to Moon,* Book Co. of America, 1965; *Barney Crome,* Book Co. of America, 1966; *Superbaby,* Nash Publishing, 1970. Contributor of fiction and articles to popular magazines.

WORK IN PROGRESS: Ransom/U.S.A., a novel.

* * *

MERILLAT, Herbert C(hristian) L(aing) 1915-

PERSONAL: Born May 7, 1915, in Winfield, Iowa; son of Christian Clarence (a businessman) and Ruth Elizabeth (Laing) Merillat. *Education:* Attended Monmouth College, 1931-33; University of Arizona, A.B., 1935; Oxford University, B.A., 1937, B.C.L., 1938, M.A., 1942; Yale Law School, graduate study, 1938-39; attended National War College, 1950-51. *Religion:* Presbyterian. *Home:* 1243 30th St. N.W., Washington, D.C. 20007. *Agent:* Harold Ober Associates, 40 East 49th St., New York, N.Y. 10017.

CAREER: Admitted to Bar of Illinois State, 1939; United States Treasury, Washington, D.C., attorney, 1939-42; *Time* Magazine, New York City, contributing editor, 1945-48; Economic Cooperation Administration and successor foreign aid agencies, Washington, D.C., London, England, and Paris, France, administrator, 1948-54; Ford Foundation, New York City and New Delhi, India, executive associate, 1955-60; American Society of International Law, Washington, D.C., executive director, 1960-63, executive vice-president, 1963-67. Visiting professor of law at University of Washington, 1966, 1968, and Arizona State University, 1969-70. *Military service:* U.S. Marine Corps Reserve, public information officer, 1942-45; became major.

MEMBER: American Society of International Law (executive director, 1960-67; member of executive council, 1967-70), International Law Association (member of executive committee, American Branch, 1967-70), Council on Foreign Relations, Association of Asian Studies, Asia Society (chairman of Washington committee, India council, 1964-67), Literary Society of Washington, Phi Beta Kappa, Sigma Alpha Epsilon, City Tavern Club, Yale Club. *Awards, honors:* Rhodes scholar, 1935-38; Ford Foundation Travel and Study Awards, 1967, 1969.

WRITINGS: The Island: A History of the First Marine Division Campaign on Guadalcanal, August 7-December 9, 1942, Houghton, 1944; (editor) *Legal Advisers and Foreign Affairs,* Oceana, 1964; *United States Law School and Latin America: Law and Development,* American Society of International Law, 1966; (editor) *Legal Advisers and International Organizations,* Oceana, 1966; *Land and the Constitution in India,* Columbia University Press, 1970; *Sculpture West and East: Two Traditions,* Dodd, 1973; *Modern Sculpture: The New Old Masters,* Dodd, 1974. Contributor of articles to newspapers, magazines, and professional journals. Editor, *International Legal Materials,* 1962-67; member of board of editors, *American Journal of International Law,* 1963-67.

WORK IN PROGRESS: Articles and books on law and politics in India; and a book on art and religion in ancient China and India.

SIDELIGHTS: Herbert Merillat has "traveled extensively" and attempts to "get to India (a main area of interest) and intermediate points as frequently as possible. He told *CA:* "I turned to writing full time in my middle fifties, in part to learn a few of those many things one never has time for in a conventional career. I enjoy trying to write simply, freshly, and directly about subjects that specialized experts tend to deal with in jargon."

* * *

MERIVALE, Patricia 1934-

PERSONAL: Born July 19, 1934, in Derby, England. *Education:* Attended Stanford University, 1951-53, and University of Frankfurt, 1953-54; University of California, Berkeley, B.A. (German), 1955; Oxford University, B.A. (English), 1958, M.A., 1962; Harvard University, Ph.D., 1962. *Office:* English Department, University of British Columbia, Vancouver, British Columbia, Canada.

CAREER: University of British Columbia, Vancouver, instructor, 1962-63, assistant professor, 1963-66, associate professor, 1966-70, professor of English, 1970—. Visiting fellow at Clare Hall, Cambridge University, and at St. Antony's College and Wolfson College, Oxford University. *Member:* Modern Language Association of America, Association of Canadian University Teachers of English, American Comparative Literature Association. *Awards, honors:* Canada Council fellowship.

WRITINGS: Pan the Goat-God: His Myth in Modern Times, Harvard University Press, 1969. Contributor of articles and reviews to scholarly journals.

WORK IN PROGRESS: Articles intended for eventual collection in a book, *Gothic Artifice and the Contemporary Artist Parable.*

BIOGRAPHICAL/CRITICAL SOURCES: Virginia Quarterly Review, summer, 1969; *Books Abroad,* winter, 1970.

* * *

MERRILL, Thomas F. 1932-

PERSONAL: Born January 5, 1932, in Maplewood, N.J.; son of Charles Earl (a broker) and Anna (Lofgren) Merrill; married Mary Jane Mong, 1957; children: Kimberly, Charles, Elizabeth, Patrick. *Education:* Princeton University, A.B., 1954; University of Nebraska, M.A., 1960; University of Wisconsin, Ph.D., 1964. *Politics:* Liberal independent. *Home:* 6 Briar Lane, Newark, Del. 19711. *Office:* Department of English, University of Delaware, Newark, Del. 19711.

CAREER: University of California, Los Angeles, assistant professor of English, 1964-66; University of Bordeaux, Bordeaux, France, Fulbright lecturer in American literature, 1966-67; De Pauw University, Greencastle, Ind., assistant professor of English, 1967-69; University of Delaware, Newark, associate professor, 1969-74, professor of English, 1974—. *Military service:* U.S. Air Force, 1954-57, 1963; became captain. *Member:* Modern Language Association of America.

WRITINGS: (Editor) *William Perkins, 1558-1602,* De Graaf, 1966; *Allen Ginsberg,* Twayne, 1969; *Christian Criticism,* Rodopi, 1976. Contributor to literary journals in America and Europe.

* * *

MERRILL, William C.   1934-

PERSONAL: Born March 2, 1934, in Webster City, Iowa; son of William N. and Anna (Lacy) Merrill; married Mavis Schnurr; children: two. *Education:* Iowa State University of Science and Technology, B.A., 1959; University of California, Berkeley, Ph.D., 1964. *Office:* Department of Economics, Iowa State University of Science and Technology, Ames, Iowa 50010.

CAREER: Iowa State University of Science and Technology, Ames, assistant professor, 1964-67, associate professor, 1967-70, professor of economics, 1970—.

WRITINGS: (With Karl A. Fox) *Introduction to Economic Statistics,* Wiley, 1970; (with Lehman B. Fletcher, Eric Graber, and Erik Thorbecke) *Guatemala's Economic Development: The Role of Agriculture,* Iowa State University Press, 1970; (with Fletcher, Randall A. Hoffman, and Michael J. Applegate) *Panama's Economic Development: The Role of Agriculture,* Iowa State University Press, 1975.

* * *

MESSER, Alfred A(mes)   1922-

PERSONAL: Born October 29, 1922, in Morristown, N.J. *Education:* Rutgers University, B.Sc., 1942; Columbia University, M.D., 1950. *Office:* WSB Radio, Atlanta, Ga. 30309.

CAREER: Presbyterian Hospital, New York City, assistant psychiatrist, 1954-58; Columbia University, New York City, assistant psychoanalyst, 1956-60; Family Mental Health Clinic, New York City, medical director, 1960-62; Emory University, Atlanta, Ga., professor of psychiatry, 1962-72; Georgia Mental Health Institute, Atlanta, chief of family research laboratories, 1968-72; currently affiliated with WSB Radio, Atlanta, Ga. Diplomate, American Board of Psychiatry and Neurology, 1957. *Military service:* U.S. Navy, 1942-46; became lieutenant. *Member:* American Psychoanalytic Association, American Association for the Advancement of Science.

WRITINGS: *The Individual in His Family,* C. C Thomas, 1970; *Your Family's Mental Health,* Douglas House, 1971. Syndicated columnist, writing "Eye on Your Family," for Hall Syndicate.

WORK IN PROGRESS: *What's Wrong with Our Country: America on an Impulse Orgy.*

* * *

MESSNER, Gerald   1935-

PERSONAL: Born March 2, 1935, in Yreka, Calif.; son of Michael Harris (a judge) and Adelaide (Wright) Messner; married Nancy Shingler (a college professor), August 17, 1963; children: Michael Harris. *Education:* Stanford University, A.B., 1956, graduate study, 1957-58; University of California, graduate study, 1956-57; Los Angeles State College (now California State University, Los Angeles), M.A., 1960. *Home:* 227 Angela Dr., Los Atos, Calif. 94022. *Office:* Canada College, 4200 Farm Hill Blvd., Redwood City, Calif. 94061.

CAREER: American River College, Sacramento, Calif.,

instructor in English, 1961-64; College of San Mateo, San Mateo, Calif., instructor in English, 1964-68; Canada College, Redwood City, Calif., instructor in English, 1968-73, director of humanities department, 1974—. Editor, Prentice-Hall, Inc., 1974—. *Member:* Modern Language Association of America, American Studies Association.

WRITINGS: (With wife, Nancy S. Messner) *Patterns of Thinking,* Wadsworth, 1968, abridged edition, 1970, 2nd edition, 1975; (editor) *Another View: To Be Black in America,* Harcourt, 1970; (with N. S. Messner) *Collection: Literature for the Seventies,* Heath, 1972; *Our Indian Heritage,* Ballantine, 1975.

WORK IN PROGRESS: *Adult Education in Humanities; Modern Church History.*

* * *

METHVIN, Eugene H.   1934-

PERSONAL: Born September 19, 1934, in Vienna, Ga.; son of Claude McKee, Jr. (an editor and publisher) and Madge (Hilburn) Methvin; married Barbara Lester; children: Helen Lester, Claudia Hilburn. *Education:* University of Georgia, B.A. (cum laude), 1955; additional study at Youngstown University, American University, and George Washington University. *Home:* 8111 Old Georgetown Pike, McLean, Va. 22101. *Office: Reader's Digest,* 1730 Rhode Island Ave. N.W., Washington, D.C. 20036.

CAREER: *Washington Daily News,* Washington, D.C., reporter, 1958-60; *Reader's Digest,* Washington Bureau, Washington, D.C., 1960—, currently a senior editor. *Military service:* U.S. Air Force, jet fighter pilot, 1955-58. *Member:* Society of Professional Journalists, Sigma Delta Chi (former president of Washington chapter), Sigma Nu.

WRITINGS: *The Riot Makers: The Technology of Social Demolition,* Arlington House, 1970; *The Rise of Radicalism: The Social Psychology of Messianic Extremism,* Arlington House, 1973.

* * *

MEYER, Agnes E(lizabeth Ernst)   1887-1970

January 2, 1887—September 1, 1970; American journalist, humanitarian, translator, and writer on social issues. Obituaries: *New York Times,* September 2, 1970; *Washington Post,* September 5, 1970; *Newsweek,* September 14, 1970; *Time,* September 14, 1970; *Current Biography,* 1970.

* * *

MEYERING, Ralph A.   1930-

PERSONAL: Born June 23, 1930, in Istanbul, Turkey; son of Harry Ralph (a professor) and Fern (Awrey) Meyering; married Joan B. Bereiter, June 14, 1956; children: Ann Elizabeth, Jay Ralph. *Education:* Mankato State College, B.S., 1952; Northwestern University, M.A., 1956; University of Iowa, Ph.D., 1961. *Home:* 215 Parkview Dr., Bloomington, Ill. 61701. *Office:* Department of Psychology, Illinois State University, Normal, Ill. 61761.

CAREER: Amerikan Orta Okulu, Kayseri, Turkey, teacher, 1952-55; high school teacher in Battle Creek, Mich., 1956-58; Illinois State University, Normal, 1961—, currently professor of psychology. Fulbright professor, Cheingmai University, Cheingmai, Thailand, 1967-68; visiting professor, University of Sydney, Sydney, Australia, 1968. *Member:* American Psychological Association, American Personnel and Guidance Association, Association for Counselor Education and Supervision, National Vocational Guidance Association, Association for Measurement and Evaluation in Guidance, American Association of University Professors, Phi Delta Kappa.

WRITINGS: Uses of Test Data in Counseling, Houghton, 1968. Editor, *Third Ear,* 1965-72.

AVOCATIONAL INTERESTS: Photography and sailing.

*   *   *

MEYERS, Cecil H(arold)   1920-

PERSONAL: Born July 18, 1920, in Solon, Iowa; son of Harold Frank (a carpenter) and Mary (Zeman) Meyers; married Corinne Freswick, June 27, 1946; children: William, Cynthia, Robert. *Education:* University of Iowa, B.A., 1947, M.A., 1948, Ph.D., 1949. *Home:* 1738 Dunedin Ave., Duluth, Minn. 55803. *Office:* Department of Economics, University of Minnesota, Duluth, Minn. 55812.

CAREER: University of Iowa, Iowa City, instructor in economics, 1948-49; University of Minnesota, Duluth Campus, assistant professor of business and economics, 1949-53, associate professor, 1953-57, professor of economics, 1957—, chairman of department, 1965-72, director of Bureau of Business and Economic Research, 1970—. *Military service:* U.S. Naval Reserve, active duty, 1942-45; served in European and African theaters; received Distinguished Unit Citation and two battle stars. *Member:* American Economic Association, American Statistical Association, American Finance Association, Association for University Business and Economic Research, Midwest Economic Association, Minnesota Economic Association (past president), Minnesota Historical Society, St. Louis County (Minn.) Historical Society.

WRITINGS: Elementary Business and Economic Statistics, Wadsworth, 1966, 2nd edition, 1970; *Handbook of Basic Graphs: A Modern Approach,* Dickenson, 1970; (contributor) *Sketches of the Past: A Bicentennial Collection,* Duluth Bicentennial Commission, 1976. Contributor to *Duluth Business Indicators and Selected Area Economic Data,* published annually by Bureau of Business and Economic Research, University of Minnesota, Duluth Campus. Contributor to periodicals, including *Review of Labor and Economic Conditions.* Editor with Glenn O. Gronseth, *Duluth Business Indicators* (monthly).

WORK IN PROGRESS: Regional economic studies.

*   *   *

MEYERS, David W.   1942-

PERSONAL: Born July 19, 1942, in Hobart, Tasmania, Australia; son of Philip T. and Margaret (Wilson) Meyers; married Jane Arthur, December 27, 1969; children: Duncan, Vanessa. *Education:* University of Redlands, B.A. (magna cum laude), 1964; University of California, Berkeley, J.D., 1967; University of Edinburgh, LL.M., 1968. *Home:* 2277 Monticello Rd., Napa, Calif. 94558.

CAREER: Rutan & Tucker (law firm), Santa Ana, Calif., trial attorney, 1968-71; Dickenson, Peatman & Fogarty (law firm), Napa, Calif., attorney, 1972—. *Member:* State Bar of California, Napa County Bar Association. *Awards, honors:* St. Andrew's Society of the State of New York fellowship at University of Edinburgh, 1967-68; Outstanding Young Men in America award, 1971.

WRITINGS: The Human Body and the Law: A Medico-Legal Study, Aldine, 1970; (contributor) *The Impact of Sci-*

ence on Society, UNESCO, 1971; (contributor) *The Dilemmas of Euthanasia,* Doubleday, 1975. Contributor to *Medico-Legal Journal* (London) and *Bio-Science* (Washington, D.C.).

WORK IN PROGRESS: An article for the *California State Bar Journal,* concerning the California Natural Death Act.

*   *   *

MICHAEL, David J.   1944-

PERSONAL: Born April 1, 1944, in Oshkosh, Wis. *Education:* University of Detroit, B.A. (cum laude), 1966; Columbia University, graduate study. *Residence:* St. Peter, Barbados. *Agent:* Paul R. Reynolds, Inc., 12 East 41st St., New York, N.Y. 10017.

AWARDS, HONORS: Mary Roberts Rinehart Foundation Award for manuscript, "Columbine," published as *A Blow to the Head.*

WRITINGS: A Blow to the Head (novel), Houghton, 1970.

WORK IN PROGRESS: Further novels.

SIDELIGHTS: "I live here [in Barbados] and swim and garden," David Michael writes, "and am doing just what I love to do; and that's my greatest achievement to date. That and straightening my teeth. I'm interested in what happens to people as nature is cut back: they always spring again—like privet—but in new and ever-changing shapes. These shapes are characters and sometimes stories and perhaps even answers."

BIOGRAPHICAL/CRITICAL SOURCES:. New York Times Book Review, March 29, 1970; *Best Sellers,* April 15, 1970.†

*   *   *

MIDDLEMAS, Robert Keith   1935-
(Keith Middlemas)

PERSONAL: Born May 26, 1935, in Alnwick, England; son of Robert James (a solicitor) and Eleanor Anne Middlemas; married Susan Tremlett, August 30, 1958; children: Sophie, Lucy, Annabel, Hugo. *Education:* Pembroke College, Cambridge, first class honors in history, 1958. *Religion:* Church of England. *Home:* Ashurst, Sussex, England. *Agent:* Peter Janson-Smith Ltd., 31 Newington Green, London N16 9PU, England. *Office:* Department of History, University of Sussex, Falmer, Brighton, England.

CAREER: House of Commons, London, England, clerk, 1958-66; University of Sussex, Falmer, Brighton, England, reader in history, 1966—. Chairman, Findon Conservation Association, 1969-72. *Military service:* British Army, Northumberland Fusiliers, lieutenant, 1953-55. Territorial Army, 1955-65. *Member:* Association of Contemporary Historians, National Rifle Association (Great Britain), Marylebone Cricket Club.

WRITINGS: Command the Far Seas: A Naval Campaign of the First World War, Hutchinson, 1961; *The Master Builders: Thomas Brassey, Sir John Aird, Lord Cowdray, Sir John Norton-Griffiths,* Hutchinson, 1963; *The Clydesiders: A Left Wing Struggle for Parliamentary Power,* Hutchinson, 1965; (author of introduction) Maureen Stafford, *British Furniture Through the Ages,* Coward, 1966; (under name Keith Middlemas; with Derek Cecil Davis) *Colored Glass,* C. N. Potter, 1968 (published in England as *Coloured Glass,* Jenkins, 1968); (under name Keith Middlemas; with John Barnes) *Baldwin* (biography of Stanley Baldwin), Weidenfeld & Nicolson, 1969, published in

America as *Life of Baldwin,* Macmillan, 1970; (editor under name Keith Middlemas) Thomas Jones, *Whitehall Diary,* three volumes, Oxford University Press, 1969; *Continental Coloured Glass,* Barrie & Rockliff, 1970; *Antique Glass in Color,* Doubleday, 1971; (under name Keith Middlemas) *The Strategy of Appeasement,* Quadrangle, 1972 (published in England as *Diplomacy of Illusion,* Weidenfeld & Nicolson, 1972); (under name Keith Middlemas) *Edward VII,* Weidenfeld & Nicolson, 1972, new edition, 1975; (under name Keith Middlemas) *Life and Times of George VI,* Weidenfeld & Nicolson, 1974; (under name Keith Middlemas) *Double Market: Art Theft and Art Thieves,* Tiptree Book Services, 1974; (under name Keith Middlemas) *Cabora Bassa: Engineering and Politics in Southern Africa,* Weidenfeld & Nicolson, 1975.

WORK IN PROGRESS: The Cult of Equilibrium: The System of British Politics 1911-65, and *Eurocommunism in France, Italy, Spain and Portugal,* both for Deutsch.

AVOCATIONAL INTERESTS: Collecting antiques and works of art; rifle shooting (member of British team competing in Canada, 1955), tennis, squash, hunting game.

BIOGRAPHICAL/CRITICAL SOURCES: Spectator, June 21, 1969, October 11, 1969; *Times Literary Supplement,* July 17, 1969.

* * *

MIDWINTER, E(ric) C(lare) 1932-

PERSONAL: Born February 11, 1932, in Sale, Lancashire, England; son of Harold and Edna (Ashworth) Midwinter; married Margaret Eley, December 28, 1964; children: Matthew, Daniel. *Education:* St. Catharine's College, Cambridge, B.A. (first class honors), 1955, M.A., 1958; University of London, Post-graduate Certificate in Education (with distinction), 1959; University of York, D.Phil., 1966; University of Liverpool, M.A.Ed., 1968. *Home:* 39 Ince Ave., Great Crosby, Liverpool 23, England. *Agent:* Murray Pollinger, 11 Long Acre, London WC2E 9LH, England.

CAREER: Teacher, lecturer, and deputy principal at schools in Manchester, Newcastle, and Liverpool, England, 1956-68; Liverpool Educational Priority Area Project, Liverpool, project director of government action-research project in education for the socially disadvantaged, 1968-71; director of Priority, Centre for Urban Community Education, Liverpool, 1971-73, Liverpool Teachers' Centre, Liverpool, principal, 1973-75; National Consumer Council, England, head of public affairs unit, 1975—. Chairman of Advisory Centre for Education, Cambridge, and educational consultant to the Home Office Community Development Projects. *Military service:* British Army, National Service, 1950-52; became sergeant. *Member:* Historical Association, Association of Teachers in Departments and Colleges of Education.

WRITINGS: Victorian Social Reform, Longmans, Green, 1968; *Law and Order in Early Victorian Lancashire,* St. Anthony's Press, 1968; *Social Administration in Lancashire, 1830-1860,* Barnes & Noble, 1969; *Nineteenth Century Education,* Longmans, Green, 1970; *Old Liverpool,* David & Charles, 1971; (editor) *Projections: An Education Priority Project at Work,* Ward, Lock, 1972; *Social Environment and the Urban School,* Ward, Lock, 1972; *Priority Education: An Account of the Liverpool Project,* Penguin, 1972; *Patterns of Community Education,* Ward, Lock, 1973; (editor) *Pre-School Priorities,* Ward, Lock, 1974; *Education and the Community,* Wiley, 1975; *Education for Sale,* in press. Also editor of *Teaching in the Urban Community School.*

Contributor: Ernest Walter, editor, *Comparative Developments in Social Welfare,* Allen & Unwin, 1972; John Raynor and Jane Harden, editors, *Cities, Communities and the Young,* Routledge & Kegan Paul, 1973; Leigh, editor, *Better Social Services,* National Council of Social Service Inc., 1973; K. Jones, editor, *Year Book of Social Policy, 1972,* Routledge & Kegan Paul, 1973; Lees and Smith, editors, *Action-Research in Community Development,* Routledge & Kegan Paul, 1975; Goodlad, editor, *Education and Social Action,* Allen & Unwin, 1975. Also contributor to *Equality and City Schools* and *Fit to Teach.*

WORK IN PROGRESS: Public Education in Late Victorian Lancashire, publication by Cambridge University Press, and several items related to Educational Priority Area work.

* * *

MIKKELSEN, Ejnar 1881(?)-1971

1881(?)—May 3, 1971; Danish arctic explorer and author. Obituaries: *New York Times,* May 5, 1971; *Washington Post,* May 6, 1971; *Time,* May 17, 1971.

* * *

MILFORD, Nancy 1938-

PERSONAL: Born March 26, 1938; daughter of Joseph Leo (an engineer) and Vivienne (Romaine) Winston; married Kenneth Milford (vice-president, Book Press), March 24, 1962; children: Matthew, Jessica Kate, Nell Susannah. *Education:* University of Michigan, B.A., 1959; Columbia University, M.A., 1964, Ph.D., 1972. *Agent:* Carl Brandt, Brandt & Brandt, 101 Park Ave., New York, N.Y. 10017.

CAREER: Columbia University, Columbia College, New York, N.Y., preceptor in English, 1968-69. Visiting professor, Briarcliff College, 1974. Juror of biographies, National Book Awards, 1973. *Awards, honors:* D.Litt., Windham College; Guggenheim fellowship, 1977-78.

WRITINGS: Zelda (biography of F. Scott Fitzgerald's wife), Harper, 1970; (contributor) Albert Gelpi and Barbara Gelpi, editors, *Adrienne Rich's Poetry,* Norton, 1975.

WORK IN PROGRESS: A biography of Edna St. Vincent Millay, for Harper.

SIDELIGHTS: Commenting on *Zelda,* Robert Emmet Long wrote: "Mrs. Milford's candor and the unusually intimate sources from which she has been able to draw make her *Zelda* a distinct and living portrait, comparable in kind and in its degree of interest to the late Andrew Turnbull's *Scott Fitzgerald. Zelda* enlarges on Turnbull's study of the Fitzgeralds, particularly on their deterioration together and apart; more amply and in greater detail than has ever been assembled before, it establishes Zelda's case."

Christopher Lehmann-Haupt reiterated: "The cumulative effect is profound and at times overwhelmingly moving. It serves to demythologize the famous Scott-Zelda saga and thereby to resurrect a portion of American literature from the burial mound of romantic legend. It fills out a missing part of F. Scott Fitzgerald's life, and make one take him more seriously both as a writer and a man. It turns what had always seemed like a tale of neurotic obsession into a richly complex love story. And, not least of all, it transforms Zelda Sayre Fitzgerald from an exotic thing into a person."

As for Nancy Milford's writing of *Zelda,* Harry T. Moore explained that "[*Zelda*] began as a master's thesis at Columbia University and Mrs. Milford spent seven years on it.

The result is what might be called an example of the "New Biography," which at its best is painstakingly thorough without smothering the subject under the weight of documentation.... It is important biographically, not only because it helps complete the picture of Zelda, but also because it increases our knowledge of Scott Fitzgerald and his work."

The subject of the "New Biography" is exemplified in Stephen Donadio's critique of *Zelda*: "Nancy Milford's biography of Zelda Fitzgerald brings us into an awareness of its subject so intense it seems unmediated by the personality of a biographer.... Mrs. Milford's decision to keep her authorial intrusions to a minimum signals her clear refusal to yield to the temptation of self-aggrandizement through omniscience or association which must suggest itself to every biographer. But there are other reasons for her obvious restraint, which takes a variety of forms: for example, the form of her watchful prose, which has the effect of keeping order without seeming to impose it. Clear-sighted and tactful, her commentary slips in and out of the confused excessive, sometimes bizarre outbursts and exchanges between the Fitzgeralds, providing perspective but not choking off the reader's own response by giving him immediate cues as to what he should think and feel.... Mrs. Milford is able to keep from losing her subject once Zelda has become manifestly psychotic. As a consequence, her biography never collapses into case history, but remains accessible as the record of a conflict which, although intensely personal and specific, transcends simple personal (and possibly idiosyncratic) considerations."

As for content and merit, Mr. Donadio wrote that "the account of Fitzgerald's weaknesses, inadequacies, and defects of character serves to deepen our sense of awe and admiration for his achievement by placing that achievement in a convincing context against which it may at last be measured. In this respect Mrs. Milford's book supersedes much of the previous biographical writing about the Fitzgeralds, writing which as a rule seems either excessively naive or lacking in its imaginative sympathies.... [Therefore] any fresh attempt to understand and judge Fitzgerald's fiction must now begin with Mrs. Milford's book."

AVOCATIONAL INTERESTS: Fencing.

BIOGRAPHICAL/CRITICAL SOURCES: Commonwealth, 1969; *New York Times*, June 8, 1970, October 28, 1972; *Washington Post*, June 12, 1970, July 7, 1970; *New York Times Book Review*, June 14, 1970; *Christian Science Monitor*, July 18, 1970; *Atlantic*, August, 1970; *Commentary*, August, 1970; *New Yorker*, August 8, 1970; *New York Review of Books*, September 24, 1970; *New York*, May 25, 1971.

* * *

MILGRAM, Gail Gleason 1942-

PERSONAL: Born June 14, 1942, in South Amboy, N.J.; daughter of John Thomas (a police chief) and Evelyn (a teacher; maiden name Lynch) Gleason; married William H. Milgram (an engineer), August 6, 1966; children: Lynn Patricia, Anne Melissa. *Education:* Georgian Court College, B.S., 1963; Rutgers University, M.Ed., 1965, Ed.D., 1969. *Home:* 15 Dobson Rd., East Brunswick, N.J. 08816. *Office:* Center of Alcohol Studies, Rutgers University, New Brunswick, N.J.

CAREER: Teacher in public schools of Sayreville, N.J., 1963-67, 1968-69; Rutgers University, New Brunswick, N.J., supervisor of Douglass College practice teachers,

1970-71, associate professor, 1971—, director of education of Center of Alcohol Studies, 1976—. Consultant, New Jersey Department of Health, Alcohol Control Program, Alcohol Education Resource Unit. Lecturer.

WRITINGS: (With Albert L. Ayars) *The Teenager and Alcohol*, Rosen Press, 1970; *The Teenager and Smoking*, Rosen Press, 1972; (with Paul Weber) *Alcohol Education Resource Unit*, New Jersey Department of Health, 1973; *The Teenager and Sex*, Rosen Press, 1974; *Alcohol Education Materials: An Annotated Bibliography*, Center of Alcohol Studies, Rutgers University, 1975; *A Discussion Leader's Guide for Hollywood Squares: Beverage Alcohol Use and Misuse*, Center of Alcohol Studies, Rutgers University, 1975; (author of introduction) A. Silverstein and V. Silverstein, *Alcoholism*, Lippincott, 1976; *Your Career in Education*, Rosen Press, 1976. Also author of pamphlets and contributor to professional journals.

* * *

MILHAVEN, John Giles 1927-

PERSONAL: Born September 1, 1927, in New York, N.Y.; son of John Michael (a securities broker) and Rose (Burns) Milhaven; married Anne Lally (a nursing administrator), May 21, 1970. *Education:* Woodstock College, A.B., 1949, M.A., 1951; Facultes Theologiques d'Enghien, Belgium, Lic. theol., 1957; University of Munich, Ph.D., 1962. *Home:* 20 Penrose Ave., Providence, R.I. 02906. *Office:* Department of Religious Studies, Brown University, Providence, R.I. 02912.

CAREER: Member of Society of Jesus (Jesuits), 1944-70; Canisius College, Buffalo, N.Y., instructor in philosophy, 1951-53; ordained a Roman Catholic priest, 1956; Fordham University, New York City, assistant professor of philosophy, 1961-65; Woodstock College, New York City, assistant professor, 1965-68, associate professor of pastoral theology, 1968-70; Brown University, Providence, R.I., visiting associate professor, 1970-71, associate professor, 1971-76, professor of religious studies, 1976—. Left Society of Jesus, withdrew from active priestly ministry to marry, 1970. *Member:* American Society of Christian Ethics, American Academy of Religion, Catholic Theological Association of America, American Association of University Professors.

WRITINGS: Toward a New Catholic Morality, Doubleday, 1970. Contributor of essays and articles to *Critic*, *Commonweal*, *Theological Studies*, *America*, *Le Supplement* (France), *American Ecclesiastical Review*, *Journal of Religious Ethics*, and other periodicals.

WORK IN PROGRESS: A book exploring the possibilities of a "Christian hedonism."

BIOGRAPHICAL/CRITICAL SOURCES: Commonweal, March 26, 1971.

* * *

MILIO, Nancy 1938-

PERSONAL: Born July 28, 1938, in Detroit, Mich.; daughter of Sam (a tool and die maker) and Filomena (La Fata) Milio. *Education:* Wayne State University, B.S., 1960, M.A., 1965; Yale University, Ph.D., 1970.

CAREER: Visiting Nurse Association, Detroit, Mich., staff nurse, 1960-61, Mom and Tots Neighborhood Center, project director, 1963-68; Children's Hospital, Cystic Fibrosis Center, Detroit, public health nurse, 1961-63; University of Michigan, College of Architecture and Design, Ann Arbor, study of early childhood facilities, research associate, 1970. Lecturer at Yale University, University of Michigan, Delhi University, New York University, and elsewhere. Member of board of directors, Community Health, Inc., New York, 1970—. Consultant to Maternal and Child Health Services, U.S. Department of Health, Education, and Welfare, 1970. *Member:* American Sociological Association, American Public Health Association (fellow).

WRITINGS: 9226 Kercheval: The Storefront that Did Not Burn, University of Michigan Press, 1970; (contributor) Vern L. Bullough and Bonnie Bullough, editors, *New Directions for Nurses,* Springer Publishing, 1970; (contributor) Frances Storlie, *Nursing and the Social Conscience,* Appleton, 1970; (contributor) A. M. Reinhardt, editor, *Family Centered Community Nursing: A Sociological Framework,* Mosby, 1971; *The Care of Health in Communities: Access for Outcasts,* Macmillan, 1975. Contributor to nursing and public health journals.

WORK IN PROGRESS: From the World of Health-Politics: A Case Study in Organizational Innovation.

SIDELIGHTS: Nancy Milio traveled in India, Japan, the Soviet Union, and Britain in 1971, to observe the training and performance of nonprofessional workers in maternal and child health and to see how similar workers might be used in a national health service program in the United States.

BIOGRAPHICAL/CRITICAL SOURCES: Detroit Free Press, December 13, 1966; *Newsweek,* March 30, 1970; *San Francisco Chronicle,* June 30, 1970; *Ann Arbor* (Mich.) *News,* July 5, 1970; *Los Angeles Times,* July 7, 1970.†

* * *

MILLAR, James R(obert) 1936-

PERSONAL: Born July 7, 1936, in San Antonio, Tex.; son of James G. (an electrical engineer) and Virginia (Harrison) Millar; married Hete Ascher (a college teacher), July 4, 1965; children: Leo, Mira. *Education:* University of Texas, B.A. (with honors), 1958; Cornell University, Ph.D., 1965; Moscow State University, exchange student, 1966. *Home:* 106 West Holmes, Urbana, Ill. 61801. *Office:* Box 30, D.K.H., University of Illinois, Urbana, Ill. 61801.

CAREER: University of Illinois, Urbana, assistant professor, 1965-70, associate professor, 1970-72, professor of economics, 1972—. Member, Academic Council of Kennan Institute for Advanced Russian Studies. *Military service:* U.S. Army, 1960; became first lieutenant. *Member:* American Association for the Advancement of Slavic Studies, Association for Evolutionary Economics, Phi Beta Kappa.

WRITINGS: (Editor) *The Soviet Rural Community: A Symposium,* University of Illinois Press, 1971. Contributor to economics journals. Editor, *Slavic Review,* and *American Quarterly of Soviet and East European Studies,* 1975—.

WORK IN PROGRESS: Writing on the economic effort of the U.S.S.R. in World War II.

* * *

MILLAR, T(homas) B(ruce)

PERSONAL: Born in Western Australia. *Education:* Royal Military College, Duntroon, Australia, graduate, 1944; University of Western Australia, B.A., 1952; University of Melbourne, M.A., 1958; University of London, Ph.D., 1960. *Home:* 7 Roebuck St., Red Hill, Canberra, Australian Capital Territory 2603, Australia. *Office:* Department of International Relations, Australian National University, Canberra 2600, Australia.

CAREER: High school teacher, 1953-58; Australian National University, Canberra, research fellow, 1962-64, fellow, 1964-66, senior fellow, 1966-68, professorial fellow, 1968—; Australian Institute of International Affairs, Canberra, director, 1969-76. *Military service:* Australian Army, 1943-50.

WRITINGS: Australia's Defence, Melbourne University Press, 1965, 2nd edition, 1969, published as *Australia's Defense,* Praeger, 1970; *The Commonwealth and the United Nations,* University of Sydney Press, 1967; (editor) *Britain's Withdrawal from Asia,* Australian National University Press, 1967; *Australia's Foreign Policy,* Angus & Robertson, 1968; (editor) *Australian-New Zealand Defence Co-operation,* Australian National University Press, 1968; *Foreign Policy: Some Australian Considerations,* Georgian House, 1972; (editor) *Australian Foreign Minister: The Diaries of R. G. Casey,* Collins, 1972.

Contributor: John Wilkes, editor, *Australian Defence and Foreign Policy,* Angus & Robertson, 1964; Norman Harper, editor, *Ferment in Asia,* Australian Broadcasting Commission, 1966; *The Year Book of World Affairs,* London Institute of World Affairs, 1967; Gordon Greenwood and Harper, editors, *Australia in World Affairs, 1961-65,* F. W. Cheshire, 1968; Roy Forward and Bob Reece, editors, *Conscription in Australia,* University of Queensland Press, 1968; Harper, editor, *Pacific Orbit,* F. W. Cheshire, 1968; *Brassey's Annual: The Armed Forces Year Book 1968,* Clowes, 1968; J.D.B. Miller, editor, *India, Japan, Australia: Partners in Asia?,* Australian National University Press, 1968; James N. Rosenau, editor, *International Politics and Foreign Policy,* Free Press (New York), 1969; *Brassey's Annual: The Armed Forces Year Book 1969,* Clowes, 1969; Charles Osborne, editor, *Australia, New Zealand and the South Pacific,* Anthony Blond, 1970; Marion W. Ward, editor, *The Politics of Melanesia,* Australian National University, 1970; Carsten Holbraad, editor, *The Nuclear Non-Proliferation Treaty and Super-Power Condominium,* Australian National University Press, 1971; Bruce Brown, editor, *Asia and the Pacific in the 1970's,* Australian National University Press, 1971; Alvin J. Cottrell and R. M. Burrell, editors, *The Indian Ocean: Its Political, Economic and Military Importance,* Praeger, 1972; Robert M. Lawrence and Joel Larus, editors, *Nuclear Proliferation Phase II,* University Press of Kansas, 1974; George H. Quester, editor, *Seapower in the 1970's,* Dunellen, 1975; Abbas Ansirie, editor, *The Persian Gulf and Indian Ocean in International Politics,* International Institute for Political and Economic Studies (Tehran), 1975. Editor of *Canberra Papers on Strategy and Defence, 1966-70.* Contributor to journals. Editor, *Australian Outlook,* 1965, 1969-70.

WORK IN PROGRESS: A book on the development of Australian foreign policy from the 1850's to the present.

* * *

MILLER, Alan W. 1926-

PERSONAL: Born October 1, 1926, in Hull, England; came to United States, 1961; son of Lewis (a rabbi) and Bessie (Champagne) Miller; married Naomi Max, June 29, 1958; children: Jonathan, Susanna, David, Adam. *Education:* Jews' College, London, B.A. (first class honors), 1947, M.A., 1948, Ph.D., 1959; Balliol College, Oxford, B.A., 1952, M.A., 1955; Leo Baeck College, Rabbinical Diploma, 1959. *Politics:* Democrat. *Home:* 40 West 86th St., New York, N.Y. 10024. *Agent:* Candida Donadio and Associates, Inc., 111 West 57th St., New York, N.Y. 10019. *Office:* Society for the Advancement of Judaism, 15 West 86th St., New York, N.Y. 10024.

CAREER: Religious education adviser, West London Synagogue, London, England, 1954-56; rabbi of reform congregation, London, 1956-61; Society for the Advancement of Judaism, New York, N.Y., rabbi, 1961—. Visiting associate professor, Brooklyn College of the City University of New York, 1972—. Lecturer in Hebrew and Midrash, Leo Baeck College, London, 1954-61. *Military service:* British Army, chaplain, 1951-54; became captain. *Member:* Authors Guild, B'nai B'rith.

WRITINGS: (Contributor) Benjamin Efron, editor, *Currents and Trends in Contemporary Jewish Thought,* KTAV, 1965; (contributor) *Black Anti-Semitism and Jewish Racism,* Richard Baron, 1969; *God of Daniel S.: In Search of the American Jew,* Macmillan, 1969. Contributor to *Saturday Review, Commentary,* and other periodicals. Member of editorial board, *Reconstructionist.*

BIOGRAPHICAL/CRITICAL SOURCES: New York Times Book Review, October 26, 1969.

*   *   *

MILLER, Alice P(atricia) McCarthy

PERSONAL: Born in Lynn, Mass.; daughter of William Henry and Julia (McCarthy) McCarthy; married Warren Hudson Miller (an insurance executive), April 3, 1942; children: Nancy, Jacqueline. *Education:* Hunter College (now Hunter College of the City University of New York), A.B.; New School for Social Research, M.S.S.; Columbia University, M.A., 1963. *Home:* 3701 Henry Hudson Pkwy., Bronx, N.Y. 10463.

CAREER: Former editor and staff writer for various publications, and substitute teacher in high schools; New York City Community College, Brooklyn, N.Y., instructor in communication arts and skills, 1960-61; Pratt Institute, Brooklyn, instructor in psychology, 1961-65; Juilliard School of Music (now Juilliard School), New York City, instructor in sociology and psychology, 1965-66; Harper & Row, New York City, free-lance writer, 1969—; instructor in sociology, Helene Fuld School of Nursing, 1973; instructor in creative writing, Riverdale Community Center, 1977—. Founding trustee, Levittown Public Library, 1950-52. *Member:* American Psychological Association, Authors Guild, Phi Beta Kappa. *Awards, honors:* Indiana University writing fellowship, 1958; merit award, Woman's Day Bicentennial Essay Contest, 1976.

WRITINGS: The Heart of Camp Whippoorwill (young people), Lippincott, 1960; *Make Way for Peggy O'Brien* (young people), Lippincott, 1961; *The Little Store on the Corner* (young people), Abelard, 1961; *In Cold Red Ink: How Term Papers Are Graded and Why* (adult), Allwyn, 1968; *It Happened in 1918* (adult), Allwyn, 1968; *A Kennedy Chronology,* Allwyn, 1968; (with husband, Warren H. Miller) *Who Shares Your Birthday?* (adult), Allwyn, 1970; (with W. H. Miller) *The 1910-1919 Decade* (adult), Allwyn, 1972; *Edmund Burke: A Biography* (young adult), Allwyn, 1976. Writer for Dave Garroway's "Today" television show, National Broadcasting Co., 1952-53. Contributor to magazines and anthologies.

SIDELIGHTS: Alice Miller wrote *CA:* "I'm interested in current movements to eliminate prejudice from books for the young but not uncritical about some of the methods being used to eradicate such prejudice. We need greater represen-

tation of the various minority groups among those who decide which manuscripts shall be published and which published books shall be purchased by school and public library systems. We need greater encouragement of writing talent among persons from many backgrounds.''

*   *   *

MILLER, Benjamin F(rank)   1907-1971

September 10, 1907—June 28, 1971; American biochemist and physician. Obituaries: *New York Times,* June 30, 1971. (See index for *CA* sketch)

*   *   *

MILLER, Charles A.   1937-

PERSONAL: Born October 27, 1937, Washington, D.C.; son of Morris (chief judge of District of Columbia Juvenile Court) and Sara (Levy) Miller. *Education:* Swarthmore College, B.A., 1959; University of Freiburg, graduate study, 1959-60; Harvard University, M.P.A., 1962, Ph.D., 1968. *Residence:* Lake Forest, Ill. *Office:* Department of Politics, Lake Forest College, Lake Forest, Ill. 60045.

CAREER: Clark College, Atlanta, Ga., assistant professor of social science and Woodrow Wilson teaching intern, 1967-70; Princeton University, Princeton, N.J., assistant professor of politics, 1970-74; Lake Forest College, Lake Forest, Ill., associate professor of politics, 1974—. *Member:* American Society for Political and Legal Philosophy, Phi Beta Kappa.

WRITINGS: The Supreme Court and the Uses of History, Harvard University Press, 1969; *A Catawba Assembly,* privately printed, 1973.

WORK IN PROGRESS: Writing on Jefferson and nature.

AVOCATIONAL INTERESTS: Classical Greece, Bach, the Appalachian Mountains.

BIOGRAPHICAL/CRITICAL SOURCES: Commonwealth, 1970.

*   *   *

MILLER, Howard S(mith)   1936-

PERSONAL: Born February 28, 1936, in Pontiac, Ill.; son of Clarence B. (a merchant) and Virginia (Smith) Miller; married Marlo Lange, June 15, 1958; children: Eric Lange, Kurt Matthew, Andrew Harrison. *Education:* Bradley University, A.B., 1958; University of Wisconsin, M.S., 1960, Ph.D., 1964. *Office:* Department of History, University of Missouri, St. Louis, Mo. 63121.

CAREER: University of Southern California, Los Angeles, assistant professor, 1964-69, associate professor of history, 1969-71; University of Missouri—St. Louis, associate professor of history, 1971—. Visiting scholar, Piedmont University Center of North Carolina, 1971. *Member:* American Historical Association, Organization of American Historians, History of Science Society, Society for the History of Technology. *Awards, honors:* Graves Award (grant) in the humanities, 1970-71; University of Southern California Associates Award for excellence in teaching, 1970.

WRITINGS: The Legal Foundations of American Philanthropy, State Historical Society of Wisconsin, 1961; (contributor) Davis D. Van Tassell and Michael Hall, editors, *Science and Society in the United States,* Dorsey, 1966; *Dollars for Research: Science and Its Patrons in Nineteenth Century America,* University of Washington Press, 1970; (contributor) George H. Daniels, editor, *Nineteenth Cen-*

tury American Science: A Reappraisal, Northwestern University Press, 1972. Contributor to *Notable American Women, 1607-1950.*†

* * *

MILLER, William Robert 1927-1970

July 3, 1927—August 10, 1970; American philosopher and theologian. Obituaries: *New York Times,* August 11, 1970; *Christian Century,* September 2, 1970. (See index for *CA* sketch)

* * *

MILLGATE, Michael (Henry) 1929-

PERSONAL: Born July 19, 1929, in Southampton, England; son of Stanley (a civil servant) and Marjorie Louisa (Norris) Millgate; married Eunice Jane Barr (a university teacher), February 27, 1960. *Education:* St. Catharine's College, Cambridge, B.A., 1952, M.A., 1956; University of Michigan, graduate study, 1956-57; University of Leeds, Ph.D., 1960. *Home:* 75 Highland Ave., Toronto, Ontario, Canada M4W 2A4. *Agent:* Peter H. Matson, Harold Matson Company, Inc., 22 East 40th St., New York, N.Y. 10016. *Office:* Department of English, University of Toronto, Toronto, Ontario, Canada M5S 1A1.

CAREER: Workers' Educational Association, tutor and organizer in South Lindsey, England, 1953-56; University of Leeds, Leeds, England, lecturer in English literature, 1958-64; York University, Toronto, Ontario, professor of English and chairman of the department, 1964-67; University of Toronto, Toronto, professor of English, 1967—. *Military service:* Royal Air Force, 1947-49. *Awards, honors:* Killam Senior Research Scholarship, University of Toronto, 1974-76.

WRITINGS: William Faulkner, Grove, 1961, Peter Smith, 1961; *American Social Fiction: James to Cozzens,* Barnes & Noble, 1964; *The Achievement of William Faulkner,* Random House, 1966; *Thomas Hardy: His Career as a Novelist,* Random House, 1971.

Editor: (And author of introduction) Alfred Tennyson, *Selected Poems,* Oxford University Press, 1963; (and author of introduction) Theodore Dreiser, *Sister Carrie,* Oxford University Press, 1965; (with Paul F. Mattheison) *Transatlantic Dialogue,* University of Texas Press, 1965; (with James B. Meriwether) *Lion in the Garden: Interviews with William Faulkner, 1926-1962,* Random House, 1968. Contributor of articles on English and American literature and of reviews to journals.

WORK IN PROGRESS: Further studies of William Faulkner and Thomas Hardy including a biography of Thomas Hardy and, with Richard L. Pardy, an edition of Hardy's collected letters.

BIOGRAPHICAL/CRITICAL SOURCES: New Yorker, June 15, 1968; *New York Times Book Review,* June 30, 1968; *New Republic,* August 31, 1968; *Contemporary Literature,* spring, 1968; *Books,* October, 1971.

* * *

MIMS, Lambert C. 1930-

PERSONAL: Born April 20, 1930, in Uriah, Ala.; married Reecie Phillips; children: Dale, Danny. *Education:* Educated in public schools of Uriah, Ala. *Religion:* Baptist. *Office:* City of Mobile, P.O. Box 1827, Mobile, Ala. 36601.

CAREER: Engaged in retail and wholesale food business,

1948-65; owner of Mims Brokerage Co., Mobile, Ala. Elected public works commissioner of Mobile, 1965, re-elected, 1969, re-elected for third term, 1973; served as mayor under Mobile's system of rotating that office among commissioners, 1968-69, second term, 1972-73, third term, 1976—. First vice-president, Alabama Baptist State Convention; trustee, Judson College. Member of board of directors, Mobile Rescue Mission; member of executive committee, Alabama League of Municipalities; member of Manpower and Income Support Committee, and National League of Cities. Speaker at conventions in United States. *Member:* American Public Works Association (director of region IV), Christian Businessmen's Committee International, Kiwanis Club, Mobile Chamber of Commerce. *Awards, honors:* Named Mobile's outstanding young man of 1965.

WRITINGS: For Christ and Country, Revell, 1969.

AVOCATIONAL INTERESTS: Restoring antique automobiles, and boating.

* * *

MINCHINTON, W(alter) E(dward) 1921-

PERSONAL: Born April 29, 1921, in Dulwich, London, England; son of Walter Edward (a clerk) and Anne (Clark) Minchinton; married Marjorie Sargood (a medical social worker), August 18, 1945; children: Paul Richard, Anne Border, Susan Clare, David Walter. *Education:* London School of Economics and Political Science, B.Sc., 1947. *Home:* 53 Homefield Rd., Exeter EX1 2QX, England. *Office:* Department of Economic History, University of Exeter, Exeter EX4 4QJ, England.

CAREER: University of Wales, University College of Swansea, assistant lecturer, 1948-50, lecturer, 1950-59, senior lecturer in history, 1959-64; University of Exeter, Exeter, England, professor of economic history and head of department, 1964—. *Military service:* British Army, Royal Signals, 1942-45; became lieutenant. *Member:* Economic History Society, Royal Economic Society, British Agricultural History Society, Royal Historical Society (fellow). *Awards, honors:* Alexander Prize of Royal Historical Society, 1953, for article, "Bristol: The Metropolis of the South West in the Eighteenth Century"; Rockefeller Foundation research fellow, 1959-60.

WRITINGS: The British Tinplate Industry: A History, Oxford University Press, 1957; *Industrial Archaeology in Devon,* Devon County Council, 1968.

Editor: *The Trade of Bristol in the Eighteenth Century,* Bristol Record Society, 1957; *Politics and the Port of Bristol in the Eighteenth Century,* Bristol Record Society, 1963; *Essays in Agrarian History,* two volume reprints edition, Augustus M. Kelley, 1968; *Industrial South Wales, 1750-1914: Essays in Welsh Economic History,* Augustus M. Kelley, 1968; *Mercantilism: System or Expediency?,* Heath, 1969; (and author of introduction) *The Growth of English Overseas Trade in the Seventeenth and Eighteenth Centuries,* Methuen, 1969, Barnes & Noble. 1970; *Wage Regulation in Pre-industrial England,* David & Charles, 1971.

WORK IN PROGRESS: Two books, *European Economic History, 1500-1916,* and *The Atlantic Slave Trade.*

* * *

MINGHI, Julian V(incent) 1933-

PERSONAL: Surname rhymes with "dinghy"; born July 26, 1933, in London, England; son of Paris and Pauline

(Millo) Minghi; married Ann Lee Loewus (a social worker), September 7, 1960; children: Monica. *Education:* University of Durham, B.A. (honors), 1957; University of Washington, Seattle, M.A., 1959, Ph.D., 1962; University of Wisconsin, graduate study, 1960. *Politics:* Independent. *Religion:* Roman Catholic. *Office:* Geography Department, University of South Carolina, Columbia, S.C. 29208.

CAREER: University of Connecticut, Storrs, 1961-64, began as instructor, became assistant professor; University of British Columbia, Vancouver, assistant professor, 1964-67, associate professor of geography, 1967-73; University of South Carolina, Columbia, professor of geography and department chairman, 1973—. Visiting assistant professor, University of Rhode Island, summer, 1964; visiting lecturer at University of Calgary, 1967, Michigan State University, 1968, and University of Washington, Queen's University of Belfast, Oxford University, and University of Newcastle, 1969. *Military service:* British Army, Royal Army Service Corps, 1952-54; served in Germany; became sergeant.

MEMBER: Association of American Geographers (member of southeastern division), American Geographical Society, National Council for Geographic Education (co-ordinator for Connecticut, 1963-64), Canadian Association of Geographers (chairman of British Columbia division, 1965-66), Association of Pacific Coast Geographers. *Awards, honors:* Canada Council grants, 1966, 1969-70; British Council visitors award, 1969.

WRITINGS: (Editor) *The Geographer and the Public Environment,* British Columbia Division, Canadian Association of Geographers, 1966; (editor with Roger E. Kasperson, and contributor) *The Structure of Political Geography,* Aldine, 1969; (editor and contributor) *Peoples of the Living Land,* Tantalus, 1972.

Contributor: Harm J. de Blij, *Systematic Political Geography,* Wiley, 1967; J. G. Nelson and M. J. Chambers, *Process and Method in Canadian Geography,* Methuen, 1969. Also contributor to *Census Data: Geographic Significance and Classroom Utility* by Borden Dent.

WORK IN PROGRESS: Problems in Political Geography, for Allyn & Bacon; research on changing frontier zones in western Europe and on the U.S.-Canadian boundary as a barrier to human interaction; research on electoral geography, especially on spatial aspects of campaigning at the urban level.

*   *   *

MINIUM, Edward W(headon) 1917-

PERSONAL: Born November 28, 1917, in Alameda, Calif.; son of Willis F. and Anna (Emerick) Minium; married Juanita Pico, July 13, 1941; children: Claudia (Mrs. David P. Smay III), Judith L. (Mrs. Jay E. Hoff). *Education:* Stanford University, A.B., 1939; University of California, Berkeley, Ph.D., 1951. *Home:* 2281 Lansford Ave., San Jose, Calif. 95125. *Office:* Department of Psychology, San Jose State University, San Jose, Calif. 95192.

CAREER: San Jose State University, San Jose, Calif., instructor, 1948-51, assistant professor, 1951-54, associate professor, 1954-58, professor of psychology, 1958—, chairman of department, 1961-66. In private practice as consultant in personnel psychology and educational research, 1950—; associate, Pacific Coast Consultants, 1955-60. *Military service:* U.S. Army Air Forces, 1943-46; became sergeant. *Member:* American Association for the Advancement of Science, American Psychological Association,

American Association of University Professors, Western Psychological Association, California Educational Research Association, Sigma Xi, Phi Kappa Phi.

WRITINGS: Statistical Reasoning in Psychology and Education, Wiley, 1970. Contributor to psychology journals.

WORK IN PROGRESS: Research in personnel psychology, statistics and experimental design, psychological probability, and education.

AVOCATIONAL INTERESTS: Music, photography, gardening, golf, oriental art.

*   *   *

MITCHELL, G(eoffrey) Duncan 1921-

PERSONAL: Born June 5, 1921, in England; son of George H. and Helen (Grimshaw) Mitchell; married Margaret Miller (a physician); children: Jeremy, Catherine. *Education:* University of London, B.Sc. (honors), 1949. *Religion:* Church of England. *Office:* Department of Sociology, Amory Building, University of Exeter, Exeter, Devonshire, England.

CAREER: University of Exeter, Exeter, England, professor of sociology and head of department. Chairman, Devon Community Housing Society. *Military service:* Royal Air Force, 1941-46; became flight lieutenant; received Order of the British Empire. *Member:* Royal Anthropological Institute (fellow).

WRITINGS: Sociology: A Study of Social Systems, University Tutorial Press, 1959, 2nd edition, 1970; *A Hundred Years of Sociology,* Aldine, 1968; *A Dictionary of Sociology,* Aldine, 1968; *Sociological Questions,* University of Exeter, 1969; (editor) *Sociology: An Outline for the Intending Student,* Humanities, 1970.

WORK IN PROGRESS: Sociology of social development; and the history of sociology.

*   *   *

MITCHELL, Margaretta 1935-

PERSONAL: Born May 27, 1935, in Brooklyn, N.Y.; daughter of Conrad William (a realtor) and Margaretta (Rice) Kuhlthan; married Frederick C. Mitchell (a publisher), May 23, 1959; children: Margaretta Anne, Catharine Francesca, Julia Warren. *Education:* Smith College, B.A. (magna cum laude), 1957. *Religion:* Episcopalian.

CAREER: Photographer; trained as a wood-engraver and also does etchings. *Member:* Phi Beta Kappa.

WRITINGS: Gift of Place, Scrimshaw Press, 1969; (with Dorothea Lange) *To a Cabin,* Grossman, 1973.

WORK IN PROGRESS: Illustrating with photographs Susan Terris' book, *The Boy Won't Wait.*

SIDELIGHTS: As a photographer, Margaretta Mitchell does studies of people, families, and children. She says that she enjoys the details of nature and "celebrates Life" in all her work.†

*   *   *

MIX, C(larence) Rex 1935-

PERSONAL: Born January 14, 1935, in Greenville, Tex.; son of Wilbur M. (a minister) and Ruth (McSpadden) Mix; married Susan Shank (a free-lance drama and dance director and choreographer), August 24, 1961; children: Helen Michelle, Meredith. *Education:* Texas Christian University, B.A., 1957, M.Div., 1961; University of Denver, Ph.D.,

1972. *Home:* 3808 Hyridge Dr., Austin, Tex. 78759. *Office:* 2704 Rio Grande 9, Austin, Tex. 78705.

CAREER: Ordained minister of Christian Church (Disciples of Christ), 1960; minister in Rosenberg, Tex., 1961-62; Texas Association of Christian Churches (now Christian Church in Texas), Fort Worth, director of Christian education, 1962-67; State University of New York College at Fredonia, instructor, 1970-72, assistant professor of speech communication, 1972-75; Texas Conference of Churches, Austin, Tex., director of Value of Life Project, 1975-77, administrative consultant, 1977-78; free-lance management and organizational development consultant, 1977—. *Member:* International Communication Association, Speech Communication Association, Texas State Speech Communication Association.

WRITINGS: (With wife, Susan S. Mix) *Toward Effective Teaching—Youth,* Christian Board of Publication and Warner Press, 1970; *God's Good Gifts to Us,* Christian Board of Publication, 1977; (with Kathy Quinn and Margaret Meyer) *Life and Death Issues,* Hogg Foundation for Mental Health, University of Texas, 1977. Contributor of articles to journals.

* * *

MIX, Susan Shank 1943-

PERSONAL: Born January 23, 1943, in Dallas, Tex.; daughter of Ralph B. (an attorney) and Pauline (Trent) Shank; married C. Rex Mix, August 24, 1961; children: Helen Michelle, Meredith. *Education:* Texas Christian University, B.A., 1965, M.A., 1967; University of Denver, doctoral candidate, 1968—. *Home:* 3808 Hyridge, Austin, Tex. 78759.

CAREER: Fredonia (N.Y.) public schools, part-time teacher of English and theater, beginning 1971; director and choreographer for Free Spirit (liturgical dance troupe), 1975—. *Member:* American Educational Theatre Association, Mortar Board.

WRITINGS: (With husband, C. Rex Mix) *Toward Effective Teaching—Youth,* Christian Board of Publication and Warner Press, 1970. Contributor to *Bethany Guide.*

WORK IN PROGRESS: With C. Rex Mix, *God's Good Gifts to Us,* for Christian Board of Publication.

* * *

MIYOSHI, Masao 1928-

PERSONAL: Born May 14, 1928, in Tokyo, Japan; son of Katsunai and Hisae Miyoshi; married Elizabeth Ann Lester, 1953; children: Kathy Michele, Owen Malcolm, Melina Cybele. *Education:* University of Tokyo, B.A., 1951; graduate study at Yale University, 1952-53, and Bennington College, 1953; New York University, M.A., 1957, Ph.D., 1963. *Office:* Department of English, University of California, Berkeley, Calif. 94720.

CAREER: Gakushuin University, Tokyo, Japan, instructor, 1951-52, lecturer in English, 1954-55; University of California, Berkeley, assistant professor, 1963-69, associate professor, 1969-73, professor of English, 1973—. Member, Humanities Research Institute, 1966-67. *Awards, honors:* University of California research professorship, 1970-71, 1975-76; Guggenheim fellowships, 1970-71, 1976.

WRITINGS: The Divided Self: A Perspective on the Literature of the Victorians, New York University Press, 1969; *Accomplices of Silence: The Modern Japanese Novel,* University of California Press, 1974. Also editor of *Wuthering Heights: The First Edition,* Bobbs-Merrill. Contributor to literary journals.

WORK IN PROGRESS: A book on the 1860 Embassy from Japan to the United States.

BIOGRAPHICAL/CRITICAL SOURCES: Times Literary Supplement, August 14, 1970.

* * *

MNACKO, Ladislav 1919-

PERSONAL: Surname is pronounced M-natch-ko; born January 29, 1919, in Val Klobouky, Czechoslovakia; married. *Politics:* Former member of Communist Party in Czechoslovakia (expelled in 1967). *Address:* c/o Molden Verlag, A-1190, Vienna, Soudgasse 33, Austria.

CAREER: Czech journalist and author, now living in exile; former editor-in-chief of *Kwlturny Zivot* at several intervals; was stripped of his Czech citizenship when he denounced anti-Semitism in his country and made an unauthorized trip to Israel in 1967; later permitted to return to Czechoslovakia but left again after the 1968 invasion by Russian military forces. *Awards, honors:* Klement Gottwald Prize (highest state award for literature in Czechoslovakia); named the outstanding writer in Czechoslovakia.

WRITINGS—Written in Slovak, with some books translated for publication the same year in Czech: *Albanska reportaz,* [Bratislava], 1950; *Vpad Rok na stavbe HUKO,* [Bratislava], 1952; *Co nebolo v novinach* (on the Communist coup d'etat, 1948), Slovenske Vydavatel'stvo Politickej Literatury, 1958; *Daleko je do Whampoa* (on China travels), Slovenske Vydavatel'stvo Politickej Literatury, 1958.

U 2 (on the U-2 incident), Statni Nakladatelstvi Politickej Literatury, 1960; *Smrt' sa vola Engelchen* (published in Czech as *Smrt si rika Engelchen*), Slovenske Vydavatel'stvo Politickej Literatury, c. 1960, translation by George Theiner published as *Death Is Called Engelchen,* Artia (Prague), 1961; *Vystavba Slovenska, 1945-1960,* edited by Kamil Gross, Vydavatel'stvo ROH, 1960; *Ja, Adolf Eichmann,* Slovenske Vydavatel'stvo Politickej Literatury, 1961; *Marxova ulica* (short stories; title means "Marx's Street"), Mlade Leta, 1962; *Oneskorene reportaze* (published in Czech as *Opozdene reportare*), Vydavatel'stvo Politickej Literatury, 1963; *Kde koncia prasne cesty* (published in Czech as *Kde donci prasne cesty*), Osveta, 1963; *Rozpraval ten kapitan* (on Danube travels; published in Czech as *Kapitan mi vypravel*), Vydavatel'stvo Politickej Literatury, 1965; *Dlha, biela prerusovana ciara* (on German travels; published in Czech as *Dlouha bila prerusovana cara*), Slovensky Spisovatel, 1965.

Nocny rozhovor (published in Czech as *Nocni rozhovor*), Vydavatel'stvo Politickej Literatury, 1966; *Jizvy zustaly,* Nase Vojsko, 1966; *Wie die Macht schmeckt* (novel; written in Slovak as "Jak chutna moc" but only excerpts were published in Czechoslovakia in two issues of the monthly *Plamen,* 1966, prior to an expurgated edition, 1968; translated into German for first complete edition), Molden (Vienna), 1967, English translation from the original Slovak by Paul Stevenson published as *A Taste of Power,* Praeger, 1967; *Die siebente Nacht* (autobiographical; written in Slovak and translated into German for initial publication), Molden, 1968, English translation from the original Slovak published as *The Seventh Night,* Dutton, 1969; *Die Aggressoren* (on Israel; written in Slovak and translated into German for initial publication), Molden, 1968.

Der Vorgang (novel), Kindler Verlag, 1970; *Genosse Muenchhausen* (satirical novel), Kindler Verlag, 1973; *Hanoi,* Holsten Verlag, 1973; *Einerwird ueberleben,* List Verlag, 1974; *Die Festrede,* List Verlag, 1976. Also author of film script of *Smrt' sa vola Engelchen (Death Is Called Engelchen).*

SIDELIGHTS: Der Vorgang was filmed for German television in 1971; an adaptation of *Einer wird ueberleben* was also filmed for German television. Some of Ladislav Mnacko's books have been translated into as many as twenty-two languages.

BIOGRAPHICAL/CRITICAL SOURCES: New York Times Book Review, May 28, 1967, September 10, 1967, October 13, 1968; *Times Literary Supplement,* June 29, 1967, June 5, 1969; *Books and Bookmen,* July, 1967; *Time,* August 11, 1967; *New York Times,* August 12, 1967, August 17, 1967, April 7, 1968; *Best Sellers,* August 15, 1967; *New York Review,* October 12, 1967, June 19, 1969; *National Review,* October 17, 1967; *L'Express* (Paris), September 8-14, 1969.

* * *

MOBERLY, R(obert) B(asil) 1920-

PERSONAL: Born January 22, 1920, in South Africa; son of Robert Hamilton (an Anglican bishop) and Rosamund (Smyth) Moberly; married Eliza Maria Hubertina Gitmans (a Dutch national), October 6, 1945; children: Elizabeth Rosamund, Robert Walter Lambert. *Education:* Attended Hertford College, Oxford, 1938-40, 1946-48; Oxford University, B.A. (first class honors), M.A. *Religion:* Church of England. *Home:* Paddock End, Manor Park, Whyteleafe, Surrey CR3 0AQ, England. *Agent:* Campbell Thomson & McLaughlin Ltd., 31 Newington Green, London N16 9PU, England. *Office:* Atomic Energy Authority, 11 Charles II St., London S.W.1, England.

CAREER: British Treasury, London, England, various posts, 1948-59; British Atomic Energy Authority, London, deputy establishments officer, 1959-69, senior staff appointment concerned with reorganization, staff structure, and manpower, 1969-72, head of industrial relations and manpower, 1972—. *Military service:* British Army, 1940-46; became major; cited for gallantry in Normandy.

WRITINGS: A War History of the Second Battalion, the Middlesex Regiment, privately printed, 1946; *Three Mozart Operas,* Gollancz, 1967, Dodd, 1968.

Librettos in English: Wagner, "Tristan und Isolde," 1966; Tchaikovsky, "Iolanta," performed at Camden Festival, 1968; Haydn, "La Fedelta Premiata," performed at Camden Festival, 1971; Mozart, "The Marriage of Figaro," "Don Giovanni," "Cosi fan tutte," and "The Magic Flute"; Verdi, "Otello"; Bartok, "Bluebeard's Castle"; Hugo Wolf, "Moerike Lieder."

WORK IN PROGRESS: A book on all the Mozart operas.

BIOGRAPHICAL/CRITICAL SOURCES: Times Literary Supplement, October 19, 1967.

* * *

MOENSSENS, Andre A. 1930-

PERSONAL: Born January 13, 1930, in Hoboken, Belgium; became U.S. citizen; son of Frans and Leontine (De Meulenaere) Moenssens; married second wife, Susan G. Gedney (an attorney), 1974; children: (first marriage) Monique Jeanne, Jacqueline Rene, Michele Lee; (second marriage)

Allan Lee, J. Frederick, William, Suzanne Marie. *Education:* Chicago-Kent College of Law, J.D. (with honors), 1966; Northwestern University, LL.M., 1967. *Office:* School of Law, University of Richmond, Richmond, Va. 23173.

CAREER: Institute of Applied Science, Chicago, Ill., head instructor in criminalistics, 1960-66; Illinois Institute of Technology, Chicago-Kent College of Law, Chicago, instructor, 1966-67, assistant professor, 1967-69, associate professor, 1969-71, professor of law, 1971-73; University of Richmond, School of Law, Richmond, Va., professor of law and director of Institute for Criminal Justice, 1973—. Lecturer at universities, continuing education programs, and elsewhere on criminal law, scientific evidence, and criminal trial practice. *Member:* American Academy of Forensic Sciences (fellow; former secretary-treasurer; former chairman of jurisprudence section; member of ethics committee, 1977-1980), International Association for Indentification, Illinois State Bar Association, Virginia State Bar, Henrico County Bar Association, Richmond Bar Association, Richmond Trial Lawyers Association, Richmond Criminal Bar Association.

WRITINGS: Legal Status of Fingerprints, Institute of Applied Science (Chicago), 1964; *Fingerprints and the Law,* Chilton, 1969; *Fingerprint Techniques,* Chilton, 1971; *Scientific Police Investigation,* Chilton, 1971; (with Inbau and Thompson) *Cases and Comments on Criminal Law,* Foundation Press, 1973; (with Moses and Inbau) *Scientific Evidence in Criminal Cases,* Foundation Press, 1973, second edition, 1978; *Direct and Cross Examination of Experts,* ASM Enterprises, 1977; *Cases and Comments on Criminal Procedure,* ASM Enterprises, 1977. General editor, *Sources of Proof in Preparing a Lawsuit,* 1976. Contributor to many journals. Editor, *Illinois Law Enforcement Officers Law Bulletin,* and *Behavioral Sciences Law Review;* editorial consultant, *Journal of Police Administration and Police Science;* former editor, *Fingerprint Identification Magazine* and *Chicago-Kent Law Review.*

WORK IN PROGRESS: Continuing research in criminal law and procedure, and in scientific evidence applications.

SIDELIGHTS: Andre Moenssens speaks French, Dutch, German, and some Portuguese and Spanish.

* * *

MOGGRIDGE, D(onald) E(dward) 1943-

PERSONAL: Born May 25, 1943, in Windsor, Ontario, Canada; son of William Robert and Doris (Livingston) Moggridge; married Janet Skelton (a research worker), July 29, 1967 (divorced, 1977). *Education:* University of Toronto, B.A. (honors), 1965; Cambridge University, M.A., 1968, Ph.D., 1970. *Politics:* Labour. *Religion:* None. *Office:* Division of Social Sciences, Scarborough College, University of Toronto, Toronto, Ontario, Canada.

CAREER: Cambridge University, Cambridge, England, research fellow at Clare College, 1967-71, junior research officer in department of applied economics, 1968-69, fellow of Clare College, 1971-72, assistant university lecturer, 1971-72, university lecturer in economics, 1973-75; University of Toronto, Toronto, Ontario, professor of economics, 1974—. *Member:* Royal Economic Society, Canadian Economics Association, American Economic Association, Economic History Association, Economic History Society, United University Club. *Awards, honors:* Woodrow Wilson fellow, 1965.

WRITINGS: The Return to Gold 1925: The Formulation of Economic Policy and Its Critics, Cambridge University Press, 1969; (editor) *The Collected Writings of John Maynard Keynes,* eleven volumes, Macmillan, 1971-77; *British Monetary Policy 1924-1931: The Norman Conquest of $4.86,* Cambridge University Press, 1972; (editor) *Keynes: Aspects of the Man and His Work,* Macmillan, 1974; *Keynes,* Macmillan, 1976; *John Maynard Keynes,* Penguin, 1976. Contributor of articles to professional journals.

WORK IN PROGRESS: More volumes of *The Collected Writings of John Maynard Keynes;* an authorized biography of Keynes.

AVOCATIONAL INTERESTS: Reading, tennis, squash, walking, wine.

* * *

MOHLER, Charles 1913-

PERSONAL: Born May 19, 1913, in Keokuk, Iowa; son of Charles Edward and Ida (Angburg) Mohler; married Hazel Dale (a professor of English), September 23, 1945; children: Charles Conrad. *Education:* University of Virginia, student, 1934; Pomona College, B.A., 1948; University of London, Certificate of Arts, 1950. *Politics:* Independent. *Religion:* Protestant. *Address:* P.O. Box 4645, Carmel, Calif. 93921. *Agent:* Philip G. Spitzer, 111-25 76th Ave., Forest Hills, N.Y. 11375.

CAREER: Rinehart & Co. (publisher), New York City, associate editor, 1951-55; W. W. Norton & Co. (publisher), New York City, associate editor, 1957-61; McGraw-Hill Book Co., New York City, editor, 1963-66; Conrad Press (editorial consultants), Carmel, Calif., director, 1970—. Teacher of fiction writing, Northwest Writing Conference, Bemidji, Minn. Writer-in-residence, Lausanne, Switzerland; writer-as-guest, Spanish Tourist Office, Madrid, Spain. Consultant, General Learning Press, 1970-74. *Military service:* U.S. Army, 1942-45; became first lieutenant; received Bronze Star, Purple Heart, and Combat Infantryman's Badge. *Member:* Authors Guild, Northern California Golf Association, San Francisco Press Club.

WRITINGS: Sextet: The Jesus Complex, McKay, 1951; *A Year of Monday Mornings,* Beacon Press, 1959; *The Hill,* Prentice-Hall, 1970. Also author of two scripts for "Daniel Boone" television series. Contributor to *Better Homes and Gardens, Reader's Digest, Sunset,* and other magazines and newspapers. Travel editor, *Game & Gossip,* 1976—.

WORK IN PROGRESS: The Fortieth Day and *The Easiest Room,* both novels; a contemporary novel set in Rowayton, Connecticut, and New York City.

SIDELIGHTS: Charles Mohler told *CA:* "I write seven days a week, 5 AM to 9 AM on fiction; then the rest of the work day goes to articles for *Game & Gossip* magazine and consulting work." Important to his writings are the works of Joseph Conrad and Walter Van Tilburg Clark, particularly Clark's *City of Trembling Leaves.* He has traveled extensively in Europe and at times lived in Italy, France, Switzerland, Spain, Portugal, and England.

AVOCATIONAL INTERESTS: Golf, theatre.

* * *

MOIR, Ronald Eugene 1928-

PERSONAL: Born November 27, 1928, in Kent, Minn.; son of Russell Eugene (a farmer) and Bella (Engebretson) Moir; married Kathleen Frickson, October 31, 1953; children:

Bradley, Monte. *Education:* North Dakota State University, B.S.E.E., 1949; University of Minnesota, M.B.A., 1956. *Politics:* Republican. *Religion:* Unitarian. *Home:* 4135 Coffman Lane, Minneapolis, Minn. 55406. *Office:* Minnesota Department of Education, 550 Cedar, St. Paul, Minn. 55101.

CAREER: Sperry Rand Corp., Univac Division, St. Paul, Minn., manager of military marketing, 1956-61; Aries Corp., Minneapolis, Minn., division manager, 1962-70; Dayton Hudson Corp., Minneapolis, manager of data processing, 1970-73; Minnesota Department of Education, St. Paul, director of School Financial Management, 1973—. Chairman, 12th Ward Republican District, 1968; member, Governor's Council on Executive Reorganization, 1968-69; chairman, 5th Congressional District, 1976-77. *Military service:* U.S. Air Force. *Member:* American Management Association, Data Processing Management Association.

WRITINGS: (With Gary Andrew) *Information-Decision Systems in Education,* Peacock Press, 1970. Contributor to *Consulting Engineer, Air Traffic Control, Computers and Automation,* and *Journal* of Minnesota Association of Educational Data Systems.

* * *

MOLE, Robert L. 1923-

PERSONAL: Born August 10, 1923, in Kissimmee, Fla.; son of H. Mikel and Ethel Lillian (McCoy) Mole; married Jeannette Rae Hogsett, September 12, 1943 (deceased); married Dolores S. Spangler, August 3, 1972; children: (first marriage) Annette Rae Mole Chapin, Roberta Lee Mole Booth, Dale Michael; (second marriage) three stepchildren. *Education:* Madison College, Madison, Tenn., B.S., 1944; Seventh-day Adventist Theological Seminary, Washington, D.C., M.A. (religion), 1946, M.D., 1957; Lutheran School of Theology, Maywood, Ill., M.A. (clinical education), 1963; American University, Washington, D.C., M.A., 1970; George Washington University, Washington, D.C., M.A. (religion and medical care), 1972; Howard University, D.S.M., 1974; additional language studies at University of California, San Diego.

CAREER: Clergyman of Seventh-day Adventist Church; foreign missionary and educator in Lebanon and Cyprus, 1946-52, including service as treasurer and associate professor of religion and history at Middle East College, Beirut, Lebanon; U.S. Navy, chaplain, 1953-76, with assignments at recruit training centers, service schools, United States Marine Units in America and overseas including two years on mainland Southeast Asia, aboard ships and in hospitals, and as Navy chaplain for Arlington National Cemetery, Washington, D.C., and for the Pentagon; currently chaplain of the Veterans Administration Bureau of Medicine and Surgery with duty at Martinez, Calif. and at the Jerry L. Pettis Memorial Veterans Hospital, Loma Linda, Calif. *Awards, honors:* National Defense Medal with Gold Star, Vietnamese Service with six combat stars, Navy Commendation Medal with valor device and star for second award, Bronze Star with valor device, U.S. Army Meritorious Medal.

WRITINGS: The Religions of South Vietnam in Faith and Fact, U.S. Government Printing Office, 1967; (with R. A. McGonigal and W. W. Newman) *Unit Leaders Personal Response Handbook,* U.S. Government Printing Office, 1967; *The Montagnards of South Vietnam: A Study of Nine Tribes,* Tuttle, 1970; *Thai Values and Behavior Patterns,* Tuttle, 1971; *Pastoral Care in Hospitalization,* Home Study

Institute (Washington, D.C.), 1974; *Please Stay with Me While I Weep,* Home Study Institute, 1976; *God Loves the Military People Also: A Brief History of Seventh-day Adventist Church and the American Military 1860-1976,* General Conference of Seventh-day Adventists (Washington, D.C.), 1977. Also author of monographs published by the U.S. Navy during the Vietnam War.

WORK IN PROGRESS: Vietnamese Time Concepts and Behavior Patterns, for Tuttle; a manuscript, *The Phat Giao Hoa Hao of South Vietnam.*

* * *

MOMBOISSE, Raymond M.   1927-

PERSONAL: Born June 16, 1927, in Petaluma, Calif.; married Mary Jane Reid; children: Michael, Steven, Mark. *Education:* University of San Francisco, B.A., 1950, J.D., 1953. *Politics:* Republican. *Religion:* Roman Catholic. *Office:* Department of Justice, Office of Attorney General, 500 Wells Fargo Bank Building, Fifth & Capitol Mall, Sacramento, Calif. 95814.

CAREER: Admitted to California Bar and to Federal Bar, 1954, and to Bar of U.S. Supreme Court, 1959; California Department of Justice, Attorney General's Office, deputy attorney general, 1954—, Criminal Division, attorney and legal adviser to State Bureau of Narcotic Enforcement, Bureau of Criminal Identification and Investigation, and Peace Officers Standards and Training Commission, 1954-67, Civil Division, attorney in government and administrative law, advisor to State Office of Economic Opportunity, 1967—. Lecturer at FBI, International Chiefs of Police, military and police training schools, conferences, and conventions; member of Riot Advisory Committee of President's Commission on Law Enforcement. *Military service:* U.S. Navy, 1945-46. *Member:* California Peace Officers Association (member of advisory committee), California Writers' Club, John A. Sutter, Jr. Memorial Committee (vice-president), Sacramento State College Citizens Advisory Council, Sutter, Comstock, and Serra Clubs (Sacramento).

WRITINGS—Books; all published by C. C Thomas: *Riots, Revolts and Insurrections,* 1967; *Community Relations and Riot Prevention,* 1967; *Industrial Security for Strikes, Riots and Disasters,* 1968; *Blueprint of Revolution: The Rebel, the Party, the Techniques of Revolt,* foreword by Ronald Reagan, 1970.

Manuals; all published by M. S. M. Enterprises, except as indicated: *Crowd Control and Riot Prevention,* State of California, 1964; *Riot Protection Checklist for Business,* 1968; *Store Planning for Riot Survival,* 1968; *Riot and Civil Emergency Guide for City and County Officials,* 1968; *Control of Student Disorders,* 1969; *Rumor Control,* 1969; *Confrontations, Riots, Urban Warfare,* 1970. Also author of manuals on jails and prisoners, state and military funerals, and riot plans for supermarkets and retail furniture stores. Contributor of numerous articles on history, law, and police techniques and procedure to various periodicals.

Producer and author of a motion picture, "Firebombs," and of a police training film, "Demonstrations and Civil Disobedience." Associate producer and author of television documentary film, "Father Junipero Serra, California's Little Giant," which won second place in the national Corinthian competition, 1964.†

* * *

MONDADORI, Arnoldo   1889-1971

November 2, 1889—June 8, 1971; Italian publisher and entrepreneur. Obituaries: *L'Express,* June 14-20, 1971; *Publishers' Weekly,* June 28, 1971; *Antiquarian Bookman,* July 5-12, 1971.

* * *

MONKA, Paul   1935-

PERSONAL: Born January 3, 1935, in New York, N.Y.; son of Philip Monka. *Education:* University of Illinois, B.S., 1956; University of California, Dominguez Hills, M.A., 1977. *Religion:* Baha'i. *Home:* 5950 Pickford St., Los Angeles, Calif. 90035. *Agent:* Mitchell J. Hamilburg Agency, 1105 Glendon Ave., Westwood, Calif. 90024.

CAREER: Builder and developer of homes and apartments, Los Angeles, Calif., 1961-65, 1976—. Motion picture producer, 1965; producer of educational films. Also has worked in radio and television. *Military service:* U.S. Army, 1956-58.

WRITINGS: Meditations in Uni Verse (young adult book with color work by Gertrude Halpern), Harper, 1969. Writer of television and screen plays.

WORK IN PROGRESS: The second and third volumes of *Meditations in Uni Verse; As One Baha'i Sees It,* a poetical view of a new world religion; two other verse works, *WHAT Is* and *The Tense Is Past,* a book of Jewish Haiku; "Verily, We Roll Along," a musical comedy revue; "Sid Arthur," a full-length comedy screenplay; "Once upon a Time," a poetic story of life's origin and development.

* * *

MONSMA, James E.   1929-

PERSONAL: Born August 11, 1929, in Grand Rapids, Mich.; son of Edwin Ype (a professor) and Frieda (Van-Wesep) Monsma; married Janice Stravers, September 15, 1956; children: James E., Jr., Frederick John, Sarah Marie. *Education:* Calvin College, A.B., 1951; Michigan State University, M.S., 1953. *Religion:* Presbyterian. *Home:* 11 Rabbit Trail Rd., Poughkeepsie, N.Y. 12603. *Office:* Decision Concepts, Inc., 415 Madison Ave., New York, N.Y. 10017.

CAREER: International Business Machines Corp., 1953-69, account representative and applied science representative in Peoria, Ill., 1958-63, customer executive instructor in Chicago, Ill., 1963-65, education research administrator in Poughkeepsie, N.Y., 1965-67, program manager in White Plains, N.Y., 1967-69; Interactive Sciences, Inc. (computer services), Brewster, N.Y., vice-president and treasurer, 1969-72; Decision Concepts, Inc. (computer services), New York, N.Y., vice-president, 1972—. *Military service:* U.S. Army, Chemical Corps, 1953-55. *Member:* Association for Computing Machinery (chairman of Poughkeepsie chapter, 1966-67), Institute of Management Sciences, Econometric Society, American Statistical Association, Society for Industrial and Applied Mathematics.

WRITINGS: (With K. F. Powell) *An Executive's Guide to Computer Concepts,* Pitman, 1969.

WORK IN PROGRESS: Investigations in the conceptual basis of information systems and the requirements of computer based foreign currency exchange systems.

* * *

MONTELL, William Lynwood   1931-

PERSONAL: Born February 18, 1931, in Tompkinsville, Ky.; son of Willie G. (a vocational supervisor) and Hazel

(Chapman) Montell; married Ruth Evelyn Jackson (a teacher), December 31, 1951; children: Monisa Elaine, William Brad. *Education:* Andrew Jackson Business University, business certificate, 1949; attended Campbellsville College, 1955-56, and University of Kentucky, 1956-57; Western Kentucky State College (now Western Kentucky University), A.B., 1960; Indiana University, M.A., 1963, Ph.D., 1964. *Religion:* Baptist. *Office:* Center for Intercultural and Folk Studies, Western Kentucky University, Bowling Green, Ky. 42101.

CAREER: High school teacher in Temple Hill, Ky., 1958-59; Campbellsville College, Campbellsville, Ky., assistant professor, 1963-64, associate professor of history and chairman of the department of social science, 1964-66, professor of history and dean of academic affairs, 1966-69; Western Kentucky University, Bowling Green, Ky., associate professor of history and folklore, assistant dean of Potter College of Liberal Arts, and coordinator of Center for Intercultural and Folk Studies, 1969-71, professor of folklore and history and director of Center for Intercultural and Folk Studies, 1971—. Commissioner, Education Commission of the Southern Baptist Convention, 1969-76. *Military service:* U.S. Navy, 1951-55. U.S. Naval Reserve, 1955-59.

MEMBER: National Education Association, American Folklore Society, Society for Ethnology and Folklore, Southern Conference of Academic Deans, South Atlantic Modern Language Association, Kentucky Folklore Society (president, 1966-70), Kentucky Education Association, Kentucky Baptist Historical Society (commissioner, 1965-70), John Edwards Memorial Foundation, Pioneer America Society.

WRITINGS: The Saga of Coe Ridge: A Study in Oral History, University of Tennessee Press, 1970; *Monroe County History, 1820-1970,* Monroe County Press, 1970; *Ghosts along the Cumberland: Deathlore in the Kentucky Foothills,* University of Tennessee Press, 1975; (editor) *Monroe County Folklife,* Monroe County Press, 1975; *Folk Medicine of the Mammoth Cave Region,* Monroe County Press, 1976; (with Michael Morse) *Kentucky Folk Architecture,* University Press of Kentucky, 1976. Contributor to *Kentucky Folklore Record, Mountain Life and Work, Abstracts of Folklore Studies, Journal of the Ohio Folklore Society, Register of the Kentucky Historical Society, Journal of American Folklore,* and *Southern Folklore Quarterly.*

WORK IN PROGRESS: The Upper Cumberland, a book which will focus on folk history, lore, and regional lifestyle, for Indiana University Press.

SIDELIGHTS: William Lynwood Montell's field research activities include recording historical legends from Negroes and whites along the upper reaches of the Cumberland River in Tennessee and Kentucky, making cross-sectional surveys of folk architectural forms across the Southern states, and intensive photographic surveys of folk architectural forms in Kentucky's Pennyroyal. He also served as a field consultant and on-film discussant for the Educational Television production, "Folk Housing in Kentucky," completed in May, 1970 with funds provided by a grant from the National Endowment for the Humanities.

Montell told *CA:* "In all of my writings I make every effort to tell the story of the people—the grass roots residents whose names never get into 'typical' history books. Additionally, I try to write in a style which these people can read and appreciate. My books are scholarly, but they are not above the heads of the laypersons."

MONTEROSSO, Carlo 1921-

PERSONAL: Born March 15, 1921, in La Spezia, Italy; son of Giuseppe Fenoglio (a company director) and Angela (Risso) Monterosso; married; children: one son. *Education:* University of Genoa. *Residence:* Rome, Italy.

CAREER: Formerly free-lance journalist in London, England, writing documentaries for British Broadcasting Corp. radio and articles for Italian periodicals; currently writing and broadcasting for radio and television in Rome, Italy. *Military service:* Italian Army, sub-lieutenant, 1941-43. *Awards, honors:* Riccardo Bonfiglio Literary Award for *Il Sale della terra.*

WRITINGS: Il Sale della terra (novel), Rizzoli, 1965, translation by Isabel Quigly published as *The Salt of the Earth,* Prentice-Hall, 1967; *Il Caso T.,* Rizzoli, 1968; *L'Odio, variazioni sul terra,* Rizzoli, 1970.

WORK IN PROGRESS: A play on Dietrich Bonhoeffer, a German pastor killed by the Nazis.

SIDELIGHTS: Carlo Monterosso writes that he "loves Bach, by whom [I] feel influenced when writing." His interest in religion and philosophy is reflected in *The Salt of the Earth,* which presents three narratives of Jesus as a human.

BIOGRAPHICAL/CRITICAL SOURCES: Book World, November 12, 1967; *Books Abroad,* winter, 1970.

* * *

MONTGOMERY, David Bruce 1938-

PERSONAL: Born April 30, 1938, in Fargo, N.D.; son of David William (a production technician) and Iva (Trask) Montgomery; married Toby Marie Franks, June 11, 1960; children: David Richard, Scott Bradford, Pamela Marie. *Education:* Stanford University, B.S. in E.E., 1960, M.B.A., 1962, M.S., 1964, Ph.D., 1966. *Politics:* Independent. *Religion:* Protestant. *Home:* 960 Wing Pl., Stanford, Calif. 94305. *Office:* Department of Business, Stanford University, Stanford, Calif. 94305.

CAREER: Massachusetts Institute of Technology, Cambridge, assistant professor, 1966-69, associate professor of management, 1969-70; Stanford University, Stanford, Calif., associate professor of management, 1970-73, professor of management, 1973-76, professor of marketing and management science, 1976—. Principal, Management Analysis Center, Cambridge, Mass., 1969—. Visiting summer professor, Indian Institute of Management, Calcutta, 1969; lecturer on strategic planning, marketing, models, and computers in United States and in Paris, London, Stockholm, Madrid, Tokyo, and other cities abroad. *Member:* Institute of Management Sciences (vice-chairman of marketing college, 1967-68, chairman, 1972-73), American Statistical Association, Econometric Society, Royal Statistical Society.

WRITINGS: (With Glen L. Urban) *Management Science in Marketing,* Prentice-Hall, 1969; (editor with Urban) *Applications of Management Science in Marketing,* Prentice-Hall, 1970; (with William F. Massy and Donald G. Morrison) *Stochastic Models of Buying Behavior,* M.I.T. Press, 1970; (editor) *Management Science: Marketing Management Models,* Institute of Management Sciences, 1971; (with others) *Consumer Behavior: Theoretical Services,* Prentice-Hall, 1973; (with George S. Day, Gerald J. Eskin, and Charles B. Weinberg) *Cases in Computer and Model Assisted Marketing: Planning,* Hewlett-Packard, 1973; (with Eskin) *Cases in Computer and Model Assisted Marketing: Data Analysis,* Hewlett-Packard, 1975. *Journal of*

Marketing Research, computer applications sub-editor, 1968-72, editorial consultant, 1972-75; department editor for marketing, *Management Science,* 1969-71; associate editor, *Journal of Marketing,* 1970-72.

WORK IN PROGRESS: Econometric analysis of marketing problems; research in modeling marketing phenomena and strategic business intelligence systems.

* * *

MONTRESOR, Beni 1926-

PERSONAL: Born March 31, 1926, in Bussolengo, Italy; son of Angelo Silvino and Maria (Fantin) Montresor. *Education:* Attended Accademia di Belle Arti, Venice, 1945-49, and Centro Sperimentale di Cinematografia, Rome, 1950-52. *Home:* 31 West 12th St., New York, N.Y. 10011.

CAREER: Newspaper film critic and author of radio plays, including adaptations of children's fairy tales, in Verona, Italy, 1945-49; set and costume designer, 1952-59, for twenty European films, including "Siegfried," 1958, and several European stage productions, such as Alberto Moravia's "Beatrice Cenci" and Paddy Chayefsky's "Middle of the Night"; came to U.S., 1960; illustrator of children's books, 1961—; set and costume designer for operas, ballet, and ·musicals, in the United States, England, and Italy, 1961—, including Samuel Barber's "Vanessa," 1961, Debussy's "Pelleas et Melisande," 1962, Anthony Tudor's ballet, "Dim Lustre," 1964, Gian-Carlo Menotti's "The Last Savage," 1964, Rodgers and Sondheim's "Do I Hear A Waltz?," 1965, Rossini's "La Cenerentola," 1965, Ponchielli's "La Giaconda," 1966, Berlioz's "Benvenuto Cellini," 1966, Menotti's "Amahl and the Night Visitors," 1968, Puccini's "Turandot," 1969, and many others; debuted as director with staging of Mozart's "The Magic Flute" at Lincoln Center, New York, N.Y., 1966. *Member:* New York Theatre Scenic Designers Union.

AWARDS, HONORS: Caldecott Medal for best children's book of year, 1964, for *May I Bring a Friend?;* knighted by Italian Government, 1966, for services to the arts; American Society of Illustrators gold medal, 1967, for *I Saw a Ship A-Sailing.*

WRITINGS—All self-illustrated juveniles: *House of Flowers, House of Stars* (picture book), Knopf, 1962; *The Witches of Venice,* Knopf, 1963; *Cinderella* (English adaptation from opera, "La Cenerentola," by Gioacchino Rossini), Knopf, 1965; *I Saw a Ship A-Sailing; or, The Wonderful Games That Only Little Flower-Plant Children Can Play* (Italianate fantasy based on Mother Goose rhymes), Knopf, 1967; *A for Angel,* Knopf, 1969.

Illustrator; all juveniles: Margaret Wise Brown, *On Christmas Eve,* W. R. Scott, 1961; Mary Stolz, *Belling the Tiger,* Harper, 1961; *The Great Rebellion,* Harper, 1961; Beatrice Schenk De Regniers, *May I Bring a Friend?* (verse), Atheneum, 1964; Gian-Carlo Menotti, *The Last Savage* (narrative version of opera), New York Graphic Society, 1964; *The Magic Flute* (based on the opera by Wolfgang Amadeus Mozart), retold by Stephen Spender, Putnam, 1966; Beatrice Schenk De Regniers, *Willy O'Dwyer Jumped in the Fire* (variations on a folk rhyme), Atheneum, 1968.

WORK IN PROGRESS: Direction of a film co-authored with James Berry, entitled *The Two Hands of Garret Parker.*

SIDELIGHTS: Beni Montresor's fascination with color was evident at an early age. In an article for *Holiday* entitled "My Verona," he tells of his childhood in that old and lovely city of "warm colors ... soft yellows, pinks, terra cotta." His grandfather often drove him "to the stationers, the little *carteleria* near the Della Pietra Bridge. It was a dark place filled with rolls of paper and books and colored pencils and many other things that seemed strange to me then (even though I had decided to be a painter when I was three)." He mentioned another major childhood influence in an interview with Joan Barthel of the *New York Times:* "Being Italian, I was practically born in the Church.... I grew up surrounded by pageantry, imagery, fantasy."

Now an internationally known set and costume designer for films, operas, and stage plays, Montresor has worked on location all over the world with directors like Federico Fellini, Roberto Rosselini, and Vitorrio de Sica. Difficulty in finding employment as a stage designer when he came to the U.S. in 1960 led him to illustrating children's books, a medium which has proved as much a showcase for his talents as the stage has been. His first self-illustrated picture book, *House of Flowers, House of Stars,* is, according to *Publishers' Weekly,* "still a favorite with American children." Beatrice Schenk De Regnier's *May I Bring a Friend?,* a verse fantasy of a boy who brings animal friends to visit the king and queen, who are in turn invited to tea at the zoo, was brilliantly illustrated by Montresor. The book was awarded the Caldecott Medal in 1965. His second solo children's book, *The Witches of Venice,* inspired the San Francisco Ballet Company production at the New York State Theatre in 1965.

Montresor seems to experience no difficulty in making the transition from designing sophisticated stage sets to writing for young children. As he told Tania Osadca of *Newsday* in 1965: "In both cases I am putting on a production—and any production needs action, color, and something to stimulate the imagination." In a review of *I Saw a Ship A-Sailing,* John Gruen of *Book World* wrote: "All manner of enchantment ... is to be found in [this book] ... which combines this artist's highly ethereal and romantic vision with an instinct for knowing which verses will elicit the best pictures.... Montresor ... brings a special fancifulness to his illustrations. His imagery is dream-like, his colors of Venetian paintings and murals, and a tapestry-like quality lends his drawings their great sense of richness and depth. His approach to the world of Mother Goose is completely personal." Composer Gian-Carlo Menotti, with whom Montresor has collaborated on several stage productions, was quoted by *Show* magazine in 1962, "It comes almost as a shock to find an artist like Beni Montresor, who, although capable of applying his amazing versatility to almost any type of spectacle, never betrays his individuality as a painter."

The Knoedler Gallery in New York City presented an exhibition of Montresor's stage designs in November of 1965.

BIOGRAPHICAL/CRITICAL SOURCES: Show, March, 1962; *Opera News,* February 8, 1964, March 23, 1968; *Newsday,* April 13, 1965; *Publishers' Weekly,* March 8, 1965; *Book Week,* March 20, 1966; *New York Times,* September 4, 1966; Jean Poindexter Colby, *Writing, Illustrating and Editing Children's Books,* Hastings House, 1967; *Book World* (children's issue), November 5, 1967; *Holiday,* August, 1968; *Vogue,* March 1, 1970.††

* * *

MOORE, James T. III 1939-
(Jimmy Moore)

PERSONAL: Born October 1, 1939; son of James T., Jr.

and Olean Moore; married Ava Jean Nelson; children: Pamela, Steve, Kimberly Lynn. *Home:* Hays Rd., Lawrenceburg, Tenn. 38464.

CAREER: Aesthetics Corp., Nashville, Tenn., vice-president and photographer, beginning 1971. Director of Civil Defense in Lawrenceburg, Tenn. *Member:* National Academy of Recording Arts and Sciences, American Federation of Television and Radio Artists, Gospel Music Association.

WRITINGS: A Value of Time (poetry), Impact Books, 1971.

WORK IN PROGRESS: Another book of poetry, which will include photographs by Moore.†

* * *

MOORE, R(obert) Laurence 1940-

PERSONAL: Born April 3, 1940, in Houston, Tex.; son of Walter Parker (an engineer) and Zoe (McBride) Moore; married Annette Hillin (deceased); married Elizabeth Anne Rogers; children: Todd Andrew, Patrick McBride, Alissa Marie, Greta Lee. *Education:* Rice University, B.A., 1962; Yale University, M.A., 1964, Ph.D., 1968. *Home:* 540 Cayuga Heights Rd., Ithaca, N.Y. 14850. *Office:* Department of History, Cornell University, Ithaca, N.Y. 14853.

CAREER: Yale University, New Haven, Conn., assistant professor of history and American studies, 1968-72; Cornell University, Ithaca, N.Y., assistant professor, 1972-74, associate professor of history, 1974—. *Member:* American Historical Association, American Association of University Professors. *Awards, honors:* Fulbright fellowship, 1966-67; J. A. Porter prize, 1968; Morse fellowship, Yale University, 1970-71; National Endowment for the Humanities fellowship, 1975-76.

WRITINGS: European Socialists and the American Promised Land, Oxford University Press, 1970; *The Emergence of an American Left: Civil War to World War I,* Wiley, 1973; *In Search of White Crows: Spiritualism, Parapsychology, and American Culture,* Oxford University Press, 1977.

WORK IN PROGRESS: Writing on intellectual deviance in the United States and the institutions of social control in a liberal society.

* * *

MOORE, Raylyn 1928-

PERSONAL: Born January 5, 1928, in Waynesville, Ohio; daughter of James Byrl and Ethelyn (Coverston) Crabbe; married Ward Moore (a writer), June 14, 1967; children: Beth Penney, Jeanne Penney, John Penney, Sara Rivkeh Moore. *Education:* Ohio State University, B.A., 1949; San Jose State College (now University), M.A., 1971. *Politics:* Independent. *Religion:* Unitarian Universalist. *Home:* 302 Park St., Pacific Grove, Calif. 93950. *Agent:* Virginia Kidd, P.O. Box 278, Milford, Pa. 18337.

CAREER: Reporter on various newspapers, including *Deseret News,* Salt Lake City, Utah, and *Prescott Courier,* Prescott, Ariz., between 1949-64; *Executive Housekeeper* (trade journal), New York, N.Y., editor, 1965-67; Monterey Peninsula College, Monterey, Calif., instructor in magazine writing, creative writing, and speculative (science) fiction, 1969—.

WRITINGS: Mock Orange (novel), Scribner, 1968; *Wonderful Wizard, Marvelous Land* (critical biography), Popular Press, 1974. Short stories have been anthologized in *The*

Best from Fantasy and Science Fiction, Science Fiction and Education, Orbit, Bad Moon Rising, The Last Dangerous Visions, Worlds Far and Near, Harper's Showcase, The Berserkers, Infinity Six, Femmes au Futur. Contributor of short stories to *Esquire, Women's Day, Magazine of Fantasy and Science Fiction, Place, Venus,* and other periodicals.

WORK IN PROGRESS: Short stories; two novels.

BIOGRAPHICAL/CRITICAL SOURCES: New York Times Book Review, April 28, 1968; *Best Sellers,* May 15, 1968.

* * *

MOORE, Raymond S. 1915-

PERSONAL: Born September 24, 1915, in Glendale, Calif.; son of Charles David and Dorothy (Holcomb) Moore; married Dorothy Nelson, June 12, 1938; children: Dennis Raymond, Dorothy Kathleen (Mrs. Bruce D. Kordenbrock), Mari Tokizaki-Limadjaja (foster daughter). *Education:* Pacific Union College, A.B., 1938; University of Southern California, M.Ed., 1946, Ed.D., 1947. *Politics:* Republican. *Religion:* Seventh-day Adventist. *Home:* Route 2, Box 553, Berrien Springs, Mich. 49103. *Office:* Hewitt Research Center, Berrien Springs, Mich. 49104.

CAREER: Teacher at public schools in California, 1938-40, principal, 1940-41, superintendent, 1945-46; Pacific Union College, Angwin, Calif., director of graduate studies and chairman, department of education and psychology, 1947-51; Nihon San-iku Gakuin College, Chiba-ken, Japan, president, 1951-56; Philippine Union College, Manila, president, 1956-57; Andrews University, Berrien Springs, Mich., chairman of department of education and psychology, 1957-60; Loma Linda University, Loma Linda, Calif., vice-president, 1960-62; Southwestern Union College, Keene, Tex., president, 1962-64; U.S. Office of Education, Washington, D.C., graduate program officer, 1964-67; The Bridge, Center for Advanced Intercultural Studies, Chicago, Ill., director, 1967-69; Andrews University, professor of higher education, 1970—. Director of Seventh-day Adventist church school system in Japan, 1951-56; coordinator of work-study committee, White House Conference on Children and Youth, 1960; executive vice-president, Cedar Springs Foundation, Loma Linda, Calif., 1964—; director, Smithsonian Conference on Intercultural Education, 1967; visiting professor, Southern Illinois University, 1967-68; co-director, First World Conference on Intercultural Education, University of Chicago, 1968; president, Hewitt Research Center, Berrien Springs, Mich., 1969—. Lecturer on higher education to various conferences and groups, including National Safety Congress, 1959, 1961, College Presidents Conference, 1967, Association for Higher Education, 1967, University of Wisconsin Conference on Developing Institutions, 1967, and Carnegie Conference on Cluster Colleges, 1968. Consultant on higher education to numerous institutions, including U.S. Office of Education, Japan Ministry of Education, Philippine Ministry of Education and Ministry of Agriculture, University of Wisconsin, Connecticut Commission on Higher Education, and Georgia State Department of Education. *Military service:* U.S. Army, 1941-46; became major.

MEMBER: American Association for Higher Education, American Association of School Administrators, American Association for the Advancement of Science, American Academy of Political and Social Science, American Men of Science, Phi Delta Kappa. *Awards, honors:* Commendation from Japanese imperial family, 1952, for work in distributive education and work-study program; Philippines congressional commendation and presidential citation, 1957.

WRITINGS: Science Discovers God, Fukuinsha, 1953; *Michibiki,* Review & Herald, 1956; *China Doctor,* Harper, 1961; (contributor) Marvin J. Taylor, editor, *Religious Education,* Abingdon, 1961; *A Guide to Higher Education Consortions,* U.S. Government Printing Office, 1967; *Consortions in American Higher Education,* U.S. Government Printing Office, 1968; (contributor) S. S. Letter, editor, *New Prospects for the Small Liberal Arts College,* Teachers College Press, 1968; *Better Late than Early,* Reader's Digest Press, 1975; *Adventist Education at the Crossroads,* Pacific Press Publishing Associations, 1976. Contributor to more than twenty college text books. Also contributor to numerous journals, including *Education Record, School and Society, National Education Association Journal,* and *Journal of Teacher Education,* to professional journals in Japan, Philippines, Germany, and Australia, and to religious periodicals.

WORK IN PROGRESS: Balanced Development of Young Children; a book on simple solutions to major problems in American education; articles on early childhood education; a book and tapes on parenthood education; inspirational books.

SIDELIGHTS: Raymond S. Moore told *CA:* "I write because I believe this is the route of optimum influence. Sound writing also requires one to dig up essential facts and thus become better informed. My philosophy is that we should do less accommodating of trends that are tending to erode our society and face up to fundamental concepts that will rebuild our society." In 1964 he led a scientific expedition to Mt. Ararat in northeastern Turkey which was jointly sponsored by the governments of the United States and Turkey. Mr. Moore speaks some Japanese and Spanish.

*   *   *

MOORE, Thomas Gale   1930-

PERSONAL: Born November 6, 1930, in Washington, D.C.; son of Charles Godwin (a naval officer) and Beatrice (McLean) Moore; married Cassandra Chrones (a college teacher), December 28, 1958; children: Charles, Antonia. *Education:* Attended Massachusetts Institute of Technology, 1949-51; George Washington University, B.A., 1957; University of Chicago, M.A., 1959, Ph.D., 1961. *Religion:* None. *Home:* 3766 La Donna, Palo Alto, Calif. 94306. *Office:* Hoover Institution, Stanford, Calif. 94305.

CAREER: Chase Manhattan Bank, New York, N.Y., foreign research economist, 1960-61; Carnegie Institute of Technology (now Carnegie-Mellon University), Pittsburgh, Pa., assistant professor of economics, 1961-65; Michigan State University, East Lansing, associate professor of economics, 1965-68; U.S. Council of Economic Advisers, Washington, D.C., senior staff economist, 1968-70; Michigan State University, professor of economics, 1970-74; Hoover Institution, Stanford, Calif., senior fellow and director of domestic studies program, 1974—. *Military service:* U.S. Navy, 1951-55. *Member:* American Economic Association, Western Economic Association, Southern Economic Association.

WRITINGS: (Contributor) *Studies in Banking Competition and the Banking Structure,* U.S. Treasury, 1966; *The Economics of the American Theater,* Duke University Press, 1968; (contributor) Walter Adams, editor, *The Structure of American Industry,* 4th edition (Moore was not associated

with earlier editions), Macmillan, 1971. Contributor to *Arts Management* and to banking and economic journals.

WORK IN PROGRESS: A study of the beneficiaries of trucking regulation.

*   *   *

MOORE, Trevor Wyatt   1924-

PERSONAL: Born July 21, 1924; son of Glendon Hazelitt (a retail executive) and Ruth Edna (Wyatt) Moore; married Marcena M. Idle, June 10, 1944; children: Marci (Mrs. J. Louis Dettling), Trevor Wyatt Dunstan II, Gregory Benedict, John Joseph, Veronica Ruth, David Michael, Martha Elizabeth, Francesca Maria, Peter Mark. *Education:* Northwestern University, student, 1947-48; Loyola University, Chicago, Ill., Ph.B., 1950; Nagoya University, Ph.D., 1960; Orthodox Seminary, New York, Th.L., 1971. *Address:* Holy Resurrection Cathedral Rectory, 1611 Wallace St., Philadelphia, Pa. 19130.

CAREER: Ordained priest of Orthodox Catholic Church, 1970; elected and consecrated Bishop of Philadelphia, Pa., 1971; elevated to Archbishop, Orthodox Catholic Archdiocese of Philadelphia, 1971; elevated to Metropolitan, 1973; became Metropolitan-Primate, Holy Eastern Orthodox Church of the United States, 1975. *Christian Art,* Chicago, Ill., editorial director, 1962-63; *Anno Domini,* Jenkintown, Pa., editor, 1963-64; *St. Joseph Magazine,* Saint Benedict, Ore., art editor, 1966-69; *WAY/Catholic Viewpoints,* San Francisco, Calif., contributing editor, 1968—; *Christian Century,* Chicago, editor-at-large, 1971—. Chairman, American Conference of Orthodox Bishops, 1976—; president, Holy Synod, Holy Orthodox Church of the American Jurisdictions, 1977—; chairman of advisory board, Hahnemann Medical College and Hospital Mental Health/Mental Retardation Center, Philadelphia, 1976—. Lecturer, World Center for Liturgical Studies. *Wartime service:* U.S. Merchant Marine, 1942-46; became senior staff officer. *Member:* Royal Society of Arts (England; fellow), American Society for Church Architecture (corporate member), Guild for Religious Architecture (associate member), Society for Priests for a Free Ministry, Episcopal Peace Fellowship, The Resistance (Philadelphia). *Awards, honors:* American College and Seminary of the Orthodox Catholic Church (New York), D.D., 1971, D.Ed., 1971, D.Th., 1972; "Old Master" honors, Purdue University, 1972; D.D. from Universidad de los Pueblos de las Americas (San Juan, P.R.), 1973, and from Church of Universal Brotherhood; Ecumenical Legion of Honor award, Temple University, 1976.

WRITINGS: Where the Action Is, World Center for Liturgical Studies, 1969; (with wife, Marcena Moore) *Sex, Sex, Sex,* Ave Maria Press and Pilgrim Press, 1969; (with Marcena Moore, Margaret O. Hyde, and others) *Science, Sex, and Reproduction,* McGraw, in press. Contributor to *Christian Century* and other periodicals.

WORK IN PROGRESS: The Holy Remnant, for Ressurection Press.

SIDELIGHTS: Trevor Moore and his wife described the troubled life of an activist family in suburbia in "Why They Ran Us Out of Jenkintown," which appeared in *Look.* They said that local harassment (their sidewalk had been painted black, the house pelted with eggs, and their children, who printed an underground newspaper, beaten at school) reached one peak after the publication of *Sex, Sex, Sex.* Eventually, total family involvement in the peace movement led to termination of the lease on their rented house and an eviction notice. Moore adds that his political activism and role of clergyman have led to work on "a theology of survival."

BIOGRAPHICAL/CRITICAL SOURCES: Look, October, 20, 1970; Christian Century, March 3, 1971.

* * *

MORAY, Neville (Peter) 1935-

PERSONAL: Surname is pronounced M'ray; born May 27, 1935, in London, England; son of Peter Albert (a businessman) and Georgette (Campbell Buller) Moray; married Gerta Glasser (an art historian), December 28, 1965. Education: Oxford University, B.A. 1957, D.Phil., 1960. Politics: "Left center." Religion: Catholic. Home: 27 Glen Oak Dr., Toronto, Ontario, Canada. Office: Department of Psychology, Scarborough College, University of Toronto, Toronto, Ontario, Canada.

CAREER: University of Hull, Hull, England, assistant lecturer in psychology, 1959-60; University of Sheffield, Sheffield, England, lecturer, 1960-66, senior lecturer in psychology, 1967-70; University of Toronto, Scarborough College, Toronto, Ontario, associate professor of psychology, 1970—. Visiting associate professor of communication biophysics, Massachusetts Institute of Technology, 1967-68. Member: Acoustical Society of America, British Psychological Society, Experimental Psychology Society, Psychonomic Society, Institute of Electrical and Electronics Engineers.

WRITINGS: Cybernetics: Machines with Intelligence, Hawthorn, 1963; An Introduction to Psychology, Blackie & Son, 1967; (contributor) Eric A. Lunzer, editor, Development in Learning, Staples, 1968; (contributor) John Cohen, editor, Psychology: An Outline, Routledge & Kegan Paul, 1968; Listening and Attention, Penguin, 1969; Attention: Selective Processes in Vision and Hearing, Academic Press, 1970; (with L. D. Reid) A Review of Models of the Air Traffic Control Systems, University of Toronto Press, 1972. Contributor to radio programs on science. Contributor of articles on religion and the philosophy of science to professional journals, and more popular articles to Listener.

WORK IN PROGRESS: A major work, Psychology of Attention; a science fiction novel, as yet untitled; and research in philosophical psychology and the psychology of grace.

SIDELIGHTS: Neville Moray is driven, he says, by "innate boundless curiosity, optimism, and enjoyment of problems rather than solutions." He has a "strong religious conviction that things make sense."†

* * *

MORENO, Francisco Jose 1934-

PERSONAL: Born January 28, 1934, in Havana, Cuba; became U.S. citizen; married; children: two. Education: University of Havana, Capacitado en Administracion Publica, 1954, Licenciado en Derecho, 1955; New York University, Ph.D., 1964. Home: 29 Washington Sq. W., New York, N.Y. 10011. Office: Department of Politics, New York University, New York, N.Y. 10003.

CAREER: New York University, New York, N.Y., instructor, 1962-64, assistant professor, 1964-67, associate professor of politics, 1967—, chairman of department of politics at Washington Square College, 1966-70. Part-time lecturer, Universidad Nacional Jose Marti, 1955-56; visiting lecturer, Universidad Catolica de Chile, 1963; Fulbright lecturer in Argentina, 1971. Military service: U.S. Army, 1956-

58. Member: American Political Science Association. Awards, honors: Research grants from Ford Foundation for field work in Dominican Republic, 1962, from Organization of American States for field work in Chile, 1963, and from National Science Foundation for field work in Spain, 1969, 1970.

WRITINGS: Legitimacy and Stability in Latin America: A Study of Chilean Political Culture, New York University Press, 1969; (editor with Ted R. Gurr) Basic Courses in Comparative Politics: An Anthology of Syllabi, International Studies Association and Sage Publications, Inc., 1970; (editor with Barbara Mitrani, and contributor) Conflict and Violence in Latin American Politics: A Book of Readings, Crowell, 1971; (contributor) Theodore L. Becker, editor, The Political Trial, Bobbs-Merrill, 1971; Between Faith and Reason: An Approach to Individual and Social Psychology, New York University Press, 1977. Contributor to South Atlantic Quarterly and to history and political science journals.

* * *

MORENTZ, Ethel Irene 1925-
(Pat Morentz)

PERSONAL: Born October 6, 1925, in Mickleys, Pa.; daughter of Jacob Paul and Ida (Lebish) Klimeck; married Paul E. Morentz (chief of psychiatry at U.S. Veterans Hospital, Martinez, Calif.), December 27, 1947; children: Ruthanne, Eileen, David. Education: Attended New York University, 1950-52, and San Jose State College (now University), 1952-53; University of California, Berkeley, A.B., 1964; Mills College, M.A., 1969. Politics: Democrat. Religion: Lutheran. Home: 285 Grizzly Peak Blvd., Berkeley, Calif. 94708. Office: Heald Business College, 2142 Broadway, Oakland, Calif. 94612.

CAREER: Heald Business College, Oakland, Calif., instructor in English and applied psychology, 1969—. Member: American Sociological Association, American Association for the Advancement of Science, Society for the Advancement of Management, California Business Education Association, Oakland Museum Association (charter member). Awards, honors: Phelan Award for Lyric Poetry, for "To John Donne."

WRITINGS: Parents Guide to Eight and Nines, Lutheran Church Press, 1964; Life's Mystery and Meaning, Lutheran Church Press, 1965. Contributor to National Antiques Review.

WORK IN PROGRESS: A study of business colleges; several articles on the application of classical philosophical writings to modern life and problems; and an article on Thomas Hooker.

SIDELIGHTS: Ethel Morentz told CA, "I was born with a relentlessly logical mind, so my teaching, writing, and counseling reflect this." She has traveled to London, Rome, and Vienna. Avocational interests: Antiques (particularly rare books), reweaving damaged antique oriental rugs for collectors and dealers, philosophy.†

* * *

MOREY, Walt(er Nelson) 1907-

PERSONAL: Born February 3, 1907, in Hoquiam, Wash.; son of Arthur Nelson (a carpenter) and Gertrude (Stover) Morey; married Rosalind Ogden (a teacher and secretary), July 8, 1934. Education: Attended schools in Oregon, Washington, Montana, and Canada; attended Benkhe Walker

Business College. *Agent:* Lenniger Literary Agency, 437 Fifth Ave., New York, N.Y. 10016.

CAREER: Millworker, construction worker, and theatre manager in Oregon and Washington during the 1930's and 1940's; shipbuilder and supervisor of burners in Vancouver, Wash., during World War II; deep sea diver and fish trap inspector in Alaska, 1951. Farmer, 1938—; director of Oregon Nut Growers; manager of Oregon Nut Growers Cooperative. *Member:* Oregon Freelance Club. *Awards, honors:* Dutton Junior Animal Book Awards, 1965, for *Gentle Ben,* and 1968, for *Kavik, the Wolf Dog;* Sequoyah Children's Book Award, 1967, for *Gentle Ben;* Northwest Bookseller's Award, 1968, Tonawanda (N.Y.) School Children's Award, 1968, Dorothy Canfield Fisher Award, 1970, and William Allen White Award, 1971, all for *Kavik, the Wolf Dog.*

WRITINGS—All juveniles, except as indicated; all published by Dutton, except as noted: (With Virgil Burford) *North to Danger* (adult book), John Day, 1954, revised and enlarged edition, Caxton, 1969; *Gentle Ben* (American Library Association Notable Book selection), 1965; *Home Is the North,* 1967; *Kavik, the Wolf Dog,* 1968; *Angry Waters,* 1969; *Gloomy Gus,* 1970; *Deep Trouble,* 1971; *Scrub Dog of Alaska,* 1971; *Canyon Winter,* 1972; *Runaway Stallion,* 1973; *Run Far, Run Fast,* 1974; *Operation Blue Bear* (adult) 1975; *Year of the Black Pony,* 1976. Contributor to men's magazines, 1930-1950, including *Saga, True, Argosy,* and others.

WORK IN PROGRESS: Books on pre-statehood Alaska, the fishing industry, and associated activities; a juvenile book on Snake River area of Oregon and Utah.

SIDELIGHTS: Jessica Jenkins calls *Home Is the North* "a story in which the fascination of the wild is inseparably bound up with the realities of living. It makes compelling reading, not only on account of its irresistible setting (a remote homestead on the Alaskan shore) but because the variety of events and the characters make it an absorbing story." Of *Kavik, the Wolf Dog,* a reviewer for the *Times Literary Supplement* writes: "Animal stories are best when they avoid attributing human qualities to the animal world. Although it is scarcely possible to make an animal the main figure in a story without using a good deal of imagination on its behalf, it can be done objectively and in a credible way. *Kavik, the Wolf Dog* by Walt Morey is a sound example of this." Helen Renthal feels that in this book "once again the author of *Gentle Ben* has worked a kind of verbal thaumaturgy, mixing some familiar ingredients with a few fresh ones and a knowledge of the Alaskan wilderness to produce an animal story that is something more than the sum of its parts."

The bear hero of Walt Morey's first children's book, *Gentle Ben,* has also been the subject of a motion picture, "Gentle Giant," Paramount, 1967, and a popular television series, "Gentle Ben." Although he began hunting at the age of five, Morey is a confirmed animal-lover who permits no hunting on the grounds of his 60-acre nut grove on the Willamette River in Oregon, which he operates with his wife.

Walt Morey was a longtime friend and companion of Virgil Burford, whose adventures as a deep-sea diver, bear hunter, prospector, and cohort of fish pirates in Alaska were chronicled in *North to Danger.* Well aware of the dangers associated with such a profession, Morey told *CA* that "Burford was lost at sea in a storm near Cordova, Alaska, June 17, 1969, while fishing commercially by himself."

BIOGRAPHICAL/CRITICAL SOURCES: Books and Bookmen, November, 1968; *Children's Book World,* November 3, 1968; *Times Literary Supplement,* June 26, 1969.

MORGAN WITTS, Max   1931-

PERSONAL: Born September 27, 1931, in Detroit, Mich.; son of George Frederick (a businessman) and Cassie (Davis) Morgan Witts; married Pauline Lawson, January 4, 1958; children: Paul, Michele. *Education:* Mount Royal College, Calgary, student, 1947-50; Academy of Radio and Television Arts, Toronto, graduate (with honors), 1952. *Residence:* London, England. *Agent:* Jonathan Clowes Ltd., 19 Jeffrey's Pl., London NW1 9PP, England.

CAREER: Has worked in the broadcasting/communications industry in Canada, the United States, Australia, Ceylon, and India; British Broadcasting Corp., London, England, executive editor of television documentary film series, 1963-72; author. *Awards, honors:* Several television awards for documentary film production; Mark Twain Award, 1970; Edgar Allan Poe Award, 1972.

WRITINGS—With Gordon Thomas; published by Stein & Day: *The Day the World Ended,* 1969; *The San Francisco Earthquake,* 1971; *Shipwreck: The Strange Fate of the Morro Castle,* 1972; *Voyage of the Damned,* 1974; *Guernica, the Crucible of World War II,* 1975 (published in England as *The Day Guernica Died,* Hodder, 1975); *Enola Gay,* 1977.

WORK IN PROGRESS: More books with Gordon Thomas.

SIDELIGHTS: Because of his past documentary film work and present research for his books allied to a penchant for travel, Max Morgan Witts has visited more than fifty countries. His books have been translated into fifteen languages. *Voyage of the Damned* was filmed by Associated General Films, and plans are underway to film *The Day the World Ended* and other of his books.

BIOGRAPHICAL/CRITICAL SOURCES: Best Sellers, April 15, 1969, September 1, 1971, January 1, 1973; *New York Times,* April 15, 1969; *Times Literary Supplement,* July 24, 1969; *Atlantic,* September, 1971; *New Yorker,* October 23, 1971; *New York Times Book Review,* June 30, 1974, February 15, 1976; *Economist,* January 24, 1976; *New Statesman,* February 13, 1976.

*   *   *

MORLAN, George K(olmer)   1904-

PERSONAL: Born May 29, 1904, in Indianapolis, Ind.; son of P. R. and Catherine (Grinsteiner) Morlan; married Blanche Silverstein, December 31, 1938; children: Joseph. *Education:* Butler University, B.A., 1926; Columbia University, M.A., 1931, Ph.D., 1936. *Politics:* Independent. *Religion:* "Sort of." *Home:* 4611 Northwest 45th St., Fort Lauderdale, Fla. 33319.

CAREER: Instructor in English (and sometimes in psychology and other subjects as well) at Pennsylvania State University, University Park, 1928-31, State University of New York at Buffalo, 1931-32, Fenn College (now Cleveland State University), Cleveland, Ohio, 1937-38, Danbury State College (now Western Conneticut State College), Danbury, Conn., 1940-41, Inter American University, San German, Puerto Rico, 1944, and Arizona State University, Tempe, 1945-46; University of Kansas City (now University of Missouri, Kansas City), Kansas City, Mo., assistant professor of psychology, 1946-47; Springfield College, Springfield, Mass., associate professor of psychology, 1947-50; Lederle Laboratories, Pearl River, N.J., coordinator of professional services, 1950-65; Michigan Technological University, Houghton, associate professor of psychology, 1965-66.

WRITINGS: America's Heritage from John Stuart Mill, Columbia University Press, 1936, reprinted, AMS Press, 1973; *Laymen Speaking,* Richard R. Smith, 1938; *How To Influence Yourself,* Berkshire Press, 1944; *Guide for Young Lovers,* A. S. Barnes, 1969. Contributor to *Printers' Ink* and to psychology and education journals.

WORK IN PROGRESS: A book about salesman in the pharmaceutical industry, tentatively entitled, *How to Stand Still on the Executive Ladder.*

SIDELIGHTS: George K. Morlan told *CA:* "John Erskine, Harold S. Latham (editor of Macmillan during its era of dominance), and Rex Stout have particularly influenced and helped me by their interest and encouragement."

He continued: "Two reviews I have especially enjoyed concerned *Laymen Speaking.* In this work I reported the views of a wide range of people on sermons: the devout, an atheist, a black prostitute, a state governor, Sally Rand, Gypsy Rose Lee, Fannie Brice, and many others. A critic . . . declared that the views of the people I interviewed were as helpful for the Christian Church as the views of African bushmen on badminton or contract bridge. This stinger amused me but I agreed more with the critic . . . who wrote that there was enough food for thought in the book to last a lifetime."

AVOCATIONAL INTERESTS: Theater, chamber music, swimming, riding a tandem bicycle with his wife ("we swim half a mile most mornings, and ride several miles on our tandem").

* * *

MORLEY, Sheridan 1941-

PERSONAL: Born December 5, 1941, in Ascot, England; son of Robert (an actor) and Joan (Buckmaster) Morley; married Margaret Gudejko (a novelist), July 18, 1965; children: Hugo, Alexis, Juliet. *Education:* Oxford University, degree in modern languages (honors), 1963; University of Hawaii, graduate study, 1963-64. *Politics:* "Reluctant liberal." *Religion:* None. *Home:* T'Gallant House, Waltham St., Lawrence, Berkshire, England. *Agent:* Curtis Brown Ltd., 1 Craven Hill, London W2 3EW, England; and John Cushman Associates, 25 West 43rd St., New York, N.Y. 10036. *Office: Punch,* 23 Tudor St., London EC4, England.

CAREER: Independent Television News, London, England, newscaster and scriptwriter, 1964-67; British Broadcasting Corporation Television Service, London, resident interviewer for television program, "Line Up," 1967-71; anchorman for television program, "Film Night," BBC-TV, 1971-72; *The Times,* London, deputy features editor, 1973-75; *Punch,* London, arts editor and drama critic, 1975—. Free-lance journalist and broadcaster. *Member:* National Union of Journalists, Buck's Club.

WRITINGS: A Talent to Amuse: A Biography of Noel Coward, Doubleday, 1969; (contributor) *The Rise and Fall of the Matinee Idol,* Weidenfeld & Nicolson, 1973; *Oscar Wilde* (biography), Holt, 1976; *Marlene Dietrich* (biography), McGraw, 1977. Contributor to *Playbill, Plays and Players, Drama,* and [London] *Times.* Regular film, theatre, and book reviewer for *Tatler, Flair, Films and Filming, Punch,* and other periodicals. Editor, Hutchinson Theatre Annuals, 1969-73; editor, Studio Vista Film Studies.

WORK IN PROGRESS: Researching a life of Gladys Cooper (his grandmother).

SIDELIGHTS: Sheridan Morley told *CA:* "[The] Coward biography, my first book, took five years to prepare and involved interviews with 300 people in England and the

U.S.A. Others [, since,] have taken less time but were equally enjoyable to write." *Avocational interests:* Travel, bookselling, talking.

BIOGRAPHICAL/CRITICAL SOURCES: Books and Bookmen, January, 1970.

* * *

MORRILL, Richard L(eland) 1934-

PERSONAL: Born February 15, 1934, in Los Angeles, Calif.; son of Robert W. (an engineer) and Lillian (Riffo) Morrill; married Joanne Cooper, December 26, 1965; children: Lee, Andrew, Jean. *Education:* Dartmouth College, B.A., 1955; University of Washington, Seattle, M.A., 1956, Ph.D., 1959. *Home:* 2837 Tenth Ave. E., Seattle, Wash. 98102. *Office:* Department of Geography, University of Washington, Seattle, Wash. 98195.

CAREER: Northwestern University, Evanston, Ill., assistant professor of geography, 1959-60; University of Washington, Seattle, 1961—, began as assistant professor, currently professor of geography. Visiting professor, University of Chicago, 1966-67. *Military service:* U.S. Army Reserve, 1958-64. *Member:* Association of American Geographers (councillor, 1971—), Institute for the Scientific Study of Population, Regional Science Association, American Civil Liberties Union, Congress on Racial Equality, American Friends Service Committee. *Awards, honors:* National Science Foundation research grant, Lund, Sweden, 1960-61; award for meritorious contribution, American Association of Geographers, 1971.

WRITINGS: Migration and the Spread and Growth of Urban Settlement, Department of Geography, University of Lund, 1965; *Spatial Organization of Society,* Wadsworth, 1970, 2nd edition, 1975; (with E. Wohlenberg) *Geography of Poverty in the United States,* McGraw, 1972.

WORK IN PROGRESS: Monographs on redistricting and the national settlement system of the United States.

* * *

MORRIS, Aldyth V. 1901-

PERSONAL: Born August 24, 1901, in Logan, Utah; daughter of Weston (a professor) and Frances (Maughan) Vernon; married Ray Morris (an architect), June 27, 1929; children: Richard V. *Education:* Agricultural College of Utah (now Utah State University), A.B., 1921; graduate study at University of Utah and University of Hawaii. *Politics:* Democrat. *Religion:* Roman Catholic. *Home:* 1028 15th Ave., Honolulu, Hawaii 96816.

CAREER: War Manpower Commission, Honolulu, Hawaii, business manager, 1943-47; University of Hawaii, Honolulu, managing editor of the University Press, 1949-65; East-West Center Press, Honolulu, editor, 1965-67. Secretary, board of directors, King's Daughters Home, Honolulu. *Member:* P.E.N. (member of executive board, Honolulu branch), National Society of Arts and Letters, National League of American Pen Women (vice-president of Honolulu branch), Dramatists Guild. *Awards, honors:* Several prizes for one-act plays.

WRITINGS—Assistant to Charles A. Moore, editor: *The Japanese Mind,* East-West Center, 1967; *The Chinese Mind,* East-West Center, 1967; *The Indian Mind,* East-West Center, 1967; *The Status of the Individual in East and West,* University of Hawaii Press, 1968.

Plays: "Carefree Tree," first produced Off-Broadway at

Phoenix Theatre, 1955; "Secret Concubine," first produced by Princeton (N.J.) Festival Players, 1956; "The Sign" (one act), first produced by the University of Hawaii Theatre Group, 1958; "The Damien Letter," first produced by Honolulu Community Theatre, Honolulu, Hawaii, 1964; "Sword and Samurai," first produced by Honolulu Community Theatre, 1966; "Tusitala: Robert Louis Stevenson in the South Pacific," produced throughout the Hawaiian Islands by the State Foundation on Culture and the Arts, 1969; "The Dragon of the Six Resemblances," first produced in Honolulu by the University of Hawaii Drama Department, 1975; "Damien," first produced in Honolulu by the University of Hawaii Drama Department, 1976. Also author of many one-act plays, including "The Wall."

BIOGRAPHICAL/CRITICAL SOURCES: Yale Review, winter, number 2, 1969.

* * *

MORRIS, Brian 1930-

PERSONAL: Born December 4, 1930, in Cardiff, Wales; son of William Robert (a naval captain) and Ellen (Shelley) Morris; married Sandra Mary James, August 18, 1955; children: Lindsay Alison Mary, Christopher Justin Robert. *Education:* Worcester College, Oxford, B.A., 1954, M.A., 1956, D.Phil., 1962. *Politics:* "I vote for the Labour Party." *Religion:* Church of England. *Home:* 9 Endcliffe Grove Ave., Sheffield 10, England. *Office:* Department of English, University of Sheffield, Sheffield 10, England.

CAREER: University of Birmingham, Birmingham, England, assistant lecturer in English, 1956-58; University of Reading, Reading, England, lecturer in English, 1958-65; University of York, Heslington, England, senior lecturer in English, 1965-70; University of Sheffield, Sheffield, England, professor of English, 1971—. *Military service:* British Army, National Service in Royal Welch Fusiliers, 1949-51; became captain. *Member:* Bibliographical Society (London), Oxford Bibliographical Society, Virgil Society, Standing Commission on Museums and Galleries.

WRITINGS: (Editor) John Ford, *The Broken Heart,* Benn, 1965, Hill & Wang, 1966; (editor) J. Ford, *'Tis Pity She's a Whore,* Benn, 1966, Hill & Wang, 1969; *John Cleveland: A Bibliography of His Poems,* Bibliographical Society (London), 1967; (editor with Elenor Withington) *The Poems of John Cleveland,* Clarendon Press, 1967; *Tide Race* (poems), Gwasg Gomer, 1976. Author of twelve television scripts produced by British Broadcasting Corp., 1964-70. Joint editor, "New Mermaid Series of Jacobean Drama"; editor, "The Mermaid Critical Commentaries." Contributor of articles on Shakespeare, Cleveland, bibliographical subjects, and music to journals.

WORK IN PROGRESS: A book on the concept of authority in Shakesperian tragedy; an edition of *The Taming of the Shrew* for "New Arden" series.

SIDELIGHTS: Brian Morris told *CA:* "As a poet I am primarily concerned with the mythology, history, politics and landscape of Wales, believing that he who earns his bread by the criticism of literature must be prepared, occasionally, to put his own neck on the block."

* * *

MORRIS, Grant Harold 1940-

PERSONAL: Born December 10, 1940, in Syracuse, N.Y.; son of Benjamin (a lawyer) and Caroline (Judelshon) Morris; married Phyllis Silberstein, July 4, 1967; children: Joshua

Oliver, Sara Benni. *Education:* Syracuse University, A.B., 1962, LL.B., 1964 (converted to J.D., 1968); Harvard University, LL.M., 1971. *Home:* 8515 Nottingham Pl., La Jolla, Calif. 92037. *Office:* School of Law, University of San Diego, Alcala Park, San Diego, Calif. 92110.

CAREER: Admitted to Bar of State of New York, and the Federal District Bar, 1964; Institute of Public Administration, New York, N.Y., recodification attorney, staff member of special project to revise and recodify Mental Hygiene Law of the State of New York, 1964-66; Wayne State University, Law School, Detroit, Mich., assistant professor, 1967-68, associate professor, 1968-70, professor of law, 1970-73, dean for academic affairs, 1971-73; University of San Diego, School of Law, San Diego, Calif., professor of law, 1973—, acting dean, 1977-78. Legal counsel to Michigan Society for Mental Health, 1970-73; San Diego County Mental Patients' Advocate, 1977—. *Member:* Phi Alpha Delta (faculty advisor, McCormick chapter), Phi Kappa Phi. *Awards, honors:* Assistant professor Research Recognition Award, Wayne State University, 1968.

WRITINGS: (Contributor) *A New Mental Hygiene Law for New York State,* Institute of Public Administration (New York), 1968; (editor and co-author) *The Mentally Ill and the Right to Treatment,* C. C Thomas, 1970; (editor with M. Norton) *Intersections of Law and Medicine,* Institute of Continuing Legal Education, 1972; (editor with Norton) *New Developments in Law/Medicine,* Institute of Continuing Legal Education, 1974; *The Insanity Defense: A Blueprint for Legislative Reform,* Lexington Books, 1975.

Contributor of articles to *Syracuse Law Review, Buffalo Law Review, University of Chicago Law Review, Wayne Law Review, University of Michigan Journal of Law Reform, California Law Review,* and other periodicals.

WORK IN PROGRESS: Research on "mental health conservatorships and jury deliberations on the effects of an insanity defense acquittal."

* * *

MORRIS, Tina 1941-

PERSONAL: Born April 8, 1941. *Education:* "Irrelevant." *Home:* 64 Meadowcroft Ave., Catterall, Preston, Lancashire, England.

CAREER: "Irrelevant."

WRITINGS: (Editor) *Victims of Our Fear,* Screeches Publications, 1964; *Flowers of Snow: City Poems,* Screeches Publications, 1964; *Whether You or I Love or Hate: Poems of Love,* Screeches Publications, 1965; *A Song of the Great Peace,* edited by Dave Cunliffe, B.B. Books, 1967; (editor with Cunliffe) *Thunderbolts of Peace and Liberation,* B.B. Books, 1969; (contributor) *New Writers VII,* Calder & Boyars, 1969; (with T. K. Metcalf) *Uncreated Stars,* B.B. Books, 1970. Contributor to journals and little magazines.

WORK IN PROGRESS: "A long-lasting love affair with trees currently drives me to express the spirit of trees (as I feel it) in many ways—prose, poetry, novels, children's books (if I keep trying, I'll get it right eventually!)."

SIDELIGHTS: Tina Morris told *CA:* "With 2 young daughters, a large food-producing garden and a vast family of assorted hairies to care for, I'm spared the effort of feeling I *ought* to be writing in any spare moments. Now, to achieve anything, I find I have to forget all the pencil-sharpening routines and really get 'stuck-in'. It's wonderful discipline!"

She added that she is "thoroughly frustrated by the publishing world. I *don't* have a stack of rejection slips but I *do* have a pile of letters from publishers praising my work then always, alas, saying that they can't/won't publish it because it isn't COMMERCIAL enough and/or short stories just don't sell. . . . My one consolation is that the writing comes first—as both joy and agony—and the attempt to get published is just a side-effect!''

The *Times Literary Supplement* reviewer states that Tina Morris' work "qualifies . . . for the dream label. Bizarre violence, rape, incest, sensations of gestation and death alternate in a planned but confusing way in a series of connecting paragraphs written in the new international avant-garde prose. . . . But despite the mannerisms Miss Morris rarely loses one's attention. This kind of dream material is becoming routine in current 'underground' literature, but she manages to evoke many of her personal nightmare images with chilling effect.''

BIOGRAPHICAL/CRITICAL SOURCES: Times Literary Supplement, August 29, 1969.

* * *

MORRIS-GOODALL, Vanne 1909-
(Vanne Morris Goodall)

PERSONAL: Born January 24, 1909, in Milford Haven, England; daughter of William (a clergyman) and Elizabeth Hornby (Legard) Joseph; married Mortimer Morris-Goodall (a company director), September 26, 1932; children: Jane (Mrs. Derek Bryceson), Judy (Mrs. Roderick Waters). *Education:* Attended Milton Mount College, Sussex, England. *Home:* 10 Durley Chine Rd., Bournemouth, England. *Agent:* Peter Janson-Smith Ltd., 31 Newington Green, Islington, London N16 9PU, England.

WRITINGS—Name indexed in most sources under Goodall: *Beyond the Rain Forest* (novel), Collins, 1967, published as *The Gold of Vala,* Fontana Books, 1970; (with Louis Seymour Bazett Leakey) *Unveiling Man's Origins: Ten Decades of Thought about Human Evolution,* Schenkman, 1969; (editor) *The Quest for Man,* preface by Julian Huxley, Praeger, 1975.

WORK IN PROGRESS: A children's book on evolution; a biography for children of her daughter, Jane Goodall.

SIDELIGHTS: Vanne Morris-Goodall accompanied her daughter, Jane, when the latter began her study of chimpanzees in the Gombe Stream chimpanzee reserve in Tanzania.

* * *

MORRISON, Claudia C(hristopherson) 1936-

PERSONAL: Born November 17, 1936, in Galveston, Tex.; daughter of Joseph Arthur (a government employee) and Edna (Crawford) Christopherson; married Michael Wogan, July 29, 1955; married second husband, Chaplain W. Morrison (a professor), August 8, 1961; children: (second marriage) Lynette, Laurie. *Education:* American University, B.A., 1957; University of Florida, M.A., 1958; University of North Carolina, Ph.D., 1964. *Politics:* Radical. *Home:* 169 Fairhaven, Pointe Claire, Quebec, Canada. *Office:* Department of English, John Abbott College, St. Anne de Bellevue, Quebec, Canada DO67O.

CAREER: Sweetbriar College, Sweetbriar, Va., assistant professor of English, 1965-66; Youngstown State University, Youngstown, Ohio, associate professor of English, 1966-69; University of Waterloo, Waterloo, Ontario, associate professor of English, 1969-72; John Abbott College, St. Anne de Bellevue, Quebec, associate professor of English, 1972—.

WRITINGS: Freud and the Critic, University of North Carolina Press, 1968.

BIOGRAPHICAL/CRITICAL SOURCES: Virginia Quarterly Review, spring, 1969.

* * *

MORRISON, Toni 1931-

PERSONAL: Born Chloe Anthony Wofford, February 18, 1931, in Lorain, Ohio; daughter of George and Ramah (Willis) Wofford; children: Ford, Slade. *Education:* Howard University, B.A., 1953; Cornell University, M.A., 1955. *Agent:* Lynn Nesbitt, International Creative Management, 40 West 57th St., New York, N.Y. 10019. *Office:* Random House, 201 East 50th St., New York, N.Y. 10022.

CAREER: Texas Southern University, Houston, instructor in English, 1955-57; Howard University, Washington, D.C., instructor in English, 1957-64; Random House, New York, N.Y., a senior editor, 1965—. Visiting lecturer, Yale University, New Haven, Conn., 1976—. *Awards, honors:* National Book Award nomination, 1975, for *Sula.*

WRITINGS: The Bluest Eye, Holt, 1969; *Sula,* Knopf, 1973; *The Black Book,* Random House, 1974; *Song of Solomon,* Knopf, 1977.

SIDELIGHTS: John Leonard writes: "Toni Morrison's *The Bluest Eye* is an inquiry into the reasons why beauty gets wasted in this country. The beauty in this case is black; the wasting is done by a cultural engine that seems to have been designed specifically to murder possibilities; the 'bluest eye' refers to the blue eyes of the blond American myth, by which standard the black-skinned and brown-eyed always measure up as inadequate. Miss Morrison expresses the negative of the Dick-and-Jane-and-Mother-and-Father-and-Dog-and-Cat photograph that appears in our reading primers, and she does it with a prose so precise, so faithful to speech and so charged with pain and wonder that the novel becomes poetry. . . . I have said 'poetry.' But *The Bluest Eye* is also history, sociology, folklore, nightmare and music. It is one thing to state that we have institutionalized waste, that children suffocate under mountains of merchanised lies. It is another thing to demonstrate that waste, to recreate those children, to live the lie and die by it. Miss Morrison's angry sadness overwhelms.''

On *Sula,* Jonathan Yardley comments: "What gives this terse, imaginative novel its genuine distinction is the quality of Toni Morrison's prose. *Sula* is admirable enough as a study of its title character, an alluring and predatory woman, and of life in the black section of a small Ohio town; but its real strength lies in Morrison's writing, which at times has the resonance of poetry and is precise, vivid and controlled throughout. . . . The most fully realized character in the novel, however, is the community of the Bottom. Toni Morrison is not a southern writer, but she has located place and community with the skill of a Flannery O'Connor or Eudora Welty. *Sula* is an intelligent and intriguing novel—and prose such as Morrison's simply does not come along very often.''

BIOGRAPHICAL/CRITICAL SOURCES: New York Times, November 13, 1970, September 6, 1977; *Newsweek,* November 30, 1970; *Washington Post,* February 3, 1974, March 6, 1974; *Contemporary Literary Criticism,* Volume IV, Gale, 1975.

* * *

MORSE, Arthur David 1920-1971

December 27, 1920—June 1, 1971; American television

writer and producer. Obituaries: *New York Times,* June 3, 1971.

* * *

MORTON, Desmond 1937-

PERSONAL: Born September 10, 1937, in Calgary, Alberta, Canada; son of R. E. A. (a brigadier general, Canadian Army) and Sylvia Cuyler (Frink) Morton; married Janet L. Smith (a political organizer), July 5, 1967; children: David, Marion. *Education:* College Militaire Royal de St-Jean, Cadet, 1954-57; Royal Military College of Canada, B.A. (honors), 1959; Oxford University, B.A., M.A.; London School of Economics and Political Science, Ph.D., 1969. *Politics:* New Democratic Party. *Home:* 3065 Lenester Dr., Unit 31, Mississauga, Ontario, Canada. *Office:* Erindale College, University of Toronto, Mississauga, Ontario, Canada L5L 1C6.

CAREER: Canadian Army, officer cadet and commissioned officer, 1954-64, rising to captain; New Democratic Party of Ontario, assistant secretary, 1964-68; University of Ottawa, Ottawa, Ontario, assistant professor, 1966-69; University of Toronto, Erindale College, Toronto, Ontario, assistant professor, 1969-71, associate professor, 1971-75, professor and academic vice-principal, 1975—. *Member:* Canadian Historical Association, Royal Canadian Military Institute, Ontario Woodsworth Foundation.

WRITINGS: Ministers and Generals: Politics and the Canadian Militia, 1868-1904, University of Toronto Press, 1970; *The Last War Drum: The Northwest Campaign of 1885,* Hakkert, 1972; (editor with R. H. Roy) *Telegrams of the Northwest Campaign, 1885,* Champlain Society, 1972; *Mayor Howland: The Citizens' Candidate,* Hakkert, 1973; *The Canadian General: Sir William Otter,* Hakkert, 1974; *N.D.P.: The Dream of Power,* Hakkert, 1974. Contributor of articles to *Canadian Historical Review, Journal of Canadian Studies, Queen's Quarterly, Social History, Saturday Night, Canadian Journal of Higher Education, The Canadian Forum,* and *Toronto Star.*

WORK IN PROGRESS: A study of politics and the development of national awareness through the Overseas Ministry and the Canadian Expeditionary Force, 1914-1919; a study of the South African War and Canada's role for the Canadian War Museum; a biography of Lieutenant General the Hon. Sam Hughes, Canadian Minister of Militia and Defence, 1911-1916; an illustrated history of Canadian trade unionism and an examination of thought in Canada.

* * *

MORTON, T(homas) Ralph 1900-

PERSONAL: Born August 18, 1900, in Greenock, Scotland; son of Robert and Marion (Stark) Morton; married Jenny Baird, June 20, 1927; children: Faith (Mrs. William Macrae Aitken), Hugh, Colin, George. *Education:* University of Glasgow, M.A., 1920, M.A. (honors), 1921; Trinity College, Glasgow, further study, 1922-25. *Politics:* Labour Party. *Home:* Monessie, by Crieff, Perthshire, Scotland.

CAREER: Presbyterian missionary in China, 1925-37; St. Columba's Church, Cambridge, England, minister, 1937-43; Community House, Glasgow, Scotland, warden, 1943-54; Iona Community, Iona and Glasgow, deputy leader, 1954-67. Honorary lecturer, University of Edinburgh, 1954-64. *Awards, honors:* D.D., University of Glasgow.

WRITINGS: Life in the Chinese Church, S.C.M. Press, 1931; *Today in Manchuria,* Friendship, 1939; *The House-*

hold of Faith: An Essay on the Changing Pattern of the Church's Life, Iona Community (Glasgow), 1951, expanded edition with chapters by Alexander Miller and John O. Nelson published as *Community of Faith,* Association Press, 1954; *The Twelve Together,* Iona Community, 1956; *The Iona Community Story,* Lutterworth, 1957; *What is the Iona Community?* (booklet), Iona Community, c. 1957; (with Mark Gibbs) *God's Frozen People,* Collins, 1964, Westminster, 1965; *Jesus: Man for Today,* Abingdon, 1970; (with Gibbs) *God's Lively People,* Westminster, 1971; *God's Moving Spirit,* Mowbray, 1973; *Knowing Jesus,* Westminster, 1974.

* * *

MOSER, Charles A. 1935-

PERSONAL: Born January 6, 1935, in Knoxville, Tenn.; son of Arthur H. (a professor) and Sarah (Ridlehoover) Moser; married Anastasia Dimitrova (a research assistant), September 14, 1968. *Education:* Yale University, B.A., 1956; Columbia University, M.A., 1958, Ph.D., 1962; Leningrad State University, additional study, 1958-59. *Politics:* Conservative Republican. *Religion:* High Episcopalian. *Home:* 2029 Freedom Lane, Falls Church, Va. 22043. *Office:* Department of Slavic Languages, George Washington University, Washington, D.C. 20006.

CAREER: Yale University, New Haven, Conn., instructor, 1960-63, assistant professor of Slavic languages, 1963-67; George Washington University, Washington, D.C., associate professor of Russian, 1967—, chairman of department of Slavic languages, 1969-74. *Member:* American Association of Teachers of Slavic and Eastern European Languages, American Association for the Advancement of Slavic Studies, Phi Beta Kappa.

WRITINGS: Antinihilism in the Russian Novel of the 1860's, Mouton, 1964; *Pisemsky: A Provincial Realist,* Harvard University Press, 1969; *A History of Bulgarian Literature, 865-1944,* Humanities, 1972; *Ivan Turgenev,* Columbia University Press, 1972. Contributor to Slavic journals.

WORK IN PROGRESS: Dimitrov of Bulgaria: A Political Biography of Dr. Georgi M. Dimitrov; a book on Denis Fonvizin.

* * *

MOSKOF, Martin Stephen 1930-

PERSONAL: Born May 18, 1930, in New York, N.Y.; son of Joseph Louis and Florence (Polesie) Moskof. *Education:* Student at City College (now City College of the City University of New York), 1948, and Black Mountain College, Black Mountain, N.C., 1951; Alfred University, B.F.A., 1952; Illinois Institute of Technology, M.S., 1954. *Home:* 337 West 76th St., New York, N.Y. 10023. *Office:* Martin Stephen Moskof & Associates, Inc., 159 West 53rd St., New York, N.Y. 10019.

CAREER: Columbia Broadcasting System, New York City, assistant art director, 1956-58; Designers Collaborative, New York City, president, 1958-60; Moskof, Morrison Associates, New York City, president, 1960-62; Martin Stephen Moskof & Associates, Inc., New York City, president, 1963—. Member, board of directors, New York State Craftsmen, Inc., 1975—. Consultant to New York State Council on the Arts. *Military service:* U.S. Army, 1954-56. *Member:* American Institute of Graphic Arts, Art Directors Club.

WRITINGS: (With Arnie Hendin) *Nude Landscapes,* University Books, 1968; (with Seymour Chwast) *Still Another Alphabet Book,* McGraw, 1969; (with Richard Hefter) *Shuffle Book,* Golden Press, 1970; (with Chwast) *Still Another Number Book,* McGraw, 1971; (with Hefter) *Everything,* Parents' Magazine Press, 1971; (with Hefter) *An Animal Shuffle Book,* Golden Press, 1971; (with Hefter) *Great Big Alphabet Book: With Lots of Pictures and Words,* Grosset, 1972; (with Chwast) *Still Another Children's Book,* McGraw, 1974; (with Hefter) *Christopher's Parade,* Parents' Magazine Press, 1974.

WORK IN PROGRESS: Three books.

AVOCATIONAL INTERESTS: Painting, sculpture.

*   *   *

MOTTRAM, Ralph Hale   1883-1971

October 30, 1883—April 16, 1971; English novelist. Obituaries: *Antiquarian Bookman,* June 24, 1971.

*   *   *

MOURELATOS, Alexander P(hoebus) D(ionysiou)   1936-

PERSONAL: Surname is pronounced Mur-el-*ahtos;* born July 19, 1936, in Athens, Greece; accepted as immigrant to United States, 1963, became citizen, 1968; son of Dionysius Alexandrou (a bank clerk) and Elia (Voutsara) Mourelatos; married Linda Oppen (a riding instructor and horse trainer), June 12, 1962. *Education:* Completed high school in Athens, Greece; Yale University, B.A. (summa cum laude), 1958, M.A., 1961, Ph.D., 1964. *Religion:* No affiliation. *Home:* 2108 Matthews Dr., Austin, Tex. 78703. *Office:* Department of Philosophy, University of Texas, Austin, Tex. 78712.

CAREER: Yale University, New Haven, Conn., instructor in philosophy, 1962-64; University of Wisconsin—Madison, junior fellow of Institute for Research in the Humanities, 1964-65; University of Texas at Austin, assistant professor, 1965-67, associate professor, 1967-71, professor of philosophy, 1971—. Member, Institute for Advanced Study, Princeton, N.J., 1967-68; fellow, Center for Hellenic Studies, 1973-74. *Member:* American Philosophical Association, American Philological Association, Society for Ancient Greek Philosophy, National Audubon Society, Sierra Club. *Awards, honors:* National Endowment for the Humanities junior fellowship, 1968; American Council of Learned Societies fellowship, 1973-74.

WRITINGS: The Route of Parmenides: A Study of Word, Image, and Argument in the Fragments, Yale University Press, 1970; *The Pre-Socratics: A Collection of Critical Essays,* Doubleday, 1974. Contributor to philology, philosophy, and metaphysics journals.

WORK IN PROGRESS: Studies on themes of metaphysics and theory of knowledge in Greek philosophy, especially pre-Socratics and Plato; studies in philosophy and linguistics.

SIDELIGHTS: Alexander Mourelatos reached Yale University as a scholarship student through a competition administered by the Institute of International Education in New York. His original goal was to study medicine, but he took the premedical program at Yale with a major in philosophy, and eventually switched to an academic career.

AVOCATIONAL INTERESTS: Playing the flute with amateur chamber music groups.

MOWAT, R(obert) C(ase)   1913-

PERSONAL: Born May 11, 1913, in Oxford, England; son of Robert Balmain (a university professor) and Mary George (Loch) Mowat; married Renee Sutton, June 14, 1942; children: David, Ann (Mrs. Robert Bruce), Anthony, Jocelyn, Fenella. *Education:* Hertford College, Oxford, B.A., 1935, M.A., 1958, D.Phil., 1970. *Home:* 20 Highfield Ave., Oxford OX3 7LR, England. *Office:* Department of Arts and Languages, Oxford Polytechnic, Oxford, England.

CAREER: Royal Naval College, Greenwich, London, England, senior lecturer in history, 1947-58; University of Ibadan, Ibadan, Nigeria, senior lecturer in history, 1958-63; Oxford Polytechnic, Oxford, England, senior and principal lecturer in history, 1963—, head of department of arts and languages, 1970—. *Military service:* British Army, 1940-46; became captain. *Member:* Historical Association, Royal Commonwealth Society.

WRITINGS: History of the World, Part 12: *1815-1865,* Odhams, 1944; *Climax of History,* Blandford, 1951; *The Message of Frank Buchman: A Study of "Remaking the World,"* Blandford, 1951, revised edition, 1953; (editor; Arthur G. Jane, translator) Oevvind Skard, *Ideological Strategy* (translation of *Ideologisk Kamp og psykologisk forsvar*), Blandford, 1955; (editor) *Report on Moral Rearmament,* Blandford, 1955; *Middle East Perspective,* Blandford, 1958, Pitman, 1959; *Ruin and Resurgence: Europe, 1939-1965,* Humanities, 1966; *Creating the European Economy,* Barnes & Noble, 1973.

WORK IN PROGRESS: A book on the partnership between western Europe and the countries of the Middle East.

*   *   *

MOWRER, Paul Scott   1887-1971

July 14, 1887—April 4, 1971; American journalist and poet. Obituaries: *New York Times,* April 7, 1971; *Washington Post,* April 7, 1971; *Variety,* April 14, 1971; *Antiquarian Bookman,* June 24, 1971. (See index for *CA* sketch)

*   *   *

MUELLER, David L.   1929-

PERSONAL: Born October 5, 1929, in Buffalo, N.Y.; son of William A. (a professor) and Mary (Fink) Mueller; married Marilyn Thompson, July 25, 1959; children: Charles David, Mary Elizabeth. *Education:* Attended Colgate University, 1947-49, and University of Heidelberg, 1949-50; Baylor University, B.A., 1951; Southern Baptist Theological Seminary, B.D., 1954; Duke University, Ph.D., 1958; further study at University of Basel, Yale University, and Harvard University. *Home:* 4908 Crofton Rd., Louisville, Ky. 40207. *Office:* Southern Baptist Theological Seminary, 2825 Lexington Rd., Louisville, Ky. 40206.

CAREER: Baptist clergyman. Baylor University, Waco, Tex., assistant professor, 1957-59, associate professor of religion, 1959-61; Southern Baptist Theological Seminary, Louisville, Ky., assistant professor, 1961-62, associate professor, 1962-77, professor of theology, 1977—. *Member:* American Academy of Religion, American Society of Church History.

WRITINGS: An Introduction to the Theology of Albrecht Ritschl, Westminster, 1969; *Makers of the Modern Theological Mind: Karl Barth,* Word Books, 1972. Contributor to *Saturday Review* and religious journals and newspapers. Book review editor, *Review and Expositor;* abstractor, *Journal of Ecumenical Studies.*

AVOCATIONAL INTERESTS: Travel, sports.

*   *   *

MUMMERY, David R. 1932-

PERSONAL: Born December 11, 1932, in Wanganui, New Zealand; son of William Rest and Gertrude Lee (Martin) Mummery; married Donna Bryner, August 13, 1966. *Education:* University of New Zealand, B.A. and LL.B., 1956, LL.M., 1960; Harvard University, LL.M., 1961; University of Virginia, S.J.D., 1966. *Home:* 10 Marsden Ave., Apt. 5, Auckland 4, New Zealand. *Office:* School of Law, University of Auckland, Auckland, New Zealand.

CAREER: New Zealand Department of Foreign Affairs, Wellington, staff member, 1955-60; Northeastern University, Boston, Mass., member of department of political science, 1962-63; University of Virginia, Charlottesville, instructor in School of Law, 1965-66; University of Auckland, School of Law, Auckland, New Zealand, senior lecturer, 1966—. *Member:* American Society of International Law.

WRITINGS: The Protection of International Private Investment: Nigeria and the World Community, Praeger, 1968. Contributor to *Proceedings* of American Society of International Law and to *American Journal of International Law.*

WORK IN PROGRESS: Work in jurisprudence and international law.

*   *   *

MUNCH, Peter A(ndreas) 1908-

PERSONAL: Surname is pronounced Munck; born December 19, 1908, in Nes, Hedmark, Norway; son of Peter Andreas (a minister) and Cathrine E. (Bull) Munch; married Helene Stephansen (an office manager), June 23, 1934; children: Cathrine (Mrs. Fred L. Snyder), Mette (Mrs. David Smith), Peter Andreas, Jr. *Education:* University of Oslo, Cand.theol., 1932, Dr.philos., 1946; also studied at Oxford University, 1933-34, University of Halle-Wittenberg, 1935-36, and University of Chicago, 1946. *Home:* 901 South Johnson Ave., Carbondale, Ill. 62901. *Office:* Department of Sociology, Southern Illinois University, Carbondale, Ill. 62901.

CAREER: University of Oslo, Oslo, Norway, university fellow in sociology (assistant professor), 1939-43, 1945-46; University of Wisconsin—Madison, research associate in sociology, 1948-49; St. Olaf College, Northfield, Minn., associate professor of sociology, 1949-51; University of North Dakota, Grand Forks, professor of sociology and anthropology and head of department, 1951-57; Southern Illinois University, Carbondale, professor of sociology, 1957-77, professor emeritus, 1977—. Visiting professor at University of Wisconsin, 1950, 1955, University of Minnesota, 1951, University of Oslo, 1961, University of Missouri, 1966, Syracuse University, 1966-67, University of Stockholm, 1970-71, and Max Weber Institute, University of Munich, 1976. Member of Norwegian scientific expedition to Tristan da Cunha in the South Atlantic Ocean, 1937-38, and field researcher there, 1964-65; also has done field work in Norway and in Norwegian settlements in Wisconsin.

MEMBER: American Sociological Association, American Anthropological Association, Society for Applied Anthropology, Royal Anthropological Institute of Great Britain and Ireland (fellow), Norwegian-American Historical Association, Midwest Sociological Association, National Geographic Society. *Awards, honors:* Rockefeller Foundation

fellow, 1946-48; research grants from National Science Foundation and other organizations.

WRITINGS: Sociology of Tristan da Cunha, Academy of Science (Oslo), 1945; *An Attempt at an Analysis of Some Sociological Terms and Concepts* (booklet), Academy of Science, 1946; *Landhandelen i Norge* (on retail trade in Norway), Halvorsen & Larsen, 1948; *A Study of Cultural Change: Rural-Urban Conflicts in Norway,* H. Aschehoug (Oslo), 1956; *The Song Tradition of Tristan da Cunha,* Anthropological Research Center, University of Indiana, 1969; (translator and editor with wife, Helene Munch) *The Strange American Way* (a collection of letters written by his grandparents), Southern Illinois University Press, 1970; *Crisis in Utopia,* Crowell, 1971. Contributor to sociology, anthropology, and folklore journals. Editor, *Sociological Quarterly,* 1961-64; member of editorial board, Norwegian-American Historical Association, 1961—.

WORK IN PROGRESS: Continued research in sociological theory and sociology of religion.

*   *   *

MUNHOLLAND, J(ohn) Kim 1934-

PERSONAL: Born November 5, 1934, in Long Beach, Calif.; son of John E. (an attorney) and Dorothy (Campbell) Munholland; married Anne Hazlehurst, June 20, 1956; children: Christopher, Sophie. *Education:* Stanford University, A.B., 1956; Princeton University, M.A., 1961, Ph.D., 1969. *Home:* 1420 Hythe St., St. Paul, Minn. 55108. *Office:* Department of History, University of Minnesota, Minneapolis, Minn. 55455.

CAREER: University of Minnesota, Minneapolis, 1963—, began as instructor, 1963-64, currently associate professor of history. *Military service:* U.S. Air Force, 1957-59; became first lieutenant. *Member:* Phi Beta Kappa.

WRITINGS: Origins of Contemporary Europe: 1890-1914, Harcourt, 1970. Contributor to *French Historical Studies.*

WORK IN PROGRESS: A study of French politics between the two world wars.

*   *   *

MUNRO, Ian S.

PERSONAL: Born in Glasgow, Scotland; son of Daniel S. (a clerk) and Emily (Sherwood) Munro; married Mary Murray Allan, June 24, 1943; children: Robin Murray. *Education:* University of Glasgow, M.A., 1945. *Home:* Braeside, Catterline, Kincardineshire, Scotland. *Agent:* S.C.O.T.T.S., 2 Clifton St., Glasgow G3 7LA, Scotland. *Office:* Department of Literature, Aberdeen College of Education, Aberdeen, Scotland.

CAREER: Aberdeen College of Education, Aberdeen, Scotland, senior lecturer in literature, 1962—. *Military service:* Royal Air Force.

WRITINGS: Leslie Mitchell: Lewis Grassic Gibbon, Oliver & Boyd, 1966; (editor and author of introduction) Lewis Grassic Gibbon, *A Scots Hairst,* Hutchinson, 1967; (author of introduction) Gibbon, *Spartacus,* Hutchinson, 1970; *The Island of Bute,* David & Charles, 1973. Writer of over twenty radio plays for British Broadcasting Corp.

WORK IN PROGRESS: Rural Schools in Scotland; radio and stage plays.

BIOGRAPHICAL/CRITICAL SOURCES: Times Literary Supplement, December 23, 1967.

MUNSON, Harold L(ewis) 1923-

PERSONAL: Born August 2, 1923, in Windham, N.Y.; son of Esmond L. (a farmer) and Gladys (Disbrow) Munson; married Evelyn C. Moore (a vocal music teacher), September 8, 1946; children: Michael, Jeffrey. *Education:* Hobart College (now Hobart and William Smith Colleges), A.B., 1947; New York College for Teachers (now State University of New York at Albany), M.A., 1948; New York University, Ed.D., 1961. *Home:* 745 Thayer Rd., Fairport, N.Y. 14450. *Office:* College of Education, University of Rochester, Rochester, N.Y. 14627.

CAREER: Social studies teacher and counselor, Cairo, N.Y., 1948-50; public school guidance director, Williamson, N.Y., 1950-54; New York State Department of Education, Albany, associate supervisor of guidance in Bureau of Guidance, 1954-59; University of Rochester, Rochester, N.Y., assistant professor, 1959-61, associate professor, 1961-66, professor of education, 1966—, chairman of department of guidance and student personnel, 1961. Vocational consultant, Social Security Administration, 1962—. Visiting professor at State University of New York Colleges at Brockport, 1967-69, and Oswego, 1969-70. *Military service:* U.S. Navy, 1944-46.

MEMBER: American Personnel and Guidance Association (life member), National Vocational Guidance Association, Association for Counselor Educators and Supervisors, American School Counselors Association, American Association for Humanistic Psychology, American Educational Research Association, New York State Personnel and Guidance Association, Genesee Valley Personnel and Guidance Association (president, 1961-62), Phi Delta Kappa.

WRITINGS: (With Hubert W. Houghton) *Organizing Orientation Activities,* Science Research Associates, 1956; *How to Set Up a Guidance Unit,* Science Research Associates, 1957; (contributor) *How to Get into College and Stay There,* Science Research Associates, 1958; *My Educational Plans,* Science Research Associates, 1959, revised edition, 1970; *Elementary School Guidance: Concepts, Dimensions, and Practice,* Allyn & Bacon, 1970; *The Foundations of Developmental Guidance,* Allyn & Bacon, 1971; (contributor) David Cook, editor, *Guidance for Education in Revolution,* Allyn & Bacon, 1971; (with Gilbert Gockley) *Career Insights and Self-Awareness Games,* Houghton, 1974; (with Gordon B. Phillips) *Career Opportunities for the Deaf,* University of Rochester, 1974.

"Guidance Activities for Teachers" series, published by Science Research Associates, all 1965: *Guidance Activities for Teachers of English; . . . of Foreign Languages; . . . of Mathematics; . . . of Science; . . . of Social Studies.* Contributor to *Encyclopedia of Careers and Vocational Guidance* and to education journals.

* * *

MURPHY, James M(artin) 1917-

PERSONAL: Born May 26, 1917, in Tucson, Ariz.; son of James S. and Alice (Duffy) Murphy; married Billie Baker, August 24, 1942; children: James W., Thomas M., Richard M. *Education:* University of Notre Dame, B.S., 1938; University of Arizona, LL.B., 1941. *Politics:* Democrat. *Religion:* Catholic. *Home:* 199 Sierra Vista Dr., Tucson, Ariz. 85719. *Office:* Murphy, Vinson & Hazlett, 1704 Tucson Federal Savings Tower, Tucson, Ariz. 85701.

CAREER: Admitted to State Bar of Arizona, later became president, 1956-57; currently attorney in Tucson, Ariz. *Military service:* U.S. Navy, 1944-47; became lieutenant junior grade.

WRITINGS: Spanish Legal Heritage in Arizona, Arizona Pioneers' Historical Society, 1966; *Laws, Courts and Lawyers: Through the Years in Arizona,* University of Arizona Press, 1969.††

* * *

MURPHY, Richard 1927-

PERSONAL: Born August 6, 1927, in County Galway, Ireland; son of William (in British Colonial Service; former mayor of Colombo, Ceylon, and governor of the Bahamas) and Elizabeth Mary (Ormsby) Murphy; married Patricia Avis, May, 1955 (divorced, 1959); children: Emily Avis. *Education:* Magdalen College, Oxford, B.A. (honors) and M.A., 1948; attended Sorbonne, University of Paris, 1955. *Home:* The New Forge, Cleggan, County Galway, Ireland.

CAREER: Author and poet. Compton Lecturer in Poetry, University of Hull, Hull, England, 1969; O'Connor Professor of Literature, Colgate University, Hamilton, N.Y., 1971. Visiting fellow, University of Reading, 1968. Visiting professor, Bard College, 1972-74; visiting lecturer, University of Princeton, 1974-75, University of Iowa, 1976-77. Writer-in-residence, University of Virginia, 1965. Adviser to a production of King Oedipus at King Abbey Theatre, Dublin, 1973. Has held many other positions including: Aide-de-camp to father, Governor of Bahamas, 1948-49; member of staff, Lloyds, London, England, 1949-50; night-watchman of a salmon river in Ireland, 1951-52; director of the English School in Canea, Crete, 1956-59; sheepfarmer in the Wicklow Mountains; skipper of a Galway Hooker, sailing off the west coast of Iceland, 1960-67. *Member:* Royal Society of Literature (fellow). *Awards, honors:* A. E. Memorial Award for Poetry, 1951; Guinness Award, 1962; Arts Council of Great Britain Awards, 1967, and 1975.

WRITINGS: The Archaeology of Love, Dolmen Press, 1955; *Sailing to an Island,* Faber, 1963, Chilmark, 1964; *The Battle of Aughrim,* Knopf, 1968; *High Island,* Faber, 1974, Harper, 1975. Also author of *The Woman of the House,* 1959, and *The Last Galway Hooker,* 1961. Poetry has appeared in various periodicals, including *Listener, New Statesman, Encounter, London Magazine, Listen, New Review, Envoy, Irish Times, Yale Review,* and in many anthologies. Contributor of poems and articles to *New York Review of Books;* contributor of poetry reviews to *Spectator* and *Times Literary Supplement.*

SIDELIGHTS: Chad Walsh finds Richard Murphy "very much out of step with the times in several ways. For one thing, he goes in for long narrative poems. More importantly, he reveals very little about himself; like Shakespeare, he seems to set his scenery and characters on the stage, and then withdraw into the audience to behold their action. Perhaps most damnably of all, he has a very strong sense of history, and the rootedness of the present in the past—a sensibility that the age mapped by McLuhan does not encourage." *The Battle of Aughrim,* Daniel Hoffman writes, "is surely one of the most deeply felt and successfully rendered interpretations of history in modern Irish verse, and in poetry in English in our generation." Walsh believes that "part of Mr. Murphy's power comes from his sense of sharing sundered worlds: English and Irish, and (vicariously) African and European. But mostly one remembers him for the lyrical loveliness and narrative movement of his long, sustained poems. He is the most important Irish poet now coming along, and very possibly a major figure in the entire English-speaking world.'' *The Battle of Aughrim* has been published in French.

BIOGRAPHICAL/CRITICAL SOURCES: Book World, November 3, 1968; *New York Times Book Review,* March 2, 1969; *Poetry,* July, 1969.

* * *

MURPHY, Robert (William)   1902-1971

August 27, 1902—July 13, 1971; American author, editor, and naturalist. Obituaries: *New York Times,* July 14, 1971; *Antiquarian Bookman,* August 2-9, 1971; *Publishers' Weekly,* September 6, 1971. (See index for *CA* sketch)

* * *

MURRAY, Robert A.   1929-

PERSONAL: Born June 16, 1929, in Craig, Neb.; son of Wallace Pierce (a wholesaler) and Clara (Lunn) Murray; married Marian D. Gray (a teacher), June 14, 1961; children: William, Laura, David. *Education:* Wayne State College, Wayne, Neb., A.B., 1952; Kansas State University of Agriculture and Applied Science, M.S., 1956. *Politics:* Republican. *Address:* P.O. Box 6467, Sheridan, Wyo.

CAREER: Teacher prior to 1958; National Park Service, historian at various parks and museums, 1958-68; Western Interpretive Services, Sheridan, Wyo., director, 1968—. Former consultant, World Film Service Ltd., and Learning Corp of America. *Military service:* U.S. Army, 1947-50. *Member:* Council on Abandoned Military Posts, U.S.A., Wyoming Historical Society, Montana Historical Society. *Awards, honors:* Carnegie fellow in international affairs at University of Wyoming, 1960; Cumulative Service Award, Wyoming Historical Society, 1970.

WRITINGS: Fort Laramie's Historic Buildings, Fort Laramie Historical Association, 1965; *Pipestone: A History,* Pipestone Indian Shrine Association, 1965; *Pipes on the Plains,* Pipestone Indian Shrine Association, 1968; (editor) E. S. Topping, *Chronicles of the Yellowstone,* Ross & Haines, 1968; *Military Posts in the Powder River Country,* University of Nebraska Press, 1968; *The Army on Powder River,* Old Army Press, 1969; *Citadel on the Santa Fe Trail,* Old Army Press, 1970; *Miners' Delight, Investor's Despair,* Piney Creek Press, 1972; *Fort Laramie, Visions of a Grand Old Post,* Old Army Press, 1974; *Military Posts of Wyoming,* Old Army Press, 1975. Contributor to Denver Westerners *Roundup* and western history journals.

WORK IN PROGRESS: A history of the headquarters of Department of the Platte, 1866-1898; a reference guide to U.S. military posts.

* * *

MUSGROVE, Philip   1940-

PERSONAL: Born September 4, 1940, in Dallas, Tex.; son of Gordan Bass (an accountant) and Retha (a psychologist; maiden name, Anthony) Musgrove; married Zina Pisarko; children: Antonina. *Education:* Haverford College, B.A., 1962; Princeton University, M.P.A., 1964; Massachusetts Institute of Technology, Ph.D., 1974. *Office:* Brookings Institution, 1775 Massachusetts Ave. N.W., Washington, D.C. 20036.

CAREER: Brookings Institution, Washington, D.C., research associate in economics, 1964-68, 1971—, consultant, 1968-70.

WRITINGS: (With Joseph Grunwald) *Natural Resources in Latin American Development,* Johns Hopkins Press, 1970; *The General Theory of Gerrymandering: Professional Papers in American Politics,* Sage Publications, 1977; *Income and Spending of Urban Families in Latin America,* Brookings Institution, 1978.

Contributor: *Energy and U.S. Foreign Policy,* Ballinger, 1974; *Latin America's New Internationalism,* Praeger, 1976; *Patterns in Household Demand and Saving,* Oxford University Press, 1977. Contributor to *Proceedings* of American Institute of Mining, Metallurgical and Petroleum Engineers, 1971, and to *Annals of Economic and Social Measurement.* Contributor of articles to *Journal of Political Economy* and *Review of Economics and Statistics.*

WORK IN PROGRESS: Studies on income distribution in Latin America and on the consequences of demographic change in the U.S. economy to 2025.

* * *

MUSSER, Joseph L.   1936-
(Joe Musser)

PERSONAL: Born August 15, 1936, in Chicago, Ill.; son of Joseph R. and Nellie (Weathers) Musser; married Nancy Green, July 29, 1956; children: Kerry, Kevin, Bruce, David, Laurinda. *Home:* 2712 Capri Ct., Rockford, Ill. 61111. *Office:* 128 Kishwaukee St., Rockford, Ill. 61104.

CAREER: Worked for newspaper in Rockford, Ill., 1952-61, and for WMBI Radio, Chicago, Ill., 1961-66; freelance writer and producer, 1966-72, 1974-75; Bibles for the World, Wheaton, Ill., vice-president, 1972; Four Most Productions, Inc., Wheaton, president, 1973; Quadrus Communications, Rockford, general manager, 1975—. Assistant director, Bedford Center for Creative Study, Glen Ellyn, Ill., 1968—. *Military service:* Illinois National Guard, 1954-62; became staff sergeant. *Member:* Fellowship of Christians in the Arts, Media and Entertainment. *Awards, honors:* His radio drama, ''Dawn at Checkpoint Alpha,'' received the first prize in radio competition at 1966 Festival of Arts in Birmingham, Ala.

WRITINGS—All published by Zondervan, except as indicated: (Editor) *Voice of the Morning* (novel), 1968; *Behold a Pale Horse* (novel), 1970; (editor) *Black and Free,* 1968; (editor) *Words of Revolution,* 1972; (editor) *H. Mjorud Biography,* Creation House, 1974; (co-author) *Joni,* 1976. Also author of a screenplay. ''The Rapture,'' 1972. Writer of radio plays and of scripts for promotional films and TV.

WORK IN PROGRESS: A second novel and the film adaptation of that novel; two nonfiction books.

* * *

MYERS, Caroline Elizabeth Clark   1887-

PERSONAL: Born July 14, 1887, in Morris, Pa.; daughter of Charles Edgar and Elizabeth (Boyd) Clark; married Garry Cleveland Myers (editor-in-chief of *Highlights for Children*), June 26, 1912 (died July 19, 1971); children: John Edgar, Elizabeth (Mrs. Kent L. Brown), Garry C. (deceased). *Education:* Bloomsburg State College, graduate, 1905; further study at Ursinus College, 1907-08, Juniata College, 1912-13, Merrill-Palmer Institute, 1930-31, and Columbia University, summers, 1931-34. *Residence:* Milanville, Pa. 18443. *Office: Highlights for Children,* 803 Church St., Honesdale, Pa. 18431.

CAREER: Director of parent education and family life at Cleveland Welfare Federation, Cleveland, Ohio, and instructor in family life and child development at Cleveland College of Western Reserve University (now Case Western Reserve University), Cleveland, 1931-41; *Highlights for Children* (juvenile periodical; formerly *Children's Activities)*, Honesdale, Pa., associate editor of *Children's Activities,* 1941-46, co-founder, managing editor and vice-president, 1946—. Summer instructor, University of Washington, Seattle, 1938-41; instructor, Oregon State University, 1942. Leader of public forums for U.S. Office of Education, 1937. *Member:* National Council on Family Relations. *Awards, honors:* Laura Spellman Rockefeller scholarship, 1930; Distinguished Service Award from Bloomsburg State College, 1953; Freedoms Foundation National Award, 1976.

WRITINGS: (With husband, Garry Cleveland Myers) *Measuring Minds* (examiner's manual), Newson, 1921; (with G. C. Myers) *The Language of America* (lessons in elementary English and citizenship for adults), Newson, 1921; (with G. C. Myers) *My Work Book in Arithmetic,* Harter Publishing, 1929; (with G. C. Myers) *Homes Build Persons,* Dorrance, 1950; (compiler) *Jumbo Holiday Handbook: Creative Suggestions from "Highlights for Children",* Highlights for Children, 1963; (with G. C. Myers) *Your Child and You,* Hewitt House, 1969; (editor) *Children's Own Stories,* Highlights for Children, 1970; (compiler) *First Steps in Getting Ready to Read,* Highlights for Children, 1972; (compiler) *More Creative Craft Activities,* Highlights for Children, 1973. Contributor to professional publications.

* * *

MYERS, Gerald E(ugene) 1923-

PERSONAL: Born June 19, 1923, in Central City, Neb.; son of Harold W. (a teacher) and Mary (Ferguson) Myers; married Martha Coleman (a professor of dance), August 7, 1948; children: Curt. *Education:* Haverford College, B.A., 1947; Brown University, M.A., 1949, Ph.D., 1954. *Office:* Graduate Center, City University of New York, 33 West 42nd St., New York, N.Y. 10036.

CAREER: Smith College, Northampton, Mass., instructor in philosophy, 1950-52; Williams College, Williamstown, Mass., instructor, 1952-55, assistant professor of philosophy, 1955-61; Kenyon College, Gambier, Ohio, associate professor of philosophy, 1961-65; Long Island University, C. W. Post Campus, Brookville, N.Y., professor of philosophy, 1965-67; City University of New York, professor of philosophy at Queens College, Flushing, N.Y., 1967-69, and at Graduate Center, New York, N.Y., 1969—. *Member:* American Philosophical Association.

WRITINGS: (Editor) *Self, Religion, and Metaphysics,* Macmillan, 1961; *Self: Introduction to Philosophical Psychology,* Pegasus, 1969; *The Spirit of American Philosophy,* Putnam, 1970.

* * *

MYERS, Martin 1927-

PERSONAL: Born December 7, 1927, in Toronto, Ontario, Canada; son of Max and Esther (Friedman) Myers; married Colleen Sue Croll, June 25, 1955; children: Lori Sue, Marshall Bradley. *Education:* University of Toronto, B.A., 1951; Johns Hopkins University, M.A., 1969.

CAREER: Self-employed communications consultant in Toronto, Ontario.

WRITINGS: The Assignment, Harper, 1970.

WORK IN PROGRESS: A novel, a filmscript, short pieces, and poetry.

BIOGRAPHICAL/CRITICAL SOURCES: Best Sellers, February 1, 1971; *Christian Science Monitor,* March 18, 1971.††

* * *

NAGEL, James (Edward) 1940-

PERSONAL: Born May 20, 1940; son of Ray (a farmer) and May (Fjeldseth) Nagel; married Gwen Lindberg (an English instructor). *Education:* Moorhead State College, B.A., 1962; Pennsylvania State University, M.A., 1964, Ph.D., 1971. *Home:* 131 North Second St., Breckenridge, Minn. 56520. *Office:* Department of English, Northeastern University, 360 Huntington Ave., Boston, Mass. 02115.

CAREER: Moorhead State College, Moorhead, Minn., instructor in English, 1965-68; Northeastern University, Boston, Mass., assistant professor, 1971-74, associate professor of English, 1974—. Fulbright lecturer in New Zealand, 1977; lecturer on world-wide tour, 1977. *Member:* Modern Language Association of America.

WRITINGS: (Compiler) *Vision and Value: A Thematic Introduction to the Short Story* (text edition), Dickenson, 1970; (editor) *Critical Essays on "Catch-22",* Dickenson, 1974; *Sarah Orne Jewett: A Reference Guide,* G. K. Hall, 1977; (editor) *American Fiction: Historical and Critical Essays,* Northeastern University Press, 1977.

Contributor of articles to literary journals. Bibliographer for *MLA International Bibliography;* editor, *Studies in American Fiction.*

WORK IN PROGRESS: A critical book on the fiction of Stephen Crane.

AVOCATIONAL INTERESTS: Tennis, swimming, hiking, raising rare cats.

* * *

NAGI, Saad Z. 1925-

PERSONAL: Born April 30, 1925, in Menufiah, Egypt; became U.S. citizen, 1963; son of Faried and Hamida (Shinaishin) Nagi; married Jane Kay Gonder, September 15, 1957; children: Mari Karima, Mazen Gonder, Omar Faried. *Education:* University of Cairo, B.Sc., 1947; Syracuse University, graduate study, 1953; University of Missouri, M.S., 1954; Ohio State University, Ph.D., 1958. *Home:* 5455 Indian Hill, Dublin, Ohio 43017. *Office:* Department of Sociology, Ohio State University, Columbus, Ohio 43210.

CAREER: Egyptian Government, Cairo, research specialist, 1947-50; U.S. Point IV Program, Ashmoun, Egypt, extension specialist, 1950-53; Ohio State University, Columbus, assistant professor, 1959-63, associate professor, 1963-64, professor of sociology, 1964—. Consultant on research programs to U.S. Government agencies, including Social Security Administration, Social and Rehabilitation Services Administration, Office of Child Development, and Department of Health, Education and Welfare. *Member:* American Sociological Association (fellow), American Statistical Association, American Association for the Advancement of Science, American Public Health Association. *Awards, honors:* Fulbright grant, 1953-54; National Rehabilitation Association, award for outstanding contributions through research on disability, 1970, Mary Switzer fellow, 1976.

WRITINGS: Disability and Rehabilitation: Legal, Clinical, and Self-Concepts and Measurement, Ohio State University Press, 1969; (editor with Ronald Corwin) *The Social Contexts of Research,* Wiley, 1972; *Disability Policies and*

Programs: Organizations, Clients and Decision-Making, Ohio State University Press, in press; *Child Maltreatment in the United States: Cry for Help and Organizational Response,* Columbia University Press, in press. Contributor to professional journals.

*   *   *

NAISMITH, Marion (Overend)   1922-

PERSONAL: Born May 5, 1922, in Glasgow, Scotland; daughter of Alexander Liddell and Rose (Carnegie) Naismith. *Education:* Attended secondary school in Scotland. *Home:* West Lodge, Mellerstain, Gordon, Berwickshire, Scotland.

CAREER: Former positions include insurance inspector, librarian, and publicity officer in a whisky distillery; currently curator of Mellerstain, the home of Lord Binning in Berwickshire, Scotland. Novelist. *Military service:* Women's Royal Naval Service (Wren), driver, World War II. *Member:* Romantic Novelists' Association.

WRITINGS—Novels; all published by Hurst & Blackett: *Prelude to Darkness,* 1965; *A Handful of Miracles,* 1966; *The Morning of the Year,* 1967; *Most Eloquent Music,* 1968; *A Dream of Unicorns,* 1968; *The Rainbow Chasers,* 1969; *Johnny Moonbeam,* 1970.

SIDELIGHTS: Paperback rights have been sold on all of Marion Naismith's books for publication in Norway, Italy, France, and Denmark. *Avocational interests:* Travel, painting.

BIOGRAPHICAL/CRITICAL SOURCES: Books and Bookmen, May, 1968.

*   *   *

NAKAYAMA, Shigeru   1928-

PERSONAL: Born June 22, 1928, in Amagasaki, Japan; son of Suketo and Satoko (Ishido) Nakayama; married Motoko Watanabe, July 8, 1962; children: Yuka, Shin. *Education:* University of Tokyo, B.Sc., 1951; Harvard University, Ph.D., 1959. *Home:* 3-7-11, Chuo, Nakano, Tokyo, Japan. *Office:* College of General Education, University of Tokyo, Komaba, Meguro, Tokyo, Japan.

CAREER: Heibonsha (publishers of encyclopedias), Tokyo, Japan, member of editorial staff, 1951-55; University of Tokyo, Tokyo, lecturer in astronomy, 1960—. *Member:* Academie Internationale d'Histoire des Sciences, History of Science Society, International Council for Science Policy Studies.

WRITINGS: Senseijutsu (title means "Astrology"), Kinokuniya, 1964; *A History of Japanese Astronomy,* Harvard University Press, 1969; *Nihon no Tenmongaku* (title means "Japanese Astronomy"), Iwanami, 1972; (editor) *Chinese Science,* M.I.T. Press, 1973; (editor) *Science and Society in Modern Japan,* M.I.T. Press, 1974; *Rekishi toshite no Gakumon,* Chuo Koron, 1974; *Nihonjin no Kagakkkan* (title means "Japanese Views of Science"), Sogensha, 1977. Member of editorial board, *Journal for the History of Astronomy, Dictionary of Scientific Biography,* and *East Asian Science Series.*

WORK IN PROGRESS: Diffusion of Copernicanism in the Far East.

SIDELIGHTS: Shigeru Nakayama writes: "It is due to the laziness of English speaking people that our major works have not translated into English yet, and alas! 'English imperialism' is still dominating in this world."

NARANG, Gopi Chand   1931-

PERSONAL: Born January 1, 1931, in Dukki, Baluchistan, India; son of Dharam Chand (a civil servant) and Tekan (Bai) Narang; married Tara Rani (a teacher); children: Arun. *Education:* Panjab University, B.A. (honors in Persian), 1950; University of Delhi, M.A. (honors in Urdu), 1954, Ph.D., 1958, Diploma in Linguistics, 1961. *Home:* D 252 Sarvodaya Enclave, New Delhi-17, India. *Office:* Department of Urdu, Jamia Millia University, New Delhi-25 India.

CAREER: University of Delhi, Delhi, India, 1957-74, began as lecturer, associate professor of Urdu language and literature, 1961-74; Jamia Millia University, New Delhi, India, professor of Urdu and chairman of department, 1974—. Visiting professor in department of Indian studies, University of Wisconsin, 1963-65, 1968-70. Regular broadcaster on All India Radio and Delhi Television; general secretary, All India National Forum of Writers; member of board of directors, Jamia Publishing House. Member of Indian Government delegation to 27th Orientalist International Congress, University of Michigan, 1967. *Member:* Urdu Association of India (member of executive committee), American Oriental Society, Linguistic Society of America, Modern Language Association of America, Association for Asian Studies, Linguistic Society of India, Royal Asiatic Society of London (fellow), All India P.E.N. *Awards, honors:* Ghalib Prize of Indian Government for best scholarly work of 1962, for *Urdu Masnawiyan;* Commonwealth fellowship, 1963; Urdu Academy Prize, 1972, for *Karbal Katha ka Lisaniyati Mutaliya;* Mir Award for total literary services, 1976.

WRITINGS: (Editor) *Miraj ul-Ashiqeen,* Azad Kitab Ghar, 1957; *Teaching Urdu as a Foreign Language,* Azad Kitab Ghar, 1960, 2nd edition, 1963; *Urdu Masnawiyan,* Maktaba Jamia, 1962; *Karkhandari Dialect of Delhi Urdu,* Munshi Ram Manohar Lal, 1963; (edtior) *Adabi Tahreerin,* Sab Ras Kitab Ghar, 1964; *Readings in Literary Urdu Prose,* University of Wisconsin Press, 1968; (editor) *Manshurat,* Anjuman taraqqi-e-Urdu, 1968; (co-author) *Karbal Katha ka Lisaniyati Mutaliya,* Maktaba Shahrah, 1970; (editor) *Aemughan-e-Malik,* Maktaba Jamia, 1973; (editor) *Imla Namah,* Urdu Development Board, 1974; *Puranon ki Kahaniyan,* National Book Trust (India), 1976.

WORK IN PROGRESS: An anthology of Urdu short stories in English translation; an outline of Urdu phonology; *Lisaniyati Tajziye.*

*   *   *

NASH, James E(dward)   1933-

PERSONAL: Born February 16, 1933, in New York, N.Y.; son of James Edward and Catherine (Callahan) Nash. *Education:* Studied five days at Manhattan College and two months at City College (now City College of the City University of New York). *Home:* 108 South Elliott Pl., Brooklyn, N.Y. 11217.

CAREER: Worked ten years for a now-defunct direct mail house and then in the order department of Fulfillment Associates, Inc. (direct mail company), Farmingdale, N.Y., 1965-70; New York State Civil Service employee, 1972—, working in the areas of taxation, drug abuse, housing, and currently working in the Department of Mental Health. *Military service:* U.S. Army, 1953-55; served eighteen months in Germany.

WRITINGS—Novels: *Poor Teddy Black,* Harper, 1970; *The Last of Ellman,* Harper, 1971.

WORK IN PROGRESS: A novel about the 25-hour day and democracy as a religion.

SIDELIGHTS: In writing, James Nash says that he has no control of his material. "When I set out to write something serious (*Poor Teddy Black*), it turns out funny and when I set out to write something funny (*The Last of Ellman*), it turns out serious."

*   *   *

NASH, June (Caprice)   1927-

PERSONAL: Born May 30, 1927, in Salem, Mass.; daughter of Joseph (a carpenter) and Josephine (Salloway) Bousley; married second husband, Herbert Menzel, July 1, 1972; children: (first marriage) Eric, Laura. *Education:* Barnard College, B.A., 1948; University of Chicago, M.A., 1953, Ph.D., 1960. *Home:* 100 Bleecker St., New York, N.Y. 10012. *Office:* Department of Anthropology, City College of the City University of New York, New York, N.Y. 10031.

CAREER: Chicago Teachers College-North (now Illinois Teachers College, Chicago-North), Chicago, Ill., assistant professor of anthropology, 1961-63; Yale University, New Haven, Conn., assistant professor of anthropology, 1964-68; New York University, New York City, associate professor of anthropology, 1968-72; City College of the City University of New York, New York City, faculty member of anthropology department, 1972—. *Member:* American Anthropological Association, American Ethnological Society, American Association of University Professors, Sigma Chi. *Awards, honors:* Guggenheim fellowship; Fulbright-Hays grant; National Institute of Mental Health fellowships, 1960-61, 1964-65; Social Science Research Council grant, 1969, for research in Bolivia.

WRITINGS: Living with Nats: An Analysis of Animism in Burman Village Social Relations, Yale University Press, 1966; *In the Eyes of the Ancestors: Belief and Behavior in a Mayan Community,* Yale University Press, 1970; *Social Structure in Amatenago del Valle: An Activity Analysis,* Centro Intercultural de Documentacion (Cuernavaca, Mexico), 1970; (editor with Helen Safa) *Sex and Class in Latin America,* Praeger, 1976; *Basilia dos Mujeres Indiginas,* Instituto Indigenas, 1976; (editor with others) *Popular Participation in Social Change: Cooperatives, Collectives, and Nationalized Industry,* Aldine, 1976; *Ideology and Social Change in Latin America,* Gordon & Breach, 1977; *He Agotado mi Vida en la Mina,* Nueva Vision, in press. Contributor to journals in the United States and Latin America.

WORK IN PROGRESS: A series of books on the developing consciousness of industrial workers, based on biographies and interviews with tin miners in Bolivia.

SIDELIGHTS: June Nash is interested in film-making as an added "dimension of reality" in anthropological field studies. She filmed the life of a miner in Bolivia while working there the summer of 1971.

*   *   *

NASH, (Frediric) Ogden   1902-1971

August 19, 1902—May 19, 1971; American poet and humorist. Obituaries: *New York Times,* May 20, 1971; *Washington Post,* May 21, 1971; *Time,* May 31, 1971; *Publishers' Weekly,* May 31, 1971; *Antiquarian Bookman,* June 7-14, 1971. (See index for *CA* sketch)

*   *   *

NATHAN, David   1926-

PERSONAL: Born December 9, 1926, in Manchester, England; son of Joseph and Doris (Ingleby) Nathan; married Norma Ellis, March 31, 1957; children: Paul, John. *Education:* Nathan describes his education as "rudimentary." *Politics:* Socialist. *Religion:* None. *Home:* 20 The Mount, Wembley Park, Middlesex, England. *Agent:* John Farquharson Ltd., 15 Red Lion Sq., London WC1R 4QW, England.

CAREER: Copyboy on newspaper in Manchester, England, 1942-44; reporter on newspapers in Lancashire, England, 1947-49, and Nottingham, England, 1949-52; *Daily Mail,* London, England, syndication news editor, 1952-54; *Daily Herald & Sun* (formerly *Daily Herald*), London, reporter, 1955-60, theater critic, 1960-69; *Jewish Chronicle,* London, arts and entertainments editor and theatre critic, 1970—. *Military service:* Royal Navy, 1944-47. *Member:* National Union of Journalists, Writers Guild.

WRITINGS: (With Freddie Hancock) *Hancock: A Biography,* Kimber & Co., 1969; *The Freeloader,* W. H. Allen, 1970; *The Laughtermakers,* P. Owen, 1971; "Human Interest" (television play), produced by Granada, 1977. Writer of comedy television scripts for "That Was the Week That Was," "Not So Much a Programme," "BBC 3," and "At the 11th Hour." Wrote screenplay of his novel, *The Freeloader,* for production by Associated British.

WORK IN PROGRESS: A television play.

*   *   *

NEAL, Sister Marie Augusta   1921-

PERSONAL: Born June 22, 1921, in Brighton, Mass. *Education:* Emmanuel College, Boston, Mass., A.B., 1942; Boston College, A.M., 1953; Harvard University, Ph.D., 1963. *Office:* Department of Sociology, Emmanuel College, 400 The Fenway, Boston, Mass. 02115.

CAREER: Roman Catholic religious, member of Sisters of Notre Dame de Namur. High school teacher in diocese of Boston, Mass., 1946-53; Emmanuel College, Boston, 1953—, began as instructor, professor of sociology and chairman of department, 1963—. Summer lecturer, Cornell University, 1966; visiting professor at University of California, Berkeley, 1968-69, and Harvard University Divinity School, 1973-75. Consultant and research director, Conference of Major Religious Superiors of Women's Institutes in the United States, 1966-68. Area chairman, Massachusetts Governor's Commission on the Status of Women, 1964-67; member of Archidiocesan Commission on Human Rights, Boston, 1966—, and Catholic Commission on Intellectual and Cultural Affairs, 1970—; director, South African Catholic Education Study, 1970-71. Member of advisory board, U.S. Catholic Conference of Bishops.

MEMBER: American Sociological Association, Association for the Sociology of Religion (member of executive council, 1962-64; vice-president, 1965-66, president, 1971-72), Society for the Scientific Study of Religion (member of executive council, 1975-77), National Liturgical Conference (member of board), Association of Urban Sisters (member of advisory board, 1968—), Phi Beta Kappa, Kappa Gamma Pi.

WRITINGS: Values and Interests in Social Change, Prentice-Hall, 1965; *Sociotheology of Letting Go,* Paulist/Newman, 1977.

Contributor: Sister Maryellen Muckenhirn, editor, *The Changing Sister,* Fides, 1965; L. V. Luzbetak, editor, *The Church in the Changing City,* Divine Word Publications, 1966; Eugene Grollmes, editor, *Vows but No Walls,* B. Herder, 1967; Muckenhirn, editor, *The New Nuns,* New

American Library, 1967; Robert N. Bellah and William G. McLoughlin, editors, *Religion in America: II (Daedelus)*, Houghton, 1968; William C. Bier, editor, *Woman in Modern Life*, Fordham University Press, 1968; Thomas M. McFadden, editor, *American Theological Perspective*, Seabury, 1976; Anne Marie Gargner, editor, *Women and Catholic Priesthood*, Paulist/Newman, 1976. Contributor to *New Catholic Encyclopedia* and to professional journals. Associate editor, *Sociological Analysis*, 1964; contributing editor, "Sisters' Forum," in *National Catholic Reporter*, 1964-66.

WORK IN PROGRESS: Research on women's religious institutes.

SIDELIGHTS: Sister Marie Neal writes: "Essay writing inserts itself with an urgency into my on-going systematic research on the changing structures of religious orders of women, that is my major monograph preoccupation. The essays address the wider issues of the changing structures of modern society in world perspective but especially how the moral quality of American life affects the life chances of third world people."

*   *   *

NEARING, Helen K(nothe)   1904-

PERSONAL: Born February 23, 1904, in New York, N.Y.; daughter of Frank K. (a businessman) and Maria (Obreen) Knothe; married Scott Nearing, December 12, 1947. *Education:* Studied violin privately at home and abroad. *Home:* Harborside, Me. 04642.

CAREER: Since 1932 she and her husband have been farming and writing, first on a subsistence farm in Pikes Falls, Vermont and more recently in Maine.

WRITINGS—With husband, Scott Nearing, except as indicated: *The Maple Sugar Book: Being a Plain, Practical Account of the Art of Sugaring*, John Day, 1950, published as *The Maple Sugar Book: Together with Remarks on Pioneering as a Way of Living in the Twentieth Century*, Schocken, 1971; *Living the Good Life: Being a Plain, Practical Account of a Twenty Year Project in a Self-Subsistent Homestead in Vermont*, Social Science Institute (Harborside, Me.), 1954, published as *Living the Good Life: How to Live Sanely and Simply in a Troubled World*, introduction by Paul Goodman, Schocken, 1970; *USA Today: Reporting Extensive Journeys and First-Hand Observations*, Social Science Institute, 1955; *The Brave New World*, Social Science Institute, 1958; *Socialists Around the World*, Monthly Review Press, 1958; (sole author) *The Good Life Album of Helen and Scott Nearing*, Dutton, 1974. Author with husband of pamphlet, *Our Right to Travel*, Social Science Institute, circa 1959.

BIOGRAPHICAL/CRITICAL SOURCES: New Republic, September 12, 1970, May 15, 1971; *Newsweek*, September 14, 1970; *Harper's*, November, 1970; *Boston Globe*, November 1, 1970; *Chicago Tribune*, November 26, 1970; *Best Sellers*, December 1, 1970; *Time*, January 18, 1971, April 28, 1971; *Washington Post*, June 3, 1971.

*   *   *

NEDERHOOD, Joel H(oman)   1930-

PERSONAL: Born December 22, 1930, in Grand Rapids, Mich.; son of Arthur William (a manufacturer) and Dean (Homan) Nederhood; married Mary Lou Steigenga; children: Maria Louise, Carol Lorraine, David Joel. *Education:* Calvin College, A.B., 1952; Calvin Theological Seminary, B.D., 1957; Free University of Amsterdam, Th.D., 1959.

Home: 18507 Locust St., Lansing, Ill. 60438. *Office:* 6555 West College Dr., Palos Heights, Ill. 60463.

CAREER: Clergyman of Christian Reformed Church; "Back to God Hour" (broadcast), Palo Heights, Ill., director and speaker, 1960—. *Military service:* U.S. Army, 1952-54.

WRITINGS: The Church's Mission to the Educated American, Eerdmans, 1960; *God Is Too Much* (young adult book), Tyndale, 1968; *The Holy Triangle*, Baker Book, 1970. Also author of *Radio Pulpit*. Editor of *Today*.

*   *   *

NEEDLEMAN, Jacob   1934-

PERSONAL: Born October 6, 1934, in Philadelphia, Pa.; son of Benjamin and Ida (Seltzer) Needleman; married Carla Satzman (a potter), August 30, 1959; children: Raphael, Eve. *Education:* Harvard University, B.A., 1956; University of Freiburg, graduate study, 1957-58; Yale University, Ph.D., 1961. *Residence:* San Francisco, Calif. *Agent:* Harold Matson Co., Inc., 22 East 40th St., New York, N.Y. 10016. *Office:* Department of Philosophy, San Francisco State University, San Francisco, Calif. 94132.

CAREER: West Haven Veterans Administration Hospital, West Haven, Conn., clinical psychology trainee, 1960-61; Rockefeller Institute, New York, N.Y., research associate, 1961-62; San Francisco State University, San Francisco, Calif., 1962—, began as assistant professor, 1962-66, became associate professor, 1966, currently professor of philosophy, chairman of department, 1968-69. Visiting scholar, Union Theological Seminary, 1967-68. *Member:* American Philosophical Association, American Academy of Religion. *Awards, honors:* Fulbright scholarship in Germany, 1957-58; Fels Foundation fellowship in Munich, 1959; Society for Religion in Higher Education grant, 1967-68; grants from Marsden Foundation and Ella Lyman Cabot Trust for research for *The New Religions*.

WRITINGS: Being in the World, Basic Books, 1963, published with new introduction, Torchbooks, 1968; (translator) Erwin Straus, *The Primary World of Senses*, Free Press, 1963; (contributor of translation) *Essays on Ego Psychology*, International Universities Press, 1964; (co-editor) *Care of Patients with Fatal Illness*, New York Academy of Sciences, 1969; (contributor) Austin H. Kutscher, editor, *Death and Bereavement*, C. C Thomas, 1969; *The New Religions*, Doubleday, 1970; *Religion for a New Generation*, Macmillan, 1973, 2nd edition, 1976; *The Sword of Gnosis*, Penguin, 1973; *Sacred Tradition and Present Need*, Viking, 1974; *A Sense of the Cosmos*, Doubleday, 1975; *On the Way to Self Knowledge*, Knopf, 1976. General editor, "Penguin Metaphysical Library." Contributor of articles and reviews to journals in his field.

WORK IN PROGRESS: In Search of Christianity, an analysis of modern Christianity's search for its own mystical tradition.

SIDELIGHTS: Jacob Needleman told *CA:* "I write to people who, like myself, are searching for a way to maintain or return to the questions of the heart that a child puts to the universe: who am I? why am I on earth? how can I find out the meaning of my life? Some time ago I discovered how easy it was to forget these questions when surrounded by sophisticated books and other people's opinions and the promises of clever theorists. I seem to feel my humanity only when I come closer to this search and if anything of that is expressed in my writing I am very glad."

NEFF, Renfreu (de St. Laurence) 1938-

PERSONAL: Born May 5, 1938, in Paris, France; daughter of James F. (a diplomat) and Elizabeth (Adams) de St. Laurence. *Education:* Attended Bennington College. *Religion:* Quaker. *Residence:* New York, N.Y. *Agent:* Ronald Hobbs Literary Agency, 22 West 48th St., Suite 800, New York, N.Y. 10036.

CAREER: Occasional jobs of "mercifully brief duration," including assistant to a Broadway stage designer and photographer's assistant; fashion model in New York and Paris for Coco Chanel and Pierre Cardin; also worked as photographic model; now a full-time writer.

WRITINGS: The Living Theatre: USA, Bobbs-Merrill, 1970. Contributor of fiction, nonfiction, reviews, and interviews to many periodicals, including *Cavalier, Realist, Sipario, Oz, Queen,* and *Rolling Stone;* worked on assignment for *Newsweek, Esquire,* and *Playboy.* Regular contributor to the alternate, or underground, media.

WORK IN PROGRESS: Two books, *The Cosmania Papers,* a "fiction piece on the soft drug scene"; and an untitled work dealing with the individuals and influences that have helped to shape the present revolutionary movement.

BIOGRAPHICAL/CRITICAL SOURCES: Cue, October 31, 1970; *Variety,* December 9, 1970.†

* * *

NEGROPONTE, Nicholas Peter 1943-

PERSONAL: Born December 1, 1943; son of Dmitri John (a shipowner) and Catherine (Coumantaros) Negroponte; married Elaine Ann Audet (an antique dealer), July 28, 1968; children: Dmitri Serge. *Education:* Massachusetts Institute of Technology, B.Arch., 1965, M.Arch., 1966. *Home:* 178 Ivy St., Brookline, Mass. 02147. *Office:* Room 9-518, Massachusetts Institute of Technology, 77 Massachusetts Ave., Cambridge, Mass. 02139.

CAREER: Massachusetts Institute of Technology, Cambridge, instructor, 1966-68, assistant professor, 1968-72, associate professor of architecture, 1972—. Visiting professor, Yale University, spring, 1970, University of California, Berkeley, winter, 1973, University of Michigan, winter, 1975. Research associate, International Business Machines Corp., 1966-69. Member of editorial board, North Holland Publishing Co., 1974. *Awards, honors:* Three awards for the graphics of *The Architecture Machine.*

WRITINGS: The Architecture Machine: Toward a More Human Environment, M.I.T. Press, 1970; *Soft Architecture Machines,* M.I.T. Press, 1975; (editor) *Computer Aids to Design and Architecture,* Mason & Lipscomb, 1975.

Contributor: Murray Milne, editor, *Computer Graphics on Architecture and Design,* Yale University School of Architecture, 1968; Gary T. Moore, editor, *Emerging Methods in Design and Planning,* M.I.T. Press, 1970; Nigel Cross, editor, *Design Participation,* Academy Editions, 1972; Edward Allen, editor, *The Responsive House,* M.I.T. Press, 1974; Issac L. Auerbach, editor, *1974 Best Computer Papers,* Petrocelli Books, 1974; William Spillers, editor, *Basic Questions of Design Theory,* American Elsevier, 1974; Yona Friedman, *Toward a Scientific Architecture,* M.I.T. Press, 1975. Also contributor to *Future Impact of Computers and Information Processing,* edited by Michael Dertouzos and Joel Moses, 1977. Contributor to *Technology Design, Architectural Review, Werk, Architectura, Architecture and Urbanism, Techniques and Architecture, Technology Review, Canadian Architect,* and other journals.

NEIMARK, Anne E. 1935-

PERSONAL: Born October 3, 1935, in Chicago, Ill.; daughter of Robert M. and Anita (Bronner) Loeb; married Paul G. Neimark (a writer), June 13, 1955; children: Jill, Todd, Jeff. *Education:* Attended Bryn Mawr College, 1953-55. *Home:* 851 Yale Lane, Highland Park, Ill. 60035.

AWARDS, HONORS: Friends of American Writers first prize for a juvenile book, 1970, for *Touch of Light.*

WRITINGS: Touch of Light: The Story of Louis Braille (juvenile), Harcourt, 1970; *Sigmund Freud: The World Within* (young adult), Harcourt, 1976. Contributor of more than 100 articles and stories to juvenile magazines, including *Highlights for Children* and *Jack and Jill;* author of articles for teachers' manuals and educational publishers, including *Encyclopaedia Britannica* and Science Research Associates.

WORK IN PROGRESS: A young people's biography of Edgar Cayce.

* * *

NELSON, Cordner (Bruce) 1918-

PERSONAL: Born August 6, 1918, in San Diego, Calif.; son of Albert (a produce dealer) and Uradel (Bruce) Nelson; married Mary Kenyon, February 4, 1941; children: Elizabeth, Rebecca Nelson French, Nancy. *Education:* University of the Pacific, A.B., 1940; University of Oklahoma, graduate study, 1946-47. *Politics:* "A necessary evil." *Religion:* "Unattached." *Address:* Box 6476, Carmel, Calif. 93921.

CAREER: Track & Field News, Los Altos, Calif., editor, covering hundreds of track meets and seven Olympic Games, 1948-70, founding editor, 1970—. *Military service:* U.S. Army, 1941-45; became major; received China-Burma-India theater combat star. U.S. Army Reserve, 1945-68; retired as colonel. *Member:* Authors League of America. *Awards, honors:* Inducted into United States Track and Field Hall of Fame, 1975.

WRITINGS: The Jim Ryun Story, Tafnews, 1967; *The Miler* (novel), S. G. Phillips, 1969; *Track & Field: The Great Ones,* Pelham Books, 1970; *Runners and Races: 1500/Mile,* Tafnews, 1973. Also author of *Distance Running* and *How to Train.*

WORK IN PROGRESS: A work tentatively entitled *Engineering the Good Life.*

SIDELIGHTS: Cordner Nelson told *CA:* "After half a lifetime of writing short stories (only two dozen published), thousands of track and field articles (unread by a huge majority), several novels (all except two still unsold), and a current play (apparently not as funny as I think), I have turned to what I know best and will do the most good in the world. It is a self-help compendium of efficient techniques for improving your life. I call it *Engineering the Good Life,* but it probably should be called, *How to Wash Your Own Brain.* I feel a need to help people, and I expect it to be one of the most popular books ever offered because it has exciting value for anyone interested in himself. In fact, if I retain this confidence for another year, I may cash in by publishing it myself. But even if it sells poorly, my own life has already benefited greatly from it. I wish I had read something similar forty years ago."

AVOCATIONAL INTERESTS: Reading, tennis, conversation.

NELSON, Geoffrey K. 1923-

PERSONAL: Born August 8, 1923, in Dereham, Norfolk, England; son of William John (a malthouse fireman) and Florence (Pitcher) Nelson; married Irene Griggs, July 31, 1955; children: Elizabeth, Christopher, Rosemary, David. Education: University of Liverpool, Certificate in Social Science, 1950; Shoreditch College of Education, Teacher's Certificate, 1954; University of London, B.Sc., 1958, M.Sc., 1961, Ph.D., 1967. Home: 32 Clun Rd., Birmingham B31 1NU, England. Office: Department of Sociology, Birmingham Polytechnic, Birmingham, England.

CAREER: Besides teaching, has been employed in social work, agriculture, and civil service; Westwood School, March, Cambridgeshire, England, teacher, 1956-62; Bournville College, Birmingham, England, assistant lecturer in sociology, 1962-64; Birmingham Polytechnic, Birmingham, lecturer, 1964-69, senior lecturer, 1969-75, principal lecturer in sociology, 1975—. Part-time tutor, Wolsey Hall, Oxford University, 1961—. Honorary fellow, Institute for the Study of Worship and Religious Architecture University of Birmingham, 1969—. Military service: Home Guard, 1940-45. Member: British Sociological Association, American Sociological Association, Society for the Scientific Study of Religion, British Association for the Advancement of Science (secretary of sociology section, 1968—), University of London Convocation (chairman of West Midland branch, 1967—).

WRITINGS: Spiritualism and Society, Schocken, 1969; (with Rosemary A. Clews) Mobility and Religious Commitment, University of Birmingham, 1971; (contributor) A. Bryman, editor, Religion in the Birmingham Area, University of Birmingham, 1975; History of Modern Spiritualism, Spiritualists' National Union, 1976. Contributor to Sociological Review, Journal for the Scientific Study of Religion, Review of Religious Research, and to sociology journals, and contributor of articles on local history and religion to newspapers and popular magazines; had poetry published in little literary magazines during the 1940's.

WORK IN PROGRESS: A sociological study of the process of religion evolution; empirical research on religion and community life.

SIDELIGHTS: Geoffrey Nelson wrote to CA: "My published work is largely in the field of the sociology of religion, and takes the form of theoretical discussion and reports on empirical research. As a sociologist who is also a spiritualist and a Christian, I hope that my work will contribute to our understanding of religion."

BIOGRAPHICAL/CRITICAL SOURCES: Times Literary Supplement, June 26, 1969; J. Milton Yinger, The Scientific Study of Religion, Macmillan, 1970.

*   *   *

NELSON, John Howard 1929-
(Jack Nelson)

PERSONAL: Born October 11, 1929, in Talladega, Ala.; son of Howard Alonzo (a salesman) and Barbara Lena (O'-Donnell) Nelson; married Virginia Dare Dickinson, August 4, 1951 (divorced, 1974); married Barbara Joan Matusow, December 7, 1974; children: (first marriage) Karen Dare, John Michael, Steven Howard. Education: Georgia State University, student, 1953-57; Harvard University, student, 1961-62. Politics: Democrat. Home: 4528 Van Ness St., Washington, D.C. 20016. Agent: Sterling Lord Agency, 660 Madison Ave., New York, N.Y. 10021. Office: Los Angeles Times, 1700 Pennsylvania Ave., Washington, D.C. 20006.

CAREER: Biloxi Daily Herald, Biloxi, Miss., reporter, 1947-51; Atlanta Constitution, Atlanta, Ga., reporter, 1952-65; Los Angeles Times, Los Angeles, Calif., bureau chief in Atlanta, Ga., 1965-70, investigative reporter in Washington, D.C., 1970-75, Washington bureau chief, 1975—. Military service: U.S. Army, 1951-52; became sergeant. Member: White House Press Correspondents Association, Reporters Committee for Freedom of the Press (member of executive committee), Federal City Club, Gridiron Club, Sigma Delta Chi. Awards, honors: Pulitzer Prize for local reporting, 1960; named one of the ten outstanding young men in America by U.S. Junior Chamber of Commerce, 1960; Nieman fellow at Harvard University, 1961-62; Drew Pearson Award for investigative reporting, 1975.

WRITINGS—Under name Jack Nelson: (With Gene Roberts, Jr.) The Censors and the Schools, Little, Brown, 1963; (with Jack Bass) The Orangeburg Massacre, World Publishing, 1970; (with Ronald J. Ostrow) The FBI and the Berrigans, Coward, 1973; Captive Voices: High School Journalism in America, Schocken, 1974.

SIDELIGHTS: Stephen Pollak, former Assistant U.S. Attorney General in charge of Civil Rights, has called The Orangeburg Massacre, an account of the fatal confrontation between police and black students at South Carolina State College in February, 1968, "the best picture yet of the anatomy of an American campus tragedy." Pollak considers Nelson and Bass "two of this country's most outstanding investigative reporters.... Drawing upon the federal investigative files, interviews of most of the participants (except the governor and the chief of the State Law Enforcement Division who refused their request), and their attendance at the trial itself, the authors set out for the first time the facts of what really happened at Orangeburg. The result is a gripping narrative of the inexorable march of the event itself and, thereafter, the investigations and trial." "The book can be highly recommended," writes Charles Dollen in a review for Best Sellers, "not only because it puts events there in their true historical perspective, but also because it has a valuable commentary on a very current issue."

BIOGRAPHICAL/CRITICAL SOURCES: Nation, September 28, 1970; Time, October 26, 1970; Best Sellers, November 15, 1970; New Republic, November 21, 1970; Washington Post, November 30, 1970; Commonweal, December 25, 1970.

*   *   *

NELSON, Martha 1923-

PERSONAL: Born January 19, 1923, in Merigold, Miss.; daughter of Ira C. (an office manager) and Louise (Felder) Rushing; married Carl R. Nelson (a minister), May 15, 1943; children: Patricia (Mrs. Gary A. James), Nancy (Mrs. James K. Liner), Rebecca (Mrs. L. Kent Payne, Jr.). Education: Attended Delta State College, 1940-42, Mississippi College, 1946-47, and Southwestern Baptist Theological Seminary. Religion: Southern Baptist. Address: P.O. Box 355, Pelahatchie, Miss. 39145.

CAREER: Homemaker, free-lance writer, and conference leader. Member: National League of American Pen Women, Denver Women's Press Club, Mississippi Press Women. Awards, honors: National League of American Pen Women Biennial award, 1974, for A Woman's Search for Serenity, 1976, for Police Wife: How to Live with the Law and Like It; Service to Humanity award, Mississippi College.

WRITINGS: The Christian Woman in the Working World, Broadman, 1970; (contributor) J. Allen Petersen, editor, The

Marriage Affair, Tyndale House, 1971; *A Woman's Search for Serenity,* Broadman, 1972; *On Being a Deacon's Wife,* Broadman, 1973; (contributor) Evelyn R. and J. Allen Petersen, editors, *For Women Only,* Tyndale House, 1974; (contributor) George W. Knight, editor, *The Christian Home of the Seventies,* Broadman, 1974; (with Pat James) *Police Wife: How to Live with the Law and Like It,* C. C Thomas, 1975; *This Call We Share,* Broadman, 1977.

* * *

NELSON, Oliver W(endell) 1904-

PERSONAL: Born December 11, 1904, in Saxon, Wash.; son of Nels Peter (a farmer) and Caroline (Christensen) Nelson; married Vera Bohlke, June 16, 1928; married second wife, Dorothy J. Buchanan, October 2, 1976; children: (first marriage) Ardelle E. (Mrs. Donald A. Leach), Darrell L. *Education:* Western Washington State College, student, 1922-24; University of Washington, Seattle, B.A., 1933, M.A., 1939, Ph.D., 1949. *Politics:* Independent. *Religion:* Protestant. *Home:* 4758 45th Ave. N.E., Seattle, Wash. 98105.

CAREER: Teacher of English, speech, and drama in public schools in Washington, 1924-38; Central Washington State College, Ellensburg, assistant professor of speech, 1939-43; State Office of Public Instruction, Olympia, Wash., supervisor of education for handicapped children, 1943-45; University of Washington, Seattle, assistant professor, 1948-53, associate professor of speech, 1953-70, associate professor emeritus, 1970—, acting chairman of department, 1962-64. *Member:* American Association of University Professors, Speech Association of America, Western Speech Association, Washington State Speech Association, Phi Delta Kappa, Tau Delta Alpha. *Awards, honors:* Distinguished Service Award, Washington State Speech Association, 1970.

WRITINGS: (With Dominic A. LaRusso) *Oral Communication in the Secondary School Classroom,* Prentice-Hall, 1970. Contributor to speech journals.

WORK IN PROGRESS: A historical novel about the adventures of a young Danish immigrant couple in America in the late nineteenth century.

* * *

NELSON, Richard K(ing) 1941-

PERSONAL: Born December 1, 1941, in Madison, Wis.; son of Robert King (a state employee) and Florence (Olson) Nelson; married Carol A. Burch (a teaching assistant), August 8, 1969 (divorced); married Kathleen H. Mautner. *Education:* University of Wisconsin, B.S., 1964, M.S., 1968; University of California, Santa Barbara, Ph.D., 1971. *Home address:* General Delivery, Tenakee Springs, Alaska 99841.

CAREER: University of California, Santa Barbara, research fellow in anthropology, 1968-71; University of Hawaii, Honolulu, assistant professor of anthropology, 1971-72; Memorial University of Newfoundland, St. Johns, assistant professor of anthropology, 1972-73; University of Alaska, College, research associate, 1973-77. Member of field expeditions to Kodiak Island, Alaska, 1961, Anangula Island in the Aleutians, 1963, and four extended ethnographic field studies among Alaskan Eskimos and Indians.

WRITINGS: Alaskan Eskimo Exploitation of the Sea Ice Environment, Arctic Aeromedical Laboratory, U.S. Air Force, 1966; *Hunters of the Northern Ice,* University of Chicago Press, 1969; *Hunters of the Northern Forest,* Uni-

versity of Chicago Press, 1973; (co-author) *Kuuvangmiit: Contemporary Subsistence Living in the Latter Twentieth Century,* in press.

WORK IN PROGRESS: Co-author, *People of the Gates,* completion expected in 1977; *Tareogmiut: Hunters of the Arctic Sea,* 1977; *In the Watchful Land,* 1978.

* * *

NERHOOD, Harry W(arren) 1910-

PERSONAL: Born May 13, 1910, in Pennsylvania Furnace, Pa.; son of Warren Wesley (a machinist) and Minnie V. (Carper) Nerhood; married Allie Leona Wilson, March 19, 1932. *Education:* Findlay College, B.A., 1936; Ohio State University, M.A., 1937, Ph.D., 1939. *Religion:* Quaker. *Home:* 11738 East Hillview Ct., Whittier, Calif. 90601.

CAREER: Whittier College, Whittier, Calif., associate professor, 1939-56, professor of history and chairman of department, 1956-75. *Member:* American Historical Association, American Association for the Advancement of Slavic Studies, Pacific Historical Association (member of book awards committee, 1977-80), Far Western Slavic Society, Phi Alpha Theta.

WRITINGS: (Compiler) *To Russia and Return: An Annotated Bibliography of Travelers' English-Language Accounts of Russia from the Ninth Century to the Present,* Ohio State University Press, 1968. Also co-editor of *Russia Observed* (ninety-four travel accounts), 1971.

SIDELIGHTS: Harry W. Nerhood has traveled extensively in Russia and the rest of Europe; in 1956-57 he spent fifteen months on a world trip.

BIOGRAPHICAL/CRITICAL SOURCES: New York Times Book Review, June 29, 1969.

* * *

NESS, Gayl D(eForrest) 1929-

PERSONAL: Born March 19, 1929, in Los Angeles, Calif.; son of Neil Howard (an engineer) and Esther (Hallgren) Ness; married Jeannine R. Aimont, 1955; children: Marc A., Eric H., Ian T., Shanta T. *Education:* University of California, Berkeley, B.A., 1952, M.A., 1957, Ph.D., 1961; University of Copenhagen, Graduate Diploma, 1956. *Politics:* Democrat. *Religion:* None. *Home:* 1301 South Forest, Ann Arbor, Mich. 48104. *Office:* Department of Sociology, University of Michigan, Ann Arbor, Mich. 48104.

CAREER: Institute of Current World Affairs, New York, N.Y., fellow in Southeast Asia, 1961-64; University of Michigan, Ann Arbor, assistant professor, 1964-66, associate professor, 1966-71, professor of sociology, 1971—. Consultant in population programs in Asia, UNESCAP Population Division, Bangkok, Thailand, 1972—. *Military service:* U.S. Army, Ordnance Corps, 1953-55. *Member:* American Sociological Association, Association for Asian Studies.

WRITINGS: Bureaucracy and Rural Development in Malaysia, University of California Press, 1967; (editor) *The Sociology of Economic Development: A Reader,* Harper, 1970.

WORK IN PROGRESS: Research on political and administrative aspects of population planning, with special reference to Malaysia and the Philippines.

SIDELIGHTS: Gayl Ness has spent a total of four and one-half years in Southeast Asia, three and one-half as a fellow, and the last year doing research on population programs.

NEUFELD, Rose 1924-

PERSONAL: Born August 20, 1924, in New York, N.Y.; daughter of Isaak (a furrier) and Sara (Merzer) Goldman; married William Neufeld (a documentary filmmaker), October 12, 1962. *Education:* Hunter College (now Hunter College of the City University of New York), B.A., 1946; New York University, M.A., 1951.

CAREER: New York (N.Y.) Board of Education, special education teacher, 1960—.

WRITINGS: Reading Fundamentals for Teenagers, John Day, 1963; *Beware the Man without a Beard, and Other Greek Folk Tales* (juvenile), Knopf, 1969; *More Reading for Teenagers,* John Day, 1971.

WORK IN PROGRESS: A reading workbook for high school students, for John Day.†

* * *

NEUTRA, Richard Joseph 1892-1970

April 8, 1892—April 16, 1970; Austrian-born American architect. Obituaries: *New York Times,* April 18, 1970; *Current Biography,* 1970. (See index for *CA* sketch)

* * *

NEVILLE, Pauline 1924-

PERSONAL: Born April 23, 1924, in Castle Douglas, Scotland; daughter of James Annet (a clergyman) and Marjory (Kingsford-Pawling) Fisher; married Michael Forrester (a major general and director of infantry, British Army), October, 1947; married second husband, Richard Neville (with Lloyds Insurance), September, 1963; children: (first marriage) Simon, Nicholas. *Education:* Attended Queen Anne's School, Reading, England. *Politics:* Liberal. *Religion:* Church of England. *Home:* Flat 4, 24 Sussex St., London SW1V 4RW, England. *Agent:* Richard Scott Simon, 32 Collegecross, London N1 1RP, England.

CAREER: Writer. Served for five years with First Aid Ambulance Service during World War II.

WRITINGS—All published by Hamish Hamilton: *My Father's House* (autobiographical), 1969; *Voyage of a Life,* 1971; *The Cousins,* 1973; *Blackwater,* 1974. Regular contributor to *Homes and Gardens* and other magazines.

SIDELIGHTS: In Pauline Neville's memoir (not to be confused with Philip Kunhardt Jr.'s more recently published *My Father's House* and several other books with the same title) she tells of her childhood as the daughter of a witty Irish clergyman. She tells it "engagingly," according to the *New Statesman.* "Her father kept the house door open day and night, wept occasionally in the pulpit, lulled babies to sleep by booming the psalms at them, and took the family for merry Irish holidays.... This remarkable father even encouraged his children to doubt, and discuss difficulties."

Mrs. Neville mentions with some surprise that she continues to receive communications from the United States about *My Father's House,* although it has been published only in England. One of the communications was from the *Christian Science Monitor* seeking permission to quote five hundred words from the book.

Mrs. Neville has traveled widely and did not begin her writing until after her two sons had gone away to boarding school. Writing to *CA* about her present circumstances, she says "that life and how we live it is my interest." She adds that her "sons now live free of me in what I hope to be the right sense, and ... I am alone again, and writing. I must

agree with the quote from James Baldwin that 'we write because we are incomplete if we do not do so' and simply have to accept the loneliness that so often comes with it."

BIOGRAPHICAL/CRITICAL SOURCES: New Statesman, February 21, 1969.

* * *

NEVINS, (Joseph) Allan 1890-1971

May 20, 1890—March 5, 1971; American historian and educator. Obituaries: *New York Times,* March 6, 1971; *Time,* March 15, 1971; *Newsweek,* March 15, 1971; *Publishers' Weekly,* March 22, 1971; *Antiquarian Bookman,* May 17, 1971. (See index for *CA* sketch)

* * *

NEVINS, Edward M(ichael) 1938-

PERSONAL: Born July 6, 1938, in New York, N.Y.; son of Michael Edward and Eva (Demas) Nevins; married Dorothy Spivack, October 1, 1960; children: Edward Michael II. *Education:* Attended public schools in New Jersey, New York, and Vermont. *Agent:* Henry Evans, P.O. 1241R, Morristown, N.J. 07960.

CAREER: Employed by various firms in airline industry in New York, N.Y. and Washington, D.C. since 1958, including British Overseas Airways and Swiss Air; partner in a firm developing desert areas for tourism in Jordan, 1964—; operator of camel caravans on educational tours in the desert, 1964—. *Military service:* U.S. Army, Infantry, 1956-58. *Member:* Explorers Club (New York).

WRITINGS: (With Theon Wright) *World without Time: The Bedouin,* photographs by Nevins, John Day, 1969. Contributor to *Explorers Journal.*†

* * *

NEWLOVE, Donald 1928-

PERSONAL: Born March 28, 1928, in Erie, Pa.; son of Durwood Samuel (an outdoorsman) and Marvel Marie (Carris) Newlove; married Norma Jean Sandberg, 1953 (divorced, 1960); married Jaqueline Rayfeld (a teacher), November 24, 1967 (divorced, 1975); married Nancy Irene Semonian; children: (first marriage) Stuart Ernest (Newlove) Anderson. *Education:* Attended Jamestown Community College and Pennsylvania State University, completed sophomore year; "mostly self-educated and by exemplary older friends." *Agent:* Helen Brann Agency, 14 Sutton Pl. S., New York, N.Y. 10022.

CAREER: Jamestown *Sun,* Jamestown, N.Y., reporter-photographer, 1959-60; Virginia Kirkus Service, New York City, book reviewer, 1962-67; McCall Publishing Co., New York City, reader, editor, 1970; trumpet player, 1970—; Virginia Kirkus Service, book reviewer, 1974—. *Military service:* U.S. Marine Corps, 1945-46. U.S. Air Force, 1953-56.

WRITINGS—Novels: *The Painter Gabriel,* McCall Publishing, 1970; *Leo and Theodore,* Dutton, 1972, revised edition published with *The Drunks* as *Sweet Adversity,* Avon, 1978; *The Drunks,* Dutton, 1974, revised edition published with *Leo and Theodore* as *Sweet Adversity,* Avon, 1978. Contributor of articles and short stories to *Esquire, Evergreen Review, Realist,* and *Workshop in Non-Violence Magazine.* Contributing editor, *Esquire.*

WORK IN PROGRESS: A novel, *Eternal Life;* a nonfiction work, *Alcohol and Genius;* a collection of his magazine articles, tentatively entitled *Little Dreamland.*

SIDELIGHTS: Donald Newlove told *CA* that "the most profound influence on my work and life was beginning recovery from alcoholism at 38, which reinvigorated my spirit beyond measure and gave my work a new spine. During my drinking career, I wrote eight books, each worse than the one before, and all eight are now in my trunk, forever. Writing and sale of my first published novel coincided with sobriety, or beginning sobriety. I'm now 49 and have not had a drug stronger than coffee or nicotine in over five years. My God, the difference!"

Robert Hughes, in a review for *Time,* called *The Painter Gabriel* "one of the best fictional studies of madness, descent and purification that any American has written since Ken Kesey's *One Flew Over the Cuckoo's Nest.* Donald Newlove clearly set out to write a first novel about demoniac society. He has produced a combined morality play and grimoire, or devil's horn-book, in which every creature is experienced with hilarious or dreadful concreteness."

Leo and Theodore and *The Drunks* are also about descent and, if not purification, at least the chance of salvation. In these symbolic novels, the bizarre protagonists, who seem to represent all of us, are often rendered humorous. Probably influenced by Newlove's own experiences with alcoholism, the two novels are about alcoholic Siamese twins. *The Drunks* is described by a *New Yorker* reviewer as "probably the most clear-eyed and moving—and certainly one of the most honest—books ever written about alcoholics." Leo and Theodore were born in upstate New York on the day the stock market crashed; they dream of becoming jazz musicians and are alcoholics by the time they are in junior high school. As Walter Clemons notes: "This sounds like a perfectly terrible idea for a novel, combining the direst possibilities of two kinds of bathos, the symbolic grotesque and the young-man-with-a-horn saga. Donald Newlove is able to make it work: his twins—goofy, raunchy and appealing—are irrefutably alive."

The Drunks finds the twins, approaching thirty, on the lower East side of New York City, living in what Frederich Busch describes as "the huge sweaty sordidness of the down-and-out life in the East Village and adjacent blood banks, hospitals and Alcoholics Anonymous waiting rooms." Their alcoholism worsens and their story becomes that much more depressing. As Clemons remarks in a later review of *The Drunks*: "Their binges used to be boyish fun; now vomiting, impotence and D.T.'s accompany them. As they approach 30, self-deceiving failed artists, they are pulled toward death by the stresses of divided personality and indissoluble twinship."

The twins' symbolic descent to hell is depicted in both these novels. Clemons calls their world "an inferno whose inhabitants down everything from Sterno to Polynesian Jade aftershave lotion." Busch continues the Dantean comparison: "The twins spiral down to hell, through cowardice, poverty, disease, terror, until, after a siege worse than usual, they reveal the split-self about which the novel is concerned: Teddy takes barbiturates, Leo amphetamines. They nearly lose their minds. . . . Newlove's use of Siamese twins as character and metaphor, his willingness to take the chance (his art is one of the risks) pays off. The experience is so horrible that we sigh with relief to find, in the last section, that the twins may, now, have actually stuck to their A.A. resolves." And yet salvation is not that easy. Despite the speeches, affirmations, and prayers of the reformed alcoholics (Leo and Teddy included), and after the closing of the A.A. meeting with the mass recitation of the Lord's Prayer, Busch continues, "we hear (the last line of the novel) 'Boy,

that should hold 'em for twenty-four hours.' So we know that there is no sure salvation or very much strength. There is no way back for (or from) the self-destroying self.''

These novels work largely because of Newlove's unusual style and sense of humor. Newlove is willing to take risks which make his books interesting—and absorbing. The *Publishers Weekly* reviewer says of *The Drunks:* "Dipping into Newlove is a bit like hearing Charles Ives for the first time. One is disoriented by the dissonance, cross rhythms, cacophony, relieved at the occasional bursts of the familiar. And if Ives doesn't permit the listener's ears to be lulled, Newlove doesn't permit the wandering eye. Attention is demanded and received." Newlove prefers dialogue without quotation marks which, as Clemons notes, "is no inconvenience when the talk leaps off the page as clearly as his does." The *New Yorker* reviewer of *The Drunks* writes: "Mr. Newlove takes incredible risks, and his cannonball style is more than a little demanding; not content with the problems inherent in writing about drunkenness (or, for that matter, Siamese twins), he adds the handicap of having Teddy's front teeth knocked out in an accident, so that a full quarter of the book is filled with his lisped dialogue. But the sheer inventiveness and strength of his writing turns risk into triumph, drunken monologues into subtle satire, A.A. meetings into riveting dramas, and what in another writer might be bathos into brilliant comedy."

Donald Newlove told *CA* that he prefers his revised edition of the novels, *Sweet Adversity.* He writes: "Paperback republication allows me to . . . bring each page way up close to the reader's face. When I wrote them they were the best I could do; now I hope they're less literary and more reader-welcoming."

BIOGRAPHICAL/CRITICAL SOURCES: Esquire, August, 1970; *New York Times,* October 6, 1970; *Time,* January 25, 1971, January 29, 1973; *New Yorker,* January 27, 1973, December 9, 1974; *Book World,* February 11, 1973; *Newsweek,* February 19, 1973, November 11, 1974, December 30, 1974; *Publishers Weekly,* August 19, 1974; *New York Times Book Review,* October 27, 1974; *Contemporary Literary Criticism,* Volume VI, Gale, 1976.

* * *

NEWMAN, Aubrey N. 1927-

PERSONAL: Born December 14, 1927, in London, England; married; children: three daughters, one son. *Education:* University of Glasgow, M.A. (honors), 1949; Wadham College, Oxford, B.A. (honors), 1953, M.A., D.Phil., 1957. *Religion:* Jewish. *Home:* 33 Stanley Rd., Leicester, England. *Office:* Department of History, University of Leicester, Leicester, England.

CAREER: University of London, Bedford College, London, England, research fellow, 1954-55, research assistant, 1955-59; University of Leicester, Leicester, England, 1959—, began as assistant lecturer, currently reader in modern history. *Military service:* Royal Air Force, flying officer, 1949-51. *Member:* Royal Historical Society (fellow).

WRITINGS: The Parliamentary Diary of Sir Edward Knatchbull, 1722-30, Royal Historical Society, 1963; *The Stanhopes of Chevening: A Family Biography,* St. Martin's, 1969; (editor with Helen Miller) *A Bibliography of English History, 1485-1760,* Historical Association, 1970; *The Parliamentary Lists of the Early Eighteenth Century: Their Compilation and Use,* Leicester University Press, 1973; *A Commentary on . . . the Records of the Borough of Leicester,* Leicester University Press, 1974; *The United Syn-*

agogue, 1870-1970, Routledge & Kegan Paul, 1976. Contributor of articles and reviews to historical journals and to *Jewish Chronicle* and *European Judaism.*

WORK IN PROGRESS: A biography of George II; a biography of the Duke of Newcastle; with A. T. Milne, a supplement to Pargellis and Medley's *Bibliography of British History 1714-1789.*

AVOCATIONAL INTERESTS: Sitting on committees.

BIOGRAPHICAL/CRITICAL SOURCES: Spectator, February 28, 1969; *Punch,* March 12, 1969.

* * *

NEWSOME, Arden J(eanne) 1932-
(Jeanne Sebastian)

PERSONAL: Born July 27, 1932, in Philadelphia, Pa.; daughter of Sebastian John (an electrical engineer) and Leonora (Kupusciensky) Bokeeno (Italian spelling is Bocchino); married Robert Newsome (a production employee of Pillsbury Co.), April 4, 1953; children: Michael, Donna, Christopher. *Education:* Attended Pierce Business School, Philadelphia, 1950-51. *Politics:* Democrat. *Religion:* Episcopalian. *Home address:* Box 142, Route 1, East Greenville, Pa. 18041. *Agent:* Elyse Sommer, Inc., Box E, 962 Allen Lane, Woodmere, N.Y. 11598.

WRITINGS—For young people: *Spoolcraft,* Lothrop, 1970; *Cork and Wood Crafts,* Lion Press, 1970; (self-illustrated) *Crafts and Toys from around the World,* Messner, 1971; (self-illustrated) *Make It with Felt: An Art and Craft Book,* Lothrop, 1972; (self-illustrated) *Egg Craft,* Lothrop, 1973; *Egg Decorating, Plain and Fancy,* Crown, 1973; (self-illustrated) *Button Collecting and Crafting,* Lothrop, 1976. Author of regular columns for *Popular Handicrafts* and *Stitch and Sew,* occasionally using the pseudonym Jeanne Sebastian. Contributor to *Better Homes and Gardens Christmas Book, McCall's Needlework & Crafts, Child Life, Highlights for Children,* and *Venture.*

WORK IN PROGRESS: Native American Crafts, for Lothrop.†

* * *

NEWSOME, George L(ane), Jr. 1923-

PERSONAL: Born October 5, 1923, in Bessemer, Ala.; son of George Lane (in industrial management) and Mary V. (Mobbs) Newsome; married Martha Merchant, 1947; children: George Lane III, Mary Virginia, Elizabeth Ann. *Education:* University of Alabama, B.S., 1949, M.A., 1950; Yale University, Ph.D., 1956. *Home:* 145 Tuxedo Rd., Athens, Ga. 30601. *Office:* University of Georgia, Athens, Ga. 30602.

CAREER: Teacher in Alabama high schools, 1950-53; University of Bridgeport, Bridgeport, Conn., lecturer, 1954-55, assistant professor, 1955-57, associate professor of the history and philosophy of education, 1957-58; University of Georgia, Athens, associate professor, 1958-63, professor of philosophy of education and head of department, 1963—. Guest professor, New Haven State Teachers College (now Southern Connecticut State College), 1955, 1957; guest lecturer, Trinity College (Conn.), summer, 1954, Northern Illinois University and University of the Pacific, both summer, 1970. *Military service:* U.S. Army, 1943-46. *Member:* Philosophy of Education Society (secretary-treasurer, 1964-66; program chairman, 1967-68), American Philosophical Association, American Educational Research Association, International Platform Association, Southern Society of Philos-

ophy of Psychology, Southeastern Philosophy of Education Society (president, 1962-63), Phi Kappa Phi, Kappa Delta Pi.

WRITINGS: (With D. B. Gowin and others) *An Experimental Study of Part-Time Faculty, Members,* Fund for the Advancement of Education, 1958; *Philosophical Perspectives,* Center for Continuing Education and University of Georgia Press, 1961; (editor) *Philosophy of Education 1968,* Philosophy of Education Society, 1968; (editor with William T. Blackstone) *Education and Ethics,* University of Georgia Press, 1969.

Contributor: Hobert W. Burns and Charles J. Brauner, editors, *Philosophy of Education,* Ronald, 1962; Joe Park, editor, *Selected Readings in Philosophy of Education,* Macmillan, 1963; John Martin Rich, editor, *Readings in the Philosophy of Education,* Wadsworth, 1966; Clarence W. Walton and Richard Eells, *The Business System,* Macmillan, 1967; Christopher J. Lucas, editor, *What Is Philosophy of Education,* Macmillan, 1968; Ronald T. Hyman, editor, *Contemporary Thought on Teaching,* Prentice-Hall, 1971. Contributor of more than thirty articles to academic journals. Member of editorial advisory committee, *Teacher Education Quarterly,* 1957-58, and publications committee, Philosophy of Education Society, 1959-60.

* * *

NEWTON, Kenneth 1940-

PERSONAL: Born April 15, 1940, in London, England; son of Kenneth (a teacher) and Ann (Templeton) Newton; married Diana Smith (a research sociologist), September 7, 1968; children: one daughter. *Education:* University of Exeter, B.A. (with honors), 1962; University of Cambridge, Ph.D., 1965. *Politics:* "Yes." *Religion:* "No." *Home:* 11 Fugelmere Close, Birmingham 15, England. *Office:* Nuffield College, Oxford University, Oxford OX1 1NF, England.

CAREER: University of Birmingham, Birmingham, England, lecturer in political sociology, 1965-73; American Council of Learned Societies fellow, University of Wisconsin, 1973-74; Oxford University, Nuffield College, Oxford, England, research fellow, 1974—. Visiting European scholar, University of Pittsburgh, 1972. *Member:* Philosophy of Science Association, American Sociological Association, American Political Science Association.

WRITINGS: (Editor with Sonya Abrams) *Opportunities after O-Level,* Penguin, 1965; *The Sociology of British Communism,* Fernhill, 1969; *Second City Politics: Democratic Processes and Decision-Making in Birmingham,* Oxford University Press, 1976. Author of a series of papers on municipal government and politics. Contributor of articles to *Cambridge Opinion, British Journal of Political Science, Journal of Politics, Policy and Politics, Political Studies,* and *Sociology.*†

* * *

NICHOLS, R(oy) Eugene 1914-

PERSONAL: Born August 27, 1914, in Terre Haute, Ind.; son of James and Louisa (Williams) Nichols; married Winnifred Lynch (an educator), July 3, 1949; children: Lynette Kay, Celeste Traci. *Education:* Mental Science Institute and School of Philosophy, Denver, M.Sc.B., 1948; Institute of Religious Science, Los Angeles, R.Sc.M., 1952; University of California, Los Angeles, student, 1952; College of Divine Metaphysics, Indianapolis, D.D., 1953. *Home:* 6394 East Floyd Dr., Denver, Colo. 80222. *Office:* Science of

Mind Church, 4670 East 17th Ave. Pkwy., Denver, Colo. 80220.

CAREER: Minister-director of Religious Science churches in Phoenix, Ariz., 1952-53, Riverside, Calif., 1953-59, and Denver, Colo., 1959-66; Science of Mind Church and School of Esoteric Christianity, Denver, minister-director, 1966—. Founder-director, Institute of Mental Cybernetics, Denver, 1970—. *Member:* International New Thought Alliance, Society for Psychical Research (London), Association for Research and Enlightenment. *Awards, honors:* M.Sc.D., Mental Science Institute, 1950; R.Sc.D., Institute of Religious Science, 1956.

WRITINGS: The Science of Mental Cybernetics, Parker Publishing, 1970; *The Science of Higher Sense Perception,* Parker Publishing, 1972; *Esoteric Keys to Personal Power,* CSA Press, 1976.

WORK IN PROGRESS: Picture Yourself a Winner.

SIDELIGHTS: R. Eugene Nichols told *CA:* "My books have come out in foreign editions, not because they entertain, but because they feature self-help techniques that guide the individual in tapping his full mental and spiritual potentialities." *The Science of Mental Cybernetics* has been translated into Japanese and Spanish. *The Science of Higher Perception* has been translated into German.

* * *

NICHOLSEN, Margaret E(sther) 1904-

PERSONAL: Born December 7, 1904, in Blue Earth, Minn.; daughter of Jacob N. (a lawyer) and Annie (McBride) Nicholsen. *Education:* Carleton College, B.A., 1926; Columbia University, B.S. in L.S., 1927; University of Chicago, M.A., 1940. *Religion:* Congregational. *Home:* 731 Simpson St., Evanston, Ill. 60201.

CAREER: Bemidji State Teachers College (now Bemidji State College), Bemidji, Minn., head librarian, 1927-39; librarian for U.S. Army Library Service, 1941-43; high school librarian in Austin, Minn., 1946-47; Morton Township High School and Junior College, Cicero, Ill., director of libraries, 1949-51; Evanston Township High School, Evanston, Ill., head librarian, 1951-64. *Military service:* U.S. Naval Reserve (WAVES), 1943-46; became lieutenant commander. *Member:* American Library Association, League of Women Voters, Evanston Historical Society (secretary, 1960-69 and 1971-73).

WRITINGS: People in Books, H. W. Wilson, 1969, supplement, 1977. Contributor to library journals.

* * *

NICHOLSON, Shirley J. 1925-

PERSONAL: Born January 8, 1925, in Little Rock, Ark.; daughter of Franc Irving (a salesman) and Shirley (Paris) Mullen; married William M. Nicholson (a psychologist), February 17, 1957; children: Carol, Patty. *Education:* University of California, Los Angeles, B.A., 1957; Newark State College, Teacher Certification, 1968; Montclair State College, Teacher Certification, 1977. *Religion:* Episcopalian. *Home:* 45 Fairview Ave., South Orange, N.J. 07079.

CAREER: Prospect Hill School, Newark, N.J., teacher of science, 1963-68; Newark Museum, Newark, talks for children, 1968-74; Glen Ridge Schools, Glen Ridge, N.J., teaching children with learning disabilities, 1974—. *Member:* Theosophical Society, New Jersey Association of Independent Schools, Phi Beta Kappa.

WRITINGS: Nature's Merry-Go-Round (juvenile), Theosophical Publishing, 1969. Contributor to *Main Currents in Modern Thought.*

* * *

NICOLSON, I(an) F(erguson) 1921-

PERSONAL: Born February 22, 1921, in Portree, Isle of Skye, Scotland; son of Angus and Isabel (Macdougall) Nicolson; married Doreen Florence Tabor, September 15, 1945; children: John, Catherine, Alexander, Ian. *Education:* Victoria University of Manchester, B.A., 1940; Trinity College, Cambridge, further study, 1950-51. *Home:* 95 Hillside Ter., St. Lucia, Brisbane, Queensland 4067, Australia. *Office:* Department of Government, University of Queensland, Brisbane, Queensland 4067, Australia.

CAREER: H. M. Colonial Administrative Service, assignments in Nigeria and Malaya, 1947-62; University of Manchester, Manchester, England, Simon research fellow, department of government, 1962-64; University of Queensland, Brisbane, Australia, senior lecturer, 1965-70, reader in department of government, 1971—. *Military service:* British Army and Indian Army, 1940-47; served in India, Assam, Burma, and Germany. *Member:* Royal Institute of Public Administration, Australian Political Science Association.

WRITINGS: (Contributor) L. F. Blitz, editor, *The Politics and Administration of Nigerian Government,* Praeger, 1965; (contributor) J. P. Mackintosh, *Nigerian Government and Politics,* Northwestern University Press, 1966; *The Administration of Nigeria, 1900-1960: Men, Methods, and Myths,* Oxford University Press, 1969; (editor with C. A. Hughes) *Pacific Polities,* Pitman, 1972.

WORK IN PROGRESS: Research for a political biography of Sir Hugh Clifford; also a (heretical) book on administration.

BIOGRAPHICAL/CRITICAL SOURCES: Spectator, March 14, 1970.

* * *

NIEBUHR, Reinhold 1892-1971

June 21, 1892—June 1, 1971; American philosopher, theologian, and minister. Obituaries: *New York Times,* June 2, 1971; *Time,* June 14, 1971; *L'Express,* June 14-20, 1971; *Christian Century,* June 16, 1971; *National Review,* June 29, 1971. (See index for *CA* sketch)

* * *

NIELSEN, Eduard 1923-

PERSONAL: Born May 8, 1923; son of Charles (a clergyman) and Bothilde Nielsen; married Dora Margrethe Levinsen (a social worker), December 30, 1947; children: Bo, Anne, Eva, Pia. *Education:* Attended University of Copenhagen, 1941-47. *Home:* 4 Vasehojvej, DK2920, Charlottenlund, Denmark. *Office:* Theological Faculty, University of Copenhagen, Kobmagergade 44-46, Copenhagen, Denmark.

CAREER: University of Aarhus, Theology Faculty, Aarhus, Denmark, assistant teacher, 1949-55; University of Copenhagen, Theological Faculty, Copenhagen, Denmark, professor of Old Testament exegesis, 1956—. *Military service:* Danish Army, 1948-49.

WRITINGS: Oral Tradition: A Modern Problem in Old Testament Introduction, S.C.M. Press, 1954; *Shechem: A Traditio-Historical Investigation* (thesis at University of

Aarhus), G.E.C. Gad (Copenhagen), 1955, revised edition, 1959; *Haandskriftfundene i Juda Oerken* (on the Dead Sea scrolls), G.E.C. Gad, 1956; (editor) *Doedehavs teksterne* (on the Dead Sea Scrolls), G.E.C. Gad, 1959; *Grundrids af Israels Historie* (on history of Israel), University of Copenhagen Press, 1959; (editor with Bent Noack) *Gads danske Bibel leksikon* (Bible dictionary), two volumes, G.E.C. Gad, 1965; *De ti bud: En traditionshistorisk skitse,* University of Copenhagen Press, 1965, translation by David J. Bourke from the German edition published as *The Ten Commandments in New Perspective: A Traditio-Historical Approach,* Allenson, 1968; *Deuterosakarja,* G.E.C. Gad, 1970; *Det gamle Israels religion* (on the religion of Israel), G.E.C. Gad, 1971.

* * *

NIEVERGELT, Jurg 1938-

PERSONAL: Born June 6, 1938, in Lucerne, Switzerland; son of Albert and Hedwig Nievergelt; married Teresita Quiambao (a librarian), February 14, 1965; children: Mark Andrew, Derek. *Education:* Swiss Federal Institute of Technology, Diploma, 1962; University of Illinois, Ph.D., 1965. *Home:* 507 West Michigan, Urbana, Ill. 61801. *Office:* Department of Computer Science, University of Illinois at Urbana-Champaign, Urbana, Ill. 61801.

CAREER: University of Illinois at Urbana-Champaign, assistant professor, 1965-68, associate professor, 1968-72, professor of computer science and mathematics, 1972—. Professor, Swiss Federal Institute of Technology, Zurich, 1975-78. *Member:* Association for Computing Machinery, Institute of Electrical and Electronics Engineers, Sigma Xi, Phi Kappa Phi.

WRITINGS: (Editor with Don Secrest) *Conference on Emerging Concepts in Computer Graphics,* University of Illinois Press, 1967, published as *Emerging Concepts in Computer Graphics,* W. A. Benjamin, 1968; (editor with Michael Faiman) *Pertinent Concepts in Computer Graphics,* University of Illinois Press, 1969; (with J. C. Farrar and E. M. Reingold) *Computer Approaches to Problems in Mathematics,* Prentice-Hall, 1975; (with Reingold and N. Deo) *Combinatorial Algorithms: Theory and Practice,* Prentice-Hall, 1977.

* * *

NILES, D(aniel) T(hambyrajah) 1908-1970

May 4, 1908—July 17, 1970; Ceylonese minister and theologian. Obituaries: *New York Times,* July 18, 1970; *Christian Century,* August 12, 1970.

* * *

NIXON, William R(ussell) 1918-

PERSONAL: Born March 17, 1918, in Phillipsburg, N.J.; son of Grace (Morris) Nixon; married Mary N. Reilly, October 26, 1966; children: William R., Jr., Marygrace. *Education:* Lafayette College, B.A., 1948; Lehigh University, M.A., 1950. *Residence:* Macungie, Pa. *Office:* Sport Seating Co., Inc., Emmaus, Pa. 18049.

CAREER: School administrator in Pennsylvania, 1948-50; in sales management, American Seating Co., 1951-60; Clopay Corp., Cincinnati, Ohio, general manager, 1960-64; C.I.T. Educational Buildings, Inc., New York, N.Y., vice-president, 1964-68; Educational Marketing Associates, Clinton, N.J., president, 1968-71; Sport Seating Co., Inc., Emmaus, Pa., executive vice-president, 1972—. *Military*

service: U.S. Army Air Forces, 1942-45; served in Southwest Pacific; became technical sergeant; received six battle stars.

WRITINGS: The School Market, Macmillan, 1968. Contributor to educational journals.

WORK IN PROGRESS: A mini-novel, *Second Son,* which is a religious science fiction treatment of the second coming of Jesus Christ.

* * *

NOLTING, Orin F(rederyc) 1903-

PERSONAL: Born April 19, 1903, in Kearney, Mo.; son of Edward and Emelia (Hessell) Nolting; married Mamie Irene Siebert, December 25, 1927. *Education:* University of Kansas, A.B., 1926; Syracuse University, M.S., 1929; University of Chicago, graduate study, 1936. *Religion:* Protestant. *Home:* 5921 West 78th St., Prairie Village, Kan. 66208.

CAREER: University of Kansas, Lawrence, secretary of Municipal Reference Bureau, 1926-27; Municipal Research Commission, Syracuse, N.Y., secretary, 1928-29; International City Managers' Association, original headquarters in Chicago, Ill., now in Washington, D.C., assistant director, 1929-56, executive director, 1956-67, executive director emeritus, 1967-71; Public Administration Service, Chicago, Ill., member of board of directors, 1956-67, chairman of board, 1967-68, special assistant to the president, 1968—. Teacher of evening courses at Northwestern University and University of Chicago; lecturer at National Chengchi University, Taipei, and Tokyo Metropolitan University, 1969; adjunct professor, Park College, 1977. Part-time secretary, National Committee on Urban Transportation, 1954-60; International Union of Local Authorities, The Hague, U.S. member of executive committee, 1957-59, vice-president, 1959-71; member, U.S. Census Advisory Committee on State and Local Government Statistics, 1959-61; member of Traffic Conference, National Safety Council, 1959-67; chairman, Committee for International Municipal Cooperation, 1962-65; consultant on public administration programs in Thailand, Philippines, and Korea, U.S. Agency for International Development, 1969. Member of Citizen's Board, University of Chicago, 1947-61; member, Johnson County (Kan.) Charter Commission, 1975-76; consultant to mayor and council of Prairie Village, Kan., 1976—. *Member:* Royal Institute of Public Administration (England), International City Management Association (honorary member), Society of Town Clerks of England and Wales (honorary member), American Society for Public Administration, Pi Sigma Alpha. *Awards, honors:* Grand Cross of the Order of Merit of Germany, 1973.

WRITINGS: Municipal Insurance, Municipal Reference Bureau, University of Kansas, 1927; (with Clarence E. Ridley) *The City Manager Profession,* University of Chicago Press, 1934; *Management Methods in City Government,* International City Managers' Association, 1942; *Post-entry Training in the Public Service in Western Europe,* International City Managers' Association, 1962; *Progress and Impact of the Council-Manager Plan,* Public Administration Service, 1969.

Author of other shorter monographs on municipal problems and government, and two on libraries, *Mobilizing Total Library Resources for Effective Service,* American Library Association, 1969, and *The Administration of a Public Affairs Library,* Public Administration Service, 1970. Contributor to *Encyclopedia Americana, Encyclopaedia Britannica, The Municipal Year Book, 1976,* and public management journals. Co-editor, *Municipal Year Book,* 1934-67; *Public Management,* managing editor, 1929-56, editor, 1956-67.

SIDELIGHTS: Nolting has made more than twenty trips to Europe since 1953, and he spent three months in the South Pacific and Southeast Asia, 1969.

BIOGRAPHICAL/CRITICAL SOURCES: Public Management, June, 1968.

* * *

NOONAN, Lowell G(erald) 1922-

PERSONAL: Born February 11, 1922, in San Francisco, Calif.; son of Gerald F. (in construction industry) and Claire E. (Lando) Noonan; married Mary J. Westfall, September 2, 1949; children: Claire E., Louise L. *Education:* San Francisco State College (now University), A.B., 1944; Stanford University, M.A., 1946; University of California, Berkeley, Ph.D., 1951. *Home:* 20444 Acre St., Canoga Park, Calif. 91306. *Office:* Department of Political Science, California State University, Northridge, Calif. 91324.

CAREER: Pennsylvania State University, University Park, instructor in political science, 1948-49; University of Southern California, Los Angeles, associate professor of political science, 1949-60; California State University, Northridge, professor of political science, 1960—. *Military service:* U.S. Army, field artillery and military police, 1942-45. *Member:* American Political Science Association, Western Political Science Association. *Awards, honors:* Fund for the Advancement of Education, fellow, 1952-53; Fulbright faculty scholar in France, 1957-58; Fulbright lecturer at University of Innsbruck (Austria), 1966-67; Creative Scholarship, California State Colleges, 1970-71.

WRITINGS: (Contributor) Clifford A. L. Rich, editor, *European Politics and Government: A Comparative Approach,* Ronald, 1962; *France: The Politics of Continuity in Change,* Holt, 1970. Contributor to *Journal of Politics, Western Political Quarterly, World Affairs Quarterly,* and other journals.

WORK IN PROGRESS: French politics and government.

* * *

NORDHOLM, Harriet 1912-

PERSONAL: Born December 7, 1912, in Red Wing, Minn.; daughter of Harry N. (an engineer) and Margretha (Von Bargen) Nordholm. *Education:* MacPhail College, B.M., 1934; summer graduate study at University of Minnesota and University of Colorado, 1946-48; Northwestern University, M.M., 1950. *Politics:* Republican. *Religion:* Lutheran. *Home:* 5001 Alhambra Cir., Coral Gables, Fla. 33146. *Office:* M319C, University of Miami, Coral Gables, Fla. 33124.

CAREER: Music teacher and supervisor at Minn. public schools in Red Wing, 1934-36, Windom, 1936-40, Montevideo, 1940-41, and Austin, 1941-51; Michigan State University, East Lansing, assistant professor of music education, 1951-56; Boston University, Boston, Mass., associate professor of music education, 1956-57; University of Miami, Coral Gables, Fla., professor of music education, 1957—. Summer guest lecturer at University of Minnesota, University of Wisconsin, Northwestern University, and other universities. *Member:* Music Educators National Conference, Florida Music Education Association, Sigma Alpha Iota, Pi Kappa Lambda (national vice-president, 1970—), Kappa Delta Pi, P.E.O. Sisterhood.

WRITINGS: (With Carl O. Thompson) *Keys to Teaching Elementary Music,* Paul A. Schmitt Music Co., 1949; *Singing and Playing,* Mills Music, 1951; *The Christmas Story,* Mills Music, 1952; (with Ruth V. Bakewell) *Keys to Teaching Junior High School Music,* Paul A. Schmitt Music Co., 1953; (with James L. Mursell and others) *Music for Living,* two books, Silver Burdett, 1956; "Birchard Opera" series, twenty-four operas with guides, Summy-Birchard, 1966; *Singing in the Elementary Schools,* Prentice-Hall, 1966; (with Robert W. John) *Learning Music: Musicianship for the Elementary Classroom Teacher,* Prentice-Hall, 1970. Contributor to music education journals.

WORK IN PROGRESS: Humanities in the Elementary School.

AVOCATIONAL INTERESTS: International travel, reading, bridge.†

* * *

NORLING, Bernard 1924-

PERSONAL: Born February 23, 1924, in Hunters, Wash.; son of Thomas Frederick and Catherine (Lucey) Norling; married Mary Pupo (a librarian), January 31, 1948. *Education:* Gonzago University, B.A., 1948; Bard College, student, 1943-44; Hamilton College, student, 1944; Washington & Lee University, student, 1945; University of Notre Dame, M.A., 1949, Ph.D., 1955. *Home:* 504 East Pokagon, South Bend, Ind. 46617. *Office:* Department of History, University of Notre Dame, Notre Dame, Ind. 46556.

CAREER: University of Notre Dame, Notre Dame, Ind., instructor, 1950-55, assistant professor, 1955-61, associate professor, 1961-75, professor of history, 1975—, assistant chairman of department, 1965-67, 1968-71, acting chairman, 1967-68. *Military service:* U.S. Army, Medical Corps, 1943-46; became sergeant. *Member:* American Historical Association, Catholic Historical Association, Midwestern Conference on British Studies, Indiana Academy of the Social Sciences. *Awards, honors:* Thomas Madden Award for outstanding teacher of freshmen, University of Notre Dame, 1968.

WRITINGS: Towards a Better Understanding of History, University of Notre Dame Press, 1960; *Timeless Problems in History,* University of Notre Dame Press, 1970; (with Charles Poinsatte) *Understanding History through the American Experience,* University of Notre Dame Press, 1976. Contributor to *Collier's Encyclopedia* and *Catholic Encyclopedia;* contributor of articles and reviews to *Review of Politics, Catholic Historical Review, Dusquesne Review, Mid-America, Ave Maria, St. Louis Globe-Democrat, History Teacher.*

WORK IN PROGRESS: Medical history.

SIDELIGHTS: Bernard Norling's primary interests are medical and military history, with special reference to modern Europe, and historiography, the subject of his three published works. He told *CA:* "I have always been interested in history, mostly from idle curiosity, I suppose. Once I began teaching, I became quite interested in that, particularly in how to improve the quality of my own performances since much college and university teaching is not done with either remarkable interest or skill. To many students history is dull or meaningless or both, mostly because they have never had any but 4th-rate courses in the subject. I have always been eager to remedy this, insofar as any one person can."

NORMAN, Adrian R(oger) D(udley) 1938-

PERSONAL: Born October 10, 1938, in Alverstoke, Hampshire, England; son of Edward Dudley (a captain in the Royal Navy) and Aileen L. (Piper) Norman; married Katherine Redwood, September 22, 1962; children: Roger H., Fiona M. *Education:* Clare College, Cambridge, B.A., 1962, M.A., 1966; Columbia University, M.B.A., 1967. *Politics:* Tory. *Religion:* Atheist. *Home:* Bramble House, Bramble Lane, Clanfield, Portsmouth PO8 ORT, England. *Agent:* Curtis Brown Ltd., 1 Craven Hill, London W2 3EW, England.

CAREER: Atomic Weapons Research Establishment, Aldermaston, England, engineer officer, 1957-63; International Business Machines Ltd., London, England, systems engineer, 1964-69; L. Messel & Co. (stockbrokers), London, computer manager, 1969-71; consultant, Interbank Research Organisation, 1971-73; Arthur D. Little Ltd., London, management sciences consultant, 1973—. *Member:* British Institute of Management (associate member), British Computer Society (fellow), Beta Gamma Sigma.

WRITINGS: (With James Martin) *The Computerized Society,* Prentice-Hall, 1970. Contributing editor, *Handbook of Security,* 1975. Co-author of British Broadcasting Corp. television program, "The Invasion of Privacy."

WORK IN PROGRESS: Computer Assisted Crime, for McGraw-Hill (England).

BIOGRAPHICAL/CRITICAL SOURCES: Observer Review, January 3, 1971.

*   *   *

NORMAN, Maxwell H(erbert) 1917-

PERSONAL: Born July 27, 1917, in New York, N.Y.; married Enid Somers Kass, December 24, 1948; children: Seth Michael, Tod Howard. *Education:* City College (now City College of the City University of New York), student, 1935-37; Ohio University, B.A., 1947; Arizona State University, M.A., 1955. *Politics:* Democrat. *Home:* 170 Diana, Apt. 34, Leucadia, Calif. 92024.

CAREER: U.S. Air Force, Williams Air Force Base, Academic Training Department, Chandler, Arizona, director of Navigation Section, 1951-55; Young Construction Company, Scottsdale, Arizona, vice-president of marketing, 1956-61; Phoenix College, Phoenix, Ariz., director of Reading Center, 1964-75. *Military service:* U.S. Army Air Forces, 1941-45; became first lieutenant; received Air Medal with three oak-leaf clusters and Distinguished Flying Cross. *Member:* National Education Association, International Reading Association, American Association of University Professors, Desert Area Reading Council (board member), Arizona Education Association.

WRITINGS: Successful Reading: Key to Our Dynamic Society, Holt, 1968, 2nd edition, 1975; *Reading Effectively,* Holt, 1969, 2nd edition, 1976; *How to Read and Study for Success at College,* Holt, 1971; (editor) *College Students Look at the 21st Century,* Winthrop Publishing, 1972; *Dimensions of the Future: Alternatives for Tomorrow,* Holt, 1974.

BIOGRAPHICAL/CRITICAL SOURCES: Arizona Republic, July 23, 1969.

*   *   *

NORTON, Joseph L(ouis) 1918-

PERSONAL: Born September 6, 1918, in Albany, N.Y.; son of Arden L. and Jessie (Van Schaick) Norton; married Ruth P. McCarthy (a nurse educator), April 5, 1947; children: Deborah J. (Mrs. Ira Colby). *Education:* St. Lawrence University, B.A. (cum laude), 1940, M.A., 1941; Syracuse University, Ph.D., 1950. *Home:* 10 Eberle Rd., Latham, N.Y. 12110. *Office:* 220 School of Education, State University of New York at Albany, 1400 Washington Ave., Albany, N.Y. 12222.

CAREER: St. Lawrence University, Canton, New York, assistant to dean in placement, 1940-41; underwriter trainee in Boston, Mass., 1941-42; public school teacher in Tannersville, N.Y., 1946; Syracuse University, Syracuse, N.Y., teaching assistant, 1947-49; Michigan State University, East Lansing, assistant professor of psychology and counselor, 1949-51; Knox College, Galesburg, Ill., associate professor of psychology and director of Counseling and Placement, 1951-53; Alfred University, Alfred, N.Y., professor of educational psychology, 1953-63; State University of New York at Albany, professor of education, 1963—. Visiting professor at Syracuse University, 1953, University of Wyoming, 1958, Utah State University, 1961, Central Washington State College, 1961, and University of British Columbia, 1966. Member of board of managers, New York State Congress of Parents and Teachers, 1952-62; Albany County Mental Health Association, vice-president, 1968-71, member of board of directors. Consultant, Bureau of Appeals, Social Security Administration, United States Office of Health, Education and Welfare, 1962-69. *Military service:* U.S. Army, Corps of Engineers, 1942-45; became captain.

MEMBER: American Psychological Association (fellow), American Personnel and Guidance Association, American Association of University Professors, National Gay Task Force (secretary, 1976—), Association of Counselor Educators of New York (secretary, 1964-66), New York State Personnel and Guidance Association (vice-president for committees, 1968-69; president, 1970-71), Psychological Association of Northeastern New York, Sigma Xi, Phi Beta Kappa.

WRITINGS: (Contributor) Raymond G. Kuhlen and George G. Thompson, editors, *Psychological Studies of Human Development,* Appleton, 1952; (contributor) Gail F. Farwell and H. J. Peters, editors, *Guidance Readings for Counselors,* Rand McNally, 1960; (with Paul F. Hooker) *Some Characteristics of Four Year College Students, Junior College Students, and Drop-Outs: A Summary* (pamphlet), Bureau of Guidance, New York State Education Department (Albany), 1968; (editor) *On the Job,* Doubleday, 1971; (contributor) Herman J. Peters and James C. Hansen, editors, *Vocational Guidance and Career Development,* Macmillan, 1971. Contributor to *Vocational Guidance Quarterly, Journal of Counseling Psychology, Personnel and Guidance Journal, Journal of Genetic Psychology, New York Parent-Teacher,* and other journals. Editor, American College Personnel Association's *Personnel-O-Gram,* 1955-56.

AVOCATIONAL INTERESTS: Skiing.

*   *   *

NOVOGROD, R(eevan) Joseph 1916-

PERSONAL: Born August 10, 1916, in Providence, R.I.; son of David and Lillian (Asher) Novogrod. *Education:* Brown University, A.B., 1938, M.A.T., 1960; Harvard University, M.A., 1949; New York University, Ph.D., 1966; John Jay College of Criminal Justice of the City University of New York, M.A. candidate, 1971—. *Politics:*

Independent. *Religion:* Judaism. *Home:* 135 Hillside Ave., Providence, R.I. 02906; and 27 Monroe Pl., Brooklyn Heights, N.Y. 11201. *Office:* Department of Public Administration, Long Island University, Brooklyn, N.Y. 11201.

CAREER: Formerly worked for city, state, and federal agencies in fields of personnel management, organizational analysis, and general administrative operations; Long Island University, Brooklyn, N.Y., instructor, 1960-61, assistant professor, 1961-67, associate professor, 1967-73, professor of public administration, 1973—, director of criminal justice programs, 1976. Consultant to governor of Rhode Island on state prison system, 1972, and to Rhode Island Department of Community Affairs. *Member:* American Society for Public administration. *Awards, honors:* Founders Day Award, New York University, 1966.

WRITINGS: (With Marshall E. Dimock and Gladys O. Dimock) *Casebook in Public Administration,* Holt, 1969. Contributor to *Collier's Yearbook;* contributor to *Federal Probation* and other journals.

WORK IN PROGRESS: Crime and Punishment in America: Rhetoric and Reality.

* * *

NUTTALL, Jeff   1933-
(Peter Church, Homoras)

PERSONAL Born July 8, 1933, in Clitheroe, Lancashire, England; son of Kenneth (a teacher) and Hilda (Addison) Nuttall; married Jane Louch, July, 1954; children: Sara, Daniel, Toby, Timmy Willy. *Education:* Graduated from Herford School of Art, 1951, and Bath Academy of Art, 1953. *Politics:* Anarchist. *Religion:* "Dionysian." *Home:* 17 West Croft, Wyke, Bradford, Yorkshire, England. *Office:* Leeds College of Art, Leeds, Yorkshire, England.

CAREER: Teacher in secondary modern schools in England, 1956-68; Bradford College of Art, Bradford, England, lecturer in fundamental studies department, 1968-70; Leeds College of Art, Leeds, England, lecturer in fine arts, 1970—. Has worked as a writer, painter, cartoonist, jazz band trumpeter and pianist; in the forefront of the London Underground of the late 1950's and early 1960's, edited a mimeographed literary journal, *My Own Mag.* Participant in various political campaigns, especially in the British Campaign for Nuclear Disarmament. *National service:* Royal Army Education Corps.

WRITINGS—Poetry: (With Keith Musgrove) *The Limbless Virtuoso,* Writers Forum, 1963; *Songs Sacred and Secular,* privately printed, 1964; *Pieces of Poetry,* Coptic Press, 1965; *Poems I Want to Forget,* Turret Books, 1965; *Journals,* Unicorn Bookshop, 1968; (with Alan Jackson and William Wantling) *Penguin Modern Poets 12,* Penguin (Harmondsworth), 1968; *Love Poems,* Unicorn Bookshop, 1969; *Poems 1963-69,* Fulcrum Press, 1970; *Selected Poems,* Horizon Press, 1970; *Objects,* Trigram, 1976; *Sun Barbs,* Poet and Peasant, 1976.

Prose: *Come Back Sweet Prince* (novelette), Writers Forum, 1966; *The Case of Isobel and the Bleeding Foetus* (fiction), Beach Books Text and Documents, 1967; *Mr. Watkins Got Drunk and Had to Be Carried Home* (fiction), Writers Forum, 1968; *Oscar Christ and the Immaculate Conception* (fiction), Writers Forum, 1968; *Bomb Culture* (social criticism), MacGibbon & Kee, 1968, Delacorte, 1969; *Pig* (fiction), Fulcrum Press, 1969; *The Fox's Lair,* Aloes, 1974; *The House Party* (fiction), Basilike, 1975; *Man, Not Man,* Unicorn, 1975; *The Anatomy of My Fath-*

er's Corpse, Basilike, 1975; *Fatty Feedemalls Secret Self,* Jack Press, 1975; *Snipe's Spinster,* Calder & Boyars, 1975. Scriptwriter for The People Show, an Underground theatre group which has appeared throughout the United Kingdom. Contributor of poetry and prose to various underground newspapers and magazines.

WORK IN PROGRESS: Mandy's Book, poetry; *Common Factors and Vulgar Factions,* a social study, for Routledge & Kegan Paul; *The Patriarchs; The Gold Hole; Love and Death and Arthur Twist,* portrait of comedian Frank Randle, for Routledge & Kegan Paul; *Applied Poetry,* two volumes.

SIDELIGHTS: A reviewer for *Newsweek* regards *Bomb Culture* as a "guidebook" to the Underground, one in which "war, violence, brutality and destructive imagination are the central energies Nuttall locates in his inventory of postwar theater, music, painting, poetry and popular culture." Lewis Bates of *Punch,* on the other hand, believes the book is too esoteric for the "common reader," calling it "an invaluable record of recent frenzies from the inside." "To Nuttall and the children of the Bomb," writes George Thayer of the *Washington Post,* "the past is irrelevant and the future nonexistent: The world is so impossible to them that the only reality is now—instant gratification and wisdom through the use of drugs, withdrawal into anarchy and mysticism." Thayer faults Nuttall for his too subjective listing of Allen Ginsberg, William Burroughs, R. D. Laing, Tim Leary, Criton Tomazos, Alexander Trocchi and The Beatles as "the major artistic impulses of the new culture"; he states rather that these have been major influences on Nuttall himself.

Nuttall has perhaps been most closely associated with William Burroughs. According to a 1967 *Life* article by Barry Farrell entitled "The Other Culture," *My Own Mag* was an important vehicle for beginning Underground writers and "the principal mouthpiece for William Burroughs." Nuttall was instrumental in publishing Burroughs' letters and experiments in "cut-up writing" in the early Underground days. Nuttall told Farrell in 1966: "'Burroughs, all of us—we're decaying men, for God's sake. We're all decaying, clearly. Playing around with drugs, playing around with every possible sexual deviation. . . . But the curious, impressive thing is that so many artists are able to go through these things as intelligent men—not as totally unprincipled sensual men. If you go through these things to some purpose, it can be even noble. It's as if, with your own rot, you refuel and invigorate—you fertilize this very scorched earth for those yet to come.'"

BIOGRAPHICAL/CRITICAL SOURCES: Life, February 17, 1967; *Punch,* November 27, 1968; *New Statesman,* November 29, 1968; *Books and Bookmen,* February, 1969; *London Magazine,* February, 1969, November, 1969; *Newsweek,* August 4, 1969; *Washington Post,* August 22, 1969; *Saturday Review,* August 23, 1969; *Poetry,* February, 1971.

* * *

OAKLEY, Don(ald G.)   1927-

PERSONAL: Born November 3, 1927, in Pittsburgh, Pa.; son of William Hageman (an accountant) and Mildred (Koerner) Oakley; married Gertrude Acklin, 1958; children: Glenn William. *Education:* Attended Carnegie Institute of Technology (now Carnegie-Mellon University), 1945-46; Western Reserve University (now Case Western Reserve University), B.A., 1951; University of Chicago, M.A., 1955. *Home:* 258 Parkview Dr., Aurora, Ohio 44202.

CAREER: Newspaper Enterprise Association, Cleveland, Ohio, and New York, N.Y., 1957—, chief editorial writer, 1964—. *Military service:* U.S. Army, Paratroops, 1946-47. *Awards, honors:* Meeman Award for newspaper series on conservation, 1964; Friends of American Writers Award, 1971, for *Two Muskets for Washington.*

WRITINGS: Two Muskets for Washington (juvenile novel), Bobbs-Merrill, 1970.

*   *   *

OCHS, Robert J. 1930-

PERSONAL: Surname rhymes with "folks"; born January 22, 1930, in Wichita, Kan.; son of Leo A. (a personnel manager) and Helen (Phillips) Ochs. *Education:* Attended University of Louvain, 1951-52; Loyola University, Chicago, Ill., M.A., 1958; University of Innsbruck, Licentiate in Theology, 1962; Catholic Institute of Paris, Doctorate in Theology, 1969. *Home:* 795 Colusa, El Cerrito, Calif. 94530. *Office:* 1735 LeRoy, Berkeley, Calif. 94709.

CAREER: Roman Catholic priest, member of Society of Jesus (Jesuits), 1952—; Jesuit School of Theology, Chicago, Ill., assistant professor of theology, 1968-73; Jesuit School of Theology, Berkeley, Calif., assistant professor of theology, 1976—. *Member:* American Academy of Religion. *Awards, honors:* Fulbright scholarship in Belgium, 1951-52; American Association of Theological Schools grant, 1970, 1971.

WRITINGS: (Translator with others from the German) Karl Rahner and Joseph Ratzinger, *The Episcopate and the Primacy,* Herder & Herder, 1962; *The Death in Every Now,* Sheed, 1969; *God Is More Present than You Think,* Paulist/Newman, 1971.

WORK IN PROGRESS: A book on the discernment of spirits, using exercises and insights from various Eastern and Western spiritual disciplines.

SIDELIGHTS: Robert J. Ochs told *CA:* "So many people complain that they cannot say what they mean, but the real difficulty is that people are not able to mean what they say. Actually, few of us have any idea what we mean, what we are meant to say. To search out this meaning is to embark on a mystic quest. Only at the end can we say something will hear vast quantities of true words spoken, without being nourished by any of them, because nobody means them. We can scarcely imagine how they would sound meant."

*   *   *

O'CONNELL, Daniel Patrick 1924-

PERSONAL: Born July 7, 1924, in New Zealand; son of Daniel Patrick (a civil servant) and Magdalen (Roche) O'Connell; married Renate von Kleist-Drenow, September 21, 1957; children: Maurice, Maria-Christina, Sean, Mary-Caroline, Patrick. *Education:* University of Auckland, B.A. and LL.B., 1946, LL.M., 1947; Trinity College, Cambridge, Ph.D., 1951. *Religion:* Roman Catholic. *Home:* Powder Hill House, Boars Hill, Oxford, England. *Office:* All Souls College, Oxford University, Oxford, England.

CAREER: University of Adelaide, Adelaide, South Australia, professor of international law and diplomacy, 1953-72; Oxford University, Oxford, England, Chichele Professor of Public International Law and fellow of All Souls College, 1972—. Visiting lecturer or professor at Harvard University, Georgetown University, Yale University, and Universities of London, Manchester, Paris, Geneva, and Vienna. Consultant to several Pacific, African, and Caribbean governments. *Military service:* Royal Australian Naval Reserve;

present rank, commander. *Member:* Institut de Droit International (associate), International Law Association, International Association of Cultural Freedom. *Awards, honors:* Knight of Grace and Devotion, Order of Malta; LL.D. from Cambridge University, 1969; D.C.L. from Oxford University, 1974.

WRITINGS: The Law of State Succession, Cambridge University Press, 1956; *International Law,* Oceana, 1965; (editor) *International Law in Australia,* Stevens & Sons, for Australian Institute of International Affairs, 1965; *State Succession in Municipal Law and International Law,* Cambridge University Press, 1967; *Richlieu,* Weidenfeld & Nicolson, 1968, World Publishing, 1969; *Opinions on Imperial Constitutional Law,* Law Book Company of Australasia, 1970; *The Influence of Laws on Seapower,* Manchester University Press, 1975.

WORK IN PROGRESS: Research in seventeenth-century diplomatic history and in law of the sea.

BIOGRAPHICAL/CRITICAL SOURCES: Observer Review, May 19, 1968; *Punch,* June 26, 1968; *Times Literary Supplement,* September 19, 1968; *Best Sellers,* April 1, 1969; *Books and Bookmen,* July, 1969.

*   *   *

O'CONNOR, John (Morris) 1937-

PERSONAL: Born September 21, 1937, in Evanston, Ill.; son of John Morris (an attorney) and Clare (Merrick) O'Connor; married Mary Bittner, December 31, 1960 (divorced); married Miranda Ind, August 14, 1971; children: Emily Bittner. *Education:* Attended Georgetown University, 1955-56; Cornell University, B.A., 1959; Harvard University, M.A., 1962, Ph.D., 1965. *Home:* 2450 Overlook Rd., Cleveland Heights, Ohio 44106. *Office:* Department of Philosophy, Case Western Reserve University, Cleveland, Ohio 44106.

CAREER: Vassar College, Poughkeepsie, N.Y., instructor, 1964-66, assistant professor of philosophy, 1966-68; Case Western Reserve University, Cleveland, Ohio, assistant professor, 1968-70, associate professor of philosophy, 1970—. *Member:* American Philosophical Association. *Awards, honors:* Woodrow Wilson fellow, 1959.

WRITINGS: (Editor with Frank Tillman and Bernard Berofsky) *Introductory Philosophy,* Harper, 1967, 2nd edition, 1971; (editor) *Modern Materialism,* Harcourt, 1969; (editor with Samuel Gorovitz and others) *Moral Problems in Medicine,* Prentice-Hall, 1976.

WORK IN PROGRESS: Determinism and moral responsibility.

AVOCATIONAL INTERESTS: Sports, crossword and jigsaw puzzles, and music (organized Committee to Preserve the Cleveland Orchestra).

*   *   *

O'DANIEL, Janet 1921-

PERSONAL: Born January 17, 1921, in Ithaca, N.Y.; daughter of Howard Leighton (a county clerk) and Edith (Clark) O'Daniel; married Louis E. Cicchetti (proprietor of a music store), May 9, 1941; children: Amy, Nancy. *Education:* Attended Ithaca College. *Politics:* Democrat. *Home:* 89 Birchwood Ave., Nyack, N.Y. 10960. *Agent:* Roberta Pryor, International Creative Management, 40 West 57th St., New York, N.Y. 10019.

CAREER: Ithaca Journal, Ithaca, N.Y., reporter, 1939-41;

Altoona Tribune, Altoona, Pa., reporter and then city editor, 1942-44.

WRITINGS: (With Lillian Ressler) *Touchstone,* Rinehart, 1947; (with Ressler) *The City beyond Devil's Gate,* Random House, 1950; *O Genesee,* Lippincott, 1957; *The Cliff Hangers,* Lippincott, 1961; *Garrett's Crossing* (juvenile), Lippincott, 1969; *A Part for Addie* (juvenile), Houghton, 1974.

WORK IN PROGRESS: A novel about early New York City.

SIDELIGHTS: Janet O'Daniel told *CA:* "I've written for both adults and children, but the things I've done for children were especially fun. I always felt I was doing them more for myself than for anybody else. Right now I've just finished a story about a cat named Macduff. It may never see the light of public print, but I have it, so to speak. It's mine, and Macduff is my cat, no matter what, because I've created him. Which makes me reflect that probably nothing is going to turn out really great unless it pleases you, the author, first of all. You have to satisfy yourself and then hope that readers will see it your way. So when anybody asks me what age my books are written for, I have to say, 'Oh, about my age.'"

O'Daniel continued: "I always like to work in the morning when thoughts are fresh and unscrambled. I do this upstairs in a little room that looks out over the Hudson River. But late in the day when dinner is cooking on the stove, I sit at the kitchen table and think about what the next day's work is going to be, and make notes and plan ahead. I have three cats that help me with this, and an old beagle."

* * *

O'DAY, Edward Francis 1925-

PERSONAL: Born April 27, 1925, in Portsmouth, Va.; son of Edward Francis (a career Marine officer) and Marian (Herring) O'Day; married Kay M. Allison, March 26, 1961; children: Danny, Mike, Kevin, Sean, Brenda. *Education:* University of Florida, B.S., 1952, M.A., 1954, Ph.D., 1956. *Home:* 3106 Via Luiseno, Alpine, Calif. 92001. *Office:* Department of Psychology, San Diego State University, San Diego, Calif. 92182.

CAREER: Veteran's Administration Hospital, Gulfport, Miss., clinical psychologist, 1954-55; Veteran's Administration Mental Hygiene Clinic, Miami, Fla., clinical psychologist, 1955-56; Bell Telephone Laboratories, Inc., Murray Hill, N.J., member of technical staff, 1956; Foundation for Research on Human Behavior, Ann Arbor, Mich., program associate, 1956-57; San Diego State University, San Diego, Calif., assistant professor, 1957-62, associate professor, 1962-66, professor of psychology, 1966—. Director of research project in psychology, San Diego State University, 1958-60. Training consultant, U.S. Naval Weapons Center, China Lake, Calif., 1961-66. *Military service:* U.S. Maritime Service, 1943-48. *Member:* American Psychological Association, Psychometric Society.

WRITINGS: Assessing Managerial Potential, Foundation for Research on Human Behavior, University of Michigan, 1958; *Physical Quantities and Units: A Self Instructional Programmed Manual,* Prentice-Hall, 1967; *Programmed Instruction and How to Use It in Educational Applications,* Prentice-Hall, 1968; (with others) *Programmed Instruction: Techniques and Trends,* Appleton, 1970.

WORK IN PROGRESS: Psychology: Principles and Implications.

ODIER, Daniel 1945-

PERSONAL: Born May 17, 1945, in Geneva, Switzerland; son of J. P. (a businessman) and Doris (Kenny) Odier; married Nell Gotkovsky (a violinist). *Education:* Ecole Superieure de Journalisme, Paris, diplome, 1966; Ecole des Hautes Etudes Internationales, Paris, diplome, 1967; Ecole des Hautes Etudes Sociales, Paris, diplome, 1967. *Religion:* Buddhist. *Home:* 9 Grande Rue, 78610 Auffargis, France.

CAREER: Journal de Geneve, London, England, art critic, 1967-68; free-lance writer for *Tribune De Geneve* and *Gazette De Lausanne,* Geneva, Switzerland, and for *Le Magazine Litteraire* and *La Quinzaine Litteraire,* Paris, France, 1968—. Lecturer on literary subjects.

WRITINGS: Transparences (poems), Perret-Gentil, 1964; *Le soleil dans la poche* (poems), Perret-Gentil, 1965; *Rouge,* Editions 317, 1967; (with William Burroughs) *Entretiens,* P. Belfond, 1969, translation by Odier published as *The Job,* Grove, 1970; *Sculptures tantriques du Nepal,* Editions du Rocher, 1971; *Le Voyage de John O'Flaherty* (novel), Seuil, 1972; *Les mystique orientales,* Denoel, 1972; *Nuit contre nuit* (poems), Oswald, 1972; *La Voie sauvage* (novel), Seuil, 1974; *Nirvana/Tao,* R. Laffont, 1974; *Nepal,* Seuil, 1975; *Ming* (novel), R. Laffont, 1976; *Splendor Solis* (novel), Stock, 1976; *L'annee du lievre* (novel), R. Laffont, 1978.

WORK IN PROGRESS: A novel about the history of the Swiss from the beginning to 1918 for R. Laffont.

SIDELIGHTS: Daniel Odier spent a year in meditation in a Tibetan monastery. He lives at present on a farm near Paris, but is always traveling. His major interest is music. Odier's work has been translated and published in numerous foreign editions. His novel *Le Voyage de John O'Flaherty* has been adapted for a motion picture.

BIOGRAPHICAL/CRITICAL SOURCES: New Yorker, July 18, 1970.

* * *

OEHSER, Paul H(enry) 1904-

PERSONAL: Surname is pronounced *O*-zher; born March 27, 1904, in Cherry Creek, N.Y.; son of Henry Christian (a farmer) and Agnes (Abbey) Oehser; married Grace M. Edgbert (an artist), October 4, 1927; children: Gordon Vincent, Richard Edgbert. *Education:* Greenville College, A.B., 1925; also studied at University of Iowa, summer, 1924, and took graduate courses at intervals at American University, 1925-30. *Politics:* Democrat. *Home:* 9012 Old Dominion Dr., McLean, Va. 22101. *Office:* National Geographic Society, Washington, D.C. 20036.

CAREER: U.S. Department of Agriculture, Bureau of Biological Survey, Washington, D.C., assistant editor, 1925-31; Smithsonian Institution, Washington, D.C., editor, U.S. National Museum, 1931-50, chief of Editorial Division, 1946-50, chief of Editorial and Publication Division and public relations officer, 1950-66; National Geographic Society, Washington, D.C., editor of scientific publications, 1966—. Member of board of directors, Greater Washington Educational Television Association, Westminster School, Annandale, Va., 1967—, and Horne of England, Ltd., 1967—.

MEMBER: Wilderness Society (member of governing council, 1964—; vice-president, 1976—), Thoreau Society (president, 1961), American Ornithologists' Union, Washington Academy of Sciences (fellow), Columbia Historical Society, Philosophical Society of Washington, Literary Society of Washington (corresponding secretary and treasurer,

1972—), Biological Society of Washington, Washington Biologists' Field Club (president, 1964-67), History of Science Club, Lake George (N.Y.) Historical Association, Arlington County (Va.) Historical Society, Cosmos Club (president, 1974), Palaver Club. *Awards, honors:* Cosmos Club Distinguished Service Award, 1968.

WRITINGS: Sons of Science: The Story of the Smithsonian Institution and Its Leaders, Henry Schuman, 1949, reprinted, Greenwood Press, 1968; *Fifty Poems,* Sherwood House (Washington, D.C.), 1954; *The Smithsonian Institution,* Praeger, 1970. Editor, *Proceedings of the Eighth American Scientific Congress,* 1940, twelve volumes; general editor, *The United States Encyclopedia of History,* 1967-68. Contributor of articles, reviews, and verse to journals, encyclopedias, and newspapers. Managing editor, *Journal of the Washington Academy of Sciences,* 1939-59; editor, *Arlington Historical Magazine,* 1939-62, and *Bulletin* of the Cosmos Club, 1951-69.

WORK IN PROGRESS: The Witch of Scrapfaggot Green and Other Folderol, a collection of light verse, essays, fables, epitaphs, and country poems.

*   *   *

OESTERREICHER, John M.   1904-

PERSONAL: Born February 2, 1904, in Stadt Liebau, Austria (Stadt Liebau is now in Czechoslovakia); naturalized U.S. citizen; son of Nathan and Ida (Zelenka) Oesterreicher. *Education:* University of Vienna, medical student, 1922-24, later theology student; University of Graz, Lic.theol., 1928, State Certificate, 1936. *Home:* Seton Hall University, South Orange, N.J. 07079. *Office:* Institute of Judaeo-Christian Studies, Seton Hall University, South Orange, N.J. 07079.

CAREER: Jewish-Catholic scholar and Roman Catholic priest; appointed papal chamberlain with title of monsignor, 1961, appointed honorary prelate, 1967; Waehringer Maedchen Realgymnasium, Vienna, Austria, professor of religion, 1935-38; Manhattanville College of the Sacred Heart, New York, N.Y., research professor of sacred theology, 1944-53; Seton Hall University, Institute of Judaeo-Christian Studies, South Orange, N.J., director, 1953—. Danforth lecturer at Columbia University, 1962, and University of Miami, 1963; also has lectured in Germany, Italy, England, and Austria. Secretariat for Christian Unity, Rome, consultor, 1961-68; member of subcommittee for Catholic-Jewish Concerns, Ecumenical and Interreligious Affairs of Archdiocese of Newark, N.J.

MEMBER: Catholic Biblical Association, Society of Biblical Literature, Catholic Theological Society, Catholic Commission on Intellectual and Cultural Affairs, Council on Religion and International Affairs, American Professors for Peace in the Middle East. *Awards, honors:* Brotherhood Award of Congregation Agudath Achim, Taunton, Mass., 1963; LL.D., Incarnate Word College, 1967; D.H.L., Canisius College, 1968.

WRITINGS: Racisme-Antisemitisme-Antichristianisme, Editions de la Maison Francaise (New York), 1943; *Walls Are Crumbling: Seven Jewish Philosophers Discover Christ,* foreword by Jacques Maritain, Devin-Adair, 1952 (published in England as *Seven Jewish Philosophers Discover Christ,* Hollis & Carter, 1953), abridged edition published as *Five in Search of Wisdom,* University of Notre Dame Press, 1967; (translator) Richard Baumann, *To See Peter: A Lutheran Minister's Journey to the Eternal City,* McKay, 1953; (with others) *The Gospel of Jesus the Christ,* Seton Hall

University Press, 1962; *Der Papst und die Juden* (booklet), Paulus Verlag, 1962; *The Israel of God,* Prentice-Hall, 1963; *Auschwitz, the Christian and the Council,* Palm Publishers, 1965; (contributor) *Concilium,* Paulist Press, 1967; (contributor) *American Participation in the Second Vatican Council,* Sheed, 1967; *Der Baum und die Wurzel,* Herder (Freiburg), 1968; (contributor) *Commentary on the Documents of Vatican II,* Herder & Herder, 1969; *The Rediscovery of Judaism,* Institute of Judaeo-Christian Studies, Seton Hall University, 1971.

Editor and author of preface: Edward Flannery, *The Anguish of the Jews,* Macmillan, 1965; Edward Synan, *The Popes and the Jews in the Middle Ages,* Macmillan, 1965.

Author of preface: Justus George Lawler, *The Christian Imagination,* Newman, 1955; Rene Aigrain and Ome Englebert, *Prophecy Fulfilled,* McKay, 1958; Claude Tresmontant, *Essay on Hebrew Thought* (translation of *Essai sur la pensee hebraique*), Desclee, 1960.

General editor and contributor, *The Bridge: A Yearbook of Judaeo-Christian Studies,* Herder & Herder, for Institute of Judaeo-Christian Studies, Volume I, 1955, Volume II, 1957, Volume III, 1959, Volume IV, 1962, Volume V, 1970. Writer of other Institute publications; also author of four Institute Teshuvah papers, *Salute to Israel, Internationalization of Jerusalem?, Jerusalem the Free,* and *The Anatomy of Contempt.* Contributor to *Die Erfuellung, Dublin Review, Orate Fratres, Pax Romana, America, Today's Family,* and other theological and secular periodicals.

WORK IN PROGRESS: Jesus and the Rabbis.

SIDELIGHTS: Oesterreicher's *Walls Are Crumbling* has been published in six countries, with translations in French, Dutch, Spanish, and Japanese.

BIOGRAPHICAL/CRITICAL SOURCES: St. Jude, June 1960; *New York Post,* December 14, 1964; *Advocate,* October 7, 1965.

*   *   *

OETTINGER, Elmer R(osenthal, Jr.)   1913-

PERSONAL: Born November 24, 1913, in Wilson, N.C.; son of Elmer Rosenthal (a merchant) and Pearl (Lichtenstein) Oettinger; married Mary Elizabeth Brown (a social worker), September 22, 1940; children: Elmer Rosenthal III, Kenneth Brown. *Education:* University of North Carolina, A.B., 1934, LL.B., 1939, M.A., 1952, Ph.D., 1966; Columbia University, graduate study, 1935. *Home:* 58 Oakwood Dr., Chapel Hill, N.C. 27514. *Office:* Institute of Government, University of North Carolina, Chapel Hill, N.C. 27514.

CAREER: Attorney in private practice in Wilson, N.C., and radio and television news commentator in Raleigh, N.C., 1940-42; American Institute of Banking, Washington, D.C., instructor in commercial law, 1941-42; attorney in private practice in Wilson, N.C., 1946; radio and television commentator and news director in Raleigh, N.C., 1946-52; University of North Carolina at Chapel Hill, instructor in English, 1952-56, lecturer in department of radio, television, and motion pictures, 1956-60, instructor in government, 1960-66, associate professor of public law and government, 1966-73, professor of public law and government, 1973—, assistant director of Institute of Government, 1962—. Member of Operating Reserve, U.S. Information Agency, 1957—; chairman, North Carolina Bench-Bar-Press-Broadcasters Law Enforcement Committee, 1965—, and special committee on Uniform Privacy Act, National Conference of Commissioners on Uniform State Laws, 1976—. Task Force on Criminal Justice and the Public, chairman, 1965—, consultant, 1969-71; member of Governor's Council on Aging, 1971—, Governor's Study Commission on Automobile Insurance, 1971, 1973—, and North Carolina Youth Advisory Council, 1976—.. *Military service:* U.S. Naval Reserve, active duty, 1952-55; became lieutenant.

MEMBER: American Judicature Society, Society of Cinema Studies (national secretary, 1960-61), American Association of University Professors, Modern Language Association of America, North Carolina Press Association, North Carolina Bar Association, Chapel Hill-Durham Torch Club (president, 1965-66).

WRITINGS: Copyright Law and Copying Practices, Institute of Government, University of North Carolina, 1968; (editor) *Administration of Criminal Justice,* Southern Regional Education Board, 1968; *The News Media and the Courts,* Bench-Bar-Press, 1969, 2nd edition, 1972; (with Edwin Maurice Braswell) *Color Me Straight: Fables on Life, Law, and Justice,* North Carolina News Media–Administration of Justice Council, 1972; (with Braswell) *Truths and Consequences: Fables on Life, Law, and Justice,* North Carolina News Media-Administration of Justice Council, 1972; (editor) *Cable Television in North Carolina,* Institute of Government, University of North Carolina, 1973. Author of plays, "Pied Piper," "Boxcar," "Nothing Ever Happened," "Designed for Justice," and "Picture Window." Contributor of many articles to law and other journals. Editor, *Popular Government* (publication of Institute of Government, University of North Carolina), 1962-74.

WORK IN PROGRESS: A handbook, *An Official's Guide to Parliamentary Procedure;* a novel, *The Dreamer;* another book, *The Shining Dark.*

* * *

OGDEN, Samuel R(obinson) 1896-

PERSONAL: Born July 19, 1896, in Elizabeth, N.J.; son of Samuel Robinson (a realtor) and Ella (Loney) Ogden; married Mary Campbell, January 21, 1921; children: Samuel Robinson III, Duncan G. *Education:* Swarthmore College, A.B., 1920; University of Grenoble, student, 1919. *Residence:* Landgrove, Vt. *Mailing address:* P.O. Londonderry, Vt. 05148.

CAREER: Worked in family real estate business in Elizabeth, N.J., 1920-29; since then has been a builder, teacher, blacksmith, town official, state legislator, and writer, living in Landgrove, Vt. Member of Vermont Legislature, 1935-47; former chairman of Vermont Development Commission; member of board of directors, New England Council. Civic posts include presidency of Vermont Symphony Association. *Military service:* U.S. Army, Infantry, World War I and World War II; became captain; received Croix de Guerre and Gold Star.

WRITINGS: How to Grow Food for Your Family, A. S. Barnes, 1942; *This Country Life,* A. S. Barnes, 1946; *The New England Vegetable Garden,* Countryman Press, 1957; *Vermont's Year* (verse), Tuttle, 1967; (editor) *America the Vanishing: Rural Life and the Price of Progress,* Stephen Green Press, 1969; *Step by Step to Organic Vegetable Growing,* Rodale Press, 1971; *Pan and Griddle Cakes,* Stephen Greene Press, 1973. Writer of weekly column, "Sparks from the Forge," for *Bennington Banner.* Contributing editor, *Vermont Life.*

WORK IN PROGRESS: A biography of Abraham Prescott.

AVOCATIONAL INTERESTS: Music and growing vegetables.

* * *

OH, John Kie-chiang 1930-

PERSONAL: Born November 1, 1930, in Seoul, Korea; son of Sung Jun and Duk Cho (Kim) Oh; married Bongwan Cho (an assistant professor in East Asian history), September 5, 1959; children: Jane, Marie, James. *Education:* Seoul National University, law student; Marquette University, B.S., 1957; Columbia University, additional study, 1957-58; Georgetown University, Ph.D., 1962. *Home:* 2231 West Apple Tree Rd., Milwaukee, Wis. 53209. *Office:* Political Science Department, Marquette University, Milwaukee, Wis. 53233.

CAREER: Korean Mission to United Nations, New York, N.Y., press attaché, 1957-58; College of St. Thomas, St. Paul, Minn., assistant professor of political science, 1962-66; Marquette University, Milwaukee, Wis., associate professor, 1966-71, professor of political science and chairman of department, 1971—. *Military service:* Republic of Korea Army, 1950-53; became captain. *Member:* American Political Science Association, Association for Asian Studies, International Studies Association, World Affairs Council, Midwest Conference on Asian Affairs (president, 1970-71), Midwest Political Science Association, Pi Sigma Alpha, Kappa Tau Alpha.

WRITINGS: Korea: Democracy on Trial, Cornell University Press, 1968. Contributor of articles and reviews to professional journals.

* * *

O'HARA, Charles E. 1912-

PERSONAL: Born August 6, 1912, in New York, N.Y.; son of James F. and Anna (Lehane) O'Hara; married Frances Schulz, June 19, 1940; children: William Tycho, Brendan Linus, Gregory Leo, Charles E., Jr., Martina. *Education:* St. Peter's College, A.B., 1934, M.S., 1936; New York University, M.S., 1938. *Religion:* Roman Catholic. *Home:* 284 Burns St., Forest Hills, N.Y. 11375.

CAREER: St. Peter's College, Jersey City, N.J., instructor in physics, 1934-38; New York (N.Y.) Police Department, with Detective Division, 1940-62; National Criminological Research Institute, New York, N.Y., director, 1965—. Director of training, Suburban Officers' Training School, Western Reserve University (now Case Western Reserve University), 1955-56. *Military service:* U.S. Air Force, 1952-55; became major; received Medal of Valor.

WRITINGS: (With James W. Osterburg) *An Introduction to Criminalistics,* Macmillan, 1949; *Fundamentals of Criminal Investigation,* C. C Thomas, 1956, 4th edition, 1976; *Photography in Law Enforcement,* Eastman Kodak Co., 1959; (with Harry Soederman and John Joseph O'Connell) *Modern Criminal Investigation,* 5th edition (not associated with earlier editions), Funk, 1961; (reviser) Burtis C. Bridges, *Practical Fingerprinting,* 2nd edition, Funk, 1963. Contributor to *Encyclopaedia Britannica.*

WORK IN PROGRESS: Application of information theory to criminal investigation; establishment of an organization or system to make available to indigent defendants in criminal cases the services of expert scientific witnesses.†

OKAMOTO, Shumpei 1932-

PERSONAL: Born January 2, 1932, in Japan; son of Fukumatsu and Satoki (Nakahira) Okamoto; married Ellen Begemann, July 1, 1961; children: Karl, Eugene. *Education:* Aoyama Gakuin University, B.A. (economics), 1954; Anderson College, B.A. (history), 1959; Columbia University, M.I.A., 1962, Certificate of East Asian Institute and Ph.D., 1969. *Home:* 6830 Wayne Ave., Philadelphia, Pa. 19119. *Office:* Department of History, Temple University, Philadelphia, Pa. 19122.

CAREER: Temple University, Philadelphia, Pa., associate professor of history, 1968—. Research associate of East Asian Institute, Columbia University, 1971-72. *Member:* American Historical Association, Association for Asian Studies, Japan Association for International Politics.

WRITINGS: The Japanese Oligarchy and the Russo-Japanese War, Columbia University Press, 1970; (editor with Dorothy Borg) *Pearl Harbor As History: Japanese-American Relations, 1931-1941,* Columbia University Press, 1973.

WORK IN PROGRESS: A book on the 1905 Peking Conference; a biography of Ishibashi Tanzan.

AVOCATIONAL INTERESTS: Music, travel.

*   *   *

OKONJO, Chukuka 1928-

PERSONAL: Born June 21, 1928, in Ogwashi-Uku, Nigeria; son of Adigwe and Mgbolie (Okocha) Okonjo; married Kamene Ofunne (a research fellow), July 12, 1953; children: Ngozi, Chukuemeka, Ikechukwu, Njideka, Chukuka, Jr., Onyema. *Education:* University of Ibadan, Diploma, 1949; University of London, B.Sc., 1951; University of Erlangen-Nuernberg, M.Sc. (mathematics) and M.Sc. (economics), 1960; University of Cologne, Dr.rer.nat., 1962. *Office:* Department of Economics, University of Nigeria, Nsukka, Nigeria.

CAREER: Ibadan Boys High School, Ibadan, Nigeria, principal and teacher of mathematics and science, 1952-55; University of Ibadan, Ibadan, lecturer, 1962-64, senior lecturer, 1964-67, director of Centre for Population Studies and of professional certificate course in statistics, 1966-67; University of Nigeria, Nsukka, senior lecturer in economics, 1967—, head of department, 1970—. Regional economic development adviser, United Nations Economic Commission for Africa, 1963. *Member:* Nigerian Economic Society (vice-president), German Mathematical Association, International Union for the Scientific Study of Population.

WRITINGS: (Contributor) P. C. Lloyd, A. L. Mabogunje, and B. Awe, editors, *The City of Ibaden,* Cambridge University Press, 1967; (editor with John Cope Caldwell and contributor) *The Population of Tropical Africa,* Columbia University Press, 1968. Contributor to African studies journals.

WORK IN PROGRESS: The Demographic Transition in Africa: The Process of Urbanisation; and *Economic Statistics of Nigeria: Location Theory and Indigenous Economics.*

SIDELIGHTS: Chukuka Okonjo has visited in the United States as well as in most countries of East, West, and North Africa and western Europe.†

*   *   *

OKPAKU, Joseph (Ohiomogben) 1943-

PERSONAL: Surname is pronounced Or-pah-koo; born March 24, 1943, in Lokoja, Nigeria; came to United States in 1962; son of Alfred (a postmaster) and Victoria Odakai (Johnson) Okpaku; married Sheila Rush (an attorney-at-law), July 18, 1971; children: Joseph Ohiomogben. *Education:* Northwestern University, B.S., 1965; Stanford University, M.S., 1966, Ph.D. candidate in dramatic literature and theatre history, 1969—; University of Warsaw, research fellow, 1969. *Politics:* None. *Home and office:* 444 Central Park W., New York, N.Y. 10025.

CAREER: Bemis Brothers, Inc., Minneapolis, Minn., efficiency analyst, 1965; Mobil Internationational, New York City, engineering intern, 1966; *Journal of the New African Literature and the Arts,* New York City, founder, editor, and publisher, 1966—; The Third Press-Joseph Okpaku Publishing Co., New York City, president and publisher, 1969—; Sarah Lawrence College, Bronxville, N.Y., associate professor of literature, 1970—. Instructor in African literature, Stanford University, 1969. *Member:* African Studies Association (member of executive board, 1971—), International P.E.N., National Writers Club. *Awards, honors:* BBC drama award, 1967, for "The Virtues of Adultery."

WRITINGS: "The Virtues of Adultery" (drama), first broadcast by British Broadcasting Corp., 1967; *Under the Iroko Tree* (novella), published in *Literary Review,* 1968; (with Verna Sadock) *Verdict!: The Exclusive Picture Story of the Trial of the Chicago 8* (drawings by Sadock, commentary by Okpaku), Third Press, 1970; (editor) *New African Literature and the Arts* (selections from *Journal of the New African Literature and the Arts),* Third Press, Volume I, 1970, Volume II, 1970, Volume III, 1973; (editor) *Nigeria, Dilemma of Nationhood: An African Analysis of the Biafran Conflict,* Greenwood Press, 1971; *Superfight Two: Joseph Muhammad Ali vs. Joe Frazer–The Exclusive Picture Story,* Third Press, in press. Also author of plays, "The Two Faces of Anirejouritse," 1965, "Born Astride the Grave," 1966, "The King's Son; or, After the Victory Was Lost," 1966, "The Presidents: The Frogs on Capital Hill," 1967, and of a narrative pantomime, "The Silhouette of God." Contributor to *World Development,* edited by Helene Castel. Contributor to *Chicago Sun-Times, Africa Report, Presence Africaine, UNESCO, Frankfurter Allgemeine Zeitung,* and other periodicals.

WORK IN PROGRESS: African Mythology; Anatomy of the White American Male.

SIDELIGHTS: According to a recent *Publishers' Weekly* article on small Black presses in the United States, "Okpaku's decision to abandon engineering in favor of writing was based on ideology, on the conviction that 'Africa is being led astray by Western "experts" who dominate African cultural life.'"

The article goes on to say that "Okpaku formulated plans for a book publishing arm of his *Journal* [now a highly respected quarterly on African humanities] while still a graduate student at Stanford. 'I thought there was a need for a book publishing dialog in the humanities that was controlled by an African, not by the Paris or London publishing houses that now dominate African publishing.'" Founder of The Third Press in 1968, Okpaku plans to publish ten to twelve new titles a year, including a series of children's books.

BIOGRAPHICAL/CRITICAL SOURCES: Publishers' Weekly, March 15, 1971.†

OLMSTED, Lorena Ann 1890-

PERSONAL: Surname is pronounced Alm-sted; born August 26, 1890, in Coronado, Calif.; daughter of Rosslyn Alonzo (an engineer) and Clara Belle (Keyes) Wood; married George Howerton Olmsted, June 28, 1911 (deceased); children: Audrey Doris (Mrs. John J. O'Connor). Education: Educated in Mendocino County, Calif. Politics: Republican. Religion: Christian Science. Home: 2049 35th St., Sacramento, Calif. 95817.

CAREER: Worked in her husband's printing shop for twenty-six years; presently a full-time writer. Member: California Writer's Club.

WRITINGS—Young adult novels; all published by Bouregy, except as indicated: Death Walked In, 1960, Cover of Darkness, 1961, Setup for Murder, 1962, Footsteps of the Cat, 1963, To Love a Stranger, 1966, Always a Bridesmaid, 1967, Many Paths of Love, 1970, Christie Comes Through, 1971; Faces of Danger, 1972; Return to Peril, Lenox Hill, 1972; Dorothea's Revenge, Lancer Books, 1972; To Trust a Stranger, 1973; Small Town Girl, 1973; Many Paths of Love, Bantam, 1973; A Touch of Fear, 1974; Dangerous Memory, 1974; The Fateful Promise, Dell, 1974; Trouble in Paradise, 1975; Journey into Adventure, 1977. Contributor of short stories and articles, mostly historical, to periodicals.

SIDELIGHTS: Lorena Olmsted told CA: "There are really two reasons for keeping my nose to the grind-stone (typewriter). First, I am a native of California and . . . I think it is a wonderful place, so many of my articles, most of them, are about the early days and about wild life. . . . Second, when I became a widow I was faced with doing something or killing time. I had written a few articles and confessions so I got out my typewriter and started to work. . . . Recently I was asked to try a child's book. I did and I loved it. No telling where I will go from here."

* * *

OLSEN, Marvin E(lliott) 1936-

PERSONAL: Born April 18, 1936, Hamilton, N.Y.; son of Edward Gustave and Faith (Eliott) Olsen; married Katherine Melchiors (a social worker), September 8, 1956; children: Lawrence, Steven, David. Education: Grinnell College, B.A., 1957; University of Michigan, M.A., 1958, Ph.D., 1965. Home: 527 Bellevue Way S.E., No. 307, Bellevue, Wash. 98004. Office: Battelle Human Affairs Research Centers, 4000 Northeast 41st St., Seattle, Wash. 98105.

CAREER: University of Michigan, Ann Arbor, instructor in sociology, 1963-65; Indiana University, Bloomington, assistant professor, 1965-69, associate professor, 1969-74, professor of sociology, 1974-75, director of Institute of Social Research, 1970-74; Battelle Human Affairs Research Centers, Seattle, Wash., senior research scientist, 1974—. Affiliate professor, University of Washington, 1975—. Visiting summer professor at University of Oregon, 1967, and at University of Washington, 1970; visiting professor, Uppsala University, Uppsala, Sweden, 1971-72. Military service: U.S. Air Force, 1958-62; became captain. Member: American Sociological Association, World Future Society, Society for the Study of Social Problems, Pacific Sociological Association, Phi Beta Kappa, Phi Kappa Phi.

WRITINGS: The Process of Social Organization, Holt, 1968; (editor) Power in Societies, Macmillan, 1970; Social Aspects of Energy Conservation, Northwest Energy Policy Project, 1977. Contributor to sociology journals. Book review editor, American Sociological Review, 1968-71.

WORK IN PROGRESS: The Process of Social Organization: Power in Social Systems, for Praeger; Participatory Pluralism: Comparative Studies of Political Participation and Influence.

* * *

OLSON, Helen Kronberg

PERSONAL: Born in Mt. Angel, Ore.; daughter of Paul and Leopoldena Kronberg; married Anthony Perillo (deceased); married John Harold Olson (a representative for an electronics company); children: (first marriage) Paul Anthony Perillo. Education: Mt. Angel College, B.S., 1952. Politics: Democrat. Home: 20739 Hazelnut Ridge Rd. N.E., Scotts Mills, Ore. 97375.

CAREER: Marion County Welfare, Salem, Ore., child welfare caseworker, 1960-63; Oregon State Hospital, Salem, social worker, 1964-65; art and elementary school teacher in Marion County, Ore.; full-time writer and Christmas tree farmer.

WRITINGS: Stupid Peter and Other Tales: New Stories to Read Together (original children's folk tales), Random House, 1970; (contributor) The Real Book of First Stories (anthology), edited by Dorothy Haas, Rand McNally, 1974; (contributor) The Princess Book (anthology), edited by Haas, Rand McNally, 1975; (contributor) The Witch Book (anthology), edited by Haas, Rand McNally, 1976. Also author of an unpublished children's book; contributor of short stories to Humpty Dumpty, Children's Playmate, Encyclopaedia Britannica, Scholastic Magazine, Adventure, and other periodicals.

WORK IN PROGRESS: A children's mystery novel; a wilderness suspense novel.

AVOCATIONAL INTERESTS: Painting, sculpting, and hiking.

BIOGRAPHICAL/CRITICAL SOURCES: Silverton Appeal Tribune, November 26, 1970; Statesman (Salem), December 13, 1970; The Oregonian, December 19, 1970.

* * *

OLSON, Robert G(oodwin) 1924-

PERSONAL: Born May 8, 1924, in Minneapolis, Minn.; son of Goodwin Carl (a salesman) and Mary Helen (Hutchins) Olson. Education: University of Minnesota, B.A., 1943; Columbia University, additional study, 1946-48; Sorbonne, University of Paris, Docteur d'universite, 1953; University of Michigan, Ph.D., 1957. Politics: "Independent radical (left)." Religion: None. Home: 222 East 30th St., New York, N.Y. 10016. Office: Department of Philosophy, Long Island University, Brooklyn, N.Y. 11201.

CAREER: Associated Press, St. Paul, Minn., copy editor, 1940-43; Grolier Society, New York City, staff editor, 1946-48; U.S. Office of Military Government, Berlin, Germany, historian, 1948-49; Lycee Jacques Decour, Paris, France, instructor in English, 1949-53; Ripon College, Ripon, Wis., assistant professor of philosophy, 1953-56; University of Michigan, Ann Arbor, instructor in philosophy, 1956-58; Columbia University, New York City, assistant professor of philosophy, 1958-61; Rutgers University, New Brunswick, N.J., associate professor, 1961-65, professor of philosophy, 1965-69, chairman of department, 1961-69; Long Island University, Brooklyn Center, Brooklyn, N.Y., professor of philosophy and chairman of department, 1969—. Military service: U.S. Army Air Forces, 1943-46; became sergeant. Member: American Philosophical Association, American Association of University Professors.

WRITINGS: An Introduction to Existentialism, Dover, 1962; The Morality of Self-Interest, Harcourt, 1965; A Short Introduction to Philosophy, Harcourt, 1967; Meaning and Argument, Harcourt, 1969; Ethics: A Short Introduction, Random House, 1977. Contributor to Encyclopedia of Philosophy and to professional journals.

WORK IN PROGRESS: A General Theory of Meaning.

* * *

OMARI, T(hompson) Peter   1930-

PERSONAL: Born November 3, 1930, in Mpraeso, Ghana; son of Thomas Ameyaw (an educator and computer programmer) and Felicia (Gyanewa) Omari; married Theodora Pontillas (a computer programmer), June 13, 1956; children: Thomas Kwame, Rosina Ama, Nina Akua. Education: Central State University, Wilberforce, Ohio, B.Sc. (magna cum laude), 1952; University of Wisconsin, M.Sc., 1953, Ph.D., 1955. Home address: P.O. Box 3005, Addis Ababa, Ethiopia. Office: Office of the Executive Secretary, United Nations Economic Commission for Africa, Addis Ababa, Ethiopia.

CAREER: University of Wisconsin—Madison, research associate, 1955-56; Department of Social Welfare and Community Development, Accra, Ghana, mass education officer, 1956-58; University of Ghana, Accra, lecturer, 1958-62, senior lecturer in sociology, 1962-63; United Nations Economic Commission for Africa, Addis Ababa, Ethiopia, social affairs officer and head of Social Development Section, 1963-69; United Nations Headquarters, New York, N.Y., social affairs officer, Regional and Community Development Section, 1969-71; United Nations Economic Commission for Africa, special assistant to the executive secretary, 1971—. Consultant to Dag Hammarskjold Foundation, Uppsala, Sweden, 1968—, and Swedish International Development Agency, Stockholm, 1968—. Director of international conference and seminars on problems of African development.

WRITINGS: Marriage Guidance for Young Ghanians, Thomas Nelson, 1962; (with St. Clair Drake) Social Work in West Africa, Government Printer (Accra), 1962; A Basic Course in Statistics for Sociologists, University of Ghana Bookshop (Legon), 1962; Kwame Nkrumah: The Anatomy of an African Dictatorship, Africana Publishing (New York), 1970.

Contributor: Pierre wan den Berghe, Africa: Social Problems of Change and Conflict, Chandler Publishing, 1965; Bernard Farber, editor, Kinship and Family Organization, Wiley, 1966; Sven Hammell, Refugee Problems in Africa, Scandinavian Institute of African Studies, 1967; Olle Nordberg and others, editors, Action for Children, Dag Hammarskjord Foundation, 1975. Editor and author of most titles, "United Nations Social Welfare Services in Africa," a series of monographs.

WORK IN PROGRESS: Marriage and Family in Africa; Applied General Statistics; and a study of problems in development of Africa.

* * *

O'NEILL, Carlotta Monterey   1888-1970

December 28, 1888—November 18, 1970; American actress and widow of Eugene O'Neill. Obituaries: New York Times, November 21, 1970.

O'NEILL, William F.   1931-

PERSONAL: Born April 8, 1931, in Long Beach, Calif.; son of Jack P. and Laurene (Hutton) O'Neill; married Beverly Lewis (a professor), November 21, 1952; children: Teresa Lynn. Education: California State College at Long Beach (now University), B.A., 1951, M.A., 1952; University of Southern California, Ph.D., 1958. Home: 32 57th Pl., Long Beach, Calif. 90803. Office: Department of Education, University of Southern California, Los Angeles, Calif. 90007.

CAREER: University of Southern California, Los Angeles, assistant professor, 1961-63, associate professor, 1963-68, professor of educational philosophy, 1968—. Military service: U.S. Naval Reserve, 1952-54. Member: American Educational Research Association, Philosophy of Education Society, Comparative Education Society, Far Western Philosophy of Education Society, Phi Delta Kappa.

WRITINGS: (Editor) Selected Educational Heresies: Some Unorthodox Views Concerning the Nature and Purposes of Contemporary Education, Scott, Foresman, 1969; Readin, Ritin and Rafferty, Glendessary, 1969; With Charity toward None: An Analysis of Ayn Rand's Philosophy, Philosophical Library, 1971; (with George Demos) Education under Duress, Lucas Brothers, 1971.

WORK IN PROGRESS: Approaches to Philosophy, a textbook.

* * *

ONO, Chiyo   1941-

PERSONAL: Born February 26, 1941, in Tokyo, Japan; daughter of Rei (a noh player) and Ryuko Kondoh; married Yoh Ono (master of a training ship), August 7, 1960; children: Sayuri. Education: Fuji Women's College, 1962. Home: 8-406, Jingumae 6-25, Shibuya Ku, Tokyo, Japan.

WRITINGS: (And illustrator) Watashi no Geta (juvenile), Shiko-Sha Co. (Tokyo), 1969, translation published as Which Way, Geta?, Thomas Nelson, 1970; Maigoni natta Ohmu, Shiko-Sha Co., 1970; Itodenwa, Shiko-Sha Co., 1971.

* * *

OOST, Stewart Irvin   1921-

PERSONAL: Surname rhymes with "toast"; born May 20, 1921, in Grand Rapids, Mich.; son of Jacob John and Bessie Ola (Stewart) Oost. Education: University of Chicago, A.B., 1941, M.A., 1947, Ph.D., 1950; Yale University, graduate studies, 1943-44. Politics: Republican. Religion: Methodist. Home: 9652 South Seeley Ave., Chicago, Ill. 60643. Office: Department of History, University of Chicago, 1050 East 59th St., Chicago, Ill. 60637.

CAREER: Starr Commonwealth for Boys, Albion, Mich., teacher, 1941-42; Southern Methodist University, Dallas, Tex., instructor, 1948-50, assistant professor, 1950-54, associate professor of history, 1954-59; University of Chicago, Chicago, Ill., associate professor, 1959-64, professor of ancient history in departments of history and classical languages and literature, 1965—. Consultant on Greek and Roman history, Encyclopaedia Britannica, 1969—. Military service: U.S. Army, 1942-46; became first sergeant. Member: American Historical Association, American Catholic Historical Association, American Philological Association, Phi Beta Kappa. Awards, honors: Ford Foundation fellow in Italy, 1955-56.

WRITINGS: Roman Policy in Epirus and Acarnania in the

Age of the Roman Conquest of Greece, Southern Methodist University Press, 1954; *Galla Placidia Augusta: A Biographical Essay,* University of Chicago Press, 1968. Contributor to *Encyclopedia Americana* and to classical and philology journals. Associate editor, *Classical Philology,* 1959—.

WORK IN PROGRESS: Research in the history of Greece in the fourth and third century, B.C.

* * *

OOSTHUIZEN, Gerhardus C(ornelis) 1922-

PERSONAL: Born June 18, 1922, in Alexandria District, South Africa; son of Carel Adam (a farmer) and Anna Johanna (Potgieter) Oosthuizen; married Anna Cornelia Opperman (a medical practitioner); children: Carel, Rudolf, Gerhardus. *Education:* University of Stellenbosch, B.A., 1941, M.Th., 1953; University of South Africa, M.A., 1946, Ph.D., 1955; Union Theological Seminary, New York, N.Y., S.T.M., 1958; Free University, Amsterdam, Netherlands, Th.D., 1958. *Home:* 2 Jamieson Dr., Westville, Durban, South Africa. *Office:* University of Durban-Westville, Private Bag X54001, Durban, South Africa.

CAREER: Ordained minister of Dutch Reformed Church, 1944; pastor of church in Bulawayo, Rhodesia, 1950-56, and Queenstown, South Africa, 1956-59; University of Fort Hare, Alice, Cape Province, South Africa, professor of missiology and church history, 1959-68; University of Durban-Westville, Durban, South Africa, professor of missiology, 1969-71, professor of religious studies, 1972—. Visiting professor in West Berlin, 1966-67, and the Netherlands, 1970-71. Former mayor of Alice, Cape Province. *Military service:* South African Air Force, chaplain, 1944-46; became captain. *Member:* International Association for Missiological Studies, International Association for the History of Religions, International Association for the Study of Prehistoric Religions and Ethnology, South African Academy for Arts and Science, Missiological-Anthropological Research Association.

WRITINGS: Theological Discussions and Confessional Developments in the Churches of Asia and Africa, Wever (Netherlands), 1958; *Die kerk in gistende Afrika en Asie,* Lovedale Pers (South Africa), 1960; *Delayed Action,* Gollancz, 1961; *The Theology of a South African Messiah,* E. J. Brill, 1967; *Post-Christianity in Africa: A Theological and Anthropological Study,* Eerdmans, 1968; *Shepherds of Lovedale: A Life for Southern Africa,* Keartlands, 1970; (contributor) *World Mission Handbook,* Lutterworth, 1970; *Theological Battleground in Asia and Africa,* Humanities, 1972; (editor) *The Ethics of Tissue Transplantation,* Howard Timmins (Cape Town), 1974; *Pentecostal Penetration into the Indian Community in Metropolitan Durban,* Human Sciences Research Council (Pretoria), 1975; *Moving to the Waters,* Bethesda Publications, 1975; *Iconography of Religions: Afro-Christian Religions,* E. J. Brill, 1977; (editor) *Euthanasia in South Africa,* Howard Timmins (Cape Town), 1977. Contributor of articles to religion journals in the Netherlands, Germany, Switzerland, South Africa, South East Asia, and the United States.

SIDELIGHTS: In addition to English and Afrikaans, Gerhardus Oosthuizen has some competency in Dutch, Zulu, Xhosa, German, Hebrew, and Latin.

* * *

OPIE, John 1934-

PERSONAL: Born July 31, 1934, in Chicago, Ill.; son of John (an engineer) and Vlasta (Rytirova) Opie; married Lora Jean Watson, August 6, 1955; children: John, Christopher, Stephen, Maria. *Education:* De Pauw University, B.A., 1956; Union Theological Seminary, New York, B.D., 1959; University of Chicago, M.A., 1961, Ph.D., 1963. *Office:* Department of History, Duquesne University, Pittsburgh, Pa. 15219.

CAREER: Ordained minister of United Presbyterian Church, U.S.A.; University of Illinois at Urbana-Champaign, director of experimental program in religion, 1963-65; Duquesne University, Pittsburgh, Pa., assistant professor, 1965-67, associate professor, 1967-71, professor of history, 1971—. Visiting professor at Pittsburgh Theological Seminary, 1966—. *Member:* American Historical Association, Organization of American Historians, American Society of Church History, Society for Reformation Research. *Awards, honors:* American Philosophical Society research grant, 1966.

WRITINGS—Editor and author of introduction: *Jonathan Edwards and the Enlightenment,* Heath, 1969; *Americans and Environment: The Controversy over Ecology,* Heath, 1971. Contributor of articles and reviews to scholarly journals and popular periodicals. Member of editorial staff, *Journal of Ecumenical Studies,* 1966-68; bibliographer, *American Quarterly,* 1967—.

WORK IN PROGRESS: The Ecological Eye, for Scribner.†

* * *

OPITZ, Edmund A. 1914-

PERSONAL: Born February 11, 1914, in Worcester, Mass.; son of Ernest Edmund (a businessman) and Olga (Lundgren) Opitz; married Helen Ralston, May 27, 1946; children: Claudia, Elaine. *Education:* Maryville College, Maryville, Tenn., A.B., 1936; Starr King School for the Ministry, Th.B., 1939. *Politics:* Republican. *Religion:* Congregationalist. *Home:* 137 Longview Ave., White Plains, N.Y. 10605. *Office:* Foundation for Economic Education, Irvington, N.Y. 10533.

CAREER: Harrisburg Academy, Harrisburg, Pa., teacher, 1942-43; field director in India, American Red Cross, 1944-46; Second Congregational Parish, Hingham, Mass., minister, 1946-51; Spiritual Mobilization, Los Angeles, Calif., conference director, 1951-55; Foundation for Economic Education, Irvington, N.Y., senior staff member, 1955—.

WRITINGS: The Powers That Be, Foundation for Social Research, 1956; (editor) *The Kingdom without God,* Foundation for Social Research, 1956; *Religion and Capitalism: Allies, Not Enemies,* Arlington House, 1970; (editor) Albert Lax, *Consumer's Capitalism and the Immutable Laws of Economics,* Hallberg, 1970. Contributor of articles and reviews to a variety of periodicals.

BIOGRAPHICAL/CRITICAL SOURCES: National Review, July 28, 1970; *University Bookman,* winter, 1971.

* * *

OPPENHEIMER, Martin 1930-

PERSONAL: Born 1930, in Soest, Germany; came to United States, 1937; married Sara A. Crookston (a social worker), July 21, 1961; children: Miriam, Joel. *Education:* Temple University, B.S., 1952; Columbia University, M.A., 1953; University of Pennsylvania, Ph.D., 1963. *Office:* Department of Sociology, Livingston College, Rutgers University, New Brunswick, N.J.

CAREER: Part-time instructor at Pennsylvania State University, Ogontz Campus, 1959, and Drexel Institute of Technology (now Drexel University), Philadelphia, Pa., 1960; Temple University, Community College, Philadelphia, instructor in social science, 1961-63; Haverford College, Haverford, Pa., assistant professor of sociology, 1964-65; Bryn Mawr College, Bryn Mawr, Pa., lecturer in sociology, 1965-66; Vassar College, Poughkeepsie, N.Y., assistant professor of sociology, 1966-68; Lincoln University, Lincoln University, Pa., associate professor of sociology and chairman of department of sociology and anthropology, 1968-70; Rutgers University, Livingston College, New Brunswick, N.J., associate professor of sociology and chairman of department, 1970—. Guest professor, John F. Kennedy Institute, Free University of Berlin, summer, 1976. Social science in Office of Development Coordinator, City of Philadelphia, 1959; associate director of studies program, American Friends Service Committee, 1963-64. *Military service:* U.S. Army, 1953-55; served in England. *Member:* American Sociological Association, Society for the Study of Social Problems, American Association of University Professors, Eastern Sociological Society.

WRITINGS: (With George Lakey) *A Manual for Direct Action,* Quadrangle, 1965; *The Urban Guerrilla,* Quadrangle, 1969; (editor) *The American Military,* Aldine-Atherton, 1971.

Contributor: *Problems and Prospects of the Negro Movement,* Wadsworth, 1968; *Riots and Rebellion: Civil Violence in the Urban Community,* Sage Books, 1968; *Nonviolent Direct Action,* Corpus Books, 1969; *Interpreting Education: A Sociological Approach,* Appleton, 1971; *Radical Democracy,* Grossman, 1971; *Radical Conflict,* Little, Brown, 1971; *Radical and Ethnic Relations,* Crowell, 1972. Also author of *The Black Revolt,* 1971. Contributor of articles and reviews to *Nation, New Politics, Mankind* (India), *Bulletin,* and others.

WORK IN PROGRESS: With John C. Leggett and Irving Louis Horowitz, *American Working Class in the 1970's,* for Transaction Books.

BIOGRAPHICAL/CRITICAL SOURCES: New Republic, May 24, 1969; *New Yorker,* June 21, 1969.

*   *   *

O'REILLY, John (Thomas)   1945-

PERSONAL: Born May 23, 1945, in Boston, Mass.; son of William F. (a laborer) and Helen E. (Sullivan) O'Reilly. *Education:* St. Louis University, B.A., 1966, M.A., 1970. *Politics:* Independent-Liberal. *Religion:* Catholic. *Agent:* Richard Palmer, 32-69 38th St., Long Island City, N.Y. 11103.

CAREER: Ordained Roman Catholic priest, 1970; Contemporary Mission, St. Louis, Mo., vice-president, beginning 1966. Advisor, St. Louis Detention Center.

WRITINGS: (With Patrick Berkery and Joseph Valentine) *A New Catholic Catechism,* Stein & Day, 1970; *Voices of Change: Religious Life as Was and Could Be,* Herder, 1970.

WORK IN PROGRESS: Two books, one about priesthood, and the other concerning "faith."†

*   *   *

O'REILLY, Robert P.   1936-

PERSONAL: Born June 17, 1936; son of Joseph Michael (a welder) and Marie (Blakesley) O'Reilly; married Cecelia Hale, July 12, 1959; children: Mark, Anne, Patrice, Robert, Katherine. *Education:* University of Buffalo (now State University of New York at Buffalo), B.S., 1959; Cornell University, M.S., 1966, Ph.D., 1969. *Home:* 1709 Tilton Dr., Silver Spring, Md. 20902. *Office:* Montgomery County Public Schools, 850 Hungerford Dr., Rockville, Md. 20850.

CAREER: Affiliated with New York State Education Department, Albany; currently director of the Department of Research and Evaluation, Montgomery County Public Schools, Rockville, Md. *Member:* International Reading Association, American Psychological Association, American Educational Research Association, National Council on Measurement in Education, Northeast Educational Research Association, Phi Delta Kappa, Phi Kappa Phi.

WRITINGS: (Editor and major contributor) *Racial and Social Class Isolation in the Schools: Implications for Educational Policy and Programs,* Praeger, 1970; *Comprehensive Achievement Monitoring,* Educational Technology Publications, 1975. Contributor to psychology and education journals.

WORK IN PROGRESS: A textbook on reading comprehension testing, for Educational Technology Publications; research on new methods for assessing reading comprehension based on the cloze technique.

*   *   *

ORNA, Mary Virginia   1934-

PERSONAL: Born July 4, 1934, in Newark, N.J.; daughter of Edward Joseph (an accountant) and Julia (Lebert) Orna. *Education:* Chestnut Hill College, B.S., 1955; Fordham University, M.S., 1958, Ph.D., 1962; Catholic University of America, M.A., 1967. *Politics:* Democrat. *Home:* 29 Castle Pl., New Rochelle, N.Y. 10801. *Office:* Department of Chemistry, College of New Rochelle, New Rochelle, N.Y. 10805.

CAREER: Roman Catholic nun; Academy of Mount St. Ursula, Bronx, N.Y., teacher of chemistry, 1958-62; College of New Rochelle, New Rochelle, N.Y., 1966—, began as assistant professor, currently associate professor of chemistry. Lecturer, Bronx Community College, 1961-62. *Member:* American Chemical Society, Society for Social Responsibility in Science, Society for Applied Spectroscopy. *Awards, honors:* American Cyanamid Co. award for excellence in teaching.

WRITINGS: Cybernetics, Society, and the Church, Pflaum, 1969. Contributor to *Downside Review, Front Line, Cross and Crown, Journal of Chemical Education,* and other journals.

*   *   *

ORR, Daniel   1933-

PERSONAL: Born May 13, 1933, in New York, N.Y.; son of Robert Connell (an engineer and accountant) and Lillian (Nagle) Orr; married Mary Lee Hayes, October 4, 1957; children: Rebecca, Matthew, Sara. *Education:* Oberlin College, A.B., 1954; University of Michigan, graduate study, 1954; Princeton University, M.A., 1956, Ph.D., 1960. *Politics:* Republican. *Home:* 8941 Nottingham Pl., La Jolla, Calif. 92037. *Office:* Department of Economics, University of California, San Diego, La Jolla, Calif. 92037.

CAREER: Procter & Gamble Co., Cincinnati, Ohio, operations analyst, 1956-58; Amherst College, Amherst, Mass., assistant professor of economics, 1960-61; University of Chicago, Graduate School of Business, Chicago, Ill., assistant professor of mathematical economics, 1961-65; University of California, San Diego, La Jolla, associate professor, 1965-68, professor of economics, 1968—. Visiting associate professor of economics, Northwestern University, 1966; visiting professor of economics, University of Nottingham, 1972. Consultant to RAND Corp., 1963-65 and U.S. Treasury, 1966—. *Military service:* U.S. Army Reserve, 1957. *Member:* American Economic Association, Econometric Society. *Awards, honors:* Ford Foundation fellowship, 1962; Walgreen Foundation award, 1963; National Science Foundation grants, 1966-68, 1968-71, 1971—.

WRITINGS: Cash Management and the Demand for Money, Praeger, 1971; *Property, Markets, and Government Intervention: A Textbook in Microeconomic Theory and Its Current Applications,* Goodyear Publishing, 1976. Contributor to economics journals.

* * *

ORTIZ, Alfonso A(lex) 1939-

PERSONAL: Born April 30, 1939, in San Juan Pueblo, N.M.; son of Sam and Lupe (Naranjo) Ortiz; married Margaret Davisson, July 26, 1961; children: Juliana, Elena, Antonico. *Education:* University of New Mexico, A.B., 1961; University of Chicago, M.A., 1963, Ph.D., 1967. *Politics:* Liberal. *Religion:* Pagan. *Home:* 830 East Zia Rd., Santa Fe, N.M. 87501. *Office:* Department of Anthropology, University of New Mexico, Albuquerque, N.M. 87131.

CAREER: Pitzer College, Claremont, Calif., assistant professor of anthropology, 1966-67; Princeton University, Princeton, N.J., assistant professor, 1967-70, associate professor of anthropology, 1970-74; University of New Mexico, Albuquerque, professor of anthropology, 1974—. Member, National Humanities Faculty, 1974—. Fellow, Center for Advanced Study in the Behavioral Sciences, 1977-78. Consultant to Xerox Corp., 1968, Ford Foundation, 1969-70, and John Hay Whitney Foundation, 1971. President, Association on American Indian Affairs, 1973; member of advisory council, Native American Rights Fund. *Member:* American Anthropological Association (fellow), Royal Anthropological Institute (fellow), Current Anthropology (associate). *Awards, honors:* Guggenheim fellowship, 1975-76.

WRITINGS: The Tewa World: Space, Time, Being, and Becoming In a Pueblo Society, University of Chicago Press, 1969; (editor) *New Perspective on the Pueblos,* University of New Mexico Press, 1972; (compiler with wife, Margaret D. Ortiz) *To Carry Forth the Vine,* Columbia University Press, 1977. Contributor to anthropology journals.

WORK IN PROGRESS: Editing Southwestern volumes of *Handbook of American Indians,* publication by Smithsonian Institution Press.

* * *

OSBORN, Catherine B. 1914-

PERSONAL: Born June 16, 1914, in Cleveland, Ohio; daughter of Clarence Powers (a professor) and Sarah (Babbitt) Bill; married James W. Osborn (a physician), June 16, 1939; children: Lawrence W., Edward M. *Education:* Bryn Mawr College, B.A., 1935, M.A., 1939. *Religion:* Episcopalian. *Home:* Cobble Hill, Falls Village, Conn. 06031.

CAREER: Teacher at Garrison Forest School, Garrison, Md., 1936-38, and Harley Country Day School, Rochester, N.Y., 1939-40, 1944-45; Case Western Reserve University, Cleveland, Ohio, lecturer, 1953-59, assistant professor of Romance languages and assistant dean of Flora Stone Mather College, 1959-69.

WRITINGS: (With Margaret Waterman) *Papa Gorski* (novel after Balzac's *Pere Goriot*), Harcourt, 1969. Contributor to *American Scholar, PMLA,* and *French Review.*

WORK IN PROGRESS: You Bet She Can Fly, a true juvenile story about one of our early aviators; a work on "the changing meaning of reality in the 19th century French short story."

* * *

OSKAMP, Stuart 1930-

PERSONAL: Born May 31, 1930, in Oak Park, Ill.; son of Alfred Stuart (a professor) and Catharine (Willard) Oskamp; married Barbara Harvey, December 26, 1955 (divorced, 1972); married Catherine Cameron, December 18, 1973; children: David, Karen. *Education:* Grinnell College, B.A. (with honors), 1951; Stanford University, Ph.D., 1960. *Office:* Department of Psychology, Claremont Graduate School, Claremont, Calif. 91711.

CAREER: Center for Advanced Study in the Behavioral Sciences, Stanford, Calif., assistant psychologist, 1956; Stanford University, Stanford, assistant psychologist, 1957-59; Veterans Administration Hospital, Palo Alto, Calif., trainee in clinical psychology, 1957-59; Veterans Administration Mental Hygiene Clinic, San Francisco, Calif., trainee in clinical psychology, 1959-60; Claremont Graduate School, Claremont, Calif., assistant professor, 1960-64, associate professor, 1964-70, professor of psychology, 1970—. Research psychologist, Palo Alto Medical Research Foundation, Palo Alto, Calif., 1960; U.S. Peace Corps, Hilo, Hawaii, field assessment officer, 1963; Tri-City Mental Health Authority, Pomona, Calif., psychologist, 1964-66; research associate at Institute of Social Research, University of Michigan, 1966-67 and University of Bristol, Bristol, England, 1971. American Psychological Association visiting scientist, 1967-68. *Military service:* U.S. Naval Reserve, 1951-55; became lieutenant. *Member:* American Psychological Association, Society for the Psychological Study of Social Issues, Western Psychological Association, Phi Beta Kappa, Sigma Xi.

WRITINGS: (With R. M. Suinn) *The Predictive Validity of Projective Measures: A Fifteen-Year Evaluative Review of Research,* C. C Thomas, 1969; (contributor) L. S. Wrightsman, *Social Psychology in the Seventies,* Brooks/Cole, 1972, 2nd edition, 1977; *Attitudes and Opinions,* Prentice-Hall, 1977. Contributor to psychology journals. Advisory editor, *Journal of Consulting and Clinical Psychology,* 1969—.

WORK IN PROGRESS: Research on attitudes, social issues, experimental social psychology, and on the factors affecting success in contraceptive planning.

SIDELIGHTS: Stuart Oskamp told *CA:* "One of my most satisfying activities is working with individual graduate students to plan and design research projects which are both rigorous and relevant to important questions. Though all of my work runs the theme of applying social psychological methods and findings to the solution of social problems and public policy issues . . . other satisfying moments have come in reaching for high standards in my avocational activities such as choral and solo singing, photography, and coaching my son's and daughter's soccer teams."

* * *

OSSERMAN, Richard A. 1930-

PERSONAL: Born May 31, 1930, in New York, N.Y.; son

of Harold A. (a dentist) and Letty (Tonkonogy) Osserman; married Gwen Stalberg, July 11, 1954 (divorced); married Linda Adler, April 15, 1974; children: Eric, Joel, Steven, Robert. *Education:* Hobart College, A.B., 1951; Columbia University, J.D., 1954; New York University, LL.M. in taxation, 1961. *Home:* 333 Central Park W., New York, N.Y. 10025.

CAREER: Attorney specializing in tax law, New York, N.Y., 1956—, with the law firm of Weisman, Celler, Allan, Spett, Sheinberg, 1956-72, and with Pryor, Cashman, Sherman and Flyns, 1972—. *Military service:* U.S. Army, 1954-56. *Member:* Federal Bar Council Association of the Bar of the City of New York.

WRITINGS: (With Joseph Ruskay) *Halfway to Tax Reform,* Indiana University Press, 1970.

WORK IN PROGRESS: Tax Shelters, for Indiana University Press.

BIOGRAPHICAL/CRITICAL SOURCES: New York Times, November 29, 1970.

* * *

OSSOWSKA, Maria 1896-

PERSONAL: Born January 16, 1896, in Warsaw, Poland; married Stanislaw Ossowski (a professor at University of Warsaw), July 1, 1924 (died November 7, 1963). *Education:* University of Warsaw, Ph.D., 1921. *Home:* Krasinskiego 16m 32, Warsaw, Poland.

CAREER: University of Warsaw, Warsaw, Poland, 1932-63, began as privatdocent, became professor of sociology, 1945-63. Lecturer at Barnard College, 1960, and University of Pennsylvania, 1967; occasional lecturer in Brussels and Liege. *Member:* Polish Sociological Association. *Awards, honors:* Prize of the Polish Scientific Association for *Podstawy nauki o moralnosci;* prize of the A. Jurzykowski Foundation (New York).

WRITINGS: Podstawy nauki o moralnosci (title means "The Foundation of a Science of Morals"; includes summary in French), Panstwowe Wydawnictwo Naukowe, 1945, 4th edition, 1966; *Moralnoc mieszczanska* (title means "The So-Called Bourgeois Morality"; includes summaries in Russian and English), Ossolinskich, 1956; *O pewnych przemianach etyki walki* (booklet on changes in the ethics of fighting), Ksiazka & Wiedza, 1957; *Socjologia moralnosci: Zarys zagadnien* (title means "Sociology of Morals"; includes summary in English), Panstwowe Wydawnictwo Naukowe, 1963, 2nd edition, 1969; *Mysl moralna Oswiecenia angielskiego* (title means "Moral Thought in the English Enlightenment"; includes summary in English), Panstwowe Wydawnictwo Naukowe, 1966; *Moralnose i speleczenstwo,* edited by Maria Ofierska and Maria Dietl, Panstwowe Wydawnictwo Naukowe, 1969; *Social Determinants of Moral Ideas* (lectures; includes parts of *Socjologia moralnosci),* University of Pennsylvania Press, 1970; *Normy moralne: Proba systematyzacji* (title means "Moral Norms: A Tentative Systematization"), Panstwowe Wydawnictwo Naukowe, 1970, 2nd edition, 1971; *Ethos rycerski i jego odmiany,* Panstwowe Wydawnictwo Naukowe, 1973. Also author of *Wzor obywatela w ustroju demokratycznym* (booklet on civil rights and democracy), 1946, and *Motywy Postepowania: Z zagadnien psychologii moralnosci* (title means "Human Motivations"; includes summary in English), 1948, 2nd edition published by Ksiazka i Wiedza, 1958.

SIDELIGHTS: Maria Ossowska spent 1921-22 in Paris,

and studied in England, 1934-35. In addition to her native language, she is competent in German, Russian, Latin, Greek, French, and English.†

* * *

OSTROW, Joanna 1938-

PERSONAL: Born March 20, 1938, in New York, N.Y.; daughter of Benjamin (a journalist) and Dora (Lubin) Ostrow; married Robin MacDonald (a British lecturer), December 17, 1959 (divorced); children: Jennie, Sally. *Education:* Queens College (now Queens College of the City University of New York), A.B., 1958; Stanford University, graduate study, 1959-60. *Home:* R.R. 2, North Gower, Ontario, Canada K0A 2T0.

CAREER: Riding teacher at various times; lived in Scotland for eight years, where she organized and ran pre-school play groups and prenatal training courses in rural areas. *Member:* Phi Beta Kappa. *Awards, honors:* " ... *In The Highlands since Time Immemorial"* selected by *Time* as one of Year's Best Books, 1970.

WRITINGS: ... *In the Highlands since Time Immemorial* (novel), Knopf, 1970 (published in England as *In the Highlands,* Hamilton, 1970). Stories included in *Stanford Short Stories,* 1959 and *Best American Short Stories,* 1968, and published in *Massachusetts Review* and *New Yorker.* Contributor, as free-lance journalist, to British Broadcasting Corp. programs, and to *Scotsman* and *Guardian.*

WORK IN PROGRESS: A novel set in Canada.

SIDELIGHTS: "Joanna Ostrow is one of those writers who seem to have been born with every insight, every comma in place," a *Time* reviewer states. "Her book lies far beyond such usual first-novel adjectives as 'promising.' A classically perfect little story, it polarizes an encounter between the frantic present and an almost still-life past. ... She is in the presence of death, and she knows it. Her achievement is to show that when tradition dies, it can affect the swinging young even more than the hidebound old."

Her long residence in Scotland left Ostrow "very U.K.-oriented." Her other vital interests: "Country life and the problems of ecology and environmental pollution; dogs, horses, that kind of thing; 'the north,' in literature for instance, a continuing interest." She has been thinking of children's literature as a subject, especially with northern myth-patterns or fantasy involved, and would like to spend time in Finland. "The natural world/the tradition of myth and fantasy [are] of prime importance in my work," she adds. "Contradictory, but there it is."

BIOGRAPHICAL/CRITICAL SOURCES: New York Times, April 3, 1970; *New York Times Book Review,* June 7, 1970; *Time,* June 29, 1970, January 4, 1971.†

* * *

OTTEN, Charlotte M(arie) 1915-

PERSONAL: Born May 23, 1915, in Sheboygan, Wis.; daughter of Robert E. (a pharmacist) and Aurabelle (Blake) Otten. *Education:* Carleton College, B.A., 1937; University of Chicago, M.A., 1951; University of Michigan, Ph.D., 1961. *Politics:* "Conservationist." *Religion:* "Conservationist." *Office:* Department of Anthropology, Northern Illinois University, DeKalb, Ill. 60115.

CAREER: University of Minnesota, Minneapolis, instructor in laboratory medicine, 1958-60, instructor in anthropology, 1960; University of Wisconsin, Madison, instructor, 1960-62, assistant professor of anthropology, 1962-67; Northern Illinois University, DeKalb, associate professor, 1967-70, professor of anthropology, 1970—. Visiting professor, University of Chicago, 1971.

MEMBER: International Association of Human Biologists, American Anthropological Association (fellow), American Association of Physical Anthropologists, Society for the Study of Human Biology, American Association for the Advancement of Science, American Society of Human Genetics, Society for Social Biology, Royal Anthropological Institute, Sigma Xi. *Awards, honors:* National Institutes of Health and National Institute of Dental Research training grants, 1964-66; National Science Foundation research grants, 1966-67, 1967-68.

WRITINGS: (Editor) *Anthropology and Art: Readings in Cross-Cultural Aesthetics,* National History Press, 1971; (compiler) *Aggression and Evolution,* Xerox College Publishing, 1973. Contributor to anthropology journals and to *Journal of Dental Research.*

WORK IN PROGRESS: Research on "sex differences, especially with regard to spacial perception," and on behavior genetics, primitive art, the role of art in culture, and acculturation in aesthetics; a textbook on ethnographic art.

* * *

OTTO, Calvin P. 1930-

PERSONAL: Born April 19, 1930, in Detroit, Mich.; son of John E. (a chef) and Myrtle (Soncrant) Otto; married Patricia Reed, March 16, 1954; children: Sharon, James. *Education:* University of Michigan, B.B.A., 1958. *Religion:* Methodist. *Home:* 124 Elm St., Bennington, Vt. 05201. *Office:* Wood Flong Corp., Davis St., Hoosick Falls, N.Y. 12090.

CAREER: Bolt Beranek & Newman, Inc. (science research and development firm), Cambridge, Mass., director of education and training services, 1963-71; Wood Flong Corp., Hoosick Falls, N.Y., president and chairman of board, 1971—. Managing director, Joseph Batchelon Ltd. Chairman of archives, Town of Sudbury, 1970-71. *Military service:* U.S. Army, 1950-53; became sergeant first class. *Member:* American Society of Training Directors, Sudbury Historical Society, Ephemera Society (founder and chairman of North America branch).

WRITINGS: (With Rollin Glaser) *The Management of Training,* Addison-Wesley, 1970; *Public Occurrences: The First American Newspaper,* Americana Classics, 1975; *Treaty of Paris, 1783,* Americana Classics, 1976; (contributor) *Shires of Bennington,* Bennington Museum, 1976; (contributor) *Battle of Bennington,* Bennington Museum, 1977.

* * *

OTTO, Wayne (R.) 1931-

PERSONAL: Born October 22, 1931, in Fremont, Wis.; son of Henry F. (a mechanic) and Edna (Wohlt) Otto; married Shirley Bergen (an administrative assistant), October 13, 1953; children: Eleni. *Education:* Wisconsin State College at River Falls (now University of Wisconsin—River Falls), B.S., 1953; University of Wisconsin, M.S., 1958, Ph.D., 1961. *Politics:* Independent. *Religion:* Eclectic. *Home:* 4161 Cherokee Dr., Madison, Wis. 53711. *Office:* Research and Development Center, University of Wisconsin, 1025 West Johnson St., Madison, Wis. 53706.

CAREER: University of Oregon, Eugene, assistant pro-

fessor of education, 1961-64; University of Georgia, Athens, associate professor of education, 1964-65; University of Wisconsin—Madison, professor of education, 1965—, associate director, Research and Development Center, 1975—. Senior researcher, Institute for Research on Teaching, Michigan State University, 1976—. *Military service:* U.S. Marine Corps, 1953-55; became sergeant. *Member:* International Reading Association, National Reading Conference, American Educational Research Association.

WRITINGS: (With R. A. McMeneny and R. J. Smith) *Corrective and Remedial Teaching,* Houghton, 1966, revised edition, 1973; (with David Ford) *Teaching Adults to Read,* Houghton, 1967; (with Karl Koenke) *Remedial Teaching,* Houghton, 1969; (with Richard J. Smith) *Administering the School Reading Program,* Houghton, 1970; *Focused Reading Instruction,* Addison-Wesley, 1975; *New Linguistic Readers,* Bobbs-Merrill, 1975; *Speedway: The Action Way to Speed Read,* HyCite, 1975; (with Robert D. Chester) *Objective Based Reading,* Addison-Wesley, 1976; (editor with others) *Reading Problems: A Multidisciplinary Approach,* Addison-Wesley, 1977; *READ: An Adaptation of the Wisconsin Design for Disabled Readers,* 1977. Also author of *Wisconsin Design for Reading Skill Development,* National Computer Systems, 1971-77. Executive editor, *Journal of Educational Research.*

WORK IN PROGRESS: With others, *Basic Reading Skills for Adults,* for Steck; *Read: An Adaptation of the Wisconsin Design for Disabled Readers; How to Teach Reading,* for Addison-Wesley.

* * *

OVERSTREET, Harry Allen 1875-1970

October 25, 1875—August 17, 1970; American psychologist and educator. Obituaries: *New York Times,* August 18, 1970; *Time,* August 31, 1970; *Current Biography,* 1970. (See index for *CA* sketch)

* * *

OVERY, Paul 1940-

PERSONAL: Born February 14, 1940, in Dorchester, Dorset, England; son of Arthur Frederick (a salesman) and Joan (Major) Overy. *Education:* King's College, Cambridge, B.A., 1962, M.A., 1965. *Home:* 92 South Hill Park, London N.W.3, England. *Agent:* John Johnson, 12-13 Henrietta St., London WC2E 8LF, England.

CAREER: Teacher at schools in London, England, 1962-64; Brixton College of Further Education, London, assistant lecturer, 1964-65; art critic for *Listener,* 1966-68, and *Financial Times,* 1968-70; *New Society* (magazine), London, books editor, 1970-71; art critic for *The Times,* London, 1973—. Tutor, Royal College of Art. Visiting lecturer at colleges of art in England, 1966-70. *Member:* International Association of Art Critics, National Union of Journalists. *Awards, honors:* Scholarship from Italian Government to Florence and Rome, 1970.

WRITINGS: Edouard Manet, Purnell & Sons, 1967; *De Stijl,* Dutton, 1969; *Kandinsky: The Language of the Eye,* Praeger, 1969. Author of script and presenter of BBC educational television series, "The Visual Scene since 1945," 1969, of BBC Open University programs, "Art as Performance" and "Artists' Films," 1976. Contributor to art journals and to *Times, Times Literary Supplement, New York Times, New Society, Studio International, Arts Canada,* and *British Journal of Photography.* Editor, *Axle* (quarterly), 1962-63.

WORK IN PROGRESS: The Mechanization of Man: Art, Technology and Politics, 1908-1933, for Paul Elek; a novel, *Before the War.*

AVOCATIONAL INTERESTS: Photography, walking, and fishing.

BIOGRAPHICAL/CRITICAL SOURCES: New Society, December 11, 1969; *Observer,* December 14, 1969; *Art and Artists,* January, 1970; *Architectural Review,* June, 1970; *Times Literary Supplement,* September 9, 1970.

*   *   *

OWEN, Lewis   1915-

PERSONAL: Born December 10, 1915, in Scranton, Pa.; son of Emerson David (a publicist) and Mabelle (Cochrane) Owen; married Esther Howell, October 14, 1939; children: Richard Lewis, Patricia Lynne (Mrs. Richard Schuler). *Education:* Educated in Hackensack, N.J. *Home:* 508 Summit Ave., Oradell, N.J. 07649. *Agent:* Paul R. Reynolds, Inc., 12 East 41st St., New York, N.Y. 10017; (historical slide talks) Ann Lewis Program Service, 97 Port Washington Blvd., Roslyn, N.Y. 11576.

CAREER: McCann-Erickson, Inc. (advertising agency), New York City, 1939-57, began as advertising writer, became associate creative director; Donahue & Coe, Kudner Agency, New York City, creative director and vice-president, 1957-60; Ogilvy & Mather, New York City, account supervisor, 1960-68; left advertising in early 1969 "to make a living in more pleasant ways"; now conducts a print-publishing business specializing in nineteenth-century woodcuts and engravings, manufactures plaques with Victorian ephemera, runs a mail order firm; along with his variety of businesses ("Lewis Owen's Things"), he writes, lectures on the stock market, and on Revolutionary War history, and is a business consultant. *Military service:* U.S. Army Air Forces, 1943-46; became sergeant. *Member:* American Revolution Round Table of New Jersey (chairman), Bergen County Historical Society, Cross and Cockade, Company of Military Historians, Lions International.

WRITINGS: Washington's Final Victory, K/S Historical Publications, 1967; *How Wall Street Doubles My Money Every Three Years: The No-Nonsense Guide to Steady Stock Market Profits,* Geis, 1969; *The Indian-Lover,* Bantam, 1975; *The Revolutionary Struggle in New Jersey,* New Jersey Historical Commission, 1976.

WORK IN PROGRESS: Swamp Fighter.

SIDELIGHTS: Lewis Owen told *CA:* "A lifetime of the disciplines of writing advertising that had to (1) attract and hold attention, (2) provide information and (3) trigger some kind of response trained me unconsciously for my present chief occupation. This is the creating of a rather unusual type of historical fiction: packed with fact and totally accurate in its events and in the picture it gives of the people and their times. Weaving a strong thread of romantic and dramatic continuity into the warp of history is a difficult but rewarding task. Turning out a story that will also attract readers who don't give a darn about such history is, of course, even more difficult. Sales and the low 'return' rate of my novel, *The Indian-Lover,* seem to indicate I've managed it pretty well.

"To satisfy more fully my own desire to present an accurate historic picture—and to answer the usually unspoken question of the reader as to what was fiction and what fact, I add a frank 'epilogue' which spells this out completely and tells what really happened subsequent to the novel's close. This approach indicates my strong feeling that distortion need not be the handmaiden of drama. The American Revolution, which is my theater, has outstanding cloth to fit any dramatic need. It should be cut and sewn skillfully but never replaced by tinsel and plastic. And if I didn't feel so strongly about this I wouldn't risk sounding stuffy by spelling it out with so outrageous a metaphor."

*   *   *

OWENS, Robert Goronwy   1923-

PERSONAL: Born June 13, 1923, in West Haven, Conn.; son of Goronwy William and Irene (Brennan) Owens; married Barbara Perkins (a teacher), February 21, 1950; children: Shellie, Sydney. *Education:* University of Connecticut, B.A., 1945, Ph.D., 1955; Columbia University, M.A., 1950. *Home:* 175 Columbia Heights, Brooklyn, N.Y. 11201. *Office:* School of Education, Brooklyn College of the City University of New York, Brooklyn, N.Y. 11210.

CAREER: Central School, Errol, N.H., teaching headmaster, 1945-47; principal of Broad Brook School, East Windsor, Conn., 1947-54, and of elementary schools in West Hartford, Conn., 1954-63; State University of New York at Buffalo, assistant professor of education, 1963-65; Brooklyn College of the City University of New York, Brooklyn, N.Y., associate professor, 1965-69, professor of education, 1969—, associate professor of education administration, 1969-75, coordinator of Advanced Certificate Program in Educational Administration and Supervision. Consultant in secondary education to India Ministry of Education on Fulbright and U.S. State Department awards, 1960-61. *Member:* American Association of School Administrators, American Education Research Association, National Conference of Professors of Educational Administration, Phi Delta Kappa.

WRITINGS: (Editor with others) *Summer School Programs in Transition,* Western New York School Study Council, State University of New York at Buffalo, 1965; (with Lawrence T. Alexander, Stephen Lockwood, and Carl Steinhoff) *A Demonstration of the Use of Simulation in the Training of School Administrators,* Division of Teacher Education, City University of New York, 1967; (with Steinhoff) *Organizational Climate in the More Effective Schools,* Division of Teacher Education, City University of New York, 1968; *A Regular Meeting of the Board,* State University of New York at Albany, 1968; *Organizational Behavior in Schools,* Prentice-Hall, 1970; (with Steinhoff) *Administering Change in Schools,* Prentice-Hall, 1976.

Contributor of articles to *Overview, Connecticut Teacher, American School Board Journal, Journal of Educational Administration, Group and Organization Studies,* and other education journals.

WORK IN PROGRESS: A revised edition of *Organizational Behavior in Schools,* for Prentice-Hall.

AVOCATIONAL INTERESTS: Sailing, skiing, horseback riding, cooking.

*   *   *

PACAUT, Marcel   1920-

PERSONAL: Born October 30, 1920, in Lyons, France; son of Edouard and Henriette (Dumont) Pacaut; children: Francoise, Anne. *Education:* University of Lyons, Licence es lettres, Aggregation. *Home:* 3 rue Duquesne, Lyons 69006, France. *Office:* Department of History, University of Lyons, 86 rue Pasteur, Lyons 69, France.

CAREER: University of Paris, Sorbonne, Paris, France, assistant in history, 1948-52; professor of history at a lycee in Paris, 1952-56; University of Lyons, Lyons, France, professor of history of the Middle Ages, 1956—, director of Institute of Political Studies, 1967—. Secretary, International Commission on Comparative Ecclesiastical History. *Military service:* French Resistance Forces, 1943-44.

WRITINGS: *L'Iconographie chretienne,* Presses Universitaires de France, 1952; *Alexandre III: Etudes sur la conception du pouvoir pontifical dans sa pensee et dans son oeuvre,* Vrin, 1956; *Louis VII et les elections episcopales dans le royaume de France,* Vrin, 1957; *La Theocratie: L'Eglise et le pouvoir au moyen age,* Aubier, 1957; *Les Institutions religieuses,* translation by Bernard Denvir published as *The Churches of the West,* Walker & Co., 1963; (with Paul M. Bouju) *Le Monde contemporain, 1945-1963,* A. Colin, 1964, 3rd revised and updated edition, 1968; *Louis VII et son royaume,* S.E.V.P.E.N., 1964; *Guide de l'etudiant en histoire medievale,* Presses Universitaires de France, 1968; *Frederic Barberousse,* Fayard, 1967, translation by A. J. Pomerans published as *Frederick Barbarossa,* Scribners, 1970; (with Jacques Rossiaud) *L'Age roman,* Fayard, 1968; *Les Structures politiques de l'Occident medieval,* A. Colin, 1969; *Les Ordres monastiques et religieuse au moyen age,* Nathan, 1970; *Histoire de la Papauté des origines au Concile de Trente,* Fayard, 1976.

* * *

PAHER, Stanley W(illiam) 1940-

PERSONAL: Surname sounds like "payer"; born January 20, 1940, in Las Vegas, Nev.; son of Stanley M. (a motel owner) and Dorothy (Betts) Paher. *Education:* Sacramento State College (now California State University, Sacramento), B.A., 1965; University of Nevada, Reno, M.A., 1969. *Politics:* Republican. *Religion:* Church of Christ. *Office:* Nevada Publications, P.O. Box 15444, Las Vegas, Nev. 89114.

CAREER: Writer; worked part-time as real estate salesman and research assistant, 1963-68. Staff aide to congressional candidates in general election, 1968, and special election, 1969; Florida College, Temple Terrace, news director, 1971-73; Nevada Publications, Las Vegas, publisher of regional books, 1971—. *Military service:* U.S. Navy, aviation storekeeper, 1958-60. *Member:* Western History Association, Nevada Historical Society (life member). *Awards, honors:* American Association of State and Local History merit award, for *Nevada Ghost Towns and Mining Camps.*

WRITINGS: *Nevada Ghost Towns and Mining Camps,* Howell-North Books, 1970; *Northwestern Arizona Ghost Towns,* Gateway Press, 1970; *Las Vegas, As It Began, As It Grew,* Nevada Publications, 1971; *Ponderosa Country,* Nevada Publications, 1972; *Death Valley Teamsters,* Nevada Publications, 1972; *Death Valley Ghost Towns,* Nevada Publications, 1973; *Nevada Bibliography,* Nevada Publications, 1974; *Colorado River Ghost Towns,* Nevada Publications, 1976; (editor with others) *Nevada Official Bicentennial Book,* Nevada Publications, 1976. Author of weekly column in *Las Vegas Sun.* Contributor to *American West* and *Nevada.*

SIDELIGHTS: In addition to extensive travel in the southwestern deserts in the United States for research on his books, Stanley W. Paher has visited more than two dozen foreign countires, including "considerable hitch-hiking in Southern Europe" and some travel in Asia. Paher told *CA:* "I find book publishing more fascinating than book writing ... [and] practical politics equally interesting." He finds that "biblical archaeology and details on religious movements, especially historical, hold much fascination" for him. He adds: "The Bible is the only source of religious truth; a close study of the text in both English and Greek has been influential in my life."

AVOCATIONAL INTERESTS: Reading articles on economics, history, sociology, geography, politics, religion, and business. Paher clips and classifies news items, articles, quips, and anecdotes; he has assembled more than 55,000 items in fourteen years of this hobby.

* * *

PAICE, Margaret 1920-

PERSONAL: Surname rhymes with "race"; born in 1920, in Brisbane, Queensland, Australia; daughter of Sydney (an engineer) and Violet (Burman) Cantle; married Hubert W. Paice, January 10, 1941 (died, 1956); married Wilfred L. Harriss (a high school teacher), January 16, 1960 (died, 1975); children: (first marriage) Jeannette (Mrs. Peter Lloyd), Peter W.; (second marriage) Christopher. *Education:* Studied at National Art School, Sydney, for one year, and at Royal Art Society School for one year. *Home:* 4 Paulwood Ave., North Springwood, New South Wales 2777, Australia.

CAREER: Commercial artist with firm in Sydney, Australia, 1957-60; illustrates and writes books for children. *Member:* Australian Society of Authors, New South Wales Children's Book Council, Fellowship of Australian Writers, Society of Women Writers, V.I.E.W. Club.

WRITINGS—All self-illustrated for children: *Mirram,* Angus & Robertson, 1955; *Namitja,* Angus & Robertson, 1956; *Valley in the North,* Angus & Robertson, 1957; *The Lucky Fall,* Angus & Robertson, 1958; *A Joey for Christmas,* Angus & Robertson, 1960; *The Secret of Greycliffs,* Angus & Robertson, 1961; *Over the Mountain,* Angus & Robertson, 1964; *The Bensens,* Collins, 1968; *They Drowned a Valley,* Collins, 1969; *The Morning Glory,* Collins, 1971; *Run to the Mountains,* Collins, 1972; *Dolan's Roost,* Collins, 1974; *Jackey-Jackey,* Collins, 1976; *Shadow of Wings,* Collins, 1977. Contributor of short stories to magazines.

Illustrator: Anne E. Wells, *Tales from Arnhem Land,* Angus & Robertson, 1959; Clarice Morris, *A Handbook of Australian Wild Flowers,* Angus & Robertson, 1961; Stella Sammon, *The Lucky Stone,* Methuen, 1969; Wells, *Rain in Arnhem Land,* Angus & Robertson, 1961; Wells, *Skies of Arnhem Land,* Angus & Robertson, 1964.

WORK IN PROGRESS: A history of transport in Australia, for Collins.

SIDELIGHTS: Margaret Paice told *CA:* "Friends have sometimes said to me: 'When are you going to stop writing for children and write proper books?' Meaning, of course adult fiction. Well, as far as I am concerned children's books are 'proper books.' They take just as much work and care—probably more. You can't get away with shoddy writing when you're dealing with children, nor with dishonesty in any shape or form. I find a child's natural curiosity will make him want to understand what you are trying to say; but his mind is sharp as a tack—he will see straight through any sort of sham."

AVOCATIONAL INTERESTS: Reading, painting, drawing, travelling.

PALAZZO, Anthony D. 1905-1970
(Tony Palazzo)

April 7, 1905—September 10, 1970; American illustrator and author of children's books. Obituaries: *New York Times*, September 12, 1970. (See index for *CA* sketch)

*   *   *

PALM, Goeran 1931-

PERSONAL: Born February 3, 1931, in Uppsala, Sweden; son of Samuel E. (a vicar) and Valborg (Ekman) Palm; divorced. *Education:* University of Uppsala, B.A., 1956. *Politics:* "Not organized. Socialist." *Home:* Surbrunnsgatan 31 B, 11348 Stockholm, Sweden.

CAREER: Newpaperman, 1955; adult education teacher in the Swedish countryside, and editor of a Stockholm literary magazine, 1955-58; literary critic for several newspapers in Sweden, 1950-65; free-lance writer and journalist, 1965—. Social activist, working with independent left wing groups in Sweden. Factory worker, Ericsson Company, Stockholm, 1970-71. *Member:* Swedish Writers' Union, P.E.N. *Awards, honors:* Several Swedish literary prizes.

WRITINGS: (Compiler with Folke Isaksson) *Femtio-Talslyrik* (title means "Poems from the Fifties"), Bonnier, 1960; *Hundens Besoek* (title means "The Dog's Visit"; poems), Norstedt, 1961; *Vaeriden ser dig* (title means "World Looks at You"; poems), Norstedt, 1964; (editor with Lars Baeckstroem) *Sweden Writes* (collection of Swedish poetry and prose in English), Prisma and Swedish Institute, 1965; *En Oraettvis betraktelse* (political essays), Norstedt, 1966, translation by Verne Moberg published as *As Others See Us*, Bobbs-Merrill, 1968; *Sjaelens furir och andra dikter*, Norstedt, 1967; *Indoktringeringen i Sverige* (title means "Indoctrination in Sweden"; essays), Norstedt, 1968; *Vad kan man gora?* (essays and poems), Norstedt, 1969; *Varfoer har naetterna inga namn?* (title means "Why Have the Nights No Names?"), Norstedt, 1971; *Ett ar pa LM and Bokslut fran LM* (two industrial reports), Foerfattarfoerlaget, 1972; *Dikter pa vers och prosa* (poems in verse and prose), Norstedt, 1976; *The Flight from Work*, translated by Patrick Smith, Cambridge University Press, 1977.

WORK IN PROGRESS: "A satirical dictionary for people who want to know how to think and write to succeed (or at least to be accepted) in the kingdom of Sweden."

SIDELIGHTS: Goeran Palm wrote *As Others See Us*, according to one reviewer, before he had ever set foot outside of Europe. He has since traveled in the Middle East, North Africa, and West Africa.

BIOGRAPHICAL/CRITICAL SOURCES: Best Sellers, December 1, 1968.

*   *   *

PALMER, (Nathaniel) Humphrey 1930-

PERSONAL: Born November 6, 1930, in Keighley, England; son of William Nathaniel (a teacher) and Dorothy (Procter) Palmer; married Elizabeth Packiam Theophilus (a lecturer), December 20, 1956; children: Jeremy Mohan. *Education:* Christ Church, Oxford, B.A. (in classics and philosophy; first class honors), 1953, M.A., 1956, B.A. (in theology), 1958; University of Wales, Ph.D., 1966. *Office:* Philosophy Department, University College, University of Wales, Cardiff, Wales.

CAREER: Christ Church College, Kanpur, India, lecturer in philosophy and English, 1956-58; University of Wales,

University College, Cardiff, assistant lecturer, 1958-60, lecturer, 1960-68, senior lecturer, 1968-74, reader in philosophy, 1974—, assistant dean of Faculty of Theology, 1968-70. Lecturer, Madras Christian College, 1962-64. External examiner in theology, University of Bristol. *Military service:* National service as conscientious objector, 1953-55.

WRITINGS: (With wife, Elizabeth Palmer) *Common Tamil Words,* Ravi & Co., for Christian Literature Society, 1964; *The Logic of Gospel Criticism,* St. Martin's, 1968; (translator from the German) L. Nelson, *Progress and Regress in Philosophy,* Basil Blackwell, Volume I, 1970, Volume II, 1971; *Analogy,* St. Martin's, 1973. Contributor to *Listener, Spectator,* and to philosophy and theology journals.

WORK IN PROGRESS: The logic of presuppositions, with special reference to Collingwood.

AVOCATIONAL INTERESTS: Simple gadgetry.

*   *   *

PALMER, John A. 1926-

PERSONAL: Born May 22, 1926, in Spokane, Wash.; son of Cary Alfred (a director of immigration) and Blanche (Trussell) Palmer. *Education:* University of Washington, Seattle, B.A., 1950; Cornell University, M.A., 1952, Ph.D., 1962. *Home:* 1301 South Atlantic, Monterey Park, Calif. 91754. *Office:* Office of Academic Affairs, California State University, Los Angeles, Calif. 90032.

CAREER: Cornell University, Ithaca, N.Y., instructor in English, 1955-59, 1960-62; California State University, Los Angeles, assistant professor, 1962-65, associate professor, 1965-70, professor of English, 1970—, chairman of department, 1967-70, dean of Letters and Science, 1969-70, vice-president for academic affairs, 1970—. *Military service:* U.S. Navy, 1943-46. *Member:* Modern Language Association of America, American Association of University Professors.

WRITINGS: Joseph Conrad's Fiction: A Study in Literary Growth, Cornell University Press, 1968; *Twentieth Century Interpretations of "The Nigger of the Narcissus,"* Prentice-Hall, 1969.

WORK IN PROGRESS: An analytic history of the English novel; and a study of metaphysical attitudes in American poetry.

*   *   *

PALUMBO, Dennis J(ames) 1929-

PERSONAL: Born November 18, 1929, in Chicago, Ill.; son of Richard Anthony and Nora (Griffin) Palumbo; married Sachiko Onishi, April, 1954; children: Jean, Susan, Dennis E., Linda. *Education:* University of Chicago, M.A., 1958, Ph.D., 1960. *Home:* 7623 West 10th St., Indianapolis, Ind. 46224. *Office:* School of Public and Environmental Affairs, Indiana University, 1232 West Michigan Ave., Indianapolis, Ind. 46202.

CAREER: Michigan State University, East Lansing, assistant professor of social science, 1960-61; University of Hawaii, Honolulu, assistant professor of political science, 1962-63; University of Pennsylvania, Philadelphia, associate professor of political science, 1963-66; Brooklyn College of the City University of New York, Brooklyn, N.Y., professor of political science, 1966-76, director of graduate program in urban administration, 1971-74, director of undergraduate-graduate program of urban administration and information science, 1973-76; Indiana University,

School of Public and Environmental Affairs, Indianapolis, professor of public and environmental affairs, 1976—, chairman of policy and administrative faculty, 1976—. Visiting professor, Columbia University, summer, 1971. Research associate, Council of State Governments, Chicago, Ill., 1959-60; associate researcher, Legislative Reference Bureau, Honolulu, Hawaii, 1962-63. Director, Research Center in Comparative Politics and Administration, Brooklyn College of the City University of New York. *Military service:* U.S. Air Force, Intelligence, 1950-54; became sergeant. *Member:* American Political Science Association, American Public Health Association, American Society of Public Administration. *Awards, honors:* I.D.A. Noyes scholarship, University of Chicago, 1959-60; U.S. Department of Health, Education, and Welfare, Public Health Service Research Grant, 1967-69.

WRITINGS: Statistics in Political and Behavioral Science, Appleton, 1969, 2nd edition, Columbia University Press, 1977; (contributor) Daniel Elazar, and others, editors, *Cooperation and Conflict,* F. E. Peacock, 1969; *American Politics,* Appleton, 1973; (contributor) Stuart Nagel, editor, *Policy Studies and the Social Sciences,* Lexington Books, 1975; (contributor) Fred Greenstein and Nelson Polsby, editors, *Handbook of Political Science,* Addison-Wesley, 1976; (contributor) Nagel, editor, *Modeling in Criminal Justice,* Sage Publications Inc., 1977. Contributor to *Urban Affairs, Quarterly, Public Administration Review, American Political Science Review, Commonweal, Intellect, Crime and Delinquency,* and *American Journal of Politics, American Journal of Public Health.*

WORK IN PROGRESS: American Criminal Justice; Analyzing Public Policy; Public Affairs Data System for Urban Management and Policy Evaluation; The New York City Financial Crisis: Significance for Other Cities; Urban Policy: A Bibliography.

SIDELIGHTS: Dennis J. Palumbo wrote *CA:* "I write because I enjoy it, because it is the best way to reach a large number of people, because I believe I have something important to say, and because I love words. But most important, writing enables me to see, almost as if I were an objective observer of myself, how I have improved over the years. Although much of my writing has been technical thus far, I expect to get better and believe my best years are yet to come. One can always look forward to doing the truly great work, even if it never happens."

* * *

PALUSCI, Larry 1916-

PERSONAL: Born May 22, 1916, in Camden, N.J.; son of Vincent (a painter) and Giovanini (Frosoni) Palusci; married Patricia Bottalico, November 2, 1935; children: Joanne (Mrs. Roy L. Holben). *Education:* Attended University of Pennsylvania. *Religion:* Roman Catholic.

CAREER: Larry Palusci Associates (retail management training), Newark, Del., owner, 1965-71; Arlen Properties, Mannix Division, New York, N.Y., general division manager, beginning 1971. Occasional instructor in retailing, University of Delaware, Newark.

WRITINGS: Profitable Retailing of Building Supplies: A Working Manual, Cahners, 1969. Contributor to *Building Supply News.*††

* * *

PAPANDREOU, Margaret C. 1923-

PERSONAL: Surname is pronounced Pa-pan-*dray*-ou; born September 30, 1923, in Oak Park, Ill.; daughter of Douglas G. and Hulda (Pfund) Chant; married Andreas George Papandreou (a professor), August 30, 1951; children: George, Sophia, Nicholas, Andreas. *Education:* University of Minnesota, B.A., 1946, M.P.H., 1955. *Residence:* Athens, Greece.

CAREER: Hennepin County Tuberculosis Association, Minneapolis, Minn., public relations work, 1946-47; Chant, Inc. (public relations agency), Minneapolis, Minn., head, 1947-49; U.S. Public Health Service, roving health educator, 1949-51.

WRITINGS: Nightmare in Athens, Prentice-Hall, 1970. Contributor of articles and reviews to periodicals.

WORK IN PROGRESS: Children's books—a series with socialist concepts.

SIDELIGHTS: Margaret Papandreou writes: "My political 'education' in Athens, and the role of the U.S. in developments there, from 1959-1968, motivated me to write my first book, and the ones I am working on now. My writing . . . is politically motivated. I want to contribute what I can to the anti-imperialist struggle."

* * *

PAPPAS, George 1929-

PERSONAL: Born January 25, 1929, in Boston, Mass.; son of Christos (a priest) and Jennie (Georgacopoulos) Pappas; married Marilyn Rafkin (a college teacher), June, 1953; married second wife, Sarah Hughes (a professor in junior college); children: Thomas, Jane. *Education:* Massachusetts College of Art, B.S., 1952; Harvard University, M.A., 1953; Massachusetts Institute of Technology, graduate study, 1952-53; Pennsylvania State University, D.Ed., 1957. *Politics:* Liberal. *Home:* 413 Park Ridge Ave., Temple Terrace, Fla. 33617. *Office:* Art Department, University of South Florida, Tampa, Fla. 33620.

CAREER: Junior and senior high school art teacher in Needham, Mass., 1953-54; Iowa State Teacher's College (now University of Northern Iowa), Cedar Falls, instructor in art, 1953-54; Pennsylvania State University, University Park, part-time instructor, 1955-56, assistant professor, 1956-60, associate professor of art education and art, 1960-66; University of South Florida, Tampa, associate professor of art education and art, 1966—, chairman of department of art education, 1968-73, chairman of art department, 1973—. Artist, with eighteen one-man shows, 1957—, including showings at Pennsylvania State University, 1957, 1962, 1965, Kanegis Gallery, Boston, and de Cordova Museum, Lincoln, Mass., 1958, Purdue University, 1963, Philadelphia College of Art, 1968, and at other colleges and universities; work represented in more than fifty exhibitions, including Pennsylvania Academy of Fine Arts, 1960-61, Detroit Institute of Arts, 1960, Chautaqua National Jury Show, 1963, National Small Painting Show, 1964, and Boston Museum of Fine Arts, 1966. *Member:* College Art Association, National Art Education Association. *Awards, honors:* Awards for painting, including Chautaqua National Jury Show, 1964, 1965, and Florida Craftsmen, 1967.

WRITINGS: (With Vadomillen and Adams) *Design: Its Form and Function,* Pennsylvania State University Press, 1960; (compiler) *Concepts in Art and Education: An Anthology of Current Issues,* Macmillan, 1970. Contributor to art and education journals. Contributing editor, *School Arts.*

PARADIS, Marjorie (Bartholomew)   1886(?)-1970

1886(?)—July 2, 1970; American novelist, playwright, and short story writer. Obituaries: *New York Times,* July 8, 1970; *Antiquarian Bookman,* September 7-14, 1970.

*   *   *

PARK, Peter   1929-

PERSONAL: Born September 3, 1929, in Inchon, Korea; son of Kyungsan and Pooyoung (Kim) Park; married Donna Singer (a teacher), May 24, 1963; children: Susan, Samuel, Phoebe. *Education:* Columbia University, B.A., 1953; Yale University, M.A., 1955, Ph.D., 1958. *Politics:* Independent. *Religion:* None. *Home:* 31 Dryads Green, Northampton, Mass. 01060. *Office:* Department of Sociology, University of Massachusetts, Amherst, Mass. 01002.

CAREER: Harvard University, Cambridge, Mass., Social Science Research Council fellow, 1957-58; Yale University, New Haven, Conn., research assistant, Center for Alcohol Studies, 1958-61; Sociological Research Institute of Alcohol Studies, Helsinki, Finland, research associate, 1961-62; University of Massachusetts, Amherst, assistant professor, 1962-67, associate professor, 1967-72, professor of sociology, 1972—. *Member:* American Sociological Association, American Statistical Association, Population Association of America, Psychometric Society.

WRITINGS: Sociology Tomorrow, Pegasus, 1969, revised edition published as *Sociology Tomorrow: An Evaluation of Sociological Theories of Science,* 1977.

WORK IN PROGRESS: Sociology of counterculture.†

*   *   *

PARKER, Derek   1932-

PERSONAL: Born May 27, 1932, in Looe, Cornwall, England; son of George Nevin (an agriculturist) and Ivy Vashti (Blatchford) Parker; married Julia Louise Lethbridge (a consultant astrologer), July 27, 1957. *Education:* Attended schools in England until seventeen. *Politics:* Labour. *Religion:* Agnostic. *Home:* 37 Campden Hill Towers, London W11 3QW, England; and Severalls, Foxton, Cambridgeshire SG8 6RP, England. *Agent:* David Higham Associates Ltd., 5 Lower John St., Golden Square, London W1R 4HA, England.

CAREER: Cornishman, Penzance, Cornwall, England, reporter, 1949-54; *Western Morning News,* Plymouth, Devonshire, England, drama critic, 1955-57; TWW-TV, Cardiff, Wales, interviewer and newscaster, 1957-58; free-lance writer and broadcaster, London, England, 1958—. Has made innumerable broadcasts on British radio and television; introduces "The Paperback Programme" weekly for the BBC World Service; lecturer on the history of astrology and on contemporary and classical English poetry. *Member:* Radiowriters' Association, Society of Authors, Royal Academy of Dancing (member of grand council), Royal Literary Fund (member of executive committee).

WRITINGS: The Fall of Phaethon (poems), Zebra Press (Exeter), 1954; (with Paul Casimir) *Company of Two* (poems), Zebra Press, 1955; *Byron and His World,* Vanguard, 1968; (editor with John Lehmann) *Selected Letters of Edith Sitwell,* Macmillan, 1970; *Astrology in the Modern World,* Taplinger, 1970; *The Question of Astrology,* Eyre & Spottiswoode, 1970; (with wife, Julia Parker) *The Compleat Astrologer,* McGraw, 1971; (with J. Parker) *The Compleat Lover,* McGraw, 1972; (editor) *Sacheverell Sitwell: A Symposium,* Bertram Rota, 1975; *John Donne and His World,*

Thames & Hudson, 1975; *Familiar to All,* J. Cape, 1975; (with J. Parker) *The Natural History of the Chorus Girl,* Bobbs-Merrill, 1975; *The Immortals,* McGraw, 1976.

Contributor: Charles Causley, editor, *Peninsula,* Mac-Donald & Co., 1957; Borestone, editor, *Best Poems of 1965,* Pacific Books, 1966; Arthur Russell, editor, *Ruth Pitter: Homage to a Poet,* Rapp & Whiting, 1969. Editor, *Poetry Review,* 1965-70.

WORK IN PROGRESS: The Isle Is Full of Noises: British Broadcasting, a Personal History, for David & Charles; with Julia Parker, a history of British operetta and musical comedy, for Chappell.

SIDELIGHTS: Derek Parker wrote *CA,* "An author who wishes to write serious books must (unless subsidised by university grants) pay for the time to be spent on them by writing good sellers." *The Compleat Astrologer* has sold over a million copies in nine languages, including Japanese.

*   *   *

PARKER, Robert Allerton   1889(?)-1970

1889(?)—June 14, 1970; American biographer and writer on popular religious movements. Obituaries: *New York Times,* June 15, 1970; *Antiquarian Bookman,* September 7-14, 1970.

*   *   *

PARKIN, Alan   1934-

PERSONAL: Born November 3, 1934, in King's Lynn, England; son of Henry Raymond (a journalist) and Mary (Bodiley) Parkin; married Lily Mack, December 13, 1965; children: Natasha, Sergei. *Education:* Peterhouse, Cambridge, B.A., 1958. *Home:* 88 Moreland Ct., Church Walk, Finchley Rd., London N.W.2, England. *Office:* Henrion Design Associates, 35 Pond St., London N.W.3, England.

CAREER: Architects Journal, London, England, production editor, 1959-60; Henrion Design Associates, London, associate, 1961—. Tutor in postgraduate graphics, Central School of Art and Design, London, 1968-69; special investigator of computer-based atlas mapping, Reader's Digest Association Ltd., London, 1968-69. *Military service:* Royal Air Force, National Service, 1953-55. *Awards, honors:* Research grant from Italian Government, 1958-59; two first prizes for fabric and wallpaper design in Sanderson Centenary Competition, London, 1959.

WRITINGS: (With F.H.K. Henrion) *Design Coordination and the Corporate Image,* Reinhold, 1967. Contributor of exhibits and an article to catalogue, *Cybernetic Serendipity,* 1968; also contributor to design journals.

WORK IN PROGRESS: Work in the general mathematical treatment of graphics on a very broad front, with special reference to computer graphics.††

*   *   *

PARKINSON, Michael   1944-

PERSONAL: Born August 11, 1944; son of John (a bus driver) and Margaret (Corrin) Parkinson; married Frances Anderson (a secondary school teacher), July 9, 1966. *Education:* University of Liverpool, B.S. (with honors), 1965; University of Manchester, M.A. (with distinction), 1968. *Politics:* Radical. *Religion:* None. *Office:* Department of Political Theory, Social Studies Building, University of Liverpool, Liverpool L69 3BX, England.

CAREER: University of Liverpool, Liverpool, England, resident fellow, 1967-70, lecturer in political theory and institutions, 1970—. Visiting associate professor, Washington University, 1972-73.

WRITINGS: The Labour Party and the Organization of Secondary Education, 1918-65, Humanities, 1970. Also author of a research report, *Politics of Urban Education,* University of Liverpool, 1973. Contributor of articles to *Political Studies.*

WORK IN PROGRESS: A study of English local political parties.†

* * *

PARR, Lucy 1924-
(Laura Carroll)

PERSONAL: Born July 25, 1924, in Kanab, Utah; daughter of Eustace Josiah (a rancher) and Geneva (Esplin) Chamberlain; married Robert Emmet Parr (a college professor and writer), May 21, 1945. *Education:* Attended Utah schools. *Politics:* Republican. *Religion:* Mormon. *Home:* 845 Garfield Ave., Salt Lake City, Utah 84105.

CAREER: Worked as a cashier for several years in Hollywood, Calif., and Salt Lake City, Utah; writer. *Awards, honors: Instructor* Stories for Children Award, 1965, for "That Pesky Crow."

WRITINGS: Pioneer and Indian Stories (for children and young people), Bookcraft, 1969; *Family Christmas Stories,* Bookcraft, 1973; *Not of the World: A Living Account of the United Order* (adult), Horizon, 1975; *True Stories of Mormon Pioneer Courage,* Horizon, 1976. Contributor of more than 250 short stories, articles, and verse to over fifty juvenile, teen, and adult magazines, some of them published under the pseudonym Laura Carroll.

WORK IN PROGRESS: Juvenile novels about wagon trains and life among the Indians; short stories.

SIDELIGHTS: Lucy Parr told *CA:* "I began writing because of my keen interest in American history, particularly the history of the Southwest. From the beginning, I have been very careful in researching for my stories and books, giving attention to the smallest details. Thus, time spent in research fills a large part of my writing schedule. But I have repeatedly found that this care with facts has paid off in achieving a reputation as a careful writer. It is my desire to create respect for our pioneers, to show the faith and courage which they exhibited in building our country. My most satisfying writing project to date is *Not of the World: A Living Account of the United Order.* This is the true story of an interesting period in the history of the West. Under the guidance of Brigham Young, the 'Mormons' established cooperative ventures, attempting to live in unity in temporal matters as well as in spiritual. A few communities achieved remarkable success in the venture. I have had the satisfaction of seeing this book well-accepted by those whose ancestors lived in the United Order and by others who have an interest in the book's historical value.

"My advice to aspiring writers is to find something which truly interests and excites them, something that can be of lasting value, then give it their time and enthusiasm. My husband and I decided many years ago that we must make a choice between writing and watching television. We chose writing, and have not regretted the decision. I have attempted to set definite work schedules for my writing, but find too many other demands infringing on my time. I find that I can set long-range goals and stay with them more successfully than to set a schedule of a certain number of hours per day or week. My time is somewhat limited for keeping up with the current literary scene, but much of what I do read alarms me with its cynicism about our country—past, present, and future. But I have been accused of being an optimist. I am also disappointed by the degrading language and moral tone of much of today's 'literature.' "

* * *

PARRISH, Michael E. 1942-

PERSONAL: Born March 4, 1942, in Huntington Park, Calif.; son of Emerson W. and Mabel (Weidemann) Parrish; married Caryl Smith, April, 1963; children: Scott David, Stephanie Lynn. *Education:* University of California, Riverside, B.A. (with high honors), 1964; Yale University, M.A., 1966, Ph.D., 1968. *Politics:* Democrat. *Religion:* Unitarian Universalist. *Home:* 1115 Aloha Dr., Encinitas, Calif. *Office:* Department of History, University of California, San Diego, P.O. Box 109, La Jolla, Calif. 92037.

CAREER: University of California, San Diego, La Jolla, assistant professor, 1968-73, associate professor of history, 1973—. *Member:* American Historical Association, Organization of American Historians. *Awards, honors:* Woodrow Wilson fellow, 1964-65.

WRITINGS: Securities Regulation and the New Deal, Yale University Press, 1970; (contributor) Richard Traina and Armin Rappaport, editors, *Source Problems in American History,* Macmillan, 1971.

WORK IN PROGRESS: A biography of Felix Frankfurter.†

* * *

PARSONS, James Bunyan 1921-

PERSONAL: Born October 31, 1921, in Shelbyville, Tenn.; son of James Bunyan and Alma (Raby) Parsons. *Education:* Fresno State College (now California State University, Fresno), A.B., 1943; University of California, Berkeley, M.A., 1948, Ph.D., 1954; attended Yenching University, Peking, China, 1949-50. *Home:* 4899½ Glenwood Dr., Riverside, Calif. 92501. *Office:* Department of History, University of California, Riverside, Calif. 92502.

CAREER: University of California, Riverside, assistant professor, 1954-61, associate professor, 1961-68, professor of history, 1968—. Visiting assistant professor of history, Stanford University, 1959-60; visiting professor of history, Simon Fraser University, Burnaby, British Columbia, 1967-68. *Military service:* U.S. Naval Reserve, active duty, 1942-46; became lieutenant junior grade. *Member:* American Historical Association, Association for Asian Studies. *Awards, honors:* Fulbright fellow in China, 1948-49; Social Science Research Council grant, 1957-58; American Council of Learned Societies grant, 1967, 1972.

WRITINGS: (Contributor) Charles O. Hucker, editor, *Chinese Government in Ming Times: Seven Studies,* Columbia University Press, 1969; *The Peasant Rebellions of the Late Ming Dynasty,* University of Arizona Press, 1970; (editor and contributor) *Papers in Honor of Professor Woodbridge Bingham: A Festschrift for His Seventy-fifth Birthday,* Chinese Material Center (Taipei), 1976. Contributor to oriental studies journals.

WORK IN PROGRESS: A monograph dealing with the Ming dynasty bureaucracy, completion expected in 1980.

SIDELIGHTS: In addition to two years in China, James Parsons spent one year in Japan, and two years in Taiwan doing research on the history of the Ming dynasty.

PARSONS, Kermit Carlyle 1927-

PERSONAL: Born July 15, 1927, in Cleveland, Ohio; son of Kermit Carlyle and Emma (Siebert) Parsons; married Janice Patten, June 30, 1951; children: John Everett, Stephen Carl, Kathrine Ingram. *Education:* Miami University, Oxford, Ohio, B.Arch., 1951; Cornell University, M.R.P., 1953. *Politics:* Democrat. *Religion:* Presbyterian. *Home:* 1604 Dryden Rd., R.D. 2, Freeville, N.Y. 13068. *Office:* Sibley Hall, Cornell University, Ithaca, N.Y. 14850.

CAREER: City Planning Commission, Cleveland, Ohio, city planner in urban renewal section, 1953-56, head of community planning section, 1956-57; Cornell University, Ithaca, N.Y., assistant professor, 1957-60, associate professor, 1960-65, professor of city and regional planning, 1965—, chairman of department, 1964-71, dean, College of Architecture, Art and Planning, 1971—. Visiting professor, University of Puerto Rico, 1969-70; visiting lecturer at University of Washington, Seattle, Western Reserve University (now Case Western Reserve University), 1966, University of Puerto Rico, 1966-68, and Harvard University, 1967-68. Private consulting practice in city, urban renewal, and university planning, 1957—. Consultant to Ford Foundation, 1970-76; consultant on campus planning for University of Ife, twenty-two campuses of State University of New York, and to other universities and cities. *Military service:* U.S. Naval Reserve, active duty, 1945-46.

MEMBER: American Institute of Planners (president, New York upstate chapter, 1966-67; member of executive committee, 1967-68), National Association of Housing and Redevelopment Officials, American Society of Planning Officials, Society for College and University Planning (president, 1966-68), Association for Institutional Research (associate), Regional Science Association, Urban Land Institute, Society of Architectural Historians. *Awards, honors:* Ford Foundation public affairs research grant, 1961-62; Cornell University faculty research grant, 1962-64; Ford Foundation study-travel grant, 1969; Woodrow Wilson International Center for Scholars fellow, 1977.

WRITINGS: An Annotated Bibliography on University and Medical Center Planning and Development, Council of Planning Librarians, 1962, 2nd revised edition, 1969; (contributor) C. Wentworth Eldredge, editor, *Taming Megalopolis,* Doubleday-Anchor, 1967; *The Cornell Campus: A History of Its Planning and Development,* Cornell University Press, 1968; (with Jon Lang) *An Annotated Bibliography on University Planning and Development,* Society for College and University Planning, 1968; (with others) *Public Land Acquisition for New Communities and the Control of Urban Growth: Alternative Strategies,* New York State Urban Development Corp., 1973; (with Pierre Clavel) *National Growth Policy: An Institutional Perspective,* National Science Foundation, Office of Science and Technology Policy, 1977. Contributor to professional journals.

WORK IN PROGRESS: With Georgia K. Davis, writing a chapter on educational planning, for *Local Planning Administration.*

*   *   *

PARTRIDGE, Frances 1900-

PERSONAL: Born March 15, 1900, in London, England; daughter of William Cecil (an architect) and Margaret (Lloyd) Marshall; married Ralph Partridge, February, 1933 (deceased); children: Lytton Burgo. *Education:* Newnham College, Cambridge, graduated with honors, 1921. *Politics:* Liberal. *Religion:* None. *Home:* 16 West Halkin St., London S.W.1, England.

CAREER: Engaged in bookselling, 1921-28; translator. *Member:* Society of Authors, Botanical Society of the British Isles.

WRITINGS: (Editor with husband, Ralph Partridge) *The Greville Memoirs, 1814-1860,* eight volumes, Macmillan, 1938.

Translator from the Spanish: Mercedes Ballesteros de Gailbrois, *Nothing Is Impossible,* Harvill, 1956; Vincent Blasco-Ibanez, *Blood and Sand,* Elek, 1958; Blasco-Ibanez, *The Naked Lady,* Elek, 1959; Miguel A. Asturias, *The President,* Atheneum, 1963; Jose L. Aranguren, *Human Communication,* McGraw, 1967; Pedro L. Entralgo, *Doctor and Patient,* McGraw, 1969; Alejo Carpentier, *War of Time,* Knopf, 1970; Rita Guibert, *Seven Voices,* Knopf, 1973; Carpentier, *Reasons of State,* Knopf, 1976.

Translator from the French: Iovleff Bornet, *Something to Declare,* Harvill, 1957; Joseph Kessel, *The Enemy in the Mouth,* Hart-Davis, 1961; Gabrielle Estivals, *A Gap in the Wall,* Collins, 1963; Raymond Cogniat, *Seventeenth-Century Painting,* Viking, 1964; Vassily Photiades, *Eighteenth-Century Painting,* Viking, 1964; Olivier Beigbeider, *Ivory,* 1965; Pierre Nordon, *Conan Doyle: A Biography,* J. Murray, 1966, Holt, 1967; Jacques Bonssard, *The Civilization of Charlemagne,* McGraw, 1967; Gilbert Martineau, *Napoleon's St. Helena,* J. Murray, 1968, Rand McNally, 1969; Martineau, *Napoleon Surrenders,* J. Murray, 1974; Martineau, *Napoleons Last Journey,* J. Murray, 1976. Also translator of magazine articles from French and Spanish.

SIDELIGHTS: Frances Partridge told *CA:* "As a translator from Spanish and French I began out of interest in these two languages, and have continued mainly because the problem of combining fidelity to my original and the working of good English, which does not read as a translation, has always absorbed me. I think the standard of translation is extremely low, partly because it is work that needs much . . . care, and (being very badly paid) does not generally get it."

AVOCATIONAL INTERESTS: Music (plays violin in an amateur orchestra and is an opera- and concert-goer), collecting and identifying wild flowers, reading (particularly history, memoirs, philosophy, biography).

*   *   *

PASCAL, Anthony H(enry) 1933-

PERSONAL: Born July 10, 1933, in Los Angeles, Calif.; son of Paul E. (a businessman) and Rose (Farber) Pascal; married Barbara Edelberg (an art gallery director), February 3, 1956; children: Amy, Jennifer. *Education:* University of California, Los Angeles, B.A. (highest honors), 1955; Columbia University, Ph.D., 1967. *Home:* 12243 Falkirk Lane, Los Angeles, Calif. 90049. *Office:* RAND Corp., 1700 Main St., Santa Monica, Calif. 90406.

CAREER: RAND Corp., Santa Monica, Calif., researcher and research supervisor, 1958-61, 1962-65, program director, Human Resource Studies, 1967—; U.S. Department of Commerce, Economic Development Administration, director of research, 1966-67. Research and administrative associate, Commission on Fiscal System of Venezuela, 1958; member, Secretary's Task Force on the Organization of Social Services, Department of Health, Education and Welfare, 1968-69. Visiting professor of economics, University of Nuevo Leon, Monterrey, Mexico, 1961-62; lecturer in economics, University of California, Los Angeles,

1964—; director of summer Institute of Regional Development, Williams College, 1966; visiting professor of economics, Stanford University, 1970, 1971, 1972; visiting scholar, University of California, Los Angeles, 1972-73; visiting scientist, St. Olaf College, spring, 1972.

MEMBER: American Economic Association, Western Regional Science Association (president, 1970-71), Western Economic Association, Inter-University Committee on Urban Economics, Phi Beta Kappa. *Awards, honors:* Annual Economics Research Award, Bank of Mexico, 1963.

WRITINGS—All published by Rand Corp., except as indicated: (Contributor) *The Fiscal System of Venezuela,* Johns Hopkins Press, 1959; (co-author) *The Economic Structure of North Eastern Mexico,* University of Nuevo Leon, 1963; (co-author) *An Appraisal of U.S. Capital Assistance to Less Developed Countries,* 1964; (with J. H. Niedercorn) *Resume of the Rand Conference on Urban Economics,* 1964; *The Economics of Housing Segregation,* 1965; *Reconnaissance for the War on Poverty,* 1965.

(With Nancy E. Hausner) *Criteria for the Location of Federal Regional Facilities,* 1966; *New Directions in Regional Research and Policy,* 1967; (editor and contributor) *Cities in Trouble: An Agenda for Urban Research,* 1968; (with Stephen J. Carroll) *Youth and Work: Toward a Model of Lifetime Economic Prospects,* 1969.

(Editor and contributor) *Thinking About Cities: New Perspectives on Urban Problems,* Dickenson, 1970; (contributor) *Social Welfare Forum,* Columbia University Press, 1970; (contributor) John P. Crecine and Louis H. Masotti, editors, *Financing the Metropolis,* Sage Publications, 1970; (contributor) *Symposium in Benefit Cost Analysis,* English Universities Press, 1971; *Enhancing Opportunities in Job Markets: Summary of Research and Recommendations for Policy,* 1971; (editor and contributor) *Population Change and Public Resource Requirements: The Impact of Future U.S. Demographic Trends on Education, Welfare and Health Care,* 1972; (editor and contributor) *Racial Discrimination in Economic Life,* Heath, 1972; (contributor) *Cities and Regions,* Longman, 1973; (contributor) R. Morris and others, editors, *Centrally Planned Social Change,* University of Illinois Press, 1974.

(Editor and contributor) *Programs for Mid-Life Redirection of Careers,* 1975; (editor and contributor) *Innovations in Career Education,* 1975; *Analysis of the School Preferred Reading Program in Selected Los Angeles Minority Schools,* 1976; (co-author) *Youth Policy in Transition,* 1976; (co-author) *Indicators of Justice,* Heath, 1977. Contributor to *Public Interest, Annals of Regional Science, Policy Sciences,* and *American Economic Review.* American editor, *Urban Studies;* member of editorial board, *Journal of Urban Economics* and *Review of Regional Studies;* editor, *North American Journal of Urban Studies.*

SIDELIGHTS: Anthony Pascal lists his professional interests as poverty, employment, welfare problems, race relations, population distribution, vocational education and the theory of policy and program analysis. *Avocational interests:* Film making, graphics.

BIOGRAPHICAL/CRITICAL SOURCES: Time, November 7, 1969.

* * *

PASCHAL, George H., Jr. 1925-

PERSONAL: Born August 22, 1925, in San Antonio, Tex.; son of George H. (a doctor) and Mary Louise (Steele) Pas-

chal; married Olive A. Hill (a social studies teacher), November 1, 1959. *Education:* Attended Texas A&I University, 1944; Trinity University, San Antonio, Tex., B.A., 1947, M.A., 1956; Louisiana State University, Ph.D., 1967; additional graduate study at University of Texas, Columbia University, and Texas Tech University. *Politics:* Republican ("usually"). *Religion:* Presbyterian. *Home:* 214 Primera Dr., San Antonio, Tex. 78212. *Office:* Department of History, Trinity University, 715 Stadium Dr., San Antonio, Tex. 78212.

CAREER: Teacher of blind students (at elementary level) and at high school in Texas, 1958-59; Trinity University, San Antonio, Tex., instructor in American history, 1963—. *Member:* American Historical Association, Bexar County Historical Association (past president).

WRITINGS: (With J. A. Benner) *One Hundred Years of Challenge and Change: A History of the Synod of Texas of the United Presbyterian Church in the U.S.A.,* Principia Press, 1968.

WORK IN PROGRESS: Footprints in the Sands of Time, a series of little-known but colorful historical figures; *A New Life of Jim Bowie.*

* * *

PASQUIER, Marie-Claire 1933-

PERSONAL: Born July 7, 1933, in Paris, France; daughter of Marcel and Lucile (Doumer) Pasquier; children: Emmanuel. *Education:* Sorbonne, University of Paris, Licence d'anglais, 1953, Agregation d'anglais, 1958; Cornell University, M.A., 1955. *Home:* 38 rue de Richelieu, Paris, 75001, France. *Agent:* Simone Benmussa, Theatre d'Orsay, 7 Quai A. France, Paris, 75008, France. *Office:* Universite de Paris X, Nanterre, France.

CAREER: University of Paris, Faculte de Nanterre, Nanterre, France, assistant teacher of twentieth-century English and American literature, 1965—. Has also taught in Algiers. *Awards, honors:* Fulbright scholar in United States.

WRITINGS: (Translator into French) Sidney Cohen, *The Beyond Within: The LSD Story,* Gallimard, 1965; (editor with Nicole Rougier and Bernard Brugiere) *L'Angleterre d'aujourd'hui par les textes,* Armand Colin, 1967, revised edition, 1974; (with Rougier and Brugiere) *Le Nouveau theatre anglais,* Armand Colin, 1969; (adapter and translator into French with Simone Benmussa) Edward Bond, *Lear,* Bourgois, 1975; *Le Theatre americain d'aujourd'hui,* Presses Universitaires de France, 1976. Contributor of articles to *Les Cahiers de Renaud—Barrault* and *Le Monde des Livres,* and translation to *Les Temps Modernes* and *Digraphe;* also has written for television. Contributing editor, *Theatres.*

WORK IN PROGRESS: Gertrude Stein, for state doctoral thesis; *Le Roman americain contemporain* for Presses Universitaires de France.

BIOGRAPHICAL/CRITICAL SOURCES: London Magazine, November, 1968.

* * *

PASSEL, Anne W(onders) 1918-
(Anne Wonders)

PERSONAL: Born September 12, 1918, in Baltimore, Md.; daughter of Darcy V. (a lawyer) and Hazel (Miller) Wonders; married Howard B. Passel (a professor and artist), August 22, 1942; children: Paul H. D., Jonathan C. *Educa-*

tion: Mount Holyoke College, A.B. (cum laude), 1940; University of the Pacific, M.A., 1964, Ph.D., 1967. *Office:* Department of English, California State College, 9001 Stockdale Hwy., Bakersfield, Calif. 93309.

CAREER: Former writer and editor on *Evening Post,* Charleston, S.C., *Philadelphia Inquirer,* Philadelphia, Pa., *Junior League* (magazine), and for McGraw-Hill, Inc. and Robbins Publishing Co.; former advertising copywriter in San Diego, Calif., and Washington, D.C.; University of the Pacific, Stockton, Calif., instructor, 1966-67, assistant professor of English, 1967-69; Fresno State College (now California State University, Fresno), Bakersfield Center, associate professor of English, 1969-70; California State College, Bakersfield, associate professor, 1970-72, professor of English, 1972—. *Member:* National League of American Pen Women, Bronte Society (England), Phi Kappa Phi.

WRITINGS: Poems 68, Crafton Press, 1968; *Jane Eyre by Charlotte Bronte* (book notes), Barnes & Noble, 1969. Contributor to journals. Writes poetry and magazine articles under name Anne Wonders.

WORK IN PROGRESS: A novel, *No Third Way;* a critical study, *Emily Bronte,* for Twayne English Authors series; a novel, *Up Cycle;* a research project, *Time in the Novel.*

SIDELIGHTS: Anne Passel has lived in France and traveled extensively in western Europe.

*   *   *

PAST, Ray(mond Edgar) 1918-

PERSONAL: Born December 14, 1918, in Jamestown, N.D.; son of Alvin E. and Frances (Tabler) Past; married Frances Paracca, September 23, 1942; children: Alvin W. *Education:* University of Pennsylvania, A.B., 1941; University of Texas, M.A., 1947, Ph.D., 1950. *Politics:* Democrat. *Religion:* "Not affiliated." *Home:* 3244 Louisville Ave., El Paso, Tex. 79930. *Office:* Department of Linguistics, University of Texas, El Paso, Tex. 79968.

CAREER: University of Texas, Main University (now University of Texas at Austin), instructor in English, 1950-51; Texas A&M University, College Station, assistant professor of English, 1951-52; University of Texas at El Paso, assistant professor, 1952-57, associate professor, 1957-61, professor of English, 1961-67, professor of linguistics, 1967—, chairman of department, 1971—. *Military service:* U.S. Navy, 1941-46; became lieutenant. *Member:* Teachers of English to Speakers of Other Languages, Modern Language Association of America, National Council of Teachers of English.

WRITINGS: (With Maria de Dozal) *Say It in English,* Volume I, W. C. Brown, 1968, Volume II, Kendall/Hunt, 1971, Volume III, Kendall/Hunt, 1972; *Language as a Lively Art,* published with exercise manual, W. C. Brown, 1970. Contributor of articles on language and linguistics to journals.

*   *   *

PASTORE, Nicholas 1916-

PERSONAL: Born November 2, 1916, in New York, N.Y.; son of Antonio and Maria (Altieri) Pastore. *Education:* City College (now City College of the City University of New York), B.S., 1940; Columbia University, Ph.D., 1948. *Home:* 56 Seventh Ave., New York, N.Y. 10011. *Office:* Department of Psychology, Queens College of the City University of New York, Flushing, N.Y. 11367.

CAREER: Long Island University, Brooklyn Center, Brooklyn, N.Y., instructor in psychology, 1948-51; Queens College of the City University of New York, Flushing, N.Y., instructor, 1951-56, assistant professor, 1956-60, associate professor, 1960-66, professor of psychology, 1966—. *Member:* American Psychological Association, American Association for the Advancement of Science.

WRITINGS: The Nature Nurture Controversy, King's Crown Press, 1949; *Selective History of Theories of Visual Perception: 1650-1950,* Oxford University Press, 1971. Contributor of more than sixty articles to *Science, Scientific American,* and psychology journals.

WORK IN PROGRESS: Writing on visual and cognitive processes, history of psychology, and sociology of knowledge.

SIDELIGHTS: Nicholas Pastore told *CA,* "In my current writings I am motivated in extending the relevance of concepts drawn from gestalt psychology in the understanding and resolution of historical as well as contemporary issues in human psychology." *Avocational interests:* Tennis.

*   *   *

PATAI, Raphael 1910-

PERSONAL: Surname rhymes with "Hawaii"; born November 22, 1910, in Budapest, Hungary; came to United States in 1947, naturalized in 1951; son of Joseph (a writer) and Edith (Ehrenfeld) Patai; married Naomi Tolkowsky, June, 1940; married second wife, Frances Pollack (a teacher), August 30, 1969; children: (first marriage) Ofra Jennifer (Mrs. William H. Wing), Daphne. *Education:* Attended University of Breslau, 1930-31 and Rabbinical Seminary, Breslau, 1930-31; University of Budapest, Ph.D., 1933; Rabbinical Seminary, Budapest, Rabbinical Diploma, 1936; Hebrew University of Jerusalem, Ph.D., 1936. *Home:* 39 Bow St., Forest Hills, N.Y. 11375.

CAREER: Hebrew University of Jerusalem, Jerusalem, Israel (then Palestine), instructor in Hebrew, 1938-42; research fellow in ethnology, 1943-47; Palestine Institute of Folklore and Ethnology, Jerusalem, director of research, 1944-48; Dropsie College for Hebrew and Cognate Learning (now Dropsie University), Philadelphia, Pa., professor of anthropology, 1948-57; Herzl Institute, New York City, director of research, 1956-71; Herzl Press, New York City, editor, 1957-71; Fairleigh Dickinson University, Rutherford, N.J., professor of anthropology, 1966-76. Consultant on Middle East, United Nations Secretariat, 1951; director, Syria-Jordan-Lebanon Research Project, Human Relations Area Files, Inc., 1955-56. Field researcher, Viking Fund, 1948; fellow, Bureau of Applied Social Research, Columbia University, 1948. Visiting lecturer in anthropology, Columbia University, 1948, 1954-56, 1960-61, New School for Social Research, 1948, New York University, 1951-53, and Princeton University, 1952-54; visiting professor of anthropology, University of Pennsylvania, 1948-49 and Ohio State University, 1956; visiting professor of Jewish studies, Brooklyn College of the City University of New York, 1971-72. Executive secretary, Israel Institute of Technology, 1942-43; president, American Friends of Tel Aviv University, 1956-68. *Member:* American Anthropological Association (fellow), Council of American Folklore Society, Royal Anthropological Institute. *Awards, honors:* Bialik Prize, Tel Aviv Municipality, 1936; Anisfield-Wolf Award in Race Relations, 1976; Bernard H. Marks Jewish History Award, 1976.

WRITINGS: Shire Yisrael Berekhyah Fontanella (title

means "The Poems of Israel Fontanella"), [Budapest], 1933; *Ha-Mayim* (title means "Water"), [Tel-Aviv], 1936; *Ha-Sapanuth ha'ivrith* (title means "Jewish Seafaring"), [Jerusalem], 1938; *Adam we-adamah* (title means "Man and Earth"), two volumes, Hebrew University Press Association, 1942-43; *Historical Traditions and Mortuary Customs of the Jews of Meshhed*, [Jerusalem], 1945; *On Culture Contact and Its Working in Modern Palestine*, American Anthropological Association, 1947; *Mada' ha-adam* (title means "The Science of Man"), two volumes, [Tel-Aviv], 1947; *Man and Temple in Ancient Jewish Myth and Ritual*, Thomas Nelson, 1947, 2nd edition, Ktav Publishing, 1967; *Israel between East and West: A Study in Human Relations*, Jewish Publications Society, 1953, 2nd edition, Greenwood Press, 1970; *Jordan, Lebanon, and Syria: An Annotated Bibliography*, Human Relations Area Files Press, 1957; *The Kingdom of Jordan*, Princeton University Press, 1958; *Cultures in Conflict: Three Lectures on the Socio-Cultural Problems of Israel and Her Neighbors*, Theodore Herzl Institute, 1958, 2nd edition published as *Cultures in Conflict: An Inquiry into the Socio-Cultural Problems of Israel and Her Neighbors*, Herzl Press, 1961; *Sex and Family in the Bible and the Middle East*, Doubleday, 1959; *Family, Love and the Bible*, MacGibbon & Kee, 1960; (with David de Sola Pool and Abraham Lopes Cardozo) *The World of the Sephardim*, Herzl Press, 1960; *Golden River to Golden Road: Society, Culture, and Change in the Middle East*, University of Pennsylvania Press, 1962, 3rd edition, 1969, paperback edition published as *Society, Culture and Change in the Middle East*, 1971; (with Robert Graves) *Hebrew Myths: The Book of Genesis*, Doubleday, 1964; (author of introduction and notes) Angelo Solomon Rappaport, *Myth and Legend of Ancient Israel*, three volumes, Ktav Publishing, 1966; *The Hebrew Goddess*, Ktav Publishing, 1968; *The Tents of Jacob: The Diaspora Yesterday and Today*, Prentice-Hall, 1971; *Myth and Modern Man*, Prentice-Hall, 1972; *The Arab Mind*, Scribners, 1973; (with Jennifer P. Wing) *The Myth of the Jewish Race*, Scribners, 1975.

Editor: (With Zvi Samuel Wohlmuth) *Mivhar ha-sipur ha-eretz-yisraeli* (title means "Israeli Short Stories"), two volumes, [Jerusalem], 1938, third edition, 1956; (and translator) Erich Brauer, *Yehude Kurdistan* (title means "The Jews of Kurdistan"), [Jerusalem], 1947; Farid Aouad, M. M. Bravmann, and others, *The Republic of Syria*, Human Relations Area Files Press, 1956; *The Hashemite Kingdom of Jordan*, Human Relations Area Files Press, 1956; Farid Aouad and others, *Jordan*, Human Relations Area File Press, 1957; *Current Jewish Social Research*, Theodor Herzl Foundation, 1958; (with Francis Lee Utley and Dov Noy) *Studies in Biblical and Jewish Folklore*, Indiana University Press, 1960; *The Complete Diaries of Theodor Herzl*, five volumes, Herzl Press, 1961; (and author of introduction) *Women in the Modern World*, Free Press, 1967; *Encyclopedia of Zionism and Israel*, two volumes, McGraw, 1971. Editor, *The Herzl Year Book*, Herzl Press, 1958-71.

WORK IN PROGRESS: The Jewish Mind.

SIDELIGHTS: Raphael Patai has traveled widely in the Middle East and Europe, and speaks English, German, French, Hungarian, Hebrew, and Arabic. He indicated to *CA* his "scholarly specialization [is] in the anthropology of the ancient Near East, the modern Middle East, Israel, [and] the Jews."

PATAPOFF, Elizabeth 1917-

PERSONAL: Born October 9, 1917, in Salem, Ore.; married Abrum J. Patapoff, 1953; children: three. *Education:* Willamette University, B.A., 1939; Columbia University, graduate study, 1948. *Home:* 1820 Southeast 38th Ave., Portland, Ore. 97214. *Office:* KOAP-TV, 2828 Southwest Front St., Portland, Ore. 97201.

CAREER: Former teacher in Oregon public schools and assistant for children's traveling libraries, Oregon State Library, Salem; Oregon School of the Air, KOAC-AM, Corvallis, director, 1949-56, 1958-65; KRVM-FM (Eugene school system radio station), Eugene, Ore., program director, 1957-58; Oregon Educational Broadcasting, KOAP-TV, Portland, producer-writer, 1965—. *Member:* Oregon Historical Society, Oregon Council for Women's Equality, Oregon State Employees Association.

WRITINGS: (With Margaret Weeks Adair) *Folk Plays for Social Studies*, John Day, 1971. Writer of radio and television scripts for Oregon Educational Broadcasting.

SIDELIGHTS: Elizabeth Patapoff told *CA* that her interest in plays for young people, which began with radio script writing, combined naturally with her interest in puppetry. Patapoff "tried to help fill the great need for youthful plays ... specifically aimed at diversity ... plays with varied formats, special effects, tales from around the world."

*   *   *

PATTERSON, Charlotte (Buist) 1942-
(Charlotte Buist)

PERSONAL: Born February 25, 1942, in Grand Rapids, Mich.; daughter of Samuel (a physician) and Ruth (Roelofs) Buist; married Thomas Patterson (a real estate broker), March 13, 1968. *Education:* University of Michigan, B.S., 1964; DePaul University, graduate study, 1965-68; University of Colorado, Pediatric Nurse Practitioner, 1969; Antioch College, Denver, Colo., M.Ed., 1974. *Home:* 384 Hollyberry Lane, Boulder, Colo. 80303.

CAREER: Children's Memorial Hospital, Chicago, Ill., public health nurse coordinator in Developmental Clinic, 1965-67; Children's Medical Center, Dallas, Tex., public health nurse coordinator, 1968-69; Denver Visiting Nurse Service, Denver, Colo., public health coordinator for Denver Developmental Evaluation Center and pediatric nurse practitioner at Denver General Hospital, 1969-71; teacher at Boulder Day Nursery, Boulder, Colo., 1972-74, and Raggedy Ann Preschool, Boulder, 1974-76; Boulder County Department of Social Services, Boulder, child development consultant, 1976—; The Maple Tree (therapeutic preschool), Boulder, co-director, 1976—. Member of board of directors, Human Services, Inc.; legislative chairman, Boulder Resources for the Education of Young Children. *Member:* National Association for Education of Young Children, Colorado Council for Exceptional Children.

WRITINGS: (Under name Charlotte Buist; with Jerome Schulman) *Toys and Games for Educationally Handicapped Children*, C. C Thomas, 1969; (with Leslie Segner) *Ways to Help Babies Grow and Learn: Activities for Infant Education*, World Press, 1970.

*   *   *

PATTERSON, Elizabeth C.

PERSONAL: Born in Clarkville, Red River County, Tex.; daughter of Clifton A. (an operator of cotton mills and gins) and Eva (Smith) Chambers; married Andrew Patterson (a professor of chemistry at Yale University), June 6, 1940; children: Ellen C. (Mrs. Jonathan C. Brown), Andrew Muir, Elizabeth L., Katharine C. *Education:* University of Texas, B.A., 1937, M.A., 1940; graduate study at University of Michigan, 1938, Mount Holyoke College, 1938-39, and Oxford University, 1966-67. *Home:* 175 East Rock Rd., New Haven, Conn. 06511. *Office:* Department of Physics, Albertus Magnus College, New Haven, Conn. 06511.

CAREER: Between 1940 and 1948 held a number of full and part-time teaching posts at various colleges where her husband was stationed; Albertus Magnus College, New Haven, Conn., 1958—, began as lecturer, professor of physics, 1970—. *Member:* American Association of Physics Teachers, American Physical Society, American Association for the Advancement of Science, History of Science Society, British Society for the History of Science, Connecticut Academy of Arts and Sciences, Phi Beta Kappa, Sigma Xi, Iota Sigma Pi, Mortar Board. *Awards, honors:* National Science Foundation, science faculty fellowship, 1967, and summer conference fellowship; American Philosophical Society grants, 1969, 1973.

WRITINGS: John Dalton and the Atomic Theory: The Biography of a Natural Philosopher, Doubleday, 1970. Contributor to professional journals.

WORK IN PROGRESS: Preparing a biography of Mrs. Somerville, and a bio-bibliography of nineteenth-century British scientific women.

*   *   *

PATTERSON, Raymond R. 1929-

PERSONAL: Born December 14, 1929, in New York, N.Y.; son of John Tollie and Mildred (Clemens) Patterson; married Boydie A. Cooke, November, 1957; children: Anna. *Education:* Lincoln University, Lincoln University, Pa., A.B., 1951; New York University, M.A., 1956; summer study at Wagner College, Columbia University, and Hunter College (now Hunter College of the City University of New York). *Home:* 2 Lee Ct., Merrick, N.Y. 11566. *Office address:* Black Poets Reading, Inc., Box 575, New York, N.Y. 10027.

CAREER: Youth House for Boys, New York City, children's supervisor, 1956-58; Benedict College, Columbia, S.C., instructor in English, 1958-59; New York (N.Y.) public schools, junior high school teacher of English and reading, 1959-68; City College of the City University of New York, New York City, lecturer in English, 1968—. Director, Black Poets Reading, Inc., New York City. *Military service:* U.S. Army, 1951-53. *Awards, honors:* Borestone Mountain poetry awards, 1950; National Endowment for the Arts discovery grant, 1969-70.

WRITINGS: (With Lawrence Sykes) *Get Caught: A Photographic Essay,* Verge Publications, 1964; *Twenty-six Ways of Looking at a Black Man and Other poems,* Award Books, 1969; (contributor) William Heyen, editor, *American Poets in 1976,* Bobbs-Merrill, 1976. Author of syndicated weekly column on Negro history, "From Our Past," for *New York Citizen-Call, New Jersey Herald News,* and *Buffalo Empire Star,* 1960-62.

WORK IN PROGRESS: A collection of poems; a book on word origins; *The Battle at Milliken's Bend* (possible title), a Civil War novel.

*   *   *

PATTISON, O(live) R(uth) B(rown) 1916-

PERSONAL: Born November 11, 1916, in Pittsburgh, Pa.;

daughter of James Wilson (a clergyman) and Olive (a chiropractor; maiden name, Roberts) Brown; married John B. Pattison (retired colonel, U.S. Air Force, and presently a high school administrator), July 11, 1938; children: John Barkley III. *Education:* University of Pittsburgh, B.S. in Ed., 1938. *Religion:* Baptist.

CAREER: Teacher of English at Chung Kung High School, Taipei, Taiwan, and teacher of the gospels at Taiwan Theological College, Taipei, 1962-63. American chairman, Chinese Air Force Orphanage, 1962; director, Friendship Corps (volunteers teaching English language in Taiwan high schools), 1963.

WRITINGS: The Undelivered, Revell, 1969.

WORK IN PROGRESS: A novel, tentatively entitled *Rest, My Daughter.*

SIDELIGHTS: O.R.B. Pattison has also lived in Panama, Afghanistan, the Philippines, and Okinawa, and has traveled in more than twenty-five other countries of Asia, Middle East, Africa, Europe, and North and Central America. She received a letter of commendation from the Air Force for her efforts in furthering Afghan-American friendship during her husband's tour as air attache at the American Embassy in Kabul, Afghanistan, 1950-53.

BIOGRAPHICAL/CRITICAL SOURCES: St. Petersburg Evening Independent, April 3, 1970.††

*   *   *

PAUL, Judith Edison 1939-
(Judith Edison)

PERSONAL: Born May 26, 1939, in Grand Rapids, Mich.; daughter of Arthur Perry (a farmer) and Marion (Weaver) Edison; married Thomas Clayton Paul (an educator), April 12, 1969; children: Mary Joe, Tobianne. *Education:* Michigan State University, B.S., 1961; University of Wisconsin, M.A., 1962, further graduate study, summers, 1964, 1965. *Politics:* Republican. *Religion:* Congregationalist. *Home:* 253 South Jefferson, Lancaster, Wis. 53813. *Office:* Southwest Wisconsin Vocational and Technical Institute, Bronson Blvd., Fennimore, Wis. 53805.

CAREER: Gateway Technical Institute, Kenosha, Wis., marketing instructor and program chairman, beginning 1962; currently teaching fashion merchandising and marketing at Southwest Wisconsin Vocational and Technical Institute, Fennimore. *Member:* National Education Association, Wisconsin Association of Distributive Educators, Wisconsin Education Association.

WRITINGS—Under name Judith Edison, with Kenneth Mills: *Checker-Cashier,* South-Western, 1969; *Create Distinctive Displays,* Prentice-Hall, 1974.

WORK IN PROGRESS: With Kenneth Mills, *Retail Sales Simulation,* for Prentice-Hall.

*   *   *

PAULDEN, Sydney (Maurice) 1932-

PERSONAL: Born September 6, 1932, in Eccles, England; son of Abe (a grocer) and Polly (Wallis) Paulden; married Mirkka-Liisa Levonius (secretary for her husband), December 1, 1956; children: Raymond Levonius, Kai Andrew, Jan Eric. *Education:* Downing College, Cambridge, B.A., 1954, M.A., 1959. *Politics:* None. *Religion:* None. *Home:* "Windsmoor," the Ridges, Finchampstead, Berkshire, England.

CAREER: Hulton Press Ltd., London, England, industrial

editor, 1956-59; Envoy Journals Ltd., London, editorial director, 1959-68. *Military service:* British Army, 1954-56; became sergeant. *Awards, honors:* Winston Churchill Memorial Trust fellowship, 1969.

WRITINGS: Plan Your Export Drive, Arlington Books, 1965; (with Colin McMillan) *Export Agents: A Complete Guide to Their Selection and Control,* Cahners, 1968, 2nd edition published as *Sales Manager's Guide to Selection and Control of Export Agents,* 1969; (with Bill Hawkins) *Whatever Happened at Fairfields?,* Gower Press, 1969; *Market Europe—The Trendsetters,* British National Export Council, 1971; *Hardy Heating International* (produced as a series of ten television programs by British Broadcasting Corp., 1971), BBC Publications, 1971; *Yan and the Gold Mountain Robbers* (juvenile; produced as a television program by British Broadcasting Corp., 1976), Abelard, 1975; *Yan and the Firemonsters* (juvenile), Abelard, 1976. Also author of *Joint Export Marketing Groups,* 1973. Regular contributor to *Times* (London), *Guardian, Financial Times* and *Computer Weekly.* Consultant editor, *Export Direction.*

WORK IN PROGRESS: Two more children's books, *Yan and the Battle for Bergania* and *Yan and the Power of the Wizards.*

SIDELIGHTS: Sydney Paulden told *CA:* "Whatever is written should be enjoyable to read and easily digestible. This applies to fiction and non-fiction. . . . Children's book writing is not so far removed from business book writing. I want my children's books to be exciting adventures that, at the same time, convey a sense of more profound implications." He is fluent in French and German and has varying degrees of competency in Spanish, Italian, Swedish, and Finnish.

* * *

PAWLEY, Thomas Desire III 1917-

PERSONAL: Born August 5, 1917, in Jackson, Miss.; son of Thomas Desire, Sr. (a teacher) and Ethel (Woolfolk) Pawley; married Ethel Louise McPeters (an elementary teacher), August 14, 1941; children: Thomas IV, Lawrence. *Education:* Virginia State College, A.B., 1937; University of Iowa, M.A., 1939, Ph.D., 1949; University of Missouri, additional study, 1957. *Home:* 1014 Lafayette, Jefferson City, Mo. 65101. *Office:* Department of Speech and Theatre, Lincoln University, Jefferson City, Mo. 65101.

CAREER: Prairie View State College (now Prairie View Agricultural and Mechanical College), Prairie View, Tex., instructor in theater, 1939-40; Lincoln University, Jefferson City, Mo., instructor, 1940-43, assistant professor, 1943-49, associate professor, 1949-53, professor of English, 1953-58, head of department of English and speech, 1958-69, head of department of speech and theatre, 1969—, chairman of Division of Humanities and Fine Arts, 1967—. Summer instructor, Atlanta University, 1939, 1940, 1941, 1943, 1944; visiting professor, University of California, Santa Barbara, 1968, Northern Illinois University, and University of Iowa, 1976. President, Jefferson City Library Board, 1970-72. *Member:* National Association of Dramatic and Speech Arts (president, 1953-55), American Educational Theatre Association (advisory council member, 1953-55), Alpha Phi Alpha (director of educational activities, 1967-73), Iota Sigma Lambda, Omicron Delta Kappa. *Awards, honors:* First prize in Jamestown and Virginia Corp. playwriting contest, 1954.

WRITINGS: Jedgement Day (one-act play), Dryden, 1941; (with William Reardon) *The Black Teacher and the Dramatic Arts,* Negro Universities Press, 1970.

Unpublished plays: "Messiah," produced, 1954; "F.F.V.," produced, 1963.

Also author of play, "The Tumult and the Shouting," produced in 1969 and published in *The Black Theatre, 1847-1974,* edited by James Hatch and Ted Shine, Free Press, 1974. Contributor of articles, poetry, and book reviews to journals and magazines.

* * *

PAWLOWSKI, Gareth L. 1939-

PERSONAL: Born September 11, 1939, in Memphis, Tenn.; son of Steve J. (U.S. Navy, retired) and Christine (Baldwin) Pawlowski. *Education:* Attended public schools in Memphis, Tenn., Honolulu, Hawaii, and Alameda, Calif. *Politics:* Democrat. *Religion:* Protestant. *Residence:* Burbank, Calif.

CAREER: Joined the U.S. Navy on completing high school in 1959, served as radioman aboard the "USS Ticonderoga," 1959-62, and participated in the Laos, Quemoy-Matsu, and Vietnam operations; employed in blueprint control room, Lockheed California Co., Burbank, 1963—. *Awards, honors—Military:* Armed Forces Expeditionary Medal (twice), Vietnam Service Medal with bronze star, National Defense Service Medal.

WRITINGS: Flat-Tops and Fledglings: A History of American Aircraft Carriers, A. S. Barnes, 1971.

WORK IN PROGRESS: Air Raid Pearl Harbor: This Is No Drill, for A. S. Barnes; a definitive history of The Beatles in Liverpool and Hamburg, 1960-1963.

SIDELIGHTS: Gareth Pawlowski first became interested in naval history at an early age while living in Hawaii, where he "boarded every ship that entered Pearl Harbor during the Korea conflict." It took him a little more than four years, working evenings, to complete the 500-page *Flat-Tops and Fledglings,* mainly because of the research involved.

AVOCATIONAL INTERESTS: Rusty (his dog), collecting items of historical importance ("someday my house will look like a small museum").

* * *

PAYNE, Michael 1941-

PERSONAL: Born January 17, 1941, in Dallas, Tex.; son of Fred G. and Jocie M. (Lundberg) Payne; married second wife, Laura Asherman, December 26, 1973; children: (first marriage) Jeffrey Michael. *Education:* Attended University of California, Berkeley, 1958-59, 1961; Southern Oregon College, B.A., 1962; University of Oregon, Ph.D., 1969. *Home:* 308 Harrison Ave., Lewisburg, Pa. 17837. *Office:* Department of English, Bucknell University, Lewisburg, Pa. 17837.

CAREER: Medford Senior High School, Medford, Ore., English teacher, 1962-63; University of Oregon, Eugene, English instructor, assistant director of English composition, 1966-69; Bucknell University, Lewisburg, Pa., assistant professor, 1969-74, associate professor of English, 1974—. Writer for Oregon Curriculum Study Center, 1966, 1969; fellow, Folger Shakespeare Library, 1973. *Member:* Modern Language Association of America, Shakespeare Association of America, American Association of University Professors. *Awards, honors:* National Endowment for the Humanities fellow, 1974; Lindback Award for Distinguished Teaching, 1976.

WRITINGS: (Editor with Glen Love) *Contemporary Es-*

says on Style, Scott, Foresman, 1969; Irony in Shake-speare's Roman Plays, University of Salzburg, 1974; (contributor) Perspectives on Hamlet, Bucknell University Press, 1976. Contributor of articles to University Review, Renaissance, English Journal, Modern Fiction Studies, Bucknell Review, Essays in Criticism, Blake Newsletter, Shakespeare Quarterly, CEA Critic, Journal of General Education, College Literature, and Style. Associate editor, Bucknell Review.

WORK IN PROGRESS: A study of myth in the works of William Blake.

* * *

PEARSON, Scott Roberts 1938-

PERSONAL: Born March 13, 1938, in Madison, Wis.; son of Carlyle Roberts (a physician and surgeon) and Edith Hope (Smith) Pearson; married Sandra Carol Anderson, September 12, 1962; children: Sarah Roberts, Elizabeth Hovden. Education: University of Wisconsin, B.S., 1961; University of Grenoble, Diploma, 1964; Johns Hopkins School of Advanced International Studies, M.A., 1965; Harvard University, Ph.D., 1969. Home: 691 Miranda Ave., Stanford, Calif. 94305. Office: Food Research Institute, Stanford University, Stanford, Calif. 94305.

CAREER: U.S. Peace Corps, teacher of African history and geography at Sokoto Training College, Sokoto, Nigeria, 1961-63; Stanford University, Food Research Institute, Stanford, Calif., assistant professor, 1968-74, associate professor of economics, 1974—. Staff economist, Commission on International Trade and Investment Policy, Washington, D.C., 1970-71. Consultant at intervals, U.S. Agency for International Development, 1965—, and International Bank for Reconstruction and Development, 1971—. Military service: U.S. Army Reserve, 1956-64. Member: American Economic Association, American Agricultural Economics Association, African Studies Association, Association for the Advancement of Agricultural Sciences in Africa, American Academy of Political and Social Science, Phi Beta Kappa. Awards, honors: Research grant from Social Science Research Council and American Council of Learned Societies, 1971-72.

WRITINGS: (Contributor) John D. Montgomery and Arthur Smithies, editors, Public Policy, Harvard University Press, 1966; (contributor) Carl K. Eicher and Carl Leidholm, editors, Growth and Development of the Nigerian Economy, Michigan State University Press, 1970; Petroleum and the Nigerian Economy, Stanford University Press, 1970; (with John Cownie and others) Commodity Exports and African Economic Development, Heath, 1974; (contributor) E. W. Erickson and Leonard Waverman, editors, The Energy Question, University of Toronto Press, 1974. Contributor to journals in his field.

WORK IN PROGRESS: Research on political economy of the rich in West Africa.

* * *

PECK, Ruth L. 1915-

PERSONAL: Born May 2, 1915, in Hamden, Conn.; daughter of Gilbert C. (a builder) and Mary A. (Penn) Peck. Education: Teachers College of Connecticut (now Central Connecticut State College), B.A., 1936; New Haven State Teachers College (now Southern Connecticut State College), M.A., 1951; University of Connecticut, sixth year certificate, 1957; additional studies at Columbia University and

Yale University. Home: 66 Brown St., Hamden, Conn. 06518.

CAREER: Elementary teacher in Hamden, Conn., 1936-71; Southern Connecticut State College, New Haven, instructor and supervisor of student art teachers, 1971-75. Member: National Education Association, National Art Education Association, Connecticut Education Association, Connecticut Arts.

WRITINGS: (With Robert S. Aniello) What Can I Do for an Art Lesson, Parker Publishing, 1966; (with Aniello) Art Lessons on a Shoestring, Parker Publishing, 1968; (with Helen E. Peck) Art and Language Lessons for the Elementary Classroom, Parker Publishing, 1969; Art Lessons that Teach Children about Their Natural Environment, Parker Publishing, 1973; Best of the Teacher's Art and Crafts Workshop, Parker Publishing, 1974. Author and editor, Teacher's Arts and Crafts Workshop, 1968—.

WORK IN PROGRESS: A book of art lessons for the elementary teacher.

SIDELIGHTS: Ruth L. Peck is a direct descendant of one of the original settlers of New Haven, Conn., and of William Penn. Avocational interests: Stamp collecting, gardening.

* * *

PEEL, Malcolm Lee 1936-

PERSONAL: Born June 12, 1936, in Jeffersonville, Ind.; son of Frank Peyton (a career military man) and Ella (Ditsler) Peel; married Ruth Ann Nash, June 18, 1960; children: Noel Carol, Drew George. Education: Indiana University, A.B., 1957; Louisville Presbyterian Seminary, B.D., 1960; Yale University, M.A., 1962, Ph.D., 1966; University of Utrecht, graduate study, 1962-63; University of Michigan, post-doctoral research, summer, 1968; Claremont University, graduate study, summer, 1969, 1970; Howard University, graduate study, 1971; University of Chicago, graduate study, 1974. Home: 3918 Wenig Rd. N.E., Cedar Rapids, Iowa 52402. Office: Department of Philosophy and Religion, Coe College, Cedar Rapids, Iowa 52402.

CAREER: Lycoming College, Williamsport, Pa., assistant professor of religion, 1965-69; Coe College, Cedar Rapids, Iowa, assistant professor, 1969-70, associate professor and chiarman of department of philosophy and religion, 1970—, chairperson, core program in liberal arts, 1973-74. Director, Center for Computer-Oriented Research, Society of Biblical Literature, 1970-72. Member: Society of Biblical Literature, American Academy of Religion, American Association of University Professors, Claremont Graduate School Institute for Antiquity and Christianity (corresponding and research member). Awards, honors: American Philosophical Society grants, summer, 1968, 1969, 1970; National Endowment for the Humanities, fellowship, 1971-72, curriculum development grant, 1974; Guggenheim fellow, 1972-73; Fulbright travel grant, 1973.

WRITINGS: (Editor with Carsten Colpe) Yale Gnosticism Seminar in 1963, Yale Divinity School, 1963; The Epistle to Rheginos: A Valentinian Letter on the Resurrection, Westminster, 1969. Also author of Gnosis and Auferstehung, 1974, and The Teachings of Silvanus, 1975. Contributor of articles and book reviews to theological journals in the United States and the Netherlands.

WORK IN PROGRESS: Two translations of newly-discovered Coptic Gnostic documents, for E. J. Brill; Basic Gnostic Bibliography, for E. J. Brill; preparing a monograph, *Whither the Quest?: The Historical Jesus in Modern Research;* research on teaching about religion in public schools of Iowa.

SIDELIGHTS: Malcolm Lee Peel told *CA:* "The theologian who writes and receives support for the task is never without a measure of divine pressure to produce. 'From him to whom much has been given, much will be required.'"

*   *   *

PELL, Arthur R.   1920-

PERSONAL: Born January 22, 1920, in New York, N.Y.; son of Harry and Rae (Meyers) Pell; married Erica Frost (a music teacher), May 19, 1946; children: Douglas, Hilary. *Education:* New York University, B.A., 1939, M.A., 1944; Cornell University, Professional Diploma, 1943. *Home and office:* 111 Dietz St., Hempstad, N.Y. 11550.

CAREER: Eagle Electric Manufacturing Co., Long Island, N.Y., personnel manager, 1946-50; North Atlantic Construction Co., New York City, personnel manager, 1950-53; Harper Associates (personnel consultants), New York City, vice-president, 1953-73; consultant in human resources management in New York City, 1975—. Professor of management in evening classes, City College of the City University of New York, 1947-67. Adjunct professor of management, New York University, 1960—, and St. John's University, 1971—. *Military service:* U.S. Army, 1942-46; became warrant officer. *Member:* American Society for Personnel Administration, American Society for Training and Development, National Employment Association.

WRITINGS: Placing Salesmen, Impact Publishers, 1963; (with Wlater Patterson) *Fire Officers Guide to Leadership,* privately printed, 1963; *Placing Executives,* Impact Publishers, 1964; *Police Leadership,* C. C Thomas, 1967; (with Maxwell Harper) *How to Get the Job You Want after Forty,* Pilot Books, 1967; *Recruiting and Selecting Personnel,* Simon & Schuster, 1969; (with Harper) *Starting and Managing an Employment Agency,* U.S. Small Business Administration, 1971; *Advancing Your Career* (home study program), Management Games Institute, 1971; *Recruiting, Training and Motivating Volunteer Workers,* Pilot Books, 1973; *Be a Better Employment Interviewer,* Personnel Publications, 1974, revised edition, 1976; (with Wilma Rogalin) *Women's Guide to Management Positions,* Simon & Schuster, 1975; (with Albert Furbay) *The College Student Guide to Career Planning,* Simon & Schuster, 1975; *Managing through People,* Simon & Schuster, 1975. Also author of numerous pamphlets and cassette taped programs on personnel subjects. Contributor of more than one hundred articles to trade and professional magazines, including syndicated newspaper series, "When Your Husband Loses His Job," 1971; columnist on personnel subjects, *Placement.*

WORK IN PROGRESS: Enriching Your Life, The Dale Carnegie Way, for Simon & Schuster; *Career Paths for Business Administration Majors,* for McKay.

SIDELIGHTS: Arthur Pell told *CA:* "My mission in life and work is to utilize my God-given talents to help others to identify, develop and make the most of their capabilities in their work and in their lives. My books have all been written with this mission in mind. My hope is that readers of my writings will be able to apply what they read to their careers and those other aspects of their daily activities so that they will be able to achieve a higher degree of self-actualization than they might have before reading these books."

PELLETIER, Ingrid   1912-

PERSONAL: Born March 27, 1912; daughter of Otto Eric (a carpenter) and Alina (Matson) Tast; married Emil George Pelletier (a railroad foreman), May 20, 1933 (died April 17, 1977); children: Janice I. Pelletier Lindemood, Gerald E., Joyce A. Pelletier Peterson, Gene O. *Education:* Attended public schools in Duluth, Minn. *Religion:* Lutheran. *Home:* 9595 Stark Rd., Duluth, Minn. 55810.

CAREER: J. C. Penney Co., Duluth, Minn., former office worker and clerk for ten years.

WRITINGS: Daughter of Lapland (juvenile), illustrations by Carolyn Cather Tierney, Putnam, 1970.

WORK IN PROGRESS: Ghost of Island Lake, a juvenile; short stories for religious and youth magazines.

AVOCATIONAL INTERESTS: Music, sports, fishing, outdoor life.

*   *   *

PELTON, Robert W(ayne)   1934-
(Tiffany Arthur, Kevin Martin, Robert W. Martin, Mark Milton, Robert Notlep, Devi Sonero)

PERSONAL: Born January 9, 1934, in Perry, N.Y.; son of Daniel Mitchell (a detective) and Ruth Lois (Collister) Pelton; divorced. *Education:* Attended Columbia University, 1953-54, University of Hawaii, 1955-56, University of Southern Mississippi, 1963-64, and Long Beach City College, 1966-68. *Home address:* P.O. Box 2381, Knoxville, Tenn. 37917. *Agent:* Al Zuckerman, Writers House, Inc., 132 West 31st St., New York, N.Y. 10001.

CAREER: Litton Industries (engineering firm), Pascagoula, Miss., marine engineer, 1957-63; Barnes & Reinecke (engineering firm), Chicago, Ill., architect, 1963-64; M. Rosenblatt & Sons (marine consultants), San Francisco, Calif., marine designer, 1964-67; Forster Design (marine consultants), Long Beach, Calif., marine engineer, 1967-68; currently full-time writer and lecturer. Consultant, Queen Mary Hotel-Museum project, 1968. *Military service:* U.S. Navy, 1951-54; received Silver Star, Bronze Star, and Purple Heart. *Member:* International Graphoanalysis Society, Toastmasters International. *Awards, honors:* Toastmaster of the Year Award, 1963, 1964.

WRITINGS: (Under pseudonym Robert W. Martin) *Love Guide by Handwriting Analysis,* Brandon House, 1968; (under pseudonym Robert Notlep) *The Autograph Collector: A New Guide,* Crown, 1969; (under pseudonym Tiffany Arthur) *Astrology in the Age of Aquarius,* Tower, 1970; *Beautiful Hair for Everyone,* Workman Publishing, 1970; *What Your Handwriting Reveals,* Hawthorn, 1970; *Complete Book of Voodoo,* Putnam, 1972; *One Hundred and One Things You Should Know about Marijuana,* Western Islands, 1972; *Your Future–Your Fortune,* Fawcett, 1973; *Voodoo Secrets–A through Z,* A. S. Barnes, 1973; *Voodoo Charms and Talismans,* Drake, 1973; *Lost Secrets of Astrology,* Nash Publishing, 1973; *Handwriting and Drawings Reveal Your Child's Personality,* Hawthorn, 1973; *Meatless Cooking the Natural Way,* A. S. Barnes, 1974; *Natural Baking the Old-Fashioned Way,* A. S. Barnes, 1974; (with Karen Carden) *Snake Handlers: God Fearers? Or Fanatics?,* Thomas Nelson, 1974; *Ancient Secrets of Fortunetelling,* A. S. Barnes, 1976; *Compleat Booke of Ancient Astrological Secrets,* A. S. Barnes, 1976; (with Keith Cottam) *Writer's Research Handbook,* A. S. Barnes, 1976; *Religious Revolving Puzzles,* Standard Publishing, 1976; *Natural Cooking the Old-Fashioned Way,* A. S. Barnes, 1976; (with

Merabe Hoke) *Bible Pinwheel Puzzles,* edited by J. Westers, Standard Publishing, 1976; *Bible Oddities,* CSS Publishing, 1976; (with Carden) *In My Name Shall They Cast Out Devils,* A. S. Barnes, 1976; (with Carden) *The Persecuted Prophets,* A. S. Barnes, 1976; *Women of the Bible Quiz Book,* CSS Publishing, 1977; *The Devil and Karen Kingston,* Portals Press, 1977; *Confrontations with the Devil,* A. S. Barnes, 1977; (with G. M. Farley) *Satan Unmasked,* Portals Press, 1978.

Under pseudonym Kevin Martin: *How to Go to High School or College by Mail,* Fell, 1969; *The Complete Gypsy Fortune-Teller,* Putnam, 1970; *Telling Fortunes with Cards: A Guide to Party Fun,* A. S. Barnes, 1970; *Compleat Booke of White Magic,* A. S. Barnes, 1976.

Under pseudonym Mark Milton: *Free for Teens,* Ace Books, 1969; *Free for Housewives,* Ace Books, 1970; *Handwriting Analysis,* Tower, 1970; *Guide to Numerology,* Tower, 1970.

Under pseudonym Devi Sonero: *Phrenology: Secrets Revealed by Your Face and Head,* Tower, 1970; *Secrets of Hypnotism,* Tower, 1970.

Contributor to numerous magazines, including *Horoscope Guide, Lookout, Law and Order, Police Times, Occult, American Astrology, Your Personal Astrology, Astrology Guide, Medical Dimensions, Coronet, Today's Health In the Know,* and *Modern Man.*

SIDELIGHTS: Robert W. Pelton told *CA:* "I began writing while an architect on a part-time basis, for 3 years, then quit the job to write full-time. I wrote and contracted 6 books during that 3 year period, [and] have now written full-time for about 10 years. . . .

"I write for days and weeks on end, then take a short trip, or just quit and relax for a few days. . . . My advice to aspiring writers: never quit. Simply be persistent and mass query publishers with your ideas for both books and articles. Keep your material going out to editors and never take a rejection personally, or as an indication that your work is not good enough to be put into print."

Pelton hopes that his "Karen Kingston book (case history of a recent exorcism on a retarded child who was cured) will be made into a movie." Many of his books have been translated and are in print in over fifteen countries.

*   *   *

PEMBERTON, Madge   188(?)-1970

188(?)—September 23, 1970; British playwright. Obituaries: *Stage,* October 1, 1970; *Variety,* October 7, 1970.

*   *   *

PENNEY, J(ames) C(ash)   1875-1971

September 16, 1875—February 12, 1971; American department store chain founder. Obituaries: *New York Times,* February 13, 1971; *Newsday,* February 13, 1971.

*   *   *

PERCY, William A., Jr.   1933-

PERSONAL: Born December 10, 1933, in Memphis, Tenn.; son of William A. and Anne (Dent) Percy. *Education:* Princeton University, student, 1951-53, A.M., 1962, Ph.D., 1964; University of Tennessee, A.B., 1957; University of Naples, Certificate, 1958-59; Cornell University, M.A., 1960. *Office:* Department of History, University of Massachusetts, Boston, Mass. 02116.

CAREER: Louisiana State University, Baton Rouge, assistant professor of history, 1962-66; University of Missouri, St. Louis, associate professor of history, 1966-68; University of Massachusetts, Boston, associate professor, 1968-73, professor of history, 1973—. Visiting associate professor, Washington University, 1967; visiting professor, Northeastern University, Boston, Mass., 1969-77. *Military service:* U.S. Army, interpreter, 1953-56. *Member:* American History Association, Mediaeval Academy of America, Renaissance Society of America (South Central conference), American Numismatic Society (fellow). *Awards, honors:* Bursa di Studia, Italian government, 1958-59; Grants-in-aid from Louisiana State University for study at Widener Library, summers, 1964, 1965, and for University of Missouri, University of North Carolina, and Duke University, summer, 1966.

WRITINGS: (With Jerah Johnson) *The Age of Recovery: Europe in the Fifteenth Century,* Cornell University Press, 1970. Contributor to *People's Encyclopedia.* Contributor to *Louisiana History, American Historical Review, Speculum, Manuscripta, Italian Quarterly.*

WORK IN PROGRESS: (With Edward W. Fox) *Western Civilization,* for Prentice Hall.

*   *   *

PERERA, Victor   1934-

PERSONAL: Born April 12, 1934, in Guatemala City, Guatemala; son of Salomon (a businessman) and Tamar (Nissim) Perera; married Padma Hejmadi (a writer), August 8, 1960 (divorced, 1974). *Education:* Brooklyn College (now Brooklyn College of the City University of New York), B.A., 1956; University of Michigan, M.A., 1958. *Religion:* Jewish. *Address:* P.O. Box 653, Capitola, Calif. 95010. *Agent:* Raines & Raines, 475 Fifth Ave., New York, N.Y. 10017.

CAREER: United Nations, New York City, interpreter-trainee, 1959; University of Michigan, Ann Arbor, pre-doctoral teaching fellow in English and Spanish literature, 1959-63; *New Yorker,* New York City, member of editorial staff, 1963-66; Vassar College, Poughkeepsie, N.Y., lecturer in English, 1968-70; University of California, Santa Cruz, visiting lecturer in creative writing, 1971—. *Member:* Authors Guild, Friends of the MacDowell Colony. *Awards, honors:* Major essay prize in Avery and Jule Hopwood Awards at University of Michigan, 1961; several fellowships at Yaddo and MacDowell Colony.

WRITINGS: The Conversion (novel), Little, Brown, 1970; *The Loch-Ness Monster-Watchers* (non-fiction), Capra, 1974. Contributor of short stories and articles to *Commentary, Partisan Review, New York, Vogue, Harper's, Atlantic, Saturday Review, New York Times,* and other periodicals. Also has done translations of the works of Neruda, Asturias, and other Latin American writers for periodicals. Contributing editor, *Present Tense,* 1974—.

WORK IN PROGRESS: Rites of Passage, a novel; *The Gray Whale,* a children's book; a collection of essays, several of them previously published and some new.

SIDELIGHTS: Victor Perera writes: "My two chief reasons for writing, when the baser worldly motives are pared away: I write to know better the soul within me, to see, to be illuminated. I write to find my peers, other seekers who strive to become part of a regenerative process in a time of destruction and decay."

He adds that he is a devoted tennis player and has "an amateur interest in Indian (i.e. Hindu and Jain), Greek, Mayan, Inca, and Aztec archaeology, and have tramped about a good many sites of these old civilizations in the past decade.'' Perera has traveled extensively in India, the Far East, South America, and in western Europe, particularly in Spain.

BIOGRAPHICAL/CRITICAL SOURCES: Time, June 29, 1970; *Best Sellers,* July 1, 1970.

* * *

PEREZ, Joseph F(rancis) 1930-

PERSONAL: Born September 19, 1930, in Nice, France; naturalized U.S. citizen; son of Antonio (a tailor) and Teresa (DeSantis) Perez; married Geraldine Boudreau, September 4, 1954; children: Joseph, Jr., Kathleen, Christopher, Monique. *Education:* University of Connecticut, A.B., 1954, Ph.D., 1959; Boston University, Ed.M., 1956. *Politics:* Democrat. *Religion:* Roman Catholic. *Home:* 446 Chesterfield Rd., Leeds, Mass. 01053. *Office:* Department of Psychology, Westfield State College, Westfield, Mass. 01085.

CAREER: Director guidance psychology in public schools of Massachusetts, 1959-61; Veterans Administration Psychiatric Hospital, Northampton, Mass., counseling psychologist, 1961-63; Westfield State College, Westfield, Mass., professor of psychology and chairman of department, 1963—. Consulting psychologist to Northampton (Mass.) public schools, 1964—, and to Roman Catholic Diocese of Springfield, Mass. *Military service:* U.S. Army, 1950-52. *Member:* American Psychological Association, Massachusetts Psychological Association.

WRITINGS: Couseling: Theory and Practice, Addison-Wesley, 1965; (editor with others) *General Psychology: Readings in Human Relations,* Van Nostrand, 1967; *The Initial Counseling Contact,* Houghton, 1968; (with Alvin Cohen) *Mom and Dad Are Me: The Study of a Disturbed Adolescent,* Brooks-Cole, 1969.

* * *

PERIN, Constance

PERSONAL: Born in Pontiac, Mich. *Education:* University of Chicago, B.A., 1950, A.M., 1972; University of Pennsylvania, M.C.P., 1966; University College, London, additional study, 1968-69; American University, Ph.D., 1975. *Home:* 1451 East 55th St., Chicago, Ill. 60615.

CAREER: University of Chicago, Chicago, Ill., research assistant with National Opinion Research Center, 1951-52; Kling Studios, Inc., Chicago, senior staff writer, 1952-55; Harold Cabot & Co., Boston, Mass., advertising copywriter, 1956-57; Citizens Advisory Committee for Cambridge, Mass., assistant to director, 1957-58; Adams, Howard & Greeley (planning consultants), Brookline, Mass., assistant to resident planner, 1958-62; American Institute of Planners, New York, N.Y., director of publications, 1962-67; U.S. Department of Housing and Urban Development, Washington, D.C., program evaluation officer and assistant director of Presidential Task Force on Suburban Problems, 1967-68; University of Chicago, member of research staff, Office of Physical Planning and Construction, 1969-70; fellow of Adlai Stevenson Institute of International Affairs, 1970-71; Library of Congress, Washington, D.C., consultant to Congressional Research Service, 1972-73; Institution and Public Decisions, Resources for the Future, Washington, D.C., senior research associate, 1973-76. Visiting lecturer at several universities,

including University of Illinois at Chicago Circle, University of Illinois, Urbana, 1972, Portland State University, 1973, and University of Texas at Austin, 1975. Ford Foundation fellow, University of Chicago. Has conducted lecturers and seminars to various universities, including Princeton University, Texas A & M University, University of Cincinnati, and New York University. Consultant to many groups and companies, including National Academy of Sciences, Potamac Institute, 1976, Rouse Co., and American Institute of Architects. *Member:* American Anthropological Association (fellow), National Academy of Science, Environmental Design Research Association (member of board of directors, 1974-77). *Awards, honors:* Fulbright scholar in London, 1968-69; Ford Foundation travel grant, 1968-69, 1977; Guggenheim fellowship, 1977-78.

WRITINGS: With Man in Mind: An Interdisciplinary Prospectus for Environmental Design, M.I.T. Press, 1970; *Everything in Its Place: Social Order And Land Use in America,* Princeton University Press, 1977.

Contributor: William Mitchell, editor, *Environmental Design Research and Practice,* University of California, Los Angeles, 1972; Jon Lang and others, editors, *Designing for Human Behavior,* Dowden, 1974; Basil Honikman, editor, *Responding to Social Change,* Halstead, 1975; Bela C. Maday, editor, *Anthropology and Society,* Anthropological Society of Washington, 1975. Contributor to planning journals, including *Journal of the American Institute of Planners.*

* * *

PERLS, Frederick S. 1894(?)-1970
(Fritz Perls)

1894(?)—March 14, 1970; German-born author and co-founder of Gestalt school of psychotherapy. Obituaries: *New York Times,* March 17, 1970; *Time,* March 30, 1970.

* * *

PERRETT, Bryan 1934-

PERSONAL: Born July 9, 1934; son of Thomas Edgar and Ellen (Nicholson) Perrett; married Anne Catherine Trench, August 13, 1966. *Education:* Educated in Liverpool, England. *Home:* 7 Maple Ave., Burscough, near Ormskirk, Lancashire, England. *Office:* Griffiths & Armour, 101 Derby House, Liverpool 2, England.

CAREER: Bentalls Ltd. (department store), Kingston, Surrey, England, trainee buyer, 1955-56; Lloyds Brokers, London, England, broker, 1956-60; Griffiths & Armour (insurance broker), Liverpool, England, broker and claims adjustor, 1960—. *Military service:* British Army, 1952-54. Territorial Army, 1954-67. Army Emergency Reserve, Royal Tank Regiment, 1967—; current rank, captain; awarded Territorial Decoration, 1970. *Member:* Insurance Institute of Liverpool.

WRITINGS: Fighting Vehicles of the Red Army, Ian Allen, 1969, Arco, 1970; *NATO Armour,* Ian Allen, 1971; *The "Valentine" in North Africa, 1942-43,* Ian Allen, 1972; *The "Matilda",* Ian Allen, 1973; *The "Churchill",* Ian Allen, 1974; *Through Mud and Blood,* foreword by Field Marshal Sir Michael Carver, R. Hale, 1975; *Armoured Operations in Burma, 1942-1945,* R. Hale, in press. Also author of a monograph on armour and the Russian officer published in *Army Quarterly.* Contributor of articles to *U.S. Army Defense Review, Military Modelling, Battle;* contributor of stories to *Battle, War Picture Libraries, IPC.*

WORK IN PROGRESS: Research for possible books on the Anglo-Turkish War of 1914-1918, Banastre Tarleton, the infamous British Cavalry leader, and the Chesapeake campaign of 1814; an article of the battle of Meiktila and the destruction of the Japanese Burma Area Army; a series of articles on forgotten armoured engagements; a series of articles on major tactical blunders.

SIDELIGHTS: Bryan Perrett told *CA:* "I took up writing as an antidote to excessive spare time when Harold Wilson's Labour Government virtually disbanded the Territorial Army in 1967. My first two books were written simply to fill a gap in the market, but subsequent works all have one thing in common, i.e. the correction of an imballance in the published history of Royal Armoured Corps operations 1939/45. Whilst much had been written on the operations carried out by armoured division, almost nothing was available on tank brigades whose job it was to support infantry operations. . . .

"So far, my work has been confined to a narrow field, and although this is widening steadily, I am not sure that I can offer anything more than the obvious advice to aspiring writers of military history. One may receive many conflicting opinions concerning the conduct of any one operation, since this is seen by every man from a different standpoint. . . . It is the historian's duty to sift the merits of the case impartially, and to write what he believes to be the honest truth. Trust no one source—experts are frequently wrong, particularly as to detail; famous names are quite as capable of making mistakes as anyone else. To obtain the truth, one must play the Devil's Advocate with one's own sources, until one is absolutely satisfied that they are accurate; any historian who does less faces the uncomfortable prospect of living with his mistakes. . . .

"I do not believe that any writer can succeed without the most ruthless self discipline. The military historian in particular must establish an iron routine for himself, and maintain his effort until he has achieved his object. Waiting for inspiration and working by fits and starts will not finish the job—like any artist, you are working because an inner drive compels you to do so. If that drive is so weak that you are unable to apply yourself continuously, I think you would do well to find some other way of passing your time.

"Finally, remember that criticism is only another man's opinion. It can be constructive or destructive, and should be assessed in its turn as to whether it contains merit. There is an element of the frustrated performer in most critics, and one should not become either unduly depressed or elated by what they say."

*   *   *

PERRY, Kenneth I.   1929-

PERSONAL: Born March 2, 1929, in Salt Lake City, Utah; son of Ivan and Hannah Laurie (Hair) Perry. *Education:* Attended Universite de Paris, Sorbonne, 1951; Brigham Young University, A.B., 1954; University of Michigan, M.A., 1959, Ph.D., 1966; Auburn University, M.Pol.Sci., 1975. *Politics:* Republican. *Religion:* Church of Jesus Christ of Latter-day Saints. *Home:* 1660 North LaSalle, Apt. 2301, Chicago, Ill. 60614. *Office:* Department of French, University of Illinois at Chicago Circle, Chicago, Ill. 60680.

CAREER: Duke University, Durham, N.C., instructor in French, 1962-65; University of Illinois at Chicago Circle, Chicago, associate professor of French, 1965—. *Military service:* U.S. Air Force; became colonel. *Member:* Modern Language Association of America, American Association of Teachers of French, American Council of Teachers of For-

eign Languages, Societe des Professeurs de Francais en Amerique.

WRITINGS: (With Donald O. Oscarson) *Six Sent South* (musical), Deseret Press, 1959; (contributor) *Chicago Circle Studies,* University of Illinois at Chicago Circle, 1967; *The Religious Symbolism of Andre Gide,* Mouton & Co., 1969, Humanities, 1970; (editor) *"La Chamade": A Supplementary Reader,* text edition, Prentice-Hall, 1970; (editor) Francoise Sagan, *Le Cheval evanoui* [suivi de] *L'Echarde,* Prentice-Hall, 1971. Contributor of articles to *Air University Professional Studies* and *Kentucky Romance Quarterly.*

WORK IN PROGRESS: Critical analysis of the "Nouveau Roman" leading to a book on the optics, perspectives, and reader approach to the new novel.

*   *   *

PERRY, Phillip M.   1948-

PERSONAL: Born November 29, 1948, in Beaver, Pa. *Education:* University of Notre Dame, B.A., 1970. *Office:* Phillip M. Perry Associates, 1600 Broadway, New York, N.Y. 10019.

CAREER: Founder and president, Phillip M. Perry Associates (communications firm), New York, N.Y. *Military Service:* U.S. Army, 1971—, serving in Infantry as first lieutenant.

WRITINGS: (Compiler and contributor) *Mad Windows,* Literature Press, 1969; *The Warlock* (narrative poem), Dustbooks, 1971; *Security for Schools and Centers,* Creative Book Co., 1976.

WORK IN PROGRESS: Garlandia, a novel.

*   *   *

PESEK, Ludek   1919-

PERSONAL: Born April 26, 1919, in Kladno, Czechoslovakia; son of Ludvik (a clerk) and Anna (Cihakova) Pesek; married Bozena Raymannova (a secretary), August 22, 1953. *Education:* Studied in Czechoslovakia at a classical gymnasium, 1932-39, and at Academy of Arts, Prague, 1939-46. *Home:* Rohrhaldenstrasse 8, 8712 Staefa, Switzerland.

CAREER: Painter and illustrator. Collaborator in fields of astronomy and geology with National Geographic Society, Washington, D.C. *Military service:* Czechoslovak Army, 1946-47. *Member:* Czechoslovak Union of Artists. *Awards, honors:* First prize in European Literary Club contest, 1948, for *Drazba; Die Mondexpedition* was on the honor list of best German books for youths, 1967; Der deutsche Jugendbuch-Preis, 1971, for *Die Erde ist nahe.*

WRITINGS: Lide v Kameni (novel; title means "People Among the Stones"), Lukasik (Ostrava), 1946; *Tahouni* (novel; title means "Draught-Horses"), European Literary Klub (Prague), 1947; *Drazba* (novel; title means "Auction"), European Literary Klub, 1948; *Lebanon* (travel book), Artia (Prague), 1965; *Die Mondexpedition* (youth novel), Paulus-Verlag (West Germany), 1967, translation published as *Log of a Moon Expedition,* Knopf, 1969; *Die Erde ist nahe* (novel; title means "The Earth Is Near"), Bitter Verlag (West Germany), 1971; *Nur Ein Stein* (novel; title means "Only a Stone"), Beltz Verlag (West Germany), 1972; *Preis Der Beute* (title means "Price of the Prey"), Beltz Verlag, 1973; *An Island for Two* (novel), Bradbury, 1975; *Flug In Die Welt von Morgen* (science-fiction; title means "A Flight into the World of Tomorrow"), Bitter Verlag, 1975; *Messung Des Unermesslichen* (non-fiction; title means "Measurement of Immeasurable"), Bitter Verlag, 1976; *Falle fuer Perseus* (novel; title means "A Trap for Perseus"), Beltz Verlag, 1976. Also author of picture books with commentary by Josef Sadil, published in Czechoslovakia by Artia and then translated and subsequently published in England; author with Peter Ryan, a series of nonfiction books. Also illustrator of a series of popular-scientific filmstrips on geology, paleontology, and planetology.

WORK IN PROGRESS: Job, 23, a novel from the end of World War II.

SIDELIGHTS: Ludek Pesek's novel, *Drazba,* was banned by the Union of Writers in Prague. His science-based books have had much wider circulation than his novels—*The Moon and the Planets* was translated for publication in Denmark, Netherlands, France, Germany, Italy, Japan, Mexico, and the Soviet Union, and *Mondexpedition* also was published in Italian and Dutch editions and *The Earth is Near* has been translated into nine languages. Pesek has made numerous study trips in European countries, and in the United States, Middle East, Central Asia, Egypt, and Tunis. He speaks English fluently.

* * *

PESIN, Harry 1919-

PERSONAL: Born October 16, 1919, in New York, N.Y.; son of Abraham (a businessman) and Lena (Bachman) Pesin; married Betty Klein, February 20, 1944; children: Arthur, Alan, Richard. *Education:* City College (now City College of the City University of New York), B.B.A., 1942. *Address:* P.O. Box 350, Rancho Santa Fe, Calif. 92607. *Office:* Pesin, Sydney & Bernard Advertising, Inc., 509 Madison Ave., New York, N.Y. 10022.

CAREER: Lester L. Wolff Advertising, New York City, public relations director, 1947; Rockmore Co., New York City, vice-president and creative director, 1948-60; David J. Mendelsohn, New York City, senior vice-president and creative director, 1961-63; Pesin, Sydney & Bernard Advertising, Inc., New York City, president and creative director, 1963—. *Military service:* U.S. Army, 1942-45; became second lieutenant. *Member:* American Society of Magazine Photographers, Copy Club. *Awards, honors:* Art Director's Club of New York award; 1960, 1968, 1970; Communication Arts award, 1968; American Institute of Graphic Arts award, 1970; Power of Print Award, *Time* Magazine, 1970.

WRITINGS—All published by Perspective: (With son, Alan Pesin) *My Little Brother Gets Away with Murder,* photographs by author, 1958; *The Acropolis Is a Nice Place to Visit but I Wouldn't Want to Live in the Eiffel Tower,* photographs by author, 1963; *Sayings to Run an Advertising Agency By,* 1966; *2½ Hours with Judy in the Nude,* photographs by author, 1967; (with son, Richard Pesin) *My Father, the Cigar Smoker,* 1967; *Quit Your Job and Run Away to Europe with the Wife and Kids,* 1968; *Why Is a Crooked Letter* (fiction), 1969; *Welcome, Stranger and Partners* (fiction), 1974; *Sayings on Running the Human Race,* 1975. Author of a weekly column, "I Say," for *Back Stage,* 1963-64.

WORK IN PROGRESS: Loneliness Makes Strange Bedfellows, a novel.

SIDELIGHTS: Founder of his own advertising agency in 1963, Harry Pesin keeps total creative control over the ads his company produces. He conceives, writes, and photographs campaigns at his home in Rancho Santa Fe, California, although the ad agency is located in New York City.

Pesin relaxes by writing aphorisms. About his last book of maxims, *Sayings on Running the Human Race,* Robert Kirsch of the *Los Angeles Times* said, "Aphorists are alive and flourishing . . . Harry Pesin divides his gall into three parts . . . clever . . . sage, succinct . . . ."

* * *

PETERS, J. Ross 1936-

PERSONAL: Born March 11, 1936, in Abbotsford, British Columbia, Canada; son of Henry Terence and Olive (Green) Peters. *Education:* University of British Columbia, B.Comm., 1958; Indiana University, M.B.A., 1959; McGill University, Ph.D., 1968. *Politics:* Conservative. *Religion:* Anglican. *Home:* 150 Carlyle Ave., Town of Mount Royal, Quebec, Canada H3R 1S9. *Office:* Royal Bank of Canada, P.O. Box 6001, Montreal, Quebec, Canada H3C 3A9.

CAREER: Sun Life Assurance of Canada, Montreal, Quebec, investment assistant, 1960-63; Morgan, Ostiguy & Hudon, Inc. (investment dealers), Montreal, director of research, 1968-71; vice-president for economics, Crang & Ostiguy, 1971-74; Royal Bank of Canada, Montreal, senior economist, 1974—. *Member:* Canadian Association of Business Economists, Montreal Economics Association. *Awards, honors:* Newcomen Award for material contributions to history, 1964.

WRITINGS: Economics of the Canadian Corporate Bond Market, McGill-Queen's University Press, 1970.

* * *

PETERSON, Agnes F(ischer) 1923-

PERSONAL: Born March 8, 1923, in Berlin, Germany; daughter of Hermann O. L. (a professor of biochemistry) and Ruth (Seckels) Fischer; married Louis J. Peterson (a professor), December 22, 1954. *Education:* University of Toronto, B.A., 1945; Radcliffe College, M.A., 1949. *Home:* 362 Yerba Buena Ave., Los Altos, Calif. 94022. *Office:* Hoover Institution, Stanford University, Stanford, Calif. 94305.

CAREER: National Film Board of Canada, Ottawa, Ontario, research assistant, 1945-48; California Historical Society, San Francisco, library assistant, 1949-52; Stanford University, Hoover Institution on War, Revolution and Peace, Stanford, Calif., circulation and reference assistant, 1952-54, Central and Western European Collection, acting curator, 1954-59, curator, 1959—. *Member:* American Historical Association, Conference Group on German Politics, Society for French Historical Studies, California Historical Society.

WRITINGS—Compiler: (With Grete Heinz) *NSDAP Hauptarchiv* (guide to Hoover Institution microfilm collection), Hoover Institution, 1964; (with Gabor Erdelyi) *German Periodical Publication* (checklist of German language serials and series currently received in Stanford University libraries), Hoover Institution, 1967; (with Heinz) *The French Fifth Republic: Establishment and Consolidation, 1958-1965* (annotated bibliography of holdings at the Hoover Institution), Hoover Institution, 1970; *Western Europe* (survey of holdings at the Hoover Institution), Hoover Institution, 1970; (with Heinz) *The French Fifth Republic: Continuity and Change, 1966-1970,* Hoover Institution, 1974; (with Bradley F. Smith) *Heinrich Himmler: Geheimredern, 1933-1945,* Propylaeen Verlag, 1974. Contributor of reviews to *History* and other periodicals.

PETERSON, Edward N(orman) 1925-

PERSONAL: Born August 27, 1925, in St. Joseph, Mo.; son of Roscoe Dillon and Rachel (White) Peterson; married Ursula Martha Schmidt, August 29, 1946; children: John Edward, Michael Paul. *Education:* St. Joseph Junior College, St. Joseph, Mo, A.A., 1948; University of Wisconsin, B.A., 1950, M.A., 1951, Ph.D., 1953. *Politics:* Democrat. *Home:* 936 West Maple St., River Falls, Wis. 54022. *Office:* Department of History, University of Wisconsin, River Falls, Wis. 54022.

CAREER: Eastern Kentucky State College (now University), Richmond, assistant professor, 1953-54; University of Wisconsin—River Falls, professor of history, 1954—, chairman of department, 1962—. *Military service:* U.S. Army, 1944-47. *Member:* American Historical Association, American Association of University Professors, Conference Group on German Politics, Phi Beta Kappa. *Awards, honors:* Grants from Alexander von Humboldt Foundation, 1963-64, 1966, Wisconsin State University, 1963-64, 1966, National Endowment for the Humanities, 1969-70, and Social Science Research Council, 1970-71.

WRITINGS: Hjalmar Schacht: For and Against Hitler, Christopher, 1954; *The Limits of Hitler's Power,* Princeton University Press, 1969. Contributor to *Der Staat* (Berlin) and professional journals in America.

WORK IN PROGRESS: A book on occupation policy in Germany; writing on power and strategy of World War II.

BIOGRAPHICAL/CRITICAL SOURCES: Virginia Quarterly Review, summer, 1970.

*   *   *

PETERSON, Harold 1939-

PERSONAL: Born September 14, 1939, in Chicago, Ill.; son of Rolland Harold (a public accountant) and Kathleen (Morphy) Peterson. *Education:* Harvard University, A.B., 1961; graduate study at Utah State University, 1969-70, and University of Denver, 1977-78. *Politics:* "Radical conservative, Jeffersonian liberal." *Religion:* Protestant.

CAREER: Time, Inc., New York, N.Y., staff writer on *Sports Illustrated,* 1961-69; Utah State University, Logan, university writer, 1969-70; Time, Inc., staff writer, 1970-75; California State University, Long Beach, head of magazine journalism sequence, 1976-77.

WRITINGS: The Last of the Mountain Men, Scribner, 1969, revised edition published as *The Last of the Mountain Men: The True Story of a Living American Legend,* 1975; *The Man Who Invented Baseball,* Scribner, 1973; (with others) *Solo,* Playboy Press, 1974.

WORK IN PROGRESS: A political novel; a Utopian modern or future-set novel; an already controversial book dealing with sexuality and liberation.

BIOGRAPHICAL/CRITICAL SOURCES: Chicago Tribune Book World, August 3, 1969; *Newsweek,* August 11, 1969.

*   *   *

PETERSON, James Allan 1932-

PERSONAL: Born October 11, 1932, in Redfield, S.D.; son of Paul Waldemar and Ruby (Collins) Peterson; married Neysa Marion McCall (a registered nurse), March 23, 1957; children: Sheryl, Kathleen, Susan. *Education:* Dakota State College, Madison, S.D., B.S.Ed., 1958; attended University of South Dakota, Vermillion, 1961; South Dakota State

University, Brookings, M.Ed., 1962; Boston University, Ed.D., 1968. *Home:* 45 White Birch Lane, Williston, Vt. 05495. *Office:* College of Education and Social Services, University of Vermont, Burlington, Vt. 05401.

CAREER: Arlington High School, Arlington, S.D., director of music, 1958-60, director of music and guidance, 1960-62; Dakota State College, Madison, S.D., music instructor, 1962; Boston University, Boston, Mass., National Defense Education Act field work supervisor, 1962-63, counseling practicum superviser, 1963-66; University of Vermont, College of Education and Social Services, Burlington, associate professor and chairman, programs in counseling and guidance and student personnel services in higher education, 1966-74, professor of organizational and human resource development, 1974—. Visiting lecturer at Florida State University, Tallahassee, Fla., 1963, University of Rhode Island, Kingston, R.I., 1965-66. Member of executive committee of the Family Education Center of Greater Burlington, 1971. *Military service:* U.S. Navy, 1953-57. *Member:* American Personnel and Guidance Association, American School Counselor Association, Association for Counselor Education and Supervision, American Psychological Association, American Society for Adlerian Psychology, Vermont Personnel and Guidance Association, Kappa Sigma Iota.

WRITINGS: (Editor) Rudolf Dreikurs, *Understanding Your Children* (study guide for a television course), University of Vermont, 1968; *Counseling and Values: A Philosophical Examination,* International Textbook Co., 1970.

WORK IN PROGRESS: A book on the meaning of vocation; revising *Counseling and Values.*

AVOCATIONAL INTERESTS: Music, sports, camping, fishing, hunting, hiking, skiing.

*   *   *

PETERSON, William S(amuel) 1939-

PERSONAL: Born June 14, 1939, in Black River Falls, Wis.; son of Bert S. and Juanita (Thompson) Peterson; married Eileen J. Lester, June 5, 1961; children: Heather E., Glenn E. *Education:* Walla Walla College, B.A. (cum laude), 1961; University of Wisconsin, M.A., 1962; Northwestern University, Ph.D., 1968. *Office:* Department of English, University of Maryland, College Park, Md. 20742.

CAREER: Andrews University, Berrien Springs, Mich., instructor, 1962-64, 1966-67, assistant professor, 1967-70, associate professor of English, 1970-71; University of Maryland, College Park, associate professor, 1971-76, professor of English, 1976—. *Member:* Modern Language Association of America, American Association of University Professors, Lewis Carroll Society of North America, Browning Institute (vice-president), Research Society for Victorian Periodicals. *Awards, honors:* Grants from American Council of Learned Societies, 1969, and Newberry Library, 1970, both for research on Mrs. Humphry Ward; grants from Huntington Library, 1973, University of Maryland General Research Board, 1974, and American Philosophical Society, 1974, all for research on Robert Browning.

WRITINGS: Interrogating the Oracle: A History of the London Browning Society, Ohio University Press, 1970; *Robert and Elizabeth Barrett Browning: An Annotated Bibliography, 1951-1970,* Browning Institute, 1974; *Victorian Heretic: Mrs. Humphry Ward's "Robert Elsmere",* Leicester University Press, 1976. Contributor of articles to *Victorian Newsletter, Bulletin of the New York Public Li-*

brary, Times Literary Supplement, and other publications. Editor, *Browning Institute Studies.*

WORK IN PROGRESS: Editing the correspondence between Robert Browning and F. J. Furnivall; a catalogue and index of fiction published in Victorian periodicals.

* * *

PETRAS, John W. 1940-

PERSONAL: Born February 17, 1940, in Ashland, Wis.; son of John and Angeline (Sedlar) Petras; married Lynne Wilhelm, November 26, 1960 (divorced, 1977); children: Christopher, Stephanie. *Education:* Northland College, B.A., 1962; University of Connecticut, M.A., 1964, Ph.D., 1966. *Office:* Department of Sociology, Central Michigan University, Mount Pleasant, Mich. 48859.

CAREER: Central Michigan University, Mount Pleasant, assistant professor, 1966-67, associate professor, 1967-69, professor of sociology, 1969—. *Member:* International Society for the Study of the History of the Behavioral and Social Sciences, American Sociological Association, American Association of Sex Educators, Counselors, and Therapists, Sex Information and Education Council of the United States, North Central Sociological Association, Michigan Education Association, Michigan Sociological Society.

WRITINGS: George Herbert Mead: Essays on His Social Philosophy, Teachers College Press, 1968; (editor with James E. Curtis) *Introduction to the Sociology of Knowledge,* Praeger, 1970; (contributor) Tamotsu Shibutani, editor, *Human Nature and Collective Behavior: Papers in Honor of Herbert Blumer,* Prentice-Hall, 1970; *Sexuality in Society,* Allyn & Bacon, 1973; *Sex: Male-Gender: Masculine,* Alfred Publishing, 1975; (with Bernard N. Meltzer and Larry T. Reynolds) *Symbolic Interactionism: Genesis, Varieties, Criticisms,* Routledge & Kegan Paul, 1975; *The Social Meaning of Human Sexuality,* Allyn & Bacon, 1977; (with Janice Reynolds and L. T. Reynolds) *Critiques of Sociological Theory,* Alfred Publishing, 1978. Contributor of about thirty articles to sociology journals in the United States and Europe.

WORK IN PROGRESS: With Charlotte O'Kelly, *Sex Role Differences: A Sociological Critique of Biologically Based Models.*

* * *

PFAU, Hugo 1908-

PERSONAL: Surname pronounced "fow"; born March 7, 1908, in Kreutzlingen, Switzerland; naturalized U.S. citizen, 1913; son of Richard (a barber) and Bertha (Kaegi) Pfau; married Irene Solomon (a teacher), July 27, 1935; children: Richard Anthony, Raymond Lawrence. *Education:* Attended New York University, 1925; State University of New York at Stony Brook, B.A., 1971. *Politics:* Republican. *Religion:* "Formally—Methodist; informally—Pantheist." *Home:* Little Bull Court, Centerport, N.Y. 11721.

CAREER: LeBaron, Inc., designer and member of sales staff of New York City branch, 1923-30, designer and member of sales staff of Detroit, Mich. branch, 1930-31; Hempstead Motors, Hempstead, N.Y., member of sales staff, 1932-34; Parker, Wilder & Co., New York City, textile executive, 1934-50; self-employed manufacturers' representative, 1950-68; full-time writer, 1968—. *Military service:* New York National Guard, infantry, 1928-31. *Member:* Society of Automotive Historians, Pierce-Arrow Society, Stony Brook Alumni Association, Veterans Association of

the Seventh Regiment, Lions International (Northport-Centerport chapter).

WRITINGS: The Custom Body Era, A. S. Barnes, 1971; *The Coachbuilt Packard,* Dalton Watson, 1973. Contributor of articles to *Motor Trend, Arrow, Classic Car, Cars and Parts, Automobile Quarterly,* and *Special Interest Autos.*

WORK IN PROGRESS: A revised edition of *The Custom Body Era.*

SIDELIGHTS: Hugo Pfau told *CA:* "I personally designed some distinguished automobiles of the 1920/30 period and have written primarily about these and the works of others of that time whom I knew personally." Among his designs are a prototype convertible top, the first Packard convertible roadster, several Rolls Royces, and the Isotta Franchini sport Phaeton. He has also designed Lincolns for Edsel Ford and Al Jolson. Pfau adds: "I am also considering writing on politics, bureaucracy, travel, and the theater, with each of which I have had some experience."

* * *

PFEFFER, Susan Beth 1948-

PERSONAL: Born February 17, 1948, in New York, N.Y.; daughter of Leo (a lawyer and professor) and Freda (a librarian; maiden name, Plotkin) Pfeffer. *Education:* New York University, B.A., 1969. *Home:* 17 Benton Ave., Middletown, N.Y. 10940.

*WRITINGS—*Juvenile novels: *Just Morgan,* Walck, 1970; *Better than All Right,* Doubleday, 1972; *Rainbows and Fireworks,* Walck, 1973; *The Beauty Queen,* Doubleday, 1974; *Whatever Words You Want to Hear,* Walck, 1974; *Marly the Kid,* Doubleday, 1975; *Kid Power,* F. Watts, 1977.

AVOCATIONAL INTERESTS: U.S. movie history.

BIOGRAPHICAL/CRITICAL SOURCES: New York Times Book Review, November 12, 1972.

* * *

PHELPS, Jack 1926-

PERSONAL: Born February 15, 1926, in Guymon, Okla.; son of E. W. (a farmer) and Nettie (Foreman) Phelps; married Mary G. Hale, May 28, 1946; children: Jacqueline, Judy, Janet, Jon. *Education:* Panhandle Agricultural and Mechanical College (now Oklahoma Panhandle State College of Agriculture and Applied Science), B.S., 1948; Western State College of Colorado, M.A., 1954; Oklahoma State University of Agriculture and Applied Science, Ed.D., 1963. *Office:* Department of Mathematics, Northwestern State College, Alva, Okla. 73717.

CAREER: Teacher of mathematics, coach, and principal of public elementary and high schools in Oklahoma, 1948-61; Oklahoma State University, Stillwater, extension teacher, 1962-63; Southwestern State College, Weatherford, Okla., assistant professor of mathematics, 1963-66; Northwestern State College, Alva, Okla., professor of mathematics and chairman of department, 1966—. *Military service:* U.S. Army Air Forces, 1943-45. *Member:* Mathematical Association of America, National Council of Teachers of Mathematics, National Education Association, Oklahoma Council of Teachers of Mathematics, Oklahoma Education Association.

WRITINGS: Elementary Mathematics: Theory and Practice, Brooks/Cole, 1970.

WORK IN PROGRESS: Fundamental Mathematics: Theory and Practice, for Brooks/Cole; and an article for *O.E.A. Magazine,* "Discovery: Antidote for Apathy."

PHILLIPS, William

PERSONAL: Born in New York, N.Y.; son of Edward and Marie (Berman) Phillips; married Edna Greenblatt (an education consultant), May 15, 1933. *Education:* City College (now City College of the City University of New York), B.S., 1928; New York University, M.A., 1930; Columbia University, graduate study, 1930-31. *Residence:* New York, N.Y. *Office:* Department of English, Rutgers University, 191 College Ave., New Brunswick, N.J. 08903; and *Partisan Review,* 522 Fifth Ave., New York, N.Y. 10036.

CAREER: Partisan Review, New Brunswick, N.J., founding editor, 1934—. New York University, New York City, instructor in English, 1929-32; associate professor of English at Columbia University, New York City, 1945, and New York University, 1960-63; Rutgers University, New Brunswick, N.J., professor of English, 1963—. Visiting lecturer at Sarah Lawrence College, 1951-54, 1956-57, and at New School for Social Research and University of Minnesota, 1953. Former consulting editor for Dial Press, Inc., Criterion Books, Inc., and Random House; now consulting editor for Chilmark Press, Inc. Member of board of directors, American Committee for Cultural Freedom, 1958-68; member, New Jersey Governor's Commission on the Arts, 1964-68; chairman, Coordinating Council of Literary Magazines, 1967—. *Member:* Authors League of America, American Association of University Professors, P.E.N. *Awards, honors:* Rockefeller Foundation grants, 1957, 1960.

WRITINGS—Editor, except as indicated: *Great American Short Novels,* Dial, 1946; (with Philip Rahv) *The Partisan Reader, 1934-1944,* Dial, 1946; *The Stories of Dostoevsky,* Dial, 1946; *The New Partisan Reader, 1945-1953,* Harcourt, 1953; (with Rahv) *The Avon Book of Modern Writing,* Numbers I-II, Avon, 1953, Number III published as *The Berkley Book of Modern Writing,* Berkley Publishing, 1953; *Art and Psychoanalysis,* Criterion, 1957; *The Partisan Review Anthology,* Holt, 1962; (author) *A Sense of the Present* (essays, stories, and reviews), Chilmark, 1967. Contributor of articles to *Commentary, Partisan Review, Encounter, New York Review of Books, Nation, New Republic, Kenyon Reivew, Horizon, Twentieth Century,* and other American and English literary and cultural magazines; also contributor to newspapers.

WORK IN PROGRESS: Working on intellectual and personal memoir.

SIDELIGHTS: Publication of *A Sense of the Present* has focused attention on a thirty-year career during which William Phillips, as a founding editor of *Partisan Review,* "has been fighting the threat to culture in a world of middle-browism and academicism," writes Arnold Beichman, who continues: "[Phillips] is a tolerant man . . . far more editor than polemicist [whose] magazine has reflected and directed the movement for modernity while also safeguarding the best of the traditional." Theodore Solotaroff writes that "the coherence of Phillips' career derives from his loyalty to advanced thought and writing. . . . He is more concerned with revealing the potentialities of literature and society than in protecting its norms and standards. But, though a modernist and a socialist, Phillips is no bohemian or activist, and, as his fiction makes clear, he approaches the issues of liberation, whether political or literary, with the skepticism of the veteran intellectual whose final honor lies in not being taken in. The result is a tone of quiet outspokenness. . . . Relevance of judgment is the highest virtue."

Phillips has been criticized as being concerned only with the "new," and James Degnan accuses him of overrating the "nonsense" of certain writers, but Solotaroff continues, "These essays are, in effect, position papers by an editor/critic who has one foot in the avant-garde tradition of the past and who is looking for the more solid ground in contemporary writing on which to station the other."

BIOGRAPHICAL/CRITICAL SOURCES: Christian Science Monitor, February 21, 1968; *New York Times Book Review,* March 24, 1968; *New Republic,* April 6, 1968; *Commentary,* June, 1968; *Choice,* Volume V, July, 1968; *Kenyon Review,* Volume XXX, number 5, 1968.

* * *

PHIPPS, William E(ugene) 1930-

PERSONAL: Born January 28, 1930, in Waynesboro, Va.; son of Charles Henry (a clergyman) and Ruth (Patterson) Phipps; married Martha Ann Swezey, December 21, 1954; children: Charles, Anna, Ruth. *Education:* Davidson College, B.S., 1949; Union Theological Seminary, Richmond, Va., B.D., 1952; University of St. Andrews, Ph.D., 1954; University of Hawaii, M.A., 1963. *Home:* Lincoln Ave., Elkins, W.Va. 26241. *Office:* Davis and Elkins College, Elkins, W.Va. 26241.

CAREER: Presbyterian clergyman; Peace College, Raleigh, N.C., professor of Bible, 1954-56; Davis and Elkins College, Elkins, W.Va., professor of religion and philosophy and chairman of department, 1956—. *Military service:* U.S. Army Reserve, 1955-63; became first lieutenant. *Member:* American Philosophical Association, American Academy of Religion, American Association of University Professors, West Virginia Philosophical Society (president, 1968-69), Phi Alpha Theta, Rotary.

WRITINGS: Was Jesus Married?: The Distortion of Sexuality in the Christian Tradition, Harper, 1970; *The Sexuality of Jesus: Theological and Literary Perspectives,* Harper, 1973; *Recovering Biblical Sensuousness,* Westminster, 1975. Contributor to *New York Times* and to religious journals.

WORK IN PROGRESS: A publication "that focuses on the ways in which distinguished Christian theologians down through history have dealt with human sexuality."

BIOGRAPHICAL/CRITICAL SOURCES: Christian Century, November 25, 1970, March 3, 1971, April 28, 1971.

* * *

PICCARD, Joan Russell

PERSONAL: Surname is accented on second syllable; born in Pennsylvania; daughter of Charles Regnier and Ruth (Pownall) Russell; married Donald Louis Piccard (a balloon builder), December 30, 1946 (divorced); children: Ruth Elizabeth Piccard Klauber, Mary Louise, Wendy Leigh. *Education:* Attended Augustana College, Sioux Falls, S.D., 1963-65; Orange Coast College, A.A., 1971. *Religion:* Reared a Quaker, now an Episcopalian. *Residence:* Newport Beach, Calif. 92660.

CAREER: Artist and writer, with many years of interest in aeronautics and ballooning. *Member:* Arts Patrons of Newport Beach.

WRITINGS: Adventure on the Wind (for young readers), illustrations by Hollis Williford, Nash Publishing, 1971. Contributor to magazines.

WORK IN PROGRESS: The Ballooning Game (proposed title); a technical book.

AVOCATIONAL INTERESTS: Oil painting, print-making, horseback riding, swimming, tennis, sailing, travel, drama.†

* * *

PIERARD, Richard Victor 1934-

PERSONAL: Born May 29, 1934, in Chicago, Ill.; son of Jack P. and Diana F. (Russell) Pierard; married Charlene Burdett, June 15, 1957; children: David Edward, Cynthia Kay. *Education:* Los Angeles State College of Applied Arts and Sciences (now California State University, Los Angeles), B.A., 1958, M.A., 1959; University of Hamburg, graduate student, 1962-63; University of Iowa, Ph.D., 1964. *Politics:* Democrat. *Religion:* Baptist. *Home:* 1101 Maple Ave., Terre Haute, Ind. 47804. *Office:* Department of History, Indiana State University, Terre Haute, Ind. 47809.

CAREER: University of Iowa, Iowa City, instructor in history, 1964; Indiana State University, Terre Haute, assistant professor, 1964-67, associate professor, 1967-72, professor of history, 1972—. Visiting professor at Greenville College, 1972-73, and Regent College, 1975. *Military service:* U.S. Army, 1954-56; served in Japan. *Member:* American Historical Association, Conference on Faith and History (secretary-treasurer, 1967—), Conference Group for Central European History, Evangelical Theological Society, American Association of University Professors, American Society of Missiology, Phi Alpha Theta. *Awards, honors:* Fulbright scholar at University of Hamburg, 1962-63.

WRITINGS: (With Robert G. Clouse and Robert D. Linder) *Protest and Politics: Christianity and Contemporary Affairs,* Attic Press, 1968; *The Unequal Yoke: Evangelical Christianity and Political Conservatism,* Lippincott, 1970; (with Clouse and Linder) *The Cross and the Flag,* Creation House, 1972; (with Linder) *Politics: A Case for Christian Action,* Inter-Varsity Press, 1973; (with Linder) *The Twilight of the Saints: Christianity and Civil Religion in Modern America,* Inter-Varsity Press, 1977; (contributor) T. Dowley, editor, *The Lion Handbook of Christian History,* Lion Press, 1977. Author of pamphlet, *Sylvanus F. Bowser,* published by Fort Wayne (Ind.) Public Library, 1964. Contributor to *Baker's Dictionary of Christian Ethics,* 1973, and *The New International Dictionary of the Christian Church,* 1974; also contributor to *Eternity, Tanzania Notes and Records, Race, Evangelical Quarterly, Reformed Journal, Christianity Today,* and other journals.

WORK IN PROGRESS: Writing on the German colonial society, the relationship between theological and political conservatism, social concern and Christianity, and civil religion.

* * *

PIERCE, Ruth (Ireland) 1936-

PERSONAL: Born September 14, 1936, in Cleveland, Ohio; daughter of Thomas Saxton (an author and lecturer) and Mildred (Locke) Ireland; married David Merwyn Pierce (an attorney), June 20, 1959 (divorced). *Education:* Vassar College, B.A., 1958; attended San Francisco State College (now University), 1963-64; University of California, Berkeley, M.S.W., 1966. *Politics:* Democrat. *Home and office:* 2730 Webster St., Berkeley, Calif. 94705.

CAREER: Clinical social worker licensed by State of California; director of a research project for Planned Parenthood, Oakland, Calif., 1965; Florence Crittenton Home, San Francisco, Calif., psychiatric social worker, 1966-68. Volunteer, Suicide Prevention program in San Francisco, 1966-69. *Member:* Academy of Certified Social Workers.

WRITINGS: Single and Pregnant, Beacon Press, 1970, 2nd edition with preface and revised appendix, 1971.

* * *

PIET, John H(enry) 1914-

PERSONAL: Born September 2, 1914, in Grand Rapids, Mich.; son of Reinder and Gezina (Brinkman) Piet; married C. Wilma Vander Wende, June 30, 1939; children: John Judson, David Lee. *Education:* Hope College, B.A., 1936; Princeton Theological Seminary, student, 1936-37; Western Theological Seminary, B.D., 1939; Hartford Seminary Foundation, S.T.M., 1940; Union Theological Seminary-Columbia University, Ph.D., 1952. *Politics:* Republican ("loosely"). *Religion:* Protestant. *Home:* 1140 Hazel Ave., Waukazoo, Holland, Mich. 49423. *Office:* Western Theological Seminary, Holland, Mich. 49423.

CAREER: Voorhees College, Vellore, South India, vice-president, 1941-55; Arcot Theological Seminary, Vellore, professor of religion, 1955-60; Western Theological Seminary, Holland, Mich., professor of Bible and missions, 1960—. *Member:* American Association of Biblical Studies, Association of Professors of Missions, Mid-West Professors of Missions.

WRITINGS: Leaflet Evangelism, Christian Literature Society for India (Madras), 1950; *A Logical Presentation of the Saiva Siddhanta Philosophy,* Christian Literature Society for India, 1952; *The Road Ahead: A Theology for the Church in Mission,* Eerdmans, 1970; *The Key to the Good News,* Eerdmans, 1974.

Illustrator: Fredrik Franklin, *Indien Serfarmot,* Triangelforlaget (Stockholm), 1951; Franklin, *Intervuju met Indien,* Triangelforlaget, 1955; Dorothy Clarke Wilson, *Dr. Ida: The Story of Dr. Ida Scudder of Vellore,* McGraw, 1959.

Contributor to *International Review of Missions, Church Herald, Eternity, The N.C.C. Review, India, Reformed Review.*

WORK IN PROGRESS: What Other Faiths Can Teach Me as a Christian: Hinduism, Islam, Buddhism, Communism, and Secularism; The Key to the Good News Bible.

SIDELIGHTS: John H. Piet has conducted tours around the world and to Africa. He speaks and reads Tamil, Dutch, German, and reads French, Greek, Hebrew, and Latin. *Avocational interests:* Photography, sailing.

* * *

PILARSKI, Laura 1926-

PERSONAL: Born December 10, 1926, in Niagara Falls, N.Y.; daughter of Joseph and Mary (Pytko) Pilarski. *Education:* Syracuse University, B.A., 1948. *Religion:* Roman Catholic. *Home:* Kornelius-strasse 3, 8008 Zurich, Switzerland; and 2245 Welch Ave., Niagara Falls, N.Y.

CAREER: Milwaukee Journal, Milwaukee, Wis., general news reporter, 1949-60; assistant to Associated Press correspondent, Warsaw, Poland, 1963; McGraw-Hill World News, chief correspondent in Zurich, Switzerland, 1964—. *Member:* Overseas Press Club, Foreign Press Association of Switzerland, Phi Beta Kappa, Theta Sigma Phi. *Awards, honors:* Milwaukee Press Club Award, 1957.

WRITINGS—Juvenile: They Came from Poland, Dodd, 1969; *Tibet: Heart of Asia,* Bobbs-Merrill, 1974. Contributor to *National Geographic.*

PILBROW, Richard (Hugh) 1933-

PERSONAL: Born April 28, 1933, in Beckenham, Kent, England; son of Arthur Gordon and Marjorie (Haywood) Pilbrow; married former spouse Viki Brinton (a casting director), July 12, 1958; married Molly Friedel; children: (first marriage) Abigail, Fred, Sandra. *Education:* Attended public schools in England. *Office:* Theatre Projects Ltd., 10 Long Acre, London WC2E 9LN, England.

CAREER: Lighting designer, producer, and theatre consultant; Theatre Projects Ltd., London, England, chairman, 1958—; director of New Shakespeare Theatre Company. *Member:* Royal Society of Arts (fellow), Association of British Theatre Technicians, Society of British Theatre Lighting Designers (vice-chairman), United Scenic Artists, Society of West End Theatre Managers, Garrick Club.

WRITINGS: Stage Lighting, Van Nostrand, 1970.

*   *   *

PILISUK, Marc 1934-

PERSONAL: Born January 19, 1934, in New York, N.Y.; son of Louis and Charlotte (Feterholtz) Pilisuk; married Phyllis E. Kamen, June 17, 1956; children: Tammy, Jeffrey. *Education:* Queens College (now Queens College of the City University of New York), B.A. (with honors), 1955; University of Michigan, M.A., 1956, Ph.D., 1961. *Home:* 494 Cragmont, Berkeley, Calif. 94708. *Office:* School of Public Health, University of California, Berkeley, Calif. 94720.

CAREER: U.S. Veterans Administration Hospital, Dearborn, Mich., psychological trainee, 1956-57; consultant in clinical psychology, Michigan Children's Aid Society, 1957-58; University of Michigan, Ann Arbor, trainee in diagnostics and therapy at Children's Psychiatric Hospital, 1958-60, lecturer in psychology, 1960-65, assistant professor of psychology in nursing, associate research psychologist at Mental Health Research Institute, 1961-65, consultant, Institute for Social Research, 1965-70; Oberlin College, Oberlin, Ohio, assistant professor of psychology, 1961; Purdue University, West Lafayette, Ind., associate professor of administrative sciences and psychology, 1965-67; University of California, Berkeley, visiting associate professor, 1967-68, professor-in-residence, School of Social Welfare, 1969-72, director of National Institute of Mental Health training program. 1970-75, professor-in-residence, School of Public Health, 1972—. Staff member, Pacific Children and Family Counseling Center, Oakland, Calif., 1975—; consultant, Berkeley Community and Mental Health Consultation Services.

MEMBER: International Studies Association, Inter-American Society of Psychology, American Psychological Association (fellow), American Orthopsychiatric Association, American Sociological Association, American Association for the Advancement of Science, American Academy of Political and Social Science, American Association of University Professors, American Civil Liberties Union, Society for the Psychological Study of Social Issues (member of council), New York Academy of Sciences, Sigma Xi, Psi Chi. *Awards, honors:* U.S. Public Health Service fellowship, 1955-56; Society for Psychological Study of Social Issues award, 1965, for essay, *Is There a Military-Industrial Complex Which Prevents Peace?;* Sigma Xi research award for "Psychology of Conflict."

WRITINGS: (With Thomas Hayden) *Is There a Military-Industrial Complex Which Prevents Peace?: Consensus and Countervailing Power in Pluralistic Systems,* Mental Health Research Institute, University of Michigan, 1964; (with J. Alan Winter, R. Chapman, and N. Hass) *Honesty, Deceit, and Timing in the Display of Intentions,* Herman C. Krannert Graduate School of Industrial Administration, Purdue University, 1966; (with Edward Overstreet) *Simulation Models of Sequential Choices in the Prisoner's Dilemma,* Institute for Research in the Behavioral, Economic, and Management Sciences, Purdue University, 1968; (compiler with Robert Perrucci) *The Triple Revolution: Social Problems in Depth,* Little, Brown, 1968; (editor with Perrucci) *Triple Revolution Emerging: Social Problems in Depth,* Little, Brown, 1971; (editor with wife, Phyllis Pilisuk) *Poor Americans: How the White Poor Live* [and] *Poor Americans: The Dynamics of Change,* two volumes, Aldine, 1971; *International Conflict and Social Policy,* Prentice-Hall, 1971.

Contributor: W. Isard and J. Wolpert, editors, *Papers,* Volume I, of (International) Peace Research Society, Chicago Conference, 1963; *Proceedings* of IX Inter-American Congress of Psychology, 1964; W. G. Bennis and others, editors, *Interpersonal Dynamics: Essays in Human Interaction,* Dorsey, 1964; *Papers,* Volume V, of (North American) Peace Research Society, Philadelphia Conference of 1965, 1966; L. Menashe and R. Radosh, editors, *Teach-Ins: U.S.A., Reports, Opinions, Documents,* Praeger, 1967; Paul Swingle, editor, *Experiments in Social Psychology,* Academic Press, 1968; R. Abelson and others, editors, *Theories of Cognitive Consistency,* Rand McNally, 1968; R. Buckhout and others, editors, *Toward Social Change,* Harper, 1970; Kenneth Boulding, editor, *Peace and the War Industry,* Aldine, 1970; Donald Michael, editor, *The Future Society,* Aldine, 1970; Richard Ofshe, editor, *Interpersonal Behavior in Small Groups,* Prentice-Hall, 1971. Contributor of articles and reviews to numerous psychology and sociology journals, including *Journal of Clinical Psychology, Psychonomic Science, Sociometry, Behavioral Science, Journal of Conflict Resolution, Journal of Personality and Social Psychology, Canadian Forum, Trans-action, American Journal of Orthopsychiatry, Harvard Educational Review, Journal of Social Work Education,* and *New University Thought.*

Author of several scientific papers, many unpublished, presented before psychology and sociology conferences and symposia. Associate editor of *Journal of Conflict Resolution,* 1966-71; editorial consultant for *Sociometry,* 1969-71.

WORK IN PROGRESS: Research in community mental health, youth involvement, alienation and drug abuse, social power and contemporary social movements, psychology and social policy.

SIDELIGHTS: Marc Pilisuk claims to be "a founder of the first Teach-In." He told *CA* that "his biases are in favor of conflict, against academic mandarins and the cybernetic state."

*   *   *

PINKERTON, Robert E(ugene) 1882-1970

March 12, 1882—February 19, 1970; American novelist and short story writer. Obituaries: *New York Times,* February 21, 1970; *Antiquarian Bookman,* March 16, 1970.

*   *   *

PINKETT, Harold T(homas) 1914-

PERSONAL: Born April 7, 1914, in Salisbury, Md.; son of

Levin W. (a minister) and Catherine (Richardson) Pinkett; married Lucille Cannady (a social science analyst), 1943. *Education:* Morgan State College, A.B., 1930; University of Pennsylvania, A.M., 1938; Columbia University, graduate study, 1939-40; American University, Ph.D., 1953. *Politics:* Democrat. *Religion:* Methodist. *Home:* 5741 27th St. N.W., Washington, D.C. 20015. *Office:* National Archives, Washington, D.C. 20408.

CAREER: High school teacher of Latin in Baltimore, Md., 1936-38; Livingstone College, Salisbury, N.C., professor of history and government, 1938-39, 1941-42; National Archives, Washington, D.C., junior archivist, 1942-43, supervisory archivist, 1946-59, chief of agriculture record branch, 1959-62, senior appraisal archivist, 1962-68, deputy director of Records Appraisal Division, 1968-71, chief of natural resources branch, 1971—. Lecturer at American University, Howard University, University of Maryland, and other universities. *Military service:* U.S. Army, Signal Corps, 1943-46; served in Europe, the Philippines, and Japan; became technical sergeant.

MEMBER: Society of American Archivists (fellow), American Historical Association, Organization of American Historians, Forest History Society (president, 1976—), Association for the Study of Negro Life and History, Agricultural History Society. *Awards, honors:* Commendable Service Award, National Archives, 1964, 1970; Book Award of Agricultural History Society, 1968, for manuscript of *Gifford Pinchot: Private and Public Forester.*

WRITINGS: Gifford Pinchot: Private and Public Forester, University of Illinois Press, 1970; (editor with Frank B. Evans) *Research in the Administration of Public Policy,* Howard University Press, 1975. Contributor to archivist and historical journals. Editor, *American Archivist,* 1968—; member of editorial board of *Prologue* (journal of the National Archives).

* * *

PINKWATER, Daniel Manus 1941-

PERSONAL: Born November 15, 1941, in Memphis, Tenn.; son of Philip (a ragman) and Fay (Hoffman) Pinkwater; married Jill Schutz (author and illustrator), October 12, 1969. *Education:* Bard College, B.A., 1964. *Politics:* Taoist. *Religion:* Republican. *Home:* 22 Hudson Pl., Hoboken, N.J. 07030.

CAREER: Formerly taught art to children; worked as a fine artist; exhibited prints; travelled; currently writer and illustrator of children's books.

WRITINGS—All juveniles; self-illustrated except as noted: *The Terrible Roar,* Knopf, 1970; *Bear's Picture,* Holt, 1972; *Wizard Crystal,* Dodd, 1973; *Fat Elliot and the Gorilla,* Four Winds, 1974; *Magic Camera,* Dodd, 1974; *Wingman,* Dodd, 1975; *Blue Moose,* Dodd, 1975; *Three Big Hogs,* Seabury, 1975; *Lizard Music,* Dodd, 1976; *Around Fred's Bed* (illustrations by Robert Mertens), Prentice-Hall, 1976; *The Big Orange Splot,* Hastings House, 1976; *Superpuppy* (illustrations by wife, Jill Pinkwater), Seabury, 1977; *The Blue Seed Thing,* Prentice-Hall, 1977; *The Hoboken Chicken Emergency,* Prentice-Hall, 1977; *Fat Men from Space,* Dodd, 1977; *The Last Guru,* Knopf, in press.

WORK IN PROGRESS: Currently finishing two books, *Moose Two,* and *Captain Moonlight;* another children's novel, and other projects.

SIDELIGHTS: Daniel Pinkwater operated a puppy training school, 1974-76, with his wife, Jill. He wrote to *CA,* "Have abandoned fine art as a profession. Prefer writing for children." He is a member of the Subud spiritual brotherhood. *Avocational interests:* Formerly many things—now everything.

* * *

PINSKY, Robert 1940-

PERSONAL: Born October 20, 1940, in Long Branch, N.J.; son of Milford Simon (an optician) and Sylvia (Eisenberg) Pinsky; married Ellen Bailey, December 30, 1961; children: Nicole, Caroline Rose. *Education:* Rutgers University, B.A., 1962; Stanford University, Ph.D., 1966. *Home:* 26 Leighton Rd., Wellesley, Mass. 02181. *Office:* Department of English, Wellesley College, Wellesley, Mass. 02181.

CAREER: University of Chicago, Chicago, Ill., assistant professor of humanities, 1966-67; Wellesley College, Wellesley, Mass., associate professor of English, 1967—. *Awards, honors:* Stegner Fellowship in Creative Writing, Stanford University.

WRITINGS: Landor's Poetry, University of Chicago Press, 1968; *Sadness And Happiness* (poems) Princeton University Press, 1975; *The Situation of Poetry,* Princeton University Press, 1977. Contributor of articles and poems to *American Review, American Poetry Review, Antaeus, Poetry, Shenandoah,* and *Yale Review.*

WORK IN PROGRESS: Poems.

SIDELIGHTS: Of his poetry Robert Pinsky says: "I tend naturally to write in images and atmospheres—the pathetic streets and ocean front of my home town, for example. On the other hand, a strong ambition in my poems has been to resist the general prejudice against abstract statement; the poems try to get at the profoundly emotional, obsessive side of such supposedly ordinary activities as playing tennis or watching passers-by from a parked car. I am interested in the truth of such things not symbolically, but actually. I would like to write a poetry which could contain every kind of thing, while keeping all the excitement of poetry." Pinsky lived in London, England, 1970-71.

* * *

PIRIE, N(orman) W(ingate) 1907-

PERSONAL: Born July 1, 1907; son of George Pirie (a painter); married Antoinette Patey, 1931. *Education:* Attended Emmanuel College, Cambridge. *Politics:* Left. *Religion:* None. *Office:* Rothamsted Experimental Station, Harpenden, Hertfordshire, England.

CAREER: Biochemical Laboratory, Cambridge, England, demonstrator, 1932-40; Rothamsted Experimental Station, Harpenden, England, virus physiologist, 1940-46, head of biochemistry department, 1947—. *Member:* Royal Society (fellow, 1949—), Council for Civil Liberties, Pugwash.

WRITINGS—Editor: (With Arnold Ashley Miles) *The Nature of the Bacterial Surface* (symposium of Society for General Microbiology, April, 1949), Blackwell Scientific Publications, 1949; (with Frederic Le Gros Clark) *Four Thousand Million Mouths: Scientific Humanism and the Shadow of World Hunger,* Oxford University Press, 1951; (with J. B. Cragg) *The Numbers of Man and Animals* (symposium held September 24-25, 1954), Oliver & Boyd for the Institute of Biology, 1955; *The Biology of Space Travel: Symposium,* Hafner, 1961; *Food Resources: Conventional and Novel,* Penguin, 1969, 2nd edition, 1976; *Leaf Protein: Its Agronomy, Preparation, Quality, and Use,* Basil Blackwell, 1971.

PISAR, Samuel 1929-

PERSONAL: Born March 18, 1929, in Bialystock, Poland; came to U.S., 1953; naturalized, 1961, by special act of Congress; son of David (a businessman) and Helen (Suchowolski) Pisar; married Norma Marmorston, December 30, 1955; married second wife, Judith Frehm, September 2, 1971; children: (first marriage) Helaina, Alexandra; (second marriage) Leah. *Education:* Queens College, University of Melbourne, LL.B., 1953; Harvard University, LL.M., S.J.D., 1956; University of Paris, Doctor of Law, 1967. *Home:* 23 Square de l'Avenue Foch, Paris 16, France. *Office:* 68 Boulevard de Courcelles, Paris 17, France.

CAREER: Admitted to Bars of Washington, D.C., and California; senior partner, International Law Firm, Paris, France and Washington, D.C. Member of President's Task Force on Foreign Economic Policy, 1961; adviser to U.S. Department of State; counsel to UNESCO; barrister-at-law at Gray's Inn, London, England, and at Conseil Juridique, Paris. *Member:* American Bar Association, American Judicature Society, American Society of International Law.

WRITINGS: Coexistence and Commerce: Guidelines for Transactions between East and West, McGraw, 1970; *Les Armes de la Paix,* Denoeel (Paris), 1971. Contributor of numerous articles on economic, financial and legal subjects to *Harvard Law Review* and other American, British, and French periodicals.

SIDELIGHTS: According to David Schoenbrun, *Coexistence and Commerce* "received warm prepublication comments from a broad spectrum of American leaders, including Henry Ford, Thomas Watson, and Senators Fulbright, Javits and Kennedy." Schoenbrun believes the book is "timely, cogent, and persuasive" at this point of "the so-called detente" between East and West. He points out that Pisar, having endured imprisonment in Nazi concentration camps during the war, and subsequently having served "with the United Nations and the State Department, and as consultant and witness to Congressional committees, until he achieved his present eminent position in the field of international law," is particularly qualified to offer "the general public . . . authoritative, specific, and compelling answers" to the problems of coexistence.

Schoenbrun is especially appreciative of "the scope and depth of [Pisar's] study, which ranges through the political, economic, diplomatic, legal, social, and commercial aspects of transactions between West and East." In regard to U.S. motives for trade with the Soviet Union, "Pisar concedes that American concern about building up a rival is legitimate. He gently remarks, however, that we tend to exaggerate our fears and impose more restrictions on trade than are needed. . . . In a conclusion . . . [he] presents an eighty-point plan covering the entire range of trade enterprises" which is not "some kind of panacea, a magic formula for instant peace . . . but, rather, a practical, hard-headed, highly professional set of proposals."

BIOGRAPHICAL/CRITICAL SOURCES: Saturday Review, September 19, 1970; *Chicago Tribune,* September 20, 1970; *New York Times,* November 15, 1970; *Wall Street Journal,* April 28, 1971.

*　　*　　*

PITCHER, Robert W(alter) 1918-

PERSONAL: Born October 26, 1918, in Grand Rapids, Mich.; son of Harry Lewis (an accountant) and Louise (Morrison) Pitcher; married Adretta K. Atchinson, August 21, 1943; children: James Robert, Judith Kay (Mrs. William Gelvin II). *Education:* Alma College, A.B. (summa cum laude), 1946; Northern Baptist Seminary, M.R.E., 1949; University of Michigan, Ph.D., 1953. *Religion:* Methodist. *Home:* 55 Barrett Rd., Apt. 437, Berea, Ohio 44017. *Office:* Department of Psychology, Baldwin-Wallace College, Berea, Ohio 44017.

CAREER: Baldwin-Wallace College, Berea, Ohio, assistant professor, 1952-55, associate professor, 1955-59, professor of psychology, 1959—, chairman of department, 1955-59, dean of students, 1959-65, vice-president for student affairs, 1965-69. Director, Educational Development Center, 1963—. Vice-president, Discover Yourself, Inc., 1972—. Consultant, Council for the Advancement of Small Colleges, 1972—. *Member:* American Psychological Association, American Personnel and Guidance Association, National Association of Student Administrators, Association for Supervision and Curriculum Development.

WRITINGS: (With Babette Blaushild) *Why College Students Fail,* Funk, 1970.

WORK IN PROGRESS: Underachievement at college level; academic support programs for colleges.

SIDELIGHTS: Robert W. Pitcher told *CA* that his "primary attention since 1963 has been focused upon the diagnosis and solutions to academic underachievement." He adds: "[I] have designed programs and trained faculty in Mid-Appalachia College Council, Florida Community Colleges, University of Detroit, etc."

*　　*　　*

PITT, David C(harles) 1938-

PERSONAL: Born August 15, 1938, in Wellington, New Zealand; son of Maurice Simeon (a teacher) and Elizabeth (Hyams) Pitt; married Carol Haigh, February 13, 1959; children: Jerome Manuel, Sara Elizabeth, Devra Simone, Joshua Dan, Danielle Chana, Joseph Joel, Lisa Monique. *Education:* University of New Zealand, B.A., 1961; Oxford University, B.Litt., 1963, D.Phil., 1965. *Office:* Department of Sociology, University of Auckland, Auckland, New Zealand.

CAREER: University of Victoria, Victoria, British Columbia, assistant professor of anthropology and sociology, 1966-67; University of Waikato, Hamilton, New Zealand, professor of sociology and head of department, 1968-71; University of Auckland, Auckland, New Zealand, professor of sociology, head of department, and chairman of European Studies Committee, 1971—. Consultant to International Labor Organization, 1968-70, to UNESCO, 1970-71, to United Nations, Center for Development Planning (New York), 1972-75, to UNESCAP (Bangkok), 1972—, to International Union for the Conservation of Nature (Switzerland), 1976—. *Member:* International Sociological Association (member of council, 1970—), Royal Anthropological Institute, American Sociological Association, British Sociological Association, American Anthropological Association.

WRITINGS: Tradition and Economic Progress in Samoa: A Case Study in the Role of Traditional Social Institutions in Economic Development, Clarendon Press, 1970; *Historical Documents in Anthropology and Sociology,* Holt, 1972; (with C. Macpherson) *Emerging Pluralism,* Longman, 1975; *Social Dynamics of Development,* Pergamon, 1976; (editor) *Development from Below: Anthropologists & Development Situations,* Aldine, 1976; (editor) *Social Class in New Zealand,* Longman, 1977. Contributor to professional journals.

WORK IN PROGRESS: Writing on the sociology of economic development, ethnic relations, social stratification, rural society, population, and mountains.

AVOCATIONAL INTERESTS: Mountains, boating, viticulture, travel.

* * *

PLACET, Leroi 1901-1970

December 4, 1901—February 13, 1970; American novelist, short story writer, and playwright. Obituaries: *New York Times,* February 17, 1970.

* * *

PLANT, Raymond 1945-

PERSONAL: Born March 19, 1945, in Grimsby, Lincolnshire, England; son of Stanley (a fireman) and Marjorie (East) Plant; married Katherine Sylvia Dixon; children: Nicholas Augustine, Matthew Benedict, Richard Jonathan. *Education:* King's College, London, B.A. (honors in philosophy), 1966. *Politics:* Labour Party. *Religion:* Anglican. *Home:* 81 Manley Rd., Manchester, Lancashire, England. *Office:* Department of Philosophy, University of Manchester, Manchester, Lancashire, England.

CAREER: University of Manchester, Manchester, England, lecturer in philosophy, 1967—. *Member:* Aristotelian Society.

WRITINGS: Social and Moral Theory in Casework, Humanities, 1970; *Hegel: Through Philosophy to Community,* Allen & Unwin, 1973; (contributor) C. B. Cox and A. E. Dyson, editors, *The Twentieth Century Mind,* Oxford University Press, 1971; *Community and Ideology,* Routledge & Kegan Paul, 1974; *Political Philosophy and Social Welfare,* Routledge & Kegan Paul, in press. Contributor to *New Left Review.*

* * *

PLATT, Jennifer (Ann) 1937-

PERSONAL: Born February 23, 1937, in Bingham, Nottinghamshire, England; daughter of Christopher James (an accountant) and Alma (Collins) Platt; married Charles M. Goldie (a university lecturer), March 30, 1967. *Education:* Cambridge University, B.A. (first class honors), 1958; Barnett House, Oxford, Diploma in Public and Social Administration, 1959; University of Leeds, graduate study, 1960-61; University of Chicago, M.A., 1964. *Religion:* Agnostic. *Home:* 98 Beaconsfield Villas, Brighton BN1 GHE, Sussex, England. *Office:* Department of Sociology, University of Sussex, Brighton BN1 9QN, Sussex, England.

CAREER: Cambridge University, Cambridge, England, junior research officer in sociology in department of applied economics, 1961-64; University of Sussex, Brighton, England, lecturer, 1964-76, reader in sociology, 1976—. *Member:* British Sociological Association, American Sociological Association.

WRITINGS: (With John H. Goldthorpe, David Lockwood, and Frank Bechhofer) *The Affluent Worker: Industrial Attitudes and Behaviour,* Cambridge University Press, 1968; (with Goldthorpe, Lockwood, and Bechhofer) *The Affluent Worker: Political Attitudes and Behaviour,* Cambridge University Press, 1968; (with Goldthorpe, Lockwood, and Bechhofer) *The Affluent Worker in the Class Structure,* Cambridge University Press, 1969; (contributor) M. D. Yudkin, editor, *General Education,* Allen Lane, 1969; *Social Re-*

search in Bethnal Green, Macmillan, 1971; *Realities of Social Research,* Sussex University Press, 1976. Contributor of articles and reviews to sociology journals.

WORK IN PROGRESS: Research on the sociology of sociology; sociology of the antique trade.

* * *

PLUMMER, Alfred 1896-

PERSONAL: Born November 2, 1896, in London, England; son of Alfred (a builder) and Adelaide Elizabeth (Silverton) Plummer; married Minnie D. Goodey, 1919 (died, 1972); married Elsie Evelyn M. Fellingham, 1973. *Education:* Trinity College, Dublin, B.A. (honors), 1920; London School of Economics and Political Science, M.Sc. (by research), 1928; Oriel College, Oxford, B.Litt. (by research), 1929. *Home:* Warmington, Black Heath, Wenhaston, Suffolk, England. *Office:* Worshipful Company of Weavers, 53 Romney St., Westminster, London S.W.1, England.

CAREER: University College (now University of Southampton), Southampton, England, lecturer in department of commerce, 1920-25; Ruskin College, Oxford, England, vice-principal and lecturer in economics, 1925-37; City of Birmingham Commercial College, Birmingham, England, head of department of economics and social studies and acting principal, 1937-38; South West Essex Technical College, Walthamstow, England, head of department of commerce, languages, and social studies, 1938-43, vice-principal and headmaster of Technical High School, 1944-45; Forest Training College, Walthamstow, director, 1945-49; London County Council, London, England, inspector of further education, 1949-60, staff inspector, 1960-63; Worshipful Company of Weavers, London, honorary librarian, 1964—. *Military service:* British Army, Artillery, 1915-17; served in France; became second lieutenant.

WRITINGS: Exercises in Economics, Pitman, 1929, 4th edition, 1967; *Labour's Path to Power,* Richards, 1930; *The World in Agony: An Economic Diagnosis,* Griffin & Co., 1932; (editor and author of introduction) *The Witney Blanket Industry,* George Routledge, 1934; (contributor) *Great Democrats,* Nicholson & Watson, 1934; *International Combines in Modern Industry,* Pitman, 1934, 3rd edition, 1951; *New British Industries in the Twentieth Century,* Pitman, 1937; *Raw Materials or War Materials?,* Gollancz, 1937; (with Richard E. Early) *The Blanket Makers, 1660-1969: A History of Charles Early and Marriott (Witney) Ltd.,* Augustus Kelley, 1969; *Bronterre: A Political Biography of Bronterre O'Brien, 1804-1864,* Allen & Unwin, 1971; *The London Weavers' Company, 1600-1970,* Routledge & Kegan Paul, 1972. Contributor to *Encyclopaedia of the Social Sciences* and to journals.

SIDELIGHTS: The Worshipful Company of Weavers of London, Alfred Plummer points out, is the oldest of all the London livery companies, descended from a guild of twelfth-century weavers. The company still possesses a royal charter granted by Henry II in 1155.

* * *

PLUMMER, Beverly J. 1918-

PERSONAL: Born December 6, 1918, in Chicago, Ill.; daughter of Ray C. (a draftsman) and Mary Irene (Burns) Watson; married John Plummer, Jr. (a teacher), April 18, 1941; children: John III, Christopher, Roxanne. *Education:* Attended public schools, and took occasional university courses ("for the sheer fun of it"). *Home:* 630 Grove St., De

Kalb, Ill. 60115. *Agent:* Julie Fallowfield, McIntosh & Otis, Inc., 475 Fifth Ave., New York, N.Y. 10017.

CAREER: Carnegie Steel, Gary, Ind., photographer, 1942-44; folksinger for ten years; writer, 1960—.

WRITINGS: Give Every Day a Chance, Putnam, 1970; *Earth Presents: How to Make Beautiful Gifts from Nature's Bounty,* Atheneum, 1974; *Fragrance: Now to Make Natural Soaps, Scents, and Sundries,* Atheneum, 1975. Contributor to *Illustrated Library of Arts and Crafts,* Fuller & Dees, 1974. Also contributor of articles on folk arts, folk music, travel, and crafts to periodicals. Author of folk music column, "Sing Out," 1965-66.

WORK IN PROGRESS: Collecting information on the history of folk instruments of North America, with a book expected to result; doing laboratory work on handmade papers made from a wide variety of plant material ("A chapter in *Earth Presents* is devoted to handmade papers and I plan to expand on what was begun there").

SIDELIGHTS: Beverly Plummer told *CA:* "Not having had a college education to determine what it is I'm best suited to do, I've had the freedom to do almost anything I pleased. Whatever it is I do, I keep coming back to my interest in folk-life. I love seeing evidence of a person's inventiveness—the ability to make something out of nothing. In studying folk music and folk life, one sees men and women making funny songs about all the things in life that are too ridiculous and too frightening to face as realities. One sees dyes being made from sunflower seeds, mattresses out of cornshucks, banjos out of a turtle shell or gourds. Contraptions and contrivances made for farming when our country was being settled are so beautiful."

AVOCATIONAL INTERESTS: Making body ornaments out of stones, seeds, nuts, feathers, beans, papier mache, and antique beads.

*   *   *

POGGI, Emil J.   1928-
(Jack Poggi)

PERSONAL: Surname rhymes with "*oh*-gee"; born June 14, 1928, in Oakland, Calif.; son of Emilio J. (a salesman) and Josephine (Gian) Poggi; married Jeanlee Mathey (a teacher), January 14, 1967. *Education:* University of San Francisco, B.A., 1950; Harvard University, M.A., 1951; Columbia University, Ph.D., 1964. *Politics:* Liberal. *Religion:* "Don't know." *Home:* 90 Valentine Ave., Glen Cove, N.J. 11542. *Agent:* Gunther Stuhlmann, 65 Irving Pl., New York, N.Y. 10003. *Office:* Department of Theater and Film, C. W. Post Center, Long Island University, Greenvale, Long Island, N.Y.

CAREER: Free-lance actor and director, 1955-63; Long Island University, C. W. Post Center, Greenvale, N.Y., professor of theater arts, 1963—, former chairman of department. Part-time instructor at Cooper Union and Manhattan School of Music, 1956-63. *Military service:* U.S. Army, 1951-53; became second lieutenant. *Member:* Actors' Equity Association.

WRITINGS—Under name Jack Poggi: *Theater in America: The Impact of Economic Forces, 1870-1967,* Cornell University Press, 1968. Contributor of articles on acting, *The Drama Review, Ventures in Research,* and *Actor Training.*

WORK IN PROGRESS: From Improvisation to Text: A Guide for Actors; stage adaptations of works by Dostoevsky; new translations of Chekhov.

SIDELIGHTS: Emil J. Poggi told *CA:* "I do a lot of different things: acting, teaching, writing, translating. I think a fascination with acting as a process lies at the heart of all of them. I am particularly interested in how the written word comes to life on stage—that's mainly what I teach and write about—and even when I translate a play I find myself acting all the lines in my head before putting them down on paper."

*   *   *

POGREBIN, Letty Cottin   1939-

PERSONAL: Surname is pronounced *Po*-greb-in; born June 9, 1939, in New York, N.Y.; daughter of Jacob (an attorney) and Cyral (designer; maiden name, Halpern) Cottin; married Bertrand B. Pogrebin (an attorney), December 8, 1963; children: Abigail and Robin (twins), David. *Education:* Brandeis University, B.A. (cum laude), 1959. *Office: Ms.* Magazine, 370 Lexington Ave., New York, N.Y. 10017. *Agent:* Wendy Weil, Julian Bach Literary Agency, Inc., 3 East 48th St., New York, N.Y. 10020.

CAREER: Simon & Schuster, Inc., New York City, part-time secretary and assistant, 1957-59; Coward-McCann, Inc., New York City, editorial assistant, 1959-60; Sussman & Sugar (advertising), New York City, copywriter, 1960; Bernard Geis Associates (publishers), New York City, director of publicity, advertising, and subsidiary rights, 1960-70, vice-president, 1970, consultant, 1970; *Ms.* (magazine), editor, 1971—. Lecturer on women's issues. Member of board of directors of Ms. Foundation, and of Action for Children's Television; consultant to ABC television program, "Free to Be . . . You and Me." *Member:* National Organization for Women, National Women's Political Caucus (founding member), Women's Equity Action League, Author's Guild. *Awards, honors:* Women in Communications "Sound of Success" Award, and Clarion Award, 1974, for *Ladies Home Journal* columns.

WRITINGS: How to Make It in a Man's World, Doubleday, 1970; *Getting Yours: How to Make the System Work for the Working Woman,* McKay, 1975. Also author of monthly column "The Working Woman" for the *Ladies Home Journal,* 1971—. Contributor to *Good Housekeeping, Cosmopolitan, Variety,* and other periodicals.

WORK IN PROGRESS: Raising a Free Child in a Sexist Society, a guide to non-sexist child rearing, completion expected in 1977.

SIDELIGHTS: Letty Pogrebin told *CA:* "My major areas of interest are feminism, women and employment, children (particularly the psychology and sociology of childrearing), politics and women's status, family life."

BIOGRAPHICAL/CRITICAL SOURCES: New York Times, April 15, 1970; *New Republic,* June 13, 1970; *Time,* December 20, 1971.

*   *   *

POIGNANT, Raymond   1917-

PERSONAL: Born December 26, 1917, in Morainvilliers, Seine-et-Oise, France; son of Jules (a baker) and Marie (Beaufourd) Poignant; married Suzanne Auxionnaz, December 19, 1939; children: Bernard. *Education:* Ecole Nationale d'Administration (advanced civil service college), Paris, graduate, 1949. *Home:* 2 avenue du Vert Bois, 92410 Ville d'Avray, Hauts-de-Seine, France. *Office:* Conseil d'Etat, Place du Palais-Royal, 75001 Paris, France.

CAREER: Conseil d'Etat, Paris, France, observer, 1949-51, technical adviser in the office of the Minister of National

Education, 1951-54, the Secretary of State, 1954-55, and the Minister of National Education, 1956-58, maitre des requetes, 1958-63; United Nations Educational, Scientific and Cultural Organization (UNESCO), Paris, senior staff member and vice-president of council of consultants, International Institute for Educational Planning, 1963-69, director of International Institute for Educational Planning, 1969-74; Conseil d'Etat, councillor, 1974—. Other French posts include chief rapporteur of School and University Committee of the General Commisariat of the Plan, 1958-61, 1962-65, general secretary of Inter-Ministerial Committee for the Reform of Medical Studies, 1958-63, and member of national committee of the National Scientific Research Centre, 1959-70. *Awards, honors:* Officier de la Legion d'honneur; Officier de l'ordre national du Merite; Commandeur des Palmes academiques; Chevalier des Arts et Lettres; Chevalier de la Sante publique.

WRITINGS: (With Christopher Freeman and Ingvar Svennilson) *Science, Economic Growth, and Government Policy,* Organization for Economic Co-operation and Development, 1963; *L'Enseignement dans les pays du Marche commun: Etude comparative,* National Institute of Pedagogy (Paris), 1965, translation published as *Education and Development in Western Europe, the United States, and the U.S.S.R.: A Comparative Study,* Teachers College Press, 1969; (with Jacques Hallak) *Les Aspects financiers de l'enseignement dans les pays africains d'expression francaise,* International Institute for Educational Planning, 1966; (director and co-author of study) *Planification de l'education in U.R.S.S.,* International Institute for Educational Planning, 1967; *The Relation of Educational Plans to Economic and Social Planning,* International Institute for Educational Planning, 1967; *Education in Industrialized Countries,* translation by Noel Lindsay, Nijhoff, 1973.

*   *   *

POINDEXTER, David 1929-

PERSONAL: Born January 30, 1929, in Hood River, Ore.; son of Dean C. (a Methodist clergyman) and Anna L. (Porter) Poindexter; married Marian J. Sayre (a writer), December 25, 1952; children: James David. *Education:* Willamette University, B.A., 1951; Boston University, S.T.B., 1957. *Home:* 10 Cottage Pl., Cresskill, N.J. 07626.

CAREER: Ordained to Methodist ministry, 1954; pastor in Newton, Mass. and Portland, Ore., 1954-65; National Council of Churches, Broadcasting and Film Commission, New York City, director of utilization, 1965-68, director of promotion services, 1968-70; Population Communication Center, New York City, director, beginning 1970. *Member:* Council on International Nontheatrical Events (secretary), National Association of Educational Broadcasters, Association for Educational Communication Technology, New York Film Association (former vice-president).

WRITINGS—With wife, Marian J. Poindexter: *Come In, World,* Friendship, 1970; *Junior Teacher's Guide on How the Word Gets Around,* Friendship, 1970. Contributing editor and TV cclumnist, *Together;* member of editorial board, *Ecology Today.*

SIDELIGHTS: David Poindexter told *CA,* "At present I am at work to bring to bear the communication resources of the United States on the population crisis, and its related crucial issues." *Avocational interests:* Travel, family, and "most of all travel with my family."††

POINDEXTER, Marian J(ean) 1929-

PERSONAL: Born April 5, 1929, in Denison, Iowa; daughter of James E. (a railroad man) and Grace (Lee) Sayre; married David Poindexter, December 25, 1952; children: James David. *Education:* Willamette University, B.A., 1951; Boston University, M.Ed., 1956. *Religion:* United Methodist. *Home:* 10 Cottage Pl., Cresskill, N.J. 07626.

CAREER: Booth Hospital, Boston, Mass., social service caseworker, 1953; Auburndale Congregational Church, Boston, director of Christian education, 1954-57; Parkrose Heights Methodist Church, Portland, Ore., director of Christian education, 1958-64; now full-time writer.

WRITINGS—With husband, David Poindexter: *Come In, World,* Friendship, 1970; *Junior Teacher's Guide on How the Word Gets Around,* Friendship, 1970. Also author of filmstrip, "The Group Way of Teaching," Television, Radio and Film Commission (T.R.A.F.C.O., Nashville). Feature writer for United Methodist curriculum materials and *Spectrum.*††

*   *   *

POINSETT, Alex(ander) Ceasar 1926-

PERSONAL: Born January 27, 1926, in Chicago, Ill.; son of Alexander A. and Ardele L. (Prindle) Poinsett; married Norma R. Miller (a high school teacher and librarian), August, 1951; children: Pierrette, Mimi, Alexis Pierre. *Education:* University of Illinois, B.S., 1952, M.A., 1953; University of Chicago, graduate study, 1954—. *Politics:* Independent. *Religion:* Unitarian. *Home:* 8532 South Wabash Ave., Chicago, Ill. 60619. *Office:* Johnson Publishing Co., 820 South Michigan Ave., Chicago, Ill. 60616.

CAREER: Johnson Publishing Co., Chicago, Ill., 1953—, began as assistant editor, now senior staff editor. Former board member, First Unitarian Church, Chicago, Ill. *Military service:* U.S. Navy, 1944-47. *Member:* Black Unitarian Universalist Caucus (Chicago chairman, 1968-70). *Awards, honors:* J. C. Penney—University of Missouri Journalism Award, 1968, for article "Ghetto Schools: An Educational Wasteland."

WRITINGS—All published by Johnson Publishing Co. (Chicago), unless otherwise noted: *Common Folk in an Uncommon Cause,* Liberty Baptist Church, 1962; (contributor) *The Negro Handbook,* 1966; (contributor) *The White Problem in America,* 1966; (contributor) *The Black Revolution,* 1970; *Black Power Gary Style: The Making of Mayor Richard Gordon Hatcher,* 1970; (contributor) *Ebony Pictorial History of Black America,* 1971. Contributor to *Ebony.*

SIDELIGHTS: Alex Poinsett wrote an influential 1958 story leading to the commutation of the death sentence of Jimmy Wilson, an Alabama black man given the death penalty for a $1.95 robbery. As a journalist he has traveled more than one million miles, visiting such places as Haiti, Kenya, and the Soviet Union.

*   *   *

POLATNICK, Florence T. 1923-

PERSONAL: Born March 30, 1923, in New York, N.Y.; daughter of William and Esther (Herschkowitz) Tambor; married Samuel Polatnick (executive director of New York City high schools), February 28, 1942; children: Stephen, Margaret, Michael. *Education:* Brooklyn College (now Brooklyn College of the City University of New York),

B.A., 1943; New School for Social Research, M.A., 1952; Yeshiva University, M.S., 1960. *Residence:* Plainview, N.Y.

CAREER: New York Journal of Commerce, New York City, economic researcher and reporter, 1943-44; *Quonset News,* New York City, founder and editor, 1946-48; *Plainview Herald,* Plainview, N.Y., founder and editor, 1955-57; Central School District 2, Syosset, N.Y., teacher of social studies, 1960—. *Member:* National Council for the Social Studies, New York State Council for the Social Studies, League of Women Voters. *Awards, honors:* Howard L. Pierson Distinguished Service Medal; National Council for Geographic Education outstanding teacher award, 1971.

WRITINGS: (With Alberta L. Saletan) *Shapers of Africa* (juvenile), Messner, 1969; *Zambia's President: Kenneth Kaunda* (juvenile), Messner, 1972.

WORK IN PROGRESS: A novel; articles on economic subjects, travel, education, and youth.

BIOGRAPHICAL/CRITICAL SOURCES: Best Sellers, November 1, 1969.

* * *

POLKING, Kirk 1925-

PERSONAL: Born December 21, 1925, in Covington, Ky.; daughter of Henry (a salesman) and Mary (Hull) Polking. *Education:* Studied in evening courses at American University, 1944, and at University of Cincinnati and Xavier University at intervals, 1944—. *Politics:* Independent. *Religion:* Roman Catholic. *Home:* 5450 Beechmont, Cincinnati, Ohio 45230. *Office:* F & W Publishing Co., 9933 Alliance Rd., Cincinnati, Ohio 45210.

CAREER: U.S. War Department, Washington, D.C., administrative assistant, 1943-45; F & W Publishing Co., Cincinnati, Ohio, editorial assistant on *Modern Photography* and *Writer's Digest,* 1948-52, circulation manager of *Farm Quarterly,* 1952-57; free-lance writer, 1957-63; F & W Publishing Co., editor of *Writer's Digest,* 1963-73, editor of *Artists Market,* 1973-75, director of Writer's Digest School, 1976—. *Member:* Author's Guild, National League of American Pen Women, Women in Communications. *Awards, honors:* Women in Communications Headliner Award, 1970.

WRITINGS: Let's Go with Lewis and Clark, Putnam, 1963; *Let's Go with Henry Hudson,* Putnam, 1964; *Let's Go See Congress at Work,* Putnam, 1966; *Let's Go to an Atomic Energy Town,* Putnam, 1968; (editor with Jean Chimsky) *The Beginning Writer's Handbook,* Writer's Digest, 1971; (editor) *How to Make Money in Your Spare Time by Writing,* Cornerstone Library, 1971; *The Private Pilot's Dictionary and Handbook,* Arco, 1974. Editor or co-editor, *The Writer's Market,* 1964-71.

WORK IN PROGRESS: New home study courses in writing.

AVOCATIONAL INTERESTS: Flying (obtained private pilot's license in 1968).

* * *

POLLACK, Cecelia 1909-

PERSONAL: Born February 28, 1909, in Russia; naturalized U.S. citizen; daughter of Louis and Bess (Ezikoff) Cohen; married Harry Pollack (owner of a book business), May 1, 1943; children: Alexandra. *Education:* Hunter College (now Hunter College of the City University of New York), B.A., 1930; City College (now City College of the City University of New York), M.S. in Ed., 1960; New York University, Ph.D., 1966. *Home:* 56-31 175th St., Flushing, N.Y. 11365. *Office:* Department of Special Education, Herbert H. Lehman College of the City University of New York, Bronx, N.Y. 10468.

CAREER: Certified as psychologist and as teacher of the physically handicapped in New York State; elementary teacher in New York City public schools for fourteen years; Northside Center for Child Development, New York City, remedial reading therapist, 1961-62; Northside School, Levittown, N.Y., teacher of children with minimal cerebral dysfunction, 1961-63; New York University, New York City, part-time instructor in special education department, 1964-68; Maimonides Community Mental Health Services, New York City, director of learning rehabilitation services, 1966-70; Herbert H. Lehman College of the City University of New York, New York City, associate professor, 1970-74, professor in special education department, 1974-77, director of Intersensory Learning Center, 1977—. Member, Council for Exceptional Children. *Member:* International Reading Association, American Psychological Association, American Orthopsychiatric Association, Orton Society. *Awards, honors:* Grant from Sidney L. Green Foundation for Adolescent and Child Psychiatry, 1968-70.

WRITINGS—All published by Book-Lab, except as indicated: *Phonic Readiness Kit,* 1967; *The Intersensory Reading Method,* 1967; (with Patrick Lane) *The Hip Reader* (for non-reading teenagers), 1969; *Composing Language: Steps,* Macmillan, 1974. Contributor to education journals.

* * *

POLLAK, Kurt 1919-

PERSONAL: Born July 25, 1919, in Vienna, Austria; son of Julius (a head clerk) and Aloisia (Suwald) Pollak; married Lisa Bank, June 20, 1944; children: Ariane. *Education:* Attended University of Berlin and University of Danzig; University of Vienna, M.D., 1944. *Home:* Kreillerstrasse 165, Munich 82, Federal Republic of Germany.

CAREER: Deutsche Bundeswehr, wartime service and medical training, 1938-45; intern in hospital for displaced persons, Bad Hofgastein, Austria, 1945-47; general practitioner in Henndorf am Wallersee, Austria, 1947-56; Deutsche Bundeswehr, medical officer, 1956—, with current rank of colonel. *Member:* Internationale Paracelsus-Gesellschaft (Salzburg), Gesellschaft fuer Wehrmedizin und Wehrpharmazie (Bonn).

WRITINGS: Wetter und Klima als Krankheitsursachen, Butzon & Bercker, 1951; *Der neue Hausarzt,* Andreas-Verlag, 1951; *Der Naturarzt,* Verlag Neues Leben, 1953; *Krebs ist heilbar,* Humboldt-Taschenbuecher, 1954; *Lexikon der guten Ernaehrung,* Humboldt-Taschenbuecher, 1954; *Arterienverkalkung,* Paracelsus-Verlag, 1956; *Wie die Medizin hilft,* Bertelsmann, 1957; *Bertelsmann aerztlicher Ratgeber,* Bertelsmann, 1958; *Sanitaetsfibel,* Verlag Offene Worte, 1959; *Gesundheits-und Diatkochbuch,* Mary Hahns Kochbuchverlag, 1961; *Die Juenger des Hippokrates,* Econ Verlag, 1963; *Der Schluessel zur Medizin von heute,* Econ Verlag, 1965; *Wissen und Weisheit der alten Aerzte,* Econ Verlag, 1968; *Die Heilkunde der Antike,* Econ Verlag, 1969, translation and revision by E. Ashworth Underwood published as *The Healers,* Thomas Nelson, 1969; *Knaurs Gesundheits-lexicon,* Droemer-Knaur, 1970; *Knaurs Lexicon der modernen Medizin,* Droemer-Knaur, 1972; (with U. H. Peters) *Vom Kopfschmerz kann man sich befreinen,*

Kindler, 1976; *Der Hausarzt,* Mosaik Verlag; 1976. Editor, *Jahrbuch der Wehrmedizin.*

BIOGRAPHICAL/CRITICAL SOURCES: Punch, March 6, 1968.

* * *

POLLARD, Jack 1926-

PERSONAL: Born July 31, 1926, in Sydney, New South Wales, Australia; son of John Hume (a tailor) and Grace (Griffiths) Pollard; married Barbara Anne Broadbent (a journalist), March 29, 1958; children: James, John, Katharine, Louise. *Education:* Attended school in Sydney, Australia. *Politics:* Liberal. *Religion:* Church of England. *Home and office:* 7 Selwyn St., Wollstonecraft, Sydney, New South Wales, Australia. *Agent:* Paul R. Reynolds, Inc., 12 East 41st St., New York, N.Y. 10017.

CAREER: Journalist with *Sydney Daily Telegraph,* Sydney, Australia, 1940-43; foreign correspondent for Australian newspapers, 1947-56; executive editor of K. G. Murray Ltd. (magazine chain), Sydney, Australia, 1959-65; full-time writer and editor of sports books, 1965—; Pollard Publishing Co., Sydney, Australia, owner, 1969—. Adviser on outdoor and sporting books to several Australian publishers. *Military service:* Australian Army, 1943-46; mainly assigned to army newspapers; became sergeant. *Member:* Australian Publishers' Association, Australian Journalists' Association. *Awards, honors:* Several Australian Book Week commendations.

WRITINGS: Meet the Kangaroos: Introducing the 1948/49 Australian Rugby Team, Hotspur Publishing, 1949; *Penny Arcade* (novel), Muller, 1956; (with Lew Hoad) *The Lew Hoad Story,* Prentice-Hall, 1958 (published in England as *My Game,* Hodder & Stoughton, 1958); *Advantage Receiver,* Muller, 1960; *The Roughrider: The Story of Lance Skuthorpe,* Lansdowne Press, 1962, published as *The Horse Tamer,* Pollard Publishing, 1970; (with Rodney George Laver) *How to Play Winning Tennis,* Pelham Books, 1964, published as *How to Play Championship Tennis,* Macmillan, 1965; (with John Williams Raper) *The Johnny Raper Rugby League Book,* K. G. Murray, 1965; (with Bruce Devlin) *Play Like the Devil,* Angus & Robertson, 1967; (with Don Talbot) *Swimming to Win,* Pelham, 1967, Hawthorne, 1969; *The Ampol Book of Sporting Records,* Pollard Publishing, 1968, 2nd edition published as *Ampol's Australian Sporting Records,* 1969, 3rd edition published as *Ampol's Sporting Records,* 1971. Also author of *Keith Miller on Cricket* (as told to Pollard), c. 1963.

Editor or compiler: *Cricket—the Australian Way,* N. Kaye, 1961, 2nd revised edition, 1967; *This Is Rugby League,* Lansdowne Press, 1962, 2nd edition published as *Rugby League—the Australian Way,* 1970; *Lawn Bowls—the Australian Way,* Lansdowne Press, 1962; *Swimming—Australian Style,* Lansdowne Press, 1963; *Lawn Tennis—the Australian Way,* Lansdowne Press, 1963, 2nd edition, 1971; *The Australian Surfrider,* K. G. Murray, 1963, revised edition published as *The Surfrider,* K. G. Murray, 1965, Taplinger, 1968; *Straight Shooting,* K. G. Murray, 1963, 2nd revised edition, 1967; *High Mark: The Complete Book on Australian Football,* K. G. Murray, 1964, 2nd edition, 1967; *Six and Out: The Legend of Australian Cricket,* Lansdowne Press, 1964; *Horses and Horsemen: Wild Bush Horses, Thoroughbreds and the Men Who Rode Them,* Lansdowne Press, 1966; *One for the Road: Stories of Racetrack, Trials, Pioneer, Veteran, Vintage and Outback Motoring in Australia and New Zealand,* Angus & Robertson, 1966, Tri-

Ocean, 1967; *The Scream of the Reel,* Lansdowne Press, 1966; *Birds of Paradox: Birdlife in Australia and New Zealand,* Lansdowne Press, 1967; *Wild Dogs, Working Dogs, Pedigrees and Pets,* Lansdowne Press, 1968; *Australian and New Zealand Fishing,* International Publishing Service, 1969; *The Pictorial History of Australian Horse Racing,* Paul Hamlyn, 1971; *How to Ride a Surfboard,* Pollard Publishing, 1972.

Compiler for Gregory's Guides and Maps firm: *Gregory's Australian Guide to Bowls,* 2nd edition (Pollard was not associated with earlier edition), 1963; *Gregory's Australian Fishing Guide,* 2nd edition, 1963 (Pollard was not associated with earlier edition), 4th edition, 1965; *Gregory's Australian Guide to Hunting and Shooting,* 1963; *Gregory's Australian Guide to Golf,* 2nd edition (Pollard was not associated with earlier edition), 1964; *Gregory's Australian Guide to Camping and Caravans,* 1964; *Gregory's Guide to Rugby League,* 1965.

Contributor and editorial adviser to Australian editions of *World Book Encyclopedia.* Contributor to magazines and newspapers.

SIDELIGHTS: Cricket is Jack Pollard's perennial love, although he is regarded as a world authority on lawn tennis and has covered nine Wimbledons, five British Open gold championships, and countless international rugby matches. He says that his work "is fairly remote to U.S. readers," although most of his books have been available in America through Sportshelf & Soccer Associates the same year as their publication in Australia, and several stories from the books have been serialized in *Sports Illustrated* and *Esquire.* Sales of his books now exceed 500,000 copies. Many of them have been published in England and New Zealand as well as in Australia; three books have been translated into Japanese, and others into German, Dutch, and Italian. In 1969, Pollard himself became a publisher.†

* * *

POLLARD, T(homas) E(van) 1921-

PERSONAL: Born February 1, 1921, in Mackay, Australia; son of Harold Stanley (an accountant) and Hilda Maud (Evans) Pollard; married Noela Esme Verdun Thomas, February 24, 1945; children: Gwennyth Noela (Mrs. Cleland Robin McLay), Sandra Elizabeth (Mrs. Gray Spence Townsend), Margaret Anne. *Education:* University of Sydney, B.A., 1941, B.D. (honors), 1948; attended United Faculty of Theology, 1945-47; University of St. Andrews, Ph.D., 1956. *Home:* 50 Evans St., Opoho, Dunedin, New Zealand. *Office:* Theological Hall, Knox College, Dunedin, New Zealand.

CAREER: Ordained Presbyterian minister, 1949; parish minister of congregations in New South Wales, Australia, 1949-52, 1957-62; St. Andrew's College, Sydney, New South Wales, acting principal, 1953; University of Sydney, Sydney, New South Wales, instructor in New Testament, 1958-62; University of Otago, Dunedin, New Zealand, lecturer in New Testament, 1962—, dean of faculty of theology, 1967-69, 1973-75; Knox College, Dunedin, New Zealand, professor of New Testament Studies, 1962—. Special invitation lecturer, University of St. Andrew's, 1969; visiting scholar, Corpus Christi College, Cambridge, England, 1975. Secretary, Committee on Inter-Church Aid, 1956-58. *Military service:* Royal Australian Air Force, 1942-45. *Member:* Sydney Fellowship of Biblical Studies (president, 1958-59), Studiorum Novi Testamenti Societas.

WRITINGS: Johannine Christology and the Early Church,

Cambridge University Press, 1970. Contributor to *New South Wales Presbyterian, Outlook, Forum, Theological Review, Scottish Journal of Theology, New Testament Studies, Studia Patristica, Vigiliae Christianae, Expository Times, Colloquim,* and other theological journals.

WORK IN PROGRESS: General research in New Testament and Patristic Exegesis of the New Testament; and a translation of works by Eusebius of Caesarea, *contra Marcellum* and *de Ecclesiastica Theologia,* with commentary.

SIDELIGHTS: T. E. Pollard told *CA* that he has an "interest in [the] historical development of theology in the first five centuries A.D. . . . [My] motivation in research and writing is to increase knowledge of early historical theology and to contribute to ecumenical discussion." He has a reading knowledge of Hebrew, Latin, Greek, French, German, Italian, and Spanish. *Avocational interests:* Bowls, gardening, and music.

* * *

POLLOCK, James K(err) 1898-1968

May 25, 1898—October 4, 1968; American diplomat, educator, and political scientist. Obituaries: *Detroit News,* October 5, 1968; *Detroit Free Press,* October 8, 1968. (See index for *CA* sketch)

* * *

POLOME, Edgar (Ghislain) C(harles) 1920-

PERSONAL: Surname is pronounced Polo-*may;* born July 31, 1920, in Brussels, Belgium; son of Marcel Felicien (a linotypist) and Berthe (Henry) Polome; married Julia Josephine Schwindt, July 22, 1944 (died May 29, 1975); children: Monique, Andre. *Education:* Free University of Brussels, B.A., 1940, Ph.D., 1949; Catholic University of Louvain, M.A., 1943. *Home:* 2701 Rock Ter., Austin, Tex. 78704. *Office:* Department of Oriental and African Languages and Literatures, University of Texas, P.O. Box 8058, Austin, Tex. 78712.

CAREER: Athenee Adolphe Max, Brussels, Belgium, instructor in Germanic languages, 1942-54; Belgian Broadcasting Services, Brussels, professor of Dutch, 1954-56; State University of the Belgian Congo and Ruanda-Urundi, Elizabethville, Katanga, professor of linguistics, 1956-61; University of Texas at Austin, visiting associate professor, 1961-62, professor of linguistics and Germanic languages, 1962—, director of Center for Asian Studies, 1963-72, head of department of Oriental and African languages and literatures, 1969-76. Fulbright-Hays professor of linguistics, University of Kiel, 1968. Team director in Tanzania, Ford Foundation Survey of Language Use and Language Teaching in Eastern Africa, 1969-70. Trustee, American Institute of Indian Studies, 1965—.

MEMBER: American Oriental Society, Association for Asian Studies, African Studies Association, Linguistics Society of America, American Anthropological Association, Modern Language Association of America, Societe de Linguistique de Paris, Indogermanische Gesellschaft. *Awards, honors:* Fulbright-Hays scholar in Germany, 1968.

WRITINGS: (Contributor) Werner Winter, editor, *Evidence for Laryngeals,* Mouton & Co., 1965; (contributor) Henrik Birnbaum and Jaan Puhvel, editors, *Ancient Indo-European Dialects,* University of California Press, 1966; *Swahili Language Handbook,* Center for Applied Linguistics, 1967; (contributor) Joshua A. Fishman, Charles A. Ferguson and J. Das Gupta, editors, *Language Problems of*

Developing Nations, Wiley, 1968; (editor and contributor) *Old Norse Literature and Mythology: A Symposium,* University of Texas Press, 1969; (contributor) George Cardona, Henry M. Hoenigswald, and Alfred Senn, editors, *Indo-European and Indo-Europeans,* University of Pennsylvania Press, 1970; (contributor) Jaan Puhvel, editor, *Myth and Law among the Indo-Europeans,* University of California Press, 1970; (contributor) W. H. Whiteley, editor, *Language Use and Social Change,* Oxford University Press, 1971; (contributor) Dell Hymes, editor, *Pidginization and Creolization of Languages,* Cambridge University Press, 1971; (contributor) Frans van Coetsem and Herbert L. Kufner, editors, *Toward a Grammar of Proto-Germanic,* Tuebingen, Niemeyer, 1972; (co-editor with Sirarpi Ohannessian and Charles Ferguson, and contributor) *Language Surveys in the Developing Nations,* Center for Applied Linguistics, 1974; (contributor) Gerald James Larson, editor, *Myth in Indo-European Antiquity,* University of California Press, 1974; (co-editor with M. A. Jazayery and Winter) *Linguistic and Literary Studies in Honor of Archibald A. Hill,* Peter de Ridder, 1976. Contributor to proceedings of linguistic conferences, to festschrifts, and to journals in America and abroad. Also contributor to a special issue of *The Conch,* 1972. Co-editor, *Journal of Indo-European Studies,* and *Journal of Creole Studies.*

WORK IN PROGRESS: With C. P. Hill and H. David Barton, *Language in Tanzania,* for Oxford University Press (Nairobi); translating four volumes of *Comparative Germanic Grammar,* published by the Russian Academy of Sciences.

SIDELIGHTS: Edgar Polome is fluent in French, Dutch, and German, has a practical command of Swahili, and a reading knowledge of Italian, Swedish, and Danish. In addition, he teaches Sanskrit, Buddhistic Pali, Hittite, Avestan, Old Persian, and Gothic, also offering courses in the comparative grammar of Indo-Iranian, Greek, Latin, Germanic, and Bantu languages, as well as comparative religion. His research in the Congo (four years) and in East Africa (a year and a half) was concentrated on the Bantu languages, especially Swahili and sociolinguistics. He has traveled in more than twenty countries of Africa, Europe, and Asia.

He wrote to *CA:* "My main interest is in language and culture, both in present day African and in the Ancient Indo-European world. As a result of my education as a comparative linguist and of my long stays in Central and East Africa, the focus of my attention is on the relation of language to the structure of society and on the impact of religious factors on sociolinguistic behavior."

* * *

POMERANTZ, Joel 1930-

PERSONAL: Born February 8, 1930, in Brooklyn, N.Y.; son of Max and Eva (Litvack) Pomerantz. *Education:* City College (now City College of the City University of New York), B.S.S., 1950. *Religion:* Jewish. *Home and office:* Grossinger Hotel, Grossinger, N.Y. 12734.

CAREER: Public relations work, currently with Grossinger Resort, Grossinger, N.Y.

WRITINGS: Jennie and the Story of Grossinger's, Grosset, 1970.

BIOGRAPHICAL/CRITICAL SOURCES: Variety, June 10, 1970.†

POMPIAN, Richard O(wen) 1935-

PERSONAL: Born July 17, 1935, in Chicago, Ill.; son of Bertram Edwin (a swimming-pool builder) and Molly (Pumpian) Pompian; married Rita Beyers (an assistant professor in English at Pace University), December 20, 1970. *Education:* University of Michigan, A.B. and Certificate in Journalism, 1958, Internship Certificate in Advertising, 1961; New York University, M.B.A. (with distinction), 1965, Certificate in Graphics, 1967, Certificate in Television, 1968, Certificate in Computer Programming and Systems, 1970, further graduate study in psychology at New School for Social Research, 1965, 1968-69; studies in musicianship, and private studies in voice. *Home:* 300 Riverside Dr., New York, N.Y. 10025. *Office:* 420 Lexington Ave., New York, N.Y. 10017.

CAREER: Dancer-Fitzgerald-Sample, Inc., New York City, advertising copywriter, 1960-68; Davis, Mayer & Joyce, Englewood, N.J., advertising consultant, 1968-69; Mitchell Barkett Advertising, Inc., New York City, vice-president, 1970; Pompian Advertising, Inc., New York City, president, 1970—. Lecturer in advanced writing, Pace University, 1974. Consultant in writing to American Telephone and Telegraph Co., 1976—; consultant and writer for other advertising agencies in New York City. *Military service:* U.S. Army, 1958-60; became first lieutenant. *Member:* National Association of Television Arts and Sciences, Sigma Delta Chi.

WRITINGS: Advertising (juvenile), F. Watts, 1970; (editor) *The Rhythm Book* (music textbook), Associated Music Publishers, 1971. Also contributing editor of *Africa and the Arab World*, Sadlier. Editor, *The Northeast Gazette,* 1976—.

WORK IN PROGRESS: Preparing a series of articles on business writing; writing with wife, Rita Pompian, a follow-up text to *Working Sentences* by R. L. Allen and Rita L. Pompian.

AVOCATIONAL INTERESTS: Riflery, skiing, music, photography, psychology, language.

* * *

PONICSAN, Darryl 1938-

PERSONAL: Surname is pronounced *Pahn*-i-son; born May 26, 1938, in Shenandoah, Pa.; son of Frank G. (a merchant) and Anne (Kuleck) Ponicsan; married Katie Hardison, April 8, 1966 (divorced, 1977); children: Dylan. *Education:* Muhlenberg College, A.B., 1959; Cornell University, M.A., 1965. *Residence:* Los Angeles, Calif. *Agent:* Ned Brown, Inc., 407 North Maple Dr., Beverly Hills, Calif. 90210.

CAREER: Teacher of English at high school in Owego, N.Y., 1959-62; social worker for Los Angeles County, Los Angeles, Calif., 1965, and teacher of English in Los Angeles schools, 1965-66; La Canada High School, La Canada, Calif., teacher of English, 1966-69. *Military service:* U.S. Navy, 1962-65. *Member:* Authors Guild.

WRITINGS: The Last Detail (novel; alternate Literary Guild selection), Dial, 1970; *Goldengrove* (novel), Dial, 1971; *Andoshen, Pa.* (novel), Dial, 1973; *Cinderella Liberty* (novel), Harper, 1973; *The Accomplice* (novel), Harper, 1975; *Tom Mix Died for Your Sins* (biographical novel), Delacorte, 1975; *The Circus from Stoney Flats* (novel), Delacorte, 1977.

SIDELIGHTS: Yvette Schmitt calls the characters in *The Last Detail* "uneducated, tough, uncultured career sailors, but their warmth and affection come through, and readers become really involved with them—the innocent victims of the military and a heartless society." Ponicsan's characters are believable because, as he told *CA,* "as a writer I exist only in the pages of my books."

Film rights to *The Last Detail* were sold to Columbia Pictures for $100,000 and a percentage of profits, paperback rights were sold to New American Library for $150,000, and foreign publishing rights have been sold in England, Japan, Spain, Italy, and Germany. *Cinderella Liberty* was made a film by Twentieth Century-Fox.

BIOGRAPHICAL/CRITICAL SOURCES: Variety, March 6, 1970; *New York Times Book Review,* October 18, 1970.

* * *

PONTIERO, Giovanni 1932-

PERSONAL: Born February 10, 1932, in Cambuslang, Lanarkshire, Scotland; son of Federico (a restauranteur) and Concetta (Fraioli) Pontiero. *Education:* University of Glasgow, M.A. (second class honors), 1960, Ph.D., 1962. *Home:* 3, The Grove, Didsbury, Manchester 20 8RG, England. *Office:* Department of Spanish and Portuguese Studies, University of Manchester, Manchester M13 9PL, England.

CAREER: University of Paraiba, Joao Pessoa, Paraiba, Brazil, head of department of English studies and director of studies at Institute of English Culture, 1960-61; University of Manchester, Manchester, England, assistant lecturer, 1962-64, lecturer in Latin American literature, 1964-66; University of Liverpool, Liverpool, England, lecturer in Latin American literature, 1966-70; University of Manchester, lecturer in Latin American literature, 1970—. *Member:* International Association of Hispanists, International Association of Ibero-American Literature, Society for Latin American Studies (founder-member), National Association of Hispanists, Hispanic and Luso-Brazilian Councils, Latin American Society (University of Manchester; honorary member). *Awards, honors:* Leverhulme award for research in Brazil, 1967; Camoens Prize for translation, 1968; Rio Branco Essay Award, 1970; travel awards for research in Latin America from the Brazilian Embassy, Anglo-Brazilian Society (London), Carnegie Foundation (Edinburgh), and Parry Funds (Universities of Liverpool and Manchester).

WRITINGS: (Editor, and author of critical introduction and notes) Florencio Sanchez, *La gringa and Barranca Abajo* (drama), Las Americas, 1969; (editor, and author of critical introduction and notes) *An Anthology of Brazilian Modernist Poetry*, Pergamon, 1969. Also author of *The Poetry of Manuel Bandeira* (an interpretive study), and of *The Vampire of Curitiba: Dalton Trevisan and the Pursuit of Decadence* (an interpretive study). Translations of stories and poems by Carlos Martinez Moreno, Clarice Lispector, Manuel Bandeira, Renata Pallottini, Nelida Pinon, and Lygia Fagundes Teles are included in *New Directions, Anthology No. 20,* 1968, *Anthology of Modern Poetry Translations,* J. Cape, and others. Contributor of entries on Latin American authors to *20th Century Writing,* Hamlyn, 1969, and *Modern Authors,* Wilson, 1971, 1976. Contributor of articles and reviews in English and Spanish to professional journals in Europe and the Americas.

WORK IN PROGRESS: A study and translation of Nelida Pinon's *The House of Passion;* a monograph, *The Poetry of Carlos Drummond de Andrade;* a series of articles on Manuel Bandeira's prose writings.

POOL, David de Sola   1885-1970

May 16, 1885—December 1, 1970; English-born American rabbi, theologian, and author of books on Judaica. Obituaries: *Publishers' Weekly,* December 14, 1970.

*   *   *

POORE, Charles (Graydon)   1902-1971

August 20, 1902—July(?), 1971; Mexican-born American author and book reviewer. Obituaries: *Detroit News,* July 27, 1971; *Newsday,* July 28, 1971.

*   *   *

POPE, Ray   1924-

PERSONAL: Born August 12, 1924, in King's Lynn, Norfolk, England; son of Harry (a harbor master) and Dorothy Pope; married; wife's name, Elizabeth Ellen (a teacher of domestic science); children: Rachela, Glenn, Mark. *Education:* Attended Goldsmiths' College, London, 1947-49. *Politics:* "The British are shy politically!" *Religion:* Church of England. *Home:* "The Vatican," 49 High St., Marshfield, Chippenham, Wiltshire, England.

CAREER: Chippenham High School for Girls, Chippenham, England, teacher of geography, beginning 1966. Currently working as long distance lorry driver, as well as author of children's books. *Military service:* Royal Navy, radio operator, 1942-45.

WRITINGS—All juvenile books; published by Macdonald & Co., except as indicated: *Strosa Light,* Hart-Davis, 1965, Childrens Press, 1970; *Nut Case,* Methuen, 1966; *Salvage from Strosa,* Hart-Davis, 1967, Childrens Press, 1970; *The Drum,* Macmillan (London), 1968; *Desperate Breakaway,* Hart-Davis, 1969, Childrens Press, 1970; *One's Pool,* Macmillan (London), 1969; *The Model-Railway Men,* 1970; *"Is It Always Like This?,"* 1970; *Telford and the American Visitor,* 1970; *The Model-Railway Men Take Over,* 1971; *Hayseed & Co.,* Methuen, 1972; *Telford's Holiday,* 1972; *Telford and the Festiniog Railway,* 1973; *Telford Saves the Line,* 1974; *Telford Goes Dutch,* 1976; *Telford Tells the Truth,* 1977.

WORK IN PROGRESS: Trilogy on possession by spirits; an adventure story with trucking background.

SIDELIGHTS: One's Pool and *Hayseed & Co.* have been featured on British television; *Nut Case* has been published in Italy, *"Is It Always Like This?"* in Germany, and *Desperate Breakaway* in Spain.

BIOGRAPHICAL/CRITICAL SOURCES: Times Literary Supplement, June 26, 1969, April 16, 1970, July 20, 1970; *Books and Bookmen,* September, 1969.

*   *   *

POPE, Robert G(ardner)   1936-

PERSONAL: Born August 13, 1936, in Newton, Mass.; son of Daniel Stuart, Jr. (a salesman) and Marguerite (Jones) Pope; married Dorothy Root, June 28, 1958; children: Cynthia, Christopher, Elizabeth. *Education:* Marietta College, B.A., 1960; Yale University, Ph.D., 1967. *Religion:* Episcopalian. *Home:* 236 Parker Ave., Buffalo, N.Y. 14214. *Office:* Department of History, State University of New York, Buffalo, N.Y. 14222.

CAREER: University of Massachusetts, Amherst, assistant professor of history, 1965-68; State University of New York at Buffalo, associate professor of history, 1968—; ordained Episcopal priest. *Military service:* U.S. Marine Corps, 1954-

57; became sergeant. *Member:* Organization of American Historians.

WRITINGS: The Half-Way Covenant: Church Membership in Puritan New England, Princeton University Press, 1969; (editor) *The Notebook of the Rev. John Fiske, 1644-1676,* Colonial Society of Massachusetts, 1974, 2nd edition, Essex Institute, 1975.

WORK IN PROGRESS: Society, Security, and Persecution.

*   *   *

POPENOE, David   1932-

PERSONAL: Surname is pronounced *Pop*-en-oe; born October 1, 1932, in Los Angeles, Calif; son of Paul (a family life specialist) and Betty (Stankovitch) Popenoe; married Katharine Sasse, July 18, 1959; children: Rebecca, Julia. *Education:* Antioch College, A.B., 1954; University of Pennsylvania, M.C.P., 1958, Ph.D., 1963. *Politics:* Democrat. *Religion:* Religious Society of Friends (Quaker). *Home:* 150 Loomis Ct., Princeton, N.J. 08540. *Office:* Douglass College, Rutgers University, New Brunswick, N.J. 08903.

CAREER: Philadelphia (Pa.) Redevelopment Authority, program planner, 1956-58; Newark (N.J.) Central Planning Board, senior planner, 1958-59; Rutgers University, New Brunswick, N.J., assistant director of research and education, Urban Studies Center, 1961-64, director of academic affairs, Urban Studies Center, 1965-69, associate professor of urban planning at Livingston College, 1967-69, associate professor of sociology at Douglass College, 1969—. Adjunct professor of public administration, New York University, 1964-65, 1967-68; lecturer in department of sociology, University of Pennsylvania, 1965-69; visiting professor, University of Stockholm (Sweden), 1972-73, 1974. *Military service:* U.S. Army, 1954-56.

MEMBER: International Sociological Association, American Sociological Association, American Institute of Planners, American Association of University Professors, Eastern Sociology Society, Society for the Advancement of Scandinavian Studies.

WRITINGS: (Editor) *The Urban-Industrial Frontier: Essays on Social Trends and Institutional Goals in Modern Communities,* Rutgers University Press, 1969; (editor with Robert Gutman) *Neighborhood, City and Metropolis: An Integrated Reader in Urban Sociology,* Random House, 1970; *Sociology* (introductory text), third edition, Prentice-Hall, 1977; *The Suburban Environment: Sweden and the United States,* University of Chicago Press, 1977.

Contributor: Ralph Blasingame and Leonard Grunt, editors, *Research on Library Services in Metropolitan Areas,* Graduate School of Library Service, Rutgers University, 1967; P. P. Indik and F. K. Berrien, editors, *People, Groups and Organizations,* Teachers College Press, 1968; Paul Meadows and Ephraim H. Mizruchi, editors, *Urbanism, Urbanization, and Change: Comparative Perspectives,* Addison-Wesley, 1969; Marcia P. Effrat, editor, *The Community: Approaches and Applications,* Free Press, 1974.

Contributor of articles and reviews in the area of sociology, urban studies, and social planning to professional journals. Editor with Robert Gutman of a special issue of *American Behavioral Scientist* devoted to urban studies, February, 1963; also editor of *Urban Education,* April, 1971. Member of editorial board, "Studies in Comparative International Development" series, 1969—; associate review editor, *Journal of the AIP* (American Institute of Planners), 1968—;

member of editorial committee, *Journal of the Community Development Society,* 1969—.

* * *

POPPER, Frank J. 1944-

PERSONAL: Born March 26, 1944, in Chicago, Ill.; son of Hans (a physician) and Lina (Billig) Popper; married Deborah Epstein, August 9, 1968; children: two. *Education:* Haverford College, A.B. (with high honors), 1965; Massachusetts Institute of Technology, graduate study, 1965-66; Harvard University, M.P.A., 1968, Ph.D., 1972. *Home and office:* 1719 East 54th St., Chicago, Ill. 60615.

CAREER: Twentieth Century Fund, New York, N.Y., research associate, 1968-69; Public Administration Service, Chicago, Ill., research associate, 1971-73; American Society of Planning Officials, Chicago, senior research associate, 1973-74; Twentieth Century Fund Project on the Politics of State Land-Use Planning, Chicago, director, 1975—.

WRITINGS: The President's Commissions, Twentieth Century Fund, 1970; (co-author) *Urban Nongrowth: City Planning for People,* Praeger, 1976. Contributor to political science, city planning, environmental, and medical journals, as well as to major government reports.

WORK IN PROGRESS: A book tentatively entitled *The Politics of Land-Use Reform,* completion expected 1978.

* * *

PORTER, Thomas E. 1928-

PERSONAL: Born January 13, 1928, in Cleveland, Ohio; son of Emmett Thomas (a safety engineer) and Mary (Connell) Porter. *Education:* Loyola University, Chicago, Ill., A.B., 1949, M.A. (English), 1954; West Baden College, L.S.T., 1959; Catholic University of America, M.A. (drama), 1960; University of North Carolina, Ph.D., 1964. *Office:* Office of the Dean, University of Detroit, Detroit, Mich. 48221.

CAREER: Roman Catholic priest of the Jesuit order; Colombiere College, Clarkston, Mich., dean, 1965-67; University of Detroit, Detroit, Mich., associate professor, 1967-72, professor of English, 1972—, acting dean, 1973-75, dean, 1975—. Trustee of University of Detroit and of Community Development Training Institute, Detroit; member of board of trustees, Marquette University, 1973—. *Member:* Modern Language Association of Michigan, Michigan Conference of Teachers of English. *Awards, honors:* Charles Carpenter Fries Award, Michigan Council of English, 1971.

WRITINGS: Myth and Modern American Drama, Wayne State University Press, 1969.

WORK IN PROGRESS: A book on theory and interpretation of the film; a book on dramatic theory.

* * *

PORTER, W(alter) Thomas, Jr. 1934-

PERSONAL: Born January 8, 1934, in Corning, N.Y.; son of Walter Thomas (a minister) and Mary (Brookes) Porter; married Dixie Jo Thompson, April 3, 1959; children: Kimberlee, Douglas, Jane-Amy Elizabeth. *Education:* Rutgers University, B.S., 1954; University of Washington, Seattle, M.B.A., 1959; Columbia University, Ph.D., 1964. *Religion:* Congregationalist. *Office:* Touche Ross & Co., Financial Center, Seattle, Wash. 98161.

CAREER: Touche, Ross, Bailey & Smart, associate consultant, 1959-61, manager, 1964-66; University of Washington,

Graduate School of Business Administration, Seattle, associate professor, 1966-71, professor of management information systems, 1971-74; North European Management Institute, Oslo, Norway, visiting professor of management control, 1974-75; Touche Ross & Co., Seattle, partner, 1975—. Member of board of directors, Universal Security Life Insurance Co., Computer Audit Systems, Inc., and Dynafacts, Inc. Research consultant, American Institute of Certified Public Accountants. *Military service:* U.S. Army, 1955-57; became first lieutenant. *Member:* American Institute of Certified Public Accountants, Beta Gamma Sigma.

WRITINGS: Auditing Electronic Systems, Wadsworth, 1966; (contributor) *Accounting and the Computer,* American Institute of Certified Public Accountants, 1966; (contributor) Gordon B. Davis, editor, *Auditing and EDP,* American Institute of Certified Public Accountants, 1968; (contributor) J. B. Bower and W. R. Welke, editors, *Financial Information Systems: Selected Readings,* Houghton, 1968; (with J. C. Burton) *Auditing: A Conceptual Approach,* Wadsworth, text edition, 1970; *EDP: Controls and Auditing,* Wadsworth, 1971; (with D. Alkire) *Wealth—How to Achieve It,* Reston, 1976. Contributor of about thirty articles to accounting and management journals.

SIDELIGHTS: W. Thomas Porter writes: "The circumstances surrounding my last book were quite different from my previous three. My interest was to write a how-to-do it book about a topic of general interest—personal financial planning. Because of this, the writing seemed easier although early morning blocks of time were still required to complete the manuscript.... I strongly recommend discipline and adherence to a schedule in writing; without it all sorts of activities become more important."

* * *

POSPIELOVSKY, Dimitry V. 1935-

PERSONAL: Born January 13, 1935, in Rovno, Poland (now Ukrainian Soviet Socialist Republic); became a Canadian citizen; son of Vladimir (a physician) and Marianna (Ushinsky) Pospielovsky; married Mirjana Dobrovich, June 21, 1960; children: Darya, Andrei, Bogdan. *Education:* Attended Russian schools until 1949; Sir George Williams University, B.A., 1957; University of Frankfurt, part-time study, 1957-58; University of London, graduate study at School of Slavonic and East European Studies, 1959-61, and London School of Economics and Political Science, part-time, 1962-67, M.Phil., 1967. *Politics:* "Christian-personalist." *Religion:* Orthodox. *Home:* 50 Blackacres Blvd., London, Ontario, Canada N6G 2G6. *Office:* Department of History, University of Western Ontario, London, Ontario, Canada.

CAREER: Free-lance journalist, 1957-59, working for *Posev* and Radio Free Russia in West Germany and elsewhere in Europe; British Broadcasting Corp., London, England, program assistant in Russian section, 1959-65, research analyst on Soviet and East European affairs at Central Research Unit, 1965-67; Stanford University, Stanford, Calif., research associate at Hoover Institution and lecturer in Russian for university scientists, 1967-69; Radio Liberty Committee, Munich, Germany, senior research analyst on Soviet matters, 1969-72; University of Western Ontario, London, assistant professor, 1972-75, associate professor of Russian history, 1975—.

WRITINGS: (Compiler and translator with Keith Bosley and Janis Sapiets) *Russia's Other Poets* (clandestine poetry), Longmans, Green, 1968, Praeger, 1969; *Russian Po-*

lice Trade Unionism: Experiment or Provocation?, Weidenfeld & Nicolson, 1971; *Soviet Society and Uncensored Thought: 1956-1976*, Nordland, 1977. Writer of about a hundred scripts in Russian for British Broadcasting Corp., mostly on historical and historico-economic subjects. Contributor to *The 1968 Yearbook on International Communist Affairs*, Hoover Institution, 1969, and *Handbook on the Soviet Union and Eastern Europe*, Anthony Blond, 1970; also contributor of more than twenty articles to *Soviet Studies, Russian Review, Canadian Slavonic Papers, L'est*, and other journals.

WORK IN PROGRESS: "A book on the fate of the Orthodox Church under the Soviet regime with special attention to: a. inter-influence of the position of the Church in the Soviet Union with the currents and policies of the Russian emigre Church groups; b. the development and trends of the Orthodox-Christian *samizdat* in the post-Stalin era."

SIDELIGHTS: Dimitry Pospielovsky writes: "As a youth I hoped to devote my life to Russia, my country of origin. Hence in my college days I first studied 'Western' social sciences (to contribute them to the future Russia of my dreams), followed by the intense study of the internal Soviet scene and its intellectual and spiritual emancipatory processes, along with the study of Russian history.

"With age I came to realize that the duty of a Christian is to serve the concrete man in that space and time in which one happens to be, and that the dehumanization process is a universal contemporary illness springing in both parts of the world from one and the same source: materialism, hedonism, relativism in ethics and morality.

"I have therefore turned to the teaching profession and to writing on Russia for the Western reader. The cataclysmic experience of Russia, having reached the lowest depths of the abyss precipitated by class hatred and atheist amoralism, I believe, has an important lesson to teach the 'West'. I consider it my duty to help as much as possible to transmit this lesson and message to the continuously shrinking free part of humanity."

BIOGRAPHICAL/CRITICAL SOURCES: New York Times, May 10, 1969.

*   *   *

POSTEN, Margaret L(ois)   1915-

PERSONAL: Born March 28, 1915, in Villisca, Iowa; daughter of Harry C. (a farmer) and Glenna (Fisher) Williams; married C. Leonard Posten (a building contractor and farmer), February 21, 1936; children: Pamela Ann (Mrs. Robert Abel), Johnnie L. *Education:* Tarkio College, associate degree in elementary education (highest honors), 1933; Northwest Missouri State College (now Northwest Missouri State University), B.S. (honors), 1968. *Religion:* Methodist. *Residence:* Villisca, Iowa 50864.

CAREER: Teacher in public schools in Iowa, 1933-56; Villisca Community School, Villisca, Iowa, elementary teacher, 1956—. 4-H Club leader, 1951-56; Sunday school children's superintendent, 1951-56, 1972-73. *Member:* Progress Club, Book Forum (vice-president, 1969-71; president, 1971-74), Auxiliary of Good Samaritan Nursing Home, Wesleyan Service Guild. *Awards, honors:* Teacher of the Year, Villisca Community Schools, Iowa, 1970.

WRITINGS—All juvenile; all published by Denison, except as indicated: *This Is the Place: Iowa*, Iowa State University Press, 1965, 3rd edition, 1970; *Lucky You!*, 1966; *The Gold Seekers: The Story of Hernando de Sota,* 1967;

Maggie and Friend, 1969; *Symbols of Democracy,* 1971; *Skill Sheets for Individualized Reading,* 1976. Contributor to *Villisca Review* and *Encyclopaedia Britannica* reading series.

WORK IN PROGRESS: Short stories for children.

SIDELIGHTS: Margaret L. Posten told *CA:* "I love kids but in my teaching I find a lack of their taking responsibility is the main thing I have to fight. I try to impress on children that a democracy can survive if only our youth assume responsibilities (our democracy becomes less democratic each year)." Mrs. Posten has traveled in all fifty states, Canada, and Mexico. She writes: "I'd rather travel than eat!"

*   *   *

POSTER, John B.   1939-

PERSONAL: Born July 8, 1939, in Chicago, Ill.; son of Joseph (an executive) and Jeannette (Ochs) Poster; married Madeleine Rosen (an artist), April 29, 1969. *Education:* University of Chicago, B.A., 1961, M.A.T., 1963, Ph.D., 1971. *Home:* 432 Fourth St., Palisades Park, N.J. 07650. *Office:* Fordham University, Lincoln Center, Room 1114, New York, N.Y. 10023.

CAREER: Instructor in education, University of Chicago, Chicago, Ill., beginning 1970; currently associate professor and program coordinator in Division of Administration, Policy, and Urban Education, Fordham University, New York City. Educational consultant, National Teacher Corps, 1976. *Member:* American Political Science Association, National Council for the Social Studies, American Educational Research Association, Organization of American Historians, Phi Delta Kappa.

WRITINGS: (With Mark M. Krug and William B. Gillies III) *The New Social Studies: Analyses of Theory and Materials,* F. E. Peacock, 1970.

WORK IN PROGRESS: The Politics of State Educational Finance Reform.

*   *   *

POTHAN, Kap   1929-

PERSONAL: Surname is pronounced *Poth*-an; born March 18, 1929, in Dannevirke, New Zealand; son of Lawrence Valentine (a builder) and Joyce (Lee) Pothan; married Janet Munro (an office assistant), July 26, 1952; children: Kenneth Scott, Cherrie Janet. *Education:* New Zealand Survey Board, Diploma of Registration as Land Surveyor, 1953. *Home and office:* 83 Walker St., North Sydney 2060, New South Wales, Australia. *Agent:* Curtis Brown Ltd., P.O. Box 19, Paddington, Sydney, New South Wales 2021, Australia; and John Cushman Associates, Inc., 25 West 43rd St., New York, N.Y. 10036.

CAREER: K. A. Pothan & Associates (consulting surveyors), Sydney, New South Wales, Australia, principal. *Member:* Australian Institution of Surveyors, New Zealand Institute of Surveyors, Australian Society of Authors, Australian Writers Guild, Jaguar Drivers' Club.

WRITINGS—Novels: *A Time to Die,* Jacaranda, 1967; *The Shame of the Shikaree,* Jacaranda, 1968. Also author of *The Naked Hours,* Jacaranda.

WORK IN PROGRESS: Three novels, *The Seventh Capsule, Shades of Grey,* and *Build Me a Mountain;* poems and songs.

AVOCATIONAL INTERESTS: Contemporary art, cars, sailing, football.†

POTHOLM, Christian Peter II   1940-

PERSONAL: Born November 14, 1940, in Hartford, Conn.; son of Harold Christian (a builder) and Ella (Carlsen) Potholm; married Sandra Quinlan, September 14, 1964; children: Erik Dodds, Pebbles Alexandra. *Education:* Bowdoin College, A.B. (magna cum laude), 1962; Fletcher School of Law and Diplomacy, A.M., 1964, M.A.L.D., 1965, Ph.D., 1967. *Office:* Department of Government and Legal Studies, Bowdoin College, Brunswick, Me. 04011.

CAREER: Dartmouth College, Hanover, N.H., instructor in political science, 1966-67, assistant professor of African politics and international relations, 1967-68; Vassar College, Poughkeepsie, N.Y., assistant professor of international relations, 1968-70; Bowdoin College, Brunswick, Me., assistant professor, 1970-75, associate professor, 1975-77, professor of government, 1977—, chairman of department, 1975-77. Visiting summer professor, College of the Virgin Islands, 1970. *Member:* American Political Science Association, African Studies Association, Phi Beta Kappa. *Awards, honors:* Outstanding Educators of America award, 1971; Rockefeller Foundation fellowship, 1974.

WRITINGS: Four African Political Systems, Prentice-Hall, 1970; (co-editor) *Southern Africa in Perspective,* Free Press, 1972; *Swaziland: The Dynamics of Political Modernization,* University of California Press, 1972; (co-editor) *Focus on Police,* Wiley, 1976; *Liberation and Exploitation: The Struggle for Liberation,* University Press of America, 1976. Contributor to *Crowell-Collier Yearbook,* 1968-70; also contributor of more than eighty articles and reviews to journals.

WORK IN PROGRESS: Two books, one on African politics and the other on American politics.

SIDELIGHTS: Christian Potholm lived and traveled in Europe, 1962-63, and did research in Africa, England, and Europe (including Portugal, Greece, and Switzerland).

*   *   *

POTTER, David   1915-

PERSONAL: Born May 12, 1915, in New York, N.Y.; son of Herman and Esther (Burston) Potter; married Matilda Braverman, June 10, 1940; married second wife, Marjorie Bond (a college professor), June 12, 1965; children: (first marriage) William Clark, Ellen Claire. *Education:* Rutgers University, B.S., 1937, A.M., 1939; Northwestern University, student, summers, 1940-43; Columbia University, Ph.D., 1943. *Politics:* Democrat. *Religion:* Unitarian. *Residence:* Idyllwild, Calif.

CAREER: Rutgers University, New Brunswick, N.J., instructor, 1938-40, assistant professor of speech, 1946-49; Columbia University, New York, N.Y., instructor in speech, 1940-43; University of Akron, Akron, Ohio, professor of speech and head of department, 1949-50; Michigan State University, East Lansing, associate professor of speech, 1950-60; Southern Illinois University, Carbondale, professor of speech, 1960-77, professor emeritus, 1977—. Instructor, American Banking Institute, 1938-39, 1947-49; visiting professor, New York University, 1948-49. *Military service:* U.S. Army, Communications, 1944-46; became sergeant. *Member:* American Association of University Professors, American Speech Association, Speech Communication Association, International Communication Association, Central States Speech Association.

WRITINGS: Debating in the Colonial Chartered Colleges: An Historical Survey, Bureau of Publications, Teacher's College, Columbia University, 1944; (editor) *Argumentation and Debate: Principles and Practices,* Dryden, 1954; (with Joel Moss and Herbert F. A. Smith) *Photosituations: A Technique for Teaching,* Burgess, 1963; (with Martin P. Andersen) *Discussion in Small Groups: A Guide to Effective Practice,* Wadsworth, 1963, 3rd edition, 1976; (editor with Gordon L. Thomas) *The Colonial Idiom,* Southern Illinois University Press, 1969. General editor, *Landmarks in Rhetoric and Public Address,* Southern Illinois University Press, 1963—. Contributor of articles and reviews to *Speech Teacher, Quarterly Journal of Speech,* and other professional journals.

WORK IN PROGRESS: A chapter on colonial town meetings for a book on colonial public address.

SIDELIGHTS: David Potter told *CA* that he is "particularly interested in interpersonal relations, rhetorical theory, contemporary public address, and residential education for adults." He has traveled extensively in Europe, North Africa, Japan, Australia, and New Zealand.

*   *   *

POUILLON, Fernand   1912-

PERSONAL: Born May 14, 1912, in Cancon, Lot-et-Garonne, France; son of Alexis (an engineer) and Fernande (Moreau) Pouillon; married Andree Autran, 1935; married second wife, Helen Maslov, 1962; married third wife, Gin Audibert (a painter), March 20, 1969; children: (first marriage) Marguerite (Mrs. Diego Masson), Anne-Marie (Mrs. Jacques Morhange), Claude (Mrs. Juan Masson), Francois, Catherine. *Education:* Ecole Nationale Superieure des Beaux Arts, Diplome d'architecte, 1942. *Politics:* None. *Religion:* Muslim. *Home and office:* Villa les Arcades, Diar el Mahcoul, Algiers, Algeria.

CAREER: Architect, 1936—, with major works in Europe, Asia, and Africa. Chief architect for reconstruction, and consulting architect to the French Government on reconstruction, 1949-56; also architect for the Algerian Government. *Military service:* French Army, volunteer in Mountain Artillery, 1939-45. *Awards, honors:* Chevalier of the Legion of Honor, 1945; Officer of the Peruvian Order of Merit, 1961.

WRITINGS: Ordonnances, privately printed, 1955; *Maitre d'oeuvre* (issued in portfolio), F. de Nobele, 1962; *Les Pierres Sauvages* (novel), Editions du Seuil, 1964, translation by Edward Gillott published as *The Stones of the Abbey,* Harcourt, 1970 (published in England as *The Stones of Le Thoronet,* J. Cape, 1970); *Abbayes cisterciennes,* privately printed, 1967; *Memoires d'un architecte* (autobiography), Editions du Seuil, 1968.

WORK IN PROGRESS: Dictionnaire d'Architecture; monographs on Aix-en-Provence and its environs and on Les Baux de Provence.

AVOCATIONAL INTERESTS: Sailing, hunting, fishing.††

*   *   *

POWDERMAKER, Hortense   1900-1970

December 24, 1900—June 15, 1970; American anthropologist and educator. Obituaries: *New York Times,* June 17, 1970; *Time,* June 26, 1970; *Current Biography,* 1970. (See index for *CA* sketch)

POWELL, G. Bingham, Jr. 1942-

PERSONAL: Born February 8, 1942, in Salem, Ore.; son of G. Bingham (a savings officer) and Gretchen (Spencer) Powell; married V. Patricia Lee, August 23, 1963 (divorced, 1974); married Lynda L. Watts, June 5, 1975; children: (first marriage) Elizabeth, Suzanne, Katrin. *Education:* Princeton University, B.A., 1963; Stanford University, M.A., 1964, Ph.D., 1968. *Office:* Department of Political Science, University of Rochester, Rochester, N.Y. 14627.

CAREER: University of California, Berkeley, assistant professor of political science, 1968-70; University of Rochester, Rochester, N.Y., assistant professor, 1970-73, associate professor of political science, 1973—. *Member:* American Political Science Association. *Awards, honors:* Woodrow Wilson fellowship, 1963-64; Danforth fellowship, 1963-67.

WRITINGS: (With Gabriel A. Almond) *Comparative Politics: A Developmental Approach,* Little, Brown, 1966; *Social Fragmentation and Political Hostility: An Austrian Case Study,* Stanford University Press, 1970; (contributor) G. Almond, Scott Flanigan, and Robert Mundt, *Crisis, Choice and Change,* Little, Brown, 1973; (contributor) Sidney Verba and Lucien W. Pye, *The Citizen and Politics,* Greylock, 1976; (with Almond) *Comparative Politics: System, Process, and Policy,* Little, Brown, 1977. Contributor of articles to *American Political Science Review, American Journal of Political Science,* and *Comparative Politcs.*

WORK IN PROGRESS: "A book applying theories of individual and group behavior to the explanation of political conflict in contemporary democracies; a research project on the comparative role of electoral processes in political representation."

*   *   *

POWELL, Margaret 1907-

PERSONAL: Born October 30, 1907, in Hove, Sussex, England; daughter of Harry (a decorator) and Florence Maud (Langley) Steer; married Albert Edward Powell (a milkman), 1932; children: Harry, David, Philip. *Education:* Attended elementary school in Hove, Sussex, England. *Politics:* "Variable, according to what Prime Minister is in." *Home:* 222 Old Shoreham Rd., Hove, Sussex, England.

CAREER: Won a scholarship to grammar school (high school), but had to go to work at thirteen as a bath-chair pusher; laundry worker at fourteen; entered domestic service as a kitchen-maid at fifteen and worked up to cook; daily charwoman, 1941-68; after publication of first book in June, 1968, "didn't need to go out to work—for which heaven be praised." Lecturer to women's guilds and institutes, 1968—; has made a number of radio and television appearances.

*WRITINGS—*All published by P. Davies, except as indicated: *Below Stairs,* 1968, Dodd, 1970; *Climbing the Stairs* (autobiographical), 1969; *Margaret Powell Cookery Book,* 1970; *The Treasure Upstairs* (autobiographical), 1970; *Margaret Powell's London Season,* 1972; *Sweetmaking for Children,* Piccolo Books, 1972.

All published by M. Joseph: *My Mother and I,* 1973; *Margaret Powell in America,* 1973; *Margaret Powell's Common Market,* 1974; *Albert My Consort,* 1975; *Margaret Powell Down Under,* 1976; *Bringing Up Children,* 1977.

SIDELIGHTS: Below Stairs was applauded by British critics. "They are right," Neil Millar writes in the *Christian Science Monitor.* "The book is salty and unpretentious.... The rules were loaded against her [Margaret Powell's] happiness, but she played the game by the rules and won. Always outwardly deferential to the gentry, alert, cautious, comradely among her fellow-workers, she survived—indeed, flourished—partly because she was a bit odd. She read books."

Margaret Powell still reads books ("I'm keen on acquiring an education"), studying for A-level examination in history. In 1966 she passed her O-level examination in English grammar, and in 1967 passed the A-level examination in English literature. Her three sons were sent to the university.

BIOGRAPHICAL/CRITICAL SOURCES: Christian Science Monitor, April 25, 1970; *New Yorker,* April 25, 1970.

*   *   *

POWELL, Reed M(adsen) 1921-

PERSONAL: Born September 11, 1921, in Provo, Utah; son of Verner Ammon (an engineer) and Edith Hannah (Madsen) Powell; married Kathryn Ann Richards, July 17, 1945; children: Reed M., Jr., Diane, Laurie, Blythe, Susan. *Education:* Brigham Young University, B.S., 1946, M.S., 1947; Michigan State University, Ph.D., 1951; Harvard University, additional study, 1957-58. *Religion:* Church of Jesus Christ of Latter-day Saints. *Office:* Office of the Dean, California State Polytechnic University, 3801 West Temple Ave., Pomona, Calif. 91768.

CAREER: University of Oklahoma, Norman, instructor, 1950, assistant professor, 1951-56, associate professor of sociology, 1956-57, chairman of department, 1955-57; National University of Guatemala, Guatemala, Smith Mundt Professor, 1957-58; University of California, Los Angeles, associate director of executive programs and conferences, 1959-65; Ohio State University, Columbus, professor, director of research, and associate dean of College of Administrative Science, 1956-74; California State Polytechnic University, Pomona, dean of School of Business Administration and director of University Business Development Center, 1974—. Visiting professor, University of San Carlos, 1957; visiting lecturer, Harvard University, 1958-59; visiting summer professor, University of Southern California, 1959. Member of international scientific advisory board, Macmillan Ltd., London, England; member of advisory council, U.S. Senate; member and chairman, National Advisory Council to U.S. Small Business Administration, and other committees. Has given testimony before the U.S. Senate Small Business Committee and before the Joint Economic Committee of the Congress. Consultant to government agencies, industry, and universities.

MEMBER: Academy of Management (chairman of social policy research and action committee, 1969—), National Association of Purchasing Management (vice-chairman for management development, 1968—), American Sociological Association (fellow), Industrial Relations Research Association, National Council for Small Business Management Development, International University Contact for Management Education, Beta Gamma Sigma. *Awards, honors:* Special award for teaching efficiency from University of Oklahoma, 1952, and University of San Carlos, 1957.

WRITINGS: (Contributor) Harry Knudsen, Jr., editor, *Human Elements of Administration: Cases and Simulation Exercises,* Holt, 1963; (contributor) John Glober and Ralph Hower, editors, *The Administrator,* 4th edition (Powell did not contribute to earlier editions), Irwin, 1963; *Race, Religion, and the Promotion of the American Executive,* College of Administrative Science, Ohio State University, 1969; (co-editor and contributor) *Management Problems in Social*

Policy and Social Action Programs, Ohio State University, 1973. Contributor to *Cowles Comprehensive Encyclopedia* and to more than twenty management and sociology periodicals.

WORK IN PROGRESS: Continuing study of the executive promotion process in American business corporations.

* * *

PRAGER, Arthur

PERSONAL: Born in New York, N.Y. *Residence:* Sag Harbor, N.Y. *Agent:* Daniel M. O'Shea, Jr., 108 East 82nd St., New York, N.Y. 10028. *Office:* 7 Washington Square N., New York, N.Y. 10003.

CAREER: Attache at U.S. Embassy, Taipei, Taiwan and U.S. Consulate, Hong Kong, 1955-59; New York University, New York City, assistant professor of air science, 1959-62; Office of the Mayor, New York City, member of staff, 1962—. Consultant to Twentieth Century-Fox Film Corp. and Book-of-the-Month Club. *Military service:* U.S. Army Air Forces, 1943-46; became captain; received Distinguished Flying Cross.

WRITINGS: Rascals at Large: Or, the Clue in the Old Nostalgia, Doubleday, 1971. Contributor of articles and reviews to *Saturday Review* and *American Heritage.*

* * *

PRAGO, Albert 1911-

PERSONAL: Born November 16, 1911, in New York, N.Y.; son of William and Celia (Leibowitz) Prago. *Education:* City College (now City College of the City University of New York), B.S.S., 1934; Hofstra University, M.A., 1964; further study at New School for Social Research, Queens College (now Queens College of the City University of New York), Flushing, N.Y., and City University (now City College of the City University of New York); Union Graduate School, Ph.D., 1976. *Home:* 138-15 Franklin Ave., Flushing, N.Y. 11355. *Agent:* Curtis Brown Ltd., 60 East 56th St., New York, N.Y. 10022.

CAREER: Affiliated with Jefferson School of Social Sciences, 1944-56; Hofstra University, Hempstead, N.Y., instructor in history, 1964-69; Kingsboro Community College, Brooklyn, N.Y., instructor in history, 1965-68; Cornell University, New York State School of Industrial and Labor Relations, New York City, adjunct lecturer in history, 1969—, senior extension associate, 1972-74; New York Institute of Technology, New York City, instructor in history, 1969-72. *Member:* American Historical Association.

WRITINGS: The Revolutions in Spanish America: The Independence Movements of 1808-1825, Macmillan, 1970; *Strangers in Their Own Land: A History of Mexican Americans,* Scholastic Book Services, 1973.

WORK IN PROGRESS: Readings in American Labor History, for New York State School of Industrial and Labor Relations; *A History of the Organization of the Unemployed, 1929-1935.*

* * *

PRATT, Keith L(eslie) 1938-

PERSONAL: Born January 27, 1938, in London, England; son of William Thomas (a lecturer) and Doris (Nash) Pratt; married Sondra Elizabeth Ingham, April 15, 1963; children: Rachel, Lucy Clare, Timothy Damian. *Education:* University College, Durham, B.A. (first class honors), 1962, Diploma in Education, 1963. *Religion:* Church of England. *Home:* 47 Willowtree Ave., Gilesgate Moor, Durham City, County Durham, England. *Office:* School of Oriental Studies, University of Durham, Elvet Hill, Durham City, County Durham, England.

CAREER: Elwick Road Junior Boys' School, Hartlepool, England, teacher, 1963-64; University of Durham, Durham, England, Spalding Lecturer in Chinese Language and Civilization, 1964—. Extramural examiner in Chinese, University of London, 1970, 1971; teacher of Chinese subjects to adult extramural classes. Member, Universities' China Committee (London). *Military service:* Royal Air Force, 1957-59.

WRITINGS: Visitors to China: Eyewitness Accounts of Chinese History, Macmillan, 1968, revised and enlarged edition, Praeger, 1970; *Peking in the Early Seventeenth Century,* Oxford University Press, 1971; *China: An Index to European Visual and Aural Materials,* Crosby Lockwood Staples, 1973. Writer of television series, "Land of the Living Dragon," produced by Independent Television Authority, 1969; also author of two filmstrips with notes, "Past and Present: China," 1973, and "The Arts of China," 1975, both for Visual Publications.

WORK IN PROGRESS: Research on the transmission of music from China to Korea in the T'ang and Sung periods.

AVOCATIONAL INTERESTS: Reading, especially sinology and general history, badminton, gardening, and music.

BIOGRAPHICAL/CRITICAL SOURCES: Best Sellers, November 15, 1970.

* * *

PRESTON, Nathaniel Stone 1928-

PERSONAL: Born March 1, 1928, in Boston, Mass.; son of Jerome and Iva (Stone) Preston; married Ravida Kennedy, November 22, 1958; children: Emily, Andrew, Sarah. *Education:* Boston University, A.B., 1950; University of Pennsylvania, M.A., 1951; Princeton University, Ph.D., 1960. *Religion:* Episcopalian. *Home:* 5212 Partridge Lane N.W., Washington, D.C. 20016. *Office:* Department of Government, American University, Washington, D.C. 20016.

CAREER: West Virginia University, Morgantown, visiting instructor in government, 1953-55; Tufts University, Medford, Mass., instructor in government, 1957; Boston College, Boston, Mass., lecturer in government, 1957-58; Trinity College, Hartford, Conn., instructor in government, 1959-61; American University, Washington, D.C., assistant professor, 1961-63, associate professor, 1963-67, professor of government, 1967—, director, Washington semester program, 1962-73, vice-president for academic affairs, 1973-76. Member of Canada-U.S. Committee, U.S. and Canadian Chambers of Commerce, 1976—. Member of corporation, Squam Lakes Science Center, 1971—. *Wartime service:* U.S. Merchant Marine, 1945. *Member:* American Association for Higher Education, American Political Science Association, Phi Beta Kappa, Pi Sigma Alpha, Cosmos Club, Squam Lakes Association (Holderness, N.H.; director, 1972—). *Awards, honors:* Named to Collegium of Distinguished Alumni, Boston University.

WRITINGS: Politics, Economics and Power: Ideology and Practice Under Capitalism, Socialism, Communism and Fascism, Macmillan, 1967; (editor) *The Senate Institution,* Von Nostrand, 1969. Contributor to journals in his field.

WORK IN PROGRESS: A research project on socialist movements and ideas in Australia, Canada, and New Zealand as compared to the United States.

PREWITT, Kenneth 1936-

PERSONAL: Born March 16, 1936, in Alton, Ill.; son of Carl K. and Louise (Carpenter) Prewitt; married Anne Biggar, September 6, 1963; children: Jennifer Ann, Geoffrey Douglas. *Education:* Southern Methodist University, B.A., 1958; Washington University, St. Louis, M.A., 1959; Stanford University, Ph.D., 1963. *Home:* 5739 South Blackstone, Chicago, Ill. 60637. *Office:* National Opinion Research Center, University of Chicago, Chicago, Ill. 60637.

CAREER: Washington University, St. Louis, Mo., assistant professor of political science, 1963-64; Makerere University College, Kampala, Uganda, visiting professor of political science, 1964-65; University of Chicago, Chicago, Ill., 1964—, began as assistant professor and senior study director, National Opinion Research Center, currently professor of political science and director, National Opinion Research Center. Research associate in political science, Stanford University, 1968-69; also taught at Institute of Development Studies, University of Nairobi, Nairobi, Kenya, 1970-72. *Member:* American Political Science Association, Association for the Advancement of Science.

WRITINGS: (Editor with Louis Knowles) *Institutional Racism in America,* Prentice-Hall, 1969; (with Richard E. Dawson) *Political Socialization: An Analytic Study,* Little, Brown, 1969; *Recruitment of Political Leaders: A Study of Citizen-Politicians,* Bobbs-Merrill, 1970; *Education and Political Values,* East African Publishing House, 1971; *Labyrinths of Democracy,* Bobbs-Merrill, 1973.

BIOGRAPHICAL/CRITICAL SOURCES: Washington Post, February 24, 1970.

*   *   *

PRICE, R(onald) F(rancis) 1926-

PERSONAL: Born June 24, 1926, in Hondon, Wales; son of John and Marguerite E. M. Price; married Erika R. Flack (an art teacher in a training college), 1960. *Education:* Attended University College of South West, Exeter (now University of Exeter), 1948-52; University of London, External B.Sc., 1951, Ph.D., 1969. *Home:* 48 Copley Park, Streatham, London S.W.16, England. *Office:* School of Education, La Trobe University, Bundoora, Victoria 3083, Australia.

CAREER: Taught biology in a technical college, physics at an English-language school in Sofia, Bulgaria, educational psychology at University College of Cape Coast, Cape Coast, Ghana, and then English at a foreign language institute in Peking, China, 1965-67; La Trobe University, Bundoora, Victoria, Australia, 1967—, began as lecturer, currently senior lecturer in comparative and international education. *Military service:* British Army, 1944-48; served in Mideast Command. *Member:* Institute of Biology, Comparative Education Society in Europe (British section).

WRITINGS: A Reference Book of English Words and Phrases for Foreign Science Students, Pergamon, 1966; *Education in Communist China,* Praeger, 1970.

WORK IN PROGRESS: Research on education in China, and on a comparative study of communist education in China and the U.S.S.R.

AVOCATIONAL INTERESTS: Swimming, table tennis, listening to all kinds of music other than "pop."

*   *   *

PRICHARD, Nancy S(awyer) 1924-

PERSONAL: Born March 9, 1924, in Owosso, Mich.; daughter of Morgan Rowland and Helen (Stone) Gilbert; married Thomas B. Davis, June 9, 1945; married second husband, Kenneth D. Prichard (a travel agent), December 9, 1954; children: (first marriage) Thomas Morgan Davis. *Education:* University of Washington, Seattle, B.A., 1952, M.A., 1954. *Home:* 806 Oakland, Apt. 201, Urbana, Ill. 61801. *Office:* National Council of Teachers of English, 1111 Kenyon Rd., Urbana, Ill. 61801.

CAREER: Shoreline Community College, Seattle, Wash., instructor, 1964-65, assistant professor, 1965-66, associate professor, 1967-68, professor of English, 1968-71; National Council of Teachers of English, Urbana, Ill., assistant executive secretary, 1969-74, associate executive secretary, 1974—. *Military service:* U.S. Navy Women's Reserve, WAVES, link trainer operator, 1944-46. *Member:* Conference on College Composition and Communication (member of executive committee, 1967-69), National Junior College Committee (chairman, 1968-69), American Association of University Professors, Pacific Northwest Conference on English in the Two-Year College (chairman of executive committee, 1967-69), Phi Beta Kappa.

WRITINGS: (Editor with John E. Struger, J. David Wright, and Alexander Maxwell) *Voices,* Houghton, 1970. Contributor to literary and educational journals.

*   *   *

PRICKETT, (Alexander Thomas) Stephen 1939-

PERSONAL: Born June 4, 1939, in Freetown, Sierra Leone; son of William Ewart and Barbara (Lyne) Prickett; married Diana Mabbutt, 1966; children: Ruth. *Education:* Trinity Hall, Cambridge, B.A. and M.A., 1961, Ph.D., 1967; University College, Oxford, Dip.Ed., 1962. *Home:* 3 Dymocks Manor, East End Lane, Ditchling, Sussex, England. *Office:* Arts Bldg., University of Sussex, Brighton, Sussex, England.

CAREER: Methodist College, Uzuakoli, East Nigeria, English teacher, 1962-64; University of Sussex, Brighton, Sussex, England, lecturer in English, 1967—, proctor, 1971-72, sub-dean, School of English and American Studies, 1972—. Visiting lecturer in English, Smith College, Northampton, Mass., 1970-71.

WRITINGS: Do It Yourself Doom, Gollancz, 1962; *Coleridge and Wordsworth: The Poetry of Growth,* Cambridge University Press, 1970; (co-editor) *Cambridge New Architecture,* 3rd edition (Prickett was not associated with the earlier editions), International Textbook, 1970; *Wordsworth and Coleridge: The Lyrical Ballads,* Edward Arnold, 1975; *Romanticism and Religion: The Tradition of Coleridge and Wordsworth in the Victorian Church,* Cambridge University Press, 1976.

WORK IN PROGRESS: Victorian Fantasy.

BIOGRAPHICAL/CRITICAL SOURCES: Times Literary Supplement, October 2, 1970.

*   *   *

PRINCE, Alison 1931-

PERSONAL: Born March 26, 1931, in Kent, England; daughter of Charles (a bank official) and Louise (David) Prince; married Goronwy Siriol Parry (a teacher), December 26, 1957; children: Samantha, Andrew, Benjamin. *Education:* Slade School of Art, London, Diploma in Fine Art, 1952; Goldsmiths' College, London, Art Teacher's Diploma, 1954. *Politics:* None. *Religion:* Agnostic. *Home:* Hill Farm, Elmswell, Suffolk, England.

CAREER: Head of school art department in London, England, 1954-58; adult education art teacher in Bromley, Kent, England, 1960—. *Member:* Royal Society of Painter-Etchers and Engravers, International P.E.N.

WRITINGS—For children, except as indicated: *The Joe Annual,* Polystyle Publications, 1968, 1969, 1970, 1971; *Joe and the Horse,* British Broadcasting Corp., 1969; *The House on the Common,* Methuen, 1969, Farrar, Straus, 1970; (self-illustrated) *The Red Alfa,* Methuen, 1971, published as *The Red Jaguar,* Atheneum, 1972; (with Joan Hickson) *Joe and the Nursery School,* British Broadcasting Corp., 1972; (with Hickson) *Joe Moves House,* British Broadcasting Corp., 1972; *The Doubting Kind* (for teenagers), Methuen, 1976; *Whosaurus? Dinosaurus!,* Studio Vista, 1976. Television series for British Broadcasting Corp. include "Joe," with a second film series of that name started in 1971, "Jackanory," "War Stories," and "Watch with Mother." Contributor to *Times Educational Supplement.*

WORK IN PROGRESS: A book for teenagers, *The Turkey's Nest,* for Methuen.

SIDELIGHTS: Alison Prince's interests embrace everything related to her work—films, music, art, children, schools, and animals. She likes writing for children "because they are honest and they read a book because they want to read it, not because they want to be seen reading it." She told *CA* that she is now interested in farming ("rearing calves commercially") as well as writing.

* * *

PRINGLE, Laurence P. 1935-
(Sean Edmund)

PERSONAL: Born November 26, 1935, in Rochester, N.Y.; son of Laurence Erin (a realtor) and Marleah (Rosehill) Pringle; married Judith Malanowicz (a librarian), June 23, 1962 (divorced, 1970); married Alison Newhouse (a freelance editor), July 14, 1971; children: (first marriage) Heidi, Jeffrey, Sean. *Education:* Cornell University, B.S., 1958; University of Massachusetts, M.S., 1960; Syracuse University, graduate study, 1960-62. *Residence:* West Nyack, N.Y. 10994.

CAREER: High school science teacher in Lima, N.Y., 1961-62; American Museum of Natural History, *Nature and Science* (children's magazine), New York, N.Y., associate editor, 1963-65, senior editor, 1965-67, executive editor, 1967-70; free-lance writer, editor, and photographer, 1970—. Faculty member, New School for Social Research, 1976—.

WRITINGS—Juvenile, except as noted: *Dinosaurs and Their World,* Harcourt, 1968; *The Only Earth We Have,* Macmillan, 1969; (editor) *Discovering the Outdoors: A Nature and Science Guide to Investigating Life in Fields, Forests, and Ponds,* Natural History Press, 1969.

(Editor) *Discovering Nature Indoors: A Nature and Science Guide to Investigations with Small Animals,* Natural History Press, 1970; *From Field to Forest,* World Publishing, 1970; *In a Beaver Valley,* World Publishing, 1970; *One Earth, Many People: The Challenge of Human Population Growth,* Macmillan, 1971; *Ecology: Science of Survival,* Macmillan, 1971; *Cockroaches: Here, There and Everywhere,* Crowell, 1971; *This Is a River,* Macmillan, 1971; *From Pond to Prairie,* Macmillan, 1972; *Pests and People,* Macmillan, 1972; *Wild River* (adult book), photographs by the author, Lippincott, 1972; *Estuaries: Where Rivers Meet the Sea,* Macmillan, 1973; *Into the Woods: Exploring the Forest Ecosystem,* Macmillan, 1973; *Follow a Fisher,*

Crowell, 1973; *Twist, Wiggle, and Squirm: A Book about Earthworms,* Crowell, 1973; *Recycling Resources,* Macmillan, 1974.

Energy: Power for People, Macmillan, 1975; *City and Suburb: Exploring an Ecosystem,* Macmillan, 1975; *Chains, Webs, and Pyramids: The Flow of Energy in Nature,* Crowell, 1975; *Water Plants,* Crowell, 1975; *The Minnow Family: Chubs, Dace, Minnows, and Shiners,* Morrow, 1976; *Listen to the Crows,* Crowell, 1976; *Our Hungry Earth: The World Food Crisis,* Macmillan, 1976; *Death Is Natural,* Four Winds, 1977; *The Hidden World: Life under a Rock,* Macmillan, 1977; *The Controversial Coyote: Predation, Politics, and Ecology,* Harcourt, 1977; *The Gentle Desert: Exploring an Ecosystem,* Macmillan, 1977; *Animals and Their Niches: How Species Share Resources,* Morrow, 1977; *The Economic Growth Debate: Are There Limits to Growth?* (adult book), F. Watts, 1977.

Contributor to *Audubon, Ranger Rick's Nature Magazine, Highlights for Children,* and *Smithsonian,* sometimes under the pseudonym Sean Edmund.

BIOGRAPHICAL/CRITICAL SOURCES: New York Times, November 9, 1969; *Saturday Review,* January 23, 1971.

* * *

PROCTOR, Charles S(heridan) 1925-

PERSONAL: Born March 12, 1925, in Westminster, Tex.; son of Irl Sheridan (a credit manager) and Mary (West) Proctor. *Education:* Southern Methodist University, B.A.S., 1950, M.F.A., 1967. *Religion:* Methodist. *Home:* 1129 North Beckley Ave., Dallas, Tex. 75203. *Office:* Communication Department, University of Texas, Arlington, Tex. 76010.

CAREER: Actor, 1950-57; appeared in Broadway productions in New York, N.Y., at Margo Jones Repertory Theatre in Dallas, Tex., and on network television programs in California and New York; worked for Eastman Kodak Co. in California, 1957-63; Tarleton State College (now University), Stephenville, Tex., instructor in speech, 1967-69; University of Texas at Arlington, assistant professor, 1969-73, associate professor of speech, 1973—, chairman of department of communication, 1974—. *Military service:* U.S. Army Air Forces, 1943-45; became staff sergeant; received Distinguished Flying Cross, and Air Medal with two oak-leaf clusters. *Member:* National Speech Communication Association.

WRITINGS: (With Winifred T. Weiss) *Umphrey Lee: A Biography,* Abingdon, 1971.

* * *

PROCTOR, Elsie 1902-

PERSONAL: Born September 16, 1902; daughter of Alexander (an accountant) and Rosetta (Stevens) Proctor. *Education:* University of Liverpool, B.S. (biology); Oxford University, Diploma in Education. *Home:* The Homestead, 29 Sandringham Rd., Hunstanton, Norfolk, England.

CAREER: Prior to 1937 taught in girls' grammar schools and in a co-educational grammar school; senior lecturer in biology at a teacher training college in Bedford, England, 1937-61. Lecturer at numerous educational institutions. *Member:* Royal Society for the Protection of Birds (fellow), Soroptimist International Federation (past president of London and Eastern Counties branch).

WRITINGS—All published by A. & C. Black, except as indicated: "Looking at Nature" series (juvenile), Book 1, 1961, Book 2, 1961, Book 3, 1963, 2nd edition, 1971, Book 4, 1965, published in one volume, 1965, 2nd edition, 1969; *Natural Science: A Teacher's Handbook*, 1966; *Nature Themes*, Evans Brothers, 1975. Contributor to *Nature* and *Teachers World*.

WORK IN PROGRESS: Research on umbelliferae, on hibernation, and on pioneer plants.

SIDELIGHTS: The omnibus edition of the "Looking at Nature" series has been translated into Dutch. *Avocational interests:* Wildlife photography, visiting game reserves in South Africa.

BIOGRAPHICAL/CRITICAL SOURCES: *Times Literary Supplement*, June 26, 1969.

* * *

PROCTOR, Thelwall 1912-

PERSONAL: Born May 31, 1912, in Long Beach, Calif.; son of Thelwall Newby and Bessie (True) Proctor. *Education:* Pomona College, A.B., 1935; University of California, Berkeley, M.A., 1938, Ph.D., 1962. *Politics:* "Hereditary democrat." *Religion:* "Romantic agnostic." *Home:* 2970 Greenbriar Lane, Arcata, Calif. 95521. *Office:* Department of English, California State University, Humboldt, Arcata, Calif. 95521.

CAREER: San Francisco State College (now University), San Francisco, Calif., instructor in English, 1946-50; University of Maryland, College Park, instructor in English, 1952-57; California State University, Humboldt, Arcata, Calif., associate professor, 1959-68, professor of English, 1968-75, professor emeritus, 1975—. *Military service:* U.S. Army, 1942-46. *Member:* American Association of University Professors, American Association of Teachers of Slavic and East European Languages, American Association for the Advancement of Slavic Studies, Philological Association of the Pacific Coast, Far Western Slavic Association, Phi Beta Kappa.

WRITINGS: *Dostoevskij and the Belinskij School of Literary Criticism,* Mouton & Co. (The Hague), 1969, Humanities, 1970. Contributor of reviews and articles to periodicals.

WORK IN PROGRESS: Translations of Soviet plays.

* * *

PROSTANO, Emanuel Theodore, Jr. 1931-

PERSONAL: Born October 12, 1931, in New Haven, Conn.; son of Emanuel Theodore, Sr., and Violet (Matthews) Prostano; married Joyce Scala (a library media specialist), November 27, 1952; children: Stephen, Loren Joy. *Education:* Southern Connecticut State College, B.S., 1953; Yale University, M.S., 1955; University of Connecticut, Ph.D., 1962. *Religion:* Roman Catholic. *Home:* 42 Harrison Dr., Hamden, Conn. 06514. *Office:* Division of Library Science and Instructional Technology, Southern Connecticut State College, New Haven, Conn. 06515.

CAREER: Hartford Public Schools, Hartford, Conn., coordinator of library media service, 1966-69; Southern Connecticut State College, New Haven, Conn., associate professor, 1969-74, professor of library science and director of Division of Library Science and Instructional Technology, 1974—. Chairman, Public Library Board, Hamden, Conn., 1970-72; vice-president, Southern Connecticut Library Council, 1971-72. *Military service:* U.S. Army, 1954.

Member: American Library Association, Association for Educational Communications and Technology, New England Library Association, New England Educational Media Association, Connecticut Educational Media Association, Connecticut Library Association.

WRITINGS: *School Media Programs: Case Studies in Management,* Scarecrow, 1970, 2nd edition, 1974; (with wife, Joyce S. Prostano) *School Library Media Center,* Libraries Unlimited, 1971; *AV Media and Technology in Libraries: Collected Readings,* Libraries Unlimited, 1972; (with Martin Piccirillo) *Law Enforcement: A Selected Bibliography,* Libraries Unlimited, 1974.

WORK IN PROGRESS: Second edition of *School Library Media Center; The Learning Resource Programs in the Community College,* for Libraries Unlimited.

* * *

PROWN, Jules David 1930-

PERSONAL: Born March 14, 1930, in Freehold, N.J.; son of Max M. and Matilda (Cassileth) Prown; married Shirley Martin, June 23, 1956; children: Elizabeth Anderson, David Martin, Jonathan, Peter Cassileth, Sara Peiter. *Education:* Lafayette College, A.B., 1951; Harvard University, A.M. (fine arts), 1953, Ph.D., 1961; University of Delaware, A.M. (early American culture), 1956. *Home:* 103 Tyler City Rd., Orange, Conn. 06477. *Office address:* Box 2009, Yale Station, New Haven, Conn. 06520.

CAREER: Harvard University, Cambridge, Mass., assistant to director of Fogg Art Museum, 1959-61; Yale University, New Haven, Conn., instructor, 1961-64, assistant professor, 1964-67, associate professor, 1967-71, professor of the history of art, 1971—, curator of Garvan and related collections of American art at Yale Art Gallery, 1963-68. Visiting lecturer, Smith College, 1966-67. Director, Center for British Art at Yale, New Haven, 1968-76; member of board of directors, Arts Council of Greater New Haven, 1973-75, College Art Association, 1975—; member of executive board, American Society for Eighteenth-Century Studies, 1973-76, National Humanities Institute, New Haven, 1975—; member of board of trustees, Heritage Foundation, Deerfield, Mass., 1971-75, Whitney Museum of American Art, 1975—; member of advisory commission, National Portrait Gallery, Washington, D.C., 1969-74, and of numerous other advisory committees and councils.

MEMBER: College Art Association, American Association of University Professors, American Antiquarian Society, Association of Art Museum Directors, Colonial Society of Massachusetts, New Haven Colony Historical Society (member of board of directors, 1965-70). *Awards, honors:* Guggenheim fellow, 1964-65; Blanche Elizabeth MacLeish Billings Award of Yale University, 1966; A.M., Yale University, 1971; Benjamin Franklin fellow, Royal Society of Arts, 1972—.

WRITINGS: *John Singleton Copley,* two volumes, Harvard University Press, 1966; (contributor) *The Visual Arts in Higher Education,* College Art Association of America, 1966; (author of foreword) Theodore Sizer, *The Works of Colonel John Trumbull,* revised edition, Yale University Press, 1967; *American Painting,* Volume I: *From Its Beginning to the Armory Show,* Skira, 1969; (author of preface) Kathryn C. Buhler and Graham Hood, *American Silver in the Yale University Art Gallery: Garvan and Other Collections,* Yale University Press, 1970.

Publications include two exhibition catalogues, *John Sin-*

gleton Copley, October House, 1965, and *American Art from Alumni Collections,* Yale University Art Gallery, 1968. Contributor to various art journals. Member of editorial board, *American Quarterly,* 1965-69.

BIOGRAPHICAL/CRITICAL SOURCES: Atlantic, December, 1969; *Christian Science Monitor,* December 4, 1969; *Nation,* December 28, 1970.

* * *

PROXMIRE, William 1915-

PERSONAL: Born November 11, 1915, in Lake Forest, Ill.; son of Theodore Stanley (a doctor) and Adele (Flanigan) Proxmire; married Ellen Hodges (an author), December 1, 1956; children: Theodore Stanley, Elsie Stillman, Douglas Clark. *Education:* Yale University, B.A., 1938; Harvard University, M.B.A., 1940, M.P.A., 1948. *Politics:* Democrat. *Religion:* Episcopalian. *Home:* 4613 East Buckeye Rd., Madison, Wis. 53704. *Agent:* Donald MacCampbell, Inc., 12 East 41st St., New York, N.Y. 10017. *Office:* Senate Office Building, Washington, D.C. 20510.

CAREER: Reporter for *Capital Times,* 1949, and *Madison Union Labor News,* 1950, both Madison, Wis.; assemblyman, Wisconsin State Legislature, 1951-52; Artcraft Press, Waterloo, Wis., president, 1953-57; U.S. Senate, Washington, D.C., senator from Wisconsin, 1957—, serving on Appropriations Committee, Defense Production Committee, Banking and Currency Committee, and numerous other congressional committees and subcommittees; chairman of Senate Banking Committee, Joint Economic Committee, Consumer Credit Subcommittee, and others. Unsuccessful Democratic candidate for governor of Wisconsin, 1952, 1954, 1956. *Military service:* U.S. Army, served in Counter-intelligence Corps, 1941-46; became first lieutenant. *Member:* American Legion, Madison Press Club.

WRITINGS: Can Small Business Survive?, Regnery, 1964; *Report from Wasteland: America's Military-Industrial Complex,* foreword by Paul H. Douglas, Praeger, 1970; *Uncle Sam—The Last of the Bigtime Spenders,* Simon & Schuster, 1972; *You Can Do It!,* Simon & Schuster, 1973.

SIDELIGHTS: In a March, 1971 *Time* article entitled "William Proxmire, the Giant Killer," the Wisconsin senator was described as "a loner and a maverick who disdains the Senate 'club' way of conducting business." After ten years of campaigns against appropriations for development of the controversial supersonic transport aircraft, William Proxmire was the key figure in the bill's defeat. His "reputation as one of the chief watchdogs of Government waste" is well-earned; *Time* noted that the kind of tenacity he displayed in rallying opposition to the SST has made him "the bane of defense contractors, pork-barreling colleagues and consumer frauds."

Report from Wasteland is a telling account of government waste in military spending and cost-overruns. In a review of the book A. John Giunta writes: "This book points out that the taxpayers of the country have been footing the bill for billions of dollars of cost-overruns. In one case alone, the C5A military transport plane, the cost-overrun reached $2 billions." Giunta adds that this figure "is almost ten times the amount budgeted for urban mass transit and high-speed ground transportation programs in the Department of Transportation. It is almost three times the amount budgeted for law enforcement, the administration of justice, and civil rights." Harrison Brown writes in a review that "the military-industrial complex emerged as a result of the vicious circle of the cold war." Proxmire's *Report from Wasteland,*

he continues, "is particularly valuable for the insights he gives the reader concerning the position of Congress in the system. The picture of frustration and helplessness he presents suggests that the system will not be changed either quietly or easily."

In *Uncle Sam—The Last of the Bigtime Spenders,* Proxmire continues his denouncement of government spending practices and suggests alternatives to create a more cost-effective bureaucracy. However, as Giunta explains, he expands his criticism to include not only the military-industrial complex—"the most publicized form of governmental squandering—but also well-meaning and humanitarian programs such as Medicare and Housing. . . . This book should have top priority on the reading list of every concerned citizen and taxpayer."

BIOGRAPHICAL/CRITICAL SOURCES: New Republic, April 25, 1970; *Best Sellers,* May 1, 1970, December 1, 1972; *New York Times Book Review,* May 24, 1970; *Time,* June 8, 1970, March 29, 1971; *Atlantic,* December, 1970; *Publishers Weekly,* August 21, 1972; *National Review,* October 13, 1972; *Progressive,* February, 1973; *Booklist,* February 15, 1973; *Choice,* April, 1973; *Public Administration Review,* January, 1974.

* * *

PRYCE, Roy 1928-

PERSONAL: Born October 4, 1928, in Burton on Trent, Staffordshire, England; son of Thomas and Madeleine (Fiddler) Pryce; married Sheila Griffiths, July 18, 1954; children: Susan Elizabeth, Charlotte Anne, Lucy Catherine. *Education:* Emanuel College, Cambridge, M.A., 1954, Ph.D., 1954. *Office:* Commission of the European Communities, 200 rue de la Loi, 1040 Brussels, Belgium.

CAREER: Oxford University, St. Antony's College, Oxford, England, research fellow, 1955-57; London Delegation of the High Authority of the European Coal and Steel Community, press and information officer, 1957-59; Joint Press and Information Service of the European Communities, head of office, London, 1959-64; University of Sussex, Brighton, England, professorial fellow and founding director of Centre for Contemporary European Studies, 1965-73; Commission of the European Communities, Directorate General for Information, Brussels, Belgium, director, 1973—. Visiting professor and member of academic board, College of Europe, Brugge, Belgium, 1965-71. Trustee, Federal Trust for Education and Research. *Military service:* British Army, National Service, 1946-48.

MEMBER: University Association for Contemporary European Studies (founder; secretary, 1970-71), International Political Science Association. *Awards, honors:* Italian Government scholarship for research in Italy, 1952-53; Rockefeller Foundation fellowship for research in Brussels, 1964-65.

WRITINGS: The Italian Local Elections, 1956, Chatto & Windus, 1957, St. Martin's, 1958; *The Political Future of the European Community,* Marshbank, in association with Federal Trust, 1962; (contributor) Peter Hall, editor, *Labour's New Frontiers,* Deutsch, 1964; (contributor) John Calmann, editor, *Western Europe: A Handbook,* Praeger, 1967; (with John Pinder) *Europe after de Gaulle: Towards the United States of Europe,* Penguin, 1969; *Politics of the European Community,* Rowman & Littlefield, 1973. Contributor to Purnell's *History of the XXth Century,* to *Encyclopaedia Britannica,* and to journals, including *Parliamentary Affairs* and *Government and Opposition.* Joint editor, Macmillan's

"Studies in Contemporary Europe" series. Member of advisory council, *Journal of Common Market Studies*.

* * *

PUHVEL, Jaan 1932-

PERSONAL: Surname is pronounced *Puh*-vel, given name sounds like "yawn"; born January 24, 1932, in Tallinn, Estonia; naturalized U.S. citizen; son of Karl (a civil engineer) and Meta Elisabeth (Paern) Puhvel; married Sirje Madli Hansen (a research immunologist), June 4, 1960; children: Peter Jaan. *Education:* Received secondary education in Sweden; McGill University, B.A., 1951, M.A., 1952; Harvard University, Ph.D., 1959. *Politics:* Democrat. *Home:* 15739 High Knoll Rd., Encino, Calif. 91316. *Office:* Department of Classics, University of California, Los Angeles, Calif. 90024.

CAREER: McGill University, Montreal, Quebec, lecturer in classic, 1955-56; University of Texas at Austin, instructor in classical languages, 1957-58; University of California, Los Angeles, assistant professor, 1958-61, associate professor of classics and Indo-European linguistics, 1961-64, professor of Indo-European studies, 1964—, director of Center for Research in Languages and Linguistics, 1962-67, chairman of department of classics, 1968—. *Member:* Linguistic Society of America, American Oriental Society, American Philological Association, Association for the Advancement of Baltic Studies (president, 1971-72). *Awards, honors:* American Council of Learned Societies fellow, 1961-62; Officer First Class of Order of the White Rose (Finland), 1967; Guggenheim fellow, 1968-69.

WRITINGS: (Reviser with others, under direction of Joshua Whatmough) *Pierre Guiraud: Bibliographie critique de la statistique linguistique*, Editions Spectrum (Utrecht), 1954; *Laryngeals and the Indo-European Verb*, University of California Press, 1960; (editor with Henrik Birnbaum, and contributor) *Ancient Indo-European Dialects*, University of California Press, 1966; (editor) *Substance and Structure of Language*, University of California Press, 1969; (editor and contributor) *Myth and Law among the Indo-Europeans: Studies in Indo-European Comparative Mythology*, University of California Press, 1970; (editor with Ronald Stroud) *California Studies in Classical Antiquity*, eight volumes, University of California Press, 1976.

Contributor: Ernst Pulgram, editor, *Studies Presented to Joshua Whatmough*, Mouton & Co., 1957; E. L. Bennett, editor, *Mycenaean Studies*, University of Wisconsin Press, 1964; Werner Winter, editor, *Evidence for Laryngeals*, Mouton & Co., 1965; George Cardona and others, editors, *Indo-European and Indo-Europeans*, University of Pennsylvania Press, 1970. Contributor to other festschrifts and symposia. Contributor to *Encyclopaedia Britannica, Encyclopedia Americana, Books Abroad, Western Folklore* and to philological, linguistic, and literary journals in United States and abroad.

WORK IN PROGRESS: Hittite Etymological Dictionary, in two volumes; studies in Indo-European comparative mythology, in collaboration with Georges Dumezil.

SIDELIGHTS: In addition to his native language, Jaan Puhvel is competent in Finnish, Swedish, French, German, Greek, Latin, and Sanskrit.†

* * *

PURKEY, William Watson 1929-

PERSONAL: Born August 22, 1929, in Shenandoah, Va.;

married Imogene Ellen Hedrick, May, 1951; children: William Watson, Jr., Cynthia Ann. *Education:* University of Virginia, B.S., 1957, M.Ed., 1958, Ed.D., 1964. *Religion:* Christian (Disciples of Christ). *Office:* School of Education, University of North Carolina, Greensboro, N.C. 27411.

CAREER: Junior high school teacher of social studies, Chatham, N.J., 1958-61; University of Virginia, Charlottesville, psychologist with McGuffy Reading Clinic, 1962, instructor in education, 1963-64; University of Florida, College of Education, Gainesville, assistant professor, 1964-67, associate professor, 1967-70, professor of psychological foundations of educations, 1970-76; University of North Carolina at Greensboro, School of Education, professor, 1976—. *Military service:* U.S. Air Force, 1951-55. *Member:* American Psychological Association, American Educational Research Association, American Association for Humanistic Psychology, American Association of University Professors, North Carolina Psychological Association (fellow), Phi Delta Kappa, Kappa Delta Pi.

WRITINGS: Self Concept and School Achievement, Prentice-Ha!!, 1970; (with D. L. Avila and A. W. Combs) *Helping Relationships: Basic Concepts for the Helping Professions*, Allyn & Bacon, 1971; (editor with Avila and Combs) *The Helping Relationship Sourcebook*, Allyn & Bacon, 1971, 2nd edition, 1977; *Inviting School Success*, Wadsworth, 1978. Contributor of fifty-four articles and monographs to educational journals. Editor-in-chief, *University of Virginia Education Review*, 1963-64.

* * *

PUTCAMP, Luise, jr. 1924-

PERSONAL: First syllable of surname rhymes with "foot"; born March 9, 1924, in San Diego, Calif.; daughter of William Jennings (a sales engineer) and Luise (Zimmermann) Putcamp; married Robert H. Johnson (managing editor, Associated Press), February 24, 1945; children: Robert Hersel III, Luise Robin, Jan Leah, Stephanie Neale, Jennifer Anne. *Education:* Attended Phoenix Junior College, 1942-43, and Southern Methodist University, 1946-47. *Politics:* None. *Religion:* Self-Realization Fellowship. *Home and office:* 1 Strawberry Hill Ave., Apt. 6B, Stamford, Conn. 06902.

CAREER: Arizona Republic, Phoenix, reporter, 1940-43; KOY, Phoenix, Ariz., news and continuity writer, 1943-44; *Miami Beach Sun*, Miami Beach, Fla., wire editor, 1944, 1946; WINX, Washington, D.C., night news editor, 1945; *Dallas News*, Dallas, Tex., copy writer and book columnist, 1946-51; *Dallas Times Herald*, Dallas, book editor, 1951-52; KRLD-TV, Dallas, script writer, 1953-54; free-lance copy writer and publicity agent for advertising agencies in Dallas, 1954, 1959; *Ogden Standard-Examiner*, Ogden, Utah, book columnist, 1956-57; *Indianapolis News*, Indianapolis, Ind., columnist and feature writer, 1961-62; Associated Press, Dallas, string correspondent, 1964-65; Operation LIFT, Dallas, center supervisor-teacher, 1965-66; *Dallas Times Herald*, book editor, 1968-69; educational filmstrip writer, Pathescope Educational Films, Inc., 1973-74; *Advocate* (magazine), Stamford, Conn., editor, 1976—. Volunteer publicity work for Junior Players Guild, Cosette Faust Newton Foundation, Theosophical Society, Creative Arts Center of Dallas, Self Realization Fellowship, United Way of Stamford, and Child Care Center of Stamford.

MEMBER: Women in Communications, Texas Institute of Letters, Poetry Society of Texas, Press Club of Dallas (charter member, 1951), Theta Sigma Phi. *Awards, honors:*

Kaleidograph Award, Kaleidograph Press, 1952, for *Sonnets for the Survivors, and Other Poems;* Christopher Award, 1955, for short story "The Miracle at Derrick, Texas."

WRITINGS: Sonnets for the Survivors, and Other Poems, Kaleidograph Press, 1952; (author of introduction) Merritt Mauzey, *The Cotton-Farm Boy,* Abelard, 1953; *The Christmas Carol Miracle* (originally published as short story in *Good Housekeeping,* December, 1954), Abingdon, 1970; *The Night of the Child* (verse/dialogue version of Christmas story), Word Inc., 1971. Also author of "The Miracle at Derrick, Texas" (serialized story), syndicated by Associated Press, 1970-71, and "Loud Sounds, Soft Sounds" (original filmscript), 1970. Contributor to *Fate, Exploring the Unknown, Writer's Digest, American Weekly, Retail Bookseller, Reporter, Good Housekeeping, Glamour,* and other periodicals.

WORK IN PROGRESS: Two books, *Lalla and the Kali Yuga,* an English version of verses of fourteenth-century Kashmiri yogi poet, Lal Ded, and *The Tantric Artifact,* a Gothic novel.

SIDELIGHTS: Luise Putcamp, jr., told *CA:* "*Sonnets for the Survivors* [is] an elegy for the young dead of World War II (or any war) dedicated to my brother, William J. Putcamp, Jr., who was killed in a B-29 crash in 1945. . . . *The Christmas Carol Miracle* was written on the last minute plea of a friend, Gerry Johnson, who had a Dallas TV program and needed a Christmas reading, in 1953. *The Night of the Child* was written in 1957 as a Christmas cantata libretto because I heard my choir-singer husband singing cantata words that seemed stilted and pretentious."

Putcamp has done research for Irving Wallace's books, *The Twenty-Seventh Wife, The Prize,* and *The Three Sirens* in Utah, Mexico, Texas, Arizona, New Mexico, and other states, and has covered Stamford's "Charity Year" for Carl Bakal's forthcoming book about charity. She has also done scripts for various organizations in Dallas, Indianapolis, and Salt Lake City.

*   *   *

PUTNAM, Jackson K(eith)   1929-

PERSONAL: Born February 10, 1929, in Emmons County, N.D.; son of Hugh Gordon (a farmer) and Lucille (Jackson) Putnam; married Patricia Lenora Harris, May 29, 1965; children: Roy Justice, Zona Marlene, Zreata Michelle, Mike Jerome. *Education:* University of North Dakota, B.S., 1952, M.A., 1956; Stanford University, Ph.D., 1964. *Politics:* Democrat. *Home:* 16202 Cairo Cir., Placentia, Calif. 92670. *Office:* Department of History, California State University, Fullerton, 800 North State College Blvd., Fullerton, Calif. 92634.

CAREER: Oregon State University, Corvallis, instructor, 1958-62, assistant professor of history, 1962-65; California State University, Fullerton, assistant professor, 1965-68, associate professor, 1968-72, professor of history, 1972—. *Military service:* U.S. Army, 1952-54. *Member:* American Historical Association, Organization of American Historians, Western History Association, Western Literature Association, California Historical Society.

WRITINGS: Old Age Politics in California: From Richardson to Reagan, Stanford University Press, 1970; (with others) *Essays on Western History in Honor of Elwyn B. Robinson,* University of North Dakota Press, 1970. Contributor to *Pacific Historical Review, North Dakota Quarterly, Southern California Quarterly,* and *Western Historical Quarterly.*

WORK IN PROGRESS: The Westward Impulse: An Interpretive History of the American West; Western History and the Western Novel.

SIDELIGHTS: Jackson K. Putnam told *CA:* "I'm interested especially in the relationship of history to the behavioral science disciplines on the one hand and to the humanities on the other. I wish to investigate the possibilities of the historian both learning from and contributing to these allied fields."

*   *   *

PYKE, Helen Godfrey   1941-

PERSONAL: Born February 16, 1941, in Grand Rapids, Minn.; daughter of George Slater (a farmer) and Julia (Steiner) Godfrey; married Ted Pyke (teacher), November 27, 1966; children: Gregory. *Education:* Walla Walla College, B.A. *Politics:* "Mostly Republican." *Religion:* Seventh-day Adventist. *Home address:* Route 1, Bryant, Ala. 35958.

CAREER: Elementary teacher in Bemidji, Minn., 1959-61, in Detroit Lakes, Minn., 1963-64; free lance writer in Bemidji, Minn., 1964-71, in Bryant, Ala., 1971—.

WRITINGS—All published by Southern Publishing: *A Sword Unsheathed* (juvenile), 1970; *A Wind to the Flames,* illustrated by J. William Myers, Jr., 1973; (with Gertrude V. Pyke) *Student Nurse,* 1977. Contributor to Sunday school papers.

WORK IN PROGRESS: Maggie, a horse story set in California in 1910.

SIDELIGHTS: Helen Godfrey Pyke began writing while living in a log cabin in northern Minnesota. "[I] lived off the land with no well or electricity until [my] marriage in 1966," she says. "[I] enjoy gardening and other vigorous outdoor work. At present we are taming five acres on Sand Mountain in northeastern Alabama."†

*   *   *

PYLYSHYN, Zenon W(alter)   1937-

PERSONAL: Surname is pronounced *Pi*-li-shin; born August 25, 1937, in Montreal, Quebec, Canada; son of George and Ann (Dackow) Pylyshyn; married Linda Mae Illingworth, June 31, 1962; children: Sonia Rae, Joel Ernest. *Education:* McGill University, B.Eng., 1959; University of Saskatchewan, M.Sc., 1961, Ph.D., 1963. *Home:* 530 St. James St., London, Ontario, Canada N5Y 3P3. *Office:* Department of Psychology, University of Western Ontario, London 72, Ontario, Canada.

CAREER: University of Western Ontario, London, assistant professor, 1966-69, associate professor of psychology and computer science, 1970—. Traveling fellow, Ontario Mental Health Foundation, 1969; fellow, Foundations' Fund for Research in Psychiatry, Stanford University, 1970. *Member:* Canada Psychological Association, American Psychological Association, Association for Computing Machinery. *Awards, honors:* Canadian Council senior fellow in engineering, science, and medicine, 1964-66.

WRITINGS: (Editor) *Perspectives on the Computer Revolution,* Prentice-Hall, 1970. Contributor to psychology, computer, and medical journals.

WORK IN PROGRESS: New Foundations for Cognitive Psychology, a book-length monograph.

SIDELIGHTS: Zenon W. Pylyshyn told *CA:* "I am interested in exploring the question of how thoughts, images and knowledge are represented in the mind. I believe that significant progress on these ancient questions can be made with the aid of intellectual techniques which have their origin in computer science."

*   *   *

QUAMMEN, David   1948-

PERSONAL: Born February 24, 1948, in Cincinnati, Ohio; son of W. A. and Mary (Egan) Quammen. *Education:* Yale University, B.A., 1970; Oxford University, B.Litt., 1973. *Home:* 204 East Pine, No. 6, Missoula, Mont. 59801. *Agent:* A. Watkins, Inc., 77 Park Ave., New York, N.Y. 10016.

CAREER: Writer.

WRITINGS: To Walk the Line (novel), Knopf, 1970. Also author of a screen adaptation of *Absalom, Absalom!,* neither published nor produced.

WORK IN PROGRESS: Second Samuel, a novel based on events surrounding the death of William Faulkner.

SIDELIGHTS: David Quammen describes *To Walk the Line* as dealing "with the birth, growth, and death of a friendship between a white ivy leaguer and a black militant, and is intended to map the gradual convergence of two radically different consciousnesses. As a first draft, it came at the reader in alternating chapters of first person narration by Tyrone, the black, and John, the white. . . . [My novel then] went into a straight third person narrative form, and became more modest and, I think, more honest in the process. I was probably not bringing off the projection of Tyrone's consciousness, and in the final form I am not pretending to. The more striking overall affect was sacrificed to greater tightness, reality, and (hopefully) line-by-line, thought-by-thought integrity."

BIOGRAPHICAL/CRITICAL SOURCES: Best Sellers, December 15, 1970.

*   *   *

QUANDT, William B.   1941-

PERSONAL: Born November 23, 1941, in Los Angeles, Calif.; son of William C. (a teacher) and Dorothy (Bauer) Quandt; married Anna Spitzer, June 21, 1964. *Education:* Stanford University, B.A., 1963; Massachusetts Institute of Technology, Ph.D., 1968. *Home:* 4515 MacArthur Blvd., Washington, D.C. 20007. *Office:* National Security Council Staff, Old Executive Office Building, Washington, D.C. 20506.

CAREER: RAND Corp., Santa Monica, Calif., member of research staff, 1968-72; National Security Council, Washington, D.C., member of staff, 1972-74; University of Pennsylvania, Philadelphia, member of department of political science, 1974-77; National Security Council, member of staff, 1977—. Lecturer in department of political science, University of California, Los Angeles, 1968, 1971. *Member:* American Political Science Association.

WRITINGS: Revolution and Political Leadership: Algeria, 1954-1968, M.I.T. Press, 1969; *The Comparative Study of Political Elites,* Sage Publications, 1970; *The Politics of Palestinian Nationalism,* University of California Press, 1973; *Decade of Decisions: American Policy Toward the Arab-Israeli Conflict, 1967-1977,* University of California Press, 1977.

WORK IN PROGRESS: Research on U.S. policy in the Middle East.

BIOGRAPHICAL/CRITICAL SOURCES: Nation, Au-

gust 31, 1970; *Times Literary Supplement,* November 13, 1970.

*   *   *

QUIGLEY, Joan
   (Angel Star)

PERSONAL: Born in Kansas City, Mo.; daughter of John B. and Zelda (Marks) Quigley. *Education:* Vassar College, B.A. *Home:* 1055 California St., San Francisco, Calif. 94108. *Agent:* Bill Berger Associates, Inc., 44 East 58th St., New York, N.Y. 10022.

CAREER: Astrologer, 1953—. *Member:* American Federation of Astrologers, Junior League of San Francisco.

WRITINGS: (Under pseudonym Angel Star) *Astrology for Teens,* Bantam, 1968; *Astrology for Adults,* Holt, 1969; *Astrology for Parents of Children and Teenagers,* Prentice-Hall, 1971.

WORK IN PROGRESS: A novel.

AVOCATIONAL INTERESTS: Tennis, bridge, art history.

*   *   *

QUINN, A(lexander) James   1932-

PERSONAL: Born April 8, 1932, in Cleveland, Ohio; son of Alex J. and Mary (Garvey) Quinn. *Education:* Attended St. Charles College, 1950-52, St. Mary Seminary, 1952-58, John Carrol University, 1956-58; St. John Lateran University, Rome, J.C.D., 1962; Cleveland State University, J.D., 1972. *Home:* 1027 Superior Ave., Cleveland, Ohio 44114.

CAREER: Ordained Roman Catholic priest; Catholic Diocese of Cleveland, Cleveland, Ohio, chancellor, 1969-74, financial and legal secretary, 1974—. Member of board of trustees, Council for Economic Opportunities.

WRITINGS—All published by Alba, except as indicated: *Censorship: Federal and Church Law,* Catholic Book Agency (Rome), 1962; (with James A. Griffin) *Thoughts for Our Times,* 1969; *Thoughts for Sowing: Reflections on the Liturgical Readings for Sundays and Holy Days,* 1970; *Ashes from the Cathedral,* 1972. Contributor to *Family* and *Pastoral Life.*

WORK IN PROGRESS: Occasional Thoughts.

*   *   *

RAAB, Robert Allen   1924-

PERSONAL: Born August 23, 1924, in Cleveland, Ohio; son of Albert Sam and Emma (Horowitz) Raab; married Marjorie Deena Klein (a guidance counselor), April 10, 1951; children: Daniel Warren, Joel Stephen. *Education:* University of Cincinnati, B.A., 1947; Hebrew Union College, Cincinnati, M.H.L., 1950, D.H.L., 1959, D.D., 1975; Post Graduate Center for Mental Health, graduate of Pastoral Counseling Program, 1977; Ackerman Institute, additional study, 1977—. *Home:* 3235 Waterbury Dr., Wantagh, N.Y. 11793. *Office:* Suburban Temple, 2900 Jerusalem Ave., Wantagh, N.Y. 11793.

CAREER: Ordained rabbi, 1950; assistant rabbi of temple in Chicago, Ill., 1949-50; rabbi of temple in McKeesport, Pa., 1954-62; Suburban Temple, Wantagh, N.Y., rabbi, 1962—. Instructor in sociology, Nassau Community College, Garden City, N.Y., 1969-71, and Five Towns College, Merrick, N.Y.; lecturer on his travels in Russia and Israel. Dean, National Federation of Temple Youth. *Military ser-*

vice: U.S. Air Force, chaplain, 1951-53. Member: Central Conference of American Rabbis, New York Board of Rabbis, New York Federation of Reformed Rabbis, Nassau-Suffolk Association of Rabbis, Long Island Association of Reformed Rabbis (president, 1968-69).

WRITINGS: The Teenager and the New Morality, Rosen Press, 1970; Coping with Death, Rosen Press, 1978.

* * *

RABIE, Jan 1920-

PERSONAL: Born November 14, 1920, in George, South Africa; son of Johannes W. (a teacher) and Susanna (Le Roux) Rabie; married Marjorie Wallace (a painter), January 5, 1955. Education: University of Stellenbosch, B.A., 1939, M.A., 1944; Sorbonne, University of Paris, graduate study, 1950. Politics: "Loyal rebel." Religion: "Born Protestant." Address: P.O. Box 4618, Cape Town, South Africa. Agent: Jeannette Zimmerman, 152 West 58th St., New York, N.Y. 10019.

CAREER: Teacher of languages in South Africa, 1945-47; radio announcer in Cape Town, South Africa, 1955-58. Member: Suid-Afrikaanse Akademie.

WRITINGS: A Man Apart (novel), Macmillan, 1969.

In Afrikaans: 21 (short stories), Balkema, 1966; Bolandia (a trilogy of historical novels), Human & Rousseau, 1964-66; Polemika (polemic writings), John Malherbe, 1966; Klipweig, Human & Rousseau, 1970.

WORK IN PROGRESS: Ark, a novel about the human crisis in South Africa.

AVOCATIONAL INTERESTS: The sea, space travel, mountaineering, music.

BIOGRAPHICAL/CRITICAL SOURCES: New York Times Book Review, June 29, 1969; Books Abroad, winter, 1971.

* * *

RABINOWITZ, Alan 1927-

PERSONAL: Born January 18, 1927, in New York, N.Y.; son of Aaron (in real estate) and Clara (Greenhut) Rabinowitz; married Andrea Wolf (a psychiatric social worker), December 2, 1951; children: Eric W., Peter MacG., Martha L., Katherine W. Education: Yale University, M.B.A., 1950; Massachusetts Institute of Technology, Ph.D., 1969. Politics: Democrat. Home: 3400 East Laurelhurst Dr., Seattle, Wash. 98105. Office: Department of Urban Planning, University of Washington, Seattle, Wash. 98195.

CAREER: Employed as consultant in urban economics and in related positions, 1950-59; Arthur D. Little, Inc., Cambridge, Mass., member of staff, 1959-63; Urban Survey Corp., Cambridge, Mass., president, 1963-69; Boston Redevelopment Authority, Boston, Mass., administrator of program planning and finance, 1969-71; University of Washington, Seattle, professor of urban planning and chairman of department, 1971—. Fellow, Harvard-M.I.T. Joint Center for Urban Studies, 1969. Military service: U.S. Naval Reserve, active duty, 1945-46, 1952-54. Member: American Institute of Planners.

WRITINGS: Municipal Bond Finance and Administration, Interscience, 1969. Contributor to planning journals.

* * *

RACKMAN, Emanuel 1910-

PERSONAL: Born June 24, 1910, in Albany, N.Y.; son of David and Anna (Mannesovtich) Rackman; married Ruth Fischman, December 28, 1930; children: Michael I., Bennett M., Joseph R. Education: Columbia University, B.A., 1931, LL.B., 1933, Ph.D., 1953; Yeshiva University, Rabbinical Certificate, 1934. Office: Fifth Avenue Synagogue, 5 East 62nd St., New York, N.Y. 10021.

CAREER: Rabbi in Glen Cove, N.Y., 1930-36, in Lynbrook, N.Y., 1936-46, and in Far Rockaway, N.Y., 1946-67; Fifth Avenue Synagogue, New York, N.Y., rabbi, beginning 1967. Yeshiva University, professor of political philosophy and jurisprudence, 1969-71, provost, 1970-71; consultant on Jewish studies to the chancellor, City University of New York. Member of executive committee, Jewish Agency; chairman of Commission on Jewish Chaplaincy, National Jewish Welfare Board, 1972-75. Military service: U.S. Army Air Forces, chaplain, 1943-46; military aide to commander of European theater's special advisor on Jewish affairs, 1946; became major; received Army Commendation Ribbon with oak-leaf cluster. U.S. Air Force Reserve, beginning 1946; retired as colonel.

MEMBER: Rabbinical Council of America (president, 1958-60), Religious Zionists of America (former vice-president), Association of Jewish Chaplains of the Armed Forces (president, 1948-50), New York Board of Rabbis (president, 1955-57), Phi Beta Kappa. Awards, honors: D.D., Yeshiva University, 1961.

WRITINGS: Israel's Emerging Constitution 1948-51, Columbia University Press, 1955; Sabbaths and Festivals in the Modern Age, Yeshiva University, 1961; Jewish Values for Modern Man (essays), Jewish Education Committee and Philosophical Library, 1959, published with additional essays, 1962; One Man's Judaism and Other Essays, Philosophical Library, 1970. Author of weekly column, Jewish Week. Contributor of articles to Jewish periodicals and reviews to scholarly journals. Associate editor, Tradition (quarterly).

* * *

RADEL, John J(oseph) 1934-

PERSONAL: Surname rhymes with "cradle"; born August 22, 1934, in Long Branch, N.J.; son of John Joseph and Gertrude (McCarthy) Radel; married Kerstin Margareta Palmgren, December 21, 1957; children: Gunnar John, Mark Christopher, James Oliver, Bengt Andrew. Education: Seton Hall University, B.A., 1960, M.A., 1963. Politics: "Registered Republican (with Independent Voting Habits)." Religion: Roman Catholic.

CAREER: Parsippany High School, Parsippany, N.J., teacher of Chinese, English, and social studies, 1963-67, 1970—; Parsippany-Troy Hills School District, Parsippany, director of Title III Center, 1967-70, instructor in Afro-Asian history, 1970—. Member of faculty, Institute of Far Eastern Studies, Seton Hall University, 1964. Military service: U.S. Marine Corps, 1953-56; became sergeant. Member: National Education Association, Chinese Language Teachers Association, American Academy of Political and Social Science, New Jersey Education Association, Morris County Council of Educational Associations, Parsippany-Troy Hills Education Association (executive vice-president).

WRITINGS: The Asian World, Creative Education Press, 1971. Contributor to Senior Scholastic. Associate editor, Journal of Chinese Language Teachers of America Association.

WORK IN PROGRESS: A book on secondary education in America.††

*   *   *

RADIMSKY, Ladislaw   1898-1970
(Petr Den)

April 3, 1898—September 9, 1970; Czech diplomat, editor, essayist, and short story writer. Obituaries: *New York Times,* September 12, 1970; *Washington Post,* September 14, 1970; *Books Abroad,* spring, 1971.

*   *   *

RAEF, Laura (Gladys) C(auble)

PERSONAL: Born in Walnut Grove, Mo.; daughter of William Arthur (a construction worker) and Edna May (Fox) Cauble; married William Raef (a businessman); children: Sharon Ann. *Education:* Burge Hospital School of Nursing, R.N., 1934; attended College of San Mateo and San Francisco State College (now University), 1956-58. *Politics:* Republican. *Religion:* Christian Scientist. *Home and office:* 965 San Marcos Cir., Mountain View, Calif. 94040.

CAREER: Metropolitan Life Insurance Co., San Francisco, Calif., industrial nurse, 1948-57; writer. *Member:* California's Writers' Club (Berkeley).

WRITINGS—All published by Bouregy: *Symphony in the Sky,* 1970; *Nurse in the News,* 1970; *Nurse in Fashion,* 1972; *Nurse Jan and the Legacy,* 1974; *Miracle at Seaside,* 1975; *Waikiki Nurse,* 1976. Contributor of feature articles to *Christian Science Monitor* and children's and women's stories to various newspapers and magazines.

*   *   *

RAITT, A(lan) W(illiam)   1930-

PERSONAL: Born September 21, 1930, in Morpeth, Northumberland, England; son of William (a headmaster) and May (Davison) Raitt; married Lia Noemia Rodrigues; children: Suzanne, Claire, Correia. *Education:* Magdalen College, Oxford, B.A., 1951, M.A., 1955, D.Phil., 1957. *Home:* 17 Harbord Rd., Oxford, England. *Agent:* Curtis Brown Ltd., 1 Craven Hill, London W2 3EW, England. *Office:* Magdalen College, Oxford University, Oxford, England.

CAREER: Oxford University, Oxford, England, fellow of Magdalen College, 1952-55, fellow and tutor in French at Exeter College, 1955-66, fellow and tutor in French at Magdalen College, 1966—.

WRITINGS: (Editor and author of introduction and notes) *Balzac: Short Stories,* Oxford University Press, 1964; *Life and Letters in France,* Volume III: *The Nineteenth Century,* Thomas Nelson, 1965; (editor with P. G. Castex) Villiers de l'Isle-Adam, *Le Pretendant,* Corti, 1965; *Villiers de l'Isle-Adam et le mouvement symboliste,* Corti, 1965; *Prosper Merimee,* Eyre & Spottiswoode, 1970, Scribner, 1971. Contributor to scholarly journals.

WORK IN PROGRESS: With J. M. Bellefroid and P. G. Castex, a critical edition of the complete works of Villiers de l'Isle-Adam.

AVOCATIONAL INTERESTS: Music, tennis, watching soccer, wasting time.

BIOGRAPHICAL/CRITICAL SOURCES: Atlantic, June, 1970; *New Republic,* January 30, 1972.

RAKOSI, Matyas   1892-1971

1892—February 5, 1971; Hungarian Communist party leader and author of books on his country. Obituaries: *New York Times,* February 6, 1971; *L'Express,* February 15-21, 1971.

*   *   *

RAMANUJAN, Molly   1932-
(Shouri Ramanujan; Shouri Daniels)

PERSONAL: Born July 2, 1932, in Kerala, India; daughter of Chacko and Leah (Mikhail) Daniels; married Attipat Krishnaswami Ramanujan (a poet and professor of linguistics), June 7, 1962; children: Krittika (daughter), Krishnaswami (son). *Education:* University of Bombay, B.A. (honors), 1955, M.A., 1957; Indiana University, graduate study, 1961-62, summer, 1964; University of Chicago, presently doctoral candidate. *Home:* 5629 Dorchester Ave., Chicago, Ill. 60637.

CAREER: Started out as a journalist and worked on *Deccan Herald* (English-language newspaper), Bangalore, India, but "found it meaningless"; taught English literature at Sophia College, Bombay, India, 1957, Lady Shri Ram College, Delhi, India, 1958-64, Delhi University, Delhi, 1971-73, and at Kennedy-King College, Chicago, Ill., 1974-76. *Awards, honors:* Smith-Mundt and Fulbright grants for study in United States, 1961-62.

WRITINGS: (Under name Shouri Ramanujan) *Haladi Meenu* (originally written in English as "The Yellow Fish" translated into Kannada by her husband, A. K. Ramanujan, for publication in India), Manohar Grantha Mala, 1967; (under name Shouri Daniels) *Salt Doll,* Vikas, 1978. Portions of "The Yellow Fish" have been published in English in *Chicago Review,* 1968, and in *Experiments in Prose,* Swallow Press, 1969; portions of *Salt Doll* have been published in *Tri-Quarterly,* winter, 1974, *Primavera,* and *Femina,* January, 1976. Contributor to *Femina, Carleton Miscellany,* and to newspapers in India; author of book reviews for Indian P.E.N., 1956-57.

WORK IN PROGRESS: A book of short stories; essays on *Passage to India;* a book-length essay, *Jubilate Agno.*

SIDELIGHTS: Molly Ramanujan told *CA:* "I am interested in 'characters,' my writing has to be about what it is to be some particular person. My earliest literary passion was for *Hamlet.* I tore the play out, bound it, tied it to my wrist, and was never seen without it. I have read very few books seriously, but these few I chew, digest, and make my own. I take the movies seriously. I am excited about anything that seems to be a new way of doing things, especially in narrative techniques. I have discovered that I am incurably sane. Not in the least bit mad.

"In 'The Yellow Fish,' I tried to present the point of view of both men and women, but in *Salt Doll* I tried to write exclusively from a woman's point of view. Now I am trying to work out a pre-Romantic neutral point of view. In the book of short stories, I hope to write exclusively from the point of view of an old-fashioned man. I wrote *Salt Doll* from 1968 to 1970, and revised it and rewrote it for another two years. I originally wrote it for Saul Bellow who was kind enough to read several drafts. For four years after that I did nothing but teach. . . . I have now started spending several hours at the typewriter, and am turning out a short story each month. My new publisher, Vikas, distributes in the United States, and though I expect the book [of short stories] to be banned in India, I'm sure it will find many readers here."

Publication of *Haladi Meenu* caused something of a furor in

Kannada, according to the *Chicago Review*. Mrs. Ramanujan, who sometimes uses the Indian name of Shouri instead of Molly, has also lived in Aden, Arabia. She and her husband return to India every other year.

* * *

RAMSETT, David E. 1942-

PERSONAL: Born May 12, 1942, in Viroqua, Wis.; son of Arnold and Beulah (Wintz) Ramsett; married Maureen Dawn Rude, August 25, 1962; children: Teena Renee, Dean David, Jodi Leigh. *Education:* Luther College, B.A., 1965; University of Oklahoma, M.A., 1966, Ph.D., 1968. *Home:* 2814 South Tenth, Grand Forks, N.D. 58201. *Office:* Department of Economics, University of North Dakota, Grand Forks, N.D. 58201.

CAREER: University of Northern Iowa, Cedar Falls, assistant professor of economics, 1968-70; University of North Dakota, Grand Forks, associate professor, 1970-72, professor of economics, 1972—, chairman of department, 1976—. Director, North Dakota Council on Economic Education. *Military service:* U.S. Army, 1960-62. *Member:* American Economic Association, Beta Gamma Sigma, Omicron Delta Epsilon (president of Oklahoma chapter, 1967-68).

WRITINGS: Regional Industrial Development in Central America, Praeger, 1969. Contributor to *Journal of Economic Education, Journal of Experimental Education, College and University Teaching,* and other professional journals.

WORK IN PROGRESS: Resource Allocation within Universities; Ecology, Energy, and the Growth Crisis.

SIDELIGHTS: David Ramsett has traveled to Mexico and Central America to research his writings.

* * *

RAND, Clayton (Thomas) 1891-1971

May 25, 1891—February 26, 1971; American columnist, editor, and publisher. Obituaries: *New York Times,* February 27, 1971; *Washington Post,* March 1, 1971. (See index for CA sketch)

* * *

RANDHAWA, Mohinder Singh 1909-

PERSONAL: Born February 2, 1909, in Zira, Ferozepore, India; son of Sher Singh and Shrimati Bachint (Kaur) Randhawa; married Shrimati Iqbal Kaur; children: S. S. (son), Asha (Mrs. R. Glassey), J. S. (son). *Education:* Forman Christian College, F.Sc. (medical), 1926; Government College, Lahore, B.Sc. (honors), 1929, M.Sc. (honors), 1930; Punjab University, D.Sc., 1955. *Religion:* Sikh. *Home:* Garden House, Garden Colony, Kharar, near Chandigarh, India.

CAREER: Joined Indian Civil Service as an assistant magistrate, 1934, and held magistrate's post in various parts of Uttar Pradesh, 1934-41; deputy commissioner, Rae Bareli, Uttar Pradesh, 1942-45; secretary of Indian Council of Agricultural Research, New Delhi, 1945-46; deputy commissioner, Delhi, 1946-48, and in Ambala, Punjab, 1948-49; additional director-general and then director-general of rehabilitation, Punjab, Jullundur, 1949-51; commissioner of Ambala Division, Punjab, 1951-53; development commissioner, Punjab, 1953-55; vice-president of Indian Council of Agricultural Research, New Delhi, 1955-60; adviser on

Natural Resources, Planning Commission, 1961-64; special secretary, Ministry of Food and Agriculture, 1964-66; chief commissioner, Chandigarh Union Territory, 1966-68; vice-chancellor of Punjab Agricultural University, Ludhiana, 1968-76. Chairman of Lalit Kala Akademi, Chandigarh, and of advisory committee to Chandigarh Museum.

MEMBER: National Academy of Sciences (president), Northern India Science Association (president), Association of Vice-Chancellors of Agricultural Universities in India, Phycological Society (India; past president), All-India Fine Arts and Crafts Society (president).

WRITINGS: Zygnemaceae (monograph on algae), Indian Council of Agricultural Research, 1934, Academic Press, 1959; *The Art of E. H. Brewster and Achsah Brewster,* Kitabistan, 1944; *Beautifying India,* Rajkamal Publications, 1950; *Out of the Ashes: Study of the Rehabilitation of Refugees in East Punjab,* Public Relations Department (Punjab), 1954; *National Extension Service and Community Projects in Punjab,* Community Projects Administration (Punjab), 1955; *The Krishna Legend in Pahari Painting,* Lalit Kala Akademi, 1956; *Flowering Trees in India,* Indian Council of Agricultural Research, 1957, 2nd edition published as *Beautiful Trees and Gardens,* 1961, abridged edition published as *Flowering Trees,* National Book Trust (New Delhi), 1965, Verry, 1969; *Agriculture and Animal Husbandry in India,* Indian Council of Agricultural Research, 1958, revised edition, 1962; *Agricultural Research in India: Institutes and Organisations,* Indian Council of Agricultural Research, 1958, 2nd revised edition, 1963, International Publications Service, 1970; *Basohli Painting,* Ministry of Information and Broadcasting (New Delhi), 1959.

Kangra Paintings of the Bhagavata Purana, National Museum of India, 1960; *Kangra Paintings on Love,* National Museum of India, 1962; (editor) *An Anthology of Great Thoughts,* Atma Ram, 1962; *Kangra* (in Punjabi), Nav Yuga Press (Delhi), 1963; *Kangra Paintings of the Gita Govinda,* National Museum of India, 1963; *The Cult of Trees and Tree-Worship in Buddhist-Hindu Sculpture,* All-India Fine Arts and Crafts Society, 1964; *Kangra Paintings of the Bihari Sat Sai,* National Museum of India, 1966; *Kangra Ragamala Paintings,* National Museum of India, 1970; *Kumaon Himalayas,* Oxford Book Co. (New Delhi), 1970; *Travels in the Western Himalayas,* Thompson Press (Delhi), 1974; *Gardens Through the Ages,* Macmillan, 1976.

Co-author: (With others) *Developing Village India: Studies in Village Problems,* edited by U. N. Chatterjee, Imperial Council of Agricultural Research, 1946, revised edition, Orient Longmans, 1951; (with others) *Farmers of India,* Volumes I-IV, Indian Council of Agricultural Research, 1959-68; (with Prem Nath Hindi) *Punjab, Himachal Pradesh, Jammu and Kashmir,* Indian Council of Agricultural Research, 1959; (with others) *Madras, Andhra Pradesh Mysore and Kerala,* Indian Council of Agricultural Research, 1961; (with Jagjit Singh, A. K. Dey, and Vishnu Mittre) *Evolution of Life,* Council of Scientific and Industrial Research (New Delhi), 1968; (with John Kenneth Galbraith) *Indian Painting: The Scene, Themes and Legends,* Houghton, 1968.

Booklets and pamphlets: *Kangra Valley Painting,* Ministry of Information and Broadcasting, 1954; *Beautifying Cities of India,* Indian Council of Agricultural Research, 1961; *Natural Resources of India: A Brief Statement,* Planning Commission, Government of India, 1963; *Chamba Painting,* Lalit Kala Akademi, 1967, International Publications Service, 1970.

Editor-in-chief, "Monographs on Algae" series, Indian Council of Agricultural Research; also editor-in-chief of *Roopa-Lekha* (journal of All-India Fine Arts and Crafts Society), and of *Everyday Science* (journal of Northern India Science Association).

SIDELIGHTS: Indian Painting, the book that Randhawa produced with America's former ambassador to India, John Kenneth Galbraith, was well received in this country. Eliot Fremont-Smith, writing in the *New York Times,* called it "an unusually personal and engaging volume, obviously born of enthusiasm." Galbraith and Randhawa, India's leading art historian, put together a gallery of thirty-five paintings done between 1600 and 1820. The result, in Fremont Smith's view, "is extremely informative, delightful, enchanting in the proper meaning of that cosmeticized word, and it offers what will be for many a first, dazzling look at a robust and beautiful art." According to *Book World,* Randhawa collected what observers had to say about the court life and the social settings which inspire Indian painting, and Galbraith organized the findings into a continuous narrative.

BIOGRAPHICAL/CRITICAL SOURCES: Book World, October 13, 1968; *New York Times,* November 8, 1968; *New Yorker,* December 21, 1968.

*   *   *

RANGA, N. G.   1900-

PERSONAL: Born November 7, 1900, in Nidubrolu, Andhra Pradesh, India; son of Nagaiah and Atchamamba Ranga; married; wife's name, Bharathidevi. *Education:* Oxford University, B.Litt., Diploma in Political Science and Economics, Diploma in Sociology. *Politics:* Congress Party. *Religion:* Hindu. *Home:* Nidubrolu, Andhra Pradesh, India. *Office:* Indian Peasants' Institute, Nidubrolu, Andhra Pradesh, India.

CAREER: Professor of economics at Pachiayappa's College, Madras, India, 1927-30; economic adviser to Madras Government, 1928-30; co-founder of All-India Kisan Sammelan (Rural People's Federation), 1929; member of Indian Parliament, 1935—; member of national executive, Indian National Congress Party, 1946-51; resigned from the Congress and from All-India Kisan Sammelan when Communists moved in, and formed the Bharat Krishikar Lok Party, 1951; rejoined Indian National Congress, 1955, and served as general secretary of the Congress Party in Parliament, 1958-59; founder-president of the Swatantra Party (largest single party in opposition in the Indian Parliament until 1971), 1959—. Founder-member of International Agricultural Producers, 1946-49; vice-president of National Cooperative Union, 1955-60. Represented India at International Labor Organization, 1948, and at UNESCO, 1969. *Member:* International Peasants' Union, Indian Council of World Affairs, Indian Parliamentary Union, Foreign Affairs Association of India (founding president, 1951—), Gandhi Smriti (North Delhi; member of executive committee, 1972—).

WRITINGS—In English: *Economic Organisation of Indian Villages,* Taraporewala Sons, Volume I, 1926, Volume II, 1930; *The Economics of Handloom,* Taraporewala Sons, 1930; *The Tribes of the Nilgiris,* [Bezwada, India], 1934; *The Modern Indian Peasant,* Kisan Publications, 1936; *Kisan Hand Book,* Kisan Publications, 1938; *Peasants and Congress,* All India Kisan Publications, 1939; (with Swami Sahajanad Saraswathi) *History of Kisan Movement,* All India Kisan Publications, 1939; *Outlines of National Revolutionary Path,* Hind Kitabs, 1945; *The Colonial and Coloured Peoples: A Programme for Their Freedom and Prog-*

ress, Hind Kitabs, 1946; *Revolutionary Peasants,* Amrit Book Co., 1949; *Credo of World Peasantry,* Indian Peasants' Institute, 1957; (with P. R. Paruchuri) *The Peasant and Co-operative Farming: A Socio-Economic Study,* Indian Peasants' Institute, 1958; *Storm Bursts on the Peasantry,* Indian Peasants' Institute, 1959; *Self-Employed Sector: Their Constructive Role in Planned Economy,* Indian Peasants' Institute, 1959; *Freedom in Peril,* Indian Peasants' Institute, 1961; *Fight for Freedom* (autobiography), Verry, 1968. Also author of *Bapu (Gandhi) Blesses,* 1970, *Agony of Solace,* and *Distinguished Acquaintances,* two volumes, 1977.

Other, short publications in English include: *Four Crore Artisans Hail the Gandhian Plan,* Hind Kitabs, 1945; *The Plan and the Peasant: An Appraisal of the Second Five Year Plan,* Indian Peasants' Institute, 1956; *Panchayat Landlordism versus Peasant Economy,* Indian Peasants' Institute, 1958.

Author of six books published only in Telugu, including a novel (title means "Harijan Leader"), 1934. A number of his books in English also were published in Telugu.

SIDELIGHTS: Described as a leftist with anti-Communist views, N. G. Ranga fought long for peasant proprietorship of land. In the earlier days of India's freedom fight (1930-47), he was imprisoned on six occasions by the British. Between 1948 and 1964 Ranga visited the United States five times. He met with President Truman in 1949 to press for economic aid to developing countries, had talks with Eleanor Roosevelt in 1952 and 1954, and has urged American publishers to provide popular literature on democracy at low prices. He has toured in Europe (including the Iron Curtain countries), Canada, Australia, New Zealand, Japan, Burma, and other Asian countries.

*   *   *

RAPPAPORT, Eva   1924-

PERSONAL: Born April 7, 1924; daughter of Paul (a physician) and Gisella (Jaeger) Stein; married Dov Rappaport (a sociologist; formerly director of a sanitarium), January 31, 1945; children: Elana, Leslie Joan, Jesse. *Education:* Cooper Union Art School, Diploma in Fine Arts, 1944; student at New School for Social Research, 1944-46, and Art Students' League, 1945-46; Jewish Theological Seminary of America, Teachers Certificate, 1953. *Politics:* Liberal. *Religion:* Non-affiliated. *Home:* The Kings Valley Animal Family, Route 2, Box 62, Monmouth, Ore. 97361. *Agent:* Bertha Klausner, 71 Park Ave., New York, N.Y. 10016.

CAREER: Free-lance designer and artist, doing advertising and window display, interior design, graphics, sculpture in hardwoods, and color woodcuts, 1944-46; Forsyte Gallery, Los Angeles, Calif., director, 1948-51; Temple Beth-El, Great Neck, N.Y., art director, 1951-55; free-lance photographer and writer, 1967—. Exhibitor of slides and speaker on behalf of Guide Dogs for the Blind, Inc., San Rafael, Calif. *Member:* America Association of Zoological Parks and Aquariums, American Goat Society, National Pygmy Goat Association (founding director and secretary), Collie Club of America, American Smooth Collie Club, Guide Dogs for the Blind, German Shepherd Dog Club of America, Pacific Northwest Collie Club.

WRITINGS: Banner, Forward! The Pictorial Biography of a Guide Dog, Dutton, 1969. Contributor of photographs and articles to periodicals. Editor, *Pygmy Goat Memo.*

WORK IN PROGRESS: Research and photography at the

foster care nursery of the Los Angeles Zoo for a fully-illustrated book, *Tender and Tame: Children of the Zoo,* for ages ten and up; a book on life with otters, toucans, and other animals in the author's collection.

SIDELIGHTS: Eva Rappaport told *CA:* "We moved to Oregon in 1970 with a truck full of our city animals: dogs, cats, otters, toucan, rabbits, chinchillas, rats, ducks, chicken, raven, and a dairy goat kid. More accurately, we fled from Los Angeles, from city zoning restrictions, and from neighbors who insisted that civilized life left no room for animals. We named our new place, a 160-some acre farm, The Kings Valley Animal Family, and advisedly so. Our neighbors now were sheepmen and cattle ranchers who refer to all animals as 'livestock' and to dogs as 'stock dogs' or 'marauders.' But in our setting, all the animals are members of the family. We raise our calves, kids, goslings, puppies, kittens—the youngsters of all species—with the same awareness of early developmental influences as we applied to the raising of our children. We have not only the power, but also the responsibility, to control the circumstances and learning conditions that will shape the young animals' personalities, to the end that they will become responsive, non-competitive, cooperative creatures that can (and like to) live peaceably among their own and with other species.

"In line with our interest in inter-species cooperation, we have concentrated on breeding Smooth Collies—bright, socially responsible dogs whose chief aim seems to be to keep the entire farm population happy and safe in their assigned places. While I enjoy writing for young people, who are far less prejudiced or opinionated about animals than adults, the chronicle about animal interaction on the farm will be a book for older readers. We will want to convince them that animals do indeed communicate; that 'dumbness' has survival value; and that some knowledge of biology helps in gaining an understanding of behavior—be it animal or human."

* * *

RAPPAPORT, Sheldon R(aphael) 1926-

PERSONAL: Born April 19, 1926, in Jacksonville, Fla.; son of Maurice and Fay (Farber) Rappaport; married Florence Ward, March 2, 1950; married second wife, Shirley Ruby, August 29, 1969; children (first marriage) Bruce, Lisa; stepchildren: Carol, Linda, Barbara. *Education:* Temple University, A.B., 1946, A.M., 1947; Washington University, St. Louis, Mo., Ph.D., 1950; attended Philadelphia Association for Psychoanalysis, 1958-61. *Home address:* Poplar Cove, Box 140, Onancock, Va. 23417. *Office address:* Effective Educational Systems, Inc., Box 140, Onancock, Va. 23417.

CAREER: Diplomate in Clinical Psychology of American Board of Professional Psychology; Alton State Hospital, Alton, Ill., psychologist, 1948, supervising psychologist, 1948-51; in private practice as psychologist, 1951-64; Jefferson Medical College, Philadelphia, Pa., research associate in psychiatry, 1964-66; Pathway School, Norristown, Pa., president, 1961-70; licensed clinical psychologist, Virginia State Board of Medicine; Effective Educational Systems, Onancock, Va., president, 1970—. Senior psychologist, Embreeville State Hospital, 1951-52; psychologist in department of psychiatry, Albert Einstein Medical Center, Philadelphia branch, 1951-55; research associate in psychiatry, Hahnemann Medical College and Hospital, 1955-60; medical research scientist in children's unit, Eastern Pennsylvania Psychiatric Institute, 1960-66. Member of task force, Joint Commission on Mental Health of Children, 1968-69; member, Pennsylvania State Teacher Education

Advisory Committee, 1964-70; member of advisory council, Action for Brain-Injured Children, 1970-74; member of advisory board, Grove School; member of advisory board, Darell Harmon Resource Center, 1975—. Consultant, National Resource Center of Pennsylvania, 1971; consultant, President's National Advisory Council on Supplementary Centers and Services, 1973-74.

MEMBER: American Psychological Association (fellow), American Association for the Advancement of Science (fellow), American Orthopsychiatric Association (fellow), Society for Projective Techniques and Personality Assessment (fellow), American Academy of Psychotherapists, Virginia Psychological Association, New York Academy of Sciences, Sigma Xi.

WRITINGS: (Editor) *Childhood Aphasia and Brain Damage,* Livingston, Volume I: *A Definition,* 1964, Volume II: *Differential Diagnosis,* 1965, Volume III: *Habilitation,* 1967; (contributor) William M. Cruickshank, editor, *The Teacher of Brain-Injured Children: A Discussion of the Bases for Competency,* Syracuse University Press, 1966; *Public Education for Children with Brain Disfunction,* Syracuse University Press, 1969.

(Contributor) Margaret Robb, editor, *Foundations and Practices in Perceptual Motor Learning,* American Alliance for Health, Physical Education, and Recreation, 1971; (contributor) Cruickshank and Daniel P. Hallahan, editors, *Perceptual Learning Disabilities in Children,* Volume I, Syracuse University Press, 1975; (contributor) Hallahan and James M. Kauffman, editors, *Teaching Children with Learning Disabilities: Personal Perspectives,* C. E. Merrill, 1976. Also contributor to *Sharing Educational Success,* National Advisory Council on Supplementary Centers and Services, 1974. Contributor to professional journals. Member of editorial advisory board, *Journal of Learning Disabilities,* 1967—.

* * *

RASKIN, Herbert A(lfred) 1919-

PERSONAL: Born April 21, 1919, in Detroit, Mich.; son of Samuel (a businessman) and Mary Lea (Drews) Raskin; married Ann Frankel, March 14, 1942; children: Judith (Mrs. Jeffrey Rycus), Linda, Barbara, Gregory. *Education:* University of Michigan, A.B., 1940, M.S.P.H., 1941; Wayne University (now Wayne State University), M.D., 1949. *Religion:* Jewish. *Home:* 4660 Pickering Rd., Birmingham, Mich. 48010. *Office:* 20100 Civic Center Dr., Southfield, Mich. 48076.

CAREER: Licensed to practice medicine in Michigan, 1950; Wayne County General Hospital, Eloise, Mich., intern, 1949-50; Veteran's Hospital, Dearborn, Mich., neuropsychiatric resident, 1950-51, 1952-53; Detroit General Hospital (formerly Detroit Receiving Hospital), chief resident in psychiatry, 1953-54; private practice of general psychiatry and psychoanalysis, Detroit, Mich., 1954-68, Southfield, Mich., 1968—. Wayne State University, Detroit, Mich., instructor, 1954-57, adjunct professor, 1957-73, clinical professor of psychiatry, 1973—. Council on Mental Health Committee on Drug Dependence and Alchoholism, American Medical Association, member, 1963-73, chairman, 1970-73. Has served on various civic, municipal, state, and federal governmental committees and projects, including Detroit Department of Health Narcotics Clinic (medical director, 1954-58), Michigan Department of Mental Health Task Force on Revision of Mental Health Statutes, 1964-66, Joint Committee Advisory to Federal Bureau of Narcotics, U.S. Department of the Treasury, 1965-68, Committee on Problems of Drug Dependence, and Narcotic Addict Rehabilitation Coordinating Organization (executive advisor and member of board of directors, 1969—).

MEMBER: American Psychiatric Association (fellow, president of Michigan District branch, 1967), American Medical Association, American Academy of Psychoanalysis (fellow), American College of Psychoanalysts (charter fellow), American Academy of Psychiatry and Law (charter member), American College of Psychiatrists (fellow), American Association for the Advancement of Science, Michigan Society of Psychiatry and Neurology (president, 1967), Michigan State Medical Society, Michigan Association of Law and Psychiatry (president, 1969), Michigan Society for Mental Health, Detroit Psychoanalytic Society and Institute, New York Academy of Sciences, Sigma Xi.

WRITINGS: (Contributor) Howard Franklin Conn, editor, *Current Therapy, 1960,* Saunders, 1960; (contributor) Melvin H. Belli, editor, *Trial and Tort Trends of 1966,* Coiner, 1968; (with Henry Krystal) *Drug Dependence: Aspects of Ego Functioning,* Wayne State University Press, 1970. Contributor to *Journal* of the American Medical Association, *American Journal of Psychiatry, Inventory,* and other professional journals.

* * *

RATIGAN, William 1910-

PERSONAL: Born November 7, 1910, in Detroit, Mich.; son of Bernard Joseph (a Great Lakes engineer and automobile dealer) and Bertie (Laing) Ratigan; married Eleanor Dee Eldridge (a librarian and author), September 12, 1935; children: Patricia Lee (Mrs. Arthur A. Ranger), Anesta Colleen (Mrs. Arthur J. Pelton), Bobbie Laing (deceased), Shannon Leitrim (son). *Education:* University of Chattanooga (now University of Tennessee at Chattanooga), A.B., 1935; Michigan State University, M.A., 1961, Ph.D., 1963, post-doctoral study, 1969. *Residence:* Charlevoix, Mich. *Office address:* Dockside Press, Box 1, Charlevoix, Mich. 49720.

CAREER: National Broadcasting Co., continuity director and producer in Denver, Colo., 1937-40, supervisor of Far East listening post, 1940-42, managing news editor, Western Division, and supervisor of commentators and war correspondents in Pacific Theater of Operations, 1942-45, news editor and script writer, first United Nations Conference, San Francisco, Calif., 1945; free-lance writer, 1946—; Dockside Press, Charlevoix, Mich., founder and proprietor, 1954—; former teacher and guidance director at Charlevoix public schools. Senior extension lecturer, Michigan State University, 1962—; visiting lecturer at various times since 1965 at Florida State University, University of Wisconsin—Milwaukee, and University of Miami, Coral Gables; former journalism instructor at University of California, Los Angeles. Member-at-large, U.S. Advisory Council on Naval Affairs, 1959. Consultant on technical development of Great Lakes craft, Smithsonian Institution. *Member:* Phi Kappa Phi, Blue Key (president), Hollywood Authors Club. *Awards, honors:* California Chaparral Poetry Prize, 1944; adopted chief of Ottawa Tribe, given name Opwa-naniian Kanotong (Interpreter of Dreams), 1957.

WRITINGS: Soo Canal! (shorter version originally published in *Country Gentleman* as "Gangway for Tomorrow"), Eerdmans, 1954, 2nd edition, 1968; *Young Mister Big: The Story of Charles Thompson Harvey,* Eerdmans, 1955; (editor and author of introduction) Henry Wadsworth Longfellow, *The Song of Hiawatha,* centennial facsimile edition, Eerdmans, 1955; *The Adventures of Captain McCargo* (fiction), Random House, 1956; *Straits of Mackinac! Crossroads of the Great Lakes,* Eerdmans, 1957; *Tiny Tim Pine,* Eerdmans, 1958; *The Adventures of Paul Bunyon and Babe,* Eerdmans, 1958; *The Blue Snow,* Eerdmans, 1958; *The Long Crossing,* Eerdmans, 1959; *Highways over Broad Waters: Life and Times of David B. Steinman, Bridgebuilder,* Eerdmans, 1960; *Great Lakes Shipwrecks and Survivals,* Eerdmans, *Carl D. Bradley* edition, 1960, *Daniel J. Morrell* edition, 1969, *Edmund Fitzgerald* edition, 1977; (with Buford Stefflre, and others), *Theories of Counseling,* McGraw, 1965, 2nd edition, 1972. Work featured in *A Literary Map of Michigan.* Contributor to *School Counseling: A View from Within* (yearbook), American School Counselor Association, 1967, to *Encyclopedia Americana,* and to magazines and professional journals, including *Saturday Evening Post.*

WORK IN PROGRESS: Research on the Great Lakes, early Americana, the Civil War, and other projects.

SIDELIGHTS: William Ratigan described *Great Lakes Shipwrecks and Survivals* as "an ongoing chronology of Great Lakes shipping and issues in navigation." Each edition is dedicated to the memory of a lost boat and her crew. Ratigan's Dockside Press is a converted fish shanty. The working pressmark of his press is collected in books about private presses around the world. His home is on Coast Guard Hill overlooking the Charlevoix harbor lights, with a view of the scenes that have inspired a number of his books. Ratigan's papers have become part of the Michigan Historical Collections at the University of Michigan.

* * *

RATTENBURY, Arnold (Foster) 1921-

PERSONAL: Born October 5, 1921, in Hankow, China; son of Harold Burgoyne (a missionary) and Emily (Ewins) Rattenbury; married Simonette Cooper-Willis (an anthropologist researcher), April 3, 1946; children: Emma Caroline, Adam Benedick. *Education:* Attended St. John's College, Cambridge, 1939-40. *Agent:* Curtis Brown Ltd., 1 Craven Hill, London W2 3EW, England.

CAREER: Editor of *Our Time* and *Theatre Today* (magazines), London, England, 1944-49; free-lance journalist and designer, 1949—; exhibition designer, London, 1960—. *Military service:* British Army, 1940-44. *Awards, honors:* British Arts Council grant, 1969, for work on *The Birth, Life and Lingering Death of Humbug.*

WRITINGS: (Editor and author of introduction) Emily Bronte, *Wuthering Heights,* Saturn Press, 1947; *Second Causes* (poems), Chatto & Windus, 1969; *Exhibition Design: Theory and Practice,* Van Nostrand, 1971; *Man Thinking* (poems), Byron Press, 1972.

WORK IN PROGRESS: The Birth, Life, and Lingering Death of Humbug, a study of nonconformist conscience in England in the eighteenth and nineteenth centuries, for Chatto & Windus.

BIOGRAPHICAL/CRITICAL SOURCES: London Magazine, October, 1969.†

* * *

RAUCHER, Herman 1928-

PERSONAL: Surname is pronounced *Row*-sher; born April 13, 1928, in New York, N.Y.; son of Benjamin Brooks and Sophie (Weinshank) Raucher; married Mary Kathryn Martinet, April 20, 1960; children: Jacqueline Leigh, Jennifer

Brooke. *Education:* New York University, B.S., 1949. *Religion:* Hebrew. *Residence:* Cos Cob, Conn. *Address:* c/o Arthur B. Greene, 230 Park Ave., New York, N.Y. 10017.

CAREER: Advertising writer in Hollywood, Calif., for Twentieth Century-Fox, 1950-54, and Walt Disney, 1954-55; worked at Calkins & Holden (advertising), New York City, 1956-57; Reach, McClinton (advertising), New York City, vice-president, creative director, member of board of directors, 1957-63; Maxon (advertising), New York City, vice-president, creative director, 1963-64; Gardner (advertising), New York City, vice-president, creative director, 1964-65; Benton & Bowles (advertising), New York City, consultant, 1965-67. *Military service:* U.S. Army, 1950-52; became second lieutenant. *Member:* Writers Guild of America, Dramatists Guild, Authors League of America.

WRITINGS—Screenplays: "Sweet November," Warner Bros., 1968; "Can Heironymus Merkin Ever Forget Mercy Humppe and Find True Happiness?," Regional Film Distributors, 1969; "Watermelon Man," Columbia, 1970; "Summer of '42," Warner Bros., 1971; "Class of '44" (sequel to "Summer of '42"), Warner Bros., 1972; "Ode to Billy Joe," Warner Bros., 1976. Writer of original television dramas for "Studio One," "Alcoa Hour," and "Goodyear Playhouse," 1956-58.

Novelizations of screenplays: *Watermelon Man,* Ace Books, 1970; *Summer of '42,* Putnam, 1971; *A Glimpse of Tiger,* Putnam, 1971; *Ode to Billy Joe,* Dell, 1976.

AVOCATIONAL INTERESTS: "Amorphic and everchanging."

BIOGRAPHICAL/CRITICAL SOURCES: Punch, July 29, 1970; *Best Sellers,* March 1, 1971; *Washington Post,* March 15, 1971; *Commonweal,* May 21, 1971; *Atlantic,* July, 1971.

*   *   *

RAUDIVE, Konstantin   1909-

PERSONAL: Given name sometimes appears as Konstantins; born April 30, 1909, in Uppsala, Sweden; son of Vincente and Rosalia (Locis) Raudive. *Education:* Attended University of Paris, 1934, and University of Edinburgh, 1937; University of Madrid, Doctor of Arts, 1936; University of Uppsala, Fil.lic., 1953. *Religion:* Roman Catholic. *Home:* Roemerweg 9, 7812 Bad Krozingen, Federal Republic of Germany.

CAREER: Author; in recent years also experimenter in parapsychology. *Member:* Die Gemeinschaft fuer Psychologie. *Awards, honors:* First prize of Swiss Union for Parapsychology, 1969.

WRITINGS: Die Memoiren des Sylvester Perkons (novel trilogy written in Latvian as "Silvestra Perkona memurai" and translated into German for initial publication; title means "The Memoirs of Sylvester Perkons"), Verlag Rost & Dietrich, 1946-48, 2nd edition, published in one volume as *Helligkeit und Zwielicht: Die Aufzeichnungen des Bildhauers Sylvester Perkons* (title means "The Brightness and the Twilight"), Jolis Verlag, 1966; *Der Chaosmensch und seine Ueberwindung: Betrachtungen ueber die Tragik unserer Zeit* (philosophical treatise; title means "The Chaosman and His Subdual"), Maxmilian Dietrich, 1951; *Das unsichtbare Licht* (novel; title means "The Invisible Light"), Thomas-Verlag, 1956; *Sapni un isteniba: Meditacijas par Don Kochota temu* (title means "Dreams and Reality: Meditations on Cervantes' Don Quixote"), Skirmanta apgads (Chicago), 1956; *Asche und Glut* (novel

written in German and Latvian as "Pelni un kvele"; title means "Ashes and Glow"), Dieva zimogs, 1953, Maxmilian Dietrich, 1961; *Unhoerbares wird hoerbar: Auf den Spuren einer Geistarwelt, Beitrag zur experimentellen Parapsychologie,* Otto Reichl, 1968, translation by Nadia Fowler published as *Breakthrough: An Amazing Experiment in Electronic Communication with the Dead,* edited by Joyce Morton, Taplinger, 1971; *Ueberleben wir den Tod?,* Verlag Der Leuchter Reichl, 1973. Also author of *Noladetas dveseles* (novel in two volumes; title means "The Damned Souls"), 1948, and *Un piedod mums . . .* (novel; title means "And Forgive Us Our Trespasses"), 1959.

WORK IN PROGRESS: Further parapsychological research.

SIDELIGHTS: Konstantin Raudive is competent in German, Swedish, Russian, French, Spanish, English, and the Baltic languages.

BIOGRAPHICAL/CRITICAL SOURCES: Aleksis Rubulis, *Baltic Literature,* University of Notre Dame Press, 1970; *Light* (London), spring, 1970, summer, 1971; *Sunday Express,* March 28, 1971; *Psychic News,* April 3, 1971; *New Scientist and Science Journal,* April 15, 1971; *Irish Times,* July, 1971.†

*   *   *

RAVIELLI, Anthony   1916-

PERSONAL: Born July 1, 1916, in New York, N.Y.; son of Peter (a sculptor) and Letizia (Cacacce) Ravielli; married Georgia Ann Weber, May 3, 1954; children: Jane, Ellen, Anthony, Jr. *Education:* Attended Cooper Union, 1932-35, and Art Students League, 1936. *Home and office:* 79 Lolly Lane, Stamford, Conn. 06903.

CAREER: Frances Buente Advertising Agency, New York, N.Y., assistant art director, 1932-34; art director, Superior Litho Co., 1934-37, and Otto Freund Studios, 1937-42, both New York. Illustrator of adult and children's books; exhibited with American Institute of Graphic Arts (A.I.G.A.) Children's Book Show, New York, 1955-57, and other shows; represented in permanent collections of National Club, Augusta, Ga., Officers Club, Governors Island, N.Y., and Fort Niagara, Niagara Falls, N.Y. *Military service:* U.S. Army, 1942-45. *Member:* Authors League of America. *Awards, honors:* A.I.G.A. Children's Book Show award, 1955-57.

WRITINGS—All self-illustrated juveniles: Wonders of the Human Body, Viking, 1954; *An Adventure in Geometry,* Viking, 1957 (published in England as *An Adventure with Shapes,* Phoenix House, 1960); *The World is Round,* Viking, 1963; *The Rise and Fall of the Dinosaurs,* Parents' Magazine Press, 1963; *Elephants, the Last of the Land Giants,* Parents' Magazine Press, 1965; *From Fins to Hands: An Adventure in Evolution,* Viking, 1968; *What Is Bowling?,* Atheneum, 1975; *What Is Golf?,* Atheneum, 1976; *What Is Tennis?,* Atheneum, 1977.

Illustrator: Kate Shippen, *Men, Microscopes and Living Things,* Viking, 1955; Ben Hogan and Herbert Warren Wind, *Five Lessons: The Modern Fundamentals of Golf,* A. S. Barnes, 1957; Don Carter, *Ten Secrets of Bowling,* Viking, 1958; Sybil Sutton-Vane, *The Story of Eyes,* Viking, 1958; Charles Robert Darwin, *Voyage of the Beagle,* abridged and edited by Millicent E. Selsam, Harper, 1959; Martin Gardner, *Relativity for the Million,* Macmillan, 1962; Isaac Asimov, *The Human Body,* Houghton, 1963; Isaac Asimov, *The Human Brain,* Houghton, 1963; H. Chandler

Elliott, *The Shape of Intelligence*, Scribner, 1969; Robert T. Jones, *Bobby Jones on the Basic Golf Swing*, Doubleday, 1969; Dick Aultman, *Square-to-Square Golf Swing*, Golf Digest, 1970; Navin Sullivan, *Controls in Your Body*, Lippincott, 1971; John Jacobs and Ken Bowden, *Practical Golf*, Quadrangle, 1972; Carl Lohren and Larry Dennis, *One Move to Better Golf*, Quadrangle, 1975; Dick Aultman and Ken Bowden, *The Methods of Golf's Masters*, Coward, 1975; Byron Nelson and Larry Dennis, *Shape Your Swing the Modern Way*, Simon & Schuster, 1976; Memmler, *The Human Body in Health and Disease*, Lippincott, 1977.

WORK IN PROGRESS: Evolution of the Human Brain.

AVOCATIONAL INTERESTS: Paleontology, photography, golf, wood-working.

BIOGRAPHICAL/CRITICAL SOURCES: David Harris Russell, Mary Agnella Gunn, and others, *The Ginn Basic Reading Program, Junior High-School Series: Achievement Through Reading*, Ginn, 1965; Henry Thompson Fillmer and others, *Composition Through Literature*, American Book Co., 1967; Diana Klemin, *The Illustrated Book: Its Art and Craft*, C. N. Potter, 1970.

* * *

RAWORTH, Thomas Moore 1938-
(Tom Raworth)

PERSONAL: Surname is pronounced *ray*-worth; born July 19, 1938.

WRITINGS—Poetry, except as indicated; all published under name Tom Raworth: *Weapon Man*, Goliard Press, 1965; *The Relation Ship*, Goliard Press, 1966; *Continuation*, Goliard Press, 1966; (with John Esam and Anselm Hollo) *Haiku*, Trigram, 1968; *The Big Green Day*, Trigram, 1968; *Betrayal* (novel), Trigram, 1969; *A Serial Biography* (novel), Fulcrum Press, 1969; *Lion Lion*, Trigram, 1970; (translator with others) *The Penguin Book of South American Verse*, Penguin, 1971; *Moving*, Cape Goliard, 1971; (with John Ashberry and Lee Harwood) *Penguin Modern Poets 19*, Penguin, 1971; *Pleasant Butter*, Sand Project Press, 1972; *Act*, Trigram, 1973; *Back to Nature*, Joe DiMaggio Press, 1973; *Ace*, Goliard Press, 1974; *Bolivia*, Secret Books, 1974; *Cloister*, Sand Project Press, 1975; *Common Sense*, Zephyrus Image, 1975; *The Mask*, Poltroon Press, 1976; *Log Book* (prose), Poltroon Press, 1977. Also author of film script, "A Plague on Both Your Houses," 1967.

BIOGRAPHICAL/CRITICAL SOURCES: New Statesman, December 13, 1968, November 14, 1969, December 4, 1970; *London Magazine*, February, 1969.

* * *

RAWSON, Clayton 1906-1971
(Great Merlini)

August 15, 1906—March 1, 1971; American magician and mystery story writer. Obituaries: *Newsday*, March 3, 1971; *Variety*, March 10, 1971. (See index for *CA* sketch)

* * *

RAY, Mary (Eva Pedder) 1932-

PERSONAL: Born March 14, 1932, in Rugby, England; daughter of William John (a teacher) and Dora (Moule) Ray. *Education:* Attended Birmingham College of Art and Crafts, 1950-52; College of the Ascension, Birmingham, England, London Diploma of Social Studies, 1954. *Religion:* Church of England. *Home:* Pandora, 24 Richmond Dr., Herne Bay, Kent, England.

CAREER: Church social worker in Sheffield, England, 1957-61; old people's welfare worker for Warwickshire County Council, 1961-62; civil servant in Birmingham and London, England, 1962—.

WRITINGS: The Voice of Apollo, J. Cape, 1964, Farrar, Strauss, 1966; *The Eastern Beacon*, J. Cape, 1965, Farrar, Straus, 1967; *Standing Lions*, Faber, 1968, Meredith, 1969; *Spring Tide*, Faber, 1969; (with John Philip Ray) *The Victorian Age*, Heinemann, 1969; *Living in Earliest Greece*, Faber, 1969; *Shout against the Wind*, Faber, 1970; *A Tent for the Sun*, Faber, 1971; *The Ides of April*, Faber, 1974; *Sword Sleep*, Faber, 1975; *Beyond the Desert Gate*, Faber, 1977.

SIDELIGHTS: Mary Ray told *CA:* "Since I was a child of about six I have never felt any strangeness or distance about what I have learned about the people of Greece and Rome and of earlier civilizations. I was at home in the periods in the way that some people are at home in a place or a country. I started writing about Roman Britain, because I knew what the places looked like, and for me it is important that the three strands of actual geographical firsthand knowledge, historical research and imagination should all be as strong as I can make them. After I was able to go to Greece regularly I particularly enjoyed writing about the people who had lived there. I became fascinated by what was the same for me—smells and weather and mountains and ants, and what was quite different—slavery, pain and the worship of different Gods. Looking back I can see that certain themes are usually important in my books. Creative people have a habit of turning up as characters, as making things—from jam to fine art—is very important to me, and my creative people often have to fight to be able to practice their skills as in my experience one does in real life. I also enjoy writing about the very old and the very young, which is a hangover from working in residential homes for mothers and babies and the old when I was a social science student. I am also obsessed by a theme very common in children's books—and how and when, when one is young, you become able to come to terms with what life brings. I suppose this is because for children's writers their own childhood is still very alive. We remember the things that it was painful to learn, what we had to fight for and what we had to accept; the characters in our books follow where we went or the way we wish we had gone."

* * *

RAY, Talton F. 1939-

PERSONAL: Born October 9, 1939, in St. Louis, Mo.; son of E. Lansing (a journalist) and Miriam (Francis) Ray; married Lilli Doberstein, August 7, 1963; children: Justina, Nicola. *Education:* Stanford University, B.A., 1961; Columbia University, M.A., 1967. *Home:* 1120 Fifth Ave., New York, N.Y. 10028. *Office:* Ford Foundation, 320 East 43rd St., New York, N.Y. 10017.

CAREER: ACCION en Venezuela (community development), director of field operations, 1961-64; Chase Manhattan Bank, New York City, credit analyst, 1967-68; Ford Foundation, New York City, administrative officer, 1968—.

WRITINGS: The Politics of the Barrios of Venezuela, University of California Press, 1969.

* * *

REACH, James 1910(?)-1970

1910(?)—March 5, 1970; American playwright, novelist, and short story writer. Obituaries: *New York Times*, March 7, 1970; *Antiquarian Bookman*, March 23, 1970.

REDDIN, W(illiam) J(ames) 1930-

PERSONAL: Born May 10, 1930, in London, England; now a Canadian citizen; married Mary Kathleen Zillioux. *Education:* University of New Brunswick, B.A., 1955; Harvard University, M.B.A., 1957; Massachusetts Institute of Technology, Sloan fellow, 1963-64. *Address:* Box 1012, Fredericton, New Brunswick, Canada.

CAREER: Canadian Army, active force, 1948-51, served in Militia, 1951-61, retired as major; University of New Brunswick, Fredericton, full-time faculty member in business administration, 1957-73; currently visiting fellow, Oxford Management Centre, Oxford, England. *Member:* World Future Society, American Sociological Association, Society for the Psychological Study of Social Issues.

WRITINGS: Successful Spending, Saving, and Investing: A Practical Guide for Canadians, McGraw, 1964; *Problems in Economic and Business Statistics for Canadian Students,* Tribune Press, 1965, 2nd edition (with R. Lim), 1971; *Campus Countdown,* McGraw, 1967; *Managerial Effectiveness,* McGraw, 1970; *Effective Management by Objectives,* McGraw, 1971.

* * *

REDKEY, Edwin S(torer) 1931-

PERSONAL: Born September 19, 1931, in Washington, D.C.; son of William Henry (a rehabilitation administrator) and Lucile (Storer) Redkey; married Nancy Lee Jenks (an author), June 22, 1963; children: David Henry, Elizabeth. *Education:* University of Washington, Seattle, B.A., 1954; Princeton Theological Seminary, B.D., 1960; Yale University, M.A., 1964, Ph.D., 1967. *Office:* Department of History, State University of New York College at Purchase, Purchase, N.Y. 10577.

CAREER: Ordained clergyman of United Presbyterian Church, U.S.A., 1960; Middlebury College, Middlebury, Vt., lecturer in religion and acting chaplain, 1960-62; Yale University, New Haven, Conn., dean of Trumbull College, 1965-68, lecturer in American studies, 1966-67, assistant professor of history and American studies, 1967-68; University of Tennessee, Knoxville, associate professor of history, 1968-71; State University of New York College at Purchase, associate professor of history and dean of students, 1971—. *Military service:* U.S. Navy, aviator, 1954-57; became lieutenant junior grade. *Member:* American Historical Association, Organization of American Historians, Association for the Study of Negro Life and History, African Studies Association, American Studies Association (president, Kentucky-Tennessee chapter, 1970-71).

WRITINGS: Black Exodus: Black Nationalist and Back-to-Africa Movements, 1890-1910, Yale University Press, 1969; (editor) *Respect Black: Writings and Speeches of Bishop Henry McNeal Turner,* Arno, 1971.

WORK IN PROGRESS: A biography of Bishop Henry McNeal Turner, for Oxford University Press; continuing research in the history of back-to-Africa movements and in black nationalism.

* * *

REED, Barry Clement 1927-

PERSONAL: Born January 28, 1927, in San Francisco, Calif.; son of Clement Barry and Julia A. (Donahue) Reed; married Marie T. Ash, June 2, 1951; children: Debra, Marie, Barry, Susan. *Education:* Holy Cross College, B.S., 1949; Boston College, L.L.B., 1954. *Politics:* Democrat. *Religion:* Roman Catholic. *Home:* 41 Cushing Rd., Westwood, Mass. 02090. *Office:* 101 Tremont St., Boston, Mass. 02108.

CAREER: Admitted to the Bar of the State of Massachusetts; trial lawyer in Boston, Mass., 1955—. *Military service:* U.S. Army, 1945-47; became staff sergeant.

WRITINGS—With Elliott L. Sagall: *The Heart and the Law: A Practical Guide to Medicolegal Cardiology,* Macmillan, 1968; *The Law and Clinical Medicine,* Lippincott, 1970. Contributor to *American Bar Association Journal* and other periodicals and newspapers.

WORK IN PROGRESS: A novel with a medical-legal background involving malpractice.

SIDELIGHTS: Barry Reed indicates an interest in both law and medicine and in historical novels. He told *CA:* "If I had my 'druthers' I would rather teach English literature in some small co-ed college than trying corporate-merger cases or doing heart transplants."

* * *

REED, Betty Jane 1921-

PERSONAL: Born August 6, 1921, in Pittsburgh, Pa.; daughter of Charles August and Barbara (Miller) Reed. *Education:* University of Minnesota, B.S., 1951, M.A., 1954. *Politics:* Independent. *Religion:* Lutheran. *Home:* 4401 Columbus Ave. S., Minneapolis, Minn. 55407.

CAREER: Minneapolis (Minn.) public schools, first grade teacher, 1951-65, director of Community Resource Volunteers department, 1965—. *Member:* Association for Childhood Education, National Education Association, National Council of Teachers of English, Women in Education, Minnesota Education Association, Minnesota Association of Volunteer Directors, Minneapolis Area Council of Teachers of English, Pi Lambda Theta.

WRITINGS—"Early Reading" series, all published by Denison: *Are You a Kangaroo?,* 1969; *A Horse of Course,* 1969; *Flyin' with a Lion,* 1969; *More Mom for Tom,* 1969; *Laugh with a Giraffe,* 1969; *A Rabbit with a Special Habit,* 1971; *Mouse in the House,* 1971; *They Left the Moon Too Soon,* 1972; *Such a Fuss for a Hippopotamus,* 1974; *A Knapsack for Jack,* in press.

WORK IN PROGRESS: Six books for Denison's "Early Reading" series, tentatively entitled *Zoom on Mr. Gloom's Broom, A Hullabaloo in the Zoo, A Ghost for a Host, Double Trouble with a Bubble, This Cat Is Like That,* and *Thinkin' about Lincoln.*

SIDELIGHTS: Betty Jane Reed told *CA:* "As a first and second grade teacher, I became aware of two factors that eventually started me writing. First of all, I learned that rhyming words help children learn and read and, secondly, that libraries were very lacking in rhyming books of interest to young children." She goes on to say: "My first story was written to make a point in a mental health television program I was doing as part of a health series on educational television. I did a series at first grade level, one at second and one at third. In the first grade one I used my story, "Tommy's Problem." After the broadcast I had so many letters and calls asking where the story could be purchased that I decided to put it into book form and that's how it all started. That story, now titled, *More Mom for Tom,* actually started my writing of rhyming books for children."

AVOCATIONAL INTERESTS: Reading, poetry, making rock jewelry, and travel ("do lots of the former but little of the latter").

REED, Edward W(ilson) 1913-

PERSONAL: Born September 5, 1913, in Galatia, Ill.; son of William E. and Ota (Abney) Reed; married Anna L. Isherwood, August 20, 1938; children: Alan K. *Education:* Southern Illinois University, B.Ed., 1936; University of Illinois, M.A., 1937, Ph.D., 1947. *Home:* 2775 North West Forest Ave., Beaverton, Ore. 97005.

CAREER: Instructor in public schools in Illinois, 1937-41; University of Louisville, Louisville, Ky., assistant professor of economics, 1941-43; University of Illinois, Urbana, assistant professor of economics, 1946-47; University of Arkansas, Fayetteville, professor of economics, 1948-52; City National Bank, Fort Smith, Ark., president, 1952-58; University of Oregon, Eugene, John B. Rogers Professor of Banking and Finance, 1958-68; U.S. National Bank of Oregon, Portland, senior vice-president and economist, 1968—. Visiting summer professor, Banking School of the South, Louisiana State University, 1960—, and Pacific Coast Banking School, Seattle, Wash., 1962—. Member, Economic Research Center, University of Hawaii, 1960. Consultant, U.S. National Bank of Oregon, 1962—. *Military service:* U.S. Navy, 1942-46; became lieutenant commander, U.S. Naval Reserve, 1946—. *Member:* National Association of Business Economists, American Economic Association, American Finance Association, Western Economic Association, Western Finance Association (president). *Awards, honors:* Outstanding Professor in School of Business Administration, University of Oregon, 1966-69.

WRITINGS: Inter-jurisdictional Tax Problems, [Urbana], 1947; *Comparative Analysis of Arkansas Tax System,* University of Arkansas, College of Business Administration, 1951; *Recent Attempts to Improve Property Tax Administration in Selected States,* University of Arkansas, College of Business Administration, 1951; *Comparative Analysis of Arkansas State Expenditures,* University of Arkansas, College of Business Administration, 1952; (with Henry M. Alexander) *The Government and Finance of Counties in Arkansas,* University of Arkansas, College of Business Administration, 1953; *Consumer Financing Costs and Practices in Hawaii,* Economic Research Center, University of Hawaii, 1960; *Resort Financing in Hawaii,* Economic Research Center, University of Hawaii, 1960; *Commercial Bank Management,* Harper, 1963; *Personal Bankruptcies in Oregon,* University of Oregon, Bureau of Business and Economic Research, 1967; (with Donald L. Woodland) *Cases in Commercial Banking,* Appleton, 1970; (with Richard V. Cotter, Edward K. Gill, and Richard K. Smith) *Commercial Banking,* Prentice-Hall, 1976.

WORK IN PROGRESS: A revised edition of *Cases in Commercial Banking* with Donald L. Woodland and Peter S. Rose for Prentice-Hall.

* * *

REEDY, George E(dward) 1917-

PERSONAL: Born August 5, 1917, in East Chicago, Ind.; son of George Edward (a news correspondent) and Mary (Mulvaney) Reedy; married Lillian Greenwald, March 22, 1948; children: Michael Andrew, William James. *Education:* University of Chicago, B.A., 1938. *Politics:* Democrat. *Religion:* Episcopalian. *Home:* 2307 East Newberry Blvd., Milwaukee, Wis. 53233. *Agent:* Michael Hamilburg, 1104 South Robertson Blvd., Los Angeles, Calif. 90035. *Office:* College of Journalism, Marquette University, Milwaukee, Wis. 53233.

CAREER: United Press, Washington, D.C., senate corre-

spondent, 1938-42, 1946-51; U.S. Senate, Washington, D.C., committee consultant, 1951-52, staff director of Democratic Policy Committee, 1952-60; Office of the Vice-President, Washington, D.C., special assistant to Vice-President Lyndon B. Johnson, 1961-64; The White House, Washington, D.C., press secretary, 1964-65, aide to President Johnson, 1965-66; Struthers Research & Development Corp., Washington, D.C., president, 1966-68; The White House, special assistant and consultant to President Johnson, 1968-69; Pegram Lecturer, Brookhaven National Radiation Laboratory, 1971; State University of New York, New York, N.Y., adjunct professor of political science, 1971-72; Marquette University, Milwaukee, Wis., dean, College of Journalism, 1972-76, Distinguished Lucius W. Nieman Professor of Science, 1977—. President and director, Struthers Scientific and International Corp; vice-president and director, Struthers Wells Corp. Fellow, Woodrow Wilson International Center for Scholars, 1968-72. Member of numerous government committees and boards of enquiry including, President's National Advisory Committee on Selective Service, 1966-67, and President's National Advisory Committee on Marine Science and Engineering Resources, 1967—. *Military service:* U.S. Army Air Forces, 1942-46; became captain. *Member:* American Academy of Political and Social Science.

WRITINGS: Who Will Do Our Fighting for Us?, World Publishing, 1969; (contributor) *Friendly Adversaries: The Press and Government,* Marquette University Press, 1969; *The Twilight of the Presidency,* New American Library, 1970; *The Presidency in Flux,* Columbia University Press, 1971. Contributor of articles and syndicated series to *New York Times, Annals of the American Academy of Political and Social Sciences, Newsday, Washington Post,* and other publications.

WORK IN PROGRESS: A book on oceanography, for World Publishing; also writing on Latin America, politics, and government.

BIOGRAPHICAL/CRITICAL SOURCES: Washington Post, July 26, 1969; *Virginia Quarterly Review,* spring, 1970; *Christian Science Monitor,* June 3, 1970; *New York Times Book Review,* August 23, 1970.

* * *

REES, Albert (Everett) 1921-

PERSONAL: Born August 21, 1921, in New York, N.Y.; son of Hugo R. and Rosalie (Landman) Rees; married Candida Kranold, July 15, 1945; married second wife, Marianne Russ, June 22, 1963; children: (first marriage) David; (second marriage) Daniel, Jonathan. *Education:* Oberlin College, B.A., 1943; University of Chicago, M.A., 1947, Ph.D., 1950. *Home:* 32 Turner Ct., Princeton, N.J. 08540. *Office:* 3 Nassau Hall, Princeton University, Princeton, N.J. 08540.

CAREER: Roosevelt College (now Roosevelt University), Chicago, Ill., instructor in economics, 1947-48; University of Chicago, Chicago, Ill., assistant professor, 1948-54, associate professor, 1954-61, professor of economics and chairman of department, 1961-66; Princeton University, Princeton, N.J., professor of economics, 1966—, provost, 1975—. Research associate, National Bureau of Economic Research, 1953-54; staff member, Council of Economic Advisers, 1954-55; fellow, Center for Advanced Study in the Behavioral Sciences, 1959-60. Member of board of directors, Social Science Research Council, 1966—; member, New Jersey Public Employment Relations Commission, 1968-69.

Member: American Economic Association, Industrial Relations Research Association.

WRITINGS: Real Wages in Manufacturing, 1890-1914, Princeton University Press, 1961; (editor with Earl J. Hamilton and Harry G. Johnson) *Landmarks in Political Economy,* University of Chicago Press, 1962; *The Economics of Trade Unions,* University of Chicago Press, 1962; (with George P. Shultz) *Workers and Wages in an Urban Labor Market,* University of Chicago Press, 1970; *Economics of Work and Pay,* Harper, 1973.

Contributor: *Interpreting the Labor Movement,* Industrial Relations Research Association, 1952; *The Measurement and Behavior of Unemployment,* Princeton University Press, 1957; Philip D. Bradley, editor, *The Public Stake in Union Power,* University Press of Virginia, 1959; *Wages, Prices, Profits, and Productivity,* final edition, American Assembly, Graduate School of Business, Columbia University, 1959; *The Price Statistics of the Federal Government,* National Bureau of Economic Research, 1961. Contributor of about twenty articles to economic, labor relations, and business journals. Editor, *Journal of Political Economy,* 1954-59; associate editor, *International Encyclopedia of the Social Sciences,* 1962-67.

* * *

REES, Ioan Bowen 1929-
(Ioan Rhys)

PERSONAL: Rees and the Welsh form of his surname, Rhys, rhyme with "peace"; born January 13, 1929, in Dolgellau, Wales; son of Aurfryn Mudie (a schoolmaster) and Kate Olwen (Parry) Rees; married Margaret Wynn Meredith, March 14, 1959; children: Dafydd Gwyrfai Bowen, Catrin Non Bowen, Gruffudd Maredudd Bowen. *Education:* Queen's College, Oxford, B.A., 1952, M.A., 1956; Law Society's School, University of London, Solicitor of the Supreme Court, 1956; University of Birmingham, further study, 1967. *Politics:* Welsh nationalist/radical. *Religion:* Congregationalist. *Home:* Tal-Sarn, Llanllcchid, Bangor, Wales. *Office:* County Offices, Caernarvon, Gwynedd, Wales.

CAREER: Lancashire County Council, Lancashire, England, assistant solicitor, 1956-58; Cardiff City Council, Cardiff, Wales, 1958-65, with final post as chief prosecuting solicitor; Pembrokeshire County Council, Haverfordwest, Wales, deputy clerk of the council and deputy clerk of the peace, 1965-73; first county secretary of the new county of Dyfed, Wales, 1973; county secretary of Gwynedd, Wales, 1973—. *Military service:* British Army, 1947-49; became sergeant instructor. *Member:* Royal Institute of Public Administration, Society of County Secretaries (chairman of Welsh panel), Honourable Society of Cymmrodorion, Club Alpin Suisse. *Awards, honors:* Haldane Medal of Royal Institute of Public Administration, 1968, for his essay, "Local Government in Switzerland."

WRITINGS: Galwad y Mynydd (in Welsh), Dryw, 1961; *The Welsh Political Tradition,* Plaid Cymru, 1963, 2nd edition, 1975; *Dringo Mynyddoedd Cymru* (in Welsh), Dryw, 1965; (under name Ioan Rhys, with Gwynfor Evans, Hugh MacDiarmid, and Owen Dudley Edwards) *Celtic Nationalism,* Routledge & Kegan Paul, 1968; *Government by Community,* Benn, 1971; *The Welsh Language Today,* Gomer, 1973; *Mynyddoedd* (in Welsh), Gomer, 1975. Contributor of articles on government, Welch questions, and mountaineering, and of Welsh poetry to periodicals.

WORK IN PROGRESS: A book on government in Switzerland; a travel book on the Grisons in Switzerland.

BIOGRAPHICAL/CRITICAL SOURCES: New Statesman, December 13, 1968; *Times Literary Supplement,* February 2, 1969; *New Society,* July 15, 1971; *Municipal Review,* December, 1971; *Political Quarterly,* October/December, 1971; *New York Times,* July 5, 1973.

* * *

REEVES, C(harles) Thomas 1936-

PERSONAL: Born August 25, 1936, in Tacoma, Wash.; son of Clifford (a laborer) and Dorothy (Christ) Reeves; married Kathleen Garrison, February 1, 1958; children: Kirsten, Elizabeth, Margaret. *Education:* Pacific Lutheran University, B.A. (with honors), 1958; University of Washington, Seattle, M.A., 1961; University of California, Santa Barbara, Ph.D., 1966. *Home:* 5039 Cynthia Lane, Racine, Wis. 53406. *Office:* Department of History, University of Wisconsin—Parkside, Kenosha, Wis. 53140.

CAREER: University of Colorado, Boulder, assistant professor of history, 1966-70; University of Wisconsin—Parkside, Kenosha, associate professor, 1970-73, professor of history, 1973—. *Member:* American Historical Association, Organization of American Historians. *Awards, honors:* Research grants from El Pomar Foundation, 1968, 1970, American Philosophical Society, 1970, 1975, Eleanor Roosevelt Institute, 1975, and National Endowment for the Humanities, 1976.

WRITINGS: Freedom and the Foundation: The Fund for the Republic in the Era of McCarthyism, Knopf, 1969; (editor) *Foundations under Fire,* Cornell University Press, 1970; (editor) *McCarthyism,* Dryden, 1973; *Gentleman Boss: The Life of Chester Alan Arthur,* Knopf, 1975. Contributor to history journals and *Nation.*

WORK IN PROGRESS: A biography of Senator Joseph R. McCarthy, for Stein & Day.

* * *

REEVES, Elton T(raver) 1912-

PERSONAL: Born September 23, 1912, in Rigby, Idaho; son of Aames Marshall and Bertha (Traver) Reeves; married Lois Bashor, November 25, 1936; married second wife, Elsie Wolfinger, August 18, 1962; children: (first marriage) Delores (Mrs. Kenneth R. Blackman), Rosemary (Mrs. David Sonnikson). *Education:* University of Idaho, B.S., 1932; University of Washington, Seattle, M.A., 1938; Louisiana State University, additional study, 1959-61. *Religion:* Lutheran. *Home:* 4859 Sheboygan Ave., No. 304, Madison, Wis. 53705. *Office:* University of Wisconsin, Room 321, 432 North Lake St., Madison, Wis. 53706.

CAREER: Medical representative, American Cyanamid Corp., Lederle Laboratories Division, 1948-54; Kaiser Aluminum & Chemical Corp., industrial relations posts at plants in four locations, 1954-63; Warwick Electronics, Inc., Chicago, Ill., corporate training director, 1963-64; Boeing Co., Seattle, Wash., management development coordinator, 1964-69; University of Wisconsin—Madison, assistant professor, 1969-72, associate professor, 1972-76, professor of management, 1976—. *Military service:* U.S. Naval Reserve, one year. *Member:* American Society for Training and Development.

WRITINGS—All published by the American Management Association: *Management Development for the Line Manager,* 1969; *Dynamics of Group Behavior,* 1970; *So You Want to Be a Supervisor!,* 1971; *So You Want to Be a Manager!,* 1971; *So You Want to Be an Executive!,* 1971; *How to*

Get Along with (Almost) Everybody, 1973; *Practicing Effective Management,* 1975. Contributor to journals.

AVOCATIONAL INTERESTS: Golf, bowling, bridge.

* * *

REGHABY, Heydar 1932-

PERSONAL: Born December 16, 1932, in Teheran, Persia (now Iran); son of Ahmad and Akram (Allalah) Reghaby. *Education:* University of Teheran, law degree, 1954; Columbia University, M.A., 1959; Free University of Berlin, Ph.D., 1963. *Home:* 6270 Colby St., Oakland, Calif. 94618. *Office:* Department of Philosophy, San Jose State University, San Jose, Calif. 95114.

CAREER: Columbia University, New York, N.Y., special lecturer in philosophy, 1964-66; Ball State University, Muncie, Ind., assistant professor of philosophy, 1965-66; University of Oklahoma, Norman, assistant professor of philosophy, 1966-67; San Jose State University, San Jose, Calif., assistant professor of philosophy, 1967—. Assistant professor, University of California Extension, Berkeley, 1967—.

WRITINGS: Die Revolutionaere und konservative Aspekte in der Philosophie des Volksgeistes (Ph.D. dissertation), Federal Republic of Germany, 1963; *Philosophy and Freedom,* Philosophical Library, 1970; (editor and contributor) *Philosophy of the Third World,* Deganawidah-Quetzalcoatl University, 1974.

Books in Persian: *Asemane Ashk* (poetry; title means "The Sky of Tears"), Khayyam Publishing Co. (Teheran), 1950; *Naghushaye Khatar* (title means "Bells of Danger"), Khayyam Publishing Co., 1951; *Parchame Seh Rang* (title means "The Three Colored Flag"), Khayyam Publishing Co., 1952; *Khaterate Maygoon* (novel; title means "Memories of Maygoon"), Mohsen Publishing Co. (Teheran), 1952; *Shahrezad* (poetry), Khayyam Publishing Co., 1953; *Shaere Shahre Shoma* (title means "The Poet of Your City"), Amirkabir Publications (Teheren), 1970; *Mossadegh va Movazenehe Manfi* (title means "Mossadegh and the Negative Political Balance"), Iranian National Front Publication, 1972.

WORK IN PROGRESS: On the Paths of Infinity: A Scientist-Philosopher Dialogue.

* * *

REID, Anthony 1916-

PERSONAL: Born February 8, 1916, in Wadebridge, Cornwall, England; son of Robert Archer George (a bank manager) and Elsie (Rickard) Reid; married Beatrice Elliot Jackson, May 8, 1954; children: Phaon Michael. *Education:* University of London, B.A., 1955. *Religion:* Humanist. *Home:* Lake Dawn, Avon Castle Dr., Ringwood, Hampshire, England. *Office:* c/o Barclays Bank, 53 The Grove, West Southbourne, Bournemouth, England.

CAREER: Bank manager. *Military service:* Royal Air Force, 1940-46; became flying officer; received Distinguished Service Certificate (twice). *Member:* Private Libraries Association, Heraldry Society. *Awards, honors: Engraved Bookplates, 1950-70* was named one of the Fifty Best Books of the Year by National Book League, London.

WRITINGS: Laughter in the Sun: A Mediterranean Adventure, Bles, 1952; *A Checklist of the Book Illustrations of John Buckland Wright, Together with a Personal Memoir,* Private Libraries Association (London), 1968; *Ralph Chubb, the Unknown,* Private Libraries Association, 1971;

(with Mark Severin) *Engraved Bookplates, 1950-70,* Private Libraries Association, 1972.

WORK IN PROGRESS: With his wife, Betty Reid, a series of six historical novels for children, the first five titled *The Hounds of Garamantes, The Brigands of Alta Montana, The Horses of Sybaris, The Heroes of Far Contray,* and *The Ships of Polynikes;* also currently researching books on aspects of heraldry.

SIDELIGHTS: Anthony Reid has a private library of private pressbooks and modern first editions on homosexuality and other topics, including the "finest collection in existence" on John Buckland Wright, Ralph Chubb, and George Ives. Reid's latest book, *Engraved Bookplates, 1950-70,* was the subject of a color television program for the British Broadcasting Corporation, and was chosen to represent Britain in the European Book Fair at Leipzeig. He was a resident of Italy for three years.

* * *

REID, R(obert) W(illiam) 1933-

PERSONAL: Born April 20, 1933, in Cleckheaton, England; son of Harry and Nancy (Senior) Reid; married Penelope Ann Mckay (a publisher); children: Camilla, Matthew. *Education:* Christ Church, Oxford, M.A., 1956; Queen's University at Kingston, M.Sc., 1959; Queens' College, Cambridge, Ph.D., 1961. *Home:* 22 Colet Gardens, London W.14, England. *Agent:* Curtis Brown, 1 Craven Hill, London W2 3EW, England.

CAREER: British Broadcasting Corp., London, England, television producer, 1961-69, head of science and features department, 1969-72. *Military service:* British Army, Royal Tank Regiment, 1956-58; became lieutenant.

WRITINGS: The Spectroscope, Weidenfeld & Nicolson, 1965; *Tongues of Conscience: Weapons Research and the Scientists' Dilemma,* Walker & Co., 1969 (published in England as *Tongues of Conscience: War and the Scientist's Dilemma,* Constable, 1969); *Marie Curie,* Saturday Review Press, 1974; *Microbes and Men,* Saturday Review Press, 1974; *My Children, My Children,* Harcourt, 1977.

BIOGRAPHICAL/CRITICAL SOURCES: Times Literary Supplement, July 5, 1974; *New York Times,* June 19, 1974.

* * *

REILE, Louis 1925-

PERSONAL: Surname rhymes with "steel"; born June 13, 1925, in San Antonio, Tex.; son of Louis and Theresa (Haass) Reile. *Education:* St. Mary's University, B.A. (cum laude), 1949; University of Fribourg, additional study, 1957-61; Johns Hopkins University, M.A., 1965. *Politics:* "Active." *Home:* 1 Camino Santa Maria, San Antonio, Tex. 78284. *Office:* St. Mary's University, San Antonio, Tex. 78284.

CAREER: Roman Catholic priest of Marianist Order (S.M.); Provencher College, St. Boniface, Manitoba, teacher of English, 1953-56; teacher of English at secondary school in St. Louis, Mo., 1956-57; St. Mary's University, San Antonio, Tex., assistant professor, 1965-71, associate professor of English and cinema, 1971—. *Military service:* U.S. Naval Reserve, World War II. *Member:* National Council of Teachers of English, Association of University Film Professors, Texas Council of Teachers of English, Marianist Writers Guild, San Antonio Motion Picture Council.

WRITINGS: Battle and Brother Louis, Newman, 1959; Running Giant, Maryhurst Press, 1966; Films in Focus, Abbey Press, 1970. Also author of Winding Flows the River, 1975.

WORK IN PROGRESS: The Person, the Arts, and the Church; Sex, Violence, and Nudity in Cinema; a textbook on poetry analysis and one on cinema and criticism; The Roaring and the Roasting, a book of 101 reviews of 1965-70 films; a popular book on religion today, The Cross for Now; critical essays on plays of William Shakespeare.

*　　*　　*

REILLY, Francis E(agan)　1922-

PERSONAL: Born November 26, 1922, in Buffalo, N.Y.; son of Thomas Edward (a machinery operator) and Kathryn (Eagan) Reilly. Education: Spring Hill College, B.S., 1946; Woodstock College, S.T.L., 1954; Saint Louis University, Ph.D., 1959. Home and office: Ateneo de Manila, Quezon City, Philippines.

CAREER: Entered Society of Jesus (Jesuits), 1940, ordained priest, 1953; Ateneo de San Pablo, San Pablo City, Philippines, high school teacher, 1947-50; San Jose Seminary, Quezon City, Philippines, teacher of philosophy and dean of seminary, 1959-66; Ateneo de Manila, Quezon City, teacher of philosophy, 1967-71; Canisius College, Buffalo, N.Y., teacher of philosophy, 1971-72; Ateneo de Manila, teacher of philosophy, 1972—. Member: Metaphysical Society of America.

WRITINGS: The Really Real: Elements of Metaphysics, Jesuit Educational Association of the Philippines, 1962; Charles Peirce's Theory of Scientific Method, Fordham University Press, 1970. Contributor of reviews to Philippine Studies.

*　　*　　*

REJAUNIER, Jeanne　1934-

PERSONAL: Born April 19, 1934, in Garden City, Long Island, N.Y.; daughter of Edward W. and Harriet (Wright) Rejaunier; married Edson C. Newquist, April, 1974 (separated); children: Vadine Rejaunier Newquist. Education: Vassar College, A.B., 1956; additional study at Sorbonne, University of Paris, at University of Pisa, and at University of California, Los Angeles. Religion: "Born Episcopal but am universal in thinking." Home: 1226 North Havenhurst, Hollywood, Calif. 90046. Agent: Ziegler-Ross, Tennant, 9255 Sunset Blvd., Beverly Hills, Calif.

CAREER: Has been a free-lance actress and model in New York, Hollywood, and Europe, and television script writer. Treasurer, North America Silica Corp. Member: Actors' Equity Association, Screen Actors Guild, American Federation of Television and Radio Artists, Dramatists Guild, Writers Guild of America, West.

WRITINGS: Astrology and Your Sex Life, Century Books, 1965; The Beauty Trap (novel), Trident, 1969; (with L. A. Horstman) Astrology for Lovers, Pocket Books, 1971; The Motion and the Act, Nash Publishing, 1972.

WORK IN PROGRESS: The Return of the Woman.

*　　*　　*

REMARQUE, Erich Maria　1898-1970

June 22, 1898—September 25, 1970; German-born American novelist and playwright. Obituaries: New York Times, September 26, 1970; Washington Post, September 26, 1970;

Newsweek, October 5, 1970; Time, October 5, 1970; Books Abroad, spring, 1971.

*　　*　　*

RENFIELD, Richard L.　1932-

PERSONAL: Born April 30, 1932, in Staten Island, N.Y.; married Marilyn Lewis (a physician). Education: Harvard University, B.A. (magna cum laude), 1953; University of Maryland, M.A., 1959; American University, Ph.D., 1965. Home: 2200 Leeland Dr., Falls Church, Va. 22043. Office: International Monetary Fund, 700 19th St. N.W., Washington, D.C. 20431.

CAREER: Institute for the Study of the USSR, Munich, Germany, translator, 1953-54; National Education Association, Washington, D.C., intern with Committee on International Relations, 1957-58, associate secretary of Educational Policies Commission, 1958-67; Communications Satellite Corp., Washington, D.C., interim communications satellite committee and Intelsat affairs department, 1967-70; International Monetary Fund, Washington, D.C., reviser-translator, 1974—. Teacher of Seminar in Soviet education, George Washington University, 1965-66; summer instructor at Institute of World Affairs, Salisbury, Conn., 1966, and American University, 1967. Member of board of directors, Futures for Children, 1968—. Military service: U.S. Army, Intelligence, 1955-57. Member: Phi Beta Kappa.

WRITINGS: (Translator) Fyodor Dostoevsky, Winter Notes on Summer Impressions, Criterion, 1955; If Teachers Were Free, Acropolis Books, 1969. Co-author of sixteen monographs for Educational Policies Commission of National Education Association, 1958-67. Contributor to New York Times, Yale Review, European Community, and other publications.

SIDELIGHTS: Richard L. Renfield wrote CA: "I wrote If Teachers Were Free because I believe a country with such an education system would come as close to Utopia as a human society can. I long for my own children to go to such schools and to live in such a society. I translate because I love languages above all human inventions, thanks to the high school language teacher who introduced them to me."

*　　*　　*

RENN, Thomas E(dward)　1939-
(Jeremy Strike)

PERSONAL: Born November 8, 1939, in Welch, W.Va.; son of Ernest Edward and Dorothy (Strike) Renn. Education: University of Toledo, B.A., 1962. Politics: Republican. Religion: Episcopalian.

CAREER: Flournoy & Gibbs, Inc., Toledo, Ohio, director of radio-television advertising, 1962-66; Savage Communications, Inc., Toledo, director of advertising, 1966-69; currently living in Europe.

WRITINGS: (Under pseudonym Jeremy Strike) A Promising Planet, Ace Books, 1970.††

*　　*　　*

RESNIK, Henry S.　1940-

PERSONAL: Born April 3, 1940, in New Haven, Conn.; son of Howard B. (a lawyer and financier) and Muriel (Spitzer) Resnik. Education: Yale University, B.A., 1962, M.A.T., 1963.

CAREER: High school teacher of English in Great Neck, N.Y., 1963-65. Awards, honors: Rockefeller Foundation grant and Thomas Skelton Harrison Foundation grant, 1968, to write *Turning on the System: War in the Philadelphia Public Schools.*

WRITINGS: Turning on the System: War in the Philadelphia Public Schools, Pantheon, 1970. Contributor of articles and reviews to *Saturday Review, Vogue,* and other magazines.

WORK IN PROGRESS: Magazine articles.

AVOCATIONAL INTERESTS: "Magic, mysticism, communes, tripping, travel, yoga, sailing, skiing, jogging, bicycling, women, women's liberation, revolution, counter culture, music, guitar, movies, media, children, money, survival, death, dropping out, organic food—not in order of importance; this varies from day to day."††

* * *

REVELL, Peter 1929-

PERSONAL: Born May 23, 1929, in Surrey, England; son of John (a builder) and Dorothy (King) Revell; married Francess Monaghan, February 28, 1953; children: Alison Francess, Graham Aidan. *Education:* University College, London, B.A., 1952; University of Western Ontario, M.A., 1964; University of Wales, Ph.D., 1974. *Home:* 126 Watford Rd., St. Albans, Hertfordshire, England.

CAREER: National Central Library, London, England, trainee librarian, 1952-53; University of Reading Library, Reading, England, assistant librarian, 1954-55; University of London, London, England, assistant librarian, Institute of Historical Research, 1956-57; London Public Library and Art Museum, London, Ontario, assistant librarian, 1957-62, head of West reference department, 1962-65, head of arts and sciences department, 1965-66; University College of South Wales and Monmouthshire, University of Wales, Cardiff, senior assistant librarian, 1966-75; University of London, Westfield College, London, England, chief librarian, 1975—. *Military service:* Royal Air Force, 1947-49. *Member:* Library Association (United Kingdom; fellow), English Association, British Association for American Studies. *Awards, honors:* Fellowship of the Library Association, 1957.

WRITINGS: James Whitcomb Riley, Twayne, 1970; (coeditor) *A Catalogue of the Tennyson Collection in the Library of University College, Cardiff,* University College, University of Wales (Cardiff), 1972; *Fifteenth-Century English Prayers and Meditations: A Descriptive List of Manuscripts in the British Library,* Garland Publishing, 1975. Contributor to library journals and to *Alphabet* and *Fiddlehead.*

WORK IN PROGRESS: Paul Laurence Dunbar.

* * *

REYNOLDS, G. Scott 1925-

PERSONAL: Born June 26, 1925, in Atlanta, Ga.; son of George Edwin and Josephine (Sullivan) Reynolds; married Carolyn Walden, November 5, 1948; children: Scott Edward, Ryan Winfield, Keith Walden. *Education:* Took courses equivalent to two years of college. *Religion:* Methodist. *Home:* 4376 Jett Rd. N.W., Atlanta, Ga. 30327. *Agent:* Scott Meredith Literary Agency, Inc., 845 Third Ave., New York, N.Y. 10022. *Office:* Lenox Towers West, Suite 1632, 3390 Peachtree Rd. N.E., Atlanta, Ga. 30326.

CAREER: Owner of self-service laundry business in Atlanta, Ga., 1947-60; Francis I. DuPont, Atlanta, account executive, 1961-62; Reynolds & Co. (investments and insurance counseling), Atlanta, owner, 1963—. *Military service:* U.S. Army Air Forces, 1943-45. *Member:* National Association of Securities Dealers, American Risk and Insurance Association, Authors Guild. *Awards, honors: The Mortality Merchants* was cited by *Library Journal* as one of the fifty best business books of 1968-69.

WRITINGS: The Mortality Merchants: The Legalized Racket of Life Insurance and What You Can Do about It, McKay, 1968.

WORK IN PROGRESS: A revised edition of *The Mortality Merchants.*

BIOGRAPHICAL/CRITICAL SOURCES: Book World, May 12, 1968; *Best Sellers,* May 15, 1968.†

* * *

REZMERSKI, John Calvin 1942-

PERSONAL: Surname is pronounced Rez-*mer*-ski; born January 15, 1942, in Kane, Pa.; son of John James and Augusta (Dickinson) Rezmerski; married Mary K. Naegle, January 22, 1966; children: Marysia, Nicholas, Peter. *Education:* Gannon College, B.A., 1963; John Carroll University, M.A., 1965; University of Kansas, further graduate study, 1965-67. *Politics:* "Utopian." *Religion:* "Animist." *Home:* 217 West Locust, St. Peter, Minn. 56082. *Office:* Department of English, Gustavus Adolphus College, St. Peter, Minn. 56082.

CAREER: Gustavus Adolphus College, St. Peter, Minn., associate professor of English, 1967—. *Awards, honors:* Devins Memorial Award in Kansas City Poetry Contest, 1969, for *Held for Questioning;* National Endowment for the Arts creative writing fellowship, 1973.

WRITINGS: Held for Questioning (poems), University of Missouri Press, 1969; *An American Gallery* (poems), Three Rivers Press, 1977.

Poems have been anthologized in *25 Minnesota Poets,* Nodin Press, 1975, *Minnesota Poets in the Schools Anthology,* 1976, and *Heartland II,* Northern Illinois University Press, 1976. Contributor to poetry magazines, including *Chelsea, Kansas Write-In,* and *Poetry Northwest.*

WORK IN PROGRESS: Several books of poems, including a book of epigrams, *Solipsisms;* two science fiction novels; a poetry textbook.

BIOGRAPHICAL/CRITICAL SOURCES: Chelsea Review, December, 1969.

* * *

RICE, Eugene F(ranklin), Jr. 1924-

PERSONAL: Born August 20, 1924, in Lexington, Ky.; son of Eugene F. (a civil engineer) and Lula (Piper) Rice; married Charlotte Bloch (an art historian), August 26, 1952; children: Eugene, John, Louise. *Education:* Harvard University, B.A., 1947, M.A., 1948, Ph.D., 1953; Ecole Normale Superieure, Paris, France, graduate study, 1951-52. *Home:* 560 Riverside Dr., New York, N.Y. 10027. *Office:* Department of History, Columbia University, New York, N.Y. 10027.

CAREER: Harvard University, Cambridge, Mass., instructor in history and general education, 1953-55; Cornell University, Ithaca, N.Y., assistant professor, 1955-59, associate professor, 1959-63, professor of history, 1963-64; Columbia University, New York, N.Y., professor of history, 1964—, chairman of department, 1970-73. Member, Institute for Advanced Study, Princeton, N.J., 1962-63; resident, American Academy in Rome, 1974-75. *Military service:* U.S. Army, 1942-45; became staff sergeant. *Member:* American Historical Association, Society for Reformation Research, Renaissance Society of America (executive director, 1970—). *Awards, honors:* Guggenheim fellow, 1959-60; Fulbright research grant, 1959-60; American Council of Learned Societies research grant, 1962-63; American Academy of Arts and Sciences fellowship, 1974; National Endowment for the Humanities senior fellowship, 1974-75.

WRITINGS: The Renaissance Idea of Wisdom, Harvard University Press, 1958; *The Foundations of Early Modern Europe, 1460-1559,* Norton, 1970; *The Prefatory Epistles of Jacques Lefevre d'Etaples and Related Texts,* Columbia University Press, 1971. Contributor to scholarly journals.

WORK IN PROGRESS: The Humanist Idea of Christian Antiquity; several chapters for Harper's *Columbia History of the World;* and also writing on problems in Renaissance intellectual history.

SIDELIGHTS: Eugene F. Rice is able to work in French, Spanish, Italian, German, and Latin.

* * *

RICE, Inez 1907-

PERSONAL: Born September 16, 1907, in Portland, Ore.; daughter of Herman Richard (a physician) and Clara (Schroeder) Biersdorf; married Stephen O. Rice (a research engineer), February 26, 1931; children: Carole (Mrs. Douglas Hanau), Joan (Mrs. William McHugh), Stephen Edgar. *Education:* Oregon State University, B.S., 1929. *Politics:* Republican. *Home:* 8110 El Paseo Grande, Apt. 308, La Jolla, Calif. 92037.

CAREER: Author of children's fiction. *Member:* Authors Guild, Kappa Delta Pi. *Awards, honors: The March Wind* was an honor book in *New York Herald Tribune* Children's Spring Book Festival Awards, 1957; Author Award, New Jersey Teachers of English, 1964, for *A Long Long Time.*

WRITINGS—Juvenile books: *The March Wind,* Lothrop, 1957; *A Long Long Time,* Lothrop, 1964; *A Tree This Tall,* Lothrop, 1970; *Signposts,* Houghton, 1971, 2nd edition, 1974.

SIDELIGHTS: Inez Rice says of her work: "To me the creativity of writing for children is moving backward and forward in time over facts and through illusions. I have always believed that a writer of children's fiction was really writing for the child in himself (or herself). Everyone has bits and pieces of the child he once was, hidden carefully away. In thoughtful moments he may slip back alone to ponder the strange wisdom and the haunting magic of the past."

* * *

RICE, Joseph Peter 1930-

PERSONAL: Born December 30, 1930; son of Joseph Peter and Marie (Glaser) Rice; married June Elaine Center, June 16, 1961; children: Linda Leslie, April Anne, Catherine Jennifer, Joseph Peter, Jr. *Education:* American International College, B.A., 1953; Springfield College, M.Ed., 1954; University of Connecticut, Ph.D., 1959; N.S.F. grant at University of California, Davis, 1959; University of California, Santa Barbara, graduate student, 1960; Stanford University, credential in school psychology, 1961. *Religion:* Episcopal. *Home address:* P.O. Box 783, Homewood, Lake Tahoe, Calif. 95718. *Office:* California Mini-Corps, 1919 21st St., Room 203, Sacramento, Calif. 95814.

CAREER: Served externship at Holyoke Child Guidance Clinic, Holyoke, Mass., 1954; Mitchell College, New London, Conn., director of student services, 1954-56; served internship at Norwich State Hospital, Norwich, Conn., 1956; Fresno City College, Fresno, Calif., instructor in psychology, psychometrist at Department of Vocational Rehabilitation, Calif., 1956-58; Yuba College, Marysville, Calif., testing officer, 1958-60; Lompoc Unified School District, Lompoc, Calif., psychologist, director of Pupil Personnel Services, 1960-62; California State Department of Education, Sacramento, Calif., Bureau for Mentally Exceptional Children, consultant, 1962-68, chief, 1968-71; associate commissioner of education, Commonwealth of Massachusetts, 1971-74; California Mini-Corps, Sacramento, associate director of California Migrant Teacher Corps, 1974—.

MEMBER: American Personnel and Guidance Association, American Psychological Association, California Association of School Psychologists, California Teachers Association, Council for Exceptional Children.

WRITINGS: A Comparative Study of the Guidance Program in the Private and Public Junior College, University of Connecticut, 1959; (with P. D. Plowman) *California Project Talent: Revised Guidelines for Establishing and Evaluating Programs for Mentally Gifted Minors,* California State Department of Education, 1964; (with Plowman) *California Project Talent: Identification and Case Study,* California State Department of Education, 1964; (with Plowman) *California Project Talent: Final Report, Western Conference,* California State Department of Education, 1967; *The Gifted: Developing Total Talent,* C. C Thomas, 1970.

Contributor to *Clearing House, California Journal of Educational Research, Personnel and Guidance Journal, California Schools, California Education, School and Society, Exceptional Children,* and other educational journals. Author, with P. D. Plowman, of *The Gifted Pupil,* a newsletter of programs for mentally gifted minors, published by the California State Department of Education, Volumes I, II, and III, 1965, 1966, and 1967. Also author of annual reports for United States Office of Education on various programs and evaluations of California State Department of Education, 1974-76.

* * *

RICE, Otis K(ermit) 1919-

PERSONAL: Born June 6, 1919, in Hugheston, W.Va.; son of Charles Orion (a timberman) and Mary Catherine (Belcher) Rice. *Education:* Attended West Virginia Institute of Technology, 1935-40; Morris Harvey College, B.S., 1943, A.B. (magna cum laude), 1944; West Virginia University, M.A., 1945; University of Kentucky, Ph.D., 1960. *Politics:* Democrat. *Residence:* Hugheston, W.Va. 25110. *Office:* Division of Humanities and Sciences, West Virginia Institute of Technology, Montgomery, W.Va. 25136.

CAREER: Teacher and principal in public schools of Kanawha County, W.Va., 1938-57; West Virginia Institute of Technology, Montgomery, assistant professor, 1957-59, associate professor, 1959-60, professor of history, 1960—, chairman of department of history and social sciences, 1962—, director of Division of Humanities and Sciences, 1968—, acting dean, summer, 1969, chairman of humanities division, 1972—. Visiting summer professor at Morris Harvey College, 1961, 1968, and Marshall University, 1963, 1964, 1966, 1967; Danforth associate, 1968—. Member, West Virginia Antiquities Commission, 1968-70, and of West Virginia Historic Road Markers Advisory Board, 1970—.

MEMBER: American Historical Association, American Association for State and Local History, Organization of American Historians, Southern Historical Association, Western Historical Association, West Virginia Historical Society (president, 1955-56; treasurer, 1959-69), West Virginia Historical Association of Professional Historians (president, 1970-71), Phi Alpha Theta, Kappa Delta Pi. *Awards, honors:* American Association for State and Local History summer research grants, 1961, 1965.

WRITINGS: The Allegheny Frontier: West Virginia Beginnings, 1730-1830, University Press of Kentucky, 1970; *West Virginia: The State and Its People,* McClain Printing Co., 1972; *Frontier Kentucky,* University Press of Kentucky, 1975.

Author of introduction to reprint editions published by McClain Printing Co.: John Stuart, *Narrative of the Indian Wars and Other Occurrences,* 1971; John J. Jacob, *A Biographical Sketch of the Life of the Late Captain Michael Cresan,* 1971; Joseph Doddridge, *Logan: The Last of the Race of Shikellemus, Chief of the Cayuga Nation,* 1971. Contributor of major articles on the state of West Virginia to *Dictionary of American History, Encyclopedia of Southern History, Book of Knowledge, Collier's Encyclopedia,* and *Merit Students Encyclopedia;* contributor of about fifty articles and reviews to historical journals. Book review editor, *West Virginia History,* 1971—.

WORK IN PROGRESS: A book tentatively entitled *West Virginia,* for University Press of Kentucky.

*　　*　　*

RICH, Elizabeth 1935-

PERSONAL: Born June 13, 1935, in Portland, Me.; daughter of Mulford Edward and Elsie (McCausland) Rich. *Education:* Attended Wheaton College, Norton, Mass., 1953-55; Barnard College, B.A., 1958. *Home:* 17 Rue Gros, Paris 75016, France. *Office:* Trans World Airlines, Inc., Hanger 12, John F. Kennedy International Airport, Jamaica, N.Y. 11430.

CAREER: Harvard University, Cambridge, Mass., secretary at Center for International Affairs, 1958-60; U.S. Air Force, director (as civilian) of service club in France, 1960-62; Trans World Airlines, New York City, flight attendant, 1963—. Fulbright analyst, Institute for International Education, New York City, 1962-66.

WRITINGS: Flying High: What It's Like to Be an Airline Stewardess, Stein & Day, 1970, revised edition, 1972; *Flying Scared: Why We Are Being Skyjacked and How to Put a Stop to It,* Stein & Day, 1972.

WORK IN PROGRESS: With Cynthia Glacken, *The Travel Book.*

*　　*　　*

RICH, Michael B(enjamin) 1935-

PERSONAL: Born June 6, 1935, in New York, N.Y.; son of Harry Porter and Frieda (Harris) Rich; married Abbe Benenson, October 14, 1960; children: Jaime, Johsua Michael. *Education:* Haverford College, B.A., 1954.

CAREER: Newsweek, New York, N.Y., general promotion manager, beginning 1968. Director, Champion Sports, Inc.; president, Professional Players School. *Member:* International Advertising Association, Media Promotion Group, U.S. Naval Institute, Copeia.

WRITINGS: (With Elaine Tarkenton) *A Wife's Guide to Pro Football,* Viking, 1969; (with Charline Gibson) *A Wife's Guide to Baseball,* Viking, 1970; (with Jane West) *A Wife's Guide to Pro Basketball,* Viking, 1970. Contributor to *Gebraus Graphic, Seventeen,* and *World Federalist.*

WORK IN PROGRESS: Three books, *A Wife's Guide to NHL Hockey, A Wife's Guide to Driving,* and *The Brotherhood of Basketball;* a television show.

BIOGRAPHICAL/CRITICAL SOURCES: Book World, November 9, 1969.††

*　　*　　*

RICHARD, Adrienne 1921-

PERSONAL: Born October 31, 1921; daughter of Leslie MacDonald (a printer) and Marguerite (Brown) Gooder; married James Richard (a management consultant), April 22, 1943; children: James, Daniel, Randall. *Education:* University of Chicago, A.B., 1943; further study at Writers Workshop, University of Iowa, 1948-50, and Boston College, 1969—. *Politics:* Independent. *Religion:* "Eclectic." *Home:* 45 Chiltern Rd., Weston, Mass. 02193.

MEMBER: National League of American Pen Women. *Awards, honors: Pistol* was runner-up for the Golden Spur Award of Western Writers of America, 1970, and designated "notable" by the American Library Association; Newbery Award and National Book Award nominations in children's literature, 1974, for *Wings.*

WRITINGS—Young adult novels: *Pistol,* Little, Brown, 1969; *The Accomplice,* Little, Brown, 1973; *Wings,* Little, Brown, 1974; *Into the Road,* Little, Brown, 1976. Contributor of articles, travel sketches, short stories, and book reviews to magazines and newspapers.

WORK IN PROGRESS: A young adult novel, *The Island on the Edge of the Sky;* an adult novel, *I, Eighty;* more travel sketches, articles, and short stories.

SIDELIGHTS: Adrienne Richard wrote *CA:* "The human and historical role of stories and storytelling has become a central interest. I am more and more convinced that the narrative story is a deeply needed response to a frightening, unknowable world vastly larger and more complex than any individual or any society. A story needn't be reassuring in its meaning to serve this purpose in the modern world. Story as form may be enough—now I am getting out where I don't know the answers. Irony and ambiguity may be deep-running disservices. Is it really a dirty joke to be born to die? I am asking the question. Answers next time—or perhaps more questions."

Richard's other interests are in traditional societies, the arts, the integration of mind and body, fruit and vegetable gardening, and always stories and storytelling, myths, and folktales.

BIOGRAPHICAL/CRITICAL SOURCES: Book World, November 9, 1969; *New York Times Book Review,* November 30, 1969, January 12, 1975.

*　　*　　*

RICHARDS, Lawrence O. 1931-
(Larry Richards)

PERSONAL: Born September 25, 1931, in Milan, Mich.; son of Vivian S. and Charlotte M. (Zeluff) Richards; married Marla M. Hafner, July 24, 1955; children: Paul, Joy, Timothy. *Education:* University of Michigan, B.A., 1958; Dallas Theological Seminary, Th.M., 1962; Northwestern University, Ph.D., 1972. *Politics:* Independent. *Religion:*

Protestant. *Home:* 14411 North Sixth St., Phoenix, Ariz. 85022.

CAREER: Scripture Press Publications, Wheaton, Ill., editor, 1962-65; Wheaton College, Graduate School, Wheaton, Ill., assistant professor of Christian education, 1965-72; Renewal Research Associates, Phoenix, Ariz., president, 1972—. Consultant, Scripture Press Publications, 1965—. *Military service:* U.S. Navy, 1951-55. *Member:* Phi Beta Kappa.

WRITINGS—Published by Moody: (Editor) *The Key to Sunday School Achievement,* 1965; *Creative Bible Teaching,* 1970; *Teaching Youth Asks Books,* 1971; *You, the Teacher,* 1972; (with Elsiebeth McDaniel) *You and Children,* 1973; *You and Youth,* 1973; *You, the Parent,* 1974; *You and Adults,* 1974; (with McDaniel) *You and Preschoolers,* 1975; *You and Teaching: Leader's Guide,* 1975.

Published by Standard Publishing; edited by Marian Bennett: *Helping My Child Know Jesus,* 1975; *Helping My Child Love,* 1975; *Helping My Child Memorize Scripture,* 1975; *Helping My Child Obey,* 1975; *Helping My Child Overcome Fears,* 1975; *Helping My Child Pray,* 1975; *Helping My Child Share,* 1975; *Helping My Family Worship,* 1975.

Published by Zondervan: *A New Face for the Church,* 1970; *Creative Bible Study,* 1971; *Youth Ministry: Its Renewal in the Local Church,* 1972; (with Marvin Keene Mayers) *Reshaping Evangelical Higher Education,* 1972; *Sixty-Nine Ways to Start a Study Group and Keep It Growing,* 1973; *Three Churches in Renewal,* 1975; *A Theology of Christian Education,* 1975.

Under name Larry Richards; published by David Cook: *Freedom Road,* edited by Timothy E. Udd, 1976; *Let Day Begin,* 1976; *The Servant King,* 1976; *Years of Darkness: Days of Glory,* 1977; *Edge of Judgement,* 1977; *The Great Adventure,* 1977; *Regions Beyond,* 1977; *Springtime Coming,* 1978.

Published by Moody: *Are You for Real?,* 1968; *How Far Can I Go?,* 1969; *Is God Necessary?,* 1969; *How Do I Fit In?,* 1970; *What's in It for Me?,* 1970; *Youth Asks: A Leader's Guide,* 1971.

Published by Victor: *One Way,* 1972; *Science and the Bible . . . Can We Believe Both?,* 1973; *Becoming One in the Spirit,* 1973; *You Can Be Transformed!,* 1973; *Born to Grow: For New and Used Christians,* 1974; *How to Understand the Old Testament without Being a Seminary Student,* 1974; *What You Should Know about the Bible,* 1974; *The Complete Christian: Insights for Life from the Book of Hebrews,* 1975; *Christ's Mission on Earth,* 1975. Author of column in *Action Magazine.*

WORK IN PROGRESS: Measuring learning outcomes in religious education; examining restructuring of seminary educational systems and approaches.

SIDELIGHTS: Lawrence O. Richards told *CA* that he does "much speaking in [the] fields of church renewal, youth, and church education," and that "these represent major concerns, especially the development of [a] theological base for church renewal and restructuring of the church toward New Testament patterns. At present [I am] also heavily involved in rethinking the education of ministers to equip them for ministry in the renewal church. I write from a distinctively conservative and evangelical viewpoint (theologically.)"†

*   *   *

RICHARDSON, Alan   1923-

PERSONAL: Born December 4, 1923, in Letchworth, Hert-

fordshire, England; son of John Sibley (an inventor) and Henrietta (Stevens) Richardson; married Faith May Clayton (an actress), August 22, 1953; children: June Muriel, Catherine Henrietta. *Education:* University of Western Australia, B.A. (honors) and Diploma in Clinical Psychology, 1953; University of London, Ph.D., 1956. *Home:* 75 Beatrice Rd., Dalkeith 6009, Western Australia. *Office:* University of Western Australia, Nedlands, Western Australia.

CAREER: Signals Development and Research Establishment, Hampshire, England, draftsman, 1942-45; Torville Holiday Camp, Devonshire, England, manager, 1945-46; University of London, London, England, assistant lecturer, 1953-56; University of Western Australia, Nedlands, senior lecturer, 1957-69, reader in psychology, 1970—. Chairman of advisory board, Perth Marriage Guidance Council, 1969. *Military service:* British Army, 1946-48; became second lieutenant. *Member:* Australian Psychological Society (fellow). *Awards, honors:* Carnegie Commonwealth travel grant, 1963; visiting fellowship at Australian National University, 1966.

WRITINGS: Mental Imagery, Springer Publishing, 1969; *Man in Society,* Heinemann, 1974; *British Immigrants and Australia,* Australian National University Press (Canberra), 1974. Contributor of more than forty articles to professional journals.

WORK IN PROGRESS: Adult Human Psychology: The Experiential Dimension.

*   *   *

RICHARDSON, H(arold) Edward   1929-

PERSONAL: Born July 13, 1929, in Woodstock, Ky.; son of Samuel and Marcella (Osborne) Richardson; married Antonia Calvert, 1953; children: Shawn Edward, Jill Calvert. *Education:* Eastern Kentucky University, A.B., 1952, M.A. (education), 1954; University of Southern California, M.A. (English), 1961, Ph.D., 1963. *Home:* 1442 Cherokee Rd., Louisville, Ky. 40204. *Office:* Department of English, University of Louisville, Louisville, Ky. 40208.

CAREER: High school and junior college instructor, 1952-56; Fullerton Junior College, Fullerton, Calif., instructor in English, 1956-63; Eastern Kentucky University, Richmond, associate professor, 1963-65, professor of English, 1965-68, chairman of department, 1965-67; University of Louisville, Louisville, Ky., professor of English, 1968—. Visiting professor at California State University, Los Angeles, 1967, 1971, and University of Southern California, summer, 1968. Editorial consultant, Prentice-Hall. *Member:* Modern Language Association of America, National Council of Teachers of English, American Studies Association, South Atlantic Modern Language Association, Louisville and Lexington Civil War Round Table, Kentucky Historical Society, Madison County Historical Society, Phi Delta Phi. *Awards, honors:* Distinguished Alumni Award, Eastern Kentucky University, 1976.

WRITINGS: William Faulkner: The Journey of Self-Discovery, University of Missouri Press, 1969; *How to Think and Write,* Scott, Foresman, 1971; (with Frederick B. Shroyer) *Muse of Fire: Approaches to Poetry,* Knopf, 1971; *Cassius Marcellus Clay: Firebrand of Freedom,* University Press of Kentucky, 1976. Contributor of articles and reviews to academic journals.

WORK IN PROGRESS: Hemingway and "The Sun Also Rises": A Study in Depth; further biographical and fictional work on Cassius Marcellus Clay (1810-1903); research and writing in American literature, American cultural history, and American poetry.

SIDELIGHTS: H. Edward Richardson wrote to *CA:* "The best writing, I think, is a pure rendering of the imagination, when the mind breaks free of all corrupting motivations, those subordinate concerns that hammer so persistently on the modern mind. It is a coming to terms with one's self, what one has to say; but it is more: a naked appraisal of the naked self before a mercilessly clear, well-lighted mirror.

"In my own experience, not big things, but little things of the living past well up and become both incentive and substance. Such was the origin of the Cassius Marcellus Clay biography, which commenced with my memory as a very young boy of the old men around the Madison County Courthouse. These senior citizens of various ages, some few Civil War veterans, gathered there on warm summer days to whittle cedar sticks and tell stories. When the talk turned to the colorful 'Cash' Clay, Lincoln's minister to Russia, the whittling stopped; for his life was a crucible of volatile national issues, including emancipation. Knives and canes became punctuation marks as the old men grew eloquent, their faces all aglow behind saffron-tinctured beards, their eyes burning under bushy white brows—a sudden excitement in the hot air."

AVOCATIONAL INTERESTS: Golf, Americana, American history.

BIOGRAPHICAL/CRITICAL SOURCES: College English, December, 1962; *Books and Bookman,* February, 1965; *American Literature,* March, 1970; *Los Angeles Herald-Examiner,* March 15, 1970; *South Atlantic Quarterly,* summer, 1970; *Louisville Times,* April 23, 1976.

*　*　*

RICHARDSON, Harry W(ard) 1938-

PERSONAL: Born December 8, 1938, in Batley, Yorkshire, England; son of George (a builder) and Lena (Wright) Richardson; married Margaret Gatiss, August 22, 1960; children: Paul Antony, Clare Francesca, Matthew Philip. *Education:* University of Manchester, B.A. (first class honors), 1959, M.A., 1961. *Home:* 12 Leycroft Close, Canterbury, Kent, England.

CAREER: University of Aberdeen, Aberdeen, Scotland, assistant lecturer in economics, 1960-62; University of Newcastle upon Tyne, Newcastle upon Tyne, England, lecturer in economics, 1962-64; University of Strathclyde, Glasgow, Scotland, lecturer in economics, 1964-65; University of Aberdeen, senior lecturer in economics, 1966-68; University of Kent at Canterbury, England, director of Centre for Research in the Social Sciences, beginning 1969. Visiting professor, University of Pittsburgh, 1971, 1973.

WRITINGS: Economic Recovery in Britain, 1932-1939, Weidenfeld & Nicolson, 1967; (with Derek Howard Aldcroft) *Building in the British Economy between the Wars,* Allen & Unwin, 1968; *Regional Economics: Location Theory, Urban Structure and Regional Change,* Praeger, 1969; *Elements of Regional Economics,* Penguin, 1969; (with Aldcroft) *The British Economy, 1870-1939,* Macmillan (London), 1969, Humanities, 1970; (editor) *Regional Economics: A Reader,* St. Martin's, 1970; *Urban Economics,* Penguin, 1971; *Input-Output and Regional Economics,* Wiley, 1972; *Regional Growth Theory,* Wiley, 1973; *The Economics of Urban Size,* Lexington Books, 1973; *Economic Aspects of the Energy Crisis,* Lexington Books, 1975; *Regional Development Policy and Planning in Spain,* Lex-

ington Books, 1975; (with others) *Housing and Urban Spatial Structure: A Case Study,* Lexington Books, 1975; *The New Urban Economics: And Alternatives,* Academic Press, 1977. Contributor to business and history journals.

WORK IN PROGRESS: Research in urban and regional economics and in quantitative economic theory.

BIOGRAPHICAL/CRITICAL SOURCES: Observer Review, April 4, 1967; *Listener,* June 29, 1967; *Times Literary Supplement,* July 9, 1970.†

*　*　*

RICHARDSON, James F(rancis) 1931-

PERSONAL: Born June 19, 1931, in New York, N.Y.; married Marie Balfe (a teacher), June 28, 1958; children: Moira, Pierce, Kieran, Margaret, John. *Education:* Iona College, B.A., 1952; Georgetown University, graduate study, 1954-55; New York University, Ph.D., 1961. *Home:* 470 Merriman Rd., Akron, Ohio 44303. *Office:* Department of History, University of Akron, Akron, Ohio 44325.

CAREER: Teacher of English and history in New York, N.Y., 1955-59; Rockland Community College, Suffern, N.Y., assistant professor of history, 1960-63; Newark College of Engineering, Newark, N.J., assistant professor, 1963-66, associate professor of history, 1966-67; University of Akron, Akron, Ohio, 1967—, began as associate professor, currently professor of history and urban studies. New York University, instructor, summer, 1960, visiting assistant professor, summers, 1962, 1963. *Military service:* U.S. Army, 1952-54; became sergeant. *Member:* American Historical Association, Organization of American Historians, American Studies Association.

WRITINGS: The New York Police: Colonial Times to 1901, Oxford University Press, 1970; (editor) *The American City,* Xerox College Publishing, 1972; (editor with Raymond A. Mohl) *The Urban Experience,* Wadsworth, 1973; *Urban Police in the United States,* Kennikat, 1974. Contributor to *New York Historical Society Quarterly.*

WORK IN PROGRESS: A History of Politics and Public Policy, Cleveland, 1900-1930.

AVOCATIONAL INTERESTS: Three cushion billiards.

BIOGRAPHICAL/CRITICAL SOURCES: Virginia Quarterly Review, autumn, 1970.

*　*　*

RICHARDSON, Jeremy John 1942-

PERSONAL: Born June 15, 1942, in Bridgnorth, England; son of Samuel Radcliffe (an insurance broker) and Sarah (Hill) Richardson; married Anne Philippsen (a librarian), April 15, 1967. *Education:* University of Keele, B.A. (honors), 1964; University of Manchester, M.A., 1965, Ph.D., 1970. *Politics:* Conservative. *Religion:* Church of England. *Home:* 17 Camborne Crescent, Westlands, Newcastle, Staffordshire, England. *Office:* Department of Politics, University of Keele, Keele, Staffordshire, England.

CAREER: University of Keele, Keele, Staffordshire, England, lecturer in politics, 1966—. Member, Newcastle-under-Lyme Borough Council, 1970—. *Member:* Political Studies Association, Association of University Teachers.

WRITINGS: The Policy Making Process, Routledge & Kegan Paul, 1969, Humanities, 1970; *Campaigning for the Environment,* Routledge & Kegan Paul, 1974; *Pressure Groups in Britain,* Rowman & Littlefield, 1974. Contributor to journals of political affairs.

WORK IN PROGRESS: Policy Analysis in the United Kingdom and Sweden.

AVOCATIONAL INTERESTS: Mountain walking.

* * *

RICHARDSON, Kenneth Ridley 1934-

PERSONAL: Born June 12, 1934, in Manchester, England; son of Thomas Ridley and Mabel (Shepherd) Richardson; married Sallyann Blair (a lecturer), October 9, 1965; children: Mark, Matthew, Nicholas, Sara. *Education:* Corpus Christi College, Cambridge, B.A., 1956, M.A., 1961, M. Phil, 1976. *Home:* 4 Riverside Villas, Portsmouth Rd., Long Ditton, Surrey, England. *Office:* School of Liberal Studies, Kingston Polytechnic, Kingston-upon-Thames, Surrey KT1 2EE, England.

CAREER: Chambers's Encylopaedia, London, England, member of editorial staff, 1957-61; various lectureships in England and Australia, 1962-71; Kingston Polytechnic, Kingston-upon-Thames, Surrey, England, principal lecturer in liberal studies, 1971—.

WRITINGS: (Editor) *Twentieth Century Writing: A Reader's Guide to Contemporary Literature,* George Newnes, 1969, Transatlantic, 1970.

WORK IN PROGRESS: The Major Novels of Lawrence Durrell.

SIDELIGHTS: Kenneth Richardson lists as his major areas of vocational interest, the influence of scientific ideas on contemporary fiction and literature in education.

* * *

RICHARDSON, Richard Judson 1935-

PERSONAL: Born February 16, 1935, in Poplar Bluff, Mo.; son of Jewell Judson and Fern (Watson) Richardson; married Sammie Sue Cullum, 1961; children: Jon Mark, Anna Cecile, Ellen Elizabeth, Megan Leigh. *Education:* Harding College, B.S., 1957; Trinity College, Dublin, graduate study, 1957-58; Tulane University, M.A., 1961, Ph.D., 1967. *Home:* 1701 Fountainridge, Chapel Hill, N.C. 27514. *Office:* Department of Political Science, University of North Carolina, Chapel Hill, N.C. 27514.

CAREER: Tulane University, New Orleans, La., instructor in political science, 1963-64; Western Michigan University, Kalamazoo, assistant professor, 1965-67, associate professor of political science, 1967; University of Hawaii, Honolulu, associate professor of political science, 1967-68; University of North Carolina at Chapel Hill, associate professor, 1968-72, professor of political science, 1972—, associate chairman, 1973, chairman of department, 1975—. Consultant, Hawaii State Constitutional Convention, 1967-68. *Member:* American Political Science Association, Southern Political Science Association, Midwest Political Science Association. *Awards, honors:* Edward S. Corwin Award, American Political Science Association, 1967; Tanner Award for distinguished teaching, University of North Carolina at Chapel Hill, 1972.

WRITINGS: (With Kenneth N. Vines) *The Politics of Federal Courts: Lower Courts in the United States,* Little, Brown, 1970; (with Marian Irish and James Prothro) *The Politics of American Democracy,* 6th edition (Richardson was not affiliated with earlier editions), Prentice-Hall, 1977. Contributor to academic journals.

WORK IN PROGRESS: A study of the victimization of crime in North Carolina; and a study of blacks in southern trial courts.

RICHARDSON, Robert (Dale, Jr.) 1934-

PERSONAL: Born June 14, 1934, in Milwaukee, Wis.; son of Robert Dale (a clergyman) and Lucy (Marsh) Richardson; married Elizabeth Hall, November 7, 1959; children: Elizabeth, Anne. *Education:* Harvard University, B.A., 1956, Ph.D., 1961. *Home:* 2455 South Jackson St., Denver, Colo. 80210. *Office:* Department of English, University of Denver, Denver, Colo. 80210.

CAREER: Harvard University, Cambridge, Mass., instructor in English, 1961-63; University of Denver, Denver, Colo., assistant professor, 1963-68, associate professor, 1968-72, professor of English, 1972—, head of department, 1968-73. *Member:* Modern Language Association of America, American Studies Association, American Association of University Professors, American Civil Liberties Union, Phi Beta Kappa. *Awards, honors:* Huntington Libraries fellow, 1973-74.

WRITINGS: Literature and Film, Indiana University Press, 1969; (with Burton Feldman) *The Rise of Modern Mythology,* Indiana University Press, 1972. Contributor of articles and reviews to professional journals. *Denver Quarterly,* associate editor, 1967-76, book review editor, 1976—; member of editorial board, *Western Review.*

WORK IN PROGRESS: A book on mythology and American literature; a study of Henry David Thoreau.

BIOGRAPHICAL/CRITICAL SOURCES: New Republic, October 25, 1969; *Books Abroad,* spring, 1971.

* * *

RICHMOND, Julius B(enjamin) 1916-

PERSONAL: Born September 26, 1916, in Chicago, Ill.; son of Jacob and Anna (Dayno) Richmond; married Rhee Chidekel, June 3, 1937; children: Barry J., Charles Allen, Dale Keith (deceased). *Education:* University of Illinois, B.S., 1937, M.S. and M.D., 1939. *Home:* 79 Beverly Rd., Chestnut Hill, Mass. 02135. *Office:* Judge Baker Guidance Center, 295 Longwood Ave., Boston, Mass. 02115; and U.S. Department of Health, Education, and Welfare, Washington, D.C.

CAREER: Cook County Hospital, Chicago, Ill., intern, 1939-41, resident, 1941-42, 1946; Municipal Contagious Disease Hospital, Chicago, resident, 1941; University of Illinois, College of Medicine, Chicago, professor of pediatrics, 1946-53, director of Institute for Juvenile Research, 1952-53; State University of New York Upstate Medical Center, Syracuse, professor of pediatrics and chairman of department, 1953-65, dean of the faculty, 1965-70; Harvard University, Medical School, Cambridge, Mass., professor of child psychiatry and human development, 1971—; Children's Hospital Medical Center, Boston, Mass., psychiatrist-in-chief, 1971—; Judge Baker Guidance Center, Boston, director, 1971—; U.S. Department of Health, Education, and Welfare, Washington, D.C., assistant secretary for health, 1977—. Diplomate, American Board of Pediatrics. Member of expert advisory panel on maternal and child health, World Health Organization, 1963—; director, Project Headstart, Office of Economic Opportunity, 1965—; member of health research facilities scientific review committee, National Institute of Health, 1968; member of committee on basic research in education, National Research Council-National Academy of Sciences, 1968—. Consultant to Office of Health Affairs, U.S. Office of Economic Opportunity. *Military service:* U.S. Army Air Forces, 1942-46; became captain.

MEMBER: American Pediatric Society, American Psychiatric Association (distinguished fellow), American Public Health Association, Child Welfare League of America (vice-president, 1960-65), Institute of Medicine, Society for Pediatric Research, American Academy of Child Psychiatry (honorary member), American Orthopsychiatric Association (member of board of directors, 1963-65; vice-president, 1966-67), Society for Research in Child Development (president, 1967-69), American Medical Association (member of council on mental health, 1960-70), American Academy of Pediatrics, American Psychosomatic Society, Sigma Xi, Alpha Omega Alpha, Phi Eta Sigma. *Awards, honors:* Merkle scholar in medical science, 1948; *Parents' Magazine* award for outstanding service to children, 1966; Agnes Bruce Greig School award, 1966; C. Anderson Aldrich award, American Academy of Pediatrics, 1966; Distinguished Service award, U.S. Office of Economic Opportunity, presented at the White House, 1967; Martha May Eliot award, American Public Health Association, 1970.

WRITINGS: (With Morris Green) *Pediatric Diagnosis,* Saunders, 1962; (contributor) *Textbook of Pediatrics,* 8th edition (not associated with earlier editions), Saunders, 1964; *Currents in American Medicine: A Developmental View of Medical Care and Education,* Harvard University Press, 1969; (collaborator) Norman W. Houser, *Drugs: Facts on Their Use and Abuse,* Scott, Foresman, 1969; (collaborator) Andre Blanzaco, *VD: Facts You Should Know,* Lothrop, 1970; (with others) *Health and Growth,* Scott, Foresman, 1971; (collaborator) Houser, *About You and Smoking,* Scott, Foresman, 1971. Contributor of articles to professional journals.

* * *

RICHTER, Dorothy 1906-

PERSONAL: Born September 20, 1906, in Glenbeulah, Wis.; daughter of Frederick Alvin (a farmer) and Daisy (Barber) Baumann; married Julius Richter (an attorney), September 5, 1935; children: Juliann. *Education:* Attended Los Angeles Art Institute, 1926-28; Milwaukee State Teacher's College (now University of Wisconsin—Milwaukee), B.E., 1932. *Religion:* Methodist. *Home:* 282 East Tenth St., Fond du Lac, Wis. 54935.

WRITINGS: Fell's Guide to Hand Puppets and How to Make and Use Them, Fell, 1970; *Make Your Own Soap! Plain and Fancy,* Doubleday, 1974. Contributor to art and women's magazines.

WORK IN PROGRESS: Books on arts and crafts; researching handmade paper and handbound books.

* * *

RICKMAN, Geoffrey (Edwin) 1932-

PERSONAL: Born October 9, 1932, in Cherat, Pakistan; son of Charles Edwin (a professional soldier) and Ethel (Hill) Rickman; married Anna Wilson, April 18, 1959; children: Elizabeth Jane, David Edwin. *Education:* Oxford University, B.A. (first class honors), 1955, Diploma in Classical Archaelogy, 1958; Brasenose College, Oxford, M.A., 1958; Queen's College, Oxford, D.Phil., 1965. *Politics:* None. *Religion:* None. *Home:* 56 Hepburn Gardens, St. Andrews, Fife, Scotland. *Office:* Department of Ancient History, University of St. Andrews, St. Andrews, Fife, KY16 9AJ, Scotland.

CAREER: Henry Francis Pelham student at British School in Rome, Italy, 1958-59; Oxford University, Queen's College, Oxford, England, junior research fellow in Roman history and archaeology, 1959-62; University of St. Andrews, St. Andrews, Scotland, university lecturer, 1962-68, senior lecturer in ancient history and head of department, 1968—. *Military service:* British Army, Intelligence Corps, 1955-57. *Member:* Society of Antiquaries of London (fellow), Society for Promotion of Hellenic Studies, Society for Promotion of Roman Studies (council member, 1970—).

WRITINGS: Roman Granaries and Store Buildings, Cambridge University Press, 1971.

WORK IN PROGRESS: A book on the corn supply of Rome; research on other aspects of Roman history, art, architecture, and archaeology.

* * *

RIEGER, Shay 1929-

PERSONAL: Born November 24, 1929; married Silas Rieger, May 22, 1950 (divorced). *Education:* Studied at Art Students' League of New York and privately with Ibram Lassaw. *Politics:* Democrat. *Religion:* Jewish. *Home:* 30 Horatio St., New York, N.Y. 10014.

CAREER: Sculptor. *Member:* Artists Equity Association, National Association of Women Artists.

WRITINGS—Self-illustrated juveniles: *The Bronze Zoo,* Scribner, 1970; *The Stone Menagerie,* Scribner, 1970; *Animals in Clay,* Scribner, 1971; *Animals in Wood,* Scribner, 1971; *Our Family,* Lothrop, 1972; *Gargoyles, Monsters, and Other Beasts,* Lothrop, 1972. Also author of filmscripts, "The Bronze Zoo," 1977, "The Clay Circus," 1977, and "The Good Omen," 1978.

WORK IN PROGRESS: Heads of Stone and Feet of Clay; Religious Sculptures Then and Now.

BIOGRAPHICAL/CRITICAL SOURCES: Christian Science Monitor, March 13, 1971.

* * *

RIENITS, Rex 1909-1971

April 17, 1909—April 30, 1971; Australian journalist, playwright, and screenwriter. Obituaries: *Antiquarian Bookman,* June 7-14, 1971. (See index for *CA* sketch)

* * *

RIGDON, Raymond M. 1919-

PERSONAL: Born February 23, 1919; son of Raymond (a minister) and Emma Lou (Champion) Rigdon; married Doris Davis, May 28, 1948; children: Rebecca Ann, Robert Lee. *Education:* Mercer University, A.B., 1939; Southern Baptist Theological Seminary, M.Div., Ph.D., additional study at George Peabody College for Teachers, 1951-52, and Columbia University, 1956. *Home:* 6700 Currywood Dr., Nashville, Tenn. 37205.

CAREER: Christian educator; minister of education at Baptist church in Louisville, Ky., 1948-49; Southern Baptist Convention, Nashville, Tenn., editor for Baptist Sunday School Board, 1949-69, director of extension department, Southern Baptist Seminaries, 1969—. *Military service:* U.S. Army Air Forces, Combat Intelligence, World War II; served in the central Pacific theater. *Member:* National Association of Adult and Continuing Education, Society for Advancement of Continuing Education for Ministry, Tennessee Adult Education Association.

WRITINGS: (With Howard P. Colson) *Understanding Your Church's Curriculum,* Broadman, 1969; *Learning Is for Life,* Broadman, 1971. Also contributor to *Writing for the Religious Market,* Association Press. Contributor of articles to educational and religious periodicals.

* * *

RIGG, H(enry) K(ilburn) 1911-
(Henry Kilburn)

PERSONAL: Born January 11, 1911, in Newcastle, Del.; son of John (a clergyman) and Frances (Kilburn) Rigg; married Marjorie Matthai; children: Judith Hutchinson, John. *Education:* Educated in Alexandria, Va. *Politics:* Republican. *Religion:* Episcopalian. *Home:* Holly Beach Farm, Annapolis, Md. 21403. *Office:* Rigg's Marine Appraisals Ltd., 222 Severn Ave., Annapolis, Md. 21404.

CAREER: New Yorker, New York, N.Y., yachting editor, 1935-39; *Skipper Magazine,* Annapolis, Md., editor, 1952-68, publisher, 1968-71. Owner, Rigg's Marine Appraisals Ltd., Annapolis. *Military service:* U.S. Coast Guard, 1942-46; retired as commander; received Bronze Star. *Member:* Cruising Club of America, Ocean Cruising Club, Royal Ocean Racing Club, Annapolis Yacht Club.

WRITINGS: (Editor) *Tales of the Skipper,* Barre, 1968; *Rigg's Handbook of Nautical Etiquette,* Knopf, 1971. Contributor to yachting magazines.

WORK IN PROGRESS: Other books.

* * *

RIKON, Irving 1931-

PERSONAL: Born August 24, 1931, in Brooklyn, N.Y.; son of Joseph and Dorothy Rikon. *Education:* Columbia University, student; Illinois Institute of Technology, B.S., 1953, O.D., 1954. *Address:* c/o D. Rikon, Coventry East, Century Village, West Palm Beach, Fla. 33401.

CAREER: Private practice in optometry, West New York, N.J., 1954-69; teacher of American government and Asian history. Member of board of directors, Fort Lee Adult School of Education, Fort Lee, N.J. *Military service:* U.S. Army, 1954-56. *Member:* Toastmasters International, Forum Club of the Palm Beaches.

WRITINGS: Peace as It Can Be, Philosophical Library, 1970; "The Man Who Ate People Raw" (play), produced Off-Broadway, 1975. Did play adaptation of Lewis Carroll's *Alice in Wonderland,* for live actors and puppets, produced Off-Broadway, 1960. Also has written under several undisclosed pseudonyms. Newspaper columnist, "Write on with Rikon," featuring play reviews and celebrity interviews.

WORK IN PROGRESS: A novel; a non-fiction sequel to *Peace as It Can Be;* and "a non-fiction informal work that will take a fond look at some of the people in my community, this, a sociological study of national import."

SIDELIGHTS: Irving Rikon wrote *CA:* "I'm interested in government, politics, religion, briefly, anything that helps to explain people and nature: how they are, what they are, why they are, were, or will be, and what we can or cannot do to influence their future directions." He continued: "The older I get, the more I realize I can stop writing about the same as I can willingly cease breathing. A lonely lifestyle, I have rather a greater gregariousness than four walls can describe. But I write out of total conviction: My mind is unique, and I have worthy things to say, plus the ability to say them. I write both for myself and for an audience, for my readers with a certain love that only those walls may know." He spent 1970 and 1971 traveling around the world.

RILEY, James F. 1912-

PERSONAL: Born May 2, 1912, in Settle, Yorkshire, England; son of Frederic (an engineer) and Elizabeth (Harris) Riley; married Marina Fraser, April 29, 1943; children: Marina Elizabeth, Alastair James, Honor Marjorie, Paul Adrian Fraser. *Education:* University of Edinburgh, M.B. and Ch.B. (honors), F.R.C.S., 1938, D.M.R.T., 1948; University of St. Andrews, Ph.D., 1959. *Office:* Royal Infirmary, Dundee, Scotland.

CAREER: Royal Infirmary, Dundee, Scotland, consultant radiotherapist, 1947—. Reader in experimental medicine, University of Dundee, Dundee, Scotland. *Military service:* Royal Army Medical Corps, 1945-46; served in Indian Mobile Surgical Unit. *Member:* Royal Society of Edinburgh (fellow). *Awards, honors:* Shared with G. B. West the prize of American Association of Dermatologists for research on histamine in mast cells; Claude Bernard Medal of University of Montreal for research on mast cells.

WRITINGS: The Hammer and the Anvil: A Tribute to Michael Faraday, Dalesman Publishing, 1954; *The Mast Cells* (foreword by Sir Henry Dale), E. & S. Livingstone, 1959; *Introducing Biology,* Penguin, 1967.

WORK IN PROGRESS: Further research on mast cells and carcinogenesis in mice.

AVOCATIONAL INTERESTS: Collecting pictures and books, especially early books on atomic physics and on evolution.

* * *

RIMEL, Duane (Weldon) 1915-
(Peter Biggs, Eric Leggett, Andre Lemir, Rex Weldon)

PERSONAL: Surname is pronounced *Rye*-mel; born February 21, 1915, in Asotin, Wash.; son of Pearl Guy (a painter) and Florence (Wilsey) Rimel; married Ruth McClure (a secretary), September 2, 1944; children: Duane, Jr., William L., Kay, James Arthur. *Education:* Attended public schools in Asotin, Wash. *Politics:* Democrat. *Residence:* Lewiston, Idaho.

CAREER: Once a full-time professional jazz pianist, and still plays with small groups or solo on week ends; also former bartender, liquor store clerk, salesman for a department store and wholesale oil company, proofreader on a daily newspaper, and night clerk in a hotel; reporter for *Clarkston Herald,* Clarkston, Wash., 1942-47; editor of *Valley News* (weekly), Lewiston, Idaho, 1954; as a writer he calls himself "more of a commercial scribbler than an author." Former commissioner, Federal Housing Committee, Asotin County, Wash.; president, Lewiston Central Labor Council, 1952-53; secretary-treasurer, Musician's Local 664, Lewiston, 1952-59. *Member:* Elks.

WRITINGS: The Curse of Cain, McKay, 1945; *Motive for Murder,* Kemsley Newspapers, 1945; *The Jury Is Out,* Kemsley Newspapers, 1947; *Death Call,* Novel Books, 1961; *Hot Package,* Novel Books, 1961; *The River Is Cold,* Vega Books, 1962; (contributor) August Derleth and James Turner, editors, *Selected Letters, Volume IV: H. P. Lovecraft,* Arkham, 1976.

Under pseudonym Rex Weldon; all published by Brandon House: *Party Wife,* 1967; *Shy One,* 1967; *Wife for the Taking,* 1967; *Your Wife for Mine,* 1967; *No Bed of Her Own,* 1968; *Limit for Laura,* 1968; *Lavendar House,* 1968; *Try Me Again,* 1968; *Wake Up, My Love,* 1968; *Three Women for Curt,* 1969.

Author of about eighty other paperback books under various pseudonyms, published by Bee-Line Books, Greenleaf Classics, Saber Books, Merit Books, Midwood Books, United Graphics, and Publisher's Export Co., 1962-71; forty-one paperbacks for Carlyle Communications, Inc., 1972-76. Poem included in *Dark of the Moon,* edited by August Derleth, Arkham House, 1947, and in *Arkham Collector,* 1967. Verse, short stories and novellas have been published in magazines, including *Progressive Youth, Weird Tales, Future Fiction, Jungle Stories,* and other pulps; articles, some illustrated with his own photographs, have appeared in *Author and Journalist, Idaho Outdoor Guide,* and *Portland Oregonian.*

WORK IN PROGRESS: Tales of Old Asotin, a collection of published reminiscences about his home town; a collection of the verse he has published over a twenty-five-year period; "several modern suspense books to feature an already established hero, detective extraordinary, Mark Jason"; a modern suspense novel, *It All Came Down;* a long quasibiographical novel, *The Talisman;* and a long novel about the distant future is planned.

SIDELIGHTS: Duane Rimel is a self-taught musician and writer, and an amateur anthropologist. He was a former correspondent of the late Howard P. Lovecraft, and the latter's letters to Rimel are in the Lovecraft collection at Brown University Library, some of which have been published.

Rimel wrote to *CA:* "H. P. Lovecraft had a tremendous influence during the short time of the correspondence, 1934-37, but I was much too young and immature at the time to appreciate it." He continued, "In the sixties a correspondence with August Derleth proved encouraging and enlightening, but the authors who influenced me most, just from reading them, are James Cain, Raymond Chandler, John Steinbeck, William Faulkner, Thomas Wolfe, Aldous Huxley and George Orwell." His advice to aspiring writers is: "Make sure you have sufficient talent to succeed. Try a reliable agent." Of his own work he says: "I write best in the early morning, with lots of coffee and cigars. The only things I have written that I feel have any real artistic merit are several early weird poems. Much of the rest is commercial, some of it junk."

BIOGRAPHICAL/CRITICAL SOURCES: August Derleth and James Turner, editors, *Selected Letters, Volume IV: H. P. Lovecraft,* Arkham, 1976.

*   *   *

RINEHART, Stanley Marshall, Jr.   1897-1969

August 18, 1897—April 26, 1969; American editor and publisher. Obituaries: *New York Times,* April 27, 1969.

*   *   *

RING, Alfred A.   1905-

PERSONAL: Born January 25, 1905, in Beuthen, Germany; naturalized U.S. citizen; son of Salo and Elizabeth (Wolfson) Ring; married Elsie B. Bardusch, July 30, 1932 (died December 21, 1973); married Emily Stevens Maclachlan, April 20, 1975; children: (first marriage) Katharine Elizabeth (Mrs. Edward Shepperd), Georgia Ann (Mrs. Alan Rolfe). *Education:* New York University, B.S. (magna cum laude), 1942, M.B.A., 1944, Ph.D., 1947. *Politics:* Republican. *Religion:* Episcopalian. *Address:* Box 13535, University Station, Gainesville, Fla. 32601.

CAREER: Westchester Lighting Co., Mount Vernon, N.Y., senior estimator, 1932-42; New York University,

New York, N.Y., instructor in economics, 1943-47, lecturer in Graduate School of Economics, 1945-47; University of Florida, Gainesville, professor of real estate and university appraiser, 1947-70, chairman of department of real estate and urban land studies, 1960-70; Noram Secured Income N.V. (Netherlands), independent valuer, 1970—. Appraiser, Certified Veterans Administration, 1955-65; appraiser, consultant, and expert witness in federal and state courts. Public utilities consultant, H. Zinder & Associates, Washington, D.C., 1970—. Lecturer, Wichita State University, 1971-72, and Portland State University, 1972. Member of board of directors, Long Cove Point Association; member of advisory board, British American Investment Fund. *Member:* American Economic Association, American Institute of Real Estate Appraisers, Society of Real Estate Appraisers, National Tax Association, Tax Institute of America, Florida Association of Realtors (honorary member), Gainesville Board of Realtors, Beta Gamma Sigma, Lambda Alpha.

WRITINGS: (With Philip A. Benson and Nelson L. North) *Real Estate Principles and Practices,* 4th edition (Ring was not associated with earlier editions), Prentice-Hall, 1954, 8th edition (with Jerome Dasso), 1977; *Real Estate Questions and Practice Problems,* Prentice-Hall, 1955, published as *Questions and Problems in Real Estate Principles and Practices,* 1960, 4th edition, 1977; *The Valuation of Real Estate,* Prentice-Hall, 1963, 2nd edition, 1970; *Study Guide for Real Estate Principles,* Prentice-Hall, for U.S. Armed Forces Institute, 1969; (with Dasso) *Fundamentals of Real Estate,* Prentice-Hall, 1977. Contributor to *Encyclopedia Americana;* contributor of more than thirty articles to real estate and economics journals.

SIDELIGHTS: Real Estate Principles and Practices, which Alfred Ring coauthored, is, after fifty-five years, in his words "still the leading text in its field." He attributes its success to the ability of its author to "take his reader literally by the hand and to guide him with interest-like Alice in Wonderland-through the maze of specialized knowledge." Mr. Ring believes a sense of humor, "the interjection of occasional remarks that under or overstate a cause" is important even to the creation of a textbook. He comments, "To this day a sense of humor has proven an excellent anchor that prevents drifting into nothingness."

*   *   *

RISTE, Olav   1933-

PERSONAL: Born April 11, 1933, in Volda, Norway; son of Olav (a headmaster) and Bergliot (Meidell) Riste; married Ruth Pittman (a cyto-technician), June 15, 1964. *Education:* University of Oslo, Cand.philol., 1959; St. Antony's College, Oxford, D.Phil., 1963. *Home:* Husarveien 18, Billingstad 1362, Norway.

CAREER: United Nations, New York, N.Y., special interne, 1956-57; Norwegian Armed Forces, War Historical Department, Oslo, Norway, civil historian, 1964—. Occasional lecturer, University of Oslo, 1964—; research fellow, Harvard University, 1967-68; visiting professor, Free University of Berlin, 1972-73. *Military service:* Norwegian Army, Signal Corps, one year.

WRITINGS: The Neutral Ally: Norway's Relations with Belligerent Powers in the First World War, Humanities, 1965; (editor, and author with Johannes Andenaes and Magne Skodvin) *Norway and the Second World War,* J. G. Tanum, 1966; (with Berit Noekleby) *Norway 1940-1945: The Resistance Movement,* International Publication Service,

1970; 'London-regjeringa': Norge i krigsalliansen 1940-1945, Volume I: 1940-1942, Proevetid, Det Norske Samlaget, 1973. Contributor to historical journals.

WORK IN PROGRESS: A study of the Norwegian Government-in-exile and its cooperation with the Allies, 1940-45, Volume II.

* * *

RITCHIE, Edwin 1931-
(Voltaire Lewis)

PERSONAL: Born January 8, 1931, in Long Island, N.Y.; son of Lewis E. and Amy (Smith) Ritchie. Education: Attended Pratt Institute; studied fine art at American School of Design and Grand Central School of Art, New York, N.Y. Politics: Independent. Religion: Agnostic.

CAREER: Worked in advertising and public relations and held various positions in New York, N.Y.; international citizen in conference and public relations division of United Nations for one year; author of weekly column, "Park Bench," 1965—. Military service: Served briefly in U.S. Merchant Marine.

WRITINGS: A Rose in December (novel), Courthouse Press, 1967, published as A Light in Eden, 1971; (under pseudonym Voltaire Lewis) Godiva Marlow, Courthouse Press, 1968; (under pseudonym Voltaire Lewis) Insomniacs' Cabaret, Courthouse Press, 1970.

Author of a tribute to President John F. Kennedy, "Elegy for November 22nd, 1963," published in various periodicals in America and abroad. Contributor of fiction to various periodicals and flying publications, and of poetry to local weekly newspapers.

WORK IN PROGRESS: A novel about "the human condition at seventeen."

SIDELIGHTS: According to the biographical data contained in the 1971 Courthouse edition of A Light in Eden (originally entitled A Rose in December), Edwin Ritchie claims that "with some eighty appearances in a decade in most leading national magazines and newspapers, he should be the best-known writer of Letters To The Editor in the USA."

Ritchie also claims that Erich Segal's Love Story bears a striking similarity to his own novel. "In view of the manufactured hubbub about a current best-seller called Love Story," Ritchie wrote in his June 4, 1970, "Park Bench" column, "I must instruct the interested that Segal's book distinctly resembles my own carefully disguised autobiographical novel, A Rose in December, which was published in a limited and unreviewed clothbound edition in 1967 and which was all but quietly sold out, in some cases to a campus audience.... There are of course differences, relating usually to what appear to be thoughtful rearrangements of props and settings and themes, but these may be seen in retrospect to be manifestly superficial as contrasted with the duplications, which remain conspicuous—too much so to be coincidental."

AVOCATIONAL INTERESTS: Painting, music, psychology.†

* * *

ROBBINS, Martin 1931-

PERSONAL: Born July 10, 1931, in Denver, Colo.; son of Sam M. (a businessman) and Evelyn (Bricker) Robbins. Education: University of Colorado, B.A. (cum laude), 1952;

State University of Iowa, M.A., 1959; Brandeis University, Ph.D., 1968. Religion: Jewish. Office: Radcliffe Institute, Cambridge, Mass. 02138.

CAREER: Public relations feature writer at State University of Iowa, 1959-61, and Yeshiva University, 1960; Northeastern University, Boston, Mass., assistant professor of English, 1963-73; Harvard College, Cambridge, Mass., teacher of writing, 1973-76; currently member of faculty at Radcliffe Institute, Cambridge. Senior Fulbright-Hays lecturer, National University of Buenos Aires, 1973; visiting associate professor of drama, Boston University, 1974; teacher of short story writing, Boston College, 1974. Public relations director, Aspen Music Festival, 1953, 1954. Gives poetry readings, lecture-recitals, and song recitals; appearances on WHDH-TV, WGBH-TV, and WBZ, as lecturer, discussant, singer, and interviewer. Member: P.E.N., New England Poetry Club.

WRITINGS—Poetry: A Refrain of Roses, Alan Swallow, 1965; A Reply to the Headlines: Poems 1965-70, Swallow Press, 1970.

Plays: "The Seasons of His Mercies: John Donne at St. Paul's, Christmas, 1624," first produced in Boston at Church of the Advent, December 21, 1969; "The Revolution Starts Inside" (one-act), first produced in Boston at Northeastern University, April 23, 1970; "Mussorgsky on Seeing the Pictures at an Exhibition" (dramatic monologue with music and choreography), first performed at Northeastern University, April 3, 1971; "To Form a More Perfect Union" (a dramatic oratorio), first performed at College of William and Mary, December 4, 1976.

Translator: Schumann, "A Woman's Life and Love," first performed by Margot Blum Schevill, 1969; Liederkreis, Eichendorff, 1970; Scores and Sketches (music textbook), Addison-Wesley, 1971; Gottfried Benn, Countermeasures, in press.

Contributor to Saturday Review, New York Times, New York Herald Tribune, San Francisco Review, West Coast Review, Yankee, Chelsea, English Language Notes, Art International, Boston Globe, New Republic, Harvard Magazine, and Colorado Quarterly. Assistant editor, Labor Weekly.

WORK IN PROGRESS: A full length play, "Windows"; a book, Shakespeare's Sweet Music; "A Memorial to the Innocents."

AVOCATIONAL INTERESTS: Fishing, hiking.

* * *

ROBERTS, Allen 1914-

PERSONAL: Born February 20, 1914, in New York, N.Y.; son of Maurice (a theater director) and Emma (Michaelson) Roberts; married Mildred Stern (a physical therapist). Education: New York University, A.B., 1936. Politics: Democrat. Home: 110-34 73rd Rd., Forest Hills, N.Y. 11375. Agent: Albert Zuckerman, 303 West 42nd St., New York, N.Y. 10036.

WRITINGS: The Turning Point: The Assassination of Louis Barthou and King Alexander I of Yugoslavia, St. Martin's, 1970; Web of Intrigue (biography of Admiral Welhelm Canaris), Moore Publishing, in press. Record columnist, Long Island Entertainer. Regular contributor of articles to Soho Weekly News; contributor to national magazines.

WORK IN PROGRESS: A biography of the conductor, Leopold Stokowski.

AVOCATIONAL INTERESTS: Music, playing the piano.

ROBERTS, Brian 1930-

PERSONAL: Born March 19, 1930, in London, England; son of Henry Albert (an engineer) and Edith (Watts) Roberts. *Education:* St. Mary's College, Twickenham, England, Teacher's Certificate, 1955; University of London, Diploma in Sociology, 1958. *Religion:* Roman Catholic. *Home:* Gum Tree Cottage, Teubes Rd., Kommetjie, Cape, South Africa. *Agent:* Marie Rodell, 141 East 55th Street, New York, N.Y. 10022.

CAREER: Teacher in England and South Africa, 1958-67; free-lance writer. *Military service:* Royal Navy, 1949-53.

WRITINGS: Ladies in the Veld, J. Murray, 1965; *Cecil Rhodes and the Princess,* Lippincott, 1969; *Churchills in Africa,* Taplinger, 1971; *The Diamond Magnates,* Scribner, 1972; *The Zulu Kings,* Scribner, 1974. Contributor to newspapers and magazines in England and South Africa.

WORK IN PROGRESS: A history of Kimberly, South Africa's diamond city.

BIOGRAPHICAL/CRITICAL SOURCES: Observer Review, July 6, 1969, November 20, 1970; *Times Literary Supplement,* July 31, 1969; *New York Times,* August 5, 1969; *Books and Bookmen,* September, 1969.

*   *   *

ROBERTS, Derrell C(layton) 1927-

PERSONAL: Born May 24, 1927, in Ocilla, Ga.; son of William C. (a farmer) and Marie (Sandifer) Roberts; married Leta Faye Hammond, August 17, 1955; children: Ree, Marianna, Danalee. *Education:* Georgia Southern College, B.S., 1949; George Peabody College, M.A., 1950; University of Georgia, Ph.D., 1958. *Politics:* Democrat. *Religion:* Baptist. *Home:* 1202 Sherwood Dr., Dalton, Ga. 30720. *Office:* Office of the President, Dalton Junior College, Dalton, Ga. 30720.

CAREER: Assistant principal in public school in Tifton, Ga., 1949-55; Georgia State College of Business Administration (now Georgia State University), Atlanta, instructor in history, 1957-58; Florida Southern College, Lakeland, associate professor of history and chairman of department, 1958-63; Mobile College, Mobile, Ala., professor of history and chairman of department of social science, 1963-66; Kennesaw Junior College, Marietta, Ga., professor of history and dean of the College, 1966-70; Dalton Junior College, Dalton, Ga., president of college, 1970—. *Military service:* U.S. Army, 1946-47. *Member:* Southern Historical Association, Georgia Historical Society, Florida Historical Society.

WRITINGS: Joseph E. Brown and the Politics of Reconstruction, University of Alabama Press, 1973. Contributor to *Georgia Historical Quarterly, Florida Historical Quarterly, Georgia Review, Negro History Bulletin, Alabama Historical Quarterly, Atlanta Economic Review, Wesleyan Quarterly Review, Atlanta Historical Bulletin,* and other journals.

WORK IN PROGRESS: Research in the area of state legislatures and social welfare, and in social welfare in the reconstruction era.

*   *   *

ROBERTS, I(olo) F(rancis) 1925-

PERSONAL: Born July 9, 1925, in Liverpool, England; married Menai Pritchard; children: Nia F. *Education:* University College of North Wales, B.Sc. (honors), 1946, M.Sc., 1961. *Office:* Department of Education, University of Keele, Keele, Staffordshire, England.

CAREER: Raine's Foundation School for Boys, Stepney, London, England, chemistry master, 1947-50; Sir Thomas Jones School, Amlwch, Anglesey, Wales, senior science master, 1950-56; Flintshire Technical College, Flintshire, Wales, lecturer in chemistry, 1956-62; University of Keele, Keele, Staffordshire, England, lecturer, 1962-70, senior lecturer in education, 1970—. *Member:* Royal Institute of Chemistry (fellow).

WRITINGS: (With Leonard M. Cantor) *Further Education in England and Wales,* Routledge & Kegan Paul, 1969, 2nd edition, 1972; *Crystals and Their Structures,* Methuen, 1974. Contributor to science journals.

*   *   *

ROBERTS, Joan Ila 1935-

PERSONAL: Born June 26, 1935, in Salt Lake City, Utah; daughter of Wallace B. and Ila Roberts. *Education:* University of Utah, B.A. (with honors), 1957; Columbia University, M.A., 1960, Ed.D., 1970. *Address:* 444 North 12th W., Salt Lake City, Utah (permanent); and 235 Waring Rd., Syracuse, N.Y.

CAREER: University of Utah, Salt Lake City, English teaching assistant, 1956-57; Herrold Associates Management Consultants, New York City, consultant, supervisor of testing, 1958-61; Columbia University, Teachers College, New York City, trainer and research assistant in Group Dynamics Workshop for Rehabilitation Counselors, 1961; research staff member, Teachers for East Africa, Columbia University, University of London, London, England, and Makerere College, Kampala, Uganda, 1961-63; Hunter College of the City University of New York, New York City, research associate, Teacher Resources for Urban Education, 1964-67; University of Wisconsin—Madison, assistant professor in department of educational policy studies, 1968-75; State University of New York Upstate Medical Center, Syracuse, associate professor, 1976—. Adjunct associate professor, Syracuse University, 1976—.

MEMBER: American Anthropological Association, American Association of University Women, American Psychological Association, American Sociological Association, Council on Anthropology and Education, Society for Applied Anthropology, Society for the Psychological Study of Social Issues, National Organization for Women (member of national committee to review projects on sexism and education), Syracuse University Women's Studies Committee.

WRITINGS: (Editor) *School Children in the Urban Slum: Readings in Social Science Research* (originally published in experimental offset printing edition as *School Children in the Urban Slum: A Book of Readings in Social Psychology for Teachers,* Hunter College of the City University of New York, 1965), Free Press, 1967, 2nd edition, 1968; *Scene of the Battle: Group Behavior in Urban Classrooms* (originally published in experimental offset printing edition as *Group Behavior in Urban Classrooms,* Hunter College of the City University of New York, 1968), Doubleday, 1970; (editor) *Beyond Intellectual Sexism: A New Woman, A New Reality,* McKay, 1976, (editor with Sherrie K. Akinsanya) *Educational Patterns and Cultural Configurations: The Anthropology of Education,* McKay, 1976; (editor with Akinsanya) *Schooling in the Cultural Context: Anthropological Studies of Education,* McKay, 1976. Also author of two monographs, *The Training of American Teachers for Work Overseas* and *The Selection of American Teachers for Work Overseas,* both 1964.

Contributor of articles to *Comparative Education Review,*

Nursing Forum, Nursing Outlook, Canadian Nurse, Women in Higher Education, Female Studies, Theory into Practice, and *Interchange.*

WORK IN PROGRESS: A book tentatively entitled *The Ethos of Learning.*

* * *

ROBERTS, Myron 1923-

PERSONAL: Born September 6, 1923, in Los Angeles, Calif.; son of Harry and Rose (Kessler) Roberts; married Estelle Caloia, 1944; children: Cathy, Victoria. *Education:* Los Angeles State College (now California State University, Los Angeles), B.A., 1949, M.A., 1967. *Home:* 1054 West Via Romales, San Dimas, Calif. 91773. *Office:* Department of English, Chaffey College, Alta Loma, Calif. 91701.

CAREER: Reporter for *Honolulu Star Bulletin,* Honolulu, Hawaii, *Los Angeles Examiner,* Los Angeles, Calif., and *Savannah Morning News,* Savannah, Ga.; teacher of history and English in California junior and senior high schools, 1949-55; Chaffey College, Alta Loma, Calif., associate professor of English, 1956—. Executive secretary to Lieutenant Governor of California, 1962-64. Has worked as general manager and columnist, Advertiser-Press Newspapers, Hawthorne, Calif. Frequently appears on radio and television public affairs shows. *Military service:* U.S. Army Air Forces, 1942-45.

WRITINGS: A Nation of Strangers and Other Essays, W. C. Brown, 1967; (with Lincoln Haynes and Sasha Gilien) *The Begatting of a President,* Ballantine, 1969; *The Roots of Rebellion,* W. C. Brown, 1970; (with Michael Malone) *Pop to Culture* (English literature text), Holt, 1971; *Writing under Thirty* (English literature text), Scott, Foresman, 1971; (with John Moore) *American Politics,* Macmillan, 1976. Columnist, *Theater Arts,* 1969—. Contributor to *Saturday Review, West Magazine,* and to U.S. Information Service publications abroad. Associate editor, *Los Angeles Magazine,* 1960-71; former editor and publisher, *West Covina News* and *Manhattan Beach Tide;* former editor, *Pomona Today.*

SIDELIGHTS: Myron Roberts, Lincoln Haynes, and Sasha Gilien printed and marketed *The Begatting of a President* themselves when their "ugly child," as one local distributor called the book, failed to find a market. Ultimately California reviewers began to notice the book, but the trio claims that forty-four New York publishers turned them down before Ballantine offered a contract. Since then *The Begatting* has been produced as a comedy record with Orson Welles as narrator and condensed for United Features syndication to newspapers.

* * *

ROBERTSON, Constance (Pierrepont Noyes) (Dana Scott)

PERSONAL: Born in Niagara Falls, Canada; daughter of Pierrepont Burt and Corinna (Kinsley) Noyes; married Miles E. Robertson, August 18, 1918 (died, 1972). *Education:* Attended University of Wisconsin. *Home:* Kenwood, Oneida, N.Y. 13421. *Agent:* Curtis Brown Ltd., 575 Madison Ave., New York, N.Y. 10022.

CAREER: Writer. *Member:* Author's League, English Speaking Union, Onondaga Historical Association, Oneida County Historical Society, Madison County Historical Society, Kappa Kappa Gamma.

WRITINGS—All novels, except as indicated: *Enchanted Avenue,* Longmans, Green, 1931; (under pseudonym Dana Scott) *Five Fatal Letters,* Farrar & Rinehart, 1937; *Seek-no-Further,* Farrar & Rinehart, 1938; *Salute to the Hero,* Farrar & Rinehart, 1942; *Fire Bell in the Night,* Holt, 1944; *The Unterrified,* Holt, 1946; *The Golden Circle,* Random House, 1951; *Six Weeks in March,* Random House, 1953; *Go and Catch a Falling Star,* Random House, 1957; (editor and author of introduction) *Oneida Community: An Autobiography, 1851-1876,* Syracuse University Press, 1970.

WORK IN PROGRESS: Editing *Oneida Community: The Breakup, 1876-1881,* for Syracuse University Press; a third volume of the history of the Oneida Community.

SIDELIGHTS: The granddaughter of John Humphrey Noyes, founder of the Oneida Community in New York, Mrs. Robertson uses the setting of her native state as a background for her historical novels. Most critics find her books accurate in detail and scholarship. The *New Yorker* reviewer called *The Unterrified* "a monumental work of historical investigation and a fine novel, lit by very subtle discernment." Others appreciate the style with which Mrs. Robertson presents a period in American life. Jane Cobb believes that she "brings sympathy and understanding to most of her characters, and a wholesome dislike to those who deserve it. She has written paragraphs of real beauty about weather and landscape without slowing the pace of her story." Mary Ross agrees. "A prosaic setting and a situation fraught with ignoble emotions provide a base from which rises, wholly credibly, a story that frequently achieves the spaciousness of poetry."

BIOGRAPHICAL/CRITICAL SOURCES: New York Times, October 25, 1931, July 31, 1938, March 29, 1942, April 30, 1944, June 16, 1946, November 4, 1951, January 18, 1953, July 28, 1957; *Books,* November 1, 1931, January 24, 1938, March 29, 1942; *Saturday Review,* July 30, 1938, March 28, 1942, June 15, 1946, November 24, 1951, January 24, 1953, August 10, 1957; *New Yorker,* March 28, 1942, June 22, 1946; *Atlantic,* May, 1942; *Commonweal,* May 26, 1944, July 12, 1946; *Christian Science Monitor,* June 28, 1946; *Chicago Sunday Tribune,* January 18, 1953; *New York Herald Tribune,* January 18, 1953, August 11, 1957.

* * *

ROBERTSON, E(smonde) M(anning) 1923-

PERSONAL: Born May 1, 1923, in Reigate, London; son of Manning Durdin and Nora Kathrine (Parsons) Robertson; married Aline Helene Herrmann, September 2, 1963; children: Patrick Otto. *Education:* University of Edinburgh, student, 1950. *Religion:* Episcopalian. *Home:* "Crendon" 4, Chevening Rd., Chipstead, Sevenoaks, Kent, England. *Office:* Department of International History, London School of Economics and Political Science, University of London, London WC2A 2AE, England.

CAREER: Cabinet Office, Historical Section, London, England, researcher, 1951-55; Institut fuer Zeitgeschichte, Munich, Germany, researcher, 1958-61; Queens University, Belfast, Northern Ireland, lecturer, 1962-63; University of Edinburgh, Edinburgh, Scotland, lecturer, 1963-70; University of London, London School of Economics and Political Science, London, lecturer in international history, 1971—. *Military service:* British Army, 1942-47; became warrant officer.

WRITINGS: Barbarossa (monograph), Cabinet Office, 1952; *Hitler's Plans for the Invasion of Russia* (monograph), Cabinet Office, 1952; *Hitler's Pre-War Policy and Military Plans, 1933-39,* Longmans, Green, 1963; (contributor)

G. Rossini, editor, *L'Europa fra la due Guerre,* [Turin], 1966; *The Origins of the Second World War: Historical Interpretations,* St. Martin's, 1970. Contributor to European journals.

WORK IN PROGRESS: Mussolini as Empire Builder, 1932-1936, for Macmillan; *The Breakdown of British Rule in Ireland, 1912-1922.*

SIDELIGHTS: In a review of *Origins of the Second World War,* James Joll called E. M. Robertson's work "an important and interesting book which confirms the view that Hitler's immediate plans both in foreign and military policy were short-term ones, even though his terrifying long-term aims were inflexibly pursued behind the opportunism of the day-to-day policies which misled his opponents."

AVOCATIONAL INTERESTS: Russian icons, Bavarian history.

BIOGRAPHICAL/CRITICAL SOURCES: New York Review of Books, February 15, 1968.

* * *

ROBERTSON, Roland 1938-

PERSONAL: Born August 7, 1938, in Norwich, Norfolk, England; son of Bernard Hugh and Ivy (Bristowe) Robertson; married Jennifer Shaw, April 15, 1961; children: Mark, Thomas, Joel. *Education:* University of Southampton, B.Sc. (honors), 1960; London School of Economics and Political Science, student, 1960-61; University of Leeds, student, 1961-62. *Politics:* Social Democrat. *Religion:* None. *Home:* 909 South Negley, Pittsburgh, Pa. 15232. *Office:* Department of Sociology, University of Pittsburgh, Pittsburgh, Pa. 15260.

CAREER: University of Leeds, Leeds, England, assistant lecturer, 1962-64, lecturer in sociology, 1964-65; University of Essex, Colchester, England, lecturer in sociology, 1965-67; University of Pittsburgh, Pittsburgh, Pa., associate professor, 1967-70, adjunct professor, 1970-73, professor of sociology, 1973—. Professor of sociology and head of department, University of York, 1970-74; Distinguished Visiting Professor, Chinese University of Hong Kong, 1971. *Member:* American Sociological Association, Society for the Scientific Study of Religion.

WRITINGS: (With John Peter Nettl) *International Systems and the Modernization of Societies,* Basic Books, 1968; (editor) *The Sociology of Religion: Selected Readings,* Penguin, 1969; *The Sociological Interpretation of Religion,* Schocken, 1970; (with Laurie Taylor) *Deviance, Crime and Socio-Legal Control,* Fred B. Rothman, 1973; *Meaning and Change,* Blackwell, 1977. Contributor to *American Sociological Review, American Journal of Sociology, British Journal of Sociology, Sociological Review, History and Theory, Journal of Conflict Resolution, Population Studies, New Society, Political Studies,* and other journals. Editor, *Clarion,* 1960-61; member of editorial board, *Journal of Mathematical Sociology,* 1969-72, *Sociological Analysis,* 1975-78.

WORK IN PROGRESS: Culture and Cultural Change, for Blackwell and Harper; *Identity and Authority,* for Blackwell; *Georg Simmel,* for Blackwell.

SIDELIGHTS: Roland Robertson lists his "main vocational interests" as sociology of religion, contemporary sociological theory, history of ideas, international relations, and philosophical anthropology.

ROBINSON, Daniel Sommer 1888-

PERSONAL: Born October 19, 1888, in North Salem, Ind.; son of William Matthews (a lawyer) and Lucretia (Cassity) Robinson; married Oma Glasburn (a former teacher, and genealogical writer), June 6, 1912; children: Daniel Sommer, Jr. (deceased), Joan (Mrs. Charles R. Clark), Sydney Caroline Robinson Charles. *Education:* Butler University, B.A., 1910; Yale University Divinity School, M.A., 1911, B.D. (magna cum laude), 1912; University of Breslau, graduate study, 1912-13; Harvard University, Ph.D., 1917. *Politics:* Republican. *Home:* 3640 Homeland Dr., Los Angeles, Calif. 90008.

CAREER: Congregational minister with pastorates in Billings, Mont., 1913-14, and Newport, N.H., 1917-18; University of Wisconsin—Madison, instructor, 1919-20, assistant professor of philosophy, 1920-22; Miami University, Oxford, Ohio, professor of philosophy and head of department, 1922-29; Indiana University, Bloomington, professor of philosophy and head of department, 1929-39; Butler University, Indianapolis, Ind., president, 1939-42; University of Southern California, Los Angeles, professor of philosophy and director of School of Philosophy, 1946-54, director emeritus, 1954—. Bethany College, Bethany, W.Va., John Hay Whitney Visiting Professor, 1954-55, distinguished service professor, 1955-58; Hill Family Foundation Lecturer at Macalester College and Hamline University, 1956-57. Member, Indiana State Board of Education, 1940-41; member, Indiana State Historical and Library Board, 1940-42. Delegate, Ninth International Congress of Philosophy, Paris, France, 1937. *Military service:* U.S. Navy, chaplain, 1917, 1942-46; became commander.

MEMBER: American Philosophical Association (president, 1942-44), International Phenomenological Society, Military Chaplains Association of the U.S.A. *Awards, honors:* Dwight traveling fellow of Yale University Divinity School in Germany, 1912-13; Litt.D., Marietta College, 1937.

WRITINGS: The Principles of Reasoning, Appleton, 1924, 3rd revised edition, 1947; *The God of the Liberal Christian,* Appleton, 1926; *An Introduction to Living Philosophy,* Crowell, 1932; *Political Ethics,* Crowell, 1935; *The Principles of Conduct: An Introduction to Theoretical and Applied Ethics,* Appleton, 1948; *Critical Issues in Philosophy,* Christopher, 1955; *Royce and Hocking: American Idealists,* Christopher, 1968.

Editor: *Illustrations of the Methods of Reasoning,* Appleton, 1927; *An Anthology of Recent Philosophy* (twentieth-century philosophy), Crowell, 1929, reprinted, 1976; *An Anthology of Modern Philosophy* (1500-1900), Crowell, 1931; *Powell Lectures at Indiana University,* First Series, 1937, Second Series, 1938, Third Series, 1939; *Royce's Logical Essays,* W. C. Brown, 1951; Reinhold F. A. Hoernle, *Studies in Philosophy,* Allen & Unwin, 1952, Harvard University Press, 1953; Heinrich Gomperz, *Philosophical Studies,* Christopher, 1953; *The Story of Scottish Philosophy,* Exposition Press, 1961.

Contributor: *The Nature of Religious Experience: Essays in Honor of Douglas Clyde Macintosh,* Harper, 1937; *Philosophic Thought in France and the United States,* University of Buffalo Press, 1950; *Philosophy, Religion and the Coming of World Civilization: Essays in Honor of William Ernest Hocking,* Nijhoff, 1966.

Translator: Georg Wobbermin, *The Christian Belief in God,* Yale University Press, 1918; (with Theophil Menzel) Georg Wobbermin, *The Nature of Religion,* Crowell, 1935. Contributor of articles and essays to journals. Book review editor, *Philosophy and Phenomenological Research.*

* * *

ROBINSON, Jean O. 1934-

PERSONAL: Born August 19, 1934, in La Crosse, Wis.; daughter of Henry Adam (a hardware merchant) and Amanda (Lueck) Kroner; married Donald W. Robinson (an art director), March 12, 1955; children: Lindsey Jean, Carol Elizabeth. *Education:* Wisconsin State College—La Crosse (now University of Wisconsin—La Crosse), student, 1953-54. *Religion:* Lutheran. *Home:* 18 Mercer Hill Rd., Ambler, Pa. 19002.

CAREER: WKBT Television, La Crosse, Wis., copywriter, 1954-55; KTRI Radio, Sioux City, Iowa, copywriter, 1955-56; KSTP Radio & Television, Minneapolis, Minn., copywriter, 1956-57; has also worked as a librarian in La Crosse, Wis., and in Minneapolis, Minn., where she was a church librarian for six years; writer for children.

WRITINGS: Francie (juvenile novel), Follett, 1970; *The Secret Life of T. K. Dearing,* Seabury, 1973; *The Strange, But Wonderful Cosmic Awareness of Duffy Moon,* Seabury, 1974; *The Mystery of Lincoln Detweiler and the Dog Who Barked Spanish,* Follett, 1977. Writer of two hundred career guidance pamphlets for teen-agers, published by Finney. Contributor of short stories and articles to *Ingenue, Child Life, Coed, Jack and Jill, American Girl, Modern Bride, Lady's Circle, Weight Watchers, Girltalk, Camping Journal, Organic Gardening and Farming, Midnight,* and other periodicals.

WORK IN PROGRESS: Another juvenile novel and articles for magazines.

SIDELIGHTS: Special adaptations of *The Secret Life of T. K. Dearing,* 1975, and *The Strange, But Wonderful Cosmic Awareness of Duffy Moon,* 1976, were produced for ABC-TV afterschool programming.

* * *

ROBINSON, T(homas) M(ore) 1936-

PERSONAL: Born November 4, 1936, in Durham, England; son of Alban Bainbridge (an engineer) and Emilia (Tolmie) Robinson; married Judith Ann Kirby (an editor), August 11, 1964. *Education:* University of Durham, B.A. (first class honors), 1961; research at Jesus College, Oxford, 1961-62, 1963-64, and Sorbonne, University of Paris, 1962-63; Oxford University, B.Litt., 1965. *Office:* Department of Philosophy, University of Toronto, Toronto, Ontario, Canada.

CAREER: University of Calgary, Calgary, Alberta, assistant professor of philosophy and classics, 1964-67; University of Toronto, Toronto, Ontario, visiting associate professor of classics at University College, 1967-68, associate professor of philosophy in the university, 1968—, associate professor of classics at Trinity College, 1971—, associate chairman of philosophy department, 1974-77. Visiting professor, Columbia University, summer, 1967. *Member:* American Philological Association, Canadian Philosophical Association, Classical Association of Canada (member of council, 1969-76).

WRITINGS: Plato's Psychology, University of Toronto Press, 1970; (contributor) J. P. Anton and G. L. Kustas, editors, *Essays in Ancient Greek Philosophy,* State University of New York Press, 1971; (contributor) J. King-Farlow and W. R. Shea, editors, *Values and the Quality of Life,* [New York], 1976. Contributor to *Encyclopedia of World Biography;* contributor of more than twenty articles and about forty reviews to professional journals. Member of editorial board, *Computer Studies,* 1967-74; *Phoenix,* review editor, 1968-70, associate editor, 1970-71, editor, 1971-76.

SIDELIGHTS: T. M. Robinson reads Latin, classical and modern Greek, French, German, Spanish, Portuguese, Italian. *Avocational interests:* Verse translation, particularly of Italian and classical Greek lyric poetry; radio broadcasting (CBC) on topics concerning the history of ideas.

* * *

ROBOTTOM, John 1934-

PERSONAL: Born January 8, 1934, in Birmingham, England; son of Albert (an engineer) and Kathleen (Carlisle) Robottom; married Molly Barber (a lecturer), November 11, 1956; children: Ellen, Sally, Robert. *Education:* University of Birmingham, B.A. (honors), 1956. *Home:* 282 Robin Hood Lane, Birmingham B28 0EQ, England.

CAREER: Teacher in secondary schools, 1956-65; Bingley College of Education, Yorkshire, England, lecturer in history, 1966-68; Crewe College of Education, Crewe, England, senior lecturer, 1968-73, principal lecturer in history, 1973-76; British Broadcasting Corp., Midland's Division, education officer, 1976—.

WRITINGS: Modern China: China in Revolution, Longmans, Green, 1967, published as *China in Revolution,* McGraw, 1969; *Modern Russia,* Longmans, Green, 1969; (editor) *Making the Modern World,* Longmans, Green, 1970; *Twentieth Century China,* Wayland, 1971; *Nineteenth Century Britain,* Longman, 1976.

WORK IN PROGRESS: Source material for study of Russian and European history; *History of Caribbean,* a textbook; *History of Twentieth Century Britain,* a textbook.

* * *

ROBSON, B(rian) T(urnbull) 1939-

PERSONAL: Born February 23, 1939, in South Shields, England; son of Oswell and Doris Lowes (Ayre) Robson; married Glenna Conway, 1973. *Education:* St. Catharine's College, Cambridge, B.A., 1961, M.A., 1964, Ph.D., 1965. *Office:* Fitzwilliam College, Cambridge University, Cambridge, England.

CAREER: University of Wales, University College of Wales, Aberystwyth, lecturer in geography, 1964-67; Cambridge University, Fitzwilliam College, Cambridge, England, lecturer in geography, 1967—. *Member:* Institute of British Geographers. *Awards, honors:* Commonwealth Fund of New York fellowship, Harkness Foundation, 1967-68.

WRITINGS: Urban Analysis: A Study of City Structure with Special Reference to Sunderland, Cambridge University Press, 1969; *Urban Growth: An Approach,* Methuen, 1973; *Urban Social Areas,* Oxford University Press, 1975. Contributor of articles to *Urban Studies, Area,* and other periodicals. Honorary editor of *Transactions of the Institute of British Geographers.*

WORK IN PROGRESS: Research project on the role of local authorities in the provision of housing and social facilities in British towns.

AVOCATIONAL INTERESTS: Antiquarian maps and early town plans.

ROBSON, John M(ercel)   1927-

PERSONAL: Born May 26, 1927, in Toronto, Ontario, Canada; son of William R. M. and Christina (Sinclair) Robson; married Ann Provost Wilkinson (an associate professor of history), August 8, 1953; children: William, John, Ann Christine. *Education:* University of Toronto, B.A., 1951, M.A., 1953, Ph.D., 1956. *Home:* 28 McMaster Ave., Toronto, Ontario, Canada M4V 1A9. *Office:* Department of English, Victoria College, University of Toronto, Toronto, Ontario, Canada.

CAREER: University of British Columbia, Vancouver, instructor in English, 1956-57; University of Alberta, Edmonton, assistant professor of English, 1957-58; University of Toronto, Victoria College, Toronto, Ontario, assistant professor, 1958-61, associate professor, 1961-66, professor of English, 1966—, principal of college, 1971-76. *Member:* Canadian Association of University Teachers, Association of Canadian University Teachers of English, British Studies Association, Victorian Studies Association, Research Society for Victorian Periodicals, Royal Society of Canada (fellow). *Awards, honors:* Fellowships from Humanities Research Council (Canada), Canada Council, and Guggenheim Foundation.

WRITINGS: (Editor) Edmund Burke, *An Appeal from the New to the Old Whigs,* Bobbs-Merrill, 1961; (editor) *The Collected Works of J. S. Mill,* University of Toronto Press, Volumes II-III: *Principles of Political Economy,* 1965, Volumes IV-V: *Essays on Economics and Society,* 1967, Volume X: *Essays on Ethics, Religion, and Society,* 1969, Volumes VII and VIII: *System of Logic,* 1973, Volumes XVII and XVIII: *Essays on Politics and Society,* 1977; *The Improvement of Mankind: The Social and Political Thought of J. S. Mill,* University of Toronto Press, 1968; *The Hmnnn Retort,* New Press, 1970; (editor and contributor) *Rhetoric: A Unified Approach to English Curricula,* Ontario Institute for Studies in Education, 1971. Also author, with others, of *Word Games for Families that Are Still Speaking to One Another,* 1975. Contributor of chapters to books, articles and reviews to journals. Editor, *Mill News Letter.*

WORK IN PROGRESS: Completing an edition of about twenty-five volumes of the works of John Stuart Mill; and a rhetorical study of contemporary communications and of nineteenth-century literature.

\   *   *   *

ROBY, Pamela A.   1942-

PERSONAL: Born November 17, 1942, in Milwaukee, Wis. *Education:* University of Denver, B.A. (with honors), 1964; Syracuse University, M.A., 1966; New York University, Ph.D., 1971. *Office:* Kresge College, University of California, Santa Cruz, Calif. 95064.

CAREER: Public school teacher in Denver, Colo., 1964; Russell Sage Foundation, New York City, research assistant, 1967-69; New York University, New York City, instructor, 1966-70, assistant professor of sociology, 1970-71; George Washington University, Washington, D.C., assistant professor of sociology and research associate of Center for Manpower Policy Studies, 1970-71; Brandeis University, Waltham, Mass., assistant professor of sociology, 1971-73; University of California, Santa Cruz, Kresge College, associate professor, 1973-77, professor of sociology and community studies, 1977—. *Member:* American Sociological Association, Society for the Study of Social Problems (member of board of directors), International Sociological Association (member of research council), Sociologists for Women in

Society, American Educational Research Association, National Association on Early Childhood Development, Phi Beta Kappa, Alpha Kappa Delta. *Awards, honors:* Ford Foundation grants, 1971, 1976; Russell Sage Foundation grants, 1973, 1974.

WRITINGS: (With Seymour Michael Miller) *The Future of Inequality,* Basic Books, 1971; (editor) *Child Care: Who Cares?, Foreign and Domestic Early Childhood Policies,* Basic Books, 1973; (editor) *The Poverty Establishment,* Prentice-Hall, 1974.

*   *   *

ROCHE, George Charles III   1935-

PERSONAL: Born May 16, 1935, in Denver, Colo.; son of George Charles, Jr. (an entrepreneur) and Margaret (Stewart) Roche; married June Bernard, February 11, 1955; children: George Charles IV, Muriel Ellen, Margaret Clare. *Education:* Regis College, Denver, Colo., B.S., 1956; University of Colorado, M.A., 1961, Ph.D., 1965. *Home:* 189 Hillsdale St., Hillsdale, Mich. 49242. *Office:* Office of the President, Hillsdale College, Hillsdale, Mich. 49242.

CAREER: Colorado School of Mines, Golden, professor of history and philosophy, 1964-66; Foundation for Economic Education, Irvington, N.Y., director of seminars, 1966-71; Hillsdale College, Hillsdale, Mich., president, 1971—. Member of board of trustees, Foundation for Economic Education; member of board of directors, Culver Educational Foundation; chairman of academic advisory council, Charles Edison Memorial Youth Board; member of national advisory board, Young Americans for Freedom. Textbook evaluator, *America's Future. Military service:* U.S. Marine Corps, 1956-58; became first lieutenant. *Member:* American Historical Association, American Academy of Political and Social Science, Mont Pelerin Society, Young Presidents' Organization, American Association of Presidents of Independent Colleges and Universities (first vice-president), Philadelphia Society. *Awards, honors:* Freedom Leadership Award, Freedom Foundation, 1972.

WRITINGS: American Federalism, Foundation for Economic Education, 1967; *Power,* Foundation for Economic Education, 1968; *Education in America,* Foundation for Economic Education, 1969; *Legacy of Freedom,* Arlington House, 1969; *Frederic Bastiat: A Man Alone,* Arlington House, 1971; *The Bewildered Society,* Arlington House, 1972; *The Balancing Act: Quota Hiring in Higher Education,* Open Court, 1974. Contributor of articles to periodicals.

BIOGRAPHICAL/CRITICAL SOURCES: Detroit News, September 17, 1972.

*   *   *

ROCHMIS, Lyda N(onne)   1912-

PERSONAL: Born February 5, 1912, in New York, N.Y.; daughter of Abraham Simon (an engineer) and Berta H. (Simkin) Pinkus; married Max Rochmis (divorced); children: Paul G. *Education:* Hunter College (now Hunter College of the City University of New York), A.B., 1930; Radcliffe College, A.M. (magna cum laude), 1931.

CAREER: Teacher in public schools in New York, N.Y., 1937—. *Member:* Speech Association of Eastern States, New York State Speech Association, New York City Speech Association (former president).

WRITINGS: (With Dorothy Doob) *Speech Therapy: A Group Approach for Schools and Clinics,* John Day, 1970.

Contributor of articles to professional journals. Former editor, New York City Speech Association *Bulletin*.†

* * *

ROCKLEY, L(awrence) E(dwin) 1916-

PERSONAL: Born August 11, 1916, in Leicester, England; son of Arthur Edwin (an electrical engineer) and Laura (Norman) Rockley; married Margaret Joan Gray, February 10, 1940; children: Anne Cathryn (Mrs. Nigel R. Hopkins), Richard David. *Education:* Attended University College, Leicester (now University of Leicester) and Leicester College of Technology, 1933-38; B.Com. (London), 1948; Warwick University, M.Phil. *Religion:* Methodist. *Home:* Charnwood, 121 Windy Arbour, Kenilworth, Warwickshire, England. *Office:* Lanchester Polytechnic, Coventry, England.

CAREER: Leicester Electricity Undertaking, Leicester, England, senior assistant, 1946-47; City Treasurer's Office, Leicester, principal assistant and deputy chief internal auditor, 1947-56; National Coal Board, Warwickshire, England, area chief auditor, 1957-60; Lanchester Polytechnic, Coventry, England, 1960—, began as lecturer, principal lecturer in business finance, 1965—. Lecturer, British Productivity Council; consultant to business firms. *Military service:* British Army, 1940-46; became major. *Member:* Institute of Municipal Treasurers and Accountants (associate), British Institute of Management (associate). *Awards, honors:* Annual "Book of the Year" Award, Society of Commercial Accountants, 1971, for *Finance for the Non-Accountant;* Social Science Research Council grant to do research for Ph.D. dissertation.

WRITINGS: Production Control Information, Kynoch Press, 1965; *Capital Investment Decisions,* Business Books Ltd., 1968; *Finance for the Non-Accountant,* Business Books Ltd., 1970, 2nd edition, 1976; *Non-Accountant's Guide to Finance,* Business Books Ltd., 1972; *Investment for Profitability,* Business Books Ltd., 1972; *Non-Accountant's Guide to the Balance Sheet,* Business Books Ltd., 1973; *Public and Local Authority Accounts,* Heinemann, 1975; *The Meaning of Balance Sheets and Company Reports,* Business Books Ltd., 1975. Contributor to business journals.

* * *

ROCKWELL, Thomas 1933-

PERSONAL: Born March 13, 1933, in New Rochelle, N.Y.; son of Norman (an artist) and Mary (Barstow) Rockwell; married Gail Sudler (an artist), July 16, 1955; children: Barnaby, Abigail. *Education:* Bard College, B.A., 1956. *Home address:* R.D.3, Lauer Rd., Poughkeepsie, N.Y. 12603. *Agent:* Joan Raines, Raines & Raines Agency, 475 Fifth Ave., New York, N.Y. 10017.

AWARDS, HONORS: Mark Twain Award, California Young Readers' Medal, and Golden Archer Award, all 1975; South Carolina Children's Book Award, Massachusetts Children's Book Award, Sequoyah Award, and Nene Award, all 1976.

*WRITINGS—*Juveniles: *Rackety-Bang,* illustrations by wife, Gail Rockwell, Pantheon, 1969; *Norman Rockwell's Hometown,* illustrations by father, Norman Rockwell, Windmill Books, 1970; *Humpf!,* illustrations by Muriel Batherman, Pantheon, 1971; *Squawwwk!,* illustrations by G. Rockwell, Little, Brown, 1972; *How to Eat Fried Worms,* illustrations by Emily McCully, F. Watts, 1973; *The Neon*

Motorcycle, illustrations by Michael Horen, F. Watts, 1973; *The Portmanteau Book,* illustrations by G. Rockwell, Little, Brown, 1974; *Hiding Out,* illustrations by Charles Molina, Bradbury, 1974; *Tin Cans,* illustrations by Saul Lambert, Bradbury, 1974; *The Thief,* illustrations by G. Rockwell, Delacorte, 1977.

* * *

RODALE, J(erome) I(rving) 1898-1971

August 16, 1898—June 7, 1971; American organic farmer, author, and publisher. Obituaries: *Washington Post,* June 9, 1971; *Antiquarian Bookman,* July 5-12, 1971; *Organic Gardening,* August, 1971.

* * *

RODBERG, Lillian 1936-
(Lillian R. Boehme)

PERSONAL: Born April 15, 1936, in Vineland, N.J.; daughter of Henrik Nils (an interior designer of churches) and Katherine (Nitsch) Rodberg; married Walter K. Boehme (divorced); children: Kathleen Anne, Carroll Stephen, Kirsten Yvonne. *Education:* Attended Rutgers University, 1953-54. *Politics:* "Laissez-faire capitalism." *Religion:* Atheist. *Home:* 211 Crestmont Terrace, Collingswood, N.J. 08108.

CAREER: Industrial Landscape Maintenance, Wenonah, N.J., bookkeeper-secretary, 1954-66, office manager, 1967-69, secretary, 1970-71; owner, Lillian R. Boehme Correspondence Service, 1962-67; *The Libertarian,* Wenonah, editor and co-owner, 1965-71; *The Review of News,* Belmont, Mass., editorial assistant, 1971-72, economics columnist, 1972-75; Grounds Care, Wenonah, manager and designer, 1972-75; W. B. Saunders Co., Philadelphia, Pa., medical manuscript editor, 1975—.

WRITINGS: (Under name Lillian R. Boehme) *Carte Blanche for Chaos,* Arlington House, 1970. Author of a weekly column, "Economics," in *The Review of the News,* 1971-75; contributing reviewer, *Books for Libertarians,* 1972-75. Contributor of feature articles to *The Review of the News* and *American Opinion,* 1972-75.

WORK IN PROGRESS: A fantasy novel, tentatively entitled *The Tanstaafl Caper;* a study on the nature and function of government; several monographs on the work of popular novelists, including Marcia Davenport and Dorothy L. Sayers.

SIDELIGHTS: Lillian Rodberg told *CA:* "[My] principal vocational interest, as a writer, is the application of a philosophy based on man's nature as a rational being (meaning, man's nature as a being whose conceptual faculty is his basic means of survival) to specific current cultural phenomena and political events." *Avocational interests:* Music (Chopin, Rachmaninoff, Scott Joplin, and Janis Ian), photography, interior decorating, house plants, cats, landscape designing, and cooking.

* * *

RODGERS, Brian 1910-

PERSONAL: Born May 25, 1910, in Bangor, Northern Ireland; son of Arthur Silcock (a company secretary) and Mary (Mahaffey) Rodgers; married Barbara Stancliffe (a university lecturer), June 26, 1950. *Education:* London School of Economics and Political Science, B.Sc., 1947. *Politics:* "Not a member of any political party. I vote Labour." *Religion:* Quaker. *Home:* Old Vicarage, Goostrey, Crewe, Cheshire, England.

CAREER: Began his career in commerce and then engaged in social work; University of Manchester, Manchester, England, 1947-73, began as assistant lecturer, senior lecturer in social administration, 1959-73. Chairman, Congleton Rural District Council, 1970-71. Consultant, World Council of Churches. *Member:* Manchester Literary and Philosophical Society (past president), Manchester Statistical Society.

WRITINGS: (Contributor) Lady Stocks, *Fifty Years in Every Street,* Manchester University Press, 1964; (with others) *British Association Survey of Manchester,* Manchester University Press, 1964; *Battle against Poverty,* Volume I: *From Pauperism to Human Rights,* Routledge & Kegan Paul, 1968, Humanities, 1969, Volume II: *Towards a Welfare State,* Routledge & Kegan Paul, 1969; *J. S. Mill: The Avignon Years,* Manchester Literary and Philosophical Society, 1975. Contributor to professional journals.

WORK IN PROGRESS: A study of the life of John Stuart Mill; writing on problems concerning concepts of liberty, research on the growth of social policy in Great Britain.

AVOCATIONAL INTERESTS: Painting (especially landscapes) and ornithology.

*   *   *

RODINI, Robert J(oseph)   1936-

PERSONAL: Born August 2, 1936, in Albany, Calif.; son of Joseph and Mary (Marsala) Rodini; married Eleanor Morgan, September 3, 1962; children: Elizabeth, Mark. *Education:* University of California, Berkeley, B.A., 1958, M.A., 1960, Ph.D., 1967; also studied at Middlebury College, 1958, and University of Florence, 1960. *Home:* 1632 Adams St., Madison, Wis. 53711. *Office:* 618 Van Hise Hall, University of Wisconsin, Madison, Wis. 53706.

CAREER: University of Wisconsin—Madison, instructor, 1965-66, assistant professor, 1966-69, associate professor, 1969-76, professor of French and Italian, 1976—. Resident director, Indiana-Wisconsin Junior Year in Bologna, Italy, 1971-72. *Member:* Modern Language Association of America, Renaissance Society of America, American Association of Teachers of Italian, Midwest Modern Language Association. *Awards, honors:* Fulbright fellowship, 1960-61; American Council of Learned Societies fellowship, 1976-77.

WRITINGS: Antonfrancesco Grazzini: Poet, Dramatist and "Novelliere," 1503-1584, University of Wisconsin Press, 1970; (translator) Donald M. Anderson, editor, *A Renaissance Alphabet,* University of Wisconsin Press, 1971; (editor) Giuseppe Berto, *Le Opere di Dio,* Houghton, 1976.

WORK IN PROGRESS: Theatre and Spectacle in Medicean Florence.

*   *   *

RODRIGUES, Jose Honorio   1913-

PERSONAL: Born September 20, 1913, in Rio de Janeiro, Brazil; son of Honorio Jose (a businessman) and Judith (Pacheco) Rodrigues; married Leda Boechat (a lawyer and writer), March 3, 1941. *Education:* University of Brazil, LL. and Soc.Sc.Bach., 1937. *Religion:* Roman Catholic. *Home:* Rua Paul Redfern 23, Apt. CO1, Rio de Janeiro, Guanabara ZC-37, Brazil.

CAREER: National Library, Division of Publications, Rio de Janeiro, Brazil, director, 1946-58; National Archives, Rio de Janeiro, director, 1958-64; Institute of International Relations, Rio de Janeiro, executive director, 1963—. Professor of diplomatic history and the history of Brazil, Instituto Rio Branco, Brazilian Ministry of Foreign Affairs, 1946-56; professor of history, University of the State of Guanabara, 1953—; visiting professor at University of Texas, 1963-64, 1966, and at Columbia University, spring, 1970. Member of Commission on Textbooks on Brazil History, Brazilian Ministry of Foreign Relations; member of National Council on Geography, Brazil Institute of Geography and Statistics; Pan American Institute of Geography and History, vice-president of Commission of Historical Bibliography, 1959—, Brazil's delegate to meetings in Ecuador, 1959, and Argentina, 1961. Participant in international colloquiums on Luso-Brazilian studies in Washington, D.C., 1950, at Harvard University, 1966, and in other countries.

MEMBER: Instituto Historico e Geografico Brasileiro, Sociedade Capistrano de Abreu (president), Academia Portuguesa de Historia, Royal Historical Society (London), Academy of American Franciscan History (Washington, D.C.), Nederlandsche Maatschapij voor Letterkunde (Utrecht); and other professional organizations. *Awards, honors:* Erudition Prize of Brazil Academy of Letters, 1937, for manuscript of *Civilizacao Holandesa no Brasil;* Rockefeller Foundation research fellowship in United States, 1943-44; British Council grant for a month in England, 1950.

WRITINGS: (With Joaquim Ribeiro) *Civilizacao Holandesa no Brasil,* Companhia Editora Nacional, 1940; (author of introduction, notes, and bibliography) Johan Nieuhof, *Memoravel Viagem Maritima e Terrestre ao Brasil,* Livraria Martins, 1942; *Teoria da Historia do Brasil,* Instituto Progresso Editorial, 1949, two-volume 2nd edition, Companhia Editoria Nacional, 1957; *Historiografia e Bibliografia do Domino Holandes no Brasil,* Instituto Nacional do Livro, 1949.

Noticia de Varia Historia, Livraria Sao Jose, 1951; *A Pesquisa Historica no Brasil: Sua evolucao e problemas atuais,* Instituto Nacional do Livro, 1952; *O Continente do Rio Grande,* Edicoes Sao Jose, 1954; (author of preface and notes) Capistrano de Abreu, *Capitulos de Historia Colonial,* 4th revised edition, Livraria Briguiet, 1954; *Brasil: Periodo Colonial,* Instituto Panamericano de Geografia e Historia, 1957; *Historiografia del Brasil: Siglo XVI,* Instituto Panamericano de Geografia e Historia, 1957; *Indice Anotado da Revista do Instituto do Ceara,* Imprensa Universitaria do Ceara, 1959.

Indice Anotado da Revista do Instituto Arquelogico, Historico e Geograficao Pernambucano, 1961; *Brasil e Africa: Outro Horizonte,* Editora Civilizacao Brasileira, 1961, two-volume 2nd edition, 1964, translation by Richard A. Mazzara and Sam Hileman published as *Brazil and Africa,* University of California Press, 1965; *Aspiracoes Nacionais: Interpretacao Historico-Politica,* Editora Fulgor, 1963, 2nd edition, 1965, translation by Ralph Edward Dimmick published as *The Brazilians: Their Character and Aspirations,* University of Texas Press, 1967; *Historiografia del Brasil: Siglo SVII,* Instituto Panamericano de Geografia e Historia, 1963; (contributor) A. R. Lewis and T. F. McGann, editors, *The New World Looks at Its History,* University of Texas Press, 1963; *Conciliacao e Reforma no Brasil: Interpretacao Historico-Politica,* Editora Civilizacao Brasileira, 1965; *Historia e Historiadores do Brasil,* Editora Fulgar, 1965; (contributor) A. M. Halpern, editor, *Policies Toward China: Views from Six Continents,* McGraw, 1965; *Interesse Nacional e Politica Externa,* Editora Civilizacao Brasileira, 1966; *Vida e Historia,* Editora Civilizacao Brasileira, 1966; *Historia e Historiografia,* Editora Vozes, 1970; *O Parlamento e a Evolucao Nacional: Introducao Historica,*

1826-1840, Senado Federal, 1972; *A Assembleia Constituinte de 1823,* Editora Vozes, 1974; *Independencia: Revolucao e Contra-Revolucao,* five volumes, Livraria Francisco Alves Editora, 1975-76; *Historia, Corpo do Tempo,* Editora Perspectiva, 1976.

Editor and author of preface; official publications: (Also author of notes and bibliography) *Os Holandeses no Brasil,* Instituto do Acucar e do Alcool, 1942; *Catalogo da Colecao Visconde de Rio Branco,* two volumes, Instituto Rio Branco, 1950; Jose Maria da Silva Paranhos, *Cartas ao Amigo Ausente,* Instituto Rio Branco, 1953; *Correspondencia de Capistrano de Abreu,* three volumes, Instituto Nacional do Livro, 1954-56. Also editor and author of preface of *Anais da Biblioteca Nacional,* Volumes LXVI-LXXIV, *Documentos Historicos da Biblioteca Nacional,* Volumes LXXI-CX, and *Publicacoes do Arquivo Nacional,* Volumes XLIII-L.

Author of preface: J. E. Pohl, *Viagem ao interior do Brasil empreendida nos anos de 1817 a 1821,* Instituto Nacional do Livro, 1951; Daniel de Carvalho, *Estudos e Depoimentos,* Jose Olimpio, 1953; Guilherme Piso, *Historia Natural e Medica da India Ocidental,* Instituto Nacional do Livro, 1957.

Editor, *Revista Brasileira de Politica Internacional,* Volumes XXIV-XXX. Contributor to scholarly reviews, literary supplements, and daily newspapers; there have been separate reprints of fourteen of his articles first published in *Verbum, Revista de Historia, Hispanic American Historical Review, Journal of African History,* and other journals. Member of editorial committee, *Revista de Historia de American* (publication of Pan American Institute of Geography and History), 1953—; associate editor, *Hispanic American Historical Review,* Duke University Press, 1957-61; member of editorial advisory board, *Historical Abstracts* (Munich), 1961—.

WORK IN PROGRESS: A modern history of Brazil, for publication by Praeger in the United States and Weidenfeld & Nicolson in England.

SIDELIGHTS: In addition to Spanish and Portuguese, Jose Rodrigues speaks French, Italian, and English and reads German and Dutch.

BIOGRAPHICAL/CRITICAL SOURCES: Revista Chilena de Historia y Geografia, January-June, 1953; Leda Boechat Rodrigues, *Bibliografia de Jose Honorio Rodrigues,* [Rio de Janeiro], 1956; *Times Literary Supplement,* September 22, 1966.

* * *

ROEMING, Robert Frederick 1911-

PERSONAL: Born December 12, 1911, in Milwaukee, Wis.; son of Ferdinand August (a machinist) and Wanda E. (Radtke) Roeming; married Alice Mae Voss, August 30, 1941; children: Pamela Alice. *Education:* University of Wisconsin, B.A., 1934, M.A., 1936, Ph.D., 1941. *Politics:* "Conservative in political organization, but a perpetual dissenter." *Home:* 6078 North Oakland Hills Rd., Nashotah, Wis. 53058. *Office:* Department of French and Italian, University of Wisconsin—Milwaukee, Milwaukee, Wis. 53201.

CAREER: University of Wisconsin—Milwaukee, instructor, 1936-43; D. C. Heath and Co., Lexington, Mass., representative, 1943-46; University of Wisconsin—Milwaukee, assistant professor, 1946-50, associate professor, 1950-56, professor of French and Italian, 1956—, associate dean of College of Letters and Science, 1957-62, director of depart-

ment of language laboratories, 1964-70, acting director, 1969-70, director of Center for Twentieth Century Studies, 1970-74. Lecturer, Wisconsin State Radio Network program, "Black French Literature," 1977; lecturer and researcher in France, Germany, Italy, Spain, England, Rumania, Brazil, Uruguay, Argentina, Chile, Peru, and Caribbean Islands. Member of Wisconsin State Board of Nursing, 1977-81. *Member:* Modern Language Association of America (member of committee on ERIC, 1966-70; member of index committee, 1970—), American Association of Teachers of French, American Association of Teachers of Italian, National Association of Language Laboratory Directors (charter member), American Comparative Literature Association (member of organizing committee), Association for Higher Education (member of organizing committee), American Council on the Teaching of Foreign Languages (consultant to organizing committee, 1966-67), Northeast Conference on Foreign Languages, Central States Conference on Foreign Languages (member of organizing committee), Caribbean Studies Association, Verband Deutscher Schriftsteller der Gewerckschaft Druck und Papier (German Writers Union; only member with United States residence). *Awards, honors:* Palmes Academiques, Chevalier, 1965, Officer, 1973; National Endowment for the Humanities grants, summers, 1976 and 1977.

WRITINGS: (With Charles E. Young) *Introduction to French,* Heath, 1951; (editor) *Camus: A Bibliography,* University of Wisconsin Press, 1968, 6th edition, 1977; (editor) *Generating Literary Appreciation,* University of Wisconsin—Milwaukee, 1971; (editor) *Creating Awareness through Poetry,* University of Wisconsin—Milwaukee, 1972; (editor) *Perspectives on Criminal Justice,* University of Wisconsin—Milwaukee, 1974; (editor) *Cultural Diversity and Ethnic Alienation,* University of Wisconsin—Milwaukee, 1974. Managing editor, *Modern Language Journal,* 1963-70.

WORK IN PROGRESS: With Alain Bosquet, *Ideological Influences on Twentieth Century Poetry,* an anthology; a collection of his own articles on foreign language learning; further studies on Camus; translations of Grenier's *Camus* and *Interviews with Louis Foncet.*

AVOCATIONAL INTERESTS: Tennis, conservation.

BIOGRAPHICAL/CRITICAL SOURCES: Books Abroad, summer, 1969.

* * *

ROES, Nicholas 1926-

PERSONAL: Surname is pronounced as "rose"; born April 24, 1926, in North Bergen, N.J.; children: Nicholas, Jr., Frank, Louis. *Education:* Studied at New York University, 1948-50, and Columbia University, 1950-52. *Home:* 15 West Church Rd., Saddle River, N.J. 07458.

CAREER: A shorthand prodigy trained by the founder of the Gregg System, he taught shorthand as an extra duty in the Army and later was a court reporter in the District Attorney's Office, New York City; secretary to ad agency president, later writer for publishing accounts and mail order ads; Ted Bates & Co., Inc. (advertising), New York City, vice-president and senior creative supervisor. President, Cathedral Guild, Inc. *Military service:* U.S. Army, infantryman, later secretary to a general; received three battle stars.

WRITINGS: (With William E. Kennedy) *The Space Flight Encyclopedia,* Follett, 1968. Contributor of detective stories, articles on shorthand, and military biographies to periodicals.

WORK IN PROGRESS: Outlines for further books in Follett's "Vest Pocket Handbooks" series; scripts for television programs and television commercials.

AVOCATIONAL INTERESTS: Swimming, horseback riding, military projects, criminology, music ("play drums and trumpet badly").

* * *

ROGAN, Donald L(ynn) 1930-

PERSONAL: Born June 16, 1930, in Staunton, Va.; son of Charles Earnest (a printer) and Jane Whyte (Batts) Rogan; married Sarah Anne Larew (a high school teacher), August 25, 1954; children: Edward, John, Peter, Lynn. *Education:* Morris Harvey College, A.B., 1951; General Theological Seminary, New York, N.Y., M.Div., 1954, further study, 1962-65; St. Augustine's College, Canterbury, England, Diploma, 1960. *Politics:* Democrat. *Home address:* Box 371, Gambier, Ohio 43022. *Office:* Department of Religion, Kenyon College, Gambier, Ohio 43022.

CAREER: Episcopal clergyman; Trinity Church, Morgantown, W.Va., rector, 1956-62; St. Hilda's and St. Hugh's School, New York, N.Y., chairman of religious studies, 1964-65; Kenyon College, Gambier, Ohio, assistant professor, 1965-67, associate professor and chaplain, 1968-72, professor of religion and chairman of department, 1973—. *Member:* American Association of University Professors, American Academy of Religion.

WRITINGS: Campus Apocalypse: The Student Search Today, Seabury, 1969; (contributor) *Violence–A Study in the Ethics of Action,* Xerox College Publishing, 1971. Contributor to religious journals.

WORK IN PROGRESS: The Anatomy of Superstition.

* * *

ROGERS, David 1930-

PERSONAL: Born April 17, 1930, in Boston, Mass.; son of Herman (a merchant) and Helen (Novack) Rogers; married Theresa Falaguerra (a researcher in sociology), September 2, 1960; children: Edward David, Alex Emanuel. *Education:* Harvard University, A.B., 1953, Ph.D., 1960; Princeton University, graduate study, 1953-54. *Politics:* Democrat. *Religion:* Jewish. *Home:* 875 West End Ave., New York, N.Y. 10025. *Agent:* Oliver Swan, Paul R. Reynolds, Inc., 12 East 41st St., New York, N.Y. 10017. *Office:* Graduate School of Business Administration, New York University, New York, N.Y. 10003.

CAREER: Columbia University, New York City, assistant professor of sociology, 1959-62; New York University, Graduate School of Business Administration, New York City, assistant professor, 1962-65, associate professor, 1965-70, professor of sociology and management, 1970—. Visiting project director, Russell Sage Foundation, 1971-72; project director and senior research associate, Institute of Public Administration, 1973-74. Consultant, Human Resources Administration and Los Angeles Urban Coalition; consultant and member of educational task force, New York Urban Coalition. *Member:* American Sociological Association, Eastern Sociological Society.

WRITINGS: 110 Livington Street: Politics and Bureaucracy in the New York City School System, Random House, 1968; *An Exploratory Study of Inter-Organizational Relations,* U.S. Department of Labor, 1969; (co-author) *Sociology and the Business Establishment,* Russell Sage Foundation, 1970; *Inter-Organizational Relations and Inner City*

Manpower Programs, Graduate School of Business Administration, New York University, 1971; *The Management of Big Cities: Interest Groups and Social Change Strategies,* Sage Publications, 1971; (with Gordon Bultena and Vince Webb) *Public Response to Planned Environmental Change,* Department of Sociology, Iowa State University, 1973; (editor with Willis D. Hawley) *Improving the Quality of Urban Management,* Sage Publications, 1974; *Inventory of Educational Improvement Efforts in the New York City Public Schools,* Teachers College, Columbia University, 1977. Contributor to *Saturday Review* and to social science journals.†

* * *

ROHRBOUGH, Malcolm J(ustin) 1932-

PERSONAL: Born August 3, 1932, in Cambridge, Mass.; son of George Irwin (an educator) and Martha Fraser (Waugh) Rohrbough; married Barbara Jean Gustine, December 16, 1961 (divorced, February 25, 1977); children: Elizabeth Fraser, Justin Anthony, Peter Malcolm. *Education:* Harvard University, A.B., 1954; University of Wisconsin, M.A., 1958, Ph.D., 1963; University of Melbourne, graduate study, 1960-61. *Politics:* Democrat. *Home:* 420 Ferson Ave., Iowa City, Iowa 52240. *Office:* Department of History, University of Iowa, Iowa City, Iowa 52240.

CAREER: Princeton University, Princeton, N.J., instructor in history, 1962-64; University of Iowa, Iowa City, assistant professor, 1964-68, associate professor of history, 1968—. *Military service:* U.S. Marine Corps, 1954-56; became first lieutenant. *Member:* Organization of American Historians, Western History Association. *Awards, honors:* Fulbright scholar at University of Melbourne, 1960-61.

WRITINGS: The Land Office Business: The Settlement and Administration of American Public Lands, 1789-1837, Oxford University Press, 1968. Also author of *The First American Frontier: People, Societies, and Institutions in the Trans-Appalachian West, 1775-1850,* 1977.

WORK IN PROGRESS: A history of Aspen, Colorado, from 1880-1918.

AVOCATIONAL INTERESTS: Ornithology, camping, summers on the New England coast.

* * *

ROHRMAN, Nicholas L(eroy) 1937-

PERSONAL: Born April 25, 1937, in Indianapolis, Ind.; son of Leroy N. (a factory foreman) and Mary E. (O'Callaghan) Rohrman; married Carol A. Cunningham, December 7, 1959; children: Lisa, Melinda. *Education:* Butler University, A.B., 1959; Miami University, Oxford, Ohio, M.A., 1964; Indiana University, Ph.D., 1967. *Politics:* "Occasionally." *Religion:* "Druid." *Office:* Department of Psychology, Colby College, Mayflower Hill, Waterville, Me. 04901.

CAREER: Bucknell University, Lewisburg, Pa., assistant professor of psychology, 1967-69; Florida State University, Tallahassee, assistant professor of psychology, 1969-77; Colby College, Waterville, Me., professor of psychology and chairman of department, 1977—. Democratic county committeeman, Union County, Pa., 1968-69. *Military service:* U.S. Air Force, 1959-62; became first lieutenant. *Member:* American Association for the Advancement of Science, American Association of University Professors, American Psychological Association, Linguistic Society of America, Sigma Xi, Psychonomic Society. *Awards, honors:* National Science Foundation grants, 1968, 1970.

WRITINGS: (With Wendell Irving Smith) *Human Learning,* McGraw, 1970. Contributor to *Psychological Reports, Psychonomic Science,* and other journals. Member of editorial board, *Journal to Verbal Learning and Verbal Behavior.*

WORK IN PROGRESS: Continuing research into the psychological organization of linguistic information.

* * *

ROONEY, Patrick C. 1937-

PERSONAL: Born May 23, 1937, in Chicago, Ill.; son of Bernard H. and Carmella (Capilupo) Rooney. *Education:* Attended Loras College, 1955-57; Pontifical Faculty of Philosophy, River Forest, Ill., Ph.L., 1960; Aquinas Institute of Theology, Dubuque, Iowa, M.A., 1963; International Center for Studies in Religious Education, Brussels, Belgium, Diplome de Catechese, 1966.

CAREER: High School religion teacher in Oak Park, Ill., 1966-67; University of Notre Dame, South Bend, Ind., instructor in education, beginning 1967. *Member:* Religious Education Association, Society for the Scientific Study of Religion.

WRITINGS: (Editor with James M. Lee) *A Social Science Approach to Religious Education,* Pflaum/Standard, 1970; (editor with Lee) *Toward a Future for Religious Education,* Pflaum/Standard, 1970.†

* * *

ROOSE-EVANS, James 1927-

PERSONAL: Born November 11, 1927, in England; son of Jack and Catherine Owen (Morgan) Roose-Evans. *Education:* Oxford University, B.A., 1952, M.A., 1957. *Politics:* None. *Religion:* Christian. *Residence:* Wales and London. *Agent:* David Higham Associates Ltd., 5-8 Lower John St., Golden Square, London W1R 4HA, England.

CAREER: Maddermarket Theatre, Norwich, England, artistic director, 1954-55; Julliard School of Music, New York, N.Y., member of faculty, 1955-56; Royal Academy of Dramatic Art, London, England, staff member and judge, 1957-62; Hampstead Theatre Club, London, England, founder and artistic director, 1959-71. Artistic director, Pitlochry Festival Theatre, Scotland, 1960; resident director, Belgrade Theatre, Coventry, 1960; director, Stage Two, a theatre workshop and research center. Lecturer. Adjudicator, National Union of Students Drama Festival, 1970, and National Drama Festival of Zambia, 1973. Member, drama committee and dance committee, Welsh Arts Council; member, combined arts panel, Southeast Wales Arts Association; council member, Welsh Dance Theatre. Director of many West End productions, including *Under Milk Wood, Cider with Rosie, Private Lives, The Happy Apple, An Ideal Husband,* and *Spitting Image;* also directed *Oedipus* at Greek Contemporary Theatre, Athens. Director of documentary films, "The Female Messiah," 1975, and "The Third Adam," 1976, both for British Broadcasting Corp. *National service:* Royal Army Educational Corps, 1947-49. *Member:* Garrick Club. *Awards, honors:* Arts Council bursary to Finland, 1968; "The Female Messiah" was chosen by British Broadcasting Corp. as its entry for the 1975 Italia Prize.

WRITINGS: (Adaptor) *The Little Clay Cart,* Elek Books, 1965; *Directing a Play: James Roose-Evans on the Art of Directing and Acting,* Theatre Arts Inc., 1968; (author of introduction) Andrew Sinclair, *Adventures in the Skin Trade*

(based on the novel by Dylan Thomas), New Directions, 1968; *Experimental Theatre: From Stanislavsky to Today,* Universe Books, 1970, revised and enlarged edition, 1974; (contributor) Richard Brown, editor, *Actor Training Two,* Drama Book Specialists, 1976; *London Theatre: From the Globe to the National,* Phaidon, 1977.

Juveniles; all published by Deutsch: *The Adventures of Odd and Elsewhere,* 1971; *The Secret of the Seven Bright Shiners,* 1972; *Odd and the Great Bear,* 1973; *Elsewhere and the Gathering of the Clowns,* 1974; *The Return of the Great Bear,* 1975; *The Secret of Tippity-Witchit,* 1976; *The Lost Treasure of Wales,* 1977. Contributor to *Financial Times, Drama,* and other periodicals.

WORK IN PROGRESS: The Within-God, a book on meditation.

SIDELIGHTS: About the Hampstead Theatre, James Roose-Evans says: "We believe in a theatre that is at home with everyone and is a home to everyone; a theatre that can bring a sense of fulfillment or a sense of shock. Audiences will not be bored but exhilarated; not passive but involved. The theatre unites us in a communal experience. No longer shut in his separate house before his separate television set, cut off one from the other, but brought together, made one."

Roose-Evans visits America twice a year, lecturing and conducting workshops. Students also come from American colleges to study at his workshop in London.

In *Directing a Play,* Roose-Evans attempted to transfer his experience as a director to textbook form. Norman Marshall believes he has succeeded admirably. "He writes with a tremendous verve which conveys all the excitement as well as the anguish of bringing a play to life. I wish every amateur director would read this book—and a good many professionals as well."

BIOGRAPHICAL/CRITICAL SOURCES: Camden Journal, February-March, 1968; *Drama,* winter, 1968; *New York Times,* June 3, 1970.

* * *

ROSE, Carl 1903-1971

1903—June 21, 1971; American cartoonist and illustrator. Obituaries: *New York Times,* June 22, 1971; *New Yorker,* July 3, 1971.

* * *

ROSE, Constance Hubbard 1934-

PERSONAL: Born July 20, 1934, in Cambridge, Mass. *Education:* Rollins College, B.A., 1955; Boston University, A.M., 1961; Harvard University, Ph.D., 1968.

CAREER: Houghton Mifflin Co. (publisher), Boston, Mass., editorial work, 1956-58; Ginn & Co. (publisher), Boston, editorial work, 1961-62; instructor in Romance languages at junior colleges in Massachusetts, 1961-64; Brandeis University, Waltham, Mass., instructor in Spanish, 1967-69; University of Pittsburgh, Pittsburgh, Pa., assistant professor of Spanish and comparative literature, beginning 1969. *Member:* Modern Language Association of America, American Association of University Professors, American Association of University Women, Renaissance Society of America, Association Internacional de Hispanistas, Phi Sigma Iota, Phi Society. *Awards, honors:* National Endowment for the Humanities junior fellow, 1972-73; American Philosophical Society research grant, 1973.

WRITINGS: Alonso Nunez de Reinoso: The Lament of a

Sixteenth-Century Exile, Fairleigh Dickinson University Press, 1970; (editor and author of introduction with F.M. Rogers and L. G. Cohen) *Antonio Enriquez Gomez: "Fernan mendes Pinto": Comedia famoso en dos partes,* Acta Universitatis Conimbrigensis (Coimbra Portugal), 1971. Contributor to *Revue de Litterature Comparee, Romanische Forschungen,* and other scholarly journals.

WORK IN PROGRESS: With Steven Hess, an anthology of sixteenth-century Spanish drama; and a long-range project on literature of exile—works of Spain's Golden Age published or written outside of Spain.†

* * *

ROSE, Elinor K(iess) 1920-

PERSONAL: Born 1920, in Edon, Ohio; daughter of David Theodore (an optometrist) and Bertha (Twichell) Kiess; married Dana Rose, December 25, 1935 (deceased); children: Stuart Rex, Douglas Dana, Bruce Geoffrey. *Education:* Hillsdale College, A.B. and B.S. (cum laude). *Religion:* Methodist. *Home:* 25560 Dundee Rd., Royal Oak, Mich. 48070.

CAREER: Writer of light verse (quatrains) syndicated to newspapers by Allied Features Syndicate, 1952—. Professional lecturer; member of staff of Oakland University-Detroit Women Writers Writers Conference, 1963—; participant in Writer-in-Residence program, Michigan Council for the Arts; judge in Scholastic Writing Awards and other contests. Member of board of women commissioners and board of trustees, Hillsdale College. *Member:* Detroit Women Writers, Detroit Press Club, Women in Communication. *Awards, honors:* Achievement award, Hillsdale College, 1955; Writer of the Year Award of Detroit Women Writers, 1959; national achievement award, Kappa Kappa Gamma, 1968.

WRITINGS: Relax, Chum, Five Oaks Press, 1955; *Sugar and Spice,* Five Oaks Press, 1959; *Rhyme & Reason,* Simon & Schuster, 1967. Poems included in *Childhood in Poetry,* Gale, 1968, and *Fun and Laughter,* Reader's Digest; poems included in and editor with others of *Echoes from the Moon,* 1976. Contributor of articles and verse to *Reader's Digest, Saturday Evening Post, Christian Herald, Good Housekeeping, Wall Street Journal,* and other magazines and newspapers.

SIDELIGHTS: Elinor Rose told *CA* that she is a "people watcher." She finds subjects for her verse listening to all kinds of people, trying to absorb and translate a variety of experiences and moods. "Since I principally work in the tight form of the quatrain," she writes, "technique is of enormous importance. I spend 40 hours a week writing, revising. The wastebasket by my desk is, alas, always crammed."

* * *

ROSEN, Winifred 1943-

PERSONAL: Born October 16, 1943, in Columbia, S.C.; daughter of Victor H. (a psychoanalyst) and Elizabeth (a modern dancer and dance therapist; maiden name, Ruskay) Rosen. *Education:* New York University, B.A., M.A. *Home:* 200 East 64th St., 29-C, New York, N.Y. 10021. *Agent:* Anita Gross, International Famous Agency, Inc., 1301 Avenue of the Americas, New York, N.Y. 10019.

CAREER: High school teacher in New York, N.Y., 1965-68; Dial Press, Inc., New York, N.Y., editorial assistant, 1970. *Member:* Phi Beta Kappa.

WRITINGS—All juvenile: *Marvin's Manhole,* Dial, 1970; *Ralph Proves the Pudding,* Doubleday, 1972; *Hiram Makes Friends,* Four Winds Press, 1974; *The Hippopotamus Book,* Golden Press, 1975; *Henrietta: The Wild Woman of Borneo,* Four Winds Press, 1975; *Cruisin' for a Bruisin'* (novel), Knopf, 1976; *Dragons Hate to be Discrete,* Knopf, in press; *Henrietta and the Day of the Iguana,* Four Winds Press, in press.

WORK IN PROGRESS: A novel for Knopf.

AVOCATIONAL INTERESTS: Fabric design, embroidery, music.

* * *

ROSENBERG, Bruce A(lan) 1934-

PERSONAL: Born July 27, 1934, in New York, N.Y.; son of Howard Alyne (an attorney) and Jeanne (Whiteson) Rosenberg; married Gloria I. Brocato, June 11, 1959; married second wife, Mary Kay Hammond, September 15, 1972; children: (first marriage) Eric Peter, Seth Allan. *Education:* Attended Alfred University, 1952-54; Hofstra University, B.A., 1955; Pennsylvania State University, M.A., 1962; Ohio State University, Ph.D., 1965. *Religion:* Jewish. *Office:* Department of English, Brown University, Providence, R.I. 02912.

CAREER: University of Wisconsin—Milwaukee, instructor in English, 1962; University of California, Santa Barbara, assistant professor of English, 1965-67; University of Virginia, Charlottesville, assistant professor of English, 1967-69; Pennsylvania State University, University Park, associate professor of English, beginning 1969; currently affiliated with departments of English and American civilization, Brown University, Providence, R.I. *Military service:* U.S. Army, Ordnance, 1955-57; became first lieutenant. *Member:* Modern Language Association of America, American Folklore Society, Mediaeval Academy of America, California Folklore Society. *Awards, honors:* American Council of Learned Societies fellow, 1967-68; Chicago Folklore Prize, 1970; James Russell Lowell Prize of Modern Language Association of America; fellow, Newberry Library, summer, 1971; National Endowment for the Humanities fellow, 1972-73.

WRITINGS: (Editor) *The Folksongs of Virginia,* University Press of Virginia, 1969; *The Art of the American Folk Preacher,* Oxford University Press, 1970; (editor with Jerome Mandel) *Medieval Literature and Folklore Studies,* Rutgers University Press, 1970; *Custer and the Epic of Defeat,* Pennsylvania State University Press, 1974. Contributor to *Centennial Review, Genre, Philological Quarterly, Publications of the Modern Language Association,* and other journals.

BIOGRAPHICAL/CRITICAL SOURCES: Commonweal, December 25, 1970; *Virginia Quarterly Review,* winter, 1971.

* * *

ROSENBERG, Ethel (Clifford)
(Eth Clifford, Ruth Bonn Penn)

PERSONAL: Married David Rosenberg (a publisher), October 15, 1941; children: Ruthanne. *Agent:* Scott Meredith Literary Agency, Inc., 845 Third Ave., New York, N.Y. 10022.

CAREER: David-Stewart Publishing Co., Indianapolis, Ind., editor and writer, 1959—. *Awards, honors:* Honorable mention, Indiana Authors' Awards, 1960, for Arizona Highways Nature-Adventure Books; Friends of American Writers Award, 1973, for *Year of the Three-Legged Deer.*

WRITINGS—Under name Eth Clifford; all juveniles: *The Year of the Second Christmas,* Bobbs-Merrill, 1959; *Red Is Never a Mouse* (selected one of the 100 best books of year by *New York Times* and *Saturday Review*), Bobbs-Merrill, 1960; (with Willis Peterson) *Wapiti, King of the Woodland,* Follett, 1961; *A Bear Before Breakfast,* Putnam, 1962; *A Bear Can't Bake a Cake For You,* E. C. Seale, 1962; (with Raymond Carlson) *The Wind Has Scratchy Fingers,* Follett, 1962; *Ground Afire: The Story of Death Valley,* Follett, 1962; *Pigeons Don't Growl and Bears Don't Coo,* E. C. Seale, 1963; *The Witch That Wasn't,* E. C. Seale, 1964; *Living Indiana History: Heartland of America,* David-Stewart, 1965; *Why Is an Elephant Called an Elephant?,* Bobbs-Merrill, 1966; (with others) *War Paint and Wagon Wheels: Stories of Indians and Pioneers,* David-Stewart, 1968; *The King Who Was Different,* Bobbs-Merrill, 1969; *Show Me Missouri,* Unified College Press, 1975.

All published by Houghton: *The Year of the Three Legged Deer,* 1972; *Search for the Crescent Moon,* 1973; *Burning Star,* 1974; *The Wild One,* 1974; *The Curse of the Moonraker,* 1977. Also author of *The Blue Dog, and Other Stories, The Almost Ghost, and Other Stories, The Flying Squirrels, and Other Stories, Look at the Moon,* and *Tommy Finds a Seed,* all juveniles published by Lyons & Carnahan.

Under name Eth Clifford with husband, David Rosenberg, under pseudonym David Clifford: *No Pigs, No Possums, No Pandas* (juvenile), Putnam, 1961; *Your Face Is a Picture* (juvenile), E. C. Seale, 1963.

Under pseudonym Ruth Bonn Penn: *Mommies Are For Loving* (juvenile), Putnam, 1962; *Unusual Animals of the West* (juvenile), Follett, 1962; *Simply Silly* (juvenile), E. C. Seale, 1964.

Adult books: *Go Fight City Hall,* Simon & Schuster, 1949; *Uncle Julius and the Angel with Heartburn,* Simon & Schuster, 1951; (with Molly Picon) *So Laugh a Little,* Messner, 1962.

Excerpts from various works included in *Best Humor Annual, 1949-50,* edited by Louis Untermeyer and R. E. Shikes, Holt, 1951, and other anthologies. Contributing editor, *Compton's Illustrated Science Dictionary,* Compton, 1967, and *Compton's Dictionary of Natural Sciences,* Encyclopaedia Britannica, 1966.

SIDELIGHTS: Ethel Rosenberg told *CA:* "The author of children's books is often regarded as someone who is essentially lazy and has chosen the 'easy' way to put a story down on paper. 'You write books for children? Have you ever thought of writing *seriously?'* Yes. I want to write seriously, and for the most part, that's why I write for young adult readers. They bring freshness and vitality and excitement to their reading; they love a good story. As critics, they are keen and probing and exacting. When they ask questions, they want precise answers. If they take exception to something you've written, you hear about it. They can pin you to the wall with one of your own sentences. The youngsters who write this author almost always sign their letters 'with love from your friend.' That's why I keep on writing children's books . . . somewhere out there I know I have many friends."

*   *   *

ROSENBERG, George S(tanley)   1930-

PERSONAL: Born February 20, 1930, in New York, N.Y.; son of David S. (a lawyer) and Sarah (Shapiro) Rosenberg; married Ruth Herzberg, October 2, 1951; children: William, Jonathan, Joshua. *Education:* University of Chicago, B.A., 1951; Columbia University, M.A., 1953, Ph.D., 1960. *Office:* Department of Sociology, Case Western Reserve University, Cleveland, Ohio 44106.

CAREER: Carnegie Institute of Technology (now Carnegie-Mellon University), Pittsburgh, Pa., assistant professor of sociology, 1957-61; Bureau of Social Science Research, Washington, D.C., research associate, 1961-67; Case Western Reserve University, Cleveland, Ohio, associate professor, 1967-73, professor of sociology, 1973—. *Military service:* U.S. Army, 1953-55. *Member:* American Sociological Association, Gerontological Society, Eastern Sociological Society.

WRITINGS: The Worker Grows Old: Poverty and Isolation in the City, Jossey-Bass, 1970; (contributor) Herbert Otto, editor, *The Family in Search of a Future: Alternate Models for Moderns,* Appleton, 1970; (with D. F. Anspach) *Working Class Kinship,* Heath, 1973. Contributor to *Journal of Gerontology, Journal of Marriage and the Family, Sociological Focus.*

WORK IN PROGRESS: A book, tentatively entitled *Essays in the Sociology of Old Age;* a book about kinship and economy from a theoretical point of view.

*   *   *

ROSENBLATT, Stanley M.   1936-

PERSONAL: Born July 10, 1936, in Brooklyn, N.Y.; son of Isidore (a businessman) and Mary (Stern) Rosenblatt; divorced; children: Brad. *Education:* Attended University of Florida, 1954-55; University of Miami, B.A. (magna cum laude), 1957, J.D., 1960. *Politics:* Independent. *Religion:* Jewish. *Office:* 66 West Flagler St., Miami, Fla. 33130.

CAREER: Granat, Rosenblatt & Roemer (law firm), Miami Beach, Fla., partner, 1960-65; Rosenblatt & Roemer (law firm), Miami, Fla., president, specializing in jury trial cases, 1965-70; Stanley M. Rosenblatt, P.A., Miami, trial specialist, 1970—. Special lecturer, Florida Circuit Judges Conference, 1976; lecturer, Continuing Legal Education series, Florida Bar Association. *Member:* Association of Trial Lawyers of America, Academy of Florida Trial Lawyers.

WRITINGS: The Divorce Racket, Nash Publishing, 1969; *Instant Divorce,* Award Books, 1970; *Justice Denied,* Nash Publishing, 1971; *Malpractice and Other Malfeasances,* Lyle Stuart, 1977.

*   *   *

ROSENBLOOM, Joseph R.   1928-

PERSONAL: Born December 5, 1928, in Rochester, N.Y.; son of Morris D. (a shoe-cutter) and Pearl (Vinik) Rosenbloom; married Cordelia Sherman, 1952; children: Deborah, Eve, Dena. *Education:* Attended College of Wooster, 1946-47; University of Cincinnati, B.A., 1950; Hebrew Union College, Cincinnati, B.H.L., 1952, M.H.L., 1954, D.H.L., 1957; Eden Seminary, D.Min., 1974. *Home:* 541 Purdue, St. Louis, Mo. 63130. *Office:* Department of Classics, Washington University, St. Louis, Mo. 63130.

CAREER: Rabbi; University of Kentucky, Lexington, instructor in department of ancient languages and literature, 1956-61; Temple Emanuel, St. Louis, Mo., rabbi, 1961—; Washington University, St. Louis, adjunct professor of classics, 1961—. *Member:* Society of Biblical Literature, National Association of Professors of Hebrew, American Oriental Society, American Historical Association, American Jewish Historical Society, American Association of University Professors. *Awards, honors:* American Philosophical Society grant to study in Morocco, summer, 1965; Merrill Foundation grant for research in England, 1968.

WRITINGS: (Compiler) *A Biographical Dictionary of Early American Jewry,* University of Kentucky Press, 1960; *Dead Sea Isaiah Scroll: A Literary Analysis,* Eerdmans, 1970; *A Living Faith* (sermons and lectures), Temple Emanuel (St. Louis), 1970. Contributor to *Revue de Qumran, America,* and to historical and Jewish journals.

WORK IN PROGRESS: Two books, *Conversion to Judaism through History* and *Jews and Arabs through History;* research on a reinterpretation of the first book of Samuel and on the relationship between Jews and Arabs, Judaism and Islam.

* * *

ROSENBLUM, Marc J.   1936-

PERSONAL: Born July 27, 1936, in Brooklyn, N.Y.; son of William and Henrietta (Feld) Rosenblum; married Ruth Plager (an editor), September 5, 1967 (divorced, 1974). *Education:* Hunter College of the City University of New York, A.B., 1963, M.A., 1964; University of Minnesota, Ph.D., 1971. *Politics:* Democrat. *Religion:* Jewish. *Home:* 2915 Connecticut Ave. N.W., Washington, D.C. 20008. *Office:* International Research Institute, American Institutes for Research, 3301 New Mexico Ave. N.W., Washington, D.C. 20016.

CAREER: Hunter College of the City University of New York, instructor in economics, 1964-66, summer, 1967; University of Minnesota, Minneapolis, research fellow in industrial relations, 1970-71; John Jay College of Criminal Justice of the City University of New York, assistant professor of economics, 1971-76; International Research Institute, American Institutes for Research, Washington, D.C., research scientist, 1976—. Consultant to U.S. Senate Special Committee on Aging, 1976-77, and U.S. Equal Employment Opportunity Commission, 1977. *Military service:* U.S. Army, 1958-60. *Member:* Industrial Relations Research Association.

WRITINGS: How a Market Economy Works, Lerner, 1970; *Economics of the Consumer,* Lerner, 1970; *The Stock Market,* Lerner, 1970. Also author of working papers for U.S. Senate, Special Committee on Aging. General editor, Lerner's "The Real World of Economics" series of eleven high school texts. Contributor of articles and reviews to journals. Member of editorial advisory board, *Industrial Gerontology,* 1977.

* * *

ROSENSTONE, Robert A(llan)   1936-

PERSONAL: Born May 12, 1936, in Montreal, Quebec, Canada; son of Louis (a businessman) and Anne (Kramer) Rosenstone. *Education:* University of California, Los Angeles, B.A., 1957, Ph.D., 1965. *Office:* California Institute of Technology, Pasadena, Calif. 91109.

CAREER: Los Angeles Examiner, Los Angeles, Calif., reporter and copy editor, 1960; *Los Angeles Times,* Los Angeles, public relations work, 1961-62; University of Oregon, Eugene, assistant professor of history, 1965-66; California Institute of Technology, Pasadena, assistant professor, 1966-69, associate professor, 1969-75, professor of history, 1975—. Summer professor, University of Califor-

nia, Los Angeles, 1966; visiting professor of American studies, Kyushu University, and Seinan Gakuin University, Fukuoka, Japan, 1974-75. *Military service:* California National Guard, 1961-67; active duty in U.S. Army, 1962. *Member:* Phi Beta Kappa. *Awards, honors:* Old Dominion Fund grant, 1969-70; American Philosophical Society travel grant, 1970; Fulbright-Hays senior lecturer, 1974-75, in Fukuoka, Japan; Silver Medal from Commonwealth Club of California, 1975, for *Romantic Revolutionary: A Biography of John Reed;* National Endowment for the Humanities summer grant, 1977.

WRITINGS: (Editor) *Protest from the Right,* Glencoe Press, 1968; *Crusade of the Left: The Lincoln Battalion and the Spanish Civil War,* Pegasus, 1970; (contributor) *The New Music,* Dutton, 1970; (co-editor) *Seasons of Rebellion: Protest and Radicalism in Recent America,* Holt, 1972; (co-author) *Los cantos de la conmocion: Veinte anos de rock,* Tusquets (Barcelona), 1974; *Romantic Revolutionary: A Biography of John Reed,* Knopf, 1975. Contributor to *New Republic, The Progressive,* and to historical journals. Co-editor, "Protest in the Sixties" issue of *Annals* of the American Academy of Political and Social Science, March, 1969.

WORK IN PROGRESS: Study of Japanese-American cultural relations in the nineteenth century.

SIDELIGHTS: Romantic Revolutionary: A Biography of John Reed has been translated into Italian.

BIOGRAPHICAL/CRITICAL SOURCES: Nation, April 6, 1970; *New Republic,* September 20, 1975; *New York Times Book Review,* November 2, 1975; *Reviews in American History,* June, 1976.

* * *

ROSENTHAL, Bernard G(ordon)   1922-

PERSONAL: Born February 3, 1922, in Chicago, Ill.; son of Benjamin J. and Sonia (Gordon) Rosenthal; married Judith Straka, September 22, 1957; children: Amy, Mark. *Education:* Northwestern University, B.S. (with distinction), 1942; Princeton University, M.A., 1943, Ph.D., 1944. *Home:* 801 Hinman Ave., Evanston, Ill. 60616. *Office:* Department of Psychology, Illinois Institute of Technology, Chicago, Ill. 60616.

CAREER: Princeton University, Princeton, N.J., instructor in psychology, 1947-48; University of Chicago, Chicago, Ill., assistant professor of psychology, 1948-54; Harvard University, Cambridge, Mass., lecturer and research associate in psychology, 1957-60; Illinois Institute of Technology, Chicago, professor of social psychology, 1964—. Consultant in research study, Chicago State Hospital, Chicago, 1955-56; co-chairman of Greater Boston Committee for a Sane Nuclear Policy, 1959-60; chairman of Greater Illinois Faculty Committee on Vietnam, 1965-66. *Wartime service:* U.S. War Department, Morale Services Division, 1944-45. *Member:* American Psychological Association, American Association for Humanistic Psychology (midwestern regional chairman, 1966-68), American Association of University Professors, Phi Beta Kappa, Sigma Xi, Princeton Club of Chicago.

WRITINGS: Images of Man, Basic Books, 1971; (contributor) Blank and Gottsegen, editors *Confrontation: Encounters in Self and Inter-Personal Relations,* Macmillan, 1971; *Von der Armut der Psychologie: Und wie ihr Abzuhelfen ware,* Ernst Klett Verlag (Stuttgart), 1974.

Author of thirty scientific papers. *Human Context* (an international journal), co-editor, 1968-76, executive editor of American editorial board.

WORK IN PROGRESS: Studies and research papers on various social psychological subjects, including the effect of size on behavior of groups, a system of conceptual and empirical designs for studies of the effects of crowding on behavior and affect, the development of attitudes toward money in rich and poor children; a book, tentatively entitled *Social and Psychological Conditions for the Optimization of Human Behavior;* a paper entitled "Humanistic and Middle-Class Psychology, Social-Economic Reality and Social Change."

AVOCATIONAL INTERESTS: Tennis, music, walking, manual construction and labor, swimming; travel in Europe, North Africa, Central America.

* * *

ROSIER, Bernard 1931-

PERSONAL: Born October 23, 1931, in Melun, France; married Anne Scheid (a psychologist), February 15, 1958; children: Benedicte, Claire, Bruno, Marc. *Education:* Institut National Agronomique, Paris, Ingenieur Agronome, 1955; Centre d'Etude des Programmes Economiques, Paris, Dipl.C.E.P.E., 1964; University of Grenoble, Sc.D., 1967; Faculte des Sciences economiques de France, Agrege de Sciences economiques, 1970. *Home:* Le Petit Roquefavour, Aix-en-Provence, France. *Office:* University of Aix-Marseille, Place Victor Hugo, 13331 Marseille Cedex 3, France.

CAREER: Societe Grenobloise d'Etudes et d'Applications Hydrauliques, Grenoble, France, director of studies, 1958-61; Institut National Agronomique, Paris, France, assistant master in agricultural development and planning, 1961-67; University of Grenoble, Faculty of Economic Sciences, Grenoble, faculty member, 1967-74, professor, 1970-74; University of Aix-Marseille, Faculty of Economic Sciences, Marseille, France, professor, 1974—. Professor, Institut des Sciences Politiques, Paris.

WRITINGS: (With Rene Dumont) *Nous allons a la famine,* Editions du Seuil, 1966, translation published as *The Hungry Future,* Praeger, 1969; *Agriculture moderne et socialisme: Une experience yougoslave,* Presses Universitaires de France, 1968; *Structures agricoles et developpement economique,* Mouton, 1969; (editor and co-author) *Modeles de Planification decentralisee,* Presses Universitaires de Grenoble, 1973; *Croissance et crise capitalistes,* Presses Universitaires de France, 1975. Contributor to economics journals in France and Belgium.

WORK IN PROGRESS: A book on agricultural development in growth theory and social dynamics; and research on comparative models of development and transition to socialism.

* * *

ROSS, Alec 1926-

PERSONAL: Born March 19, 1926, in San Francisco, Calif.; son of Henry and Ida (Moses) Ross. *Education:* University of California, Berkeley, B.A., B.L.S., 1952; University of Kansas, M.A., 1956. *Home:* 1121 Winsor Ave., Piedmont, Calif. 94610. *Office:* Department of English, Contra Costa College, San Pablo, Calif. 94806.

CAREER: Contra Costa College, San Pablo, Calif., English instructor, 1963—. *Member:* National Council of Teachers of English, California Association of Teachers of English, Central California Council of Teachers of English (member of board of directors, 1968-72).

WRITINGS: (With Helen Kocher) *Success with Sentences,* Macmillan, 1966; (with Kocher) *From Outline to Essay,* Macmillan, 1968; *Talking Is Speech,* Macmillan, 1968; *Writing to Be Read,* Holt, 1969; *Words for Work: Writing Fundamentals for Technical-Vocational Students,* Houghton, 1970; (with David Plant) *Writing Police Reports,* Motorola, 1977. Also author, with Plant, of a film script, "Report Writing," produced by Motorola, 1976.

WORK IN PROGRESS: A textbook on research writing.

SIDELIGHTS: Alec Ross told *CA:* "My major interest is in clear communication in every field of endeavor. The film script and textbook on police report writing are not far removed from the more traditional 'English books' I have done. Good writing is good writing, no matter what the field."

* * *

ROSS, Eric (De Witt) 1929-

PERSONAL: Born February 24, 1929, in Moncton, New Brunswick, Canada; son of David De Witt (a grocer) and Clara May (Wells) Ross. *Education:* University of New Brunswick, B.A. (honors), 1951, M.A., 1954; University of Edinburgh, Ph.D., 1962. *Home address:* Box 1625, Sackville, New Brunswick, Canada. *Office:* Department of Geography, Mount Allison University, Sackville, New Brunswick, Canada.

CAREER: Worked for Canadian Government before entering the academic field; University of Victoria, Victoria, British Columbia, assistant professor of geography, 1962-68; Bishop's University, Lennoxville, Quebec, professor of geography and head of department, 1968-72; Mount Allison University, Sackville, New Brunswick, professor of geography and head of department, 1972—. Visiting professor at Laval University, Quebec City, Quebec, 1966-67, and University of Edinburgh, Edinburgh, Scotland. *Member:* Canadian Association of Geographers, American Association of Geographers.

WRITINGS: Beyond the River and the Bay: Some Observations on the State of the Canadian Northwest in 1811 with a View to Providing the Intending Settler with an Intimate Knowledge of That Country, University of Toronto Press, 1970. Writer of about two dozen scripts for radio.

WORK IN PROGRESS: Books on Canada in the 1840's, and on off-shore islands of Nova Scotia.

* * *

ROSS, Joel E(lmore, Jr.) 1922-

PERSONAL: Born September 23, 1922, in Clinton, S.C.; son of Joel Elmore, Sr. (a railroad station master) and Cora Clyde (Cox) Ross; married Carol Piscitelli, November 21, 1946; children: Joel III, Beverly, Gregory, Mary, Susan. *Education:* Yale University, A.B., 1946; George Washington University, M.B.A., 1959, D.B.A., 1961. *Home:* 2767 Spanish River Rd., Boca Raton, Fla. 33432. *Office:* Department of Management, Florida Atlantic University, Boca Raton, Fla. 33432.

CAREER: U.S. Navy, 1946-63, attended Naval War College, 1961-62, became commander; retired from service, 1963; Merrimack College, Andover, Mass., professor of management and dean of business, 1963-64; Florida Atlantic University, Boca Raton, Fla., professor of management, chairman of department, 1964—. Visiting lecturer at University of Rhode Island, 1961-62, and University of Virginia, 1962-63. Platform speaker at conventions and seminars. *Member:* Society of Management Information Systems,

Academy of Management, Southern Economic Association, American Association of University Professors.

WRITINGS: Management by Information System, reference edition, Prentice-Hall, 1970; (with R. G. Murdick) *Information Systems for Modern Management,* text edition, Prentice-Hall, 1971, 2nd edition, 1975; (with M. Kami) *Corporate Management in Crisis: Why the Mighty Fall,* Prentice-Hall, 1973; (with Murdick) *Management Update: The Answers to Obsolescence,* American Management Association, 1973; *M.I.S. in Action,* West Publishing, 1975; *Modern Management and Information Systems,* Reston, 1976; *Managing Productivity,* Reston, 1977. Also author of *Crisis in Management: Causes and Cures.*

Author of government research studies and monographs, and over fifty closed circuit instructional television programs. Contributor of articles to *Journal of Systems Management, Computers and Automation, Management Accounting,* and other journals.

WORK IN PROGRESS: "Currently involved in research on strategic planning which will result in a professional book."

SIDELIGHTS: Joel Ross wrote to *CA:* "Increasing proliferation of books and publications in Business Management area demands that someone orchestrate theory and practice. I have attempted to do this in an applied approach for the practitioner."

*   *   *

ROSS, Leonard M(ichael) 1945-

PERSONAL: Born July 7, 1945, in Los Angeles, Calif.; son of William and Pauline (Lieberman) Ross. *Education:* Attended Reed College, 1959-62; University of California, Los Angeles, B.A., 1963; Yale University, LL.B., 1967, Ph.D. candidate in economics, 1967—. *Office:* Department of Business Management, California State Polytechnic University, 380 West Temple Ave., Pomona, Calif. 91768.

CAREER: Harvard University, Law School, Cambridge, Mass., Thayer teaching fellow, 1970-71; Columbia University, Law School, New York, N.Y., assistant professor of law, beginning 1971; currently affiliated with department of business management, California State Polytechnic University, Pomona, Calif. Executive director of Council for Policy Evaluation, New York, N.Y. Member of mayor's panel on public utilities, New York, N.Y. Consultant for President's Task Force on Communications Policy, President's Commission on Campus Unrest, Rand Corp., Arthur D. Little, Inc., New England Economic Research Foundation, and Sloan Commission on Cable Television.

WRITINGS: (With David Kendall) *The Lottery and the Draft: Where Do I Stand,* Harper, 1970; (with Peter Passell) *Communications Satellite Tariffs for Television* (monograph), International Broadcast Institute, c. 1972; (with Passell) *The Retreat from Riches: Affluence and Its Enemies,* Viking, 1973; (with Passell) *The Best,* Farrar, Straus, 1974; *Economic and Legal Foundations of Cable Television,* Sage Publications, 1974.

Contributor of articles and reviews to *New Republic, New York Times Book Review, Trans-Action, Saturday Review, Harvard Law Review,* and other periodicals. Editor-in-chief, *Yale Law Journal,* 1966-67.

WORK IN PROGRESS: Research in a number of national policy areas, including health, educational finance, fiscal policy, automobile insurance; research on Latin American politics and political sociology.†

ROSS, Thomas B. 1929-

PERSONAL: Born September 2, 1929, in New York, N.Y.; son of Henry M. (a businessman) and Evelyn (Timothy) Ross; married Gunilla Ekstrand, January 2, 1963; children: Maria, Anne, Kristina. *Education:* Yale University, B.A., 1951; Harvard University, graduate study, 1964. *Religion:* Roman Catholic. *Home:* 2911 P St. N.W., Washington, D.C. 20007. *Agent:* Sterling Lord Agency, 660 Madison Ave., New York, N.Y. 10015. *Office:* 1901 Pennsylvania Ave., Washington, D.C. 20006.

CAREER: Chicago Sun-Times, Chicago, Ill., reporter in Washington, Beirut, and Paris, 1958-70, Washington bureau chief, 1970—. *Military service:* U.S. Navy, 1951-54; became lieutenant junior grade. *Awards, honors:* Nieman fellow at Harvard University, 1964.

WRITINGS: (With David Wise) *The U-2 Affair,* Random House, 1962; (with Wise) *The Invisible Government,* Random House, 1964; (with Wise) *The Espionage Establishment,* Random House, 1967.

BIOGRAPHICAL/CRITICAL SOURCES: Book World, November 5, 1967; *New York Times,* November 26, 1967; *New York Review,* December 7, 1967; *New Yorker,* January 6, 1968; *Observer Review,* July, 1968.

*   *   *

ROSSI, Alfred 1935-

PERSONAL: Born August 18, 1935, in Chicago, Ill.; son of Alfred (a fireman) and Levia (Rossi) Rossi; married Helen Slingsby, September 9, 1961; children: Paul, Damian, Anthony. *Education:* Loyola University, Chicago, B.S., 1957; University of Kansas, M.A., 1960; University of Minnesota, Ph.D., 1965. *Politics:* Independent. *Religion:* Roman Catholic. *Home:* 1429 Cornell Dr., Davis, Calif. 95616. *Office:* Department of Dramatic Art, University of California, Davis, Calif. 95616.

CAREER: Worked as actor in various professional theatres in California, Illinois, Indiana, and Wisconsin; Tyrone Guthrie Theatre, Minneapolis, Minn., actor and director, 1963; Institute for Advanced Studies in Theatre Arts, New York, N.Y., director, 1964; University of California, Davis, associate professor of dramatic art, 1965—. Director, Colorado Shakespeare Festival, Pacific Conservatory of Performing Arts, Santa Maria and Solvang, Berkeley Stage Co., and at "La Biennale" in Venice, Italy. Administrative director, University of California, Davis Professional Resident Theatre, 1966-71; assistant director, Mark Taper Forum, 1970. Film and television actor; has appeared in "Streets of San Francisco," "Serpico," "Most Wanted," "Dirty Mary, Crazy Larry," and "Escape to Witch Mountain." *Military service:* U.S. Air Force, 1957-58. U.S. Air Force Reserve, 1959-63. *Member:* American Federation of Television and Radio Artists, Actors' Equity Association, Screen Actors' Guild. *Awards, honors:* McKnight Foundation fellowship, 1961-63; Rockefeller grant, 1964; Humanities Institute fellowship, 1968; Creative Arts grants, 1973, 1976.

WRITINGS: Minneapolis Rehearsals: Tyrone Guthrie Directs Hamlet, University of California Press, 1970; *Astonish Us in the Morning: Tyrone Guthrie Remembered,* Hutchinson, 1977. Contributor to *Drama Critique* and *Drama Survey.*

SIDELIGHTS: Alfred Rossi told *CA:* "It was a great thrill to speak with so many of the great artists of the theatre who worked with Sir Tyrone Guthrie over the years. These included Lord Laurence Olivier, Sir Alec Guinness, Sir John

Gielgud, Dame Sybil Thorndike, Anthony Quayle, and Robert Morley."

*   *   *

ROSZAK, Betty 1933-

PERSONAL: Born May 31, 1933, in New York, N.Y.; married Theodore Roszak, June 1, 1956; children: Kathryn. *Education:* University of California, Los Angeles, B.A., 1955; University of California, Berkeley, M.L.S., 1956. *Residence:* London, England.

CAREER: Miss Fine's School, Princeton, N.J., librarian, 1956-58; San Diego State College (now University), San Diego, Calif., reference librarian, 1958-59; University of California, Berkeley, residence halls librarian, 1963-64; KPFA, Pacifica Foundation network, Berkeley, Calif., dance critic and overseas correspondent, 1965—; writer, 1965—. *Member:* Phi Beta Kappa.

WRITINGS: (Editor with husband Theodore Roszak) *Masculine/Feminine: Readings in Sexual Mythology and the Liberation of Women,* Harper, 1970. Contributor to *Peace News, Manas, Ballet Review, Liberation,* and *Daily Californian.* Former editorial assistant, *Peace News.*

WORK IN PROGRESS: Studying aspects of sexual oppression, false dualisms, psychology of wholeness, form and movement, organicist biology, anarchy and pacifism, mystical socialism, and "much more."

SIDELIGHTS: Betty Roszak told *CA:* "My mentors are Leo Tolstoy, Vaslav Nijinsky, Isadora Duncan, Lewis Mumford, Bela Bartok, Lancelot Law Whyte, Paul Klee, Martha Graham, William Blake, Thomas Merton, e.e. cummings. . . ."†

*   *   *

ROTHENBERG, Jerome 1924-

PERSONAL: Born February 6, 1924, in New York, N.Y.; son of Gabriel and Rose (Goldberg) Rothenberg; married Winifred Barr (a teacher), July 11, 1948; children: Ellen, Beth, Robert. *Education:* Columbia University, B.A., 1945, M.A., 1947, Ph.D., 1954. *Home:* 100 Upland Rd., Waban, Mass. *Office:* Department of Economics, E 52-355, Massachusetts Institute of Technology, Cambridge, Mass. 02139.

CAREER: Amherst College, Amherst, Mass., instructor in economics, 1949-54; University of Massachusetts, Amherst, instructor in economics, 1953-54; University of California, Berkeley, assistant professor of economics, 1954-57; University of Chicago, Chicago, Ill., assistant professor of economics, 1957-60; Northwestern University, Evanston, Ill., associate professor, 1960-62, professor of economics, 1962-66; Massachusetts Institute of Technology, Cambridge, professor of economics, 1966—, fellow of Harvard-M.I.T. Joint Center for Urban Studies, 1968—. Academic visitor, London School of Economics, 1973-74. Fellow, Center for Advanced Study in the Behavioral Sciences, 1956-57; visiting fellow, Nuffield College, Oxford University, 1965-66. Consultant to Resource Management Corp., 1967—, and to U.S. Department of Housing and Urban Development, 1967—, U.S. Department of Transportation, World Bank, and Harbridge House Inc. *Military service:* U.S. Army, 1943.

MEMBER: American Economic Association, Econometric Society, Phi Beta Kappa. *Awards, honors:* Ford Foundation faculty research fellow, 1965-66; National Institute of Public Affairs fellowship; research grants from Brookings Institution and National Science Foundation.

WRITINGS: The Measurement of Social Welfare, Prentice-Hall, 1961; *Economic Evaluation of Urban Renewal,* Brookings Institution, 1967; (editor with Matthew Edel) *Readings in Urban Economics,* Macmillan, 1972; (editor with Ian Heggie) *Transport and the Urban Environment,* Macmillan, 1974; (editor with Heggie) *The Management of Water Quality and the Environment,* Macmillan, 1974.

Contributor: *Public Finance,* Pitman, 1959; *The Economics of Medical Care,* University of Michigan Press, 1964; Robert Dorfman, editor, *Measuring Benefits of Government Investments,* Brookings Institution, 1965; Julius Margolis, editor, *The Public Economy of Urban Communities,* Resources for the Future, 1965; Sherman Krupp, editor, *The Structure of Economic Science,* Prentice-Hall, 1966; Roland McKean, editor, *Issues in Defense Economics,* National Bureau of Economic Research, 1967; James M. McKie, editor, *Social Responsibility and the Business Predicament,* Brookings Institution, 1974; Ronald Grieson, editor, *Public and Urban Economics,* Lexington, 1976; A. Brown and E. Neuberger, editors, *Urban Analysis in Market and Non-Market Economics,* Praeger, 1976; Brown and Neuberger, editors, *Comparative Analysis of Internal Migration,* Academic Press, 1976; W. Oates, editor, *The Political Economy of Multi-Level Government,* Lexington, 1976; T. N. Clark, editor, *Citizen References and Urban Public Policy: Models, Measures, Uses,* Sage Publications, 1976; Gregory Ingram, editor, *Residential Locations and Urban Housing Markets,* National Bureau of Economic Research, 1977; Samuel Bernstein, editor, *Selected Readings in Quantitative Urban Analysis,* Pergamon, 1977. Contributor to *Encyclopedia of the Social Sciences;* contributor of about sixty articles to economics journals.

WORK IN PROGRESS: Studies on intra-metropolitan location of economic activities, on optimum public expenditures and tax policy in metropolitan areas, on theoretical and econometric models of the metropolitan housing market, on models of metropolitan land use and development, on the economics of pollution and congestion, on urban transportation policy, on urban problems in developing areas, and on government regulation in the U.S. copper industry.

BIOGRAPHICAL/CRITICAL SOURCES: Virginia Quarterly Review, spring, 1968.

*   *   *

ROUGIER, Louis (Auguste Paul) 1889-

PERSONAL: Born April 10, 1889, in Lyons, France; son of Louis (a doctor) and Marguerite (Trillat) Rougier; married Lucie Herzka, December 26, 1942. *Education:* University of Lyons, Agrege de philosophie, 1914; Sorbonne, University of Paris, Docteur es lettres, 1920. *Home:* 354 rue Saint-Honore, Paris, France.

CAREER: Professor at University of Besancon, 1924-39, and University of Caire, France, 1934-36; Foundation Edouard Herriot, Lyons, France, professor of history of religions, 1938-39; New School for Social Research, New York, N.Y., associate professor, 1941-43. Visiting professor, l'Institute universitaire de hautes etudes internationales and University of Geneva, both Geneva, Switzerland. *Member:* Mont Pelerin Society, and numerous other scientific societies. *Awards, honors:* Rockefeller Foundation fellowship, 1933; Prix de l'Academie des sciences morales et politiques, 1968; prix l'Academie francaise, 1971.

WRITINGS: La Materialisation de l'energie (essay), Gauthier-Villars (Paris), 1919, revised and enlarged edition published as *La Matiere et l'energie selon la theorie de la relativite et la theorie des quanta*, 1921, translation of revised edition by Morton Masius published as *Philosophy and the New Physics*, P. Blakiston's Son & Co., 1921; *Les Paralogismes du rationalisme: Essai sur la theorie de la connaissance*, F. Alcan (Paris), 1920; *La Philosophie geometrique de Henri Poincare*, F. Alcan, 1920; *La Structure des theories deductives*, F. Alcan, 1921; *En marge de Curie, de Carnot et d'Einstein*, Chiron (Paris), 1922; *La Scolastique et le thomisme*, Gauthier-Villars, 1925; *Celse; ou, Le Conflit de la civilisation antique et du christianisme primitif*, Editions du Siecle (Paris), 1926; *La Mystique democratique, ses origines, ses illusions*, E. Flammarion (Paris), 1929.

L'Origine astronomique de la croyance pythagoricienne en l'immortalite celeste des ames, Geuthner, 1932; *La Mystique sovietique*, Equilibres (Brussels), 1934; *Les Mystiques politiques contemporaines et leurs incidences internationales*, Librairie du Recueil Sirey (Paris), 1935; *Actes de Congres International de Philosophie Scientifique*, Hermann, 1936; *Les Mystiques economiques: Comment l'on passe des democraties liberales aux etats totalitaires*, Librarie de Medicis (Paris), 1938; *Le Colloque Walter Lippmann*, Librairie de Medicis, 1939; *Creance morale de la France*, L. Parizeau (Montreal), 1945; *Les Accords Petain-Churchill: Histoire d'une mission secrete*, Beauchemin (Montreal), 1945, revised and enlarged edition published as *Mission secrete a Londres: Les Accords Petain-Churchill*, Editions du Cheval Aile (Geneva), 1946; *Pour une politique d'amnistie* (brochure; originally published in *Ecrits de Paris*, March, 1947, as "Psychanalyse du peuple francais"), l'Enseigne du Cheval Aile, 1947; *La Defaite des vainqueurs*, La Diffusion du Livre (Brussels), 1947; *La France en marbre blanc: Ce que le monde doit a la France*, Editions du Cheval Aile, 1947; *La France jacobine*, La Diffusion de Livre, 1947; *De Gaulle contre De Gaulle*, Editions du Triolet (Paris), 1948.

La France est-elle un etat de droit?: De la legalite du gouvernement de Vichy, C.E.P.S. (Paris), 1950; *La France a la recherche d'une constitution*, Recueil Sirey, 1952; *Les Accords secrets franco-britanniques de l'autonme 1940: Histoire et imposture*, Grasset (Paris), 1954; *Traite de la connaissance*, Gauthier-Villars, 1955; *La Critique biblique dans l'antiquite: Marcion et Fauste de Mileve*, Cercle Ernest Renan (Paris), 1958; *La Religion astrale des Pythagoriciens*, Presses Universitaires de France, 1959; *La Metaphysique et le langage*, Flammarion, 1960; *La Civilisation occidentale et le christianisme*, Cercle Ernest Renan, 1960; *L'Erreur de la democratie francaise*, Editions L'Esprit Nouveau (Paris), 1963; *La Revolution philosophique due aux progres des sciences et ses consequences religieuses*, Cercle Ernest Renan, 1965; (translator and author of introduction) Aulus Cornelius Celsus, *Discours vrai contre les Chritiens*, J. Pauvert (Paris), 1965; *Histoire d'une faillite philosophique: La Scolastique*, J. Pauvert, 1966; *L'Incompatibilite due christianisme avec la vie paienne*, Cercle Ernest Renan, 1968; *Le Genie de l'Occident: Essai sur la formation d'une mentalite*, R. Laffont, 1969, translation published as *The Genius of the West*, Nash Publishing, 1971; *La Genise des dogmes chritiens*, Editions Albin Michel, 1972; *Le Conflit du Christianisme primitif et de la civilisation antique*, Copernic, 1976.

WORK IN PROGRESS: Du Paradis a l'Utopie; studies in logic, epistemology, history of religions, and history of civilizations.

BIOGRAPHICAL/CRITICAL SOURCES: Adriano Tilgher, *Relativistes contemporains: Einstein, Oswald Spengler, Louis Roughier, Vainhinger*, F. Alcan, 1922; P. Descoqs, *Thomisme et scolastique*, Archives de Philosophie, 1927; Lorenzo Giusso, *Il ritorno di Fausto: Oswald Spengler, Louis Rougier*, [Naples], 1937; Raymundo Pardo, *El Caracter evolutivo de la razon en la epistomologia de L. Rougier*, [Buenos Aires], 1954.

*   *   *

ROUGIER, Nicole 1929-

PERSONAL: Born August 29, 1929, in Paris, France; daughter of Louis F. (in advertising) and Denyse (Goddard) Rougier; divorced; children: Denis Lenoir. *Education:* Sorbonne, University of Paris, License d'anglais, 1958, Agregation d'anglais, 1961. *Home:* 23 rue des Longs Pres, 92100 Boulogne-sur-Seine, France. *Office:* Institut d'Anglais, University of Paris VII, 10 rue Charles V, 75004 Paris, France.

CAREER: Teacher in a secondary school, Paris, France, 1961-63; Sorbonne, University of Paris, Paris, France, 1963—, assistant at English Institute, 1963-65, assistant teacher at English Institute, 1965—. *Member:* Syndicat National de l'Enseignement Superieur (secretary of English section, 1967-69), Societe des Anglicistes de l'Enseignement Superior.

WRITINGS: (Editor with Marie-Claire Pasquier and Bernard Brugiere) *L'Angleterre d'aujord'hui par les textes*, Armand Colin, 1967; (editor with Pasquier and Brugiere) *Le Nouveau theatre anglais*, Armand Colin, 1969; (with F. Ducrocq and A. Valdin-Guillou) *Youth in Contemporary Britain*, Masson, 1972.

WORK IN PROGRESS: Research on women's studies.

BIOGRAPHICAL/CRITICAL SOURCES: London Magazine, November, 1968.

*   *   *

ROUSCULP, Charles G(ene) 1923-

PERSONAL: First syllable of surname rhymes with "now"; born December 17, 1923, in Lima, Ohio; son of Harold Charles and Arta Marie (Morris) Rousculp; married Alice S. Koenig, June 9, 1946; children: Kathy K. (Mrs. Michael A. Ryan). *Education:* Ohio State University, B.S., 1949, M.A., 1952. *Religion:* Lutheran. *Home:* 545 East Weisheimer Rd., Columbus, Ohio 43214. *Office:* Worthington Schools, 300 West Granville Rd., Worthington, Ohio 43085.

CAREER: State of Ohio Treasury, Columbus, assistant cashier, 1947-49; Worthington (Ohio) public schools, teacher of English and history, 1949—, coordinator of English, 1966-74. Test writer, Ohio State University, Bureau of Educational Research and Service, 1963-68; consultant, Battelle Memorial Institute, 1969—, School Management Institute, 1969-71; platform speaker, 1968—. *Military service:* U.S. Marine Corps, 1942-45; became sergeant; wounded on Iwo Jima; received Purple Heart. *Member:* National Education Association, National Council of Teachers of English, Ohio Education Association, Central Ohio Education Research Council, Phi Delta Kappa. *Awards, honors:* Named Ohio's Teacher of the Year by a committee representing the State Department of Education and other educational groups, 1968; Ohioana Book Award in nonfiction, 1970, for *Chalk Dust on My Shoulder*.

WRITINGS: Chalk Dust on My Shoulder (autobiographical), C. E. Merrill, 1969; (co-author) *Increasing the Effectiveness of Educational Management: Appraising Teacher Performance*, Battelle Memorial Institute, 1970.

Author of full-length science fiction play, "The Mantis House." Contributor of articles and poems to journals.

WORK IN PROGRESS: Rip-off in Hamelin, a critique of educational change since the 1960's.

BIOGRAPHICAL/CRITICAL SOURCES: Best Sellers, March 15, 1969; *Saturday Review,* May 17, 1969.

* * *

ROUSE, Richard H(unter) 1933-

PERSONAL: Born August 14, 1933, in Boston, Mass.; son of Hunter and Dorothy (Husmert) Rouse; married Mary Ames, September 7, 1959; children: Thomas, Andrew. *Education:* University of Iowa, B.A., 1955; University of Chicago, M.A., 1957; Cornell University, Ph.D., 1963. *Home:* 11444 Berwick St., Los Angeles, Calif. 90049. *Office:* Department of History, University of California, Los Angeles, Calif. 90024.

CAREER: Cornell University, Ithaca, N.Y., reference librarian, 1957-58; Harvard University, Cambridge, Mass., assistant curator of manuscripts for Houghton Library, 1962-63; University of California, Los Angeles, assistant professor, 1963-69, associate professor, 1969-75, professor of history, 1975—, associate director of Center for Medieval and Renaissance Studies, 1967-68. Member, Comite International de Paleographie, 1973—. *Member:* Mediaeval Academy of America, Medieval Association of the Pacific (president, 1970). *Awards, honors:* American Council of Learned Societies fellow, 1972-73.

WRITINGS: (Editor) *Guide to Serial Bibliographies for Medieval Studies,* University of California, 1969; (with wife, M. A. Rouse) *Preachers, Florilegia and Sermons: Studies on the Manipuluo Florum,* University of Toronto, in press. Co-editor of *Viator,* published by the Center for Medieval and Renaissance Studies.

* * *

ROUSSEAU, George Sebastian 1941-

PERSONAL: Born February 23, 1941, in New York, N.Y.; son of Hyman V. (a social welfare worker) and Esther (Zacuto) Rousseau. *Education:* Amherst College, B.A., 1962; Princeton University, M.A., 1964, Ph.D., 1966; University of London, postdoctoral study, 1967. *Home:* 2424 Castilian Dr., Los Angeles, Calif. 90068. *Office:* Department of English, University of California, 405 Hilgaard Ave., Los Angeles, Calif. 90024.

CAREER: Harvard University, Cambridge, Mass., instructor in English, 1966-68; University of California, Los Angeles, professor of English, 1968—. *Member:* British Society for the History of Science, Royal Society of Medicine (fellow), Royal Society of Arts (fellow), Modern Language Association of America, American Society of Eighteenth-Century Studies, History of Science Society, Augustan Reprint Society. *Awards, honors:* Woodrow Wilson fellowship, 1966.

WRITINGS: (With Marjorie Hope Nicolson) *The Long Disease My Life: Alexander Pope and the Sciences,* Princeton University Press, 1968; (editor and author of introduction) John Hill, *Hypochondriasis,* University of California Press, 1969; (editor) *Twentieth-Century Interpretations of the Rape of the Lock* (essay collection), Prentice-Hall, 1969; (editor and contributor) *The Augustan Milieu: Essays Presented to Louis A. Landa,* Clarendon Press, 1970; (with Neil Rudenstine) *English Poetic Satire: Wyatt to Byron,* Holt, 1971; *Oliver Goldsmith: The Critical Heritage,* Routledge &

Kegan Paul, 1974; (editor) *Organic Form,* Routledge & Kegan Paul, 1974; *The Ferment of Knowledge,* Cambridge University Press, in press. Contributor of about fifty articles and reviews to professional journals. Advisory editor, *Journal of the History of Ideas,* and others; reviewer for *New York Times Book Review* and *Times Literary Supplement,* 1974—.

WORK IN PROGRESS: Writing a biography of Sir John Hill, a little-known eighteenth-century medical and scientific figure; a critical study about the role of the passions in post-Renaissance European and English literature.

* * *

ROWE, Jeanne A. 1938-

PERSONAL: Born February 22, 1938, in New York, N.Y. *Education:* Syracuse University, B.A., 1959. *Office:* Franklin Watts, Inc., 845 Third Ave., New York, N.Y. 10022.

CAREER: Franklin Watts, Inc. (publishers), New York, N.Y., publicity director for adult trade books, 1961-65, editor, adult trade books, 1965-67, editor, juvenile nonfiction, 1967—.

WRITINGS—Juvenile: City Workers, F. Watts, 1969; *A Trip through a School,* F. Watts, 1969; *An Album of Presidents,* F. Watts, 1969; *An Album of Martin Luther King, Jr.,* F. Watts, 1970; *United Nations Workers: Their Jobs, Their Goals, Their Triumphs,* F. Watts, 1970.†

* * *

RUBADEAU, Duane O. 1927-

PERSONAL: Born January 7, 1927, in Jefferson, Wis.; married Lois Ann Rentmeester; children: Ronald, Thomas, David, Paul, Jon, Susan. *Education:* City College of San Francisco, A.A., 1952; San Francisco State College (now University), B.A. (with honors), 1956; Washington State University, M.S., 1959; University of Rochester, Ed.D., 1967. *Home:* 62 Drake St., Sault Ste. Marie, Ontario, Canada. *Office:* Department of Psychology, Algoma College, Sault Ste. Marie, Ontario, Canada.

CAREER: U.S. Naval Radiological Defense Laboratory, San Francisco, Calif., research associate, 1947-57; Montana State College (now University), Bozeman, assistant professor of psychology, 1959-62; Muskingum College, New Concord, Ohio, assistant professor of psychology, 1962-63; State University of New York College at Geneseo, assistant professor, 1963-67, associate professor of psychology, 1967-69, chairman of educational psychology, 1966-69; Algoma College (affiliate of Laurentian University of Sudbury), Sault Ste. Marie, Ontario, associate professor of psychology and acting chairman of department, 1969—. Visiting associate professor, Eastman School of Music, University of Rochester, 1966-68. Registered psychologist, Ontario. Co-director, Canadian Psychological Specialists; member of board of directors, Sault Ste. Marie chapters of Association for Children with Learning Disabilities and Canadian Mental Health Association.

MEMBER: National Society for the Study of Education, American Association for the Advancement of Science, Human Ecological Society, International Society for Nonverbal Therapy, National Council on Measurement in Education, Canadian Association of University Teachers, Ontario Confederation University Faculty Association, Sigma Xi, Psi Chi. *Awards, honors:* Outstanding Professor Award, Montana State College, 1962.

WRITINGS: (Editor with Irene J. Athey) *Educational Implications of Piaget's Theory,* Ginn, 1970. Publications include *Child Observation Outline,* Multiprint, Inc., 1968. Also author of *A Guide to Elementary Statistics* and editor, with Athey, of *Readings on the Psychology of Jean Piaget.* Contributor to New York State Department of Education publications and to journals.

WORK IN PROGRESS: Editing with A. J. Heitzman, *Controlling Classroom Behaviour: The Application of Behaviour Modification Procedures.*†

* * *

RUBENSTEIN, Richard E(dward) 1938-

PERSONAL: Born February 24, 1938, in New York, N.Y.; son of Harold S. (in textiles) and Jo (Feldman) Rubenstein; married Elizabeth Marsh, August 26, 1962 (divorced); married Brenda Libman, September 21, 1975; children: (first marriage) Alec Louis, Matthew Robert. *Education:* Harvard University, B.A., 1959, J.D., 1963; Oxford University, M.A.Juris., 1961. *Politics:* Radical. *Religion:* Jewish. *Home:* 2108 Sherman Ave., Evanston, Ill. 60201. *Agent:* Richard Curtis, 156 East 52nd St., New York, N.Y. 10022. *Office:* Department of Political Science, Roosevelt University, 430 South Michigan Ave., Chicago, Ill. 60605.

CAREER: Steptoe & Johnson (law firm), Washington, D.C., attorney, 1963-67; Adlai Stevenson Institute, Chicago, Ill., assistant director, 1967-70; Roosevelt University, Chicago, associate professor of political science, 1969—. Fulbright visiting professor, Universite de Provence, France, 1976-77. Professorial lecturer, Malcolm X Community College, Chicago, 1969-70. Consultant, National Advisory Commission on Causes and Prevention of Violence, 1968-69. *Member:* Phi Beta Kappa. *Awards, honors:* Rhodes Scholar at Oxford University, 1959-61.

WRITINGS: (Editor with Robert M. Fogelson) *Mass Violence in America,* Arno, 1969; (contributor) Jerome H. Skolnick, *The Politics of Protest,* Ballantine, 1969; *Rebels in Eden: Mass Political Violence in the United States,* Little, Brown, 1970; Martin Meyerson, editor, *The Conscience of the City,* Braziller, 1970; R. Aya and N. Miller, editors, *The New American Revolution,* Free Press, 1971; *Left Turn: Origins of the Next American Revolution,* Little, Brown, 1973; (editor) *Great Courtroom Battles,* Playboy Press, 1973; *Seeds of Struggle: American Farmers and the Rise of Agribusiness,* Arno, 1975.

BIOGRAPHICAL/CRITICAL SOURCES: Nation, April 6, 1970; *Time,* April 20, 1970; *Christian Science Monitor,* July 3, 1970.

* * *

RUBIN, Isadore 1912-1970

June 5, 1912—July 31, 1970; American author and editor of sex education books. Obituaries: *New York Times,* August 3, 1970. (See index for *CA* sketch)

* * *

RUCHELMAN, Leonard I. 1933-

PERSONAL: Born June 28, 1933, in Brooklyn, N.Y.; son of Jacob (a businessman) and Sarah (Rosenblum) Ruchelman; married Diana G. Hoffberger, February 12, 1961; children: Lauren, Charles. *Education:* Brooklyn College (now Brooklyn College of the City University of New York), B.A., 1954; Columbia University, Ph.D., 1965. *Religion:* Jewish. *Office:* Department of Government, Lehigh University, Bethlehem, Pa. 18015.

CAREER: West Virginia University, Morgantown, visiting assistant professor of political science, 1962-64; Alfred University, Alfred, N.Y., assistant professor, 1964-67, associate professor of political science, 1967-69, chairman of department, 1968-69; Lehigh University, Bethlehem, Pa., associate professor of government, 1969—, director of urban studies, 1972—. *Military service:* U.S. Army, 1954-56. *Member:* American Political Science Association, American Association of University Professors.

WRITINGS: (Editor) *Big City Mayors: The Crisis in Urban Politics,* Indiana University Press, 1970; *Political Careers: Recruitment through the Legislature,* Fairleigh Dickinson University Press, 1970; (editor) *Who Rules the Police?,* New York University Press, 1973; *Police Politics: A Comparative Study of Three Cities,* Ballinger, 1974. Contributor of articles to *Midwest Journal of Political Science* and *Western Political Quarterly.*

WORK IN PROGRESS: Editing *City Manager Politics: Power and Administration in the Urban Community.*

SIDELIGHTS: Leonard I. Ruchelman told *CA* that his "interest is in the area of urban leadership and executive leadership generally. Surprisingly, there is a dearth of scholarly material on these subjects and I am trying to fill the gap."†

* * *

RUDHYAR, Dane 1895-
(Daniel Chenneviere)

PERSONAL: Born March 23, 1895, in Paris, France; came to United States in 1916, naturalized in 1926; married Malya Contento, June 9, 1930; married second wife, Eya Fechin, June 27, 1945 (divorced, 1954); married third wife, Gail Tana Whittall, March 27, 1964 (divorced, 1976); married fourth wife, Leyla Rasl, 1977. *Education:* Studied at Sorbonne, University of Paris, and at Paris Conservatoire, 1912. *Home:* 3635 Lupine Ave., Palo Alto, Calif. 94303.

CAREER: Once secretary to French sculptor Francois Auguste Rodin; lecturer for fifty years in Europe and the United States. Composer; his orchestral works in polytonal style, "Poemes Ironiques" and "Vision Vegetale," were performed at New York Metropolitan Opera Festival, 1917; did scenic music for Hollywood Pilgrimage plays, 1920, 1922; has written, numerous orchestral and piano works. *Member:* International Composers Guild (founding member), American Composers Alliance. *Awards, honors:* Received prize of Los Angeles Philharmonic, 1922, for the symphonic poem, "Soul Fire."

WRITINGS: (Under pseudonym Daniel Chenneviere) *Claude Debussy et son oeuvre* (booklet), A. Durand & Fils, 1913; *Rhapsodies* (poems in French), [Ottawa], 1919; *The Astrology of Personality: A Re-formulation of Astrological Concepts and Ideals,* Lucis, 1926, edition with a new preface, Servire (The Hague), 1963, edition with a new preface, Doubleday, 1970; *The Rebirth of Hindu Music,* Theosophical Publishing, 1928; *Toward Man* (poems), limited autographed edition, Seven Arts, 1928.

Art as Release of Power (seven essays published separately as a series, 1928-29), Hamsa Publications, 1930; *White Thunder,* limited edition, Hazel Dreis Editions, 1938, new edition, Seed Center, 1976; *New Mansions for New Men,* Lucis, 1938; *The Faith That Gives Meaning to Victory,* Foundation for Human Integration, 1942; *The Pulse of Life: New Dynamics in Astrology,* McKay, 1943, new edition, Shambala Publishing, 1970; *Modern Man's Conflicts: The Creative Challenge of a Global Society,* Philosophical Library, 1948.

Gifts of the Spirit, New Age Press, 1956; *La Roc enflamme: Le renouvellement des grand images de la tradition chretienne,* Editions de la Baconniere, 1960, enlarged English translation by the author published as *Fire Out of the Stone: A Reinterpretation of the Basic Image of the Christian Tradition,* Servire, 1963; *Astrological Study of Psychological Complexes and Emotional Problems,* Servire, 1966; *The Lunation Cycle: A Key to the Understanding of Personality,* Servire, 1967; *The Rhythm of Human Fulfillment,* Seed Publications, 1968; *Of Vibrancy and Peace* (poems), Servire, 1968; *Practice of Astrology,* Servire, 1968; *Birth Patterns for a New Humanity: A Study of Astrology Cycles Structuring the Present World Crisis,* Servire, 1969.

The Planetarization of Consciousness, Servire, 1970, revised edition, ASI Publications, 1977; *Directives for New Life,* Seed Publications, 1971; *The Astrological Houses,* Doubleday, 1972; *Rania: An Epic Narrative,* Unity Press, 1973; *Return from No Return: A Paraphysical Novel,* Seed Center, 1974; *An Astrological Mandala,* Random House, 1974; *The Astrology of America's Destiny,* Random House, 1975; *The Sun Is Also a Star: The Galactic Dimension of Astrology,* Dutton, 1976; *Occult Preparations for a New Age,* Quest Books, 1976; *Culture, Crisis and Creativity,* Quest Books, 1977; *Astrology and the Modern Psyche,* C.R.C.S. Publications, 1977. Also author of *Triptych,* published by Servire.

Published music: "Three Paens for Piano," published in *New Music,* 1919; "Granites," published in *New Music,* 1935; "Five Stanzas for Strings' Ensemble," published in *New Music,* 1938; "Prophetic Rite," Mercury Music Corp., 1956. Other orchestral works include "The Surge of Fire," "Ouranos," and "Threshold"; piano works include "Tetragrams" (nine), "Pentagrams" (four), and "Syntony."

SIDELIGHTS: Dane Rudhyar reports that he is writing constantly at his home in Palo Alto, California, and is lecturing, giving seminars, and working with young people. His music is being revived and performed again in California and Minnesota; his piano music has recently been recorded by William Masselos, Michael Sellers, and Marcia Mikulak. There have been recent exhibits of his paintings at Long Beach University and the Minneapolis University Gallery.

* * *

RUDNIK, Raphael 1933-

PERSONAL: Born April 30, 1933, in New York, N.Y.; son of Charles (a poet) and Amalia (Rossfield) Rudnik. *Education:* Bard College, B.A., 1955; Columbia University, M.A., 1968; further graduate study at City University of New York. *Home:* Sarphatipak 109, Amsterdam, Netherlands.

CAREER: Bureau of Child Welfare, New York City, social investigator, 1957; Federation of Jewish Philanthropies and United Jewish Appeal, both New York City, publicist, 1958-63; Monarch Press (college texts), New York City, writer and editor, 1963-68; City University of New York, teacher at graduate center, 1968-69; lecturer on contemporary American poetry. *Awards, honors:* Yaddo fellowship, 1963; Delmore Schwartz Memorial Poetry Award, first recipient, 1970; Guggenheim fellowship, 1970-71; Jacob Glatstein Memorial Award, *Poetry* Magazine, 1975; Creative Artists Public Service Award, 1975.

WRITINGS: Pre-Twentieth Century American Poetry (college review text), Monarch Press, 1964; *A Lesson from the Cyclops and Other Poems,* Random House, 1969; (contributor of translations) Irving Howe, editor, *A Treasury of Yiddish Poetry,* Holt, 1969; *In the Heart or Our City,*

Random House, 1973. Contributor to *Centennial Review, New Directions 16, Quarterly Review of Literature, Stony Brook, Sumac,* and *New Yorker.*

WORK IN PROGRESS: Two new collections of poetry, *Frank 207,* and *Five Minutes in Green-Haired Ireland;* a work combining both poetry and prose, *Silver Ship.*

SIDELIGHTS: Raphael Rudnik says that the "raw, and sometimes the final substance" of his poetry "depends a good deal on being surprised into realizations by *seeing.*" For that reason living in a great city is important to him. For several years he has lived in Amsterdam. Rudnik has also traveled in Hungary, France, Ireland, and Yugoslavia.

BIOGRAPHICAL/CRITICAL SOURCES: Contemporary Literary Criticism, Volume VII, Gale, 1977.

* * *

RUESCHHOFF, Phil H. 1924-

PERSONAL: Born January 15, 1924, in Grinnell, Kan. *Education:* University of Nebraska, B.F.A., 1950; Pennsylvania State University, M.Ed., 1952, D.Ed., 1959. *Office:* 109 Bailey Hall, University of Kansas, Lawrence, Kan. 66044.

CAREER: Instructor in music and art in Danneborg public schools, 1946-47; University of Nebraska, Lincoln, coordinator of Fine Art Extension, 1952-59; University of Kansas, Lawrence, associate professor, 1960-64, professor of art education and chairman of department, 1964—. Member, Western Arts Council, 1964-66. Consultant, University of Washington School of Art and Dallas (Tex.) public schools, 1969-70. *Military service:* U.S. Army, World War II; served in Europe; received Air Medal and Purple Heart. *Member:* National Art Education Association, Western Arts Association, Kansas Art Education Association, Delta Phi Delta, Phi Delta Kappa.

WRITINGS: (With M. Evelyn Swartz) *Teaching Art in the Elementary Schools: Enhancing Visual Perception,* Ronald, 1969.

WORK IN PROGRESS: An elementary art education series.

* * *

RUNKEL, Philip J(ulian) 1917-

PERSONAL: Born June 25, 1917, in La Crosse, Wis.; son of Kenneth E. and Bernice (Hanan) Runkel; married Margaret West, April 26, 1943. *Education:* Central State Teachers College (now University of Wisconsin—Stevens Point), B.S., 1939; University of Michigan, M.A., 1954, Ph.D., 1956. *Office:* Center for Educational Policy and Management, University of Oregon, Eugene, Ore. 97403.

CAREER: West High School, Madison, Wis., teacher of geometry and general science, 1940-41; engineering draftsman, Panama Canal, Canal Zone, 1941-44, 1946-48; La Boco High School, Canal Zone, supervising teacher, 1948-51; University of Illinois, Urbana, 1955-64, began as research assistant professor, professor of educational psychology and member of Bureau of Educational Research, 1963-64; University of Oregon, Eugene, professor of psychology and research associate, Center for Educational Policy and Management, 1964—. Licensed psychologist, state of Oregon. *Military service:* U.S. Army, Corps of Engineers, 1944-46.

MEMBER: International Association of Applied Social Scientists, American Educational Research Association, American Psychological Association (fellow), Society for

General Systems Research, National Training Laboratories, American Association of University Professors. *Awards, honors:* Douglas McGregor Memorial Award (shared with R. A. Schmuck and Daniel Langmeyer), 1969, for "Improving Organizational Problem-Solving in a School Faculty," published in *Journal of Applied Behavioral Science*.

WRITINGS: (Editor with wife, Margaret Runkel, and Roger Harrison, and contributor) *The Changing College Classroom,* Jossey-Bass, 1969; (with R. A. Schmuck) *Organizational Training for a School Faculty,* Center for the Advanced Study of Educational Administration, University of Oregon, 1970; (with J. E. McGrath) *Research on Human Behavior: A Systematic Guide to Method,* Holt, 1972; (with Schmuck, S. L. Saturen, R. T. Martell, and C. B. Derr) *Handbook of Organization Development in Schools,* National Press Books, 1972. Contributor to academic journals.

WORK IN PROGRESS: Co-authoring, with W. H. Wyant, W. E. Bell, and Margaret Runkel, *Organizational Specialists in a School District: Four Years of Innovation;* writing a revised edition of *Handbook of Organization Development in Schools.*

* * *

RUPP, Richard H(enry) 1934-

PERSONAL: Born November 16, 1934, in Indianapolis, Ind.; son of Virgil Richard and Henrietta (Wiskirchen) Rupp; married Mary Grove, June 15, 1963; children: Elizabeth, Christopher, Nicholas, Matthew, Daniel. *Education:* University of Notre Dame, B.A., 1956, M.A., 1957; Indiana University, Ph.D., 1964. *Politics:* Moderate Republican. *Religion:* Roman Catholic. *Home address:* Route 5, Box 159A, Boone, N.C. 28607. *Office:* Graduate School, Appalachian State University, Boone, N.C. 28608.

CAREER: Gilmour Academy, Gates Mills, Ohio, instructor, 1957-58; Georgetown University, Washington, D.C., assistant professor of English, 1961-68; University of Miami, Coral Gables, Fla., assistant professor of English, 1968-72; Brooklyn College of the City University of New York, Brooklyn, N.Y., associate professor of English, 1972-74; Appalachian State University, Boone, N.C., dean of graduate school, 1975—. *Member:* Modern Language Association of America, South Atlantic Modern Language Association, National Council of University Research Administrators.

WRITINGS: Celebration in Postwar American Fiction, 1945-1967, University of Miami Press, 1970. Also author of television scripts for "You and Your Parish Council," produced in August, 1970, and "Christmas in the Arts," produced December 20, 1970.

Editor: (And author of critical notes) Nathaniel Hawthorne, *The Marble Faun,* Bobbs-Merrill, 1971; *Critics on Whitman,* University of Miami Press, 1972; *Critics on Dickinson,* University of Miami Press, 1972. Contributor of articles to *Midwest Quarterly, Commonweal, Dissertation Abstracts, Xavier University Studies, Sewanee Review, Journal of Historical Studies,* and *Southern Humanities Review.*

WORK IN PROGRESS: A study of fifteen major American novels, 1900-1940, stressing concepts of action; a study of freedom and order in nineteenth-century American fiction.

AVOCATIONAL INTERESTS: Liturgical renewal, ecumenism, the relationship between literature and theology, experimental communities, landscape architecture and urban design, music, tennis, swimming, fishing, and travel.

BIOGRAPHICAL/CRITICAL SOURCES: Books Abroad, winter, 1971.

* * *

RUST, Richard Dilworth 1937-

PERSONAL: Born September 4, 1937, in Provo, Utah; son of Richard Dexter and Alta (Cutler) Rust; married Patricia Brighton, March 18, 1960; children: Beverly Ann, Pamela, David. *Education:* Brigham Young University, B.S., 1961; University of Wisconsin, M.S., 1962, Ph.D., 1966. *Religion:* Church of Jesus Christ of Latter-day Saints (Mormon). *Home:* 414 Thornwood Rd., Chapel Hill, N.C. 27514. *Office:* Department of English, University of North Carolina, Chapel Hill, N.C. 27514.

CAREER: University of North Carolina at Chapel Hill, assistant professor, 1966-71, associate professor of American literature, 1971—. Senior Fulbright lecturer, University of Heidelberg, 1971-72. *Member:* Modern Language Association of America, American Studies Association, South Atlantic Modern Language Association, Southeastern American Studies Association.

WRITINGS: (Editor) *Glory and Pathos: Responses of Nineteenth-Century American Authors to the Civil War,* Holbrook, 1970; (editor) Washington Irving, *Astoria, or Anecdotes of an Enterprize beyond the Rocky Mountains,* Twayne, 1976. Contributor to academic journals.

WORK IN PROGRESS: An edition of James Fenimore Cooper's *The Pathfinder,* for the State University of New York Press.

* * *

RUTHERFORD, Meg 1932-

PERSONAL: Born July 23, 1932, in Sydney, New South Wales, Australia; daughter of Norman (a grazier) and Joan (Bassett) Rutherford; married Amis Stuart Goldingham (an accountant), March 19, 1966. *Education:* Attended National Art School, Sydney, 1955-58; Slade School of Art, London, Diploma in Fine Art, 1961. *Home:* Bracondale, 3 Baring Crescent, Beaconsfield, Buckinghamshire, England.

CAREER: Sculptor who "strayed into the book trade"; presently illustrating almost full time. *Awards, honors: The Beautiful Island* was named one of the fifty best books of 1969 by the American Institute of Graphic Arts, and the British edition was cited at the Frankfurt Book Fair as one of the best examples of English book production, 1970.

WRITINGS: (Self-illustrated) *The Beautiful Island* (juvenile), Doubleday, 1969; (self-illustrated) *A Pattern of Herbs,* Allen & Unwin, 1975, Doubleday, 1976.

* * *

RYAN, Alan 1940-

PERSONAL: Born May 9, 1940; son of John William (an accountant) and Ivy (Tickle) Ryan; married Joanna Frances (a psychologist), July 28, 1962 (divorced); married Kathleen Alyson Lane, November 21, 1972; children: (second marriage) Sadie Jane. *Education:* Balliol College, Oxford, B.A., 1962. *Politics:* Labour. *Religion:* None. *Home:* Haymakers, Stanton, St. John, Oxford, England. *Agent:* A. D. Peters, 10 Buckingham St., Adelphi, London WC2N 6BU, England. *Office:* New College, Oxford University, Oxford, England.

CAREER: University of Keele, Keele, England, lecturer in philosophy, 1963-66; University of Essex, Colchester, England, lecturer in politics, 1966-69; Oxford University, New

College, Oxford, England, fellow and tutor in politics, 1969—. Visiting professor of political science, City University of New York, 1967-68; visiting professor of government, University of Texas, 1972; visiting professor of politics, University of California, Santa Cruz, 1977. Visiting fellow, Australian National University, 1974.

WRITINGS: John Stuart Mill, Pantheon, 1970; *The Philosophy of the Social Sciences,* Pantheon, 1971; (editor) *Philosophy of Social Explanation,* Oxford University Press, 1973; *J. S. Mill: An Author-Guide,* Routledge & Kegan Paul, 1975.

WORK IN PROGRESS: Property and Political Theory, completion expected in 1977.

BIOGRAPHICAL/CRITICAL SOURCES: Listener, July 9, 1970.

* * *

RYAN, Kevin 1932-

PERSONAL: Born October 7, 1932, in Mt. Vernon, N.Y.; married, 1964; children: one. *Education:* University of Toronto, B.A., 1955; Columbia University, M.A., 1960, summer graduate study, 1962; Stanford University, Ph.D., 1966; Harvard University, postdoctoral study, 1970-71.

CAREER: High school English teacher in Suffern, N.Y., 1959-63; Stanford University, Stanford, Calif., instructor in education, 1965-66; University of Chicago, Graduate School of Education, Chicago, Ill., assistant professor and director of master of arts in teaching program, 1966-69, director of teacher trainers program, 1969-72, associate dean of training program, 1972-73, associate professor of education, beginning 1973. Instructor, Naval Officer's Candidate School, summer, 1963. Member of administrative policy commission, ERIC-Clearinghouse Teacher Education, U.S. Office of Education, 1973. Consultant, Commission for Public School Personnel Policies in Ohio, 1971-73. *Military service:* U.S. Naval Reserve, 1955-59; active duty, 1959-65; became lieutenant. *Member:* American Educational Research Association, American Association of Colleges for Teacher Education, Association for Supervision and Curriculum Development, Phi Delta Kappa. *Awards, honors:* Alfred North Whitehead fellow at Harvard University, 1970-71.

WRITINGS: (With Dwight William Allen) *Microteaching,* Addison-Wesley, 1969; (editor) *Don't Smile until Christmas: Accounts of the First Year of Teaching,* University of Chicago Press, 1970; (contributor) J. L. Olivero and E. G. Buffe, editors, *Educational Manpower,* Indiana University Press, 1970; (contributor) Robert Maidment, editor, *Criticism, Conflict, and Change: Readings in American Education,* Dodd, 1970; (author of foreword) James Lewis, Jr., *Differentiating the Teaching Staff,* Parker Publishing, 1971; (with James M. Cooper) *Those Who Can Teach,* Houghton, 1972, 2nd edition, 1975; (compiler with Cooper) *Kaleidoscope: Selected Readings in Education,* Houghton, 1972, 2nd edition, 1975; (contributor) Cooper, editor, *Differentiated Staffing,* Saunders, 1972; (editor) *Teacher Education,* University of Chicago Press, 1975; (editor with David E. Purpel) *Moral Education,* McCutchan, 1976. Also author of *Technical Skills of Teaching,* multimedia teaching materials published by General Learning Corp. Contributor to education journals.†

* * *

RYAN, Robert Michael 1934-

PERSONAL: Born September 19, 1934, in Jennertownship,

Pa.; married; three children. *Education:* Attended St. Mary's College, St. Mary, Ky., 1952-53; Eastern Kentucky University, A.B., 1959; graduate student at Morehead State University, 1960-62; University of Tennessee, M.S.S.W., 1965; University of Denver, D.S.W., 1972. *Home:* 3665 Paris Blvd., Westerville, Ohio 43081. *Office:* College of Social Work, Ohio State University, Columbus, Ohio 43210.

CAREER: Junior high science, math, world history, and government teacher in Kentucky schools, 1959; Western State Hospital, Hopkinsville, Ky., social work trainee, 1962; Southern Kentucky Comprehensive Care Center, Bowling Green, Ky., community mental health worker, 1965; Western Kentucky University, Bowling Green, assistant professor of sociology, 1966; Southern Regional Education Board, Atlanta, Ga., director of Social Welfare Manpower Project, 1969; currently associate professor in the College of Social Work, Ohio State University, Columbus. Kentucky Welfare Association, member, 1962-69, district vice-president, 1965; Christian County Mental Health Clinic, Hopkinsville, part-time administrative director, 1965; social work consultant for Southern Kentucky Comprehensive Care Center, Bowling Green, 1967-69, Rough River Area Council, Project Head Start, Health Service, Hardinsburg, Ky., and Kentucky Institute for Community Development, Lexington, Ky., 1968, Southern Kentucky Economic Opportunity Council, Bowling Green, 1969, Southern Regional Education Board, 1970, Social Welfare Manpower Project, 1971; management consultant, Middletown (Ohio) Mental Health Center, 1975-76, Harding Hospital (Ohio), 1976-77; curriculum consultant, University of Pennsylvania, School of Social Work, 1975-76; planning consultant, Ohio Department of Mental Health, 1976. Technical assistant in Egypt for United States Agency for International Development, 1977; member of advisory committee, Title VII Project, Florida State University School of Social Work, Tallahassee, Fla., 1969—. *Member:* National Association of Social Workers (chairman of Western Kentucky District, 1969), Council on Social Work Education, University of Tennessee Alumni Association, School of Social Work (member of board of directors, 1968-70, 1972—).

WRITINGS: Social Welfare Field Experience for Field Instructors, Department of Sociology and Anthropology, Western Kentucky University, 1968; (with Robert W. Klenk) *The Practice of Social Work,* Wadsworth, 1970, 2nd edition, 1974; (contributor) Parker Oborn, editor, *Consultation: A Review of the Literature,* Social Welfare Research Institute (Denver), 1971; (with Harold McPheeters) *A Core of Competence for Baccalaureate Social Welfare and Curricular Implications,* Southern Regional Education Board, 1971; *The Human Services Organization: A Proposed Model,* College of Administrative Science, Ohio State University, 1975; (contributor with McPheeters) Beulah Compton and Burt Galaway, editors, *Social Work Processes,* Dorsey, 1975; (with Gwendolyn C. Gilbert) *Beyond Ain't It Awful,* College of Administrative Science, Ohio State University, 1976; (contributor) *Social Work in Practice,* National Association of Social Workers, 1976; (contributor) *The Field Experience in Education for Management in Social Welfare,* University of Pennsylvania Press, 1976; (contributor with Gilbert) Dolores Norton and Samuel Miller, editors, *Sourcebook on Educating for Social Work Practice in a Pluralistic Society,* Council on Social Work Education (New York), in press.

Editor: *Tri-State Workshop on the Multiple Career Line Concept in Social Welfare,* Southern Regional Education Board, 1970; *Issues in Implementing an Undergraduate*

Social Welfare Program, Southern Regional Education Board, 1970; Creative Curricula in Undergraduate Social Welfare Education, Southern Regional Education Board, 1970. Contributor to Administration in Mental Health and other periodicals.

* * *

RYAN, Thomas Richard 1897-

PERSONAL: Born October 7, 1897, in Union City, Ind.; son of John Francis and Catherine (Kelly) Ryan. Education: Studied at St. Joseph's College, Rensselaer, Ind., and St. Charles Seminary, Celina, Ohio. Home: St. Joseph's College, Rensselaer, Ind. 47979.

CAREER: Roman Catholic priest; former teacher in a number of Catholic high schools and academies, most recently at Vincentian Academy, Pittsburgh, Pa.; former faculty member of Brunnerdale Seminary, Canton, Ohio.

WRITINGS: The Sailor's Snug Harbor: Studies in Brownson's Thought, Westminster Press, 1952; (editor) Orestes Augustus Brownson, Saint-Worship and the Worship of Mary, St. Anthony Guild Press, 1963; Orestes A. Brownson (biography), Our Sunday Visitor Press, 1976.

WORK IN PROGRESS: The Life and Letters of Orestes Augustus Brownson.

* * *

RYDER, Ellen 1913-

PERSONAL: The name Ellen Ryder is a pseudonym; born December 20, 1913, in New York, N.Y.; daughter of an American lawyer and an English actress; married several times; children: five (two deceased). Education: Attended a private school in England; Ecole Britannique, Paris, France, diploma. Politics: Left wing. Religion: Quaker. Agent: Curtis Brown Ltd., 1 Craven Hill, London W2 3EW, England.

CAREER: Currently a painter.

WRITINGS: The Red Baize Door, Hutchinson, 1964; Kate, Hutchinson, 1967; The Forest Pool, Hutchinson, 1968.

SIDELIGHTS: Ellen Ryder (the name "ensures my privacy") writes: "When I was young, I traveled and had adventures. My ideas were avant-garde. I liked art, languages, love and talk. Now I live quietly in rural surroundings, always trying to know and understand more, and labouring, too, in the house and garden as I am very practical."

BIOGRAPHICAL/CRITICAL SOURCES: Times Literary Supplement, March 23, 1967; Books and Bookmen, April, 1968.

* * *

RYKEN, Leland 1942-

PERSONAL: Born May 17, 1942, in New Sharon, Iowa; son of Frank (engaged in farming) and Eva (Bos) Ryken; married Mary Graham, August 22, 1964; children: Philip Graham, Margaret Lynn, Nancy Elizabeth. Education: Central College (now Central University of Iowa), B.A., 1964; University of Oregon, Ph.D., 1968. Politics: Independent. Religion: Presbyterian. Home: 1118 North Howard, Wheaton, Ill. 60187. Office: Department of English, Wheaton College, Wheaton, Ill. 60187.

CAREER: Wheaton College, Wheaton, Ill., professor of English, 1968—.

WRITINGS: The Apocalyptic Vision in "Paradise Lost," Cornell University Press, 1970; The Literature of the Bible, Zondervan, 1974; (contributor) Kenneth Gros Louis, editor, Literary Interpretations of Biblical Narratives, Abingdon, 1974. Editor of Heroes of Genesis, Heroines of the Bible, Parables and Portraits of the Bible, for Literature of the Bible, Inc., 1976, 1977. Contributor to scholarly journals.

WORK IN PROGRESS: A book on literature in Christian perspective; articles on Milton, the Bible as literature, and Christianity and literature.

BIOGRAPHICAL/CRITICAL SOURCES: Virginia Quarterly Review, summer, 1970.

* * *

RYZL, Milan 1928-

PERSONAL: Surname is pronounced Ree-zal; born May 22, 1928, in Prague, Czechoslovakia; son of Josef and Anna (Bilkova) Ryzl; married Jirina Souckova, November 14, 1951; children: Radim, Daniel. Education: Charles University, Prague, Czechoslovakia, Ph.D., 1952. Office address: P.O. Box 9459, Westgate Station, San Jose, Calif. 95157.

CAREER: College for Nurses, Kladno, Czechoslovakia, instructor, 1952-53; Research Institute for Perfection of Materials, Prague, Czechoslovakia, research chemist, 1953-60; Czechoslovakia Academy of Science, Prague, scientific assistant to vice-president, 1960-62; left Czechoslovakia for political reasons and came to U.S. in 1967 on immigration visa; Institute for Parapsychology, Durham, N.C., research associate, 1967-68; lecturer and professor of parapsychology at various universities in California, 1969—. Corresponding research associate, Parapsychology Laboratory, Duke University, Durham, 1963. Member: Parapsychological Association, Society for Psychical Research (London), American Society for Psychical Research, Assoziatione Italiana Scientifica di Metapsichica. Awards, honors: McDougall Award, Institute for Parapsychology, 1963, for distinguished work in parapsychology.

WRITINGS: Parapsychology: A Scientific Approach, Hawthorn, 1970; Hypnose und ASW (title means "Hypnosis and ESP"), Ramon F. Keller (Geneva), 1971; ASW-Phaenomene (title means "ESP-Phenomena"), Ramon F. Keller, 1972; Jesus, Ramon F. Keller, 1973; ASW-Training (title means "ESP-Training"), Ariston (Geneva), 1975. Contributor of articles to International Journal of Parapsychology, Journal of Parapsychology, and Grenzgebiete der Wissenschaft (Austria).

WORK IN PROGRESS: Research in hypnosis and ESP; and studies in parapsychology and its philosophical and religious implications.

SIDELIGHTS: Because of his extensive travels and two decades of experience in psychical research in Eastern Europe, Milan Ryzl is considered one of the leading authorities in the Western World on parapsychology behind the Iron Curtain. A linguist who is proficient in Russian, German, French, and Dutch, in addition to his native Czech, he also has reading knowledge of several Slavonic languages. Ryzl is credited with being the first author to publish scientific material on parapsychology in Communist Europe.

* * *

SACHS, Mendel 1927-

PERSONAL: Born April 13, 1927, in Portland, Ore.; son of Samuel (a rabbi) and Florence (Farber) Sachs; married Yetty Herman, June 22, 1952; children: Robert, Daniel,

Carolyn, Michael. *Education:* University of California, Los Angeles, A.B., 1949, M.A., 1950, Ph.D., 1954. *Home:* 95 Carriage Cir., Williamsville, N.Y. 14221. *Office:* Department of Physics, State University of New York, Buffalo, N.Y. 14214.

CAREER: University of California, Livermore, physicist in radiation laboratory, 1954-56; Lockheed Missiles and Space Co., Palo Alto, Calif., research scientist, 1956-61; San Jose State College (now University), San Jose, Calif., assistant professor of physics, 1957-61; McGill University, Montreal, Quebec, research professor of physics, 1961-62; Boston University, Boston, Mass., associate professor of physics, 1962-66; State University of New York at Buffalo, professor of physics, 1966—. *Military service:* U.S. Navy, 1945-46. *Member:* British Society for the Philosophy of Science, Sigma Xi.

WRITINGS: Solid State Theory, McGraw, 1963; (contributor) R. Cohen and M. Wartofsky, editors, *Boston Studies in the Philosophy of Science,* Humanities, 1968; *The Search for a Theory of Matter,* McGraw, 1971; *The Field Concept in Contemporary Science,* C. C Thomas, 1973; (contributor) C. A. Hooker, editor, *Contemporary Research in the Foundations and Philosophy of Quantum Theory,* D. Reidel, 1973; *Ideas of the Theory of Relativity,* Wiley, 1974.

Contributor of articles to *Nuovo Cimento, British Journal for Philosophy of Science, La Recherche, International Journal of Theoretical Physics, Synthese, Philosophy and Phenomenological Research, Nature, Annals of Physics, Physics Today, Physical Review,* and *American Journal of Physics.* Member of editorial board, *International Journal of Theoretical Physics.*

WORK IN PROGRESS: Research in general relativity applied to astronomical and elementary particle problems, foundations of quantum theory, and philosophy and history of science.

* * *

SAGALL, Elliot L. 1918-

PERSONAL: Born July 6, 1918, in Chelsea, Mass.; son of Barnard (a dentist and physician) and Rose (Ansel) Sagall; married Annette Y. Turn, June 16, 1944; children: Richard Joel, Ronald David. *Education:* Harvard University, A.B. (magna cum laude), 1939, M.D. (cum laude), 1943. *Politics:* Independent. *Religion:* Jewish. *Home:* 178 Old Farm Rd., Newton, Mass. 02159. *Office:* 454 Brookline Ave., Boston, Mass. 02215.

CAREER: Beth Israel Hospital, Boston, Mass., intern, then resident, 1943-45, clinical fellow in medicine, 1947-48, presently associate physician in Medical Service; private practice as physician, specializing in cardiology, Boston, 1948—. Harvard University Medical School, Boston, clinical instructor in medicine, 1948-76, assistant clinical professor of medicine, 1976—; Tufts University Medical School, Medford, Mass., clinical instructor in medicine, 1949-55; Boston University School of Law, Boston, lecturer in law and legal medicine, 1969-71; Boston College School of Law, Boston, instructor in legal medicine, 1970—. Lecturer for Massachusetts Continuing Legal Education, Inc., and Practising Law Institute, New York. Member of consultant staff, Brookline Hospital; member of consultant staff at other hospitals in the Boston area; regional medical and rehabilitation consultant, Insurance Co. of North America. Diplomate of National Board of Medical Examiners, 1944, and American Board of Internal Medicine, 1950, with certification in cardiovascular diseases, 1959. *Military service:* U.S. Army, Medical Corps, captain, 1945-47.

MEMBER: American College of Cardiology (fellow), American Medical Association, American Academy of Compensation Medicine (fellow), American Heart Association (fellow; founding member of committee on stress, strain and heart disease; member of clinical council of cardiology), American Society of Law and Medicine (co-founder, 1973; president, 1973—), Massachusetts Medical Association (fellow), Massachusetts Heart Association (member of board of directors, 1969—), Massachusetts Society of Examining Physicians (member of executive board, 1967-69; vice-president, 1969-71; president, 1971-73), Phi Beta Kappa, Alpha Omega Alpha.

WRITINGS: (With J. E. F. Riseman) *Electrocardiogram Clinics,* Macmillan, 1958; (with Riseman) *Cardiac Arrhythmias: Electrocardiography, Diagnosis, Treatment,* Macmillan, 1963; (with Barry Clement Reed) *The Heart and the Law: A Practical Guide to Medicolegal Cardiology,* Macmillan, 1968; (with Reed) *The Law and Clinical Medicine,* Lippincott, 1970; (editor with Irl Lucas) *Malpractice Hazards in Cardiology,* Massachusetts Heart Association, 1974. Contributor to *Legal Medicine Annual,* 1970-75; contributor of more than a hundred articles to scientific and medico-legal journals. Former medical editor, *Trial Magazine* of American Trial Lawyers Association; executive editor, *Medicolegal News;* executive editor and editor of Medicolegal Reference Library Section, *American Journal of Law and Medicine;* member of board of editors, *Journal of Sportsmedicine.*

WORK IN PROGRESS: The Medicolegal Reference Library.

* * *

SAGENDORPH, Robb Hansell 1900-1970

November 20, 1900—July 4, 1970; American farmer and publisher. Obituaries: *New York Times,* July 6, 1970; *Newsweek,* July 20, 1970; *Antiquarian Bookman,* July 20-27, 1970; *Current Biography,* 1970. (See index for *CA* sketch)

* * *

SAGER, Clifford J. 1916-

PERSONAL: Born September 28, 1916, in New York, N.Y.; son of Max and Lena (Lipman) Sager; married Marjorie Weiss; married second wife, Ruth L. Garsson; children: Barbara (Mrs. Dickson Parsons), Philip, Anthony, Rebecca. *Education:* Pennsylvania State University, B.S., 1937; New York University, M.D., 1941. *Office:* 65 East 76th St., New York, N.Y. 10021.

CAREER: Licensed to practice medicine in New York, New Jersey, and California; Montefiore Hospital, New York City, intern, 1941-42; Bellevue Hospital, New York City, fellow in psychiatry, 1942, 1946-48; New York Medical College, New York City, director of therapeutic service and associate dean of Postgraduate Center for Mental Health, 1948-60, professor of psychiatry and director of partial hospitalization programs, family treatment and study unit, 1966-70; Metropolitan Hospital, New York City, attending psychiatrist, 1960-70; Mount Sinai Medical School, New York City, clinical professor of psychiatry, 1970—; Beth Israel Medical Center, New York City, associate director, department of psychiatry (family and group therapy), and attending physician; Gouverneur Hospital, New York City, chief of applied behavioral sciences and attending physician, 1971-74; Jewish Family Services, New York City, psychiatric director, 1974—. *Military service:* U.S. Army, medical corps, 1942-46; became captain.

MEMBER: American Psychiatric Association, American Medical Association, Academy of Psychoanalysis, American Orthopsychiatric Association, American Group Psychotherapy Association (member of board of directors, 1962—; president, 1968-70), Society of Medical Psychoanalysts (president, 1960-61), American Board of Psychology and Neurology, Eastern Society for Sex Therapy (president, 1976-77), New York Society for Clinical Psychiatry.

WRITINGS: (Contributor) Alfred H. Rifkin, editor, *Schizophrenia in Psychoanalytic Office Practice,* Grune, 1957; (author of introduction) John G. Howells, *The Theory and Practice of Family Psychiatry,* C. C Thomas, 1963; (contributor) Jules Masserman, editor, *Current Psychiatric Therapies,* Grune, 1965; (contributor) Silvano Arieti, editor, *American Handbook of Psychiatry,* Volume III, Basic Books, 1966; (contributor) Alfred M. Freedmand and H. I. Kaplan, editors, *Comprehensive Textbook of Psychiatry,* Williams & Wilkins, 1967; (contributor) S. E. Waxenberg, Thomas L. Brayboy, S. Slipp, and Barbara R. Waxenberg, editors, *Progress in Community Mental Health,* Grune, 1969; (with Brayboy and B. Waxenberg) *The Black Ghetto Family in Therapy: A Laboratory Experiment,* Grove, 1970; *Progress in Group and Family Therapy,* Brunner, 1972; *Marriage Contracts: Hidden Sources of Intimate Relationships,* Brunner, 1976. Contributor to *Mental Hygiene, American Journal of Psychotherapy, Journal of Neurological and Mental Diseases, Psychoanalytic Review, International Journal of Group Psychotherapy, American Journal of Orthopsychiatry, Journal of Psychology, Journal of Medical Education, American Journal of Psychiatry, Family Process,* and other professional journals. Member of editorial board, *Family Process, American Journal of Orthopsychiatry, International Journal of Group Psychotherapy,* and *Divorce;* editor, *Journal of Sex and Marital Therapy.*

WORK IN PROGRESS: Various articles on marriage and sex for professional journals.

*   *   *

SAGESER, A(delbert) Bower   1902-

PERSONAL: Born December 31, 1902, in Chambers, Neb.; son of M. L. (a farmer) and L. Mae (Clausen) Sageser; married Ruth F. Fancher, 1927; children: Sandra Jean (Mrs. Michael Clark). *Education:* Wayne State College, Wayne, Neb., A.B., 1925; University of Nebraska, M.A., 1930, Ph.D., 1934. *Politics:* Independent. *Religion:* Methodist. *Home:* 721 Midland Ave., Manhattan, Kan. 66502. *Office:* Department of History, Kansas State University, Manhattan, Kan. 66502.

CAREER: George Washington University, Washington, D.C., research fellow, 1930-31; University of Missouri, Columbia, visiting instructor in history, 1933-34; Southern Oregon College, Ashland, visiting professor of history, 1936; College of Emporia, Emporia, Kan., professor of history, 1936-37; Kansas State University, Manhattan, associate professor, 1938-41, professor of history, 1941—. *Member:* American Historical Association, Organization of American Historians, American Association of University Professors (president of Kansas Conference, 1968-69), Western Historical Society, Kansas Historical Society (president, 1966-67), Nebraska Historical Society, Phi Kappa Phi, Phi Alpha Theta, Pi Sigma Alpha, Phi Delta Kappa, Kiwanis Club.

WRITINGS: The First Two Decades of the Pendleton Act, University of Nebraska Press, 1936; (contributor) John D. Bright, *Kansas: The First Century,* Volumes I-II, Lewis Historical Publishing, 1956; *Joseph L. Bristow: Kansas Progressive,* University of Kansas Press, 1968. Contributor to *Encyclopaedia Britannica,* about twenty-five articles to history journals, and seventy book reviews to professional journals. Guest editor of special issue of *Journal of the West,* devoted to irrigation and conservation, January,1968.

WORK IN PROGRESS: Contributing to a book on Kansas in honor of Nyle Miller.

AVOCATIONAL INTERESTS: Golf.

*   *   *

ST. CYR, Margaret   1920-

PERSONAL: Born September 18, 1920, in Manchester, N.H.; daughter of Louis J. and Anna (O'Donnell) Nordle; married Arthur J. St. Cyr, July 7, 1941 (died, 1968); children: Gail (Mrs. Raymond Ayotte), Patricia. *Education:* Attended public schools in Manchester, N.H.; graduated from Manchester Central High School, 1939. *Religion:* Roman Catholic. *Home:* 8 Palomino Lane, Bedford, N.H. 03102.

CAREER: Secretary; news editor for Poetry Society of New Hampshire, 1969-74. Lecturer. *Member:* Authors Guild, Authors League of America, Poetry Society of New Hampshire, Manchester Writers Club, Manchester Association for Retarded Children. *Awards, honors:* First prize for essay in a statewide competition, New Hampshire Federation of Women's Clubs.

WRITINGS: The Story of Pat (*Catholic Digest* Book-of-the-Month selection, July, 1970; condensation published in *Catholic Digest,* July, 1970), Paulist-Newman, 1970.

Contributor of articles and features to local magazines, *New Hampshire Profiles* and *New Hampshire Echoes,* as well as photojournalistic pieces in the *Manchester Union-Leader Daily.*

WORK IN PROGRESS: A sequel to *The Story of Pat;* a research paper, "Deinstitutionalization . . . Good or Bad?"

SIDELIGHTS: Mrs. St. Cyr writes that her book "covers nineteen years of our daughter's life, years which have left us poignantly aware of how much is left to do for our academically limited children, our mentally retarded." Mrs. St. Cyr told *CA:* "I strongly feel that my optimism stems from my Irish/Scandinavian heritage. A father who grew up in a land where the sun shines at MIDNIGHT could not help but make for a philosophy that 'nothing is impossible.' It was his encouragement and teachings which kept me writing and submitting Pat's story during those long ten years." One of Mrs. St. Cyr's goals is "to have some of my family-type fiction published."

Mrs. St. Cyr was featured on a 30-minute television show broadcast by NBC on December 13, 1970. The interview, with Fr. James Lloyd of the Paulist Fathers, was part of the Sunday "Inquiry" series. She has also appeared on the "Sonya Hamlin Show," on Boston TV, and Educational TV in New Hampshire.

AVOCATIONAL INTERESTS: Photography and writing light verse.

*   *   *

SAKS, Katia   1939-

PERSONAL: Born October 23, 1939, in Lima, Peru; daughter of Henrik (a chemist) and Consuelo (Yepez) von Saxe; married Ronald R. Fieve (a physician and professor of psychiatry at Columbia-Presbyterian Medical Center), December 28, 1963; children: Lara, Vanessa. *Education:* Attended College Francais, Lima, Peru, and Chatham College, Pittsburgh, Pa. *Politics:* Democrat. *Religion:* Roman Catholic. *Residence:* New York, N.Y.

CAREER: McGraw-Hill Book Co., New York, N.Y., assistant to editor of International Division, 1965-67.

WRITINGS: La Rifa, Morrow, 1968.

Novels in Spanish: *Su Majestad el destino,* Salas (Lima), 1956; *La Leyenda de todos y de nadie,* Ausonia (Lima), 1957; *La Mojigata,* Ausonia, 1958; *Los Titeres,* Italprint (Lima), 1960.

WORK IN PROGRESS: A novel, as yet untitled.

*   *   *

SALES, M(ary) E(ileen)   1936-

PERSONAL: Born October 14, 1936, in Boscombe, Hampshire, England; daughter of Stanley Barrett (a pharmaceutical chemist) and Phyllis (Sherrington) Sales; married Richard Morley (an economist), September 3, 1969. *Education:* Oxford University, B.A. (honors), 1958; University of London, B.Sc. (economics), 1966. *Home:* 3 Wood View, Shincliffe, Durham City, County Durham, England.

CAREER: General Medical Council, London, England, administrative assistant, 1959-63; British Foreign Office, London, research assistant, 1963-65; University of Durham, Durham, England, research assistant, 1966-69, research fellow in Middle East politics, 1969-71.

WRITINGS: (Compiler with Charles Henry Dodd) *Israel and the Arab World,* Barnes & Noble, 1970.

WORK IN PROGRESS: A book on the administration of the Arab States of Syria during the French mandate; research on contemporary society and politics of Syria.†

*   *   *

SALKELD, Robert J.   1932-

PERSONAL: Born July 26, 1932, in Glen Rock, N.J.; son of Charles Feagles and Doris (Cheney) Salkeld. *Education:* Attended California Institute of Technology, 1950-52; Princeton University, A.B., 1954; Harvard University, M.B.A., 1956. *Politics:* Republican. *Home:* 30228 Morning View Dr., Malibu, Calif. 90265.

CAREER: Ramo-Wooldridge Corp., Los Angeles, Calif., administrative assistant, 1956-58; Space Technology Labs, Inc., Los Angeles, assistant project engineer, 1958-60; Aerospace Corp., Los Angeles, manager of Advanced Manned Systems, 1960-63; United Aircraft Corp., Los Angeles, technical director, Military and Space Systems Planning, 1963-67; R. J. Salkeld and Associates, president, consultant to United Aircraft, Aerospace Corp., Aerojet-General, and National Aeronautics and Space Administration, 1967-71; Systems Development Corp., Santa Monica, Calif., planning director, 1971-75, consultant, 1975—. Patentee in the field of strategic missiles and space vehicles. *Member:* American Association for the Advancement of Science (fellow), American Institute of Aeronautics and Astronautics (associate fellow), American Astronautical Society (senior member), British Interplanetary Society (fellow).

WRITINGS: War and Space, foreword by B. A. Schriever, Prentice-Hall, 1970. Author of numerous technical papers, many of them published in the *American Institute of Aeronautics and Astronautics Journal.*

WORK IN PROGRESS: A second edition of *War and Space.*

SALZANO, F(rancisco) M(auro)   1928-

PERSONAL: Born July 27, 1928, in Cachoeira do Sul, Brazil; son of Francisco (a medical doctor) and Onelia (Pertille) Salzano; married Thereza Torres, March 20, 1952; children: Felipe, Renato. *Education:* Federal University of Rio Grande do Sul, Sc.Bach., 1950, licentiate, 1952, Priv.Doc., 1960; University of Sao Paulo, fellow, 1951, Ph.D., 1955. *Home:* Venancio Aires, 1092, Apt. 11, Porto Alegre, Rio Grande do Sul, Brazil. *Office:* Departamento de Genetica, Caixa Postal 1953, Porto Alegre, Rio Grande do Sul, Brazil.

CAREER: Federal University of Rio Grande do Sul, Porto Alegre, Rio Grande do Sul, Brazil, instructor, 1952-60, assistant professor, 1960-67, associate professor of genetics, 1967—, Institute of Natural Sciences, researcher, 1952-62, head of genetics section, 1963-68, director, 1968-71. Rockefeller Foundation fellow, 1956-57. *Member:* International Association of Human Biologists (secretary-general, 1974-80), Latin American Genetics Society (member of board, 1972-76), Brazilian Society of Genetics (president, 1966-68), Brazilian Society for the Advancement of Science (member of council, 1961-77), Brazilian Academy of Sciences. *Awards, honors:* Silver medal of Sociedade Brasileira pora o Progresso da Cieucia, 1973, for distinguished service to the sciences in Brazil.

WRITINGS: O Problema das especies cripticas: Estudos no sub-grupo bocainensis (Drosophila), Instituto de Ciencias Naturais, Universidade Federal do Rio Grande do Sul, 1956; *Estudos geneticos e demograficos entre os indios do Rio Grande do Sul,* Instituto de Ciencias Naturais, Universidade Federal do Rio Grande do Sul, 1961; (with Newton Freire-Maia) *Populacoes brasileiras: Aspectos demograficos, geneticos e antropologicos,* Companhia Editora Nacional and Universidade de Sao Paulo, 1967, English adaptation published as *Problems in Human Biology: A Study of Brazilian Populations,* text editon, Wayne State University Press, 1970; (editor) *The Ongoing Evolution of Latin American Populations,* C. C Thomas, 1970; (editor) *The Role of Natural Selection in Human Evolution,* North-Holland, 1975.

Also author or co-author of over 270 scientific papers published in journals and books in Brazil, Mexico, the United States, Europe, and India.

WORK IN PROGRESS: Research in human genetics, including population structure and polymorphisms, chromosome aberrations, problems of medical interest, and studies on twins.

SIDELIGHTS: F. M. Salzano told *CA* that he was at first involved with research in animal genetics; after a one-year stay at the human genetics department of the University of Michigan, he became interested in human genetics. He has traveled extensively in Brazil's interior, because of Indian group studies.

*   *   *

SAMKANGE, Stanlake (John Thompson)   1922-

PERSONAL: Born March 11, 1922, in Mariga, Rhodesia; son of T. D. (a clergyman) and Grace C. Samkange; married Tommie Anderson (a professor of psychology), February 6, 1958; children: Stanlake John Mudavanhie, Harry Mushore Anderson. *Education:* University College of Fort Hare, B.A., 1948; University of South Africa, B.A. (honors), 1951; Indiana University, M.Sc. in Ed., 1958, Ph.D., 1968. *Politics:* African Nationalist. *Religion:* Methodist. *Office:* Department of African-American Studies, Northeastern University, 360 Huntington Ave., Boston, Mass. 02115.

CAREER: Director of companies in Salisbury, Rhodesia, 1958-65; honarary organizing secretary, Nyatsime College, Rhodesia; presently associated with department of African-American studies, Northeastern University, Boston, Mass. *Awards, honors:* Herskovits Award from African Studies Association, 1970, for *Origins of Rhodesia.*

WRITINGS: The Chief's Daughter Who Would Not Laugh, Longmans, Green, 1964; *On Trial for My Country,* Humanities, 1966; *Origins of Rhodesia,* Prager, 1968; *African Saga,* Abingdon, 1971; *The Mourned One,* Heinemann, 1975; *Year of the Uprising,* Heinemann, 1977.

WORK IN PROGRESS: Africans under Rhodes; Among Them Yanks.

* * *

SAMMIS, John 1942-
(Patrick Russell)

PERSONAL: Born June 22, 1942; son of Fred Rutledge (a publisher) and Mary Ruth (Townsend) Sammis; married Susan Field (an editor and writer), August 26, 1966. *Education:* Bowdoin College, A.B. *Politics:* Independent. *Religion:* "Same as politics." *Home:* 6 Rebel Rd., Westport, Conn. 06880.

CAREER: Rutledge Books, Inc., New York, N.Y., associate publisher, beginning 1965. *Member:* American Contract Bridge League, Bowdoin Club of New York, Briard Club of America.

WRITINGS: (With Earl Weaver), *Winning,* Morrow, 1972; (with Johnny Bench), *Catching and Power Hitting,* Viking, 1975.

Under pseudonym Patrick Russell: *Going Going Gone* (juvenile), Doubleday, 1967; *The Tommy Davis Story* (juvenile), Doubleday, 1969.

WORK IN PROGRESS: A book of hockey fiction.

AVOCATIONAL INTERESTS: Platform tennis (nationally ranked), baseball, softball, tennis, football, ice hockey, bowling, basketball, golf, bridge; dogs, especially his own champion Briards.†

* * *

SANBORN, Ruth Cummings 1917-

PERSONAL: Born April 10, 1917, in Bradford, N.H.; daughter of Lloyd Roswell (a businessman) and A. Dorothy (Smith) Cummings; married Arthayer R. Sanborn, Jr. (a Baptist minister), August 19, 1939; children: David (deceased), Peter, Stephen, Philip, Ann. *Education:* Simmons College, B.S.; Columbia University, Teachers College, graduate study. *Home:* 522 Avenue A, Melbourne Beach, Fla. 32951.

CAREER: Teacher at schools at Nyack, N.Y., 1957-61, and New York City, 1961-64; Katharine Gibbs School, New York City, teacher of business education, 1964-69, director of secretarial studies, 1969-71, curriculum manager, 1971-72; Reinforcement Learning, Inc., Englewood Cliffs, N.J., business education consultant and editor, 1973—. Owner of craft shop, Indialantic, Fla. *Member:* American Association of University Women, National Business Teachers Association, Eastern Business Teachers Association.

WRITINGS: (With husband, Arthayer R. Sanborn) *Do You Hear Me God?,* Judson, 1968; (with A. R. Sanborn) *Next Stop Grand Central* (poems), Judson, 1969. Contributor to church and business education periodicals.

WORK IN PROGRESS: With Arthayer R. Sanborn, research for a biography of Edward Hopper, the artist; a book fo contemporary verse, *Old Age Is Not for Sissies;* research for *Crafts for the Elderly.*

* * *

SANCTUARY, Gerald 1930-

PERSONAL: Born November 22, 1930, in Bridport, England; son of John C. T. (a physician) and Maisie (Brooks) Sanctuary; married Rosemary L'Estrange, July 28, 1956; children: Celia, Nigel, Thomas, Charles, Sophie. *Education:* Attended Bryanston School, Blandford, England, and Law Society's School of Law, London. *Home:* 100 Fishpool St., St. Albans, Hertfordshire, England. *Office:* The Law Society, Chancery Lane, London, England.

CAREER: Hasties (attorneys), London, England, partner, 1957-63; National Marriage Guidance Council, London, field secretary, 1963-65, national secretary, 1965-69; Sex Information and Educational Council of the U.S. (SIECUS), New York, N.Y., director for international services, 1969, executive director, 1969-71; The Law Society, London, secretary of professional and public relations, 1971—. Speaker at conferences on the family and marriage in Europe, Africa, and United States; assisted in formation of Family Service Council of Kenya, 1967. Liveryman and honorary legal adviser, Guild of Air Pilots and Air Navigators of London; freeman of City of London. *Military service:* Royal Air Force, 1953-55. *Member:* American Association of Marriage Counselors (clinical member).

WRITINGS: Marriage under Stress, Verry, 1968; (with Constance Whitehead) *Divorce—and After: A Handbook for the Divorced and Separated,* Gollancz, 1970; *Before You See a Solicitor,* Oyez, 1973. Contributor to journals.

AVOCATIONAL INTERESTS: Amateur drama (has played seven Shakespearean roles and many other parts).

* * *

SANDERS, Pieter 1912-

PERSONAL: Born September 21, 1912, in Schiedam, Netherlands; son of Pieter (an architect) and Ina (Habraken) Sanders; married June 24, 1937; wife's name, Ida; children: Pieter, Frederieke (Mrs. Willard B. Taylor), Martijn. *Education:* University of Leiden, law student, 1930-34, Ph.D., 1945. *Religion:* Protestant. *Home:* 134 Burg. Kanppertlaan, Schiedam, Netherlands.

CAREER: Admitted to bar, 1936; private law practice, 1936-59; Netherlands School of Economics, Rotterdam, professor of corporation law, 1959—. Member of board of directors, K.L.M. (Royal Dutch Airlines), Ryn Schelde Verolme Shipyards, OGEM, and other corporations. Trustee of Museum Boymans van Beuningen, Rotterdam, and Stedelyh Museum, Amsterdam.

WRITINGS: Aantasting van arbitrale vonnissen (on arbitration and award in the Netherlands), Tjeenk Willink, 1940; (rapporteur general for International Association of Lawyers) *Arbitrage International Commercial: International Commercial Arbitration,* Nijhoff, Volume I, 1956, Volume II, 1960, Volume III, 1965; *Het Nationaal Steun Fonds: Bijdrage tot de geschiedenis van de financiering van het verzet, 1941-1945* (on World War II finance in the Netherlands; includes summary in English), Nijhoff, 1960; *Europaeische Aktiengesellschaft* (on corporation law in European Economic Community countries), Staatsdrukkerijen Uitgeverijbedrijf, 1967; (editor) *International Arbitration: Liber ami-*

corum for Martin Domke, Nijhoff, 1968; *European Stock Corporation: Text of Draft Statute with Commentary*, Commerce Clearing House, 1969; *N.V. and B.V. ter nieuwe ondernewingirecht*, Kluwer, 1976; *Trends in the Field of International Commercial Arbitration, Hague Academy Lectures, 1975*, Nijhoff, 1976; (editor) *Yearbook on Arbitration*, Kluwer, 1976; (editor) *Yearbook on Arbitration*, Kluwer, 1977.

WORK IN PROGRESS: A chapter on arbitration for *Encyclopedia of Comparative Law;* editing *Yearbook on Arbitration,* for Kluwer; *Dutch Company Law.*

AVOCATIONAL INTERESTS: Comparative art (modern, African, pre-Columbian).

* * *

SANDERS, Stephen (Jesse, Jr.) 1919-

PERSONAL: Born November 10, 1919, in Salisbury, N.C.; son of Stephen Jesse, Sr. and Pattie (Mann) Sanders; married Mildred McCormick, March 31, 1944 (divorced, 1964); children: Stephen Jesse III. *Education:* Attended Pfeiffer College, 1938. *Religion:* Crownist. *Address:* P.O. Box 3743, Carmel, Calif. 93921.

CAREER: U.S. Army, 1942-50, served with Infantry, Military Police, and Counter Intelligence, became captain, attended various army schools, including Army Language School, Monterey, Calif.; worked for *Clarion-Ledger* and *Jackson Daily News*, Jackson, Miss., 1952-59, became national advertising manager; founder and president of Stephen J. Sanders, Inc. (export-import firm), Jackson and Vicksburg, Miss., 1960-65; founder and president of Fellowship of the Crown (religious order), Montreat, N.C., 1967—. Founder and chairman of Foreign Trade Committee of Jackson (Miss.) Chamber of Commerce, 1961-62; secretary of board of governors, Mississippi World Trade Council, 1962-63. *Member:* National Fourth Infantry Division Association, Twenty-second Infantry Association. *Awards, honors—*Military: Bronze Star Medal with oak-leaf cluster; combat infantryman's badge. Civilian: E. Flag and Certificate, presented by President John F. Kennedy, 1962, for "outstanding contributions to U.S. Export Expansion Program."

WRITINGS: To Him Who Conquers, Doubleday, 1970.

WORK IN PROGRESS: A definitive history of Jesus of Nazareth; and an autobiography.

SIDELIGHTS: Stephen Sanders told *CA:* "My major interest now, and my vocation, is serving as spiritual director to those persons entering the higher stages of spiritual awareness known best as Illumination and Union. This interest is due to a cataclysmic religious experience in November, 1963. My book ... relates some of the results of this experience and the ministry that developed out of it. The vocation involves the establishment of a global religious order titled Fellowship of the Crown."

* * *

SANDLER, Irving (Harry) 1925-

PERSONAL: Born July 22, 1925, in New York, N.Y.; son of Harry (a teacher) and Anna (Robin) Sandler; married Lucy Freeman (a professor of art history), September 4, 1958; children: Catherine Harriet. *Education:* Attended Franklin and Marshall College, 1943-44; Temple University, B.A., 1948; University of Pennsylvania, M.A., 1950; New York University, Ph.D., 1976. *Home:* 100 Bleecker St., New York, N.Y. 10012. *Office:* Department of Art Education, State University of New York College at Purchase, Purchase, N.Y. 10577.

CAREER: Tanager Gallery, New York City, director, 1956-59; *Art News*, New York City, senior critic, 1956-62; *New York Post*, New York City, art critic, 1961-64; New York University, New York City, instructor in art history, 1963-72; State University of New York College at Purchase, Purchase, N.Y., professor of art history, 1972—. President of board of directors, Committee for the Visual Arts, New York City. Consultant, National Endowment for the Arts. *Military service:* U.S. Marine Corps, 1943-46; became second lieutenant. *Member:* International Association of Art Critics (president of American section, 1959—), College Art Association, Institute for the Study of Art in Education. *Awards, honors:* Tona Shepard grant to travel in Germany and Austria, 1960; Guggenheim fellow, 1965-66.

WRITINGS: (With E. C. Goossen and Robert Goldwater) *Three American Sculptors*, Grove, 1959; (contributor) B. H. Friedman, editor, *School of New York: Some Younger Artists*, limited edition, Grove, 1960; *Paul Burlin* (exhibit catalogue), American Federation of Arts, 1962; (contributor) Maurice Tuchman, *American Sculpture of the Sixties*, New York Graphics Society, 1967; *The Triumph of American Painting: A History of Abstract Expressionism*, Praeger, 1970; (contributor) *Contemporary Art, 1942-1972: Collection of the Albright-Knox Art Gallery*, Praeger, 1973; (contributor) Gregory Battcock, editor, *New Ideas in Art Education*, Dutton, 1973; (contributor) Dore Ashton and others, editors, *The Hirshhorn Museum and Sculpture Garden*, Abrams, 1974. Contributor to *Saturday Review* and art journals. Art critic and contributing editor, *Art in America*, 1971—.

WORK IN PROGRESS: Further writing on contemporary art.

* * *

SARANO, Jacques 1920-

PERSONAL: Born July 19, 1920; married Cecile Delhomme (died, 1966); married, 1971; children: (first marriage) three. *Education:* University of Lyons, A.E.H.L., Licence de Philosophe. *Home:* 12 Rue la Fontaine, Valence 26, France.

CAREER: Physician specializing in gastrointestinal disorders. *Military service:* Parachutist with British Special Air Service in World War II; received Croix de Guerre.

WRITINGS: La guerison, P.U.F., 1955; *La culpabilite*, A. Colin, 1957; *Medecine et Medecins*, Editions du Seuil, 1959; *Essai sur la signification du corps*, Delachaux & Niestle, 1963, translation by James H. Farley published as *The Meaning of the Body*, Westminster, 1966; *La Douleur*, Editions de l'Epi, 1965, translation by Dennis Pardee published as *The Hidden Face of Pain*, Judson, 1970; *L'equilibre humain*, Editions du Centurion, 1966; *Connaissance de soi, connaissance d'autri*, Editions du Centurion, 1967; *Homme et sciences de l'homme*, Editions de l'Epi, 1968; *La Solitude humaine*, Editions du Centurion, 1969; *La sexualite liberee*, Editions de l'Epi, 1969; *Rester et devenir soi-meme*, Editions du Centurion, 1970; *Reussir sa vie*, Editions du Centurion, 1971; *La Separation*, Le Centurion, 1972; *Le defi de l'esperance*, Le Centurion, 1973; *Nos liens de dependance*, Le Centurion, 1975; *Relation avec les malades*, Le Centurion, 1977. Contributor to other books and to periodicals.

SIDELIGHTS: Nine of Jacques Sarano's books have been translated into other languages.

SARGEANT, Winthrop 1903-

PERSONAL: Born December 10, 1903, in San Francisco, Calif.; son of Winthrop (secretary, California Academy of Sciences) and Geneve (a painter; maiden name, Rixford) Sargeant; married Ellery Allen, 1927; married second wife, Georgia Graham, 1937; married third wife, Jane Smith (a painter), December 23, 1955. *Education:* Attended high school in San Francisco, where he also studied violin and composition privately; continued his musical studies in Europe, 1923-26, mainly under Carl Prohaska, Vienna, and Lucien Capet, Paris. *Politics:* "Neutral; hope for a better world." *Religion:* Theravada Buddhist. *Office: New Yorker,* 25 West 43rd St., New York, N.Y. 10036.

CAREER: Violinist in San Francisco Symphony Orchestra, 1921-23, New York Symphony Orchestra, 1926-28, and New York Philharmonic (under Toscanini), 1928-30; gave up violin in 1930 and "converted myself into a writer"; music critic for *Brooklyn Eagle,* 1934-36, and *New York American,* 1936-37; *Time,* New York City, music editor, 1937-39, general writer, 1939-45; *Life,* New York City, senior writer, 1945-49, roving correspondent, 1946-49, and contributor until 1952; *New Yorker,* New York City, music critic and writer, 1949—. In earlier years did arrangements for Broadway musicals, composed scores for modern dance groups, and taught musical composition; has been a Sanskrit scholar for more than twenty-five years. *Member:* Century Association, Coffee House Club (both New York). *Awards, honors:* Citation for distinguished contribution to music from National Association for American Composers and Conductors.

WRITINGS: Jazz, Hot and Hybrid, Arrow Editions, 1938, third revised and enlarged edition published as *Jazz: A History,* Da Capo Press, 1976; *Geniuses, Goddesses, and People* (includes biographical sketches originally published in *Life,* 1944-48), Dutton, 1949; *Listening to Music* (anthology of criticism), Dodd, 1958, reprinted, Greenwood, 1977; *Humility, Concentration and Gusto: A Profile of Marianne Moore* (booklet), Pratt Adlib, 1960; *In Spite of Myself* (personal memoirs), Doubleday, 1970. Contributor to *Nation, Theatre Arts Monthly, Saturday Evening Post, American Mercury, Ladies' Home Journal,* and other national magazines, and to music journals, including *Musical Quarterly.*

WORK IN PROGRESS: A new translation from the Epic Sanskrit, for Doubleday; continuing research in ths Sanskrit language and the history and mythology of India.

SIDELIGHTS: Winthrop Sargeant originally wanted to be a symphony conductor, but succeeded, he says, "only in being a symphony orchestra violinist, which did not satisfy me." In his memoir, *In Spite of Myself,* which was written twenty years before publication, he told *CA,* "he reveals that psychoanalysis brought relief from a crippling neurosis which, for a time, prevented him from writing." A great deal of his magazine writing has concerned foreign countries; he has covered Europe from Greece to Finland, spent many months in India, and traveled in Southeast Asia. He is "reasonably fluent in—though by no means a master of—French, German, Italian, Spanish, and, nowadays, Sanskrit."

BIOGRAPHICAL/CRITICAL SOURCES: Winthrop Sargeant, *In Spite of Myself,* Doubleday, 1970; *Newsweek,* July 20, 1970; *New York Times Book Review,* July 26, 1970; *New Yorker,* September 5, 1970; *New York Times,* December 31, 1970.

SARGENT, Lyman Tower 1940-

PERSONAL: Born February 9, 1940, in Rehoboth, Mass.; son of Stanley Morse (a clergyman) and Doris (Tower) Sargent; married Patricia McGinnis (a high school teacher), December 27, 1961 (divorced); children: Evan Charles. *Education:* Macalester College, B.A., 1961; University of Minnesota, M.A., 1962, Ph.D., 1965. *Home:* 1102 North Hanley Rd., St. Louis, Mo. 63130. *Office:* Department of Political Science, University of Missouri—St. Louis, St. Louis, Mo. 63121.

CAREER: University of Wyoming, Laramie, instructor in political science, 1964-65; University of Missouri—St. Louis, assistant professor, 1965-70, associate professor, 1970-75, professor of political science, 1975—, chairman of department, 1969-71, 1975—. *Member:* International Political Science Association, American Political Science Association, Political Studies Association of the United Kingdom, Canadian Political Science Association, American Society for Political and Legal Philosophy, Conference for the Study of Political Thought (St. Louis area coordinator, 1969—), International Association for Philosophy of Law and Social Philosophy (American section), American Association of University Professors, American Studies Association, Science Fiction Research Association, American Civil Liberties Union, Midwest Political Science Association, Northeast Political Science Association, Southern Political Science Association, Western Political Science Association, Missouri Political Science Association.

WRITINGS: Contemporary Political Ideologies: A Comparative Analysis, Dorsey, 1969, 3rd edition, 1975; (with Thomas Zant) *Techniques of Political Analysis: An Introduction,* Wadsworth, 1970; *New Left Thought: An Introduction,* Dorsey, 1972. Contributor to *Minus One, Anarchy, Journal of General Education, Annals of Iowa, Futurist, Comparative Literature Studies, Political Theory, Extrapolation, Science Fiction Studies,* and *Minnesota Review.* Editor, *Newsletter* of Conference for the Study of Political Thought, 1970—.

WORK IN PROGRESS: Research on utopian literature and anarchism.

*   *   *

SARNO, Ronald A(nthony) 1941-

PERSONAL: Born September 26, 1941, in Jersey City, N.J.; son of Anthony Vincent (an accountant) and Philomena (Pilla) Sarno. *Education:* Attended Bellarmine College, Plattsburgh, N.Y., 1959-63, and Weston College, 1963-66; Boston College, A.B., 1965, M.A., 1966; Woodstock College, M.Div., 1972; New York University, candidate for Ph.D., 1975—. *Politics:* Democrat. *Home:* 52 Charles St., Little Ferry, N.J. 07643. *Office:* 703 Main St., Paterson, N.J. 07506.

CAREER: Parochial high school teacher of English and religion, New York, N.Y., 1966-69; St. Peter's College, Jersey City, N.J., lecturer on mass media, 1970; facilitator, high school human relations workshops, National Conference of Christians and Jews, 1968-71; U.S. Christian Life Communities, Paterson, N.J., national college moderator, 1970-75, east region representative, 1975—. Associate director, St. Ignatius Retreat House, Manhasset, N.Y., 1972-75; lecturer on New Testament, St. John's University, Jamaica, N.Y., 1975; administrative assistant in department of pediatrics, St. Joseph's Hospital and Medical Center, Paterson, N.J., 1976—. *Member:* International Platform Association, Loyola Christian Life Community.

WRITINGS: Achieving Sexual Maturity, Paulist/Newman, 1969; *Let Us Proclaim the Mystery of Faith,* Dimension Books, 1970; *The People of Hope,* Liguorian, 1971; *The Cruel Caesars: Their Impact on the Early Church,* Alba, 1976. Also editor of *Liturgical Handbook for CLC's,* 1974, and author of *Prayers for Modern, Urban, Uptight Man.* Contributor to *Jesuit Yearbook;* contributor of about twenty-five articles to *America, Chicago Studies,* and other periodicals. Assistant editor, *Sacred Heart Messenger,* 1967; contributing editor, *National Jesuit News,* 1971-72.

WORK IN PROGRESS: A textbook with Fr. Len Badia, *Contemporary Catholic Issues;* planning dissertation on mass media and its effect over the centuries on religious education.

SIDELIGHTS: Ronald Sarno told *CA:* "I always feel slightly outdated when writing because I really believe that media have far more influence on people today than print. However, I have also found that my writing has always received an appreciative, if limited audience. I am in the unusual position of telling print-oriented readers how much influence the non-print media have on their lives, especially on religious and philosophical opinions."

*　　*　　*

SARRE, Winifred Turner 1931-

PERSONAL: Surname rhymes with "car"; born October 17, 1931, in Adelaide, South Australia; daughter of George Bawden (a businessman) and Grace (Loughlin) Turner; married Brian Sarre (a retail jeweler); March 1, 1952; children: Deborah, Warwick, Airlie. *Education:* University of Adelaide, B.A., 1953, Dip.Ed., 1974. *Religion:* Reorganized Church of Jesus Christ of Latter-day Saints. *Home:* 6 Taylor Ter., Rosslyn Park 5072, South Australia.

CAREER: High school teacher of English literature and French in Adelaide, South Australia, 1969—. As a singer has appeared on radio and television in Adelaide. *Member:* Alliance Francaise.

WRITINGS: If with All Your Heart, Herald House (Independence, Mo.), 1969. Also author of *Growing with God's Help,* Herald House. Has translated into French about one hundred hymns and other materials for use in French Polynesia.

WORK IN PROGRESS: A religious education course for her church, and a book on pioneer women in Australia, both for Herald House.

*　　*　　*

SAVORY, Teo

PERSONAL: Given name is pronounced Tay-o; born in Hong Kong; daughter of Lambert and Elizabeth (Lyons) Dunbar; married Alan Brilliant (director and co-owner of Unicorn Press), February 20, 1958. *Education:* Studied with private tutors in Hong Kong; attended Royal College of Music, London, Paris Conservatoire, and University of London. *Address:* P.O. Box 309, West Stockbridge, Mass. 01266. *Office:* Unicorn Press, P.O. Box 3307, Greensboro, N.C. 27402.

CAREER: Novelist, poet, and translator; Unicorn Press, *Unicorn Journal,* Santa Barbara, Calif., general editor, 1968-72, now based in Greensboro, N.C., editor, 1972—.

WRITINGS—Novels, except as noted: *The Landscape of Dreams,* Braziller, 1960; *The Single Secret,* Braziller, 1961; *A Penny for the Guy,* Gollancz, 1963, published as *A Penny for His Pocket,* Lippincott, 1964; *To a High Place,* Unicorn Press, 1971; *A Clutch of Fables* (short fiction), Unicorn Press, 1976; *Stonecrop: The Country I Remember,* Unicorn Press, 1977.

Poetry; all published by Unicorn Press: *The House Wrecker,* 1967; *Traveler's Palm,* 1967; *Snow Vole,* 1968; *Transitions,* 1971; *Dragons of Mist and Torrent,* 1974.

Translator; all published by Unicorn Press, except as noted: *Corbiere,* 1967; *Prevert I,* 1967; *Prevert II,* 1967; *Supervielle,* 1967; *Michaux,* 1967; *Jammes,* 1967; *Guillevic,* 1968; *Queneau,* 1971; *Guenter Eich,* 1971; Katrina von Hutten, *Eleven Visitations,* [Munich], 1971; (with Ursula Mahlendorf) Horst Bienek, *The Cell,* 1972; Guillevic, *Selected Poems,* Penguin, 1974; Guillevic, *Euclidians,* 1975; (with Vo-Dinh) Nhat Hanh, *Zen Poems,* 1976.

General editor, Unicorn French Series, Unicorn German Series, and Unicorn Keepsake European Series, 1967—.

WORK IN PROGRESS: Anthology of French poetry; various translations from the Vietnamese; another novel.

*　　*　　*

SAWEY, Orlan (Lester) 1920-

PERSONAL: Surname rhymes with "joy"; born May 8, 1920, in Grit, Mason County, Tex.; son of Francis Bennett (a farmer) and Catherine Lavinia (Gary) Sawey; married Nina Geneva Ewing, April 2, 1942; children: Sara Catherine, Bennett Charles, Timothy Ewing. *Education:* Texas College of Arts and Industries (now Texas A & I University), B.A., 1942; University of Texas, M.A., 1947, Ph.D., 1953. *Politics:* "Skeptic." *Religion:* Church of Christ. *Home:* 823 South 23rd St., Kingsville, Tex. 78363. *Office:* Department of English, Texas A & I University, Kingsville, Tex. 78363.

CAREER: Texas A & I University, Kingsville, instructor, 1947-50, assistant professor of English, 1952-55; Harding College, Searcy, Ark., associate professor, 1955-56, professor of English, 1956-58; Lincoln Memorial University, Harrogate, Tenn., professor of English and head of department, 1958-60; University of Virginia, Clinch Valley College, Wise, professor of English and chairman of department, 1960-62; Appalachian State University, Boone, N.C., professor of English, 1962-65; Pan American College, Edinburg, Tex., professor of English and head of department, 1965-69, director of Division of Arts and Sciences, 1966-68; Texas A & I University, professor of English, 1969—, chairman of department, 1971-75. Preacher of Church of Christ, 1942—. Guitarist and folk singer for more than forty years. *Military service:* U.S. Army, Medical Department, 1942-46; became technical sergeant.

MEMBER: American Folklore Society, Western Historical Association, Western American Literature Association, Southwestern American Literature Association, South Central Modern Language Association, Texas Folklore Society, Friends of Arizona Folklore, Montana Historical Association, Texas Council of College Teachers of English, Texas Association of College Teachers.

WRITINGS: Bernard DeVoto, Twayne, 1969. Also editor with wife, Nina Sawey, *She Hath Done What She Could: The Reminiscences of Hettie Lee Ewing,* [Dallas], 1974. Contributor to literary and folklore journals.

WORK IN PROGRESS: Charles A. Siringo, for Twayne.

SAXTON, Josephine (Mary) 1935-

PERSONAL: Born June 11, 1935, in Halifax, Yorkshire, England; daughter of Ernest and Clarice Lavinia (Crowther) Howard; married Geoffrey Banks (an artist), October, 1958; married second husband, Colin Saxton (an artist), September, 1961; children: (first marriage) Simon Howard; (second marriage) Matthew Colin, Naomi Josephine. *Education:* Attended secondary school in England and studied art for one year. *Politics:* "Never." *Religion:* "Never." *Home:* Ivy House, G, Daintry St., Leek, Staffordshire, England.

WRITINGS—Novels: *The Hieros Gamos of Sam and An Smith,* Doubleday, 1969; *Vector for Seven,* Doubleday, 1970; *Group Feast (at Cora's),* Doubleday, 1971. Contributor to several anthologies, including *Again, Dangerous Visions,* Doubleday, 1973, *New Dimensions,* Walker & Co., and *Orbit* and *Alchemy Academe,* both published by Doubleday. Contributor of short stories to magazines, mainly science fiction periodicals, and essays to *Idler.*

SIDELIGHTS: Josephine Saxton writes: "I am not even yet competent in English and never expect to be competent in any other language, but would choose Welsh if I decided to learn.... I like gardening and making and wearing clothes, cooking, dancing. I like hot sun, and do not distinguish between sane/insane/visionary—these are meaningless terms. I have no fixed beliefs; I am only sure that I can be sure of nothing. I loathe slugs but have one thing in common with them—a passion for fresh garden vegetables and strawberries."

BIOGRAPHICAL/CRITICAL SOURCES: Publishers' Weekly, October 5, 1970.

*　　*　　*

SAXTON, Lloyd 1919-

PERSONAL: Born September 28, 1919, in Loveland, Colo.; son of Oliver George and Alice (Andersen) Saxton; married Nancy Roberts, December 17, 1955; children: Perry, Jay, Barbara. *Education:* University of California, Berkeley, A.B. (English), 1942, A.B. (psychology), 1954; San Francisco State College (now San Francisco State University), M.A., 1955; University of the Pacific, Ph.D., 1957. *Politics:* Democrat. *Religion:* Protestant. *Home:* 57 Hatzic Ct., Larkspur, Calif. 94939.

CAREER: College of San Mateo, San Mateo, Calif., psychologist, 1955; University of the Pacific, Stockton, Calif., assistant professor of psychology, 1957-58; American Academy of Asian Studies, San Francisco, Calif., professor of psychology, 1958-63. Psychologist in private practice, San Francisco, Calif., 1957-70, Larkspur, Calif., 1970—. *Member:* American Psychological Association, American Association of Marriage and Family Counselors, American Association for the Advancement of Science, American Association of University Professors, California State Psychological Association, Mensa, International Carinita Sailing Association.

WRITINGS: The Individual, Marriage, and the Family, Wadsworth, 1968, 3rd edition, 1977; (compiler) *The Individual, Marriage, and the Family: Current Perspectives,* Wadsworth, 1970; (editor with W. Kaufmann) *The American Scene: Social Problems of the 70's,* Wadsworth, 1971; *Student Guide,* Wadsworth, 1977.

AVOCATIONAL INTERESTS: Small-boat sailing, tennis, chess, music, ballet, Go.

SAY, Allen 1937-

PERSONAL: Born August 28, 1937; son of Masako Moriwaki; married Deirdre Myles, April 18, 1974. *Education:* Studied at Aoyama Gakuin, Tokyo, Japan, three years, Chouinard Art Institute, one year, Los Angeles Art Center School, one year, University of California, Berkeley, two years, and San Francisco Art Institute, one year. *Home:* 2934 Larkin St., San Francisco, Calif. 94109.

CAREER: Commercial photographer and illustrator.

WRITINGS: (Illustrator) Brother Antoninus, *A Canticle to the Waterbirds,* EIZO Press, 1968; (illustrator) Wilson Pinney, editor, *Two Ways of Seeing,* Little, Brown, 1971; (self-illustrated) *Dr. Smith's Safari,* Harper, 1972; (self-illustrated) *Once under the Cherry Blossom Tree,* Harper, 1974; (self-illustrated) *The Feast of Lanterns,* Harper, 1976.

WORK IN PROGRESS: Writing a novel, *The Ink Keeper's Apprentice;* illustrating *Magic and the Night River,* by Eve Bunting.

AVOCATIONAL INTERESTS: Fly fishing.

*　　*　　*

SCARF, Maggie 1932-
(Maggi Scarf)

PERSONAL: Born May 13, 1932, in Philadelphia, Pa.; daughter of Benjamin and Helen (Rotbin) Klein; married Herbert E. Scarf (a professor at Yale University), June 23, 1953; children: Martha, Elizabeth, Susan. *Education:* Attended Temple University, 1950-53, Stanford University, 1955-56, and Southern Connecticut State College, 1963-64. *Politics:* Democratic. *Religion:* Jewish. *Home:* 88 Blake Rd., Hamden, Conn. 06517. *Agent:* Brandt & Brandt, 101 Park Ave., New York, N.Y. 10017.

CAREER: Writer. *Awards, honors:* Nieman fellow at Harvard University, 1975-76; fellow at Center for Advanced Study in the Behavioral Sciences, 1976-77.

WRITINGS: (Under name Maggi Scarf) *Meet Benjamin Franklin* (juvenile), Random House, 1968; *Antarctica: Exploring the Frozen Continent* (juvenile), Random House, 1970; *Body, Mind, Behavior,* New Republic, 1976. Contributor to *New York Times, Psychology Today, New Republic, Redbook, Cosmopolitan,* and *New York Times Book Review.*

WORK IN PROGRESS: "A book about depression, as it manifests itself in women, from a life-cycle viewpoint."

SIDELIGHTS: Maggie Scarf writes: "I have been greatly influenced by the advice of a friend, Bernard Malamud. I once asked him about his own writing habits, and he gave me the most valuable advice I have ever received: That is, that one should set aside an amount of time—a specific number of hours per day—and go to it on a daily basis, for five or six or seven days per week *at* that designated time. He remarked that although one might feel more or less 'inspired' or energetic on a particular day, the actual quality of the production didn't vary in concert with one's mood. And I've found this to be the case. The best advice that any writer can ever give or receive has to do, I believe, with strategies for creating self-discipline."

*　　*　　*

SCHACHT, Richard (Lawrence) 1941-

PERSONAL: Surname pronounced "shocked"; born December 19, 1941, in Racine, Wis.; son of Robert H. and Alice (Munger) Schacht; married Marsha Clinard (a psychiatric social worker), August 17, 1963; children: Eric, Marshall. *Education:* Harvard University, B.A., 1963; Princeton University, M.A., 1965, Ph.D., 1967; University of Tuebingen, graduate study, 1966-67. *Home:* 1406 West Park Ave., Champaign, Ill. 61820. *Office:* Department of Philosophy, University of Illinois, Urbana, Ill. 61801.

CAREER: University of Illinois, Urbana, assistant professor, 1967-71, associate professor of philosophy, 1971—. *Member:* American Philosophical Association.

WRITINGS: Alienation, Doubleday, 1970; *Hegel and After: Studies in Continental Philosophy between Kant and Sartre,* University of Pittsburgh Press, 1975.

WORK IN PROGRESS: Nietzsche, a study of his philosophy.

* * *

SCHAEREN, Beatrix 1941-

PERSONAL: Born September 1, 1941, in Schleitheim, Switzerland; daughter of Gerhard Paul and Anne (Steiger) Huber; married Fritz Schaeren (secretary of an appeals court), March 26, 1966; children: Fritzli, Simon Andreas. *Education:* Attended art school for one year, and textile design school for three and one-half years. *Religion:* Protestant.

CAREER: Stoffels AG, St. Gall, Switzerland, art designer, 1960-63; painter and writer.

WRITINGS: (Self-illustrated) *Gigin und Till,* Artemis Verlag, 1968, translation by Roseanna Hoover published as *Gigin and Till,* Atheneum, 1969; *Tillo,* Artemis Verlag, 1972.

WORK IN PROGRESS: More children's books.†

* * *

SCHAM, Alan (Myron) 1937-

PERSONAL: Born May 9, 1937, in Sterling, Ill.; son of Irving and Matilda (Stoler) Scham; married Juliana Leslie Hill, September 6, 1963; children: Sarah Elizabeth Rose, Emma Sofia Anne. *Education:* University of California, Berkeley, A.B., 1965; University of Durham, Durham, England, Ph.D., 1968. *Home:* 4699 East State St., Hermitage, Pa. 16146. *Office:* Department of History, Youngstown State University, Youngstown, Ohio 44503.

CAREER: University of California, Riverside, associate in department of history, 1968-69; Southern Connecticut State College, New Haven, assistant professor of modern French history, 1969-76; Youngstown State University, Youngstown, Ohio, faculty member in history department, 1977—. Free-lance writer and researcher, 1976—. *Member:* American Historical Association, Society for French Historical Studies, French Colonial Historical Society (president, 1974-76), Authors Guild. *Awards, honors:* American Philosophical Society summer research grant, 1970.

WRITINGS: Lyautey in Morocco: Protectorate Administration, 1912-1925, University of California Press, 1970.

WORK IN PROGRESS: A book on an aspect of French colonialism in Africa; a biography of Emile Zola; with R. L. Hill, a history of a Sudanese battalion in the Franco-Mexican War.

SIDELIGHTS: Alan Scham told *CA:* "Writing is a two-way venture. The author is a teacher; he also learns from his own research. I am fascinated (perhaps the word is 'haunted') by history and men's lives. How does such and such an event occur, who are the protagonists, what are the events in their lives that have made this possible? I suppose if I were to sum up the most important factor involved in my own work, I would say it is 'curiosity', curiosity to learn the full truth behind the hopes, thoughts and acts of the people who share history with us, and make it what it is."

* * *

SCHAPSMEIER, Edward L(ewis) 1927-

PERSONAL: Born February 8, 1927, in Council Bluffs, Iowa; son of Henry Louis and Lena Marie (Stallman) Schapsmeier; married Juanita G. Santos, June 13, 1971; children: Diana. *Education:* Concordia Teachers College, Seward, Neb., B.S., 1949; University of Nebraska, M.S., 1952; University of Southern California, Ph.D., 1965. *Home:* 15 Sunset Rd., Bloomington, Ill. 61701. *Office:* Department of History, Illinois State University, Normal, Ill. 61761.

CAREER: Hawthorne (Calif.) public schools, teacher, 1954-64; University of Southern California, Los Angeles, lecturer in history, 1964-65; Ohio State University, Columbus, instructor in history, 1965-66; Illinois State University, Normal, associate professor, 1966-69, professor of history, 1969—. Visiting professor of history, Illinois Wesleyan University, Bloomington, 1970-71. *Member:* American Historical Association, Agricultural History Society, American Political Science Association, Organization of American Historians, Rural Sociological Society, Midwest Political Science Association, Illinois State Historical Association, Wisconsin-Northern Illinois American Studies Association.

WRITINGS—With brother, Frederick H. Schapsmeier: *Henry A. Wallace of Iowa: The Agrarian Years, 1910-1940,* Iowa State University Press, 1969; *Walter Lippmann: Philosopher-Journalist,* Public Affairs Press, 1969; *Prophet in Politics: Henry A. Wallace and the War Years, 1940-1965,* Iowa State University Press, 1971; *Ezra Taft Benson and the Politics of Agriculture: The Eisenhower Years, 1953-1961,* Interstate Press, 1975; *Encyclopedia of American Agricultural History,* Greenwood Press, 1976. Also author of *Abundant Harvests: The Story of American Agriculture,* 1974. Regional editor, *Journal of the West.*

WORK IN PROGRESS: With Frederick H. Schapsmeier, *Dictionary of American Political Parties and Civic Action Groups.*

SIDELIGHTS: Edward L. Schapsmeier and his twin brother, Frederick, believe history is best presented and taught via biography. They have selected both liberals and conservatives for their joint biographies of "those individuals who influenced the course of history through personal courage and dedicated service." They emphasize that they do not attempt to glorify or debunk, but to present a critical analysis.

* * *

SCHAPSMEIER, Frederick H(erman) 1927-

PERSONAL: Born February 8, 1927, in Council Bluffs, Iowa; son of Henry Louis and Lena Marie (Stallman) Schapsmeier. *Education:* Creighton University, student, 1945-47; Concordia Teachers College, Seward, Neb., B.S., 1949; University of Nebraska, M.S., 1953; University of Southern California, Ph.D., 1965. *Politics:* Independent. *Religion:* Protestant. *Home:* 22 East New York Ave., Oshkosh, Wis. 54901. *Office:* Department of History, University of Wisconsin, Oshkosh, Wis. 54901.

CAREER: Principal and teacher in public schools in

Omaha, Neb. and Glendale, Calif., 1956-62; University of Southern California, Los Angeles, lecturer, 1963-64, assistant professor of American history, 1964-65; University of Wisconsin—Oshkosh, associate professor, 1965-70, professor of history, 1970—. *Military service:* U.S. Army, 1944-45. *Member:* American Historical Association, Organization of American Historians, Agricultural History Society, American Political Science Association, American Studies Association, Western Historical Association, Phi Alpha Theta. *Awards, honors:* Outstanding Educator Award, Wisconsin Academy of Arts, Letters, and Science, 1971.

WRITINGS—With brother, Edward L. Schapsmeier: *Henry A. Wallace of Iowa: The Agrarian Years, 1910-1940,* Iowa State University Press, 1969; *Walter Lippmann: Philosopher-Journalist,* Public Affairs Press, 1969; *Prophet in Politics: Henry A. Wallace and the War Years, 1940-1965,* Iowa State University Press, 1971; *Ezra Taft Benson and the Politics of Agriculture: The Eisenhower Years, 1953-1961,* Interstate Press, 1975; *Encyclopedia of American Agricultural History,* Greenwood Press, 1976. Contributor to *Historian, Social Studies, Agricultural History, Journal of the West, Ohio History, Annals of Iowa,* and *Midwest Quarterly.* Associate editor, *Journal of the West,* 1968—.

WORK IN PROGRESS: With Edward L. Schapsmeier, *Dictionary of American Political Parties and Civic Action Groups.*

SIDELIGHTS: Frederick H. Schapsmeier told *CA:* "In order to make history relevant, my brother and co-author and I seek to emphasize the personal aspect in our writing. Thus we use the media of political biography to reveal the interrelationship with policy making and the personal background of the historical figures involved. Men make history, not inanimate forces beyond our control. Historical events cannot be understood without understanding the men involved."

* * *

SCHEFFER, Victor B(lanchard) 1906-

PERSONAL: Born November 27, 1906, in Manhattan, Kan.; son of Theophilus (a biologist) and Celia E. (Blanchard) Scheffer; married Beth MacInnes, October 12, 1935; children: Brian M., Susan E. (Mrs. Robert Irvine), Ann B. (Mrs. William Carlstrom). *Education:* University of Washington, Seattle, B.S., 1930, M.S., 1932, Ph.D., 1936. *Home:* 14806 Southeast 54th St., Bellevue, Wash. 98006.

CAREER: U.S. Fish and Wildlife Service, biologist in Olympia and Seattle, Wash., and Fort Collins, Colo., 1937-69. Lecturer, University of Washington, Seattle, 1966, 1967, 1968, 1971, and 1972. Chairman, Marine Mammal Commission, 1973-76. *Member:* American Society of Mammalogists, Wildlife Society, Wilderness Society, Nature Conservancy, National Wildlife Foundation, National Audubon Society. *Awards, honors:* John Burroughs Medal, 1970, for *The Year of the Whale.*

WRITINGS: Seals, Sea Lions, and Walruses, Stanford University Press, 1958; *The Year of the Whale,* Scribner, 1969; *The Year of the Seal,* Scribner, 1970; *The Little Calf,* Scribner, 1970; *The Seeing Eye,* Scribner, 1971; *A Voice for Wildlife,* Scribner, 1974; *A Natural History of Marine Mammals,* Scribner, 1976.

BIOGRAPHICAL/CRITICAL SOURCES: Time, August 15, 1969; *Best Sellers,* September 1, 1969; *New Yorker,* September 20, 1969; *New York Times,* November 5, 1970.

SCHEIBE, Karl E(dward) 1937-

PERSONAL: Born March 5, 1937, in Belleville, Ill.; son of John Henry and Esther (Friesen) Scheibe; married Elizabeth Mixter (an admissions officer), September 10, 1961; children: David Sawyer, Robert Daniel. *Education:* Trinity College, Hartford, Conn., B.S., 1959; University of California, Berkeley, Ph.D., 1963. *Home:* 11 Long Lane, Middletown, Conn. 06457. *Office:* Department of Psychology, Wesleyan University, Middletown, Conn. 06457.

CAREER: Wesleyan University, Middletown, Conn., assistant professor, 1963-67, associate professor, 1967-73, professor of psychology, 1973—. Visiting professor, University of Brasilia, 1968; Fulbright fellow, Catholic University, Sao Paulo, 1972-73. Consultant to National Science Foundation. Member of board of fellows, Trinity College, Hartford, Conn. *Member:* American Psychological Association, American Association for the Advancement of Science, American Association of University Professors, Sociedade Interamericana de Psicologia, Eastern Psychological Association, New England Psychological Association, Phi Beta Kappa. *Awards, honors:* Woodrow Wilson fellowship.

WRITINGS: Beliefs and Values, Holt, 1970.

WORK IN PROGRESS: A psychological study of national identity.

* * *

SCHERER, F(rederic) M(ichael) 1932-

PERSONAL: Born August 1, 1932, in Ottawa, Ill.; son of Walter King (a merchant) and Margaret (Lucey) Scherer; married Barbara Silbermann, August 17, 1957; children: Thomas M., Karen A., Christina A. *Education:* University of Michigan, A.B., 1954; Harvard University, M.B.A., 1958, Ph.D., 1963. *Home:* 110 Sixth St., Wilmette, Ill. 60091. *Office:* Department of Economics, Northwestern University, Evanston, Ill. 60201.

CAREER: Harvard University, Graduate School of Business Administration, Boston, Mass., member of faculty, 1958-63; Princeton University, Princeton, N.J., assistant professor of economics, 1963-66; University of Michigan, Ann Arbor, associate professor, 1966-69, professor of economics, 1969-72; International Institute of Management, Berlin, Germany, social research fellow, 1972-74; U.S. Federal Trade Commission, Bureau of Economics, Washington, D.C., director, 1974-76; Northwestern University, Evanston, Ill., professor of economics, 1976—. Consultant on national security policy, technological change, the patent system, and antitrust matters. *Military service:* U.S. Army, 1954-56. *Member:* American Economic Association, Federation of American Scientists. *Awards, honors:* Lanchester Prize of Operations Research Society of America, 1964, for *The Weapons Acquisition Process: Economic Incentives.*

WRITINGS: (With others) *Patents and the Corporation,* privately printed, 1958, revised edition, 1959; (with M. J. Peck) *The Weapons Acquisition Process: An Economic Analysis,* Division of Research, Harvard Business School, 1962; *The Weapons Acquisition Process: Economic Incentives,* Division of Research, Harvard Business School, 1964; *Industrial Market Structure and Economic Performance,* Rand McNally, 1970; (with others) *The Economics of Multi-Plant Operation: An International Comparisons Study,* Harvard University Press, 1975. Contributor to economic and technology journals.

WORK IN PROGRESS: Thorough revision of *Industrial Market Structure and Economic Performance.*

SCHIER, Donald (Stephen) 1914-

PERSONAL: Born September 10, 1914, in Fort Madison, Iowa; son of Frank Stephen and Marcella (Kenny) Schier. *Education:* University of Iowa, B.A., 1936; Columbia University, M.A., 1938, Ph.D., 1941. *Politics:* None. *Religion:* None. *Home:* 717 East Second St., Northfield, Minn. 55057. *Office:* Department of Modern Languages, Carleton College, Northfield, Minn. 55057.

CAREER: Bemidji State College, Bemidji, Minn., instructor in French and English, 1939-41; Illinois Institute of Technology, Chicago, instructor in French, English, and Spanish, 1940-41, 1946; Carleton College, Northfield, Minn., assistant professor, 1946-49, associate professor, 1949-53, professor of French, 1953—. Visiting professor, University of Wisconsin, 1964-65. *Military service:* U.S. Army, Signal Corps, 1941-46; became captain. *Member:* Modern Language Association of America, American Association of Teachers of French, American Association of University Professors, Midwest Modern Language Association, Minneapolis Society of Fine Arts, Phi Beta Kappa.

WRITINGS: Louis-Bertrand Castel, Torch Press, 1941; (editor with Scott Elledge) *The Continental Model: Selected French Critical Essays of the Seventeenth Century in English Translation,* University of Minnesota Press, 1960, revised edition, Cornell University Press, 1970; (editor) Bertrand LeBovier de Fontenelle, *Nouveaux Dialogues des morts,* University of North Carolina Press, 1965, revised edition, 1974. Contributor to academic journals.

WORK IN PROGRESS: Writing on Andre Morellet and on Michel Butor.

AVOCATIONAL INTERESTS: Playing violin, reading detective stories.

* * *

SCHIFFRIN, Harold Z. 1922-

PERSONAL: Born September 26, 1922, in Rochester, N.Y.; son of William (an insurance agent) and Lillian (Harris) Schiffrin; married Ruth Kett (a biochemist), October 17, 1948; children: Meira, Yael (daughters). *Education:* University of California, Berkeley, B.A., 1944, M.A., 1956; University of Rochester, B.A., 1946; Hebrew University of Jerusalem, Ph.D., 1961. *Religion:* Jewish. *Home:* 8 Qorot Haittim, Jerusalem, Israel. *Office:* Department of Chinese Studies, Hebrew University, Jerusalem, Israel.

CAREER: Hebrew University of Jerusalem, Jerusalem, Israel, 1965—, began as senior lecturer, currently associate professor of Chinese studies, dean for overseas students, 1968-70, chairman of department of Chinese studies, 1969—. *Military service:* U.S. Army, 1943-46; became sergeant. *Member:* Association for Asian Studies. *Awards, honors:* Co-winner of John K. Fairbank Prize of American Historical Association, 1969, for *Sun Yat-sen and the Origins of the Chinese Revolution.*

WRITINGS: Sun Yat-sen and the Origins of the Chinese Revolution, University of California Press, 1968.

WORK IN PROGRESS: Another book on Sun Yat-sen; studies in Chinese intellectual history and Chinese nationalism.

BIOGRAPHICAL/CRITICAL SOURCES: Book World, April 6, 1969.

SCHILLACI, Peter Paul 1929-
(Anthony Schillaci)

PERSONAL: Born August 13, 1929, in Chicago, Ill.; son of Thomas Guy and Mary (Macaluso) Schillaci. *Education:* Attended Michigan State University and University of Illinois; Loyola University, Chicago, Ill., Ph.B., 1950; Aquinas Insitute of Philosophy and Theology, M.A., 1958; Pontifical University Angelicum, Rome, Italy, Ph.D., 1960. *Politics:* Democrat.

CAREER: Entered Dominican Order, 1951; ordained priest with religious name of Anthony Schillaci, 1958; Aquinas Institute of Philosophy and Theology, River Forest, Ill., assistant professor of metaphysics, 1961-67; Fordham University, Bronx, N.Y., assistant professor of communications, 1967-69; presently teaching at Union Theological Seminary and New School for Social Research, both in New York, and Seton Hall University, South Orange, N.J. Visiting summer professor, University of San Francisco, 1968. Member of National Film Study Project; associate of National Center for Film Study; member of award committee, National Catholic Office for Motion Pictures. Lecturer on film arts at conferences around the country. *Military service:* U.S. Army, 1944-47. *Member:* American Catholic Philosophical Association, University Film Association, Christian Preaching Conference, New York Film Society, Society of Priests for a Free Ministry.

WRITINGS: (Under name Anthony Schillaci) *Movies and Morals,* Fides, 1968; (contributor) Ed Wakin, editor, *Controversial Conversations with Catholics,* Pflaum, 1969; (under name Anthony Schillaci; editor with John Culkin) *Films Deliver: Teaching Creatively with Film,* Citation, 1970; (contributor) James McKendree Wall, editor, *Three European Directors,* Eerdmans, 1973. Has structured twenty film series, principally on religious themes. Writer of television series, "Film and Society," thirty programs for National Educational Television. Contributor to *Saturday Review, New City, Catholic Mind, Drama Critique, Listening,* and other periodicals.

WORK IN PROGRESS: Cinema as Cultural Myth, book version of television series, "Film and Society," for Pflaum.

AVOCATIONAL INTERESTS: Photography and sports (especially sailing).†

* * *

SCHILLER, Herbert I(rving) 1919-

PERSONAL: Born November 5, 1919, in New York, N.Y.; son of Benjamin F. (a jeweler) and Gertrude (Perner) Schiller; married Anita L. Rosenbaum (a research librarian), November 5, 1946; children: Daniel T., P. Zachary. *Education:* City College (now City College of the City University of New York), B.S.S. (cum laude), 1940; Columbia University, M.A., 1941; New York University, Ph.D., 1960. *Politics:* Independent. *Religion:* None. *Home:* 7109 Monte Vista, La Jolla, Calif. 92037. *Office:* Department of Communications, Third College, University of California, San Diego, Box 109, La Jolla, Calif. 92093.

CAREER: Economist with U.S. Government, including Office of Military Government, Berlin, Germany, 1941-42, 1945-48; City College (now City College of the City University of New York), New York, N.Y., lecturer in economics, 1949-59; Pratt Institute, Brooklyn, N.Y., instructor, 1950-53, assistant professor, 1953-60, associate professor, 1960-62, professor of economics and chairman of department of social studies, 1962-63; University of Illinois, Urbana, visiting research associate professor, 1961-62, research associate professor, 1963-66, research professor of economics and communication, 1966-70; University of California, San Diego, La Jolla, professor of communications, 1970—. Visiting fellow, Institute for Policy Studies, Washington, D.C., 1967-68; visiting professor, Hebrew University of Jerusalem, 1969; visiting professor, University of Amsterdam, 1973-74. Lecturer in "World Today" series, Brooklyn Institute of Arts and Science, 1961-67. *Military service:* U.S. Army, 1942-45.

MEMBER: International Association for Mass Communication Research, American Association for the Advancement of Science, Phi Beta Kappa. *Awards, honors:* Ford Foundation fellow, summer, 1963.

WRITINGS: (Contributor) Lloyd D. Musolf, editor, *Communications Satellites in Political Orbit,* Chandler Publishing, 1968; (contributor) J. Sherwood Weber, editor, *Good Reading,* New American Library, 1968; *Mass Communications and American Empire,* Kelley, 1969; (editor with J. D. Phillips) *Superstate: Readings in the Military-Industrial Complex,* University of Illinois Press, 1970; *The Mind Managers,* Beacon Press, 1973; *Communications and Cultural Domination,* International Arts & Sciences Press, 1976. Contributor of about fifty articles and reviews to *Nation, Antioch Review,* and professional periodicals. Editor, *Quarterly Review of Economics and Business,* 1966-70.

WORK IN PROGRESS: A book on the "international knowledge industry."

*   *   *

SCHLEINER, Winfried 1938-

PERSONAL: Born October 19, 1938, in Mannheim, Germany; son of Johann (an engineer) and Anne-Marie (Koehler) Schleiner; married Louise Gittings, August 3, 1968; children: Anne Marie, Christa. *Education:* Universitaet Kiel, Staatsexamen, 1964; Brown University, M.A., 1965, Ph.D., 1968. *Religion:* Roman Catholic. *Home:* 1004 West 8th St., Davis, Calif. 95616. *Office:* English Department, University of California, Davis, Calif. 95616.

CAREER: Max Plank Schule, Kiel, Germany, junior teacher and assessor in English and French, 1968-70; Rhode Island College, Providence, assistant professor of English, 1970-73; University of California, Davis, assistant professor, 1973-75, associate professor of English, 1975—.

WRITINGS: The Imagery of John Donne's Sermons, Brown University Press, 1970. Contributor of articles to *Literatur in Wissenschaft und Unterricht; Studies in Philology, English Language Notes, Zeitschrift fuer Anglistik und Amerikanistik,* and other periodicals.

WORK IN PROGRESS: Studies of Renaissance literature and emblems.

*   *   *

SCHLEPP, Wayne Allen 1931-

PERSONAL: Born July 8, 1931, in Mobridge, S.D.; son of John (a laborer) and Elma (Oberlander) Schlepp; married Kate Vosberg, February 21, 1955; children: Vaughan Roydon. *Education:* Northern State College, Aberdeen, S.D., B.Sc., 1953; University of London, B.A. (honors), 1961, Ph.D., 1964. *Home:* Apt. 3-H, 20 Prince Arthur Ave., Toronto, Ontario, Canada M5R 1B1. *Office:* Department of East Asian Studies, University of Toronto, Toronto, Ontario, Canada M5S 1A5.

CAREER: University of Wisconsin—Madison, assistant professor, 1964-68, associate professor of Chinese and chairman of department of East Asian languages and literatures, 1968-73; University of Toronto, Toronto, Ontario, professor of East Asian studies, 1973—. *Military service:* U.S. Army, 1953-56. *Awards, honors:* National Endowment for Humanities grant, 1967; American Council of Learned Societies research fellow, 1967-68.

WRITINGS: San-Ch'u: Techniques and Imagery, University of Wisconsin Press, 1970.

*   *   *

SCHLEUNES, Karl A(lbert) 1937-

PERSONAL: Surname is pronounced *shloy*-ness; born April 21, 1937, in Kiel, Wis.; son of Henry F. and Adelia (Eickhoff) Schleunes; married Brenda Pursel (a free-lance writer), August 15, 1964; children: Anna Frederika. *Education:* Lakeland College, B.A., 1959; University of Minnesota, M.A., 1961, Ph.D., 1966. *Religion:* Protestant. *Office:* Department of History, University of North Carolina, Greensboro, N.C. 27412.

CAREER: University of Illinois, Chicago, assistant professor of modern European history, 1965-71; University of North Carolina at Greensboro, associate professor of history, 1971—. *Member:* International Studies Association, American Historical Association. *Awards, honors:* Fulbright fellow, 1961-62; Leo Baeck Institute fellowship, 1964; National Foundation for Jewish Culture fellowship, 1964-65; Social Science Research Council grant, 1971; National Endowment for the Humanities research grant, 1973.

WRITINGS: The Twisted Road to Auschwitz: Nazi Policy toward German Jews, 1933-39, University of Illinois Press, 1970. Contributor to journals.

WORK IN PROGRESS: Nazi Propaganda, and *German Educational History.*

*   *   *

SCHMITZ, Dennis 1937-

PERSONAL: Born August 11, 1937, in Dubuque, Iowa; son of Anthony and Roselyn (Schwartz) Schmitz; married Loretta D'Agostino, August 25, 1960; children: Anne, Sara, Martha, Paul. *Education:* Loras College, B.A., 1959; University of Chicago, M.A., 1961. *Religion:* Roman Catholic. *Home:* 1348 57th St., Sacramento, Calif. 95819. *Office:* Department of English, California State University, Sacramento, Calif. 95819.

CAREER: Illinois Institute of Technology, Chicago, instructor in English, 1961-62; University of Wisconsin—Milwaukee, instructor in English, 1962-66; California State University, Sacramento, Calif., assistant professor, 1966-70, associate professor of English, 1970—. *Awards, honors:* Discovery Award of Young Men's Hebrew Association Poetry Center, New York, N.Y., 1968; Big Table Series of Younger Poets Award, 1969, for manuscript of *We Weep for Our Strangeness;* National Endowment for the Arts fellowship grant, 1976.

WRITINGS: We Weep for Our Strangeness (poems), Big Table Publishing, 1969; *Double Exposures* (poems), Triskelion Press, 1971; *Goodwill, Inc.* (poems), Ecco Press, 1976. "The Poetry of Dennis Schmitz" appears on tape in McGraw's "Sound Seminars," 1970.

SCHNACKENBURG, Rudolf 1914-

PERSONAL: Born January 5, 1914, in Kattowitz, Germany; son of Leopold (an engineer) and Anna (Christ) Schnackenburg. *Education:* University of Breslau, Dr. theol., 1937; University of Munich, Habilitation for New Testament Exegesis, 1947. *Home:* Erthalstrasse 22d, 87 Wuerzburg, Federal Republic of Germany. *Office:* Seminar fuer neutestament Exegese, Universitaet Wuerzburg, 87 Wuerzburg, Neue Universitaet, Sanderring 2, Federal Republic of Germany.

CAREER: Roman Catholic priest; University of Dillingen, Dillingen, Germany, assistant professor, 1952-55; University of Bamberg, Bamberg, Germany, ordinary professor, 1955-57; University of Wuerzburg, Wuerzburg, Germany, professor of New Testament exegesis and biblical theology, 1957—. Former consultor to Pontifical Bible Commission and to Secretariat for Promoting Christian Unity (Rome); member of Pontifical Theological Commission and of a number of ecumenical groups. Lecturer at University of Notre Dame, fall, 1965, and participant in various congresses in the United States. *Member:* Studiorum Novi Testamenti Societas (president, 1966-67), Society of Biblical Literature (honorary member). *Awards, honors:* Dr.theol.h.c., Innsbruck University, 1970.

WRITINGS: Die Johannesbriefe, Herder (Freiburg), 1953, 5th edition, 1975; *Die sittliche Botschaft des Neuen Testamentes,* Max Hueber, 1954, revised and enlarged German edition, 1962, translation of revised edition by J. Holland-Smith and W. J. O'Hara published as *The Moral Teaching of the New Testament,* Herder, 1965; *Gottes Herrschaft und Reich,* Herder, 1959, translation by John Murray published as *God's Rule and Kingdom,* Herder & Herder, 1963, 2nd enlarged edition, 1968.

La theologie du Nouveau Testament, Desclee de Brouwer (Brussels), 1961, translation by David Askew published as *New Testament Theology Today,* Herder & Herder, 1963; *Baptism in the Thought of St. Paul: A Study in Pauline Theology,* Herder & Herder, 1964; *Von der Wahrheit die freimacht,* A. Pustet (Munich), 1964, translation by Rodelinde Albrecht published as *The Truth Will Make You Free,* Herder & Herder, 1966; *Das Johannesvangelium,* Herder, Volume I, 1965, Volume II, 1971, Volume III, 1975, translation of Volume I by Kevin Smith published as *The Gospel According to St. John,* Herder & Herder, 1968; *Present and Future: Modern Aspects of New Testament Theology* (lecture series), University of Notre Dame Press, 1966; *Die Kirche im Neuen Testament: Ihre Wirklichkeit und theologische Deutung,* ihr Wesen und Geheimnis, Herder, 1966, translation by W. J. O'Hara published as *The Church in the New Testament,* Herder & Herder, 1965; *Das Evangelium nach Markus,* Patmos-Verlag, Volume I, 1966, Volume II, 1971, translation published as *The Gospel According to St. Mark,* Herder & Herder, 1970; *Christliche Existenz nach dem Neuen Testament,* Koesel-Verlag, Volume I, 1967, Volume II, 1968, translation by F. Wieck published in two volumes as *Christian Existence in the New Testament,* University of Notre Dame Press, 1968; *Schriften zum Neuen Testament,* Koesel-Verlag, 1971. Editor, *Biblische Zeitschrift,* 1957—.

WORK IN PROGRESS: Kommentar zum Brief an die Ephesen, fur: Evangelisch-Katholischer Kommentar zum Neuen Testament (Zurich-Neukirchen).

BIOGRAPHICAL/CRITICAL SOURCES: Christian Century, February 26, 1969.

SCHNEEBAUM, Tobias 1921-

PERSONAL: Born March 25, 1921, in New York, N.Y.; son of Jacob (a grocer) and Rebecca (Ehrenfreund) Schneebaum. *Education:* Attended City College (now City College of the City University of New York), 1939-41. *Politics:* Democrat. *Home:* 29 Stuyvesant St., New York, N.Y. 10003. *Agent:* Don Congdon, Harold Matson Co., Inc., 22 East 40th St., New York, N.Y. 10016.

CAREER: Irma Jonas School of Painting, Ajijic, Mexico, teacher, 1949-50; cook and dishwasher on freighter traveling to Alaska, Japan, and Korea, 1951-52; has held various jobs, from folding to managing, with a greeting card company in New York City, on and off, 1954—; painter, exhibiting about every other year at Peridot Gallery, New York City. *Military service:* U.S. Army Air Forces, 1942-45. *Awards, honors:* Fulbright fellow, 1955.

WRITINGS: Keep the River on Your Right (nonfiction), Grove, 1969.

Illustrator: Vance Bourjaily, *The Girl in the Abstract Bed,* Tiber Press, 1954; Mary Britton Miller, *Jungle Journey,* Pantheon, 1964.

WORK IN PROGRESS: Writing a book, *Tell Me, Wild Man, Are You the Dalai Lama?.*

SIDELIGHTS: Keep the River on Your Right is Tobias Schneebaum's memoir of a trip he made to Peru to study art in 1955. He traveled by himself through the jungle and lived for several months with primitive peoples, including a tribe of cannibals. He has painted on other trips in Central America, Asia, southern Europe, and Africa.

BIOGRAPHICAL/CRITICAL SOURCES: New York Times, September 12, 1969; *New York,* September 15, 1969; *Book World,* September 21, 1969; *New York Times Book Review,* November 16, 1969; *Commonweal,* February 20, 1970; *Books,* October, 1971.

* * *

SCHNEIDAU, Herbert N. 1935-

PERSONAL: Born August 26, 1935, in New Orleans, La.; son of Herbert D. (an executive) and Bess (Cartledge) Schneidau; married Barbara Ott, July 29, 1961; children: Gregory, Gretchen. *Education:* Dartmouth College, B.A., 1957; Princeton University, M.A., 1960, Ph.D., 1963. *Politics:* "Deradicalized." *Religion:* "Yahwist." *Home:* 1424 Alameda Padre Serra, Santa Barbara, Calif. 93103. *Office:* Department of English, University of California, Santa Barbara, Calif. 93106.

CAREER: Duke University, Durham, N.C., instructor in English, 1961-63; State University of New York at Buffalo, assistant professor, 1963-68, associate professor of English, 1968-70; University of California, Santa Barbara, associate professor, 1971-75, professor of English, 1975—.

WRITINGS: Ezra Pound: The Image and the Real, Louisiana State University Press, 1969; *Sacred Discontent: The Bible and Western Tradition,* Louisiana State University Press, 1976. Contributor to academic journals.

* * *

SCHNEIDER, Herman 1905-

PERSONAL: Born May 31, 1905, in Kreschov, Poland; son of Louis (a tailor) and Leah (Feldman) Schneider; married Natalie Shmerler, August 19, 1931 (divorced, 1941); married Nina Zimet (a writer), June 29, 1941; children: (first marriage) Robert; (second marriage) Susan Schneider Colchie,

Lucy; (stepson) Steven. *Education:* Free Academy (now City College of the City University of New York), B.S., 1928, M.S., 1930. *Religion:* Jewish. *Home:* 21 West 11th St., New York, N.Y. 10011.

CAREER: New York (N.Y.) public schools, teacher, 1928-48, science supervisor, 1948-53; Bank St. College, New York, N.Y., member of faculty, 1941-46. Consultant for fifty-two filmstrips associated with the *Heath Science Series* published by University Films, Inc. *Member:* National Education Association, National Science Teachers Association, American Association for the Advancement of Science (fellow), Council for Elementary Science International, Association for the Education of Teachers in Science, National Association of Science Writers, New York Academy of Science. *Awards, honors:* Litt.D., Fairleigh Dickinson University, 1967.

WRITINGS: Everyday Machines and How They Work, Whittlesey House, 1950; *Everyday Weather and How It Works,* Whittlesey House, 1951, 3rd edition, 1963; (compiler with Julius Schwartz) *Growing Up with Science Books* [New York], c. 1959; *How Scientists Find Out,* McGraw, 1976.

With wife, Nina Schneider; all juveniles: *How Big Is Big?: From Stars to Atoms, a Yardstick for the Universe,* W. R. Scott, 1946, revised edition, 1959; *Let's Find Out,* W. R. Scott, 1946; *Now Try This,* W. R. Scott, 1947, published as *Now Try This to Move a Heavy Load: Push, Pull and Lift,* 1963 (published in England as *Push, Pull, and Lift,* Brockhampton Press, 1960); *Let's Look inside Your House: A Picture-Science Book about Water, Heat and Electricity,* W. R. Scott, 1948; *How Your Body Works,* introduction by Milton I. Levine, W. R. Scott, 1949.

Let's Look under the City: Water, Gas, Waste, Electricity, Telephone, W. R. Scott, 1950, revised edition, 1954; *Plants in the City,* John Day, 1951, revised edition, Faber, 1953; *You among the Stars,* W. R. Scott, 1951; *Follow the Sunset,* Doubleday, 1952; *Rocks, Rivers and the Changing Earth: A First Book about Geology,* W. R. Scott, 1952; *Your Telephone and How It Works,* Whittlesey House, 1952, 3rd edition, 1965; *More Power to You: A Short History of Power from the Windmill to the Atom,* W. R. Scott, 1953, also published as *More Power to You: From Windmills to Atomic Energy,* E. M. Hale, 1953; *Science Fun with Milk Cartons,* Whittlesey House, 1953; *Heath Elementary Science,* Heath, Book 1: *Science for Work and Play,* Book 2: *Science for Here and Now,* Book 3: *Science Far and Near,* Book 4: *Science in Your Life,* Book 5: *Science in Our World,* Book 6: *Science for Today and Tomorrow,* 1954-55, 2nd edition published as *Heath Science Series,* with additional titles, Book 7: *Science in the Space Age,* Book 8: *Science and Your Future,* 1961, 3rd edition, 1968 (series published in England as *Elementary Science,* Harrap, 1954-55, 2nd edition, 1961), 4th revised edition, 1973; *Let's Find Out about Electricity* (includes kit to make working models of a telegraph set, lighthouse, 4-way traffic signal, and TV theatre), Grosset, 1956; *Let's Find Out about the Weather* (includes kit to make working models of a barometer, weather vane, air current and air speed indicators, humidity gauge, and weather house), Grosset, 1956; (editor) Eunice Holsaert, *Life in the Arctic,* Harvey House, 1957; (editor) Eunice Holsaert, *Life in the Tropics,* Harvey House, 1957.

Science around You, Harrap, 1966; *Science Fun with a Flashlight,* McGraw, 1975; *Science Fun for You in a Minute or Two,* McGraw, 1975.

SCHNEIDER, Nina 1913-

PERSONAL: Born January 29, 1913, in Antwerp, Belgium; daughter of Menassa and Helen (Silber) Zimet; married Solomon Chernowitz, August 15, 1931; married second husband, Herman Schneider (a writer), June 29, 1941; children: (first marriage) Steven; (second marriage) Susan Schneider Colchie, Lucy. *Education:* Brooklyn College (now Brooklyn College of the City University of New York), B.A. (magna cum laude), 1940. *Politics and religion:* "Peace on Earth." *Home:* 21 West 11th St., New York, N.Y. 10011.

CAREER: Teacher, librarian, reviewer, editor. *Member:* Authors League of America, Authors Guild, P.E.N.

WRITINGS: Hercules, the Gentle Giant, Roy, 1947; *While Susie Sleeps,* W. R. Scott, 1948.

With husband, Herman Schneider; all juveniles: *How Big Is Big?: From Stars to Atoms, a Yardstick for the Universe,* W. R. Scott, 1946, revised edition, 1959; *Let's Find Out,* W. R. Scott, 1946; *Now Try This,* W. R. Scott, 1947, published as *Now Try This to Move a Heavy Load: Push, Pull and Lift,* 1963 (published in England as *Push, Pull, and Lift,* Brockhampton Press, 1960); *Let's Look inside Your House: A Picture-Science Book about Water, Heat and Electricity,* W. R. Scott, 1948; *How Your Body Works,* introduction by Milton I. Levine, W. R. Scott, 1949.

Let's Look under the City: Water, Gas, Waste, Electricity, Telephone, W. R. Scott, 1950, revised edition, 1954; *Plants in the City,* John Day, 1951, revised edition, Faber, 1953; *You among the Stars,* W. R. Scott, 1951; *Follow the Sunset,* Doubleday, 1952; *Rocks, Rivers and the Changing Earth: A First Book about Geology,* W. R. Scott, 1952; *Your Telephone and How It Works,* Whittlesey House, 1952, 3rd edition, 1965; *More Power to You: A Short History of Power from the Windmill to the Atom,* W. R. Scott, 1953, also published as *More Power to You: From Windmills to Atomic Energy,* E. M. Hale, 1953; *Science Fun with Milk Cartons,* Whittlesey House, 1953; *Heath Elementary Science,* Heath, Book 1: *Science for Work and Play,* Book 2: *Science for Here and Now,* Book 3: *Science Far and Near,* Book 4: *Science in Your Life,* Book 5: *Science in Our World,* Book 6: *Science for Today and Tomorrow,* 1954-55, 2nd edition published as *Heath Science Series,* with additional titles, Book 7: *Science in the Space Age,* Book 8: *Science and Your Future,* 1961, 3rd edition, 1968 (series published in England as *Elementary Science,* Harrap, 1954-55, 2nd edition, 1961), 4th revised edition, 1973; *Let's Find Out about Electricity* (includes kit to make working models of a telegraph set, lighthouse, 4-way traffic signal, and TV theatre), Grosset, 1956; *Let's Find Out about the Weather* (includes kit to make working models of a barometer, weather vane, air current and air speed indicators, humidity gauge, and weather house), Grosset, 1956; (editor) Eunice Holsaert, *Life in the Arctic,* Harvey House, 1957; (editor) Eunice Holsaert, *Life in the Tropics,* Harvey House, 1957.

Science around You, Harrap, 1966; *Science Fun with a Flashlight,* McGraw, 1975; *Science Fun for You in a Minute or Two,* McGraw, 1975.

Contributor of poems to *Mademoiselle, Nation,* and *New American Review.* Editor, juvenile books, Virginia Kirkus Bookshop Service; columnist, *Instructor* Magazine.

WORK IN PROGRESS: A novel, *The Woman Who Lived in a Prologue.*

SIDELIGHTS: Mrs. Schneider told *CA:* "I have always been interested in books—reading them and writing them. From the time, early in my teens, that I read Malory's *Morte d'Arthur* in the five big old volumes, I became interested in language. I worked on the school newspaper, edited my college magazine, taught English poetry and when I had so many children I didn't know what to do, I worked in their City and County library. I have never stopped loving poetry and especially Shakespeare.... [and] I taught English at Hofstra University. I began to write books for children to answer questions asked by my children and the children with whom I worked at the City and County School.''

BIOGRAPHICAL/CRITICAL SOURCES: Huck and Young, *Children's Literature in the Elementary School,* Holt, 1961; Muriel Fuller, editor, *More Junior Authors,* H. W. Wilson, 1963; *The Children's Bookshelf,* Child Study Association of America, Bantam, 1965; Nancy Larrick, *A Teacher's Guide to Children's Books,* Merrill, 1966; Nancy Larrick, *A Parent's Guide to Children's Reading,* 3rd edition, Doubleday, 1969.

* * *

SCHNEIDER, William, Jr. 1941-

PERSONAL: Born November 20, 1941, in Rockville Centre, N.Y.; son of William (a business executive) and Jane (Law) Schneider. *Education:* Villanova University, B.S.; New York University, Ph.D., 1968. *Politics:* Republican. *Religion:* Roman Catholic. *Home:* 17 Buckminster Rd., Rockville Centre, N.Y. 11570. *Office:* Hudson Institute, Quaker Ridge Rd., Croton-on-Hudson, N.Y. 10520.

CAREER: Hudson Institute, Croton-on-Hudson, N.Y., economist, 1968—; staff member of the U.S. Senate and U.S. House of Representatives, 1971—. Ship's radio officer, U.S. Merchant Marine. *Member:* American Economic Association, Econometric Society, Institute for Strategic Studies (London).

WRITINGS: (Editor with Johan J. Holst) *Why ABM? Policy Issues in the Missile Defense Controversy,* Pergamon, 1969; *Food, Foreign Policy and Raw Materials Cartels,* Craine, Russak, 1976; (co-author) *Arms, Men, and Military Budgets: Issues for Fiscal Year 1977,* Craine, Russak, 1976.

WORK IN PROGRESS: Defense Policy in the 1970s; research concerning future military technology and arms control.

AVOCATIONAL INTERESTS: Amateur radio.

BIOGRAPHICAL/CRITICAL SOURCES: National Review, July 29, 1969.

* * *

SCHNEIER, Edward V(incent), Jr. 1939-

PERSONAL: Surname rhymes with "fire"; born May 25, 1939, in Bronx, N.Y.; son of Edward Vincent (a steel importer) and Lillian (Buhr) Schneier; married Janice Bernier, June 16, 1960 (divorced, 1974); children: Andrew, Katherine. *Education:* Oberlin College, B.A., 1960; Claremont Graduate School, M.A., 1961, Ph.D., 1963. *Politics:* Democrat. *Religion:* None. *Home:* 1 Harrison St., New York, N.Y. 10013. *Office:* Department of Political Science, City College of the City University of New York, New York, N.Y. 10031.

CAREER: Brookings Institution, Washington, D.C., research fellow, 1963-64; Johns Hopkins University, Baltimore, Md., assistant professor of political science, 1964-65; Princeton University, Princeton, N.J., assistant professor of political science, 1965-68; City College of the City Univer-

sity of New York, New York, N.Y., assistant professor, 1968-71, associate professor of political science, 1971—. Fellow, National Humanities Institute, University of Chicago, 1977-78. Legislative assistant to Senator Birch Bayh of Indiana, 1963-64; New York State elections supervisor for National Broadcasting Company News, 1969-70; co-founder, Movement for a New Congress, 1970. Member, American-Jewish Committee. *Member:* American Political Science Association, Professional Staff Congress, Downtown Independent Democrats, Staten Island Democratic Association, Village Independent Democrats, Pi Sigma Alpha.

WRITINGS: (Editor) *Policy-Making in American Government,* Basic Books, 1969; (with Julius Turner) *Party and Constituency: Pressures on Congress,* Johns Hopkins Press, 1970; (with William Murphy) *Vote Power,* Prentice-Hall, 1970; (contributor) Jon Rosenbaum, editor, *Vigilante Politics,* University of Pennsylvania Press, 1976. Contributor to *Nation, Society Bulletin of the Atomic Scientists,* and other periodicals.

WORK IN PROGRESS: Toward a Theory of Congress; with Bertram Gross, *The Legislative Struggle.*

* * *

SCHNELL, George A(dam) 1931-

PERSONAL: Born July 13, 1931, in Philadelphia, Pa.; son of Earl Blackwood and Emily (Bernheimer) Schnell; married Mary Lou Williams, June 21, 1958; children: David, Douglas, Thomas. *Education:* West Chester State College, B.S., 1958; Pennsylvania State University, M.S., 1960, Ph.D., 1965. *Politics:* Democrat. *Religion:* Reformed Church. *Home:* 1 North Manheim Blvd., New Paltz, N.Y. 12561. *Office:* Department of Geography, Hamner House 1, State University of New York College at New Paltz, New Paltz, N.Y. 12561.

CAREER: State University of New York College at New Paltz, assistant professor, 1962-65, associate professor, 1965-68, professor of geography, 1968—, chairman of department, 1969—. Visiting professor, University of Hawaii, summer, 1966. *Military service:* U.S. Army, 1952-54. *Member:* Association of American Geographers, National Council on Geographic Education, Pennsylvania Academy of Science. *Awards, honors:* National Science Foundation summer fellow, 1965.

WRITINGS: (Editor with George J. Demko and Harold M. Rose) *Population Geography: A Reader,* McGraw, 1970; (with Kenneth Corey and others) *The Local Community,* Macmillan, 1971; (contributor) Q. H. Stanford, editor, *The World's Population: Problems of Growth,* Oxford University Press (Canada), 1972; (contributor) *Readings on West Virginia and Appalachia,* Kendall-Hunt, in press. Contributor to geography and other professional journals.

* * *

SCHOENBERGER, Walter Smith 1920-

PERSONAL: Born November 19, 1920, in Pittsburgh, Pa.; son of Homer (a businessman) and Alice (Smith) Schoenberger; married Maralyn Morton (a social worker), February 2, 1952; children: Karen. *Education:* University of Pittsburgh, A.B., 1950, M.A., 1953; Fletcher School of Law and Diplomacy, M.A., 1954, Ph.D., 1963. *Politics:* Democrat. *Religion:* Swedenborgian. *Home:* 25 College Heights, Orono, Me. 04473. *Agent:* Gerard McCauley Agency, Inc., 551 Fifth Ave., New York, N.Y. 10017. *Office:* Department of Political Science, University of Maine, 33 North Stevens, Orono, Me. 04473.

CAREER: Tufts University, Medford, Mass., instructor in international relations and American government, 1954-56; University of Maine, Orono, instructor, 1956-59, assistant professor, 1959-63, associate professor, 1963-67, professor of political science, 1967—. *Military service:* U.S. Naval Reserve, naval aviator on active duty, 1942-46, Organized Reserve, 1946-54; became lieutenant; received Air Medal (twice). *Member:* American Political Science Association, International Studies Association, American Association of University Professors.

WRITINGS: Decision of Destiny, Ohio University Press, 1970.

WORK IN PROGRESS: U.S. Policy Toward China, 1945-1971; other studies on current world problems.

*   *   *

SCHOENHERR, Richard Anthony 1935-

PERSONAL: Born January 11, 1935, in Center Line, Mich.; son of Edward Anthony (a car salesman) and Irene (Grobbel) Schoenherr; married Judith Ann Woods, December 11, 1970. *Education:* Sacred Heart Seminary, Detroit, Mich., A.B. (with honors), 1957; St. John's Provincial Seminary, Plymouth, Mich., S.T.B., 1961; University of Chicago, M.A., 1967, Ph.D., 1970. *Politics:* Liberal Democrat. *Residence:* Madison, Wis. *Office:* Department of Sociology, University of Wisconsin, Madison, Wis. 53706.

CAREER: Ordained Roman Catholic priest, 1961; Saint Benedict's Church, Pontiac, Mich., associate pastor, 1961-64; Saint Sabina Church, Chicago, Ill., part-time assistant pastor, 1964-70; University of Chicago, Chicago, Comparative Organizational Research Program, National Science Foundation fellow and senior research assistant, project director for Employment Security Agency Study, 1966-68, National Opinion Research Center, associate study director, 1969-70, senior study director, 1970-71, research associate and assistant professor of sociology, 1971; University of Wisconsin—Madison, assistant professor, 1971-75, associate professor of sociology, 1976—. Consultant, Sisters Advisory Council, Priests Senate, Archdiocese of Detroit, 1969. *Member:* American Sociological Association, American Catholic Sociological Society, Society for the Scientific Study of Religion, Association for the Sociology of Religion.

WRITINGS: (With Peter M. Blau) *The Structure of Organizations,* Basic Books, 1971; (with Andrew M. Greeley) *American Priests,* National Opinion Research Center, University of Chicago, 1971.

Contributor: *Renewal through General Chapters,* Canon Law Society of America, 1967. Contributor of articles and reviews to *Public Personnel Review, American Journal of Sociology,* and other periodicals.

WORK IN PROGRESS: Study of the organizational structure of dioceses and religious communities of the Roman Catholic Church.

*   *   *

SCHOEPFLIN, George A. 1939-

PERSONAL: Born November 24, 1939, in Budapest, Hungary; son of Gyula and Katalin (Balazs) Schoepflin; married C. Jane O. Morton (a journalist), January, 1966; children: Julia Krisztina Macduff, Sophia Elisabeth Macduff, Katherine Alexandra Macduff. *Education:* University of Glasgow, M.A., 1960, LL.B., 1962; College of Europe, Certificate in European Studies, 1963. *Home:* 71 Chester Rd., London N.19, England. *Office:* London School of Eco-

nomics and School of Slavonic and East European Studies, University of London, London W.C.2, England.

CAREER: Royal Institute of International Affairs, London, England, research assistant, 1963-67; British Broadcasting Corp., External Services, London, research assistant, 1967-73, 1974-76; University of London, School of Slavonic and East European Studies, Hayter fellow, 1973-74, London School of Economics and School of Slavonic and East European Studies, lecturer in East European political institutions, 1976—.

WRITINGS: (Editor) *The Soviet Union and Eastern Europe: A Handbook,* Praeger, 1970.

WORK IN PROGRESS: A book on nationalism and nationalist ideologies in eastern Europe.

SIDELIGHTS: George Schoepflin wrote to *CA:* "Thurber got it right. To put *cogito ergo sum* in preference to *non sum qualis eram* is like putting Descartes before Horace."

*   *   *

SCHOER, Lowell A(ugust) 1931-

PERSONAL: Born January 7, 1931, in Fairmont, Minn.; son of Albert (a laborer) and Malinda (Huse) Schoer; married Corinne Hoefker, May 31, 1954; children: Renee, Alan, Jonathon, Darren. *Education:* Bethany College, Mankato, Minn., student, 1949-51; University of Iowa, B.A., 1958, M.A., 1959, Ph.D., 1961. *Politics:* Democrat. *Religion:* Lutheran. *Home address:* R.R.2, Iowa City, Iowa 52240. *Office:* College of Education, University of Iowa, Iowa City, Iowa 52240.

CAREER: University of Iowa, Iowa City, assistant professor, 1961-64, associate professor, 1964-67, professor of educational psychology, 1967—. *Military service:* U.S. Navy, 1953-57. *Member:* American Psychological Association, American Educational Research Association, Sigma Xi, Phi Delta Kappa.

WRITINGS: Recent Research in Written Composition, National Council of Teachers of English, 1963; *An Introduction to Statistics and Measurement,* Allyn & Bacon, 1966, revised edition published as *Statistics and Measurement: A Programmed Introduction,* 1971; (with Henry H. Albers) *Programmed Organization and Management Principles,* Wiley, 1966; *Test Construction: A Programmed Guide,* Allyn & Bacon, 1970; *Writing the Classroom Test,* Allyn & Bacon, in press.

WORK IN PROGRESS: A book on educational psychology, completion expected in 1978.

*   *   *

SCHOLES, Marie V(ielmetti) 1916-

PERSONAL: Born November 20, 1916, in Norway, Mich.; daughter of Max (a grocer) and Mary (Scavarda) Vielmetti; married Walter Vinton Scholes (a history professor; deceased), June 21, 1941. *Education:* University of Michigan, B.A., 1939, M.A., 1940. *Home:* 1515 Ross, Columbia, Mo. 65201.

CAREER: Writer.

WRITINGS: (With husband, Walter V. Scholes) *The Foreign Policies of the Taft Administration,* University of Missouri Press, 1970.†

*   *   *

SCHOMP, Gerald 1937-

PERSONAL: Surname is pronounced Skomp; born February 6, 1937, in Toledo, Ohio; son of Harvey L. (a professional gambler) and Henrietta (Dusseau) Schomp; married Janice M. Hall, August 5, 1962; children: Craig, Diane, Eileen, Brian, Dane. *Education:* University of Toledo, B.B.A., 1959, M.A., 1961; Syracuse University, graduate study. *Politics:* "Damned independent." *Religion:* Catholic. *Residence:* Miami, Fla. *Agent:* Jay Garon-Brooke Associates, 415 Central Park W., New York, N.Y. 10025. *Office:* G.A.C. Properties, Inc., 7880 Biscayne Blvd., Miami, Fla. 33138.

CAREER: Creative Programs, Toledo, Ohio, creative writer, 1963-64; WSUN-TV, St. Petersburg, Fla., promotion manager, 1964-65; John Birch Society, state coordinator for southern Florida, 1965-67; Bishop Verot High School, Fort Meyers, Fla., teacher, 1967-69; G.A.C. Properties, Inc., Miami, Fla., editor, 1969—. *Member:* Florida Magazine Association.

WRITINGS: The Political Assassination of Robert A. Taft, Allegiance Books, 1967; *Birchism Was My Business,* Macmillan, 1970; *Overcoming Anxiety: A Christian Guide to Personal Growth,* St. Anthony Messenger Press, 1976; *Alcohol, Its Use, Abuse and Therapy,* Our Sunday Visitor, 1977.

WORK IN PROGRESS: Two novels, *The Lovable Hate-Monger,* and *Underneath It All.*

SIDELIGHTS: Gerald Schomp told *CA:* "As a writer I wish to become a successful *moralist,* making social commentary through the medium of fiction in particular. I am especially anxious to expose hypocrisy wherever I see it (which is about everywhere these days). I am somewhat of a rebel by nature and I am willing to run contrary to the popular wind—in fact, I think I am fated to enrage people in the future with whatever I write. But whatever I write, there will be a strong moral lesson in it, woven into entertainment so as to be able to reach a mass audience."†

*   *   *

SCHOOR, Gene 1921-

PERSONAL: Surname is pronounced Shore; born July 26, 1921, in Passaic, N.J.; son of Bernard and Marie (Winstone) Schoor; married Frances Stampler (a nursery school consultant), September, 1942. *Education:* Miami University, Coral Gables, Fla., B.P.E., 1938. *Home:* 75 Bank St., New York, N.Y. 10014.

CAREER: Athletic instructor at New York University, New York City, 1938-39, University of Minnesota, Minneapolis, 1939-41, and City College (now City College of the City University of New York), New York City, 1941-42; professional writer. Owner of New York restaurant, Gene Schoor Steak House. *Military service:* U.S. Navy, public relations, 1942-45. *Awards, honors:* Awards from Boys' Club of America for *Joe Di Maggio: The Yankee Clipper, The Jim Thorpe Story, Young John Kennedy, The Army-Navy Game,* and *Young Robert Kennedy.*

WRITINGS: (Editor) Samuel Nisenson, *Giant Book of Sports,* Garden City Publishing, 1948; *Picture Story of Franklin Delano Roosevelt,* Fell, 1950; *The Thrilling Story of Joe Di Maggio,* Fell, 1950; *General Douglas MacArthur: A Pictorial Biography,* Rudolph Field, 1951; *Sugar Ray Robinson,* Greenberg, 1951; (with Henry Gilfond) *The Jim Thorpe Story: America's Greatest Athlete,* Messner, 1951; (with Gilfond) *Red Grange: Football's Greatest Halfback,* Messner, 1952; (with Gilfond) *The Story of Ty Cobb: Baseball's Greatest Player,* Messner, 1952; (with Gilfond) *Casey*

Stengel: Baseball's Greatest Manager, Messner, 1953; (with Gilfond) *Christy Mathewson: Baseball's Greatest Pitcher,* Messner, 1953; (with Gilfond) *The Ted Williams Story,* Messner, 1954; *The Leo Durocher Story,* Messner, 1955; *Joe Di Maggio: The Yankee Clipper,* Messner, 1956; *The Pee Wee Reese Story,* Messner, 1956; (with Gilfond) *The Jack Dempsey Story,* Nicholas Kaye, 1956; *Jackie Robinson: Baseball Hero,* Putnam, 1958; *Bob Turley: Fireball Pitcher,* Putnam, 1959; *Mickey Mantle of the Yankees,* Putnam, 1959; *Roy Campanella: Man of Courage,* Putnam, 1959.

Lew Burdette of the Braves, Putnam, 1960; *Willy Mays: Modest Champion,* Putnam, 1960; *The Red Schoendienst Story,* Putnam, 1961; *Bob Feller: Hall of Fame Strikeout Star,* Doubleday, 1962; (editor) *A Treasury of Notre Dame Football,* Funk, 1962; *Young John Kennedy,* Harcourt, 1963; (editor) *The Army-Navy Game: A Treasury of the Football Classics,* Dodd, 1967; *Courage Makes the Champion,* Van Nostrand, 1968; *Young Robert Kennedy,* McGraw, 1969.

Football's Greatest Coach: Vince Lombardi, Doubleday, 1974; (with Robert J. Antonacci) *Track and Field for Young Champions,* McGraw, 1974; (with wife, Fran Schoor) *Luechow's German Festival Cookbook,* Doubleday, 1976; *The Story of Yogi Berra,* Doubleday, 1976.

SIDELIGHTS: Gene Schoor went to Miami University on an athletic scholarship and was on the university boxing team for three years. As an amateur boxer he won eighteen city, state, and national championships.

BIOGRAPHICAL/CRITICAL SOURCES: New York Times Book Review, November 9, 1969.†

*   *   *

SCHORR, Alvin L. 1921-

PERSONAL: Surname rhymes with "more"; born April 13, 1921, in New York, N.Y.; son of Louis and Tillie (Godiner) Schorr; married Ann Girson (a social researcher), August 21, 1948; children: Jessica Lee, Kenneth L., Wendy Lauren. *Education:* City College (now City College of the City University of New York), New York, N.Y., B.S.S., 1941; Washington University, St. Louis, Mo., M.S.W., 1943; additional study at Bryn Mawr College and University College, London. *Religion:* Jewish. *Home:* 45 Gramercy Park, New York, N.Y. 10010. *Office:* Community Service Society, 105 East 22nd St., New York, N.Y. 10010.

CAREER: Caseworker and executive in family service and other social agencies, 1943-58; U.S. Social Security Administration, Washington, D.C., family life specialist, later director of long-range research, 1958-65; U.S. Office of Economic Opportunity, Washington, D.C., director of research and planning, 1965-66; U.S. Department of Health, Education, and Welfare, Washington, D.C., deputy assistant secretary, 1966-68; Brandeis University, Waltham, Mass., professor at Florence Heller School for Graduate Studies in Social Welfare, Washington, D.C., 1968-70; New York University, Graduate School of Social Work, New York City, dean, 1970-73; currently affiliated with Community Service Society, New York City. Visiting professor at London School of Economics and Political Science, University of London; visiting lecturer at University of North Carolina. Consultant to "model cities" programs on income maintenance. *Member:* National Association of Social Workers, American Public Welfare Association, International Conference on Social Welfare. *Awards, honors:* Senior Fulbright scholar in England, 1962-63; Michael

Schwerner award, 1974, for leadership in civil rights; Doctor of Humane Letters, Adelphi University, 1976.

WRITINGS: Filial Responsibility in the Modern American Family, U.S. Government Printing Office, 1960; *Slums and Social Insecurity,* U.S. Government Printing Office, 1963; *Social Security and Social Services in France,* U.S. Government Printing Office, 1965; *Poor Kids,* Basic Books, 1966; *Explorations in Social Policy,* Basic Books, 1968; *Children and Decent People,* Basic Books, 1974; *Jubilee for Our Times,* Columbia University Press, 1977.

BIOGRAPHICAL/CRITICAL SOURCES: New York Times Book Review, January 5, 1969; *Commonweal,* April 25, 1969.

* * *

SCHORR, Jerry 1934-

PERSONAL: Born October 1, 1934, in New York, N.Y.; son of Morris and Minnie (Klein) Schorr; married Judith R. Kramer, November 26, 1960; children: Stephen Paul. *Education:* New York University, B.S., 1959; M.B.A., 1962, further graduate study. *Home:* 5700 Arlington Ave., Riverdale, N.Y. 10471. *Office:* Eastern Airlines, 10 Rockefeller Plaza, New York, N.Y. 10020.

CAREER: ASR Corp., New York City, market researcher, 1960-61; REA Express, New York City, distribution consultant, 1961-65; Eastern Airlines, New York City, director of cargo marketing development, 1965—. *Military service:* U.S. Army, 1954-56. *Member:* Operations Research Society of America, National Council of Physical Distribution Management.

WRITINGS: (With M. Alexander and R. Franco) *Logistics in Marketing,* Pitman, 1969. Contributor of articles on distribution analysis to journals.††

* * *

SCHRANK, Jeffrey 1944-

PERSONAL: Born February 8, 1944, in Milwaukee, Wis.; son of Harry and Irene (Schmidt) Schrank; married Louise Welsh (a teacher), August 15, 1970. *Education:* St. Mary's University, San Antonio, Tex., B.A., 1966; University of Notre Dame, M.A., 1972. *Home:* 145 Brentwood, Palatine, Ill. 60067.

CAREER: Teacher in parochial schools in Chicago, Ill., 1966-69, and St. Louis, Mo., 1969-70; free-lance writer, 1971—. President, Learning Seed Co., 1975—.

WRITINGS: Media in Value Education: A Critical Guide, Argus Communications Co., 1970; *Communication; Destiny; Revolution; Violence,* Silver Burdett, 1970; *Teaching Human Beings: 101 Subversive Activities for the Classroom,* Beacon Press, 1972; *Freedom: Now and When,* Winston Press, 1972; *Feelings: Exploring Inner Space,* Paulist/Newman, 1973; *TV Action Handbook,* McDougal, Littell, 1974; *The Learning Seed Catalog,* Beacon Press, 1974; *Deception Detection,* Beacon Press, 1975; *Understanding Mass Media,* National Textbook Co., 1976; *Snap Crackle and Popular Taste,* Dell, 1977. Editor, *Media Mix Newsletter,* 1970—.

* * *

SCHROETER, Louis C(larence) 1929-

PERSONAL: Surname is pronounced Shray-ter; born December 13, 1929, in St. Louis, Mo.; son of Clarence E. (a pharmacist) and Eleanor (Schindler) Schroeter; married Ju-

lann Griffin, June 7, 1952; children: John Louis, Lois Celeste, Julie Ann, Robert Louis. *Education:* St. Louis College of Pharmacy, B.S., 1952, M.S., 1956; University of Wisconsin, Ph.D., 1959. *Politics:* Republican. *Religion:* Roman Catholic. *Home:* 5371 Colony Woods Dr., Portage, Mich. 49081. *Office:* Upjohn Co., Kalamazoo, Mich. 49001.

CAREER: Schroeter Pharmacy, St. Louis, Ill., pharmacist, 1947-52; St. Louis College of Pharmacy, St. Louis, Mo., instructor in pharmacy, 1952-53; Firmin Desloge Hospital, St. Louis, Mo., pharmacist, 1955-56; Upjohn Co., Kalamazoo, Mich., research associate, 1959-63, head of pharmacy applied research, 1963-69, assistant manager of Pharmacy Research Unit, 1969-70, manager, 1970; Merck Sharp & Dohme, West Point, Pa., executive director of pharmaceutical research and development, 1970-73; Upjohn Co., vice-president for pharmaceutical manufacturing, 1973—. Kauffman Memorial Lecturer, Ohio State University, 1969. Holder of four medical patents. *Military service:* U.S. Army, 1953-55.

MEMBER: American Pharmaceutical Association, Academy of Pharmaceutical Sciences (fellow; vice-president, 1967-68), Sigma Xi, Rho Chi, Phi Lambda, Phi Sigma. *Awards, honors:* W. E. Upjohn Award of Upjohn Co., 1968; Distinguished Service to Pharmacy Award, St. Louis College of Pharmacy Alumni, 1968.

WRITINGS: (Contributor) *Remington's Pharmaceutical Sciences,* 13th edition (Schroeter was not associated with earlier editions), Mack Publishing, 1965, 14th edition, 1970; *Sulfur Dioxide: Applications in Foods, Beverages, and Pharmaceuticals,* Pergamon, 1966; *Ingredient X: The Production of Effective Drugs,* Pergamon, 1969; *Organization Elan,* American Management Association, 1970; (contributor) *How Modern Medicines Are Developed,* Futura Publishing, 1977.

WORK IN PROGRESS: A book on the development of self-discipline, *Ring of Iron;* a philosophical work on Stoicism.

* * *

SCHROETTER, Hilda Noel 1917-
(Hilda Bloxton Noel, Jr.)

PERSONAL: Surname rhymes with "better"; born October 11, 1917, in Lynchburg, Va.; daughter of Jesse Cleveland (a shoe designer and salesman) and Hilda (Bloxton) Noel; married Samuel T. Schroetter, Jr. (a college history instructor), June 27, 1944. *Education:* Randolph-Macon Woman's College, B.A., 1938; University of Virginia, M.A., 1946. *Politics:* Democrat ("on local, state, and national levels"). *Religion:* Episcopalian. *Home:* #300, 100 West Franklin St., Richmond, Va. 23220.

CAREER: Teacher of English and history in Virginia public schools, 1938-45; *Bristol Herald-Courier,* Bristol, Va., reporter, 1946-47; Virginia World War II History Commission, Richmond, editorial assistant, 1947-50; *Bristol Herald-Courier,* stringer, writing reviews and advertising columns, 1950-52; Station WINA, Charlottesville, Va., copy chief, 1952-54; University of Virginia, Charlottesville, editor of university catalogs, 1954-66; Virginia Commonwealth University, Richmond, member of adjunct faculty of Evening College, teaching English and journalism, 1966—. Free-lance editor for K. S. Giniger Co., Inc. (publisher), for Ohio University Press, and for religious organizations and educational associations. Member, Council of the Virginia Museum; member of the executive board, Associates of the James Branch Cabell Library. *Member:* Poetry Society of

Virginia, Virginia Writers Club, Historic Richmond Foundation (member of board), Woman's Club (Richmond), Democratic Woman's Club (Richmond).

WRITINGS—Editor: (And author of preface) *Flowers from St. Francis,* Golden Press, 1967; (and author of preface) *Prayers from the Bible,* Golden Press, 1967; *Great Thoughts from Luther,* Collins, 1968; *Great Thoughts of Freedom,* Collins, 1968; *Great Thoughts from Wesley,* Collins, 1968; *Great Thoughts from Knox,* Collins, 1968; Louis Rubin, *Forecasting the Weather,* F. Watts, 1970. Contributor of reviews to *Chicago Tribune Magazine of Books* and *Richmond Times-Dispatch.* Wrote under maiden name, Hilda Bloxton Noel, Jr., while in college.

*   *   *

SCHUH, G(eorge) Edward 1930-

PERSONAL: Born September 13, 1930, in Indianapolis, Ind.; son of George Oscar Edward (a farmer) and Viola May (Lentz) Schuh; married Maria Ignez Angeli, May 23, 1965; children: Audrey Marie, Susan Marie, Tanya Marie. *Education:* Purdue University, B.S., 1952; Michigan State University, M.S., 1954; University of Chicago, M.A., 1958, Ph.D., 1961. *Home:* Route 9, Arrowhead, Lafayette, Ind. 47906. *Office:* Center for Public Policy and Public Administration, Purdue University, Lafayette, Ind. 47907.

CAREER: Purdue University, Lafayette, Ind., 1959—, currently director of Center for Public Policy and Public Administration. Honorary professor, Agricultural University, Vicosa, Minas Gerais, Brazil, 1965; agriculture program adviser, Ford Foundation, Rio de Janeiro, Brazil, 1966-72; senior staff economist, President's Council of Economic Advisers, 1974-75; director, National Bureau of Economic Research, 1976—. *Military service:* U.S. Army, 1954-56; became sergeant. *Member:* American Agricultural Economics Association (director), American Academy of Arts and Sciences (fellow), Econometric Society, American Economic Association, International Association of Agricultural Economists, Brazilian Society of Agricultural Economists.

WRITINGS: (With Eliseu R. Alves) *The Agricultural Development of Brazil,* Praeger, 1970; *Research on Agricultural Development in Brazil,* Agricultural Development Council, 1970; *The Development of Paulista Agriculture,* Secretariat of Agriculture (Sao Paulo, Brazil), 1972. Contributor to agricultural economics journals.

*   *   *

SCHULTZ, Duane P(hilip) 1934-

PERSONAL: Born February 15, 1934, in Baltimore, Md.; son of George Philip (an engineer) and Virginia (Ford) Schultz; married Sydney Ellen Olman, June 17, 1962. *Education:* Johns Hopkins University, A.B., 1955; Syracuse University, M.A., 1957; American University, Ph.D., 1962. *Office:* Department of Psychology, University of North Carolina, Charlotte, N.C. 28205.

CAREER: Martin Co., Baltimore, Md., human factors engineer, 1958-60; American University, Washington, D.C., instructor in psychology, 1960-61; Westinghouse Corp., Air Armaments Division, Baltimore, senior human factors engineer, 1961; Institute for Defense Analyses, Washington, D.C., scientist, 1962; University of Virginia, Mary Washington College, Fredericksburg, assistant professor of psychology, 1963-66; University of North Carolina at Charlotte, associate professor, 1966-69, professor of psychology,

1969—. Visiting professor, University of Groningen, 1970. *Military service:* U.S. Army, 1957.

MEMBER: American Psychological Association, American Association of University Professors, Eastern Psychological Association, Southeastern Psychological Association. *Awards, honors:* Research grants from National Institute of Mental Health, 1962, and from Office of Naval Research, 1963-71.

WRITINGS: Panic Behavior, Random House, 1964; *Sensory Restriction: Effects on Behavior,* Academic Press, 1965; *A History of Modern Psychology,* Academic Press, 1969, 2nd edition, 1975; (compiler) *Psychology and Industry,* Macmillan, 1970; (editor) *The Science of Psychology: Critical Reflections,* Appleton, 1970; *Psychology and Industry Today,* Macmillan, 1973; *Theories of Personality,* Brooks/Cole, 1976; *Growth Personality: Models of the Healthy Personality,* Van Nostrand, 1977. Contributor of more than twenty articles to psychology journals.†

*   *   *

SCHULZ, David A. 1933-

PERSONAL: Born April 17, 1933, in St. Louis, Mo.; son of Jonathan H. (in real estate) and Bertha Stella (Renick) Schulz; married Helene Alice Robertson, August 31, 1957; children: Lisa Mariah, Allison Lee. *Education:* Princeton University, A.B., 1954; Protestant Episcopal Theological Seminary in Virginia, B.D., 1960; Washington University, St. Louis, Mo., M.A., 1965, Ph.D., 1968. *Politics:* Independent. *Office:* Department of Sociology, Pennsylvania State University, University Park, Pa. 16802.

CAREER: American Zinc Co., field geologist, 1956-57; ordained to priesthood of Episcopal Church, 1961; curate of church in Kirkwood, Mo., 1961-62; Washington University, St. Louis, Mo., lecturer, 1964-67; Pennsylvania State University, University Park, assistant professor of sociology, 1967—. *Military service:* U.S. Army, 1954-56. *Member:* American Sociological Association, Society for the Study of Social Problems, Eastern Sociological Society. *Awards, honors:* Bobbs-Merrill Award, 1965; National Science Foundation institutional grant, 1968.

WRITINGS: Coming Up Black: Patterns of Ghetto Socialization, Prentice-Hall, 1968; *The Changing Family: Its Function and Future,* Prentice-Hall, 1972, second edition, 1976; (with Stanley Rodgers) *Marriage, the Family, and Personal Fulfillment,* Prentice-Hall, 1975; (with Robert A. Wilson) *Urban Sociology,* Prentice-Hall, in press. Contributor to sociology journals. Book review editor, *Journal of Marriage and the Family,* 1968-74.

*   *   *

SCHULZ, John E. 1939-

PERSONAL: Born March 12, 1939, in Evanston, Ill.; son of Carl William (a lawyer) and Cornelia (Ernst) Schulz. *Education:* Princeton University, A.B., 1961 (spent junior year at University of Paris); Yale University, LL.B., 1968. *Politics:* "Eclectic." *Religion:* "Existentialist humanist." *Office:* School of Law, University of Southern California, Los Angeles, Calif.

CAREER: Groton School, Groton, Mass., teacher of French, 1962-65; University of Southern California, Los Angeles, professor of law, 1968—. Summer associate of the law firms of Sidley & Austin, Chicago, Ill., 1965, and Mayer, Friedlich, Spiers, Tierney, Brown & Platt, Chicago, 1967; research-writer for Ralph Nader, Washington, D.C., summer, 1968. Member of board of directors, Association of California Consumers; vice-president of board of directors, Los Angeles Neighborhood Legal Service Society, 1968-69. *Member:* Association of American Law Schools, Order of the Coif.

WRITINGS: (With Edward F. Cox and Robert C. Fellmeth) *The Nader Report on the Federal Trade Commission,* preface by Ralph Nader, Richard W. Baron, 1969. Editor-in-chief, *Military Law Reporter,* 1973—.

WORK IN PROGRESS: Research on the Selective Service law and on American revolutionary history and rhetoric.

AVOCATIONAL INTERESTS: French literature, music (rock blues, baroque, and contemporary).†

* * *

SCHUSTER, Max Lincoln 1897-1970

March 2, 1897—December 20, 1970; Austrian-born American editor and publisher. Obituaries: *Variety,* December 23, 1970; *Newsweek,* January 4, 1971; *Publishers' Weekly,* January 4, 1971; *Time,* January 4, 1971.

* * *

SCHUYLER, Keith C. 1919-

PERSONAL: Surname is pronounced Skyler; born June 10, 1919, in Berwick, Pa.; son of Glenn W. and G. Ethel (Kirchner) Schuyler; married Eloise Jean Helt, January 17, 1942; children: Keith C., Jr., Brian J., Bradley K. *Education:* Attended high school in Berwick, Pa. *Politics:* Republican. *Religion:* Episcopalian. *Home address:* R.D.2, Berwick, Pa. 18603. *Office:* 123 West Front St., Berwick, Pa. 18603.

CAREER: Berwick Enterprise, Berwick, Pa., reporter, photographer, and became city editor, 1937-51; flight instructor and charter pilot in Berwick, 1946-49; Chamber of Commerce, Berwick, executive secretary, 1951-55; Connecticut Mutual Life Insurance Co., agent in Berwick, 1955—; freelance writer, mainly on sports. *Military service:* U.S. Army Air Forces, 1942-45; commander of B-24 on bombing missions over Germany; became first lieutenant. *Member:* Authors Guild, Outdoor Writers of America (former member of board), National Rifle Association (member of board), Trout Unlimited, Pennsylvania Outdoor Writers Association (past president), Veterans of Foreign Wars, American Legion, Masons.

WRITINGS: Lures: The Guide to Sport Fishing, Stackpole, 1955; *Elusive Horizons,* A. S. Barnes, 1969; *Archery: From Golds to Big Game,* A. S. Barnes, 1970; *Bow Hunting for Big Game,* Stackpole, 1974. Columnist, "Fins, Furs & Feathers," *Berwick Enterprise,* 1938—, "About Hunting & Fishing," *V.F.W. Magazine,* 1952—, "Straight from the Bowstring," *Pennsylvania Game News,* 1963—.

* * *

SCHWARTZ, Lita Linzer 1930-

PERSONAL: Born January 14, 1930, in New York, N.Y.; daughter of Aaron Jerome (a manufacturer) and Dorothy (Linzer) Linzer; married Melvin Jay Schwartz (a business executive), June 18, 1950; children: Arthur Lee, Joshua David, Frederic Seth. *Education:* Hunter College (now Hunter College of the City University of New York), student, 1947; Vassar College, A.B., 1950; Temple University, Ed.M., 1956; Bryn Mawr College, Ph.D., 1964. *Home:* 411 Lodges Lane, Elkins Park, Pa. 19117. *Office:* Department of Educational Psychology, Pennsylvania State University, Ogontz Campus, Abington, Pa. 19001.

CAREER: Psychological Service Center, Philadelphia, Pa., staff psychologist, 1957-62; Pennsylvania State University, Ogontz Campus, Abington, part-time instructor in psychology, 1961-66, assistant professor, 1966-71, associate professor, 1971-76, professor of educational psychology, 1976—. Private practice in diagnostic evaluations and counseling, 1964—. Summer lecturer, Temple Universtiy, 1959. *Member:* American Psychological Association, Council for Exceptional Children, American Educational Research Association, Society for Personality Assessment, National Education Association, Association for Children with Learning Disabilities, American Association of University Professors, Pennsylvania Psychological Association (secretary of Academic Division, 1968-69), Philadelphia Society of Clinical Psychologists (member of executive board, 1968-69, 1970-71; secretary, 1975-76). *Awards, honors:* New York Philanthropic Humanitarian Award, 1973.

WRITINGS: (Editor) *Current Concerns in Educational Psychology,* Selected Academic Readings, 1968, revised edition, 1970; *American Education: A Problem-Centered Approach,* Holbrook, 1969, 2nd edition, 1974; *Educational Psychology: Focus on the Learner,* Holbrook, 1972, 2nd edition, 1977; *The Exceptional Child: A Primer,* Wadsworth, 1975. Contributor to psychology journals.

WORK IN PROGRESS: With N. Isser, *The American School and the Melting Pot.*

* * *

SCHWARTZBERG, Julie 1943-

PERSONAL: Born July 19, 1943, in New York, N.Y.; daughter of Murray and Anne (Shearer) Schwartzberg. *Education:* Queens College of the City University of New York, B.A., 1964; Columbia University, M.A., 1966, Ed.D. candidate, 1969—. *Office:* Department of Social Studies, Teachers College, Columbia University, New York, N.Y.

CAREER: Queens Junior High School 204, New York City, physical education teacher, 1964-65; Population Council, New York City, research assistant, 1965-66; Hilltop Junior School, Nyack, N.Y., social studies teacher, 1967-69; Columbia University, Teachers College, New York City, instructor in social studies, 1969—. Consultant, New York City Public Schools, summer, 1970; leader for workshop in values clarification, fall, 1971. *Member:* National Council for the Social Studies, New York State Council for the Social Studies.

WRITINGS: (With George W. Carey) *Teaching Population Geography: An Ecological Interdisciplinary Approach,* Teachers College Press, Columbia Universtiy, 1969.†

* * *

SCHWARTZMANN, Mischa 1919-

PERSONAL: Given name is pronounced Me-sha; born June 15, 1919, in Feodosiya, Russia; son of Leo and Sarah (Rozonski) Schwartzmann; married Sharon Lynn Wilson, August 4, 1956; children: Ethan, Sarah. *Education:* University of Washington, Seattle, B.A., 1949; San Francisco State College (now University), M.A., 1959; University of California, Berkeley, Administrative Credential, 1965. *Politics:* Independent. *Religion:* Hebrew. *Home:* 6809 Collton Blvd., Oakland, Calif. 94611. *Office:* Division of Language Arts, Chabot College, 2555 Hesperian Blvd., Hayward, Calif. 94545.

CAREER: High school teacher in Edmonds, Wash., 1951-56; Coalinga Community College, Coalinga, Calif., instructor in English, 1960-63; Chabot College, Hayward, Calif., instructor in English, 1963—. *Military service:* U.S. Army, Infantry, 1943-45; became sergeant; received Purple Heart and Bronze Star. *Member:* California Teachers Association, Western College Reading Association.

WRITINGS: (With Thomas D. Kowalski) *Through the Paragraph: A Visual Approach to Reading Imporvement,* Prentice-Hall, 1969. Contributor to education journals.

WORK IN PROGRESS: Reading I, a remedial text, for publication by Winthrop; editing *The Inner Space: The World of the Student,* an anthology of poems, plays, articles, and stories for W. C. Brown.†

* * *

SCHWARZ, Richard W(illiam) 1925-

PERSONAL: Born September 12, 1925, in Wataga, Ill.; son of George William (a farmer) and Mildred (Imschweiler) Schwarz; married Joyce Anderson, June 11, 1950; children: Constance Kay, Richard Paul, Dwight Luther. *Education:* Emmanuel Missionary College, B.A., 1949; University of Illinois, M.S., 1953; University of Michigan, M.A., 1959, Ph.D., 1964. *Politics:* Republican. *Religion:* Seventh-day Adventist. *Home:* 229 North Maplewood Dr., Berrien Springs, Mich. 49103. *Office:* Department of History, Andrews University, Berrien Springs, Mich. 49104.

CAREER: Broadview Academy, La Grange, Ill., librarian, 1949-53; Adelphian Academy, Holly, Mich., librarian, 1953-55; Andrews University, Berrien Springs, Mich., instructor, 1955-58, assistant professor, 1958-63, associate professor, 1963-68, professor of history and chairman of department, 1968—. Guest lecturer, Michigan State University Extension Service, 1967. *Military service:* U.S. Naval Reserve, 1944-46. *Member:* American Historical Association, Organization of American Historians, Association of Seventh-day Adventist Historians, Phi Beta Kappa, Phi Alpha Theta.

WRITINGS: John Harvey Kellogg, M.D., Southern Publishing, 1970. Contributor of book reviews to *Seminary Studies* and *Library Journal* and articles to *Illinois State Historical Journal, Adventist Heritage,* and *Spectrum.* Editor, *Seventh-day Adventist Historians Newsletter,* 1968—.

WORK IN PROGRESS: A college textbook on the history of the Seventh-day Adventist Church.

SIDELIGHTS: Richard W. Schwarz, whose life-long interest has been teaching, has co-directed two student study tours of Europe. He spent over ten years in research for his biography and several articles on John Harvey Kellogg, and is a frequent speaker on Kellogg at historical societies.

* * *

SCHWARZSCHILD, Bettina 1925-

PERSONAL: Born June 14, 1925, in Germany; daughter of Feiwel and Sima (Sipper) Freireich; married Arthur Schwarzschild (a traffic manager), January 30, 1949; children: Michael, Jane. *Education:* Brooklyn College (now Brooklyn College of the City University of New York), student, 1943-46. *Religion:* Jewish. *Home:* 83-15 98th St., Woodhaven, N.Y. 11421.

WRITINGS: The Not-Right House: Essays on James Purdy, University of Missouri Press, 1969.

WORK IN PROGRESS: A book of essays on the adventure story; additional essays on James Purdy to be added to *The Not-Right House;* a fictional account of life in Nazi Germany as seen through the eyes of a six-year-old, based on her own childhood recollections.

SCOPES, John T. 1900-1970

August 3, 1900—October 21, 1970; American schoolteacher and subject of the "monkey trial" of 1925. Obituaries: *New York Times,* October 23, 1970; *Washington Post,* October 23, 1970.

* * *

SCOTT, George (Edwin) 1925-

PERSONAL: Born June 22, 1925, in Leyton, Essex, England; son of George Benjamin (an insurance agent) and Florence (Burch) Scott; married Shelagh Maw, December 22, 1947; children: Susan Francesca, Alexander Michael, Daniel Matthew. *Education:* New College, Oxford, B.A. (honors), 1948. *Politics:* Liberal. *Home:* 26 Vineyard Hill Rd., London S.W.19, England.

CAREER: Started as journalist with *Northern Echo,* 1941-42, and *Yorkshire Post,* 1942-43; *Daily Express,* London, England, journalist, 1948-53; *Truth* (political review), London, 1953-57, deputy editor, 1954, editor, 1954-57; interviewer and commentator for British Broadcasting Corp., London, and for independent television companies, 1956—. Chairman of Political Division, British Liberal Party, 1962-63; stood unsuccessfully as Liberal parliamentary candidate from Middlesbrough East, March, 1962, from Middlesbrough West, June, 1962 and from Wimbledon, 1964. *Military service:* Royal Naval Volunteer Reserve, 1943-46; became sub-lieutenant. *Member:* Royal Institute of International Affairs, Society of Authors, British Academy of Film and Television Arts, Media Society, Reform Club (London).

WRITINGS: Time and Place (autobiographical), Staples, 1956; *The R.C.'s: A Report on Roman Catholics in Britain Today,* Hutchinson, 1967; *Reporter Anonymous* (centennial history of London's Press Association), Hutchinson, 1968; (with Leslie Smith) *Woman Alone,* Elm Tree Press, 1971; *The Rise and Fall of the League of Nations,* Hutchinson, 1974. Author of television documentary about Pope Paul, "The Sixth Paul," produced in 1968. Contributor to British magazines and newspapers, including *Economist, Punch,* and *Spectator.* Founding editor of *Oxford Viewpoint* while at New College; editor, *Listener,* 1974—.

AVOCATIONAL INTERESTS: Cricket ("still play, after a portly fashion, every summer weekend").

BIOGRAPHICAL/CRITICAL SOURCES: Punch, March 15, 1967; *Times Literary Supplement,* March 23, 1967; *Books and Bookmen,* April, 1968.

* * *

SCOTT, James C(ampbell) 1936-

PERSONAL: Born December 2, 1936, in Mount Holly, N.J.; son of Parry Mason (a physician) and Augusta (Campbell) Scott; married Louise Goehring (an art historian), September 2, 1961; children: Mia, Aaron, Noah. *Education:* Williams College, B.A., 1958; graduate study at University of Rangoon, 1958-59, and Institut des Etudes Science Politiques, Paris, 1959-60; Yale University, M.A., 1963, Ph.D., 1967. *Religion:* Society of Friends. *Residence:* Durham, Conn. *Office:* Department of Political Science, Yale University, New Haven, Conn. 06520.

CAREER: Wesleyan University, Middletown, Conn., instructor in political science, 1967; University of Wisconsin—Madison, assistant professor of political science, 1967-76; Yale University, New Haven, Conn., professor of political science, 1976—. *Member:* American Political Science Association, Association for Asian Studies, Phi Beta Kappa. *Awards, honors:* Ford Foundation foreign area fellowship to study in Malaysia, 1964-66; National Science Foundation post-doctoral fellow, 1968; National Institute of Mental Health postdoctoral fellow, 1971; National Endowment for the Humanities senior fellowship, 1975-76.

WRITINGS: Political Ideology in Malaysia, Yale University Press, 1968; *Comparative Political Corruption,* Prentice-Hall, 1971; *The Moral Economy of the Peasant: Rebellion and Subsistence in Southeast Asia,* Yale University Press, 1976. Contributor to political science journals.

WORK IN PROGRESS: Research on peasant culture and politics, peasant rebellion, the peasantry in Southeast Asia, and the experience of powerlessness and dependency.

* * *

SCOTT, Mel(lier Goodin) 1906-

PERSONAL: Born May 2, 1906, in New Orleans, La.; son of Mellier Goodin (a cotton broker) and Ada (Buckingham) Scott; married Geraldine Knight (a landscape architect), February 25, 1939. *Education:* University of California, Los Angeles, B.A., 1927; graduate study at University of California, Berkeley, 1928-29, and University of Southern California, 1930-31. *Politics:* Democrat. *Religion:* None. *Home:* 1130 Sterling Ave., Berkeley, Calif. 94708.

CAREER: Hollywood Citizen-News, Hollywood, Calif., chief editorial writer, 1935-39; Los Angeles County Housing Authority, Los Angeles, Calif., director of public relations, 1940-41; National Resources Planning Board, Pacific Southwest Office, Berkeley, Calif., research associate, 1942-43; Citizens Planning Council, San Jose, Calif., executive director, 1943-45; Department of City Planning, San Francisco, Calif., consultant, 1947; San Francisco, Calif. Unified School District, consultant, 1948; University of California, Berkeley, lecturer in department of city and regional planning, 1950-68, research associate, Institute of Governmental Studies, 1961-69. President, Citizens for Regional Recreation and Parks (San Francisco Bay area), 1961-63. *Member:* American Society of Planning Officials (honorary life member).

WRITINGS: Cities Are for People, Pacific Southwest Academy, 1942; *Metropolitan Los Angeles: One Community,* Haynes Foundation, 1949; *Guide for Planning Recreation Parks in California,* California Committee on Planning for Recreation, Park Areas and Facilities, 1956; *San Francisco Bay Area: A Metropolis in Perspective,* University of California Press, 1959; *The Future of San Francisco Bay,* Institute of Governmental Studies, University of California, Berkeley, 1963; *Partnership in the Arts,* Institute of Government Studies, University of California, Berkeley, 1963; *American City Planning since 1890,* University of California Press, 1969; *The States and the Arts,* Institute of Governmental Studies, University of California, Berkeley, 1971.

WORK IN PROGRESS: A book on selected hill towns in Tuscany and Umbria, Italy, under the auspices of Friends of the Earth, with photographs by Richard Kauffman.

SIDELIGHTS: Mel Scott wrote *CA* that since his retirement early in 1970, Scott and his wife have been "making two trips annually, one in United States, the other in Europe, studying urban design, art, and architecture." They have visited almost every section of the United States and many areas in England, France, Spain, Portugal, Italy, Greece, Switzerland, and the Netherlands.

SCOVILLE, Herbert, Jr. 1915-

PERSONAL: Born March 16, 1915, in New York, N.Y.; son of Herbert, Sr. and Orlena (Zabriskie) Scoville; married Ann Curtiss, June 26, 1937; children: Anthony Church, Thomas Welch, Nicholas Zabriskie, Mary Curtiss. *Education:* Yale University, B.S., 1937; Cambridge University, graduate work in physical chemistry, 1937-39; University of Rochester, Ph.D., 1942. *Home and office:* 6400 Georgetown Pike, McLean, Va. 22101.

CAREER: National Defense Research Committee, Washington, D.C., began as assistant chemist, became associate chemist, handled a variety of research contracts in chemical warfare in various locations, 1941-45; Atomic Energy Commission, Los Alamos Scientific Laboratory, Calif., senior scientist, 1946-48; U.S. Department of Defense, technical director of Armed Forces Special Weapons Project in Virginia, 1948-55; Central Intelligence Agency, Washington, D.C., 1955-63, began as assistant director of scientific intelligence, became deputy director for research; U.S. Arms Control and Disarmament Agency, Washington, D.C., assistant director for Science and Technology, 1963-69; Carnegie Endowment for International Peace, New York, N.Y., director of Arms Control Program, 1969-71. Member of Killian Committee, Technological Capabilities Panel, 1955; member of Air Force Science Advisory Board, 1955-62; member of U.S. delegation to the Geneva Conference, 1958; chairman of U.S. delegation to NATO Disarmament Experts' Meetings, 1966-68, and of U.S. delegations to Japan, Australia, and South Africa on the Non-Proliferation Treaty, 1967-68. Consultant to President's Science Advisory Committee, 1957-63, Arms Control and Disarmament Agency, 1969-73, and Safeguard Committee of Atomic Energy Commission, 1970-73. Member of board of trustees, Berkshire, Litchfield Environmental Conservancy Council, Inc., 1970—.

MEMBER: Federation of American Scientists (chairman of Committee on Strategic Arms, 1970—), Public Welfare Foundation (member of board of directors), Council of Foreign Relations, Sigma Xi, Cosmos Club (Washington, D.C.), Century Club (New York).

WRITINGS: (With Robert Osborn) *Missile Madness,* Houghton, 1970; *Toward a Strategic Arms Limitation Agreement,* Carnegie Endowment, 1970; (contributor) Boskey and Willrich, editors, *Nuclear Proliferation: Prospects for Control,* Dunellen, 1970; (contributor) *The Future fo the Sea-Based Deterrent,* MIT Press, 1973; (contributor) Willrich and Rhidelander, editors, *SALT: The Moscow Agreements and Beyond,* Free Press, 1974.

Contributor of articles on national security to *Scientific American, New Republic, Foreign Affairs, Foreign Policy,* and other periodicals.

WORK IN PROGRESS: Research in arms control.

AVOCATIONAL INTERESTS: Travel and trout fishing.

* * *

SCOVILLE, James G(riffin) 1940-

PERSONAL: Born March 19, 1940, in Amarillo, Tex.; son of Orlin James (an economist) and Carol (Griffin) Scoville; married Judith Nelson, June 11, 1962; children: Nathan James. *Education:* Oberlin College, A.B., 1961; Harvard University, A.M., 1963, Ph.D., 1965. *Home:* R.R. 1, Sydney, Ill. 61877. *Office:* Department of Labor and Industrial Relations, University of Illinois, 504 East Armory Ave., Champaign, Ill. 61820.

CAREER: Harvard University, Cambridge, Mass., instructor in economics, 1964-65; International Labour Office, Geneva, Switzerland, economist, 1965-66; Harvard University, assistant professor of economics, 1966-69; University of Illinois, Champaign, associate professor, 1969-75, professor of economics and labor and industrial relations, 1975—. Consultant to U.S. Department of Labor, International Labour Office, and Agency for International Development. *Member:* American Economic Association, Industrial Relations Research Association.

WRITINGS: The Job Content of the U.S. Economy, McGraw, 1969; *Perspectives on Poverty and Income Distribution,* Heath, 1971; *Manpower and Occupational Analysis: Concepts and Measurements,* Heath, 1972; (editor with Adolf Fox Sturmthal) *The International Labor Movement in Transition,* University of Illinois Press, 1973. Contributor to economics and industrial relations journals.

WORK IN PROGRESS: Research on labor markets in less developed countries and on the growth and development of labor organizations.

* * *

SEABOUGH, Ed(ward Ellis) 1932-

PERSONAL: Born October 27, 1932, in Aurora, Mo.; son of Robert Holmes (a minister) and Maurgarite (Ellis) Seabough. *Education:* Southwest Baptist College, A.A., 1952; Southwest Missouri State College (now University), B.S., 1954; Southwestern Baptist Theological Seminary, M.R.Ed., 1956. *Religion:* Baptist. *Home:* 6558 Roswell Rd. N.W., Atlanta, Ga. 30328. *Office:* Baptist Home Mission Board, 1350 Spring St. N.W., Atlanta, Ga. 30309.

CAREER: Baptist Convention of Oregon-Washington, Portland, Ore., secretary of department of student work, 1956-60; Baptist Sunday School Board, Nashville, Tenn., consultant to student department, 1960-68; Baptist Home Mission Board, Atlanta, Ga., associate secretary of department of missionary personnel, 1968—.

WRITINGS: After the Riot and Other Debris, Broadman, 1969; *Babble On . . . and Other Ruins,* Broadman, 1970; *New Day on the Hudson,* Baptist Home Mission Board, 1970; *So You're Going to College,* Broadman, 1974; (with John Hendrix) *The Festival of Night and Light,* Broadman, 1975. Also author of *The Lyrics of Ed Seabough.* Writer of religious songs for youth and of multimedia dramas for nationwide student religious conferences. Contributor to religious publications for high school and college youth.

WORK IN PROGRESS: Seeing the Truth, a book of contemporary visual poetry; *Pilgrimage,* a book on personal renewal in the Christian faith.†

* * *

SEAMAN, Barbara 1935-

PERSONAL: Born September 11, 1935, in New York, N.Y.; daughter of Henry Jerome (a public welfare administrator) and Sophie (a high school English teacher; maiden name, Kimels) Rosner; married Gideon Seaman (a psychiatrist), January 13, 1957; children: Noah Samuel, Elana Felicia, Shira Jean. *Education:* Oberlin College, B.A., 1956; Columbia University, Advanced Science Writing Certificate, 1968. *Politics:* Independent. *Religion:* Jewish. *Home:* 300 West End Ave., New York, N.Y. 10023. *Agent:* McIntosh & Otis, Inc., 475 Fifth Ave., New York, N.Y. 10017; (lectures) National Student Association, 2115 S St., Washington, D.C. 20008.

CAREER: Hamilton County Welfare Department, Cincinnati, Ohio, caseworker in Children's Services Division, 1956-57; free-lance writer, 1960-65; *Brides,* New York City, columnist, 1964-66; *Ladies' Home Journal,* New York City, columnist and contributing editor, 1965-69; *Family Circle,* New York City, child care and education editor, 1970-73; lecturer on women and women's health matters. Vice-president, Women's Medical Center, New York City, 1971-73; co-founder, Women's Health Lobby, 1975—. Has appeared on more than two hundred radio and television discussion and seminar programs. Member of advisory council, Feminist Press, 1975—; member of advisory boards of many women's organizations including Women's History Library, 1973—; member of steering committee, New York Women's Forum, 1974—. Judge for various journalism awards. *Member:* Society of Magazine Writers, National Association of Science Writers, Authors Guild, National Organization of Women, National Council on Family Relations, American Civil Liberties Union, Overseas Press Club of America, Education Writers Association. *Awards, honors:* Ford Foundation Early Admissions scholar.

WRITINGS: The Doctors' Case against the Pill, Peter H. Wyden, 1969; *Free and Female: The Sex Life of the Contemporary Woman,* Coward, 1972; (author of foreword) Louise Lacey, *Lunaception: A Feminine Odyssey into Fertility and Contraception,* Coward, 1974; (with husband, Gideon Seaman) *How to Get Off the Pill and Hormones and Be Better than Ever,* Atheneum, 1976; (with G. Seaman) *Women and the Crisis in Sex Hormones,* Rawson Associates, 1977. Contributor to newspapers and magazines; writer of radio and television scripts, poetry, and song lyrics.

SIDELIGHTS: Many of Barbara Seaman's books and articles have been published in Spanish, German, Dutch, Turkish, Japanese, Hebrew, and other languages.

BIOGRAPHICAL/CRITICAL SOURCES: Washington Post, January 24, 1970.

* * *

SEARIGHT, Mary W(illiams) 1918-

PERSONAL: Born January 4, 1918, in Cordell, Okla.; daughter of John Quitman (a rigger) and Grace (Giles) Williams; married Harold Newton Mock, December 15, 1946 (deceased); married Paul James Searight (owner of an office supply store), June 13, 1953; children: (first marriage) Gregory Newton; (second marriage) Sara Ann. *Education:* St. Francis Hospital School of Nursing, San Francisco, Calif., Diploma, 1940; University of California, San Francisco, B.S. (with honors), 1960, M.S., 1961; University of California, Berkeley, extension courses, 1961-65. *Home:* 50 Fairlie Dr., Santa Rosa, Calif. 95401. *Office:* Department of Nursing, California State College, Sonoma, Rohnert Park, Calif.

CAREER: Nurse at Tulare County Hospital, Tulare, Calif., 1940-42, at Kaiser Shipbuilding Co., Richmond, Calif., 1942-45, at Puunene Plantation Hospital, Puunene, Maui, Hawaii, 1945-46; Fairmont (Alameda County) Hospital, San Leandro, Calif., head nurse and out-patient clinic supervisor, 1948-50; U.S. Veterans Administration Hospital, Fresno, Calif., staff nurse and evening supervisor, 1950-52; nurse in ophthalmologist's office, Berkeley, Calif., 1952-54; Contra Costa Health Department, Pleasant Hill, Calif., clinic nurse, 1954-55; Concord Community Hospital, Concord, Calif., part-time staff nurse, 1955-61; Merritt College, Oakland, Calif., instructor in nursing, 1962-66; University of California, School of Nursing, San Francisco, lecturer and project director, 1966-68; director of nursing workshops and consultant, 1967-71; California State College, Sonoma, Rohnert Park, professor of nursing and chairperson of department, 1971—. Visiting summer lecturer, University of Minnesota, 1970-71. Sonoma County Comprehensive Health Planning, member of executive committee, coordinating committee, and board of directors, 1970.

MEMBER: American Nurses' Association, American Association of Colleges of Nursing, American Association of University Professors, American Association of University Women, California Nurses' Association, Sonoma County Nurses' Association, Sigma Theta Tau. *Awards, honors:* California Nurses' Association Lulu Hassenplug Award for distinguished achievement in nursing education, 1975.

WRITINGS: Your Career in Nursing (juvenile), Messner, 1970; (editor and contributor) *The Second Step: Baccalaureate Education for Registered Nurses,* F. A. Davis, 1976. Writer of reports on nursing education; contributor to nursing journals.

WORK IN PROGRESS: The second edition of *Your Career in Nursing;* more articles relating to nursing.

AVOCATIONAL INTERESTS: Home decorating, gourmet cooking, gardening, hiking, fishing.

* * *

SEARLE, Kathryn Adrienne 1942-
  (Kathryn)

PERSONAL: Born July 3, 1942, in Lytham, Lancashire, England; daughter of Charles William (a bank manager) and Margaret (Baxter) Marsh; married Keith Searle (a company director), November 20, 1970. *Education:* Westwood Castle Training College, graduate (with distinction in art), 1963. *Home:* 75 Sudbourne Rd., London S.W.2, England.

CAREER: Formerly a primary teacher in Oxfordshire and Cheshire, England; presently employed as a commercial artist with an advertising company in London, England. Work as an artist includes painting, drawing, and sculpture.

WRITINGS—Self-illustrated children's books under name Kathryn: *James,* Basil Blackwell, 1966; *James and the Hat,* Basil Blackwell, 1967; *James and Lucy,* Basil Blackwell, 1968.

WORK IN PROGRESS: A cartoon strip based on the James and Lucy characters in her books.

SIDELIGHTS: Kathryn Searle told *CA:* "I first came to write stories from my experiences in teaching five-to-six-year olds. We never seemed to have enough story material. I felt there was a need for more books of a suitable size to show to a small group whilst telling the story, therefore the pictures were of great importance to help hold that interest. In my own books the characters emerged pictorially first and the story wound 'round them."

Two stories, with pictures, about James were used on the British Broadcasting Corp. television program, "Playschool."†

* * *

SEARS, David O'Keefe 1935-

PERSONAL: Born June 24, 1935, in Urbana, Ill.; son of Robert R. (a professor) and Pauline (a professor; maiden name, Snedden) Sears; married 1961; children: Juliet Alison, Olivia Erin. *Education:* Stanford University, A.B., 1957; Yale University, Ph.D., 1961. *Office:* Department of Psychology, University of California, Los Angeles, Calif. 90024.

CAREER: University of California, Los Angeles, assistant professor, 1961-67, associate professor, 1967-71, professor of psychology and political science, 1971—. Visiting lecturer, Harvard University, 1967-68; visiting professor, University of California, Berkeley, 1972-73.

WRITINGS: (With R. E. Lane) *Public Opinion,* Prentice-Hall, 1964; (with J. L. Freedman and J. M. Carlsmith) *Social Psychology,* Prentice-Hall, 1970; (with J. B. McConahay) *Politics of Violence,* Houghton, 1973.

* * *

SEARS, Pauline Snedden 1908-

PERSONAL: Born July 5, 1908, in Fairlee, Vt.; married Robert R. Sears (a college administrator), 1932; children: two. *Education:* Stanford University, A.B., 1930; Columbia University, M.A., 1931; Yale University, Ph.D., 1939. *Home:* 1770 Bay Laurel Dr., Menlo Park, Calif. 94025. *Office:* School of Education, Stanford University, Stanford, Calif. 94305.

CAREER: Harvard University, Cambridge, Mass., research associate in education, 1948-53; Stanford University, Stanford, Calif., assistant professor, 1953-58, professor of education, 1958—. Instructor at Yale University and University of Iowa. *Member:* American Psychological Association, American Educational Research Association, Society for Research in Child Development.

WRITINGS: The Effect of Classroom Conditions on the Strength of Achievement Motive and Work Output of Elementary School Children, Stanford University, 1963; (with Vivian S. Sherman) *In Pursuit of Self-Esteem: Case Studies of Eight Elementary School Children,* Wadsworth, 1965; (editor) *Intellectual Development,* Wiley, 1971; (contributor with A. Barbee) J. Stanley, W. George, and C. Solano, editors, *The Gifted and the Creative: Fifty Year Perspective,* Johns Hopkins Press, 1977. Also contributor to *National Society for the Study of Education Yearbook on the Gifted Child,* 1977.

* * *

SEAVER, Paul S(iddall) 1932-

PERSONAL: Born March 19, 1932, in Philadelphia, Pa.; son of Benjamin and Madge (Tompkins) Seaver; married Kirsten Andresen, June 11, 1956; children: Hannah, David. *Education:* Haverford College, B.A., 1955; Harvard University, M.A., 1956, Ph.D., 1965. *Home:* 3638 Bryant St., Palo Alto, Calif. 94306. *Office:* Department of History, Stanford University, Stanford, Calif. 94305.

CAREER: Reed College, Portland, Ore., instructor in history, 1962-64; Stanford University, Stanford, Calif., assistant professor, 1964-70, associate professor of history, 1970—. *Member:* American Historical Association, Historical Association (England), American Society for Church History, American Association of University Professors. *Awards, honors:* Guggenheim fellowship.

WRITINGS: The Puritan Lectureships, 1560-1662, Stanford University Press, 1970; (editor and author of introduction) *Seventeenth-Century England: Society in an Age of Revolution,* F. Watts, 1976.

* * *

SEAY, James 1939-

PERSONAL: Born January 1, 1939, in Panola County, Miss.; son of James E. and Lucie Belle (Page) Seay; married

Lee Smith, June 17, 1967; children: Joshua Field, Turlington Page. *Education:* University of Mississippi, B.A., 1964; University of Virginia, M.A., 1966. *Office:* Department of English, University of North Carolina, Chapel Hill, N.C. 27514.

CAREER: Virginia Military Institute, Lexington, instructor in English, 1966-68; University of Alabama, University, assistant professor of English, 1968-71; Vanderbilt University, Nashville, Tenn., assistant professor of English, 1971-74; University of North Carolina at Chapel Hill, lecturer in English, 1974—. Has read poetry at various colleges and universities. Member of 1967 William Faulkner Foundation Fiction Award Committee. *Awards, honors:* Southern Literary Festival Prize, 1964; Academy of American Poets Poetry Prize, University of Virginia, 1966; Emily Clark Balch Prize, 1968.

WRITINGS: Let Not Your Hart (poems), Wesleyan University Press, 1970; *Water Tables,* Wesleyan University Press, 1974. Work represented in *Best Poems of 1968: Borestone Mountain Poetry Awards,* edited by Lionel Stevenson and others, Pacific Books, 1969, and *Hero's Way: Contemporary Poems in the Mythic Tradition,* edited by John A. Allen, Prentice-Hall, 1971. Contributor to *Virginia Quarterly Review, Nation, Southern Review, American Review,* and *Esquire.*

WORK IN PROGRESS: Another collection of poetry.

* * *

SEE, Carolyn 1934-

PERSONAL: Born January 13, 1934, in Pasadena, Calif.; daughter of George Newton Bowland (a writer) and Kate (Sullivan) Laws; married Richard Edward See (an anthropologist), February 27, 1954; married second husband, Tom Sturak (an editor and teacher), April 11, 1960; children: (first marriage) Lisa; (second marriage) Clara. *Education:* Los Angeles State College of Applied Arts and Sciences (now California State University, Los Angeles), B.A., 1957; University of California, Los Angeles, M.A., 1961, Ph.D., 1963. *Politics:* ''Peace and Freedom.'' *Home:* 21643 Hodgson Circle Dr., Topanga, Calif. 90290. *Agent:* Monica McCall, International Creative Management, 40 West 57th St., New York, N.Y. 10019.

CAREER: Associate professor of English at Loyola University of Los Angeles, Los Angeles, Calif. *Member:* Modern Language Association of America.

WRITINGS: The Rest Is Done with Mirrors (novel), Little, Brown, 1970; *Blue Money,* McKay, 1973. Regular contributor to *TV Guide;* also contributor to *Atlantic, Los Angeles Times Magazine, McCall's,* and *Ms.*

WORK IN PROGRESS: A novel, *Mothers, Daughters;* a ''cheerful novel about divorce.''

SIDELIGHTS: ''I am an expert witness in pornography trials—on the side of pornography,'' Carolyn See writes. ''Lived in Europe, Mexico, Newfoundland. Obsessed by poverty and the freakish. Managed an apartment house in the slums, live alone now in a primitive cabin. E. M. Forster is the best, the only novelist.''

* * *

SEGAL, Harold S. 1903-

PERSONAL: Born June 28, 1903, in St. John, New Brunswick, Canada; son of Simon (a rabbi) and Minnie Segal; married Dorothy Milstein, November 27, 1949; children: Diane Susan. *Education:* Attended Lafayette College, 1920-21; Bates College, B.A., 1924. *Home:* 190 Shore Dr. S., Miami, Fla. 33133.

CAREER: Began career in journalism, with editorial positions including copy desk chief, city editor, news editor, editorial writer, and columnist on newspapers in Pennsylvania, Maine, New York, and New Jersey; later executive of a chain of retail stores; currently manager of family properties. *Member:* Phi Beta Kappa.

WRITINGS: The Secret of Love and Happy Marriage, Branden Press, 1970.

WORK IN PROGRESS: The Devil's Work, a mystery novel; *Fun with Puns,* a book of original puns.

* * *

SEGAL, Robert M. 1925-

PERSONAL: Born August 29, 1925, in Newark, N.J.; son of Sol and Pauline (Fishman) Segal; married Beverly E. Gechman (a speech pathologist), June 21, 1953; children: Alicia, Paula, Beth. *Education:* University of Wisconsin, B.A., 1950; University of Pittsburgh, M.S.W., 1952; Brandeis University, Ph.D., 1969. *Home:* 3252 Bluett Dr., Ann Arbor, Mich. 48105. *Office:* Institute for the Study of Mental Retardation and Related Disabilities, University of Michigan, 130 South First St., Ann Arbor, Mich. 48109.

CAREER: Welfare Planning Council, Miami, Fla., planning consultant, 1962-66; University of Michigan, Ann Arbor, associate professor in School of Social Work, program director for social work, Institute for the Study of Mental Retardation and Related Disabilities, and associate of University Hospital, 1969—. Director of project on serving the aging and aged developmentally disabled, U.S. Department of Health, Education, and Welfare. Member of board of directors, Washtenaw Association for Retarded Children, 1969-71. *Military service:* U.S. Army, 1946-48. *Member:* National Association of Social Workers, American Association on Mental Deficiency.

WRITINGS: Mental Retardation and Social Action: A Study of the Associations for Retarded Children as a Force for Social Change, C. C Thomas, 1970; (contributor) William Cruickshank, editor, *Cerebral Palsy: A Developmental Disability,* 3rd edition, Syracuse University Press, 1976. Writer and producer of television films, ''The Emotionally Disturbed Child'' and ''Mental Retardation: A National Problem.''

SIDELIGHTS: Robert Segal writes: ''The reason I began writing was the pressure I began to feel from the University. 'Perish or publish' was a real message so I began to share my ideas with my colleagues and soon found I enjoyed the writing experience as it forced me to pull together many of my scattered thoughts in the field of mental retardation.''

* * *

SEGRAVE, Edmond 1904-1971

October 4, 1904—March 28, 1971; British editor. Obituaries: *Bookseller,* April 3, 1971; *Publishers' Weekly,* April 12, 1971; *Antiquarian Bookman,* June 24, 1971.

* * *

SEIB, Kenneth Allen 1938-

PERSONAL: Surname rhymes with ''tribe''; born March 27, 1938, in Shelby, Ohio; son of Frank and Grace (Wanamaker) Seib; married Lorna Jane Maddocks (an editorial consultant), July 6, 1966. *Education:* Ashland College, B.A., 1960; Columbia University, M.A., 1961; University of Pittsburgh, Ph.D., 1966. *Politics:* Democrat. *Religion:* None. *Home:* 1314 East Santa Ana, Fresno, Calif. 93704. *Office:* Department of English, California State University, Fresno, Calif. 93740.

CAREER: Illinois State University, Normal, assistant professor of English, 1963-66; University of Maryland, European Division, lecturer in English, 1966-68; California State University, Fresno, 1968—, began as assistant professor, currently professor of English, chairman of English department, 1977—. Fulbright professor at Ruhr-Universitat, Bochum, West Germany, 1970-71, and University of Bergen, Norway, 1971. *Member:* Modern Language Association of America, American Association of University Professors, Authors Guild, United Professors of California. *Awards, honors:* Woodrow Wilson fellow, 1960-61; Andrew Mellon fellowship, 1962-63.

WRITINGS: James Agee's "A Death in the Family": A Critical Commentary, Study Master Publications, 1965; *Albert Camus' "The Plague": A Critical Commentary,* Study Master Publications, 1966; *James Agee: Promise and Fulfillment,* University of Pittsburgh Press, 1969. Contributor of articles to *Commonweal, Critique, Essays in Literature, Studies in American Fiction,* and other journals.

WORK IN PROGRESS: "The Slow Death of Fresno State College: Power and Politics in the University," a manuscript; a book on the use of cinematic techniques by American authors.

SIDELIGHTS: Kenneth Seib writes: "I consider myself a teacher who writes when he has something to say, and otherwise has the good sense to remain silent, which is not always the case. But I feel that writing informs my teaching, so I generally keep something in my typewriter and try to write a variety of things, including fiction and poetry, so that the experiences will allow me to convey more about those kinds of writing to my students. I hope to continue doing the same in the future."

* * *

SEIDENBAUM, Art(hur) 1930-

PERSONAL: Surname is pronounced *Sigh*-den-bohm; born May 4, 1930, in New York, N.Y.; son of William George (in advertising) and Lida (Aretsky) Seidenbaum; married Judith Weiner (a teacher), June 14, 1951 (divorced, 1973); married Patricia Lee Houser, June 20, 1974; children: (first marriage) Kyle (son), Kerry (daughter). *Education:* Northwestern University, B.S.; Harvard University, graduate study, 1951-52. *Residence:* Los Angeles, Calif. *Agent:* Ned Brown, 315 South Beverly Dr., Beverly Hills, Calif. 90210. *Office: Los Angeles Times,* 202 West First St., Los Angeles, Calif. 90053.

CAREER: Life, New York, N.Y., reporter, 1955-59, correspondent in Los Angeles, Calif., 1959-61; *Saturday Evening Post,* Philadelphia, Pa., West Coast bureau chief in Los Angeles, 1961-62; *Los Angeles Times,* Los Angeles, columnist on environment and sociology, 1962—. Host, "City Watchers," KCET, Los Angeles, 1966-76. *Military service:* U.S. Navy, 1952-55; became lieutenant.

WRITINGS: Confrontation on Campus: Student Challenge in California, Ritchie, 1969; *This Is California: Please Keep Out,* Peter H. Wyden, 1975. Contributor to *Esquire, McCall's, West, Los Angeles Magazine,* and other periodicals.

SEIDLER, Grzegorz Leopold 1913-

PERSONAL: Born September 18, 1913, in Stanislawow, Poland; son of Teodor (a lawyer) and Eugenia (Dawidowicz) Seidler; married Alina Bogusz (an editor), March 1, 1968. *Education:* Jagiellonian University, Doctorate, 1938; additional study at University of Vienna and Oxford University. *Home:* Raabego 7m, 17 Lublin, Poland. *Office:* Faculty of Law, Marie Curie-Sklodowska University, 20-080 Lublin, Plac Litewski 3, Poland.

CAREER: Jagiellonian University, Cracow, Poland, lecturer in history of philosophy, 1945-50; Marie Curie-Sklodowska University, Lublin, Poland, chair of philosophy of law, 1950—, rector, 1959-69; Polish Cultural Institute, London, England, director, 1969-71. *Awards, honors:* Banner of Labour II (state decoration); honorary doctorate, Maria Curie-Sklodowska University and Academy of Economics, Cracow.

WRITINGS: Technika prac parlamentarnych, privately printed, 1938; *O istocie wladzy panstwowej,* Ksiegarnia Powszechna (Krakow), 1946; *Ewolucja problemow budzetowych w polskin prawie konstytucyjnym* (booklet), Ksiaznica (Krakow), 1946; *Rozwazania nad norma ustrojowa,* Ksiaznica, 1947; *Wladza ustawodawcza i wykonawcza,* Swiat i Wiedza (Krakow), 1948; *Teoria panstwa i prawa,* Pantswowe Wydawnictwo Naukowe (Krakow), 1951; *Wspolczesne kierunki w nauce prawa,* Panstwowe Wydawnictwo Naukowe, 1951; *Mysl polityczna Starozytnosci,* Wydawnictwo Literackie (Krakow), 1955, 3rd edition, 1961; *Doktryny prawne imperializmu,* Panstwowe Wydawnictwo Naukowe, 1957, 2nd edition, 1962; *Soziale Ideen in Byzanz,* Akademie-Verlag (Berlin), 1960; *Mysl polityczna Sredniowiecza,* Wydawnictwo Literackie, 1961; *The Emergence of the Eastern World,* Oxford University Press, 1968; *Mysl polityczna czasow nowozytnych,* Wydawnictwo Literackie, 1972; *Przedmarksowska mysl polityczna,* Wydawnictwo Literackie, 1974. Contributor to *Slavic Review* and journals in Poland and Germany. Editor-in-chief, *Annales* of Marie Curie-Sklodowska University, 1955—.

WORK IN PROGRESS: Allegories and Symbols as Factors Shaping Consciousness.

SIDELIGHTS: Grzegorz Seidler told *CA:* "My studies aim at achieving a broad synthesis, so that the history of political thought would become fairly coherent and focused on principal evolutionary tendencies. In my opinion studies in the history of political thought of necessity lead to a comparison of our own value system and our ideas with those of the past. Only a past that is united with the present is significant in the shaping of human consciousness which is always being formed in the present."

Seidler's *Doktryny prawne imperializmu* was published in Czech, Ukrainian, Russian, Hungarian, and Bulgarian translations; several of his other books have also appeared in translation.

* * *

SEIDMAN, Harold 1911-

PERSONAL: Born July 2, 1911, in Brooklyn, N.Y., son of Joseph A. (a lawyer) and Rebecca (Duchowney) Seidman. *Education:* Brown University, A.B. (summa cum laude), 1934, M.A., 1935; Yale University, Ph.D., 1940. *Office:* Department of Political Science, University of Connecticut, Storrs, Conn. 06268.

CAREER: New York (N.Y.) Department of Investigation, director of research, 1938-43; U.S. Bureau of the Budget,

Washington, D.C., administrative analyst and government corporation specialist, 1943-61, acting chief, Office of Management and Organization, 1961-64, assistant director of Bureau, 1964-68; National Academy of Public Administration, Washington, D.C., scholar-in-residence, 1968-71; University of Connecticut, Storrs, professor of political science, 1971—. Visiting professor, Syracuse University, 1969. University of Leeds, Leeds, England, political science research fellow, 1971, visiting professor, 1972-75. Lecturer at George Washington University, 1952-53, and University of Southern California, 1962. Federal coordinator for Alaska and Hawaii transitions to statehood; consultant to Colombia, 1950, United Nations, 1953, 1959, 1966, Guatemala, 1957, Turkey, 1961, Vietnam, 1967, and to Economic Commission for Africa, and President's Council on Executive Organization.

MEMBER: National Academy of Public Administration, American Political Science Association, American Society for Public Administration, International Institute of Administrative Sciences, Phi Beta Kappa.

WRITINGS: Labor Czars: A History of Labor Racketeering, Liveright, 1938; *Investigating Municipal Administration,* Institute of Public Administration, 1941; (with S. D. Goldberg) *The Government Corporation,* Public Administration Service, 1953; *Politics, Position, and Power: The Dynamics of Federal Organization,* Oxford University Press, 1970, 2nd edition, 1975; (contributor) *New Political Economy,* Macmillan, 1975. Contributor to *Encyclopaedia Britannica* and to public affairs journals.

WORK IN PROGRESS: Research on administration of public enterprise.

BIOGRAPHICAL/CRITICAL SOURCES: Political Quarterly, January/March, 1971; *American Political Science Review,* Volume LXV, 1971.

* * *

SEIDMAN, Hugh 1940-

PERSONAL: Born August 1, 1940, in Brooklyn, N.Y.; son of Monas (a real estate manager and broker) and Susan (Grossman) Seidman. *Education:* Massachusetts Institute of Technology, student, 1957-58; Polytechnic Institute of Brooklyn, B.S. (cum laude), 1961; University of Minnesota, M.S., 1964; Columbia University, M.F.A. (with distinction), 1969. *Home:* 463 West St., Apt. D-1016, New York, N.Y. 10014.

CAREER: Lecturer at in-service seminars for elementary and secondary school teachers, Nassau County Board of Cooperative Educational Services, 1969, 1970; instructor at private poetry workshops, 1970—; poet-in-residence, City College of the City University of New York, 1972-75; writer-in-residence, Wilkes College, 1975; faculty member, New School for Social Research, New York City, 1976—. Visiting poet at local high schools, 1970-72, and at Yale University, 1971, 1973; coordinator of poetry readings and workshops, 1971-73. Judge, Barnard College poetry contest, 1971, and Calliope Poetry Society poetry contest, 1973; cooperating sponsor, Great Lakes Colleges Art Program, 1972; consultant on selection process, Creative Artists Program Services poetry grants, 1974-76, and Academy of American Poets Walt Whitman Award, 1975; panelist, coordinating Council of Literary Magazines small press grants, 1975. *Member:* Authors Guild, Authors League of America, P.E.N. *Awards, honors:* Yale Series of Younger Poets prize, 1969, for *Collecting Evidence;* National Council on the Arts "Discovery Grant" for poetry, 1970; Cultural Council Foundation grant for poetry, 1971; National Endowment for the Arts creative writing fellowship, 1972-73; Yaddo fellow, 1972; MacDowell Colony fellow, 1974, 1975.

WRITINGS: Collecting Evidence (poems), Yale University Press, 1970; *Blood Lord* (poems), Doubleday, 1974. Contributor of poems to various periodicals, including *Atlantic, New American Review, Poetry, Salmagundi, Nation,* and *Caterpillar.* Poetry represented in many anthologies, including: *One Hundred American Poems,* edited by Selden Rodman, New American Library, 1970; *Inside Outer Space: New Poems of the Space Age,* edited by Robert Vas Dias, Doubleday, 1970; *A Caterpillar Anthology,* edited by Clayton Eshleman, Doubleday, 1971; *American Poetry Anthology,* edited by Daniel Halpern, Avon, 1975. Co-editor of the poetry magazine, *Equal Time.*

WORK IN PROGRESS: Several volumes of poetry.

SIDELIGHTS: Hugh Seidman told *CA:* "I was academically trained in mathematics and physics which might be perhaps of interest to any poet being, as he is, concerned with energy and form. The evidence of the poem is obviously the universe—*being*—wherever it is found. The Buddhists and contemporary physicists have demonstrated the illusion of matter, although this consideration can only take full weight when it is joined to a reverence for the LIVING as in the work of Wilhelm Reich."

Peter Davison of *Atlantic Monthly* said of Seidman: "In his initial book [*Collecting Evidence*] he has achieved the first necessary thing as a poet: faced down his feelings. . . . His work is full of frustration, anger, images of desecration and rebellion. . . . It is exciting to see someone discovering the essential materials of poetry and, often, mastering them." "His poems may be disturbed but, like Seidman," writes a reviewer for the *Seattle Times,*"they are in the world, of the world, and reading one is like holding a squirming thing in one's hand . . . one knows that it is alive and, because one feels it, that oneself is alive as well."

BIOGRAPHICAL/CRITICAL SOURCES: University Review, November-December, 1970; *Atlantic Monthly,* January, 1971; *Seattle Times,* January 10, 1971; *New York Review of Books,* May 6, 1971; *East Village Other,* May 18, 1971; *Herald,* May 30, 1071; *Poetry,* August, 1971.

* * *

SELDES, Gilbert (Vivian) 1893-1970
(Lucien Bluphocks, Sebastian Cauliflower, Foster Johns, Vivian Shaw)

January 3, 1893—September 29, 1970; American critic, essayist, editor, and early authority on the popular arts. Obituaries: *New York Times,* September 30, 1970; *Newsday,* October 1, 1970; *Washington Post,* October 1, 1970; *Variety,* October 7, 1970; *Newsweek,* October 12, 1970; *Time,* October 12, 1970; *Books Abroad,* spring, 1971. (See index for *CA* sketch)

* * *

SELDIN, Maury 1931-

PERSONAL: Born February 27, 1931, in Los Angeles, Calif.; married Rachel Reisner, August 29, 1954; children: Susan Amy, Judith Ann. *Education:* University of California, Los Angeles, B.S., 1953, M.B.A., 1957; Indiana University, D.B.A., 1960. *Home:* 8044 Cindy Lane, Bethesda, Md. 20034. *Office:* School of Business Administration, American University, Washington, D.C. 20016.

CAREER: University of Southern California, Los Angeles,

assistant professor of finance and real estate, 1960-65; American University, School of Business Administration, Washington, D.C., associate professor, 1965-68, professor of business administration, 1968—, director of program in real estate and urban development, 1968-74, acting dean, 1974-75. President and member of board of directors, Homer Hoyt Institute, 1968—.

MEMBER: American Real Estate and Urban Economics Association (vice-president, 1970-71; president, 1971-72), Urban Land Institute, Lambda Alpha, Rho Epsilon, Beta Gamma Sigma. *Awards, honors:* Fellowships from Equitable Life Assurance Society of America, 1963, Chase Manhattan Bank, 1965, and Mortgage Bankers Association of America.

WRITINGS: (With Richard H. Swesnik) *Real Estate Investment Strategy,* Wiley, 1970; (contributor) Harry A. Golman, editor, *Financing Real Estate Development,* American Institute of Architects, 1974; *Land Investment,* Dow Jones-Irwin, 1975; (with Michael Sumichrast) *Housing Analyses,* Dow Jones-Irwin, 1977. Writer of monographs and study reports published by Homer Hoyt Institute, National Park Service, U.S. Small Business Administration, and U.S. Forest Service. Contributor to real estate and allied journals.

WORK IN PROGRESS: Studies of the urban development process which emphasize public policy influences on land development; also studies in real estate decision making, especially with regard to investment; editing *The Real Estate Handbook,* for Dow Jones-Irwin.

*   *   *

SELIGMAN, Ben B(aruch) 1912-1970

November 20, 1912—October 23, 1970; American Jewish economist and author. Obituaries: *New York Times,* October 25, 1970. (See index for *CA* sketch)

*   *   *

SELSAM, Howard 1903-1970

June 28, 1903—September 7, 1970; American lecturer, educator, scholar, and writer on Marxism. Obituaries: *New York Times,* September 9, 1970.

*   *   *

SERRANO PLAJA, Arturo 1909-

PERSONAL: Born December 23, 1909, in El Escorial, Spain; son of Arturo and Florinda (Plaja) Serrano; married Claude Bloch (divorced); married Ingrid Kruse, July 12, 1969; children: (first marriage) Carlos. *Education:* Instituto Cardenal Cisneros, Madrid, Spain, B.A. 1926, licentiate, 1934. *Home:* 2911 Kenmore Pl., Santa Barbara, Calif. 93105. *Office:* Spanish Department, University of California, Santa Barbara, Calif. 93106.

CAREER: Spanish teacher in various high schools in Paris, France, 1954-61; Spanish instructor at University of Wisconsin—Madison, 1961-63, University of Minnesota, Minneapolis, 1963-68 and University of California, Santa Barbara, 1968—.

WRITINGS: Destierro infinito (poetry), Heroe (Madrid), 1936; *El Hombre y el trabajo* (poetry), Hora de Espana (Barcelona), 1938; *Del cielo y del escombro* (includes "El Capitan Javier," "Del cielo y del escombro," "Juanito el tonto," "El Duque y su perro," and "El Inventor de la calle del Rey"), Ediciones Nuevo Romance (Buenos Aires), 1942;

Chant a la liberte (poetry), Charlot (Algiers), 1943; *Los Misticos* (comparative studies in mysticism), Atlantida (Buenos Aires), 1943; *Antonio Machado,* Schapire (Buenos Aires), 1944; *Espana en la edad de oro,* Atlantida, 1944; *Libro de el Escorial,* Poseidon (Buenos Aires), 1944; *El Realismo espanol* (essay), Patronato Hispano-Argentino de Cultura (Buenos Aires), 1944; *El Greco,* Poseidon, 1945; *Manuel Angeles Ortiz* (includes a poem by Rafael Alberti), Poseidon, 1945; *Versos de guerra y paz* (poetry), Nova (Buenos Aires), 1945; *Don Manuel de Leon,* Emece (Buenos Aires), 1946; *Escultura espanola, desde los origenes hasta el siglo XVIII,* Rosario (Rosario), 1946; *Les Mains fertiles* (poetry), Charlot (Paris), 1947; *Phokas el americano* (poetry), Nova, 1948; *Galop de la destinee* (poetry), written in Spanish but translated into French by Emmanuel Robles and Alice Ahrweiler for original publication, P. Seghers (Paris), 1954, published in Argentina as *Galope de la suerte, 1945-1956,* Losada (Buenos Aires), 1958; *La Mano de Dios pasa por este perro: Cadena de blanco-spirituals para matar el tiempo como Dios manda,* Ediciones Rialp (Madrid), 1965; *El Arte comprometido y el compromiso del arte,* Ayma (Barcelona), 1967; *Realismo "magico" en Cervantes Don Quijote, visto desde Tom Sawyer y El Idiota,* Gredos (Madrid), 1967, translation by Robert S. Rudden published as *"Magic" Realism in Cervantes' Don Quixote: As Seen through Tom Sawyer and The Idiot,* University of California Press, 1970.

Editor or translator: (Compiler and author of prologue) *Hijo del alba: Villancicos, canciones, ensaladillas y coloquios pastoriles de nochebuena,* Imprenta Lopez (Buenos Aires), 1943; (translator) Elie Faure, *Descubrimiento del Archipielago,* Poseidon, 1944; (translator) Andre Gide, *Trozos escogidos,* Poseidon, 1945; (editor) *Antologia de los misticos espanoles,* Schapire, 1946; (editor) *Es la religion el opio del pueblo?* (essays), Porrua (Madrid), 1976. Poems anthologized in several collections, including *La Poesie espagnole,* P. Seghers, 1963, and *Thirty Spanish Poems of Love and Exile,* translated by Kenneth Rexroth, City Lights, 1968.

WORK IN PROGRESS: A novel, *La Cacatua atmosferica,* to be published in Mexico; *Los alamos oscuros,* a poetical anthology of his works.

BIOGRAPHICAL/CRITICAL SOURCES: Alicia Raffucci de Lockwood, *Cuatro poetas de la generacion del 36,* University of Wisconsin, 1966, revised edition, Editorial Universitaria (Puerto Rico), 1974; Johannes Lechner, *El Compromiso en la poesia espanola del siglo XX,* Universitaire Pres, Leiden, 1968.

*   *   *

SETH-SMITH, Michael 1928-

PERSONAL: Born June 11, 1928, in Surrey, England; son of Edward and Joan (Ridley) Seth-Smith; married Elizabeth Palmer, August 22, 1955; married second wife, Mary Dennis, December 7, 1967; children: Alexandra, Philippa, Camilla. *Education:* Attended public schools in England. *Politics:* Conservative. *Religion:* Church of England. *Home:* Sylvans, Tilford Rd., Farnham, Surrey, England. *Agent:* Ursula Winant, Winant Towers Ltd., Furnival St., Chancery Lane, London, England.

CAREER: Private secretary to the governor of Western Australia, 1951-53; Christopher & Co., London, England, wine merchants, 1957—. Horse race commentator for British Broadcasting Corp., Independent Television Authority, and Jockey Club, 1953—.

WRITINGS: (With John Lawrence, Roger Mortimer, and Peter Willett) *The History of Steeplechasing,* M. Joseph,

1966; *Bred for the Purple,* Frewin Publishers, 1969; *Lord Paramount of the Turf,* Faber, 1971; *Life and Times of Steve Donoghue,* Faber, 1973; *The Long Haul,* Hutchinson, 1974; *International Stallions and Stallions,* Foulsham, 1975; *History of Cresta Run,* Foulsham, 1976. Also author of *Two Hundred Years of Richard Johnson and Nephew,* 1972. Contributor to *Tatler* and to horse-racing journals. Editor, *British Racehorse,* 1977.

WORK IN PROGRESS: A history of Prix de l'Arc de Triomphe.

BIOGRAPHICAL/CRITICAL SOURCES: Times Literary Supplement, July 24, 1969.

* * *

SEXTON, Virginia Staudt 1916-
(Virginia Staudt)

PERSONAL: Born August 30, 1916, in New York, N.Y.; married Richard Sexton (a member of the English faculty at Fordham University). *Education:* Hunter College (now Hunter College of the City University of New York), B.A. (cum laude), 1936; Fordham University, M.A., 1941, Ph.D., 1946, additional study, 1949-51; Columbia University, additional study, 1952-53. *Religion:* Roman Catholic. *Home:* 188 Ascan Ave., Forest Hills, N.Y. 11375. *Office:* Herbert H. Lehman College of the City University of New York, Bedford Park Blvd., Bronx, N.Y. 10468.

CAREER: Elementary teacher in Bronx, N.Y., 1936-39; Department of Welfare, New York City, clerk, 1939-44; Notre Dame College (now Notre Dame College of St. John's University), Staten Island, N.Y., instructor, 1944-48, associate professor of psychology, 1948-52, chairman of department, 1946-52; City University of New York, New York City, member of faculty of Hunter College, 1953-68, began as instructor, became professor of psychology at Hunter College, 1967-68, professor of psychology at Herbert H. Lehman College, 1968—. Lecturer at Seton Hall University, 1947-52, 1954-55, and at Long Island University, spring, 1948. Chairman, New York State Board for Psychology, New York State Department of Education, 1976. Member of advisory council on psychology, New York State Department of Education, 1968-71.

MEMBER: American Psychological Association (fellow; secretary-treasurer of division 24, 1969-71), American Association for the Advancement of Science (fellow), International Council of Psychologists (fellow), American Historical Association, American Catholic Psychological Association (president, 1964-65), International Organization for Study of Group Tensions, Academy of Religion and Mental Health, Interamerican Society of Psychology, Psychology and Law Society, American Association of University Professors, American Association of University Women, American Association of Women Psychologists, Women's Equity Action League, Eastern Psychological Association, New York Academy of Sciences (fellow; chairman of division of psychology, 1965-67; chairman of history, philosophy, and ethics of science and technology section), New York State Psychological Association (president, 1967-68), Albertus Magnus Guild, Phi Beta Kappa, Sigma Xi, Psi Chi, Delta Kappa Gamma, Eta Sigma Phi. *Awards, honors:* Ford Foundation faculty fellow, 1952-53; New York State Department of Mental Hygiene summer psychiatric fellow, 1959, 1960.

WRITINGS: (Under name Virginia Staudt; with Henry Misiak) *Catholics in Psychology: A Historical Survey,* McGraw, 1954; (with Misiak) *History of Psychology: An Overview,* Grune, 1966; (contributor) N. J. Pallone, editor, *Readings for Catholic Counselors,* National Catholic Guidance Conference, 1966; (contributor) W. C. Bier, editor, *Women in the Modern World,* Fordham University Press, 1968; (with Misiak) *Historical Perspectives in Psychology,* Brooks/Cole, 1971; (with Misiak) *Phenomenological, Existential and Humanistic Psychologies: A Historical Survey,* Grune, 1973; (editor with Misiak) *Psychology around the World,* Brooks/Cole, 1976. Contributor of about thirty-five articles to professional journals, and of twenty-three biographies to *New Catholic Encyclopedia.* Associate editor, *Psychological Abstracts,* 1961-62; book review editor, *Newsletter of American Catholic Psychological Association.*

WORK IN PROGRESS: Revision of *History of Psychology: An Overview,* with Misiak; writing a chapter on psychology for *Introduction to Psychology.*

* * *

SEYERSTED, Per

EDUCATION: Harvard University, M.A.; University of Oslo, Dr.philos. *Office:* American Institute, University of Oslo, Oslo 3, Norway.

CAREER: University of Oslo, Oslo, Norway, lecturer, 1968-73, professor of American literature, 1973—, director of American Institute, 1973—. *Member:* Nordic Association for American Studies (chairman, 1973—).

WRITINGS: (Editor) *Gilgamesj* (Norwegian edition of the epic), Cappelen, 1967; *Kate Chopin: A Critical Biography,* American Institute, University of Oslo, 1969, Louisiana State University Press, 1970; (editor and author of introduction) *The Complete Works of Kate Chopin,* two volumes, foreword by Edmund Wilson, Louisiana State University Press, 1970. Contributor of articles and chapters to books and journals.

SIDELIGHTS: Reviewing both Seyersted's biography of Kate Chopin and his edition of her complete works, Daniel Aaron states: "The simultaneous publication of Per Seyersted's critical biography of Kate Chopin and his edition of her complete works is a literary event that ought to make more of a noise than it probably will. . . . Seyersted's sensitive and sensible interpretation of this extraordinarily talented author, together with two volumes of her writing (some of it hitherto unpublished) should allow readers with or without his intelligent assistance to evaluate the results of his literary excavation. . . . His enthusiasm for her best work may lead his readers to expect too much from her more pedestrian efforts. But his solid and unpretentious biography is not likely to be superseded. He has given Kate Chopin a habitation and a name. He has demonstrated that if she is no Emily Dickinson, she is considerable enough to swell a scene or two. Now there can be no excuse for confining her to a footnote in our still patchy literary annals."

BIOGRAPHICAL/CRITICAL SOURCES: New York Times Book Review, February 8, 1970; *New Yorker,* March 14, 1970; *American Literature,* March, 1971.

* * *

SHAFF, Albert L(averne) 1937-

PERSONAL: Born March 31, 1937, in Brainard, Minn.; son of Floyd Laverne and Betty Mona (Tolles) Shaff; married Teresa Ann Russeth, August 11, 1967 (divorced); children: Kari Ann. *Education:* Bemidji State College, B.S., 1961; graduate study at University of Missouri, 1964-67, University of Bonn, 1969-70, and Free University of Berlin, 1972.

Politics: Social-Democrat. *Home:* 3496 Pilgrim Lane, Plymouth, Minn. 55441. *Office:* 10635 36th Ave. N., Plymouth, Minn.

CAREER: High school teacher and coach in Thief River Falls, Minn., 1961-64, and in Robbinsdale, Minn., 1964—. *Military service:* U.S. Army, paratroops, 1954-58; became second lieutenant. *Member:* American Federation of Teachers, Minnesota Federation of Teachers, Southern Christian Leadership Conference. *Awards, honors:* Fulbright teacher exchange grant to Germany, 1968.

WRITINGS: The Student Journalist and the Critical Review, Rosen Press, 1969. Regular contributor to *Minneapolis Tribune ;* salaried correspondent for Sun Newspapers. Editor, *Rostrum* (opinion magazine for Robbinsdale [Minn.] Federation of Teachers).

WORK IN PROGRESS: With Gael Pierce, *Teachers, Tyrants, and Other Misfits; Robin's Flight,* a novel.

*   *   *

SHALOFF, Stanley   1939-

PERSONAL: Born October 10, 1939, in Bronx, N.Y.; son of Isidore and Yolanda (Simon) Shilofsky. *Education:* City College (now City College of the City University of New York), B.A., 1960; Northwestern University, M.A., 1962, Ph.D., 1967. *Politics:* Democrat. *Religion:* Jewish. *Home:* 4849 Connecticut Ave. N.W., Apt. 828, Washington, D.C. 20008. *Office:* Office of the Historian, Bureau of Public Affairs, U.S. Department of State, Washington, D.C. 20520.

CAREER: Wisconsin State University—Oshkosh, instructor, 1964-67, assistant professor, 1967-69, associate professor of history, 1970-75; U.S. Department of State, Bureau of Public Affairs, Office of the Historian, Washington, D.C., historian, 1976—. Visiting lecturer in history, University of Ghana, Legon, 1968-69; visiting associate professor of African American studies, University of Maryland Baltimore County, 1972-73; visiting associate professor, University of Wisconsin—Madison, 1974-75; associate professorial lecturer, George Washington University, spring, 1977. *Member:* African Studies Association, American Historical Association, Phi Beta Kappa, Phi Alpha Theta. *Awards, honors:* National Endowment for the Humanities research fellow, 1969-70.

WRITINGS: Reform in Leopold's Congo, John Knox, 1970. Contributor of articles to historical journals in Britain, France, Ghana, and the United States. Book review editor, *Societas—A Review of Social History.*

WORK IN PROGRESS: Writing research material on political development in the Gold Coast, 1928-46.

*   *   *

SHANAHAN, William J.   1935-

PERSONAL: Born September 18, 1935, in Chicago, Ill.; son of Joseph F. (an accountant) and Dorothy (Ferguson) Shanahan; married Mary K. Mihajlov, April 15, 1961 (divorced); married Patricia Ruth Mayer, January 16, 1972; children: (first marriage) Josephine, Paul, William, Jr. *Education:* Loyola University, Chicago, Ill., B.S., 1957, Ph.D., 1966; attended training programs on alcoholism at Ohio Dominican College, 1974-75 and Rutgers University, 1975. *Religion:* Roman Catholic. *Home:* 7790 Clark State Rd., Blacklick, Ohio 43004.

CAREER: Mundelein College, Chicago, Ill., instructor in English, 1962-65; Idaho State University, Pocatello, assis-

tant professor, 1965-68, associate professor of English, 1968-70; Globe Book Co., Inc., New York, N.Y., representative, 1971-72, editorial director of Learning Trends, Inc., 1972-73; Charles E. Merrill Publishing Co., Columbus, Ohio, managing editor of language arts division, 1973-74; Columbus Health Department, Division on Alcoholism, Columbus, occupational consultant, 1974-76; National Council on Alcoholism, Labor-Management Taskforce, Cincinnati, Ohio, consultant, 1976—. *Military service:* U.S. Army, 1958-59. *Member:* Association of Labor-Management Alcoholism Consultants of America, Ohio Association of Alcohol Programs, Jefferson Township Civic Association.

WRITINGS: (Editor with Wilbur Huck) *The Modern Short Story,* American Book Co., 1969; (with Charles Herbert Kegel) *Lyric Poems on Twelve Themes,* Scott, Foresman, 1970. Author of musical comedy, "The Major and the Millionaire." Contributor of short stories, articles and reviews to *Ave Maria, Cadence, Catholic World, Intermountain Observer, Iota,* and other periodicals.

WORK IN PROGRESS: Editing Foster Lane's *Logbook,* a personal history of American aviation.

AVOCATIONAL INTERESTS: Music, particularly jazz of the 1930's and 1940's.

*   *   *

SHANK, David Arthur   1924-

PERSONAL: Born October 7, 1924; son of Charles Lewis (an engineer) and Crissie (Yoder) Shank; married Wilma Hollopeter, August 11, 1948; children: Michael Stephen, Crissie, Rachel. *Education:* Goshen College, B.A., 1948, B.D., 1953; Eastern Baptist Theological Seminary, M.Div., 1968; University of Notre Dame, graduate study, 1967-68. *Politics:* Independent.

CAREER: Mennonite Board of Missions and Charities, Elkhart, Ind., minister and missionary, 1950—, former pastor of Evangelical church in Rixensart, Belgium. *Wartime service:* Civilian Public Service as conscientious objector. *Member:* Fellowship of Reconciliation.

WRITINGS—All published by Herald Press: (Contributor) *From the Mennonite Pulpit,* 1965; *Who Will Answer?,* 1969; *His Spirit First,* 1971; (co-author) *Mission Strategy* (pamphlet), 1971. Contributor to religious periodicals. Member of editorial board, *Concern.*

WORK IN PROGRESS: Research on the Flemish Mennonite artist, Karel van Mander.†

*   *   *

SHAPIRO, Irving   1917-

PERSONAL: Born August 23, 1917, in Brooklyn, N.Y.; son of Isidor (a pharmacist) and Bessie (Hecht) Shapiro; married Rosalind L. Roth (a laboratory technician), September 14, 1941; children: Deanne Ruth, Susan Ellen, Joyce Anne. *Education:* New York University, J.D., 1942, A.B., 1946. *Home:* 75-08 180th St., Flushing, N.Y. 11366. *Office:* St. Vincent's College, St. John's University, Jamaica, N.Y. 11439.

CAREER: New York State Supreme Court, Brooklyn, court clerk, 1949-74; St. John's University, Jamaica, N.Y., associate professor of criminal justice, 1974—. Lecturer for Practising Law Institute, 1966, 1967, 1968, Prep Institute, 1969, and City of New York Personnel Department, 1970. Instructor of court career courses at various institutions. *Military service:* U.S. Army, 1943-46; became master sergeant; received Army Commendation Medal. *Member:* American Judicature Society, American Bar Association, National Council on Crime and Delinquency, Supreme Court Historical Society.

WRITINGS: Dictionary of Legal Terms, Gould Publications, 1968; *Criminal Law of New York,* Prep Institute, 1969. Editor of annual editions of *Code of Criminal Procedure, New York, Civil Practice Law and Rules, New York,* and *Penal Law, New York,* 1965-73. Contributor to legal journals; also writes whimsical articles and stories for children, "chiefly unpublished."

WORK IN PROGRESS: Court Management, reading and understanding legal documents.

AVOCATIONAL INTERESTS: Carpentry, cabinet-making, refinishing antique furniture, and golf.

* * *

SHAPIRO, Nat 1922-

PERSONAL: Born September 27, 1922, in New York, N.Y.; son of Dewey (a salesman) and Rose (Harap) Shapiro; married Vera Miller (a research director), December 30, 1949; children: Amy. *Education:* Attended Brooklyn College (now Brooklyn College of the City University of New York), 1940-41. *Home:* 75 Central Park W., New York, N.Y. 10023.

CAREER: Mercury Records, New York City, national director of promotion, 1948-50; Broadcast Music, Inc., New York City, public relations representative, 1954-55; Columbia Records, New York City, director, international artists and repertoire, 1956-66. Assembled creative elements of Broadway musical, "Hair," 1968, personal and business representative of "Hair" company, 1968—; co-creator of Off-Broadway musical, "Jacques Brel Is Alive and Well and Living in Paris," 1967. *Military service:* U.S. Army, Signal Corps, 1942-45. *Member:* Music Library Association, National Academy of Recording Arts and Sciences.

WRITINGS—Editor: (With Nat Hentoff) *Hear Me Talkin' to Ya,* Rinehart, 1955 (published in England as *Hear Me Talkin' to Ya: The Story of Jazz by the Men Who Made It,* P. Davies, 1955); (with Hentoff) *The Jazz Makers,* Rinehart, 1958; *Popular Music: An Annotated Index of American Popular Songs,* Adrian Press, Volume I: *1950-59,* 1964, Volume II: *1940-49,* 1965, Volume III: *1960-64,* 1967, Volume IV: *1930-39,* 1968, Volume V: *1920-29,* 1969, Volume VI: *1965-69,* 1973.

WORK IN PROGRESS: An Encyclopedia of Quotations about Music, for Doubleday.

SIDELIGHTS: Nat Shapiro told *CA* he has produced about 100 record albums for Columbia, Philips, Vanguard, Epic, and other companies, including recordings for Marlene Dietrich, Barbra Streisand, Yves Montand, Lotte Lenya, Michel Legrand, Mahalia Jackson, Lena Horne, Miles Davis, and Juliette Greco.

* * *

SHARKANSKY, Ira 1938-

PERSONAL: Born November 25, 1938, in Fall River, Mass.; son of Eugene Louis (a pharmacist) and Beatrice (Mines) Sharkansky; married Ina Goldberg, August 21, 1960; children: Stefan Michael, Erica Jean. *Education:* Wesleyan University, Middletown, Conn., B.A., 1960; University of Wisconsin, M.S., 1961, Ph.D., 1964. *Office:* Department of Political Science, University of Wisconsin, Madison, Wis. 53706.

CAREER: Assistant professor of political science at Ball State University, Muncie, Ind., 1964-65, at Florida State University, Tallahassee, 1965-66, and at University of Georgia, Athens, 1966-68; University of Wisconsin—Madison, associate professor, 1968-71, professor of political science, 1971—; Hebrew University of Jerusalem, Jerusalem, Israel, professor of political science, 1975—. Visiting professor, University of North Carolina, summer, 1967. *Member:* American Political Science Association. *Awards, honors:* Woodrow Wilson fellowship, 1960-61; Social Science Research Council fellowship, 1966-68.

WRITINGS: Spending in the American States, Rand McNally, 1968; *The Politics of Taxing and Spending,* Bobbs-Merrill, 1969; *Regionalism in American Politics,* Bobbs-Merrill, 1969; (editor) *Policy Analysis in Political Science: A Reader,* Markham, 1969; *Public Administration: Policy-Making in Government Agencies,* Markham, 1970, 3rd edition, Rand McNally, 1975; (editor with Richard I. Hofferbert) *State and Urban Politics: Readings in Public Policy,* Little, Brown, 1970; *The Routines of Politics,* Van Nostrand, 1970; (with Robert Lineberry) *Urban Politics and Public Policy,* Harper, 1971, 2nd edition, 1974; *The Maligned States,* McGraw, 1972; *The United States: A Study of a Developing Country,* McKay, 1975; (with Donald S. Van Meter) *Politics and Policy in American Government,* McGraw, 1975. Contributor of about thirty-six articles and reviews to political science and social science journals. Member of editorial board, *Journal of Politics, Social Science Quarterly, American Politics Quarterly,* and *Publius—Journal of Federalism.*

WORK IN PROGRESS: Policy-Making in Israel.

* * *

SHARP, Dolph 1914-
(Dolph Shapiro)

PERSONAL: Born April 4, 1914, in Hempstead, N.Y.; son of Benjamin L. (a businessman) and Lillian (Cooper) Sharp; married Roslyn Bernstein (a piano teacher), November 1, 1940; children: Miriam, Deborah, Naomi, Elizabeth Eve. *Education:* University of Michigan, A.B., 1936; New York University, special courses, 1936-37; University of Arizona, special courses, 1941-42. *Home and office:* 3394 Blair Dr., Los Angeles, Calif. 90028.

CAREER: Began as a reporter/columnist on weekly newspapers in Long Island, N.Y., 1936-40; free-lance magazine and advertising writer, 1940—; Carson/Roberts Agency, Los Angeles, Calif., advertising copywriter, 1959-63; Sony-Superscope, advertising manager, copy chief, and publicity director, 1963-67.

WRITINGS: The Other Ark (juvenile), Putnam, 1969; *Ludwig Von Wolfgang Vulture,* Price, Stern, 1973; *I'm O.K., You're Not So Hot,* Warner Brothers, 1975. Also author of radio scripts. Anthologized in *Best American Short Stories, 1948,* edited by Martha Foley and David Burnett, Houghton, 1948. Contributor to *Colliers, Coronet, Esquire, Woman's Day, True, Argosy, Reader's Digest, Travel and Leisure,* and to university quarterlies.

WORK IN PROGRESS: Writing a major trilogy on creation in the ultimate destruction of civilization, completion expected, 1990.

SIDELIGHTS: Dolph Sharp has traveled in the U.S., Canada, and Mexico.

SHARP, Donald Bruce   1938-

PERSONAL: Born May 18, 1938, in Portales, New Mexico; son of Robert T. and Gladys (Shahan) Sharp. Education: Eastern New Mexico University, B.A., 1961; University of Alaska, M.A., 1963; University of Chicago, graduate study, 1971. Politics: Independent. Religion: None.

CAREER: Maunaolu College, Maui, Hawaii, English and speech instructor, 1963-65; Caulfield Grammar School, Melbourne, Australia, English master, 1965-66; Hawaii Pacific College, Honolulu, librarian, 1966-67; Illinois Institute of Technology, Chicago, English and speech instructor, 1967-69; Carlow College, Pittsburgh, Pa., librarian, beginning 1969. Member: Pittsburgh World Affairs Council, University Center for Rational Alternatives.

WRITINGS: (Editor) Commentaries on Obscenity, Scarecrow, 1970. Contributor of articles to American Scholar, Library Binder, and English Education.

WORK IN PROGRESS: A textbook unifying composition and literature for use in freshman English classes; and another text unifying composition and speech.

AVOCATIONAL INTERESTS: Automobile restoration, carpentry.††

*   *   *

SHARP, James Roger   1936-

PERSONAL: Born August 8, 1936, in Troy, Kan.; son of Francis Wilson and Shirley (Carlson) Sharp; married Nancy Anne Weatherly (a journalist), December 18, 1957; children: Sandra Lynn, Matthew Edward. Education: University of Missouri, A.B., 1958, M.A., 1960; University of California, Berkeley, Ph.D., 1966. Home: 140 Westminster Ave., Syracuse, N.Y. 13210. Office: History Department, Syracuse University, Syracuse, N.Y. 13210.

CAREER: Syracuse University, Syracuse, N.Y., assistant professor, 1966-70, associate professor of history, 1970—. Military service: U.S. Army Reserve, active duty, 1958-59; became captain. Member: American Historical Association, Organization of American Historians, Southern Historical Association. Awards, honors: American Philosophical Society grant, 1967; Social Science Research Council grant, 1968; National Endowment for the Humanities fellow, 1970-71.

WRITINGS: The Jacksonians Versus the Banks: Politics in the States after the Panic of 1837, Columbia University Press, 1970. Contributor of reviews to San Francisco Chronicle, Oakland Tribune, and to professional journals.

WORK IN PROGRESS: Research for a book, tentatively entitled The Jeffersonians' Conception of Party: The Development of the Idea of a Loyal Opposition.

AVOCATIONAL INTERESTS: Jogging; reading current fiction, old classics, political literature, and history; skiing, ice skating, and basketball.

*   *   *

SHARP, Laure M(etzger)   1921-

PERSONAL: Born April 10, 1921, in Frankfurt, Germany; became U.S. citizen; daughter of Fred and Harriet (Isenburger) Metzger; married Samuel L. Sharp (a college professor), 1947; children: Deborah, Daniel, Susan. Education: University of Grenoble, law studies, two years; Hunter College (now Hunter College of the City University of New York), B.A., 1944; American University, M.A., 1958. Home: 6405 East Halbert Rd., Bethesda, Md. 20034. Office:

Bureau of Social Science Research, Inc., 1990 M St. N.W., Washington, D.C. 20036.

CAREER: Research analyst in U.S. Office of Strategic Service and U.S. Department of State, Washington, D.C., 1944-47; U.S. Department of Labor, Washington, D.C., survey statistician, 1950-53; Bureau of Social Science Research, Inc., Washington, D.C., research associate, 1953-56; District of Columbia Tuberculosis Association, Washington, D.C., research director, 1956-59; Bureau of Social Science Research, Inc., senior research associate and assistant director, 1959—. Consultant to National Institutes of Health, 1951-61, National Society of Professional Engineers, 1952—, Langley Porter Clinic, Berkeley, Calif., Federal Trade Commission, 1974, and National Institute for Drug Abuse, 1976—. Member: World Association for Public Opinion Research (member of executive council, 1974-76), American Sociological Association, American Educational Research Association, American Association for Public Opinion Research.

WRITINGS: Two Years after the College Degree: Work and Further Study Patterns, U.S. Government Printing Office, 1963; Training for Occupational Skills in the Washington Metropolitan Area, Bureau of Social Science Research, 1963; (with Albert D. Biderman) The Employment of Retired Military Personnel, Bureau of Social Science Research, 1966; (with Raymond A. Bauer and Richard S. Rosenbloom) Second-Order Consequences: A Methodological Essay on the Impact of Technology, M.I.T. Press, 1969; Education and Employment: The Early Careers of College Graduates, Johns Hopkins Press, 1970; (with Gene Petersen and Thomas F. Drury) Southern Newcomers to Northern Cities: Work and Social Adjustments in Cleveland, Praeger, 1976. Contributor to professional journals.

*   *   *

SHARPE, Mitchell R(aymond)   1924-

PERSONAL: Born December 22, 1924, in Knoxville, Tenn.; son of Mitchell R. (a salesman) and Katie Grace (Hill) Sharpe; married Virginia Ruth Lowry, December 21, 1952; children: Rebecca, Rachel, David. Education: Auburn University, B.S., 1949, M.A., 1954; Emory University, graduate study, 1954-55. Religion: Unitarian Universalist. Home: 7302 Chadwell Rd., Huntsville, Ala. 38502.

CAREER: U.S. Army Missile Command, Huntsville, Ala., technical writer, 1955-60; Marshall Space Flight Center, Huntsville, technical writer and historian, 1960-74. Consultant, National Air and Space Museum, Washington, D.C., 1965—, and Alabama Space and Rocket Center, 1967—. Military service: U.S. Army, 1943-46, 1950-52. U.S. Army Reserve, 1952—; current rank, lieutenant colonel. Member: National Association of Science Writers, Company of Military Historians, Society for the History of Technology, British Interplanetary Society (fellow), Societe d'Astronautique Francaise. Awards, honors: Robert H. Goddard Essay Awards in the history of rocketry, 1968 and 1975; Tsiolkovsky Gold Medal of USSR, 1973.

WRITINGS: (With F. I. Ordway and J. P. Gardner) Basic Astronautics: An Introduction to Space Science, Engineering, and Medicine, Prentice-Hall, 1962; (with Ordway, Gardner, and R. C. Wakeford) Applied Astronautics, and Introduction to Space Flight, Prentice-Hall, 1963; (contributor) Ernst Stuhlinger and others, editors, Astronautical Engineering and Science, from Peenemunde to Planetary Space. McGraw, 1963; (contributor) Ordway, editor, Advances in Space Science and Technology, Academic Press,

Volume VII, 1964 (Sharpe not associated with earlier volumes), Volume VIII, 1965; *Living in Space: The Astronaut and His Environment,* Doubleday, 1969; *Yuri Gagarin: First Man into Space,* Strode, 1969; *Satellites and Probes: The Development of Unmanned Space Flight,* Doubleday, 1970; (with C. C. Adams and Ordway) *Dividends from Space,* Crowell, 1971; *"It Is I, Seagull": Valentina Tereshkova, First Woman in Space,* Crowell, 1975. Author of U.S. Army manuals. Contributor to *Encyclopaedia Britannica Year Book,* 1963-76, *Compton's Encyclopedia, Encyclopedia of World Biography,* and to journals. Associate editor, *Space Journal,* 1957-59.

WORK IN PROGRESS: A history of rocketry from the thirteenth century through the early twentieth century; a book on the biological rhythms of life; a study of the German scientists who came to the United States with Wernher von Braun.

SIDELIGHTS: Mitchell R. Sharpe told *CA:* "As a boy in Knoxville, Tenn., I read every book I could get my hands on, at home, in school, or in the public library. As I grew older, I began collecting a library; and I now have almost 2000 books of my own. To be a serious writer, a person must be a serious reader." Sharpe went on to say: "My paternal grandfather and his brothers were great talkers, especially when small children were around them. They spun tales only a little less tall than those of Davy Crockett, but they fascinated me by the hour. I suppose that oral literature and the ability to communicate with children are two of the things I learned early, long before I ever thought of becoming a writer."

AVOCATIONAL INTERESTS: Photography (often illustrates his own work).

* * *

SHAW, John MacKay 1897-

PERSONAL: Born May 15, 1897, in Glasgow, Scotland; came to America with his parents in 1911; became a U.S. citizen in 1922; son of Neil (a carpenter) and Catherine Ann (Mackenzie) Shaw; married Lillian Reamer, June 19, 1926; children: Cathmar Jeanne (Mrs. James William Prange), John Bruce. *Education:* "Scottish schools to age 14. Self-educated from that point on, with some help from the University of Pennsylvania's Wharton School." *Politics:* Republican. *Religion:* Presbyterian. *Home:* 915 Gardenia Dr., Tallahassee, Fla. 32303. *Office:* Robert Manning Strozier Library, Florida State University, Tallahassee, Fla. 32306.

CAREER: On leaving school trained himself to become a shorthand secretary; Mitten Management, Inc. (city transportation), Philadelphia, Pa., vice-president, 1925-29; American Telephone & Telegraph Co., New York, N.Y., 1930-59, assistant vice-president, 1944-59. Florida State University, Robert Manning Strozier Library, Tallahassee, curator (voluntary) of Childhood in Poetry Collection, which he gave to the library, 1960—. Board member and chairman of initial gifts, Community Chest of the Oranges (N.J.), 1940-50; member of national council, Boy Scouts of America, 1947-66. Board member, Joint Council of Economic Education, 1948-55, and National Information Bureau. Occasional lecturer to business groups on advertising, public relations, and marketing subjects. *Military service:* U.S. Army, 1917-19; ambulance driver in Second Battle of the Marne and Meusse-Argonne Offensive. *Member:* American Library Association, Bibliographical Society of America, The Manuscript Society, Public Relations Society of New York (cofounder and second chairman, 1945; honorary member), St.

Andrew's Society of State of New York (member of board of managers, 1955-59), St. Andrew's Society of Tallahassee (president, 1976) Grolier Club (New York). *Awards, honors:* Honorary doctorate, Florida State University, 1972.

WRITINGS: The Poems, Poets and Illustrators of St. Nicholas Magazine, 1873-1943, An Index, Robert M. Strozier Library, Florida State University, 1965; *The Things I Want* (poems written for his own children three decades earlier), Friends of Florida State University Library, 1967; *Childhood in Poetry: A Catalogue, with Biographical and Critical Annotations, of the Books of English and American Poets Comprising the Shaw Childhood in Poetry Collection in the Library of Florida State University,* ten volumes, Gale, 1968-76; *Zumpin* (more poems for children), Friends of Florida State University Library, 1969; *The Dilemma of the Modern University Library "Ex Libris",* Emory University, 1975. Writer of notes for exhibition catalogue, *The Parodies of Lewis Carroll and Their Originals,* Florida State University, 1960, and editor of exhibition catalogue, *What the Poets Have to Say About Childhood,* Florida State University, 1966. An unpublished manuscript, "Life of Thomas Eugene Mitten of Philadelphia (1874-1929)" is in the Free Library of Philadelphia. Contributor to *Bell Telephone Magazine,* 1933-59.

SIDELIGHTS: Writing poems for his own children in the mid-thirties led John Shaw to begin studying and collecting the works of others ("the power of poetry in the training of the child mind was early impressed on me because of the experience of my own childhood," he says). This leisure-time hobby resulted in a collection of more than ten thousand volumes which includes, besides first editions, numerous anthologies, periodicals, biographies, and other reference works. He made a gift of the collection to Florida State University because he "did not wish his well-loved books" to be scattered to the four winds or embalmed on the storage shelves of a library not in a position to prepare an adequate delineation of the collection. At Robert Manning Strozier Library, the Shaw Collection (now over 20,000 volumes) is housed separately in a new wing. Shaw's Bell System papers—reports, speeches, memoranda, and letters—are on deposit with the Communications Museum at the University of Wisconsin.

AVOCATIONAL INTERESTS: Golf.

BIOGRAPHICAL/CRITICAL SOURCES: Journal of Library History, July, 1966; *Antiquarian Bookman,* December 22-29, 1969.

* * *

SHAW, W. David 1937-

PERSONAL: Born July 2, 1937, in Ottawa, Ontario, Canada; son of William Edward (a pharmacist) and Helen Mabel (Graburn; a teacher) Shaw; married Carol Ann Robinson, September 20, 1969; children: Cathy Ann. *Education:* University of Toronto, B.A., 1959; Harvard University, A.M., 1960, Ph.D., 1963. *Religion:* Anglican. *Home:* 18 McNairn Ave., Toronto, Ontario, Canada M5M 2H5. *Office:* N.A.B. 302, Department of English, University of Toronto, Toronto, Ontario, Canada M5S 1K7.

CAREER: Cornell University, Ithaca, N.Y., assistant professor of English, 1963-69; University of Toronto, Victoria College, Toronto, Ontario, associate professor, 1969-75, professor of English, 1975—. Visiting associate professor, University of California, Riverside, 1968-69. *Member:* Modern Language Association of America.

WRITINGS: The Dialectical Temper: The Rhetorical Art of Robert Browning, Cornell University Press, 1968; *Tennyson's Style,* Cornell University Press, 1976.

WORK IN PROGRESS: Poetic theory and practice in the nineteenth century.

* * *

SHEEHAN, Neil 1936-

PERSONAL: Born October 27, 1936, in Holyoke, Mass.; son of Cornelius Joseph (a farmer) and Mary (O'Shea) Sheehan; married Susan M. Margulies (a staff writer under the name Susan Sheehan on *New Yorker* and author of *Ten Vietnamese*), March 30, 1965; children: Maria Gregory, Catherine Fair. *Education:* Harvard University, B.A. (cum laude), 1958. *Home:* 4505 Klingle St. N.W., Washington, D.C. 20016. *Agent:* Robert Lescher, 155 East 71st St., New York, N.Y. 10021. *Office:* New York Times, 1920 L St. N.W., Washington, D.C. 20036.

CAREER: United Press International, bureau chief, Saigon, Vietnam, 1962-64; *New York Times,* New York, N.Y., news staff, 1964—, as reporter in New York, 1964, foreign correspondent in Indonesia, 1965, and Vietnam, 1965-66, Pentagon correspondent, Washington, D.C., 1966-68, White House correspondent, 1968-69, special investigative reporter, Washington, D.C., 1969—. *Military service:* U.S. Army, 1959-62; received Army Commendation Medal. *Awards, honors:* Silver Medal of the Poor Richard Club of Philadelphia, 1964; Louis M. Lyons Award for conscience and integrity in journalism, 1964.

WRITINGS: The Arnheiter Affair, Random House, 1971.

BIOGRAPHICAL/CRITICAL SOURCES: Detroit News, February 20, 1972; *Time,* March 6, 1972; *Variety,* June 28, 1972.

* * *

SHELDON, Sidney 1917-

PERSONAL: Born February 11, 1917, in Chicago, Ill.; son of Otto (a salesman) and Natalie (Marcus) Sheldon; married Jorja Curtright (an actress), March 28, 1951; children: Mary. *Education:* Attended Northwestern University one year.

CAREER: Creator, producer, and writer of television shows, Los Angeles, Calif., 1963—. Productions include the "Patty Duke Show," "I Dream of Jeannie," and "Nancy." *Military service:* U.S. Army Air Forces, 1941. *Awards, honors:* Academy Award ("Oscar") of Academy of Motion Picture Arts and Sciences, 1948, for screenplay, "The Bachelor and the Bobby-Soxer"; Antoinette Perry Award ("Tony"), 1956, for book for "Redhead."

WRITINGS—All published by Morrow: *The Naked Face* (novel), 1970; *The Other Side of Midnight,* 1974; *A Stranger in the Mirror,* 1976.

Plays: (Adaptor with Ben Roberts) "The Merry Widow" (operetta), first produced on Broadway at Majestic Theatre, August 4, 1943; "Jackpot," first produced on Broadway at Alvin Theatre, January 13, 1944; "Dream with Music," first produced on Broadway at Majestic Theatre, May 18, 1944; "Alice in Arms," first produced on Broadway at National Theatre, January 31, 1945; (with Dorothy and Herbert Fields, and David Shaw) "Redhead" (musical), first produced on Broadway at 46th St. Theatre, February 5, 1959; "Roman Candle," first produced on Broadway at Cort Theatre, February 3, 1960.

Films: "The Bachelor and the Bobby-Soxer," RKO, 1947; (with Albert Hackett and Frances Goodrich) "Easter Parade" (musical), Metro-Goldwyn-Mayer, 1948; "Annie Get Your Gun" (from musical produced on Broadway), Metro-Goldwyn-Mayer, 1950; "Rich, Young, and Pretty" (musical), Metro-Goldwyn-Mayer, 1951; (and director) "Dream Wife," Metro-Goldwyn-Mayer, 1953; "Anything Goes" (musical), Paramount, 1956; "Never Too Young," Paramount, 1956; (and director) "The Buster Keaton Story," Paramount, 1957; "Billy Rose's Jumbo," Metro-Goldwyn-Mayer, 1962.

SIDELIGHTS: Over five million copies of *The Other Side of Midnight* have been sold to date, and a *Publishers' Weekly* reviewer has estimated that Sheldon's latest novel, *A Stranger in the Mirror,* will sell just as fast. *The Other Side of Midnight* was made into a film with the same title.

BIOGRAPHICAL/CRITICAL SOURCES: Publishers' Weekly, November 19, 1973, December 30, 1974, July 7, 1975, January 24, 1977; *New York Times Book Review,* January 27, 1974, May 2, 1976; *Newsweek,* June 13, 1977; *Time,* June 20, 1977; *New Yorker,* July 11, 1977.

* * *

SHEPARD, Leslie Albert 1929-
(Leslie A. Juhasz)

PERSONAL: Surname changed from Juhasz to Shepard, 1967; born September 27, 1929, in Budapest, Hungary; son of William P. (an author) and Mary (Christianus) Juhasz. *Education:* Fordham University, B.A., 1954; New York University, M.A., 1959, Ph.D., 1968. *Politics:* Liberal. *Residence:* Pullman, Wash. *Office:* Washington State University, Pullman, Wash. 99163.

CAREER: New York University, New York, N.Y., instructor in English, 1961-65; Washington State University, Pullman, assistant professor, 1968-73, associate professor of English and foreign languages, 1973—. Free-lance textbook editor for Appleton-Century-Crofts, Inc., 1967. *Member:* American Association of University Professors.

WRITINGS—Under name Leslie A. Juhasz; reprinted editions are under name Leslie Shepard: *The Major Works of Thomas Mann,* Monarch, 1965; *"No Exit," "The Flies," and Other Works by Sartre,* Monarch, 1965; *William Faulkner's "As I Lay Dying": A Critical Commentary,* Monarch, 1965; *Dostoyevsky's "Notes from the Underground,"* Monarch, 1965; *William Faulkner's "Light in August": A Critical Commentary,* Monarch, 1965; *A History of French Literature,* Monarch, 1966; *Leo Tolstoy's "War and Peace,"* Barrister Publishing, 1966; *Balzac's "Eugenia Grandet" and "Pere Goriot,"* Monarch, 1966.

Has written a language course for radio, and done translations. Contributor of articles to professional journals.

SIDELIGHTS: Leslie Shepard spent his formative years in war-time Europe. In his twenties he was drawn to the French existentialists, and currently is interested in surrealism and structural criticism. He is competent in French, Italian, German, and Latin in addition to his native Hungarian.

* * *

SHEPARD, Richmond 1929-

PERSONAL: Born April 24, 1929, in New York, N.Y.; son of B. John (a chemist, lawyer, and importer) and Gladys (Marshall) Shepard; married Sykes Equen, July, 1956; married second wife, Hadria Brown, January 1, 1960; children: (second marriage) Armina, Vonda, Rosetta, Luana. *Educa-*

tion: Emory University, student, 1946-48; Adelphi University, B.A., 1951; California State College (now University), Los Angeles, M.A., 1969. *Religion:* Jew (Subud). *Home:* 17241 Hatteras St., Encino, Calif. 91316.

CAREER: Mime, actor, director and author of films and plays, and teacher; Pantomime Art Theatre, New York City, director, 1952-56; Theatre Workshop, Los Angeles, Calif., director, 1957-58; Living Theatre, New York City, instructor in mime, 1960-63; Professional Theatre Workshop, Hollywood, Calif., teacher of mime and acting, 1965-71; Los Angeles Civic Light Opera Co., Los Angeles, instructor in mime and acting, 1966-71; California State University, Los Angeles, associate professor of theatre, 1968-70. Instructor, Princeton University, 1962; instructor in mime, United States International University (formerly California Western University), 1966-68. Director of Mime Troupe, 1952—, and Los Angeles Improvisational Group, "The L.A. Cabaret," 1967—. Appeared in over one hundred television programs as a mime and an actor, including "Kojak," "The F.B.I.," "Merv Griffin," and "Dinah Shore"; director of fourteen Off-Broadway plays, six short films, one feature film. *Member:* Screen Actors Guild, American Federation of Television and Radio Artists, Mime Guild (founder, 1971). *Awards, honors:* Annual Showbusiness Award, 1956, for Mime Company; Charles Filmmakers Award, 1962, for short, "Afternoon of a Fannette."

WRITINGS: "Reality, Mr. Kaufman" (filmscript), 1970; (with Peter Tevis) "The Merry Weed" (filmscript), 1971; "The End of the Rainbow" (filmscript; based on the novel by Charles G. Finney), 1971; "Two Views of Mirais" (play), first produced in Los Angeles at Professional Theatre Workshop, 1971; *Mime: The Technique of Silence,* Drama Book Specialists, 1971.

Also author of "From the Monastery to the Sugar Cube" (a book on mysticism), "Tap-Tap Ruthy—In the Web" (novel), and "'I've Come to Save You!' '. . . Wait a Minute . . .'" (novel), as yet unpublished.

WORK IN PROGRESS: Creating Comedy; Mime Plays; Mime: Advanced Techniques and Style; several film projects.

SIDELIGHTS: Richmond Shepard has been called "America's foremost mime." He told *CA:* "I work primarily in the theatre—writing, performing, and directing—stage, and films. Also [I] am interested in the esoteric—[I] belong to the spiritual brotherhood of Subud." *Avocational interests:* Archaeology ("especially pre-history"), anthropology, raising tropical fish ("have the only balanced aquariums in L.A. area—no filters, aerators, etc.—self-sustaining little lakes in each tank").

BIOGRAPHICAL/CRITICAL SOURCES: Doug Hunt and Keri Hunt, *Pantomime: The Silent Theatre,* Atheneum, 1964.

* * *

SHEPARDSON, Mary (Thygeson) 1906-

PERSONAL: Born May 26, 1906, in St. Paul, Minn.; daughter of Nels Marcus (a lawyer) and Sylvie G. (Thompson) Thygeson; married Dwight E. Shepardson (a physician), 1942 (deceased). *Education:* Sorbonne, University of Paris, Certificate in French Civilization (honors), 1927; Stanford University, A.B. (with great distinction), 1928, M.A., 1956; University of California, Berkeley, Ph.D., 1960. *Politics:* Democrat. *Religion:* Protestant.

Home address: Box 25, Star Route, Redwood City, Calif. 94062. *Office:* Department of Anthropology, San Francisco State University, San Francisco, Calif.

CAREER: University of Chicago, Chicago, Ill., research associate, 1961-67; San Francisco State University, San Francisco, Calif., associate professor of anthropology, 1967-73, professor emeritus, 1973—. *Member:* American Anthropological Association (fellow), American Ethnological Society, Southwestern Anthropological Association, Phi Beta Kappa. *Awards, honors:* National Science Foundation post-doctoral fellow, 1960-61; National Institute of Mental Health research grants, 1962-64, 1965-67.

WRITINGS: Navajo Ways in Government: A Study in Political Process, American Anthropological Association, 1963; (with Blodwen Hammond) *The Navajo Mountain Community: Social Organization and Kinship Terminology,* University of California Press, 1970; (contributor) Keith Basso and Morris Opler, editors, *Studies in Apachean Culture and Ethnology,* University of Arizona Press, 1971. Contributor to anthropology journals.

WORK IN PROGRESS: Navajo Ways in Law.

* * *

SHEPHARD, Roy J(esse) 1929-

PERSONAL: Born May 8, 1929, in London, England; son of Jesse (a civil servant) and Esther Rose (Cummins) Shephard; married Muriel Neve Cullum, August 18, 1956; children: Sarah Elizabeth, Rachel Judith. *Education:* London University, Guy's Hospital Medical School, B.Sc. (first class honors), 1949, M.B.B.S. (honors), 1952, Ph.D., 1954, M.D., 1959. *Politics:* Liberal. *Religion:* United Church of Canada. *Home:* 42 Tollerton Ave., Willowdale, Ontario, Canada. *Office:* University of Toronto, 150 College St., Toronto, Ontario, Canada.

CAREER: University of Cincinnati, Cincinnati, Ohio, assistant professor of applied physiology, 1956-58; U.K. Ministry of Defence, Chemical Defence Experimental Establishment, Porton Down, Wiltshire, England, principal scientific officer, 1958-64; University of Toronto, Toronto, Ontario, professor of applied physiology, 1964—. Consultant, Toronto Rehabilitation Centre, Gage Research Institute (Toronto), and Universite du Quebec a Trois Rivieres. *Military service:* Royal Air Force, 1954-56; became flight lieutenant.

MEMBER: Canadian Physiological Society, Canadian Association for Health, Physical Education, and Recreation, Canadian Association of Sports Sciences (president, 1970-71), American Physiological Society, American Association for Health, Physical Education, and Recreation, American College of Sports Medicine (fellow; board member, 1970—; president, 1975-76), United Kingdom Physiological Society, British Medical Association, Ergonomics Research Society, Medical Research Society. *Awards, honors:* University of London, post-graduate fellowship, 1952-53; Fulbright research fellowship, 1956-58; Phillip Noel Baker prize, UNESCO.

WRITINGS: Endurance Fitness, University of Toronto Press, 1969, 2nd edition, 1976; (editor) *Frontiers of Fitness,* C. C Thomas, 1971; (with others) *Fundamentals of Exercise Testing,* World Health Organization, 1971; *Alive Man: Physiology of Physical Activity,* C. C Thomas, 1972; *Men At Work: Applications of Ergonomics to Performance and Design,* C. C Thomas, 1974; (editor with S. Itoh) *Circumpolar Health,* University of Toronto Press, 1976. Editor of *Pro-*

ceedings of International Symposium on Physical Activity and Cardiovascular Disease, Canadian Medical Association, 1967. Also author of over three hundred technical papers, including more than forty for the United Kingdom Chemical Defence Experimental Establishment, twelve for the Flying Personnel Research Committee of the Royal Air Force, and over forty reports and reviews for various medical and physiological societies, conferences, and international symposia.

Contributor: Dorothy S. Dittmer and R. M. Grebe, editors, *Handbook of Respiration,* American Physiological Society, 1958; Dittmer and Grebe, editors, *Handbook of Circulation,* American Physiological Society, 1959; C. N. Davies, editor, *Inhaled Particles and Vapours,* Pergamon, 1961; Davies, editor, *Ergonomics of the Respirator,* Pergamon, 1961; P. L. Altman and Dorothy S. Dittmer, editors, *Handbook of Environmental Biology,* Federation of American Societies for Experimental Biology, 1965; R. Goddard, editor, *The Effects of Altitude on Physical Performance* (proceedings of international symposium), Athletic Institute, 1967. Contributor to *Encyclopaedia of Sports Medicine,* edited by L. Larson. Also contributor of over 140 scientific articles to more than fifty medical journals, including *British Heart Journal, Ergonomics, Journal of Physiology, Thorax, Archives of Environmental Health* (A.M.A.), *Canadian Medical Association Journal, British Journal of Industrial Medicine, Arbeitsphysiologie, International Journal of Air Pollution, Journal of Aerospace Medicine, Poumon Coeur, Malattie Cardiovasculari, South African Medical Journal, Journal of Sports Medicine and Fitness* (Italy), *Research Quarterly,* and *Internationale Zeitschrift fuer angewandte Physiologie.*

WORK IN PROGRESS: Frontiers of Physical Activity and Child Health for Pelican (Quebec City), and *The Fit Athlete* for Oxford University Press; research on exercise and cardio-respiratory health.

SIDELIGHTS: Roy Shephard told *CA* that he has "visited many parts of the world to study inter-relations of physical activity, health and environment and present the results of his research to international conferences; one of the most fascinating of these excursions was to study the fitness of Eskimos in the Northern Arctic."

* * *

SHEPPARD, Mary

PERSONAL: Born in Winston-Salem, N.C.; daughter of Robah Wilson (a salesman) and Myrtle (Moore) Stimson; married James Robert Sheppard (vice-president of a veneer mill), May 18, 1944; children: James Robert, Jr., Randolph Stimson. *Education:* Elon College, student, 1935-36. *Religion:* Methodist. *Home:* 980 Wellington Rd., Winston-Salem, N.C. 27106.

WRITINGS—Novels: *Devil Dunes,* Arcadia House, 1969; *The Humming Precipice,* Lenox Hill, 1970; *Strangers in the Sun,* Lenox Hill, 1972. Contributor to *Ford Times, Popular Mechanics,* and religious magazines.

WORK IN PROGRESS: A Gothic novel, *His Brother's Keeper.*†

* * *

SHERET, Rene (Dundee) 1933-

PERSONAL: Surname is pronounced *Share*-it; born January 9, 1933, in Buffalo, N.Y.; son of Andrew Dundee (a jeweler) and Martha (Bensley) Sheret; married Marion

Wagner, May 1, 1955; children: Mark, Steven, Nora. *Education:* Art Center College of Design, B.P.A. (with honors), 1954. *Home:* 6933 Varna Ave., Van Nuys, Calif. 91405.

CAREER: Advertising art director and graphic designer for General Dynamics, San Diego, Calif., 1957-59, Frye & Smith Printing, San Diego, 1960-62, Barnes Chase Advertising, San Diego, 1963-64, Lennon & Newell Advertising, San Francisco, Calif., 1965, Copley Newspapers, La Jolla, Calif., 1966-67, and MacManus, John & Adams Advertising, Los Angeles, Calif., 1968-69; Rene Sheret Design, Los Angeles, owner, 1970—. Writer and illustrator of children's books. *Military service:* U.S. Navy, 1955-57.

WRITINGS—Self-illustrated juveniles: *Dutch,* Bobbs-Merrill, 1970; *What If You Heard?,* Bobbs-Merrill, 1970; *Dutch and the Jewel Robbers,* Bobbs-Merrill, 1973.†

* * *

SHERIDAN, James F(rancis), Jr. 1927-

PERSONAL: Born September 28, 1927, in Fall River, Mass.; son of James F. (a salesman) and Anne (Garvey) Sheridan; married Peggy Bishir, June 15, 1954; married second wife, Nancy Damuth (a psychometrist), August 30, 1961; children: (first marriage) Sue, James; (second marriage) Michael. *Education:* Allegheny College, B.A., 1950; Pennsylvania State University, M.A., 1954; University of Illinois, Ph.D., 1957. *Home:* 361 Sherman St., Meadville, Pa. 16335. *Office:* Department of Philosophy, Allegheny College, Meadville, Pa. 16335.

CAREER: Ohio University, Athens, instructor, 1957-59, assistant professor of philosophy, 1960-62; St. Cloud State College, St. Cloud, Minn., associate professor of philosophy, 1962-65; Allegheny College, Meadville, Pa., associate professor, 1965-68, professor of philosophy, 1968—. *Military service:* U.S. Navy, 1945-46. U.S. Army, 1952-54. *Member:* American Philosophical Association, Metaphysical Society of America. *Awards, honors:* Research grants from Hill Foundation, 1962, and from Ford Foundation, summer, 1969 and 1970.

WRITINGS: Sartre: The Radical Conversion, Ohio University Press, 1969; *Once More: From the Middle,* Ohio University Press, 1972. Contributor to philosophy journals.

WORK IN PROGRESS: Nature and Nature—A Phenomenological Inquiry, and *Psyche,* an essay in philosophical psychology.

* * *

SHERMAN, Bernard 1929-

PERSONAL: Born February 21, 1929, in Chicago, Ill.; son of Abe Sherman (a merchant); married Marilyn Roiter, March 18, 1951; children: Mitch, Aviva, Rachel. *Education:* Roosevelt University, B.A., 1951; Northwestern University, M.A., Ph.D., 1966. *Home:* 9525 North Kenneth, Skokie, Ill. 60076. *Office:* Roosevelt University, 430 South Michigan Blvd., Chicago, Ill. 60605.

CAREER: Roosevelt University, Chicago, Ill., assistant professor, 1957-66, associate professor, 1966-70, professor of education, 1970—. *Military service:* U.S. Army, 1953-55. *Member:* Association for Teacher Education.

WRITINGS: The Invention of the Jew: Jewish-American Education Novels, 1917-1964, Yoseloff, 1969. Former reviewer, *Chicago Jewish Forum* (now defunct).

SHERMAN, Philip M(artin) 1930-

PERSONAL: Born July 10, 1930, in Norwalk, Conn.; son of Robert and Anne (Margulies) Sherman; married Doris Gottlieb (a teacher), April 3, 1955; children: Judith, Alan, Emily. *Education:* Cornell University, B.Eng. Physics, 1952; Yale University, M.E., 1956, Ph.D., 1959. *Home:* 471 Claybourne Rd., Rochester, N.Y. 14618. *Office:* Xerox Corp., Xerox Sq., Rochester, N.Y. 14644.

CAREER: Sperry Gyroscope Co., Great Neck, N.Y., engineer, 1952-55; Yale University, New Haven, Conn., instructor in electrical engineering, 1957-59; Bell Telephone Laboratories, Inc., Murray Hill, N.J., department head and supervisor, 1959-69; Xerox Corp., Rochester, N.Y., manager, 1969—. Part-time faculty member in graduate school of management, University of Rochester. *Member:* Institute of Electrical and Electronics Engineers, Association for Computing Machinery, Society for Management Information Systems.

WRITINGS: Programming and Coding Digital Computers, Wiley, 1963; (co-author) *Algorithms, Computation, and Mathematics,* Stanford University Press, 1965; (co-author) *Physical Design of Communications Equipment,* Prentice-Hall, 1969; *Techniques in Computer Programming,* Prentice-Hall, 1970.

SIDELIGHTS: Philip Sherman's work has been translated and published in Japanese, Spanish, and Polish.

* * *

SHERMAN, Richard B. 1929-

PERSONAL: Born November 16, 1929, in Somerville, Mass.; son of James B. and Hilda L. (Ford) Sherman; married Hanni Fey (a teacher), June 13, 1952; children: Linda C., Alan T. *Education:* Harvard University, A.B., 1951, Ph.D., 1959; University of Pennsylvania, M.A., 1952. *Home:* 205 Matoaka Ct., Williamsburg, Va. 23185. *Office:* Department of History, College of William and Mary, Williamsburg, Va. 23185.

CAREER: Pennsylvania State University, State College, instructor in history, 1957-60; College of William and Mary, Williamsburg, Va., assistant professor, 1960-65, associate professor, 1965-70, professor of history, 1970—. University of Stockholm, Fulbright professor of American history, 1966-67. *Military service:* U.S. Army, 1952-54; became sergeant. *Member:* American Historical Association, Organization of American Historians, American Association of University Professors.

WRITINGS: (Editor) *The Negro and the City,* Prentice-Hall, 1970; *The Republican Party and Black America: From McKinley to Hoover, 1896-1933,* University Press of Virginia, 1973. Contributor to *New England Quarterly, Mid-America, Phylon, Historisk Tidskrift,* and other journals.

* * *

SHERWOOD, Hugh C. 1928-

PERSONAL: Born February 9, 1928, in Boston, Mass.; son of Carlton M. (a professional fund-raiser) and Ann (Glover) Sherwood. *Education:* Yale University, B.A., 1948; Columbia University, M.S., 1950. *Religion:* Congregational. *Home:* Apt. L6, 105 North Broadway, White Plains, N.Y. 10603.

CAREER: Medical Economics, Oradell, N.J., associate editor, 1955-59; free-lance writer, New York City, 1960-62; *Business Management,* Greenwich, Conn., managing editor, 1963-69; *Finance,* New York City, assistant managing editor, 1969; free-lance writer, Pleasantville, N.Y., 1970-75. Chairman of 1948 class, Yale Alumni Fund Agents, 1964-74; director, Yale Alumni Fund, 1965-70. *Military service:* U.S. Marine Corps, 1951-54; became staff sergeant. *Member:* Society of Magazine Writers. *Awards, honors:* George Washington Honor Medal of Freedoms Foundation, 1953, for essay, "What America Means to Me"; National Media Award of Family Service Association of America, 1964, for article, "Should Employers Meddle in Family Problems?"

WRITINGS: The Journalistic Interview, Harper, 1969, revised edition, 1972; *How to Invest in Bonds,* Walker & Co., 1974; *How Corporate and Municipal Debt Is Rated: An Inside Look at Standard & Poor's Rating System,* Wiley, 1976. Contributor to *Nation's Business, Industry Week, Town and Country, Coronet, Pageant, Family Circle, New York Times Sunday Magazine,* and other publications. Contributing editor, *Dental Management,* 1970-75, *Industry Week,* 1971—.

SIDELIGHTS: Hugh Sherwood wrote to *CA* that he enjoys the labor of writing because "I like to explain complex subjects clearly and succinctly to other people. Nonetheless, I basically write to please myself. I reason that if I can understand a complex subject, I can explain it to other people." *Avocational interests:* Sports (as spectator and participant), reading, movie-going.

* * *

SHERWOOD, John J(oseph) 1933-

PERSONAL: Born May 17, 1933, in San Francisco, Calif.; married Rosemary Francisco, November 15, 1956; children: Todd Canfield, Janet Lynn, Mark Adam. *Education:* Stanford University, B.A., 1959; University of Michigan, Ph.D., 1962. *Home:* 2617 Covington St., West Lafayette, Ind. 47906. *Office:* Department of Administrative Sciences, Krannert Graduate School of Management, Purdue University, Lafayette, Ind. 47907.

CAREER: Instructor in psychology at University of Michigan, Ann Arbor, and assistant professor of psychology at Eastern Michigan University, Ypsilanti, 1962-63; Carleton College, Northfield, Minn., assistant professor of psychology, 1963-64; Purdue University, Lafayette, Ind., assistant professor, 1964-66, associate professor, 1966-70, professor of psychology and administrative sciences, 1970—, chairman of University Senate, 1970—. Visiting professor, Harvard University, 1972-73. Adjunct professor in the Union Graduate School of the Union for Experimenting Colleges and Universities at Antioch College. Fellow and member of board of directors, National Training Laboratories Institute. Consultant to industry and governmental agencies. *Military service:* U.S. Army, Medical Corps, 1955-57.

MEMBER: International Association of Applied Social Scientists, American Sociological Association (fellow), American Psychological Association, Society for the Psychological Study of Social Issues, Society for the Study of Social Problems, American Association of University Professors, American Civil Liberties Union, Sigma Xi. *Awards, honors:* National Institute of Mental Health grant and U.S. Office of Education research grant, 1962; Purdue Research Foundation grants, summers, 1964-68; Society for the Psychological Study of Social Issues research grant, 1968.

WRITINGS: (Editor with R. V. Wagner, and contributor) *The Study of Attitude Change,* Brooks/Cole, 1969; (contributor) P. E. Converse, editor, *Measures of Social Psycholog-*

ical Attitudes, Institute for Social Research, University of Michigan, 1969; (editor with H. L. Fromkin) *Integrating the Organization,* Free Press, 1971; (contributor) C. G. McClintock, editor, *Experimental Social Psychology,* Holt, 1971; (editor with H. L. Fromkin) *Intergroup and Minority Relations,* University Associates, 1976. Contributor to professional journals.

* * *

SHIBLES, Warren 1933-

PERSONAL: Born July 10, 1933, in Hartford, Conn.; son of Stanley Neil and Jean (Russell) Shibles; married Patricia Pell, August, 1957; married second wife, Carolyn Foster, 1976; children: (first marriage) Garth, Kirsten, Eric. *Education:* University of Connecticut, B.A., 1958; University of Colorado, M.A., 1963; Indiana University, graduate study, 1963-66. *Religion:* "Philosopher-Atheist." *Address:* Box 342, Whitewater, Wis. 53190. *Office:* Department of Philosophy, University of Wisconsin, Whitewater, Wis. 53190.

CAREER: Parsons College, Fairfield, Iowa, lecturer in philosophy, 1966-67; University of Wisconsin—Whitewater, assistant professor of philosophy and chairman of department, 1967—; Language Press, Whitewater, director, 1970—. *Military service:* U.S. Army, 1953-55. *Member:* American Philosophical Association, American Association of University Professors, Writers Association. *Awards, honors:* University of Wisconsin research grant, 1974-75.

WRITINGS: Philosophical Pictures, Language Press, 1969; Wittgenstein, *Language and Philosophy,* Language Press, 1969; *Models of Ancient Greek Philosophy,* Vision Press, 1971; *An Analysis of Metaphor,* Mouton, 1971; *Metaphor: An Annotated Bibliography and History,* Language Press, 1971; *Death,* Language Press, 1974; *Emotion,* Language Press, 1974.

Contributor of over thirty articles to journals including *International Review of History and Political Science, Journal of the Indian Academy of Philosophy, American Rationalist,* and *University of South Florida Language Quarterly;* also contributor to various poetry journals and anthologies.

WORK IN PROGRESS: A book on an analysis of humor; a series of books on philosophy for children.

SIDELIGHTS: Warren Shibles told *CA:* "My goal is to promote honest, open, inquiry and to inquire and clarify the most relevant aspects of knowledge for understanding, humanism and to live an aesthetic life. Most people, however, seem to refuse to inquire and even to oppose it."

* * *

SHIKES, Ralph E. 1912-

PERSONAL: Born September 20, 1912, in Boston, Mass.; son of David (a realtor) and Rebecca Charlotte (Herson) Shikes; married Elizabeth Todd, February 10, 1940; married second wife, Ruth Collins, September 19, 1958; children: (first marriage) Katherine Todd; (second marriage) Jennifer Collins. *Education:* Harvard University, A.B. (magna cum laude), 1933. *Politics:* Independent. *Home:* 16 West 77th St., New York, N.Y. 10024.

CAREER: Associated with American Book Co., New York City, 1934-38, Viking Press, New York City, 1938-41, Limited Editions Club, New York City, 1941-42, and Office of War Information, Washington, D.C., 1942-43; Editorial Projects, Inc., New York City, president, 1952-58; Science & Medicine Publishing Co., New York City, president, 1958-73. Member of board of directors, Bill of Rights Foun-

dation. *Military service:* U.S. Army, 1943-45; editor of *Daily Pacifican. Member:* National Association of Science Writers, American Association for the Advancement of Science, American Federation of Arts, Print Council of America, American Institute of Graphic Arts.

WRITINGS: Slightly Out of Order, Viking, 1958; *The Indignant Eye: The Artist as Social Critic in Prints and Drawings From the 15th Century to Picasso,* Beacon Press, 1969; (contributor) *The Artist in the Service of Politics,* M.I.T. Press, 1977. Also author with Paula Hays Harper, *Camille Pissarro: Biography of an Artist,* 1977. Editor of numerous anthologies. Managing editor, *The Washington Spectator.*

* * *

SHILLING, N(ed) 1924-

PERSONAL: Born June 11, 1924, in Walton, Ind.; married in 1955. *Education:* Purdue University, B.S., 1949; Columbia University, M.A., 1955, Ph.D. (economics), 1964. *Office:* Department of Management Science, Pennsylvania State University, University Park, Pa. 16801.

CAREER: Columbia University, New York, N.Y., lecturer in statistics, 1958-61; Pennsylvania State University, University Park, 1961—, assistant director of research center, 1961-68, currently professor of statistics. Consultant to Pennsylvania Department of Commerce, 1964-65 and to Public Defender, State of New Jersey, 1970-71. *Military service:* U.S. Army, 1942-45; became sergeant. *Member:* American Economic Association, American Statistical Association, Institute of Management Science, Risk Theory Seminar.

WRITINGS: (With Louis Winnick) *American Housing and Its Use: The Demand for Shelter Space,* Wiley, 1957; *Excise Taxation of Monopoly,* Columbia University Press, 1969.

WORK IN PROGRESS: The use of mathematical models in business and administrative decision-making.†

* * *

SHINGLETON, Royce (Gordon, Sr.) 1935-

PERSONAL: Born October 25, 1935, in Stantonsburg, N.C.; son of Wiley Thomas (a merchant and farmer) and Lossie (Vick) Shingleton; married Ruth Bennett (a medical records librarian), June 10, 1962; children: Royce Gordon, Jr., Justin Thomas. *Education:* East Carolina University, B.S., 1958; Appalachian State University, M.A., 1964; Florida State University, Ph.D., 1971. *Home:* D-27, 6851 Roswell Rd. N.E., Atlanta, Ga. 30328. *Office:* Department of History, Georgia State University, Atlanta, Ga. 30303.

CAREER: Dinwiddie High School, Dinwiddie, Va., history and English teacher, 1960-61; Greene Central High School, Snow Hill, N.C., social studies teacher, 1961-63; Lees-McRae College, Banner Elk, N.C., dean of men, 1964-65; Georgia State University, Atlanta, history instructor, 1968—. *Military service:* U.S. Army, 1958-60; served as administrative assistant in West Germany. *Member:* American Historical Association, Southern Historical Association, Phi Alpha Theta.

WRITINGS: (Editor) *America in the Making,* text edition, McCutchan, 1969. Contributor to *Proceedings* of American Philosophical Society; also contributor of articles to various history journals.

WORK IN PROGRESS: Descent on Dixie: Rural Life in the Old South as Seen by Britons.

AVOCATIONAL INTERESTS: Tennis, water skiing, camping††

* * *

SHIPMAN, David 1932-

PERSONAL: Born November 4, 1932, in Norwich, England; son of Alfred Herbert and Edith (Deeks) Shipman. *Education:* Attended Merton College, Oxford, 1954-55. *Agent:* Laurence Pollinger Ltd., 18 Maddox St., London W1R OEU, England.

CAREER: Assistant sales manager for publishers Victor Gollancz Ltd., and Methuen & Co. Ltd., London, England, 1955-61; representative in Europe for U.S. publisher, Curtis Circulation, 1961-63; free-lance European representative for several British publishers, 1964-66; writer and film historian, 1968—. Guest lecturer on cinema, University of East Anglia, 1972.

WRITINGS: The Great Movie Stars: The Golden Years, Crown, 1970; *The Great Movie Stars: The International Years,* Angus & Robertson, 1972, St. Martin's, 1973; *Brando,* Doubleday, 1975.

WORK IN PROGRESS: A history of the cinema in two volumes, for McKay.

* * *

SHIRE, Helena (Mary) Mennie 1912-

PERSONAL: Born June 21, 1912, in Aberdeen, Scotland; daughter of John Henderson and Jane (Rae) Mennie; married Edward S. Shire (a reader in physics at Cambridge University and fellow of King's College), March 31, 1936; children: Alisoun (Mrs. David Gardner-Medwin), John, Christine (Mrs. Brian Bromwich). *Education:* University of Aberdeen, M.A. (first class honors), 1933; Newnham College, Cambridge, B.A., 1935, M.A., 1937; London School of Economics and Political Science, graduate study, 1941-43. *Religion:* Church of Scotland. *Home:* 2 Bulstrode Gardens, Cambridge CB3 OEN, England. *Office:* Robinson College, Cambridge University, Cambridge CB2 1ST, England.

CAREER: University of London, London, England, lecturer in medieval literature at Queen Mary College, 1941-44, lecturer in English for foreigners at London School of Economics and Political Science, 1941-44; Cambridge University, Cambridge, England, member of faculty of English, 1951—, associate college lecturer in English at King's College, 1954—, fellow of Robinson College, 1975—. *Member:* Scottish Text Society (member of council), Saltire Society (president of Cambridge branch). *Awards, honors:* Carnegie Trust for Universities of Scotland senior research fellow in arts, 1961-63; grant for travel in America, 1971.

WRITINGS: (Editor with Kenneth Elliott) *Music of Scotland, 1500-1700,* Volume XV of *Musica Britannica,* Royal Musical Association, 1957; (editor) *Alexander Montgomerie: A Selection from His Songs and Poems,* Oliver & Boyd, for Saltire Society, 1960; *Song, Dance and Poetry of the Court of Scotland under King James VI,* Cambridge University Press, 1969; (editor with Marion Stewart) *King Orpheus, Sir Colling, The Brother's Lament, and Litel Musgray,* Ninth of May, 1973.

Editor of three small volumes issued in limited editions under the imprint Ninth of May (imprint used by Mrs. Shire and Sebastian Carter, printer): *Poems from Panmure House* (three poems transcribed from *The Commonplace-book,* compiled from about 1630 onwards), 1960; *Sir Robert Ayton: A Choice of Poems and Songs,* 1961; *The Thrissil, the Rois,* *and the Flour-de-lys* (unpublished poems of sixteenth-century Scotland), 1962; *The Sheath and the Knife or Leesome Brand,* 1974.

Translator of songs and plays from the Polish. Contributor to *Literature and Western Civilization.* Also contributor to *Saltire Review, Les Fetes de la Renaissance, Music and Letters,* and other journals.

WORK IN PROGRESS: A sequel to *Song, Dance and Poetry of the Court of Scotland,* on music and poetry of pre-Reformation Scotland and contemporary Europe; also writing on song in seventeenth-century Scotland, on Spenser, and on Gavin Douglas; translating Polish folk-songs and twentieth-century Polish drama into Scots or English.

SIDELIGHTS: Helena Shire was instigator in 1950 of the research project Musica Scotica, to discover and collate all manuscripts and early printed records of art-song of Scotland. She has made research trips to France, Portugal, and Poland to observe folk and religious festivals, and has done library research in the United States.

* * *

SHISSLER, Barbara J(ohnson) 1931-

PERSONAL: Born August 12, 1931, in Roanoke, Va.; daughter of Willis Morton (an electrical engineer) and Kathryn (Bradford) Johnson; married John Lewis Shissler, Jr. (deceased); married Lewis H. Nosanow (a doctor); children: (first marriage) John Lewis III, Ada Holland. *Education:* Smith College, A.B., 1951; Western Reserve University (now Case Western Reserve University), M.A., 1957. *Home:* 7610 Glendale Rd., Chevy Chase, Md. 20015. *Office:* Educational Division, National Archives, Washington, D.C.

CAREER: Cleveland Museum of Art, Cleveland, Ohio, managing editor of *Journal of Aesthetics and Art Criticism,* 1957-62; Minneapolis Institute of Arts, Minneapolis, Minn., editor of publications and director of documents program, 1963-72; University of Minnesota Art Gallery, Minneapolis, director, 1972-76; National Archives, Washington, D.C., director of Division of Education, 1976—. Leader of several museum tours abroad.

WRITINGS: Sports and Games in Art (juvenile), Lerner, 1966; *The Worker in Art* (juvenile), Lerner, 1970; *The New Testament in Art* (juvenile), Lerner, 1970; *American Period Rooms at the Minneapolis Institute of Arts,* Minneapolis Institute of Arts, 1970. Contributor to *Catalogue of European Paintings in the Minneapolis Institute of Arts.*

* * *

SHNEIDMAN, Edwin S. 1918-

PERSONAL: Born May 13, 1918, in York, Pa.; son of Louis (a merchant) and Manya (Zukin) Shneidman; married Jeanne Keplinger, October 1, 1944; children: David William, Jonathan Aaron, Paul Samuel, Robert James. *Education:* University of California, Los Angeles, A.B., 1938, M.A., 1940; University of Southern California, M.S., 1947, Ph.D., 1948. *Home:* 11431 Kingsland St., Los Angeles, Calif. 90066. *Office:* University of California, 760 Westwood Plaza, Los Angeles, Calif. 90024.

CAREER: Veterans Administration Neuropsychiatric Hospital, Los Angeles, Calif., clinical psychologist, 1949-54, chief of research in psychological service, 1954-58; Suicide Prevention Center, Los Angeles, co-director, 1958-66; National Institute of Mental Health, Bethesda, Md., chief of Center for Studies of Suicide Prevention, 1966-69; Harvard

University, Cambridge, Mass., visiting professor of psychology, 1969; Center for Advanced Study in the Behavioral Sciences, Stanford, Calif., fellow, 1969-70; University of California, Los Angeles, professor of medical psychology in department of psychiatry, 1970—. University of Southern California, School of Medicine, research associate, 1955—, associate professor, 1961-64, professor of psychology, 1964-66; Harvard University, U.S. Public Health Service special research fellow, 1961-62; Johns Hopkins University, School of Medicine, lecturer, 1967-69; George Washington University, School of Medicine, clinical professor, 1967-69. American Board of Examiners in Professional Psychology, diplomate, 1954, vice-president, 1966. Veterans Administration Hospitals, Los Angeles, consultant, 1970—. *Military service:* U.S. Army Air Forces, 1942-45; became captain.

MEMBER: American Psychological Association (fellow), American Association of Suicidology (president, 1968), Society for Projective Techniques and Personality Assessment (president, 1962). *Awards, honors:* Harold M. Hildreth Memorial Award of American Psychological Association, 1966.

WRITINGS: (Editor) *Thematic Test Analysis,* Grune, 1951; (editor with N. L. Farberow) *Clues to Suicide,* McGraw, 1957; (editor with Farberow) *The Cry for Help,* McGraw, 1961; (editor) *Essays in Self-Destruction,* Science House, 1967; (editor) *On the Nature of Suicide,* Jossey-Bass, 1969; (with Farberow and R. E. Litman) *The Psychology of Suicide,* Science House, 1970; *Deaths of Man,* Quadrangle, 1973; (editor) *Death: Current Perspectives,* Mayfield, 1976; (editor) *Suicidology: Contemporary Developments,* Grune, 1976. Editor, *Suicide and Life-Threatening Behavior,* 1970—.

WORK IN PROGRESS: Studies on attitudes toward death in America today, and on death and the death certificate.

*   *   *

SHORT, Robert Stuart 1938-

PERSONAL: Born May 13, 1938, in London, England; son of Charles Stanley (a journalist) and Edith Audrey (Pulford) Short; married Virginia Ann Page (a writer), June 25, 1965; children: Octavia Alice. *Education:* Trinity Hall, Cambridge, B.A., 1959, Diploma of Education, 1961, M.A., 1964; University of Sussex, Ph.D., 1965. *Politics:* Socialist. *Home:* 5 St. Giles Ter., Norwich NR1 2NS, England. *Office:* School of European Studies, University of East Anglia, Norwich, England.

CAREER: Tulse Hill School, Brixton, London, England, teacher, 1959-60; Ecole Colbert, Paris, France, teacher of English, 1961-62; University of Hull, Hull, England, assistant lecturer, 1965-67; University of East Anglia, Norwich, England, senior lecturer, 1967—. Vice-chairman, Norfolk Contemporary Arts Society. Committee member, Norfolk and Norwich Film Theatre, 1970—.

WRITINGS: (With Roger Cardinal) *Surrealism: Permanent Revelation,* Dutton, 1970. Contributor to *Journal of Contemporary History, Art and Artists,* and others.

WORK IN PROGRESS: *The Surrealist Revolution,* for Weidenfeld & Nicolson; *Beauty and the Beast,* for Elek.

*   *   *

SHU, Austin Chi-wei 1915-
(Chi-wei, Yang-jen)

PERSONAL: Born May 14, 1915, in Anhwei, China; son of Feng-i and Shih (Ch'en) Shu; married Hsiang-teh Fang,

August 25, 1920; children: Lester, Peter. *Education:* Boone University, B.L.S., 1942; National Anhwei University, B.A., 1944; Ministry of Education, China, M.A., 1945; University of Chicago, graduate study, 1969. *Home:* 703-208 Cherry Lane, East Lansing, Mich. 48823. *Office:* Michigan State University Library, East Lansing, Mich. 48823.

CAREER: National Central Library, Nanking, China, head cataloger, 1945-50; Taiwan Provincial Library, Taipei, China, department head, 1950-58; Nanyang University Library, Singapore, head cataloger, 1958-63; East West Center Library, Honolulu, Hawaii, senior cataloger, 1963-67; Michigan State University, International Library, East Lansing, bibliographer, 1967—. *Member:* International Association of Orientalist Librarians, Association of Asian Studies.

WRITINGS: (Compiler and translator with William W. L. Wan) *Twentieth Century Chinese Works on Southeast Asia: A Bibliography,* East West Center, 1968; (compiler) *Modern Chinese Authors: A List of Pseudonyms,* Asian Studies Center, Michigan State University, 1969, revised edition, Chinese Materials and Research Aids Service Center of Association of Asian Studies, 1971; (compiler) *On Mao Tsetung: A Bibliographic Guide,* Asian Studies Center, Michigan State University, 1972; (compiler) *Lei-Shu: Old Chinese Reference Works,* Chinese Materials and Research Aids Service Center of Association of Asian Studies, 1973; (compiler) *Modern Japanese Authors in Area Studies: A Namelist,* Chinese Materials Center, Inc., 1976-77.

WORK IN PROGRESS: China's Great Proletarian Cultural Revolution, 1966-69: A Bibliographic Guide; Afro-Asian Relations Bibliography.

*   *   *

SHULMAN, Alix Kates 1932-

PERSONAL: Born August 17, 1932, in Cleveland, Ohio; daughter of Samuel S. and Dorothy (Davis) Kates. *Education:* Bradford Junior College, A.A., 1951; Western Reserve University (now Case Western Reserve University), B.A., 1953; graduate study at Columbia University, 1953-54, and New York University, 1960-61. *Residence:* New York, N.Y. *Agent:* Ellen Levine, Curtis Brown Ltd., 575 Madison Ave., New York, N.Y. 10022.

CAREER: Writer. Teacher of creative writing at New York University.

WRITINGS: (Contributor) *Women's Liberation: A Blueprint for the Future,* Ace Books, 1970; (editor) *The Traffic in Women and Other Essays,* Times Change Press, 1970; (contributor) Vivian Gornick and B. K. Moran, editors, *Women in Sexist Society: Studies in Power and Powerlessness,* Basic Books, 1971; *Memoirs of an Ex-Prom Queen* (novel), Knopf, 1972; (editor) *Red Emma Speaks: Selected Writings and Speeches of Emma Goldman,* Random House, 1972; *Burning Questions* (novel), Knopf, 1978.

Juveniles: *Bosley on the Number Line,* McKay, 1970; *Awake or Asleep,* Addison-Wesley, 1971; *To the Barricades: The Anarchist Life of Emma Goldman,* Crowell, 1971; *Finders Keepers,* Bradbury, 1972. Contributor to numerous periodicals, including *Redbook, Evergreen Review, New York Times Book Review, Ms., Village Voice,* and *Aphra.*

SIDELIGHTS: In a review of *Memoirs of an Ex-Prom Queen,* Sara Blackburn writes: "I want to praise this novel for its intentions, which are to give a straight, obviously autobiographical portrait of the oppressive aspects of growing up as a white, middle-class female in America, lightened and relieved by the inclusion of all the self-flagellating humor that goes along with it. But until the very end of the book, where Alix Kates Shulman gives us a devastating picture of her heroine as wife and mother that will arouse everything from enormous empathy to rage and panicky denial from every woman reader, this novel is a smashing disappointment. And that is chiefly because it is actually more a memoir of a middle-class Jewish girlhood than it is a book about being female and thus tracked into American womanhood.''

However, Lucy Rosenthal calls *Memoirs of an Ex-Prom Queen* a "remarkable first novel . . . in many ways a breakthrough book, innovative both in its rendering of the feminine experience and in its quite perfect marriage of thesis to art.'' Marilyn Bender writes that Alix Shulman "seems to have drawn pique from Norman Mailer . . . [and anyone] who pricks the crocodile skin of Mailer—that boring boor of fearful knighthood—deserves more than a faint round of applause. These 'Memoirs' scale no lyrical or imaginative peaks, but they rate a bravo as a consciousness-raising attempt.''

BIOGRAPHICAL/CRITICAL SOURCES: Commonweal, May 21, 1971; *New York Times Book Review*, April 23, 1972; *New York Times*, April 25, 1972; *Washington Post*, May 13, 1972; *Saturday Review*, May 20, 1972; *Detroit News*, June 25, 1972; *Contemporary Literary Criticism*, Volume II, Gale, 1974.

* * *

SHULMAN, Arnold 1914-

PERSONAL: Born April 12, 1914, in Philadelphia, Pa.; son of Edward N. (a merchant) and Anna (Leshner) Shulman; married Mary Frances Johnson, 1943; children: Diane (Mrs. Carl Dapaleo), Warren, Amy, Lynn (Mrs. Stephen M. Moorman). *Education:* Attended Emory University, 1931-32; University of Georgia, J.D., 1936. *Religion:* Jewish. *Home:* 1420 Stephens Dr. N.E., Atlanta, Ga. 30329.

CAREER: In private practice as an attorney in Atlanta, Ga., 1937—. *Military service:* U.S. Army, 1941-46; became captain. *Member:* American Bar Association, Georgia State Bar Association, Atlanta Bar Association, Lawyers Club Atlanta.

WRITINGS: (With Wiley H. Davis) *Georgia Practice and Procedure,* Harrison Co., 1948, 4th edition (with Warren S. Schulman), 1975. Also author of numerous legal articles and papers.

* * *

SHULMAN, Frank Joseph 1943-

PERSONAL: Born September 20, 1943, in Boston, Mass.; son of Murray (a civil engineer) and Edna (Altman) Shulman. *Education:* Harvard University, A.B. (magna cum laude), 1964; additional study at Hebrew University of Jerusalem, 1964-65, and Inter-University Center for Japanese Language Studies, 1967-68; University of Michigan, M.A. (East Asian studies), 1968, M.A. (library science), 1969, doctoral candidate, 1974—. *Office:* East Asia Collection, McKeldin Library, University of Maryland, College Park, Md. 20742.

CAREER: University of Michigan, Center for Japanese Studies, Ann Arbor, bibliographer and librarian, 1970-75; University of Maryland, McKeldin Library, College Park, head of East Asia Collection, 1976—. Library consultant to the Groupe d'Etudes et de Documentation sur le Japon Con-

temporain, Ecole Pratique des Hautes Etudes, 1974. *Member:* International Association of Orientalist Librarians, Association for Asian Studies, American Historical Association, European Association for Japanese Studies, Middle East Librarians' Association, Japan-American Society of Washington, D.C., Interchange for Pacific Scholarship.

WRITINGS: (Editor and compiler) *Japan and Korea: An Annotated Bibliography of Doctoral Dissertations in Western Languages, 1877-1969,* American Library Association, 1970; *Doctoral Dissertations on South Asia, 1966-1970: An Annotated Bibliography Covering North America, Europe and Australia,* Center for South and Southeast Asian Studies, University of Michigan, 1971; (editor and compiler with Leonard Gordon) *Doctoral Dissertations on China: A Bibliography of Studies in Western Languages, 1945-1970,* University of Washington Press, 1972; *American and British Doctoral Dissertations on Israel and Palestine in Modern Times,* Xerox University Microfilms, 1973; (with Robert Ward) *Allied Occupation of Japan, 1945-1970: An Annotated Bibliography of Western-Language Materials,* American Library Association, 1974; *Doctoral Dissertations on Japan and Korea, 1969-1974,* University Microfilms International, 1976. Contributor of numerous articles, book reviews, reports, and papers to professional journals, including *Journal of Asian Studies, Monumenta Nipponica, Library Quarterly, Journal of Korean Affairs, Asian Studies Professional Review,* and many others. Assistant editor, *Bibliography of Asian Studies* of the Association for Asian Studies.

WORK IN PROGRESS: Doctoral Dissertations on China, 1971-1975, for the University of Washington Press; *Doctoral Dissertations in Jewish Studies and Related Subjects, 1945-1979: A Bibliography of Jewish History and Civilization,* for Greenwood Press; *Doctoral Dissertations on Southeast Asia, 1968-1975: An Annotated Bibliography of International Research,* for University of Michigan; *A Classified Bibliography of Western-Language Articles Relating to Japan Published in Periodicals and Other Collective Publications since 1945; A Guide to Reviews of Books about China, Japan and Korea Reviewed in Western-Language Periodicals since 1945.*

SIDELIGHTS: Frank Shulman has a reading knowledge (good to excellent) of Dutch, French, German, Hebrew, and Yiddish, in addition to Japanese. Shulman has long been interested in the subject of Japan's postwar economic and political relations with the Middle East. He has a very extensive personal library collection on Asia.

* * *

SHUMWAY, Floyd M(allory, Jr.) 1917-

PERSONAL: Born September 8, 1917, in New York, N.Y.; son of Floyd Mallory, Sr. (a business executive) and Mary Elvira (Spencer) Shumway; married Margaret Frances Rabling, June 27, 1942 (divorced, 1960); married Emma Jean Clifton, July 1, 1960; children: (first marriage) Spencer Thomas, Jean Todd, Peter Mallory. *Education:* Yale University, B.A., 1939; Columbia University, M.A., 1965, Ph.D., 1968. *Religion:* Episcopalian. *Home:* 157 East 82nd St., New York, N.Y. 10028. *Office:* School of General Studies, Columbia University, New York, N.Y. 10027.

CAREER: Prentice-Hall, Inc., New York City, editorial assistant, 1940-41; John David, Inc. (men's clothing stores), New York City, floorman, 1941-42; Liberty Mutual Insurance Co., New York City, employee in claims department,

1942-43; General Electric Co., Bridgeport, Conn. and Chicago, Ill., began as clerk, became sales executive, 1943-52; partner in Shumway-Fresen Co. (manufacturer's agency), Chicago, 1952-58; R. H. Wilson Co. (management consultants), Mountain Lakes, N.J., associate, 1955-60; Remsen-Whitney Publishing Corp., Manhasset, N.Y., vice-president and editor, 1961-62; Rutgers University, Douglass College, New Brunswick, N.J., history instructor, 1968; Columbia University, New York City, instructor, 1968, assistant professor, 1969-70, adjunct associate professor of history, 1976—, assistant dean of School of General Studies, 1970-73, associate editor of "John Jay Papers," 1973-76. *Member:* American Historical Association, St. Nicholas Society, Sons of the American Revolution, General Society of Sons of the Revolution.

WRITINGS: (With John E. Pomfret) *Founding the American Colonies, 1583-1660,* Harper, 1970; *Seaport City: New York in 1776,* South Street Seaport Museum, 1975; (with Richard B. Morris) *John Jay: The Making of a Revolutionary, 1745-1780,* Harper, 1975. Editor of *NATO Journal,* Remsen-Whitney, 1961-62.

* * *

SHUTE, R(eginald) Wayne 1933-

PERSONAL: Born April 25, 1933, in Tuberose, Saskatchewan, Canada; son of Reginald A. and Clara Irene (Barge) Shute; married Lorna Claire Hart, August 3, 1959; children: Christian Wayne, Jonathan Wayne, Nancy Alice, Leslie Jean, Gordon Reginald, Marianne. *Education:* Brigham Young University, B.S., 1955; M.Ed., 1959; University of Southern California, Ed.D., 1964. *Politics:* Republican. *Home:* 768 East 3800 N., Provo, Utah 84601.

CAREER: Mormon missionary in Samoa, 1955-58; Brigham Young University, Provo, Utah, chairman of University's California Center, Los Angles, 1961-64, assitant professor, Graduate School of Education, 1964, assistant dean of Division of Continuing Education, 1964-68; Church of Jesus Christ of Latter-day Saints, president of Samoa Mission, Apia, Western Samoa, 1968-71. *Member:* National University Extension Association, Professors of Adult Education.

WRITINGS: (Compiler) *His Servants Speak: Excerpts From Devotional Addresses Given at Brigham Young University by General Authorities of the Church of Jesus Christ of Latter-day Saints,* Bookcraft, 1966; *For Adults Only: A Lifetime of Learning,* Deseret, 1968. Contributor to *Improvement Era* (Salt Lake City).†

* * *

SHUTE, Wallace B. 1911-

PERSONAL: Born June 4, 1911, in London, Ontario, Canada; son of Richard J. and Elizabeth (Treadgold) Shute; married Eileen Elizabeth Radcliff, October 9, 1937. *Education:* University of Western Ontario, B.A. (honors), 1933, M.D., 1936. *Religion:* Protestant. *Home:* 300 Island Park Dr., Ottawa, Ontario, Canada.

CAREER: Gynecologist and obstetrician in private practice, Ottawa, Ontario. Staff member of Ottawa Civic Hospital and Riverside Hospital. Diplomate, American Board of Obstetrics and Gynecology, 1942. Has made several tours of university centers in Europe, two sponsored by the Canadian Government, to present the Shute parallel obstetrical forceps and other surgical techniques he developed. *Military service:* Royal Canadian Medical Corps, 1945-46; became major.

MEMBER: Royal College of Obstetricians and Gynecologists, Royal College of Surgeons of Canada (fellow), American Society of Abdominal Surgeons (fellow), American College of Surgeons (fellow), Royal Society of Medicine (Canada; fellow), Royal Society of Medicine (London), Society of Obstetricians and Gynecologists of Canada, American Association for the Advancement of Science, Canadian Society for the Study of Fertility, New York Academy of Sciences, Canadian Writers Foundation.

WRITINGS: Christus, Herald House, 1971. Writer and narrator of film, "Shute Parallel Obstetrical Forceps." Contributor to medical journals.

WORK IN PROGRESS: Continuing research and invention in the field of medicine.

* * *

SIELLER, William Vincent 1917-

PERSONAL: Surname is pronounced *Seal*-er; born January 5, 1917, in Norfolk, Conn.; son of Peter J. and Mary (Murphy) Sieller. *Education:* Attended Syracuse University, 1938-41 and Trinity College, Hartford, Conn., 1943; University of Buffalo, B.A., 1948; Canisius College, A.M., 1952; University of Hartford, C.A.G.S., 1959. *Religion:* Roman Catholic. *Home:* Ashpohtag Rd., Norfolk, Conn. 06058. *Office:* Department of Modern Languages, Northwestern Connecticut Community College, Winsted, Conn. 06098.

CAREER: University of Buffalo (now State University of New York at Buffalo), instructor in English, 1946-48; Canisius College, Buffalo, instructor, 1948-53, assistant professor of English, 1953-55; Pearson School, Winsted, Conn., teacher of English, 1956-66; Northwestern Connecticut Community College, Winsted, assistant professor, 1966-67, associate professor of English, 1967—, director of arts and sciences, 1967-70. *Member:* Poetry Society of America.

WRITINGS—Poetry: This Transient Hour, Falmouth House, 1939; *Let Him Return,* Falmouth House, 1960; *Green Water for a Granite Valley,* Golden Quill, 1970; *Beyond All Seasons,* Golden Quill, 1971; *Gather Back the Dream,* Golden Quill, 1973. Poems have been included in *John Masefield: Poet Laureate* (a bibliography) and in anthologies; contributor of several hundred poems to literary quarterlies and to *New York Times, New York Herald Tribune, Christian Science Monitor,* and *Sign.*

* * *

SILBER, William L. 1942-

PERSONAL: Born November 26, 1942, in New York, N.Y.; son of Joseph F. (a businessman) and Pauline (Rothstein) Silber; married Lillian Frank, January 26, 1964; children: Jonathan, Daniel, Tammy. *Education:* Yeshiva University, B.S., 1963; Princeton University, Ph.D., 1966. *Office:* Department of Economics, New York University, 100 Trinity Pl., New York, N.Y. 10006.

CAREER: Council of Economic Advisors, Executive Office of the President, Washington, D.C., senior staff economist, 1970-71; New York University, New York, N.Y., associate professor, 1971-74, professor of economics and finance, 1974—. Consultant to various government agencies. *Member:* American Economic Association.

WRITINGS: (With L. S. Ritter) *Money,* Basic Books, 1970, 2nd revised edition, 1977; *Portfolio Behavior of Financial Institutions,* Holt, 1970; *Principles of Money Banking and Financial Markets,* Basic Books, 1974, revised edition,

1977; *Financial Innovation*, Heath, 1975. Contributor of articles to professional journals.

* * *

SILLS, Ruth C(urtis)

PERSONAL: Born in New York, N.Y.; daughter of Charles Stuart (a civil engineer) and Catherine (Curtis) Frank; married H. Donald Sills (a lawyer), May 18, 1932; children: Charles Frank. *Politics:* Non-partisan. *Religion:* Presbyterian. *Home:* 3 East 69th St., New York, N.Y. 10021.

CAREER: Active in civic and philanthropic organizations in New York, N.Y.; president of board, Kidney Foundation of New York, 1964-65; chairman of board, Development Council of Cabrini Health Care Center; member of board of New York Heart Association, Pearl S. Buck Foundation, and Waldemar Medical Research Foundation; vice president, National Muscular Dystrophy Association; trustee of Metropolitan chapter, National Hemophilia Foundation; vice-chairman of New York committee, National Easter Seal Society for Crippled Children and Adults, 1965-68; chairman of Pan American Fiesta, 1965, Spring Festival of Fragrance, 1965-68, and other benefits. Past president of Women's Service League. *Member:* York Club. *Awards, honors:* Awards for service to the handicapped from National Easter Seal Society for Crippled Children and Adults, Kidney Foundation, Pearl S. Buck Foundation, and Hemophilia Foundation.

WRITINGS: Sweet Bitter Charity, John Day, 1970.

WORK IN PROGRESS: A collection of short stories; a sequel to *Sweet Bitter Charity*.

* * *

SILVAROLI, Nicholas J. 1930-

PERSONAL: Born December 4, 1930, in Buffalo, N.Y.; son of Nicholas Amrigo and Caroline (De Paula) Silvaroli; married Margaret M. Masterson (a teacher), August 22, 1952 (divorced May 12, 1975); children: Diane, Christine, Pamela. *Education:* State Teacher's College (now State University of New York at Fredonia), B.A., 1953; State University College of Education at Buffalo (now State University of New York at Buffalo), M.A., 1960; Syracuse University, Ed.D., 1963. *Politics:* Independent. *Religion:* Unitarian Universalist. *Home:* 999 East Baseline, Tempe, Ariz. 85282. *Office:* College of Education, Arizona State University, Tempe, Ariz. 85281.

CAREER: Teacher in public schools of Williamsville, N.Y., 1956-60; Arizona State University, Tempe, director of Reading Center, 1964, associate professor, 1965-70, professor of education, 1970—. Director of annual migrant teacher institutes in Arizona. *Military service:* U.S. Army, 1953-55; became sergeant. *Member:* International Reading Association (chairman of committee on automation in reading), National Society for the Study of Education, National Committee for Research in Education, Phi Delta Kappa.

WRITINGS: Classroom Reading Inventory, W. C. Brown, 1966; (with John C. Edwards) *Reading Improvement Program*, W. C. Brown, 1968; (with William D. Sheldon) *This Cool World* (young adult book), Allyn & Bacon, 1970. Writer of "Motivating Communication," instructional film series, for Crowell Collier.

WORK IN PROGRESS: Revision of an oral language text entitled *Oral Language Evaluation*.

AVOCATIONAL INTERESTS: Flying (private pilot with visual flight rules rating), playing the piano (former member of a musician's local union).

* * *

SIMIC, Charles 1938-

PERSONAL: Born May 9, 1938 in Yugoslavia; came to United States in 1949; son of George (an engineer) and Helen (Matijevic) Simic; married Helene Dubin (a dress designer), October 25, 1965; children: Anna. *Education:* New York University, B.A., 1966. *Politics:* None. *Religion:* Eastern Orthodox. *Address:* Old Mountain Rd., Northwood, N.H. 03261. *Office:* Department of English, University of New Hampshire, Durham, N.H.

CAREER: Aperture (photography magazine), New York, N.Y., editorial assistant, 1966-74; University of New Hampshire, Durham, associate professor of English, 1974—. *Military service:* U.S. Army, 1961-63. *Awards, honors:* P.E.N. International Award for Translation, 1970; Guggenheim fellowship, 1972-73; National Endowment for the Arts fellowship, 1974-75; Edgar Allen Poe Award, 1975; National Institute of Arts and Letters and American Academy of Arts and Letters Award, 1976.

WRITINGS—Poetry: *What the Grass Says*, Kayak, 1967; *Somewhere among Us a Stone Is Taking Notes*, Kayak, 1969; *Dismantling the Silence*, Braziller, 1971; *White*, New Rivers Press, 1972; *Return to a Place Lit by a Glass of Milk*, Braziller, 1974; *Biography and a Lament*, Bartholemew's Cobble (Hartford, Conn.), 1976; *Charon's Cosmology*, Braziller, 1977.

Translator: Ivan V. Lalic, *Fire Gardens*, New Rivers Press, 1970; Vasko Popa, *The Little Box*, Charioteer Press, 1970; *Four Modern Yugoslav Poets*, Lillabulero (Ithaca, N.Y.), 1970; (and editor with Mark Strand) *Another Republic*, Viking, 1976.

Poetry represented in anthologies, including: *The Young American Poets*, edited by Paul Carroll, Follett, 1968; *The Contemporary American Poets*, edited by Mark Strand, World Publishing, 1969; *Major Young American Poets*, edited by Al Lee, World Publishing, 1971; *America a Prophesy*, edited by George Quasha and Jerome Rothenberg, Random House, 1973; *Shake the Kaleidoscope: A New Anthology of Modern Poetry*, edited by Milton Klonsky, Pocket Books, 1973; *The New Naked Poetry*, edited by Stephen Berg and Robert Mezey, Bobbs-Merrill, 1976; *The American Poetry Anthology*, edited by Daniel Halpern, Avon, 1976.

Contributor of poetry to *New Yorker, Poetry, Nation, Esquire, Chicago Review, Minnesota Review, Field, Iowa Review, Seneca Review, Choice, Antaeus, American Poetry Review, New Republic, Antioch Review*, and many other periodicals.

SIDELIGHTS: Charles Simic's poetry has been compared to that of Mark Strand, W. S. Merwin, and even Sylvia Plath. Some reviewers find that he is more influenced by Vasco Popa, one of the Yugoslavian poets whose work he has translated. James Atlas writes that Simic "draws on the practices of Surrealism, but his work owes more to East European poetry, with its emphasis on a condensed, sombre, even ballad-like language." Atlas also mentions Simic's translations of Popa, "with whom he has obvious affinities; his poems possess the same incantatory powers, the same cunning and story-telling art."

Common objects are presented in Simic's poetry in an almost mystical fashion. Robert Shaw writes: "Simic surrounds the most homely objects with halos of strangeness. Human beings figure in his work only indirectly, in relation to these odd totems: a knife, fork, or spoon, an ax, a stone, a needle.... His mordant focusing on common objects, of course, only leads him closer to the human essence. With a pitiless reductionism he strips away the artificialities of civilization, and often prophesies a return to a harsh natural existence."

Describing the world of Simic's poetry, Paul Zweig writes: "Simic's poetic landscape is intensely cared for, as a peasant cares for meadows which have been coaxed and humanized by centuries of labor. It is not only a pun to say that Simic's poems are profoundly cultivated, if we define culture as an act of conciliation which turns the Furies into goddesses of harvest. Culture in this sense becomes a form of magic.... Simic speaks, in his poems, with garrulous ease, charming us into complicity with the spirits which are at his beck and call. Too late, we discover that the poet's garrulous voice has taken us further than we knew; that Simic's humble mysteries have a sharp and hidden edge...."

BIOGRAPHICAL/CRITICAL SOURCES: Poetry, March, 1972, February, 1975; *Village Voice,* April 4, 1974; *Choice,* March, 1975; *Virginia Quarterly Review,* spring, 1975; *Contemporary Literary Criticism,* Volume VI, Gale, 1976.

* * *

SIMKIN, C(olin) G(eorge) F(rederick)   1915-

PERSONAL: Born January 18, 1915, in Dunedin, New Zealand; son of George Russel (a salesman) and Lilian (Fleury) Simkin; married Margaret Elisa Armstrong, May 18, 1939 (died, 1969). *Education:* University of Otago, Dunedin, New Zealand, M.A., 1937; Oxford University, D.Phil., 1949. *Home:* 29/3 Bariston Ave., Cremorne, New South Wales 2090, Australia. *Office:* Department of Economics, University of Sydney, Sydney, New South Wales 20006, Australia.

CAREER: University of Canterbury, Christchurch, New Zealand, 1939-45, began as lecturer, became senior lecturer; University of Auckland, Auckland, New Zealand, 1946-69, became professor of economics; University of Sydney, Sydney, New South Wales, Australia, professor of economics, 1969—. Visiting Commonwealth professor, University of Essex, 1966-67. Consultant at various periods, United Nations Economic Commission for Asia and the Far East, 1961-65. *Military service:* Royal New Zealand Air Force, 1942-45; became flying officer. *Member:* Economic Society of Australia and New Zealand (vice-president of Sydney branch, 1970), Australian and New Zealand Association for the Advancement of Science (president of economic section, 1970).

WRITINGS: The Instability of a Dependent Economy, Oxford University Press, 1950; *The Traditional Trade of Asia,* Oxford University Press, 1968; *Economics at Large,* Weidenfeld & Nicolson, 1968; (editor) *Currier & Ives Prints: An Illustrated Checklist,* revised edition (Simkin was not associated with earlier edition), Crown, 1970. Member of editorial board, *Economic Record,* 1946—.

WORK IN PROGRESS: The Contemporary Trade of Asia, for Oxford University Press; *Economic Development in Southeast Asia.*

AVOCATIONAL INTERESTS: Chamber music, gardening, and swimming.

BIOGRAPHICAL/CRITICAL SOURCES: Yale Review, autumn, 1969.†

* * *

SIMMONS, Dawn Langley
(Gordon Langley Hall)

PERSONAL: Formerly Gordon Langley Hall; born in Heathfield, Sussex, England; now U.S. citizen; adopted child of the late British actress Margaret Rutherford and her husband, Stringer Davis; married John-Paul Simmons (a captain of a shrimp boat and sculptor), January 23, 1969; children: Bathsheba Marjorie (deceased), Natasha Manigault Paul; Barry (stepson). *Education:* Educated privately in England. *Politics:* Democrat. *Religion:* Anglican. *Home:* 390 Main St., Catskill, N.Y. 12414.

CAREER: Journalist and free-lance writer, previously under name of Gordon Langley Hall. Work includes feature stories about the British royal family and some of America's first ladies and their families; covered Queen Elizabeth's tour of Nigeria for the *New York Mirror,* and Princess Margaret's Caribbean tours and her marriage in Westminster Abbey for the *Boston Globe.* Obituary editor, *Winnipeg Free Press,* 1949-53; society editor, *Nevada Daily Mail,* 1953-56; executive editor, Gordon Langley Hall News Service & Syndicate, New York City, 1956. Former curator, Isabel Lydia Whitney Memorial Art Gallery, Charleston, S.C. *Member:* Society for Theatre Research, Authors League of America.

WRITINGS: A Rose for Mrs. Lincoln: A Biography of Mary Todd Lincoln, Beacon Press, 1970; *Man into Woman: A Transsexual Biography,* Icon Books (London), 1970; *All for Love* (autobiographical), Star Books, 1975.

Under name Gordon Langley Hall: *Saraband for a Saint: A Modern Morality Play in Two Acts,* Exposition Press, 1954; *Me Papoose Sitter,* Crowell, 1955; *The Gypsy Condesa* (novel), Macrae, 1958; *Princess Margaret: An Informal Biography,* Macrae, 1958; *Peter Jumping Horse* (juvenile), Lutterworth, 1959, Holt, 1961; *The Enchanted Bungalow* (biography), [Brighton, England], 1959, Southern Publishing Co., 1960; *Golden Boats from Burma,* Macrae Smith, 1961; *Peter Jumping Horse at the Stampede* (juvenile), Lutterworth, 1961, Holt, 1962; *The Two Lives of Baby Doe* (biography), Macrae, 1962; *Vinnie Ream: The Story of the Girl Who Sculptured Lincoln,* Holt, 1963; *The Sawdust Trail: The Story of American Evangelism,* Macrae, 1964; *Osceola* (biography), Holt, 1964; (with Ann Pinchot) *Jacqueline Kennedy: A Biography,* Fell, 1964; *Dear Vagabonds: The Story of Roy and Brownie Adams,* photographs by Roy B. Adams, Tara Books, 1964; *Mr. Jefferson's Ladies,* Beacon Press, 1966; *Lady Bird and Her Daughters,* Macrae, 1967; *William, Father of the Netherlands,* Rand McNally, 1969. Contributor to *Cincinnati Enquirer, Kwik* (Belgium), and *Country Editor.*

WORK IN PROGRESS: A book about the Carter family; a juvenile work; a novel.

SIDELIGHTS: Reviewing *A Rose for Mrs. Lincoln: A Biography of Mary Todd Lincoln,* W. H. Archer writes: "If an honest portrait of Abraham Lincoln's often grossly maligned wife has been long overdue, it is at last provided by this scrupulously researched biography of a tragic but appealing figure....Writing in a charmingly unpremeditated style, this biographer has achieved a balanced presentation of all factors involved in a complex story, while bringing alive for her readers the way American people thought and lived from the 1840's through the 1860's."

A *Publishers' Weekly* reviewer summarizes Dawn Simmons' own story, *Man into Woman: A Transsexual Autobiography,* in this way: "Born with a pre-natal genital defect the author spent the first 30 years of her life wrongly sexed as a male. Then in 1968 her body began to undergo some drastic changes. After several careful examinations her doctors advised her to enter the Gender Identification Clinic at Johns Hopkins Hospital, where she underwent surgery to correct the genital defect. In this autobiography the author tells of her life when she was Gordon Langley Hall, her writing career, her operation, and finally her marriage. . . ."

BIOGRAPHICAL/CRITICAL SOURCES: Dawn Langley Simmons, *Man into Woman: A Transsexual Autobiography,* Icon Books, 1970; *Sunday Times* (London), November 7, 1970; *Best Sellers,* November 15, 1970; *Publishers' Weekly,* July 15, 1971; Simmons, *All for Love,* Star Books, 1975.

* * *

SIMMONS, J(erry) L(aird)   1933-

PERSONAL: Born August 16, 1933; son of Earl and Lola (Hoyt) Simmons; married Nola Cox (a dianetic counselor), May 28, 1957; children: Christopher, David. *Education:* State University of Iowa, B.A., 1959, Ph.D., 1963. *Religion:* Scientology. *Office:* Scientology South Bay Mission, 607 South Pacific Coast Hwy., Redondo Beach, Calif. 90277.

CAREER: University of Illinois, Urbana, assistant professor of sociology, 1962-65; University of California, Santa Barbara, assistant professor of sociology, 1965-68; University of California, Davis, assistant professor of sociology, 1968-70; presently director of Scientology South Bay Mission.

WRITINGS: (With George J. McCall) *Identities and Interactions,* Free Press, 1966; (with Barry Winograd) *It's Happening: A Portrait of the Youth Scene Today,* Marc-Laird, 1966; *Marihuana: Myths and Realities,* Branden Press, 1968; (with McCall) *Issues in Participant Observation,* Addison-Wesley, 1969; *Deviants,* Glendessary, 1969.

WORK IN PROGRESS: Writing on Scientology.

BIOGRAPHICAL/CRITICAL SOURCES: New Republic, April 1, 1967.

* * *

SIMMONS, Matty   1926-

PERSONAL: Born October 3, 1926, in Brooklyn, N.Y.; son of Irving Benjamin and Kate (Sharp) Simmons; married Lee Easton (a publisher, editor, and author), February 26, 1952; children: Michael, Julie, Andrew. *Education:* City College (now City College of the City University of New York), student, 1944-45. *Politics:* Independent. *Religion:* Jewish. *Residence:* New York, N.Y. *Office:* 21st Century Communications, 635 Madison Ave., New York, N.Y. 10022.

CAREER: Author and editor. Employed as newspaper reporter, 1944-45, and public relations consultant, 1947-58; Diners' Club, New York City, executive vice-president, and editor of *Diners' Club Magazine,* 1950-67; 21st Century Publishing Co., New York City, chairman of the board, 1967—, chief executive officer of subsidiary, *National Lampoon,* 1970—, producer of "National Lampoon Lemmings," 1972-74, and "National Lampoon Show," 1974—. Chairman of the board, San Francisco Warriors, 1963; president of Bravo Inc., and executive editor of *Bravo Magazine,* 1965-66. Engaged in racing and breeding harness horses, 1960-70.

Chairman of fund raising, Columbia Grammar School, 1964-66. *Military service:* U.S. Army, 1945-47. *Member:* Standard Bred Owners Association, United States Trotting Association, Wayfarer's Club (president, 1966-67).

WRITINGS: (With Don Simmons) *On the House,* Coward, 1955; (editor) *The Diners' Club Drink Book,* Doubleday, 1961, revised edition published as *The New Diners' Club Drink Book,* New American Library, 1969; (editor with Sam Boal) *The Best of the "Diners' Club Magazine,"* Regents Publishing, 1962 (published in England as *Diners' Delight: The Best of the "Diners' Club Magazine,"* Souvenir Press, 1963); *The Card Castle* (novel), Putnam, 1970; (editor) *Medical Reports from "Weight Watchers Magazine,"* New American Library, 1975. Editor, *Weight Watchers Magazine,* 1968-75; former editor, *Signature.*

WORK IN PROGRESS: A second novel.†

* * *

SIMMS, D(enton) Harper   1912-

PERSONAL: Born December 21, 1912, in Alamogordo, N.M;. son of J. Denton (a clergyman) and May (Harper) Simms; married Effie M. Fite, June 8, 1936; children: Katharine Idell (Mrs. Frank E. Conway), Marilyn Dannelle (Mrs. Mark J. Daniels). *Education:* Attended Park College, 1929-30, 1931-32; University of Missouri, A.B., 1936, B.J., 1936. *Religion:* Presbyterian. *Home:* 1111 Morningside N.E., Albuquerque, N.M. 87110.

CAREER: U.S. Department of Agriculture, Soil Conservation Service, information specialist and regional information division director, Albuquerque, N.M., 1936-51, director of Information Division, Washington, D.C., 1951-68. *Military service:* U.S. Navy, 1944-46; became lieutenant. *Member:* Soil Conservation Society of America, Outdoor Writers Association of America, Phi Beta Kappa. *Awards, honors:* Superior Service Award, U.S. Department of Agriculture, 1959; American Motors Conservation Award, 1967.

WRITINGS: The Soil Conservation Service, Praeger, 1970; (with William Reed, Ray Brandes, and others) *Troopers West,* Frontier Heritage, 1970. Also author of ten educational cartoon booklets for the Soil Conservation Society of America, William C. Popper Co., 1966-71. Contributor of articles on outdoor subjects to newspapers, and of articles to retirement magazines. Former editor of *Corral Dust* (a western history periodical).

WORK IN PROGRESS: More environment cartoon booklets.

SIDELIGHTS: Concerning his environmental cartoon booklets D. Harper Simms wrote to *CA;* "I believe this is a medium that reaches, better than many others, the young people who will soon be making crucial decisions on environmental matters."

* * *

SIMMS, Willard S.   1943-

PERSONAL: Born February 22, 1943, in Denver, Colo.; son of Evan Willard (a livestock show manager) and Thirza Simms; married Janet Catriona MacDonald-Lucas, September 27, 1969. *Education:* University of Denver, B.A., 1965; University of Oklahoma, M.F.A., 1967. *Home:* 1304 South Columbine, Denver, Colo. 80210. *Agent:* Robert Freedman, 101 Park Ave. S., New York, N.Y. 10017.

CAREER: Exhibits manager, National Western Stock Show, Denver, Colo. Playwright; television writer; historical writer. Commissioned to write the official State Historical Drama for Colorado. *Member:* Colorado Author's League. *Awards, honors:* Fellowship to Rocky Mountain Writer's Workshop at University of Colorado; Shubert playwriting fellowship at University of Oklahoma.

WRITINGS—Plays; published by Dramatists Play Service: *The Acting Lesson,* 1967; *The Passing of an Actor,* 1968; *Miss Farnsworth,* 1969; *Two's a Crowd,* 1970.

Published by Pioneer Drama Service: *The Wizard of Oz in the Wild West,* 1973; *Alice in Wonderland,* 1974; *Thursday Meets the Wolfman,* 1975; *Jim Bridger: Mountain Man,* 1976; *King Midas and the Magic Touch,* 1977; *An Evening with King Kong and Friends,* 1977.

Also author of eleven episodes of "The Spirit of '76", national television series for children, produced by M. G. Animation, 1975, and of twelve segments of "Time: Alive," sponsored by National Endowment for the Humanities and Denver Public Library, 1976-77.

WORK IN PROGRESS: "Goodwill Blues," a two-act play.

SIDELIGHTS: Willard S. Simms writes: "An author in the late twentieth century faces a difficult task. He must be able to personalize a world that grows more impersonal daily. He must be able to write truthfully and openly, putting down as much of himself as his talent will allow. Yet he cannot forget that we write to entertain ourselves as well as to entertain our audience, and the greatest joy comes when we succeed at both. Writing chooses us more than we choose it. Thus our problem becomes—how do we choose to live with it?"

*   *   *

SIMON, Andre (Louis)   1877-1970

February 28, 1877—September 5, 1970; French-born authority and writer on food and wines. Obituaries: *New York Times,* September 6, 1970.

*   *   *

SIMON, Henry W(illiam)   1901-1970

October 9, 1901—October 1, 1970; American editor, music and literary critic, and Shakespearean scholar. Obituaries: *New York Times,* October 3, 1970; *Variety,* October 7, 1970; *Time,* October 19, 1970; *Books Abroad,* spring, 1971. (See index for *CA* sketch)

*   *   *

SIMON, Joseph H.   1913-
(Joe Simon)

PERSONAL: Born October 11, 1913, in Rochester, N.Y.; son of Harry (a tailor) and Rose (Kurland) Simon; married, May 18, 1946; wife's name, Harriet; children: Jon, James, Melissa, Gail, Lori. *Education:* Attended Syracuse University. *Politics:* Independent. *Religion:* Jewish. *Home:* 11 Arbutus Lane, Stony Brook, N.Y. 11790.

CAREER: Rochester Journal American, Rochester, N.Y., artist-writer, 1933-36; *Syracuse Journal American,* Syracuse, N.Y., art editor, writer, 1936-38; *Syracuse Herald,* Syracuse, artist-writer, 1938-39; Harvey Publications, New York City, editor, 1945—. Editor for Goodman Publications and Crestwood Publications, 1946-68, National Periodicals and Pyramid Publications, 1968-70, all in New York City. Publisher, Mainline Publications and Pastime Publications; art director, Bursten, Phillips & Newman Advertising, Great Neck, N.Y. *Military service:* U.S. Coast Guard, 1942-45.

WRITINGS—Under name Joe Simon; all self-illustrated: *Incurably Sick,* Avon, 1962; *Look Who's Talking,* W.W.R., Inc., 1964; *A Funny Thing Happened to Me on the Way to Tel Aviv,* All American Printing Co., 1967; (editor) *Ensicklopedia,* Pyramid Publications, 1970.

Creator of Captain America and many other comic book heroes; originator of "Young Romance" comic books and *Sick* Magazine.

WORK IN PROGRESS: A self-illustrated book on dog breeding for the family, entitled *Home Bred;* memoirs of the early years of comic books.

AVOCATIONAL INTERESTS: Breeding great danes; politics.

BIOGRAPHICAL/CRITICAL SOURCES: Jules Feiffer, *The Great Comic Book Heroes,* Dial, 1965.††

*   *   *

SIMON, Ulrich E(rnst)   1913-

PERSONAL: Born September 21, 1913, in Berlin, Germany; son of James Martin (a composer) and Anna (Levy) Simon; married Jean Westlake (a teacher), December 29, 1949; children: Sophia, Martin, Peter. *Education:* King's College, London, B.D., 1938; University of London, M.Th., 1944. *Home:* 11 Anson Rd., London N7 ORB, England. *Office:* King's College, University of London, Strand, London W.C.2, England.

CAREER: Priest of Church of England, rector in Upton, Buckinghamshire, 1942-45, and Millbrook, Bedfordshire, 1950-54; University of London, King's College, London, England, assistant professor, 1954-58, professor in department of theology, chair in Christian Literature, 1958—. Visiting professor, St. Mary's University, Baltimore, Md., 1969-70. Examiner in British universities. Trustee, Kinkardine Foundation. *Member:* Society of Old Testament Studies, London Society for the Study of Religions. *Awards, honors:* Fellow of King's College, University of London, 1958; D.D., University of London, 1960.

WRITINGS: A Theology of Crisis, Allenson, 1948; *A Theology of Salvation,* Allenson, 1953; *Heaven in the Christian Tradition,* Harper, 1958; *The Ascent to Heaven,* Barrie & Rockliff, 1961; *The End Is Not Yet,* Nisbet, 1963; *Theology Observed,* Epworth, 1966; *A Theology of Auschwitz,* Gollancz, 1967; *The Trial of Man,* Mowbray, 1973; *Story and Faith,* S.P.C.K., 1975. Contributor to *Dictionary of Christian Ethics;* regular reviewer for *Times Literary Supplement, Theology,* and other journals.

WORK IN PROGRESS: Sitting in Judgement: Interpretation of History 1913-63; and *Job's Diary.*

SIDELIGHTS: Ulrich Simon is bilingual in German (his native language) and English, and competent in French, Latin, Greek, and Hebrew. *Avocational interests:* Mountaineering, swimming, playing violin (especially chamber music).

BIOGRAPHICAL/CRITICAL SOURCES: Times Literary Supplement, October 26, 1967.

*   *   *

SIMSOVA, Sylva   1931-

PERSONAL: Born February 24, 1931, in Prague, Czechoslovakia; children: Cyril, Debora. *Education:* University College, London, F.L.A., 1957, M.Phil., 1975. *Office:* School of Librarianship, Polytechnic of North London, 207-225 Essex Rd., London N1 3PN, England.

CAREER: Islington Public Library, London, England, junior assistant, 1951-55; Hackney Public Library, London, senior assistant, 1955-58; Stoke Newington Public Library, London, branch librarian, 1958-60; Finchley Public Library, London, district librarian, 1960-64; Polytechnic of North London, London, assistant lecturer, 1964-66, lecturer, 1966-70, senior lecturer in librarianship, 1971—. *Member:* Library Association.

WRITINGS—Published by Shoe String, except as noted: (Editor) *Lenin, Krupskaia and Libraries,* translation by G. Peacock and Lucy Prescott, 1968; (editor) *Nicholas Rubakin and Bibliopsychology,* translation by Monique MacKee and Peacock, 1968; (with MacKee) *A Handbook of Comparative Librarianship,* 1970, 2nd revised and enlarged edition, Bingley, 1975; (with A. D. Burnett and R. K. Gupta) *Studies in Comparative Librarianship,* Library Association, 1973.

Contributor: J. S. Kujoth, editor, *Libraries, Readers and Book Selection,* Scarecrow, 1969; J. S. Kujoth, editor, *Reading Interests of Children and Young Adults,* Scarecrow, 1970; B. Katz and R. Burgess, editors, *Library Lit. 4: The Best of 1974,* Scarecrow, 1975. Contributor to *Assistant Librarian, Library Association Record, Library World, Books and Bookmen, Bookseller, Libri, Journal of Librarianship, International Library Review,* and other professional journals.

WORK IN PROGRESS: Research on the subjective dimensions of readability; a book on the problems of library service to ethnic groups.

SIDELIGHTS: Sylva Simsova told *CA:* "The guiding theme of my work is the relationship between the library and its users both in the social and individual aspect." She lists her professional interests as comparative librarianship, library services to ethnic groups, and the psychology of reading. *Avocational interests:* Bringing up children and sharing their interests, hiking, camping, open air life, reading, music and other cultural pursuits, philosophy, and psychology.

* * *

SINGER, Joy Daniels   1928-

PERSONAL: Born February 22, 1928, in New York, N.Y.; daughter of Maurice B. and Anna (Kleegman) Daniels; married Jack Singer (a program director for American Broadcasting Co.), 1955; children: Meriamne, Daniel, Richard. *Education:* Cornell University, B.A., 1948; Sorbonne, University of Paris, graduate study, 1949. *Politics:* Democratic. *Religion:* Jewish. *Home:* 49 West 87th St., New York, N.Y. 10024. *Office:* 8th Floor, 15 West 44th St., New York, N.Y. 10036.

CAREER: Advertising copywriter at various agencies in New York, N.Y., including March Advertising and Franklin Spier. Wrote scripts for Canadian television show, "Magistrate's Court," 1969-70.

WRITINGS: My Mother, the Doctor, Dutton, 1970.

WORK IN PROGRESS: A novel.

SIDELIGHTS: Joy Daniels Singer started writing "because there was a great story in my family and it had to be told." During the past few years most of her creative interests have been concentrated on renovating a brownstone in New York's urban renewal area. *Avocational interests:* Skiing, the theater, traveling "anywhere."

BIOGRAPHICAL/CRITICAL SOURCES: Best Sellers, March 15, 1970; *New York Times Book Review,* June 14, 1970.

* * *

SIRAGELDIN, Ismail A(bdel-Hamid)   1930-

PERSONAL: Surname is pronounced Se-*ra*-gel-deen; born August 1, 1930, in Cairo, Egypt; son of Abdelhamid J. (a lawyer) and Ayesha (Radwan) Sirageldin; married Hanaa A. Noah, April 28, 1958; children: Kamal, Camelia, Sherif. *Education:* University of Cairo, B.Sc., 1954; University of Toronto, M.S.A., 1962; University of Michigan, Ph.D., 1967. *Office:* Department of Economics, Johns Hopkins University, Baltimore, Md. 20036.

CAREER: Agricultural engineer and farmer in United Arab Republic, 1954-55; Japanese External Trade Recovery Organization-Middle East, Cairo, Egypt, assistant manager for market research, 1956-60; University of Michigan, Institute for Social Research, Ann Arbor, member of research staff in economic behavior, 1964-65, assistant study director, 1966-67; Johns Hopkins University/Government of Pakistan, West Pakistan Research and Evaluation Center, Lahore, chief adviser, 1967-68, 1969-70; Johns Hopkins University, Baltimore, Md., assistant professor, 1967-70, associate professor of population and economics, 1970—. Consultant on population to United Nations, World Bank, and Ford Foundation. *Member:* American Economic Association, Econometric Society, Royal Economic Society, American Statistical Association, American Association of University Professors, Population Association of America.

WRITINGS: (With James N. Morgan and Nancy Baerwaldt) *Productive Americans: A Study of How Individuals Contribute to Economic Growth,* Institute for Social Research, University of Michigan, 1966; *Non-Market Components of National Income,* Survey Research Center, University of Michigan, 1969; (editor) *Research in Human Capital and Development: An Annual Compilation of Research,* Volume I, Jai Press, 1977. Contributor to population and economics journals.

WORK IN PROGRESS: Evaluation of the Pakistan Family Planning Program based on a national study; the measurement of income and welfare as related to family size and decisions; study of economic incentives in population planning.†

* * *

SIRE, James W(alter)   1933-

PERSONAL: Born October 17, 1933, in Inman, Neb.; son of Walter Guy and Elsie (Mulford) Sire; married Marjorie Ruth Wanner (a laboratory technician), June 14, 1955; children: Carol, Eugene, Richard, Ann. *Education:* University of Nebraska, B.A., 1955; Washington State University, M.A., 1958; University of Missouri, Ph.D., 1964. *Religion:* Christian. *Office:* Inter-Varsity Press, 5206 Main, Downers Grove, Ill. 60515.

CAREER: University of Missouri, Columbia, instructor in English, 1958-64; Nebraska Wesleyan University, Lincoln, assistant professor, 1964-66, associate professor of English, 1966-68; Inter-Varsity Press, Downers Grove, Ill., editor, 1968—. Part-time associate professor at Northern Illinois University, 1969-70 and Trinity College, Deerfield, Ill., 1971-75; visiting summer professor at University of Nebraska, 1966, and University of Missouri, 1967. *Military service:* U.S. Army, Ordnance, 1955-57; became first lieutenant. *Member:* Modern Language Association of America, Conference on Christianity and Literature, Milton Society, American Scientific Affiliation.

WRITINGS: (With Robert Beum) *Papers on Literature: Models and Methods,* Holt, 1970; *Program for a New Man,* Inter-Varsity Press, 1973; *Jeremiah, Meet the Twentieth Century,* Inter-Varsity Press, 1975; *The Universe Next Door,* Inter-Varsity Press, 1976.

*   *   *

SISK, John P(aul) 1914-

PERSONAL: Born March 25, 1914, in Spokane, Wash.; son of Paul John (a postal clerk) and Rose (Freitag) Sisk; married Gwen Annette Servick, August 20, 1951; children: Eric, Mary, Gavin, Toner, Teresa, Paule. *Education:* Gonzaga University, A.B., 1936, M.A., 1939; University of Washington, Seattle, graduate study, 1950. *Politics:* Democrat. *Religion:* Roman Catholic. *Home:* West 201 26th Ave., Spokane, Wash. 99203. *Office:* Department of English, Gonzaga University, East 502 Boone Ave., Spokane, Wash. 99202.

CAREER: MWAK Construction Co., Coulee Dam, Wash., clerk, 1936-38; Gonzaga University, Spokane, Wash., instructor, 1939-42, assistant professor, 1946-52, associate professor, 1952-63, professor of English, 1963—, chairman of department, 1963-67. Consultant, National Endowment for the Humanities, 1975, 1976. *Military service:* U.S. Army Air Forces, 1942-46; became captain; received Commendation Ribbon. *Member:* Philological Association of the Pacific Coast. *Awards, honors:* Carl Foreman Award of Harcourt, Brace & Highroads Productions, 1961, for best short novel, "A Trial of Strength"; LL.D. from Gonzaga University, 1961; senior fellowship, National Endowment for the Humanities, 1972-73.

WRITINGS: Person and Institution, Fides, 1970. Contributor of critical essays and reviews to *Commonweal, Atlantic, Commentary, New York Times Book Review, Harper's, The American Scholar, Worldview, The Shakespeare Quarterly,* and other periodicals and newspapers.

WORK IN PROGRESS: A study of contemporary American culture, especially as it is expressive of the recurring conflict between conservative and liberal forces (portions of this work have been published in magazines).

SIDELIGHTS: John Sisk wrote to *CA:* "I write in order to clear up the bothersome confusions in my mind and because, as Hemingway has put it, 'if I do not write a certain amount I do not enjoy the rest of my life.'"

*   *   *

SIZER, John 1938-

PERSONAL: Born September 14, 1938, in Grimsby, England; son of John Robert (a docks foreman) and Mary (Hawley) Sizer; married Valerie Davies, October 10, 1965; children: Richard John, Stuart James, Jonathan Matthew. *Education:* Attended Grimsby College of Technology, 1954-61; University of Nottingham, B.A., 1964. *Home:* 37 Beacon Rd., Loughborough, England. *Office:* Department of Management Studies, Loughborough University of Technology, Loughborough, England.

CAREER: Clover Dairies Ltd., Grimsby, England, assistant accountant, 1958-61; G.K.N. Ltd., Smethwick, England, financial analyst, 1964-65; University of Edinburgh, Edinburgh, Scotland, lecturer in accounting, 1965-68; London Graduate School of Business Studies, London, England, senior lecturer in accounting, 1968-70; Loughborough

University of Technology, Loughborough, England, professor of financial management, 1970—. *Member:* Institute of Cost and Management Accountants, American Accounting Association, British Institute of Management. *Awards, honors:* Leverhulme Prize, Institute of Cost and Management Accountants.

WRITINGS: An Insight into Management Accounting, Penguin, 1969; *Case Studies in Management Accounting,* Longman, 1974. Contributor to management and accounting journals.

WORK IN PROGRESS: Research on the accountant's role in pricing decisions and on life cycle costing and performance indicators in higher education.

*   *   *

SKIDMORE, Max J(oseph Sr.) 1933-

PERSONAL: Born December 25, 1933, in Springfield, Mo.; son of Joseph Franklin and Gladys (Watt) Skidmore; married Patricia Bassett, April 15, 1954 (divorced); married Charlene Campbell, June 20, 1976; children: (first marriage) Max Joseph, Jr. *Education:* Southwest Missouri State College (now University), B.S. and B.S. in Education, 1956; University of Missouri, M.Ed., 1956; attended Brookings Institution, 1959-60; University of Minnesota, Ph.D., 1964. *Politics:* Democrat. *Religion:* Unitarian. *Residence:* Springfield, Mo. *Office:* Department of Political Science, Southwest Missouri State University, Springfield, Mo. 65802.

CAREER: Teacher in Missouri public schools, 1954-55; superintendent of schools, Climax Springs, Mo. 1956-57; Department of Health, Education and Welfare, Washington, D.C., Social Security Administration, management analyst, 1959-62, Office of Commissioner of Social Security, administrative assistant, 1962-64, U.S. Office of Education, program review officer, 1964-65; University of Alabama, Tuscaloosa, associate professor of political science, director of American studies program, 1965-68; Southwest Missouri State University, Springfield, Mo., professor of political science and head of department, 1968—. Visiting professor at University of Colorado, Colorado Springs, summer, 1968, and University of Nebraska at Omaha, summer, 1972. Consultant to various municipalities and educational institutions.

MEMBER: American Political Science Association, American Studies Association, American Academy of Political and Social Science, American Association of University Professors, Mid-Continent American Studies Association (president, 1976-1977), Southeastern American Studies Association (executive board member, 1966-68), Southern Political Science Association, Western Political Science Association, Missouri Political Science Association (president, 1971-72), Council on Human Relations (Tuscaloosa; member of board of directors, 1966-68).

WRITINGS: Medicare and the American Rhetoric of Reconciliation, University of Alabama Press, 1970; *Word Politics: Essays on Language and Politics,* James Freel, 1970; (with Marshall Carter Wanke) *American Government,* St. Martin's, 1974, 2nd edition, 1977; *The Core of American Political Thought,* St. Martin's, 1977.

Contributor of articles and reviews to *Mississippi Quarterly, School and Community, American Quarterly, Phi Delta Kappan, Progressive, Greek Review of Social Research, American Studies, Political Science Quarterly,* and other periodicals. Member of editorial board, *American Studies,* 1972—.

WORK IN PROGRESS: Additional work on language and

politics, political thought, and American politics; "I am even guilty, occasionally, of poetry."

SIDELIGHTS: Max J. Skidmore told *CA* that his "central motivation in writing [is] human and non-human survival and the development of human potential . . . [which implies] two fundamental considerations: political and ecological (i.e., to provide survival at a humane level). . . . Basic to these considerations are the paradoxical needs to prevent community or governmental actions that stifle individual potential, and the prevention of the excesses of possessive individualism that stifle community potential (and even community and individual awareness of the difficulties)."

*   *   *

SKIPWITH, Sofka   1907-

PERSONAL: Born October 23, 1907, in St. Petersburg (now Leningrad) Russia; daughter of Prince Peter and Countess Sophy (a physician, licensed pilot, and eventually an emigre taxi driver in Paris; maiden name, Bobrinsky) Dolgorouky; married Leo Zinovieff (an army major; deceased); married second husband, Grey d'Estoteville Skipwith (killed flying with the Royal Air Force, 1942); children: (first marriage) Peter, Ian; (second marriage) Patrick. *Education:* Attended schools in many countries of Europe. *Politics:* Humanist. *Religion:* Humanist. *Home:* Bradford Cottage, near Bisland, Bodmin, Cornwall, England.

CAREER: Born into Russian nobility, the princess fled with her family in 1919 to England, in the suite of the Dowager Empress, who was welcomed by relatives, King George V and Queen Mary; during World War II she was caught in France by the German Occupation and was interned there for three years; secretary to Sir Laurence Olivier, 1933-39, and to the Old Vic Theatre Company, 1944-47; manager of a travel agency, 1950-60.

WRITINGS: Sofka (autobiography), Hart-Davis, 1968; *Eat Russian,* David & Charles, 1972.

Translator: Princess Wolkonsky, *Way of Bitterness,* Macmillan, 1935; *History of Costume,* Hyperion, 1938; A. F. Polovtsoff, *Favourites of Catherine the Great,* Jenkins, 1940; "A Dam Against an Ocean" (translation and adaptation of Marguerite Duras' novel, *Un Barrage contre le Pacifique*), for British Broadcasting Corp., 1962. Translator and abridger of articles from Russian periodicals for *London Magazine,* 1968—.

BIOGRAPHICAL/CRITICAL SOURCES: Listener, December 5, 1968.

*   *   *

SLATER, Mary Louise   1923-

PERSONAL: Born September 3, 1923, in East St. Louis, Ill.; daughter of Roy and Anna E. Severns; married Albert L. Slater (a missionary), February 14, 1947; children: Suzanna, Jan Marie. *Education:* Shurtleff College, Alton, Ill., B.M.E.; Central Baptist Theological Seminary, M.R.E., 1951. *Home:* Tharigoppala, via Mustiala, Jangaon Taluk, Warangal District, Andhra Pradesh, South India.

CAREER: American Baptist foreign missionary in South India, 1952—, doing general missionary service, 1952-64, and working on community development in an interior village, 1966—.

WRITINGS: Children's Lessons: Broadly Graded Sunday School Lessons for Villages, India Sunday School Union, Volume I, 1963, Volume II, 1964; *Future Maker in India:*

The Story of Sarah Chakka, Friendship, 1968. Contributor of articles and children's stories to American Baptist Convention publications.

WORK IN PROGRESS: Writing on various aspects of life in India, including the role of women in villages, and the bondage of malnutrition and illiteracy in which village children still are living.†

*   *   *

SLEATOR, William (Warner III)   1945-

PERSONAL: Born February 13, 1945, in Havre de Grace, Md.; son of William Warner, Jr. (a professor) and Esther (Kaplan) Sleator. *Education:* Harvard University, B.A., 1967. *Religion:* None.

CAREER: Originally music was his primary interest, but work as assistant to artist Blair Lent led to his writing for children; he had studied piano for twelve years, the cello for five, and worked for several years as an accompanist for ballet classes, with one year at the Royal Ballet School in London, England; also composer of scores for ballets and amateur films and plays. *Awards, honors:* Fellowship at Bread Loaf Writers' Conference, 1969.

WRITINGS: The Angry Moon, illustrations by Blair Lent, Little, Brown, 1970; *Blackbriar* (juvenile novel), illustrations by Lent, Dutton, 1972; *Run* (mystery), Dutton, 1973; *House of Stairs* (science fiction), Dutton, 1974; *Among the Dolls,* illustrations by Trina Schart, Dutton, 1975; (with William H. Redd) *Take Charge: A Personal Guide to Behavior Modification,* Random House, 1977. Writer of musical score for animated film, "Why the Sun and Moon Live in the Sky," also in collaboration with Lent.

WORK IN PROGRESS: With Lent, a children's novel and several picture books, both original and adaptations from folklore.†

*   *   *

SLOAN, James Park (Jr.)   1944-

PERSONAL: Born September 22, 1944, in Greenwood, S.C.; son of James Park and Alice Catherine (Gaines) Sloan; married Jeannette Carol Pasin (an artist and book illustrator), July 27, 1968; children: Eugene Blakely, Anna Jeannette. *Education:* Harvard University, B.A., 1968. *Politics:* None. *Religion:* None. *Residence:* Oak Park, Ill. *Office:* Department of English, University of Illinois at Chicago Circle, Chicago, Ill. 60680.

CAREER: Writer; previously employed as teacher of English and accounting and director of business schools; faculty member of English department, University of Illinois at Chicago Circle, 1972—. *Military service:* U.S. Army, paratroops, 1964-67; became sergeant. *Awards, honors:* Army Commendation Medal; Vietnamese Medal of Honor; Great Lakes Colleges Association New Writer's Award, 1971, for *War Games.*

WRITINGS: War Games, Houghton, 1971; *The Case History of Comrade V.* (novel), Houghton, 1972. Contributor to *Harvard Advocate.*

WORK IN PROGRESS: Research or reading on linguistics, physics, anthropology, astronomy, mathematics, and logic.

SIDELIGHTS: Discussing his views on writing, James Park Sloan states: "For *War Games* I had an idea of the places and events to be described, but I kept them purposefully vague until the protagonist encountered them. I have found that excessive planning causes aridity. A story known only in vague outline seems to grow out of the tone of narration, inventing its own details. . . . The question of *form*— the overall structure of a novel—is for me the most exciting and underdeveloped area of modern fiction. Innovative form is far rarer than splashy language or even action. Modern readers, in fact, are a bit deadened to language and action."

Reviewing Sloan's novel *The Case of Comrade V.*, a *New York Times* reviewer writes that "the stimulation of this cerebral thriller lies in the way Mr. Sloan keeps collapsing reality around us; and that despite its somewhat hyperintellectual quality and the overtrickiness of its ending, I lay awake after finishing it, trying to figure out who in it is sane, and who is crazy; what is sanity, what is madness."

AVOCATIONAL INTERESTS: Basketball, tennis.

BIOGRAPHICAL/CRITICAL SOURCES: Saturday Review, February 27, 1971; *Best Sellers*, March 1, 1971; *Writer*, November, 1971; *New York Times*, April 13, 1972.†

*   *   *

SMALL, Melvin   1939-

PERSONAL: Born March 14, 1939, in New York, N.Y.; son of Herman Z. and Ann (Ashkenazy) Small; married Sara Jane Miller, October 23, 1958; children: Michael, Mark. *Education:* Dartmouth College, B.A., 1960; University of Michigan, M.A., 1961, Ph.D., 1965. *Home:* 1815 Northwood, Royal Oak, Mich. 48073. *Office:* History Department, Wayne State University, Detroit, Mich. 48227.

CAREER: Wayne State University, Detroit, Mich., assistant professor, 1965-70, associate professor, 1970-75, professor of history, 1976—. Visiting assistant professor, University of Michigan, summer, 1968; visiting professor, Aarhus University, Aarhus, Denmark, 1972-74. *Member:* American Historical Association, Organization of American Historians, Society for Historians of American Foreign Relations, Peace Science Society (member of executive council, 1976-79). *Awards, honors:* Fellow, Center for Advanced Study in the Behavioral Sciences, 1969-70; study fellowship, American Council of Learned Societies, 1969-70.

WRITINGS: (Editor) *Public Opinion and Historians*, Wayne State University Press, 1970; (with J. David Singer) *The Wages of War*, Wiley, 1972.

Contributor: James N. Rosenau, editor, *International Politics and Foreign Policy*, Free Press, 1969; Francis A. Beer, editor, *Alliances*, Holt, 1970; Julian R. Friedman and others, editors, *Alliances in International Politics*, Allyn & Bacon, 1970; James Short and Marvin Wolfgang, editors, *Collective Violence*, Aldine, 1972; William Coplin and Charles Kegley, editors, *Analyzing International Relations*, Praeger, 1975; Alexander De Conde, editor, *Dictionary of the History of American Foreign Policy*, Scribner, in press. Contributor to journals in his field.

WORK IN PROGRESS: American Attitudes towards Russia, 1939-1944.

*   *   *

SMART, (Roderick) Ninian   1927-

PERSONAL: Born May 6, 1927, in Cambridge, England; son of William Marshall (a professor) and Isabel (Carswell) Smart; married Libushka Clementina Baruffaldi, July 17, 1954; children: Roderick, Luisabel, Caroline, Peregrine. *Education:* Oxford University, B.A., 1951, B.Phil. and M.A., 1954. *Politics:* Labour. *Religion:* Church of England.

Home: Westbourne Ho, Westbourne Rd., Lancaster, England. *Office:* Department of Religious Studies, University of Lancaster, Lancaster, England.

CAREER: University College of Wales, Aberystwyth, assistant lecturer, 1952-55; University of London, King's College, London, England, lecturer in the history and philosophy of religion, 1956-61; University of Birmingham, Birmingham, England, H. G. Wood Professor of Theology, 1961-67; University of Lancaster, Lancaster, England, professor of religious studies, 1967—. Visiting lecturer in philosophy, Yale University, 1955-56; visiting lecturer, Banaras Hindu University, summer, 1960; Teape lecturer, University of Delhi, 1964; visiting professor, University of Wisconsin, 1965. *Military service:* British Army, Intelligence Corps, 1945-48; served overseas in Ceylon; became captain. *Member:* Aristotelian Society, Athenaeum Club (London).

WRITINGS: Reasons and Faiths, Routledge & Kegan Paul, 1958; *A Dialogue of Religions*, S.C.M. Press, 1960; (editor) *Historical Selections in the Philosophy of Religion*, Harper, 1962; *Philosophers and Religious Truth*, S.C.M. Press, 1964, 2nd edition, 1969; *Doctrine and Argument in Indian Philosophy*, Allen & Unwin, 1964; *The Teacher and Christian Belief*, James Clarke, 1966; *Secular Education and the Logic of Religion*, Faber, 1968; *The Yogi and the Devotee*, Allen & Unwin, 1968; *The Religious Experience of Mankind*, Scribner, 1969; *The Philosophy of Religion*, Random House, 1970, 2nd revised edition, 1976; *The Concept of Worship*, Macmillan, 1972; *The Phenomenon of Religion*, Macmillan, 1973; *The Science of Religion and the Sociology of Knowledge*, Princeton University Press, 1974; *Mao*, Collins, 1974; *The Long Search*, BBC Publications, 1977. Contributor to philosophy and theology journals. Editorial consultant, BBC-TV series, "The Long Search."

WORK IN PROGRESS: A book on Christianity, to be published by Collins and Harper.

SIDELIGHTS: Ninian Smart told *CA:* "I have tried in my writings to illuminate problems of philosophy and the history and nature of religion and religions. When I have the ideas I usually write fast. *The Concept of Worship* was written in eight days in Princeton in 1971. But sometimes I do a lot of revision. Though some of the stuff is technical I believe in clarity. I write best in my wife's home in North Italy: the sun seems to warm the brain."

AVOCATIONAL INTERESTS: Cricket, painting.

BIOGRAPHICAL/CRITICAL SOURCES: New York Times Book Review, February 9, 1969, July 16, 1969; *Commonweal*, April 4, 1969; *Christian Century*, May 7, 1969.

*   *   *

SMELSER, William T(aylor)   1924-

PERSONAL: Born July 14, 1924, in Kahoka, Mo.; son of Joseph N. (a teacher) and Susie (Hess) Smelser; married Betty Ward, September 10, 1951; children: Claudia, Lisa. *Education:* University of California, Berkeley, B.A., 1949, M.A., 1950, Ph.D., 1957. *Home:* 235 Trinity Ave., Kensington, Calif. 94708. *Office:* School of Social Welfare, University of California, Berkeley, Calif. 94720.

CAREER: University of California, Berkeley, clinical field supervisor, 1956-57, research psychologist, 1957-63, visiting instructor, 1959-60, lecturer in social welfare, 1963—. Instructor, San Francisco State College (now University), 1958-59. Psychotherapist, California Medical Clinic, 1960—; clinical psychologist, Permanete Medical Group, Oakland, Calif. *Military service:* U.S. Army, 1943-45. *Member:* Phi Beta Kappa, Sigma Xi.

WRITINGS: (Editor with brother, Neil Joseph Smelser) *Personality and Social Systems,* Wiley, 1963, 2nd edition, 1970. Contributor to psychology journals.

WORK IN PROGRESS: Research in sociology and personality theory.†

* * *

SMILEY, Virginia Kester 1923-

PERSONAL: Born February 21, 1923, in Rochester, N.Y.; daughter of Harold P. and Isabell (Fleming) Kester; married Robert P. Smiley (a gravure engraver), September 8, 1945; children: Suzanne, Kimberly. *Education:* Attended public schools in Rochester, N.Y. *Politics:* Republican. *Religion:* Protestant. *Home:* 669 Webster Rd., Webster, N.Y. 14580.

CAREER: Worked in Rochester, N.Y., as a telephone operator, 1941-42, secretary at a hospital, 1942-43, and in the offices of Hickok Manufacturing Co., 1943-44, and Birdseye-Snyder Co., 1944-45; currently full-time writer. *Member:* Mystery Writers of America, Genessee Valley Writers (former secretary).

WRITINGS—All published by Bouregy, except as noted: *Little Boy Navaho* (juvenile), Abelard, 1954; *The Buzzing Bees* (juvenile), Abelard, 1956; *Swirling Sands,* Dodd, 1958; *Nurse Kate's Mercy Flight,* Ace Books, 1968; *A Haven for Jenny,* 1970; *High Country Nurse,* 1970; *Under Purple Skies,* 1972; *Guest at Gladehaven,* Dell, 1972; *Mansion of Mystery,* Dell, 1973; *Nurse for Morgan Acres,* 1973; *Nurse of the Grand Canyon,* 1973; *Cove of Fear,* 1974; *Nurse for the Civic Center,* 1974; *Libby Williams, Nurse Practitioner,* 1975; *Liza Hunt, Pediatric Nurse,* 1976; *Nurse Delia's Choice,* 1977. Contributor of short stories to juvenile and teen magazines.

SIDELIGHTS: Virginia Smiley told *CA:* "I write 'light' nurse romances, and 'light' mystery, suspense romances because I believe there is a need for this type of book . . . something to pick up and read easily in an evening, in a bus, on a plane etc. I think, with so many adult type novels being published, there is a need for 'clean' stories. . . . I do an occasional juvenile because I enjoy writing for the young. Whenever I find a fan letter from a child in my mailbox the hours I spend glued to the typewriter are worthwhile."

* * *

SMITH, Barry D(ecker) 1940-

PERSONAL: Born June 12, 1940, in Harford, Pa.; son of Clinton T. (a school administrator) and Gretchen (Decker) Smith; married Elizabeth Wormley, June 15, 1963; children: Douglas Alan, Debra Lynne. *Education:* Pennsylvania State University, B.S., 1962; Bucknell University, M.A., 1964; University of Massachusetts, Ph.D., 1967. *Home:* 12206 Valerie Lane, Laurel, Md. 20810. *Office:* Department of Psychology, University of Maryland, College Park, Md. 20742.

CAREER: Assistant professor of psychology, University of Massachusetts, summer, 1967; University of Maryland, College Park, assistant professor, 1967-71, associate professor of psychology, 1971—. *Member:* American Psychological Association, Psychonomic Society.

WRITINGS: (With R. C. Teevan) *Motivation,* McGraw, 1967; (with H. J. Vetter) *Theoretical Approaches to Personality,* Appleton, 1971; (compiler with Vetter) *Personality Theory: A Source Book,* Appleton, 1971. Also editor of *Anxiety: Theory and Research.*

WORK IN PROGRESS: A handbook based on research in psychophysiology; research in psychological and physiological habituation, personality variables in psychophysiology, and other studies.†

* * *

SMITH, Catherine C. 1929-
(Kay Smith)

PERSONAL: Born August 8, 1929, in Geneva, Ill.; daughter of Frederick and Evalyn (Nesbitt) Collier; married Rufus E. Smith, Jr. (a district marshall), December 6, 1951; children: Patricia Diane. *Education:* University of Miami, Coral Gables, Fla., B.A., 1950. *Religion:* Presbyterian. *Home:* 7521 Southwest 53rd Pl., Miami, Fla. 33143.

CAREER: Dade County public schools, Miami, Fla., home and hospital teacher, 1952-54, 1966—. *Member:* Beaux Arts (associate member), Mortar Board. *Awards, honors:* First place for children's writing, Southeast Writers Conference, 1971.

WRITINGS: (Under name Kay Smith) *Parakeets and Peach Pies* (juvenile), Parents' Magazine Press, 1971. Contributor to *Humpty Dumpty.*

WORK IN PROGRESS: Stories for children; designing bulletin board materials and other visual aids for Trend Enterprises.

* * *

SMITH, Charles E(dward) 1904-1970

June 8, 1904—December 16, 1970; American authority and writer on jazz. Obituaries: *Newsday,* December 18, 1970; *Variety,* December 23, 1970; *Publishers' Weekly,* January 18, 1971.

* * *

SMITH, David Elvin 1939-

PERSONAL: Born February 7, 1939, in Bakersfield, Calif.; son of Elvin William (a clerk) and Dorothy (McGinnis) Smith; married Alice De Swarte (a teacher), August 15, 1970; children: Julia, Suzanne. *Education:* University of California, Berkeley, B.S., 1960, San Francisco Medical Center, M.D., M.S., 1964. *Politics:* Democrat. *Religion:* Unitarian. *Home:* 321 Crestmont, San Francisco, Calif. 94131. *Office:* Haight-Ashbury Free Clinic, 1698 Haight St., San Francisco, Calif. 94117.

CAREER: University of California, San Francisco Medical Center, assistant clinical professor of toxicology, 1967—; Haight-Ashbury Free Clinic, San Francisco, founder and medical director, 1967—.

WRITINGS: The New Social Drug: Medical, Legal and Cultural Perspectives on Marijuana, Prentice-Hall, 1970; *Love Needs Care: A History of San Francisco's Haight-Ashbury Free Clinic,* Little, Brown, 1971; *The Free Clinic: Community Approaches to Health Care and Drug Abuse,* Stash Press, 1972; *It's So Good, Don't Even Try It Once: Heroin in Perspective,* Prentice-Hall, 1973; *Drugs in the Classroom,* Mosby, 1973; *Upper and Downers,* Prentice-Hall, 1974; *Barbiturate Use and Abuse,* Behavioral Publications, 1976. Founder and editor, *Journal of Psychedelic Drugs,* 1967—.

BIOGRAPHICAL/CRITICAL SOURCES: Washington Post, June 6, 1970; *National Review,* December 15, 1970.

SMITH, David M(arshall)   1936-

PERSONAL: Born July 16, 1936, in Birmingham, England; son of James Marshall and Elizabeth (McIlquam) Smith; married Margaret Ruth Harrup (a sociologist), August, 1961; children: Michael, Tracey. *Education:* University of Nottingham, B.A., 1958, Ph.D., 1961. *Politics:* Socialist. *Religion:* None. *Home:* 41 Traps Hill, Laughton, Essex, England. *Office:* Department of Geography, Queen Mary College, University of London, Mile End Rd., London E1 4NS, England.

CAREER: Staffordshire County Planning and Development Office, England, research assistant, 1961-63; University of Manchester, Manchester, England, lecturer in geography and planning, tutor in extramural studies, 1963-66; Southern Illinois University, Carbondale, visiting assistant professor, 1966-67, associate professor of geography, 1967-70; University of Florida, Gainesville, associate professor of geography and urban studies, 1970-72; University of London, Queen Mary College, London, England, professor of geography, 1973—. Visiting lecturer, Natal College for Advanced Technical Education, Durban, South Africa, and Witwatersrand College for Advanced Technical Education, Johannesburg, South Africa, 1972-73; visiting associate professor, University of New England, 1973. Affiliated with Anglo-Soviet Cultural Exchange, 1977. Consultant to Ministry of Public Building and Works and National Buildings Record, 1961-66, Regional Development Service of Greek Government, 1965-66, South East Lancashire and North East Cheshire Transportation Study, 1966, city of Tampa, Fla., 1971-72, and government of Peru, 1976. *Member:* Association of American Geographers, Institute of British Geographers, Regional Science Association, Regional Studies Association. *Awards, honors:* American Philosophical Society research awards, 1967, 1968, and 1970.

WRITINGS: The Industrial Archaeology of the East Midlands, David & Charles, 1965; *Industrial Britain: The North West,* David & Charles, 1969; *Industrial Location: An Economic Geographical Analysis,* text edition, Wiley, 1971; *The Geography of Social Well-being in the United States,* McGraw, 1973; (with wife, Margaret R. Smith) *The United States: How They Live and Work,* David & Charles, 1973; *Patterns in Human Geography,* David & Charles, 1975; *Human Geography: A Welfare Approach,* St. Martin's, 1977.

Contributor to journals of geography, regional planning, and social studies, including *East Midland Geographer, Journal of Industrial Archaeology, Regional Studies, Environment and Planning,* and *Tijdschrift voor Economische en Sociale Geografie.* Editor of "Industrial Britain" series, David & Charles, 1965—.

SIDELIGHTS: David M. Smith told *CA* that his "main motivation for writing, apart from the need for personal expression, is to make some small contribution to the understanding of the relationship between economic development and social well-being. . . . Contemporary American society is preoccupied with the production of goods and the exploitation of resources, and overlooks the unhappy human consequences of unrestricted free business enterprise. The need for the collective planning of a new and more just society has never been more clear."

*   *   *

SMITH, Dorothy Valentine   1908-

PERSONAL: Born September 24, 1908, in Staten Island, N.Y.; daughter of John Frederick (an insurance executive and banker) and Abbie (Crocheron) Smith. *Education:* Educated in Staten Island, N.Y. *Politics:* Republican. *Religion:* Episcopalian. *Home:* 1213 Clove Rd., Staten Island, N.Y. 10301. *Agent:* Muriel Fuller, P.O. Box 193, Grand Central Station, New York, N.Y. 10017.

CAREER: Writer. Member of board of directors, Girl Scout Council of Greater New York, 1942-52; Society for Seamen's Children, member of board of managers, 1947-69, first vice-president, 1965-69; vice-president, Richmond Opera, 1959-61; member of film estimate board, Motion Picture Association of America, 1959-62; president, Visiting Nurse Association of Staten Island, 1959-72; Richmondtown Restoration, Inc., an incorporator, 1961, trustee, 1961—, vice-president, 1968—, chairman of board of trustees, 1973—; trustee, Stanley-Timolat Foundation, 1967—; second vice-president, Washington Headquarters Association, Inc., 1973—.

MEMBER: Society of Architectural Historians, National Trust for Historic Preservation, Victorian Society of America, American Association for State and Local History, English-Speaking Union, National Historical Society, Daughters of Founders and Patriots of America, Daughters of the American Revolution, Foundation for Modern Art, Huguenot Society, New York Genealogical and Biographical Society, New York Historical Society (life member), Long Island Historical Society, Municipal Art Society of New York, Staten Island Historical Society (life member), Preservation Society of Charleston, S.C. *Awards, honors:* Wagner College, Distinguished Service Award, 1958, Distinguished Citizenship Award, 1966; Woman of Achievement in International Women's Year, Staten Island Community College, 1975; citation for Distinguished Service to the Community and the Nation, General Federation of Women's Clubs, 1977.

WRITINGS: (With Theodora DuBois) *Staten Island Patroons* (booklet), Staten Island Historical Society, 1961; *This Was Staten Island,* Staten Island Historical Society, 1968; *Staten Island: Gateway to New York,* Chilton, 1970. Contributor to *Notable American Women, 1677-1950;* contributor of historical articles to *New York Times, Staten Island Advance,* and other publications. Editor, *Empire State DAR News,* 1953-56; national chairman, *DAR Magazine,* 1966-71.

WORK IN PROGRESS: Theodosia, a biography of Theodosia Burr; *Passion Is the Wind,* a novel based on the Polly Bodine murder trials; *Our Sixty Feet of Daughters,* the biography of a noted eighteenth-century New England family, completion expected in 1978.

*   *   *

SMITH, Florence Margaret   1902-1971
(Stevie Smith)

1902—March 7, 1971; English poet, novelist, and illustrator. Obituaries: *Books and Bookmen,* June, 1971; *Antiquarian Bookman,* June 24, 1971. (See index for *CA* sketch)

*   *   *

SMITH, Harmon L.   1930-

PERSONAL: Born August 23, 1930, in Ellisville, Miss.; son of Harmon L. (a clergyman) and Mary (O'Donnell) Smith; married Bettye Watkins, August 21, 1951; children: Pamela Lee, Amy Joanna, Harmon L. III. *Education:* Millsaps College, A.B., 1952; Duke University, B.D., 1955, Ph.D., 1962. *Residence:* Durham, N.C. *Office:* Divinity School, Duke University, Durham, N.C. 27706.

CAREER: Minister of Grace Church in Burlington, N.C., 1955-59; Duke University, Divinity School, Durham, N.C., assistant dean, 1959-65, assistant professor of Christian ethics, 1962-68, associate professor of moral theology, 1968-73, professor of moral theology, 1973—, professor of community health sciences, 1974—. Member of board of directors, North Carolina Council on Human Relations. *Military service:* U.S. Naval Reserve, 1948-52. *Member:* American Society of Christian Ethics, American Academy of Religion, Society for Values in Higher Education. *Awards, honors:* American Association of Theological Schools faculty fellow; Duke Endowment research fellow; Cooper Foundation research fellow, 1968-69; research fellow at St. Barnabas Hospital for Chronic Diseases, 1973.

WRITINGS: (With John C. Bennett and others) *Storm over Ethics,* United Church Press, 1967; (with Louis W. Hodges) *The Christian and His Decisions,* Abingdon, 1969; *Ethics and the New Medicine,* Abingdon, 1970; (with Daniel T. Gianturco) *The Promiscuous Teenager,* C. C Thomas, 1974.

Contributor: G. H. Shriver, editor, *American Religious Heretics,* Abingdon, 1966; Larry M. Lance, editor, *Proceedings of the Population Workshop on Who Shall Live and How?,* University of North Carolina, Institute for Urban Studies and Community Service, 1971; J. Philip Wogaman, editor, *The Population Crisis and Moral Responsibility,* Public Affairs Press, 1973; I. S. Cooper, M. Riklan, and R. S. Snider, editors, *The Cerebellum, Epilepsy, and Behavior,* Plenum Press, 1974; K. J. Struhl and P. R. Struhl, editors, *Ethics in Perspective,* Random House, 1974; Robert L. Perkins, editor, *Abortion: Pro and Con,* Schenkman, 1974; V. O. Stumpf, editor, *The Harnett County Forum,* Campbell College Press, 1975; L. W. Hodges, editor, *Social Responsibility: Journalism, Law, Medicine,* Washington and Lee University, 1976. Contributor to *Christian Century, Religion in Life, London Quarterly,* and other journals.

WORK IN PROGRESS: A book on William Temple.

AVOCATIONAL INTERESTS: Golf, playing the guitar, European travel.

* * *

SMITH, (Oliver) Harrison 1888-1971

August 4, 1888—January 8, 1971; American editor and critic. Obituaries: *Publishers' Weekly,* January 18, 1971.

* * *

SMITH, K(ermit) Wayne 1938-

PERSONAL: Born September 15, 1938, in Newton, N.C.; son of Harold Robert (a clerk) and Hazel (Smith) Smith; married Audrey Kennedy, December 19, 1958; children: Stuart Wayne. *Education:* Wake Forest University, B.A., 1960; Princeton University, M.A., 1962, Ph.D., 1964; University of Southern California, postgraduate study, 1965. *Office:* 8480 Beverly Blvd., Los Angeles, Calif. 90048.

CAREER: United States Military Academy, West Point, N.Y., assistant professor of political science and economics, 1963-66; U.S. Department of Defense, Washington, D.C., special assistant on systems analysis to assistant secretary of defense, 1966-69; RAND Corp., Santa Monica, Calif., program manager of defense studies, 1969-70; National Security Council, Washington, D.C., director of program analysis, 1970-72; Dart Industries, Los Angeles, Calif., vice-president of group planning, 1972-73, president of resort develop-

ment group, 1973—. Member of visitors commission, Brookings Institution, 1971—; member of visitors board, Wake Forest University, 1972—. Former consultant to U.S. Department of Defense, Office of Emergency Preparedness, and RAND Corp. *Military service:* U.S. Army, 1963-66; became captain. *Member:* American Political Science Association, American Society of Public Administration, Institute for Strategic Studies, Council on Foreign Relations, Phi Beta Kappa, Omicron Delta Kappa.

WRITINGS: (Contributor) Joint Economic Committee, *The Analysis and Evaluation of Public Expenditures: The PPB System,* U.S. Government Printing Office, 1969; (contributor) Robert H. Haveman and Julius Margolis, editors, *Public Expenditures and Policy Analysis,* Markham, 1970; (with Alain C. Enthoven) *How Much Is Enough?: Shaping the Defense Program, 1961-69,* Harper, 1971. Contributor to *Foreign Affairs* and *Interplay.*

AVOCATIONAL INTERESTS: Golf, handball, and painting.

BIOGRAPHICAL/CRITICAL SOURCES: New Republic, February 20, 1971; *Time,* March 15, 1971; *Nation,* May 17, 1971.†

* * *

SMITH, Lee L. 1930-

PERSONAL: Born February 14, 1930, in Frederick, Md.; son of Eugene B. (a machinist) and Freda (Spurrier) Smith; married Duane Virts, July 3, 1952; children: Teri Lee, Robin Roxanne, Melinda Susan. *Education:* Towson State College, B.S. in Ed., 1952; George Washington University, M.A. in Ed., 1958; George Washington University, Ed.D., 1971. *Home:* 10360 Cullen Ter., Columbia, Md. 21043. *Office:* Howard County Public Schools, 8045 Route 32, Columbia, Md. 21044.

CAREER: Frederick (Md.) public schools, elementary principal, 1957-76; currently supervisor of staff development for Howard County Public Schools. *Military service:* U.S. Army, 1952-54; became staff sergeant. *Member:* National Association of Elementary-School Principals, Association for Supervision and Curriculum Development, National Council of Staff Developers, Maryland Congress of Parents and Teachers (life member).

WRITINGS: A Practical Approach to the Nongraded Elementary School, Parker Publishing, 1968; *Teaching in a Nongraded School,* Parker Publishing, 1970; *Jack Out of the Box: Practical Guide to the Open Classroom,* Parker Publishing, 1974.

AVOCATIONAL INTERESTS: Singing with choral groups, fishing, woodworking, camping.

* * *

SMITH, LeRoi Tex 1934-
(LeRoi Ugama, Charles Scott Welch)

PERSONAL: Born January 1, 1934, in Cleveland, Okla.; son of Carlos Debs and Esther (Welch) Smith; married Margaret Hamilton, September 18, 1955; children: Scott Storm, Shawna Starr, Stacey Sonnet, Sierra Shelley. *Education:* Student at Idaho State University, one year, at Ricks College, one year, and at Montana State University, two years. *Politics:* Independent. *Religion:* Church of Jesus Christ of Latter-day Saints. *Home:* 216 Pinon St., Lake of the Woods, Calif. 93225. *Office address:* Cherokee Publishing Co., P.O. Box 278, Frazier Park, Calif. 93225.

CAREER: Played professional baseball briefly with St. Louis Browns; *Hot Rod* (magazine), Los Angeles, Calif., editor, 1957-64; free-lance writer, 1964—; field director, National Hot Rod Association, 1960-65; editor, Professional Press, 1967-70, and Brock Publications, 1971-73; editorial director, TRM Publications, 1969-71, and Challenge Publications, 1973-77; Cherokee Publishing Co., Frazier Park, Calif., publisher, 1975—. *Military service:* U.S. Air Force, pilot, 1953-57; became first lieutenant.

WRITINGS: How to Fix Up Old Cars (young adult), Dodd, 1968; *We Came In Peace,* Classic Press, 1969; (with W.R.C. Shedenhelm), *The Complete Volkswagen Book,* Petersen, 1969; (editor) *Basic Bodywork and Painting,* Petersen, 1969; *Complete Book of Engine Swapping, Number 2,* Petersen, 1969; *Karting,* Arco, 1971; *Make Your Own Hot Rod,* Dodd, 1971; *Fixing Up Motorcycles,* Dodd, 1974; *Money-Savers Do-It-Yourself Car Repair,* Macmillan, 1975. Columnist for *Rod & Custom* and *Popular Hot Rodding,* and contributor of about 125 illustrated articles annually to periodicals in the automotive, aviation, and space fields.

WORK IN PROGRESS: Restoring Cars, and *Hanggliding,* both for Dodd. *Don't Call 'Em Hot Rods,* for Cherokee Publishing; a novel on drag racing.

SIDELIGHTS: LeRoi Smith, whose family Cherokee name is Ugama, is active in National American Indian affairs and speaks the Cherokee language.

BIOGRAPHICAL/CRITICAL SOURCES: Best Sellers, February 1, 1969.

* * *

SMITH, Merriman 1913-1970

February 10, 1913—April 13, 1970; American journalist and political analyst. Obituaries: *New York Times,* April 14, 1970. (See index for *CA* sketch)

* * *

SMITH, Norman F. 1920-

PERSONAL: Born July 18, 1920, in Waterbury, Conn.; son of Fred S. (an executive) and Clara K. (Zehnder) Smith; married Evelyn R. Bishop (administrative assistant in NASA public affairs office), January 25, 1962; children: Douglas W., Gail C. *Education:* Purdue University, B.S. in M.E., 1941; University of Houston, graduate courses in education, 1968—. *Politics:* Independent. *Religion:* None.

CAREER: National Aeronautics and Space Administration, aeronautical research scientist in Langley Research Center, Hampton, Va., 1941-62, technical assistant to director of engineering and development at Manned Spacecraft Center, Houston, Tex., 1962-70; currently full-time writer. Licensed pilot with instrument rating. President, Virginia Association for Retarded Children, 1960; vice-president, National Association for Retarded Children, 1961-63. *Member:* Writers Guild of America, American Association for the Advancement of Science.

WRITINGS: (Editor with Paul E. Purser and Maxine A. Fayet) *Manned Spacecraft: Engineering Design and Operation,* Fairchild, 1964; *Uphill to Mars, Downhill to Venus: The Science and Technology of Space Travel,* Little, Brown, 1970; *Wings of Feathers, Wings of Flame: The Science and Technology of Aviation,* Little, Brown, 1972; *Energy and Environment,* Steck, 1974; *The Atmosphere,* Steck, 1975; *Sun Power,* Coward, 1976; *Space: What's Out There?,* Coward, 1976; *Moonhopping through Our Solar System,* Coward, 1977; *The Inside Story of Metals,* Mes-

sner, in press. Writer of six educational films on space mechanics for Teaching Films of Houston. Contributor to *Rotarian, Air Facts, Science Teacher,* and other journals.

WORK IN PROGRESS: Co-authoring a junior high school physical science textbook; science filmstrips.

BIOGRAPHICAL/CRITICAL SOURCES: Best Sellers, April 1, 1970.†

* * *

SMITH, Pauline C(oggeshall) 1908-

PERSONAL: Born December 14, 1908, in Randolph, Iowa; husband deceased; children: Patricia Gail Lewis. *Education:* Attended Municipal University of Omaha (now University of Nebraska at Omaha), University of California, Los Angeles, Glendale College, and Ventura College. *Politics:* Democrat. *Religion:* None. *Home:* 1923 Linda Vista, Ventura, Calif. 93003.

CAREER: Free-lance writer. *Member:* Mystery Writers of America. *Awards, honors:* Mystery Writers of America award, 1972, for short story, "My Daughter Is Dead."

WRITINGS: Confess for Cash, Pilot Books, 1960; *Frigid Web,* Newsstand Library, 1960; *Nothing but the Blood,* Chicago Paperback, 1962; *Hold Yourself Dear* (teen book), Messner, 1965; *The End of the Line,* A. S. Barnes, 1970. Short stories represented in numerous anthologies, including *The Best Detective Stories of the Year* and *Mystery Writers of America.* Contributor of more than eight hundred short stories to magazines, including *Antaeus* and *Alfred Hitchcock's Mystery Magazine.*

WORK IN PROGRESS: Short stories; a young people's novel; a juvenile work; research on a project involving the mentally ill.

SIDELIGHTS: Pauline Smith's short stories have been reprinted in foreign languages and in Braille, and adapted for the screen and radio.

* * *

SMITH, Perry McCoy 1934-

PERSONAL: Born December 16, 1934, in West Point, N.Y.; son of Perry McCoy (an army officer) and Mary Emily Smith; married Connor Cleckley Dyess, May 9, 1959; children: Perry McCoy, Jr., Serena Connor. *Education:* U.S. Military Academy, B.S., 1956; Columbia University, Ph.D., 1967. *Religion:* Episcopalian.

CAREER: U.S. Air Force, regular officer, 1956—, with present rank of colonel; former associate professor of political science, U.S. Air Force Academy, Colorado Springs, Colo. Served as combat pilot in Vietnam, 1968-69; director of electives programs at National War College, Washington, D.C., 1970-71. Member of All-American Lacrosse Team, 1956; assistant lacrosse coach and chief scout for U.S. Air Force Academy, 1966-70. *Member:* Order of Daedalians. *Awards, honors:* Distinguished Flying Cross (twice), Bronze Star Medal, Air Medal with ten oak-leaf clusters.

WRITINGS: The Air Force Plans for Peace 1943-45, Johns Hopkins Press, 1970.

BIOGRAPHICAL/CRITICAL SOURCES: Washington Post, April 14, 1970.††

* * *

SMITH, Rodney P(ennell), Jr. 1930-

PERSONAL: Born February 27, 1930, in Magnolia, Ark.;

son of Rodney P. and Molly Ailene (Cobb) Smith; married Elaine Campbell; children: Melissa, Penn. *Education:* University of Arkansas, M.A., 1952; Yale University, Advanced Certificate in Large Systems Management, 1971; graduate study at Yale University and Florida State University, received Ph.D., 1971. *Home:* 5587 W. W. Kelly Rd., Tallahassee, Fla. 32301.

CAREER: University of Arkansas, Fayetteville, instructor in English, 1952; teacher and administrator in Arkansas public schools, 1953-58; teacher and principal in Florida public schools, 1959-63; Florida State Department of Education, Tallahassee, consultant on English, 1963-67, executive director of curriculum and instruction department, 1967-70, assistant bureau chief, 1970—. Teacher of humanities and head of department, Lake Sumter Junior College, 1961-63; visiting professor, Stetson University, 1961, 1962, and Florida Presbyterian College, 1963. Lecturer on tour in Britain, 1969. *Member:* National Council of Teachers of English, Institute for Educational Leadership, American Association of University Professors, American Association of School Administrators.

WRITINGS: Creativity in the English Program, National Council of Teachers of English, 1970; *Differentiated Staffing,* Prentice-Hall, 1972. Writer of a videotape series on psychology and governmental management. Former editor, *Elementary English.*

WORK IN PROGRESS: A book on teaching written composition in kindergarten through grade school, for Silver Burdette.

SIDELIGHTS: Rodney Smith, Jr. told *CA* that his "poetry has never been published. Instead [I have] focused on teaching writing in the public schools, creativity research, and input to the education bureaucracy of many large states."

*   *   *

SMITH, Samuel   1904-

PERSONAL: Born December 24, 1904, in Meretz, Lithuania; came to U.S. in 1906, naturalized in 1914; son of Louis (a merchant) and Lillian (Samuelson) Smith. *Education:* Attended Harvard University, 1921-24; New York University, B.S., M.A., Ph.D., 1933. *Politics:* Democrat. *Religion:* Hebrew. *Home address:* R.D. 1, Box 220, Monroe, N.Y. 10950.

CAREER: A. Smith & Bros., importers, New York City, partner, 1924-30; music teacher in New York, 1934-35; research assistant, New York State Board Regents Inquiry, 1937-38; Acorn Publishing Co., New York City, research director, 1939-41; superintendent, National Education Programs, 1941-43; editor, Dryden Press, 1944, Hinds, Hayden & Eldredge, 1945-49, both New York City; Barnes & Noble, Inc., New York City, editor-in-chief, 1950-69. *Member:* Phi Delta Kappa, Masons.

WRITINGS: (Editor with others) *An Outline of Educational Psychology,* Barnes & Noble, 1934, 6th edition, 1970; (with Robert K. Speer) *Supervision in the Elementary School,* Dryden, 1938; (with Arthur W. Littlefield and others) *Best Methods of Study: A Practical Guide for the Student,* Barnes & Noble, 1938, 2nd edition, published as *An Outline of Best Methods of Study,* 1951, 4th edition, published under original title, 1970; (with Speer and George R. Cressman) *Education and Society: An Introduction to Education for a Democracy,* Dryden, 1942; (editor with Bernard Joseph Stern) *Understanding the Russians: A Study of So-*

viet Life and Culture, Barnes & Noble, 1947; (with others) *Atlas of Human Anatomy,* 5th edition, edited by M. F. Ashley Montagu, Barnes & Noble, 1959, 6th edition, 1961; *Read it Right and Remember What You Read,* Barnes & Noble, 1970.

Research director and co-author of National Achievement Tests, 1939—; general editor of "College Outline" series and "Everyday Handbook" series, 1956—. Also editor of a series of biographies of educators published by Twayne.

WORK IN PROGRESS: A text based on the series of biographies of educators.

*   *   *

SMITH, Varrel Lavere   1925-

PERSONAL: Born July 4, 1925, in Tacoma, Wash.; son of Edwin U. (a farmer) and Amanda (Jensen) Smith; married Elaine Knutson (a teacher), March 17, 1950; children: Laraine, Barbara, Carol, Alan, Richard. *Education:* Pacific Lutheran University, B.A., 1950; University of Washington, Seattle, graduate courses.

CAREER: Elementary teacher in Puyallup, Wash., 1950-53; elementary and secondary teacher in Federal Way, Wash., 1955—. *Military service:* U.S. Navy, 1942-46; received Asiatic Pacific Medal with one battle star.

WRITINGS: Their Majesties and Other Folk, A. S. Barnes, 1970.

WORK IN PROGRESS: Research for a popular history of the French monarchy; a novel centering on a suburban county sheriff.

BIOGRAPHICAL/CRITICAL SOURCES: Christian Science Monitor, January 6, 1970.††

*   *   *

SMITH, Wesley E.   1938-

PERSONAL: Born April 2, 1938, in Chicago, Ill.; son of Edward L. and Frances (Yoder) Smith; married Primrose Clerie, May 28, 1965; children: Lisa, Konda. *Education:* Greenville College, Greenville, Ill., B.A., 1962.

CAREER: Full Life Crusade, St. John's, Mich., president, 1966—.

WRITINGS: Mission Impossible, Tyndale, 1969; *Gateway to Power,* Whitaker House, 1973. Also author of *The Jesus People.*

AVOCATIONAL INTERESTS: Photography (filmed and produced a travelogue on Haiti).†

*   *   *

SMITH, William I.   1932-

PERSONAL: Born September 13, 1932, in Denver, Colo.; son of Charles (a physician) and Ruth (McGrew) Smith. *Education:* University of Denver, A.B., 1955, M.A. (counseling and guidance), 1958, M.A. (librarianship), 1968. *Home:* 1640 Beeler St., Apt. 201, Aurora, Colo. 80010.

CAREER: Free-lance writer.

WRITINGS: Guidelines to Classroom Behavior, Book-Lab, 1970. Contributor to juvenile publications, mystery magazines, and education journals.

*   *   *

SMITHERS, Peter Henry Berry Otway   1913-

PERSONAL: Born December 9, 1913, in Moor Allerton,

Yorkshire, England; son of Harry O. (a lieutenant colonel, British Army, and justice of the peace) and Ethel (Berry) Smithers; married Dojean Sayman (an American), 1943; children: two daughters. *Education:* Magdalen College, Oxford, B.A. (first class honors), 1934, M.A., 1937, D.Phil., 1954. *Address:* CH-6911 Vico Morcote, Switzerland.

CAREER: Called to the Bar, Inner Temple, 1936, and joined Lincoln's Inn, 1937; rural district councillor, Winchester, England, 1946-49; Conservative member of Parliament for Winchester Division of Hampshire, 1950-64, with posts as Parliamentary Private Secretary, Colonial Office, 1951-59, United Kingdom delegate to United Nations General Assembly, 1960-62, and Parliamentary Under-Secretary of State, Foreign Office, 1962-64; Secretary General of Council of Europe, 1964-69; presently senior fellow of United Nations Institution for Teaching and Research. Chairman, Conservative Overseas Bureau, 1956-59; vice-president, European Assembly of Local Authorities, 1959-62. Chairman, British-Mexican Society, 1952-55. *Military service:* Royal Naval Volunteer Reserve, 1939-45; became lieutenant commander; served in Naval Intelligence Division of the Admiralty, as assistant naval attache at the British Embassy, Washington, D.C., and then as acting naval attache for Mexico, Central American republics, and Panama. *Member:* Carlton Club (London), Metropolitan Club (New York). *Awards, honors:* Chevalier de la Legion d'Honneur; Orden Mexicana del Aguila Azteca; Honorable Doctor of Jurisprudence, Zurich, 1969; Alexander von Humboldt gold medal, 1969; knighted by Queen Elizabeth, 1970.

WRITINGS: Life of Joseph Addison, Oxford University Press, 1954, 2nd edition, 1968.

*   *   *

SNAPE, R(ichard) H(al)   1936-

PERSONAL: Born December 9, 1936, in Melbourne, Australia; son of Richard (an accountant) and Hazel Elizabeth (Knapp) Snape; married Yvonne Claire Stewart, February 6, 1960; children: Richard Gordon, Fiona Claire, Matthew David. *Education:* University of Melbourne, B.Comm. (with honors), 1958; London School of Economics, Ph.D., 1962. *Office:* Department of Economics, Monash University, Melbourne, Victoria, Australia 3168.

CAREER: University of Melbourne, Melbourne, Victoria, Australia, tutor in economics, 1959-60; Monash University, Melbourne, Victoria, lecturer, 1962-65, senior lecturer, 1966-69, reader in economics, 1969-71, professor of economics, 1971—, chairman of department of economics, 1975—. Member of Priorities Review Staff, Government of Australia, 1973-74. *Member:* Economic Society of Australia and New Zealand. *Awards, honors:* Nuffield fellow, 1967-68.

WRITINGS: International Trade and the Australian Economy, Longmans, Green, 1969, 2nd edition, Longman, 1973; (editor with I. A. McDougall) *Studies in International Economics,* North-Holland Publishing, 1970. Contributor to *Economic Record, Oxford Economic Papers, Journal of Political Economy,* and *Economica.*

WORK IN PROGRESS: A study of the effects of taxes and subsidies on international trade.

*   *   *

SNIPES, Wilson Currin   1924-

PERSONAL: Born March 15, 1924, in Rocky Mount, N.C.;

son of Ralph Vincent (a master mechanic) and Annie May (Parham) Snipes; married Juanita Krentzman, August 28, 1950; children: Caroline Malcolm, Wilson Currin, Jr. *Education:* University of the South, B.A., 1948; Florida State University, M.A., 1950; Stanford University, graduate study, 1951-52; Vanderbilt University, Ph.D., 1957. *Office:* Department of English, Virginia Polytechnic Institute, 204 Williams Hall, Blacksburg, Va. 24061.

CAREER: Instructor in English at Admiral Farragut Academy, St. Petersburg, Fla., 1948-49, Delta State College, Cleveland, Miss., 1950-51, and University of Florida, Gainesville, 1954-57; Converse College, Spartanburg, S.C., professor of English, 1957-61, chairman of department, 1957-59, dean of College of Arts and Sciences, 1959-61; Mercer University, Macon, Ga., professor of English, 1961-66; Virginia Polytechnic Institute, Blacksburg, professor of English, 1966—, head of department, 1966-76. American Heritage Lecturer, 1963-64. Member of advisory board, Spartanburg Mental Health Clinic, 1960-61, and Museum of Arts and Sciences, Macon, 1965-66. Consultant to secondary school curriculum development in English, Kentucky and West Virginia, 1967-68. *Military service:* U.S. Naval Reserve, 1942—; active duty in Supply Corps, 1943-47; presently captain attached to Naval Reserve Unit.

MEMBER: Modern Language Association of America, National Council of Teachers of English, College English Association, Conference on College Composition and Communication, American Association of University Professors, Southern Humanities Conference (chairman of planning committee, 1970; chairman of Conference, 1971-72), South Atlantic Modern Language Association, North Carolina-Virginia Council of Teachers of English, Virginia Association of Teachers of English, Virginia Education Association, Virginia Humanities Conference (vice-president, 1970-71; president, 1971-72).

WRITINGS: (Editor) *Essays on Language,* Mercer University, 1962; *Writer and Audience: Forms of Non-Fiction Prose,* Holt, 1970. Writer of research reports for U.S. Navy. Contributor of articles to professional journals and poems to *Folio, Bitterroot, Maelstrom,* and other periodicals.

*   *   *

SNIVELY, W(illiam) D(aniel), Jr.   1911-

PERSONAL: Born February 9, 1911, in Rock Island, Ill.; son of William Daniel and Mary (Wills) Snively. *Education:* Augustana College, Rock Island, Ill., student, 1930-32; University of Illinois, A.B., 1934; Northwestern University, M.B., 1937, M.D., 1938. *Religion:* Roman Catholic. *Home address:* Rocky Glen Farm, R.R.1, Box 277, Evansville, Ind. 47712. *Office:* Department of Life Sciences, University of Evansville, Evansville, Ind. 47701.

CAREER: Cincinnati General Hospital, Cincinnati, Ohio, intern, 1937-38; Children's Memorial Hospital, Chicago, Ill., assistant resident, 1938-39; private practice of medicine in Rock Island, Ill., 1939-41; Mead Johnson & Co., Evansville, Ind., medical consultant, 1947-49, medical director, 1949-54, vice-president and medical director, 1954-60, executive vice-president, 1960-65, vice-president for medical affairs, 1965-66, vice-president for medical affairs, Mead Johnson International, 1967-68; Bristol-Meyers Co., International Division, Evansville, Ind., vice-president for medical information, 1968-69, consultant, 1969—; University of Evansville, Evansville, Ind., professor of life sciences, 1970—. Visiting professor, University of Alabama Medical Center. Member of staff of St. Mary's Hospital and Deaconess Hospital, both Evansville. Member of Indiana Governor's Commission on Medical Education. *Military service:* U.S. Navy and U.S. Marines, 1941-46; major portion of time was spent as flight surgeon with U.S. Marines; became commander, 1945.

MEMBER: American Medical Association, American College of Physicians (fellow; life member), American Medical Writers' Association (fellow; president, 1964-65; trustee, 1965—), Sociedad de Pediatria de El Salvador (honorary member), Sociedad Pediatrica del Centro (Mexico City; honorary member), Indiana Historical Society, Kentucky Historical Society, Illinois State Historical Society, Phi Beta Kappa, Sigma Xi, Filson Club (Louisville), Evansville Petroleum Club, Union League Club of Chicago.

AWARDS, HONORS: Billings Gold Medal, American Medical Association, 1956; Distinguished Service Award, American Medical Writers' Association, 1963; Ross Award, American Academy of General Practice, 1963, for one of two most significant articles published in *GP* in 1962; other awards for medical exhibits and medical writing.

WRITINGS: (With M. J. Sweeney) *Fluid Balance Handbook for Practitioners,* C. C Thomas, 1956; *Sea Within: The Story of Our Body Fluid,* Lippincott, 1960; (editor and contributor) *Body Fluid Disturbances,* Grune, 1962; (with Norma Metheny) *Nurse's Handbook of Fluid Balance,* Lippincott, 1967, 2nd edition, 1974; (with Louanna Furbee) *Satan's Ferryman: A True Tale of the Old Frontier,* Ungar, 1968; *The Patient and Fluid Balance* (text for nurses and technicians), Lippincott, 1969; (with Jan Thuerbach) *The Sea of Life,* McKay, 1969; (with Thuerbach) *Healing beyond Medicine,* Parker Publishing, 1972; (with D. R. Beshear) *Textbook of Pathophysiology,* Lippincott, 1972.

Contributor: Robert Turell, editor, *Diseases of the Colon and Anorectum,* two volumes, Saunders, 1959; Turell, editor, *The Surgical Clinics of North America,* Lippincott, 1960; Elmer W. Weber, editor, *Health and the School Child,* C. C Thomas, 1964; H. S. Shirkey, editor, *Pediatric Therapy,* Mosby, 1969; Charles Varga and others, *Handbook of Pediatric Medical Emergencies,* 4th edition (Snively was not associated with earlier editions), Mosby, 1968.

Monographs: *Pageantry of the English Language* (reprint of series running in eight editions of *Bulletin of the AMWA*), Mead Johnson Laboratories, 1964; *My Father,* Rose Valley Press, 1964; *Profile of a Manager: A Descriptive Approach* (booklet), Lippincott, 1965; *The Golden Mean,* National Research Bureau, 1968.

Contributor of more than eighty articles to journals and some lay magazines. Member of editorial advisory board, *Familiar Medical Quotations,* Little, Brown; member of medical advisory board, *Medical Group News;* member of editorial board, *Journal of the Indiana State Medical Association.*

AVOCATIONAL INTERESTS: Early American history, exploring, water sports.

BIOGRAPHICAL/CRITICAL SOURCES: Best Sellers, September 1, 1969.

*   *   *

SNODGRASS, Milton M(oore)   1931-

PERSONAL: Born July 9, 1931, in Linesville, Pa.; son of Clifford Marshall (a farmer) and Anna (Moore) Snodgrass; married Jean I. Seiders, June 9, 1951; children: Linda Jane, Ronald Duane. *Education:* Edinboro State College, student, 1948-49; Pennsylvania State University, B.S., 1951; Purdue

University, M.S., 1955, Ph.D., 1956. *Home:* 1984 Crescent Dr., Las Cruces, N.M. 88001. *Office:* Department of Agricultural Economics and Agricultural Business, New Mexico State University, Las Cruces, N.M. 88003.

CAREER: Purdue University, Lafayette, Ind., assistant professor, 1956-59, associate professor, 1959-64, professor of agriculture economics, 1964-67; California State Polytechnic University, Pomona, professor of international agriculture, chairman of department, and coordinator of overseas educational programs, 1969-72; New Mexico State University, Las Cruces, professor of agricultural economics and agricultural business, 1972—. Visiting professor, Kasetsart University, Bangkok, Thailand, 1964-65; campus administrator, U.S. Technical Assistance Program to Tanzania, East Africa, 1967-70. *Military service:* U.S. Air Force, 1951-53; became staff sergeant. *Member:* American Agricultural Economics Association, American Economic Association, International Association of Agricultural Economists, Association of U.S. University Directors of International Agricultural Programs, Sigma Xi.

WRITINGS—With L. T. Wallace: *Agriculture, Economics, and Growth,* Appleton, 1964, 2nd edition, 1970; *Agriculture, Economics, and Resource Management,* Prentice-Hall, 1975.

*   *   *

SNYDER, Cecil K., Jr.   1927-

PERSONAL: Born March 31, 1927, in Tyrone, Pa.; son of Cecil K. (a pipefitter) and Martha Flarence (Walls) Snyder; married Joyce Hildebrand (an elementary teacher), December 20, 1947; children: Cecil K. III, Arden, Justine. *Education:* Pennsylvania State University, B.A., 1950, M.A., 1961, Ph.D., 1968; Columbia University, M.A., 1950. *Politics:* Libertarian. *Religion:* No affiliation. *Home:* 20345 Stanford Ave., Riverside, Calif. 92507. *Agent:* Harold Matson Co., Inc., 22 East 40th St., New York, N.Y. 10016. *Office:* Department of English, California State Polytechnic University, Pomona, Calif. 91766.

CAREER: Nationwide Insurance Companies, claims adjuster in Columbus, Ohio, 1950-56; lecturer in English at Santa Ana College, Santa Ana, Calif., 1961-62, University of California, Riverside, 1962-69, and University of California, Los Angeles, 1964-66; California State Polytechnic University, Pomona, lecturer in English, 1968—. Writer. *Military service:* U.S. Army, 1945-46; became sergeant. *Awards, honors:* Spur Award of Western Writers of America for best first western novel of 1969, *Big with Vengeance.*

WRITINGS: Big with Vengeance, Ballantine, 1969.

WORK IN PROGRESS: Jackstraw, a novel; with son, Cecil K. Snyder III, a science fiction novel, *Mutiny on the Magellan.*

SIDELIGHTS: Cecil Snyder, Jr., writes: "There have been about forty million titles printed since Gutenberg pulled his first impression. A man reading a book per day seven days a week all through an adult life of sixty years could only read about 22 thousand titles, not even 1/1,000th of the total available. Yet we keep on writing books. Why? I'll be damned if I know. I think in my case it's the last refuge of the lone scoundrel. You may need a publisher. You may think you need an agent. But you don't need *anyone's* help in that little upstairs backroom of the mind where the dark act is done, where the thing, foul or fair, is made."

SNYDER, Eloise C(olleen) 1928-

PERSONAL: Legally adopted mother's maiden surname; born May 13, 1928, in Hazleton, Pa.; daughter of Michael J. (a policeman) and Mildred (Snyder) Bartos. *Education:* Lycoming College, B.A., 1952; Pennsylvania State University, M.A., 1953, Ph.D., 1956. *Politics:* Independent. *Religion:* Protestant. *Home:* 621 East Irwin Ave., State College, Pa. 16801. *Office:* Department of Sociology, Pennsylvania State University, University Park, Pa. 16802.

CAREER: Pennsylvania State University, University Park, part-time instructor in sociology and part-time researcher, 1955-56; Southern Illinois University, Carbondale, instructor, 1956-57, assistant professor, 1957-63, associate professor of sociology, 1963-67; University of South Carolina, Columbia, visiting professor of sociology, 1967-68; Columbia College, Columbia, S.C., professor of sociology, 1968-70; Pennsylvania State University, University Park, professor of sociology, 1970—. Special consultant to juvenile delinquency task force, South Carolina Governor's Commission on Crime, 1969-70, and to South Carolina Legislative Committee on Juvenile Delinquency, 1969-70. President of South Carolina Council on Family Relations, 1969-70. *Member:* American Sociological Association. *Awards, honors:* Fellowship of Inter-University Council on Social Gerontology, summer, 1959.

WRITINGS: (With Herman Lantz) *Marriage: An Examination of the Man Woman Relationship* and *Teacher's Manual,* Wiley, 1962, revised edition of both, 1969.

WORK IN PROGRESS: Research on jury decision-making and on deviant behavior; a book on women's studies.

*   *   *

SNYDERMAN, Reuven K. 1922-

PERSONAL: Born July 6, 1922, in Philadelphia, Pa.; son of Harry S. and Ann (Koss) Snyderman; married December 6, 1960; wife's name, Adrienne E.; children: (previous marriage) Peri, Lisa, Scott. *Education:* University of Pennsylvania, A.B., 1943, M.D., 1946. *Politics:* Nonpartisan. *Religion:* Jewish. *Home:* 24 Balcort Dr., Princeton, N.J. 08540. *Office:* 253 Witherspoon St., Princeton, N.J. 08540.

CAREER: Licensed to practice medicine in Pennsylvania, 1948, in New York State, 1954, and in New Jersey, 1973; certified by American Board of Plastic and Reconstructive Surgeons, 1957. Intern and resident at U.S. Naval hospitals, 1946-47, 1948-49; assistant resident in surgery, then resident or special fellow at hospitals in New York City, 1949-53; Sloan-Kettering Institute, New York City, assistant director of experimental surgery, 1954-56, assistant clinician, 1956—, head of experimental plastic surgery section, 1958-63, and of transplantation section, 1963—; Memorial Hospital, New York City, member of staff, 1954, associate attending surgeon in plastic and reconstructive surgery, 1967—; New York Hospital, New York City, member of staff, 1967—, associate attending surgeon, 1968—; Medical Center at Princeton, Department of Surgery, Section of Plastic and Reconstructive Surgery, Princeton, N.J., attending surgeon, 1973—; Raritan Valley Hospital, Greenbrook, N.J., chief of Division of Plastic Surgery, 1975—. Cornell University Medical College, instructor, 1954-61, clinical assistant professor, 1961-68, clinical associate professor of plastic surgery, 1968—; instructor in surgery, Columbia University, College of Physicians Surgeons, 1955-64; assistant clinical professor of surgery, New York University, School of Medicine, 1964-68; clinical professor of plastic surgery, College of Medicine and Dentistry of New Jersey Medical School,

Rutgers University, 1975—; physician and consultant in plastic surgery, Veterans Administration Hospital, Lyons, N.J., 1975—. Former attending or visiting surgeon at Bellevue Hospital, New York University Hospital, and other hospitals. *Military service:* U.S. Naval Reserve, 1942-67; active duty, 1942-45, 1946-49; retired as lieutenant, 1967.

MEMBER: American Medical Association, American Association of Plastic Surgeons (fellow), American Society of Plastic and Reconstructive Surgeons, Plastic Surgery Research Council, Webster Society of Plastic Surgery, Israel Association of Plastic Surgeons (honorary fellow), New York State Medical Society, New York Cancer Society, New York County Medical Society. *Awards, honors:* Award of Honor from New York Chapter of Hadassah, 1968.

WRITINGS: (Contributor) J. M. Converse, editor, *Reconstructive Plastic Surgery,* Saunders, 1964; (with Nancy Rosenberg) *New Parts for People: The Story of Medical Transplants* (teen book), Norton, 1969; (editor) *Symposium on Neoplastic and Reconstructive Problems of the Female Breast,* Volume VII, Mosby, 1973; (contributor) Stephen Gallager, editor, *Early Breast Cancer: Detection and Treatment,* Wiley, 1975; (contributor) *A Plastic Surgeon's Involvement in the Breast Tumor Problem,* Georg Thieme Verlag (Stuttgart), 1975; (contributor) Robert M. Goldwyn, editor, *Plastic and Reconstructive Surgery of the Breast,* Little, Brown, 1976. Contributor to medical journals, including *Journal of the American Medical Association, Plastic and Reconstructive Surgery, Transplantation Bulletin, Annals of the New York Academy of Sciences, Journal of the National Cancer Institute,* and *New York State Journal of Medicine.*

BIOGRAPHICAL/CRITICAL SOURCES: Saturday Review, June 28, 1969.

*   *   *

SOBILOFF, Hy(man J.) 1912-1970

December 16, 1912—August(?), 1970; American industrialist, film producer, poet, and philanthropist. Obituaries: *New York Times,* August 13, 1970.

*   *   *

SOBOLEV, Leonid (Sergeevich) 1898-1971

July 20, 1898—February 17, 1971; Russian novelist, essayist, and journalist. Obituaries: *Publishers' Weekly,* March 1, 1971.

*   *   *

SOLBERG, Gunard 1932-

PERSONAL: Born August 15, 1932, in Chicago, Ill.; son of Gunard Jensen (an inventor) and Olga (Olsen) Solberg; married Gloria West, March 21, 1951; married second wife, Kris Sikes, January 19, 1962; married third wife, Renee-Alexis Strong, May 1, 1976; children: (first marriage) Gunard Scott, Katla West; (second marriage) Signe Johanna; (third marriage) Amalia Janne. *Education:* University of Wisconsin, B.S., 1955; University of California, Berkeley, graduate study, 1957-59. *Address:* c/o Soladay, P.O. Box 384, San Anselmo, Calif. 94960. *Agent:* William Morris Agency, 1350 Ave. of the Americas, New York, N.Y. 10019.

CAREER: San Rafael School District, San Rafael, Calif., high school teacher of English, 1964-76; Singapore American School, Republic of Singapore, English teacher, 1976—.

WRITINGS: Shelia, Houghton, 1969. Also co-author of two film scripts.

WORK IN PROGRESS: A novel which explores the Wovoka ("Ghost Dance Messiah") legend.

SIDELIGHTS: Shelia was produced as a motion picture under the title "Honky" by Stonehenge Co.

* * *

SOLBERT, Romaine G. 1925-
(Ronni Solbert)

PERSONAL: Born September 7, 1925, in Washington, D.C.; daughter of Oscar N. and Elizabeth (Abernathy) Solbert. *Education:* Vassar College, B.A. (with honors), 1946; Cranbrook Academy of Art, M.F.A., 1948. *Home:* 29 South Main, Randolph, Vt. 05060. *Agent:* Marilyn E. Marlow, Curtis Brown Ltd., 575 Madison Ave., New York, N.Y. 10022.

CAREER: Painter, sculptor, and free-lance illustrator of children's books. Had a one-woman exhibition at Museum of Modern Art, New York, 1959; work has been shown in more than twenty group exhibitions, including the Corcoran Biennial and exhibitions at Detroit Institute of Arts, Rochester Memorial Art Gallery, and Corning Glass Center Museum. *Awards, honors:* Fulbright fellowship to India, 1952.

WRITINGS—Under name Ronni Solbert: (Editor with Jean Merrill and illustrator) Issa, *A Few Flies and I* (haiku), Pantheon, 1969; (author and illustrator) *32 Feet of Insides,* Pantheon, 1970; (author and photographer) *I Wrote My Name on the Wall,* Little, Brown, 1971; *The Song that Sings Itself,* Bobbs-Merrill, 1972.

Illustrator under name Ronni Solbert: Jean Merrill, *Henry, the Hand-Painted Mouse,* Coward, 1951; Jean Merrill, *The Woover,* Coward, 1952; Jean Merrill, *Boxes,* Coward, 1953; Jean Merrill, *The Tree House of Jimmy Domino,* Oxford University Press, 1955; Jean Merrill, *The Travels of Marco,* Knopf, 1956; Henry Chafetz, *The Lost Dream,* Knopf, 1956; Gwendolyn Brooks, *Bronzeville Boys and Girls,* Harper, 1957; Elizabeth Johnson, *The Little Knight,* Little, Brown, 1957; Jean Merrill, *A Song for Gar,* Whittlesey House, 1957; Elizabeth Low, *Mouse, Mouse, Go Out of My House,* Little, Brown, 1958; Henry Chafetz, *The Legend of Befana,* Houghton, 1958; Audrey McKim, *Andy and the Gopher,* Little, Brown, 1959; Aline Havard, *Run Away Home,* Lothrop, 1959; Jean Merrill and Eunice Holsaert, *Outer Space,* Henry Holt, 1959; Kay Boyle, *The Youngest Camel,* Harper, 1959.

Jean Merrill, *Blue's Broken Heart,* Whittlesey House, 1960; Jean Merrill, *Shan's Lucky Knife,* W. R. Scott, 1960; Jean Merrill, *Emily Emerson's Moon,* Little, Brown, 1960; Parvati Thampi, *Geeta and the Village School,* Doubleday, 1960; Marion Garthwaite, *Mario,* Doubleday, 1960; Elizabeth Johnson, *The Three-in-One-Prince,* Little, Brown, 1960; Elizabeth Low, *Snug in the Snow,* Little, Brown, 1963; Jean Merrill, *The Superlative Horse,* W. R. Scott, 1963; Jean Merrill, *High, Wide and Handsome,* W. R. Scott, 1964; Jean Merrill, *The Pushcart War,* W. R. Scott, 1964; *The Nile,* Garrard, 1964; Adele De Leeuw, *Indonesian Legends and Folk Tales,* Thomas Nelson, 1964; Henry Chafetz, *Thunderbird and Other Stories,* Pantheon, 1965; Mary Neville, *Woody and Me,* Pantheon, 1966; Virginia Haviland, *Told in Sweden,* Little, Brown, 1966; Jean Merrill, *The Elephant Who Liked to Smash Small Cars,* Pantheon, 1967; Jean Merrill, *Red Riding,* Pantheon, 1968; Jean

Merrill, *The Black Sheep,* Pantheon, 1969; Jean Merrill, *Mary, Come Running,* McCall, 1970; Giose Rimanelli and Paul Pinsleur, *Pictures Make Poems,* Pantheon, 1972; Mary Hohau, *Nuts to You and Nuts to Me,* Knopf, 1974; Salley Hovey Wriggins, *White Monkey King,* Pantheon, 1977.

* * *

SOLL, Ivan 1938-

PERSONAL: Born March 29, 1938, in Philadelphia, Pa.; son of Hyman and Betty (Pearlstein) Soll; married Sandra Levowitz (a graphicist, painter, and art teacher), June 14, 1964. *Education:* Princeton University, A.B., 1960, Ph.D., 1966; graduate study at Harvard University, 1960-61, and University of Munich, 1961-62. *Home:* 1711 Summit Ave., Madison, Wis. 53705. *Office:* 85 Bascom Hall, University of Wisconsin, Madison, Wis. 53706.

CAREER: University of Wisconsin—Madison, instructor, 1964-66, assistant professor, 1966-69, associate professor, 1969-73, professor of philosophy, 1973—. Reviewer of manuscripts for publishers, including Nijhoff, McGraw-Hill, Princeton University Press, and Cornell University Press. Lecturer on philosophy to numerous groups in North America, South America, and Europe. *Member:* American Philosophical Association, International Hegel Society, Institute for Research in the Humanities in Madison (fellow), Phi Beta Kappa. *Awards, honors:* Woodrow Wilson fellowship, 1960-61; Fulbright fellowship, 1961-62; research grants from University of Wisconsin graduate school, 1966, 1967, 1970, 1972, 1974, and 1976; American Council of Learned Societies travel grant, 1972; Counsel for European Studies travel grant, 1972; Spencer Foundation grant, 1973; National Endowment for the Humanities Younger Humanist grant, 1974.

WRITINGS: An Introduction to Hegel's Metaphysics, University of Chicago Press, 1969; (contributor) Robert C. Soloman, editor, *Nietsche,* Doubleday, 1973; (contributor) *Anais do VIII Congresso Interamericano de Filosofia,* Instituto Brasileiro de Filosofia (Sao Paulo), 1974. Also contributor to *World Book Encyclopedia,* 1967-70, and to *Das Hegel Jarbuch,* 1974. Contributor of articles on philosophy to periodicals, including *Philosophical Review, Journal of Philosophy,* and *New Republic.*

WORK IN PROGRESS: Reviews and articles on philosophy for publication in journals and anthologies.

* * *

SOLNICK, Bruce B. 1933-

PERSONAL: Born September 7, 1933, in New York, N.Y.; son of Morris and Rose (Sobin) Solnick; married Arlene Stroll (a teacher), December 26, 1959; children: Helene Laura. *Education:* New York University, A.B., 1954, A.M., 1955, Ph.D., 1960. *Home:* 60 Meadowland St., Delmar, N.Y. 12054. *Office:* Department of History, State University of New York at Albany, 1400 Washington Ave., Albany, N.Y. 12222.

CAREER: New York University, New York City, instructor in history, summers, 1957-59; Hunter College (now Hunter College of the City University of New York), New York City, instructor in history, 1959-61; State University of New York at Albany, assistant professor, 1961-64, associate professor of history, 1964—. Visiting summer professor, New York University, 1964, 1968; visiting professor, Union University, Union College, Schenectady, N.Y., 1970. *Member:* American Historical Association, Conference on

Latin American History, Society for the History of Discoveries, Latin American Studies Association, Instituto Historico e Geografico Brasileiro, Societe d'Histoire d'Outremer. *Awards, honors:* Postdoctoral fellow at John Carter Brown Library, Brown University, 1968.

WRITINGS: (Contributor) Ronald Hilton, editor, *The Movement Toward Latin American Unity,* Praeger, 1969; *The West Indies and Central America to 1898,* Knopf, 1970. Also contributor to *Revista do Instituto Historico e Geografico Brasileiro,* 1970. Executive editor, *Terrae Incognitae,* 1967—.

* * *

SOLOMON, Margaret C(laire) 1918-

PERSONAL: Born November 27, 1918, in Enid, Okla.; daughter of David H. M. (a Presbyterian minister) and Candace (Morrison) Boyle; married Marland R. Solomon, December 30, 1949 (divorced); children: Stephen, Stuart. *Education:* San Diego State College (now University), student, 1956-58; University of Hawaii, B.A., 1960; University of California Berkeley, M.A., 1961; Claremont Graduate School, Ph.D., 1967. *Politics:* Liberal Democrat. *Religion:* "Protestant Agnostic." *Home:* 212 Hawaii Loa St., Honolulu, Hawaii 96821. *Office:* English Department, University of Hawaii, Honolulu, Hawaii 96822.

CAREER: Worked as income tax consultant in Los Angeles, Calif., 1945-46, and in finance department, U.S. Navy, Kodiak, Alaska, 1950-51; Bill Jack Scientific Instrument Co., Solana Beach, Calif., cost accountant, 1953-56; freelance writer in San Diego, Calif., and Honolulu, Hawaii, 1957-59; Pacific and Asian Affairs Council, Honolulu, Hawaii, administrative assistant, 1959-60; University of Hawaii, Honolulu, instructor in English, 1961-64; La Verne College, La Verne, Calif., instructor in English, 1965; University of Hawaii, assistant professor, 1966-69, associate professor, 1969-74, professor of English, 1974—. Participant at five James Joyce International Symposia, Dublin, Trieste, Paris, 1967, 1969, 1971, 1973, 1975. Senior guest lecturer, St. Peter's College, Oxford, England, 1971. Working guest at Yaddo (artist's retreat), 1975. Drug clinic volunteer, Waikiki Ministry, 1968-69. *Member:* Modern Language Association of America, James Joyce Foundation (trustee), American Association of University Professors, National Education Association. *Awards, honors:* Woodrow Wilson fellow, 1960-61; University of Hawaii Foundation travel awards, 1967, 1969, American Council of Learned Societies travel award, 1975.

WRITINGS: Eternal Geomater: The Sexual Universe of Finnegans Wake, Southern Illinois University Press, 1969.

Contributor: Maurice Harmon, editor, *The Celtic Master,* Dolmen Press (Dublin), 1969; Louis Bonnerot, editor, *Ulysses: Cinquante Ans Apres,* Editions Didiers (Paris), 1974; Michael Bengal and Fritz Senn, editors, *A Conceptual Guide to Finnegan's Wake,* Pennsylvania State University Press, 1974; John Unterecker and Kathleen McGrony, editors, *Yeats, Joyce, and Beckett,* Bucknell University Press, 1976. Contributor to academic journals.

WORK IN PROGRESS: A book entitled, *The Nature of the Creative Process.*

SIDELIGHTS: Margaret Solomon wrote to *CA:* "Good literary criticism is always creative. A creative critic cannot be, and should not pretend to be, absolutely objective. His/her 'truth' is colored by a very personal reading, and that reading ought to acknowledge the critic's own creative

unconscious. Creative criticism involves pain, similar to that of the artist himself, in that the critic is re-creating his/her self in the process of discovering the development or disintegration of the artist's self through the artist's *corpus.* One begins to know intimately the artist in the works—a person who may resemble very little the writer others know biographically. A creative critic soon learns that the sources of art are in that part of early childhood that is unremembered in rational consciousness; they are pre-linguistic, a condition preceding discourse. These sources are always in tension—in dynamic conflict—with the writer's words."

AVOCATIONAL INTERESTS: Acting in university and community theaters.

BIOGRAPHICAL/CRITICAL SOURCES: Virginia Quarterly Review, summer, 1970; *James Joyce Quarterly,* summer, 1970; *Modern Fiction Studies,* summer, 1970; *A Wake Newslitter,* June, 1970; *West Coast Review,* October, 1970; *Language and Literature,* January, 1971.

* * *

SOMERVILLE, Mollie

PERSONAL: Born in New York, N.Y.; divorced; children: Richard C. J., Margaret Ann S. Fernandez. *Education:* Attended Cornell University and Columbia University. *Residence:* 1414 Seventeenth St. N.W., Washington, D.C. 20036.

CAREER: Participant, Conference on Women in the Era of the American Revolution, George Washington University, 1975; lecturer to student groups, patriotic and hereditary societies, and organizations related to American history. *Member:* Authors Guild, National League of American Pen Women (Alexandria branch), Association for the Preservation of Virginia Antiquities, Manuscript Society (Washington, D.C. branch).

WRITINGS: Alexandria, Virginia: George Washington's Home Town (guidebook), Newell-Cole, 1966; *Washington Walked Here: Alexandria on the Potomac,* Acropolis Books, 1970; (contributor) *Alexandria: A Composite History,* Volume I, Alexandria Bicentennial Commission, 1975. Also author of *Women and the American Revolution,* 1974. Contributor to periodicals, including *DAR Magazine.*

WORK IN PROGRESS: A survey of historical buildings owned by the National Society, Daughters of the American Revolution, 1890 to the present.

* * *

SOMMER, John 1941-

PERSONAL: Born August 26, 1941, in New York, N.Y.; son of Richard L. and Margaret N. Sommer; married Wendy Solmssen, January 24, 1970. *Education:* Wesleyan University, Middletown, Conn., B.A., 1963; Johns Hopkins University School of Advanced International Studies, M.A., 1968. *Home:* 2941 Macomb St. N.W., Washington, D.C. 20008. *Office:* Overseas Development Council, 1717 Massachusetts Ave. N.W., Washington D.C. 20036.

CAREER: International Voluntary Services, working on education program and as team leader in Vietnam, 1963-67; consultant to U.S. Senate Judiciary Subcommittee on Refugees, lecturer for U.S. Information Service and U.S. Foreign Service Institute, and escort-interpreter for U.S. Department of State, Washington, D.C., during 1966-68; newsletter editor for United Methodist Church, Washington, D.C., 1968; Ford Foundation, New York, N.Y., training associate in Asia Program, 1969, assistant representative for India, Sri Lanka, and Nepal, New Delhi, India, 1970-75; Overseas Development Council, Washington, D.C., fellow, 1975—.

WRITINGS: (With Don Luce) *Viet Nam: The Unheard Voices,* foreword by Edward M. Kennedy, Cornell University Press, 1969; *U.S. Voluntary Aid to the Third World: What Is Its Future,* Overseas Development Council, 1975. Contributor of articles to *Newark News,* Newark, N.J., 1963-67, *Saturday Review,* 1969, and to other publications.

WORK IN PROGRESS: The Rich, the Poor, and American Philanthropy; and another book on U.S. aid to the Third World.

BIOGRAPHICAL/CRITICAL SOURCES: Saturday Review, June 28, 1969; *New York Times Book Review,* July 20, 1969; *New York Times,* October 10, 1969.

*   *   *

SONENBLUM, Sidney   1924-

PERSONAL: Born December 2, 1924, in Vienna, Austria; son of Morris (a businessman) and Anna (Zuckerman) Sonenblum. *Education:* New York University, B.A., 1948; Columbia University, M.A., 1951, Ph.D., 1954. *Religion:* Jewish. *Office:* Sidney Sonenblum, Consultants, 494 Tuallitan Rd., Los Angeles, Calif. 90049.

CAREER: U.S. Government, Washington, D.C., economist, 1951-54; National Planning Association, Washington, D.C., economist, 1955-69; University of California, Los Angeles, economist, 1969-77; Sidney Sonenblum, Consultants, Los Angeles, economic consultant, 1977—. *Military service:* U.S. Army, 1942-45. *Member:* American Economic Association, American Statistical Association, Regional Science Association.

WRITINGS: Local Impact of Foreign Trade, National Planning Association, 1960; (with Werner Svi Hirsch) *Selecting Regional Information for Government Planning and Decision-Making,* Praeger, 1970; *Governing Urban America in the 1970s,* Praeger, 1972; *Local Government Program Budgeting,* Praeger, 1974; *How Cities Provide Services,* Ballinger, 1977. Contributor to professional journals.

WORK IN PROGRESS: Energy and Economic Growth; research on economic development, energy, and public economics.

SIDELIGHTS: Sidney Sonenblum told *CA:* "After a number of years of writing to a technical and research oriented audience, I have decided to change direction. I am now seeking to apply my research and am writing to those in government and the private sector who implement programs and decide policy."

*   *   *

SONSTROEM, David   1936-

PERSONAL: Born April 11, 1936, in Bristol, Conn.; son of Arthur M. and Lillian (Meyer) Sonstroem; married Anne McKinnon (a clinical psychologist), June 13, 1964; children: Eric, Sara. *Education:* Amherst College, A.B., 1958; Harvard University, M.A., 1959, Ph.D., 1965. *Home:* 247 Codfish Falls Rd., Storrs, Conn. 06268. *Office:* Department of English, University of Connecticut, Storrs, Conn. 06268.

CAREER: University of Connecticut, Storrs, assistant professor, 1965-68, associate professor of English, 1969—.

WRITINGS: Rossetti and the Fair Lady, Wesleyan University Press, 1970. Contributor to *North American Review, Victorian Studies, Midwest Quarterly, Modern Language Quarterly, Victorian Poetry, PMLA, Victorian Newsletter,* and others.

*   *   *

SOULE, George (Henry, Jr.)   1887-1970

June 11, 1887—April 14, 1970; American economist, editor, and labor authority. Obituaries: *New York Times,* April 15, 1970; *Time,* April 27, 1970; *Antiquarian Bookman,* May 4-11, 1970; *Current Biography,* 1970. (See index for *CA* sketch)

*   *   *

SPACH, John Thom   1928-

PERSONAL: Born March 5, 1928, in Winston-Salem, N.C.; son of William Mathias (a furniture manufacturer) and Evelyn (Thom) Spach. *Education:* United States Military Academy, West Point, N.Y., cadet, 1947-49; Duke University, B.A., 1955. *Address:* P.O. Box 2503, Winston-Salem, N.C. 27102. *Agent:* James Oliver Brown, James Brown Associates, Inc., 22 East 60th St., New York, N.Y. 10022.

CAREER: Employed in sales or advertising, 1955—; formerly with Proctor & Gamble, *Furniture South,* and Alderman's, High Point, N.C.; South Carolina sales manager of Hunter Publishing Co., Winston-Salem, N.C., beginning 1968; managing editor, *Sports Digest of North Carolina,* Winston-Salem, 1973—. *Military service:* U.S. Army, Counter-Intelligence Corps, 1951-53.

WRITINGS: Time Out from Texas (novel), Blair, 1970.†

*   *   *

SPACHE, Evelyn B(ispham)   1929-

PERSONAL: Born August 15, 1929, in Sarasota, Fla.; married Charles Schoonover, 1951; married second husband, George D. Spache, October 29, 1967; children: (first marriage) Raymond, Margo. *Education:* Florida Southern College, B.S., 1951; University of Florida, M.A., 1959. *Religion:* Presbyterian. *Home:* 4163 Shell Rd., Sarasota, Fla. 33581. *Office:* University of South Florida, Tampa, Fla. 33620.

CAREER: Teacher in public schools of Sarasota, Fla., 1951-53, 1956-63; Wee Wisdom Nursery School, Gainesville, Fla., director, 1954-56; Florida Southern College, Lakeland, assistant professor of education, 1963-65; Jacksonville University, Jacksonville, Fla., assistant professor of education, 1965-70; University of South Florida, Tampa, professor of reading, 1972—. Secretary and treasurer, Spache Educational Consultants, Inc., 1973—. Consultant to School of Education, Johannesburg, South Africa, 1966; instructor at Provincial Summer School, Halifax, Nova Scotia, 1969. *Member:* Association for Childhood Education International, International Reading Association, National Reading Conference, Florida Reading Council, Delta Kappa Gamma.

WRITINGS: (With husband, George D. Spache) *Reading in the Elementary School,* 2nd edition (Evelyn Spache was not associated with the first edition), Allyn & Bacon, 1969, 4th edition, 1977; *Reading Activities for Child Involvement,* Allyn & Bacon, 1972, 2nd edition, 1976; *Concepts and Inquiry: Vocabulary Building Exercises,* Allyn & Bacon, 1975; (with Robert Ruddell) "Pathfinder" series, Allyn & Bacon, 1977. Also author of *Puzzlers to Teach Phonics,* and *Puzzlers to Teach Vocabulary Books,* Instructor Publications, 1976.

SPACKS, Barry 1931-

PERSONAL: Born February 21, 1931, in Philadelphia, Pa.; son of Charles (a merchant) and Evelyn (Schindler) Spacks; married Patricia Meyer (a teacher and writer), June 10, 1955; children: Judith. *Education:* University of Pennsylvania, B.A., 1952; Indiana University, M.A., 1956; Cambridge University, additional study, 1956-57. *Politics:* "Humane." *Religion:* "Same as politics." *Home:* 16 Abbott St., Wellesley, Mass. *Office:* Massachusetts Institute of Technology, Massachusetts Ave., Cambridge, Mass. 02139.

CAREER: University of Florida, Gainesville, assistant professor, 1957-59; Massachusetts Institute of Technology, Cambridge, professor of literature, 1960—. *Military service:* U.S. Army, Signal Corps, 1952-54. *Awards, honors:* St. Botolph's Arts Award, 1971, for fiction and poetry.

WRITINGS: The Sophomore (novel), Prentice-Hall, 1968; *The Company of Children* (poems), Doubleday, 1969; *Orphans* (novel), Harper Magazine Press, 1972; *Something Human* (poems), Harper Magazine Press, 1972; *Teaching the Penguins to Fly* (poems), David R. Godine, 1975. Contributor to *Hudson Review, New Yorker, Poetry, Atlantic Monthly,* and other magazines.

WORK IN PROGRESS: A collection of poems, entitled *Like a Prism;* a novel, *The Only Poet.*

SIDELIGHTS: "Spacks is going to make a place for himself," said Miller Williams, and, with both a successful volume of poems and a well-received novel, it would seem that he is well on his way. "No synopsis [of *The Sophomore*] can do justice to Spack's technical skill and comic inventiveness," H. S. Resnick wrote. "Spacks . . . [can] run the gamut of style, from put-on to Existentialist drama to pathos, without being inconsistent. This is characteristic of the growing number of writers who attempt to touch the heart of reality by calling attention to their own artifice, but Spacks is more successful than most."

Williams called *The Company of Children* "one of the best first collections of poetry to come off the presses in a long while." Spack's book, he writes, "has all the qualities that have characterized the finest poetry of any culture at any time—it creates a fragile illusion of conversational speech; it builds around a recognizable and imaginable situation. The poet obviously cares about the world he lives with and has touched it." Spacks is unafraid of meaning, Williams concludes, "not embarrassed to be moved by the world and does not hide from it behind the transparent masks of obscurantism, abstractionism, and new directionism."

Marie Borroff, writes of a later collection of Barry Spacks poetry, *Something Human,* "There is a recurrent humor, always rooted in affection. . . . The basic mood is hopeful, lighthearted; poems end in easings of tension, outward motions of release . . . we see literal event modulate effortlessly into myth."

BIOGRAPHICAL/CRITICAL SOURCES: Saturday Review, March 9, 1968, June 14, 1969; *Observer Review,* February 16, 1969; *Spectator,* February 21, 1969; *Virginia Quarterly Review,* summer, 1969; *Yale Review,* autumn, 1972.

* * *

SPANGENBERG, Judith Dunn 1942-
(Judy Dunn)

PERSONAL: Born October 6, 1942, in New Jersey; daughter of T. C. Tristram and Phoebe (a photographer; maiden name, Pierson) Dunn; married Thomas Craig Spangenberg (an advertising executive), December 18, 1965; children: Tyler Craig. *Education:* Sweet Briar College, B.S., 1964. *Religion:* Protestant. *Home:* 129 R.D. 2, New Canaan, Conn. 06840.

CAREER: J. C. Penny Co., New York City, copywriter, 1964-65; Ogilvy & Mather Advertising Agency, New York City, editor of house organ, 1966-67.

WRITINGS—Juvenile books under name Judy Dunn: *Things,* Doubleday, 1968; *Feelings,* Creative Educational Society, 1971; *Having Fun,* Creative Educational Society, 1971; *Animal Friends,* Creative Educational Society, 1971; *Friends,* Creative Educational Society, 1971; *Our Time Is Now* (poetry) Hallmark, 1973; *The Little Duck,* Random House, 1976. Poems were published in a number of journals, 1961-66.

* * *

SPATZ, Jonas 1935-

PERSONAL: Born September 2, 1935, in Brooklyn, N.Y.; son of Simon and Anna (Stahl) Spatz; married Lois Settler (an associate professor of classics), June 10, 1962. *Education:* Brooklyn College (now Brooklyn College of the City University of New York), B.A., 1958; New York University, M.A., 1960; Indiana University, Ph.D., (with honors), 1964. *Home:* 5426 Holmes, Kansas City, Mo. 64110. *Office:* Department of English, University of Missouri, Kansas City, Mo. 64110.

CAREER: Brooklyn College of the City University of New York, Brooklyn, N.Y., instructor in English, 1964-66; University of Missouri—Kansas City, assistant professor, 1966-69, associate professor of English, 1969—. *Military service:* U.S. Air Force, active duty, 1959, active reserve, 1959-65. *Member:* Modern Language Association of America.

WRITINGS: Hollywood in Fiction: Some Versions of the American Myth, Humanities, 1969, revised edition, 1970.

Contributor; all published by Everett Edwards: Warren Graham French, editor, *The Thirties: Fiction, Poetry, and Drama,* 1967; French, editor, *The Forties: Fiction, Poetry, and Drama,* 1969; French, editor, *The Twenties: Fiction, Poetry, Drama,* 1975. Also contributor to *Texas Studies in Language and Literature,* 1974.

WORK IN PROGRESS: An essay on Sinclair Lewis' *Arrowsmith;* Mary Shelley's *Frankenstein;* and a book on unconscious motivation in nineteenth century literature.

* * *

SPEAIGHT, George Victor 1914-

PERSONAL: Surname is pronounced Spate; born September 6, 1914, in Bishop's Hatfield, England; son of Frederick William and Emily (Elliot) Speaight; married Mary Mudd (schools officer of London Museum), 1946; children: Anthony Hugh, Margaret Isabella Mary. *Education:* Attended Haileybury and Imperial Service College. *Politics:* "Radical conservative liberal." *Religion:* "Progressive Roman Catholic." *Home:* 6 Maze Rd., Kew Gardens, Richmond, Surrey, England.

CAREER: George Rainbird Ltd. (publishers), London, England, editorial director. *Member:* British Puppet and Model Theatre Guild (vice-president), Union Internationale de la Marionette (member of honor), Society for Theatre Research (chairman), International Federation for Theatre Research.

WRITINGS: Juvenile Drama: The History of the English Toy Theatre, Macdonald & Co., 1946, revised and enlarged edition published as *The History of the English Toy Theatre,* Plays, Inc., 1969; *The History of the English Puppet Theatre,* De Graff, 1955, revised edition published as *Punch and Judy: A History,* Plays, Inc., 1970; (editor) *The Memoirs of Charles Dibdin the Younger,* Society for Theatre Research, 1956; (editor) *Bawdy Songs of the Early Music Hall,* David & Charles, 1975.

BIOGRAPHICAL/CRITICAL SOURCES: Spectator, April 18, 1969; *Punch,* July 1, 1970.

* * *

SPEARS, Jack 1919-

PERSONAL: Born December 23, 1919, in Fort Smith, Ark.; son of Clifford G. (an accountant) and Josephine (Ferguson) Spears; married Helen Jeanne Jackson (a realtor), May 14, 1942; children: Jack, Jr., Richard Thomas. *Education:* University of Arkansas, B.S. (with honors), 1941. *Politics:* Republican. *Religion:* Methodist. *Home:* 6208 South Utica, Tulsa, Okla. 74136. *Office:* Tulsa County Medical Society, 750 Utica Square Medical Center, Tulsa, Okla. 74114.

CAREER: Tulsa County Medical Society, Tulsa, Okla., executive director, 1941—. *Member:* American Cancer Society (former member of board of directors of Tulsa County Unit), American Association of Medical Society Executives (former member of board of directors), Tulsa County Public Health Nursing Association, Tulsa-Lakes Area Tuberculosis and Health Association, Tulsa Press Club.

WRITINGS: Hollywood: The Golden Era, A. S. Barnes, 1971; *The Civil War on the Screen and Other Essays,* A. S. Barnes, 1976. Contributor to *Films in Review.*

WORK IN PROGRESS: An untitled book on the social history of the films of the twenties.

AVOCATIONAL INTERESTS: Collecting motion picture memorabilia, including old silent films, rare books and magazines, and stills.

* * *

SPECHT, Ernst Konrad 1926-

PERSONAL: Born February 16, 1926, in Altenkirchen, Germany; son of Arnold and Kate (Stock) Specht; married Ingrid Juergensen, 1962. *Education:* Educated at Universities of Bonn, Koeln, and Goettingen, 1946-52, and Oxford University, 1952-53. *Office:* University of Bonn, Bonn, Germany.

CAREER: University of Bonn, Bonn, Germany, docent in philosophy, 1961—. *Member:* Deutsche Psychoanalytische Vereinigung.

WRITINGS: Der Analogiebegriff bei Kant und Hegel, Koelner Universitats-Verlag, 1952; *Die Sprachphilosophischen und ontologischen Grundlagen im Spaetwerk Ludwig Wittgensteins,* Koelner Universitats-Verlag, 1963, translation by D. E. Walford published as *The Foundations of Wittgenstein's Late Philosophy,* Barnes & Noble, 1969; (editor with Ingeborg Heidemann and Manfred Kleinschneider) *Einheit und Sein: Gottfried Martin zum 65* (philosophy addresses and lectures), Koelner Universitats-Verlag, 1966; *Sprache und Sein: Untersuchungen zur sprachanalytischen Grundlegung der Ontologie,* de Gruyter, 1967.

WORK IN PROGRESS: Research on Wittgenstein and on psychoanalysis and philosophy.†

SPECTOR, Jack J. 1925-

PERSONAL: Born October 2, 1925, in Bayonne, N.J.; son of Abraham (in insurance business) and Sarah (Hartstein) Spector; married Helga Gisela Dolezal, August 2, 1962; children: Robert Mark, Elisabeth, Erik Andrew. *Education:* City College (now City College of the City University of New York), B.S., 1956; Columbia University, M.A., 1959, Ph.D., 1964. *Home:* 28 Spring St., Somerset, N.J. 08873. *Office:* Department of Art, Rutgers University, New Brunswick, N.J. 08903.

CAREER: Teacher of art in junior and senior high schools in New York, N.Y., 1956-59; Rutgers University, New Brunswick, N.J., instructor, 1962-64, assistant professor, 1965-67, associate professor, 1967-71, professor of art history, 1972—, director of junior year in France program, 1971-73. *Member:* College Art Association, American Association of University Professors, Phi Beta Kappa. *Awards, honors:* Fulbright fellow in Paris, 1968; American Council of Learned Societies grant, 1969.

WRITINGS: The Murals of Eugene Delacroix at Saint-Sulpice, College Art Association, 1967; *The Aesthetics of Freud,* Praeger, 1972; *Delacroix's Death of Sardanapalus,* Penguin, 1974. Contributor to art journals.

WORK IN PROGRESS: A textbook on twentieth-century art; research on the death of Marat; further research on Delacroix, Freud, and Magritte.

* * *

SPENCER, Ann 1918-

PERSONAL: Born June 13, 1918, in New Hope, Pa.; daughter of Robert Carpenter (an artist) and Margaret (an architect; maiden name Fulton) Spencer; married Louis Simon (a teacher and writer), October 26, 1946. *Education:* Studied at Ecole Sevigne, Paris, 1932-33, Holmquist School, New Hope, Pa., 1934-35, and at Art Student's League, New York, N.Y., 1936-38. *Politics:* Democrat. *Religion:* Protestant. *Home:* 4550 West Speedway, Tucson, Ariz. 85705. *Agent:* Diarmuid Russell, Russell & Volkening, Inc., 551 Fifth Ave., New York, N.Y. 10017.

CAREER: Artist in New York City, until 1956, and in Tucson, Ariz., 1956—. Has exhibited with Associated American Artists in New York City, at Santa Barbara Art Museum, and at Rosequist Galleries, Tucson.

WRITINGS—Self-illustrated: The Cat Who Tasted Cinnamon Toast, Knopf, 1969.

* * *

SPENCER, Warren F(rank) 1923-

PERSONAL: Born January 27, 1923, in Swan Quarter, N.C.; son of Carroll B. (a lawyer) and Lucille (Mann) Spencer; married Elizabeth Toth (an artist), September 7, 1947; children: Lucille Mann, Carroll B. *Education:* Attended University of Florida, 1942-43; Georgetown University, B.S.S. (cum laude), 1947; University of Pennsylvania, M.A., 1949, Ph.D., 1955. *Politics:* Democrat. *Religion:* Episcopalian. *Home:* 290 Fortson Dr., Athens, Ga. 30601. *Office:* Department of History, University of Georgia, Athens, Ga. 30601.

CAREER: Salem College, Winston-Salem, N.C., instructor, 1950-54, assistant professor of history, 1954-56; Old Dominion College (now University), Norfolk, Va., assistant professor, 1956-57, associate professor, 1957-61, professor of history, 1962-67, chairman of department, 1961-62, 1963-

67, chairman of Division of Social Studies, 1962-63; University of Georgia, Athens, professor of French history, 1967—. Visiting scholar, Duke University, summer, 1952. *Military service:* U.S. Army, 1943-45; served in North Africa, Italy, and Austria; received four battle stars. U.S. Air Force Reserve, 1949—; present rank, major. *Member:* Society for French Historical Studies, American Historical Association, Southern Historical Association (program chairman, European history section, 1970), Phi Alpha Theta. *Awards, honors:* American Philosophical Society grants, 1958, 1970, 1975; Old Dominion College, Outstanding Faculty Award, 1961-62, and Outstanding Honors Professor Award, 1977.

WRITINGS: (With Lynn M. Case) *The United States and France: Civil War Diplomacy,* University of Pennsylvania Press, 1970; (contributor) Nancy Nichols Barker and Marvin Brown, editors, *Diplomacy in an Age of Nationalism: Essays in Honor of Lynn Marshall Case,* Nijhoff, 1971. Contributor to *Revue d'Histoire diplomatique* and regional history journals.

WORK IN PROGRESS: Writing *Confederate Navy in Europe,* publication by University of Georgia Press; and doing research for a full-scale biography of Edouard Drouyn de Lhuys, French foreign minister and diplomat.

* * *

SPINELLI, Marcos 1904-1970

1904—May 18, 1970; Brazilian-born American novelist and short story writer. Obituaries: *New York Times,* May 20, 1970; *Antiquarian Bookman,* June 1-8, 1970; *Publishers' Weekly,* June 29, 1970; *Books Abroad,* spring, 1971.

* * *

SPINNEY, J(ohn) D(avid) 1912-
(David Spinney)

PERSONAL: Born October 23, 1912, in Fareham, England; son of Eugene and Hilda (Ramsay) Spinney. *Education:* Christ's College, Cambridge, M.A. (honors), 1934. *Religion:* Church of England. *Home:* The Old Cottage, Iwerne Minster, Blandford, Dorsetshire, England.

CAREER: Claysmore School, Iwerne Minster, Blandford, England, senior history master, 1935—. *Military service:* Royal Naval Volunteer Reserve, 1940-45. *Member:* Society for Nautical Research (council member), Royal Naval Volunteer Reserve Officer's Association.

WRITINGS—Under name David Spinney: *Rodney* (biography), Allen & Unwin, 1969, U.S. Naval Institute, 1970. Contributor under name J. D. Spinney to *Blackwood's Magazine* and *Mariner's Mirror.*

BIOGRAPHICAL/CRITICAL SOURCES: Spectator, October 11, 1969.

* * *

SPINRAD, William 1917-

PERSONAL: Born August 13, 1917, in New York, N.Y.; son of Max (a garment worker) and Esther (Lax) Spinrad; married Leah Babitz (a teacher), December 23, 1953 (deceased); children: Mark, Pauline. *Education:* City College (now City College of the City University of New York), New York, N.Y., B.S.S., 1941; Columbia University, M.A., 1950, Ph.D., 1955. *Home:* 48 McLoughlin St., Glen Cove, N.Y. *Office:* Department of Sociology, Adelphi University, Garden City, N.Y. 11530.

CAREER: Queens College (now Queens College of the City University of New York), Flushing, N.Y., instructor in criminology, 1952; Hofstra University, Hempstead, N.Y., instructor in sociology, 1954-55; Rutgers University, New Brunswick, N.J., began as instructor, became assistant professor of sociology, 1955-61, teaching at College of Arts and Sciences, Newark, 1955-58, and at University College, New Brunswick, 1956-61; Paterson State College (now The William Paterson College of New Jersey), Wayne, N.J., associate professor of social science, 1959-65; Adelphi University, Garden City, N.Y., professor of sociology, 1965—. Also taught at New York University, spring, 1957, Brooklyn College of the City University of New York, summers, 1960-62, City College of the City University of New York, evening classes, 1962-64, School of Industrial and Labor Relations, Cornell University, fall, 1972, and John Jay College of Criminal Justice of the City University of New York, fall, 1973. *Military service:* U.S. Army, 1942-45. *Member:* American Sociological Association, American Association of University Professors, American Civil Liberties Union, American Federation of Teachers, American Association for Public Opinion Research, Society for the Study of Social Problems, Eastern Sociological Society.

WRITINGS: Civil Liberties, Quadrangle, 1970.

Contributor: *Blue Collar World,* Prentice-Hall, 1964; William Glaser and David Sills, editors, *Government of Associations: Selections from the Behavioral Sciences,* Bedminster, 1966; Reinhard Bendix and Seymour M. Lipset, editors, *Class, Status, and Power,* 2nd edition, Free Press, 1966; Robert Gutman and David Popenoe, editors, *Neighborhood, City, and Metropolis,* Random House, 1970; Baidya N. Varma, editor, *The New Social Sciences,* Greenwood Press, 1976; Rhoda L. Goldstein and W. V. Roye, editors, *Interracial Bonds,* Emerson Hall, in press. Also contributor to *Sociology of Sport: A Contemporary Anthology,* edited by James H. Humphrey, Appleton. Contributor of articles and reviews to sociology journals.

WORK IN PROGRESS: A book on public opinion.

BIOGRAPHICAL/CRITICAL SOURCES: Christian Century, October 7, 1970.

* * *

SPOELSTRA, Nyle (Ray) 1939-

PERSONAL: Born October 12, 1939, in Fairplay, Colo.; son of Lyle W. (a teacher) and E. Marie (Hughes) Spoelstra; married Betsy E. Boesel, June 21, 1963. *Education:* Southern Methodist University, student, 1957-59; University of Colorado, B.A., 1961; University of Wisconsin, Ph.D., 1969. *Office:* Department of Economics, Indiana University, Bloomington, Ind. 47405.

CAREER: Indiana University, Bloomington, Ind., assistant professor of economics, 1968—. Midwest Universities Consortium for International Activities adviser to National Institute of Development Administration, Bangkok, Thailand.

WRITINGS: (Editor with Joseph Theodore Morgan and contributor) *Economic Interdependence in Southeast Asia* (proceedings of a conference held in Bangkok, 1967), University of Wisconsin Press, 1969.

WORK IN PROGRESS: Studies on education and development, on private business sector in Thailand, and on trade and investment patterns in Southeast Asia.††

* * *

SPRADLEY, James P. 1933-

PERSONAL: Born December 19, 1933, in Baker, Ore.; son

of Francis William and Nanette Laura Spradley; married Barbara A. Walton (an educator), August 23, 1956; children: Sheryl, Deborah, Laura. *Education:* Los Angeles City College, A.A., 1954; Fresno State College (now California State University, Fresno), B.A., 1960; University of Washington, Seattle, M.A., 1963, Ph.D., 1967. *Home:* 1980 Goodrich Ave., St. Paul, Minn. 55105. *Office:* Department of Anthropology, Macalester College, St. Paul, Minn. 55105.

CAREER: Seattle Pacific College, Seattle, Wash., instructor in anthropology, 1963-68; University of Washington, Seattle, assistant professor of psychiatry and anthropology, 1966-69; Macalester College, St. Paul, Minn., associate professor, 1969-73, professor of anthropology, 1973—. *Member:* American Anthropological Association (fellow). *Awards, honors:* American Anthropological Association, Stirling Award in Culture and Personality.

WRITINGS: Guests Never Leave Hungry: The Autobiography of James Sewid, a Kwakiutl Indian (based on interviews with Sewid), Yale University Press, 1969; *You Owe Yourself a Drunk: An Ethnography of Urban Nomads,* Little, Brown, 1970; (editor with David McCurdy) *Conformity and Conflict,* Little, Brown, 1971, 3rd edition, 1977; *Culture and Cognition,* Crowell, 1972; (with Brenda Mann) *The Cocktail Waitress,* Wiley, 1975.

BIOGRAPHICAL/CRITICAL SOURCES: Saturday Review, June 21, 1969.

* * *

SPRAGUE, Richard E. 1921-

PERSONAL: Born August 27, 1921, in Philadelphia, Pa.; son of Hugh A. (a civil engineer) and Ethel (Dodd) Sprague; married Constance Campbell, February 3, 1945; married second wife, Gloria Triguba (a purchasing and finance officer), June 14, 1969; children: Peter C., Anne D., Abbye, Sherry, Jeffrey, Robert. *Education:* Purdue University, B.S.E.E., 1942. *Politics:* Independent. *Office:* Personal Data Services, 193 Pinewood Rd., Hartsdale, N.Y. 10530.

CAREER: Computer Research Corp., Hawthorne, Calif., vice-president, 1950-54; National Cash Register Co., Hawthorne, director of sales, 1954-55; Teleregister Corp., Stamford, Conn., manager, 1955-60; Touche, Ross, Bailey & Smart, New York City, partner, 1960-68; Personal Data Services Corp., Hartsdale, N.Y., president, 1968—; Bionics Inc., Minneapolis, Minn., eastern marketing manager, 1969-71; Litton Industries, Morristown, N.J., special markets manager in Advanced Retail Systems division, 1971-72; Pitney Bowes-Alpex, Danbury, Conn., special markets development manager, 1972-73; Payment Systems, Inc., New York City, director of research in Payment Systems Research Program, 1974; Singer Business Machines, New York City, member of international marketing staff, 1974-75; consultant on international payment systems to Battelle Memorial Institute, Frankfurt, Germany, and Columbus, Ohio, 1975—; National Commission on Electronic Fund Transfers, Washington, D.C., senior staff member and manager, International Program, 1976-77. President, Sprague Research and Consulting; consulting associate, Technology Management, Inc. Consultant to WOFAC Co.; consultant on the photographic evidence of the John F. Kennedy assassination, for the U.S. House of Representatives Select Committee on Assassinations. *Military service:* U.S. Naval Reserves, 1944-46; became lieutenant junior grade. *Member:* Assocation for Computing Machinery, Society for Management Information Systems, Institute of Management Sciences, Institute of Electrical and Electronic

Engineers. American Management Association, National Committee to Investigate Assassinations (director).

WRITINGS: Electronic Business Systems: Management Use of On-line–Real-Time Computers, Ronald, 1962; *Information Utilities,* Prentice-Hall, 1969; *The Taking of America 1-2-3,* Sprague Publications, 1976. Also author with Dick Russell, *In Search of the Assassins,* 1977. Contributor to periodicals. Contributing editor, *Computers and Automation.*

WORK IN PROGRESS: Various books on assassinations; and a book on personalized information systems.

* * *

SPRINGER, Bernhard J. 1907(?)-1970

1907(?)—December 26, 1970; German-born American editor and publisher. Obituaries: *New York Times,* December 30, 1970; *Publishers' Weekly,* January 11, 1971; *Antiquarian Bookman,* January 18, 1971.

* * *

STACEY, Margaret 1922-

PERSONAL: Born March 27, 1922, in London, England; daughter of Conrad Eugene (a printer) and Grace Priscilla (Boyce) Petrie; married Frank Arthur Stacey (a university professor), May 20, 1945; children: Patricia, Richard, Kate, Peter, Michael. *Education:* London School of Economics and Political Science, B.Sc. (Econ.), 1943. *Politics:* Labour. *Religion:* Agnostic. *Home:* 20 Honeypot Lane, Husbands Bosworth, Nr. Lutterworth, Leicester LE17 6LY, England. *Office:* Department of Sociology, University of Warwick, Coventry CV4 7AL, England.

CAREER: Royal Ordnance Factory, Glasgow, Scotland, labor officer, 1943-44; Oxford University, Oxford, England, tutor, 1944-51; University College of Swansea, Singleton Park, Swansea, Wales, research officer, 1961-62, research fellow, 1962-63, lecturer, 1963-70, senior lecturer in sociology, 1970-74; University of Warwick, Coventry, England, professor of sociology, 1974—, chairperson of department, 1974—. Member, Welsh Hospital board, 1970-74, General Medical Council, 1976—. *Member:* British Sociological Association (honorary general secretary, 1968-70; vice-chairperson, 1975—).

WRITINGS: Tradition and Change: A Study of Banbury, Oxford University Press, 1960; (contributor) K. J. Hilton, editor, *The Lower Swansea Valley Project,* Longmans, Green, 1967; *Methods of Social Research,* Pergamon, 1969; (editor) *Comparability in Social Research,* Heinemann, 1969; (editor) *Hospitals, Children, and Their Families: The Report of a Pilot Study,* Routledge & Kegan Paul, 1970; (with others) *Power, Persistence and Change: A Second Study of Banbury,* Routledge & Kegan Paul, 1975. Also editor of *Sociology of the WHS,* a sociological review monograph for the University of Keele.

WORK IN PROGRESS: Co-author with M. Price of *Women and Power* for Tavistock Publications; editor with others, *Health Care and Health Knowledge,* and *Health Care and Health Policy;* author and editor with others, *Beyond Separation: Further Perspectives on Children in Hospital.*

SIDELIGHTS: Margaret Stacey told *CA:* "[My] main concern [is] with the individual and society; currently [I am] most interested in its specification to the patient in hospitals, but this interest also led to locality studies undertaken. [My] husband and children [are] a main matter of life importance;

[my] work and writing have been undertaken as possible within this consideration.''

* * *

STACY, Donald L. 1925-

PERSONAL: Born September 3, 1925, in New Jersey; son of George (a painter) and Irene (Conway) Stacy; married wife, Bernice (an artist), June 15, 1953; children: Sherah Anne. Education: Studied at Newark School of Fine Art, 1941-42, Art Students' League, New York, 1947-53, University of Paris, 1953-54, and University of Aix-Marseille, 1954-55. Home: 17 East 16th St., New York, N.Y. 10003.

CAREER: Artist; teacher of art in New York, N.Y. at Institute of Modern Art of Museum of Modern Art, 1957-70, at New School for Social Research, 1967—, and at Stacy-Studio-Workshop, 1969—. Works have been exhibited in the United States, Europe, and Japan. Consultant to design department, U.S. Plywood, 1968-69. Military service: U.S. Naval Construction Battalion (Seabees), 1943-46; served in the South Pacific two years. Member: Foundation for Integrative Education, World Institute, American Institute for Conservation of Art Works. Awards, honors: Fulbright grants for study and painting in France, 1953, 1954-55.

WRITINGS: (Self-illustrated) The Runaway Dot (juvenile), Bobbs-Merrill, 1969; Experiments in Art (juvenile), Four Winds Press, 1976. Contributor to National Encyclopedia, to publications of the World Institute, and of book reviews to American Journal of Art Therapy. Former art editor, Fields within Fields; former member of editorial board, Main Currents in Modern Thought.

WORK IN PROGRESS: The Voice of Painting.

* * *

STADE, George 1933-

PERSONAL: Born November 25, 1933, in New York, N.Y.; son of Kurt Herman (a hairdresser) and Eva (Aronson) Stade; married Dorothy Fletcher, December 16, 1956; children: Bjorn, Eric, Nancy, Kirsten. Education: St. Lawrence University, B.A., 1955; Columbia University, M.A., 1958, Ph.D., 1965. Politics: None. Religion: None. Home: 430 West 116th St., New York, N.Y. 10027. Office: Department of English, Columbia University, New York, N.Y. 10027.

CAREER: Rutgers University, New Brunswick, N.J., instructor in English, 1960-63; Columbia University, New York, N.Y., assistant professor, 1963-68, associate professor, 1968-70, professor of English, 1970—, chairman of department, 1968-75. Member: P.E.N., Modern Language Association of America, National Council of Teachers of English, National Book Critics Circle.

WRITINGS: Robert Graves, Columbia University Press, 1966; (editor with F. W. Dupee) Selected Letters of E. E. Cummings, Harcourt, 1969; (editor) Six Modern British Novelists, Columbia University Press, 1974; (editor) Six Contemporary British Novelists, Columbia University Press, 1976. Contributor of poems, articles, fiction, and reviews to journals.

WORK IN PROGRESS: A novel; a book on popular fiction.

BIOGRAPHICAL/CRITICAL SOURCES: New Republic, June 7, 1969; Newsweek, June 9, 1969; Saturday Review, July 5, 1969; Book World, July 6, 1969.

STADTMAN, Verne A. 1926-

PERSONAL: Born December 5, 1926, in Carrizozo, N.M.; son of Walter William (an insurance agent) and Minnie Ethel (Reece) Stadtman; married Jackolyn Carol Byl, August 26, 1949; children: Kristen Karen, Rand Theodore, Judith Dayna Stadtman-Miller, Todd Alan. Education: University of California, Berkeley, A.B., 1950. Politics: Democrat. Home: 638 Peralta Ave., Berkeley, Calif. 94707. Office: Carnegie Council on Policy Studies in Higher Education, 2150 Shattuck Ave., Berkeley, Calif. 94704.

CAREER: California Alumni Association, Berkeley, Calif., managing editor of California Monthly, 1950-64; University of California, Berkeley, centennial editor, 1964-69; Carnegie Commission on Higher Education, Berkeley, editor and staff associate, 1969-72, associate director and editor, 1972-73; Carnegie Council on Policy Studies in Higher Education, Berkeley, associate director and editor, 1973—. Military service: U.S. Army, 1945-47. Member: Education Writers Association, American Association of Higher Education, American Alumni Council (director of alumni publications, 1960-62; president, 1963-64), Editorial Projects for Education (president, 1962-63; trustee), Faculty Club, University of California, Sigma Delta Chi. Awards, honors: Alumni Publishing Service Award of American Alumni Council, 1969; Alumnus Service Award of California Alumni Association, 1970; American Council on Education Book of the Year Award, 1973, for Academic Transformation: Seventeen Institutions Under Pressure.

WRITINGS: California Campus, Howell-North Books, 1960; (editor) Centennial Record of the University of California, University of California Press, 1967; The University of California, 1868-1968, McGraw, 1970; (editor with David Riesman) Academic Transformation: Seventeen Institutions Under Pressure, McGraw; 1973. General editor of more than 100 publications of Carnegie Commission on Higher Education and of Carnegie Council on Policy Studies in Higher Education; supervising editor for books of others, including Ansel Adams and Nancy Newhall, Fiat Lux, and Albert Pickerell and May Dornin, Pictorial History of University of California.

WORK IN PROGRESS: Research on adult higher education and undergraduate curriculum in American higher education.

* * *

STAHL, Ben(jamin) 1910-

PERSONAL: Born September 7, 1910, in Chicago, Ill.; son of Benjamin Franklin (in real estate) and Grace (Meyer) Stahl; married Ella Lehocky, December 19, 1936; children: (prior marriage) Benjamin F., Gail; (present marriage) Regina, David F. A. Education: Attended public schools in Chicago. Politics: Republican. Religion: Protestant. Home and studio: Apdo. 421, San Miguel de Allende, GTO. Mexico.

CAREER: Artist; illustrator for national magazines, 1933—; co-founder and adviser, Famous Artists Schools (F.A.S.) International, Westport, Conn., 1949—. Has taught painting at School of the Art Institute of Chicago and American Academy of Art. Had one-man shows sponsored by Society of Illustrators, 1945, and Sarasota Art Association, 1950, and other numerous shows here and abroad; exhibitor at National Academy of Art, Carnegie invitational, and other shows; work includes paintings of fifteen scenes of the Way of the Cross for Catholic Bible and Catholic Press, and paintings for Sarasota Museum of the Cross (he designed the building). Member of Florida State Art Commission. *Military service:* U.S. Air Force, civilian with Special Services, 1959. *Member:* Society of Illustrators, Artists and Writers (New York), Players (New York), Sarasota Art Association (vice-president, 1953), Westport Artists (founder and first president). *Awards, honors:* Saltus Gold Medal of National Academy of Design, 1949; Sequoia Award for best children's book, 1965, for *Blackbeard's Ghost;* more than forty other national awards.

WRITINGS: Blackbeard's Ghost (novel; self-illustrated), Houghton, 1965; *The Secret of Red Skull* (illustrations by son, Ben F. Stahl), Houghton, 1971. Also author of "Journey into Art with Ben Stahl," an educational television series produced by the South Carolina Educational Television Network. Contributor to Famous Artists Schools textbooks. Contributor to *Saturday Evening Post* and illustrator of over eight hundred of its stories, beginning 1937; illustrated all of the "Hornblower" serials by Forrester.

WORK IN PROGRESS: A novel, *Triad,* about artists and art.

SIDELIGHTS: Blackbeard's Ghost was adapted for a film starring Peter Ustinov and produced by Walt Disney Productions, 1965.

Ben Stahl wrote to *CA:* "The current scene in writing I believe is as good as it ever was. God help writing if it goes the way of painting, with multitudes of undisciplined Sunday writers whose work is horrible. I would also see some kind of law which made it a serious offense for any writer who attempted to write about painting. Let writers write about writing and painters do the writing bit on painting."

*   *   *

STALLYBRASS, Oliver (George Weatherhead) 1925-

PERSONAL: Born March 11, 1925, in Heswall, Cheshire, England; son of Clare Oswald (a doctor) and Irene (Weatherhead) Stallybrass; married Gunnvor Sannerud (a design consultant), July 8, 1948; children: Anne, Michael. *Education:* Attended School of Oriental and African Studies, London, 1943-44; Clare College, Cambridge, B.A. (second class honors), 1951; University College, London, Postgraduate Diploma in Librarianship, 1954. *Politics:* "No party loyalties." *Religion:* None (humanist). *Home and office:* 106 Westwood Hill, London S.E. 26, England.

CAREER: Portsmouth Grammar School, Portsmouth, England, English master, 1951; London Library, London, England, staff, 1952-53, 1954-64, chief cataloger, 1958-61, deputy librarian, 1961-64; Secker & Warburg Ltd. (publishers), London, editor and advertising manager, 1964-66; Royal Institution of Great Britain, London, librarian and publications officer, 1966-67. *Military service:* British Army, 1944-47; became sergeant. *Member:* Translators Association, National Book League, Society of Authors, London Library.

WRITINGS: (With Emil Gelenczei and Roland Sallay) *The Ben-Oni Defence,* British Chess Magazine, 1966; (editor and contributor) *Aspects of E. M. Forster* (fifteen essays written for Forster's ninetieth birthday), Harcourt, 1969; (editor with Alan Bullock, and contributor) *The Harper Dictionary of Modern Thought,* Harper, in press.

Translator: Axel Jensen, *Epp,* Chatto & Windus, 1967; Knut Hamsun, *Victoria,* Farrar, Straus, 1969; (with David Hamblyn) Milan Kundera, *The Joke,* Coward, 1969; *Four Screenplays* ("The Passion of Joan of Arc," "Vampire,"

"Day of Wrath," "The Word"), Indiana University Press, 1970; Rolf Doecker, *Marius,* Harcourt, 1970; Sven Plovgaard, editor, *Public Library Buildings,* Library Association (London), 1971; (with Roger Greaves) Pierre Leprohon, *The Italian Cinema,* Praeger, 1972; Johan Borgen, *The Red Mist,* Calder & Boyars, 1973; Niels Jensen, *Days of Courage,* Harcourt, 1973 (published in England as *When the Land Lay Waste,* Methuen, 1973); (with wife, Gunnvor Stallybrass) Knut Hamsun, *The Wanderer,* Farrar, Straus, 1975; Erik Sletholt, *Wild and Tame,* Duckworth, 1976.

Indexer of many books, including *The Collected Essays, Journalism and Letters of George Orwell,* four volumes, Harcourt, 1968. Contributor of poems, articles, and reviews to *Guardian, Listener, New Statesman, Indexer, Times Literary Supplement, Spectator, Correspondence Chess,* and other British journals and newspapers. Editor, *Link,* 1958-62, *Proceedings of the Royal Institution of Great Britain,* 1966-67, and *Asian Affairs: Journal of the Royal Central Asian Society,* 1969-70.

WORK IN PROGRESS: Editing the Arbinger Edition of the complete works of E. M. Forster, for Edward Arnold; with wife, Gunnvor Stallybrass, translating Knut Hamsun's *The Women at the Pump,* for Farrar, Straus.

BIOGRAPHICAL/CRITICAL SOURCES: New Statesman, January 17, 1969; *Book World,* February 2, 1969; *Saturday Review,* February 15, 1969; *New Yorker,* February 15, 1969.

*   *   *

STALVEY, Lois Mark   1925-

PERSONAL: Born August 22, 1925, in Milwaukee, Wis.; daughter of Aloyisius Leo and Gertrude Katherine (Wolf) Mark; married Conrad J. Stawski, November 13, 1943; married second husband, Bennett Stalvey, Jr. (a government executive), May 14, 1955 (divorced, 1977); children: (second marriage) Bennett III, Noah Wolf, Sarah Lois. *Education:* Attended public schools in Milwaukee, Wis. *Politics:* Democrat. *Religion:* "Protestant-Agnostic." *Home:* Presidential Apartments, City Line Ave., Philadelphia, Pa. 19131. *Agent:* Harold Ober Associates, Inc., 40 East 49th St., New York, N.Y. 10017. *Office:* Community College of Philadelphia, 34 South 11th St., Philadelphia, Pa. 19107.

CAREER: Lois Mark & Associates (advertising firm), Milwaukee, Wis., president, 1946-54; McCann-Erickson (advertising firm), Chicago, Ill., television and radio writer and producer, 1954-55; consultant, Ramsdell-Buckley, 1962-70; currently instructor in creative writing and news reporting at Community College of Philadelphia, Philadelphia, Pa. Member of steering committee, Panel of American Women, 1961—; state advisory committee member, U.S. Civil Rights Commission, 1965-71. Also lecturer at colleges and civic groups nationally. *Member:* Society of Magazine Writers, Authors Guild. *Awards, honors:* Erma Proetz Award, 1949; Philadelphia Human Relations Commission Award, 1971.

WRITINGS: The Education of a WASP, Morrow, 1970; *Getting Ready: The Education of a White Family in Inner-City Schools,* Morrow, 1974. Contributor to *Reader's Digest, Woman's Day, Good Housekeeping,* and other periodicals. Book reviewer, *St. Louis Post Dispatch,* 1970—.

WORK IN PROGRESS: The Education of a Woman, completion expected in 1977.

SIDELIGHTS: Lois Stalvey told *CA:* "[It was] a happy accident that experience in advertising combined with involvement in civil rights ... enable[d] me to write, in lay terms, of personal experiences. Also, writing fit in perfectly with [a] full-time job as [a] housewife and mother of three—making me able to write *to* other 'average women' with similar life experiences. Now that my children are grown, teaching writing to college students in an inner-city community college fills needs for me and, I believe, for my students. My book-in-progress, *The Education of a Woman* will explore the 'happy accidents' that have provided a satisfying life as a writer and a woman.''

BIOGRAPHICAL/CRITICAL SOURCES: Washington Post, June 6, 1970; *Best Sellers,* July 1, 1970.

* * *

STARKIE, Enid 1903(?)-1970

1903(?)—April 21, 1970; Irish biographer and authority on French literature and poetry. Obituaries: *New York Times,* May 2, 1970; *Antiquarian Bookman,* May 25, 1970; *Books Abroad,* spring, 1971. (See index for *CA* sketch)

* * *

STAVE, Bruce M(artin) 1937-

PERSONAL: Born May 17, 1937, in New York, N.Y.; son of Bernard R. (an attorney) and Mildred (Silberman) Stave; married Sondra T. Astor (a public official), June 16, 1961; children: Channing M. L. *Education:* Columbia University, A.B., 1959, M.A., 1961; University of Pittsburgh, Ph.D., 1966. *Politics:* Independent Democrat. *Home:* Merrow Road—The Broadway, Coventry, Conn. 06238. *Office:* Department of History, University of Connecticut, Storrs, Conn. 06268.

CAREER: Samuel Lubell Associates, New York, N.Y., and Washington, D.C., political pollster (intermittently), 1958-64; University of Bridgeport, Bridgeport, Conn., instructor, 1965-66, assistant professor of history, 1966-70; University of Connecticut, Storrs, assistant professor, 1970-71, associate professor, 1971-75, professor of history, 1975—. Fulbright professor of American history in India, 1968-69. Guest fellow and visiting lecturer in history, Yale University, fall, 1976. *Member:* American Historical Association, Organization of American Historians, Oral History Association, Social Science History Association, Immigration History Society, Academy of Political Science, American Association of University Professors, New England Historical Association, Association for the Study of Connecticut History, Connecticut Civil Liberties Union (board member, 1967-68), Fairfield County (Conn.) Civil Liberties Union (chairman, 1967-68), Greater Hartford (Conn.) Civil Liberties Union (vice-chairman, 1971-72), Northeastern Connecticut Civil Liberties Union (founder and board member, 1972—, president, 1975-76). *Awards, honors:* National Endowment for the Humanities fellowship, 1974.

WRITINGS: The New Deal and the Last Hurrah: Pittsburgh Machine Politics, University of Pittsburgh Press, 1970; (editor) *Urban Bosses, Machines, and Progressive Reformers,* Heath, 1972; (editor with D. L. Ashby) *The Discontented Society,* Rand McNally, 1972; (editor and contributor) *Socialism in the Cities,* Kennikat, 1975. Contributor of articles and reviews to periodicals. *Journal of Urban History,* member of editorial board, 1974-76, associate editor, 1977—.

WORK IN PROGRESS: The Making of Urban History, for Sage Publications, Inc.; a research project entitled ''20th Century Hartford: Urban & Suburban Competition & Development.''

AVOCATIONAL INTERESTS: Travel, photography.

STAVENHAGEN, Rodolfo 1932-

PERSONAL: Born August 29, 1932, in Frankfurt, Germany; citizen of Mexico; son of Kurt (a businessman) and Lore (Gruenbaum) Stavenhagen; married Maria Eugenia Vargas (an anthropologist), October 13, 1931; children: Marina, Andrea. *Education:* University of Chicago, B.A., 1951; University of Mexico, M.A., 1958; University of Paris, Ph.D., 1965. *Home:* Guadalupe 46, Lomas de San Angel Inn, Mexico 20, D.F., Mexico. *Office:* Department of Sociology, El Colegio de Mexico, Apdo. 20-671, Mexico City 20, D.F., Mexico.

CAREER: National University of Mexico, Mexico, beginning 1956, began as instructor, became professor; Latin American Center for Research in the Social Sciences, Rio de Janeiro, Brazil, general secretary, 1962-65; International Institute for Labour Studies, Geneva, Switzerland, senior staff associate, 1969-71; El Colegio de Mexico, Mexico City, director of department of sociology, 1972—. *Member:* International Social Science Council, Latin American Social Science Council, Latin American Sociological Association, Latin American Faculty of Social Sciences (president), Society for Applied Anthropology.

WRITINGS: Classes, Colonialism and Acculturation, Social Science Institute, Washington University, 1965; *Las Clases sociales en las sociedades agrarias,* Siglo XXI (Mexico), 1969, translation by Judy Hellman published as *Social Classes in Agrarian Societies,* Doubleday, 1975; (editor) *Agrarian Problems and Peasant Movements in Latin America,* Doubleday, 1970; *Sociologia y subdesarrollo,* Nuestro Tiempo, 1971; (co-author) *Estructura agraria y desarrollo agricola en Mexico,* Fondo de Cultura Economica (Mexico), 1974.

Contributor: *Neolatifundismo y explotacion de Emiliano Zapata a Anderson, Clayton & Co.,* Nuestro Tiempo (Mexico), 1968. Contributor of articles to various scholarly journals.

WORK IN PROGRESS: Sociological research on problems of development, especially agrarian problems, in Latin America and particularly in Mexico; study of social movements in Latin America.

* * *

STAVIS, Ben(edict) 1941-

PERSONAL: Born October 19, 1941, in Washington, D.C. *Education:* Haverford College, B.A., 1963; Columbia University, M.A., 1966, Ph.D., 1973. *Home:* 10 Freese Rd., Ithaca, N.Y. 14850. *Agent:* Lucy Kroll Agency, 390 West End Ave., New York, N.Y. 10024. *Office:* Center for International Studies, Cornell University, 170 Uris Hall, Tower Rd., Ithaca, N.Y. 14853.

CAREER: Currently research associate at the Center for International Studies and Program on Policies for Science and Technology in Developing Nations, Cornell University, Ithaca, N.Y. Member of national staff, McCarthy for President Campaign, 1968. *Member:* National Academy of Sciences, American Society for Public Administration, American Political Science Association, Association for Asian Studies.

WRITINGS: We Were the Campaign: New Hampshire to Chicago for McCarthy, Beacon Press, 1969; *People's Communes and Rural Development in China* (monograph), Cornell Rural Development Committee, 1974; *Making Green Revolution: The Politics of Agricultural Development in China* (monograph), Cornell Rural Development

Committee, 1975; *The Politics of Agricultural Mechanization in China,* Cornell University Press, 1978. Contributor to *China Quarterly, Asian Survey, Social Scientist,* and other periodicals.

SIDELIGHTS: Stavis served as personnel director for several hundred young staffers in the McCarthy campaign. *Newsweek* called his book "the best account of the campaign to date.... A perceptive and honest personal testament of daily life in the 'Children's Crusade,' of the internecine feuds between national and local staffs and the individual struggles for power within an organization where power was considered grotesque." Since then he has done extensive research on rural development in China, where he visited in 1972. He is fluent in Mandarin Chinese and French.

BIOGRAPHICAL/CRITICAL SOURCES: National Review, February 16, 1969; *New York Times,* October 20, 1969; *Newsweek,* October 27, 1969; *New York Times Book Review,* November 23, 1969; *Nation,* February 2, 1970.

* * *

STEBBINS, Robert A(lan) 1938-

PERSONAL: Born June 22, 1938, in Rhinelander, Wis.; son of William N. (a business executive) and Dorothy (Guy) Stebbins; married Karin Y. Olson, January 11, 1964; children: Paul, Lisa, Christi. *Education:* Macalester College, B.A., 1961; University of Minnesota, M.A., 1962, Ph.D., 1964. *Politics:* None. *Religion:* None. *Home address:* P.O. Box 1056, Cochrane, Alberta, Canada. *Office:* Department of Sociology, University of Calgary, Calgary, Alberta, Canada.

CAREER: Presbyterian College, Clinton, S.C., associate professor of sociology, 1964-65; Memorial University of Newfoundland, St. John's, assistant professor, 1965-68, associate professor of sociology and chairman of department of sociology and anthropology, 1968-73; University of Texas at Arlington, professor of sociology, 1973-76; University of Calgary, Calgary, Alberta, professor of sociology and chairman of department, 1976—. President, St. John's Symphony Orchestra, 1968-69. *Military service:* Minnesota National Guard, 1956-64; became staff sergeant. *Member:* American Sociological Association, Canadian Sociology and Anthropology Association, Pacific Sociological Association, International Sociological Association, Society for the Study of Social Problems, International Society of Bassists (chairman of amateur division, 1974—). *Awards, honors:* Canada Council leave fellowship, 1971-72; National Endowment for the Humanities summer stipend, 1976.

WRITINGS: Commitment to Deviance: The Nonprofessional Criminal in the Community, Greenwood Press, 1971; *The Disorderly Classroom: Its Physical and Temporal Conditions,* Memorial University of Newfoundland, 1974; *Teachers and Meaning,* E. J. Brill, 1975. Contributor of articles, several of them on sociological aspects of jazz, to sociology journals in United States, Canada, and England. Member of editorial board, *Canadian Review of Sociology and Anthropology,* 1970-73; associate editor, *Journal of Jazz Studies,* 1973—; member of publications committee, Society for the Study of Social Problems, 1976-79.

WORK IN PROGRESS: The Amateur: On the Margin between Work and Leisure.

AVOCATIONAL INTERESTS: Playing double bass ("serious hobby").

STEBEL, S(idney) L(eo) 1924-
(Leo Bergson)

PERSONAL: First syllable of surname rhymes with "tea"; born June 28, 1924; son of Abe H. and Anna (Wicliski) Stebel; married Jan Mary Dingler (an artist), September 10, 1954; children: Patricia Anne. *Education:* University of Southern California, B.A., 1949. *Religion:* None. *Residence:* Los Angeles, Calif. *Agent:* Don Congdon, Harold Matson Co., Inc., 22 East 40th St., New York, N.Y. 10016.

CAREER: University of Southern California, Los Angeles, editor of *Alumni Review,* 1954-56; in advertising and public relations in Los Angeles, Calif., 1956-64; full-time writer, 1964—. Executive script consultant, Australian Film Corp., 1975; member of public relations council, University of Southern California. *Military service:* U.S. Army Air Forces, Ordnance; became sergeant; received unit commendation and two battle stars. *Member:* Authors Guild, Writers Guild of America (West), Film Society.

WRITINGS: (Under pseudonym Leo Bergson; with Robert McMahon) *The Widowmaster,* Fawcett, 1967; *The Collaborator,* Random House, 1968; "The Way Out" (play), first produced at Actors Studio West, 1974; *The Vorovich Affair,* Viking, 1975 (published in England as *Narc,* Constable, 1976); "Dreams of Marianne" (play), produced, 1975. Author with Robert Weverka of motion picture script, "The Revolution of Antonio de Leon"; author of a one-man show for Henry Fonda, "Fathers against Sons," which toured the United States, 1970-71. Columnist, "The Avant-Garde," in *Los Angeles Times,* 1959. Editor, *Copy* (literary quarterly), 1949.

WORK IN PROGRESS: Travels with Patricia, a book on America outside the major American cities, first published in installments in *West; Help, the Paranoids Are After Me,* a farce.

BIOGRAPHICAL/CRITICAL SOURCES: Santa Ana Register, August 18, 1968; *New York Times Book Review,* August 25, 1968; *Los Angeles Times,* June 22, 1969; *Punch,* November 12, 1969.

* * *

STEDMAN, R(aymond) William 1930-

PERSONAL: Born June 8, 1930, in Rochester, Pa.; son of Raymond Henry and Marie Louise (Sewall) Stedman; married Rita Eileen Manning, September 9, 1959; children: Eric Raymond, Craig William, Erin Leigh. *Education:* Westminster College, New Wilmington, Pa., A.B., 1952; University of Southern California, M.A., 1953, Ph.D., 1959. *Home:* 444 Merion Dr., Newtown, Pa. 18940. *Office:* Bucks County Community College, Newtown, Pa. 18940.

CAREER: University of Southern California, Los Angeles, assistant to the president, administrator of educational broadcasting, and lecturer in department of telecommunications, 1952-62; University of Florida, Gainesville, assistant professor of journalism and communication and television director, 1962; Rollins College, Winter Park, Fla., associate professor of communication and head of department, 1963-64; Nassau Community College, Garden City, N.Y., associate professor of speech, 1964-65; Bucks County Community College, Newtown, Pa., professor of English and associate dean for communication, 1965—. Chief announcer and news director, KTHE-TV, Los Angeles, 1953-54; producer-host of "Trojan Digest," Columbia Broadcasting System radio, 1956-62. *Military service:* U.S. Army Reserve, 1954-65; became first lieutenant. *Member:* National Academy of Television Arts and Sciences, Speech Communication Association, American Association of University Professors.

WRITINGS: The Serials: Suspense and Drama by Installment, University of Oklahoma Press, 1971, revised edition, 1977; *A Guide to Public Speaking,* Prentice-Hall, 1971. Writer of scripts for "Trojan Digest" and free-lance feature programs for Armed Forces Radio and Television Service. Contributor of reviews to *Journal of Broadcasting.*

WORK IN PROGRESS: Shadow of the Indian; The American Indian: A Narrative History for Young People.

BIOGRAPHICAL/CRITICAL SOURCES: Los Angeles Times, February 16, 1958, September 18, 1960, February 11, 1962; *Trenton Times,* March 16, 1967, February 11, 1968, May 30, 1971; *Variety,* March 24, 1971; *Mademoiselle,* May, 1971; *Journal of the West,* April, 1972; *Television Quarterly,* May-June, 1976.

*   *   *

STEELE, Wilbur Daniel   1886-1970

March 17, 1886—May 26, 1970; American short story writer, novelist, and playwright. Obituaries: *New York Times,* May 27, 1970; *Washington Post,* May 28, 1970; *Publishers' Weekly,* June 29, 1970; *Books Abroad,* spring, 1971.

*   *   *

STEEN, Malcolm Harold   1928-
   (Mike Steen)

PERSONAL: Born February 16, 1928, in Monroe, La.; son of Euel Miley (a rancher) and Juanita (MacDaniel) Steen. *Education:* Attended Northeast Louisiana University, 1944-46; Louisiana State University, B.A., 1948. *Politics:* "Variable." *Home:* 1302 Park Ave., Monroe, La. *Office:* 2351 Teviot St., Los Angeles, Calif. 90039.

CAREER: Film actor in Hollywood, Calif., 1956—, and dialogue director, 1960—; Villanova Preparatory School, Ojai, Calif., teacher of English and coach, 1970-71; assistant professor of English at Northeast Louisiana University, Monroe, 1974, and University of New Orleans, New Orleans, La., 1975. *Military service:* U.S. Naval Air Corps, 1952-54. *Member:* American Federation of Television and Radio Artists, Screen Actors' Guild, Actors' Equity Association.

WRITINGS—Under name Mike Steen: *A Look at Tennessee Williams,* Hawthorn, 1969; *The Biography of Pandro S. Berman,* American Film Institute, 1972; *Hollywood Speaks,* Putnam, 1974. Writer of two screenplays, "Hero in Exile" and "Conquest by Blood," both as yet unproduced.

WORK IN PROGRESS: Two novels.

SIDELIGHTS: Steen lived and worked in Spain, 1962-64.

*   *   *

STEFFAN, Truman Guy   1910-

PERSONAL: Born February 20, 1910, in Bellwood, Pa.; son of Truman J. and Nellie (Teale) Steffan; married Esther Sigman, August 27, 1938. *Education:* Dickinson College, B.A., 1931; University of Wisconsin, M.A., 1933, Ph.D., 1937. *Office:* English Department, Parlin Hall, University of Texas, Austin, Tex. 78712.

CAREER: Graduate assistant and later instructor in English at University of Wisconsin—Madison, 1931-38; instructor in English, University of Texas at Austin, 1938-42, and Navigation Naval Flight Preparatory School, Austin, 1942-44;

University of Texas at Austin, instructor, 1944-46, assistant professor, 1946-49, associate professor, 1949-61, professor of English, 1961—. *Member:* Modern Language Association of America, Conference of College Teachers of English, Phi Beta Kappa. *Awards, honors:* University of Texas Research Institute grants, 1947, 1965.

WRITINGS: (Author of Volume I, and editor with W. W. Pratt of Volumes II-III) *Byron's Don Juan,* four volumes, University of Texas Press, 1957, 2nd edition, 1970; (editor) *Lord Byron's "Cain": Twelve Essays and a Text with Variants and Annotations,* University of Texas Press, 1969; (editor with others) Lord Byron, *Don Juan,* Penguin, 1973. Also author of a monograph, *From Cambridge to Missolonghi: Byron Letters at the University of Texas,* 1972. Contributor of more than twenty-five articles to scholarly journals. Member of editorial advisory board, *Studies in Romanticism,* 1961—.

BIOGRAPHICAL/CRITICAL SOURCES: New York Review of Books, October 22, 1970.

*   *   *

STEIN, Arthur (Benjamin)   1937-

PERSONAL: Born August 25, 1937, in Philipsburg, Pa.; son of Samuel and Mary (Abelson) Stein; married Karen Friedman (a teacher at University of Rhode Island), July 1, 1964; children: Lisa, Jody. *Education:* Pennsylvania State University, M.A., 1959; University of Melbourne, graduate study, 1959-60; University of Pennsylvania, M.A., 1963, Ph.D., 1965; University of California, Berkeley, postdoctoral study, 1968. *Home:* 66 Ledgewood Rd., Kingston, R.I. 02881. *Office:* Department of Political Science, University of Rhode Island, Kingston, R.I. 02881.

CAREER: Pennsylvania State University, University Park, visiting assistant professor, 1964-65; University of Rhode Island, Kingston, assistant professor, 1965-67, associate professor, 1968-74, professor of political science, 1974—. *Member:* American Political Science Association, Association for Asian Studies, American Association of University Professors, Phi Beta Kappa. *Awards, honors:* Fulbright fellowship at University of Melbourne, 1959-60; Woodrow Wilson fellowship, 1961-63; National Defense Foreign Language fellow, 1967-68.

WRITINGS: India's Reaction to the Hungarian Revolution: An Appraisal, University of Rhode Island, 1967; *India and the Soviet Union: The Nehru Era,* University of Chicago Press, 1969; *American-Soviet Relations: Some Thoughts on the Future,* University of Rhode Island, 1970; (with Robert G. Weisbord) *Bittersweet Encounter: The Afro-American and the American Jew,* Greenwood Press, 1970. Contributor of articles and reviews to political science and Asian studies journals.

WORK IN PROGRESS: Study of concepts of social justice and political change in the United States, India, the U.S.S.R., and China; work on human consciousness.†

*   *   *

STEIN, Calvert   1903-

PERSONAL: Born April 6, 1903, in Newcastle-on-Tyne, England; came to United States in 1912, naturalized in 1919; son of Harry (a tailor) and Lily (Phillips) Stein; married Lucille H. Weinstein (a psychiatric social worker), November 26, 1929; children: Eleanor M. (Mrs. Aaron M. Leavitt), Mildred J. (Mrs. Harold Sobel). *Education:* Tufts University, pre-med certificate, 1924, M.D., 1928; Northeastern

University, LL.B., 1938; graduate study at Columbia University, Yale University, and Harvard University. *Politics:* Independent. *Religion:* Reform Judaism. *Home:* 71 Meadowbrook Rd., Longmeadow, Mass. 01106. *Agent:* Barthold Fles Literary Agency, 507 Fifth Ave., New York, N.Y. 10017.

CAREER: Licensed to practice medicine in California and Massachusetts; diplomate, National Board of Medical Examiners, 1929; certified by American Board of Psychiatry and Neurology, 1936 (psychiatry), 1937 (neurology). Highland Hospital, Oakland, Calif., intern, 1928-29; Livermore Sanatorium, Livermore, Calif., resident, 1929; general practice in Oakland, and Berkeley, Calif., 1929-31; senior resident in psychiatry, neurology, and child guidance at Monson State Hospital and Springfield Hospital, 1931-38; private practice in counseling and psychosomatic medicine, in Springfield, Mass., 1938-75. Consulting neuropsychiatrist, Springfield Hospital, 1938—; official consultant and examiner, U.S. Civil Service, U.S. Railroad Retirement Board, Veteran's Administration, and U.S. Armed Forces Entrance and Examining Station, 1946; consultant, Westover Air Force Base, 1958-65. Springfield College, Springfield, Mass., lecturer in neurology and psychiatry, Graduate School, 1939, 1948—, visiting associate professor, 1967—; lecturer, American International College, 1949-51; visiting professor of clinical psychiatry at Medical College of South Carolina, 1970. *Military service:* U.S. Naval Reserve, medical corps, 1941-46; became captain.

MEMBER: American Medical Association, American Academy of Neurology (fellow), American Psychiatric Association (life fellow), American Society of Clinical Hypnosis (president, 1971-72), American Society of Group Psychotherapy and Psychodrama (president, 1962-64), Springfield Society of Clinical Hypnosis (president, 1970-71), Maimonides Medical Association (president, 1961), Massachusetts Medical Association, Sinai Temple (president, 1947-49). *Awards, honors:* First prize, New England Psychiatric Society, for original research in epilepsy, 1936.

WRITINGS—All published by C. C Thomas, except as indicated: *Nothing to Sneeze At,* privately printed, 1951; *Hidden Springs of Human Action,* privately printed, 1952; *Practical Psychotherapeutic Techniques,* 1968; *Practical Psychotherapy in Nonpsychiatric Specialties,* 1969; *Practical Family and Marriage Counseling,* 1969; *Practical Pastoral Counseling,* 1970; (author of foreward) Fredericka Freytag, *The Body Image in Gender Orientation Disturbances,* Vantage, 1977. Contributor of over seventy clinical case studies, book reviews, and articles to medical journals. Contributing editor, *Group Psychotherapy,* 1962-75.

WORK IN PROGRESS: Two books, *Sexual Behavior in Biblical Times,* and *How to Hang Loose When You're Uptight.*

AVOCATIONAL INTERESTS: Handicrafts, gardening, and music.

* * *

STEIN, Mini

PERSONAL: Born in Port Elizabeth, South Africa; daughter of Benjamin (a businessman) and Bluma (Sendzul) Stein. *Education:* Studied drama and piano in Port Elizabeth, South Africa, prior to 1939, and took courses at New York University, 1954. *Religion:* Jewish. *Residence:* New York, N.Y.

CAREER: Writer, 1948—; broadcaster on radio and televi-

sion in South Africa and New York, and storyteller. Broadcasts include series of her own South African stories on WNYC, New York, and on WFUV-FM, South Africa; also has presented programs for children on U.S. networks and appeared on the Jack Paar, Steve Allen, and other shows; as storyteller, 1950—, has given programs of her own stories, rhymes, and songs on educational television and radio, in schools and hospitals, and at the Children's Zoo in New York (initiated the zoo programs as a volunteer). *Member:* Authors Guild, American Society of Composers, Authors and Publishers.

WRITINGS—For children: *God and Me,* Peggy Cloth Books, 1960; *We Help Daddy,* Golden Press, 1962; *Two Oxen for Lobola,* S. Story International, 1964; *Mort the Mascot Mouse,* Hallmark, 1968; *Majola: A Zula Boy,* Messner, 1969; *Puleng of Lesotho,* Messner, 1969. Her songs were published as *My Little World,* Sam Fox Publishing, 1956, and recorded under the same title, MGM Records, 1957. Feature stories have been published by Associated Press and NEA News Syndicate and in *American Home, Pageant, Today's Woman, Modern Baby, New York Times Magazine,* and other periodicals.

WORK IN PROGRESS: A children's book on African music, for Messner; fun stories for children; adapting *Two Oxen for Lobola* for a dance drama.†

* * *

STEINBERG, Erwin R(ay) 1920

PERSONAL: Born November 15, 1920, in New Rochelle, N.Y.; son of Samuel (a women's clothes cutter) and Lea (Neumann) Steinberg; married Beverly Mendelson, August 15, 1954; children: Marc W., Alan J. *Education:* Attended City College (now City College of the City University of New York), 1937-38, and Plattsburgh State Normal School (now State University of New York College at Plattsburgh), 1938-40; New York College for Teachers (now State University of New York at Albany), B.S., 1941, M.S., 1942; New York University, Ph.D., 1956. *Home:* 1376 Sheridan Ave., Pittsburgh, Pa. 15206. *Office:* Department of English, Carnegie-Mellon University, Pittsburgh, Pa. 15213.

CAREER: Carnegie-Mellon University, Pittsburgh, Pa., instructor, 1946-49, assistant professor, 1949-55, associate professor, 1955-61, professor of English, 1961-75, professor of English and interdisciplinary studies, 1975—, dean of Margaret Morrison Carnegie College, 1960-73, dean of College of Humanities and Social Sciences, 1965-75, chairman of board, Carnegie-Mellon Education Center, 1968-75. Communications consultant to various companies in Pennsylvania, New York, and California, and to Educational Testing Service, 1963-67, U.S. Office of Education, 1963-64, Learning Institute of North Carolina, 1965, and American Institutes for Research, 1965-66. Visiting scholar, Center for Advanced Study in the Behavioral Sciences, 1970-71; member, Commission of Scholars, Board of Higher Education, State of Illinois, 1974—. *Military service:* U.S. Army Air Forces, 1943-46; became sergeant. *Member:* National Council of Teachers of English, Conference on College Composition and Communication, Modern Language Association, Kappa Delta Pi, Phi Delta Kappa, Phi Kappa Phi. *Awards, honors:* Carnegie Teaching Award, 1956; Distinguished Alumnus, State University of New York at Albany, 1969; Alumnus of the Year, State University of New York College at Plattsburgh, 1971.

WRITINGS: (With William M. Schutte) *Communication in Business and Industry,* Holt, 1960; (editor with Schutte)

Personal Integrity, Norton, 1961; (with Schutte) *Communication Problems from Business and Industry,* Encyclopaedia Britannica Films, 1961; (editor) *The Rule of Force,* Norton, 1962; *Needed Research in the Teaching of English,* U.S. Department of Health, Education, and Welfare, Office of Education, 1963; (with others) *Curriculum Development and Evaluation in English and Social Studies,* Carnegie Institute of Technology, 1964; (editor with Lois S. Josephs and contributor) *English Education Today,* Noble, 1970; (editor with Alan M. Markman) *English Then and Now: Readings and Exercises,* Random House, 1970; *The Stream of Consciousness and Beyond in "Ulysses",* University of Pittsburgh Press, 1973.

Contributor: G. Kerry Smith, editor, *Current Issues in Higher Education,* Association of Higher Education, 1963; A. J. McCaffrey, editor, *Implications of Research, Development, and Experimentation in American Education,* American Textbook Publishers Institute, 1964; M. E. Manty, editor, *New Theology—Number One,* Macmillan, 1964; Michael Shugrue, editor, *Patterns and Models for Teaching English,* National Council of Teachers of English, 1964; D. H. Russell, editor, *Research Design and the Teaching of English,* National Council of Teachers of English, 1964; Gary Tate, editor, *Reflections on High School English,* University of Tulsa, 1965; *Educationally Disadvantaged Students,* Council on Social Work Education, 1968; P. F. Neumeyer, editor, *Twentieth Century Interpretations of "The Castle",* Prentice-Hall, 1969; (with W. M. Schutte) T. F. Stanley and B. Benstock, editors, *Approaches to "Ulysses",* University of Pittsburgh Press, 1970; Fritz Senn, editor, *New Light on Joyce from the Dublin Symposium,* Indiana University Press, 1972.

General editor, "Insight" series, Noble, 1968-73. Contributor to many periodicals and journals, including *Literature and Psychology, Modern Fiction Studies, James Joyce Review, James Joyce Quarterly, Style, College English, Quarterly Journal of Speech, English Journal, Educational Forum, Clearing House, Journal of Engineering Education, University Quarterly, PMLA,* and *American Journal of Orthopsychiatry.*

WORK IN PROGRESS: The Stream-of-Consciousness Technique in the Modern Novel, completion expected in 1978; *Ambiguity in the Works of Franz Kafka,* completion expected in 1980; *Archetype and Myth in Modernist Literature,* completion expected in 1980.

* * *

STEINER, Gerolf 1908-
(Justus Andereich, Harald Stuempke, Trotzhard Wiederumb)

PERSONAL: Born March 22, 1908, in Strasbourg, Alsace-Lorraine (then German territory, but restored to France, 1919); son of Karl Theodor and Katharina (Frick) Steiner; married Renate du Mesnil de Rochemont, November 27, 1954; children: Ursula, Friederike, Alfred, Berthold, Irmtrud, Wolfram, Dietrich. *Education:* University of Heidelberg, Dr. in Sciences, 1931. *Home:* 10 Schwarzwaldhochstr, D756 Gaggenau-Freiolsheim, West Germany. *Office:* Universitaet Fridericiana, Kaiserstrasse 12, D75 Karlsruhe, West Germany.

CAREER: University of Heidelberg, Heidelberg, Germany, assistant in zoology laboratory, 1931-35; Food Cold Storage Investigating Laboratory, Karlsruhe, Germany, scientific collaborator, 1935-39; Darmstadt Institute of Technology (a university), Darmstadt, Germany, assistant

professor of zoology, 1939-47; University of Heidelberg, assistant professor of zoology, 1950-62; Baden Institute of Technology (Universitaet Fridericiana), Karlsruhe, Germany, professor of zoology and director of zoology laboratory, 1962-73. *Member:* German Zoologists Association, Deutscher kaltetech Verein (German refrigeration engineers association), Gesellschaft Deutscher Naturforscher und Aerzte.

WRITINGS: (Under pseudonym Harald Stuempke) *Bau und Leben der Rhinogradentia,* Gustav Fischer, 1961, translation by Leigh Chadwick published as *The Snouters: Form and Life of the Rhinogrades,* Natural History Press, for American Museum of Natural History, 1967; *Wort-Elemente der wichtigsten zoologischen Fachausdruecke* (pamphlet on zoology terminology), Gustav Fischer, 1962; *Das zoologische Laboratorium* (title means "The Zoological Laboratory"), Schweizebart, 1963; (under pseudonym Justus Andereich) *Nebenergebnisse aus 1001 Sitzungen* (title means "Byproducts from 1001 Sessions"), Moos, 1968; (under pseudonym Trotzhard Wiederumb) *Wie werde ich Diktator* (title means "How to Become a Dictator"), Moos, 1968; *Zoomorphologie in umrissen* (title means "Zoomorphology in Outlines, An Atlas on Eumetazoa"), Gustav Fischer, in press. Contributor of articles to scientific and popular periodicals.

SIDELIGHTS: The Snouters, about a fictitious order of mammals, includes a bibliography of equally fictitious citations. Steiner told *CA* that in the book he was applying the "laws of evolution on a strange model, i.e. animals walking on their noses; [it is] in some respects a 'serious' joke." Steiner's hobby is painting and drawing; he drew a caricature for *CA,* depicting himself with enigmatic smile, a few tufts of hair, and a bow tie tucked under his chin.

* * *

STEINKE, Peter L(ouis) 1938-

PERSONAL: Born June 18, 1938, in Glen Cove, N.Y.; son of Arthur F. (a minister) and Marguerite (Frankel) Steinke; married Carolyn Joyce Wagner (a teacher), June 14, 1963; children: Rene, Timothy, Krista. *Education:* Concordia Senior College, Fort Wayne, Ind., B.A., 1960; Presbyterian School of Christian Education, M.A., 1967; Concordia Seminary, St. Louis, Mo., M.Div., 1969; Chicago Theological Seminary, D.Rel., 1971. *Politics:* Independent. *Home:* 349 St. Cloud, Friendswood, Tex. 77546.

CAREER: Ordained to Lutheran ministry, 1964; minister in Chester, Va. and Villa Park, Ill., 1964-70; executive director, Jonus House, 1972-74; Hope Lutheran Church, Friendswood, Tex., pastor, 1974—.

WRITINGS: Right, Wrong, or What?, Concordia, 1970; *Is There Life after Thirty?,* Augsburg, 1971; *Whose Who,* Concordia, 1973; *With Eyes Wide Open,* Concordia, 1974.

WORK IN PROGRESS: Big Blooming Buzzing Confusion.

SIDELIGHTS: Peter L. Steinke told *CA* that he is interested in the areas of religion and mental health, and family life.

* * *

STEIRMAN, Hy 1921-

PERSONAL: Surname is pronounced Steer-man; born November 11, 1921, in Montreal, Quebec; came to United States in 1948, naturalized in 1958; son of Bernard (a policeman) and Rose (Rosen) Steirman; married Ruth Kravitz (a social worker), January 2, 1947; children: Beryl Kaye, Andrew Robin. *Education:* Attended McGill University, 1946-48, and Columbia University, 1948-49. *Politics:* Democrat. *Religion:* Jewish. *Home:* 1 Chesterfield Rd., Scarsdale, N.Y. 10583.

CAREER: Stearn Publications, New York City, editorial director, 1950-53; Hillman Periodicals, New York City, editor, 1954-57; Warner Communications, New York City, Division of Coronet Communications, president, 1958-72, Division of Paperback Library, publisher, 1960-72; Steirman Communicators, Inc., New York City, editor and publisher, beginning 1973; president and publisher, *Family Health* (magazine), 1974—; publisher, *Weight Watchers Magazine,* 1975—. Chairman of the board, Ralmar TV Sports Productions; publishing adviser, Palestine Economic Commission. Vocational teacher, Fox Meadow School, 1966-72; member of school system evaluation committee, Scarsdale (N.Y.) Public Schools, 1971. *Military service:* Royal Canadian Air Force, 1940-45; served two tours on antisubmarine patrol; became flight lieutenant; mentioned in dispatches. *Member:* Periodical and Book Association (past president), Overseas Press Club, Warbirds of the RAF, National Council for a Responsible Firearms Policy (member of board of directors).

WRITINGS: (With Glenn D. Kittler) *Triumph: The Incredible Saga of the First Transatlantic Flight,* Harper, 1961; *Strike Terror,* Paperback Library, 1968; *Good News, Bad News, Agnews,* Paperback Library, 1969; *Cry of the Hawk,* Paperback Library, 1970.

WORK IN PROGRESS: Hudson Bay Episode, a novel; *The Publisher.*

SIDELIGHTS: Hy Steirman lists his interests as "[trying] to keep America from turning to the right politically; photography, antique collecting and repairing; writing humorous limericks; fighting the big corporate battle." By way of autobiography, he says that "a kid born and bred in the depression never stops being hungry. He works. If he's lucky, he works at something he enjoys. I love writing, editing, publishing, and teaching." The Steirman-Kittler book *Triumph* has been translated into about twenty languages for distribution by the U.S. Information Service.†

* * *

STEISS, Alan Walter 1937-

PERSONAL: Born February 15, 1937, in Woodbury, N.J.; son of Walter and Martha (Schroeder) Steiss; married Patricia McClintock, June 13, 1959; children: Carol Jean, Darren Christopher, Todd Alan. *Education:* Bucknell University, A.B. (sociology) and A.B. (psychology), 1959; University of Wisconsin, M.A., 1966, Ph.D. (urban and regional planning), 1969. *Home:* 1397 Locust St., Blacksburg, Va. 24060. *Office:* College of Architecture and Urban Studies, Virginia Polytechnic Institute and State University, Blacksburg, Va. 24061.

CAREER: State of New Jersey, Division of State and Regional Planning, Trenton, assistant planner, 1960-61, senior planner, 1961-62, principal planner, 1962-63, supervising planner, 1963-64, section chief, 1964-65; Virginia Polytechnic Institute and State University, Blacksburg, assistant professor, 1967-69, associate professor, 1969-72, professor, 1972—, assistant director of Center for Urban and Regional Studies, 1968-69, director, 1969-70, chairman of Division of Environmental and Urban Systems, 1969-75, associate dean for research and graduate studies, 1974—. Lecturer at Rider College, 1963-64, New York University, 1964, Georgia In-

stitute of Technology, 1968-70. Member of firm, Planning Sciences Organization, 1967-73, and Anthony J. Catanese & Associates, 1973; principal investigator, National Training and Development Service Urban Management Curriculum Development Project, 1976—. Consultant to Trust Territory of the Pacific, 1968, State of Hawaii, 1974—, and to other state and industrial groups.

MEMBER: American Institute of Planners (chairman of committee on programs for planning students, 1960-64), Association of Collegiate Schools of Planning (member of executive committee, 1970-71, secretary, 1971-72), American Association of University Professors, National Urban Coalition, Urban America, Inc., Psi Chi, Lambda Alpha, Lambda Chi Alpha, Tau Delta Rho. *Awards, honors:* Named one of Outstanding Young Men in America by U.S. Junior Chamber of Commerce, 1970; named Outstanding Educator of America, 1972; Teaching Excellence Award, 1975.

WRITINGS: (With James Collins and George McKnight) *The Setting for Regional Planning in New Jersey,* New Jersey Department of Conservation and Economic Development, 1961; (with Collins) *An Open Space Plan for New Jersey,* New Jersey Department of Conservation and Economic Development, 1963; (with Harold F. Wise, Henry Fagin, and Edward Schten) *Planning Administration,* Wisconsin Department of Resource Development, 1966; *A Framework for Planning in State Government,* Council of State Governments, 1968; (with Anthony J. Catanese) *Systemic Planning: Theory and Application,* Heath, 1970; (contributor) James T. Murray, editor, *Dynamic Factors in Transportation,* Duke University Press, 1970; (contributor) *Handbook for Regional Research and Regional Planning,* Akademie fur Raumforschung and Landesplanung, 1970; (with Charles Burchard and F. D. Regetz) *A Public Service Option for Architectural Curricula,* Association of Collegiate Schools of Architecture, 1971; *Public Budgeting and Management,* Heath, 1972; *Urban Systems Dynamics,* Heath, 1974; *Models for the Analysis and Planning of Urban Systems,* Heath, 1974; *Administracion y Presupuestos Publicos,* Editorial Diana, 1974; (with John Dickey, Michale Harvey, and Bruce Phelps) *Dynamic Change and the Urban Ghetto,* Heath, 1975; *Local Govern-Finance: Capital Facilities Planning and Debt Administration,* Heath, 1975; *Performance Administration,* Heath, 1977. Writer of other research reports on land use and urban planning. Contributor of more than forty articles to planning and urban affairs journals in the United States and Europe.

WORK IN PROGRESS: Public Budgeting and Accounting for Local Government, with Leo Herbert; *Public Policy/Program Analysis and Evaluation,* with Greg Daneke; case study workbook on public finance and budgeting.

* * *

STEMP, Isay 1922-

PERSONAL: Surname originally Stempnitzky; born September 10, 1922, in Russia; son of Isaac (a businessman) and Tema Lea Stempnitzky; married Naomi Kramer, June 25, 1950; children: Sarah E., Ruth G., Leo I., Morris W. *Education:* Massachusetts Institute of Technology, B.S., 1945, M.S.E.E., 1946; New York University, graduate work in business administration, 1955-58. *Home:* 336 Redmont Rd., West Hempstead, N.Y. 11552. *Office:* Stemp & Co., Inc., 275 Madison Ave., New York, N.Y. 10016.

CAREER: Isomet Co., Newtonville, Mass., president, 1950-54; J. A. Deknatel & Son, Inc., Queens Village, N.Y., general manager, 1954-59; Carter, Berlind & Weill, Inc., New York City, director of corporate finance department, 1961-67; Stemp & Co., Inc., New York City, president, 1967—. Lecturer on finance in Europe and South America. *Member:* American Finance Association, American Economic Association, American Management Association, Mathematical Association of America, Sigma Xi, Tau Beta Pi.

WRITINGS: Corporate Growth Strategies, American Management Association, 1969. Also author of *Finance and Accounting for Non-Financial Executives,* 1977.

WORK IN PROGRESS: Case studies in mergers and acquisitions; memoirs of a merger-maker; also writing on valuation of enterprises.

* * *

STENT, Gunther S(iegmund) 1924-

PERSONAL: Surname changed legally at time of naturalization; born March 28, 1924, in Berlin, Germany; came to United States in 1940, naturalized in 1945; son of George and Elizabeth (Karfunkelstein) Stensch; married Inga Loftsdottir (a music teacher), October 27, 1951; children: Stefan-Loftur. *Education:* University of Illinois, B.S., 1945, Ph.D., 1958. *Home:* 145 Purdue Ave., Berkeley, Calif. 94708. *Office:* Department of Molecular Biology, University of California, Berkeley, Calif. 94720.

CAREER: University of California, Berkeley, assistant research biochemist, 1952-56, associate professor, 1957-58, professor of bacteriology and virology, 1959-63, professor of molecular biology, 1963—. Member of genetics panel, National Institutes of Health, 1959-64, and National Science Foundation, 1965-69. *Member:* American Academy of Arts and Sciences, Max Planck Gesellschaft. *Awards, honors:* National Research Council Merck fellow in biology, 1948-50; American Cancer Society fellow at University of Copenhagen, and Pasteur Institute, Paris, 1950-52; National Science Foundation senior fellow, 1960-61; Guggenheim fellow, 1969-70.

WRITINGS: (Editor) *Papers on Bacterial Viruses,* Little, Brown, 1960, 2nd edition, 1965; *Molecular Biology of Bacterial Viruses,* W. H. Freeman, 1963; (editor with J. Cairns and J. D. Watson) *Phage and the Origins of Molecular Biology,* Cold Spring Harbor Laboratory, 1967; *The Coming of the Golden Age: A View of the End of Progress,* Natural History Press, 1969; *Molecular Genetics,* W. H. Freeman, 1971. Contributor to scientific journals. Member of editorial board, *Zeitschrift fuer Vererbungslehre,* 1962-71, *Genetics,* 1963-68, *Journal of Molecular Biology,* 1965-69, *Annual Reviews of Genetics,* 1965-69, and *Annual Reviews of Microbiology,* 1966-70.

SIDELIGHTS: Reviewing *The Coming of the Golden Age,* a *New Yorker* critic writes: "It is Professor Stent's thesis . . . that the end of progress in all artistic and intellectual disciplines is now clearly in view. . . . He feels we will tend toward a sort of technological Polynesia . . . [the] arguments are so closely constructed and his style so lucid that his brief book is marvellous to read—and, indeed, he may even be right."

BIOGRAPHICAL/CRITICAL SOURCES: New Yorker, February 7, 1970; *Nation,* October 19, 1970.

* * *

STEPHENS, Thomas M. 1931-

PERSONAL: Born June 15, 1931, in Youngstown, Ohio;

son of Thomas J. and Mary (Hanna) Stephens; married Evelyn Kleshock, July 1, 1955. *Education:* Youngstown University, B.S., 1955; Kent State University, M.Ed., 1957; University of Pittsburgh, Ph.D., 1966. *Home:* 1753 Blue Ash Pl., Columbus, Ohio 43229. *Office:* College of Education, Ohio State University, 1945 North High, Columbus, Ohio 43210.

CAREER: Teacher and psychologist in public schools in Warren and Niles, Ohio, 1955-58; Montgomery County Schools, Dayton, Ohio, school psychologist, 1958-60; Ohio Department of Education, Columbus, Ohio, educational specialist, 1960-62, administrator of programs for gifted and slow learning children, 1962-64, Title I-E.S.E.A. state coordinator, 1965-66; University of Pittsburgh, Pittsburgh, Pa., associate professor of education, 1966-70; Ohio State University, Columbus, 1970—, began as associate professor, currently professor of education and chairman of exceptional children department. Consultant to U.S. Office of Education, Council for Exceptional Children, and school districts in seven states, 1966—. Co-director of national evaluation of Project Follow Through, 1967-68. *Member:* American Psychological Association, Council for Exceptional Children, Council for Children with Behavioral Disorders (president, 1971-72), Phi Delta Kappa.

WRITINGS: (Contributor, and editor with Walter B. Barbe) *Educating Tomorrow's Leaders,* Ohio Department of Education, 1961; (contributor, and editor with Barbe) *Attention to the Gifted Child a Decade Later,* Ohio Department of Education, 1962; (contributor, and editor with A. R. Gibson) *Pathways to Progress,* Ohio Department of Education, 1963; (contributor, and editor with Gibson) *Acceleration and the Gifted,* Ohio Department of Education, 1963; (editor with S. J. Bonham) *Mental Health Planning in Education,* Ohio Department of Education, 1964; (contributor) D. L. Cleland and Elaine Vilschek, editors, *Progress and Promise in Reading Instruction,* University of Pittsburgh, 1966; (editor with A. T. Jersild, Jerome Kagan, and Richard Alpert) *Three Views of Human Behavior,* Ohio Department of Education, 1967; (contributor) James Miller, editor, *Teaching Migrant Children,* Ohio Department of Education, 1969; *Directive Teaching of Children with Learning and Behavioral Handicaps,* C. E. Merrill, 1970, 2nd edition, 1976; *Implementing Behavior Approaches in Elementary and Secondary Schools,* C. E. Merrill, 1975; *Teaching Skills to Children with Learning and Behavioral Disorders,* C. E. Merrill, 1977.

Monographs; all published by Ohio Department of Education, except as noted: *Ohio's Academically Gifted, 1960-61,* 1961; *A Look at Ohio's Gifted-Status Study,* 1962; *Some Problems in the Definition and Identification of Gifted High School Students,* 1962; (with Gibson) *Ohio's Academically Gifted, 1961-62,* 1962; (with Bonham) *Psychological Evaluation and Screening Procedures for Slow Learning Children,* 1963; (with H. N. Menapace and C. E. Grover) *Orthopedically Handicapped Children in Ohio Public Schools,* 1964; (with H. McPherson) *Developing a Work Experience Program for Slow Learning Youth,* 1964; (with Marvin Kurfurst) *The National Evaluation of Project Follow Through, 1967-68,* School of Education, University of Pittsburgh, 1969; *Using Behavioral Approaches with Delinquent Youth and Implications for Vocational Assessment: A Selected Review,* University of Pittsburgh, 1970.

Contributor to *Journal of School Psychology, Exceptional Children, Public School Digest, Journal of Educational Psychology, Ohio's Health, Clearinghouse,* and other journals. Book review editor, *Journal of School Psychology;*

associate editor, *Behavior Disorders* and *Exceptional Children.*

WORK IN PROGRESS: Mainstreaming Handicapped Children, for Wiley.

SIDELIGHTS: Thomas Stephens writes, "[I have a] great concern about the increasing failure of our educational and social institutions to help children and youth to become competent, happy and self-sufficient citizens."

* * *

STEPHENS, W(illiam) P(eter)   1934-

PERSONAL: Born May 16, 1934, in Penzance, Cornwall, England; son of Alfred Cyril William Joseph and Jennie Eudora (Trewavas) Stephens. *Education:* Attended Cambridge University, 1952-57, University of Lund, 1957-58, University of Strasbourg, 1965-67, and University of Muenster, 1966-67; Cambridge University, M.A., 1961, B.D., 1971; University of Strasbourg, Docteur es sciences religieuses, 1967. *Home:* 61 Northover Rd., Bristol BS9 3LQ, England. *Office:* Wesley College, University of Bristol, Bristol, BS10 7QD, England.

CAREER: Hartley Victoria College, Manchester, England, assistant tutor in New Testament, 1958-61; University of Nottingham, Nottingham, England, Methodist chaplain, 1961-65; minister of Methodist church in Shirley, Croydon, England, 1967-71; Hartley Victoria College, holder of Ranmoor Chair of Church History, 1971-73; University of Bristol, Wesley College, Bristol, England, holder of Randles Chair of Historical and Systematic Theology, 1973—. Fernley Hartley Lecturer, 1972; James A. Gray Lecturer at Duke University, 1976. Chairman of Shirley Group of Churches, 1969-70, Croydon Anti-Apartheid Group, 1970-72, and Withington World Development Movement, 1972-73. Member of Bristol City Council. *Member:* Society for Study of Theology (secretary, 1963—), British Roman Catholic-Methodist Commission, Conference of European Churches (member of advisory committee).

WRITINGS: The Holy Spirit in the Theology of Martin Bucer, Cambridge University Press, 1970; *Faith and Love* (sermons), Epworth, 1971. Also author of many articles on churches in Eastern and Western Europe.

WORK IN PROGRESS: The Theology of Ulrich Zwingli.

SIDELIGHTS: W. P. Stephens is competent in French, German, Swedish, Hebrew, Latin, and Greek.

* * *

STEPHENS, W(illiam) Richard   1932-

PERSONAL: Born January 2, 1932, in Ashburn, Mo.; son of G. Lewis (a merchant and farmer) and Helen M. (Williamson) Stephens; married Arlene M. Greer, June 28, 1952; children: Richard, Kendell, Kelli. *Education:* Greenville College, B.S., 1953; University of Missouri, M.Ed., 1957; Washington University, St. Louis, Mo., Ed.D., 1964. *Politics:* Democrat. *Religion:* Christian. *Office:* Greenville College, Greenville, Ill. 62246.

CAREER: High school teacher in Sturgeon, Mo., 1955-57; Greenville College, Greenville, Ill., assistant professor, 1957-61, associate professor of education, 1963-64, chairman of Division of Education, 1963-64; Indiana State University, Terre Haute, assistant professor, 1964-67, associate professor of education, 1967-70; Indiana University, Bloomington, professor of history of education, 1970-71; Greenville College, vice-president for academic affairs, and dean of

faculty, 1971—. Summer instructor, Washington University, St. Louis, Mo., 1962-63. *Military service:* U.S. Army, 1953-55. *Member:* History of Education Society, Philosophy of Education Society, Society of Professors of Education (associate editor of publications, 1968-71), Midwest History of Education Society (president, 1972), Central States Faculty Colloquium (chairman, 1969—), Ohio Valley Philosophy of Education Society (secretary-treasurer, 1967-70). *Awards, honors:* National Vocational Guidance Association Award of Merit, 1973, for *Social Reform and the Origins of Vocational Guidance, 1890-1925.*

WRITINGS: The Teacher Education Guide, Greenville College, 1961; (contributor) George C. Stoumbis and Alvin W. Howard, editors, *Schools for the Middle Years,* International Textbook Co., 1969; *Social Reform and the Origins of Vocational Guidance: A Study of Intellectual and Social Forces Which Have Shaped the Guidance Idea in American Education, 1890-1925,* National Vocational Guidance Association, 1970; (contributor) William Joyce and John R. Lee, editors, *Readings in Elementary Social Studies,* Allyn & Bacon, 1970; (with William Van Til) *Education in American Life,* Houghton, 1972. Contributor to *World Topics Yearbook,* 1973-76. Editor, *Proceedings* of the Ohio Valley Philosophy of Education Society Annual Meeting, 1968, 1969, 1970, all volumes published by Indiana State University; also editor of *Insights* (an occasional paper for John Dewey Society for the Study of Education and Culture), 1972—. Contributor to education journals.

* * *

STERLING, Robert R.   1931-

PERSONAL: Born May 16, 1931, in Bugtussle, Okla.; son of Riley Paul (a farmer) and Lillian (Newman) Sterling; married Margery Stoskopf, May 2, 1954; children: Robert, Kimberly. *Education:* University of Denver, B.S., 1956, M.B.A., 1958; University of Florida, Ph.D., 1964. *Religion:* Quaker. *Home:* 4431 Mt. Vernon, Houston, Tex. 77006. *Office:* Rice University, Houston, Tex. 77001.

CAREER: Harpur College (now State University of New York at Binghamton), assistant professor of social science, 1963-66; Yale University, New Haven, Conn., science faculty fellow, 1966-67; University of Kansas, Lawrence, associate professor, then professor of business administration, 1967-70, Arthur Young Distinguished Professor, 1970-74; Rice University, Houston, Tex., Jessee Jones Distinguished Professor, 1974—. *Member:* American Accounting Association (vice-president, 1975—), Accountants for Public Interest (director), International Association for Research on Income and Wealth, American Association of University Professors. *Awards, honors:* National Science Foundation faculty fellow; Gold Medal of American Institute of Certified Public Accountants for best research published in English, 1968, for "The Going Concern: An Examination" in *Accounting Review.*

WRITINGS: Theory of the Measurement of Enterprise Income, University Press of Kansas, 1969; (editor with William F. Bentz) *Accounting in Perspective,* South-Western, 1971; (editor) *Asset Valuation and Income Determination,* Scholars Book Co., 1971; (editor) *Research Methodology in Accounting,* Scholars Book Co., 1972; (editor) *Institutional Issues in Public Accounting,* Scholars Book Co., 1974. Writer of papers on accounting and research methodology. Book review editor, *Accounting Review.*†

STERN, Robert A. M. 1939-

PERSONAL: Born May 23, 1939, in New York, N.Y.; son of Sidney S. and Sonya (Cohen) Stern; married Lynn Solinger, May 22, 1966; children: Nicholas S. G. *Education:* Columbia University, B.A., 1960; Yale University, M.Arch., 1965. *Home:* 101 Central Park W., New York, N.Y. 10023.

CAREER: Robert A. M. Stern & John S. Hagmann (architects and designers), New York City, partner, 1969—. Columbia University, School of Architecture, New York City, lecturer, 1970-72, assistant professor, 1972—. Vice-president, Cunningham Dance Foundation, 1969-73; member of building committee, Whitney Museum; trustee, American Federation of Arts.

WRITINGS: 40 Under 40 (catalog), American Federation of Arts, 1966; *New Directions in American Architecture,* Braziller, 1969; *George Howe: Toward a Modern Architecture,* Yale University Press, 1975.

WORK IN PROGRESS: Post-Modernism.

*   *   *

STEVENS, Edward 1928-

PERSONAL: Born November 28, 1928, in Boston, Mass.; son of Edward (an accountant) and Alice (Murphy) Stevens. *Education:* Woodstock College, A.B., 1952, S.T.L., 1960; Fordham University, M.A., 1955; St. Louis University, Ph.D., 1965. *Office:* Department of Philosophy, Canisius College, Buffalo, N.Y. 14208.

CAREER: Teacher at Brooklyn Preparatory School, Brooklyn, N.Y., 1953-54, and Xavier High School, New York, N.Y., 1954-56; St. Louis University, St. Louis, Mo., part-time instructor in philosophy, 1963-65; Canisius College, Buffalo, N.Y., 1965—, began as assistant professor, currently associate professor of philosophy. *Member:* American Philosophical Association, American Association of University Professors, American Management Association.

WRITINGS—All published by Paulist/Newman: *Making Moral Decisions,* 1969; *Oriental Mysticism,* 1972; *The Morals Game,* 1974; *The Religion Game: American Style,* 1976. Contributor to sociology, education, and religious periodicals.

WORK IN PROGRESS: Writing on business ethics.

*   *   *

STEVENS, Eleanour V(irginia) 1926-

PERSONAL: Born April 15, 1926, in Somerville, Mass.; daughter of Walter Beckwith (a business administrator) and Virginia (Gilmore) Stevens. *Education:* Indiana University, B.S., 1956, M.B.A., 1957; University of Illinois, Ph.D., 1966. *Politics:* Republican. *Religion:* Protestant. *Home:* 168 Yale Ave., Fort Collins, Colo. 80521. *Office:* Department of Management, Colorado State University, Fort Collins, Colo. 80521.

CAREER: Colorado State University, Fort Collins, professor of management, 1957—. Visiting professor of management, University of Missouri, 1969-70. *Member:* American Academy of Management, American Association of University Women, American Business Women's Association. *Awards, honors:* Ford Foundation Fellowship, 1962.

WRITINGS: (With J. L. McKeever) *Casettes in Human Relations,* W. C. Brown, 1968; (with Ronald A. Wykstra) *Labor Law and Public Policy,* Odyssey, 1970; (with Wykstra) *American Labor and Manpower Policy,* Odyssey, 1970.

WORK IN PROGRESS: Selected Readings in Human Relations, with J. L. McKeever, R. D. Steade, and G. J. Francis, for Kendall/Hunt.

*   *   *

STEVENS, Franklin 1933-
(Steve Franklin)

PERSONAL: Born October 31, 1933, in Camden, N.J.; son of Franklin P. and Virginia (Mitchell) Stevens; married. *Education:* Attended public schools in Summit, N.J. *Home:* Old King's Hwy., Stone Ridge, N.Y. 12484. *Agent:* Mary Yost Associates, 141 East 55th St., New York, N.Y. 10022.

CAREER: Writer.

WRITINGS: (Under pseudonym Steve Franklin) *The Malcontents,* Doubleday, 1970; *If This Be Treason: Your Sons Tell Their Own Stories of Why They Won't Fight for Their Country,* Peter H. Wyden, 1970; (under pseudonym Steve Franklin) *The Chickens in the Airshaft,* Doubleday, 1972; *Dance as Life: A Swan with American Ballet Theatre,* Harper, 1976.

WORK IN PROGRESS: Last Call, a novel; *Giulliano,* an novel; *The Expendable Man,* a mystery-thriller.

SIDELIGHTS: Franklin Stevens told *CA:* "I write mysteries, non-fiction, and journalism in order to support myself while I write novels. I write novels because it is the most deeply rewarding activity I know of." Stevens has lived in Paris and has traveled in Europe, Morocco, most of the United States, and Martinique.

BIOGRAPHICAL/CRITICAL SOURCES: Best Sellers, December 15, 1970; *Nation,* May 24, 1971.

*   *   *

STEWART, Daniel K(enneth) 1925-

PERSONAL: Born July 14, 1925, in East Lansing, Mich.; son of Earle H. and Frieda M. Stewart; married August 5, 1947; children: four. *Education:* Michigan State University, B.A., 1949, M.A., 1952, Ph.D., 1959. *Home:* 14 Golf View Pl., De Kalb, Ill. 60115. *Office:* Department of Marketing, Northern Illinois University, De Kalb, Ill. 60115.

CAREER: Michigan State University, East Lansing, instructor, 1955-61, assistant professor of natural science, 1961-62; Campbell-Ewald Co. (advertising), Detroit, Mich., consultant, 1961-62, research account executive, 1962-67, director of basic science unit, 1967-69, consultant, 1969-70; University of Illinois, Urbana, visiting professor of advertising, 1969-70; Northern Illinois University, De Kalb, associate professor of marketing, 1970—. *Member:* American Psychological Association, Institute for the Study of Human Knowledge, Business/Professional Advertising Association, Advertising Club of Chicago. *Awards, honors:* National Institute of Mental Health grant for research on the laws of logic involved in communication, 1960-62; *Advertising Age* fellowship for media workshop, Chicago, 1972; American Academy of Advertising special award for first editor of *Journal of Advertising,* 1975.

WRITINGS: The Psychology of Communication (textbook), Funk, 1969. Contributor of about thirty articles to various scholarly journals. Editor, *Journal of Advertising,* 1972-75.

WORK IN PROGRESS: Advertising and Consumer Behavior, a textbook; *Legal and Social Aspects of Advertising,* a textbook; *Procedure Manual for Advertising Evaluation;* three major research projects.

SIDELIGHTS: Daniel K. Stewart wrote *CA:* "The basic problem we face in the social and behavioral sciences today is their overwhelming domination by philosophical materialism. The theories which govern their methodologies and experimental designs are ontologically restricted to physical phenomena—the crudest example being the recently discarded theory of behaviorism. Indeed, it is this materialistic bias in the human sciences that accounts for the anthropomorphic empiricism demonstrated in their research methodology. We need scientists who understand that man is more than an animal, and whose research will explore hypotheses based on this assumption."

The Psychology of Communication has been translated into Spanish and Portuguese.

*   *   *

STEWART, Donald H(enderson) 1911-

PERSONAL: Born June 27, 1911, in Des Moines, Iowa; son of Fred Henderson (a teacher) and Lillian (Hanke) Stewart; married Joann Evans (a mutual funds representative), December 27, 1948; children: Douglas Evans, David Frederick, Deborah Claralynn, Donna Joan. *Education:* Drake University, B.A., 1934, M.A., 1935; University of Iowa, graduate study, summer, 1935; Columbia University, Ph.D., 1950; postdoctoral study at University of Utrecht, summer, 1950, University of the Americas, summer, 1951, and Harvard University, 1953-54. *Home:* 13 Warren St., Cortland, N.Y. 13045. *Office:* Department of History, State University of New York, Cortland, N.Y. 13045.

CAREER: Des Moines Register & Tribune, Des Moines, Iowa, clerk in auditing department, 1928-30; high school and junior college teacher in Osceola, Iowa, 1935-37; Union College, Barbourville, Ky., began as assistant professor, became associate professor of history, 1940-42, 1946-47; Drake University, Des Moines, Iowa, assistant professor, 1947-51, associate professor of history, 1951-56; State University of New York College at Cortland, associate professor, 1956-57, professor of history, 1957-75, Distinguished Teaching Professor of American History, 1975—, chairman of department of social studies, 1959-63. Fulbright professor, University of Muenster, 1954-55. *Military service:* U.S. Army, 1942-46; became captain. U.S. Army Reserve, 1948-67; became lieutenant colonel.

MEMBER: American Historical Association, Organization of American Historians, American Association of University Professors, Cortland County Historical Society, Phi Beta Kappa, Phi Alpha Theta, Kappa Delta Pi. *Awards, honors:* Ford Foundation faculty fellow at Harvard University, 1953-54; State University of New York research awards, 1959-63.

WRITINGS: (With R. A. Brown) *A Student Guide to the American Story,* McGraw, 1956; (with others) *Concise Dictionary of American Biography,* Scribner, 1964; *The Opposition Press of the Federalist Period,* State University of New York Press, 1969. Author of introductions to several reprints of history books. Contributor of twenty articles to *McGraw-Hill Encyclopedia of World Biography,* 1973. Contributor of articles and reviews to professional journals.

WORK IN PROGRESS: A survey text on the American Civil War; research on newspapers and the adoption of the Federal Constitution.

SIDELIGHTS: Donald Stewart told *CA:* "Earlier experience on a newspaper gave me an interest in and a conviction as to the importance of the media in America. My writing efforts have been largely directed toward showing that this significance has been characteristic even in our early history as a nation."

AVOCATIONAL INTERESTS: Sports (on a dilettante or spectator basis), photography, philately, music appreciation.

*   *   *

STEWART, James Brewer 1940-

PERSONAL: Born August 8, 1940, in Cleveland, Ohio; son of Richard H. (an attorney) and Marian (Brewer) Stewart; married Dorothy Carlson, June 26, 1965; children: Rebecca Ann, Jennifer Lynn. *Education:* Dartmouth College, B.A., 1962; Case Western Reserve University, M.A., 1966, Ph.D., 1968. *Home:* 1835 Fairmount Ave., St. Paul, Minn. 55101. *Office:* Department of History, Macalester College, St. Paul, Minn. 55101.

CAREER: Carroll College, Waukesha, Wis., assistant professor of American history, 1968-69; Macalester College, St. Paul, Minn., assistant professor, 1969-72, associate professor of American history, 1972—, chairman of department, 1972—. *Member:* American Historical Association, Organization of American Historians, Association for the Study of Negro Life and History, Southern Historical Association.

WRITINGS: Joshua R. Giddings and the Tactics of Radical Politics, Press of Case Western Reserve University, 1970; *Holy Warriors: The Abolitionists and American Slavery,* Hill & Wang, 1976. Contributor to historical journals.

WORK IN PROGRESS: A biography of Wendell Phillips.

*   *   *

STEWART, Philip Robert 1940-

PERSONAL: Born May 21, 1940, in Kansas City, Mo.; son of Robert N. (an office manager) and Lucile (Soule) Stewart; married Joan Elizabeth Hinde (a teacher), January 31, 1970. *Education:* Yale University, B.A., 1962, Ph.D., 1967. *Home:* 522 Wofford Rd., Durham, N.C. 27707. *Office:* Department of Romance Languages, Duke University, Durham, N.C. 27706.

CAREER: Yale University, New Haven, Conn., instructor in French, 1966-68; Harvard University, Cambridge, Mass., assistant professor of French, 1968-72; Duke University, Durham, N.C., associate professor of French, 1972—. *Member:* American Society for Eighteenth-Century Studies, Societe Francaise d'Etudes du 18e Siecle, American Association of Teachers of French.

WRITINGS: Imitation and Illusion in the French Memoir-Novel, 1700-1750: The Art of Make-Believe, Yale University Press, 1969; *Le Masque et la parole: Le Langage de l'amour au dix-huitieme siecle,* Jose Corti (Paris), 1973; (editor) Prevost, *Cleveland,* critical edition, Presses Universitaires de Grenoble, 1977.

WORK IN PROGRESS: Essays on early French novels.

*   *   *

STEWART, Vincent (Astor, Jr.) 1939-

PERSONAL: Born May 13, 1939, in San Augustine, Tex.; son of Vincent A. (a sales manager) and Nay Deen (Flournoy) Stewart; married Judith McVicker, September 3, 1965; children: Cassandra Gray, Carleton Flournoy. *Education:* Tulane University, student, 1957-59; Stephen F. Austin State College (now University), B.A., 1961, M.A., 1962; University of Iowa, graduate student, 1962-64. *Politics:* Democrat. *Religion:* Episcopalian. *Office:* Department of English, Lock Haven State College, Lock Haven, Pa. 17745.

CAREER: Northeast Missouri State Teachers College (now Northeast Missouri State University), Kirksville, assistant professor of English, 1964-66; Virginia Polytechnic Institute, Blacksburg, instructor in English, 1966-68; Lock Haven State College, Lock Haven, Pa., associate professor of English, 1968—. Visiting lecturer, Stephen F. Austin State College (now University), summer, 1964; consultant in creative writing, Hawaii State Department of Education, summer, 1967. *Member:* Modern Language Association of America, National Council of Teachers of English.

WRITINGS: Words for the Builder (poems), Brush Mountain Press, 1966; (with Steven Roth) *Small Deceits,* Lock Haven Chapbooks, 1968; *Three Dimensions of Poetry: An Introduction,* Scribner, 1969. Contributor of poems to *Maelstrom, Voices, Hudson Review, Appalachian Review, Laurel Review, Blue Guitar, New Athenaeum,* and other journals.

WORK IN PROGRESS: With Richard A. Reed, an edition of *The Daily Meditations of Philip Pain; What Words for the Pawnbroker?,* a collection of poems; a critical study of the nature of poetry, incorporating new advances in prosodic study.†

*   *   *

STEYER, Wesley W. 1923-

PERSONAL: Born July 15, 1923, in Carleton, Neb.; son of Carl W. (a farmer) and Emma (Fegesack) Steyer; married Audrey Lietsch (a teacher), August 20, 1950; children: James K., Mark W. *Education:* Doane College, B.A. (cum laude), 1951; University of Nebraska, graduate student, 1953-54; University of Arizona, M.B.A., 1959. *Politics:* Republican. *Religion:* Brethren Church. *Home:* 1770 Longview, Stockton, Calif. 95207. *Office:* Department of Business, San Joaquin Delta College, Stockton, Calif. 95204.

CAREER: Teacher in public schools of Sumner, Neb., 1951-53; General Mills, Inc., Kankakee, Ill., accountant, 1954-58; San Joaquin Delta College, Stockton, Calif., 1959—, currently faculty member in department of business. *Military service:* U.S. Navy, 1944-46. *Member:* National Education Association, California Business Education Association, California Teachers Association.

WRITINGS: (With James Anthony Saxon) *Basic Principles of Data Processing,* Prentice-Hall, 1967, 2nd edition, 1970.

WORK IN PROGRESS: Accounting principles teaching tapes.†

*   *   *

STIERLIN, Helm 1926-

PERSONAL: Born March 12, 1926, in Mannheim, Germany; son of Paul (a civil engineer) and Elsbeth (Schoeningh) Stierlin; married Satuila Zanolli (a psychotherapist), June 10, 1965; children: Larissa, Saskia. *Education:* Studied philosophy and medicine at Universities of Heidelberg, Freiburg, and Zurich, 1946-63; University of Heidelberg, Ph.D., 1951, M.D., 1953. *Home:* Kappellenweg 19, 69 Heidelberg, West Germany. *Office:* University of Heidelberg, Heidelberg, West Germany.

CAREER: Staff member at various psychiatric hospitals and research institutes in Switzerland and the United States, 1953-74; National Institute of Mental Health, Bethesda, Md., acting chief of family study section, Adult Psychiatry Branch, 1969-74; University of Heidelberg, Heidelberg, West Germany, professor and chief psychoanalyst, 1974—. Private practice as psychoanalyst; assistant professor of psychiatry at Johns Hopkins University, 1969-74; associate professor of psychiatry at University of Maryland, 1972-74. Lecturer in Europe, Australia, New Zealand, and the Far East.

WRITINGS: Der gewalttaetige Patient, S. Karger (New York and Basel), 1956; *Conflict and Reconciliation: A Study in Human Relations and Schizophrenia,* Science House, 1969; *Das Tun des Einen ist das Tun des Anderen,* Suhrkamp, 1971; *Separating Parents and Adolescents,* Quadrangle, 1974; *Adolf Hitler: A Family Perspective,* Psychohistory Press, 1976; *Psychoanalyses and Family Therapy,* Jason Aronson, 1977; (co-author) *Das erste Familiengesprach,* Klett, 1977; *Wurzelin des Bosen,* Suhrkamp, 1978; *Delegation und Familie,* Suhrkamp, 1978. Also editor of *Texte zur Familiendynamik,* Klett. Contributor of about forty articles, mainly to scientific journals in America, Germany and France. Editor with J. Duss-von Werdt, *Famliendynamik.*

WORK IN PROGRESS: Research in schizophrenia and adolescence, and the problems of the family.

AVOCATIONAL INTERESTS: Philosophy and literature.

*   *   *

STOCKTON, Adrian James 1935-
(Jim Stockton)

PERSONAL: Born April 10, 1935, in Keighley, Yorkshire, England; son of Frederick John (a sound engineer) and Isobel (Smith) Stockton; married Valerie Watkins (a translator), July 28, 1962 (divorced, 1974); children: Eve. *Education:* Left school at fourteen. *Politics:* ''Unpolitical.'' *Home:* c/o Antoinette Madden, 34 rue Dauphine, Paris, France 75006. *Agent:* John Johnson, 51-54 Gresham Buildings, 12-13 Henrietta St., London WC2E 8LF, England. *Office:* c/o Stone & Webster Atlantic Corp., Sonatrach Module 1, Hassi R'Mel, Ghardia, Algeria.

CAREER: Seaman in British Merchant Service, 1952-54; served with Royal Air Force in Egypt and Cyprus, 1954-56; export clerk for Massey-Ferguson Ltd., Coventry, England, 1956-59; says that he has had ''occupations too numerous to detail,'' 1959—, working in a factory and also gardening for rent-free accommodation. He states, ''Economic situation in UK determined pattern of life to survive in the 70's.'' He has worked with Northrop-Page Inc., INTS Project, Iran, 1971-74, Williams International, Hassi R'Mel-Skikkda Pipeline, Algeria, 1974-75, Reliant Co., Khaliffa Olympic Stadium, Doha, Qatar, 1975-76, and with Stone & Webster Atlantic Corp., Hassi R'Mel, Algeria, 1977—.

WRITINGS: Runaway (autobiographical), Hutchinson, 1968.

WORK IN PROGRESS: The Ghost of the Airport Lounge, a book based on personal experiences; *A High Street Love Affair,* a book of poetry composed over the past twenty years.

SIDELIGHTS: Adrian James Stockton wrote *CA:* ''All human experience is important to me. Whilst I have to buy time to write by working on overseas contracts, sometimes in appalling conditions, I do not regret the hours spent away from a typewriter. I am building a fund of material and look forward to an early retirement.'' He lists influences: Celine, Miller, Lowry, and Agee.

BIOGRAPHICAL/CRITICAL SOURCES: Stockton,

Runaway, Hutchinson, 1968; *Books and Bookmen*, November, 1968.

* * *

STOKES, Jack (Tilden) 1923-

PERSONAL: Born August 26, 1923, in Sullivan, Ind.; son of Sherman Hays (a miner) and Elizabeth (Robbins) Stokes; married Bettie Johnson (a teacher), May 1, 1948; children: Deirdre, Tamara, Shaun, Jay T. *Education:* Indiana State University, B.A., 1950; University of Illinois, M.A., 1952; Southern Illinois University, Ph.D., 1970. *Home:* 518 South Charles, Belleville, Ill., 62221. *Office:* Belleville Area College, Belleville, Ill. 62221.

CAREER: Teacher in public schools in Basin, Wyo. and Oblong, Ill., 1950-61; Belleville Area College, Belleville, Ill., teacher of speech and drama, 1961—. *Military service:* U.S. Army, 1943-46. *Member:* Illinois State Speech and Theatre Association. *Awards, honors:* William C. Ball English Prize, Indiana State University, 1950.

WRITINGS: Wiley and the Hairy Man (juvenile), Macrae, 1970; (contributor) Betty Jean Lifton, editor, *Contemporary Children's Theatre*, Avon, 1974. Has written ten full-length plays, several children's plays and numerous drama choir pieces, which have been produced at the Oblong (Illinois) Township High School, Belleville (Illinois) Township High School-West, Belleville Area College, and Southern Illinois University-Carbondale.

WORK IN PROGRESS: Several children's plays and readers theatre pieces.

SIDELIGHTS: Jack Stokes wrote *CA:* "I am sure that I sometimes write to conceal what I think I am and to project what I want others to think I am. Always I write to find out what I am—to discover what it is like in that hairy jungle that I peep into only when I am dreaming. I write to give voice to the person or persons imprisoned in me that no one—including me—glimpses in my other public acts. I write to publish—and, as a playwright, I am happy to say, I am published every time a play of mine is enacted before an audience large or small."

AVOCATIONAL INTERESTS: Music.

* * *

STONE, Donald (Adelbert), Jr. 1937-

PERSONAL: Born June 29, 1937, in Hackensack, N.J.; son of Donald Adelbert and Julie (Cardin) Stone. *Education:* Haverford College, A.B., 1959; Yale University, Ph.D., 1963. *Office:* 201 Boylston Hall, Harvard University, Cambridge, Mass. 02138.

CAREER: Yale University, New Haven, Conn., instructor in French, 1962-63; Harvard University, Cambridge, Mass., instructor, 1963-65, assistant professor, 1965-69, professor of French, 1969—. *Member:* American Association of Teachers of French, Renaissance Society. *Awards, honors:* Guggenheim fellow, 1968-69.

WRITINGS: Handbook for French Composition, Prentice-Hall, 1965, 2nd edition, 1969; (editor) *Tristan et Iseut*, Prentice-Hall, 1966; *Ronsard's Sonnet Cycles: A Study in Tone and Vision*, Yale University Press, 1966; (editor) *Four Renaissance Tragedies*, Harvard University Press, 1966; *France in the Sixteenth Century*, Prentice-Hall, 1969; *From Tales to Truth*, V. Klostermann, 1973; *French Humanist Tragedy*, Manchester University Press, 1974. Contributor to *Esprit Createur, Studi Francesi,* and other language journals.

STONE, Robert B. 1916-

PERSONAL: Born February 26, 1916, in New York, N.Y.; son of David and Freida (Corenthal) Blustein; married Athalie Titman, 1950; married second wife, Lola Solomon, March 13, 1953; children: (second marriage) Dennis. *Education:* Massachusetts Institute of Technology, S.B., 1937. *Home and office:* 1022 Prospect St., Honolulu, Hawaii 96822. *Agent:* Curtis Brown Ltd., 575 Madison Ave., New York, N.Y. 10022.

CAREER: Writer. Publisher of house plans magazines, Huntington, Long Island, N.Y., 1950-59; public relations work, specializing in school and community relations, Huntington, Long Island, 1960-69. Conductor of awareness and sensitivity workshops sponsored by Huntington Public Library and other Huntington groups. Founder, past president, and director (1957-69) of Huntington Township Mental Health Clinic; past president, Huntington Town Forum. *Military service:* U.S. Army, Signal Corps, 1943-45; became master sergeant. *Member:* National School Public Relations Association, Authors Guild, Long Island Public Relations Association.

*WRITINGS—*With Sidney Petrie, except as indicated: (With Samuel Paul) *Complete Book of Home Modernizing*, Stuttman, for Literary Guild, 1953; (with Paul) *Homes for Living*, Simmons-Boardman, 1953; *How to Reduce and Control Your Weight with Self-Hypnotism*, Prentice-Hall, 1964; *Martinis and Whipped Cream*, Parker Publishing, 1965; *How to Strengthen Your Life with Mental Isometrics*, Parker Publishing, 1966; *What Modern Hypnotism Can Do For You*, Hawthorn, 1968; (with Christopher R. Vagts) *Anatomy of a Teacher Strike*, Parker Publishing, 1969; *The Lazy Lady's Easy Diet*, Parker Publishing, 1969; *The Truth about Hypnotism*, Frewin, 1969; *The Miracle Diet for Fast Weight Loss*, Parker Publishing, 1970; (with Christopher Hills) *Conduct Your Own Awareness Sessions*, New American Library, 1971; (sole author) *Jesus Has a Man in Waikiki: The Story of Bob Turnbull*, Revell, 1973; *Hypo-Dietetics*, Peter H. Wyden, 1975; (with Connie Haines) *For Once in My Life*, Warner Paperback, 1976; (sole author) *The Power of Miracle Metaphysics*, Parker Publishing, 1976; (with L. L. Schneider) *Old Fashioned Health Remedies that Work Best*, Prentice-Hall, 1977; (sole author) *The Magic of Psychotronic Power*, Prentice-Hall, 1978. Architectural editor, *Popular Science Do-It-Yourself Encyclopedia*, 1954.

SIDELIGHTS: Robert Stone says that he has "evolved from home improvement, to body improvement, to mind improvement" and is "getting close to the human spirit."†

* * *

STOOPS, John A(lbert) 1925-

PERSONAL: Born March 10, 1925, in Tarentum, Pa.; son of Charles Crawford (a teacher) and Ella Mae (Street) Stoops; married Muriel Brugger, August 2, 1947; children: Cathy Allen, John Albert, Jr., Judy Lynn, Charles Billingsley. *Education:* California State College, California, Pa., B.S. in Ed., 1948; University of Pennsylvania, M.S., 1949, Ed.D., 1960. *Home:* 454 Linden St., Coopersburg, Pa. *Office:* Institute of Educational Studies and Evaluation, 524 Brodhead Ave., Lehigh University, Bethlehem, Pa. 18015.

CAREER: Public school teacher in Claymont, Del., 1948-53; senior high school principal and then assistant superintendent of education in Langhorne, Pa., 1954-62; Lehigh University, Bethlehem, Pa., instructor in graduate courses, 1959-61, professor, 1962-76, Distinguished Professor of Educational Philosophy, 1976—, head of department of education, 1962-65, dean of School of Education, 1966-76, director of Institute for Educational Studies and Evaluation, 1976—. *Military service:* U.S. Navy, 1943-47; became ensign. *Member:* National Education Association, American Association of Colleges for Teacher Education, American Association of School Administrators. *Awards, honors:* Cosmos Club grant for research, Lehigh University, 1967; Hillman Award for distinguished teaching and service, Lehigh University, 1969.

WRITINGS: (With others) *The Extended School Year,* American Association for Supervision and Curriculum Development, 1960; *The Community College in Higher Education,* Lehigh University Press, 1966; *Religious Values in Education,* Interstate, 1967; *The Education of the Inner Man,* Interstate, 1969; *Education and Philosophies of Mind,* Lehigh University Press, 1969; *Philosophy and Education in Western Civilization,* Interstate, 1971; *Histories of Education from Sumeria to Modern Times,* Lehigh University Press, 1975.

WORK IN PROGRESS: Freedom and the Restoration of American Education, for Council for Educational Freedom in America.

SIDELIGHTS: John A. Stoops wrote *CA:* "I believe the two major problems facing American education are the absence of qualitative determinants and the absence of freedom. The most important educational writing of the last quarter of the twentieth century are those which examine educational evaluation and the pervasive involvement of government in educational matters."

*   *   *

STORY, Edward M.   1921-

PERSONAL: Born February 12, 1921; son of Harry M. (a utility executive) and Nancy E. (Henley) Story. *Education:* University of Tennessee, B.S., 1942; New York University, M.B.A., 1953; Berkeley Divinity School, S.T.B., 1966.

CAREER: Cunningham & Walsh, Inc. (advertising), New York, N.Y., vice-president, 1956-63; ordained to ministry of the Protestant Episcopal Church; Trinity Episcopal Church, Lincoln, Ill., rector, beginning 1968. *Member:* Rotary Club, Elks Club, Masons.

WRITINGS: (With James B. Simpson) *Long Shadows of Lambeth X: A Critical Eyewitness Account of the Tenth Decennial Conference of Anglican Bishops,* McGraw, 1969. Contributor to religious publications. Editor, *Springfield Churchman,* Springfield, Ill., 1968—.

WORK IN PROGRESS: Writing on the changing structure of the church.

BIOGRAPHICAL/CRITICAL SOURCES: Washington Post, November 15, 1969.††

*   *   *

STORY, Jack Trevor   1917-

PERSONAL: Born March 20, 1917, in Bengeo, England; son of James (a house painter and cook) and Rhoda (Dyball) Story; children: Jacqueline, Christine, Peter, Jennifer, Caroline, Lee, Lindsay, Lorel. *Education:* Attended night school in radio and electronics for seven years. *Politics:* "Lenny Bruce and Orwellian." *Religion:* "Varies." *Home:* 18 East Heath Rd., London N.W. 3, England.

CAREER: Writer, 1951—.

WRITINGS: The Trouble with Harry, T. V. Boardman, 1949, Macmillan, 1950; *Protection for a Lady,* Laurie, 1950;

Green to Pagan Street, Harrap, 1952; *The Money Goes Round and Round,* Redman, 1958; *Mix Me a Person* (mystery), W. H. Allen, 1959, Macmillan, 1960; *Man Pinches Bottom,* W. H. Allen, 1962; *Live Now, Pay Later,* Secker & Warburg, 1963; *Something for Nothing,* Secker & Warburg, 1963; *Urban District Lover,* Secker & Warburg, 1964; *I Sit in Hanger Lane,* Secker & Warburg, 1968; *Dishonourable Member,* Secker & Warburg, 1969; *One Last Mad Embrace,* Allison & Busby, 1970; *Hitler Needs You,* Allison & Busby, 1971; *Little Dog's Day,* Allison & Busby, 1971; *The Wind in the Snottygobble Tree,* Allison & Busby, 1971; *Letters to an Intimate Stranger,* Allison & Busby, 1972; *Company of Bandits,* Baker Press, 1972; *Crying Makes Your Nose Run,* Bruce & Watson, 1973; *Story on Crime,* Baker Press, 1975; *Morag's Flying Fortress,* Hutchinson, 1976. Also author of twenty Sexton Blake detective novels for Sexton Blake Library, 1951-61. Writer of film, television, and radio scripts. Contributor of short stories to magazines.

WORK IN PROGRESS: Two novels, *The Screwrape Lettuce* and *The Miracle Man.*

SIDELIGHTS: Jack Trevor Story wrote *CA:* "Like a steam engine that burns steam, I am a self-generating writer. Stories either get in the way or give you some kind of dramatic target which you smack from time to time. After suffering a broken heart and 3 stone weight loss I woke up one morning in 1973 with a line in my head: 'It was the kind of morning when everything rhymed.' It was the kind of line to start a book. My miseries were phasing out. One trouble: I had no book to write. Weeks later I get myself two good themes. 'American flyers during the war took off pissed [drunk]. It was not safe to be on the runway—they took girls aboard, f— over Hamburg.' That sounded like a story. My Flying Fortress gets shot down on such an orgy, crashes in what the crew believe to be occupied Belgium. In fact they have crossed the North Sea and are in England, a few miles from home base. They dismount a machine gun and wipe out a platoon of British Home Guards, believing them to be Germans, then steal a boat off a Suffolk beach and start back for Germany—thinking it's England. They get picked up by an enemy vessel and end the war in the cage. After the war, survivors go searching for their mistake. Good story? Right. With it I had my second theme. The captain, Alec Ranger, is now an electronics engineer who has been spying for NATO and has discovered that thalidomide and its horrors is really a genicidal remnant of Hitler's plans for the Jews. This has been brainwashed out of Alec's head when the story opens.

"When the reviews of *Morag's Flying Fortress* come out, such a dramatic and ingenious story has got to sell film rights for at least one hundred thousand dollars?" However, a reviewer for the *Sunday Telegraph* interpreted the story somewhat differently than Mr. Story had intended. The critic wrote: "When his great love Maggie ran away to Brussels, Jack Trevor Story lamented her on Saturdays in the *Guardian* for several years; it must have been terribly trying for her.

"*Morag's Flying Fortress* purports to be a spy story; Maggie, though still fled to Brussels, has become Sandra; the deserted lover has become an electronics engineer called Alec Ranger . . . this funny and likeable book, full of energy and rudeness and mistrust of the human race, is really a roundabout and complicated daydream of getting Maggie/Sandra back. Readers will wonder how she can resist such overtures."

Mr. Story commented that he believed the reviewer "missed the point." Similarly, he believed the point was missed with

The Wind in the Snottygobble Tree. He explained that "the plot dealt with the kidnapping of the Pope in order to replace him with a Mafia man. When they get him—he is electrocuted through his own piss—they discover that he is already mafiosa; Lucky Luciano, no less. Another great movie, surely? Uh uh." Mr. Story was frustrated with reviewers who interpreted it as a book about a travel agent bored with his job and thus instigates a world wide espionage organization with himself as boss. "The Pope was never mentioned in any review of the book," he added.

"In *Little Dog's Day*," Mr. Story continued, "my chief protagonists are forced to escape from a tyrannised Big Brother society by hi-jacking an airliner and taking it to the only remaining free country in the world, Iceland." He wrote that a *Guardian* reviewer thought this book was about a man who, in searching for his lost poodle, played a trombone through the streets of the city. Mr. Story concluded that "this and these are the best sidelights I can shed upon myself as a writer; they say it all."

BIOGRAPHICAL/CRITICAL SOURCES: Punch, November 27, 1968; *Sunday Telegraph,* October 24, 1976.

* * *

STRAHL, Leonard E. 1926-

PERSONAL: Born May 21, 1926, in Pittsburgh, Pa.; son of Samuel (a businessman) and Alice (Sokolsky) Strahl; married Rosemary Zeske (an author), October 23, 1954; children: Debra, Stephanie, Scott. *Education:* Studied at Julliard School of Music, 1947-49, Carnegie Institute of Technology (now Carnegie-Mellon University), 1950-51, University of Pittsburgh, 1951-52, and National Psychological Association for Psychoanalysis, 1968-69. *Politics:* Democrat. *Religion:* Unitarian Universalist. *Office:* Alfred Angelo, Inc., 1385 Broadway, New York, N.Y.

CAREER: Sales manager for Federal Industrial Manufacturing Co., Pittsburgh, Pa., and American Dynamics Corp., Philadelphia, Pa., 1957-59; Magna-Bond, Inc. (plastics manufacturers), Bala Cynwyd, Pa., marketing director, 1959-62; Business Dynamics Corp. (consultants), Philadelphia, president, 1961-63; Alfred Angelo, Inc. (manufacturers of bridal wear), New York, N.Y., sales and promotion director, 1963—. Conducted radio program, "Let's Take a Look at Business," on WIFI-FM, 1962-63. Member of Joint Council for Mental Health Services, New York, N.Y. *Military service:* U.S. Army, 1944-46. *Member:* National Psychological Association for Psychoanalysis, Bridal and Bridesmaids Apparel Association (vice-president).

WRITINGS: Meaning Business, Bobbs-Merrill, 1969.

WORK IN PROGRESS: A book about women, for Bobbs-Merrill.†

* * *

STRAND, William K. 1931-

PERSONAL: Born March 16, 1931, in Seattle, Wash.; son of William (a contractor) and Sybil (Claussen) Strand; married Constance Schaenen, December 29, 1955; children: John William, James Nelson, David Edward, Peter Keith. *Education:* Yale University, B.Eng., 1953; Stanford University, M.S. in C.E. 1957. *Home address:* Box 415, Millington, N.J. 07946. *Office:* Stone & Webster Management Consultants, Inc., 90 Broadway, New York, N.Y. 10004.

CAREER: Stone & Webster Management Consultants, Inc., New York, N.Y., 1957—, currently vice-president. Passaic Township (N.J.) Board of Education, member,

1962-78, vice-president, 1965-67, president, 1967-68; Morris County (N.J.) Educational Services Commission, member, 1973-77, president, 1976-77. *Military service:* U.S. Naval Reserve, Civil Engineer Corps, active duty, 1953-56; became lieutenant junior grade. *Member:* North American Society of Corporate Planning, American Industrial Development Council.

WRITINGS: (With J. D. Coughlan) *Depreciation: Accounting, Taxes, & Business Decisions,* Ronald, 1969. Contributor of book reviews to *Jersey Journal,* 1965-66.

AVOCATIONAL INTERESTS: European travel; English, Scottish, Irish, and Welsh folk music.

* * *

STRAUSS, Werner 1930-

PERSONAL: Born April 2, 1930, in Hannover, Germany; son of Alfred (an importer) and Ilse (Plaut) Strauss; married Jennifer Wallace (a university lecturer), June 10, 1958; children: Simon Charles, Jonathan Werner, Nicholas James. *Education:* University of Melbourne, B.Chem.E., 1953, M.Sc., 1957, D.App.Sc., 1974; University of Sydney, M.E., 1956; University of Sheffield, Ph.D., 1959. *Home:* 9 Moore St., Hawthorn, Victoria 3122, Australia. *Office:* University of Melbourne, Parkville, Victoria 3052, Australia.

CAREER: Commonwealth Scientific and Industrial Research Organisation, research officer in Melbourne and Sydney, Australia, 1955-60; University of Melbourne, Parkville, Australia, 1960—, began as lecturer, reader in industrial science, 1965—. Consultant, Westinghouse Electric Corp., Pittsburgh, 1967—. *Member:* Institution of Chemical Engineers (London; fellow), Royal Australian Chemical Institute (fellow), Clean Air Society, Air Pollution Control Association, Institution of Engineers (Australia).

WRITINGS: Industrial Gas Cleaning, Pergamon, 1966, 2nd edition, 1975; (editor) *Air Pollution Control,* Wiley, Volume I, 1971, Volume II, 1972. Editor, *Clean Air.*

WORK IN PROGRESS: Editing Volume III of *Air Pollution Control; Air Pollution,* for E. Arnold.

* * *

STRAVINSKY, Igor 1882-1971

June 17, 1882—April 6, 1971; Russian-born composer and musical giant. Obituaries: *New York Times,* April 7, 1971; *Washington Post,* April 7, 1971; *Time,* April 19, 1971.

* * *

STRAWSON, John 1921-

PERSONAL: Born January 1, 1921, in London, England; son of Cyril Walter (a headmaster) and Nellie (Jewell) Strawson; married Baroness Wilfried von Schellersheim, December 29, 1960; children: Viola, Carolin. *Education:* Attended Christ's College, Finchley, England. *Religion:* Church of England. *Home:* The Old Rectory, Boyton, Wiltshire, England. *Office:* Westland Aircraft, Ltd., Yeovil, Somerset, England.

CAREER: British Army, 1940—, with current rank of major general. Assigned to 4th Hussars, 1942-50, 1952-54, 1956-58, British Staff College, 1951-52, and U.S. Armored Center, Fort Knox, Ky., 1954-56; instructor at British Staff College, 1958-60; with War Office, 1960-62; commanding Queen's Royal Irish Hussars, 1963-65; commanding 39th Infantry Brigade, 1966-68; at Imperial Defence College, 1969; chief of staff, Supreme Headquarters Allied Powers in Europe

(SHAPE), Casteau, Belgium, 1970-72, at headquarters of United Kingdom Land Forces, 1972-76; Westland Aircraft, Ltd., Yeovil, Somerset, England, head of Cairo office, 1976—. *Member:* Cavalry Club (London). *Awards, honors*—Military: Bronze Star Medal (United States), 1946; Order of the British Empire, 1964; Commander of the Bath, 1975.

WRITINGS: The Battle for North Africa, Scribner, 1969; *Hitler's Battles for Europe,* Scribner, 1971 (published in England as *Hitler as Military Commander,* Batsford, 1971); *The Battle for the Ardennes,* Batsford, 1972; *Battle for Berlin,* Scribner, 1974. Contributor to *Times* (London), *Blackwood's Magazine,* and other publications.

WORK IN PROGRESS: A book on military interaction on the Western Front in the winter of 1944-45; a light book on life in a British cavalry regiment.

AVOCATIONAL INTERESTS: All forms of sport, particularly horses and hunting.

BIOGRAPHICAL/CRITICAL SOURCES: Bookseller, May 15, 1971.

* * *

STRAYER, Barry L. 1932-

PERSONAL: Born August 13, 1932, in Moose Jaw, Saskatchewan, Canada; son of Carl John (a farmer) and Nina (Carr) Strayer; married Eleanor Staton, July 2, 1955; children: Alison Lee, Jonathan Mark Staton, Colin James. *Education:* University of Saskatchewan, B.A., 1953, LL.B., 1955; Oxford University, B.C.L., 1957; Harvard University, S.J.D., 1966. *Home:* 504 Driveway, Ottawa, Ontario, Canada K1S 3N4. *Office:* Department of Justice, Ottawa, Ontario, Canada.

CAREER: University of Saskatchewan, College of Law, Saskatoon, Saskatchewan, professor of law, 1962-70 (on leave of absence, 1968-70); Government of Canada, Ottawa, Ontario, director of constitutional review section, Privy Council Office, 1968-72; Department of Justice, Ottawa, director of Constitutional Law Section, 1972-74, assistant deputy minister of justice, 1974—. *Member:* Institute of Public Administration of Canada, Law Society of Saskatchewan.

WRITINGS: Judicial Review of Legislation in Canada, University of Toronto Press, 1968. Contributor to legal and public administration journals.

* * *

STRICKLAND, Phil D. 1941-

PERSONAL: Born October 17, 1941, in Abilene, Tex.; son of Dallas Dowell (a businessman) and Sybil (Schrimsher) Strickland; married Carolyn Ruth Bone; children: Shannon Michelle, Delaine Patrice. *Education:* University of Texas, B.A., 1963, J.D., 1966; Southwestern Baptist Theological Seminary, graduate study, 1966-67. *Religion:* Baptist. *Office:* Christian Life Commission, Baptist General Convention of Texas, Dallas, Tex.

CAREER: Assistant to lieutenant governor of Texas, Austin, 1965, 1966; Irby & McConnico (law firm), Fort Worth, Tex., associate, 1967; Baptist General Convention of Texas, Dallas, associate secretary of Christian Life Commission, 1967—. Member of executive board, Project Equality of Texas and Inter-Racial Baptist Institute, Dallas; member, Texas United Community Services. *Member:* American Bar Association, National Conference on Social Welfare, Amer-

ican Judicature Society, American Academy of Political and Social Science, Academy of Political Science, Texas Bar Association, Dallas Bar Association.

WRITINGS: (With W. S. Garmon) *How to Fight the Drug Menace,* Broadman, 1970; (contributor) John Hendrix, editor, *Invitation to Dialogue: The Professional World,* Broadman, 1970; (with Ben E. Loring, Jr. and Dunn) *Endangered Species,* Broadman, 1976. Also contributor to *Politics: A Guidebook for Christians,* edited by James M. Dunn, 1970. Contributor to periodicals.

* * *

STRONG, Anna Louise 1885-1970

November 24, 1885—March 29, 1970; American-born journalist, critic, and advocate of communism. Obituaries: *New York Times,* March 30, 1970; *Washington Post,* March 30, 1970; *Current Biography,* 1970.

* * *

STUART, Simon (Walter Erskine) 1930-

PERSONAL: Born August 22, 1930, in Nutley, Sussex, England; son of the seventh Earl Castle Stewart and Eleanor Guggenheim (an American); married Deborah Mounsey, 1973; children: Thomas, Corin, Tristram. *Education:* Trinity College, Cambridge, M.A., 1953, Diploma of Education, 1954. *Politics:* Non-aligned. *Religion:* Atheist. *Home:* 16 Neville Dr., London N.2, England.

CAREER: Teacher of English at King's School, Canterbury, England, 1954-57, Stowe School, Buckinghamshire, England, 1958-61, and Haberdashers' Aske's School, Elstree, England, 1961—. *Military service:* Scots Guards, 1949-50; served in Malaya; became second lieutenant.

WRITINGS: (Editor) Philip O'Connor, *The Memoirs of a Public Baby,* Faber, 1958; *Say: An Experiment in Learning,* Thomas Nelson, 1969. A poem has been anthologized in *New Measure 10,* edited by Peter Jay, 1969. Contributor of reviews to *Times Education Supplement.*

WORK IN PROGRESS: The nature of literary creativity as illuminated by recent psychoanalytical findings.

SIDELIGHTS: During vacations Simon Stuart has worked abroad—on the docks in Helsinki, mining in Greece, and farming in Austria. He also made an expedition to the Skolt Lapps in Finland. "Now," he says, "I'm content to study wildlife—as an old-fashioned field naturalist with a smattering of biochemistry and ecology."

BIOGRAPHICAL/CRITICAL SOURCES: Books and Bookmen, November, 1968; *New Statesman,* May 23, 1969; *Jewish Quarterly,* summer, 1969; *Guardian,* June 12, 1969; *Times Literary Supplement,* October 16, 1969.

* * *

STUBBS, John C(aldwell) 1936-

PERSONAL: Born August 5, 1936, in Philadelphia, Pa.; son of Thomas H. (an engineer) and Elizabeth (Caldwell) Stubbs; married June Neiman, February 14, 1959; children: Leda. *Education:* Yale University, A.B., 1958 (spent junior year at University of Paris); Princeton University, Ph.D., 1963. *Politics:* Democrat. *Religion:* Society of Friends (Quaker). *Home:* 8 Carriage Way, Champaign, Ill. 61820. *Office:* Department of English, University of Illinois, Urbana, Ill. 61801.

CAREER: University of Wisconsin—Madison, instructor in English, 1962-64; University of Illinois, Urbana, assistant professor, 1964-70, associate professor of English, 1970—, executive secretary of department, 1974—. Fulbright lecturer in Copenhagen, Denmark, 1970-71, and in Rome, Italy, 1977. *Member:* American Studies Association, Modern Language Association of America, Midwest Studies Association.

WRITINGS: The Pursuit of Form: A Study of Hawthorne and the Romance, University of Illinois Press, 1970. Contributor of articles to literary journals.

WORK IN PROGRESS: Federico Fellini: A Reference Guide, for G. K. Hall.

* * *

STULTZ, Newell M(aynard) 1933-

PERSONAL: Born June 13, 1933, in Boston, Mass.; son of Irving W. (a clergyman) and Marjorie (MacEachern) Stultz; married Elizabeth Olckers, April 6, 1958; children: Elliot, Amy. *Education:* Dartmouth College, B.A., 1955; Boston University, A.M., 1960, Ph.D., 1965. *Religion:* Unitarian Universalist. *Home:* 371 New Meadow Rd., Barrington, R.I. 02806. *Office:* Department of Political Science, Brown University, Providence, R.I. 02912.

CAREER: Northwestern University, Evanston, Ill., assistant professor of political science, 1964-65; Brown University, Providence, R.I., assistant professor, 1965-68, associate professor, 1968-73, professor of political science, 1973—, associate dean of Graduate School, 1970-74, department chairman, 1974—. *Military service:* U.S. Navy, 1956-59; became lieutenant junior grade. *Awards, honors:* Fulbright fellow in South Africa, 1955-56; Ford Foundation fellow in South Africa, 1962-64; Rhodes University research fellow, 1971-72; Rockefeller Foundation fellow in South Africa, 1976-77.

WRITINGS: (With Gwendolen M. Carter) *South Africa's Transkei: The Politics of Domestic Colonialism,* Northwestern University Press, 1967 (published in England as *The Politics of Domestic Colonialism,* Heinemann, 1967); (editor with Marion E. Doro) *Governing in Black Africa: Perspectives on New States,* Prentice-Hall, 1970; *Afrikaner Politics in South Africa, 1934 to 1948,* University of California Press, 1974 (published in South Africa as *The Nationalists in Opposition, 1934 to 1948,* Human & Rousseau, 1975); *Who Goes to Parliament?,* I.S.E.R., Rhodes University, 1975.

WORK IN PROGRESS: Transkei, in Separatist Perspective.

* * *

STUPAK, Ronald J(oseph) 1934-

PERSONAL: Born November 28, 1934, in Allentown, Pa.; son of Frank John (a tailor) and Rose (Sisko) Stupak; married Dolores Sarmir, June 14, 1958; children: Valeska Celina. *Education:* Moravian College, B.A. (summa cum laude), 1961; Ohio State University, M.A., 1964, Ph.D., 1967. *Politics:* Democrat. *Home:* 2651 East Barracks Rd., Charlottesville, Va. 22901. *Office:* Federal Executive Institute, Charlottesville, Va. 22903.

CAREER: Employed as a clerk and sales planner in Allentown, Pa., 1952-55, 1961-62; Miami University, Oxford, Ohio, instructor, 1966-67, assistant professor, 1967-70, associate professor, 1970-74, professor of political science, 1974-75, chairman of Graduate Studies Committee, 1970-73; Federal Executive Institute, Charlottesville, Va., professor, 1975—, associate director, 1976. Visiting assistant professor of national security studies, Ohio State University, 1969.

Military service: U.S. Army, signal corps, 1955-57. *Member:* American Political Science Association, American Academy of Political and Social Science, American Society of Public Administration, International Studies Association, Ohio Economics and Political Science Association, Greater Cincinnati Council for Social Studies, Pi Sigma Alpha, Phi Sigma Tau, Omicron Delta Kappa. *Awards, honors:* Miami University summer research grant, 1968; Most Outstanding and Effective Teacher, Miami University, 1970; "Outstanding Young Men of America" award, 1970; Ford Foundation faculty fellow, 1973.

WRITINGS: (Editor with Richard U. Sherman, Jr.) *Reading in National Security Policy,* two volumes, Ohio State University Mershon Library, 1963; *The Shaping of Foreign Policy: The Role of the Secretary of State as Seen by Dean Acheson,* Odyssey, 1969; (contributor) Kenneth S. Pederson and Gary C. Byrne, editors, *Politics in Western Europe: Patterns and Problems,* Wiley, 1971; (contributor) Frank B. Horton, editor, *Comparative Defense Policy,* 3rd edition, Johns Hopkins Press, 1974; *American Foreign Policy: Assumptions, Processes, and Projections,* Harper, 1976; (co-author) *Understanding Political Science: The Arena of Power,* Alfred Publishing, 1977. Contributor to *ORBIS, International Review of History and Political Science, International Behavioural Scientist, Studies on the Soviet Union, Sociologia Internationales, Australian Outlook, Journal of Human Relations, Foreign Service Journal,* and other periodicals.

WORK IN PROGRESS: On Organizational Behavior; a book on the role of assistant secretaries; articles on educational theories.

SIDELIGHTS: Ronald Stupak told *CA:* "The really exciting area in higher education today is in the realm of adult education, continuing education, and short courses. It seems as if a revolution is occurring among adults who are become aware of the need for continued growth and adjustment through educational renewal programs—both on and off the traditional educational/campus centers."

* * *

SUBA, Susanne

PERSONAL: Born in Budapest, Hungary; daughter of Miklos (a painter) and May Suba. *Education:* Graduate of Pratt Institute. *Home:* 1019 Third Ave., New York, N.Y. 10021.

CAREER: Free-lance painter and illustrator, with solo exhibitions of illustrations at Weatherspoon Galleries, Greensboro, N.C. and University of North Carolina, 1976.

WRITINGS—Self-illustrated: The Man with the Bushy Beard and Other Tales (juvenile), Viking, 1969; *The Monkeys and the Pedlar,* Viking, 1970.

Illustrator: Gladys Malvern, *Dancing Star,* Messner, 1942; Carl A. Withers, *A Rocket in My Pocket,* Holt, 1948; Mary Mian, *The Merry Miracle,* 1949; John Mason Brown, *Morning Faces,* McGraw, 1949; Helen McLean, *There's No Place like Paris,* Doubleday, 1951; Gerald Heard, *Gabriel and the Creatures,* Harper, 1952; Virginia Haviland, *Favorite Fairy Tales Told in Germany,* Little, Brown, 1959; Peggy Mann, *That New Baby,* Coward, 1967; Robert Burch, *The Hunting Trip,* Scribner, 1971; Sylvia Cassedy and P. M. Thampi, *Moon Uncle, Moon Uncle,* Doubleday, 1973; Margaret Davidson, *Five True Dog Stories,* Scholastic Book Services, 1976; Ruth Belov Gross, *Dangerous Adventure,* Scholastic Book Services, 1976.

SUCHLICKI, Jaime 1939-

PERSONAL: Born December 8, 1939, in Havana, Cuba; U.S. citizen; son of Salomon (a businessman) and Ana (Greinstein) Suchlicki; married Carol Meyer, January 26, 1964; children: Michael Ian, Kevin Donald, Joy Michelle. *Education:* Attended University of Havana, 1959-60; University of Miami, A.B. (cum laude), 1964, M.A., 1965; Texas Christian University, Ph.D., 1967. *Home:* 8800 Southwest 54th Ter., Miami, Fla. 33165. *Office:* Center for Advanced International Studies, University of Miami, 1217 Dickinson Dr., Coral Gables, Fla. 33124.

CAREER: University of Miami, Coral Gables, Fla., assistant professor, 1967-70, professor of history, 1970—, Center for Advanced International Studies, research associate, 1967-70, associate director, 1970—. *Member:* Conference on Latin American History, Latin American Studies Association, Phi Alpha Theta, Phi Iota Pi.

WRITINGS: (Contributor) Robert E. McNicoll, editor, *Latin American Panorama,* Putnam, 1968; (contributor) Donald K. Emmerson, editor, *Students and Politics in Developing Nations,* Praeger, 1968; *The Cuban Revolution: A Documentary Bibliography, 1952-1968,* Center for Advanced International Studies, University of Miami, 1968; *University Students and Revolution in Cuba, 1920-1968,* University of Miami Press, 1969; (editor) *Cuba, Castro and Revolution,* University of Miami Press, 1972; *Cuba: From Columbus to Castro,* Scribner, 1974. Contributor to *Encyclopedia of World Biography,* McGraw, 1970, and to professional journals.

*   *   *

SUDA, Zdenek 1920-

PERSONAL: Born October 7, 1920, in Pelhrimov, Czechoslovakia; son of Ludvik (director of an agricultural cooperative) and Marie (Chudoba) Suda; married Maria Kerstens, August 23, 1952; children: Maria Svatava, Sybilla Adriana, Petra Mojmira, Ludvik Zdenek. *Education:* Charles University, Ph.D., 1948; University of Geneva, License es sciences economiques, 1950; College of Europe, Certificat d'etudes europeenes, 1951. *Home:* 15 Highmeadow Rd., Pittsburgh, Pa., 15215. *Office:* Department of Sociology, University of Pittsburgh, Pittsburgh, Pa. 15260.

CAREER: European Federalist Movement, France, West Germany, and United States, executive officer, 1951-68; University of Pittsburgh, Pittsburgh, Pa., associate professor of sociology, 1968—.

WRITINGS: La division internationale socialiste du travail, Sijthoff, 1967; *The Czechoslovak Socialist Republic,* edited by Jan F. Triska, Johns Hopkins Press, 1969; (editor with Jiri Nehnevajsa) *Czechoslovakia 1968: The Spring that Turned into Autumn,* XYZYX Publication, 1971; *History of the Communist Party of Czechoslovakia,* Hoover Institution, 1977. Contributor to *Est & Ouest* (Paris), *Neue Zuercher Zeitung, American Sociological Review,* and other publications.

WORK IN PROGRESS: Research on the disintegrative processes within totalitarian control structures; comparative research on social changes occasioned by modernization.

SIDELIGHTS: Zdenek Suda speaks, reads, and writes French and German in addition to Czech and English; he also reads Italian, Dutch, Russian, and Spanish.

*   *   *

SUINN, Richard M(ichael) 1933-

PERSONAL: Surname is pronounced "swin"; born May 8, 1933, in Honolulu, Hawaii; son of Maurice B. C. and Edith (Wong) Suinn; married Grace D. Toy (an artist), July 26, 1958; children: Susan, Randall, Stacy, Bradley. *Education:* Attended University of Hawaii, 1951-53; Ohio State University, B.A. (summa cum laude), 1955; Stanford University, M.A., 1957, Ph.D., 1959. *Home:* 808 Cheyenne Dr., Fort Collins, Colo. 80521. *Office:* Department of Psychology, Colorado State University, Fort Collins, Colo. 80521.

CAREER: Intern in psychology in Veterans Administration hospitals in Palo Alto, Calif., San Francisco, Calif., and Dayton, Ohio, 1955-58; Stanford University, Stanford, Calif., counselor, 1958-59, School of Medicine, research associate, 1964-66, research consultant, summer, 1967; Whitman College, Walla Walla, Wash., assistant professor of psychology, 1959-64, acting head of department of psychology, 1962; University of Hawaii, Honolulu, associate professor of psychology, 1966-68; Colorado State University, Fort Collins, professor of psychology and head of department of psychology, 1968—. Visiting professor, Central Washington State College, summers, 1961-64, University of Washington, summer, 1963, and University of Vera Cruz, summer, 1971; visiting lecturer, San Jose State College (now University), spring, 1965. Coordinator, Rehabilitation Counseling Training Program, University of Hawaii, 1966-68; team psychologist, U.S. and Nordic ski teams, Winter Olympics, 1976. Psychological consultant, State of Washington, 1961-64; psychological consultant and supervisory faculty member, Queen's Hospital Mental Health Clinic and Psychoanalytic Training Center, 1966-68; consultant, Veterans Administration Training Program, 1970, State University of New York at Stony Brook, 1970, Gateway Center, 1970.

MEMBER: American Psychological Association (fellow), American Association for the Advancement of Behavior Therapy, Western Psychological Association, Phi Beta Kappa, Sigma Xi, Psi Chi. *Awards, honors:* Grants from National Institute of Mental Health, 1963, University Research Council, 1964, Pacific Biomedical Research Center, 1966, Faculty Improvement Committee, 1969, Biomedical Sciences Support grant, 1969, U.S. Office of Education, 1970, 1971, State of Colorado, 1971; visiting scientist, National Science Foundation and American Psychological Association, 1973.

WRITINGS: (Contributor) Gardner Lindzey and Calvin S. Hall, editors, *Theories of Personality: Primary Sources and Research,* Wiley, 1965; (with William L. Dauterman) *The Stanford Ohwaki-Kohs Tactile Block Design Intelligence Test for the Blind,* Western Psychological Services, 1968; (with Stuart Oskamp) *The Predictive Validity of Projective Measures: Research on Projective Tests; A Fifteen Year Evaluation Review of Research,* C. C Thomas, 1969, 2nd edition, 1975; *The Fundamentals of Behavior Pathology,* Wiley, 1970; (with Richard G. Weigel) *The Innovative Psychological Therapies,* Harper, 1975; (with Weigel) *The Innovative Medical Therapies,* University Park Press, 1976. Contributor to *Contemporary Psychology, Behavior Therapy, Journal of Clinical Psychology, Journal of Abnormal and Social Psychology, Journal of Consulting Psychology, Group Psychotherapy, Journal of General Psychology, Lancet, Journal of Human Relations, Psychiatric Quarterly, Psychology Today,* and other professional journals.

WORK IN PROGRESS: Research in innovations in behavior therapy.

SIDELIGHTS: Richard Suinn told *CA:* "My vocational choice has been in the academic field, with current duties involving administrative responsibilities, graduate and undergraduate teaching, research and writing. [My] major research has been in the field of improving behavior therapy approaches. I have been responsible for devising a form of psychotherapy which can eliminate tensions and conflicts within as short as four hours of treatment. The most fun has been to modify behavior therapy to be applicable for training athletes; at the end of such treatment, the university's ski team won the team trophy, the men's trophy, and the women's trophy, and I like to believe that I had some valid role in the 1976 Winter Olympics."

* * *

SUITS, Daniel B(urbidge) 1918-

PERSONAL: Born June 27, 1918, in St. Louis, Mo.; son of Hollis E. (a businessman) and Dorothy (Halyburton) Suits; married Adelaide Boehm, February 14, 1942; children: Evan, Holly (Mrs. Michael N. Kazarinoff). *Education:* University of Michigan, A.B., 1940, M.A., 1941, Ph.D., 1949. *Religion:* Quaker. *Home:* 220 Atlantic Ave., Santa Cruz, Calif. 95060. *Office:* Merrill College, University of Califo﹖ ﹖ia, Santa Cruz, Calif. 95064.

CAREER: University of Michigan, Ann Arbor, instructor, 1947-50, assistant professor, 1950-52, 1953-55, associate professor, 1955-59, professor of economics, 1959-70, acting chairman of department, 1960; University of California, Santa Cruz, visiting professor, 1969-70, professor of economics at Merrill College, 1970—, deputy provost of the college, 1971—. Research associate, National Board of Economic Research, 1952-53, and Center of Economic Research, Athens, Greece, 1962-63; visiting professor at Kyoto University and Doshisha University, 1958, and at University of Hawaii, summer, 1966. Member of advisory panel for economics, National Science Foundation, 1963-65; consultant to Secretary of the Treasury, 1961-70, President's Council of Economic Advisers, 1963-69, U.S. Arms Control and Disarmament Agency, 1964, and International Monetary Fund, 1968—. *Wartime service:* Conscientious objector, assigned to Civilian Public Service with U.S. Forest Service, 1942-46. *Member:* American Economic Association, Econometric Society (fellow), American Statistical Association (fellow), American Association for the Advancement of Science, Phi Kappa Phi.

WRITINGS: Statistics: An Introduction to Quantitative Economic Research, Rand McNally, 1963; *The Theory and Application of Econometric Models,* Center of Economic Research (Athens), 1963; *An Econometric Model of the Greek Economy,* Center of Economic Research (Athens), 1964; (with others) *Impacts of Monetary Policy,* Prentice-Hall, 1964; (author of introduction) Lewis Schipper, *Consumer Discretionary Behavior,* North-Holland Publishing, 1964; *Applied Econometric Forecasting and Policy Analysis,* Centro de Economia e Financas (Lisbon), 1967; *Principles of Economics,* and *Study Guide,* Harper, 1970, 2nd edition, 1973.

Contributor: Emile Benoit and K. E. Boulding, editors, *Disarmament and the Economy,* Harper, for Center for Research on Conflict Resolution, University of Michigan, 1963; Robert A. Gordon and Lawrence R. Klein, editors, *Readings in Business Cycles,* Irwin, for American Economic Association, 1965; James S. Duesenberry and others, editors, *The Brookings Quarterly Econometric Model of the United States,* Rand McNally, 1965; Reuben Slesinger and Mark Perlman, editors, *Contemporary Economics,* 2nd edition, Allyn & Bacon, 1966; Robert Ferber, editor, *Determi-*

nants of Investment Behavior, National Bureau of Economic Research, 1967; Arnold Zeller, editor, *Readings in Economic Statistics and Econometrics,* Little, Brown, 1968.

Contributor of more than fifty articles and reviews to professional journals in this country and abroad.

WORK IN PROGRESS: Measurement of economic relationships and the use of statistical methods in economic analysis and forecasting.†

* * *

SULLIVAN, Alvin 1942-

PERSONAL: Born October 24, 1942, in Pascagoula, Miss.; son of John Gaston and Martha (Trawick) Sullivan. *Education:* Tulane University, B.A., 1964; Southern Illinois University, M.A., 1968; St. Louis University, Ph.D., 1972. *Politics:* Democrat. *Religion:* Christian. *Home:* 2305 West Delmar, Godfrey, Ill. 62035. *Office:* Department of English, Southern Illinois University, Edwardsville, Ill. 62025.

CAREER: Teacher of English at high schools in Louisiana and Illinois, 1964-67; Southern Illinois University at Edwardsville, 1968—, began as instructor, currently associate professor of English. *Member:* Modern Language Association of America.

WRITINGS: (With Nicholas Joost) *D. H. Lawrence and "The Dial",* Southern Illinois University Press, 1970; (compiler with Joost) *An Index to "The Dial",* Morris Library, Southern Illinois University, 1971. Contributor to literary journals. Editor, *Papers on Language and Literature.*

WORK IN PROGRESS: Research on D. H. Lawrence and modern British poetry.

AVOCATIONAL INTERESTS: Travel, gardening, photography.

* * *

SULLIVAN, James L(enox) 1910-

PERSONAL: Born March 12, 1910, in Silver Creek, Miss.; son of James Washington (a contractor) and Mary Ellen (Dampeer) Sullivan; married Velma Scott, October 22, 1935; children: Mary Beth (Mrs. Bobby Ray Taylor), Martha Lynn (Mrs. James M. Porch, Jr.), James David. *Education:* Mississippi College, B.A., 1932, D.D., 1948; Southern Baptist Theological Seminary, Th.M., 1935. *Politics:* Democrat. *Home:* Route 4, Mt. Juliet, Tenn. 37122. *Office address:* P.O. Box 167, Hermitage, Tenn. 37076.

CAREER: Ordained to the Baptist ministry, 1930; pastor of Baptist churches in Boston, Ky., 1932-33, Beaver Dam, Ky., 1933-38, Ripley, Tenn., 1938-40, Clinton, Miss., 1940-42, Brookhaven, Miss., 1942-46, Nashville, Tenn., 1946-50, and Abilene, Tex., 1950-53; executive secretary of Baptist Sunday School Board, Nashville, 1953—, Broadman Press, Nashville, 1953—, and Convention Press, Nashville, 1955—. Member of board of trustees, Union University, Cumberland College, Southern Baptist Theological Seminary, Hardin-Simmons University, Midstate Baptist Hospital, Tenn., and Hendrick Memorial Hospital, Tex. *Member:* Baptist World Alliance (member of executive council; president, 1975—), Rotary Club (Ripley, Tenn.), Lions Club (Brookhaven, Miss.), Kiwanis Club, (Abilene, Tex.).

WRITINGS: Your Life and Your Church, Convention Press, 1950; *John's Witness to Jesus,* Convention Press, 1965; *Memos for Christian Living* (selections from his column, "Facts and Trends"), compiled by Gomer R. Lesch, Broadman, 1966; *Reach Out,* compiled by Lesch, Broadman, 1970; *God Is My Record,* Broadman, 1975. Also author of *Rope of Sand with Strength of Steel,* 1974. Author of a column, "Facts and Trends," in the *Newsletter* of the Southern Baptist Convention Sunday School Board, 1957—. Contributor of articles to various religious publications.

*   *   *

SULLIVAN, Martin (Richard Preece) 1934-

PERSONAL: Born August 28, 1934, in Maymyo, Burma; son of Cecil Stephens (an army officer) and Nancy (Preece) Sullivan; married Anthea Boyle, May 11, 1963; children: Marc, Rebecca, Emma. *Education:* Attended Wellington College, Berkshire, England, and University of Southern California, Los Angeles. *Politics:* Conservative (Britain); Liberal (Canada). *Religion:* Anglican. *Home:* Shortgrove Hall, Newport, Essex, England.

CAREER: Gazette, Montreal, Quebec, reporter, 1956-59; public relations officer, Hilton of Canada, 1959-60; Canadian Broadcasting Corp., Toronto, Ontario, television news editor, 1961-63; Time, Inc., New York, N.Y., bureau chief in Montreal, Quebec, 1963-68, economic correspondent in Beverly Hills, Calif., 1969-70; affiliated with Wood Gundy Ltd. (investment banking), London, England and Paris, France, 1972—. *Military service:* British Army, Light Infantry, 1952-54; served in Germany and West Africa; became lieutenant. *Member:* Authors Guild, Society for Advancement of Management, Montreal Racket Club, Ski Club of Great Britain, Laurentian Zone Ski Club, Kandahar Ski Club, Royal Automobile Club, Pall Mall (London).

WRITINGS: Mandate 68: The Year of Pierre Elliott Trudeau, Doubleday, 1968. Contributor to Canadian magazines and to *Sports Illustrated* and *Life.*

*   *   *

SULLIVAN, Peggy (Anne) 1929-

PERSONAL: Born August 12, 1929, in Kansas City, Mo.; daughter of Michael C. (a florist) and Ella (O'Donnell) Sullivan. *Education:* Clarke College, Dubuque, Iowa, A.B., 1950; Catholic University of America, M.S. in L.S., 1953; graduate study at University of Virginia, 1960-62, and University of Maryland, 1962-63; University of Chicago, certificate of advanced study, 1969, Ph.D., 1972. *Politics:* Independent. *Religion:* Roman Catholic. *Home:* 953 West Montana, Chicago, Ill. 60614.

CAREER: Kansas City (Mo.) Public Library, assistant children's librarian, 1952-53; Enoch Pratt Free Library, Baltimore, Md., children's librarian and school services specialist, 1953-59; Arlington County (Va.) Public Library, children's work supervisor, 1959-61; Montgomery County Schools, Rockville, Md., library specialist, 1961-63; American Library Association, Chicago, Ill., project director, 1963-1969; University of Pittsburgh, Graduate School of Library and Information Sciences, Pittsburgh, Pa., assistant professor, 1971-73; director, Office for Library Personnel Resources, American Library Association, 1973-74; University of Chicago, Graduate Library School, Chicago, associate professor and dean of students, 1974-77; Chicago Public Library, Chicago, director of branch and regional libraries, 1977—. Instructor at Catholic University of America, 1958, 1962-63, Drexel Institute, 1961, University of Maryland, 1961-62, Rutgers University, 1967, Syracuse University, 1968, University of Chicago, 1969, and Rosary College, 1969-70. Consultant to nineteen NDEA and Higher Education Act institutes. *Member:* American Library Association, Special Libraries Association, Illinois Library Asso-

ciation, Association of Educational Communications Technology, Chicago Library Club, Beta Phi Mu. *Awards, honors:* Tangley Oaks Fellowship, 1968.

WRITINGS: The O'Donnells, Follett, 1956; *Impact: The School Library and the Instructional Program,* American Library Association, 1967; (editor) *Realization: The Final Report of the Knapp School Libraries Project,* American Library Association, 1968; *Many Names for Eileen* (juvenile), Follett, 1969; *Problems in School Media Management,* Bowker, 1971; *Carl H. Milam and the American Library Association,* H. W. Wilson, 1976; *Opportunities in Librarianship and Information Science,* Vocational Guidance Manuals, 1977. Regular reviewer, *School Library Journal,* 1958—; also has done reviews for *Baltimore Sun, Critic, Washington Post, Chicago Tribune,* and *Library Quarterly;* filmstrip reviewer, *Instructor,* 1972-77.

*   *   *

SULLY, (Lionel Henry) Francois 1927-1971

August 7, 1927—February 23, 1971; French journalist and writer on Vietnam. Obituaries: *Washington Post,* February 24, 1971. (See index for *CA* sketch)

*   *   *

SUMMERS, Gene F(ranklin) 1936-

PERSONAL: Born December 28, 1936, in Whitewater, Mo.; son of Glenn W. and Lauara (Weisenstein) Summers; children: Teresa Lee, James, Jon, Robert. *Education:* Attended Southeast Missouri State College (now University), 1954-55; University of Tennessee, B.S., 1959, Ph.D., 1962. *Politics:* Democrat. *Religion:* Methodist. *Home:* 4314 Sheffield Rd., Madison, Wis. 53711. *Office:* Department of Rural Sociology, University of Wisconsin, 610 Walnut St., Madison, Wis. 53706.

CAREER: Indiana State University, Terre Haute, instructor, 1962-63, assistant professor of sociology, 1963-64; University of Illinois, Urbana, assistant professor of sociology, 1965-70; University of Wisconsin—Madison, associate professor, 1970-75, professor of sociology, 1976—. Visiting professor, Vanderbilt University, summers, 1963, 1964. *Member:* American Sociological Association, Rural Sociological Society, Midwest Sociological Society, Southern Sociological Society. *Awards, honors:* National Institute of Mental Health postdoctoral fellowship, University of Wisconsin, 1964-65.

WRITINGS: (With C. L. Folse, R. L. Hough, and J. T. Scott) *Before Industrialization,* University of Illinois Press, 1970; (editor) *Attitude Measurement,* Rand McNally, 1970; *Industrial Invasion of Nonmetropolitan America,* Praeger, 1976. Contributor to *Social Forces, Rural Sociology, Educational and Psychological Measurement, Sociological Quarterly, Multivariate Behavioral Research, Review of Religious Research, Sociological Methodology, Planning, Small Town, Growth and Change, Journal of the Community Development Society,* and *Rural America.*

*   *   *

SUMMERSCALES, William 1921-

PERSONAL: Born August 5, 1921, in Silsden, Yorkshire, England; son of Edmund (a painter) and Margaret (Newns) Summerscales; married Ruth B. Sickler, September 8, 1945 (divorced, 1969); married Elpida Tsonides, May 31, 1970; children: Marjorie B. Summerscales Wright, Stephen Tracy (deceased). *Education:* Eastern Nazarene College, B.A.,

1944; San Francisco Theological Seminary, M.Div., 1956; University of Toronto, M.A., 1966; Columbia University, Ph.D., 1969. *Home:* 400 West 119th St., New York, N.Y. 10027. *Office:* Teachers College, Columbia University, New York, N.Y. 10027.

CAREER: Clergyman of United Presbyterian Church in the U.S.A.; parish minister in California and Canada, 1945-60; Presbyterian Board of Education, Philadelphia, Pa., director of adult education, 1960-67; Columbia University, Teachers College, New York, N.Y., administrative associate in Division of Educational Institutions and Programs, 1967-69, director of placement, 1969—, associate professor of education, 1971—, director of Institutional Development, 1972—. Member, San Mateo County (Calif.) Planning Commission, 1958-60. *Member:* American Association of Junior Colleges, American Association of School Administrators, American Educational Research Association, American Association for Higher Education, Phi Delta Lambda.

WRITINGS: Affirmation and Dissent: Columbia's Response to the Crisis of World War I, Teachers College Press, 1970; *Jesus: The Four Gospels in a Single Narrative in Modern English,* Simon & Schuster, 1974. Contributor to educational journals.

WORK IN PROGRESS: Research in American social history and higher education.

SIDELIGHTS: William Summerscales told *CA:* "For good or ill, much of my writing time is devoted to memos, reviews, correspondence these days. Important though some of this may be, the craftsmanship required for serious writing projects is the one exercise that is needed to keep alive in one's mind the moral significance of language. The occasional writing of unpublished poetry has occasionally filled the vacuum."

* * *

SUMNER, Cid Ricketts 1890-1970

September 27, 1890—October 15, 1970; American novelist and short story writer. Obituaries: *Newsday,* October 16, 1970; *Washington Post,* October 16, 1970; *Variety,* October 21, 1970; *Time,* October 26, 1970. (See index for *CA* sketch)

* * *

SUND, Robert B(ruce) 1926-

PERSONAL: Born January 24, 1926, in Los Angeles, Calif.; son of Neily and Esther (Norton) Sund. *Education:* Reed College, B.A., 1950; Stanford University, M.A., 1952, Ed.D., 1959; Oregon State University, M.S., 1960. *Home:* 27 Alles Dr., Greeley, Colo. 80631. *Office:* Department of Science Education, University of Northern Colorado, Greeley, Colo. 80639.

CAREER: University of Northern Colorado, Greeley, professor of science of education, 1960—. Member of board of directors, Colorado Tuberculosis and Respiratory Diseases Association. *Military service:* U.S. Army, 1943-46, 1950-51; became sergeant. *Member:* National Association for Research in Science Teaching, National Science Teachers Association, American Humanistic Psychological Association, National Association of Biology Teachers (member of board of directors, 1963-65), Phi Delta Kappa (president of University of Northern Colorado chapter, 1969-70). *Awards, honors:* University of Northern Colorado, scholar of the year, 1974, outstanding educator of the year, 1975.

WRITINGS: (With Arthur Carin) *Teaching Science through Discovery,* C. E. Merrill, 1964, 3rd edition, 1975;

(with Leslie W. Trowbridge) *Discovery Teaching in Science,* C. E. Merrill, 1966, 2nd edition, 1970; (with Trowbridge) *Teaching Science by Inquiry in the Secondary Schools,* C. E. Merrill, 1967, 2nd edition, 1973; (with Trowbridge, Bill W. Tillery, and Kenneth V. Olson) *Elementary Science Teaching Activities: A Laboratory Approach,* C. E. Merrill, 1967; (with Albert Piltz) *Creative Teaching of Science in the Elementary School,* Allyn & Bacon, 1968, 2nd edition, 1974.

Elementary Science Discovery Lessons: Physical Science, Allyn & Bacon, 1970; *Elementary Science Discovery Lessons: Biological Science,* Allyn & Bacon, 1970; (with Trowbridge and Tillery) *Elementary Science Discovery Lessons: Earth Science,* Allyn & Bacon, 1970; (with Carin) *Teaching Modern Science,* C. E. Merrill, 1971, 2nd edition, 1975; *Science for Human Values—Grades 3, 4, 5, and 6,* Follett, 1972; (with Anthony J. Picard) *Behavioral Objectives and Evaluation Measures: Science and Mathematics,* C. E. Merrill, 1972; (with Rodger W. Bybee) *Becoming a Better Elementary Science Teacher: A Reader,* C. E. Merrill, 1973; (with Trowbridge) *Student-Centered Teaching in the Secondary School,* C. E. Merrill, 1974; (with others) *Investigate and Discover: Elementary Science Lessons,* Allyn & Bacon, 1975; (with Ankney Sund) *Piaget for Educators: A Multimedia Program,* C. E. Merrill, 1976. Contributor of numerous articles to professional journals.

WORK IN PROGRESS: A multi-media package on questioning and listening techniques.

SIDELIGHTS: Robert B. Sund told *CA:* "I am particularly interested in preparing teachers to be more humane. I have been involved in a ghetto school project to try to provide a program of science instruction more relevant to these students and teachers and more sympathetic to their needs. I have also given many workshops on humanistic education, creativity, questioning and listening techniques, and Piagetian theory."

* * *

SUNDQUIST, James L(loyd) 1915-

PERSONAL: Born October 16, 1915, in West Point, Utah; son of Frank Victor and Freda (Carlson) Sundquist; married Beth Ritchie (a park administrator), December 25, 1937; children: Erik L., Mark L., James K. *Education:* Attended Weber State College, 1932-34, and Northwestern University, 1934-35; University of Utah, B.S., 1939; Syracuse University, M.S. in P.A., 1941. *Home:* 3016 North Florida St., Arlington, Va. 22207. *Office:* Brookings Institution, 1775 Massachusetts Ave. N.W., Washington, D.C. 20036.

CAREER: Tribune, Salt Lake City, Utah, reporter, 1935-39; U.S. Bureau of the Budget, Washington, D.C., administrative analyst, 1941-47, 1949-51; U.S. Army, European Command, director of management control in Berlin, Germany, 1947-49; U.S. Office of Defense Mobilization, Washington, D.C., reports and statistics officer, 1951-53; assistant to chairman, Democratic National Committee, 1953-54; assistant secretary to the governor of New York, 1955-56; U.S. Senate, Washington, D.C., administrative assistant to Senator Clark (Pennsylvania), 1957-62; U.S. Department of Agriculture, Washington, D.C., deputy under-secretary, 1963-65; Brookings Institution, Washington, D.C., senior fellow, 1965—. *Member:* American Society for Public Administration, American Political Science Association, National Academy of Public Administration.

WRITINGS: Politics and Policy: The Eisenhower, Kennedy, and Johnson Years, Brookings Institution, 1968; (with

David W. Davis) *Making Federalism Work,* Brookings Institution, 1969; (editor) *On Fighting Poverty: Perspectives from Experience,* Basic Books, 1969; *Dynamics of the Party System,* Brookings Institution, 1973; *Dispersing Population: What America Can Learn from Europe,* Brookings Institution, 1975. Contributor of articles to journals.

WORK IN PROGRESS: Research for a book on Congressional-executive balance of power.

BIOGRAPHICAL/CRITICAL SOURCES: New Yorker, August 23, 1969.

*   *   *

SUTTON, S(tephanne) B(arry)   1940-

PERSONAL: Born March 10, 1940, in Cleveland, Ohio; daughter of Melvin S. (a chemist) and June (Strahota) Sutton. *Education:* Wells College, B.A., 1960. *Home:* 113 Commonwealth Ave., Boston, Mass. 02116.

CAREER: Biographer. Harvard University, Cambridge, Mass., honorary research fellow at Arnold Arboretum, 1970-74.

WRITINGS: (Compiler) *A Cumulative Index to the Nine Volumes of the Symbolae Antillanae,* Arnold Arboretum of Harvard University, 1965; *Through the Arnold Arboretum,* [Boston], 1968; *Charles Sprague Sargent and the Arnold Arboretum,* Harvard University Press, 1970; (editor) *Civilizing American Cities: A Selection of Frederick Law Olmstead's Writings on City Landscapes,* M.I.T. Press, 1971; *The Arnold Arboretum: The First Century,* Nimrod, 1971; *In China's Border Provinces: The Turbulent Career of Joseph Rock, Botanist-Explorer,* Hastings House, 1974; *Cambridge Reconsidered: 3 1/2 Cents on the Charles,* M.I.T. Press, 1976.†

*   *   *

SUTTON-SMITH, Brian   1924-

PERSONAL: Born July 15, 1924, in New Zealand; son of Ernest James and Nita (Sutton) Sutton-Smith; married Shirley L. Hicks, January 6, 1953; children: Katherine, Mark, Leslie, Mary, Emily. *Education:* University of Wellington, B.A., 1946, M.A., 1948, Diploma of Education, 1952; University of New Zealand, Ph.D., 1954. *Home:* 62 Beechwood Ter., Yonkers, N.Y. 10705. *Office:* Box 119, Psychology Department, Teachers College, Columbia University, New York, N.Y. 10027.

CAREER: Bowling Green State University, Bowling Green, Ohio, professor of psychology, 1956-67; Columbia University, Teachers College, New York, N.Y., professor of psychology and education, 1967—. Adjunct professor, New York University; visiting professor, Clark University, 1963-64. *Member:* American Psychological Association, Society for Research in Child Development, American Folklore Society, American Association for Health, Physical Education and Recreation. *Awards, honors:* Fulbright scholar at University of California, Berkeley, 1952-53.

WRITINGS: Our Street (juvenile), A. H. & A. W. Reed, 1952; *Smitty Does a Bunk* (juvenile), Price-Milburn, 1959; *The Games of New Zealand Children,* University of California Press, 1959; (with B. G. Rosenberg) *The Sibling,* Holt, 1970; (with E. M. Avedon) *The Study of Games,* Wiley, 1971; (with R. E. Herron) *Child's Play,* Wiley, 1971; (with Rosenberg) *Sex and Identity,* Holt, 1972; *The Folkgames of Children,* University of Texas Press, 1972; (with wife, Shirley Sutton-Smith) *How to Play with Your Children,* Hawthorn, 1974; (editor) *Classics in Play and Games,* Arno, 1976; *The Cobbers* (juvenile), Price-Milburn, 1976.

WORK IN PROGRESS: The Folk Stories of Children; The Filmmaking of Children.

BIOGRAPHICAL/CRITICAL SOURCES: Diner's Club Magazine, November 16, 1970; *Contemporary Psychology,* June, 1971.

*   *   *

SWAIN, Donald C(hristie)   1931-

PERSONAL: Born October 14, 1931, in Des Moines, Iowa; son of George Christie (a Presbyterian minister) and Irene (Alsop) Swain; married Lavinia Lesh (a teacher), March 5, 1955; children: Christie, Cynthia. *Education:* University of Dubuque, B.A., 1953; University of California, Berkeley, M.A., 1958, Ph.D., 1961. *Religion:* Presbyterian. *Home:* 561 Woodmont Ave., Berkeley, Calif. 94708. *Office:* Office of the Academic Vice-President, 713 University Hall, University of California, Berkeley, Calif. 94720.

CAREER: University of California, Berkeley, assistant research historian, 1961-63; University of California, Davis, assistant professor, 1963-67; associate professor, 1967-70, professor of history, 1970-75, academic assistant to the chancellor, 1967-68, 1970, vice-chancellor for academic affairs, 1972-75; University of California System, Berkeley, academic vice-president, 1975—. *Military service:* U.S. Navy, 1953-56; became lieutenant junior grade. *Member:* American Historical Association, Organization of American Historians. *Awards, honors:* William Best Hesseltine Award, Wisconsin State Historical Society, 1967.

WRITINGS: Federal Conservation Policy, 1921-1933, University of California Press, 1963; (co-editor) *The Politics of American Science: 1939 to the Present,* Rand McNally, 1965; *Wilderness Defender: Horace M. Albright and Conservation,* University of Chicago Press, 1970. Contributor to professional journals.

WORK IN PROGRESS: Conservation Policy in the New Deal, completion expected in 1980.

BIOGRAPHICAL/CRITICAL SOURCES: American Forests, April, 1970; *American West,* July, 1970; *Journal of American History,* September, 1970; *Living Wilderness,* winter, 1970-71.

*   *   *

SWAN, Berta W(aterhouse)   1928-

PERSONAL: Born February 13, 1928, in Lynchburg, Va.; daughter of Richard Green (a physician) and Berta (White) Waterhouse; married Charles Karns Swan, Jr. (a bakery executive), September 1, 1950; children: Charles Karns III, Laura Lee, Richard Henry. *Education:* University of Tennessee, B.A., 1950. *Religion:* Presbyterian. *Home:* 7812 Corteland Dr., Knoxville, Tenn. 37919.

CAREER: Writer. *Member:* National League of American Pen Women, Tennessee Woman's Press and Author's Club.

WRITINGS: Dark Side of Glory, Zondervan, 1969.

SIDELIGHTS: Dark Side of Glory has been translated into German.

*   *   *

SWANSON, Bert E(lmer)   1924-

PERSONAL: Born August 15, 1924, in Tacoma, Wash.; son of Lars M. (a crane operator) and Enis (Ronman) Swanson; married Jean Mills, January 28, 1950; married second wife, Edith Pinkus (a research associate), November 4, 1969; children: (second marriage) Fran, Genie, Amy. *Education:*

George Washington University, B.A., 1950; University of Oregon, M.A., 1956, Ph.D., 1959. *Politics:* Democrat. *Religion:* Unitarian Universalist. *Home:* 1419 Northwest 48th Ter., Gainesville, Fla. *Office:* Department of Political Science, University of Florida, Gainesville, Fla. 32601.

CAREER: Assistant to Senator Richard Neuberger of Oregon, 1955-57; University of Oregon, Eugene, instructor in political science, 1958-59; Hunter College of the City University of New York, New York, N.Y., instructor in political science, 1959-61; Sarah Lawrence College, Bronxville, N.Y., 1961-71, began as instructor, became professor of political sociology and chairman of social science faculty, director of Institute for Community Studies, 1965-69; University of Florida, Gainesville, professor of political science and urban studies, 1971—. Lecturer at Pratt Institute, 1961-64, and Brooklyn College of the City University of New York, 1961-65; visiting professor at New York University, 1965-66.

MEMBER: American Political Science Association, American Sociological Association, Society for General Systems Research, American Educational Research Association, Pi Sigma Alpha. *Awards, honors:* Danforth fellow at Syracuse University, summers, 1959, 1960; Woodrow Wilson Award, American Political Science Association, 1965, for *The Rulers and the Ruled: Political Power and Impotence in American Communities;* Twentieth Century Fund fellowship in public service, 1967.

WRITINGS: (With Robert S. Hirschfield and others) *Selected Readings in Political Science,* Hunter College, 1960; (with Robert H. Connery and David Deener) *Mental Health in Metropolitan Areas,* Institute of Public Administration (New York), 1961; (editor) *Current Trends in Comparative Community Studies,* Community Studies, 1962; (with Robert E. Agger and Daniel Goldrich) *The Rulers and the Ruled: Political Power and Impotence in American Communities,* Wiley, 1964, abridged edition published as *The Rulers and the Ruled,* Duxbury, 1972; *The Struggle for Equality: School Integration Controversies in New York City,* Hobbs-Dorman, 1966; *Decision-Making in the School Desegregation-Decentralization Controversies,* Institute for Community Studies, Sarah Lawrence College, 1969; *The Concern for Community in Urban America,* Odyssey, 1970; (with Louis Harris) *Black-Jewish Relations in New York City,* Praeger, 1970; (with wife, Edith Swanson) *Community Analysis: Social, Economic, and Political Profiles,* Consortium on Community Crisis, Cornell University, 1970; (with Harold Williams) *The Revitalization of Stump Creek,* Institute on Man and Science, 1975; (with Edith Swanson) *Discovering the Community: Comparative Analysis of Social, Political, and Economic Change,* Irvington Press, 1976; (with Richard Cohen) *The Small Town in America: A Guide for Study and Community Development,* U.S. Office of Education, 1976.

Contributor: Paul Tillett, editor, *Inside Politics,* Oceana, 1962; Robert Cahill and Stephen Hencley, editors, *The Politics of Education in the Local Community,* Interstate, 1964; William J. Gore and Leroy C. Hodapp, editors, *Change in the Small Community,* Friendship, 1967; Howard E. Freeman, Sol Levine, and Leo G. Reider, editors, *Handbook of Medical Sociology,* Prentice-Hall, 1970; Ray Brown, editor, *The Citizenry and the Hospital,* Duke University Press, 1974; Edward Hassinger and Larry Whiting, editors, *Rural Health Services,* Iowa State University Press, 1976; Donald Freeman, editor, *An Introduction to Political Science,* Free Press, 1977. Contributor of articles and reviews to journals.

WORK IN PROGRESS: The ABC's of the Local School System; The Tenuous Bonds of Town and Gown.

* * *

SWANSON, Edward I. 1923-

PERSONAL: Born September 14, 1923, in Providence, R.I.; son of John Edward and Edith O. (Lundquist) Swanson; married Wilma D. Butler, June 20, 1953; children: David Edward, Peter Nelson, Hanna Christina (deceased). *Education:* Worcester Polytechnic Institute, B.S. in Mechanical Engineering, 1944; Episcopal Theological School, Cambridge, Mass., B.D., 1949. *Politics:* Democratic. *Home:* 4105 Dana Ct., Kensington, Md. 20795. *Office:* General Commission on Chaplains and Armed Forces Personnel, 5100 Wisconsin Ave. N.W., Suite 310, Washington, D.C. 20016.

CAREER: Episcopal priest; vicar of parishes in North Scituate, R.I., Foster, R.I., and rector of churches in Clinton, Mass. and West Roxbury, Mass., 1949-66; Protestant Episcopal Church, Office of the Bishop for the Armed Forces, New York, N.Y., civilian coordinator, 1966-71, General Commission on Chaplains and Armed Forces Personnel, Washington, D.C., editor of *Link* and *Chaplain* magazines and director of publications, 1971—, director, 1974. *Military service:* U.S. Naval Reserve, active duty as ensign in Naval Ordnance Laboratory, 1944-45.

WRITINGS: Ministry to the Armed Forces, General Commission on Chaplains and National Catholic Community Service, 1968; *Serviceman's Prayer Book,* World Publishing, 1970.

AVOCATIONAL INTERESTS: Music (especially light opera), photography, gardening, reading.

* * *

SWANSON, Walter S. J. 1917-

PERSONAL: Born August 7, 1917, in Adrian, Mich.; son of Swan (a salesman) and Anna L. (Nordquist) Swanson; married Rosamond E. Sanderson, 1937; children: Jan. *Education:* Attended high school in Lansing, Mich., and took courses at University of California, Los Angeles. *Religion:* Protestant. *Home:* 8110 El Paseo Grande, La Jolla, Calif. 92037.

CAREER: Copley Newspapers, La Jolla, Calif., executive, 1954-75. *Awards, honors:* Special distinction citation in Sergel Awards, administered by University of Chicago, 1970, for play "Negerinde!"

WRITINGS: The Thin Gold Watch (biography of Ira C. and James S. Copley), Macmillan, 1964, revised paperback edition, Copley Newspapers, 1971; *Bread Loaf* (play; first produced as "The Good Priests" at School of Performing Arts, California Western University), privately printed, 1967; *The Happening* (novel), A. S. Barnes, 1970. Also author of a play, "Negerinde!" (originally entitled "The First Bad Sojourns of Young Miss Truth"), published in full in *Massachusetts Review,* autumn, 1970.

WORK IN PROGRESS: Plainsong, a love story based on research dealing with the moderately retarded; *T Square,* a novel with a plot based on counter-terrorism.

SIDELIGHTS: Walter Swanson writes: "Lo, it is only seven years since my *The Happening* was published, with its unexplicit "Deep Throat" background. I supposed then—and I knew the words had I wanted to write it otherwise!—that mystery and pathos and lovingkindness could dwell in such themes, not just sensationalism. But look what has happened since—not just "Deep Throat" itself, with its simpering bow to Freud, but darker things, even animalism and child exploitation. Against such trends, must a writer vie to be explicit? Or shall he or she dare continue to write of life as the majority still know it—life that holds a hope of love, or at least a hint of it?"

* * *

SWATRIDGE, Irene Maude Mossop
(Irene Mossop; pseudonyms: Fay Chandos, Virginia Storm, Jan Tempest; Theresa Charles, a joint pseudonym)

PERSONAL: Born in Woking, Surrey, England; daughter of Robert (a solicitor) and Maude B. (Eyre) Mossop; married Charles John Swatridge (a farmer and novelist), June 16, 1934. *Education:* Educated privately. *Politics:* Conservative. *Religion:* Church of England. *Home:* Middlecombe, Beeson, Kingsbridge, Devonshire, England. *Agent:* S. Walker Literary Agency, 199 Hampermill Lane, Oxhey, Watford, Hertfordshire WD1 4PJ, England.

CAREER: Novelist; she and her husband farm on the south Devonshire coast, keeping a dairy herd and raising sheep. *Member:* Romantic Novelists' Association, National Farmers' Union, Royal Society for the Prevention of Cruelty to Animals, National Canine Defence, Women's Institute.

WRITINGS—Under name Irene Mossop: *Prunella Plays the Game,* Low, 1929; *Vivien of St. Val's,* Shaw, 1931; *Charm's Last Chance,* Nisbet, 1931; *Feud in the Fifth,* Low, 1933; *Hilary Leads the Way,* Warne, 1933; *The Taming of Pickles,* Shaw, 1933; *Fifth at Cliff House,* Warne, 1934; *Four V's,* Warne, 1934; *Well Played, Juliana,* Low, 1934; *Chris in Command,* Low, 1935; *Play Up! Pine House,* Ryerson, 1935; *Theresa on Trial,* Warne, 1935; *Luck of the Oakleighs,* Warne, 1936; *Gay Adventure,* Warne, 1937; *Nicky, New Girl,* Low, 1938.

Under pseudonym Fay Chandos; all published by Mills & Boon: *No Limit to Love,* 1937; *No Escape from Love,* 1937; *Man of My Dreams,* 1937; *Before I Make You Mine,* 1938; *Wife for a Wager,* 1938; *Gay Knight I Love,* 1938; *All I Ask,* 1939; *Another Woman's Shoes,* 1939; *When Three Walk Together,* 1939; *The Man Who Wasn't Mac,* 1939; *Husband for Hire,* 1940; *You Should Have Warned Me,* 1940; *When We Two Parted,* 1940; *Substitute for Sherry,* 1940; *Women Are So Simple,* 1941; *Only a Touch,* 1942; *Awake, My Love!,* 1942; *A Letter to My Love,* 1942; *Eve and I,* 1943; *A Man to Follow,* 1943; *Away from Each Other,* 1944; *Made to Marry,* 1944; *Just a Little Longer,* 1944; *Last Year's Roses,* 1945; *A Man for Margaret,* 1946; *When Time Stands Still,* 1946; *Three Roads to Romance,* 1946; *Home Is the Hero,* 1946; *Because I Wear Your Ring,* 1947; *Cousins May Kiss,* 1947; *Lost Summer,* 1948; *Since First We Met,* 1948; *June in Her Eyes,* 1949; *For a Dream's Sake,* 1949; *Fugitive from Love,* 1950; *There Is a Tide,* 1950; *This Time It's Love,* 1951; *Now and Always,* 1951; *First and Favourite Wife,* 1952; *Families Are Such Fun,* 1952; *Leave It to Nancy,* 1953; *The Other One,* 1953; *Find Another Eden,* 1953; *Just before the Wedding,* 1954; *Doctors Are Different,* 1954; *Husbands at Home,* 1955; *Hibiscus House,* 1955; *So Nearly Married,* 1956; *Romantic Touch,* 1957; *Partners Are a Problem,* 1957; *Model Girl's Farm,* 1958; *Nan and the New Owner,* 1959; *Wild Violets,* 1959; *Where Four Ways Meet,* 1961; *Sister Sylvan,* 1962; *Two Other People,* 1964; *Don't Give Your Heart Away,* 1966; *Strangers in Love,* 1966; *Farm by the Sea,* 1967; *The Three of Us,* 1970; *Sweet Rosemary,* 1972.

Under pseudonym Virginia Storm: *A Match Is Made,* Mills & Boon, 1948, published as *The Ugly Prince,* Arcadia House, 1950; *Cinderella Had Two Sisters,* Mills & Boon, 1948, Arcadia House, 1950; *First I Must Forget,* Arcadia House, 1951.

Under pseudonym Jan Tempest; published by Mills & Boon, except as noted: *Stepmother of Five,* 1936; *Someone New to Love,* 1936; *Be Still, My Heart!,* 1936; *Kiss—and Forget,* 1936; *Believe Me, Beloved,* 1936; *All This I Gave,* 1936; *If I Love Again,* 1937; *No Other Man,* 1937; *Grow Up, Little Lady!,* 1937; *Carey, Come Back!,* 1937; *Face the Music—for Love,* 1938; *Man—and Waif,* 1938; *Because My Love Is Come,* 1938; *When First I Loved,* 1938; *Hiliary in His Heart,* 1938; *Say You're Sorry,* 1939; *My Only Love,* 1939; *Uninvited Guest,* 1939; *I'll Try Anything Once,* 1939; *Top of the Beanstalk,* 1940; *The Broken Gate,* 1940; *Why Wouldn't He Wait!,* 1940; *Little Brown Girl,* 1940; *Always Another Man,* 1941; *The Moment I Saw You,* 1941; *The Unknown Joy,* 1941; *Ghost of June,* 1941; *No Time for a Man,* 1942; *Romance on Ice,* 1942; *If You'll Marry Me,* 1942; *A Prince for Portia,* 1943; *Wife after Work,* 1943; *The Long Way Home,* 1943; *"Never Again!" Said Nicola,* 1944; *The One Thing I Wanted,* 1944; *Utility Husband,* 1944; *Westward to My Love,* 1944; *Love While You Wait,* 1944; *Not for This Alone,* 1945; *To Be a Bride,* 1945; *The Orange Blossom Shop,* 1946; *Happy with Either,* 1946; *House of the Pines,* 1946, Ace Books, 1968; *Bachelor's Bride,* 1946; *Lovely, though Late,* 1946; *Close Your Eyes,* 1947; *Teach Me to Love,* 1947; *How Can I Forget?,* 1948; *Shortcut to the Stars,* 1949; *Never Another Love,* 1949, Arcadia House, 1950; *Promise of Paradise,* Gramercy Publishing, 1949.

Nobody Else—Ever, 1950; *Now and Always,* Arcadia House, 1950; *Until I Find Her,* Arcadia House, 1950; *Two Loves for Tamara,* 1951; *Open the Door to Love,* 1952; *Without a Honeymoon,* 1952; *Happy Is the Wooing,* 1952; *Meet Me by Moonlight,* 1953; *Give Her Gardenias,* 1953; *Enchanted Valley,* 1954; *First-Time of Asking,* 1954; *Ask Me Again,* 1955; *Where the Heart Is,* 1955; *For Those in Love,* 1956; *Wedding Bells for Willow,* 1956; *Craddock's Kingdom,* 1957; *Will Not Now Take Place,* 1957; *Because My Love Is Come,* 1958; *Youngest Sister,* 1958; *Because There Is Hope,* 1958; *Romance for Rose,* 1959; *Stranger to Love,* 1960; *Mistress of Castlemount,* 1961; *The Turning Point,* 1961; *That Nice Nurse Nevin,* 1963; *The Madderleys Married,* 1963; *The Flower and the Fruit,* 1964; *The Way We Used to Be,* 1965; *The Lonesome Road,* 1966; *Meant to Meet,* 1967; *Lyra, My Love,* Moody, 1969.

With husband, Charles Swatridge, under joint pseudonym Theresa Charles; all published by Longmans, Green: *The Distant Drum,* 1940; *My Enemy and I,* 1941; *Happy Now I Go,* 1947; *To Save My Life,* 1948; *Man-Made Miracle,* 1949.

All published by Cassell: *Burning Beacon,* 1950; *At a Touch I Yield,* 1952; *Fairer than She,* 1953; *My Only Love,* 1954; *Kinder Love,* 1955; *Ultimate Surrender,* 1958; *A Girl Called Evelyn,* 1959.

All published by R. Hale: *No Through Road,* 1960; *House on the Rocks,* 1962; *Ring for Nurse Raine,* 1962; *Widower's Wife,* 1963; *Nurse Alice in Love,* 1964; *Patient in Love,* 1964; *The Man for Me,* 1965; *How Much You Mean to Me,* 1966; *Proud Citadel,* 1967; *The Way Men Love,* 1967; *The Shadowy Third,* 1968; *From Fairest Flowers,* 1969; *Wayward as the Swallow,* 1970; *Second Honeymoon,* 1970; *My True Love,* 1971; *Therefore Must Be Loved,* 1972; *Castle Kelpiesloch,* 1973; *Nurse by Accident,* 1974; *The Flower and the Nettle*, 1975; *Trust Me, My Love*, 1975; *One Who Remembers*, 1976; *Rainbow after Rain*, 1977; *Crisis at St. Chad's*, 1977.

Contributor of serials and short stories to British periodicals.

SIDELIGHTS: Irene Swatridge told *CA:* "Before I could read or write, I was 'making up stories', as I called it in my childhood, and it has been one of the greatest joys of my life as far back as I can remember. As soon as I could write, I was spending my pocket-money on exercise books in which to record my stories and verses. To this day, I write in pencil in exercise books.

"My first published stories, written as a schoolgirl and sent out to editors in my best handwriting, were mainly about animals and wild life. They found a ready market and I had soon sold enough to enable me to buy a typewriter. I taught myself to type, and then wrote and typed out a number of full length girls' school stories.

"From the beginning, I was happiest when I was writing about places and people I knew well and about emotions I had experienced. I was resolved not to attempt a novel until I was really and truly in love. Being the offspring of a supremely happy marriage, I firmly believe that 'some marriages are made in Heaven.' My own marriage has certainly been one of them.

"My deep love for animals, flowers, trees and the countryside, shared by my husband, has strengthened over the years, and we are glad to be able to do something towards conservation on this picturesque stretch of the Devon coast.

"Many of our novels have appeared in nineteen different languages. They are especially popular in France and Norway. Recently, two Theresa Charles novels were made into a serial for French television."

* * *

SWEENEY, James B(artholomew) 1910-

PERSONAL: Born July 7, 1910, in Philadelphia, Pa.; son of Anthony J. (a hotel owner) and Bertha (Collins) Sweeney; married Helen Ver (a lieutenant in U.S. Navy), December 2, 1944; children: Frank James. *Education:* Villanova University, B.S., 1932; attended University of Pennsylvania, School of Industrial Art, Philadelphia, University of Oklahoma, and University of Florida. *Home:* 7205 Burtonwood Dr., Alexandria, Va. 22307. *Agent:* Daniel Norvell, 3710 First Rd. S., Arlington, Va. 22204.

CAREER: Served four years with U.S. Merchant Marine before enlisting in Pennsylvania National Guard, 1940; U.S. Army, 1941-50, became regimental sergeant major, 1941, commissioned second lieutenant, Infantry, 1942, later transferred to staff of *Yank* (Army weekly); U.S. Air Force, officer, 1950-65, with duty as combat reporter during Korean War. *Member:* International Association of Boating Writers, International Oceanographic Foundation, National Press Club, National Rifle Association. *Awards, honors*—Military: Bronze Star (received as combat reporter in Korea), and sixteen other military medals. Civilian: Various medals and awards from Japanese government, Georgia Sheriff's Association, and for organizing, coaching, and managing youth markmanship rifle teams.

WRITINGS: Pictorial History of Oceanographic Submersibles, Crown, 1970; *Pictorial History of Sea Monsters and Other Dangerous Marine Life*, Crown, 1972; *Vessels for Underwater Exploration*, Crown, 1973; (with Peter R. Limburg) *102 Questions and Answers about the Sea*, Messner, 1975. Contributor of articles and stories to periodicals.

SIDELIGHTS: James Sweeney lived in many countries during his career in the military, including Japan, Germany, North Africa, England, Greece, and Turkey.

* * *

SWIFT, Mary Grace 1927-

PERSONAL: Born August 3, 1927, in Bartlesville, Okla.; daughter of Frank William (an engineer) and Helen (Moran) Swift. *Education:* St. Mary's College, Notre Dame, Ind., student, 1945-47; Creighton University, B.S. (cum laude), 1956, M.A., 1960; University of Notre Dame, Ph.D., 1967; language study at Universities of Kansas, Colorado, Michigan, Illinois, St. Louis University, and at L'Institut Catholique, Paris, France. *Home address:* c/o Ursuline Convent, Paola, Kan. 66071. *Office:* Department of History, Loyola University, New Orleans, La. 70118.

CAREER: Member of the Ursuline order of nuns; teacher in elementary schools in Kansas, 1947-56, and in secondary schools in Kansas and Oklahoma, 1957-61; Loyola University, New Orleans, La., 1966—, began as assistant professor, currently associate professor of European and Russian history. *Member:* American Association for the Advancement of Slavic Studies. *Awards, honors:* National Defense Education Act fellow, 1962-64; National Defense Foreign Languages fellow, 1968, 1969.

WRITINGS: The Art of the Dance in the U.S.S.R., University of Notre Dame Press, 1968; *A Loftier Flight*, Wesleyan University Press, 1974; (editor) *With Bright Wings: A Book of the Spirit*, Paulist/Newman, 1976. Contributor of articles to dance magazines and of reviews to professional journals.

* * *

SWIFT, W. Porter 1914-

PERSONAL: Born September 9, 1914, in Albany, N.Y.; son of Cyrus Burgess and Georgia May (Fisher) Swift; married Jean MacPherson, June 22, 1943; children: Diane Stuart (Mrs. Stephen O. Hand), Neil Randolph, Frank Douglas. *Education:* New York College for Teachers (now State University of New York at Albany), A.B., 1936, A.M., 1938; Cornell University, Ph.D., 1947. *Home:* 3 Murray St., Binghamton, N.Y. 13905.

WRITINGS: General Psychology, McGraw, 1969; (coauthor) *Psychology: Human Relations and Motivation*, McGraw, 1975. Author of two Office of War Training manuals, 1942, and series of occupational monographs for New York State Department of Education. Personnel research editor, *Personnel Journal*, 1959-68.

* * *

SWOPE, George S(teel) 1915-

PERSONAL: Born October 30, 1915, in Huntingdon, Pa.; son of Earl Barras and Letty (Steel) Swope; married Caryl Harrison, September 6, 1947; children: George Steel, Jr., Lucy J. *Education:* Yale University, B.A., 1939; University of Chicago, M.B.A., 1948. *Home:* 325 Glenwood Rd., Lake Forest, Ill. 60045. *Office:* Manplan Consultants, 20 North Wacker Dr., Chicago, Ill. 60606.

CAREER: Inland Steel Co., Chicago, Ill., assistant secretary and assistant director of industrial relations, 1946-57; SMC Corp., Syracuse, N.Y., director of industrial relations and organization planning and assistant to senior vice-president, 1957-60; Crane Co., Chicago, director of industrial relations and organization and member of corporate operating committee, 1960-62; Manplan Consultants (management consultants), Chicago, partner, 1962—. President of board of trustees, Allendale School, Lake Villa, Ill. *Military service:* U.S. Army, 1941-46; became first lieutenant. *Member:* American Compensation Association, Chicago Club, Onwentsia Club (Lake Forest).

WRITINGS: Interpreting Executive Behavior, American Management Association, 1970; *Dissent: The Dynamic of Democracy,* Amacom Division, American Management Association, 1972. Also author of research report, "2001 Oddessey of Pay Price Productivity," Manplan Consultants, 1976. Contributor to business journals.

*　　*　　*

SYBURG, Jane 1927-

PERSONAL: Surname is pronounced See-burg; born August 29, 1927, in Des Moines, Iowa; daughter of Robert John and Alice (Duffy) Mitchell; married Frederic W. Syburg (a professor of drama), June 17, 1950; children: Nancy, Robert, Ellen. *Education:* Clarke College, Dubuque, Iowa, A.B., 1949; University of Notre Dame, M.A., 1969. *Religion:* Catholic. *Home:* 918 Whitehall Dr., South Bend, Ind. 46615. *Office:* Department of English, St. Joseph High School, South Bend, Ind.

CAREER: Teacher of religion to high school students in South Bend, Ind., 1958-68; St. Mary's Academy, South Bend, teacher of English and chairman of department, 1959-76; St. Joseph High School, South Bend, teacher of English and chairman of department, 1976—. *Member:* National Council of Teachers of English.

WRITINGS: (Editor) *People* (anthology), Fides, 1968; *Teaching High School Religion through Literature* (teacher's manuals to accompany *People* and subsequent books *Principles, Partners,* and *Pilgrims*), Fides, Volume I, 1968, Volume II, 1969, Volume III, 1970, Volume IV, 1971; (editor) *Principles* (anthology), Fides, 1969; (editor) *Partners* (anthology), Fides, 1970; (editor) *Pilgrims* (anthology), Fides, 1971.

*　　*　　*

SYKES, (Richard) Adam 1940-

PERSONAL: Born May 29, 1940, in London, England; son of Richard Lawrence and Nancy (Bailey) Sykes. *Education:* Attended Winchester College, London, 1953-58; Oxford University, B.A. (honors in English), 1961. *Religion:* Church of England. *Home:* Barley Hill House, Nuffield, Oxfordshire, England.

CAREER: Leo-Burnett-LPE Ltd., London, England, advertising executive, 1964.

WRITINGS—Compiler with Iain Sproat: *The Wit of Sir Winston,* Frewin Publishers, 1965; *The Wit of Westminster,* Frewin Publishers, 1967; *The Wit of the Law,* Frewin Publishers, 1968.†

*　　*　　*

SYKES, Christopher (Hugh) 1907-
(Richard Waughburton, a joint pseudonym)

PERSONAL: Born November 17, 1907, in Menethorpe, Yorkshire, England; son of Mark (a member of Parliament) and Edith Violet (Gorst) Sykes; married Camilla Georgiane Russell (a translator of gardening books and gardening correspondent for *Times Literary Supplement*), October 26, 1936; children: Mark Richard. *Education:* Attended Sorbonne,

University of Paris, 1926, and Christ Church, Oxford, 1926-28. *Politics:* "Floating voter." *Religion:* Roman Catholic. *Home:* Swyre House, Swyre, Dorchester, Dorsetshire, England. *Agent:* A. D. Peters & Co., 10 Buckingham St., London WC2N 6BU, England.

CAREER: Honorary attache at British Embassies in Berlin, Germany, 1928-29, and Tehran, Persia (now Iran), 1930-31; since his aim at that time was to be an Orientalist, he spent another extended period in Iran before World War II, and then returned there as second secretary of the British Embassy, Tehran, 1941-43, and as special correspondent of the *Daily Mail,* covering the Persian Azerbaijan Campaign, 1946; British Broadcasting Corp., London, England, script writer, producer, and member of program committee, 1946-68, deputy controller of Third Programme, 1948. Member, London Library Committee, 1965—. *Military service:* British Army, 1939-41, 1943-45; served at Middle East Headquarters, Cairo, 1940-41, and as intelligence officer in airborne corps, 1943-45; became major; mentioned in dispatches and received Croix de Guerre. *Member:* Royal Society of Literature (fellow), Royal Geographical Society, Literary Society, White's Club.

WRITINGS: (With Robert Byron, under joint pseudonym Richard Waughburton) *Innocence and Design,* Macmillan, 1935; *Wassmus: The German Lawrence,* Longmans, Green, 1936; (self-illustrated) *Stranger Wonders: Tales of Travel,* Longmans, Green, 1937; *High-Minded Murder,* Home & van Thal, 1944; *Four Studies in Loyalty* (essays), Collins, 1946, Sloane, 1948; *Answer to Question 33* (novel), Sloane, 1948; *Character and Situation* (short stories), Collins, 1949, Knopf, 1950; *Two Studies in Virtue,* Knopf, 1953; *A Song of a Shirt* (fiction), Verschoyle, 1953; *Dates and Parties* (fiction), Collins, 1955; *Orde Wingate* (biography), World Publishing, 1959; *Albert and Emerald; or, How They Saved the Nation* (juvenile), Hollis & Carter, 1961; *Crossroads to Israel,* World Publishing, 1965; *Troubled Loyalty,* Collins, 1968, published as *Tormented Loyalty: The Story of a German Aristocrat Who Defied Hitler,* Harper, 1969; *Nancy: The Life of Lady Astor,* Harper, 1972; *Evelyn Waugh: A Biography,* Little, Brown, 1975. Literary editor, *New English Review,* 1948-49.

SIDELIGHTS: Christopher Sykes' father was one of Lloyd George's main advisers on Oriental affairs, 1916-19, and was largely instrumental in bringing about the Balfour Declaration, hence the origin of the son's early interest in the Islamic world and Zionism. This Orientalist interest has colored most of Sykes' writing, he says. He has also been influenced "by almost every book I have read, not excluding contemptible ones." He believes the most vital of all vital subjects "is the question whether European civilisation will survive.... Of all contemptible contemporaries the worst are those who have abandoned hope and climbed onto the barbarian bandwagon, pretending to enjoy the music."

BIOGRAPHICAL/CRITICAL SOURCES: New Statesman, November 29, 1968; *Spectator,* December 13, 1968; *Christian Science Monitor ,* July 3, 1969; *New Yorker,* July 12, 1969.

*　　*　　*

SYLVESTER, Dorothy 1906-

PERSONAL: Born July 12, 1906, in Crewe, England; daughter of Albert (an accountant) and Florence (Dean Bray) Sylvester; married William Taylor, July, 1971. *Education:* University of Liverpool, B.A. (honors in geography), 1927, diploma in education, 1928, M.A., 1930. *Religion:*

Methodist. *Home:* High Beach, 15 Park Dr., Wistaston, near Crewe, Cheshire, England.

CAREER: University of Durham, Durham, England, lecturer in geography at colleges of the university, 1930-44; University of Manchester, Manchester, England, 1944-66, began as senior lecturer, became reader in geography. *Member:* Royal Geographical Society (fellow), Institute of British Geographers; and numerous county historical archaeological societies.

WRITINGS: Map and Landscape, George Philip & Son, 1952; (editor with Geoffrey Nulty) *The Historical Atlas of Cheshire,* Cheshire Community Council, 1958; (contributor) Robert W. Steel and Richard Lawton, editors, *Liverpool Essays in Geography,* Longmans, Green, 1967; *The Rural Landscape of the Welsh Borderland: A Study in Historical Geography,* Macmillan (London), 1969; *A History of Cheshire,* Darwen Finlayson, 1971. Contributor to geography journals, local history journals, and newspapers.

WORK IN PROGRESS: A History of Gwynedd, for Phillimore.

AVOCATIONAL INTERESTS: Photography.

BIOGRAPHICAL/CRITICAL SOURCES: Times Literary Supplement, July 24, 1969.

* * *

SYRED, Celia 1911-

PERSONAL: First syllable of surname rhymes with "my"; born April 10, 1911, in Westbury-on-Severn, Gloucestershire, England; daughter of Charles (an actor) and Georgina (an actress; maiden name, France) Whitlock; married Errol Syred (a farmer), April 20, 1952 (deceased). *Education:* Royal College of Art, A.R.C.A., 1934; additional study at Cheltenham School of Art. *Politics:* None. *Religion:* Church of England. *Home:* 19 Old South Rd., Bowral, New South Wales 2576, Australia.

CAREER: Taught art at colleges and art schools in England and Wales, 1934-55; author of children's books. *Member:* Australian Society of Authors. *Awards, honors:* Highly commended by Children's Book Council of Australia, 1967, for *Cocky's Castle,* 1977, for *Hebe's Daughter.*

WRITINGS—Youth books: *Cocky's Castle,* Angus & Robertson, 1966; *Baker's Dozen,* Angus & Robertson, 1969; *An Innkeeper,* Oxford University Press, 1970; *A Printer,* Oxford University Press, 1971; *Hebe's Daughter,* Hodder & Stoughton, 1976.

WORK IN PROGRESS: A youth book about eighteenth-century Scotland, particularly the Jacobite rising; research into cheese-making in the southern highlands of New South Wales.

SIDELIGHTS: Baker's Dozen was translated into Spanish. *Avocational interests:* Modern embroidery.

BIOGRAPHICAL/CRITICAL SOURCES: Times Literary Supplement, June 26, 1969.

* * *

SZANIAWSKI, Jerzy 1886-1970

1886—March 16, 1970; Polish journalist and playwright. Obituaries: *Antiquarian Bookman,* April 6-13, 1970; *Books Abroad,* spring, 1971.

* * *

TABACHNIK, Abraham B(er) 1902-1970

August 22, 1902—June 13, 1970; Russian-born American

Yiddish essayist and poet. Obituaries: *New York Times,* June 16, 1970; *Books Abroad,* spring, 1971.

* * *

TAKAHASHI, Akira 1932-

PERSONAL: Born September 18, 1932, in Sapporo City, Japan; son of Tomoji and Mitsuko Takahashi; married Mitsuko Hirao, October 10, 1961; children: Asako (daughter), Itsuro (son). *Education:* University of Tokyo, B.A., 1955, M.A., 1957, Ph.D., 1968. *Office:* Institute of Oriental Culture, University of Tokyo, Hongo, Bunkyo-Ku, Tokyo, Japan.

CAREER: Institute of Developing Economies, Tokyo, Japan, senior research officer, 1961-68; University of Tokyo, Institute of Oriental Culture, Tokyo, lecturer, 1968-71, associate professor of geography, 1971—. Fulbright exchange professor at State University of New York at Oswego, 1969-70, and University of Kansas, Lawrence, 1970-71. *Member:* Association of Japanese Geographers, Association of Economic Geographers, Japanese Society of Ethnology.

WRITINGS: Chubu Ruson no beisaku noson (title means "A Rice-Growing Village in Central Luzon"), Institute of Developing Economies (Tokyo), 1965, translation published as *Land and Peasants in Central Luzon: Socio-Economic Structure of a Bulacan Village,* Institute of Developing Economies, 1969, same translation published as *Land and Peasants in Central Luzon: Socio-Economic Structure of a Philippine Village,* East-West Center Press, 1970; (with Morio Ohno) *Village Communities in Asia,* Tokyo University Press, 1969. Also author of *Ringyo kikai jiten,* 1958, and co-author with Iwai Shinji of *Netsukokasei jushi to sono kako,* 1964.

WORK IN PROGRESS: Studies of the socio-economic structure of village communities in the Philippines, India, and Japan, and of the formation and significance of agricultural laborers in India and the Philippines.†

* * *

TALLCOTT, Emogene

PERSONAL: Born in Parish, N.Y. *Education:* Oswego State Normal School (now State University of New York College at Oswego), student; Columbia University, B.S. and M.A. *Home:* 7573 West Main St., Port Leyden, N.Y. 13433.

CAREER: Teacher, principal, and supervisor at elementary schools in Garden City, N.Y., 1925-43; engaged in educational reorganization for Office of Military Government in Germany for three years; spent two years as educational technician with the International Cooperation Administration in Paraguay; producer of educational television programs in Watertown, N.Y., for three years. *Member:* National League of American Pen Women, American Association of University Women, Delta Kappa Gamma.

WRITINGS: Glacier Tracks (juvenile), Lothrop, 1970.

WORK IN PROGRESS: Research for a juvenile science book about continental movements, tentatively entitled *These Shifting Continents;* research for a revision of *Glacier Tracks.*

AVOCATIONAL INTERESTS: Photography, geology, sewing, oil painting, dramatics, anthropology of the early peoples of North America.

TALMON, Shemaryahu 1920-

PERSONAL: Surname is pronounced Tal-*mon;* born May 28, 1920, in Poland; son of Litmann and Hella (Ell) Zelmanowicz; married Yonina Garber (a professor), November 17, 1948 (deceased); married Penina Moraq (a lecturer), March 18, 1969; children: (first marriage) Efrath, Tamar; (second marriage) Nogah, Tammy. *Education:* Hebrew University of Jerusalem, M.A., 1945, Ph.D., 1955. *Religion:* Jewish. *Home:* 5 Smuts St., Jerusalem, Israel. *Office:* Faculty of Humanities, Hebrew University, Jerusalem, Israel.

CAREER: University of Leeds, Leeds, England, lecturer in Semitic studies, 1950-51; University of Tel-Aviv, Tel-Aviv, Israel, lecturer in Bible studies, 1953-55; Hebrew University of Jerusalem, Jerusalem, Israel, instructor, 1955-57, lecturer in Bible studies, 1958-61; Brandeis University, Waltham, Mass., professor of Near Eastern studies, 1961-63; Hebrew University of Jerusalem, senior lecturer, 1963-66, associate professor, 1966-74, Magnes Professor of Bible Studies, 1974—, rector of University College, Haifa, 1968-69, dean of faculty of the humanities, 1975—. Visiting professor, Harvard University, 1970-71; Foster Visiting Professor of Bible Studies, Brandeis University, 1971-72. *Military service:* Israeli Defence Army, Infantry, 1948-49; became captain. *Member:* Israel Exploration Society, Israel Historical Society, Israel Society of Bible Research, Society of Old Testament Study (Great Britain), Society of Biblical Literature (United States), American Oriental Society, American Schools of Oriental Research, World Association of Jewish Studies.

WRITINGS: (Editor) *Selections from the Pentateuch in the Samaritan Version,* Hebrew University, 1957; (editor with M. Avi-Yonah and A. Malamat) *Views of the Bible World* (in English and Hebrew), International Publishers, Volume II, 1959, Volume III, 1960; (editor) *Textus: Annual of the Hebrew University Bible Project,* Magnes Press of Hebrew University, Volume IV, 1964, Volume V, 1966, Volume VI, 1967, Volume VII, 1969, Volume VIII, 1973; *Darkhe ha-sipur ba-Mikra* (on the Bible as literature), Akademon, Hebrew University, 1965; (editor) *Toldot nosah ha-Mikra ba-mehkar he-hadish* (readings on the history of the Bible text in recent literature; chiefly in English), Akademon, Hebrew University, 1966; (author of introduction) Roman-Francois Butin, *The Ten Nequdoth of the Torah,* Ktav Publishing, 1969; *The Old Testament Text: The Cambridge History of the Bible,* Volume I, edited by P. R. Akroyd and C. F. Evans, Cambridge University Press, 1970; (editor with F. M. Cross) *Qumran and the History of the Biblical Text,* Harvard University Press, 1975.

Contributor to *Encyclopaedia Biblica, Hebrew Bible Dictionary, Enciclopedia de la Biblica, Interpreter's Dictionary of the Bible,* and *Theologisches Woerterbuch zum Alten Testament.* Contributor of more than eighty articles and a number of reviews to journals in Israel, United States, England, Netherlands, and Italy.

WORK IN PROGRESS: The Covenanters from the Judean Desert, a sociological analysis; *The Biblical Narrative,* an introduction to biblical prose literature; a critical edition of the Book of Jeremiah.

*   *   *

TAMARIN, Alfred H. 1913-

PERSONAL: Born May 31, 1913, in Hudson, N.Y.; son of Abraham and Fanny (Naishtat) Tamarin; married Shirley Glubok (an author); children: Susan (Mrs. Alain Eluard). *Education:* New York University, B.A. (with honors), 1934. *Residence:* New York, N.Y.

CAREER: Theatre Guild, New York City, director of advertising and public relations, 1942-45; United Artists, New York City, vice-president for music and recording, 1956; Inflight Motion Pictures, New York City, vice-president, 1961-68. Lecturer, National Endowment for the Humanities, Princeton, N.J., and Metropolitan Museum of Art, New York City. *Member:* Authors Guild, Perstare et Praestare, Phi Beta Kappa. *Awards, honors:* Best Nonfiction award from *Horn Book* and Northeast Library Association, 1976, for *Voyaging to Cathay.*

WRITINGS—All juveniles, except as indicated: (Editor) *Revolt in Judea: The Road to Masada* (adult), Four Winds, 1968; (editor) *Benjamin Franklin: An Autobiographical Portrait,* Macmillan, 1969; (abridged and adapted from translation by John Addington Symonds) *The Autobiography of Benvenuto Cellini,* Macmillan, 1969.

Japan and the United States: The Early Encounters, 1791-1860, Macmillan, 1970; *Firefighting in America,* Macmillan, 1971; *We Have Not Vanished: Eastern Indians of the United States,* Follett, 1974; *Ancient Indians of the Southwest,* Doubleday, 1975; (with wife, Shirley Glubok) *Olympic Games in Ancient Greece,* Harper, 1975; (with S. Glubok) *Voyaging to Cathay,* Viking, 1976.

SIDELIGHTS: Alfred Tamarin told *CA:* "My interest in history, and some of the puzzling unanswered questions which hang over it, and my wife's concern for art and art history join in our viewing the same events from two different points of view, both of which get into our books. To me art is a window on history. To her history is a backdrop for the art. Both are combined in the words and illustrations of our books."

AVOCATIONAL INTERESTS: Photography (photographed most color covers and inside illustrations for his wife's series of art books for children).

*   *   *

TAMEDLY, Elisabeth L. 1931-

PERSONAL: Born July 4, 1931, in Berlin, Germany; daughter of Michael F. (a superintendent of education) and Hertha (Lejeune) Tamedly; married Andrew Lenches (a civil engineer), March 20, 1966. *Education:* Attended University of Zurich, 1954-56; University of Munich, Dip.econ., 1958; Institut Universitaire de Hautes Etudes Internationales, Geneva, Ph.D., 1968. *Religion:* Protestant. *Office:* Department of Economics, Pepperdine University, Malibu, Calif. 90265.

CAREER: Pepperdine University, Los Angeles, Calif., 1968—, began as assistant professor, currently associate professor of economics.

WRITINGS: Socialism and International Economic Order, Caxton, 1969.

WORK IN PROGRESS: Research in international economics, Eurodollars and international banking.

AVOCATIONAL INTERESTS: Music, literature, and outdoor activities.

*   *   *

TAMIR, Max Mordecai 1912-

PERSONAL: Born May 17, 1912, in Haifa, Israel; came to United States, 1943; son of Matatyahu and Hanna (Horowitz) Tamir; married Vicki Levy (a writer and translator),

July 6, 1956; children: Edith-Varda, AaDean-Neer (son). *Education:* Sorbonne, University of Paris, Ph.D., 1939. *Home:* 785 West End Ave., New York, N.Y. 10025.

CAREER: City of New York, N.Y., director in Department of Traffic, 1952-57; president, Directomat, Inc., 1957-66; City of New York, director of planning and research in Transportation Administration, 1967—. *Wartime service:* Served with French underground during World War II. *Member:* American Institute of Planners, Institute of Traffic Engineers, Society of Munic Engineers, Association of Architects and Engineers in Israel. *Awards, honors:* Academie-des-Beaux-Arts-de-Paris Award, 1939, for *Les Expositions internationales a travers les ages.*

WRITINGS: Les Expositions internationales a travers les ages, Galerie Jeanne Bucher, 1939; (with wife, Vicki Tamir) *Wall Street on the Hudson: A Treatise for the Stage in Four Acts and Prologue, or a Play without Guts and Blood,* Opus Publishing, 1970. Also author of *La Mer Morte et une ville a son bord,* 1937. Contributor to *McGraw's Encyclopedia of World Drama* and to *Gazette des Beaux-Arts.*

SIDELIGHTS: Max Tamir invented the Directomat machine, and built the Pal Pavilion at the International Fair in Paris, 1937.

* * *

TAMIR, Vicki 1924-

PERSONAL: Born July 17, 1924, in Sofia, Bulgaria; daughter of Eliezer Isaac (a businessman) and Regina (Graciani) Levy; married Ernst Julisch, 1949 (deceased); married Max Mordecai Tamir (a city planner), July 6, 1956; children: Edith-Varda, AaDean-Neer (son). *Education:* University of Sofia, law degree, 1947; attended University of Basel, 1947-48. *Home:* 785 West End Ave., New York, N.Y. 10025.

CAREER: Free-lance translator, writer, and foreign-language researcher. *Military service:* Israeli Army, 1948.

WRITINGS: Idei i dela (title means "Ideas and Deeds"; a Zionist anthology), Zionist Organization, 1947; (with husband, Max Tamir) *Wall Street on the Hudson: A Treatise for the Stage in Four Acts and Prologue, or a Play without Guts and Blood,* Opus Publishing, 1970. Also author of *Jews in Limbo: Bulgaria and Her Jews.* Contributor of articles on German, Russian, Spanish, Bulgarian, and other drama to *McGraw's Encyclopedia of World Drama.* Editorial assistant and regular contributor, *Atlas* (magazine).

WORK IN PROGRESS: Two philosophical novels set in Switzerland and Israel; researching Ladino (sixteenth-century Castilian/Hebrew dialect) and the Sephardic past for possible translation and editing of a Ladino lexicon.

SIDELIGHTS: Vicki Tamir told *CA:* "In writing, syntax, vocabulary and style are marginal. What counts more than anything else, is a belief in the sovereignty of the human spirit over matter, and the ability to reflect this belief, in one form or another, in one's work." She speaks German, French, Spanish, Hebrew, and Portuguese, as well as English and her native Bulgarian.

* * *

TART, Charles T(heodore) 1937-

PERSONAL: Born April 29, 1937, in Morrisville, Pa.; son of Charles Samuel (a musician) and Alma (Pfleger) Tart; married Judith Ann Bamburger, February 11, 1958; children: Catherine Lucinda, David Theodore. *Education:* Attended Massachusetts Institute of Technology, 1955-57, and

Duke University, 1957-58; University of North Carolina, B.A., 1960, M.A., 1962, Ph.D., 1963. *Religion:* Church of the Awakening. *Office:* Department of Psychology, University of California, Davis, Calif. 95616.

CAREER: Radio engineer for commercial broadcasting stations, 1956-59; Stanford University, Stanford, Calif., lecturer in psychology, 1964-65; University of Virginia, School of Medicine, Charlottesville, instructor in psychiatry, 1965-66; University of California, Davis, assistant professor, 1966-69, associate professor, 1969-74, professor of psychology, 1974—. Diplomate in Experimental Hypnosis, American Board of Examiners in Psychological Hypnosis.

MEMBER: American Association for the Advancement of Science, American Society of Clinical Hypnosis (former fellow), Association for the Psychophysiological Study of Sleep, Parapsychological Association (former member of council), Parapsychological Research Group, Inc. (director of research; member of board), Society for Clinical and Experimental Hypnosis (fellow). *Awards, honors:* Research grants from U.S. Public Health Service, 1963-65, 1967-71; citation by Society for Clinical and Experimental Hypnosis, 1966, for best paper on hypnosis research.

WRITINGS: (Editor) *Altered States of Consciousness: A Book of Readings,* Wiley, 1969; *On Being Stoned: A Psychological Study of Marijuana Intoxication,* Science & Behavior Books, 1971; (editor) *Transpersonal Psychologies,* Harper, 1975; *States of Consciousness,* Dutton, 1975; *The Application of Learning Theory to Extrasensory Perception,* Parapsychology Foundation, 1975; (with P. Lee, D. Galin, R. Ornstein, and A. Deikman) *Symposium of Consciousness,* Viking, 1975; *Learning to Use Extrasensory Perception,* University of Chicago Press, 1976.

Contributor: W. B. Webb, editor, *Sleep: An Experimental Approach,* Macmillan, 1968; R. Cavanna and M. Ullman, editors, *Psi and Altered States of Consciousness,* Parapsychology Foundation, 1968; M. Kramer, editor, *Dream Psychology and the New Biology of Sleep,* C. C Thomas, 1969; R. Cavanna, editor, *Psi Favorable States of Consciousness,* Parapsychology Foundation, 1970; R. Monroe, editor, *Journeys beyond Death,* Doubleday, 1971; J. White, editor, *The Highest State of Consciousness,* Doubleday, 1971. Also contributor to E. Fromm and R. Shor, editors, *Current Trends in Hypnosis Research,* and L. Bourne and B. Ekstrand, editors, *Human Action: An Introduction to Psychology.* Contributor of more than seventy articles to professional journals.

WORK IN PROGRESS: Government-supported research on hypnosis, sleep, and dreams.

SIDELIGHTS: Charles Tart told *CA:* "I am concerned with helping to alert academic psychology so [that] it deals with real human problems and potentialities, such as psychedelic drugs, mystical experience, survival [after] death, ESP, genuine encounter, love, and the like, instead of [with] rats. . . . I want to develop research methods that show . . . that you can be spiritual and precise and technological, thus spanning the full range of human potentialities instead of one extreme or the other."

* * *

TASHJIAN, Virginia A. 1921-

PERSONAL: Surname is pronounced *Tash*-jun; born September 20, 1921, in Brockton, Mass.; daughter of Vahan H. and Zvart (Shushian) Agababian; married James H. Tashjian (a journalist and editor), January 14, 1946; children:

Douglas (nephews) Kenneth, Roy. *Education:* Simmons College, B.S., 1943, M.L.S., 1969. *Politics:* Independent. *Religion:* Armenian Apostolic. *Home:* 278 Belmont St., Watertown, Mass. 02172. *Office:* Newton Free Library, 414 Centre St., Newton, Mass. 02158.

CAREER: Newton Free Library, Newton, Mass., branch librarian, 1943-67, assistant director, 1967-70, director, 1970—. Instructor at Bridgewater State College, 1969—, and at Framingham State College, 1972—. Lecturer on children's literature at Boston College, Harvard University, and Providence College. Book reviewer and storyteller for civic groups. *Member:* American Library Association, National Education Association, Women's National Book Association, Roundtable of Children's Librarians (chairman, 1967-69), New England Library Association, Massachusetts Library Association (member of executive board, 1970—; president, 1973-75). *Awards, honors:* American Library Association listed *Once There Was and Was Not* as an honor book, 1966.

WRITINGS—Juveniles: Sing and Pray: A Book of Armenian Hymns and Prayers, McLaughlin & Reilly, 1961; *Once There Was and Was Not: Armenian Tales Retold* (based on stories by H. Toumanian), Little, Brown, 1966; *Juba This and Juba That,* Little, Brown, 1969; *Three Apples Fell from Heaven: Armenian Folktales Retold,* Little, Brown, 1971; *Miller-King* (play), Ginn, 1971; *With a Deep Sea Smile,* Little, Brown, in press. Contributor to *Armenian Weekly, Boston Globe,* and *Washington Post.*

WORK IN PROGRESS: A collection of children's tales; a pictorial history of Armenia.

AVOCATIONAL INTERESTS: Travel, music, theater, gardening.

* * *

TATTERSALL, Lawrence H(olmes) 1933-

PERSONAL: Born February 26, 1933, in London, England; son of Lawrence (a chartered surveyor) and Phyllis M. (Holmes) Tattersall; married Jill M. Buddin (a medical practitioner), September 15, 1959; children: Jane, Luke, Toby. *Education:* Attended schools in England. *Politics:* None. *Religion:* None. *Home:* 38 Cherry Tree Rd., Sheffield S11 9AB, Yorkshire, England. *Office:* Lawrence Tattersall, Chartered Surveyors, 66 Leopold St., Sheffield S1 3RT, Yorkshire, England.

CAREER: Lawrence Tattersall, Chartered Surveyors, Sheffield, Yorkshire, England, apprentice, 1950-55, partner, 1957—. *Military service:* Royal Artillery, 1955-57; became second lieutenant. Territorial Volunteer Reserve, 1957-73; retired as lieutenant colonel. *Member:* Royal Institution of Chartered Surveyors (fellow).

WRITINGS: The Haven (novel), Secker & Warburg, 1969.

BIOGRAPHICAL/CRITICAL SOURCES: Spectator, March 28, 1969.

* * *

TAUBR, Paul Raymond 1937-

PERSONAL: Surname is pronounced *taw*-ber; born May 3, 1937, in Detroit, Mich.; son of Joseph Henry (a civil engineer) and Mary Taubr; married Marcia Vesely, July, 1968. *Education:* College of St. Thomas, St. Paul, Minn., B.A., 1959; University of Minnesota, M.A., 1970, Ph.D., 1973. *Home:* 4821 Elliot Ave. S., Minneapolis, Minn. 55417.

CAREER: Actuarial trainee with insurance firm in Minne-

apolis, Minn., 1959-60; Cleveland State University, Cleveland, Ohio, professor of English and education, 1971-74; consultant, Illinois Office of Education, 1974-77; currently information analyst, Foundation for Health Care Evaluation, Minneapolis.

WRITINGS: (With Mansoor Alyeshmerni) *Working with Aspects of Language,* Harcourt, 1970, 2nd edition, 1975; *Code Elaboration among Minneapolis Sixth-Grade Children: Variation with Interviewer,* University of Minnesota Press, 1973.

* * *

TAYLOR, John G(erald) 1931-

PERSONAL: Born August 18, 1931, in Hayes, Kent, England; son of William (a philosopher) and Elsie (Kershaw) Taylor; married Patricia Kenney, June 5, 1954; children: Geoffrey, Frances, Robin, Susan. *Education:* Mid-Essex Technical College, B.Sc. (first class honors), 1950; Christ's College, Cambridge, B.Sc. (first class honors), 1952, B.A. (first class honors), 1953, M.A., 1955, Ph.D., 1956. *Home:* 13 Charlbury Rd., Oxford, England. *Agent:* Ates Orga, International Authors Agency, Wadhurst, Sussex, England. *Office:* Department of Mathematics, Kings College, University of London, London WC1E 7HU, England.

CAREER: Institute for Advanced Study, Princeton, N.J., Commonwealth Fund fellow, 1956-58; Cambridge University, Cambridge, England, research fellow of Christ's College, 1958-59, university lecturer in mathematics, 1959-60, senior research fellow of Churchill College, 1963-64; Rutgers University, New Brunswick, N.J., professor of physics, 1964-66; Oxford University, Oxford, England, faculty lecturer at Mathematical Institute and fellow of Hertford College, 1966-67; University of London, Queen Mary College, London, England, senior lecturer, 1967-68, reader in physics, 1968-69; University of Southampton, Southampton, England, professor of physics, 1969-71; University of London, Kings College, London, professor of mathematics, 1971—. Visiting research associate professor, University of Maryland, summer, 1958; visiting scientist at Laboratoire de Physique, Orsay, France, 1960, and at Research Institute for Advanced Studies, Baltimore, Md., 1961; visiting member at Institute for Advanced Study, Princeton, 1961, 1962, and at Courant Institute of Mathematical Sciences, New York University, 1962. Actor, appearing on television, stage, radio, and in films; also gives poetry readings in England.

MEMBER: American Physical Society, British Institute of Physics (fellow), Actors Equity (England), Cambridge Philosophical Society (fellow). *Awards, honors:* Adams Prize of Cambridge University, 1959.

WRITINGS: Quantum Mechanics: An Introduction, Allen & Unwin, 1970; *Physics: An Introduction,* Kahn & Averill, 1971; *The Shape of Minds to Come,* Weybright & Talley, 1971; *The New Physics,* Basic Books, 1971; *Black Holes: The End of the Universe?,* Souvenir Press, 1973, Random House, 1974; *New Worlds in Physics,* Faber, 1974; *Special Relativity,* Oxford University Press, 1975; *Superminds: An Enquiry into the Paranormal,* Macmillan, 1975. Author of stage play, "Are You All There?," first performed at Churchill College, Cambridge, England, 1963, and of two science fiction plays for radio, "Survival of the Fittest" and "Take Me to Your Leader." Contributor of more than seventy articles to scientific journals and the more popular science magazines in Europe and the United States. Associate editor, *Journal of Mathematical Physics,* 1967-70; editor, *Rapid Results in Particle Physics,* 1971—.

WORK IN PROGRESS: The Death of Britain, on pollution; The Search for Elementarity, explaining the elementary particles; Return to Earth, a science fiction novel; Love Lyrical, Love Barody, a book of poems; research on the brain to understand the physical basis of thought, and on non-linear quantum field theories to understand the basis of matter.†

* * *

TAYLOR, William L. 1937-

PERSONAL: Born January 20, 1937, in Paterson, N.J.; son of William Amos (a mail clerk) and Myrtle (Leonhard) Taylor; married Joan Leighton, August 18, 1962; children: Nancy. Education: Bates College, B.A., 1958; Rice University, M.A., 1960; Brown University, Ph.D., 1968. Home address: Rural Route 1, Box 142, Center Harbor, N.H. 03226. Office: Department of History, Plymouth State College, Plymouth, N.H. 03264.

CAREER: Plymouth State College, Plymouth, N.H., instructor, 1967-68, assistant professor, 1968-71, associate professor of history, 1971—, and director of Institute for New Hampshire Studies. Vice-chairman, New Hampshire American Revolution Bicentennial Commission. Member, Center Harbor Conservation Commission. Member: Organization of American Historians, American Association of University Professors.

WRITINGS: A Productive Monopoly: The Effect of Railroad Control on the New England Coastal Steamship Lines, 1870-1916, Brown University Press, 1970. Contributor, Encyclopedia Americana Annual Yearbook, 1976. Contributor to historical journals. Member of editorial review board, Historical New Hampshire.

* * *

TEKEYAN, Charles 1927-

PERSONAL: Born April 15, 1927, in New York, N.Y.; son of Arthur (an owner of a small factory) and Rose (Ischilian) Tekeyan; married Ruth Bell, 1947 (divorced, 1953); married Birgit Ahlstrom, March 29, 1961 (divorced, 1976); children: Arthur, Rose. Education: Attended Columbia University but mainly self-educated through "the works of other writers." Address: Box 416, Cathedral Station, New York, N.Y. 10025.

CAREER: Writer; held jobs as a librarian, car salesman, copy writer, and proof reader ("At the time I held these positions I considered them temporary, hoping to return to writing full time. But some of them, for financial reasons, went on for years.") Military service: U.S. Army, 1945-46.

WRITINGS: The Passionate Tennis Player, and Other Stories, Pastoral-Universe, 1949; New York Is All Ours, Beekman, 1956; The Revelations of a Disappearing Man (novel), Doubleday, 1971. Contributor of stories to more than a dozen magazines and articles to New York Times.

WORK IN PROGRESS: Two novels.

SIDELIGHTS: Critical reaction to Tekeyan's writing has been mixed. A New Yorker reviewer describes The Passionate Tennis Player, and Other Stories as "five sprightly but disembodied stories by a young writer whose impressive flair for the precise use of language is offset by his nebulous situations and by the determined whimsicality of many of his characters." A Springfield Republican reviewer however, found the stories "interestingly told in a light, semihumorous vein, with a depth of meaning which will make the serious reader do a little thinking."

Tekeyan told CA: "The thousands of books I have read, even the ones of low quality, have all been important to me. And the thousands of people I have met through the years have been equally important. Not knowing why we lived and died, I thought I could find out from books and people. By writing I thought I could also find out from myself. I was eleven when I began to write, contributing short pieces to an Armenian-American publication from Boston called The Hairenik Weekly. Many years have passed and I am still trying to learn 'The Secret' from others and from myself. At last it is within my grasp.

"Every year less people are reading. We cannot put the blame entirely on TV. Writers must not let the reader lose his patience by forcing him to tolerate their wordiness, cleverness, their silliness and solemness, their obfuscations, pomposities and other stylistic indulgences. The reader wants to see if today's serious writers have anything important to tell him. He knows he has very little time because there are so many distractions and uncertainties in his life. Writers have to come to the point—and they have to make the point a new one and not the same old stuff. Otherwise, people will be reading only Gothic novels and other trivial books one of these days."

BIOGRAPHICAL/CRITICAL SOURCES: New Yorker, August 6, 1949; Springfield Republican, August 14, 1949; New York Times, August 14, 1949, April 4, 1971; Commonweal, September 16, 1949; Crozer Quarterly, January, 1950; Publishers' Weekly, January 11, 1971.

* * *

TEMPLE, Nigel (Hal Longdale) 1926-

PERSONAL: Born January 21, 1926, in Lowestoft, Suffolk, England; son of Sydney and Honor (Tucker) Temple; married Judith Tattersill, August 4, 1955; children: Richard Longdale, Sidney Anne. Education: Farnham School of Art, N.D.D., 1951; Sheffield College of Art, A.T.D., 1953. Home: Cheltenham, Gloucestershire, England. Office: Department of Visual Studies, Gloucestershire College of Education, Gloucester, England.

CAREER: Sheffield College of Art, Yorkshire, England, teacher of art, 1953-55; Wakefield College of Art, Yorkshire, England, teacher of art, 1955-58; Gloucestershire College of Education, Gloucester, England, head of department of visual studies, 1959—. Associate of various community groups concerned with man-made environment. Practising painter with exhibitions in England and West Germany. Military service: Royal Air Force, 1944-48. Member: Society of Architectural Historians of Great Britain, Society of Authors, Royal West of England Academy (associate member). Awards, honors: National Society for Art Education fellowship, 1964.

WRITINGS: Farnham Inheritance, Herald Press (Farnham, Surrey), 1956, 2nd edition, 1965; Farnham Buildings and People, Herald Press, 1963, 2nd edition, Phillimore, 1973; (editor) Seen and Not Heard: A Garland of Fancies for Victorian Children, Dial, 1970; Blaise Hamlet (guide), National Trust, 1975. Also author of a filmstrip series "Looking at Things," Visual Publications, 1968. Contributor of articles and reviews to periodicals, including House and Garden, Country Life, and Architectural Review.

WORK IN PROGRESS: Aspects of eighteenth- and nineteenth-century landscape and cottage architecture.

AVOCATIONAL INTERESTS: Development of nineteenth-century commercial book production and illustration.

TERRELL, John Upton 1900-

PERSONAL: Born December 9, 1900, in Chicago, Ill.; son of William John and Alice (Shaul) Terrell; married Donna McManus. *Home:* 115 East Live Oak Ave., San Gabriel, Calif. 91776.

CAREER: Newspaper reporter, Washington correspondent and war correspondent. Writer of historical fiction and non-fiction. *Awards, honors:* Silver Medal of Commonwealth Club of California, 1963, for *Journey into Darkness;* Western Heritage Award of National Cowboy Hall of Fame and Western Heritage Center, 1964, for outstanding western nonfiction book, *Furs by Astor.*

WRITINGS: The Little Dark Man (novel), Reilly & Lee, 1934; *Adam Cargo* (novel), Reilly & Lee, 1935; *Sunday Is the Day You Rest* (novel), Reilly & Lee, 1939; *Plume Rouge: A Novel of the Pathfinders,* Viking, 1942; *Journey into Darkness,* Morrow, 1962 (published in England as *Journey into Darkness: Cabeza de Vaca's Expedition across North America, 1528-36,* Jarrolds, 1964); *Furs by Astor,* Morrow, 1963; *Black Robe: The Life of Pierre-Jean De Smet, Missionary, Explorer, Pioneer,* Doubleday, 1964; *War for the Colorado River,* two volumes, Arthur H. Clark, 1965; (with George Walton) *Faint the Trumpet Sounds: The Life and Trial of Major Reno,* McKay, 1966; *Pueblo of the Hearts,* Best-West, 1966; *Traders of the Western Morning: Aboriginal Commerce in Pre-Columbian North America,* Southwest Museum, 1967; *The Six Turnings: Major Changes in the American West, 1806-1834,* Arthur H. Clark, 1968; *Zebulon Pike: The Life and Times of an Adventurer,* Weybright, 1968; *Estevanico the Black,* Westernlore, 1968; *La Salle: The Life and Times of an Explorer,* Weybright, 1968; *The Man Who Rediscovered America: A Biography of John Wesley Powell,* Weybright, 1969; *Navajos: The Past and Present of a Great People,* Weybright, 1970; *Bunkhouse Papers,* illustrations by Lorence Bjorklund, Dial, 1971; *American Indian Almanac,* World Publishing, 1971; *Apache Chronicle,* World Publishing, 1972; *Land Grab: The Truth about the "Winning of the West",* Dial, 1972; *Pueblos, Gods and Spaniards,* Dial, 1973; *Sioux Trail,* McGraw, 1974; (with wife, Donna M. Terrell) *Indian Women of the Western Morning: Their Life in Early America,* Dial, 1974; *The Plains Apache,* Crowell, 1975.

For younger readers; all published by Duell, Sloan & Pearce, unless otherwise indicated: *The Key to Washington,* Lippincott, 1962; *The United States Department of the Interior: A Story of Rangeland, Wildlife and Dams,* 1963; *The United States Department of the Treasury: A Story of Dollars, Customs and Secret Agents,* 1963; *The United States Department of State: A Story of Diplomats, Embassies and Foreign Policy,* 1964; *The United States Department of Health, Education, and Welfare: A Story of Protecting and Preserving Human Resources,* 1965; *The United States Department of Justice: A Story of Crime, Courts and Counterspies,* 1965; *The United States Department of Commerce: A Story of Industry, Science and Trade,* 1966; *The United States Department of Agriculture: A Story of Food, Farms and Forests,* 1966; *The United States Department of Defense: A Story of the War to Preserve Freedom,* Meredith, 1967; *The United States Post Office Department: A Story of Letters, Postage and Mail Fraud,* Meredith, 1968; *The United States Department of Labor: A Story of Workers, Unions and the Economy,* Meredith, 1968; *The Discovery of California,* illustrations by W. K. Plummer, Harcourt, 1970; *Search for the Seven Cities: The Opening of the American Southwest,* illustrations by W. K. Plummer, Harcourt, 1970.

BIOGRAPHICAL/CRITICAL SOURCES: Best Sellers, February 1, 1969; *New Yorker,* September 13, 1969; *Washington Post,* September 16, 1969, January 20, 1974; *New York Times Book Review,* October 5, 1969.

* * *

TERRIS, Susan 1937-

PERSONAL: Born May 6, 1937, in St. Louis, Mo.; daughter of Harold W. (a realtor) and Myra (Friedman) Dubinsky; married David Warren Terris (a stockbroker), August 31, 1958; children: Daniel, Michael, Amy. *Education:* Wellesley College, A.B., 1959; San Francisco State College (now University), M.A., 1966. *Politics:* Democrat. *Religion:* Jewish. *Home:* 11 Jordan Ave., San Francisco, Calif. 94118. *Agent:* Marilyn Marlow, Curtis Brown, Ltd., 575 Madison Ave., New York, N.Y. 10022.

CAREER: Teacher of writing workshops at University of California Extension.

WRITINGS—Juveniles; all published by Doubleday, except as indicated: *The Upstairs Witch and the Downstairs Witch,* 1970; *The Backwards Boots,* 1971; *On Fire,* 1972; *The Drowning Boy,* 1972; *Plague of Frogs,* 1973; *Pickle,* Four Winds Press, 1973; *Whirling Rainbows,* 1974; *Amanda, the Panda, and the Redhead,* 1975; *The Pencil Families,* Greenwillow, 1975; *No Boys Allowed,* 1976; *The Chicken Pox Papers,* F. Watts, 1976. Contributor of book reviews to *New York Times.*

WORK IN PROGRESS: Two juvenile books, *Two P's in a Pod,* for Greenwillow, and *No Scarlet Ribbons,* for F. Watts.

* * *

TERRY, Edward D(avis) 1927-

PERSONAL: Born May 19, 1927, in Eclectic, Ala.; son of W. J. (an educator) and Venola (Davis) Terry; married Marilyn Landers. *Education:* University of Alabama, B.S., 1949, M.A., 1953; National University of Mexico, graduate study, 1951; University of North Carolina, Ph.D., 1958. *Home:* 22 El Dorado E., Tuscaloosa, Ala. 35401. *Office address:* Box 1422, University, Ala. 35486.

CAREER: Sullins College, Bristol, Va., instructor in Spanish, 1953-55; Southern Methodist University, Dallas, Tex., assistant professor of Spanish, 1958-62; University of Tennessee, Knoxville, assistant professor of Romance languages, 1962-64; University of Alabama, University, associate professor, 1964-70, professor of Romance languages, 1970—, director of Latin American studies program, 1966-72. *Military service:* U.S. Army Air Corps, 1945-46; became sergeant. *Member:* Latin American Studies Association, American Association of Teachers of Spanish and Portuguese, Instituto International de Literatura Iberoamericana, South Atlantic Modern Language Association, Southeastern Conference on Latin American Studies (secretary-treasurer, 1970-73; president-elect, 1975-76; president, 1976-77), Phi Eta Sigma, Beta Gamma Sigma, Sigma Delta Pi.

WRITINGS: (Editor) *Artists and Writers in the Evolution of Latin America,* University of Alabama Press, 1969; (co-editor and contributor) *Yucatan: A World Apart,* University of Alabama Press, 1977. Contributor to language journals. Editor, *South Eastern Latin Americanist,* 1970-73.

WORK IN PROGRESS: A book, tentatively entitled *The Academia Espanola and the American Language Academies: Their Foundation and Subsequent Activities.*

TERRY, Robert H(arold)   1935-

PERSONAL: Born January 9, 1935, in Mansfield, Pa.; son of Harold E. (a pharmacist) and Gertrude (Hewitt) Terry; married Shirley Ann Flohr (a teacher), May 21, 1955; children: Paula Ann, Mickie Marie. *Education:* Mansfield State College, B.S., 1956; Shippensburg State College, M.Ed., 1963; American University, M.A., 1967, Ph.D., 1972. *Home:* 114 Locust Lane, Dillsburg, Pa. 17019. *Office:* History Department, York College, York, Pa. 17405.

CAREER: York College, York, Pa., 1965—, began as assistant professor of history, currently associate professor of international relations and chairman of department of history and international relations. Lay speaker in the United Methodist Church. *Military service:* U.S. Navy, 1956-58. *Member:* American Historical Association, American Association of University Professors, National Council of Social Studies, Latin American Historical Association, American Academy of Political and Social Science.

WRITINGS: Comparative Readings on Latin America, McCutchan, 1969. Also author of *A Salute to the Bicentennial,* and *Bicentennial Essays on York 1976,* both 1976.

AVOCATIONAL INTERESTS: Travel, camping, various youth oriented activities.

*   *   *

THAKUR, Shivesh Chandra   1936-

PERSONAL: Born March 31, 1936, in Bihar, India; son of Trilok Narian (a farmer and landowner) and Sonaclai (Tha) Thakur; married first wife, Chandraprabha, May 22, 1954 (died, 1968); married second wife, Philippa Tilley (a secondary school teacher), March 14, 1969; children: Sunita, Ravi N., Sanjay K. *Education:* University of Patna, B.A. (honors), 1954, M.A., 1956; University of Durham, Ph.D., 1966; Oxford University, Diploma in History and Philosophy of Science, 1966. *Office:* Department of Philosophy, University of Surrey, Guildford, Surrey GU2 5XH, England.

CAREER: University of Patna, Bihar, India, lecturer in philosophy, 1956-59; University of Ranchi, Ranchi, Birgar, India, lecturer in philosophy, 1959-63, 1966-67; University of Victoria, Wellington, New Zealand, lecturer in philosophy, 1967-69; University of Auckland, Auckland, New Zealand, senior lecturer in philosophy, 1969-72; University of Surrey, Surrey, Guildford, England, professor of philosophy, 1973—. Part-time lecturer in philosophy, University of Durham, 1963-65; visiting professor of religion and Larwill Lecturer, Kenyon College, 1972. *Member:* Aristotelian Society, Mind Association, Royal Institute of Philosophy. *Awards, honors:* Commonwealth Scholar, 1963-66.

WRITINGS: Christian and Hindu Ethics, Allen & Unwin, 1969, published as *Christian and Hindu Ethics: Two Religions Compared,* Hillary, 1970; (contributing editor) *Philosophy and Psychical Research,* Allen & Unwin, 1976. Contributor to *Philosophical Quarterly, Philosophical Studies, International Philosophical Quarterly, Dialectics and Humanism,* and *Australiasian Journal of Philosophy.*

WORK IN PROGRESS: Problems regarding religious language.

SIDELIGHTS: Shivesh Chandra Thakur told *CA:* "What can one man contribute to the world? But perhaps every little drop counts!"

THEINER, George   1927-
(Jonathan George, a joint pseudonym)

PERSONAL: The "Th" in surname is pronounced as "T"; born November 4, 1927, in Prague, Czechoslovakia; son of Jan (a printing works executive) and Hermina (Mueller) Theiner; married Anna Helis, March 6, 1954; children: Anna, Paul. *Education:* Attended Leamington College, England, 1940-44, and London College of Printing, 1944-45. *Agent:* David Higham Associates, Ltd., 5-8 Lower John St., London W1R 4HA, England. *Office:* George Weidenfeld & Nicolson, Ltd., 11 St. John's Hill, London SW11 1XA, England.

CAREER: Czechoslovak News Agency, Prague, Czechoslovakia, editor, 1946-50; began translating Czech and Slovak literature as a spare-time hobby, 1950; Pedagogical Publishing House, Prague, production assistant, 1954-56; Artia Publishing House, Prague, English editor, 1956-62; free-lance writer and translator in Prague, 1962-68; left Czechoslovakia after Russian invasion of 1968, moved to England; George Weidenfeld & Nicolson, Ltd. (publishers), London, England, administrative editor, 1969—. *Military service:* Czechoslovak Army, 1950-53; served in Silesian coal mines as "enemy of the State." *Awards, honors:* Czechoslovak Writers Union prize for translations of Czech literature, 1968.

WRITINGS: (With John Burke, under joint pseudonym Jonathan George) *The Kill Dog,* Doubleday, 1970; *The Secret Vysocany Congress: Proceedings and Documents of the Extraordinary Fourteenth Congress of the Communist Party of Czechoslovakia, 22 August 1968,* Allen Lane, 1971.

Translator from Czech or Slovak: Jan Vladislav, *Persian Fables* (retold), Spring Books, 1960; *Death Is Called Engelchen,* Artia Publishing House (Prague), 1961; *A Dog's Life,* Artia Publishing House, 1962; Arnoust Lustig, *Night and Hope,* Dutton, 1962; Vaclav Jan Stanek, *Introducing Birds,* Golden Pleasure Books (London), 1963; Stanek, *Pictorial Encyclopedia of the Animal Kingdom,* Crown, 1963; (and editor) *The Monkey King,* Hamlyn, 1964; *That Particular Fault . . . ,* Artia Publishing House, 1964; Vladimir Hulpach, *American Indian Tales and Legends,* Hamlyn, 1965; *Seven Short Stories,* Orbis Publishing House (Prague), 1966; Arnost Lustig, *Dita Sax,* Hutchinson, 1966; *Modern Fairy Tales,* Hamlyn, 1967; (with Ian Milner) Miroslav Holub, *Selected Poems,* Penguin, 1967; Karel Jalovec, *German and Austrian Violin-Makers,* edited by Patrick Hanks, Tudor, 1967; Klara Jarunkova, *Don't Cry for Me,* Four Winds, 1968; *Slovak Short Stories,* Orbis Publishing House, 1969; (and compiler) *New Writing in Czechoslovakia* (fiction), Penguin, 1969; Frantisek Tichy, *The Drawings of Frantisek Tichy,* notes by Vojtech Volauka, Hamlyn, 1969; Vladimir Hulpach, Emanuel Frynta, and Vaclav Cibula, *Heroes of Folk Tale and Legend,* Hamlyn, 1970; *European Tales and Legends,* Hamlyn, 1970; *Diary of a Counter-Revolutionary,* McGraw, 1970; Jan Vladislav, *Italian Fairy Tales,* Hamlyn, 1971; (with Ewald Osers) *Three Czech Poets: Vitezslav Nezval, Antonin Bartusek, Josef Hanslik,* Penguin, 1971.

Also author of several original children's stories and translator from the Czech and Slovak of several art books, children's books, film scripts, radio plays, short stories, and poems. Translations of poems have appeared in *Modern Poetry in Translation, Art and Literature, City Lights Journal, Stand,* and other English and American periodicals.

WORK IN PROGRESS: Translating from the Czech, *The Sorrow of Lieutenant Boruvka.*

SIDELIGHTS: George Theiner told *CA:* "I have wanted to write ever since I was at school, literature and languages being my favourite subjects. On returning to Prague from England after the war I became a journalist, running an English news service for CTK and giving this up when decent journalism became impossible owing to the changed political circumstances.... I have always wanted to travel, but in pre-Dubcek Czechoslovakia this was virtually impossible for a non-Party man known to have liberal and pro-Western views. It was a great achievement when, in 1962 through the good offices of the Writers Union, I was able to come to England for the first time since the war for the publication of Arnost Lustig's collection of short stories about the Terezin ghetto, *Night and Hope,* which I translated.... I left Czechoslovakia with my family after the Russian invasion [in 1968] and have settled in London.... I am also interested in the theatre and films."†

* * *

THEODORSON, George A. 1924-

PERSONAL: Born October 19, 1924, in New York, N.Y.; son of Achilles George (a writer) and Anna D. (Debos) Theodorson; married Lucille Ann, September 6, 1950; children: Carol Jean Ann. *Education:* Cornell University, B.A., 1950, M.A., 1951, Ph.D., 1954. *Religion:* Presbyterian. *Home:* 259 East Waring Ave., State College, Pa. 16802. *Office:* Department of Sociology, Pennsylvania State University, University Park, Pa. 16802.

CAREER: University of Buffalo, Buffalo, N.Y., instructor, 1954-55, assistant professor of sociology, 1955-56; Pennsylvania State University, University Park, assistant professor, 1956-60, associate professor, 1960-66, professor of sociology, 1966—. Fulbright lecturer, University of Rangoon, 1958-59; Fulbright professor, University of Vienna, 1962-63. Member of selection committee, American Field Service in Austria, 1962-63. *Military service:* U.S. Army, 1943-46; served in Asiatic-Pacific theater. *Member:* American Sociological Association (fellow), Burma Research Society (life member), Eastern Sociological Society. *Awards, honors:* Smith-Mundt grant, 1958-59; research grants from Pennsylvania State University, 1957-58, 1959-64.

WRITINGS: (Editor and contributor) *Studies in Human Ecology,* Row, Peterson & Co., 1961; (with father, Achilles Theodorson) *Modern Dictionary of Sociology,* Crowell, 1969; (editor with N. S. Timasheff) *Sociological Theory: Its Nature and Growth,* 4th edition (Theodorson was not associated with earlier editions), Random House, 1976.

Contributor: Joseph S. Roucek, editor, *Contemporary Sociology,* Philosophical Library, 1958; Peter Heintz, editor, *Die Soziologie der Entwicklungslander,* Kiepenheuer & Witsch, 1962; Llewellyn Z. Gross, editor, *Sociological Theory: Inquiries and Paradigms,* Harper, 1967. One of his articles, "Romanticism and Motivation to Marry in the United States, Singapore, Burma, and India," has been reprinted in six other books. Contributor of more than fifty articles and reviews to foreign professional journals in America.

WORK IN PROGRESS: A book on social ecology and a book on the sociology of American society.

SIDELIGHTS: George A. Theodorson has traveled widely in Asia, the Middle East, and Europe. Editions of Theodorson's books have been published in German, Italian, Spanish, and Arabic. *Avocational interests:* Southeast Asian art, plant ecology, American archaeology.

THEOHARIS, Athan George 1936-

PERSONAL: Born August 3, 1936, in Milwaukee, Wis.; son of George A. and Adeline (Konop) Theoharis; married Nancy Artinian, August 21, 1966; children: Jeanne Frances, George Thomas, Elizabeth Armen. *Education:* University of Chicago, A.B., 1956, A.B., 1957, A.M., 1959, Ph.D., 1965. *Politics:* Democrat. *Religion:* Greek Orthodox. *Home:* 8527 North Lane, Fox Point, Wis. *Office:* Department of History, Marquette University, Milwaukee, Wis. 53233.

CAREER: Texas A&M University, College Station, instructor in history, 1962-64; Wayne State University, Detroit, Mich., assistant professor of history, 1964-68; Staten Island Community College of the City University of New York, Staten Island, N.Y., associate professor of history, 1968-69; Marquette University, Milwaukee, Wis., associate professor, 1969-76, professor of American history, 1976—. *Member:* American Historical Association, Academy of Political Science, Organization of American Historians, American Civil Liberties Union, National Committee for a Sane Nuclear Policy (national board member), University of Chicago Alumni (board, 1968-70). *Awards, honors:* Truman Institute for National and International Affairs summer research grants, 1965, 1966; Wayne State University research grant, 1967; Marquette University research grant, 1970; Institute for Humane Studies grant, 1971; American Bar Association Gavel awards.

WRITINGS: Anatomy of Anti-Communism, Hill & Wang, 1969; (with others) *The Yalta Myths: An Issue in U.S. Politics, 1945-1955,* University of Missouri Press, 1970; *Seeds of Repression: Harry S. Truman and the Origins of McCarthyism,* Quadrangle, 1971; (contributor) *Politics and Policies of the Truman Administration,* Quadrangle, 1970; (contributor) *Public Opinion and Historians,* Wayne State University Press, 1970; (co-editor) *The Specter,* New Viewpoints, 1974; (contributor) *Men, Women and Issues in American History,* Dorsey, 1975; (co-author) *Twentieth Century United States,* Prentice-Hall, 1978. Contributor to *New University Thought* and other journals.

WORK IN PROGRESS: Internal security policy, 1936-76; compiling and editing files of FBI important internal security cases and federal surveillance policy.

AVOCATIONAL INTERESTS: Sports.

BIOGRAPHICAL/CRITICAL SOURCES: New York Times, March 7, 1971; *New York Review of Books,* March 11, 1971; *American Political Science Review,* spring, 1976.

* * *

THIELE, Colin (Milton) 1920-

PERSONAL: Surname is pronounced Tee-lee; born November 16, 1920, in Eudunda, South Australia; son of Carl Wilhelm (a farmer) and Anna (Wittwer) Thiele; married Rhonda Gill (a teacher and artist), March 17, 1945; children: Janne Louise (Mrs. Geoffrey Minge), Sandra Gwenyth. *Education:* University of Adelaide, B.A., 1941, Diploma of Education, 1947; Adelaide Teachers College, Diploma of Teaching, 1942. *Home:* 24 Woodhouse Crescent, Wattle Park, South Australia 5066, Australia. *Office:* Wattle Park Teachers Centre, Wattle Park, South Australia 5066, Australia.

CAREER: South Australian Education Department, English teacher and senior master at high school in Port Lincoln, 1946-55, senior master at high school in Brighton, 1956; Wattle Park Teachers College, Wattle Park, South Australia, lecturer, 1957-61, senior lecturer in English, 1962-63, vice-principal, 1964, principal, 1965-73; director, Murray Park College of Advanced Education, 1973; Wattle Park Teachers Centre, Wattle Park, principal, 1973—. Commonwealth Literary Fund lecturer on Australian literature; speaker at conferences on literature and education in Australia and United States. *Military service:* Royal Australian Air Force, 1942-45.

MEMBER: Australian College of Education (fellow), Australian Society of Authors (vice-president, 1965), English Teachers Association (president, 1957), South Australian Fellowship of Writers (president, 1961). *Awards, honors:* W. J. Miles Poetry Prize, 1944, for *Progress to Denial;* Commonwealth Jubilee Literary Competitions, first prize in radio play section, for "Edge of Ice," and first prize in radio feature section, both 1951; South Australian winner in World Short Story Quest, 1952; Fulbright scholar in United States and Canada, 1959-60; Grace Leven Poetry Prize, 1961, for *Man in a Landscape;* Commonwealth Literary Fund fellowship, 1967-68; a number of commendations in Australian Children's Book Council awards.

WRITINGS—All published by Rigby, except as indicated: *Progress to Denial* (poems), Jindyworobak, 1945; *Splinters and Shards* (poems), Jindyworobak, 1945; *The Golden Lightning* (poems), Jindyworobak, 1951; (editor) *Jindyworobak Anthology* (verse), Jindyworobak, 1953; *Man in a Landscape* (poems), 1960; (editor with Ian Mudie) *Australian Poets Speak,* 1961; *The Sun on the Stubble* (novel), 1961; (editor) *Favourite Australian Stories,* 1963; (editor, and author of commentary and notes) *Handbook to Favourite Australian Stories,* 1964; *In Charcoal and Conte* (poems), 1966; *The Rim of the Morning* (short stories), 1966; *Heysen of Hahndorf* (biography), 1968, Tri-Ocean, 1969; *Barossa Valley Sketchbook,* illustrations by Jeanette McLeod, Tri-Ocean, 1968; *Labourers in the Vineyard* (novel), 1970; *Selected Verse (1940-1970),* 1970; *Coorong,* photographs by Mike McKelvey, 1972; *Range without Man: The North Flinders,* 1974; *The Little Desert,* photographs by Jocelyn Burt, 1975; *Grains of Mustard Seed,* South Australia Education Department, 1975; *Heysen's Early Hahndorf,* 1976; *The Bight,* photographs by McKelvey, 1976.

Children's books and school texts; all published by Rigby, except as indicated: *The State of Our State,* 1952; (editor and annotator) *Looking at Poetry,* Longmans, Green, 1960; *Gloop the Gloomy Bunyip* (children's story in verse; also see below), Jacaranda, 1962; (editor with Greg Branson) *One-Act Plays for Secondary Schools,* Books 1-2, 1962, one-volume edition of Books 1-2, 1963, Book 3, 1964, revised edition of Book 1 published as *Setting the Stage,* 1969, revised edition of Book 2 published as *The Living Stage,* 1970; *Storm Boy,* 1963, Rand McNally, 1966, new edition, with illustrations by Robert Ingpen, 1974; (editor with Branson) *Beginners, Please* (anthology), 1964; *February Dragon* (children's novel), Tri-Ocean, 1965; *Mrs. Munch and Puffing Billy,* 1967, Tri-Ocean, 1968; *Yellow-Jacket Jock,* illustrations by Clifton Pugh, F. W. Cheshire, 1969; *Blue Fin* (children's novel), 1969, Harper, 1974; *Flash Flood,* 1970; *Flip Flop and Tiger Snake,* 1970; *Gloop the Bunyip* (children's story in verse; contains material from *Gloop the Gloomy Bunyip*), 1970; (editor with Branson) *Plays for Young Players* (for primary schools), 1970; *The Fire in the Stone,* 1973, Harper, 1974; *Albatross Two,* 1974, published as *Fight Against Albatross Two,* Harper, 1976; *Uncle Gustav's Ghosts,* 1974; *Magpie Island,* 1974; *The Hammerhead Light,* 1976.

Plays: "Burke and Wills" (verse), first performed at Adelaide Radio Drama Festival, 1949, and published in full in *On the Air,* edited by P. R. Smith, Angus & Robertson, 1959; "Edge of Ice" (verse), first performed on radio, 1952; "The Shark Fishers" (prose), first performed, 1954; "Edward John Eyre" (verse), first performed at Adelaide Radio Drama Festival, 1962.

Author of other verse plays for radio, and radio features, documentaries, children's serials, and schools broadcasts programs; national book reviewer for Australian Broadcasting Commission. His poetry and short stories have appeared in many anthologies and journals; also contributor of articles and reviews to periodicals.

SIDELIGHTS: Colin Thiele's children's story *Storm Boy* was made into a feature film in 1976. His books have been translated into German, Russian, and Afrikaans.

BIOGRAPHICAL/CRITICAL SOURCES: Australian Book Review, Children's Supplement, 1964, 1967, 1969; *Kirkus,* January 1, 1966; *New York Times Book Review,* May 1, 1966; *Young Readers Review,* September, 1966; *Bulletin of the Center for Children's Books,* Volume XX, November, 1966; *Childhood Education,* Volume XLIII, December, 1966, Volume XLIII, April, 1967; *Books and Bookmen,* July, 1968.

* * *

THIER, Herbert D(avid) 1932-

PERSONAL: Born February 27, 1932, in New York, N.Y.; son of Benjamin and Hannah (Greenberg) Thier; married Marlene Bach, December 19, 1954; children: Maura, Lynne, Holli. *Education:* New York College for Teachers (now State University of New York at Albany), B.A., 1953, M.A. 1954; New York University, Ed.D., 1962. *Home:* 142 Hodges Dr., Moraga, Calif. 94556. *Office:* Lawrence Hall of Science, University of California, Berkeley, Calif. 94720.

CAREER: Teacher of general science and physics at high school in Long Beach, N.Y., 1954-58; science coordinator and physics teacher at high school in Nishkayuna, N.Y., 1958-59; New Brunswick (N.J.) public schools, director of secondary education, 1959-62; Falls Church (Va.) public schools, assistant superintendent, 1962-63; University of California, Berkeley, assistant director of Science Curriculum Improvement Study, 1963—, director of Adapting Science Materials for the Blind, 1969—, co-director of Instructional Strategies for Outdoor Biology Project, 1972—, director of Individualized Research Project, 1972—. Visiting professor, Simon Fraser University, summer, 1972, and Tel Aviv University, summer, 1974. Consultant to Israel Elementary Science Project, Tel Aviv University, summer, 1970, and to various school systems and universities. *Member:* National Association for Research in Science Teaching, Association for Education of Teachers in Science, National Science Teachers Association, Phi Delta Kappa.

WRITINGS: (With Robert Karplus) *A New Look at Elementary School Science,* photographs by authors, Rand McNally, 1967; *Teaching Elementary School Science: A Laboratory Approach,* Heath, 1970.

Teacher's manuals, all written with Karplus and published by Science Curriculum Improvement Study, University of California, Berkeley: *Interaction and Systems: A Science Unit for the Primary Grades,* 1963; *Material Objects: A Science Unit for the Primary Grades,* 1964; *Energy Sources,* 1969. Consulting editor, "Professional Growth for Teachers" series, Croft Publications.

THIERAUF, Robert J(ames) 1933-

PERSONAL: Born July 25, 1933, in Covington, Ky. Education: Xavier University, Cincinnati, Ohio, B.S.B.A., 1958, M.B.A., 1960; Ohio State University, Ph.D., 1966. Home: 535 Fairway Lane, Cincinnati, Ohio 45228. Office: Department of Management and Information Systems, Xavier University, Cincinnati, Ohio 45207.

CAREER: Lybrand, Ross Brothers & Montgomery, public accountant in Cincinnati, Ohio, 1958-60, consultant to New York office, 1960-63; certified public accountant, state of Ohio, 1963; Xavier University, Cincinnati, chairman of department of management and information system, 1965—. Member: American Institute of Certified Public Accountants, American Institute of Decision Sciences, Institute of Management Science, Academy of Management, Association for Computing Machinery.

WRITINGS: Richard A. Grosse, editor, Decision Making Through Operations Research, Wiley, 1970, 2nd edition, 1975; Data Processing for Business and Management, Wiley, 1973; Systems Analysis and Design of Real-Time Management Information Systems, Prentice-Hall, 1975; (with others) Management Principles and Practices: A Contingency and Questionnaire Approach, Wiley, 1977.

*   *   *

THOMAS, Donald F. 1913-

PERSONAL: Born September 30, 1913, in Woodsboro, Md.; son of F.I.M. (a minister) and Mabel E. (Fritz) Thomas; married Helen B. McBride (a librarian), August 31, 1939; children: Grace H. Education: Attended Findlay College, 1931-33; Franklin and Marshall College, A.B., 1937; Eastern Baptist Theological Seminary, B.D., 1942, Th.M., 1943, Th.D., 1945. Residence: Covina, Calif.

CAREER: Clergyman of American Baptist Convention; pastor in Philadelphia, Pa., 1938-50, and in Portland, Ore., 1950-58; American Baptist Home Mission Society, Valley Forge, Pa., program associate, 1958-63; American Baptist Seminary of the West, Covina, Calif., professor of pastoral theology, beginning 1963, vice-president, 1966. Member: Society for the Advancement of Continuing Education for Ministry.

WRITINGS: The Church in the Home, Judson, 1960; The Deacon in a Changing Church, Judson, 1969.

WORK IN PROGRESS: The Layman at Worship; and Leadership in the Congregation.†

*   *   *

THOMAS, Henry 1886-1970

1886—December 25, 1970; American biographer, publisher, and educator. Obituaries: New York Times, December 26, 1970; Newsday, December 28, 1970; Publishers' Weekly, January 18, 1971; Books Abroad, spring, 1971.

*   *   *

THOMAS, Theodore L. 1920-
(Ted Thomas; Leonard Lockard, a pseudonym)

PERSONAL: Born April 13, 1920, in New York, N.Y.; married Virginia Kent Paton, July 18, 1947; children: Lenore Webster, Jefferson Webster, Alexandra Webster. Education: Massachusetts Institute of Technology, S.B., 1947; Georgetown University, J.D., 1953. Politics: Republican. Religion: Presbyterian. Home: 1284 Wheatland Ave., Lancaster, Pa. 17603.

CAREER: American Cyanamid Co., chemical engineer in Stamford, Conn., 1947-50, patent lawyer in Washington, D.C., 1950-55; Armstrong Cork Co., Lancaster, Pa., patent lawyer, 1955—. Chairman of Lancaster Zoning Board of Adjustment, 1966-70 and Lancaster Narcotics and Dangerous Drugs Committee, 1970-71. Military service: U.S. Army, 1943-46; became first lieutenant. Member: American Association for the Advancement of Science, American Bar Association, American Patent Law Association, Philadelphia Patent Law Association, Underwater Explorer's Club.

WRITINGS—Novels: (With Kate Wilhelm) The Clone, Berkley Publishing, 1965; (under name Ted Thomas; with Wilhelm) Year of the Cloud, Doubleday, 1969. Contributor to twenty short story anthologies; contributor of about seventy-five short stories and articles to magazines, some under pseudonym Leonard Lockard. Author of "Science for Everybody," semi-weekly column in Stamford Advocate, 1949—.

WORK IN PROGRESS: A novel.

*   *   *

THOMSEN, Moritz 1915-

PERSONAL: Born August 3, 1915, in Los Angeles, Calif.; son of Charles M. (a businessman) and Marie (Titus) Thomsen; divorced. Education: Attended University of Washington, Seattle, 1936, University of Oregon, 1937, 1938, and Columbia University, 1939. Politics: Democrat. Address: c/o Embajada de los Estados Unidos, Peace Corps, Quito, Ecuador.

CAREER: Farmer in California, 1945-64; Peace Corps volunteer, 1965—, farming in Ecuador. Military service: U.S. Army Air Force, 1941-45; became captain; received Distinguished Flying Cross and Air Medal. Awards, honors: Governor's Award, state of Washington, for Living Poor.

WRITINGS: Living Poor: A Peace Corps Chronicle, University of Washington Press, 1970; On the River of Emeralds, Houghton, 1978.

BIOGRAPHICAL/CRITICAL SOURCES: New Republic, November 29, 1969.

*   *   *

THOMSON, David 1912-1970

January 13, 1912—February 24, 1970; English educator, critic, and authority on modern politics and law. Obituaries: New York Times, February 25, 1970; Antiquarian Bookman, March 16, 1970. (See index for CA sketch)

*   *   *

THOMSON, Irene Taviss 1941-
(Irene Taviss)

PERSONAL: Born December 10, 1941, in New York, N.Y.; daughter of David and Ruth (Geller) Taviss; married Michael G. R. Thomson (a physicist), February 8, 1974; children: Kenneth. Education: Brooklyn College (now Brooklyn College of the City University of New York), B.A. (summa cum laude), 1962; Harvard University, Ph.D., 1967. Home: 42 Orion Rd., Berkeley Heights, N.J. 07922. Office: Department of Social Sciences, Fairleigh Dickinson University, Madison, N.J. 07940.

CAREER: Harvard University, Cambridge, Mass., research associate, Harvard University Program on Technology and Society and head of information center for the program, 1966-72, lecturer in sociology department, 1972-74;

Fairleigh Dickinson University, Madison, N.J., assistant professor in social sciences department, 1975—. Has conducted summer seminars and taught courses at Brooklyn College (now Brooklyn College of the City University of New York) and Massachusetts Institute of Technology. *Member:* American Sociological Association, Phi Beta Kappa, Alpha Kappa Delta.

WRITINGS—All published under the name, Irene Taviss: (Editor) *The Computer Impact,* Prentice-Hall, 1970; (editor with Everett Mendelsohn and Judith Swazey) *Human Aspects of Biomedical Innovation,* Harvard University Press, 1971; *Our Tool-Making Society,* Prentice-Hall, 1972; (contributor) Robin Marris, editor, *The Corporate Society,* Wiley, 1974; (contributor) Laurence Tribe, Corinne Schelling, and John Voss, editors, *When Values Conflict: Essays on Environmental Analysis, Discourse, and Decision,* Ballinger, 1976. Contributor to sociology journals.

* * *

THOMSON, James C(laude), Jr. 1931-

PERSONAL: Born September 14, 1931, in Princeton, N.J.; son of James Claude (a missionary in China and Japan) and Margaret Seabury (Cook) Thomson; married Diana Dodge Duffy Butler, December 19, 1959; stepchildren: two. *Education:* Attended University of Nanking, 1948; Yale University, B.A., 1953; Clare College, Cambridge, B.A. (first class honors in history), 1955, M.A., 1959; Harvard University, Ph.D., 1961. *Home:* 21 Sibley Ct., Cambridge, Mass. 02138. *Office:* Nieman Foundation for Journalism, 48 Trowbridge St., Cambridge, Mass. 02138.

CAREER: Held posts in Washington, D.C., 1959-64, as assistant to Representative Bowles of Connecticut, 1959-60, special assistant to Under Secretary of State, 1961, special assistant to the President's special representative and adviser on African, Asian, and Latin American affairs, 1961-63, special assistant to Assistant Secretary of State for Far Eastern Affairs, 1963-64, and staff member of National Security Council, the White House, 1964-66; Harvard University, Cambridge, Mass., assistant professor of history, 1966-70, lecturer, 1970—, associate, Institute of Politics, 1966-72; curator, Nieman Foundation for Journalism, Cambridge, Mass., 1972—. Director, National Committee on U.S.-China Relations. Trustee, Yale-in-China Program, Yale University. and Lawrenceville School. *Military service:* U.S. Army Reserve, Military Intelligence, 1950-56; became sergeant. *Member:* Association for Asian Studies, Council on Foreign Relations, Phi Beta Kappa, Scroll and Key. *Awards, honors:* Honorary scholar of Clare College, Cambridge University; Council on Foreign Relations international affairs fellow, 1969-70.

WRITINGS: (Editor) *Seventy-five: A Study of a Generation in Transition,* Yale University Press, 1953; (contributor) *No More Vietnams? The War and the Future of American Foreign Policy,* Harper, for Stevenson Institute of International Affairs, 1968; (contributor) *Who We Are: An Atlantic Chronicle of the United States and Vietnam 1966-1969,* Little, Brown, 1969; *While China Faced West: American Reformers in Nationalist China, 1928-1937,* Harvard University Press, 1969. Contributor to *Papers on China,* Volume XI, Harvard University Press, 1957; contributor of articles and reviews to *China Quarterly, Atlantic, New Republic, Washington Post, Boston Globe, New York Times,* and other publications. Chairman of editorial board, *Yale Daily News,* 1952-53; member of editorial board, *Foreign Policy.*

WORK IN PROGRESS: Studies in the American-East-Asian relationship.

SIDELIGHTS: James Thomson lived in China and Japan, 1933-40, in China, 1948-49, and traveled in Asia in 1961, 1962, 1966, 1969. He has also traveled as a government official, scholar, and tourist in Europe, the Middle East, and Africa.

* * *

THOMSON, Keith 1912-

PERSONAL: Born August 16, 1912, in London, England; son of Bernard Home (an artist) and Margaret (Scholfield) Thomson; married Virginia Wood (an interior designer), May 4, 1956; children: Holly, Marie, William, Max. *Education:* Oxford University, B.A., 1933. *Religion:* Church of England. *Home:* Kenfield Hall, Canterbury, Kent, England. *Agent:* Curtis Brown Ltd., 1 Craven Hill, London W2 3EW, England.

CAREER: York Festival of the Arts, York, England, artistic director, 1950-52; ESSO Petroleum Co., London, England, editor and assistant manager of public relations, 1953-67. Editorial and film consultant. *Military service:* British Army, Intelligence, 1939-45; became lieutenant colonel. *Awards, honors:* Order of the British Empire for service to the arts.

WRITINGS: The Dance of the Sun (novel), MacGibbon & Kee, 1968. Author of scripts for radio and documentary films. Contributor to periodicals.

WORK IN PROGRESS: A novel with proposed title, *Dream of a Lily White Boy;* research for commentary on the recently discovered Gospel of St. Thomas.

AVOCATIONAL INTERESTS: Dairy farming, Indonesia, mysticism ("what a curious combination," Thomson comments).

* * *

THORPE, Donald W(illiam) 1928-

PERSONAL: Born August 24, 1928, in Westwood, Calif.; son of Frederick William and Emma (Cornutt) Thorpe; married Evelyn Francis Burton, June 24, 1954; married second wife, Barbara Jane Fifield (a postal employee), March 28, 1970; children: (first marriage) William, Donald, Jonathon, Jennifer; (second marriage) Ryan, Rachel. *Education:* Los Angeles Valley College, A.A., 1962.

CAREER: Lumberman, seaman, and cowboy, 1944-49; served in U.S. Army, 1949-56, retired as master sergeant; muralist and commercial artist in Los Angeles, Calif., 1956-58; Bechtel Corp., Vernon, Calif., graphics designer and coordinator, beginning 1958; Historical Aviation Research, Norwalk, Calif., aviation research consultant, 1965—. Graphics director, Movie World, Buena Park, Calif., 1970. Model builder and aviation researcher; aviation historical consultant for Revell, Inc., and Twentieth Century-Fox, 1958—, with advisory work including the film, "Tora! Tora! Tora!"; technical adviser, Air Force Museum and Air Museum. *Member:* International Plastic Modelers Society, American Aviation Historical Society, Society of Luftwaffe Historians. *Awards, honors:* Literary achievement award of International Plastic Modelers Society, 1970.

WRITINGS: (Self-illustrated) *Japanese Army Air Force Camouflage and Markings, World War II,* Aero, 1968; (editor and illustrator) Edward Maloney, *Luftwaffe Aircraft and Aces,* Air Museum Publications, 1969; *The Air Museum*

Collection, Air Museum Publications, 1969; (self-illustrated) *Japanese Naval Air Forces Camouflage and Markings, World War II*, Aero, 1977. Also author of *Courage Comes in All Colors*, 1973, and co-author of *The Zero Fighter*. Author of dramatic scripts for Revell, Inc., 1967—. Managing editor, Air Museum Publications, 1969-72; associate editor, *Air Combat*.

WORK IN PROGRESS: The Air Forces of the Eastern European Nations, 1914-1969; editing and illustrating Robert Mikesh's *The Presidential Aircraft;* research on the contributions of the black races to aviation and aerospace progress, for a series of volumes directed to the child, the young adult, and the serious historian.†

*　　*　　*

TIBBETTS, Orlando L(ailer), Jr. 1919-

PERSONAL: Born April 9, 1919, in Portland, Me.; son of Orlando Lailer and Ruby (Wilkinson) Tibbetts; married Phyllis Jones, June 25, 1941; children: Roger, Douglas, Faith (Mrs. Dexter Benedict), Judith (Mrs. Dwight Foster). *Education:* Gordon College, A.B., 1940; Andover Newton Theological School, B.D., 1943, S.T.M., 1952, D.Min., 1973. *Home:* 16 Maple St., South Windsor, Conn. 06074. *Office:* 100 Bloomfield Ave., Hartford, Conn. 06105.

CAREER: Ordained to ministry of Baptist Church, 1943; Baptist Seminary, Mexico City, Mexico, founder, and president, 1947-53; pastor of Baptist churches in Ohio, 1953-63; Boston Baptist City Mission Society, Boston, Mass., executive minister, 1963-68; Massachusetts Council of Churches, Boston, executive minister of Metropolitan Boston Commission, 1968-70; American Baptist Churches of Connecticut, Hartford, executive minister, 1971—. Chaplain, Home for Unwed Mothers, Boston; treasurer, Boston Industrial Mission; member of board of directors, North Conway Institute. *Member:* American Protestant Hospital Association, National Council of Churches, Association of Council Secretaries, Massachusetts Conference on Social Welfare, Iona Community (Scotland; associate member). *Awards, honors:* D.D. from Rio Grande College, Rio Grande, Ohio.

WRITINGS—All published by Judson: *The Reconciling Community*, 1969; *Sidewalk Prayers*, 1971; *More Sidewalk Prayers*, 1973.

AVOCATIONAL INTERESTS: Music (plays a number of instruments), painting in oils.

*　　*　　*

TICHENOR, Tom 1923-

PERSONAL: Born February 10, 1923; son of Jacob Marshall (an educator) and Emma (a dressmaker; maiden name, Moore) Tichenor. *Education:* Attended George Peabody College for Teachers, 1946-48. *Religion:* Baptist. *Home:* 310 Thompson Lane, Nashville, Tenn. 37211.

CAREER: Puppeteer, actor, and writer. First appeared with his own marionettes, in "Puss in Boots," Nashville Public Library, Nashville, Tenn., November, 1938; Nashville Public Library, puppeteer, general consultant, and director of children's entertainment, 1947-60, artistic advisor for the children's department of the new Nashville Public Library building, 1964; WKNO-TV (educational television), Memphis, Tenn., 1957-60, children's director, creating among other programs a weekly series of folk and fairy tales; creator of puppets for Broadway musical, "Carnival," 1961-62; WNBC-TV, New York City, performer on "Birthday House," 1964-67; Nashville Public Library, puppeteer,

1967—. Designer of stuffed animals for Bantam; former costume and dress designer. *Military service:* U.S. Army, 1943-45. *Member:* American Federation of Television and Radio Artists, Screen Actors Guild, Actors' Equity Association, Puppeteers of America.

WRITINGS—Children's books: *Folk Plays for Puppets* (five plays and directions for making puppets, scenery, and stage setting for each), Abingdon, 1959; *Smart Bear*, Abingdon, 1970; *Sir Patches and the Dragon*, Aurora, 1971; *Tom Tichenor's Puppets*, Abingdon, 1971; *Tom Tichener's Christmas Tree Crafts*, Lippincott, 1975.

Children's plays: "Night of the Full Moon," first produced in Nashville at Nashville Circle Theatre, May, 1957; "Trip to the Moon," first produced in United States, January, 1958; "Seven at One Blow," first produced in United States, October, 1959; "The Three Spinners," first produced in United States, December, 1959; "The Dancing Princesses," first produced in Nashville at Nashville Children's Theatre, December 10, 1960; (adaptor) "The Moon Maiden" (Chinese folk tale), first produced in New York at Museum of the City of New York's Puppet Exhibition, May 22, 1962. Contributor of stories, plays, poems, and articles to various periodicals, including *Good Housekeeping*.

SIDELIGHTS: Tom Tichenor writes: "I wanted to act, but shyness kept me from taking part in school plays. Then when I discovered puppetry I could act and not be exposed. Naturally the puppet shows needed plays, so I wrote them. Before long I was writing radio scripts and acting, not only on radio, but in Children's Theatre productions.... When I am forced to make a talk I always stress the importance of cultivating the imagination and having a dream. Plus patience, determination and lots of plain old drudgery. For all my so-called living in a world of make-believe, none of it would come true if I didn't spend those long, hard hours in my workroom. It is the puppets and characters in my books that lead carefree lives and laugh through every adversity. Would that I had their attitude."

*　　*　　*

TIERNEY, Kevin (Hugh) 1942-

PERSONAL: Born September 22, 1942, in Bristol, England; son of Hugh John (a chartered accountant) and Margaret Ellis (Davies) Tierney. *Education:* St. John's College, Cambridge, B.A., 1964, LL.B., 1965; Yale University, LL.M., 1967, M.A., 1968. *Home:* 213 West Lake Rd., Penn Yan, N.Y. 14527.

CAREER: Donovan, Leisure, Newton & Irvine (law firm), New York, N.Y., associate lawyer, 1969-70. Writer.

WRITINGS: Courtroom Testimony: A Policeman's Guide, Funk, 1970; *How to Be a Witness*, Oceana, 1972. Contributor to *New Law Journal* and *New Republic*.

WORK IN PROGRESS: A biography of Clarence Darrow, for Crowell.

SIDELIGHTS: Kevin Tierney writes: "Above all, I value clarity and precision in language; the greatest literary sin is incomprehensibility. In both fact and fiction, I favor a spare, uncluttered style. I try to avoid mere word-spinning and am brutal in editing my own rough drafts.

"I work best at a typewriter (on which I am self-taught and very inaccurate) and have often wondered if I should be reincarnated as a journalist. I work well to a deadline, but it must be absolutely hard and fast with no possibility of extension. I admire both Henry Mencken and Malcolm Muggeridge as stylists and gadflies, though I profoundly disagree with the former's opinion that there is (or ought to be) an 'American' language distinct from English; for myself, I rejoice in the commonality of the Anglo-American literary tradition.''

* * *

TIGHE, Donald J. 1928-

PERSONAL: Surname is pronounced as "tie"; born December 3, 1928, in Youngstown, Ohio; son of Francis William (a steel-mill roller) and Nellie (Dillon) Tighe; married Ardelia Snead, June 4, 1952; children: Jennifer, William, Julia, Donna Jo. *Education:* Attended Bluefield College, 1948-49; Concord College, B.S.Ed., 1952; West Virginia University, M.A., 1952; additional graduate study at Pennsylvania State University, 1956, University of Maryland, 1961, and University of London, 1975. *Home:* 1020 Tuckaseegee Trail, Maitland, Fla. 32751. *Office:* Department of Communications, Valencia Community College, Orlando, Fla. 32802.

CAREER: Concord College, Athens, W.Va., assistant professor of English, 1953-60; Millersville State College, Millersville, Pa., associate professor of English, 1960-63; St. Petersburg Junior College, St. Petersburg, Fla., assistant chairman of department of English, 1963-73; Valencia Community College, Orlando, Fla., chairman of communications department, 1973—. *Military service:* U.S. Navy, 1946-47. *Member:* National Council of Teachers of English, Conference on College Composition and Communication.

WRITINGS: (With Alan Casty) *Staircase to Writing and Reading: A Rhetoric and Anthology,* Prentice-Hall, 1969, 2nd edition, 1974; (editor with Lloyd Flanigan) *Source, Idea, Technique: A Writer's Reader,* Holbrook, 1969, 2nd edition, 1974; (editor) *Ways of Communicating: An Anthology,* Winthrop, 1971, 2nd edition, 1973.

WORK IN PROGRESS: A freshman rhetoric textbook, for Prentice-Hall.

* * *

TILLINGHAST, Richard 1940-

PERSONAL: Born November 25, 1940, in Memphis, Tenn.; son of Raymond Charles (a mechanical engineer) and Martha (Williford) Tillinghast. *Education:* University of the South, Sewanee, Tenn., A.B., 1962; Harvard University, A.M., 1963, Ph.D., 1970. *Home:* 88 Walnut Ave., Corte Madera, Calif. 94925. *Office:* Department of English, College of Marin, Kentfield, Calif. 94904.

CAREER: University of California, Berkeley, assistant professor of English, 1968-73; affiliated with College of Marin, currently teaching in the college program at San Quentin State Prison. *Awards, honors:* Woodrow Wilson fellow, 1962-63; Creative Arts Institute, University of California, Berkeley, 1970.

WRITINGS: Sleep Watch (poems), Wesleyan University Press, 1969; (contributor) *Ten American Poets,* Carcanet Press, 1974.

SIDELIGHTS: Robert Watson finds Tillinghast's speech to be "quiet, modest, witty, while he talks about the oddness of the ordinary experiences of life. . . . The title of this collection, *Sleep Watch,* is very accurate, for a large number of his poems are about sleeping and waking, about the operation of the mind. The experiences he presents have the quality of a collage or surrealistic film: waking states of mind shift to dream states, to memories, memories seem to merge with fantasy or vision.''

BIOGRAPHICAL/CRITICAL SOURCES: Poetry, December, 1970.

* * *

TIMASHEFF, Nicholas S. 1886-1970

November 22, 1886—March 9, 1970; Russian-born American sociologist, educator, and authority on the Russian Orthodox Church. Obituaries: *New York Times,* March 10, 1970. (See index for *CA* sketch)

* * *

TINDALL, Kenneth (Thomas) 1937-

PERSONAL: Born January 26, 1937, in Los Angeles, Calif.; son of Kenneth Verlin and Ferdeythyl (Leemans) Tindall; married Tove Skjerning; married second wife, Marianne Dohm; children: (first marriage) Seth. *Education:* Attended public school in Newark, N.J. *Religion:* Danish Lutheran. *Address:* c/o Schwarck Dalgas, Boulevard 48, 2000 Copenhagen F., Denmark.

CAREER: Writer. Previous employment includes positions as advertising clerk in Detroit, Mich., factory worker in Jersey City, N.J., Copenhagen, Denmark, and Long Island, N.Y., handyman in Galway, Ireland, magazine salesman in Paris, France, farm worker in Jutland, caretaker and folk musician in Copenhagen, and street-peddler and postal clerk in New York City; currently translator and letter-carrier in Copenhagen. *Military service:* U.S. Navy, 1954-56.

WRITINGS: Vindharpen, Hans Reitzel (Copenhagen), 1967, translation published as *Great Heads,* Grove, 1969. Unpublished writings include: short stories, "Sea Urchins"; poetry, "The Boonkeeper"; two novels, "The Head Wars" and "The Banks of the Sea."

WORK IN PROGRESS: A new novel; poetry; another book of short stories; an essay on "Love in the sight of God, from the Danish word Asyn."

SIDELIGHTS: Kenneth Tindall writes: "Never do anything you don't believe in or that you really don't want to do, or that you know is wrong. My dad always said that if you build a better mousetrap the world will beat a path to your door, and so I live where I want to live and write what I want to write, avoiding professionalism and literary scenes. I am most inspired and write best when with a woman and working at a regular job, and in everyday contact with ordinary people. I write from fullness of feeling, because my cup runneth over, the giving that is the desiring of one's beloved. My writing is lyrical and strong.''

* * *

TINDALL, P(eggy) E(leanor) N(ancy) 1927-

PERSONAL: Born May 11, 1927, in Woking, Surrey, England; daughter of William Sidney (a local government official) and Annie (Ginger) White; married Thomas Edward Tindall (an inspector of education in Rhodesia), July 8, 1951. *Education:* University of Bristol, B.A. (honors), 1948, Certificate of Education, 1949; University of London, further study, 1962. *Office:* Department of History, University College of Rhodesia, Salisbury, Southern Rhodesia.

CAREER: Teacher in Bristol and Bedford, England, 1949-51; teacher in Rhodesia at African secondary schools, 1953, at teacher training institutions, 1961, and at European secondary schools, 1963-64; University College of Rhodesia, Salisbury, lecturer in African history, 1966—. *Member:* Central African Historical Association (treasurer, 1966—), Prehistory Society (Salisbury).

WRITINGS: (With husband, Thomas E. Tindall) *A History of Africa,* Longmans, Green, 1959, 2nd edition, 1965; (with T. E. Tindall) *A History of the Commonwealth,* Longmans, Green, 1959; (with others) *Junior Secretary History Course,* Longmans, Green, 1961; *A History of Central Africa,* Praeger, 1968; *Discovering African History,* Longmans, Green, 1970; *Discovering World History,* Longman, 1971. Contributor to archaeology, museum, and educational publications in Africa.

WORK IN PROGRESS: Revising several textbooks; research in early Bantu expansion and allied problems.

AVOCATIONAL INTERESTS: Archaeology (has dug at several sites in Africa), brass rubbing, and pottery.†

* * *

TITUS, Eve 1922-
(Nancy Lord)

PERSONAL: Born July 16, 1922, in New York, N.Y.; divorced; children: Richard Keen. *Education:* Attended New York University. *Agent:* McIntosh & Otis, Inc., 22 East 40th St., New York, N.Y. 10016.

CAREER: Free-lance author and lecturer. Director and originator of the annual "Storybook Writing Seminar," Miami, Fla. and Houston, Tex., 1964—. *Member:* Authors League, Womens National Book Association, Mystery Writers of America. *Awards, honors:* Twice runner-up for the Caldecott Award.

WRITINGS—Illustrations by Paul Galdone, except as indicated: *Anatole,* Whittlesey House, 1956; *Anatole and the Cat,* Whittlesey House, 1957; *Basil of Baker Street,* Whittlesey House, 1958; (under pseudonym Nancy Lord) *My Dog and I* (Junior Literary Guild selection), McGraw, 1958; *Anatole and the Robot,* Whittlesey House, 1960; *Anatole over Paris,* Whittlesey House, 1961; *The Mouse and the Lion,* illustrations by Leonard Weisgard, Parents' Magazine Press, 1962; *Basil and the Lost Colony,* Whittlesey House, 1964; *Anatole and the Poodle,* Whittlesey House, 1964; *Anatole and the Piano,* McGraw, 1966; (adapted from the Japanese) *The Two Stonecutters,* illustrations by Yoko Mitsuhashi, Doubleday, 1967; *Anatole and the Thirty Thieves,* McGraw, 1969; *Mr. Shaw's Shipshape Shoeshop,* illustrations by Larry Ross, Parents' Magazine Press, 1970; *Anatole and the Toyshop,* McGraw, 1970; *Basil and the Pygmy Cats,* McGraw, 1971; *Why the Wind God Wept,* illustrations by James Barkley, Doubleday, 1972; *Anatole in Italy,* McGraw, 1973; *Basil and the Lost Colony,* Hodder & Stoughton, 1975; *Basil in Mexico,* McGraw, 1976.

WORK IN PROGRESS: Researching ancient legends of Mexico, particularly those of Yucatan, with Mayan background.

SIDELIGHTS: Eve Titus was originally a professional concert-pianist giving piano recitals in New York, Florida, Arkansas, Texas, Jamaica, and Mexico. She has also cruised the Caribbean on ships as a concert pianist. *Anatole* and *Anatole and the Piano* have been made into films. Mrs. Titus's original manuscripts are in the Case Collection at Wayne State University, Detroit, Michigan.

BIOGRAPHICAL/CRITICAL SOURCES: Huck and Young, *Children's Literature in the Elementary School,* Holt, 1961; *The Children's Bookshelf,* Child Study Association of America, Bantam, 1965; *Books for Children, 1960-1965,* American Library Association, 1966; Nancy Larrick, *A Parent's Guide to Children's Reading,* 3rd edition, Doubleday, 1969.†

TOBIAS, Richard C(lark) 1925-

PERSONAL: Born October 10, 1925, in Xenia, Ohio; son of Raymond L. (a farmer) and Cathryn (Eckerle) Tobias; married Barbara Nitche (an editor), June 16, 1949; children: Leslie, Alan Clark, Emily. *Education:* Attended Miami University, Oxford, Ohio, 1943-44; Ohio State University, B.Sc., 1948, M.A., 1951, Ph.D., 1957. *Home:* 5846 Darlington Rd., Pittsburgh, Pa. 15217. *Office:* Department of English, University of Pittsburgh, Pittsburgh, Pa. 15213.

CAREER: University of Colorado, Boulder, instructor in English, 1952-55; Ohio State University, Columbus, faculty assistant, 1955-57; University of Pittsburgh, Pittsburgh, Pa., instructor, 1957-59, assistant professor, 1959-64, associate professor, 1964-69, professor of English, 1969—. Regional associate, American Council of Learned Societies, 1961-63. *Military service:* U.S. Army, Infantry, 1944-46; served in Europe; received Purple Heart, Bronze Star, and two battle stars. *Member:* Modern Language Association of America (member of executive committee of Victorian division), American Association of University Professors, Catch Society of America. *Awards, honors:* Charles E. Merrill fellow in humanities, summer, 1962.

WRITINGS: The Art of James Thurber, Ohio University Press, 1970. Compiler of "Annual Bibliography of Victorian Studies" for *Victorian Studies,* 1959-74, and "Year's Work in Victorian Poetry" for *Victorian Poetry,* 1962—. Editorial associate, *Victorian Poetry,* 1965—; editor, *Victorian Studies,* 1974—.

WORK IN PROGRESS: A biography of Manx poet T. E. Brown (1830-1897), for Twayne.

* * *

TOBIAS, Tobi 1938-

PERSONAL: Born September 12, 1938, in New York, N.Y.; daughter of William S. (a doctor) and Esther (Meshel) Bernstein; married Irwin Tobias (a college professor), September 4, 1960; children: Anne, John. *Education:* Barnard College, B.A., 1959; New York University, M.A., 1962.

CAREER: Hudson Review, New York City, managing editor, 1959-60; free-lance writer, 1970—; *Dance Magazine,* New York City, contributing editor, 1971-76, associate editor, 1976—.

WRITINGS: Maria Tallchief, Crowell, 1970; *Marian Anderson,* Crowell, 1972; *A Day Off,* Putnam, 1973; *Isamu Noguchi: The Life of a Sculptor,* Crowell, 1974; *The Quitting Deal,* Viking, 1975; *Arthur Mitchell,* Crowell, 1975; *Moving Day,* Knopf, 1976; *An Umbrella Named Umbrella,* Knopf, 1976; *Petey,* Putnam, 1977; *That's a Good Question,* Children's Press, 1977; *Chasing the Goblins Away,* Warne, 1977; *The Man Who Played Accordian Music behind Closed Apartment House Doors,* Knopf, 1978. Contributor to oral history program of the Dance Collection, Lincoln Center Library of the Performing Arts, and to the television series, "Dance in America"; also contributor to *New York Times, New York Times Book Review,* and *Stagebill.*

WORK IN PROGRESS: Dancers' Voices, for Knopf.

* * *

TODSICHER, J(ohn) Edgar 1926-

PERSONAL: Born December 26, 1926, in Yahoo, Kan.; son of Andrew Jackson (an itinerant preacher) and Thelma (Thanatogenes) Todsicher; married Inocencia B. Engkopf, June 26, 1944 (divorced, 1972); married Amelia Whitbread,

July 4, 1973; children: (first marriage) John Wayne, Carrie Nation (Mrs. Gerry C. Mander), Bob Jones, Aimee Semple, Mercury and Apollo (twin sons; deceased), Richard Spiro; (second marriage) Cosmo Milhous. *Education:* Attended God's Peace and Power Baptist Seminary, 1944; Gopher Junction Community College, A.A., 1947; also studied Kranshaw Correspondence Course in salesmanship, 1949, and attended Betsy Barnes Business College, Gopher Junction, 1951. *Politics:* "Right-wing middle-of-the-road conservative." *Religion:* True Believer. *Residence:* Dearborn, Mich. *Office:* Caveat Emptor Life Insurance, 22702 Clairwood, St. Clair Shores, Mich. 48080.

CAREER: Employed as door-to-door vacuum cleaner salesman in Haggard County, Kan., 1950-51; Heep Collection Agency, St. Louis, Mo., collector, 1952-56; Eddie Scheister's Used Parts and Service (used car dealer), St. Louis, Mo., salesman, 1956-59, in charge of training salesmen, 1959-62; Sado & Miasma Life Insurance, Inc., Grand Rapids, Mich., broker, 1963-69; Caveat Emptor Life Insurance, Detroit, Mich., founder and president, 1969—. Organizer of evangelical meetings for Amazing Grace Baptist Union throughout southern U.S., 1952-62; founder and treasurer of Metropolitan Church of True Believers, Detroit, Mich. *Military service:* U.S. Army, chaplain's assistant, 1947-49.

MEMBER: International Society of Missionaries (charter member), National Association of Church of True Believers (member of board of directors, 1970—), National Gunshooters Ltd., American Association to Make George Lincoln Rockwell a Saint, Southern Academy of Holy Writers, Anti-Bussers of the Midwest (vice-president of Pontiac, Mich., chapter, 1970—), Traditionalists of America (president of Dearborn chapter). *Awards, honors:* Sons of Business award, 1968, for outstanding service to the life insurance community; George Lincoln Rockwell Memorial award, Sweet Jesus Press, 1970, for "True Belief" series.

WRITINGS: The Christian Car Salesman: Moral Merchandising (booklet), Betsy Barnes Business Press, 1958; (with father, Andrew Jackson Todsicher) *Armageddon Trilogy,* Schweinkopf Publishers, Book 1: *Armageddon and You,* 1959, Book 2: *Armageddon Revisited,* 1961, Book 3: *Son of Armageddon,* 1961; *Redemption in Our Time: How Life Insurance Can Save America,* Palm Tree Press, 1975.

"True Belief" series, all published by Sweet Jesus Press: *The First Book of True Believers,* 1964; *Total Immersion and True Belief,* 1964; *True Belief and Your Children,* 1965; *True Belief and the Evils of Fluoridation,* 1966; *True Belief and Communism,* 1966; *True Belief and LSD,* 1967; *True Belief and Perversion,* 1967; *True Belief and Woman's Place,* 1968; *True Belief and Your Operation,* 1970; *The Moon Walk and True Belief,* 1970; *True Belief and America's Deteriorating Morals,* 1971; *True Belief and the Necessity of Repealing the Nineteenth Amendment,* 1972; *True Belief and Your Divorce,* 1972; *True Belief and Salvation through Remarriage,* 1973.

WORK IN PROGRESS: True Belief and the Evils of Sex Education; Life Insurance and the Hereafter: How You Can Collect on Your Own Policy.

SIDELIGHTS: J. Edgar Todsicher told *CA:* "The combination of the Free Enterprise system and Christian morality is the only way towards national and individual salvation. This is the very heart of our strength. I believe that we are Number One in the world and that we must remain Number One, pouring out our wealth and showing other countries how to live. . . . We must follow in the footsteps of our fore-

fathers, and re-embrace the idea of a competitive and holy spirit guiding our country to newer and greater heights of truth, justice, and bold economic action. To those young people of today who would question our values I say 'For shame!' The 'tearer downers' of this country want to make us think that we can't do anything better, more efficiently, and more righteously than any other nation in the world. They are always pointing out what's wrong with us. In my books I hope I have exposed them for what they are—Country without reservation and fear of the contempt of atheistic doubting Thomases." Todsicher lists as influences Dale Carnegie, Norman Vincent Peale, and John Wayne. He hopes to seek political office in the near future.

AVOCATIONAL INTERESTS: Guns, hunting, fishing, and the Bible.

BIOGRAPHICAL/CRITICAL SOURCES: Seymour Slarom, *A Christian Interpretation of "The Armageddon Trilogy,"* Sweet Jesus Press, 1963; *Supremacist Quarterly,* spring, 1968; *Yahoo* (Kan.) *Herald,* November 17, 1970.

*   *   *

TOERNQVIST, (Per) Egil   1932-

PERSONAL: Surname is pronounced Turn-kvist; born December 19, 1932, in Uppsala, Sweden; son of Einar P. G. and Marit (Sjoevall) Toernqvist; married Marguerite Verschuur (an author of children's books), December 10, 1960; children: Torbjoern, Marit, Saskia. *Education:* Uppsala University, Swedish doctors degree in comparative literature, 1969. *Home:* Evertslaan 14, Bussum, Netherlands. *Office:* Skandinavisch Seminarium, Jodenbreestraat 23, Amsterdam, Netherlands.

CAREER: University of Amsterdam, Amsterdam, Netherlands, professor of Scandinavian studies, 1969—. *Military service:* Swedish Air Force, 1952-53. *Member:* Swedish-Dutch Association (Amsterdam; chairman, 1971-73). *Awards, honors:* American Council of Learned Societies fellowship, 1965-66.

WRITINGS: (Editor) *Drama och teater,* Almqvist & Wiksell (Stockholm), 1968; *A Drama of Souls: Studies in O'-Neill's Super-Naturalistic Technique* (dissertation), Almqvist & Wiksell (Uppsala), 1968, Yale University Press, 1970; (editor) *Ibsens dramatik,* Wahlstroem & Widstrand (Stockholm), 1971; *Svenska Dramastrukturer,* Prisma (Stockholm), 1973; *Bergman och Strindberg,* Prisma, 1973. Contributor of more than thirty articles on drama to literary journals.

WORK IN PROGRESS: Theoretical problems related to the analysis of drama.

SIDELIGHTS: Egil Toernqvist told *CA* that, in addition to his native Swedish, he has a reading or speaking knowledge of Norwegian, Danish, Dutch, German, French, Latin, and Old Icelandic.

*   *   *

TOLL, Seymour I.   1925-

PERSONAL: Born February 19, 1925, in Philadelphia, Pa.; son of Louis D. and Rose E. Toll; married Jean Barth, June 25, 1951; children: Emily B., Elizabeth T., Martha A., Constance N. F. *Education:* Attended Cornell University, 1942-43; Yale University, B.A. (magna cum laude), 1948, LL.B., 1951; attended University of Oslo, summer, 1947. *Home:* 453 Conshohocken State Rd., Cynwyd, Pa. 19004. *Office:* Suite 2040, 1845 Walnut St., Philadelphia, Pa. 19103.

CAREER: Member of Bars of New York, Pennsylvania, and U.S. Supreme Court; law clerk to Irving R. Kaufman, 1951-52; Hartman & Craven, New York City, associate in general practice of law, 1952-55; Richter, Lord, Toll & Cavanaugh, Philadelphia, Pa., senior partner, 1955-65; independently engaged in research, travel, and writing, 1965-68; Richter, Lord, Toll, Cavanaugh, McCarty & Raynes, Philadelphia, senior member, 1968-69; Seymour I. Toll, Philadelphia, trial and appellate practice and consultant in the field of urban planning law, 1970-74; Toll & Ebby, Philadelphia, founding partner, 1975—. Founding partner, Toll & Armstrong, Publishers, 1970—. Lecturer in department of planning, Yale University, 1966-67. President, Citizens' Council on City Planning, Philadelphia, 1967-69; public director and member of executive committee, Philadelphia Housing Development Corp., 1967—. *Military service:* U.S. Army, combat infantryman, 1943-45; wounded during Battle of the Bulge; received Purple Heart, two battle stars.

MEMBER: American Bar Association, Pennsylvania Bar Association, Philadelphia Bar Association, Phi Beta Kappa, Yale Club of Philadelphia, Franklin Inn Club. *Awards, honors:* American Philosophical Society grant for work on *Zoned American.*

WRITINGS: Zoned American, Grossman, 1969. Author of two zoning reports published by Citizens' Council on City Planning, Philadelphia. Contributor to legal journals.

WORK IN PROGRESS: A children's book (fiction) about the dehumanizing tendencies of today's world.

AVOCATIONAL INTERESTS: American literary expatriates of the 1920's, music (especially Mozart), still photography, the coast of Maine.

*   *   *

TOLSTOY, Dimitry 1912-

PERSONAL: Born November 8, 1912, in Moscow, Russia; son of Michael and Eileen May (Hamshaw) Tolstoy-Miloslavsky; married Frieda Mary Wicksteed, June 30, 1934 (marriage dissolved); married second wife, Natalie Deytrikh, February 28, 1943; children: (first marriage) Nikolai, Natasha; (second marriage) Tania, Andrew. *Education:* Attended Wellington College, Berkshire, England; Trinity College, Cambridge, B.A., 1934, M.A., 1965. *Address:* c/o Barclay's Bank Ltd., 137 Brompton Rd., London S.W.3, England.

CAREER: Called to the Bar of Gray's Inn, London, England, 1937; barrister-at-law, London, 1937—; Queen's counsel, 1959—. President of Cambridge Union, England, 1935. Lecturer in divorce, Inns of Court School of Law, London, 1952-68.

WRITINGS: Law and Practice of Divorce and Matrimonial Causes, Sweet & Maxwell, 1946, 7th edition published as *Tolstoy on Divorce,* 1971; *The Matrimonial Causes Act, 1965,* Sweet & Maxwell, 1966; (contributor) *Supreme Court Practice: 1950-1970,* Sweet & Maxwell, 1971. Contributor to legal periodicals.

*   *   *

TOMPKINS, E(dwin) Berkeley 1935-

PERSONAL: Born January 26, 1935, in Philadelphia, Pa.; son of John Kirby (a printing executive) and Hazel (Fenton) Tompkins; married Sally Lou Kress, August 25, 1956; children: Alicia Kress, Edwin Berkeley, Jr., Benjamin Fenton. *Education:* Yale University, B.A. (magna cum laude), 1957; University of Pennsylvania, M.A., 1960, Ph.D., 1963. *Of-*

fice: National Historical Publications Commission, National Archives Building, Washington, D.C. 20408.

CAREER: Philadelphia Maritime Museum, Philadelphia, Pa., director, 1961; Stanford University, Stanford, Calif., lecturer in history and director of summer sessions, 1963-68, senior fellow at Hoover Instituion of War, Revolution and Peace, 1968-71; State of Delaware, Dover, director of historical and cultural affairs, 1971-73; National Historical Publications Commission, Washington, D.C., executive director, 1973—. Lecturer, Institute of American History, summer, 1966. *Member:* American Historical Association, Organization of American Historians, American Academy of Political and Social Science, American Studies Association, U.S. Naval Institute, Society of Historians of American Foreign Relations, English-Speaking Union, Phi Beta Kappa. *Awards, honors:* Joint fellowship of National Trust for Historic Preservation, Colonial Williamsburg, American Association for State and Local History, and American Association of Museums, 1963.

WRITINGS: Anti-Imperialism in the United States: The Great Debate, 1890-1920, University of Pennsylvania Press, 1970; (editor) *Peaceful Change in Modern Society,* Hoover Institution, 1971; (editor) *The United Nations in Perspective,* Stanford University Press, 1972. Contributor of more than sixty articles, essays, and reviews to newspapers, popular periodicals, and professional journals. Member of editorial board, *Peace and People.*

WORK IN PROGRESS: The United States in the Twentieth Century; Opposition to Empire: A Comparative Study of the British and American Experience; a biography of Ambassador Hugh S. Gibson.

AVOCATIONAL INTERESTS: Tennis, sailing, swimming, hiking, riding, photography, bridge, music.†

*   *   *

TOMPKINS, Jane P(arry) 1940-

PERSONAL: Born January 18, 1940, in New York, N.Y.; daughter of Henry T. and Lucille (Reilly) Parry; married Daniel P. Tompkins, September 7, 1963 (divorced); married E. Daniel Lartain, November, 1975. *Education:* Bryn Mawr College, B.A., 1961; Yale University, M.A., 1962, Ph.D., 1966. *Home:* 624 North 22nd St., Philadelphia, Pa. 19130. *Office:* Department of English, Temple University, Philadelphia, Pa. 19122.

CAREER: Connecticut College, New London, instructor, 1966-67, assistant professor of English, 1967-68; Greater Hartford Community College, Hartford, Conn., assistant professor of English, 1969-70; Temple University, Philadelphia, Pa., visiting assistant professor, 1970-77, associate professor of English, 1977—.

WRITINGS: (Editor) *Twentieth Century Interpretations of "The Turn of the Screw" and Other Tales,* Prentice-Hall, 1970. Contributor to academic journals.

WORK IN PROGRESS: The Reader's Experience of Nineteenth-Century American Fiction.

*   *   *

TOMPKINS, Julia (Marguerite Hunter Manchee) 1909-
(Marguerite Neilson)

PERSONAL: Born December 3, 1909, in London, England; daughter of Arthur Hunter (a coffee importer) and Emily May (Wood) Neilson; married John Frederick Charles

Tompkins (a civil servant), August 9, 1941. *Education:* Attended schools in London and Croydon, England, until 1927. *Politics:* "Disillusioned Labour to Conservative." *Religion:* "Anglican if anything. Mainly Questioning." *Home:* 78 Littleheath Rd., South Croydon CR2 7SD, Surrey, England. *Agent:* Laurence Pollinger Ltd., 18 Maddox St., London WIR OEU, England.

CAREER: Shorthand-typist in various positions, mainly civil service, 1928-41, 1955-72. Writer. *Member:* Society of Women Writers and Journalists, Romantic Novelist's Association, Croydon Writers' Circle.

WRITINGS: Stage Costumes and How to Make Them, Plays, 1969; *More Stage Costumes and How to Make Them,* Pitman, 1975, published as *Easy-to-Make Costumes for Stage and School,* Plays, 1976.

Novels; under pseudonym Marguerite Neilson; all published by Wingate: *My Only Love, My Only Hate,* 1973; *The Dark Path,* 1976; *The Bride of Alderburn,* 1976. Contributor of short stories and articles to women's magazines.

WORK IN PROGRESS: A Gothic novel; a book about cats.

SIDELIGHTS: "I have always been interested in the theatre, particularly costume plays, and primarily Shakespeare," Julia Tompkins writes. She explained that *Stage Costumes and How to Make Them"* was the outcome of four years as costume supervisor with the Croydon Histrionic Society (founded 1878 and of near-professional standard).... I made many of the costumes myself, working direct from designer's sketches. Those costumes which I did not actually make, I cut out, and farmed out with instructions for the various stages of assembly. While doing this work, I had to evolve a way of cutting period costume from present day patterns...."

Her first novel, *My Only Love, My Only Hate,* is the story of Romeo and Juliet, while *The Dark Path* and *The Bride of Alderburn* are Gothic romances set in the early part of this century, with a hint of the supernatural. She says that she is a "sluttish housewife," with the philosophy that publishers want words, so the dust can wait.

BIOGRAPHICAL/CRITICAL SOURCES: Drama, spring, 1969.

* * *

TOWNSEND, Elsie Doig 1908-

PERSONAL: Born October 15, 1908, in Far West, Mo.; daughter of Samuel Miller (a teacher) and Florence (a teacher; maiden name, Wildermuth) Andes; married James Doig, August 19, 1934 (deceased); married O. Wendell Townsend (in sheetmetal work), August 17, 1946; children: (first marriage) Beverly, Marjorie and Marilyn (twins), James and Joan (twins). *Education:* Attended Graceland College and Western Montana College; Central Missouri State College (now University), B.S., 1934; Montana State University, M.S., 1960; additional study at University of Montana and University of Missouri at Kansas City. *Religion:* Reorganized Church of Jesus Christ of Latter-day Saints. *Home:* 3141 Santa Fe Ter., Independence, Mo. 64055.

CAREER: Teacher in Montana rural schools, 1927-29, 1931-34, in Manhattan, Mont., 1941-42; high school music and English teacher in Ennis, Mont., 1942-43, Three Forks, Mont., 1943-45, Knobnoster, Mo., 1945-57, Bozeman, Mont., 1948-55, and Fort Osage, Mo., 1956-57, 1958-61; Metropolitan Junior College, Kansas City, Mo., teacher of

English, 1961-71, chairman of communications department, 1969-70; currently full-time author. Has lectured throughout the United States, and been interviewed on national television. *Member:* American Association of University Professors, Good Government League, National Council of Teachers of English, Delta Kappa Gamma.

WRITINGS—All published by Herald House: *None to Give Away,* 1970; *Always the Frontier,* 1972; *If You Would Learn, Go Teach,* 1973; *6+1=One,* in press. Contributor to *Daily Bread, Stepping Stones,* and other journals. Edited *Seminar* (teachers bulletin) for five years.

SIDELIGHTS: Elsie Townsend wrote to *CA:* "Having tried for so many years to teach students to write, I wanted to see whether I could express myself accurately enough that I would transmit an experience, would make real images, would communicate so that the reader would share with me in my emotions. Mark Twain is perhaps my model. I am not ashamed of using the episodic style, in imitation of his writing—perhaps. His terse, crisp descriptions fascinate me. Hemingway's objective style is an inspiration for me. To let a reader learn of a character through his speech, his actions, the words of another character is my goal.

"To aspiring authors I would say what I have often said to my college students: Write something. Don't wait for a proper beginning. Just start to write. Save all you write. Write of something that is near and dear to you—something that you are familiar with. Don't let friends—a reader—discourage you."

BIOGRAPHICAL/CRITICAL SOURCES: Maple Woods News, January 15, 1971; *Kansas City Star,* October 1, 1973.

* * *

TOWNSEND, Peter (Wooldridge) 1914-

PERSONAL: Born November 22, 1914, in Rangoon, Burma; son of Edward Copleston (a lieutenant colonel, Indian Army, and a member of Burma Legislative Council) and Gladys (Hatt-Cook) Townsend; married Rosemary Pawle, 1941 (divorced, 1952); married Marie-Luce Jamagne, 1959; children: (first marriage) Giles, Hugo; (second marriage) Marie-Isabelle, Marie-Francoise, Pierre. *Education:* Attended Haileybury College and at Royal Air Force College. *Religion:* Church of England. *Home:* La Mare aux Oiseaux, 78116 Saint Leger-en-Yvelines, France.

CAREER: Royal Air Force, 1935-56, retiring as group captain (colonel), 1956; pilot in torpedo squadron, Singapore, 1936-37; commander of fighter squadron during Battle of Britain, 1939-41; equerry to King George VI, 1944-52, and deputy master of the Royal household, 1950; equerry to Queen Elizabeth, 1952-53; air attache in Brussels, Belgium, 1953-56; writer, traveler, public relations counselor and wine exporter, 1956-71; currently full-time author and journalist. *Awards, honors*—Military: Distinguished Service Order, 1941; Distinguished Flying Cross and bar; mentioned in dispatches. Civil: Commander of Royal Victorian Order, 1947; Officer of Legion of Honor (France), Officer of Order of Orange Nassau (Netherlands), Chevalier of Order of Dannebrog.

WRITINGS: Earth, My Friend (autobiographical travelogue), Hodder & Stoughton, 1959, Coward, 1960; *Un Duel d'aigles: R.A.F. contre Luftwaffe,* Laffont, 1969, published as *Duel of Eagles,* Simon & Schuster, 1970; *The Last Emperor: Decline and Fall of the British Empire,* Weidenfeld & Nicolson, 1975, published as *The Last Emperor: An Intimate Account of George VI and the Fall of His Empire,*

Simon & Schuster, 1976. Contributor of articles to newspapers and magazines.

WORK IN PROGRESS: An untitled autobiography to be published by Simon & Schuster.

SIDELIGHTS: Peter Townsend made a global tour (detailed in *Earth, My Friend*) in 1956-58. On the first leg of his trip, which altogether covered 57,000 miles, he drove from Brussels to Singapore, then through Australia and New Zealand. He traveled in Red China and Japan by air and rail, drove from Vancouver to Charleston, S.C., covered Mexico and Panama by road and boat, and then drove from Caracas to Santiago to Rio de Janeiro, and through Africa from Cape Town to Algiers. Townsend traveled to the United States on business for several years, and lived there during 1964 and 1965. He returned as an information emmissary for United Artists' film, "The Battle of Britain," and again in 1971 on a promotion tour for his book, *Duel of Eagles*.

BIOGRAPHICAL/CRITICAL SOURCES: Earth, My Friend, Hodder & Stoughton, 1959; *Look,* March 3, 1959; *Saturday Review,* June 25, 1960, March 13, 1971; *Variety,* September 10, 1969; *Duel of Eagles,* Simon & Schuster, 1970; *National Observer,* February 15, 1970; *Times Literary Supplement,* October 23, 1970; *Atlanta Journal,* January 13, 1971; *Newsday,* January 20, 1971; *Time,* January 25, 1971; *Best Sellers,* February 1, 1971; *Washington Post,* September 29, 1971; *New York Times,* January 21, 1977.

* * *

TRACY, Theodore J(ames) 1916-

PERSONAL: Born January 2, 1916, in Chicago, Ill.; son of Theodore James (a jeweler) and Honor Evelyn (Higgins) Tracy. *Education:* Loyola University, Chicago, A.B. (honors), 1938, M.A., 1942; Bellarmine School of Theology (then at West Baden College), S.T.L., 1951; Princeton University, M.A., 1954, Ph.D., 1962. *Politics:* "A radical independent." *Home:* 6525 Sheridan Rd., Chicago, Ill. 60626. *Office Address:* Department of Classics, University of Illinois, P.O. Box 4348, Chicago Circle, Chicago, Ill. 60680.

CAREER: Entered Society of Jesus (Jesuits), 1939, ordained priest, 1950; Loyola Academy, Chicago, Ill., instructor in Latin, Greek, and English, 1943-47; Xavier University, Cincinnati, Ohio, instructor in classics, 1955-56; Loyola University, Chicago, instructor in classics and ancient philosophy, 1956-60, assistant professor, 1960-67, associate professor of classical studies, 1967-70, chairman of department, 1960-67, member of board of trustees, 1958-60, 1972—; University of Illinois at Chicago Circle, associate professor of classics, 1970—. Member of board of directors, Chicago Archdiocesan Adult Education Program, 1959-63, Jesuit School of Theology, Chicago, 1975—; member of Latin achievement committee, College Entrance Examination Board, 1969-72. Consulting member, Institute for Encyclopedia of Human Ideas on Ultimate Reality and Meaning.

MEMBER: American Philological Association, Archaeological Institute of America, American Classics League, Society for Ancient Greek Philosophy, Classical Association of the Middle West and South, Chicago Classical Club (president, 1963-65), Society of Medical History of Chicago (member of governing board, 1971—), Blue Key, Pi Gamma Mu. *Awards, honors:* John Harding Page Fellow in Classics, Princeton, 1956; Fulbright fellow in Italy, 1960-61; distinguished professor of the year, Loyola University, Chicago, 1970.

WRITINGS: Physiological Theory and the Doctrine of the Mean in Plato and Aristotle, Loyola University Press (Chicago), 1969; (contributor) M. Marcovich, editor, *Illinois Classical Studies,* Volume I, University of Illinois Press, 1975. Contributor to *Theological Studies, Classical World, Classical Outlook,* and other periodicals.

WORK IN PROGRESS: Research on the interaction of ancient Greek philosophy and science, for example, the influence on Plato on Galen; several projects in Greek and Roman literature and archeology.

SIDELIGHTS: Theodore Tracy wrote to *CA:* "As a Catholic priest and college teacher, [I am] much concerned with the changes in contemporary society and the Church, especially as they affect young people. [I] find teaching in these times an exciting, challenging, and hopeful enterprise." He has traveled and lived in Europe, Middle East, West Africa, and West Indies.

AVOCATIONAL INTERESTS: Water sports, painting, film, and theater.

* * *

TRACZ, Richard Francis 1944-

PERSONAL: Surname is pronounced *tray*-see; born January 14, 1944; son of Boley John (a businessman) and Frances Delores (Yoda) Tracz. *Education:* Rockhurst College, Cl.A.B. (with honors), 1965; University of Kansas, M.A., 1967. *Politics:* Independent. *Religion:* Catholic. *Home:* 7047 Freemont St., Dallas, Tex. 75231. *Office:* Southern Methodist University, Dallas, Tex. 75222.

CAREER: University of Kansas, Lawrence, assistant instructor, 1956-67; Tarrant County Junior College, Fort Worth, Tex., instructor in English, 1967-69; Southern Methodist University, Dallas, Tex., instructor in discourse and literature, 1969—. *Member:* National Council of Teachers of English, Modern Language Association, College English Association, Conference of College Teachers of English, Conference on College Composition and Communication, South Central Modern Language Association, Dallas Symphony Orchestra League.

WRITINGS: (Compiler with C. Jeriel Howard) *The Responsible Man: Essays, Short Stories and Poems,* Canfield Press, 1970, 2nd edition, 1975; (with Howard) *TEMPO: A Thematic Approach to Sentence/Paragraph Writing,* Canfield Press, 1971; *--30--A Journalistic Approach to Freshman Composition,* Goodyear Publishing, 1973; *CONTACT: A Textbook in Applied Communications,* Prentice-Hall, 1974; *Writing Effective Paragraphs,* Winthrop Publishing, 1976.

WORK IN PROGRESS: An individualized instruction text for remedial English.

* * *

TREBING, Harry M(artin) 1926-

PERSONAL: Born September 14, 1926, in Baltimore, Md.; son of Harry A. (a chemist) and Bess (Shore) Trebing; married Joyce Christie, 1958; children: Evan, David. *Education:* University of Maryland, B.A., 1950, M.A., 1952; University of Wisconsin, Ph.D., 1958. *Religion:* Protestant. *Home:* 4568 Manitou Dr., Okemos, Mich. 48864. *Office:* Graduate School of Business Administration, 6H Berkey Hall, Michigan State University, East Lansing, Mich. 48824.

CAREER: University of Maryland, College Park, instructor in economics, 1951-52; University of Nebraska, Lincoln, assistant professor of economics, 1957-62; Indiana University, Bloomington, associate professor of public utilities and transportation, 1962-66; Michigan State University, East Lansing, professor of economics and director of Institute of Public Utilities, 1966—. Federal Communications Commission, supervisory industry economist in Common Carrier Bureau, 1963-65, chief of Economic Studies Division, 1965-66. Consultant to President's Task Force on Communications Policy, 1968, Cabinet Committee on Price Stability, Council of Economic Advisors, 1968-69, and Canadian Task Force for the Study of the Regulation of Telecommunications, 1969-70. Chief economist, U.S. Postal Rate Commission, 1971-72; conference administrator for Annual Regulatory Studies Program, National Association of Regulatory Utility Commissioners, 1973—; member, Committee on Telecommunications, National Academy of Engineering, National Research Council, 1974—. *Military service:* U.S. Naval Reserve, 1945-46.

MEMBER: American Economic Association (past president of Transportation and Public Utilities Group), Association for Evolutionary Economics (past president), Midwest Economics Association, Midwest Business Administration Association, Economics Society of Michigan, Beta Gamma Sigma. *Awards, honors:* University of Nebraska summer research fellow, 1958; National Science Foundation grant, 1976-78.

WRITINGS—Editor: *Performance Under Regulation,* Institute of Public Utilities, Michigan State University, 1968; (with R. H. Howard) *Rate of Return Under Regulation: New Directions and Perspectives,* Institute of Public Utilities, Michigan State University, 1969; *The Corporation in The American Economy,* Quadrangle, 1970; *Essays on Public Utility Pricing and Regulation,* Institute of Public Utilities, Michigan State University, 1971; (and author of introduction) *New Dimensions in Public Utility Pricing,* Michigan State University, Bureau of Business and Economic Research, 1976.

Contributor: (With Manley R. Irwin) H. Edward English, editor, *Telecommunications for Canada,* Methuen (Canada), 1973; William G. Shepherd and Thomas G. Gies, editors, *Regulation in Further Perspective,* Ballinger, 1974; (with W. H. Melody) Michael W. Klass and Shepherd, editors, *Regulation and Entry,* Michigan State University, Bureau of Business and Economic Research, 1976; W. J. Samuels, editor, *The Chicago School of Political Economy,* Association for Evolutionary Economics, and Michigan State University, Bureau of Business and Economic Research, 1976; Werner Sichel, editor, *Salvaging Public Utility Regulation,* Lexington Books, 1976. Publications include several government reports on communications and regulated industries. Contributor to professional journals. Member of editorial board, *Nebraska Journal of Economics and Business,* 1961-62, and *Land Economics,* 1969—.

WORK IN PROGRESS: Competition and Regulatory Reform in the Energy Utilities, a project funded by the National Science Foundation.

* * *

TREFETHEN, Florence 1921-

PERSONAL: Born September 18, 1921, in Philadelphia, Pa.; daughter of Otto and Emma (Paessler) Newman; married Lloyd MacGregor Trefethen (a professor at Tufts University), May 17, 1944; children: Gwyned, Lloyd Nicholas. *Education:* Bryn Mawr College, A.B., 1943; Cambridge University, M.Litt., 1950. *Home and office:* 23 Barberry Rd., Lexington, Mass. 02173.

CAREER: Johns Hopkins University, Operations Research Office, Chevy Chase, Md., operations analyst, 1950-54; Tufts University, Medford, Mass., instructor in English, 1959-66; free-lance editor, 1966—. Lecturer, Northeastern University, 1967-69, Radcliffe Institute, 1969-70, 1972-73. Book editor, Harvard University, East Asian Research Center, 1974—. *Military service:* U.S. Naval Reserve, WAVES, 1943-45 became lieutenant junior grade. *Member:* Poetry Society of America, New England Poetry Club, Washington Poets Association. *Awards, honors:* Consuelo Ford Award, Poetry Society of America, 1975; Power Dalton Award, New England Poetry Club, 1976.

WRITINGS: (Editor with Joseph McCloskey, and contributor) *Operations Research for Management,* Volume I, Johns Hopkins Press, 1954; *Writing a Poem,* Writer, Inc., 1970, revised edition, 1975. Columnist, "The Poet's Workshop" in *Writer Magazine,* 1968—. Contributor of poetry to *Poetry Miscellany, Christian Science Monitor, Pacific Search,* and other periodicals.

WORK IN PROGRESS: Poetry and fiction.

SIDELIGHTS: Operations for Research Management has been translated into French, Spanish, Italian, Portuguese, Serbo-Croat, and Japanese.

* * *

TRIESCHMAN, Albert E(well) 1931-

PERSONAL: Born September 20, 1931, in Baltimore, Md.; son of Albert Ewell (a lawyer) and Charlotte (Borcherding) Trieschman; married Nancy Eaton (an early childhood educator), June 25, 1955; children: Thomas, Karl, Matthew. *Education:* Franklin and Marshall College, A.B. (magna cum laude), 1951; Harvard University, Ph.D., 1960. *Politics:* Democrat. *Religion:* Unitarian Universalist. *Home:* 1968 Central Ave., Needham, Mass. 02192. *Office:* School of Medicine, Harvard University, Cambridge, Mass. 02138.

CAREER: Baltimore Department of Public Welfare, Baltimore, Md., caseworker in foster home care, 1953-55; Children's Hospital, Boston, Mass., staff psychologist in psychiatry department, 1958-61, supervising psychologist, 1961-76; Walker Home and School, Needham, Mass., director, 1962—; Harvard University, Medical School, Cambridge, Mass., member of faculty, 1970—. Lecturer in graduate program, Clark University, 1968-70; guest lecturer at University of Michigan, University of Minnesota, University of Chicago, and elsewhere. Member of task force, U.S. Joint Commission on Mental Health of Children, 1968. Board member of a number of child-serving community agencies. *Member:* American Orthopsychiatric Association, American Psychological Association, Council for Exceptional Children, Massachusetts Psychological Association, Massachusetts Conference on Social Welfare, Phi Beta Kappa, Phi Alpha Theta, Pi Gamma Mu.

WRITINGS: (With James K. Whittaker and Larry K. Brendtro) *The Other Twenty-Three Hours: Child Care Work with Emotionally Disturbed Children in a Therapeutic Milieu,* Aldine, 1969; (with Whittaker) *Children Away from Home: A Source Book in Residential Treatment,* Aldine-Atherton, 1972; (contributor) Richard Heidenreich, editor, *Urban Education,* College Reading, 1972. Contributor, Chamberlin and Cate, editors, *Administration Education and Change,* published by Kendall/Hunt. Contributor to *New York Times* and to professional journals.

WORK IN PROGRESS: A book for parents about child management; an article on violent children.

TRIMBLE, Martha Scott 1914-

PERSONAL: Born May 27, 1914, in Fort Collins, Colo.; daughter of Edgar Harrison and Flora May (Clark) Trimble. *Education:* Colorado State College A & M (now Colorado State University), B.S., 1936; University of Colorado, M.A., 1940; summer study at Bread Loaf School of English, 1941, University of Iowa, 1942, and Harvard University, 1963. *Politics:* Republican. *Religion:* Episcopalian. *Home:* 1909 Stover St., Fort Collins, Colo. 80521. *Office:* 337 Liberal Arts Building, Colorado State University, Fort Collins, Colo. 80521.

CAREER: High school English teacher in Akron, Colo., 1936-39; Ft. Lewis School (now Ft. Lewis College), Durango, Colo., instructor, 1939-40; Colorado State University, Fort Collins, instructor in English, 1940-43; employed part-time with Larimer County Court and KCOL Radio, Fort Collins, 1946-61, until surgery restored her normal hearing; Colorado State University, instructor, 1961-65, assistant professor, 1965-71, associate professor, 1971-77, professor of English, 1977—. *Military service:* U.S. Naval Reserve, WAVES, 1943-46; became lieutenant senior grade. *Member:* Modern Language Association of America, National Council of Teachers of English, Conference on College Composition and Communication, American Association of University Professors, Western Literature Association, (treasurer, 1966—), Rocky Mountain Modern Language Association, Colorado Language Arts Society, Delta Kappa Gamma, Phi Kappa Phi.

WRITINGS: Programmed Review of English, Harper, Unit I: *Spelling,* Unit II: *Diction,* Unit III: *Writing,* all 1969; *N. Scott Momaday* (monograph), Boise State College, 1973.

WORK IN PROGRESS: Two textbooks, one historical account, and a novel.

*　　　*　　　*

TRINKAUS, Charles (Edward) 1911-

PERSONAL: Born October 25, 1911, in Brooklyn, N.Y.; son of Charles E. (an insurance man) and Frances M. (Krueger) Trinkaus; married Sarah Elizabeth Marks (a pianist and music teacher), April 6, 1949; children: John Aaron (deceased), Peter Mark. *Education:* Wesleyan University, Middletown, Conn., B.A., 1933; Columbia University, Ph.D., 1940. *Politics:* Independent liberal. *Religion:* "Inactive; Methodist parents." *Home:* 1831 Coronada Dr., Ann Arbor, Mich. 48103. *Office:* Department of History, University of Michigan, Ann Arbor, Mich. 48104.

CAREER: Sarah Lawrence College, Bronxville, N.Y., faculty member, 1936-70, professor of cultural history, 1950-70, director of foreign studies, 1969-70, director of summer sessions in Florence, Italy, 1966-71, faculty trustee, 1964-68; University of Michigan, Ann Arbor, professor of history, 1970—. Visiting professor, New York University, 1948, Graduate School of Long Island University, 1951-52, and University of California, Los Angeles, 1976; associate in university seminars, Columbia University, 1944—, secretary of Renaissance Seminar, 1960-68, chairman, 1968-70. Consultant to American Council of Learned Societies and to publishers. *Member:* American Historical Association, American Council of Learned Societies (member of selection board, 1970-72), Mediaeval Academy of America, Renaissance Society of America (council member; president, 1973-75). *Awards, honors:* American Council of Learned Societies humanities fellow, 1965-66; cited as an alumnus distinguished as a teacher and scholar by Wesleyan Univer-

sity, 1965; National Endowment for the Humanities senior fellow, 1972-73.

WRITINGS: Adversity's Noblemen: The Italian Humorists on Happiness, Columbia University Press, 1940, reprinted with new preface, Octagon, 1965; *In Our Image and Likeness: Humanity and Divinity in Italian Humanist Thought,* two volumes, University of Chicago Press, 1970; (editor with Heiko A. Oberman) *The Pursuit of Holiness in Late Medieval and Renaissance Religion,* E. J. Brill, 1974. Also author of *Graduate Study in an Undergraduate College,* 1956. Contributor to *Encyclopedia of World Art;* contributor of articles on Renaissance and Reformation thought to scholarly journals.

WORK IN PROGRESS: A general cultural history of the Renaissance.†

*　　　*　　　*

TRINKNER, Charles L. 1920-

PERSONAL: Born May 25, 1920, in Green Bay, Wis.; son of Charles L. (an engineer) and Minnie (Vissers) Trinkner; married Marian Rumph (a school administrator). *Education:* University of Florida, B.A., 1950, M.Ed., 1951, Ed.S., 1956; Louisiana State University, M.S.L.S., 1954. *Religion:* Protestant. *Home:* 4770 Peacock Dr., Pensacola, Fla. 32504.

CAREER: Teacher, librarian, and audiovisual specialist in Florida public schools, 1949-55; North Texas State University, Denton, instructor in department of library science and educational bibliographer, 1955-56; University of Texas, Arlington, librarian, 1956-57; Arkansas State College (now University), State University, assistant professor of library science and library director, 1957-58; Pensacola Junior College, Pensacola, Fla., director of library services, instructor in library science, Ficus library administrator, 1958-68; owner, librarian, and editor of publications, Gull Point Press, 1968—. Research assistant, University of Florida, 1949-50. Resident librarian, Appalachian State University, summer, 1960. Visiting summer professor at Texas Woman's University, 1955, and University of Oregon, 1963; visiting lecturer at University of Illinois, summer, 1964. Director of workshops, Utah State University, summer, 1964, and University of Montana, summer, 1965. Member, West Florida Library Board, 1964-67. *Military service:* National Guard, 1939-40. U.S. Marine Corps, 1940-45; served in South Pacific; received six battle stars. U.S. Marine Corps Reserves, 1946-56; became lieutenant.

MEMBER: American Library Association, National Education Association (life member), Association for Higher Education, American Association of University Professors, American Historical Society, American Association of State and Local History, Bibliographic Society of America, Association of College and Research Libraries, Southwest Library Association, Louisiana State Library Association, Southeastern Library Association, Florida Library Association, Florida Education Association (life member), Escambia County Library Association, Escambia Education Association, University of Florida Alumni Association, Southern Historical Society, Florida Historical Society, Pensacola Historical Society, Kappa Delta Pi, Alpha Phi Omega, Psi Chi, Phi Delta Kappa, Beta Phi Mu, Beta Alpha, Alpha Kappa Delta.

WRITINGS—Editor or compiler: *Better Libraries Make Better Schools,* Shoe String, 1962; *Basic Books for Junior College Libraries: 20,000 Vital Titles,* Colonial Press (Northport, Ala.), 1963; (with wife, Marian R. Trinkner)

Guidance for Better Schools, Colonial Press, 1963; *Library Services for Junior Colleges,* American Southern Publishing (Northport, Ala.), 1964; *Florida Lives: The Sunshine State Who's Who,* Historical Record Association, 1966; *Teaching for Better Use of Libraries,* Shoe String, 1970; (author) *Evaluation Guide for Junior College Libraries,* Gull Point Press, 1971. Also author of *The Collegiate Reference Handbook,* Scarecrow. Contributor to *Encyclopedia of Library and Information Science* and to professional journals.

AVOCATIONAL INTERESTS: Swimming, horseshoes, collecting antiques, playing the concertina, juggling.

* * *

TRIPODI, Tony 1932-

PERSONAL: Born November 30, 1932, in Sacramento, Calif.; son of Nicholas and Christana (Grandinetti) Tripodi; married Roni Ann Roberts (a social worker); children: Lee Anna, Anthony Carroll, David Elliot, Stephen Joseph, Rachel Ann Newman (stepdaughter). *Education:* University of California, Berkeley, A.B., 1954, M.S.W., 1958; Columbia University, D.S.W., 1963. *Politics:* Independent. *Religion:* No preference. *Home:* 330 Hazelwood, Ann Arbor, Mich. 48103. *Office:* School of Social Work, University of Michigan, Ann Arbor, Mich. 48104.

CAREER: California Department of Mental Hygiene, Sacramento, research technician, 1958-59; California Youth Authority, Sacramento, research analyst, 1959-60; Brooklyn College (now Brooklyn College of the City University of New York), Brooklyn, N.Y., research associate in department of psychology, 1963-65; Columbia University, School of Social Work, New York, N.Y., assistant professor of social research, 1963-65; University of California, School of Social Welfare, Berkeley, assistant professor of social welfare, 1965-66; University of Michigan, School of Social Work, Ann Arbor, professor of social work, 1966—. Evaluation consultant, San Francisco State College (now University), Institute of Social Sciences, 1965-66; evaluation consultant, monitor, and technical assistant specialist, U.S. Office of Economic Opportunity, 1966-68; associate director and research consultant, Family and School Consultation Project, Ann Arbor, 1969-74. *Military service:* U.S. Naval Reserve, 1954-62. *Member:* Academy of Certified Social Workers, National Association of Social Workers, American Psychological Association, California Scholarship Organization (life member), Phi Theta Kappa (life member).

WRITINGS: (With James Bieri, Alvin Atkins, Scott Briar, Robin Lehman, and Henry Miller) *Clinical and Social Judgment,* Wiley, 1966; (with Phillip Fellin and Meyer) *The Assessment of Social Research,* F. E. Peacock, 1969; (editor with Fellin and Meyer) *Exemplars of Social Research,* F. E. Peacock, 1969; (contributor) P. B. Warr, editor, *Thought and Personality: A Book of Readings,* Penguin, 1970; (with Fellin and Irwin Epstein) *Social Program Evaluation,* F. E. Peacock, 1971; (with Fellin, Epstein, and Roger Lind) *Social Workers at Work,* F. E. Peacock, 1972, 2nd edition, 1976; *Uses and Abuses of Social Research in Social Work,* Columbia University Press, 1974. Has done editorial work and contributed articles and reviews to a number of professional journals.

WORK IN PROGRESS: With Irwin Epstein, *Research Techniques for Program Planning Monitoring and Evaluation,* for Columbia University Press.

TRIPP, Eleanor B(aldwin) 1936-

PERSONAL: Born May 27, 1936, in Boston, Mass.; daughter of William V., Jr. (in investment business) and Nell (Baldwin) Tripp; married Robert S. November (director of Development Planning, *New York Times*), August 17, 1969; children: two sons. *Education:* Smith College, B.A., 1958; London School of Economics and Political Science, further study, 1958-59; Columbia University, M.A., 1966. *Home:* 73 Walworth Ave., Scarsdale, N.Y. 10583.

CAREER: Teacher in Corte Madera, Calif., 1960-61, and Cambridge, Mass., 1961-64; Columbia University, New York City, lecturer on American immigration, periodically, 1966-69; New York State Museum and Science Service, New York City, script writer, 1968-69; New Lincoln School, New York City, seventh grade teacher, 1969-70. Trustee, American Museum of Immigration, New York City, 1974—.

WRITINGS: To America (teen book), Harcourt, 1969.

AVOCATIONAL INTERESTS: Reading, travel, the theater, photography; outdoor activities, including tennis and skiing.

* * *

TRIVAS, A(lexander) Victor 1894-1970

July 9, 1894—April 12, 1970; Russian-born film writer, director, and author of books about Russia. Obituaries: *New York Times,* April 13, 1970; *Variety,* April 15, 1970. (See index for *CA* sketch)

* * *

TROTTER, Sallie (W. B.) 1915-

PERSONAL: Born August 31, 1915, in Glasgow, Scotland; daughter of Alexander G. (a clergyman) and Mary Castle (Brown) Paisley; married Frank Melrose Trotter (chief assistant Solicitor of Scotland), June 14, 1943 (died September 12, 1950); married John M. Crawford (a former civil servant), September, 1962 (divorced, 1972); married Raymond Taylor, October, 1976; children: (first marriage) James J. M.; (second marriage) Frank P. *Education:* University of Edinburgh, M.A. and Post-Graduate Diploma in Social Studies, 1938; State registered nurse, 1942. *Religion:* Church of England. *Home:* 1 Bryn Asapl Cottapes, Upper Denbigh Rd., St. Asapl, Clwyd, North Wales. *Office:* Shell Island Crafts, 36 Abbey St., Rbye, Clwyd, North Wales.

CAREER: Organizer for Health Education, Edinburgh, Scotland, 1953; Department of Attorney General, Toronto, Ontario, Canada, adult probation officer, 1953-55; governor of women's prisons at Toronto and Brampton, Ontario, 1955-57; Surrey County Council, Public Health Department, Kingston upon Thames, England, chest care almoner, 1957-60; Home Office and National Association of Discharged Prisoners Societies, London, England, senior welfare officer at Wandsworth Prison (first woman social worker in Britain to serve inside all-male prison), 1960-62; Kingston Hospital, Kingston upon Thames, home warden, 1970-72; Chaworth Approved School for Girls, Ottershaw, Surrey, England, house mistress, 1972-74; Shell Island Crafts (gift shop), Rbye, Clwyd, North Wales, proprietor, 1974—. *Military service:* Queen Alexandra's Royal Naval Nursing Service (Reserve), 1943-44; became lieutenant. *Member:* Society of Authors, International P.E.N., Ex-Canadian Authors' Society.

WRITINGS: Royal Paladin (novel), Serif Books, 1950; *Farewell, Brave Folly* (novel), R. Hale, 1969; *No Easy*

Road: A Study of the Theories and Problems Involved in the Rehabilitation of the Offender, Allen & Unwin, 1970.

WORK IN PROGRESS: The Bonny Earl (tentative title) a novel on the political and religious intrigues which lead to the murder of James Stewart, Earl of Moray; Birth of a Nightingale, a nursing autobiography.

SIDELIGHTS: Sallie Trotter wrote to CA that the purpose behind her book on criminology is "to show value of first hand professional experience of criminals versus theories, and [to] awaken opinions."

A Guardian reviewer states: "Prisons, prisoners, and the rehabilitation of offenders—these are subjects which all too often are debated with more emotionalism than experience. This is why Sallie Trotter's study of the theories and problems involved in the rehabilitation of offenders is valuable and challenging."

AVOCATIONAL INTERESTS: Music of all kinds and nationalities, singing, dancing, embroidery, crochet, knitting, tapestry and rug-making, antiques and Eastern rugs.

BIOGRAPHICAL/CRITICAL SOURCES: Daily Telegraph, September 30, 1960; Scotsman, November 2, 1960; Christian Science Monitor, January 20, 1961; Woman, October, 1961; Times Literary Supplement, November 2, 1967; Guardian, December 12, 1969, February, 1970; Evening News (London), January, 1970; Books, February, 1970.

*　　*　　*

TRUESDALE, C(alvin) W(illiam) 1929-

PERSONAL: Born March 27, 1929; son of Cavour Langdon (retired president of a plastics company) and Isabel (Hardie) Truesdale; married Joan Wurtele, March 25, 1950; children: Anna, Hardie, Stephanie. Education: University of Washington, Seattle, B.A., 1951, Ph.D., 1957. Home: 90 Oxford Place, Staten Island, New York, 10301. Office: Department of Humanities, Cooper Union, Cooper Sq., New York, N.Y. 10003.

CAREER: University of New Mexico, Albuquerque, instructor in English, 1954-55; Virginia Military Institute, Lexington, assistant professor of English, 1956-62; Macalester College, St. Paul, Minn., assistant professor of English, 1962-67; New Rivers Press, New York City, founder and director, beginning 1967; currently adjunct professor of humanities, Cooper Union, New York City.

WRITINGS: In the Country of a Deer's Eye [or] En el pais del ojo de venado (poetry; bilingual edition), translated into Spanish by Otto-Raul Gonzalez, El Corno Emplumado (Mexico), 1966; The Loss of Rivers, Azazel Books (Denver), 1967; Moon Shots (poetry; originally published in limited edition as El Hombre: La Guerra), lithographs by Lucas Johnson, Mexican Art Annex (New York), 1968; (translator from the Yugoslavian; with Charles Simic) Ivan V. Lalic, Fire Gardens, New Rivers, 1970; The Masters of Knives, Hamman Publishing, 1971; Plastic Father, Fragments Books, 1971; Cold Harbors, Latitudes Press, 1974; (with Robert Bonazzi and Carlos Isla) Domingo (poem: a bilingual edition), Latitudes Press, 1974; Doctor Vertigo, Wyrd Press, 1976. Contributor of poetry and essays to various magazines. Editor, Minnesota Review, 1971—.

WORK IN PROGRESS: A collection of poems entitled Pope John's Motel to be completed 1978.

SIDELIGHTS: In a Minnesota Review article on Truesdale's poetry, Roy Arthur Swanson describes "two kinds of sadness, one of which is "creative sadness," which "predis-

poses an individual to humanity—and predisposes an artist to express it for humanity." Swanson writes that Truesdale's personal knowledge of tragedy has been translated into "a concept of melancholy derived from sense-data" in his poetry. "'The Face of Sable Island' is, for example, 'The luminous, scarred face of humanity/Acknowledging himself'. . . . The words are not cleverly disposed or timed to mechanistic clicks. They, like those of the best cubistic poetry, lack oily academic ingenuity but not soft, quiet, denotative precision. . . . Truesdale, like Wordsworth, reacts to nature as a tertium comparationis between a controlled personal sadness and 'the still sad music of humanity.'"

Swanson also points out that "one of Truesdale's most effective images is geography . . . Truesdale insists, 'I have always wanted to see with more than just my eyes; in my effort to fix a place poetically, I also need to think and sound out its geography.' He does not mean merely that he needs to think about a place's geography; he needs, literally, to think a place's geography. And by sounding out a place's geography he means, again, not merely probing it but also giving it sound: combining earth song with mind music." Charles Baxter, in a separate article, also mentions the visionary quality of Truesdale's poems, which "strain toward . . . perfect seeing, so that the reader, victim of smokescreen and blow-up alike, may finally observe with a deer's eye."

BIOGRAPHICAL/CRITICAL SOURCES: Minnesota Review, summer, 1967, Number 3, 1968; The Little Magazine, summer, 1971.

*　　*　　*

TRYON, Thomas 1926-
(Tom Tryon)

PERSONAL: Born January 14, 1926, in Hartford, Conn.; son of Arthur Lane (a clothier) and Elizabeth (Lester) Tryon; divorced. Education: Yale University, B.A., 1949. Home: 145 Central Park West, New York, N.Y. 10023. Agent: Arthur Riley, 32 Shadow Hill Rd., Ridgefield, Conn. 06877.

CAREER: Actor and writer; has appeared in films "Moon Pilot," 1960, "The Longest Day," 1962, "The Cardinal," 1964, "In Harm's Way," and others. Military service: U.S. Navy.

WRITINGS:—All novels; published by Knopf: The Other, 1971; Harvest Home (Literary Guild selection), 1973; Lady, 1974; Crowned Heads, 1976. Author of "The Other" (screenplay; based on his novel of same title), for Twentieth Century-Fox, 1972. Also author of unpublished work, "What Is the Answer, What Was the Question?"

SIDELIGHTS: For many years a successful actor, Thomas Tryon decided that acting was not a satisfying enough career so he turned to writing—something that he found very fulfilling and enjoyable.

Although Tryon made the switch to writing years ago and has published four novels, people still think of him as "Tom Tryon the Actor." "I even changed my name to 'Thomas' to steer people away from that Hollywood image," Tryon writes. "But no—no matter what I do, no matter how many books I write, it's always good old 'Tom' on TV shows and interviews. . . . It is very difficult for people to allow me to be a writer, because they have slotted me as an actor."

Tryon writes of his first novel, The Other: "I hadn't been long into it when I realized I had something. I knew if I finished the book that I had something, that it would be published, that it would make some kind of a mark. I did know that something had happened . . . the book was an act of faith, it really was."

Talking about the four novels he has written, Tryon writes: "I think the danger in writing or in being considered a 'best-selling author' is that you can as easily get typed in that as in acting. I waged a long battle in Hollywood for 15 years or something to avoid getting typed as an actor. By the same token, I don't want to be typed as a writer of thrillers." *Harvest Home* was adapted into a "Made-for-TV" movie.

BIOGRAPHICAL/CRITICAL SOURCES: Life, May 14, 1971; *Philadelphia Inquirer,* November 17, 1974; *Times-Picayune,* November 23, 1974; *Contemporary Literary Criticism,* Volume III, Gale, 1975.

* * *

TRYTHALL, J(ohn) W(illiam) D(onald) 1944-

PERSONAL: Surname is pronounced *Try*-thall; born October 10, 1944, in Washington, D.C.; citizen of the United Kingdom; son of John Douglas (a rear-admiral in the Royal Navy) and Elizabeth (Donald) Trythall; married Joanna Colquhoun (a secretary), June 29, 1968. *Education:* Balliol College, Oxford, B.A., 1965; attended St. Anthony's College, Oxford, 1965-68. *Home:* 7 Belle Vue Ter., York YO1 5AZ, England. *Office:* Department of History, University of York, Heslington, York YO1 5DD, England.

CAREER: University of York, York, England, lecturer in history, 1969—. Part-time tutor for the Open University, England, 1971.

WRITINGS: Franco: A Biography, Hart-Davis, 1970, published as *El Caudillo: A Political Biography of Franco,* McGraw, 1970. Contributor to *History of the Second World War* magazine.

WORK IN PROGRESS: A history of the Franco regime in Spain (1936-1975).

BIOGRAPHICAL/CRITICAL SOURCES: Times Literary Supplement, May 28, 1970; *Best Sellers,* November 1, 1970; *Listener,* December 17, 1970.

* * *

TSATSOS, Jeanne 1909-

PERSONAL: Given name in Greek is Ioanna, variant spelling of surname, Tsatsou; born January 4, 1909, in Smyrna (now Izmir), Turkey; Greek citizen; daughter of Stelios (a professor of international law at University of Athens) and Despina (Teneleides) Seferiades; married Constantine D. Tsatsos (president of the Hellenic Republic and a writer), June, 1930; children: Despina (Mrs. Constantine Mylonas), Theodora (Mrs. Alexander Simeonides). *Education:* University of Athens, doctorate in law, 1930. *Religion:* Greek Orthodox. *Home:* 9 Kydathineon, Athens 119, Greece.

CAREER: Involved in relief and resistance activities in Greece during and after World War II; chairman of Liberal Party organization for the civic rights and education of Greek women, 1949-51; represented her country on committees at the United Nations General Assembly, 1966; as the wife of a man involved in the government of Greece for more than a decade, she has also worked with numerous social service organizations. Member of Greek branch, International Social Service; member of national board, Greek Girl Scouts. *Awards, honors:* Military Medal for distinguished service; Golden Cross of Benevolence; first prize for biography, National Award, 1974, for *O adelfos mou Giorgos Seferis.*

WRITINGS—All published by Hestia Bookstore-J. D. Collaros, except as indicated: *Phylla Katoches* (title means "Leaves from the Occupation"), 1965, second edition, 1966, translation by Jean Demos published as *The Sword's Fierce Edge: A Journal of the Occupation of Greece, 1941-1944,* Vanderbilt University Press, 1969; *Logia Siopis* (poems; title means "Words of Silence"), 1968; *Atmito Fos* (poems; title means "The Indivisible Light"), 1969; *Athenais, Aelia Eudocia Augusta* (biography), 1970; *Elegos* (poems; title means "Elegy"), 1971; *O adelfos mou Giorgos Seferis* (biography; title means "My Brother George Seferis"), 1973; second edition, 1975; *Gymnos Tichos* (poems; title means "The Naked Wall"), 1975. Also author of *Executed during the Occupation,* 1947.

WORK IN PROGRESS: A book of poems.

SIDELIGHTS: Jeanne Tsatsos kept a journal throughout the years of the Italo-German occupation. From time to time she dropped the pages of the journal into a tin box buried in her garden, so that sometime her children might read them and also because she considered it an obligation to commemorate what she had witnessed. She is a sister of the Nobel prize-winning poet, George Seferis.

Her work *Phylla Katoches* about the German occupation has been translated and published in French.

BIOGRAPHICAL/CRITICAL SOURCES: Figaro Literaire (Paris), June 26-July 8, Number 1106; *Southern Humanities Review,* winter, 1971.

* * *

TUCCILLE, Jerome 1937-

PERSONAL: Surname pronounced too-*chilly;* born May 30, 1937, in New York, N.Y.; son of Salvatore J. (a taxi owner) and Virginia (Marano) Tuccille; married Marie Winkler, January 23, 1965; children: Jerome, Christine. *Education:* Manhattan College, B.S., 1959. *Politics:* "Anarchist-Libertarian." *Religion:* None. *Residence:* Tarrytown, N.J. *Agent:* Collier Associates, 280 Madison Ave., New York, N.Y.

CAREER: Writer. Broker for Merrill Lynch, Pierce, Fenner & Smith Inc., 1975—. *Military service:* U.S. Marine Corps, 1957-63; became sergeant.

WRITINGS: Radical Libertarianism: A Right Wing Alternative, Bobbs-Merrill, 1970; *It Usually Starts with Ayn Rand* (novel), Stein & Day, 1971; *Here Comes Immortality,* Stein & Day, 1973; *Who's Afraid of 1984,* Arlington House, 1975; *Everything the Beginner Needs to Invest Wisely,* Arlington House, 1977. Contributor of articles to *New York Times, Libertarian Forum, Nation, National Review,* and other newspapers and periodicals.

WORK IN PROGRESS: A novel.

AVOCATIONAL INTERESTS: Travel (Australia, Europe), tennis, squash, and "politics generally."

BIOGRAPHICAL/CRITICAL SOURCES: National Review, October 6, 1970; *Nation,* November 16, 1970.

* * *

TUCKER, Helen 1926-

PERSONAL: Born November 1, 1926, in Raleigh, N.C.; daughter of William Blair and Helen (Welch) Tucker; married William Thad Beckwith, January 9, 1971. *Education:* Wake Forest University, B.A., 1946; Columbia University, graduate study, 1957-58. *Religion:* Episcopalian. *Home:* 2930 Hostetler St., Raleigh, N.C. 27609. *Agent:* William

Morris Agency, Inc., 1350 Avenue of the Americas, New York, N.Y. 10019.

CAREER: Reporter on newspapers in Burlington, N.C., 1946-47, Twin Falls, Idaho, 1948-49, and Boise, Idaho, 1950-51; KDYL Radio, Salt Lake City, Utah, copywriter, 1951-52; WPTF Radio Co., Raleigh, N.C., copy supervisor, 1953-55; *Raleigh Times,* Raleigh, reporter, 1955-57; Columbia University Press, New York, N.Y., editorial assistant, 1959-60; North Carolina Museum of Art, Raleigh, director of publicity, 1967-70. *Awards, honors:* Distinguished Alumni award, Wake Forest University, 1971.

WRITINGS—All published by Stein & Day: *The Sound of Summer Voices* (novel), 1969; *The Guilt of August Fielding,* 1971; *No Need of Glory,* 1972; *The Virgin of Lontano,* 1973.

BIOGRAPHICAL/CRITICAL SOURCES: Best Sellers, November 15, 1969; *Book World,* May 12, 1970.

*   *   *

TUCKER, (Allan) James 1929-
(David Craig)

PERSONAL: Born August 15, 1929, in Cardiff, Wales; son of William Arthur and Violet Irene (Bushen) Tucker; married Marian Roberta Craig (a teacher), July 17, 1954; children: Patrick, Catherine, Guy, David. *Education:* University College of South Wales and Monmouthshire, B.A., 1951. *Home:* 5 Cefncoed Rd., Cardiff, Wales. *Agent:* Campbell, Thompson, & McLaughlin, 31 Newington Green, London N16 9PU, England.

CAREER: Journalist on various newspapers in Britain, 1954—, and author; University College of South Wales and Monmouthshire, Cardiff, Wales, tutor in English literature, 1967—. *Military service:* Royal Air Force, 1951-53; became flying officer.

WRITINGS: Equal Partners, Chapman & Hall, 1960; *The Right Hand Man,* Chapman & Hall, 1960; *Burster,* Gollancz, 1966; *Honourable Estates* (nonfiction), Gollancz, 1966; *The Novels of Anthony Powell,* Macmillan, 1976.

Under pseudonym David Craig; all published by Stein & Day: *The Alias Man,* 1968; *Message Ends,* 1969; *Contact Lost,* 1970; *Young Men May Die,* 1970; *A Walk at Night,* 1971; *The Squeeze,* 1974.

Writer of television and radio documentaries. Contributor to *Punch, Spectator, Sunday Times,* and *New Review.*

*   *   *

TUELL, Jack Marvin 1923-

PERSONAL: Born November 14, 1923, in Tacoma, Wash.; son of Frank Harry (a funeral director) and Anne (Bertelson) Tuell; married Marjorie Beadles (a teacher), June 17, 1946; children: Jacqueline (Mrs. Roger Richter), Cynthia, James. *Education:* University of Washington, B.S., 1947, J.D., 1948; Boston University, S.T.B., 1955; University of Puget Sound, M.A., 1961. *Religion:* United Methodist. *Home:* 15088 Southwest Trillium Lane, Beaverton, Ore. 97005.

CAREER: Admitted to the Bar of Washington State, 1948; attorney, Edmonds, Wash., 1948-50; ordained minister of United Methodist Church, 1955; pastor in Tewksbury, Mass., 1952-55, Tacoma, Wash., 1955-61; United Methodist Church, Everett, Wash., district superintendent, 1961-67; United Methodist Church, Vancouver, Wash., pastor, 1967-72, bishop, 1972—. Member of board of trustees, University of Puget Sound, 1961-72, Vancouver Memorial Hospital, 1967-72, Willamette University, 1972—, Alaska Methodist

University, 1972—. Member of Human Relations Commission, City of Vancouver, 1970-72. *Military service:* U.S. Army Air Forces, 1943-45. *Member:* Rotary International, Tacoma U.S.O. (president, 1960-61), Vancouver YMCA, Vancouver Seamen's Center (vice-president, 1971). *Awards, honors:* D.D., Pacific School of Religion, 1966.

WRITINGS: The Organization of the United Methodist Church, Abingdon, 1970, revised edition, 1977. Author of handbook, "Organizing for Ministry," for United Methodist Church.

*   *   *

TURLINGTON, Bayly 1919-

PERSONAL: Born September 14, 1919, in Norfolk, Va.; son of S. James (a lawyer) and Florence Bayly (Browne) Turlington; married Anne Apperson, July 1, 1950; children: Bayly Fielding, Anne Bowman. *Education:* University of the South, B.A., 1942; Johns Hopkins University, Ph.D., 1949. *Politics:* Republican. *Home:* High Tor, Sewanee, Tenn. 37375. *Office:* Department of Classical Languages, University of the South, Sewanee, Tenn. 37375.

CAREER: Smith College, Northampton, Mass., instructor in classics, 1949-50; University of the South, Sewanee, Tenn., assistant professor, 1950-54, associate professor, 1954-60, professor of classics, 1960—, head of department, 1954—, secretary of board of trustees, 1967—, marshal for University Faculties, 1953-68. *Military service:* U.S. Army, 1942-46; became captain. *Member:* American Philological Association, Tennessee Philological Association (president, 1968-69), Phi Beta Kappa, Omicron Delta Kappa, Pi Gamma Mu.

WRITINGS: Socrates: The Father of Western Philosophy (juvenile), F. Watts, 1969. Contributor to classical journals.

*   *   *

TURNER, Dean (Edson) 1927-

PERSONAL: Born May 24, 1927, in Tyrone, Okla.; son of Jesse Lee (a barber) and Cora Mae Turner; married Nancy Margaret Roche (a rehabilitation counselor), August 12, 1965. *Education:* Attended Baylor University, 1945-46; Centro de Estudios Universitarios, Mexico City, B.A., 1955, Adams State College, M.Ed., 1956; University of Texas, Ph.D., 1966. *Home:* 1857 13th Ave., Greeley, Colo. 80631. *Office:* Department of History and Philosophy of Education, University of Northern Colorado, Greeley, Colo. 80631.

CAREER: Ordained minister in Disciples of Christ Church, 1967; University of Northern Colorado, Greeley, professor of philosophy of education and human relations, 1966—. Chairman, Starving Children's Fund. *Military service:* U.S. Army, 1950-52.

WRITINGS: Lonely God, Lonely Man: A Study in the Relation of Loneliness to Personal Development, Philosophical Library, 1960; *The Autonomous Man: An Essay in Personal Identity and Integrity,* Bethany Press, 1970; *Commitment to Care: An Integrated Philosophy of Science, Education, and Religion,* Devin-Adair, 1977; *The Einstein Myth,* Devin-Adair, 1977; (editor) *The Ives Papers,* Devin-Adair, 1977; *Krinkle Nose: A Prayer of Thanks,* Devin-Adair, 1977.

WORK IN PROGRESS: Researching materials for book to be entitled *Teaching for a New Generation.*

SIDELIGHTS: Dean Turner has traveled extensively in Asia, Europe, and Central America.

BIOGRAPHICAL/CRITICAL SOURCES: Christian Century, May 5, 1971.

*   *   *

TURNER, L(eonard) C(harles) F(rederick) 1914-

PERSONAL: Born August 29, 1914, in Johannesburg, South Africa; son of Leonard Robinson (a publicity agent) and Henrietta (Chapman) Turner; married Olive M. Evans, November 17, 1945; children: Caroline, Penelope. Education: University of the Witwatersrand, B.A. (first class honors), 1937, M.A. (with distinction), 1939. Home: 79 Springvale Dr., Weetangera, Canberra, Australian Capital Territory, Australia. Office: Department of History, Royal Military College, Canberra, Australian Capital Territory, Australia.

CAREER: South African Official War History Project, Pretoria, chief narrator, 1946-49, assistant editor, 1949-56; University of New England, Armidale, New South Wales, Australia, lecturer, 1956-59, senior lecturer, 1959-62, associate professor of history, 1962-68; University of New South Wales, Canberra, Australian Capital Territory, Australia, professor of history on Faculty of Military Studies, Royal Military College, 1968—. Visiting professor, Queens University at Kingston, 1963. Military service: British Army, 1939-45; became major. Member: Academy of Social Sciences (Australia; fellow). Awards, honors: Carnegie travel grant to United States, 1963.

WRITINGS: (With J.A.I. Agar-Hamilton) Crisis in the Desert, May-July 1942, Oxford University Press, 1952; (editor) General F. W. von Mellinthin, Panzer Battles 1939-45, Cassell, 1955, University of Oklahoma Press, 1956; (with Agar-Hamilton) The Sidi Rezeg Battles, 1941, Oxford University Press, 1957; (with H. R. Gordon-Cumming and J. E. Betzler) War in the Southern Oceans, 1939-45, Oxford University Press, 1961; The First World War, F. W. Cheshire, 1967; The Coming of the First World War, F. W. Cheshire, 1968; Origins of the First World War, Norton, 1970; The Great War, 1914-1918, F. W. Cheshire, 1971; The American Civil War and Reconstruction, F. W. Cheshire, 1971; Napoleon and Europe, F. W. Cheshire, 1973; (contributor) Historical Discipline and Culture in Australasia, University of Queensland Press, 1977. Contributor to military and historical journals.

AVOCATIONAL INTERESTS: Flying (held private pilot's license, 1962-69).

*   *   *

TURNER, Morrie 1923-

PERSONAL: Born December 11, 1923, in Oakland, Calif.; son of James G. (a Pullman porter) and Nora (Spears) Turner; married Letha M. Harvey; children: Morrie A. Politics: Democrat. Home: 1 Kelton Ct. 2-H, Oakland, Calif. 94611.

CAREER: Oakland Police Department, Oakland, Calif., police clerk, 1950-64; syndicated cartoonist, King Features Syndicate, New York, N.Y., 1965-74, Register and Tribune Syndicate, Des Moines, Iowa, 1972—. Teacher of cartooning, Lavey College (Calif.) and San Mateo College (Calif.), both 1971-72. Member of board of directors, Volunteer Bureau of Alameda County and Oakland Young Men's Christian Association. Vice-chairman of Media Forum, White House Conference on Children, 1970. Military service: U.S. Army Air Forces, 1943-46. Member: Magazine Cartoonists Guild, National Cartoonists Society, California Writers Club. Awards, honors: Brotherhood Award of National Conference of Christians and Jews; Intergroup Relations Award of B'nai B'rith Women; Alameda County Teachers Association Layman of the Year award.

WRITINGS—All published by Signet, except as noted: Black and White Coloring Book, Troubador, 1969; Wee Pals, 1969; Nipper, Westminster, 1970; Kid Power, 1970; Freedom Is . . ., Judson Press, 1970; Wee Pals: Right On, 1971; Nipper's Secret Power, Westminster, 1971; Wee Pals: Getting It All Together, No. Four, 1972; Wee Pals: Doing Their Thing, 1973; Wee Pals No. Five, 1973; (with wife, Letha Turner) Famous Black Americans, Judson Press, 1973; Wee Pals: Book of Knowledge, 1974; Wee Pals: Staying Cool, 1974; Wee Pals: Happy Birthday America!, 1975. Also author of Wee Pals: Rainbow Power, and of Wee Pals: God Is Groovy. Author of "Kid Power," an animated television series for American Broadcasting Companies, Inc., and of the animated film "Who Do You Think Should Belong to the Club?".

WORK IN PROGRESS: A series of school readers.

SIDELIGHTS: Morrie Turner lectures in schools and colleges on the subject of cartooning, and teaches a course in cartooning in night school.

*   *   *

TURNER, Richard E(ugene) 1920-

PERSONAL: Born April 8, 1920; son of Frederick Alworth (an oil producer) and Florence (Foster) Turner; married Patricia Ann Hayes (a bank teller), September 14, 1947; children: Scott Foster, Drew Hayes, Brett Alexander. Education: Principia College, B.A., 1947. Politics: Republican. Religion: Protestant. Home: 636 South Shields, Fort Collins, Colo. 80521. Agent: Stanley M. Ulanoff, 17 The Serpentine, Roslyn, Long Island, N.Y. 11576.

CAREER: S. W. Hayes Hatcheries, Centralia, Ill., general manager, 1947-52; Harmony Guest Ranch, Estes Park, Colo., owner-operator, 1953-63; architectural consultant and planner, Fort Collins, Colo., 1963-67; full-time writer, 1967—. Has held a working interest in oil production in East Texas, 1951—. Military service: U.S. Army Air Forces, 1942-45; U.S. Air Force, 1951-54; fighter pilot in Europe and later Asian theater; became colonel; received Silver Star, Distinguished Flying Cross with oak-leaf cluster, Air Medal with 35 oak-leaf clusters, Presidential Unit Citation with cluster, five battle stars, and Croix de Guerre with palme. Member: American Fighter Aces Association (vice-president, 1969-70).

WRITINGS: Big Friend, Little Friend: Memoirs of a World War II Fighter Pilot, Doubleday, 1969 (published in England as Mustang Pilot, Kimber & Co., 1969).

WORK IN PROGRESS: A biography of James H. Howard, Medal of Honor winner.

BIOGRAPHICAL/CRITICAL SOURCES: New York Times Book Review, December 14, 1969.††

*   *   *

TURNER, (Clarence) Steven 1923-

PERSONAL: Born April 18, 1923, in Baton Rouge, La.; son of Calvin Murphy (a bricklayer) and Mary (Wright) Turner; married Dean Harding, November 27, 1943; married second wife, Jean Kay Tyrrell (an elementary school teacher), December 31, 1953; children: (first marriage) David Harding; (second marriage) Brenda Jean, Deborah Ann. Education:

Southern Methodist University, B.A., 1948, M.A., 1950; University of Texas, Ph.D., 1962. *Politics:* Democrat. *Religion:* Methodist. *Home:* 613 Westview Ter., Arlington, Tex. 76013. *Office:* Department of English, University of Texas, Arlington, Tex. 76010.

CAREER: Instructor in English at General Beadle State Teacher's College (now Dakota State College), Madison, S.D., 1953-54, Michigan Technological University, Houghton, 1954-55, Pennsylvania State University, Pottsville Campus, 1955-57, and University of Texas at Austin, 1957-60; University of Texas at Arlington, associate professor, 1960-64, professor of American literature, 1964—. *Military service:* U.S. Navy, 1940-46, 1950-52; became chief aviation photographer. *Member:* Modern Language Association of America.

WRITINGS: A Measure of Dust (novel), Simon & Schuster, 1970; *George Milburn,* Steck, 1970. Fiction editor, *Arlington Quarterly,* 1967-70.

WORK IN PROGRESS: A novel, *To Shun the Heaven.*

AVOCATIONAL INTERESTS: Physical exercise.

BIOGRAPHICAL/CRITICAL SOURCES: New York Times Book Review, May 24, 1970; *Best Sellers,* June 15, 1970.

*   *   *

TURNEY, Alfred W(alter)   1916-

PERSONAL: Born August 6, 1916, in Miss.; son of Walter Alfred and Hazel (Waddell) Turney; married Sarah Chidester (a psychologist), July 12, 1957; children: Mia. *Education:* Attended University of Maryland, Kansas State University, and University of Heidelberg, 1938-63; University of New Mexico, B.A., 1965; M.A., 1966, Ph.D., 1969. *Home:* 1529 Pine Ave., Weatherford, Okla. 73096. *Office:* Department of Social Sciences, Southwestern Oklahoma State University, Weatherford, Okla. 73096.

CAREER: U.S. Army, career officer, 1938-63, retired from army with rank of lieutenant colonel; Southwestern Oklahoma State University, Weatherford, assistant professor, 1968-70, associate professor of history, 1970—. During World War II served in Europe in combat; in subsequent years served in military intelligence. *Member:* Southern Historical Association. *Awards, honors:* Bronze Star Medal.

WRITINGS: Disaster at Moscow: Van Bock's Campaigns, 1941-42, University of New Mexico Press, 1970.

WORK IN PROGRESS: Completing a research project pertaining to the displacement of millions of peoples in Europe during and after World War II.

SIDELIGHTS: Alfred Turney told *CA:* "As a retired military officer, I am interested in military affairs and in the military posture of the United States. As a college professor, I am interested in furthering the study of modern history, especially the brutal, inhumane aspects of modern warfare, which most historians tend blissfully to ignore. (That is probably because most of them never experienced the horrors of war at first hand, as I have.)"

*   *   *

TUTTLE, William M., Jr.   1937-

PERSONAL: Born October 7, 1937, in Detroit, Mich.; son of William M. (a surgeon) and Geneva (Duvall) Tuttle; married Linda Stumpp, December 12, 1959 (divorced); children: William M. III, Catharine Terry, Andrew Sanford. *Education:* Denison University, B.A., 1959; University of Wis-

consin, M.A., 1964, Ph.D., 1967. *Politics:* None. *Religion:* Unitarian Universalist. *Home:* 1116 Tennessee St., Lawrence, Kan. 66044. *Office:* Department of History, University of Kansas, Lawrence, Kan. 66045.

CAREER: Historian for recent U.S. history, Study of American Education, Princeton, N.J., 1965-67; University of Kansas, Lawrence, assistant professor, 1969-70, associate professor, 1970-75, professor of American history, 1975—. Senior fellow in Southern and Negro history, Johns Hopkins University, Baltimore, Md., 1969-70. *Military service:* U.S. Air Force, 1959-62; became first lieutenant; received Air Force Commendation Medal. *Member:* Society of American Historians, American Historical Association, Organization of American Historians, Association for the Study of Afro-American Life and History. *Awards, honors:* Harry S. Truman Library Institute research grant, 1968; Award of Merit for State History, Illinois State Historical Society, 1971; American Council of Learned Societies grant-in-aid, 1972; research fellowship, Harvard University, 1972-73; Younger Humanist fellowship, National Endowment for the Humanities, 1972-73; Award of Merit, American Association of State and Local History, 1972; grants-in-aid, Lilly Endowment, 1975, 1976; Tom L. Evans grant, Harry S. Truman Library Institute, 1975-76; John Simon Guggenheim Memorial fellow, 1975-76.

WRITINGS: Race Riot: Chicago in the Red Summer of 1919, Atheneum, 1970; *W.E.B. DuBois,* Prentice-Hall, 1973.

Contributor: Richard Resh, editor, *Black America: Confrontation and Accommodation in the Twentieth Century,* Heath, 1969; Thomas R. Frazier, editor, *Afro-American History: Primary Sources,* Harcourt, 1970; Milton Cantor, editor, *Black Labor in America,* Negro Universities Press, 1970; John Bracey and others, editors, *Black Workers and Organized Labor,* Wadsworth, 1971; Kenneth Jackson and Stanley Schultz, editors, *American History: Urban Perspective,* Knopf, 1971. Contributor to history journals.

WORK IN PROGRESS: A history of violence in twentieth-century United States; a biography of James B. Conant, completion expected in 1977.

*   *   *

TYDINGS, Joseph D(avies)   1928-

PERSONAL: Born May 4, 1928, in Asheville, N.C.; son of Millard E. (a former U.S. Senator) and Eleanor (Davies) Tydings; married Terry Lynn Huntingdon, August 20, 1955; children: Mary Campbell, Millard E. II, Emlen Davies, Eleanor Davies, Paige Crowley, Alexandra. *Education:* University of Maryland, B.A., 1951, LL.B., 1953. *Politics:* Democrat. *Religion:* Episcopalian. *Home:* Oakington, Havre de Grace, Md. 21078. *Office:* 1120 Connecticut Ave., Washington, D.C. 20036.

CAREER: Admitted to the Bar of State of Maryland, 1952; Tydings, Sauerwein, Benson & Boyd (law firm), Baltimore, Md., associate, 1952-57; Maryland House of Delegates, Annapolis, member from Harford County, 1955-61; Tydings & Rosenburg (law firm), Baltimore, partner, 1958-61; U.S. Attorney for District of Maryland, 1961-64; U.S. Congress, Washington, D.C., senator from Maryland, 1965-71; Danzansky, Dickey, Tydings, Quint & Gordon (law firm), Washington, D.C., partner, 1971—. Delegate, Interpol Conference, Helsinki, Finland, and International Penal Conference, Bellagio, Italy, 1963. President, Joe Davies Scholarship Foundation. Member of board of regents, University of Maryland; member of board of trustees, McDonogh School. *Military service:* U.S. Army, 1946-48.

MEMBER: American Bar Association, Federal Bar Association, District of Columbia Bar Association, Maryland Bar Association, Harford County Bar Association, Baltimore City Bar Association, Phi Eta Sigma, Phi Kappa Phi, Omicron Delta Kappa, Phi Kappa Sigma, Scabbard and Blade.

WRITINGS: Born to Starve, Morrow, 1970, published as *Born to Starve: It Is Not Too Late to Help Millions of People Doomed to Live in Poverty, Hunger and Despair,* 1971. Contributor to *Harper's* and *Saturday Evening Post.*

SIDELIGHTS: During Joseph Tydings' unsuccessful re-election campaign in 1970, Alex Campbell charged that a "storm that is being worked up against [Tydings] in his state is contrived by the gun lobby in part because he is a liberal, and people who fear and hate liberal views readily believe that Tydings is plotting to disarm them so as to leave them helpless prey of vaguely glimpsed powers of evil. . . . Meanwhile, Tydings' efforts to protect poor and black people from the criminals who prey on them are rudely rebuffed."

Defeated in part by the gun lobby and by identification as one sympathetic to the actions of radical students, Tydings, while in office, espoused a variety of causes in addition to gun control laws and opposition to the Indochina War. He sponsored and supported various forms of legislation to protect the rights of minority and poor people, pushed for legislation tougher on organized crime and more lenient on first time drug offenders and drug addicts. His book, *Born to Starve,* as described by Alex Campbell, "says that 5.4 million American women who are poor don't want large families and do want family planning assistance, but fewer than 800,000 can get it." The reaction to his book by many of what Campbell terms "less rational accusers" was a mixture of "blacks [who] say he's a rich white who aims to sterilize the black poor [and] others [who] profess shock at his proposal to leave abortion 'to individual conscience.'"

Another significant aspect of Tydings' political career is his emphasis on the importance of the Constitution as a protector of civil liberties. In an article in which he opposed an attempt to hold a new national constitutional convention, he stated: "Our individual liberties—based squarely on the Constitution—are the pride and envy of the world. It is disgraceful that a last-gasp attempt to perpetuate malapportionment should threaten our fundamental charter. It is shocking that this strategem has gone so far while most of us—including most of us in Congress—weren't looking. There is yet time for this to be halted and reversed. The time is now."

BIOGRAPHICAL/CRITICAL SOURCES: Saturday Evening Post, June 17, 1967; *New Republic,* June 27, 1970; *Life,* August 28, 1970; *Nation,* September 28, 1970; *Newsweek,* October 19, 1970.

* * *

TYLER, Ronnie C(urtis) 1941-

PERSONAL: Born December 29, 1941, in Temple, Tex.; son of Jasper J. and Melba (James) Tyler; married. *Education:* Temple Junior College, A.A., 1962; Abilene Christian College, B.S.E., 1964; Texas Christian University, M.A., 1966, Ph.D., 1968. *Home:* 3418 Worth Hills Dr., Fort Worth, Tex. 76109. *Office address:* Amon Carter Museum of Western Art, P.O. Box 2365, Fort Worth, Tex. 76101.

CAREER: Austin College, Sherman, Tex., assistant professor of history, 1967-69; Amon Carter Museum of Western Art, Fort Worth, Tex., curator of history and director of publications, 1969—. *Member:* American Historical Association, American Association of Museums, Organization of American Historians, Conference on Latin American History, Latin American Studies Association, Western History Association, Southwestern Council on Latin American Studies, Texas State Historical Association. *Awards, honors:* Carroll Award, for *Vision, Destiny—War!;* Tullis Award, for *The Big Bend.*

WRITINGS: Joseph Wade Hampton, Editor and Individualist, Texas Western Press, 1969; *Vision, Destiny—War!: Manifest Destiny and the Mexican War,* Steck, 1970; (editor with Lawrence R. Murphy) *Slave Narratives of Texas,* Encino Press, 1971; *Santiago Vidaurri and the Confederacy,* Texas State Historical Association, 1973; *The Mexican War: A Lithographic Record,* Texas State Historical Association, 1973; *The Cowboy,* Ridge Press, 1975; *The Big Bend: The Last Texas Frontier,* National Park Service, 1975; *The Image of America in Caricature and Cartoon,* Amon Carter Museum, 1975. Contributor to history journals.

WORK IN PROGRESS: The Rodeo Photographs of John Stryker, for Encino Press.

* * *

TYLER, Stephen A(lbert) 1932-

PERSONAL: Born May 8, 1932, in Hartford, Iowa; son of Guy Earle (a farmer) and Beatrice V. (Slack) Tyler; married Martha S. Grosskop, June 15, 1962. *Education:* Simpson College, B.A., 1957; Stanford University, M.A., 1962, Ph.D., 1964. *Home:* 3106 Bluebonnet, Houston, Tex. 77025. *Office:* Department of Anthropology, Rice University, Houston, Tex. 77001.

CAREER: University of California, Davis, assistant professor of anthropology, 1964-67; Tulane University, New Orleans, La., associate professor of anthropology, 1967-70; Rice University, Houston, Tex., professor of anthropology and linguistics, 1970—. Visiting summer professor, University of California, Berkeley, 1966. Anthropological field work in South India, 1963-64. *Military service:* U.S. Air Force, 1952-56. *Member:* American Anthropological Association, Linguistic Society of America, Association for Asian Studies.

WRITINGS: Koya: An Outline Grammar, University of California Press, 1969; (editor) *Cognitive Anthropology,* Holt, 1969; (editor) *Concepts and Assumptions of Contemporary Anthropology,* University of Georgia Press, 1970; *India: An Anthropological Perspective,* Goodyear Publishing, 1973. Contributor to journals. Associate editor, *Annual Reviews: Anthropology.*

WORK IN PROGRESS: The Said and Unsaid: An Introduction to Language and Culture.

* * *

TYTELL, John 1939-

PERSONAL: Born May 17, 1939, in Antwerp, Belgium; son of Charles and Lena (Ganopolski) Tytell; married Mary Ellen Gregori (a photographer), May 28, 1967. *Education:* City College (now City College of the City University of New York), B.A., 1961; New York University, M.A., 1963, Ph.D., 1968. *Home:* 69 Perry St., New York, N.Y. 10014. *Office:* Department of English, Queens College of the City University of New York, Flushing, N.Y. 11367.

CAREER: Queens College of the City University of New York, Flushing, N.Y., lecturer, 1964-69, assistant professor, 1969-74, associate professor of English, 1974—. *Member:* Modern Language Association of America, Phi Beta Kappa. *Awards, honors:* National Endowment of the Humanities fellowship, 1974.

WRITINGS: (Editor with Harold Jaffe) *The American Experience: A Radical Reader,* Harper, 1970; (editor with Jaffe) *Affinities: A Short Story Anthology,* Crowell, 1970; *Naked Angels: The Lives and Literature of the Beat Generation,* McGraw, 1976. Contributor to *American Scholar, Partisan Review, Studies in the Novel,* and other professional journals; contributor of poetry to little magazines, including *Partisan Review, Fiddlehead,* and *Galley Sail Review.*

*   *   *

UBLE, T(homas) R(alph) O(bermeyer)   1931-

PERSONAL: Surname rhymes with "bubble"; born January 1, 1931, in White Plains, N.Y.; son of William Obermeyer Edward and Beatrice (Hasty) Uble; married Iris Nancyann Rush, October, 1955; children: Mortimer R. *Education:* Attended Academy of Data Processing, 1951-52; Seyburn Institute of Technology, B.S., 1953. *Home:* 4309 Nottingham, Detroit, Mich.

CAREER: Radical Techniques, Inc., Revere, N.J., head of key punch department, 1954-55; Soft Wear Unlimited, Upsala, N.Y., head programmer, 1955-63; New Day Co., Sylvanopolis, N.J., manager of computer composition department, 1963-64, vice-president, 1964-67, president, 1967—.

WRITINGS: Symbolic Ambience in the Automation Approach, Fairweather, 1959; *Facilitating the Understanding of Human Behavior in Relation to Computer Dynamics,* New Day, 1963; *How to be Responsive to Change in Methods, Goals, Points of View,* New Day, 1964; *Applying Computer Techniques to Publishing,* New Day, 1966; *Eliminating the Human Factor,* New Day, 1967; *The Struggle to Oblivion,* Pap Press, 1970.

SIDELIGHTS: Uble told *CA:* "Computers are my life; they have brought me happiness, fame, and fortune. I consider my 1967 book the answer to the ills of today's world."

*   *   *

UEHLING, Carl Theodore   1927-

PERSONAL: Born May 10, 1927, in Passaic, N.J.; son of Carl Reinhold (an insurance broker) and Wilhelmina (Kohn) Uehling; married Jean Arlene Kniseley (a teacher), June 18, 1949; children: Carl, Mark, Blair, Earl. *Education:* Gettysburg College, A.B., 1946; Lutheran Theological Seminary at Gettysburg, B.D., 1949; also attended Columbia University. *Politics:* Republican. *Home:* 7145 Crittenden St., Philadelphia, Pa. 19119. *Office: Lutheran* Magazine, 2900 Queen Lane, Philadelphia, Pa. 19129.

CAREER: Ordained a Lutheran minister, 1949; served pastorates at Lutheran churches in Elizabeth, N.J., 1949-53, Newark, N.J., 1953-59, Akron, Ohio,1959-65, and Chicago, Ill., 1965-69; *Lutheran* Magazine, Philadelphia, Pa., articles editor, 1969—. *Member:* National Lutheran Editors and Managers Association (vice-president).

WRITINGS: Blood, Sweat, and Love: The Circus Kirk Story, Fortress, 1970; *The Middle Years: Prime Time,* Lutheran Church Press, 1970; *Prayers for Public Worship,* Fortress, 1972; *Prayers for Lay Ministry,* Fortress, 1974. Contributor of articles to various church publications.

ULLMAN, James Ramsey   1907-1971

November 24, 1907—June 20, 1971; American author, adventurer, playwright, and producer. Obituaries: *New York Times,* June 21, 1971; *Time,* July 5, 1971; *Antiquarian Bookman,* July 5-12, 1971. (See index for *CA* sketch)

*   *   *

ULRICH, Betty Garton   1919-

PERSONAL: Born October 28, 1919, in Indianapolis, Ind.; daughter of Harry Wasson (a physician) and Nora (Davis) Garton; married Louis Ulrich (a minister), January 5, 1946; children: Barbara, James, Ruth, John, David. *Education:* University of Wisconsin—Madison, B.A., 1942. *Home:* 1608 Deerwood Dr., South St. Paul, Minn. 55075.

CAREER: National Lutheran Council, Student Service Department, Chicago, Ill., field secretary, 1942-46; Augsburg College, Minneapolis, Minn., teacher of Old and New Testaments and Christian ethics, 1946-47; Grand Forks High School, Grand Forks, N.D., Latin and English teacher, 1958; began writing full-time in 1963.

WRITINGS: A Way We Go, Concordia, 1970; *Every Day with God,* Augsburg, 1972. Also author of *How to Help Your Minister Get Ahead.* Contributor of articles, short stories, and poems to various periodicals.

WORK IN PROGRESS: A novel set in the future, tentatively entitled *Second Eve.*

BIOGRAPHICAL/CRITICAL SOURCES: Grand Forks Herald, April 29, 1956; *Sun* (South St. Paul, Minn.), April 23, 1969.

*   *   *

UNGER, Marvin H.   1936-

PERSONAL: Born October 22, 1936, in Syracuse, N.Y.; son of Nathan H. (a contractor) and Betty (Simon) Unger; married Jane Desmon, October 22, 1967 (divorced). *Education:* University of Buffalo (now State University of New York at Buffalo), B.A., 1958; State University of New York at Buffalo, M.Ed., 1964, Ed.D., 1970; also studied at Syracuse University, 1960, San Francisco State College (now University), 1964, and Stanford University, 1966. *Religion:* Jewish.

CAREER: Science teacher in Savannah, N.Y., 1958-60; chemistry teacher in Buffalo, N.Y., 1960-64; Peace Corps volunteer, teaching in Liberia, 1964-66; Buffalo (N.Y.) Board of Education, administrative assistant, 1966-68. *Member:* Society for Educational Administration.

WRITINGS: Pawpaw, Foofoo and Juju: Reflections of a Peace Corps Volunteer, Citadel, 1968; *Softly, Softly Catch a Monkey* (juvenile), Scholastic Book Services, 1968. Abstractor for *Educational Administration Abstracts,* 1969.†

*   *   *

UNRUH, Glenys Grace (Green)   1910-

PERSONAL: Born November 29, 1910, in Burrton, Kan.; daughter of Howard L. (a postal employee) and Kate (a businesswoman; maiden name, Saylor) Green; married Adolph Unruh (a professor of education), May 24, 1932; children: Marla Kay Lee, Shirley Jo (Mrs. Charles A. Herrick), Janet Lynn. *Education:* Wichita State University, A.B., 1933; Washington University, St. Louis, M.A., 1955; St. Louis University, Ph.D., 1972. *Religion:* Protestant. *Home:* 151 North Bemiston Ave., Clayton, Mo. 63105.

CAREER: Elementary and secondary teacher for ten years in Kansas, Colorado, and Missouri public schools; University City Public Schools, University City, Mo., assistant superintendent for curriculum and instruction, 1962—. Local project director, Comprehensive School Improvement for Ford Foundation; member of teams representing U.S. at international conferences on education. *Member:* National Education Association, Association for Supervision and Curriculum Development (ASCD; president, 1974-75).

WRITINGS: (Editor) *New Curriculum Developments,* ASCD-NEA, 1965; (editor with Robert R. Leeper) *Influences in Curriculum Change,* ASCD-NEA, 1967; *Innovations in Secondary Education,* Holt, 1970, 2nd edition, 1974; *Responsive Curriculum Development: Theory and Action,* McCutchan, 1975. Contributor to *Social Education, Educational Leadership, Today's Education, NEA Journal, School and Community,* and other education journals.

*   *   *

UNSWORTH, Walter   1928-
(Walt Unsworth)

PERSONAL: Born December 16, 1928, in Littleborough, Lancashire, England; married Dorothy Winstanley, 1952; children: Gail, Timothy Duncan. *Education:* Attended Wigan Technical College, 1942-47, and Chester College, 1949-51; Licentiate of the College of Preceptors (L.C.P.), 1956. *Home:* 16 Briarfield Rd., Worsley, Manchester M28 4GQ, England.

CAREER: Taught in Wednesfield, Staffordshire, and in Horwich, Lancashire, England; Worsley Walkden Secondary School, Worsley, Lancashire, England, head of physics department, 1957-73; editor, *Climber & Rambler* (magazine), 1974—. Managing editor and partner, Cicerone Press (publishers of specialist mountaineering booklets); at one time a professional mountain-climbing instructor during summer months. *Military service:* British Army, Royal Artillery, 1947-49; served in Malta and Libya. *Member:* Alpine Club, Association of British Members of the Swiss Alpine Club, British Mountaineering Council (member of executive committee), Wayfarer's Club.

WRITINGS: The Young Mountaineer, Hutchinson, 1959; *A Climber's Guide to Pontesford Rocks,* Wilding & Son, 1962; *The English Outcrops,* Gollancz, 1964; *Matterhorn Man: The Life of Edward Whymper,* Gollancz, 1965; (contributor) *The Mountaineer's Companion,* Eyre & Spottiswoode, 1966; (contributor) *Miscellany Four,* Oxford University Press, 1967; *Tiger in the Snow: The Life and Adventures of A. F. Mummery,* Gollancz, 1967; *Because It Is There: Famous Mountaineers 1840-1940,* Gollancz, 1968; *The Devil's Mill* (juvenile novel), Gollancz, 1968; *The Book of Rock-Climbing,* Arthur Barker, 1968; (compiler) *Otztal Alps: A Selection of Climbs* (climbing guide), West Col Productions, 1969; *North Face: The Second Conquest of the Alps,* Hutchinson, 1969.

Whistling Clough (juvenile novel), Gollancz, 1970; (with R. B. Evans) *The Southern Lakes* (climbing guide), Cicerone Press, 1971; *Portrait of the River Derwent,* R. Hale, 1971; *The High Fells of Lakeland,* R. Hale, 1972; *Colour Book of the Lake District,* Batsford, 1974; *Colour Book of the Peak District,* Batsford, 1974; *Grimsdyke* (juvenile novel), Gollancz, 1974; *Encyclopaedia of Mountaineering,* R. Hale, 1975. Also author of *Everest 72,* the official booklet of the British Mount Everest Expedition, 1972. Contributor of articles and reviews to magazines, mountaineering journals, and newspapers, including some in the United States and Australia.

WORK IN PROGRESS: Lakeland Pilgrimage, for Batsford; definitive history of Mt. Everest, for Penguin.

SIDELIGHTS: Walter Unsworth has climbed all the Alps, where he still spends five or six weeks every summer. His other major hobbies are photography and industrial archaeology. His youth books are mainly for older children but he says that they "are not beyond the understanding of a reasonably intelligent adult, as well!"

BIOGRAPHICAL/CRITICAL SOURCES: New Statesman, November, 1968; *Listener,* November 14, 1968; *Times Literary Supplement,* October 16, 1969, October 30, 1970.

*   *   *

UNTERMEYER, Jean Starr   1886-1970

May 13, 1886—July 12, 1970; American poet and former wife of Louis Untermeyer. Obituaries: *New York Times,* July 29, 1970; *Books Abroad,* spring, 1971.

*   *   *

UPHOFF, Norman Thomas   1940-

PERSONAL: Born July 22, 1940, in Madison, Wis.; son of Walter Henry (a professor) and Mary Jo (Weiler) Uphoff; married Marguerite Helen McKay (a physician); children: Elisabeth, Jonathan. *Education:* Attended University of Cologne, 1958-59; University of Minnesota, B.A., 1963; Princeton University, M.P.A., 1966; University of California, Berkeley, Ph.D., 1970. *Religion:* Society of Friends (Quaker). *Home:* 16 Cedar Lane, Ithaca, N.Y. 14850. *Office:* Department of Government, Cornell University, Ithaca, N.Y. 14850.

CAREER: University of California, Berkeley, research political scientist, Institute of International Studies, working on Ghana aid project, 1967-69; Cornell University, Department of Government and Center for International Studies, Ithaca, N.Y., professor of government, 1970—. Consultant on Nigeria project, Education and World Affairs, New York, 1966. *Member:* American Political Science Association, American Civil Liberties Union, Phi Beta Kappa.

WRITINGS: (With Ilchman) *The Political Economy of Change,* University of California Press, 1969; (with Raphael Littauer) *The Air War in Indochina,* Beacon Press, 1972; *The Political Economy of Development: Theoretical and Empirical Contributions,* University of California Press, 1972; *The Student Internationals,* Scarecrow, 1973. Also author with Milton Esman, *Local Organization for Rural Development: Analysis of Asian Experience,* 1974.

WORK IN PROGRESS: The Politics of Development and Experience in Nkrumah's Ghana: Contradicting the Politics of "Modernization" and "Political Order"; comparative research on rural local organization and political participation, with special reference to Sri Lanka.

*   *   *

U'REN-STUBBINGS, Hilda   1914-
(Hilda Uren Stubbings, Hilda U'Ren, Hilda Uren)

PERSONAL: Born December 14, 1914, in Connor Downs, Cornwall, England; daughter of John Percival and Florence Mary (Williams) Uren; married George A. Stubbings, 1935; children: Robert George, Carl Herbert, Katharine Beatrice Mott, Suzanne Joyce Willis. *Education:* Stetson University, B.A., 1960, M.A. (American studies), 1962, M.A. (English), 1965; Florida State University, graduate study, 1963; Vanderbilt University, Ph.D., 1968; George Peabody College for Teachers, M.L.S., 1977. *Address:* Box 881, George Peabody College for Teachers, Nashville, Tenn. 37203; and R. 1, Box 40A, Beaver Creek, Ore. 97004.

CAREER: Willamette University, Salem, Ore., assistant professor of English, 1968-70; Portland State University, Division of Continuing Education, Portland, Ore., bibliographical consultant, 1974-76; Vanderbilt University, Nashville, Tenn., researcher in collections department, 1976—. Bibliographical consultant. *Member:* Modern Language Association of America, American Association of Teachers of Spanish and Portuguese, American Library Association, Phi Beta Kappa.

WRITINGS—Under name Hilda Uren Stubbings: (Compiler) *Renaissance Spain in Its Literary Relations with England and France: A Critical Bibliography,* Vanderbilt University Press, 1969. Several articles have been published under variations of the author's name. Contributor to *Christian Science Monitor* and *An Baner Kernewek* (St. Austell, Cornwall, England).

WORK IN PROGRESS: Annotated comparative bibliographies in Spanish and Celtic literature and in literary thematology; bibliography of scholarly works about women; informal essays on Cornwall and Cornish customs; a bibliography on medieval and Renaissance women; a history of books and libraries during World War II.

SIDELIGHTS: Hilda U'Ren-Stubbings told *CA:* "Before I knew better, I thought that bibliography was a dry-as-dust discipline. But now I see that it has a mystique of its own that is seductive. It is an intensely social activity, paradoxically carried on in general solitude in the deep recesses of libraries. The social aspect can be expressed metaphorically: the compiler is a hostess at a grand feast to which guests of like mind have been invited. One of the hostess' pleasant roles is that of introducing newcomers into this convivial and august society. (Among the newcomers, too, may be publishers!) The guests already there, of course, are the scholars whose works are listed in the bibliography who are meeting these authors and their works for the first time. They have a great deal in common, so the party should be a big success. What hostess does not wish this for every party?

"My conversion to bibliography has led me, also, into a preoccupation with the history of books and libraries (and printing). These are a part of our lives we take so much for granted that bringing new perspectives on them to the general reader can offer much to both the reader and the author. In this perspective, too, the role of the publisher, who is often criticized for his crass commercialism, can be seen as indispensable to the preservation of our book heritage which is at once so fragile and yet so enduring."

AVOCATIONAL INTERESTS: Classical music.

*   *   *

URZIDIL, Johannes   1896-1970

February 3, 1896—November 2, 1970; Czechoslovakian journalist and critic. Obituaries: *New York Times,* November 4, 1970; *Newsday,* November 5, 1970; *Washington Post,* November 5, 1970; *Time,* November 16, 1970; *Books Abroad,* spring, 1971.

*   *   *

USHER, Dan   1934-

PERSONAL: Born May 15, 1934, in Montreal, Quebec, Canada; son of Abe and Rose (Leventhal) Usher; married Samphan Chayarahs, June 27, 1962; children: Ann, David.

Education: McGill University, B.A., 1955; University of Chicago, Ph.D., 1960. *Religion:* Jewish. *Home:* 153 Collingwood, Kingston, Ontario, Canada. *Office:* Department of Economics, Queen's University, Kingston, Ontario, Canada.

CAREER: United Nations Economic Commission for Asia and the Far East, assistant economic affairs officer in Bangkok, Thailand, 1960-61; University of Manchester, Manchester, England, research fellow, 1961-63; Oxford University, Nuffield College, Oxford, England, research fellow, 1963-66; Columbia University, Graduate School of Business, New York, N.Y., assistant professor of economics, 1966-67; Queen's University at Kingston, Kingston, Ontario, associate professor, 1967-69, professor of economics, 1969—. Consultant, Canadian International Development Agency, 1969; consultant in Malaysia, Harvard Development Advisory Service, 1974. *Member:* International Association for Research in Income and Wealth, Canadian Economic Association, American Economic Association.

WRITINGS: The Price Mechanism and the Meaning of National Income Statistics, Clarendon Press, 1968. Contributor to economic journals.

WORK IN PROGRESS: Research in economic theory and national income.

*   *   *

USHER, Stephen   1931-

PERSONAL: Born September 25, 1931, in Swansea, Wales; son of George and Gwendoline (Hounsell) Usher; married Anna Olive Hopkins (a lecturer in mathematics at University of London), January 23, 1959; children: Mark, Alan. *Education:* University College of Swansea, Wales, B.A. (first class honors in classics), 1951, M.A., 1953; University College, London, Ph.D., 1955. *Home:* 9 Willow Walk, Englefield Green, Egham, Surrey, England. *Office:* Royal Holloway College, University of London, Englefield Green, Egham, Surrey, England.

CAREER: Victoria University of Wellington, Wellington, New Zealand, lecturer in classics, 1957-60; University of London, Royal Holloway College, Englefield Green, Surrey, England, lecturer, 1960-73, senior lecturer in classics, 1973—. *Military service:* Royal Air Force, Education Corps, 1955-57; became flying officer. *Member:* Hellenic Society, Classical Association.

WRITINGS: The Historians of Greece and Rome, Hamish Hamilton, 1969, Taplinger, 1970; (contributor) John Higginbotham, editor, *Greek and Latin Literature,* Barnes & Noble, 1969; (editor and translator) Dionysius of Halicarnassus, *Critical Essays,* two volumes, Heinemann, 1974—. Contributor of articles on Isocrates and Lysias to classical journals.

AVOCATIONAL INTERESTS: Music (oboe playing), chess, bridge, squash rackets, tennis, ornithology.

BIOGRAPHICAL/CRITICAL SOURCES: Books and Bookmen, June, 1969; *Times Literary Supplement,* July 17, 1969.

*   *   *

VADAKIN, James C(harles)   1924-

PERSONAL: Born March 8, 1924, in Lima, Ohio; son of James Charles and Grace (Miller) Vadakin; married Ann Willoughby, January 14, 1946; children: Jeffrey. *Education:* Denison University, B.A., 1946; Harvard University,

M.B.A., 1947; Cornell University, Ph.D., 1952. *Politics:* Democrat. *Religion:* Protestant. *Home:* 1450 Ancona Ave., Coral Gables, Fla. 33146. *Office:* Department of Economics, University of Miami, Coral Gables, Fla. 33124.

CAREER: University of Miami, Coral Gables, Fla., associate professor, 1947-49, 1950-57, professor of economics, 1957—, chairman of department, 1961-65, coordinator of Cuban Economic Research Project, 1961—. Arbitrator in labor-management disputes, 1950—; member of panel of arbitrators, Federal Mediation and Conciliation Service and National Mediation Board. *Military service:* U.S. Navy, Supply Corps, 1943-46; became lieutenant junior grade. *Member:* American Economic Association, National Academy of Arbitrators (member of board of governors, 1967-70), American Arbitration Association, Industrial Relations Research Association, Southern Economic Association (Florida correspondent), Harvard Club (Miami; vice-president, 1966-69).

WRITINGS: Family Allowances: An Analysis of Their Development and Implications, University of Miami Press, 1958; *Children, Poverty and Family Allowances,* Basic Books, 1968. Contributor of articles on labor relations and social welfare to periodicals, including *New Republic, Public Interest.*

WORK IN PROGRESS: A textbook on labor relations, for McGraw.

BIOGRAPHICAL/CRITICAL SOURCES: Commonweal, March 14, 1969.

* * *

VAJDA, Stephan 1926-

PERSONAL: Born March 19, 1926, in Budapest, Hungary; son of Ferenc and Maria (Oesterreicher) Vajda; married Eva Szana (a translator), 1949. *Education:* Attended University of Budapest. *Religion:* Roman Catholic. *Home and office:* 9 Bergler Strasse, 21, Vienna, Austria.

CAREER: Abandoned his law studies to become a journalist in Hungary; currently a free-lance writer and art director for television and films for Schoenbrunn Film, Vienna, Austria. *Member:* Oesterreichische Gesellschaft fuer Literatur (Austrian literary society). *Awards, honors:* Georg Mackensen Preis, 1963, for best short story published in Germany; Austrian Ministry of Education awards, 1963, 1964.

WRITINGS: L'Accident (novel), Stock (Paris), 1961; *Budapest AA 338* (novel), Doubleday, 1963. Short stories included in *Anthologie Aldo Martello Milano,* [Italy], 1961, and *Anthologie Neff Verlag Wien,* [Austria], 1963. Author of plays in German for the stage, screen, and television.

WORK IN PROGRESS: A novel for publication by Hoffmann & Campe (Hamburg).†

* * *

VALSAN, E. H. 1933-

PERSONAL: Born August 30, 1933, in Trichur, India; son of E. M. Hariharan and M. K. Narayani; married Srilakshmi Cheruvari, May, 1974. *Education:* University of Madras, B.A., 1953; University of Nagpur, M.A., 1956; Indiana University, Ph.D., 1967. *Politics:* None. *Home:* 19 Bustan, Flat 52, Cairo, Egypt. *Office:* American University in Cairo, 113 Sharia Kasr El-aini, Cairo, Egypt.

CAREER: University of Nagpur, Nagpur, India, lecturer in public administration, 1956-62, acting head of department of

public administration and local self-government, 1958-59; East-West Center, Institute of Advanced Projects, Honolulu, Hawaii, international development research fellow, 1964-66; Indiana University, Bloomington, instructor in political science, 1966-67; American University in Cairo, Cairo, Egypt, assistant professor, 1967-69, associate professor of public administration, 1969-73, professor of management and political science, 1973—. Secretary, World University Service, 1960-62. *Member:* Working Groups on Ethics in Public Administration and on Public Enterprises, International Institute of Administrative Sciences, International Studies Association, Indian Institute of Public Administration (secretary of Nagpur chapter, 1960-62), American Society for Public Administration, Eastern Regional Organization for Public Administration. *Awards, honors:* Student Government Award for Outstanding Teacher, American University in Cairo, 1969, 1970, 1971.

WRITINGS: Community Development Programs and Rural Local Government: Comparative Case Studies of India and the Philippines, Praeger, 1970. Contributor to *Studies in Family Planning,* published by Population Council; also contributor to *Philippine Journal of Public Administration, Labour World, Mathrubhoomi, East-West Center Review,* and *Middle East Management Review.*

WORK IN PROGRESS: Development Administration in Egypt: 1952-1970; and *Leadership for Development: A Theoretical Essay.*

SIDELIGHTS: E. H. Valsan lists his major vocational interests as teaching and research in development administration, and research in the administrative problems of family planning programs. He told *CA:* "The efforts of the rural populations all over the world to improve their lot are major sources of motivation for my studies. The concluding chapter in my book, is, hopefully, only the beginning of an enquiry into the whole realm of developmental leadership." Valsan has traveled extensively in Asia, Europe, the Middle East, and North America.

* * *

VANCE, John Holbrook 1920-
(Jack Vance)

PERSONAL: Born August 28, 1920, in San Francisco, Calif.; son of Charles Albert (a rancher) and Edith (Hoefler) Vance; married Norma Ingold, August 24, 1946; children: John Holbrook II. *Education:* University of California, Berkeley, B.A., 1942. *Politics:* "Above and between Left and Right." *Religion:* None. *Home:* 6383 Valley View Rd., Oakland, Calif. *Agent:* Kirby McCauley, 220 East 26th St., New York, N.Y. 10010.

CAREER: Writer. Worked briefly at one point for Twentieth Century-Fox. *Awards, honors:* Edgar Allan Poe Award, Mystery Writers of America, 1961, for *The Man in the Cage;* Hugo Award, World Science Fiction Convention, 1964, for *The Dragon Masters* and 1967, for *Last Castle;* Nebula Award, Science Fiction Writers of America, 1967, for *Last Castle.*

WRITINGS: The Man in the Cage, Random House, 1960; *Valley of the Flame,* Ace Books, 1964; *The Fox Valley Murders,* Bobbs-Merrill, 1966; *The Pleasant Grove Murders,* Bobbs-Merrill, 1967; *The Deadly Isles,* Bobb-Merrill, 1969.

Under name Jack Vance: *The Dying Earth,* Hillman, 1950; *Vandals of the Void,* Winston, 1953; *The Space Pirate,* Toby Press, 1953; *To Live Forever,* Ballantine, 1956; *Take*

My Face, Avalon, 1957; *Big Planet,* Ace Books, 1957; *Slaves of the Klau,* Ace Books, 1958; *The Languages of Pao,* Avalon, 1958.

The Five Gold Bands [and] *The Dragon Masters,* Ace Books, 1962; *The Star King,* Berkley Publishing, 1964; *The Houses of Iszm* [and] *Son of the Tree,* Ace Books, 1964; *Future Tense,* Ballantine, 1964; *The Killing Machine,* Berkley Publishing, 1964; *Space Opera,* Pyramid Publications, 1965; *Monsters in Orbit* [and] *The World between and Other Stories,* Ace Books, 1965; *The Brains of Earth* [and] *The Many Worlds of Magnus Ridolph,* Ace Books, 1966; *The Blue World,* Ballantine, 1966; *The Eyes of the Overworld,* Ace Books, 1966; *The Palace of Love,* Berkley Publishing, 1967; *The Last Castle* [and] *World of the Sleeper,* the latter by Tony R. Wayman, Ace Books, 1967; *Eight Fantasms and Magics: A Science Fiction Adventure,* Macmillan, 1969; *Emphyrio,* Doubleday, 1969.

The Worlds of Jack Vance, Ace Books, 1973; (contributor) *Three Trips in Time and Space: Original Novellas of Science Fiction,* Hawthorn Books, 1973; *Bad Ronald,* Ballantine, 1973; *The Gray Prince,* Bobbs-Merrill, 1974; *Showboat World,* Pyramid Publications, 1975; *The Best of Jack Vance,* Pocket Books, 1976; *Mask: Thaery,* Berkley Publications, 1976.

"Planet of Adventure" series; published by Ace Books: *City of the Chasch,* 1968; *Servants of the Wankh,* Ace Books, 1969; *The Dirdir,* 1969; *The Pnume,* 1970.

"Durdane" cycle; published by Dell: *The Anome,* 1973; *The Brave Free Men,* 1973; *The Asutra,* 1974.

"Alastor" cycle; published by Ballantine: *Trullion: Alastor 2262,* 1973; *Marune: Alastor 933,* 1975; *Wyst: Alastor 1716,* in press.

Author of television scripts for "Captain Video." Contributor of fiction to periodicals.

WORK IN PROGRESS: The first book in the "Demon Prince" series.

BIOGRAPHICAL/CRITICAL SOURCES: Best Sellers, June 15, 1966, November 1, 1967, May 1, 1968; *Saturday Review,* June 25, 1966, October 28, 1967, August 30, 1969; *New York Times Book Review,* July 3, 1966, September 10, 1967, May 25, 1969; *Booklist,* March 1, 1970, July 1, 1976; *Magazine of Fantasy and Science Fiction,* April, 1970; *Times Literary Supplement,* July 16, 1970; *Village Voice,* June 13, 1974; *Psychology Today,* June, 1975; *Observer,* April 4, 1976; *Kirkus Review,* August 15, 1976.

*   *   *

VANCE, Samuel 1939-

PERSONAL: Born March 15, 1939, in Douglas County, Ga.; son of Julius (a post office employee) and Essie (Lovett) Vance; married June 20, 1962; wife's name, Barbara (divorced); children: Gary Duryea. *Education:* Attended high school, 1956-69. *Religion:* Baptist.

CAREER: U.S. Army, 1960-69, leaving service as staff sergeant; Grady Memorial Hospital, Atlanta, Ga., computer program analyst, beginning 1969. *Awards, honors*—Military: Purple Heart and Silver Star.

WRITINGS: The Courageous and the Proud, Norton, 1970.

WORK IN PROGRESS: A novel tentatively entitled *Triumph without Glory.*

AVOCATIONAL INTERESTS: Photography, swimming, fishing.††

VANDENBERG, Donald 1931-

PERSONAL: Born August 4, 1931, in Milwaukee, Wis.; son of Richard Arthur (a police officer) and Elsie (Scheamann) Vandenberg; married Erma Jean Pinkston, May 19, 1955; children: Marta, Donald, Sara. *Education:* Maryville College, Maryville, Tenn., B.A., 1958; University of Wisconsin, M.A., 1961; University of Illinois, Ph.D., 1966. *Politics:* None. *Religion:* None. *Home:* 12 Salisbury St., Indooroopilly, Queensland, Australia 4068. *Office:* University of Queensland, Brisbane, Queensland, Australia 4067.

CAREER: High school English teacher in Whitehall, Mich., 1960-62; University of Calgary, Calgary, Alberta, assistant professor of education, 1965-68; Pennsylvania State University, University Park, associate professor of philosophy of education, 1968-72; faculty member at University of Calgary, 1972-73, and University of California, Los Anegles, 1973-76; University of Queensland, Brisbane, Queensland, Australia, reader in education, 1976—. *Military service:* U.S. Navy, 1949-53. *Member:* Philosophy of Education Society, John Dewey Society, Society for Phenomenology and Existential Philosophy, Society of Professors of Education.

WRITINGS: (Editor) *Teaching and Learning,* University of Illinois Press, 1969; (editor) *Theory of Knowledge and Problems of Education,* University of Illinois Press, 1969; *Being and Education: An Essay in Existential Phenomenology,* Prentice-Hall, 1971; (contributor) D. Denton, editor, *Existentialism and Phenomenology in Education,* Teachers College Press, 1974; (contributor) D. Nyberg, editor, *The Philosophy of Open Education,* Routledge & Kegan Paul, 1975. Contributor to education journals. Reviewer, *Educational Forum.*

WORK IN PROGRESS: The Philosophy of Learning.

*   *   *

VanDerBEETS, Richard 1932-

PERSONAL: Born December 6, 1932, in Los Angeles, Calif.; son of Richard McClellen and Ruth (Nye) VanDerBeets; married Marlene Balogh, July 23, 1959 (divorced); children: Dirk, Scott, Ruth, Mark. *Education:* San Jose State College (now University), B.A., 1959; University of Idaho, M.A., 1961; University of the Pacific, Ph.D., 1973. *Home:* 998 Meridian Ave., San Jose, Calif. 95126. *Office:* Department of English, San Jose State University, San Jose, Calif. 95114.

CAREER: Instructor in English at University of Idaho, Moscow, 1963-64, Menlo College, Menlo Park, Calif., 1964-65, and Robert College, Istanbul, Turkey, 1965-66; San Jose State University, San Jose, Calif., assistant professor, 1966-74, associate professor of English, 1974—. *Military service:* U.S. Navy, 1952-56. *Member:* Modern Language Association of America, American Studies Association, American Association of University Professors.

WRITINGS: A Guide to Henry James's "The Ambassadors," Barnes & Noble, 1969; (editor with James Keith Bowen) *American Short Fiction: Readings and Criticism,* Bobbs-Merrill, 1970; (editor with Bowen) *"Adventures of Huckleberry Finn": An Edition,* Scott, Foresman, 1970; (editor with Bowen) *A Critical Guide to Herman Melville,* Scott, Foresman, 1971; *Drama: A Critical Collection,* Harper, 1972; *Classic Short Fiction,* Bobbs-Merrill, 1972; *Held Captive by Indians,* University of Tennessee Press, 1973. Contributor to literature journals. Co-editor, *American Literature Abstracts,* 1967-72.

WORK IN PROGRESS: Three books, *The Indian Captivity Narrative, An American Genre,* and *The Indian in American Literature, 1607-1783.*

*   *   *

VAN DER SLIK, Jack R(onald) 1936-

PERSONAL: Born December 14, 1936, in Kalamazoo, Mich.; son of Julius Henry (a tool and die salesman) and Cornelia (Koopsen) Van Der Slik; married Gertrude Jane Bonnema, June 29, 1963; children: Franci Lynn, Gary Jon, Randall Martin. *Education:* Calvin College, A.B., 1958; Western Michigan University, A.M., 1961; Michigan State University, A.M., 1966, Ph.D., 1967. *Religion:* Christian Reformed. *Home:* 45 Hillcrest Dr., Carbondale, Ill. 62901. *Office:* Department of Political Science, Southern Illinois University, Carbondale, Ill. 62901.

CAREER: Junior high school teacher in California Christian schools, 1958-60; high school teacher in Colorado Christian schools, 1961-62; Southern Illinois University, Carbondale, Ill., assistant professor, 1967-71, associate professor of political science, 1971—, acting chairperson of department, 1975, associate dean of College of Liberal Arts, 1975—. Visiting associate professor, Calvin College, 1972-73. Research fellow, Illinois Legislative Council, Springfield, 1969-70. *Member:* American Political Science Association, Midwest Political Science Association, Southern Political Science Association, Southwestern Social Science Association.

WRITINGS: (Editor) *Black Conflict with White America: A Reader in Social and Political Analysis,* C. E. Merrill, 1970; (editor with Stephen V. Monsma) *American Politics: Research and Readings,* Holt, 1970; (with David Kenney and Samuel J. Pernacciaro) *Roll Call!: Patterns of Voting in the Sixth Illinois Constitutional Convention,* University of Illinois Press, 1975; *American Legislative Processes,* Crowell, 1977.

Contributor of articles to *Social Science Quarterly, Business and Government Review, Political Science Quarterly, American Journal of Political Science,* and *Journal of Political Science.*

WORK IN PROGRESS: A study of citizen witnesses who have appeared before committees of the U.S. House of Representatives.

*   *   *

VANDERWOOD, Paul J.

PERSONAL: Born in Brooklyn, New York; son of Joseph and Mildred (Horstman) Vanderwood. *Education:* Bethany College, Bethany, W.Va., B.A., 1950; New York University, graduate study, 1953-54; Memphis State University, M.A., 1957; University of Texas, Ph.D., 1970. *Home:* 6851 Mohawk St., San Diego, Calif. 92115. *Office:* Department of History, San Diego State University, San Diego, Calif. 92115.

CAREER: Memphis Press-Scimitar, Memphis, Tenn., reporter, 1954-63; Peace Corps evaluator, 1963; San Diego State University, San Diego, Calif., 1969—, began as assistant professor, currently associate professor of history. *Military service:* U.S. Army, 1951-63; became lieutenant. *Member:* American Historical Association.

WRITINGS: Night Riders of Reelfoot Lake, Memphis State University Press, 1969. Contributor of articles and reviews to newspapers and scholarly journals.

WORK IN PROGRESS: "A book on the role of the con-

stabulary in a modernizing nation with emphasis on Mexico; a book on the relationship between Hollywood and the Federal Government with emphasis on how various forces mold the characterizations of historical figures in cinema."

*   *   *

VAN DE VALL, Mark 1923-

PERSONAL: Born January 20, 1923, in Heiloo, Netherlands; divorced; children: Renee, Monique. *Education:* Municipal University of Amsterdam, B.A., 1950, M.A., 1955, Ph.D., 1963. *Office:* Department of Sociology, University of Leyden, Stationsweg 46, Leyden, Netherlands.

CAREER: State University of New York at Buffalo, professor of sociology, 1963-77; University of Leyden, Leyden, Netherlands, professor of sociology, 1977—. Research fellow at Department of Health, Education and Welfare, Washington, D.C., 1969-71; visiting professor at University of Leyden, Netherlands, 1971. Associate, Kirschner Associates, Inc., Albuquerque and Washington, D.C. *Member:* International Industrial Relations Association, American Sociological Association, Industrial Relations Research Association, American Association of University Professors.

WRITINGS: De Vakbeweging in de Welvaartsstaat, J. A. Boom (Meppel), 1963, translation published as *Labor Organizations: A Macro- and Micro-Sociological Analysis on a Comparative Basis,* Cambridge University Press, 1970.

Contributor: H. Matthes, editor, *Soziologie and Gesellschaft in den Niederlanden,* Luchterhand Verlag (Neuwied/Rhein), 1965; Milton Albrecht, editor, *Studies in Sociology,* Buffalo Studies, 1967; Desmond Graves, editor, *Management Research: A Cross-Cultural Perspective,* Jossey Bass, 1973; Frank Baker and H. C. Schulberg, editors, *Program Evaluation in the Health Fields,* Behavioral Publications, 1977. Contributor to *Proceedings* of 17th and 22nd annual meetings of Industrial Relations Research Association. Contributor of over thirty articles and reports on sociological and political science subjects, in Dutch, German, French, and English, to periodicals.

WORK IN PROGRESS: With Charles D. King, *Roads to Industrial Democracy: Workers' Participation in Great Britain, West Germany and Yugoslavia;* with Cheryl Bolas, *Policy Research: Methodology and Utilization,* a research monograph.

*   *   *

VAN DYKE, Jon M. 1943-

PERSONAL: Born April 29, 1943, in Washington, D.C.; son of Stuart H. (a diplomat and economist) and Eleanora (Markham) Van Dyke. *Education:* Yale University, B.A., 1964; Harvard University, J.D., 1967. *Office:* School of Law, University of Hawaii, Honolulu, Hawaii 96822.

CAREER: Catholic University of America, Washington, D.C., assistant professor of law, 1967-69; California Supreme Court, San Francisco, law clerk to chief justice, 1969-70; affiliated with Center for the Study of Democratic Institutions, Santa Barbara, Calif., 1970-71; University of California, Hastings College of the Law, San Francisco, 1971-76, began as associate professor, became professor; University of Hawaii, School of Law, Honolulu, professor, 1976—. *Member:* American Society of International Law, U.S. Institute on Human Rights.

WRITINGS: North Vietnam's Strategy for Survival, Pacific Books, 1972; *Jury Selection Procedures: Our Uncer-*

tain Commitment to Representative Panels, Ballinger, 1977. Contributor of numerous articles to legal and professional publications.

WORK IN PROGRESS: Casebook on International Law; an article on land problems in Hawaii.

* * *

Van DYKE, Lauren A.   1906-

PERSONAL: Born November 24, 1906, in Sioux City, Iowa; son of Heiman (a contractor) and Mabel (Crouch) Van Dyke; married Mildred Wade, May 30, 1933; children: Gardner. *Education:* Morningside College, A.B., 1928; University of Missouri, M.A., 1934, Ph.D., 1941. *Politics:* Democrat. *Religion:* Methodist. *Home:* Route 6, Iowa City, Iowa. *Office:* School of Education, University of Iowa, Iowa City, Iowa 52240.

CAREER: Teacher in Lohrville, Iowa, 1928-30; principal-superintendent in Monroe City, Mo., 1930-35; high school principal in Sedalia, Mo., 1935-38; Missouri State Department of Education, Jefferson City, assistant superintendent, 1938-41; University of Iowa, Iowa City, assistant professor, 1941-68, professor and associate dean of education, 1968—. Fulbright lecturer, University of Santo Tomas, 1949-50. *Member:* National Education Association, American Association of School Administrators, National Association of Secondary-School Principals, North Central Association of Colleges and Secondary Schools (president, 1967-68), Rotary, Masons. *Awards, honors:* Distinguished Service Award in Education, University of Missouri, 1965.

WRITINGS: (With Earl McGrath) *Toward General Education,* Macmillan, 1948; *General Education in the Philippine Public High Schools,* U.S. Educational Foundation, 1950; (with K. B. Hoyt) *The Drop-Out Problem in Iowa High Schools,* University of Iowa, 1958; (with Lester W. Anderson) *Secondary School Administration,* Houghton, 1963, revised edition, 1973. Also author of a number of handbooks on various aspects of public schools in Missouri.

* * *

VAN HECKE, B(resee) C(oleman)   1926-

PERSONAL: Born November 9, 1926, in Fairview, Mont.; son of Floran Louie (an evangelist) and Quay (Whitley) Van Hecke; married Timandra Courtney, November 9, 1949 (deceased). *Education:* Attended San Francisco City College for two years. *Politics:* Republican. *Religion:* Interdenominational.

CAREER: Owner and manager of a real estate firm in Los Angeles, Calif. *Military service:* U.S. Navy, 1946-48.

WRITINGS: (With Ray Lee) *Gangsters and Hoodlums: The Underworld in the Cinema,* A. S. Barnes, 1971; (with Lee) *The Detectives,* A. S. Barnes, 1971.

WORK IN PROGRESS: Studies of the history of wars, religion, and Shakespeare in films; and a book about "the royal family of Hollywood," the Barrymores.

SIDELIGHTS: B. C. Van Hecke told *CA* that he is "considered a movie historian," and owns a library of 40,000 movie stills, from both the silent and sound eras. He has also "done extensive research for various writers . . . some of this for Mr. George Jessel."†

* * *

Van HOOK, Roger Eugene   1943-

PERSONAL: Born February 7, 1943, in Long Beach, Calif.;

son of Beverly Eugene (an engineer) and Yvonne (Barnett) Van Hook; married Diane Gracia Ohman. *Education:* Long Beach City College, A.A., 1964; California State College at Long Beach (now California State University, Long Beach), A.B., 1966, M.A., 1968. *Politics:* Democrat. *Religion:* Unitarian Universalist. *Home:* 735 Carmel Ave., Seal Beach, Calif. 90740. *Office:* Long Beach City College, Long Beach, Calif. 90808.

CAREER: Long Beach City College, Long Beach, Calif., associate professor of speech communication, 1967—. President, Creative Promotions, Long Beach, 1969. *Member:* National Education Association, California Teachers Association, Teachers Association of Long Beach, American Association of University Professors.

WRITINGS: (With Julie McElhiney) *Comprehensive Rhetorical Guidelines,* McCutchan, 1969; *Communicate* (textbook), Kendall/Hunt, 1976.

* * *

VANN, J(erry) Don   1938-

PERSONAL: Born January 17, 1938, in Weatherford, Tex.; son of John Robert (an engineer) and Ruby (Wood) Vann; married Dolores Warden, June 11, 1958; children: John Christopher Alan, Vanessa. *Education:* Texas Christian University, B.A., 1959, M.A., 1960; Texas Technological College (now Texas Tech University), Ph.D., 1967. *Home:* 811 West Oak, Denton, Tex. 76201. *Office:* Department of English, North Texas State University, Denton, Tex. 76203.

CAREER: North Texas State University, Denton, instructor, 1964-67, assistant professor, 1967-71, associate professor of literature, 1971—. *Member:* Modern Language Association of America, Modern Humanities Research Association, Research Society for Victorian Periodicals. *Awards, honors:* American Philosophical Association research grant, 1971.

WRITINGS: (With James T. F. Tanner) *Samuel Beckett: A Checklist,* Kent State University Press, 1969; *Graham Greene: A Checklist of Criticism,* Kent State University Press, 1970; (editor) *Critics on Henry James,* University of Miami Press, 1971. Contributor to professional journals. Bibliographer, Research Society for Victorian Periodicals.

WORK IN PROGRESS: Dickens and the Reviewers, researched in British Museum Library.

* * *

Van NESS, Peter   1933-

PERSONAL: Born March 26, 1933, in Paterson, N.J. *Education:* Williams College, B.A., 1955; University of California, Berkeley, M.A., 1961, Ph.D., 1967. *Office:* Graduate School of International Studies, University of Denver, Denver, Colo. 80210.

CAREER: University of Denver, Graduate School of International Studies, Denver, Colo., assistant professor, 1966-70, associate professor of international studies, 1970—. Associate of Center for Chinese Studies, University of Michigan. Member of board of directors, National Committee on United States-China Relations. *Awards, honors:* Woodrow Wilson International Center for Scholars fellowship, Smithsonian Institution, 1973-74.

WRITINGS: Revolution and Chinese Foreign Policy: Peking's Support for Wars of National Liberation, University of California Press, 1970.

WORK IN PROGRESS: People's China and the Third World: A Political Economy of Maoist Foreign Policy, 1949-1969, with Satish Raichur.

SIDELIGHTS: Revolution and Chinese Foreign Policy has been published in a Spanish edition.

* * *

van OORT, Jan 1921-
(Jean Dulieu)

PERSONAL: Born April 13, 1921, in Amsterdam, Netherlands; married M. M. Sijmons (his assistant in production of puppet films), July 8, 1943; children: Dorinde, Annelies, Francesco. *Education:* Studied at Conservatorium for Music, Amsterdam, 1935-40. *Home:* de Genestetlaan 18, Soest, Netherlands.

CAREER: Violinist in Amsterdam, Netherlands, playing for opera orchestra, 1941-44, and with Concertgebouw Orkest, 1944-46; free-lance writer and illustrator, radio actor, and puppeteer, 1946—; currently writing the scripts, making the puppets, and doing the animation as producer of puppet films for television. *Member:* Vereniging van Letterkundigen (writer's organization; member of board, 1960-65), Maatschappy van Letterkunde, P.E.N. *Awards, honors:* Prize from Youth Friends Association (New York), 1956, and Diploma of Merit in International Hans Christian Andersen Awards, 1958, both for *Francesco; Paulus de hulpsinterklaas* was named best children's book of the year in the Netherlands, 1962; Edison award for best recording for children, 1962.

WRITINGS—All under pseudonym Jean Dulieu; all self-illustrated: *Het winterboek van Paulus,* Arbeiderspers, 1948; *Francesco* (biography of Saint Francis of Assisi), van der Peet, 1956; *Paulus en Kenarrepoere,* van der Peet, 1957; *Paulus en Priegeltje,* van der Peet, 1957; *De verrassing,* van der Peet, 1959; *Het Ei,* van der Peet, 1959; *Het klaaghemd,* van der Peet, 1959.

Puntnik en andere verhalen, van der Peet, 1960; *Paulus de hulpsinterklaas,* Ploegsma, 1962; *Paulus en Eucalypta,* Ploegsma, 1962; *Paulus en het Levenswater,* Ploegsma, 1962; *Paulus en Joris het vispaard,* Ploegsma, 1962; *Paulus en Mol,* Ploegsma, 1962, translation by Marian Powell published as *Paulus and Mole,* World's Work (England), 1965; *Paulus en Wawwa,* Ploegsma, 1962; *Paulus en de 3 rovers,* Ploegsma, 1963, translation by Powell published as *Paulus and the Three Robbers,* World's Work, 1965; *Paulus en Pieter,* Ploegsma, 1963; *Paulus en Salomo,* Ploegsma, 1963, translation by Powell published as *Paulus and Solomon,* World's Work, 1965; *Paulus en het draakje,* 1964; *Paulus en de Eikelmannetjes,* Ploegsma, 1965, translation by the author, assisted by T.D.R. Thomason and Patricia Tracy Lowe, published as *Paulus and the Acornmen,* World Publishing, 1966; *Paulus en schipper Makreel,* Ploegsma, 1964; *Poetepoet,* Ploegsma, 1965; *Kevertje Plop,* van Goor Zonen, 1966, translation by the author, assisted by Thomason and Lowe, published as *The Adventures of Beetlekin the Brave,* World Publishing, 1966.

Het Eukelknijn, Holkema en Warendorf, 1970; *Japie de Eenhoorn,* Holkema en Warendorf, 1970; *Het Oliebollenfeest,* Holkema en Warendorf, 1970; *De Rokomobiel,* Holkema en Warendorf, 1970; *Heksenvakantie,* Holkema en Warendorf, 1970; *De reus Worrelsik,* Holkema en Warendorf, 1970; *De Beren,* Holkema en Warendorf, 1971; *Het Boomspook,* Holkema en Warendorf, 1971; *De Bruiloft,* Holkema en Warendorf, 1971; *De Bergbouters,* Holkema en Warendorf, 1971.

Scripts include 750 short radio plays for children, and forty puppet films for television. Creator and illustrator of a daily comic strip appearing in *Vrije Volk* (Amsterdam) for more than twelve years; writer of weekly illustrated stories for *Eva* (Leiden) for six years, and for *Margriet* (Amsterdam) for two years; currently author and illustrator of a daily comic strip appearing in twenty journals; also author and illustrator of stories for *Bobo* (weekly publication); contributor of more than 150 illustrated short stories to *Kris Kras* (children's journal published in Amsterdam).

SIDELIGHTS: Jan van Oort's books also have been translated for publication in Indonesia, Sweden, South Africa, Japan, and Germany.

* * *

VAUGHAN, Harold Cecil 1923-

PERSONAL: Born October 26, 1923, in New York, N.Y.; son of Harold Cecil and Anna (Gosler) Vaughan. *Education:* Columbia University, A.B., 1943, M.A., 1947, graduate study, 1947-48. *Politics:* Democrat. *Religion:* None. *Home:* 2200 North Central Rd., Fort Lee, N.J. 07024.

CAREER: Brooklyn Friends School, Brooklyn, N.Y., teacher of history and social studies, 1950-59; Ridgewood Board of Education, Ridgewood, N.J., teacher of history and social studies, 1959—. Lecturer to many organizations, including Colonial Dames, Daughters of the American Revolution, Contemporary Club, Junior League of New York, and Long Island Historical Association. *Military service:* U.S. Army Air Force, 1943-44.

WRITINGS—Youth books; all published by F. Watts: *The Citizen Genet Affair, 1793: A Chapter in the Formation of American Foreign Policy,* 1970; *The Hayes-Tilden Election of 1876: A Disputed Election in the Gilded Age,* 1971; *The XYZ Affair, 1797-98: The Diplomacy of the Adams Administration and an Undeclared War with France,* 1972; *The Monroe Doctrine, 1823,* 1973; *The Colony of Georgia,* 1975; *The Versailles Treaty, 1919,* 1975; *The Constitutional Convention, 1787: The Beginning of Federal Government in America,* 1976.

WORK IN PROGRESS: Currently doing research on a book concerning the Declaration of Independence.

SIDELIGHTS: Harold Vaughan has traveled extensively throughout Europe, Canada, and the United States.

* * *

VAUGHAN, Paul 1925-

PERSONAL: Born October 24, 1925, in Brixton, London, England; son of Albert George (an association secretary) and Ada Rose (Stocks) Vaughan; married Barbara Prys-Jones, August 11, 1951; children: Kate Amanda, Timothy Owain, Matthew David, Lucy Elizabeth. *Education:* Wadham College, Oxford, B.A., 1944, M.A., 1948. *Politics:* "Lifetime Supporter of Labour Party." *Religion:* Agnostic. *Home:* 17 Courthope Rd., Wimbledon, London S.W.19, England; and Lower Draintewion, Llandinam, Montgomeryshire, Wales. *Agent:* A. P. Watt & Son, 26-28 Bedford Row, London WC1R 4HL, England.

CAREER: British Medical Association, London, England, chief press officer, 1959-64; free-lance journalist, London, 1964-70; *World Medicine,* London, deputy editor, 1970-73; free-lance journalist, London, 1973—. Appears on radio and television, presenting "Kaleidoscope," "Horizon," and other programs. *Military service:* British Army, 1944-47; became sergeant. *Member:* Medical Journalists Association (deputy chairman, 1967-71, chairman, 1971-73), Association of British Science Writers, National Union of Journalists.

WRITINGS: Doctors Commons, Heinemann, 1959; *Family Planning,* Queen Anne Press, 1969; *The Pill on Trial,* Coward, 1970. Contributor to newspapers and journals.

SIDELIGHTS: Paul Vaughan has made numerous radio and television broadcasts in England, including "Kaleidoscope," a regular radio program, and "Horizon," a regular television presentation. *Avocational interests:* Playing the clarinet, reading, movies, enjoying the Welsh countryside.

*   *   *

VELVEL, Lawrence R.   1939-

PERSONAL: Born September 7, 1939, in Chicago, Ill.; son of Herman R. and Ann (Molin) Velvel; married Louise Rose, June 17, 1962; children: Douglas, Kathryn. *Education:* University of Michigan, B.A., 1960, J.D., 1963. *Office:* School of Law, Catholic University of America, Washington, D.C. 20017.

CAREER: U.S. Department of Justice, Washington, D.C., attorney, 1963-66; assistant to Senator William Proxmire of Wisconsin, Washington, D.C., 1966; University of Kansas Law School, Lawrence, assistant professor, 1966-69, associate professor, 1969-70, professor of law, beginning 1970; currently affiliated with School of Law, Catholic University of America, Washington, D.C. *Member:* American Society of International Law (member of Civil War panel), Lawyers Committee on American Policy Towards Vietnam (member of consultative council), National Committee on Preventive Detention, Legal Action Fund for Peace, Constitutional Lawyers' Committee on Undeclared War (founder and chairman), Order of the Coif.

WRITINGS: (Contributor) R. A. Falk, *The Vietnam War and International Law,* Princeton University Press, 1969; *Undeclared War and Civil Disobedience: The American System in Crisis,* Dunellen, 1970; (contributor) John M. Wells and Maria Wilhelm, editors, *The People vs. Presidential War,* Dunellen, 1970; (contributor) H. A. Bosmajian, *The Principles and Practice of Freedom of Speech,* Houghton, 1971. Contributor to law reviews. Former assistant editor, *University of Michigan Law Review.*

WORK IN PROGRESS: Systemic Problems; and a book on the recent work of the U.S. Supreme Court.†

*   *   *

VENABLE, Tom C(alvin)   1921-

PERSONAL: Born December 1, 1921, in Bowling Green, Ky.; son of Calvin Earl (a pharmacist) and Nina (Stone) Venable; married Helen Botts (a librarian), October 9, 1943; children: Tom Calvin, Jr., Bonnie (Mrs. Ed Chickadaunce), Bradford. *Education:* Western Kentucky University, A.B. and M.A., 1947; George Peabody College for Teachers, Ph.D., 1953. *Politics:* Democratic. *Religion:* Presbyterian. *Home:* 90 Heritage Dr., Terre Haute, Ind. 47803. *Office:* Indiana State University, Terre Haute, Ind. 47809.

CAREER: Murray State University, Murray, Ky., faculty member, 1950-51, 1952-56, started as assistant professor, became associate professor; Kentucky State Department of Education, Frankfort, supervisor, 1951-52; Indiana State University, Terre Haute, professor of education, 1956-68, assistant dean, 1968—. *Military service:* U.S. Army Air Forces, 1942-45; became first lieutenant.

WRITINGS: Patterns of Secondary School Curriculum, Harper, 1958; *Philosophical Foundations of Curriculum,* Rand McNally, 1967.

*   *   *

VENTURI, Marcello   1925-

PERSONAL: Born April 21, 1925, in Lucca, Italy; son of Ugolino and Adelina (Della Nina) Venturi; married Camilla Salvago Raggi (a writer), February 10, 1960. *Education:* Studied foreign languages at University of Milan. *Religion:* Roman Catholic. *Home:* Villa Campale, Molare, Italy 15074. *Agent:* Eric Linder, Corso Matteotti 3, Milan, Italy 20121.

CAREER: Journalist in Italy, 1948-56; Giangiacomo Feltrinelli (publishers), Milan, Italy, literary adviser, 1956-64. *Awards, honors:* Premio Viareggio, 1952, for *Dalla Sirte a casa mia;* Premio Saint Vincent, 1957, for journalism; Premio Puccini-Senigallia, 1965, for *Gli anni e gli inganni;* Premio Chianciano, 1967, for *L'appuntamento;* Premio Bancarellino, 1967, for *L'ultimo veliero;* Premio Civinini, 1970, for *Piu lontane stazioni.*

WRITINGS: Dalla Sirte a casa mia, Macchia, 1952; *Il treno degli Appennini,* Einaudi, 1956; *Vacanza tedesca,* Feltrinelli, 1959; *L'ultimo veliero,* Einaudi, 1961; *Bandiera bianca a Cefalonia,* Feltrinelli, 1963, translation by William Clowes published as *The White Flag,* Anthony Blond, 1966, Vanguard, 1969; *Gli anni e gli inganni,* Feltrinelli, 1965; *L'appuntamento,* Rizzoli, 1967; *Piu lontane stazioni,* Rizzoli, 1970; *Terra di nessuno,* Rizzoli, 1975.

WORK IN PROGRESS: A novel about his own personal experiences in the country of Monferrato (Piemonte), and his training as a farmer among a species in extinction such as Italian laborers during the last twenty years.

SIDELIGHTS: Marcello Venturi left the Communist Party "after the Hungarian facts and the revelations on Stalinism." The recurrent theme of many of his novels is war. "I dare say this is the fact which most appeals to me," he explains, "especially in regard [to] man as victim of violence." This is also the theme of his latest novel, *Terra di nessuno,* in which, he continues, "there is a young man, born during the last world-war, who does not know whether his father is a German or an American soldier, and in his quest of an identity ends up by committing an absurd crime."

*   *   *

VERGARA, Joseph R.   1915-

PERSONAL: Born July 13, 1915, in New York, N.Y.; son of Rosario (a shoemaker) and Lena (Corio) Vergara; married Mildred A. Olson, May 27, 1944. *Education:* City College (now City College of the City University of New York), B.A., 1937; Stanford University, additional study. *Home:* 8630 Sancho St., Hollis, N.Y. 11423.

CAREER: Professional piano player, New York City, 1933-40; Harper & Row, Publishers, Inc., New York City, editor, specializing in general non-fiction, 1946—. Instructor in Extension Division, City College (now City College of the City University of New York), 1950-54. *Military service:* U.S. Army, Signal Corps, 1942-46; became second lieutenant. *Member:* Authors Guild, Hundred Million Club (vice-president, 1960-61), Dutch Treat Club.

WRITINGS: Love and Pasta, Harper, 1968. Contributor to *Encyclopedia Americana* and *Grolier's Encyclopedia;* also contributor to *Reader's Digest, Catholic Digest,* and *Publishers' Weekly.*

WORK IN PROGRESS: A second autobiographical book with an Italian immigrant background.

SIDELIGHTS: Joseph R. Vergara travels extensively in Europe and Near East for material as well as pleasure. He is competent in French, Spanish, and Italian. He says *Love and Pasta* was suggested by Barzini's *The Italians.*

BIOGRAPHICAL/CRITICAL SOURCES: The House of Harper, Harper, 1967; *New York Post,* June 29, 1968.

* * *

VESAAS, Tarjei 1897-1970

1897—March 15, 1970; Norwegian poet, novelist, playwright, and short story writer. Obituaries: *New York Times,* March 16, 1970; *Antiquarian Bookman,* April 6, 1970; *Books Abroad,* spring, 1971.

* * *

VETTER, Harold J. 1926-

PERSONAL: Born March 31, 1926, in Buffalo, N.Y.; son of Harold John (a clerical worker) and Gladys (Bates) Vetter; married Virginia Rose, April 24, 1964. *Education:* University of Buffalo (now State University of New York at Buffalo), B.A. (summa cum laude), 1949, Ph.D., 1955. *Agent:* Harry Altshuler, 225 West 86th St., New York, N.Y. 10024. *Office:* Department of Criminal Justice, University of South Florida, Tampa, Fla. 33620.

CAREER: University of Maryland Overseas Program, assistant professor of psychology in European Division, 1955-58, lecturer in Far East Division, 1959-63; Sophia University, Japan, lecturer in International Division, 1963-64; University of Maryland, College Park, assistant professor, 1964-68, associate professor of psychology, 1964-69; Florida State University, Tallahassee, associate professor of criminology, 1969-71; Loyola University, New Orleans, La., professor of psychology, 1971-74, chairman of department, 1972-74; University of South Florida, Tampa, director of graduate studies in department of criminal justice, 1974—. Former Peace Corps field assessment officer and Neighborhood Youth Corps project director. Consultant to U.S. Veterans Administration, 1965-72, and to Maryland Department of Public Hygiene, 1965-67. Member of Florida Governor's Commission Task Force on Law Enforcement. *Military service:* U.S. Navy, 1942-46. *Member:* American Psychological Association, Linguistic Society of America, American Association of University Professors, Phi Beta Kappa.

WRITINGS: Women of the Swastika, Regency Press, 1963; *Mutiny at Koje Island,* Tuttle, 1965; (editor) *Language Behavior in Schizophrenia,* C. C Thomas, 1968; *Language Behavior and Communication: An Introduction,* F. E. Peacock, 1969; *Language Behavior and Psychopathology,* Rand McNally, 1969.

(With B. D. Smith) *Personality Theory: A Sourcebook,* Appleton, 1970; *Psychology of Abnormal Behavior,* Ronald, 1972; (with Jack Wright, Jr.) *Introduction to Criminology,* C. C Thomas, 1972, 2nd edition, 1977; (with Richard Howell) *Language in Behavior,* Behavioral Publications, 1975; (with C. E. Simonsen) *Criminal Justice in America: The System, the Process, the People,* Saunders, 1976; (with Ira Silverman) *The Nature of Crime,* Saunders, 1977. Consulting editor to *Journal of Psycholinguistic Research* and to International Textbook Co.

SIDELIGHTS: Harold Vetter's first two books grew out of travel and residence in Europe and the Far East, 1955-64. *Avocational interests:* Sailing.

VICHAS, Robert P. 1933-

PERSONAL: Surname is pronounced *Vick*-us; born September 26, 1933; son of Peter (a businessman) and Idalene (Cooper) Vichas; married Dolores M. Flores Castellon, June 26, 1965. *Education:* Louisiana State University, B.S., 1965; University of the Americas, Mexico City, Mexico, M.A., 1966; University of Florida, Ph.D. and Certificate in Latin American Studies, 1967; Institut Universitaire de Hautes Etudes Internationales, Geneva, Switzerland, Diplome, 1972. *Home address:* P.O. Box 341266, Miami, Fla. 33134.

CAREER: Dunn & Bradstreet, Inc., New York, N.Y., financial analyst, 1957-63; East Carolina University, Greenville, N.C., assistant professor of economics and finance, 1967-68; West Georgia College, Carrollton, associate professor of economics, 1968-72. Visiting professor of economics and business, University Jose Simeon Canas, San Salvador, 1970. Former director and vice-president, Executive Management Consultants. *Member:* American Finance Association, Financial Management Association, Order of the Cross Society, Miletus Society, Life Insurance Truth Society, Beta Gamma Sigma. *Awards, honors:* Ford Foundation grant for research in Nicaragua; Fulbright-Hays senior lecturer.

WRITINGS: (Editor with W. Glenn Moore and contributor) *Coeval Economics: A Book of Readings,* McCutchan, 1970; *Getting Rich in Commodities, Currencies, or Coins,* Arlington House, 1975; (contributor) V. Orval Watts, editor, *Politics vs. Prosperity,* Pendell, 1976. Contributor to *West Georgia Review* and *Choice.*

WORK IN PROGRESS: Handbook of Financial Mathematics, Formulas, and Tables, for Prentice-Hall.

* * *

VIGUERS, Ruth Hill 1903-1971
(Ruth A. Hill)

July 24, 1903—February 3, 1971; American editor, lecturer, critic, and authority on children's literature. Obituaries: *Publishers' Weekly,* March 1, 1971; *Antiquarian Bookman,* June 24, 1971. (See index for *CA* sketch)

* * *

VILLA-GILBERT, Mariana 1937-

PERSONAL: Born February 21, 1937, in Croydon, Surrey, England; daughter of Walter (a consulting engineer) and Ada Mary (Hill) Villa-Gilbert. *Education:* Attended high school in Berkshire, England, and then studied art in London, 1954-57. *Home:* 28 St. Martin's Rd., Canterbury, Kent, England. *Agent:* Herbert van Thal, London Management Ltd., 235-241 Regent St., London W1A 2JT, England.

CAREER: Novelist; sales assistant in record shops in London and Canterbury, England, 1957—.

WRITINGS—Novels: *Mrs. Galbraith's Air,* Chatto & Windus, 1963; *My Love All Dressed in White,* Chatto & Windus, 1964; *Mrs. Cantello,* Chatto & Windus, 1966; *A Jingle Jangle Song,* Chatto & Windus, 1968; *The Others,* Chatto & Windus, 1970; *Manuela: A Modern Myth,* Chatto & Windus, 1973. Contributor of record reviews to periodicals.

WORK IN PROGRESS: An untitled novel which "might be described as a variation on the Adam and Eve theme."

SIDELIGHTS: Mariana Villa-Gilbert told *CA:* "No one thing started me writing. I was always a writer—before I could read even. It's a way of seeing things, a way of life. I don't really think about what I will achieve as a writer. I just have to write, and each book is like a first book—the same problems every time. I don't know many writers: I need the stimulation, rather, of other sorts of people. But one instinctively withdraws, I think, from relationships: one has to remain 'outside'. I am impatient with those who assume one has done everything one's characters have done, or been everything one's characters have been. The author's role is a passive one: he's a sort of computer, always processing information. One is, I believe, born experienced. One's perceptions, too, run at a level others might have to artificially induce: one is 'high' all the time.

"... I enjoy writing about both men and women, but feel that I express myself best through my male characters. But I have first to develop a character—the rest comes after. Some of his facets are my own perhaps, some not. I then create around him (or her) a situation, which I examine in depth. This is my metier: a couple of characters, and a situation. There are many sorts of situations I want to write about. I don't know if I'll achieve them all, since I am a slow writer and am obliged for financial reasons to hold down a regular job. . . . Personally, I find a regular job a hindrance. I believe in any case that all the books I will write . . . are already complete inside me. . . . A writer is born and not made. I think it harmful that he must take on work he does not want but has to have. As a writer, he already has a full-time job. Since, however, I must have another job I chose something not in any way related to writing (or to any of the arts) that I might conserve creative energy.

"I should like enough money to travel, of which I've not done enough. Not because I believe in its broadening effects—one has to be 'open' to these things to start with—but because I've a yet unsatisfied appetite for foreign places, the East in particular. . . . I don't think of money as something important—health is of major importance, and time. Time for one's work as a writer, and time in which to absorb the matter one's work demands—to 'stop and stare.'"

AVOCATIONAL INTERESTS: Photography, music (mainly early European and Oriental), target shooting, walking, being out of doors.

BIOGRAPHICAL/CRITICAL SOURCES: Books and Bookmen, May, 1968; *New Statesman,* October 23, 1970; *Punch,* November 25, 1970.

* * *

VINCENT, Jack 1904-

PERSONAL: Born March 6, 1904, in Richmond, Surrey, England; son of William George (a stockbroker) and Edith (Burridge) Vincent; married Mary Russell, April 13, 1934; children: John, Thamar Vincent Fletcher. *Education:* Educated in England. *Religion:* Church of England. *Home address:* "Firle," Box 44, Mooi River 3300, Natal, South Africa.

CAREER: Farmer in Sussex, England, and later in Natal, South Africa, 1921-29; British Museum (Natural History), London, England, field collector and explorer in Africa, 1930-34; managing director of Zanzibar Distillers Ltd. and Central Line Sisal Estates Ltd. in Zanzibar and Tanganyika, 1935-37; farmer at Mooi River, Natal, South Africa, 1938-39, 1945-48; Natal Parks, Game and Fish Preservation Board, Pietermaritzburg, Natal, South Africa, director, 1949-63, editor, 1967-69, assistant director, 1970-75. Liaison officer and secretary of Survival Service Commission, International Council for Bird Preservation and International

Union for Conservation of Nature, Morges, Switzerland, 1964-67. *Military service:* South African Forces, 1939-42, British Army, 1942-45; became lieutenant colonel.

MEMBER: Royal Geographical Society (fellow), British Ornithologist Union (corresponding member), American Ornithologists' Union (corresponding member), South African Ornithological Society (president, 1961-63, 1968-69), South African Wild Life Protection and Conservation Society (life member), Zoological Society of London (fellow), Old Blues Club, Victoria Club. *Awards, honors:* Member, Order of the British Empire; World Wildlife Fund Gold Medal, 1973; Knight, Order of the Golden Ark, 1973.

WRITINGS: Birds of Northern Mozambique, Witherby, 1936; *A Check List of the Birds of South Africa,* Cape Times, 1952; *Red Data Book of the International Union for Conservation of Nature,* Volume II, [Switzerland], 1966; (with James Fisher and Noel Simon) *Wildlife in Danger,* Studio Books, 1969 (published in England as *The Red Book,* Collins, 1969). Contributor to ornithological journals. Editor of *Ostrich,* 1947-53; also editor of *Lammergeyer* and all publications of the Natal Parks Board, 1967-75.

WORK IN PROGRESS: Research into the biology of the Lammergeyer Gypaetus Barbatus; *History of the Natal Parks, Game and Fish Preservation Board.*

SIDELIGHTS: Jack Vincent traveled overland from the southern tip of South Africa to the western tip of West Africa studying grass warblers of the genus Cisticola, 1930-31. The following year he became the first person to climb and explore the Namuli Mountains of northern Portuguese East Africa, and in 1933-34 did extensive exploring and collecting in previously unvisited areas of the western Congo and northern Angola.

* * *

VISCOTT, David S(teven) 1938-

PERSONAL: Born May 24, 1938, in Boston, Mass.; son of Hiram (a pharmacist) and Shirley (Levy) Viscott; married Judith Ann Finn (a figure skater), July 12, 1959 (divorced); children: Elizabeth, Penelope, Jonathan. *Education:* Dartmouth College, A.B., 1959; Tufts University, M.D., 1963. *Home:* 13 Draper Rd., Wayland, Mass. *Office:* School of Medicine, Boston University, Boston, Mass. 02115.

CAREER: Barnes Hospital, St. Louis, Mo., intern, 1963-64; University Hospital, Boston, Mass., resident in psychiatry, 1964-67; Boston University, School of Medicine, Boston, instructor in psychiatry, 1967—. President of Sensitivity Games, Boston, 1970—. *Member:* American Psychiatric Association, Authors Guild, Authors League, Royal Society for Health, New York Academy of Science (fellow), Massachusetts Medical Society, Phi Sigma Delta. *Awards, honors:* Mosby Book Award, 1963, for research as a medical student; Law Medicine Institute fellow, 1967-68.

WRITINGS: Labyrinth of Silence (novel), Norton, 1970; *Feel Free,* Peter H. Wyden, 1971; *Winning,* Peter H. Wyden, 1972; *The Making of a Psychiatrist,* Arbor House, 1973; *Dorchester Boy: Portrait of a Psychiatrist as a Very Young Man,* Arbor House, 1973; *How to Live with Another Person,* Arbor House, 1974; *The Language of Feelings,* Arbor House, 1976; (with Jonah Kalb) *What Every Kid Should Know,* Houghton, 1976; *Risking,* Simon & Schuster, 1977. Contributor of articles to *Psychiatry, Archives of General Psychiatry, Bulletin of Tufts New England Medical Center, Cosmopolitan, Marketing Age, New Woman, Today's Health.*

WORK IN PROGRESS: The Making of a Psychiatrist II; Natural Therapy; a collection of essays; an art book on Oriental Rugs; filmscripts, poetry, and a novel.

SIDELIGHTS: David Viscott told *CA:* "I first began writing when I was about eight. . . . Throughout grade and secondary school I experimented with different forms, always attracted to dialogue, the drama, musical settings for spoken voice and the short story. My artistic interest was mainly music and perhaps the greatest influence on my writing is still music. I am most concerned with the sound of the spoken word. I read aloud everything I write to myself and always have. At Dartmouth I was in English Honors and edited the literary magazine. Honors English was closely copied from the Cambridge Don system and for two years I studied the English language from Beowulf to Virginia Woolf and became steeped in the English tradition. With this background I entered Tufts medical school and of course quickly published, wrote scientific papers on my own cancer research and eventually drifted into psychiatry. . . .

"I write sporadically, but I am always gathering material. I have day books in which I keep a running account of ideas. When I am working on a book the day book will contain first draft material. Often it contains lists of errands. When I write I can sit at the typewriter 6 to 10 hours a day, the highest output I have is around 20,000 words per day. There are months when I don't write at all."

*   *   *

VITAL, David 1927-

PERSONAL: Surname originally Grossman; adopted surname is pronounced Vee-*tal;* born April 10, 1927, in London, England; son of Meir (a journalist) and Barbara (DePorte) Grossman; married Alisa Waxman (a musician), May 1, 1957; children: Tamar, Adam Elie, Ruth. *Education:* Oxford University, B.A., 1951, M.A., 1956, D.Phil., 1966. *Religion:* Jewish. *Home:* 75 Rehov Hazorea, Kfar Shmaryahu, Israel. *Office:* Department of Political Science, University of Haifa, Mount Carmel, Haifa, Israel.

CAREER: Journalist in Israel, 1952-54; government service in Israel, 1954-66; University of Sussex, Brighton, England, lecturer in international relations, 1966-68; Bar-Ilan University, Ramat-Gan, Israel, associate professor of political studies, 1968-71, Winston Churchill Professor of International Relations, 1969-71, professor of political studies, 1971-72; University of Haifa, Haifa, Israel, professor of political science, 1972—. Visiting professor at University of California, Los Angeles, 1969, and University of Jerusalem, 1969-70; visiting fellow at Australian National University, 1974, and Wolfson College, Oxford University, 1974-75. Member of Senate Standing Committee and Board of Governors, University of Haifa, 1972-74. *Military service:* British Army, 1945-48. Israel Defense Forces, Reserves, 1953—. *Member:* Institute for Strategic Studies (London), Political Studies Association (United Kingdom).

WRITINGS: The Inequality of States: A Study of the Small Power in International Relations, Oxford University Press, 1967; *The Making of British Foreign Policy,* Praeger, 1968; *The Survival of Small States; Studies in Small Power/Great Power Conflict,* Oxford University Press, 1971; *The Origins of Zionism,* Oxford University Press, 1975. Contributor to *Economist, Jerusalem Post, World Politics, International Affairs, International Journal, Journal of Contemporary History, Commentary, Government and Opposition, Political Science Quarterly,* and *Times Literary Supplement.*

WORK IN PROGRESS: A history of the Zionist movement; and foreign policy analysis.

SIDELIGHTS: The Inequality of States has been translated into Spanish, and *The Survival of Small States* has been translated into Spanish and Hebrew.

*   *   *

VITELLI, James R(obert) 1920-

PERSONAL: Born November 15, 1920, in Trenton, N.J.; son of James Robert and Grace (Commini) Vitelli; married Alice Carter (an artist), July 3, 1943; children: Karen Donne, Jefferson Blake, Eloise Adams, Stephen James, Lillian Clemens. *Education:* College of Wooster, A.B., 1942; University of Pennsylvania, M.A., 1948, Ph.D., 1955. *Home:* 100 Pennsylvania Ave., Easton, Pa. 18042. *Office:* Department of English, Lafayette College, Easton, Pa. 18042.

CAREER: Lafayette College, Easton, Pa., instructor, 1950-55, assistant professor, 1955-60, associate professor, 1960-68, professor of English, 1968—, chairman of program in American civilization, 1960—, Jones Lecturer, 1960. Fulbright lecturer, University of Trieste, 1956-58; visiting lecturer in American literature, University of Bombay, 1964-65; U.S. Department of State specialist in India, summer, 1969. Director, Easton School Board, 1954-55. *Military service:* U.S. Naval Reserve, active duty, 1942-46; became lieutenant junior grade. *Member:* Modern Language Association of America, American Studies Association, American Association of University Professors.

WRITINGS: (Editor and author of introduction) *An Amazing Sense: Selected Poems and Letters of Emily Dickinson,* Popular Prakashan (Bombay), 1966; *Van Wyck Brooks,* Twayne, 1969; (author of introduction) *The Ordeal of Mark Twain,* Dutton, 1970; (author of introduction) *Three Essays on America,* Dutton, 1970; *Van Wyck Brooks: A Reference Guide,* G. K. Hall, 1976.

WORK IN PROGRESS: Randolph Bourne: A Critical Study; a book on the idea of tradition in American literature.

*   *   *

VIVANTE, Paolo 1921-

PERSONAL: Born September 30, 1921, in Rome, Italy; son of Leone and Elena (de Rosis) Vivante. *Education:* Attended University of London, 1939; Pembroke College, Oxford, B.A. (honors), 1947; University of Florence, Degree in Classics, 1948. *Home:* 1235 Sault St. Louis, La Prairie, Quebec, Canada. *Office:* McGill University, 522 Leacock Building, Montreal, Quebec, Canada.

CAREER: High school teacher of Greek, Latin, and Italian literature in Montepulciano, Cortona, and Florence, Italy, 1948-52; University of Texas, Main University (now University of Texas at Austin), assistant professor of classics, 1963-66; McGill University, Montreal, Quebec, assistant professor, 1966-67, associate professor of classics, 1967—. Visiting lecturer in classics, Hebrew University of Jerusalem, 1958-60. *Military service:* British Army, 1941-45.

WRITINGS: The Homeric Imagination: A Study of Homer's Poetic Perception of Reality, Indiana University Press, 1970. Contributor to classical journals in the United States and Italy.

WORK IN PROGRESS: Writing on Greek poetry and language.

VIZZARD, John Anthony 1914-
(Jack Vizzard)

PERSONAL: Born June 14, 1914, in San Francisco, Calif.; son of James Leo (an insurance agent) and Mary (Flaherty) Vizzard; married Margaret M. Meere, 1943; children: James Terrance, John Anthony, Jr., Kathleen M. *Education:* Attended University of Santa Clara, 1933-35; Gonzaga University, 1935-38, M.A., Ph.L. *Politics:* Eclectic. *Religion:* "No formal religion." *Agent:* Don Congdon, Harold Matson Co., Inc., 22 East 40th St., New York, N.Y. 10016.

CAREER: Jesuit seminarian prior to 1943; Motion Picture Association of America, Inc., Production Code Administration, Los Angeles, Calif., censor, 1944-68, assistant director of Production Code Administration, 1955-68; involved in real estate, 1968—, first with Boise-Cascade Corp., and more recently with a private brokerage firm in Encino, Calif. Member of foreign committee, Academy of Motion Picture Arts and Sciences.

WRITINGS—Under name Jack Vizzard: *See No Evil: Life Inside a Hollywood Censor,* Simon & Schuster, 1970. Contributor to *Variety* and other trade publications.

BIOGRAPHICAL/CRITICAL SOURCES: Best Sellers, April 15, 1970; *Harper's,* April, 1970; *National Observer,* May 11, 1970; *New York Times Book Review,* July 19, 1970.††

*   *   *

VOLBACH, Walther R(ichard) 1897-

PERSONAL: Born December 24, 1897, in Mainz, Germany; naturalized American citizen; son of Fritz (a composer and conductor) and Kaethe (Ginsberg) Volbach; married Claire Neufeld, December 27, 1924. *Education:* Studied at University of Tuebingen, 1916-18, and University of Munich, 1918-19; University of Muenster, Ph.D., 1920. *Politics:* Liberal. *Religion:* Roman Catholic. *Home:* 378-D, Northampton Rd., Amherst, Mass. 01002.

CAREER: Deutsches Theater, Berlin, Germany, assistant director, 1920-22; stage director of municipal theaters in Zurich, Kiel, and Danzig, of state theaters in Berlin and Stuttgart, and of Volkstheater and Volksoper in Vienna, 1922-36; Marquette University, Milwaukee, Wis., assistant professor of dramatics, 1939-41; Cleveland Institute of Music, Cleveland, Ohio, director of opera, 1941-42; Texas Christian University, Fort Worth, professor of drama and director of theater and opera, 1946-58, professor of theater and chairman of department of theater arts, 1958-65; University of Massachusetts, Amherst, visiting professor of theater history and play directing, 1965-71. Stage director for St. Louis Grand Opera Association, 1940, and Fort Worth Opera Association, 1946. *Member:* American Society for Theatre Research. *Awards, honors:* Theatre Library Association, 1969, for *Adolphe Appia.*

WRITINGS: Problems of Opera Production, Texas Christian University Press, 1953, revised edition, Archon Books, 1967; *Adolphe Appia, Prophet of the Modern Theatre: A Profile,* Wesleyan University Press, 1968; *Memoirs of Max Reinhardt's Theatres, 1920-1922,* University of Pittsburgh, 1972. Contributor to theater journals.

WORK IN PROGRESS: Translating Adolphe Appia's essays and scenarios.

SIDELIGHTS: Walther Volbach is fluent in French in addition to German; speaks some Italian. *Avocational interests:* History, philosophy, reading novels.

VOLZ, Carl (Andrew) 1933-

PERSONAL: Born October 7, 1933, in Faribault, Minn.; son of Oswald Samuel and Louise (Werling) Volz; married Lydia Anna Rittmann, August 17, 1958; children: Carol, Martin, Stephen, Katherine, Michael. *Education:* Concordia College, St. Paul, Minn., A.A., 1953; Concordia Seminary, St. Louis, Mo., B.A., 1955, B.D., 1958, S.T.M., 1959; Washington University, St. Louis, Mo., M.A., 1961; Fordham University, Ph.D., 1966. *Office:* Luther Theological Seminary, 2375 Como Ave. W., St. Paul, Minn. 55108.

CAREER: Clergyman of Lutheran Church; Concordia College, Bronxville, N.Y., instructor in history, 1959-62; minister of Lutheran church in Yonkers, N.Y., 1962-64; Concordia Seminary, St. Louis, Mo., assistant professor, 1964-73, associate professor of ancient church history, 1973-74, regristrar, 1969-71; Luther Theological Seminary, St. Paul, Minn., associate professor of ancient church history, 1974—, dean of students, 1975-76. *Member:* American Society of Church History, American Historical Association, Mediaeval Academy of America, Lutheran Academy for Scholarship, Concordia Historical Institute, Phi Beta Kappa. *Awards, honors:* John W. Behnken postdoctoral award and American Association of Theological Schools award, 1971, for sabbatical year in Cambridge, England.

WRITINGS: Teaching the Faith: New Perspectives on Luther's Catechism, Lutheran Education Society, 1967; *The Church of the Middle Ages: Growth and Change, 600-1400,* Concordia, 1970. Managing editor, *Dialog* (theological quarterly).

WORK IN PROGRESS: Research for a project on the nature of religious toleration in the late Middle Ages.

*   *   *

VON HILSHEIMER, George E(dwin III) 1934-

PERSONAL: Born August 15, 1934, in West Palm Beach, Fla.; son of George Edwin, Jr. (a builder) and Ruth Virginia (Peebles) Von Hilsheimer; married Dian Kirk (an artist); married second wife, Catherine Munson (a teacher), December 27, 1969; children: (first marriage) David Dean, Dana Germaine, Oliver, George IV. *Education:* University of Miami, B.A., 1955; graduate study at University of Chicago, 1956, Washington University, 1957, and University of Maryland, 1958. *Politics:* "Reactionary Republican."

CAREER: Ordained minister in Religious Order of Humanitas, 1957; Church of the Brotherhood, Orange City, Fla., minister, 1964; Green Valley School and Psychiatric Hospital, Orange City, Fla., superintendent, beginning 1963. President, Growth Institutes, Inc. *Military service:* U.S. Army, 1957-59. *Member:* American Association for the Advancement of Science, Association for Children with Learning Disabilities, National Association for the Education of Young Children, American Society for Humanistic Education (chairman), Council for Children with Behavioral Disorders, National Rifle Association. *Awards, honors:* B.D., Free Religious Association, 1957.

WRITINGS: (Contributor) Helen Huus, editor, *Values for a Changing America,* University of Pennsylvania Press, 1966; *First Abacus,* Humanitas Books, 1966; *How Many?,* Humanitas Books, 1966; *Is There a Science of Behavior?,* Humanitas Books, 1967; *How to Live with Your Special Child: A Handbook for Behavioral Change,* Acropolis Books, 1970, revised edition published as *Understanding Young People in Trouble: A Practical Guide for Parents and Teachers,* 1974; (contributor) S. Repo, editor, *This Book Is about Schools*, Pantheon, 1971; *Allergy, Toxins, and the Learning-Disabled Child*, Academic Therapy Publications, 1974. Contributor of over seventy articles to professional journals. Editor, *Human Learning*.

WORK IN PROGRESS: And There Ain't No Teacher Any More; Green Valley: A Democratic Approach to Child Rearing; and *The Revolting Christian*.

SIDELIGHTS: George E. Von Hilsheimer told *CA* that he was interested in "community, intentional or otherwise, how schooling has replaced learning and education . . . the curious growth of psychiatry, psychology, social work and the like as replacement for religious faith, despite the equal lack of scientific evidence for them." He ran the first integrated school in Florida and says that he "had a school burned by rednecks in North Carolina, trained and led many of the first S.N.C.C. and similar workers in the deep South."

AVOCATIONAL INTERESTS: Tri-hull sailing.†

* * *

VON MOLNAR, Geza (Walter Elemer) 1932-

PERSONAL: Born August 5, 1932, in Leipzig, Germany; naturalized U.S. citizen; son of Elemer (a publisher) and Annelies (Jolowicz) Von Molnar; married Barbara Baten, November 24, 1957; children: Karen, Anina. *Education:* Hunter College (now Hunter College of the City University of New York), B.A., 1958; Stanford University, M.A., 1960, Ph.D., 1966. *Office:* Department of German, Northwestern University, Evanston, Ill. 60201.

CAREER: Northwestern University, Evanston, Ill., instructor, 1963-66, assistant professor, 1966-68, associate professor of German, 1968—, chairman of department, 1970-74. Visiting professor, Dartmouth University, 1974-75. *Military service:* U.S. Air Force, 1950-54. *Awards, honors:* American Council of Learned Societies grant, 1973-74.

WRITINGS: Novalis' "Fichte Studies": The Foundations of His Aesthetics, Mouton & Co., 1970. Contributor of articles to *PMLA, German Life and Letters, Unterrichtspraxis,* and *Euphorion*. Editor, *Versuche zu Goethe*.

WORK IN PROGRESS: A comprehensive monograph on Novalis.

* * *

VON UNRUH, Fritz 1885-1970

May 10, 1885—November 28, 1970; German novelist and playwright. Obituaries: *Newsday*, November 30, 1970; *Variety*, December 2, 1970; *Books Abroad*, spring, 1971.

* * *

WADE, Carlson 1928-

PERSONAL: Born June 7, 1928; son of Arthur (a writer) and Lena (Franks) Wade. *Address:* Room 707, 12 East 41st St., New York, N.Y. 10017.

CAREER: Literary agent, New York, N.Y., 1949—. *Member:* American Medical Writers Association.

WRITINGS—With Edward Podolsky: *Erotic Symbolism*, Epic, 1960; *Transvestism Today*, Epic, 1960, *Sexual Sadism*, Epic, 1961; *Nymphomania*, Epic, 1961; *Exhibitionism*, Epic, 1961; *Sexual Masochism*, Epic, 1961; *Voyeurism*, Epic, 1961.

Other books: *The Key to Nutrition*, Key Publishing Co., 1963; *The Key to Delicious Cooking*, Key Publishing Co.,

1963; *Helping Your Health with Enzymes*, Parker Publishing, 1966; (with Albert Reissner) *Dictionary of Sexual Terms*, Associated Booksellers, 1967; *The Natural Way to Health through Controlled Fasting*, Parker Publishing, 1968; *Instant Health: The Nature Way*, Award Books, 1968; *Magic Minerals: Key to Better Health*, Parker Publishing, 1968; *Carlson Wade's Gourmet Health Foods Cookbook*, Parker Publishing, 1969, published as *Carlson Wade's Health Food Recipes for Gourmet Cooking*, Arc Books, 1971; *Natural and Folk Remedies*, Parker Publishing, 1970; *The Natural Laws of Healthful Living: The Bio-Nature Health Rhythm Program*, Parker Publishing, 1970; *Rejuvenation Vitamin*, Award Books, 1970; *Emotional Health and Nutrition*, Award Books, 1971; *Health Tonics, Elixirs, and Potions for the Look and Feel of Youth*, Parker Publishing, 1971. Also author of *Home Repairs Made Easy, Be Your Own Carpenter, Be Your Own Plumber,* and *Tropical Fish*, all published by Key Publishing Co. Editor, *Parker Natural Health Bulletin*.

* * *

WAGENHEIM, Kal 1935-

PERSONAL: Born April 21, 1935, in Newark, N.J.; son of Harold and Rozlon (Heller) Wagenheim; married Olga Jimenez, June 10, 1961; children: David, Maria-Dolores. *Education:* Rutgers University, student, 1953-54, 1956, 1959; State University of New York at Buffalo, graduate study. *Religion:* Jewish.

CAREER: Newark Star-Ledger, Newark, N.J., part-time sports reporter, 1953-54, 1956-58; Prudential Insurance Co., Newark, N.J., copywriter, 1956-60; Keuffel & Esser Engineering Products, Hoboken, N.J., technical writer, 1960-61; reporter for weekly periodicals and radio announcer for WKYN, San Juan, Puerto Rico, 1961-63; free-lance writer on Caribbean affairs, also translator and researcher, Puerto Rico, 1963-68; University of Puerto Rico, Rio Piedras, editor of scientific publications for Nuclear Center, 1968-70; *Buffalo Evening News*, Buffalo, N.Y., reporter, beginning 1970. Co-founder and co-editor of *San Juan Review* (monthly), 1963-66, and *Caribbean Review* (quarterly), 1968—; part-time correspondent for *New York Times*, 1967-70. *Military service:* U.S. Army, 1954-56.

MEMBER: Authors Guild, American Newspaper Guild, Overseas Press Club of Puerto Rico (member of board of directors, 1968-70). *Awards, honors:* Overseas Press Club of Puerto Rico Award, 1969, for best story published off-island (in *New York Times*); recipient with Barry Bernard Levine of grant from the Plumstock Foundation to support publication of *Caribbean Review*, 1969.

WRITINGS: Puerto Rico: A Profile, Praeger, 1971, revised edition, 1976; (editor) *Puerto Rican Short Stories*, Institute of Puerto Rican Culture, 1971; (translator) Ricardo Alegria, *Discovery, Conquest and Colonialization of Puerto Rico*, Institute of Puerto Rican Culture, 1971; (editor with wife, Olga Jimenez de Wagenheim) *The Puerto Ricans: A Documentary History*, Praeger, 1973; *Clemente: The Life of Roberto Clemente*, foreward by Wilfrid Sheed, Praeger, 1973; *Babe Ruth: His Life and Legend*, Praeger, 1974; *A Survey of Puerto Ricans on the U.S. Mainland in the 1970's*, Praeger, 1975; *Paper Gold: How to Hedge against Inflation by Investing in Postage Stamps*, Peter H. Wyden, 1976.

Contributor of more than one hundred news articles to *New York Times* and other articles to *Nation, New Leader, New Republic,* and *Liberation*. Has sold cartoon ideas to *New Yorker, Playboy,* and other magazines.

WORK IN PROGRESS: Translating *La Charca,* a novel, by Manuel Zeno Gandia; translating and researching for Oscar Lewis, for his forthcoming book *Six Women.†*

*   *   *

WAGNER, Ruth H(ortense) 1909-

PERSONAL: Born August 6, 1909, in Ankeny, Iowa; daughter of William L. (a contractor) and Anna (Hutton) Wagner. *Education:* Attended Grinnell College, 1926-28, and Drake University, summers, 1928-30; University of Iowa, B.A., 1931; University of Denver, M.A., 1957. *Politics:* Republican. *Religion:* Protestant.

CAREER: Teacher in primary schools, Whitefish Bay, Wis., 1931-40; Scott, Foresman & Co., Chicago, Ill., editorial assistant and reading consultant, 1941-44; *Midland Schools,* Des Moines, Iowa, associate editor, 1945-54; *Kansas Teacher,* Topeka, Kan., managing editor, 1954-56; American Academy for Girls, Istanbul, Turkey, instructor, 1957-60; Friendship Press (National Council of Churches), New York, N.Y., editor-director of children's publications, 1960-67; free-lance writer, 1967—. *Member:* National Education Association (life member), National League of American Penwomen.

WRITINGS—All published by C. R. Gibson, except as indicated: (With Ivah Green) *Put Democracy to Work,* Schuman, 1952, revised edition (sole author), Abelard, 1961; *Iowa Beautiful Land,* Klipto Publishing, 1954; (compiler) *Garlands for Mother,* 1968; (editor and compiler) *For I Am with You,* 1969; (compiler) *Follow Your Star,* 1969; (compiler) *Our Precious Baby,* 1970; *Jewels of Inspiration,* 1970; *Jewels of Comfort,* 1970; *Jewels of Faith,* 1970; *Jewels of Friendship,* 1970; *Jewels of Home,* 1970; *Jewels of Love,* 1970; (compiler) *Bouquets for Mother,* 1974. Contributor to education and religious journals.†

*   *   *

WAGNER, Stanley P(aul) 1923-

PERSONAL: Born March 22, 1923, in Ambridge, Pa.; son of Stephan and Anna (Wojtkowski) Wagner; married Diana Mills, October 20, 1945; children: Kathleen Anne (Mrs. William J. Meyers). *Education:* Attended University of North Carolina at Chapel Hill, 1943, and American University, Shrivenham, England, 1945; University of Pittsburgh, B.A., 1947, M.A., 1949, Ph.D., 1953. *Religion:* Episcopalian. *Home:* 230 South Francis Ave., Ada, Okla. 74820. *Office:* Office of the President, East Central State Oklahoma University, Ada, Okla.

CAREER: Muskingham College, New Concord, Ohio, instructor, 1949-52, assistant professor of political science, 1952-53; Allegheny College, Meadville, Pa., assistant professor of political science, 1954-62; Oklahoma City University, Oklahoma City, chairman of departments of history and political science, 1962-64, associate dean of College of Arts and Sciences, 1964-68; Minnesota State College, St. Paul, vice-chancellor for academic affairs, 1968-69; East Central State Oklahoma University, Ada, president of college, 1969—. Counselor at guidance clinic, Allegheny College, summers, 1954-68. *Military service:* U.S. Army, 1942-45. *Member:* American Political Science Association, Taft Institute of Practical Politics (director, 1967—), Rotary International, Ada (Okla). Chamber of Commerce.

WRITINGS: The End of the Revolution, A. S. Barnes, 1970. Contributor of articles and reviews to *Polish American Studies, Social Science, Oklahoma City Magazine, Choice,*

Midwest Journal of Political Science, Journal of Modern History, and other journals.

*   *   *

WAGONER, Harless D. 1918-

PERSONAL: Born April 13, 1918, in Shelbyville, Ind.; son of David (a horseman) and Jessie (Steirs) Wagoner; married Josephine Tedeschi (a research analyst), September 23, 1944. *Education:* Butler University, A.B. (magna cum laude), 1941; University of Wisconsin, M.A., 1942; Catholic University of America, B.L.S., 1948; American University, Ph.D., 1967. *Politics:* Democrat. *Religion:* None.

CAREER: U.S. Government, Washington, D.C., archivist with War Production Board (later Civilian Production Administration), 1942-47, National Security Resources Board, 1948-51, and National Production Authority, 1951-53; Records Engineering, Inc., Washington, D.C., analyst, 1954-55; U.S. Department of Defense, Fort Meade, Md., management analyst and historian, beginning 1955. *Member:* Economic History Association, Society for the History of Technology, United Nations Association, National Wildlife Association, Greater Washington Education Television Association.

WRITINGS: U.S. Machine Tools Industry 1900-1950, M.I.T. Press, 1968.

WORK IN PROGRESS: Classified research and writing in fields of communications and electronics.

AVOCATIONAL INTERESTS: The history, languages, and problems of American Indians (North and South America), problems of other minority or disadvantaged groups, conservation, pollution control.††

*   *   *

WAHKING, Harold L(eroy) 1931-

PERSONAL: Surname is pronounced *Way*-king; born August 23, 1931, in Louisville, Ky.; son of LeRoy James (in real estate business) and Sarah Jessamine (English) Wahking; married Barbara Jean Knadler (a teacher), June 21, 1954; children: Walter, Diane. *Education:* University of Louisville, B.C.E., 1954, M.A. (psychology), 1960; Southern Baptist Theological Seminary, B.D. and M.A. (theology), 1961. *Politics:* Independent. *Religion:* Southern Baptist. *Home address:* R.R. 3, Georgetown, Ky. 40324.

CAREER: Eastern State Hospital, Lexington, Ky., chaplain, 1961-65; Georgetown College, Georgetown, Ky., assistant professor of psychology and pastoral counselor, 1965-71; Eckerd College, St. Petersburg, Fla., director of Career and Personal Counseling Service, 1971-76; director, Network of Christian Counseling Centers, St. Petersburg, Fla. Training consultant, International Business Machines, Lexington, Ky., 1967—. Lecturer at colleges and local churches. *Military service:* U.S. Navy, 1954-56; became lieutenant, junior grade. *Member:* Association for Clinical Pastoral Education, Kentucky Psychological Association, Central Kentucky Regional Mental Health-Mental Retardation Board.

WRITINGS: Being Christlike, Broadman, 1970; *The Single Student's Guide to Sex, Love and Marriage,* Broadman, 1971. Also author of *Break Free to Win.* Contributor to *Baptist Student, Adult Leader, Collage, Inscape,* and *Search.*

SIDELIGHTS: Harold Wahking told *CA:* "My general area of interest is in the psychology of religion, the use of theological and psychological concepts to better help people live a life of spontaneous, open, joyful meaning. I do a good bit of private counseling and psychotherapy in which I assist people in utilizing the insights of theology and psychology to help themselves. I write partly to show the high correlation between psychology and theology and to thereby make the point that theology is a behavioral science, not merely a belief structure."

* * *

WAKEFIELD, Sherman Day 1894-1971

July 12, 1894—May 23, 1971; American editor, bibliographer, and author of works on Abraham Lincoln. Obituaries: *Antiquarian Bookman,* July 5-12, 1971.

* * *

WAKEHAM, Irene 1912-

PERSONAL: Born June 28, 1912, in Watford, England; daughter of William Henry (a minister) and Mabel (Pringle) Wakeham. *Education:* Emmanuel Missionary College (now Andrews University), Secretarial Diploma, 1931, B.A., 1934; University of Southern California, M.A., 1939; Stanford University, Ph.D., 1965. *Politics:* Independent. *Religion:* Seventh-day Adventist. *Office:* Antillian College, P.O. Box 118, Mayaquez, Puerto Rico 00708.

CAREER: Teacher of English, commerce, and French at various Seventh-day Adventist academies in Ohio and California, 1934-41, and at Hawaiian Mission Academy, Honolulu, 1941-45; Pacific Union College, Angwin, Calif., instructor in English and French, 1945-46; Philippine Union College, Manila, head of department of English, 1946-54, and 1965-70; Mountain View College, Malaybalay, Bukidnon, Philippines, head of department of English and registrar, 1954-64; Oakwood College, Huntsville, Ala., head of department of English, 1971-75; Loma Linda University, Loma Linda, Calif., professor of English and linguistics, 1975-77; Antillian College, Mayaquez, Puerto Rico, chairman of department of English, 1977—. *Member:* National Council of Teachers of English, Teachers of English to Speakers of Other Languages, Linguistic Society of the Philippines.

WRITINGS: Strictly Confidential, Pacific Press, 1955; *Oral English,* Philippine Publishing House, 1956, 3rd edition, 1963; *Though the Heavens Fall* (short stories), Southern Publishing, 1970. Contributor of articles to religious periodicals and educational journals.

* * *

WAKSTEIN, Allen M. 1931-

PERSONAL: Born August 12, 1931, in Boston, Mass.; son of David (a painter) and Betty (Soloman) Wakstein; married Marilyn Mishkin (a professor of English), August 14, 1955; children: Gary S., Julie A. *Education:* University of Massachusetts, B.A., 1956; University of Illinois, M.A., 1958, Ph.D., 1961. *Politics:* Democrat. *Religion:* Jewish. *Home:* 17 Ridgefield Dr., Framingham, Mass. 01701. *Office:* Department of History, Boston College, Chestnut Hill, Mass. 02167.

CAREER: Ithaca College, Ithaca, N.Y., assistant professor of history, 1961-63; Boston College, Chestnut Hill, Mass., associate professor of history, 1963—. *Military service:* U.S. Army, 1953-55. *Member:* Organization of American Historians, American Historical Association, American Association of University Professors.

WRITINGS: (Editor) *The Urbanization of America: An Historical Anthology,* Houghton, 1970. Contributor to historical journals.

WORK IN PROGRESS: The Emergence and Growth of a Metropolis: A Case Study of the Boston Metropolitan Area.

* * *

WALKER, Philip Mitchell 1943-

PERSONAL: Born November 21, 1943, in Anderson, S.C.; son of Leonard L. and Ethel (Mitchell) Walker; married Joyce Maresca (a college instructor), August 19, 1967. *Education:* Yale University, B.S., 1966; Massachusetts Institute of Technology, S.M., 1968; Georgetown University Law Center, graduate study.

CAREER: International Business Machines (IBM) Corp., Raleigh, N.C., engineer, 1966; Mitre Corp., Bedford, Mass., member of technical staff, 1967; Office of the Secretary of Defense, Washington, D.C., systems analyst, 1968-70. Consultant to U.S. Department of Justice, 1968, Arthur D. Little, Inc., 1970—, Federal Communications Commission, 1971—, Office of Telecommunications Policy, 1971—, Executive Office of the President, beginning 1971. *Military service:* U.S. Army Reserve, 1969-70; became first lieutenant; received Joint Service Commendation Medal, 1970. *Member:* Association for Computing Machinery, Institute of Electrical and Electronics Engineers.

WRITINGS: (With Stuart L. Mathison) *Computers and Telecommunications: Issues in Public Policy,* Prentice-Hall, 1970; (contributor) N. Abramson and F. Kuo, editors, *Computer Communication Networks,* Prentice-Hall, 1975.†

* * *

WALL, Joseph Frazier 1920-

PERSONAL: Born July 10, 1920, in Des Moines, Iowa; son of Joseph Frazier (a veterinarian) and Minnie (Patton) Wall; married Beatrice Mills, April 16, 1944; children: April Ane (Mrs. Richard Mulloy), Joseph Frazier, Julia Mills. *Education:* Grinnell College, B.A., 1941; Harvard University, M.A., 1942; Columbia University, Ph.D., 1951. *Politics:* Democrat. *Home:* 1409 Broad St., Grinnell, Iowa 50112. *Office:* Department of History, Grinnell College, Grinnell, Iowa 50112.

CAREER: Grinnell College, Grinnell, Iowa, instructor, 1947-51, assistant professor, 1951-55, associate professor, 1955-57, professor of history, 1957—, James Morton Roberts Professor of History, 1960-61, Parker Professor of History, 1961—, Earl Strong Distinguished Professor of History, 1972—, chairman of department, 1954-57, 1963-64, chairman of Division of Social Studies, 1956-57, 1959-60, chairman of division of history, philosophy, and math, 1965-66, chairman of faculty, 1966-69, dean of the college, 1969-73. Fulbright scholar, University of Edinburgh, 1957-58; Fulbright professor, University of Gothenburg, 1964-65; visiting professor, Brown University, 1972. Member of state board, Iowa Civil Liberties Union, 1950-57, 1962—; trustee, Stewart Public Library, Grinnell, 1968—. *Military service:* U.S. Naval Reserve, active duty, 1942-46; became lieutenant.

MEMBER: American Historical Association, Society of American Historians, Organization of American Historians, American Association of University Professors (state chairman, 1955-56), American Conference of Academic Deans, Commission on Higher Education, American Civil Liberties Union, Western History Association, Phi Beta Kappa, Sigma Delta Chi. *Awards, honors:* Honorable mention, John

H. Dunning Prize of American Historical Association, 1956, for *Henry Watterson;* Bancroft Prize of Columbia University and Iowa Library Association prize for literature, both 1971, for *Andrew Carnegie.*

WRITINGS: Henry Watterson: Reconstructed Rebel, Oxford University Press, 1956; (with Robert Parks) *Freedom,* Iowa Farm Bureau Federation Press, 1956; *Andrew Carnegie,* Oxford University Press, 1970; (editor with Richard Lowitt) *Interpreting Twentieth-Century America,* Crowell, 1973.

WORK IN PROGRESS: The Unmaking of a Revolution: The Election of 1872; a biography of Alfred I. DuPont.

SIDELIGHTS: Joseph Wall told *CA:* "During the past several years when I have served as both college administrator and professor, I have had little time for even my major professional interests: historical research and writing, and no time at all for my avocational interests in travel, reading and just being lazy in the sun." Now that he is no longer serving in an administrative position he hopes to "return to what I like best: teaching, writing and hopefully some extra-curricular reading."

BIOGRAPHICAL/CRITICAL SOURCES: New York Times, October 3, 1970; *Christian Century,* October 7, 1970; *Washington Post,* November 18, 1970; *National Review,* February 9, 1971.†

*   *   *

WALLACE, Barbara Brooks

PERSONAL: Born in Soochow, China; daughter of Otis Frank (a businessman) and Nicia E. Brooks; married James Wallace, Jr. (in U.S. Air Force), February 27, 1954; children: James. *Education:* Attended schools in Hankow, Tientsin, and Shanghai, China, Baguio, Philippines, and Claremont, Calif.; attended Pomona College, 1940-41; University of California, Los Angeles, B.A., 1945. *Religion:* Episcopalian. *Home:* 2708 George Mason Pl., Alexandria, Va. 22305. *Agent:* Johnson & Thompson, 28th & O St., Washington, D.C.

MEMBER: National League of American Pen Women, Children's Book Guild of Washington, D.C., Alpha Phi. *Awards, honors:* National League of American Pen Women juvenile book award, 1970, for *Claudia.*

WRITINGS—All published by Follett, except as indicated: *Claudia* (juvenile), 1969; *Andrew the Big Deal* (juvenile), 1971; *Trouble with Miss Switch,* Abingdon, 1971; *Victoria,* 1972; *Can Do, Missy Charlie,* 1974; *The Secret Summer of L.E.B.,* 1974; *Julia and the Third Bad Thing,* 1975; *Palmer Patch,* 1976; *Hawkins,* Abingdon, 1977.

WORK IN PROGRESS: Two books for young readers.

*   *   *

WALLACE-HADRILL, D(avid) S(utherland)   1920-

PERSONAL: Born January 12, 1920, in Bromsgrove, Worcestershire, England; son of Frederic (a schoolmaster) and Norah (White) Wallace-Hadrill; married Vera Tracey Monks, April 25, 1947; children: Peter John, Mary, Benjamin, Robert Gordon. *Education:* Corpus Christi College, Oxford, B.A. (honors), 1941, M.A., 1945; University of Manchester, B.D. (with distinction), 1944, D.D., 1960. *Politics:* Socialist. *Home:* Kennedy's House, Aldenham School, Elstree, Hertfordshire, England.

CAREER: Ordained clergyman of Church of England, 1943; curate in Manchester and London, 1943-47; vicar of Holy Cross, Hornchurch, Essex, 1947-50; chaplain of Aldenham School, Elstree, Hertfordshire, 1950-55; vicar of Eston, Yorkshire, 1955-62; housemaster at Aldenham School, 1962—.

WRITINGS: Eusebius of Caesarea, Mowbray, 1960; *The Greek Patristic View of Nature,* Barnes & Noble, 1968. Contributor to theological journals, including *Harvard Theological Review.*

WORK IN PROGRESS: The Christian Rationalists of Antioch; and *The Latin Patristic View of Nature.*

BIOGRAPHICAL/CRITICAL SOURCES: Spectator, January 3, 1968.††

*   *   *

WALLHAUSER, Henry T.   1930-

PERSONAL: Born May 29, 1930, in Newark, N.J.; son of George Marvin and Isabel (Towne) Wallhauser; married Rachel Roberts, May 19, 1956; children: James R., Sarah R. *Education:* University of Pennsylvania, B.A., 1952; Columbia University, M.S., 1958. *Politics:* Republican. *Religion:* Protestant. *Home:* 56 Mountain Ave., Millburn, N.J. *Office:* Briod & Wallhauser, Inc., 60 Park Pl., Newark, N.J.

CAREER: Briod & Wallhauser, Inc. (public relations), Newark, N.J., public relations counselor, 1969—. *Military service:* U.S. Army, Counter-Intelligence Corps, 1952-55; became sergeant.

WRITINGS: Pioneers of Flight (juvenile), Hammond, Inc., 1969. Regular music columnist, *Newark Star-Ledger.*

WORK IN PROGRESS: Mad Mission, a juvenile aviation adventure; the airplane's role in Pershing's expedition to Mexico.

AVOCATIONAL INTERESTS: Sailing, literature.

*   *   *

WALTERS, A(lan) A(rthur)   1926-

PERSONAL: Born June 17, 1926, in Leicester, England; son of James Arthur and Clarabel (Heywood) Walters; married Audrey Elizabeth Claxton, March 30, 1950; children: Louise. *Education:* University College, Leicester, B.Sc. (London), 1951; Nuffield College, Oxford, further study, 1951-52. *Home:* 4 Sutherland House, Marloes Rd., London W8, England. *Office:* London School of Economics and Political Science, University of London, Houghton St., London WC2A 2AE, England.

CAREER: University of Birmingham, Birmingham, England, lecturer in econometrics, 1952-61, professor and head of department of econometrics and social statistics, 1961-68; University of London, London School of Economics and Political Science, London, England, Cassel Professor of Economics, 1968—. Visiting professor of economics, Northwestern University, 1958-59, and Massachusetts Institute of Technology, 1966-67. Economic advisor to Secretary of State for Health and Social Security, 1970—; consultant to governments of Israel, Singapore, and Malaysia. Governor, Centre for Environmental Studies, 1971—. Director, Economists Bookshop. Member, Commission on London's Third Airport, 1968-70. *Member:* Reform Club (London), Econometric Society (fellow). *Awards, honors:* Gerstenberg prize.

WRITINGS: The Theory and Measurement of Private and Social Cost of Highway Congestion, Faculty of Commerce and Social Science, University of Birmingham, 1959; *A Survey of Statistical Production and Cost Functions,* Faculty of Commerce and Social Science, University of Birmingham, 1959; (with N. J. Kavanagh) *Demand for Money in the U.K., 1877-1962,* Faculty of Commerce and Social Science, University of Birmingham, 1964; (with Mitchell Harwitz, George Dalton, and R. W. Clower) *Growth Without Development,* Northwestern University Press, 1966; *Integration in Freight Transport,* Transatlantic, 1968; *The Economics of Road User Charges,* Johns Hopkins Press, for International Bank for Reconstruction, 1968; *An Introduction to Econometrics,* Macmillan (London), 1969, 2nd edition, Norton, 1970; (with Esra Bennathan) *Economics of Ocean Freight Rates,* Praeger, 1969; *Money in Boom and Slump,* Institute of Economic Affairs, 1969, 3rd edition, 1971, Transatlantic, 1969; (editor) *Money and Banking: Selected Readings,* Penguin, 1973; (with others) *Government and the Land,* Institute of Economic Affairs, 1974; *Noise and Prices,* Clarendon Press, 1975; (with J. H. Wood) *Commercial Bank Loan and Investment Behavior,* Wiley, 1975. Author or co-author of a number of pamphlets on money, inflation, and transportation economics. Contributor of articles to *American Economic Review, Econometrica, Economic Journal, Economica,* and *Journal of Political Economy.* Managing editor, *Review of Economic Studies,* 1971; member of editorial board of *Journal of Money Credit and Banking* and *Urban Economics.*†

* * *

WALTERS, Robert S(tephen) 1941-

PERSONAL: Born October 6, 1941, in Houston, Tex.; son of Robert King (an engineer) and Harriett (Fuller) Walters; married Linda Fisher, August 22, 1964; children: Christopher Scott, Claire Suzanne. *Education:* University of Michigan, B.A., 1963, M.A., 1964, Ph.D., 1967. *Home:* 102 Hawthorne Rd., Pittsburgh, Pa. 15221. *Office:* Department of Political Science, University of Pittsburgh, Pittsburgh, Pa. 15260.

CAREER: Brookings Institution, Washington, D.C., research fellow, 1966-67; University of Michigan, Ann Arbor, Horace H. Rackham postdoctoral research fellow, 1967-68; University of Pittsburgh, Pittsburgh, Pa., assistant professor, 1968-73, associate professor of political science, 1973—, chairman of department, 1976—. *Member:* Pi Sigma Alpha, Phi Kappa Phi.

WRITINGS: American and Soviet Aid: A Comparative Analysis, University of Pittsburgh Press, 1970; (with David Blake) *The Politics of Global Economic Relations,* Prentice-Hall, 1976. Contributor to journals of international affairs.

WORK IN PROGRESS: U.S. commodity policy.

* * *

WALTON, Clyde C(ameron) 1925-

PERSONAL: Born March 8, 1925, in Chicago, Ill.; son of Clyde C. (a clerk) and Helen L. (Williams) Walton; married Anne Hoover, December 27, 1947; children: James R., Jean Anne, Julia Lee. *Education:* Cornell College, Mount Vernon, Iowa, B.A., 1949; University of Chicago, M.A., 1950. *Politics:* Democratic. *Religion:* Methodist. *Home:* 1128 Northern Ct., DeKalb, Ill. 60115. *Office:* University Library, Northern Illinois University, DeKalb, Ill. 60115.

CAREER: University of Iowa, Iowa City, library assistant in charge of serials-reserve, 1950-51, curator of rare books, university archivist, and instructor in bibliography, 1951-55, assistant professor and head of reference department, 1955-56; Illinois State Historical Society, Springfield, executive director and head of Illinois State Historical Library, 1956-67; Northern Illinois University, DeKalb, director of libraries, 1967—. Secretary, Illinois Civil War Centennial Commission, 1959-65. Chairman of council, Conference of Midwest Universities (athletic), 1970—. Springfield Central Area Development Association, director, 1960-67, president, 1963-64; member, Capitol City Plan Commission, 1965-67. *Military service:* U.S. Army, 1943-45; became sergeant; received Bronze Star, Purple Heart, and Combat Infantryman Badge.

MEMBER: American Library Association (life member), Abraham Lincoln Association (secretary, 1963-67; director, 1967—), U.S. Grant Association (director and secretary, 1959—), Illinois State Historical Society (director, 1968), Illinois Library Association (life member), Rotary Club. *Awards, honors:* Litt.D., Lincoln College, 1956.

WRITINGS—Editor, except as noted: *The Indian War of 1864,* St. Martin's, 1960; *An Illinois Gold Hunter in the Black Hills,* Illinois State Historical Society, 1960; *Private Smith's Journal,* Donnelley, 1963; *Behind the Guns: The History of Battery I,* Southern Illinois University Press, 1965; (author) *Mr. Lincoln Opens His Mail,* Illinois State Historical Society, 1967; *An Illinois Reader,* Northern Illinois University Press, 1970. Writer of historical pamphlets and exhibit catalogues; contributor to encyclopedias and historical journals. Founder and editor, *Civil War History* (University of Iowa), 1955-59; former editor, *Journal of the Illinois State Historical Society,* 1956-67.

WORK IN PROGRESS: A study of the administration of a Civil War infantry regiment; and a documentary history of Illinois.

AVOCATIONAL INTERESTS: Fishing, particularly for trout; fly tying, hunting, camping, college athletics.

* * *

WALZ, Edgar 1914-

PERSONAL: Born April 13, 1914, in Freeman, S.D.; son of Philip (a farmer and merchant) and Elizabeth (Maag) Walz; married Esther Klawitter, March 12, 1937; children: Evelyn (Mrs. Donald F. Johnson). *Education:* Concordia College, St. Paul, Minn., graduated, 1933; studied at Northern State Teacher's College (now Northern State College), Aberdeen, S.D., University of South Dakota, and Dakota Wesleyan University, 1942-46; Concordia Seminary, St. Louis, Mo., B.A., 1946, B.D., 1956; Ball State University, M.A., 1956; Indiana University, Ed.D., 1961. *Politics:* Republican. *Home:* 1915 Colony Dr., Fort Wayne, Ind. 46825. *Office:* Concordia Senior College, 6600 North Clinton, Fort Wayne, Ind. 46825.

CAREER: Ordained to Lutheran ministry, 1938; pastor in Norris, S.D., Lebanon, S.D., and Mitchell, S.D., 1937-46; teacher in public school in Fort Wayne, Ind., 1946-51; Concordia Junior College, Fort Wayne, instructor in psychology and business manager, 1951-57; Concordia Senior College, Fort Wayne, instructor in psychology and business administration, and business manager, 1957—, acting dean of administration, 1965—. Financial aid officer, Concordia Senior College. Conducted workshops for pastors, teachers, and laymen, in Fort Wayne, Ind., St. Louis, Mo., St. Paul, Minn., 1962-65. Participant in conference presentations at Southern Ohio Pastor's Conference and Northern Indiana Pastor's Conference, 1962. Consultant to congregations in St. Louis, Mo., Fort Wayne, Ind., and South Bend, Ind. *Member:* Walther League (former president of South Dakota District).

WRITINGS: Church Business Methods: A Handbook for Pastors and Leaders of the Congregation, Concordia, 1970. Contributor to *Journal of Business Education, College and University Business,* and *Lutheran Education.*

SIDELIGHTS: Edgar Walz told *CA:* "[My] experiences as a parish minister toward the end of the 'Depression' and at the beginning of World War II led to an intense interest in business as this affects the life and work of churches. Consequently study and experience led to . . . the writing of *Church Business Methods* and continued research in an attempt to assist ministers and lay officers of churches in 'minding the church's business.'"

* * *

WANDESFORDE-SMITH, Geoffrey Albert 1943-

PERSONAL: Born November 2, 1943, in Wardle, Lancashire, England; son of Leslie (a merchant) and Marjorie (Fitton) Smith; married Margaret Wandesforde, November 26, 1969. *Education:* Attended Bury Grammar School, Lancashire, England, 1952-62; University of Nottington, B.A. (honors), 1965; University of Washington, Seattle, M.A., 1967, Ph.D., 1970. *Office:* Department of Political Science, University of California, Davis, Calif. 95616.

CAREER: University of California, Davis, assistant professor, 1970-74, associate professor of political science and environmental studies, 1974—, associate dean, 1975-76. Consultant, Assembly Committee on Natural Resources, California legislature, 1971-72. *Member:* International Union for the Conservation of Nature and Natural Resources, American Political Science Association, American Society for Public Administration, American Academy of Political and Social Science, American Association for the Advancement of Science, Policy Studies Organization. *Awards, honors:* California Water Center research grant, 1970-72; National Science Foundation research grant, 1971-73.

WRITINGS: (With Robert Warren) *Federal-State Development Planning: The Federal Field Committee for Development Planning in Alaska,* Department of Political Science, University of Washington, 1969; (editor with Richard A. Cooley, and contributor) *Congress and the Environment,* University of Washington Press, 1970; (with Laurence Baxter and Edmond Costantini) *Regional Agency Voting Behavior: The Tahoe Experience,* Institute of Government Affairs, University of California, 1974. Contributor to *Stanford Law Review* and *Natural Resources Journal;* reviewer for *Seattle Post-Intelligencer.*

WORK IN PROGRESS: Studies on the political and administrative aspects of environmental and resource management policy in the Pacific Coast states; and a study of the Council on Environmental Quality.†

* * *

WARD, David 1938-

PERSONAL: Born July 8, 1938, in Manchester, England; son of Horace (a shopkeeper) and Alice (Harwood) Ward; married Judith Barbara Freifeld, June 11, 1964; children: Michael John Harry, Peter Frank Benjamin. *Education:* University of Leeds, B.A. (first class honors), 1959, M.A., 1961; University of Wisconsin, Ph.D., 1963. *Home:* 1202 Edgehill Dr., Madison, Wis. 53705. *Office:* Department of Geography, Science Hall, University of Wisconsin, Madison, Wis. 53706.

CAREER: Carleton University, Ottawa, Ontario, lecturer

in geography, 1963-64; University of British Columbia, Vancouver, British Columbia, assistant professor of geography, 1964-66; University of Wisconsin—Madison, associate professor, 1966-71, professor of geography, 1971—, chairman of department, 1974-77. *Member:* Association of American Geographers (honorary secretary and chairman of West Lakes Division, 1967-69; councillor-at-large, 1975-78), Institute of British Geographers, Economic History Association, Economic History Society. *Awards, honors:* Fulbright travel award, 1960; Keikhofer Distinguished Teaching Award, University of Wisconsin—Madison, 1962; Guggenheim fellowship, 1970-71; American Council of Learned Societies fellowship, 1977-78.

WRITINGS: Cities and Immigrants: A Geography of Change in Nineteenth Century America, Oxford University Press, 1971.

Editor of monograph series, published by Association of American Geographers, 1972-76. Contributor of articles to *Annals* of the Association of American Geographers, *Economic Geography, Geographical Analysis, Geographical Magazine,* and other periodicals. Editor for the Americas, *Journal of Historical Geography.*

WORK IN PROGRESS: A book, *Ethnicity Redefined: The Changing Geography of Pluralism in American Cities.*

* * *

WARD, (John Stephen) Keith 1938-

PERSONAL: Born August 22, 1938, in Hexham, Northumberland, England; son of John (a director) and Evelyn (Simpson) Ward; married Marian Trotman (a teacher), June 22, 1963; children: Fiona Caroline, Alun James Kendal. *Education:* University of Wales, B.A., 1962; Linacre College, Oxford, B.Litt., 1967. *Office:* Department of Philosophy of Religion, King's College, University of London, Strand, London WC2R 2LS, England.

CAREER: University of Glasgow, Glasgow, Scotland, lecturer in logic, 1964-66, lecturer in moral philosophy, 1966-69; University of St. Andrews, St. Andrews, Scotland, lecturer in moral philosophy, 1969-71; University of London, King's College, London, England, lecturer in philosophy of religion, 1971—. *Military service:* Royal Air Force, 1956-58; served in Strategic Air Command.

WRITINGS: Fifty Key Words in Philosophy, Lutterworth, 1968, John Knox, 1969; *Ethics and Christianity,* Humanities, 1970; *The Development of Kant's View of Ethics,* Basil Blackwell, 1972; *The Concept God,* St. Martin's, 1975; *The Christian Way,* S.P.C.K., 1976; *The Divine Image: The Foundations of Christian Morality,* S.P.C.K., 1976. Contributor of articles to journals in his field.

WORK IN PROGRESS: A book on religious language and experience.

BIOGRAPHICAL/CRITICAL SOURCES: Times Literary Supplement, October 23, 1970.†

* * *

WARD, Ritchie R(unyan) 1906-

PERSONAL: Born April 6, 1906, in Medicine Lodge, Kan.; son of Frank Cooper and Mary (Ritchie) Ward; married Claire C. Marshall, August 23, 1933 (died November 18, 1974); children: William A. R. *Education:* Attended University of California, Los Angeles, 1923-25; University of California, Berkeley, B.S., 1927, M.J. (journalism), 1966. *Politics:* Liberal Republican. *Religion:* Episcopalian. *Home:* 93 El Toyonal Rd., Orinda, Calif. 94563.

CAREER: Hawaiian Sugar Planters' Association, Honolulu, assistant chemist, 1929-34; Shell Development Co., Emeryville, Calif., manager of technical information services, 1934-62; University of California, Berkeley, public information writer in Office of Engineering Research, 1965-67. Member of Commission on the International Federation for Documentation, National Academy of Sciences, 1961-63. *Member:* American Association for the Advancement of Science, California Writer's Club (director, 1976—.)

WRITINGS: Practical Technical Writing, Knopf, 1968; *The Living Clocks,* Knopf, 1971; *Into the Ocean World,* Knopf, 1974. Contributor of about forty sketches of scientists, engineers, and technical administrators to *Current Biography,* 1963-65, 1971—. Also contributor of popular science articles to *Natural History, Horizon, Ecolibrium,* and *Smithsonian Magazine.*

WORK IN PROGRESS: Our Living World, a book for the general reader on the high probability of life beyond the earth, with authoritative scientific support for the thesis.

SIDELIGHTS: Ritchie Ward told *CA:* "I hope to intrigue the non-specialist general reader with the detective-story quality of scientific discovery, with the objective of leading him to see great scientists as the human beings that they are, and how their discoveries affect the lives of all of us in a complex and difficult world."

* * *

WARD, William Arthur 1921-

PERSONAL: Born December 17, 1921, in Oakdale, La.; son of Albert Winfred and Laura (Williams) Ward; married Virginia Ella Bell (a public school administrator), June 30, 1945; children: J. Craig, David Bell, Lisa Diane. *Education:* McMurry College, B.Sc., 1948; Oklahoma State University of Agriculture and Applied Science, M.Sc., 1949; further additional study at University of Texas, summers of 1950, 1951, and North Texas State University, part-time, 1957-61. *Religion:* Methodist. *Home:* 2141 Green Hill Circle, Fort Worth, Tex. 76112. *Office:* Texas Wesleyan College, Fort Worth, Tex. 76105.

CAREER: Schreiner Institute, Kerrville, Tex., director of public relations, 1949-55; Texas Wesleyan College, Fort Worth, assistant to the president, 1955—. Member of board, Fort Worth Library, Tarrant County Chapter of the American Red Cross, and Longhorn Council, Boy Scouts of America. *Military service:* U.S. Army, 1942-46; served in Asiatic-Pacific theater, 1945-46. *Member:* American College Public Relations Association, Religious Public Relations Council, Sigma Delta Chi, Phi Delta Kappa, Rotary Club of Fort Worth (president, 1970-71). *Awards, honors:* LL.D. from Oklahoma City University, 1962.

WRITINGS: Thoughts of a Christian Optimist, Droke, 1968; (compiler and editor) *For This One Hour,* Droke, 1969; (compiler and editor) *Prayer Is . . .,* Droke, 1969; *Fountains of Faith,* Droke, 1971. Writer of regular column, "Ward's Words," in *Quote,* and daily front-page column, "Think It Over," in *Fort Worth Star-Telegram.*

WORK IN PROGRESS: Today Well Lived, The Wisdom of Discovering Yourself, and other books containing his maxims, which he calls "pertinent proverbs."

* * *

WARDEN, G(erard) B(ryce) 1939-

PERSONAL: Born August 1, 1939, in Pittsburgh, Pa.; son of James B. (a banker) and Emily (Bryce) Warden. *Education:* Yale University, B.A., 1961, M.A., 1962, Ph.D., 1966.

CAREER: U.S. Grant Foundation, New Haven, Conn., chairman of English department, 1959-61; Educational Development Center, Cambridge, Mass., consultant, 1965-67; Princeton University, Princeton, N.J., instructor in American history, 1966-69; Yale University, New Haven, Conn., assistant professor of American history, 1970-75; Harvard University, Cambridge, Mass., fellow in law and history, 1975-76. Director, Connecticut Council for the Social Studies, 1973-75. Consultant, Corporation for Public Broadcasting, 1971.

WRITINGS: (With E. S. Morgan and N. Plessner) *The Making of the American Revolution,* Educational Services, Inc., 1967; *Boston, 1689-1776,* Little, Brown, 1970. Assistant editor of *Papers of Benjamin Franklin,* Yale University Press, 1970-75.

WORK IN PROGRESS: A history of New England; early American legal history.

* * *

WARDROPER, John (Edmund) 1923-

PERSONAL: Born December 10, 1923, in Duncan, British Columbia, Canada; son of Wilfrid Strickland (a farmer) and Mathilda (Lythall) Wardroper; married Patricia Carr, September 25, 1953; children: Ann, Michael, Mark. *Education:* University of British Columbia, B.A., 1948. *Home:* 60 St. Paul's Rd., London N.1, England.

CAREER: Reporter for *Cowichan Leader,* Duncan, British, Columbia, 1941-43, and *Daily Colonist,* Victoria, British Columbia, 1943-45; *News-Herald,* Vancouver, British Columbia, desk man, 1948-49; sub-editor on *Sunderland Echo,* Sunderland, England, 1949, *Liverpool Post,* Liverpool, England, 1950, *Daily Express,* London, England, 1951-64, *Sun,* London, 1964-70, and *Sunday Times,* London, 1970—. *Member:* National Union of Journalists, Society of Authors.

WRITINGS: (Editor) *Love and Drollery: A Selection of Amatory, Merry and Satirical Verse of the 17th Century,* Barnes & Noble, 1969; *Jest upon Jest* (selections from English jestbooks, 1485-1800), Routledge & Kegan Paul, 1970; *Demaundes Joyous* (riddle book of 1511), Gordon Fraser, 1971; *Kings, Lords and Wicked Libellers: Satire and Protest, 1760-1857,* J. Murray, 1973; *The Caricatures of George Cruikshank,* Gordon Fraser, 1977.

* * *

WARNER, Harry, Jr. 1922-

PERSONAL: Born December 19, 1922, in Chambersburg, Pa.; son of Harry B. (an accountant) and Margaret Caroline (Klipp) Warner. *Education:* Attended public schools in Hagerstown, Md. *Politics:* Independent. *Religion:* Lutheran. *Home:* 423 Summit Ave., Hagerstown, Md. 21740. *Office:* Herald-Mail Co., 25-31 Summit Ave., Hagerstown, Md. 21740.

CAREER: Office clerk for railroad, 1942; *Morning Herald,* Hagerstown, Md., reporter, 1943-62, city editor, 1962-71; *Morning Herald* and *Daily Mail,* Hagerstown, columnist, 1971—; free-lance writer and photographer. *Member:* National Fantasy Fan Association (founding member and former chairman), Fantasy Amateur Press Association (former president, vice-president, and secretary-treasurer), Cosmic Circle, Futurian Federation of the World. *Awards, honors:* Hugo Awards for best writer of non-profit science fiction, World Science Fiction Convention, 1969, 1971.

WRITINGS: All Our Yesterdays: An Informal History of Science Fiction Fandom in the Forties, Advent, 1969; *A*

Wealth of Fable, Fanhistorica Press, in press. Contributor of short stories and novelettes to science fiction magazines, articles for press syndicates, and stories and articles to amateur journals.

SIDELIGHTS: Harry Warner told *CA* that he has had a "life-long interest in science fiction and fantasy fiction, as well as in the fandoms that have grown up around these forms of literature, expressed principally as [a] collector of books and magazines, writer for professional and amateur publications, [and editor for] . . . amateur publications regularly since 1938."

* * *

WARNER, W(illiam) Lloyd 1898-1970

October 26, 1898—May 23, 1970; American sociologist and educator. Obituaries: *New York Times,* May 24, 1970; *Washington Post,* May 25, 1970; *Antiquarian Bookman,* June 15, 1970. (See index for *CA* sketch)

* * *

WARTOFSKY, (William) Victor 1931-

PERSONAL: Born June 15, 1931, in New York, N.Y.; son of Harry and Sadie (Gondelman) Wartofsky; married Tamar Chachik (a teacher), February, 1957; children: Leora, Ari, Alona. *Education:* George Washington University, student, 1950-52; American University, B.A., 1963. *Religion:* Jewish. *Home:* 8507 Wild Olive Dr., Potomac, Md. 20854. *Agent:* Curtis Brown, Ltd., 575 Madison Ave., New York, N.Y. 10022.

CAREER: United Press International, Washington, D.C., reporter, 1954-60; B'nai B'rith, Washington, D.C., writer and publicist, 1960; National Institute of Health, Bethesda, Md., writer, 1961—. *Military service:* U.S. Army, 1952-54.

WRITINGS: Mr. Double and Other Stories (short story collection), Joshua Chachik Publishing Co., 1967; *Meeting the Pieman* (novel), John Day, 1971; *Year of the Yahoo* (novel), John Day, 1972. Contributor of short stories to periodicals.

WORK IN PROGRESS: Suit without Pockets, a novel about a Jewish fraternal organization; *The Passage,* a novel about a scientific search for the human soul.

SIDELIGHTS: Victor Wartofsky says that he is influenced by "almost every contemporary writer I have read. . . . Although I can't say with certainty which ones had more of an impact than others, I especially enjoy reading Malamud and Petrakis because of their feeling for the human condition, their simplicity of language, and their storytelling ability. They seem to get to the core of Faulkner's statement that there's nothing worth writing about except the human heart in conflict with itself. I believe that a serious writer should also show the need for people to be better than they are."

BIOGRAPHICAL/CRITICAL SOURCES: Best Sellers, January 1, 1971.

* * *

WARWICK, Jack 1930-

PERSONAL: Born September 9, 1930, in Huddersfield, England; son of Alfred (an engineer) and Margaret (Tobin) Warwick; married H. Clare Shoosmith (a journalist), May 15, 1954; children: Genevieve, Brigid, Jacqueline. *Education:* Oxford University, B.A. (honors), 1953; University of Western Ontario, M.A., 1959, Ph.D., 1963. *Home:* 20 Highbourne Rd., Toronto, Ontario, Canada. *Office:* Department

of French Literature, York University, Toronto, Ontario, Canada.

CAREER: Huron College, London, Ontario, instructor in French, 1959-60; University of Western Ontario, London, instructor, 1960-61, lecturer, 1961-63, assistant professor of French and Spanish, 1963-68; McMasters University, Hamilton, Ontario, associate professor of French and social sciences, 1968-70; York University, Toronto, Ontario, associate professor, 1970-72, professor of French, 1972—. *Military service:* British Army, 1948-50; became second lieutenant. *Member:* Association Internationale des Etudes Francaises, Association des Professeurs de Francais des Universites Canadiennes (president, 1976-78). *Awards, honors:* Canada Council senior fellowship for research, 1966-67.

WRITINGS: The Long Journey: Literary Themes of French Canada, University of Toronto Press, 1968. Contributor to *Canadian Literature, Revue de l'Institut de Sociologie* (Brussels), and other French and English journals.

WORK IN PROGRESS: Research in Counter-Reformation thought and imagination, and in the application of literature to social and ideological question in Canada.

BIOGRAPHICAL/CRITICAL SOURCES: Books Abroad, autumn, 1968.

* * *

WASHINGTON, Gladys J(oseph) 1931-
(Gladys J. Curry)

PERSONAL: Born March 4, 1931, in Houston, Tex.; daughter of Eddie and Anita (Malbrough) Joseph; divorced; married Elton Washington. *Education:* Texas Southern University, B.A., 1952, M.A., 1955; Tulane University, graduate study, 1964-67. *Home:* 1422 Richmond Ave., Houston, Tex. 77006. *Office:* Department of English, Texas Southern University, Houston, Tex. 77004.

CAREER: Southern University and Agricultural and Mechanical College, New Orleans, La., associate professor of English, 1962-70; Texas Southern University, Houston, assistant professor of English, 1970—. *Member:* Modern Language Association of America, National Council of Teachers of English, South Central Modern Language Association, Alpha Kappa Mu.

WRITINGS—Under name Gladys J. Curry: (Editor) *Viewpoints from Black America,* Prentice-Hall, 1970. Contributor to *Roots* (Texas Southern University literary magazine).

WORK IN PROGRESS: A proposed comprehensive anthology of black drama in America.

SIDELIGHTS: Gladys Washington told *CA:* "My major area of vocational interest within the field of English is Afro-American literature. . . . My book, *Viewpoints from Black America,* was conceived out of the need for a reading text that concerned itself with the prose of black writers. At the time of its conception, no such text existed. . . . As a college teacher, I feel that the most vital issue today exists in American education. There is a dire need for a recognition of the contribution of black people to American culture and a subsequent incorporation of such contributions into educational textbooks on all levels."

AVOCATIONAL INTERESTS: Drama (has been affiliated with amateur theatre groups).

WATERHOUSE, Charles 1924-

PERSONAL: Born September 22, 1924, in Columbus, Ga.; son of Harry Howard (a mechanic) and Bertha (Rassmussen) Waterhouse; married Barbara Andersen, June 6, 1948; children: Jane, Amy. *Education:* Attended Newark School of Fine and Industrial Art, 1947-50. *Religion:* Protestant. *Home:* 67 Dartmouth St., Edison, N.J. 08817.

CAREER: Free-lance illustrator, in both black and white and color, for national publications and accounts, including *Argosy, Outdoor Life, Scholastic, Readers Digest,* Boy Scouts of America, American Legion, Prudential Insurance, Bell Telephone, and the U.S. Army, Navy, Air Force, and Marine Corps, for Associated Press news features, and for textbooks, juvenile books, and book jackets. Instructor of illustration at Newark School of Fine and Industrial Art, Newark, N.J. *Military service:* U.S. Marine Corps, 1943-46; received Presidential Unit Citation and Purple Heart. *Member:* Society of Illustrators, Salmagundi Club (Naval Art Cooperation and Liaison Committee artist), Company of Military Historians, U.S.M.C. Combat Correspondents.

WRITINGS: Vietnam Sketchbook Drawings from Delta to DMZ, Tuttle, 1968; *Vietnam War Sketches from the Air, Land and Sea,* Tuttle, 1970.

Illustrator: Bette Ward Widney, *The Mystery of the Wheat Pirates* (juvenile), Vanguard, 1968; Leslie Waller, *Mountains* (juvenile), Grosset, 1969; Barbara Kaye Greenleaf, *Forward March to Freedom: A Biography of A. Phillip Randolph* (juvenile), Grosset, 1971; Nathan Shalit, *Cup and Saucer Chemistry* (juvenile), Grosset, 1972; Charles Richard Smith, *Marines in the Revolution: A History of the Continental Marines in the American Revolution, 1775-1783,* History and Museums Division, U.S. Marine Corps, 1975.

WORK IN PROGRESS: Strategic Air Command (SAC) sketchbook of the artist in Alaska, *Have Brush, Will Travel.*

BIOGRAPHICAL/CRITICAL SOURCES: American Artist, September, 1968.

*　　*　　*

WATKIN, David (John) 1941-

PERSONAL: Born April 7, 1941, in Salisbury, England. *Education:* Trinity Hall, Cambridge, M.A., 1966, Ph.D., 1967. *Office:* Faculty of Architecture and History of Art, Cambridge University, 1 Scroope Ter., Cambridge, England.

CAREER: Cambridge University, Cambridge, England, fellow of Peterhouse, 1970—, librarian of the Faculty of Architecture and History of Art, 1967-72, lecturer in history of art, 1972—. *Member:* Athenaeum Club. *Awards, honors:* Alice Davis Hitchcock Medallion, Society of Architectural Historians of Great Britain, 1975, for *The Life and Work of C. R. Cockerell, R.A.*

WRITINGS: Thomas Hope, 1769-1831, and the Neo-Classical Idea, J. Murray, 1968, Transatlantic, 1970; *The Life and Work of C. R. Cockerell, R.A.,* A. Zwemmer, 1974.

*　　*　　*

WATSON, James Gray 1939-

PERSONAL: Born June 16, 1939, in Baltimore, Md.; son of William Gray (a physician) and Margaret (Meister) Watson; married Ann Boyles, April 20, 1963; children: William Gray II, Richard Boyles. *Education:* Bowdoin College, A.B., 1961; University of Pittsburgh, M.A., 1963, Ph.D., 1968.

Home: 1344 East 19th St., Tulsa, Okla. 74120. *Office:* Faculty of Letters, University of Tulsa, Tulsa, Okla. 74104.

CAREER: University of Pittsburgh, Pittsburgh, Pa., assistant dean, 1968-69; University of Tulsa, Tulsa, Okla., assistant professor, 1969-75, associate professor of English, 1976—. *Member:* Modern Language Association of America, American Association of University Professors, South Central Modern Language Association.

WRITINGS: The Snopes Dilemma: Faulkner's Trilogy, University of Miami Press, 1970.

WORK IN PROGRESS: Research in modern American fiction, especially the short stories of Ernest Hemingway and William Faulkner.

*　　*　　*

WATTS, (Anna) Bernadette 1942-
(Bernadette)

PERSONAL: Born May 13, 1942, in Northampton, England; daughter of Bert (a surveyor) and Josephine (Roberts) Watts; children: Hywell. *Education:* Maidstone College of Art, National Diploma in Design. *Politics:* Socialist. *Religion:* None. *Home:* "Little Dowles", Stone St., Kent, England.

CAREER: Free-lance illustrator and author. *Awards, honors:* Premio Graphico (Bologna, Italy), 1969, for illustrations in James Reeves' *One's None;* Best New Childrens Book award, 1975, for *Little Red Riding Hood.*

WRITINGS—All juvenile; author and illustrator under name Bernadette: *Hans the Miller Man,* McGraw, 1969 (published in England as *Hans Millerman,* Oxford University Press, 1969); *Varenka,* Nord-Sud-Verlag, 1971, Putnam, 1972; *Mother Holly* (retelling of Brothers Grimm tale), Crowell, 1972; Caroline Rubin, editor, *The Proud Crow,* Albert Whitman, 1975; *Brigette and Ferdinand: A Love Story* (originally entitled *The Little Flute Player*), Prentice-Hall, 1976.

Illustrator under name Bernadette Watts: Brothers Grimm, *Little Red Riding Hood,* Oxford University Press, 1968, World Publishing, 1969; Ruth Ainsworth, *Look, Do and Listen,* F. Watts, 1969; James Reeves, editor, *One's None: Old Rhymes for New Tongues,* F. Watts, 1969; Alfred Tennyson, *Lady of Shallott,* F. Watts, 1969; Reinhold Ehrhardt, *Kikeri, or The Proud Red Rooster,* World Publishing, 1969; Kathleen Arnott, *Animal Folk Tales around the World,* Blackie & Son, 1970, Walck, 1971; Brothers Grimm, *Jorinda and Joringel,* World Publishing, 1970; Rhoda D. Power, *The Big Book of Stories from Many Lands,* F. Watts, 1970; Ehrhardt, *Die Turmuhr,* Nord-Sud-Verlag, 1971; George Mendoza, *The Christmas Tree Alphabet Book,* World Publishing, 1971; Brothers Grimm, *Frau Holle,* Nord-Sud-Verlag, 1972; Brothers Grimm, *Haensel und Gretel,* Nord-Sud-Verlag, 1973. Also illustrator of *Cinderella,* C. A. Watts, *Snow White,* C. A. Watts, and *The Lord's Prayer,* Parents Magazine Press. Also illustrated little "zig-zag" books for Kauffmann Verlag, posters, book jackets, and educational materials.

WORK IN PROGRESS: Writing more children's short stories; *Ashputtel,* and two other full color books.

SIDELIGHTS: Bernadette Watts has a great interest in the people of Africa, their culture, music, and stories, and spent four months in South Africa in 1969. She attends the Bologna and Frankfurt book fairs annually, and also visits other European countries regularly. Watts told *CA:* "Interested, more and more, in producing books toward the universal understanding of all peoples in the world.'' She is also currently interested in illustrating small books for schools in the Welsh language.

BIOGRAPHICAL/CRITICAL SOURCES: Young Readers Review, October, 1969.

* * *

WATTS, Reginald John 1931-

PERSONAL: Born January 28, 1931, in Essex, England; son of Wilford John Lionel (a marine surveyor) and Julia Doris (Wheeler) Watts; married Susan Roscoe Cushman (a teacher), 1960; children: Charlotte Amelia Roscoe, Marcus Redmayne. *Education:* Attended Bishop's Stortford College, 1944-49. *Politics:* Tory. *Religion:* Church of England. *Home:* 37 Talbot Rd., London W.2, England. *Office:* Burson-Marsteller Ltd., 25 North Row, London W.1, England.

CAREER: Burson-Marsteller Ltd. (public relations consultants), London, England, vice-president, 1970-77, chairman, 1977—. *Member:* Institute of Journalists, Institute of Public Relations, Institute of Directors (fellow), Carlton Club, Hurlinsham Club.

WRITINGS: Reaching the Consumer: The Elements of Product Public Relations, Business Books, 1970; *The Businessman's Guide to Marketing*, Business Books, 1972. Also co-author of *Good Will: The Wasted Asset.*

WORK IN PROGRESS: Public Relations for Top Management to be published by Croner.

* * *

WAYNE, Doreen

PERSONAL: Born in Hull, England; daughter of David (a company director) and Jane Juggler; married Jerry Wayne (an actor and producer), July 4, 1967. *Education:* Educated in Manchester, England. *Residence:* London, England. *Agent:* Eric Glass Ltd., 28 Berkeley Sq., London W1X 6HD, England.

CAREER: Worked as a typist and bookkeeper in London, England, 1961-63, then formed her own company to phototype scripts for film companies and theatrical producers.

WRITINGS: Love Is a Well Raped Word (novel), Frewin, 1968; *The Love Strike*, W. H. Allen, 1971.

WORK IN PROGRESS: Filmscript for *Love Is a Well Raped Word.*

BIOGRAPHICAL/CRITICAL SOURCES: Books and Bookmen, January, 1969.†

* * *

WAYNE, Jerry 1919-

PERSONAL: Born July 24, 1919, in Buffalo, N.Y.; son of David (a realtor) and Anna (Schneider) Krauth; married Cathie Scheninger, June 19, 1941; married second wife, Doreen Juggler, July 4, 1967; children: (first marriage) Jeffrey. *Education:* Attended University of Buffalo (now State University of New York at Buffalo) and Ohio State University. *Residence:* London, England. *Agent:* Eric Glass Ltd., 28 Berkeley Sq., London W1X 6HD, England.

CAREER: Actor and singer in New York City, 1943-61; producer in New York City and London, England, 1963—.

WRITINGS: The Arabian Nights of Samuel Arnstein, Frewin, 1968; *The Bad Back Book*, Delacorte, 1972.

WORK IN PROGRESS: Filmscript for *The Arabian Nights of Samuel Arnstein.*

BIOGRAPHICAL/CRITICAL SOURCES: Books and Bookmen, January, 1969.†

* * *

WEBB, Eugene 1938-

PERSONAL: Born November 10, 1938, in Santa Monica, Calif.; son of Eugene, Jr. and Marguerite (Rufi) Webb; married Marilyn Domoto, June 4, 1964; children: Alexandra Mariko. *Education:* University of California, Los Angeles, B.A., 1960; Columbia University, M.A., 1962, Ph.D., 1965. *Religion:* Episcopalian. *Home:* 6911 57th Ave. N.E., Seattle, Wash. 98115. *Office:* Comparative Literature Program, University of Washington, Seattle, Wash. 98195.

CAREER: Simon Fraser University, Burnaby, British Columbia, assistant professor of English, 1965-66; University of Washington, Seattle, assistant professor, 1966-70, associate professor, 1970-75, professor of comparative literature and comparative religion, 1975—. *Member:* Modern Language Association of America, Phi Beta Kappa. *Awards, honors:* Woodrow Wilson fellowship, 1960.

WRITINGS—All published by the University of Washington Press: *Samuel Beckett: A Study of His Novels*, 1970; *The Plays of Samuel Beckett*, 1972; *The Dark Dove: The Sacred and Secular in Modern Literature*, 1975. Contributor to literary journals.

WORK IN PROGRESS: A book on the religious thought of Eric Voepelin.

SIDELIGHTS: Eugene Webb is competent in French, German, Latin, Greek, and Italian (listed in descending order of his competence).

* * *

WEBB, Rozana 1908-

PERSONAL: Born March 31, 1908, in Memphis, Tenn.; daughter of William Donaldson and Aubrey Leota Amelia (Hill) Sprigg; married Ernest Webb, May 27, 1926 (died, 1975); children: Dorothy Rose. *Education:* Educated in private and public schools. *Politics:* ''Regularly Democrat. . . . Vote Independent.'' *Religion:* Anglican. *Address:* P.O. Box 467, Visalia, Calif. 93277.

CAREER: Writer. Instructor in creative writing, 1967—. Lecturer to and organizer of poetry workshops; western representative, South and West, Inc.; former assistant editor, 7 Poets Press. *Member:* Centro Studi e Scambi Internazionali, Composers, Authors, and Artists of America, Parent-Teacher Association, Chaparral National Writers, San Joaquin Artists and Writers Association, Women's Club, Tulare County Cotton Wives. *Awards, honors:* Golden Pegasus Award, California Poets, 1969, for ''Treasures of the Sea''; Silver Trophy, South & West, Inc., 1970.

WRITINGS—All poetry: *The Thirteenth Man*, 7 Poets Press, 1962; *The Monsoon Breeds*, Border Press, 1965; *Eternal the Flow*, South & West, 1966; *Coffee Break*, South & West, 1967; *The Way*, South & West, 1969; *The Ghost Walkers*, South & West, 1974. Work represented in several anthologies, including *To Each His Song*, edited by Lilith Lorraine, Different Press, 1958, *New Orlando*, edited by Anca Vrborska, New Orlando Publications, 1958, and *Poetry Dial*, edited by Lourine White, Piggot Banner Press, 1962. Contributor of poetry, articles, and short stories to many periodicals, including *South & West, Voices, Quest, Nimrod, Tangent, Poetry India*, and *Wisconsin Poetry*. Editor, *Bollweevil.*

WORK IN PROGRESS: A book of poetry featuring the American Indian; revising first and third sections of *The Thirteenth Man;* a new collection of writings.

SIDELIGHTS: Rozana Webb told *CA:* "[I] started writing in first grade. [I] combined poetry, stories, and art. [I] still use my own art work to illustrate my books. . . . I make frequent trips to various states and to schools in our area, to give poetry workshops and talks on poetry NOW. My travel madness is Anywhere, U.S.A. [I] am sort of in love with this land of ours. [I] haven't seen nearly enough of it. . . . I read about other places, but have not had time to make the foreign scene. . . . I would like to go to the moon." She adds: "Writing can be done in the home and is therefore the perfect vocation for me. I like being a woman and a wife. All this 'lib' jazz is for the birds who just couldn't cut it in the very tough job of making a home."

AVOCATIONAL INTERESTS: Painting, oriental art, research into the past and future, and driving "somewhat over the speed limit."

* * *

WEBBER, Ross A. 1934-

PERSONAL: Born July 18, 1934, in New Rochelle, N.Y.; son of Richard (an engineer) and Muriel (Arkels) Webber; married Mary Louise Foradora, September 29, 1956; children: Sarah Ruth, Judith Mary, Gregory Ross, Jennifer Louise, Stephen Andrew. *Education:* Princeton University, B.S.M.E. (with honors), 1956; Columbia University, Ph.D., 1965. *Religion:* Roman Catholic. *Home:* 206 Horse Shoe Ct., Cherry Hill, N.J. 08034. *Office:* Management Department, Wharton School, University of Pennsylvania, Philadelphia, Pa. 19175.

CAREER: Eastman Kodak Co., Rochester, N.Y., industrial engineer, 1956-59; University of Pennsylvania, Wharton School, Philadelphia, lecturer, 1964-65, assistant professor, 1965-69, associate professor, 1969-76, professor of management, 1976—. Has conducted management training programs for public and business groups. *Military service:* U.S. Navy, 1956-59.

WRITINGS: (With David R. Hampton and Charles E. Summer) *Organization Behavior and the Practice of Management,* Scott, Foresman, 1968; *Culture and Management: Text and Readings in Comparative Management,* Irwin, 1969; *Time and Management,* Van Nostrand, 1972; *Management: Basic Elements of Managing Organizations,* Irwin, 1975. Contributor to business and psychology journals.

* * *

WEBER, Alfons 1921-

PERSONAL: Born July 26, 1921, in Zurich, Switzerland; son of Leo and Ida (Buergisser) Weber; married Margrit Ritschel, October 17, 1954; children: Elizabeth, Dagmar, Bernard, Beda. *Education:* Studied at University of Zurich and University of Vienna; University of Basel, M.D., 1949, advanced study in pediatrics and child psychiatry, 1949-58. *Politics:* None. *Religion:* Roman Catholic. *Home:* Im Roetel 19c, 6300 Zug, Switzerland. *Office:* Children's Hospital, 8032 Zurich, Switzerland.

CAREER: Physician specializing in pediatrics, Zug, Switzerland, 1958-65; Children's Hospital, Zurich, Switzerland, chief of department of child psychiatry, 1965—; University of Zurich, Faculty of Medicine, Zurich, assistant professor of child psychiatry, 1970—. *Military service:* Swiss Army, Sanitary Troops, with rank of major. *Member:* Swiss Society for Paediatry, Swiss Society for Child Psychiatry, Swiss Society for Psychosomatic Medicine, International Society for Psycho-Endocrinology.

WRITINGS: Elisabeth wird gesund (juvenile), Ex Libris Verlag, 1969, translation published as *Elizabeth Gets Well,* Crowell, 1970 (published in England as *Lisa Goes to Hospital,* Blackie & Son, 1970).

WORK IN PROGRESS: A textbook on child psychiatry; research on the effects of television in childhood, on problems of hospitalization in childhood, and in psychoendocrinology.

AVOCATIONAL INTERESTS: Painting, literature.

* * *

WEBER, Lenora Mattingly 1895-1971

October 1, 1895—January 29, 1971; writer of books and short stories for children. Obituaries: *Publishers' Weekly,* February 15, 1971. (See index for *CA* sketch)

* * *

WEBSTER, David 1930-

PERSONAL: Born April 14, 1930, in Philadelphia, Pa.; son of Harold Shoemaker (an engineer) and Grace (Gourley) Webster; married Winifred Wightman, April 15, 1961; children: Douglas, Jocelyn. *Education:* Rutgers University, B.S., 1952; Harvard University, graduate study, 1958. *Politics:* Republican. *Religion:* Protestant. *Home:* Todd Pond Rd., Lincoln, Mass. 01773.

CAREER: Junior high school science teacher, Lebanon, N.H., 1955-57; director of science, Lincoln (Mass.) Public Schools, 1957-61; National Science Foundation, Elementary Science Study, Newton, Mass., staff writer, 1961-67; science consultant to Wellesley (Mass.) Public Schools, 1967—. *Military service:* U.S. Army, 1952-54; became second lieutenant.

WRITINGS—For young people: *Brain-Boosters,* Natural History Press, 1966; *Crossroad Puzzles,* Natural History Press, 1967; *Snow Stumpers,* Natural History Press, 1968; *Towers,* Natural History Press, 1971; *Track-Watching,* F. Watts, 1972; *Photo-Fun,* F. Watts, 1973; *How to Do a Science Project,* F. Watts, 1974; *Let's Find Out about Mosquitoes,* F. Watts, 1974; *More Brain-Boosters,* Doubleday, 1975; *Shadow Science,* Doubleday, 1976; *Science Projects with Eggs,* F. Watts, 1976. Contributor of articles to magazines. Author of "Brain-Booster" column in *Nature and Science.* Has written several film loop programs at Ealing Corp. and developed activities for a new Ginn Science Textbook Series, grades 1-8.

BIOGRAPHICAL/CRITICAL SOURCES: New York Times Book Review, November 5, 1967, November 3, 1968.

* * *

WEINBERG, Kerry

PERSONAL: Born in Germany, near the French border. *Education:* Teachers College, Wuerzburg, Germany, B.A.; Hebrew University of Jerusalem, English Diploma; Temple University, M.A., 1957; New York University, doctoral candidate; graduate study at Princeton University, Columbia University, New School for Social Research, and State University of New York. *Address:* P.O. Box 342, Spring Valley, N.Y. 10977.

CAREER: Teacher of English at high school in Tel-Aviv, Israel, prior to 1954; East Ramapo Central School District,

Spring Valley, N.Y., high school teacher of English, Latin, French, German, and Hebrew, 1956—. Part-time teacher of English and German at community colleges in New York area.

WRITINGS: T. S. Eliot and Charles Baudelaire, Mouton, 1969, Humanities, 1970; (co-author) *Emuna/Horizonte,* Emuna Verlag (Frankfurt), 1972. Contributor of articles to periodicals in Europe and United States, including *Die Unterrichtspraxis, Die Neucren Sprachen, Classical Outlook,* and *New York Teacher.*

WORK IN PROGRESS: A critical study in the field of English-French comparative literature.

SIDELIGHTS: Kerry Weinberg told *CA:* "In my teens, my interests were divided among literature (especially poetry-writing), math and music. Fate led me to concentrate on literature. I hope to be able, in the foreseeable future, to devote some time to fiction-writing." *Avocational interests:* The theatre, music, travel, water sports, gardening.

*   *   *

WEINBERGER, Paul E. 1931-

PERSONAL: Born January 17, 1931, in Vienna, Austria; son of Julius and Sophie (Glass) Weinberger; married Dorothy Zegart, April 10, 1960; children: Ellis, Joel, Benjamin. *Education:* San Francisco State College (now University), B.A. (cum laude), 1951; University of California, Berkeley, M.S.W., 1958; University of Southern California, D.S.W., 1966. *Religion:* Jewish. *Agent:* Gerard McCauley Agency, Inc., 159 West 53rd St., New York, N.Y. 10019. *Office:* School of Social Work, San Diego State University, San Diego, Calif. 92115.

CAREER: American-Israeli Shipping Co., New York, N.Y., statistical and editorial work, 1951-52; Great American Insurance Co., San Francisco, Calif., audit reviewer and casualty underwriter, 1952-56; Family Service Bureau, Oakland, Calif., caseworker, 1958-60; Alameda County (Calif.) Public Welfare Department, senior child welfare worker, 1960; Marianne Frostig School for Educational Therapy, Los Angeles, Calif., chief social worker, 1960-62; Mount Sinai Hospital, Los Angeles, research associate, department of child psychiatry, 1962-63; Children's Home Society of California, Los Angeles, research associate, 1963-65; University of Southern California, School of Social Work, Los Angeles, lecturer, 1964-65; San Francisco State College (now University), San Francisco, Calif., associate professor of welfare, 1965-68; San Diego State University, School of Social Work, San Diego, Calif., professor of social work, 1968—. Research and administrative consultant to state hospitals and to Headstart programs in California. Member of Western Region advisory board, American Jewish Congress. *Member:* Council on Social Work Education.

WRITINGS: (Editor and contributor) *Perspectives on Social Welfare,* Macmillan, 1969, 2nd edition, 1974; (contributor) Alfred Kadushin, editor, *Child Welfare Services: A Sourcebook,* Macmillan, 1970. Contributor to social work and Jewish journals.†

*   *   *

WEINER, Irving B(ernard) 1933-

PERSONAL: Born August 16, 1933, in Grand Rapids, Mich.; son of Jacob H. (a businessman) and Mollie (Laevin) Weiner; married Frances Shair, June 9, 1963; children: Jeremy H., Seth H. *Education:* University of Michigan,

A.B., 1955, M.A., 1957, Ph.D., 1959. *Home:* 2742 Belvoir Blvd., Shaker Heights, Ohio 44122. *Office:* Office of the Dean of Graduate Studies, Case Western Reserve University, Cleveland, Ohio 44106.

CAREER: U.S. Veterans Administration, clinical trainee, 1956-58; University of Michigan, Ann Arbor, Bureau of Psychological Service, counselor, 1957-59; University of Rochester, Rochester, N.Y., instructor in psychiatry, 1959-62, senior instructor, 1962-64, assistant professor, 1964-67, associate professor, 1967-69, professor of psychiatry, pediatrics, and psychology, 1969-72, head of Division of Psychology, University Medical Center, 1968-72; Case Western Reserve University, Cleveland, Ohio, professor of psychology and chairman of department, 1972-77, dean of graduate studies, 1976—. Diplomate, American Board of Professional Psychology. Advisory editor, John Wiley & Sons. *Member:* American Association for the Advancement of Science, American Psychological Association, Society for Personality Assessment, Society for Adolescent Medicine, Eastern Psychological Association, New York Academy of Sciences, Phi Beta Kappa, Sigma Xi, Phi Kappa Phi.

WRITINGS—All published by Wiley, except as indicated: *Psychodiagnosis in Schizophrenia,* 1966; *Psychological Disturbances in Adolescence,* 1970; (with Marvin Goldfried and George Stricker) *Rorschach Handbook of Clinical and Research Applications,* Prentice-Hall, 1971; (with David Elkind) *Child Development,* 1972; *Principles of Psychotherapy,* 1975; *Clinical Methods in Psychology,* 1976. Editor, "Wiley Series on Psychological Disorders" and "Wiley Series on Personality Processes."

*   *   *

WEINIG, Jean Maria 1920-
(Mother Mary Anthony, Sister Mary Anthony Weinig)

PERSONAL: Born May 19, 1920, in New York, N.Y.; daughter of Anthony Joseph (a businessman) and Elizabeth L. (O'Brian) Weinig. *Education:* Rosemont College, B.A., 1942; Fordham University, M.A., 1951, Ph.D., 1957. *Home and office:* Rosemont College, Rosemont, Pa. 19010.

CAREER: Entered Society of the Holy Child Jesus (congregation of teaching religious), 1940, and took her vows as Mother Mary Anthony, 1942 (in 1968 the order changed the form of name used by its members and she became Sister Mary Anthony Weinig); teacher at Catholic high school in Suffern, N.Y., 1943-56; Rosemont College, Rosemont, Pa., 1956—, began as instructor, professor of English, 1970—. *Member:* Modern Language Association of America, College English Association, American Association of University Professors, Pennsylvania College Teachers of English. *Awards, honors:* American Philosophical Society research grant, 1965; Danforth associate, 1968.

WRITINGS: (Under name Mother Mary Anthony) *Fire in the Well* (poems), published as special (entire) issue of *South and West,* summer, 1966. Also author of a collection of poems, "Rain in the Chimney," published in *South and West,* 1972. Contributor of articles to literary journals and poetry to about twenty periodicals, including *Commonweal, Southern Humanities Review,* and *Approach;* regular abstracter, *Abstracts of English Studies;* regular reviewer, *Best Sellers* and *Choice.*

WORK IN PROGRESS: One or more editions of Coventry Patmore's uncollected prose and a book on Patmore, for Twayne; a third collection of her own poems.

BIOGRAPHICAL/CRITICAL SOURCES: Poetry Review, summer, 1967.

*   *   *

WEINSTEIN, Robert A. 1914-

PERSONAL: Born October 9, 1914, in Philadelphia, Pa.; son of Max (a salesman) and Pearl (Guss) Weinstein; married Vivian R. Levin (a teacher and administrator), August 29, 1939; children: David M. *Home:* 1253 South Stanley Ave., Los Angeles, Calif. 90019.

CAREER: Ward Ritchie Press, Los Angeles, Calif., graphic designer, 1949—, executive vice-president, 1968-76. Research associate of maritime history at Bernice Bishop Museum, Honolulu, Hawaii, and Los Angeles County Museum of Natural History. Southern California representative, San Francisco Maritime Museum. Consultant to American Heritage Publishing Co., Oakland Museum, and other museums, and to Special Collections Department Library, University of California at Los Angeles. *Military service:* U.S. Army, 1942-46; served in Europe. *Member:* Western History Association, California Historical Society, Historical Society of Southern California (first vice-president), San Diego Historical Society, Zamarano Club, Rounce and Coffin Club, Mendocino County Historical Society, American Association for State and Local History (member of bicentennial commission), Maritime Museum Association of San Diego (member of board of directors), The Westerners, Los Angeles Corral.

WRITINGS: (Editor with Ruth I. Mahood) *Photographer of the Southwest, Adam Clark Vroman*, Ritchie, 1961; (illustrator and editor with John H. Kemble) Richard H. Dana, Jr., *Two Years before the Mast*, Ritchie, 1964; (with Russell E. Belous) *Will Soule: Indian Photographer at Fort Sill, 1869-74*, Ritchie, 1968; (editor with William Webb) *Dwellers at the Source*, Viking, 1973; (editor with David Phillips) *The West: An American Experience*, Regnery, 1975; (with Larry Booth) *The Collection, Care and Use of Historical Photographs*, American Association for State and Local History, 1977. Also editor with Phillips, *The Taming of the West*, for Regnery. Contributor of articles and reviews to journals, including *American West* and *American Heritage*. Graphics editor, *American West*; art director, *California Historical Society Quarterly*.

WORK IN PROGRESS: The Unknown Daguerreotype View of the California Gold Rush, 1848-1851; a book on Charles Robert Pratsch, a photographer in Grays Harbor, Washington; a book on the Indians of the Southwest.

*   *   *

WEIR, Molly 1920-

PERSONAL: Born March 17, 1920, in Glasgow, Scotland; daughter of Thomas (an engineer) and Jeannie (Clark) Weir; married Alexander Hamilton (a shipbroker). *Education:* Attended University of Glasgow. *Politics:* Conservative. *Religion:* Protestant. *Residence:* Pinner, Middlesex, England.

CAREER: Actress and writer, Has appeared in revues and plays in the theatre, in films, and on radio and television, including roles in "Scrooge," starring Albert Finney, Sir Alec Guinness, and Dame Edith Evans, released in America, 1970, and in "One of Our Dinosaurs Is Missing," starring Helen Hayes and Peter Ustinov, for Walt Disney, 1975. Speaker with Associated Speakers, London, 1970—. Member of National Trust, 1960—. *Member:* National Film Society (actress member), B.B.C. Club (actress member).

WRITINGS—All published by Hutchinson, except as indicated: *Molly Weir's Recipes*, Collins, 1960; *Shoes Were for Sunday* (early autobiography), 1970; *Best Foot Forward*, 1972; *A Toe on the Ladder*, 1973; *Stepping into the Spotlight*, 1975. Contributor, *Woman's Hour Anthology*, 1971. Columnist in *People's Journal* (Scottish weekly), 1960—; contributor to other newspapers, magazines, and to British Broadcasting Corp. radio and television (as writer as well as actress).

WORK IN PROGRESS: Another volume of autobiography, taking up where *Stepping into the Spotlight* left off.

SIDELIGHTS: Molly Weir told *CA*, "My books have practically all derived from people urging me to write them! When I spoke to the Women's Press Club in London, the top journalists of the capital immediately urged me to get my childhood memories between hard covers. And that's how all those autobiographies began. I'm now on the fifth, for I write in great detail of the people and circumstances around me everywhere. They're not just about me, they're about life and times wherein I moved and worked."

*   *   *

WEISHEIT, Eldon 1933-

PERSONAL: Born January 13, 1933, in Clayton, Ill.; son of Harry (a farmer) and Edna (Gamm) Weisheit; married Carolyn Pomerenke (a teacher), August 15, 1954; children: Dirk, Timothy, Wesley. *Education:* Concordia Theological Seminary, Springfield, Ill. (now Fort Wayne, Ind.), completed six-ye.. program, 1962. *Politics:* "Independent Democrat." *Home:* 252 Ironwood, Bloomington, Ill. 60108.

CAREER: Ordained to Lutheran ministry, 1962; Trinity Lutheran Church, McComb, Miss., pastor, 1962-65; Lutheran Church of the Epiphany, Montgomery, Ala., pastor, 1965-71; *Lutheran Witness*, St. Louis, Mo., associate editor, 1971-75; Trinity Lutheran Church, Roselle, Ill., pastor, 1976—. Member of board of governors, Concordia Historical Institute; member of children's script committee, Lutheran Television. *Military service:* U.S. Navy, 1952-56.

WRITINGS—All published by Concordia: *Sixty-One Worship Talks for Children*, 1968; *Sixty-One Gospel Talks for Children*, 1969; *Excuse Me, Sir*, 1971; *The Preacher's Yellow Pants*, 1973; *The Zeal of His House* (a history of the Missouri Synod of the Lutheran Church), 1973; *Moving*, 1974; "To the Kid in the Pew" series (chapel talks), three books, 1974-76; *Should I Have an Abortion?*, 1976; *Abortion: Resources for Pastoral Counseling*, 1976; *A Sermon Is More Than Words*, 1977; "The Gospel for Kids," series, Volume I, 1977. Also author of scripts for radio programs, including "The Lutheran Hour," "Day by Day with Jesus," and "Portals of Prayer." Regular contributor to *Lutheran Witness;* contributor of poetry to *This Day* and *Christian Century;* contributor to *Concordia Pulpit, Lutheran Standard*, and *My Devotions.* Editor, *Advance* (magazine), 1972-75.

WORK IN PROGRESS: The second volume in "The Gospel for Kids" series; *Worship Is an Active Verb.*

SIDELIGHTS: Eldon Weisheit told *CA:* "After almost five years as a full-time writer/editor, I am again a parish pastor using writing as a way to extend my ministry. The work as an editor gave me an opportunity to expand my writing experience. But being back in the parish gives me the opportunity to be closely related to people and to write to the joys and sorrows I see in the lives of others. I have heard it said that a good writer can't speak and a good speaker can't write, but I am trying to combine the two. In addition to the frequent need for public speaking in a parish, I often have speaking engagements outside my own congregation. I am working to combine the discipline of writing clear and concise sentences and the warmth and personal involvement of public speaking.''

AVOCATIONAL INTERESTS: Running (six miles a day).

BIOGRAPHICAL/CRITICAL SOURCES: Lutheran Witness, September, 1970.

*   *   *

WEISSTUB, D(avid) N(orman)   1944-

PERSONAL: Born October 26, 1944, in Port Arthur, Ontario, Canada; son of Irvin Elijah (a physician and writer) and Clara (Lerner) Weisstub; married Lola Rosamund Rasminsky (a musician), June 9, 1968. *Education:* Columbia University, B.A., 1963; University of Toronto, M.A., 1965; Yale University, J.D., 1970. *Religion:* Jewish. *Home:* 38 Dunvegan Rd., Toronto, Ontario, Canada. *Office:* Room 320, Osgoode Hall Law School, York University, 4700 Keele St., Downsview, Ontario, Canada M3J 2R5.

CAREER: York University, Osgoode Hall Law School, Downsview, Ontario, assistant professor of jurisprudence, 1970—. Visiting Hoyt Fellow, Yale University, 1971. Member of executive committee, Federal Government Task Force on Privacy, 1971-72; chairman, International Conference on Law, Growth, and Technology, Centro Intercultural de Documentacion, Mexico, 1972; chairman, Gerstein Lecture Series, Toronto, 1972; member of panel on minority rights, National Conference on Law, 1972; member of advisory panel, Royal Commission on Violence and the Media, 1975. Visiting associate professor of psychiatry, Clarke Institute of Psychiatry, 1976-77. Lecturer to numerous universities and groups, including Yale University, 1969-70, Department of Interdisciplinary Studies, University of Toronto, 1971-72, 1972-73, Oxford University, 1973, Ontario Psychiatric Association, 1974, Canadian Bar Association, 1975, Harvard Law School, 1975, and McMaster University Medical School, 1976. Legal consultant, Ontario College of Physicians and Surgeons, 1975; forensic consultant, Clarke Institute of Psychiatry, 1976. *Awards, honors:* Province of Ontario Government Fellowship, 1964-67; James C. Cumming Fellowship, 1965-66; Canada Council doctoral fellowship, 1965-68; scholarship to The Hague Academy of International Law, 1968.

WRITINGS: Heaven Take My Hand (poems), McClelland & Stewart, 1968; (with C. C. Gottlieb) *Privacy and Computers,* Department of Computer Science, University of Toronto, 1972; (editor and contributor) *Law, Growth, and Technology: Proceedings of the Cuernavaca Conference,* Centro Intercultural de Documentacion Institute Press, 1972; (editor) *Law and Psychiatry: Cases and Materials,* Osgoode Hall Law School, 1974, third edition, 1976; (editor) *Creativity and the University,* [Toronto], 1975; (editor) *Law and Policy,* Osgoode Hall Law School, 1976. Also contributor of poems to *Anthology of Literature,* McGraw (Canada). Contributor of articles on law to *Journal of Law and Science, Administrative Law Review, American Journal of Legal Medicine,* and *University of Toronto Law Journal.* Contributor of poetry to periodicals, including *Canadian Forum, Dimension, Canadian Journal of Theology,* and *Queen's University Quarterly.*

WORK IN PROGRESS: Law and Telos: Some Historical Reflections on the Nature of Authority; Confidentiality, Privacy and Mental Health; with G. Sawyer and G. Sharpe,

Canadian Medical Law; with A. Kontos, *The Foundations of Western Legal Theory;* a second volume of verse.

BIOGRAPHICAL/CRITICAL SOURCES: Canadian Forum, December, 1968; *Fiddlehead,* number 79, March-April, 1969.

*   *   *

WEITZ, John   1923-

PERSONAL: Born May 25, 1923, in Berlin, Germany; naturalized U.S. citizen, 1943; son of Robert and Hedy (Jakob) Weitz; married second wife, Susan Kohner (an actress), August 31, 1964; children: (first marriage) Karen (Mrs. Richard Curtis), Robert; (second marriage) Paul John, Christopher John. *Education:* Attended St. Paul's School, London, England, 1936-39. *Residence:* New York, N.Y. *Office:* John Weitz Designs, 40 West 55th St., New York, N.Y. 10019.

CAREER: Migrated to England with his parents during the Hitler regime; after leaving school in London, was apprenticed to a British dressmaker; came to America and became a designer of women's sportswear; designer with various companies until 1954; John Weitz Designs, New York, N.Y., founder and designer of men's fashions produced by manufacturers in the United States, Europe, and Japan, 1954—. *Military service:* U.S. Army, 1943-46. *Awards, honors: Sports Illustrated* award, 1959; Today award from National Broadcasting Co., 1960; Caswell Massey awards, 1963-66; *Harpers Bazaar* medallion, 1966; Coty Award, 1974.

WRITINGS: The Value of Nothing (novel), Stein & Day, 1970; *Man in Charge* (nonfiction), Macmillan, 1974.

WORK IN PROGRESS: A novel about a German-Jewish refugee.

SIDELIGHTS: Leonard Sloane writes: ''John Weitz has never been bashful about offering his opinions. When he moved from designing women's clothes to designing men's clothes he had no hesitancy in stating that he was 'bored to tears' with the type of male clothing then on the market. When he began licensing American and foreign companies to produce merchandise bearing his label, he made no bones about telling the press and public why his apparel surpassed that of his rivals in function as well as fashion. And when his name and face became familiar enough to people in the right circles, he became a frequent visitor on radio and television shows, where he promulgated his didactic views among a wider audience.''

In a review of *The Value of Nothing,* Margaret Crimmins says: ''Whatever the criticisms of New York fashion designer John Weitz's first novel, he can't be accused of making it up out of whole cloth. *The Value of Nothing* is too candid—and depressing—a look at the clawing of people scrambling up the slippery fashion pedestal to be imaginary.'' Sidney Blackmore believes that the novel ''is compulsive reading and [Weitz's] couture associates must be very busy, at this moment, flicking through the novel in an attempt to match characters with people in the real world. For an outsider, it is an interesting insight into the luxurious rag-trade, but in the end one feels that it has all been said before.''

Sloane feels that *Man in Charge* ''is a further extension of Mr. Weitz's strongly expressed ideas about male grooming. But attire is just one part of this slight, conversational, fast-reading book. For equally strong are the attitudes he expresses about a variety of subjects, like body care, manners, and travel. And it all adds up to an enjoyable visit with a man who has much to say about how other men can better express their good taste.''

John Weitz told *CA:* "The modern man must never look as if he is of any specific nationality. The jet plane has wiped away all those differences. Modern clothes must be featherweight, easy to pack, wrinkle-proof. They must contour themselves to the body without heavy interlining or darting of stiff fabrics. I have eliminated most of these Victorian hangovers. I think that dandyism is a joke in the 1970s. I believe that a man should take his time to develop his own style and to become truly well-dressed. Function must always precede fashion and I am as interested in construction as in styling. Most of all, a man must always look healthy and fit and scrubbed. And he must wear his clothes as if they are old and valued friends.''

Mr. Weitz was chosen for the International Best Dressed List in 1967, and he was elected to the Best Dressed Hall of Fame in 1971. *The Value of Nothing* has been translated into four languages.

AVOCATIONAL INTERESTS: Formerly automobile racing (he drove at Sebring in 1955, 1956, and 1957), tennis, and sailing.

BIOGRAPHICAL/CRITICAL SOURCES: New York Times, February 14, 1970, December 23, 1974; *Washington Post,* May 11, 1970; *New York Times Book Review,* June 28, 1970; *Books and Bookmen,* April, 1971.

* * *

WEITZMAN, Alan 1933-

PERSONAL: Born October 29, 1933, in Cincinnati, Ohio; son of Isadore and Ella (Lisner) Weitzman; married Carole Tayler, November 22, 1970. *Education:* University of Cincinnati, B.A., 1955; Hebrew Union College-Jewish Institute of Religion, ordained in conjunction with M.A., 1960; summer graduate study at Harvard University and Hebrew University, Jerusalem, Israel. *Home:* 50 North Fourth St., Reading, Pa. 19601. *Office:* c/o Shengold Publishers, Inc., 45 West 45th St., New York, N.Y. 10036.

CAREER: Indianapolis Hebrew Congregation, Indianapolis, Ind., assistant rabbi, 1960-64; Temple Oheb Sholom, Reading, Pa., rabbi, 1964—. Member of executive committee and vice-chairman of Social Action Cabinet, Berks County Ministerium; member of advisory board, Mental Health and Mental Retardation Association, and member of executive committee of Mental Health Association, both Berks County, Pa.; member of board of Fellowship House and Jewish Community Center, vice-president of Police Athletic League, and member of clergy committee of Planned Parenthood, all in Reading, Pa. *Member:* Central Conference of American Rabbis.

WRITINGS: Living Symbols Past and Present, Shengold, 1969. Contributor of articles to *Jewish Examiner, Jewish Exponent,* and *Jewish Post and Opinion.*

* * *

WELDON, (Nathaniel) Warren (Jr.) 1919-

PERSONAL: Born June 14, 1919, in Warren County, N.C.; son of Nathaniel Warren and Ethel Hicks (Buffaloe) Weldon; married Anne Keith Skaggs, June 14, 1952 (divorced); children: Nathaniel Warren III. *Education:* Attended Davidson College, 1936-37; Oberlin College, B.A., 1940; Harvard University, M.B.A., 1942; American Theatre Wing, New York, N.Y., student-actor, 1947-50. *Home:* 82 Irving Pl., New York, N.Y. 10003.

CAREER: New London Players (summer theatre), New London, N.H., owner, producer, and director, 1948-54; J. Walter Thompson Co., New York City, staff of television department, 1956-61; Rado Watch Co., New York City, general manager, 1965-66. *Military service:* U.S. Naval Reserve, active duty, 1942-46; became lieutenant commander. *Member:* Dramatists Guild of the Authors League of America, The Players, Masons.

WRITINGS: A Happy Medium: The Life of Caroline Randolph Chapman, Prentice-Hall, 1970.

Author of plays, "Prince Consort," 1952, "Shadow Boxing," 1955, "Out of the Blue," 1956, and "What's a Little Murder among Friends," 1962. Author of filmscript, "Instant Love," 1963.

WORK IN PROGRESS: Living with a Foot on Both Sides, a collaboration with Judith Richardson Haimes on Warren Weldon's life and psychic work; and untitled novel.

AVOCATIONAL INTERESTS: Classical music (piano particularly), bridge, reading, travel.

* * *

WELLBORN, Charles 1924-

PERSONAL: Born September 24, 1924, in Alto, Tex.; son of Charles Floyd (an attorney) and Ethel (Swanzy) Wellborn; married Elizabeth Hood, March 3, 1951; children: Gary Marshall, Jon Richard. *Education:* Baylor University, B.A., 1946, M.A., 1950; Southwestern Baptist Theological Seminary, B.D., 1950; Duke University, Ph.D., 1964. *Politics:* Democrat. *Home:* 1625-37 Centerville, Tallahassee, Fla. 32303. *Office:* Williams Building, Florida State University, Tallahassee, Fla. 32306.

CAREER: Baptist clergyman, 1950—; Baylor University, Waco, Tex., instructor, 1946-48, assistant professor of religion, 1950-51; University Baptist Church, Waco, senior minister, 1951-61; Campbell College, Buies Creek, N.C., associate professor of religion, 1964-65; Florida State University, Tallahassee, associate professor, 1965-69, professor of religion, 1969—. Fellow, King's College, University of London. Consultant on managerial ethics, U.S. Civil Service Commission, 1967—; consultant for southeastern United States, Associate Consultants for Education Abroad, London, England. *Military service:* U.S. Army, 10th Mountain Division, 1943-45; became technical sergeant; received Bronze Star with oak-leaf cluster.

MEMBER: American Academy of Religion, Society for the Scientific Study of Religion, Association for the Coordination of University Religion Affairs (member of executive committee, 1967-69), Sigma Alpha Epsilon. *Awards, honors:* Named Outstanding Young Man of Texas by U.S. Junior Chamber of Commerce, 1953.

WRITINGS: (Editor) *Youth Speaks,* Broadman, 1947; *This Is God's Hour,* Broadman, 1950; *The Challenge of Church Membership,* Convention Press, 1955; (editor) *Challenge to Morality,* Florida State University Press, 1966; *Twentieth Century Pilgrimage: Walter Lippmann and the Public Philosophy,* Louisiana State University Press, 1969; (with George Bedell and Leo Sandon) *Religion in America,* Macmillan, 1975. Contributor to religion journals.

WORK IN PROGRESS: Religion and Politics in the South; and *Sex Attitudes of the College Student.*

SIDELIGHTS: Charles Wellborn has traveled extensively in Europe, with some travel in the Middle East and Latin America. *Avocational interests:* Playwriting, community theatricals.

BIOGRAPHICAL/CRITICAL SOURCES: Christian Century, October 15, 1969.

* * *

WELLS, Helen 1910-
(Francine Lewis)

PERSONAL: Name legally changed; born March 29, 1910, in Danville, Ill.; daughter of Henry M. and Henrietta (Basch) Weinstock. *Education:* New York University, B.S. (with honors), 1934; Programming and Systems Institute, New York, diploma, 1969; New York University, School of Continuing Education, student, 1962—. *Home:* 345 East 57th St., New York, N.Y. 10022. *Agent:* McIntosh & Otis, Inc., 475 Fifth Ave., New York, N.Y. 10017.

CAREER: Full-time professional writer. Institute of Children's Literature, Redding Ridge, Conn., instructor, 1976—. Four-year volunteer escorting Latin-American visitors to U.S., Rockefeller Institute of Inter-American Affairs. *Member:* Author's Guild, Mystery Writers of America (member of board of directors, 1970-77; national secretary, 1973-75), Women's National Book Association.

WRITINGS: The Girl in the White Coat, Messner, 1953; *Escape by Night: A Story of the Underground Railroad,* Winston, 1953; *A Flair for People,* Messner, 1955; *Adam Gimbel, Pioneer Trader,* McKay, 1955; *Introducing Patti Lewis, Home Economist,* Messner, 1956; *A City for Jean,* Funk, 1956; *Barnum, Showman of America,* McKay, 1957; *Doctor Betty,* Messner, 1969.

"Cherry Ames" series, all published by Grosset: *Cherry Ames, Student Nurse,* 1943; *Cherry Ames, Army Nurse,* 1944; *Cherry Ames, Chief Nurse,* 1944; *Cherry Ames, Senior Nurse,* 1944; *Cherry Ames, Private Duty Nurse,* 1945; *Cherry Ames, Flight Nurse,* 1945; *Cherry Ames, Veterans' Nurse,* 1946; *Cherry Ames, Visiting Nurse,* 1947; *Cherry Ames, Cruise Nurse,* 1948; *Cherry Ames, Boarding School Nurse,* 1955; *Cherry Ames, Department Store Nurse,* 1956; *Cherry Ames, Camp Nurse,* 1957; *Cherry Ames' Book of First Aid and Home Nursing,* 1959; *Cherry Ames at Hilton Hospital,* 1959; *Cherry Ames, Island Nurse,* 1960; *Cherry Ames, Rural Nurse,* 1961; *Cherry Ames, Staff Nurse,* 1962; *Cherry Ames, Companion Nurse,* 1964; *Cherry Ames, Jungle Nurse,* 1965; *Mystery in the Doctor's Office,* 1966; *Ski Nurse Mystery,* 1968; *Mystery of Rogue's Cave,* 1972.

"Vicki Barr" series, all published by Grosset: *Silver Wings for Vicki,* 1947; *Vicki Finds the Answer,* 1947; *Hidden Valley Mystery,* 1948; *The Secret of Magnolia Manor,* 1949; *Peril over the Airport,* 1953; *The Search for the Missing Twin,* 1954; *The Mystery of the Vanishing Lady,* 1954; *The Ghost at the Waterfall,* 1956; *The Clue of the Gold Coin,* 1958; *The Silver Ring Mystery,* 1960; *The Clue of the Carved Ruby,* 1961; *The Mystery of Flight 908,* 1962; *The Brass Idol Mystery,* 1964.

Under pseudonym Francine Lewis; "Polly French" series, all published by Whitman Publishing: *Polly French of Whitford Hight,* 1952; *Polly French Finds Out,* 1953; *Polly French Takes Charge,* 1954; *Polly French and the Surprising Stranger,* 1955.

SIDELIGHTS: Helen Wells told *CA:* "A course in playwriting taught me a very great deal about how to construct a story. I never expect to write a play for the theater—but it is no accident that my stories 'play', and several have been dramatized on radio and television."

Helen Wells' travels have included Spain, France, Italy, Switzerland, England, Ireland, Scotland, Mexico, Brazil, Finland, and the Scandinavian countries. The "Cherry Ames" and "Vicki Barr" series have been published in Canada, Britain, Norway, Sweden, Denmark, Finland, Iceland, Japan, France, Italy, Holland, and Bolivia.

* * *

WENDE, Philip 1939-

PERSONAL: Surname is pronounced Wendy; born January 9, 1939, in Ogdensburg, N.Y.; son of Ernest Andrew (an engineer) and Doris (Northrup) Wende; married Janet Dant, 1958; married second wife, Beverly Heacock, September 1, 1962; children: (second marriage) Christopher, Jill, Seth. *Education:* Attended University of Tennessee, 1958, and Ringling School of Art, 1959-61. *Politics:* "Constantly changing."

CAREER: Free-lance artist and illustrator.

WRITINGS—Self-illustrated juveniles: *Hector the Dog Who Loves Fleas,* Singer, 1967; *The Rhinoceros Who Loves Trees,* Singer, 1967; *Hector Has a Flea Circus,* Singer, 1969; *Bird Boy,* Cowles, 1970.

Illustrator: Al Perkins, *Hugh Lofting's Doctor Dolittle,* Beginner Books, 1968; Michael O'Donoghue, *The Incredible Thrilling Adventures of the Rock,* Random House, 1968; Robert Littell, *Gaston's Ghastly Green Thumb,* Cowles, 1969; Littell, *Left and Right with Lion and Ryan,* Cowles, 1969; George Mendoza, *The Hunter, the Tick, and the Gumberoo,* Cowles, 1971.

"Picture Dictionaries" series; written by S. Alan Cohen; published by Random House, 1970: *Animal Kingdom Dictionary; Let's Pretend Dictionary; Playmates Dictionary; Tell Me Why Dictionary; Up and Away Dictionary.*

SIDELIGHTS: Philip Wende says he writes and illustrates books for children, not for "mothers, fathers, critics, distributors, salesmen, and other persons whose motives are questionable."†

* * *

WENNER, Manfred W. 1936-

PERSONAL: Born October 2, 1936, in Basel, Switzerland; naturalized U.S. citizen; son of Wilhelm K. (a research chemist) and Gisela M. (Schreiner) Wenner; married Lettie M. McSpadden, April 3, 1961; two children. *Education:* Oberlin College, B.A., 1956; Johns Hopkins University, School of Advanced International Studies, M.A., 1958, Ph.D., 1965; graduate study at Free University of Berlin, 1958-59, and University of California, Berkeley, 1959-61. *Religion:* None. *Home:* 124 Thrush Lane, Naperville, Ill. 60540. *Office:* Department of Political Science, Northern Illinois University, De Kalb, Ill. 60115.

CAREER: Atlantic Research Corp., Washington, D.C., research assistant, 1964; Legislative Reference Service, Washington, D.C., foreign policy analyst, 1964-66; Wisconsin State University—Oshkosh, assistant professor of political science, 1966-69, chairman of department of international studies, 1967-69; Northern Illinois University, De Kalb, associate professor of political science, 1969—. Lecturer, U.S. Department of State, Foreign Service Institute, 1964-66; visiting assistant professor, University of California, Berkeley, 1969; visiting associate professor, University of Washington, Seattle, 1971, Salzburg College (Austria), 1972. *Member:* American Political Science Association, International Political Science Association, Middle East Studies Association, Mid-West Political Science Association.

WRITINGS: (Co-author) *Soviet Foreign Aid Policies*, Atlantic Research Corp., 1965; *Modern Yemen, 1918-1966*, Johns Hopkins Press, 1967; (co-author) *Governments and Politics of the Contemporary Middle East*, Dorsey, 1970; (co-author) *Political Elites and Political Development in the Middle East*, Schenkman, 1975; (co-author) *Comparative Human Rights*, Johns Hopkins Press, 1976. Contributor to *Worldmark Encyclopedia of the Nations*, 1967, 1971, and to journals and newspapers, including Middle Eastern newspapers.

WORK IN PROGRESS: A study of modern separatist movements, tentatively entitled *Political Disintegration in the Modern World;* further studies in comparative judicial behavior.

SIDELIGHTS: Manfred Wenner is competent in Arabic and French in addition to German.

* * *

WERKLEY, Caroline E(lsea)

PERSONAL: Born in Clinton, Mo.; daughter of Luther (a railroad employee) and Caroline (Hutton) Elsea; married John Gerard Werkley, June 7, 1938 (deceased); children: Christopher. *Education:* Attended Moberly Junior College, 1931-33; University of Missouri—Columbia, B.J. 1935; Long Island University, M.L.S., 1966. *Religion:* Methodist. *Home:* Wyndon Apartments, Apt. A-302, Wynnewood, Pa. 19096. *Office:* Department of Anthropology, University Museum, University of Pennsylvania, 33rd and Spruce Sts., Philadelphia, Pa. 19104.

CAREER: University of Pennsylvania, Philadelphia, research librarian in department of anthropology, 1966—. *Member:* American Library Association, Manuscript Society, Missouri Historical Society.

WRITINGS: *Mister Carnegie's Lib'ary*, American Heritage Press, 1970. Contributor to library journals and popular magazines, including *Esquire, American Heritage,* and *Smithsonian.*

BIOGRAPHICAL/CRITICAL SOURCES: *Antiquarian Bookman*, January 18, 1971.

* * *

WERNER, Victor 1894-

PERSONAL: Born September 22, 1894, in Brooklyn, N.Y.; son of Charles A. (owner of motion picture theaters) and Cathrine Marie (Frisk) Werner; married Geraldine Thompson. *Education:* George Washington University, A.A., 1958, B.B.A., 1963. *Home:* 7418 Holly Ave., Takoma Park, Md. 20012.

CAREER: Conducted classes in memory improvement at branches of Young Men's Christian Associations, 1916-17, and for Brooklyn Edison Co., Brooklyn, N.Y., 1922-23; Werner Motor Freight Co., Reading, Pa., owner and manager, 1923-27; Cranford Co. (builders and contractors), Brooklyn, office manager, 1927-31; administrative officer for state and local government agencies, New York, N.Y., 1932-38; Federal Civil Service employee, 1939-64, working in Washington, D.C., as management analyst with Treasury Dept., 1939-40, War Dept., 1940-43, Office of Civilian Defense, 1943-45, War Assets Administration, 1945-49, Department of the Navy, 1949-51, and Department of the Army, 1951-64. Conducts classes in memory improvement for government agencies and lectures on his memory methods. *Military service:* U.S. Army, Ordnance, 1917-19; served overseas with American Expeditionary Forces and

Army of Occupation. *Member:* Veterans of Foreign Wars, Danish Club (Washington, D.C.). *Awards, honors:* Certificate of Merit, Office of Civilian Defense, 1945; Army Certificate of Achievement, 1964; Army Patriotic Civilian Service Award, 1966.

WRITINGS: *Short-Cut Memory*, Cowles, 1968. Also writer of memory methods material. Contributor of articles to *Federal Times, Retirement Living, Army Times, Navy Times, Air Force Times, Family Circle, Toastmaster International Magazine,* and *National Enquirer.* Associate editor, *V.F.W. Bulletin*, Kings County, N.Y., 1934-35.

WORK IN PROGRESS: *Adventures in ESP.*

SIDELIGHTS: Victor Werner told *CA*, "Sharing a talent is a blessing. It is psychic income. You can't put it in a bank or buy anything with it, but . . . it is a wonderful feeling to be able to say, 'Today I helped someone.'" *Avocational interests:* People, stockmarket, reading.

BIOGRAPHICAL/CRITICAL SOURCES: *Washington Evening Star*, February 21, 1963, June 24, 1964, May 7, 1969, September 1, 1976; *Washington Post Magazine*, June 20, 1965.

* * *

WERSBA, Barbara 1932-

PERSONAL: Born August 19, 1932, in Chicago, Ill.; daughter of Robert and Lucy Jo (Quarles) Wersba. *Education:* Bard College, B.A., 1954; studied acting at Neighborhood Playhouse and at the Paul Mann Actors Workshop; studied dance with Martha Graham. *Home:* 101 Gedney St., Nyack, New York 10960. *Agent:* McIntosh & Otis, Inc., 475 Fifth Ave., New York, N.Y. 10017.

CAREER: Was an actress from the ages of 12 to 27, working in radio and television, summer stock, Off-Broadway, and touring companies; full-time writer, 1960—. Summer lecturer at New York University. *Awards, honors:* Deutscher Jugend Buchpreis, 1973, for *Run Softly, Go Fast.*

WRITINGS—Published by Atheneum, except as noted: *The Boy Who Loved the Sea*, Coward, 1961; *The Brave Balloon of Benjamin Buckley*, 1963; *The Land of Forgotten Beasts*, 1964; *A Song for Clowns*, 1965; *Do Tigers Ever Bite Kings?*, 1966; *The Dream Watcher*, 1968; *Run Softly, Go Fast*, 1970; *Let Me Fall before I Fly*, 1971; *Amanda, Dreaming*, 1973; *The Country of the Heart*, 1975; "The Dream Watcher" (play; adaptation of her novel of the same title), produced in Westport, Conn. at the White Barn Theatre, 1975; *Tunes for a Small Harmonica*, Harper, 1976. Regular reviewer of children's books for the *New York Times.*

WORK IN PROGRESS: Poetry.

BIOGRAPHICAL/CRITICAL SOURCES: *Young Readers' Review*, November, 1968; *Children's Literature Review*, Volume III, Gale, 1977.

* * *

WERSTEIN, Irving 1914(?)-1971

1914(?)—April 7, 1971; American author of children's books and works on Americana. Obituaries: *New York Times*, April 9, 1971; *Publishers' Weekly*, April 26, 1971; *Antiquarian Bookman*, June 24, 1971.

* * *

WERTHEIMER, Richard F(rederick) II 1943-

PERSONAL: Born November 27, 1943, in Washington,

D.C.; son of Richard Frederick (an editor) and Elizabeth (Butts) Wertheimer; married Alyce Joan Arena, July 24, 1965; children: Wendy Rae, Amy Lorraine. *Education:* Columbia University, A.B., 1965; University of Maryland, Ph.D., 1971. *Religion:* Unitarian Universalist. *Home:* 7729 Beech Tree Rd., Bethesda, Md. 20034. *Office:* Urban Institute, 2100 M St. N.W., Washington, D.C. 20037.

CAREER: Urban Institute (nonprofit research organization), Washington, D.C., senior research associate, 1968—. Lecturer in economics, University of Maryland, 1971—. *Member:* American Economic Association.

WRITINGS—Published by Urban Institute: *The Monetary Rewards of Migration within the United States,* 1970; (coauthor) *Planning, Allocation, and Control in a Decentralized Manpower Program* (monograph), 1971; (co-author) *Policy Exploration through Microanalytic Simulation,* 1976; (co-author) *The Impact of Demographic Change on the Distribution of Earned Income and the AFDC Program: 1975-1985,* 1976. Contributor to economics journals.

WORK IN PROGRESS: Income Adequacy and the Elderly; The Cost and Distribution of Benefits of Welfare Reform.

AVOCATIONAL INTERESTS: Gardening, jogging.

*   *   *

WESSLER, Ruth Ann   1938-

PERSONAL: Born March 17, 1938, in Kendallville, Ind.; daughter of William Thomas (a purchasing agent) and Ruth (Schwalm) Cotter; married Richard Wessler (a psychologist), December 4, 1965. *Education:* Grinnell College, A.B., 1960; Washington University, St. Louis, Mo., A.M., 1962, Ph.D., 1965.

CAREER: Washington University, St. Louis, Mo., research associate in Social Science Institute, 1965-69, and in Graduate Institute of Education, 1968-69, clinical psychologist in Child Guidance Clinic, 1968; Parsons College, Fairfield, Iowa, clinical psychologist, beginning 1969. *Member:* American Psychological Association, Midwestern Psychological Association, Sigma Xi.

WRITINGS: (With Jane Loevinger and Carolyn Redmore) *Measuring Ego Development,* Jossey-Bass, 1970. Contributor to *American Educational Research Journal.*†

*   *   *

WESTMAN, Wesley C(harles)   1936-

PERSONAL: Born February 19, 1936, in Schuyler, Neb.; son of Meade Levi (an architect) and Violet (Abbott) Westman; married Noelene Raiford, December 21, 1957; children: Mark Phillip, Charlene Ann. *Education:* Attended College of William and Mary, 1954-55, 1961-62; University of Virginia, B.A., 1961; University of Wisconsin—Madison, M.S., 1963, Ph.D., 1965. *Home:* 101 Four Mile Rd., West Hartford, Conn. 06117. *Office:* Hartford Dispensary, 45 Retreat Ave., Hartford, Conn. 06106.

CAREER: Eastern State Hospital, Williamsburg, Va., psychology student, 1961-62; Petersburg Training School, Petersburg, Va., psychologist, 1964; Western Behavioral Science Institute, La Jolla, Calif., pre-doctoral fellow, 1964; Rehabilitation Research and Training Center, Institute, W.Va., planning director, 1965-66; Vocational Rehabilitation Planning Project, Hartford, Conn., project director, 1966-68; clinical psychologist in private practice, West Hartford, 1967—; Hartford Dispensary, Methadone Mainte-

nance Treatment Program, Hartford, executive director, 1971—. Consultant to poverty programs, state mental health and drug addiction programs in New York and Connecticut. *Military service:* U.S. Marine Corps, 1955-58; became sergeant. *Member:* American Psychological Association, National Rehabilitation Association.

WRITINGS: The Drug Epidemic: What It Means and How to Combat It, Dial, 1970. Contributor of articles to *Journal of Rehabilitation.*

WORK IN PROGRESS: A book about a social bartering system in which people can get what they want without money entitled *The People Plan; Cultures in Conflict: A Study of Poverty and Delinquency in Appalachia.*

SIDELIGHTS: Wesley Westman wrote to *CA:* "I am a psychologist and write to understand myself and the people that I work for, my patients. Requiring myself to sit down and write what I *think* I understand very often indicates to me how little I really do know. This in turn requires me to think through that issue or situation again until I am able to communicate it effectively on paper. Based on this experience, I have a suggestion to beginning writers. Write down what seems clear and understandable to you, then get a number of people to read it and ask precise questions of anyone who doesn't understand any part of it. This 'reality testing' will improve your writing."

*   *   *

WESTMORELAND, Reg(inald Conway)   1926-
(Ward Conway)

PERSONAL: Born October 31, 1926, in Navarro, Tex.; son of Mark Arthur (a barber) and Grace B. (Knight) Westmoreland; married Mary Nell Burns, February 9, 1949; children: Linda, Lisa, David. *Education:* North Texas State University, B.A., 1947, M.A., 1956; University of Missouri, Ph.D., 1961. *Religion:* Church of Christ. *Home:* 1916 Cornell Lane, Denton, Tex. 76201. *Office:* Department of Journalism, North Texas State University, Denton, Tex. 76203.

CAREER: Dallas Times Herald, Dallas, Tex., sports makeup editor and columnist, 1947-55; Abilene Christian College, Abilene, Tex., director of publications, associate professor of journalism, 1955-64; North Texas State University, Denton, director of news and public service, 1964-66, associate professor, 1964-69, professor of journalism, 1969—, director of journalism graduate studies, 1970—, chairman of department of journalism, 1974—. *Military service:* U.S. Army Active Reserve, 1949-62; became captain. *Member:* Association for Education in Journalism, Sigma Delta Chi, Kappa Tau Alpha, Texas Association of College Teachers.

WRITINGS: How to Write for Newspapers, Car-Teach, Inc., 1967; *A Guide to Church Publicity,* Sweet Publishing Co., 1971. Author of numerous articles for Texas daily newspapers, AP, UPI, and various periodicals. Editor and publisher, *Texas Press Messenger;* Sunday editor, *Columbia Missourian,* summers, 1959-60.

WORK IN PROGRESS: The Dallas Times Herald, 1879-1961.

AVOCATIONAL INTERESTS: Gardening, mass communications.

*   *   *

WESTON, Burns H.   1933-

PERSONAL: Born November 5, 1933, in Cleveland, Ohio;

son of S. Burns (an attorney) and Simonne (Humphrey) Weston; married Hanna Elisabeth Bergmann (a teacher), February 21, 1958 (divorced); children: Timothy Bergmann, Rebecca Burns. *Education:* Attended Oberlin Conservatory of Music, 1952-53, University of Edinburgh, 1954-55; Oberlin College, B.A., 1956; Yale University, LL.B., 1961, J.S.D., 1970. *Home:* 416 North Linn St., Iowa City, Iowa 52240. *Office:* College of Law, University of Iowa, Iowa City, Iowa 52240.

CAREER: New Haven Redevelopment Agency, legal assistant to deputy director and general counsel, 1959-60; Paul, Weiss, Rifkind, Wharton and Garrison, New York, N.Y., law clerk, 1960, associate attorney, 1961-64; University of Iowa, Iowa City, assistant professor, 1966-67, associate professor, 1967-69, professor of law, 1969—. Director, Center for World Order Studies, 1972—, on leave, 1976-78; senior fellow and director, Transnational University Program, Institute for World Order, 1976—. International law consultant, Naval War College, 1968, 1969; visiting adjunct professor, Grinnell College, 1974. *Member:* International Law Association, International Studies Association, American Society of International Law (member of executive council), Procedural Aspects of International Law Institute (member of advisory council), American Association of University Professors, Lawyers Committee on American Policy Towards Vietnam (member of consultative council).

WRITINGS: International Claims: Postwar French Practice, Syracuse University Press, 1971; (with Richard B. Lillich) *International Claims: Their Settlement by Lump Sum Agreements,* two volumes, Syracuse University Press, 1975; (with Richard A. Falk) *International Law and World Order: An Introductory Problem-Oriented Coursebook,* West Publishing, 1977.

Contributor: Richard S. Miller and Roland Jonathan Stanger, editors, *Essays on Expropriations,* Ohio State University Press, 1967; Richard A. Falk and Cyril E. Black, editors, *The Future of the International Legal Order 36,* Volume II, Princeton University Press, 1970; Richard B. Lillich, editor, *The Valuation of Property under International Law,* Procedural Aspects of International Law Institute, 1971; (and editor with W. Michael Reisman) *Toward World Order and Human Dignity: Essays in Honor of Myres S. McDougal,* Free Press, 1976. Contributor of articles and reviews to several law reviews and to *Proceedings* of the American Society of International Law. Member of board of editors, *American Journal of International Law.*

WORK IN PROGRESS: Two books, *International Law and the Deprivation of Foreign Wealth,* and *Global Interdependence and Human Survival—An Introduction to World Order Education.*

* * *

WHEAT, Leonard F. 1931-

PERSONAL: Born November 13, 1931, in Sioux City, Iowa; son of Leonard B. (an educator) and Gertrude (Wieland) Wheat; married Janis Knudsen (picture editor, National Geographic Society), May 9, 1964 (divorced, 1977). *Education:* University of Minnesota, Duluth Campus, B.A., 1952; University of Minnesota, M.A.P.A., 1954; Harvard University, Ph.D., 1958. *Politics:* Independent. *Religion:* None. *Home:* 1911 Stirrup Lane, Alexandria, Va. 22308. *Office:* Economic Development Administration, U.S. Department of Commerce, Washington, D.C.

CAREER: Minnesota Department of Taxation, St. Paul, research analyst, 1954-55; U.S. Department of the Navy,

Washington, D.C., program analyst, 1958-59; U.S. Bureau of the Budget, Washington, D.C., budget examiner, 1959-66; U.S. Department of Commerce, Washington, D.C., transportation officer with Office of Regional Economic Development, 1966-68, economist with Economic Development Administration, 1968—. *Member:* Society of Government Economists, American Economic Association, American Society for Public Administration.

WRITINGS: Paul Tillich's Dialectical Humanism: Unmasking the God above God, Johns Hopkins Press, 1970; *Regional Growth and Industrial Location,* Heath, 1973; *Urban Growth in the Nonmetropolitan South,* Heath, 1976.

WORK IN PROGRESS: A study of the determinants of county labor force participation rates, unemployment rates, and median family income.

SIDELIGHTS: A reviewer writes of Leonard Wheat's book *Paul Tillich's Dialectical Humanism:* "Though an economist by profession, Wheat writes a thorough, well documented, and well argued polemic, charging that Tillich's 'God above the God of theism' is really a covert symbol for humanity as man's ultimate concern. Tillich's thought proceeds dialectically: man's original affirmation of God (the initial Yes) is undercut by Tillich's attack on all supernaturalism (the No), but the original transcendent meaning ... with respect to God is retained and refocused on man (the final Yes).... Recommended as a responsible and provocative critique which must be reckoned with."

AVOCATIONAL INTERESTS: History of religion and comparative religions, hiking, canoeing.

BIOGRAPHICAL/CRITICAL SOURCES: Choice, May, 1971.

* * *

WHEATLEY, Jon (James) 1931-

PERSONAL: Born August 4, 1931, in Surrey, England; now a Canadian citizen; son of James Edgar (a businessman) and Margery (Cotterall) Wheatley. *Education:* McGill University, B.A., 1952; University of British Columbia, M.A., 1957; University of London, Ph.D., 1962. *Home:* 555 St. Giles Rd., West Vancouver, British Columbia, Canada. *Office:* Dean of Graduate Studies Office, Simon Fraser University, Burnaby, British Columbia, Canada V5A 1S6.

CAREER: Queen's University, Kingston, Ontario, lecturer, 1962-63, assistant professor, 1963-64, associate professor of philosophy, 1964-65; University of California, Santa Barbara, professor of philosophy, 1966-71; Simon Fraser University, Burnaby, British Columbia, professor of philosophy and dean of graduate studies, 1971—. British Council visitor, United Kingdom, 1964; visiting professor at San Francisco State College (now University), San Francisco, Calif., 1968. *Military service:* Royal Canadian Air Force; became flying officer. *Member:* Mind Association, Aristotelian Society, American Philosophical Association, Canadian Philosophical Association (member of board), Association of the Universities and Colleges of Canada (member of board).

WRITINGS: Language and Rules, text edition, Humanities, 1970; *Prolegomena to Philosophy,* text edition, Wadsworth, 1970; (contributor) *Symposium on J. L. Austin,* [London], 1970. Contributor of articles to philosophical journals, including *American Philosophical Quarterly, Theoria, Analysis, Canadian Journal of Linguistics, Queen's Quarterly, Mind, Linguistic Reporter,* and *Memorias* of the XIII Congreso Internacional de Filosofia. Author of numerous addresses presented to philosophical societies and congresses.

WORK IN PROGRESS: Two books, *The Concept of Rationality,* and *Chinese Cooking.*

SIDELIGHTS: Jon Wheatley described himself for *CA* as "an analytic philosopher with a literary bent; I also work in linguistics with computers."

* * *

WHEELER, Douglas L. 1937-

PERSONAL: Born July 19, 1937, in St. Louis, Mo.; son of Russell Charles (a dentist) and Lucille (Wengler) Wheeler; married Katherine Wells, June 13, 1964; children: Katherine Gladney, Lucille Lanphier. *Education:* Dartmouth College, A.B., 1959; Boston University, M.A., 1960, Ph.D., 1963. *Politics:* Independent. *Religion:* United Church of Christ. *Home:* 27 Mill Rd., Durham, N.H. 03824. *Office:* Department of History, Social Science Center, University of New Hampshire, Durham, N.H. 03824.

CAREER: Morgan State College, Baltimore, Md., part-time lecturer in history, 1965; University of New Hampshire, Durham, assistant professor, 1965-69, associate professor, 1969-75, professor of history, 1975—. Professional consultant to U.S. Department of State on Portugal and Africa, 1974, 1976. Assistant to curator, Missouri Historical Society, St. Louis, summer, 1960. *Military service:* U.S. Army Reserve, active duty as first lieutenant, 1963-65. *Member:* African Studies Association, American Association of University Professors, Central Africa Historical Association (Salisbury, Rhodesia), Phi Alpha Theta. *Awards, honors:* Senior Key Award (faculty) for 1969, University of New Hampshire; Gulbenkian Foundation (Portugal) grants.

WRITINGS: (With M. Rene Pelissier) *Angola,* Praeger, 1971. Contributor of articles and reviews on African history to *Foreign Affairs, Christian Science Monitor* and other professional journals; also has done translations of Portuguese articles.

WORK IN PROGRESS: A modern history of Angola; a history of the first Portuguese Republic, 1910-1926; a modern history of Portugal; a book on Portugal in Angola in the nineteenth century; studies in Mozambique history.

SIDELIGHTS: Douglas Wheeler speaks Spanish in addition to Portuguese, and reads French. *Avocational interests:* Reading, old movies, watching athletic games and sports.

* * *

WHEELER, Mary Jane
(Mary Jane Fowler, Mary Jane Simonson)

PERSONAL: Divorced; children: Penny (Mrs. Carl Buick), Diane (Mrs. Richard Williams), Deborah, Laurie, Heidi, Daniel. *Education:* Attended Grand Rapids Junior College, Michigan State University, University of Michigan, and Mundelein College. *Politics:* Liberal-independent. *Religion:* Unitarian Universalist. *Home:* 1674 Hollenbeck, Apt. 22, Sunnyvale, Calif. 94087.

CAREER: Former writer and editor for Fideler Co., Grand Rapids, Mich., Bobbs-Merrill Co., Inc., Indianapolis, Ind., Harper & Row Publishers, Inc., New York, N.Y., and Scott, Foresman & Co., Glenview, Ill.

WRITINGS: (Under pseudonym Mary Jane Simonson) *Cowboy without a Horse,* Benefic, 1970; (under pseudonym Mary Jane Simonson) *Cowboy on the Mountain,* Benefic, 1970; (under pseudonym Mary Jane Fowler; with Peg Fisher) *Colonial America,* Fideler, 1974.

WHEELER, Molly 1920-

PERSONAL: Born October 26, 1920, in Surrey, England; daughter of Harry (a banker) and Violet (Wilks) Wheeler. *Education:* Attended Croham Hurst School, South Croydon, Surrey, 1927-37. *Politics:* "Not interested in modern politics." *Religion:* Church of England. *Home:* 4 Grove Rd., Newbury, Berkshire, England. *Agent:* J. F. Gibson's Literary Agency, 4-5 Vernon House, Sicilian Ave., London WC1 2QH, England.

CAREER: Cost clerk for Surrey County Council, 1941-42, and for Coulsdon & Purley U.D.C., 1944-65; Borough of Croydon, London, England, clerical assistant, 1965-66; Hampshire County Council, senior clerk, 1966—.

WRITINGS: By Sword or Fire, Harrap, 1967; *The Farthermost Fort,* Dent, 1969.

SIDELIGHTS: Molly Wheeler writes: "I am very fond of exploring Iron Age hill forts and Roman remains. I am a member of the Sealed Knot, which reenacts English Civil War battles; members wear seventeenth-century costume, and use copies of antique weapons. I am a voracious reader of classical literature (in translation) and particularly admire Plato."

BIOGRAPHICAL/CRITICAL SOURCES: Times Literary Supplement, June 26, 1969.

* * *

WHIPPLE, James B. 1913-

PERSONAL: Born May 31, 1913, in Lowell, Mass.; son of Herbert F. and Helen (Stevens) Whipple; married Florence E. Corkum (a teacher), September 3, 1947; children: Jonathan B., Judith H. *Education:* Dartmouth College, A.B., 1936; Western Reserve University (now Case Western Reserve University), M.A., 1948, Ph.D., 1951. *Politics:* Democrat. *Religion:* Unitarian Universalist. *Home:* 7 Hawthorn Rd., Marblehead, Mass. 01945. *Office:* Department of History, Bunker Hill Community College, Charlestown, Mass.

CAREER: Cleveland Welding Co., Bicycle Division, Cleveland, Ohio, service manager, 1936-42; Western Reserve University (now Case Western Reserve University), Cleveland, Ohio, instructor in history, 1950-53; Center for the Study of Liberal Education for Adults (foundation affiliated with University of Chicago, Chicago, Ill., prior to 1964 and with Boston University, Boston, Mass., 1964-68), began as staff associate, became assistant director and associate director, 1953-68; New Directions for Education (consulting firm), Marblehead, Mass., senior partner, 1968-73; Bunker Hill Community College, Charlestown, Mass., associate professor of history, 1973—. *Military service:* U.S. Army, 1942-46; served in Europe with 5th Infantry Division; became captain; received five battle stars and Bronze Star Medal. *Member:* Adult Education Association of the U.S.A., American Historical Association, Organization of American Historians, American Association of University Professors, Corinthian Yacht Club.

WRITINGS: (With Peter E. Siegle) *New Directions in Programming for University Adult Education,* Center for the Study of Liberal Education for Adults, 1957; (contributor) *Adult Education as a Field of Professional Study,* Adult Education Association, 1964; (contributor) *The Continuing Task: Reflections on Purpose in Higher Continuing Education,* Center for the Study of Liberal Education for Adults, 1967; *A Critical Balance: History of CSLEA,* Center for the Study of Liberal Education for Adults, 1967; (with Kenneth Haygood, Freda H. Goldman, and Peter E. Siegle) *Liberal*

Education Reconsidered: Relfections on Continuing Education for Contemporary Man, Syracuse University Publications in Continuing Education, 1969; (contributor) Doris S. Chertow, editor, *University and Community Service: Perspectives for the Seventies,* Syracuse University Publications in Continuing Education, 1970; *Community Service and Continuing Education: A Literature Review,* Syracuse University Publications in Continuing Education, 1970. Contributor to education journals.

AVOCATIONAL INTERESTS: Sailing, skiing, stamp collecting, gardening.

* * *

WHITAKER, C(leophaus) S(ylvester), Jr. 1935-

PERSONAL: Born February 21, 1935, in Pittsburgh, Pa.; son of Cleophaus Sylvester (a mortician) and Edith (McColes) Whitaker; married Jeanne Theis, August 18, 1956 (divorced, 1964); children: Mark Theis, Paul McColes. *Education:* Swarthmore College, B.A. (with high honors), 1956; Princeton University, M.A., 1958, Ph.D., 1964. *Home:* 222 South Second Ave., Highland Park, N.J. 08904.

CAREER: Princeton University, Princeton, N.J., instructor, 1960-61, lecturer in politics, 1961-62; University of California, Los Angeles, assistant professor, 1962-68, associate professor, 1968-69, professor-designate of politics, 1969, associate dean of student and academic affairs in Graduate Division, 1964-67; Princeton University, professor of politics and public affairs, beginning 1969, chairman of Afro-American studies program, 1969-70. Member of advisory board of International Affairs Division, American Friends Service Committee, and Zenith Books. *Member:* American Political Science Association, International Studies Association, African Studies Association. *Awards, honors:* Social Science Research Council fellow in England and Nigeria, 1958-60.

WRITINGS: (Contributor) J. S. Coleman and Carl G. Rosberg, editors, *Political Parties and National Integration in Tropical Africa,* University of California Press, 1964; (contributor) Gwendolen M. Carter, editor, *National Unity and Regionalism in Eight African States,* Cornell University Press, 1966; *The Politics of Tradition: Continuity and Change in Northern Nigeria, 1945-1965,* Princeton University Press, 1969. Contributor to political affairs journals.

WORK IN PROGRESS: Editing *Continuity in Change: Traditional Influences in New States,* for Anchor Books.

BIOGRAPHICAL/CRITICAL SOURCES: Marvin Weisbord, *Some Form of Peace,* Viking, 1968.†

* * *

WHITAKER, Rod 1931-
(Nicholas Seare)

PERSONAL: Born June 12, 1931, in Granville, N.Y.; married Diane Brandon. *Education:* University of Washington, Seattle, B.A., 1959, M.A., 1960; Northwestern University, Ph.D., 1966. *Home:* 1419 Newning Ave., Austin, Tex. 78704. *Office address:* P.O. Box 7158, University of Texas, Austin, Tex. 78712.

CAREER: Dana College, Blair, Neb., chairman of department of speech and drama, 1963-66, head of Division of Communications, 1965-66; currently associate professor, University of Texas at Austin. Director and designer for the professional theater, television, and films. Consultant to Prentice-Hall, Inc., for books on film. *Military service:* U.S. Navy, 1949-53. *Awards, honors:* Special award at Riata Film Festival and *Esquire* Award, both for "Stasis"; Gold Medal at Atlanta Film Festival, for "Cinemania."

WRITINGS: The Language of Film, Prentice-Hall, 1970; (under pseudonym Nicholas Seare) *1339 ... Or So: Being an Apology for a Pedlar,* Harcourt, 1975.

WORK IN PROGRESS: Directing the compilation of a cross index of the American cinema.

BIOGRAPHICAL/CRITICAL SOURCES: Cavalier, April, 1968; *Films on the Campus,* A. S. Barnes, 1970.†

* * *

WHITE, Howard Ashley 1913-

PERSONAL: Born September 28, 1913, in Cloverdale, Ala.; son of John Parker (a grocer) and Mabel (Hipp) White; married Maxcine Feltman, June 17, 1952; children: Ashley Feltman, Howard Elliott. *Education:* Tulane University of Louisiana, B.A., 1946, M.A., 1952, Ph.D., 1956. *Home:* 6280 Paseo Canyon Dr., Malibu, Calif. 90265. *Office:* Pepperdine University, Malibu, Calif. 90265.

CAREER: Ordained to ministry of Church of Christ, 1930; minister of several congregations of Church of Christ in U.S., including New Orleans, La., 1941-52, Nashville, Tenn., Los Angeles, Calif., 1957-63; David Lipscomb College, Nashville, Tenn., professor of history and head of department, 1953-58; Pepperdine University, Malibu, Calif., professor of history and head of department, 1958-69, dean of undergraduate studies, 1966-69, executive vice-president, 1970—. Co-founder and director, Pepperdine Year in Europe, Heidelberg, Germany, 1963-64. *Member:* Organization of American Historians, Southern Historical Association. *Awards, honors:* Montgomery Prize in history, Tulane University of Louisiana, 1946.

WRITINGS: The Freedman's Bureau in Louisiana, Louisiana State University Press, 1970. Member of editorial staff, *Twentieth Century Christian.*

SIDELIGHTS: Howard White has lived in Germany for a year, and has traveled to other European countries. He told *CA,* "I am chiefly interested in Christian education, in which cause I serve at Pepperdine University...."

* * *

WHITE, James W. 1941-

PERSONAL: Born August 22, 1941, in Cleveland, Ohio; son of Edwarda (Williams) White Van Benschoten and stepson of Birney Mills Van Benschoten (an attorney); married Marion Sullivan, January 7, 1967; children: James Van Benschoten. *Education:* Princeton University, A.B. (with highest honors), 1964; Stanford University, M.A., 1965, Ph.D., 1969. *Home:* 209 Hill St., Chapel Hill, N.C. 27514. *Office:* Department of Political Science, University of North Carolina, Chapel Hill, N.C. 27514.

CAREER: Stanford University, Stanford, Calif., lecturer and research associate, 1968-69; University of North Carolina at Chapel Hill, assistant professor, 1969-73, associate professor of political science, 1973—. Visiting professor of law, Kyoto University (Japan), 1977. *Member:* American Political Science Association, Association for Asian Studies, Committee of Concerned Asian Scholars, Phi Beta Kappa. *Awards, honors:* Woodrow Wilson fellow; grants from National Science Foundation, Social Science Research Council, and Japan Foundation.

WRITINGS: The Sokagakkai and Mass Society, Stanford University Press, 1970; (contributor) Gabriel Almond, Scott

Flanagan, and Robert Mundt, editors, *Crisis, Choice, and Change,* Little, Brown, 1973; (co-editor) *Social Change and Community Politics in Urban Japan,* Institute for Research in the Social Sciences, 1976.

WORK IN PROGRESS: A study of political implications of cityward migration in Japan.

AVOCATIONAL INTERESTS: Rugby, karate (holds first degree black belt).

* * *

WHITE, John Wesley 1928-

PERSONAL: Born September 15, 1928, in Saskatchewan, Canada. *Education:* Moody Bible Institute, graduate, 1950; Wheaton College, Wheaton, Ill., B.A., 1952; Oxford University, D.Phil., 1963. *Office:* Richmond College, Toronto, Ontario, Canada.

CAREER: Associate evangelist with Billy Graham, traveling to one hundred countries, 1964—; Richmond College, Toronto, Ontario, chancellor, 1967—.

WRITINGS: Re-entry: Striking Parallels Between Today's News Events and Christ's Second Coming, Zondervan, 1970; *Mission Control,* Zondervan, 1971; *Re-entry II,* Zondervan, 1971; *Future Hope,* Creation House, 1974; *The Runaway,* Crescendo, 1976; *The Land Columbus Loved,* Gordon Press, 1976. Also author of *Everywhere Preaching the Gospel,* 1969.

WORK IN PROGRESS: Recovery, for Zondervan.†

* * *

WHITE, William Luther 1931-

PERSONAL: Born July 7, 1931, in Clay City, Ind.; married Patricia Ann Orr (on administrative staff at Illinois State University), 1955; children: Lucinda Kay, Christopher William, Duncan Mark. *Education:* DePauw University, A.B. (cum laude), 1953; Garrett Theological Seminary, B.D., 1957; Northwestern University, M.A., 1957, Ph.D., 1968. *Home:* 1205 Westview Dr., Normal, Ill. 61761. *Office:* Department of Religion, Illinois Wesleyan University, Bloomington, Ill. 61701.

CAREER: Clergyman of United Methodist Church; Methodist Temple, Evansville, Ind., minister of Christian education, 1957-62; Illinois Wesleyan University, Bloomington, chaplain and professor of religion, 1963—. Representative of Methodist Board of Education at White House Conference on Children and Youth, 1961. Trustee, Citizen Exchange Corps (New York City). *Member:* National Association of College and University Chaplains, American Association of University Professors, National Campus Ministry Association, Christians Associated for Relations with Eastern Europe (secretary), Church Society for College Work, Spiritual Frontiers Fellowship.

WRITINGS: The Image of Man in C. S. Lewis, Abingdon, 1969. Contributor to religious journals.

* * *

WHITTLESEY, Susan 1938-

PERSONAL: Born October 25, 1938, in Pittsfield, Mass.; daughter of William Augustus (vice-president of Northeast Utilities) and Margaret (Gage) Whittlesey; married Thomas Anthony Wolf (an international economist), September 13, 1969; children: Thomas Whittlesey Wolf, Edward Downing Wolf, Caroline Tilden Wolf. *Education:* Smith College, B.A. (cum laude), 1960. *Politics:* Democratic. *Home:* 2188

Tremont Rd., Columbus, Ohio 43221. *Agent:* Carl Brandt, Brandt & Brandt, 101 Park Ave., New York, N.Y. 10017.

CAREER: Berkshire Eagle, Pittsfield, Mass., editor assistant, summers, 1959, 1960; Bunka Gakuin (high school and college), Tokyo, Japan, teacher of English and director of dramatics, 1960-61; *Peace Corps Volunteers* (magazine), Washington, D.C., assistant editor, 1962-63; Reader's Digest Condensed Book Club, New York, N.Y., associate editor, 1964-71.

WRITINGS—Juvenile: *U.S. Peace Corps: The Challenge of Good Will,* Coward, 1963; *Vista: Challenge to Poverty,* Coward, 1970. Writer of "Ohayo from Ohio," a comedy in simple English produced at Bunka Gakuin, Tokyo, 1962, and several dramatic adaptations of plays, including "Peter Pan," "Little Women," and "Human Comedy," produced at the same school.

WORK IN PROGRESS: "A children's book based on travels with my small children in Austria and Germany, where we have just lived for three years."

SIDELIGHTS: Susan Whittlesey wrote to *CA:* "I feel I have hardly begun. I have notebooks full of ideas. This is my decade to inspire my own small children—three of them 5½ and under. So the notebooks get thicker—but the time draws nearer when I can devote more hours to them. Writing nonfiction (which my books are) is for me, a craft. But to write fiction is to make art. I hope to go in that direction."

BIOGRAPHICAL/CRITICAL SOURCES: Best Sellers, November 15, 1970.

* * *

WIDMER, Emmy Louise 1925-

PERSONAL: Born December 25, 1925, in Frankfurt-am-Main, Germany; daughter of George (an engineer) and Magdalena (Schmidt) Numrich; children: Mark G. *Education:* New York University, Washington Square College of Arts and Sciences, A.B., 1947, Ed.D., 1963; State University of New York, M.S., 1952. *Office:* College of Education, Florida Atlantic University, Boca Raton, Fla. 33432.

CAREER: Kindergarten and primary teacher in public and private schools in Rochester, N.Y., New York, N.Y., and East Stroudsburg, Pa., 1949-51, 1956-59; East Stroudsburg State College, East Stroudsburg, Pa., demonstration teacher and supervisor in Campus Laboratory School, 1959-61, assistant professor of education, 1961-62; New York University, New York, N.Y., instructor and supervisor of student teachers, 1962-63; Temple University, Philadelphia, Pa., assistant professor of education, 1963-65; University of Miami, Miami, Fla., associate professor of education, 1965-67; Florida Atlantic University, Boca Raton, professor of education and coordinator of early childhood program, 1967—, interim dean of College of Education, 1975-77. Visiting professor at New York University and Barry College, Miami, Fla.; director of NDEA (National Defense Education Act) Institute at University of Miami; consultant for Palm Beach, Broward, and Dade Counties, Kindergarten, Headstart and Migrant Programs, and National Teacher Corps Program, all in Florida; delegate to 1970 White House Conference on Children and member of Ad Hoc Advisory Committee; member, State Department Committees on Migrant Education and Early Childhood Education; member, board of directors, Community Coordinated Child Care of Palm Beach County.

MEMBER: International Platform Association, Association for Childhood Education International, American Association of Elementary-Kindergarten-Nursery Educators, National Association on Education of Young Children, Day Care Association of America, Kappa Delta Pi, Delta Kappa Gamma. *Awards, honors:* Founders Day Award for outstanding scholarship, New York University, 1964.

WRITINGS: The Critical Years: Early Childhood Education at the Crossroads, International Textbook Co., 1970. Contributor: Dorothy Fenton Westley-Gibson, compiler, *Social Foundations of Education,* Free Press, 1967; Joe L. Frost, editor, *Early Childhood Education Rediscovered,* Holt, 1968; *A Guide: Early Childhood Education in Florida Schools,* Florida State Department, 1969; *Kindergarten: Who? What? Where?,* Southern Association on Children Under Six and Georgia State Department, 1969. Also contributor to, Hass and Wiles, editors, *Readings in Elementary School Teaching,* 1968, and *Community Education,* 1975. Contributor of articles to *Elementary School Journal, Young Children, Florida Education, Peabody Journal of Education,* and *Childhood Education.*

AVOCATIONAL INTERESTS: Travel, music, swimming, tennis, hiking, camping, boating, and literature.

* * *

WIERSMA, Stanley M(arvin) 1930-
(Sietze Buning)

PERSONAL: Born July 15, 1930, in Orange City, Iowa; son of Samuel (a farmer) and Hermina (Peters) Wiersma; married Irene Hanenburg, July 11, 1955; children: Samuel Christian, Robert Mouw. *Education:* Calvin College, A.B., 1951; University of Wisconsin, M.Sc., 1956, Ph.D., 1961. *Politics:* Democrat. *Religion:* Christian Reformed Church. *Home:* 1330 Logan S.E., Grand Rapids, Mich. 49506. *Office:* Department of English, Calvin College, Grand Rapids, Mich. 49506.

CAREER: High school English teacher in Hull, Iowa, 1951-52; Calvin College, Grand Rapids, Mich., instructor, 1959-61, assistant professor, 1961-63, associate professor, 1963-67, professor of English, 1967—. Fulbright lecturer, Free University of Amsterdam, 1968-69; summer lecturer at Grand Valley State College, 1963-65, University of Idaho, 1968. *Military service:* U.S. Army, 1953-54. *Member:* Modern Language Association of America, Conference on Christianity and Literature, Workgroup Christian Writers (vice-president).

WRITINGS: Christopher Fry, Eerdmans, 1970; (with Merle Meeter) *Contrasting Christian Approaches to Teaching Literature* (monograph), Calvin College, 1970; (translator) Gerrit Achterberg, *A Tourist Does Golgotha and Other Poems,* Begin Press, 1972. Also author of numerous poems on the Dutch ethnic past under the pseudonym Sietze Buning. Contributor to literature journals.

WORK IN PROGRESS: Catching the Dove in Flight: An Exercise in Literary Criticism; and a full-length work on Christopher Fry.

* * *

WIESEN, Allen E. 1939-

PERSONAL: Born May 5, 1939, in New York, N.Y.; son of Irving (a businessman) and Estelle (Schwartz) Wiesen; married Terry Newberg, April 30, 1966 (divorced, 1969); married Susan Matsuo, September, 1972. *Education:* Hunter College of the City University of New York, B.A., 1961; University of Florida, M.A., 1963, Ph.D., 1965. *Politics:* Independent. *Home:* 2837 Evergreen Pt. Rd., Bellevue, Wash. 98004.

CAREER: Veteran's Administration Hospital, Augusta, Ga., intern in clinical psychology, 1964-65; Fircrest School, Seattle, Wash., head of psychology department, 1965-69; private practice in clinical psychology, Seattle, 1966-68; Seattle Public Schools, Seattle, consultant and behavioral specialist, 1969—. *Member:* American Psychological Association, Puget Sound Psychological Association. *Awards, honors:* U.S. Public Health Fellowships, 1963, 1964.

WRITINGS: (With Merle L. Meacham) *Changing Classroom Behavior: A Manual for Precision Teaching,* International Textbook Co., 1969; (with William Getzetal) *Fundamentals of Crisis Counseling,* Heath, 1974; *Positive Therapy,* Nelson-Hall, 1977. Contributor to psychology journals.

WORK IN PROGRESS: Positive Parenting.

SIDELIGHTS: Allen Wiesen told *CA:* "Clinical experience has led me to view man as capable of increasing control of his destiny. In *Positive Therapy* I assume the existential position that 'life offers two alternatives. Positive and Negative.' Positive therapy is the systematic selection of life over death."

* * *

WILCOX, R(uth) Turner 1888-1970

April 29, 1888—June 3, 1970; American designer, artist, and author of books on costume. Obituaries: *Publishers' Weekly,* July 13, 1970. (See index for *CA* sketch)

* * *

WILENTZ, Theodore 1915-
(Ted Wilentz)

PERSONAL: Born March 15, 1915, in New York, N.Y.; son of Samuel and Celia (Levitt) Wilentz; married Esther Simonds; married second wife, Joan Steen (a science writer), June 25, 1965; children: (second marriage) David Thomas, John Eric Karl. *Education:* New York University, B.A., 1935, graduate study, 1936. *Politics:* Independent Democrat. *Religion:* Jewish. *Home:* 228 Everit, New Haven, Conn. 06511. *Office:* Yale University Cooperative, 77 Broadway, New Haven, Conn. 06520.

CAREER: Book-Art, New York City, vice-president, 1937-41; Eighth Street Bookshop, New York City, co-owner, 1947-68; publications manager, Sierra Club, 1968-70; Gotham Book Mart, New York City, vice-president, 1970-72; Discovery Bookshop, New York City, owner, 1972-73; Yale University Cooperative, New Haven, Conn., manager of book department, 1973—. Co-publisher and co-editor, Corinth Books, 1960—. *Military service:* U.S. Army, 1941-45; became captain. *Member:* American Booksellers Association, National Book Committee, Booksellers League of New York (president, 1970-73).

WRITINGS: (Editor, under name Ted Wilentz; with Tom Weatherly) *Natural Process: An Anthology of New Black Poetry,* Hill & Wang, 1970. Contributor to *TriQuarterly.*

WORK IN PROGRESS: Bohemia: The Avant-Garde and the Alternative Culture.

SIDELIGHTS: Wilentz told *CA:* "I have always considered writing the highest form of art. Perhaps because I have not written much myself I have been involved with writers and with editing and publishing. To me the most exciting aspect of writing is the avant-garde because it changes the old and signals the new and leaves it to reader and critic to judge what is both new and good. In co-editing Corinth

Books . . ., I have been primarily involved in poetry because it has been in poetry that new social and literary ideas and attitudes have found primary expression.''

* * *

WILFORD, John Noble 1933-

PERSONAL: Born October 4, 1933, in Camden, Tenn.; son of John Noble (a minister) and Pauline (Hendricks) Wilford; married Nancy Watts, December 25, 1966; children: Nona. Education: University of Tennessee, B.S. (magna cum laude), 1955; Syracuse University, M.A., 1956; Columbia University, additional graduate study, 1961-62. Religion: Protestant. Home: 232 West 10th St., New York, N.Y. 10014. Office: New York Times, 229 West 43rd St., New York, N.Y. 10036.

CAREER: Wall Street Journal, New York City, reporter, 1956-61; Time, New York City, contributing editor, 1962-65; New York Times, New York City, aerospace reporter, 1965-73, assistant national editor, 1973-75, director of science news, 1975—. Director, Corpcom Services, Inc. Military Service: U.S. Army, Counter Intelligence Corps, 1957-59. Member: Overseas Press Club, Aviation/Space Writers Association, Sigma Delta Chi. Awards, honors: Ford Foundation fellow in international affairs, 1961-62; Aviation/Space Writers Association book award, 1970, for We Reach the Moon; G. M. Loeb Achievement Award, University of Connecticut, 1972; Press Award, National Space Club, 1974.

WRITINGS: (Contributor) Harrison E. Salisbury, editor, The Soviet Union: The Fifty Years, Harcourt, 1967; We Reach the Moon, Bantam, 1969, expanded hardcover edition, Norton, 1969. Contributor to magazines and newspapers.

SIDELIGHTS: Since 1965 John Noble Wilford has covered space exploration, from the Gemini Project and Apollo flights, through the unmanned flights to the planets.

BIOGRAPHICAL/CRITICAL SOURCES: New York Times, July 16, 1969.

* * *

WILHELM, Walt 1893-

PERSONAL: Born February 27, 1893, in Trenton, Mo.; son of William Sherman (a miner) and Dora Jane (Duncan) Wilhelm; married Minerva Beatrice Melvin, May 14, 1924 (died, 1967); married Muriel Blanche Johnson, 1971; children: (first marriage) Rowena Beatrice (Mrs. William F. Stucky). Education: Self-educated (first attended a school in Mackay, Idaho, in 1900, then schools in Columbia, Calif., 1903, Washoe Valley, Nev., 1905, Battle Mountain, Nev., 1907, and Long Beach, Calif., briefly in 1911). Politics: Republican. Religion: ''Make my own.'' Home: 301 Yermo Rd., Box 9, Yermo, Calif. 92328.

CAREER: Former blacksmith, working as a civilian blacksmith for sixteen years with U.S. Marine Corps Supply units and four years with U.S. Army.

WRITINGS: Last Rig to Battle Mountain, Morrow, 1970. Archery (magazine), contributor of articles, 1943-74, author of regular column, ''It's a Fact,'' until 1974. Also contributor of stories to Archery World, Field & Stream, Desert Magazine, Northern Sportsman, and several newspapers.

WORK IN PROGRESS: Two books dealing mainly with the Mojave Desert of California, Nevada, and Arizona, from 1870 to the present; a book of short-stories and poems.

SIDELIGHTS: Walt Wilhelm started to write in 1938. He says: ''What little I know about the craft I learned from Erle Stanley Gardner, a friend and exploring pal of 40 years. I . . . do a lot of research on the desert, some for my books, some looking for artifacts of prehistoric man that roamed the deserts in bygone days. I got started in this archaeology craft about twelve years ago when the late Dr. Leaky started a dig in the Calico Mountains looking for artifacts of the Ice Age Man that he thought could have lived in this section of the desert nineteen thousand years ago.''

* * *

WILKEN, Robert L(ouis) 1936-

PERSONAL: Born October 20, 1936, in New Orleans, La.; son of Louis F. (an investment broker) and Mabel (Rayl) Wilken; married Carol Faith Weinhold, June 4, 1960; children: Gregory, Jonathan. Education: Attended Concordia College, Austin, Tex., 1953-55; Concordia Seminary, B.A., 1957, B.D., 1960; University of Chicago, M.A., 1961, Ph.D., 1963. Religion: Lutheran. Home: 308 LaMonte Ter., South Bend, Ind. 46616. Office: Department of Theology, University of Notre Dame, Notre Dame, Ind. 46556.

CAREER: Deutsche Akademische Austauschdienst, Heidelberg, Germany, postdoctoral fellow, 1963-64; Lutheran Theological Seminary, Gettysburg, Pa., assistant professor of history, 1964-67; Fordham University, New York, N.Y., assistant professor of history, 1967-71; University of Notre Dame, Notre Dame, Ind., associate professor of history of Christianity, 1972—, director of graduate studies. Visiting professor, St. Mary's Seminary, Baltimore, 1971-72. Member: American Historical Association, Society for Religion in Higher Education (fellow), American Academy of Religion, American Society of Church History, American Association of University Professors. Awards, honors: German Academic Exchange Service fellow, 1963-64.

WRITINGS: Judaism and the Early Christian Mind: A Study of Cyril of Alexandria's Exegesis and Theology, Yale University Press, 1971; The Myth of Christian Beginnings: History's Impact on Belief, Doubleday, 1971; (editor) Aspects of Wisdom in Judaism and Early Christianity, University of Notre Dame Press, 1975. Also author of lectures, ''Abraham in the Early Christian Interpretation'' (cassette tape), Instructional Media Center, Concordia Seminary (St. Louis), 1972. Contributor to periodicals. Associate editor, Una Sancta.†

* * *

WILKINSON, Doris Yvonne 1936-

PERSONAL: Born June 13, 1936, in Lexington, Ky.; daughter of Howard Thomas and Regina (Cowherd) Wilkinson. Education: University of Kentucky, B.A., 1958; Case Western Reserve University, M.A., 1960, Ph.D., 1968. Politics: ''No political affiliation.'' Religion: Unitarian Universalist. Home: 1600 Grand Ave., St. Paul, Minn. 55105. Office: Department of Sociology, Macalester College, St. Paul, Minn. 55101.

CAREER: Kent State University, Kent, Ohio, instructor in sociology and anthropology, 1961-63; Carnegie-Mellon University, Pittsburgh, Pa., instructor in sociology and anthropology and research associate, 1966-67; University of Kentucky, Lexington, assistant professor of sociology, 1967-70; Macalester College, St. Paul, Minn., 1970—, began as associate professor, currently professor of sociology. Visiting associate professor, Columbia University, 1969; member of task force on national parks in urban America, Conservation

Foundation, 1971-72; member, Minnesota Humanities Commission, 1973—. *Member:* American Sociological Association, American Association of University Professors, American Orthopsychiatric Association, Society for the Study of Social Problems, Phi Delta Kappa, Alpha Kappa Delta. *Awards, honors:* Woodrow Wilson fellowship, 1959-61; named one of three outstanding women faculty members at University of Kentucky, 1969; Social Science Research Council award, 1975.

WRITINGS: Workbook for Introductory Sociology, Burgess, 1968; (editor) *Black Revolt: Strategies of Protest,* McCutchan, 1969; (editor) *Black Male/White Female,* Schenkman, 1975; (editor with R. Taylor) *The Black Male in America,* Nelson-Hall, 1976; *Social Structure and Assassination,* Schenkman, 1976. Contributor to *British Journal of Sociology, Sociological Focus, International Journal of Comparative Sociology, Phylon, International Behavioural Scientist, Sociological Quarterly, Political Scientist, Youth and Society, Journal of Black Studies,* and *American Sociologist.*

WORK IN PROGRESS: Research on sexual and racial variables in psychiatry, and on images of women in twentieth-century fiction.

AVOCATIONAL INTERESTS: Piano, creative writing.

* * *

WILLENSKY, Elliot 1933-

PERSONAL: Born July 11, 1933, in New York, N.Y.; son of Morris (a merchant) and Fannie (Eisenstein) Willensky; children: Marc Isaac, Diana Gwen. *Education:* Attended Cooper Union, 1950-53; Yale University, M.Arch., 1955. *Home and office:* 52 Clark St., Brooklyn, N.Y. 11201.

CAREER: Registered architect in New York and other states. Architectual designer and administrator with architectural firms in New York City, 1955-65; Cornell University, College of Architecture, associate professor of architecture and director of New York City Program, 1963-68; New York City Parks, Recreation, and Cultural Affairs Administration, New York City, director of design, 1968, deputy administrator for development, 1968-70; High Rock Park Conservation Center, Staten Island, N.Y., director, 1971-76. Arts consultant to On-Site Urban Communications Program for New York City, 1970-72, Frederick Law Olmstead 150th Anniversary Exhibition feasability study, 1971, and to Young Filmmakers/Video Arts-Film Forum feasability study for Mediacenter, 1977.

MEMBER: American Institute of Architects (secretary of New York chapter, 1964-65), American Association of Museums, Society for Industrial Archeology, Long Island Historical Society (director, 1974—), Frederick Law Olmstead Association (vice-president, 1972—). *Awards, honors:* Award of merit of Municipal Art Society of New York, 1969, for *A.I.A. Guide to New York City,* and 1976, for programs at High Rock Park Conservation Center; Design Award of *Industrial Design Magazine,* 1969, for Parks, Recreation, and Cultural Affairs (P.R.C.A.) Urban Outdoor Graphics Program; Arnold W. Brunner Scholarship from American Institute of Architects (New York chapter), 1975.

WRITINGS: (Editor with Norval C. White) *A.I.A. Guide to New York City,* New York Chapter, American Institute of Architects, 1967, 2nd revised edition, Macmillan, 1978. Also author of *Guide to Developing a Neighborhood Marker System* and *An Urban Information System for New York City,* both for the Museum of the City of New York, 1972.

WORK IN PROGRESS: A book on "hidden" New York, those elements of the physical city which are normally not noticed by the observer because they are too high up, behind real or imagined barriers, or beneath one's feet.

* * *

WILLIAMS, Barry 1932-

PERSONAL: Born April 20, 1932, in Brighton, England; son of Gwynfryn Evans (a police detective-superintendent) and Eiluned (Rowlands) Williams; married Margaret Ann Wiles (a teacher), April 10, 1954; children: Sara Beverley, Amanda Jane. *Education:* University of Bristol, B.A. (honours in history), 1953. *Home:* Cynara, Kington Magna, Gillingham, Dorsetshire, England.

CAREER: History master at a grammar school in Penistone, Yorkshire, England, 1957-63; Clee Humberstone Foundation School, Lincolnshire, England, senior history master, 1964-69; Gillingham School, Gillingham, Dorsetshire, England, head of history department and sixth form master, 1969-72; Sherborne School for Girls, Dorsetshire, England, university adviser and head of history side, 1971—. History adviser to Education Division, Rank Film Organization, 1962-70. *Military service:* Royal Air Force, flying officer, 1953-56. *Member:* Historical Association (secretary of Grimsby branch, 1967-69).

WRITINGS—All published by Longmans, Green prior to 1971, Longman 1971 and after, except as indicated: *The Struggle for Canada,* 1967, revised edition, 1968, published as *The Struggle for North America,* McGraw, 1969; *Modern Japan,* 1968, published in an enlarged edition as *Emerging Japan,* McGraw, 1969; *Asia: Food and People,* 1970; *Japan,* 1970; *Congo Tragedy,* 1970; *South Africa,* 1970; *Modern Africa, 1870-1970,* 1970, revised edition, 1976; (contributor) *The Teaching of History in Secondary Schools,* Cambridge University Press, 1975; (contributor) G. Uden, editor, *Longman Illustrated Companion to World History,* 1976; *France, 1870-1975,* 1978. Also author of *The First Industrial Revolution* and *Transport,* ten packs of resource evidence, 1973-74.

Teachers' handbooks for Encyclopædia Britannica films: *The Vikings,* 1964; *The Industrial Revolution,* 1965; *The Second World War,* 1966; *The Age of Exploration,* 1967; *The French Revolution,* 1967. Author of two motion picture synopses for Rank Film Organization, "Lord and Vassal" and "Africa in the last Eighty Year," both 1967.

* * *

WILLIAMS, Byron (Leigh) 1934-

PERSONAL: Born July 4, 1934, in Inglewood, Calif.; son of Ralph Darby (a missionary) and Jewyl (Stoddard) Williams; married Irene Chipurnoi, September 4, 1968. *Education:* Attended University of Wichita, 1955-56, and Los Angeles City College, 1957-58, 1961-62. *Politics:* Independent. *Religion:* None.

CAREER: Electronics technician for Boeing, Bendix, and International Business Machines Corp. (IBM), 1955-59; technical writer in electronics industry, 1959-62; free-lance writer in New York, N.Y., 1962-66, and in Forest Knolls, Calif., 1966—. Director of a theater workshop in Mill Valley, Calif. *Military service:* U.S. Navy, 1951-55.

WRITINGS—All juvenile; published by Parents' Magazine Press: *Cuba: The Continuing Revolution,* 1969; *Continent in Turmoil,* 1971; *Puerto Rico: Commonwealth, State, or Nation?,* 1972. Contributor of short stories to magazines.

WORK IN PROGRESS: A novel, *The Six Books of Clayton Olney;* research in California history and in current Latin American upheavals.

AVOCATIONAL INTERESTS: Motorcycle touring in Europe, Mexico, Canada, and the United States; flying.†

* * *

WILLIAMS, C(lifford) Glyn 1928-

PERSONAL: Born February 23, 1928, in Letterston, Pembrokeshire, Wales; son of Arthur James (a laborer) and Annie (Morgans) Williams; married Penelope Cleghorn (a vocation guidance counselor), February 2, 1964 (divorced March 16, 1977); married Nancy Hammons (an executive secretary), March 25, 1977; children: (first marriage) Karen, Andrew. *Education:* University College of Wales, Aberystwyth, B.A., 1956; University of Manchester, M.A., 1958; University of Virginia, Ph.D., 1962. *Home:* 201 Tyborne Circle, Columbia, S.C. 29210. *Office:* Department of Economics, University of South Carolina, Columbia, S.C. 29208.

CAREER: Assistant professor of economics at Queens College, Charlotte, N.C., 1960-61, University of Alberta, Edmonton, 1961-63, Indiana University, Bloomington, 1963-66, and Boston College, Boston, Mass., 1966-69; University of South Carolina, Columbia, associate professor, 1969-73, professor of economics, 1973—. *Member:* American Economic Association, Royal Economic Society, Industrial Relations Research Association, Omicron Delta Epsilon. *Awards, honors:* Fulbright travel scholarship.

WRITINGS: Technological Change in the Railway Industry, Canadian Ministry of Labour, 1968; *Labor Economics: The Changing Labor Scene,* Wiley, 1970; *An Analysis of Civilian Labor Force and Civilian Employment Changes in South Carolina During the 1960's,* University of South Carolina Press, 1973; *Employment and Labor Force in South Carolina in 1980: State and Economic Relationships,* University of South Carolina Press, 1974. Contributor to economics journals.

WORK IN PROGRESS: Survey of postwar views of economists on the role of labor unions in inflation; research on the influence of off-shore manufacturing on corporate employment practices and corporate performance in the United States; analysis of wage structures in U.S. manufacturing industries.

* * *

WILLIAMS, David A. 1922-

PERSONAL: Born February 18, 1922, in Pittsburgh, Pa.; son of Walter L. and Esther (Haney) Williams; married Ruth B. Coropoff (a teacher), November 2, 1949; children: Julie, Norman, Janet. *Education:* University of California, Los Angeles, B.A., 1949, M.A., 1951; University of Southern California, Ph.D., 1963. *Home:* 144 Glendora Ave., Long Beach, Calif. 90803. *Office:* Department of History, California State University, Long Beach, Calif. 90801.

CAREER: Began as teacher in Los Angeles County (Calif.) public schools; California State College (now California State University), lecturer in history at Long Beach campus, 1961-62, and at Los Angeles campus, 1962-64, assistant professor of history at Fullerton campus, 1964-65; California State University, Long Beach, 1965—, began as associate professor, currently professor of history. *Military service:* U.S. Army, 1944-46; became staff sergeant. *Member:* American Historical Association, Organization of American

Historians, California Historical Society, Historical Society of Southern California.

WRITINGS: David C. Broderick: A Political Portrait, Huntington Library, 1969; *California, the Golden State,* Doubleday, 1972. Contributor to professional journals.

* * *

WILLIAMS, Edward Francis 1903-1970
(Lord Francis-Williams)

March 10, 1903—June 5, 1970; British author, journalist, and television commentator. Obituaries: *New York Times,* June 6, 1970; *Current Biography,* 1970.

* * *

WILLIAMS, Edward G. 1929-

PERSONAL: Born November 3, 1929, in Fayetteville, N.C.; son of Alonza S. and Blanche (Beebe) Williams. *Education:* Norfolk State College, student, 1948-50; City College of the City University of New York, B.A., 1966, M.A., 1977. *Politics:* Independent Democrat. *Religion:* Methodist. *Home:* 801 West End Ave., Apt. 5BB, New York, N.Y. 10025.

CAREER: United Nations, New York City, supervisor of staff of typists in procurement department, 1959-63; *New York Herald Tribune* (later *World Journal Tribune*), New York City, traffic manager in promotion department and writer of promotional material, 1963-67; S. R. Leon Advertising Agency, New York City, director of traffic department, 1967; free-lance writer, 1967—. *Military service:* U.S. Navy, 1950-54. *Member:* P.E.N., Writers Guild.

WRITINGS: Not Like Niggers (novel), St. Martin's, 1969. Three short stories anthologized in *A Galaxy of Black Writing,* Moore Publishing, 1970. Contributor of articles to *Christian Science Monitor.*

WORK IN PROGRESS: Worlds in Collision: The Black Man and Reconstruction; a collection of short stories, not yet titled; *Footsteps and Shadows,* the second novel of a trilogy; a three-act play, "Great Day for a Funeral."

AVOCATIONAL INTERESTS: Music, the theater, films.

BIOGRAPHICAL/CRITICAL SOURCES: New York Times Book Review, November 9, 1969.

* * *

WILLIAMS, Geoffrey (John) 1943-

PERSONAL: Born September 1, 1943, in Redruth, Cornwall, England; son of Thomas Kenneth and Vera (Matthews) Williams. *Education:* St. Edmund Hall, Oxford, B.A. (with honors). *Home:* Medlyn Moor Farm, Perkellis, Helston, Cornwall, England. *Agent:* A. P. Watt & Son, 26/28 Bedford Row, London WC1R 4HL, England.

CAREER: St. Bernard's School, New York, N.Y., master in charge of geography, 1965-67; built 57-foot ketch "Sir Thomas Lipton" and won Singlehanded Transatlantic Yacht Race, 1968; Ocean Youth Club (educational charity for boys and girls), England, executive director, 1969-76, also director of club boatyard and responsible for construction of world's largest fleet of fiberglass 72-foot sailing ketches, 1970—. Trustee, National Maritime Museum, Greenwich, England, 1971-75; elected member of Cornwall county council, 1972-75. *Awards, honors:* Named Britain's Outstanding Young Man of the Year, 1968; honorary research fellow at University of Exeter.

WRITINGS: Sir Thomas Lipton Wins, P. Davies, 1969, Lippincott, 1970. Also author of a report for I.B.M. International and R.T.Z. Ltd. on personal development of young people at school and work, and of a report for Cornwall Conservation Forum on the implications of oil in the Celtic Sea. Contributor to yachting journals and Daily Telegraph.

WORK IN PROGRESS: A research project on low-cost windmills for rural houses and farm.

SIDELIGHTS: Geoffrey Williams told CA that he was "impressed by Meadows' Limits to Growth and frustrated by the inertia of politics," and as a result he has "opted for a life of self sufficiency and organic husbandry on a small farm."

*   *   *

WILLIAMS, Herbert (Lloyd) 1932-

PERSONAL: Born September 8, 1932, in Aberystwyth, Wales; son of Richard David (a painter and decorator) and Minnie Esther (Jones) Williams; married Dorothy Maud Edwards, November 13, 1956; children: Peter, David, Alan, Mary, John. Education: Attended public schools in Aberystwyth, Wales. Home: 107 Pantbach Rd., Rhiwbina, Cardiff, Wales.

CAREER: Welsh Gazette, Aberystwyth, Wales, reporter, 1951-53; Reading Standard, Reading, England, reporter, 1953; Cambrian News, Aberystwyth, reporter and sub-editor, 1953-56; South Wales Echo, Cardiff, reporter, industrial correspondent, then sub-editor, 1956-60; Scottish Daily Mail, Edinburgh, Scotland, sub-editor, 1960-61; South Wales Echo, chief feature writer, 1961-72; Birmingham Evening Mail, Birmingham, England, features sub-editor, 1972-73; general programmes producer, British Broadcasting Corp., Wales, 1973—.

WRITINGS: Too Wet for the Devil (poems), Outpost, 1962; The Dinosaurs (poems), Triskel Press, 1966; The Trophy (poems), Christopher Davies, 1967; A Lethal Kind of Love (verse play), John Jones, 1968; Battles in Wales, John Jones, 1975; Come Out Wherever You Are, Quartet, 1977. Poetry anthologized in Welsh Voices, edited by Bryn Griffiths, Dent, 1967, The Lilting House: An Anthology of Anglo-Welsh Poetry, 1917-67, edited by J. Stuart Williams and M. Stephens, Dent, 1969, Corgi Poets 1, edited by Dannie Abse, Corgi, 1971, and Dragon's Hoard, edited by Sam Adams and Guilym Rees Hughes, Gomer Press, 1976.

WORK IN PROGRESS: A non-fiction book about the stage-coach days in Wales, for Stewart Williams; a revision of the novel, Dear Laura, Bloody Laura.

*   *   *

WILLIAMS, Lawrence K(enneth) 1930-

PERSONAL: Born March 8, 1930, in Bellows Falls, Vt.; son of Freeman and Francis (Orth) Williams; married Jean E. Starliper, 1955. Education: Tufts University, B.A. (cum laude), 1952; University of Illinois, M.A., 1954; University of Michigan, Ph.D., 1960. Home: 412 Highland Rd., Ithaca, N.Y. 14850. Office: New York State School of Industrial and Labor Relations, Cornell University, Ithaca, N.Y. 14850.

CAREER: University of Michigan, Ann Arbor, study director, survey research center of Institute for Social Research, 1960-61; Cornell University, New York State School of Industrial and Labor Relations, Ithaca, assistant professor, 1961-64, associate professor, 1964-70, professor of organizational behavior, 1970—. Military service: U.S. Army, 1954-

56. Member: Industrial Relations Research Association, American Psychological Association, Sigma Xi. Awards, honors: Fulbright fellow in Peru, 1967-68.

WRITINGS: (Contributor) Computer Technology—Concepts for Management, Industrial Relations Counselors, 1964; (contributor) Automation, Education and Human Values, School & Society Books, 1965; (contributor) B. P. Indik and F. K. Berrien, editors, People, Groups and Organizations, Teachers College Press, 1968; (with William F. Whyte) Toward an Integrated Theory of Development, New York State School of Industrial and Labor Relations, 1968. Contributor to other symposia and to social science and psychology journals.

*   *   *

WILLIAMS, Stirling B(acot), Jr. 1943-

PERSONAL: Born March 28, 1943, in Memphis, Tenn.; son of Stirling Bacot (a salesman) and Virginia (Kendrick) Williams. Education: University of Mississippi, B.A.E. (magna cum laude), 1965, M.Ed., 1966, Ed.D., 1968. Home: 4426 Willowgrove Cove, Memphis, Tenn. 38116.

CAREER: Memphis (Tenn.) city schools, high school teacher of English, 1966-67; University of Mississippi, University, instructor in education, 1967-68; Memphis city schools, administrative intern, 1968-69, assistant principal of Overton High School, 1969-74, 1974-76, vice-principal, Briarcrest High School, 1976—. Special consultant, Mississippi State Department of Education, 1967-68; assistant director of secondary education, Briarcrest Baptist School System. Member: National Association of Secondary School Principals, American Association of School Administrators, Association for Supervision and Curriculum Development, Tennessee Association for Supervision and Curriculum Development, Tennessee Association of Secondary School Principals, Phi Delta Kappa, Kappa Delta Pi.

WRITINGS: (Editor with Joseph Linfield Miller of 1st edition; author with Jerry Hal Robbins of subsequent editions) The Administration of Public Education in Mississippi, School of Education, University of Mississippi, 1966, 3rd edition, 1969; (with Robbins) Administrator's Manual of School Plant Administration, Mississippi State Department of Education, 1968, 2nd edition, Interstate, 1970; (with Robbins) School Custodian's Handbook, Mississippi State Department of Education, 1968, 2nd edition, Interstate, 1970; (with Robbins) Student Activities in the Innovative School, Burgess, 1969; (contributor) L. C. Deighton, Encyclopedia of Education, Macmillan, 1971.

WORK IN PROGRESS: A text on English composition for high school and college students.

*   *   *

WILLIAMS, T(erence) C(harles) 1925-

PERSONAL: Born April 30, 1925, in Pontllanfraith, Wales; son of Frederick Charles and Evelyn (Munn) Williams; married Gwynneth Henry, August 28, 1928; children: Nicholas Charles. Education: Attended University College of Wales, Aberystwyth and Jesus College, Oxford. Permanent home address: Old Weir House, St. Peter St., Marlow, Buckinghamshire, England. Office: Department of Philosophy, University of Guelph, Guelph, Ontario, Canada.

CAREER: Royal Air Force, 1944-67; University of Guelph, Guelph, Ontario, 1969—, began as assistant professor, currently associate professor of philosophy.

WRITINGS: The Concept of the Categorical Imperative,

Clarendon Press, 1968; (contributor) *Proceedings of the Ottawa Conference on Kant,* [Ottawa], 1976.

WORK IN PROGRESS: Research on Kant's critical philosophy, particularly in relation to problems presented by findings in the area of parapsychology.

* * *

WILLIAMSON, Craig (Burke) 1943-

PERSONAL: Born August 26, 1943, in Lafayette, Ind.; son of Gerald H. (an accountant) and Helen (Sheets) Williamson; married Susan Greenawalt, September 4, 1968. *Education:* Stanford University, B.A., 1965; Harvard University, M.A., 1966; University of Pennsylvania, Ph.D., 1973. *Address:* c/o Citadel Press, 120 Enterprise Ave., Secaucus, N.J. 07094.

CAREER: American Friends Service Committee, Philadelphia, Pa., volunteer worker in Tanzania, East Africa, 1966-67. *Awards, honors:* Woodrow Wilson fellowship; Danforth fellowship.

WRITINGS: African Wings (poetry), Citadel, 1969; (translator from the French) L. S. Senghor, *Selected Poems/Poesies Choisies,* Collings, 1976; (editor) *The Old English Riddles of the Exeter Book,* University of North Carolina Press, 1977.

WORK IN PROGRESS: More poetry.

SIDELIGHTS: Craig Williamson speaks French and Swahili.

* * *

WILLIAMSON, Robin (Martin Eyre) 1938-

PERSONAL: Born July 27, 1938, in Limassol, Cyprus; son of Henry Martin (a managing director) and Ruth (Lyons) Williamson; married Priscilla Hatch-Barnwell, January 24, 1970; children: Jonathan Martin Eyre. *Education:* Magdalen College, Oxford, B.A. (second class honors), 1961, Postgraduate Diploma in History and Philosophy of Science, 1963.

CAREER: Dataskil Ltd. (computer software firm), London, England, manager, beginning 1963. *Member:* British Computer Society.

WRITINGS: (With Anthony Chandor and John Graham) *Penguin Dictionary of Computers,* Penguin, 1970; (with Chandor and Graham) *Practical Systems Analysis,* Hart-Davis, 1970, Putnam, 1971. Also author, with J.W.S. Carmichael, of *The Barnwell System: A Computer Systems Case Study,* Allen & Unwin.††

* * *

WILLIS, Wayne 1942-

PERSONAL: Born September 5, 1942, in Nashville, Tenn.; son of Clark Miller (an insurance salesman) and Georga (Sain) Willis; married Dorothy Sue Jones (a teacher), June 7, 1969; children: Damon Blake, Justin Kane. *Education:* Abilene Christian College, B.A., 1964, M.A., 1966; Vanderbilt University, B.D., 1969; Memphis Institute of Medicine and Religion, Certified Hospital Chaplain, 1970. *Home:* 3910 Riveroaks Circle, Louisville, Ky. 40222.

CAREER: First Presbyterian Church, Marianna, Ark., minister, 1970-75; Norton Children's Hospitals, Louisville, Ky., pediatrics chaplain, 1975—. *Member:* Association for Clinical Pastoral Education, Association for Rational Thinking, College of Chaplains (fellow).

WRITINGS: Communicating Christ in the Inner City: A Handbook for Teachers of Disadvantaged Children, R. B. Sweet, 1970. Contributor to religious journals and nursing journals.

* * *

WILLRICH, Ted L. 1924-

PERSONAL: Born May 30, 1924, in Dexter, Iowa; son of Charles E. (a businessman) and Clara (Marsh) Willrich; married Lida Lawrence, March 20, 1947; children: Kathleen J., Rebecca L. *Education:* Iowa State University of Science and Technology, B.S., 1949, Ph.D., 1961; Oklahoma State University of Agriculture and Applied Science (now Oklahoma State University), M.S., 1952. *Religion:* Lutheran. *Office:* Department of Agriculture, Oregon State University, Corvallis, Ore. 97331.

CAREER: Veterans' Institutional-on-Farm Training program, instructor in Dexter, Iowa, and self-employed farmer, 1949-51; Iowa State University of Science and Technology, Ames, 1952-71, became professor of agricultural engineering and Extension agricultural engineer; Oregon State University, Corvallis, professor of agricultural engineering, 1971—. Registered professional engineer in Iowa, 1953; lecturer and speaker on rural environment engineering, mainly concerned with animal waste management. *Military service:* U.S. Army, 1943-46; spent eighteen months in Europe with 42nd Infantry (Rainbow) Division.

MEMBER: American Society of Agricultural Engineers, Soil Conservation Society of America, Water Conditioning Association International (honorary member), Sigma Xi, Phi Kappa Phi, Alpha Zeta, Gamma Sigma Delta, Epsilon Sigma Phi. *Awards, honors:* Named Iowa Farmer, Future Farmers of America, 1942; U.S. Department of Agriculture Superior Service Award, 1967, for work on public affairs task force; four awards from American Society of Agricultural Engineers for entries in educational aids competition.

WRITINGS: (Contributor) *Agriculture and the Quality of Our Environment,* American Association for the Advancement of Science, 1967; (with N. W. Hines) *Water Pollution Control and Abatement,* Iowa State University Press, 1967; (with others) *Private Water Systems,* Iowa State University Midwest Plan Service Publication, 1968; (with W. B. Buck and C. J. Ruehle) *Effects of Water Quality on Animal Health and Productivity* (annotated bibliography), Water Conditioning Research Council, 1968; (editor with George E. Smith, and contributor) *Agricultural Practices and Water Quality,* Iowa State University Press, 1970. Author of Iowa State University Extension Service pamphlets and contributor to International Water Quality Symposium proceedings.

WORK IN PROGRESS: Research in the area of pollutants of agricultural origin.

* * *

WILSON, Andrew 1923-

PERSONAL: Born December 6, 1923, near Canterbury, England; son of Andrew J. and Florence (Spindler) Wilson; married Eva-Maria Mendelssohn (a literary agent), January 29, 1949. *Education:* Exeter College, Oxford, M.A., 1949. *Politics:* Liberal. *Religion:* Agnostic. *Home:* 44 Fitzalan Rd., London N.W.3, England. *Agent:* Bolt & Watson Ltd., 8 Storey's Gate, London S.W.1, England. *Office: The Observer,* 8 St. Andrew's Hill, London E.C.4, England.

CAREER: Worked for *Daily Express,* London, England,

and as personal assistant to Lord Beaverbrook, 1950-52; member of staff of eastern European news desk, British Broadcasting Corp., 1953-60; *The Observer,* London, England, chief African correspondent, mainly in the Congo, 1960-62, defense and aviation correspondent, 1963—, associate editor, 1972—. *Military service:* British Army, Royal Armoured Corps, 1941-46; became captain; received Military Cross. *Member:* Royal Institute of International Affairs, International Institute for Strategic Studies (London), Royal United Institute for Defence Studies.

WRITINGS: Flame Thrower, Kimber & Co., 1956; (translator with wife, Eva Wilson) *The Schlieffen Plan,* Oswald Wolff, 1958; *North from Kabul,* Allen & Unwin, 1961; *The Bomb and the Computer,* Barrie & Rockliff, 1968, Delacorte, 1969; (editor) *The Observer Atlas of World Affairs,* Mitchell-Beazley, 1971; *The Concorde Fiasco,* Penguin, 1973.

SIDELIGHTS: Andrew Wilson is an "engineer manque and a poet manque who once could speak Persian but now speaks only English, bad German and French." He adds that all of his "books are an excuse for not finishing a novel begun in 1949."

* * *

WILSON, Ernest Charles 1896-

PERSONAL: Born March 30, 1896, in Fargo, N.D.; son of Joseph and Villa Mabel (Wheeler) Wilson. *Education:* Unity School of Christianity, ordained, 1934; College of Divine Metaphysics, Indianapolis, Ind., D.D., 1935. *Politics:* Republican. *Home:* Vista del Rio II, 700 East Eighth St., Kansas City, Mo. 64106. *Office:* 707 West 47th, Kansas City, Mo. 64112.

CAREER: Ordained a minister, 1916; founder and secretary of Harmonial Institute, San Diego, Calif. 1918; appointed pastor of Unity Society of Practical Christianity, Kansas City, Mo., 1934-38; director of West Coast Unity, 1938, and founder and pastor of Christ Church Unity, 1938-65, both Los Angeles, Calif.; Unity Society of Practical Christianity, pastor, 1965-76, pastor emeritus, 1976—. Conducted daily radio program in Kansas City, Mo., 1927-38, Sunday radio program over KLAC, Los Angeles, 1938-65, and daily television program over KLAC-TV, Los Angeles, 1949-54; appeared as a weekly regular on "Betty White Show" over National Broadcasting Co. network, 1955, and as a daily regular on "Jack Wheeler Show," KTTV, 1958-59; made several guest appearances on Columbia Church of the Air and local and network stations. *Member:* Unity Ministers' Association (president, 1947), International New Thought Alliance (president, 1948), Masons (Minneapolis, Kansas City, and Los Angeles). *Awards, honors:* Doctor of Suggestive Therapeutics, Weltmer Institute, Nevada, Mo., 1928; D.D., Unity School of Practical Christianity, 1976.

WRITINGS—All published by Unity School of Christianity, except as indicated: *The Simple Truth,* Harmonial Publishers, 1920; *You and the Universe: A Book of Numbers,* Harmonial Publishers, 1922; *The Sunlit Way,* 1924, revised edition, 1941; *Adventures in Prosperity,* 1928; *The Contemplation of Christ,* 1934; *Ernest C. Wilson's Master Class Lessons,* first series, 1935, published as *The Great Physician,* 1945; *Have We Lived Here Before?,* 1936; *The Song of Life: An Interpretation of the 23rd Psalm* (greeting booklet), 1937; *The Protecting Presence: An Interpretation of the 91st Psalm,* (greeting booklet), 1937.

Sons of Heaven, Unity Classics, 1941; *Many Mansions,* Unity Classics, 1946; *Every Good Desire,* Unity Classics,

1948, reprinted, G. K. Hall, 1974; *The Other Half of the Rainbow,* Unity Classics, 1952; *Have You Lived Other Lives?,* Prentice-Hall, 1956; *Soul Power,* Unity Books, 1963; *The Week That Changed the World,* Unity Books, 1968; *The Emerging Self,* Unity Books, 1970; *Like a Miracle,* Unity Books, 1971. Contributor of articles and verse to numerous periodicals.

WORK IN PROGRESS: Preparing memoirs.

* * *

WILSON, Kenneth L(ee) 1916-

PERSONAL: Born July 2, 1916, in Pittsburgh, Pa.; son of Charles Emerson and Mary Elizabeth (Markel) Wilson; married Juanita Carpenter, June 20, 1941; children: Mrs. Emily Sue Wilson Carter, Mrs. Sally Jean Wilson Siler, David Lee, James Kenneth. *Education:* Houghton College, student, 1937-41; Butler University, A.B., 1941. *Politics:* Independent. *Home:* 63 Benedict Ave., White Plains, N.Y. 10603. *Office: Christian Herald,* 40 Overlook Dr., Chappaqua, N.Y. 10514.

CAREER: Ordained minister of Disciples of Christ, 1941; David C. Cook Publishing Co., Elgin, Ill., managing editor of *Boys World* (magazine), 1941-42; American Baptist Publication Society, Philadelphia, Pa., editor of *'Teens* (magazine), 1942-49; *Christian Herald* (magazine), Chappaqua, N.Y., associate editor, 1949-53, managing editor, 1953-60, executive editor, 1960-67, editor, 1967—. Member of board of directors of Mustard Seed, Inc., Glendale, Calif., and Christian Children's Fund, Richmond, Va.; president, Penney Retirement Community, Penney Farms, Fla.; president, Associated Church Press, Chicago, Ill., 1970-71. *Awards, honors:* Litt.D., Houghton College, 1957.

WRITINGS: Angel at Her Shoulder: Lillian Dickson and Her Taiwan Mission, Harper, 1964; *Have Faith without Fear,* Harper, 1970; *All Things Considered,* Christian Herald Books, 1977.

Editor; children's picture books published by American Baptist Publication Society, except as indicated: *Hero of Burma* (adapted from *Waste-Basket Surgery*), 1943; *Adventure in Burma* (biography of Gordon S. Seagrave), 1944; *Tom Hardy, P,K.,* 1945; *Bible Boyographies,* 1945; *Tom Hardy, Explorer,* 1947; *The Man with Twenty Hands,* Friendship Press, 1948. Contributor to religious periodicals.

SIDELIGHTS: Kenneth Wilson told *CA:* "I began writing for magazines when I was 12. To me, writing is a way for me to get to know myself. My intent is always to express a new thought (or an old idea in a new way), never to say what has already been said." The *Publisher's Weekly* reviewer calls *All Things Considered* "refreshingly unpretentious" and adds: "Wilson doesn't preach 'sin'; he neither pushes nor implores. Good-humoredly he ticks off his own foibles and failures ... while somehow managing to avoid sermonizing or talking 'down'."

Angel at Her Shoulder has been published in England, Switzerland, and Finland; it has also been translated into Chinese and published in Taiwan.

BIOGRAPHICAL/CRITICAL SOURCES: Christian Century, December 23, 1970; *Publisher's Weekly,* December 6, 1976.

* * *

WILSON, Pat 1910-

PERSONAL: Born October 25, 1910; daughter of Alfred

Lakin; married Oliver Godfrey Wilson, 1934; children: Mike, Robin, Briony (Mrs. Richard Jenkins), Bridget (Mrs. Stuart Carter). *Education:* Attended secondary school in England. *Politics:* "Usually vote Tory." *Religion:* None. *Home:* 66 Marwood Dr., Great Ayton, Middlesborough, Cleveland TS9 6PO, England.

CAREER: Secretary in a tuberculosis dispensary, 1927-33; director of a small foundry, 1949—; part-time lecturer at Longlands College of Further Education, Middlesborough, England. *Awards, honors:* Co-winner of prize for play, "3 Sheep, 2½ Kangaroos"; Dublin Theatre Festival Award, 1970, for "Thy Kingdom Come."

WRITINGS—Plays: *A Summer's Tale* (three-act), Evans, 1968; *Four for a Boy,* HUB Publications, 1970; *Enchanted Pantomime,* HUB Publications, 1970; *Funeral Tea,* HUB Publications, 1971, Performance Publishing, 1973; *Ballet Who?,* Performance Publishing, 1972; *One More Time,* Performance Publishing, 1972; *The Little Miracle,* HUB Publications, 1972; *Get It All Together,* Performance Publishing, 1973; *The Adventures of Pinocchio,* HUB Publications, 1973; *The Snow Queen,* HUB Publications, 1973; *Christmas Eve at the Mortuary,* HUB Publications, 1973; *Mix Up at the Mortuary,* Performance Publishing, 1973; *Mixed Bag,* Performance Publishing, 1973; *Rectory Return,* HUB Publications, 1973; *The Reunion,* HUB Publications, 1974; *Send Us Victorias,* HUB Publications, 1974; *Rummage Rip-off,* Performance Publishing, 1974; *New Broom,* HUB Publications, 1974; *Heavenly High Rise,* Performance Publishing, 1975; *Queen Bee,* Performance Publishing, 1975; *Christmas Cake and Chipatees,* HUB Publications, 1975; *The Tektite,* HUB Publications, 1975; *Thy Kingdom Come,* HUB Publications, 1975; *Wedding Picture Mixture,* Performance Publications, 1976; *Ashes to Ashes, Crumb to Crumb,* Performance Publishing, 1976. Also writer of one-act plays, a television series sold but not produced, a passion play, and two booklets of poems.

SIDELIGHTS: Pat Wilson writes: "Having had a hard and curious life, [I] write mostly comedy and farce—as I believe that people always try to carry on normally whatever hits them—and the idiotic 'keep to the norm' can be pricelessly funny!" *Avocational interests:* Tracing cup and ring marks, archeaology.

BIOGRAPHICAL/CRITICAL SOURCES: Drama, spring, 1969.

*   *   *

WINCH, Peter G(uy)   1926-

PERSONAL: Born January 14, 1926, in London, England; son of William Edward (an insurance agent) and Gertrude (Gifford) Winch; married Erika Neumann, January 4, 1948; children: Christopher, David. *Education:* St. Edmund Hall, Oxford, B.A., 1949, B.Phil., 1951. *Office:* King's College, University of London, Strand, London WC2R 2LS, England.

CAREER: University of Wales, University College of Swansea, Swansea, Wales, 1951-64, began as assistant lecturer, became lecturer, senior lecturer in philosophy, 1959-64; University of London, London, England, reader in philosophy at Birkbeck College, 1964-67, professor of philosophy at King's College, 1967—. Visiting professor, University of Rochester, 1961-62, and University of Arizona, 1970. Member of editorial board for philosophy, Basil Blackwell & Mott Ltd. *Military service:* Royal Navy, 1944-46; became petty officer. *Member:* Royal Institute of Philosophy (council member), Mind Association, Aristotelian Society (council member, 1965-67).

WRITINGS: The Idea of a Social Science and Its Relation to Philosophy, Humanities, 1958; *Moral Integrity: Inaugural Lecture in the Chair of Philosophy Delivered at King's College, London, 9 May 1968,* Basil Blackwell, 1968; (editor) *Studies in the Philosophy of Wittgenstein,* Humanities, 1969; *Ethics and Action,* Routledge & Kegan Paul, 1972. Contributor to philosophy journals. Editor, *Analysis,* 1965-71.

SIDELIGHTS: The Idea of a Social Science and Its Relation to Philosophy has been translated into German, Portuguese, and Italian.

BIOGRAPHICAL/CRITICAL SOURCES: Times Literary Supplement, October 16, 1969; *Listener,* January 22, 1970; Alan Ryan, *The Philosophy of the Social Sciences,* Macmillan, 1970.†

*   *   *

WINDHAM, Douglas M(acArthur)   1943-

PERSONAL: Born September 5, 1943, in St. Petersburg, Fla.; son of Hoyt and Ruby (Hattaway) Windham; married Jeannette Poirer, April 27, 1963; children: Karen Adele, Douglas, Jr. *Education:* Florida State University, B.A. (cum laude), 1964, M.A., 1967, Ph.D., 1969. *Office:* Department of Economics, University of Chicago, 5835 Kimbark Ave., Chicago, Ill. 60637.

CAREER: Florida A. & M. University, Tallahassee, part-time assistant professor, 1967-68, assistant professor of economics, 1968-69; University of North Carolina, Greensboro, assistant professor of economics, 1969-72; North Carolina Council on Economic Education, executive director, 1971-72; Ford Foundation, project specialist in Malaysia, 1972-74; University of Chicago, Chicago, Ill., associate professor of education and member of department of economics, 1974—. Consultant on economics education to North Carolina State Department of Public Instruction, 1970, Entrance Examination Board, 1970-71, and to Greensboro Tax Study Commission, 1971. *Member:* American Economic Association, Southern Economic Association, American Educational Research Association.

WRITINGS: (With Marshall Rudolph Colberg) *The Oyster-Based Economy of Franklin County, Florida,* U.S. Department of Health, Education and Welfare, 1965; (with Colberg and T. Stanton Dietrich) *The Social and Economic Values of Apalachicola Bay, Florida,* Federal Water Pollution Control Administration, 1968; *Redistributive Effects of Public Higher Education in Florida* (monograph), Department of Economics and Business Administration, University of North Carolina, Greensboro, 1969; *Education, Equality and Income Redistribution: A Study of Public Higher Education,* Heath, 1970.

Contributor: *Proceedings* of the Oyster Culture Workshop, University of Georgia and Georgia Game and Fish Commission, 1967; *Governmental Research Bulletin,* Political Research Institute, Florida State University, 1969. Contributor of articles to journals and periodicals, including *Rivista Internazionale di Scienze Economiche e Commerciali, Journal of Political Economy,* and *Mississippi Valley Journal of Business and Economics.*

WORK IN PROGRESS: Books on the economics of educational financing, the economics of student aid, and state/local tax reorganization.†

*   *   *

WING, J. K.   1923-

PERSONAL: Born October 22, 1923. *Education:* University of London, M.D., and Ph.D. *Office:* London School of Hygiene, Keppel St., London WC1E 7HT, England; and Institute of Psychiatry, De Crespigny Park, Denmark Hill SE5 8AF, England.

CAREER: Medical Research Council, Social Psychiatry Unit, London, England, director, 1965—; Institute of Psychiatry, Denmark Hill, England, and London School of Hygiene, London, England, professor of social psychiatry, 1970—. Consultant psychiatrist, Maudsley Hospital, London, England. *Military service:* Royal Naval Volunteer Reserve, 1941-45; became lieutenant.

WRITINGS: (With G. W. Brown, M. Bone, and B. Dalison) *Schizophrenia and Social Care,* Oxford University Press, 1966; (with Brown) *Institutionalism and Schizophrenia,* Cambridge University Press, 1970; (with J. E. Cooper and N. Sartorius) *Description and Classification of Psychiatric Syndromes,* Cambridge University Press, 1974.

Editor: *Early Childhood Autism,* Pergamon, 1966; (with H. Hare) *Psychiatric Epidemiology,* Oxford University Press, 1970; (with R. Bransby) *Psychiatric Case Registers,* H.M.S.O., 1970; (with A. M. Hailey) *Evaluating a Community Psychiatric Service,* Oxford University Press, 1972.

WORK IN PROGRESS: Investigation of social factors in causation and treatment of psychiatric disorders.

* * *

WINGLER, Hans M(aria) 1920-

PERSONAL: Born January 5, 1920, in Constance, Germany; son of Hans (a merchant) and Gertrud (Lange) Wingler; married Hedwig Tax (an assistant professor of philosophy), November 20, 1969; children: (first marriage) Lothar, Angelika; (present marriage) Johannes. *Education:* Studied history of art and archaeology at University of Frankfurt and University of Vienna. *Home:* Heerstrasse 68, D-1000 Berlin 19, West Germany. *Office:* Bauhaus-Archive, Schloss-Strasse 1, Berlin 19, West Germany.

CAREER: University of Frankfurt, Frankfurt am Main, Germany, assistant at Institute of Art History, 1945-49; Harvard University, Cambridge, Mass., research fellow at Busch-Reisinger Museum, 1957-58; art critic and scholar, 1957—; Bauhaus-Archive, director in Darmstadt, West Germany, 1960-71, director in Berlin, West Germany, 1971—. Lecturer at Illinois Institute of Technology, University of Amsterdam, and at other schools and museums in Europe and South America. *Member:* Association Internationale des Critiques d'Art, International Commission of Museums, Deutscher Werkbund. *Awards, honors:* Award of the Republic of Austria, 1956, for *Oskar Kokoschka: Das Werk des Malers.*

WRITINGS: Oskar Kokoschka: Das Werk des Malers, Galerie Welz, 1956, translation by Frank S. C. Budgen and others published as *Oskar Kokoschka: The Work of the Painter,* Galerie Welz, also Faber (London), 1958; *Kokoschka-Fibel,* Galerie Welz, 1957, translation by Peter George published as *Introduction to Kokoschka,* Thames & Hudson, 1958; (with Friedrich Welz) *Oskar Kokoschkas: Das Druckgraphische Werk,* Verlag Welz, 1975.

Editor: (And author of foreword) *Die Bruecke: Kunst im Aufbruch,* Buchheim-Verlag, 1954; *Ernst Ludwig Kirchner: Holzschnitte,* Buchheim-Verlag, 1954; *Oskar Kokoschka: Kuenstler und Poeten,* Buchheim-Verlag, 1954; *Der Blaue Reiter,* Buchheim-Verlag, 1954; (and author of introduction) *Der Sturm,* Buchheim-Verlag, 1955; (and author of epilogue) Johann von Goethe, *Walpurgisnacht,* Buchheim-Verlag,

1955; *Oskar Kokoschka: Schriften, 1907-1955,* Langen-Mueller, 1956; *Oskar Kokoschka: Ein Lebensbild in zeitgenoessischen Dokumenten,* Langen-Mueller, 1956, enlarged paperback edition published as *Oskar Kokoschka: Ein Lebensbild,* Ullstein, 1966; *Wie sie einander sahen: Moderne Maler im Urteil ihrer Gefaehrten,* Langen-Mueller, 1957; Ludwig Meidner, *Hymnen und Laesterungen,* Langen-Mueller, 1959; *Oskar Kokoschka: Die traeumenden Knaben und andere Dichtungen* (booklet), Galerie Welz, 1959.

Das Bauhaus, 1919-1933: Weimar, Dessau, Berlin, Rasch, 1962, enlarged edition published as *Das Bauhaus, 1919-1933: Weimar, Dessau, Berlin und die Nachfolge in Chicago seit 1937,* Rasch, 1968, translation by Wolfgang Jabs and Basil Gilbert, edited by Joseph Stein, published as *The Bauhaus: Weimar, Dessau, Berlin, Chicago,* M.I.T. Press, 1969; *Die Mappenwerke "Neue europaeische Graphik,"* Kupferberg, 1965, translation by Gerald Onn published as *Graphic Work from the Bauhaus,* New York Graphic Society, 1969; Walter Gropius, *Die neue Architektur und das Bauhaus,* Kupferberg, 1965; Paul Klee, *Paedagogisches Skizzenbuch,* Kupferberg, 1965; Oskar Schlemmer, Laszlo Moholy-Nagy and Farkas Molnar, *Die Buehne im Bauhaus,* Kupferberg, 1965; Theo van Doesburg, *Grundbegriffe der neuen gestaltenden Kunst,* Kupferberg, 1966; Gottfried Semper, *Wissenschaft, Industrie und Kunst,* Kupferberg, 1966; Walter Gropius, *Apollo in der Demokratie,* Kupferberg, 1967; Ludwig Hilberseimer, *Berliner Architektur der Zwanziger Jahre,* Kupferberg, 1967; Laszlo Moholy-Nagy, *Malerei, Fotografie, Film,* Kupferberg, 1967; Laszlo Moholy-Nagy, *Von Material zu Architektur,* Kupferberg, 1968; Oskar Schlemmer, *Der Mensch,* Kupferberg, 1969; Gyorgy Kepes, *Die Sprache des Sehens,* Kupferberg, 1970; Serge Chermayeff and Christopher Alexander, *Gemeinschaft und Privatbereich,* Kupferberg, 1971; Piet Mondrian, *Neue Gestaltung,* Kupferberg, 1974; Walter Gropius, *Bauhausbauten Dessau,* Kupferberg, 1974; J. J. P. Oud, *Hollandische Architektur,* Kupferberg, 1976.

Editor of various Bauhaus-Archive publications and a Bauhaus catalogue. Contributor to *Encyclopaedia Britannica, Kindlers Malerei-Lexikon,* and other collections.

BIOGRAPHICAL/CRITICAL SOURCES: Spectator, August 9, 1967; *New Republic,* October 11, 1969; *Newsweek,* December 15, 1969; *New York Review of Books,* January 1, 1970; *Commentary,* March, 1970; *Times Literary Supplement,* April 16, 1970.

* * *

WINNER, Anna K(ennedy) 1900-

PERSONAL: Born November 15, 1900, in Nashville, Tenn.; daughter of Robert Ross (a dentist) and Estella (Fisher) Freeman; married Evans Hawthorne Winner (an accountant), April 18, 1927 (divorced, 1934); children: Evans Hawthorne, Jr., Elaine. *Education:* University of Arizona, B.A., 1919; additional courses in languages at Columbia University, 1922-23, Hunter College (now Hunter College of the City University of New York), 1925-27, University of Pennsylvania, 1951-52. *Politics:* Independent. *Religion:* "Independent, Buddhist modified by science." *Home:* 253 South Ninth St., Philadelphia, Pa. 19107.

CAREER: High school teacher of French, Spanish, and Latin in Claremore, Okla., 1920-21; New York Telephone Co., New York City, mathematician, 1922-24; Hannah More Academy, Reisterstown, Md., teacher of French and Spanish, 1924; Chase National Bank, New York City, assistant translator in foreign department, 1925-28; *Biological*

Abstracts, Philadelphia, Pa., translator and transcriber, 1930-32, writer of taxonomic abstracts, 1943-65, and part-time writer of abstracts, 1965—.

WRITINGS: The Basic Ideas of Occult Wisdom, Theosophical Publishing, 1970.

WORK IN PROGRESS: Background for the Study of Human Evolution: Selected Abstracts of Pertinent Publications.

SIDELIGHTS: Anna K. Winner told *CA* that she maintains a "'private card-file encyclopedia on human evolution' which contains personal abstracts of publications on fossil finds and theories about evolution, dating from the first primate fossil find in 1836, and numbering well over two thousand abstracts of 250-300 words each . . . to which additions are being made constantly." Since childhood her major interest has been the biological and spiritual progress of the human race, and she came to believe in reincarnation as a logical hypothesis for the evolution of consciousness.

She continued: "Writing long letters to a score or more of people on my 'communications network,' including some 'adopted' or 'spiritual' children and grandchildren, occupies a good deal of time and energy. . . . Trying to keep up with important publications connected with theosopy, psychical research, and 'occult wisdom' in general also consumes time."

She is fluent in the Romance languages, and has studied German, Russian, Swedish, Danish, Esperanto, Hindi, Urdu, and Sanskrit. *The Basic Ideas of Occult Wisdom* has been translated into Spanish (but not published in that language) and is being translated into Hebrew.

AVOCATIONAL INTERESTS: Classical music (she makes tapes for friends from a collection of eight hundred classical records), reading science fiction.

* * *

WINNIKOFF, Albert 1930-

PERSONAL: Born July 22, 1930, in Vancouver, British Columbia, Canada; son of immigrants from the Russian Ukraine, Morris (a tailor, later operator of a grocery store and laundry business) and Eva (Hoffman) Winnikoff; married Lillian Haaxma, July 8, 1952; children: Joel, Marc. *Education:* University of California, Berkeley, B.A., 1953. *Politics:* Democrat. *Religion:* Jewish. *Home:* 29046 Cliffside Dr., Malibu, Calif. 90265.

CAREER: With $3,000 savings, started a laundry business with his father in Los Angeles, Calif., and operated it, 1954-56; Douglas Aircraft, El Segundo, Calif., 1956-59, began as technical writer, became manager of technical publications for Xerox Data Systems in 1966; Data Products Corp., Woodland Hills, Calif., manager of technical publications, 1969—. Started buying acreage in Malibu in 1958, and is owner of income property, homes, and land in Malibu and Santa Monica, as well as president of three land investment corporations and general partner of five land companies in Sun City, Agoura, and Malibu. Total holdings are valued in excess of $2,000,000.

WRITINGS: The Land Game: How to Make a Fortune in Land Investment, Lyle Stuart, 1970; (with Burt Prelutsky) *Sell, Sell, Sell, or How to Make $100,000 a Year,* Barlenmir, 1977.

BIOGRAPHICAL/CRITICAL SOURCES: Press Democrat, Santa Rosa, Calif., September 20, 1970; *St. Petersburg Times,* St. Petersburg, Fla., January 8, 1971.

WINSTON, Eric V(on) A(rthur) 1942-

PERSONAL: Born April 16, 1942, in Savannah, Ga.; son of Daniel P. and Pearl (Williams) Winston. *Education:* Morehouse College, B.A., 1963; Atlanta University, M.S. in L.S., 1965; Michigan State University, Ph.D., 1972. *Home:* 1956 Lac du Mont Dr., Haslett, Mich. 48840. *Office:* College of Urban Development, Michigan State University, East Lansing, Mich. 48823.

CAREER: Michigan State University, East Lansing, urban affairs bibliographer, 1969-70, assistant to dean of College of Urban Development, 1970—, director of Office of Student Affairs. Member of Michigan Black Democratic Party Caucus, 1971; chairman of board, Urban Resources Systems, Haslett, Mich., 1971—. *Military service:* U.S. Army, 1966-68. *Member:* American Library Association, National Association of Black Urban and Ethnic Directors, Kappa Alpha Psi.

WRITINGS: (Compiler with Marilyn Terzise) *Directory of Urban Affairs Information and Research Centers,* Scarecrow, 1970.

WORK IN PROGRESS: Research on library service to the urban disadvantaged.†

* * *

WINSTON, Sarah 1912-
(Sarah E. Lorenz)

PERSONAL: Born December 15, 1912, in New York, N.Y.; daughter of Henry (a manufacturer and inventor) and Esther (Lorenz) Rosenblum; married Keith Winston (a businessman), June 11, 1932 (died, 1970); children: Neil R., David L. *Education:* Attended New York University, two years and Barnes Foundation, Merion, Pa., 1966-69, 1970-71. *Home:* 1838 Rose Tree Lane, Havertown, Pa. 19083.

CAREER: Taught dancing in earlier years; free-lance writer. *Member:* National League of American Pen Women (Philadelphia branch), National League of Women Voters (public relations chairman of Haverford branch, 1951), Friends of the Barnes Foundation. *Awards, honors:* First prize, biennial contest, National League of American Pen Women, for *Our Son, Ken,* and for *Everything Happens for the Best,* 1972.

WRITINGS: (Under pseudonym Sarah E. Lorenz) *And Always Tomorrow,* Holt, 1963; (under pseudonym Sarah E. Lorenz) *Our Son, Ken,* Dell, 1969; *Everything Happens for the Best,* Yoseloff, 1969; *Not Yet Spring,* Golden Quill, 1976. Contributor of articles, some with husband, to newspapers and magazines for a number of years; poetry has been published in literary magazines and in newspapers. *And Always Tomorrow* and *Everything Happens for the Best* have been recorded as talking books for the blind and physically handicapped.

WORK IN PROGRESS: Guess Who in the Zoo, Guess Who on the Farm, Guess Who in the Bird World, series of photographic children's books.

AVOCATIONAL INTERESTS: Oil painting.

* * *

WINTER, Klaus 1928-

PERSONAL: Born August 15, 1928; son of Albert (an architect) and Ellen (Grimm) Winter. *Education:* Studied architecture two years, and then graphic art for three years at art academies in Weimer and Karlsruhe, Germany. *Home and studio:* 64 Am alten Berg, Goetzenhain, Germany.

CAREER: Free-lance artist; has shared a studio and worked with Helmut Bischoff, 1951—; their joint works were shown at a two-man exhibition at Klingspor Museum, Offenbach, Germany, 1968, and at Gallery 303, New York, N.Y., December, 1968. *Member:* Bund Deutscher Buchkuenstler, Bund Deutscher Designer. *Awards, honors:* Nine of the Winter-Bischoff books have received awards in the annual competition for the fifty best illustrated German books; other joint awards include first prize in the international contest for illustrations of *Grimm's Fairy Tales,* 1962, Deutscher Jugendbuchpreis for graphic design, 1965, for *Hoppla Hoppla Bauersmann,* honorable mention at the Biennial of Graphic Art in Bratislava, 1967, for *Trari Trara der Somer ist da.*

WRITINGS—Picture books with Helmut Bischoff: (Text by Helga Mauersberger) *Die Sonne,* Otto Maier, 1958, translation published as *The Sun,* F. Watts, 1961; (verse by H. D. Huebsch) *Foerster Pribam,* Gerhard Stalling, 1959, translation published as *Forester Pfeffer,* F. Watts, 1960; (adaptation of story by Theodoor van Hoytema) *Die glueck-lichen Eulen,* Georg Lentz, 1962, new edition, Julius Beltz, 1966, translation and adaptation by Linda R. Edelberg published as *The Happy Owls,* Lion Press, 1967; *Mool,* Herder Verlag, 1962 (translation published as *Mole,* Holt); *Kuck-uck, Kuckuck Rufts aus dem wald,* Herder Verlag, 1964; *Hoppla Hoppla Bauersmann,* Julius Beltz, 1964, new edition, 1966, translation published as *Hoppla, Hoppla Farm-erman,* Childrens Press, 1966; Hans A. Halbey, editor, *Fabeln aus aller Welt,* Julius Beltz, 1965 (translation published as *Fables from Many Lands,* Knopf); *Alte und neue Kinderspiele,* Chemische Fabrik Goedecke (Freiburg), 1965; *Kennst du Silberland,* Julius Beltz, 1966, translation published as *The King and the Parrot and Other Fables,* Knopf, 1969.

Illustrator with Bischoff: Edelgard von Bethusy Huc, *End-station Australien,* Steingruben Verlag, 1961; Lothar Fecher, *Der bunte Rabe,* Druckfarbenfabriken Gebr. Schmidt, 1963; Heinrich Fuhrer, *Aus meinem Jaegerruck-sack,* Waldkircher Verlagsanstalt, 1963; Carl Orff, *Weih-nachtsgeschichte,* Julius Beltz, 1965; Orff, *El, das Soll tun Frau Nachtigall,* Julius Beltz, 1965; Orff, *Das Huhn Ga-gackt, die Ente Quackt,* Julius Beltz, 1965; Orff, *Trari Trara der Somer ist da,* Julius Beltz, 1967; Heinz Grothe, *Das neue Narrenschiff: Schwaenke und Anekdoten aus vier Jahrhunderten,* Goverts Verlag, 1967.

Readers and textbooks designed and illustrated with Helmut Bischoff: Theo Schreiber and Gerhard Velthaus, *Meine Fibel,* Klett, 1966; Heiner Schmidt and Bernhard Weisger-ber, *Weinheimer Lesebuch,* Julius Beltz, 1967; Rudolf Feus-tel, Rosemarie Reinhardt, and Hermine Schaefer, *Unsere neue Welt,* Klett, 1967. Illustrator with Bischoff of *Unser Liederbuch,* by Peter Fuchs and *Lesebuch,* by Hans Hein-rich Plickat and Ursula Schiebel, both for Klett. Also illus-trator with Bischoff of calendars commissioned by German industrial firms, a farmer's almanac, and a series of monthly weather forecasts.

SIDELIGHTS: Winter and Bischoff, who is the younger by two years, studied at the same art schools and work in such cooperation that the results appear to have been done by one personality. Their principal medium is the hand-printed illus-tration, for which they use linoleum and other materials, or processes similar to monotype. According to Hans A. Hal-bey, director of the museum in Offenbach, Germany, they "preserve the aura of original craftsmanship even in large editions. . . . The persuasive force [of their books] lies in the picture."†

WINTERICH, John   1891-1970

May 25, 1891—August 15, 1970; American bibliophile, edi-tor, and book collector. Obituaries: *New York Times,* Au-gust 17, 1970.

* * *

WINTERS, Donald L(ee)   1935-

PERSONAL: Born August 11, 1935, in Fort Dodge, Iowa; son of Charles Worth (a worker in the meat industry) and Viola (Griep) Winters; married Raena Wagner, September 3, 1960; children: Ann Marie, Alison Le. *Education:* At-tended Fort Dodge Junior College, 1953-54; State College of Iowa (now University of Northern Iowa), B.A., 1957, M.A., 1963; University of Wisconsin, Ph.D., 1966. *Home:* 6426 Currywood, Nashville, Tenn. 37205. *Office:* Depart-ment of History, Vanderbilt University, Nashville, Tenn. 37235.

CAREER: University of Northern Iowa, Cedar Falls, assis-tant professor, 1966-69, associate professor of history, 1969-70; Vanderbilt University, Nashville, Tenn., associate pro-fessor of history, 1970—. *Member:* American Historical Association, Organization of American Historians, Eco-nomic History Association, Agricultural History Society, Southern Historical Association. *Awards, honors:* Book Award of Agricultural History Society, 1969, for manuscript of *Henry Cantwell Wallace as Secretary of Agriculture, 1921-24.*

WRITINGS: Henry Cantwell Wallace as Secretary of Agri-culture, 1921-24, University of Illinois Press, 1970. Contrib-utor to historical journals.

WORK IN PROGRESS: A history of land tenancy in Iowa, 1880-1920.†

* * *

WINTLE, Anne
(Olivia Ellis, Anne Francis)

PERSONAL: Born in London, England; daughter of Wil-liam (an accountant) and E. O. (Beecham) Senior-Ellis; mar-ried Francis Julian Wintle (a film and television producer), October 26, 1943; children: Christopher Simon, Justin Bee-cham. *Education:* Educated in private schools. *Politics:* Liberal. *Religion:* None. *Home:* 6 Hamilton House, 1 Hall Rd., London NW8 9RA, England.

WRITINGS—Under pseudonym Olivia Ellis: *Golden Grain,* Stanley Paul, 1944; *The Profitable Strangers,* Stanley Paul, 1947; *Rainbow in My Hand,* Stanley Paul, 1947.

Under pseudonym Anne Francis: *Paulette* (novel), Dent, 1956; *A Guinea a Box* (biography of her great-grandfather, Thomas Beecham), R. Hale, 1968.

Co-author of short documentary films and a feature film, "Snowball"; writer of plays for British Broadcasting Corp. and contributor to television series, "Probation Officer" and "Human Jungle." Contributor to magazines and news-papers, including *Lady, Iceland Review,* and *Christian Sci-ence Monitor;* literary critic for *Books and Bookmen.*

WORK IN PROGRESS: Several plays.

SIDELIGHTS: Anne Wintle told *CA:* "One hot summer's day when I was eight my father settled me in a cool part of the garden and told me to write a story. I began with a tale of a boy, a castle, and an ogre, and only stopped when dusk sedimented down. The mental sense of relief, and release, was marvellous, and ever since I have been a writer. The story was submitted to Children's Hour, B.B.C., and broadcast the following year.

"Advice to aspiring authors? The golden one of writing what one knows about. Study the authors who make the most personal appeal. Simplify, unclutter, prune, and never be affected by failure. Aim for a specific market, but finally be true to what the great Icelandic author, Halldor Laxness, has called 'the one true flame.' With regard to the contemporary scene, I must deplore the decline of the novel, though doubtless, and in due course, it will surface to full value again."

AVOCATIONAL INTERESTS: Traveling, opera, Hatha Yoga, dancing.

BIOGRAPHICAL/CRITICAL SOURCES: Books and Bookmen, April, 1968.

* * *

WINTTERLE, John F(rancis) 1927-

PERSONAL: Born February 14, 1927, in Vicksburg, Mich.; son of Theries Delos (a social worker) and Angeline (McArdle) Wintterle; married Kathleen M. Mathieus, 1960; children: Rachel. *Education:* Attended Southern Oregon College, 1947-49; University of Oregon, B.S., 1951, M.S., 1953, Ph.D., 1959; University of California, Berkeley, M.A., 1956. *Office:* Department of History, San Jose State University, San Jose, Calif. 95114.

CAREER: Teacher at Menlo School and College, Menlo Park, Calif., 1952-53, and in Long Beach, Calif., 1959-63; San Jose State University, San Jose, Calif., instructor, 1964-65, assistant professor, 1965-68, associate professor of history, 1968—. *Military service:* U.S. Navy, 1944-46. *Member:* American Historical Association, Organization of American Historians.

WRITINGS: (Editor with Richard Cramer and Billie Jensen) *American Humor,* two volumes, Spartan Bookstore, San Jose State College, 1970; (with Cramer) *Portraits of Nobel Laureates in Peace* (juvenile), Abelard, 1971.

WORK IN PROGRESS: Editing *Humor of the Civil War,* with Richard Cramer and Billie Jensen; and a study of the hero in America's best-selling novels from 1650 to the present.†

* * *

WIRTH, John D(avis) 1936-

PERSONAL: Born June 17, 1936, in Dawson, N.M.; son of Cecil W. (a school administrator) and Virginia (Davis) Wirth; married Nancy Farwell Meem, June 22, 1960; children: Peter Farwell, Timothy Corbin, Nicholas Newhall. *Education:* Harvard University, B.A., 1958; Stanford University, Ph.D., 1966. *Politics:* Democrat. *Religion:* Episcopalian. *Home:* 37 Park Dr., Atherton, Calif. 94025. *Office:* Department of History, Stanford University, Stanford, Calif. 94305.

CAREER: Stanford University, Stanford, Calif., assistant professor, 1966-72, associate professor of history, 1972—, director of Center for Latin American Studies, 1975—. *Military service:* U.S. Army Reserve, 1958-64. *Member:* American Historical Association, Conference on Latin American History, Latin American Studies Association. *Awards, honors:* Bolton Memorial Prize, 1971; Pacific Coast Council on Latin American Studies Prize, 1971.

WRITINGS: The Politics of Brazilian Development, 1930-1954, Stanford University Press, 1970; *Minas Gerais in the Brazilian Federation, 1889-1937,* Stanford University Press, 1977.

WORK IN PROGRESS: A study of Brazilian legal culture in the twentieth century.

SIDELIGHTS: John D. Wirth told *CA,* "With my first book translated into Portugese, I am proud to be one of the Brazilianists, a small group which is privileged to interpret one of the world's most fascinating societies, contemporary Brazil."

* * *

WISWALL, F(rank) L(awrence), Jr. 1939-

PERSONAL: Born September 21, 1939, in Albany, N.Y.; son of Frank Lawrence (a lawyer) and Clara (Chapman) Wiswall; married Priscilla Ann Gwyn, December 26, 1961; children: Anne Chapman, Frank Lawrence III. *Education:* Colby College, B.A., 1962; Cornell University, J.D., 1965; Clare College, Cambridge, Ph.D., 1967. *Politics:* Republican. *Religion:* Episcopalian. *Home:* Meadow Farm, Castine, Me. 04421. *Office:* Burlingham, Underwood, Wright, White & Lord, 25 Broadway, New York, N.Y. 10004.

CAREER: Admitted to Bar of the State of Maine, 1965, Bar of the U.S. Supreme Court, 1968, and Bar of the State of New York, 1968; Burlingham, Underwood, Wright, White & Lord (admiralty law firm), New York, N.Y., proctor and advocate in admiralty, 1967—. Legal advisor, Bureau of Maritime Affairs, Republic of Liberia, 1968—. Trustee, Castine Community Hospital, Castine, Me. *Member:* American Bar Association, Maritime Law Association of the U.S., Selden Society, Society for Legal History, American Society of International Law, Society for Nautical Research, Association of Average Adjusters. *Awards, honors:* Yorke Prize, Cambridge University, 1968.

WRITINGS: The Development of Admiralty Jurisdiction and Practice Since 1800, Cambridge University Press, 1971. Contributor of articles to law journals.

WORK IN PROGRESS: Co-authoring with G. H. Robinson a new multi-volume edition of the standard practice work, *Robinson on Admiralty,* for Matthew Bender.

SIDELIGHTS: F. L. Wiswall told *CA,* "I write about the two professions from which I earn my living: the Sea and its Law."††

* * *

WITTKE, Carl (Frederick) 1892-1971

November 13, 1892—May 24, 1971; American historian and author. Obituaries: *Washington Post,* May 26, 1971; *New York Times,* May 26, 1971.

* * *

WITTREICH, Joseph Anthony, Jr. 1939-

PERSONAL: Surname is pronounced *Wit-*trick; born July 23, 1939, in Cleveland, Ohio; son of Joseph Anthony (a supervisor) and Mamie (Pucel) Wittreich. *Education:* University of Louisville, B.A., 1961, M.A., 1962; Western Reserve University (now Case Western Reserve University), Ph.D., 1966. *Home:* 320 South 16th St., Philadelphia, Pa. 19102. *Office:* Department of English, University of Maryland, College Park, Md. 20742.

CAREER: University of Wisconsin—Madison, assistant professor, 1966-70, associate professor, 1970-74, professor of English, 1974-76; University of Maryland, College Park, professor of English, 1977—. Guest lecturer, California

State University, Los Angeles, summer, 1970, and fall, 1972. Member of advisory board of editors, *Blake Studies,* 1968—, *Literary Monographs,* 1971—, *Genre,* 1973—, and *Milton and the Romantics. Member:* Modern Language Association of America, Milton Society of America (member of executive committee), Blake Foundation of America (member of board of directors), Renaissance Society. *Awards, honors:* American Philosophical Society fellowship, 1967; Henry E. Huntington fellowship, 1968, 1976; Folger fellowship, 1971, 1974; National Endowment for the Humanities fellowship, 1974, 1976; Newberry Library fellowship, 1974; Wisconsin Institute for Research in the Humanities fellowship, 1975.

WRITINGS: (Editor) *The Romantics on Milton: Formal Essays and Critical Asides,* Press of Case Western Reserve University, 1970; (author of introduction) William Hayley, *Life of Milton,* 2nd edition, Scholars Facsimiles & Reprints, 1970; (editor and author of introduction) *Early Lives of William Blake, 1806-1910,* Scholars Facsimiles & Reprints, 1970; (editor) *Calm of Mind: Tercentenary Essays on "Paradise Regained" and "Samson Agonistes,"* Press of Case Western Reserve University, 1971; (editor with Stuart Currant, and contributor) *Blake's Sublime Allegory: Essays on "The Four Zoas," "Milton," and "Jerusalem,"* University of Wisconsin Press, 1973; (contributor) John T. Shawcross and Michael Lieb, editors, *Achievements of the Left Hand: Essays on John Milton's Prose Work,* University of Massachusetts Press, 1974.

Angel of Apocalypse: Blake's Idea of Milton, University of Wisconsin Press, 1975; (editor and contributor) *Milton and the Line of Vision,* University of Wisconsin Press, 1975; (contributor) John T. Shawcross and others, editors, *Milton Encyclopedia,* Bucknell University Press, 1976; (contributor) Balachandra Raja, editor, *Homage to Milton,* University of Georgia Press, 1976. Editor with Eric Rothstein of two monographs, *Medieval and Renaissance Literature,* and *Thackeray, Hawthorne, Melville, and Dreiser,* published by University of Wisconsin Press, 1975. Contributor of numerous articles and essays to journals, including *PMLA, Blake Studies, Studies in Philology, English Language Notes, Milton Quarterly, Milton Studies, Bucknell Review, Keats-Shelley Journal,* and *Huntington Library Quarterly;* contributor of reviews to journals, including *Genre, Renaissance Quarterly, Seventeenth-Century News, Blake Newsletter,* and *Journal of English and German Philology.* Guest editor, *Blake Studies,* 1972; editor, *Literary Monographs,* 1973-74.

WORK IN PROGRESS: Visionary Poetics: Milton's Tradition and His Legacy; Milton: Revolutionary Artist.

*   *   *

WOESSNER, Nina C.   1933-

PERSONAL: Born June 21, 1933, in Oyster Bay, N.Y. *Education:* State Teachers College (now State University of New York College at New Paltz), B.S., 1955, State University of New York at Albany, M.S., 1968. *Home:* 50 Presidential Plaza, Syracuse, N.Y. 13202.

CAREER: Teacher in public schools in Oyster Bay, N.Y., 1955, Colonie, N.Y., 1957, and Delmar, N.Y., 1959; Fayetteville-Manlius Schools, Manlius, N.Y., teacher of reading, 1968—. *Member:* International Reading Association, National Education Association, New York State Teachers Association.

WRITINGS—Juveniles compiled with William D. Sheldon; all published by Allyn & Bacon: *The Big Ones,* 1968; (and

with Warren Wheelock) *With It,* 1971; (and with Wheelock) *The Time Is Now,* 1971; *Coming Through,* 1972; *How It Is,* 1972; *Making the Scene,* 1972; *On the Spot,* 1972.†

*   *   *

WOLDENDORP, R(ichard)   1927-

PERSONAL: Born January 1, 1927; son of Gerad (a hotelier) and Marie (Spijkerman) Woldendorp; married Lynette Dockery, October 19, 1962; children: Yolanta, Gemma, Eva (all daughters). *Education:* Attended a technical school in the Netherlands for five years. *Religion:* Roman Catholic. *Home:* Binbrook Pl., Darlington, Western Australia 6070, Australia. *Agent:* (Photographs) Alan Faley Ltd., P.O. Box 223, Narrabeen, New South Wales 2101, Australia.

CAREER: Australian Tourist Committee, Victoria, Australia, free-lance photographer, 1966—; also does other free-lance photographic work in Australia and Southeast Asia. *Awards, honors:* Transfield Book of the Year Award, 1970.

WRITINGS: (With Peter Slater) *The Hidden Face of Australia,* Thomas Nelson, 1968; (illustrator) *A Million Square: Western Australia,* text by Thomas A. G. Hungerford, International Publications Service, 1969; (with Tony Johns) *Indonesia,* Thomas Nelson, 1972. Also author and illustrator of *Western Australia,* 1977.

*   *   *

WOLF, Arnold Jacob   1924-

PERSONAL: Born March 19, 1924, in Chicago, Ill.; son of Max A. (a tailor) and Nettie (S.) Wolf; married Lois Blumberg (a teacher), November 26, 1953; children: Jonathan, Benjamin, Sara. *Education:* University of Chicago, A.A., 1942, additional study, 1955-58; University of Cincinnati, B.A., 1945; Hebrew Union College, Cincinnati, M.H.L. and Rabbi, 1948. *Politics:* Socialist. *Home:* 35 High, New Haven, Conn. 06510. *Office:* Yale Hillel, Yale Station, Box 1904A, New Haven, Conn. 06520.

CAREER: Assistant rabbi in Chicago, Ill., 1948-55; instructor in Bible, College of Jewish Studies, Chicago, Ill.; Congregation Solel, Highland Park, Ill., rabbi, 1957-72; Yale Hillel, New Haven, Conn., director, 1972—. First rabbinical director of camp institutes, National Federation of Temple Youth and Chicago Federation of Temple Youth; former vice-president, Religion and Labor Seminary Foundation. Conductor of radio and television programs, "Reflections," "Vision," and "Answers," in Chicago. *Military service:* U.S. Navy, chaplain; served in Korea. *Member:* Chicago Board of Rabbis. *Awards, honors:* Brotherhood Award of National Conference of Christians and Jews, 1962.

WRITINGS: Challenge to Confirmands: An Introduction to Jewish Thinking (for teen-agers), Scribe, 1963, 3rd edition, 1967; (editor) *Rediscovering Judaism: Reflections on a New Theology,* Quadrangle, 1965; *What Is Man?,* Bloch Publishing, for B'nai B'rith, 1969. Contributor to *Christian Century, Religious Digest, Commentary,* and other journals. Former editor, *Sh'ma* (publication of Chicago Board of Rabbis).

*   *   *

WOLF, Charlotte (Elizabeth)   1926-

PERSONAL: Born September 14, 1926, in Boulder, Colo.; daughter of Marion Guy (a carpenter) and Ethel (Thomas) Rosetta; married Rene Arthur Wolf (an army engineer), September 3, 1952; children: Christopher, Michele. *Education:* University of Colorado, B.A., 1949, M.A., 1959; University of Minnesota, Ph.D., 1968. *Home:* 45 Park Ave., Delaware, Ohio 43015. *Office:* Department of Sociology, Ohio Wesleyan University, Delaware, Ohio 43015.

CAREER: University of Colorado, Boulder, instructor, 1949-50; George Washington University, Washington, D.C., part-time instructor, 1954-55; University of Maryland, lecturer in Tokyo, Japan, 1959-62, and Ankara, Turkey, 1965-67; St. Mary College, Xavier, Kan., instructor, 1962-63; Colorado State University, Fort Collins, assistant professor of sociology, 1968-69; Temple Buell College, Denver, Colo., assistant professor of sociology, 1969-74; Ohio Wesleyan University, Delaware, Ohio, associate professor of sociology and chairman of department, 1974—. *Member:* American Sociological Association, American Academy of Political and Social Science, American Association for the Advancement of Science, American Association of University Professors, Sociologists for Women in Society (co-founder), Pacific Sociological Association, Midwest Sociological Society, National Organization for Women (president of Denver chapter, 1970-72).

WRITINGS: Garrison Community: A Study of an Overseas American Military Colony, Greenwood Press, 1970; (contributor) Ray Mohan and Arthur Wilke, editors, *Community Theory and Social Change,* Greenwood Press, 1977; (contributor) Joseph Roucek, editor, *Social Control,* Greenwood Press, 1977. Also author of *The Social Psychology of Minority Groups.* Author of professional monographs and contributor of articles to various periodicals.

* * *

WOLF, George D(ugan) 1923-

PERSONAL: Born June 4, 1923, in Corry, Pa.; son of Sol W. and Norah (Dugan) Wolf; married Margaret McNeil, March 31, 1948; children: Nancy McNeil, Susan Norah, Linda Carol. *Education:* Dickinson Junior College (now Lycoming College), graduate; Muskingum College, B.A., 1947; Bucknell University, M.A., 1953; University of Pennsylvania, Ph.D., 1964. *Politics:* Republican. *Religion:* Presbyterian. *Home:* 304 Deerfield Rd., Camp Hill, Pa., 17011. *Office:* Pennsylvania State University, Capitol Campus, Middletown, Pa. 17057.

CAREER: High school teacher of English and history in Pennsylvania, 1948-56; Lycoming College, Williamsport, Pa., instructor in history, 1954-56; Lock Haven State College, Lock Haven, Pa., associate professor, 1957-64, professor of history, 1964-66; Pennsylvania State University, Capitol Campus, Middletown, associate professor, 1966-69, professor of history and American studies, 1969—, head, division of humanities, social sciences, and education, 1971-73, dean of faculty, 1973—. Member of Republican executive committee, Clinton County, 1963-66; special assistant to Governor William W. Scranton, 1965-66; consultant to Lieutenant Governor Raymond J. Broderick, 1967-70; historian for Pennsylvania Constitutional Convention, 1967-68; member of Board of State College and University Directors, 1970-71. Township supervisor, Pine Creek Township, 1959-61. *Military service:* U.S. Army, 1943.

MEMBER: American Historical Association, American Studies Association, Organization of American Historians, American Association of University Professors, American Association for Higher Education, Pennsylvania Historical Association (member of council). *Awards, honors:* Fellowship from National Center for Education in Politics, 1965-66; research grants from Pennsylvania State University, 1967-70.

WRITINGS: State Constitutional Revision, Department of Public Instruction, State of Pennsylvania, 1968; *The Fair Play Settlers of the West Branch Valley, 1769-1784,* Pennsylvania Historical and Museum Commission, 1969; *Pennsylvania's Constitutional Revision,* National Municipal League, 1969. Author of index for Reference Manual No. 9, Pennsylvania Constitutional Convention, 1967, and introduction and index for *Debates of the Pennsylvania Constitutional Convention,* 1969. Contributor of articles and reviews to journals.

WORK IN PROGRESS: Squire Scranton, Pragmatist.

BIOGRAPHICAL/CRITICAL SOURCES: Lycoming College Bulletin, fall, 1967.

* * *

WOLFF, Geoffrey (Ansell) 1937-

PERSONAL: Born November 5, 1937, in Los Angeles, Calif.; son of Arthur Saunders (an engineer) and Rosemary (Loftus) Wolff; married Priscilla Porter, August 21, 1965; children: Nicholas Hinckley, Justin Porter. *Education:* Princeton University, A.B. (summa cum laude), 1961; attended Churchill College, Cambridge, 1963-64. *Politics:* Independent. *Religion:* None. *Home:* Prickly Mountain, Warren, Vt. 05674. *Agent:* Robert Lescher, 155 East 71st St., New York, N.Y. 10021.

CAREER: Robert College, Istanbul, Turkey, lecturer in comparative literature, 1961-63; Istanbul University, Istanbul, lecturer and chairman of department of American Civilization, 1962-63; *Washington Post,* Washington, D.C., book editor, 1964-69; Maryland Institute, College of Art, Baltimore, lecturer in aesthetics, 1965-69; Corcoran School of Art, Washington, D.C., lecturer, 1968-69; *Newsweek,* New York City, book editor, 1969-71; Princeton University, Princeton, N.J., visiting lecturer in creative arts, 1970-71, 1972-74; *New Times,* New York City, book editor, 1974. Visiting lecturer in English literature at Middlebury College, 1976. Senior fellow, National Endowment of the Humanities, 1974-75. *Awards, honors:* Woodrow Wilson fellow, 1961-62, 1963-64; Fulbright scholar, 1963-64; Guggenheim fellowship in creative writing, 1971-72.

WRITINGS: Bad Debts (novel), Simon & Schuster, 1969; *The Sightseer* (novel), Random House, 1974; *Black Sun: The Brief Transit and Violent Eclipse of Harry Crosby* (biography), Random House, 1976; *Inklings* (novel), Random House, 1977. Contributor of essays and reviews to *American Scholar, New Leader, New Republic, Atlantic Monthly, Saturday Review,* and other periodicals.

WORK IN PROGRESS: The Duke of Deception, a biography of his father, a confidence man, for Random House.

SIDELIGHTS: Several critics, including Richard Brickner, are of the opinion that the chief impact of *Bad Debts,* Wolff's first novel, lies in its "bitterly comic" scenes rather than in its "emotional thrust" as a novelistic whole. "*Bad Debts* has scenes in it that make one wince in delighted discomfort," Brickner writes. "[It] is a novel with honest-to-God touchstones in it, a novel to be recommended for virtues rare enough that one is grateful for even their qualified appearance. . . . The entire Washington section of the book is marvelous, humanly letter-perfect." According to John Leonard of the *New York Times,* the novel "deals wittily with a collection of people as unappetizing as Miss Porter's ship of fools, people whose possibilities appear to have been poisoned at the source, as though birth itself were a fatal wound. Looking at them through Mr. Wolff's savage eye is like being trapped at a disastrous dinner party, or being one among a dozen conscripts in a malfunctioning elevator.... It is a novel about credit, and its logic is that dreams deferred end in violence, but not even violence can always serve as a vehicle of recognition. Satire there is of a surgical sort, and an unrelenting war on thingness as psychic dispersion, on buying (or owing) as a cry for help."

Isa Kapp notes that Wolff himself "apparently took a careful estimate of the deposits in his creative bank, and made a cautious investment" in writing *Bad Debts;* "[it] achieves a gray naturalism of the soul that makes the pages of Theodore Dreiser seem positively to rock with romance." Kapp details Wolff's tallying up of bad (emotional) debts among the members of Freeman's family and says: "There is something too mathematical about all this, something intellectualized—reverbrating [sic] the grotesqueries of Nathaniel West, but without his nervous sincerity, the inflection and oppressed manner of Saul Bellow, but without his conscience and vitality.... In the novels of Kafka, there is a strange anonymity in the characters, an unnatural vacant space around them—but we can, through our identification with their situations, endow them with specific lifelike qualities. In *Bad Debts,* the furnishings and the lifelike qualities are abundant, but we endow them with an anonymous terror. This frightening little novel gives us more of a clue of what hell, rather than earthly life, may really be like." Jack Kroll called *Bad Debts* a "compassionate study of creatures whose behavioral absurdity defines a human dislocation that goes deeper than morals or ethics.... Wolff's characters ... are all deplorable misfits, moral and psychic mutants. But Wolff goes beyond this to evoke a sharp sense of a certain kind of madness endemic in the modern world, and localized here in the figure of Benjamin.... Something radical about our time lives in the figure of Benjamin Freeman."

In a later book, *Black Sun: The Brief Transit and Violent Eclipse of Harry Crosby,* Wolff creates a biography of Harry Crosby. Harry Crosby was the wealthy, well born, poet, publisher and founder of the Black Sun Press who killed himself in a spectacular and sensational fashion at the age of thirty-one. Of Crosby, Wolff writes that "death was a goal [Crosby] ran toward full tilt. He was a poet of final stanzas, or so he liked to believe, and that last shot was no more than a punctuation point, a dot smaller than his finest fingernail, a hard period, dull stop." A reviewer from *Booklist* remarked, "All the riddles of [Harry] Crosby's life and death are not solved in Wolff's biography, but some cogent explanations for an eccentric and unstable personality are advanced."

AVOCATIONAL INTERESTS: Photography, both still and motion picture.

BIOGRAPHICAL/CRITICAL SOURCES: New York Times, November 12, 1969; *Newsweek,* November 17, 1969; *Washington Post,* November 22, 1969; *New Yorker,* November 22, 1969; *Book World,* November 23, 1969; *New Leader,* January 5, 1970; *Christian Science Monitor,* January 8, 1970; *New York Times Book Review,* February 1, 1970; *Booklist,* September 15, 1976.

*   *   *

WOLFRAM, Walter A.   1941-

PERSONAL: Born February 15, 1941, in Philadelphia, Pa.; son of Carl (a laborer) and Johana (Waltering) Wolfram; married Margaret Linder, July 17, 1963; children: Tyler, Todd, Terry, Tanya. *Education:* Wheaton College, Wheaton, Ill., B.A., 1963; Hartford Seminary Foundation, M.A., 1966, Ph.D., 1969. *Politics:* Independent. *Religion:* Protes-

tant. *Office:* Center for Applied Linguistics, 1611 North Kent St., Arlington, Va. 22209.

CAREER: Center for Applied Linguistics, Arlington, Va., research associate, 1967—. Special lecturer at Trinity College, Washington, D.C., 1967—, Georgetown University, 1969-71, and Federal City College, 1971—. *Member:* Linguistic Society of America, American Anthropological Association.

WRITINGS: (With Roger W. Shuy and William K. Riley) *Field Techniques in an Urban Language Study,* Center for Applied Linguistics, 1968; *A Sociolinguistic Description of Detroit Negro Speech,* Center for Applied Linguistics, 1969; *Sociolinguistic Aspects of Assimilation: Puerto Rican English in New York City,* Center for Applied Linguistics, 1974; *The Study of Social Dialects in American English,* Prentice-Hall, 1974; (with Donna Christian) *Appalachian Speech,* Center for Applied Linguistics, 1976.

WORK IN PROGRESS: Indian English, completion expected in 1978.

*   *   *

WOLOCH, Isser   1937-

PERSONAL: Born October 16, 1937, in New York, N.Y.; son of Nathan M. and Edith (Kramer) Woloch; married Nancy Spelman (an historian), July, 1962; children: David, Alexander. *Education:* Columbia University, A.B., 1959; Princeton University, M.A., 1961, Ph.D., 1965. *Home:* 50 West 97th St., New York, N.Y. 10025. *Office:* Department of History, Columbia University, New York, N.Y. 10027.

CAREER: Indiana University, Bloomington, Ind., lecturer, 1963-64, assistant professor of history, 1964-66; University of California, Los Angeles, assistant professor of history, 1966-69; Columbia University, New York, N.Y., associate professor, 1969-75, professor of history, 1975—. Member, Institute for Advanced Studies, Princeton University, 1973-74. *Member:* American Historical Association, Society for French Historical Studies, Phi Beta Kappa. *Awards, honors:* Woodrow Wilson fellowship, 1959-60; American Council of Learned Societies fellowship, 1973-74.

WRITINGS: Jacobin Legacy: The Democrat Movement under the Directory, Princeton University Press, 1970; (editor) *The Peasantry in the Old Regime: Conditions and Protests,* Holt, 1970; (co-author) *The Western Experience,* Knopf, 1974. Contributor to *Encyclopedia Americana;* contributor of articles to *Journal of Modern History, Journal of Interdisciplinary History,* and *Reviews in European History.*

WORK IN PROGRESS: The French Veteran, from the Revolution to the Restoration.

*   *   *

WOLTERS, Raymond   1938-

PERSONAL: Born July 25, 1938, in Kansas City, Mo.; son of Raymond Martin and Margaret (Reilly) Wolters; married Mary McCullough, June 23, 1962; children: Jeffrey, Kevin. *Education:* Stanford University, B.A., 1960; University of California, Berkeley, M.A., 1962, Ph.D., 1967. *Home:* 702 Dallam Rd., Newark, Del. 19711. *Office:* Department of History, University of Delaware, Newark, Del. 19711.

CAREER: University of Delaware, Newark, instructor, 1965-67, assistant professor, 1967-70, associate professor, 1970-75, professor of history, 1975—. *Member:* Organization of American Historians, American Historical Association, Association for the Study of Negro Life and History. *Awards, honors:* American Council of Learned Societies grant, 1970; National Endowment for the Humanities fellowship, 1971-72; American Philosophical Society grant, 1974.

WRITINGS: Negroes and the Great Depression: The Problem of Economic Recovery, Greenwood Press, 1970; *The New Negro on Campus: Black College Rebellion of the 1920's,* Princeton University Press, 1975; (contributor) John Braeman, editor, *The New Deal,* Ohio State University Press, 1975.

WORK IN PROGRESS: Strife and Contention: Factionalism among Black Leaders, 1900-1940, completion expected in 1980.

* * *

WONNACOTT, Ronald J(ohnston) 1930-

PERSONAL: Born September 11, 1930, in London, Ontario, Canada; son of Gordon and Murial (Johnston) Wonnacott; married Eloise Howlett, September 11, 1954; children: Douglas, Robert, Cathy Anne. *Education:* University of Western Ontario, B.A., 1955; Harvard University, A.M., 1957, Ph.D., 1959. *Religion:* United Church of Canada. *Home:* 171 Wychwood Park, London, Ontario, Canada. *Office:* Department of Economics, University of Western Ontario, London, Ontario, Canada N6A 3K7.

CAREER: University of Western Ontario, London, assistant professor, 1958-61, associate professor, 1961-64, professor of economics, 1964—, chairman of department, 1969-72. Visiting associate professor, University of Minnesota, 1961-62. Consultant to Stanford Research Institute, Resources for the Future, Economic Council of Canada, and other groups. *Military service:* Royal Canadian Naval Reserve, 1951-55; became lieutenant. *Member:* Canadian Economics Association, American Economic Association, Econometric Society.

WRITINGS: Canadian-American Dependence: An Interindustry Analysis of Production and Prices, North-Holland Publishing, 1961; (with Grant L. Reuber) *The Cost of Capital in Canada,* Resources for the Future, 1961; *Manufacturing Costs and the Comparative Advantage of United States Regions,* University of Minnesota, 1963; (with Gordon Paul Wonnacott) *Free Trade Between the U.S. and Canada,* Harvard University Press, 1967; (with David E. Bond) *Trade Liberalization and the Canadian Furniture Industry,* University of Toronto Press, for Private Planning Association of Canada, 1968; (with G. P. Wonnacott) *U.S.-Canadian Free Trade,* Canadian-American Committee, 1968; (with Thomas Wonnacott) *Introductory Statistics,* Wiley, 1969, 3rd edition, in press; (with T. Wonnacott) *Econometrics,* Wiley, 1970; (with T. Wonnacott) *Introductory Statistics for Business and Economics,* Wiley, 1972, 2nd edition, in press; *Canada's Trade Options,* Economic Council of Canada, 1975. Contributor to economics journals.

AVOCATIONAL INTERESTS: Golf, skiing, tennis.

* * *

WOOD, Allen W(illiam) 1942-

PERSONAL: Born October 26, 1942, in Seattle, Wash.; son of Forrest Elmer (a supervisor at Boeing Aircraft Co.) and Alleen (Blumberg) Wood; married Rega Clark, June 20, 1965. *Education:* Reed College, B.A., 1964; Yale University, M.A., 1966, Ph.D., 1968. *Home:* 206 University Ave., Ithaca, N.Y. 14850. *Office:* Philosophy Department, Cornell University, Ithaca, N.Y. 14850.

CAREER: Cornell University, Ithaca, N.Y., assistant professor, 1968-73, associate professor of philosophy, 1973—. Visiting assistant professor, University of Michigan, 1973—. *Awards, honors:* Cornell Society for Humanities summer fellowship, 1970.

WRITINGS: Kant's Moral Religion, Cornell University Press, 1970.

WORK IN PROGRESS: A translation of Kant's *Lectures on Philosophical Theology* with a critical essay, "Kant's Rational Theology"; a book on Karl Marx, for Routledge & Kegan Paul's "Arguments of the Philosophers" series, completion expected in 1979; research on Rousseau's philosophy of morality and society, on Marx's concept of practice, freedom, and social ideals, and on religious belief in St. Anselm, Hume, and Kierkegaard.

* * *

WOOD, Barry 1940-

PERSONAL: Born June 18, 1940, in Toronto, Ontario, Canada; son of Albert (a custodian) and Daisy (Bell) Wood; married Sharilyn Mulligan (a specialist in primary education), December 19, 1964; children: Colin Gerald Orion, Michael William Joseph. *Education:* University of Toronto, B.A., 1963; University of British Columbia, M.A., 1968; Stanford University, Ph.D., 1974. *Religion:* "Studiously unaffiliated." *Home:* 4365 Harvest Lane, Houston, Tex. 77004; and R.R. 1, Bethany, Ontario, Canada (summer). *Office:* Department of English, University of Houston, Houston, Tex. 77004.

CAREER: Secondary school teacher of English, Scarborough, Ontario, 1964-66; University of Houston, Houston, Tex., instructor, 1972-74, assistant professor, 1974-77, associate professor of English, 1977—. *Member:* Modern Language Association of America, Thoreau Society.

WRITINGS: (Author of notes and critical commentary) Mark Twain, *Huckleberry Finn* (high school edition), Clarke, Irwin, 1968; *The Magnificent Frolic,* Westminster, 1970; *The Only Freedom,* Westminster, 1972. Contributor of articles and reviews to *PMLA, Canadian Literature, New England Quarterly, Contemporary Literature,* and *Critique.*

WORK IN PROGRESS: The Central Experience, a book length study of integrating experiences in various areas of human life based on the paradigm of "religious" experience; a full study of Ralph Waldo Emerson's thought, tentatively entitled *Unbounded Empire;* writing the notes for the Harvard edition of *Representative Men,* Volume IV of Ralph Waldo Emerson's *Collected Works;* extensive manuscript holdings, along with journals and notebooks of local history and folklore about the hamlet of Lifford (which no longer exists) in Ontario which "seems headed for publication as a book of stories and anecdotes, perhaps in a context of Canadian pioneer history."

SIDELIGHTS: Barry Wood told *CA:* "Writers to whom I keep returning are Norman Berrill (*Man's Emerging Mind*), Teilhard de Chardin (*The Phenomenon of Man*) and Whitehead (*Process and Reality*). The strongest personal influences on my thinking have come from Northrop Frye, at the University of Toronto, and Alan Watts (1915-1973), author of numerous books and a general interpreter of Zen Buddhism in the west. From about 1964 Watts was the major shaper of my thought and style, as *The Magnificent Frolic* and *The Only Freedom* might suggest; moreover, Watts provided the kind of encouragement in 1967 needed to get my first book into publishable form. My personal contact with Frye dates to 1963, and his approach to religious literature has influenced me ever since. Frye's archetypal and mythic approaches to literary criticism which continue to appear in published form have asserted themselves in my own thinking and writing since 1975 and will continue to hold an important place in my development as a literary critic.

"Since 1973 I have spent 3 months each year at Lifford, Ontario, restoring a 100-year-old octagonal farmhouse which stands on a family farm of 125 acres. In addition to this project, which exercises my fondness for carpentry, I have found my initial interest in tracing family roots in the area now expanded into a manuscript and folklore collection and local history of Lifford and the surrounding area."

* * *

WOOD, Christopher (Hovelle) 1935-
(Rosie Dixon, Oliver Grape, Timothy Lea, Penny Sutton)

PERSONAL: Born November 5, 1935, in London, England; son of Walter Leonard and Audrey (Hovelle) Wood; married Jane Patrick, July 21, 1962; children: Caroline Sarah, Adam Sebastian Hovelle, Benjamin Nicholas Hamilton. *Education:* Cambridge University, M.A., 1960. *Politics:* "Pink Conservative." *Religion:* Church of England. *Agent:* Deborah Rogers, 29 Goodge St., London W1P 1FD, England. *Office:* Masius Wynne Williams, 2 St. James Sq., London S.W.1, England.

CAREER: British Colonial Office, plebiscite organizer in Southern Cameroons, West Africa, 1960-61; Masius Wynne Williams, London, England, account executive, 1961—. *Military service:* British Army, Royal Artillery, served in Cyprus; became second lieutenant. *Member:* Institute of Practitioners in Advertising, Royston Rugby Club.

WRITINGS: Make It Happen to Me, Constable, 1969, published as *Kiss Off,* Sphere Books, 1970; *'Terrible Hard,' Says Alice,* Constable, 1970; *John Adam, Samurai,* Arlington Books, 1971; *John Adam in Eden,* Sphere Books, 1973.

Under pseudonym Rosie Dixon; all published by Futura Publications, except as noted: *Confessions of a Gym Mistress,* 1974; *Confessions of a Night Nurse,* 1974; *Confessions from a Package Tour,* 1975; *Confessions of a Lady Courier,* 1975; *Confessions from an Escort Agency,* 1975.

Under pseudonym Oliver Grape: *Crumpet Voluntary,* 1974; *It's a Knock-Up!,* 1975.

Under pseudonym Timothy Lea: *Confessions of a Window Cleaner,* Sphere Books, 1971; *Confessions from a Holiday Camp,* Sphere Books, 1972; *Confessions of a Driving Instructor,* Sphere Books, 1972; *Confessions from a Hotel,* Sphere Books, 1973; *Confessions from the Clink,* Sphere Books, 1973; *Confessions of a Film Extra,* Sphere Books, 1973; *Confessions of a Travelling Salesman,* Sphere Books, 1973; *Confessions from a Health Farm,* 1974; *Confessions from the Pop Scene,* 1974, published as *Confessions of a Pop Performer,* 1975; *Confessions of a Private Soldier,* Sphere Books, 1974; *Confessions from the Shop Floor,* 1975; *Confessions of a Long Distance Lorry Driver,* 1975; *Confessions of a Plumber's Mate,* 1975; *Confessions of a Private Dick,* 1975.

Under pseudonym Penny Sutton: *The Stewardesses,* Sphere Books, 1973; *The Stewardesses Down Under,* Sphere Books, 1973; *Jumbo Jet Girls,* 1974; *I'm Penny, Fly Me,* 1975.

BIOGRAPHICAL/CRITICAL SOURCES: Observer Review, September 7, 1969, July 5, 1970; *Books,* October, 1969.†

* * *

WOOD, James E(dward), Jr. 1922-

PERSONAL: Born July 29, 1922, in Portsmouth, Va.; son of James Edward and Elsie Elizabeth (Bryant) Wood; married Alma Leacy McKenzie, August 12, 1943; children: James Edward III. *Education:* Carson-Newman College, B.A., 1943; Southern Baptist Theological Seminary, B.D., 1947, Th.M., 1948, Ph.D., 1957; Columbia University, M.A., 1949; also studied at University of Tennessee, 1943-44, Yale University, 1948-49, and Naganuma School of Japanese Studies, Tokyo, 1950-51. *Politics:* Democrat. *Home:* 1324 North Illinois St., Arlington, Va. 22205. *Office:* 200 Maryland Ave. N.E., Washington, D.C. 20002.

CAREER: Baptist clergyman and educator, 1942—; Seinan Gakuin University, Fukuoka, Japan, professor of religion and literature, 1950-55; Baylor University, Waco, Tex., assistant professor, 1955-57, associate professor, 1957-59, professor of history of religions and director of J.M. Dawson Studies in Church and State, 1959-72, chairman of church-state studies, 1965-72; executive director, Baptist Joint Committee on Public Affairs, 1972—. Member of Commission on Religious Liberty and Human Rights, Baptist World Alliance, 1965—. Editor-in-chief, Markham Press, Baylor University, 1970-72.

MEMBER: American Academy of Religion, American Society of Church History, National Council on Religion and Public Education (secretary), Public Education and Religious Liberty (member of executive committee), American Society of International Law, American Civil Liberties Union (president of Waco, Tex. chapter, 1969-72), Planned Parenthood (president of Waco, Tex. chapter, 1971-72), Texas Civil Liberties Union (member of board, 1969-72), Washington Council (member of executive committee), Phi Eta Sigma, Pi Kappa Delta, Alpha Psi Omega, Rotary International.

WRITINGS: A History of American Literature: An Anthology, Kenkyusha (Japan), 1952; (with E. Bruce Thompson and Robert T. Miller) *Church and State in Scripture, History, and Constitutional Law,* Baylor University Press, 1958; (contributor) *We Hold These Truths,* Protestants and Other Americans United, 1964; (editor and contributor) Joseph Martin Dawson, *A Thousand Months to Remember: An Autobiography,* Baylor University Press, 1964; (contributor) *The Teacher's Yoke: Essays Honoring Henry Trantham,* Baylor University Press, 1964; *The Problem of Nationalism in Church-State Relationships,* Herald Press, 1969; (editor and contributor) *Jewish-Christian Relations in Today's World,* Baylor University Press, 1971; (editor and contributor) *Baptists and the American Experience,* Judson Press, 1976; *Nationhood and the Kingdom,* Broadman Press, 1977. Contributor and resource editor, *The Encyclopedia of Modern Christian Missions,* Nelson, 1967; contributor of more than one hundred articles and reviews to professional journals. Editor, *Journal of Church and State,* 1959-72.

WORK IN PROGRESS: Baptists and Religious Liberty.

SIDELIGHTS: James E. Wood is competent in Greek, Hebrew, Latin, and French in addition to Japanese. He has traveled in Africa, Europe, Asia, Mexico, the South Pacific, New Zealand, and Australia.

WOOD, Leon J. 1918-

PERSONAL: Born October 6, 1918, in Middleville, Mich.; son of Clyde Earl (a minister) and Effa (Porter) Wood; married Helen DeNise, August 21, 1942; children: James Lee, Carol Joan, Marilyn Ruth. *Education:* Calvin College, A.B., 1941; Calvin Theological Seminary, Th.B., 1943, Th.M., 1949; Michigan State University, Ph.D., 1963. *Home:* 2722 Durham Ave. N.E., Grand Rapids, Mich. 49505. *Office:* Grand Rapids Baptist Bible College and Seminary, 1001 East Beltline Ave. N.E., Grand Rapids, Mich. 49505.

CAREER: Ordained to ministry of Baptist Church, 1943; pastor in Paw Paw, Mich., 1943-45; Grand Rapids Baptist Bible College and Seminary, Grand Rapids, Mich., professor of Old Testament, 1945—, dean of education, 1950-61, dean of seminary, 1961—. *Member:* Evangelical Theological Society.

WRITINGS—All published by Zondervan, except as indicated: *Is the Rapture Next?*, 1956; *Elijah, Prophet of God*, Regular Baptist Press, 1968; *A Survey of Israel's History*, 1970; *A Commentary on Daniel*, 1973; *The Bible and Future Events*, 1973; *Distressing Days of the Judges*, 1975; *The Holy Spirit and the Old Testament*, 1976. Also author of two study guides on Old Testament readings.

*   *   *

WOOD, Leslie A(lfred) 1930-

PERSONAL: Born June 13, 1930, in Huntington, Ind.; son of Ralph W. (a professor) and Roxie (Kerns) Wood; married Ruth Elaine Baker, August 1, 1954; children: Jeffrey Allen, Pamela Jean, Sara Ruth. *Education:* Ball State University, B.S., 1952; Western Reserve University (now Case Western Reserve University), M.A., 1957; Stanford University, Ed.D., 1962. *Religion:* Christian. *Office:* Department of Education, Indiana University—Purdue University at Indianapolis, 902 North Meridian, Indianapolis, Ind. 96204.

CAREER: Secondary teacher in Huntington, Ind., 1952-53; Fruehauf Trailer Co., Fort Wayne, Ind., employment manager, 1953-54; Thompson-Ramo Wooldrige, Cleveland, Ohio, production control, 1954-55; secondary teacher in Euclid, Ohio, and in Glendale, Calif., 1955-59; Stanford University, Stanford, Calif., instructor, 1959-62; University of Toledo, Toledo, Ohio, director of student field experiences, 1962-65; Indiana University at Bloomington, School of Education, associate professor of social studies and secondary curriculum, 1969-70; Indiana University—Purdue University at Indianapolis, chairman of secondary education, 1970—. Consultant to school systems in California, West Virginia, Ohio, Kentucky, and Indiana.

MEMBER: National Education Association, National Council for the Social Studies (chairman of publications committee, 1969), Association for Supervision and Curriculum Development, American Association of University Professors, Phi Delta Kappa, Pi Gamma Mu. *Awards, honors: A Guide to Human Rights Education* was selected as one of the twenty best books in education published in 1969 by National Education Association and Phi Lambda Theta.

WRITINGS: (Editor with E. J. Nussell) *Readings in Educating the Disadvantaged*, NDEA Institute, 1965; (with Paul E. Hines) *A Guide to Human Rights Education*, National Council for the Social Studies, 1969; *Contemporary Strategies in Teaching Social Studies*, Cooperative Educational Research Laboratory, 1970. Contributor to academic journals. Editor, *California Social Science Review*, 1962; member of advisory board, *Social Education*, 1976-78.

*   *   *

WOODS, George A(llan) 1926-

PERSONAL: Born January 26, 1926, in Lake Placid, N.Y.; son of George Joseph (a storekeeper) and Ann (Van Nostrand) Woods; married Nancy Kirkwood Shaw, January 31, 1948; children: Gail, Catherine, George, Regina, Martha, Christopher, Philip, Valerie, Andrew, Martin, Pauline, Timothy, Sarah, Eric. *Education:* Fordham University, B.S.S., 1950. *Politics:* Democrat. *Religion:* Roman Catholic. *Home:* 11 Central Ave., Demarest, N.J. 07627.

CAREER: Worked for *New York Times Book Review*, New York City, "in all capacities," 1951-63; *New York Times*, New York City, children's book editor, 1963—. Lecturer in children's literature, Fordham University, 1976, and Marymount College, 1977. Judge, Catholic Press Association, 1959-67; Demarest Public Library, Demarest, N.J., trustee, 1969-70, vice-president, 1970-73. Councilman in Demarest, N.J., 1973-75. *Military service:* U.S. Army, 1944-46; became sergeant. U.S. Army Reserve, 1948-53; became second lieutenant.

WRITINGS: (Author of foreword) Henry Augustus Shute, *Brite and Fair*, new edition, Noone House, 1968; *Vibrations*, Harper, 1970; *Catch a Killer*, Harper, 1972. Contributor to *Encyclopedia Americana Yearbooks;* also contributor of numerous articles to *New York Times* and *Wilson Library Bulletin*.

BIOGRAPHICAL/CRITICAL SOURCES: Sunday Record (Hackensack, N.J.), February 7, 1971.

*   *   *

WOODS, William Crawford 1944-

PERSONAL: Born March 30, 1944, in Philadelphia, Pa.; son of Arthur Roy (a lawyer) and Louise (Crawford) Woods; married Mary Van Nice, October 28, 1968 (separated). *Education:* University of North Carolina, student, 1964-65; George Washington University, B.A., 1966; Johns Hopkins University, M.A., 1969. *Politics:* None. *Religion:* "Variable." *Home:* c/o 5607 Durbin Rd., Bethesda, Md. 20014. *Agent:* Candida Donadio & Associates, 111 West 57th St., New York, N.Y. 10019. *Office:* Longwood College, Farmville, Va. 23901.

CAREER: Peabody Conservatory, Baltimore, Md., instructor in English, 1968; *Washington Post*, Washington, D.C., rock music critic, 1969-70; Otto Preminger (Sigma Productions), Hollywood, Calif., screen writer, 1970; *Washington Post*, television critic, 1970-71; currently member of English and philosophy faculty, Longwood College, Farmville, Va. *Military service:* U.S. Army, 1966-68; broadcast specialist, Far East Network, Tokyo. *Member:* Authors Guild, College English Association. *Awards, honors: The Killing Zone* was included on *New York Times* best fiction list, 1970; fellowship at Bread Loaf Writers' Conference, 1971.

WRITINGS: The Killing Zone (novel), Harper, 1970. Contributor of short stories to *Esquire, Carolina Quarterly, New American Review*, and other periodicals.

WORK IN PROGRESS: A book of short stories.

BIOGRAPHICAL/CRITICAL SOURCES: Washington Post, September 12, 1970; *Newsweek*, November 30, 1970; *New Yorker*, January 23, 1971.

WOOLFOLK, Josiah Pitts   1894-1971
(Jack Woodford)

March 25, 1894—May 16, 1971; American author, motion picture scenarist, and ex-convict. Obituaries: *Washington Post,* May 19, 1971.

* * *

WOOLMAN, David S.   1916-
(Lawdom Vaidon)

PERSONAL: Born August 30, 1916, in Columbus, Ohio; son of Harlan (a manufacturer) and La Nelle (Humke) Woolman. *Education:* Attended Indiana University, 1935-36; DePauw University, B.A., 1950; Stanford University, additional study, 1950. *Address:* c/o Wise and Azukas, 1015 Washington, Hoboken, N.J. 07302.

CAREER: Free-lance journalist in Tangier, Morocco, 1952—. *Military service:* U.S. Army Air Forces, 1940-46. U.S. Air Force, 1946-47, 1950-52; served more than three years in the Caribbean and India; became captain.

WRITINGS: Rebels in the Rif, Stanford University Press, 1968; (under pseudonym Lawdom Vaidon) *Tangier: A Different Way,* Scarecrow, 1977. Contributor of feature and travel articles to U.S. newspapers and articles to journals.

WORK IN PROGRESS: An autobiographical novel; a study of Western "bad men".

SIDELIGHTS: As a small boy in 1923, David Woolman was enthralled by newspaper accounts of the Abd el Krim Rebellion then flourishing in Morocco; *Rebels in the Rif* is a history of that martial episode. Woolman says that he speaks "ghastly Spanish and mere menu French, but am not tortured by my deficiency here [in Morocco]." He has made two leisurely trips around the world, has epicurean tastes in food and wine, and plays table tennis for exercise ("have been northern Morocco champion for seven years, although that's not saying very much"), and "recently spent an ebullient year in Colombia."

* * *

WORDSWORTH, Jonathan   1932-

PERSONAL: Born November 28, 1932, in London, England; son of Andrew and Helen (Fletcher) Wordsworth; married Ann Sherratt (a lecturer at St. Hugh's College, Oxford), June 26, 1958; children: Thomas, Charles, Henry, Samuel. *Education:* Brasenose College, Oxford, B.A. (first class honors), 1955. *Politics:* "White liberal." *Religion:* Atheist. *Home:* Old Vicarage, Warborough, Oxford, England. *Agent:* A. D. Peters, 10 Buckingham St., London WC2N 6BU, England. *Office:* Exeter College, Oxford University, Oxford, England.

CAREER: Oxford University, Exeter College, Oxford, England, fellow and lecturer in English literature, 1957—. Visiting assistant professor, Cornell University, 1966-67, 1970. Trustee, Wordsworth Archives, Dove Cottage, Grasmere, England. *Military service:* "Brief and inglorious." *Member:* Modern Language Association of America.

WRITINGS: The Music of Humanity: A Critical Study of Wordsworth's "Ruined Cottage," Harper, 1969; (editor with Beth Darlington) *Bicentenary Wordsworth Studies in Memory of John Alban Finch,* Cornell University Press, 1970. Contributor to *Times Literary Supplement.*

WORK IN PROGRESS: A chronological edition of Wordsworth's poetry, 1787-1807, for Harper; editing with M. H. Abrams and Stephen Gill, a critical edition of Wordsworth's

Prelude, including texts of 1799, 1805, and 1850, for Norton; *The Visionary Gleam: Aspiration and Achievement in Wordsworth's Great Decade.*

AVOCATIONAL INTERESTS: Collector of Wordsworth and contemporary books and manuscript materials, and late eighteenth-century watercolors.

* * *

WORONOFF, Jon   1938-

PERSONAL: Born January 19, 1938, in New York, N.Y.; son of Jules and Sophie (Tabor) Woronoff. *Education:* New York University, B.A., 1959; University of Geneva, Diploma of Interpreters School, 1962, License in Political Science of Graduate Institute of International Studies, 1966. *Home:* 340 East 64th St., New York, N.Y. 10021.

CAREER: Free-lance interpreter and translator for United Nations and other organizations working in Europe, Africa, Asia, and United States, 1962-73; managing director, Interlingua Language Services Ltd., 1973—. *Member:* Association Internationale des Interpretes de Conference, African Studies Association.

WRITINGS: Organizing African Unity, Scarecrow, 1970; *West African Wager,* Scarecrow, 1972. Editor, "African Historical Dictionaries" series, Scarecrow, 1974—. Contributor to *Africa Report* and other African studies journals.

WORK IN PROGRESS: A comparative study of economic development.

* * *

WORRALL, Olga (Nathalie)   1906-

PERSONAL: Born November 30, 1906, in Cleveland, Ohio; daughter of John Gabriel (a Russian Orthodox priest) and Elizabeth (Karanczay) Ripich; married Ambrose Alexander Worrall (a writer), June 7, 1928; children: Ambrose K., Alexander M. (twins, both deceased). *Education:* Graduate of Cleveland Business University, 1925, and Cleveland Commercial School, 1927. *Religion:* Russian Orthodox and Methodist. *Home:* 1208 Havenwood Rd., Baltimore, Md. 21218.

CAREER: Commercial teacher in Baltimore high schools, 1942-50; New Life Clinic, Mt. Washington United Methodist Church, Baltimore, Md., associate director and writer, lecturer, instructor, 1950—; K. & W. Enterprises, Inc., Baltimore, senior vice-president, inventor, and designer, 1964—. Member of board, E.S.P. Foundation, and Autogenics Institute Foundation, Inc. Member of consulting board, Ernest Holmes Research Foundation; consultant, Research Spiritual Healing Science of Mind. *Member:* American Society for Psychical Research, Academy of Parapsychology Medicine, Churches Fellowship for Psychical Studies (London), Spiritual Frontiers Fellowship, Order of St. Luke (England), Hillside Garden Club (Baltimore; former officer).

WRITINGS: How to Start a Healing Service, privately printed, 1957; (with husband, Ambrose Alexander Worrall) *The Gift of Healing: A Personal Story of Spiritual Therapy,* Harper, 1965; (with A. A. Worrall) *Miracle Healers,* New American Library, 1968; (with A. A. Worrall and Will Oursler) *Explore Your Psychic World,* Harper, 1970; (with Harold Sherman) *Your Power to Heal,* Fawcett, 1972; (with Edwina Cerutti) *Olga Worrall: Mystic with the Healing Hands,* Harper, 1975. Contributor of articles to *Science of Mind, Fate Magazine,* and other periodicals.

SIDELIGHTS: Olga Worrall told *CA:* "Since I am gifted in psychic abilities such as clairvoyance, etc. and spiritual healing, I am interested in the scientific research approach into parapsychological demonstrations motivated by personal experiences, especially in the areas of proving immortality and spiritual healing."

BIOGRAPHICAL/CRITICAL SOURCES: Will Oursler, *The Healing Power of Faith,* Hawthorn, 1957.

* * *

WOSMEK, Frances 1917-
(Frances Brailsford)

PERSONAL: Born December 16, 1917, in Popple, Minn.; daughter of Frank J. (a farmer) and Rebecca (Fenton) Wosmek; divorced; children: Brian, Robin. *Education:* Attended Wadena Teachers Training College, Wadena, Minn., and Meinzinger's Art School, Detroit, Mich. *Religion:* "Beyond the limitations of any special creed." *Home:* 90 West St., Beverly Farms, Mass. 01915.

CAREER: School teacher in rural Minnesota; designer of greeting cards; also has done layout and advertising art; presently free-lance designer and writer.

WRITINGS—All juveniles: (Self illustrated) *Sky High,* John Martin's House, 1949; (self illustrated) *Twinkle Tot Tales,* Lowe, 1949; (self illustrated) *Cuddles and His Friends,* Lowe, 1949; (illustrator) Edith May Lowe, *Throughout the Day,* John Martin's House, 1949; (illustrator) Rosemary Smith Fitzgerald, *Bobby and Buttons,* Garden City Books, 1949; (illustrator) Josephine Van Dolzen Pease, *One, Two, Cock-a-doodle-do,* Rand McNally, 1950; (under name Frances Brailsford) *In the Space of a Wink,* illustrations by Ati Forberg, Follett, 1969; (self illustrated) *A Bowl of Sun,* Children's Press, 1976. Also author of *Little Dog, Little Dog,* and illustrator of *Go to Sleep Book* for Rand McNally. Contributor of poems to *Christian Science Monitor* and *North Shore Examiner.*

WORK IN PROGRESS: Writing; designing toys, fabrics, and cards.

SIDELIGHTS: Frances Wosmek wrote *CA:* "A career in creative endeavors such as mine is the precarious unfolding of a human life ... an attempt to be true to oneself in as honest an expression as possible, in the face of every possible obstruction which is thrown in one's path. Our society believes itself to be a practical one, and is impatient with the "frills". It is the artist's task to prove, in time, that all else springs from art and without it (in whatever form) there could only be a collapse of forms. . . . So, which is the real?"

* * *

WRENN, Robert L. 1933-

PERSONAL: Born August 7, 1933, in Palo Alto, Calif.; son of C. Gilbert (a psychologist) and Kathleen (La Raut) Wrenn; married Margaret McKenzie (a ceramicist), December 29, 1956; children: Lisa, Susie, David. *Education:* Macalester College, A.B. (cum laude), 1955; Ohio State University, M.A., 1959, Ph.D., 1962. *Home:* 1222 Big Rock Rd., Tucson, Ariz. 85718. *Office:* Department of Psychology, University of Arizona, Tucson, Ariz. 85721.

CAREER: Ohio State University, Columbus, counselor, University Counseling Bureau, 1960-62; University of Arizona, Tucson, counseling psychologist, Student Counseling Bureau, 1962—, assistant professor of education and psychology, 1963-66, associate professor of psychology, 1967-75, professor of psychology, 1975—. Counseling psycholo-

gist, University of California, Berkeley, summer, 1966. President of board of trustees, Tucson Community School, 1969-70. *Military service:* U.S. Army, 1955-57. *Member:* International Association of Counseling Services (president, 1977-78), American Psychological Association, American Personnel and Guidance Association, Arizona State Psychological Association (secretary-treasurer, 1966-69; president, 1970). *Awards, honors:* National Institute of Mental Health demonstration grant, 1967.

WRITINGS: (Editor) *Basic Contributions to Psychology: Readings,* Wadsworth, 1966, revised edition, 1970; (with R. A. Ruiz) *The Normal Personality: Issues to Insights,* Brooks-Cole, 1970; (with Reed A. Mencke) *Being: The Psychology of Self,* Science Research Associates, 1975. Contributor to psychology journals.

AVOCATIONAL INTERESTS: Playing jazz piano.

* * *

WRIGHT, Charles 1935-

PERSONAL: Born August 25, 1935, in Hardin County, Tenn. *Education:* Davidson College, B.A., 1957; University of Iowa, M.F.A., 1963. *Home:* 1771 Thurston Dr., Laguna Beach, Calif. 92651. *Office:* Department of English, University of California, Irvine, Calif. 92664.

CAREER: University of California, Irvine, 1966—, began as assistant professor, currently professor of English. Fulbright lecturer in Venice, Italy, 1968-69. *Military service:* U.S. Army, Intelligence Corps, 1957-61. *Member:* P.E.N. American Center. *Awards, honors:* Fulbright scholar at University of Rome, 1963-65; Eunice Tietjens Award, *Poetry* Magazine, 1969; Guggenheim fellow, 1975; Edgar Allan Poe Award, Academy of American Poets, 1976, for *Bloodlines;* Melville Cane Award, Poetry Society of America, 1976, for *Bloodlines;* Academy-Institute Award, American Academy and Institute of the Arts, 1977.

WRITINGS—Poetry; published by Wesleyan University Press, except as indicated: *The Dream Animal* (chapbook), House of Anansi (Toronto), 1968; *The Grave of the Right Hand,* 1970; *The Venice Notebook,* Barn Dream Press, 1971; *Hard Freight,* 1973; *Bloodlines,* 1975; *China Trace,* 1977.

WORK IN PROGRESS: New poems.

SIDELIGHTS: The writer for *Kirkus Reviews* calls *The Grave of the Right Hand* the work of a "sensitive, accomplished poet ... a new talent." Although the reviewer comments that "when Wright speaks naturally, his voice is fresh and moving," he also found the diction "Too often marred by stilted vocables and syntactical turns" which might benefit from "a careful and generous pruning." X.J. Kennedy disagrees by saying that Wright "proved his command of impeccable phrasing and finely detailed imagery" in this book.

Of *Hard Freight* Kennedy writes, "Too many of the poems wear the structure of a list—of things merely enumerated and intoned." John N. Morris's first impression is that the book seems like a "journey in a time machine, a visit to the 'fifties." Comparing *Hard Freight* and *The Grave of the Right Hand,* Morris notes: "No single poem here has quite the permanent and classic weight of 'The Grave of the Right Hand,' the title poem of Wright's earlier collection. But I couldn't have said of that book, as I can of this one, that I everywhere admire the exactness of these verses, composed, line by absolute line, of associations at once strange and just." Peter Meinke calls this collection "hard poems to get into" but further comments that "Wright's strangely lit and colored landscapes create a cumulative effect, disturbing and hypnotic."

In a review of *Bloodlines,* the *Choice* reviewer comments, "Wright emerges as a major American poet; the promise of his previous work is richly fulfilled." John Morris compares Wright to Berryman, and *Choice* also calls *Bloodlines* possibly "the best poetic sequence since John Berryman's *Dream Songs.*" Helen Vendler found "flaws, caused mostly by a sensibility that has to split off a part of itself in order to get a poem written, so that the abstractions can't get sufficiently biographical, and the recollections can't get sufficiently abstract." She adds, however, that the two longest sequences in *Bloodlines* "have the single indispensable quality for poetry—a self-sustaining language, where meaning scarcely matters till the second time around. . . . A poem has an independent life where language and meaning are inseparable and in his lucky moments, Wright . . . lives in that unstable synthesis."

BIOGRAPHICAL/CRITICAL SOURCES: Kirkus Review, February 1, 1970; *New Republic,* November 24, 1973; *New York Times Book Review,* February 17, 1974, September 7, 1975; *Hudson Review,* spring, 1974, autumn, 1975; *Sewanee Review,* spring, 1974; *Choice,* September, 1975; *Contemporary Literary Criticism,* Volume VI, Gale, 1976.

* * *

WRIGHT, Edward A(rlington) 1906-

PERSONAL: Born January 25, 1906, in Mount Pleasant, Iowa; son of Fred David (a hardware merchant) and Clara (Holland) Wright; married Louise Wellman, June 12, 1940. *Education:* Iowa Wesleyan College, student, 1924-27; University of Iowa, B.A., 1928, M.A., 1930; also studied summers at University of California, Los Angeles, University of London, and University of Michigan. *Politics:* Democrat. *Religion:* Methodist Episcopal. *Home:* 350 South Fuller Ave., Apt. 11-C, Los Angeles, Calif. 90036.

CAREER: Toured the Midwest as an impersonator, 1922, and played the Chautauqua Summer Circuit and the Lyceum Winter Circuit as a student of Elias Day, 1922-32; Marshalltown Junior College, Marshalltown, Iowa, instructor in speech and theater, 1930-37; Denison University, Granville, Ohio, professor of theater, 1937-67, founder and director of Denison Summer Theatre, 1947-53; California State University, Long Beach, professor of theater, 1967-74, professor emeritus, 1974—. Fulbright lecturer at universities in Tokyo, 1959-60. Appearing solo, he has given more than five thousand performances of a program of character sketches and impersonations in the United States, Canada, Europe, and the Far East; acted in summer stock, 1933-46; troop entertainer with American Theatre Wing during World War II; director at Cain Park Theatre, Cleveland, and Playhouse on the Green, Worthington, Ohio; producer of plays for overseas tours for Department of Defense for ten years; during one sabbatical leave he appeared on radio for a year in "Gang Busters," "David Harum," "Parson Jim," and other network programs.

MEMBER: International Platform Association (president, 1963-66), The Players (New York), National Theatre Conference (treasurer, 1950-65; member of board of directors, 1955-67), American Educatonal Theatre Association, Sigma Phi Epsilon. *Awards, honors:* Citations from U.S. Department of State for entertaining troops during World War II and for taking play groups to the Far East and Europe; D.F.A., Iowa Wesleyan College, 1961; the Edward A.

Wright Theatre Arts scholarship was established in his honor at Denison University by his students, 1962; Certificate of Merit, *Dictionary of International Biography,* 1970, for distinguished service as actor, author, director, and teacher of theatre.

WRITINGS: Primer for Playgoers, Prentice-Hall, 1957, 2nd edition (with Lenthiel Downs), 1969; *Understanding To-day's Theatre,* Prentice-Hall, 1959, revised edition, 1974. Also author of series of sketches, "Americans You Do Not Read About in the Newspapers," for British Broadcasting Corp.

* * *

WRIGHT, (Philip) Quincy 1890-1970

December 28, 1890—October 17, 1970; American diplomat, educator, and authority on international law. Obituaries: *New York Times,* October 18, 1970; *Washington Post,* October 19, 1970; *Current Biography,* 1970. (See index for *CA* sketch)

* * *

WRIGHT, Sylvia 1917-

PERSONAL: Born January 21, 1917, in Berkeley, Calif.; daugher of Austin Tappan (a law professor at University of California, Berkeley, and writer) and Margaret G. (Stone) Wright; married Paul J. Mitarachi (an architect), May 21, 1959; children: John Paul Mitarachi. *Education:* Bryn Mawr, A.B., 1938. *Politics:* Democrat. *Religion:* None. *Home:* 120 Deepwood Dr., Hamden, Conn. 06517. *Agent:* Elizabeth McKee, Harold Matson Co., Inc., 22 East 40th St., New York, N.Y. 10016.

CAREER: After college, worked for Farrar & Rinehart in New York, N.Y., and for the U.S. Office of War Information in New York, London, Paris, and Munich; following World War II, worked for the features department of *Harper's Bazaar,* and later free-lanced for the U.S. Information Service.

WRITINGS: Get Away from Me with Those Christmas Gifts, McGraw, 1957; *A Shark-Infested Rice Pudding,* Doubleday, 1969. Contributor to magazines and newspapers.

WORK IN PROGRESS: A biography of some nineteenth-century New England women.

SIDELIGHTS: Sylvia Wright has some writers in her background, "as well as a number of people who wrote books." In the first group were her father, Austin Tappan Wright, whose long novel of an imaginary country, *Islandia,* she cut and edited for posthumous publication, and her grandmother, Mary Tappan Wright, who published several novels.

She says that she turned from humor (her first book) to the novel "not because the world of the forties and fifties was funnier than the world of the sixties, but because fiction now seems more direct. . . . Maybe there is a new humor somewhere, but I haven't yet discovered it."

Miss Wright adds that there is nothing unusual about her, except that she has twenty-five ribs and that she uses "the anomalous cervical rib for filling up gaps in conversations at parties, and distracting doctors." She and her husband live in a house he designed, set on a trap rock hill looking over the city of New Haven to the Sound and distant Long Island. Her husband's family owns two places in Greece, an apartment in Athens and a house on the island of Siphnos, both of which they visit occasionally.

WROTH, Lawrence Counselman 1884-1970

January 14, 1884—December 25, 1970; American bibliographer, librarian, and historian of printing and the book trade. Obituaries: *Publishers' Weekly,* January 11, 1971; *Antiquarian Bookman,* January 18, 1971.

* * *

WULLSTEIN, L(eroy) H(ughes) 1931-

PERSONAL: Born November 23, 1931, in Nampa, Idaho; son of Leroy H. (a federal executive) and Maud (Ziegler) Wullstein; married Betty Mills, April 17, 1956; children: Kathryn Lee, Kristen Marie. *Education:* University of Utah, B.S., 1957; Oregon State University, M.S., 1961, Ph.D., 1965. *Office:* Biology Department, University of Utah, Salt Lake City, Utah 84112.

CAREER: University of British Columbia, Vancouver, assistant professor of soil science, 1964-66; University of Utah, Salt Lake City, assistant professor, 1966-70, associate professor of biology, 1970—. Lecturer in United Kingdom under auspices of National Research Council of Canada, 1965. Consultant to U.S. Bureau of Mines and Brookhaven National Laboratories. *Military service:* U.S. Army Reserve, 1951-59. *Member:* American Association for the Advancement of Science, Sigma Xi. *Awards, honors:* National Science Foundation/American Society of Soil Science travel and lecture award, Australia, 1968; Fulbright fellow in Ireland, 1972-73.

WRITINGS: Man, Environment and Survival, University of Utah Press, 1971. Also author of more than twenty-five published research papers.

WORK IN PROGRESS: Research on nitrogen transformation in the environment and the biochemistry of nitrogen fixation.

* * *

WYATT, David K(ent) 1937-

PERSONAL: Born September 21, 1937, in Fitchburg, Mass.; son of Kenneth Hall (a journalist) and Rebecca (Chasteney) Wyatt; married Alene Wilson, July 15, 1959; children: Douglas Stewart, Andrew Richard, James Wilson. *Education:* Harvard University, A.B., 1959; Boston University, M.A., 1960; Cornell University, Ph.D., 1966. *Religion:* Episcopalian. *Home:* 415 Warren Rd., Ithaca, N.Y. 14850. *Office:* Department of History, McGraw Hall, Cornell University, Ithaca, N.Y. 14853.

CAREER: School of Oriental and African Studies, University of London, London, England, lecturer in history, 1964-68; University of Michigan, Ann Arbor, assistant professor of history, 1968-69; Cornell University, Ithaca, N.Y., associate professor, 1969-75, professor of history, 1975—, director of Southeast Asia Program, 1976—. *Member:* Association for Asian Studies, Royal Asiatic Society (Malaysian branch), Siam Society, Koninklijk Instituut voor Taal-, Land- en Volkenkunde (Netherlands), American Historical Association. *Awards, honors:* Ford Foundation foreign area training fellowships, 1960-61, 1962-64; National Endowment for the Humanities senior fellowship, 1974-75.

WRITINGS: (Editor) *The Nan Chronicle,* Southeast Asia Program, Cornell University, 1966; *The Politics of Reform in Thailand: Education in the Reign of King Chulalongkorn,* Yale University Press, 1969; (with Andries Teeuw) *Hikayat Patani: The Story of Patani,* Nijhoff, 1970; (with David J. Steinberg and others) *In Search of Southeast Asia: A Modern History,* Praeger, 1971; *The Crystal Sands: The*

Chronicles of Nagara Sri Dharrmaraja, Southeast Asia Program, Cornell University, 1975; (editor) *The Short History of the Kings of Siam,* The Siam Society, 1975. Contributor to *Encyclopaedia Britannica, Dictionary of World History,* and other reference volumes, and to journals of Asian studies.

WORK IN PROGRESS: A book on the history of the Thai peoples.

SIDELIGHTS: David Wyatt did historical research in Thailand in 1962-63, 1966 and 1976, and in Laos in 1972. He is able to carry out his research in seven languages—Thai, Lao, Burmese, Pali, French, German, and Dutch.

* * *

WYLDER, Delbert E(ugene) 1923-

PERSONAL: Born October 5, 1923, in Jerseyville, Ill.; son of Robert Maines (a banker) and Blanche (Coulthard) Wylder; married Jean Williams, June 5, 1948; married second wife, Edith Perry Stamm (a professor of literature), July 15, 1965; children: (first marriage) Stephen John, William Creighton; (stepchildren) Paul Stamm Wylder, Philip Stamm Wylder. *Education:* Attended Coe College, 1941-42, and University of Illinois, 1942; National University of Mexico, summer study, 1946, 1947; University of Iowa, B.A., 1948, M.F.A., 1950, Ph.D., 1968. *Religion:* None. *Home:* 104 South Ninth St., Murray, Ky. 42071. *Office:* Department of English, Murray State University, Murray, Ky. 42071.

CAREER: Bradley University, Peoria, Ill., instructor in English, 1950-52; University of Iowa, Iowa City, instructor in communication skills, 1952-58; Sandia Corp., Albuquerque, N.M., technical writer, 1958-61, consultant, 1963-65; University of New Mexico, Albuquerque, instructor and director of freshman English, 1961-65; Utah State University, Logan, Utah, assistant professor of American literature, 1965-66; Colorado State University, Fort Collins, assistant professor of American literature, 1966-68; Bemidji State College, Bemidji, Minn., associate professor of American literature, 1968-69; Southwest State University, Marshall, Minn., professor of literature and American language, 1969-77; Murray State University, Murray, Ky., professor of English and chairman of department, 1977—. *Military service:* U.S. Army Air Forces, 1942-45; fighter pilot in Italy; became second lieutenant; received Air Medal with three oak-leaf clusters. *Member:* Modern Language Association of America, Society for the Study of Southern Literature, Western Literature Association (president, 1967; member of executive council, 1969-72), Rocky Mountain Modern Language Association, Midwest Modern Language Association.

WRITINGS: (With W. L. Garner and D. G. Pugh) *Reading Factual Prose,* Scott, 1956; (with John C. Gerber and Jeffrey Fleece) *Toward Better Writing,* Prentice-Hall, 1968; *Hemingway's Heroes,* University of New Mexico Press, 1969. Author of pamphlet on Emerson Hough in Steck-Vaughn "Southwest Writers" series. Contributor to literary reviews. Associate editor, *Western American Literature,* 1966-68, member of editorial advisory board, 1968.

WORK IN PROGRESS: Emerson Hough, for Twayne; continuing research in Western American literature ("concerned about the lack of attention paid to good western writers like Edward Abbey and William Eastlake").

WYLDER, Edith (Perry) 1925-

PERSONAL: Born February 15, 1925, in Akron, Ohio; daughter of Beverly Francis and Maude (Greenwood) Perry; married William F. Stamm, October, 1952; married second husband, Delbert E. Wylder (a professor of American literature), July 15, 1965; children: (first marriage) Paul, Philip. *Education:* Student at Ohio Wesleyan University, 1942-43, and University of Arizona, 1943-44; University of Akron, B.A., 1947; University of New Mexico, M.A., 1949, Ph.D., 1967. *Politics:* Democrat. *Home:* 104 South Ninth St., Murray, Ky. 42071. *Office:* Department of English, Murray State University, Murray, Ky. 42071.

CAREER: University of New Mexico, Albuquerque, instructor in English, 1963-65; Colorado State University, Fort Collins, instructor in English, 1966-68; Bemidji State College, Bemidji, Minn., assistant professor of English, 1968-69; Southwest State University, Marshall, Minn., assistant professor, 1968-71, associate professor, 1971-73, professor of English literature, 1973-77; Murray State University, Murray, Ky., professor of English, 1977—. *Member:* Modern Language Association of America, Western Literature Association, Midwest Modern Language Association.

WRITINGS: The Last Face: Emily Dickinson's Manuscripts, University of New Mexico, 1971.

WORK IN PROGRESS: The Restitution of Idolatry: Emily Dickinson's Poetry.

*　　*　　*

WYSS, Thelma Hatch 1934-

PERSONAL: Born November 17, 1934, in Bancroft, Idaho; daughter of A. Wilder (a rancher) and Agatha Pratt (Van Orden) Hatch; married Lawrence Frederick Wyss (an interior designer), December 18, 1964; children: David Lawrence. *Education:* Brigham Young University, B.S., 1957. *Religion:* Church of Jesus Christ of Latter-day Saints (Mormon). *Home:* 1119 Stansbury Way, Salt Lake City, Utah 84108.

CAREER: Glamour (magazine), New York, N.Y., assistant production manager, 1959-60; high school teacher of English in Salt Lake City, Utah, 1961-66. *Member:* Utah State Historical Society.

WRITINGS: Star Girl (youth book), Viking, 1967.

BIOGRAPHICAL/CRITICAL SOURCES: Book World, March 3, 1968.

*　　*　　*

YAHIL, Leni

PERSONAL: Surname is pronounced Ya-*khil;* born in Duesseldorf, Germany; daughter of Ernst (a judge) and Helene (Simon) Westphal; married Chaim Yahil (an Israeli diplomat and chairman of the Broadcasting Authority), 1942 (died, 1974); children: Amos, Jonathan (killed in Israel's Six-Day War, 1967). *Education:* Hebrew University of Jerusalem, M.A., 1940, Ph.D., 1964. *Office:* Haifa University, Mount Carmel, Haifa, Israel.

CAREER: Technion (Israel Institute of Technology), Haifa, Israel, lecturer in humanities, 1965-67; University College, Haifa, lecturer in modern Jewish history, 1965-68; Hebrew University of Jerusalem, Jerusalem, Israel, office for overseas students staff member, 1968-70; Haifa University, Haifa, faculty member, 1971—, associate professor, 1976—. *Member:* Historical Society of Israel, World Union of Jewish Studies, Association of Jewish Studies (United States; member of executive board).

WRITINGS: Hatsalat ha-Yehudim be-Denyah (in Hebrew with English summary), Magnes Press of Hebrew University of Jerusalem, 1966, translation by Morris Gradel published as *The Rescue of Danish Jewry,* Jewish Publication Society, 1969; (contributor) P. Bagge, editor, *Hilsen til Haestrup,* Odense Universitetsforlag, 1969; (contributor) D. Asheri and J. Schatzman, editors, *Scripta Hierosolymitana,* Magnes Press of Hebrew University of Jerusalem, 1972; (contributor) B. Vago and G. L. Mosse, editors, *Jews and Non-Jews in Eastern Europe, 1918-1945,* Wiley, 1974; (contributor) *Holocaust,* Keter Publishing House, 1974. Contributor to *Encyclopaedia Judaica.* Contributor of articles to Hebrew journals, *Wiener Library Bulletin,* and *Jewish Social Studies.*

WORK IN PROGRESS: Concise History of the Holocaust, 1932-1945, two volumes, for Uetev Publishing House.

SIDELIGHTS: Leni Yahil lived in the Scandinavian countries, where her husband was ambassador for Israel, in 1956-59. She has traveled extensively in Europe, and visited the United States and South Africa. She speaks English and some French, and reads Danish, Swedish, Norwegian and Dutch. Her interests include politics, social problems, literature, and all aspects of Jewish life.

BIOGRAPHICAL/CRITICAL SOURCES: Commentary, October, 1967; *Jewish Social Studies,* April, 1971.

*　　*　　*

YAMAGUCHI, Marianne (Illenberger) 1936-

PERSONAL: Born January 10, 1936, in Cuyahoga Falls, Ohio; daughter of Arthur Max (a lawyer) and Esther (Lind) Illenberger; married John Tohr Yamaguchi (an economic consultant, demographer, and writer), September 10, 1960; children: Esme Turid, Kara Elizabeth. *Education:* Bowling Green State University, student, 1954-57; Rhode Island School of Design, B.F.A., 1960. *Home:* Flat 1, 44 Milson Rd., Cremorne Point, New South Wales, 2090, Australia.

CAREER: High school art teacher in Australia.

WRITINGS—Self-illustrated: (Compiler) *Finger Plays,* Holt, 1970.

Illustrator: Tohr Yamaguchi, *The Golden Crane,* Holt, 1963; T. Yamaguchi, *Two Crabs in the Moonlight,* Holt, 1965; Yoshika Uchida, *The Sea of Gold,* Scribner, 1965; J. R. Larson, *Palace in Bagdad,* Scribner, 1966; Eric C. Rolls, *Running Wild,* Angus & Robertson, 1973; Rolls, *The River,* Angus & Robertson, 1974.

WORK IN PROGRESS: Writing and illustrating a book.

SIDELIGHTS: The Yamaguchis lived in New York City for seven years before his work took them to Australia.†

*　　*　　*

YAVETZ, Zvi 1925-

PERSONAL: Name sometimes appears as Zwy Yawetz; born April 26, 1925, in Cernowitz, Russia; son of Leo and Amalia (Yavetz) Zucker. *Education:* Attended Hebrew University of Jerusalem, 1944-50, Ph.D., 1955; St. Antony's College, Oxford, additional study, 1954-55, 1960-61, 1962-63. *Religion:* Jewish. *Home:* University Ave. 89, Tel Aviv, Israel. *Office:* Tel Aviv University, Tel Aviv, Israel.

CAREER: Tel Aviv University, Tel Aviv, Israel, professor of ancient history. *Military service:* Israeli Army; became captain.

WRITINGS: (Editor and translator) *Mered Spartakus,* [Tel-Aviv], 1957; *Peshute ha-'am be-Romi* (title means

"Abolition of Debts in Rome"), [Tel-Aviv], 1958; *Plebs and Princeps* (translation of *Hamon u-manhigim be-Romi*, 1965), Oxford University Press, 1969; (editor with H. Avni) *Madrikh bibliyografi la-moreh le-historyah be-vet-ha-sefer ha tokhon* (bibliographical guide for history teachers), [Jerusalem], 1960; *Kesar ve-kesarizm* (title means "Caesar and Caesarism"), [Tel Aviv], 1971; *Caesar in der offertlichen meinung* (in German), [Duesseldorf], 1978.

WORK IN PROGRESS: Two books in English, one on the Flavians and one on the Roman plebs, both for Weidenfeld & Nicolson.

BIOGRAPHICAL/CRITICAL SOURCES: Times Literary Supplement, July 17, 1969.

* * *

YELLEN, Sherman 1932-

PERSONAL: Born February 25, 1932, in New York, N.Y.; married Joan Fuhr, June 12, 1952; children: Nicholas. *Education:* Bard College, B.A., 1952.

CAREER: Playwright. *Awards, honors:* Wilton E. Lockwood prize, Bard College, 1950, for creative writing; Hallmark Award for television drama, 1961, for play, "Time Out of Marble"; Prize Medal Award of The Theatre Club for best play by an American author, 1971; Tony Award nominee, 1971, for book for the musical, "The Rothschilds."

WRITINGS—Television plays: "Day before Battle," produced on "Studio One" series, CBS-TV, 1956; "Cry of Angels," produced on "Hallmark Hall of Fame" series, NBC-TV, 1963; "The Ghostbreakers," produced on NBC-TV, 1964; "Dr. Jekyll and Mr. Hyde Musical Special," produced on NBC-TV, 1973. Also author of television play, "Time Out of Marble."

Plays: (Author of sketch, "Delicious Indignities") "Oh! Calcutta!" (musical revue), first produced Off-Broadway at Eden Theatre, June 15, 1969; (author of book) "The Rothschilds" (musical), first produced in Detroit at Fisher Theatre, August 11, 1970, produced on Broadway at Lunt-Fontanne Theatre, October 19, 1970. Also author of screenplay, "The Day They Shook the Plum Tree," for Avco Embassy Pictures Corp.

WORK IN PROGRESS: A drama, "New Gods for Lovers"; a musical play, "Vicky."

BIOGRAPHICAL/CRITICAL SOURCES: New York Times, June 18, 1969; *Variety,* August 13, 1970, October 21, 1970, March 14, 1973; *Detroit Free Press,* September 6, 1970; *Christian Science Monitor,* October 26, 1970; *Cue,* October 31, 1970; *New York,* November 2, 1970; *Newsweek,* November 2, 1970; *Nation,* November 16, 1970; *New Leader,* November 16, 1970.†

* * *

YETMAN, Norman R(oger) 1938-

PERSONAL: Born January 10, 1938, in New York, N.Y.; son of Norman Charles (a minister) and Lucile (Darling) Yetman; married Anne Bishop, July 25, 1964; children: Barbara Jill, Norman Douglas. *Education:* Attended Colgate University, 1956-57; University of Redlands, B.A., 1960; University of Pennsylvania, M.A., 1961, Ph.D., 1969. *Politics:* Democrat. *Religion:* Protestant. *Home:* 1621 New Hampshire, Lawrence, Kan. 66044. *Office:* Department of Sociology, University of Kansas, Lawrence, Kan. 66044.

CAREER: University of Redlands, Redlands, Calif., instructor in sociology, 1962-63; University of Kansas, Law-

rence, assistant professor, 1966-71, associate professor of American studies and sociology, 1971—. *Member:* American Sociological Association, Organization of American Historians, American Studies Association, Midwest Sociological Society, Midcontinent American Studies Association (vice-president, 1970-71; president, 1971-72). *Awards, honors:* Woodrow Wilson fellow, 1960; Danforth fellow, 1960; Johns Hopkins University senior research fellow, 1972-73.

WRITINGS: (Editor) *Life under the "Peculiar Institution,"* Holt, 1970, published as *Voices from Slavery: Personal Accounts from the Slave Narrative Collection,* 1970; (editor with C. Hoy Steele) *Majority and Minority: The Dynamics of Racial and Ethnic Relations,* Allyn & Bacon, 1971, 2nd edition, 1975. Contributor of book reviews to professional journals. Associate editor, *American Studies.*

WORK IN PROGRESS: Sociology: Social Change and Social Process, with George Ritzer and Kenneth C. W. Kemmeyer.

* * *

YONEMURA, Margaret V. S. 1928-

PERSONAL: Born September 30, 1928, in Wales; U.S. citizen. *Education:* University of London, B.Sc., 1951; Columbia University, M.A., 1957, Ed.D., 1965. *Office:* Department of Professional Education, State University of New York, Binghamton, N.Y. 13901.

CAREER: Irvington House, Irvington on Hudson, N.Y., kindergarten teacher, then director of early elementary school, 1957-65; Queens College of the City University of New York, Flushing, N.Y., assistant professor of education and acting director of Early Childhood Center, 1965-66; Columbia University, Teachers College, New York City, assistant professor of education, 1966-68; Queens College of the City University of New York, associate professor of education, 1968-69; Bank Street College of Education, New York City, chairman of graduate program, 1969-73; State University of New York at Binghamton, professor of education, 1973—. Summer resource consultant, University of Hawaii, 1968 and 1970. *Member:* National Association for the Education of Young Children, American Educational Research Association, Association for Supervision and Curriculum Development, Child Study Association of America, Organisation Mondiale pour l'Education Prescolaire, Association for Childhood Education International (national chairperson, task force on re-orienting values, 1977-80).

WRITINGS: (With Ruth Hamlin and Rose Mukerji) *Schools for Disadvantaged Young Children,* Teachers College Press, 1967; *Developing Language Programs for Young Disadvantaged Children,* Teachers College Press, 1969; (contributor) Charlotte Winsor, editor, *Dimensions of Language Experience,* Agathon Press, 1975; (contributor) B. Spodek, editor, *Teaching Practices: Re-examining Assumptions,* National Association for the Education of Young Children, 1977. Contributor to professional journals.

* * *

YORBURG, Betty 1926-

PERSONAL: Born August 27, 1926, in Chicago, Ill.; daughter of Max (a storekeeper) and Hannah (Bernstein) Gitelman; married Leon Yorburg (a physician), June 23, 1946; children: Harriet, Robert. *Education:* University of Chicago, Ph.B., 1945, M.A., 1948; New School for Social Research, Ph.D., 1968. *Home:* 8 Meadow Marsh Lane, Old

Greenwich, Conn. *Office:* Department of Sociology, City College of the City University of New York, New York, N.Y. 10031.

CAREER: City College of the City University of New York, New York, N.Y., 1967—, began as assistant professor, currently associate professor of sociology. *Member:* American Sociological Association, Eastern Sociological Association.

WRITINGS: Utopia and Reality: A Collective Portrait of American Socialists, Columbia University Press, 1969; *The Changing Family,* Columbia University Press, 1973; *Sexual Identity: Sex Roles and Social Change,* Wiley, 1974; *The New Women,* C. E. Merrill, 1976.

* * *

YORK, Herbert (Frank) 1921-

PERSONAL: Born November 21, 1921, in Rochester, N.Y.; son of Herbert Frank and Nellie (Lang) York; married Sybil Dunford, September 28, 1947; children: Rachel Dunford, Cynthia Dunford; stepchildren: David Winters. *Education:* University of Rochester, B.S., 1942, M.S., 1943; University of California, Berkeley, Ph.D., 1949. *Home:* 6110 Camino de la Costa, La Jolla, Calif. 92037. *Office address:* Department of Physics, University of California at San Diego, P.O. Box 109, La Jolla, Calif. 92037.

CAREER: University of California, Berkeley, physicist in Radiation Laboratory, 1943-54, assistant professor of physics in the university, 1951-54, associate director of Radiation Laboratory and director of Livermore Weapon Development Laboratory, 1954-58; Institute for Defense Analyses, Washington, D.C., director of research, Advanced Research Projects Division, 1958; U.S. Department of Defense, Washington, D.C., chief scientist, Advanced Research Projects Agency, 1958, director of defense research and engineering, 1958-61; University of California at San Diego, La Jolla, chancellor, 1961-64, 1970-72, professor of physics, 1965—, dean of graduate studies, 1969-70. Member of scientific advisory board, U.S. Air Force, 1953-57, of ballistic missile advisory committee, Secretary of Defense, 1955-58, of science advisory panel, U.S. Army, 1956-58, of President's Science Advisory Committee, 1957-58, 1964-68, and of general advisory committee, U.S. Arms Control and Disarmament Agency, 1961-69; member of board of trustees of Aerospace Corp., 1961-76, and Institute for Defense Analyses, 1964.

MEMBER: Federation of American Scientists, American Physical Society, International Academy of Astronautics, American Academy of Arts and Sciences, Phi Beta Kappa, Sigma Xi. *Awards, honors:* D.Sc., Case Institute of Technology (now Case Western Reserve University), 1960; Lawrence Award, U.S. Atomic Energy Commission, 1962; LL.D., University of San Diego, 1964; L.H.D., Claremont Graduate School, 1971.

WRITINGS: Race to Oblivion: A Participant's View of the Arms Race, Simon & Schuster, 1970; (editor) *Readings in Arms Control,* W. H. Freeman, 1973; *The Advisors: Oppenheimer, Teller and the Superbomb,* W. H. Freeman, 1976. Author of articles on scientific topics, and on arms and arms control matters.

* * *

YOST, F(rank) Donald 1927-

PERSONAL: Born June 23, 1927, in Minneapolis, Minn.; son of Frank Herman (a clergyman, professor, and editor) and Esther May (Zimmer) Yost; married Lois Lamborn Scott (an elementary teacher), July 10, 1949; children: Robert Scott, Patricia Lynn. *Education:* Attended Columbia Union College, 1944-46; Andrews University, B.A., 1949; American University, M.A., 1961; Syracuse University, Ph.D., 1974. *Home:* 9309 Lynmont Dr., Adelphi, Md. 20783. *Office:* General Conference of Seventh-day Adventists, Takoma Park, Washington, D.C. 20012.

CAREER: Seventh-day Adventist Church, ministerial intern (licensed minister), Battle Creek, Mich., 1949-50; Review & Herald Publishing Association, Washington, D.C., editorial assistant, 1950-52, assistant editor of *Youth's Instructor,* 1952-56; General Conference of Seventh-day Adventists, Washington, D.C., editor of *MV Program Kit,* 1957-61; Newbury Park Academy, Newbury Park, Calif., instructor in English and journalism, 1961-64; Southern Missionary College, Collegedale, Tenn., assistant professor of journalism, 1964-67; Review & Herald Publishing Association, associate editor of *Review & Herald,* 1967-69, editor of *Insight,* 1969-71, associate book editor, 1971-73; General Conference of Seventh-day Adventists, archivist, 1973-75, director of archives and statistics, 1975—. *Member:* Society of American Archivists.

WRITINGS: Writing for Adventist Magazines, Southern Publishing, 1968. Contributor to religious magazines and *Journalism Quarterly.*

AVOCATIONAL INTERESTS: Flying (private pilot), collecting stamps, computers and information retrieval.

* * *

YOST, Nellie Snyder 1905-

PERSONAL: Born June 20, 1905, in North Platte, Neb.; daughter of Albert Benton and Grace (McCance) Snyder; married David Harrison Yost, July 6, 1929 (deceased); children: Thomas Snyder. *Education:* Graduate of Maxwell High School in Nebraska, 1923. *Politics:* Republican. *Religion:* Baptist. *Home and office:* 1505 West D. St., North Platte, Neb. 69101.

CAREER: Rural school teacher in McPherson County, Neb., 1925-26; cashier at Miller's Department Store, Salem, Ore., 1927-29; president of Fort McPherson Centennial Pageant, 1961—. Spent eight months on staff of *North Platte Telegraph* for special 1967 edition. Member of Nebraska Poet Laureate Commission, 1974, and Nebraska Hall of Fame Commission, 1974. *Member:* Altrusa International, American National Cowbelles, National Cowboy Hall of Fame, Western Writers of America (secretary-treasurer, 1971—), Western History Association, Westerners International (Buffalo Bill Corral; secretary, 1969-70), Nebraska Writers Guild (secretary, 1956-58; vice-president, 1966-69; president, 1969-71), Nebraska State Historical Society (2nd vice-president, 1970—), Lincoln County Historical Society (former vice-president and member of board of directors), Western Heritage Center (Oklahoma City), P.E.O. *Awards, honors:* Western Writers of America, Golden Spur, for best non-fiction western of 1969, *Boss Cowman,* Golden Saddleman, 1975, for "bringing dignity and honor to the history and legends of the West"; Eyes on Nebraska award, Nebraska Optometric Association, 1970.

WRITINGS: (With father, Albert Benton Snyder) *Pinnacle Jake,* Caxton, 1951; (with John Leakey) *The West That Was: From Texas to Montana,* Southern Methodist University Press, 1958; (with mother, Grace McCance Snyder) *No Time On My Hands,* Caxton, 1963; *Call of the Range: Story of the Nebraska Stock Growers Association,* Sage Books,

1966; (editor) *Boss Cowman: The Recollections of Ed Lemmon, 1857-1946,* University of Nebraska Press, 1969; *Medicine Lodge: The Story of a Kansas Frontier Town,* Swallow Press, 1970; (editor) Clark Fuller, *Pioneer Paths,* Purcells, 1974; (editor) Bartlett Richards, *Defender of the Grasslands,* Nebraska State Historical Society, 1977; *Buffalo Bill in North Platte,* Swallow Press, 1977; *Before Today,* Holt County Historical Society, 1977. Contributor of short western features to *Christian Herald, Western Horseman,* and other periodicals. Author of script for 1963 Fort McPherson Pageant.

WORK IN PROGRESS: A Man as Big as the West, a biography of Ralph Hubbard.

SIDELIGHTS: Nellie Yost was born in a sodhouse in northwest Lincoln County, Nebraska, and has spent most of her life on either her parents' or her husband's ranch. She lists as interests history, travel, and horseback riding, and told *CA* she is "the first and only woman ever to serve on the board [of the Nebraska State Historical Society] in its 99 year history." Nellie Yost went on to say: "I will never live long enough to put on paper a fraction of the absorbing history of our magnificent Great Plains area, but it is a satisfaction to me to know that some of it will be left behind for posterity—some that would never have been recorded if I had not taken the time and effort to hunt it up and write it down—only a small addition perhaps to what many others have done, but nevertheless an addition, a portion that would not have been preserved if I had not done it. Far too much has already been irretrievably lost because no one put it into words, on paper, while there was still time. It has been a labor of love."

BIOGRAPHICAL/CRITICAL SOURCES: Roundup (Western Writers of America), September, 1969; *North Platte Telegraph,* November 20, 1969; *Omaha World-Herald,* September 6, 1970.

*   *   *

YOUNG, Al 1939-

PERSONAL: Born May 31, 1939, in Ocean Springs, Miss.; son of Albert James (a professional musician and auto worker) and Mary (Campbell) Young; married Arlin Belch (a free-lance artist), October 8, 1963; children: Michael James. *Education:* Attended University of Michigan, 1957-61; Stanford University, fellow in creative writing, 1966-67; University of California, Berkeley, B.A., 1969. *Politics:* Independent. *Religion:* "Free Thinker." *Home:* 373 Oxford St., Palo Alto, Calif. 94306. *Agent:* Lynn Nesbit, International Creative Management, 40 West 57th St., New York, N.Y. 10019. *Office:* Creative Writing Center, Stanford University, Stanford, Calif. 94305.

CAREER: Free-lance musician, playing guitar and flute, and singing professionally throughout the United States, 1957-64; Radio Station KJAZ-FM, Alameda, Calif., disk jockey, 1961-65; San Francisco Museum of Art, San Francisco, Calif., writing instructor, 1967-69; Berkeley Neighborhood Youth Corps, Berkeley, Calif., writing instructor and language consultant, 1968-69; Stanford University, Stanford, Calif., Henry James Lecturer in Creative Writing, 1969—. Vice-president, Yardbird Publishing Cooperative. Lecturer and speaker at numerous universities throughout the country. *Member:* American Association of University Professors, Committee of Small Magazine Editors and Publishers, Authors Guild, Authors League, Writers Guild of America, Sigma Delta Pi. *Awards, honors:* Wallace E. Stegner Fellowship in Creative Writing, 1966-67; Joseph

Henry Jackson Award of San Francisco Foundation, 1969, for *Dancing;* National Arts Council Award for poetry, 1969-70; California Association of Teachers of English Special Award, 1973; Guggenheim fellowship, 1974; National Endowment for the Arts fellowship, 1975.

WRITINGS—All published by Holt, except as noted: *Dancing* (poems), Corinth Books, 1969; *Snakes* (novel), 1970; *The Song Turning Back into Itself* (poems), 1971; *Who Is Angelina?* (novel), 1975; *Geography of the Near Past* (poems), 1976; *Sitting Pretty* (novel), 1976. Work is represented in numerous anthologies, including *The Heath Introduction to Poetry,* Heath, 1975, and *How Does a Poem Mean?,* edited by John Ciardi and Miller Williams, Houghton, 1976. Contributor of articles, short stories, and poetry to *Audience, California Living, New Times, Rolling Stone, Evergreen Review, Encore, Journal of Black Poetry,* and others. Editor with Ishmael Reed, *Yardbird Reader;* west coast editor, *Changes.*

WORK IN PROGRESS: A new novel and a book of poems.

SIDELIGHTS: Al Young's first novel has been acclaimed by several reviewers, including Martin Levin and L. E. Sissman, as an authentic exploration of the experiences of a jazz-oriented black youth growing up in a middle American city. However, as Young has said, in writing *Snakes* he has tried "to go beyond the old socio-racial cliches and formulae that the average reader has not only come to expect but *demand* from contemporary black novelists. I have attempted in this work of fiction to construct what might be called a prose-movie centered in the emerging consciousness of a black teenager out of the urban Midwest, Detroit, who is more concerned with the meaning of life than with being either black or a musician or 'one of the boys' or 'hip.' I hoped also to capture some of the more elusive and lyrical rhythms and melodies of Afro-American speech, a language that has only recently begun to be studied and appreciated seriously."

Gregg Thomas Weinlein reviews one of Young's later books, *Geography of the Near Past:* "Without becoming sentimental, Young writes of his tender relationship with his wife and his son, a relationship that represents the fulfillment of his own existence. The affection, concern and understanding he exhibits in his love poems are like well executed escapes from the cold realities of life, but these poems also hit home in an ironic way because Young is not looking for escape, but rather further involvement and indulgence. Even Young's low key poems have an air of consolation, a hidden assurance that one can indeed make it out of the mire of existence."

Young told *CA:* "I write out of spiritual need. I consider it a religious experience. It has been an essential part of my life since I was nine years old. When I finish a novel I feel I have imparted what I know about life up to that time. [But] I don't want to reach the point where I think I have it all figured out. My influences stem from living rather than from literary traditions."

AVOCATIONAL INTERESTS: Contemporary mythology, popular culture, and mysticism.

BIOGRAPHICAL/CRITICAL SOURCES: Stanford Observer, March, 1970; *California Living* (Sunday supplement of *San Francisco Chronicle/Examiner*), May 3, 1970; *New York Times Book Review,* May 17, 1970; *Time,* June 29, 1970; *New Yorker,* July 11, 1970; *Kite,* June 9, 1976; *Peninsula Magazine,* June, 1976.

YOUNG, Ian (George) 1945-

PERSONAL: Born January 5, 1945, in London, England; son of George Roland and Joan (Morris) Young. *Education:* Attended Malvern Collegiate Institute, 1957-63, and University of Toronto, 1964-67, 1970-71. *Politics:* Libertarian. *Home and office:* 315 Blantyre Ave., Scarborough, Ontario, Canada.

CAREER: Writer and publisher. Director of Catalyst Press, 1969—. *Member:* League of Canadian Poets, Libertarians for Gay Rights. *Awards, honors:* Canada Council awards, 1969, 1972, 1974, 1976; Ontario Arts Council awards, 1970, 1975.

WRITINGS—All poetry: *White Garland: 9 Poems for Richard,* Cyclops, 1969; *Year of the Quiet Sun,* Anansi, 1969; *Double Exposure,* New Books, 1970, new edition, Crossing Press, 1974; (with Richard Phelan) *Cool Fire: 10 Poems by Ian Young and Richard Phelan,* Catalyst, 1970; (with Phelan) *Lions in the Stream,* Catalyst, 1971; *Some Green Moths,* Catalyst, 1972; (editor) *The Male Muse: A Gay Anthology,* Crossing Press, 1973; *Invisible Words,* Missing Link, 1974; *The Male Homosexual in Literature* (bibliography), Scarecrow, 1975; *Common-Or-Garden Gods,* Catalyst, 1976. Work represented in many anthologies including *T.O. Now: The Young Toronto Poets,* Anansi, 1968, *Poets of Canada 1969,* Rae-Art, 1969, *Fifteen Winds,* edited by Alred W. Purdy, Ryerson, 1969, and *Notes for a Native Land: A New Encounter with Canada,* edited by Andy Wainwright, Oberon Press, 1969. Contributor to *Canadian Forum, Canadian Poetry, Cyclops, Descant, Edge, Fiddlehead, The Fifth Page, Gargoyle, Gayokay, Hearse, Luv, One, Pandora's Bag, Quarry, Random, Satyrday, Seven, Sunyata, Variety, Writ,* and other periodicals and magazines. Translator of Count Jacques d'Adelsward Ferson, *Curieux d'amour,* London, 1970. Book review editor, *Option,* 1973—; contributing editor, *Gay Sunshine,* 1975—.

WORK IN PROGRESS: Poems, articles, fiction.

SIDELIGHTS: Ian Young told *CA:* "I write what I call an objectivist poetry (that is, poetry which has as its prime reference an objective reality, an object or event in the material world). What is often referred to as 'irony' in this sort of writing is in fact an unexpected but appropriate and revealing relationship or juxtaposition of things, images, events or states of being, in a taut and meaningful way to illuminate, to bring a subtle and perhaps hidden aspect of a situation or condition, into awareness.... This is why I write: to bring into consciousness, to make connections, and thus to gain better control of my reality and to help others gain better control of theirs. When someone tells me a poem of mine has brought something into focus or shown him something that he *almost* knew but couldn't quite 'put his finger on,' I know the poem has been successful for that person: it has caused that personal metamorphosis which art should create.

"Much of my writing and publishing activity has reflected my involvement in the Gay liberation and libertarian/anarchist movements. My book publishing company, Catalyst, is especially interested in the work of Gay writers and Canadian writers, and we are eager to read manuscripts of all sorts, particularly fiction and poetry."

BIOGRAPHICAL/CRITICAL SOURCES: Saturday Night, February, 1970; *Margins,* 1975; *Gay News* (London), 1975; *Quill & Quire,* July, 1976; *Gay Examiner* (London), 1976.

YOUNG, Richard E(merson) 1932-

PERSONAL: Born July 12, 1932, in Owosso, Mich.; son of William Charles (a jeweler) and Katherine (Middaugh) Young; married Ann Elizabeth Albert, August 29, 1953; children: Jonathan Field, Lynn Mikell, David Thurston. *Education:* University of Michigan, B.A. (with honors), 1954, Ph.D., 1964; University of Connecticut, M.A., 1956. *Home:* 1309 Fountain, Ann Arbor, Mich. 48103. *Office:* Department of Humanities, University of Michigan, Ann Arbor, Mich. 48109.

CAREER: University of Michigan, Ann Arbor, instructor in English in College of Engineering, 1956-64, assistant professor, 1964-67, associate professor, 1967-71, professor of English, 1971—, chairman of department of humanities, 1971-76, research associate, Center for Research on Language and Language Behavior, 1965-69. *Member:* Modern Language Association of America, National Council of Teachers of English, Conference on College Composition and Communication (member of executive committee, 1966-69), Rhetoric Society of America (member of board of directors, 1969-71, 1976-78). *Awards, honors:* Distinguished Service Award, College of Engineering, University of Michigan, 1968.

WRITINGS: (With A. L. Becker and K. L. Pike) *Rhetoric: Discovery and Change,* Harcourt, 1970; (contributor) Gary Tate, editor, *Teaching Composition,* Texas Christian University Press, 1976. Contributor to language and education journals.

WORK IN PROGRESS: Research on rhetoric and systematic problem-solving.

* * *

YOUNG, Richard Phillip 1940-

PERSONAL: Born July 21, 1940, in Milwaukee, Wis.; son of Robert John (a salesman) and Phyllis (Meyers) Young; married Nancy Newcomer (a writer), November 15, 1963; children: Thomas Jarrett. *Education:* Lawrence College (now University), B.A., 1963; Northwestern University, M.A.T., 1963; attended Edinburgh University, 1963-64; Stanford University, M.A., 1968, Ph.D. candidate, 1969—. *Office:* Department of Political Science, State University of New York, Binghamton, N.Y. 13901.

CAREER: Delta College, University Center, Mich., instructor in history and political science, 1965-67; San Jose State College (now University), San Jose, Calif., lecturer in political science, 1969-70; Stanford University, Stanford, Calif., assistant professor of political science, 1970-71; State University of New York at Binghamton, lecturer in political science, 1971—. Consultant to National Advisory Commission on Civil Disorders, 1967. *Member:* American Political Science Association.

WRITINGS: (Editor) *Roots of Rebellion: The Evolution of Black Politics and Protest since World War II,* Harper, 1970; (compiler with Edward S. Greenberg) *American Politics Reconsidered: Power and Inequity in American Society,* Duxbury, 1973. Contributor of articles to *Western Political Quarterly, Encounter,* and other periodicals.

WORK IN PROGRESS: Social Change and Black Militancy.†

* * *

YOUNG, Robert Doran 1928-

PERSONAL: Born March 12, 1928, in Philadelphia, Pa.;

son of Earl Melroy (a certified public accountant) and Emma (Doran)Young; married Louisa Anna Grace, June 28, 1952; children: Linda L., David E., Carol S. *Education:* Eastern Baptist College and Seminary, B.A. and B.D., 1953; University of Pennsylvania, M.A., 1953; Temple University, Ph.D., 1968. *Politics:* Democrat. *Home:* 803 Spruce Ave., West Chester, Pa. 19380.

CAREER: Westminster Presbyterian Church, West Chester, Pa., minister, 1966—. Instructor in Hinduism and Buddhism, Eastern Baptist College. *Member:* American Academy of Political and Social Science.

WRITINGS: Encounter with World Religions, Westminster, 1970; *Freedom, Responsibility, and God,* Harper, 1975. Contributor to *Journal of School Health.*†

*   *   *

YUDELL, Lynn D.   1943-

PERSONAL: Surname is pronounced Yu-*dell;* born April 30, 1943, in New York, N.Y.; daughter of Milton H. (a physician) and Lili (Ebenstein) Yudell. *Education:* Boston University, B.F.A., 1965; Yale University, M.F.A., 1967. *Office:* Children's Museum, Jamaica Plain, Mass. 02130.

CAREER: Cambridge Seven Associates (architectural firm), Cambridge, Mass., graphic designer, 1967-68; Designs and Devices, Boston, Mass., partner, 1968-71; Children's Museum, Jamaica Plain, Mass., graphic designer, 1971—. Teacher of bookbinding seminar, Boston University, 1971. Consultant to Boston Redevelopment Authority, 1970-71, and Institute of Contemporary Art, Boston.

WRITINGS—Self-illustrated: *Make a Face* (juvenile), Little, Brown, 1970.

WORK IN PROGRESS: A book about body movement, probably for preschool children.

AVOCATIONAL INTERESTS: Crafts, particularly weaving and bookbinding.†

*   *   *

YUDKIN, Leon Israel   1939-

PERSONAL: Born September 9, 1939, in Northampton, England; son of Solomon and Ada (Mankin) Yudkin; married Meirah L. Goss (a lecturer), August 29, 1967. *Education:* University College, London, B.A., 1960, M.A. (with distinction), 1963. *Politics:* Non-party. *Religion:* Jewish. *Home:* 4 Kersal Crag, Singleton Rd., Salford M70 WL, England. *Office:* Department of Hebrew, University of Manchester, Manchester, Lancashire, England.

CAREER: University of London, London, England, lecturer in modern Hebrew, 1964-65; University of South Africa, Pretoria, lecturer in Judaica, 1965-66; University of Manchester, Manchester, England, lecturer in modern Hebrew, 1966—.

WRITINGS: Isaac Lamdan: A Study in Twentieth Century Hebrew Poetry, Cornell University Press, 1970; (editor with B. Tammuz) *Meetings with the Angel,* Deutsch, 1973; *Escape into Siege,* Routledge & Kegan Paul, 1974; *U.Z. Greenberg: On the Anvil of Hebrew Poetry,* Hebrew Publishing, 1975. Contributor of articles and columns to Jewish periodicals, including *Zionist Record, Jewish Chronicle, European Judaism, Jewish Quarterly, Federation Chronicle* (South Africa), *Moz ayim* (Israel), *Modern Hebrew Literature* (Israel), *Books Abroad* (United States), and *Jewish Spectator* (United States).

WORK IN PROGRESS: History of the Hebrew novel in the twentieth century.

YUDKIN, Michael D(avid)   1938-

PERSONAL: First syllable of surname rhymes with "good"; born July 30, 1938, in Middlesex, England; son of John (a university professor) and Emily (Himmelweit) Yudkin; married Patricia Nabarro (a statistician), June 26, 1966; children: Benjamin, Ruth. *Education:* Attended Eton College, 1952-56; Cambridge University, B.A., 1959, M.A., 1963, Ph.D., 1963. *Office:* Department of Biochemistry, Oxford University, Oxford, England.

CAREER: Harvard University, Cambridge, Mass., Harkness fellow, 1962-64; Oxford University, Oxford, England, fellow and tutor, University College, 1965—, university lecturer in biochemistry, 1966—.

WRITINGS: (Contributor) Frank Raymond Leavis, *Two Cultures: The Significance of C. P. Snow,* Chatto & Windus, 1962, Pantheon, 1963; (editor and contributor) *General Education: A Symposium on the Teaching of Non-Specialists,* Allen Lane, 1969, Fernhill, 1971; (with Robin Offord) *Harrison's Guidebook to Biochemistry,* Cambridge University Press, 1971; (with Offord) *Comprehensible Biochemistry,* Longman, 1973, Houghton, 1975. Contributor of articles on biochemical subjects to journals and magazines.

*   *   *

ZAINU'DDIN, Ailsa (Gwennyth)   1927-

PERSONAL: Surname is pronounced Zine-*oo*-din; born April 8, 1927, in Melbourne, Australia; daughter of Boyd Kyle (a teacher) and Thelma Beryl (Roberts) Thomson; married, December 10, 1956; husband's name Zainu'ddin (a teacher and translator); children: Nurel Zainila, Lisa Zafrina (both daughters). *Education:* Attended Methodist Ladies College, Melbourne; Melbourne University, B.A. (with honors), 1948, M.A., 1954, B.Ed., 1961. *Office:* Education Faculty, Monash University, Clayton, Victoria, 3168 Australia.

CAREER: Melbourne University, Melbourne, Australia, history tutor, 1948-51, 1961-64; Canberra University College, Canberra, Australia, research assistant in history department, 1951-54; Ministry of Education, English Language Inspectorate, Jakarta, Indonesia, teacher, 1954-56; Monash University, Melbourne, Australia, lecturer in education, 1965—. *Member:* Australian and New Zealand History of Education Society, Australian Indonesian Association (Victoria), Australian Society of Authors, Victoria Historical Association, Immigration Reform Group, Victorian Women Graduates Association.

WRITINGS: How to Cook Indonesian Food, Australian Indonesian Association, 1964-66; *A Short History of Indonesia,* Cassell (Melbourne) 1968, Praeger, 1970; (author and translator) *Songs of Indonesia,* music by Helen McMahon, Heinemann (Melbourne), 1969; (contributor) D. Johnson, editor, *The Making of the Modern World,* Volume I, Benn, 1971; (with husband, Zainu'ddin) *Indonesia,* Angus & Robertson, 1973, McGraw, 1975; *Indonesia,* Longman (Australia), 1975.

Contributor of articles to *Melbourne Studies in Education;* editor, newsletter of Volunteer Graduate Association, 1956-62, newsletter of Australian Indonesian Association, 1964-66.

WORK OF PROGRESS: A history of the Methodist Ladies College in Melbourne.

SIDELIGHTS: Ailsa Zainu'ddin told *CA:* "My writing on Indonesia has been motivated by a desire to introduce Indonesia and Indonesians to their next-door neighbours in Australia. It is less an attempt to see ourselves as others see us than to see others as they see themselves.... Now I am moving away from my concern with Indonesia to a concern with the role of women in society as I see considerable parallels between racism, colonialism and sexism." She has traveled in Indonesia, Malaysia, Philippines, Japan, United States, England, and the Netherlands.

BIOGRAPHICAL/CRITICAL SOURCES: Ivan Southall, *Indonesia Face to Face,* Lansdowne, 1964.

* * *

ZANER, Richard M(orris) 1933-

PERSONAL: Born September 20, 1933, in Duncan, Ariz.; son of Irving Morris and Ruth (Cosper) Zaner; married Junanne Head (an artist and sculptor), November 9, 1956; children: Melora Lou, Andrew William Dorion. *Education:* University of Houston, B.S. (summa cum laude), 1957; New School for Social Research, New York, M.A., 1959, Ph.D., 1961. *Home:* 9620 Meadowhill, Dallas, Tex. 75238. *Office:* Department of Philosophy, Southern Methodist University, Dallas, Tex. 75275.

CAREER: New School for Social Research, New York, N.Y., member of philosophy faculty, 1960-61; University of Houston, Houston, Tex., member of faculty, 1961; Lamar State College, Beaumont, Tex., assistant professor of philosophy, 1961-64; Trinity University, San Antonio, Tex., assistant professor, 1964-65, associate professor of philosophy, 1965-67; University of Texas at Austin, associate professor of philosophy, 1967-71, National Endowment for the Humanities fellow, 1969; State University of New York at Stony Brook, professor of philosophy and humanities, and chairman of Division of Social Sciences and Humanities, 1971-73; Southern Methodist University, Dallas, Tex., Easterwood Professor of Philosophy, 1973—. Visiting assistant professor, New School for Social Research, 1964; adjunct professor at University of Texas at Galveston, 1973—, and University of Texas at Dallas, 1975—; visiting professor, University of Missouri—Columbia, 1976, 1977. *Military service:* U.S. Air Force, 1951-54; became sergeant; received Distinguished Flying Cross, three Air Medals. *Member:* American Philosophical Association, Society for Phenomenology and Existential Philosophy, Metaphysical Society, American Association of University Professors, American Civil Liberties Union, Southwestern Philosophical Society (member of executive committee, 1965, 1967), Texas Association of College Teachers, Society for Health and Human Values, Institute of Human Values in Medicine (member of board of directors, 1977—).

WRITINGS: The Problem of Embodiment: Some Contributions to a Phenomenology of the Body, Humanities, 1964; *The Way of Phenomenology: Criticism as a Philosophical Discipline,* Pegasus, 1970; (editor) Alfred Schutz, *Reflections on the Problem of Relevance,* Yale University Press, 1970; (translator from the German with H. Tristam Engelhardt, Jr.) Alfred Schutz and Thomas Luchman, *The Structures of the Life-World,* two volumes, Northwestern University Press, 1973. Also translator of Dilthey's *Die Geistige Welt,* 1977.

Contributor of articles and reviews to *Philosophy and Phenomenological Research, Social Research, Psychological Review, Journal of Existentialism,* and other philosophy journals. Member of board of editors: *Journal for Phenomenological Psychology, Southern Journal of Philosophy, Human Studies, Journal of Medicine and Philosophy, Teaching Philosophy, Research in Phenomenology,* and *Philosophy of Sport.*

SIDELIGHTS: Richard Zaner told *CA:* "Besides my regular types of activities in the University setting, and with my own research into issues pertaining to self, self/other, and the social, especially as these relate to medicine, I am deeply concerned with pursuing certain ideas in poetry; I also indulge myself in sculpture (wood) and hand-carved pipes."

* * *

ZEA, Leopoldo 1912-

PERSONAL: Born June 30, 1912, in Mexico City, Mexico; son of Leopoldo, Sr. and Luz (Aguilar) Zea; married Elena Prado Vertiz, May 14, 1943; children: Alejandra, Irene, Leopoldo, Elena, Marcela, Francisco. *Education:* National Autonomous University of Mexico, M.Ph., 1943, Ph.D., 1944. *Home:* Cerro Tuera 74, Oxtopuleo, Mexico 20 D.F. *Office:* Center for Latin American Studies, National Autonomous University of Mexico, Ciudad Universitaria, Villa Obregon, Mexico, 20 D.F.

CAREER: Escuela Nacional Preparatoria, Mexico City, Mexico, instructor in philosophy, 1942-47; Universidad Nacional de Mexico, Mexico City, professor of philosophy, 1944—, dean of department, beginning 1966; El Colegio de Mexico, Mexico City, professor of philosophy, beginning 1946; National Autonomous University of Mexico, Villa Obregon, Mexico, director of faculty of philosophy and letters, 1966-70, currently director of Center for Latin American Studies. Head of department of intellectual cooperation and university studies, Secretary of Public Education, Mexico, 1953-54; secretary of permanent commission, UNESCO, Consejo Consultivo, Mexico, 1953-54; director of cultural relations, Secretary of Exterior Relations, Mexico, special deputy and plentipotentiary, 1960-66. Member of Official Mission sent by Mexican Government on good-will visit to Africa, 1961; Panamerican Institute of Geography and History, National History Commission, vice-president, 1961—, president of committee on History of Ideas in America. Participant in various government seminars, congresses, and expositions all over Latin America and Europe; lecturer in philosophy at numerous universities and government institutions throughout the world.

MEMBER: International Institute of Political Philosophy, International Academy of Political Sciences, Inter-American Society of Philosophy (life member), Iberian-American Society of Philosophy, Peruvian Society of Philosophy (honorary member), Mexican Congress of History (honorary member), European Society of Culture (Venice; honorary member). *Awards, honors:* Justo Sierra prize, *El Universal* (Mexico City), 1944, for *Apogeo y decadencia del positivismo en Mexico;* Grand Official of the Order "Al Merito de la Repubblica Italiana," 1963; awarded Bandera Yogoslava con Corona de Oro en Collar, 1963; Commander, Legion d'Honneur (France), 1964; Grand Official of the Order "Al Merito por Servicios Distinguidos" (Peru), 1966.

WRITINGS: Supebus Philosophus, El Colegio de Mexico, 1942; *El Positivismo en Mexico,* El Colegio de Mexico, 1943, 2nd edition, Studium, 1953; *Apogeo y decadencia del positivismo en Mexico,* El Colegio de Mexico, 1944; *En torno a una filosofia americana,* El Colegio de Mexico, 1946; (editor and author of introduction) Max Ferdinand Scheler, *Hombre y cultura,* Secretaria de Educacion Publica (Mexico), 1947; *Ensayos sobre filosofia en la historia del Centro de Estudios Filosoficos de la Universidad Nacional de Mexico,* Stylo (Mexico), 1948; *Dos etapas del pensamiento en Hispanoamerica: Del romanticismo al positivismo,* El Colegio de Mexico, 1949, translation by James H.

Abbott and Lowell Dunham published as *The Latin-American Mind*, University of Oklahoma Press, 1963.

Conciencia y posibilidad del mexicano, Porrua y Obregon (Mexico), 1952; *La Filosofia como compromiso, y otros ensayos*, Fondo de Cultura Economica (Mexico), 1952; *America como conciencia*, Cuadernos Americanos (Mexico), 1953; *El Occidente y la conciencia de Mexico*, Porrua y Obregon, 1953; *La Conciencia del hombre en la filosofia: Introduccion a la filosofia*, Imprenta Universitaria, 1953, 2nd edition, 1960; *La Filosofia en Mexico*, two volumes, Libro-Mex (Mexico), 1955; *America en la conciencia de Europa*, Los Presentes (Mexico), 1955; *Esquema para una historia de las ideas en Iberoamerica*, Imprenta Universitaria, 1956; *Del liberalismo a la revolucion en la educacion mexicana*, Instituto Nacional de Estudios Historicos de la Revolucion Mexicana, 1956, published with *Problema cultural de America Latina* as *Dos ensayos* (also see below); *Las Ideas en Iberoamerica en el siglo XIX*, Instituto de Historia de la Filosofia y del Pensamiento Argentino, Universidad Nacional de La Plata (La Plata), 1957; *America en la historia*, Fondo de Cultura Economica, 1957, 2nd edition, Revista de Occidente (Madrid), 1969; *La Cultura y el hombre de nuestros dias*, Imprenta Universitaria, 1959.

Latinoamerica y el mundo (lectures), Universidad Central de Venezuela (Caracas), 1960; *Dos ensayos: Del Liberalismo a la revolucion* [y] *Problema cultural de America Latina*, Universidad de Carabobo (Valencia, Venezuela), 1960; *Democracias y dictaduras en Latinoamerica*, [Merida], 1960; *Antologia del pensamiento social y politico de America Latina*, Union Panamericana (Washington, D.C.), 1964; *El Pensamiento latinoamericano*, Formaca (Mexico), 1965; *America Latina y el mundo*, Editorial Universitaria de Buenos Aires, 1965, tranlation by Frances K. Hendricks and Beatrice Berler published as *Latin America and the World*, introduction by Maria del Carmen Millan, University of Oklahoma Press, 1969; *Latinoamerica en la formacion de nuestro tiempo*, Cuadernos Americanos, 1965; (compiler and author of prologue) *Antologia de la filosofia americana contemporanea*, Costa-Amic (Mexico), 1968; (with others) *Caracteristicas de la cultura nacional* (seminar organized by the Instituto de Investigaciones Sociales, Mexico, April, 1968), Universidad Nacional Autonoma de Mexico, 1969.

La Filosofia americana como filosofia sin mas, Siglo XXI (Mexico), 1970; *Dialectica de la conciencia americana*, Alianza Editorial, 1976; *Latinoamerica terler mundo*, Extemporaneos (Mexico), 1977.

Contributor: F.S.C. Northrop, *Ideological Differences and World Order*, Yale University Press, 1949; *Interrelations of Cultures*, UNESCO, 1953; *Philosophy in the Mid-Century*, Institut International de Philosophie (Florence), 1959; Guy Metraux, editor, *Nineteenth-Century World*, New American Library, 1963; *Estudios de historia de la filosofia en la filosofia en Mexico*, Universidad Nacional Autonoma de Mexico, 1963; Stanley Robert Ross, editor, *Is the Mexican Revolution Dead?*, Knopf, 1966; Morris David Forkosch, editor, *Essays in Legal History in Honor of Felix Frankfurter*, Bobbs-Merrill, 1966. Contributor of articles and essays to *El Hijo Prodigo, Filosofia y Letras, Dianoia, Excelsior, Cuadernos Americanos, La Republica, Foro Internacional, El Comercio* (Lima), *Cahiers d'Histoire Mondiale* (Paris), *La Prensa* (Buenos Aires), *Papel Literario* (Caracas), *Marcha* (Montevideo), *O Globo* (Brazil), and numerous other Mexican and foreign periodicals.

Member of board of editors, *Journal of the History of Ideas* (New York), 1959—; director, *Historia de las Ideas en America* (Quito), 1959—.

ZEHNLE, Richard F(rederick) 1933-

PERSONAL: Born May 18, 1933, in New York, N.Y.; son of Frederick Raymond (an accountant) and Agnes (Cavanagh) Zehnle; married Joyce Marie Robicheaux (an assistant professor), September 14, 1968; children: Natanya Marie. *Education:* University of Dayton, B.A., 1954; Universite de Fribourg, Switzerland, S.T.L., 1964; Ecole Biblique, S.S.D., 1967. *Religion:* Roman Catholic.

CAREER: St. Louis University, Divinity School, St. Louis, Mo., assistant professor of Biblical literature, 1967-68; McMaster University, Hamilton, Ontario, assistant professor of religion, 1968-69; Canisius College, Buffalo, N.Y., assistant professor of religion, beginning 1969. *Member:* Society of Biblical Literature, American Academy of Religion.

WRITINGS: The Making of the Christian Church, Fides, 1969; *Peter's Pentecost Discourse: Tradition and Lukan Reinterpretation in Peter's Speeches of Acts Two and Three*, Abingdon, 1971.

WORK IN PROGRESS: Jesus: The Man and His Mission.

SIDELIGHTS: Richard F. Zehnle told *CA* that his "current research has shifted to the occult and the paranormal, thanks to a course I'm giving on magic and witchcraft."†

*   *   *

ZELVER, Patricia (Farrell) 1923-
(Patricia Farrell)

PERSONAL: Born September 28, 1923, in Long Beach, Calif.; daughter of Frank Parnell (a lawyer) and Katherine (Robinson) Farrell; married Alvin Zelver (a city planning consultant), January 8, 1948; children: Nicholas, Michael. *Education:* University of Oregon, student, 1941-43; Stanford University, B.A., 1946, M.A., 1948. *Residence:* Portola Valley, Calif.

WRITINGS: (Under name Patricia Farrell; with Carolyn Kauffman) *If You Live with Little Children* (nonfiction), Putnam, 1957; *The Honey Bunch* (novel), Little, Brown, 1970; *The Happy Family* (novel), Little, Brown, 1972. Work represented in *O. Henry Prize Collection of Short Stories*, edited by William Abrahams, Doubleday, 1972, 1973, 1975, 1977. Contributor of short stories for both children and adults to magazines, including *McCall's, Cosmopolitan, Redbook, Story, Atlantic, Esquire, Virginia Quarterly*, and *Pacific Spectator*.

WORK IN PROGRESS: A novel, *The Crime of Mrs. Markall.*

SIDELIGHTS: Patricia Zelver writes: "I have been writing as long as I can remember. Perhaps it's a form of addiction. I do feel that fiction can provide a form of insight into the human different from (and often more imaginative and profound) psychological treatises, Self Help books, and the Film."

BIOGRAPHICAL/CRITICAL SOURCES: New York Times Book Review, January 25, 1970.

*   *   *

ZENTNER, Peter 1932-

PERSONAL: Born August 13, 1932, in Prague, Czechoslovakia; son of Francis and Gertrude (Fischer) Zentner; married Carola Mosse (a journalist), September 20, 1963; children: Victoria, Adam, Laurence, Marcus, Quentin. *Education:* Gonville and Caius College, Cambridge, M.A., 1954. *Home:* 38 Woodland Gardens, London N.10, England.

CAREER: Procter & Gamble, Newcastle, England, brand manager, 1954-58; Greenlys Advertising, London, account executive, 1958-59; Envoy Journals Ltd., London, director, 1960-70; international marketing consultant, 1970—.

WRITINGS: East-West Trade: A Practical Guide to Selling in Eastern Europe, Parrish, 1967. Contributor to Times (London), Financial Times, and to business journals.

BIOGRAPHICAL/CRITICAL SOURCES: Times Literary Supplement, October 26, 1967.

* * *

ZIADEH, Nicola A(bdo) 1907-

PERSONAL: Born December 2, 1907, in Damascus, Syria; son of Lebanese parents, Abdo and Elen (Asad) Ziadeh; married Margarite Shahwan, April 18, 1944 (died August 28, 1974); children: Raid, Basim. Education: Attended Arab College, Jerusalem, 1921-24; University College, London, B.A. (honors), 1939; School of Oriental and African Studies, London, Ph.D., 1949. Religion: Christian. Home and office: American University of Beirut, Beirut, Lebanon.

CAREER: Arab College, Jerusalem, Palestine (now Israel), lecturer in history, 1939-47; officer in charge of organization teaching illiterates in Arab villages, Palestine, 1947-48; Cambridge University, Cambridge, England, lector in Arabic, 1948-49; American University of Beirut, Beirut, Lebanon, professor of Arab history, 1949-73, professor emeritus, 1973—. Assistant director of education, Cynenaica, 1949. Visiting professor, Harvard University, 1957, 1962-63. Secretary general, Mediterranean Social Research Council, 1965-70. Member of board of management, Beirut College for Women, 1968-70. Member: Mediaeval Academy of America, American Oriental Society.

WRITINGS: Urban Life in Syria under the Early Mamluks, Greenwood Press, 1953; Whither North Africa, Institute of Islamic Studies, Muslim University (Aligarh), 1957; Syria and Lebanon, Praeger, 1957; Sanusiyah: A Study of the Revivalist Movement in Islam, E. J. Brill, 1958; Origins of Nationalism in Tunisia, Faculty of Arts and Sciences, American University of Beirut, 1962; Damascus under the Mamluks, University of Oklahoma Press, 1964.

Author of books in Arabic: Ruwwad al-Sharq al'Arabi (on Arab countries), 1943; Al-Qawmiyh wa-al-'Urubah (on Arabism), 1945; Libya wa-Tunis wa-al-Jaza'ir (on Libya, Tunisia, and Algeria), 1952; Al-Rahhalat al-Arab (on travellers), 1957; Muhadarat fi tarikh Libiya (on Libya), 1958; Lamahat min tarikh al-'Arab (on Arab history), 1961; Al-Jughrafiyah wa-al-rahalat 'Inda al-'Arab (on Arab geographers), 1962; Tunis fi 'ahd al-himayah (on French occupation of Tunisia, 1881-1956), 1963; Al-Hisbah wa-al-muhtasib (on Muhtasib), 1963; Mundun 'Arabiyah (on cities and towns of Arab countries), 1965; Safahat Maghribiyah (on North Africa), 1966; Libya fi al-'usur al-hadithah (on Libyan history), 1966; (editor) Libya sanat 1948, 1966; Dirasat fi al-thawrah al-Arabiyah al-kubra (Near Eastern history), c. 1968; Ghandi, tahiyah min Lubnan (essays), 1970.

WORK IN PROGRESS: Research on cultural development in North Africa in the nineteenth century and on external confrontations of Islam, 1100-1400 A.D.

* * *

ZIEGER, Robert H. 1938-

PERSONAL: Born August 2, 1938, in Englewood, N.J.; son of John H. (a laboratory technician) and Grace (Harman) Zieger; married Gay Pitman (a teacher and an author), June 30, 1962; children: Robert E. Education: Montclair State College, B.A., 1960; University of Wyoming, M.A., 1961; University of Maryland, Ph.D., 1965. Politics: Democrat. Religion: Unitarian Universalist. Home: 24660 Manistee, Oak Park, Mich. 48237. Office: Department of History, Wayne State University, Detroit, Mich. 48202.

CAREER: University of Wisconsin—Stevens Point, assistant professor, 1964-68, associate professor of history, 1968-73; Kansas State University, Manhattan, associate professor of history, 1973-77; Wayne State University, Detroit, Mich., professor of history, 1977—. Member: American Historical Association, Organization of American Historians.

WRITINGS: Republicans and Labor, 1919-1929, University Press of Kentucky, 1969; Madison's Battery Workers, 1934-52: A History of Federal Labor Union 19587, New York State School of Industrial and Labor Relations, Cornell University, 1977. Contributor to historical journals.

* * *

ZIJDERVELD, Anton C(ornelis) 1937-

PERSONAL: Surname is pronounced Zy-der-veld; born November 21, 1937, in Malang, Indonesia; son of Jacobus Hendrik and Charlotte (Moulijn) Zijderveld; married Angelika Dissmann, May 25, 1967; children: Gabriele Maria, Susanne Micheline, Christiaan Robert. Education: University of Utrecht, B.D., 1960, M.Th., 1963; Hartford Seminary Foundation, Hartford, Conn., S.T.M., 1964; University of Leyden, Ph.D., 1966. Home: 52 Goirleseweg, Tilburg, Netherlands. Office: Faculty of Social Science, Tilburg University, 225 Hogeschoollaan, Tilburg, Netherlands.

CAREER: Wagner College, Staten Island, N.Y., assistant professor of sociology, 1966-68; Sir George Williams University, Montreal, Quebec, associate professor of sociology, 1968-70; Tilburg University, Tilburg, Netherlands, professor of sociology, 1971—.

WRITINGS: Institutionalisering: Een studie over het methodologisch dilemma der sociale wetenschappen, Hilversum, 1966, second edition, 1976; The Abstract Society: A Cultural Analysis of Our Time, Doubleday, 1970, translation published in Germany as Die Abstrakte Gesellschaft, Fischer Verlag, 1973; Sociologie van de zotheid: De humor als sociaal verschijnsel (title means "Sociology of Folly: Humor as Social Phenomenon"), Meppel, 1971, translation published in Germany as Humor und Gesellschaft, Styria Verlag, 1976; De Theorie van het symbolisch interactionisme (title means "The Theory of Symbolic Interactionism"), Meppel, 1973, second edition, 1975; De relativite it van kennis en werkelvekheid: Inleiding tot de kennis-sociologie (title means "The Relativity of Knowledge and Reality: Introduction to the Sociology of Knowledge"), Meppel, 1974.

WORK IN PROGRESS: A book on the social and political functions of the late-medieval court jester.

AVOCATIONAL INTERESTS: Music (pianist), literature, the theater.

* * *

ZIMMER, Timothy W. L. 1947-

PERSONAL: Born May 29, 1947, in Jackson, Mich.; son of Walter Willard (a minister) and Catherine (Cilley) Zimmer. Education: Attended Earlham College, 1965-67, 1969, Miami University, Oxford, Ohio, 1969-70. Politics: Pacifist. Religion: Pacifist.

WARTIME SERVICE: Conscientious objector; served two years in federal prison for refusal to cooperate with the military system. *Member:* Institute for Studies in Nonviolence (Oxford, Ohio), World Without War Council, Midwest (peace interne and director of resources).

WRITINGS: Letters of a C.O. from Prison, Judson Press, 1969.

WORK IN PROGRESS: Prison Journal.

SIDELIGHTS: Timothy Zimmer told *CA,* "I am an absolute pacifist, opposed to all forms of violence against human beings and to all forms of coercive activity by men and states."

BIOGRAPHICAL/CRITICAL SOURCES: Earlham Review, spring, 1967.†

* * *

ZIMMERMAN, Velma E. 1902-

PERSONAL: Born August 14, 1902, in Doe Run, Mo.; daughter of Carl Frederick and Ida Bell (Jones) Zimmerman. *Education:* Southeast Missouri State College (now University), Teacher Certificate, 1925; University of Missouri, B.S. in Ed., 1936; additional study at Washington University, St. Louis, Mo., and at George Peabody College for Teachers. *Home:* 1201 Burgess Ave., Crystal City, Mo. 63019.

CAREER: Elementary teacher in Farmington, Mo., 1923-24, Desloge, Mo., 1925-26, Leadwood, Mo., 1926-30, South Beloit, Ill., 1930-35, and Crystal City, Mo., 1936-67. *Member:* Missouri State Teachers' Association, Missouri Writer's Guild, American Association of University Women (charter member of Jefferson County branch), Jefferson County Writers (president), Delta Kappa Gamma.

WRITINGS: Tee Wee Mouse, Pageant, 1952; *Cotton Patch Andy,* State Publishing Co. (St. Louis), 1961; *Come with Me from A to Z,* Denison, 1968; *Nosey Blacky,* Denison, 1969; *Blue Coat Larry,* Denison, in press. Children's stories, articles on crafts and education topics, poems, quizzes, and puzzles have been published in about fifty magazines, including *Child Life, Jack & Jill, Highlights for Children, Poet's Reed,* and *Montana Poetry Quarterly;* one of her poems was included in the anthology, *American Sonnets and Lyrics.*

WORK IN PROGRESS: Devotional material and fiction for children eight to twelve years old.

AVOCATIONAL INTERESTS: Travel, photography, ceramics, and needlework.

BIOGRAPHICAL/CRITICAL SOURCES: Jefferson Republic (De Soto, Mo.), August 15, 1968.

* * *

ZINTZ, Miles V(ernon) 1918-

PERSONAL: Born July 16, 1918, in Plano, Iowa; son of William Edward and Ivy (Scott) Zintz; married Mary Estalee Hatley, March 9, 1946; children: Mary Elizabeth, Audrey Estalee. *Education:* Iowa State Teachers College (now University of Northern Iowa), B.A., 1939; University of Iowa, M.A., 1941, Ph.D., 1949. *Home:* 3028 Marble Ave. N.E., Albuquerque, N.M. 87106. *Office:* School of Education, University of New Mexico, Albuquerque, N.M.

CAREER: Teacher in public schools in Iowa and Illinois, 1936-42; Iowa State Teachers College (now University of Northern Iowa), Cedar Falls, associate professor of education, 1946-57; University of New Mexico, Albuquerque,

professor of education, 1957—. *Military service:* U.S. Army, 1942-46; became sergeant. *Member:* National Education Association, International Reading Association, Council for Exceptional Children, Phi Delta Kappa.

WRITINGS: Education across Cultures, W. C. Brown, 1963, 2nd edition, Kendall/Hunt, 1969; *Corrective Reading,* W. C. Brown, 1966, 3rd edition, 1977; *The Reading Process: The Teacher and the Learner,* W. C. Brown, 1970, 2nd edition, 1975; (with F. F. Bowren) *Reading in Adult Basic Education,* W. C. Brown, 1977.

* * *

ZISKIND, Sylvia 1906-

PERSONAL: Born January 12, 1906, in Philadelphia, Pa.; daugher of Israel and Sara (Starkman) Goldberg; married David Ziskind (an attorney at law), June 5, 1931; children: Ellen (Mrs. Robert J. Berg), Jane (Mrs. Raymond Carhart). *Education:* Cummock School of Expression, Los Angeles, diploma, 1927; University of California, Berkeley, B.A., 1930; University of Southern California, M.A., 1937; Immaculate Heart College, Los Angeles, M.A. in L.S., 1962. *Politics:* Democrat. *Home:* 2339 Silver Ridge Ave., Los Angeles, Calif. 90039.

CAREER: Cumnock School of Expression, Los Angeles, Calif., teacher, 1933-35; teacher in Washington, D.C. schools, 1936-40; Bellflower High School, Bellflower, Calif., librarian, 1949-62; Immaculate Heart College, Los Angeles, associate professor, 1962-72, acting dean, 1971-72. Lecturer in library science at Univeristy of Southern California, summers, 1973, 1974, 1975. *Member:* American Library Association, League of Women Voters, California Library Association (president of southern district, 1965), California Association of School Librarians (president of southern section, 1960), Special Libraries Association, Zeta Phi Eta.

WRITINGS: Reference Readiness, Shoe String Press, 1971, revised edition, 1977; *Telling Stories to Children,* H. W. Wilson, 1976. Contributor of articles to *Wilson Library Bulletin, California School Libraries, School Libraries, Journal of Education for Librarianship, Library Journal,* and *Catholic Educator,* and of reviews to *Choice.*

SIDELIGHTS: Sylvia Ziskind told *CA* she is interested in the theatre, an avocation which dates from the 1930's, when she "acted and directed in the little theatre movement. My interest in story telling most probably stems from those early years." *Avocational interests:* Gardening and reading.

* * *

ZNEIMER, John (Nicolas) 1925-

PERSONAL: Born July 3, 1925, in Chicago, Ill.; son of Nicolas and Marion (Gundeck) Zneimer; married Eileen Hess, October 28, 1949; children: Cary, John, Maud, Peter. *Education:* Attended Ripon College, 1942-43, 1946-48, B.A., 1948; Columbia University, M.A., 1950; University of Wisconsin, Ph.D., 1966. *Home:* 7406 Colorado Ave., Hammond, Ind. 46323. *Office:* Department of English, Indiana University Northwest, Gary, Ind. 46408.

CAREER: Coe College, Cedar Rapids, Iowa, instructor in English, 1950-52; self-employed real estate broker, Hammond, Ind., 1955-64; Indiana University Northwest, Gary, lecturer, 1964-66, assistant professor, 1966-69, chairman of department of English, 1968-70, associate professor of English, 1969—. *Military service:* U.S. Army Air Forces, 8th Air Force, navigator, 1943-46; became first lieutenant. *Member:* Modern Language Association of America.

WRITINGS: The Literary Vision of Liam O'Flaherty, Syracuse University Press, 1970.

* * *

ZUCKER, Jack 1935-

PERSONAL: Born January 23, 1935, in Brooklyn, N.Y.; son of Morris (a salesman) and Elsie (Wachtel) Zucker; married Helen Goldberg (a writer), August 23, 1957; children: Laurie, Elizabeth. *Education:* City College (now City College of the City University of New York), B.A. (cum laude), 1957; New York University, M.A., 1961, further courses, 1961-65. *Home:* 624 South Fox Hills Dr., No. 203, Bloomfield Hills, Mich. 48013.

CAREER: Teacher of English in Jackson Heights, N.Y., 1959-61; Ohio State University, Columbus, assistant instructor in English, 1961-62; Newark State College, Newark, N.J., assistant professor of English, 1962-65; Babson Institute of Business Administration, Babson Park, Mass., assistant professor of English, 1965-68; Marietta College, Marietta, Ohio, assistant professor of English, 1968-70; Phillips Academy, Andover, Mass., instructor in English, 1970-76. Teacher of creative writing, Cambridge Center for Adult Education, 1967-68. *Military service:* U.S. Army Reserve, 1958-64. *Member:* Poetry Society of America, New England Poetry Club. *Awards, honors:* Second prize in Island Contest (poetry) sponsored by Harvard University, 1966; fellowships to Suffield Writer's Conference, 1966, and Mont Chateau Writer's Conference, 1969; John Masefield Prize for Narrative Poetry, 1976; Ruth Fox Prize, 1976.

WRITINGS: (With I. Konigsberg) *Critical Thinking: An Anthology for Composition,* Macmillan, 1969. Poetry has been published in *Epos, Folio, Laurel Review, Trace, Literary Review, Southern Poetry Review, Esquire,* and other literary reviews.

WORK IN PROGRESS: A collection of his own poetry.

* * *

ZUCKER, Paul 1888-1971

August 14, 1888—February 14, 1971; German-born American architect, educator, and author of books on architecture. Obituaries: *Publishers' Weekly,* March 8, 1971. (See index for *CA* sketch)

* * *

ZYTOWSKI, Donald G(lenn) 1929-

PERSONAL: Born June 10, 1929, in St. Louis, Mo.; son of Dewey C. and Hilda (Henning) Zytowski; married Lois Remley, August 21, 1959; children: Carl, Eric. *Education:* Harris Teachers College, A.B.Ed., 1952; Washington University, St. Louis, Mo., M.S., 1957, Ed.D., 1965. *Home:* 2304 Northwestern, Ames, Iowa 50010. *Office:* Department of Psychology, Iowa State University of Science and Technology, Ames, Iowa 50010.

CAREER: Iowa State University of Science and Technology, Ames, assistant professor, 1965-69, professor of psychology and psychologist in student counseling service, 1969—. *Member:* American Psychological Association, American Personnel and Guidance Association, Sigma Xi, Phi Delta Kappa.

WRITINGS: (Editor) *Vocational Behavior: Readings in Theory and Research,* Holt, 1968; *Psychological Factors in Career Development,* Houghton, 1970; *Contemporary Approaches to Interest Measurement,* University of Minnesota Press, 1973.

WORK IN PROGRESS: Vocal Communication in Counseling.